THE BILLBOARD

ILLUSTRATED ENCYCLOPEDIA OF

ROCK

This revised, updated, and expanded paperback edition published in 2003 by
Billboard Books
An imprint of Watson-Guptill Publications
A division of VNU Business Media, Inc
770 Broadway
New York
NY 10003

Published in the UK by Virgin Books Ltd

Text © MUZE UK Ltd 2002
UNDER LICENSE FROM MUZE INC

Library of Congress Cataloguing-in-Publication data for this title can be
obtained from the Library of Congress

Library of Congress Control Number 2002109287
ISBN: 0-8230-7701-2

Printed in Italy

First printing 2003
1 2 3 4 5 6 7 8 9/09 08 07 06 05 04 03

CREDITS
EPM/MUZE Project Editor: Nic Oliver.

With special thanks to Colin Larkin and Sue Pipe at Muze/EPM, KT Forster
and Carolyn Thorne at Virgin Books.

First edition designed and produced by Flame Tree Publishing
A part of The Foundry Creative Media Company Ltd
ART DIRECTION: Nick Wells
DESIGNER SECOND EDITION: Sue Michniewicz
PICTURE RESEARCH: Frances Banfield; Lizzie Clachan

The typography used in this book is based on the classic versions of Baskerville, Futura and Trajan

THE BILLBOARD ILLUSTRATED ENCYCLOPEDIA OF ROCK

Billboard Books
An imprint of Watson-Guptill Publications/New York

HOW TO USE THIS BOOK

The entries in this book are arranged in alphabetical order to cover the best of rock and pop music from the birth of rock 'n' roll. Specific genres like R&B, blues, country, hip hop and rap are included, but only where they directly impact on the broader music scene, e.g. bluesman John Lee Hooker is included whereas blues roots artist Lead Belly is not.

The entries have been edited down by Nic Oliver from the updated version of the text already published in the EPM (*Encyclopedia Of Popular Music*, edited and compiled by Colin Larkin) most of which also appear in the *Virgin Concise Encyclopedia of Popular Music* also by Colin Larkin. We have tried to retain the flavour and comprehensiveness of this original work, but the creation of an illustrated version out of a much bigger, words-only reference work has necessitated some, not always desirable, shortcuts.

The selection of the entries out of the many thousands of possibilities does represent our own, much argued-over view of what's happening and what happened. Inevitably, during the making of the book some artists didn't make the final selection: next time we'll look at them all again.

MAIN ENTRIES

- There is no simple solution to the surprisingly complex issue of alphabetical order: individuals are listed by surname, i.e. Lennon, John, but Alice Cooper on the other hand can be found under 'A' because it is used both by the band and the individual; however, Iggy Pop is categorized under Pop, Iggy because this is his own, adopted, name. There are some historical curiosities like Puff Daddy being found under Combs, Sean 'Puffy', because this is how he started, with only recent releases as Puff Daddy.
- Bands such as the Kinks, whose names start with 'the', are found under the main part of their name because 'the' is simply a prefix.
- The names of artists or bands appearing in bold means that they have their own entry elsewhere in this Encyclopedia.
- The names of albums, EPs, books, newspapers, magazines, television and radio programmes, stage plays, musicals and films are all in italics. Major works of classical music are also in italics.
- Individual song titles appear in single quotation marks.
- An artist's year of birth is given wherever possible. In spite of exhaustive research we cannot find everyone's details for a number of reasons: birth certificates for the 20s, 30s and 40s are difficult to come by; many artists, particularly post-punk, seem prone to giving false names and dates of birth as a matter of fashion.

SIDE BARS

- These provide a snapshot of each artist or band. They provide a quick way of sampling their tastes and influences and refer you ➤ to other entries in the Encyclopedia. They also include main albums and further details of collaborators, connections, influences and further references where space permits. The full listing of albums, books, videos and films appears in the final pages of the book in comprehensive and, necessarily, microscopic detail.

- An entry with no side bar information means that a band/artist has released no albums, or only compilations.

Albums – up to three of the artist's key albums including compilations are included in the side bars. In many cases recent anthologies give a superb overview of an artist's career and will lead the reader to the main catalogue.

Collaborators – those people who have worked with the artist, i.e. producers, prominent session players, duet partners etc.

Connections – significant bands to which the artist previously belonged, actors they have worked with, bands who share the same label, associations/movements the artist has been involved with etc.

Influences – some of the people who have affected the artist either personally or musically. These influences sometimes include poets, authors or events.

Further References – usually one film, video or book. These often include films or videos the artist has starred in, composed for, or which have been made about their life and books either written by or about the artist. The complete list appears in the end matter.

END MATTER

- We have tried to provide a complete listing of albums, compilations, films, videos and books. Due to limitations of space, some compilations by major record companies have been included at the expense of budget versions.
- Albums, videos and films with alternative names in different parts of the world appear with both titles; for instance the 1964 Ray Charles film *Blues For Lovers* was also known as *Ballad In Blue*.

ALBUM RATINGS

The star-rating system used in this book has been retained from the original *Encyclopedia Of Popular Music*, which combined author Colin Larkin's experienced ear with that of many critics, reviewers and fans.

The ratings are carefully made, and consequently you will find we are very sparing with 5 Star and 1 Star albums.

★★★★★ **Outstanding in every way.** A classic and therefore strongly recommended. No comprehensive record collection should be without this album.

★★★★ **Excellent.** A high-standard album from this artist and therefore highly recommended.

★★★ **Good.** Good by the artist's usual standards and therefore recommended.

★★ **Disappointing.** Flawed or lacking in some way.

★ **Poor.** An album to avoid unless you are a completist.

A NOTE ON RECORD SALES

Originally an album could attain gold status only by the amount of money it made; fluctuating prices created a need for a new system and, from 1974 onwards, albums and singles started to be judged by how many copies were sold as follows:

US SINGLES

Gold Singles – sales of 1,000,000 copies pre-1989; 500,000 copies post-1989.
Platinum Singles – sales of 2,000,000 copies pre-1989; 1,000,000 copies post-1989.

US ALBUMS

1958–74:
Gold Albums – sales of $1,000,000.
Post-1974:
Gold Albums – sales of 500,000 copies.
Platinum Albums – sales of 1,000,000 copies.

UK SINGLES

Silver Singles – sales of 200,000 copies.
Gold Singles – sales of 400,000 copies.
Platinum Singles – sales of 600,000 copies.

UK ALBUMS

Silver Albums – sales of 60,000 copies.
Gold Albums – sales of 100,000 copies.
Platinum Albums – sales of 300,000 copies.

PICTURE ACKNOWLEDGEMENTS

www.lfi.co.uk: 6, 8(r), 9, 11, 12(bl), 16, 22(l), 23, 24(bl), 29(r), 29(b), 34(l), 35(l), 36(r), 37(bl), 40(l), 41, 42(bc), 43(t), 44, 48(l), 50(r), 51(t), 51(b), 54(b), 55(l), 60, 64(t), 64(bl), 66(r), 78(t), 81, 87(r), 97, 98, 101, 105, 108(r), 109(r), 111(t), 115(b), 116(l), 118, 128(r), 130(l), 136(r), 139, 140, 143(b), 146, 149, 152(b), 154(r), 156(b), 158(bl), 160(t), 164, 166(l), 166(r), 169, 172, 184(c), 187(t), 187(bl), 189, 191, 193(r), 203(r), 205, 206(r), 208(l), 210(l), 214(r), 227(r), 228, 231, 233(r), 241, 246, 250, 253, 255, 257, 258, 262, 267(l), 268(br), 269(r), 274(r), 275(br), 276, 285(r), 286, 289(b), 292, 298, 299, 302(b), 305(t), 305(b), 306(t), 307, 310, 316(l), 318, 326, 327(l), 331, 332(l), 332(r), 333, 334, 344, 346(r), 352, 354(r), 356, 357(r), 400. R.E. Aaron 293, E. Adebari 21(t), M. Alan 353(bl), L. Anderson 18, M. Anker 251, Archive 126(tr), R. Baras 227(l), 260, C. Barritt 153(l), 195, A. Boot 7, 161, A. Butt 280(r), K. Callahan 13(t), 35(r), 221(l), 235, 303, R.J. Capak 295(l), A. Catlin 54(t), 89(r), 248(r), J.M. Cole 134(b), P Conty 87(l), P. Cox 77(t), 184(tr), 263(l), 309(r), 317(r), 336, K. Cummins 69(l), 103(l), 132(r), 149, 184(r), 190(t), 200, 320(c), 327(r), 346(l), 358(t), J. Davy 96(t), S. DeBatselier 273, G. De Guire 92, G. De Roos 125, G. De Sota 85(l), Mike Diver 162, 283(r), A. Dixon 63, N. Elgar 237(r), Fienstein 322(r), D. Fisher 119(l), 222(b), 225(r), 242(r), 297, 313(l), F. Forcino 19, 296(l), S. Fowler 129(l), 171(l), 312, 328, 357(l), Goedefroit 107(b), 261, J. Goedefroit 94(r), F.R. Griffin 135(r), 182(l), 341, Griffin 108(l), 174(l), 197(r), 215, 277(r), 313(r), C. Gunther 73(c), 127(br), 173, 282(r), Hein/Topline 26(r), 247, J. Hicks 28(b), J. Hughes 234(l), W. Idele 45(l), I. Jennings 27, A. Keidis 278(l), G. Knaeps 71(l), 122, 131(b), 148(r), 265(l), D. Koppel 65, K. Kulish 64(br), 68(l), L. Lawry 317(l), P. Loftus 31(t), 145(l), J. Macoska 288, R. Marino 10(b), 10(r), 13(b), 109(l), 338, 347, C. Mason 49, 294, 349, P. Mazel 287, 330, K. Mazur 20(r), 77(b), 168(r), 188(t), 248(l), 280(l), 348, L. McAffee 308, P. Mountain 252(l), I. Musto 42(bl), 61(r), 208(r), 213(t), 222(t), 282(l), T. Paton 102, A. Phillips 236, D. Picerno 138, Prior 197(l), N. Preston 243, M. Putland 221(r), S. Rapport 43(b), 120(r), 289(t), 316(r), 351, K. Regan 47, 123(l), 234(r), D. Ridgers 38(bc), 82(r), 99, 100(b), 153(r), 211, 272, 339(l), J. Roca 223(l), W. Roelen 30(t), T. Sheehan 14, 56(r), 74(b), 86(l), 217, 270(r), 306(r), 314, 319, H. Snitzer 301(l), M. Stringer 110, G. Swaine 112, 279, 290, 311(l), 324(r), 335(br), G. Swenie 193(l), S. Thomann 325, G. Tucker 253(r), K. Weingart 239, R. Wolfson 171(t), 220, 226. **Steve Gillett, London**: 15, 48(r), 59(l), 61(l), 89(bl), 136(l), 179(l), 188(b), 204, 284(br), 358(b),. **Angela Lubrano, London**: 17, 21(bl), 26(l), 40(r), 74(t), 89(t), 96(br), 131(t), 175, 194, 207(l), 229(br), 234, 252(r), 271, 275(bl), 340. **Jeff Tamarkin, New Jersey**: 75, 83(l). **Star File Photo Agency, London**: 32, 72(r), 217(l), B. Gruen 198, 212(l), J. Mayer 155(l), 201, C. Pulin 124, 295(r), L. Seifert 121(b), J.J. Sia 185(l), B. Wentzell 177, V. Zuffante 58, 113, 267(r). **Ebet Roberts, New York**: 25(t), 31(r), 106(c), 144(b), 158(tr), 178(l), 186, 219(r), 266(r), 335(bl), 350. **Redferns, London**: 76, 88, 104, G.A. Baker Archives 53, 70, P. Bergen 111(b), 216, 296(r), F. Costello 33(l), 33(r), 183(r), N. Crane 278(r), G. Davis 203(l), 219(l), 321, I. Dickson 281, J. Douglas 68(r), A. Edwards 329, N. Elder 256(l), B. Engl 212(r), P. Ford 142, 230, 265(r), Fotex 100(tc), P. Frank 315, Gems 114(c), 115(t), B. Gwinn 192, M. Hatchett 240, M. Hutson 209, 229(t), 264, 277(l), 309(l), S. Idriss 133(l), J.M. International 116(r), M. Linseen 160(b), H. Madden 134(t), M. Ochs Archives 259, D. Redfern 143(t), 153(t), 174(r), 183(l), 213(b), 343(l), E. Roberts 178(r), 343(r), 354(t), N.J. Sims 82(l), 202, 233(l), 302(t), 304. **All Action**: 123(br), S. Meaker 12(t), 62(r), P. Ramey 121(t), J. Thomas 165(br)

All Album images courtesy of Foundry Arts and Foundry Arts/John Stickland, with thanks to all the record companies and publicity/management agencies who supplied and gave their permission to use promotional photographs and record and CD sleeves in the book.

Every effort has been made to contact copyright holders. If any omissions do occur the publisher would be delighted to give full credit in subsequent reprints and editions.

Key to picture locations
l – Left, r – Right, c – Centre, t – Top, b – Bottom, tr – Top right, tl – Top left,
tc – Top centre, br – Bottom right, bl – Bottom left, bc – Bottom centre

A FLOCK OF SEAGULLS

New wave electro-pop group from Liverpool, England. The band – Mike Score (b. 1957; keyboards/vocals), Ali Score (drums/vocals), Paul Reynolds (b. 1962; guitar) and Frank Maudsley (b. 1959; bass) – followed an adventurous EP with *A Flock Of Seagulls*, a splendid example of futurist pop that included 'I Ran (So Far Away)' (US Top 10, 1982). *Listen* was another infectious collection of songs, but the Top 10 single 'Wishing (If I Had A Photograph Of You)' was their only UK success. Reynolds departed after *The Story Of A Young Heart*, and following one further album (1986's *Dream Come True*) the band disintegrated. Score has periodically revived the band with new musicians, issuing an album in 1995 and continuing to tour into the new millennium.

A TRIBE CALLED QUEST

US male rap group formed in Manhattan, New York, USA, by Q-Tip (b. Jonathan Davis, 1970), Ali Shaheed Muhammad (b. 1970), Phife Dog (b. Malik Taylor, 1970) and Jarobi. Their 1989 debut, 'Description Of A Fool', was followed by the hits 'Bonita Applebum' and 'Can I Kick It?', the latter a typically refined jazz/hip-hop cross. As members of the Native Tongues Posse (with **Queen Latifah** and the Jungle Brothers) they were promoters of the Africentricity movement that aimed to make US Africans aware of their heritage, a theme emphasized in their music. *People's Instinctive Travels And The Paths Of Rhythm*, recorded as a trio following the departure of Jarobi, was more eclectic, whereas *Low End Theory* saw them return to their roots with a more bracing, harder funk sound, aided by jazz bassist Ron Carter. By *Midnight Marauders* there were allusions to the rise of gangsta rap, although they maintained the optimism predominant on their debut. *Beats, Rhymes And Life* was released in 1996 following a three-year hiatus. This US chart-topper offered highly philosophical lyrics, reflecting Q-Tip's conversion to Islam. Following one further album the individual members elected to concentrate on solo work. Q-Tip reinvented himself as a salacious mack figure on his 1999 solo debut, *Amplified*. The title of his sophomore album, *Kamaal The Abstract*, referred to his new Islamic name, Kamaal Fareed.

A-HA

Formed in early 1983, this Norwegian pop rock band features Morten Harket (b. 1959; lead vocals), Magne Furuholmen (b. 1962; keyboards/vocals) and Pål Waaktaar (b. 1961; guitar/vocals). The trio's melodic brand of Europop was perfectly represented by their debut single 'Take On Me', which reached US number 1 and UK number 2 in 1985. A world tour and a series of hits ensued, including the UK chart-topper 'The Sun Always Shines On TV', 'Train Of Thought', 'Hunting High And Low', 'I've Been Losing You' and 'Cry Wolf'. In 1987, Waaktaar composed the theme for the James Bond film *The Living Daylights* with John Barry and, in 1988, after two pop albums, the trio attempted a more serious work with *Stay On These Roads*. In 1989, Harket starred in the film *Kamilla Og Tyven* and recorded a one-off single with Bjorn Eidsvag.

A-Ha found further UK chart success in 1990 with a revival of the **Everly Brothers**' 'Crying In The Rain', but following the release of 1993's slow-selling *Memorial Beach* the trio embarked on their own projects. Harket enjoyed great success in Scandinavia as a solo artist, while Furuholmen formed Timbersound with Kjetil Bjerkestrand and Waaktaar played with his wife Lauren in the New York-based Savoy. The trio reunited as A-Ha in the late 90s to record the well-received *Minor Earth/Major Sky*.

A1

If at first you don't succeed keep on trying, should be the motto of this UK boy band. Mark Read (b. 1978), Ben Adams (b. 1981), Norwegian-born Christian Ingebrigtsen (b. 1977), and Paul Marazzi (b. 1975) were brought together in 1998 by the management team of Tim Byrne and Vicky Blood. The four members, who compose most of their own material, signed a lucrative recording and publishing deal with Columbia Records in February 1999. They debuted in June with 'Be The First To Believe', a catchy slice of pure pop co-written with Peter Cunnah of D:Ream that broke into the UK Top 10. The Top 5 follow-ups, 'Summertime Of Our Lives' and 'Everytime'/'Ready Or Not', were not enough to establish the quartet in the ultra-competitive boy-band market. Facing oblivion in 2000, they were rescued by the chart-topping success of their lame cover version of **A-Ha**'s 80s hit 'Take On Me'. The R&B-styled follow-up, 'Same Old Brand New You', was a far superior track which deservedly gave the quartet their second UK chart-topper in November. Tragedy beset A1 the following March, when four teenage girls were crushed to death during an in-store appearance at a shopping mall in Jakarta, Indonesia. The quartet bounced back in 2002 with the excellent acoustic track, 'Caught In The Middle'.

AALIYAH

b. Aaliyah Dana Haughton, 1979, d. 2001. Although she grew up in Detroit, Michigan, Aaliyah pronounced Ah-Lee-Yah ('highest, most exalted one' in Swahili), initially came to attention as part of the 'new jill swing' movement in the mid-90s. Her early career was fostered by **R. Kelly**, and 1994's debut *Age Ain't Nothing But A Number* included the US Top 10 singles 'Back & Forth' and 'At Your Best (You Are Love)'. She travelled to Kelly's home in Chicago for the sessions while she was still a student at the Detroit High School of the Performing Arts. After breaking her partnership with Kelly, Aaliyah released 1996's superior follow-up, *One In A Million*, on which she worked with hotshot producer Timbaland. Soundtrack work followed, with contributions to *Anastasia* ('Journey To The Past') and *Dr. Dolittle* ('Are You That Somebody?'). Aaliyah also began filming on her screen debut in *Romeo Must Die*. 'Try Again', taken from the movie soundtrack, went to the top of the US singles chart in June 2000. The following year's self-titled third album saw Aaliyah publically bidding farewell to her teenage years and fashioning a bold new sound with collaborator **Timbaland**.

Tragedy struck in August 2001 when, after filming a video in the Bahamas, the small light aircraft carrying Aaliyah and her entourage crashed shortly after taking off. Her third album posthumously climbed to the number 1 position in America, while in the UK 'More Than A Woman' reached the top of the singles chart in January 2002. *Queen Of The Damned*, the movie the singer had been filming at the time of her death, was completed posthumously.

ABBA

The acronym ABBA, coined in 1973, represented the coming together of four leading figures in Scandinavian pop. Agnetha Fältskog (b. 1950) had achieved pop success in her native Sweden with 'Jag Var Sa Kar' (1968). Fältskog teamed up with fellow Swede Björn Ulvaeus (b. 1945; ex-Hootenanny Singers) and released a few records overseas as Northern Lights, before joining Benny Andersson (b. 1946; ex-Hep Stars) and Norwegian solo singer Anni-Frid Synni-Lyngstad aka Frida (b. 1945).

Under the guidance of Swedish svengali Stig Anderson (b. 1931, d. 1997), Ulvaeus and Andersson joined forces for one album, Lycka. The marriage of Ulvaeus and Fältskog, followed by that of Andersson and Lyngstad, laid the romantic and musical foundations of ABBA. In 1973, the quartet (now known as Björn & Benny, Agnetha & Anni-Frid) represented their country in the Eurovision Song Contest with the infectious 'Ring Ring'. They succeeded the following year as ABBA, with the more polished 'Waterloo', which not only won the contest, but topped the UK charts and infiltrated the US Top 10.

The middling success of the re-released 'Ring Ring' and singalong 'I Do, I Do, I Do, I Do, I Do' provided little indication of the chart domination that was to follow. In 1975, ABBA returned with the worldwide hit 'SOS', a powerhouse pop production highlighted by immaculately executed counter harmonies and an infectiously melodic arrangement. This classic ABBA sound was evident on their first trilogy of consecutive UK chart-toppers, 'Mamma Mia', 'Fernando' and 'Dancing Queen'. The last also brought them their only US number 1 and precipitated their rise to pop superstardom with sales unmatched since the golden age of the **Beatles**. Between 1977 and 1978, ABBA celebrated a second trilogy of UK chart-toppers ('Knowing Me, Knowing You', 'The Name Of The Game' and 'Take A Chance On Me'), enhanced by some of the finest promotional videos of the period. *ABBA: The Movie* was released at this time, although in retrospect it is remarkable only for being an early outing by director Lasse Hallström.

The group began the 80s with two more UK number 1s, 'The Winner Takes It All' and 'Super Trouper', taking their UK chart-topping tally to nine in just over six years. Depite the dissolution of both marriages in the group, they maintained a high profile for a while – eclipsing the car manufacturers Volvo as Sweden's largest earners of foreign currency. However, in 1982 they elected to rest the group. Fältskog and Frida embarked on solo careers, but found chart success elusive. Ulvaeus and Andersson enjoyed a productive relationship with Tim Rice, culminating in London's West End musical *Chess*.

In 1992 a well-publicized 70s fashion and music boom gave fuel to countless (misguided) rumours of an ABBA re-formation. Seven years later, *Mamma Mia!*, a stage musical based on the songs of ABBA, opened in London to excellent reviews. The Australian band Bjorn Again also enjoyed great success touring with a set composed entirely of faithful ABBA cover versions.

ABC

This UK band are dominated by the stunning vocal range and songwriting skills of lead singer Martin Fry (b. 1958). The band was formed after Fry interviewed electronic musicians Mark White (b. 1961; guitar) and Stephen Singleton (b. 1959; saxophone) for his fanzine *Modern Drugs*. Fry took artistic control of their outfit, Vice Versa, changing the name to ABC and steering the music towards a more 'poppy' course. The band was completed by bass player Mark Lickley and drummer David Robinson, although the latter was soon replaced by David Palmer (b. 1961).

Their 1981 debut, 'Tears Are Not Enough', made the UK Top 20, followed by three Top 10 hits with 'Poison Arrow', 'The Look Of Love' and 'All Of My Heart'. Their pristine pop songs were displayed on the superb *The Lexicon Of Love*. This Trevor Horn-produced UK number 1 album was a formidable collection of melodramatic pop love songs. However, the failure of *Beauty Stab* to emulate the debut's success resulted in a personnel upheaval, which by 1984 left only Fry and White remaining from the original line-up. They continued as ABC using session musicians and changing their image for *How To Be A . . . Zillionaire!*. The new-look ABC enjoyed particular success in the USA, with 'Be Near Me' reaching the Top 10 and '(How To Be A) Millionaire' the Top 20.

Fry became seriously ill in 1986 and was absent for great lengths of time owing to treatment for Hodgkin's disease. He teamed up with White once more for 1987's memorable UK Top 20/US Top 5 hit 'When Smokey Sings'. Later albums failed to match the success of their debut, and by the mid-90s only Fry remained from the original line-up. *Skyscraping* was a good attempt at recreating the band's peak, but sounded dated. Since the album's release Fry has continued to lead ABC on the 80s revival circuit.

AC/DC

This theatrical Australian hard-rock band was formed in 1973 by Scottish-born Malcolm Young (b. 1953; rhythm guitar). Young, whose elder brother George had already achieved Australian stardom in **Easybeats**, enlisted his younger brother Angus (b. 1955; guitar). Their sister later suggested that Angus wear his school uniform on stage, a gimmick that became their trademark. In 1974, the Youngs and vocalist Dave Evans (b. ????) moved to Melbourne. Another Scotsman, Bon Scott (b. Ronald Scott, 1946, d. 1980; ex-Valentines, Fraternity), graduated from being the band's chauffeur to vocalist when Dave Evans refused to go on stage in 1974. The AC/DC line-up which welcomed him had already recorded a single, 'Can I Sit Next To You Girl', but it was his voice that graced their first two albums, *High Voltage* and *T.N.T.*. The latter featured new members Mark Evans (b. 1956; bass) and Phil Rudd (b. 1954; drums). Both sets were produced by George Young and his writing partner, Harry Vanda (ex-Easybeats). Neither album was issued outside Australia, though Britain's Atlantic Records did offer a selection of material from both as *High Voltage* in 1976. These albums brought them to the attention of Atlantic Records, who relocated the band to London in 1976. Evans, tired of touring, was replaced by Englishman Cliff Williams (b. 1949; ex-Home) in 1977.

Once AC/DC began to tour outside Australia, the band quickly amassed a cult following, as much for the unashamed gimmickry of their live show as for their furious, frequently risqué brand of hard rock. *Let There Be Rock* broke them as a UK chart act, its contents including the perennial crowd-pleaser, 'Whole Lotta Rosie'. However, it was 1979's *Highway To Hell* that established them as international stars. This, the band's first album with producer Mutt Lange, also proved to be their last with Bon Scott. On 19 February 1980, after a night of heavy drinking, he was left unconscious in a friend's car, and was later found dead, having choked on his own vomit.

Scott's death threatened the band's future, but his replacement former Geordie lead singer Brian Johnson (b. 1947) proved more than equal to the task. His first album with the band, *Back In Black*, reached number 1 in the UK and Australia, and spawned the hit 'Rock 'n' Roll Ain't Noise Pollution'. In 1981 *For Those About To Rock (We Salute You)* topped the US charts for three weeks. After 1983's *Flick Of The Switch*, drummer Phil Rudd left to become a helicopter pilot. He was replaced by Simon Wright (b. 1963; ex-A II Z), who in turn departed to join Dio in 1990. His replacement was Chris Slade (b. 1946; ex-**Manfred Mann's Earth Band**).

AC/DC maintained an increasingly relaxed schedule through the 80s, touring to support each album release. When Malcolm Young was unfit to tour in 1988 his cousin, Stevie Young (ex-Starfighters), temporarily deputised. Paul Greg also stepped in for Cliff Williams on the US leg of the band's 1991 tour. A year earlier *The Razor's Edge* had been one of the more successful albums of their later career, producing a UK Top 20 hit, 'Thunderstruck'. In 1992, they issued a live album, whose attendant single, 'Highway To Hell', made the UK Top 20. With Brian Johnson long having buried the ghost of

Bon Scott, the band shows no signs of varying its winning musical formula, and in 1994 were buoyed by the return of Rudd to the line-up. The following year's *Ballbreaker* marked a powerful return after a lengthy break from recording. The ensuing *Bonfire* box set, meanwhile, served as a fitting memorial to Bon Scott. The band greeted the new millennium in typical style with the 'business-as-usual' recording, *Stiff Upper Lip*.

ADAM AND THE ANTS

Formed in 1977, the band comprised Adam Ant (b. Stuart Leslie Goddard, 1954; vocals, guitar), backed by Lester Square (guitar), Andy Warren (bass, vocals) and Paul Flanagan (drums). Heavily influenced by the **Sex Pistols**, they used bondage gear and sado-masochistic imagery in their live act and repertoire. The line-up was relatively *ad hoc* between 1977 and 1979, with Mark Ryan (b. Mark Gaumont) replacing Square (who joined the **Monochrome Set**, as Andy Warren would later do) and colourful manager Jordan (b. Pamela Rooke) occasionally taking vocals. Other members included drummers Kenny Morris and Dave Barbe, guitarists Johnny Bivouac and Matthew Ashman (d. 1995), and bass player Leigh Gorman. The band released one studio album, *Dirk Wears White Sox*, but it was poorly received.

At the end of the decade, Adam Ant sought the advice of **Sex Pistols** manager Malcolm McLaren, who suggested a radical shift in musical policy and a daring new look. In 1980, the group abandoned their leader to form McLaren's newsworthy **Bow Wow Wow**, but with a fresh set of Ants – Marco Pirroni (b. 1959; guitar, vocals), Kevin Mooney (bass, vocals) and two drummers, Terry Lee Miall (b. Terry Day, 1958) and Merrick (b. Christopher Hughes, 1954) – Adam reinvented himself. Out went the punk riffs and bondage, replaced by a sound heavily influenced by the Burundi Black drummers. With Adam's Apache war paint and colourful, piratical costume, the new-look band enjoyed three UK hits in 1980, culminating in the number 2 'Ant Music'. With his striking looks and clever use of costume, Adam Ant was a natural pin-up. His portrayal of a highwayman ('Stand And Deliver') and pantomime hero ('Prince Charming') brought two UK number 1s and ushered in an era of 'New Pop', where fancy dressing-up and catchy, melodic songs without a message became the norm. In 1981, Mooney was replaced by Gary Tibbs (b. 1958). Having dominated the Ants since 1977, it came as little surprise when, following January 1982's number 3 hit 'Ant Rap', Adam announced that he was dissolving the unit to go solo.

ADAM ANT

The multi-talented Adam Ant (b. Stuart Leslie Goddard, 1954) began his career leading Adam And The Ants. He also starred in Derek Jarman's film *Jubilee*, with singer **Toyah**. Adam went solo in early 1982, retaining his old musical partner Marco Pirroni, and relaunched himself with 'Goody Two Shoes', which hit UK number 1 in June. 'Friend Or Foe' followed, hitting UK number 5; thereafter the spell was broken. **Phil Collins** was recruited as producer to halt Adam's sudden decline and the pantomime-influenced 'Puss In Boots' duly made the UK Top 5. However, the revival was only temporary, and by the end of 1983 Ant's chart career was practically non-existent. The original god of New Pop seemed commercially bankrupt, his place taken by new idols. Even an appearance at Live Aid in 1985 with 'Vive Le Rock' only produced a number 50 UK chart entry and Adam returned adroitly to acting, relocating to America in the process.

A return to England and a surprise chart comeback in 1990 with 'Room At The Top' appeared a lucky strike which did not seriously distract the singer from his thespian pursuits. A new album in 1995, promoted by concert appearances in London, provoked further media saturation and good reviews, but little in terms of sales. The next time Ant made the news was in a distressing series of incidents in the London area in January 2002, following which he was legally confined at the Royal Free Hospital under the 1983 Mental Health Act.

ADAMS, BRYAN

The unpretentious Adams (b. 1959) developed into the most popular mainstream Canadian artist of the late 80s and 90s, although he remains better known for several romantic ballads rather than his rock songs. After recording an album with Sweeney Todd, Adams' solo career commenced in 1978 when he began writing songs with Jim Vallance (ex-Prism). These early collaborations were recorded by **Loverboy**, **Bachman-Turner Overdrive** and **Bonnie Tyler** among others. In 1979, Adams signed a contract with A&M Records, putting together a band which included Vallance on drums, with Ken Scott (lead guitar) and Dave Taylor (bass). Their debut single, 'Let Me Take You Dancing', was followed by a self-titled album. The follow-up, *You Want It, You Got It*, scraped into the US charts. *Cuts Like A Knife* (1983) was Adams's breakthrough, reaching US number 8 and going platinum. It saw Vallance replaced by Mickey Curry, though the former maintained his songwriting partnership with Adams. The first single from the album, 'Straight From The Heart', also made the US Top 10, and two follow-up singles, 'Cuts Like A Knife' and 'This Time', reached the Top 20 and Top 30 respectively. *Reckless* returned the singer to the Top 10 and reached UK number 7. 'Run To You' fared well on both sides of the Atlantic, as did 'Somebody'.

Adams scored a US number 1 in 1985 with 'Heaven'. The same year he appeared at Live Aid and co-wrote (with Vallance) the Canadian benefit record for Ethiopia, 'Tears Are Not Enough'. The defiant and celebratory 'Summer Of '69' returned him to the US Top 10 and he ended a successful year duetting with **Tina Turner** on 'It's Only Love'. *Into The Fire* became a US/UK Top 10 hit, boasting songs of a more political bent, informed by Adams' charity work and tours for Amnesty International. It also saw the last Adams/Vallance songwriting collaboration, and the end of a five-album tenure with producer Bob Clearmountain. 'Heat Of The Night' provided Adams with his fifth US Top 10 hit, although subsequent single releases fared less well. He contributed to records by **Mötley Crüe**, **Belinda Carlisle**, Charlie Sexton and others and guested at 1988's Nelson Mandela birthday party concert at Wembley Stadium.

All was eclipsed, however, by his contribution to the 1991 movie *Robin Hood: Prince Of Thieves*. The soundtrack single, '(Everything I Do) I Do It For You', was a phenomenal chart success, staying at UK number 1 for 16 weeks –

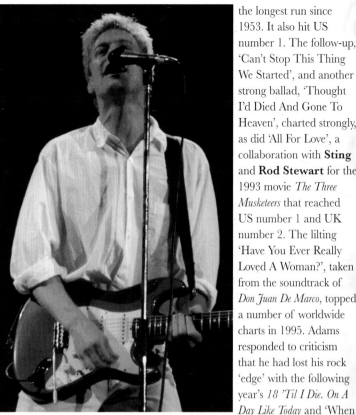

the longest run since 1953. It also hit US number 1. The follow-up, 'Can't Stop This Thing We Started', and another strong ballad, 'Thought I'd Died And Gone To Heaven', charted strongly, as did 'All For Love', a collaboration with **Sting** and **Rod Stewart** for the 1993 movie *The Three Musketeers* that reached US number 1 and UK number 2. The lilting 'Have You Ever Really Loved A Woman?', taken from the soundtrack of *Don Juan De Marco*, topped a number of worldwide charts in 1995. Adams responded to criticism that he had lost his rock 'edge' with the following year's *18 'Til I Die*. *On A Day Like Today* and 'When You're Gone' a high-profile duet with Melanie C. from the Spice Girls that reached UK number 3 in December 1998 and spent 10 weeks in the Top 10 – helped re-establish his commercial profile.

ADAMS, RYAN

Adams' (b. David Ryan Adams, 1974) first foray into music was with high-school punk band Patty Duke Syndrome. However, first experiences of love-turned-sour converted Adams to country and folk as he searched for a musical genre which could embody his feelings. In this spirit, **Whiskeytown** was the band Adams formed in 1994 with Caitlin Cary, Phil Wandscher, Eric 'Skillet' Gilmore and Steve Grothman. After only two albums and beset by personnel changes, the band began to disintegrate. Adams' image as a latter-day hell-raiser served him well, however, and his popularity survived the demise of the band.

After a period of introspection, he began working on his own songs. He teamed up with **Emmylou Harris** for a tribute album to his hero **Gram Parsons**, which featured their duet of 'Return Of The Grievous Angel'. However, it was the emotional impetus of the split with a girlfriend that led to his first solo album in autumn 2000, the Dylanesque *Heartbreaker*, recorded in collaboration with Ethan Johns. Adams credits Johns with organising Harris's appearance on 'Oh My Sweet Carolina', a particularly melodic and soulful track. The melancholy tone, complete with harmonica, could not totally crush the infectious energy underlying the whole album, in large part owing to the gutsy guitar licks. His sophomore release, *Gold*, was a highly ambitious and breathtakingly consistent work which helped confirm Adams as the alternative country artist with the most potential to break into the mainstream.

ADAMSON, BARRY

Manchester, England-born Adamson (b. 1958) was the original bass player with acclaimed post-punk outfit **Magazine**, and has also been a member of **Visage** and **Nick Cave**'s Bad Seed. His solo output has largely been in the field of instrumental music intended for films. His debut EP, *The Man With The Golden Arm* (1988), included the first of his spectacular cover versions of James Bond

film themes. The title track was also included on *Moss Side Story*, the soundtrack to a non-existent *film noir* about the Manchester suburb, which presaged his later scores. *Delusion* allowed Adamson to garnish a real film with his music; since then he has been in constant demand by a variety of directors. His seductive mood pieces and instrumentals stand by themselves without any visual, situation-specific stimuli. The excellent *Soul Murder*, dominated by Adamson's trademark keyboard surges, earned him a Mercury Prize nomination in 1992, a feat he repeated in 1994 with *The Negro Inside Me*. Following the release of 1996's *Oedipus Schmoedipus*, Adamson was forced to undergo major hip surgery. He returned to recording to provide music for David Lynch's *Lost Highway* and to release *As Above, So Below*, on which he handled his own vocals for the first time. In 2001 he collaborated with Finnish duo Pan Sonic on *Motorlab #3*.

ADVERTS

The Adverts were fronted by vocalist Tim 'TV' Smith and Gaye Advert (b. Gaye Atlas, 1956; bass, vocals), with Howard Pickup (b. Howard Boak, 1951, d. 1997; guitar) and Laurie Driver (drums). **Damned** guitarist Brian James was so impressed by their performance that he offered them a support slot, and introduced them to Stiff Records. Their debut, 'One Chord Wonders', was well received and its follow-up, 'Gary Gilmore's Eyes', was a macabre but euphoric slice of punk pop that catapulted the Adverts into the UK Top 20 in August 1977. One of the first punk acts to enjoy commercial success, the quartet also boasted the first female punk star in Gaye Advert.

Despite tabloid newspaper publicity, 'Safety In Numbers' failed to chart, although its successor, 'No Time To Be 21', reached number 38. Their debut album, *Crossing The Red Sea With The Adverts*, was barely recorded before Driver was ousted and replaced by former Chelsea/Generation X drummer John Towe, who left shortly afterwards, succeeded by Rod Latter. Changing record labels, personnel problems and unsuitable production dogged their progress, while *Cast Of Thousands* went largely ignored.

On 27 October 1979, with a line-up comprising Smith, Dave Sinclair (drums), Mel Weston (keyboards), Eric Russell (guitar) and bass player Colin Stoner (ex-Doctors Of Madness), the Adverts gave their last performance, at Slough College of Art. Smith went on to record with TV Smith's Explorers and as a solo artist.

AEROSMITH

One of America's most popular hard-rock acts, Aerosmith formed in the Boston, Massachusetts area in 1970 when vocalist Steven Tyler (b. Steven Victor Tallarico, 1948) joined guitarist Joe Perry (b. Anthony Joseph Perry, 1950) in a **Cream**-styled rock combo. Together with Tom Hamilton (b. 1951; bass), Joey Kramer (b. 1950; drums) and Ray Tabano (guitar), the band's original line-up was complete. Tabano was quickly replaced by Brad Whitford (b. 1952). After their first gig, at the Nipmuc Regional High School, the band took the name Aerosmith. Their popularity grew, and a triumphant gig at Max's Kansas City led to a recording contract with Columbia Records.

In 1973, Aerosmith secured a minor chart placing with their self-titled debut album. Its attendant single, 'Dream On', peaked at number 59 (it became a Top 10 hit in 1976). *Get Your Wings* introduced a fruitful working relationship with producer Jack Douglas, culminating in the highly successful *Toys In The Attic*, which sold in excess of six million copies worldwide. *Rocks* achieved platinum status and Aerosmith maintained their pre-eminent position with *Draw The Line* and the powerful *Live! Bootleg*. Tyler's physical resemblance to Mick Jagger, and his foil-like relationship with guitarist Perry, also inspired comparisons with the **Rolling Stones**, with whom they shared several musical reference points.

In 1978, Aerosmith appeared in the ill-fated *Sgt. Pepper's Lonely Hearts Club Band* movie, and although their version of 'Come Together' reached the US Top 30, tension between Tyler and Perry proved irreconcilable. The guitarist left the band following the disappointing *Night In The Ruts* and subsequently founded the Joe Perry Project. Jimmy Crespo joined Aerosmith in 1980, but the following year Whitford left to pursue a new musical career. Rick Dufay debuted on *Rock In A Hard Place*, but this set failed to capture the fire of the band's classic recordings.

Contact between the remaining band members and Perry and Whitford was re-established during a 1984 tour. Antagonisms were set aside and the following year the quintet's most enduring line-up was performing together again. *Done With Mirrors*, their debut for new label Geffen Records, was a tentative first step, after which Tyler and Perry rid themselves of their notorious drug and alcohol dependencies. In 1986 they accompanied **Run-DMC** on 'Walk This Way', an Aerosmith song from *Toys In The Attic* and a former US Top 10 entry. The collaboration, which reached US number 4, rekindled interest in Aerosmith's career and helped push rap music into the mainstream.

Permanent Vacation became one of their bestselling albums, and the first to make an impression in the UK, while the highly-acclaimed *Pump* and *Get A Grip* emphasized their revitalization. The band spent an age recording 1997's *Nine Lives*, which marked a return to their old label Columbia. The following September they achieved their first US number 1 with the Diane Warren-penned 'I Don't Want To Miss A Thing', taken from the soundtrack of the movie *Armageddon*. The song stayed at the top for four weeks and also provided the band with their first UK Top 5 single.

The new century saw Aerosmith as sharp as ever, with *Just Push Play* proving to be another strong album in a career that now spans four decades. Those wishing to immerse themselves in this extraordinary band should invest in the impressive 13-CD box set *Box Of Fire*.

AFGHAN WHIGS

From Cincinnati, Ohio, USA and original stalwarts of the Sub Pop Records empire, Afghan

Whigs gained prominence as favoured proponents of grunge, although the traditional nature of much of their recorded output progressively belied this tag. The band was formed in the late 80s by Rick McCollum (b. 1965; guitar), Steven Earle (b. 1966; drums), John Curley (b. 1965; bass) and Greg Dulli (b. 1965; vocals, guitar). Dulli first met Curley in jail, where they were being held overnight for, respectively, urinating in front of a police officer and drug-dealing. When Afghan Whigs provoked the interest of the major labels, Dulli insisted that he produce their records and direct their videos. Their major-label debut, 1993's *Gentlemen*, concerned familiar Afghan Whigs subjects: alienation and the seedier side of life. One of the songs, 'My Curse', was so personal that Dulli could not sing it himself – instead employing Marcy Mays of Scrawl.

Earle was subsequently replaced by Paul Buchignani as the band's soul influence came to the fore on *Black Love* and *1965*. The latter featured new drummer Michael Horrigan and proved to be one of 1998's outstanding releases. In December, Dulli was beaten up and temporarily left in a coma after a concert in Austin, Texas. The Afghan Whigs broke up in February 2001, with Dulli going on to record with the Twilight Singers.

AFRIKA BAMBAATAA

The influence of Afrika Bambaataa (b. Kevin Donovan, 1960) on rap's development is pivotal. He was the founding father of his native New York's Zulu Nation, whose name was inspired by the movie *Zulu*, and the code of honour and bravery of its black participants. Zulu Nation (and its head) helped transform the gangs of the late 70s into the hip-hop crews of the early 80s. By 1980, Bambaataa was the pre-eminent hip-hop DJ in New York. He made his recording debut the same year, producing two versions of 'Zulu Nation Throwdown' for Cosmic Force and Soul Sonic Force. Signing to the independent label Tommy Boy Records, he made his first own-name release in 1982, as Afrika Bambaataa And The Jazzy Five, with 'Jazzy Sensation' (based on Gwen Guthrie's 'Funky Sensation'). It was followed by 'Planet Rock', a wholly synthesized record, this time based on **Kraftwerk**'s 'Trans-Europe Express'. It took hip-hop music far beyond its existing street-rhyme and percussion-break format. The contribution of Arthur Baker and John Robie in programming the track's beats is also highly significant, for in turn they gave birth to the electro-rap movement which dominated the mid-80s and paved the way for the popularization of dance music.

'Looking For The Perfect Beat' continued the marriage of raw lyrics and synthesized electro-boogie, and was another major milestone for the genre. The follow-up album, *Beware (The Funk Is Everywhere)*, included a take on the **MC5**'s 'Kick Out The Jams' (produced by **Bill Laswell**). Bambaataa also recorded an album as part of Shango, backed by Material members Laswell and Michael Beinhorn. Never a man to stay in one place for long, Bambaataa went on to record two vastly different and unexpected singles – 'World Destruction' with ex-**Sex Pistols** vocalist John Lydon, and 'Unity' with **James Brown**.

Bambaataa fell out of the limelight in the latter half of the 80s, as new generations of disc jockeys and rappers stepped forward with their own innovations and fresh beats. He re-formed Soul Sonic Force in the mid-90s to record *Lost Generation*, and continues to DJ and record new material on a regular basis.

AGUILERA, CHRISTINA

Aguilera (b. 1980) was one of several US teen pop stars to rise to huge popular acclaim in the late 90s. Of Irish and Ecuadorian descent, Aguilera began performing at school talent shows, before making her first professional appearance at the age of eight on the nationally syndicated *Star Search* show. She joined Disney's *Mickey Mouse Club* at the age of 12, appearing alongside future pop stars JC Chasez and Justin Timberlake of **'N Sync**, and **Britney Spears**.

Aguilera spent two years with the *Mickey Mouse Club* before moving to Japan to record 'All I Wanna Do', a hit duet with local pop star Keizo Nakanishi.

Back in the USA in early 1998, Aguilera recorded 'Reflection' for the soundtrack of Disney's full-length animation *Mulan*. Her rapid ascent to stardom continued when she signed to RCA Records shortly afterwards. 'Genie In A Bottle', a lightweight urban track with an infectious hookline, went to the top of the US charts in July 1999 and ended the year as the biggest-selling US single. Aguilera's self-titled debut entered the US album chart at number 1 in September. A month later 'Genie In A Bottle' entered the UK singles chart at number 1.

Aguilera proved herself a genuine rival for Spears' teen-pop crown when she returned to the top of the US charts in January 2000 with 'What A Girl Wants' and again in October with 'Come On Over Baby (All I Want Is You)'. In a shrewd marketing ploy, she then released a Spanish-language collection of her hits, *Mi Reflejo*, and the seasonal *My Kind Of Christmas*. Aguilera enjoyed a transatlantic chart-topper the following summer with a cover version of LaBelle's 'Lady Marmalade', recorded with **Lil' Kim**, **Mya** and **Pink** for the soundtrack of the movie *Moulin Rouge*.

AIR

Purveyors of delightfully retro electronic space pop, former architect Nicolas Godin (bass, guitar, vocoder, percussion) and mathematician Jean-Benoit Dunckel (keyboards, clavinet, synthesizer) both originate from Versailles, France. They met at college, where Godin joined Dunckel in indie rock band Orange, alongside future producer Alex Gopher. After a period spent concentrating on their respective studies, Dunckel and Godin reunited as Air and began forging a new electronic direction, signing to the Paris-based Source label. They released several singles, including the *Modulor Mix* EP in

November 1995 and the *Casanova 70* EP in August 1996. These early tracks were collected on the *Premiers Symptomes* compilation.

Godin and Dunckel then decamped to an abandoned eighteenth-century chateau outside Paris to record their debut, *Moon Safari*. Produced on an eight-track console, the album juxtaposed lush instrumentals and effortless electro-pop with vocals by Godin and Paris-based American singer Beth Hirsch. The album's retro feel was heightened by Dunckel and Godin's use of mini-Moog and vocoder, and the romantic themes of space travel and stargazing. The duo was subsequently commissioned to compose the original score for Sophie Coppola's acclaimed film adaptation of *The Virgin Suicides*. Their sophomore studio album, *10,000 Hz Legend*, was recorded in Paris and Los Angeles. Released in May 20001, the album's restless experimentalism drew a mixed response from critics still enamoured by the lush textures of *Moon Safari*.

ALABAMA

Statistically the biggest US country rock act of the 80s and 90s, Alabama were originally formed in 1969 as Young Country by cousins Randy Owen (b. 1949; vocals, guitar) and Teddy Gentry (b. 1952; bass, vocals), with Jeff Cook (b. 1949; vocals, guitar). Changing their name to Wild Country, they recorded for several small labels in the 70s before adopting the moniker Alabama in 1977. A sequence of hits followed the success of 'I Wanna Be With You Tonight', at which point they recruited drummer Mark Herndon (b. 1955).

After 1980's 'My Home's In Alabama' reached the US Country Top 20 they signed to RCA Records. Country chart-toppers followed with 'Tennessee River', 'Why Lady Why' and 'Feels So Right'; later singles, such as 'Love In The First Degree', acquired crossover pop success. Of their five platinum albums during the 80s, the most successful was *40 Hour Week*.

In 1995, Alabama celebrated its 15th anniversary with sales of over 50 million albums, and the Academy Of Country Music's Artist Of The Decade Award for their work in the 80s. 'Sad Lookin' Moon' in February 1997 took their total of country number 1s to a remarkable 41, as their worldwide record sales topped 58 million. Despite an increasingly formulaic sound, they remain a major live attraction.

ALBION COUNTRY BAND

This volatile traditional UK folk ensemble was founded in 1972 by defecting Steeleye Span bassist Ashley Hutchings (b. 1945). Royston Wood (b. 1935; vocals), American Sue Draheim (b. 1949; fiddle) and Steve Ashley (b. 1946; guitar) completed the new venture, alongside Simon Nicol (b. 1950; guitar) and Dave Mattacks (b. 1948; drums), two of Hutchings' former colleagues from **Fairport Convention**. The early line-up disintegrated six months after its inception and a caretaker unit, which included **Richard Thompson**, fulfilled outstanding obligations. Hutchings, Nicol and new drummer Roger Swallow then pieced together a second Country Band with folk acolytes **Martin Carthy** (b. 1940), Sue Harris (b. 1949) and John Kirkpatrick (b. 1947). Their lone album, *Battle Of The Field*, recorded in 1973, was withheld until 1976, and only issued following public demand. Hutchings, Nicol and Mattacks were reunited in the Etchingham Steam Band, a part-time outfit formed to support Shirley Collins. The group subsequently evolved into the Albion Dance Band. *Lark Rise To Candleford* was a typical project, an adaptation of Flora Thompson's novel set to music.

The group entered the 80s as the Albion Band, retaining a mixture of traditional and original material. Musicians continued to arrive and depart with alarming regularity, and by the end of the 80s the personnel tally easily exceeded one hundred. On one occasion in 1980, the entire band quit *en masse*, forming the critically acclaimed Home Service. Throughout, Ashley Hutchings has remained at the helm, ensuring the dogged individuality of this legendary band is carried on into the new millennium.

ALEXANDER, ARTHUR

US-born Alexander's (b. 1940, d. 1993) recordings have been covered extensively. 'Anna (Go To Him)', a US R&B Top 10 hit, and 'You Better Move On' were covered by the **Beatles** and the **Rolling Stones** respectively, while 'A Shot Of Rhythm And Blues' became an essential British beat staple (notably by **Johnny Kidd**). Alexander's subsequent work was produced in Nashville, where his poppier perceptions undermined the edge of his earlier work. Later singles included 'Go Home Girl' and the haunting 'Soldier Of Love'. A pop hit was secured with 'Every Day I Have To Cry Some' (1975), but success remained short-lived.

For many years Alexander worked as a bus driver, but began to perform again in 1993 – *Lonely Just Like Me* was his first album in 21 years. He signed a new recording and publishing contract in May 1993, suffering the cruelest fate when he collapsed and died the following month, three days after performing in Nashville with his new band.

ALICE COOPER

US star Alice Cooper (b. Vincent Damon Furnier, 1948) became known as the 'master of shock rock' during the 70s and remains a popular hard-rock artist into the new millennium. Furnier, who grew up in Phoenix, Arizona, began playing with local groups in the mid-60s. Teaming up with Michael Bruce (b. 1948; guitar), Dennis Dunaway (b. 1948; bass), Glen Buxton (b. 1947, d. 1997; guitar) and Neal Smith (b. 1947; drums), Furnier invented an androgynous, outrageously attired character to attract attention and the band played deliberately abrasive rock music with the intention of shocking and even alienating those attending their concerts. In 1969, the Alice Cooper Band found a kindred spirit in **Frank Zappa**, who signed them to his new Straight Records label. They recorded two albums, *Pretties For You* and *Easy Action*, before switching to Warner Brothers Records in 1970. By that time Cooper had taken on more extreme tactics in his live performances, using a guillotine and electric chair as stage props and a live snake as part of his wardrobe.

As the band and its singer built a reputation as a bizarre live act, their records began to sell in greater quantities. In 1971 'Eighteen' reached US number 21; in 1972, the rebellious 'School's Out' made the US Top 10 and UK number 1. A streak of bestselling albums followed: the transatlantic number 1 *Billion Dollar Babies*, then *Muscle Of Love*, *Alice Cooper's Greatest Hits* and *Welcome To My Nightmare*, all of which reached the US Top 10. The last was his first true solo album as the band fractured and Furnier officially adopted the Alice Cooper name as his own. The late 70s saw the singer becoming a Hollywood celebrity and appearing in movies such as *Sextette* and *Sgt. Pepper's Lonely Hearts Club Band*. In 1978, Cooper admitted chronic alcoholism and underwent treatment; *From The Inside*, with songs co-written by Bernie Taupin, reflected on the experience. His band continued touring, and between 1979 and 1982 featured ex-**Iron Butterfly** lead guitarist Mike Pinera (b. 1948).

Cooper continued recording into the early 80s with diminishing results. In 1986, after a four-year recording absence, he signed to MCA Records, but neither of his two albums for that label reached the US charts. In 1989, *Trash*, his first album for Epic Records, returned him to the Top 40 and yielded the transatlantic hit single 'Poison'. *Hey Stoopid* found him accompanied by **Joe Satriani**, Steve Vai and Slash and Axl Rose from **Guns N'Roses**, while his 90s tours saw Cooper drawing a new, younger audience who considered him a heavy metal pioneer. This impression was immortalized by Cooper's memorable cameo appearance in *Wayne's World*. Cooper has maintained a healthy touring schedule, while his first studio album of the new millennium, *Brutal Planet*, was considered by many to be his best collection of material since the late 80s.

ALICE IN CHAINS

Formed in 1987 in Seattle, USA, by Layne Staley (b. 1967, d. 2002; vocals) and Jerry Cantrell (b. 1966; guitar, vocals) with Mike Starr (bass) and Sean

Kinney (b. 1966; drums). Alice In Chains developed a sound which mixed **Black Sabbath**-style riffing with Staley and Cantrell's unconventional vocal arrangements and strong songwriting. After dispensing with their early moniker, Fuck, the band became Alice In Chains, a name coined by Staley for 'a parody heavy metal band that dressed in drag'.

Their 1990 debut, *Facelift*, received excellent reviews but took off slowly. Boosted by US touring, 'Man In The Box' became an MTV favourite, and the album went gold in 1991. The band then released the gentler *Sap* EP. *Dirt* was a dark, cathartic work with many personal lyrics, including 'Rooster' (about Cantrell's father's Vietnam War experience), which became a live centrepiece, but critical attention focused on a sequence of songs referring to Staley's past heroin problems. Despite the controversy, *Dirt* was the critics' album of the year in many metal magazines, entering the US charts at number 6. 'Would?' became a hit, boosted by the band's appearance playing the song in the movie *Singles*.

Michael Inez (b. 1966) replaced Starr as the band embarked on a sell-out tour of Europe and the USA. In 1994, *Jar Of Flies* became the first EP to top the US album charts. Staley put together a side-project, Mad Season, with Pearl Jam's Mike McCready and Screaming Trees' Barrett Martin, amid rumours that Alice In Chains had split. In 1994, gigs, including Woodstock II were cancelled, due to Staley's 'health problems'. The band managed a further album and performed for MTV on an *Unplugged* special, but Cantrell's solo debut (*Boggy Depot*) and the release of three compilation sets

raised further doubts about the future of Alice In Chains. Tragically, Staley was found dead on 19 April 2002 of a heroin overdose.

ALIEN ANT FARM

This nu-metal outfit was formed in Riverside, California, USA in 1996 by Dryden Mitchell (vocals), Terry Corso (guitar), Tye Zamora (bass) and Mike Cosgrove (drums). Their strange moniker arises from Corso's concept of humanity being watched by aliens like a child watching his ant farm. Their cheekily named debut *Greatest Hits*, was released on the band's own Chick Music imprint in 1999. A recording contract with **Papa Roach**'s New Noize imprint followed, giving Alien Ant Farm all the benefits of the label's distribution deal with the major DreamWorks. *ANThology*, released in March 2001, received good reviews and made inroads into the US national chart. The second single from the album, a quirky cover version of **Michael Jackson**'s 'Smooth Criminal', with an excellent promotional video pastiching the singer's physical mannerisms, helped push the album into the upper regions of the *Billboard* 200 album chart.

ALL ABOUT EVE

Originally called the Swarm, All About Eve emerged on the late-80s UK gothic scene. Julianne Regan (vocals; ex-Gene Loves Jezebel) and Tim Bricheno (b. 1963; guitar, ex-Aemotti Crii), provided much of the band's material. After various early personnel changes, the rhythm section was stabilized with Andy Cousin (bass; ex-Aemotti Crii) and Mark Price (drums). Given encouragement by rising stars **The Mission** (for whom Regan had sung backing vocals), All About Eve developed a solid following. Regan's predilection for white-witchcraft, mysticism and tarot cards provided a taste of the exotic with a mixture of goth rock and 70s folk. Early singles 'Our Summer' and 'Flowers In Our Hair' achieved great success in the UK independent charts.

After signing to Mercury Records, they secured a Top 10 hit with 'Martha's Harbour' in July 1988. Both the band's albums reached the UK Top 10, but in 1990 a rift between Bricheno and the other band members resulted in his departure to join the **Sisters Of Mercy**. The recruitment of **Church** guitarist Marty Willson-Piper on a part-time basis revitalized the band's drive, although the subsequent album, *Touched By Jesus*, enjoyed only middling success. A stormy dispute with Phonogram Records saw All About Eve leave the label in 1991 and sign to MCA. After releasing *Ultraviolet*, the band split, with Cousin joining the Mission. Regan formed Mice in 1995, recruiting Cousin, Price and Willson-Piper among others.

To the delight of their diehard fans, Regan, Willson-Piper and Cousin embarked on an impromptu acoustic tour as All About Eve in early 2000. The highlights were captured on the two volumes of *Fairy Light Nights*.

ALL SAINTS

Initially promoted as a sassier version of the **Spice Girls**, this London, England-based all-female vocal group was formed as a duo in 1993 by Shaznay Lewis (b. 1975) and Melanie Blatt (b. 1975). Taking their name from the street in which their London recording studio was based, they signed with ZTT Records and released one unsuccessful single, 'If You Wanna Party'. By 1995

they had been joined by Canadian-born sisters Nicole Marie (b. 1974) and Natalie Jane Appleton (b. 1973). They were eventually signed by London Records in November 1996. Their debut, 'I Know Where It's At', was released in August 1997. Recorded in Washington and London, the predominantly mid-paced collection of songs that comprised their debut album held few surprises and betrayed little sign of invention beyond the central principle of cloning a successful formula. The single 'Never Ever' was, however, hugely successful reaching UK number 1; it also climbed to number 4 in the US later in the same year. The follow-up single, pairing cover versions of the **Red Hot Chili Peppers**' 'Under The Bridge' and LaBelle's 'Lady Marmalade', was another UK chart-topper in May 1998. They achieved a third consecutive UK number 1 in September 1998 with 'Booty Call'.

Although they were rarely out of the media spotlight, the quartet's new single 'Pure Shores', produced by **William Orbit** and featured on the soundtrack of the Leonardo DiCaprio movie *The Beach*, didn't appear until February 2000. While Lewis was busy in the recording studio writing material for their new album, the three other band members made their acting debut in David A. Stewart's *Honest*. Orbit's distinctive sound was again in evidence on *Saints & Sinners*, which was premiered by the excellent UK chart-topping single 'Black Coffee'.

Following the cancellation of their 2001 UK tour and ongoing disputes between the four members, it was announced that All Saints had been put 'on ice' for the immediate future. Chief songwriter Lewis embarked on solo work, while Blatt appeared on the Artful Dodger's UK hit single 'Twentyfourseven'.

ALLISON, LUTHER

The fourteenth of 15 children, US guitarist Allison (b. 1939, d. 1997) spent his youth working with his siblings in the local cotton fields. He also sang with a family gospel group before moving to Chicago in 1951. Around 1957, he formed his own band with his brother Grant. They gigged occasionally under the name of the Rolling Stones and later the Four Jivers. After a year, the group disbanded and Allison went on to work with Jimmy Dawkins, Magic Slim, Magic Sam, **Muddy Waters**, **Little Richard**, **Freddie King** and others until the mid-60s.

In 1967, he recorded a session for Bill Lindemann, later issued by the collector label Delmark. He toured California, recording as accompanist to Sunnyland Slim and Shakey Jake Harris. He made his first album under his own name in 1969. In the early 70s, he recorded for Motown Records' subsidiary label, Gordy, and from the late 70s spent much of his time in France, living and working for a large and faithful following. He recorded for many labels, usually funk or **Jimi Hendrix**- and **Rolling Stones**-influenced rock.

In the late 80s Allison recorded two well-received albums, *Serious* and *Soul Fixin' Man*. By the mid-90s he was reaching a peak, winning W. C. Handy awards and experiencing financial success with *Blue Streak*. This Indian summer of his career was cruelly cut short when, in July 1997, he was diagnosed as having lung cancer; he died just over a month later. His son, Bernard Allison, released his debut album shortly before his father's death.

ALLMAN BROTHERS BAND

Formed in Georgia, USA, in 1969 by guitarist Duane Allman (b. Howard Duane Allman, 1946, d. 1971), the band included his brother Gregg (b. 1947; keyboards, vocals), 'Dickie' Betts (b. Forrest Richard Betts, 1943; guitar), Raymond Berry Oakley (b. 1948, d. 1972; bass), Butch Trucks (b. Claude Hudson Trucks Jnr; drums) and Jai 'Jaimoe' Johnny Johanson (b. John Lee Johnson, 1944; drums). Duane and Gregg Allman were members of pop/soul ensemble Hour Glass, which broke up when demo tapes for a projected third album were rejected by their record company. Duane then found employment at the Fame studio, where he participated in several sessions, for **Aretha**

Franklin, **Wilson Pickett** and **King Curtis**, prior to instigating this new sextet. The band were soon established as a popular live attraction. Their first two albums, *The Allman Brothers Band* and *Idlewild South*, were marked by strong blues-based roots, while a two-album set, *Live At The Fillmore East*, showcased the band's emotional fire. The set brought the band to the brink of stardom, while Duane's reputation as an outstanding slide guitarist was enhanced by his contribution to **Derek And The Dominos'** *Layla And Other Assorted Love Songs*.

Tragedy struck on 29 October 1971, when Duane was killed in a motorcycle accident. The remaining members completed *Eat A Peach*, which consisted of live and studio material, before embarking on a mellower direction with the US chart-topper *Brothers And Sisters*. A second pianist, Chuck Leavell (b. 1950), was added to the line-up, but just as the band recovered its momentum, Berry Oakley was killed in a road accident, on 11 November 1972. Gregg Allman (who later married **Cher**, twice) and Betts embarked on solo careers while Leavell, Johanson and new bassist Lamar Williams (b. 1947, d. 1983) formed Sea Level. After a notorious drugs trial in 1976, in which Gregg testified against a former road manager, the other members vowed never to work with the vocalist again, but a reconstituted 1978 line-up included Allman, Betts and Trucks. *Enlightened Rogues* was a commercial success, but subsequent albums fared less well and in 1982 the Allman Brothers Band split for a second time.

In 1989, a new line-up – Gregg Allman, Betts, Trucks, Warren Haynes (guitar, vocals), Douglas Allen Woody (b. 1956, d. 2000; bass) and Johnny Neel (keyboards) – spawned the credible **Seven Turns**. Neel left the band and the remaining sextet made *Shades Of Two Worlds*. Mark Quinones (percussion) joined for *An Evening With The Allman Brothers Band* in 1992. Their 1994 album, *Where It All Begins*, was recorded live in the studio, with production by Allman Brothers Band veteran Tom Dowd. Further studio work followed, but it is as a touring unit that the band retains its remarkable popularity. Woody and Haynes left in April 1997 to join Gov't Mule. New members Derek Trucks (guitar) and Oteil Burbridge (bass) were subsequently added to the line-up. Betts was sacked in early 2000 and released a solo album, *Let's Get Together*, the following year.

ALMOND, MARC

Following the demise of **Soft Cell** and their adventurous offshoots Marc And The Mambas and Marc And The Willing Sinners, Almond (b. Peter Marc Almond, 1956) embarked on a solo career with 1984's *Vermin In Ermine*. *Stories Of Johnny*, released the following year, was superior and displayed Almond's undoubted power as a torch singer. Prior to the album's release, he reached the UK Top 5 in a disco-inspired duet with **Bronski Beat** entitled 'I Feel Love (Medley)'. The single combined two **Donna Summer** hits ('I Feel Love' and 'Love To Love You Baby') with snatches of John Leyton's 'Johnny Remember Me', all sung in high register by fellow vocalist Jimmy Somerville. The controversial *Mother Fist And Her Five Daughters* did little to enhance Almond's career, which seemed commercially in the descendent by the time of the singles compilation.

Almond's old commercial sense was emphasized by the opportune revival of 'Something's Gotten Hold Of My Heart' with **Gene Pitney**. This melodramatic single was sufficient to provide both artists with their first number 1s as soloists. Almond returned in 1990 with a cover album of **Jacques Brel** songs and *Enchanted*, which featured the singer's usual flamboyant style complemented by flourishes of flamenco guitar and violin. In 1992, Almond reached the UK Top 5 with a revival of David McWilliams' 'The Days Of Pearly Spencer'. The same year he staged an extravagant comeback concert at the Royal Albert Hall, documented on *12 Years Of Tears*. In contrast, *Absinthe: The French Album* was a strikingly uncommercial set that saw the singer performing Baudelaire and Rimbaud poems.

Almond returned to the cold electronic sounds of the 80s with 1996's *Fantastic Star* and 1999's *Open All Night*, the latter released on his own Blue Star

label. His profile was further raised in the new millennium by news of a Soft Cell reunion, and the release of the excellent *Stranger Things*. This collaboration with Icelandic producer Johann Johannson was widely regarded to be the singer's strongest release since *Absinthe*.

ALTERED IMAGES

Formed in 1979, this Scottish pop ensemble featured Clare Grogan (b. 1962; vocals), Johnny McElhone (b. 1963; bass), Tony McDaid (guitar) and Michael 'Tich' Anderson (drums). Before their recorded debut, Grogan landed a starring role in the acclaimed film *Gregory's Girl*. In 1980, Altered Images toured with **Siouxsie And The Banshees** and subsequently employed bass player Steve Severin as producer. Another champion of their work was influential UK disc jockey John Peel. Their BBC radio sessions secured a contract with Epic Records, and two unsuccessful singles followed – the early 80s indie classic 'Dead Pop Stars' and 'A Day's Wait'. With the addition of guitarist Jim McInven, the band completed their debut, *Happy Birthday*, in 1981. The infectious title track, produced by Martin Rushent, soared to UK number 2, establishing the elfin Grogan as a punkish Shirley Temple. 'I Could Be Happy' and 'See Those Eyes' were also hits, but the band's second album, *Pinky Blue*, was badly received.

Grogan took on a more sophisticated, adult image for 1983's *Bite*. Anderson and McInven were replaced by Stephen Lironi (guitar, drums), while new producers Tony Visconti and Mike Chapman were brought in to oversee the album. The experiment brought another Top 10 hit, 'Don't Talk To Me About Love', but the group disbanded shortly afterwards. Grogan pursued an acting career (notably on UK television in *Red Dwarf* and *EastEnders*, and more recently as an MTV presenter), recorded an unreleased solo album, and reappeared fronting new group Universal Love School. McElhone went on to play with Hipsway and **Texas**.

AMEN

This California, USA-based outfit has transformed their underground status into mainstream success by ladling their high-energy take on nu-metal with venomous helpings of raw punk attitude. The band was formed in Los Angeles in 1994 by Casey Chaos (vocals) and Paul Fig (guitar). A veteran of the Californian scene, Chaos had enjoyed a brief spell with Christian Death and recorded with his own hardcore outfit, Disorderly Conduct. Drummer Shannon Larkin (ex-**Ugly Kid Joe**) and two former members of Snot, guitarist Sonny Mayo and John 'Tumor' Fahnestock, completed the line-up that recorded Amen's independent-label debut, *Slave*.

Three years later the band achieved their major breakthrough when their second album was overseen by leading nu-metal producer Ross Robinson, and marketed through the partnership between his I Am imprint and Roadrunner Records. Chaos allegedly shed real blood during recording sessions in an attempt to recreate the near-anarchic energy of the band's live shows. Relations with Roadrunner fell apart after several violent incidents, and not long afterwards the band found themselves the beneficiaries of I Am's new distribution contract with Virgin Records. Robinson assumed the production reins once more for the recording of the band's wonderfully titled sophomore set *We Have Come For Your Parents*, released in October 2000. Fig left the band the following November.

AMEN CORNER

Formed in Cardiff, Wales, this R&B-styled septet comprised Andy Fairweather-Low (b. 1950; vocals), Derek 'Blue Weaver' (b. 1949; organ), Neil Jones (b. 1949; guitar), Clive Taylor (b. 1949; bass), Alan Jones (b. 1947; baritone saxophone), Mike Smith (b. 1947; tenor saxophone) and Dennis Byron (b. 1949; drums). After reaching the UK Top 20 with 'Gin House Blues' (1967), the band swiftly ploughed more commercial ground with 'World Of Broken Hearts', 'Bend Me, Shape Me' and 'High In The Sky'. They subsequently moved from Decca Records to Andrew Loog Oldham's Immediate Records label and enjoyed their only UK number 1 with '(If Paradise Is) Half As Nice' in 1969. Following one final UK Top 5 hit, 'Hello Suzie', they split. Fairweather-Low, Blue Weaver, Byron and Taylor subsequently formed Fairweather, before the singer embarked on a solo career and Weaver joined the **Strawbs**. The brass section became Judas Jump.

AMERICA

Formed in the late 60s by the offspring of American service personnel stationed in the UK, America comprised Dewey Bunnell (b. 1951, England), Dan Peek (b. 1950, USA) and Gerry Beckley (b. 1952, USA). Heavily influenced by **Crosby, Stills And Nash**, the trio employed similarly strong counter-harmonies backed by acoustic guitar. Their first single, 'A Horse With No Name', proved a massive UK hit and, with backing by Warner Brothers Records and management by former UK underground disc jockey Jeff Dexter, the single topped the US charts. The debut album, *America*, fitted perfectly into the soft-rock style of the period and paved the way for a series of further hits including 'I Need You', 'Ventura Highway', 'Tin Man' and 'Lonely People'. David Geffen eventually took over the running of their affairs. With former **Beatles** producer **George Martin**, the trio returned to US number 1 in 1975 with the melodic 'Sister Golden Hair'.

In 1977, Peek left to concentrate on more spiritual material, in the wake of his conversion to Christianity. America continued as a duo, and returned to form in 1982 with the Russ Ballard-produced *View From The Ground*, which included the US Top 10 hit 'You Can Do Magic'. The duo's subsequent efforts no doubt please their existing fans, but have failed to make any new converts to what essentially remains dated, mid-70s west-coast rock.

AMERICAN MUSIC CLUB

One of their country's most undervalued bands, San Francisco's American Music Club was formed by **Mark Eitzel** (b. 1959; vocals, guitar), with Danny Pearson (b. 1959; bass), Tim Mooney (b. 1958; drums), Vudi (b. Mark Pankler, 1952; guitar) and occasionally Bruce Kaphan (b. 1955; steel guitar). From his earliest appearances, Eitzel's onstage demeanour rivalled the extravagances of **Iggy Pop**. In the early days he was also a fractious heavy drinker, until the day American Music Club signed to a major label after several acclaimed independent albums. Before this, he had left the band twice, once after the tour to support 1987's *Engine*, and once after *Everclear*. He also temporarily fronted Toiling Midgets. Following *Everclear*, in 1991, *Rolling Stone* magazine elected Eitzel their Songwriter Of The Year.

Mercury was the band's debut for a major record label – song titles such as 'What Godzilla Said To God When His Name Wasn't Found In The Book Of Life' illustrated that Eitzel's peculiar lyrical scenarios were still intact. *San Francisco* brought further acclaim but little commercial reward, and Eitzel elected to go solo in 1995. The other members later recorded as Clodhopper.

AMON DÜÜL II

This inventive act evolved out of a commune based in Munich, Germany. The collective split into two factions in 1968, following an appearance at the Essen Song Days Festival where they supported the Mothers Of Invention and the Fugs. The political wing, known as Amon Düül, did record four albums, but Amon Düül II was recognized as the musical faction. Renate Knaup-Krötenschwanz (vocals, percussion), John Weinzierl (guitar, bass), Falk Rogner (organ), Dave Anderson (bass), Dieter Serfas (drums), Peter Leopold (drums) and Shrat (percussion) completed *Phallus Dei* in 1969 with the aid of Christian Burchard (vibes) and Holger Trulzsh (percussion). A double set, *Yeti*, proved more popular, combining space-rock with free-form styles. Serfas, Shrat and Anderson quit (the latter joined Hawkwind before forming Amon Din); Lothar Meid from jazz-rock collective Utopia, left and rejoined Amon Düül II on several occasions, while producer Olaf Kubler often augmented live performances on saxophone.

Chris Karrer (guitar, violin) joined Weinzierl and Renate on another two-album package, *Dance Of The Lemmings*, which featured shorter pieces linked together into suites. The melodic *Carnival In Babylon* was succeeded by *Wolf City*. By that point Amon Düül II were at the vanguard of German rock, alongside **Can, Faust** and **Tangerine Dream**. *Vive La Trance* was a marked disappointment and the band's tenure at United Artists Records ended with the budget-priced *Live In London*, recorded during their 1972 tour. *Lemmingmania* compiled various singles recorded between 1970 and 1975. *Hijack* and *Made In Germany* showed a band of dwindling power and four members, including Renate and Rogner, left on the latter's release. Weinzierl quit the line-up after *Almost Alive*, leaving Karrer to lead the ensemble through 1978's *Only Human*.

Amon Düül II was officially dissolved in 1980, although within a year several founding musicians regrouped for the disappointing *Vortex*. Weinzierl kept the name upon moving to Wales where, with Dave Anderson, he completed *Hawk Meets Penguin* and *Meetings With Menmachines*, the latter credited to Amon Düül (UK). Karrer, Renate, Weinzierl and Leopold reunited in 1989 to play at Robert Calvert's memorial concert in London, and again, in 1992, in order to protect the rights to the Amon Düül II name. That secured, they recommenced recording with Lothar Meid. Recent judicious live material from their golden era is a timely reminder of the band at the peak of its creative powers.

AMOS, TORI

Amos (b. Myra Ellen Amos, 1963) was enrolled in Baltimore's Peabody Institute as a five-year-old prodigy. In 1980, aged 17, she released (as Ellen Amos) 'Baltimore'/'Walking With You' on the MEA label (named after her own initials). She

favoured cover versions such as **Joni Mitchell**'s 'A Case Of You', Billie Holiday's 'Strange Fruit' and **Bill Withers**' 'Ain't No Sunshine', later staples of her live set. Amos then adopted the first name Tori, after a remark that she didn't 'look much like an Ellen, more like a Tori'.

Amos then moved to front rock band Y Kant Tori Read, but the production and material did her few favours. Amos lowered her profile for a while after this undignified release, though she did appear on albums by **Al Stewart** and Stan Ridgway. She also persevered in writing her own songs, and eventually a tape reached Atlantic Records' co-chairman, Doug Morris. Deciding that her sound would not be to the taste of the average American FM-listener, he sent Amos to the UK, and East West Records.

Amos moved to London in 1991 and played small-scale gigs around the capital. Her 'debut' EP, *Me And A Gun* (1991), tackled the emotive topic of her rape by an armed 'fan' as she drove him home after a gig. An acclaimed debut album, *Little Earthquakes*, followed in 1992. Much of the following year was spent writing and recording a second album with co-producer Eric Rosse. The result, *Under The Pink*, included a guest appearance from Trent Reznor (**Nine Inch Nails**). 'Cornflake Girl' reached UK number 4 in January 1994, and Amos was heralded in the press, alongside Polly Harvey (**PJ Harvey**) and **Björk**, as part of a new wave of intelligent, literate female songwriters. This was cemented with the release of the sexually charged *Boys For Pele*, although it was Armand Van Helden's remix of 'Professional Widow' which provided Amos with a UK number 1 hit.

Several of the songs on the follow-up, *From The Choirgirl Hotel*, were informed by Amos's recent miscarriage. The album proved to be her most mature and musically adventurous to date, Amos recording with a full band for the first time. A prolific songwriting burst led to the release of the double *To Venus And Back* the following year. The eclectic *Strange Little Girls* was a bold project on which Amos attempted some interesting cover versions, including the **Beatles**' 'Happiness Is A Warm Gun', the **Stranglers** 'Strange Little Girl' and **Eminem**'s '97 Bonnie & Clyde'.

ANASTACIA

(b. Anastacia Newkirk, 1973) This Los Angeles, California, USA-based soul diva was raised in Chicago but relocated to New York as a teenager. She enrolled at Manhattan's Professional Children's School at the age of 14, but before too long was immersing herself in the city's dance music scene at Club 1018. Her first claim to fame was as a dancer for hire, making regular appearances on MTV's *Club MTV* and featuring in a couple of videos for urban duo **Salt-N-Pepa**. A frustrating spell as a session vocalist followed, before an appearance on the MTV talent show *The Cut* brought her to the attention of several major labels. A recording contract with the Epic Records

subsidiary *Daylight* followed in March 1999. The singer collaborated with leading American producer/writers on her debut *Not That Kind*, but the album's highly commercial blend of soul, dance and pop proved more popular in Europe than her homeland. Both 'I'm Outta Love' and the title track became huge club and pop hits, with particular attention being paid to the singer's remarkably powerful vocals, which are reminiscent of **Chaka Khan** and **Tina Turner** at their peak. *Freak Of Nature* followed in 2001.

AND YOU WILL KNOW US BY THE TRAIL OF DEAD

Sporting a cumbersome but entirely appropriate moniker, this Austin, Texas, USA-based noise-rock outfit has gained notoriety for its chaotic live shows while pursuing sonic perfection on their studio recordings. Multi-instrumentalists Jason Reece (guitar, drums, vocals) and Conrad Keely (guitar, drums, vocals) first met as high-school students in Oahu, Hawaii. After a short spell in Olympia, Washington, the duo relocated to Austin, Texas, where they joined up with Kevin Allen (guitar) and Neil Busch (bass, samples). After several cassette-only releases, the quartet signed a recording contract with King Coffey's Trance Syndicate Records label and recorded 1998's self-titled debut. Critical comparisons to **Sister**-era **Sonic Youth** and hardcore legends **Fugazi** were pretty close to the mark, but despite all its *Sturm und Drang* the album did lack some of the band's dramatic live energy. Following the closure of Trance Syndicate, the quartet was picked up by leading independent label Merge Records for Madonna before signing a major-label deal with Interscope Records. They debuted for the label in 2002 with *Source Tags & Codes*.

ANDERSON, LAURIE

A product of New York's avant-garde art scene, Anderson (b. Laura Phillips Anderson, 1950) eschewed her initial work as a sculptor in favour of performing. *The Life And Times Of Josef Stalin*, which premiered at Brooklyn's Academy of Music in 1973, was a 12-hour epic containing many of the audio-visual elements the artist brought to her music. *Big Science* included the eight-minute vocoder-laden 'O Superman' (1981), a cult hit in Europe that reached UK number 2. *Mr. Heartbreak* featured contributions from **Peter Gabriel** and writer William Burroughs, while her sprawling five-album set, *United States*, chronicled an ambitious, seven-hour show. *Home Of The Brave* resumed the less radical path of her second album and was co-produced by former **Chic** guitarist Nile Rodgers. The guests on 1994's *Bright Red* included **Lou Reed**, with whom Anderson would subsequently begin a personal relationship. *The Ugly One With The Jewels* captured a live performance of Anderson reading from her book *Stories From The Nerve Bible*, which examines her experience of travelling in the Third World. Her next project was *Songs And Stories From Moby Dick*, an ambitious show based on Herman Melville's famous novel. *Life On A String*, Anderson's first studio album in over six years, was released in autumn 2001.

ANIMALS

Formed in Newcastle-upon-Tyne, England, in 1963, when vocalist Eric Burdon (b. 1941), joined local R&B band the Alan Price Combo, the Animals comprised **Alan Price** (b. 1941; piano), Hilton Valentine (b. 1943; guitar), John Steel (b. 1941; drums) and Chas Chandler (b. Bryan James Chandler, 1938, d. 1996; bass). Their raucous and exciting stage act made them an integral part of the fast-burgeoning London club scene. Produced by Mickie Most, they debuted with 'Baby Let Me Take You Home', followed by their version of Josh White's 'The House Of The Rising Sun', a song about a New Orleans brothel. Despite Columbia Records' fears the track was too long (at

four-and-a-half minutes), it leapt to the top of the worldwide charts. The combination of Valentine's simplistic guitar introduction and Price's shrill organ complemented Burdon's remarkably mature and bloodcurdling vocal.

Over the next two years the Animals had seven further transatlantic hits. Their choice of material was exemplary and many of their hits contained thought-provoking lyrics, from the angst-ridden 'I'm Crying' to the frustration and urban despair of Cynthia Weil and Barry Mann's 'We Gotta Get Out Of This Place'. During this time Price departed (reportedly suffering from a fear of flying), and was replaced by Dave Rowberry from the Mike Cotton Sound. Steel left in 1966, replaced by Nashville Teens drummer Barry Jenkins (b. 1944). The new band scored with 'Its My Life' and 'Inside Looking Out'.

By 1967, Burdon and Valentine had become totally immersed in psychedelia, musically and chemically. This alienated them from the rest of the Animals, leading to the band's disintegration. Chandler went on to discover and manage the **Jimi Hendrix** Experience. Burdon, however, retained the name and reappeared as Eric Burdon And The New Animals. Having moved to the USA, they courted the west-coast sound. 'San Franciscan Nights' perfectly echoed the moment, while 'Monterey' eulogized the Monterey Pop Festival of 1967. A number of musicians passed through the New Animals, notably John Weider, Vic Briggs, Danny McCulloch, **Zoot Money** and Andy Summers.

The group eventually disbanded at the end of 1968. The original line-up regrouped twice, in 1977 and 1983, but on both occasions new albums were released to an indifferent public. For the 1983 revival tour it was reported that Valentine had become so rusty on the guitar that a lead guitarist was recruited. Valentine and Steel continue to gig on the pub circuit as Animals II.

ANKA, PAUL

A prolific songwriter and child prodigy, Canadian Anka (b. 1941) became a 50s teen idol. He hit the music scene in 1957 with the self-written 'Diana', which reached UK and US number 1, selling a reported 10 million copies worldwide. This was followed by a series of hits such as 'You Are My Destiny', 'Put Your Head On My Shoulder' and 'Puppy Love'. Pubescent worries and condescending parents were familiar themes and contributed to his success. As the 50s wound to a close, he moved away from teen ballads and planned for a long-term future as a songwriter. His 'It Doesn't Matter Anymore' was a posthumous UK number 1 for **Buddy Holly** in 1959. By this time Anka had begun an acting career, appearing in *Let's Rock* and *Girls Town*, the latter of which included the huge US hit 'Lonely Boy'. In 1962, he starred in the more serious *The Longest Day*.

During the 60s, the former teen star was in demand on the nightclub circuit and a regular at New York's Copacabana and Los Angeles' Coconut Grove. The success of **Donny Osmond**, who took 'Puppy Love' to the top in Britain, kept Anka's early material alive for a new generation. Songwriting success continued, most notably with **Frank Sinatra**'s reading of his lyric to 'My Way' and **Tom Jones**'s million-selling 'She's A Lady'. In the 70s, Anka returned to US number 1 with '(You're) Having My Baby', a risqué duet with his protégé Odia Coates. A spree of hits followed and, in 1983, Anka was back in the charts with 'Hold Me Till The Mornin' Comes'. He continued to play lucrative seasons in Las Vegas and Atlantic City, and toured Europe in 1992 for the first time in 25 years. In 1996 he released his first album aimed at the Latin market, with some of his greatest hits sung in Spanish and duetting with artists such as **Celine Dion**, **Julio Iglesias** and Jose Luis Rodriguez.

ANTHRAX

New York, USA-based thrash-metal outfit was formed in 1981 by Scott 'Not' Ian (b. Scott Rosenfeld, 31 December 1963; rhythm guitar) and Dan Lilker (bass). After a series of personnel changes, Ian and Lilker were joined by Neil Turbin (vocals), Dan Spitz (guitar) and Charlie Benante (drums). Managed by

Johnny Zazula, head of the independent Megaforce Records, the quintet released *Fistful Of Metal* in 1984. Despite its tasteless sleeve, the album garnered fair reviews and was a small but steady seller. Lilker soon left Anthrax to join Nuclear Assault, and was replaced by Frank Bello. His departure was followed by that of Turbin, whose initial replacement, Matt Fallon, was quickly succeeded by Joey Belladonna (b. 1960). This line-up released the *Armed And Dangerous* EP in 1985, and signed to Island Records. *Spreading The Disease* was well received, and the band's European profile was raised considerably by their support slot on **Metallica**'s Damage Inc tour. *Among The Living* established Anthrax in the speed-metal scene, producing UK hits in 'I Am The Law' and 'Indians'. A humorous rap song, 'I'm The Man', became both a hit and a favourite encore. However, *State Of Euphoria* was a patchy affair, with the band suffering a media backlash over their image until live work restored their reputation. *Persistence Of Time*, a dark and relentless work, produced another hit – **Joe Jackson**'s 'Got The Time' – and *Attack Of The Killer B's*, which was essentially a collection of b-sides, became one of Anthrax's most popular albums. This was followed by a hit collaboration with **Public Enemy**, 'Bring The Noise', which led to the bands touring together.

After Anthrax signed a new contract with Elektra Records, Belladonna was fired, replaced by ex-Armored Saint frontman John Bush. *Sound Of White Noise*, released in 1993, was hailed as the band's finest hour, a post-thrash *tour de force* of power metal with bursts of hardcore speed. In 1995, Anthrax began work on *Stomp 442*, an unremittingly brutal collection of hardcore and metal. However, Spitz was ejected from the band just prior to recording. In 1998 Ian guested on **Tricky**'s *Angels With Dirty Faces*, shortly before Anthrax broke a three-year silence with *Volume 8 - The Threat Is Real*.

APHEX TWIN

The Aphex Twin (b. Richard James, 1971) was born in Ireland but raised in Cornwall, England. Over the course of the 90s James, under a variety of names, became one of the leading exponents of 'intelligent techno', 'ambient techno' and other terms invented to describe his brand of electronic music.

He began making music in his early teens, and debuted on the Mighty Force label in 1991 with 'Analogue Bubblebath'. His breakthrough release came on the R&S Records label the following year with 'Didgeridoo'. Much of his work from around this time such as 'Phloam' and 'Isopropanol' was built from incredibly abrasive sounds, but a different style by which he became more widely known emerged on the album *Selected Ambient Works '85 - '92*. The *On* EP (1993) followed his signing to Warp Records on a permanent basis, under a contract which licenses material to Sire Records in the US. *Selected Ambient Works Vol 2* was not as well received as its predecessor, but by this point James was highly sought-after for his remixing skills. His prodigious recorded output included material issued under the pseudonyms Polygon Window on Warp Records (*Surfing On Sine Waves*), Caustic Window ('Joyrex J5', 'Joyrex J4') on Rephlex Records – a label he co-owns – and sundry other releases by Blue Calx, GAK and PCP.

... *I Care Because You Do* and the EPs *Ventolin* and *Donkey Rhubarb* were followed in 1996 by *Richard D. James Album*, on which his usual combination of caustic noises and forlorn textures were set beside more varied rhythms than usual, showing the influence of drum 'n' bass. *The Come To Daddy* and *Windowlicker* EPs moved further into this genre, and were accompanied by controversial and genuinely disquieting videos directed by Chris Cunningham. James also recorded the score to Cunningham's short film *Flex*, before breaking a long album silence in 2001 with the double set, *Drukqs*.

APHRODITE'S CHILD

Formed in Greece during 1967, Aphrodite's Child comprised Egyptian-born Demis Roussos (b. 1946; vocals), alongside Greek musicians Evanghelos Odyssey Papathanassiou (b. 1943; keyboards), Anargyros 'Silver' Koulouris (guitar) and Lucas Sideras (b. 1944; drums). Minus Koulouris, who was obliged to stay in Greece to complete military service, they enjoyed a massive European hit with 1968's haunting ballad 'Rain And Tears'. Further European hits 'I Want To Live' and 'Let Me Love, Let Me Live' followed, although the band only enjoyed cult status in the UK and America. The conceptual *666: The Apocalypse Of John*, released in 1972 and featuring original guitarist Koulouris, marked an artistic peak. Roussos subsequently found international fame as a purveyor of MOR material while Papathanassiou achieved notable solo success as **Vangelis**.

APPLE, FIONA

Growing up in a dysfunctional New York family, Apple (b. Fiona Apple Maggart, 1977) soon discovered the impetus to articulate frustrations, which would eventually result in widespread comparisons to **Alanis Morissette** for her 1996 debut, *Tidal*.

Apple began writing her own material at an early age, as a means of coping with shyness, a lack of confidence about her appearance and her rape ordeal at the age of 12. She found solace in the poetry of Maya Angelou, which she maintains was her biggest influence. Her debut album was the result of songs recorded on a cheap tape recorder in her bedroom, which a friend played to a Columbia Records' executive.

In 1997, Apple won the Best New Artist accolade at the MTV Awards. Her relationship with magician David Blaine raised her media profile, although the couple split up while Apple was recording her sophomore collection. The title of this album runs to an astonishing 90 words, but is commonly abbreviated as *When The Pawn ....* When all the fuss regarding its title had died down, the album proved to be another challenging collection of singer-songwriter material, albeit less accessible than her debut.

ARGENT

When 60s pop group the **Zombies** disintegrated, keyboardist Rod Argent (b. 1945) wasted no time in forming a band that would enable his dexterity as pianist and songwriter to flourish. The unit included Russ Ballard (b. 1945; guitar, vocals), Bob Henrit (b. 1944; drums) and Jim Rodford (b. 1941; bass). Their critically acclaimed debut contained Ballard's 'Liar', a song that became one of their concert regulars. *All Together Now* contained the exhilarating 'Hold Your Head Up' which became a transatlantic Top 5 hit. *In Deep* produced another memorable hit with 'God Gave Rock 'N' Roll To You' (a 1992 hit for **Kiss**). Ballard left in 1974 to pursue a solo career and his place was taken by two new members, John Verity (b. 1949; guitar, bass, vocals) and John Grimaldi (b. 1955; cello, mandolin, violin). Argent disbanded in 1976, with their leader going on to establish himself as a successful record producer and session player.

ARMATRADING, JOAN

The Armatrading family moved from the West Indies to Birmingham, England, in 1958, and Joan (b. 1950) taught herself to play piano and guitar. She met Pam Nestor when they were working in a touring cast of the hippie musical *Hair*. Armatrading and Nestor worked as a songwriting team, before Armatrading released her 1972 debut, *Whatever's For Us*. The album was a

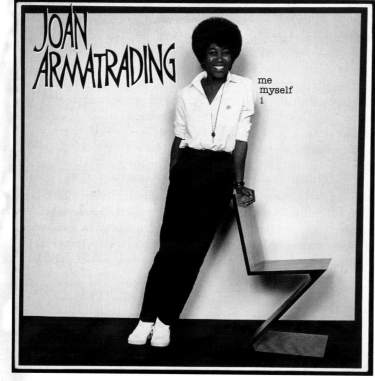

greater critical than commercial success and Armatrading and Nestor dissolved their partnership soon afterwards.

By 1975, Armatrading was signed to A&M Records worldwide. However, *Back To The Night* was unsuccessful and it was not until 1976 and *Joan Armatrading*, the first of four album produced by Glyn Johns, that she hit the limelight. It made the UK Top 20, and includes her only UK Top 10 hit 'Love And Affection'. *Show Some Emotion* became her first album to reach the UK Top 10. In 1979, her partnership with Johns ended with *Steppin' Out*, a live album recorded in the USA, which did not chart on either side of the Atlantic.

Me Myself I was Armatrading's first album to reach the US Top 40. It also returned her to the UK Top 10, and included two minor UK hit singles: the title track and 'All The Way From America'. *Walk Under Ladders* featured the celebrated Jamaican rhythm section of Sly Dunbar and Robbie Shakespeare, while *The Key* included 'Drop The Pilot', her second-biggest UK hit single. Later that year, a 'Best Of' album, *Track Record*, made the UK Top 20. *Sleight Of Hand*, Armatrading's first self-produced album, was her least successful album in commercial terms since her debut, stalling outside the UK Top 30 and charting even lower in the USA. *The Shouting Stage* from 1988 was her most impressive album for some time, but like the follow-up, *Hearts And Flowers*, demonstrated that even though the quality of Armatrading's output was seldom less than exemplary, it rarely achieved its commercial desserts.

By the 90s Armatrading had reached a plateau in her career that was slightly below the top echelon in commercial terms, but enabled her to continue recording with reasonable success. In 1994 she signed to RCA Records after many years with A&M, and released *What's Inside* the following year. Armatrading is to be applauded for remaining unpretentious, and is also in the enviable position of being able to choose her own touring and recording timetable. She has also contributed her services to a number of charitable concerts, such as the Prince's Trust, the 1988 Nelson Mandela Concert and Amnesty International. She was awarded an MBE in October 2001.

ARNOLD, P. P.

Arnold (b. Patricia Arnold, 1946) first came to prominence in 1966 as a member of **Ike And Tina Turner**'s backing group, the Ikettes. Relocating

to England from America, she was signed to Andrew Loog Oldham's Immediate Records label, and was backed on tour by the Nice. Her exceptional version of **Cat Stevens**' 'The First Cut Is The Deepest', was a UK Top 20 hit in 1967 and she enjoyed a second major hit in 1968 with Chip Taylor's 'Angel Of The Morning', arranged by future **Led Zeppelin** bass player John Paul Jones. Highly regarded among her musical peers for the power and clarity of her voice, Arnold's first two albums were produced by Mick Jagger (the second in conjunction with **Steve Marriott**). Arnold repaid Marriott's production work by contributing powerful vocals to the **Small Faces**' hit 'Tin Soldier'.

Never quite hitting the big time, Arnold began increasingly to concentrate on acting, appearing in such musicals as *Catch My Soul*, *Jesus Christ Superstar* and *Starlight Express*. After years of session work, she returned to the UK charts in 1989, fronting the Beatmasters on 'Burn It Up', and in 1998 with retro-popsters **Ocean Colour Scene**. Recent session work includes albums with **Paul Weller** and **Oasis**.

ARRESTED DEVELOPMENT

Rap collective from Atlanta, Georgia, USA, headed by Speech (b. Todd Thomas, 1968). He met DJ Headliner (b. Timothy Barnwell, 1967) while they were students in Atlanta. Speech, then known as DJ Peech, had already formed Disciples Of Lyrical Rebellion, a proto-gangsta outfit, which evolved into Secret Society. They changed the name to Arrested Development and found new members, including Aerle Taree (b. Taree Jones, 1973; vocals), Montsho Eshe (b. Temelca Garther, 1974; dancer), and Rasa Don (b. Donald Jones, 1968; drums). They developed an Afrocentric outlook, and all moved into the same house while maintaining their own daytime jobs. Afterwards, spiritualist Baba Oje (b. 1932), whom Speech had known as a child, was added as the group's symbolic head man.

Cited by many critics as the most significant breakthrough of 1992, 'Tennessee', 'People Everyday' and 'Mr. Wendal' confirmed their commercial status. Their debut album embraced a number of issue-based narratives, 'Mama's Always On The Stage' a feminist treatise, and 'Children Play With Earth', an exhortation for children to get back in touch with the natural world. They released the live album *Unplugged* with a 17-person line-up. A second album, *Zingalamaduni*, Swahili for 'beehive of culture', emerged in 1994, once again extending their audience beyond the hip-hop cognoscenti. As well as introducing new vocalist Nadirah, plus DJ Kwesi Asuo and dancer Ajile, it

saw the departure of Taree who had gone back to college. The album was a commercial failure, and the members of the band went their separate ways at the end of 1995. Speech embarked on a solo career.

ART OF NOISE

Formed in 1983, UK-based pop experimentalists Art Of Noise were the first artists to be signed to Trevor Horn's ZTT Records. The nucleus of the ensemble

was Horn, Anne Dudley (keyboards, arrangements), J. J. Jeczalik (keyboards, production) and Gary Langan (various instruments, production), with input from writer Paul Morley. The band achieved early success as dancefloor favourites in America with the inventive *Into Battle With The Art Of Noise* E.P. At the end of 1984, they reached the UK Top 10 with 'Close (To The Edit)', an inspired mix of hip-hop rhythms and vocal effects. After falling out with ZTT the band moved to China Records, and from then on their career consisted chiefly of working with other artists. A revival of 'Peter Gunn' with **Duane Eddy** hit the UK Top 10, followed by a collaboration with the television cartoon-animated character Max Headroom on 'Paranoimia'. Their finest and most bizarre backing role, however, was reserved for **Tom Jones** who made a Top 10 comeback with a version of **Prince**'s 'Kiss'.

Having enjoyed several years of quirky chart success, Art Of Noise split in 1990, with Dudley going on to enjoy particular success as a soundtrack composer. She reunited with Horn and Morley in the late 90s to record a new Art Of Noise album, *The Seduction Of Claude Debussy*, on which the trio were joined by the experienced Lol Creme.

ASH

Formed in County Down, Northern Ireland, Ash began to make headway in 1994, playing sprightly, youthful punk pop. Rick 'Rock' McMurray (b. 1975; drums), Tim Wheeler (b. 1977; vocals, guitar) and Mark Hamilton (b. 1977; bass) were still at school when their single, 'Jack Names The Planets', was released in a limited edition of 1,000 copies. Their appeal easily translated to an American alternative climate and they landed a recording contract with Reprise Records. In the UK they signed to Infectious Records.

A seven-song mini-album was recorded in Wales in 1994, with **Oasis** producer Owen Morris. 'Girl From Mars' reached UK number 11, followed by 'Angel Interceptor', the Top 10 singles 'Goldfinger' and 'Oh Yeah', and their chart-topping debut album *1977*, its title inspired by the release date of the movie *Star Wars*. It rose straight to UK number 1, although the expected US success was not forthcoming.

The band added a new member in 1997 when guitarist Charlotte Hatherley (b. 1977) joined from Nightnurse. They returned to the UK Top 10 with the title song of the movie *A Life Less Ordinary*. Introduced by the frenetic single 'Jesus Says', 1998's *Nu-Clear Sounds* saw the band move

towards a harder-edged alternative sound. It was another three years before they were finally ready to release a follow-up album, which was premiered by the retro-pop swagger of 'Shining Light'. *Free All Angels* mixed the raw pop charm of the band's debut with the polished production of *Nu-Clear Sounds*.

ASHFORD AND SIMPSON

Nickolas 'Nick' Ashford (b. 1942) and Valerie Simpson (b. 1946) met in the choir of Harlem's White Rock Baptist Church. Having recorded unsuccessfully as a duo, they joined Jo 'Joshie' Armstead, at the Scepter/Wand label where their compositions were recorded by Ronnie Milsap ('Never Had It So Good'), Maxine Brown ('One Step At A Time'), the **Shirelles** and Chuck Jackson. Their 'Let's Go Get Stoned' gave **Ray Charles** a number 1 US R&B hit in 1966. Ashford and Simpson then joined **Holland/Dozier/Holland** at Motown Records where their best-known songs included 'Ain't No Mountain High Enough', 'You're All I Need To Get By', 'Reach Out And Touch Somebody's Hand' and 'Remember Me'. Simpson also began 'ghosting' for Tammi Terrell when the latter became too ill to continue her partnership with **Marvin Gaye**, and she sang on part of the duo's *Easy* album.

In 1971, Simpson embarked on a solo career, but two years later she and Ashford were recording together for Warner Brothers Records. The couple, who married in 1974, enjoyed success with 'It Seems To Hang On' (1978) and 'Found A Cure' (1979), alongside production for Diana Ross (*The Boss*) and **Gladys Knight** (*The Touch*). Their status was further assured in 1984 when 'Solid' became an international hit single. Although their commercial success had dried up by the end of the 80s, Ashford and Simpson remain one of soul's quintessential partnerships. In 1996 they collaborated with poet Maya Angelou on *Been Found*, and received The Founder's Award from ASCAP.

ASIA

A supergroup formed in 1981 by well-known musicians from UK art-rock bands, Asia originally comprised John Wetton (b. 1949; vocals), Geoff Downes (b. 1952; keyboards), Steve Howe (b. 1947; guitar) and Carl Palmer (b. 1950; drums, percussion). Wetton had recently left the progressive band UK; Howe and Downes had just abandoned **Yes** and Palmer had left **Emerson, Lake And Palmer**. The band's self-titled debut album was dismissed by critics, but stayed at the top of the US charts for nine weeks. 'Heat Of The Moment' reached the US Top 5, but while the follow-up album *Alpha* reached the US Top 10 its sales failed to match those of the debut. Wetton was replaced by Greg Lake (b. 1948), another Emerson, Lake And Palmer alumnus. A live television concert from Japan drew over 20 million US viewers in late 1983, but Lake's voice turned out to be unsuited to the band's material, and he was replaced by the returning Wetton. Ongoing personality clashes saw Howe leaving during recording sessions for a third album, with Canadian Mandy Meyer (b. Armand Meyer, 1960) brought in as his replacement. The comparatively low chart position of 1985's *Astra* precipitated the band's dissolution.

A series of abortive reunions culminated in Wetton and Palmer playing a series of European dates with various musicians. They were joined by Downes and Pat Thrall for a series of further dates to promote *Then & Now*, a compilation of new and old material. Wetton and Palmer subsequently moved on to other projects, leaving Downes as the sole remaining founder member. He inaugurated a new era for the band by forming a songwriting partnership with John Payne (bass, vocals). The partnership has continued to release new studio albums, with the creative highpoint being 1996's *Arena*.

ASIAN DUB FOUNDATION

Asian Dub Foundation was formed in 1993 at the Community Music centre in Farringdon, London, England, which had been established by jazz drummer John Stevens. The inaugural sound-system line-up featured two of the centre's teachers, Dr Das (b. Aniruddha Das; bass) and Pandit G (b. John Pandit; DJ/mixer), and one of their students, Master D (b. Deedar Zaman; vocals). Chandrasonic (b. Steve Chandra Savale; guitar), Bubble-E (dancer), and Sun-J (DJ/keyboards) had been added to the line-up by 1995. The same year the band released *Facts & Fictions*, which clearly demonstrated the influence of Jamaican dub on their sound, a combination of ragga, garage punk and traditional Indian ragas. They continued touring, proving especially popular in Europe where their follow-up, *R.A.F.I. (Real Areas For Investigation)*, was released in France. The band enjoyed media interest when **Primal Scream** acknowledged them as the best live act in England, and a major label contract with London Records soon followed. The band's credibility with the indie genre was further enhanced when they collaborated with Primal Scream on the protest single 'Free Saptal Ram'. A variety of television appearances followed to promote the single, 'Change'. Their second album was then remixed and re-released as *Rafi's Revenge*, paying lip service to the Pakistani-born Bollywood singer Mohamed Rafi. The follow-up *Community Music* tore into the complacent heart of contemporary England on tracks such as 'Real Great Britain', 'Crash', and 'Memory War'.

ASLEEP AT THE WHEEL

Ray Benson (b. 1951; guitar, vocals), Christine O'Connell (b. 1953; vocals), Lucky Oceans (b. Reuben Gosfield, 1951; steel guitar), Floyd Domino (piano) and Leroy Preston (rhythm guitar, drums) formed the core of this protean western swing-styled unit. Initially based in West Virginia, they moved to Texas, and a more receptive audience, in the wake of their 1973 debut. They had a US Top 10 single the same year with 'The Letter That Johnny Walker Read' and won a Grammy for their version of Count Basie's 'One O'Clock Jump'. Despite undoubted live appeal and an appearance in the rock movie *Roadie*, the band's anachronistic style has hampered more widespread success. The Bob Wills tribute album released in 1993 featured several guest artists, including **Willie Nelson**, Chet Atkins, **Merle Haggard** and **Dolly Parton**. A similar affair appeared in 1999, with contributions from **Mark Chesnutt**, **Dwight Yoakam** and even the **Manhattan Transfer**.

ASSOCIATES

Scottish vocalist Billy MacKenzie (b. 1957, d. 1997) and Alan Rankine formed the Associates in 1979. After a minor-label recording of **David Bowie**'s 'Boys Keep Swinging', they were signed to Fiction Records, where they released the

critically acclaimed *The Affectionate Punch*. They formed their own Associates label (distributed by Sore/WEA) and enjoyed a UK Top 10 chart breakthrough with 'Party Fears Two'. Further Top 30 hits followed with 'Club Country' and '18 Carat Love Affair'/'Love Hangover', but MacKenzie became involved in other projects and split with Rankine in 1983. The following year MacKenzie reconvened the Associates but, following several very low chart entries, was dropped from WEA in 1988. In 1990, he returned with *Wild And Lonely*, which was stylistically similar to the earlier work. The disappointing follow-up, *Outernational*, was released under MacKenzie's own name.

An abortive reunion with Rankine took place in 1993, after which McKenzie retired from the music business for several years to concentrate on breeding dogs. In 1996, he signed to Nude and demoed new material written in collaboration with Steve Aungle. Following a bout of depression after his mother's death, MacKenzie was found dead at his parents' home in January 1997. Several posthumous releases made available the new recordings he was working on at the time of his death.

ASSOCIATION

This psychedelic pop harmony outfit was formed in the mid-60s by Gary Alexander (lead vocals), Russ Giguere (guitar, vocals), Brian Cole (d. 1972; bass, vocals), Jim Yester (guitar, vocals), Ted Bluechel (drums) and Terry Kirkham (keyboards). After 'Babe I'm Gonna Leave You' and a folk-rock version of **Bob Dylan**'s 'One Two Many Mornings', they found success in 1966 with Tandyn Almer's 'Along Comes Mary' (US Top 10). Terry Kirkham gave them their first US number 1 with 'Cherish', while their debut album, *And Then ... Along Comes*, displayed their harmonic talent. The Association's image was ambiguous: genuinely psychedelic in spirit, they also sang ballads, appeared in smart suits and largely wrote their own material. Another US chart-topper, 'Windy', was followed by a number 2 with 'Never My Love'.

Never candidates for the hip elite, the band failed to attract a devoted following and by the late 60s their sales were dwindling, with 'Everything That Touches You' their last US Top 20 single. Losing ground and major-label status, they released a soundtrack for the movie *Goodbye Columbus* in 1969. Giguere was replaced by keyboard player Richard Thompson the following year. A reasonable 'comeback' album, *Waterbeds In Trinidad* (1972), brought new hope, but the death of founder-member Coles from drug abuse accelerated their eventual move onto the revivalist circuit.

ASTLEY, RICK

Astley (b. Richard Paul Astley, 1966) played with several local bands in his native Lancashire, England, before being discovered by producer Pete Waterman. In 1987 he recorded 'Learning To Live' with Ochi Brown and was part of Rick And Lisa who released 'When You Gonna' for RCA Records. He also sang on the UK number 1 'Let It Be' by Ferry Aid. His solo 'Never Gonna Give You Up' became the biggest UK single of 1987 and his debut album, *Whenever You Need Somebody*, also reached UK number 1, selling over one million copies. When Astley was launched in the USA in 1988, he was an instant success, topping the US charts with his first two singles. Under the wing of his producers **Stock, Aitken And Waterman**, Astley achieved seven UK and four US Top 10 singles.

Despite the fact that he possessed one of the most excellent voices in pop music he became a target for the UK media who saw him as a puppet of his producers. Astley eventually left the winning production and writing team and resurfaced in 1991 with *Free*. 'Cry For Help', which he had co-written and produced, put him back into the Top 10 on both sides of the Atlantic. Astley left RCA in 1993, and very little was heard of him until he signed a new recording contract with Polydor Universal in May 2001. His first studio album in almost ten years, *Keep It Turned On*, was released in Germany in December that year.

ASWAD

Reggae group formed in London, England, in 1975, featuring Guyanan-born Brinsley Forde (vocals, guitar), George 'Ras Levi' Oban (bass), Angus 'Drummie Zeb' Gaye (drums), Jamaican-born Donald 'Benjamin' Griffiths (vocals), and Courtney Hemmings. Taking their name from the Arabic word for black, they attempted a fusion of Rastafari with social issues more pertinent to London. *Aswad*, which highlighted the plight of the immigrant Jamaican, was well received. A more ethnic approach was evident on the superior follow-up, *Hulet*. The departure of Oban, who was replaced by Tony 'Gad' Robinson did little to diminish their fortunes. Forde appeared in the movie *Babylon*, with Aswad's 'Warrior Charge' on its soundtrack.

A brief change of label saw the band record two albums for CBS Records, before returning to Island Records for *Live And Direct*, recorded at London's Notting Hill Carnival in 1982. In 1984, they reached the UK charts with 'Chasing The Breeze' and a cover of the Maytals' '54-46 (That's My Number)'. The excellent *To The Top* was followed by *Distant Thunder*. The latter was a launching-pad for a significant stylistic overhaul and the shift to lightweight funk and soul made them UK chart stars. The album bore a 1988 UK number 1 in 'Don't Turn Around' which, coupled with their riveting live act, made them major stars. 'Shine' reached the UK Top 5 in 1994, while the attendant *Rise And Shine* reached the *Billboard* Reggae Top 10. Further albums received a more muted commercial and critical response. Nevertheless, Aswad remain one of the UK's most popular reggae acts.

AT THE DRIVE-IN

This El Paso, Texas, USA-based band emerged from cult underground status to become one of the most talked about American rock act since the mid-90s heyday of **Nirvana** and **Rage Against The Machine**. At The Drive-In was formed in 1994 by the core partnership of Cedric Bixler (b. 1974; vocals) and Jim Ward (b. 1976; guitar). Their debut single, December 1994's 'Hell Paso', was released on the band's own Western Breed label. Puerto Rican bass player Omar Rodriguez (b. 1975) was added to the line-up shortly afterwards. They released a second single, 'Alfaro Vive, Carajo!', in June 1995 before hooking up with the tiny independent label Flipside Records. The low-budget *Acrobatic Tenement* managed to capture some of the energy of their live shows on record and, with confidence growing, Bixler, Ward and Rodriguez were joined by Paul Himojos (b. 1975; bass) and Lebanese drummer Tony Hajjar (b. 1974). Rodriguez switched to guitar to accommodate Himojos, but a short period of upheaval saw Ward quit during recording sessions for the six-track EP, *El Gran Orgo*. He returned to the band in time to play on the 'live' studio recording *In/Casino/Out*.

The following year the band toured Europe for the first time. After the release of the *Vaya* EP the band was signed to the new DEN Records label which shortly afterwards merged with the **Beastie Boys**' Grand Royal Records label. *Relationship Of Command*, recorded with leading nu-metal

producer Ross Robinson, saw the band's searing take on hardcore punk, art-noise and straightforward rock 'n' roll reaching new heights. Shortly afterwards, they announced that they were embarking on an extended hiatus. Bixler and Rodriguez went on to record with Mars Volta and De Facto.

ATLANTA RHYTHM SECTION

The cream of the studio musicians from Georgia, USA, the Atlanta Rhythm Section came together in 1970 after working at a **Roy Orbison** recording session. The band – Dean Daughtry (b. 1946; keyboards), Robert Nix (drums), J. R. Cobb (b. 1944; guitar), vocalist Rodney Justo (replaced after the first album by Ronnie Hammond), Barry Bailey (b. 1948; guitar) and Paul Goddard (b. 1945; bass) – recorded two albums for Decca Records in 1972, neither of which made an impact.

Their first album for new label Polydor Records, 1974's *Third Annual Pipe Dream*, only reached US number 74 and the next two albums fared worse, but in 1977 'So Into You' reached the US Top 10, as did the attendant *A Rock And Roll Alternative*. Their follow-up, *Champagne Jam*, went to the Top 10 in 1978, together with 'Imaginary Lover', after which Nix was replaced by Roy Yeager (b. 1946). The band's last hit on Polydor was a 1979 remake of 'Spooky', a song with which Cobb and Daughtry had been involved when they were with their former band, **Classics IV**. A switch to Columbia Records in 1981 gave the band one last chart album, *Quinella*, and a US Top 30 single, 'Alien', after which they faded from the national scene. The Atlanta Rhythm Section have continued to perform to a loyal audience, although they have only recorded sporadically in subsequent decades.

ATOMIC KITTEN

Andy McCluskey, who enjoyed several pop hits of his own in the 80s with **OMD**, is the musical mastermind behind this Liverpool, England-based girl

23

group. Natasha Hamilton (b. 1982) joined original duo Kerry Katona (b. 1980) and Liz McLarnon (b. Elizabeth Margaret McLarnon, 1981) in May 1999 as the previous moniker Automatic Kittens was abandoned in favour of the snappier Atomic Kitten. The trio embarked on the usual course to teen stardom, supporting boy band 911, visiting Japan, and doing the dreaded school tour. Vibrant live performances and McCluskey's undiminished ability to write a good tune boosted the fortunes of the trio's first two singles for Innocent Records. 'Right Now' reached UK number 10 in December 1999. 'See Ya' was more successful, debuting at number 6 the following April. Two more singles followed before the release of *Right Now*. Katona left the group in February 2001 to have a baby, and was replaced by Jenny Frost (b. 1978). Shortly afterwards 'Whole Again', the fifth single from the group's debut album, took up residency at the top of the UK singles chart for four weeks. The trio's cover version of the **Bangles**' 'Eternal Flame' topped the UK charts in August.

ATOMIC ROOSTER

Formed in 1969 at the height of the UK progressive rock boom, the original Rooster line-up comprised Vincent Crane (b. 1943, d. 1989; organ), Nick Graham (bass) and Carl Palmer (b. 1950; drums). After only one album, however, the unit fragmented, with Graham joining Skin Alley and Palmer founding **Emerson, Lake And Palmer**. Crane and new members John Cann (guitar, vocals) and Paul Hammond (drums) released *Death Walks Behind You*, followed in 1971 by the UK hit singles 'Tomorrow Night' and 'The Devil's Answer'. With Pete French (from Cactus) the trio recorded *In Hearing Of*, then split.

The irrepressible Crane recruited new members, guitarist Steve Bolton, bass player Bill Smith, drummer Rick Parnell and established singer Chris Farlowe (b. John Henry Deighton, 1940). A shift towards blue-eyed soul won few new fans, however, and Crane finally dissolved the band in 1974. He

returned in 1979 with Preston Hayman (drums), but their two albums were anti-climatic. In 1983, Crane accepted an invitation to record and tour with **Dexys Midnight Runners**, appearing on 1985's *Don't Stand Me Down*. Tragically he committed suicide in 1989.

AUTEURS

Truculent UK indie stars the Auteurs were spearheaded by Luke Haines (b. 1967; vocals, guitar), alongside Glenn Collins (b. 1968; drums) and Alice Readman (bass). Both Haines and Readman had performed with minor indie band the Servants. In 1992, they released 'Showgirl' – notable for Haines' impressive use of language (instructed by film, music and theatre) the focal point. Joined by cellist James Banbury, the Auteurs' debut album was lavishly praised and they missed out on the 1993 Mercury Music Prize by just one vote. *Now I'm A Cowboy* continued the pattern of press eulogy and public indecisiveness, on a set soaked with Haines' class obsessions. *After Murder Park* was produced by Steve Albini, whose previous credits included **Nirvana**'s *In Utero* and the **Pixies**' *Surfer Rosa*.

Haines then put the Auteurs on hold and released an uneven album as Baader-Meinhof. He later formed Black Box Recorder with singer Sarah Nixey and guitarist John Moore (ex-**Jesus And Mary Chain**), before re-forming the Auteurs for 1999's *How I Learned To Love The Bootboys*. The prolific Haines has subsequently recorded with Black Box Recorder again, provided the soundtrack to Paul Tickel's *Christie Malry's Own Double Entry*, and released his solo debut, *The Oliver Twist Manifesto*.

AVERAGE WHITE BAND

This soul-influenced Scottish outfit evolved from several local beat groups, with Alan Gorrie (b. 1946; bass, vocals) joined by Hamish Stuart (b. 1949; guitar, vocals), Owen 'Onnie' McIntyre (b. 1945; guitar), Malcolm 'Mollie' Duncan (b. 1945; saxophone), Roger Ball (b. 1944; saxophone, keyboards) and Robbie McIntosh (b. 1950, d. 1974; drums). Although their 1973 debut, *Show*  *Your Hand*, showed promise, it was not until the band was signed to Atlantic Records that its true potential blossomed. *AWB* was a superb collection, the highlights including a spellbinding version of the **Isley Brothers**' 'Work To Do', and the rhythmic original instrumental 'Pick Up The Pieces' (US number 1/UK Top 10). *AWB* topped the US album charts, but this euphoric period was halted abruptly in 1974 by the tragic death of Robbie McIntosh after an accidental heroin overdose. He was replaced by Steve Ferrone (b. 1950; ex-Bloodstone).

The new line-up secured further success with 'Cut The Cake', but subsequent releases proved more formulaic. A pairing with singer **Ben E. King** (Benny And Us), and the late 70s singles 'Walk On By' and 'Let's Go Round Again', were more inventive. The Average White Band retired during much of the 80s as the members pursued individual projects. Hamish Stuart later surfaced in **Paul McCartney**'s *Flowers In The Dirt* touring group, and was unavailable when the band re-formed in 1989. The resulting *Aftershock* featured Gorrie, Ball and McIntyre alongside singer Alex Ligertwood (ex-**Santana**) and multi-instrumentalist Eliot Lewis. Further line-up changes followed the release of 1997's *Soul Tattoo*, with founding member Ball retiring from touring.

AYERS, KEVIN

Ayers (b. 1944) spent part of his childhood in Malaysia before returning to his native Kent, England. A founder member of **Soft Machine**, this talented singer-songwriter abandoned the group in 1968.

His debut album, *Joy Of A Toy*, nonetheless bore a debt to his former colleagues, all of whom contributed to this innovative collection. In 1970, Ayers formed the Whole World, featuring saxophonist Lol Coxhill, guitarist **Mike Oldfield** and pianist/ arranger David Bedford. *Shooting At The Moon*, a radical, experimental release, was a landmark in British progressive rock. Coxhill left the Whole World shortly afterwards and his departure precipitated their demise. Oldfield and Bedford contributed to *Whatevershebringswesing*, but Ayers never quite fulfilled his undoubted potential, despite moments of inspiration

on *Bananamour*. A high-profile appearance at London's Rainbow Theatre resulted in June 1, 1974, on which Ayers was joined by **John Cale**, **Nico** and **Brian Eno**. Unfortunately, later albums such as *Sweet Deceiver*, *Yes We Have No Mañanas*, *So Get Your Mañanas Today* and *Rainbow Takeaway* were lower profile, interspersed by prolonged holidays in the singer's beloved Spain.

Despite this reduced public profile and a prolonged creative lull during the mid-80s, Ayers retains a committed cult following and has continued to follow his highly personal path throughout subsequent decades. His occasional studio forays include the well-received *Falling Up* and *Still Life With Guitar*, and he has appeared with long-standing admirers Ultramarine and the Liverpool-based outfit, the Wizards Of Twiddly.

AZTEC CAMERA

Scottish pop outfit formed in 1980 by songwriter Roddy Frame (b. 1964; vocals), with Campbell Owens (bass) and Dave Mulholland (drums). A regular turnover of band members ensued while Frame put together the songs that made up 1983's debut, *High Land, Hard Rain*. Three singles in the UK independent charts on the influential Postcard Records label, had already made the band a critics' favourite, but this album of light acoustic songs was a memorable work, with 'Oblivious' reaching UK number 18. Excellent songs such as the uplifting 'Walk Out to Winter' and the expertly crafted 'We Could Send Letters' indicated a major talent in the ascendant. The **Mark Knopfler**-produced *Knife* broke no new ground, but, now signed to WEA Records, the band was pushed on to the world stage to promote the album. Frame retreated back to Scotland following the tour, re-emerging in 1987 with *Love*. This introverted yet over-produced album showed Frame's continuing development, with **Elvis Costello**-influenced song structures. Its comparative failure was rectified the following year with two further UK hits, 'How Men Are' and the Top 5 'Somewhere In My Heart'. As a result, *Love* belatedly became a substantial success climbing to Number 10 in the UK album chart.

Frame returned in 1990 with the acclaimed *Stray*, which included a duet with Mick Jones on the bitter 'Good Morning Britain'. Frame then delivered *Dreamland* (recorded with composer Ryûchi Sakamoto) and *Frestonia*, strong collections of emotionally direct, honest songs that rivalled Aztec Camera's debut of a decade earlier. The group disintegrated in 1996 as Frame worked on a solo project, *The North Star*, which was eventually released in late 1998 on the Independiente Records label.

B-52'S

The quirky B-52's songs show many influences, including 50s' rock 'n' roll, punk and commercial dance music. Formed in Georgia, USA, in 1976, the group took their name from the bouffant hairstyle, worn by Kate Pierson (b. 1948; organ, vocals) and Cindy Wilson (b. 1957; guitar, vocals). The line-up was completed by Cindy's brother Ricky (b. 1953, d. 1985; guitar), Fred Schneider (b. 1951; keyboards, vocals) and Keith Strickland (b. 1953; drums). The lyrically bizarre but musically thunderous 'Rock Lobster' led to them being signed to Island Records in the UK. Their debut, *B-52's*, became a strong seller and 'Rock Lobster' was a belated US hit in 1980. Subsequent albums continued to defy categorization, their love of melodrama and pop culture running side by side and helping to establish the band on the American campus circuit.

Tragically Ricky Wilson died of AIDS, but the band continued, reaching a commercial peak in 1989 with the ebullient 'Love Shack'. In 1992 the group parted company with Cindy Wilson and recorded *Good Stuff* with producers Don Was and Nile Rodgers. The B-52's achieved huge commercial success in 1994 with the theme song to *The Flintstones*. Schneider recorded a solo album in 1996, while Wilson rejoined in 1998 as the band embarked on a tour to support that year's hits collection.

B. BUMBLE AND THE STINGERS

US group formed by pop svengali Kim Fowley. Their 'Bumble Boogie' (1961), an adaptation of Rimsky-Korsakov's 'The Flight Of The Bumble Bee', reached US number 21. The following year's 'Nut Rocker' only reached US number 23, but this propulsive instrumental – an irreverent reading of Tchaikovsky's *Nutcracker Suite* – soared to UK number 1 and, 10 years later, again reached the Top 20. The group – B. Bumble (b. R.C. Gamble), Terry Anderson (guitar), Jimmy King (rhythm guitar) and Don Orr (drums) – completed a UK tour in 1962.

BABES IN TOYLAND

US female rock trio formed in 1987, comprising Kat Bjelland (b. Katherine Bjelland, 1963; vocals, guitar), Michelle Leon (bass) and Lori Barbero (b. 1961; drums, vocals). A debut album was recorded live with overdubbed vocals. After signing to WEA Records, they recorded the mini-album *To Mother*. In 1992 Leon was replaced by Maureen Herman (b. 1965) and their next album, *Fontanelle*, received favourable reviews. When the band took a break in 1993, Barbero formed her own label, Spanish Fly, while Bjelland worked with her husband Stuart Gray on two projects, Crunt and KatSu.

Babes In Toyland reconvened in time for the Lollapalooza tour, and 1995's *Nemesisters* included memorable cover versions of Sister Sledge's 'We Are Family' and Eric Carmen's 'All By Myself' alongside original compositions such as 'Memory' and 'Scherezadian 22'. Herman was replaced by Dana Cochrane in 1996. Her former bandmates have subsequently concentrated on other projects, with Babes On Toyland put on extended hiatus. Bjelland, Barbero and bass player Jessie Farmer played a live show in Minneapolis on 25 November 2000, which was captured for posterity on the following year's *Minneapolism*.

BABYBIRD

The alter ego of Sheffield, England-based artist Stephen Jones (b. 1962). Jones recorded over 400 songs as four-track demos, going on to use several dozen of them across his self-released albums, between July 1995 and August 1996. The albums quickly acquired a cult following. In 1996, Jones signed to Echo Records and assembled a live band for the first time, with whom he recorded *Ugly Beautiful*, a 'debut' received with mixed emotions by critics but lapped up by the public on the back of the surprise UK Top 5 hit 'You're Gorgeous'.

BABYFACE

📀 Albums
For The Cool In You (Epic 1993)★★★
➤ p.360 for full listings
🎵 Collaborators
L.A. Reid
📻 Connections
Manchild
🎻 Further References
Video: *Babyface: A Collection Of Videos* (Epic 1990)

BACHARACH, BURT

📀 Albums
Casino Royale film soundtrack (RCA 1967)★★★
Butch Cassidy And The Sundance Kid film soundtrack (A&M 1970)★★★
with Elvis Costello *Painted From Memory: The New Songs Of Bacharach & Costello* (Mercury 1998)★★★
➤ p.360 for full listings
🎵 Collaborators
Elvis Costello ➤ p.100
Dionne Warwick ➤ p.344
Hal David
Mack David
Bob Hilliard
Carole Bayer Sager
🎻 Further References
Video: *A Tribute To Burt Bacharach & Hal David* (Aviva International 2001)

Jones proved himself an able, if, confrontational live performer, but the commercial failure of his second major label album, *There's Something Going On*, indicated that his dalliance with the charts may have been a brief one. He published his first novel in 2000, shortly before the release the surprisingly upbeat solo collection, *Bugged*.

BABYFACE

Babyface (b. Kenneth Edmonds, 1959) began performing in the mid-70s in the funk outfit Manchild, although his achievements as a songwriter and producer throughout the late 80s and 90s, especially with L.A. Reid, sometimes overshadowed his subsequent solo efforts. He enjoyed great success with such artists as **Boyz II Men** (Edmonds wrote and produced the massive US chart-topper 'End Of The Road'), **Bobby Brown** and **Toni Braxton**. Since splitting with Reid in the mid-90s, Babyface's main success has been as a producer and writer of film soundtracks, with *The Bodyguard* and *Waiting To Exhale* both going multi-platinum.

Edmonds looked set to stake his claim as a solo artist of note in the mid-90s, with 'When Can I See You' winning a Grammy award in 1995. His solo albums continued to disappoint, however, relying on guest artists to boost his own rather unremarkable voice. Following an unplugged MTV set and a seasonal release, Babyface signed a new recording contract with Arista Records. His debut for the label featured collaborations with **Snoop Dogg** and the **Neptunes**.

BACHARACH, BURT

Composer and arranger Bacharach (b. 1928) was raised in New York. A jazz aficionado, he played in various ensembles during the 40s. After his discharge from the army, he worked as a pianist, arranger and conductor for a number of artists, including Vic Damone, Steve Lawrence, Polly Bergen and the Ames Brothers. From 1956–58, Bacharach worked as musical director for Marlene Dietrich, and registered his first hit as a composer with the Five Blobs' 'The Blob' (written for a horror b-movie), written in tandem with Mack David. A more fruitful partnership followed when Burt was introduced to Mack's brother, Hal David. In 1958, Bacharach and David placed their first hit with 'The Story Of My Life', a US Top 20 single for Marty Robbins. Greater success followed with Perry Como's 'Magic Moments' (UK number 1/US number 4). However, Bacharach and David did not work together exclusively until 1962. In the meantime, Bacharach found a new songwriting partner, Bob Hilliard, with whom he composed several recordings for the **Drifters**.

During the early 60s, Bacharach and David wrote for many successful US and UK artists. Frankie Vaughan's 'Tower Of Strength' gave them their third UK number 1, as well as another US Top 10 hit, in a version by Gene McDaniels. **Gene Pitney** achieved two of his early hits with the duo's '(The Man Who Shot) Liberty Valance' and 'Twenty-Four Hours From Tulsa'. From 1962 onwards, the formidable writing team steered **Dionne Warwick**'s career with an array of hit songs including 'Don't Make Me Over', 'Anyone Who Had A Heart', 'Walk On By', 'Message To Michael', 'I Say A Little Prayer' and 'Do You Know The Way To San Jose?'. They also maintained a quotient of UK number 1s thanks to first-class cover versions by **Cilla Black** ('Anyone Who Had A Heart'), **Sandie Shaw** ('(There's) Always Something

There To Remind Me'), the **Walker Brothers** ('Make It Easy On Yourself') and Herb Alpert ('This Guy's In Love With You'). Bacharach's melodies and the deftness of touch neatly complemented David's soul-tortured, romantic lyrics.

The duo were also popular as composers of film scores. *What's New, Pussycat* brought them an Oscar nomination and another hit when **Tom Jones** recorded the title song. Further hits and Academy Award nominations followed for the films *Alfie* and *Casino Royale* (which featured 'The Look Of Love'). Finally, in 1969, a double Oscar celebration was achieved with the score from *Butch Cassidy And The Sundance Kid* and its award-winning 'Raindrops Keep Fallin' On My Head'. The duo then completed their own musical, *Promises, Promises*, the enormously successful show enjoying a lengthy Broadway run.

In 1970, Bacharach wrote the **Carpenters**' hit 'Close To You' yet, remarkably, he did not enjoy another chart success for over 10 years. An acrimonious split from Hal David, the break-up of Bacharach's marriage and the loss of his most consistent hitmaker, Dionne Warwick, were all factors. Worse followed when his musical *Lost Horizon* was a commercial disaster.

It was not until 1981 that Bacharach's dry run ended, when he met a lyricist of genuine commercial fire – future wife Carole Bayer Sager. Their Oscar-winning 'Arthur's Theme' (co-written with Peter Allen and singer **Christopher Cross**) made the charts. The couple provided hits for **Roberta Flack** ('Making Love') and **Neil Diamond** ('Heartlight'). In 1986, Bacharach placed two US number 1s, 'That's What Friends Are For' (an AIDS charity record by Warwick and 'Friends' – **Elton John**, **Gladys Knight** and **Stevie Wonder**) and 'On My Own' (**Patti LaBelle** and **Michael McDonald**). In the late 80s, Bacharach and Sager wrote film songs such as 'They Don't Make Them Like They Use To' (*Tough Guys*), 'Everchanging Time' (*Baby Boom*), and 'Love Is My Decision' (*Arthur 2: On The Rocks*), for which he also wrote the score.

In 1992, when Bacharach and Sager separated, he and David finally reunited. Their songs included 'Sunny Weather Lover' for Warwick's new album. In 1994, a musical revue, *Back To Bacharach And David*, opened in New York, and the following year BBC Television transmitted a major film profile, *Burt Bacharach: … This Is Now*, which was narrated by **Dusty Springfield**. His albums were reissued in response to a tremendous upsurge of interest in easy-listening music among young people in the mid-90s, and he made a cameo appearance in the hit movie *Austin Powers: International Man Of Mystery*.

In 1998, Bacharach collaborated with **Elvis Costello** on *Painted From Memory*, a finely crafted collection of ballads bearing the unmistakable trademarks of its

creators: Bacharach's deft romantic touch, coupled with the quirky, realistic style of Costello. Among the album's highlights were 'God Give Me Strength', which featured in the 1996 movie, *Grace Of My Heart*. Another of the numbers, 'I Still Have That Other Girl', won a 1999 Grammy Award. In the same year, Bacharach and David contributed some songs to the Bette Midler movie *Isn't She Great*.

BACHELORS

Formed in 1958 as the Harmony Chords then as the Harmonichords, this group originally featured brothers Conleth (b. 1941) and Declan Cluskey (b. 1942) and John Stokes (b. Sean James Stokes, 1940). The Dublin, Eire-born trio initially worked as a mainstream folk act, all three playing harmonicas. In 1961, Decca Record's A&R head Dick Rowe signed them and suggested their new name. With the assistance of producer Shel Talmy, the trio scored a UK Top 10 hit with a revival of the Lew Pollack/ Erno Rapee song 'Charmaine' (1963). After three unsuccessful follow-ups they struck again with a string of easy-listening pop hits including several revivals. In 1966, they revealed their former folk roots and surprisingly completely outmaneuvered **Simon And Garfunkel** by taking 'The Sound Of Silence' to UK number 3.

 In later years, the Bachelors achieved success on the cabaret circuit with a line-up that remained unchanged for 25 years. In 1984, John Stokes left after a dispute with the Cluskey brothers. After taking legal action he received compensation. His replacement was Peter Phipps, who stayed with the second generation **New Bachelors** until 1993. The Cluskey brothers have continued to tour and record as a duo.

BACHMAN-TURNER OVERDRIVE

Canadian hard-rock band formed by Randy Bachman (b. 1943; guitar, vocals; ex-**Guess Who**). In 1970, Bachman had recorded a solo album before forming Brave Belt with his brother Robbie (drums), C. F. 'Fred' Turner (b. 1943; bass, vocals) and Chad Allan (b. Allan Kobel; keyboards). Brave Belt recorded two unsuccessful albums in 1971–72, after which Allan was replaced by another Bachman brother, Tim. In 1972 the new band took its new name and, in 1973, signed to Mercury Records. Their self-titled debut made a minor impact in the USA and Canada. After constant US touring, *Bachman-Turner Overdrive II* provided their breakthrough, reaching US number 4 and yielding the number 12 hit 'Takin' Care Of Business'. Tim Bachman then departed, replaced by Blair Thornton (b. 1950). *Not Fragile* (1974) topped the US album charts and provided the US number 1/UK number 2 'You Ain't Seen Nothing Yet'. *Four Wheel Drive* (1975) was the band's last Top 10 recording, although they continued to release singles and albums until the end of the 70s.

 Randy Bachman departed in 1977 and was replaced by Jim Clench. The following year the band officially changed its name to B.T.O., but could not revive its earlier fortunes. In 1984, Randy Bachman, Tim Bachman and C. F. Turner regrouped, with ex-Guess Who drummer Gary Peterson, and released a second self-titled album. Tim Bachman continued to lead a version of the band before several other original members returned to tour in the early 90s. Randy Bachman subsequently left the band once more to concen-

trate on his songwriting career. Turner, Thornton, Rob Bachman and new member Randy Murray have continued to keep the band's name alive on the concert circuit. The quartet returned to the studio in 1996 to re-record some of the band's classic material and five new tracks for *Trial By Fire*.

BACKSTREET BOYS

Formed in Orlando, Florida, USA, in the mid-90s, this popular white vocal quintet comprises Kevin Scott Richardson (b. 1972), Nicholas Gene Carter (b. 1980), Brian 'B-rok' Littrell (b. 1975), A. J. McLean (b. Alexander James McLean, 1978) and Howie D. (b. Howard Dwaine Dorough, 1973). Their success began in 1995 when the single 'We've Got It Goin' On' became a substantial hit in Germany, and eventually charted in the rest of mainland Europe. Further success followed in the UK, with 'Get Down (You're The One For Me)' and reissues of 'We've Got It Goin' On' and 'I'll Never Break

Your Heart' breaking into the Top 20. Their self-titled debut album repeated this success, although it was only made available in Europe, as was the 1997 follow-up, *Backstreet's Back*. 'Everybody (Backstreet's Back)' became another huge hit, and was instrumental in breaking the group in the US when it reached number 4 in June 1998.

 Further huge hits followed with 'Quit Playing Games (With My Heart)' and 'As Long As You Love Me'. Their self-titled US debut, compiling tracks from the European albums, went on to become the third best-selling record of 1998 in that country. They topped the UK singles chart in May 1999 with a new single, 'I Want It That Way', which also proved an enduringly popular US Top 10 radio hit. *Millennium* was a predictable success, topping the US album charts at the start of June 1999 and selling two million copies in just over three weeks. The group's popularity showed no sign of waning over the following year, with a string of hit singles followed by the bestselling *Black & Blue*, which topped the US charts in November 2000. They were forced to cancel several concert dates the following summer when McLean checked into an alcohol rehabilitation centre.

BAD BRAINS

This black American hardcore punk and dub reggae outfit was formed in 1978 by HR (b. Paul Hudson; vocals), his brother Earl Hudson (drums), Dr. Know (guitar) and Darryl Aaron Jenifer (bass). Little studio material remains from the band's early period, though 'Pay To Cum' and 'Big Takeover' are regarded as punk classics. They continued through the 80s, until HR went solo. In 1988, he was temporarily replaced by ex-**Faith No More** vocalist Chuck Mosley, while Mackie Jayson (ex-Cro-Mags) took over on drums. In 1994, **Madonna** offered them a place on her Maverick label, with HR returning to the fold. *God Of Love*, produced by Ric Ocasek (ex-**Cars**), concentrated more on dub and rasta messages than hardcore. In 1995, HR left the band after assaulting fellow members. He was subsequently arrested at the Canadian border and charged with a drugs offence. The band was then dropped by Maverick, but have continued touring and recording under the new moniker Soul Brains.

BAD COMPANY

Heavy-rock band formed in the UK in 1973, with a line-up comprising **Paul Rodgers** (b. 1949; vocals, ex-**Free**), Simon Kirke (b. 1949; drums, vocals, ex-Free), Mick Ralphs (b. 1944; guitar, vocals, ex-**Mott The Hoople**) and Boz Burrell (b. Raymond Burrell, 1946; bass). Bad Company were akin to a blues-based supergroup, with strong vocals placed beside tough melody lines and hard riffing. Their debut album

was well-received and a string of albums through the 70s brought them chart success in both their homeland and in the US. They achieved singles success with several powerful songs, notably 'Can't Get Enough' and 'Feel Like Makin' Love'.

Following almost a decade of extensive gigging and regular albums, the band split up in 1983. A new line-up, with former Ted Nugent vocalist Brian Howe replacing Rodgers, came together for *Fame And Fortune*. The late 80s/early 90s Bad Company, with Ralphs and Kirke joined by Rick Wills (bass) and Dave Colwell (rhythm guitar), enjoyed further US success with 'If You Needed Somebody', 'Walk Through Fire' and 'How About That'. The band has continued playing into the new millennium, although their studio releases are a pale shadow of their earlier work.

BAD MANNERS

Formed in 1976 as Stoop Solo & The Sheet Starchers, this unit came to be known as Buster Bloodvessel And His Bad Manners and then simply Bad Manners when the UK 2-Tone ska revival was at its peak. Featuring the exuberant Buster Bloodvessel (b. Douglas Trendle, 1958; vocals), Gus 'Hot Lips' Herman (trumpet), Chris Kane (saxophone), Andrew 'Marcus Absent' Marson (saxophone), Winston Bazoomies (harmonica), Brian 'Chew-it' Tuitti (drums), David Farren (bass), Martin Stewart (keyboards) and Louis 'Alphonzo' Cook (guitar), Bad Manners enjoyed a string of UK hits in the early 80s. The catchy 'Ne-Ne Na-Na Na-Na Nu-Nu' was followed by 11 UK chart entries, including four Top 10 hits 'Special Brew', 'Can Can', 'Walking In The Sunshine' and 'My Girl Lollipop'. In the late 80s Bloodvessel formed Buster's All-Stars to motivate the other members of Bad Manners into doing something. In recent years he has toured occasionally with the band, as well as trying his hand as an hotelier at the appropriately named Fatty Towers in Margate, Kent.

BAD RELIGION

US hardcore band formed in 1980 by Greg Graffin (vocals), Brett Gurewitz (guitar), Jay Lishrout (drums) and Jay Bentley (bass). They debuted with the poorly produced *Bad Religion* on Epitaph Records, formed by Gurewitz. Pete Finestone took over as drummer in 1982. *How Could Hell Be Any Worse?* created local and national interest, but *Into The Unknown* disillusioned fans when the emphasis shifted to slick keyboard textures. In 1984, Greg Hetson and Tim Gallegos took over guitar and bass, while Gurewitz took time out due to drink and drug problems. A comeback EP, *Back To The Known*, was better received and, in 1987, Gurewitz rejoined while Hetson worked with former band Circle Jerks. They signed a major-label contract with Atlantic Records in 1993, but Gurewitz retired the following year to look after Epitaph, which was enjoying success with **Offspring** and others. *The Gray Race* was recorded by Graffin, Hetson, Bentley, Brian Baker (guitar) and Bobby Schayer

(drums). Gurewitz guested on their final album for Atlantic, 2000's *The New America*, and returned full-time on *The Process Of Belief*.

BADFINGER

This Welsh group evolved from the Iveys, who recorded unsuccessfully for Apple Records. Comprising Pete Ham (b. 1947, d. 1975; vocals), Mike Gibbins (b. 1949; drums) and Englishmen Tom Evans (b. Thomas Evans, 1947, d. 1983; guitar) and Joey Molland (b. 1947; bass), the quartet debuted with the transatlantic hit 'Come And Get It', composed by label boss **Paul McCartney**. 'No Matter What' was a transatlantic Top 10 hit and by the beginning of the 70s, Badfinger were something of an Apple house band. They appeared on three solo **Beatles** recordings (*All Things Must Pass*, 'It Don't Come Easy' and *Imagine*) as well as appearing at **George Harrison**'s Bangla Desh benefit concert.

In 1972, Nilsson enjoyed a transatlantic chart topper with the Ham/Evans ballad 'Without You', but subsequently Badfinger failed to exploit their full potential. By the time of their final Apple recording, *Ass*, Molland was writing over half their songs, but he left soon after. The band recruited Bob Jackson (b. 1949; vocals, keyboards), but tragedy struck a year later when Pete Ham hanged himself after a long period of personal and professional worries. Consequently, the band split.

Nearly four years later, Molland and Evans re-formed the band, but still commercial success proved elusive and in November 1983 history repeated itself when Evans committed suicide. Following the discovery of some home recorded tapes, two complete albums of Ham's songs were issued in the late 90s.

BADLY DRAWN BOY

This maverick UK artist (b. Damon Gough, 1970) established a cult following on the strength of two EPs on his own label, Twisted Nerve. The releases provoked something of an A&R bidding war before Gough signed to XL Records for a reputedly six-figure sum. Further EPs followed before the release of Gough's highly anticipated debut album, the aptly-titled *The Hour Of Bewilderbeast*. Over 18 sprawling tracks Gough managed to weave his disparate influences into a quietly compelling whole. His sound has a sparse, lo-fi quality and the music features repetitive guitar melodies, strong percussion and Gough's ethereal vocals. The album won the UK's Mercury Music Prize in September 2000, but Gough continued to attract criticism for his notoriously amateurish live shows.

Badly Drawn Boy returned in April 2002 with the exceptional soundtrack to the movie adaptation of Nick Hornby's *About A Boy*. Gough clearly has talent, with, or maybe one day without, his ridiculous woollen hat.

BADU, ERYKAH

Badu (b. Erica Wright, 1971) is an uncompromising American neo-soul performer. Before turning solo, she performed alongside her cousin Free in the group Erykah Free. Her 1997 debut *Baduizm* was largely self-written, and was co-produced with Bob Power, and friends and colleagues from her days on the Memphis music scene. The album, which fluctuated between warm jazz textures and hip-hop and soul rhythms, won critical praise and earned Badu two Grammy Awards.

A strong live performer, Badu took the unusual step of releasing a concert album only a few months after her debut. Featuring several tracks from *Baduizm* alongside cover versions and one new song, the excellent 'Tyrone', *Live!* was another high-quality release from this exceptional singer. Badu then took an extended hiatus to concentrate on raising her son, although she guested on hits by Busta Rhymes ('One') and the Roots (the Grammy Award-winning 'You Got Me'), and made cameo appearances in the movies *Blues Brothers 2000* and *The Cider House Rules*. She returned to the charts in autumn 2000 with the hit single 'Bag Lady', taken from her eagerly awaited sophomore set, *Mama's Gun*.

BAEZ, JOAN

US born Baez's (b. 1941) appearance at the 1959 Newport Folk Festival established her as a vibrant interpreter of traditional material. Her first four albums featured American and British ballads, but as the civil rights campaign intensified, she became increasingly identified with the protest movement. Her reading of 'We Shall Overcome', first released on *In Concert/Part 2*, achieved anthem status. The album also featured **Bob Dylan**'s 'Don't Think Twice, It's All Right'. The duo subsequently toured together, becoming romantically involved, and over the years Baez interpreted many of Dylan's songs. Baez also covered work by contemporary writers including **Phil Ochs**, brother-in-law Richard Farina, **Tim Hardin** and **Donovan**.

Baez founded the Institute for the Study Of Nonviolence, and in 1968 married David Harris, a peace activist who was later imprisoned for draft resistance. They divorced in 1972, but Baez's commitment to peace resulted in jail on two occasions for participation in anti-war rallies.

Although her cover version of the **Band**'s 'The Night They Drove Old Dixie Down' was a US hit in 1971, Baez found it hard to maintain a consistent commercial profile. Her devotion to politics continued and 1973's *Where Are You Now, My Son?* included recordings made in North Vietnam. Six years later she founded Humanitas International, a rapid-response human rights group that was instrumental in rescuing the boat people. She has received numerous awards and honorary doctorates for her work.

Diamonds And Rust, released in 1975, brought further musical success and the title track, the story of her relationship with Dylan, presaged their reunion, in the legendary Rolling Thunder Revue. That, in turn, inspired the self-penned album, *Gulf Winds*, on which her songwriting continued to develop. On 1989's *Speaking Of Dreams*, which celebrated 30 years of performing, she duetted with **Paul Simon**, **Jackson Browne** and the Gipsy Kings. Her 1992 release *Play Me Backwards* was in the smooth country-rock genre, and subsequent albums releases have dallied with African rhythms and sounds.

BAKER, GINGER

This brilliantly erratic UK drummer was already an experienced musician when he formed **Cream** with **Eric Clapton** and **Jack Bruce** in 1967. Baker (b. Peter Baker, 1939) had drummed with trad-jazz bands, working with Terry Lightfoot, Acker Bilk, **Alexis Korner**'s Blues Incorporated and the Graham Bond Organization. After Cream, Baker joined Steve Winwood, Ric Grech and Clapton in **Blind Faith**, followed by the ambitious Airforce. Baker then left Britain to live in Nigeria, where he cultivated an interest in African music and built his own recording studio (**Wings**' *Band On The Run* was recorded there). He formed Nigerian band Salt and recorded with Fela Kuti.

In 1973, Baker returned to Britain and formed the Baker

Gurvitz Army. His solo album *11 Sides Of Baker* was justifiably panned in 1977, but he returned with *Energy* in 1979, briefly joined **Atomic Rooster**, **Hawkwind** and later formed Ginger Baker's Nutters. In 1986, he played on **Public Image Limited**'s UK Top 20 hit 'Rise'. In 1994, he joined Jack Bruce and Gary Moore and, as BBM, they released an accomplished and satisfying album. Baker has since returned to his first love, jazz, recording with Bill Frisell and Charlie Haden.

BAKER, LAVERN

US singer Baker (b. Delores Williams, 1929, d. 1997) was discovered in 1947 in a Chicago nightclub by bandleader Fletcher Henderson. Although still a teenager, she won a contract with the influential OKeh Records, later securing a contract with Atlantic Records. 'Tweedle Dee' reached both the US R&B and pop charts in 1955. It sold in excess of one million copies, as did 'Jim Dandy' in 1957. In 1959, she enjoyed a number 6 pop hit with 'I Cried A Tear' and throughout the decade remained one of black music's leading performers. Although eclipsed by newer acts during the 60s, she enjoyed success with 'Saved' (**Leiber And Stoller**), and 'See See Rider'. Baker's final chart entry came with 'Think Twice', a 1966 duet with **Jackie Wilson**.

While entertaining US troops in Vietnam, she became ill and went to the Philippines to recuperate. She stayed there for 22 years, reviving her career at New York's Village Gate club in 1991. She was elected to the US Rock And Roll Hall Of Fame and starred in the Broadway musical *Black And Blue* in the early 90s. Sadly, ill-health made her final years miserable.

BALDRY, LONG JOHN

Beginning his career playing folk and jazz in the late 50s, this UK singer (b. 1941) toured with **Ramblin' Jack Elliott** before moving into R&B. After a spell with Blues Incorporated, he joined Cyril Davies' R&B All Stars, then fronted the Hoochie Coochie Men, which also included **Rod Stewart**. Baldry and Stewart also joined forces in Steam Packet, featuring Brian Auger and Julie Driscoll. After a brief period with Bluesology (including a young **Elton John**), Baldry went solo to record straightforward pop. He took 'Let The Heartaches Begin', a despairing ballad, to UK number 1 in 1967. His chart career continued with the Olympic Games theme 'Mexico', which also made the UK Top 20. By the end of the 60s, the hits had ceased and another change of direction was ahead: furs and a beard replaced suits and neat haircuts, as Baldry attempted to establish himself with a new audience. With production assistance from Rod Stewart and Elton John, he recorded *It Ain't Easy*, but it

BAEZ, JOAN

Albums
Farewell Angelina (Vanguard 1965)★★★★
Diamonds And Rust (A&M 1975)★★★★
p.360 for full listings

Collaborators
Bob Dylan ➤ p.126
Paul Simon ➤ p.300

Further References
Book: *Daybreak: An Intimate Journey*, Joan Baez
Film: *Don't Look Back* (1967)

BAKER, GINGER

Albums
Falling Off The Roof (Atlantic 1996)★★★★
p.360 for full listings

Collaborators
Jack Bruce ➤ p.67
Eric Clapton ➤ p.89
Bill Frisell
Charlie Haden

Connections
Blind Faith ➤ p.50
Cream ➤ p.104
Airforce
Baker Guervitz Army
BBM
Blues Incorporated
Graham Bond Organisation

BAKER, LAVERN

Albums
LaVern Baker (Atlantic 1957)★★★★
Rock And Roll With LaVern (Atlantic 1957)★★★★
Blues Ballads (Atlantic 1959)★★★★
p.360 for full listings

Collaborators
Jackie Wilson ➤ p.349

BALDRY, LONG JOHN

Albums
Lookin' At Long John (United Artists 1966)★★★
Right To Sing The Blues (Stony Plain 1997)★★★
p.360 for full listings

Collaborators
Rod Stewart ➤ p.316

Connections
Bluesology
Steam Packet

failed to sell. After a troubled few years in the USA he emigrated to Canada, where he performed on the club circuit. In the early 90s his voice was used as Robotnik on the *Sonic The Hedgehog* computer game. Since then, from his base in the USA, he has continued to perform in blues clubs, recording occasionally.

BANANARAMA

Keren Woodward (b. 1961), Sarah Dallin (b. 1961) and Siobhan Fahey (b. 1958, Eire) formed Bananarama in 1980. After singing at parties and pubs in their native London, the trio were recorded by former **Sex Pistols'** drummer Paul Cook on the Swahili Black Blood cover version 'Ai A Mwana'. The single caught the attention of **Fun Boy Three** vocalist Terry Hall and Bananarama backed his trio on their revival of 'It Ain't What You Do, It's The Way That You Do It'. The Fun Boy Three subsequently backed Bananarama on their cover version of the Velvelettes' 'Really Saying Something', which reached the UK Top 5 in 1982.

Bananarama had a strong visual image and a refreshingly unaffected approach to choreography. They also retained considerable control over their careers. A tie-up with producers Tony Swain and Steve Jolley brought them UK Top 10 hits with 'Shy Boy', 'Na Na Hey Hey Kiss Him Goodbye' and 'Cruel Summer', while 'Robert De Niro's Waiting' reached the Top 3. They tackled more serious matters in 'Rough Justice', a protest song on the political situation in Northern Ireland.

A lean period followed before Bananarama joined **Stock, Aitken And Waterman** for a remake of **Shocking Blue**'s 'Venus', which brought them a US number 1 in 1986. Their biggest UK hit followed with the glorious 'Love In The First Degree'. In 1987 Fahey left, married **Eurythmics**' David A. Stewart and formed **Shakespears Sister**. Her replacement, Jacquie O'Sullivan, went solo in 1991 leaving Woodward and Dallin to continue as a duo. Their last chart entry was 'More, More, More' in spring 1993. The original line-up re-formed in 1998 to record a cover version of **ABBA**'s 'Waterloo' for UK Channel Four's *Eurotrash* Eurovision tribute. Dallin and Woodward went on to record a new album, *Exotica*, which was released in France in 2001.

BAND

When the Band emerged in 1968 with *Music From Big Pink*, they were already a seasoned and cohesive unit. Four of the group, Canadians **Robbie Robertson**

(b. Jaime Robbie Robertson, 1943; guitar, vocals), Richard Manuel (b. 1943, d. 1986; piano, drums, vocals), Rick Danko (b. 1942, d. 1999; bass, vocals) and Garth Hudson (b. Eric Hudson, 1937; organ, keyboards), had embraced rock 'n' roll during its first flush of success. One by one they joined the Hawks, a backing group formed by **Ronnie Hawkins**, which included American Levon Helm (b. Mark Levon Helm, 1940; drums, vocals).

'Bo Diddley' (1963) was a major Canadian hit and the following *Mojo Man* featured Helm on vocals for 'She's 19' and 'Farther Up The Road'. The quintet then left Hawkins and toured America's small-town bars before settling in New York.

Robertson, Helm and Hudson backed blues singer John Hammond Jnr on his debut single, 'I Wish You Would' (1964), before supporting **Bob Dylan** on his Electric 1966 world tour. They later recorded the famous *The Basement Tapes* in Dylan's Woodstock retreat. *Music From Big Pink* placed traditional American music in an environment of acid-rock and psychedelia; its woven, wailing harmonies suggested the fervour of sanctified soul, while the instrumental pulse drew inspiration from carnivals, country and R&B. *The Band* confirmed the quintet's unique qualities, with Robertson emerging as principal songwriter.

It contained several classics – 'Across The Great Divide', 'The Unfaithful Servant' and 'The Night They Drove Old Dixie Down' – as well as 'Rag Mama Rag', an ebullient UK Top 20 hit. The Band then resumed touring, the perils of which were chronicled on *Stage Fright*. In 'The Rumor' they created one of the era's most telling portraits, yet the band's once-seamless sound had grown increasingly formal, a dilemma that increased on *Cahoots*. It was followed by a warm in-concert set, *Rock Of Ages*, arranged by **Allen Toussaint**, and *Moondog Matinee*, a selection of favourite cover versions.

In 1974, the Band backed Dylan on *Planet Waves* and undertook the extensive tour, documented on *Before The Flood*. The experience renewed their creativity and *Northern Lights-Southern Cross*, their strongest set since *The Band*, included 'Acadian Driftwood', one of Robertson's most evocative compositions. However, the band split the following year after a gala performance (*The Last Waltz*) in San Francisco. The many guests included Dylan, **Eric Clapton**, **Muddy Waters**, **Van Morrison**, **Neil Young**, **Joni Mitchell** and **Paul Butterfield**, and the event was the subject of Martin Scorsese's film of the same name.

The Band completed contractual obligations with *Islands*, a somewhat tepid set. Helm then pursued a career as a performer and actor; Danko recorded a solo album; while Hudson played session appearances. Robertson scored soundtracks to several Scorsese films, but refused to join the Band reunions of 1984 and 1985 (he was replaced by Jim Weider). A third tour ended in tragedy when Manuel hanged himself in a motel room. His death inspired 'Fallen Angel' on Robertson's 'comeback' album, but he still refused to join his colleagues when they regrouped again in 1991 with Weider, Randy Ciarlante (drums, vocals) and Richard Bell (keyboards). This line-up released three new studio albums during the 90s. Danko passed away in his sleep in December 1999.

BANGLES

Known as the Colours, the Bangs and finally the Bangles, this Los Angeles, California, USA-based quartet mastered the art of melodic, west coast, guitar-based pop. The band was formed in 1981 by Susanna Hoffs (b. 1962; guitar, vocals), Debbi Peterson (b. 1961; drums, vocals), Vicki Peterson (b. 1958; guitar, vocals) and Annette Zilinskas (bass, vocals). The Bangles' first recordings were made on their own Downkiddie label and then for Miles Copeland's Faulty Products, which resulted in the eponymous mini-album.

On signing to CBS Records in 1983, Zilinskas departed and was replaced by former **Runaways** member Michael Steele (b. 1954; bass, vocals). 'Hero Takes A Fall' failed to chart, but their interpretation of Kimberley Rew's 'Going Down To Liverpool' scraped into the UK singles listing and their debut album, *All Over The Place*, achieved a minor US chart placing.

However it was the US/UK number 2 hit 'Manic Monday' (written by **Prince**) and the success of *Different Light* that really won an audience. Their gorgeous interpretation of Jules Shear's 'If She Knew What She Wants' showed touches of mid-60s **Mamas And The Papas**, while 'Walk Like An Egyptian' gave the band a US number 1/UK number 3 hit. Their version of **Simon And Garfunkel**'s 'Hazy Shade Of Winter', which was featured in the movie *Less Than Zero*, reached US number 2 in 1988.

Everything included 1989's transatlantic number 1 hit 'Eternal Flame'. Featuring lead vocals from Hoffs, the song was viewed by the other band members as an unnecessary departure from the Bangles' *modus operandi*, with its use of string backing and barely any instrumental contribution from them. Internal conflict led to the decision to dissolve the band at the end of the year. Hoffs embarked on a lukewarm solo career, while the remaining members failed to make any impact with their respective projects. They re-formed in 2000 for live dates and had further exposure in 2001 when **Atomic Kitten** took their cover version of 'Eternal Flame' to the top of the UK charts.

BAR-KAYS

Formed in Memphis, Tennessee, USA by Jimmy King (guitar), Ronnie Caldwell (organ), Phalon Jones (saxophone), Ben Cauley (trumpet), James Alexander (bass) and Carl Cunningham (drums) were originally known as the River Arrows. Signed to Stax Records, the Bar-Kays were groomed as that label's second-string house band by **Booker T. And The MGs**' drummer Al Jackson. They were **Otis Redding**'s touring backing group, and the tragic plane crash that took Redding's life in 1967 also claimed King, Caldwell, Jones and Cunningham. Alexander, who missed the flight, put together a new line-up with Cauley, the sole survivor of the accident, recruiting Harvey Henderson (saxophone), Ronnie Gordon (keyboards), Michael Toles (guitar), Willie Hall (drums) and Roy Cunningham (drums). Further personnel changes saw Cauley, Cunningham, Gordon and Toles dropping out and the addition of vocalist Larry Dodson and keyboardist Winston Stewart. The new line-up pursued a funk-based direction on their own releases. 'Son Of Shaft' reached the US R&B Top 10 in 1972, whereas 'Shake Your Rump To The Funk', 'Move Your Boogie Body' and 'Freakshow On The Dancefloor' were aimed at the disco market. Dodson, Henderson and Stewart carried the band's name into the 90s, but the latter two called it a day in 1993, leaving Dodson to carry on with original member James Alexander and several new recruits.

BARCLAY JAMES HARVEST

This UK progressive rock band was formed by Stewart 'Woolly' Wolstenholme (b. 1947; keyboards, vocals), John Lees (b. 1947; guitar, vocals), Les Holroyd (b. 1948; bass, vocals) and Mel Pritchard (b. 1948; drums). The band became one of Harvest Record's first signings. Their blend of melodic 'underground' music was initially acclaimed, although commercial success eluded them for years. Their early albums featured the mellotron and they were able to combine earthy guitar with harmony vocals. 'Mockingbird' from 1971's *Once Again*

became the albatross around their necks, with the orchestrated classical style leaving the band open to sniping critics. Fortunes changed when they signed with Polydor Records in 1974, releasing *Everyone Is Everybody Else*, and in 1976 they reached the UK charts with *Octoberon*. After 1978's *XII*, Wolstenholme left to embark on a solo career. Barclay James Harvest's live *Concert For The People*, recorded in Berlin, became their most commercially successful record in the UK. In Germany the band are major artists, while in Britain their loyal followers are able to view, with a degree of satisfaction, that Barclay James Harvest rode out the criticism and stayed on their chosen musical path without compromise

BARDENS, PETER

An accomplished organist, Bardens (b. 1945, England, d. 2002, USA) was a founder member of the Cheynes, before a brief spell in **Them**. By 1966 he was fronting the club-based Peter B's, which included drummer Mick Fleetwood and guitarist **Peter Green**. They recorded 'If You Wanna Be Happy', before being absorbed into Shotgun Express, a soul-inspired revue featuring **Rod Stewart**. Bardens later formed the short-lived Village, before releasing his first solo album, *The Answer* (1970). This informal selection featured Peter Green, under the pseudonym 'Andy Gee'. Peter Bardens was more focused and showcased the artist's touring group.

In 1972 Bardens formed Camel, remaining with this successful unit for six years before going solo again with *Heart To Heart*. He later divided his time between session work and crafted adult rock and new-age material, exemplified on his US-charting 1987 release *Seen One Earth* and 1991's *Water Colors*. In 1994 he formed Mirage with several leading prog rock musicians, including ex-bandmate Andy Ward and Dave Sinclair. Bardens succumbed to lung cancer in January 2002.

BARENAKED LADIES

Canadian group formed in 1988 by songwriters Steven Page (b. 1970; guitar, vocals) and Ed Robertson (b. 1970; guitar, vocals). Brothers Jim (b. 1970; bass, keyboards) and Andrew Creeggan (b. 1971; congas) and Tyler Stewart (b. 1967; drums) were soon added to the line-up. Their debut album, *Gordon*, sold half a million copies in Canada. Their melodic pop, with its strong harmonies and string-driven acoustics, was evident on songs such as 'Be My Yoko Ono' and 'If I Had A Million Dollars'. Their self-deprecating humour and high energy make for an entertaining live show, captured on 1996's *Rock Spectacle*. They bounced back into the commercial spotlight in 1998 with the infuriatingly catchy US chart-topping single 'One Week'. The attendant *Stunt* was also a success. The follow-up, *Maroon*, was a mixed attempt to introduce a touch of levity to Page and Robertson's songwriting formula.

BARRETT, SYD

UK-born Barrett (b. Roger Keith Barrett, 1946) acquired his 'Syd' sobriquet at school, where his friends included **Roger Waters** and Dave Gilmour. Later, while an art student in London, Barrett played in the aspiring R&B act the Hollering Blues. Meanwhile Waters had formed his own group and invited Barrett to join. They took the name the Pink Floyd Sound from an album featuring blues musicians Pink Anderson and Floyd Council. Having dropped their suffix, **Pink Floyd** became part of London's nascent 'underground' scene.

Barrett was their principal songwriter, composing the hits 'Arnold Layne' and 'See Emily Play', as well as the bulk of *The Piper At The Gates Of Dawn*.

Barrett's child-like, often naive compositional style was offset by his highly original playing. An impulsive, impressionistic guitarist, his unconventional use of feedback, slide and echo did much to transfer the mystery and imagery of Pink Floyd's live sound into a studio equivalent. Sadly an indulgence in hallucinogenic drugs led to a disintegration in Barrett's mental health (reflected on 'Apples And Oranges'). Dave Gilmour joined in 1968, prompting suggestions that Barrett would retire from live work and concentrate solely on songwriting. Instead, he departed the following April. Within a month Barrett began a solo album. Gilmour took a keen interest in the sessions. In June he suggested that he and Waters should produce some tracks, and the rest of the album was completed in three days. *The Madcap Laughs* is an artistic triumph, on which Barrett's fragile vocals and delicate melodies create a hypnotic, ethereal atmosphere. It contains some of his finest performances, notably 'Octopus', which was issued as a single, and 'Golden Hair', a poem from James Joyce's *Chamber Music* set to a moving refrain.

In 1970 Barrett began recording a second album with Gilmour as producer. *Barrett* was more assertive, but less poignant, than its predecessor. It included the chilling 'Rats', one of the singer's most vitriolic performances. Barrett completed a session for BBC Radio 1's 'Sounds Of The Seventies', but despite declaring himself 'totally together', he was becoming a recluse. The following year he put together Stars, but after a few live gigs in Barrett's native Cambridge he failed to surface for their next date and shows were cancelled.

Pink Floyd included a tribute to Barrett, 'Shine On You Crazy Diamond', on the bestselling 1975 release *Wish You Were Here*, but regrettably Barrett's precarious mental state precluded any further involvement in music. *Opel* comprised unissued masters and alternate takes, enhancing his reputation for startling, original work as evinced by the affecting title track, bafflingly omitted from *The Madcap Laughs*. Barrett, by now living back in Cambridge with his mother, pronounced his approval of the project when it was

completed in 1988. Although he suffers from diabetes, rumours of Barrett's ill-health tend to be exaggerated. He simply lives quietly and prefers to forget his past musical career.

BARRY, JEFF

Barry (b. 1938, USA) began his career as a singer, recording for RCA Records and Decca Records between 1959 and 1962. He enjoyed concurrent success as a songwriter, most notably with 'Tell Laura I Love Her', a US Top 10 hit for Ray Peterson and a UK number 1 for Ricky Valance. In 1961, Barry was contracted to Trinity Music, for whom he completed over 100 compositions and gained experience in arranging, producing and recording demos. Ellie Greenwich, who he later married, proved to be the most enduring of his many collaborators. Together they wrote 'Maybe I Know' (Leslie Gore) and 'Do Wah Diddy Diddy' (**Manfred Mann**) and, as the Raindrops, recorded the US Top 20 hit 'The Kind Of Boy You Can't Forget'. However, they are best known for their work with Phil Spector, including 'Da Doo Ron Ron' and 'Then He Kissed Me' (the Crystals), 'Be My Baby' and 'Baby, I Love You' (the Ronettes) and 'River Deep – Mountain High' (Ike And Tina Turner). The duo wrote and co-produced releases for the **Dixie Cups**, **Shangri-Las** and **Neil Diamond**. When their marriage ended in 1965, Barry resumed his recording career but achieved greater success in partnership with singer Andy Kim, writing, producing and performing for the Archies' cartoon series. His work with Greenwich has rightly stood the test of time, having reached the pinnacle of stylish pop music during the 60s.

BARTHOLOMEW, DAVE

An American producer, arranger, songwriter, bandleader and artist, Bartholomew (b. 1920) produced and co-wrote most of **Fats Domino**'s major hits for Imperial Records. Bartholomew performed in marching bands, formed his first band in New Orleans in the late 40s and backed **Little Richard** on early recordings. In 1948, Bartholomew discovered Domino in New Orleans and introduced him to Imperial. They collaborated on 'The Fat Man' (1950), which became the first of over a dozen hits co-authored by the pair and produced by Bartholomew. Bartholomew's other credits included Smiley Lewis's 'I Hear You Knocking' and 'One Night' (later a toned-down hit for **Elvis Presley**), Lloyd Price's 'Lawdy Miss Clawdy', and records for Earl King, Roy Brown, Huey 'Piano' Smith, Robert Parker, Frankie Ford and Snooks Eaglin. In 1963, Imperial was sold to Liberty Records, at which point Bartholomew left.

In 1972, **Chuck Berry** reworked Bartholomew's 'My Ding-A-Ling', and achieved his only US number 1. In 1981, Bartholomew recorded a Dixieland album and in the 90s was involved with occasional special events such as the New Orleans Jazz & Heritage Festival. He was inducted into the Rock And Roll Hall Of Fame in 1991.

BASEMENT JAXX

This respected, UK-based DJing and production duo comprises Felix Buxton and Simon Ratcliffe. Setting out to rediscover the original feeling of early Chicago house music they began by holding illegal parties in Brixton, south London, in 1994. Their unique cocktail of influences (rap, funk, ragga, disco and garage, all given a deep house twist) has been described as 'punk garage' and has found a devoted audience in their native London and beyond (especially in Japan, Canada, Australia and the USA), where their DJing skills have been in demand. Their Basement Jaxx club nights in London never fail to fill venues.

Following the release of the club classics 'Fly Life' and 'Samba Magic', the duo signed to highly successful XL Records in 1998. Their first single for the label, 'Red Alert', released in April 1999, received much praise and radio airplay in the UK and US, and broke into the UK Top 5. The single's critical and commercial success was repeated by the follow-up, 'Rendezvous', and the attendant *Remedy*. The duo's faces were rarely not on the covers of hip music and style magazines during 1999 and many pundits were naming them as the saviours of truly inventive dance music. *Rooty*, titled after the duo's underground parties in London, was released to even greater acclaim in July 2001.

BASSEY, SHIRLEY

After touring the UK in revues and variety shows, Bassey (b. 1937) had her first UK hit with the calypso-styled 'Banana Boat Song' (1957), followed by 'Kiss Me Honey Honey, Kiss Me'. The unique Bassey phrasing started to emerge in 1959 with the UK chart-topper 'As I Love You', and continued through to the mid-70s in songs including 'As Long As He Needs Me', 'You'll Never Know', 'What Now My Love', 'I (Who Have Nothing)' and 'For All We Know'. The Welsh singer's rise to the top was swift and by the early 60s she was headlining in New York and Las Vegas. In 1964, she had a US hit with 'Goldfinger', and she also sang the James Bond themes for *Diamonds Are Forever* and *Moonraker*. In 1969, she moved to Switzerland but continued to play major concert halls throughout the world.

In 1976, the American Guild Of Variety Artists voted her 'Best Female Entertainer'. The following year she received a Britannia Award for the 'Best Female Solo Singer In The Last 50 Years'. In 1981, Bassey announced her semi-retirement, but continued to appear occasionally throughout the 80s and recorded a few albums. In one of pop's more unlikely collaborations, she was teamed with Swiss electro-pop duo **Yello** in 1987 for 'The Rhythm Divine'.

In the following decade Bassey proved herself to be an enduring, powerful and exciting act, performing hits such as 'Big Spender', 'Nobody Does It Like Me' and 'What Kind Of Fool Am I'. In 1993, she received the CBE. After celebrating her 60th birthday with nine sell-out concerts at London's Royal Festival Hall (among other locations), and on television in *Happy Birthday, Shirley*, she duetted with **Chris Rea** on the clubland hit "Disco' La Passione'. It was the title song from her first feature film, written and scored by Rea, in which she played herself. In 1997, Bassey reinvented herself once more, and was back in the UK Top 20 with 'History Repeating', a collaboration with big beat artists the **Propellerheads**. Two years later, *The Birthday Concert* album was nominated for a Grammy Award.

In the year 2000, Bassey embarked on her Millennium Tour and also played Las Vegas for the first time in a decade. In the same year, she was created a Dame Commander of the Most Excellent Order of the British Empire.

BATT, MIKE

UK songwriter Batt (b. 1950) began his career as an in-house music publisher and songwriter, before moving into production, working on albums by Hapshash And The Coloured Coat and the Groundhogs. In 1973 he discovered a hit-making machine: *The Wombles*, a children's television programme that spawned a number of hit singles. He continued to produce for other artists, including the **Kursaal Flyers**, **Steeleye Span** and Linda Lewis. He released eponymous orchestral albums, including portraits of the **Rolling Stones**, **Bob Dylan**, **Simon And Garfunkel**, **George Harrison**, **Elton John** and **Cat Stevens**. As a soloist, Batt hit number 4 with 'Summertime City' in 1975, and Art Garfunkel took his 'Bright Eyes' (from the movie *Watership Down*) to number 1 in 1979. Since then, Batt has continued to write for films and musicals, including David Essex's 'A Winter's Tale' (lyrics by Tim Rice). His stage musical, *The Hunting Of The Snark*, opened in London in 1991 but closed just seven weeks later.

Batt worked in both the classical and pop music fields during the 90s and relaunched the Wombles. In summer 2001, he was commissioned to write the UK Conservative Party's election campaign theme ('Heartlands'). In August of the same year, he was badly injured in a car crash in Spain.

BAUHAUS

Originally known as Bauhaus 1919, this UK quartet featured Peter Murphy (vocals), Daniel Ash (vocals, guitar), David Jay, aka David J., (b. David Jay Haskins; vocals, bass) and Kevin Haskins (drums). Within months of forming, they recorded their 1979 debut single, the nine-minute gothic anthem 'Bela Lugosi's Dead'. They recorded for various independent labels – Small Wonder, Axix, 4AD Records and Beggars Banquet Records – and recorded four albums in as many years, of which 1981's *Mask* proved the most accessible. They had a cameo appearance in the movie *The Hunger*, starring David Bowie, and later took advantage of the Bowie

connection to record a copy of 'Ziggy Stardust', their only UK Top 20 hit. The group disbanded in 1983. Murphy briefly joined **Japan**'s Mick Karn in Dali's Car; the remaining three members soldiered on as Love And Rockets. The original members reunited in the mid-90s for several live dates in Los Angeles, which led to a fully-fledged reunion tour in 1998. *Gotham Live 1998* captured the band's performance at New York's Hammerstein Ballroom.

BAY CITY ROLLERS

Formed during 1967 in Edinburgh, Scotland, the Bay City Rollers were created as a **Beatles** covers band based around brothers Derek (b. 1955; drums) and Alan Longmuir (b. 1953; bass). After meeting entrepreneur Tam Paton, they played on the Scottish circuit until breaking into the UK Top 10 in 1971 with 'Keep On Dancing', produced by Jonathan King. The single proved a one-off and for the next couple of years the band struggled. After various personnel shuffles, the Longmuirs added another three Edinburgh musicians: Les McKeown (b. 1955; vocals), Stuart 'Woody' Wood (b. 1957; guitar) and Eric Faulkner (b. 1955; guitar). Striking a chord with teenage and pre-pubescent fans in search of pin-up pop stars, they enjoyed a run of UK hits, including 'Remember (Sha La La)', 'Shang-A-Lang', 'Summerlove Sensation' and 'All Of Me Loves All Of You'. In 1975, they enjoyed two consecutive UK number 1s – 'Bye Bye Baby' and 'Give A Little Love' and topped the US charts with 'Saturday Night'.

Line-up changes followed with the arrival of Ian Mitchell and Billy Lyall, but over the next three years disaster struck. McKeown was charged with reckless driving after hitting and killing a 75-year-old widow, and Faulkner and

Longmuir attempted suicide. Paton was subsequently jailed for committing indecent acts with underage teenagers, Mitchell starred in a pornographic movie and Lyall died from an AIDS-related illness in 1989. A tawdry conclusion to one of the most famous teenybop acts in British pop history.

When Faulkner attempted to re-form the band in 1992, unemployed music fan David Gates stole their guitars and hid them in a derelict house. He later claimed in court that he was attempting to 'save the world from the Bay City Rollers'.

BEACH BOYS

The Beach Boys were formed in California, USA, in 1961 by brothers Brian (b. 1942), Carl (b. 1946, d. 1998) and Dennis Wilson (b. 1944, d. 1983), their cousin Mike Love (b. 1941), and schoolfriend Al Jardine (b. 1942). Brian's songwriting ability and Dennis's fondness for surfing culminated in 'Surfin'', a minor hit which brought the group a recording contract with Capitol Records. Over the next 18 months the Beach Boys had 10 US hits and released four albums of surfing and hot-rod songs. (David Marks, who temporarily replaced Jardine while he attended dentistry college, featured on the covers of many of the group's early records.) However their punishing workload began to affect Brian, who was additionally writing material for **Jan And Dean**.

In 1963, the Beach Boys hit the UK via 'Surfin' USA', which mildly interrupted the Merseybeat domination of the charts. The predominantly working-class image of the British beat-group scene was at odds with the clean and wholesome west-coast lifestyle portrayed by the Beach Boys. During 1964, a further four albums were released, culminating in the *Christmas Album* – eight albums in just over two years, six of which were arranged and produced by Brian, in addition to his having written 63 out of the 84 songs. However, the **Beatles** had begun to dominate the US charts, and in their wake the British invasion took place. This drove Brian to compete against the Beatles, gaining some pyrrhic revenge, when in 1966 the Beach Boys were voted number 1 group worldwide by the UK music press (the Beatles came second).

Wilson's maturity as a composer was developing with classics like 'I Get Around', 'California Girls' and 'God Only Knows', and the quality of albums such as *Summer Days And Summer Nights!!* and *Today* was extremely high. Many of Wilson's songs portrayed his own insecurity as an adolescent and songs such as 'In My Room', 'Wouldn't It Be Nice' and 'Girl Don't Tell Me' found a receptive audience who could relate to the lyrics. While their instrumentals were average, the vocal combination was immaculate: both Carl and Brian had perfect pitch, even though Brian was deaf in one ear (reputedly from his father's beatings).

In private the 'musical genius' was working on his self-intended masterpiece, *Pet Sounds*. It was released in 1966 to outstanding reviews but, for no explicable reason, poor sales. Brian was devastated when it only reached US number 10, and was mortified when the Beatles' *Sgt. Peppers Lonely Hearts Club Band* was released a year later. He had already experienced two nervous breakdowns and retired from performing with the group, turning instead to barbiturates. Publicly he was briefly replaced by Glen Campbell (b. 1936), then by Bruce Johnston. Yet through this turmoil the Beach Boys rose to their peak at the end of 1966 with 'Good Vibrations'. They then embarked on a major European tour, releasing 'Heroes And Villains' (lyrics by Van Dyke Parks). Brian meanwhile attempted a counter-attack on the Beatles, with a project to be known as *Smile*. This became the band's albatross, although it was never officially released. The painstaking hours spent on this project is now one of pop's legendary tales. Parts of the material surfaced on their next three albums, and further tracks appeared on other collections up until 1971.

Conflict between Brian and the rest of the band was also surfacing. Love in particular wanted to continue with their immaculate pop music, and argued that Brian was getting too 'far out'. Indeed, Brian's reclusive nature, fast-increasing weight and growing dependence on drugs added fuel to Love's argument. *Smiley Smile* in 1967 and *Wild Honey* the following year were comparative failures. Their music had lost its cohesiveness and their mentor and guiding light had by now retreated to his bed. In Europe the group were still having hits, and even had a surprise UK chart-topper in 1968 with 'Do It Again', with Love's nasal vocals taking the lead on a song harping back to better times.

In 1969, the Beach Boys left Capitol in a blaze of litigation. *Sunflower* was an artistic triumph but a commercial disaster, to which Dennis contributed four songs including 'Forever'. Over the next year they set about rebuilding their US credibility, having lost ground to the new-wave bands from San Francisco. They toured constantly, and the arrival of *Surf's Up* in 1971 completed their remarkable renaissance. The record's ecological stance was years ahead of its time, and critics were unanimous in their praise.

As Dennis co-starred with James Taylor in the cult road movie *Two-Lane Blacktop*, Brian's life was deteriorating into mental instability. Miraculously the band were able to maintain their career despite shifting personnel. The  addition of Ricky Fataar, Blondie Chaplin and Daryl Dragon gave the band a fuller sound, culminating in *Holland*, for which the entire Beach Boys organization (including wives and children) moved to Holland for eight months. A year later, *Endless Summer*, a compilation, unexpectedly rocketed to the top of the US charts, reinforcing Love and Jardine's theory that all anybody wanted of the Beach Boys was surfing and car songs. With the addition of James William Guercio (ex-**Chicago**), the band enjoyed major concert tour success, and ended 1974 as *Rolling Stone*'s 'Band of the Year'. *Spirit Of America*, another compilation of earlier tracks, stayed on the US charts for almost a year. Meanwhile, Brian's physical and mental health had

only moderately well. At the same time the Beach Boys released 'Kokomo', included in the Tom Cruise movie *Cocktail*; unexpectedly it went to US number 1. In 1990, the rest of the group took Brian to court in an alleged attempt to wrest his $80 million fortune from him: maintaining he was insane and unable to look after himself. He defended the case but eventually accepted a settlement, which stipulated that he sever links with his controversial doctor/guru Eugene Landy. He was then officially sacked/resigned and proceeded to get back monies which had been pouring in from his back catalogue. However, Mike Love then issued a writ to Brian claiming he co-wrote 79 songs with him, including 'California Girls', 'I Get Around' and 'Surfin' USA'. In 1993 the band continued to tour, and during 1994 mutterings were heard that the pending lawsuit would be settled, as Love and Brian were at least speaking to each other. Late that year it was announced that a substantial settlement had been made to Love.

In 1995 a thin, handsome, recently remarried Wilson began working with Love, but no new material was forthcoming. Carl Wilson underwent treatment for cancer in 1997, tragically losing his battle the following year. Since his death there have been two rival bands touring under the Beach Boys moniker, one led by Mike Love with Bruce Johnston. The other goes under the banner Beach Boys, Family And Friends, and is led by Al Jardine together with Brian's daughters Wendy and Carnie and Jardine's two sons Matt and Adam. Jardine started litigation in 2001 claiming that Love has no right to use the name 'Beach Boys'. The continuing absence of Brian, who is concentrating on his solo career, casts a major shadow on the group.

BEASTIE BOYS

This famed white rap trio was formed in New York, USA around Adam 'MCA' Yauch (b. 1967; vocals), Mike 'D' Diamond (b. 1965; vocals), Adam 'King Adrock' Horovitz (b. 1966; vocals, guitar), and John Berry (guitar) and Kate Schellenbach (who both departed after the hardcore *Polly Wog Stew* EP). The 1983 EP *Cooky Puss* offered the first evidence of rap, and friend and sometime band member, Rick Rubin signed them to his fledgling Def Jam Records label. Their debut revealed a collision of bad attitudes, spearheaded by the raucous single, '(You Gotta) Fight For Your Right (To Party)'. There was nothing self-conscious or sophisticated about the lyrics, just complaints about their parents confiscating their pornography or telling them to turn the stereo down. However, 1986's *Licensed To Ill* became the first rap album to top the US charts and by the time 'No Sleep Till Brooklyn' and 'She's On It' charted, the band had become a *cause célèbre*. Their stage shows regularly featured caged, half-naked females, while their Volkswagen pendants resulted in a crime wave, with fans stealing from vehicles throughout the UK.

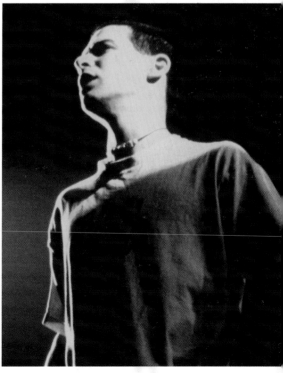

deteriorated further and he was undergoing therapy. However in 1976, *15 Big Ones* scored a hit with **Chuck Berry**'s 'Rock And Roll Music'. The publicity centred on a tasteless 'Brian Is Back' campaign, with the now obese Wilson being unwillingly pushed into the spotlight.

In 1977, the band signed a recording contract with CBS Records (reputedly worth $8 million) on the terms that Brian contributed at least four new songs and a total of 70 per cent of the material for each album. The first album was the patchy *LA (Light Album)*, which nevertheless produced a sizeable hit with Al Jardine's 'Lady Lynda'. The next official Beach Boys work was *Keeping The Summer Alive*, a poor album, made without Dennis (by now he had a serious cocaine habit which hampered the recording of his excellent solo album *Pacific Ocean Blue*). By 1980 only Love and Jardine survived from the original line-up. Carl delivered his first solo album, a beautifully sung, well-produced record that flopped. One track, 'Heaven', later became a regular part of the Beach Boys' repertoire.

In 1982, Brian Wilson was officially dismissed, and was admitted to hospital, weighing a massive 320 pounds. A year later, Dennis was tragically drowned while diving from his boat. His death snapped his brother out of his stupor, and Brian gradually re-emerged to participate onstage. A clean and healthy-looking band graced the back of *The Beach Boys*. Following this collection, and without a recording contract, they decided to concentrate on touring the world. In 1987, they teamed up with rap act the Fat Boys for a remake of the Surfaris' 'Wipe Out'.

In 1988, Brian returned with the solo album for which his fans had waited over 20 years. The critics and fans loved it, but sadly the album sold

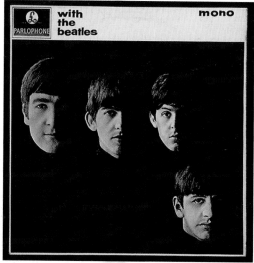
After a break for solo projects, the band reunited in 1989, but the public had forgotten them. *Paul's Boutique* (co-produced by the Dust Brothers) remains one of rap's most overlooked pieces a complex reflection of pop culture which is infinitely subtler than their debut. *Check Your Head* saw them returning to their thrash roots and in the meantime the trio had invested wisely, setting up their own magazine, studio and label, Grand Royal. During this period Yauch had become a Buddhist, speaking out in the press against US trade links with China because of the latter's annexation of Tibet. In 1994, he set up the Milarepa Fund to raise funds and public awareness of the situation in Tibet, and organized the hugely successful Tibetan Freedom Concerts from 1996 to 1998.

Ill Communication, their debut for Grand Royal, was another voyage into Beastie Boys thuggism. *The In Sound From Way Out!* was a collection of b-sides and instrumental takes, and merely a taster for 1998's *Hello Nasty*. A return to a more sparse, rap-dominated sound, the album topped the charts on both sides of the Atlantic. Grand Royal, which had enjoyed eight years of critical and commercial success, was forced to close down in September 2001.

BEAT (UK)

Founded in England in 1978, the original Beat comprised Dave Wakeling (b. 1956; vocals, guitar), Andy Cox (b. 1960; guitar), David Steele (b. 1960; bass) and Everett Morton (b. 1951; drums). Local pub-circuit success led to them being signed to the Two-Tone label and the Beat expanded to include punk rapper Ranking Roger (b. Roger Charlery, 1961) and Jamaican saxophonist Saxa. Their ska/pop fusion led to their debut single, a cover version of Smokey Robinson's 'Tears Of A Clown', reaching the UK Top 10. They then formed their own label, Go Feet, and enjoyed a run of UK hits. 'Mirror In The Bathroom' and 'Best Friend' worked both as observations on personal relationships and more generalized putdowns of the 'Me' generation. The band's political awareness led to 'Stand Down Margaret' (about British Prime Minister Margaret Thatcher). Their debut album, 1980's *I Just Can't Stop It*, included several hit singles. Within a year, however, their pop-based style was replaced by a stronger reggae influence. *Wha'ppen?* and *Special Beat Service* were well received, but the run of hits temporarily evaporated. By 1982, Saxa had retired, replaced by Wesley Magoogan. The Beat continued to tour extensively, but their dissolution was imminent. Their career ended with a cover version of Andy Williams' 60s hit, 'Can't Get Used To Losing You', which gave the band their biggest UK hit.

Ranking Roger and Dave Wakeling went on to form General Public while Cox and Steele recruited Roland Gift to launch the **Fine Young Cannibals**.

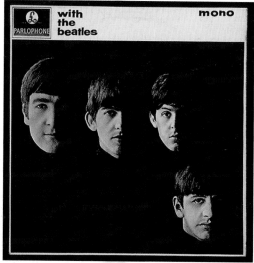

BEATLES

The phenomenon that became the Beatles began in Liverpool, England, in 1957, when teenager Paul McCartney (b. James Paul McCartney, 1942) auditioned as guitarist for the Quarry Men, a skiffle group led by John Lennon (b. 1940, d. 1980). Within a year, 15-year-old guitarist George Harrison (b. 1943, d. 2001) was recruited, alongside Stuart Sutcliffe (b. 1940, d. 1962). After a brief spell as Johnny And The Moondogs, the band rechristened themselves the Silver Beetles. In 1960, they played before impresario Larry Parnes, winning the dubious distinction of a support slot on a tour of Scotland with autumnal idol Johnny Gentle. Later that year the group were renamed the

Beatles. A full-time drummer, Pete Best (b. 1941) was recruited and they secured a residency at Bruno Koschminder's Indra Club in Hamburg, honing their repertoire of R&B and rock 'n' roll favourites during six-hour-sets.

Already, the musical/lyrical partnership of Lennon/McCartney was bearing fruit, anticipating a body of work unparalleled in modern popular music. The image of the group was also changing, most noticeably with their fringed haircuts or, as they were later known, the 'mop-tops', the creation of Sutcliffe's German fiancée Astrid Kirchherr. The first German trip ended when the under-age Harrison was deported in 1960 and the others lost their work permits. Afterwards the group reassembled for regular performances at Liverpool's Cavern Club and briefly returned to Germany, where they performed at the Top Ten club and backed Tony Sheridan on 'My Bonnie'. Meanwhile, Sutcliffe decided to leave, staying in Germany to paint. McCartney then took up the bass guitar.

In 1961, Brian Epstein became the Beatles' manager. Despite his enthusiasm, several major record companies passed up the group, although they were granted an audition with Decca Records in 1962. After some prevarication, the label rejected the band in favour of Brian Poole And The Tremeloes. The tragic news that Stuart Sutcliffe had died in Hamburg of a brain haemorrhage, took the Beatles back to Germany. While there, they began playing at Hamburg's Star Club. Shortly afterwards Epstein found a Beatles convert in EMI Records producer George Martin, who signed the group to Parlophone; three months later, Best was sacked – he looked the part, but his drumming was poor. His replacement was Ringo Starr (b. Richard Starkey, 1940), the extrovert and locally popular drummer from Rory Storm And The Hurricanes.

At the end of 1962, the Beatles reached the UK charts with their debut, 'Love Me Do'. The single was far removed from the traditional 'beat combo' sound, and the use of Lennon's harmonica made the song stand out. On 13 February 1963 the Beatles appeared on UK television's *Thank Your Lucky Stars* to promote 'Please Please Me'; they were seen by six million viewers. The single, with its distinctive harmonies and infectious group beat, soon topped the UK charts and signalled the imminent overthrow of the solo singer in favour of an irresistible wave of Mersey talent. From this point, the Beatles progressed artistically and commercially with each successive record. After seven weeks at the top with 'From Me To You', they released 'She Loves You' – the catchphrase 'Yeah, Yeah, Yeah' was echoed in frequent newspaper headlines. The single hit number 1, retreated, then returned to the top seven weeks later as Beatlemania gripped the nation. The Beatles became a household name. 'She Loves You' was replaced by 'I Want To Hold Your Hand', which had UK advance sales of over one million and entered the charts at number 1.

Until 1964, America had proven a barren ground for British pop artists. The Beatles changed that. 'I Want To Hold Your Hand' was helped by the band's television appearance on the *Ed Sullivan Show* and soon surpassed

UK sales. By April, they held the first five places in the *Billboard* Hot 100, while in Canada they boasted nine records in the Top 10.

By 1965, Lennon and McCartney's writing had matured to a startling degree and their albums were relying less on other material. Their first two films, *A Hard Day's Night* and *Help!*, were not the usual pop celluloid cash-ins but were witty and inventive; they achieved critical acclaim as well as box-office success. The same year also saw the Beatles awarded MBEs for services to British industry and the release of their first double-sided number 1, 'We Can Work It Out'/'Day Tripper'.

At Christmas 1965, the Beatles released *Rubber Soul*, an album that was not a collection of would-be hits or favourite cover versions, as the previous releases had been, but a startlingly diverse collection, ranging from the pointed satire of 'Nowhere Man' to the reflective 'In My Life'. Pointers to their future styles included Harrison's use of sitar on 'Norwegian Wood' – that same year, the **Byrds**, the **Yardbirds** and the **Rolling Stones** also incorporated Eastern-influenced sounds into their work. Significantly George Harrison also wrote two major songs for *Rubber Soul*, 'Think For Yourself' and 'If I Needed Someone' (later a hit for the **Hollies**).

During 1966, the Beatles continued performing their increasingly complex arrangements before scarcely controllable fans, but the novelty of fandom was wearing frustratingly thin. By the summer, the group were exhausted and defeated. They played their last official performance at Candlestick Park, San Francisco, on 29 August.

The gloriously elaborate harmonies and charmingly prosaic theme of 'Paperback Writer' were another step forward, followed by a double-sided chart topper, 'Yellow Submarine'/'Eleanor Rigby'. The attendant album *Revolver* was equally varied, with Harrison's caustic 'Taxman', McCartney's plaintive 'For No One' and Lennon's drug-influenced 'I'm Only Sleeping' and the mantric and then-scary 'Tomorrow Never Knows'. The latter has been described as the most effective evocation of a LSD experience ever recorded.

After 1966, the Beatles retreated into the studio. 'Penny Lane'/ 'Strawberry Fields Forever', their first release for over six months, broke their long run of consecutive UK number 1s – it was kept off the top by Engelbert Humperdinck's 'Release Me'. Nevertheless, this landmark single brilliantly captured the talents of Lennon and McCartney. It was intended to be the jewel in the crown of their next album, but by the summer of 1967 they had sufficient material to release 13 new tracks on *Sgt. Peppers Lonely Hearts Club Band*. This turned out to be no mere pop album, but a cultural icon embracing pop art, garish fashion, drugs, instant mysticism and freedom from parental control. Although the Beatles had previously experimented with collages on *Beatles For Sale* and *Revolver*, they took the idea further on the sleeve of *Sgt. Pepper* which included photos of every influence on their lives that they could remember. The album had a gatefold sleeve, cardboard cut-out figurines, and, for the first time on a pop record, printed lyrics. The music had evolved too: instead of the traditional breaks between songs, one track merged into the next, linked by studio talk, laughter, electronic noises and animal sounds. The album closed with the epic 'Day In The Life', the Beatles' most ambitious work to date, featuring what Lennon described as 'a sound building up from nothing to the end of the world'.

While *Sgt. Peppers Lonely Hearts Club Band* topped the album charts, the group appeared on a live television broadcast playing 'All You Need Is Love'. The following week it entered many of the world's charts at number 1; but there was sadness, too – on 21 August 1967, Brian Epstein was found dead, from a cumulative overdose of the drug carbratol. With spiritual guidance from the Maharishi Mahesh Yogi, the Beatles took Epstein's death calmly and decided to proceed without a manager. The first fruits of their post-Epstein labour was the film *Magical Mystery Tour*, screened on UK television on Boxing Day 1967. The phantasmogorical movie received mixed reviews, but nobody could complain about the music.

In 1968, the Beatles became increasingly involved with running their company, Apple Corps (alongside a mismanaged boutique that came and went). The first Apple single, 'Hey Jude', was a warm-hearted ballad that progressed over its seven-minute duration into a rousing singalong finale. Their fourth film, *Yellow Submarine*, was a cartoon, and the graphics were acclaimed as a landmark in animation. The soundtrack album was half instrumental, with George Martin responsible for some interesting orchestral work. Only four new proper Beatles tracks were included, among them 'Hey Bulldog', 'Only A Northern Song' and 'It's All Too Much'. With their prolific output, the group crammed the remainder of their most recent material onto a double album, *The Beatles* (now known as *The White Album*), released in a stark white cover. The album revealed that the four musicians were already working in isolated neutrality.

Despite continued commercial success, the Beatles' inability as business executives was becoming apparent from the parlous state of Apple, to which Allen Klein attempted to restore some order. At the end of the decade, they released the transatlantic chart-topper 'Get Back', a return-to-roots venture which featured Billy Preston on organ. Cameras were present at their next recording sessions, as they ran through dozens of songs, many of which they had not played since Hamburg. A select few also witnessed the band's last 'public' performance on the rooftop of the Apple head-quarters in Savile Row, London. Amid the uncertainty of 1969, the Beatles enjoyed their final UK number 1 with 'The Ballad Of John And Yoko', on which only Lennon and McCartney performed.

In a sustained attempt to cover the increasing cracks, the Beatles reconvened for *Abbey Road*. The accompanying single coupled Lennon's 'Come Together' with Harrison's 'Something'. The latter gave Harrison the kudos he deserved; it has become the second-most covered Beatles song (the most popular is 'Yesterday'). The single reached only UK number 4, the band's lowest chart position since 1962.

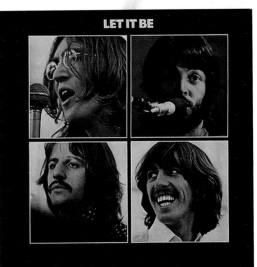

LET IT BE

With various solo projects coming up, the Beatles stumbled through 1970, their disunity emphasized in the depressing film *Let It Be*, which shows Harrison and Lennon clearly unhappy about McCartney's attitude towards the band. The subsequent album, finally pieced together by producer Phil Spector, was a controversial and bitty affair. It included an orchestrated 'Long And Winding Road' which provided their final US number 1, and there was their last official single, 'Let It Be', which entered the UK charts at number 2, only to drop to number 3 the following week, the final sad anti-climax before the inevitable split. The acrimonious dissolution of the Beatles, like that of no other band before or since, symbolized the end of an era that they had dominated and helped create.

John Lennon's tragic murder in 1980 put an end to speculation of any reunions, but in 1995, the first volume of *Anthology* was released. A collection of 52 previously unreleased out-takes and demo versions recorded between 1958 and 1964, plus eight spoken tracks taken from interviews. The album was accompanied by an excellent six-part television series, made with the help of Harrison, McCartney and Starr, and by the release of the new singles 'Free As A Bird' and 'Real Love' (Lennon's original demo vocals on both tracks were backed vocally and instrumentally by the other three Beatles). The critical reaction to *Anthology 2* and *Anthology 3* was equally strong. Further Beatles activity has included the release of a remixed *Yellow Submarine* in 1999, and the bulky *Anthology* book the following year. Harrison lost his battle with cancer in November 2001.

The most successful recording act of the twentieth century in the USA, with album sales of over 106 million, the Beatles are universally and unconditionally adored.

BEAU BRUMMELS
Formed in San Francisco, USA in 1964 by vocalist Sal Valentino (b. Sal Spampinato, 1942) with Ron Elliott (b. 1943; guitar, vocals), Ron Meagher (b. 1941; bass) and John Petersen (b. 1942; drums). Playing a staple diet of current hits and material by the **Beatles** and **Searchers**, the Beau Brummels enjoyed a committed local following. Declan Mulligan (b. Eire; guitar) subsequently joined. Signed to local label Autumn Records, the quintet enjoyed early US hits with 'Laugh Laugh' and 'Just A Little'. Their first two albums fused folk, country and R&B, with Valentino's deep, tremulous delivery providing an unmistakable lead. Mulligan left in 1965, but the Beau Brummels continued to make progress and moved to Warner Brothers Records. New member Don Irving was featured on their disappointing next collection, *Beau Brummels 66*. Irving and Petersen both left (the latter later joined **Harpers Bizarre**) and the remaining trio completed the exquisite *Triangle*. Meagher left in 1967, leaving Elliott and Valentino to complete *Bradley's Barn*, an early excursion into country rock, before separating. Valentino issued three solo singles before founding Stoneground. Elliott completed *The Candlestickmaker*, formed the disappointing Pan, then undertook session work.

The original Beau Brummels regrouped in 1974, although Meagher was replaced by Dan Levitt. *Beau Brummels* was an engaging collection, but progress halted in 1975 when Petersen left for a Harpers Bizarre reunion. Peter Tepp provided a temporary replacement, but the project was abandoned. The Beau Brummels have since enjoyed several short-lived resurrections. Archive recordings have kept the band's name and music alive.

BEAUTIFUL SOUTH
This highly literate UK pop outfit grew from the ashes of the **Housemartins**. The original line-up featured vocalists Paul Heaton (b. 1962) and David Hemingway (b. 1960), who recruited Sean Welch (b. 1965; bass), Briana Corrigan (vocals), David Stead (b. 1966; drums) and Heaton's new co-writer, David Rotheray (b. 1963; guitar). Continuing an association with Go! Discs, their first single was 'Song For Whoever' which reached UK number 2 in 1989. *Welcome To The Beautiful South* (1989) was critically praised and 'A Little Time' (1990) became their first number 1 single.

A writer able to deal with emotive subjects in an intelligent and forthright manner, Heaton's next topic was alcoholism in 'Old Red Eyes Is Back'. However, Corrigan objected to the lyrics of '36D' (a song about topless models) and left the band after *0898: Beautiful South*. Her replacement, Jacqueline Abbott (b. 1973), was introduced on a cover version of Fred Neil's 'Everybody's Talkin'', and more fully on *Miaow*. The singles collection, *Carry On Up The Charts* dominated the UK chart listings in late 1994 and early 1995.

'Rotterdam' and 'Don't Marry Her', from *Blue Is The Colour*, continued the band's run of hit singles. Heaton worked with his old Housemartins colleague Norman Cook aka **Fatboy Slim** on 1998's *Quench*, which featured the UK number 2 hit single 'Perfect 10'. Abbott departed company with the band shortly after the release of 2000's *Painting It Red*. The following year, Heaton released his solo debut, *Fat Chance*, under the pseudonym Biscuit Boy Aka Crackerman.

BECK
Beck Hansen (b. 1970) rose swiftly to prominence in 1994 with his exhilarating marriage of folk and guitar noise. His guitar-playing was inspired by the blues of Mississippi John Hurt, which he would deliver with improvised lyrics while busking. After dropping out of school at 16, Hansen played his first gigs in between sets at LA clubs. His music was now a *pot-pourri* of diverse influences – street hip-hop, Delta blues, Presbyterian hymns, punk with scat lyrics – and the whole was beginning to take shape as he released his first single, 'MTV Makes Me Want To Smoke Crack'.

'Loser', produced with hip-hop technician Karl Stephenson, was finally released after a year's delay. Critics called it an anthem for doomed youth. The major labels swooped for his signature which Geffen Records won, although Beck had already set in motion two independent records – 'Steve Threw Up' for Bong Load and *A Western Harvest Field By Moonlight*, on Fingerpaint Records. Geffen's contract allowed Beck to continue recording material for other companies. *Mellow Gold*, the debut album for Geffen was one of three albums released in 1994, alongside *Stereo Pathetic Soul Manure* on LA's Flipside independent, and a collaboration with Calvin Johnson of Beat Happening, emerged on K Records. *Odelay* (1996) was Beck's next major release and reaped numerous Album Of The Year awards in the music press. It spawned several successful singles, including 'Where It's At' and a Noel Gallagher (**Oasis**) remix of 'Devil's Haircut'.

His major-label follow-up *Mutations* was originally planned for release on Bong Load, but its downbeat charms were still impressive for what was effectively a stopgap collection. Beck returned to the mix-and-match style of *Odelay* on 1999's soul-influenced *Midnite Vultures*, which confirmed him as without doubt one of America's most original musical talents.

BECK, JEFF

UK-born Beck (b. 1944) was a competent pianist and guitarist by the age of 11. His first band was the locally acclaimed Tridents, before he replaced guitarist Eric Clapton in the Yardbirds, silencing sceptical fans with his guitar pyrotechnics utilizing feedback and distortion. The tension between Beck and joint lead guitarist Jimmy Page was finally resolved during a US tour in 1966: Beck walked out and never returned. His solo career was launched in 1967 with 'Hi-Ho Silver Lining', featuring his trademark guitar solo. The record was a UK Top 20 hit and has re-entered the charts on several occasions. The follow-up, 'Tallyman', was also a minor hit, but Beck's ambitions lay in other directions. The Jeff Beck Group, formed in 1968, consisted of Beck, Rod Stewart (vocals), Ron Wood (bass), Nicky Hopkins (piano) and Mickey Waller (drums). *Truth* was a major US success, resulting in the band undertaking a number of arduous tours. *Cosa Nostra Beck-Ola* enjoyed similar success, although Stewart and Wood had by now departed for the Faces. Beck contributed some sparkling guitar and received equal billing with Donovan on the hit single 'Goo Goo Barabajagal (Love Is Hot)'.

Following an 18-month period of recuperation after a car accident, Beck formed another group with Cozy Powell, Max Middleton and Bob Tench. This unit recorded two albums, *Rough And Ready* and *Jeff Beck Group*. In 1973, Beck formed the trio Beck, Bogert And Appice with two former members of Vanilla Fudge. Soon afterwards, he introduced yet another musical dimension, this time forming an instrumental band. The result was the excellent *Blow By Blow*, a million-seller as was its follow-up, *Wired*, on which he combined rock, jazz and blues.

After a three-year hiatus, Beck returned in 1980 with *There And Back*. During the 80s, his appearances were sporadic, though he did work with Tina Turner, Robert Plant and Jimmy Page and toured with Rod Stewart. *Flash* was a commercial failure, but the release of a box set in 1992, chronicling Beck's career, was a fitting tribute. His next project was *Crazy Legs*, a tribute to the music of Gene Vincent.

Beck returned in 1999 with a new studio album, *Who Else!*, which received glowing reviews but failed to sell. The album's interesting experiments with electronica were repeated on the impressive follow-up, *You Had It Coming*.

BEE GEES

Hugely successful UK trio comprising twins Maurice and Robin Gibb (b. 1949) and their elder brother Barry (b. 1946). All three members were born in the Isle Of Man, and performed regularly in Manchester before the family emigrated to Australia in 1958. The boys began performing as a harmony trio and, christened the Bee Gees, an abbreviation of Brothers Gibb, they signed to the Australian label Festival Records, releasing a series of singles written by Barry. While 'Spicks And Specks' was topping the Australian charts, the brothers were on their way to London to audition for Robert Stigwood. This led to a record contract with Polydor and the swift release of 'New York Mining Disaster, 1941'. The single with its evocative, intriguing lyrics and striking harmony provoked premature comparison with the Beatles and gained the trio a UK hit. During this period, Australians Colin Peterson (drums) and Vince Melouney (guitar) joined.

The Bee Gees' second UK single, 'To Love Somebody', failed to reach the Top 40 but by 1967, the group had their first UK number 1 with 'Massachusetts'. They experimented with different musical styles and briefly followed the Beatles and the Rolling Stones along the psychedelic road, but their progressive forays confused their audience, and the double album *Odessa* failed to match the work of their major rivals. Their singles remained adventurous, with the unusual tempo of 'World' followed by the neurotic romanticism of 'Words'. Both singles hit the UK Top 10 but signs of commercial fallibility followed with the relatively unsuccessful double a-side 'Jumbo'/'The Singer Not The Song'. The group next turned to the heart-rending 'I've Gotta Get A Message To You', their second UK number 1 and sixth consecutive US Top 20 hit. The group then showed their talent as composers, penning the Marbles' Top 10 UK hit 'Only One Woman'.

Internal bickering led to a year of chaos, but after reuniting in 1970 they went on to have two major US hits with 'Lonely Days' and the chart-topping 'How Can You Mend A Broken Heart'. Yet, despite transatlantic hits in 1972 with 'My World' and 'Run To Me', the group's appeal diminished to an all-time low and three hitless years. Eventually they teamed up with famed US producer Arif Mardin, resulting in *Mr. Natural*. The album indicated a noticeable R&B/soul influence which was extended on 1975's *Main Course*. Now living in Miami, the Gibbs gathered together a formidable backing unit and burst back onto the music scene with 'Jive Talkin'', which zoomed to US number 1 and brought them back to the UK Top 10.

The trio were perfectly placed to promote and take advantage of the underground dance scene in the USA, and their next album, *Children Of The World*, went platinum; 'You Should Be Dancing' reached US number 1 and 'Love So Right', hit number 3. The trio's soundtrack contributions also provided massive hits for Yvonne Elliman ('If I Can't Have You') and Tavares ('More Than A Woman'). The Bee Gees' reputation as the new gods of the discotheque was consummated on the movie soundtrack *Saturday Night Fever*, which sold in excess of 30 million copies. The group achieved a staggering run of six consecutive chart toppers: 'How Deep Is Your Love', 'Stayin' Alive', 'Night Fever', 'Too Much Heaven', 'Tragedy' and 'Love You Inside Out'. Their grand flurry continued with the movie *Grease*, for which they produced the chart-topping title track by Frankie Valli. Ill-advisedly the group then took the starring role in the movie *Sgt. Pepper's Lonely Hearts Club Band*. The film proved an embarrassing detour for both the brothers and their co-star Peter Frampton.

As the 70s ended the Bee Gees increasingly switched towards production. Although they released *Spirits Having Flown* (1979) and *Living Eyes* (1981), greater attention was being focused on their chart-topping younger brother Andy. With the group's activities on hold, Barry emerged as the most prolific producer and songwriter. He duetted with Barbra Streisand on 'Guilty'

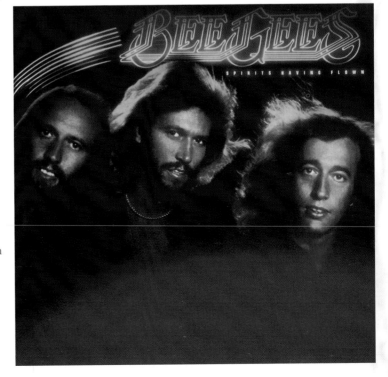

and composed and sang on **Dionne Warwick**'s 'Heartbreaker'. The brothers also wrote 'Islands In The Stream' (**Kenny Rogers/Dolly Parton**) and **Diana Ross**'s 'Chain Reaction'. The group reunited in 1987 for the hugely successful *ESP*. Their 'comeback' single 'You Win Again' was warmly received by usually hostile critics and gave the group their fifth UK number 1.

Looking back over the Bee Gees' career, one cannot fail to be impressed by the sheer diversity of their talents and their remarkable ability continually to reinvent themselves. Like that other great family group, the Beach Boys, they have shown controlled dignity in surviving family feuds, dissension, tragic death, harsh criticism and changes in musical fashion, and their work represents one of the richest tapestries in the entire history of modern popular music. This appeared to be recognized at the 1997 BRIT Awards, which was followed by a glut of press and television promotion for *Still Waters*, which became a sizeable commercial hit. The brothers' remarkable creativity showed no sign of waning on the much publicized follow-up, *This Is Where I Came In*. They were rewarded with CBEs in January 2002's New Year's Honours List.

BELL, ARCHIE, AND THE DRELLS

This US vocal soul group was formed by Archie Bell (b. 1944), with James Wise (b. 1948) and Willie Parnell (b. 1945). By their first record in 1967, the group comprised Bell, Wise, Huey 'Billy' Butler and Joe Cross. 'Tighten Up', originally a b-side, sold in excess of three million copies and reached US number 1, whilst Bell, who had been drafted into the army, was recuperating from a wound received in Vietnam. The Drells continued recording with producers Gamble And Huff, although for live performances fake 'Archie Bells' were enlisted. These sessions produced three more hits: 'I Can't Stop Dancing', 'Doin' The Choo-Choo' (both 1968) and '(There's Gonna Be A) Showdown' (1969). Paradoxically, the singles were less successful once Bell left the forces. 'Here I Go Again' was a belated UK hit in 1972.

In 1975, the group enjoyed several R&B successes on Gamble And Huff's TSOP/ Philadelphia International label, including 'Let's Groove (Part 1)' and 'Soul City Walk'. Archie Bell recorded a solo album in 1981 and charted with 'Any Time Is Right'. He still actively pursues a singing career.

BELL, FREDDIE, AND THE BELLBOYS

This US rock 'n' roll six-piece outfit was led by Freddie Bell (b. 1931; vocals). Their repertoire included a version of Willie Mae Thornton's 'Hound Dog', recorded for the Teen label in 1955. **Elvis Presley** saw them performing live the following year, inspiring his own version of the song. The same year, the Bellboys appeared in the first rock 'n' roll movie, *Rock Around The Clock*, and were the first US rock act to tour the UK, supporting Tommy Steele. 'Giddy Up A Ding Dong' reached UK number 4, while other singles included 'The Hucklebuck', 'Teach You To Rock' and 'Rockin' Is My Business'. They appeared in another film, *Get Yourself A College Girl*, in 1964. Bell now lives in Las Vegas for most of the year and tours the world in the remaining weeks.

BELLAMY BROTHERS

American brothers Howard (b. 1946) and David Bellamy (b. 1950) began their career in pop and soul, but latterly became one of the leading country acts of the 80s and 90s. They formed Jericho in 1968, but disbanded three years later, to begin writing songs for other artists (David's 'Spiders And Snakes' was a Top 3 hit for Jim Stafford). In 1976, the Bellamy Brothers reached US number 1 and the UK Top 10 with 'Let Your Love Flow'. In 1979, 'If I Said You Had A Beautiful Body (Would You Hold It Against Me)?' became the first of 10 country chart singles for the group and reached the UK Top 3. By the late 80s, the brothers were recording country hits on a regular basis. They were also one of the first country acts to launch an artist-owned label, inaugurating Bellamy Brothers Records in 1992.

BELLE AND SEBASTIAN

Formed at an all-night café in Glasgow, Scotland in early 1996, and named after a cult 60s television show, Belle And Sebastian's original line-up comprised Stuart Murdoch (vocals, guitar, piano), Stuart David (bass), Stevie Jackson (guitars, harmonica, vocals), Richard Colburn (drums), Chris Geddes (keyboards, guitar), Isobel Campbell (cello) and Sarah Martin (violin, stylophone). After the limited edition, mail-order-only *Tigermilk* sold out within a month of its May 1996 release, the band were signed to London independent Jeepster Records. Within 10 days a second album had been completed.

The band's dark tones and Murdoch's quirky, sometimes **Morrissey**-esque lyrics found favour in alternative circles as far afield as San Francisco and especially France. Part-time trumpeter Mick Cooke was made a full-time member of the band in 1997. With their ever-increasing success on the US independent charts, the band were able to finalize an American deal with Matador Records, releasing *The Boy With The Arab Strap* the following year. The album earned the band a surprise BRIT Award for Best British Newcomer. Stuart David (as Looper) and Isobel Campbell (as the Gentle Waves) also released solo records. The following year, David had his debut novel, *Nalda Said*, published and left to concentrate on Looper full time. His former bandmates returned in June 2000 with *Fold Your Hands Child, You Walk Like A Peasant*.

BELLY

Based in Rhode Island, USA, Belly was formed in 1991 by Tanya Donelly (b. 1966; vocals, guitar), Thomas Gorman (b. 1966; guitar), Chris Gorman (b. 1967; drums) and Fred Abong (bass). Donelly, along with half-sister Kristin Hersh, was a founding member of Throwing Muses. She had also worked with the Breeders before moving on to Belly. Abong was replaced in quick succession by Leslie Langston and then Gail Greenwood (b. 1960).

Belly debuted with the EPs *Slow Dust* and *Gepetto*, followed by *Star*. *The Feed The Tree* EP gave the band an unlikely chart hit and helped propel the album to number 2 in the UK charts. *King* was recorded with producer Glyn Johns, and featured writing contributions from Tom Gorman and Greenwood for the first time. The band split in 1996, with Donelly embarking on an erratic solo career and Greenwood joining L7.

BEN FOLDS FIVE

Formed in North Carolina, USA, the misleadingly named Ben Folds Five comprised Ben Folds (piano, vocals), Robert Sledge (bass) and Darren Jessee (drums). Their eponymous 1995 debut album displayed the trio's offbeat, ever-inventive style, with many listeners failing to notice the absence of guitar player. Their live shows were also breathtaking. The excellent follow-up *Whatever And Ever Amen* used wry humour to temper its sad tales of broken relationships. In 1998, Folds collaborated with the band's producer Caleb Souther and John Marc Painter on the side project Fear Of Pop. The Ben Folds Five returned in 1999 with *The Unauthorized Biography Of Reinhold Messner*, another challenging but rewarding collection. The trio announced the end of the Ben Folds Five at the end of the following year. Folds released his solo debut, *Rockin' The Surburbs*, in September 2001.

BENATAR, PAT

After training as an opera singer Benatar (b. Patricia Andrzejewski, 1953) became a major hit-maker in the early 80s, adept at both mainstream rock and powerful ballads. Her 1979 debut *In The Heat Of The Night*, produced by Mike Chapman, spawned three US chart singles. *Crimes Of Passion*, which later won a Grammy Award for Best Female Rock Vocal Performance, rose to US number 2, while the hard-rocking 'Hit Me With Your Best Shot', became her first *Billboard* Top 10 single.

Precious Time (1981) reached US number 1 and, although no Top 10 singles resulted, Benatar won another Grammy for 'Fire And Ice'. In 1983, 'Love Is A Battlefield', one of two new studio tracks on *Live From Earth*, reached US number 5, as did 'We Belong' (1984) from *Tropico*. The former single belatedly reached the UK Top 20 in 1985. That same year, 'Invincible', from the movie *Legend Of Billie Jean*, reached the US Top 10, but *Seven The Hard Way* indicated a decline in popularity. A compilation album, *Best Shots*, was released in 1987. Although moderately successful in her homeland, it became a major hit in Europe, putting her into the UK Top 10 album chart for the first time. The blues-influenced *True Love* was a commercial and critical disaster, and subsequent albums have seen Benatar struggling to regain lost sales.

BENNETT, TONY

The son of an Italian father and American mother, Bennett (b. Anthony Dominick Benedetto, 1926) became a talented artist, exhibiting in New York, Paris and London. His tenor voice (which deepened over the years) led Bennett to sing during service with the US Army's entertainment unit in World War II. After the army, he worked in clubs as Joe Bari before being spotted by Bob Hope, who changed his name to Tony Bennett.

In 1950, he was signed to Columbia Records and a year later topped the US chart with 'Because Of You' and 'Cold, Cold Heart'. Other 50s hits, mostly backed by the Percy Faith Orchestra, included 'Rags To Riches', 'Stranger In Paradise' (from *Kismet*) and 'In The Middle Of An Island'. His 1958 recording *Basie Swings–Bennett Sings* was a precursor to Bennett's later jazz-based work.

In 1962, he made a chart comeback with 'I Left My Heart In San Francisco' (which won a Grammy Award) and a sell-out Carnegie Hall concert, which was released as a double-album set. He continued his long association with pianist/arranger Ralph Sharon, and frequently featured cornet soloist Bobby Hackett. Bennett made the 60s singles charts with contemporary songs such as 'I Wanna Be Around', 'The Good Life' and 'If I Ruled The World'. In the 70s, he recorded for several different labels, including sessions with jazz musicians Ruby Braff and Bill Evans.

In 1991, Bennett celebrated 40 years in the business with a concert in London. In 1993 and 1994 he was awarded Grammys for Best Traditional Pop Performance for *Perfectly Frank* and *Steppin' Out*. He also won over a younger audience following a string of unusual guest appearances, including a slot on the *David Letterman Show*, an *Unplugged* session for MTV, and a live set at the UK's Glastonbury Festival. Studio albums during this period included well-received tributes to Billie Holiday and Duke Ellington.

BENSON, GEORGE

This US guitarist and singer (b. 1943) played in various R&B outfits in the 50s, and recorded 'It Should Have Been Me' in 1954. By 1965 he was an established jazz guitarist, having worked with Brother Jack McDuff, Herbie Hancock and, crucially, Wes Montgomery (whose repertoire was drawn from pop, light classical and other non-jazz sources). Further testament to Benson's prestige was the presence of Hancock, Earl Klugh, Miles Davis, Joe Farrell and other jazz musicians on his early albums.

From 1971's *Beyond The Blue Horizon*, an arrangement of Jefferson Airplane's 'White Rabbit' was a turntable hit and, after *Bad Benson* reached the US album lists, the title song of *Supership* cracked European charts. Benson signed to Warner Brothers Records, winning Grammy awards with 1976's *Breezin'* and its memorable 'This Masquerade'. Profit from revivals of 'On Broadway' (a US Top 10 single from 1978's *Weekend In LA*), film themes such as 'The Greatest Love Of All' (from the *The Greatest*), and the million-selling *Give Me The Night* allowed Benson to revisit his jazz roots via 1987's excellent *Collaboration* with Earl Klugh.

In the mid-90s Benson moved to the GRP Records label, debuting with the excellent *That's Right*. The follow-up *Standing Together* was a disappointing contemporary R&B collection, and Benson wisely returned to instrumentals on *Absolute Benson*. Benson is one of a handful of artists who have achieved major critical and commercial success in different genres, and this pedigree makes him one of the most respected performers of the past 30 years.

BENTON, BROOK

A stylish, mellifluent singer, Benton (b. Benjamin Franklin Peay, 1931, d. 1988) began recording in 1953, but his first major hit came in 1959, after forging a songwriting partnership with Clyde Otis and Belford Hendricks. 'It's Just A Matter Of Time' reached the US Top 3, followed by 'So Many Ways' (1959), 'The Boll Weevil Song' (1961) and 'Hotel Happiness' (1962). Duets with Dinah Washington, 'Baby (You've Got What It Takes)', a million-seller, and 'A Rockin' Good Way (To Mess Around And Fall In Love)', topped the R&B listings in 1960. His releases encompassed standards, blues and spirituals, while his compositions were recorded by **Nat 'King' Cole**, Clyde McPhatter and Roy Hamilton.

Later releases failed to recapture his previous success, but by the end of the decade, he rose to the challenge of younger acts with a series of excellent recordings for Atlantic Records' Cotillion subsidiary. His languid, atmospheric version of 'Rainy Night In Georgia' (1970) was an international hit. Benton continued to record for myriad outlets during the 70s, including Brut, Stax and MGM. Sadly he died of pneumonia while weakened by spinal meningitis, aged 56.

BERLIN

Los Angeles, USA-based AOR outfit formed in 1977 as a new wave/electro pop group by John Crawford (b. 1960; bass, synthesizer). He was joined on the band's 1980 debut, on their own Zone H label, by Virginia Macolino (vocals), Terri Nunn (b. 1961; backing vocals), Jo Julian (b. 1948; synthesizer), Chris Velasco (guitar) and Dan Van Patten (drums). They signed to I.R.S. Records in the USA, but managed only one single before breaking up in 1981. Crawford formed a new band with Nunn, David Diamond (guitars), Ric Olsen (b. 1956; guitar), Matt Reid (b. 1958; keyboards) and Rod Learned (drums). The 1982 mini-album *Pleasure Victim* was followed by *Love Life*. They gained a US Top 30 hit with 'No More Words', before the line-up changed to Crawford, Nunn and Rob Brill (b. 1956; drums). In 1986, the trio had a transatlantic number 1 with 'Take My Breath Away', the theme song to the movie *Top Gun*. It re-entered the charts in 1988 and reached the UK Top 3 on reissue in 1990. Follow-up singles fared less well and the band broke up for a second time in the late 80s. Nunn released a solo album, and has resurrected Berlin for a number of nostalgia tours.

BERRY, CHUCK

Chuck Berry (b. Charles Edward Anderson Berry, 1926) learned guitar while in his teens, a period blighted by a three-year spell in Algoa Reformatory for armed robbery. On his release, Berry undertook several jobs while pursuing part-time spots in St. Louis bar bands. In 1951, he purchased a tape recorder to capture ideas for compositions and, the following year, joined Johnnie Johnson (piano) and Ebby Hardy (drums) in the houseband at the Cosmopolitan Club. The trio became a popular attraction, playing a mixture of R&B, country and standards. The guitarist also fronted his own group, the Chuck Berry Combo.

In 1955, **Muddy Waters** advised Berry to approach Chess Records, resulting in a recording deal and 'Maybellene'. It topped the R&B chart and reached US number 5. Berry enjoyed further US R&B hits with 'Thirty Days' and 'No Money Down', before producing a stream of classics: 'Roll Over Beethoven', 'Too Much Monkey Business' and 'Brown-Eyed Handsome Man'. His subsequent releases read like a lexicon of pop history: 'School Days', 'Rock And Roll Music', 'Sweet Little Sixteen', 'Johnny B. Goode', and 'Let It Rock'. Berry drew from both country and R&B and based his vocal style on **Nat 'King' Cole**. Both the **Beatles** and **Rolling Stones** acknowledged their debt to Berry and the **Beach Boys** rewrote 'Sweet Little Sixteen' as 'Surfin' USA'.

Between 1955 and 1960, Berry enjoyed 17 R&B Top 20 entries and appeared in the movies *Go, Johnny, Go!*, *Rock Rock Rock* and *Jazz On A Summer's Day*. However, on 28 October 1961, he was convicted of 'transporting an underage girl across state lines for immoral purposes' and served 20 months. He emerged just as 'Memphis Tennessee' (1963), recorded in 1958, reached the UK Top 10. He wrote several compositions during his incarceration, including 'Nadine', 'No Particular Place To Go', 'You Never Can Tell' and 'The Promised Land', each of which reached the UK Top 30.

Inevitably his chart success waned and, in 1966, he sought vainly to regenerate his career by moving from Chess to Mercury Records. He returned to Chess in 1969, with 'Tulane'. *Back Home* and *San Francisco Dues* were cohesive selections

and in-concert appearances showed a renewed purpose. Dave Bartholomew's ribald 'My Ding-A-Ling' topped both the US and UK charts and was his biggest – and his last major – hit. Despite new recordings, Berry became confined to the revival circuit.

Berry's legal entanglements resurfaced in 1979 when he was imprisoned for income-tax evasion. Upon release he embarked on a punishing world tour, but with little result. In 1986, the artist celebrated his 60th birthday with gala performances in St. Louis and New York, and a documentary, *Hail! Hail! Rock 'N' Roll*. Berry was inducted into the Rock And Roll Hall Of Fame the same year.

Sadly, the 90s began with further controversy and reports of indecent behaviour at the singer's Berry Park centre. Although the incident served to undermine the individual, Berry's stature as an essential figure in the evolution of popular music cannot be overestimated.

BERRY, DAVE

With backing group, the Cruisers UK-born Berry (b. David Holgate Grundy, 1941) eventually signed to Decca Records. There he found success with a cover version of **Chuck Berry**'s 'Memphis Tennessee' in 1963. Versions of Arthur Crudup's 'My Baby Left Me' and **Burt Bacharach**'s 'Baby It's You' were minor hits, but the band's breakthrough came with Geoff Stevens' 'The Crying Game', which reached the UK Top 5 in 1964. Bobby Goldsboro's 'Little Things' and Ray Davies' 'This Strange Effect' provided further chart success, which concluded with the B. J. Thomas opus, 'Mama', in 1966. The next decade saw a resumption of Berry's recording career and he continues to tour abroad, appearing regularly on the cabaret/revivalist circuit.

BERRY, RICHARD

US singer Berry (b. 1935, d. 1997) began recording in 1953 under various names (the Hollywood Blue Jays, the Flairs, the Crowns, the Dreamers, the Pharaohs). His most famous moments on record are his bass vocal contributions to the Robins' 'Riot In Cell Block No. 9' and as 'Henry', Etta James's boyfriend, on 'Roll With Me Henry (The Wallflower)'. His claim to fame is composing the rock 'n' roll standard 'Louie Louie'. Berry recorded the song in 1956, but had to wait seven years for its success with the **Kingsmen**. The song spawned over 300 cover versions, including those by the **Kinks**, the **Beach Boys** and **Paul Revere And The Raiders**. During the 60s and 70s, Berry became a soul singer. He recorded for west-coast labels and continued performing until his death.

BETA BAND

John MacLean (sampling), Robin Jones (drums) and Steve Mason (vocals) formed this highly acclaimed UK art rock band while studying at college in Edinburgh, Scotland. With the addition of bass player Richard Greentree they began building a strong word-of-mouth reputation. Produced by Nick McCabe of the **Verve**, their debut EP *Champion Versions* appeared in July 1997. The EP's four tracks set the standard for future releases, revealing an eclectic mix of alternative and kraut rock styles with ambient dub and samples, eschewing conventional music categories in preference for a bold, experimental approach. *The Patty Patty Sound* and *Los Amigos Del Beta Bandidos* EPs drew further critical acclaim, and collected together on one album, *The 3 E.P.'s* broke into the UK Top 40. In December 1998, while the band were still recording material for their debut album, Mason released the solo EP *King Biscuit Time 'Sings' Nelly Foggit's Blues In Me And The Pharaohs*.

The band's self-titled debut employed a diverse range of musical styles to no coherent effect, although the results were

The band itself was a product of Zimbabwe's late-70s war of liberation, the name Bhundu ('bush') being chosen to commemorate the freedom fighters who fought against the white settlers in rural areas. Although occasionally embracing the traditional, rural Shona mbira ('thumb piano') music, the Bhundu Boys were altogether more eclectic and urban, drawing on the traditions of tribal people in Zimbabwe. Jit found almost immediate acceptance amongst the youth of post-independence Zimbabwe, and between 1981 and 1984 the band had four number 1s – 'Baba Munini Francis', 'Wenhamo Haaneti', 'Hatisitose' and 'Ndimboze'. *The Bhundu Boys*, *Hupenyu Hwenasi* and *Shabini*, proved equally popular.

In 1986 they moved to Britain, establishing a reputation as one of the most exciting bands in the country, helped by their incessant touring. In 1987 the band signed to WEA Records, released *Tsvimbodzemoto* and supported **Madonna** at London's Wembley Stadium. However, while the sales of the earlier *Shabini* had made the Bhundu Boys stars of the independent scene, they failed to achieve mainstream success and were dropped from WEA in 1990. Shortly afterwards, Biggie Tembo left and several members subsequently succumbed to AIDS. The Bhundu Boys re-emerged in 1991 with the live set, *Absolute Jit*, on the Discafrique label. Tragically Tembo hanged himself in 1995, a chilling epitaph for the original line-up of a once-pioneering group.

BIG AUDIO DYNAMITE

Guitarist Mick Jones (b. 1955; ex-**Clash**) formed Big Audio Dynamite (B.A.D.) in 1984 with DJ and film-maker Don Letts (keyboards/effects). They recruited Dan Donovan (keyboards) Leo Williams (bass) and Greg Roberts (drums). *This Is Big Audio Dynamite* featured cut-up funk spiced with sampled sounds, and generated the startling UK hit 'E=MC^2'. The follow-up included writing contributions from former Clash vocalist Joe Strummer. In 1988, Jones came close to death from pneumonia, which caused a delay in the release of *Megatop Phoenix*. This led to the break-up of the band and by 1990 and **Kool-Aid**, Jones had assembled a completely new line-up (B.A.D. II) featuring Nick Hawkins (guitar), Gary Stonadge (bass) and Chris Kavanagh (drums, ex-Sigue Sigue Sputnik). DJ Zonka was drafted in to provide live 'scratching' and mixing.

Following further personnel changes and a series of name changes, Jones regrouped Big Audio Dynamite in 1995 for the accomplished *F-Punk*, which mixed imported west-coast hip-hop beats with jungle textures and rock 'n' roll and reaffirmed Jones' status as an intelligent artist working on the periphery of the rock scene. Radioactive Records elected not to release the follow-up *Entering The New Ride*, although tracks have been made available by the band on their official website.

BIG BLACK

From Illinois, USA, Big Black debuted in 1983 with the six-track EP *Lungs*. Fronted by guitarist/vocalist Steve Albini, the group underwent several changes before completing *Bulldozer*. A more settled line-up was formed around Albini, Santiago Durango (guitar) and Dave Riley aka David Lovering (bass). *Atomizer* (1986) established the trio as one of America's leading independent acts, with their blend of post-hardcore, post-industrial styles. Melvin Belli replaced Durango for 1987's *Songs About Fucking*, their best-known album. However, Albini tired of his creation and dissolved Big Black before the record's release. He became a producer, working

often charming. Promotion was not helped by the band members claiming the album was 'rubbish'. They appeared to approve of the excellent follow-up *Hot Shots II*, which retained the experimental edge but achieved the completeness felt to be lacking from their debut.

BEVIS FROND

Bevis Frond is just one person: London, England-born psych rock artist Nick Saloman. In 1982, Saloman was injured in a motorcycle accident. He used the money he received in compensation to record *Miasma*. He then released *Inner Marshland* and *Triptych* on his own Woronzow Records. Reckless Records re-released his early work and provided an outlet for 1988's *Bevis Through The Looking Glass* and its follow-up *The Auntie Winnie Album*. Saloman's brand of raw, imaginative blues guitar drew many converts and *Any Gas Faster* was widely lauded. *Magic Eye* was an inconsistent collaboration with ex-Pink Fairies drummer Twink.

A tireless believer in the need for communication, Saloman set up an underground magazine, *Ptolemaic Terrascope*, in the late 80s. Like his music, it is a loyal correspondent of the UK psychedelic scene. Still a prolific songwriter, Saloman's recent albums have included *Superseeder*, an appealing blend of electric and acoustic styles, the 26-track *North Circular* and *Valedictory Songs*, the final Bevis Frond album for the time being.

BHUNDU BOYS

This ill-fated band was formed in Harare, Zimbabwe, in 1980 by Biggie Tembo (b. Rodwell Marasha, 1958, d. 1995; guitar, vocals), Rise Kagona (guitar), David Mankaba (d. 1991; bass), Shakie Kangwena (b. 1956, d. 1993; keyboards) and Kenny Chitsvatsa (drums). They achieved fame in Zimbabwe and in Britain with their idiosyncratic jit style of dance music.

43

with the **Pixies** (*Surfer Rosa*), the **Breeders** (*Pod*) and Tad (*Salt Lick*), before forming the short-lived Rapeman. He subsequently produced PJ Harvey's *Rid Of Me* and **Nirvana**'s *In Utero*. Afterwards he returned to a group format with Shellac. Durango recorded two EPs as Arsenal.

BIG BOPPER

After a spell as a DJ, the Big Bopper (b. Jiles Perry Richardson, 1930, d. 1959) won a contract with Mercury Records, releasing two unsuccessful singles in 1957. The following year, under his radio moniker The Big Bopper, he recorded 'Chantilly Lace', a rock 'n' roll classic. The follow up, 'Big Bopper's Wedding' proved popular enough to win him a place on a tour with Buddy Holly and Ritchie Valens. On 3 February 1959, a plane carrying the three stars crashed, leaving no survivors. Few of Richardson's recordings were left for posterity, though there was a posthumous album, *Chantilly Lace*, which included the rocking 'White Lightning'. In 1960, Johnny Preston took the Big Bopper's composition 'Running Bear' to number 1 on both sides of the Atlantic.

BIG COUNTRY

Stuart Adamson (b. William Stuart Adamson, 1958, d. 2001; guitar, vocals; ex-**Skids**) formed Scottish band Big Country in 1981. He recruited Canadian-born Bruce Watson (b. 1961; guitar) and, after an initial rhythm section proved incompatible, Mark Brzezicki (b. 1957; drums) and Tony Butler (b. 1957; bass). Both guitarists wove a ringing 'bagpipe' sound from their instruments and the band's debut album included the UK hits, 'Fields Of Fire (400 Miles)' and 'In A Big Country' (the latter also reached the US Top 20). 'Chance', 'Wonderland' and 'Look Away' all reached the UK Top 10, while a second collection, *Steeltown*, was also a commercial success. Their fourth album, 1988's *Peace In Our Time*, offered little new, although its leading single, 'King Of Emotion', broached the UK Top 20.

The band struggled into the early 90s, only reaching the lower end of the singles charts. Brzezicki had left the band in July 1989 and was replaced by Pat Ahern and then Chris Bell. Simon Phillips was recruited as drummer for *The Buffalo Skinners*, the band's debut for the new Compulsion label. *Without The Aid Of A Safety Net*, featuring a returning Brzezicki, failed to capture the band's exciting in-concert sound. *Eclectic* was a partially successful take on the 'unplugged' format.

Adamson relocated to Nashville in 1997, with the rest of the band joining him to record *Driving To Damascus*. In November 1999, Adamson briefly went missing, causing much furore in the media. The following year the band embarked on what they claimed was their farewell tour. Various releases in 2001 included a cover-versions album, a second rarities compilation, and a collection of 12-inch mixes. Adamson, meanwhile, began working with Marcus Hummon in the Raphaels, but was increasingly troubled by personal problems. He went missing again and was found hanged in a Hawaii hotel room in December.

BIG STAR

Formed in Memphis, Tennessee, USA, in 1971, Big Star evolved when ex-**Box Tops** singer Alex Chilton (b. 1950) joined local group Ice Water – Chris Bell (d. 1978; guitar, vocals), Andy Hummel (bass) and Jody Stephens (drums). The quartet made an impressive debut with *#1 Record*, which skilfully synthesized British pop and 60s-styled Los Angeles harmonies. The album's commercial potential was marred by poor distribution and internal friction led to Bell's departure in 1972.

The band reconvened the following year, releasing the excellent *Radio City*. Corporate apathy doomed the project and an embittered Big Star retreated following a brief, ill-starred tour on which John Lightman replaced a disaffected Hummel. Chilton and Stephens worked on a projected third album with the assistance of Steve Cropper (guitar), Jim Dickinson (piano)

and Tommy McLure (bass), but they broke up without officially completing the set. *3rd* has subsequently appeared in various guises and mixes.

In 1993, Chilton and Stephens re-formed the band (with backing from members of the Posies) for a one-off gig at Missouri University. It was so successful that they briefly toured the UK, while sporadic reunions have followed in subsequent years.

BIKINI KILL

Pioneers of the 90s radical feminist musical movement named Riot Grrrl, USA's Bikini Kill were led by the haranguing voice of Kathleen Hanna, alongside Billy Karren (guitar), Tobi Vail (drums) and Kathi Wilcox (bass). Believing that indie rock was just as sexist as mainstream rock, the band's recordings included direct takes on sexual politics. 'Rebel Girl', the band's anthem, which had already been recorded twice (once in single form with Joan Jett as producer), made a third appearance on 1993's *Pussy Whipped*. They recorded one further album before disbanding in 1998. Hanna went on to record with Le Tigre. While the initial spark of Riot Grrrl has died down, Bikini Kill remains its most vibrant legacy.

BIOHAZARD

Formed in New York, USA, in 1988, Biohazard comprised Evan Seinfeld (bass, vocals), Billy Graziadei (guitar, vocals), Bobby Hambel (guitar) and Danny Schuler (drums). An independent debut, *Biohazard*, led to a contract with Roadrunner Records in 1992. *Urban Discipline* was recorded in under two weeks on a tiny budget, but proved to be the band's breakthrough album. Blisteringly heavy with lyrics to match, it drew massive praise, as did live shows. The band recorded a well-received track with rappers Onyx for the *Judgement Night* soundtrack, while their Warner Brothers debut, *State Of The World Address*, was recorded in seven weeks. Hambel was sacked from the band in 1995 prior to the recording of *Mata Leão*. His replacement was Rob Echeverria (ex-Helmet). *No Holds Barred*, a fierce live album recorded in Europe, was followed by the band's PolyGram Records debut, *New World Disorder*. Echeverria was subsequently replaced by Leo Curley. The band's stay with a major label proved to be short, and their next studio set was released on the Steamhammer label.

BIRKIN, JANE

English actress Jane Birkin (b. 1946) turned singer as a result of her association with French composer Serge Gainsbourg. He had originally recorded a track with Brigitte Bardot entitled 'Je T'Aime ... Moi Non Plus' but as he explained at the time 'she thought it was too erotic and she was married'. Birkin had no such reservations and expertly simulated the sensual heavy breathing that gave the disc its notoriety. Originally released in the UK by Fontana Records,

the company dissociated itself from the disc's controversial matter by ceasing production while the record was number 2 in the charts. The ever-opportunistic entrepreneur Phil Solomon accepted the banned composition which was reissued on his Major Minor label and reached number 1 in 1969. 'Je T'Aime ...' re-entered the UK charts in 1974. In 1996, Birkin released an album of songs composed by her ex-partner.

BIRTHDAY PARTY

This Australian outfit began as new-wave band Boys Next Door. After one album, the band relocated to London and switched names. Birthday Party – **Nick Cave** (b. 1957; vocals), Roland S. Howard (guitar), Mick Harvey (b. 1958; guitar, drums, organ, piano), Tracy Pew (d. 1986; bass) and Phil Calvert (drums) – debuted on the 4AD Records label with 'Fiend Catcher'. Back in Australia they recorded their debut album for the Missing Links label. Barry Adamson (ex-**Magazine**), Howard's brother Harry and Chris Walsh helped out on the recording of the follow-up. After collaborating with the **Go-Betweens** on 'After The Fireworks' (as the Tuf Monks), the band moved to Berlin. Calvert was dropped (moving on to **Psychedelic Furs**), while the four remaining members worked on projects with Lydia Lunch and Einstürzende Neubauten, among others. Harvey left in 1983, temporarily replaced on drums by Des Heffner. After a final gig in Melbourne, the band split. Howard joined Crime And The City Solution alongside Harry and Harvey, who also continued in Cave's solo band the Bad Seeds.

BISHOP, ELVIN

As an aspiring guitarist, Bishop (b. 1942) frequented Chicago's blues clubs and in 1965 he joined the Big John club's house band. This group became the Paul Butterfield Blues Band. Bishop was featured on four Butterfield albums, but left in 1968 following the release of *In My Own Dream*. He was initially signed to Bill Graham's Fillmore label, but these and other early recordings achieved only local success. In 1974, he signed to Capricorn Records which favoured the hippie/hillbilly image Bishop had nurtured. Six albums followed, including *Let It Flow*, *Juke Joint Jump* and a live set, *Live! Raisin' Hell*, but it was a 1975 release, *Struttin' My Stuff*, which proved most popular. It included 'Fooled Around And Fell In Love' which reached US number 3. The featured voice was Mickey Thomas (later of **Jefferson Starship**). After Thomas's departure, Bishop's career suffered a further setback in 1979 when Capricorn filed for bankruptcy.

Although he remained a much-loved figure in the Bay Area live circuit, the guitarist's recorded output was sparse during the 80s. During then 90s Bishop signed with Alligator Records, and the series of credible albums he has recorded with the label indicates that he has found a comfortable niche.

BISHOP, STEPHEN

US singer-songwriter Bishop (b. 1951) formed his first group, the Weeds, in 1967. They recorded some **Beatles**-inspired demos in Los Angeles before disbanding. In 1976, Bishop landed a contract with ABC, via the patronage of **Art Garfunkel**. His debut, *Careless*, was much in the style of Garfunkel and featured top Los Angeles session players. It was nominated for a Grammy and, like the succeeding *Bish*, hovered in the lower reaches of the national Top 40. The accompanying singles (particularly 'On And On' from *Careless*) also fared well. The **Four Tops**, **Chaka Khan** and Barbra Streisand covered his compositions and Bishop gained studio assistance from Khan, Garfunkel, Gary Brooker, Steve Cropper, **Phil Collins** and others. He contributed to Collins' *Face Value* (1981), and composed 'Separate Lives', the Englishman's duet with Marilyn Martin, taken from the movie *White Nights*.

Bishop also wrote the theme songs to *Animal House* ('Dream Girl') and *Roadie* ('Your Precious Love' with Yvonne Elliman). He has also tried his hand at acting, although music remains his calling card. His later albums have not enjoyed the same commercial success as his 70s work.

BJÖRK

Former **Sugarcubes** vocalist, Björk (b. Björk Gudmundsdóttir, 1965), made her 'debut' in 1977, as an 11-year old prodigy, with an album of cover versions recorded in her native Iceland. Her next recording outfit was Tappi Tikarrass, who recorded two albums between 1981 and 1983. A higher-profile role was afforded via work with KUKL, who introduced her to future Sugarcubes Einar Örn and Siggi.

Björk returned to Iceland after the Sugarcubes' six-year career, recording a solo album in 1990 backed by a local be-bop group. She re-emerged in 1993 with the startling *Debut*, which came to prominence in the dance charts before crossing over to mainstream success. The album generated

four UK hit singles and a series of remixes. 'Play Dead', a collaboration with David Arnold for the soundtrack of *Young Americans*, reached UK number 12 later in the year. *Post* was a more eclectic album, ranging from the hard techno beats of 'Army Of Me', to the shimmering 'Hyperballad' and the 40s revival number 'It's So Quiet'. The latter provided the singer with her biggest UK hit, reaching number 4 in December 1993.

Now an unwilling media star, Björk made the headlines following her attack on an intrusive reporter, and through her liaison with jungle artist **Goldie**. Following a desultory remix album (*Telegram*), Björk released her third solo set, *Homogenic*. The album was notable for lyrics revealing a more personal side to the singer, reflecting on her troubled year.

Björk subsequently switched her focus to acting, winning the Best Actress award at the 2000 Cannes film festival for her role as Selma in Lars von Trier's *Dancer In The Dark*. The challenging soundtrack, *Selma Songs*, was written by Björk with Guy Sigsworth, Mark Bell and Vince Mendoza. Her next studio album, *Vespertine*, followed in August 2001.

BLACK CROWES

Brothers Chris (b. 1966; vocals) and Rich Robinson (b. 1969; guitar) formed this US rock band under the name Mr. Crowe's Garden in 1984. They were joined by Johnny Colt (b. 1966; bass), Steve Gorman (b. 1965; drums) and Jeff Cease (guitar) on their 1990 debut, *Shake Your Money Maker* – an album blending soul and uncomplicated R&B. Influenced by **Otis Redding**, they covered his 'Hard to Handle', but the record's highlight was 'She Talks To Angels', an emotive ballad about a drug addict. Their live performances drew Rolling Stones comparisons, the band's image being very much rooted in the 70s, with

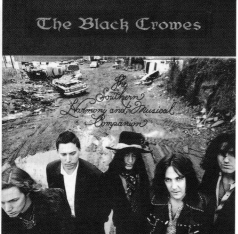

Chris Robinson's thin frame dominating the stage.

Canadian keyboard player Ed Harsch, who had played on the album, joined in 1991. Robinson collapsed suffering from exhaustion following an acoustic showcase at Ronnie Scott's in London, but recovered to participate in the band's European tour. Cease was replaced by Marc Ford (guitar, vocals; ex-Burning Tree) prior to work beginning on the band's second album. *The Southern Harmony And Musical Companion* (1992) received positive reviews. With both the album and single, 'Remedy', a success, the Black Crowes returned to the road for the hugely popular *High As The Moon* tour.

Amorica was released in 1994, although it drew more attention for its provocative cover than the musical content. Live shows saw the debut of percussionist Chris Trujillo. *Three Snakes And One Charm* was hampered by personnel changes, with both Ford and Colt leaving the band in 1997. The latter was replaced by Sven Pipien (ex-Mary My Hope). The ensuing *By Your Side* marked a welcome return to the sleazy rock 'n' roll style of their earlier albums.

In 2000, the band teamed up with **Jimmy Page** for a series of highly praised US concerts. The two final shows at the LA Amphitheater were captured for posterity on *Live At The Greek*. The band's sixth studio album, *Lions*, was generally regarded as their best since *The Southern Harmony And Musical Companion*.

BLACK FLAG

Formed in 1977 in Los Angeles, Black Flag rose to become one of America's leading hardcore groups. The initial line-up – Keith Morris (vocals), Greg Ginn (guitar), Chuck Dukowski (bass) and Brian Migdol (drums) – completed the *Nervous Breakdown* EP, but in 1979 Morris left to form the Circle Jerks. Several members joined and left before Henry Rollins (b. Henry Garfield, 1961; vocals), Dez Cadenza (guitar) and Robo (drums) joined Ginn and Dukowski for *Damaged*, the band's first full-length album. Originally scheduled for release by MCA Records, the company withdrew support, citing outrageous content, and the set appeared on the quintet's own label, SST Records. Ginn continued to lead Black Flag in tandem with Rollins and the music's power remained undiminished. Pivotal albums included *My War* and *In My Head* while their diversity was showcased on *Family Man*. The band split up in 1986 following the release of the live set, *Who's Got The 10½?*. Rollins went on to successful careers as solo performer and spoken-word artist.

BLACK GRAPE

There was immense media interest in the post-**Happy Mondays** pursuits of singer Shaun Ryder (b. 1962) and 'dancer' Bez (b. Mark Berry). Their 1995 debut as Black Grape, *It's Great When You're Straight, Yeah!*, received ecstatic reviews. The germination of Black Grape had occurred only weeks after the dissolution of the Happy Mondays. The band Ryder put together was initially named the Mondays, and included rapper Kermit (b. Paul Leveridge), guitarist 'Wags' (b. Paul Wagstaff), second guitarist Craig Gannon (ex-**Smiths**) and Martin Smith of Intastella. By the time Black Grape had taken their new name and were recording their debut album, both Smith and Gannon had departed, replaced by Danny Saber, who took on a co-writing role, Ged Lynch and Stephen Lironi (ex-**Altered Images**). The title of the album partly expressed Ryder's decision to turn away from hard drug abuse. His much-publicized 'cut-up' lyrics were present, along with his trademark scat coupling of meaningless phrases used primarily for their phonetic value. Kermit's growling raps balanced the slurring Ryder delivery perfectly and the band were rewarded with a UK number 1 album. During an eventful 1996, Black Grape toured regularly but lost the services of Bez, while Kermit announced his own side-project Man Made in 1997. With new vocalist Carl 'Psycho' McCarthy on board, the long-awaited *Stupid, Stupid, Stupid* was released to mixed reviews. Soon afterwards, both Kermit and Psycho left, reducing the band to the duo of Ryder and Saber, and the inevitable split followed. Ryder re-formed the Happy Mondays in 1999, while Kermit went on to record with Big Dog.

BLACK OAK ARKANSAS

Formed in the late 60s, Black Oak Arkansas took its name from the US town and state where singer Jim 'Dandy' Mangrum (b. 1948) was born. The other founding members were Ricky Reynolds (b. 1948; guitar), Stanley Knight (b. 1949; guitar), Harvey Jett (guitar), Pat Daugherty (b. 1947; bass) and Wayne Evans (drums). As Knowbody Else, they recorded an unsuccessful album for Stax Records in 1969. In 1971, they changed their name, signed with Atco Records and recorded a self-titled album that introduced them to the US charts. Touring steadily, their hard rock/southern boogie band built a core following. Of their 10 US-charting albums between 1971 and 1976, *High On The Hog* proved the most commercially successful, peaking at number 52. It featured the bestselling Top 30 single, 'Jim Dandy' (sung by female vocalist Ruby Starr, who reappeared on the 1976 *Live! Mutha* album).

Evans was replaced on the third album by Thomas Aldrich (b. 1950), and in 1975 Jett was replaced by James Henderson (b. 1954). The following year Black Oak Arkansas had their final chart single, 'Strong Enough To Be Gentle'. By 1977, only Mangrum remained from the original band and there was no further record success. Mangrum did, however, maintain various touring versions of the band during the 80s, as well as recording a solo album (*Ready As Hell*) in 1984. In 1999 he reunited with several original members to record *The Wild Bunch*.

BLACK REBEL MOTORCYCLE CLUB

This San Francisco, California, USA-based trio's dark psychedelic rock carries on in the great tradition of the **Velvet Underground**, although they are closer in spirit and sound to mid-80s UK bands the **Jesus And Mary Chain** and **Primal Scream**. High-school friends Robert Turner (guitar, bass, vocals) and Peter Hayes (guitar, bass, vocals), formed the band with Nick Jago (b. England; drums) in October 1998. Originally called the Elements, the trio subsequently renamed themselves after Marlon Brando's motorcycle gang in the seminal 50s movie *The Wild One*. The trio began performing around San Francisco and recorded and produced a limited-edition demo CD. They recorded their Virgin Records debut *B.R.M.C.* at their home studio and Sound City in Los Angeles. Released in April 2001, the album gained strong reviews on both sides of the Atlantic from critics enamoured of the band's aggressive guitars and haunting melodies.

BLACK SABBATH

Terry 'Geezer' Butler (b. 1949; bass), Tony Iommi (b. Anthony Frank Iommi, 1948; guitar), Bill Ward (b. 1948; drums) and Ozzy Osbourne (b. John Osbourne, 1948; vocals) grew up together in Birmingham, England. They were originally known as Earth, but changed to Black Sabbath in 1969, taking the name from the title of a cult horror film. The line-up remained unchanged until 1973 when Rick Wakeman, keyboard player for **Yes**, was drafted in to play on *Sabbath Bloody Sabbath*. During this period, Black Sabbath recorded such classic heavy rock albums as their self-titled debut and its follow-up, *Paranoid*.

By 1977 personnel difficulties were beginning to take their toll, and the music was losing some of its earlier orchestral, bombastic sheen. Ozzy Osbourne went solo the following year. He was replaced by Dave Walker (ex-

Savoy Brown), then by American Ronnie James Dio (b. Ronald Padavona, 1940), who left in 1982. Ian Gillan (b. 1945) appeared on *Born Again*, which failed to capture the original vitality of the band. By 1986 Iommi was the only original band member, alongside Geoff Nichols (keyboards), Glenn Hughes (b. 1952, vocals; ex-**Deep Purple**) and Americans Dave Spitz (bass), and Eric Singer (drums). In 1986, the surprisingly blues-sounding *Seventh Star* was released, with lyrics and music by Iommi. Hughes left, replaced by Ray Gillen (d. 1994), an American singer who failed to record anything with them. Tony Martin was the vocalist on 1987's *The Eternal Idol* and 1988's *Headless Cross*.

By 1991, the band was suffering from flagging record sales and declining credibility, so Iommi recruited original bass player Butler. Osbourne's attempts to re-form the original line-up for a 1992 tour faltered when the others demanded an equal share in the spoils. In 1994 a tribute album, *Nativity In Black*, was released, which featured appearances from all four original members. Spurred by the new interest in the band, Iommi continued to lead an ever-changing cast of personnel around the live circuit. In December 1997 the original line-up re-formed to play two live shows at the Birmingham NEC. In April, Ward suffered a heart attack, and was temporarily replaced by Vinnie Appice. The band's double album of live recordings, featuring two new studio tracks, broke into the *Billboard* Top 20 the following year.

BLACK UHURU

Formed in Jamaica by Rudolph 'Garth' Dennis, Derrick 'Duckie' Simpson and Euvin 'Don Carlos' Spencer in 1974, Black Uhuru first recorded a version of Curtis Mayfield's 'Romancing To The Folk Song' as Uhuru (Swahili for 'Freedom'). Dennis and Spencer both left and Simpson enlisted Michael Rose as lead singer with Errol Nelson singing harmonies. This line-up sang for Prince Jammy on 1977's *Love Crisis*, later reissued and retitled *Black Sounds Of Freedom*. Nelson left soon afterwards and Puma Jones (b. Sandra Jones, 1953, d. 1990) took over. This combination began work for Sly Dunbar and Robbie Shakespeare's Taxi label in 1980, and Black Uhuru mania gripped the Jamaican reggae audience. The solid bedrock of **Sly And Robbie**'s rhythms with Puma and Simpson's eerie harmonies provided a perfect counterpoint to Rose's tortured vocals as his songs wove tales of the hardships of Jamaican life. *Showcase*, later reissued as *Vital Selection*, gave equal prominence to the vocal and instrumental versions of songs such as 'General Penitentiary', 'Shine Eye Gal' and 'Abortion'.

The band's albums for Island Records continued in the same militant vein, and 1984's *Anthem* was remixed for the American market and earned a Grammy. Michael Rose left in the mid-80s for a solo career. Junior Reid took over lead vocals, but after a couple of moderately well-received albums, he too went solo. Puma Jones, who had left the band after *Brutal* and been replaced by soundalike Olafunke, died of cancer in 1990. During this period the original members reunited to tour and record. Subsequent albums proved less successful, and by the end of the decade only Simpson remained from the original line-up.

BLACK, BILL

Black (b. William Patton Black, 1926, d. 1965) was the bass-playing half of the Scotty And Bill team that backed **Elvis Presley** on his earliest live performances. He played on Presley's earliest Sun Records tracks, including 'That's All Right', and toured with Presley alongside guitarist Scotty Moore. Drummer D. J. Fontana was subsequently added to the group.

In 1959, after leaving Presley, the Bill Black Combo was formed, with Reggie Young (guitar), Martin Wills (saxophone), Carl McAvoy (piano) and Jerry Arnold (drums). The group favoured an instrumental R&B-based sound tempered with jazz. Their first chart success was 'Smokie Part 2' (1959), but it was the follow-up 'White Silver Sands' (1960) that gave the group its biggest

US hit, reaching number 9. Black retired from touring in 1962, and the group continued performing under the same name without him. They continued playing even after Black died of a brain tumour in October 1965. The Bill Black Combo achieved a total of 19 US chart singles and was still working under the leadership of bass player Bob Tucker decades later.

BLACK, CILLA

Black (b. Priscilla White, 1943) appeared as guest singer with various groups at Liverpool, England's Cavern club, and was brought to the attention of Brian Epstein. He changed her name and exploited her girl-next-door appeal. Her first single was a brassy powerhouse reworking of the **Beatles**' unreleased 'Love Of The Loved', which reached the UK Top 40 in 1963. She changed her style with **Burt Bacharach**'s 'Anyone Who Had A Heart' and emerged a ballad singer of immense power. 'You're My World' was another brilliantly orchestrated, impassioned ballad, which reached UK number 1. By this time, Black was outselling all her Merseyside rivals except the Beatles. By the end of 1964, she was one of the most successful female singers of her era and continued to release cover versions of superb quality, including the **Righteous Brothers**' 'You've Lost That Lovin' Feelin'' and **Randy Newman**'s 'I've Been Wrong Before'. In 1965, she ceased recording and worked on her only film, *Work Is A Four Letter Word*, but returned the following year with 'Love's Just A Broken Heart' and 'Alfie'.

In 1968, Black moved into television work. Throughout the late 60s, she continued to register Top 10 hits, including 'Surround Yourself With Sorrow', 'Conversations' and 'Something Tells Me'. She wound down her recording career in the 70s and concentrated on live work and television commitments, aided by her manager/husband Bobby Willis. Black entered the 90s as one of the highest-paid family entertainers in the British music business, with two major UK television shows, *Blind Date* and *Surprise! Surprise!*. In 1993, she celebrated 30 years in showbusiness with an album, video, book and television special, all entitled *Through The Years*. Her partnership with Willis was broken by his death in October 1999.

BLACK, FRANK

This US vocalist/guitarist (b. Charles Thompson IV, 1965) led the **Pixies** under the name Black Francis. He embarked on a solo career as Frank Black in 1993. His self-titled debut, featuring Nick Vincent (drums), ex-Pixies guitarist Joey Santiago and Eric Drew Feldman (guitar, saxophone; ex-Captain Beefheart's Magic Band), showed its creator's quirky grasp of pop. The sprawling *Teenager Of The Year* was Black's final record for 4AD Records. A new release on the Epic Records label failed to improve his solo standing. Backed by the Catholics (Lyle Workman, Dave McCaffrey and Scott Boutier), Black returned to indie cultdom with the rough-and-ready double whammy of *Frank Black And The Catholics* and *Pistolero*. In an even more welcome move, he enlisted Santiago as guitarist on 2001's excellent *Dog In The Sand*.

BLACK, MARY

Black (b. 1955, Eire) began singing in Dublin's folk clubs. Her self-titled recording debut reached number 4 in the Irish charts in 1983. Shortly afterwards she joined De Dannan, recording *Song For Ireland* and *Anthem* before leaving the band in 1986. During her time with De Dannan she released the gold-selling solo album, *Without The Fanfare*. In 1987 and 1988, Black was voted Best Female Artist in the Irish Rock Music Awards Poll. *No Frontiers*, apart from being one of Ireland's bestselling albums in 1989, also reached the Top 20 of the New Adult Contemporary charts in the USA.

In 1991, Black returned from an American tour in order to finish *Babes In The Wood*, released the same year. Her 1991 tours in England/Japan were efforts to reach a wider audience (until *Babes In The Wood*, her albums had not had a full distribution in Britain). Further releases on the Grapevine Records label have built on her success, culminating in *Shine* and *Speaking With The Angel* – Black's most commercial outings to date.

BLACKMORE, RITCHIE

British guitarist Blackmore (b.1945) spent his early career in Mike Dee And The Jaywalkers before joining Screaming Lord Sutch And His Savages in 1962. Within months he had switched to the Outlaws, a principally instrumental group which served as the studio houseband for producer Joe Meek. Blackmore briefly joined the group the Wild Boys in 1964, and completed an idiosyncratic solo single, 'Little Brown Jug'/'Getaway', before jumping between Neil Christian's Crusaders, the Savages and the Roman Empire. When a short-lived act, Mandrake Root, broke up in 1967, Blackmore opted to live in Hamburg, but was invited back to London in 1968 to join organist Jon Lord in **Deep Purple**. Blackmore's powerful, urgent runs became an integral part of their attraction. He left in 1975 and joined forces with the USA-based Elf to form the highly popular hard-rock attraction Ritchie Blackmore's Rainbow. He was also involved in the Deep Purple reunion undertaken in 1984, although animosity between the guitarist and vocalist Ian Gillan resulted in the latter's departure. Blackmore finally quit the band in 1994. He has subsequently recorded several albums with his new outfit, Blackmore's Night, exploring the fringes of medieval music with his own distinctive heavy edge.

BLACKWELL, OTIS

Blackwell (b. 1931, d. 2002) was one of the greatest US songwriters of the rock 'n' roll era. His first release was his own composition 'Daddy Rolling Stone', a Jamaican favourite, where it was recorded by Derek Martin. During the mid-50s, Blackwell also recorded for RCA Records and Groove before turning to writing songs for other artists. In 1956, his 'Fever' was a success for both Little Willie John and Peggy Lee. Soon 'All Shook Up' began a highly profitable association with co-writer **Elvis Presley**. The rhythmic tension of the song perfectly fitted Presley's stage persona and was his first UK number 1. 'Don't Be Cruel' (1956), 'Paralysed' (1957), 'Return To Sender' (1962) and 'One Broken Heart For Sale' followed. There was a distinct similarity between Blackwell's vocal style and Presley's, which has led to speculation that the latter adopted some of Blackwell's mannerisms. Blackwell also provided hits for **Jerry Lee Lewis** ('Breathless' and 'Great Balls Of Fire'), Dee Clark ('Hey Little Girl' and 'Just Keep It Up'), **Jimmy Jones** ('Handy Man') and **Cliff Richard** ('Nine Times Out Of Ten'). Blackwell suffered a stroke in 1991 and remained in poor health up until his death in May 2002.

BLACKWELL, ROBERT 'BUMPS'

An arranger and studio bandleader with Specialty Records, Blackwell (b. 1918, d. 1985) led a band in Seattle. He arranged and produced gospel and R&B singles for Lloyd Price and Guitar Slim and wrote a series of stage revues – Blackwell Portraits – much in the same vein as the Ziegfeld Follies. His Bumps Blackwell Jnr Orchestra featured, at various times, **Ray Charles** and **Quincy Jones**. He also worked with Lou Adler and Herb Alpert before taking over the A&R department at Specialty. In 1955, he recorded **Little Richard**'s 'Tutti Frutti' and was a key producer and songwriter in the early days of rock 'n' roll. Along with John Marascalco he wrote 'Ready Teddy', 'Rip It Up', and, with Enotris Johnson and Little Richard, 'Long Tall Sally'. Blackwell helped launch the careers of former gospel singers Sam Cooke and Wynona Carr and, after leaving Specialty, was involved in setting up Keen Records. He co-produced the title track of **Bob Dylan**'s *Shot Of Love* in 1981, one of his last pieces of work before his death from pneumonia.

BLAINE, HAL

Drummer Blaine (b. Harold Simon Belsky, 1929) claims to be the most-recorded musician in history. The Los Angeles-based session musician says he has performed on over 35,000 recordings, including over 350 that reached the US Top 10. After a stint in the army, he became a professional drummer, first with the Novelteers (also known as the Stan Moore Trio) and then with singer Vicki Young (later his first wife). At the end of the 50s he worked with Tommy Sands, then singer Patti Page and took on session work in the late 50s, beginning on a Sam Cooke record. His first Top 10 single was Jan And Dean's 'Baby Talk' in 1960. His huge discography includes drumming for Phil Spector's sessions, including hits by the Crystals, Ronettes and Righteous Brothers. He played on many of the **Beach Boys**' greatest hits and on sessions for **Elvis Presley**, the Association, Gary Lewis And The Playboys, the **Mamas And The Papas**, Johnny Rivers, the **Byrds**, **Simon And Garfunkel**, the **Monkees**, the **Carpenters**, **John Lennon**, **Ringo Starr**, **George Harrison**, the **Supremes**, **John Denver**, the **Fifth Dimension**, **Captain And Tennille**, **Cher** and hundreds of others. In the late 70s, Blaine's schedule slowed and by the 80s his involvement in the LA studio scene virtually drew to a halt. In 1990 he wrote a book about his experiences, *Hal Blaine And The Wrecking Crew*.

BLASTERS

Formed in Los Angeles in 1979, the Blasters were one of the leading proponents of the US 'roots-rock' 80s revival. The group – Phil Alvin (vocals), his songwriter brother Dave (guitar), John Bazz (bass) and Bill Bateman (drums) – debuted in 1980 with *American Music*, a critically applauded fusion of rockabilly, R&B, country and blues. In 1981, they released the Top 40 album *The Blasters*, for which pianist Gene Taylor joined and saxophonist Lee Allen guested. A live EP recorded in London followed in 1982 but it was *Non Fiction* which earned the band its greatest acclaim. Newly recruited saxophonist Steve Berlin featured on 1985's *Hard Line*. The album included backing vocals by the **Jordanaires**. Dave Alvin left to join X, and was replaced by Hollywood Fats, who died of a heart attack at the age of 32. Phil Alvin and Berlin kept a version of the group together until 1987. Both Alvin brothers have recorded solo albums and worked on other projects.

BLIGE, MARY J.

Blige (b. 1971) burst on to the US music scene with her 1992 debut, *What's The 411?*. The album's striking fusion of hip-hop and soul helped establish the singer as one of the leading talents of the new urban R&B scene, a position which she maintained for the next decade. Quality rather than quantity remains the keynote to Blige's career. *My Life* was an edgy, raw set that dealt with the break-up of her relationship with K-Ci Hailey of **Jodeci**. According to her publicity handout, *Share My World* marked 'her personal and musical rebirth'. *Mary* featured guest appearances from the artists including **Lauryn Hill**, **Eric Clapton**, **George Michael**, **Elton John** and, on the tense personal drama of 'Not Lookin'', her ex-lover Hailey. Blige maintained her impressive series of releases with 2001's *No More Drama*, featuring the US chart-topping single 'Family Affair'.

BLIND FAITH

Formed in 1969, Blind Faith were one of the earliest rock acts to earn the dubious tag 'supergroup'. **Eric Clapton** (b. Eric Patrick Clapp, 1945; guitar, vocals, ex-**Cream**), Ginger Baker (b. 1939; drums, ex-Cream), **Steve Winwood** (b. 1948; keyboards, vocals, ex-**Traffic**) and Ric Grech (b. 1945, d. 1990; bass, violin, ex-**Family**) stayed together for one highly publicized, million-selling album and a lucrative major US tour. Their debut was a free concert in front of an estimated 100,000 at London's Hyde Park in June 1969. The controversial album cover depicted a topless pre-pubescent girl holding a phallic chrome model aeroplane and included only one future classic, Clapton's 'Presence Of The Lord'.

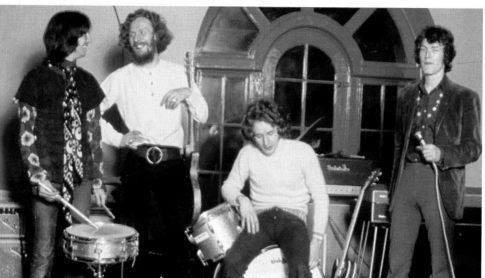

BLIND MELON

Formed by Glen Graham (drums), Shannon Hoon (vocals), Rogers Stevens (guitar), Christopher Thorn (guitar) and Brad Smith (bass), this US alternative rock band entered the US mainstream in 1993. Graham's sister Georgia, portrayed as an awkward, publicity-shy youngster adorned in a bee-suit, featured on the cover of their debut album. The image became a cult icon and helped propel the band's 1993 debut album into the US Top 5.

The highly anticipated follow-up *Soup* was less accessible than many expected, recorded in New Orleans during bouts of drug-related non-activity (Hoon confessed that he could not actually remember making the record). It was generally known that Hoon had unsuccessfully fought heroin addiction for some time, and he fatally overdosed in October 1995. *Nico* (named after Hoon's stepdaughter), was released in 1997. It was a sad, patched-together affair that the remaining members felt morally obliged to release. Thorn and Smith resurfaced three years later in Unified Theory.

BLINK-182

Based in San Diego, USA, Blink-182's highly melodic and entertaining thrash rock broke through on to the mainstream charts in the late 90s. Formed as Blink by Mark Hoppus (b. 1972; bass, vocals), Tom DeLonge (b. 1975; guitar, vocals) and Scott Raynor (drums), they began a non-stop gigging schedule on the local punk circuit. The band's full-length debut, *Cheshire Cat*, was released on the Grilled Cheese label in 1994. Shortly afterwards the trio were forced to adopt the new moniker Blink-182 following the threat of legal action by an Irish techno outfit already recording as Blink. Despite the enforced name change, the trio's popularity continued to grow largely owing to their ubiquitous presence on the skating and snow boarding scenes. They also developed a reputation for stripping naked during live shows.

A steady flow of singles and EPs confirmed both the trio's penchant for gloriously immature lyrics, and their ability to craft great tunes. Their commercial breakthrough arrived with 1997's *Dude Ranch* and the radio hit 'Dammit (Growing Up)'. Raynor was replaced by Travis Barker (b. 1975, USA) on the band's major label debut, *Enema Of The State*, which debuted in the US Top 10 in June 1999 and went on to sell over a million copies in barely two months. The album was helped by two highly catchy hits, 'What's My Name Again?' and 'All The Small Things'. Following the release of a stop-gap live set, the band confirmed the commercial appeal of their scatological punk rock when their fifth album, *Take Off Your Pants And Jacket*, debuted at the top of the US charts in June 2001.

BLODWYN PIG

British band formed when Mick Abrahams (b. 1943; guitar) left **Jethro Tull**. Abrahams, fluid playing blended well with the rest of the band, Jack Lancaster (saxophone), Andy Pyle (bass) and Ron Berg (drums). Their 1969 debut *Ahead Rings Out* contained a mixture of various styles of progressive blues. The second album showed great moments, notably Abrahams' punchy 'See My Way' and Lancaster's long pieces such as 'San Francisco Sketches'. However, Abrahams departed and was replaced by Pete Banks (b. 1947). Now led by Lancaster, the new line-up adopted the name Lancaster's Bomber, and finally Lancaster. Four years later, Abrahams and Lancaster re-formed Blodwyn Pig with Pyle and ex-Jethro Tull drummer Clive Bunker (b. 1946), but it became evident that their day was long past.

Abrahams resurrected the group in the 90s to play club dates, performing new material with Bunker, Pyle and Dick Heckstall-Smith. He has subsequently recorded new studio material with various personnel.

BLONDIE

Blondie was formed in New York City in 1974 when Deborah Harry (b. 1945; vocals), Chris Stein (b. 1950; guitar), Fred Smith (bass) and Bill O'Connor (drums) abandoned the revivalist Stilettos for an independent musical direction. Progress was undermined by the departure of Smith for **Television** and the loss of O'Connor, but when James Destri (b. 1954; keyboards), Gary Valentine (bass) and Clement Burke (b. 1955; drums) joined Harry and Stein, the band secured a recording contract with Private Stock Records and released their self-titled debut in 1976.

After internal disputes, Valentine left and the arrival of Frank Infante (guitar) and Englishman Nigel Harrison (bass) triggered the band's most consistent period. *Plastic Letters* contained two UK Top 10 hits: 'Denis' and '(I'm Always Touched By Your) Presence Dear', while *Parallel Lines* included the UK chart-topping 'Heart Of Glass' and 'Sunday Girl' (the former also reached US number 1). *Eat To The Beat* spawned the UK chart-topper 'Atomic'. 'Call Me', produced by Giorgio Moroder, was taken from the soundtrack of *American Gigolo* and reached UK/US number 1. *Autoamerican* provided two further US chart toppers in 'The Tide Is High' and 'Rapture'. The former, originally recorded by reggae group the Paragons, also reached UK number 1.

Despite their commercial ascendancy, Blondie was beset by internal difficulties, as the media increasingly focused on Harry and the distinction between the band's name and her persona became increasingly blurred. After the release of her solo album, *Koo Koo*, *The Hunter* became Blondie's final recording. Stein's ill-health (a genetic disease, pemphigus vulgaris) brought an

attendant tour to a premature end and both he and Harry, his partner, absented themselves from full-time performing.

Harry later resumed her solo career and sang with the Jazz Passengers before re-forming Blondie in 1997 with Stein, Burke and Destri. A high media profile helped push 'Maria', a classic slice of late-70s power pop, to the top of the UK charts in February 1999. *No Exit*, although it was also a commercial success, was more disappointing.

BLOOD, SWEAT AND TEARS

The jazz/rock excursions made by Blood, Sweat And Tears offered a refreshing change to 60s guitar-dominated rock. The band was conceived by Al Kooper (b. 1944; keyboards/vocals), together with Steve Katz (b. 1945; guitar), Randy Brecker (b. 1945; saxophone) and Jerry Weiss. Kooper departed soon after their debut album *Child Is The Father To The Man* and Brecker and Weiss were replaced by Chuck Winfield (b. 1943; trumpet) and Lew Soloff (b. 1944; trumpet). English vocalist David Clayton-Thomas (b. David Thomsett, 1941) was added to the line-up on *Blood Sweat & Tears*, which topped the US album charts, sold millions of copies, won a Grammy Award and spawned three major worldwide hits: 'You've Made Me So Very Happy', 'Spinning Wheel' and 'And When I Die'. The following two albums were both considerable successes, with their gutsy brass arrangements, occasional biting guitar solos and Clayton-Thomas's growling vocal delivery. Following *BS&T4*, Clayton-Thomas departed for a solo career, resulting in a succession of lead vocalists, including Jerry LaCroix (b. 1943). The band never regained their former glory, even following the return of Clayton-Thomas, although 1975's *New City* reached the US album charts. The supper-club

circuit ultimately beckoned with the Blood, Sweat And Tears name continuing in one guise or another behind Clayton-Thomas.

BLOODHOUND GANG

This US alternative rock group was formed by Jimmy Pop Ali (vocals) and Lupus (guitar). The original line-up made their debut with 1994's *Dingleberry Haze* EP, which was released on the independent Cheese Factory label. The sample-heavy *Use Your Fingers* was licensed to Columbia Records, but the band, with Evil Jared (bass), Spanky G (drums) and DJ Q-Ball added to the line-up, returned to independent status for *One Fierce Beer Coaster*. However, when their 1996 single, 'Fire Water Burn', began to attract regular airplay on rock stations, the band found itself moving to a major, Geffen Records, once again. Their second album was reissued in amended form, and immediately made an impact on the US Top 100. Song titles included 'Kiss Me Where It Smells Funny' and 'I Wish I Was Queer So I Could Get Chicks', revealing a schoolboy level of humour which had begun to wear thin by the time the band released their third album, *Hooray For Boobies*, in December 1999. The album nevertheless struck a chord with fans of other non-politically correct acts and was a huge commercial success.

BLOOMFIELD, MIKE

For many, Bloomfield (b. 1944, d. 1981) was the finest white blues guitarist America has so far produced. Although signed to Columbia Records in 1964 as the Group (with Charlie Musslewhite and Nick Gravenites), it was his emergence in 1965 as the guitarist in the **Paul Butterfield Blues Band** that brought him to public attention. Bloomfield was **Bob Dylan**'s lead electric guitarist at Newport, and again on the seminal *Highway 61 Revisited*. On leaving Butterfield in 1967, Bloomfield formed Electric Flag, although he left shortly afterwards. *Super Session*, recorded with **Stephen Stills** and **Al Kooper**, became his biggest seller and led to a short but lucrative career with Kooper, but it was five years before his next satisfying work appeared, *Triumvirate*, with John Paul Hammond and Dr. John. Plagued with a long-standing drug habit he occasionally supplemented his income by scoring music for pornographic movies. He also wrote soundtracks for *The Trip* (1967), *Medium Cool* (1969) and *Steelyard Blues* (1973). In 1975, he was cajoled into forming KGB with Ric Grech, Barry Goldberg and Carmine Appice. The album was a disaster and Bloomfield resorted to playing mostly acoustic music. He had a prolific period between 1976 and 1977, releasing five albums, the most notable being the critically acclaimed *If You Love These Blues, Play 'Em As You Please*. Another burst of activity occurred shortly before his death from a suspected drug overdose, when three albums-worth of material was recorded.

BLOW MONKEYS

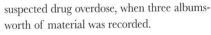

Led by Dr Robert (b. Bruce Robert Howard, 1961; guitar), this UK political pop band took their name from Australian slang for Aboriginal didgeridoo players. He was joined by Tony Kiley (b. 1962; drums), Neville Henry (saxophone) and Mick Anker (b. 1957; bass). They recorded for RCA Records in 1984 but made no headway in the UK charts until 1986 with 'Digging Your Scene', one of the earliest songs about AIDS; the track also broke into the US Top 20. The following January they had their biggest UK hit with the number 5 single 'It Doesn't Have To Be This Way'. The politically-charged '(Celebrate) The Day After You', featuring the voice of

Curtis Mayfield, was banned by the BBC. 'You Don't Own Me' appeared on the successful *Dirty Dancing* soundtrack and minor hits followed. In 1989, Dr Robert recorded a duet (under his own name) with soul singer Kym Mazelle. The Blow Monkeys' last hit was 1990's 'Springtime For The World'. Following the break-up of the band Dr Robert worked with **Paul Weller** and started a solo career.

BLUE AEROPLANES

Since forming in Bristol, England, in the early 80s, the Blue Aeroplanes have had endless line-up changes, but have maintained their original aim to involve a large number of musicians in an almost communal manner. The nucleus of the band originally revolved around vocalist Gerard Langley, his brother John (drums, percussion), Nick Jacobs (guitar), Dave Chapman (multi-instrumentalist) and dancer Wojtek Dmochowski. Individuals such as Angelo Bruschini (guitar, bass, organ), John Stapleton (tapes), Ruth Coltrane (bass, mandolin), Ian Kearey (guitar, banjimer, harmonium), Rodney Allen (guitar), Simon Heathfield (bass) and Caroline Halcrow (guitar) have all contributed. After *Bop Art* (1984), the band recorded several well-received EPs, succeeded by their second album, *Tolerance*. Their third set, *Spitting Out Miracles*, surfaced in 1987. All were characterized by Langley's monotone verse and a deluge of instruments and sounds hinged around the guitar.

The band made their major-label debut with 1990's *Swagger*, an album which suggested a more direct, straightforward approach. In 1991, the line-up – Langley, Bruschini, Dmochowski, Allen, Paul Mulreany (drums; ex-Jazz Butcher), Andy McCreeth, Hazel Winter and Robin Key – released *Beatsongs*, co-produced by **Elvis Costello** and Larry Hirsch. The fresh-sounding *Life Model* featured Gerard Langley joined by Marcus Williams (bass, ex-Mighty Lemon Drops) and Susie Hugg (vocals). Following a 10th anniversary tour, *Rough Music* proved to be their best album since *Beatsongs*, but commercial success became elusive. After a long hiatus, the band re-emerged in 2000 with the excellent *Cavaliers*.

BLUE CHEER

San Francisco, USA-based band formed by Dickie Peterson (b. 1948; vocals, bass), Leigh Stephens (guitar) and Paul Whaley (drums). Taking their name from a brand of LSD, they made an immediate impact with *Vincebus Eruptum*, which featured cacophonous interpretations of **Eddie Cochran**'s 'Summertime Blues' (US number 14) and Mose Allison's 'Parchman(t) Farm'. *Outside Inside* was completed in the open air when high volume levels destroyed their studio monitors. Leigh Stephens was replaced by Randy Holden during the sessions for *New! Improved!*. Bruce Stephens (bass) and Ralph Burns Kellogg (keyboards) were added to the line-up when Holden also departed during the protracted recording sessions. *Blue Cheer* unveiled a reconstituted line-up of Peterson, Kellogg and Norman Mayell (drums, guitar). Gary Yoder was added to the line-up on *The Original Human Being*, a 1970 recording which featured the atmospheric, raga-influenced 'Babaji (Twilight Raga)', the band's most cohesive work.

Blue Cheer was dissolved in 1971 but was re-formed in 1979 by Peterson and Whaley. *The Beast Is Back* featured Petersen, Whaley and guitarist Tony Rainer. Peterson and Whaley have continued to pursue the band's original bombastic vision on subsequent recordings.

BLUE NILE

Blue Nile was formed in Glasgow, Scotland, in 1981, featuring Paul Buchanan (vocals, guitar, synthesizers), Robert Bell (synthesizers) and Paul Joseph Moore (piano, synthesizers). Their debut, 'I Love This Life', was followed by 1984's highly praised *A Walk Across The Rooftops*. It was five years before the follow up,

Hats, continued the shimmering legacy of its predecessor. In the 90s the band journeyed to California to record backing vocals for **Julian Lennon**, eventually working with Robbie Robertson and several others. They signed a contract with Warner Brothers Records in 1993. The greatly anticipated *Peace At Last* was highly praised but only a modest success.

BLUE ÖYSTER CULT

Blue Öyster Cult sprang from the musical ambitions of rock writers Sandy Pearlman and Richard Meltzer. Based in New York, USA, they put together a band – known variously as the Soft White Underbelly and Oaxaca – to perform their songs. By 1969 the unit, now dubbed the Stalk-Forrest Group, established around Eric Bloom (b. 1944; guitar, vocals), Donald 'Buck Dharma' Roeser (b. 1947; guitar, vocals), Allen Lanier (b. 1946; keyboards, guitar), Joe Bouchard (b. 1948; bass, vocals) and Albert Bouchard (drums). They completed a single, 'What Is Quicksand', before becoming Blue Öyster Cult. Early releases combined **Black Sabbath**-styled riffs with obscure lyricism, which engendered an 'intelligent heavy metal' tag. 'Career Of Evil' from *Secret Treaties* – co-written by Patti Smith – showed an increasing grasp of commercial hooklines, which flourished on 1976's international **Byrds**-sounding hit, '(Don't Fear) The

Reaper'. Smith continued her association with the band on *Agents Of Fortune* and added 'Shooting Shark' to the band's repertoire for *Revolution By Night*. Fantasy writer Michael Moorcock contributed to *Mirrors* and *Cultosaurus Erectus*. The release of the live *Some Enchanted Evening* brought the band's most innovative era to an end, despite the hit 'Joan Crawford Has Risen From The Grave', drawn from *Fire Of Unknown Origin*. Rick Downey replaced Al Bouchard in 1981, while Joe Bouchard left at the end of the decade to form Deadringer. Lanier, Bloom and Roeser reconvened in 1998 to record *Heaven Forbid*, their first studio album in ten years. They were joined by Danny Miranda (bass) and Bobby Rondinelli (drums).

BLUE, DAVID

(b. Stuart David Cohen, 1941, d. 1982) Having left the US Army, Blue arrived in Greenwich Village in 1960 hoping to pursue an acting career, but was drawn instead into the nascent folk circle. As David Blue he was signed to the influential Elektra Records label in 1965 and released *Singer/Songwriter Project*, a joint collaboration with Richard Farina, Bruce Murdoch and Patrick Sky. His first full-scale collection in 1966 exhibited a rudimentary charm. Several acts recorded the singer's compositions, but it was two years before a second album appeared. *23 Days In December* showcased a more mellow performer, before a further release recorded in Nashville, *Me, S. David Cohen*, embraced country styles.

Another hiatus ended in 1972 when Blue was signed to the emergent Asylum Records label, and his first album for the company, *Stories*, was the artist's bleakest, most introspective selection. Subsequent releases included *Nice Baby And The Angel* and *Com'n Back For More*, but although his song, 'Outlaw Man', was covered by the **Eagles**, Blue was unable to make a significant commercial breakthrough. He resumed acting later in the decade and made memorable appearances in **Neil Young**'s *Human Highway* and Wim Wenders' *The American Friend*. His acerbic wit was one of the highlights of Dylan's *Renaldo And Clara* movie, but this underrated artist died in 1982 while jogging in Washington Square Park.

BLUES BROTHERS

Formed in 1978, this US act was centred on comedians John Belushi (b. 1949, d. 1982) and Dan Aykroyd (b. 1952). Renowned for contributions to the satirical *National Lampoon* team and television's *Saturday Night Live*, the duo formed this 60s-soul-styled revue as a riposte to disco. Assuming the epithets Joliet 'Jake' Blues (Belushi) and Elwood Blues (Aykroyd), they embarked on live appearances with the assistance of a backing group – Steve Cropper (guitar), Donald 'Duck' Dunn (bass) and Tom Scott (saxophone). *Briefcase Full Of Blues* topped the US charts, a success that in turn inspired the movie *The Blues Brothers* (1980). An affectionate, if anarchic, tribute to soul and R&B, this featured cameo appearances by **Aretha Franklin**, **Ray Charles**, **John Lee Hooker** and **James Brown**. Belushi's death from a drug overdose in 1982 brought the original concept to a premature end, since which time Aykroyd has continued a successful acting career. Several of the musicians, including Cropper and Dunn, later toured and recorded as the Blues Brothers Band. The original Blues Brothers have also inspired numerous copy-cat/tribute groups. In 1991, interest in the concept was again boosted with a revival theatre production in London's West End. A new movie was released in 1998, with Belushi's role taken by John Goodman.

BLUES MAGOOS

Formed in New York, USA in 1964 and initially known as the Trenchcoats and then the Bloos Magoos, the founding line-up was Emil 'Peppy' Thielhelm (b. 1949; vocals, guitar), Dennis LaPore (lead guitar), Ralph Scala (b. 1947; organ, vocals), Ronnie Gilbert (b. 1946; bass) and John Finnegan (drums). By the end of the year LaPore and Finnegan had been replaced by Mike Esposito and Geoff Daking. The Blues Magoos quickly became an important part of the emergent Greenwich Village rock scene, enjoying one notable hit, '(We Ain't Got) Nothin' Yet' (1966), which reached US number 5. Its garage-band snarl set the tone for *Psychedelic Lollipop*, which contained several equally virulent selections. After *Basic Blues Magoos* (1968), they broke up.

Thielhelm then fronted a revamped line-up featuring John Leillo (vibes, percussion), Eric Kaz (keyboards), Roger Eaton (bass) and Richie Dickon (percussion). They completed *Never Goin' Back To Georgia* and, with session musicians and no Eaton, the disappointing *Gulf Coast Bound*. The original line-up of the Blues Magoos reunited for a live performance at Cavestomp 2000.

BLUES PROJECT

The Blues Project was formed in New York, USA in the mid-60s by guitarist Danny Kalb, with Tommy Flanders (vocals), Steve Katz (b. 1945; guitar), Andy Kulberg (b. 1944; bass, flute), Roy Blumenfeld (drums) and Al Kooper (b. 1944; vocals, keyboards). They established themselves as the city's leading electric blues band, a prowess demonstrated on their debut, *Live At the Cafe Au-Go-Go*. Flanders went solo and the resultant five-piece embarked on *Projections*. Before *Live At The Town Hall* was issued, Kooper left to form **Blood, Sweat And Tears**, where he was subsequently joined by Katz. Kalb also quit, but Kulberg and Blumenfeld added Richard Greene (b. 1945; violin), John Gregory (guitar, vocals) and Don Kretmar (bass, saxophone) for a fourth collection, *Planned Obsolescence*.

The new line-up subsequently changed their name to Seatrain, but in 1971, Kalb reclaimed the erstwhile moniker and recorded two further albums with Flanders, Blumenfeld and Kretmar. This version of the band was supplanted by a reunion of the *Projections* line-up for a show in Central Park, after which the Blues Project name was abandoned.

BLUES TRAVELER

New York, USA blues-rock quartet formed in the mid-80s by singer/harmonica player John Popper, originally under the name the Blues Band. Joined by Brendan Hill (drums), Chan Kinchla (guitar) and Bobby Sheehan (bass), the quartet changed their name to Blues Traveler and recorded their debut at the end of 1989. The band was befriended at an early stage by Paul Shaffer, band leader and arranger for the David Letterman television show. Letterman's sponsorship of the band stretched to over a dozen appearances in their first four years of existence. In 1992, Popper was involved in a motorcycle accident which left him injured. *Save His Soul*'s release was consequently delayed, but Popper took the stage again in 1993, in a wheelchair. Chuck Leavell joined Paul Shaffer in contributing to *Four*, which sold over four million copies. *Straight On Till Morning* was another critical and commercial success. Popper recorded the solo *Zygote* in 1999, but also had to undergo emergency angioplasty. In August, Sheehan was found dead in his New Orleans home. He was replaced by guitarist Chan Kinchla's brother, Tad, on the band's new studio release, *Bridge*.

BLUNSTONE, COLIN

Blunstone (b. 1945), former lead vocalist of the **Zombies**, possesses a unique voice and two of his performances with his former band, 'She's Not There' and 'Time Of The Season', are established as 60s pop classics.

Blunstone started a promising solo career as Neil MacArthur and then reverted to his own name with *One Year* in 1971. *Ennismore* was his finest work, and included two UK chart hits, 'How Could We Dare To Be Wrong' and 'I Don't Believe In Miracles'. After two further albums Blunstone kept a low profile, although he appeared on four Alan Parsons Project albums. He resurfaced in 1981 with **Dave Stewart**'s hit remake of Jimmy Ruffin's 'What Becomes Of The Broken Hearted', and the following year had a minor hit with **Smokey Robinson**'s 'Tracks Of My Tears'. During the 80s he attempted further commercial success with Keats, but the group folded shortly after their debut album.

In 1995, Blunstone's various live BBC recordings, an excellent compilation, and a new studio album, *Echo Bridge*, were released within the space of a few months. Blunstone participated in the assembly of *Zombie Heaven* in 1997, a superlative CD box set of the Zombies' work. Reunited with Argent, they toured together and produced *Out Of The Shadows* in 2001.

BLUR

Blur were formed in London, England, while Damon Albarn (b. 1968; vocals), Alex James (b. 1968; bass) and Graham Coxon (b. 1969; guitar) were students.

Drummer Dave Rowntree (b. 1964) joined later. The band was initially called Seymour, and within a year the quartet had signed to Food Records, run by ex-**Teardrop Explodes** keyboard player David Balfe and *Sounds* journalist Andy Ross, who suggested the name Blur.

Playing vibrant 90s-friendly pop with a sharp cutting edge, Blur's debut release, 'She's So High' sneaked into the UK Top 50. With the band displaying a breezy confidence in their abilities, 'There's No Other Way' reached UK number 8 in 1991. This success continued when *Leisure* entered the UK charts at number 2. A relatively fallow period followed and Blur seemed set to disappear with the same alacrity with which they had established themselves. *Modern Life Is Rubbish* was presented to their record company but rejected, Balfe insisting that Albarn should write at least two more tracks. The resultant songs, 'For Tomorrow' and 'Chemical World', were the album's singles. When it finally emerged in 1993, its sales profile failed to match that of its predecessor or expectations, but touring rebuilt confidence. The 'new' model Blur saw fruition in 1994 with 'Girls & Boys', the first single from what was to prove the epoch-making *Parklife*. This set borrowed liberally from the **Beatles**, the **Small Faces**, the **Kinks**, the **Jam** and **Madness**, topped off by Albarn's knowing, cockney delivery.

The UK press attempted to concoct an **Oasis** versus Blur campaign when both bands released singles on the same day in 1995. In the event, Blur won the chart battle (with 'Country House'), although Oasis took over the headlines on a daily basis. Following the lukewarm reception given to *The Great Escape*, Blur quietly retreated to Iceland to work on new material. The result of their labour was 'Beetlebum' and *Blur*, both UK chart-toppers. The harder sound (evident on the thrashy 'Song 2') owed a substantial debt to US alternative rock, and eventually broke the band in that country.

In 1998, Coxon launched his own label, Transcopic, and released his solo debut. The band returned in 1999 with the chart-topping *13*, which was overseen by producer William Orbit. The band's dismissive treatment of their pre-Blur back catalogue on the subsequent tour indicated a desire to erase the past and forge a new identity, although the new 'Music Is My Radar' on 2000's compilation set was hardly groundbreaking.

In the meantime, Coxon released a second solo album while Albarn branched out into soundtrack work and collaborated with comic artist Jamie Hewlett and several leading hip-hop producers to create the manufactured cartoon band, the Gorillaz. He also travelled to Mali to record with traditional musicians. The results were later collated into an album, *Mali Music*.

BO STREET RUNNERS
Formed in 1964 in England, the Bo Street Runners comprised John Dominic (vocals), Gary Thomas (lead guitar), Royston Fry (keyboards), Dave Cameron (bass) and Nigel Hutchinson (drums). After recording a self-financed EP, they were accepted to appear on the television show *Ready, Steady, Go!*, in the show's talent contest; they won, securing a deal with Decca Records. 'Bo Street Runner' became their debut single, but despite the publicity, it failed to chart. Glyn Thomas and Tim Hinkley replaced Hutchinson and Fry, while Dave Quincy joined as saxophonist. 'Tell Me What You're Gonna Do' and 'Baby Never Say Goodbye' (for Columbia Records) ensued. Thomas was then replaced by Mick Fleetwood, and Quincy departed for Chris Farlowe. The reshaped Bo Street Runners released a cover version of the **Beatles**' 'Drive My Car' in 1966. Fleetwood was replaced by Alan Turner and then by Barrie Wilson, and when Dominic opted to manage the group, Mike Patto joined as vocalist. The group disbanded late in 1966, after which Patto recorded a solo single, 'Can't Stop Talkin' 'Bout My Baby'. The b-side, 'Love', was the final Bo Street Runners' recording.

BOB AND EARL
Bobby Day (b. Bobby Byrd, 1932) formed the 50s rock 'n' roll outfit the Hollywood Flames, which featured Earl Lee Nelson. Day then secured a solo hit with 'Rockin' Robin' before briefly joining Nelson in the original Bob And Earl. Bob Relf replaced Day when the latter resumed his own career. The **Barry White**-produced 'Harlem Shuffle', their best-known song, was released in 1963. A minor hit in the USA, upon reissue it reached UK number 7

in 1969. Bob And Earl had one more hit, the prophetically titled 'Baby It's Over' (1966). Nelson recorded under the name of Jay Dee for Warner Brothers Records in 1973, and also as Jackie Lee, charting in the USA with 'The Duck' (1965), 'African Boo-Ga-Loo' (1968) and 'The Chicken' (1970). Relf wrote Love Unlimited's 1974 hit 'Walking In The Rain'. A new duo, Earl and Bobby Garrett, recorded together, and individually, during the 70s.

BOLAN, MARC
Bolan (b. Mark Feld, 1947, d. 1977) began singing during the mid-60s folk boom. As 'Toby Tyler', he completed several unsuccessful demos before reportedly creating his new surname from (Bo)b Dy(lan). 'The Wizard' (1965), revealed an early penchant for pop mysticism whereas 'The Third Degree', was indebted to R&B. B-side 'San Francisco Poet' gave the first airing to Bolan's distinctive, tremulous warble, evinced on his third single, 'Hippy Gumbo'. A series of demos was undertaken at this point, several of which surfaced on *The Beginning Of Doves* (1974) and, with overdubs, on *You Scare Me To Death* (1981), but plans for a fourth single were postponed. Frustrated at his

commercial impasse, the artist joined John's Children in 1967. He composed their best-known single, 'Desdemona', but left after a matter of months to form **Tyrannosaurus Rex**. Here Bolan gave full range to the 'underground' poetic folk mysticism, redolent of author J. R. R. Tolkien. The unit evolved into T. Rex three years later. Between 1970 and 1973 this highly popular attraction enjoyed a run of 10 consecutive UK Top 5 singles. After a lean period, a contemporary television series, *Marc*, revived a flagging public profile. This ascendancy ended abruptly when Bolan was killed in a car crash in 1977.

BOLTON, MICHAEL

Bolton (b. Michael Bolotin, 1954) became one of America's most successful rock balladeers of the late 80s and early 90s. He recorded his first single in 1968 and a couple of solo albums, all released under his birth name. In the late 70s, he became lead singer with hard-rock band Blackjack, but their two albums sold poorly. Turning to songwriting and a solo career, Bolton had greater success as a composer, providing Laura Branigan with the 1983 hit 'How Am I Supposed To Live Without You', co-written with Doug James.

He changed his name to Bolton in 1983 and, as a solo performer, persevered with a heavy-rock approach; it was not until he shifted to a soul-ballad style on *The Hunger* that he had his own first Top 20 single, 'That's What Love Is All About' (1987). From that point on Bolton had a series of blue-eyed soul hits that included a US chart-topping version of 'How Am I Supposed To Live Without You' in 1990, as well as 'How Can We Be Lovers' and the 1991 successes 'Love Is A Wonderful Thing' and 'Time, Love And Tenderness'. He topped the US charts for the second times with a cover version of Percy Sledge's 'When A Man Loves A Woman'. In 1995 he resurfaced with a UK hit single 'Can I Touch You ... There?' and a greatest

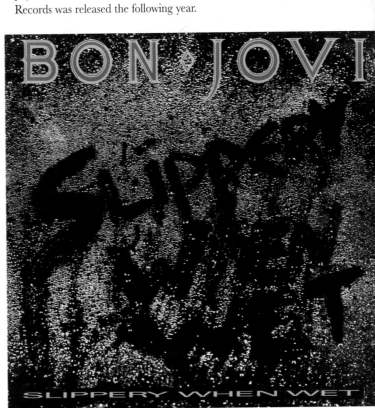

hits package. After the commercial failure of *All That Matters*, Bolton reappeared in the late 90s, performing quasi-operatic material. Years of litigation with the **Isley Brothers** ended in January 2001 when Bolton was ordered to pay them over $5 million in a plagiarism lawsuit. His first recording for Jive Records was released the following year.

BON JOVI

Commercial hard-rock band formed in New Jersey, USA and fronted by Jon Bon Jovi (b. John Francis Bongiovi Jnr, 1962; vocals) with Richie Sambora (b. 1959; guitar), David Bryan (b. David Rashbaum, 1962; keyboards), Tico Torres (b. 1953; drums) and Alec John Such (b. 1956; bass). By 1983, a recording contract with PolyGram Records resulted in a self-titled debut and *7800 Degrees Fahrenheit*. Both albums were greeted with cynicism by the media, which was already reticent at the prospect of the band's manicured image and formularized heavy rock. However, *Slippery When Wet* was the biggest-selling rock album of 1987 and 'Wanted Dead Or Alive', 'You Give Love A Bad Name' and 'Livin' On A Prayer', were US and European hits. *New Jersey* contained 'Living In Sin', a Jon Bon Jovi composition which owed a debt to his hero **Bruce Springsteen**.

An extended hiatus saw Jon Bon Jovi release his solo debut, a quasi-soundtrack of songs inspired by the movie *Young Guns II*. The commercial incentive to return to Bon Jovi was hard to resist, though, and the band reunited in 1992 to record *Keep The Faith*. The slick ballad, 'Always', confirmed their renaissance by becoming a chart fixture in 1994. The lacklustre *These Days* included the hit single 'This Ain't A Love Song'. Jon Bon Jovi began to nurture an acting career in the 90s with roles in *Moonlight And Valentino* and *The Leading Man*, and enjoyed solo success with 1997's *Destination Anywhere*. The band regrouped two years later to record their new album, *Crush*.

BONDS, GARY 'U.S.'

Having initially sung in various gospel groups, Bonds (b. Gary Anderson, 1939) embraced secular music upon moving to Norfolk, Virginia. A successful spell in the region's R&B clubs resulted in a contract with local entrepreneur Frank Guida,

whose production gave Bonds' releases their distinctive sound. 'New Orleans' set the pattern for the artist's recordings, reaching an apogee on 'Quarter To Three', a US chart-topper and the singer's sole million-seller. Bonds enjoyed similar-sounding hits in 1961–62, but his career then declined. He toured the revival circuit until 1978, when long-time devotee **Bruce Springsteen** joined the singer on-stage during a live engagement. Their friendship resulted in *Dedication*, produced by Springsteen and Little Steven. The former contributed three original songs to the set, one of which, 'This Little Girl', reached the US Top 10 in 1981. Their collaboration was maintained with *On The Line*, followed by Bonds' self-produced *Standing In The Line Of Fire*. Little was heard of him in the 90s, other than a cameo appearance with other musical artists in the movie *Blues Brothers 2000*.

BONE THUGS-N-HARMONY

Formed in Ohio, USA, in 1993, Bone Thugs-N-Harmony was one of the most successful 90s rap outfits to break into the mainstream. The band features Layzie Bone (b. Steve Howse, 1977), Bizzy Bone (b. Bryon McCane, 1976), Krayzie Bone (b. Anthony Henderson, 1974), Wish Bone (b. Charles Scruggs, 1977) and Flesh-n-Bone (b. Stan Howse), and were 'discovered and nurtured' by the founder of Ruthless Records, the late Eazy-E. Their 1994 debut EP, *Creeping On Ah Come Up*, spent over 70 weeks in *Billboard*'s Top 200 album chart, with sales of over four million. The following year's *E. 1999 Eternal* went to number 1 in the same album chart, selling over 330,000 copies in its first week of release.

The quintet returned in 1997 with the overindulgent double disc *The Art Of War*, which stretched its lyrical and musical conceits far too thinly. In the late 90s, the group concentrated on developing artists signed to their own Mo Thug Records label. Bizzy, Krayzie and Flesh-n-Bone also released commercially and critically successful solo albums. The quintet reunited to record *BTNHResurrection*, which debuted at US number 2 in March 2000, before resuming their solo careers.

BONEY M

In 1976, German-based producer/composer Frank Farian invented a group to front a single he had already recorded, 'Baby Do You Wanna Bump?'. The Carribean-born line-up comprised Marcia Barrett (b. 1948; vocals), Bobby Farrell (b. 1949; vocals), Liz Mitchell (b. 1952; vocals) and Maizie Williams (b. 1951; vocals). Between 1976 and 1977, the group enjoyed four UK Top 10 hits with 'Daddy Cool', 'Sunny', 'Ma Baker' and 'Belfast'. Their peak period was 1978, when the chart-topping 'Rivers Of Babylon'/'Brown Girl In The Ring' spent 40 weeks in the UK chart. Its follow-up, 'Rasputin', climbed to number 2 and Boney M ended 1978 with the festive chart-topper 'Mary Boy's Child – Oh My Lord'. They experienced phenomenal success in Europe (over 50 million total sales). The singalong 'Hooray Hooray It's A Holi-Holiday' and 'Gotta Go Home'/'El Lute' were their last Top 20 hits.

Farrell was fired in 1981 and replaced by Reggie Tsiboe. He rejoined the group for 1985's *Eye Dance*, but the following year Boney M split up. The original line-up reconvened two years later to promote a remix compilation. With tensions running high between the group members, Mitchell left to join Tsiboe in Farian's rival version of Boney M. The ensuing court case ruled that all four original members were entitled to perform as Boney M, with Mitchell's version being acknowledged as the 'official' version. By 1994 there were three versions of the group in existence, keeping the Boney M name alive on the cabaret circuit.

BONO, SONNY

Bono (b. Salvatore Bono, 1935, d. 1998) started out as director of A&R at Specialty Records. He co-wrote 'She Said Yeah' for Larry Williams, later covered by the Rolling Stones, and pursued a recording career under numerous aliases, including Don Christy, Sonny Christy and Ronny Sommers. Phil Spector inspired Bono to found the Rush label, but he achieved fame when 'Needles And Pins', a collaboration with Jack Nitzsche, was recorded by Jackie DeShannon and the Searchers.

In 1963 Bono married Cherilyn Sarkisian La Pierre (Cher) and they worked as a duo, first as Caesar & Cleo, then Sonny And Cher. In 1965 they enjoyed an international smash with 'I Got You Babe', written, arranged and produced by Bono. His subsequent solo projects included 'Laugh At Me' (US/UK Top 10) and 'The Revolution Kind'. His lone album, *Inner Views*, was a commercial failure and Bono subsequently abandoned solo recordings. Although Sonny and Cher ended the personal partnership in 1974, they continued to host a television show. Bono later concentrated on an acting career, on television and in films, notably *Hairspray* (1988). Now a confirmed Republican, he was voted mayor of Palm Springs in 1988, and in 1994 won the House of Representatives seat for the town. Sadly he died in 1998, the victim of a skiing accident.

BONZO DOG DOO-DAH BAND

Formed as the Bonzo Dog Dada Band in 1965 by art students Vivian Stanshall (b. 1943, d. 1995; vocals, trumpet, devices) and Rodney Slater (b. 1941; saxophone), this eccentric ensemble also included Neil Innes (b. 1944; vocals, piano, guitar), Roger Ruskin Spear (b. 1943; props, devices, saxophone) and 'Legs' Larry Smith (b. 1944; drums). Various auxiliary members, including Sam Spoons (b. Martin Stafford Ash, 1942), Bob Kerr and Vernon Dudley Bohey-Nowell (b. 1932), augmented the line-up. In 1966, two singles, 'My Brother Makes The Noises For The Talkies' and 'Alley Oop', reflected their transition from trad jazz to pop and in 1967 they released their debut, *Gorilla*. Kerr and others had already left for the rival New Vaudeville Band, but the Bonzos secured a residency on the British television children's show *Do Not Adjust Your Set*.

The band featured in the **Beatles'** film *Magical Mystery Tour*, performing the memorable 'Death Cab For Cutie', and in 1968 secured a UK Top 5 hit with 'I'm The Urban Spaceman' (produced by **Paul McCartney** under the pseudonym Apollo C. Vermouth). Further albums, *The Doughnut In Granny's Greenhouse* and *Keynsham*, displayed an endearing eclecticism while displaying a rock-based bent. Newcomers Dennis Cowan (b. 1947), Dave Clague and Joel Druckman toughened their live sound. They disbanded in 1970, but a reconvened line-up completed *Let's Make Up And Be Friendly* in 1972. Both Stanshall and Innes went on to enjoy mixed solo career. Sadly, the former died in a house fire in 1995.

BOO RADLEYS

Formed in 1988 in Liverpool, England by Sice (b. Simon Rowbottom, 1969; guitar, vocals), Martin Carr (b. 1968; guitar), Timothy Brown (b. 1969; bass) and Steve Drewitt (drums), the Boo Radleys took their name from a character in the novel *To Kill A Mockingbird*. Their 1990 debut, *Ichabod And I*, demonstrated their adherence to the guitar-blasted sound of My Bloody Valentine and Dinosaur Jr.

Drewitt was replaced by Robert Cieka (b. 1968), just as the Boo Radleys signed to Rough Trade Records for the EP *Every Heaven*. A move to Creation Records was rewarded with *Everything's Alright Forever*, which broke them out of the indie ghetto. *Giant Steps* saw the band producing a set that retraced the grandeur of Merseybeat, bringing them several Album Of The Year awards in the UK. An evident attempt to wrest chart domination away from **Oasis** or **Blur**, 1993's *Wake Up* lacked the usual chaotic experimentalism, replaced instead by sweeping vistas of orchestrated pop and the perky UK hit, 'Wake Up Boo!'. The experimental spirit of the Boo Radleys was captured in the follow-ups, *C'Mon Kids* and *Kingsize*, but both albums were commercial failures. The band announced they were splitting up in January 1999. Carr resurfaced the following year under the moniker Brave Captain, releasing material on the Wichita label.

BOOKER T. AND THE MGS

Formed in Memphis, Tennessee, USA, in 1962 as a spin-off from the Mar-Keys, this instrumental outfit comprised session men Booker T. Jones (b. 1944; organ), Steve Cropper (b. 1941; guitar), Lewis Steinberg (b. 1933; bass) and Al Jackson Jnr (b. 1934, d. 1975; drums). 'Green Onions', their first hit, evolved out of a blues riff. Its simple, smoky atmosphere, punctuated by Cropper's cutting guitar, provided the blueprint for a series of excellent records.

In 1964, Steinberg was replaced on bass by Donald 'Duck' Dunn (b. 1941). The new line-up's intuitive interplay became the bedrock of classic Stax, the foundation on which the label and studio sound was built. The quartet appeared on all the company's notable releases, including 'In The

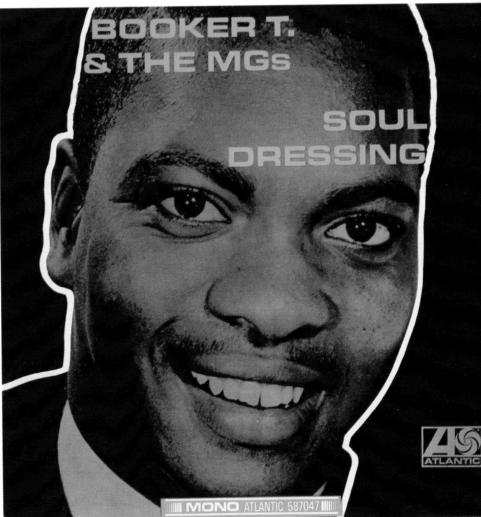

Midnight Hour' (Wilson Pickett), 'Hold On I'm Comin'' (Sam And Dave) and 'Walkin' The Dog' (Rufus Thomas). Although Jones divided his time between recording and studying, the MGs charted consistently in their own right. 'Hang 'Em High' (1968) and 'Time Is Tight' (1969) were both US Top 10 singles and 'Melting Pot' (1971) reached the Top 50.

The MGs split in 1971, but in 1973 Jackson and Dunn put together a reconstituted group with Bobby Manuel and Carson Whitsett. Jackson worked for Al Green and Syl Johnson, but was shot dead in his Memphis home in 1975. Cropper set up his TMI studio/label. He latterly rejoined Dunn, drummer Willie Hall and the returning Jones for *Universal Language*. Cropper and Dunn also played in the movie *The Blues Brothers* in 1980. 'Green Onions' was reissued and became a Top 10 hit in 1979. They were inducted into the Rock And Roll Hall Of Fame in 1992. In 1994, Jones, Cropper and Dunn recorded their first album in seventeen years, *That's The Way It Should Be*.

BOOMTOWN RATS

Formed in 1975, this Irish band comprised Bob Geldof (b. Robert Frederick Zenon Geldof, 1954; guitar, vocals), Garry Roberts (b. 1954; vocals, guitar), Gerry Cott (guitar), Johnnie Fingers (b. John Moylett, 1956; keyboards), Pete Briquette (b. Patrick Cusack, 1954; bass) and Simon Crowe (drums). They named themselves after **Woody Guthrie**'s term for oilfield workers in his autobiography, *Bound For Glory*.

Before moving to London, the band signed to the recently established Ensign Records. Their self-titled debut, a UK chart success, included 'Looking After No. 1' and 'Mary Of The 4th Form', both of which reached the UK Top 20. The following *A Tonic For The Troops* featured the biting 'She's So Modern' and the quirky 'Like Clockwork'. A third hit from the album, the acerbic urban protest 'Rat Trap', secured them their first UK number 1. *The Fine Art Of Surfacing* coincided with their finest moment, 'I Don't Like Mondays' – the harrowing true-life story of an American teenage girl who went to school with a shotgun and killed her headmaster and a janitor and wounded several of her classmates. The UK chart-topping single proved almost impossible to match, despite the energetic follow-up, 'Someone's Looking At You'. The Rats were still hitting the UK Top 5, though, and released an understated comment on Northern Ireland in 'Banana Republic'.

By 1982 they had fallen from critical and commercial grace, and their subsequent recordings seemed *passé*. For Geldof, more important work lay ahead with the founding of Band Aid and his work on relieving famine in Africa. The Rats performed at the Live Aid concert (1985) before bowing out the following year at Dublin's Self Aid benefit.

BOSTON

As a result of home-made demos recorded by the enterprising Tom Scholz (b. 1947), one of the finest US AOR albums of all time was created. Fran Sheehan (b. 1949; bass), Brad Delp (b. 1951; guitar, vocals), Barry Goudreau (b. 1951; guitar) and Sib Hashian (b. 1949; drums) joined Scholz, and the name

Boston was adopted. Their 1976 debut was a US Top 3 album which sold 16 million copies in the USA alone and spent two years in the US charts. The memorable single 'More Than A Feeling' contained all the ingredients of adult-orientated rock: upfront guitar, powerful lead vocal and heavy bass and drums. Two years later the band repeated the formula with *Don't Look Back*, which also topped the US charts.

A long-running court battle between Scholz and CBS Records delayed the release of any further material. Goudreau, tired of the delay, released a solo album before quitting to form Orion The Hunter. Boston, in the guise of Scholz and Delp, returned in 1986 with *Third Stage*, which spawned two further US hit singles, 'Amanda' (number 1) and 'We're Ready', and became the band's third chart-topping album. *Walk On*, with Scholz the sole remaining member of the original line-up, was a disappointment, although it still reached the US Top 5. Delp returned to the Boston fold in 1994, and although they continue to play live, no new studio album has been forthcoming.

BOW WOW WOW

Formed in London in 1980 by former **Sex Pistols** manager Malcolm McLaren, Bow Wow Wow comprised former **Adam And The Ants** members David Barbe (b. David Barbarossa, Mauritius; drums), Matthew Ashman (d. 1995) and Leigh

Gorman (bass). This trio was called upon to back McLaren's latest protégée, 14-year-old Annabella Lwin (b. Myant Myant Aye, Burma).

Bow Wow Wow debuted with 'C30, C60, C90, Go'. Its follow-up, the cassette-only *Your Cassette Pet*, featured eight tracks in an EP format. Although innovative and exciting, the group received limited chart rewards with EMI Records. After signing with RCA Records, however, McLaren promoted the band with a series of publicity stunts, amid outrageous talk of paedophiliac pop as jailbait Lwin had her head shaven into a Mohican and appeared in tribal clothes. Further controversy ensued when she was photographed semi-nude on an album sleeve pastiche. A UK Top 10 hit followed in 1981 with 'Go Wild In The Country', a frenzied, almost animalistic display of sensuous exuberance. An average cover version of 'I Want Candy' also clipped the Top 10, but by then McLaren was losing control of his concept. Singer Lieutenant Lush was briefly recruited and threatened to steal the limelight from McLaren's *ingénue* so was subsequently ousted, only to reappear in Culture Club as Boy George. In 1983, amid uncertainty and disillusionment, Bow Wow Wow folded. The backing group briefly soldiered on as the Chiefs Of Relief, while Lwin took a sabbatical, reappearing in 1985 for an unsuccessful solo career. Ashman died in 1995 following complications from diabetes. In 1997, a new version of the band, including Lwin and Gorman, toured America.

BOWIE, DAVID

The mercurial Bowie (b. David Robert Jones, 1947) underwent a veritable odyssey of career moves and minor crises before establishing himself as a major performer on the UK music scene. He began playing saxophone during his teens, initially with school groups. In the early 60s, his style was decidedly orthodox – all mod clothes and R&B riffs. Over the next few years, he went through a succession of backing groups including the King Bees, the Manish Boys, the Lower Third and the Buzz. In 1966, he changed his surname because of the emergence of Davy Jones of the **Monkees**. He also came under the wing of manager Kenneth Pitt, who nurtured his career for the remainder of the decade. A contract with the fashionable Decca Records subsidiary Deram saw Bowie achieve high-profile publicity, but subsequent singles and a well-promoted debut album failed to sell. Bowie even attempted a cash-in novelty number, 'The Laughing Gnome'. In 1969, he finally broke through with the UK Top 10 hit 'Space Oddity', released to coincide with the American Moon launch. Unfortunately, Bowie seemed unable to follow up the single with anything similarly clever.

A remarkable series of changes in Bowie's life, both personal and professional, occurred in 1970, culminating in him swapping Kenneth Pitt for the more strident Tony De Fries. Amid this period of flux, Bowie completed his first major work, an extraordinary album entitled *The Man Who Sold The World*. With musical assistance from Mick Ronson, drummer Mick Woodmansey and producer Tony Visconti on bass, Bowie employed an arrestingly heavy sound, aided by the eerie synthesizer work of Ralph Mace to embellish his chillingly dramatic vocals. The package was completed with a striking cover revealing Bowie lounging seductively in a flowing dress.

With the svengali-like De Fries aggressively promoting his career, Bowie signed to RCA Records and completed *Hunky Dory* in 1971. The album was lighter in tone than its predecessor, with Bowie reverting to acoustic guitar on some tracks and exploring a more commercial, yet still intriguing, direction with tributes to **Bob Dylan** and the **Velvet Underground**. Up until this point, Bowie had experimented with diverse ideas, themes and images that coalesced effectively, though not necessarily coherently. The complete fusion was revealed in 1972 on *The Rise And Fall Of Ziggy Stardust And The Spiders From Mars*, a startling concept album which promoted Bowie to the premier ranks of the rock scene.

Bowie seemed to have the Midas touch and his production talents brought rewards for his old hero **Lou Reed** (*Transformer* and 'Walk On The Wild Side') and a resurrected **Mott The Hoople**, who had their first hit with

Bowie's 'All The Young Dudes'. The track 'Oh! You Pretty Things' (from *Hunky Dory*) had already provided a hit for Peter Noone and an equally unlikely artist, **Lulu**, enjoyed a Top 10 smash courtesy of 'The Man Who Sold The World'. Meanwhile, Bowie had undertaken a world tour and achieved a UK number 1 with *Aladdin Sane*, another concept work which centred on global destruction. While still at his peak, Bowie shocked the rock world on 4 July 1974 by announcing his retirement. It later transpired that it was not Bowie who was retiring, but his Ziggy Stardust persona.

After recording a US-broadcast television special entitled *The 1980 Floor Show*, Bowie produced *Diamond Dogs*. Having failed to receive permission to use the title *1984*, he nevertheless adapted George Orwell's famous novel, but without the familiar sound of the Spiders From Mars and the cutting guitar work of Mick Ronson. A massive tour of USA and Canada saw the 'Diamond Dogs' spectacle at its most excessive and expansive. Bowie's popularity was as great as ever in the mid-70s, when he effectively righted the wrongs of history by taking 'Space Oddity' to number 1, six years after its initial UK chart entry. He also enjoyed his first US number 1, 'Fame', which featured the voice and co-composing skills of **John Lennon**. The song appeared on *Young Americans*, which saw the emergence of a new Bowie, successfully tackling Philadelphia soul. Bowie also worked on Nicholas Roeg's film *The Man Who Fell To Earth*, in which he was given the leading role of the displaced alien.

Bowie's next persona was the Thin White Duke, the icy character who came to life on *Station To Station*. He relocated to France and then Berlin with **Brian Eno** and **Tony Visconti** for a cycle of albums which displayed Bowie at his least commercial and most ambitious. *Low* and *Heroes* (both 1977), were predominantly instrumental works whose mood was strongly influenced by Eno's minimalist electronics. Surprisingly, segments from each album found their way on to a live album, *Stage*. Following a best-forgotten appearance in the movie *Just A Gigolo*, Bowie concluded his collaborative work with Eno on 1979's *Lodger*. Generally regarded as the least impressive of the Eno trilogy, it nevertheless contained some strong songs.

Bowie's thespian pursuits continued with a critically acclaimed starring role in the Broadway production of *The Elephant Man*. He also released a new album which leaned closer to the rock mainstream. *Scary Monsters (And Super Creeps)* was adventurous, with its modern electro-pop and distorted electric guitar, provided by former King Crimson helmsman Robert Fripp. The album contained the reflective 'Ashes To Ashes', which included references to one of Bowie's earlier creations, Major Tom. It was his first UK number 1 since 'Space Oddity'.

The early 80s saw Bowie taking on a series of diverse projects, including an appearance in Bertolt Brecht's *Baal*, surprise chart collaborations with **Queen** ('Under Pressure') and **Bing Crosby** ('Peace On Earth'/'Little Drummer Boy') and two more starring roles in the films *The Hunger* and *Merry Christmas, Mr. Lawrence*. A switch from RCA to EMI saw Bowie release his most commercial work since the early 70s with *Let's Dance* (1983), produced by Nile Rodgers of **Chic**. The title track gave Bowie his third solo UK number 1 and effectively revitalized his recording career. He had two further hits that year, both narrowly missing UK number 1: 'China Girl' and 'Modern Love'. *Let's Dance* was quickly followed by the anti-climactic *Tonight*, which attracted universally bad reviews but managed to spawn a hit single with 'Blue Jean'. During 1985, Bowie was chiefly in demand as a collaborator, first with the Pat Metheny Group on 'This Is Not America' (from the film *The Falcon And The Snowman*) and next with Mick Jagger on a reworking of Martha And The Vandellas' 'Dancing In The Street' for Live Aid.

His next venture, the much-publicized movie *Absolute Beginners*, divided the critics, but its strong title track provided Bowie with a major hit. He also starred in the fantasy film *Labyrinth* and sang the theme of the anti-nuclear war cartoon *When The Wind Blows*. In 1987, Bowie teamed up with former classmate Peter Frampton for the 'Glass Spider' tour. The attendant album, *Never Let Me Down*, was poorly received. Never predictable, Bowie decided to put a group together in 1989 and called upon the services of Reeves Gabrels (guitar), Tony Sales (bass) and Hunt Sales (drums) – the two brothers had worked with **Iggy Pop** and **Todd Rundgren**. The unit took their name from the title song of their new album, *Tin Machine*, a set that displayed some good, old-fashioned guitar work, occasionally bordering on heavy metal. It was an interesting experiment, but neither the album or the follow-up did much to increase Bowie's critical standing in the late 80s.

Black Tie White Noise, released in 1993, was his strongest album in years and entered the UK charts at number 1. In 1995, Bowie signed a major recording contract with Virgin Records America. His first release was *1. Outside*, a collaboration with Brian Eno that received mixed reviews and disappointing sales. The industrial noise-rock and techno-inspired *Earthling* was another mixed bag, but showed the artist willing to take chances in his 50th year. In 1998, Bowie, ever looking towards the future, launched the first

artist-created Internet service provider, Bowienet. In 1999, he worked and recorded with **Placebo**, and returned to a more conventional style of songwriting on *'hours ...'*. In December 2001 the singer announced the launch of his independent label, ISO. He released *Heather* in 2002.

BOX TOPS

Formed in 1965, this Memphis, Tennessee, USA-based quintet – Alex Chilton (b. 1950; guitar, harmonica, vocals), Gary Talley (b. 1947; lead guitar), Billy Cunningham (b. 1950; rhythm guitar), John Evans (bass) and Danny Smythe (drums) – sprang to fame when their debut single, 'The Letter', became an international hit and US chart-topper. Their appeal lay in Chilton's raspy delivery and Dan Penn's complementary production, a combination repeated on further successes, 'Neon Rainbow', 'Cry Like A Baby', 'Soul Deep' and 'Choo-Choo Train'. Rick Allen (b. 1946) replaced Evans in 1968, but the band's gifted singer remained its focal point. They broke up in 1969, with Chilton reappearing in the critically acclaimed **Big Star**. A one-off reunion took place in Los Angeles in 1997.

BOY GEORGE

During the early 80s Boy George (b. George O'Dowd, 1961) became a regular on the London, England, New Romantic club scene. He appeared, briefly, in Malcolm McLaren's Bow Wow Wow. A meeting with former disc jockey Mikey Craig (b. 1960; bass) resulted in the forming of In Praise of Lemmings. After the addition of former **Adam And The Ants** drummer Jon Moss

(b. 1957) and Roy Hay (b. 1961; guitar, keyboards), the group was renamed **Culture Club**. Boy George's appetite for publicity and media manipulation seemed endless, but it was his involvement with drugs that brought his downfall when a visiting New York keyboard player, Michael Rudetski, died of a heroin overdose while staying at George's London home.

George's public renouncement of drugs coincided with the dissolution of Culture Club and the launch of a solo career. His debut, a cover of the **Bread**/ Ken Boothe hit, 'Everything I Own', (1987), gave him his first UK number 1 since Culture Club's 'Karma Chameleon' in 1983. He formed his own record label, More Protein, in 1989, and fronted a band, Jesus Loves You, reflecting his new-found spiritual awareness and love of reggae and soul. Releases with the E-Zee Possee, meanwhile, demonstrated his increasing involvement in the UK's club scene.

His pop career was revived in 1992 by a cover version of 'The Crying Game', which was featured in the hit movie of the same name. *Cheapness And Beauty* was a blend of punky glam pop, at odds with his perceived 90s image of fading superstar. Its release date in 1995 coincided with the publication of the artist's self-deprecating autobiography. By now recognized as a leading club DJ, George contributed vocals to a drum 'n' bass version of 'Police And Thieves', released by London dance collective Dubversive in 1998. He has also produced, often in collaboration with Pete Tong, several mix compilations for the Ministry Of Sound label.

The singer returned to his New Romantic days in a new musical, *Taboo*, which opened at The Venue in London on 29 January 2002. The cast performed new songs written by George specifically for the show.

BOYZ II MEN

This US close-harmony soul group enjoyed an almost unprecedented level of success during the early 90s, beginning with 1991's Top 3 single, 'Motownphilly'. Wanya 'Squirt' Morris (b. 1973), Michael 'Bass' McCary (b. 1972), Shawn 'Slim' Stockman (b. 1972) and Nathan 'Alex-Vanderpool' Morris (b. 1971) formed the band in 1988. Michael Bivins of Bell Biv Devoe took the group under his wing and brought them to Motown Records. Their debut album sold over seven million copies. The soundtrack song 'End Of The Road' topped the US charts for a mammoth 13 weeks in 1992 and provided the quartet with a UK chart-topper. Their winning formula was repeated with uncanny accuracy in 1994, the follow-up album becoming a huge hit. It spawned three of the best-selling singles in US chart history, with 'I'll Make Love To You' (at the top for 14 weeks), 'On Bended Knee' (at the top for 6 weeks) and 'One Sweet Day' (with **Mariah Carey**, number 1 for an astonishing 16 weeks). Following the release of *Evolution*, the quartet also set up their own label, Stonecreek. After a three-year hiatus they launched *Nathan Michael Shawn Wanya* on to a market now saturated with a new generation of R&B vocal groups. The quartet's brand of smooth, inoffensive soul, though classy as always, struggled to make a commercial impact in a less discerning and more sexually explicit climate.

BOYZONE

This quintet of unaffected young Irish men were tailored for mainstream success by manager/promoter Louis Walsh. Mikey Graham (b. 1972) and Keith Duffy (b. 1974) were recruited from their jobs as mechanics, Shane Lynch (b. 1976) from an architecture course, while Ronan Keating (b. 1977) and Stephen Gately (b. 1976) were enlisted directly from school. Their debut single, a cover version of the **Detroit Spinners**' 'Working My Way Back To You' released in November 1993, launched the group in Ireland, but their UK breakthrough came with a cover of the **Osmonds**' 'Love Me For A Reason'. *Said And Done,*

released in August 1995, included three other hit singles, 'Key To My Life', 'So Good' and their Christmas cover version of **Cat Stevens**' 'Father And Son'.

With the demise of **Take That** in 1996 and the rise of numerous 'boy bands', Boyzone moved to the head of the pack, with further hit singles including 'Coming Home Now' and a cover version of the **Bee Gees**' 'Words', their first UK number 1. Further UK hits followed with 'A Different Beat' (number 1), 'Isn't It A Wonder', 'Picture Of You', a cover version of **Tracy Chapman**'s 'Baby Can I Hold You', and 'All That I Need' (number 1). The Andrew Lloyd-Webber/Jim Steinman-penned 'No Matter What', taken from the musical *Whistle Down The Wind*, became the band's first million-selling single. *A Different Beat* and *Where We Belong* followed in the footsteps of their debut album by entering the UK charts at number 1, and their charity cover version of Billy Ocean's 'When The Going Gets Tough' topped the UK singles chart for two weeks in March 1999.

Keating worked hard to establish himself away from the band, recording solo material and presenting the prime-time UK talent show *Get Your Act Together*. He has also enjoyed success as a manager/promoter, with his protégés **Westlife** enjoying a string of UK chart-topping singles. His cover version of Keith Whitley's country hit 'When You Say Nothing At All', taken from the soundtrack of *Notting Hill*, topped the UK charts in August 1999. He and Gately both released successful solo albums the following year but denied rumours that Boyzone had split up.

BRADY, PAUL

A member of Dublin, Eire-based R&B group the Kult, Brady (b. 1947), later embraced folk music with the Johnstons. He subsequently joined the much-respected traditional unit Planxty, where he met Andy Irvine. *Andy Irvine/Paul Brady* prefaced Brady's solo career, which began with the much-lauded *Welcome Here Kind Stranger* (1978). The singer abandoned folk in 1981 with *Hard Station*, which included the Irish chart-topping single 'Crazy Dreams'. *True For You* followed a prolific period in which Brady toured, supporting **Dire Straits** and **Eric Clapton**. Tina Turner's versions of 'Steel Claw' and 'Paradise Is Here' cemented Brady's reputation as a songwriter. He collaborated with **Mark Knopfler** on the soundtrack to *Cal*, before completing a strong live album, *Full Moon*. *Trick Or Treat* was recorded under the aegis of former **Steely Dan**

producer, Gary Katz. **Bonnie Raitt**, an admirer of Brady's work, gave his career a significant boost by including two of his songs on her 1991 album *Luck Of The Draw*. Brady enlisted outside help in the shape of Ronan Keating, Connor Reeves, **Carole King** and Will Jennings on 2000's *Oh What A World* – his first album in over five years.

BRAGG, BILLY

Bragg (b. Steven William Bragg, 1957) made his name in the 80s as one of the most committed left-wing political performers on the UK music scene. After forming the ill-fated punk group Riff Raff, Bragg briefly joined the British Army (Tank Corp), before buying his way out for a solo musical career. Bragg undertook a maverick tour of the concert halls of Britain, ready at a moment's notice to fill in as support for almost any act. His lyrics, full of passion, anger and wit, made him a truly original character. Managed by Peter Jenner, his 1983 debut *Life's A Riot With Spy Vs Spy* reached the UK Top 30, while the follow-up *Brewing Up With Billy Bragg*, reached number 16. At Bragg's insistence, the albums were kept at a below average selling price.

Omnipresent at political rallies, and benefits, particularly during the 1984 Miners' Strike, Bragg produced powerful pro-Union songs and the EP title track, 'Between The Wars'. He was instrumental in creating the socialist musicians collective 'Red Wedge', including pop luminaries **Paul Weller**, Junior Giscombe and **Jimmy Somerville**.

Despite the politicizing, Bragg was still able to pen classic love songs such as 'New England', which **Kirsty MacColl** took into the UK Top 10 in 1985, and 'Levi Stubbs' Tears', which appeared on 1986's *Talking With The Taxman About Poetry*. In 1988, his cover of the **Beatles**' 'She's Leaving Home', shared a double A-side single release with **Wet Wet Wet**'s 'With A Little Help From My Friends', which resulted in a UK number 1. In 1991 Bragg issued his most commercial work, *Don't Try This At Home*, which featured a shift towards personal politics, most noticeably on the witty hit single 'Sexuality'. *William Bloke*, released after a five-year hiatus, was less angry and more ironic, displaying an almost graceful confidence and maturity.

The following year he collaborated with **Woody Guthrie**'s daughter on a musical project to interpret several of the hundreds of completed lyrics bequeathed by the great American folk singer. Working with American country rockers Wilco, Bragg fashioned a respectful testament to Guthrie that avoided nostalgia and easy sentiment. A second Guthrie collection was released the following year. Bragg resumed his solo career in 2002 with *England, Half-English*, recorded with his regular backing band the Blokes.

BRAN VAN 3000

This sprawling, highly eclectic Canadian outfit were formed by Montreal-based video director and part-time DJ James 'Bran Man' Di Salvio. Musical director Di Salvio and co-producer 'EP' Bergen were joined in the initial line-up of Bran Van 3000 by vocalists Sara Johnston and Jayne Hill, but gradually recruited a large cast of Montreal musicians for recording and touring purposes. Experienced rapper Steve 'Liquid' Hawley, guitarist Nick Hynes, bass player Gary McKenzie, drummer Rob Joanisse, and vocalist Stèphane Moraille were brought on board to augment the band's sample-heavy mixture of sprightly indie pop melodies, club beats, trip-hop sprawl, and cheesy lounge music.

Their debut *Glee* was originally released in spring 1997 on the Audioworks label, but the following year's international release contained several new songs and different versions of many tracks owing to licensing problems. 'Drinking In LA', featuring Moraille's soulful vocal chorus juxtaposed with Di Salvio's ranting verses, reached number 3 when re-released in the UK

in August 1999, thanks to its prominent use in a Rolling Rock beer advertisement. Di Salvio and his cohorts teamed up with Mike D of the **Beastie Boys** to record the follow-up *Discosis*.

BRAND NEW HEAVIES

Simon Bartholomew and Andy Levy formed this London, England based outfit in 1985. Joined by drummer Jan Kincaid and keyboardist Ceri Evans, they had one failed contract with Acid Jazz Records, who tried to launch them as a 'rare-groove' outfit, before they joined with US label Delicious Vinyl. The latter's management put them in touch with N'Dea Davenport who had provided backing vocals for **George Clinton** and Bruce Willis. Word spread throughout the USA and they were sampled heavily on a number of early 90s rap records; in return many rap artists guested on their second album, *Heavy Rhyme Experience: Vol. 1*. Ceri Evans left in 1992 to undertake production work and record as Sunship.

The Brand New Heavies' huge success in the US with the single 'Never Stop' was soon mirrored in the UK, with the singles 'Dream On Dreamer' and 'Midnight At The Oasis' reaching the Top 20 in 1994. Soul artist Siedah Garrett became the new lead singer in 1997 after Davenport's departure the previous year for a solo career. They enjoyed further chart success the same year when their cover version of Carole King's 'You've Got A Friend' broke into the UK Top 10. Garrett was replaced by Carleen Anderson following the release of the studio set, *Shelter*.

BRANDY

Among the best of the crop of female urban singers to emerge in the mid-90s, Brandy (b. Brandy Norwood, 1979) soon established herself as a multi-media star. She appeared in the ABC television situation comedy *Thea* as a teenager,

and in 1994 released her self-titled debut album. It included the successful crossover singles, 'I Wanna Be Down' and 'Baby'. Brandy also appeared in the hugely popular television show *Moesha*, and her second album was recorded during breaks from filming. Her spiky duet with fellow soul singer Monica on 1998's 'The Boy Is Mine' was a huge-selling US number 1, spending 13 weeks at the top of the *Billboard* Hot 100 and becoming the all-time number one female duet in US chart history. The single also reached number 2 in the UK and sold over 3 million copies worldwide. The attendant *Never S-A-Y Never*, was disappointingly bland, but follow-up single, 'Top Of The World' was another transatlantic hit single and 'Have You Ever?', written by Diane Warren, topped the Hot 100 in January 1999. The same year, Brandy made her acting debut in the horror movie *I Still Know What You Did Last Summer*. She returned to the music scene in 2002 with the Rodney Jerkins-produced transatlantic hit single 'What About Us?'. The jarring rhythms of the single were sadly absent on the mundane *Full Moon*.

BRAXTON, TONI

Braxton (b. 1968) was signed to Arista Records in 1990, with her four sisters, as the Braxtons. 'The Good Life' brought them to the attention of producers L.A. Reid and Babyface, who provided her with solo successes such as 'Another Sad Love Song' and 'You Mean The World To Me'. Though described as the 'new Whitney Houston', Braxton's vocal talent also found an audience in club circles, and her 1993 debut album sold more than two million copies. She won a Grammy for Best New Artist the same year. *Secrets* repeated the success of her debut, particularly in her homeland, where it spent 92 weeks on the chart.

Surprisingly, in light of her previous commercial success, Braxton filed for bankruptcy in January 1998 following litigation with her record company. She returned in style two years later with *The Heat* which included the Rodney Jerkins-penned Top 5 hit 'He Wasn't Man Enough'.

BREAD

Bread was formed in 1969 when David Gates (b. 1940), a leading Los Angeles session musician, produced an album for the Pleasure Faire, a band which included vocalist/guitarist Rob Royer. Songwriter James Griffin contributed several compositions to the set and the three aspirants then decided to pool resources. All were assured multi-instrumentalists, and although not a commercial success, their 1969 debut album established a penchant for melodious soft-rock. Mike Botts augmented the line-up for *On The Water*, which included the million-selling US chart-topper 'Make It With You', while *Manna* spawned a further gold disc with 'If', later successfully revived by actor/singer Telly Savalas. Royer was replaced by keyboard veteran Larry Knechtel, but Bread's smooth approach was left unruffled as they achieved further international success with , 'Baby I'm-A Want You' (1971), 'Everything I Own' and 'Guitar Man' (both 1972). Increasing friction between Gates and Griffin led to the band's collapse. The combatants embarked on solo careers while Botts joined the Linda Ronstadt Band, but they reconvened in 1976 for *Lost Without Your Love*, the title track of which reached the US Top 10. Guitarist Dean Parks joined when Griffin resumed his independent direction. A court ruling banned Gates from recording or touring as Bread until an ongoing legal dispute with Griffin over the use of the band name was resolved. Gates elected to go solo, scoring a US Top 20 hit in 1978 with 'Goodbye Girl'. The original line-up regrouped in 1996–97 for a brief tour.

BREEDERS

Restless with her subordinate role in the **Pixies**, Kim Deal (b. 1961; guitars, vocals, synthesizers) forged this spin-off project with Throwing Muses guitarist Tanya Donelly (b. 1966). The name Breeders, a derogatory term used by homosexuals to describe heterosexuals, had been the name of a band Deal fronted prior to the Pixies, with her twin sister Kelley.

Deal and Donelly were joined by English bass player Josephine Wiggs (b. Josephine Miranda Cordelia, 1965) on *Pod*. Britt Walford from Kentucky hardcore group Slint drummed on the record under the pseudonym Shannon Doughton. The line-up was then augmented by Kelley Deal (guitar, vocals) on the four-track EP *Safari*, but despite critical and commercial acclaim the Breeders remained a sideline.

Following the Pixies' bitter split, Deal rekindled the band in 1993. Donelly had left to form Belly, but Wiggs rejoined the Deal twins and Jim MacPherson (b. 1966; drums) on *Last Splash*. Less abrasive than its predecessor, this revealed Deal's encompassing mock C&W, grunge-styled instrumentals and ballads. In 1996, Kelley Deal underwent drug rehabilitation and left for The Last Hard Men before forming the Kelley Deal 6000. Wiggs also left to concentrate on the Josephine Wiggs Experience, while Kim Deal formed the short-lived Amps.

Rumours of Kim Deal reuniting with the original band continued to circulate in the 90s, although the only material to surface was a cover version, 'Collage', recorded for *The Mod Squad* soundtrack. The Deal sisters recruited new personnel to play several live shows in 2001, and returned to the studio with Steve Albini to record their new album, *Title Tk*.

BREL, JACQUES

Brel (b. 1929, d. 1978) began a career in Paris, France in the 50s as a singing composer. Impresario Jacques Canetti presented him regularly at Pigalle's Theatre Des Trois Baudets, where he was accompanied by his guitar and a small backing band. His performances, embracing fierce anger, romanticism and world-weariness, captivated the audiences and his popularity increased after 'Quand On N'A Que L'Amour'. Other domestic hits included 'La Valse À Mille Temps', 'Les Bourgeois', 'Les Dame Patronesse' and 'Les Flamandes'. His lyricism remained intrinsically Gallic until 1957's *American Debut*, from which a substantial English-speaking following grew.

Brel strongly influenced the output of such diverse wordsmiths as **Leonard Cohen**, **David Bowie** and **Scott Walker**. He reached a global market by proxy when his material was translated, as instanced by the Kingston Trio's 1964 rendition of 'Le Moribond' as 'Seasons In The Sun' (a UK number 1 for Terry Jacks a decade later), and the evolution of 'If You Go Away' into a cabaret standard. He played two sell-out Carnegie Hall shows but was keener on developing his film career with *Les Risques Du Métier* and *La Bande À Bonnet*.

Brel eventually withdrew to Polynesia, returning only fleetingly to Paris for one-take recording sessions, but his work remained in the public eye through a three-year Broadway run of the musical *Jacques Brel Is Alive And Well And Living In Paris* (later a film). Brel's death from cancer was marked by a million-selling compilation album.

BRICKELL, EDIE

This US artist (b. 1966) got her first break as a vocalist in 1985, when she was asked to front local jazz-influenced band the New Bohemians. As their popularity grew they signed to Geffen Records as Edie Brickell And The New Bohemians. *Shooting Rubberbands At The Stars* went platinum in the USA, where it reached number 4 in 1988. 'What I Am', the attendant single, reached the

US Top 10. The band's second album *Ghost Of A Dog* was not as successful as their debut, and little was heard of Brickell until her solo *Picture Perfect Morning* (1994). The album was produced by Roy Halee and **Paul Simon** (her husband since June 1992). She reunited with the New Bohemians in 1999 to record the independent release, *The Live Montauk Sessions*.

BRINSLEY SCHWARZ

The initial line-up of this UK band – Brinsley Schwarz (guitar, vocals), Barry Landerman (organ, vocals), **Nick Lowe** (b. 1949; bass, vocals) and Pete Whale (drums) – played together as Kippington Lodge. Bob Andrews replaced Landerman in 1968 and the following year they recruited new drummer Billy Rankin, and renamed themselves in deference to their lead guitarist.

Their debut, *Brinsley Schwarz*, was pleasant but undemanding, although *Despite It All* showed more promise. A second guitarist, Ian Gomm (b. 1947), was added prior to *Silver Pistol*, arguably the band's most unified and satisfying release. *Nervous On The Road* featured 'Don't Lose Your Grip On Love', while '(What's So Funny 'Bout) Peace, Love and Understanding', later revived by **Elvis Costello**, made its debut on *The New Favourites Of Brinsley Schwarz*. The group broke up in 1975. Schwarz and Andrews later joined Graham Parker And The Rumour, while Gomm and Lowe went solo.

BRONSKI BEAT

Formed in 1983, this Anglo-Scottish band comprised Jimmy Somerville (b. 1961; vocals), Steve Bronski (keyboards) and Larry Steinbachek (keyboards). After establishing themselves in London's gay community, the trio were signed to London Records. 'Smalltown Boy' drew attention to Somerville's falsetto vocal, which became the hallmark of their sound. The single climbed to UK number 3 and the follow-up, 'Why?' broke into the Top 10. By the end of 1984, Somerville was well-known as a tireless homosexual rights campaigner. *The Age Of Consent* met with a mixed reaction in the music press, but a sprightly cover of George Gershwin's 'It Ain't Necessarily So' scaled the charts. In 1985, the band teamed up with **Marc Almond** for an extraordinary version of **Donna Summer**'s 'I Feel Love', interwoven with the refrains of 'Love To Love You Baby' and 'Johnny Remember Me'. The single reached the UK Top 3 in April 1985, but at the end of the month Somerville left the band. He resurfaced in the **Communards**, before relocating to San Francisco. Bronski Beat found a replacement in John Jon (b. John

Foster) and initially enjoyed some success. The catchy 'Hit That Perfect Beat' returned them to the Top 3 and two further albums followed. The impetus was gradually lost, however, although Bronski Beat carried on into the 90s with new vocalist Jonathan Hellyer.

BROOKS, ELKIE

Brooks (b. Elaine Bookbinder, 1946) began her career touring the UK during the early 60s with the Eric Delaney Band. Her early records included versions of 'Hello Stranger' and 'The Way You Do The Things You Do'. In 1970, she joined Dada, a 12-piece jazz-rock act featuring **Robert Palmer** (vocals) and Pete Gage (guitar). These three artists subsequently formed the core of Vinegar Joe, a popular soul/rock act.

That band dissolved in 1974, and Brooks embarked on a solo career. She enjoyed two UK Top 10 hits with 'Pearl's A Singer' and 'Sunshine After The Rain' (both 1977), but her once-raucous approach became increasingly tempered by MOR trappings. 'Fool (If You Think It's Over)' and 'Nights In White Satin' (both 1982) enhanced the singer's reputation for dramatic cover versions, but 'No More The Fool', composed by Russ Ballard, revived her contemporary standing, reaching the UK Top 5 in 1986. An attendant album achieved double-gold status, while *Bookbinder's Kid* emphasized this revitalization with further songs by Ballard and material by Bryan Adams.

By the 90s Brooks was firmly established as one of Britain's leading live performers. Her studio albums during this decade were pleasant but unremarkable recordings which never achieved the creative heights of her work during the 70s.

BROOKS, GARTH

Brooks (b. Troyal Garth Brooks, 1962) started out in Oklahoma night clubs before signing to Capitol Records with producer Allen Reynolds. His 1989 debut had a western swing and country feel and included a revival of a Jim Reeves' 'I Know One'. *No Fences* was even better, and included his concert-stopping 'Friends In Low Places'. The album sold ten million copies in the USA. *Ropin' The Wind* sold four million copies in its first month of release and topped both the US pop and country charts. His version of **Billy Joel**'s 'Shameless' was a US country number 1, as were 'The Thunder Rolls', 'Two Of A Kind' and 'Working On A Full House'.

After a brief break for fatherhood, Brooks re-emerged with a Christmas record, *Beyond The Season*. The follow-up *The Chase* moved away from the honky-tonk style of his debut towards a 70s-orientated soft-rock sound. *Fresh Horses* was his first album to have simultaneous worldwide release, and an international hit came with 'She's Every Woman'. In 1995, he took over his own business affairs with the help of his wife Sandy.

In 1997, Brooks released *Sevens*, which debuted at number 1 in the *Billboard* pop and country charts with pre-orders of more than five million. His worldwide album sales reached 81 million the following year, making him the all-time biggest-selling solo artist in the world. Brooks shocked the country establishment in 1999 when he recorded an entire pop album under the pseudonym of Chris Gaines, a character in his forthcoming movie *The Lamb*. Sales for the album were disappointing and a swift return to straight-forward country songs ensued.

BROS

Twins Matthew and Luke Goss (vocals) were born in London, England in 1968. Along with Scottish school-friend Craig Logan (b. 1969; guitar) they formed a group named Cavier before changing the name to Bros. Securing the services of **Pet Shop Boys** manager Tom Watkins and producer Nicky Graham, they scraped into the UK charts in 1987 with 'I Owe You Nothing'. Well groomed and ambitious, the trio soon attracted a fanatical teenage fan following. Their second single, 'When Will I Be Famous' was promoted aggressively and climbed to number 2. 'Drop The Boy' soon followed, again just missing the number 1 spot. By now established as *the* teen idols of 1988, the trio's first single 'I Owe You Nothing' was re-promoted and reached number 1. A string of UK Top 10 singles followed, including 'I Quit', 'Cat Among The Pigeons', 'Too Much', 'Chocolate Box' and 'Sister'. Fortunes gradually took a downward turn. In 1989 Logan was ousted and Bros became embroiled in an acrimonious legal battle with their manager. Written off as mere teenybop fodder, they actively pursued a more serious direction and returned to the UK Top 20 with 'Are You Mine?' and the album *Changing Faces* in 1991. By 1993 the phenomenon had passed, with the twins now separated. Matt pursued a solo career while Luke Goss turned to acting, enjoying success as a stage actor and appearing as Nomak in *Blade II*.

BROTHERHOOD OF MAN

Pop vocal act formed in London, England in 1969 by songwriter Tony Hiller. The lead singer was veteran session man Tony Burrows (ex-Ivy League, **Flowerpot Me**n, **Edison Lighthouse**) and the band's first success was Hiller's 'United We Stand', a UK Top 10 hit in 1970. With changing personnel, the Brotherhood Of Man continued to record, unsuccessfully, for Deram Records and Dawn Records in the early 70s until, in 1976, they represented the UK in the Eurovision Song Contest. Appearing as an **ABBA**-inspired male/female quartet led by Martin Lee, Lee Sheridan, Sandra Stevens and Nicky Stevens, Brotherhood Of Man's breezy rendition of 'Save Your Kisses For Me' won the competition and became an international hit. A series of UK successes followed, including the number 1s 'Angelo' and 'Figaro'. Thereafter, their popularity dwindled and by the 80s Brotherhood Of Man was relegated to the lucrative though uninspiring scampi-and-chips nightclub circuit, although 'Lightning Flash' in 1982 was a minor hit.

BROUDIE, IAN

As well as piloting the successful 90s pop band the **Lightning Seeds**, Broudie (b. 1958) has established himself as one of the UK's most talented pop producers. He started out in the 70s with the O'Boogie Brothers (with future **Culture Club** drummer Jon Moss) and subsequently joined Big In Japan, Merseyside's primal punk band. Broudie then moved on to the Opium Eaters, with Pete Wylie, Budgie and Paul Rutherford (future star of **Frankie Goes To Hollywood**). They never recorded. His next band was the Original Mirrors, formed with Steve Allen (of Deaf School), who secured a contract with Mercury Records. Despite two albums, the band had collapsed by the beginning of the 80s and Broudie moved into production. The first record he produced, **Echo And The Bunnymen**'s 'Rescue', was their first UK Top 20 single. In 1983, he formed Care, with ex-Wild Swans singer Paul Simpson. Broudie returned to production in 1986 for the **Icicle Works**' *If You Want To Defeat Your Enemy Sing His Song*.

Broudie inaugurated the Lightning Seeds in 1989 to record their UK Top 20 debut single, 'Pure'. They went on to enjoy success with 'The Life Of Riley', 'Lucky You', 'Change', 'Perfect' and 'Ready Or Not'. In 1996, Broudie composed England's anthem for soccer's European championship, 'Three Lions' (recorded with comedians David Baddiel and Frank Skinner), which reached number 1 in the UK chart. He repeated the feat with the revamped 'Three Lions 98' in June 1998, released to coincide with England's World Cup challenge.

BROUGHTON, EDGAR BAND

Popular on London, England's underground scene, this anarchic band comprised Edgar Broughton (b. 1947; guitar, vocals), Steve Broughton (b. 1950; drums, vocals) and Arthur Grant (bass, guitar, vocals). Edgar's growling voice was often compared to that of Captain Beefheart. During the Blind Faith free concert in Hyde Park in June 1969, the Broughtons incited the crowd to a frenzy with 'Out Demons Out'. They expanded to a four-piece for 1971's self-titled third album, employing ex-**Pretty Things** guitarist Victor Unitt. Despite airplay from John Peel, the political and sexual themes of their songs had dated by the early 70s. Unitt had left by the time the band recorded *Bandages* for the NEMS label in 1975. Prevented from recording by managerial problems, the band made a low-key return in 1979 – now billed simply as the Broughtons. During subsequent decades, the Broughtons could still be found performing as part of late-60s revival shows and on the London pub circuit.

BROWN, ARTHUR

UK vocalist Brown (b. 1944) fronted a succession of bands in London before moving to Paris in 1966, where he honed a theatrical and visual image. He contributed two songs to *La Curee*, a Roger Vadim film starring Jane Fonda. In 1967, he formed the first Crazy World Of Arthur Brown with Vincent Crane (b. 1943, d. 1989; organ), Drachen Theaker (drums) and, later, Nick Greenwood (bass). They were quickly adopted by the 'underground' audience, where Brown's facial make-up, dervish dancing and fiery helmet earned them immediate notoriety. The band scored a UK number 1 in 1968 with the compulsive 'Fire'. The attendant album, *The Crazy World Of Arthur Brown*, contained many stage favourites, including 'Spontaneous Apple Creation' and 'Come And Buy'.

Theaker and Crane left the band during a US tour and although Crane later returned, Carl Palmer, formerly of Chris Farlowe's Thunderbirds, joined as drummer. Brown's most successful group ended in 1969 when the newcomer and Crane formed **Atomic Rooster**. Brown moved to Dorset, where a music commune had been established. Reunited with Theaker, he completed *Strangelands*, before embarking on a new direction with *Kingdom Come*. Brown resumed a solo career in 1974, but despite a memorable cameo as the Priest in Ken Russell's *Tommy*, subsequent recordings proved disappointing.

Brown went into semi-retirement and pursued a career as a carpenter and decorator in Texas, with former Mothers Of Invention drummer, Jimmy Carl Black. In 1999 he guested with UK psychedelic revivalists **Kula Shaker**, still with his helmet of fire.

BROWN, BOBBY

A former member of New Edition, Brown (b. 1969) emerged in the late 80s as the king of the new urban sound, swingbeat. On his debut album he was joined by Larry Blackmon and John Luongo, but it was the follow-up set, and the seamless production technique of Teddy Riley and L.A. Reid and Babyface, that pushed him up the charts. Cuts such as the US number 1 'My Prerogative' were infectious dance workouts. Further US Top 5 singles included 'Roni', 'Every Little Step', 'On Our Own', and 'Humpin' Around', while a collaboration with Glenn Medeiros, 'She Ain't Worth It', topped the charts in summer 1990.

Brown married **Whitney Houston** in 1992, and made tentative steps into acting. In 1995, 'Two Can Play That Game' reached the UK Top 5, following which he began working again with New Edition on the successful reunion album, *Home Again*. A new Bobby Brown album appeared at the end of 1997 amid rumours of marital strife and bad behaviour.

BROWN, FOXY

Naming herself after the eponymous Pam Grier character in the cult blaxploitation movie, Brown (b. Inga Marchand, 1979) began her rapid rise to fame with an appearance on **LL Cool J**'s 1995 single 'I Shot Ya'. Her provocative rap on Jay-Z's 'Ain't No Nigga' established her highly sexual and ultra-confident persona, which came as a breath of fresh air on the male-dominated hip-hop scene. A major-label scramble for her signature ended when Def Jam Records signed her in March 1996. Production maestros Trackmasters oversaw her debut set, *Ill Na Na*. Almost overnight Brown had become a powerful female icon, revolutionizing hip-hop with her sexually explicit lyrics and provocative image. She also appeared with Nas, AZ and Nature as part of rap supergroup the Firm, whose Mafia-inspired debut was released the following year.

Now a bona-fide rap superstar, Brown's *Chyna Doll* went straight in at number 1 on the *Billboard* album chart in February 1999, despite the failure of the single 'Hot Spot'. She was rarely out of the headlines following the album's release, with a number of highly controversial incidents leading many to wonder if Brown would continue in the music business. True to form, she blasted the doubters away with the release of *Broken Silence* in 2001.

BROWN, IAN

Formerly the lead vocalist with seminal UK indie-rock outfit the **Stone Roses**, few expected Brown (b. 1963) to launch a viable solo career following the bad-natured disintegration of the former band. Brown signed a deal with Polydor Records on the understanding that his debut album would be released in its original unadorned, demo-quality state. The label's faith in the artist was rewarded when 'My Star' debuted at UK number 5 in January 1998, and *Unfinished Monkey Business* entered the UK album chart at number 4. Brown's resurrection suffered a setback when he was charged with a public-order offence at Manchester airport, following an incident on a flight from Paris on 13 February. He was given a four-month custodial sentence following his conviction in October, but was released in December. He celebrated with a guest lead vocal on U.N.K.L.E.'s 'Be There', which reached the UK Top 10 the following February. His second solo collection, *Golden Greats*, included the UK Top 5 single, 'Dolphins Were Monkeys'. Brown confirmed his status as the most musically committed ex-Stone Roses member with the adventurous and clever *Music Of The Spheres*.

BROWN, JAMES

After a chequered adolescence, including a conviction for theft at the age of 16, the legendary US singer James Brown (b. 1928) joined the Gospel Starlighters, who evolved into the Flames after embracing R&B. In 1955 their demo of 'Please Please Please' saw them signed to the King/Federal company. A re-recorded version of the song was issued in 1956. Credited to 'James Brown And The Famous Flames', it reached number 5 in the US R&B list. Further releases fared poorly until 1958, when 'Try Me' rose to US R&B number 1. However, it was 1963's *Live At The Apollo*, that established the singer; raw, alive and uninhibited, it confirmed Brown as *the* voice of black America. His energetic songs, such as 'Night Train' and 'Shout And Shimmy', contrasted with slower sermons such as 'I Don't Mind' and 'Bewildered', but it was the orchestrated weepie, 'Prisoner Of Love' (1963), that gave Brown his first US Top 20 pop single.

Throughout the 60s, Brown recorded increasingly unconventional songs, including 'Papa's Got A Brand New Bag', 'I Got You (I Feel Good)', 'It's A Man's Man's Man's World' and 'Money Won't Change You'. In 1967, Alfred Ellis replaced Nat Jones as Brown's musical director and 'Cold Sweat' introduced further radical refinements to the group's presentation. It was followed by a string of hits, including 'Say It Loud – I'm Black And I'm Proud' (1968), 'Mother Popcorn' (1969), and 'Get Up (I Feel Like Being A) Sex Machine' (1970). In 1971, Brown moved to Polydor Records and unveiled a new backing band, the JBs. Led by Fred Wesley, it featured such seasoned players as Maceo Parker and St. Clair Pinckney. However, as the decade progressed, his work became less compulsive and the advent of disco saw a decline in Brown's popularity.

He returned with a vengeance in 1986, the year he was inducted into the Rock And Roll Hall Of Fame, with 'Living In America'. An international hit, it was followed by two R&B Top 10 entries, 'How Do You Stop' (1987) and 'I'm Real' (1988). However, the resurrection was abruptly curtailed in 1988 when the singer was imprisoned for illegal possession of drugs and firearms, aggravated assault and failure to stop for the police. Sentenced to six-and-a-half years' imprisonment, Brown was released in February 1991.

During the 90s Brown continued to have further problems with the law and faced an ongoing battle to quit drugs. Despite his personal problems, he is still seen as one of the most dynamic performers in American music and a massive influence on most forms of black music – soul, hip-hop, funk, R&B and disco.

BROWN, JOE

Brown (b. Joseph Roger Brown, 1941) has sustained a career for over 40 years as a cheerful 'cockney' rock 'n' roll singer and guitarist. In 1956, he formed the Spacemen skiffle group, which became the backing group on Jack Good's television series *Boy Meets Girls* in 1959. Brown was regarded as one of the finest guitarists in the UK and his services were frequently in demand. Rechristened Joe Brown And The Bruvvers, the group joined Larry Parnes' successful stable of artists and signed to Decca Records. He first charted with 'The Darktown Strutters Ball' in 1960 and enjoyed UK Top 10 hits on the Piccadilly label in 1962–63 with 'A Picture Of You', 'It Only Took A Minute' and 'That's What Love Will Do'. He appeared in the film *What A Crazy World* and in the mid-60s starred in the hit musical *Charlie Girl*, as well as fronting his own UK television shows *Joe & Co* and *Set 'Em Up Joe*.

In the early 70s, Brown put together country-rock band Home Brew, which originally featured his wife Vicki (vocals), Dave Hynes (drums), Ray Mynott (guitar), Kirk Duncan (keyboards) and Jeff Peters (bass). A second line-up featured the Browns and Hynes joined by Tony Williams (piano, vocals), Joe Fagin (bass, vocals) and Roger McKew (guitar). Tragically, Vicki died from cancer in 1991.

Brown has occasionally appeared for other artists; in 1982 he appeared on **George Harrison**'s *Gone Troppo*. His daughter Sam Brown forged her own career as a notable rock singer and Joe released a well-received album in 1997.

BROWNE, JACKSON

Browne (b. 1948) was born in Heidelberg, Germany, but raised in Los Angeles, USA. In 1966, he joined the Nitty Gritty Dirt Band, only to leave within six months. An ensuing deal with Nina Music, the publishing arm of Elektra Records, resulted in several of Browne's songs being recorded by the label's acts, including Tom Rush. Browne had meanwhile ventured to New York, where he accompanied singer Nico during her engagement at Andy Warhol's Dom club.

A demo tape resulted in a recording deal with the newly established Asylum Records. His 1972 debut *Jackson Browne* aka *Saturate Before Using* showed increased potential, including his own readings of 'Jamaica Say You Will', 'Rock Me On The Water' and 'Doctor My Eyes', which reached the US Top 10 but was even more successful in the hands of the Jackson Five. Browne also drew plaudits for 'Take It Easy', which he wrote with Glenn Frey (the **Eagles**). Jackson's own version of 'Take It Easy' appeared on *For Everyman*, which also featured 'These Days', one of the singer's most popular early songs. The album introduced a long-standing relationship with multi-instrumentalist David Lindley, but although the punchy 'Redneck Friend' became a regional hit, the set was not a commercial success. *Late For The Sky* was a stronger collection, on which Browne offered a more contemporary perspective. *The Pretender*, produced by Jon Landau, included 'Here Come Those Tears Again' and the anthemic title track, the poignancy of which was enhanced by the suicide of Brown's wife, Phyllis, in 1976. *The Pretender* earned a gold disc and the singer's newfound commercial appeal was emphasized with *Running On Empty*, from which 'Stay' reached both the US and UK Top 20.

During the 70s, Browne pursued a heightened political profile through his efforts on behalf of the anti-nuclear lobby, for whom he organized benefit

concerts. It was 1980 before he completed a new studio album, but although *Hold On* was undeniably well-crafted, it lacked the depth of earlier work. Commitments to social causes and his personal life only increased Browne's artistic impasse and 1983's *Lawyers In Love* was a major disappointment. *Lives In The Balance*, which addressed the Reagan presidential era, showed a greater sense of accomplishment, a feature

continued on *World In Motion*. Browne's 90s comeback album, *I'm Alive*, clearly demonstrated that after more than 20 years of writing songs, it is possible to remain as sharp and fresh as ever. In marked contrast, the follow-up *Looking East* was a limp and lifeless affair.

BRUCE, JACK

Bruce (b. John Symon Asher, 1943) has utilized his bass playing to bridge free jazz and heavy rock. Born in Scotland, he moved to London to join Alexis Korner's band and then became a key member of the pioneering Graham Bond Organisation. Following brief stints with John Mayall's Bluesbreakers

and **Manfred Mann**, Bruce joined former colleague, Ginger Baker, who, together with **Eric Clapton**, formed the 60s 'supergroup' **Cream**. During his time with Cream, Bruce helped popularize the bass, an instrument that had previously not featured prominently in rock music.

Upon the break-up of Cream in 1969, Bruce released an exemplary solo album, *Songs For A Tailor*. Pete Brown's imaginative and surreal lyrics were the perfect foil to Bruce's furious and complex bass patterns. Evocative songs such as 'Theme For An Imaginary Western' and 'Weird Of Hermiston' enabled Bruce's vocal ability to shine. Throughout the early 70s, a series of excellent albums and constantly changing line-ups gave him a high profile. His involvement with Tony Williams' Lifetime and his own West, Bruce And Laing, enhanced his position in the jazz and rock worlds. A further aggregation, Jack Bruce And Friends, included jazz guitarist Larry Coryell and former **Jimi Hendrix** drummer Mitch Mitchell. Bruce added vocals to Carla Bley's *Escalator Over The Hill*, and Bley was a member of the 1975 version of the Jack Bruce Band. In 1979, he toured as a member of John McLaughlin's Mahavishnu Orchestra.

The 80s started with a new Jack Bruce Band which featured guitarist Dave 'Clem' Clempson and David Sancious. The ill-fated heavy-rock trio BLT, formed in 1981 with guitarist Robin Trower and drummer Bill Lordan, disintegrated after two albums. After a period of retirement, Bruce released *Automatic* (1987) and then the impressive *A Question Of Time*. In 1994, he formed the short-lived rock trio BBM, with Gary Moore and Baker. A new solo album was released in August 2001 and proved to be Bruce's best in many a year.

BRYANT, BOUDLEAUX

Bryant (b. Diadorius Boudleaux Bryant, 1920, d. 1987) started performing in a family band with his four sisters and brothers, playing at county fairs in Midwest America. In 1937, he began playing with the Atlanta Symphony Orchestra as well as with jazz and country music groups. In 1945, he married Felice Scaduto (b. 1925) and they began composing together, including 'Country Boy', which became a hit for Little Jimmy Dickens.

The duo then moved to Nashville as staff writers for Acuff-Rose. Among their numerous country and pop successes in the 50s were 'Have A Good Time' (Tony Bennett), 'Hey Joe' (Carl Smith and Frankie Laine), and the Eddy Arnold hits 'I've Been Thinking' and 'The Richest Man'. In 1957, the Bryants switched to material for the Everly Brothers. Beginning with 'Bye Bye Love', they supplied a stream of songs that were melodramatic vignettes of teen life. Several of them were composed by Boudleaux alone, including the wistful 'All I Have To Do Is Dream', the tough and vengeful 'Bird Dog', 'Devoted To You' and 'Like Strangers'. At this time he wrote what has become his most recorded song, the sorrowful, almost self-pitying ballad 'Love Hurts'. From the early 60s, the Bryants returned to the country sphere, composing the standard 'Rocky Top' as well as providing hits for artists such as Sonny James ('Baltimore') and Roy Clark ('Come Live With Me'). Shortly before Boudleaux's death in 1987, the Bryants were inducted into the Songwriters' Hall Of Fame.

BRYANT, FELICE

The lyricist of some of the Everly Brothers' biggest hits, Felice Bryant (b. Felice Scaduto, 1925) was a member of one of the most famous husband-and-wife songwriting teams in pop and country music. Recordings of their 750 published songs have sold over 300 million copies in versions by over 400 artists as diverse as **Bob Dylan** and Lawrence Welk. Of Italian extraction, Felice was already writing lyrics when she met Boudleaux Bryant. After their marriage in 1945 the duo wrote together. The success of 'Country Boy' for Little Jimmy Dickens led them to Nashville where they were the first full-time songwriters and pluggers. During the 50s, the Bryants' country hits were often covered by pop artists such as Al Martino, Frankie Laine and Tony Bennett.

US Top 10 hit 'If Ever You're In My Arms Again'. Soundtrack duets with **Celine Dion** ('Beauty And The Beast') and Regina Belle ('A Whole New World (Aladdin's Theme)') in 1992 provided Bryson with further chart success.

BUCKCHERRY

This sleazy US hard-rock outfit was formed in 1995 by Keith Nelson (guitar) and Joshua Todd (vocals), with Jonathan Brightman (bass) and Devon Glenn (drums) added to the line-up shortly afterwards. Fronted by the cocksure Todd, the band's blistering live show earned them a serious word-of-mouth reputation on the Los Angeles music scene. Bolstering the line-up with a second guitarist, Yogi, the band was signed to the newly-formed DreamWorks label for their 1999 debut. Their avowed intention to rescue rock 'n' roll was thrillingly realized on the opening track 'Lit Up', but the remainder of the album was a disappointment. The band's sophomore release, *Timebomb*, repeated many of the faults of the debut. The band split in summer 2002.

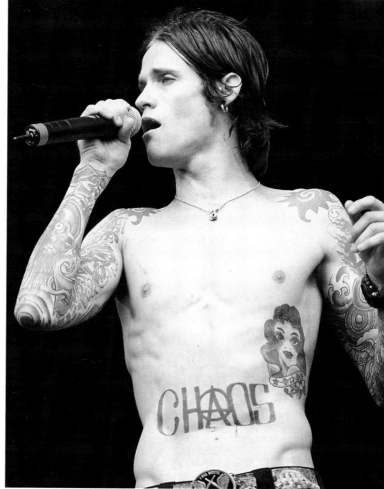

In 1957, they switched to composing teenage pop material for the **Everly Brothers**. Among the hits they supplied were 'Bye Bye Love', 'Wake Up Little Susie', 'Problems', 'Poor Jenny' and 'Take A Message To Mary'. They also composed 'Raining In My Heart' (**Buddy Holly**) and the witty 'Let's Think About Living' (Bob Luman). After the rock 'n' roll era had subsided, the Bryants returned to the country scene, composing prolifically throughout the 60s and 70s in bluegrass and American Indian folk material. Their most enduring song of this period was 'Rocky Top', first recorded by the Osborne Brothers in 1969. In the late 70s, Felice and Boudleaux recorded their own compositions for the first time.

BRYSON, PEABO

This talented soul singer and producer was a former member of Moses Dillard and the Tex-Town Display and Michael Zager's Moon Band. Between 1976 and 1978, Bryson (b. Robert Peabo Bryson, 1951) had US hits with the latter with 'Reaching For The Sky' and 'I'm So Into You'. His numerous appearances in *Billboard*'s R&B chart include 'Underground Music', 'Feel The Fire', 'Crosswinds', 'She's A Woman' and 'Minute By Minute'. 'Gimme Some Time', a 1979 duet with Natalie Cole, was the first of several successful partnerships. Despite hits with Melissa Manchester and Regina Belle, the singer is best known for his work with **Roberta Flack**, and in particular the ballad 'Tonight, I Celebrate My Love' (1983), which reached the UK Top 5. Such releases have obscured Bryson's solo career, which includes the 1984

BUCKINGHAM, LINDSEY

This US vocalist and guitarist (b. 1949) began his career as a folk singer before joining Fritz, an aspiring Bay Area rock band featuring vocalist **Stevie Nicks**. When Fritz folded in 1971, the couple formed Buckingham Nicks. Their 1973 self-titled album made little commercial impression and Buckingham undertook session work. When Bob Welch left **Fleetwood Mac** in 1974, drummer Mick Fleetwood invited Buckingham and Nicks to join as replacements. *Fleetwood Mac* and the multi-million selling *Rumours* helped established the revived band as one of the world's top-selling acts. Buckingham's skills as a singer, composer, guitarist and producer were crucial to this success. However, following the release of 1979's *Tusk*, both he and Nicks went solo.

Buckingham's 1981 debut, *Law And Order*, continued the craftsmanship displayed on earlier work, but although one of the tracks, 'Trouble', reached the US Top 10, it failed to match the profile Nicks had achieved with her first release. Both artists resumed their roles with Fleetwood Mac for *Mirage* (1982), but subsequently pursued individual paths. The title song from a second Buckingham collection, *Go Insane*, provided another US hit, and although he returned to the parent band's fold for the excellent *Tango In The Night* (1987), Buckingham officially parted from the unit the following year. A decade later, having found little in the way of solo success, he returned to work with the 1973 *Rumours* line-up of Fleetwood Mac.

BUCKINGHAMS

Formed in Chicago, USA, in 1966, the Buckinghams originally featured Dennis Tufano (b. 1946; vocals), Carl Giammarese (b. 1947; lead guitar), Dennis Miccoli (organ), Nick Fortuna (b. 1946; bass) and Jon Poulos (b. 1947, d. 1980; drums). Although their first hit, the US chart-topping 'Kind Of A Drag' was their only gold disc, they enjoyed a consistent run of US chart successes throughout 1967, achieving two further Top 10 entries with 'Don't You Care' and 'Mercy, Mercy, Mercy'. Miccoli was later replaced by Marty Grebb (b. 1946). Despite slick, commercial singles, the Buckinghams' albums showed a desire to experiment and, unable to reconcile their image and ambitions, they split in 1970. Poulos later managed several local acts, but died of drug-related causes in 1980. Tufano and Giammarese continued working as a duo, while Grebb later worked with Chicago. Fortuna and Giammarese subsequently revived the Buckinghams for nostalgia tours, making an occasional return to the recording studio.

BUCKLEY, JEFF

The son of respected singer-songwriter **Tim Buckley**, Jeff Buckley (b. Jeffrey Scott Buckley, 1966, d. 1997) first garnered attention at a Tim Buckley tribute, performing 'Once I Was'. He made appearances at several of New York's clubs, recording his 1992 debut mini-album at the Sin-é coffee-house. This tentative four-song set included two original compositions, alongside versions of **Van Morrison**'s 'The Way Young Lovers Do' and Edith Piaf's 'Je N'En Connais Pas Le Fin'. Having secured a contract with Sony Records, Buckley completed the critically acclaimed *Grace* with Michael Tighe (guitar), Mick Grondhal (bass) and Matt Johnson (drums). An expressive singer, Buckley soared and swept across this collection, which included three cover versions alongside breathtaking original material. His live appearances blended expressive readings of songs from *Grace* with an array of interpretations, ranging from Big Star ('Kanga Roo') to the **MC5** ('Kick Out The Jams'). Buckley, a gifted, melodic composer, was about to resume work on his second album when he drowned in a hazardous stretch of the Mississippi.

His final recordings were released as *Sketches (For My Sweetheart The Drunk)* in May 1998, comprising sessions recorded with Tom Verlaine and the basic four-track demos on which Buckley was working at the time of his death. Several posthumous releases have followed.

BUCKLEY, TIM

A radiant talent, Buckley (b. 1947, d. 1975) began his solo career in the folk clubs of Los Angeles, USA. He was discovered by manager Herb Cohen, who secured Buckley's recording deal with Elektra Records. His 1965 debut *Tim Buckley* introduced the artist's skills, but his vision flourished more fully on a second selection, *Goodbye And Hello*. Although underscored by arrangements now deemed over-elaborate, the set featured 'Morning Glory' – one of Buckley's most evocative compositions. With *Happy Sad* he forsook the services of long-time lyricist Larry Beckett, employing Lee Underwood (guitar) and David Friedman (vibes). This expansive style was maintained on *Blue Afternoon*

and *Lorca*, but while the former largely consisted of haunting, melodious folk-jazz performances, the latter offered a more radical, experimental direction. Its emphasis on improvization inspired the radical *Starsailor*, which included the delicate 'Song To The Siren' (revived by the UK's This Mortal Coil in 1983).

Buckley's work was now deemed uncommercial and, disillusioned, he sought alternative employment, including a spell as a chauffeur for Sly Stone. His comeback, the sexually frank *Greetings From L.A.*, marked a new-found fascination with contemporary black music. Two further albums were less well-received and in June 1975 Buckley died of a drugs overdose. Renewed interest in Buckley came in the 90s when many of his albums were well reviewed when reissued on CD, and by the critical success of his son **Jeff Buckley**.

BUFFALO SPRINGFIELD

A seminal band in the development of American country-rock and folk-rock during the 60s, although short-lived, the monumental influence of Buffalo Springfield rivals that of the **Byrds**. The original line-up of the band comprised Americans Stephen Stills (b. 1945; guitar, vocals), Richie Furay (b. 1944; guitar, vocals) and Jim Messina (b. 1947; bass), and Canadians Neil Young (b. 1945; guitar, vocals), Dewey Martin (b. 1942; drums) and Bruce Palmer (b. 1947). Furay and Stills worked together in the Au Go-Go Singers in the mid-60s, where they met Young, at the time a solo singer; they had also previously worked with Palmer in the Mynah Birds. In 1966, the quartet started a band in Los Angeles. Following a series of successful gigs at the prestigious *Whiskey A Go-Go*, they were signed to Atco Records. Ego problems were compounded by Palmer's drug problems. Eventually, Young's former associate Ken Koblun was recruited as a replacement, in turn replaced by Jim Fielder (b. 1947).

Despite a major US hit with the protest anthem 'For What Its Worth' (1967), and the release of two superb long-playing collections, Buffalo Springfield began to disintegrate within a couple of years of their formation. Young's unpredictability meant that he would sometimes not show up at gigs, or would leave the band for long periods. His main replacement was ex-Daily Flash guitarist Doug Hastings (b. 1946), although David Crosby deputized at the Monterey Pop Festival. The album *Last Time Around* was patched together by Messina after the band had broken up for the final time.

Furay later formed Poco and continued his country-rock leanings. Messina joined with Furay and later with Kenny Loggins as Loggins and Messina. Fielder joined Blood, Sweat And Tears, while Hastings joined Rhinoceros. Dewey Martin formed New Buffalo Springfield, later New Buffalo. Lastly, Young and Stills went on to mega-stardom as members of Crosby, Stills, Nash And Young and also enjoyed high-profile solo careers.

BUFFALO TOM

This melodic US alternative-rock trio was formed in 1986 by Bill Janovitz (vocals, guitar), Tom Maginnis (drums) and Chris Colbourn (bass). Their first album was produced by Dinosaur Jr's J. Mascis. By 1992's *Let Me Come Over*, the band had established a promising reputation. *Big Red Letter Day* demonstrated a more orchestrated approach to songwriting, which contrasted with the three-week sessions for 1995's *Sleepy Eyed*. Janovitz released a country-styled solo debut in 1996, backed by Joey Burns and John Convertino. Buffalo Tom reconvened for 1998's *Smitten*, a more polished collection of songs that lacked the charm of their earlier work. Janovitz's second solo album was released during an extended sabbatical for the parent band.

BUFFETT, JIMMY

After releasing several poorly produced solo albums in the early 70s, US country pop singer Buffet (b. 1946) made his breakthrough with 1974's US Top 30 hit 'Come Monday'. In 1975, newly settled in Key West, Florida, he formed the Coral Reefer Band, recording *Havana Daydreaming*. Arguably his best album, *Changes In Latitudes, Changes In Attitudes*, included the million-selling US Top 10 hit 'Margaritaville'. He continued to record prolifically, including in the contemporary rock genre, but by the late 80s his songs had begun to lack sparkle. *Hot Water* included guest appearances by **Rita Coolidge**, **James Taylor** and **Steve Winwood**, but failed to restore him to the upper reaches of the charts.

Buffett's commercial fortunes improved in the 90s, with a series of US Top 10 albums on his own Margaritaville label (also the name of his store). *Carnival* was the soundtrack to an adaptation of Herman Wouk's *Don't Stop The Carnival*, and an interesting stylistic diversion for the singer. His songs continue to reflect his Key-West lifestyle, and he remains a major concert attraction, especially in Florida, where he addresses his fans as 'Parrotheads'.

BUGGLES

Trevor Horn (b. 1949) and Geoff Downes (b. 1952) met as session musicians in 1977. Pooling their resources, they formed Buggles. Their debut, 1979's 'Video Killed The Radio Star' became Island Records' first number 1 single. Its innovative video was later used to launch MTV in the USA. The duo enjoyed three further chart entries with 'The Plastic Age', 'Clean Clean' and 'Elstree', but remained a studio group. They were invited to replace Jon Anderson and Rick Wakeman in Yes in 1980. The unlikely liaison lasted a few months before Downes departed to form **Asia**; Horn became a highly successful record producer and founded ZTT Records.

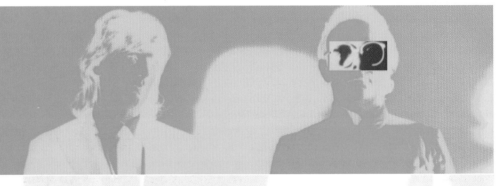

BURDON, ERIC

This English singer (b. 1941) originally came to prominence in the 60s as lead singer of the **Animals**. Following the demise of the latter-day Eric Burdon And The New Animals, he linked up with the black jazz/rock band Nite Shift, and, together with his friend Lee Oskar, they became Eric Burdon And War. 'Spill The Wine' preceded the well-received *Eric Burdon Declares War*. Both this and the follow-up, *Black Man's Burdon*, combined ambitious arrangements mixing flute with Oskar's harmonica.

In the early 70s, after parting company, War went on to become hugely successful, while Burdon's career stalled. He teamed up with Jimmy Witherspoon on *Guilty* and attempted a heavier rock approach with *Sun Secrets* and *Stop*. In 1980, Burdon formed Fire Dept in Germany, making *Last Drive*, and finally fulfilled long-standing big-screen ambitions by appearing in the movie *Comeback*, albeit as a fading rock star. Throughout the 80s Burdon continued to perform, with little recorded output, while experiencing drug and alcohol problems. His 1977 and 1983 reunion albums with the Animals were poorly received, and while his popularity in Germany continued, his profile in the UK and USA decreased.

Burdon continued to tour throughout the 90s, playing with his own I Band and Alvin Lee's *The Best Of British Blues*, and re-forming the New Animals in 1999. Ultimately, Burdon remains one of the finest white blues vocalists of our time.

BURKE, SOLOMON

From 1955–59, US R&B singer Burke (b. 1936) attempted various styles, until 'Be Bop Grandma' attracted the attention of Atlantic Records. An eclectic performer, his 'Just Out Of Reach' (1961) was a US Top 30 hit, before he began asserting a soul direction with 'Cry To Me' (1962). His sonorous voice was then heard on a succession of singles, including 'If You Need Me' (1963) and 'Everybody Needs Somebody To Love' (1964). This exceptional period culminated with 'The Price' and 'Got To Get You Off My Mind'. 'Take Me (Just As I Am)' reached the US Top 50, but Burke left Atlantic for Bell Records shortly afterwards. *Proud Mary* was a soul classic, and its title track (written by John Fogerty) charted in the USA.

The 70s saw a move to MGM Records, but Burke's work there was marred by inconsistency. The same was true of his spells at Dunhill Records and Chess Records, although his collaborations with Swamp Dogg, collected on *From The Heart*, recalled his old power. Following several strong gospel albums for Savoy, Burke's rebirth continued on *Soul Alive*. A strong studio collection, *A Change Is Gonna Come*, followed a 1987 European tour. Burke carried on recording during the 90s, releasing several worthy albums.

BURNETT, T-BONE

This Texan-born songwriter and producer (b. John Henry Burnett, 1945) started out producing Delbert And Glen and recorded a solo album for Uni as J. Henry Burnett in 1972. After touring with Delaney And Bonnie and the **B-52**'s he joined **Bob Dylan**'s Rolling Thunder Revue. He then founded the Alpha Band with Steven Soles and David Mansfield, who made three albums between 1976 and 1979. After the demise of the Alpha Band, Burnett made a rootsy solo album for Takoma. He later toured with Richard Thompson and **Elvis Costello**, releasing a 1985 single with the latter as the Coward Brothers and producing his *King Of America*.

Increasingly active as a producer, among the artists Burnett has worked with are Leo Kottke, **Los Lobos**, **Roy Orbison**, **Counting Crows**, **Bruce Cockburn**, the **Wallflowers**, **Gillian Welch**, and **Sam Phillips**, the former Christian singer who he later married. In the new millennium Burnett helped spearhead a US bluegrass revival after being commissioned by the Coen Brothers to organize the bestselling soundtrack to their *O Brother, Where Art Thou?*

BURNETTE, JOHNNY

Having attended the same high school as **Elvis Presley**, Burnette (b. 1934, d. 1964) formed a trio with his brother Dorsey Burnette (string bass) and Paul Burlison (guitar). The group recorded 'Go Mule Go' for Von Records and were subsequently signed to Coral Records, where they enjoyed a minor hit with 'Tear It Up'. After touring with Carl Perkins and Gene Vincent in 1956, they changed personnel, recruiting drummer Tony Austin. That year, the trio featured in Alan Freed's movie *Rock Rock Rock* and issued a number of singles, including 'Honey Hush', 'The Train Kept A-Rollin'', 'Eager Beaver Baby', 'Drinkin' Wine, Spo-Dee-O-Dee' and 'If You Want It Enough'.

The trio broke up in 1957 and the Burnette brothers moved on to enjoy success as songwriters, providing Rick Nelson with many of his hits. Their own releases, 'Dreamin'' and 'You're Sixteen', were transatlantic Top 10 hits, perfectly suited to Burnette's light but expressive vocal, but a series of lesser successes followed with 'Little Boy Sad', 'Big Big World', 'Girls' and 'God, Country And My Baby'. Burnette formed his own label Magic Lamp

in 1964. In August that year, he fell from his boat in California and drowned. His son Rocky subsequently achieved recording success in the 70s.

BURNING SPEAR

Jamaican Burning Spear (b. Winston Rodney, 1945) appropriated the name from former Mau Mau leader Jomo Kenyatta, then president of Kenya. He entered the music business in 1969, after **Bob Marley** organized an audition for him with Coxsone Dodd. Spear continued to make records for Dodd's Studio One until 1974, with 'Joe Frazier' (aka 'He Prayed') making the Jamaican Top 5 in 1972. In 1975, he began working with Jack Ruby and backing vocalists Rupert Wellington and Delroy Hines on the material for his breakthrough recording, *Marcus Garvey*, released in the UK in remixed form on Island Records. Rodney began to release music on his Spear label at the end of the year. *Dry & Heavy* reworked many of his Studio One classics.

In 1978, Spear parted with Island and issued *Marcus Children*, which was released in the UK as *Social Living*. In 1980, he signed to EMI Records, issuing the stunning *Hail H.I.M.*. Two excellent dubs of *Social Living* and *Hail H.I.M.* also appeared as *Living Dub Volumes 1* and *2*, mixed by engineer Sylvan Morris.

Spear has continued to tour widely and release albums on a regular basis. *Resistance*, nominated for a Grammy in 1984, was a particularly strong set. His lyrical concerns – black culture and history, Garveyism and Rasta beliefs, and universal love – have been consistently and powerfully expressed during his recording career.

BURTON, JAMES

One of the most distinguished of US rock and country guitar players, Burton (b. 1939) toured and recorded with **Rick Nelson** and **Elvis Presley** amongst others. His first recording was 'Suzie-Q', sung by Dale Hawkins in 1957. Burton performed with country singer Bob Luman before spending six years touring and recording with Nelson, perfecting a guitar sound known as 'chicken pickin''. Among the best examples of this style are 'Hello Mary Lou', 'Never Be Anyone Else But You' and the rockabilly-flavoured 'Believe What You Say'.

During the 60s and 70s, Burton made two albums of his own, one in collaboration with steel guitarist Ralph Mooney. His session work took him in contrasting directions. With pianist Glen D. Hardin (ex-**Crickets**) he was a mainstay of Elvis Presley's touring and recording band from 1969–77, but he also played a leading role in the growing trend towards country/rock fusion. Burton's most significant performances in this respect came on the albums of **Gram Parsons**, **Buffalo Springfield** and **Michael Nesmith**. He also worked with **Emmylou Harris**, **Jesse Winchester**, **Ronnie Hawkins**, **Rodney Crowell**, **J. J. Cale** and toured with **Jerry Lee Lewis**.

As a result of an accident in 1995, Burton lost the use of his hands and had to receive treatment to enable him to play the guitar again. He returned to work remarkably quickly, playing with Lewis and the Elvis Tribute Band and appearing on albums by Travis Tritt and the Tractors. He was inducted into the Rock And Roll Hall Of Fame in 2001.

BUSH

This 90s rock band, formed in London, England, found their initial success in the USA. By 1995, their debut album had become a US million-seller, while highly promoted UK artists such

as **Blur** and **Oasis** were still struggling to achieve one-tenth of those sales.

Bush had previously spent two years toiling around small London venues. *Sixteen Stone* was principally written by Gavin Rossdale (b. 1967; vocals, guitar), who had previously recorded two singles with his first band, Midnight. He formed Bush with Dave Parsons (b. 1962; bass; ex-Transvision Vamp), Robin Goodridge (drums) and Nigel Pulsford (guitar). The songs on *Sixteen Stone* dealt with issues including an IRA bomb ('Bomb'), death ('Little Things'), religious cults ('Monkey') and sex ('Testosterone'). After gaining airplay on Los Angeles' KROQ station in 1994, interest in the band snowballed and their debut had soon racked up multi-platinum status.

Steve Albini was chosen to produce their second set, *Razorblade Suitcase*, which entered the US album chart at number 1. Following in the wake was the UK, who finally recognized the band's existence by buying enough copies to put them in the album chart. *The Science Of Things* saw a marked drop in US sales. Ironically, given their past history, the band seems to be now caught up in the general malaise afflicting UK acts attempting to sell records in America. *Golden State* was a welcome return to well-structured songs.

BUSH, KATE

While still at school in her native England, Bush (b. Catherine Bush, 1958) was discovered by **Pink Floyd**'s Dave Gilmour, who was so impressed by

the imaginative quality of her songwriting that he financed demo recordings. EMI Records encouraged her to develop her writing, dancing and singing in preparation for a long-term career. The apprenticeship ended in 1978 with the release of 'Wuthering Heights', inspired by Emily Brontë's novel. It reached UK number 1. An attendant album, *The Kick Inside*, was a further example of her diversity as a songwriter. 'The Man With The Child In His Eyes' was typical of her romantic, sensual style of writing, and provided her with another Top 10 success. Bush consolidated her position with *Lionheart* and during 1979 undertook her first major tour. The live shows were most notable for her mime work and elaborate stage set, but it would be the last time the singer would tour. After guesting on **Peter Gabriel**'s 'Games Without Frontiers', Bush was back in the charts with 'Breathing' and 'Babooshka'. The latter was her most accomplished work since 'Wuthering Heights', with a clever story line and strong vocal. *Never For Ever* entered the UK album charts at number 1 and further hits followed with 'Army Dreamers' and the seasonal 'December Will Be Magic Again'.

At this point, Bush was still regarded as a mainstream pop artist, although 1982's self-produced *The Dreaming* suggested a new direction, with its experimental song structures, even though its less melodic approach alienated some critics. A comparative commercial failure, the album nevertheless proved to be highly influential on other 80s pop musicians, and in particular on Gabriel's increasingly studio-bound work.

A two-year hiatus followed, during which Bush perfected work which would elevate her to new heights in the pop pantheon. The pilot single, 'Running Up That Hill' was a dense and intriguing composition. *Hounds Of Love* revealed Bush at the zenith of her powers. Songs such as the eerily moving 'Mother Stands For Comfort' and the dramatic 'Cloudbusting' underlined her strengths, not only as a writer and singer, but as a producer. 'The Ninth Wave', fused Arthurian legend and Jungian psychology in a musical framework, part orchestral and part folk. After a hit duet with Peter Gabriel, 'Don't Give Up', Bush took an extended sabbatical to plot a follow-up album. In 1989, she returned with *The Sensual World*, in which she experimented with various musical forms, including a Bulgarian folk troupe, and adapted Molly Bloom's soliloquy from James Joyce's *Ulysses* for the enticing 'The Sensual World'.

Sadly, the music world has heard less and less of Bush in subsequent years as she has devoted her time to her own family, guitarist/partner Danny McIntosh and son Bertie. A variety of artists contributed to her sole release of the 90s, *The Red Shoes*. Though it rarely reached the creative heights of her 80s recordings, the album was a notable success for the singer in the American market. She was reported to be working on another studio album in the new millennium.

BUTTERFIELD, PAUL

US artist Butterfield (b. 1942, d. 1987) helped shape the development of blues music played by white musicians in the same way that John Mayall and Cyril Davies were doing in the UK. He sang, composed and led a series of seminal bands throughout the 60s, but it was his earthy Chicago-style harmonica-playing that gained him attention. Mike Bloomfield, Mark Naftalin, Elvin Bishop, David Sanborn and Nick Gravenites were some of the outstanding musicians that passed through his bands. His performance at the 1965 Newport Folk Festival gave him the distinction of being the man who supported **Bob Dylan**'s musical heresy by going electric. In 1973, Butterfield's new venture Better Days went on the road to a lukewarm response, and during subsequent years he struggled to find success, plagued by ill-health.

BUTTHOLE SURFERS

Formerly known as the Ashtray Baby Heads, this maverick quartet from Texas, USA, made its recording debut in 1983 with a self-titled mini-album. Gibson 'Gibby' Haynes (vocals), Paul Sneef (b. Paul Leary Walthall; guitar) and King Koffey (drums) were initially indebted to the punk/hardcore scene and employed explicit lyrics. Having endured a succession of bass players, including Kramer from Shockabilly and Bongwater, the band secured the permanent services of Jeff Pinker, alias Tooter, alias Pinkus, in 1985. Two strong albums, *Locust Abortion Technician* and *Hairway To Steven*, followed. *Digital Dump*, a house-music project undertaken by Haynes and Tooter (as 'Jack Officers'), was followed by *pioughd*, which showed their continued ability to enrage, and Paul Leary's solo, *The History Of Dogs*.

To the surprise of many, the band then signed a major-label contract with Capitol Records. The delay of *Electriclarryland* was as a result of objections received from the estate of Rodgers And Hammerstein when the band wanted to call the album *Oklahoma!*. Haines subsequently appeared alongside actor Johnny Depp in *P*, while Coffey recorded 1992's *Pick Up Heaven* as Drain on his own Trance Syndicate Records label. Following the release of 1998's *After The Astronaut*, the band signed a contract with Surfdog. Their first album for the label, *Weird Revolution*, was released in August 2001. Tagged as the sickest band in the world, they thrive on their own on-stage obscenities.

BUZZCOCKS

Formed in England in 1976, the Buzzcocks originally featured Pete Shelley (b. Peter McNeish, 1955; vocals, guitar), Howard Devoto (b. Howard Trafford; vocals), Steve Diggle (bass) and John Maher (drums). A support spot on the

Sex Pistols' infamous Anarchy tour prefaced the Buzzcocks' debut EP, *Spiral Scratch*. Devoto left in February 1977, only to resurface later that year with Magazine. A reshuffled Buzzcocks, with Shelley taking lead vocal and Garth Davies (later replaced by Steve Garvey) on bass, won a contract with United Artists. They recorded some of the finest pop-punk singles of their era, including

'Orgasm Addict', 'What Do I Get?', 'Love You More' and 'Ever Fallen In Love (With Someone You Shouldn't've)'. After three albums Shelley quit for a solo career, while Diggle re-emerged with Flag Of Convenience.

Shelley, Diggle, Garvey and Maher re-formed for a reunion tour in 1989, then again in 1990 with former **Smiths** drummer Mike Joyce replacing Maher. Their 1993 tour saw Shelley and Diggle joined by Tony Arber (bass) and Phil Barker (drums). A genuinely riveting comeback album (*Trade Test Transmissions*) added to their legacy. Further studio recordings, *All Set* and *Modern* confirmed the Buzzcocks' latterday renaissance.

In October 2000 Shelley reunited with the Buzzcocks' co-founder Devoto under the Buzzkunst moniker. The duo recorded a well-received album which owed little to their respective musical pasts.

BYRDS

Originally a trio, the Jet Set, this seminal US band was formed by Jim (Roger) McGuinn (b. James Joseph McGuinn, 1942; vocals, lead guitar), Gene Clark (b. Harold Eugene Clark, 1941, d. 1991; vocals, tambourine, rhythm guitar) and David Crosby (b. David Van Cortlandt, 1941; vocals, rhythm guitar). Ex-folkies caught up in the **Beatles** craze of 1964, they were signed to a one-off singles contract with Elektra Records which resulted in the commercially unsuccessful 'Please Let Me Love You' (released as the Beefeaters). By late 1964, the band included bass player Chris Hillman (b. 1942) and drummer Michael Clarke (b. Michael Dick, 1944, d. 1993).

Under the supervision of manager/producer Jim Dickson, the new line-up slowly and painfully began perfecting their unique brand of folk rock. In 1964, they signed to CBS Records as the Byrds, assigned to producer Terry Melcher. Their debut, 'Mr Tambourine Man', was a glorious creation, fusing

the lyrical genius of **Bob Dylan** with the harmonic and melodious ingenuity of the Beatles. The opening guitar sound, of a Rickenbacker 12-string, has been linked to the Byrds and McGuinn ever since. By 1965, the single had reached US and UK number 1. Their debut album, *Mr Tambourine Man*, was a surprisingly solid work that included four Dylan covers and some exceptionally strong torch songs from Clark. The Byrds then spent months in the studio before releasing their third single, 'Turn! Turn! Turn!' (US number 1). The album of the same name again showed Clark in the ascendant with 'The World Turns All Around Her' and 'Set You Free This Time'.

In 1966, the band had parted from Melcher and branched out to embrace raga and jazz. 'Eight Miles High' effectively elevated them to the artistic level of the Beatles and the **Rolling Stones**, but their commercial standing was blasted by a radio ban alleging that their latest hit was a 'drugs song'. The setback was worsened by Clark's abrupt departure. Continuing as a quartet, the Byrds recorded *Fifth Dimension*, a clever amalgam of hard, psychedelic-tinged pop and rich folk rock orchestration. Their chart fortunes were already waning by this time and neither the quizzically philosophical '5-D (Fifth Dimension)' nor the catchy 'Mr Spaceman' made much impression.

The pivotal year in the Byrds' career proved to be 1967, commencing with 'So You Want To Be A Rock 'N' Roll Star', complete with taped screams from their ill-fated UK tour. *Younger Than Yesterday* proved their best album yet, ably capturing the diverse songwriting skills of Crosby, McGuinn and Hillman, and ranging in material from the raga-tinged 'Mind Gardens' to the country-influenced 'Time Between' and all styles in between. Their creative ascendancy coincided with intense inter-group rivalry, culminating in the dismissal of David Crosby (later of **Crosby, Stills And Nash**). The remaining Byrds recruited

former colleague Gene Clark, who lasted a mere three weeks. Drummer Michael Clarke was dismissed soon afterwards, leaving McGuinn and Hillman to assemble the stupendous *The Notorious Byrd Brothers*. For this album, the

Byrds used recording studio facilities to remarkable effect, employing phasing, close microphone technique and various sonic experiments to achieve the sound they desired. Producer Gary Usher, who worked on this and their previous album, contributed significantly towards their ascension as one of rock's most adventurous and innovative bands. Successful readings of Gerry Goffin and Carole King's 'Goin' Back' and 'Wasn't Born To Follow' were placed alongside Byrds originals such as 'Dolphin's Smile', 'Tribal Gathering' and 'Draft Morning'.

In 1968, Hillman's cousin Kevin Kelley took over on drums and Gram Parsons (b. Ingram Cecil Connor III, 1946, d. 1973) added musical weight as singer, composer and guitarist. Under Parsons' guidance, the band plunged headlong into country, recording the much-acclaimed *Sweetheart Of The Rodeo*. A perfectly timed reaction to the psychedelic excesses of 1967, the album pre-dated Dylan's *Nashville Skyline* by a year and is generally accepted as the harbinger of country rock. However, Parsons' vocals were replaced by those of McGuinn due to contractual complications and sales were poor. Further conflict ensued when Parsons dramatically resigned on the eve of their ill-advised South Africa tour in 1968.

Late 1968 saw the Byrds at their lowest ebb, with Hillman quitting after a dispute with new manager Larry Spector. The embittered bassist soon reunited with Parsons in the **Flying Burrito Brothers**. McGuinn, meanwhile, assumed total control of the Byrds and assembled an entirely new line-up: Clarence White (b. 1944, d. 1973; vocals, guitar), John York (vocals, bass) and Gene Parsons (b. Eugene Victor Parsons, 1944; vocals, drums). York contributed to two albums, *Dr Byrds & Mr Hyde* and *Ballad Of Easy Rider*, before being replaced by Skip Battin (b. Clyde Battin, 1934). This unlikely but stable line-up lasted from 1969–72 and re-established the Byrds' reputation with the hit 'Chestnut Mare' and the bestselling (*Untitled*).

After three successive albums with their first producer Melcher, they again severed their connections with him and hurriedly attempted to record a compensatory work, *Farther Along*, which only served to emphasize their disunity. McGuinn eventually dissolved the band after agreeing to participate in a recorded reunion of the original Byrds for Asylum Records. Released in 1973, *Byrds* received mixed reviews and the band re-splintered. That same year tragedy struck when Clarence White was killed by a drunk driver and, less than three months later, Gram Parsons died from a drug overdose.

By the 80s, the individual members were either recording for small labels or touring without a record contract. Crosby, meanwhile, had plummeted into a narcotic netherworld and into prison. He emerged reformed and enthusiastic, and set about resurrecting the Byrds with McGuinn and Hillman. A five-way reunion of the Byrds, for a live album and world tour, was proposed, but the old conflicts frustrated it. However, McGuinn, Crosby and Hillman completed four songs in 1990, which were subsequently included on a boxed set featuring 90 songs. The members were each inducted into the Rock And Roll Hall Of Fame in 1991. The chance of playing together again finally elapsed with the deaths of Gene Clark later that year and Michael Clarke in 1993.

BYRNE, DAVID

Byrne (b. 1952) was born in Scotland but raised in the US. He formed **Talking Heads** in 1974 with two fellow design students, and by the early 80s they had evolved from New York's punk milieu into one of America's leading rock attractions. *My Life In The Bush Of Ghosts*, Byrne's 1981 collaboration with **Brian Eno**, was widely praised by critics for its adventurous blend of sound collages, ethnic influences and vibrant percussion, which contrasted with Byrne's ensuing solo album, *The Catherine Wheel*. The soundtrack to Twyla Tharp's modern ballet, this set was the prelude to an intensive period in the parent band's career, following which Byrne began composing and scripting a feature film. *True Stories*, which Byrne directed and starred in, was the subject of an attendant Talking Heads album. *Music For The Knee Plays*, on which Byrne worked with playwright Robert Wilson, confirmed interests emphasized in 1987 by his collaboration with Ryuichi Sakamoto and Cong Su on the soundtrack for Bertolucci's *The Last Emperor*.

Byrne continued recording with Talking Heads, but by the end of the 80s intimated a reluctance to appear live with them. Instead he assembled a 14-strong Latin-American ensemble which toured the USA, Canada, Europe and Japan to promote *Rei Momo*, while a 1991 statement established that Talking Heads were on 'indefinite furlough'. *The Forest* confirmed the artist's prodigious talent by involving European orchestral music. Byrne's Luaka Bop label, founded in 1988, established itself as a leading outlet for world music albums with a pop edge, including several devoted to Brazilian recordings. After two lacklustre rock-orientated releases, 1997's *Feelings* gained Byrne some of his best reviews for years. The album employed several guest producers, including UK trip-hop outfit Morcheeba. The follow-up *Look Into The Eyeball* was even better, a perfect fusion of exotic world rhythms and pop melody. Byrne enjoyed a surprise UK number 2 hit in April 2002, collaborating with X-Press 2 on 'Lazy'.

CABARET VOLTAIRE

Experimental, innovative, electronic outfit formed in Sheffield, England, in 1974. Stephen Mallinder (bass, vocals), Richard H. Kirk (guitar) and Chris Watson (electronics, tapes) strove to avoid the confines of traditional pop music, and their early appearances veered towards performance art. They contributed two tracks to Factory Records' 1978 double EP *A Factory Sample*, before signing to Rough Trade Records for the *Extended Play* EP. The trio continued to break new ground, using sampled 'noise', cut-up techniques (inspired by author William Burroughs) and tape loops. Watson left in 1981, with Eric Random (guitar) joining up for live work.

A series of releases on different labels preceded a joint recording contract with Some Bizzare/Virgin Records. The first fruits of this move, 'Just Fascination' and 'Crackdown', confirmed Cabaret Voltaire's new approach and signalled a drastic shift towards rhythmic dancefloor sounds (assisted by keyboard player Dave Ball's presence). 'Sensoria' ripped the dance charts apart in 1984, setting the tone for much of Caberet Voltaire's subsequent work. By 1987, they had transferred to Parlophone Records. Code introduced a more commercial dance slant, lacking the earlier, experimental approach. 'Hypnotised' (1989) reflected their visit to the house music capital, Chicago, while Kirk's highly influential single 'Testone' (1990), issued under the guise of Sweet Exorcist (with DJ Parrot, later of the All Seeing I), was pure techno. Cabaret Voltaire continued in this style with 'Keep On' and *Groovy, Laidback And Nasty*, working with some of the leading lights of the US house and techno scene. The well-received *Body And Soul* consolidated Cabaret Voltaire's pivotal position on the UK's dance scene, which they had, without fanfare, helped develop over a decade and a half. *International Language* and *The Conversation* were more minimalist pieces that appeared on their own Plastex label.

Mallinder emigrated to Australia in late 1993, which effectively spelt the end for Cabaret Voltaire as a recording unit. Kirk has continued to release challenging dance-orientated material under a variety of guises, including Electronic Eye, Sandoz, Xon, Citrus, and Richard H. Kirk.

CALE, J. J.

US artist Cale (b. Jean W. Cale, 1938) began playing guitar professionally in a 50s western swing group. With the advent of rock 'n' roll, he led Johnnie Cale And The Valentines, before attempting a career in country music. Cale

then played in a variety of bar bands, worked as a studio engineer and recorded several singles before collaborating with songwriter Roger Tillison on 1967's psychedelic album *A Trip Down Sunset Strip*.

Cale's fortunes improved dramatically when Eric Clapton recorded his 'After Midnight', a song Cale had released as a single in 1965. This led to Cale being signed to record *Naturally*. The album's laconic, almost lachrymose, delivery became a trademark, and Cale even enjoyed a US Top 30 single with 'Crazy Mama'. *Really* confirmed the high quality of the artist's compositions, but *Okie* and *Troubadour* lacked the first two albums' immediacy. The latter contained Cale's own version of 'Cocaine', another song popularized by Clapton.

Despite the inclusion of the popular 'Money Talks', Cale's two Phonogram Records albums, *Grasshopper* and *#8*, were unsuccessful. He re-emerged in 1989 with *Travel-Log*, which like most of Cale's work never strayed too far from the blueprint established on his debut. His two albums for Virgin

Records during the 90s, *Closer To You* and *Guitar Man*, were more of the same with faultless musical support.

CALE, JOHN

Welsh-born Cale (b. 1942) was studying viola and keyboards when he was introduced to electronic music. After moving to New York, he joined the Dream Syndicate, an *avant-garde* ensemble led by LaMonte Young. Cale also began playing rock and met **Lou Reed**, with whom he helped form the **Velvet Underground**. Cale remained with this highly influential band until 1968, during which time his experimental predisposition combined with Reed's grasp of pop's traditions to create a truly exciting lexicon.

Cale produced albums for Nico and for the **Stooges**, before embarking on a solo career with *Vintage Violence*. Those anticipating a radical set were pleasantly surprised by its melodic flair. *Church Of Anthrax*, a pairing with Terry Riley, and the imaginative *The Academy In Peril*, reaffirmed his experimental reputation. The haunting *Paris 1919* continued the popular style of Cale's debut and remains, for many, the artist's finest work. Cameos on albums by Nick Drake and Mike Heron preceded *Fear*, which featured **Brian Eno**. The latter also contributed to *Slow Dazzle* and appeared with Cale, Nico and Kevin Ayers on June 1, 1974. The disappointing *Helen Of Troy* was balanced by Cale's strong production work on **Patti Smith**'s debut *Horses*.

Now fêted by the punk audience, Cale's own late-70s recordings increasingly borrowed ideas rather than introducing them and he hit an artistic trough with the onstage beheading of a chicken, which led to his band walking out on him. However, *Music For A New Society* marked a renewed sense of adventure, adeptly combining the popular and cerebral. Cale continued to offer innovative music and *Words For The Dying* matched his initial work for purpose and imagination.

Songs For Drella, a 1990 collaboration with **Lou Reed** as a tribute to Andy Warhol, was lauded by critics and audiences alike. Cale was part of the Velvet Underground reunion in 1993, but old wounds between himself and Reed re-opened and Cale was soon back to recording idiosyncratic solo albums. He is also a highly respected soundtrack composer, with credits including scores for *I Shot Andy Warhol*, *Basquiat*, *American Psycho* and *Beautiful Mistake*.

CAMEO

This US soul/funk act, originally called the New York City Players, was formed in 1974 by Larry 'Mr. B' Blackmon (drums, vocals) and vocalists Tomi Jenkins and Nathan Leftenant. They recorded their debut, *Cardiac Arrest*, with various backing musicians. Subsequent albums gained modest positions in the US and UK pop charts. In 1984, 'She's Strange' gave Cameo their first UK Top 40 pop single. After the success of 1985's 'Single Life' (UK Top 20), 'She's Strange' was remixed and peaked at number 22. Having won over the UK pop market, it was not until 1986 that Cameo finally broke into the US Top 40 chart; 'Word Up' had reached number 3 in the UK, and subsequently reached number 1 in the US R&B chart and number 6 in the *Billboard* pop chart. By the 90s, however, their commercial success had dramatically waned, but they continue to tour and release the occasional new album.

CAMPBELL, GLEN

This US-born artist (b. 1936) had, by the end of the 50s, become a renowned session player and one of the finest guitarists in Hollywood. After briefly joining the Champs, he released a solo single, 'Too Late To Worry, Too Blue To Cry', which crept into the US charts. He then took on the arduous – and brief – task of replacing Brian Wilson on touring commitments with the **Beach Boys**, but he soon returned to session work and recording, enjoying a minor hit with Buffy Sainte-Marie's 'The Universal Soldier'. By 1967, his solo

career was taking off and his version of 'Gentle On My Mind' won a Grammy for Best Country & Western Recording.

Campbell's finest work was recorded during the late 60s, most notably a superb trilogy of hits written by Jimmy Webb: 'By The Time I Get To Phoenix', 'Wichita Lineman' and 'Galveston'. Campbell also began acting, starring with John Wayne in *True Grit* (1969). Further hits included 'Honey Come Back', 'It's Only Make Believe' and 'Dream Baby', followed by a film appearance in *Norwood* (1970) and a duet album with Anne Murray. His first US number 1 was 1975's 'Rhinestone Cowboy'; the second was with a version of Allan Toussaint's 'Southern Nights'. By the late 70s, he had become a C&W institution, regularly releasing albums, touring and appearing on television.

Campbell's career is most remarkable for its scope. A brilliant guitarist, star session player, first-class interpreter, television personality, strong vocalist and in-demand duettist, he has run the gamut of American music and rarely faltered.

CAMPER VAN BEETHOVEN

Witty alternative rock band formed in California, USA, in 1983. They were given their name by early member David McDaniels, though initial line-ups were frequently unstable. David Lowery (b. 1960, USA; vocals, guitar) was

originally joined by Greg Lisher (guitar), Chris Pedersen (drums), Chris Molla, Jonathan Segel (violin) and Victor Krummenacher (bass). *Telephone Free Landslide Victory* contained the live favourite 'Take The Skinheads Bowling', but the band failed to make a successful transition to major-label status, despite the fine *Our Beloved Revolutionary Sweetheart*. Their final album, 1989's *Key Lime Pie*, featured new member Morgan Fichter.

Main songwriter David Lowery finally made the deserved transition to a major band with **Cracker**. He reunited with Krummenacher and Segel in late 1999 to promote the rarities set *Camper Van Beethoven Is Dead, Long Live Camper Van Beethoven*, and to undertake a handful of live dates.

CAN

Experimental German unit founded by two classical music students, Irmin Schmidt (b. 1937; keyboards) and Holger Czukay (b. 1938; bass). Michael Karoli (b. 1948, d. 2001; guitar), Jaki Liebezeit (b. 1938; drums) and Americans David Johnson (flute) and Malcolm Mooney (vocals) rounded out the initial line-up, although Johnson left shortly after the unit began work on their debut. *Monster Movie*, released in 1969, introduced many of Can's subsequent trademarks: Schmidt's choppy, percussive keyboard style, Karoli's incisive guitar and the relentless, hypnotic pulse of its rhythm section. This line-up completed several other masters, later to appear on *Soundtracks* and *Delay 1968*, prior to the departure of Mooney. He was replaced by Japanese vocalist Kenji 'Damo' Suzuki (b. 1950). *Tago Mago*, a sprawling, experimental double set, followed. They began to explore a more precise, even ambient direction on two superb early 70s recordings, *Ege Bamyasi* and *Future Days*. Suzuki left in 1973, and although they flirted with other featured vocalists, Can carried on as a quartet on the faultless *Soon Over Babaluma*. In 1976, the band unexpectedly hit the UK Top 30 with 'I Want More'. Can was later augmented by Rosko Gee (bass) and Reebop Kwaku Baah (percussion), but the departure of Czukay hastened their demise.

Czukay pursued an influential and successful solo career with a series of excellent albums. Schmidt completed several film soundtracks, Liebezeit formed his own group, the Phantom Band, while Karoli recorded a strong solo set. The four musicians remained in close contact and a re-formed Can, complete with Malcolm Mooney, returned to the studio in 1987. The fruits of their renewed relationship appeared two years later in the shape of *Rite Time*. Can's extensive influence on the dance-music scene was celebrated in 1997 with the release of the remix CD *Sacrilege*.

CANNED HEAT

Blues/rock band formed in Los Angeles, USA in 1965 by Alan Wilson (b. 1943, d. 1970; vocals, harmonica, guitar) and Bob 'The Bear' Hite (b. 1943, d. 1981; vocals). They were joined in the initial line-up by Frank Cook (drums), Henry Vestine (b. 1944, d. 1997; guitar) and Larry Taylor (bass). Canned Heat's debut album was promising rather than inspired, but the arrival of Mexican drummer Alfredo Fito (b. Adolfo De La Parra, 1946) brought a new-found confidence, displayed on 1968's *Boogie With Canned Heat*. The set included a remake of Jim Oden's 'On The Road Again' (UK Top 10/US Top 20). A double album, *Livin' The Blues*, included a version of Charley Patton's 'Pony Blues' and a 19-minute *tour de force*, 'Parthenogenesis'.

Between 1969 and 1970, Canned Heat recorded four more albums, including a collaboration with **John Lee Hooker**, and released a documentary of their 1970 European tour. Vestine left, replaced by Harvey Mandel and the reshaped band enjoyed UK hits with a cover of Wilbert Harrison's 'Let's Work Together' (number 2) and the cajun-inspired 'Sugar Bee'. The band's new-found impetus was shattered by the suicide of Wilson in September 1970. Taylor and Mandel left to join John Mayall, while Vestine returned and Antonio De La Barreda became their new bass player. They completed *Historical Figures & Ancient Heads* before Hite's brother Richard (b. 1951, d. 2001) replaced Barreda for 1973's *The New Age*.

Personnel changes continued throughout the decade, undermining the band's strength of purpose, although spirits lifted with the release of *Human Condition*. Sadly, in April 1981, following a gig, the gargantuan Hite died of a heart attack. Despite the loss of many key members, the Canned Heat name has survived. Taylor and de la Parra now pursue the nostalgia circuit with various former members.

CANNON, FREDDY

A frantic and enthusiastic vocalist, known as the 'last rock 'n' roll star', US-born Cannon (b. Freddy Picariello, 1940) started off in Freddy Karmon And The Hurricanes and played guitar on sessions for the G-Clefs. 'Tallahassee Lassie' (1959) was released under his new name on Swan, a label part-owned by Dick Clark, who often featured Cannon on his US *Bandstand* television programme and roadshows. The single was the first of Cannon's 21 US hits over seven years. These included 'Way Down Yonder In New Orleans' (1959) and 'Palisades Park' (1962). *The Explosive! Freddy Cannon* (1960) was the first rock album to top the UK charts. He returned briefly to the charts in 1981 in the company of **Dion**'s old group, the Belmonts, with a title that epitomized his work: 'Let's Put The Fun Back Into Rock 'N' Roll'. He remains a tireless live performer.

CAPALDI, JIM

English musician Capaldi (b. 1944) made his name as drummer and lyricist with **Traffic**. He made his solo debut in 1972 with the excellent *Oh How We Danced*, but it was 1975's *Short Cut Draw Blood* which proved his finest work. The album featured two US hits, 'It's All Up To You' and a cover version of 'Love Hurts'.

After a series of poor albums, Capaldi returned to form in 1989 with *Some Came Running*, and then contributed to **Steve Winwood**'s multi-million-selling *Roll With It* and *Refugees Of The Heart*. In 1994, Traffic re-formed for a major world tour and recorded *Far From Home*. Two years later, Capaldi won a BMI Award for 'Love Will Keep Us Alive', co-written with Peter Vale and recorded by the **Eagles**. An interesting CD appeared in 1999, featuring highlights from Capaldi and old Traffic partner Dave Mason's 40,000 Headmen tour.

CAPTAIN AND TENNILLE

US-born singer Toni Tennille (b. 1943) co-wrote the 1972 rock musical *Mother Earth*. When it was staged in Los Angeles, the house band included Daryl

Dragon (b. 1942; keyboards). Tennille and Dragon then toured as part of the **Beach Boys'** backing group before writing and producing 'The Way I Want To Touch You', their first recording as Captain And Tennille. Their first hit was 'Love Will Keep Us Together' (1975), a Neil Sedaka composition which established them as MOR radio favourites. It sold a million copies, as did 'Lonely Night (Angel Face)'and 'Muskrat Love'. Following a move to the Casablanca Records label in 1979, 'Do That To Me One More Time' reached US number 1. By now, Captain And Tennille were established in television with their own primetime series, which was followed in the 80s by a daytime show hosted by Tennille with Dragon as musical director. Tennille later made solo albums of standard ballads, before reuniting with Dragon in 1995 to record *Twenty Years Of Romance*.

CAPTAIN BEEFHEART

California, USA-born Captain Beefheart (b. Don Glen Vliet, 1941) formed his first Magic Band in 1964, featuring Beefheart, Alex St. Clair Snouffer (guitar), Doug Moon (guitar), Paul Blakely (drums) and Jerry Handley (bass). A series of R&B singles failed and the band was dropped by their label, A&M Records.

Captain Beefheart reappeared on the fledgling Buddah Records label with a series of pioneering releases, including 1967's *Safe As Milk* and 1969's *Trout Mask Replica*. Crudely recorded by musical associate **Frank Zappa**, the latter contained a wealth of bizarre pieces, with Beefheart using his multi-octave range to great effect. The definitive Magic Band were present on this record: Mascara Snake (b. Victor Haydon; bass clarinet), Antennae Jimmy Semens (b. Jeff Cotton; guitar), Drumbo (b. John French; drums), Zoot Horn Rollo (b. Bill Harkelroad. 1949; guitar) and Rockette Morton (b. Mark Boston; bass, vocals). The structure and sound of many of the pieces was reminiscent of the free jazz of Ornette Coleman. A similar theme was adopted for *Lick My Decals Off, Baby* and *The Spotlight Kid*, although the latter had a more structured musical format. Beefheart also contributed vocals to 'Willie The Pimp' on Zappa's *Hot Rats*. Following *Clear Spot* and a heavy touring schedule, the Magic Band split from Beefheart to form Mallard. Beefheart signed to the UK's Virgin Records, releasing two albums, including the critically acclaimed *Unconditionally Guaranteed*. In 1975, Beefheart and Zappa released *Bongo Fury*, a live set recorded in Texas.

In latter years, Beefheart toured and recorded only occasionally and since 1982, there have been no new recordings. He is now a respected artist and sculptor.

CAPTAIN SENSIBLE

Together with Dave Vanian, Brian James and Rat Scabies, Captain Sensible (b. Raymond Burns, 1954) formed one of the UK's leading punk bands, the **Damned**. A riotous character with an unnerving sense of charm, Sensible performed at gigs dressed in various guises. The Damned were frequently inactive and Sensible formed a number of short-lived side projects before releasing 1981's *This Is Your Captain Speaking* EP.

Signed by A&M Records as a solo act, he recorded a cover version of Rodgers and Hammerstein's 'Happy Talk' (1982), and the single unexpectedly shot to UK number 1. He subsequently released two albums in close collaboration with lyricist **Robyn Hitchcock**, and had further hits with 'Wot!' and 'Glad It's All Over'. He left the Damned in 1984. He undertook a national tour the following year, as well as studio work, which culminated in the formation

of his own Deltic and Humbug labels. Sensible also played bass in the psychedelically inclined The Space Toad Experience, before joining up with Vanian in the re-formed Damned in 1996.

CARAVAN

Formed in Canterbury, England, in 1968, by Pye Hastings (b. 1947; guitar, vocals), Jimmy Hastings (flute), David Sinclair (b. 1947; keyboards), Richard Sinclair (b. 1948; bass, vocals) and Richard Coughlan (b. 1947; drums). The quintet debuted with *If I Could Do It All Over Again, I'd Do It All Over You*, but it was not until 1971's *In The Land Of Grey And Pink* that they achieved commercial success. David Sinclair then joined Matching Mole, and Steve Miller, Phil Miller and Lol Coxhill were drafted in to help record *Waterloo Lily*. Richard Sinclair left for Hatfield And The North, before David returned to a line-up featuring Hastings, Coughlan, John Perry (b. 1947; guitar), Rupert Hine (synthesizer) and Geoff Richardson (b. 1950; viola, violin). A rigorous touring schedule was punctuated by *For Girls Who Go Plump In The Night* and *Caravan And The New Symphonia*, but further personnel changes undermined the band's early progress. Although *Cunning Stunts* provided a surprise US chart entry, Caravan were increasingly confined to a rock backwater.

Pye Hastings, the Sinclairs and Coughlan reunited on 1982's *Back To Front*, but this was followed by a long period of recording inactivity, with only occasional live appearances. A flurry of activity in 1991 saw Caravan performing once more, with the addition of Richard Sinclair's amalgamation of former Caravan and Camel members undertaking a series of low-key London club dates under the name of Caravan Of Dreams. New recordings on the HTD Records label have found particular favour in Japan.

CARDIGANS

This leading Swedish rock band was formed in the small town of Jönköping in 1992 by Peter Svensson (guitar), Magnus Sveningsson (bass), and Mattias Alfheim. The latter soon left, and the new line up was completed by Bengt Lagerberg (drums), Lars Olof Johansson (keyboards), and Nina Persson (vocals). Both *Emmerdale* and *Life* were notable for their delicate, intricate melodies. Strong media coverage prompted healthy sales in Sweden, the UK and Japan. On *First Band On The Moon* they introduced elements of progressive and hard-rock guitar. The band enjoyed a huge transatlantic hit in 1997 with the re-released 'Lovefool', featured on the soundtrack to *William Shakespeare's Romeo And Juliet*. The UK hit 'My Favourite Game' provided a taster for the experimental electronic pop of *Gran Turismo*. Persson also records country-tinged material with A Camp.

CAREY, MARIAH

This US pop diva (b. 1970) enjoyed an unprecedented string of American chart-toppers that helped establish her as the most successful female solo artist of the 90s.

Carey began singing on R&B sessions in New York when she met keyboard player and songwriter Ben Margulies, who became her songwriting partner and close friend. With Carey writing the melodies and most of the lyrics, and Margulies arranging the songs, they developed a simple blend of soul, gospel and pop. Sony Music's US president Tommy Mottola signed Carey after hearing their demo. Her first single, 1990's 'Visions Of Love', was a US chart-topper and her debut album stayed at the top of the American charts for 22 weeks as the singer won 1991 Grammys for Best Female Vocalist and Best New Artist. Further US number 1s followed, including 'Love Takes Time', 'Someday', 'I Don't Wanna Cry', 'Emotions', 'I'll Be There', 'Dreamlover', 'Hero', 'Fantasy' and 'One Sweet Day'. The latter, a collaboration with **Boyz II Men**, topped the US charts for a staggering 16 weeks between 1995 and 1996. In 1998, 'My All' became Carey's thirteenth US number 1, placing her behind only **Elvis Presley** and the **Beatles** in the all-time US singles chart. Further chart-toppers followed with 'Heartbreaker' and 'Thank God I Found You'.

In 2001, Carey signed a four album, $80 million recording contract with Virgin Records. Shortly before the release of her debut for the label, *Glitter*, the soundtrack to a movie loosely based on her life, Carey was admitted to hospital suffering from mental and physical exhaustion. The album was one of the year's most high-profile failures and Carey was bought out of her Virgin contract a few weeks later.

CARLISLE, BELINDA

When her former band the Go-Go's broke up in 1985, Carlisle (b. 1958) underwent a period of physical recuperation and image remodelling, emerging as the quintessential young Californian. With artistic assistance from former band-mate Charlotte Caffey, Carlisle hit the US Top 3 with the following year's 'Mad About You'. She achieved international acclaim and a transatlantic chart-topper with the infectious 'Heaven Is A Place On Earth'. This winning formula was subsequently used for a string of albums and other chart singles such as 'I Get Weak', 'Circle In The

Sand', 'Leave A Light On' and 'We Want The Same Thing'. Carlisle's chart success tailed off in the 90s, and at the end of the decade she reunited with her former colleagues to record a new Go-Go's album.

CARLTON, LARRY

US guitarist Carlton (b. 1948) has courted rock, jazz and acoustic new-age genres with considerable success. He spent the 70s working as a session musician, playing for **Steely Dan** and on numerous **Joni Mitchell** albums. Moving away from session work, his solo debut appeared in 1978, but it was not until 1981's *Sleepwalk* that Carlton was fully accepted as a solo artist. Both *Alone But Never Alone* and *Discovery* broadened Carlton's following, while the live *Last Nite* saw a return to his jazz roots. With *On Solid Ground*, Carlton demonstrated a stronger rock influence and he was awarded Grammys in 1981 and 1987 for his version of 'Minute By Minute'.

In 1988, Carlton was shot in the neck by an intruder at his studio. After an emergency operation and many months of physiotherapy he made a full recovery. Carlton joined the GRP Records stable in 1991 and found a home that perfectly suited his music. Carlton remains a master musician with a catalogue of accessible and uplifting music that occasionally catches fire.

CARMEN, ERIC

US-born Carmen (b. 1949) first achieved success in the early 70s with the **Raspberries**. He wrote and sang lead on all their US successes: 'Go All The Way', 'I Wanna Be With You', 'Let's Pretend' and 'Overnight Sensation (Hit Record)', and was the sole member to prosper commercially when the band split in 1975.

In 1976 he scored an international hit with 'All By Myself', and went on to enjoy two further US Top 20 entries with 'Never Gonna Fall In Love Again' (1976) and 'Change Of Heart' (1978). A lean period followed before Carmen returned to the US Top 10 in 1987 with 'Hungry Eyes' (from the movie *Dirty Dancing*), and the following year 'Make Me Lose Control' reached US number 3. The only new Carmen release during the 90s was the Japan-only *Winter Dreams*. Ten tracks from *Winter Dreams* were later included on *I Was Born To Love You*, Carmen's first US studio album in over 15 years.

CARNES, KIM

Gravel-voiced US singer Carnes (b. 1945) started out with the New Christy Minstrels in the 60s, before embarking on a solo career in 1971. *Kim Carnes* (1975) brought her critical favour, although she was reaping greater success as a songwriter with her husband Dave Ellingson. **Frank Sinatra**, **Barbra Streisand** and **Kenny Rogers** all recorded her songs. In 1979, Carnes and Ellingson wrote all the material for Rogers' bestselling *Gideon*. Rogers also duetted with Carnes on the following year's US Top 5 hit 'Don't Fall In Love With A Dreamer'.

In 1981, Carnes topped the US charts for nine weeks with 'Bette Davis Eyes'. The attendant *Mistaken Identity* also reached US number 1. During 1984, she had two major hits: 'What About Me?' (with Kenny Rogers and James Ingram) and 'Make No Mistake, He's Mine' (with Barbra Streisand). Carnes returned to her country roots for 1988's *View From The House*, which featured the country chart hit 'Speed Of The Sound Of Loneliness', with **Lyle Lovett** on backing vocals. During the 90s she established herself in Nashville as a reliable hit songwriter for artists such as Reba McEntire, Tim McGraw and Trisha Yearwood, although her own recording career was limited to a 1991 Japanese album and three new tracks on a 1993 compilation.

CARPENTER, MARY-CHAPIN

Despite signing to a major Nashville label in 1986, it was five years before this US-born artist (b. 1958) made the country charts with a revival of **Gene Vincent**'s 'Right Now'. Her 1992 hit, 'I Feel Lucky', preceded the release of the excellent *Come On, Come On*. Carpenter's acceptance by a country audience was sealed later in the year when she was voted the CMA's Female Vocalist Of The Year. *Stones In The Road* brought fresh melody to an old and sometimes predictable genre. *A Place In The World* maintained her reputation in the country field, as well as gaining her a mainstream rock audience, a path she continued down with 2001's *Time*Sex*Love*.

CARPENTERS

This US brother-and-sister duo, famous for their MOR pop, featured Richard (b. 1946; piano) and Karen Carpenter (b. 1950, d. 1983; vocals, drums). Richard originally backed Karen, who was signed to the small Magic Lamp label in 1965. After winning a battle of the bands contest at the Hollywood Bowl they signed to RCA Records, but no material was issued. In 1967, the siblings teamed up with John Bettis in the short-lived Spectrum.

A&M Records president Herb Alpert heard some demos and signed them. In 1969, their debut, *Offering*, was issued, but failed to chart. It took a cover version of the **Beatles**' 'Ticket To Ride' to set their hit career in motion. A wonderful reading of **Burt Bacharach** and **Hal David**'s 'Close To You', complete with superbly understated piano arrangement, took them to US number 1 and was a worldwide hit. In 1970, they were back at US number 2 with 'We've Only Just Begun'. Throughout 1971, the duo continued with such hits as 'For All We Know', 'Rainy Days And Mondays' and 'Superstar'/ 'Bless The Beasts And Children'. They also received Grammy Awards for Best New Artist and Best Vocal Performance and launched their own television series, *Make Your Own Kind Of Music*.

Between 1972–73, 'Goodbye To Love', 'Sing' and 'Yesterday Once More' all reached the US Top 10 and 'Top Of The World' reached number 1. A cover of the **Marvelettes**' 'Please Mr Postman' brought them back to number 1 in 1974, the same year they played at the White House. There was a noticeable decline in their Top 40 performance during the second half of the 70s, with personal and health problems taking their toll. Richard became addicted to prescription drugs, entering a clinic in 1978 to overcome his problem. Karen, meanwhile, was suffering from anorexia nervosa. She completed a solo album during 1979, but it was destined to remain unreleased for many years. Thereafter, she reunited with Richard for *Made In America*, and for their final US Top 20 hit with 'Touch Me When We're Dancing'. Tragically, on 4 February 1983, Karen died from a cardiac arrest induced by her anorexia.

CARR, JAMES

This exceptional US soul singer (b. 1942, d. 2001) performed gospel in the Sunset Travellers and the Harmony Echoes before going solo on the Goldwax Records label in the 60s. It took four singles to define his style, but 'You've Got My Mind Messed Up' burned with an intensity few contemporaries could match. It was followed by the classic soul singles 'Love Attack' (1966), 'Pouring Water On A Drowning Man' (1966) and 'The Dark End Of The Street' (1967), but Carr's fragile personality was increasingly disturbed by drug abuse. 'Hold On' appeared on Atlantic Records in 1971, but by the end of the decade an impoverished Carr was recording for obscure labels and struggling to perform on stage.

Following a lengthy absence from the music scene, Carr returned in the 90s with two albums of new material and some warmly-received live performances. His troubled life was eventually brought to an end by cancer in January 2001.

CARRACK, PAUL

After **Ace** split in 1977, this UK singer (b. 1951) temporarily joined Frankie Miller's band before moving on to **Roxy Music**, appearing on *Manifesto* and *Flesh And Blood*. After recording the solo *Nightbird*, Carrack joined Squeeze as **Jools Holland**'s replacement, singing on the hit single 'Tempted' and appearing on *East Side Story*. He then teamed up with **Nick Lowe**, and released his second solo album, *Suburban Voodoo*, reaching the US Top 40 with 'I Need You'. A regular member of **Eric Clapton**'s band in the mid-80s, he was enlisted as lead singer of **Mike And The Mechanics** in 1985. His distinctive voice was heard on the hits 'Silent Running (On Dangerous Ground)' and 'The Living Years'. In 1987, he had a US Top 10 solo hit with 'Don't Shed A Tear'. *Groove Approved* was also highly successful in America.

In the 90s Carrack's career was mostly taken up with his participation with Mike And The Mechanics. He stepped outside in the mid-90s with an excellent solo album that spawned two hit singles, notably a beautiful reworking of 'How Long' and the equally fine 'Eyes Of Blue'. *Satisfy My Soul* further established the songwriting partnership Carrack has developed with former **Squeeze** colleague Chris Difford.

CARS

Formerly known as Cap'n Swing, this US band began recording as the Cars in 1977. The line-up comprised Ric Ocasek (b. Richard Otcasek, 1949; guitar, vocals), Benjamin Orr (b. Benjamin Orzechowski, 1947, d. 2000; bass, vocals), Greg Hawkes (keyboards), Elliot Easton (b. Elliot Shapiro, 1953; guitar) and David Robinson (drums). Their catchy, well-crafted pop/rock generated transatlantic hits with 'My Best Friend's Girl' and 'Drive'. In 1985 the latter song was opportunistically but tastefully used to pull at people's consciences during the Live Aid concert.

The band broke up at the end of the 80s in favour of solo work. Ocasek became busy as a record producer, while Easton toured with Creedence Clearwater Revisited. Orr formed Big People, but in October 2000 succumbed to cancer of the pancreas.

CARTER USM

This eccentric UK indie band was formed in 1987 by the curiously-monikered Jimbob (b. James Morrison, 1960) and Fruitbat (b. Leslie Carter, 1958). The duo acquired a drum machine and, taking their name from a newspaper cutting, created Carter The Unstoppable Sex Machine. The single 'Sheltered Life' made little impression, but the following 'Sheriff Fatman' (1989) was an exciting amalgam of a great riff and strident lyrics. *101 Damnations* was an innovative melting-pot of samples, ideas and tunes, shot through with a punk-inspired ethos. 'Rubbish' and 'Anytime, Anyplace, Anywhere' were followed by the controversial 'Bloodsports For All'. *30 Something* reached the UK Top 10 in 1991, but their Top 20 hit 'After The Watershed' experienced copyright problems relating to the **Rolling Stones**' 'Ruby Tuesday'.

Carter USM's later albums displayed a gradually more sophisticated approach, though the cornerstone of their appeal remained their incisive lyrics and propulsive live shows. They released *Starry Eyed And Bollock Naked*, a collection of b-sides, recruited a full-time drummer, Wez, and played a historic gig in Zagreb, Croatia – the first band to play there since the start of the civil war. Early copies of *Worry Bomb* included a live recording of the concert. The mini-album *A World Without Dave* was followed by their final recording, *I Blame The Government*, bringing to an end a most entertaining chapter in the annals of the UK's independent music scene.

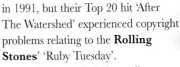

CARTER, CARLENE

This Nashville, USA-born singer (b. Rebecca Carlene Smith, 1955) is the daughter of country singers Carl Smith and June Carter and the grand-daughter of Maybelle Carter of the Carter Family. Her parents divorced and, when she was 12, her mother married **Johnny Cash**. Carlene Carter herself first married when 16 and had a daughter, but she was divorced within two years. After college she joined her mother and stepfather on the road and was featured on Johnny Cash's family album *The Junkie And The Juicehead Minus Me* in 1974. Carlene then met Jack Routh and within three months they were married. They had a son, John Jackson Routh, but they separated in 1977. Carter brought her new boyfriend, Rodney Crowell, to the UK where she made an appealing, upbeat rock album with Graham Parker And The Rumour. Crowell's song 'Never Together But Close Sometimes' was almost a UK hit, and Carter's song 'Easy From Now On' was recorded by **Emmylou Harris**.

Musical Shapes was produced by her new husband **Nick Lowe**. Her 1981 album *Blue Nun* was also produced by Lowe and featured members of Rockpile and Squeeze. The album, with such titles as 'Do Me Lover' and 'Think Dirty', was an explicit celebration of sex. Carter, whose marriage to Lowe had by now broken up, won acclaim in 1985 for her role as one of the waitresses in the London cast of the country musical *Pump Boys And Dinettes*. Her later recordings, including 1990's *I Fell In Love* and 1995's *Little Acts Of Treason*, have shown the singer moving towards the country mainstream.

CARTHY, MARTIN

UK folk legend Carthy (b. 1940) started out as an actor before becoming a skiffle guitarist and singer, with the Thameside Four, in 1959. Carthy became resident guitarist at London's top folk club the Troubadour; where he taught songs to visiting Americans including **Bob Dylan** and **Paul Simon**. They later adapted his 'Lord Franklin' and 'Scarborough Fair'. Carthy, Leon Rosselson, Ralph Trayner and Marian MacKenzie recorded as the 3 City 4 before Carthy recorded the duo album *Byker Hill* with violinist Dave Swarbrick.

From 1969 to 1972, Carthy was a member of **Steeleye Span**, with whom he first played electric guitar. Later he joined more traditional vocal group the Watersons, which included his wife Norma Waterson. In the 80s, Carthy toured and recorded with Brass Monkey, and in the following decade recorded with his daughter Eliza and Norma Waterson. In June 1998, Carthy was awarded an MBE in the Queen's Birthday Honours, and subsequently released the acclaimed *Signs Of Life*, his first solo release in almost 10 years. He also teamed up with Roger Wilson and Chris Wood to form the folk 'supergroup' Wood Wilson Carthy.

CASH, JOHNNY

After a spell in the US Army, Cash (b. 1932) auditioned as a gospel singer for Sun Records before developing his 'boom chicka boom' sound with two friends:  Luther Perkins (lead guitar) and Marshall Grant (bass). Their first record, 1955's 'Hey Porter'/'Cry! Cry! Cry!', credited to Johnny Cash And The Tennessee Two, was released in 1955 and reached number 14 on the US country charts. Carl Perkins' drummer, W. S. Holland, joined Cash in 1958, resulting in the Tennessee Three. 'I Walk The Line' reached number 17 on the US pop charts and they achieved further pop hits with 'Ballad Of A Teenage Queen', 'Guess Things Happen That Way' and 'The Ways Of A Woman In Love'. Sun Records released Cash's debut album, *Johnny Cash With His Hot And Blue Guitar*, but in 1958 the singer joined Columbia Records. His cautionary tale, 'Don't Take Your Guns To Town', sold half a million copies, but Cash's work began to suffer when he started taking hard drugs. A series of ambitious concept albums highlighted worthy causes such as the plight of the American Indian, but for all this, the drugged-up country star was a troublemaker himself. His biggest misdemeanour was starting a forest fire.

In 1963, Mexican brass was added to the ominous 'Ring Of Fire', but the single was another big pop hit. Cash's roadshow in the 60s featured Carl Perkins (who played guitar for Cash after Luther Perkins' death), the Statler Brothers and the Carter Family. One night Cash proposed to June Carter on stage and they were married in 1968. Their successful duets include 'Jackson' and 'If I Were A Carpenter'.

In 1968, Columbia released *Johnny Cash At Folsom Prison*, one of the most acclaimed live recordings of all time. The Folsom Prison concert was followed by one at San Quentin, which was filmed for a television documentary. Shortly afterwards, the humorous 'A Boy Named Sue' gave Cash his only US Top 10 pop hit and reached UK number 4. This popularity brought him his own television series (1969–71), but, despite notable guests such as **Bob Dylan** (who Cash had helped in his early days at Columbia), the show was not a great success.

By opening his own recording studios, House Of Cash, in 1972, he became even more prolific. His family joined him on the quirky *The Junkie And*

The Juicehead Minus Me and his son-in-law J. W. Routh wrote several songs and performed with him on *The Rambler*. He has always followed writers and the inclusion of **Nick Lowe**, former husband of **Carlene Carter**, and Rodney Crowell, husband of **Rosanne Cash**, into his family increased his awareness.

In 1986, Cash moved to Mercury Records and found success with the whimsical 'The Night Hank Williams Came To Town'. In 1988, he made *Water From The Wells Of Home*, with **Emmylou Harris**, the **Everly Brothers** and **Paul McCartney** among others, and his 60s composition 'Tennessee Flat-Top Box' became a US country number 1 for daughter Rosanne. During his late-80s revival, Cash was hampered by pneumonia, heart surgery and a recurrence of drug problems. He returned to the stage, however, either touring with the Carter Family or as part of the Highwaymen with **Kris Kristofferson**, Waylon Jennings and **Willie Nelson**.

In a genre now dominated by new country, Cash found it difficult to obtain record contracts in the early 90s, but released the low-key American Recordings, produced by Rick Rubin in 1994. An appearance at the Glastonbury Festival in 1994 also introduced him to a new audience. *Unchained* continued his renaissance, but more worryingly, Cash announced he was suffering from Parkinson's disease at a Flint, Michigan concert on 25 October 1997, and was hospitalized with double pneumonia soon afterwards. Later he claimed that he had Shy-Drager syndrome, although this was subsequently stated to be a wrong diagnosis. Cash actually suffers from autonomic neuropathy, a group of symptoms involving the central nervous system. Nevertheless, he was able to return to the studio to record the third instalment in Rubin's American Recordings series, *Solitary Man*.

Cash is a member of the Rock And Roll Hall Of Fame, the Country Music Hall Of Fame and the Songwriters' Hall Of Fame.

CASH, ROSANNE

The daughter of **Johnny Cash** and Vivian Liberto, and one of the pioneers of the new country movement of the late 80s. In the late 70s, Cash (b. 1955) spent a year in England working for CBS Records (her father's label) and signed a recording contract in Germany with Ariola. Cash was influenced by British punk, but on her return to Nashville, began recording with CBS as a neo-country act. She married producer Rodney Crowell in 1979, the year of her first CBS album, *Right Or Wrong*. The album included three US country hits including 'No Memories Hangin' Round' (a duet with Bobby Bare). *Seven Year Ache* went gold, reaching the Top 30 of the US pop chart and including three US country number 1s. *Somewhere In The Stars* also reached the pop Top 100 and included three country chart singles, while *Rhythm And Romance* included four US country hits. *King's Record Shop* yielded four US country number 1s including Rosanne's revival of her father's 1962 hit, 'Tennessee Flat-Top Box'. On her fifth US country number 1, 'It's A Small World', Cash duetted with Crowell. She won a Grammy in 1985 for Best Country Vocal Performance Female, and in 1988 won *Billboard*'s Top Single Artist Award.

Interiors, a hauntingly introspective album, was released after her marriage breakdown. The emotional fall-out was subsequently explored by Cash on her bleak and compelling *The Wheel*. In 1996, she demoed new material for Capitol who persuaded her to release the songs in their unadorned state, feeling the sparse arrangements complemented the introspective nature of the material. Cash also published a collection of short stories, *Bodies Of Water*.

CASSIDY, DAVID

Cassidy (b. 1950) received his big break after being cast in US television's *The Partridge Family*. Before long, the Partridge Family were registering pop hits, with Cassidy taking lead vocals on their 1970 US chart-topper, 'I Think I Love You'. Further hits followed and, in 1971, he was launched as a solo artist. Within a month he reached the US Top 10 with a revival of the Association's

talent, encouraged her and facilitated her appearance on several albums as a backing singer. Meantime, Biondi was stockpiling tapes by Cassidy and in 1991, while recording Chuck Brown And The Soul Searchers, played examples for the band's leader. Brown was immediately taken with her sound, and in 1992 Brown and Cassidy recorded *The Other Side*. The following year Cassidy had outpatient surgery for a malignant skin lesion. Early in 1994 she recorded for Blue Note Records, but, unlike the sessions with Brown, she found this musically unsatisfying. In January 1996, she appeared at Blues Alley again, a session that was recorded, but when summer came she was unwell. This time the check-up revealed advanced melanoma. In September, a tribute concert was organized at which she sang, as did Brown. She died two months later.

Cassidy's singing voice was a crystalline soprano, ideal for the pop ballads and folk songs she performed. Most of her recorded work displays a remarkable and unspoiled talent, and almost all of it has been released posthumously. In 1998, shortly after the release of the compilation *Songbird*, a couple of tracks were playlisted on UK's Radio 2. The response from listeners was considerable and sales of her back catalogue picked up. Nearly four years later, the album reached the top of the UK charts. Cassidy's entire catalogue is worthy of attention.

CAST

Much of the attention surrounding this Liverpool, England-based guitar pop band – John Power (vocals, guitar), Peter Wilkinson (bass), Keith O'Neill (drums) and Skin (b. Liam Tyson; guitar) – arose from Power having played bass in the critically revered band the **La's**. Cast debuted in 1995 with 'Finetime' (UK Top 20). Their first album, *All Change*, introduced them as one of the UK's brightest prospects, and further UK hit singles followed with 'Alright', 'Sandstorm', 'Walkaway' and the non-album track 'Flying'. It was therefore a surprise that their second album, *Mother Nature Calls*, did not create the same ripples of excitement, despite the single 'Guiding Star' reaching number 3 in June 1997. The anthemic 'Beat Mama' provided the band with yet another UK Top 10 single in summer 1999, and was followed by the critically acclaimed third album *Magic Hour*. Aware of becoming increasingly anachronistic in the urban-dominated post-millennial music scene, Powers broadened his musical repertoire on the band's fourth album, *Beetroot*. This funkier release proved to be a commercial disappointment and failed to chart.

CASTAWAYS

Formed in Minnesota, USA, in 1962, the Castaways made one appearance on the US charts in 1965 with 'Liar, Liar', a garage-rock gem marked by organ and heavily echoed vocals. Roy Hensley (guitar), Denny Craswell (drums) and Dick Roby (bass) formed the band, later recruiting Bob Folschow (guitar) and Jim Donna (keyboards). They recorded several other singles but none charted. Craswell left to join Crow in 1970, but the remaining four continued to perform together in subsequent decades.

CATATONIA

This indie-pop band was originally formed in 1992 in Cardiff, Wales, when guitarist Mark Roberts met singer Cerys Matthews (b. 1969) while she was busking acoustic outside Debenhams' department store. With the addition of Paul Jones (who had played with Roberts in Y Crifft), drummer Dafydd Ieuan (b. 1969) and keyboard player Clancy Pegg, the band recorded two EPs for the Welsh independent label Crai Records and another for the Rough Trade Records' Singles Club. With a good deal of press interest, the band relocated to London and signed to Warner Brothers Records, subsidiary Blanco y Negro. Ieuan and Pegg had left by this point, to join Super Furry Animals and Crac respectively. Owen Powell was drafted in as an additional guitarist while Aled Richards took over on drums.

'Cherish'. In 1972, he hit UK number 2 with 'Could It Be Forever'/'Cherish' and enjoyed a chart-topper with a revival of the Young Rascals' 'How Can I Be Sure'. 'Rock Me Baby' just failed to reach the UK Top 10 and peaked at US number 38. It was to be his last American hit as he began to concentrate on the UK market. This ploy was rewarded with the success of 'I'm A Clown'/'Some Kind Of Summer' (Top 3) and 'Daydreamer'/'The Puppy Song' (number 1). He recycled several well-known songs, including the **Beatles'** 'Please Please Me' and the **Beach Boys'** 'Darlin''.

By the mid-70s, his teen-idol days were drawing in, so he returned to acting, appearing in *Joseph And The Amazing Technicolor Dreamcoat*. In 1985, he made a surprise return to the UK Top 10 with the self-penned 'The Last Kiss', featuring backing vocals from **George Michael**. Two years later, he took over the lead role in Dave Clark's musical *Time*. In 1993, he appeared with his teen-idol younger brother Shaun and singer Petula Clark, in the Broadway production of *Blood Brothers*. His next major assignment was 1996's multi-million high-tech musical EFX at the MGM Grand Hotel, Las Vegas. Cassidy returned to the upper regions of the UK charts in 2001 with the album *Then And Now*.

CASSIDY, EVA

(b. 1963, d. 1996) Growing up in a musical family on the outskirts of Washington, DC, Cassidy became more involved with music and painting as a teenager. She was heard by producer Chris Biondi who, impressed by her raw

The Nursery label released a Japanese/European import collection of their singles to date, paving the way for 1996's *Way Beyond Blue*. The real commercial breakthrough in the UK came in 1998, when the topical and highly catchy 'Mulder And Scully' reached number 3. Another single from the album, 'Road Rage', debuted at number 5 in May, and *International Velvet* reached number 1 after 14 weeks on the album chart. Cerys Matthews also appeared as a guest vocalist on **Space**'s UK Top 5 single 'The Ballad Of Tom Jones'. The lush melodic ballad 'Dead From The Waist Down' preceded *Equally Cursed And Blessed*, which entered the album chart at number 1 but ultimately was a commercial disappointment. Rumours surrounding Matthews' health and the future of the band circulated around the music press prior to the release of the well-crafted *Paper Scissors Stone*. Further drama ensued in August 2001 when their major tour was cancelled, and the following month the band announced they were splitting up.

CAVE, NICK

After the **Birthday Party** disbanded, Australian vocalist Nick Cave (b. 1957) teamed up with German guitarist Blixa Bargeld (b. 1959; ex-Einstürzende Neubauten), English bass player Barry Adamson (b. 1958; ex-**Magazine**) and fellow Australian and multi-instrumentalist Mick Harvey (b. 1958). They became the Bad Seeds. Their 1984 debut *From Her To Eternity* was accompanied by a startling rendition of **Elvis Presley**'s 'In The Ghetto'. *The First Born Is Dead* followed a year later, but the Bad Seeds really made their mark with the covers album *Kicking Against The Pricks*. The subsequent *Your Funeral, My Trial* emphasized the power of his self-penned compositions. Cave's lyricism reached new heights on the taut 'The Mercy Seat' and the albums *Tender Prey* and *The Good Son*.

In 1989, Cave's first novel, *And The Ass Saw The Angel*, was published. He also made an appearance in Wim Wenders' *Wings Of Desire* (1987) and gave a powerful performance as a prison inmate in the Australian production *Ghosts Of The Civil Dead* (1989). Still prolific on the music side, Cave released the comparatively pedestrian *Henry's Dream* in 1992. It was followed by a live collection and contributions to the soundtrack of Wenders' *Faraway, So Close!* The brooding, self-obsessed *Let Love In* was recorded during an increasingly turbulent period in Cave's personal life, but was one of his finest releases. In 1995 Cave (with the Dirty Three) provided a live soundtrack to Carl Dreyer's 1928 silent classic *La Passion De Jeanne d'Arc*, while an unlikely musical coupling with **Kylie Minogue** on 'Where The Wild Roses Grow' proved to be a commercial success. This in turn spawned *Murder Ballads*, a dark concept album. *The Boatman's Call* and *No More Shall We Part* were highly accomplished and deeply personal collections which saw Cave's artistry reaching new creative heights.

CHAD AND JEREMY

Chad Stuart (b. 1943; vocals, guitar, banjo, keyboards, sitar) and Jeremy Clyde (b. 1944; vocals, guitar) met as students at London, England's Central School of Speech and Drama. Their early brand of folk-influenced pop, similar to **Peter And Gordon**, was commercially unsuccessful in their native UK. However they had four US Top 30 hits in the mid-60s, including 'Yesterday's

Gone' and 'A Summer Song'. A concept album, *Of Cabbages And Kings*, signalled a switch to progressive styles, but this ambitious and sadly neglected work was unsuccessful and the pair broke up in 1969. Clyde later pursued an acting career, while Stuart wrote for musical comedies, worked as musical director for *The Smother Brothers Comedy Hour*, and recorded with his wife Jill before moving into radio work. The duo reunited in 1983 to record a new album, and three years later appeared on the British Reinvasion tour.

CHAIRMEN OF THE BOARD

Briefly known as the Gentlemen, this Detroit, USA-based vocal quartet was instigated by General Norman Johnson (b. 1944; ex-Showmen), with Danny Woods (b. 1944), Eddie Curtis and Canadian Harrison Kennedy. Although Johnson provided the most recognizable voice, Woods and Kennedy also shared the lead spotlight. The group secured an international hit with their debut, 'Give Me Just A Little More Time', followed by the vibrant '(You've Got Me) Dangling On A String'. The group ceased recording in 1971, but singles continued to appear until 1976. Johnson subsequently enjoyed a series of late-70s R&B hits before reuniting with Woods. 'Loverboy' (1984) reflected their enduring popularity on the American beach/vintage soul music scene, and was a minor UK hit.

CHAMBERS, KASEY

Country singer Chambers (b. 1976) was brought up in a remote region of Australia. While she and her brother Nash were still very young, their parents, Bill and Diane, moved to the Nullabor Plains, and eventually took to travelling in a truck and hunting for a living. In the late 80s, they formed a family band, playing in the bars and clubs they encountered on their travels. The so-called Dead Ringer Band released several albums and had big Australian hits with Kasey's own song, 'Already Gone', and a chart-topping cover version of **Maria McKee**'s 'Am I The Only One (Who's Ever Felt This Way?)'.

Kasey Chambers' 1999 solo debut, *The Captain*, reaped numerous awards in Australia before being released worldwide to even further acclaim. Her second solo album, *Barricades & Brickwalls*, was a thoughtful collection of deep lyrical intensity which received glowing reviews.

CHAMELEONS

Formed in Manchester, England, in 1981, by Mark Burgess (vocals, bass), Reg Smithies (guitar), Dave Fielding (guitar) and Brian Schofield (drums), although the latter was soon replaced by John Lever. Early singles included 'In Shreds', 'As High As You Can Go' and 'A Person Isn't Safe Anywhere These Days'. Their *Script Of The Bridge* and *What Does Anything Mean?* basically revealed the Chameleons as a promising guitar-based outfit with a strong melodic sense. *Strange Times* was very well-received by the critics, but just as a breakthrough beckoned, their manager Tony Fletcher died, and amid the ensuing chaos, the band folded.

Spin-off bands, the Sun And The Moon, Music For Aborigines, Weaveworld and the Reegs, lacked the charm of the powerful but unrealized mother act. The Chameleons re-formed in 2000 to play some live dates. They commemorated the success of this reunion with the release of *Strip*, a collection of acoustic versions of previous recordings along with two new tracks. The quartet subsequently began work on their new studio album. *Why Call It Anything* proved to be a stunning reaffirmation of the brilliance of this unsung band.

CHANDLER, GENE

Chicago, USA-born Chandler (b. Eugene Dixon, 1937) is best remembered for his 1962 US number 1, 'Duke Of Earl'. The million-selling single featured the Dukays, a doo-wop quintet featuring Shirley Jones, James Lowe, Earl Edwards and Ben Broyles. After a brief hiatus Chandler returned with some Curtis Mayfield-penned hits, including 'Rainbow' (1963), 'Just Be True' (1964) and 'Nothing Can Stop Me' (1965). Other successes included 'There Goes The Lover', 'From The Teacher To The Preacher' (with Barbara Acklin) and 'Groovy Situation'.

During the disco boom a revitalized Chandler released the hit singles 'Get Down', 'When You're Number 1' and 'Does She Have A Friend'. He continued recording into the 80s and remains a popular live attraction.

CHANTAYS

US-based group formed in 1962 by Bob Spickard (lead guitar), Brian Carman (guitar, saxophone), Bob Marshall (piano), Warren Waters (bass) and Bob Welsh (drums). The quartet secured success with 'Pipeline' the following year; this atmospheric surfing instrumental brought a new level of sophistication to an often one-dimensional genre. It was a standard the quintet was unable to maintain and although Steve Khan replaced Welsh, the group broke up following a handful of unsuccessful releases. However, a re-formed line-up emerged during the 80s in the wake of a surfing resurgence.

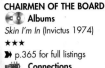

CHAPIN, HARRY

Chapin (b. 1942, d. 1981) directed the Oscar-nominated movie *Legendary Champions* in 1968, before turning to music. In 1971, he began playing clubs in his native New York, USA, with John Wallace (bass), Ron Palmer (guitar) and Tim Scott (cello). In 1972, his debut *Heads And Tales* and the six-minute single 'Taxi' enjoyed minor success. Chapin's writing strength emerged through fascinating narrative songs, often with a twist in the tale. 'W-O-L-D', about the life of a local disc jockey, went on to become an FM radio classic. At Christmas 1974, Chapin reached US number 1 with the evocative 'Cat's In The Cradle'. After a series of albums, he wrote the Broadway musical revue *The Night That Made America Famous* in the same year that he won an Emmy for his musical work on the children's television series *Make A Wish*.

During the late 70s, Chapin became increasingly involved in politics and was a delegate at the 1976 Democratic Convention. The title track to his 1980 album *Sequel* (a story sequel to 'Taxi') gave him his final US Top 30 entry. On 16 July 1981, while travelling to a benefit concert, he was killed when his car was hit by a truck. A Harry Chapin Memorial Fund was subsequently launched.

CHAPMAN, MICHAEL

Chapman (b. 1941) emerged from Britain's folk-club circuit with 1969's *Rainmaker*, which revealed a gifted songwriter and guitarist. *Fully Qualified Survivor*, which reached the UK Top 50 the following year, included the emotional 'Postcards Of Scarborough', his best-known work. Subsequent releases failed to maintain his early promise and the collapse of Criminal Records, the company responsible for several of his late 70s recordings, was a further blow. In the late 80s, Chapman recorded several cassettes for his own Homemade Records label and signed to the Coda label to perform new-age music (a tag that he reportedly despises). After recovering from a heart attack in 1991, Chapman resumed recording and hit a late peak with 1995's *Navigation* and 2000's *Americana*.

CHAPMAN, ROGER

Chapman (b. 1942) progressed from local UK bands to a sojourn in Germany in the early 60s with the (UK) Exciters. When Ric Grech left the Exciters to join the Farinas, Chapman followed. Changing their name to **Family** they returned to London in 1966 and embarked on an acclaimed recording career.

When Family broke up in 1973 the Chapman/Whitney songwriting partnership continued in *Streetwalkers*. They produced a couple of excellent hard-rock albums but split up after three years. Chapman's first solo output, *Chappo*, was well received. There was only the occasional UK gig during the following decade, although by this point Chapman was a huge draw in Germany, where he enjoyed a major hit with a cover version of **Mike Oldfield**'s 'Shadow On The Wall'. *Mail Order Magic* and *Mango Crazy* were also successful, but by the late 80s Chapman's muse appeared to have deserted him. He bounced back in the 90s with *Hybrid And Lowdown* and *Kiss My Soul*, and remains a riveting live attraction.

CHAPMAN, TRACY

US singer-songwriter Chapman (b. 1964) got her big break during Nelson Mandela's 70th birthday concert at Wembley Stadium, London, in 1988. Owing to headliner **Stevie Wonder**'s enforced walk-out, her spot was extended. Her debut album, *Tracy Chapman*, climbed to US number 1 within days, and became an international success, selling over three million copies. 'Fast Car' reached the US/UK Top 10 and 'Talkin' Bout A Revolution' became a concert favourite. She appeared with **Peter Gabriel**, **Sting** and other artists for a worldwide tour in aid of Amnesty International. Afterwards, she lost momentum with *Crossroads*, despite the album topping the UK charts. The pedestrian folk-rock material on 1992's *Matters Of The Heart* suffered as a result of Chapman's lengthy spell away from the spotlight. A three-year hiatus ensued before the release of *New Beginning*, which found a much wider audience in the USA thanks to the left-field hit, 'Give Me One Reason'. *Telling Stories* was arguably her best collection of songs since her debut, leavening her trademark self-absorption on affecting songs such as the title track and 'It's OK'.

CHARLATANS (UK)

Formed in Manchester, England by Tim Burgess (b. 1968; vocals), Martin Blunt (bass), Jon Baker (guitar), Jon Brookes (drums) and Rob Collins (b. 1963, d. 1996; keyboards), the Charlatans fused 60s melodies and Hammond-organ riffs on their 1990 debut 'Indian Rope'. A recording contract with Beggars Banquet Records led to 'The Only One I Know', a UK Top 10 hit later in the year. The band's long-playing debut, *Some Friendly*, was praised by critics and topped the UK album charts.

The band entered 1992 with guarded optimism, but *Between 10th And 11th* disappointed, Blunt suffered a nervous breakdown, Baker departed (replaced by Mark Collins) and Rob Collins was jailed as an accessory to armed robbery. *Up To Our Hips*, produced by **Steve Hillage**, repaired some of the damage. Their revival in both the singles and albums charts continued until tragedy struck in July 1996 when Collins was killed in a car crash. Martin Duffy (**Primal Scream**) was drafted in temporarily and, in 1997, keyboard player Tony Rogers was recruited for touring purposes. The glorious *Tellin' Stories* was an inspired response to the tragic events of the previous year. Rogers was brought in to the line-up as a full-time member on the band's major-label releases, *Us And Us Only* and *Wonderland*.

CHARLATANS (USA)

The first of San Francisco's 'underground' rock bands, formed in 1964 by George Hunter (autoharp, tambourine), Mike Wilhelm (guitar, vocals) and Richard Olsen (bass, clarinet, vocals). They recruited pianist Michael Ferguson and drummer Sam Linde, who was later replaced by **Dan Hicks**. By this time, the band had honed their *mélange* of blues, folk and R&B, but 'The Shadow Knows' was the sole release by this line-up. Disillusioned, Hicks, Ferguson and Hunter left. Olsen and Wilhelm persevered and in 1969 completed their sole album with Darrell De Vore (piano) and Terry Wilson (drums).

Hicks went on to form the acclaimed Dan Hicks And His Hot Licks, while Hunter's artwork graced numerous magnificent record covers including *Happy Trails* (**Quicksilver Messenger Service**), *Hallelujah* (**Canned Heat**) and *It's A Beautiful Day* (**It's A Beautiful Day**).

CHARLES AND EDDIE

California, USA-born Eddie Chacon began in local soul bands before continuing his recording career on projects with the Dust Brothers and Daddy-O, as well as releasing two solo albums. Charles Pettigrew (d. 2001) grew up in Philadelphia and went on to study jazz vocals at the Berklee College Of Music. The duo met up in New York and debuted in 1992 with the worldwide hit 'Would I Lie To You?', followed by 'NYC (Can You Believe This City)'. Both tracks were on their debut, *Duophonic*. A second album, belatedly released three years later, was a disappointingly bland collection, and following its release the duo split-up to work on solo projects. Pettigrew later sang with the Tom Tom Club on their 2000 set *The Good The Bad The Ugly*, but lost his battle with cancer the following April.

CHARLES, RAY

This US singer and pianist's marriage of gospel and R&B laid the foundations for soul music. His influence is inestimable, and his talent widely acknowledged and imitated by white artists such as **Steve Winwood**, **Joe Cocker**, **Van**

Morrison and **Eric Burdon**. Charles has been honoured with countless awards during his career including induction into the Rock And Roll Hall Of Fame in 1986, and receiving the Grammy Lifetime Achievement Award in 1987.

As a result of glaucoma, Georgia, USA-born Charles (b. Ray Charles Robinson, 1930) was completely blind by the age of seven. He learned to read and write music in braille and was proficient on several instruments by the time he left school. He began recording in 1949 playing in the style of **Nat 'King' Cole**. Three years later, Atlantic Records acquired his contract, but his early work revealed only an occasional hint of the passions later unleashed.

Charles's individual style emerged as a result of his work with Guitar Slim, whose gospel-based fervour greatly influenced Charles's thinking. This effect was fully realized in the successful 'I Got A Woman' (1954) followed by 'This Little Girl Of Mine' (1955) and 'Talkin' 'Bout You' (1957) among others. This style culminated in the thrilling call and response of 'What'd I Say' (1959). This acknowledged classic is one of the all-time great encore numbers performed by countless singers and bands in stadiums, clubs and bars all over the world. However, Charles was equally adept at slow ballads, as his 'Drown In My Own Tears' and 'I Believe To My Soul' (both 1959) clearly show.

In 1959, Charles left Atlantic for ABC Records, where he secured both musical and financial freedom. 'Georgia On My Mind' (1960) and 'Hit The Road Jack' (1961) established the artist as an international name and in 1962, *Modern Sounds In Country And Western*, a bestselling landmark collection, produced the million-selling single 'I Can't Stop Loving You'. Its success defined the pattern for Charles's career during the 60s and 70s; the edges were blunted, the vibrancy was stilled as the singer's repertoire grew increasingly inoffensive.

Charles's 80s work included more country-flavoured collections and a cameo appearance in the movie *The Blues Brothers*, but the period is better marked by his powerful appearance on the *USA For Africa* release, 'We Are The World' (1985). *My World*, released in 1993, marked a slight return to form. Of more note was Charles's return to his jazz roots with an excellent contribution on Steve Turre's 2000 recording *In The Spur Of The Moment*.

CHEAP TRICK

Rick Nielsen (b. 1946; guitar, vocals) and Tom Petersson (b. Tom Peterson, 1950; bass, vocals) first recorded as members of US group Fuse. The duo then joined Thom Mooney and Robert 'Stewkey' Antoni (both ex-Nazz), before Mooney was replaced by drummer Brad Carlson aka Bun E. Carlos (b. 1951)

and Antoni by Randy 'Xeno' Hogan and then Robin Zander (b. 1952; guitar, vocals). Their 1977 debut *Cheap Trick* introduced the band's inventive flair and striking visual image: Zander and Petersson's good looks juxtaposed with Carlos's seedy garb and Nielsen's baseball cap, bow-tie and mono-grammed sweater. The band completed *In Color* within months of their debut, offering a smoother sound with a sure grasp of melody on favourites such as 'I Want You To Want Me' and 'Hello There'. *At Budokan* followed a highly

successful tour of Japan and became the quartet's first platinum disc. *Dream Police* added little to the sound and producer George Martin barely deflected this sterility on *All Shook Up*.

A disaffected Petersson left in 1982, replaced briefly by Pete Comita, then by Jon Brant. Neither *One On One* nor the Todd Rundgren-produced *Next Position Please* halted Cheap Trick's commercial slide, but *Standing On The Edge* offered hopes of a renaissance. In 1986, 'Mighty Wings' appeared in the smash-hit movie *Top Gun* and the return of Petersson re-established the band's most successful line-up. *Lap Of Luxury* went multi-platinum when 'The Flame' reached US number 1 in 1988. *Busted* failed to scale similar heights, and their one album for Warner Brothers Records, *Woke Up With A Monster*, was completely overshadowed by the release of a sequel to the *Budokan* album the same year. The band's standing remained high among the new wave of American alternative rockers, however, and they played several dates on the 1996 Lollapalooza tour before signing with the independent label Red Ant. Their second self-titled album followed and marked a return to the thundering power-pop of their classic late-70s releases.

CHECKER, CHUBBY

Checker (b. Ernest Evans, 1941) began his musical career in 1959, when he met Kal Mann at a chicken market in his native Philadelphia. The songwriter penned Checker's debut, 'The Class'. He was given his nickname by the wife of Dick Clark, and Checker became one of several artists to enjoy the patronage of the disc jockey's influential *American Bandstand* television show and the successful Cameo-Parkway label.

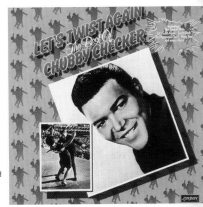

Checker achieved national fame in 1960 with 'The Twist', a compulsive dance-based performance which became an institution. The single topped the US chart in 1960 and again in 1961. 'Pony Time' (1961) became Checker's second gold disc and second US number 1, before 'Let's Twist Again' established him as an international attraction. It inspired competitive releases by the **Isley Brothers** ('Twist And Shout'), **Joey Dee And The Starliters** ('Peppermint Twist') and **Sam Cooke** ('Twisting The Night Away') while Checker mined its appeal on a surprisingly soulful 'Slow Twistin'' (with Dee Dee Sharp) and 'Teach Me To Twist' (with **Bobby Rydell**). He also recorded a slew of opportunistic singles, including 'The Fly' (1961) and 'Limbo Rock' (1962), both of which sold over one million copies. However, dance-inspired records devoted to the Jet, the Swim and the Freddie were less successful. Even so, Checker had a remarkable run of 32 US chart hits up to 1966.

Latterly, Checker was confined to the revival circuit, reappearing in 1975 when 'Let's Twist Again' re-entered the UK Top 5. The Fat Boys' 'The Twist (Yo Twist)', with Checker guesting on vocals, climbed to UK number 2 in 1988. He has continued to perform, record and maintain a profile, particularly in the music trade where he continues to remind and inform the music business that he deserves greater recognition.

CHEMICAL BROTHERS

UK DJ duo Tom Rowlands and Edward Simons met in 1989 at Manchester Polytechnic. Inspired by the UK's burgeoning dance scene, the duo named themselves the Dust Brothers and released 'Song To The Siren' in 1993. Remixes for Lionrock, **Leftfield** and **Saint Etienne** established their reputation, and they released a series of acclaimed EPs. Following the success of these records and the Sunday Social, a club that they ran in London in conjunction with Heavenly Records, they signed to Virgin Records in early 1995 as the Chemical Brothers, after the threat of legal action from the original US Dust Brothers. Their first releases included the single 'Leave Home' and the album *Exit Planet Dust* on their own subsidiary, Freestyle Dust. As well as their trademark sound of guitars, heavy breakbeats and analogue noise, the album included vocals from Beth Orton and Tim Burgess of the **Charlatans**.

In the autumn of 1996, the pair released 'Setting Sun', which featured lead vocals by **Oasis**'s Noel Gallagher, and became their first UK number 1 single. The Chemical Brothers' huge popularity was confirmed with the release of their second album, *Dig Your Own Hole*. Their 'big-beat' music became the crossover success of the year, appealing to rock and dance fans in equal measure. The number 1 single 'Block Rockin' Beats' won a Grammy Award for Best Rock Instrumental (despite featuring vocals).

Remix work for **Spiritualized**, **Mercury Rev** and the original Dust Brothers followed in 1998, as well as another mix album. The duo returned to the UK pop charts in June 1999 with the Top 5 single, 'Hey Boy Hey Girl', and the chart-topping *Surrender*. The album featured guest vocal turns from **New Order**'s Bernard Sumner, **Primal Scream**'s Bobby Gillespie and **Mazzy Star**'s Hope Sandoval. Rowlands and Simons sustained their remarkable creativity with their first album of the new millennium, *Come With Us*.

CHER

Cher (b. Cherilyn Sarkisian La Pierre, 1946) started out as a session singer, during which time she met future husband **Sonny Bono**. After two singles (as Caeser & Cleo), the duo achieved international acclaim in the late 60s as Sonny And Cher. Cher also sustained a solo career during this period, securing several hits, including a cover of the **Byrds**' 'All I Really Want To Do'. 'Bang Bang (My Baby Shot Me Down)', with its gypsy beat and maudlin violins was a worldwide smash in 1966, followed by 'I Feel Something In The Air' and 'You Better Sit Down Kids'. She also appeared in two minor 60s movies, *Good Times* (1967) and *Chastity* (1969).

In 1971, the zestful, 'Gypsies, Tramps And Thieves' and its attendant album saw Cher back in the ascendant. Two further US number 1s ('Half Breed' and 'Dark Lady') preceded her divorce from Bono. In 1975, she released the Jimmy Webb-produced *Stars* and one album with Gregg Allman, *Allman And Woman: Two The Hard Way*. By the late 70s, she had become a regular media fixture, amid speculation over her relationships with Allman, Gene Simmons (**Kiss**) and Les Dudek.

In 1981, Cher appeared on **Meat Loaf**'s 'Dead Ringer For Love' but recording took a back seat to acting. A leading role in *Come Back To The Five And Dime, Jimmy Dean, Jimmy Dean* (1982) was followed by an Oscar nomination for her role in *Silkwood* (1983). Appearances in *Mask* (1985), *The Witches Of Eastwick* (1987), *Suspect* (1987) and *Moonstruck* (1987) followed, winning an Oscar for Best Actress for the latter. The album *Cher* and its attendant transatlantic Top 10 single 'I Found Someone' began her musical comeback. The US Top 10 hits 'After All' (with Peter Cetera), 'If I Could

Turn Back Time' and 'Just Like Jesse James' preceded her 1991 UK chart-topper, 'The Shoop Shoop Song (It's In His Kiss)', the theme song to another screen appearance in *Mermaids*.

In March 1995, in the company of Chrissie Hynde, **Neneh Cherry** and **Eric Clapton**, Cher topped the UK charts with the charity single 'Love Can Build A Bridge'. The same year she did a credible cover of Marc Cohn's 'Walking In Memphis', which preceded *It's A Man's World*. Her astonishing popularity was confirmed by the world-wide hit single 'Believe', which topped the UK charts for seven weeks in late 1998 and rose to the top of the US charts the following spring. The attendant album featured notable contributions from dance gurus Junior Vasquez and Todd Terry. Oddly enough, Cher's next album, *Not.com.mercial*, was only made available through her own website. *Living Proof* repeated the *Believe* formula to lesser effect.

CHERRY, NENEH

Swedish-born Cherry (b. Neneh Mariann Karlsson, 1964) is the step-daughter of jazz trumpeter Don Cherry. She joined English post-punk band Rip, Rig And Panic in 1981 as a vocalist, later performing with several ex-members as Float Up CP. In the mid-80s she sang backing vocals for the **Slits** and **The The**.

In 1989, Cherry recorded a series of dance hits including 'Buffalo Stance', 'Manchild' and 'Kisses On The Wind'. Her debut *Raw Like Sushi*'s eclectic blend of hip-hop rhythms and pop melodies earned Cherry excellent reviews and sizeable sales figures. In 1990, Cherry contributed to the AIDS-charity collection, *Red Hot And Blue*, singing **Cole Porter**'s 'I've Got You Under My Skin', but was quiet again until the release of *Homebrew* in 1992. She reasserted herself as a commercial force in 1994 with the international hit single 'Seven Seconds', which saw her collaborating with African superstar **Youssou N'Dour**. In March 1995, in the company of Chrissie Hynde, **Cher** and **Eric Clapton**, she topped the UK charts with the charity single 'Love

Can Build A Bridge'. Family commitments meant another lengthy recording hiatus before she released *Man* in 1996. During the late 90s her studio appearances were limited to guest vocals on several big club hits, including the Dreem Teem's 'Buddy X 99'.

CHI-LITES

Formed in 1960 as the Hi-Lites, Eugene Record (b. 1940), Robert Lester, Creadel Jones and Marshall Thompson mixed doo-wop and street-corner harmony. A series of releases followed before 'I'm So Jealous' (1964) introduced their new name, Marshall And The Chi-Lites – the 'Chi' celebrating their origins in Chicago. Johnson left later that year and, with the release of 'You Did That To Me', they became the Chi-Lites. Record formed a songwriting partnership with Barbara Acklin, and together they created many of his group's finest moments. 'Give It Away' (1969) became their first US hit, followed by the wistful 'Have You Seen Her' (1971), the US number 1 'Oh Girl' (1972), 'It's Time For Love' and 'You Don't Have To Go' (1976) among others. Jones left in 1973, replaced by Stanley Anderson, then by Willie Kensey. In 1976, Record left for a short-lived solo career. David Scott and Danny Johnson replaced him but the original quartet of Record, Jones, Lester and Thompson re-formed in 1980. The title track of *Bottoms Up* (1983) became a Top 10 soul single, but further releases failed to sustain that success. Creadel Jones retired and Record left again, leaving Thompson with the Chi-Lites' name. They group remain a popular draw on the oldies circuit.

CHIC

This US group was built around Nile Rodgers (b. 1952; guitar) and Bernard Edwards (b. 1952, d. 1996; bass). They joined the Big Apple Band in 1971, backing hit group New York City on tour. Two female singers, Norma Jean Wright and Luci Martin, and drummer Tony Thompson were recruited. Wright later went solo, replaced by Alfa Anderson. They scored an immediate hit with 'Dance, Dance, Dance (Yowsah, Yowsah, Yowsah)' (1977), which introduced wit and sparkling instrumentation to the maligned disco genre. In 1978, 'Le Freak' sold over four million copies and 'Good Times' (US number 1) went gold.

Edwards and Rodgers also guested for **Sister Sledge**, **Diana Ross** and Sheila B. Devotion, but Chic's later work was treated with indifference. Edwards' solo album, *Glad To Be Here*, was a disappointment, and Rodgers' *Adventures In The Land Of Groove*, fared little better. Rodgers' then worked on **David Bowie**'s *Let's Dance* and produced **Madonna**'s *Like A Virgin*, while Edwards took control of recording the Power Station, the **Duran Duran** offshoot. Edwards also provided the backbone to **Robert Palmer**'s 1986 hit, 'Addicted To Love'.

In 1992 Rodgers and Edwards re-formed Chic, releasing 'Chic Mystique' and an album. Sadly Chic's revival looks to have ended with the death of Edwards in 1996, but their huge influence on dance music (especially its rhythms) ensures a place in pop history. Rodgers continues as a popular producer and in 1998 founded his own distribution and record label, Sumthing Else.

CHICAGO

Formed in 1966 in Chicago, USA, and initially known as the Missing Links, the Big Thing and then Chicago Transit Authority, the original line-up featured Terry Kath (b. 1946, d. 1978; guitar, vocals), Peter Cetera (b. 1944; bass, vocals), Robert Lamm (b. 1944; keyboards, vocals), Walt Perry (b. Walter Parazaider, 1945; saxophone), Danny Seraphine (b. 1948; drums), James Pankow (b. 1947; trombone) and Lee Loughnane (b. 1941; trumpet). The horn section set Chicago apart from other mid-60s rock bands and, in 1969, manager Jim Guercio landed them a contract with Columbia Records. Their 1969 debut missed the Top 10, but stayed on the US charts for 171 weeks.

In 1970, still working in the jazz-rock idiom, they released *Chicago II*, but gradually began to break away from jazz toward more mainstream pop, resulting in such light-rock staples as 'Colour My World', the 1976 transatlantic number 1 'If You Leave Me Now' and the 1982 number 1 'Hard To Say I'm Sorry'. Five consecutive Chicago albums topped the charts between 1972 and 1975.

In 1977, after *Chicago X* was awarded a Best Album Grammy, Guercio and the group parted ways. On 23 January 1978, Kath was killed by a self-inflicted accidental gunshot wound. The group continued, with Donnie Dacus joining on guitar, although he was replaced, briefly, by Chris Pinnick and then keyboardist Bill Champlin. Cetera left the group in 1985 (replaced by Jerry Scheff), embarking on a successful solo career.

Chicago enjoyed another US chart-topper in 1988 with 'Look Away'. Serraphine left the following year and DaWayne Bailey was added to the line-up. Their popularity tailed off in the 90s, despite continuing to play to appreciative audiences on the live circuit.

CHICKEN SHACK

This UK band was formed by guitarist Stan Webb and bass player Andy Silvester. The original line-up enjoyed a long residency at Hamburg's Star Club before returning to England in 1967. Christine Perfect (b. 1943; piano, vocals) then joined the line-up as did drummer Dave Bidwell. *Forty Blue Fingers Freshly Packed And Ready To Serve* was a fine balance between original songs and material by **John Lee Hooker** and **Freddie King**, to whom Webb was stylistically indebted. The quartet enjoyed two minor UK hits with 'I'd Rather Go Blind' and 'Tears In The Wind', before Perfect left for a solo career (as Christine McVie). She was replaced by Paul Raymond, but following the release of two further albums Raymond and Bidwell departed for Savoy Brown, a unit Silvester later joined.

Webb reassembled Chicken Shack with John Glascock (bass; ex-**Jethro Tull**) and Paul Hancox (drums). They completed the disappointing *Imagination Lady* before Bob Daisley replaced Glascock, but this line-up broke up in 1973 after completing *Unlucky Boy*. Webb established a completely new unit for *Goodbye Chicken Shack*, before dissolving the band to join Savoy Brown. Chicken Shack have been resurrected on several occasions in order to take advantage of the band's continued popularity on the European continent,

CHICORY TIP

Pop quartet formed in Kent, England, in 1968 by singer Peter Hewson (b. 1950), Barry Mayger (b. 1950; bass), Brian Shearer (b. 1951; drums) and Dick Foster (guitar). Foster was replaced in 1972 by Rod Cloutt (b. 1949; guitar, keyboards). 'Son Of My Father' topped the UK charts the same year and Chicory Tip rode the glam rock wagon long enough to enjoy two further UK Top 20 hits with 'What's Your Name?' (1972) and 'Good Grief Christina' (1973). In the USA, the band were marketed as Chicory.

CHIEFTAINS

The original Chieftains line-up – Paddy Moloney (b. 1938; uillean pipes, tin whistle), Sean Potts (b. 1930; tin whistle, bodhran), Michael Tubridy (b. 1935; flute, concertina, whistle) and Martin Fay (b. 1936; fiddle) – met in Eire in the late 50s as members of Ceoltoiri Cualann, a folk orchestra led by Sean O'Riada. After *Chieftains 1* (1964), the group chose to remain semi-professional and further recordings were sporadic. Sean Keane (b. 1946; fiddle, whistle), Peadar Mercier (b. 1914; bodhran, bones) and Derek Bell (b. 1935; harp,

dulcimer, oboe) joined the line-up, which then became a full-time venture. Their 1975 release *Chieftains 5* marked their debut with Island Records. The following year, Mercier was replaced by Kevin Conneff, and in 1979 Matt Molloy (flute; ex-Planxty) joined. The latter's skilled arrangements allowed the group to retain its freshness despite the many changes in personnel.

During the 80s, the group provided two film soundtracks and recorded album collaborations with James Galway and Van Morrison. In the 90s, the band found favour in the USA with *The Long Black Veil*. Subsequent releases were notable for the number of guest artists appearing alongside the Chieftains, although *Water From The Well* saw the group alone in the studio.

CHIFFONS

Formed in their native New York, USA, erstwhile backing singers Judy Craig, Barbara Lee Jones (b. 1947, d. 1992), Patricia Bennett (b. 1947) and Sylvia Peterson (b. 1946) are best recalled for 1963's international hit 'He's So Fine'. The song later acquired a dubious infamy in a plagiarism case involving George Harrison's million-selling, 'My Sweet Lord'. This battle made little difference to the Chiffons, who despite enjoying hits with 'One Fine Day' (1963) and 'Sweet Talkin' Guy' (1966), were all too soon reduced to the world of cabaret and 'oldies' nights. They did, however, record their own version of 'My Sweet Lord'.

CHILLI WILLI AND THE RED HOT PEPPERS

This leading UK pub-rock attraction was formed by Martin Stone (b. 1946; guitar, mandolin, vocals) and Phil 'Snakefinger' Lithman (b. 1949, d. 1987; guitar, fiddle, piano, vocals). Both were former members of an aspiring early 60s blues group before Stone joined the Savoy Brown Blues Band and then Mighty Baby. They were reunited on Chilli Willi And The Red Hot Peppers' 1972 debut, *Kings Of The Robot Rhythm*, an informal collection which featured blues singer Jo-Ann Kelly and several members of **Brinsley Schwarz**. The duo then recruited Paul 'Dice Man' Bailey (b. 1947; guitar, saxophone, banjo), Paul Riley (b. 1951; bass) and Pete Thomas (b. 1954; drums) and gradually became one of the UK's most compulsive live attractions. *Bongos Over Balham* failed to capture their in-concert passion and they disbanded in 1975. Thomas joined the Attractions, Riley played with Graham Parker's band, Bailey helped form Bontemps Roulez, and Stone joined the Pink Fairies. Lithman resumed an earlier association with the Residents and worked as a solo musician prior to his death from a heart attack in 1987.

CHOCOLATE WATCH BAND

US garage rock band whose original line-up – Ned Torney (guitar), Mark Loomis (guitar, vocals), Jo Kleming (organ), Richard Young (bass), Danny Phay (lead vocals) and Pete Curry (drums) – was assembled in California in 1964.

Gary Andrijasevich replaced Curry within weeks. In 1965, Torney, Kleming and Phay defected to local outfit, the Topsiders, but the latter's guitarist, Sean Tolby, joined Loomis and Andrijasevich. Dave Aguilar (vocals) and Bill Flores (bass) completed the revamped line-up whose best work includes 'Don't Need No Lovin', 'No Way Out' and 'Are

You Gonna Be There (At The Love In)'. Several Chocolate Watch Band masters featured studio musicians, while a substitute vocalist, Don Bennett, was employed on certain sessions. A disillusioned Aguilar quit the line-up prior to the release of *The Inner Mystique*. Phay resumed his place on the disappointing *One Step Beyond*. The band split up in 1970, but have occasionally re-formed in subsequent decades.

CHRISTIANS

Formed in Liverpool, England, in 1984, by Henry Priestman (b. 1955; keyboards) and the Christian brothers Roger (b. 1950), Garry (b. 1955) and Russell (b. 1956). Until then, the brothers had performed as a soul *a cappella* trio under a variety of names, most notably as Natural High. Priestman became the band's main songwriter and their combination of pop and soul earned them a string of UK hits in 1987, including 'Forgotten Town', 'Hooverville (And They Promised Us The World)', 'When The Finger Points', and 'Ideal World'.

Roger quit the band the same year, but 1988 brought further UK hits with 'Born Again' and a Top 10 cover version of the **Isley Brothers'** 'Harvest For The World'. The labours over recording *Colour* paid off when it reached UK number 1 on its first week in the chart. Subsequent singles failed to break into the top reaches of the chart, though, and 1992's *Happy In Hell* proved to be a commercial failure.

The band subsequently pursued solo projects, officially splitting up in 1997. Garry Christian released the acclaimed *Your Cool Mystery* the same year, while Priestman and Russell Christian teamed up with singer Desi Campbell in Blu-Dog. Priestman and Russell Christian reunited with Garry Christian in 1999 to play live dates and record a new Christians album. *Prodigal Sons* was released in 2002 and was backed by a UK tour.

CHRISTIE, LOU

Christie (b. Lugee Alfredo Giovanni Sacco, 1943) started out as a session singer in New York. He recorded unsuccessfully with the Classics and Lugee And The Lions, but his high falsetto ensured his 1963 solo 'The Gypsy Cried' achieved US sales in excess of one million. The following year's 'Two Faces Have I' proved equally successful. After US military service, Christie achieved a third golden disc with the US chart-topper 'Lightnin' Strikes' (1966), his vocal histrionics set against a Tamla/Motown-styled backbeat. 'Rhapsody In The Rain' (1966), was another US Top 20 entry, despite a ban for 'suggestive lyric'. In 1969, Christie had his final Top 10 hit with 'I'm Gonna Make You Mine'. A curious, almost anachronistic performer, he has spent most of the past three decades performing on the US rock 'n' roll revival circuit.

CHUCK D.

After **Public Enemy** lapsed into silence in the mid-90s, a Chuck D. (b. Carlton Douglas Ridenhour, 1960) solo album, *Autobiography Of Mistachuck*, reinforced his credentials as rap's most eloquent commentator. Media work and a book followed before Chuck D. rejoined the original line-up of Public Enemy to provide the soundtrack for Spike Lee's *He Got Game*. The singer subsequently crossed swords with Def Jam Records when he posted new Public Enemy material on the Internet, including the single 'Swindler's Lust', a blatant attack on the music industry. The group then signed up with an Internet record company, Atomic Pop, and became the first mainstream artists to release an album online.

CHUMBAWAMBA

The multi-member Chumbawamba was formed in Leeds, England and first played live in 1983. Their first single, 'Revolution', opened with the sound of **John Lennon**'s 'Imagine', before having it removed from the stereo and

smashed. The follow-up, 'We Are The World' was banned from airplay and *Pictures Of Starving Children Sell Records* used polemic to denounce the self-indulgence of Band Aid. Other targets included multinationals, apartheid and imperialism. Their discourse was made all the more articulate by the surprising diversity of music employed, from polka to ballad to thrash. *English Rebel Songs* acknowledged their place in the folk protest movement, and *Slap!* saw hope in rebellious dance music.

Somewhat abandoning their previous austerity, 'Tubthumping', their ode to alcohol, narrowly missed UK number 1 in 1997 and also made the US Top 10. The following album was much slicker than past efforts. Three years later the band released the follow-up, *WYSIWYG (What You See Is What You Get)*, which featured an unlikely cover version of the **Bee Gees**' 'New York Mining Disaster, 1941'.

CHURCH

Formed in Australia in 1980 by Englishmen Steven Kilbey (b. 1954; bass, vocals) and Marty Willson-Piper (b. 1958; guitar, vocals), Peter Koppes (b. 1955; guitar, vocals) and Nick Ward (drums). Richard Ploog (b. 1962) replaced Ward after their debut, *Of Skins And Heart*. Their 1998 release *Starfish* gained the Church college radio airplay in the USA, earning a Top 30 hit with 'Under The Milky Way'. Ploog left in 1990, replaced by Jay Dee Daugherty.

Willson-Piper released several solo albums and took on a part-time role as guitarist for **All About Eve** in 1991, appearing on their final two releases *Touched By Jesus* and *Ultraviolet*. Kilbey also recorded several solo albums and collaborated with Go-Betweens guitarist/vocalist Grant McLennan under the name Jack Frost, as well as publishing a book of poems. Peter Koppes completed an EP, *When Reason Forbids*, in 1987, and embarked on his own sequence of album releases, briefly leaving the Church in the mid-90s (1994's *Sometime Anywhere* was recorded by Kilbey, Willson-Piper and new drummer Tim Powles). The Church signed a new recording contract with Cooking Vinyl Records in the late 90s, releasing the covers collection *A Box Of Birds* and *After Everything Now This*.

CITY HIGH

This New Jersey, USA-based urban trio were the first act to be signed to Jerry Duplessis and Wyclef Jean's Booga Basement label. The one woman/two man line-up and their cool fusion of contemporary hip-hop and R&B styles inevitably drew comparisons to the **Fugees**. Formed by established producer/songwriters Robby Pardlo and Ryan Toby, singer Claudette Ortiz was brought on board at the suggestion of Duplessis and Jean. The trio enjoyed trans-atlantic success in 2001 with the gripping morality tale 'What Would You Do?', which had originally gained widespread exposure on the *Life* soundtrack. Their excellent self-titled debut was released shortly afterwards.

CLANNAD

Hailing from Co. Donegal, Eire, Clannad have successfully bridged folk and rock. The band was formed in 1968 by brothers Pól Brennan (b. Pol Ó Braonáin; guitar, vocals, percussion, flute), Ciarán Brennan (b. Ciaran Braonáin; guitar, bass, vocals, keyboards) and their twin uncles Pádraig Duggan (b. Pádraig Ó Dúgáin, 1949; guitar, vocals, mandolin) and Noel Duggan (b. Noel Ó Dúgáin; guitar, vocals). They were originally known as An Clann As Dobhar (Gaelic for a family from the townland of Dore), and although the name was soon abbreviated to Clannad the band continued to sing mainly in their native tongue at local folk festivals. Máire Brennan (b. Marie Ní Bhraonáin, 1952; harp, vocals) subsequently joined the band, who earned a recording contract with Philips Records.

The band's breakthrough success came in Germany, where they toured in 1975. The following year the band decided to commit themselves to music full-time. Máire's sister, Enya (b. Eithne Ní Bhraonáin, 1961) joined the line-up in 1980 and appeared on the transitional *Fuaim*, before leaving in 1982 to pursue a highly successful solo career. Clannad initially caught wide UK attention when they recorded the Top 5 with the theme tune for television's *Harry's Game* in 1982. In 1984, they recorded the soundtrack to UK television's *Robin Of Sherwood*. Further chart success followed with the UK Top 20 hit 'In A Lifetime' (1986), on which M·ire Brennan duetted with Bono from **U2**.

Pól Brennan left at the end of the decade to concentrate on solo work, but in his absence Clannad have continued to release enchanting and distinctive albums that have stayed true to their Celtic roots. They have been particularly successful in America, where 'Theme From Harry's Game' gained belated exposure on the movie soundtrack *Patriot Games* and a Volkswagen television commercial. Their work on the soundtrack to *The Last Of The Mohicans* also gained widespread stateside exposure. Máire Brennan, meanwhile, has established a successful solo career as a contemporary Christian artist.

CLAPTON, ERIC

The young Clapton (b. Eric Patrick Clapp, 1945, England) first played guitar with the Roosters, a local R&B group that included Tom McGuinness, later of **Manfred Mann**. In 1963, Clapton was recruited by the Yardbirds, to replace Tony Topham. Clapton stayed for 18 months; leaving when the Yardbirds took a more pop-orientated direction. Next, he joined **John Mayall**'s Bluesbreakers, with whom he made one album, the classic *Bluesbreakers*. It was with Mayall that Clapton would earn the nickname 'God'.

The formation of **Cream** in 1966, saw Clapton join **Jack Bruce** and **Ginger Baker**. Cream lasted just over two years, but their influence on rock music has been inestimable. Clapton then joined Baker, Steve Winwood and Ric Grech in **Blind Faith**. This 'supergroup' recorded one self-titled album and made a lucrative American tour. During the tour, Clapton befriended **Delaney And Bonnie**, who he later joined. He played on one album, *Delaney And Bonnie On Tour*, and three months later, absconded with three band members to make the disappointing *Eric Clapton*. The band (Jim Gordon, Bobby Whitlock and Carl Radle) formed the basis of Clapton's next project, **Derek And The Dominos**.

As Clapton struggled to overcome an engulfing heroin habit, the **Who**'s Pete Townshend organized the famous Eric Clapton At The Rainbow concert as part of his rehabilitation crusade. Clapton's appearance broke two years of silence, and he played a majestic and emotional set. Although still addicted, this represented a turning point, and he underwent treatment in London's Harley Street.

A rejuvenated Clapton released the buoyant *461 Ocean Boulevard* in 1974. Gone were the long guitar solos, replaced by relaxed vocals over shorter, more compact songs. It hit US number 1 and UK number 3 and its singles were also hits, notably a cover version of **Bob Marley**'s 'I Shot The Sheriff' (US number 1). Also included was the autobiographical 'Give Me Strength' and 'Let It Flow'. *There's One In Every Crowd* and the live *E. C. Was Here* maintained his reputation and were followed by two more major albums, *Slowhand* and *Backless*. Further singles success came with 'Lay Down Sally' and 'Promises'.

All Clapton's 80s albums sold in massive amounts and were warmly received by critics. *Journeyman*, his 1989 release, saw Clapton rediscovering the fiery guitar-work of old. His popularity undiminished, he began an annual season of concerts at London's Royal Albert Hall. The tragic death of his son Conor in 1991 halted Clapton's career for some months (resulting in the poignant hit 'Tears In Heaven'). The following year's *Unplugged* became one of his most successful albums. On it he demonstrated his blues roots, playing acoustically with his band. *From The Cradle*, an electric-blues album, was followed by the soul-influenced *Pilgrim*. He has maintained both directions, recording a wonderful album with **B. B. King** in 2000 and returning to the soul vibe on *Reptile*.

CLARK, DAVE, FIVE

One of the most popular British beat groups of the mid-60s, especially in the USA, the Dave Clark Five's career began in 1958 as a backing group for north-London singer Stan Saxon. Dave Clark (b. 1942; drums, vocals) was joined in the newly independent band by Mike Smith (b. 1943; organ, vocals), Rick Huxley (b. 1942; bass guitar), Lenny Davidson (b. 1944; lead guitar) and Denis Payton (b. 1943; saxophone). Smith's throaty vocals and Clark's incessant thumping beat were the band's most familiar trademarks. The Clark/Smith composition 'Glad All Over' proved one of the most distinctive and recognizable beat songs of its era and reached number 1 in the UK during January 1964, removing the **Beatles**' 'I Want To Hold Your Hand', from a six-week reign at the top. The national press, ever fixated with Beatles stories, pronounced in large headlines: 'Has The Five Jive Crushed The Beatles' Beat?' The Dave Clark Five took advantage of the publicity by swiftly issuing 'Bits And Pieces', which climbed to number 2. Over the next couple of years, the band's chart career in the UK was erratic at best, although they enjoyed a sizeable Top 10 hit in 1965 with 'Catch Us If You Can' ('Having A Wild Weekend' in the USA) from the film of the same name, in which they starred.

Even as their beat group charm in the UK faded, surprisingly new opportunities awaited them in the USA. A series of appearances on the *Ed Sullivan Show* saw them at the forefront of the mid-60s beat invasion and they racked up a string of million-sellers. A remarkable 17 *Billboard* Top 40 hits included 'Can't You See That She's Mine', 'Because', 'I Like It Like That' and their sole US number 1 'Over And Over'. Back in the UK, they enjoyed a belated and highly successful shift of style with the Barry Mason/Les Reed ballad, 'Everybody Knows'. Slipping into the rock 'n' roll revivalist trend of the early 70s, they charted with the medleys 'Good Old Rock 'N' Roll' and 'More Good Old Rock 'N' Roll', before bowing out in 1971.

Clark's astute business know-how had enabled the Dave Clark Five to enjoy lucrative pickings in the US market long after their beat contemporaries had faded, and he subsequently became a successful entrepreneur and multi-millionaire, both in the video market, where he purchased the rights to the pop show *Ready Steady Go!*, and onstage where his musical *Time* (starring Cliff Richard) enjoyed box office success.

CLARK, GENE

US singer-songwriter Clark (b. 1944, d. 1991) joined the New Christy Minstrels in 1963. Afterwards he teamed up with Roger McGuinn and David Crosby in the Jet Set. This trio evolved into the **Byrds**. Clark contributed significantly to their early work; classics from this period include 'Feel A Whole Lot Better', 'Here Without You' and 'Set You Free This Time'. Following the release of 'Eight Miles High' (1966), he dramatically left the group, citing fear of flying as the major cause.

With producer Jim Dickson, Clark recorded a solo album with the Gosdin Brothers, followed by two albums with Doug Dillard as Dillard And Clark. In 1968, Crosby left the Byrds and Clark re-joined, but he left within weeks. He revitalized his career with *White Light* (1971), but a lack of touring forestalled his progress. After a recorded reunion with the original Byrds in 1973, he recorded a solo album for Asylum Records. *No Other* was highly acclaimed, but sales again proved disappointing. He reunited with former colleagues McGuinn and Chris Hillman in the later 70s. The trio enjoyed brief success, but during the recording of 1980's *City*, Clark left amid some acrimony. Afterwards he mainly recorded for small labels, occasionally touring solo or with other ex-Byrds. Clark died from heart failure in 1991.

CLARK, GUY

Texas, USA-born Clark (b. 1941) worked in television and as a photographer. He briefly performed in a folk trio with K. T. Oslin, before moving to Los Angeles. Clark and writing hit songs such as 'LA Freeway', 'Desperados Waiting For A Train' and 'Texas 1947'. His 1975 debut *Old No. 1* was critically acclaimed but failed to chart on either side of the Atlantic and *Texas Cookin'*, was no more successful. *The South Coast Of Texas* and *Better Days* included the US country chart singles 'The Partner Nobody Chose' and 'Homegrown Tomatoes', but Clark's commercial rewards still failed to match the critical plaudits. After a brief hiatus, he returned to recording with *Old Friends*, appearing on **U2**'s label, Mother Records. Even with the implied patronage of U2, Clark enjoyed little more success than he had previously experienced. His contribution to American music is readily acknowledged by fellow musicians.

CLARK, PETULA

English singer Clark (b. 1932) was a child performer. By 1943, she had her own programme with an accent on wartime, morale-building songs. She made her first film in 1944 and went on to appear in over 20 feature films, including the *Huggett* series. By 1949 she was recording, and throughout the 50s had several hits. Her international breakthrough began in 1964 with Tony Hatch's 'Downtown'. It became a big hit in western Europe and reached US number 1. Clark's subsequent recordings of Hatch songs, including 'Don't Sleep In The Subway', 'My Love' and 'I Know A Place', all made the US Top 10 ('My Love' reached the top). Her recording of 'This Is My Song', written by Charles Chaplin for *A Countess From Hong Kong* (1967), reached UK number 1. In 1968, Clark revived her film career in *Finian's Rainbow*, followed by a part in MGM's 1969 remake of *Goodbye, Mr. Chips*.

Clark was by now not only a major recording star, but also an international personality, able to play all over the world in cabaret and concerts. Between 1981 and 1982, she played the part of Maria in the London revival of *The Sound Of Music*. In 1989, PYS Records issued a version of her 'Downtown', with the original vocal accompanied by 'acid house' backing. It went to UK number 10. In 1992, she toured the UK and the following year joined the cast of *Blood Brothers* on Broadway. In 1995, she played the part of Norma Desmond in the London production of *Sunset Boulevard* for six weeks while Elaine Paige was on holiday, and subsequently led the cast until the show closed in April 1997. A few months on, she was created CBE 'for services to entertainment' in the New Year's Honours List.

CLASH

The Clash at first tucked in snugly behind punk's loudest noise, the **Sex Pistols**

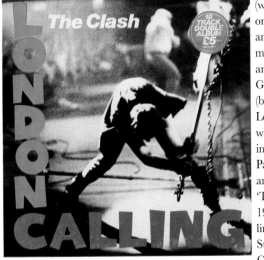

(whom they supported on the Anarchy tour), and later became a much more consistent and intriguing force. Guitarist Mick Jones (b. 1955) formed London SS in 1975, whose members included bass player Paul Simonon (b. 1956) and drummer Nicky 'Topper' Headon (b. 1955). The early Clash line-up included Joe Strummer (b. John Graham Mellor, 1952), guitarist Keith Levene and drummer Terry Chimes, but the latter two left in 1976. Jones, Simonon, Headon and Strummer signed to CBS Records, recording their brilliant 1977 debut in just three weeks. **Blue Öyster Cult**'s Sandy Pearlman produced *Give 'Em Enough Rope*, which reached UK number 2. The Clash increasingly embraced reggae elements, seemingly a natural progression from their anti-racist stance, and had a minor UK hit with '(White Man) In Hammersmith Palais' in 1978, followed by the frothy punk-pop of 'Tommy Gun', their first UK Top 20 hit. *London Calling* marked a return to almost top form, but the triple set *Sandinista!* was too sprawling. The experienced producer Glyn Johns was brought in for the snappy *Combat Rock*, recorded with Chimes after Headon abruptly left the group. 'Rock The Casbah' became a US Top 5 hit.

Jones left in 1983 (forming **Big Audio Dynamite**) and the Clash struggled, with the listless *Cut The Crap* only just breaking into the UK Top 20. Strummer finally disbanded the Clash in 1986 and turned to acting and production. In 1991, the Clash made a dramatic return to the UK charts when 'Should I Stay Or Should I Go?' was used in a Levi's jeans advertisement. The re-release reached number 1, but rumours of a reunion were misguided. A long-overdue live album was finally released in 1999 at the same time as Don Letts' compelling documentary *Westway To The World* was premiered on British television.

CLASSICS IV

Formed in Florida, USA, the Classics IV featured Dennis Yost (vocals), James Cobb (b. 1944; lead guitar), Wally Eaton (rhythm guitar), Joe Wilson (bass) and Kim Venable (drums). Seasoned session musicians, they had already worked on records by Tommy Roe, Billy Joe Royal and the Tams. Between 1968 and 1969, they enjoyed three soft-rock US hits with 'Spooky', 'Stormy' and 'Traces'. Cobb left and, despite the recruitment of guitarist Dean Daughtry (b. 1946), the loss of his songwriting proved insurmountable. Classics IV enjoyed only one more minor hit, 'What Am I Crying For' (1972). Cobb and Daughtry later formed the **Atlanta Rhythm Section**.

CLIFF, JIMMY

One of the great popularizers of reggae music, Jamaican Jimmy Cliff's (b. James Chambers, 1948) early singles, 'Daisy Got Me Crazy' (with Count Boysie) and 'I'm Sorry', were followed by the local hit 'Hurricane Hattie'. Cliff joined producer Leslie Kong in 1963, singing 'King Of Kings' and 'Dearest Beverley' in a hoarse, raucous voice. Afterwards, Cliff moved to London, England, and by 1968 was being groomed as a solo star to the underground rock market. The shift away from conventional reggae was made by a cover of **Procol Harum**'s 'Whiter Shade of Pale'. He finally broke through in 1969 with 'Wonderful World, Beautiful People'. 'Vietnam' was a small hit the following year, and was described by **Bob Dylan** as the best protest song he had heard. In local terms, however, its success was outstripped by a cover version of **Cat Stevens**' 'Wild World'.

While the albums *Jimmy Cliff, Hard Road To Travel* and particularly *Another Cycle* were short on roots credibility, his next move, as the gun-toting, reggae-singing star of *The Harder They Come* (1972), was short on nothing. Cliff's role in the film made him Jamaica's most marketable property, and its soundtrack one of the biggest-selling reggae records of all time. The crossover never happened, and Cliff's star began to wane directly as **Bob Marley** began his rise to worldwide fame.

Outside the reggae world, Cliff remains best known for writing 'Many Rivers To Cross', a massive hit for **UB40**. However, his popularity on the African continent is enormous. He is similarly venerated in South America, whose samba rhythms have helped to inform and enrich his latter-day material. His most recent studio albums highlight, as ever, his gospel-tinged delivery, offering ample evidence to dispel the widely held belief (particularly in the West) that he is a perennial underachiever.

CLIMAX BLUES BAND

Originally the Climax Chicago Blues Band, this enduring British unit was formed by Colin Cooper (b. 1939; vocals, saxophone), Peter Haycock (b. 1952; vocals, guitar), Richard Jones (bass), Arthur Wood (keyboards), Derek Holt (b. 1949; rhythm guitar) and George Newsome (b. 1947; drums). Their 1969 debut *The Climax Chicago Blues Band* evoked early **John Mayall** and Savoy Brown but *Plays On* (minus Jones and with Holt switching to bass) displayed a new-found maturity. A freer, flowing pulse and rock-based elements were reflected on *A Lot Of Bottle* and *Tightly Knit*, by which time keyboardist Anton Farmer had joined the line-up. Newsome was replaced by John Cuffley in 1973, and Jones rejoined in 1975.

The Climax Blues Band enjoyed a surprise UK number 10 hit with 'Couldn't Get It Right' the following year. The success proved temporary, although the band has continued as a popular live attraction in the following decades. Jones left in 1977, and was replaced by Peter Filleul and then George Glover. Holt was replaced by John 'Rhino' Edwards in 1982, before Roger Inniss and then Neil Simpson took over the bass slot. Jeff Rich was recruited following Cuffley's departure in 1983, but was in turn replaced by Roy Adams two years later. The long-serving Haycock was replaced the same year by Lester Hunt, leaving Cooper as the only remaining original member.

CLINE, PATSY

US-born Cline (b. Virginia Patterson Hensley, 1932, d. 1963) began her career in 1948 when she approached Wally Fowler, a noted Grand Ole Opry artist. Taken aback by her overt approach, he let her sing for him and included her in that night's show. In 1952, she met Bill Peer, a disc jockey and musician, who was touring with his band the Melody Boys And Girls. He hired her as lead vocalist. In 1953, Patsy married Gerald Cline and the following year signed a two-year recording contract with Four-Star, a Pasadena-based independent company. She made her first four recordings in 1955, under the production of pianist, guitarist and arranger Owen Bradley. 'A Church, A Courtroom And Then Goodbye' was the chosen song, but it failed to reach the country charts, nor did further recordings including 'I Love You Honey' and the rockabilly 'Stop, Look And Listen'.

In an effort to secure a country hit, she recorded 'Walkin' After Midnight', in a session that also included 'A Poor Man's Roses (Or A Rich Man's Gold)' and 'The Heart You

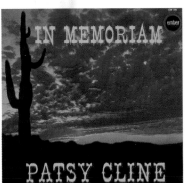

Break May Be Your Own'. The record reached country number 2 and pop number 12. Her next single, 'I Fall To Pieces', quickly became a country number 1 and peaked at pop number 12. In 1961, she completed a four-day recording session that included 'True Love', 'The Wayward Wind', 'San Antonio Rose' and her version of **Willie Nelson**'s 'Crazy' (country number 2/pop number 9). In 1962, 'She's Got You' reached country number 1 and pop number 14.

Cline's last recording session took place on 7 February 1963. On 5 March, Cline, together with country singers Cowboy Copas and Hawkshaw Hawkins, set off on a five-hundred-mile flight to Nashville, in a small aircraft piloted by Randy Hughes. Cline was killed when the aircraft crashed in woodland about a mile off Highway 70, near Camden, Tennessee. At the time of her death, Cline's recording of 'Leaving On Your Mind' was in both country and pop charts. Before the year was over, 'Sweet Dreams' and 'Faded Love' were Top 10 country and minor pop hits.

CLINTON, GEORGE

The mastermind behind the highly successful **Parliament** and **Funkadelic**, Clinton (b. 1940) found his empire crumbling at the beginning of the 80s. Restrained from recording by a breach-of-contract lawsuit and unable to meet the running expenses of his considerable organization, he found himself personally and professionally destitute. After finally settling most of his debts and overcoming a cocaine addiction, he resumed recording. With the P-Funk All Stars he secured two minor hits, 'Hydrolic Pump' and 'One Of Those Summers' (both 1982), before releasing the solo 'Loopzilla'. *Computer Games* featured several ex-Funkadelic/Parliament cohorts, including Bernie Worrell and Bootsy Collins, while 'Atomic Dog' (1983), was a US R&B number 1 single.

Clinton has continued to work as a soloist and with the P-Funk All Stars, pursuing his eclectic, eccentric vision on *Some Of My Best Jokes Are Friends* and *The Cinderella Theory*. *His Hey Man ... Smell My Finger* set featured a cameo by **Dr. Dre**, who in turn invited Clinton to guest rap on 'You Don't Wanna See Me' from Dre's collaboration with **Ice Cube**, *Helter Skelter*. As Dre and many other recent American rappers confess, they owe a great debt to Clinton, not least for their liberal use of his music. Clinton was not one to complain, however, as the young guns' heavy use of Parliament and Funkadelic samples had helped him overcome a crippling tax debt in the early 80s. Clinton's 1996 album *The Awesome Power Of A Fully Operational Mothership* was a superb blend of the Funkadelic and Parliament sounds.

CLOVER

Formed in California, USA, by bass player Johnny Ciambotti, John McFee (b. 1953; guitar, vocals), Alex Call (guitar, vocals) and Mitch Howie (drums). Originally known as the Tiny Hearing Aid Company, they became Clover in 1967. *Clover* proved their reputation as a feisty bar band, but suffered from primitive production. *Forty-Niner* was a marked improvement, but a dispirited Howie left, replaced by Huey (Louis) Lewis (b. Hugh Anthony Cregg III, 1950; vocals, harmonica), Sean Hopper (keyboards, vocals) and Mickey Shine (drums).

In 1976, the band went to Britain and accompanied **Elvis Costello** on his debut *My Aim Is True*. Despite two promising albums, Clover were unable to make a

significant breakthrough and returned to the USA in 1978, where they folded. McFee joined the **Doobie Brothers**, while Lewis and Hooper eventually achieved commercial success as **Huey Lewis And The News**.

CLOVERS

US R&B vocal ensemble formed in Washington, DC, in 1946. By 1950, the Clovers comprised John 'Buddy' Bailey (b. 1930; lead), Matthew McQuater (tenor), Harold Lucas (baritone) and Harold Winley (bass), with instrumental accompaniment from Bill Harris (b. 1925, d. 1988; guitar). In 1952, Charles White (b. 1930) became the Clovers' new lead when Buddy Bailey was drafted into the army. The following year, Billy Mitchell took over from White. Bailey rejoined in 1954 but Mitchell remained and the two alternated the leads.

The Clovers had three US R&B number 1s with 'Don't You Know I Love You', 'Fool, Fool, Fool' (both 1951) and 'Ting-A-Ling' (1952), plus four number 2 R&B hits. They only made the US pop charts twice: 'Love Love Love' (number 30, 1956) and 'Love Potion No. 9' (number 23, 1959). In 1961, the Clovers split into rival groups led, respectively, by Bailey and Lucas and the hits dried up. Various permutations of the Clovers continued to record and perform for years afterwards, particularly in the Carolinas where their brand of music was popular as 'beach music'.

COASTERS

The illustrious career of the Coasters, the pre-eminent US vocal group of the early rock 'n' roll era, was built on a remarkable body of cleverly comic R&B songs for Atco Records, fashioned by their producers, **Leiber And Stoller**. Under their direction, the Coasters exchanged the crooning of ballads favoured by most groups of the era for robust and full-throated R&B shouting.

The group was formed in 1955 by Carl Gardner (b. 1928; lead), Bobby Nunn (b. Ulysses B. Nunn, 1925, d. 1986; bass), Leon Hughes (b. Thomas Leon Hughes, 1932; tenor) and Billy Guy (b. 1936; lead, baritone). Hughes was replaced briefly in 1957 by Young Jessie (b. Obie Donmell Jessie, 1936), who in turn was replaced by ex-Flairs Cornell Gunter (b. 1938, d. 1990). In January 1958, Nunn was replaced by ex-Cadets Will 'Dub' Jones (b. Will J. Jones, 1928, d. 2000). At the start of the following year original guitar player Adolph Jacobs (b. Herman Adolph Jacobsen, 1931) was replaced by Albert 'Sonny' Forriest (b. Elbert McKinley Forriest, 1934, d. 1999), who became a contracted member of the line-up. Ex-**Cadillacs** Earl 'Speedo' Carroll (b. Gregory Carroll, 1937) replaced Gunter in mid-1961.

The Coasters first charted with 'Down In Mexico' (US R&B Top 10) in 1956, but the following year's 'Searchin''/'Young Blood' established them as major rock 'n' roll stars. Three more giant US hits by the classic line-up of Gardner, Guy, Gunter and Jones sustained their career: 'Yakety Yak', 'Charlie Brown' and 'Poison Ivy'. By the mid-60s, however, the lustre had worn off, as the hits increasingly emphasized the comic lyrics to the detriment of the music. The long-serving Gardner and Guy enjoyed a brief comeback in late 1971, when a reworking of 'Love Potion Number Nine' for the King label broke into the *Billboard* Hot 100.

The Coasters have continued in the subsequent decades as an oldies act, fracturing into several different groups playing the nostalgia circuit, although most authorities accept the Carl Gardner-led Coasters as the genuine article. Gardner, Guy, Jones and Gunter's induction into the Rock And Roll Hall Of Fame in January 1987 went some of the way towards restoring the group's tarnished image.

COCHRAN, EDDIE

Although this US artist's career was brief, during which time he had only had one major hit in the USA and topped the UK charts only once, he is now regarded as one of the finest-ever rock 'n' roll singers and an outstanding rhythm guitarist. Cochran (b. Edward Raymond Cochrane, 1938, d. 1960) began as a country singer, but soon becoming an outstanding rockabilly guitarist with his trademark Gretsch guitar.

In 1956, after his cameo performance of 'Twenty Flight Rock' in the movie *The Girl Can't Help It*, he was signed by Liberty Records. 'Sittin' In The Balcony' reached the US Top 20, but it was the following 'Summertime Blues' (1957) and 'C'mon Everybody' (1958) that have become timeless classics. Tragically, while holidaying in Britain, Cochran was killed in a car crash. Gene Vincent and Sharon Sheeley (co-writer of Cochran's posthumous hit 'Something Else') were badly injured. His biggest record was the inappropriately titled 'Three Steps To Heaven', which topped the UK chart shortly after his untimely death. Surprisingly it failed to dent the chart in the USA. 'Weekend' was another posthumous hit, and the last of his classics, another tale of simple youthful enthusiasm for life and the anticipated wild weekend.

Cochran was a dedicated musician and one of the greatest exponents of 'progressive' rock 'n' roll. It is remarkable that in a chart career of little over two years, he made such a big impression, and like **Buddy Holly** he continues to be cited as a major influence.

COCKBURN, BRUCE

Cockburn (b. 1945) has long been heralded as Canada's best-kept secret. His numerous early albums (10 from 1970–79) were tainted by a strong devotional feel, tied to their author's Christian beliefs. After a breakthrough single 'Wondering Where The Lions Are' (from 1980's *Dancing In The Dragon's Jaws*), his lyrical gaze turned to more secular matter on *World Of Wonders*. Later work embraced environmental concerns, such as 'If A Tree Falls' and 'Radium Rain', a song informed by the Chernobyl disaster. He remains enormously popular in his homeland, yet his brand of folk rock remains only a cult item elsewhere. Cockburn moved to the more sympathetic Rykodisc Records during the late 90s.

COCKER, JOE

UK-born Cocker (b. John Robert Cocker, 1944) started out in 1961 with Sheffield band the Cavaliers (later Vance Arnold And The Avengers). A one-off solo single for Decca Records flopped and Cocker went on to form the first Grease Band in 1966, with Chris Stainton (bass), Vernon Nash (piano), Dave Memmott (drums) and Frank Myles (guitar). After two years of solid club gigs, they were rewarded with a recording session. The single 'Marjorine' was a minor hit and Cocker and Stainton assembled a new Grease Band with Mickey Gee (guitar), Tommy Reilly (drums) and Tommy Eyre (keyboards). The resulting single, a remarkable cover version of the **Beatles'** 'With A Little Help From My Friends', was recorded with session musicians including **Jimmy Page** and B. J. Wilson. The single went to UK number 1 in 1968.

Cocker's debut album failed to chart in the UK but was a US hit. Cocker and his band, now featuring guitarist Henry McCullough, started touring America in 1969 and became huge stars through exposure on the *Ed Sullivan Show* and constant performing. By the end of 1969 Cocker had a further two hits with Dave Mason's 'Feelin' Alright' and Leon Russell's 'Delta Lady', together with another solid and successful album *Joe Cocker!*.

The 70s began with the famous Mad Dogs And Englishmen tour – over 60 dates were played in as many days. A subsequent film and double album were released, although it was reported that Cocker was bankrupted by the whole charade. He then slid into a drink-and-drug stupor that lasted through most of the decade. Despite this, he still managed to produce a few hits, including 'Midnight Rider', 'You Are So Beautiful' and 'Put Out The Light'. His albums were patchy, except for 1974's *I Can Stand A Little Rain*.

Apart from a minor hit guesting with the Crusaders on 'I'm So Glad I'm Standing Here Today', little was heard from Cocker until 1982, when he returned to US number 1 duetting with **Jennifer Warnes** on 'Up Where We Belong', taken from the soundtrack to *An Officer And A Gentlemen*. The ensuing *Civilized Man* was another disappointment, but three years later Cocker released the superior *Unchain My Heart*. Following the release of a couple of minor albums, Cocker re-emerged in 1994 with his best album in years, *Have A Little Faith*. He paid tribute to himself in 1996 with *Organic*, an album containing many remakes from his catalogue and illustrating Cocker's great ear for a good songwriter. In contrast, *No Ordinary World* was a lacklustre performance.

COCKNEY REBEL

Formed in England in 1973 by Steve Harley (b. Steven Nice, 1951) with Jean-Paul Crocker (violin, guitar), Paul Avron Jeffreys (b. 1952, d. 1988; bass), Milton Reame-James (keyboards) and Stuart Elliott (drums). Their debut UK hit 'Judy Teen' was a confident start after which the band was reconstructed. The most stable line-up featured Jim Cregan (guitar; ex-**Family**), George Ford (bass), Lindsay Elliott (percussion), Duncan MacKay (keyboards) and original drummer Stuart Elliott. Their first two albums remain their best works and they reached UK number 1 in 1975 with the catchy single 'Make Me Smile (Come Up And See Me)', billed as Steve Harley and Cockney Rebel. A cover version of **George Harrison**'s 'Here Comes the Sun' reached the UK Top 10 in 1976. Harley moved to America and discarded the Cockney Rebel tag for 1978's *Hobo With A Grin*, the first of several unsuccessful solo releases. He returned to the UK charts in 1986, duetting with Sarah Brightman in the title song from *The Phantom Of The Opera*. Little was heard until 1988 when a UK television commercial used one of his early hits 'Mr Soft'. In 1992 Harley returned to the UK Top 50 with the re-released 'Make Me Smile (Come Up And See Me)' and embarked on a major tour to back a new studio album. He has continued to record the occasional album, but remains primarily a live attraction.

COCTEAU TWINS

Formed in Scotland, in 1982, the Cocteau Twins originally featured Elizabeth Fraser (b. 1963), Robin Guthrie (b. 1962) and Will Heggie (bass). Able to convey an astonishing variety of moods and emotions, using words more for their sound than their meaning, Fraser's voice has become one of the most recognizable and imitated of the last two decades.

The band's debut for the 4AD Records label, *Garlands*, preceded Heggie's departure. *Head Over Heels* smoothed over the rougher edges of its predecessor with Guthrie adding layers of echo and phased drum effects. The duo was also involved in 4AD's This Mortal Coil project. Simon Raymonde (b. 1962) joined on bass and featured on two superb EPs, *Sunburst And Snowblind* and *Pearly-Dewdrops' Drops*, which dominated the UK independent charts. *Treasure* saw the

trio scaling new heights. *Victorialand*, recorded without Raymonde, had a lighter, acoustic sound. Raymonde returned for the *Love's Easy Tears* EP and *The Moon And The Melodies*, a collaboration with Harold Budd.

On *Blue Bell Knoll* it seemed the Cocteau Twins had lost their touch, but the stunning *Heaven Or Las Vegas* redeemed their reputation. 'Iceblink Luck' reached the UK Top 40 and the band resumed touring. They signed a new contract with Fontana Records in 1992 and completed the average *Four-Calendar Café*. The superior *Milk & Kisses* was preceded by two EP releases, the 'ambient' *Otherness* (with Mark Clifford of Seefeel) and the 'acoustic' *Twinlights*. The latter was accompanied by the band's first film short. The Cocteau Twins announced they were splitting up in June 1998.

COHEN, LEONARD

Canadian-born Cohen (b. 1934) started out as a novelist, with *The Favorite Game* (1963) and *Beautiful Losers* (1966) offering the mixture of sexual and spiritual longing, despair and black humour later prevalent in his lyrics. Two early songs, 'Suzanne' and 'Priests', were recorded by Judy Collins. The former was also included on *The Songs Of Leonard Cohen*, his 1967 debut. The weary loneliness portrayed by Cohen's intonation was enhanced by the barest of accompaniment. *Songs From A Room* maintained a similar pattern, but despite the inclusion of 'Story Of Isaac' and 'Bird On The Wire', lacked the commercial impact of its predecessor. Although Cohen's lugubrious delivery had slackened by *Songs Of Love And Hate*, it contained two of his finest compositions, 'Joan Of Arc' and 'Famous Blue Raincoat'.

After a four-year hiatus, *New Skin For The Old Ceremony* showed his talent was undiminished and included the disconsolate track 'Chelsea Hotel', an account of Cohen's sexual encounter with **Janis Joplin**. A second impasse in his career ended in 1977 with *Death Of A Ladies' Man*, an unlikely collaboration with **Phil Spector**. The grandiose backing tracks proved ill-fitting and Cohen later disowned the project. *Recent Songs* and *Various Positions* were underrated collections and the singer's career seemed destined to remain confined to a small, committed audience until **Jennifer Warnes** released *Famous Blue Raincoat* (1987), a commercially successful album consisting solely of Cohen's songs. His own next set, *I'm Your Man*, was afforded widespread attention and attendant live performances formed the core of a BBC television documentary. His talent was confirmed by 1992's excellent *The Future*, but Cohen spent the rest of the decade as a reclusive figure, emerging only to support the recording career of his son Adam. He returned to the studio in the new millennium to record his first album in almost a decade, *Ten New Songs*.

COLDPLAY

This UK band's inoffensive and slightly bland acoustic rock songs bear strong comparison to the hugely successful **Travis**. Coldplay was formed in 1998 by UCL students Chris Martin (b. 1977; vocals), Jon Buckland (b. 1977; guitar), Guy Berryman (b. 1978; bass) and Will Champion (b. 1978; drums). Self-financed demo sessions were productive enough to warrant the release of the *Safety* EP in May. A one-off single for Fierce Panda, 'Brothers And Sisters', broke into the UK charts at the start of 1999. The same May the band signed a major label deal with Parlophone Records. In 2000, they enjoyed breakthrough UK hits with 'Shiver', 'Yellow' and 'Trouble' and the level of hype helped propel their debut album, *Parachutes*, to the top of the UK charts in July. The band was also nominated for the Mercury Music Prize.

COLE, LLOYD

English singer-songwriter Lloyd Cole (b. 1961) emerged from the post-punk renaissance with his band the Commotions. Neil Clark (b. 1955; guitar), Blair Cowan (keyboards), Lawrence Donegan (b. 1961; bass) and Stephen Irvine (b. 1959; drums) completed the line-up responsible for 1984's *Rattlesnakes*, a

critically lauded set that introduced Cole's **Lou Reed**-inspired intonation. The attendant 'Perfect Skin' reached the UK Top 30, while the follow-up album, *Easy Pieces*, spawned two Top 20 entries in 'Brand New Friend' and 'Lost Weekend'. Unfortunately, their style seemed laboured on *Mainstream* and Cole disbanded the Commotions. The solo *Lloyd Cole* showed signs of an artistic rejuvenation, but *Don't Get Weird On Me, Babe* and *Bad Vibes*, although good in parts, failed to lift the atmosphere of bookish lyrics rendered without the requisite soul. His recent band the Negatives, with whom he recorded a self-titled album in 2000, features the occasional services of talented singer-songwriter Jill Sobule.

COLE, NAT 'KING'

The most moving aspect of Cole's (b. Nathaniel Adams Coles, 1916, d. 1965) legacy is the way his music cuts across the usual boundaries – chart-watchers and jazz aficionados, rock 'n' rollers and MOR fans can all have a good time with his music.

Cole was born in Montgomery, Alabama, USA, but the family migrated to Chicago in 1921. He learned piano by ear from his mother, and when he was 12 years old he took lessons in classical piano. Cole's first professional break came touring with the show *Shuffle Along*, a revival of the first all-black show to make it to Broadway, which he joined with his bass-playing brother, Eddie.

In 1939, stranded in Los Angeles, Cole formed an innovative trio with Oscar Moore on guitar and Wesley Prince on bass. Like **Fats Waller** in the previous generation, Cole managed to combine pleasing and humorous ditties with piano stylings that were state-of-the-art. Times had moved on, and Cole had a suave sophistication that expressed the new aspirations of the black community. In 1943 he recorded his 'Straighten Up And Fly Right' for Capitol Records – it was an instant hit and Cole's future as a pop success was assured. In 1946 'The Christmas Song' added strings, starting a process that would lead to Cole emerging as a middle-of-the-road singer, accompanied by leading arrangers and conductors. In the 40s Cole made several memorable sides with the Trio, including 'Sweet Lorraine', 'It's Only A Paper Moon', '(Get Your Kicks) On Route 66' and '(I Love You) For Sentimental Reasons'. By 1948, and 'Nature Boy' (a US number 1), on which Cole was accompanied by Frank

DeVol's Orchestra, the move away from small-group jazz, towards his eventual position as one of the most popular vocalists of the day, was well underway.

Confirmation came in 1950, when Cole, with Les Baxter conducting Nelson Riddle's lush arrangement of 'Mona Lisa', spent eight weeks at the top of the US chart with what was to become one of his most celebrated recordings. Throughout the 50s the singles hits continued to flow, mostly with ballads such as 'Too Young', 'Faith Can Move Mountains', 'Because You're Mine', 'Unforgettable', 'Pretend', 'Can't I?', 'Answer Me, My Love', 'Smile', 'The Sand And The Sea', 'A Blossom Fell', 'When I Fall In Love' and 'Star Dust'. They continued in the early 60s with 'Ramblin' Rose', 'Those Lazy-Hazy-Crazy Days Of Summer' and 'Let There Be Love'.

During the years of Cole's enormous popularity in the 'easy listening' field, jazz fans had to turn out to see him in the clubs to hear his glorious piano – an extension of the Earl Hines style that had many features of the new, hip sounds of bebop. If Cole had not had such an effective singing voice he might well have been one of bebop's leaders. Bebop was an expression of black pride, but so was Cole's career, creating opportunities for all kinds of 'sepia Sinatras' (**Charles Brown**, **Sammy Davis Jnr.** etc.), who proved that whites had no monopoly on sophistication. Though his position entailed compromises that gained him the hostility of civil rights activists in the early 60s, he was a brave and decent figure in a period when racial prejudice was at its most demeaning. He died from lung cancer in 1965.

COLE, NATALIE

The daughter of **Nat 'King' Cole**, Natalie (b. 1950) survived early pressures to emulate her father's laid-back style. Signed to Capitol Records in 1975, her debut, 'This Will Be', reached the US Top 10 and was the first of three consecutive number 1 soul singles. Natalie maintained her popularity into the 80s, but drug dependency took a professional and personal toll. In 1984, she emerged from a rehabilitation centre and began recording *Everlasting*. From this came three transatlantic hits – 'Jump Start', 'I Live For Your Love' and 'Pink Cadillac'. Further pop hits with 'Miss You Like Crazy' and 'Wild Women Do', the latter taken from the soundtrack of the movie *Pretty Woman*. In 1991, she recorded a unique tribute to her late father, a 'duet' with him on his original recording of 'Unforgettable'. The accompanying album won seven Grammy Awards, including Best Album and Song. *Unforgettable ... With Love* marked a stylistic turning point in Cole's career, with the singer moving away from the urban contemporary market and embracing the smooth jazz-pop sound of her father on subsequent albums. *Take A Look* included a superb cover version of the standard 'Cry Me A River', while her Christmas albums *Holly & Ivy* and *The Magic Of Christmas* brought new life to some old chestnuts. Her revealing autobiography was published in 2000.

COLLECTIVE SOUL

Formed in Georgia, USA, Collective Soul enjoyed commercial success in the mid-90s with several strong, hook-laden pop rock songs, including 1994's 'Shine'. After years of rejection from major labels, Ed Roland (vocals, guitar) disbanded an early line-up of the band in 1992. When radio began expressing an interest in 'Shine', he re-formed Collective Soul with his brother Dean (guitar), Ross Childress (lead guitar), Will Turpin (bass) and original drummer Shane Evans. The band's repackaged debut album became a million-seller. 'Gel' was the first single from their second album and was featured on the soundtrack to the cult movie *Jerky Boys*. Their recent recordings, although commercially successful, have been somewhat disappointing.

COLLINS, ALBERT

Texas, USA-born Collins (b. 1932, d. 1993) was a master guitarist: using non-standard tuning and slashing out blocked chords and sharp flurries of treble

notes on his Fender Telecaster. His first singles, released from 1958 onwards, were shuffle instrumentals including 'The Freeze' and 'Frosty', but it was not until the late 60s that he began singing on a regular basis. A series of splendid studio and live albums over the following years extended his basic Texas style across the boundaries of jazz and funk, establishing him as a major international blues attraction. A lull in his career was broken by 1978's *Ice Pickin'*. On this, he was supported by the Icebreakers – Larry Burton (guitar), Chuck Smith (saxophone), Casey Jones (drums), A. C. Reed (saxophone) and Alan Batts (keyboards). Two live albums, *Frozen Alive* and *Live In Japan*, emphasized Collins' charismatic stage presence. This talented man endured terminal cancer with great humility; his death at 61 was a cruel shock.

COLLINS, BOOTSY

Bootsy Collins (b. William Collins, 1951) was an integral part of the JBs, **James Brown**'s backing group after the Famous Flames. Between 1969 and

1971, Collins' distinctive basswork propelled some of the era's definitive funk anthems. Later, Collins and several others switched to George Clinton's Parliament/Funkadelic organization. The bassist's popularity inspired the formation of Bootsy's Rubber Band, a spin-off group featuring other Brown/Clinton associates. Collins' outrageous image emphasized a mix of funk and fun exemplified by 'Psychoticbumpschool' (1976), 'The Pinocchio Theory' (1977) and 'Bootzilla' (1978). Collins and the Bootzilla Orchestra were employed for the production of Malcolm McLaren's 1989 album *Waltz Darling* and by the early 90s the Rubber Band had started touring again. In the 90s he found plenty of work on hip-hop/rap projects, but his own releases have tended to be competent rather than inspired. However, a return to a major label for *Fresh Outta "P" University* produced his best work since his 70s peak.

COLLINS, EDWYN

Following the collapse of **Orange Juice**, Scottish singer Edwyn Collins (b. 1959) went solo. Both the Orange Juice producer, Dennis Bovell, and drummer Zeke Manyika were present on Collins' 1989 solo debut, *Hope And Despair*, as was **Aztec Camera**'s Roddy Frame. *Hellbent On Compromise* was a more intimate and atmospheric recording. Collins produced for other artists and worked with the Setanta Records roster before 'A Girl Like You' became the most successful instalment in his 15-year recording career, entering the Top 10 in Australia, France and the UK during 1994. Collins has since balanced production work with the occasional solo release, including 1997's *I'm Not Following You* and 2002's *Doctor Syntax*.

COLLINS, JUDY

US folk singer Judy Collins (b. 1939) was originally trained as a classical pianist. Signed to Elektra Records in 1961, her early releases emphasized her traditional repertoire, but by the release of *Judy Collins #3*, her clear soprano was tackling more contemporary material. This pivotal selection included **Bob Dylan**'s 'Farewell'. *Judy Collins' Fifth Album* was the artist's last purely folk collection, including compositions by Dylan, Richard Farina, Eric Andersen

and Gordon Lightfoot, alongside songs culled from theatre's bohemian fringes. *In My Life* embraced Jacques Brel, Bertolt Brecht, Kurt Weill and the then-unknown **Leonard Cohen**. On *Wildflowers* she introduced **Joni Mitchell** and in the process enjoyed a popular hit with 'Both Sides Now'. These releases were marked by Joshua Rifkin's string arrangements, which became a feature of her work. Her finest work, 1968's *Who Knows Where The Time Goes*, featured Stephen Stills and Van Dyke Parks. *Whales And Nightingales* was equally impressive, and included the million-selling single 'Amazing Grace'.

Although Collins' own compositions were meritorious, she was never a prolific writer. Her reliance on outside material grew increasingly problematic as the era of classic songwriters drew to a close and the artist looked to outside interests, although she did secure another international hit in 1975 with a version of Stephen Sondheim's 'Send In The Clowns'. Although subsequent recordings lack her former perception, and indeed have grown increasingly infrequent, she remains an immensely talented interpreter. In recent years Collins has shown a gift for writing novels, while the new millennium saw her launching her own label, Wildflower Records.

COLLINS, PHIL

Taking a break from his drumming and singing duties in **Genesis**, UK-born Collins (b. 1951) released his solo debut *Face Value* in 1981. The album immediately confirmed him as a songwriter of note and became an international bestseller, with the stand-out track 'In The Air Tonight' reaching UK number 2. Over the next decade Collins continued to record with Genesis while maintaining a successful solo career. *Hello, I Must Be Going* and a cover version of the **Supremes**' 'You Can't Hurry Love' were worldwide hits in 1982. He also became a highly successful record producer and session drummer, working with such artists as **John Martyn**, **Robert Plant**, **Adam And The Ants**, **Eric Clapton** and **Howard Jones**. Additionally, his specially commissioned film-soundtrack song for *Against All Odds* reached the top of the US singles chart. He played drums on Band Aid's 'Do They Know It's Christmas?' and, a few weeks later, was again near the top of the US charts duetting with Philip Bailey on the infectious 'Easy Lover'. Barely pausing for breath, he released *No Jacket Required*, which topped charts worldwide.

Collins made musical history on 13 July 1985 by appearing at both Live Aid concerts, in London, and, courtesy of Concorde, in Philadelphia. A second duet and film soundtrack, this time with Marilyn Martin for *White Nights* made 'Separate Lives' his fourth US chart-topper. In 1987 Collins starred as great train robber Buster Edwards in *Buster*. Two years later he released his fourth solo album, which immediately topped the charts and spawned further hit singles.

In the 90s, in addition to continuing with Genesis, Collins released the *Both Sides* in 1993. A transatlantic chart-topper, the album marked a return to the stark emotion of *Face Value*. The underwhelming *Dance Into The Light*, recorded after the singer had left Genesis and relocated to Switzerland, was Collins' first real failure, although the subsequent *Hits* compilation restored him to the top of the UK charts in 1998. The following year Collins composed the songs for the Disney movie *Tarzan*, enjoying particular success with the ballad 'You'll Be In My Heart', which later won the Oscar for Best Original Song. He also recorded a big band live album.

COLVIN, SHAWN

US singer Colvin played with both hard-rock and country-swing bands while at college. After a brief sojourn playing solo acoustic sessions, she relocated to New York in 1980 and appeared in off-Broadway productions such as *Pump Boys And Dinettes*, *Diamond Studs* and *Lie Of The Mind*. After straightening out her hectic personal life, Colvin set about recording her 1989 debut *Steady On*. Backed by fellow guitarist and songwriting partner John Leventhal, she pulled together arresting material with an understated approach and was awarded a Grammy for Best Folk Album. Colvin's second album was recorded with **Joni Mitchell**'s husband, Larry Klein, while 1994's *Cover Girl* was entirely comprised of non-original material. The excellent *A Few Small Repairs* was more rock-orientated. After going through a divorce, Colvin had no shortage of philosophical emotions to turn into song.

Apart from a seasonal album released in 1998, little was heard of Colvin until she returned in the new millennium with her first album of original material in over five years, *Whole New You*.

COMBS, SEAN 'PUFFY'

One of the most prosperous of a new breed of entrepreneurs in US black music, Sean 'Puffy' Combs (b, 1970) is a hugely successful hip-hop artist (under the name Puff Daddy) and noted producer for artists including **TLC** and **Mary J. Blige**. He also excels in business, with his multi-million dollar Bad Boy Entertainment empire establishing Combs as one of the leading figures in black music. Although his sample-heavy sound has been criticized for taking hip-hop too far into the mainstream, its commercial appeal is unquestionable, and by the late 90s had made Combs one of the most powerful players in American music.

Combs began his career at Andre Harrell's Uptown Records. By the age of 18, he was Uptown's head of A&R, and in 1993 he launched his own company, Bad Boy Entertainment. Quickly assembling a pool of talented R&B and hip-hop artists, Bad Boy enjoyed commercial success with artists such as Faith Evans, Craig Mack, Total and the **Notorious B.I.G.**. His involvement in the east coast/west coast gangsta-rap feud, which pitched Combs and the Notorious B.I.G. against 2Pac and Marion 'Suge' Knight's Death Row Records, was an unpleasant distraction from his seemingly unstoppable assault on both the pop and R&B charts. It was the Notorious B.I.G.'s untimely death that led to Combs' international number 1 hit 'I'll Be Missing You', which was based around a hypnotic sample of the **Police**'s 'Every Breath You Take'.

The multi-platinum *No Way Out* preceded a collaboration with Jimmy Page on the old **Led Zeppelin** track 'Kashmir', which was featured on the soundtrack to 1998's remake of *Godzilla*. *Forever* was a less effective album, with Combs' pop nous ultimately swamped by the over-cooked arrangements and gloating raps. Combs' high media profile meant his alleged involvement in a nightclub shooting incident, in December 1999, dominated the music headlines when the case was finally brought to trial in January 2001. He was acquitted in March and bizarrely announced that he was henceforth to be known as P. Diddy, under which name he released a new album in June.

COMMANDER CODY AND HIS LOST PLANET AIRMEN

Country-rock band formed in Michigan, USA, in 1967. The line-up originally featured Commander Cody (b. George Frayne IV, 1944; piano), John Tichy (lead guitar), Steve Schwartz (guitar), Don Bolton aka the West Virginia Creeper (pedal steel), Stephen Davis (bass) and Ralph Mallory (drums), though only Frayne, Tichy and Bolton remained with the group on their move to San Francisco the following year. Their debut, 1971's *Lost In The Ozone*, featured new members Billy C. Farlowe (vocals, harp), Andy Stein (b. 1948; fiddle, saxophone), Billy Kirchen (b. 1948; lead guitar), 'Buffalo' Bruce Barlow (b. 1948; bass) and Lance Dickerson (b. 1948; drums). This earthy collection covered rockabilly, western swing, country and jump R&B. Despite enjoying a US Top 10 single the following year with 'Hot Rod Lincoln', the band's allure began to fade. *Live From Deep In The Heart Of Texas* and *We've Got A Live One*

Here redressed the balance, but individual members grew disillusioned. Tichy's departure preceded an almost total desertion in 1976. The following year Cody released his first solo album, *Midnight Man*, before convening the New Commander Cody Band with Barlow and Black and recording a couple of albums for Arista Records. In later years Cody periodically teamed up with Kirchen's Moonlighters and recorded a couple of low-key albums.

COMMODORES

Formed in Alabama, USA, in 1967 by **Lionel Richie** (b. 1949; keyboards, saxophone, vocals), Thomas McClary (b. 1950; guitar), William King (b. 1949;

trumpet), Andre Callahan (drums), Michael Gilbert (bass) and Milan Williams (b. 1949; keyboards). By 1969, Callahan and Gilbert had been replaced by Walter 'Clyde' Orange (b. 1947) and Ronald LaPread. They relocated to New York and recorded an album for Atlantic Records. Subsequently released as *Rise Up* several years after the band had found fame, it included instrumental covers alongside original material.

In 1972, the Commodores secured a support slot on an American tour with the **Jackson Five**, and were signed to Motown Records. They continued to tour with the Jackson Five for three years, after which they supported the **Rolling Stones**. The instrumental 'Machine Gun' gave them their first US hit, and was followed by a string of transatlantic hits including, 'Slippery When Wet', 'Just To Be Close To You', 'Easy' and 'Too Hot To Trot'. Richie's love song 'Three Times A Lady', became a transatlantic number 1 and helped establish the Commodores as one of the 70s leading soft-soul acts. The follow-up, 'Sail On', introduced a country flavour and Richie began receiving commissions from artists such as **Kenny Rogers**. After 'Still' (1979) gave the Commodores another US pop and soul number 1, they attempted to move into a more experimental blend of funk and rock on *Heroes*, but the album was a commercial failure. This, and Richie's successful duet with **Diana Ross** on 'Endless Love', persuaded him to go solo.

Kevin Smith was brought in to replace Richie, and in 1984 McClary was replaced by English vocalist J. D. Nicholas (b. 1952; ex-**Heatwave**). The new line-up enjoyed a creative and commercial renaissance with the affecting 'Nightshift'. A new contract with Polydor Records prompted the departure of LaPread, and following 'Goin' To The Bank' (1986) the Commodores' hits began to dry up. Now reduced to a trio comprising Orange, King and Nicholas, the Commodores continue to perform to loyal fans around the world. They also manage their own Commodores Records label.

COMMUNARDS

After leaving **Bronski Beat** in 1985, Scottish vocalist Jimmy Somerville (b. 1961) teamed up with classically trained, English pianist Richard Coles (b. 1962) to form the Committee. This was changed to the Communards (borrowed from a 19th-century group of French Republicans). Their disco-styled debut 'You Are My World' reached the UK Top 30, and the follow-up 'Disenchanted' was a minor hit. The duo augmented the line-up with various backing musicians and, in 1986, reached UK number 1 with a revival of **Harold Melvin And The Blue Notes**' 'Don't Leave Me This Way', featuring vocalist Sarah Jane Morris. After 'So Cold The Night', the Communards blazed back into the UK Top 5 with their revival of **Gloria Gaynor**'s 'Never Can Say Goodbye'. Following a few minor hits, Somerville wound down the band's activities and embarked on an intermittently successful solo career.

CONCRETE BLONDE

This Hollywood, USA-based rock band was formed in 1986 by Jim Mankey (guitars), Johnette Napolitano (bass, vocals) and Harry Rushakoff (drums). The trio recorded a self-titled debut for I.R.S. Records. Bass player Alan Bloch joined prior to the recording of *Free*, allowing Napolitano to concentrate on singing. *Bloodletting* was the band's strongest album and saw the introduction of percussionist Paul Thompson (ex-**Roxy Music**). Rushakoff returned to the line-up on 1992's *Walking In London*, which included a female-sung cover version of James Brown's 'It's A Man's Man's Man's World'. *Mexican Moon* included Hispanic influences, and continued the vein of sincere, sassy and seductive rock that made the band such a welcome presence during the late 80s and early 90s. In 1995 Napolitano left to form Vowel Movement and Pretty & Twisted (with Marc Moreland), and the rest of the group decided to disband.

Napolitano and Mankey reunited in 1997 to record *Concrete Blonde Y Los Illegals* with the Los Angeles-based Los Illegals. A more permanent reunion took place in September 2001, when the duo reunited with Rushakoff to play at a benefit concert for the New York Firefighters 9-11 Disaster Relief Fund. A new studio album was released the following January.

CONLEY, ARTHUR

US-born Conley (b. 1946) first recorded as Arthur And The Corvets. He signed to his mentor **Otis Redding**'s Jotis label and released singles on Volt and Stax Records before his 'Sweet Soul Music' (1967) hit the US pop charts. A thin reworking of **Sam Cooke**'s 'Yeah Man' saw the song's original lyrics amended to pay homage to several contemporary soul singers. Although 'Funky Street' was a US Top 20 hit, Redding's tragic death forestalled Conley's progress. Minor successes followed throughout 1968 and 1969 before the singer switched to the Capricorn label in 1971. Later, Conley had a set of recordings for Swamp Dogg released, and then, having relocated to Europe, a live album recorded in Amsterdam in 1980 under his pseudonym of Lee Roberts finally emerged some eight years later.

CONTOURS

Formed as an R&B vocal group in Detroit, USA, in 1959 by Billy Gordon (lead vocals), Billy Hoggs, Joe Billingslea and Sylvester Potts. Hubert Johnson (d. 1981) joined in 1960, and it was his cousin, **Jackie Wilson**, who secured the group a contract with Motown Records. In 1962, 'Do You Love Me'

reached US number 3. Its frantic blend of R&B and the Twist dance craze also powered the following 'Shake Sherry'. Both songs heavily influenced the British beat group scene, with 'Do You Love Me' covered by **Brian Poole And The Tremeloes**, Faron's Flamingos and the **Dave Clark Five**. As the Contours' line-up went through several changes, they had occasional R&B successes with 'Can You Jerk Like Me', Smokey Robinson's 'First I Look At The Purse', and the dance number 'Just A Little Misunderstanding'. Latter-day vocalist Dennis Edwards later enjoyed success with the Temptations.

Despite Johnson's suicide in 1981, a trio consisting of Billingslea, Potts and Jerry Green carried on performing. In 1988, 'Do You Love Me' returned to the US Top 20 on the strength of its inclusion in the movie *Dirty Dancing*. Billingsea and Potts continued into the new millennium, reaping lucrative dates for their revue show and recording a studio album for the Orchard label.

COODER, RY

By age 17, US-born Cooder (b. Ryland Cooder, 1947) was part of a blues act with singer Jackie DeShannon. In 1965, he formed the short-lived Rising Sons with Taj Mahal and drummer Ed Cassidy, before going on to play on sessions with **Paul Revere And The Raiders**, **Captain Beefheart**, **Randy Newman**, **Little Feat** and the **Rolling Stones**, as well as guesting on the soundtracks of *Candy* and *Performance*.

Cooder's 1970 debut album included material by Lead Belly, Sleepy John Estes and Blind Willie Johnson, and offered a patchwork of Americana that became his trademark. The excellent *Into The Purple Valley* and the rather desolate *Boomer's Story* completed Cooder's early trilogy and, in 1974, he released the buoyant *Paradise And Lunch*. *Chicken Skin Music* embraced Tex-Mex and Hawaiian styles and featured Flaco Jiminez and Gabby Pahuini.

Cooder later embraced a more mainstream approach with *Bop Till You Drop*, an ebullient, rhythmic, yet rock-based collection, which featured several R&B standards, including 'Little Sister' and 'Don't Mess Up A Good Thing'. *Borderline* and *The Slide Area* offered similar fare, but such overtly commercial selections contrasted with Cooder's soundtrack work. The music for *The Long Riders*, *Paris, Texas* and *Crossroads* owed much to the spirit of adventure prevalent in his early work.

It was five years before Cooder released an official follow-up to *The Slide Area* and although *Get Rhythm* offered little not already displayed, it re-established a purpose to his rock-based work. In 1992, Cooder joined up with **Nick Lowe**, Jim Keltner and **John Hiatt** to record and perform under the name of Little Village. In the mid-90s he was acclaimed for his successful collaborations with V. M. Bhatt on *A Meeting By the River*, and with Ali Farka Tourè on *Talking Timbuktu*. Further accolades came in 1997 when he worked with obscure Cuban musicians as the Buena Vista Social Club. The project's surprising commercial success was due reward for both Cooder and his new musical cohorts.

COOKE, SAM

Between 1951 and 1956, US-born Cooke (b. Sam Cook, 1931, d. 1964), a former member of the Highway QCs, sang lead with the Soul Stirrers. Cooke's distinctive florid vocal style was soon obvious on 'Touch The Hem Of His Garment' and 'Nearer To Thee'. The Soul Stirrers recorded for the Specialty Records label, where the singer's popularity encouraged producer Robert 'Bumps' Blackwell to provide Cooke with pop material. 'Loveable'/

'Forever' was issued as a single in 1957, disguised under the pseudonym 'Dale Cook' to avoid offending the gospel audience. The follow-up 'You Send Me', released on the Keen label, sold in excess of two million copies and topped the US singles chart for three weeks. Cooke also had the foresight to set up his own publishing company, Kags Music, with J. W. Alexander in 1958.

Cooke left Keen for RCA Records, where original compositions such as 'Chain Gang' (1960), 'Cupid' (1961) and 'Twistin' The Night Away' (1962), displayed a pop craft later offset by such grittier offerings as 'Bring It On Home To Me' and Willie Dixon's 'Little Red Rooster'. Although RCA attempted to market him as a supper-club performer in the tradition of Sammy Davis Jnr. and **Nat 'King' Cole**, Cooke was effectively creating a new style of music – soul – by reworking the gospel anthems that remained at the heart of his music. To promote this new music, Cooke and Alexander founded the SAR and Derby labels, on which the Simms Twins' 'Soothe Me' and the **Valentinos**' 'It's All Over Now' were issued.

On 11 December 1964, following an altercation with a girl he had picked up, the singer was fatally shot by the manageress of a Los Angeles motel. The ebullient 'Shake' became a posthumous hit, but its serene coupling, 'A Change Is Gonna Come', was a more melancholic epitaph. Arguably his finest composition, its title suggested a metaphor for the concurrent Civil Rights movement. Cooke's legacy continued through his various disciples – Johnnie Taylor, who had replaced Cooke in the Soul Stirrers, bore an obvious debt, as did Bobby Womack of the Valentinos. Cooke's songs were interpreted by acts as diverse as **Rod Stewart**, the **Animals** and **Cat Stevens**, while the Rolling Stones' cover version of 'Little Red Rooster' echoed Cooke's reading rather than that of **Howlin' Wolf**. **Otis Redding**, **Aretha Franklin**, **Smokey Robinson** – the list of those acknowledging Cooke's skill is a testimony in itself.

COOLIDGE, RITA
Part-white, part-Cherokee Indian, Coolidge (b. 1944) recorded briefly before becoming a session singer for **Eric Clapton** and **Stephen Stills** among others. Stills wrote a number of songs about her including 'Cherokee', 'The Raven' and 'Sugar Babe'. In 1969–70, Coolidge toured with **Delaney And Bonnie** and Leon Russell (whose 'Delta Lady' was inspired by Coolidge), after which she was signed to A&M Records. Her debut album included the cream of LA session musicians, and was followed by almost annual releases during the 70s. Coolidge also made several albums with **Kris Kristofferson**, to whom she was married between 1973 and 1979. Her hit singles included a cover version of the **Jackie Wilson** hit '(Your Love Has Lifted Me) Higher And Higher' and **Boz Scaggs**' 'We're All Alone'. Coolidge was less active as a recording star in the 80s, although in 1983 she recorded 'All Time High' – the theme to the James Bond movie *Octopussy*. Her recent work, including the Walela recordings with her sister Priscilla Coolidge and her niece Laura Satterfield, has explored her Cherokee roots.

COOLIO
US rapper Coolio (b. Artis Ivey, 1963) started out with WC And The MADD Circle, guesting on their 1991 release, before joining the 40 Thevz. His debut solo release was 'County Line', followed by 1994's US Top 5 hit 'Fantastic Voyage'. *It Takes A Thief* went platinum and established Coolio as one of the leading crossover rap stars. 'Gangsta's Paradise', a resigned lament performed with the gospel singer L.V. and a full choir, went to US and UK number 1 and won a Grammy, in 1996, for Best Rap Solo Performance. *My Soul*, which included the hit single 'C U When U Get There', was another downbeat collection that confirmed Coolio as one of hip-hop's most interesting artists. He subsequently set up his own Crowbar label and concentrated on an acting career.

COPE, JULIAN
Welsh-born Cope (b. 1957) started out in the Crucial Three with Ian McCulloch and Pete Wylie before founding the critically acclaimed **Teardrop Explodes**. Cope went solo in 1984 with *World Shut Your Mouth*. The sleeve of his second album, *Fried*, featured a naked Cope cowering under a turtle shell and commentators drew parallels with rock casualties Roky Erickson and Syd Barrett, both of whom Cope admired A third album, *Skellington*, was rejected by his label, which resulted in Cope switching to Island Records where he enjoyed a UK Top 20 hit with 'World Shut Your Mouth'. *Saint Julian* became his bestselling album, but a tour to promote *My Nation Underground*, was abandoned when he became too ill to continue. Cope bounced back with 1991's *Peggy Suicide*. The album garnered considerable praise but he was dropped from Island after the follow-up *Jehovakill*. Later albums were issued on small labels and the artist retains a healthy cult following. He teamed up with Kevlar and Dogman to form the 'psycho metal supergroup' Brain Donor, who released *Love Peace And Fuck* in 2001.

Cope is also a respected writer, publishing two witty autobiographical volumes, the passionate *Krautrocksampler*, a study of the German 'Krautrock' bands who had such a great musical influence on him, and *The Modern Antiquarian*, a weighty guide to Great Britain's megalithic sites which Cope spent most of the 90s researching.

CORROSION OF CONFORMITY
Mid-80s American hardcore crossover band, originally known as No Labels, formed in North Carolina by Reed Mullin (drums), Woody Weatherman (guitar) and Mike Dean (bass, vocals) in 1982. *Eye For An Eye* and *Animosity* mixed hardcore speed power-riffing with heavy metal. Following the blistering mini-album *Technocracy*, with Simon Bob on vocals, Bob and Dean left. They were replaced by Karl Agell (vocals), Pepper Keenan (guitar, vocals) and Phil Swisher (bass). *Blind*, released in 1991, saw a slower, more melodic, but still fiercely heavy style. The departure of Agell and Swisher slowed the band's momentum. *Deliverance*, with Keenan taking lead vocals and Dean back in place, was a considerable departure from their hardcore musical roots. This image continued to fade as Wiseblood demonstrated an excellent grasp of 70s, heavy rock. After a four-year recording gap they returned in 2000 with *America's Volume Dealer*, once again demonstrating a continuing influence from the Allman Brothers Band and the Marshall Tucker Band.

CORRS
One of Ireland's most successful pop exports of the 90s, family group the Corrs comprise Jim (b. 1964; guitar, keyboards, backing vocals), Sharon (b. 1970; violin, vocals), Caroline (b. 1973; drums, bodhràn, keyboards, vocals) and Andrea (b. 1974; lead vocals, tin whistle). After gigging locally as a duo, Jim and Sharon Corr brought in their younger sisters Caroline and Andrea in order to audition for Alan Parker's 1991 movie *The Commitments*. Andrea secured the role of Jimmy Rabbitte's sister in the film and the others featured in bit parts. A long apprenticeship honing their repertoire, in an attempt to secure an international recording deal, was rewarded in 1994 when they were invited them to play in Boston prior to America's hosting of the soccer World Cup. While in America they signed to Atlantic Records in collaboration with the Lava and 143 labels.

The Corrs' 1995 debut, F*orgiven, Not Forgotten*, was a striking work, deftly combining traditional music with a strong pop sensibility, and enjoyed substantial worldwide sales. By now the foursome's live appearances had won a devoted following, while their model good looks ensured that they were frequently photographed in numerous magazines. Andrea Corr took time off to continue her acting career, appearing alongside **Madonna** in Alan Parker's 1996 film adaptation of *Evita* as Juan Peron's mistress. *Talk On Corners*, although it contained some traditional elements, was a much more pop-orientated album with a broader appeal. A cover version of **Fleetwood Mac**'s 'Dreams', reworked by Todd Terry, provided the Corrs with their Top 10 breakthrough hit in the UK. By June 1998 the previously modest sales of *Talk On Corners* were transformed and the work rose to number 1, going on to become the biggest-selling UK album of 1998. Remixes of 'What Can I Do', 'So Young' and 'Runaway' all reached the UK Top 10. The *MTV Unplugged* collection featured five new tracks, including the single 'Radio'. The unashamedly poppy 'Breathless' preceded *In Blue* during the summer of 2000. Neither broke any new ground, but both topped the UK charts.

COSTELLO, ELVIS

English singer-songwriter Costello (b. Declan McManus, 1954) came to prominence during the 70s at the height of the punk era. His **Nick Lowe**-produced debut, 1977's *My Aim Is True*, saw Costello shouting and crooning through a cornucopia of radical issues, producing a set that was instantly hailed by the critics. The hit single 'Watching The Detectives' contained scathing verses about wife-beating over a beautifully simple reggae beat. His new band, the Attractions (bass player Bruce Thomas, drummer Pete Thomas (b. 1954) and keyboardist Steve Nieve (b. Steven Nason), gave Costello a solid base. The excellent *This Year's Model* confirmed Costello's songwriting acumen and the almighty clout of the Attractions. *Armed Forces* was the breakthrough album, reaching number 1 in the UK and breaking into the US Top 10. 'Oliver's Army', a major hit taken from the album, was a bitter attack on the mercenary soldier, sung over a contrastingly upbeat tune.

By the end of the 70s Costello was firmly established as both performer and songwriter, with **Linda Ronstadt** and Dave Edmunds having success with his compositions. The soul-influenced *Get Happy!!* failed to repeat the sales success of *Armed Forces*, despite being a stronger album. The increasingly fraught nature of the Attractions' recording sessions informed the follow-up, *Trust*, and during the same year Costello elected to relocate to Nashville to record a country covers album, *Almost Blue*, with the Attractions and legendary producer Billy Sherrill. A version of George Jones' 'Good Year For The Roses' became the album's major hit. Released in 1982, *Imperial Bedroom* marked the creative zenith of Costello's early period with the Attractions. That year Robert Wyatt recorded arguably the best-ever interpretation of a Costello song. The superlative 'Shipbuilding' offered an imposingly subtle indictment of the Falklands War, with Wyatt's strained voice giving extra depth to Costello's seamless lyric. The next year Costello, as the Imposter, released 'Pills And Soap', a similar theme cleverly masking a bellicose attack on Thatcherism.

Two lesser albums preceded 1986's rock 'n' roll-influenced *King Of America*, with production from

T-Bone Burnett and guitar contributions from the legendary James Burton, and the introspective *Blood & Chocolate*, which saw Costello reunited with the Attractions and producer Lowe. Later in the decade he collaborated with **Paul McCartney**, co-writing a number of songs for the latter's *Flowers In The Dirt*. His first release for Warner Brothers Records was 1989's eclectic *Spike*. Another mixed bag, *Mighty Like A Rose*, preceded 1993's perplexing collaboration with the classical Brodsky Quartet in 1993. *Brutal Youth* brought him back to critical approbation and reunited him with the Attractions. *All This Useless Beauty* (again with the Attractions), although containing songs offered to or recorded by other artists, was as lyrically sharp as ever.

Costello signed a worldwide deal with PolyGram Records in 1998. Following their collaboration on the track 'God Give Me Strength', featured in the 1996 movie *Grace Of My Heart*, Costello and songwriting legend **Burt Bacharach** joined forces on 1998's *Painted From Memory*, a finely crafted collection of ballads. 'I Still Have That Other Girl' won a 1999 Grammy for Best Pop Collaboration with Vocals. Costello's cover version of Charles Aznavour's 'She' also figured prominently in the Hugh Grant/Julia Roberts film *Notting Hill* and returned the singer to the UK Top 20 in July. The following year he composed the orchestral score for Italian ballet troupe Aterballeto's adaptation of *A Midsummer Night's Dream*. A stirring collaboration with opera singer Anne Sofie Von Otter in 2001 preceded a new 'pop' album, *When I Was Cruel*.

COUNTING CROWS

California, USA-based adult rock band formed by Adam Duritz (b. 1965; vocals), David Bryson (b. 1961; guitar), Mat Malley (b. 1963; bass), Steve Bowman (drums) and Charles Gillingham (b. 1960; keyboards). Their well-received 1993 debut album, produced by T-Bone Burnett, mixed traditional rock and R&B elements with Duritz's raw delivery. The MTV rotation of 'Mr. Jones' undoubtedly augmented sales, as did critical reaction. By mid-1994 their debut had reached multi-platinum status, but at this point founding member Bowman departed to join Third Eye Blind. Ben Mize (b. 1971) and Dan Vickrey (guitar, mandolin) featured on *Recovering The Satellites*, which debuted at US number 1 in 1996. The stopgap live set, *Across A Wire: Live In New York*, reached the US Top 20 two years later. *This Desert Life* was a return to form, with the loose swagger of tracks such as 'Hanginaround' and 'Mrs Potter's Lullabye' attaining an effortless peak.

COUNTRY JOE AND THE FISH

Formed in 1965 as the Instant Action Jug Band, this popular US psychedelic band revolved around former folk singer Country Joe McDonald (b. 1942) and guitarist Barry Melton (b. 1947), the only musicians to remain in the line-up throughout its history. Their earliest recording, 'I Feel Like I'm Fixin' To Die Rag' (1965), was a virulent attack on the Vietnam War. In 1966, the expanded line-up – McDonald, Melton, David Cohen (guitar, keyboards), Paul Armstrong (bass) and John Francis Gunning (drums) – embraced electric rock with a privately pressed EP. Armstrong and Gunning were soon replaced by Bruce Barthol and Gary 'Chicken' Hirsh. This reshaped quintet recorded *Electric Music For The Mind And Body*, followed by *I-Feel-Like-I'm-Fixin'-To-Die*. Beset by internal problems, the band's third album *Here We Are Again* was completed by various musicians, including Peter Albin and Dave Getz. Mark Kapner (keyboards), Doug Metzner (bass) and Greg Dewey (drums), joined McDonald and Melton in 1969. The new line-up was responsible for the fiery final album, *C.J. Fish*.

The 'classic' line-up, which appeared on the band's first three albums, was briefly reunited between 1976 and 1977 but the resultant release, *Reunion*, was a disappointment. McDonald continues to delight old folkies and hippies and is always a popular attraction at outdoor festivals. Melton has recorded

several albums under his own name and performs with the San Francisco 'supergroup' the Dinosaurs.

COVAY, DON

US-born Covay (b. Donald Randolph, 1938) started out in his family's gospel quartet. He crossed to secular music with the Rainbows, a group that included **Marvin Gaye**, and his solo career began in 1957 as part of the **Little Richard** revue. On 'Bip Bop Bip' Covay was billed as 'Pretty Boy'. His original version of 'Pony Time' lost out to **Chubby Checker**'s version, but a further dance-oriented offering, 'The Popeye Waddle' (1962), was a hit. Solomon Burke recorded Covay's 'I'm Hanging Up My Heart For You' and **Gladys Knight And The Pips** reached the US Top 20 with 'Letter Full Of Tears'. 'See-Saw', co-written with Steve Cropper, paved the way for other exceptional singles, including 'Sookie Sookie' and 'Iron Out The Rough Spots' (both 1966). Covay's ill-fated Soul Clan (with Solomon Burke, Wilson Pickett, Joe Tex and Ben E. King) ended after one single, but his songs remained successful – **Aretha Franklin** won a Grammy Award for her performance of 'Chain Of Fools'.

Covay switched to Janus in 1971, and from there moved to Mercury Records, where he combined recording with A&R duties. Further releases appeared on Philadelphia International Records (1976), U-Von Records (1977) and Newman Records (1980), but while **Randy Crawford** and **Bonnie Raitt** resurrected his songs, Covay's own career continued to slide downhill. In 1993, the Rhythm & Blues Foundation honoured the singer-songwriter with one of its prestigious Pioneer Awards. Covay, unfortunately, was by then suffering the after-effects of a stroke. He returned to the studio at the end of the decade to record his first new album in over 25 years.

COWBOY JUNKIES

Canadians Michael Timmins (b. 1959; guitar) and Alan Anton (b. Alan Alizojvodic, 1959; bass) formed a number of unsuccessful bands before joining forces with Timmins' sister Margo (b. 1961; vocals) and brother Peter (b. 1965; drums). Calling themselves the Cowboy Junkies, they recorded 1986's *Whites Off Earth Now!!* in a private house. *The Trinity Session* was recorded with one microphone in the Church of Holy Trinity, Toronto for $250. It sold 250,000 copies in North America, largely by word-of-mouth. Michael Timmins' understated guitar alongside Margo's eerie vocals have found favour with a rock audience, and the extent of their fast-growing reputation was sufficient for them to promote the 1992 album *Black Eyed Man* at London's Royal Albert Hall. Two major-label releases followed in the mid-90s, but the band had firmly settled into such a distinctive style that it was hard to see how they could

expand their appeal to reach a wider audience. The live *Waltz Across America* documents highlights from their 1999/2000 North American tour.

COYNE, KEVIN

A former art student, psychiatric therapist and social worker, Coyne (b. 1944) pursued a singing career in English pubs and clubs, later joining London-based Siren. Coyne left the band in 1972 to complete his promising solo debut, *Case History*. His Virgin Records' debut, *Marjory Razor Blade*, emphasized Coyne's idiosyncratic talent, with his guttural country-blues delivery highlighting his lyrically raw compositions. Coyne constructed the self-effacing *Blame It On The Night* before forming a group around Zoot Money (keyboards), Andy Summers (guitar), Steve Thompson (bass) and Peter Wolf (drums) to promote *Matching Head And Feet*. This line-up also recorded *Heartburn* and were captured on the live *In Living Black And White* before being disbanded for cost purposes.

Coyne's work was not out of place in the punk era, while *Babble*, a concept album recorded in collaboration with vocalist Dagmar Krause, was a triumph. Following a nervous breakdown in 1981, Coyne parted company with Virgin. His recordings for Cherry Red Records, including *Pointing The Finger* and *Politicz*, showed an undiminished fire. In 1985 Coyne left London to base himself in Nuremberg, Germany. He formed the Paradise Band and continued to release fiercely independent records in tandem with a successful painting career. In 1993 he recorded *Tough And Sweet*, featuring his sons Robert and Eugene as backing musicians. Coyne has also developed a successful writing career, including three publications in German.

CRACKER

A rowdy update of the 70s Californian folk-rock fraternity, Cracker was formed by David Lowery (b. 1960) and guitarist Johnny Hickman following the break-up in 1989 of the former's previous band, **Camper Van Beethoven**. Their 1992 self-titled debut featured Davey Faragher (bass) and session men Jim Keltner (drums) and Benmont Tench (keyboards). Melding influences as diverse as psychedelia, country rock and delta blues, the album went on to sell over 20,000 copies. *Kerosene Hot* included the alternative rock hit 'Low', which was promoted by a stunning black-and-white video featuring Lowery boxing Sandra Bernhardt.

Faragher was replaced by Bob Rupe (ex-Silos) following the recording of *Kerosene Hat*. Three years in the making, *The Golden Age*'s move towards a more polished country-rock sound indicated Cracker's future direction, although the follow-up *Gentleman's Blues* proved to be a career high point of sorts. Brandy Wood was brought into the line-up in 1999 to replace the departing Rupe.

CRADLE OF FILTH

This outlandish band quickly became the most popular UK representatives of the Satanic black-metal revival of the early 90s. Formed in 1991 by Daniel Davey aka Dani Filth (b. 1973; vocals), John Richard (bass), Paul Ryan (guitar) and Darren (drums), the band went through the several line-up changes before the release of their 1994 debut, with Robin Eaglestone aka Robin Graves (bass), Paul Allender (guitar), Benjamin Ryan (keyboards) and Nicholas Barker (drums) added to the line-up. Visually, Cradle Of Filth adopted the black-and-white make-up known as 'corpse-paint' and funereal garb, while incorporating displays of fire-breathing and drenching themselves in blood on stage.

Following the release of their debut the band entered a tumultuous phase, with the loss of several members and problems with management and their record label. They eventually regrouped in 1996 for the mini-album *Vempire: Dark Faerytales In Phallustein*, by which time the line-up incorporated founding members Filth and Robin Graves, as well as Irish keyboard player Damien Gregori and guitarists Stuart Anstis and Jared Demeter. Their third

studio set, *Dusk ... And Her Embrace*, was released on the Music For Nations label. The album featured new guitarist Gian Pyres, who was brought in to replace Demeter. Gregori was subsequently replaced by Les 'Lecter' Smith, while Sargison and then Adrian Erlandsson replaced Barker on the *From The Cradle To Enslave* E.P. Martin Powell (ex-My Dying Bride) replaced Smith and Allender rejoined on the full-length *Midian*. The stop-gap mini-album *Bitter Suites To Succubi* was the band's last on an independent label, having recently signed to Sony Records.

CRAMER, FLOYD

Cramer (b. 1933, d. 1997), a vastly experienced Nashville session player, worked with Jim Reeves, **Elvis Presley**, Chet Atkins, **Patsy Cline**, **Roy Orbison** and Kitty Lester. His delicate rock 'n' roll sound was highlighted in his first major hit, 'Last Date' (1960). Other notable US hits included 'On The Rebound' and 'New San Antonio Rose'. In 1980, he had a major hit with the theme from television soap *Dallas*. Sadly, Cramer died from cancer in December 1997.

CRAMPS

Formed in Ohio, USA, in 1976, the original Cramps – Lux Interior (b. Erick Lee Purkhiser; vocals), 'Poison' Ivy Rorschach (b. Kirsty Marlana Wallace; guitar), Bryan Gregory (d. 2001; guitar) and his sister, Pam Balam (drums) – moved to New York and joined the emergent punk scene. Miriam Linna briefly replaced Balam, before Nick Knox (b. Nick Stephanoff) became their permanent drummer. Their first singles and debut album blended the frantic rush of rockabilly with 60s garage-band panache. Bryan Gregory departed suddenly after 'Drug Train' and Kid Congo (Powers) (b. Brian Tristan; ex-Gun Club) appeared on 1981's *Psychedelic Jungle*, but later rejoined his former band. The Cramps subsequently employed several, often female, replacements including Fur and Candy Del Mar.

Wary of outside manipulation, the Cramps continue to steer their own course by touring and recording, proving themselves the masters of their particular (limited) genre. In 1991 *Interior and Rorschach* re-emerged fronting a rejuvenated line-up with Slim Chance (bass) and Jim Sclavunos (drums). *Flamejob*, released in 1994, showed that the band had become virtually a pantomime act, a fact that their most recent album sadly confirmed.

CRANBERRIES

Dolores O'Riordan (b. 1971; vocals), Noel Hogan (b. 1971; guitar), his brother Mike (b. 1973; bass) and Feargal Lawler (b. 1971; drums), who emanate from Limerick, Eire, were originally named The Cranberry Saw Us. Their debut EP, *Uncertain*, was released in 1991 on the Xeric label, following which they signed a major-label deal with Island Records. *Everybody Else Is Doing It, So Why Can't We?* sold well in the UK, but it was in the US that the band became a hot prospect thanks to the radio success of the singles 'Dreams' and 'Linger'. The follow-up, *No Need To Argue*, featured the hit single 'Zombie', but *To The Faithful Departed* was less well-received with O'Riordan's lyrics drawing particular criticism. After an extended hiatus, the band returned with 1999's *Bury The Hatchet*, which struggled to reassert their commercial and critical status.

CRASH TEST DUMMIES

Canadian band formed in the late 80s by Brad Roberts (b. 1964; vocals, guitar), his younger brother Dan (b. 1967; bass), Benjamin Darvill (b. 1967; mandolin, harmonica, guitar), Ellen Reid (b. 1966; keyboards, accordion, vocals) and Vince Lambert (drums). Their 1991 debut, *The Ghosts That Haunt Me*, rose to Canadian number 1 on the back of the hit single 'Superman's Song'. *God Shuffled His Feet* introduced new drummer Michel Dorge (b. 1960) and was co-produced by **Talking Heads**' Jerry Harrison. Their breakthrough arrived with the quirky single 'Mmmm Mmmm Mmmm', which reached US number 12 in 1994 and was also a big European hit. Indifferent songs blighted *A Worm's Life* and *Give Yourself A Hand*, and both collections failed to sell.

In 2000, Roberts released a solo acoustic collection and suffered a near-fatal automobile accident. He spent time with a group of lobster fishermen, recuperating and contemplating one of his favourite subjects: the meaning of life. Feeling rejuvenated he assembled an all-new line-up of the Crash Test Dummies and released the impressive *I Don't Care That You Don't Mind*.

CRAWFORD, RANDY

US vocalist Randy Crawford (b. Veronica Crawford, 1952) was a regular performer at Cincinnati's nightclubs. After moving to New York, she began singing with jazz musicians, including George Benson and Cannonball Adderley. She was signed to Warner Brothers Records as a solo act, but achieved fame as the (uncredited) voice on 'Street Life', a major hit for the Crusaders in 1979. Crawford toured extensively with the group, whose pianist, Joe Sample, provided her with 'Now We May Begin', a beautiful ballad that established the singer's independent career.

As a soloist, Crawford enjoyed further successes with 'One Day I'll Fly Away' (UK number 2), 'You Might Need Somebody' and 'Rainy Night in Georgia' (both UK Top 20 hits) and her 1981 album *Secret Combination*. After a five-year respite, she returned in 1986 with the haunting UK Top 5 hit 'Almaz'. Curiously, this soulful, passionate singer has found greater success in the UK than in her homeland, and her 1989 album *Rich And Poor* was recorded in London. By the new millennium, Crawford was to be found fronting the gospel group the Kingsmen.

CRAY, ROBERT

US guitarist Cray (b. 1953) plays a mixture of pure blues, soul and rock. Although he formed his first band in 1974, it was not until 1983's *Bad Influence* that Cray's name became widely known (his debut, *Who's Been Talkin'*, failed when the record label folded). The Robert Cray Band, featuring Richard Cousins (bass), Dave Olson (drums) and Peter Boe (keyboards), made a significant breakthrough into the mainstream with 1987's *Strong Persuader*, which became the most successful blues album for over two decades. The superb *Don't Be Afraid Of The Dark* followed. *Midnight Stroll* featured a new line-up that gave Cray a tougher-sounding unit and moved him out of mainstream

blues towards R&B and soul. *Some Rainy Morning* was Cray's vocal album, accentuating his mature, sweet voice. *Sweet Potato Pie* featured the Memphis Horns on a cover of 'Trick Or Treat'. Cray moved to Rykodisc Records for 1999's *Take Your Shoes Off*, a loose-limbed and funky affair that was, to all intents and purposes, a soul record. *Shoulda Been Home* moved even further away from the blues and was a pure southern soul recording, with Cray putting his guitar aside and concentrating on his singing.

CRAZY HORSE

Crazy Horse evolved in 1969 when **Neil Young** invited Americans Danny Whitten (d. 1972; guitar) and Billy Talbot (bass), and Puerto Rican Ralph Molina (drums), all formerly of Laurel Canyon-based the Rockets, to accompany him on his second album, *Everybody Knows This Is Nowhere*. The impressive results inspired a tour, but although the band also contributed to Young's *After The Goldrush*, their relationship was sundered in the light of Whitten's growing drug dependency. *Crazy Horse*, completed with the assistance of Jack Nitzsche and **Nils Lofgren**, featured several notable performances, including the emotional 'I Don't Want To Talk About It', later revived by **Rod Stewart** and Everything But The Girl.

After Whitten died from a heroin overdose, Talbot and Molina kept Crazy Horse afloat with various members, but neither *Loose* or *At Crooked Lake* compared with their excellent debut. Reunited with Young for the mid-70s releases *Tonight's The Night* and *Zuma*, and buoyed by the arrival of American guitarist Frank 'Poncho' Sampedro, Crazy Horse reclaimed its independence with the excellent *Crazy Moon*. Their role as the ideal foil to Young's ambitions was amply proved on two blistering 1979 albums, *Rust Never Sleeps* and *Live Rust*, and each member continued to work on his

albums during the 80s. The disappointing Young/Crazy Horse collaboration *Life* was released in 1987, following which Molina, Talbot and new members Matt Piucci (guitar, vocals) and Sonny Mone (guitar) recorded the lacklustre Crazy Horse album *Left For Dead*. Molina and Talbot reunited with Sampredo and Young on two back-to-form releases, *Ragged Glory* (1991) and *Sleeps With Angels* (1994), and enjoyed further joint billing with Ian McNabb on some tracks on his excellent 1994 album *Head Like A Rock*. Crazy Horse continued to work with Young on a regular basis during the rest of the 90s and into the new millennium.

CRAZY TOWN

This Los Angeles, USA-based rapcore outfit was formed by rappers Shifty Shellshock (b. Seth Brooks Binzer, 1974) and Epic (b. Bret Mazur), guitarists Rust Epique and Trouble (b. Antonio Lorrenzo Valli), bass player Faydoedeelay (b. Doug Miller, 1976), drummer JBJ (b. James Bradley Jnr.), and DJ A.M. (b. Adam Goldstein). Mazur had worked as a producer on the underground scene for almost a decade, and originally teamed up with Binzer in the

Brimstone Sluggers. Their 1999 debut *The Gift Of Game* marked them out as one of the few acts to emerge from the metal/hip-hop crossover scene to actually sound more convincing as rappers than rockers. Rust Epique was replaced by Squirrel (b. Krayge Tyler) the following year, during which *The Gift Of Game* began its steady rise up the US charts, buoyed by the radio success of nu-metal anthems 'Toxic' and 'Butterfly'. The latter reached the top of the *Billboard* singles chart in March 2001.

CREAM

This legendary UK trio was formed in July 1966 by **Jack Bruce** (b. John Symon Asher, 1943; bass, vocals), **Eric Clapton** (b. Eric Patrick Clapp, 1945; guitar) and **Ginger Baker** (b. Peter Baker, 1939; drums). Cream were promoted in the music press as a pop group, with Clapton from **John Mayall**'s Blues-breakers, Bruce from Graham Bond's Organisation and briefly **Manfred Mann**, and Baker from the Graham Bond Organisation via **Alexis Korner**'s Blues Incorporated. Baker and Bruce had originally played together in the Johnny Burch Octet in 1962.

Cream's debut single, 'Wrapping Paper', made the lower reaches of the UK charts and was followed by 'I Feel Free', which unleashed such energy that it could only be matched by **Jimi Hendrix**. The excellent *Fresh Cream* preceeded *Disraeli Gears*, which firmly established Cream in the USA. Landmark songs such as 'Sunshine Of Your Love' and 'Strange Brew' established the trio as one of the leading attractions of their era. One disc of the two-record set *Wheels Of Fire* captured Cream live, at their inventive and exploratory best. While it sat on top of the US charts in 1968, they announced they would disband at the end of the year, after two final concerts. The famous Royal Albert Hall farewell concerts were captured on film. The posthumous *Goodbye* repeated the success of its predecessors.

Clapton and Baker went on to play together in the short-lived **Blind Faith** before, like Bruce before them, establishing solo careers, with the former going on to become one of rock's leading artists. The three members re-formed in 1993 for a one-off performance at the Rock And Roll Hall Of Fame awards in New York.

CREATION

This UK mod/pop-art act grew from beat group, the Mark Four. Kenny Pickett (b. Kenny Lee, 1942, d. 1997; vocals), Eddie Phillips (lead guitar), Mick Thompson (rhythm guitar), John Dalton (bass) and Jack Jones (drums) completed four singles under this appellation before Dalton left (for the **Kinks**) and Thompson abandoned music. Bob Garner (ex-**Merseybeats**) joined and the band became Creation. Their early singles, 'Making Time' and 'Painter Man', offered the same propulsive power as the **Who**, while Phillips' distinctive bowed-guitar sound was later popularized by **Jimmy Page**. Unfortunately, clashes between Pickett and Garner caused the singer's departure in 1967 and, although several strong records followed, they lacked the impact of earlier recordings. The band split up in February 1968, but re-formed in March around Pickett, Jones, Kim Gardner (b. 1946, d. 2001; bass) and Ron Wood (b. 1947; guitar). This realignment proved temporary and, impromptu reunions apart, Creation broke up in June 1968.

After 25 years, Pickett, Garner, Phillips and Jones re-formed the band

and made a live album, *Lay The Ghost*, followed by an all-new album (issued on Creation Records) in 1996. Pickett died the following year.

CREED

This US rock band was formed by Scott Stapp (b. 1973; vocals), Mark Tremonti (b. 1974; guitar, vocals), Brian Marshall (b. 1974; bass) and Scott Phillips (b. 1973; drums). Released in August 1998, their debut *My Own Prison*, quickly made an impact on the US *Billboard* charts, after initially being released independently six months earlier. The album reached a peak position of 22 on the US album chart, but by now the band had built up a massive live following. The follow-up, *Human Clay*, debuted at US number 1 in October 1999. Marshall left the band in August 2000, shortly before the comparatively gentle 'With Arms Wide Open' completed its long haul up the US charts to the number 1 position. The track helped raised funds for the charity of the same name. The band's third album, *Weathered*, debuted at number 1 on the US charts in December 2001, confirming Creed as one of the leading rock bands of the new millennium.

CREEDENCE CLEARWATER REVIVAL

This US rock band began performing together in 1959 as the Blue Velvets, but were renamed the Golliwogs in the mid-60s to capitalize on the current 'British Invasion'. The quartet, John Fogerty (b. 1945; guitar, vocals), Tom Fogerty (b. 1941, d. 1990; rhythm guitar, vocals), Stu Cook (b. 1945; bass) and Doug Clifford (b. 1945; drums), turned fully professional in 1967 and became Creedence Clearwater Revival.

Their debut album reflected a musical crossroads. Revamped Golliwogs tracks and new John Fogerty originals slotted alongside several rock 'n' roll standards, including 'Suzie-Q' (US number 11) and 'I Put A Spell On You'. *Bayou Country* was a more substantial affair and 'Proud Mary' reached US/UK Top 10 and went gold. More importantly, it introduced the mixture of southern Creole styles, R&B and rockabilly, through which the best of the band's work was filtered. *Green River* contained two highly successful singles, 'Green River' and 'Bad Moon Rising' (the latter reached UK number 1). They reached a peak with *Willie And The Poor Boys* and *Cosmo's Factory*. The latter included three gold singles – 'Travelin' Band', 'Up Around The Bend' and 'Looking Out My Back Door' – as well as an elongated reading of 'I Heard It Through The Grapevine'. The album deservedly became 1970's bestselling set. Relationships between the Fogerty brothers grew increasingly strained, reflected in the disappointing *Pendulum*. Although it featured their eighth gold single in 'Have You Ever Seen The Rain', the set lacked the intensity of its predecessors. Tom Fogerty went solo in 1971 and, although the remaining members continued to work as a trio, the band had lost much of its impetus. Creedence Clearwater Revival was officially disbanded in 1972.

John Fogerty began an erratic path dogged by legal and contractual disputes, although he deservedly re-emerged in 1985 with the US chart-topper *Centrefield*. Tom Fogerty left the music business in the early 80s to work in real estate, but died from tuberculosis in 1990. In 1993 the band were inducted into the Rock And Roll Hall Of Fame, although the animosity between Fogerty, Clifford and Cook was clearly evident. The dispute flared up again in 1998 when Clifford and Cook began touring as Creedence Clearwater

Revisited, with former **Cars** guitarist Elliot Easton and vocalist John Tristano included in the line-up. A live album was issued as John Fogerty attempted to stop Clifford and Cook from using the Creedence name.

CRENSHAW, MARSHALL

After portraying **John Lennon** in the stage show *Beatlemania*, Crenshaw (b. 1954) forged a solo career as a performer of the classic urban-American pop song. With an echo-laden guitar sound that harked back to the 60s, Crenshaw performed alongside his brother Robert (drums, vocals) and Chris Donato (bass, vocals). Their 1982 debut album contained Crenshaw's US hit 'Someday, Someway'. A lean period was relieved in 1986 by the success of Owen Paul's UK Top 5 cover of his 'My Favourite Waste Of Time'.

Crenshaw made film appearances in *Peggy Sue Got Married* and *La Bamba* (portraying **Buddy Holly**). Further album releases were acclaimed and, in the 90s, Crenshaw guested on tribute albums for **Nilsson**, **Arthur Alexander** and **Merle Haggard**, and contributed to the Gin Blossoms' 'Til I Hear It From You'. He broke a five-year silence with a new album in 1996, but this and ensuing releases remained strictly cult items.

CREW-CUTS

Formed in Toronto, Canada, in 1952, the Crew-Cuts were a white vocal quartet that achieved 50s success by covering black R&B songs. Their version of the Chords' 'Sh-Boom' stayed at US number 1 for nine weeks during 1954 and helped to usher in the rock 'n' roll era. The group featured Rudi Maugeri (b. 1931; baritone), Pat Barrett (b. 1931; tenor), John Perkins (b. 1931; lead) and his brother Ray (b. 1932; bass). Initially called the Canadaires, the group received its first break in the USA, where they appeared on Gene Carroll's television programme. Their first recording for Mercury Records, an original composition 'Crazy 'Bout Ya Baby', made the US Top 10. In addition to 'Sh-Boom', other Top 10 placings during 1955 were 'Earth Angel', 'Ko Ko Mo (I Love You So)' and 'Gum Drop'. The Crew-Cuts had further chart singles before moving to RCA Records in 1958. They disbanded in 1963.

CRICKETS

US group who backed **Buddy Holly** and continued to record and tour after his death. In addition to Holly, the original members were Jerry Allison (b. 1939; drums), Joe B. Mauldin (bass) and Niki Sullivan (guitar). When Holly was signed to Decca Records in 1957, it was decided that their Nashville-produced tracks should be released under two names, as Holly solo items (on Coral Records) and as the Crickets (on Brunswick Records). 'That'll Be The Day', credited to the Crickets, was their first number 1. Other Crickets' successes, with Holly on lead vocals, included 'Oh Boy', 'Maybe Baby' and 'Think It Over'. When Holly went solo in 1958, the Crickets did not accompany him on his final tour. Allison and producer Norman Petty had already begun recording independently, issuing 'Love's Made A Fool Of You' with Earl Sinks on lead vocals. On the later singles 'Peggy Sue Got Married' and 'More Than I Can Say' Sinks was replaced by Sonny Curtis (b. 1937; guitar, vocals).

'More Than I Can Say' was a hit for **Bobby Vee**, and in 1961 the Crickets moved to Vee's label, Liberty Records, recording an album with him the following year. Glen D. Hardin (b. 1939; piano) and Jerry Naylor (b. Jerry Naylor Jackson, 1939; vocals) joined at this point. The group also released a series of singles

between 1962 and 1965. These made little impact in the USA but 'Please Don't Ever Change' (a **Carole King/Gerry Goffin** number) and 'My Little Girl' were UK Top 20 hits.

There followed a five-year hiatus as Curtis and Allison worked as song-writers and session musicians. They were persuaded to re-form the Crickets in 1970, to record a rock revival album for the Barnaby label. This led to a contract with Mercury Records and an album containing mostly original country rock-style songs. During the 80s, Allison led the band for revival tours and he returned to recording in 1986 with original bass player Mauldin and newcomer Gordon Payne on guitar and vocals, releasing *Three-Piece* on Allison's own Rollercoaster label. During the 90s, the Crickets worked with **Nanci Griffith** and released a new studio album, *Too Much Monday Morning*, on the Carlton Records label.

CROCE, JIM

US musician Croce (b. 1943, d. 1973) played in various rock bands before moving into the New York folk circuit in 1967. By 1969, he and his wife Ingrid (b. 1947) were signed to Capitol Records for *Approaching Day*. Meanwhile, he continued with songwriting and secured a new contract with ABC Records. The title track to 1972's *You Don't Mess Around With Jim* was a US Top 10 hit. In July 1973, Croce topped the US charts with 'Bad, Bad Leroy Brown', but two months later he died in a plane crash at Natchitoches, Louisiana, along with guitarist Maury Mulheisen. Posthumously, he reached the US Top 10 with 'I Got A Name', which featured in the movie *The Last American Hero*. The contemplative 'Time In A Bottle' was released in late 1973 and reached US number 1. It was a fitting valediction. During 1974, further releases kept Croce's name in the US charts, including 'I'll Have To Say I Love You In A Song' and 'Workin' At The Car Wash Blues'. His son A. J. Croce began his own recording career in the 90s.

CROPPER, STEVE

A founder-member of the **Mar-Keys**, US guitarist Cropper (b. 1941) worked with several groups, the most successful of which was the Stax Records' house band **Booker T. And The MGs**. Cropper's songwriting and arranging skills were prevalent on many classic Stax performances, including 'Knock On Wood' (**Eddie Floyd**), 'In The Midnight Hour' (Wilson Pickett) and '(Sittin' On) The Dock Of The Bay' (**Otis Redding**).

Following the break-up of Booker T. And The MGs at the start of the 70s, Cropper recorded a solo album, *With A Little Help From My Friends*. After a period spent running his Memphis-based TMI studio, he relocated to Los Angles and became an in-demand session musician, featuring prominently on **Rod Stewart**'s hit album *Atlantic Crossing*. The surviving MGs were reunited following the death of drummer Al Jackson, and have since pursued a part-time schedule. Cropper also recorded with the **Blues Brothers**, although he has continued to maintain a low profile as a solo artist.

Cropper's distinctive sparse, clipped, high treble sound with his Fender Telecaster has been heard on many hundreds of singles and albums. His reluctance to hog the limelight cannot disguise the fact that he is one of the major figures in vintage soul music, both as a composer and guitarist.

CROSBY, DAVID

Hailing from a high-society Hollywood family, Crosby (b. 1941) dropped out of acting school in the early 60s to concentrate on singing. Towards the end of 1963, Crosby demoed several songs, but failing to secure a record deal, Crosby met two like-minded rock 'n' roll enthusiasts: Jim McGuinn and

Gene Clark. After forming the Jet Set, they systematically refined their unusual style for mass consumption. With the arrival of bass player Chris Hillman and drummer Michael Clarke, the Jet Set became the **Byrds**. Crosby remained with them for three years, and his rhythm guitar work, arranging skills and superb harmonic ability greatly contributed to their international success. However, his outspokenness and domineering tendencies resulted in his dismissal in 1967.

After a sabbatical in which he produced **Joni Mitchell**'s debut album, Crosby resurfaced as part of **Crosby, Stills And Nash**. Crosby wrote some of their most enduring songs including 'Guinnevere', 'Long Time Gone' and 'Déjà Vu'. During their peak period he finally recorded his solo album, *If I Could Only Remember My Name*. An extraordinary work, it was essentially a mood piece, with Crosby using guitar and vocal lines to superb effect. There were also a number of choral experiments, culminating in the eerie Gregorian chanting of 'I'd Swear There Was Somebody Here'.

Crosby continued to work with Graham Nash, Stephen Stills and Neil Young in various permutations but by the end of the decade he was alone, playing before small audiences and dependent upon heroin. In 1980, a completed album was rejected by Capitol Records and Crosby began to rely even more severely on drugs. A series of arrests for firearm offences and cocaine possession forced him into a drug rehabilitation centre but he absconded, only to be arrested again. He was imprisoned in 1985. A year later, he emerged corpulent and clean, and engaged in a flurry of recording activity with former colleagues. The decade ended with the release of a second solo album, *Oh Yes I Can*, and a strong-selling autobiography, *Long Time Gone*.

In the early 90s, Crosby worked with Stills and Nash and recorded the slick *Thousand Roads* with **Phil Collins**. In the mid-90s, with his drug-taking days well behind him, the man who had courted death so many times was given his ninth life with a new kidney. A worthy live album was issued during his convalescence in 1995 and he further celebrated being alive with the birth of a child in May that year. In August 2001 Crosby, together with his new band CPR, featuring Jeff Pevar and Crosby's long-lost son James Raymond, celebrated his 60th birthday. This landmark was one that few would have expected him to reach.

CROSBY, STILLS AND NASH

David Crosby (b. 1941; ex-**Byrds**) and **Stephen Stills** (b. 1945; ex-**Buffalo Springfield**) joined Englishman Graham Nash (b. 1942; ex-**Hollies**) in 1969.

Their eponymous debut album was a superlative achievement, containing several of the individual members' finest songs: 'Long Time Gone', 'Suite: Judy Blue Eyes', 'Lady Of The Island' and 'Wooden Ships'. Strong lyrics, solid acoustic musicianship and staggeringly faultless three-part harmonies were the mixture that they concocted and it influenced a generation of American performers. The need to perform live convinced them to extend their ranks and, with **Neil Young**, they reached an even bigger international audience as **Crosby, Stills, Nash And Young**.

Internal bickering and policy differences split the band at its peak, and although Crosby And Nash proved a successful offshoot, the power of the original trio was never forgotten. It was not until 1977 that the original trio reunited for *CSN*, a strong comeback with highlights including 'Shadow Captain', 'Dark Star' and 'Cathedral'. They toured the USA and seemed totally united, but subsequent recording sessions proved unsatisfactory and they drifted apart once more. Five years passed, during which Crosby's drug abuse alienated him from his colleagues. Stills and Nash set about recording an album, but were eventually persuaded by Atlantic Records' founder Ahmet Ertegun to bring back Crosby. He returned late in the sessions and although his contribution was not major, he did proffer one of the strongest tracks, 'Delta'. The resulting *Daylight Again* was disproportionately balanced, but the songs were nevertheless good and re-established the trio as one of the major concert attractions of the day.

Following a European tour, the trio splintered again, with Crosby incapacitated by cocaine addiction. Upon his release from prison, he reunited Crosby, Stills, Nash And Young for an album and took Crosby, Stills And Nash on the road. Unfortunately, *Live It Up*, their first recording as a trio in 10 years, was disappointing. Live concerts in the 90s and the new millennium underlined their continuing strength, although *After The Storm* was another poor studio set.

CROSBY, STILLS, NASH AND YOUNG

David Crosby (b. 1941), **Stephen Stills** (b. 1945) and Englishman Graham Nash (b. 1942) first came together in **Crosby, Stills And Nash** before recruiting Canadian Neil Young (b. 1945). The quartet appeared at Woodstock and established a format of playing two sets, one acoustic and one electric. Instant superstars, their *Déjà Vu*, was one of the biggest sellers of 1970 and included some of their finest material from a time when they were at their most inventive; there was even a US Top 10 single with their reading of **Joni Mitchell**'s 'Woodstock'.

In 1970, four demonstrators at Kent State University were shot and killed by National Guardsmen. Young wrote the protest song 'Ohio' as a result. Recorded within 24 hours of its composition, the song captured the foursome at their most musically aggressive and politically relevant. A series of concerts produced the double set *Four Way Street*, but by the time of its release in 1971 the four members had scattered to pursue solo projects.

Their cultural and commercial clout deemed it inconceivable that the quartet would not reconvene and, during 1974, they undertook a stadium tour. A second studio album, *Human Highway* was shelved prior to completion. Two years later, the Stills/Young Band appeared, a short-lived venture which floundered in acrimony and misunderstanding. By the late 70s, the Crosby, Stills, Nash And Young concept had lost its appeal to punk-influenced music critics who regarded their political idealism as naïve and their technical perfection as elitist and clinical.

In 1988, the quartet reunited for *American Dream*, a good comeback which contained some strong material including the sardonic title track, Crosby's 'Compass' and Nash's 'Soldiers Of Peace'. The

quartet regrouped once more in the late 90s to record material that was finally released on 1999's *Looking Forward*. The reviews were surprisingly favourable, and the album made a good showing in both the UK and USA. 'Stand And Be Counted' and 'No Tears Left', were a reminder that the quartet could still sing well, play like demons and above all, still rock.

CROSS, CHRISTOPHER

US singer Cross (b. Christopher Geppert, 1951) was signed to Warner Brothers Records on the strength of his songwriting talents. His 1980 debut spawned US hits in 'Ride Like The Wind' (featuring **Michael McDonald**), 'Sailing', 'Never Be The Same' and 'Say You'll Be Mine'. Cross won five Grammy Awards in 1981, including Best Album of the Year. In the same year, he sang and co-wrote – with Carole Bayer Sager, **Burt Bacharach** and Peter Allen, the theme song, 'Arthur's Theme (Best That You Can Do)' (US number 1/UK Top 10) for the hit movie *Arthur*. *Another Page* featured the popular 'Think Of Laura' (1983, US Top 10), but later years saw a decline in Cross's sales. He was dropped by Warner following the release of 1988's *Back Of My Mind*. A revamped dance version of 'Ride Like The Wind' was used by East Side Beat in late 1991 and reached the UK Top 10. Cross's subsequent releases include 1998's *Walking In Avalon*, a double album containing a new studio work and a live set.

CROW, SHERYL

Crow (b. 1962) started out on the LA session scene, playing for names including **Eric Clapton**, **Bob Dylan**, **Stevie Wonder**, **Rod Stewart**, **George Harrison**, **Don Henley**, **John Hiatt**, **Joe Cocker** and **Sinéad O'Connor**. Crow then spent 18 months backing **Michael Jackson** on his Bad world tour (the experience is chronicled in her 'What Can I Do For You').

Her 1993 debut, *Tuesday Night Music Club*, took almost a year to make an impact, despite the marginal success of 'Run Baby Run' and 'Leaving Las Vegas'. Finally 'All I Wanna Do' charted (US number 2/UK number 4), and within a couple of years the album had achieved multi-platinum status. *Sheryl Crow* retained little of the spontaneity, courage and flair of its predecessor, but still won a Grammy for Best Rock Album in 1997. Both *The Globe Sessions* and 1999's live collection provided a welcome antidote to the AOR slickness of her second album. Despite its troubled recording history, the much-delayed *C'mon C'mon* broke little new ground, opting for the singer's trademark breezy, west-coast rock sound.

CROWDED HOUSE

After the break-up of their former band Split Enz in 1984, Neil Finn (b. 1958; guitar, vocals) and Paul Hester (drums) recruited Craig Hooper (guitar) and Nick Seymour (bass) to form the Mullanes in 1986. Moving to Los Angeles, they signed to Capitol Records, changed their name to Crowded House,

and worked with producer Mitchell Froom. Hooper left and the trio's debut album was released to little fanfare, but two singles, 'Don't Dream It's Over' (number 2) and 'Something So Strong' (number 7), enjoyed US chart success in 1987. A subdued reaction to the second album failed to consolidate the band's reputation in the singles chart, despite reaching the US Top 40. English singer **Paul Young** gave Crowded House some welcome publicity in the UK by singing 'Don't Dream It's Over' at the Nelson Mandela concert at Wembley Stadium in June 1988. Neil's brother Tim Finn (b. 1952; guitar, vocals) joined the band in early 1991 and they reached the UK Top 20 with 'Fall At Your Feet' and the Top 10 with 'Weather With You'. *Woodface* also reached the UK Top 10, but in November 1991 Tim Finn decided to leave and continue with his solo career. Both brothers were awarded the OBE in 1993 for their contribution to New Zealand music. In 1996, they announced their farewell, bowing out with an excellent compilation package, including three new songs. Their emotional final performance was in Sydney on 24 November 1996. Neil Finn also embarked on a solo career.

CROWELL, RODNEY

Texan Crowell (b. 1950) started out as a songwriter at Jerry Reed's publishing company and worked with **Emmylou Harris**'s Hot Band. His 'Bluebird Wine' appeared on the singer's *Pieces Of The Sky*, 'Till I Gain Control Again' was on *Elite Hotel*, and her *Quarter Moon In A Ten Cent Town* featured his 'I Ain't Living Long Like This' and 'Leaving Louisiana In The Broad Daylight'. In 1978, he recorded his debut, *Ain't Living Long Like This*, using an all-star line-up including the Hot Band, **Ry Cooder**, Jim Keltner and **Willie Nelson**. In 1979, Crowell married **Rosanne Cash**, and subsequently produced most of her albums. In 1980 his *But What Will The Neighbors Think* included the US Top 40 single 'Ashes By Now'. *Street Language* included three US country chart singles, and established him as a country artist. *Diamonds And Dirt* spawned five US country number 1s and *Keys To The Highway* was largely recorded with country band the Dixie Pearls. *Life Is Messy* followed shortly after break-up with Cash and subsequent albums, such as *Let The Picture Paint Itself* and *Jewel Of The South*, have also chronicled his personal problems. As long as life is messy it appears Crowell will be able to write great songs, although his marriage to Claudia Church in September 1998 indicated he had found personal happiness once more. The self-financed *The Houston Kid* was regarded as one of the finest albums of Crowell's career.

CRYSTALS

Highly influential 60s US female vocal group produced by Phil Spector. The group featured Dee Dee Kennibrew (b. Dolores Henry), La La Brooks, Pat Wright, Mary Thomas and Barbara Alston. Their 1961 debut was 'There's No Other (Like My

Baby)', followed by 'Uptown' and **Gene Pitney**'s 'He's A Rebel'. The latter featured the lead vocals of Darlene Wright (Love); as Spector owned the name, he could use whoever wanted as the Crystals. The song became a US number 1 hit. La La Brooks returned to lead vocals on 'Da Doo Ron Ron' and 'Then He Kissed Me', two major 1963 hits.

The Crystals were overlooked when Spector devoted more time to the **Ronettes**, and consequently their career faltered. New members passed through, including Frances Collins, but the band were prematurely banished to the nostalgia circuit.

CULT

Formed in the UK as Southern Death Cult in 1981 by Ian Astbury (b. 1962; vocals), Haq Qureshi (drums), David 'Buzz' Burrows (guitar) and Barry Jepson (bass). The quartet debuted in 1982 with the double a-side 'Moya'/ 'Fatman', and released a self-titled album. Astbury then formed Death Cult with Ray 'The Reverend' Mondo (b. Ray Taylor-Smith; drums) and Jamie Stewart (bass), plus guitarist Billy Duffy (b. William Henry Duffy, 1961; ex-Theatre Of Hate). They debuted in 1983 with an eponymous four-track 12-inch, at which time Astbury also changed his name (he had previously been using Ian Lindsay, his mother's maiden name). Mondo swapped drumming positions with Sex Gang Children's Nigel Preston (d. 1992) before, in 1984, the band changed their name to the Cult.

The new line-up's debut, *Dreamtime*, was boosted by the anthemic 'Spiritwalker'. Another strong effort followed with 'She Sells Sanctuary', after which Preston was replaced by Les Warner (b. 1961). *Love* spawned two UK Top 20 hit singles with 'She Sells Sanctuary' and 'Rain'. *Electric* saw their transition to heavy rock completed, and was a transatlantic success. The band added bass player Kid 'Haggis' Chaos, with Stewart switching to rhythm guitar, but both Chaos and Warner left in 1988. *Sonic Temple*, recorded by Astbury, Stewart and Duffy with drummer Mickey Curry, reached both the UK and US Top 10. *Ceremony*, a retrogressive collection of songs, featured Stewart's replacement Charlie Drayton and the returning Curry. Scott Garrett played drums on *The Cult*, but the band fell apart when Astbury departed for the Holy Barbarians.

Astbury, Duffy, Sorum and Dutch bass player Martyn LeNoble (b. 1969)

re-formed the Cult in 1999, although the latter was soon replaced by Chris Wyse. Astbury released the solo *Spirit/Light/Speed* the following year, while the reinvigorated Cult worked on their debut for Lava Records, *Beyond Good And Evil*.

CULTURE CLUB

Harbingers of the so-called 'new pop' that swept through the UK charts in the early 80s, Culture Club was formed in 1981 by Boy George (b. George O'Dowd, 1961; vocals), Roy Hay (b. 1961; guitar, keyboards), Mikey Craig (b. 1960; bass) and Jon Moss (b. 1957; drums). The quartet were signed to Virgin Records in 1982 and released

a couple of non-chart singles, 'White Boy' and 'I'm Afraid Of Me' before reaching UK number 1 with the melodic 'Do You Really Want To Hurt Me?' and the Top 3 with 'Time (Clock Of The Heart)'. By this time, George was already one of pop's major talking-points with his dreadlocks, make-up and androgynous persona. *Kissing To Be Clever* lacked the consistent excellence of their singles, but was still a fine pop record. In 1983, the album climbed into the US Top 20, while their two UK hits both reached number 2. 'Church Of The Poison Mind', with guest vocalist Helen Terry, gave them another UK number 2, and was followed by the infectious 'Karma Chameleon', a transatlantic chart-topper. *Colour By Numbers* reached UK number 1 and US number 2, and the momentum was maintained through 1983–84 with strong singles such as 'Victims', 'It's A Miracle' and 'Miss You Blind', which all reached either the US or UK Top 10. In 1984, 'The War Song' hit UK number 2, but thereafter, chart performances took an increasing back seat to George's gutter-media profile. 'Move Away' was their only other Top 10 hit, and after much media attention over his self-confessed heroin addiction, Boy George announced Culture Club's demise in 1987.

George would continue to enjoy chart-topping success as a soloist and later as an in-demand DJ. A resurgence of all things eighties led to Culture Club re-forming in 1998, with the sweet reggae ballad 'I Just Wanna Be Loved' debuting at number 4 in the UK singles chart in October. Another excellent song, 'Your Kisses Are Charity', stalled outside the Top 20 the following August. Their first studio album since 1986, *Don't Mind If I Do*, was released shortly afterwards.

CURE

UK band formed in 1976 as the Easy Cure. Robert Smith (b. 1959; guitar, vocals), Michael Dempsey (bass) and Laurence 'Lol' Tolhurst (b. 1959; drums) issued the Albert Camus-inspired 'Killing An Arab' (1978) on the independent Small Wonder Records. By 1979, the Cure were attracting glowing reviews, particularly in the wake of 'Boys Don't Cry'. *Three Imaginary Boys* was also well-received, but shortly afterwards Dempsey left, replaced by Simon Gallup, and Mathieu Hartley (keyboards) also joined.

By 1980, the Cure were developing less as a pop group than a guitar-laden rock band. The atmospheric 12-inch 'A Forest' gave them their first UK Top 40 hit, while the strong *17 Seconds* reached the Top 20. In 1981, they released 'Primary', 'Charlotte Sometimes' and 'Faith' and the well-received *Pornography*, but there were internal problems. Hartley had lasted only a few months and, in 1982, Gallup was replaced by Phil Thornalley and Steve Goulding. However, they continued with 'The Walk, 'The Love Cats' (their first UK Top 10 single) and 'The Caterpillar'. Smith's gothic image (spiked hair, heavy eye make-up and crimson lipstick) and Tim Pope's videos helped establish the band's striking visual image. In 1985, the Cure released their most commercially successful album yet,

The Head On The Door, but by now the band was effectively Smith and Tolhurst, with others flitting through. The retrospective *Standing On A Beach* singles collection underlined their longevity during an otherwise quiet period preceding the release of the double *Kiss Me, Kiss Me, Kiss Me*. A two-year hiatus followed before the release of *Disintegration*. Their run of line-up changes culminated in the departure of Tolhurst (to form Presence), leaving Smith as the sole original member. By 1992, the line-up featured Smith, a reinstated Gallup, Perry Bamonte (keyboards, guitar), Porl Thompson (guitar) and Boris Williams (drums). In 1993, Thompson left and former member Tolhurst unsuccessfully sued Smith, the band and its record label for alleged unpaid royalties. The bizarre *Wild Mood Swings* hinted at Smith's personal insecurities. *Galore*, a useful follow-up to the earlier compilations, preceded 2000's excellent *Bloodflowers* which Smith claimed was to be the final Cure album.

CURVE

UK indie act featuring Toni Halliday (vocals) and Dean Garcia (guitar). They began as State Of Play and released two singles and a 1986 album, *Balancing The Scales*, before splitting up. Halliday released a solo album before reuniting with Garcia in the early 90s as Curve. Three EPs, *Blindfold*, *Frozen* and *Cherry*, were well-received by the UK indie-rock press. They recruited Debbie Smith (guitar), Alex Mitchell (guitar) and Steve Monti (drums), but two albums and a series of singles failed to build on their favourable press profile and the band eventually sundered in 1994.

Halliday collaborated with dance act **Leftfield** for 1995's 'Original' and worked with Curve producer/guitarist Andrew Moulder as Scylla, while Debbie Smith went on to join **Echobelly**. Garcia and Halliday regrouped in November 1997 with new members Rob Holliday (guitar) and Stephen Spring (drums) for live gigs and *Come Clean*. The album featured the excellent single 'Chinese Burn' (also used on a Sony Discman commercial), but showed little sign of any musical progress. Garcia later recorded as Headcase, before reuniting with Halliday for *Gift*.

CURVED AIR

UK progressive rock band formed in 1969 by Sonja Kristina (b. 1949; vocals), Darryl Way (b. 1948; violin), Florian Pilkington-Miksa (b. 1950), Francis Monkman (b. 1949; keyboards) and Rob Martin (bass). They were signed by Warner Brothers Records for an advance of £100,000. *Airconditioning* was heavily promoted and enjoyed a particular curiosity value as one of rock's first picture-disc albums. Martin was replaced by Ian Eyre and in 1971, the band enjoyed their sole UK Top 5 hit with 'Back Street Luv'. By *Phantasmagoria*, Eyre had left, replaced by Mike Wedgewood (b. 1956). Monkman and Way also left in 1972, leaving Kristina as the sole original member. The line-up changed consistently from this point onwards. Kristina and Wedgewood recruited Kirby Gregory (guitar), Eddie Jobson (b. 1955; violin, keyboards) and Jim Russell (drums) to record *Air Cut*, before Jobson left to join **Roxy**

Music. The original band members, along with new bass player Phil Kohn, reunited for a short UK tour in December 1974. Following a hiatus, during which Kristina rejoined the cast of the musical *Hair* (which she had originally left to join Curved Air), the band was reactivated with Way returning for touring purposes. The new members were Mick Jacques (guitar), Tony Reeves (bass) and Stewart Copeland (b. 1952; drums). Two further albums followed before the unit dissolved in 1977.

Kristina pursued a solo career in music and acting, Monkman went on to form Sky, while Copeland joined the immensely successful **Police**. There have been several Curved Air reunions in subsequent decades, one of which resulted in the *Alive*, 1990 release.

CYPRESS HILL

Interracial Los Angeles, USA-based rap crew featuring DJ Muggs (b. Lawrence Muggerud, 1968), vocalists B-Real (b. Louis Freese, 1970) and Sen Dog (b. Senen Reyes, 1965). As a teenager, Sen Dog, with his younger brother Mellow Man Ace, formed the prototype rap outfit, DVX, and claims to have invented the Spanglish 'lingo' style.

Cypress Hill's 1991 debut set went platinum, while the follow-up, *Black Sunday*, debuted at Number 1 in the US R&B and pop charts. The trio attracted controversy for their lyrical stance on such tracks as 'I Wanna Get High', 'Legalize It' and 'Insane In The Brain', which advocated marijuana as a cultural replacement for alcohol. However, the real reason for their widespread success lay with their blend of full and funky R&B, tales of dope and guns adding the final sheen to the laid-back beats.

Their third long-player, the dark, edgy *III: Temples Of Boom*, lost Cypress Hill their college audience but regained the respect of the hip-hop community. Sen Dog left in February 1996 to work with his punk/metal outfit SX-10 and was replaced by DJ Scandalous, who had already worked with the crew. A nine-track EP of rare remixes followed before the members concentrated on solo projects, with Muggs releasing *Muggs Presents ... The Soul Assassins Chapter 1* and B-Real working with the Psycho Realm. Cypress Hill, with Sen Dog back on board, made an impressive artistic comeback in 1998 with *Cypress Hill IV*, although the album did not reach the US Top 10. *Skull & Bones* and *Stoned Raiders* failed to re-establish their commercial standing.

D'ANGELO

R&B singer-songwriter and multi-instrumentalist D'Angelo (b. Michael Archer, 1974) released his debut album in 1995. Alongside **Ben Harper**, it saw D'Angelo celebrated as representing a return to the singer-songwriter tradition in black music following the dominance of hip-hop. D'Angelo subsequently contributed soundtrack work to the movies *Scream 2*, *Down In The Delta* and *Belly*, and duetted with **Lauryn Hill** on 'Nothing Even Matters' from her acclaimed *The Miseducation Of Lauryn Hill*. D'Angelo debuted at US number 1 in 2000 with *Voodoo*, an occasionally inspired collection of songs crafted from endless studio jams. The following year he was rewarded with Grammy Awards for Best Male R&B Vocal Performance and Best R&B Album.

D'ARBY, TERENCE TRENT

US-born D'Arby (b. 1962) started out with local funk band Touch, in 1983. His first solo single, 1987's 'If You Let Me Stay', reached the UK Top 10 and *Introducing The Hardline According To Terence Trent D'Arby* was one of the most successful debut albums of its time. *Neither Fish Nor Flesh* was a commercial and artistic failure, but the more rock-orientated *Symphony Or Damn* was better received. *Vibrator* continued the transition from smooth soul to a harder-edged sound, but failed to resurrect D'Arby's fortunes. He founded his own label Wildcard after his Sony contract ended.

DAFT PUNK

French house duo Guy-Manuel de Homem Christo (b. 1974) and Thomas Bangalter (b. 1975) originally recorded indie pop under the name Darling, before making their breakthrough in 1995 with an insanely catchy slice of techno/funk, 'Da Funk'. The re-release of 'Da Funk' by Virgin Records, and the subsequent *Homework*, broke Daft Punk to an overground audience. Bangalter's alter ego, Stardust, was responsible for 'Music Sounds Better With You', one of the club anthems of 1998. *Discovery* was a far more commercial outing, allaying the hard house grooves of the debut with plenty of highly melodic retro synth-pop such as 'One More Time' (featuring Romanthony), 'Digital Love' and 'Harder, Better, Faster, Stronger'.

DALE, DICK

US-born Dale (b. Richard Monsour, 1937) first gained popularity as a local country singer. His first record was 'Ooh-Whee-Marie' on Deltone, his father's label for whom he recorded nine singles between 1959 and 1962; 'Let's Go Trippin'' (1961) is considered to be the first instrumental surf record. He then formed the Del-Tones and sparked the surf music craze on the US west coast in the early 60s. Dale played left-handed without reversing the strings and started to fine-tune the surf-guitar style. He met Leo Fender, the inventor of the Fender guitar and amplifier line, and together they worked on designing equipment more suitable for surf guitar. *Surfer's Choice* made the national album charts and Capitol Records signed Dale in 1963; 'The Scavenger' and *Checkered Flag* made the US charts. Dale continued to record throughout the 60s and 70s, but a cancer scare which he overcame sidelined his career. His

music was rediscovered in the 80s, and in 1987 he recorded a version, with **Stevie Ray Vaughan**, of the Chantays' 'Pipeline' for the movie *Back To The Beach*. 'Misirlou' was featured in the 1994 movie *Pulp Fiction*, bringing Dale new recognition with a younger audience.

DAMNED

UK punk band formed in 1976 by **Captain Sensible** (b. Raymond Burns, 1954), Rat Scabies (b. Chris Miller, 1957; drums), Brian James (b. Brian Robertson; guitar) and Dave Vanian (b. David Letts; vocals). The band supported the **Sex Pistols** at the 100 Club just two months after forming and were then signed to Stiff Records. In 1976, they released 'New Rose', generally regarded as the first UK punk single. *Damned Damned Damned* was produced by **Nick Lowe**. Lu Edmunds joined as a second guitarist, but soon afterwards Rat Scabies quit, replaced by percussionist Jon Moss (b. 1957). *Music For Pleasure*, produced by **Pink Floyd**'s Nick Mason, was mauled by the critics. The Damned were dropped from Stiff and split in 1978.

Sensible, Vanian and Scabies formed the Doomed before becoming legally entitled to use the name Damned. Joined by Algy Ward (bass), they had their first Top 20 single, 'Love Song'. Minor hits followed. Ward was replaced by Paul Gray (ex-Eddie And The Hot Rods), before Sensible went solo in 1984 and Roman Jugg (guitar, keyboards) and Bryn Merrick (bass) joined Scabies and Vanian. In 1986, the band reached UK number 3 with a cover of Barry Ryan's 'Eloise'. The band continue to tour and record into the new millennium, sometimes with Sensible and lately without Scabies.

DANDY WARHOLS

Oregon, USA-based indie quartet formed by Peter Holmstrom (guitar), Courtney Taylor (vocals, guitar), Eric Hedford (drums, vocals) and Zia McCabe (keyboards, bass, percussion). In 1995, the quartet recorded *Dandys Rule OK* for Portland label Tim Kerr. The band's live shows and impressive debut led to a major label contract with Capitol Records. ... *The Dandy Warhols Come Down* demonstrated a knack for straightforward garage rock ('Cool As Kim Deal' and the controversial 'Not If You Were The Last Junkie On Earth'). A video was later made by famed photographer David LaChappelle. Brent De Boer replaced Hedford on the band's third album, *Thirteen Tales From Urban Bohemia*. 'Bohemian Like You' broke into the UK Top 10 in 2001 thanks to its use on a television advertisement for Vodaphone.

DANNY AND THE JUNIORS

Philadelphia, USA-based, Italian-American vocal quartet – Danny Rapp (b. 1941, d. 1983; lead vocals), Dave White (first tenor), Frank Mattei (second tenor) and Joe Terranova (baritone). Formed in 1955 as the Juvenairs, their song 'Do The Bop' came to the attention of Dick Clark, who suggested changing it to 'At The Hop'. The re-named song was released in 1957 and shot to the top of the US chart; it also reached the UK Top 3. Their only other US

Top 20 hit was the similar sounding 'Rock 'N' Roll Is Here To Stay'. White left the group in the early 60s. In the 70s, Danny And The Juniors played the 'oldies' circuit with a line-up that included Fabian's ex-backing singer Jimmy Testa. In 1976, a re-issue of 'At The Hop' returned them to the UK Top 40. Rapp was found dead in 1983 having apparently committed suicide.

DARIN, BOBBY

US singer Darin (b. Walden Robert Cassotto, 1936, d. 1973) entered the music business in the mid-50s. The pop novelty 'Splish Splash' was a worldwide hit in 1958. He also recorded in the Ding Dongs, from which sprang the Rinky-Dinks, the backing artists on 'Early In The Morning'. Darin's solo release, 'Queen Of The Hop', sold a million copies, followed by 'Plain Jane' and 'Dream Lover' (UK number 1/US number 2). Darin then became master of the supper-club circuit, marking a dramatic change of direction. 'Mack The Knife', composed by Bertolt Brecht and Kurt Weill for the musical *The Threepenny Opera*, proved a million-seller and transatlantic chart-topper and effectively raised Darin to new status as a 'serious singer'. His hit treatments of 'La Mer (Beyond The Sea)', 'Clementine', 'Won't You Come Home Bill Bailey?' and 'You Must Have Been A Beautiful Baby' revealed his ability to tackle variety material and transform it to his own ends.

In 1960, Darin moved into films, appearing in *Come September*, *Too Late Blues*, *State Fair*, and *Hell Is For Heroes*. He returned to pop with 'Multiplication' and 'Things' and recorded an album of **Ray Charles** songs. During the beat-boom era, Darin reverted to show tunes such as 'Baby Face' and 'Hello Dolly', before a 1965 folk rock hit, 'We Didn't Ask To Be Brought Here'. Successful readings of Tim Hardin and John Sebastian songs, demonstrated his potential as a cover artist. A more political direction was evident on *Born Walden Robert Cassotto* and *Commitment* and the late 60s saw Darin involved in related interests. Darin suffered from a weak heart, which finally proved fatal. He was inducted into the Rock And Roll Hall Of Fame in 1990.

DARTS

UK rock 'n' roll revival band formed by Iain Thompson (bass), John Dummer (drums), Hammy Howell (b. 1954, d. 1999; keyboards), Horatio Hornblower (b. Nigel Trubridge; saxophone) and singers Rita Ray, Griff Fender (b. Ian Collier), bass player Den Hegarty and Bob Fish. Their debut single, a medley

of 'Daddy Cool' and **Little Richard**'s 'The Girl Can't Help It', ascended the UK Top 10 in 1977, kicking off three years of entries in both the singles and albums lists that mixed stylized self-compositions ('It's Raining', 'Don't Let It Fade Away') with predominant revamps of such US hits as 'Come Back My Love', 'The Boy From New York City', 'Get It' and 'Duke Of Earl'. The exits of Hegarty, Howell and Dummer saw the end of Darts as chart contenders.

DAVE DEE, DOZY, BEAKY, MICK AND TICH

Formed in 1961 as Dave Dee And The Bostons, Dave Dee (b. David Harman, 1943; vocals), Dozy (b. Trevor Davies, 1944; bass), Beaky (b. John Dymond,

1944; guitar), Mick (b. Michael Wilson, 1944; lead guitar) and Tich (b. Ian Amey, 1944) performed rock 'n' roll spiced with comedy routines and risqué patter. They entered the UK chart in 1965 with 'You Make It Move'. Thereafter, they had an incredible run of a dozen strong chart hits, all executed with a camp flair and costume-loving theatricalism that proved irresistible before finally losing ground at the end of the 60s. Dee left for an unsuccessful solo career. The remaining quartet split after one minor hit, 'Mr President'. A couple of brief nostalgic reunions later occurred, but not enough to encourage a serious relaunch.

DAVID, CRAIG

UK born David (b. 1981) enjoyed his first success in 1999 as the smooth, soulful voice on garage act Artful Dodger's 'Re-rewind When The Crowd Say Bo Selecta', a UK number 2 crossover hit. Rising interest in the vocalist led to a deal with Wildstar Records. His first single for them, the infectious 'Fill Me In' received substantial national radio airplay and rose to the UK's number 1 spot in April 2000. David repeated the feat with '7 Days', and completed a memorable year by winning three MOBO awards two months later. During the following 12 months he began to make an impact across the Atlantic, culminating in '7 Days' breaking into the US Top 10 in February 2002.

DAVIS, SPENCER GROUP

Formed in Birmingham, England, in 1962, by Spencer Davis (b. 1941; guitar, vocals), Steve Winwood (b. 1948; guitar, organ, vocals), Muff Winwood (b. Mervyn Winwood, 1943; bass) and Pete York (b. 1942; drums).

Initially, their bluesy pop records failed to sell, but the breakthrough came with 1965's 'Keep On Running' (UK number 1). This was followed by another chart-topper, 'Somebody Help Me', and three more hits 'When I Come Home', 'Gimme Some Lovin'' and 'I'm A Man'.

Steve Winwood left to form Traffic in 1967. Muff Winwood also left, joining Island Records as head of A&R. Davis soldiered on with the addition of Phil Sawyer, and later with Ray Fenwick (guitar) and Eddie Hardin (keyboards). They had two further minor hits, 'Mr Second Class' and 'Time Seller'. After a number of line-up changes, Hardin and York departed to form their own band. The Davis/York/Hardin/Fenwick team re-formed briefly in 1973, with Charlie McCracken on bass, and made a further two albums. In the late 90s Davis was touting a new version of the band, which included York and Miller Anderson (vocals, guitar).

DAWN

Formed in 1970 by US singer Tony Orlando (b. 1944). After hearing a demo of 'Candida', Orlando recorded it himself with session vocalists Telma Hopkins (b. 1948) and Joyce Vincent (b. 1946) and hired instrumentalists. This single was attributed to Dawn. After 'Candida' and 'Knock Three Times' topped international charts, the troupe were billed as Tony Orlando And Dawn. 'Tie A Yellow Ribbon Round The Ole Oak Tree' proved *the* hit song of 1973. The trio had their last US number 1 with 'He Don't Love You', a rewrite of a Jerry Butler single.

DAYS OF THE NEW

Modern hard-rock outfit from Kentucky, USA, formed by Travis Meeks (vocals), Jesse Vest (b. 1977; bass) and Matt Taul (b. 1978; drums). With the addition of guitarist Todd Whitener (b. 1978) they recorded their 1997 debut album with **R.E.M.** associate Scott Litt. The first single to be released from the album, 'Touch, Peel And Stand', was featured heavily on MTV. Meeks, having parted company with the others members of the band (who went on to form Tantric), wrote, recorded and produced the second and third Days Of The New album on his own.

DAZZ BAND

US funk outfit formed in the mid-70s by Bobby Harris, who was joined by Pierre DeMudd and Skip Martin III (horns, vocals), Eric Fearman (guitar), Kevin Frederick (keyboards), Kenny Pettus (percussion), Michael Wiley (bass) and Isaac Wiley (drums). Coining the word 'Dazz' – 'danceable jazz' – Harris initially named the band Kinsman Dazz and had two minor US hits in 1978 and 1979. They graduated towards a less melodic funk sound, enjoying a US Top 10 hit with 'Let It Whip' (1982), which won a Grammy. Further crossover recognition proved elusive.

DB'S

US band formed in 1978 from the ashes of the Sneakers by Chris Stamey (guitars, vocals), Gene Holder (bass), Will Rigby (drums) and Peter Holsapple (keyboards). Two excellent, melodic albums failed to make any significant commercial impact, and Stamey left to resume his solo career. Jeff Beninato was brought in to help record one final album, 1987's *The Sound Of Music*. In the 1990s, Stamey and Holsapple recorded the duo set, *Mavericks*.

DE BURGH, CHRIS

Pop singer De Burgh (b. Christopher Davidson, 1948) was born in Argentina but raised in Ireland. He enjoyed commercial success in Canada, South Africa, Europe and South America, before finally breaking through in the UK in 1982 with *The Getaway*, which featured the minor hit 'Don't Pay The Ferryman'. A popular compilation set preceded 1986's 'The Lady In Red', a romantic ballad which became a worldwide hit and topped the UK charts. *Into The Light* and *Flying Colours* consolidated De Burgh's commercial status, the latter reaching the top of the UK charts. One of the singer's most notable 90s songs was 'A New Star In Heaven Tonight', a tribute to the late Diana, Princess Of Wales.

DE LA SOUL

US hip-hop act formed by Posdnous (b. Kelvin Mercer, 1969), Trugoy the Dove (b. David Jude Joliceur, 1968), and Pasemaster Mace (b. Vincent Lamont Mason Jnr, 1970). Less harsh than many of their fellow rappers, De La Soul's pleasantly lilting rhythms generated hit singles in the late 80s and early 90s with 'Me Myself And I', and 'The Magic Number', and the acclaimed *3 Feet High And Rising*. Sophomore album *De La Soul Is Dead* returned to tougher rhythms with a mellow approach that belied difficult subject matter. Subsequent albums struggled to maintain the trio's commercial status, although 2000's excellent *Art Official Intelligence: Mosaic Thump* helped reassert their reputation as hip-hop pioneers.

DEACON BLUE

Formed in Glasgow, Scotland, in 1985 when singer-songwriter Ricky Ross (b. 1957) was advised by his song publishers to find a group to perform his compositions. He was joined by James Prine (b. 1960; keyboards), Graeme Kelling (b. 1957; guitar), Ewan Vernal (b. 1964; bass) and Dougie Vipond (b. 1960; drums). Vocalist Lorraine McIntosh (b. 1964) joined after *Raintown*. 'Dignity' (1988) was the band's first UK hit, followed by 'Chocolate Girl' and 'Real Gone Kid'. *When The World Knows Your Name* topped the UK album charts in 1989. They released two more albums before splitting up in 1994. Ross embarked on a solo career before re-forming Deacon Blue in the late 90s.

DEAD BOYS

One of the first-wave punk bands in the USA, the Dead Boys were formed in 1976 by Stiv Bators (b. Stivin Bator, 1949, d. 1990; vocals), Jimmy Zero (rhythm guitar), Cheetah Chrome (b. Gene Connor; lead guitar), Jeff Magnum (bass) and Johnny Blitz (drums). They debuted with the classic *Young, Loud And Snotty*, but subsequent releases failed to match this album's impact. They split up in 1980 with Bators recording two solo albums before forming Lords Of The New Church. Bators was killed in a car crash in 1990.

DEAD CAN DANCE

Based in England, but tracing their origins to Australia, Dead Can Dance's blissful *avant-garde* pop enjoyed considerable acclaim but little commercial reward. The core duo of Brendan Perry and Lisa Gerrard debuted in 1984 with a self-titled album. Further releases demonstrated a debt to middle-eastern music, while *Aion* used Gregorian chants. *Into The Labyrinth* confirmed Perry's greater awareness of electronics and samplers. *Spiritchaser* served to validate the reason for Dead Can Dance's continuation into the 90s, the band having proved themselves to be among the most accurate cultural conductors in popular music. Unfortunately, it proved to be their final release. Gerrard collaborated with Australian keyboard player Pieter Bourke on 1998's *Duality*, and Perry released his solo debut a year later.

DEAD KENNEDYS

Legendary San Franciscan punk band featuring Jello Biafra (b. Eric Boucher, 1958; vocals), Klaus Flouride (b. Geoffrey Lyall; bass), East Bay Ray Glasser (b. Ray Pepperell; guitar) and Ted (b. Bruce Slesinger; drums). Their 1980 debut single, 'California Uber Alles', attacked the policies of Californian governor Jerry Brown. *Fresh Fruit For Rotting Vegetables* followed a broadly traditional musical format, whereas the mini-album *In God We Trust, Inc.* was full-blown thrash. *Frankenchrist* was more considered, but Biafra fell foul of the PRMC (America's 'moral guardians') over the album's artwork. *Bedtime For Democracy* was the band's final studio recording, returning to the aggressive speed of the previous mini-album. The Dead Kennedys' contribution is best measured not by the number of copy bands who subsequently sprung up around the world, but by the enduring quality of their best records and Biafra's admirable and unyielding stance on artistic censorship.

DEAD OR ALIVE

UK band formed in the early 80s by Pete Burns (b. 1959; vocals). Burns was joined by Mike Percy (bass), Steve Coy (drums) and Tim Lever (keyboards) on 1984's UK Top 30 hit, 'That's The Way (I Like It)', and the following year's chart-topper 'You Spin Me Round (Like A Record)', production team **Stock, Aitken And Waterman**'s first UK hit. The latter also entered the US Top 20. Soundalike follow-ups fared less well, and Lever and Percy left following the release of 1989's *Nude*. In the 90s, Burns and Coy found greater success abroad, especially in Japan where *Nukleopatra* was a major hit.

DEATH IN VEGAS

Formerly called Dead Elvis, Death In Vegas's aggressive, rock-edged dance-floor sound owes a huge debt to the punk ethos of 1977. Formed by DJ Richard Fearless and producer Steve Hellier, the duo announced themselves with a series of mesmerizing singles: 'Opium Shuffle', 'Dirt', 'Rocco', 'GBH' and 'Rekkit'. These were included on 1997's *Dead Elvis*, which was celebrated within both the mainstream and dance music communities for its intelligence, musical freshness and daring. Fearless contributed music to the soundtracks of *Lost In Space* and *The Acid House*, before resuming work as Death In Vegas with new partner Tim Holmes. *The Contino Sessions* featured guest vocals from **Iggy Pop** ('Aisha') and Bobby Gillespie ('Soul Auctioneer'). 'Aisha' provided Death In Vegas with a first UK Top 10 hit in 2000.

DEBARGE

US group formed in 1978 by Bunny DeBarge and her four brothers, Mark, James, Randy and El. Signed to Motown Records in 1979, they were marketed as successors to the **Jackson Five**. The group (known as the DeBarges) were launched with *The DeBarges*. 'I Like It' was a success in

the pop charts as were 'All This Love' and 'Time Will Reveal'. In 1985 they had their biggest hit – 'Rhythm Of The Night' (US number 3) from the soundtrack to *The Last Dragon*. The follow-up, 'Who's Holding Donna Now?', was almost as successful. El DeBarge went solo in 1985, and Bunny departed in 1987. Only Mark and James appeared on *Bad Boys*, by which time their commercial impetus had been lost. The group's wholesome image was ruined by the 1988 arrest and conviction of their brothers Bobby and Chico on drug charges.

DEE, JOEY, AND THE STARLITERS

US group featuring Joey Dee (b. Joseph DiNicola, 1940; vocals), David Brigati (backing vocals), Carlton Lattimore (keyboards), Willie Davis (drums), and Larry Vernieri (backing vocals). The unit took up residency at New York's Peppermint Lounge in 1960. In 1961, a year after **Chubby Checker**'s 'The Twist' topped the US chart, Dee's 'Peppermint Twist' shot to number 1 and *Doin' The Twist At The Peppermint Lounge* reached number 2. In 1962 the group, which now included a 10-piece dance team incorporating the original line-up of the **Ronettes**, starred in the low-budget movie *Hey, Let's Twist* with the soundtrack album and title track both reaching the US Top 20. They followed this with a breakneck version of the **Isley Brothers'** 'Shout', which reached number 6. Dee embarked on an abortive solo career, and opened his own club, The Starliter, in New York in 1964. He is now the spokesman of The National Music Foundation.

DEE, KIKI

UK vocalist (b. Pauline Matthews, 1947) who made her recording debut in 1963 with Mitch Murray's 'Early Night'. After a series of Phil Spector-inspired releases, Dee began covering contemporary soul hits, leading to a recording deal with Tamla/Motown Records, the first white British act to be so honoured. Artistically lauded, Dee only found commercial success after signing with **Elton John**'s Rocket Records label in 1973. He produced *Loving & Free*, spawning the UK Top 20 hit 'Amoureuse'. She had further chart success with 'I Got The Music In Me' (1974) and '(You Don't Know) How Glad I Am' (1975), fronting the Kiki Dee Band. A duet with Elton John, 'Don't Go Breaking My Heart', topped the UK and US charts in 1976. 'Star' restored her to the UK Top 20 in 1981, and three years later she appeared in the musical *Pump Boys And Dinettes*. She was nominated for a Laurence Olivier Award in 1989 after appearing in *Blood Brothers*. Another duet with Elton John, 'True Love', reached UK number 2 in 1993. Her first studio album of the decade was released in 1998.

DEEP PURPLE

UK band formed in 1968 around Chris Curtis (b. Christopher Crummey, 1941; drums; ex-**Searchers**), Jon Lord (b. 1941; keyboards), Nick Simper (b. 1945; bass) and Ritchie Blackmore (b. 1945; guitar). Curtis dropped out within days, and Rod Evans (b. 1947; vocals) and Ian Paice (b. 1948; drums) joined. *Shades Of Deep Purple* included two striking cover versions – 'Hey Joe' and the US Top 5 hit 'Hush'. *The Book Of Taliesyn* and *Deep Purple* also featured several reworkings, notably 'River Deep – Mountain High', alongside original material. In 1969, Evans and Simper were replaced by **Ian Gillan** (b. 1945; vocals) and Roger Glover (b. 1945; bass). Often acknowledged as the 'classic' Deep Purple line-up, the quintet made its album debut on *Concerto For Group And Orchestra*, recorded with the London Philharmonic Orchestra. Its successor, *Deep Purple In Rock*, established the band as a leading hard-rock attraction and 'Black Night' reached UK number 2. *Fireball* and *Machine Head* topped the album chart, the latter including 'Smoke On The Water'. The platinum-selling *Made In Japan* captured their live prowess but *Who Do We Think We Are?* marked the end of the line-up.

Gillan and Glover's departures robbed Deep Purple of an expressive frontman and imaginative arranger, although David Coverdale (b. 1951; vocals)

and Glenn Hughes (b. 1952; bass) brought a new impetus. *Burn* and *Stormbringer* reached the Top 10, but in 1975 Blackmore left to form Rainbow. Tommy Bolin (b. 1951, d. 1976; ex-**James Gang**) joined for *Come Taste The Band*, but his jazz/soul style was incompatible with the band's sound and they folded in 1976 following a farewell UK tour.

In 1984, Gillan, Lord, Blackmore, Glover and Paice reunited and completed *Perfect Strangers* and *The House Of Blue Light*. Vocalist Joe Lynn Turner (b. Joseph Linquito, 1951) was brought in for *Slaves And Masters*. Gillan rejoined in 1993 only to quit and Blackmore left in 1994, briefly replaced by Joe Satriani. Steve Morse (b. 1954; guitar), Lord, Gillan, Glover and Paice recorded the credible *Purpendicular* in 1996.

DEF LEPPARD

UK hard-rock band formed by Pete Willis (b. 1960; guitar), Rick Savage (b. 1960; bass) and Tony Kenning (drums). Originally called Atomic Mass, they became Def Leppard when Joe Elliott (b. 1959; vocals) joined. In 1978, Steve Clark (b. 1960, d. 1991; guitar) was recruited. After several gigs, the band replaced Kenning with Frank Noon, and in 1979 they recorded a debut EP after which Noon left. Rick Allen (b. 1963) became their permanent drummer. Their 1983 breakthrough *Pyromania* saw another change in the band's line-up, when Willis was sacked and replaced by Phil Collen (b. 1957). On New Year's Eve 1984, drummer Rick Allen lost his left arm in a car crash. He resumed work after he had perfected a specially designed kit which he could play with his feet. This severely delayed the recording of *Hysteria*, which eventually sold 15 million copies worldwide producing two Top 5 US singles, 'Armageddon It' and 'Pour Some Sugar On Me', and the chart-topping 'Love Bites'.

As work began on their next album, Clark was found dead in his London flat from a mixture of drugs and alcohol. Def Leppard soldiered through the recording sessions for *Adrenalize*, which topped both the US and UK charts. Replacement guitarist Vivian Campbell (b. 1962), appeared on the 1996 collection *Slang*. Three years later *Euphoria* was released.

DEKKER, DESMOND

Jamaican-born Dekker (b. Desmond Dacres, 1942) began work as a welder before finding a music mentor in Leslie Kong. In 1963, he released his first single, 'Honour Your Father And Mother', before teaming up with backing group, the Aces. Together they enjoyed 20 Jamaican number 1s during the mid- to late 60s. Dekker's James Bond-inspired '007' went into the UK charts in 1967. Two years later, 'Israelites' became the first reggae song to top the UK charts and reached the US Top 10. The follow up, 'It Mek', reached the UK Top 10.

Dekker's British success, buoyed by consistent touring, spearheaded the arrival of a number of Jamaican chart acts. A version of **Jimmy Cliff**'s 'You Can Get It If You Really Want', from the film *The Harder They Come*, reached UK number 2 and in 1975 'Sing A Little Song' reached number 16. During the 2-Tone ska/mod revival in 1980, Dekker recorded *Black And Dekker* with Graham Parker's Rumour, but the experiment was not commercially successful. *Compass Point* was his last attempt at chart action. In 1993, during

another 2-Tone revival, Dekker released *King Of Kings* with four original members of the Specials.

DEL AMITRI

Scottish pop rock band formed by Justin Currie (b. 1964; vocals, bass), Iain Harvie (b. 1962; guitar), Bryan Tolland (guitar) and Paul Tyagi (drums). Del Amitri released their debut album in 1985, a few years before they made the UK singles chart with 'Kiss This Thing Goodbye', 'Nothing Ever Happens' and 'Spit In The Rain'. The reissue of 'Kiss This Thing Goodbye' reached the US charts. Despite faltering singles success, 1992's *Change Everything* went platinum. Touring continued throughout that year while most of 1993 was spent working on *Twisted*. The 1997 release *Some Other Sucker's Parade* preceded the band's World Cup song for the Scottish soccer team, 'Don't Come Home Too Soon'. Del Amitri returned to the UK charts in 2002 with *Can You Do Me Good?*.

DEL-VIKINGS

The first successful multiracial rock 'n' roll band, the Del-Vikings were formed in 1956 by Clarence Quick (bass), Corinthian 'Kripp' Johnson (b. 1933, d. 1990; lead tenor), Samuel Patterson (lead tenor), Don Jackson (baritone) and Bernard Robertson (second tenor). Patterson and Robertson were then replaced by Norman Wright and Dave Lerchey (the first white member). Their debut 'Come Go With Me' (1957) reached US number 4. When Jackson was transferred by the Air Force, he was replaced by second white member Donald 'Gus' Backus. 'Whispering Bells' provided the group with their second US Top

10 hit. Johnson left, replaced by William Blakely, and the new line-up debuted with 'Cool Shake' (1957). Johnson then formed his own Del-Vikings with Arthur Budd, Eddie Everette, Chuck Jackson and original member Don Jackson. They released 'Willette' and 'I Want To Marry You' to little commercial recognition. Their next release was credited to the Del-Vikings And Kripp Johnson, but this did not prevent Mercury Records suing to ensure ownership; the confusion abated when Johnson rejoined the Del-Vikings in 1958. He sang lead on 'You Cheated' and 'How Could You'. Several excellent releases followed, but none revisited the chart action of old.

DELANEY AND BONNIE

Delaney Bramlett (b. 1939) started out in the Shindogs, the house band on US television's *Shindig*. He also made several unsuccessful solo singles prior to meeting Bonnie Lynn (b. Bonnie Lynn O'Farrell, 1944), who had already sung with names including Ike And **Tina Turner**. The couple's first album, *Home*, was only released in the wake of the exemplary white-soul collection *Accept No Substitute*. An expanded ensemble, featuring Bobby Keys (saxophone), Jim Price (trumpet), Bobby Whitlock (guitar), Carl Radle (bass) and Jim Keltner (drums), toured America with **Blind Faith**, while **Eric Clapton** joined them during a tour of Britain. The backing group then left for **Joe Cocker**'s *Mad Dogs And Englishmen* escapade. *To Bonnie From Delaney*, recorded with the Dixie Flyers and Memphis Horns, lacked the purpose of previous albums. After two more albums the couple's marriage soured and they broke up in 1972.

DELFONICS

Formed in Philadelphia, USA, in 1965, originally as the Four Gents, the Delfonics featured William Hart (b. 1945; tenor), Wilbert Hart (b. 1947), Randy Cain (b. 1945) and Ritchie Daniels. Their early releases appeared on local independent labels until their manager, Stan Watson, founded Philly

Groove. After Daniels' military conscription, the remaining trio recorded their debut, 'La La Means I Love You'. The hit prepared the way for several symphonic creations, including 'I'm Sorry', 'Ready Or Not Here I Come' and 'Didn't I (Blow Your Mind This Time)' (1970). Much of their sumptuous atmosphere was due to producer Thom Bell's remarkable use of brass and orchestration, but 'Trying To Make A Fool Out Of Me' (1970), the group's tenth consecutive R&B chart entry, marked the end of this relationship. In 1971, Cain was replaced by Major Harris, whose departure three years later coincided with the Delfonics' downhill slide.

DELLS

Soul vocal and close-harmony group formed in 1953 as the El-Rays. Johnny Funches (lead), Marvin Junior (b. 1936; tenor), Verne Allison (b. 1936; tenor), Lucius McGill (b. 1935; tenor), Mickey McGill (b. 1937; baritone) and Chuck Barksdale (b. 1935; bass) released one record, 'Darling Dear I Know' (1953). After a name change they recorded 'Tell The World' (1955), followed by 'Oh What A Night' (R&B number 4). In 1965 they returned to the R&B chart with 'Stay In My Corner', and a re-recorded version reached the US pop Top 10. The Dells continued to prosper through the 70s and 80s, and in the 90s contributed music to the movie *The Five Heartbeats*. Their only line-up changes occurred when Lucius McGill left the original El-Rays and, in 1958, when Funches was replaced by Johnny Carter (b. 1934).

DENNY, SANDY

Denny (b. Alexandra Elene Maclean Denny, 1947, d. 1978) began singing in folk clubs around her native London, featuring material by Tom Paxton and Jackson C. Frank alongside traditional English songs. Work from this early period was captured on the 1967 releases *Sandy And Johnny* (with Johnny Silvo) and *Alex Campbell And His Friends*. The following year, Denny spent six months as a member of the Strawbs. Their lone album together was not released until 1973, but this melodic work included the original version of her famed composition, 'Who Knows Where The Time Goes?'. In 1968, Denny joined **Fairport Convention**, recording three albums with the band before leaving to form Fotheringay. After a solitary album with the latter, Denny recorded her solo debut, 1971's *The North Star Grassman And The Ravens*. The follow-up Sandy was another memorable collection, but *Like An Old Fashioned Waltz* closed this particular period and Denny briefly rejoined Fairpoint Convention in 1974. After completing another solo album *Rendezvous*, plans were afoot to record a new Denny set in America. Tragically, a month after falling down a staircase, Denny died from a cerebral haemorrhage.

DENVER, JOHN

US singer-songwriter Denver (b. Henry John Deutschendorf Jnr., 1943, d. 1997) was 'discovered' in a Los Angeles nightclub. He initially joined the Back Porch Majority, a nursery group for the New Christy Minstrels, but soon left for the Chad Mitchell Trio, where he forged a reputation as a talented songwriter. The Mitchell Trio became known as Denver, Boise and Johnson before Denver went solo in 1969. One of his evocative compositions, 'Leaving On A Jet Plane', provided an international hit for **Peter, Paul And Mary**, and was the highlight of Denver's solo debut, *Rhymes And Reasons*. Subsequent releases, *Take Me To Tomorrow* and *Whose Garden Was This*, garnered some attention, but it was not until the release of *Poems, Prayers And Promises* that the singer enjoyed popular acclaim. 'Take Me Home, Country Roads', broached the US Top 3 and became a UK Top 20 hit for **Olivia Newton-John** in 1973. 'I'd Rather Be A Cowboy' (1973) and 'Sunshine On My Shoulders' (1974) were both gold singles, while 'Annie's Song' secured Denver's international status when it topped the UK charts. Denver had two US number 1s in 1975 with 'Thank God I'm A Country Boy' and 'I'm Sorry' and his status as an all-round entertainer was enhanced by many television spectaculars, including *Rocky Mountain Christmas*. He continued to enjoy a high profile and forged a concurrent acting career with his role in the comedy *Oh, God!*. In 1981 opera singer Placido Domingo duetted with Denver on 'Perhaps Love'. Later in the decade Denver increasingly devoted time to charitable work and ecological interests. Tragically he died in October 1997 when his private plane crashed into the Pacific Ocean.

DENVER, KARL

Scottish singer Denver (b. Angus McKenzie, 1934, d. 1998) developed a love of contrasting folk forms while travelling, and his repertoire consisted of traditional material from the Middle East, Africa and China. His flexible voice and unusual inflections brought much contemporary comment. The artist enjoyed four UK Top 10 hits during 1961–62, including 'Marcheta', 'Mexicali Rose' and 'Wimoweh'. Denver continued to enjoy minor chart success over the next two years, before turning to cabaret work. In 1989 he collaborated with the **Happy Mondays** on 'Lazyitis (One Armed Boxer)'. He was recording new material shortly before his death in 1998.

DEPECHE MODE

Starting out as an 'electro-synth' group, Depeche Mode was formed in Basildon, Essex, England, by Vince Clarke (b. 1961), Andy Fletcher (b. 1960) and Martin

Gore (b. 1961). Following a series of concerts, they were spotted by Daniel Miller, who signed them to his independent Mute Records. Recruiting Dave Gahan (b. 1962) as permanent lead vocalist, they released 'Dreaming Of Me' in 1981, which started a run of hits which totalled 23 chart entries throughout the 80s. Principal songwriter Clarke left after *Speak & Spell* to form **Yazoo**. The writing was taken over by Gore and Alan Wilder (b. 1959; synthesizer, vocals) joined in place of Clarke.

During the early 90s, their albums continued to reach the UK Top 10, and they began to sell in Europe and America, particularly after the *Violator* tour. The album presented a harder sound, informed by Gahan's patronage of the American rock scene. This was

continued on the transatlantic chart-topper *Songs Of Faith And Devotion*. In 1996, Wilder departed and Gahan was hospitalized by a suspected overdose which almost killed him. He recovered, determined to stay clean and pursue a future with the band. *Ultra* and *Exciter* were surprisingly good albums.

DEREK AND THE DOMINOS

Formed by **Eric Clapton** (b. Erick Patrick Clapp, 1945) in 1970 following his departure from **Blind Faith** and a brief involvement with **Delaney And Bonnie**. Together with Carl Radle (d. 1980; bass), Bobby Whitlock (keyboards, vocals), Jim Gordon (drums) and Duane Allman (guitar), the band recorded *Layla And Other Assorted Love Songs*. The band were only together for a year, during which time they toured small clubs in the UK and USA. In addition to the classic 'Layla', the album contained Clapton's co-written compositions mixed with blues classics such as 'Key To The Highway' and a sympathetic reading of **Jimi Hendrix**'s 'Little Wing'. The subsequent live album, recorded on their US tour, demonstrated their considerable potential.

DESCENDENTS

US punk band formed in 1978 by Frank Navetta (vocals, guitar), Tony Lombardo (vocals, bass) and Bill Stevenson (drums). They recorded 'Ride The Wild' and collaborated with singer Cecilia for six months before Milo Aukerman became their first regular vocalist. They recorded their debut, *Milo Goes To College*, with Aukerman. The title was self-explanatory, with Aukerman indeed being college-bound. The band re-formed in 1985 with Ray Cooper replacing Navetta. Doug Carrion (bass) appeared on the following year's *Enjoy!*. Aukerman and Stevenson were then joined by Karl Alvarez (bass) and Stephen Egerton (guitar) on the Descendents' swansong, *All*, which gave the name to the new band formed by the remaining members after Aukerman returned to college. He reunited with his former bandmates in 1996.

DESERT ROSE BAND

Country-rock band formed in the mid-80s by Chris Hillman (b. 1942; lead vocals, guitar), Herb Pedersen (vocals, guitar), Bill Bryson (vocals, bass), Jay Dee Maness (pedal-steel guitar), John Jorgenson (guitar, mandolin, six-string bass) and Steve Duncan (drums); who were signed to the independent Curb Records by Dick Whitehouse. Their highly accomplished self-titled first album included a reworking of 'Time Between', previously recorded by Hillman on the **Byrds**' *Younger Than Yesterday*. Subsequent albums were critical and commercial successes, but in 1991 Maness was replaced by Tom Brumley. Jorgenson left the following year, and within not long afterwards the Desert Rose Band split up.

DESHANNON, JACKIE

Highly talented US singer-songwriter DeShannon (b. Sharon Lee Myers, 1944) commenced recording in 1960 with a series of minor-label releases. Her collaborations with Sharon Sheeley resulted in several pop songs, including 'Dum Dum' and 'Heart In Hand' (Brenda Lee), and 'Trouble' (the Kalin Twins). DeShannon then forged partnerships with Jack Nitzsche ('When You Walk In The Room', the **Searchers**' 1964 hit) and **Randy Newman**. Despite some excellent singles, DeShannon's own recording career failed to achieve the heights attained with her compositions, by Helen Shapiro, **Marianne Faithfull**, the **Byrds** and the Critters. However she reached the US Top 10 with the **Burt Bacharach**/Hal David-penned 'What The World Needs Now Is Love' (1965) and 'Put A Little Love In Your Heart' reached the Top 5 four years later.

Although she continued to write and record, DeShannon was unable to sustain the same profile during the 70s and 80s, yet her songs continued to provide hits for others, notably 'Bette Davis Eyes' (**Kim Carnes** 1981), 'Breakaway' (**Tracey Ullman**, 1983) and 'Put A Little Love In Your Heart' (**Annie Lennox** and **Al Green**, 1988). In 2000 DeShannon released the anodyne *You Know Me*, her first new recording in over 20 years.

DESTINY'S CHILD

This highly successful US urban R&B vocal quartet was formed by Beyoncé Knowles (b. 1981), LeToya Luckett (b. 1981), LaTavia Roberson (b. 1981) and Kelendria Rowland (b. 1981). The quartet adopted their biblically inspired name from a chapter in the Book Of Isaiah. Signed to Columbia Records in 1997, their self-titled debut featured the Top 10 hit 'No No No', Further hits followed, including 'With Me' and 'Get On The Bus', the latter taken from the *Why Do Fools Fall In Love?* soundtrack. *The Writing's On The Wall* was premiered by 'Bills, Bills, Bills', which provided the quartet with their first US chart-topper in July 1999, and also reached the UK Top 10. Farrah Franklin and Michelle Williams joined the group in February 2000 to replace the departing Roberson and Luckett. A month later the quartet topped the US Hot 100 with 'Say My Name'. Despite ongoing personnel problems – with Franklin leaving in August – the group enjoyed further transatlantic hits with 'Jumpin', Jumpin'' and 'Independent Women Part 1'. The latter, taken from the soundtrack of *Charlie's Angels*, topped the US charts for an incredible 11 weeks. Knowles took control of songwriting and production on the ultra-slick *Survivor*.

DETROIT SPINNERS

Formed in Detroit, USA, as the Domingoes. Henry Fambrough (b. 1935), Robert 'Bobby' Smith (b. 1937), Billy Henderson (b. 1939), Pervis Jackson and George Dixon

(vocals) became the Spinners in 1961 (the prefix 'Motown' and/or 'Detroit' was added in the UK to avoid confusion with the Spinners folk group). Producer and songwriter Harvey Fuqua sang lead on the group's debut single, 'That's What Girls Are Made For', which broached the US Top 30. Dixon was then replaced by Edgar 'Chico' Edwards. 'I'll Always Love You' (1965) was a minor US hit, but it was not until 1970 that the Spinners achieved a major success with a version of **Stevie Wonder**'s 'It's A Shame' (US/UK Top 20). Edwards was replaced by G. C. Cameron, who was in turn replaced by Philippe Wynne (b. Philip Walker, 1941, d. 1984). With producer Thom Bell, the Spinners completed a series of singles including 'I'll Be Around', 'Could It Be I'm Falling In Love' and 'Then Came You' (with Dionne Warwick). 'Ghetto Child' and 'The Rubberband Man' brought international success. John Edwards replaced Wynne in 1977, but the Spinners continued to enjoy hits, notably with 'Working My Way Back To You/Forgive Me Girl' (UK number 1/US number 2). However line-up instability undermined their subsequent career.

DEUS

Formed in Belgium in the early 90s by Tom Barman (b. 1972; vocals, guitar) and Stef Kamil Carlens (bass), Julle De Borgher (drums), Klaas Janzoons (violin) and Rudy Trouvè (b. 1967; guitar). Sharing a mutual affection for the works of **Captain Beefheart** and Tom Waits, the band set about writing a wide-ranging set of songs that zig-zagged between a number of musical traditions. Their first successful single was 'Suds And Soda', followed by the similarly bracing 'Via'. The well-received *Worst Case Scenario* was released by Island Records. Group members then concentrated on their array of solo and collaborative projects. In the interim dEUS issued a mail-order-only album, *My Sister = My Clock*. Trouvè and Carlens were then replaced by Danny Mommens (b. 1973) and Craig Ward, who featured on the excellent *In A Bar, Under The Sea* and *The Ideal Crash*.

DEVO

US new-wave band formed in 1972, featuring Gerald Casale (bass, vocals), Alan Myers (drums), Mark Mothersbaugh (vocals, keyboards, guitar), Bob Mothersbaugh (guitar, vocals), and Bob Casale (guitar, vocals). Their name comes from the theory of devolution, which they presented with electronic music, using strong robotic and mechanical overtones. The visual representation and marketing exaggerated modern life and their debut album was a synthesis of pop and sarcastic social commentary. It produced their biggest UK hit, a savage take on the **Rolling Stones**' '(I Can't Get No) Satisfaction'. *Freedom Of Choice* included 'Girl You Want' and 'Whip It', the latter giving them a million-selling single. At their peak, Devo inspired and informed, but eventually began to lose momentum. *New Traditionalists* signalled a creative descent and successive albums were released to diminishing returns. *Total Devo* saw Myers replaced by David Kendrick. Mothersbaugh moved into soundtrack work.

DEXYS MIDNIGHT RUNNERS

Soul-inspired UK band formed in 1978 by Kevin Rowland (b. 1953) and Al Archer (guitar) of punk outfit the Killjoys. They recruited Pete Williams (piano, organ), Jeff Blythe (tenor saxophone), Steve Spooner (alto saxophone), Pete Saunders (piano, organ), Big Jim Paterson (trombone) and Bobby Junior (drums). Rowland brilliantly fashioned the band's image, using *Mean Streets* as an inspiration for their New York Italian docker chic. Their debut 'Dance Stance' crept into the UK Top 40, but the follow-up 'Geno' (a tribute to 60s' soul singer Geno Washington) reached number 1 in 1980. *Searching For The Young Soul Rebels* was released to critical acclaim and commercial success. 'There, There My Dear', reached UK Top 10, but the band started to fragment.

Rowland and Paterson were then joined by Seb Shelton (drums), Micky Billingham (keyboards), Paul Speare (tenor saxophone), Brian Maurice (alto saxophone), Steve Wynne (bass) and Billy Adams (guitar), and initiated their 'ascetic athlete' phase. Early 1982 saw the band augmented by a fiddle section, the Emerald Express, featuring Helen O'Hara, Steve Brennan and Roger McDuff. Rowland's latest experiment was to fuse northern soul with Irish traditional music. This shift was reflected in their new image of hoedown gypsy chic – neckerchiefs, earrings, stubble and leather jerkins. Paterson, Maurice and Speare departed after 'The Celtic Soul Brothers', but 'Come On Eileen' (1982) restored the band to the top of the UK charts and also provided them with their first US number 1.

Further hits included a cover of **Van Morrison**'s 'Jackie Wilson Said' before the band underwent a long hibernation. They returned as a quartet: Rowland, Adams, O'Hara and Nicky Gatefield, with a new image of chic shirts and ties and neatly-cut hair. *Don't Stand Me Down* received favourable reviews but sold poorly. Although Rowland and O'Hara charted again with 'Because Of You', the commercial failure led to the end of Dexys Midnight Runners in 1987. Rowland subsequently embarked on an esoteric solo career.

DIAMOND HEAD

Part of the New Wave Of British Heavy Metal, Diamond Head were formed in 1979 by Sean Harris (vocals), Brian Tatler (guitar), Colin Kimberley (bass) and Duncan Scott (drums). Several hard-rocking releases followed, including *Borrowed Time*, but during sessions for *Canterbury*, both Kimberley and Scott left. They were replaced by Merv Goldsworthy and Robbie France respectively. Unfortunately, the album was poorly received and they disbanded in 1985.

In 1991, Harris and Tatler re-formed Diamond Head with newcomers Eddie Nooham (bass) and Karl Wilcox (drums). 'Wild On The Streets' rediscovered the spirit lost in 1985. The band broke up again after a tour to support the release of their final album in 1993.

DIAMOND, NEIL

With a career as a pop hitmaker stretching across four decades, US singer Diamond (b. 1941) has veered between straightforward pop, a progressive singer-songwriter style and middle-of-the-road balladry. After college, Diamond became a full-time songwriter in 1962. 'Sunday And Me', produced by **Leiber And Stoller** for Jay And The Americans, brought his first success as a composer in 1965. The following year, his own recording 'Cherry Cherry' entered the US Top 10. In 1967 the **Monkees** had multi-million-sellers with Diamond's memorable 'I'm A Believer' and 'A Little Bit Me, A Little Bit You'. Like his own 1967 hit, 'Thank The Lord For The Night', these songs combined a gospel feel with a memorable pop melody.

After a failed attempt at a progressive-rock album (*Velvet Gloves And Spit*) he began to record in Memphis and came up with a series of catchy, and simple hits, including 'Sweet Caroline' (1969), 'Holly Holy' and two number 1s, 'Cracklin Rosie' (1970) and 'Song Sung Blue' (1972). In the mid-70s Diamond moved into film work, winning a Grammy Award for the soundtrack of *Jonathan Livingston Seagull*. His debut for CBS Records, *Beautiful Noise*, was a tribute to the Brill Building songwriting world of the 50s and 60s. In 1978, he recorded a duet with **Barbra Streisand**, 'You Don't Bring Me Flowers', which headed the US chart. Now at the peak of his success, Diamond accepted his first film-acting role in a remake of *The Jazz Singer*.

During the 80s and 90s, Diamond increasingly co-wrote material with songwriters including Gilbert Bécaud, David Foster and above all Carole Bayer Sager and **Burt Bacharach**. His 1996 release *Tennessee Moon* was a complete departure from the safe limits of AOR pop; easily his most interesting album in years, it scaled the country music charts and introduced a totally new audience to Diamond.

DIDDLEY, BO

An early boxing career spawned the sobriquet 'Bo Diddley' for this legendary US blues/R&B artist (b. Otha Ellas Bates (later known as Ellas McDaniel), 1928). In 1954, he teamed up with Billy Boy Arnold and recorded demos of 'I'm A Man' and 'Bo Diddley'. Diddley's distorted, amplified, custom-made guitar, with its rectangular shape and pumping rhythm style, became a familiar, much-imitated trademark. His jive-talking routine with 'Say Man' (US Top 20, 1959) continued on 'Pretty Thing' and 'Hey Good Lookin'' (1963). Diddley had become an R&B legend: the Pretty Things named themselves after one of his songs, while his work was covered by artists including the **Rolling Stones**, the **Animals**, **Manfred Mann**, the **Kinks** and the **Yardbirds**. Diddley subsequently jammed on albums by **Chuck Berry** and **Muddy Waters**, and appeared at rock festivals. His classic version of 'Who Do You Love' became a staple cover for a new generation of US acts, most notably **Quicksilver Messenger Service**.

In an attempt to update his image, Diddley released *The Black Gladiator* in 1969. *Where It All Begins*, produced by Johnny Otis, was the most interesting of his post-60s albums. In 1979, Diddley toured with the **Clash** and in 1984 took a cameo role in the movie *Trading Places*. In the 90s he recorded for the Code Blue label. A familiar face on the revival circuit, Diddley is rightly regarded as a seminal figure in the history of rock 'n' roll.

DIDO

The sister of **Faithless** producer Rollo Armstrong, Dido (b. Florian Cloud de Bounevialle Armstrong, 1971) sang on the dance act's 1996 debut *Reverence* and the follow-up *Sunday 8pm*. At this stage, Dido was writing her own material and had assembled an album's worth of demo tapes. Her debut, *No Angel*, was produced by Rollo and Youth and received its US release in 1999. The album combined electronic and acoustic elements to create a lush, down-tempo style. The track 'Here With Me' was used as the theme for the hit US television series *Roswell*, and 'Thank You' was sampled by rap star **Eminem** for his single 'Stan'. Phenomenal sales followed on both sides of the Atlantic.

DIFRANCO, ANI

Prolific US artist DiFranco (b. 1970) emerged in the 90s as a literate, ebullient and natural live performer, who won converts from both folk and rock audiences. Her promising 1990 debut album, like all her material released on her own Righteous Babe label, contained lyrics informed by feminist theory but never subsumed by rhetoric or preciousness. *Imperfectly* included more complex musical arrangements, incorporating viola, trumpet and mandolin. The self-produced *Dilate* was more rock-orientated, in stark contrast to her collaboration with folk legend Utah Phillips on 1996's *The Past Didn't Go Anywhere*. In a busy 1999, DiFranco released two new solo albums and another collaborative effort with Phillips. *Revelling/Reckoning*, a sprawling, musically diverse 29-track double set released in 2001, was held together by the force of DiFranco's personality and the clarity of her lyrical vision.

DILLARD AND CLARK

Doug Dillard (b. 1937; ex-Dillards) and Gene Clark (b. Harold Eugene Clark, 1944, d. 1991; ex-**Byrds**) joined forces in 1968 to form one of the first country rock groups. Backed by the Expedition – Bernie Leadon (banjo, guitar), Don Beck (dobro, mandolin) and David Jackson (string bass) – they recorded two excellent albums. The group scattered in various directions at the end of the 60s.

DILLARDS

US bluegrass group formed by brothers Rodney (b. 1942; guitar, vocals) and Doug Dillard (b. 1937; banjo, vocals), Roy Dean Webb (b. 1937; mandolin, vocals) and Mitch Jayne (b. 1930; bass). They began recording for Elektra Records in 1962. *Back Porch Bluegrass* and *The Dillards Live! Almost!* established them as one of America's leading traditional acts. *Pickin' & Fiddlin'* was recorded with violinist Byron Berline. Dewey Martin (b. 1942; drums) also joined before Doug Dillard left to work with Gene Clark (ex-**Byrds**). Herb Peterson joined in 1968 and the reshaped quartet completed *Wheatstraw Suite* and

Copperfields. Peterson was in turn replaced by Billy Rae Latham for *Roots And Branches*, on which the unit's transformation to full-scale electric instruments was complete. Drummer Paul York was now featured in the line-up, but further changes were wrought when Jayne dropped out following *Tribute To The American Duck*. Rodney Dillard has since remained at the helm of a capricious act; he was also reunited with his prodigal brother in Dillard-Hartford-Dillard, which included multi-instrumentalist John Hartford.

DINOSAUR JR

Uncompromising alternative rock band from Massachusetts, USA, originally called Dinosaur. Main songwriter J. Mascis (b. 1965; vocals, guitar), Lou Barlow (bass) and Murph (b. Patrick Murphy) evolved from hardcore band Deep Wound. During Dinosaur Jr's career, internal rifts never seemed far from the surface, while Mascis' monosyllabic press interviews and general disinterest in rock 'n' roll machinations gave the impression of 'genius anchored by lethargy'. The 1987 release *You're Living All Over Me* brought them to the attention of hippy group Dinosaur, who insisted the band change their name. Real recognition came with the release of the huge underground anthem 'Freak Scene', but its parent album, *Bug*, and attendant tour saw Barlow depart. By *Green Mind*, Dinosaur Jr had effectively become the J. Mascis show, with him playing almost all the instruments. Murphy left and *Where You Been* did not build on the commercial inroads previously forecasted. Mascis formally announced the end of Dinosaur Jr in December 1997, following the release of *Hand It Over*. He subsequently collaborated with Kevin Shields (**My Bloody Valentine**) and Bob Pollard (**Guided By Voices**) on his next project, J Mascis And The Fog, releasing the excellent *More Light*.

DION

Between 1958 and 1960 Dion And The Belmonts were one of the leading US doo-wop groups. They had nine hits in two years, including a classic reading of the Doc Pomus and Mort Shuman song 'A Teenager In Love'. Dion (b. Dion DiMucci, 1939) went solo in 1960 and had immediate US success with 'Lonely Teenager'. The following year he had two consecutive hits with 'Runaround Sue' and 'The Wanderer' and sustained an incredible output of hits – he was in the US charts for the whole of 1963. In 1964, he disappeared from the scene to fight a serious heroin addiction. Although he and the Belmonts reunited briefly in 1967, little was heard of him as a solo artist until 1968. He returned during a turbulent year in American history. His emotional 'Abraham, Martin And John' was perfectly timed and climbed to US number 4. *Dion* and two acoustic-based albums failed to sell and he reunited with the Belmonts in 1973. Two years later Phil Spector produced 'Born To Be With You'. An album of the same name failed, as did another underrated album, *The Return Of The Wanderer*, three years later. For the next few years Dion recorded sporadically, releasing two Christian-themed albums. He returned to rock 'n' roll in 1988, playing with **Bruce Springsteen** and releasing *Yo Frankie!*. He was elected to the Rock And Roll Hall Of Fame in 1989. A fresh new album was released in 2000.

DION, CELINE

Canadian chanteuse Dion (b. 1968), the youngest of 12 children, began singing in her family's touring folk group before René Angélil, a local rock manager, took over the young star's guidance. Following a series of French Canadian albums, she made her English-language debut in 1990 with *Unison*. Despite four hit singles, true international recognition proved elusive until her US number 1 soundtrack from Disney's *Beauty And The Beast*, which won an Academy Award and a Grammy. Dion's 'When I Fall In Love', the theme tune to the hit movie *Sleepless In Seattle*, was included on 1993's *The Colour Of My Love*,

alongside a US chart-topping cover version of Jennifer Rush's classic 'The Power Of Love'. 'Think Twice' (1995) spent several weeks at UK number 1 and charted in the US. The album, and its follow-up *Falling Into You*, simultaneously topped both UK and US charts and, in 1996, Dion was chosen to sing at the opening of the Olympic Games in Atlanta, USA. She also enjoyed another huge US chart-topper with 'Because You Loved Me', the theme to the movie *Up Close & Personal*. In 1997, she was back at US/UK number 1 with 'My Heart Will Go On', the theme song from the hit movie *Titanic*. She also collaborated with the **Bee Gees** on 'Immortality', and **R. Kelly** on 'I'm Your Angel', both of which were predictably international hit singles.

The singer took a break from performing in the late 90s to concentrate on conceiving a child, and gave birth to a son, Rene Charles, in January 2001. The lure of singing meant Dion was not away for long, returning in 2002 with *A New Day Has Come*.

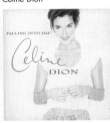

DIRE STRAITS

Scottish brothers David (b. 1952) and **Mark Knopfler** (b. 1949) joined up with bass player John Illsley (b. 1949) and drummer Pick Withers in London, England, in the 70s. Their repertoire included a basic blues progression called 'Sultans Of Swing'. It was picked up by Radio London DJ Charlie Gillett, and by the end of 1977 the band were recording their debut, *Dire Straits*, with producer Muff Winwood. The album reached US number 2. *Communiqué* sold three million copies worldwide. It missed the commercial edge of the debut but developed Knopfler's trademark of incisive, cynical lyricism. Before the recording of *Making Movies*, David Knopfler went solo, and was replaced by Hal Lindes and Alan Clark (keyboards). The album spawned a UK Top 10 single with 'Romeo And Juliet'. *Love Over Gold* was a transatlantic success, and 'Private Investigations' reached UK number 2.

Knopfler then took time off to produce **Bob Dylan**'s *Infidels* (1983) and write 'Private Dancer' for **Tina Turner**. When Dire Straits reconvened, Withers was replaced by ex-Man drummer Terry Williams. A live double set, *Alchemy Live*, filled the gap before 1985's *Brothers In Arms*. The album established them as the first real darlings of the compact-disc generation that grew out of the boom years of the 80s. It was US number 1 for nine weeks and spent three years in the UK chart, while 'Money For Nothing' reached US number 1.

The band then took another sabbatical. Mark Knopfler wrote film scores and formed an *ad-hoc* group, the Notting Hillbillies. Illsley released two poorly received solo albums. In 1991, Dire Straits announced a 'comeback' tour and the release of a new album, *On Every Street*. Following the release of another live album, and with Dire Straits on indefinite hold, Knopfler released his first solo album in 1996.

DISPOSABLE HEROES OF HIPHOPRISY

Hugely innovative US hip-hop crew formed by Rono Tse (percussion) and Michael Franti (b. 1966; vocals). They worked together for several years, most notably in *avant-garde* industrial jazz band the Beatnigs. Franti's raps on their sole album, 1992's *Hypocrisy Is The Greatest Luxury*, were articulate and challenging, breaking down his subject matter beyond the black/white rhetoric of much urban rap. In 1993, they recorded an album with author William Burroughs but, as the year closed, they split. Franti went on to enjoy further acclaim with Spearhead, while Rono worked with Oakland-based Mystic Journeymen.

DISTURBED

Chicago, USA-based nu-metal outfit comprising long-time associates Dan Donegan (guitar), Fuzz (bass), and Mike Wengren (drums), and the charismatic Dave Draiman (vocals). Draiman, who also suggested the band's name, provided an immediate focal point when he joined the three other members in 1997. *The Sickness* polished off the rough edges of their demo tape, leaving a fairly traditional metal sound with the occasional nod to electronica. In common with most of their nu-metal contemporaries the band also rattled out a desultory cover version of an 80s classic, in this case **Tears For Fears'** 'Shout'.

DIVINE COMEDY

This Irish band has been led from its inception by Neil Hannon (b. 1970), the son of the Bishop of Clogher. Hannon originally formed the band in 1989 with John McCullagh (vocals) and drummer Kevin Traynor. The trio released an indie-rock album, *Fanfare For The Comic Muse*, before Hannon struck out on his own. The prevailing influences on *Liberation* and *Promenade* included Michael Nyman, European art and Scott Walker. A breakthrough beyond critical success came in 1996 with the highly accessible *Casanova*, which put Hannon in the UK Top 20 courtesy of the singles 'Something For The Weekend' and 'The Frog Princess'. He followed this with a wondrous mini-album, *A Short Album About Love*, featuring seven heavily orchestrated new songs. Hannon, by now working with an expanded Divine Comedy line-up, also collaborated with Nyman. The Divine Comedy's final album for Setanta Records, *Fin De Siècle*, provided Hannon with his first Top 10 hit with the jaunty 'National Express'. The Divine Comedy's first album for new label Parlophone Records, 2001's *Regeneration*, eschewed the orchestral pop leanings of Hannon's previous work in favour of a more understated and rock-orientated sound.

DIXIE CHICKS

This US female trio's beguiling mixture of bluegrass, straight country and pop shook up the contemporary country scene in the late 90s. Sisters Martie Seidel (mandolin, fiddle) and Emily Erwin (banjo, dobro) founded the group in 1989 with Laura Lynch and Robin Lynn Macy. They released two bluegrass-orientated independent label albums and a Christmas single, before Macy left to form the Domestic Social Club. The more contemporary sounding *Shouldn't A Told You That* was the last recording to feature Lynch, who was replaced by new lead vocalist Natalie Maines in 1995. The new-look Dixie Chicks bounced back in 1998 with *Wide Open Spaces*, the bestselling

country album released by a group in that year. Its success was buoyed by the release of the singles 'I Can Love You Better' and 'There's Your Trouble' (a US Country number 1). The follow-up, *Fly*, which introduced a more pop-orientated style, shot to the top of the US album chart in 1999. The Top 10 single 'Goodbye Earl', a *Thelma And Louise*-style tale of two women exacting the ultimate revenge on a violent husband, became a *cause celebre* after it was banned by several male radio programmers and DJs.

DIXIE CUPS

Formed in New Orleans, USA, in 1963, the Dixie Cups featured sisters Barbara Ann (b. 1943) and Rosa Lee Hawkins (b. 1944) and their cousin Joan Marie Johnson (b. 1945). The girls formed the Meltones for a high-school talent contest in 1963 and were subsequently signed to **Leiber And Stoller**, who were then starting their own record label, Red Bird. The Dixie Cups recorded 'Chapel Of Love' in 1964. The song had failed for the Ronettes and the **Crystals**, but this time reached US number 1. Four of their follow-ups charted, including 'People Say' (number 12) and 'Iko Iko' (number 20).

DIXON, WILLIE

Mississippi, USA-born Dixon (b. 1915, d. 1992) graduated from gospel groups to form the Five Breezes with Baby Doo Caston. Their 1940 recordings blended blues, jazz, pop and vocal group harmonies. After 10 months in prison for resisting the draft, Dixon formed the Four Jumps Of Jive, before reuniting with Caston in the Big Three Trio. The trio featured vocal harmonies and the jazz-influenced guitar work of Ollie Crawford.

By 1951, Dixon was working at Chess Records as producer, A&R representative, session musician, talent scout, songwriter and, occasionally, name artist. He was largely responsible for the sound of Chicago blues on Chess and Cobra, and of the music of **Chuck Berry** and **Bo Diddley**.

He was also used on gospel sessions by Duke/Peacock. Dixon's productions of his own songs included **Muddy Waters**' 'Hoochie Coochie Man', **Howlin' Wolf**'s 'Spoonful', Diddley's 'You Can't Judge A Book By The Cover' and Otis Rush's 'I Can't Quit You Baby'.

In the 60s, Dixon teamed up with Memphis Slim to play the folk revival's notion of blues. Many British R&B bands recorded his songs, including the Rolling Stones and Led Zeppelin. After leaving Chess, Dixon went into independent production with his own labels, Yambo and Spoonful, and resumed a recording and performing career.

DJ JAZZY JEFF AND THE FRESH PRINCE

Jazzy Jeff (b. Jeffrey Townes, 1965) started DJing in the mid-70s. He met **Will Smith** aka The Fresh Prince (b. 1968) and the two secured a recording deal. Their early records included **James Brown** lifts placed next to steals from cartoon characters. In the late 80s they released million-selling teen anthems like 'Girls Ain't Nothing But Trouble'. They became the first rap act to receive a Grammy Award (for 'Parents Just Don't Understand'). *He's The DJ, I'm The Rapper* contained more accessible pop fare. Television's *The Fresh Prince Of Bel Air* augmented Smith's profile and provided an indicator of his future career. The duo picked up a second Grammy for 'Summertime' (1991), before scoring a UK number 1 with 'Boom! Shake The Room' (1993). Smith moved on to a major Hollywood career, beginning with *Six Degrees Of Separation* and continuing on to the mega-hits *Independence Day* and *Men In Black*. He also enjoys a highly successful solo career.

DJ SHADOW

DJ Shadow (b. Josh Davis) began to put together beats and samples on primitive equipment at an early age. His 1993 debut for Mo Wax Records, the atmospheric 'In/Flux'/'Hindsight', stands as a benchmark in *avant-garde* hip-hop circles. A diverse source of inspirations are apparent on further recordings 'Lost & Found' (1994) and 'What Does Your Soul Look Like' (1995). Towards the end of 1996 he released his first album, *Endtroducing ... ,* which was widely acclaimed for the way in which Davis blended hip-hop grooves with elements of jazz, rock, ambient and techno. In 1997 Shadow released a set of his tracks performed by DJ Q-Bert (renowned for his technical mastery) entitled *Camel Bob Sled Race*. Recording with old friends Blackalicious and Latyrx as Quannum, he released 1999's diversely entertaining *Spectrum*.

DMX

Marketed as a return to the chaotic, raw roots of street rap, DMX (b. Earl Simmons, 1970) became hip-hop's latest sensation during 1998 when his debut, *It's Dark And Hell Is Hot*, entered the US album chart at number 1. An impressive slice of east-coast hardcore rap, the album centred around DMX's ferocious lyrical approach. The follow-up, *Flesh Of My Flesh, Blood Of My Blood*, also reached the top of the US charts. After contributing to the Ruff Ryders' chart-topping *Ryde Or Die Vol. 1* set, DMX released his third solo album *... And Then There Was X*, another quality slice of hardcore rap and a welcome antidote to the bland hip-hop product still flooding the American market. The album followed its predecessors to the top of the US charts in 2000.

DODD, COXSONE

Dodd (b. Clement Seymour Dodd) was amongst the first in Jamaica to run his own sound system, Sir Coxsone The Down Beat, a forerunner to the mobile discos of the 60s. In the mid-50s, the supply of hard US R&B records dried up as smoother productions began to find favour in America. These were not popular in Jamaica, so the sound system operators started to make their own music. At the end of the 50s,

Coxsone's Worldisc label included local artists such as Jackie Estick, Lascelles Perkins, Clue J And His Blues Blasters and Theophilius Beckford. Dodd's productions caught the mood of the times and, from R&B to ska, he was always at the forefront. Throughout the ska era he ruled with records like 'Spit In The Sky' (Delroy Wilson), 'Hallelujah' (Maytals), 'Rude Boy Gone A Jail' (Clarendonians), 'I've Got To Go Back Home' (Bob Andy), 'Simmer Down' (the Wailers), Lee Perry tunes and dozens of fiery instrumentals by the Skatalites (the Coxsone backing group).

Dodd opened his own studio, Studio One, in the early 60s. It became the generic title for all Coxsone productions thereafter. During 1967–70, the hits flowed in a veritable deluge: by late 1966, ska's furious pace had begun to give way to the slower rocksteady beat and Dodd's raw, almost organic productions from this period formed what amounts to the foundation of reggae music in the following decades.

Younger producers, some of whom had learnt their trade while with Coxsone, began to take over in the early 70s. Nonetheless, he still produced a great deal of fine 70s music, including some of the earliest material from Horace Andy, Dennis Brown, the Wailing Souls, Burning Spear, Dennis Alcapone, Dillinger and Freddie McKay. As the dancehall style began to take hold, he was once more in full swing with recording artists such as Freddie McGregor, Sugar Minott, and DJs Michigan And Smiley and the Lone Ranger. This proved to be the final golden period for Studio One, however, and in the mid-80s Dodd closed his Brentford Road studio and relocated to New York.

DOLBY, THOMAS

Dolby (b. Thomas Morgan Robertson, 1958), a self-taught musician and computer programmer, started building his own synthesizers at the age of 18. With his own hand-built PA system he acted as sound engineer on tours by the Members, the Fall and the Passions. He co-founded Camera Cub with Bruce Wooley in 1979, before joining the Lene Lovich backing group in 1980, for whom he wrote 'New Toy'. His first solo output was 'Urges' (1981), followed by 'Europa' and 'The Pirate Twins' (both 1982). His best-known singles, 'She Blinded Me With Science' and 'Hyperactive' made the UK Top 40 and the latter reached the US Top 5; it also charted in the UK again when re-released in 1996. Dolby has produced for **Prefab Sprout** and **Joni Mitchell**, and has scored music for several films.

DOMINO, FATS

While working in a factory, Domino (b. Antoine Domino, 1928) played in local US clubs. In 1949, he was discovered by band-leader Dave Bartholomew and Imperial Records' Lew Chudd. His first recording, 'The Fat Man' (1950), hit the R&B Top 10 and launched his unique partnership with Bartholomew, who co-wrote and arranged dozens of Domino tracks over the next two decades. Domino's playing was derived from the rich mixture of musical styles found in New Orleans, including traditional jazz, Latin rhythms, boogie-woogie, Cajun and blues.

By 1955, rock 'n' roll had arrived and young white audiences were ready for Domino's music. His first pop success came with 'Ain't That A Shame' (1955), followed by 'Bo Weevil' and the catchy 'I'm In Love Again' (US Top 10). Domino's next big success came with a pre-rock 'n' roll song, 'Blueberry Hill'. Inspired by Louis Armstrong's 1949 version, Domino used his Creole drawl to

perfection. Domino had nearly 20 US Top 40 singles between 1955 and 1960, among them was the majestic 'Walking To New Orleans', a Bobby Charles composition that became a string-laden tribute to the sources of his musical inspiration. He continued to record prolifically, maintaining a consistently high level of performance. In the mid-60s, Domino recorded several albums with producers Felton Jarvis and Bill Justis, and continued to record on a regular basis in the 70s.

In 1986, Domino was inducted into the Rock And Roll Hall Of Fame, and won Hall Of Fame and Lifetime Achievement awards at the 1987 Grammys. In 1993, Domino was back in the studio recording his first sessions proper for 25 years, resulting in *Christmas Is A Special Day*.

DONEGAN, LONNIE

Scottish-born Donegan (b. Anthony Donegan, 1931) was a guitarist in a skiffle band before a spell in the army found him drumming in the Wolverines Jazz Band. After his discharge, he played banjo with Ken Colyer and then Chris Barber; with both outfits Donegan sang a couple of blues-tinged American folk tunes as a 'skiffle' break. His 1954 version of **Lead Belly**'s 'Rock Island Line' (from Barber's *New Orleans Joys*) was a US hit.

Donegan possessed an energetic whine far removed from the gentle plumminess of other UK pop vocalists. His string of familiar songs included 'Don't You Rock Me Daddy-O', 'Putting On The Style', 'Grand Coulee Dam', 'Does Your Chewing Gum Lose Its Flavour On The Bedpost Over Night', 'Jimmy Brown The Newsboy', 'Cumberland Gap' (a UK number 1), and 'Battle Of New Orleans'. He experimented with bluegrass, spirituals, Cajun and Appalachian music and, when the skiffle boom diminished, he broadened his appeal with olde-tyme music hall/pub singalong favourites, and a more pronounced comedy element – his 'My Old Man's A Dustman' (1960), sensationally entered the UK charts at number 1. Two years later, Donegan's Top 20 run ended as it had started, with a Lead Belly number ('Pick A Bale Of Cotton'); between 1956 and 1962 he had produced 34 hits.

Donegan continues to entertain and in the early 90s, touring occasionally with Chris Barber. In 1995 he was presented with an Ivor Novello Award for Outstanding Contribution To British Music. In 1998, Donegan recorded his first new album in 20 years.

DONNAS

This all-female US punk rock quartet was formed by high school students Donna A (b. Brett Anderson; vocals), Donna C (b. Torrance Castellano; drums), Donna F (b. Maya Ford; bass), Donna R (b. Allison Robertson; guitar). Originally known as Ragady Anne, and also playing as the Electrocutes, the quartet's long-playing debut was released on Super*Teem in 1996. By this time they had also recorded an Electrocutes album, *Steal Yer Lunch Money*. After graduation from high school they signed to Lookout! Records and released 1999's *Get Skintight*. In the same year, the Donnas appeared in the movies *Jawbreaker* and *Drive Me Crazy*. They celebrated reaching the legal drinking age with *Turn 21*.

DONOVAN

Adopted by the pioneering UK television show *Ready, Steady, Go!*, Scottish musician Donovan (b. Donovan Leitch, 1946) launched his career in the mid-60s with 'Catch The Wind', followed by 'Colours' and 'Turquoise'. Donovan's finest work, however, was as ambassador of 'flower power', with transatlantic hit singles like 'Sunshine Superman' and 'Mellow Yellow'. He enjoyed further hits with light material such as the calypso-influenced 'There Is A Mountain' and 'Jennifer Juniper'.

Donovan's drug/fairy tale imagery reached its apotheosis on the Lewis Carroll-influenced 'Hurdy Gurdy Man', but as the 60s closed he fell from commercial grace. His collaboration with **Jeff Beck** on 'Goo Goo Barabajagal (Love Is Hot)' showed a more gutsy approach, but during the 70s he gradually disappeared from the music scene.

In 1991, the **Happy Mondays** invited him to tour with them (he had recently become vocalist Shaun Ryder's father-in-law). He undertook a major UK tour in 1992, but *Sutras* achieved little in terms of sales.

DOOBIE BROTHERS

Formed in San Jose, USA, in 1970 by Tom Johnston (b. 1948; guitar) and John Hartman (b. 1950; drums). Original bass player Greg Murphy was quickly replaced by Dave Shogren (d. 2000) and Patrick Simmons (b. 1948; guitar) then joined. Within six months the group had become the Doobie Brothers, taken from a slang term for a marijuana cigarette. Their debut album was commercially unsuccessful and contrasted with their tougher live sound. A new bass player, Tiran Porter, and second drummer, Michael Hossack (b. 1946), joined for the excellent *Toulouse Street*, which spawned the anthem-like 'Listen To The Music'. *The Captain And Me* contained two US hits, 'Long Train Running' and 'China Grove', while *What Were Once Vices Are Now Habits*, a largely disappointing album, featured the band's first US chart-topper, 'Black Water'. Hossack was replaced by Keith Knudsen (b. 1948) for *Stampede*, which also introduced guitarist, Jeff 'Skunk' Baxter (b. 1948; ex-**Steely Dan**). In 1975, **Michael McDonald** (b. 1952; keyboards, vocals) joined, when Johnston succumbed to a recurrent ulcer problem. Although the guitarist rejoined in 1976, he left again two years later. McDonald gradually assumed control of the band's sound, instilling the soul-based perspective on *Minute By Minute* and its US number 1, 'What A Fool Believes'. Hartman and Baxter left and *One Step Closer* featured newcomers John McFee (b. 1953; guitar), Cornelius Bumpus (b. 1952; saxophone, keyboards) and Chet McCracken (b. 1952; drums). Willie Weeks subsequently replaced Porter, but by 1981 the Doobie Brothers' impetus was waning and they split the following year.

A re-formed unit, comprising the *Toulouse Street* line-up plus Bobby LaKind (congas), completed 1989's *Cycles*. They found a similar audience and 'The Doctor' made the US Top 10. In 1993, a remixed version of 'Long Train Running' put them back in the charts. McDonald also returned to the fold during this period, but by 2000's new studio album, *Sibling Rivalry*, the line-up comprised Johnston, Simmons, Hossack, Knudsen and McFee.

DOORS

In 1965, **Jim Morrison** (b. James Douglas Morrison, 1943, d. 1971) joined fellow University of California student Ray Manzarek (b. 1939; keyboards) in the R&B band Rick And The Ravens. The band was later rounded out by John Densmore (b. 1944; drums) and Robbie Krieger (b. 1946; guitar). Elektra Records signed the newly christened the Doors in 1966. *The Doors* introduced their sound: Manzarek's thin-sounding organ recalled garage-band style, but Krieger's liquid guitar playing and Densmore's imaginative drumming were already clearly evident. Morrison's striking, dramatic voice added power to the exceptional compositions, which included the pulsating 'Break On Through'. The compelling single 'Light My Fire' reached US number 1.

Strange Days showcased the exceptional 'When The Music's Over' and the quartet enjoyed further chart success with 'People Are Strange' (US Top 20), but it was 1968 before they secured another number 1 with 'Hello I Love You'. The Doors' first European tour showcased several tracks from *Waiting For The Sun*, including the declamatory 'Five To One', and a fierce protest song, 'The Unknown Soldier'. The following *The Soft Parade* was a major disappointment, although 'Touch Me' reached the US Top 5.

Commercial success exacted pressure on Morrison, whose frustration with his role as a pop idol grew more pronounced. In March 1969, following a concert in Miami, the singer was indicted for indecent exposure, public intoxication and profane, lewd and lascivious conduct. He was acquitted of all but the minor charges. Paradoxically, this furore re-awoke the Doors' creativity. *Morrison Hotel*, a tough R&B-based collection, matched the best of their early releases. Two volumes of Morrison's poetry, *The Lords* and *The New Creatures*, had been published and, having completed sessions for a new album, he left for Paris where he hoped to follow a literary career. Tragically, on 3 July 1971, Jim Morrison was found dead in his bathtub.

L.A. Woman, his final recording, is one of the Doors' finest achievements, including the superb 'Riders On The Storm'. The others continued to work as the Doors, but *Other Voices* and *Full Circle* were severely flawed and the band soon dissolved. In 1978, they supplied music to a series of poetry recitations that Morrison had taped during the *L.A. Woman* sessions; the resulting *An American Prayer* was a major success. Oliver Stone's 1991 movie biography *The Doors*, helped confirm Morrison as one of the 60s' great cultural icons.

DOVES

Manchester, England-based Doves' original incarnation Sub Sub enjoyed a UK hit in autumn 1993 when their strident house track 'Ain't No Love (Ain't No Use)' was omnipresent in clubs and on the radio. Jimi Goodwin (bass, vocals), Jez Williams (guitar, vocals) and twin Andy Williams (drums) subsequently re-invented themselves as the Doves, eschewing the sequencers and samplers that

they had previously utilized and recording a classic indie guitar album. Released in 2000, *Lost Souls* was saturated with beauty, intimacy and poignancy. The trio's second album, *The Last Broadcast*, was introduced by the UK Top 3 single 'There Goes The Fear'.

DOWNLINERS SECT

UK band formed in 1962 as the Downliners. Founder members Don Craine (b. Michael O'Donnel; vocals, rhythm guitar) and Johnny Sutton (drums) recruited Keith Grant (b. Keith Evans; bass) and Terry Gibson (b. Terry Clemson; lead guitar). Having added the 'Sect' suffix, they recorded a privately pressed EP, *A Nite In Great Newport Street*. A version of Jimmy Reed's 'Baby What's Wrong' (1964) was their first single, by which time Ray Sone (harmonica) had joined. Their musical approach was showcased on their debut album, but in 1965, they confused any prospective audience with *The Country Sect*, an album of folk and country material, and *The Sect Sing Sick Songs* EP. Sone left the band prior to recording *The Rock Sect's In*. When two pop-orientated singles, 'Glendora' and 'Cost Of Living', failed to chart, Gibson and Sutton left, replaced by Bob Taylor and Kevin Flanagan; pianist Matthew Fisher (later of Procol Harum) also joined briefly. Craine left after 'I Can't Get Away From You', after which Grant and Sutton took the unit to Sweden, where they recorded a handful of tracks before disbanding. Craine and Grant revived the Downliners Sect in 1976 in the wake of the pub-rock/R&B phenomenon, and continued to lead them throughout subsequent decades.

DR. DRE

Widely regarded as the chief architect of west-coast gangsta rap, Dr. Dre (b. Andre Young, 1965) started out as a DJ in Los Angeles. After playing with the seminal **N.W.A.** and acting as house producer for Ruthless Records, Dre confirmed rap's immersion into the mainstream with his 1992 debut *The Chronic*. His subsequent work – Eazy-E, D.O.C., Above The Law, **Snoop Doggy Dogg** and the Death Row Records label – broke new ground. The success of *The Chronic* and Dogg's *Doggystyle*, and the signing of rap's biggest new star 2Pac, briefly made Death Row one of America's most powerful labels. By 1996, however, its well documented problems culminated in Dre acrimoniously leaving to form his own Aftermath Records label. In 1998, Dre was back in the news again as co-producer on his protégè **Eminem**'s controversial breakthrough album, *The Slim Shady LP*. The following November he released his highly anticipated sophomore collection, *Dr. Dre 2001*.

DR. FEELGOOD

The most enduring act to emerge from the UK's much-touted 'pub-rock' scene, Dr. Feelgood was formed in 1971 by Lee Brilleaux (b. 1952, d. 1994; vocals, harmonica), Wilko Johnson (b. John Wilkinson; guitar), John B. Sparks (bass), John Potter (piano) and 'Bandsman' Howarth (drums). When Potter and Howarth dropped out, the remaining trio recruited John 'The Big Figure' Martin (drums). *Down By The Jetty* received critical

approbation, but the quartet only secured commercial success with *Stupidity*. Johnson was then replaced by John 'Gypie' Mayo. Dr. Feelgood then embarked on a more mainstream direction, which was only intermittently successful. 'Milk And Alcohol' (1979) was their sole UK Top 10 hit. In 1981, Johnny Guitar (b. John Crippen) replaced Mayo, while the following year Sparks and the Big Figure left. Brilleaux relaunched the band with Gordon Russell (guitar), Kevin Morris (drums) and Phil Mitchell (bass), but their audience began to dwindle. In 1993, Brilleaux was diagnosed as having lymphoma and had to break the band's touring schedule for the first time in over 20 years. He died the following year. The remaining musicians have respected his wish to keep the flame burning.

DR. HOOK

Dr. Hook And The Medicine Show began as a New Jersey, USA-based bar band with one-eyed Dr. Hook (b. Ray Sawyer, 1937; vocals), Denis Locorriere (b. 1949; guitar, vocals), George Cummings (b. 1938; lead/slide guitar), William Francis (b. 1942; keyboards) and Jay David (b. 1942; drums). They were chosen to record the score to Shel Silverstein's *Who's Harry Kellerman And Why Is He Saying These Terrible Things About Me?* (1970), and later backed Silverstein's singing on record. The band were signed to CBS Records and international success followed with 'Sylvia's Mother' and 'The Cover Of The Rolling Stone'. With Rik Elswit (b. 1945; guitar) and Jance Garfat (b. 1944; bass), they completed *Belly Up*. They were then joined by drummer John Wolters (b. 1945, d. 1997). A revival of **Sam Cooke**'s 'Only 16' was followed by the title track of *A Little Bit More*. Next came a UK number 1 with 'When You're In Love With A Beautiful Woman' from the million-selling *Pleasure And Pain*.

Throughout the 80s, Dr. Hook's chart strikes were mainly in North America, becoming more sporadic as the decade wore on. Sawyer's solo career and Locorriere's efforts as a Nashville-based songwriter had all but dissolved Dr. Hook by 1990.

DR. JOHN

Dr. John (b. Malcolm John Rebennack, 1940) is a consummate New Orleans musician, who blends funk, rock 'n' roll, jazz and R&B. He started out as a session musician, playing guitar, keyboards and other instruments. His first recording under his own name was 'Storm Warning' (1957). By 1962, Rebennack had played on countless sessions for such renowned producers as Phil Spector, Harold Battiste, H. B. Barnum and **Sonny Bono**. He also formed his own bands during the early 60s but with no success. By the mid-60s he had moved to Los Angeles, where he fused his New Orleans roots with the psychedelic sound and developed the persona Dr. John Creaux, The Night Tripper. He used an intoxicating brew of voodoo incantations and New Orleans heritage. *Gris-Gris* included 'Walk On Gilded Splinters' and inspired several similarly styled successors.

The same musical formula and exotic image were pursued on *Babylon* and *Remedies*. In 1971, Dr. John charted for the first time with *The Sun, Moon & Herbs*, followed by *Dr. John's Gumbo* and 'Iko Iko'. His biggest US hit came in 1973 with 'Right Place, Wrong Time'. The accompanying album, *In The Right Place*, was also his best seller. 'Such A Night' (1973) also charted.

Dr. John continued to record for numerous labels throughout the 70s and 80s, among them United Artists Records, Horizon and Clean Cuts. His live appearances are now less frequent, but this irrepressible artist continues his role as a tireless champion of Crescent City music. In 1997, he signed to Parlophone Records, and recorded tracks with several modern UK artists for the following year's *Anutha Zone*, which broke into the UK Top 40. A relaxed tribute to Duke Ellington followed in 1999.

DRAKE, NICK

Cult UK singer-songwriter Drake (b. 1948, d. 1974) debuted in 1969 with *Five Leaves Left*, a mature, melodic collection featuring Robert Kirby (strings), Richard Thompson (guitar) and Danny Thompson (bass). Drake's languid, almost unemotional intonation contrasted with the warmth of his musical accompaniment. *Bryter Layter* was more worldly and jazz-based, featuring Lyn Dobson (flute) and Ray Warleigh (saxophone). A bout of severe depression followed, but late in 1971 Drake resumed recording with the harrowing *Pink Moon*. Completed in two days, its stark, desolate atmosphere made for uncomfortable listening. It was three years before he re-entered a studio. On 25 November 1974, Nick Drake was found dead. The coroner's verdict was suicide.

DRIFTERS

US vocal group formed in 1953 in New York. Clyde McPhatter (b. 1932, d. 1972; tenor), Gerhart Thrasher, Andrew Thrasher and Bill Pinkney (b. 1925) achieved a number 1 R&B hit with their debut 'Money Honey', as Clyde McPhatter And The Drifters. Follow-up releases, including 'Such A Night', 'Lucille' and 'Honey Love', also proved highly successful, mixing gospel and rock 'n' roll styles. McPhatter was drafted into the armed forces in 1954; on his release he went solo. His former group enjoyed late-50s success with 'Adorable', 'Steamboat', 'Ruby Baby' and 'Fools Fall In Love', featuring a variety of lead singers including Johnny Moore (b. 1934, d. 1998). A greater emphasis on pop material ensued, but tension between the group and manager, George Treadwell, resulted in an irrevocable split.

Having fired the line-up in 1958, Treadwell, who owned the copyright to the name took on **Ben E. King** (b. 1938; tenor), Charlie Thomas (tenor), Doc Green Jnr. (d. 1989; baritone), Ellsbury Hobbs (b. 1936, d. 1996) and guitarist Reggie Kimber. They declared themselves with 'There Goes My Baby'. Further excellent releases followed, notably 'Dance With Me' (1959), 'This Magic Moment' (1960) and 'Save The Last Dance For Me' (US number 1/ UK number 2). King went solo in 1960, replaced by Rudy Lewis (b. 1935, d. 1964). The Drifters continued to enjoy hits and songs such as 'Sweets For My Sweet', 'Up On The Roof' and 'On Broadway'. Johnny Moore, who had returned to the line-up in 1963, took over the lead vocal slot after Lewis's death. 'Under The Boardwalk', recorded the day after the latter's passing, was the Drifters' last US Top 10 pop hit. Bert Berns took over production, bringing a soul-based urgency to their work 'One Way Love' and 'Saturday Night At The Movies'.

After another period in the doldrums, the Drifters' career was revitalized in 1972 when the re-releases 'At The Club' and 'Come On Over To My Place' reached the UK Top 10. British songwriters/producers Tony Macaulay, Roger Cook and Roger Greenaway fashioned a series of singles redolent of the Drifters' 'classic' era. Between 1973 and 1975, the group, still led by Moore, enjoyed six UK Top 10 hits, including 'Kissin' In The Back Row Of The Movies' and 'There Goes My First Love'. In 1982, Moore was briefly replaced by Ben E. King. They were inducted into the Rock And Roll Hall Of Fame in 1988.

DUBLINERS

Irish folk act formed in 1962 as the Ronnie Drew Group. Barney MacKenna (b. 1939), Luke Kelly (b. 1940, d. 1984), Ciaron Bourke (b. 1936, d. 1988) and Ronnie Drew (b. 1935) were known faces in Dublin's post-skiffle folk haunts. In 1964, Kelly left for England's folk scene and Bob Lynch and John Sheahan (b. 1939) joined. In 1965, the group turned professional and Kelly returned, replacing Lynch who wished to stay semi-professional. Major UK hits followed with 1967's censored 'Seven Drunken Nights' and 'Black Velvet Band'. *A Drop Of The Hard Stuff* and three of its successors charted well. A brain haemorrhage forced Bourke's retirement in 1974, and Drew's return to the ranks – after being replaced between 1975 and 1979 by Jim McCann (b. 1944) – was delayed by injuries sustained in a road accident. Kelly's ill-health (a brain tumour) saw Seàn Cannon drafted into the line-up in 1980, with Nigel Warren Green also filling in on tour. Kelly passed away in January 1984. Drew's trademark vocal was heard in 1987 on the group's 25th anniversary single, 'The Irish Rover', a merger with the **Pogues** that reached the UK Top 10. Eammon Campbell was added to the line-up in the late 80s, and in 1995 Drew left the band for the second time and was replaced by Paddy Reilly.

DURAN DURAN

This highly successful UK pop group took their name from a character in the

cult 60s movie *Barbarella*. Vocalist Simon Le Bon (b. 1958), pianist Nick Rhodes (b. 1962), guitarist Andy Taylor (b. 1961), bass player John Taylor (b. Nigel John Taylor, 1960) and drummer Roger Taylor (b. 1960) completed the most famous line-up, and charted with their 1981 debut 'Planet Earth'. The follow-up, 'Careless Memories', barely scraped into the UK Top 40, but 'Girls On Film', accompanied by a risqué Godley And Creme video featuring nude models, took them to the UK Top 10. Two albums quickly followed, as did hits like 'Hungry Like A Wolf', 'Say A Prayer' and 'Rio'. Soon they had broken into the US Top 10 and 'Is There Something I Should Know?', a gloriously catchy pop song, entered the UK charts at number 1. An impressive run of transatlantic Top 10 hits followed over the next three years, including 'New Moon On Monday', 'The Reflex' (UK/US number 1), 'The Wild Boys' and 'A View To A Kill' (a James Bond movie theme). At the peak of their success, they decided to venture into other projects, such as the Power Station and Arcadia.

In 1986, Duran Duran regrouped minus Roger and Andy Taylor, and recorded *Notorious* with producer Nile Rodgers. Pointlessly tinkering with their name (to DuranDuran) failed to restore the band's commercial fortunes. Warren Cuccurullo (b. 1956) and Sterling Campbell joined in 1989, although the latter soon departed. 'Ordinary World' became a major transatlantic hit in 1993, followed by the US Top 10 hit 'Come Undone'. The 1995 covers album *Thank You* attracted universal scorn, and two years later John Taylor left the band, leaving Le Bon and Rhodes to carry on with the long-serving Cuccurullo. Their contract with EMI ended following the record company's refusal to release *Medazzaland* in the UK. *Pop Trash*, released on the Hollywood label in 2000, was more successful. The following May, the five original members announced they were to play together for the first time in over 15 years.

DURUTTI COLUMN

UK-born Vini Reilly (b. Vincent Gerard Reilly, 1953) and his Durutti Column combined elements of jazz, electronic and folk music. Reilly (guitar), Dave Rowbotham (d. 1991; guitar), Chris Joyce (drums), Phil Rainford (vocals) and Tony Bowers (bass) featured on *A Factory Sampler* EP, but by the time of 1980's *The Return Of The Durutti Column* Reilly was the only original member left. The Durutti Column's own recordings over the next few years were a mixed batch recorded by Reilly with assistance from several musicians. This eccentric artist continued to lead the Durutti Column into the new millennium.

DURY, IAN

Dury (b. 1942, d. 2000) was stricken by polio at the age of seven. Initially he taught art before joining Kilburn And The High Roads, reinterpreting R&B numbers and later adding his own wry lyrics in a semi-spoken cockney slang. The band dissolved and the remnants formed a new line-up called the Blockheads. The most stable unit comprised Dury, Chaz Jankel (guitar, keyboards), John Turnbull (guitar), Mickey Gallagher (keyboards), Davey

Payne (saxophone), Charley Charles (drums) and Norman Watt-Roy (bass). Dury and the Blockheads' stunning debut, 1977's *New Boots And Panties*, spent more than a year in the UK album chart. Dury's brief flirtation with mainstream acceptance continued with 1979's UK chart-topper, 'Hit Me With Your Rhythm Stick'. *Do It Yourself* and *Laughter* lacked the impact of his debut. Dury continued to make records in the 80s, including the controversial 'Spasticus Autisticus', and made forays into film and television acting.

Dury developed bowel cancer in 1996, but was well enough to travel to Third World countries as UNICEF's goodwill ambassador. The cancer returned with a vengeance at the end of 1997 and Dury reunited with the Blockheads in 1998 for the warmly received *Mr. Love Pants*. Although very unwell he continued to make live appearances with the Blockheads, right until a month before his death in March 2000.

DYLAN, BOB

As a teenager, Dylan (b. Robert Allen Zimmerman, 1941) listened to R&B, **Hank Williams** and early rock 'n' roll. In 1960, Dylan adopted a persona based upon the **Woody Guthrie** romantic hobo figure of the film *Bound For Glory*; he also assumed a new voice, speaking with an Okie twang, and adopted a 'hard travellin'' appearance. Having met Jesse Fuller, a blues performer who

played guitar and harmonica simultaneously by using a harp rack, Dylan began to teach himself to do the same. Determined to be a professional musician, he set out for New York; arriving in January 1961. Dylan's impact on Greenwich Village was immediate and enormous. He captivated anyone who saw him with his energy, charisma and rough-edged authenticity, and he was signed to Columbia Records in the autumn.

Bob Dylan was a collection of folk and blues standards, often about death, sorrows and the trials of life – songs that had been in Dylan's repertoire over the past year – but it was the inclusion of two of his own compositions, notably the tribute, 'Song To Woody', that pointed the way forward. Over the next few months, Dylan wrote dozens of songs – many of them topical – and became interested in the Civil Rights movement. 'Blowin' In The Wind' (1962), was the most famous of his protest songs and was included on *The Freewheelin' Bob Dylan*. In the meantime, Dylan had written and recorded several other political songs, including 'Masters Of War' and 'A Hard Rain's A-Gonna Fall', and one of his greatest love songs, 'Don't Think Twice, It's All Right'. 'Blowin' In The Wind' recorded by **Peter, Paul And Mary** became a huge US hit, bringing Dylan's name to international attention. **Joan Baez**, already a successful folk singer, began covering Dylan songs. Soon she was introducing him to her audience and the two became lovers.

Dylan's songwriting became more astute and wordy: biblical and other literary imagery showed in songs like 'When The Ship Comes In' and 'Times They Are A-Changin''. In 1964, becoming increasingly frustrated with the 'spokesman of a generation' tag, Dylan wrote *Another Side Of Bob Dylan*. This included the disavowal of his past, 'My Back Pages', alongside newer songs such as 'Mr Tambourine Man', 'Gates Of Eden' and 'It's Alright Ma, I'm Only Bleeding'. The album was his last solo acoustic album for almost 30 years. Intrigued by the **Beatles** – he had visited London to play one concert in 1964 – and excited by the **Animals**' 'House Of The Rising Sun', he and producer Tom Wilson fleshed out some of the *Bringing It All Back Home* songs with rock 'n' roll backings, such as 'Subterranean Homesick Blues' and 'Maggie's Farm'. 'Like A Rolling Stone', was written after his final series

of UK acoustic concerts in 1965, and was commemorated in D. A. Pennebaker's documentary film *Don't Look Back*. The sound came from blues guitarist Michael Bloomfield, Harvey Brooks (bass) and Al Kooper (organ). It was producer Tom Wilson's last – and greatest – Dylan track and at six minutes, destroyed the formula of the sub-three-minute single forever. It was a huge hit.

It should have come as no surprise to those who went to see Dylan at the Newport Folk Festival on 25 July that he was now a fully fledged folk-rocker. Backed by the Paul Butterfield Blues Band, Dylan's 'new sound' was met with bewilderment and hostility, but he seemed to find the experience exhilarating and liberating. He had felt ready to quit, now he was ready to start again, to tour the world with a band. Dylan discovered the Hawks (later to become the **Band**) and they took to the road in the autumn of 1965: USA, Hawaii, Australia, Scandinavia and Britain, with a hop over to Paris in 1966. Dylan was deranged and dynamic, the group wild and mercurial. Back in America in 1966, Dylan was physically exhausted, but had to complete a film and finish *Tarantula*, an overdue book for Macmillan. He owed Columbia two more albums, and was booked to play a series of concerts right up to the end of the year.

On 29 July 1966, Dylan was injured in a motorcycle accident near his home in up-State New York. He was nursed through his convalescence by his wife, Sara – they had married in 1965 – and was visited only rarely. After several months, Dylan was joined by the Hawks, who rented a house nearby. Every day they met and played music – the final therapy that Dylan needed. A huge amount of material was recorded in the basement and, eventually, came a clutch of new compositions. Some of the songs were surreally comic: 'Please Mrs Henry', 'Quinn The Eskimo', 'Million Dollar Bash'; others were soul-searchingly introspective: 'Tears Of Rage', 'Too Much Of Nothing',

'I Shall Be Released'. Many were covered by, and became hits for, other artists and groups. Dylan's own recordings of some of the songs were not issued until 1975 (as *The Basement Tapes*).

In 1968, Dylan appeared with the Band, at the Woody Guthrie Memorial Concert at Carnegie Hall, New York. The following month *John Wesley Harding* was released. The record's final song, 'I'll Be Your Baby Tonight', was unambivalently simple and presaged the warmer love songs of *Nashville Skyline*. That album was nothing compared with the puzzlement which greeted *Self Portrait*. This double album offered mish-mash mix-ups of undistinguished live tracks, alternate takes, odd cover versions, botched beginnings and endings. *New Morning* was heralded as a 'return to form', but Dylan was restless and his appearance at the Concert For Bangla Desh benefit was his only live performance between 1970 and 1974, although he cropped up frequently as a guest on other people's albums.

In 1973, Dylan played the enigmatic Alias in Sam Peckinpah's *Pat Garrett & Billy The Kid*, for which he also supplied the soundtrack music (including 'Knockin' On Heaven's Door'). He also left CBS, having been persuaded by David Geffen to sign to Asylum, for whom he recorded the underwhelming *Planet Waves*. A US tour with the Band followed. Tickets were sold by post and attracted six million applications. The recorded evidence, *Before The Flood*, certainly oozed energy, but lacked subtlety. *Blood On The Tracks*, originally recorded in 1974, was a marked improvement. Dylan substituted some of the songs with reworked versions: 'Tangled Up In Blue', 'Idiot Wind', 'If You See Her Say Hello', 'Shelter From The Storm', 'Simple Twist Of Fate', 'You're A Big Girl Now' . . . one masterpiece followed another. Dylan had separated from Sara and this was a diary of despair.

If Dylan the writer was reborn with *Blood On The Tracks*, Dylan the performer re-emerged on the star-studded Rolling Thunder Revue. The tour hit the road in New England on 31 October 1975. Dylan – face painted white, hat festooned with flowers – was inspired, delirious, imbued with a new vitality and singing like a demon. A focal point of the Revue had been the case of wrongly imprisoned boxer Hurricane Carter and Dylan's song 'Hurricane' was included just about every night. It was also on his next album *Desire*.

In 1979, Dylan became a born-again Christian, releasing an album of

evangelical songs, *Slow Train Coming*. He played a series of powerful concerts featuring nothing but his new Christian material. The second Christian album, *Saved*, was less impressive, however, and his fervour became more muted. Gradually, old songs began to be reworked into the live set and by *Shot Of Love* and *Infidels* it was no longer clear whether or not Dylan's faith remained firm. A series of patchy albums followed, including *Empire Burlesque*, *Knocked Out Loaded* and *Down In The Groove*. In 1988, he found himself one of the **Traveling Wilburys** with **George Harrison**, **Jeff Lynne**, **Tom Petty** and **Roy Orbison** – a jokey band assembled on a whim. Their album, *Volume 1*, was a huge commercial success and Dylan's next album emerged as his best of the 80s. *Oh Mercy*, recorded informally in New Orleans and produced by Daniel Lanois, was full of strong songs. Not without its merits, the follow-up *Under The Red Sky* was for most a relative disappointment, as was the Roy-Orbison-bereft Traveling Wilburys follow-up, *Volume 3*.

Dylan's live revue (known as the Never Ending Tour) continued throughout the following decade, with his performances becoming increasingly erratic – sometimes splendid, often shambolic. Both *Good As I Been To You* and *World Gone Wrong* , were collections of old folk and blues material, performed, for the first time since 1964, solo and acoustically. *Unplugged* saw Dylan revisiting a set of predominantly 60s songs in desultory fashion. In 1997, Dylan suffered a serious inflammation of the heart muscles. He was discharged from hospital after a short time, eliciting his priceless quote to the press: 'I really thought I'd be seeing Elvis soon'. The Lanois-produced *Time Out Of Mind* was a dark and sombre recording, with Dylan reflecting over lost love and hints of death. It was his best work for many years, and although his voice continues to decline, the strength of melody and lyric were remarkable.

Dylan's first recording of the new millennium was 'Things Have Changed', the Grammy-award winning main and end-title theme for Curtis Hanson's movie *Wonder Boys*. His new studio album *Love And Theft* received further praise.

EAGLES

US country rock band formed in Los Angeles in 1971 by Bernie Leadon (b. 1947; guitar, vocals), Randy Meisner (b. 1947; bass, vocals), Glenn Frey (b. 1948; guitar, vocals) and Don Henley (b. 1947; drums, vocals). *The Eagles* contained 'Take It Easy' and 'Witchy Woman', both of which reached the US Top 20 and established their country rock sound. *Desperado* contained several of their most enduring compositions, including the emotional title track. The follow-up, *On The Border*, reasserted their commerciality. 'Best Of My Love' was their first US number 1. New guitarist Don Felder (b. 1947) was then added to the line-up. The reshaped quintet attained superstar status with the platinum-selling *One Of These Nights*. This included 'Lyin' Eyes', 'Take It To The Limit' and the title track, which topped the US charts. Leadon left in 1975, replaced by Joe Walsh (b. 1947; ex-**James Gang**). *Hotel California* topped the US album charts for eight weeks and spawned two number 1s: the title track and 'New Kid In Town'. The set sold nine million copies in its year of release. 'Please Come Home For Christmas' was their sole recorded offering for 1978. In 1979, Meisner was replaced by Timothy B. Schmit (b. 1947), but the Eagles' impetus was waning. *The Long Run* was disappointing, despite containing the US number 1 'Heartache Tonight', and the group split up in 1982.

They eventually re-formed in the mid-90s and the resulting album proved they were still one of the world's most popular acts. Their 1994–95 US tour was one of the largest-grossing on record.

EARLE, STEVE

US-born Earle (b. 1955) played acoustic guitar from the age of 11 and began singing in bars and coffee houses. He formed a back-up band, the Dukes, and was signed to CBS Records, who subsequently released *Early Tracks*. Recognition came when he and the Dukes signed to MCA Records and made a 'New Country' album, 1986's *Guitar Town*. The title track was a potent blend of country and rock 'n' roll. Earle's songs often told of the restlessness of blue-collar workers; he wrote 'The Rain Came Down' for the Farm Aid II benefit, and 'Nothing But A Child' was for an organization to help homeless children. In 1988, he released an album with a heavy-metal feel, *Copperhead Road*, which included the Vietnam saga 'Johnny Come Lately'.

After a lengthy break, allegedly to detox, Earle returned with *Train A Comin'*, featuring Peter Rowan and **Emmylou Harris**. In the mid-90s, a cleaned-up Earle started his own label, E-Squared. He also contributed to the film soundtrack of *Dead Man Walking*. Earle continued his renaissance with *I Feel Alright* and *El Corazón*, and recorded a superb bluegrass album with the Del McCoury Band. He also published the short stories collection entitled *Doghouse Roses*.

EARTH, WIND AND FIRE

Group formed in the 60s from Chicago's black music session circle. In 1969, drummer Maurice White (b. 1942) formed the Salty Peppers. The group – Verdine White (b. 1951; bass), Michael Beale (guitar), Wade Flemmons (vocals), Sherry Scott (vocals), Alex Thomas (trombone), Chet Washington (tenor saxophone), Don Whitehead (keyboards) and Yackov Ben Israel (percussion) – embraced jazz, R&B, funk and elements of Latin and ballad styles. After a couple of albums, White pieced together a second group, Earth, Wind and Fire, around Ronnie Laws (b. 1950; saxophone, guitar), Philip Bailey (b. 1951; vocals), Larry Dunn (b. Lawrence Dunhill, 1953; keyboards), Roland Battista (guitar) and Jessica Cleaves (vocals). Two 1974 releases, *Head To The Sky* and *Open Our Eyes*, established the group as an album act, while the following year 'Shining Star' reached number 1 in the US R&B and pop charts.

By the end of the decade they had regular successes with such singles as 'Fantasy', 'September', 'After The Love Has Gone' and 'Boogie Wonderland'. The line-up remained unstable, with new musicians joining periodically. Following 11 gold albums, 1983's *Electric Universe* was an unexpected commercial flop, and prompted a four-year break. A core quintet recorded *Touch The World* (1987) but they failed to reclaim their former standing. Since 1987, White has no longer toured with the band, but seemed to regain his enthusiasm with 1997's *In The Name Of Love*, a back-to-basics album recorded for new label Eagle. In March 2000, the band was inducted into the Rock And Roll Hall Of Fame.

EAST 17

UK vocal group featuring Tony Mortimer (b. 1970), Brian Harvey (b. 1974), John Hendy (b. 1971) and Terry Coldwell (b. 1974), who met at school. The band was named after their London postal code and their debut, 1993's *Walthamstow*, after their home area. With former **Bros** svengali Tom Watkins as manager they cultivated an image of youthful arrogance and 'street style' in obvious opposition to **Take That**. Their debut, 'House Of Love', became a major hit in 1992, peaking at UK number 10. 'Deep' reached the Top 5 and both 'Slow It Down' and a lacklustre cover of the **Pet Shop Boys**' 'West End Girls' made the UK Top 20. 'It's Alright' reached UK number 3 and their first two 1994 singles, 'Around The World' and 'Steam', continued their commercial ascendancy. They finally hit UK number 1 in 1994 with 'Stay Another Day'. Harvey was sacked by the band in 1997 after some ill-chosen comments about the drug ecstasy. However, the group's songwriter Mortimer left the same year to embark on a solo career. Harvey subsequently returned, and plans to relaunch the group (now known as E-17) as an urban R&B trio met with limited success. The remaining members called it a day not long afterwards, with Harvey attempting to launch himself as a solo artist.

EASTON, SHEENA

Scottish singer Easton (b. Sheena Shirley Orr, 1959) debuted with 'Modern Girl' (1979), followed by '9 To 5' which sold over a million copies in the USA (as 'Morning Train (Nine To Five)'). American success followed and Easton was given the theme to the 1981 James Bond movie *For Your Eyes Only*. Hits from her second album included 'When He Shines' and the title track, 'You Could Have Been With Me'. By now resident in California, Easton enjoyed one of her biggest hits with the controversial **Prince**-penned 'Sugar Walls'. In 1988 she switched labels to MCA, releasing *The Lover In Me*. When the title track was issued as a single it soared to number 2 on the US charts. In 1991 Easton finally became a US citizen, but during the 90s she enjoyed most success in Japan, with several of her new albums only released in that territory. By now her focus had switched towards her acting career, and in 1996 she appeared as Rizzo in the Broadway production of *Grease*. She signed a new recording contract with Universal International in 2000.

EASYBEATS

Formed in Sydney, Australia, in 1964, this beat group comprised Dutch guitarists Harry Vanda (b. Harry Vandenberg, 1947), Dick Diamonde (b. Dingeman Van Der Sluys, 1947), English vocalist Steve Wright (b. 1948), Scottish guitarist George Young (b. 1947) and English drummer Gordon 'Snowy' Fleet (b. 1946). After a series of Australian hits, including six number 1s, the group relocated to England in 1966. There they worked with top producer Shel Talmy, resulting in one of the all-time great beat singles, 'Friday On My Mind' (UK number 6). Unable to follow up this hit, the group split with Talmy during the recording of their first UK-released album. They returned to the UK charts in 1968 with 'Hello, How Are You'. Vanda and Young began writing material for other artists, and in 1969, the Easybeats split up. Ironically, they enjoyed a US hit some months later with 'St. Louis'. The group undertook a national reunion tour in 1986.

ECHO AND THE BUNNYMEN

This renowned UK band was formed in 1978 by Ian McCulloch (b. 1959), Will Sergeant (b. 1958; guitar) and Les Pattinson (b. 1958; bass), with a drum machine they christened 'Echo'. They made their vinyl debut in 1979 with 'Pictures On My Wall'/'Read It In Books'. McCulloch's brooding live performance and vocal inflections drew comparisons with **Jim Morrison**.

After signing to Korova Records (distributed by Warner Brothers Records), they replaced 'Echo' with West Indian-born Pete De Freitas (b. 1961, d. 1989). *Crocodiles* proved impressive, with a wealth of strong arrangements and compulsive guitarwork. After the less melodic 'The Puppet', the band toured extensively and issued an EP, *Shine So Hard*, which crept into the UK Top 40. *Heaven Up Here* and *Porcupine* were critically acclaimed and 'The Cutter' gave them

their biggest UK hit so far (number 8). In 1984, they charted with 'The Killing Moon' and the accompanying *Ocean Rain* reached the US Top 100.

In 1986, De Freitas was replaced by Mark Fox (ex-**Haircut 100**), but he returned within months. However, with *Echo And The Bunnymen* they began to lose their appeal, while a version of the **Doors**' 'People Are Strange' left fans and critics perplexed. In 1988, McCulloch went solo. Echo And The Bunnymen carried on with Noel Burke succeeding McCulloch, but tragically, just as they were beginning rehearsals, De Freitas was killed in a road accident. The band struggled on, recruiting new drummer Damon Reece and adding road manager Jake Brockman on guitar/synthesizer. In 1992, they released *Reverberation*, but to little effect, and they split up in the summer of the same year.

McCulloch and Sergeant reunited in 1993 as *Electrafixion*. In 1996, an announcement was made that the three remaining original members would go out as Echo And The Bunnymen once again. McCulloch, Pattinson and Sergeant released the well-received *Evergreen* in 1997. Pattinson left before the recording of their second new album, a remarkably mellow set from a band not normally associated with such a concept. The full-length *Flowers* marked a return to the trademark Echo And The Bunnymen sound, with Sergeant's guitar work to the fore.

ECHOBELLY

UK indie-pop band led by the Anglo-Asian singer Sonya Aurora Madan, with Swedish guitarist Glenn Johansson, Debbie Smith (guitar, ex-Curve), Andy Henderson (drums) and Alex Keyser (bass). After breaking the UK Top 40 in 1994 with 'I Can't Imagine The World Without Me', the band became the darlings of the British music press and began to win US support, leading to an American contract with Sony. *On* advanced their strengths, with notable songs including the hit 'Great Things'. Smith left in 1997, replaced by Julian Cooper. *Lustra* was a poorly received album that saw the band struggling to establish their musical direction. The band returned three years later with the *Digit* EP and *People Are Expensive*, both released on their own Fry Up label. By this point the departure of Harris had reduced the band to a trio.

EDDIE AND THE HOT RODS

Formed in 1975, this UK quintet originally comprised Barrie Masters (vocals), Lew Lewis (harmonica), Paul Gray (bass), Dave Higgs (guitar) and Steve Nicol (drums). After one classic single, 'Writing On The Wall', Lewis left, though he appeared on the high-energy 'Horseplay', the flipside of their cover of Sam The Sham And The Pharoahs' 'Wooly Bully'. The Rods pursued a tricky route between pub rock and punk. During 1976, the band broke house records at the Marquee Club and captured their power on a live EP. The arrival of guitarist Graeme Douglas (ex-**Kursaal Flyers**) gave them a more commercial edge and a distinctive jingle-jangle sound. 'Do Anything You Want To Do' reached the UK Top 10 and *Life On The Line* was well received. However, Douglas left, followed by Gray (who joined the **Damned**) and Masters disbanded the group for a spell. They re-formed for pub gigs and small-label appearances.

EDDY, DUANE

The simple 'twangy' guitar sound of New Yorker Duane Eddy (b. 1938) is legendary. Together with

producer Lee Hazlewood, Eddy co-wrote a deluge of hits mixed with versions of standards, using the bass strings of his Grestch guitar recorded through an echo chamber. The 1958 debut 'Movin' 'N' Groovin'' made the lower end of the US chart, and for the next six years Eddy repeated this formula with great success. His backing group, the Rebel Rousers was a tight, experienced band featuring saxophonists Jim Horn and Steve Douglas and pianist Larry Knechtel. Among their greatest hits were 'Rebel-Rouser', 'Shazam', 'Peter Gunn' and 'Theme From Dixie'. One of Eddy's most memorable hits was the superlative theme music for the movie *Because They're Young*.

Sadly, the hits dried up in 1964, and Eddy's sound dropped out of fashion. Tony Macaulay wrote 'Play Me Like You Play Your Guitar' for him in 1975, and after more than a decade he was back in the UK Top 10. He

returned to the charts in 1986, playing his 'Peter Gunn' with Art Of Noise. The following year, Jeff Lynne produced Eddy's first album for many years.

EDEN'S CRUSH

The female vocal group created by the US version of the globally successful 'reality TV' show *Popstars*. The winners – Ana Maria Lombo, Ivette Sosa, Maile Misajon, Nicole Scherzinger, and Rosanna Tavarez – were relocated to a house in Los Angeles, where they trained and rehearsed and then recorded their Sire Records/143 Records debut, with the aid of several leading pop songwriters and producers. 'Get Over Yourself' repeated the global success of the *Popstars* format, becoming the biggest-selling debut for a new group in US chart history when it was released in 2001.

EDISON LIGHTHOUSE

UK conglomeration based around singer Tony Burrows. The Tony Macaulay/Barry Mason composition 'Love Grows (Where My Rosemary Goes)' was their 1970 breakthrough, zooming to UK number 1 and the US Top 5. When Burrows moved on, his backing musicians continued under the name Edison. Macaulay, meanwhile, owned the name Edison Lighthouse and conjured up another group for recording and touring purposes.

EDMUNDS, DAVE

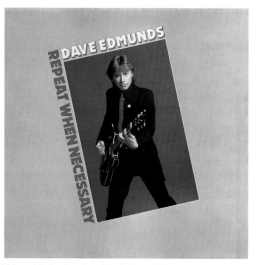

Welsh-born Edmunds (b. 1944) started out as lead guitarist of Love Sculpture. At the end of the 60s, he built his own recording studio, Rockfield, where he worked with Shakin' Stevens, the Flamin' Groovies and Brinsley Schwarz among others. Edmunds and Schwarz's bass player, **Nick Lowe**, formed a musical partnership that lasted many years. Edmunds had hits with Smiley Lewis's 'I Hear You Knocking', the Ronettes' 'Baby, I Love You' and the Chordettes' 'Born To Be With You'. *Get It* (1977) featured the fast-paced Nick Lowe composition, 'I Knew The Bride', which gave Edmunds another hit. A cover of **Elvis Costello**'s 'Girls Talk' provided Edmunds with his last major UK hit. During the 80s he worked with his own band, Rockpile, the **Fabulous Thunderbirds**, **Jeff Beck**, **Dr. Feelgood**, **k.d. lang** and **Status Quo**. In the late 90s and into the new millennium, Edmunds was a regular member of **Ringo Starr**'s All Starr Band.

EELS

Los Angeles, USA-based Eels were formed in 1995, the brainchild of the mysterious E (b. Mark Everett; vocals, guitar, keyboards). With drummer Butch Norton and bass player Tommy Walter, they released 'Novocaine For The Soul', a big college/alternative hit in 1996. However, despite their apparently conventional power-trio line-up, Eels are fascinated by sonic experimentation. Co-producer Simpson's dance background and experience of sampling expanded *Beautiful Freak*'s overall sound with hip-hop rhythm loops, earning them success in the UK as well as the US. The follow-up, *Electro-Shock Blues*, was informed by several tragedies in E's personal life. The album's fascination with mortality found beautiful expression on compelling tracks such as 'Last Stop: This Town', 'Cancer For The Cure' and 'My Descent Into Madness'. The mellow *Daisies Of The Galaxy* featured the stand-out tracks 'Mr E's Beautiful Blues' and 'It's A Motherfucker'. Everett took to dressing up as the notorious US terrorist the Unabomber to promote 2001's *Souljacker*.

808 STATE

UK acid-house band featuring Martin Price (b. 1955), Graham Massey (b. 1960), Darren Partington (b. 1969) and Andy Barker (b. 1969). Together with Gerald Simpson, they began recording as a loose electro-house collective, and rose to prominence at the end of 1989 with 'Pacific State'. *Newbuild* and *Quadrastate* helped to establish them as premier exponents of UK dance. *Ex:El* featured the vocals of New Order's Bernard Sumner on 'Spanish Heart', and Björk on 'Oops' (also a single) and 'Qmart'. They also worked with Mancunian rapper MC Tunes on *The North At Its Heights* and several singles. In 1991, Price missed their US tour, electing to work on solo projects instead. 808 State persevered with another fine album, *Gorgeous*, in 1993, which saw a new rash of collaborations. Massey occupied himself co-writing Björk's 'Army Of Me' and other material on *Post*. Martin Price departed, but *Don Solaris* finally arrived after a gap of four years. The *808:88:98* compilation included several new mixes. Since the release of this album, Massey, Partington and Barker have continued to work on new material while undertaking various remix projects.

EINSTÜRZENDE NEUBAUTEN

German experimental band Einstürzende Neubauten made their live debut in 1980. The line-up comprised Blixa Bargeld (b. Christian Emmerich, 1959; guitar, vocals), N. U. Unruh (b. Andrew Chudy, 1957; percussion), Beate Bartel and Gudrun Gut. Alexander Van Borsig (b. Alexander Hacke, 1965), an occasional contributor, joined for their first single, 'Für Den Untergang'. When Bartel and Gut left to form Malaria and Matador they were replaced by F. M. Einheit (b. Frank Struass, 1958; percussion). Their first official album was *Kollaps*, a collage of sounds created by unusual rhythmic instruments ranging from steel girders to pipes and canisters. Bass player Marc Chung (b. 1957) joined for their 1982 12-inch, 'Durstiges Tier'. *Strategien Gegen Architekturen 80=83* was compiled with Jim Thirlwell, while the band performed an ill-fated gig at London's ICA. Bargeld spent the rest of the year touring as bass player for **Nick Cave**, going on to record several studio albums as a Bad Seed.

Einstürzende Neubauten's stop-start career was revived by 1989's *Haus Der Lüge*. They set up their own Ego subsidiary to house their soundtrack work. Their 1993 album *Tabula Rasa* was another politically inclined collection exploring the reunification of Germany. It also demonstrated the band's growing commitment to conventional musical structure. *Ende Neu*, with the departed Chung replaced by Andrew Chudy, completed Einstürzende Neubauten's gradual transition to atmospheric rock band. Jochen Arbeit and Rudi Moser were added to the line-up for 2000's sparse, melodic *Silence Is Sexy*.

EITZEL, MARK

Californian songwriter Mark Eitzel (b. 1959, ex-American Music Club) recorded his first solo album in 1996. *60 Watt Silver Lining* departed from Eitzel's reputation as a despondent writer, featuring some of his most optimistic lyrics. *West* was another startling departure, with Eitzel sounding positively upbeat. The fuller sound was enriched by the participation of **R.E.M.**'s Peter Buck and the **Screaming Trees**' Barrett Martin. The follow-up was a largely acoustic affair, featuring material written before Eitzel's collaboration with Buck. He returned after a three-year hiatus with the experimental *The Invisible Man*, which used a backdrop of percussion loops and electronic samples to showcase Eitzel's typically insightful lyrics. A covers album followed.

ELASTICA

UK indie band featuring Justine Frischmann (vocals, guitar), Donna Matthews (bass), Justin Welch (drums) and Annie Holland (guitar). Elastica soon proved themselves with a series of stunning singles including 'See That Animal' (co-written with **Suede**'s Brett Anderson) and 'Waking Up', one of the most exciting singles to hit the charts in 1995, despite being a musical rewrite of the **Stranglers** 'No More Heroes'. The band's debut album included four hit singles. Numerous personnel changes then dogged Frischmann's creation. A six-track EP of new material was released to mixed reviews in 1999. The band's long-delayed second album, which by now had assumed almost mythical status, was finally released in 2000. Ironically, the tracks on *The Menace* came from a six-week burst of activity the

previous December. A collection of Radio 1 archive material, released in November 2001, proved to be a suitably patchy swansong for this erratic band.

ELBOW

Atmospheric UK rock band formed by Guy Garvey (vocals), Mark Potter (guitar), Craig Potter (keyboards), Pete Turner (bass), and Richard Jupp (drums). The quintet signed a contract with Island Records in 1998, but

was still in the process of recording their debut album when Island was taken over by Universal and their contract was terminated. The independent label Ugly Man Records released two EPs, *New Born* and *Any Day Now*, which generated renewed interest in the band. A new recording contract with V2 Records followed, as the band remixed five of the tracks from their abortive Island album and recorded six new songs for the critically acclaimed *Asleep In The Back*.

ELECTRIC FLAG

Electric Flag was formed in 1967 by Mike Bloomfield (b. 1944, d. 1981; guitar). The band featured Buddy Miles (b. George Miles, 1945; drums, vocals), Nick Gravenites (vocals), Barry Goldberg (keyboards), Harvey Brooks (bass), Peter Strazza (tenor saxophone), Marcus Doubleday (trumpet) and Herbie Rich (baritone saxophone). Their debut at the Monterey Pop Festival was a noble start, followed by the hit album, *A Long Time Comin'*, with additional members Stemziel (Stemsy) Hunter and Mike Fonfara. The band

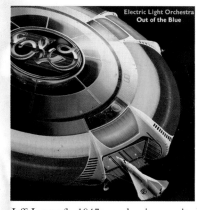

was unable to follow this release, and immediately began to dissolve. The second album was a pale shadow of their debut. Miles then left to form the Buddy Miles Express. An abortive Flag reunion produced the lacklustre *The Band Kept Playing*.

ELECTRIC LIGHT ORCHESTRA

ELO originally featured Roy Wood (b. Ulysses Adrian Wood, 1946; vocals, cello, woodwind, guitars), Jeff Lynne (b. 1947; vocals, piano, guitar) and Bev Bevan (b. 1945; drums). They completed an experimental debut set with the aid of Bill Hunt (french horn) and Steve Woolam (violin), and reached the UK Top 10 with '10538 Overture' (1972). When Woolam departed, Hugh McDowell (b. 1953), Andy Craig (cellos), Richard Tandy (b. 1948; keyboards, bass, piano, guitar) and Wilf Gibson (b. 1945; violin) were recruited. They played a series of indifferent live appearances, following which Wood took Hunt and McDowell to form Wizzard. A reshaped line-up completed *ELO II* and scored a Top 10 single with a version of 'Roll Over Beethoven'. They enjoyed a third UK hit with 'Showdown', but the ensuing 'Ma Ma Ma Ma Belle' and 'Can't Get It Out Of My Head' failed to chart in the UK, although the latter reached the US Top 10. The attendant album, *Eldorado*, went gold. By this point the band's line-up had stabilized around Lynne, Bevan, Tandy, McDowell, Kelly Grouchett (bass), Mik Kaminski (violin) and Melvyn Gale (cello). They achieved considerable commercial success with *A New World Record*, *Out Of The Blue* and *Discovery*, and between 1976 and 1981 scored an unbroken run of 15 UK Top 20 singles, including 'Telephone Line', 'Mr. Blue Sky' and 'Don't Bring Me Down'. Recurrent legal and distribution problems subsequently undermined ELO's momentum, and *Time* and *Secret Messages* lacked the verve of earlier work. Main songwriter Lynne's growing disenchantment led to him going solo and the band splitting up.

In 1991, Bevan emerged with the short-lived ELO 2. Ten years later Lynne resurrected ELO to record a new studio album, *Zoom*.

ELECTRIC PRUNES

Formed in Los Angeles, USA, in 1965, the Electric Prunes featured Jim Lowe (vocals, guitar, autoharp), Ken Williams (lead guitar), James 'Weasel' Spagnola (guitar), Mark Tulin (bass) and Quint (b. Michael Weakley; drums), although the latter was quickly replaced by Preston Ritter. The quintet debuted with the

low-key 'Ain't It Hard' before the US Top 20 hits 'I Had Too Much To Dream (Last Night)' and 'Get Me To The World On Time'. These blended the drive of garage/punk rock, the rhythmic pulse of the **Rolling Stones** and the experimentalism of the emerging psychedelic movement. Their debut album was hampered by indifferent material, but the excellent *Underground* featured some of their finest achievements. Ritter was replaced by the prodigal Quint before the remaining original members dropped out during sessions for *Mass In F Minor*. An entirely new line-up completed the lacklustre *Just Good Old Rock 'N' Roll*, and the name was then abandoned.

ELECTRONIC

Formed in England in 1989, Electronic featured Johnny Marr (b. John Maher, 1963; guitar; ex-**Smiths**) and Bernard Sumner (b. 1956; ex-**New Order**). Electronic marked Marr's move into more commercial territory. Their first single, 'Getting Away With It' (1989), featuring Neil Tennant of the **Pet Shop Boys**, reached UK number 12. Electronic capitalized on the new credibility that dance music had acquired, using 'electronic' dance rhythms and indie guitar pop. In 1991, a self-titled debut album followed two more UK Top 20 singles, 'Get The Message' and 'Feel Every Beat'. The album was also very well received, reaching UK number 2. In 1992, 'Disappointed' reached UK number 6, however *Raise The Pressure* – a blend of Pet Shop Boys harmony with the occasional hint of wah-wah pedal from Marr – was uninspiring. Sumner and Marr returned in 1999 with the more guitar-orientated *Twisted Tenderness*.

ELLIOTT, MISSY 'MISDEMEANOR'

Hip-hop/R&B songwriter Missy 'Misdemeanor' Elliott (b. Melissa Elliott) has become one of the most esteemed figures in contemporary American music, working as a recording artist, songwriter, arranger, producer, talent scout and record boss. Teaming up with her long-time collaborator Tim Mosley, aka Timbaland, Elliott signed to Elektra Records as a solo artist on the understanding that they would subsidize her own label, Gold Mind Records. In 1997, she launched her solo career with the album *Supa Dupa Fly* and attendant single 'The Rain (Supa Dupa Fly)'. In September 1998 she collaborated with Mel B from the **Spice Girls** on the one-off single, 'I Want You Back', which debuted at number 1 in the UK chart. Further writing and remixing work for **Whitney Houston** and **Janet Jackson** followed, although Elliott found time in her busy schedule to release her excellent sophomore set, *Da Real World*, in 1999. Elliott and Timbaland managed to surpass this with the

follow-up *Miss E ... So Addictive*, a stunning compendium of contemporary dance beats, urban ballads and left-field samples.

ELLIOTT, RAMBLIN' JACK

US folk singer Elliott (b. Elliott Charles Adnopoz, 1931) met **Woody Guthrie** in 1949. The pair travelled and sang together before Elliot emerged as a talent in his own right. By the early 60s he had resettled in New York, where he became an inspirational figure to a new generation of performers, including **Bob Dylan**. In 1975, Elliott was joined by Dylan during an appearance at a Greenwich Village club; he then became a natural choice for Dylan's Rolling Thunder Revue. Elliot continued his erratic but intriguing path in subsequent decades with a number of excellent releases. In 2000, his daughter directed the documentary film *The Ballad Of Ramblin' Jack*. The accompanying soundtrack album serves as a useful career retrospective.

ELY, JOE

Texan-born Ely (b. 1948) formed his first band at the age of 13, playing a fusion of country and R&B. He later joined singer-songwriters Jimmie Gilmore and George 'Butch' Hancock in the Flatlanders. In 1976, Ely's own band – Jesse Taylor (guitar), Lloyd Maines (steel drum), Gregg Wright (bass), Steve Keeton (drums) and Ponty Bone (accordion) – recorded three unsuccessful albums, *Joe Ely*, *Honky Tonk Masquerade*, and *Down On The Drag*, before Keeton was replaced by Robert Marquam and Wright by Michael Robertson for *Musta Notta Gotta Lotta*.

In 1980, the Ely Band toured extensively with the **Clash**, and released *Live Shots*. The album was no more successful than the previous three. In 1984, Ely recorded *Hi-Res*, with a completely new band of little-known musicians. By 1987, he had assembled a new band featuring David Grissom (lead guitar), Jimmy Pettit (bass) and Davis McLarty (drums). They recorded two artistically stunning albums, *Lord Of The Highway* and *Dig All Night*. In 1990, the band recorded a powerhouse live album in Austin, *Live At Liberty Lunch*. His 1995 *Letter To Laredo* was a return to his earlier sound. Ely remains one of the most completely realized artists in contemporary country music, especially in live performance, in which he excels.

EMBRACE

Led by brothers Danny (vocals) and Richard McNamara (guitar), this UK indie-pop band was founded in the late 80s. Joined by Mick Heaton (drums) and Steve Firth (bass), their debut single, 'All You Good Good People'/'My Weakness (Is None Of Your Business)', was released in a limited edition of 1,500 copies in late 1996. The first result of their pact with Hut Records was the *Fireworks* EP. The band's debut single, 'All You Good Good People', reached number 8 when it was re-released in October 1997. The band's series of excellent releases continued with the emphatic but beautiful 'Come Back To What You Know', which reached number 6 in summer 1998. Their debut album was released the same month. Despite entering the UK charts at number 1, the album was regarded by many as an anticlimax in view of the previous hype surrounding the band. *Drawn From Memory* and *If You've Never Been* failed to build on their earlier successes.

EMERSON, LAKE AND PALMER

One the most prominent rock supergroups of the early 70s, ELP comprised Keith Emerson (b. 1944; keyboards), Greg Lake (b. 1948; vocals, bass) and Carl Palmer (b. 1950; drums, percussion). They appeared at the much-publicized 1970 Isle of Wight Festival and were signed to Island Records, completing their self-titled debut album the same year. In 1971, they introduced their arrangement of Mussorgsky's *Pictures At An Exhibition*, then the concept album *Tarkus*. Extensive tours and albums followed over the next three years, including *Trilogy*, *Brain Salad Surgery* and an extravagant triple-live album. With solo outings becoming increasingly distracting, the band released one final studio album, *Love Beach*, before embarking on a farewell world tour.

In 1986, a serious re-formation was attempted. Palmer declined, so Emerson and Lake teamed up with hit drummer Cozy Powell (b. Colin Powell, 1947, d. 1998) to produce *Emerson, Lake And Powell*. When Powell quit, Palmer rejoined for a projected album in 1987, but the sessions proved fruitless. Instead, Emerson recruited Hush drummer Robert Berry for the poor-selling *To The Power Of Three*. In the early 90s, the original trio re-formed and produced *Black Moon*, followed by another live album. Whilst their concert tour was well attended, no new ground was being broken and recent new material (notably *In The Hot Seat*) is but a pale shadow of their former material.

EMF

Formed in England, in 1989, EMF featured James Atkin (b. 1969; vocals), Ian Dench (b. 1964; guitar, keyboards), Derry Brownson (b. 1970; keyboards, samples), Zac Foley (b. 1970, d. 2002; bass), Mark Decloedt (b. 1969; drums) and Milf (DJ). The band claimed EMF stood for Epsom Mad Funkers (or Ecstasy Mother Fuckers), although Parlophone Records claimed it stood for Every Mother's Favourites. They were signed to Parlophone after just four gigs and without a demo, an opportunism that was rewarded when their debut, 'Unbelievable', reached the UK Top 5 and their 1991 debut album sales exceeded two million. The band also enjoyed US success. *Stigma* disappointed, however, with sales less than one-fifth of the debut. Their label encouraged a three-year gap between 1992's *Unexplained* EP and 1995's *Cha Cha Cha*. The band returned to the charts when they teamed up with comedians Vic Reeves and Bob Mortimer on a cover of the **Monkees**' 'I'm A Believer', but having been dropped by Parlophone they decided to split up. Brownson and Atkin both went on to play with Bentley Rhythm Ace. The unit re-formed for some gigs in 2001, but Foley's death the following year marred their comeback.

EMINEM

This white US rapper (b. Marshall Bruce Mathers III, 1973) burst on to the charts in 1999 with his controversial take on the horrorcore genre. Mathers took up rapping in high school before dropping out in ninth grade, joining *ad-hoc*

EN VOGUE

🎵 **Albums**
Funky Divas (East West 1992)★★★★
➤ p.371 for full listings

ENGLAND DAN AND JOHN FORD COLEY

🎵 **Albums**
England Dan And John Ford Coley (A&M 1971)★★★
➤ p.371 for full listings

ENID

🎵 **Albums**
Something Wicked This Way Comes (Enid 1983)★★★
Tripping The Light Fantastic (Mantella 1994)★★★
➤ p.371 for full listings
✎ **Further References**
Video: *Claret Hall Farm* (Visionary 1985)

ENIGMA

🎵 **Albums**
MCMXC AD (Virgin 1990)★★★★
The Cross Of Changes (Virgin 1993)★★★★
➤ p.371 for full listings

ENO, BRIAN

🎵 **Albums**
Here Come The Warm Jets (Island 1974)★★★★
Another Green World (Island 1975)★★★★
➤ p.371 for full listings
👥 **Collaborators**
Kevin Ayers ➤ p.24
David Bowie ➤ p.59
David Byrne ➤ p.74
John Cale ➤ p.75
Robert Fripp ➤ p.152
Jah Wobble ➤ p.193
Daniel Lanois ➤ p.212
Nico ➤ p.250
Harold Budd
🎸 **Connections**
Roxy Music ➤ p.287
U2 ➤ p.335
✎ **Further References**
Video: *Imaginary Landscapes* (Mystic Fire 1991)
Books: *The Vertical Colour Of Sound*, Eric Tamm
A Year With Swollen Appendices, Brian Eno

groups Basement Productions, the New Jacks and D12. The newly named Eminem released a raw debut album in 1997 through independent label FBT. The following year's *The Slim Shady EP*, named after his sinister alter-ego, featured some vitriolic attacks on his detractors.

Eminem was then signed to Aftermath Records by label boss **Dr. Dre**, who adopted the young rapper as his protégé and acted as co-producer on Eminem's full-length debut. Dre's beats featured prominently on *The Slim Shady LP*, a provocative feast of violent, twisted lyrics, with a moral outlook partially redeemed by Eminem's claim to be only 'voicing' the thoughts of the Slim Shady character. The album was buoyed by the commercial success of the singles 'My Name Is' and 'Guilty Conscience'. He was also in the news when his mother filed a lawsuit claiming that comments made by the rapper during interviews and on *The Slim Shady LP* had caused, amongst other things, emotional distress, damage to her reputation and loss of self-esteem.

None of which harmed the sales of Eminem's follow-up album, *The Marshall Mathers LP*, which debuted at number 1 on the US album chart in 2000. By the end of the year, however, his troubled personal life and a serious assault charge had removed the gloss from his phenomenal commercial success. Despite criticism from gay-rights groups, the rapper swept up three Grammy Awards the following February. He also reunited with his D12 colleagues to record the transatlantic chart-topping *Devil's Night*.

EN VOGUE

Vocal R&B quartet comprising Dawn Robinson, Terry Ellis, Cindy Herron and Maxine Jones – formed in Oakland, California in 1988, after producers Denzil 'Denny' Foster and Thomas McElroy decided to establish their own 'girl group'. They went on to enjoy singles success with 'Hold On' and 'Lies' – the latter introduced female rapper Debbie T, and added a new, post-feminist outlook to traditional R&B. Their second album featured two **Curtis Mayfield** cover versions, and produced further hits in 'Free Your Mind'

and 'Give It Up, Turn It Loose'. Following a lengthy break from recording, during which Robinson left to pursue a solo career, they returned to a competitive market with *EV3*. After another extended hiatus the trio released the inventive *Masterpiece Theatre*.

ENGLAND DAN AND JOHN FORD COLEY

Dan Seals (b. 1950) formed a partnership with John Ford Coley (b. 1951) and they first worked as Southwest F.O.B. The name did not last, but not wanting to be called Seals And Coley, they settled on England Dan And John Ford Coley. Their first albums for A&M Records sold moderately well, but they struck gold in 1976 with a move to Big Tree Records. The single 'I'd Really Love To See You Tonight' went to number 2 in the US charts, and also reached the UK Top 30. The resulting album, *Nights Are Forever*, was a big seller and the title track, 'Nights Are Forever Without You', was another Top 10 single. They had further US hits with 'It's Sad To Belong' and 'Love Is The Answer'. When the duo split Seals, after a few setbacks, became a country star. Coley found a new partner, but their 1981 album, *Kelly Leslie And John Ford Coley*, was not a success.

ENID

Influential UK art-rockers, formed in 1974 by keyboard player Robert John Godfrey (b. 1947) with guitarists Stephen Stewart and Francis Lickerish. The founding members were joined by Glen Tollet (bass), Chris North (drums) and Dave Storey (drums). Supported by dynamic live shows, a debut album, *In The Region Of The Summer Stars*, appeared in 1976. Despite an ever-changing line-up, subsequent concept albums, rock operas and tours saw them increasing their cult audience and playing large venues. A move to Pye Records just as the label went bankrupt in 1980 broke up the band. Godfrey formed his own label, distribution and studio with Stewart. He re-formed Enid in 1983. Operating as independents, their following (known as 'The Stand') grew, and the fifth studio album, *Something Wicked This Way Comes*, was their biggest success yet. By 1988, the band's popularity appeared to have peaked, so, after two sold-out farewell gigs at London's Dominion Theatre, Godfrey split the band again. He returned to the Enid format in 1994, releasing the instrumental concept album *Tripping The Light Fantastic*. His well-publicized environmental concerns were given free reign on 1998's *White Goddess*.

ENIGMA

Ambient pop sculptors Enigma are the brainchild of Romanian pianist Michael Cretu (b. 1957). After working as a studio musician and arranger, he released his debut solo album, *Legionare* (1983). He then worked with the Moti Special, as writer, producer and keyboard player. He put together his most commercially successful project, Enigma, two years later. 'Sadeness Part 1' hit UK number 1 in 1990. The accompanying *MCMXC AD* also topped the charts and spent 57 weeks on the UK list. Gold or platinum status was attained in 25 countries. Film director Robert Evans then invited Cretu to compose the title song to *Sliver*, resulting in the release of 'Age Of Loneliness (Carly's Song)'.

After three years, he produced a follow-up. It was hardly the expected blockbuster, but 'Return To Innocence' (1994) reached UK number 9 and demonstrated his enduring appeal to the record-buying public. Subsequent albums have continued to mine Cretu's seamless fusion of new age, ambient and dance.

ENO, BRIAN

While studying at art schools in his native England, Eno (b. Brian Peter George St. Baptiste de la Salle Eno, 1948) fell under the influence of *avant garde* composers Cornelius Cardew and John Cage. Although he could not play an instrument, Eno liked tinkering with multi-track tape recorders and in 1968 wrote the limited-edition theoretical handbook, *Music For Non Musicians*. Eno joined **Roxy Music** in 1971 as a 'technical adviser', but before long his powerful visual image began to rival that of **Bryan Ferry**. He left on 21 June 1973 – the same day he began his solo career in earnest, writing 'Baby's On Fire'. Shortly afterwards, he formed a temporary partnership with Robert Fripp. In 1973, their esoteric *No Pussyfooting* was released. A tour followed and, with the entire Roxy line-up (bar Ferry) Eno completed *Here Come The Warm Jets*.

A one-off punk single, 'Seven Deadly Finns', prompted a tour with the Winkies, during which Eno's right lung collapsed. Convalescing, he visited America, recorded demos with **Television** and worked with **John Cale**. In 1974, he played alongside Cale, Kevin Ayers and Nico in London. *Taking Tiger Mountain (By Strategy)* was followed by production credits on albums by Robert Wyatt, Robert Calvert and Phil Manzanera. This led to Eno's experiments with environment-conscious music. He formed the Obscure Records label, whose third release was his own *Discreet Music*. He also completed *Another Green World*, a meticulously crafted work.

After performing in Phil Manzanera's 801, he began a fruitful alliance with David Bowie on *Low*, *Heroes* and *Lodger*. Despite that workload, he managed to complete his next solo work, *Before And After Science*. Eno then turned his attention to soundtracks before returning to ambient music. *Music For Films* was a pot-pourri of material suitable for playing while watching movies, then came *Music For Airports*. Eno also remained in demand by **Ultravox**, Cluster, Harold Budd, **Devo** and **Talking Heads**. In 1981 he released *My Life In The Bush Of Ghosts*, a pioneering collaboration with **David Byrne**, that fused 'found voices' with African rhythms.

In 1980, Eno worked with Canadian producer/engineer Daniel Lanois. Between them they produced *Voices*, by Eno's brother Roger, and a collaboration with Harold Budd, *The Plateaux Of Mirror*. This association with Lanois culminated in work on **U2**'s *The Unforgettable Fire*, *The Joshua Tree*, *Achtung Baby* and *Zooropa*. In 1990, Eno completed a collaborative album with **John Cale**, *Wrong Way Up*. The following year Eno released *My Squelchy Life*, which was withdrawn, revised, and re-released in 1992 as *Nerve Net*. It fused 'electronically-treated dance music, eccentric English pop, cranky funk, space jazz, and a myriad of other, often dazzling sounds'. In 1995, he worked with **David Bowie** on *1: Outside*, **Jah Wobble** on *Spinner* and shared composing credits with Bono, Adam Clayton and Larry Mullen Jnr. on *Passengers: Original Soundtracks 1*. His recent solo work, however, has suffered because of the huge effort he puts into producing others – little time seems to be left to give his own work creative zip.

ENYA

Enya (b. Eithne Ní Bhraonáin, 1961) is a classically trained pianist. Her keyboard-playing days for the family group **Clannad** lasted for three years, after which she was asked to record the music for the BBC television series *The Celts*. This was subsequently released as her debut album in 1987. An endearing blend of ethereal singing (in Gaelic and English) and lush synthesizers, the album was largely ignored, as was the accompanying single,

'I Want Tomorrow'. The following year Enya released *Watermark*, a work in much the same vein, and had a surprise UK number 1 with 'Orinoco Flow (Sail Away)'. Working with her long-time collaborators, Roma Ryan (lyricist) and Nicky Ryan (producer), Enya followed the chart-topper with two smaller hits, 'Evening Falls' and 'Storms In Africa Part II'. The album also enjoyed a long chart run in America, eventually attaining multi-platinum status and establishing Enya as a fixture on the new-age album chart.

She returned in the early 90s with *Shepherd Moons* which, by the mid-90s, had reached worldwide sales of 10 million. The album was hugely successful in America, and in 1993 won the Grammy for Best New Age Album. Her third collection, *The Memory Of Trees*, didn't alter the winning formula. The artist spent the remainder of the decade contributing soundtrack material to various projects, before returning to the studio to record *A Day Without Rain*. The album shot up the US and several European charts almost a year after its release, thanks to the use of the track 'Only Time' in news coverage of the terrorist attacks on the World Trade Center in New York in 2001.

EPSTEIN, BRIAN

Epstein (b. 1934, d. 1967) began his working life overseeing the North End Road Music Stores (NEMS) in Liverpool, England. In 1961, a customer requested 'My Bonnie' by a group called the **Beatles**. Epstein subsequently attended one of their gigs at the Cavern Club and, against the advice of his friends, became a pop manager. He transformed the Beatles: banned them from swearing or eating on stage, encouraged the establishment of a rehearsed repertoire and persuaded them to wear smart, grey lounge suits. In early 1962, Epstein won a record deal, thanks to the producer George Martin. During October 1962, a management contract was belatedly finalized with the Beatles – Epstein received 25 per cent of their earnings, a figure he maintained for all future signings. Weeks later, he struck a deal with music publisher Dick James, which culminated in the formation of Northern Songs, a company dealing exclusively with compositions by **John Lennon** and **Paul McCartney**. The powers agreed on a 50/50 split: half to Dick James and his partner; 20 per cent each to Lennon and McCartney, and 10 per cent to Epstein.

Long before the Beatles became the most successful entertainers in British music history, Epstein had signed his second group **Gerry And The Pacemakers**. Scouring the Cavern for further talent he soon added Tommy Quickly, the Fourmost, **Billy J. Kramer And The Dakotas**, the Big Three and **Cilla Black**. His artists dominated the UK charts throughout the year – nine number 1 hits spanning 32 weeks. One area where Epstein was deemed fallible was in the merchandizing agreements that he concluded on behalf of the Beatles.

Epstein engineered the Beatles' Hollywood Bowl concert, an event which indelibly changed rock performances. While the Beatles were conquering the New World, Epstein was expanding his empire, notably with

the career of Cilla Black; he immediately recognized her lasting charm as the gauche, unpretentious girl-next-door.

When the Beatles ceased touring, Epstein's role in their day-to-day lives was minimal. By 1967, he was losing control. Drug dependence, homosexual guilt and tabloid harrassment brought him to the verge of a nervous breakdown and he attempted suicide. In August 1967, the Beatles were attending a course in Transcendental Meditation with the Maharishi Mahesh Yogi. Brian, meanwhile, was lying dead at his London home. The inquest subsequently established death from a cumulative overdose of the sleep-inducing drug Carbatrol. Although suicide was suspected, the coroner concluded a verdict of accidental death from 'incautious self-overdoses'.

EQUALS

Twins Derv (b. 1948; vocals) and Lincoln Gordon (b. 1948; rhythm guitar), Guyanan Eddy Grant (b. 1948; lead guitar), Patrick Lloyd (b. 1948; rhythm guitar) and John Hall (b. 1947; drums) began playing together in 1965. Their best-remembered single, 'Baby Come Back', was originally recorded as a b-side (1966). The quintet's early releases made little impression until 'Baby Come Back' became a major hit in Germany (1967), and later topped the Dutch and Belgian charts. This propulsive, infectious song was then reissued in Britain, where it eventually reached number 1. Although the Equals enjoyed other hits, only 'Viva Bobby Joe' (1969) and 'Black Skinned Blue-Eyed Boys' (1970) reached the Top 10. Chief songwriter Grant went solo in 1971, after which the band underwent several personnel changes before finding security on the cabaret circuit. Their career was briefly resurrected in 1978 when Grant signed them to his Ice label for *Mystic Synster*.

ERASURE

Keyboard player and arranger Vince Clarke (b. 1961; ex-**Depeche Mode**, **Yazoo**, the Assembly) decided to undertake a new project in 1985. The plan was to record an album with 10 different singers, but after auditioning vocalist Andy Bell, Erasure was formed. The duo hit the UK chart with 'Sometimes' (1986), which reached number 2, and was followed by 'It Doesn't Have To Be Me' (1987). The following month their second album, *Circus*, reached the UK Top 10, and their popularity grew rapidly. Memorable hits such as 'Victim Of Love', 'The Circus' and 'A Little Respect' established them as serious rivals to the **Pet Shop Boys** as the world's leading vocal/synthesizer duo. Their singles and album sales continue to increase with successive releases, and *The Innocents*, *Wild!*, *Chorus* and the *Abba-Esque* EP all reached UK number 1. Subsequent releases saw a dip in the duo's popularity, however, and they took a sabbatical following 1997's *Cowboy* before recording the follow-up, *Loveboat* (2000).

ERICKSON, ROKY

Erickson (b. Roger Erkynard Erickson, 1947) came to the fore in the **13th Floor Elevators**. He composed 'You're Gonna Miss Me', the band's most popular single, before the unit broke up in 1968. Arrested on a drugs charge, Erickson faked visions to avoid imprisonment, but was instead committed to Rusk State Hospital for the Criminally Insane. On his release in 1971, he began a low-key solo career, recording several singles with new backing group, Bleib Alien. In 1980, the guitarist secured a deal with CBS Records but the resulting *Roky Erickson And The Aliens* was a disappointment.

Erickson was imprisoned in 1990 for stealing mail, but his plight inspired Sire Records' *Where The Pyramid Meets The Eye*, wherein 19 acts interpreted many of his best-known songs. Following his release from a mental institution, a grizzled Erickson recorded *All That May Do My Rhyme* one of his better efforts.

ESSEX, DAVID

UK singer Essex (b. David Cook, 1947) began singing in the mid-60s, recording a series of unsuccessful singles for a variety of labels. On the advice of manager Derek Bowman, he switched to acting, receiving his big break with the lead in the stage musical *Godspell*. His role in the 50s-inspired *That'll Be The Day* reactivated Essex's recording career and the song he composed for the film, 'Rock On', was a transatlantic Top 10 hit. During the mid-70s, he registered two UK number 1s, 'Gonna Make You A Star' and 'Hold Me Close', plus three Top 10 hits. After parting with producer Jeff Wayne, Essex continued to chart, though less successfully.

As his teen appeal waned, Essex's serious acting commitments increased, most notably with the role of Che Guevara in the stage musical *Evita*. His lead part in 1980's *Silver Dream Machine* resulted in a hit of the same title. The Christmas hit, 'A Winter's Tale', kept his chart career alive, as did the equally successful 'Tahiti', which anticipated one of his biggest projects, the elaborate musical *Mutiny!*.

Despite pursuing two careers, Essex has managed to achieve consistent success on record, in films and on stage; he is also a tireless ambassador for Voluntary Service Overseas. He was awarded an OBE in the 1999 New Year Honours list.

ESTEFAN, GLORIA

Cuban-born Estefan (b. Gloria Fajardo, 1957) originally rose to prominence in the 70s by joining Emilio Estefan in Miami Sound Machine (later Gloria Estefan And Miami Sound Machine). She married Emilio in 1978 and Miami Sound Machine recorded a sequence of Spanish-language albums during the late 70s and early 80s. They later became massively successful in the USA, Europe and Latin America with the hits 'Dr. Beat', 'Conga', 'Bad Boy', 'Rhythm Is Gonna Get You' and 'Anything For You'.

Estefan launched her solo career with 1989's *Cuts Both Ways*, three singles from which reached the US Top 10, including the number 1 'Don't

Wanna Lose You'. In 1990, her impetus was halted by a serious road accident. She returned in 1991 with *Into The Light* and an eight-month world tour. *Mi Tierra* and *Abriendo Puertas* were Spanish-language albums that distanced her somewhat from the American pop mainstream, but proved hugely popular in South America. *Destiny* was her first English-language collection for over five years, excepting the lacklustre collection of pop covers, *Hold Me, Thrill Me, Kiss Me. Gloria!* marked a welcome return to the Latin style of the Miami Sound Machine. The following year Estefan made her acting debut alongside Meryl

Streep in *Music Of The Heart*. The Spanish-language *Alma Caribeña*, meanwhile, reaped the commercial benefits of the late 90s boom in Latin music.

ETERNAL

This UK vocal quartet originally comprised lead singer Easther Bennett, her sister Vernie, Louise Nurding (b. 1974) and Kéllé Bryan. Their first two singles, 'Stay' and 'Save Our Love', made an immediate impact on the UK charts, launching the group as the teen phenomenon of 1993. These were followed by the more strident 'Just A Step From Heaven' and *Always And Forever*, which spawned six Top 20 UK hits.

Sole white member **Louise** went solo in 1995, by which time Eternal had become Britain's most successful all-female group since **Bananarama**. *Power Of A Woman* was the first serious attempt to break the group in America. *Before The Rain* suffered from a shortage of stand-out tracks, but included their first UK chart-topper, 'I Wanna Be The Only One'. Bryan left the group in late 1998, and launched a solo career the following year. The Bennett sisters released the hard-hitting 'What'cha Gonna Do' the same month, which introduced the more pronounced urban direction of their self-titled fourth album.

ETHERIDGE, MELISSA

Etheridge (b. 1961) was still a teenager when she began playing piano and guitar in various cover bands around Kansas, USA. Relocating to Los Angeles, she was spotted by Island Records chief Chris Blackwell and signed in 1986. Her break was writing the music for the movie *Weeds*. Her first album was recorded live in the studio and spawned 'Bring Me Some Water', an eventual Grammy nominee. In the early 90s, the excellent *Never Enough* won a Grammy. *Yes I Am* was a similar mix of up-tempo 'love-crazy' material. The Hugh Padgham-produced *Your Little Secret* was further confirmation of her writing talents. She won the 1996 ASCAP Songwriter of the Year award, but took a lengthy break from the music business to concentrate on her domestic arrangements. She returned in 1999 with the intimate but low-key *Breakdown*. Far more high profile was the media's obsessive interest in unearthing the biological father of her and then-partner Julie Cypher's two children. The sperm donor turned out to be David Crosby.

EURYTHMICS

David A. Stewart (b. 1952) and **Annie Lennox** (b. 1954) met in London and formed the Tourists, a band able to fuse new-wave energy with well-crafted pop songs. Following the Tourists' split, Lennox and Stewart formed the Eurythmics in 1980. Their debut *In The Garden*, a rigidly electronic-sounding album, failed to sell, but the duo persevered and made the UK charts with the synthesizer-based 'Love Is A Stranger'. The subsequent *Sweet Dreams (Are Made Of This)* spawned a number of hits, all accompanied by an imaginative series of self-produced videos. The title track made US number 1, and was followed in quick succession by a reissued 'Love Is A Stranger', 'Who's That Girl?', the celebratory 'Right By Your Side', 'Here Comes The Rain Again', and the bestselling album *Touch*.

The soundtrack to the film *1984* was poorly received, but this was remedied by the excellent *Be Yourself Tonight*, which contained less synthesized pop and more rock music, including a glorious soul duet with **Aretha Franklin** on 'Sisters Are Doin' It For Themselves'. During 1985, Lennox experienced serious throat problems, which forced the band to cancel their appearance at Live Aid. That same month, however, they enjoyed their sole UK chart topper, 'There Must Be An Angel (Playing With My Heart)'. *Revenge* included 'Missionary Man', 'Thorn In My Side' and 'The Miracle Of Love'. *Savage* maintained the standard and *We Too Are One* became their most successful album to date, staying at number 1 into 1990.

Stewart and Lennox then embarked on solo careers, with the latter enjoying particular success. She reunited with Stewart in June 1998 at a tribute concert for journalist Ruth Picardie, and again at the following year's BRIT awards, where the duo were honoured for their 'outstanding contribution' to British music. Buoyed by the successful reunion, Stewart and Lennox returned to the studio to record *Peace*.

EVERCLEAR

Comprising Art Alexakis (b. 1962; vocals, guitar), Craig Montoya (b. 1970; bass, vocals) and Scott Cuthbert (drums), Everclear were formed in Oregon, USA, in 1991. Greg Eklund (b. 1970) replaced Cuthbert on the band's 1994 debut, *World Of Noise*, which included the intriguing 'Sparkle'. It was followed by the mini-album, *White Trash Hell*, bringing in a recording contract with Capitol Records. In 1995, they released the critically lauded *Sparkle And Fade*. They repeated this success two years later with the release of the infectious and highly melodic *So Much For The Afterglow*. The clumsily titled *Songs From An American Movie Vol. One: Learning How To Smile* toned down the neo-grunge guitar rock in favour of a more eclectic approach, embracing tight harmonies, strings, and a cover version of **Van Morrison**'s 'Brown Eyed Girl'. The vitriolic pop punk collection *Songs From An American Movie Vol. Two: Good Time For A Bad Attitude*, released only four months later, helped restore the band's alternative rock credibility.

EVERLAST

White US rapper, Everlast (b. Erik Schrody) released his first single in 1988. He subsequently joined Irish American hip-hoppers House Of Pain, who enjoyed a US Top 10 smash in 1992 with the addictive 'Jump Around'. He quit the music business in 1996, but returned to recording two years later with *Whitey Ford Sings The Blues*, an impressive slow-mo fusion of hip-hop beats and folk stylings that climbed into the US Top 10. In an eventful year, Everlast had already suffered a near-fatal cardiac arrest and converted to Islam. The following year he contributed one of the stand-out tracks ('Put Your Lights On') to Santana's phenomenally successful *Supernatural*. His own *Eat At Whitey's* built on the successful acoustic blues/hip-hop template of its predecessor.

EVERLY BROTHERS

Don (b. Isaac Donald Everly, 1937) and Phil Everly (b. 1939) were child performers, appearing on their parents' (country artists Ike and Margaret) radio shows throughout the 40s. In 1957 they took Felice and Boudleaux Bryant's 'Bye Bye Love' to US number 2 and UK number 6. This was quickly followed by more irresistible Bryant songs, 'Wake Up Little Susie', 'All I Have To Do Is Dream', 'Bird Dog', 'Problems', 'So Sad' and 'Devoted To You'. By the end of the 50s they were the world's number-one vocal group. After signing with Warner Brothers Records for $1 million, they delivered the superlative 'Cathy's Clown' (written by Don). No Everly record had sounded like this before, and the echo-laden production and treble-loaded harmonies took it to US/UK number 1.

The brothers continued to release Top 10 records, surprisingly proving more popular in Britain than in their homeland. However, the advent of the beat boom pushed them out of the spotlight and while they continued to make hit records, none came near to their previous achievements. After a few years of declining fortunes, the brothers parted acrimoniously – the only time they met in the next 10 years was at their father's funeral. Both went solo, with varying degrees of success. While Don maintained a steady career, playing with Albert Lee, Phil concentrated on songwriting. 'She Means Nothing To Me' was a striking duet with **Cliff Richard** which put the Everly name back in the UK Top 10. In 1983 they hugged and made up in an emotional reunion in front of an ecstatic audience at London's Royal Albert Hall. The following year *EB84* was released and gave them another major hit with **Paul McCartney**'s 'Wings Of A Nightingale'. In 1986 they joined the Rock And Roll Hall Of Fame and now perform regularly together.

The Everly Brothers' influence on a generation of pop and rock artists is inestimable; they set a standard for close-harmony singing that has rarely been bettered and is still used as a blueprint for many of today's harmony vocalists.

EVERYTHING BUT THE GIRL

UK duo Tracey Thorn (b. 1962) and Ben Watt (b. 1962) met while students. They performed together in, and released a version of, Cole Porter's 'Night And Day' (1982). Thorn made a solo mini-album, *A Distant Shore* (1982), which was a strong seller in the UK independent charts. Watt released the critically acclaimed *North Marine Drive* the following year. In 1984, they reached the UK chart with 'Each And Everyone', which preceded the superb *Eden*. Their biggest single breakthrough came with a version of Danny Whitten's 'I Don't Want To Talk About It' (1988), which reached the UK Top 5. *The Language Of Life*, a more jazzy collection, found further critical acclaim, but the more pop-orientated follow-up, *World-wide* (1991), was released to mediocre reviews.

Watt's increasingly busy DJing schedule and Thorn's vocal contributions to trip-hop pioneers **Massive Attack**'s 1994 opus, *Protection*, demonstrated their increasing interest in the UK's dance music scene. This was reflected in the textures of *Amplified Heart*. The album was recorded following Watt's recovery from a life-threatening illness (chronicled in the quirky *Patient: The History Of A Rare Illness*). Todd Terry's remix of the track 'Missing' provided their big breakthrough, becoming a huge club hit and reaching the UK and US Top 5. The duo's new approach was confirmed on *Walking Wounded*, their Virgin Records debut, which embellished their acoustic songs with drum 'n' bass and trip-hop rhythms to stunning effect. Watt's involvement in the club scene meant that the follow-up did not appear until 1999. *Temperamental* retained some of the low-key charm of *Walking Wounded*, although three years on the duo's work sounded less groundbreaking.

EXILE

Formed in Kentucky, USA, in 1963 as the Exiles, they became Exile in 1973. In 1978, the group reached US number 1 with 'Kiss You All Over', followed by two more pop-chart singles before switching to country in 1983. At the time, the group featured J. P. Pennington (vocals, guitar), Buzz Cornelison (keyboards), Les Taylor (vocals, guitar), Marlon Hargis (vocals, keyboards), Sonny LeMaire (vocals, bass) and drummer Steve Goetzman. Their country career was more lucrative, with four successive number 1s in 1984, including 'Woke Up In Love' and 'Crazy For Your Love', and six further number 1s by 1987. Hargis was replaced by Lee Carroll in 1985 and Pennington was replaced by Paul Martin in 1989. The group signed to Arista Records in 1989, with a noticeable decline in its level of commercial success. They were dropped by the label in 1993 and broke up soon afterwards. A new version with Pennington and Taylor was on the road in 1996.

EXPLOITED

Scottish punk quartet formed in 1980 by vocalist Wattie Buchan and guitarist 'Big John' Duncan. Recruiting Dru Stix (b. Drew Campbell; drums) and Gary McCormick (bass), they signed to Secret Records in 1981 and released *Punk's Not Dead*. The band quickly earned themselves a certain low-life notoriety – songs such as 'Fuck A Mod', for example, set youth tribe against youth tribe without any true rationale – yet they were the only member of the third-generation punk set to make it on to BBC Television's *Top Of The Pops*, with 1981's 'Dead Cities'. They continue to release material on a regular basis.

EXTREME

Boston, USA-based quartet featuring Gary Cherone (b. 1961; vocals), Portuguese guitarist Nuno Bettencourt (b. 1966), Pat Badger (b. 1967; bass) and Paul Geary (b. 1961; drums). An original Extreme line-up found themselves on television in 1985, via an MTV competition, but it was the arrival of Bettencourt in 1986 and Badger in 1987 that gave them lift-off. Following a recording contract with A&M Records, the band made their vinyl debut with 'Play With Me' (from the soundtrack to *Bill And Ted's Excellent Adventure*). A self-titled debut album followed and met with widespread critical indifference. *Pornograffitti* was a stunning second release and the big break-through came when the simple acoustic ballad 'More Than Words' reached US number 1/UK number 2 in 1991. The track gave them considerable exposure beyond the heavy-metal fraternity. The band broke up following 1995's disappointing *Waiting For The Punchline*, with Cherone moving on to become lead singer with **Van Halen**.

EXTREME NOISE TERROR

Extreme Noise Terror formed in 1985 and were signed by Manic Ears Records after their first gig. Their debut was a split album with Chaos UK, and showed them in the process of twisting traditional punk influences. Along with the **Napalm Death**, they attracted the interest of **John Peel** in 1987, recording a session that was later released. Drummer Mick Harris, who had left Napalm Death to replace Extreme Noise Terror's original drummer, in turn departed. His replacement was Stick (Tony Dickens), who joined existing members Dean Jones (vocals), Phil Vane (vocals) and Pete Hurley (guitar). By 1993, the line-up included Lee Barrett (bass), Ali Firouzbakht (lead guitar) and Pig Killer (drums). Together they released *Retro-bution*, ostensibly a compilation, but nevertheless featuring the new line-up on re-recorded versions of familiar material. Pig Killer was replaced by Was shortly afterwards, but a greater shock was the departure of Vane to join Napalm Death. That band's departed vocalist Mark 'Barney' Greenway was brought in to help record *Damage 381*. Bizarrely, Vane and Greenway then swapped places once more.

FABIAN

US-born Fabian (b. Fabiano Forte Bonaparte, 1943) was 'discovered' by talent scouts Peter De Angelis and Bob Marucci in 1957. They contracted him to their Chancellor Records as a tamed **Elvis Presley**. Accompanied by the Four Dates, Fabian's first two singles – 'I'm In Love' and 'Lilly Lou' – were only regional hits, but after a string of television performances and a coast-to-coast tour, he found himself in the US Top 40 with 'I'm A Man'. Fabian's recording career peaked with 1959's million-selling 'Tiger' and *Hold That Tiger*, but his decline was as rapid as his launch. His first serious miss came with 'About This Thing Called Love' (1960), thereafter he traded his doomed musical career for one in movies, such as the 1962 war epic *The Longest Day*.

FABULOUS THUNDERBIRDS

Formed in Texas, USA, in 1977. Jimmy Vaughan (b. 1951; guitar), Kim Wilson (b. 1951; vocals, harmonica), Keith Ferguson (b. 1946, d. 1997; bass) and Mike Buck (b. 1952; drums) debuted with *The Fabulous Thunderbirds* aka *Girls Go Wild*, containing powerful original songs as well as sympathetic cover versions. Fran Christiana (b. 1951; drums; ex-**Roomful Of Blues**) replaced Mike Buck in 1980, and Preston Hubbard (b. 1953) joined after Ferguson departed. Wilson and Vaughan remained at the helm until Vaughan jumped ship in 1995. The Danny Korchmar-produced *Roll Of The Dice* was the first album with Wilson leading the band, with new lead guitarist Kid Ramos.

FACES

Formed from the ashes of defunct UK mod group the **Small Faces**. Ronnie Lane (b. 1946, d. 1997; bass), Kenny Jones (b. 1948; drums), Ian McLagan (b. 1945; organ), **Rod Stewart** (b. 1945; vocals) and Ron Wood (b. 1947; guitar) debuted in 1970 with *First Step*, which reflected their boozy, live appeal. The excellent follow-up, *Long Player*, enhanced this with its strong mix of staunch rock songs. After Stewart's solo career took off in 1971 the Faces effectively became his backing group. Although they enjoyed increasingly commercial appeal with *A Nod's As Good As A Wink ... To A Blind Horse* and a string of memorable good-time singles, there was no doubt that the focus on Stewart unbalanced the unit. Despite further hits with 'Pool Hall Richard', 'You Can Make Me Dance Sing Or Anything' and a live album, the band clearly lacked unity. In 1975, Stewart separated from the group. The band unexpectedly reunited for a one-off appearance at the BRIT Awards in 1993.

FAGEN, DONALD

New Yorker Fagen (b. 1948) joined Walter Becker in several groups. The duo then forged a career as songwriters and spent several years backing **Jay And The Americans** before forming **Steely Dan**. Steely Dan's music brilliantly combined the thrill of rock with the astuteness of jazz, but their partnership was sundered in 1981.

Fagen re-emerged the following year with *The Nightfly*, which included a cover version of the **Drifters**' 'Ruby Baby', and the close harmony-styled 'Maxine'. The long-awaited follow-up, *Kamakiriad*, was released in 1993. Fagen and Becker are currently touring and recording together again as Steely Dan.

FAIRGROUND ATTRACTION

Jazz/folk-tinged Anglo/Scottish pop band featuring Eddi Reader (b. Sadenia Reader, 1959; vocals), Mark Nevin (guitar), Simon Edwards (guitaron) and Roy Dodds (drums). Reader first linked with Nevin for the Compact Organisation sampler *The Compact Composers*, singing on two of his songs. In 1985, they built Fairground Attraction around his songs, recruiting Edwards and Dodds. Signed to RCA Records, they set about recording a debut album. The gentle skiffle of 'Perfect' topped the UK charts in 1988, but the band's promise was cut short when they split shortly afterwards. Reader went on to acting and a solo career, releasing her debut album, *Mirmama*, in 1992.

FAIRPORT CONVENTION

UK folk rock band formed in 1967 around Iain Matthews (b. Iain Matthews MacDonald, 1946; vocals), Judy Dyble (b. 1949; vocals), Ashley Hutchings (b. 1945; bass), Richard Thompson (b. 1949; guitar, vocals), Simon Nicol (b. 1950; guitar, vocals) and Martin Lamble (b. 1949, d. 1969; drums). Their self-titled debut album was a cult favourite, but sold poorly. When Dyble departed, **Sandy Denny** (b. Alexandra Denny, 1948, d. 1978) joined, bringing a traditional folk feel to their work which began to appear on the superlative *What We Did On Our Holidays*. This contained some of their finest songs, but Matthews left soon after its release, unhappy with the direction. Tragedy struck a few months later when Lamble and their friend Jeannie Franklyn were killed in a road accident.

Unhalfbricking, although not as strong as the previous album, contained excellent readings of **Bob Dylan**'s 'Percy's Song' and 'Si Tu Dois Partir' ('If You Gotta Go, Go Now'). The album charted, as did the latter Dylan number. The next album, *Liege And Lief* was astonishing. They played jigs and reels, and completed all 27 verses of the traditional 'Tam Lin'. The album featured new members Dave Swarbrick (b. 1941; violin), and Dave Mattacks (b. 1948; drums), and helped create British folk-rock in spectacular style. This change created internal problems and Hutchings left to form **Steeleye Span** and Denny departed to form Fotheringay. Dave Pegg (bass) joined and Swarbrick became lead vocalist. They wrote much of the next two albums' material before Thompson left. *Full House*, the first all-male Fairport album, was instrumentally strong with extended tracks like 'Sloth'. The concept album *Babbacombe Lee*, although critically welcomed, failed to sell and Simon Nicol left to form the Albion Country Band with Hutchings.

Sandy Denny rejoined, as did Dave Mattacks (twice), but at the end of the 70s the name was temporarily put to rest. Since their swansong in 1979, an annual reunion has taken place and is now a major event on the folk calendar. The band have no idea which ex-members will turn up! They have also continued to release albums.

FAITH NO MORE

Formed in San Francisco, USA, in 1980. Faith No More were among the first to experiment with the fusion of funk, thrash and hardcore styles. The band –

Jim Martin (b. 1961; guitar), Roddy Bottum (b. 1963; keyboards), Bill Gould (b. 1963; bass), Mike Bordin (b. 1962; drums) and Chuck Mosley (vocals) – recorded a low-budget, self-titled debut on the independent Mordam label, followed by the groundbreaking *Introduce Yourself* on Slash. It encompassed a variety of styles and was well-received by the critics. Internal disputes led to the firing of Mosley on the eve of widespread press coverage. His replacement, Mike Patton (b. 1968), was even more flamboyant and an accomplished singer. *The Real Thing* was a runaway success, with the single 'Epic' denting the US Top 10 in 1990. After Patton temporarily defected, the band finally returned with the transatlantic bestseller *Angel Dust*. However, in 1994, the ever-volatile line-up changed again as Jim Martin was ousted in favour of Trey Spruance. *Album Of The Year* received a mixed reaction, including one or two scathing reviews. In April 1998, Faith No More announced that they were disbanding. Bottum continued recording with Imperial Teen, while Patton embarked on a series of diverse projects. He also runs his own Ipecac Records label.

FAITH, ADAM

London-born Adam Faith (b. Terence Nelhams, 1940) reached the UK chart 24 times in seven years. His career opened with two chart-toppers, 'What Do You Want?' and 'Poor Me'. In a short period of time he appeared in three films, while still enjoying chart hits. In the beat era, Faith was assigned the Roulettes (featuring Russ Ballard) and songwriter Chris Andrews fed him a brief second wave of infectious beat-group hits, most notably 'The First Time'. In the mid-60s, he gave up singing and went into repertory theatre acting. He later appeared in the television shows *Budgie* and *Love Hurts*. He still works on the perimeter of the music world, and released an album in 1993.

FAITHFULL, MARIANNE

London-born Faithfull (b. 1946) began her singing career after being introduced into the **Rolling Stones**' circle. A plaintive Jagger/Richard song, 'As Tears Go By' (1964), became her debut single. It was the first of four UK Top 10 hits. Her albums reflected an impressive balance between folk and rock, but her doomed relationship with Mick Jagger undermined her ambitions as a performer. Faithfull also pursued thespian aspirations, but withdrew from the public eye following a failed suicide attempt. She re-emerged in 1976 with *Dreamin' My Dreams*, but a further period of seclusion followed. She rekindled her career three years later with the impressive *Broken English*. Faithfull's later releases followed a similar pattern, but nowhere was the trauma of her personal life more evident than on *Blazing Away*, a live album on which the singer reclaimed songs from her past. She entered a remarkable period of middle-age creativity with *Vagabond Ways* (1999) and *Kissin' Time* (2002).

FAITHLESS

This UK dance outfit is formed around the nucleus of Rollo (b. Rollo Armstrong) and Sister Bliss (b. Ayalah Bentovim). They were joined in the original line-up by rapper Maxi Jazz (b. Max Fraser), Jamie Catto, and guitarist Dave Randall, with occasional vocal input from Rollo's sister **Dido** (b. Dido Armstrong, 1971). Faithless' debut single on Rollo's Cheeky Records, 'Salva Mea', was one of the 90s' greatest and most influential house records. Its grass-roots popularity on the UK's dancefloors was emphatically confirmed when it shot straight into the UK's Top 10 upon its re-release in 1996.

Faithless' debut *Reverence* was, like the band itself, a slow-burning phenomenon, initially not selling well. On the back of subsequent Top 10 singles and a double album of remix material, however, the album went on to be certified gold in over 22 countries. The band's second album, *Sunday 8pm*, saw them developing the more ambient, meditative element of their work, but big-name DJ remixes of the singles ensured their sustained popularity in the clubs. The first single from the album, the provocatively titled 'God Is A DJ', was a UK Top 10 hit in 1998. They reasserted their club credentials with the following year's remix set and their third studio album, *Outrospective*, which included the striking single 'We Come 1'. Catto had left by this point to work on his 1 Giant Leap project.

FALL

UK indie band formed by the mercurial Mark E. Smith (b. 1957) in 1977. The first line-up – Una Baines (electric piano), Martin Bramah (guitar), Karl Burns (drums) and Tony Friel (bass) – debuted with 'Bingo Master's Breakout', a good example of Smith's surreal vision. With the independent label Step Forward, they recorded three singles, including the savage 'Fiery Jack', plus *Live At The Witch Trials*. In 1980, they signed to Rough Trade Records and released 'How I Wrote Elastic Man' and 'Totally Wired'. A series of line-up changes saw the arrival and subsequent departures of Mike Leigh, Martin Bramah and Yvonne Pawlett. The most stable line-up featured Marc Riley, Steve Hanley, Paul Hanley and Craig Scanlon.

The Fall's convoluted career produced a series of discordant, yet frequently fascinating albums, from the early menace of *Dragnet* to the chaotic *Hex Enduction Hour*. An apparent change in the band's image and philosophy occurred during 1983 with the arrival of Smith's future wife Brix. She first appeared on *Perverted By Language*, but her presence was felt more keenly when the Fall unexpectedly emerged as a potential chart act with 'There's A Ghost In My House' and a cover of the **Kinks**' 'Victoria'. On later albums such as *This Nation's Saving Grace* and *The Frenz Experiment*, they lost none of their earlier charm, but the work seemed more focused and accessible.

The band's 90s output continued successfully, helped by their hugely committed following. The estranged Brix returned to guest on *Cerebral Caustic*. Long-term bass player Steve Hanley walked out, along with two other musicians, following an onstage fight at a show in New York in April 1998. True to form,

Smith assembled a new band and returned with two excellent, thoroughly contemporary albums, *The Marshall Suite* and *The Unutterable*. Unpredictable and unique, the Fall under Smith's guidance remains one of the UK's most uncompromising bands.

FAME, GEORGIE

It took a number of years before Fame (b. Clive Powell, 1943) and his band the Blue Flames had commercial success, although he was a major force in the popularizing of early R&B, bluebeat and ska at London's Flamingo club. *Rhythm And Blues At The Flamingo* was released in 1964, followed by the UK number 1 'Yeh, Yeh'. He continued with another 11 hits, including the UK chart toppers, 'Getaway' and 'The Ballad Of Bonnie And Clyde' (his only US Top 10 single). After 'Sunny' and 'Sitting In The Park' he veered towards straight pop. While his albums showed a more progressive style his singles became lightweight and he teamed up with Alan Price to produce some catchy pop songs.

In the early 90s, he recorded a new album, *Cool Cat Blues*, and favourable reviews and regular concert appearances indicated a new phase. Fame followed this with *The Blues And Me*, an album of a similarly high standard. Since then he has worked and recorded with **Van Morrison** and **Bill Wyman** as well as gigging with his latter-day version of the Blue Flames, which features two of his sons, Tristan Powell (guitar) and James Powell (drums). Fame has reached a stage in his career where he can play what he chooses now he has reverted to his first love jazz.

FAMILY

One of Britain's leading progressive rock bands of the late 60s and early 70s, led by the vocally demonic Roger Chapman (b. 1942) with Ric Grech (b. 1946, d. 1990; violin, bass), Charlie Whitney (b. 1944; guitar), Rob Townsend (b. 1947; drums) and Jim King (flute, saxophone). Their first album was given extensive exposure on **John Peel**'s BBC radio programme and became a cult record. Following the release of their most successful album, *Family Entertainment*, Family experienced an ever-changing line-up. Grech departed, replaced in quick succession by John Weider, John Wetton and Jim Cregan. Poli Palmer (b. John Palmer, 1943) superseded Jim King in 1969, but was ultimately replaced by Tony Ashton (b. 1946, d. 2001) in 1972. Throughout this turmoil they had singles success with 'No Mules Fool', 'Strange Band', 'In My Own Time' and the infectious 'Burlesque'. Family disintegrated in 1973 after their disappointing swansong *It's Only A Movie*. Chapman and Whitney went on to form Streetwalkers.

FANNY

US female rock band formed in 1970. Jean Millington (bass, vocals), June Millington (guitar, vocals), Alice DeBuhr (drums) and Nickey Barclay (keyboards) blended driving hard rock and rock 'n' roll. In 1974, June Millington and DeBuhr were replaced by Patti Quatro (sister of **Suzi Quatro**) and Brie Brandt-Howard. None of their albums charted in the UK and their US sales were minimal. Ironically it was as the band were fragmenting in 1975 that they scored their biggest US hit, 'Butter Boy'.

FARLOWE, CHRIS

UK vocalist Farlowe (b. John Henry Deighton, 1940) started out during the 50s skiffle boom when his John Henry Skiffle Group won the all-England

championship. He then formed the original Thunderbirds, which remained semi-professional until 1962. He made his recording debut that year with the pop-oriented 'Air Travel', but failed to secure commercial success until 1966 when his version of the **Rolling Stones**' 'Out Of Time' (produced by Mick Jagger) reached UK number 1. Several minor hits followed, as well as a brace of pop/soul albums. Farlowe and the Thunderbirds remained one of the country's most impressive R&B acts, although session musicians were increasingly employed for recording purposes. In 1970, the singer founded a new group, the Hill. Their sole album, *From Here To Mama Rosa*, was not a commercial success and Farlowe joined ex-colleague Dave Greenslade in Colosseum. This powerful group disbanded in 1971, and Farlowe retired from rock. He re-emerged in 1975 with *Live!*, but during the rest of the decade failed to find a satisfactory niche for his powerful, gritty voice.

Although Farlowe gigs infrequently he can still be seen performing as a support act. He rejoined his colleagues in Colosseum in 1996 for a reunion tour and album, before resuming his solo career.

FARM

Formed in England in 1983 by Peter Hooton (b. 1962; vocals), Steve Grimes (b. 1962; guitar), Phillip Strongman (bass) and Andy McVann (drums). By 1984 John Melvin, George Maher, Steve Levy and Anthony Evans had joined, bringing with them a brass section and adding a northern-soul influence to the Farm's pop sound. Two years on, Roy Boulter, Keith Mullen (guitar) and Carl Hunter (bass) joined; the horn section departed and Ben Leach (keyboards) joined. After the flop of their fourth independent release, 'Body And Soul', the Farm started their own Produce label and had a fortuitous meeting with dance producer Terry Farley. Consequently, a cover version of the **Monkees**' 'Stepping Stone' was augmented with club beats and samples. 'Groovy Train' and 'All Together Now' swept the band into the UK Top 10, followed in 1991 by their debut album, *Spartacus*, which entered the UK charts at number 1. Unfortunately, *Love See No Colour* was bland and colourless and failed to break the UK Top 50. Help, surprisingly, came from the USA, where Seymour Stein saw some remaining commercial potential in the band. In 1994, they adopted a more orthodox guitar/bass/drums approach for their parting shot, *Hullabaloo*.

FARRELL, PERRY

This controversial icon of the alternative rock scene (b. Perry Bernstein, 1959) relocated to Los Angeles in time to catch the end of the punk-rock movement. Changing his name to Perry Farrell (equals peripheral), he formed the art-goth band Psi Com where he developed his distinctive high-pitched vocal style and charismatic stage presence. Following the disintegration of Psi Com, Farrell formed **Jane's Addiction** with Dave Navarro, Stephen Perkins and Eric Avery. The band's wildly eclectic sound and controversial stage shows helped establish alternative rock as an important and viable musical form in the late 80s.

Jane's Addiction eventually imploded in 1992, a year after Farrell inaugurated the highly successful Lollapalooza concert series. This travelling music festival was instrumental in raising the profile of alternative rock to even greater heights. At the same time, Farrell formed **Porno For Pyros** with Perkins, guitarist Peter DiStefano and bass player Martyn LeNoble. In 1997, Farrell, Navarro and Perkins re-formed Jane's Addiction for select live dates. By the end of the year, however, both Jane's Addiction and Porno For Pyros were no more and Farrell finally began work on his solo debut. *Song Yet To Be Sung*, a challenging hotchpotch of psychedelia and electronica, was released in 2001. At the same time, Farrell resumed live work with Jane's Addiction.

FATBOY SLIM

A man of many musical faces, Norman Cook's Fatboy Slim is arguably his most successful alter ego, and one which made big beat music (a combination of rock and dance music styles) a huge crossover success.

Cook began recording in the big-beat style at the Big Beat Boutique. Signing to Skint Records, Fatboy Slim's debut single was 'Santa Cruz', and was followed by further hit records, including 'Everybody Needs A 303' and the debut album *Better Living Through Chemistry*. The irresistible 'The Rockafeller Skank' brightened up the UK singles chart in 1998. 'Gangster Tripping' provided Cook with another hit single, reaching number 3, and paving the way for *You've Come A Long Way, Baby*. 'Praise You' provided Cook with his first UK number 1 single as Fatboy Slim in January 1999, and in the process dragged the album to the top of the charts. *You've Come A Long Way, Baby* also enjoyed crossover success in the USA, thanks to the prominent use of several tracks in movies including *She's All That* and *Cruel Intentions*, and advertisements for Adidas. Cook was honoured with three MTV Video Awards in September. *Halfway Between The Gutter And The Stars* was influenced by both Cook's newly-married status and the derision now accorded big beat in dance circles, with thumping big beat numbers offset by the dark house grooves of 'Star 69', 'Retox' and the **Jim Morrison**-sampling 'Sunset (Bird Of Prey)'.

FATIMA MANSIONS

Formed in 1989 by singer-songwriter Cathal Coughlan (ex-**Microdisney**) from Cork, Eire, Fatima Mansions were taken on by Kitchenware Records to record *Against Nature*. Andrías O'Gruama's guitar contributed richly to the final results, although the band was primarily a vehicle for Coughlan's lyrical invective. *Bugs Fucking Bunny* was dropped as the title of the second album in favour of *Viva Dead Ponies*. Further paranoia, bile and doses of his full-bodied vocals were poured into the mini-album *Bertie's Brochures* (1991) and *Valhalla Avenue* (1992). After a short break, Coughlan returned with 1994's *Lost In The Former West*. He also recorded two albums under the banner of Bubonique, before embarking on a solo career.

FAUST

Pioneering experimental outfit formed in Germany in 1971. Werner Diermaier, Jean Herve Peron, Rudolf Sosna, Hans Joachim Irmler, Gunther Wusthoff and Armulf Meifert released *Faust*, a conscious attempt to forge a new western 'rock' music wherein fragments of sound were spliced together to create a radical collage. Released in a clear sleeve and on clear vinyl, the album was viewed as an experimental masterpiece. *So Far* proved less obtuse,

and the unit secured a high-profile recording deal with Virgin Records. *The Faust Tapes* retailed at the price of a single (then 49p); this inspired marketing ploy generated considerable interest, but Faust's music remained non-mainstream. Despite line-up changes, Faust remained active throughout the 70s and 80s. In 1988 they reduced the price of admission to those persons arriving at live concerts with a musical instrument who were prepared to play it during the performance. *Rien*, their first album in years, was a return to ambient noise. Peron had departed by 1999's *Ravvivando*.

FEAR FACTORY

This Los Angeles, California, USA-based band mix industrial-style electronic rhythms and samples with grinding guitars and harsh vocals to create their own brutal soundscape. Formed in late 1991 by Burton C. Bell (vocals), Dino Cazares (guitar), Andrew Shives (bass) and Raymond Herrera (drums), *Soul Of A New Machine* established Fear Factory as a genuine death-metal force. *Fear Is The Mind Killer*, a mini-album of remixes by Canadian industrialists Front Line Assembly, added an industrial dance edge. The band also found a permanent bass player with the addition of Belgian Christian Olde Wolbers. *Demanufacture* was ranked as one of the definitive noise albums of 1995. Following a remix album in 1997, the band returned in 1998 with the brutal metal noisefest *Obsolete*. They also gained extensive US radio play for one of their b-sides, a cover version of **Gary Numan**'s 'Cars'. Their growing popularity was confirmed by the commercial success of *Digimortal*.

FEEDER

This highly fêted Welsh alternative-rock band was formed in 1995 by Grant Nicholas (guitar, vocals), Jon Lee (b. 1968, d. 2002; drums), and Taka Hirose (bass), and began playing under the name of Real. After signing to the Echo label later the same year, the trio changed their name to Feeder. Their early singles made little progress in the charts, but the dramatically charged 'High', gained heavy airplay on mainstream radio, and entered the UK charts at number 24 in late 1997. *Polythene*, an excellent collection of post-grunge alternative rock, saw the band receiving further high praise from the music press. They returned in March 1999 with a new single, 'Day In Day Out', followed by the supercharged 'Insomnia' and *Yesterday Went Too Soon*. The band's third full-length set *Echo Park* included the sparkling Top 5 hit 'Buck Rogers', but tragedy followed in January 2002 when Lee was found hanged at his home in Miami.

FELICIANO, JOSÉ

Feliciano (b. 1945; guitar, accordion) was born blind in Puerto Rico. He started out in 1962, performing a mixture of Spanish and American material in the folk clubs and coffee houses of Greenwich Village. Signed to RCA Records, he released 'Everybody Do The Click' before recording an impressive debut album in 1964. Its impassioned arrangements of recent hits were continued on *Feliciano!*. His first hit was a Latin treatment of the **Doors**' 'Light My Fire'. Feliciano's version of the **Bee Gees**' 'The Sun Will Shine' was a

The Dance'. The album *Bête Noire* was a notable hit, indicating that Ferry's muse was still very much alive. The covers' set *Taxi* was followed by *Mamouna*, an album of originals which suffered from a lack of sparkle. Another five-year break ensued before Ferry returned with *As Time Goes By*, on which he tackled the 30s and 40s standard songbook. Ferry reunited with Roxy Music in 2001 for a world tour, fitted in between sessions for his new studio album, *Frantic*.

FIELDS OF THE NEPHILIM

UK rock band formed in 1983 by Carl McCoy (vocals), Tony Pettitt (bass), Peter Yates (guitar) and the Wright brothers, Nod (drums) and Paul (guitar). They had two major UK independent hit singles with 'Preacher Man' and 'Blue Water' and *Dawn Razor* skimmed the UK album chart. *The Nephilim* (UK Top 20) announced the band's arrival as one of the principal rock acts of the day. They also broached the national singles chart with 'Moonchild', 'Psychonaut' and 'Summerland (Dreamed)'. In 1991 McCoy left, taking the Fields Of The Nephilim name with him. The remaining members carried on with new vocalist Alan Delaney and began gigging under the name Rubicon in the summer of 1992, leaving McCoy to unveil his version of the Nephilim (renamed Nefilim). The original band joined in the goth-rock revival by re-forming in the late 90s.

minor UK hit, but the 1970s saw RCA concentrating on Feliciano's Spanish-language material, promoted throughout Latin America. Feliciano continued to record English-language songs, notably on *Compartments*. When Motown set up its own Latin music label in 1981 Feliciano headed the roster, recording *Romance In The Night* as well as Grammy-winning Latin albums. In 1987, he signed a three-pronged deal with EMI Records to record classical guitar music and English pop as well as further Spanish-language recordings. He also pursued his jazz interests. After joining PolyGram Latino records in 1995, he released *El Americano*.

FERRY, BRYAN

UK vocalist Ferry (b. 1945) appeared with a number of local groups before forming **Roxy Music**. During their rise to fame, he plotted a parallel solo career, beginning in 1973 with *These Foolish Things*, an album of favourite cover versions. It received mixed reviews but paved the way for similar works, including **David Bowie**'s *Pin Ups* and **John Lennon**'s *Rock 'N' Roll*. Ferry continued the cover game with the less-impressive *Another Time Another Place*. A gutsy revival of Dobie Gray's 'The In Crowd' brought him a UK Top 20 hit. By 1976, Ferry had switched to R&B covers on *Let's Stick Together*. It was not until 1977 that he finally wrote an album's worth of songs for a solo work. *In Your Mind* spawned a couple of minor hits with 'This Is Tomorrow' and 'Tokyo Joe'. This was followed by the highly accomplished *The Bride Stripped Bare*, but it was another seven years before Ferry recorded solo again. The comeback, *Boys And Girls*, was stylistically similar to his work with Roxy Music and included the hits 'Slave To Love' and 'Don't Stop

5TH DIMENSION

Originally known as the Versatiles and later as the Vocals, Marilyn McCoo (b. 1943), Florence LaRue (b. 1944), Billy Davis Jnr. (b. 1940), Lamont McLemore (b. 1940) and Ron Townson (b. 1933, d. 2001) formed this soul-influenced harmony group, based in Los Angeles. Ebullient pop singles, including 'Go Where You Wanna', 'Up Up And Away' and 'Carpet Man', established their fresh voices and reached the US charts in the late 60s. After two albums they turned to Laura Nyro, whose beautiful soul-styled songs continued their success and introduced the group to the R&B charts. In 1971, they reached US number 2 with the haunting 'One Less Bell To Answer'.

In 1976, McCoo and Davis left for a successful career both as a duo and as solo artists. They had a US number 1 duet in 1976 with 'You Don't Have To Be A Star'. Townson, McLemore and LaRue carried on with new members, establishing themselves on the nightclub circuit. The original quintet briefly reunited in the early 90s for a series of concerts, touring as the Original 5th

Dimension. Townson retired from the group in 1997 due to ill-health, and passed away four years later.

FINE YOUNG CANNIBALS

English pop trio formed in 1983. Ex-Beat members Andy Cox (b. 1960; guitar) and David Steele (b. 1960; bass, keyboards) recruited Roland Gift (b. 1961; vocals) and were quickly picked up by London Records. 'Johnny Come Home', dominated by Gift's sparse and yearning vocals, reached the UK Top 10 and defined the band's sound. The following 'Blue' set out an early political agenda, attacking the Conservative government. After their debut album reached the UK Top 20, the first of a series of distinctive cover versions emerged with 'Suspicious Minds', then a radical rendition of the **Buzzcocks**' 'Ever Fallen In Love'. Their second album topped the US and UK charts and spawned five singles; 'She Drives Me Crazy' and 'Good Thing' were the most successful, both reaching US number 1.

Gift subsequently concentrated on his burgeoning acting career. Still with the ability to bounce back after long pauses, the band's 1996 compilation included new track 'The Flame'. Gift began performing solo in the late 90s and issued a solo album in 2002.

FIREBALLS

Formed in 1957 in New Mexico, USA. George Tomsco (b. 1940; guitar), Chuck Tharp (b. 1941; vocals), Danny Trammell (b. 1940; rhythm guitar), Stan Lark (b. 1940; bass) and Eric Budd (b. 1938; drums) placed 11 singles in the US charts between 1959 and 1969, beginning with the instrumental 'Torquay', although they achieved their greatest success when they teamed up with singer Jimmy Gilmer (b. 1940). In early 1963, now billed as Jimmy Gilmer And The Fireballs, they recorded 'Sugar Shack', using an unusual keyboard called a Solovox to give the record a distinctive sound. The result was one of the bestselling hits of 1963; an album of the same title also charted. Despite subsequent singles and albums, the group was unable to capitalize on that success. Their version of **Tom Paxton**'s 'Bottle Of Wine' (1968) reached US number 9 and was followed by three minor chart singles, but the Fireballs' time had clearly expired. The Fireballs continue as a popular live unit with a line-up now comprising Lark, Tomsco, Ron Cardenas and Daniel Aguilar.

FIREHOSE

Propulsive US hardcore trio formed in 1985. Mike Watt (vocals, bass) and George Hurley (drums) recruited eD fROMOHIO (b. Ed Crawford),

and debuted with the impressive *Ragin', Full-On*. *If'n* and *fROMOHIO* revealed a band that, although bedevilled by inconsistency, was nonetheless capable of inventive, exciting music. The band's variety argued against commercial fortune, but they were still signed by Columbia Records in 1991, releasing the slightly more disciplined *Flyin' The Flannel* that year. Following disappointing critical and commercial response to *Mr. Machinery Operator*, the band split in 1995.

FISH

Scottish-born Fish (b. Derek William Dick, 1958) sang for Stone Dome before auditioning for **Marillion** by writing lyrics for their instrumental 'The Web'. Marillion went from strength to strength, with Fish structuring a series of elaborately linked concept albums, which were still capable of yielding hit singles.

After the hugely successful *Clutching At Straws*, Fish began to disagree with the band about their musical direction and in 1988 he went solo. His debut album utilized stylistically diverse elements such as folk tunes and brass arrangements, but he also retained a mixture of hard rockers and ballads. In 1989, he worked with Peter Hammill on his opera *The Fall Of The House Of Usher*, but they clashed and Fish was replaced on the project by Andy Bell. His 1993 release was a desultory album of cover versions, including the **Kinks**' 'Apeman' and the **Moody Blues**' 'Question'. His 1997 album put him back in favour. A glut of fanclub releases from this period helped to sustain the singer, but after struggling for several years with his own Dick Bros label, Fish signed to Roadrunner Records. He celebrated his new recording contract with the typically bombastic *Raingods With Zippos*, but soon afterwards returned to independent-label status.

FISHBONE

Funk metal hybrid from Los Angeles, USA. Chris 'Maverick Meat' Dowd (b. 1965; trombone, keyboards), 'Dirty' Walter Kibby (b. 1964; trumpet, horn, vocals), 'Big' John Bigham (b. 1969), Kendall Jones (b. guitar), Philip 'Fish' Fisher (b. 1967; drums), John Fisher (b. 1965; bass) and Angelo Moore (b. 1965; lead vocals) debuted with a conventional metal mini-album before the more adventurous *Truth And Soul* in 1988. Subsequent recordings saw Fishbone working with rap artists, although *The Reality Of My Own Surroundings* had more in common with the hard-spined funk of Sly Stone. 'Fight The Youth' and 'Sunless Saturday' demonstrated a serious angle with socio-political, anti-racist and anti-drug lyrics, alongside their lighter more humorous songs. A transatlantic commercial breakthrough offered itself with *Give A Monkey ...*, but media coverage about Jones, who had left to join a religious cult, was damaging. Appearing on 1993's Lollapalooza tour failed to restore the band's diminishing reputation, as did a lacklustre 1996 album. A new line-up, which included Moore, Fisher and Kibby, resurfaced on the Hollywood label in 2000 with a new album.

FIVE

This UK pop quintet enjoyed widespread success in the late 90s with their polished, hip-hop inspired sound. Ritchie Neville (b. Richard Dobson, 1979), Scott Robinson (b. 1979), Richard Abidin Breen (b. 1979), Jason 'J' Brown (b. 1976) and Sean Conlon (b. 1981) all boasted stage and music backgrounds. Following in the footsteps of the **Spice Girls**, the band lived together in Surrey. Their debut single 'Slam Dunk (Da Funk)' reached the UK Top 10 in December 1997, and was followed by the Top 5 hits 'When The Lights Go Out', 'Got The Feelin'', 'Everybody Get Up' and 'Until The Time Is Through'. 'When The Lights Go Out' broke the band in the US, reaching a peak position of number 10 in August 1998. They returned to the UK charts in 1999 with the number 2 single, 'If Ya Gettin' Down', and finally achieved the top slot in October with the irresistible 'Keep On Movin''. The following July they topped the UK singles chart with an energetic cover version of **Queen**'s 'We Will Rock You'. Their third album was premiered by the chart-topping single, 'Let's Dance', but shortly afterwards 5ive announced they were splitting up.

FIVE STAR

British pop act formed by the five siblings of the Pearson family: Deniece (b. 1968), Doris (b. 1966), Lorraine (b. 1967), Stedman (b. 1964) and Delroy

(b. 1970). 'Problematic' failed to chart as did 'Hide And Seek' and 'Crazy'; however, when producer Nick Martinelli took over, 'All Fall Down' (1985) charted, followed by 'Let Me Be The One'. 'System Addict', the seventh single from *Luxury Of Life*, became the first to break the UK Top 10. 'Can't Wait Another Minute' and 'Find The Time' repeated the feat. *Silk And Steel* climbed slowly to the top of the UK charts, eventually going triple platinum and spawning several singles, including 'Rain And Shine' (UK number 2). Continued success was followed by bad investments, financial instability and alleged bankruptcy. Attempts to resurrect their career in America on Epic failed.

FLACK, ROBERTA

US singer Flack (b. 1937) was discovered singing and playing jazz in a Washington nightclub. *First Take* and *Chapter Two* garnered considerable acclaim and Flack achieved huge success with a poignant version of 'First Time Ever I Saw Your Face'. Further hits came with 'Where Is The Love' (1972), a duet with Donny Hathaway, and 'Killing Me Softly With His Song' (1973). Her cool, almost unemotional style benefited from a measured use of slow material, although she seemed less comfortable on up-tempo songs. After wavering in the mid-70s, further duets with Hathaway, 'The Closer I Get To You' (1978) and 'You Are My Heaven' (1980), showed a return to form. In the 80s, Flack enjoyed a fruitful partnership with **Peabo Bryson**, notably the hit 'Tonight I Celebrate My Love' (1983).

FLAMIN' GROOVIES

This unflinchingly self-assured act evolved from an aspiring San Francisco-based garage band, the Chosen Few. Roy Loney (b. 1946; vocals), Tim Lynch (b. 1946; guitar), Cyril Jordan (b. 1948; guitar) and George Alexander (b. 1946; bass) recruited Danny Mihm (drums) and embarked on a direction markedly different from the city's prevalent love of extended improvisation. Their official 1969 debut, *Supersnazz*, revealed a strong debt to traditional rock 'n' roll, although subsequent albums, *Flamingo* and *Teenage Head*, offered a more contemporary perspective. After *Teenage Head*, Loney and Lynch were replaced by Chris Wilson and James Farrell. The Groovies enjoyed a cult popularity in Europe and a series of superb recordings were made during a brief spell in Britain. Several of these formed the basis of *Shake Some Action*, the band's majestic homage to 60s pop. Subsequent releases relied on a tried formula where a series of cover versions disguised a lack of original songs. A reconstituted Flamin' Groovies toured Europe, Australia and New Zealand and completed a handful of new recordings, including *One Night Stand* and *Rock Juice*.

FLAMING LIPS

Formed in Oklahoma, USA, the Flaming Lips won a deserved reputation in the 80s and 90s for their discordant, psychedelia-tinged garage rock. They are led by lyricist, vocalist and guitarist Wayne Coyne (b. 1965), who was initially joined by Steven Drozd (b. 1969; drums, vocals), Ron Jones (b. 1970; guitars, vocals) and Michael Ivins (b. 1965; bass, vocals). John 'Dingus' Donahue, of **Mercury Rev** fame, was also a member during the sessions for *In A Priest Driven Ambulance*.

By the mid-90s they were at last building a substantial popular as well as critical following. A two-year break preceded the release of *Clouds Taste Metallic*, their seventh album, a typically confusing but arresting exercise in wide-eyed, skewed pop rock. Guitarist Jones departed shortly after the album was released. Reduced to a trio, the band returned with *Zaireeka*, a defiantly uncommercial 'experiment in listener participation, using multiple sound sources', whereby four separate CDs needed to be played simultaneously to hear the final mix. *The Soft Bulletin* was a far more satisfying record, representing the perfect fusion of the band's experimental urges and pop instincts.

FLEETWOOD MAC

Formed in England in 1967 by ex-**John Mayall**'s Bluesbreakers Peter Green (b. Peter Greenbaum, 1946; guitar) and Mick Fleetwood (b. 1947; drums). They secured a recording contract with Blue Horizon Records on the strength of Green's reputation as a blues guitarist. Second guitarist Jeremy Spencer (b. 1948) was recruited until another ex-Bluesbreaker, John McVie (b. 1945; bass), joined. Peter Green's Fleetwood Mac, as the band was initially billed, made its debut on 12 August 1967 at Windsor's National Jazz And Blues Festival. Their debut, *Fleetwood Mac*, reached the UK Top 5 and established a distinctive balance between Green and Spencer. The band also enjoyed two minor hits with 'Black Magic Woman' and 'Need Your Love So Bad'. *Mr. Wonderful* was another triumph, but while Spencer was content with his established style, Green extended his compositional boundaries with several haunting contributions. *Mr. Wonderful* also featured contributions from Christine Perfect (b. 1943; piano) and a four-piece horn section. Guitarist, Danny Kirwan (b. 1950) joined in 1968 and they had an immediate UK number 1 with 'Albatross', a moody instrumental.

After a couple of label changes, the band released the superb *Then Play On*. This unveiled Kirwan's songwriting talents; Spencer was notably absent from most of the sessions. Fleetwood Mac now enjoyed an international reputation, but Peter Green left the band in 1970 as his parting single, the awesome 'The Green Manalishi (With The Two Prong Crown)', became another Top 10 hit. He was replaced by Christine Perfect, now married to John McVie, on *Kiln House*. In 1971 the band was rocked for a second time when Spencer disappeared midway through an American tour – he had joined a religious sect, the Children Of God. Californian musician Bob Welch (b. 1946) was recruited. The new line-up was consolidated on *Future Games* and *Bare Trees*. Neither made much impression with UK audiences, but in America the band found a strong following.

Kirwan's chronic stage-fright led to his dismissal, replaced by Bob Weston. Vocalist Dave Walker also joined but left after eight months, having barely completed work on *Penguin*. The remaining quintet completed *Mystery To Me* before Weston was fired midway through a US tour and the remaining dates were cancelled. Welch left in 1974.

Fleetwood employed Stevie Nicks (b. 1948) and Lindsey Buckingham (b. 1949), who had already released a self-named album. This became Fleetwood Mac's most successful line-up and *Fleetwood Mac* was a promise fulfilled. The newcomers provided easy yet memorable compositions with smooth harmonies, while the British contingent gave the band its edge and power. The dramatic 'Rhiannon' gave them their first in a long line of US Top 20 singles. *Rumours* proved more remarkable still. Despite the McVies' divorce and Buckingham and Nicks splitting up, the band completed a stunning collection of exquisite songs: 'Go Your Own Way', 'Don't Stop', 'Second Hand News' and 'Dreams'.

Tusk, an ambitious double set, showed a band unafraid to experiment. An in-concert selection, *Fleetwood Mac: Live*, was released as a stopgap in 1980 and it was a further two years before a new collection, *Mirage*, appeared. Several years then passed before *Tango In The Night*, a dramatic return to form. The collection was, however, Buckingham's swansong. By that point two replacement singer/guitarists, Rick Vito and Billy Burnette (b. 1953), had joined. The new line-up debuted with the successful *Behind The Mask*. However, despite the addition of ex-**Traffic** guitarist Dave Mason (b. 1945) and Bekka Bramlett (b. 1968), *Time* failed to ignite any spark. In 1997, the famous *Rumours* line-up reunited, releasing a live album on the album's 20th anniversary.

FLEETWOODS
US doo-wop group formed in the late 50s. Gary Troxell (b. 1939), Gretchen Christopher (b. 1940) and Barbara Ellis (b. 1940) composed 'Come Softly To Me'. The haunting and catchy song shot to US number 1 and the UK Top 10. Their third release, 'Mr. Blue', was also a US number 1 and made Troxell one of the leaders in the teen-idol stakes. In the midst of their success he was drafted into the navy, his place being taken when necessary by Vic Dana. Despite Troxell's absence, the US hits continued and they totalled nine Top 40 hits between 1959 and 1963, which included the number 10 hit 'Tragedy'. The trio resurfaced in 1973 when they signed with producer Jerry Dennon; no hits came from this collaboration.

FLICKERSTICK
Alternative-rock outfit originating from Fort Worth, Texas, USA. Brandin Lea (vocals, guitar), Cory Kreig (guitar, keyboards), Fletcher Lea (bass), Rex James Ewing (guitar) and Dominic Weir (drums) had soon developed a reputation as one of the area's best live acts, with a rudimentary but highly effective multimedia show. The quintet's debut album was recorded and independently released in 2000, but their big breakthrough came about when they appeared on VH1's *Bands On The Run* reality music show, one of four unsigned bands competing for $50,000 cash, $100,000 dollars in equipment and an industry showcase. Flickerstick's outlandish pursuit of the rock 'n' roll lifestyle over the show's 15-week run helped endear them to a new audience, and they were voted the winner. A recording contract with Epic Records followed in July.

An expanded and re-mastered version of *Welcoming Home The Astronauts* was released in October.

FLOWERPOT MEN
UK group formed in 1967 by the Carter and Lewis songwriting team to exploit the flower-power boom. Their 'Let's Go To San Francisco' reached the UK Top 5 and a quartet of session vocalists – Tony Burrows, Robin Shaw, Pete Nelson and Neil Landon – then assumed the name. The group completed several well-sculpted releases, notably 'A Walk In The Sky'. An instrumental section, comprising Ged Peck (guitar), Jon Lord (organ), Nick Simper (bass) and Carlo Little (drums), accompanied the singers on tour, but this line-up was dissolved when Lord and Simper founded **Deep Purple**.

FLOYD, EDDIE
Floyd (b. 1935) was a founder-member of the Detroit-based Falcons, present on their 'You're So Fine' (1959) and 'I Found A Love' (1962). He joined the Stax Records organization in 1965, making his mark as a composer. He employed the session bands **Booker T. And The MGs** and the **Mar-Keys** and recorded 'Things Get Better' (1965), followed by the anthem-like 'Knock On Wood' (1966). Although subsequent releases were less successful, a series of powerful singles, including 'Love Is A Doggone Good Thing' (1967) and 'Big Bird' (1968), confirmed Floyd's stature both as a performer and songwriter.

When Stax went bankrupt in 1975 Floyd moved to Malaco Records, but left for Mercury Records two years later. In 1988, he linked up with William Bell's Wilbe venture and issued his *Flashback* album. In 1990, Floyd appeared live with a re-formed Booker T. And The MGs and continues to gig consistently.

FLYING BURRITO BROTHERS
Los Angeles, USA-based country-rock band formed in 1968. **Gram Parsons** (b. Ingram Cecil Connor III, 1946, d. 1973; guitar, vocals) and Chris Hillman (b. 1942; guitar, vocals) recruited 'Sneaky' Pete Kleinow (pedal steel), Chris Ethridge (bass) and various drummers. *The Gilded Palace Of Sin* allowed the founding duo's vision of a pan-American music to flourish freely. *Burrito Deluxe*, on which Bernie Leadon (b. 1947) replaced Ethridge and Michael Clarke (b. Michael Dick, 1944, d. 1993; ex-**Byrds**) became the permanent drummer, showed a group unsure of direction. Parsons went solo in 1970 and with the arrival of songwriter Rick Roberts, the Flying Burrito Brothers again asserted their high quality. The underrated *The Flying Burrito Bros* was a cohesive, purposeful set, but unfortunately, the band was again bedevilled by defections. In 1971 Leadon and Kleinow left, and Al Perkins (pedal steel), Kenny Wertz (guitar), Roger Bush (bass) and Byron Berline (fiddle) joined. *The Last Of The Red Hot Burritos* captured the excitement and power of this short-lived line-up in concert.

A bewildering series of personnel changes ensued, before the band changed direction at the start of the 80s and began to enjoy success on the country charts (as the Burrito Brothers). When this line-up faltered in the mid-80s, Kleinow reclaimed the band's original name. Further studio work followed, but by 1999's *Sons Of The Golden West* no original members remained.

FOCUS

Thijs Van Leer (keyboards, flute, vocals), Martin Dresden (bass) and Hans Cleuver (drums) backed several Dutch singers before 1969's catalytic enlistment of guitarist Jan Akkerman. The new quartet's first collective essay as recording artists was humble, but heartened by audience response Focus released a bona-fide album debut with a spin-off single, 'House Of The King'; it sold well in continental Europe. The Mike Vernon-produced *Moving Waves* embraced vocal items (in English), melodic instrumentals and the startling 'Hocus Pocus' (UK Top 20). After reshuffles in which only Van Leer and Akkerman surfaced from the original personnel, 'Sylvia' shot into the UK Top 5; *Focus III* also reached the upper echelons of the charts. An in-concert album from London and *Hamburger Concerto* both marked time artistically and, following 1975's *Mother Focus*, Akkerman left to concentrate on his parallel solo career. Van Leer elected to stick with a latter-day Focus. The 1972 line-up re-formed solely for a Dutch television special in 1990.

FOETUS

After founding his own record company, Self Immolation, in 1980, Australian émigré Jim Foetus (b. Jim Thirlwell) set about 'recording works of aggression, insight and inspiration'. Foetus released a series of albums, such as *Deaf, Ache, Hole* and *Nail*, employing a range of pseudonyms. On all his releases, Thirlwell presents a harrowing aural netherworld of death, lust, disease and spiritual decay. In 1995, Thirlwell released his first studio album in seven years, the major-label outing *Gash*, an album that led to a reappraisal of his work as one of the key figures in the development of the 'industrial' music movement. Thirlwell subsequently returned to independent-label status with his reputation and legendary status still intact.

FOGELBERG, DAN

Fogelberg (b. 1951; guitar, piano) was discovered by Nashville producer Norbert Putnam, resulting in the release of 1972's *Home Free* for Columbia Records. This highly relaxed album was notable for the backing musicians involved, including Roger McGuinn, Jackson Browne, Joe Walsh and Buffy Sainte-Marie. Despite these, the album was unsuccessful and Fogelberg was dropped by Columbia. He returned to session work, moved to Colorado, and released the charming *Souvenirs* and *Netherlands*. 'Longer' (1980) reached US number 2, and 'Same Auld Lang Syne' and 'Leader Of The Band' (both from *The Innocent Age*) reached the Top 10. The excellent *High Country Snows* saw a return to his bluegrass influences and was in marked contrast to the harder-edged *Exiles*. In the late 80s Fogelberg built a full-size studio (Mountain Bird Studio) at his ranch, enabling him to record new albums from his homebase.

FONTANA, WAYNE

After changing his name in honour of **Elvis Presley**'s drummer D. J. Fontana, Wayne (b. Glyn Ellis, 1945) was signed to the appropriately named Fontana Records. His backing group, the Mindbenders, provided a gritty accompaniment.

Their first minor hit was the unremarkable 'Hello Josephine' (1963). The group finally broke through with their fifth release, 'Um, Um, Um, Um, Um' (UK number 5). The 1965 follow-up, 'The Game Of Love', hit number 2. Thereafter the group struggled, with 'Just A Little Bit Too Late' and 'She Needs Love' their only further hits. In 1965, Fontana went solo with 'It Was Easier To Hurt Her' before finding success with the catchy 'Come On Home'. After giving up music during the early 70s, Fontana joined the revivalist circuit, although his progress was frequently dogged by personal problems.

FOO FIGHTERS

US rock band formed in 1994 by Dave Grohl (b. 1969; vocals, guitar; ex-**Nirvana**), who recruited Pat Smear (guitar), Nate Mendel (b. 1968; bass) and William Goldsmith (b. 1972; drums). Their debut, 'This Is A Call', was released on Roswell/Capitol Records. Media analysis of the band's debut album focused on tracks such as 'I'll Stick Around', which some alleged was an attack on Kurt Cobain's widow, **Courtney Love**. Detractors pointed at the similarity to Nirvana in the construction of several tracks, and Grohl's inability to match Cobain's evocation of mood. Goldsmith left during the recording of their second album, replaced by Taylor Hawkins. *The Colour And The Shape* was another hard and tough album of blisteringly paced songs, lightened by the band's great grasp of melody. Smear left the band following the album's release, and was later replaced by Franz Stahl (ex-Scream). In 1998, Grohl

recorded the soundtrack to Paul Schrader's *Touch*. Stahl left in 1999, shortly before the release of yet another strong set, *There Is Nothing Left To Lose*, the band's first album for RCA Records.

FORBERT, STEVE

US-born Forbert first recorded in 1977 for Nemperor, and was briefly heralded as the new **Bob Dylan**. Forbert's biggest commercial success came with 'Romeo's Tune' (1979, US Top 20) but after four albums his contract was terminated. For most of the 80s and 90s, Forbert was based in Nashville, songwriting and playing concerts around the South with a touring group.

FORD, FRANKIE

New Orleans rocker Frankie Ford (b. Francis Guzzo, 1939) first appeared on *Ted Mack's Amateur Hour Talent Show*, where he sang with Carmen Miranda and Sophie Tucker. In 1958 he was asked to audition for Ace Records. Subsequently, he released his first single, 'Cheatin' Woman'. Fellow musician Huey 'Piano' Smith had previously recorded a self-penned song, 'Sea Cruise'; Ford recorded a new vocal and it was released under the title *Frankie Ford With Huey 'Piano' Smith And His Clowns*. It sold over a million copies and reached the US Top 20. Ford left Ace in 1960 to form his own Spinet Records and signed to Liberty Records in 1960, but never repeated the success of 'Sea Cruise'.

Ford continued to record for obscure labels throughout the 70s. In 1971, he opened a club in New Orleans' French Quarter where he became a cabaret fixture and tourist attraction. His four recordings of 'Sea Cruise' have now sold over 30 million copies worldwide.

FOREIGNER

Transatlantic soft-rock band formed in 1976. Mick Jones (b. 1944; guitar, vocals) recruited Ian McDonald (b. 1946; guitar, keyboards, horns, vocals), Lou Gramm (b. Lou Grammatico, 1950; vocals), Dennis Elliott (b. 1950; drums), Al Greenwood (keyboards) and Edward Gagliardi (b. 1952; bass) and the band released *Foreigner*. Jones and Gramm wrote most of their material, including classics such as 'Feels Like The First Time' and 'Cold As Ice' (both US Top 10 hits). In 1979, Rick Wills (bass) replaced Gagliardi, and the following year saw the departure of McDonald and Greenwood which led to the guest appearances of Thomas Dolby and Junior Walker on *4*. The hit 'Waiting For A Girl Like You' was lifted from the album. The following 'I Want To Know What Love Is' proved to be Foreigner's greatest commercial success, topping the charts on both sides of the Atlantic in 1984–85.

In the mid-80s the members of Foreigner were engaged in solo projects. The band then released *Inside Information*, but despite containing the US Top 10 hits 'Say You Will' and 'I Don't Want To Live Without You', in many respects it was a poor record and a portent of things to come. In 1990, Gramm left the band and Jones recruited Johnny Edwards to provide vocals for *Unusual Heat*. In 1994, Jones and Gramm launched a reunited Foreigner. The band were back on the road in 1995 to promote *Mr Moonlight*. Gramm was successfully treated for a brain tumour before the band reconvened in 1999.

FORTUNES

UK beat group formed in 1963 by Glen Dale (b. Richard Garforth, 1943; vocals, guitar); Rod Allen (b. Rodney Bainbridge, 1944; bass) and Barry Pritchard (b. 1944, d. 1999; guitar). After perfecting their harmonic blend, the group recruited David Carr (b. 1943; keyboards) and Andy Brown (b. 1946; drums). Their debut, 'Summertime Summertime' passed without notice, but the following 'Caroline' was taken up as the theme song for the pirate station Radio Caroline. In 1965 the group reached the UK and US Top 10 with 'You've Got Your Troubles'. 'Here It Comes Again' and 'This Golden Ring' displayed their easy-listening appeal, but unexpectedly Dale left. The group continued and scored an unexpected US hit with 'Here Comes That Rainy Day Feeling Again' in 1971. Back in the UK, they also enjoyed their first hits in over five years with 'Freedom Come Freedom Go' and 'Storm In A Teacup' and have since sustained their career, albeit with changing personnel, on the cabaret circuit.

FOUNDATIONS

UK group formed in 1967. London record dealer Barry Class introduced the Foundations to songwriters Tony Macaulay and John Macleod, whose composition 'Baby, Now That I've Found You' became the group's debut release. The single reached UK number 1 and, eventually, US number 9; global sales exceeded three million. The group's multiracial line-up included West Indians Clem Curtis (b. 1940; vocals), Pat Burke (b. 1937; tenor saxophone/flute), Mike Elliot (b. 1929; tenor saxophone) and Eric Allandale (b. 1936, d. 2001; trombone), Londoners Alan Warner (b. 1947; guitar), Peter Macbeth (b. 1943; bass) and Tim Harris (b. 1948; drums), and Sri Lankan Tony Gomez (b. 1948; organ). They scored a second multi-million-seller in 1968 with 'Build Me Up Buttercup' and enjoyed further success with similarly styled releases, including 'Back On My Feet Again' and 'Any Old Time' (both 1968). Curtis was replaced by Colin Young (b. 1944), and the departure of Elliot signalled internal dissatisfaction. 'In The Bad Bad Old Days' (1969) returned the group to the UK Top 10, but the minor hit 'Born To Live And Born To Die' (1969), was their last chart entry. A completely new line-up later resurrected the Foundations' name with little success.

FOUNTAINS OF WAYNE

Idiosyncratic US pop duo Adam Schlesinger and Chris Collingwood originally signed a recording contract as the Wallflowers, but abandoned their claim to

the name and the proposed record never appeared. By the time they finally recorded, Schlesinger had become co-owner of Scratchie Records. The result was a self-titled collection of 12 brittle guitar pop songs. The first single from the album, 'Radiation Vibe', reached the UK Top 40. The band also achieved a flurry of publicity when their song 'That Thing You Do!' was included in the Tom Hanks movie of the same name. *Utopia Parkway*, another collection of note perfect power pop classics, was released in 1999. Schlesinger also records with Ivy.

4 NON BLONDES

San Francisco, USA-based quartet formed by Linda Perry (guitar, vocals), alongside Christa Hillhouse (bass), Roger Rocha (guitar) and Dawn Richardson (drums). Hillhouse and Perry, who begun the band, had to cancel their first-ever rehearsal on 7 October 1989 when an earthquake hit the Bay

Area. They achieved a huge transatlantic hit in 1993 with 'What's Up'. The debut album, *Bigger, Better, Faster, More!* sold half a million copies in the USA, and also topped charts in Germany and Sweden. Perry's songs quickly became the dominant force within 4 Non Blondes, and she later embarked on a solo career before branching into songwriting.

FOUR FRESHMEN

Influential vocal group formed in Indiana, USA, in 1948. Lead vocalist Bob Flanigan (b. 1926), his cousins Ross Barbour (b. 1928) and Don Barbour (b. 1929, d. 1961), and Hal Kratzsch (d. 1970) were signed to Capitol Records. Their first hit, 'It's A Blue World' (1952), reached US number 30. In 1953 Kratzsch was replaced by Ken Errair (b. 1930, d. 1968). Errair departed in 1955, replaced by Ken Albers. By that time the group had logged two more Top 40 hits, 'It Happened Once Before' and 'Mood Indigo'. Three final chart singles were issued in 1955–56. Don Barbour left in 1960, replaced by Bill Comstock (who left in 1972). Ross Barbour stayed on until 1977 and Ken Albers until 1982. Don Barbour was killed in a car crash, Kratzsch died of cancer and Errair died in a plane crash. Flanigan continues to act as manager and agent for the present day line-up, who are able to reproduce the original sound almost note-perfect.

FOUR PREPS

US vocal group formed in the early 1950s. Bruce Belland, Glen Larson, Marvin Inabnett and Ed Cobb (d. 1999) began singing together as teenagers. They were signed by Capitol Records and their first session yielded 'Dreamy Eyes' (1956), which was a minor hit. The follow-up, '26 Miles (Santa Catalina)', reached number 2 and 'Big Man' made number 3. Despite their prolific output, chart success largely eluded them. Subsequent singles failed to make the US Top 10 although the group did score a Top 10 album, *Four Preps On Campus*. Their final charting single, 1964's 'A Letter To The Beatles', parodied Beatlemania but was allegedly withdrawn from distribution upon request by the **Beatles**' management. The group continued until 1967. In 1988, the Four Preps were back on the road, with two of the original members, Belland and Cobb, being joined by David Somerville, former lead singer of the Diamonds and Jim Pike, founder of the Lettermen.

FOUR SEASONS

US vocal group formed in 1956. Vocalists **Frankie Valli** (b. Francis Castelluccio, 1937), brothers Nick and Tommy DeVito (b. 1936) and Hank Majewski were initially known as the Variatones, then the Four Lovers (they enjoyed a minor US hit with 'You're The Apple Of My Eye', composed by Otis Blackwell). After being dropped by RCA Records, they recorded a single for Epic Records, following which Valli departed briefly to pursue a solo career. Meanwhile, the Four Lovers released several records under pseudonymous names, during which Nick DeVito and Majewski departed, replaced by Nick Massi (b. Nicholas Macioci, 1935, d. 2000) and Bob Gaudio (b. 1942). The group became the Four Seasons, signed to Vee Jay Records and released 'Sherry' followed by 'Big Girls Don't Cry', 'Walk Like A Man' and 'Rag Doll', which were all US number 1s. In 1965, Massi left, replaced by Joe Long. Valli, meanwhile, was continuing to enjoy solo hits.

At the end of the decade, the group attempted to establish themselves as a more serious act with the poorly received *Genuine Imitation Life Gazette*. When Tommy DeVito left in 1970, the lucrative Four Seasons back catalogue and rights to the group name rested with Valli and Gaudio. A brief tie-up with

Motown Records saw the release of *Chameleon*, which, despite favourable reviews, sold poorly. Meanwhile, Valli was receiving unexpected UK success. While Valli was back at number 1 with 'My Eyes Adored You' (1975), the latest group line-up charted with 'Who Loves You'. Immense success followed as the group became part of the disco boom sweeping America. The nostalgic 'December 1963 (Oh What A Night)' was a transatlantic number 1 in 1976, but the following year, Valli left the group again to concentrate on his solo career. He had a US number 1 with the Barry Gibb film theme *Grease*, while the Four Seasons continued with drummer Gerry Polci on lead vocals. Valli returned to the group for a double album recorded live at Madison Square Garden.

A team-up with the **Beach Boys** on the single 'East Meets West' in 1984 was followed by a studio album, *Streetfighter*, which featured Valli. In 1990, the group was inducted into the Rock And Roll Hall Of Fame. Still going strong, Frankie Valli And The Four Seasons have become an institution whose illustrious history spans several musical eras, from the barber shop harmonies of the 50s to the disco beat of the 70s.

FOUR TOPS

Levi Stubbs (b. 1936), Renaldo 'Obie' Benson (b. 1938), Lawrence Peyton (b. 1938, d. 1997) and Abdul 'Duke' Fakir (b. 1935), first sang together at a party in Detroit in 1954 as the Four Aims. In 1956, they changed their name to the Four Tops and recorded a one-off single. After teaming up with **Holland/Dozier/Holland**, they released 'Baby I Need Your Loving', which showcased the group's strong harmonies and the gruff, soulful lead vocals of Stubbs; it reached the US Top 20. The following year, 'I Can't Help Myself', topped the charts. Holland/Dozier/Holland continued to write and produce for the Four Tops until 1967. The pinnacle of this collaboration was 'Reach Out, I'll Be There', a transatlantic hit in 1966. In 1967, the Four Tops began to widen their appeal with soul-tinged versions of pop hits, such as **Left Banke**'s 'Walk Away Renee' and Tim Hardin's 'If I Were A Carpenter'.

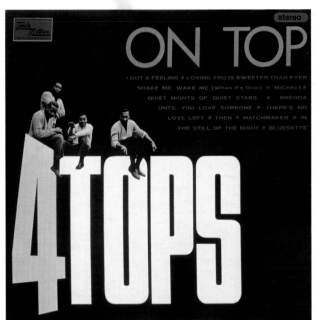

The departure of Holland, Dozier and Holland from Motown Records brought a temporary halt to the group's progress, and it was 1970 before they regained their hit status with a revival of Tommy Edwards' 'It's All In The Game'. Another revival, Richard Harris' 'MacArthur Park', brought success in 1971, while Benson also co-wrote **Marvin Gaye**'s hit 'What's Going On'.

After working with the **Moody Blues** on 'A Simple Game' (1972), the Four Tops elected to leave Motown, who were relocating to California. They signed with Dunhill Records, and restored their chart success with the theme to the movie *Shaft In Africa*, 'Are You Man Enough'. At the end of the decade, they joined Casablanca Records, and secured a soul number 1 with 'When She Was My Girl'. Subsequent releases also charted in Britain and America.

In 1983 the group performed a storming medley of their 60s hits with the **Temptations** during the Motown 25th Anniversary television special. They resigned to the label for *Back Where I Belong*, one side of which was produced by Holland/Dozier/Holland. However, disappointing sales and disputes about the group's musical direction led them to leave Motown once again. With Arista Records, they found immediate success with the singles 'Indestructible' and 'Loco In Acapulco' (both 1988), the latter taken from the soundtrack to the movie *Buster*. The Four Tops retained a constant line-up from their inception up until Peyton's death in June 1997.

FOURMOST

UK band originally known as the Blue Jays, then the Four Jays, then the Four Mosts. Brian O'Hara (b. 1942, d. 1999; lead guitar, vocals), Mike Millward (b. 1942, d. 1966; rhythm guitar, vocals), Billy Hatton (b. 1941; bass) and Dave Lovelady (b. 1942; drums) achieved momentary fame under the management wing of **Brian Epstein**. Two commercial Lennon/McCartney songs, 'Hello Little Girl' and 'I'm In Love', served as their initial a-sides, but 'A Little Lovin'' became the quartet's biggest hit (1964, UK number 6). The Fourmost's later releases veered from Motown ('Baby I Need Your Lovin'') to George Formby ('Aunt Maggie's Remedy'), but they faltered in the wake of the R&B boom. Brian O'Hara continued the name until the early 80s.

FOURPLAY

A group who have earned consistent critical praise for their blend of pop and contemporary jazz, Fourplay comprise Bob James (b. 1939; keyboards), Lee Ritenour (b. 1953; guitar), Nathan East (bass) and Harvey Mason (b. 1947; drums). Their self-titled debut album spent 31 weeks at number 1 on the US Contemporary Jazz Albums chart. Their second collection, *Between The Sheets*, also reached number 1 on the chart. The styles on their albums echo developments in pop music (particularly R&B) as well as jazz.

FRAMPTON, PETER

UK-born Frampton (b. 1950) made his name in the **Herd** and **Humble Pie**, before making his solo debut with *Wind Of Change* in 1971. He immediately set about forming a band, Frampton's Camel, to carry out US concert dates. The group featured Mike Kellie (drums), Mickey Gallagher (keyboards) and Rick

Wills (bass). Frampton was a great success in the USA, while in the UK he was commercially ignored. The following year a double set, *Frampton Comes Alive!*, reached US number 1 and stayed in the charts for two years. It became the biggest-selling live album in history and has sold over 12 million copies. The follow-up *I'm In You*, also sold in vast quantities, though not to the same scale, although 'Show Me The Way' reached the US and UK Top 10. In 1978, Frampton suffered a near-fatal car crash and when he returned in 1979 with *Where I Should Be*, his star was dwindling.

Following *The Art Of Control* Frampton 'disappeared' until 1986, when he was signed to Virgin Records and released the synthesizer-laced *Premonition*. He returned to session work thereafter. In the mid-90s, Frampton diverted his interest to the great success of his career by releasing *Frampton Comes Alive II*. In 2000, Frampton served as a musical consultant on Cameron Crowe's 70s rock biopic, *Almost Famous*.

FRANCIS, CONNIE

US-born Francis (b. Concetta Rosa Maria Franconero, 1938) began performing professionally aged 11. After winning an *Arthur Godfrey Talent Show*, she changed her name and signed to MGM Records in 1955. 'Majesty Of Love', her 10th release, a duet with Marvin Rainwater, was her first US chart entry. In 1957, she was persuaded to record the 1923 song 'Who's Sorry Now'; it reached US number 4 and UK number 1. Her other hits included 'My Happiness', 'Among My Souvenirs' and 'Stupid Cupid' (UK number 1), 'Where The Boys Are' (by Neil Sedaka and Howard Greenfield), 'Lipstick On Your Collar', 'Everybody's Somebody's Fool' (her first US number 1), 'My Mind Has A Heart Of Its Own' (US number 1), and 'Don't Break The Heart That Loves You' (US number 1).

Francis made her film debut in 1960 with *Where The Boys Are*, and followed it with similar comedy musicals such as *Follow The Boys* (1963), *Looking For Love* (1964) and *When The Boys Meet The Girls* (1965). Outdated by the 60s beat boom, she worked in nightclubs in the late 60s, and did much charity work for UNICEF and similar organizations, as well as entertaining US troops in Vietnam.

In 1974, she was the victim of a rape in her motel room after a performance. For several years afterwards she did not perform publically, and underwent psychiatric treatment. She resumed performing in 1981, returning to the same motel and an enthusiastic reception. In 1992, she was diagnosed as suffering from 'a complex illness', but in 1993 she signed a new recording contract with Sony, buoyed by the fact that her 1959 hit, 'Lipstick On Your Collar', was climbing high in the UK charts, after appearing as the title of a Dennis Potter television drama.

FRANK AND WALTERS

Three-piece band from Cork, Eire. Paul Linehan (vocals, bass), Niall Linehan (guitar) and Ashley Keating (drums) attracted immediate press attention through a debut EP on the Setanta Records label. The resulting 1992 debut album failed to fulfil critical expectations, however. 'This Is Not A Song' and 'Fashion Crisis Hits New York' offered chart hits via bigger promotion and production, and the reworked album track 'After All' narrowly failing to reach the UK Top 10. By the time the more earnest *The Grand Parade* was released, however, the fickle world of pop had moved on. An extended sojourn in the US inspired the lush, melancholic songs on 1999's *Beauty Becomes More Than Life*.

FRANKIE GOES TO HOLLYWOOD

UK pop band formed in 1980 by Holly Johnson (b. William Johnson, 1960; vocals), Paul Rutherford (b. 1959; vocals), Nasher Nash (b. Brian Nash, 1963; guitar), Mark O'Toole (b. 1964; bass) and Peter Gill (b. 1964; drums). Their debut single, 'Relax', was produced by Trevor Horn. A superb dance track with a suggestive lyric, the single was banned on BBC radio and television in

Britain. This proved the single's best marketing ploy, however, and it topped the UK charts for five weeks at the start of 1984, selling almost two million copies. The band's image of Liverpool laddishness coupled with the overt homosexuality of Johnson and Rutherford merely added to their sensationalism. The follow up, 'Two Tribes', was an awesome production built round a throbbing, infectious riff. The topical lyric dealt with the escalation of nuclear arms and the prospect of global annihilation. It entered the chart at number 1, where it stayed for nine weeks while the revitalized 'Relax' sat at number 2. *Welcome To The Pleasure Dome* contained a number of cover versions, including **Bruce Springsteen**'s 'Born To Run', **Dionne Warwick**'s 'Do You Know The Way To San Jose?' and **Gerry And The Pacemakers**' 'Ferry Cross The Mersey'. The sound was epic, glorious and critically acclaimed. The year ended with a change of style as the band enjoyed their third number 1 with the moving festive ballad 'The Power Of Love'. They became the second act in UK pop history to see their first three singles reach the top. The following year, their fourth single ('Welcome To The Pleasure Dome') stalled at number 2, and they were never again to attain their previous ascendancy.

'Rage Hard', their 1986 comeback, reached UK number 4, but seemed decidedly anti-climactic. *Liverpool* cost a small fortune to record but lacked the charm and vibrancy of its predecessor, and within a year Johnson and Rutherford had quit, effectively spelling the end of the band, although the remaining three attempted to continue with new vocalist Grant Boult. Later attempts to record as the Lads came to nothing.

FRANKLIN, ARETHA

US vocalist Franklin (b. 1942) knew the major gospel stars Mahalia Jackson and Clara Ward, who gave her valuable tutelage. At the age of 12, she left her

choir to become a featured soloist, and two years later she began recording for JVB and Checker Records. Between 1956 and 1960, her output was devotional, but the secular success of **Sam Cooke** encouraged a change of emphasis. After a dozen patchy albums with Columbia Records, a disillusioned Franklin joined Atlantic Records resulting in 'I Never Loved A Man (The Way I Loved You)' (1966). The single soared into the US Top 10. The following releases, including 'Do Right Woman – Do Right Man', 'Respect', 'Baby I Love You' and '(You Make Me Feel Like) A Natural Woman', proclaimed her 'Queen Of Soul'.

Despite Franklin's professional success, her relationship with husband and manager Ted White disintegrated, and while excellent singles such as 'Think' and 'I Say A Little Prayer' were released, others betrayed a discernible lethargy. In 1970 she was back on form with 'Call Me', 'Spirit In The Dark' and 'Don't Play That Song'. *Aretha Live At Fillmore West* restated her in-concert power and in 1972, another live appearance resulted in *Amazing Grace*, a double gospel set. Throughout the early 70s, Franklin enjoyed three R&B chart-toppers, 'Angel', 'Until You Come Back To Me (That's What I'm Gonna Do)' and 'I'm In Love'.

Sadly, the rest of the decade was marred by recordings that were at best predictable, at worst dull. However a cameo role in the movie *The Blues Brothers* rekindled her flagging career and saw a move to Arista Records. In the mid-80s, she charted with **Annie Lennox** ('Sisters Are Doin' It For Themselves') and **George Michael** ('I Knew You Were Waiting (For Me)'); the latter went to US and UK number 1 in 1987. As her 'return to gospel' *One Lord One Faith One Baptism* proved, she is still a commanding singer. A lengthy hiatus ensued before the release of 1998's impressive *A Rose Is Still A Rose*, on which Franklin co-opted the songwriting and production talents of the cream of contemporary urban music.

FRED, JOHN, AND HIS PLAYBOY BAND

During the early 60s, various versions of the Playboy Band recorded for small independent record labels, but it was not until the end of 1967 that success finally came with the international hit, 'Judy In Disguise (With Glasses)'. Fred's (b. John Fred Gourrier, 1941) blue-eyed soul vocals were evident on *Agnes English*, which included a rasping version of 'She Shot A Hole In My Soul'. By the end of the 60s the band had split-up, with Fred going on to record with a new group and work as a producer for RCS in Baton Rouge.

FREDDIE AND THE DREAMERS

UK group featuring Freddie Garrity (b. 1940; vocals), Roy Crewsdon (b. 1941; guitar), Derek Quinn (b. 1942; guitar), Pete Birrell (b. 1941; bass) and Bernie Dwyer (b. 1940; drums). Their debut, 'If You Gotta Make A Fool Of Somebody', was an R&B favourite, followed by the lighter 'I'm Telling You Now' and 'You Were Made For Me'. Further hits followed in 1964 with 'Over You', 'I Love You Baby', 'Just For You', and 'I Understand'. The group's appeal declined in the UK but early in 1965, they made a startling breakthrough in America, where 'I'm Telling You Now' topped the charts. A US Top 20 hit rapidly followed with 'Do The Freddie' (inspired by Garrity's zany stage antics). They disbanded at the end of the decade. Garrity later revived the group – with new personnel – for revival concerts.

FREE

British rock band formed in 1968. Paul Rodgers (b. 1949; vocals), Paul Kossoff (b. 1950, d. 1976; guitar), Andy Fraser (b. 1952; bass) and Simon Kirke (b. 1949; drums) gained early encouragement from **Alexis Korner**, but having completed an excellent, earthy debut album, *Tons Of Sobs*, began honing a more individual style with their second set. The powerful original songs, including 'I'll Be Creeping', showed a maturing talent. Their stylish blues rock reached its commercial peak on 1970's *Fire And Water*, containing the classic 'All Right Now' (UK number 2/US number 4).

Highway revealed a more mellow perspective highlighted by an increased use of piano at the expense of Kossoff's guitar. This was due, in part, to friction within the band and Free broke up in 1971, paradoxically in the wake of another hit, 'My Brother Jake'. They regrouped the following year when spin-off projects faltered. *Free At Last* offered some of the unit's erstwhile fire and included another UK Top 20 hit, 'Little Bit Of Love'. However,

Kossoff's increasing ill-health and Fraser's departure for the Sharks undermined any new-found confidence. Despite a final Top 10 single, 'Wishing Well', in January 1973 Free had ceased to function by July of that year. Rodgers and Kirke subsequently formed **Bad Company**.

FREED, ALAN

As an influential US disc jockey, Freed (b. 1922, d. 1965) made enemies in the music-business establishment by championing black artists. His first radio job was in 1946, playing classical records. He moved on to Ohio to play current pop material and in 1951 joined WJW Cleveland. There, Freed hosted a show consisting of R&B originals rather than white pop cover versions. Entitled *Moondog's Rock 'N' Roll Party*, the show attracted large audiences of white teenagers. His local success led him to New York and WINS in 1953. Still a champion of black artists, such as **Chuck Berry** and **Fats Domino**, Freed hosted major live shows at the Paramount Theater. However, with the rise of **Bill Haley**, **Elvis Presley** and **Pat Boone**, Freed's power as a disc jockey was weakened. In particular, he became a target of opponents of rock 'n' roll such as Columbia's A&R chief Mitch Miller. When Freed refused to play Columbia releases he was fired by WINS. Freed's arrest on a charge of inciting a riot at a Boston concert left him ill-prepared to deal with the accusations laid by a Congressional investigation in 1959. It emerged that independent labels had provided cash or publishing rights to Freed in return for the airplay they were denied by the prejudices of other radio stations. In 1962, Freed was found guilty of bribery, and this was followed by charges of tax evasion. He died of uremic poisoning in January 1965.

FRIPP, ROBERT

UK-born guitarist, composer and producer, Fripp (b. 1946) joined the **League Of Gentlemen** and later founded Giles, Giles And Fripp with brothers Pete and Mike Giles. This eccentric trio completed one album before evolving into **King Crimson**. Between 1969 and 1974, Fripp led several contrasting versions of this constantly challenging outfit, during which time he also enjoyed an artistically fruitful collaboration with **Brian Eno**.

Having disbanded King Crimson, Fripp retired from music altogether. He re-emerged in 1977, contributing to **David Bowie**'s *Heroes*, before producing and playing on **Peter Gabriel**'s second album. Fripp reconstituted King Crimson in 1981. Three well-received albums followed, during which time the guitarist pursued a parallel path leading a new League Of Gentlemen. Both units disbanded later in the decade and Fripp subsequently performed and gave tutorials under the 'League Of Crafty Guitarists' banner. He also worked with Andy Summers and David Sylvian among others, before reconvening King Crimson in the mid-90s.

FUGAZI

US hardcore band formed in the mid-80s by Ian MacKaye (vocals, guitar), Guy Picciotto (vocals, guitar), Brendan Canty (drums) and Joe Lally (bass). Fugazi ensure that door prices are kept down, mainstream press interviews are shunned and they maintain a commitment to all-age shows that shames many bands. They have forged a consistent and challenging discography. Although they have concentrated primarily on touring rather than studio efforts, each of their albums has sold over 100,000 copies, produced entirely independently within their own Dischord Records framework. In 1999 the band was filmed by Jem Cohen for the documentary *Instrument*. The attendant soundtrack album featured several unreleased studio tracks and outtakes.

FUGEES

New York, USA-based rap crew featuring **Wyclef Jean** (b. 1972), **Lauryn Hill** (b. 1975) and Pras (b. Prakazrel Michel, 1972). The trio became the most

successful crossover rap outfit of the 90s with 1996's bestselling *The Score*.

Originally signed to Ruffhouse Records in 1992 as the Tranzlator Crew, their new name was a shortened version of Refugees (inspired by Wyclef and Pras's Haitian backgrounds). All three members rapped over acoustic guitars, as well as more upbeat numbers informed by dub and reggae, on their 1994 debut *Blunted On Reality*. *The Score* was a magnificent follow-up, one of the musical highlights of 1996, and accessible enough to bring their soulful jazz-rap to a wider market. 'Ready Or Not' and reworkings of 'Killing Me Softly' (**Roberta Flack**) and 'No Woman No Cry' (**Bob Marley**) were all international hit singles, and the album achieved multi-platinum worldwide success.

Hill's pregnancy meant the trio was largely inactive during 1997, with Wyclef Jean taking the time to release a solo album. Pras and Hill later embarked on solo careers, with the latter's *The Miseducation Of Lauryn Hill* enjoying huge critical and commercial success.

FUGS

New York, USA-based band formed in 1965. The Fugs combined bohemian poetry with an engaging musical naïvety and the shock tactic of outrage. Writers Ed Sanders, Tuli Kupferberg and Ken Weaver made their recording debut on the Broadside label, which viewed their work as 'ballads of contemporary protest'. The set included poetry by William Blake alongside such tracks as 'I Couldn't Get High' and 'Slum Goddess'. The trio was supported by several musicians from the Holy Modal Rounders. Although *Tenderness Junction* featured a more proficient backing group the subject matter remained as before. *It Crawled Into My Hand, Honest*, released the following year, was another idiomatic record. They disbanded to avoid the dangers of self-parody.

Sanders and Kupferberg resumed work as the Fugs during the 80s and 90s. They attempted to hold a rival Woodstock anniversary festival in 1994 and the results were issued on a double CD in 1995.

FULLER, BOBBY

US-born Bobby Fuller (b. 1943, d. 1966) made his recording debut in 1961 with 'You're In Love'. Fuller later moved to Los Angeles where his group, the Bobby Fuller Four, became a leading attraction. In 1966, the group reached the US Top 10 with an ebullient reading of the **Crickets**' 'I Fought The Law'. This was followed up by a Top 30 hit, 'Love's Made A Fool Of You'. The singer's stature seemed assured, but on 18 July 1966, Fuller's body was discovered in a parked car in Los Angeles. His death was attributed to

asphyxia through the forced inhalation of gasoline, but further investigations as to the perpetrators remain unresolved.

FUN BOY THREE

UK band formed in 1981 by former Specials members Terry Hall (b. 1959; vocals), Neville Staples (vocals, drums) and Lynval Golding (b. 1951; guitar). Their UK Top 20 debut was the extraordinary 'The Lunatics (Have Taken Over The Asylum)'. The single effectively established the trio as both original and innovative commentators. For their follow-up, they teamed up with the then-unknown **Bananarama** for a hit revival of 'It Ain't What You Do, It's The Way That You Do It'. The Bananarama connection continued when the Fun Boy Three appeared on their hit 'Really Saying Something (He Was Really Sayin' Somethin')'. By 1982, the band were proving themselves adept at writing political songs, and reviving and remoulding classic songs. The wonderfully cynical comment on teenage love and pregnancy 'Tunnel Of Love' and the Top 10 hit 'Our Lips Are Sealed' proved the trio's last major statements. Following a second album, they split during 1983, with Hall going on to form the Colour Field and work as a solo artist.

FUN LOVIN' CRIMINALS

US hip-hop/funk crossover group formed in New York in 1993 by Huey Morgan (b. 1968; vocals, guitar), Steve Borovini (drums/programming) and Fast (b. Brian Leiser; bass, keyboards, harmonica). With samples drawn from films such as *Pulp Fiction*, obscure cover versions and lyrical narratives describing New York's criminal underclass, they soon drew comparisons to the **Beastie Boys**, among others. The excellent *Come Find Yourself* and a string of single releases (including 'Fun Lovin' Criminal', 'Scooby Snacks' and 'King Of New York') secured strong airplay in the UK, alongside a series of rave reviews for their concert appearances. *100% Colombian* downplayed the

hip-hop rhythms in favour of a soulful vibe, characterised by the Barry White tribute single, 'Love Unlimited'. The album entered the UK charts at number 3 a month later, but failed to breakthrough in their homeland, where they continue to be ignored.

Borovini was subsequently replaced by Maxwell 'Mackie' Jayson. The following year's b-side compilation *Mimosa* collected together the band's lounge-style cover versions of their own and other artist's material. *Loco* saw the trio pursuing the funk/soul vibe to great effect, and slipping in a slinky cover version of Eric B And Rakim's 'Microphone Fiend'.

FUNKADELIC

George Clinton (b. 1940) established this inventive, experimental US group from the 1969 line-up of his doo-wop group the Parliaments. Raymond Davis (b. 1940), Grady Thomas (b. 1941), Calvin Simon (b. 1942) and Clarence 'Fuzzy' Haskins (b. 1941), plus the backing group: Bernard Worrell (b. 1944; keyboards), Billy 'Bass' Nelson (b. 1951; bass), Eddie Hazel (b. 1950, d. 1992; lead guitar), Lucius 'Tawl' Ross (b. 1948; rhythm guitar) and Ramon 'Tiki' Fulwood (b. 1944; drums). The new band laced hard funk with a heady dose of psychedelia, hence the name Funkadelic (originally suggested by Nelson). Primarily viewed as an album-orientated vehicle, the group's instinctive grasp of such contrasting styles nonetheless crossed over into their singles. Although few of their singles entered the R&B Top 30, Funkadelic consistently reached the chart's lower placings. Bass sensation **Bootsy Collins** (b. William Collins, 1951, Cincinnati, Ohio, USA) was added to the line-up for the recording of 1972's **America Eats Its Young**, while teenage guitar player Michael Hampton joined up for the group's major-label debut *Hardcore Jollies*.

In 1977, Clinton moved from the Westbound label to Warner Brothers Records and in 1978 the compulsive 'One Nation Under A Groove' was a million-seller. By this point the distinctions between Funkadelic and Parliament were becoming increasingly blurred. Funkadelic secured another major hit in 1979 with '(Not Just) Knee Deep'. Three long-time associates, Haskins, Simon and Thomas, then broke away, taking the Funkadelic name with them. Despite an early R&B hit, 'Connections And Disconnections', they were unable to maintain their own direction and the group later dissolved. Now recording as the P-Funk All Stars, Clinton's 1996 album *The Awesome Power Of A Fully Operational Mothership* was a superb blend of the Funkadelic and Parliament sounds.

FURTADO, NELLY

One of the most intriguing singer-songwriters to emerge in the new millennium, this first-generation Canadian (b. 1978) was raised in British Columbia by her parents, who were originally from the Portuguese archipelago Azores. Moving to Toronto in the late 90s to work, she performed at night as one half of the hip-hop duo Nelstar and as a solo freestyler. A major label contract with DreamWorks Records was soon signed. Furtado released her debut *Whoa, Nelly!* in 2000. The album went on to become a bestseller, thanks in part to the success of the transatlantic hit single 'I'm Like A Bird'. Rooted in contemporary urban sounds, Furtado's songwriting embraces folk, trip-hop, bossa nova and reggae in a post-modern stew that is inevitably reminiscent of Beck's work.

FURY, BILLY

UK rock 'n' roll singer Fury (b. Ronald Wycherley, 1940, d. 1983) joined Larry Parnes's management stable. His debut single, 'Maybe Tomorrow' (1959) reached the UK Top 20. In 1960, he released *The Sound Of Fury*, which consisted entirely of his own songs. Fury found his greatest success with a series of dramatic ballads which, in suggesting a vulnerability, enhanced the singer's undoubted sex appeal. His stylish good looks complimented a vocal prowess, blossoming in 1961 with a cover version of Tony Orlando's 'Halfway To Paradise'. This superior single, arranged and scored by Ivor Raymonde, established a pattern that provided Fury with 16 further UK Top 30 hits. Supported initially by the Tornados, then the Gamblers, the singer showed a wider repertoire live than his label would allow on record. Bedevilled by ill-health and overtaken by changing musical fashions, Fury's final hit came

in 1965 with 'Give Me Your Word'. The following year he left Decca for Parlophone Records, debuting with 'Hurtin' Is Lovin'', but he was unable to regain his erstwhile success.

In 1971, he underwent open-heart surgery, but recovered to record 'Will The Real Man Stand Up' on his own Fury label. A second major operation in 1976 forced him to retire again, but he re-emerged at the end of the decade with new recordings of his best-known songs, and several live and television appearances. In 1981, Fury struck a new deal with Polydor Records, but his health was rapidly deteriorating and on 28 January 1983 he succumbed to a fatal heart attack.

GABRIEL, PETER

After seven years fronting **Genesis**, Gabriel (b. 1950) went solo in 1975. His first album included 'Solsbury Hill', which made the UK Top 20. The album charted in the UK and the USA, and Gabriel began a US tour, nervous of facing UK audiences. The second album made the UK Top 10 and just missed the US Top 20. It contained chiefly introspective, experimental music, but sales figures were healthy. However, Atlantic Records refused to distribute his third album in the USA, finding it too maudlin. Mercury Records stepped in and with Steve Lillywhite's production the collection was far from Atlantic's feared 'commercial suicide'. 'Games Without Frontiers' was a UK Top 5 hit, and 'Biko' (about Stephen Biko) became an anti-racist anthem. *Peter Gabriel*

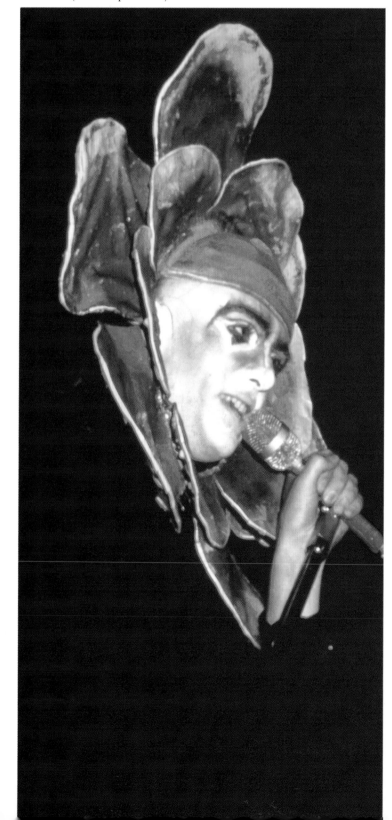

(Security) appeared more accessible. After *Peter Gabriel Plays Live*, Gabriel composed the haunting film soundtrack to *Birdy*.

Released in 1986, *So* brought commercial acceptance, containing the US number 1 'Sledgehammer'. His duet with **Kate Bush**, 'Don't Give Up', reached the UK Top 10. Throughout the 80s, Gabriel dedicated time to world music and sponsored the 1982 WOMAD (World Music And Dance) Festival. He became heavily involved in Amnesty International and recorded with **Youssou N'Dour**. They toured the USA under the banner of Conspiracy Of Hope, raising money for Amnesty. In 1989, Gabriel wrote the score for *The Last Temptation Of Christ*. Although *Us* fell short of the high standard of *So*, it put Gabriel back in the public eye. In 1999, Gabriel was commissioned to contribute music and act as musical director for the Millennium Dome show in London. The soundtrack was released the following year on the *Ovo* album.

GABRIELLE

Visually distinguished by a black eye-patch, soul diva Gabrielle (b. Louise Gabrielle Bobb, 1970) made a dramatic entrance with her UK chart-topping debut single 'Dreams' in summer 1993. The song also entered the US Top 30 later in the year. Equally accessible was the UK Top 10 follow-up, 'Going Nowhere'. During the break between her albums she gave birth to a child. The Motown Records pastiche 'Give Me A Little More Time' was a Top 5 UK hit in the spring of 1996. Further singles were less successful, before 'If You Ever', a collaboration with boy band **East 17**, reached number 2 in November. Her third collection, *Rise*, was premiered by the UK hit single 'Sunshine'. The title track, built around a hypnotic sample from **Bob Dylan**'s 'Knockin' On Heaven's Door', provided the singer with her second UK chart-topper in February 2000. 'Out Of Reach', another Top 10 hit, benefited from extensive exposure on the *Bridget Jones's Diary* soundtrack.

GALLAGHER AND LYLE

Scottish songwriters Benny Gallagher (vocals, guitar) and Graham Lyle (vocals, guitar) began their career with 'Mr. Heartbreak's Here Instead', a 1964 single for Dean Ford And The Gaylords. They later moved to London as in-house composers for Apple Records. Their 'International', was recorded by Mary Hopkin.

In 1969, they joined McGuinness Flint, for whom they wrote 'When I'm Dead And Gone' (1970) and 'Malt And Barley Blues' (1971), before leaving for an independent career. Several well-crafted albums followed, showing their flair for folk-styled melody. *Breakaway* was a commercial breakthrough, spawning 'I Wanna Stay With You' and 'Heart On My Sleeve' (both UK number 6); **Art Garfunkel** took a version of the title track into the US Top 40.

Gallagher and Lyle parted following the release of *Lonesome No More*; both have continued as successful songwriters. Lyle later found a new partner, Terry Britten, with whom he composed 'What's Love Got To Do With It' (**Tina Turner**) and 'Just Good Friends' (**Michael Jackson**).

GALLAGHER, RORY

Irish-born guitarist Gallagher (b. 1949, d. 1995) put together the blues-based rock trio Taste in 1965. When they split in 1970, Gallagher went solo, supported by Gerry McAvoy (bass) and Wilgar Campbell (drums). Campbell was replaced by Rod De'ath following the release of *Live In Europe* (with Lou Martin on keyboards). This line-up was responsible for Gallagher's major commercial triumphs, *Blueprint* and *Irish Tour '74*. De'ath and Martin left in 1978. Drummer Ted McKenna (ex-**Sensational Alex Harvey Band**) joined the ever-present McAvoy but was later replaced by Brendan O'Neill. Blues harmonica virtuoso Mark Feltham (ex-Nine Below Zero) became a full-time 'guest'.

Gallagher toured America over 30 times and the world twice, with his bottleneck guitar playing a major live attraction. He recorded with his heroes,

such as **Jerry Lee Lewis** and **Albert King**, and contributed to the work of the Fureys, Davy Spillane and Joe O'Donnell. Gallagher died following complications after a liver transplant.

GAMBLE AND HUFF

Leon Huff (b. 1942) was an established session musician; songwriter Kenny Gamble (b. 1943) was a member of the Romeos, a Philadelphia group Huff later joined. The duo produced the **Soul Survivors**' 'Expressway To Your Heart' (1967, US Top 10), followed by the Intruders' 'Love Is Like A Baseball Game'. Gamble and Huff also provided hits for Archie Bell And The Drells ('I Can't Stop Dancing'), Jerry Butler ('Only The Strong Survive') and Wilson Pickett ('Don't Let The Green Grass Fool You').

The duo formed the Neptune label, accumulating an impressive roster of acts, many of whom were retained when its successor, Philadelphia International, was founded in 1971. Philadelphia was responsible for many of the decade's finest soul singles, including 'If You Don't Know Me By Now' (**Harold Melvin And The Blue Notes**) and 'Me And Mrs Jones' (Billy Paul). Their music formed a natural stepping stone between Tamla/Motown and disco, but this pre-eminent position was undermined by a 1975 bribes-for-airplay scandal. Gamble was fined $2,500 and the pair's work suffered. Their last consistent commercial success came with Teddy Pendergrass, but the Philly-soul sound was unable to adapt to the new decade.

GANG OF FOUR

UK band formed in 1977. Jon King (vocals, melodica), Andy Gill (guitar), Dave Allen (drums) and Hugo Burnham (drums) debuted in 1978 with a three-track EP, *Damaged Goods*. Burnham's pounding, compulsive drumming and Gill's staccato, stuttering guitar work, framed their overtly political lyrics. They maintained this direction on *Entertainment!*, while introducing the interest in dance music that marked future recordings. 'At Home He's A Tourist' was issued, but encountered censorship problems over its pre-AIDS reference to 'rubbers'. Allen departed (for Shriekback), replaced by Sara Lee. *Songs Of The Free* featured the tongue-in-cheek 'I Love A Man In Uniform', which seemed destined for chart success until disappearing from radio playlists in the wake of the Falklands conflict. Burnham was fired in 1983 and a three-piece line-up completed *Hard* with session musicians. The group dissolved the following year.

King and Gill exhumed the Gang Of Four name in 1990 and released *Mall*, which did little commercially. The excellent *Shrinkwrapped*, on which the duo was joined by Dean Garcia and Steve Monti (ex-**Curve**), was to be their final release.

GAP BAND

US funk septet led by three brothers, Charles, Ronnie and Robert Wilson. After two minor US hits in 1977, they hit the R&B Top 10 with 'Shake', 'Steppin' (Out)' and 'I Don't Believe You Want To Get Up And Dance' – better known by its subtitle, 'Oops, Up Side Your Head' (1980, UK Top 10). 'Burn Rubber (Why Do You Wanna Hurt Me)' (1980), 'You Dropped A Bomb On Me' and 'Party Train' (both 1982) all topped the UK chart, while 'Big Fun' (1986) reached the UK Top 5. The trio has continued touring and

recording into the new millennium. Charles Wilson, meanwhile, remains an in-demand session vocalist.

GARBAGE

US band founded in 1994 by producer/remixers Butch Vig, Steve Marker and Duke Erikson, with Scottish singer Shirley Manson (ex-Goodbye Mr Mackenzie). Garbage's debut 'Vow' was widely acclaimed, as was 'Subhuman'; both borrowed from various traditions, notably punk, glam rock and art rock. This eclecticism was further explored on their self-titled debut album, a dark collection of songs mainly about fear, lust and envy. 'Only Happy When It Rains' charted as did a remix of 'Milk' (featuring **Tricky**) and 'Stupid Girl'.

The band's unexpected global success (especially in America) delayed the recording of their follow-up as they committed themselves to a relentless touring schedule. When *Version 2.0* finally appeared the band gained further praise for their compelling blend of slick electronic pop featuring Manson's emotive vocals. The following year the band was commissioned to write the theme tune to the new James Bond movie *The World Is Not Enough*. Their excellent third album *Beautifulgarbage* was less successful.

GARCIA, JERRY

Mercurial **Grateful Dead** guitarist Jerry Garcia (b. 1942, d. 1995) was a leading light on the west coast musical scene, credited on **Jefferson Airplane**'s *Surrealistic Pillow* as 'musical and spiritual adviser' and known locally as 'Captain Trips'. In addition to session work with the Jefferson Airplane, he worked with **David Crosby**, Paul Kantner, **Jefferson Starship**, **New Riders Of The Purple Sage**, **Crosby, Stills, Nash And Young**, as well as various spin-offs with David Grisman. Garcia played banjo and pedal-steel guitar, mastering rock 'n' roll/blues and country/bluegrass, without a hint of musical overlap. Following his heroin addiction and much publicized near-death in 1986, Garcia continued touring and recording, with the Grateful Dead and on his own. He died from a heart attack.

GARFUNKEL, ART

The possessor of one of the most pitch-perfect voices in popular music, Garfunkel (b. 1941) has had a sparse recording career since the demise of **Simon And Garfunkel**. His solo recording career actually started while he was singing with Simon as the duo Tom And Jerry, with two singles released under the name Artie Garr, 'Dream Alone' (1959) and 'Private World' (1960).

Garfunkel's successful acting career during the 70s meant his recording career was largely put on the back burner. *Angel Clare* contained 'All I Know' (US Top 10), while in the UK two of his records made number 1, 'I Only Have Eyes For You' and 'Bright Eyes' (the theme for the animated film *Watership*

Down). Simon and Garfunkel appeared together occasionally on television and on record, and in 1981 performed at the historic Central Park concert. They struggled through a world tour, opening up old wounds, until once again parting company. Since then Garfunkel has released occasional albums.

GAYE, MARVIN

The son of a minister, Gaye (b. Marvin Pentz Gay Jnr., 1939, d. 1984) left his father's church choir to team up with Don Covay and Billy Stewart in the R&B vocal group the Rainbows. In 1957, he joined the Marquees; the following year the group was taken under the wing of producer/singer Harvey Fuqua. When Fuqua moved to Detroit in 1960, Marvin went with him, becoming a session singer and vocalist for Motown Records. In 1961, Marvin married Gordy's sister, Anna, and was offered a solo recording contract. Renamed Marvin Gaye, he began his career as a jazz balladeer, but in 1962, was persuaded to record R&B, obtaining his first hit with 'Stubborn Kind Of Fellow' (R&B Top 10). In 1965, Gaye began to record in a more sophisticated style. 'How Sweet It Is (To Be Loved By You)' epitomized his new direction; it was followed by two R&B number 1s 'I'll Be Doggone' and 'Ain't That Peculiar'.

Motown teamed Gaye with their leading female vocalist, Mary Wells, for some romantic duets. When Wells left Motown in 1964, Gaye recorded with

Kim Weston until 1967; she was succeeded by Tammi Terrell. The Gaye/ Terrell partnership represented the apogee of the soul duet. In 1968 he issued the epochal 'I Heard It Through The Grapevine' – the label's biggest-selling record to date – but his career was derailed by the death of Terrell in 1970.

In 1971, the emotionally distraught Gaye emerged with a set of recordings which eventually formed his most successful solo album. He combined his spiritual beliefs with increasing concern about poverty, discrimination and political corruption in America, creating a fluid instrumental backdrop for *What's Going On*. After the soundtrack to the 'blaxploitation' thriller *Trouble Man*, Gaye shifted his attention from the spiritual to the sexual with *Let's Get It On*. He also collaborated with **Diana Ross** on a sensuous album of duets in 1973. The break-up of his marriage to Anna Gordy in 1975 delayed work on his next album. *I Want You* was merely a

pleasant reworking of *Let's Get It On*, albeit slightly more contemporary. The title track was a number 1 soul hit however, as was his 1977 disco extravaganza, 'Got To Give It Up'.

In 1980, Gaye moved to Europe where he began work on an ambitious concept album *In Our Lifetime*. When it emerged, Gaye and Motown entered into a huge dispute that led to Gaye leaving for Columbia Records in 1982. He re-emerged with 'Sexual Healing', which combined his passionate soul vocals with a contemporary electro-disco backing. *Midnight Love* offered no equal surprises, but the success of the single seemed to herald a new era in Gaye's music. The intensity of his cocaine addiction made it impossible for him to work on another album, and he fell into a prolonged bout of depression. On 1 April 1984, a violent disagreement led to Marvin Gay Snr shooting his son dead.

GAYLE, CRYSTAL

US-born Gayle (b. Brenda Gail Webb, 1951) was the sister of Loretta Lynn. In the late 60s, Gayle signed with her sister's recording label Decca Records and chose her performing name. Lynn wrote some of Gayle's first records ('Sparklin' Look Of Love', 'Mama, It's Different This Time'). Gayle first entered the US country charts in 1970 with 'I've Cried (The Blue Right Out Of My Eyes)', which was followed by 'Everybody Oughta Cry' and 'I Hope You're Having Better Luck Than Me'.

After joining United Artists Records, she was teamed with producer-songwriter Allen Reynolds and recorded his US country hit 'Wrong Road Again' (1974). Several other songwriters also supplied Gayle with excellent songs, and she had a country hit with 'Beyond You', written by herself and her lawyer/manager/husband Vassilios 'Bill' Gatzimos. Gayle entered the US country Top 10 with the title song from *Somebody Loves You*, and followed it with her first country number 1, 'I'll Get Over You'. In 1976, Gayle was voted Female Vocalist of the Year by the Academy of Country Music, but Reynolds knew there was a bigger market than country for her records. He seized the opportunity when Leigh wrote the jazz-tinged ballad 'Don't It Make My Brown Eyes Blue'. The single won Grammy Awards for Best Female Country Vocal Performance and Best Country Song. Its attendant album, *We Must Believe In Magic*, became the first million-selling album by a female country artist. In 1979, Gayle became the first US country artist to perform in China.

When I Dream was a lavish production crediting 50 musicians. British writer Roger Cook gave her a soulful ballad, 'Talking In Your Sleep' (US/UK Top 20). In 1979, Gayle signed with Columbia Records and quickly had a US pop hit with 'Half The Way'. She had three country number 1s among her 10 hits for the label, recorded an excellent version of **Neil Sedaka**'s 'The Other Side Of Me' and revived an early country record, Jimmie Rodgers' 'Miss The Mississippi And You'.

In 1982, Gayle moved to Elektra Records and worked on the soundtrack of the movie *One From The Heart* with Tom Waits. In later years, Gayle joined Capitol Records, but her commercial profile steadily declined. *Ain't Gonna Worry* reunited her with Reynolds, while Buzz Stone produced 1992's *Three Good Reasons*, a heartening return to her country roots. In the latter part of the decade, Gayle recorded two inspirational albums and a collection of **Hoagy Carmichael** songs, and began the new millennium with her first-ever album for children.

GAYNOR, GLORIA

Gaynor (b. Gloria Fowles, 1949) was discovered singing in a Manhattan nightclub by future manager, Jay Ellis. Together with producers Tony Bongiovia and Meco Monardo he created an unswerving disco backbeat-propelling such exemplary Gaynor performances as 'Never Can Say Goodbye' (1974) and 'Reach Out, I'll Be There' (1975). In 1979, the strident 'I Will

Survive' topped the UK and US charts. The song has been re-released successfully several times. The singer was too closely tied to a now-dying form (disco) and her later career suffered as a result. She bounced back in the new millennium with the club favourites 'Last Night' and 'Just Keep Thinkin' About You', and a brand new studio album

GEILS, J., BAND

US group formed in 1969. J. Geils (b. Jerome Geils, 1946; guitar), Peter Wolf (b. 1947; vocals), Magic Dick (b. Richard Salwitz, 1945; harmonica), Seth Justman (b. 1951; keyboards), Danny Klein (b. 1946; bass) and Stephan Jo Bladd (b. 1942; drums) were originally known as the J. Geils Blues Band. Their first two albums were tough, raw R&B. The following *Bloodshot* went gold in the US and *Monkey Island* reclaimed the fire and excitement of the first two albums. The group moved from Atlantic Records to EMI Records at the end of the 70s, achieving an international hit with 'Centrefold' (1982). Now divorced from its blues roots, the J. Geils Band was unsure of its direction. In 1984 Wolf went solo midway through a recording session. The group completed a final album, *You're Gettin' Even, While I'm Gettin' Old*, without him. Geils and Magic Dick reunited in the early 90s in Bluestime.

GELDOF, BOB

Irish-born Geldof (b. Robert Frederick Zenon Geldof, 1954) started out as a rock journalist in Canada. Back in Dublin, he formed Nitelife Thugs, which evolved into the **Boomtown Rats**. After a series of hits, including two UK number 1s, the group fell from favour. After appearing in the film of **Pink Floyd**'s *The Wall*, Geldof turned his attention to the dreadful famine that was plaguing Ethiopia in 1984. Shocked by horrific television pictures, Geldof organized Band Aid and wrote 'Do They Know It's Christmas?'. The charity single sold in excess of three million copies and inspired Live Aid, in which rock's elite played before a worldwide television audience of over 1,000,000,000. Geldof continued to help administer Band Aid, putting his singing career on hold for a couple of years.

After publishing his autobiography, he recorded the solo album *Deep In The Heart Of Nowhere*, which included the minor hit 'This Is The World Calling'. *The Vegetarians Of Love* included folk and cajun flavourings, but a further album was poorly received and the singer's attention began to be diverted by his extensive media interests. The acrimonious break-up of his marriage to Paula Yates also kept him in the headlines.

Geldof returned to the music scene in September 2001 with his first new recording in over eight years. A raw and brutally frank album dealing in unflinching detail with the recent emotional upheavals of Geldof's personal life, *Sex, Age & Death* was in marked contrast to his previous studio set, the relatively upbeat *The Happy Club*.

GENE

Foppish UK indie band formed in 1993 by Steve Mason (guitar), Martin Rossiter (vocals), Kevin Miles (bass) and Matt James (drums). They debuted with the double a-side 'For The Dead'/'Child's Body'. Excellent support performances to **Pulp** followed, where Rossiter's stage presence illuminated Gene's performance. Their third single, 'Sleep Well Tonight', saw them break the Top 40 and preceded the well-received *Olympian*. *To See The Lights* collected together b-sides and live recordings, acting as a stopgap for *Drawn To The Deep End*. The band was released from its Polydor contract following the release of an occasionally inspired third album. The following summer they recorded a live album at Hollywood's legendary Troubadour club. Their new studio set, *Libertine*, was released in 2001.

GENESIS

UK rock band formed at Charterhouse school. **Peter Gabriel** (b. 1950; vocals), Tony Banks (b. 1951; keyboards) and Chris Stewart (drums) joined forces with Anthony Philips (guitar, vocals) and Mike Rutherford (b. 1950; bass, vocals) from a rival group. In 1967, they sent a demo to another Charterhouse alumnus, **Jonathan King** at Decca Records; he christened the band Genesis. They recorded 'The Silent Sun' in 1968 and issued their unsuccessful debut album *From Genesis To Revelation* in 1969. After joining Tony Stratton-Smith's Charisma Records in 1970, the band recruited drummer **Phil Collins** (b. 1951).

Trespass sold poorly and, despite the addition of guitarist Steve Hackett (b. 1950), *Nursery Cryme* also failed commercially. Success on the continent brought renewed faith and eventually, with *Foxtrot*, they reached the UK Top 20. Their profile heightened with the bestselling *Selling England By The Pound* and *The Lamb Lies Down On Broadway*, but they were undermined by the shock departure of Gabriel in 1975.

Phil Collins took over as vocalist and *A Trick Of The Tail* and *Wind And Wuthering* enjoyed modest commercial success. In 1977, Hackett went solo and Genesis carried on as a trio. The more pop-orientated *And Then There Were Three* went gold and *Duke* reached UK number 1. *Abacab* reached the US Top 10 and, helped by Collins' high solo profile, they enjoyed their biggest UK hit singles with 'Mama', 'Thats All' and 'Illegal Alien'. Both *Genesis* and *Invisible Touch* topped the UK charts, while the latter also reached US number 1.

In the mid-80s, Collins went fully solo while Rutherford formed **Mike And The Mechanics**. In 1991, the trio reconvened to record and issue *We Can't Dance*; it immediately topped charts around the world. Collins opted to leave the band in March 1996 and a replacement was found in Ray Wilson (ex-Stiltskin). He was heard on 1997's *Calling All Stations*, the final Genesis recording.

GENTLE GIANT

British band formed in 1969 by the Shulman brothers, Derek (b. 1947; vocals, guitar, bass), Ray (b. 1949; vocals, bass, violin) and Phil (b. 1937; saxophone), with Kerry Minnear (b. 1948; keyboards, vocals), Gary Green (b. 1950; guitar, vocals) and Martin Smith (drums). They signed to Vertigo Records in 1970 and, with producer Tony Visconti, completed an ambitious debut album. Smith left after *Acquiring The Taste*. His replacement, Malcolm Mortimore, appeared on *Three Friends*, but a motorcycle accident forced his departure. John 'Pugwash' Weathers (b. 1947) joined for *Octopus*, but an attendant tour ended with Phil's retirement from music. The group then encountered problems in America when *In A Glass House* was deemed too uncommercial for release. *Free Hand* became their bestselling UK album; an ascendancy that faltered when *Interview* invoked the experimental style of earlier releases. *Playing The Fool* confirmed their in-concert dexterity, but subsequent albums unsuccessfully courted an AOR audience. *Civilian* was an attempt at regaining glory, but Minnear's departure signalled their demise. Gentle Giant split in 1980.

GERRY AND THE PACEMAKERS

Gerry Marsden (b. 1942; guitar, vocals), Freddie Marsden (b. 1940; drums) and John 'Les' Chadwick (b. 1943; bass) formed the Pacemakers in 1959. Les Maguire (b. 1941; piano) joined in 1961. After successful spells in German beat clubs, they became the second group signed to **Brian Epstein**. 'How Do You Do It', rejected as unsuitable by the Beatles, gave the Pacemakers a number 1 hit. Further chart-toppers 'I Like It' and 'You'll Never Walk Alone' (both 1963), followed – the group became the first act to have their first three releases reach number 1. Their lone album revealed a penchant for R&B, alongside 'Ferry Cross The Mersey' (1965), the theme song to the Pacemakers' starring film. 'I'll Be There' was their final UK Top 20 entry.

In 1967, Gerry Marsden went solo. He remained a popular figure in television and on cabaret and in 1985, following the Bradford City Football Club fire tragedy, an all-star charity recording of 'You'll Never Walk Alone' reached UK number 1. The charity re-recording of 'Ferry Cross The Mersey', for the victims of the Hillsborough crowd disaster in 1989, also reached number 1.

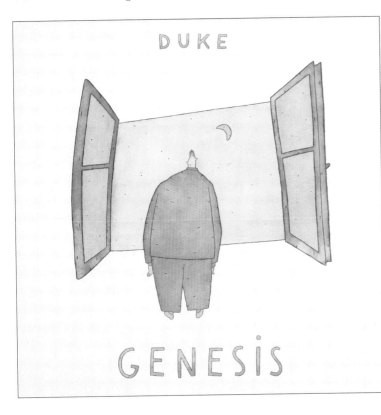

GIBBONS, STEVE

UK singer Gibbons started out in 1958 as vocalist with the Dominettes, who became the Uglys in 1962. In 1969, the Uglys split and Gibbons joined Denny Laine (ex-**Moody Blues**), Trevor Burton (ex-**Move**) and session guitarists Albert Lee and Chris Spedding in Balls. They released *Short Stories* before disbanding in 1971. Gibbons then briefly joined the Idle Race, which became the Steve Gibbons Band. The early line-up included Burton (bass), Dave Carroll and Bob Wilson on guitars, and Bob Lamb (drums). Their debut album was followed by Gibbons' UK Top 20 hit version of **Chuck Berry**'s 'Tulane' (1977), from *Caught In The Act*.

Though no longer a commercial proposition, Gibbons has remained a popular live performer, especially in the Birmingham area. Studio albums continue to appear on an infrequent basis on small UK labels.

GILL, VINCE

US-born Gill (b. Vincent Grant Gill, 1957) started out with bluegrass group Mountain Smoke. In 1975 he joined Bluegrass Alliance with Sam Bush and Dan Crary, before graduating to the Pure Prairie League, appearing on their albums *Can't Hold Back*, *Firin' Up* and *Something In The Night*. Gill then joined Rodney Crowell's backing group, the Cherry Bombs. He began his solo recording career with a six-track mini-album, *Turn Me Loose*, and a duet with **Rosanne Cash**, 'If It Weren't For Him'. In 1991, he reached the US country Top 10 with 'Pocket Full Of Gold', 'Liza Jane' and 'Look At Us', and was voted the Male Vocalist Of The Year at the 1991 Country Music Association's Annual Awards Show. In 1992, he won Male Vocalist Of The Year and Song Of The Year with 'Look At Us'. Patty Loveless and Ricky Skaggs guested on the excellent *When Love Finds You*. His 1996 release *High Lonesome Sound* explored several styles of American music. *The Key* returned him to the heart of the mainstream, gathering a number of major awards and reaching the US Top 20. In March 2000, he married singer Amy Grant. His new album, *Let's Make Sure We Kiss Goodbye*, followed a month later.

GILLAN, IAN

UK vocalist Gillan (b. 1945) formed his first band aged 16. Later, he joined **Deep Purple**, along with Welsh bass guitarist Roger Glover. They formed the legendary 'Mk II' line-up with Ritchie Blackmore, Jon Lors and Ian Paice. Gillan left in 1973, having purchased a recording studio in London, Kingsway Studios. He recorded a solo album, *Child In Time* with Ray Fenwick (guitar), Mike Moran (keyboards), Mark Nauseef (drums) and John Gustafson (bass). His next two albums featured Colin Towns (keyboards) and demonstrated a jazz-rock influence. None were particularly successful, however, and he disbanded the Ian Gillan Band in 1978.

Within a few months, he was back in the studio with Leon Genocky (drums), Steve Byrd (guitar) and John McCoy (bass) and Towns to record *Gillan* (1978). This excellent album was never released in the UK, although several of the tracks appeared on the next album, *Mr. Universe*, recorded with Pete Barnacle (drums). The album was instrumental in developing the New Wave Of British Heavy Metal, as was *Glory Road*. Now with Bernie Torme on guitar and drummer Mick Underwood, Gillan produced one of his finest albums, *For Gillan Fans Only*. After the slightly disappointing *Future Shock*, Torme left, replaced by Janick Gers, who featured on *Double Trouble* (one studio and one live album). 1982 saw the release of *Magic*, sadly the group's last recording.

Gillan then joined **Black Sabbath**, but after one album and a tour he rejoined Deep Purple. He left once more in 1989, and performed a short tour as his alter ego, Garth Rockett, before recording vocals for the Rock Aid

Armenia version of 'Smoke On The Water'. Gillan rejoined Deep Purple in 1992, recorded and toured, before yet again quitting. He recorded a 60s album with his very first band, the Javelins, before moving towards a more acoustic-based direction with 1997's *Dreamcatcher*.

GIN BLOSSOMS

US country rock band formed in 1987 by Jesse Valenzuela (b. 1962; guitar, mandolin), Bill Leen (b. 1962; bass) and Doug Hopkins (d. 1993; guitar), with the later addition of Robin Wilson (b. 1965; vocals, acoustic guitar) and Phillip Rhodes (b. 1969). Their major-label debut *New Miserable Experience* sold over four million copies in the USA. However, after struggling for years against depression and alcoholism, chief songwriter Hopkins became so unstable that he was fired. His 'Hey Jealousy' and 'Found Out About You' became major hits following his departure, and on 3 December 1993, Hopkins left a detox unit and shot himself. Scott Johnson (b. 1962) took over on guitar, but Hopkins' songwriting was more difficult to replace. Marshall Crenshaw co-wrote the hit ''Til I Hear It From You', but *Congratulations I'm Sorry* was predictably weaker. The band eventually split up in 1997, with Wilson and Rhodes going on to form the Gas Giants.

GINUWINE

Urban R&B singer Ginuwine (b. Elgin Baylor Lumpkin, 1975) met rookie producer **Timbaland** in New York, and the two recorded the unusual, synthesizer-infused R&B effort 'The Pony' together. The song attracted strong interest, and at the age of 21 Ginuwine signed with the New York-based Sony subsidiary 550 Music. He enjoyed immediate success with the release of 'Pony' which reached the US Top 10. A string of crossover hit singles followed, including 'Tell Me Do U Wanna', 'I'll Do Anything'/'I'm Sorry' and 'Only When U R Lonely'. On the strength of his work with the singer, Timbaland went on to become one of the main forces in late 90s R&B.

Ginuwine made his acting debut in November 1998, appearing in the CBS series *Martial Law*. Another stand-out Timbaland track, 1999's 'What's So Different', provided Ginuwine with his strongest single to date. The US Top 10 album *100% Ginuwine* was another showcase for his classy vocal skills and Timbaland's inventive production, featuring the huge radio hit 'So Anxious'. During the following two years, Ginuwine balanced shooting his movie debut with the recording of a new album, *The Life*.

GIRLSCHOOL

All-female heavy metal band founded by teenagers Enid Williams (bass, vocals) and Kim McAuliffe (b. 1959; guitar, vocals). Kelly Johnson (guitar, vocals) and Denise Dufort (drums) joined in 1978. Their independently

produced single, 'Take It All Away', led to a tour with **Motörhead**. Under Lemmy's sponsorship, Vic Maile produced the band's first two albums. After a minor hit with 'Race With The Devil', the group combined with Motörhead as Headgirl. They reached the UK Top 10 with the EP *St Valentine's Day Massacre*. Williams was replaced by bass player Gill Weston. Girlschool persevered with the glam-influenced *Play Dirty*. In 1984, Johnson went solo (unsuccessfully) and Girlschool added guitarist Chris Bonacci and lead singer Jacqui Bodimead; turning more towards glam rock they recorded with **Gary Glitter** in 1986. After the departure of Weston in 1987, Tracey Lamb (bass) was brought in, while McAuliffe left to work with punk singer Beki Bondage

and present the cable show *Raw Power*. Following a Russian tour supporting **Black Sabbath**, Girlschool split up. In the 90s, McAuliffe brought the group back together with Jackie Carrera.

GLITTER, GARY

UK glam rock star Glitter (b. Paul Gadd, 1944) started out in skiffle group Paul Russell And The Rebels. Then known as Paul Raven, he recorded an unsuccessful debut, 'Alone In The Night'. His cover of 'Tower Of Strength' lost out to **Frankie Vaughan**'s UK chart-topper. After unsuccessful attempts to revitalize his career, he relaunched in 1971 as Gary Glitter, complete with thigh-high boots and silver costume. His debut, 'Rock And Roll Part 2', unexpectedly reached

UK number 2 and the US Top 10. Although he failed to establish himself in America, his UK career traversed the early 70s, until the punk explosion of 1977. Among his many UK Top 10 hits were three number 1s: 'I'm The Leader Of The Gang (I Am)', 'I Love You Love Me Love' and 'Always Yours'.

An accidental drug overdose and bankruptcy each threatened to end his career, but he survived and continued to play regular UK concerts, making the occasional chart comeback. In a disturbing development, the singer was arrested in November 1997 over allegations of harbouring child pornography on his computer. He was charged the following year, and in November 1999 was found guilty and sentenced to four months in prison, following which he fled overseas.

GO WEST

UK songwriters, Peter Cox (b. 1955; vocals) and Richard Drummie (guitar, keyboard, vocals), formed Go West in 1982. They had a string of UK pop-rock hits in 1985 with 'We Close Our Eyes', 'Call Me' and 'Don't Look Down', and a successful debut album. 'One Way Street' was written for the *Rocky IV* soundtrack. The transatlantic hit 'King Of Wishful Thinking' preceded 1992's *Indian Summer*, the duo's last major success.

GO-BETWEENS

Formed in Brisbane, Australia, by songwriters Robert Forster (b. 1957; guitar, vocals) and Grant McLennan (b. 1958; bass, guitar, vocals). They first recorded as a trio with drummer Dennis Cantwell, releasing 'Lee Remick'/'Karen' (1978) and 'People Say'/'Don't Let Him Come Back' (1979). By 1979, they had recruited Tim Mustafa (drums), Malcolm Kelly (organ), but later reverted to the trio format with the addition of Lindy Morrison (b. 1951). The band briefly visited Britain to record, 'I Need Two Heads', returning to Australia to record *Send Me A Lullaby*. *Before Hollywood* garnered favourable reviews, the highlight being McLennan's evocative 'Cattle And Cane'. They later recruited Robert Vickers (b. 1959; bass) and moved to a major label. Despite *Springhill Fair* receiving critical acclaim, success still eluded them. *Liberty Belle And The Black Diamond Express* was by far their best album and the introduction of Amanda Brown (b. 1965; violin, oboe, guitar, keyboards) added an extra dimension and smoother texture to their sound. *Tallulah* reached the UK Top 100, after which Robert Vickers left, replaced by John Willsteed (b. 1957). Prior to the release of *16 Lovers Lane*, 'Streets Of Your Town' was given generous airplay, yet failed to make any noticeable chart impact. With the album also failing, Forster and McLennan elected to dissolve the Go-Betweens in 1989. They both embarked on solo careers.

In 1997, Forster and McLennan re-formed for special live dates. They subsequently teamed up with Sleater-Kinney to record the excellent new Go-Betweens set *The Friends Of Rachel Worth*.

GO-GO'S

All-female US group formed in California in 1978. **Belinda Carlisle** (b. 1958; lead vocals), Jane Wiedlin (b. 1958; rhythm guitar, vocals), Charlotte Caffey (b. 1953; lead guitar, keyboards), Elissa Bello (drums) and Margot Olaverra (bass) performed bright, infectious harmony pop songs. By their debut, *Beauty And The Beat* (US number 1), Olaverra was replaced by Kathy Valentine and Bello by Gina Schock. 'Our Lips Are Sealed' went to the US Top 20, and 'We Got The Beat' reached US number 2. *Vacation* provided a further US Top 10 hit with the title track. *Talk Show* and 'Head Over Heels' (1984) reached the US Top 20, but the over-indulgent group were starting to burn out.

The group dissolved in 1985, with Carlisle and Wiedlin subsequently pursuing successful solo careers. The Go-Go's re-formed briefly in 1990 for a benefit for the anti-fur trade organization PETA. A fuller reunion took place in 1994, after which Valentine and Schock formed the Delphines. Another reunion took place in summer 2000 for a US tour alongside the **B-52's**, with a new album released in May 2001.

GODLEY AND CREME

This UK duo began recording together in 1976. Kevin Godley (b. 1945; vocals, drums) and Lol Creme (b. 1947; vocals, guitar) had previously been involved with the Mockingbirds, Hotlegs and **10cc**. They intended to abandon mainstream pop in favour of a more elaborate project, resulting in the triple album *Consequences*. The work was lampooned in the music press, as was the duo's invention of a new musical instrument, the 'Gizmo' gadget. An edited version of the work was later issued but also failed to sell. Finally they

had a UK Top 10 hit with 'Under My Thumb', followed by 'Wedding Bells' and 'Cry', but they found their greatest success as video makers for such artists as **Visage**, **Duran Duran**, Toyah, the **Police**, **Herbie Hancock** and **Frankie Goes To Hollywood**. Creme joined the resurrected Art Of Noise in the late 90s.

GOFFIN, GERRY

Goffin (b. 1939) married fellow US songwriter **Carole King** while at New York's Queens College. In 1960, they met publisher Don Kirshner following the release of 'Oh! Neil', King's answer to **Neil Sedaka**'s 'Oh! Carol'. They joined the staff of Kirshner's company, where their early compositions included 'Will You Still Love Me Tomorrow?' (the **Shirelles**), 'Take Good Care Of My Baby' (**Bobby Vee**) and 'Up On The Roof' (the **Drifters**). Goffin also enjoyed success with Jack Keller and Barry Mann, but his compositions with King proved the most memorable. Together they wrote 'The Loco-Motion' (**Little Eva**), 'One Fine Day' (the **Chiffons**), 'I'm Into Something Good' (**Earl-Jean/Herman's Hermits**) and Aretha Franklin's '(You Make Me Feel Like) A Natural Woman', among others. However, professional and personal pressure led to their marriage ending in 1967.

Goffin enjoyed a less public profile than his successful ex-wife, however, **Blood, Sweat And Tears** recorded 'Hi De Hi', **Grand Funk Railroad** covered 'The Loco-Motion' and Carole later paid tribute to their partnership with *Pearls*, a selection of their 60s collaborations. During the 70s, Goffin worked as a producer for artists including **Diana Ross**. He recorded a solo album, *It Ain't Exactly Entertainment*, but failed to emulate King's popularity. He recorded again in 1996.

GOLD, ANDREW

US guitarist/vocalist/keyboard player Gold (b. 1951) met guitarist Kenny Edwards in Bryndle And The Rangers. The pair subsequently pursued their careers as part of **Linda Ronstadt**'s backing group. Gold also contributed to sessions for **Carly Simon**, **Art Garfunkel** and **Loudon Wainwright**. He completed his solo debut in 1975 and enjoyed a transatlantic hit with 'Lonely Boy' (1976) and a UK number 5 with 'Never Let Her Slip Away'. In the wake of the disappointing *Whirlwind*, Gold toured with Ronstadt before forming Wax with Graham Gouldman in 1986. In 1992, Undercover had a major UK hit with a dance version of 'Never Let Her Slip Away'. Gold concentrated on Nashville session work in the 90s.

GOLDEN EARRING

Formed in 1961 in the Hague, Netherlands, by George Kooymans (b. 1948; guitar, vocals) and Rinus Gerritsen (b. 1946; bass, vocals), along with Hans Van Herwerden (guitar) and Fred Van Der Hilst (drums). In 1965, they reached the Dutch Top 10 with their debut, 'Please Go'. By now, Kooymans and Gerritsen had been joined by Frans Krassenburg (vocals), Peter De Ronde (guitar) and Jaap Eggermont (drums), and they became one of the most popular 'nederbeat' attractions. Barry Hay (b. 1948; lead vocals, flute, saxophone, guitar) replaced Krassenburg in 1966, and De Ronde also left. Their first Dutch number 1, 'Dong-Dong-Di-Ki-Di-Gi-Dong' (1968), saw them branching out into Europe and the USA. Eggermont left, replaced by Cesar Zuiderwijk (b. 1948) in 1969. Their compulsive *Eight Miles High* found an international audience.

In 1972, they were invited to support the **Who** on a European tour. In 1973, they had a Dutch number 1/UK Top 10 hit with 'Radar Love' which, in 1974, reached the US Top 20. However, long term overseas success was elusive. Robert Jan Stips joined between 1974 and 1976, followed by Eelco Gelling (guitar), but by 1980 the group had reverted to Kooymans, Gerritsen, Hay and Zuiderwijk. Their reputation as a top European live act was reinforced by *Second Live*. *Cut* spawned 'Twilight Zone' (US Top 10), followed by a tour of the United States and Canada. With various members able to indulge themselves in solo projects, Golden Earring have deservedly earned themselves respect throughout Europe and America as the Netherlands' longest-surviving and successful rock group.

GOLDEN PALOMINOS

Unorthodox rock group formed in 1981 by drummer Anton Fier (ex-Pere Ubu). Their albums have featured guests such as John Lydon (the **Sex Pistols**, PiL), Michael Stipe (**R.E.M.**), Bob Mould, Richard Thompson, T-Bone Burnett and Jack Bruce. The other core band members have included Bill Laswell (bass), Nicky Skopelitis (guitar) and Amanda Kramer (vocals). For *This Is How It Feels* (1993), Fier recruited singer Lori Carson, who added both warmth and sexuality to that and the subsequent *Pure*.

GOLDIE

A distinctive visual as well as aural presence, graffiti artist, hardcore and jungle innovator Goldie (b. Clifford Price) is distinguished by the gold-inlaid front teeth from which many assume he takes his name. In fact, Goldie is an abbreviation of 'Goldilocks', a nickname he earned from his gold-dreadlocked

hip-hop days. His early musical experiences were most notably conducted as part of the Metalheads collective (later Metalheadz) on hardcore imprint Reinforced Records. The Metalheads' *Angel* EP was a major breakthrough for 'intelligent hardcore', and when offshoots of hardcore (an extreme hybrid of techno) mixed with reggae and evolved into jungle in 1993–94, Goldie found himself at the centre of the new movement. His own 'Inner City Life' single explored the possibilities of the drum 'n' bass sound of jungle, using them as

a framework for melodious vocals and other musical innovations. Similarly, the sounds contained on *Timeless*, the first jungle album released on a major label and to find mainstream approval, eschewed any notion of observing dance-music convention. The uneven *Saturnz Return* was, for all its failings, jungle's most ambitious album to date. Goldie now balances club work with a burgeoning acting career, which has included appearances in *The World Is Not Enough*, *Snatch* and the UK soap opera *EastEnders*.

GOLDFRAPP

While studying for a degree in Fine Art at Middlesex University in the early 90s, Alison Goldfrapp found her vocation in music and provided vocals on *Maxinquaye*, the award-winning debut of the UK trip-hop artist **Tricky**. She also toured with him and worked with another acclaimed UK dance music act, Orbital, before pursuing a solo career. She came into contact with the UK soundtrack composer Will Gregory in the late 90s and the pair found a shared interest in various kinds of music, such as 60s French pop, Weimar Republic cabaret as well as movie soundtracks and electronica. Recorded over a five-month period in the remote Wiltshire countryside in late 1999, her debut, *Felt Mountain*, appeared to much acclaim in 2000.

GOLDSBORO, BOBBY

US artist Goldsboro (b. 1941) first came to prominence as a guitarist in **Roy Orbison**'s touring band in 1960. In 1964, he reached the US Top 10 with the self-penned 'See The Funny Little Clown', followed by minor US hits.

International status came in 1968 with 'Honey'. The song stayed at US number 1 for five weeks and was number 2 twice: in 1968 and 1975. Goldsboro had 70s hits with 'Watching Scotty Grow' and 'Summer (The First Time)' among others. He subsequently turned to children's entertainment music, finding considerable success in later decades.

GOMEZ

This acclaimed 90s UK rock band was originally formed by four school friends from Southport, Ian Ball (guitar, harmonica, vocals), Tom Gray (guitar, keyboards, vocals), Olly Peacock (drums, percussion) and Paul Blackburn (bass). Ball met Ben Ottewell while studying at Sheffield University, inviting the fledgling vocalist to join the band. Briefly known as Gomez, Kill, Kill The Vortex, the band began recording four-track demo tapes in a Southport garage. They signed to Virgin Records subsidiary Hut. Their debut single, '78 Stone Wobble', was released in 1998, and was followed a month later by *Bring It On*. Ottewell's raw, bluesy vocals added a further touch of authenticity to the band's stylized fusion of various forms of American-roots music. *Bring It On* won the UK's Mercury Music Prize in September 1998, boosting sales past gold. A new single, 'Bring It On' (not featured on their debut), was released in June 1999. *Liquid Skin* and *In Our Gun* were mature follow-ups from a band whose brief moment in the commercial spotlight appeared to have passed.

GONG

Anarchic, experimental ensemble formed by guitarist Daevid Allen (ex-Soft Machine). Gilli Smyth aka Shanti Yoni (vocals), Didier Malherbe aka Bloomdido Bad De Grasse (saxophone/flute), Christian Tritsch aka The Submarine Captain (bass) and Pip Pyle (drums) had assisted Allen on his solo collection *Banana Moon*; Gong was formed when the musicians moved to a communal farmhouse in France, in 1971. Lauri Allen replaced Pyle as the group completed *Continental Circus* and *Camembert Electrique*: quirky, *avant-garde* music mixed with hippy-based surrealism. Subsequent releases included an ambitious 'Radio Gnome Invisible' trilogy; *Flying Teapot*, *Angel's Egg* and *You*. This saw the band reach their peak of commercial success with colourful live performances, and the addition of Steve Hillage (guitar), Mike Howlett (bass) and Tim Blake (synthesizer). Allen left in 1975 and the band abandoned his original, experimental vision for a tamer style. Within months Hillage also left, leaving Pierre Moerlen, drummer since 1973, in tenuous control. Mike Howlett left soon after and was replaced by Hanny Rowe, while Allan Holdsworth joined on guitar. After inaction in the early 80s, the

Gong name was used in performances alongside anarcho space-jazz rock group Here And Now, before being absorbed by the latter. By the late 80s and 90s, Gong was under the control of its original leader.

GOO GOO DOLLS

US rock trio formed in 1986. Robby Takac (vocals, bass), Johnny Rzeznik (vocals, guitar) and George

Tutuska (drums) began with unlikely cover versions on *Jed*, such as a version of **Creedence Clearwater Revival**'s 'Down On The Corner' and **Prince**'s 'I Could Never Take The Place Of Your Man' on *Hold Me Up*. Both albums featured unpretentious pop-punk songwriting, and the band received strong media coverage. Their commercial breakthrough came with 1995's hit single 'Name' and *A Boy Named Goo*. Their career showed signs of stalling in 1997 following litigation with their record company Warner Brothers Records and the departure of Tutuska. They were saved by the song 'Iris', which became a huge radio hit after featuring on the soundtrack of the Nicolas Cage movie *City Of Angels*. Having built up a strong following on the back of that single, the new album *Dizzy Up The Girl* climbed to number 15 on the US album chart in 1998. 'Slide' hit the US Top 10 the following January as the album continued its march to multi-platinum status. *Gutterflower*, the long-awaited follow-up to *Dizzy Up The Girl*, was released in April 2002.

GORKY'S ZYGOTIC MYNCI

One of the most idiosyncratic bands to emerge from the Welsh indie scene of the mid-90s, Gorky's Zygotic Mynci followed Super Furry Animals in getting Welsh language music on to mainstream radio. The band were formed in Carmarthen by school friends Euros Childs (vocals, keyboards), Richard James (bass) and John Lawrence (guitar), later joined by Euros Rowlands (drums) and Megan Childs (violin). Their debut album *Tatay* contained predominantly Welsh language songs, but it was the cover version of Robert Wyatt's 'O Caroline', and a track called 'Kevin Ayers', that revealed the source of the band's love of experimental whimsy. The catchy single 'Miss Trudy' gained them more critical praise and a wider audience, while 1995's *Bwyd Time* proved to be a more accessible record than the debut. Their major-label debut *Barafundle* was released in 1997 to unanimous critical praise – a beautiful and haunting blend of psychedelic pop music and quirky, original lyrics. *Gorky 5* was a less accessible, harder-edged album. The band was dropped by Fontana Records shortly afterwards, and founder-member Lawrence left the following June. Typically unfazed, the remaining quartet bounced back on the Mantra label with a series of excellent albums.

GRAND FUNK RAILROAD

US heavy rock group – Mark Farner (b. 1948; guitar), Mel Schacher (b. 1951; bass) and Don Brewer (1948; drums) – formed in 1968. Farner and Brewer had released 'I (Who Have Nothin)' (US number 46) before Schacher joined. The trio's singles made the charts but Grand Funk proved its real strength in the album market. *On Time* reached number 27, followed by the number 11 *Grand Funk*. In 1970, they became a major concert attraction, and their albums routinely reached the Top 10 for the next four years. Of those, *We're An American Band* was the biggest seller, reaching number 2. In 1971, Grand Funk became only the second group (after the **Beatles**) to sell out New York's Shea Stadium. *Live Album* reached number 5, and 1971 saw the release of *Survival* and *E Pluribus Funk*. In 1973, the group shortened its name to Grand Funk, and added a fourth member, keyboardist Craig Frost (b. 1948). They cracked the singles market with 'We're An American Band', but in 1975, with their popularity considerably diminished, the band reverted to its original name. The following year, after *Good Singin', Good Playin'* failed to reach the Top 50, Farner went solo. The others stayed together, adding guitarist Billy Elworthy and changing their name to Flint, but commercial success eluded them. Grand Funk (Farner, Brewer and bass player Dennis Bellinger) re-formed between 1981–83 and recorded *Grand Funk Lives* and *What's Funk?*. Failing to recapture former glories, they split again. The band reunited for a benefit concert for Bosnian orphans in 1997.

GRANDADDY
Based in songwriter Jason Lytle's hometown of Modesto, California, USA, Grandaddy's lo-fi slacker rock insidiously worked its way into the heart of the alternative music press during the late 90s. Around 1992, Lytle formed Grandaddy with Kevin Garcia (bass) and Aaron Burtch (drums). Jim Fairchild (guitar) and Tim Dryden (keyboards) swelled the band's ranks for 1995's seven-track cassette debut, *A Pretty Mess By This One Band*. The record attracted enough attention for the band to be able to record a full-length album. *Under The Western Freeway* was another home-produced recording. Fleshing out their lo-fi production with some odd sound-effects, songs such as the single 'Summer Here Kids' and 'A.M. 180' built around simple but winning melodies, at odds with Lytle's relentlessly downbeat lyrics. The band's excellent major-label debut followed three years later.

GRANDMASTER FLASH
Grandmaster Flash (b. Joseph Saddler, 1958) was a pivotal force in early rap music. Peter 'DJ' Jones took him under his wing, and Flash set about combining Jones' timing on the decks with the sort of records that Kool Herc was spinning. In the early 70s he discovered the way to 'segue' records smoothly together without missing a beat, highlighting the 'break' – the point in a record where the drum rhythm is isolated or accentuated – and repeating it. The complexity and speed of his method earned him the nickname Flash.

He put together a strong line-up of local talent: Grandmaster Melle Mel (b. Melvin Glover) and his brother Kid Creole (b. Nathaniel Glover), joining Cowboy. Duke Bootee (b. Ed Fletcher) and Kurtis Blow subsequently joined, but were eventually replaced by Rahiem (b. Guy Todd Williams) and Scorpio (b. Eddie Morris, aka Mr Ness). The Zulu Tribe was also inaugurated to act as security at live events: rival MCs had sprung up; Flash, Kook Herc and **Afrika Bambaataa** would hide their records from prying eyes to stop their 'sound' being pirated, and record labels were removed to avoid identifying marks.

The Furious Five debuted on 2 September 1976. Shortly afterwards they released their first record, 'Super Rappin'. Although hugely popular within the hip-hop fraternity, it failed to make commercial inroads; Flash tried again with 'We Rap Mellow' and 'Flash To The Beat'. Joe Robinson Jnr of Sugarhill Records stepped in. His wife, Sylvia, wrote and produced their subsequent record, 'Freedom'. On the back of a major tour, the first in rap's embryonic history, the single went gold. The follow-up, 'Birthday Party', was totally eclipsed by 'Grandmaster Flash On The Wheels Of Steel', a musical *tour de force*, showcasing the Flash quick-mixing and scratching skills. It, too, was overshadowed when the band recorded one of Robinson's most memorable compositions 'The Message'. In just over a month the record went platinum, yet despite the record's success Flash was receiving little money from Sugarhill, so he left for Elektra Records, taking Kid Creole and Rahiem with him. The others continued as Melle Mel and the Furious Five, scoring nearly instantly with 'White Lines (Don't Do It)'.

In the 80s Flash was largely absent until he was reunited with his Furious Five in 1987 for a **Paul Simon**-hosted charity concert in New York and again when he hosted New York's WQHT *Hot 97* show. Unfortunately, the reunion did not include Cowboy, who died in 1989 after a slow descent into crack addiction. Flash also helped out on Terminator X's *Super Bad*, which brought together many of the old-school legends. In January 2002 he released an acclaimed mix album recreating the sounds of his legendary mid-70s block parties.

GRANT LEE BUFFALO
Los Angeles, USA-based band formed in 1989 by Grant Lee Phillips (b. 1963; vocals, 12-string guitar), Paul Kimble (b. 1960; bass, keyboards) and Joey Peters (b. 1965; drums). Grant Lee Buffalo were influenced by American music 'that's based on storytelling and improvisation, blues, jazz or country'. By 1991, they had recorded 11 songs, a tape of which was passed to Bob Mould, who released 'Fuzzy' on his Singles Only Label (SOL). A month later, they had a contract with Slash Records. A debut album was recorded with Kimble producing. The songs attacked modern America's complacency and pursuit of material wealth, harking back to a golden age of American optimism. 'America Snoring' was written in response to the Los Angeles riots, and 'Stars N' Stripes' was Phillips' evocative homage to **Elvis Presley**'s Vegas period.

Mighty Joe Moon proved more restrained, but the keynote spirituality implicit in earlier recordings was maintained by 'Rock Of Ages'. The more vocally orientated *Copperopolis* broke away from the traditional rock band format by introducing pedal-steel guitar, bass clarinet and violin. Kimble left the band prior to the release of their final album *Jubilee*. Phillips (as Grant-Lee Phillips) subsequently released the low-key solo sets *Ladies' Love Oracle* and *Mobilize*.

GRANT, EDDY
West Indian-born Grant (b. Edmond Montague Grant, 1948) was 24 years old with several hits to his credit when he left the Equals to form his own production company in England. After producing other acts, he debuted with *Message Man*. Grant sang and played every note, recorded it in his own studio, and released it on his own label, Ice Records. He had developed his own sound – part reggae, part funk – pop with credibility. 'Living On The Front Line' (1979) reached UK number 11 and Grant found himself a new audience. 'Do You Feel My Love' and 'Can't Get Enough Of You' kept him in the UK Top 20. In 1982 he moved to Barbados, signed Ice Records to RCA, and reached UK number 1 with 'I Don't Wanna Dance'. 'Electric Avenue' (1983) was a transatlantic number 2, and its album *Killer On The Rampage* a big seller. The huge hits eluded him until he returned in 1988 with the anti-apartheid song 'Gimme Hope Jo'anna'.

In recent years Grant has continued recording and writing quality material, but has concentrated his efforts on building a successful music publishing company and record label in Barbados. A dance remix of 'Electric Avenue' was a huge club hit in 2001.

GRATEFUL DEAD

The enigmatic and mercurial Grateful Dead evolved in 1965. Their name was chosen from a randomly opened copy of the *Oxford English Dictionary* – the band were somewhat chemically stimulated at the time. The original line-up – **Jerry Garcia** (b. Jerome John Garcia, 1942, d. 1995; lead guitar), Bob Weir

(b. Robert Hall, 1947; rhythm guitar), Phil Lesh (b. Philip Chapman, 1940; bass), Ron 'Pigpen' McKernan (b. 1945, d. 1973; keyboards) and Bill Kreutzmann (b. 1946; drums) – were synonymous with the San Francisco acid-rock scene. In 1965, they took part in Ken Kesey's Acid Tests: Stanley Owsley manufactured the then-legal LSD and plied the band with copious amounts. This hallucinogenic opus was recorded on to tape over a six-month period, and documented in Tom Wolfe's book *The Electric Kool-Aid Acid Test*.

By the time their first album was released in 1967 they were already a huge cult band. *Grateful Dead* sounds raw today but it was a brave early attempt to capture a live concert sound on a studio album. *Anthem Of The Sun* was much more satisfying. The non-stop suite of ambitious segments, with tantalizing titles such as 'The Faster We Go The Rounder We Get' and 'Quadlibet For Tenderfeet', was an artistic success and their innovative and colourful album covers were among the finest examples of San Franciscan art (Kelley Mouse Studios). *Aoxomoxoa* contained structured songs and hints of mellowing surfaced on 'China Cat Sunflower' and the sublime 'Mountains Of The Moon'. In concert, the band were playing longer and longer sets, sometimes lasting six hours with only as many songs.

The band now added a second drummer, Micky Hart, and a second keyboard player, Tom Constanten; it was this line-up that produced *Live Dead*.

Their peak of improvisation is best demonstrated on 'Dark Star': during its 23 minutes, the music simmers, builds and explodes four times. On *Workingman's Dead* and *American Beauty*, a strong **Crosby, Stills And Nash** harmony influence prevailed. The Grateful Dead then reverted to releasing live sets, issuing a second double album closely followed by the triple, *Europe '72*. Sadly, after years of alcohol abuse, McKernan died in 1973. He was replaced by Keith Godcheaux and his vocalist wife Donna.

As a touring band the Grateful Dead continued to prosper, but their studio albums began to lose direction. The Godcheauxs left in 1979. *Go To Heaven*, with new keyboard player Brent Mydland, betrayed a hint of disco-pop and the album sleeve showed the band posing in white suits. Ironically, it was this disappointing record that spawned their first, albeit minor, success in the US singles chart with 'Alabama Getaway'. After years of drug experimentation, Garcia succumbed to heroin addiction and came close to death when he went into a diabetic coma in 1986. The joy of his survival showed in their first studio album in seven years, *In The Dark*. A stunning return to form, it resulted in a worldwide hit 'Touch Of Grey'. MTV exposure introduced them to a whole new generation of fans. *Built To Last* was dull, but they continued to play to vast audiences.

In 1990, Mydland died from a lethal combination of cocaine and morphine. His temporary replacement was **Bruce Hornsby** until Vince Welnick was recruited full-time. Garcia then became seriously ill with a lung infection. After a long spell in hospital he returned, but, on 9 August 1995, suffered a fatal heart attack. At a press conference in December the band announced that they would bury the band name along with him. Nevertheless, a staggering amount of archive material has been released, most notably with the ongoing *Dick's Picks* project.

GRAY, DAVID

Born in Manchester, England, but raised in the Welsh fishing village of Solva, Gray first aspired to being a rock performer after watching 2-Tone bands on television. Pegged as a 'crop-headed Welsh troubadour' with 'a chip on both shoulders', Gray's songs are in fact as sensitive as they are angry, and the manic energy communicated with his acoustic guitar thrash set him apart from the folkies. The singer's 1998 collection *White Ladder* (his fourth album) was recorded in his bedroom on a four-track, and several of the tracks featured heavily in the film *This Year's Love*. The album became a bestseller in Ireland and, backed by the might of East West Records, belatedly broke into the UK Top 10 the following year on the back of the Top 5 single 'Babylon'. The record's success prompted a resurgence in the singer-songwriter format. The album finally topped the UK charts in August 2001, almost three years after its initial release.

GRAY, MACY

A striking US soul singer, Gray (b. Natalie McIntyre, 1970) entranced critics and music fans alike when her debut album was released in autumn 1999. *On How Life Is* proved to be a melodic fusion of classic soul, urban R&B and hip-hop beats, rounded off by Gray's earthy rasp. Stand-out tracks included the excellent singles 'Do Something' and 'I Try'. The latter single stayed in the lower reaches of the UK Top 10 for several weeks, and finally broke Gray in her homeland the following year, climbing into the Top 5. Gray returned to the studio to record

The ID with Rick Rubin. Her incredible voice sets her apart from many of her contemporaries.

GREAT SOCIETY

Formed in 1965 by Grace Slick (b. Grace Barnett Wing, 1939; vocals, piano, guitar), her husband Jerry (drums) and his brother Darby Slick (lead guitar). David Minor (rhythm guitar) and Bard DuPont (bass) completed the original line-up, although DuPont was replaced by Peter Vandergelder (bass, saxophone). One of the first San Franciscan rock groups, they were active for 13 months and issued one single, 'Someone To Love' (later known as 'Somebody To Love'). This intriguing Darby Slick composition was adopted by **Jefferson Airplane**, the group Grace joined in 1966. The Great Society split on her departure, but two live collections, released after her fame, show rare imagination.

GREEN DAY

Alternative Californian rock act – Billy Joe Armstrong (b. 1972; vocals, guitar), Mike Dirnt (b. 1972; bass, vocals) and Tre Cool (b. Frank Edwin Wright III, 1972; drums, vocals) – formed after all three members had played in various local bands. Green Day (the name inspired by their propensity for marijuana) debuted with 1989's *1000 Hours* EP. Their debut album, *39/Smooth*, was recorded in one day. Previous drummer Kiffmeyer booked their first national tour, but then left the band to concentrate on college. Cool was asked to fill in. He wrote the comedic 'Dominated Love Song' for *Kerplunk!*, which sold over 50,000 records. Afterwards, they signed to Reprise Records. A&R man Rob Cavallo produced their third album, *Dookie*, which sold over nine million copies in the USA. Their arduous touring schedule was the chief reason for their rise, with appearances on the 1994 Lollapalooza package and the revived Woodstock event. The band were nominated in no less than four Grammy categories, and by 1995 had sold over 10 million albums worldwide, a stunning achievement for a punk-pop band. *Insomniac* and *Nimrod* confirmed their popularity. Their fourth major-label release, 2000's *Warning*, was a hugely enjoyable power-pop album.

GREEN ON RED

US band formed in 1981. Dan Stuart (guitar, vocals), Jack Waterson (bass) and Van Christian (drums) started out as the Serfers. Christian was replaced by Alex MacNicol, and Chris Cacavas added on keyboards for the first EP, *Two Bibles*, released under their new name. They attracted attention as part of the 60s-influenced 'paisley underground', but Green On Red's sound owed more to **Neil Young** and country/blues traditions. In 1984, Chuck Prophet IV joined on lead guitar. Sophisticated arrangements on *The Killer Inside Me* saw the band pushing for mainstream recognition, but shortly afterwards Waterson and Cacavas left to go solo. Prophet and Stuart forged ahead, using session

musicians for *Here Come The Snakes*. In 1991, Green On Red re-emerged with *Scapegoats*, recorded with **Al Kooper** on keyboards. Following one further Green On Red release they elected to concentrate on solo work, with Prophet's career taking off in 1993 with the well-received *Balinese Dancer*. Stuart relocated to Spain.

GREEN, AL

After a spell in the Greene Brothers, a gospel quartet, urbane singer Al Green (b. Al Greene, 1946) made his first recordings in 1960. In 1964, he helped form the Creations with Curtis Rogers and Palmer Jones. These two wrote and produced 'Back Up Train', and a 1967 R&B hit for his new group, Al Greene And The Soul Mates. Similar releases fared less well, prompting Green's decision to work solo. In 1969, he met Willie Mitchell, who took the singer to Hi Records. 'I Can't Get Next To You' (1970) was their first best-seller, previously a hit for the **Temptations**. 'Tired Of Being Alone' (1971, US number 11/UK number 4) introduced a smoother perspective. It was followed by 'Let's Stay Together' (1971), 'I'm Still In Love With You' (1972) and 'Call Me (Come Back Home)' (1973). However, following an argument, his girlfriend Mary Woodson shot herself dead in 1974. Scarred and shaken, Green's work grew increasingly predictable. The partnership with Mitchell was dissolved and Green opened his own recording studio, American Music. The first single, 'Belle', reached the US R&B Top 10; the accompanying album was a 'critics favourite', as were the later Hi collections; however further singles failed. In 1979, Green fell from a stage – he took this as a religious sign and released *The Lord Will Make A Way* (a gospel-only recording) followed by *He Is The Light*. A practising minister, he nonetheless reached the UK singles chart with the secular 'Put A Little Love In Your Heart' (1989). *Don't Look Back* (1993) was a sparkling return after many years away from recording new material.

GREEN, PETER

UK-born Peter Green (b. Peter Greenbaum, 1946) became one of several temporary guitarists in **John Mayall**'s Bluesbreakers during **Eric Clapton**'s 1965 sabbatical. When Clapton returned, Green joined Peter Bardens (organ), Dave Ambrose (bass) and Mick Fleetwood (drums) in a short-lived club band, the Peter B's. They completed one single, 'If You Wanna Be Happy'/'Jodrell Blues' (1966); the instrumental b-side showcased Green's already distinctive style. They subsequently played for Shotgun Express, backing **Rod Stewart** and Beryl Marsden, but Green left after a few weeks. He rejoined Mayall in 1966 when Clapton left to form **Cream**. Green made several contributions to the Bluesbreakers' work, most notably on *A Hard Road*.

In 1967, Green left to form **Fleetwood Mac** with Mick Fleetwood. This became one of the most popular groups of the era, developing blues-based origins into an exciting, experimental unit. However, Green grew increasingly unstable and he left in 1970; he has followed an erratic course since. His solo debut, *The End Of The Game*, was perplexing. He made sporadic session appearances but, following a cameo role on Fleetwood Mac's *Penguin*, dropped out of music altogether. In the mid-70s he was committed to mental institutions. Green returned with *In The Skies*, a light but optimistic collection. *Little Dreamer* offered a more blues-based perspective. In 1982, Green (now Greenbaum) toured unsatisfactorily with Kolors. A hastily concocted album of out-takes and unfinished demos was issued.

In 1995, **Gary Moore** recorded an album of Peter Green tracks, *Blues For Greeny*. The following year, Green showed up onstage at a Gary Moore gig. In August, he played with the Splinter Group, featuring Nigel Watson (guitar) and Neil Murray (bass), at the Guildford Blues Festival, and they issued an album in 1997. He then released *The Robert Johnson Songbook*, his first full studio album in almost two decades. Further albums have followed, demonstrating clearly that Green and his Splinter Group are serious about their music, and in particular Green's rediscovery of his pure blues roots.

GREENBAUM, NORMAN

Greenbaum (b. 1942) founded Los Angeles jug band Dr. West's Medicine Show And Junk Band, which achieved a minor hit with the novelty 'The Eggplant That Ate Chicago'. The group split in 1967 and Greenbaum retired from music to run a farm in California. In 1970, however, one of his recordings, 'Spirit In The Sky', unexpectedly scaled the US charts, reaching number 3 and later making UK number 1. Greenbaum was teased out of retirement to record a couple of albums. In 1986, the British group Doctor And The Medics revived 'Spirit In The Sky', reaching UK number 1. Despite poor health, Greenbaum has continued to write new material.

GRIFFITH, NANCI

US-born Griffith (b. 1953) grew up in a theatrical family. In 1978 her first album, *There's A Light Beyond These Woods*, was released by a local company. In 1982, *Poet In My Window* was released by another local label; like its

predecessor, it was re-released in 1986 by the nationally distributed Philo/Rounder label.

By 1984 she had met Jim Rooney, who produced *Once In A Very Blue Moon*. Following on the heels of this artistic triumph came *Last Of The True Believers*. The album became Griffith's first to be released in the UK. Signed by MCA Records, her debut album for the label was *Lone Star State Of Mind*. Attracting most attention

was Julie Gold's 'From A Distance', a song that became a standard by the 90s as covered by Bette Midler, **Cliff Richard** and many others. *Little Love Affairs* was supposedly a concept album, but major songs included 'Outbound Plane', '(My Best Pal's In Nashville) Never Mind' and 'Sweet Dreams Will Come'. *Storms*, produced by Glyn Johns (who geared the album's sound towards American radio), became Griffith's biggest seller. Although it was a sales breakthrough for Griffith, it failed to attract country audiences. *Late Night Grande Hotel* included a duet with Phil Everly, 'It's Just Another Morning Here'. The 1993 release *Other Voices, Other Rooms* was a wholehearted success artistically and commercially. Griffith interpreted some outstanding songs by artists such as **Bob Dylan** ('Boots Of Spanish Leather'), John Prine ('Speed Of The Sound Of Loneliness') and Ralph McTell ('From Clare To Here'). The exquisite *Flyer* maintained her popularity with some excellent new material. *Other Voices, Too (A Trip Back To Bountiful)* saw Griffith returning to the cover versions format once again. On 1999's *The Dust Bowl Symphony*, Griffith reinterpreted songs from her back catalogue with the help of the London Symphony Orchestra. *Clock Without Hands*, her first album to comprise largely original material since 1997, was released in 2001.

GROOVE ARMADA

This UK dance duo comprises Tom Findlay and Andy Cato. Their music is an unusual blend of influences, spanning house, big beat, Balearic, disco and funk. It combines traditional instrumentation and influences with house rhythms and technology. Their first album, *Northern Star*, was released on the London-based independent label Tummy Touch in 1998. The well-received single 'At The River', built around a Patti Page vocal sample, was also released on the label. The duo was signed to Pepper Records for their second album, *Vertigo*. Like its predecessor the album was highly praised across the music press. A re-released 'At The River' entered the Top 20 three months later. Stylish, chilled-out and making all the right musical references, Groove Armada effortlessly capture the zeitgeist of the contemporary dance music scene.

GROUNDHOGS

Formed in 1963 from struggling UK beat group the Dollarbills. Tony 'T. S.' McPhee (b. 1944; guitar), John Cruickshank (vocals, harp), Bob Hall (piano), Pete Cruickshank (bass) and Dave Boorman (drums) also adopted a 'John Lee' prefix in honour of **John Lee Hooker**, whom they subsequently backed. John Lee's Groundhogs recorded two singles before breaking up in 1966.

In 1968, they re-formed Groundhogs alongside Steve Rye (vocals, harmonica) and Ken Pustelnik (drums). They debuted with the rudimentary *Scratching The Surface*, after which Rye left. *Blues Obituary* contained 'Mistreated' and 'Express Man', which became in-concert favourites. *Thank Christ For The Bomb* cemented a growing popularity, Pustelnik left following *Who Will Save The World?* in 1972. Former Egg drummer Clive Brooks (b. 1949) was an able replacement but, despite continued popularity, subsequent recordings lacked the fire of early releases. They broke up in 1975, although McPhee maintained the name for *Crosscut Saw* and *Black Diamond*.

McPhee resurrected the Groundhogs in 1984 after interest in an archive release, *Hoggin' The Stage*. Pustelnik was one of several musicians McPhee used for touring. McPhee has in recent years appeared as a solo performer as part of a 70s nostalgia tour, together with various incarnations of his respected band.

GUESS WHO

Canada's most popular rock band of the 60s and early 70s had its roots in Chad Allan And The Reflections, formed in 1962. The original line-up consisted of Allan (b. Allan Kobel; guitar, vocals), Jim Kale (bass), Randy Bachman (b. 1943; guitar), Bob Ashley (piano) and Garry Peterson (drums). Their debut, 'Tribute To Buddy Holly', was released in 1962. Further singles followed, and by 1965 the group had become Chad Allan and the Expressions, with their cover of **Johnny Kidd And The Pirates**' 'Shakin' All Over', which hit Canadian number 1. Ashley left and was replaced by Burton Cummings, who shared lead vocal duties with Allan for a year. In 1966, the band released, *Shakin' All Over*. The words 'Guess Who?' were printed on the cover, prompting their new name. That year Allan left, replaced briefly by Bruce Decker; when he left, Cummings became chief vocalist.

In 1967, Guess Who had their first UK chart single with 'His Girl'. The following year, with financial backing from producer Jack Richardson, Guess Who recorded *Wheatfield Soul*. 'These Eyes' reached Canadian number 1 and earned the band a US contract, reaching US number 6 in 1969. That year *Canned Wheat Packed By The Guess Who* also charted.

In 1970, 'American Woman' became the Guess Who's only US number 1, and *American Woman* went to the US Top 10. In July, Bachman left the band and resurfaced with Chad Allan in Brave Belt, and again with **Bachman-Turner Overdrive**. A Guess Who album recorded while Bachman was still in the group was cancelled, and he was replaced by guitarists Kurt Winter and Greg Leskiw. Leskiw and Kale left in 1972, replaced by Don McDougall and Bill Wallace. In 1974, Winter and McDougall left, replaced by Domenic

Troiano (ex-**James Gang**). That year, 'Clap For The Wolfman' reached US number 6. It proved to be the group's final hit, and in 1975 Cummings disbanded Guess Who to go solo.

In 1979, a new Guess Who, featuring Allan, Kale, McDougall and three new members, recorded and toured, without success. Similar regroupings (minus Cummings) also failed. A 1983 Guess Who reunion aroused some interest followed by a Bachman and Cummings tour in 1987. Though various line-ups continue to tour under the Guess Who name, a successful reunion of the original members took place in the new millennium.

GUIDED BY VOICES

US alternative rock band initially led by songwriters Robert Pollard and Tobin Sprout. They debuted in 1986 with the *Forever Since Breakfast* EP, a progressive rock recording lacking in technical ability. Their first four albums similarly failed, but *Propeller* was an improvement. 'Exit Flagger' became their first genuine 'classic'. *Vampire On Titus* finally brought the band out of obscurity, while 'Static Airplane Jive' and 'Fast Japanese Spin Cycle' preceded *Bee Thousand*, arguably their best album. *Crying Your Knife Away*, followed by Box, built on their new-found popularity. *Under The Bushes, Under The Stars*, a 24-track collection of minimal pop songs, pulled away from their lo-fi roots. *Mag Earwhig!* proved to be as worthy as any previous recordings, but marked the end of the Pollard/Sprout partnership. *Do The Collapse* and *Isolation Drills* opted for a commercial, radio-friendly sound.

GUNS N'ROSES

US heavy-rock band formed in the mid-80s. Axl Rose (an anagram of Oral Sex) (b. William Bailey, 1962) and Izzy Stradlin (b. Jeffrey Isbell, 1962) met in 1984. With Tracii Guns (guitar) and Rob Gardner (drums), they formed a rock band called in turn Rose, Hollywood Rose and L.A. Guns. Soon afterwards, Guns and Gardner left, replaced by drummer Steven Adler (b. 1965) and English guitarist Slash (b. Saul Hudson, 1965). With bass player Duff McKagan (b. Michael McKagan, 1964), the band was renamed Guns N'Roses. Following a disastrous US Hell Tour '85, Guns N'Roses released an EP, *Live?!*@ Like A Suicide*, winning interest from critics and record companies. In 1986, the band signed to Geffen Records, who reissued the E.P. During 1987 they toured extensively. In 1988, Rose was kicked out but was reinstated within three days. *Appetite For Destruction* sold 20 million copies worldwide and reached US number 1 within a year. 'Welcome To The Jungle' was used on the soundtrack of the Clint Eastwood movie *Dead Pool*.

The band toured regularly – and controversially – in the US and Europe, and, in 1989, *G N' R Lies* became a transatlantic hit. However, Guns N'Roses' career was littered with incidents involving drugs, drunkenness and public-disturbance offences. In 1990, Adler was replaced by Matt Sorum

(b. 1960; ex-**Cult**), followed by Dizzy Reed (b. Darren Reed; keyboards) for a 1991 world tour. The band then released *Use Your Illusion I* and *II* – reaching US numbers 1 and 2 – preceded by a cover version of **Bob Dylan**'s 'Knockin' On Heaven's Door' from the soundtrack of *Days Of Thunder*. Further hits, 'You Could Be Mine' and 'Don't Cry', followed. Stradlin found the pressure too

much and left late in 1991 to form the Ju Ju Hounds. He was replaced by Gilby Clarke. Slash's growing reputation led to guest appearances for Dylan and **Michael Jackson**.

At the end of 1993, the covers album *The Spaghetti Incident* was issued. Duff McKagan released his debut solo album and in 1994 Gilby Clarke left. His replacement, Paul Huge, was in turn replaced by Zakk Wylde (ex-**Ozzy Osbourne**), who fell out irreconcilably with Rose before recording a note. In 1995, Stradlin was reinstated but by the end of the year Rose and Slash were again at loggerheads, and no new album was imminent. Slash confirmed Rose's departure in November 1996, reversed in February 1997 when Rose allegedly purchased the rights to the Guns N'Roses name.

In November 1999, Rose surprised everyone by contributing the industrial metal track 'Oh My God' to the soundtrack of *End Of Days*. Backed by new personnel, he embarked on *The Chinese Democracy* tour and claimed to have finally finished the band's long-awaited new album.

GUTHRIE, ARLO

Arlo (b. 1947) was the eldest son of folksinger **Woody Guthrie**. His lengthy ballad, 'Alice's Restaurant Massacre', part humorous song, part narrative, achieved popularity following his appearance at the 1967 Newport Folk

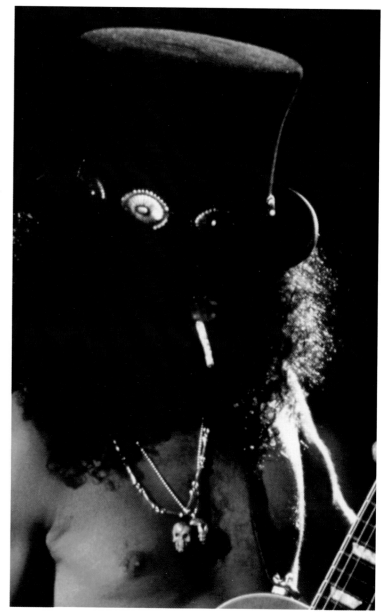

Festival. It became the cornerstone of his debut album and inspired a feature film. An early song, 'Highway In The Wind', was successfully covered by Hearts And Flowers as Arlo emerged from the shadow of his father. *Running Down The Road* indicated a new-found maturity, but Guthrie's talent truly flourished on a series of 70s recordings, notably *Hobo's Lullaby*, *Last Of The Brooklyn Cowboys* and *Amigo*. 'Presidential Rag' was a vitriolic commentary on Watergate, and 'Children Of Abraham' addressed the Arab/Israeli conflict. In 1972, Guthrie enjoyed a US Top 20 hit with 'City Of New Orleans'. Today he remains a popular figure on the folk circuit. He returned to his most famous song in 1995 with a reworked 'The Massacre Revisited'.

GUTHRIE, WOODY

A major figure of America's folk heritage. Guthrie (b. Woodrow Wilson Guthrie, 1912, d. 1967) moved to California in 1935, working on Los Angeles' KFVD radio station. Having befriended singer Cisco Houston and actor Will Geer, he established his left-wing credentials with joint appearances at union meetings and migrant labour camps. His reactions to the poverty he witnessed inspired his finest compositions, notably 'Pastures Of Plenty', 'Dust Bowl Refugees', 'Vigilante Man' and 'This Land Is Your Land'. At the end of the 30s, Guthrie travelled to New York, where he undertook a series of recordings for the folk-song archive at the Library Of Congress. The 12 discs he completed were later released commercially by Elektra Records.

Guthrie continued to traverse the country and in 1940 met Pete Seeger at a folk-song rally. Together they formed the Almanac Singers with Lee Hayes and Millard Lampell, which in turn inspired the Almanac House, a co-operative apartment in New York's Greenwich Village, which became the focus of the east-coast folk movement. In 1942, Guthrie joined the Headline Singers with Lead Belly, Sonny Terry and Brownie McGhee. He and Houston then enlisted in the merchant marines, until the end of World War II, after which Guthrie began recording again for various labels. Guthrie retained his commitment to the union movement and his prolific output continued unabated until the end of the 40s, when he succumbed to Huntington's Chorea. He was hospitalized by this lingering illness for fifteen years, until his death in 1967.

GUY, BUDDY

Louisiana-born Buddy Guy (b. George Guy, 1936) taught himself to play the blues on a home-made guitar. By the mid-50s, he was playing with leading performers, including Slim Harpo and **Lightnin' Slim**. In 1957, Guy moved to Chicago, joined the Rufus Foreman Band and became established as an artist in his own right. His first single was released the following year. Shortly afterwards he met Willie Dixon, who took him to Chess Records. As part of the company's house band he appeared on sessions by **Muddy Waters** and **Howlin' Wolf**, as well as his own recordings, most notably 'First Time I Met The Blues' and 'Stone Crazy'. Guy also established a fruitful partnership with Junior Wells featuring on the harpist's early releases, *Hoodoo Man Blues* and *It's My Life, Baby*. Guy's following albums combined classic 'Chicago' blues with contemporary soul styles, winning him attention from the rock audience. He appeared at the Fillmore auditorium and supported the **Rolling Stones** on their 1970 tour.

In 1990, he guested at **Eric Clapton**'s blues night at London's Royal Albert Hall. Guy's *Damn Right, I've Got The Blues* was recorded with the assistance of Clapton, **Jeff Beck** and **Mark Knopfler**, and the critical acclaim was further enhanced by *Feels Like Rain*. The trilogy of recent albums was completed with *Slippin' In*. *Live! The Real Deal*, was recorded with G. E. Smith and the Saturday Night Live Band. Guy represents the last strand linking the immortal Chicago bluesmen of the 1950s with the present-day contemporary blues scene.

H.P. LOVECRAFT

Chicago, USA-based band formed by George Edwards (guitar, vocals) and David Michaels (keyboards, woodwind, vocals), who debuted in 1967 with a folk rock reading of 'Anyway That You Want Me'. They were initially backed by local outfit The Rovin' Kind, until Tony Cavallari (lead guitar), Jerry McGeorge (bass) and Michael Tegza (drums) joined. *H.P. Lovecraft* fused haunting folk-based material with graphic contemporary compositions. McGeorge was replaced by Jeffrey Boyan for *H.P. Lovecraft II* before the band disintegrated. In 1970, Tegza formed Lovecraft with Jim Dolinger (guitar), Michael Been (bass) and Marty Grebb (keyboards). They completed *Valley Of The Moon*. In 1975, Tegza employed a new line-up for *We Love You Whoever You Are*, before finally laying the name to rest.

HAGGARD, MERLE

In the 30s, Haggard's (b. 1937) parents migrated from the Dustbowl to 'the land of milk and honey', California. Haggard became a tearaway who spent many years in reform schools and was later sent to San Quentin. Back in Bakersfield, California, in 1960, Haggard started performing and found work accompanying Wynn Stewart. Only 200 copies were pressed of his first single, 'Singing My Heart Out', but he made the national charts with his second, Stewart's composition 'Sing A Sad Song', for the small Tally label. Capitol Records took over his contract and reissued '(All My Friends Are Going To Be) Strangers' in 1965. The record's success prompted him to call his band the Strangers, its mainstays being Roy Nichols on lead guitar and Norm Hamlet on steel. When 'I'm A Lonesome Fugitive' became a country number 1 in 1966, it was clear that a country star with a prison record was a very commercial proposition. In 1969 a chance remark on the tour bus led to him writing 'Okie From Muskogee', a conservative reply to draft-card burning and flower power.

Around this time, Haggard wrote and recorded several glorious singles that rank with the best of country music and illustrate his personal credo: 'I Take A Lot Of Pride In What I Am', 'Silver Wings', 'Today I Started Loving You Again' and 'If We Make It Through December'. Between 1973 and 1976, Haggard achieved nine consecutive number 1 records on the US country charts. By 1990, when he moved to the Curb Records label, Haggard had notched up the incredible tally of 95 country hits on the US chart, including a remarkable 38 chart-toppers.

Although many of the new 'hat acts' of the 90s owed much to Haggard, Haggard himself became old hat for a couple of years. The reassessment of his work started with two tribute albums by contemporary performers, and some fine recent work by the man himself on his own Hag label. He also began recording for Anti, a subsidiary of the alternative label Epitaph Records, with 2000's *If I Could Only Fly* earning particular acclaim.

HAIRCUT 100

UK pop band featuring Nick Heyward (b. 1961; vocals), Les Nemes (b. 1960; bass), Graham Jones (b. 1961; guitar), Blair Cunningham (b. 1957; drums), Phil Smith (b. 1959; saxophone) and Mark Fox (b. 1958; percussion). They secured a deal with Arista Records where, produced by Bob Sargeant, their teen appeal and smooth punk-pop sound became a winning combination in 1981–82. Their debut 'Favourite Shirts (Boy Meets Girl)' reached UK number 4 and 'Love Plus One' fared even better. When Heyward left for a solo career he was replaced by Mark Fox. Subsequent singles sold poorly and, after *Paint On Paint*, they disbanded.

HALEY, BILL, AND HIS COMETS

Haley (b. 1925, d. 1981) started out in country music with the Four Aces Of Western Swing. His next group, the Saddlemen, played western swing mixed with polka. Haley's fusion of country, R&B and a steady beat was to provide the backbone of rock 'n' roll.

In 1953, Haley formed Bill Haley And His Comets. Their first single 'Crazy Man Crazy' became the first rock 'n' roll Top 20 US hit. After signing to Decca Records in 1954, Haley recorded several important songs, including 'Rock Around The Clock' – its spine-tingling guitar breaks and inspired drumming were unlike any previous recording, although initially it was only a minor hit. Haley then recorded 'Shake Rattle And Roll', whose jive-style lyrics, brilliant saxophone and upright bass brought a new sound into the US Top 20. Less important hits followed until, in 1955, 'Rock Around The Clock' was included in the controversial movie *The Blackboard Jungle*. Suddenly, it became rock 'n' roll's anthem, soaring to US/UK number 1. Haley dominated the

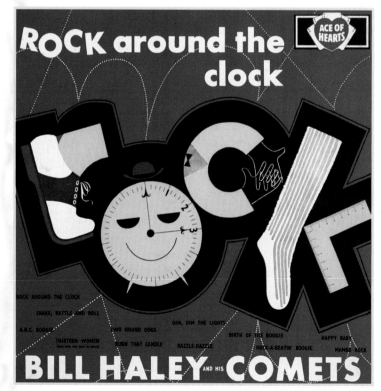

US/UK charts throughout 1955–56 with such songs as 'Rock-A-Beatin' Boogie', 'See You Later Alligator', and 'Rudy's Rock'. In 1957, he became the first rock 'n' roll star to tour abroad; he was mobbed on arrival in London.

Haley's star burned brightly for a couple of years, but once **Elvis Presley** exploded on to the scene, Haley swiftly lost his standing among his young audience. 'Rock Around The Clock' returned to the UK Top 20 in 1968 and 1974. Haley died of a heart attack in 1981.

HALF MAN HALF BISCUIT

Durable UK indie band originally formed in the mid-80s by songwriter Nigel Blackwell (vocals, guitar). He was joined by Neil Crossley (vocals, bass), Si Blackwell (guitar), David Lloyd (keyboards) and Paul Wright (drums). Thanks to disc jockey John Peel, *The Trumpton Riots* 12-inch EP (1986) stayed in the indie charts for several weeks. Inspired by cult UK television celebrities, their unforgettable song titles include '99% Of Gargoyles Look Like Bob Todd' and 'I Love You Because (You Like Jim Reeves)'. Displaying a disinterest in ambition, they turned down television appearances that clashed with their football club's home matches. They split at the peak of their success but re-formed in mid-1990 for a version of 'No Regrets'. The subsequent *McIntyre, Treadmore And Davitt* and *This Leaden Pall* continued to mine the band's parochial good humour. The band have subsequently become something of a British institution, and the quality of Blackwell's songwriting has never dipped.

HALL AND OATES

US white soul duo Daryl Hall (b. Daryl Franklin Hohl, 1949; falsetto) and John Oates (b. 1949; baritone) met in 1969. They were discovered by Tommy Mottola of Chappell Music and signed to Atlantic Records. Their three albums for the label sold few copies. The duo came to national prominence with the million-selling 'Sara Smile', on RCA Records, followed by 1977's US chart-topping 'Rich Girl'. After the unimpressive *X-Static*, the self-produced *Voices* spawned four hit singles, notably a remake of the **Righteous Brothers**' 'You've Lost That Lovin' Feelin'' and the haunting 'Every Time You Go Away'. For the next five years hit followed hit, including 'Maneater', 'I Can't Go For That (No Can Do)', 'Out Of Touch' and 'Family Man' (a **Mike Oldfield** composition).

During a three-year hiatus in the partnership, Hall recorded his second solo album. Reunited in 1988, Hall And Oates had a US Top 5 hit with 'Everything Your Heart Desires'. The 1990 hit 'So Close' added a strong rock flavour. The duo did not record together again until 1997's *Marigold Sky*, by which time their brand of white soul was out of fashion in a world of 'urban R&B'.

HALLIWELL, GERI

UK performer Halliwell (b. 1972, although her date of birth has been the subject of some conjecture) was a member of the **Spice Girls**, the pop phenomenon of the late 90s. Before joining the band her varied CV included stints as a topless model and, bizarrely, a Turkish game-show host. Although featured on the band's August 1998 UK chart-topping single, 'Viva Forever', Halliwell had actually left the band in May amid press rumours of disputes and personality clashes with the other members. Shortly afterwards she became a UN ambassador, responsible for promoting breast-cancer awareness. EMI Records won the chase for Halliwell's signature in 1998. In a bold move, Halliwell released the Shirley Bassey-styled ballad 'Look At Me' as her debut single in summer 1999. Despite the song's obvious vocal limitations, it still managed to debut at UK number 2. *Schiz-ophonic* proved to be a ragbag of musical influences. Halliwell had the last laugh, however, by going on to enjoy three consecutive UK chart-toppers with 'Mi Chico Latino', 'Lift Me Up' and 'Bag It Up'. She also published her autobiography, *If Only*. The media blitz that promoted Halliwell's second album in 2001 was dizzying even by her standards, although her drastically slim new figure disturbed some people. *Scream If You Wanna Go Faster* adopted a more straightforward pop approach, epitomized by the UK chart-topping cover version of the Weather Girls' 'It's Raining Men'.

HALLYDAY, JOHNNY

By the late 50s, French singer Johnny Hallyday (b. Jean-Philippe Smet, 1943) had become a rock 'n' roller. An apprenticeship of singing to a jukebox of US discs made him sound like an American. A 1960 radio debut led to Vogue Records contracting him for 'T'Ai Mer Follement'. After a million-selling bilingual cover of Chubby Checker's 'Let's Twist Again' (1961) and a film appearance, this svelte blond became to France what **Elvis Presley** was to the USA. *Johnny Hallyday Sings America's Rockin' Hits* indicated his future direction and his interpretations of songs such as 'The House Of The Rising Sun', 'Black Is Black', and 'Hey Joe' followed. Hallyday continued to thrive on a certain hip sensibility, manifested in his block-bookings of fashionable studios in Britain and the USA, and employment of top session musicians. Hallyday remains one of the few European rock singers to be regarded with remotely strong interest outside his own country.

HAMMILL, PETER

Hammill (b. 1948; vocals, piano, guitar) enjoyed critical acclaim as the leader of UK progressive rock band **Van Der Graaf Generator**. When they broke up in 1972, Hammill continued solo and has maintained a prolific output ever since. The quality of his work keeps mainstream artists turning to him for inspiration. He has achieved autonomy in his work – owning his studio and label – but he has never fully escaped the legacy of Van Der Graaf Generator.

HAMMOND, ALBERT

British-born Hammond began a songwriting partnership with Mike Hazelwood, a Radio Luxembourg presenter in 1966. After international success in 1968 with 'Little Arrows' for Leapy Lee, they hit in the UK with the Pipkins' 'Gimme Dat Ding'. They reached the UK Top 10 in 1969 with 'Way of Life' before moving to Los Angeles. In 1971, Hammond became the first artist contracted to the Mums label. His second single, 'It Never Rains In Southern California', sold a million in the USA. Hammond's initial triumphs have not been matched since, although subsequent songwriting hits include 'The Air That I Breathe' (with Hazelwood) for the **Hollies**, '99 Miles From LA' for **Art Garfunkel**, and 'When I Need You' (with Carole Bayer Sager) for **Leo Sayer**.

HANCOCK, HERBIE

US pianist Hancock (b. 1940) first enjoyed minor fame when a version of his 'Watermelon Man', by Mongo Santamaría, reached the US Top 10. Until the mid-60s Hancock led bands for club engagements and record dates, before joining **Miles Davis**'s quintet, with whom he stayed for more than five years. In 1968, Hancock formed a sextet with musicians including Julian Priester, Buster Williams and Eddie Henderson. Playing much Hancock material, they became one of the most popular and influential jazz-rock bands in the early 70s. From 1969, Hancock extensively used electronic keyboard instruments, including synthesizers. In 1973, the group dwindled to a quartet whose music leaned towards jazz-funk and the first album,

Headhunters, sold well into the burgeoning disco scene. His numerous disco successes included 'You Bet Your Love' (1979, UK Top 20) and *Future Shock* (with the group Material), which spawned 'Rockit' (UK Top 10/US number 1). Although Hancock's first love is jazz, he has skilfully pushed his music into other areas, creating a body of work that is breathtaking in its scope.

HANOI ROCKS

Finnish heavy rock band formed in 1980 by Michael Monroe (b. Matti Fagerholm, 1960; vocals), Nasty Suicide (b. Jan Stenfors, 1963; guitar), Andy McCoy (b. Antti Hulkko, 1962; guitar), Sam Yaffa (b. Sami Takamaki, 1963; bass), and Gyp Casino (b. Jesper Sporre; drums). They debuted with *Bangkok Shocks, Saigon Shakes, Hanoi Rocks*. They then recorded *Oriental Beat* in London. Casino was then replaced by Razzle (b. Nicholas Dingley, 1960, d. 1984). In 1983 they were signed to CBS Records, and hit the UK charts for the first and only time in 1984 with a cover version of **Creedence Clearwater Revival**'s 'Up Around The Bend'. The year ended in tragedy when Razzle was killed in a car crash in the US. In 1985 Monroe left to go solo. A near-reunion of Hanoi Rocks, featuring Monroe with Suicide and Sam Yaffa, emerged as Demolition 23 in 1993.

HANSON

Precocious group of brothers from Oklahoma, USA, who play an energetic blend of **Jackson 5**-styled harmonies and crafted pop/soul melodies. Isaac (b. 1980; guitar, piano, vocals), Taylor (b. 1983; keyboards/ vocals) and Zac Hanson (b. 1985; drums, vocals) began writing and performing in 1992. Two self-distributed CDs and extensive live performances followed. They then landed a deal with Mercury Records. Their self-penned 'MMMBop' reached US/UK number 1 in 1997. *Middle Of Nowhere* followed, recorded with 'name' producers Steve Lironi and the Dust Brothers, featuring four of their own songs alongside collaborations with established songwriters, including Barry Mann and Cynthia Weill. Further transatlantic hit singles followed with 'Where's The Love', 'I Will Come To You', and 'Thinking Of You'. *This Time Around* was a massive leap forward in maturity, but the three-year gap had seemingly lost the band a lot of fans, as sales were unexpectedly disappointing.

HAPPY MONDAYS

Few debut records could lay claim to have had the impact (or length of title) of the Happy Mondays' *Squirrel And G-Man Twenty Four Hour Party People Plastic Face Carnt Smile (White Out)*. The sextet's raw brand of urban folk, with Shaun Ryder's accented, drawled vocals, was almost universally acclaimed. From the group's formation in the early 80s the line-up remained virtually unchanged: Shaun

Ryder (b. 1962; vocals), his brother Paul (b. 1964; bass), Mark Day (b. 1961; guitar), Gary Whelan (b. 1966; drums), Paul Davis (b. 1966; keyboards) and 'Bez' (b. Mark Berry; percussion). *Bummed*, produced by Martin Hannett, was layered with diverse dance rhythms. The following year's Paul Oakenfold remix of 'Wrote For Luck' (re-titled 'WFL') crystallized the band's emergent sound, and was followed by the UK Top 10 hit 'Step On'. *Pills 'N' Thrills And Bellyaches* reached UK number 1, buoyed by strong support from Factory Records and strong media coverage. Success was tempered with unpleasant publicity, which came to a head when Shaun Ryder announced he was a heroin addict undergoing detoxification. A highly publicized strife-torn recording session in the Caribbean resulted in ... *Yes Please!*, but media interest was waning and the group split up.

The band's focal points, Ryder and Bez, eventually re-emerged in 1995 as part of a new coalition, **Black Grape**, Following the break-up of this band, Ryder re-formed the Happy Mondays for several live dates and a new recording of the **Thin Lizzy** classic 'The Boys Are Back In Town'. The 1999 line-up comprised Ryder, Paul Ryder, Bez, Gary Whelan and new member Nuts.

HARDCASTLE, PAUL

Hardcastle (b. 1957) was one of the UK dance scene's first crossover successes. His first group was First Light. After four minor solo hits, '19' (1985), a song about the Vietnam conflict utilizing spoken news reports, reached UK number 1. The follow up, 'Just For The Money', was based on the Great Train Robbery and boasted the voices of Bob Hoskins and Sir Laurence Olivier. His next success was 'Papa's Got A Brand New Pigbag' under the pseudonym Silent Underdog. In 1986, he wrote the *Top Of The Pops* theme, 'The Wizard', before switching to production for young funk band LW5 and providing remixes for various artists. Jazzmasters (with vocalist Helen Rogers) showcases his preference for smooth jazz grooves, and is particularly popular in the USA and Japan.

HARDIN, TIM

By 1964, US singer-songwriter Hardin (b. 1941, d. 1980) was a regular in New York's Greenwich Village cafés, playing a unique blend of poetic folk/blues. His poignant *Tim Hardin 1* included 'Misty Roses' (covered by Colin Blunstone). *Tim Hardin 2* featured his original version of 'If I Were A Carpenter', an international hit for **Bobby Darin** and the **Four Tops**. However, Hardin was disappointed with these releases, and his career faltered. A conceptual work, *Suite For Susan Moore And Damion* ... rekindled his former fire but his gifts then seemed to desert him. Hardin die in December 1980, almost forgotten and totally underrated, of a heroin overdose.

HARPER, BEN

US-born singer-songwriter Harper (b. 1969) soaked up a variety of musical influences, from Son House and Skip James to **Bob Marley** and **Bob Dylan** and gave his first performance at the age of 12. His acoustic guitar style came from the great folk and blues artists practised on his distinctive 'Weissenborn', a hollow-neck lap-slide guitar. In 1992, Harper played with **Taj Mahal** and performed alongside bluesman Brownie McGhee. His debut for Virgin Records earned good reviews in 1994. *Fight For Your Mind* continued to explore lyrical themes of freedom and the restraint of self-expression, alongside the deeply personal 'By My Side'. Both *The Will To Live* and *Burn To Shine* opted for a harder-edged and more commercial sound, framing Harper's superb songs in some new and unusual settings. The albums were recorded with Harper's backing band the Innocent Criminals, comprising Juan Nelson (bass), Dean Butterworth (drums), and David Leach (percussion). The unit's live power is captured on the in-concert set, *Live From Mars*.

HARPER, ROY

UK singer-songwriter Harper (b. 1941) began playing in his brother's skiffle group, before busking around Europe. On returning to England, he became resident at London's Les Cousins club. His 1966 debut *The Sophisticated Beggar* was recorded in primitive conditions, but contained the rudiments of his highly personal style. *Come Out Fighting Genghis Smith* attracted an underground audience. *Folkjokeopus* was considered patchy, unlike the follow-up *Flat, Baroque And Berserk*. Released on Harvest Records, the label allowed him considerable artistic licence. **Stormcock** featured contributions from **Jimmy Page**, who appeared on several succeeding releases including *Lifemask*, another

remarkable, if self-indulgent set, and *Valentine*. Harper's 1975 release, *HQ*, introduced Trigger, Harper's short-lived backing group: Chris Spedding (guitar), Dave Cochran (bass) and Bill Bruford (drums). Harper appeared on **Pink Floyd**'s *Wish You Were Here*, taking lead vocals on 'Have A Cigar', but his subsequent work saw him retreating to the commercial sidelines once more. Commercial success continues to elude Harper, but he retains a committed following for his passionate, articulate brand of folk rock. In the mid-90s he was often to be found performing with his son Nick, a similarly talented individual with an uncanny musical resemblance to his father.

HARPERS BIZARRE

Ted Templeman (b. Theodore Templeman, 1944; lead vocals, guitar), Dick Scoppettone (b. 1945; vocals, guitar), Dick Young (b. 1945; vocals, bass), Eddie James (vocals, guitar) and John Petersen (b. 1942; drums, vocals) formed Harpers Bizarre in 1966. A cover of **Simon And Garfunkel**'s '59th Street Bridge Song (Feelin' Groovy)' reached the US Top 20. Their first album, arranged by Leon Russell, with compositions by **Randy Newman**, proved an enticing debut. After covering Van Dyke Parks' 'Come To The Sunshine', they worked with him on a revival of Cole Porter's 'Anything Goes'. The group split in 1969. Templeman became a producer for Warner Brothers Records. Three of the original line-up reunited six years later for *As Time Goes By*.

HARRIS, EMMYLOU

US singer Harris (b. 1947) first recorded in 1970. She then met **Gram Parsons**, who needed a female partner. She appeared on his two studio albums, *GP* and *Grievous Angel*. The latter was released after Parsons' drug-related death. Parsons' manager encouraged Harris to make a solo album using the same musicians, the Hot Band. Harris released a series of excellent and often successful albums: *Pieces Of The Sky*, *Elite Hotel*, *Luxury Liner* and *Quarter Moon In A Ten Cent Town*. *Blue Kentucky Girl* was closer to pure country music than the country rock that had become her trademark, and *Roses In The Snow* was her fourth US Top 40 album. *Evangeline* and *Cimmaron* were better sellers, but a 1982 live album, *Last Date*, was largely ignored.

Harris and her third husband Paul Kennerley wrote and produced *The Ballad Of Sally Rose* and the similarly excellent *13*. Neither recaptured her previous chart heights. In 1987, Harris worked on *Trio* – a Grammy-winning collaboration with Linda Ronstadt and Dolly Parton – and her own *Angel Band*, a low-key acoustic collection. *Bluebird* was a return to form, but commercially limp. *Brand New Dance* was relatively unsuccessful, and the Hot Band was dropped in favour of bluegrass-based acoustic quintet the Nash Ramblers. However, in 1992, she was dropped by Warner Brothers Records, after 20 years.

When Harris returned in 1995, she boldly stepped away from country-sounding arrangements and recorded the stunning Daniel Lanois-produced *Wrecking Ball*. Harris described this album as her 'weird' record; the set won a Grammy in 1996 for Best Contemporary Folk Album. The live recording *Spyboy*, released in 1998, was an equally impressive summary of her career. The following year Harris teamed up with **Linda Ronstadt** on two occasions; the first time, with **Dolly Parton**, for *Trio II*, and the second for the excellent *Western Wall/The Tucson Sessions*. The majestic and highly personal song cycle *Red Dirt Girl* concentrated on her own underrated songwriting ability.

HARRIS, JET, AND TONY MEEHAN

Terence 'Jet' Harris (b. 1939; guitar) and Daniel Joseph Anthony Meehan (b. 1943; drums) began their partnership in 1959 in the **Shadows**. Meehan left in 1961 to work in Decca Records' A&R department. In 1962 Harris went solo with 'Besame Mucho'. 'The Man With The Golden Arm' gave him a UK Top 20 hit prior to reuniting with Meehan in 1963. The duo's debut, 'Diamonds', reached UK number 1, while 'Scarlett O'Hara' and 'Applejack', reached the Top 5. All featured Harris's low-tuned Fender Jaguar guitar with Meehan's punchy drum interjections. A bright future was predicted, but a serious car crash undermined Harris's confidence and the pair split up.

HARRISON, GEORGE

As the youngest member of the **Beatles**, Harrison (b. 1943, d. 2001) was constantly overshadowed by **John Lennon** and **Paul McCartney**. Although 'Don't Bother Me' (*With The Beatles*), 'I Need You' (*Help!*) and 'If I Needed Someone' (*Rubber Soul*) revealed considerable compositional talent, they were swamped by his colleagues' prodigious output. Instead, Harrison honed a distinctive guitar style and was responsible for adding the sitar into the pop lexicon.

Harrison flexed solo ambitions with the would-be film soundtrack *Wonderwall* and the trite *Electronic Sounds*, before commencing work on *All Things Must Pass*, which boasted support from **Derek And The Dominos**, **Badfinger** and Phil Spector. 'My Sweet Lord' deftly combined melody with mantra and soared to the top of the US and UK charts (Harrison was later successfully sued for plagiarism of the Chiffons' 1964 hit, 'She's So Fine'). His next project was 'Bangla Desh', a single inspired by a plea to aid famine relief. Charity concerts featuring Harrison, **Bob Dylan**, Eric Clapton and Leon Russell, were held at New York's Madison Square Garden in 1971.

Living In The Material World reached US number 1, as did 'Give Me Love (Give Me Peace On Earth)'. A disastrous US tour was the unfortunate prelude to *Dark Horse* and, his marriage to Patti Boyd now over, the set reflected its creator's depression. Subsequent releases fell short of his initial recordings, but during this period Harrison became involved with his heroes, the Monty Python comedy team, in the successful film *Life Of Brian*. In 1980, his parent label, Warner Brothers Records, rejected the first version of *Somewhere In England*, deeming its content below standard. The reshaped collection included 'All Those Years Ago', Harrison's homage to the murdered John Lennon, which featured contributions from Paul McCartney and **Ringo Starr**. The song reached the US Top 5 when issued as a single. Harrison then pursued other interests, notably with his company Handmade Films, until 1986 when he commenced work on a projected new album. Production was shared with Jeff Lynne, and Harrison's version of Rudy Clark's 'Got My Mind Set On You' reached UK number 2 and US number 1. The intentionally Beatles-influenced 'When We Was Fab' was another major success, while *Cloud Nine* proved equally popular. Harrison also played a pivotal role within the rock 'supergroup' the **Traveling Wilburys**. In 1992, he made his first tour for many years in Japan with long-time friend Eric Clapton giving him support.

Harrison co-operated with his former colleagues in the Beatles' reunion for 1995's *Anthology* series. Treatment for throat cancer cast a shadow over his personal life during the latter part of the decade, and further drama ensued on December 30 1999 when Harrison was repeatedly stabbed attempting to accost a burglar in his home. Rumours of a new album began to circulate before it was confirmed that Harrison had relapsed and was suffering from an inoperable brain tumour. He finally succumbed to the disease in November 2001.

HARRISON, WILBERT

US R&B singer Harrison (b. 1929, d. 1994) first found success in the late 50s with 'Kansas City' (US number 1). A later series of releases included 'Let's Stick Together', revived many years later by **Bryan Ferry**. Harrison continued to record, rather unsuccessfully, throughout the 60s, until 'Let's Work Together' returned him to the public eye. The song ultimately became better known with **Canned Heat**'s hit version. Its originator, meanwhile, made several excellent albums in the wake of his new-found popularity.

HARVEY, ALEX

In 1955, Scottish singer Harvey (b. 1935, d. 1982) joined saxophonist Bill Patrick in a jazz-skiffle band. The unit became the Kansas City Counts, and joined the Ricky Barnes All-Stars as pioneers of Scottish rock 'n' roll. By the end of the decade the group was known as Alex Harvey's (Big) Soul Band. Having cemented popularity in Scotland and the north of England, Harvey moved to Hamburg, where he recorded *Alex Harvey And His Soul Band*, returning to the UK a year later. Harvey dissolved the Soul Band in 1965, looking to pursue a folk-based direction. In 1967 in London, he formed Giant Moth, but the venture was a failure. Harvey took a job in the pit band for the musical *Hair*. In 1969, he released *Roman Wall Blues*, which included 'Midnight Moses', a composition Harvey took to his next outfit, the Sensational Alex Harvey Band. Harvey died in 1982.

HATFIELD, JULIANA

US singer-songwriter Hatfield (b. 1967; guitar) became a favourite of the early 90s indie media. She fronted Blake Babies before releasing a solo album which she has since denounced, finding its revelations embarrassing. Her second collection was more strident and self-assured, and featured Dean Fisher (bass) and Todd Philips (drums) in the Juliana Hatfield Three. Hatfield's breathless vocals were still apparent on 1995's *Only Everything*, which saw her retreat to solo billing. Her record company rejected her next album and this resulted in Hatfield withdrawing from the business. During her brief self-imposed exile she composed the songs that would comprise her new album, *Bed*, which appeared on the Zoe imprint. Since then she has been bursting with creativity and ideas, and in 2000 issued two new albums.

HAVENS, RICHIE

US singer Havens (b. Richard Pierce Havens, 1941) started out in gospel music, but by 1962 he was a popular Greenwich Village folk artist. A black singer in a predominantly white idiom, Havens' early work combined folk material with New York-pop inspired compositions. His soft, gritty voice and distinctive guitar playing revealed a burgeoning talent on *Mixed Bag* and *Something Else Again*. However, he established his reputation by his interpretations of songs by other acts, including the **Beatles** and **Bob Dylan**. Havens opened the Woodstock Festival with a memorable appearance. *Richard P. Havens 1983*, was arguably his artistic apogee, offering several empathic cover versions and some of the singer's finest compositions. He later established an independent label, Stormy Forest, and enjoyed a US Top 20 hit with 'Here Comes The Sun'. A respected painter, writer and sculptor, Havens also enjoys a lucrative career doing voice-overs for US television advertisements.

HAWKINS, RONNIE

US-born Hawkins (b. 1935) first recorded in Canada, producing *Rrrracket Time* with the Ron Hawkins Quartet. In 1959, he reached US number 45 with 'Forty Days' (a version of **Chuck Berry**'s 'Thirty Days'). His version of Young Jessie's 'Mary Lou' then reached US number 26. He became known as Mr. Dynamo and pioneered a dance called the Camel Walk. In 1960, Hawkins became the first rock 'n' roller to involve himself in politics with a plea for a murderer on Death Row, 'The Ballad Of Caryl Chessman' (to no avail). He later formed the Hawks, comprising Levon Helm, Robbie Robertson, Garth Hudson, Richard Manuel and Rick Danko. Their 1963 single of two Bo Diddley songs, 'Bo Diddley' and 'Who Do You Love', was psychedelia before its time. 'Bo Diddley' was a hit in Canada and Hawkins later made the country his home. The Hawks recorded for Atlantic Records, as Levon and the Hawks, before being recruited by **Bob Dylan**, as the **Band**.

Hawkins had later Canadian Top 10 hits with 'Home From The Forest', 'Bluebirds Over The Mountain' and 'Talkin' Silver Cloud Blues'. Hawkins tried acting, with a role in the disastrous movie *Heaven's Gate*. He also appeared in Bob Dylan's Rolling Thunder Revue and played 'Bob Dylan' in the movie *Renaldo And Clara*. In 1985, Hawkins joined **Joni Mitchell**, **Neil Young** and others for the Canadian Band Aid record, 'Tears Are Not Enough', by **Northern Lights**.

HAWKINS, 'SCREAMIN' JAY'

Reportedly raised by Blackfoot Indians, Hawkins (b. Jalacy Hawkins, 1929, d. 2000) became a professional pianist, playing with artists such as James Moody, Lynn Hope and Count Basie. In 1950, he began developing an act based on his almost operatic bass-baritone voice, and in 1956, Hawkins signed with Columbia's reactivated OKeh subsidiary, enjoying enormous success with his manic rendition of 'I Put A Spell On You'. The record sold over a million, becoming a rock classic and invoking hundreds of cover versions. Remaining with OKeh until 1958, Hawkins ran the gamut of his weird-but-wonderful repertoire with recordings of straight R&B songs and the bizarre 'Hong Kong', 'Alligator Wine' and 'There's Something Wrong With You'. Hawkins spent most of the 60s playing one-nighters and making occasional one-off recordings with independent labels. A brace of late-60s albums extended his idiosyncratic reputation. Hawkins continued to record and tour up until his death in February 2000, from an aneurysm following intestine surgery.

HAWKWIND

Founded in a London hippy enclave in the late 60s. Hawkwind – Dave Brock (guitar, vocals), Nik Turner (saxophone, vocals), Mick Slattery (guitar), Dik Mik (electronics), John Harrison (bass) and Terry Ollis (drums) – debuted with *Hawkwind*, produced by Dick Taylor (ex-**Pretty Things**). By 1972, the band comprised Brock, Turner, Del Dettmar (synthesizer), Lemmy (b. Ian Kilmister, 1945; bass), Simon King (drums), Stacia (dancer) and poet/writer Robert Calvert (d. 1988; vocals). Science-fiction writer Michael Moorcock deputized

part-time for Calvert. The band's science-fiction image was apparent in titles like *In Search Of Space* and *Space Ritual*. They enjoyed a freak UK number 3 in 1972 with 'Silver Machine', but this flirtation with a wider audience ended prematurely – 'Urban Guerilla' was hastily withdrawn after terrorist bombs exploded in London.

Hawkwind lost impetus in 1975 when Lemmy was fired after an arrest on drugs charges during a US tour – he subsequently formed **Motörhead**. Following the release of *Astounding Sounds, Amazing Music*, Turner was fired. Later additions Paul Rudolph, Alan Powell and Simon House also left. House joined **David Bowie**'s band and Brock, Calvert and King became the Hawklords. By 1979, they had reverted to Hawkwind and Calvert had gone solo. Dave Brock remained at the helm and new players included Huw Lloyd Langton (a guitarist on the band's debut album) and Tim Blake (synthesizer) and Alan Davey (bass). Nik Turner also reappeared.

In 1990, Hawkwind's UK popularity resurged with the growth of rave culture. *Space Bandits* reflected this new interest. It also saw the return of Simon House and the inclusion of their first female vocalist, Bridgett Wishart. Eventually reduced to a three-piece (Brock, Davey and drummer Richard Chadwick), the band became totally dance-orientated.

HAYES, ISAAC

Hayes (b. 1942) played piano and organ for several Memphis groups and recorded a few singles. In 1964, he attracted the attention of Stax Records. After session work with **Mar-Keys** saxophonist Floyd Newman, Hayes remained as a stand-in for **Booker T. Jones**. He then began songwriting with David Porter, enjoying success with **Sam And Dave**'s 'Hold On I'm Comin'' and writing for Carla Thomas and Johnnie Taylor. The remarkable *Hot Buttered Soul* established Hayes' reputation as a solo artist, but *The Isaac Hayes Movement*, *To Be Continued* and *Black Moses* were less satisfying. *Shaft* was a highly successful film soundtrack released in 1971, and its theme became an international hit single.

Hayes left Stax in 1975 following a row over royalties, setting up his Hot Buttered Soul label. Declared bankrupt in 1976, he moved to Polydor Records and then Spring Records. In 1981, he retired for five years before re-emerging with 'Ike's Rap', (US R&B Top 10). Although trumpeted as a return to form, Hayes' mid-90s albums for Pointblank Records indicated little progress. Hayes achieved cult status in the late 90s by playing Chef in the

cartoon series *South Park*. A caricature of his own loverman style, the character even returned Hayes to the top of the charts when the ribald novelty item 'Chocolate Salty Balls' reached UK number 1 in 1998.

HEALEY, JEFF

Blind since he was a year old, Canadian-born Healey (b. 1966) is a proficient multi-instrumentalist, white blues-rock guitarist and singer. In 1985, he played with Texas bluesman Albert Collins, who introduced him to Stevie Ray Vaughan. The Jeff Healey Band – Joe Rockman (bass, vocals) and Tom Stephen (drums) – was formed the same year. They released singles and videos on their own Forte label, before signing to Arista Records in 1988. *See The Light* sold nearly two million copies and a world tour followed. *Hell To Pay* tended towards hard rock and **Mark Knopfler**, **George Harrison**, **Jeff Lynne** and Bobby Whitlock guested. *Feel This* was a strong and energetic rock/blues album, while *Cover To Cover* was a collection of favourite songs by some of Healey's mentors. After a long gap Healey returned with the reassuringly blistering *Get Me Some* in 2000.

HEAR'SAY

The vocal group was created by the UK version of the globally successful 'reality TV' show *Popstars*, which adapted the concept of the original New Zealand show, but elected to create a mixed-sex act. The lucky five winners, who by this point had already recorded their Polydor Records debut with the aid of leading production/writing teams Stargate and Steelworks, were announced at the start of February 2001 as Myleene Klass (b. 1978), Suzanne Shaw (b. 1981), Noel Sullivan (b. 1980), Kimberley Marsh (b. 1976), and Danny Foster (b. 1979). The quintet played their first gig on Saturday March 10 at London's Astoria. Two days later they released 'Pure And Simple', which became the fastest-selling UK debut single since records began. Their debut album followed 'Pure And Simple' to number 1. The quintet's second single, 'The Way To Your Love', went straight to the top of the UK charts in July. A second album was rush-released later in the year in an attempt to target the lucrative Christmas market. Poor sales and internal friction prompted the departure of Marsh in January 2002. Johnny Shentall (b. Doncaster, England) beat 4,500 hopefuls in the auditions to replace her.

HEART

US rock band featuring sisters Ann (b. 1951) and Nancy Wilson (b. 1954). Ann released two singles on a local label in 1967. After a series of unreleased demos she and Nancy left for Canada, where they were joined by Steve Fossen (bass) and Roger Fisher (guitar). Michael Derosier (drums) joined later. After *Dreamboat Annie* on Mushroom Records, their second single, 'Crazy On You', brought public attention. Shortly afterwards, *Little Queen* and 'Barracuda' charted in the US. When his relationship with Nancy soured, Roger Fisher left the band. The guitar parts were covered on tour by Nancy and multi-instrumentalist Howard Leese, who became permanent. By *Private Audition*, Fossen and Derosier were also on the verge of departure, replaced by Mark Andes (ex-Spirit) and Denny Carmassi. Heart was waning, although temporarily bolstered by 'Almost Paradise ... Love Theme From Footloose' (US number 7).

In 1985, Heart joined Capitol Records, resulting in an image transformation. *Heart* reached US number 1, including 'What About Love', 'Never' and 'These Dreams' (US number 1). *Bad Animals* reached US number 2. *Brigade* included 'All I Wanna Do Is Make Love To You' (US number 1).

Both sisters then became involved in solo projects, while former companions Fossen, Roger Fisher and Derosier embarked on a new dual career with Alias. The sisters returned as Heart in 1993, backed by Schuyler Deale (bass), John Purdell (keyboards), Denny Carmassi (drums) and Howard Lease (guitar). The hit 'Will You Be There (In The Morning)' preceded *Desire Walks On*. *The Road Home*, an acoustic live album produced by John Paul Jones, marked their 20th anniversary. Nancy Wilson has subsequently been kept busy with her soundtrack work, providing instrumental scores for her husband Cameron Crowe's movies *Jerry Maguire*, *Almost Famous* and *Vanilla Sky*.

HEARTBREAKERS

Formed in New York in 1975. Richard Hell (b. Richard Meyers, 1949; bass, ex-Television) joined disaffected New York Dolls Johnny Thunders (b. Johnny Anthony Genzale Jnr., 1952, d. 1991; guitar, vocals) and Jerry Nolan (d. 1992; drums). Walter Lure (guitar, vocals) joined later. They enjoyed cult popularity and, when Hell left (replaced by Billy Rath), they moved to London and the punk scene. They supported the **Sex Pistols** on the 1976 Anarchy tour, signed to Track Records and released 'Chinese Rocks', a paean to heroin co-written by Dee Dee Ramone. **L.A.M.F.** indicated the band's strengths, but was marred by unfocused production. The Heartbreakers split in 1977, re-forming in 1978 with drummer Ty Styx. The name was dropped and resurrected several times, until Thunders was found dead in April 1991.

HEATWAVE

Although based in Britain, Heatwave was formed by Johnnie and Keith Wilder after they left the US Army. They recruited songwriter Rod Temperton, Eric Johns, Jessie Whitten, Ernest Berger and Mario Mantese. Between 1977 and 1981 they enjoyed a series of transatlantic hits, including 'Boogie Nights', 'Always And Forever' and 'Mind Blowing Decisions'. Temperton left in 1977 to concentrate on songwriting, and Heatwave's progress was marred by a series of tragedies: Whitten was stabbed to death; Mantese left after a severe car crash; and Johnnie Wilder was paralyzed as a result of another road accident. Courageously, he remained at the helm, producing and singing in the studio. Vocalist J. D. Nicholas, took his place on stage. However, Heatwave were unable to endure and in 1984 Nicholas left for the **Commodores**.

HEAVEN 17

An offshoot from the UK production company BEF, this synth-pop trio was formed by Ian Craig Marsh (b. 1956), Martyn Ware (b. 1956) and vocalist Glenn Gregory (b. 1958). '(We Don't Need This) Fascist Groove Thang' reached UK number 45 in 1981 and *Penthouse And Pavement* was a bestseller. 'Temptation', featuring guest vocalist Carol Kenyon, was a UK Top 10 hit in 1983. Predominantly a studio group, a series of albums followed. Meanwhile, the band's production services were still in demand, with Ware co-producing **Terence Trent D'Arby**'s bestselling *The Hardline According To Terence Trent D'Arby*. In 1996, they surprised the market by re-forming and recording a new studio album.

HELL, RICHARD

Hell (b. Richard Meyers, 1949) embodied the New York punk genre. In 1971, he founded the Neon Boys with guitarist Tom Verlaine, and first performed several of his best-known songs, including 'Love Comes In Spurts', in this group. The group subsequently became **Television** – Hell's torn clothing inspired Malcolm McLaren's ideas for the **Sex Pistols**. Hell left in 1975 and formed the **Heartbreakers** with Johnny Thunders and drummer Jerry Nolan. He reappeared in 1976 fronting Richard Hell And The Voidoids, with guitarists Bob Quine and Ivan Julian and drummer Marc Bell. Their debut EP appeared later that year, gaining the group underground popularity. 'Blank Generation' achieved anthem-like proportions as an apposite description of punk. A version

of the song became the title track of the Voidoids' dazzling debut album, which also featured 'Another World' and a fiery interpretation of John Fogerty's 'Walk Upon The Water'. *Blank Generation* is one of punk's definitive statements.

Hell later issued the **Nick Lowe**-produced 'The Kid With The Replaceable Head', followed by an EP and then *Destiny Street*. Quine returned, joined by **Material** drummer Fred Maher. Once again Hell withdrew from recording, opting for film work, notably Susan Seidelman's *Smithereens*. Sporadic live appearances continued, followed by *Funhunt*, a composite of three Voidoid line-ups. In 1991, Hell resumed recording in the Dim Stars, joined by Thurston Moore and Steve Shelley (**Sonic Youth**) and Don Fleming (Gumball). He subsequently concentrated on spoken-word performances and writing. His novel *Go Now* was published in 1996.

HELLOWEEN

Formed in 1984 in Hamburg, Germany and comprising Kai Hansen (guitar, vocals), Michael Weikath (guitar), Markus Grosskopf (bass) and Ingo Schwichenburg (drums). *Death Metal* was followed by *Helloween*, *Walls Of Jericho* and an EP, *Judas*. The band gained a strong following with their unique blend of high-speed power metal. After *Judas*, vocalist/frontman Michael Kiske joined. *Keeper Of The Seven Keys Part I* took a much more melodic approach. Helloween toured Europe, building a sizeable following. Hansen was then replaced by Roland Grapow. A protracted legal battle with their record company kept them out of action until 1990. They finally signed to EMI Records where *Pink Bubbles Go Ape* showed up the loss of Hansen. Kiske was dismissed, as was Ingo Schwichenberg. Andi Deris (vocals) and Ulli Kusch (drums) replaced them in time for *The Master Of The Rings*, their most successful album for several years. The band has continued to record for the Raw Power label.

HENDRIX, JIMI

Self-taught (left-handed with a right-handed guitar), Hendrix (b. Johnny Allen Hendrix, 1942, d. 1970) joined several Seattle R&B bands while still at school, before enlisting as a paratrooper. He began working with various touring revues backing, among others, **Sam Cooke** and the **Valentinos**.

In 1965, Hendrix joined struggling soul singer Curtis Knight in New York, signing a punitive contract with Knight's manager, Ed Chalpin. In 1966, Hendrix, now calling himself Jimmy James, formed a quartet which featured future **Spirit** member Randy California. They were appearing at the Cafe Wha? in Greenwich Village when Chas Chandler recognized Hendrix's extraordinary talent. Chandler persuaded Hendrix to go to London, and became his co-manager in partnership with Mike Jeffries (aka Jeffreys). Auditions for a suitable backing group yielded Noel Redding (b. 1945; bass) and John 'Mitch' Mitchell (b. 1947; drums). The Jimi Hendrix Experience debuted in France in October 1966. Back in England they released their first single, 'Hey Joe' (UK Top 10), in December. The dynamic follow-up was 'Purple Haze'. Exceptional live appearances characterized by distortion, feedback, sheer volume and Hendrix's flamboyant stage persona enhanced the group's reputation. The Experience completed an astonishing debut album. *Axis: Bold As Love* revealed a new lyrical capability, notably in the title track and the jazz-influenced 'Up From The Skies'. It completed an artistically and commercially triumphant year. Hendrix grew tired of the wild-man image however, and the last official Experience album, *Electric Ladyland*, was released in October. This extravagant double set featured contributions from Chris Wood and Steve Winwood (both Traffic) and Jack Casady (**Jefferson Airplane**), and included two UK hits, 'The Burning Of The Midnight Lamp' and 'All Along The Watchtower' – amazingly **Bob Dylan** later adopted Hendrix's interpretation.

Hendrix's life was becoming problematic – he was arrested in Toronto for possessing heroin; Chas Chandler had withdrawn from the managerial partnership and Redding and Hendrix now had irreconcilable differences. The Experience played its final concert on 29 June 1969; Hendrix subsequently formed Gypsies Sons And Rainbows with Mitchell, Billy Cox (bass), Larry Lee (rhythm guitar), Juma Sultan and Jerry Velez (both percussion). This short-lived unit closed the Woodstock Festival, during which Hendrix performed his famed rendition of the 'Star-Spangled Banner'. In October he formed an all-black group, Band Of Gypsies, with Cox and drummer Buddy Miles, intending to accentuate the African-American dimension in his music. The trio's potential was marred by pedestrian drumming and unimaginative compositions, and they split after a mere three concerts. Hendrix started work on *First Rays Of The New Rising Sun* (finally released in 1997), and later resumed performing with Cox and Mitchell.

On 18 September 1970, his girlfriend, Monika Danneman, was unable to wake Hendrix. An ambulance was called, but he was pronounced dead on arrival at hospital. The inquest recorded an open verdict, with death caused by suffocation due to inhalation of vomit. Two posthumous releases, *Cry Of Love* and *Rainbow Bridge*, mixed portions of the artist's final recordings with masters from earlier sources. Many guitarists have imitated his technique; few have mastered it and none have matched his skill. Litigation regarding ownership

of his recordings was finally resolved in 1997, when the Hendrix family won back the rights from Alan Douglas.

HENLEY, DON

Drummer and vocalist Henley (b. 1947) started out with country-rock units Four Speeds and Felicity. They completed an album under producer **Kenny Rogers**, but split up when Henley joined **Linda Ronstadt**'s touring band. This group formed the basis for the **Eagles**. Henley's distinctive voice took lead on most of this highly successful band's songs, many of which he co-composed.

When the Eagles broke up, Henley brought out *I Can't Stand Still*. 'Leather And Lace', a duet with **Stevie Nicks**, reached the US Top 10 in 1981. A songwriting partnership with guitarist Danny Kortchmar resulted in several compositions, including 'Dirty Laundry' (1982, US number 3). *Building The Perfect Beast* proved highly popular, attaining platinum status in 1985 and spawning two US Top 10 singles in 'The Boys Of Summer' and 'All She Wants To Do Is Dance'. Henley's songwriting skills were demonstrated by *The End Of The Innocence*, and in 1992 his duet with Patty Smyth 'Sometimes Love Just Ain't Enough' reached US number 2. By 1994, Henley was back with the Eagles, although he has continued to work as a solo artist.

HERD

UK band formed in 1965. Terry Clark (vocals), Andy Bown (bass, vocals, organ), Gary Taylor (guitar) and Tony Chapman (drums) were later joined by guitarist **Peter Frampton** (b. 1950). In 1967, new songwriting managers Ken Howard and Alan Blaikley promoted the reluctant Frampton to centre stage. The psychedelic 'I Can Fly' was followed by *Orpheus In The Underworld*, a UK Top 10 hit. After Virgil, Howard And Blaikley tackled Milton with 'Paradise Lost'. The Herd were marketed for teenzine consumption, with Frampton voted the 'Face of '68' by *Rave* magazine. A more straightforward hit followed with 'I Don't Want Our Loving To Die', and Howard and Blaikley were dropped in favour of Andrew Loog Oldham. Their next single, 'Sunshine Cottage', missed by a mile. Yet another manager, Harvey Lisberg, came to nothing and Frampton left to form **Humble Pie**. For a brief period, the remaining members struggled on, but to no avail.

HERMAN'S HERMITS

UK group Herman's Hermits were discovered in 1963 by manager Harvey Lisberg and his partner Charlie Silverman. The line-up emerged as Peter Noone (b. 1947; vocals), Karl Green (b. 1947; bass), Keith Hopwood (b. 1946; rhythm guitar), Lek Leckenby (b. Derek Leckenby, 1946, d. 1994; lead guitar) and Barry Whitwam (b. 1946; drums). A link with producer Mickie Most and an infectious cover of Earl Jean's 'I'm Into Something Good' brought a UK number 1 in 1964. By early 1965, the group had settled into covering 50s songs such as the Rays' 'Silhouettes' and **Sam Cooke**'s 'Wonderful World', when an extraordinary invasion of America saw them challenge the **Beatles**, selling over 10 million records in under 12 months. A non-stop stream of hits over the next two years transformed them into teen idols. Director Sam Katzman even cast them in the films *When The Boys Meet The Girls* (co-starring Connie Francis) and *Hold On!*. The hits continued until as late as 1970 when Noone finally decided to pursue a solo career. Although a reunion concert did take place at Madison Square Garden in New York in 1973, stage replacements for Noone were later employed.

HEYWARD, NICK

Heyward (b. 1961) left **Haircut 100**, in 1982, to go solo. 'Whistle Down The Wind' and 'Take That Situation' (both 1983) were similar to the style of his former band. His debut album, *North Of A Miracle*, (including 'Blue Hat For A Blue Day') won critical approval and sold well. In 1988 'You're My World' and *I Love You Avenue* failed to reach the mainstream and Heyward concentrated on his second career, graphic art. He has continued to record pleasant solo material for a small but loyal audience.

HIATT, JOHN

American singer, guitarist and songwriter, John Hiatt's (b. 1952) material has been recorded by various acts, including **Dr. Feelgood**, the **Searchers**, **Iggy Pop**, **Bob Dylan**, **Nick Lowe** and **Rick Nelson**. Hiatt started out in local R&B bands and in 1970 he signed to Epic Records, recording two albums. He left and toured solo before signing to MCA Records for two further albums. In 1980, **Ry Cooder** took him on as guitarist in his band. He played on *Borderline* and several subsequent albums and tours. Hiatt's solo album, *All Of A Sudden*, was produced by Tony Visconti and Nick Lowe. Lowe played regularly with Hiatt's band and the duo became half of a new 'supergroup' with Cooder and Jim Keltner in Little Village. Hiatt's songwriting reputation has since grown and his own recent recorded output has included two of his best albums, *Perfectly Good Guitar* and *Crossing Muddy Waters*.

HICKS, DAN

American-born former folk musician, Hicks (b. 1941) joined the **Charlatans** in 1965, replacing original drummer Sam Linde. Hicks swapped the drumkit for guitar, vocals and composing before establishing a new group, Dan Hicks And His Hot Licks, with David LaFlamme (violin) and Bill Douglas (bass). Within months, the group had reshaped around Sid Page (violin), Jaime Leopold (bass) John Weber (guitar) and singers Christina Viola Gancher and Sherri Snow. *Original Recordings* drew on country, 30s vocal jazz and quirky, deadpan humour, and included 'I Scare Myself', later revived by Thomas Dolby. Weber, Gancher and Snow dropped out, replaced by Maryann Price and Naomi Ruth Eisenberg. *Where's The Money*, recorded live at the Los Angeles Troubadour, *Striking It Rich*, with John Girton on guitar, and *Last Train To Hicksville ... The Home Of Happy Feet* completed their catalogue before Hicks went solo. During the 80s Hicks formed the Acoustic Warriors with James 'Fingers' Shupe (fiddle, mandolin) and Alex Baum (bass), with whom he continued his unique vision over the following decade. He returned to the Hot Licks band format in 2000, with the release of *Beatin' The Heat*.

HIGH LLAMAS

Formed in London, England by former **Microdisney** guitarist Sean O'Hagan. O'Hagan spent three years incubating the High Llamas' debut album. Though a low-profile release, it received several encouraging reviews. A second High Llamas album, 1994's *Gideon Gaye*, was produced on a budget of just £4,000 and released on the independent label Target Records. Again, the critical response was encouraging, enticing Sony Records to offer O'Hagan a contract. Further melodic, winsome and fresh-sounding albums have followed. *Lollo Rosso* concentrated on O'Hagan's fascination with electronica.

HILL, FAITH

Raised in the small town of Star, Mississippi, USA, this country singer (b. Audrey Faith Perry, 1967) was singing at family gatherings from the age of three. Her sparkling debut US country single, the rocking 'Wild One', topped the country charts and she followed it with a version of **Janis Joplin**'s 'Piece Of My Heart'. *Take Me As I Am* was successful, but surgery on her vocal cords delayed the making of *It Matters To Me*. The title track was a further US country chart topper in 1996. The following year, she recorded with her husband **Tim McGraw**, resulting in the number 1 hit and Country Music Association Award-winning 'It's Your Love'. The following year's *Faith* broke into the US Top 10, while the poppy 'This Kiss' climbed steadily to a peak position of 7 on the US Hot 100. The chart-topping *Breathe* followed in the footsteps of the previous album in terms of enormous success. In 2001, Hill's 'There You'll Be' was featured in the end credits of *Pearl Harbor*.

HILL, LAURYN

The multi-talented Hill (b. 1975) originally balanced an acting career which included a cameo in the Whoopi Goldberg vehicle *Sister Act 2: Back In The Habit* with her degree course and membership of the highly successful **Fugees**. Hill began work on her self-produced debut after giving birth to a son by Rohan Marley, and writing for **Aretha Franklin**'s 1998 comeback set *A Rose Is Not A Rose*. The highly acclaimed *The Miseducation Of Lauryn Hill* was released in September 1998, and was a worldwide bestseller. The lead-off singles, 'Doo Wop (That Thing)' (US number 1) and 'Ex-Factor', showcased

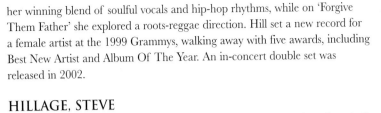

her winning blend of soulful vocals and hip-hop rhythms, while on 'Forgive Them Father' she explored a roots-reggae direction. Hill set a new record for a female artist at the 1999 Grammys, walking away with five awards, including Best New Artist and Album Of The Year. An in-concert double set was released in 2002.

HILLAGE, STEVE

Guitarist Hillage (b. 1951) played with Uriel in 1967 alongside Mont Campbell (bass), Clive Brooks (drums) and Dave Stewart (organ) (the latter trio carried on as Egg). In 1971, Hillage formed Khan with Nick Greenwood (bass), Eric Peachey (drums) and Dick Henningham, before moving on to Gong. Hillage released his first solo album, *Fish Rising*, in 1975, and began his writing partnership with long-time girlfriend Miquette Giraudy.

In the 80s, Hillage moved into production, including albums by **Robyn Hitchcock** and **Simple Minds**. In 1991 he returned to recording and live performance as leader of System 7, producing ambient dance music.

HITCHCOCK, ROBYN

UK-born Hitchcock (b. 1953) made his early reputation with the post-punk psychedelic group the **Soft Boys**. After they split in 1981 he wrote for **Captain Sensible**, before forming the Egyptians, around erstwhile colleagues Andy Metcalfe (bass), Morris Windsor (drums) and Roger Jackson (keyboards). Hitchcock's predilection for the bizarre revealed itself in titles such as 'Man With The Light Bulb Head', 'My Wife And My Dead Wife', and 'Uncorrected Personality Traits'. A move to A&M Records saw the release of *Globe Of Frogs*, which included 'Ballroom Man', a US college-radio favourite. Despite a devoted UK cult following, Hitchcock spent the early 90s concentrating on the United States (occasionally guesting with **R.E.M.**). He has also re-formed the Soft Boys and continues to release albums. In 1998, cult director Jonathan Demme filmed Hitchcock playing live in a New York department store window, later released as *Storefront Hitchcock*.

HOLE

Courtney Love (b. 1965; vocals, guitar) joined an ill-fated Sugar Baby Doll (with **L7**'s Jennifer Finch and Kat Bjelland), then a formative line-up of Bjelland's **Babes In Toyland**. In Los Angeles, she formed Hole with Caroline Rue (drums), Jill Emery (bass) and Eric Erlandson (guitar). The band's singles 'Retard Girl', 'Dicknail', and 'Teenage Whore', and favourable UK press coverage helped make Hole one of the most promising new hardcore groups of 1991. Their debut album, produced by Don Fleming and Kim Gordon (**Sonic Youth**), was followed by massive exposure supporting Mudhoney throughout Europe – with Love achieving notoriety as the first woman musician to 'trash' her guitar on stage in the UK. In 1992, Emery and Rue left the group, the same year that Love married **Nirvana** singer/guitarist Kurt Cobain. Cobain's suicide on the eve of the release of *Live Through This* practically obliterated the impact of Hole's new set, despite another startling collection of songs written with intellect as well as invective. Replacements for Emery and Rue had been found in Kristen Pfaff (bass) and Patty Schemel (drums), though Pfaff was found dead from a heroin overdose shortly after the album's release, and just two months after Cobain's death. She was replaced by Melissa Auf der Maur for Hole's 1994–95 tour, including dates in Australasia and Europe. Again Love dominated headlines with her stage behaviour. In 1997 she moved back into acting with a starring role in *The People Vs Larry Flynt*. The long-awaited *Celebrity Skin* lacked the raw abrasiveness of *Live Through This*. Auf der Maur left the band the following year to join the **Smashing Pumpkins**.

HOLLAND/DOZIER/HOLLAND

Brothers Eddie Holland (b. 1939) and Brian Holland (b. 1941), with Lamont Dozier (b. 1941) formed one of the most successful composing and production teams in popular music history. All three were prominent in the Detroit R&B scene from the mid-50s Brian Holland as lead singer with the Satintones, Eddie with the Fideltones, and Dozier with the Romeos. By the early 60s they had all become part of Berry Gordy's Motown Records concern, working as performers and as writers/arrangers. After masterminding the **Marvelettes'** 1961 smash 'Please Mr Postman', Brian and Eddie formed a production team with Freddy Gorman. In 1963, Gorman was replaced by Dozier. Over the next five years they wrote and produced records by almost all the major Motown artists, among them a dozen US number 1s. Their earliest successes came with **Marvin Gaye**, for whom they wrote 'Can I Get A Witness?', 'Little Darling', 'How Sweet It Is (To Be Loved By You)' and 'You're A Wonderful One', and **Martha And The Vandellas**, who had hits with 'Heatwave', 'Quicksand', 'Nowhere To Run' and 'Jimmy Mack'.

These achievements, however, paled alongside the team's run of success with the **Supremes**. Ordered by Berry Gordy to construct vehicles for the wispy vocal talents of **Diana Ross**, they produced 'Where Did Our Love Go?', a simplistic but irresistible slice of lightweight pop-soul. The record reached US number 1, as did its successors, 'Baby Love', 'Come See About Me', 'Stop! In The Name Of Love' and 'Back In My Arms Again'. Holland/ Dozier/Holland produced and wrote a concurrent series of hits for the **Four Tops**. 'Baby I Need Your Loving' and 'I Can't Help Myself' illustrated their stylish way with up-tempo material; '(It's The) Same Old Song' was a self-mocking riposte to critics of their sound, while 'Reach Out, I'll Be There', a worldwide number 1, pioneered what came to be known as 'symphonic soul'. The trio also found success with the **Miracles**, Kim Weston, and the **Isley Brothers**.

In 1967 they split from Berry Gordy and Motown. Legal disputes officially kept them out of the studio for several years, but they launched their own Invictus and Hot Wax labels in 1968. Hits by artists such as the **Chairmen Of The Board** and Freda Payne successfully mined the familiar vein of the trio's Motown hits, but business difficulties and personal conflicts gradually wore down the partnership in the early 70s, and in 1973 Dozier left to forge a solo career. Invictus and Hot Wax were dissolved a couple of years later. Occasional reunions by the trio have failed to rekindle their former artistic fires.

HOLLIES

Friends Allan Clarke (b. Harold Allan Clarke, 1942; vocals), and Graham Nash (b. 1942; vocals, guitar) had been singing together for a number of years in Manchester, England, when they added Eric Haydock (b. 1942; bass) and Don Rathbone (drums), to become the Fourtones and then the Deltas in 1962. With local guitar hero Tony Hicks (b. 1945) they became the Hollies, and were signed to the **Beatles'** label, Parlophone Records. Their first two singles, covers of the

Coasters '(Ain't That) Just Like Me' and 'Searchin'', both made the UK charts. Rathbone was replaced by Bobby Elliott (b. 1942) on their first album. This and their second album contained most of their live act and stayed in the UK charts, while a train of hit singles continued from 1963–74. Infectious, well-produced hits such as Doris Troy's 'Just One Look', 'Here I Go Again' and the sublime 'Yes I Will' all contained their trademark soaring harmonies.

As their career progressed, Clarke, Hicks and Nash developed into a strong songwriting team, and wrote most of their own b-sides (under the pseudonym L. Ransford). On their superb third collection, **Hollies** (1965), their talents blossomed with 'Too Many People'. Their first UK number 1 was 'I'm Alive' (1965), followed within weeks by Graham Gouldman's 'Look Through Any Window'. Early in 1966, the group enjoyed their second number 1, 'I Can't Let Go', which topped the *New Musical Express* chart jointly with the **Walker Brothers'** 'The Sun Ain't Gonna Shine Anymore'.

Haydock was sacked in 1966 and replaced by Bernie Calvert (b. 1942). The Hollies success continued unabated with Graham Gouldman's 'Bus Stop', the exotic 'Stop Stop Stop' and the poppier 'On A Carousel' and 'Carrie-Anne', all UK Top 5 hits and, finally, major hits in the USA. The Hollies embraced 'flower power' with *For Certain Because* and *Evolution*. Inexplicably, the excellent *Butterfly* (1967) failed to make either the US or UK charts. The following year, during the proposals to make *Hollies Sing Dylan*, Nash announced his departure for **Crosby, Stills And Nash**. His replacement was Terry Sylvester (b. 1947) of the Escorts. Clarke, devastated by Nash's departure, went solo after seven further hits, including 'He Ain't Heavy, He's My Brother'. The band soldiered on with the strange induction of Mikael Rickfors (b. 1948) from Sweden.

Clarke returned to celebrate the worldwide hit 'The Air That I Breathe', composed by Albert Hammond. In 1981, Sylvester and Calvert left the band, but a Stars On 45-type segued single, 'Holliedaze', was a hit and Graham Nash was flown over for the television promotion. This reunion prompted *What Goes Around*, which made the US charts. The stable line-up in the 90s featured Clarke, Elliott, Coates, Hicks and Ray Stiles. In 1993, the Hollies were given an Ivor Novello award to honour their contribution to British music. In March 2000, Carl Wayne (b. 1943; ex-**Move**) replaced Clarke.

HOLLOWAY, BRENDA

US singer Holloway (b. 1946) began her recording career in the early 60s, with producer Hal Davis. In 1964 she was spotted by a Motown Records talent scout and signed to the label later that year. Her debut, 'Every Little Bit Hurts', established her bluesy soul style, and was covered by the **Spencer Davis Group** in Britain. She enjoyed further success with 'I'll Always Love You' (1964), 'When I'm Gone' and 'Operator' (both 1965), and played on the **Beatles'** 1965 US tour. After subsequent singles, Holloway began to devote more time to songwriting with her sister Patrice, and Motown staff producer Frank Wilson, producing her 1968 single 'You've Made Me So Very Happy'. In 1968, Holloway's contract with Motown was terminated. She released a gospel album in 1983 and, in 1989, teamed with **Jimmy Ruffin** for a duet, 'On The Rebound'.

HOLLY, BUDDY

Holly (b. Charles Hardin Holley, 1936, d. 1959) was one of the first major rock 'n' roll groundbreakers, and one of its most influential artists. Holly's musical influences included both C&W music and 'race' music, or R&B. He made his first stage appearance aged five in a talent contest with his brothers; he won $5. During his Texan childhood, Holly learned to play guitar, violin and piano; in 1949 formed a bluegrass duo, Buddy And Bob, with friend Bob Montgomery.

In 1952, Buddy And Bob added Larry Welborn (bass) and were given their own radio programme, *The Buddy And Bob Show*, performing country material with occasional R&B songs. KDAV disc jockey Hipockets Duncan became the trio's manager. Further recording took place at KDAV, but no material was released. In 1954 the trio added fiddler Sonny Curtis and steel guitarist Don Guess to the group and made more recordings. That year the group, now including drummer Jerry Allison, opened concerts for **Bill Haley And His Comets** and **Elvis Presley** in Texas.

After a false start with Decca Records, Holly formed the Crickets with Allison and Niki Sullivan on rhythm guitar. On 25 February 1957, a rock 'n' roll version of Holly's 'That'll Be The Day' was recorded. The song was a revelation, containing one of the most gripping vocals and distinctive galloping riffs of any 50s record. Joe B. Mauldin joined as the Crickets' bass player following those sessions. The song was issued by Brunswick Records and with Norman Petty now as manager, the single underwent heavy promotion and reached US and UK number 1 in 1957. As the record was released, the Crickets performed at such venues as New York's Apollo Theatre and the Howard Theater in Washington, D.C., winning mostly-black audiences.

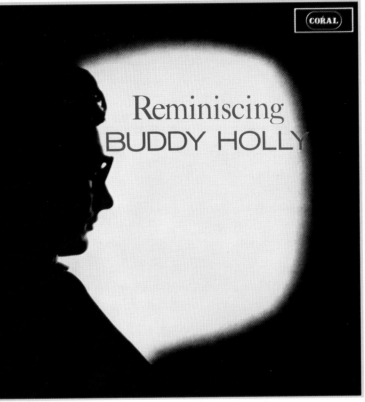

The group recorded prolifically in 1957, including classics like 'Words Of Love', 'Maybe Baby', 'Not Fade Away', 'Everyday', 'Peggy Sue' and 'Oh Boy'. Holly was innovative in the studio, making much use of new production techniques. Brunswick continued to issue recordings under the Crickets' name while Holly signed on as a solo artist to Coral Records, although most releases featured the entire group, often with other musicians and vocal group, the Picks. Holly and the Crickets only charted 11 times in the USA during their brief career and no albums charted during Holly's lifetime.

In early 1957, the Crickets recorded, then toured Australia for six days, followed by a UK tour. 'Maybe Baby' became the fourth Holly/Crickets single to chart in the USA, reaching number 17 (UK number 4). The group returned to the USA and immediately headed out on a US tour assembled by disc jockey Alan Freed, also featuring such popular artists as **Jerry Lee Lewis** and **Chuck Berry**. Coral released the frantic 'Rave On' in May and although it reached only number 37 in the USA, it made number 5 in the UK. Following the tour, Holly recorded two songs written by Bobby Darin without the Crickets; they remained unreleased but signalled an impending split between Holly and the group. While in New York Holly met Maria Elena Santiago, whom he married two months later. During that summer Holly recorded 'Heartbeat', 'Love's Made A Fool Of You' and 'Wishing'. Guitarist Tommy Allsup played on the latter two and was subsequently asked to join the Crickets.

Holly and the Crickets toured the US and Canada during October, by which time there was apparently friction between the Hollys and the Pettys. Buddy and Maria Holly travelled apart from the group between dates. After the trip, Holly announced to manager/producer Petty that he was leaving him; to Holly's surprise the other Crickets chose to leave Holly and stay with Petty. Holly allowed them use of the group's name and they continued to record without him. Meanwhile, Holly, producer Dick Jacobs and studio musicians (including a string section) recorded 'True Love Ways', 'It Doesn't Matter Anymore' (written by **Paul Anka**), 'Raining In My

Heart' and 'Moondreams'. They were held for later release while 'It's So Easy' was issued; it failed to chart in the US. 'Heartbeat' was issued in December and became the last Holly single to chart in the US during his lifetime. The superb 'It Doesn't Matter Anymore' was released posthumously and provided Holly with his only UK number 1.

In January 1959, he began assembling a band to take on the 'Winter Dance Party' tour of the US Midwest. Allsup was hired on guitar, Waylon Jennings on bass and Carl Bunch on drums. They were billed as the Crickets, despite the agreement to give Holly's former band mates that name. Also starring **Ritchie Valens**, the **Big Bopper**, **Dion** And The Belmonts and unknown Frankie Sardo, the tour began January 23 1959 in Milwaukee, Wisconsin. Following a February 2 date in Clear Lake, Iowa, Holly, Valens and the Big Bopper chartered a small plane to take them to the next date in Moorhead, Minnesota. The plane crashed minutes after take-off, killing all three stars and the pilot.

Holly's popularity increased after his death, even as late as the 80s, previously unreleased material was still being issued. In 1962, Norman Petty took some demos Holly had recorded at home in 1958 and had the instrumental group the **Fireballs** play along to them, creating new Buddy Holly records from the unfinished tapes. In 1965, *Holly In The Hills*, comprising the early Buddy And Bob radio station recordings, was released and charted in the UK. Compilation albums also charted in both the USA and the UK, as late as the 70s. During the 70s the publishing rights to Holly's song catalogue were purchased by **Paul McCartney**, who began sponsoring annual Buddy Holly Week celebrations. A 1978 film, *The Buddy Holly Story*, and a musical play *Buddy*, also commemorated his life.

HOLLYWOOD ARGYLES

In 1960 the single 'Alley-Oop' hit US number 1. It was written by Dallas Frazier, produced by Bobby Rey and featured Gary S. Paxton on vocals. At the time Paxton, part of Skip And Flip, was contracted to Brent Records, while his single was issued on Lute Records – Hollywood Argyles was created, including Paxton, Rey, Ted Marsh, Gary Webb, Deary Weaver and Ted Winters. Further singles by the Hollywood Argyles, on such labels as Paxley (co-owned by Paxton and producer Kim Fowley), failed to reach the charts.

HOLMES, DAVID

This leading Irish DJ, remixer, recording artist and soundtrack composer is a former member of the Disco Evangelists. An enormously popular DJ, Holmes found time to collaborate with former Dub Federation musicians Andy Ellison and Pete Latham as one third of the Scubadevils. He has also recorded as the Well Charged Latinos ('Latin Prayer') and 4 Boy 1 Girl Action ('Hawaiian Death Stomp'). His debut album emerged in 1995, with Sarah Cracknell (**Saint Etienne**) contributing to the quasi-James Bond theme, 'Gone', while elsewhere Holmes luxuriated in the possibilities of the long-playing format by incorporating cinematic elements, Celtic flavours and ambient guitar (provided by **Steve Hillage**). The excellent follow-up, *Let's Get Killed*, expanded on the debut's sound, and provided enough of a breakthrough for Holmes to place two singles, 'Don't Die Just Yet' and 'My Mate Paul', in the UK Top 40.

In 1998, Holmes composed his first full-length movie score for Steven Soderbergh's *Out Of Sight*. The superb *Bow Down To The Exit Sign* was recorded as the score for a screenplay in progress by Lisa Barros D'sa, with the two projects developing in tandem. It was followed by Holmes' second collaboration with Soderbergh on the director's remake of *Ocean's Eleven*.

HONEYCOMBS

Formed in London in 1963, the group was originally known as the Sherabons and comprised Denis D'ell (b. Denis Dalziel; vocals), Anne 'Honey' Lantree (drums), John Lantree (bass), Alan Ward (lead guitar) and Martin Murray (rhythm guitar), later replaced by Peter Pye. Pye Records released their debut, 'Have I The Right' – although the group were obliged to change their name. When 'Have I The Right' hit UK number 1 in 1964, the group's pop-star future seemed assured. However, a dramatic flop with the follow-up 'Is It Because' caused concern, barely saved by 'That's The Way'. The group faltered amid line-up changes and poor morale, before moving inexorably towards cabaret and the revivalist circuit.

HOOKER, JOHN LEE

Hooker (b. 1917, d. 2001) played guitar with his stepfather William Moore at dances before running away to Memphis, Tennessee, at the age of 14, where he met and played with Robert Lockwood. He then moved to Cincinnati, where he sang with gospel quartets before moving to Detroit in 1943. There he played in the blues clubs and bars at the heart of the black section, developing his unique guitar style. In 1948 he was finally given the chance to record. Accompanied only by his own electric guitar and constantly tapping foot, 'Boogie Chillen' was a surprise commercial success for Modern Records.

From the late 40s to the early 50s, Hooker recorded prolifically. His successful run with Modern produced such classics as 'Crawling King Snake', 'In The Mood', 'Rock House Boogie' and 'Shake Holler & Run'. Under a deliberately bewildering array of pseudonyms, he also released on a variety of labels. He played the R&B circuit across the country, further developing his popularity with the black-American public. In 1955, he severed his connection with Modern and began a long association with Vee Jay Records of Chicago.

By now, the solo format was deemed old-fashioned, so all of these recordings used a tight little band, often including Eddie Taylor on guitar, as well as piano and various combinations of horns. The association with Vee Jay proved very satisfactory, promoting further extensive tours. In the late 50s, Hooker appeared regularly at folk clubs and festivals. He was lionized by a new audience mainly of young, white listeners. In the early 60s his reputation grew as he was often cited by younger pop and rock musicians as a major influence. The connection with a new generation of musicians led to various 'super sessions', and bore fruit most successfully in the early 70s with the release of *Hooker 'N' Heat*, in which he played with the American rock-blues band **Canned Heat**.

Although enthusiasm for blues waned in the late 70s and early 80s, Hooker's standing has rarely faltered and he has continued to tour, latterly with the Coast To Coast Blues Band. A remarkable transformation came in 1989 when he recorded *The Healer*. This superb album featured guests on most tracks including **Bonnie Raitt**, **Los Lobos** and **Carlos Santana** on the title track. The follow-up, *Mr Lucky*, reached number 3 in the UK album charts, setting a record for Hooker, at 74, as the oldest artist to achieve that position. In his old age, Hooker was finally able to reap his long-overdue commercial reward.

This formidable artist was the last surviving giant of the real delta folk blues, and therefore represented a final touchstone with a body of music that is both rich in history and unmatched in its importance. It is a fitting tribute to the great man that he died peacefully in his sleep.

HOOTIE AND THE BLOWFISH

This hugely successful South Carolina, USA quartet was formed in the early 90s by Darius Rucker (vocals), Mark Bryan (b. 1967; guitar), Dean Felber (b. 1967; bass) and Jim 'Soni' Sonefield (b. 1964; drums). They produced a self-financed EP containing their breakthrough hit 'Hold My Hand', and sold over 50,000 copies at gigs. Their debut album, *Cracked Rear View*, followed and eventually made the US Top 10. The album became one of the most successful rock debuts of all time. A critically acclaimed tour in 1994 encompassed more than 300 dates and, at the 1995 Grammy Awards, they picked up Best New Artist and Best Pop Performance By A Group.

Any follow-up album was bound to be anti-climatic and although *Fairweather Johnson* debuted in the US chart at number 1, by the band's previous standards the album was seen as something of a flop – by anybody else's

standards it was a massive success. *Musical Chairs* failed to reach the top of the US charts, although the fall off in sales has not harmed the band's popularity as a live act. They re-affirmed their college-rock credentials with the enjoyable cover versions collection, *Scattered, Smothered & Covered*, featuring both live and studio recordings. Rucker released his solo debut, *Back To Then*, in 2002.

HOPKINS, LIGHTNIN'

One of the last great country blues singers, Hopkins' (b. Sam Hopkins, 1912, d. 1982) lengthy career began in the Texas bars and juke joints of the 20s. His work first came to prominence when, after being discovered by Sam Charters at the age of 47, *The Roots Of Lightnin' Hopkins* was released in 1959. His sparse acoustic guitar, narrated prose and harsh, emotive voice appealed to the American folk boom of the early 60s. By that time, Hopkins was re-established as a major force on the college and concert-hall circuit. In 1967 he was the

subject of an autobiographical film, *The Blues Of Lightnin' Hopkins*, which won the Gold Hugo award at the Chicago Film Festival. He experimented with a 'progressive' electric album: *The Great Electric Show And Dance*. During the 70s, he toured compulsively in the USA, Canada and, in 1977, Europe, until ill health forced him to slow down. When Hopkins died, his status as one of the major voices of the blues was assured.

HOPKINS, NICKY

A classically trained pianist, Hopkins (b. 1944, d. 1994) embraced rock 'n' roll in 1960 when, inspired by **Chuck Berry**, he joined the Savages, a seminal pre-**Beatles** group led by Screaming Lord Sutch. He later became a founder-member of Cyril Davies' R&B All Stars, before embarking on a prolific session career with appearances on recordings by the **Who**, **Dusty Springfield**, **Tom Jones**, the **Kinks**, the **Rolling Stones**, the **Jeff Beck Group**, the **Steve Miller Band**, **Quicksilver Messenger Service**, **John Lennon**, and **Jefferson Airplane** among others. Hopkins was dogged by ill-health and his death in 1994 followed complications after stomach surgery.

HORNSBY, BRUCE, AND THE RANGE

US pianist and contract songwriter, Hornsby (b. 1954) burst on to the trans-atlantic market in 1986 with the hit 'The Way It Is'. His first album featured David Mansfield (violin, mandolin, guitar), Joe Puerta (bass), John Molo (drums) and George Marinelli (guitar). Hornsby followed the first album with *Scenes From The South Side*, an even stronger collection including the powerful 'The Valley Road'. The third collection, *Night On The Town*, featured **Jerry Garcia** on guitar and, following the death of the **Grateful Dead**'s Brent Mydland in July 1990, Hornsby joined the legendary band as a temporary replacement. In addition to many session/guest appearances during the early 90s, Hornsby found time to record *Harbor Lights*, a satisfying and more acoustic-sounding

record. A new album in 1995 resorted back to the commercial-sounding formula of his debut. *Hot House* and its follow up *Spirit Trail* were both credible records, yet commercially they were disappointing.

HORSLIPS

Irish folk-rock band formed in 1970 by Barry Devlin (bass, vocals), Declan Sinnott (lead guitar, vocals), Eamonn Carr (drums, vocals), Charles O'Connor (violin, mandolin), and Jim Lockhart (flute, violin, keyboards), although Sinnott was replaced by Gus Gueist and John Fean in turn. They maintained a strong cult following, but only *The Book Of Invasions: A Celtic Symphony* reached the UK Top 40. *The Man Who Built America* received a great deal of airplay when released, but wider acceptance evaded them and the band split up in 1981.

HOT CHOCOLATE

Highly commercial UK pop band featuring Patrick Olive (b. 1947; percussion), Ian King (drums); Errol Brown (b. 1948; vocals), Tony Wilson (b. 1947; bass) and Larry Ferguson (b. 1948; piano). Apple Records signed them for a reggae version of the **Plastic Ono Band**'s 'Give Peace A Chance', and the group also provided the hit 'Think About Your Children' for Mary Hopkin. A year later, Hot Chocolate signed to RAK Records and composed **Herman's Hermits** hit 'Bet Yer Life I Do'. In 1970, Hot Chocolate enjoyed their own first hit with 'Love Is Life'.

Over the next year, Harvey Hinsley (b. 1948; guitar) and Tony Connor (b. 1948; drums) joined the group. Hot Chocolate's formidable run of UK Top 10 hits include 'I Believe (In Love)', 'Brother Louie', 'Emma', 'You Sexy Thing', 'No Doubt About It', 'Girl Crazy' and 'It Started With A Kiss'. In 1977, they reached UK number 1 with the Russ Ballard song 'So You Win Again'. The group split when Errol Brown left for a solo career in 1987. In 1997, the group sprung back into the limelight when 'You Sexy Thing' featured in the smash hit British film *The Full Monty*.

HOT TUNA

US group comprising two members of **Jefferson Airplane**, Jack Casady (bass) and Jorma Kaukonen (guitar, vocals), often using colleagues Paul Kantner (guitar) and Spencer Dryden (drums) alongside other guests. Stage appearances were initially integrated within the Jefferson Airplane's performances, but during one of

their rest periods, the duo began to appear in their own right, often with drummer Joey Covington. Hot Tuna released a self-titled debut as a duo (with harmonica player Will Scarlet guesting). By their second album, with violinist **Papa John Creach** and drummer Sammy Piazza, the line-up displayed the combination of electric and acoustic rock/blues Casady and Kaukonen had been looking for. Creach departed before *The Phosphorescent Rat*, and Piazza left to join Stoneground (he was replaced by Bob Steeler). By their sixth album they sounded like a rumbling heavy rock traditional-ragtime blues band. They maintained a hardcore following, but in the late 70s the duo split. Casady and Kaukonen reunited in the mid-80s, and returned to recording in 1991 with a workmanlike album that found little favour with the record-buying public.

HOTHOUSE FLOWERS

This folk-inspired Irish rock band originally featured Liam O Maonlai (vocals, keyboards), Fiachna O Braonain (guitar), Peter O'Toole (bass), Leo Barnes (saxophone) and Jerry Fehily (drums). Highly praised in *Rolling Stone* magazine before they had even secured a recording contract, an appearance on RTE's Saturday-night chat programme *The Late Show* led to the issue of a single on U2's Mother label, 'Love Don't Work That Way' (1987). Although commercially unsuccessful, PolyGram Records signed them. Their debut single, 'Don't Go', reached UK number 11, followed by further hits, including a cover version of **Johnny Nash**'s 'I Can See Clearly Now', 'Give It Up', and 'Movies'. Their debut album, *People*, reached UK number 2, but further albums showed little musical progression, and by 1995 O Maonlai had formed Alt with Andy White and Tim Finn. Hothouse Flowers returned in 1998 with the uninspiring *Born*.

HOUSE OF LOVE

UK-born Guy Chadwick (vocals, guitar) teamed up with Pete Evans (drums), Terry Bickers (guitar), Chris Groothuizen (bass) and Andrea Heukamp (vocals, guitar) to form the House Of Love. Their debut single, 'Shine On', was released in 1987 after which Heukamp left. 'Christine' on their debut album was rightly acclaimed, and the album was nominated the best record of 1988. Tipped as the band most likely to succeed in 1989, reinforced by the release of 'Destroy The Heart', they were signed to PhonoGram Records. The first two singles for the label, 'Never' and 'I Don't Know Why I Love You', stalled at number 41, while the album suffered huge delays. By Christmas 1989 Bickers had quit, immediately replaced by Simon Walker, and early in 1990 the long-awaited *Fontana* appeared to mixed reviews. Extensive touring followed, ending with the departure of Walker, tentatively replaced by original member Heukamp, while Bickers moved on to Levitation.

The House Of Love re-emerged in 1991 with an acclaimed EP featuring the excellent 'The Girl With The Loneliest Eyes' and in 1992 *Babe Rainbow* was released to some critical acclaim. Following *Audience Of The Mind* the band collapsed, Chadwick re-emerged a year later with the Madonnas. By 1997 he had surfaced yet again on Setanta Records as a solo artist.

HOUSEMARTINS

The Housemartins was formed by Paul Heaton (b. 1962; vocals, guitar), Stan Collimore (b. 1962; bass), Ted Key (guitar) and Hugh Whitaker (drums),

although Key was soon replaced by Norman Cook (b. 1963). Their first UK hit, 'Happy Hour' in 1986, reached number 3. Their UK Top 10 debut album *London 0 Hull 4* further established them and their *a cappella* version of 'Caravan Of Love' gave them a UK number 1.

Early in 1987 the Housemartins won the BPI award for Best Newcomers of the year. In the summer, David Hemingway (b. 1960) replaced Whitaker. An acclaimed EP, *Five Get Over Excited*, followed, after which the band displayed their left-wing politics by performing at the 'Red Wedge' concerts. They issued their final studio album, the self-mocking *The People Who Grinned Themselves To Death*. Announcing that they had only intended the Housemartins to last for three years, they split in 1988. Heaton and Hemingway found fame with the **Beautiful South**, while Cook reinvented himself under a number of dance aliases, most famously **Fatboy Slim**.

HOUSTON, WHITNEY

Whitney Houston (b. 1963, USA) followed her mother Cissy and cousin **Dionne Warwick** by beginning her career in gospel. Early performances include backing Chaka Khan, and lead vocals on the Michael Zager Band's single 'Life's A Party'. By 1983 she had signed to Arista Records; in 1984 'Hold Me', a duet with Teddy Pendergrass, crept into the US Top 50. *Whitney Houston* was released in 1984, creeping up the charts before topping them in early 1985. The singles 'You Give Good Love' and 'Saving All My Love For You' made US numbers 3 and 1 respectively; the latter also topped the charts in the UK and much of the rest of the world. 'How Will I Know' and 'Greatest Love Of All' both topped the US charts in rapid succession and Houston won a series of prestigious awards.

'I Want To Dance With Somebody (Who Loves Me)', released in 1987, was a transatlantic number 1, creating *Whitney* – the first album by a female artist to debut at number 1 on the US album charts, a feat it also achieved in the UK. The album included a version of 'I Know Him So Well' (sung with Cissy) and 'Didn't We Almost Have It All' – her fifth successive US number 1. 'So Emotional' and 'Where Do Broken Hearts Go' continued the sequence, breaking a record previously shared by the **Beatles** and the **Bee Gees**. Another series of awards followed, including Pop Female Vocal and Soul/R&B Female Vocal categories in the American Music Awards. She recorded the title track to the 1988 Olympics tribute *One Moment In Time*, while 'I'm Your Baby Tonight' put her back at number 1. Despite the relatively modest success of the album of the same name (US number 3), 'All The Man That I Need' compensated by becoming her ninth number 1.

In 1992, Houston married singer **Bobby Brown**. The same year she made her acting debut in the movie *The Bodyguard*. Four songs recorded by her were lifted from the phenomenally successful soundtrack album, including her cover version of **Dolly Parton**'s 'I Will Always Love You' (US number 1 for 14 weeks).

Houston spent most of the 90s concentrating on her acting career, but made a surprise return to the studio for 1998's *My Love Is Your Love*. Enlisting the songwriting help of **Missy 'Misdemeanor' Elliott**, **Diane Warren** and **Wyclef Jean**, the album was a confident attempt by Houston to reclaim ground lost to the new diva superstars **Mariah Carey** and **Celine Dion**. 'When You Believe', a duet with Carey taken from the animated DreamWorks movie *The Prince Of Egypt*, was a transatlantic hit. With the album selling poorly, however, Houston's fortunes were revived by the US number 2 single 'Heartbreak Hotel' and the atypical and hard-hitting 'It's Not Right But It's Okay', a US/UK Top 5 hit single.

HOWLIN' WOLF

Howlin' Wolf (b. Chester Arthur Burnett, 1910, d. 1976) was one of the most important post-war blues players. Throughout his Mississippi youth he sang at local parties and juke joints. He emulated performers like Charley Patton and Tommy Johnson, although his hoarse, powerful voice and eerie 'howling' were peculiarly his own.

Wolf met people such as Johnny Shines, Robert Johnson, and Sonny Boy 'Rice Miller' Williamson. Williamson and Wolf's half-sister Mary taught him to play harmonica, and he also experimented with the guitar. He then formed his own group and was approached by a west Memphis radio station, which brought him to the attention of Sam Phillips, who asked him to record, making separate agreements with the Bihari Brothers in California and the Chess Brothers of Chicago. Successful early recordings led to competition between these two camps but eventually he went to Chicago, where he built a powerful reputation on the club circuit, with such classics as 'Smokestack Lightning' and 'Killing Floor'. Wolf's music was a significant influence on rock and many of his best-known songs – 'Sitting On Top Of The World', 'I Ain't Superstitious', 'Killin' Floor', 'Back Door Man' and 'Little Red Rooster' – were recorded by acts as diverse as the **Doors**, **Cream**, the **Rolling Stones**, the **Yardbirds** and **Manfred Mann**. Few, however, rivalled the originals. *The London Howlin' Wolf Sessions* saw Wolf and long-serving guitarist Hubert Sumlin joined by an array of guests, including **Eric Clapton**, **Steve Winwood**, and Rolling Stones Bill Wyman and Charlie Watts. Wolf continued to tour until his death in 1976.

HUMAN LEAGUE

Formed in 1978, the initial line-up of this UK band comprised Ian Craig Marsh (b. 1956; synthesizer), Martyn Ware (b. 1956; synthesizer), Phil Oakey (b. 1955; vocals) and Addy Newton, later replaced as visual director by Adrian Wright. Their first single, 'Being Boiled', secured a tie-in deal with Virgin Records. Their debut album, *Reproduction*, sold steadily, while the EP *Holiday, '80*, won them an appearance on *Top Of The Pops*. Oakey became the focal point of the band, leading to internal friction which the chart success of *Travelogue* was unable to stem, and in late 1980, Marsh and Ware left. They went on to found **BEF** and **Heaven 17**.

Oakey chose two teenagers with no knowledge of the music business, Susanne Sulley (b. 1963) and Joanne Catherall (b. 1962), and the new line-up was completed by bass player Ian Burden (b. 1957) and ex-Rezillos guitarist Jo Callis (b. 1955). They contrasted radically with the original experimental Human League, producing a series of pure pop hits in 1981. *Dare!* sold over five million copies and the Christmas chart-topper, 'Don't You Want Me', became the biggest-selling UK single of 1981. The track went on to top the US charts, spearheading a British invasion of 'new pop' artists.

The group took a long sabbatical, releasing only a couple of hits – 'Mirror Man' and '(Keep Feeling) Fascination' – and a mini-album of dance remixes, before *Hysteria* (1984), which met a mixed response. The attendant singles, 'The Lebanon', 'Life On Your Own' and 'Louise', all reached the UK Top 20 and Oakey ended 1984 by teaming up with Giorgio Moroder for a successful single and album. Two years passed – and Wright and Callis departed – before *Crash*. The US number 1 single 'Human' was composed by producers Jam And Lewis.

Following the unsuccessful *Romantic*, the trio took an extended hiatus before returning in 1995 with *Octopus*. The hit single 'Tell Me When' retained much of the freshness and simplicity of *Dare!*. A new chapter began in 2001 with another career relaunch and a favourable critical reception for *Secrets*. Despite their erratic career, the Human League has shown a remarkable ability to triumph commercially and aesthetically, and usually at the least predictable moments.

HUMBLE PIE

Formed in 1969, this UK 'supergroup' was formed by Peter Frampton (b. 1950; guitar, vocals, ex-**Herd**), Steve Marriott (b. 1947, d. 1991; guitar, vocals, ex-**Small Faces**), Greg Ridley (b. 1947; bass, ex-**Spooky Tooth**) and Jerry Shirley (b. 1952; drums). The line-up had a UK Top 5 hit with its debut 'Natural Born Bugie'. Their first two albums blended hard-rock with several acoustic tracks, but Frampton departed for a solo career when they abandoned the latter type of material. The remaining members added former Colosseum guitarist Dave Clempson. *Smokin'* from this period was their highest-ranking UK chart album, but the band was more popular on the US live circuit. Humble Pie eventually split in 1975.

HUNTER, IAN

Hunter's (b. 1946) gravelly vocals and image-conscious looks established him as **Mott The Hoople**'s focal point. He remained their driving force until 1974, when he began a solo career. Mott guitarist Mick Ronson quit at the same time and Ronson produced and played on *Ian Hunter*, which contained Hunter's sole UK hit, 'Once Bitten Twice Shy'. After a tour as Hunter/Ronson, they parted ways. *All American Alien Boy* featured Aynsley Dunbar, David Sanborn and several members of **Queen**, but the set lacked passion. *Overnight Angels* continued this trend towards musical conservatism, although Hunter aligned himself with punk by producing *Beyond The Valley Of The Dolls* for Generation X. *You're Never Alone With A Schizophrenic* marked his reunion with Ronson and subsequent live dates were commemorated on *Welcome To The Club*. In the 90s he fronted an all-star band, Ian Hunter's Dirty Laundry, and continued to record the occasional studio album.

HÜSKER DÜ

Hüsker Dü (their name means 'Do you remember?') were formed in 1979 by Bob Mould (b. 1960; guitar, vocals), Greg Norton (bass) and Grant Hart (drums). Their melding of pop and punk influences has inspired thousands of bands. They began as an aggressive hardcore thrash band before expanding to other musical formats. Their first single, 'Statues', was released on the small Reflex label in 1981. In 1982, a debut album, *Land Speed Record*, arrived on New Alliance Records, but the EP *In A Free Land Everything Falls Apart* (1983) saw them back on Reflex. By their second EP, *Metal Circus*, Hüsker Dü had become a critics' favourite. *Zen Arcade* (1984) brought about a stylistic turning point and was followed by a non-album version of the **Byrds**' 'Eight Miles High'. A 1985 album, *New Day Rising*, maintained their reputation as a favourite of critics and college radio stations. *After Flip Your Wig* the band signed with Warner Brothers Records, and issued *Candy Apple Grey* (1986) and *Warehouse: Songs And Stories* (1987). In 1988 Hart was sacked, and the group soon disbanded. Mould and Hart continued as solo artists, before Mould formed Sugar in 1991.

HYLAND, BRIAN

A demonstration disc, recorded with Hyland's (b. 1943) high-school group the Delphis, alerted Kapp Records to his vocal talent. In 1960, his 'Itsy Bitsy Teenie Weenie Yellow Polkadot Bikini', topped the US charts. Having switched to ABC Paramount, the singer enjoyed further success with 'Let Me Belong To You' (1961; US Top 20) and 'Ginny Come Lately' (1962; UK Top 10), before securing a second gold award for 'Sealed With A Kiss'. Its theme of temporary parting was empathetic to the plight of many love-struck teenagers and the song returned to the UK Top 10 in 1975 before being revived in 1990 by Jason Donovan. Hyland continued to enjoy US chart entries, notably with 'The Joker Went Wild' and 'Run, Run, Look And See' (both 1966), and reasserted his career in 1970 with a version of the Impressions' 'Gypsy Woman'. This third million-seller was produced by long-time friend Del Shannon, who co-wrote several tracks on the attendant album. This rekindled success proved short-lived and the artist later ceased recording.

IAN, JANIS

US singer-songwriter Ian (b. Janis Eddy Fink, 1951) made an immediate impact in 1967 with the controversial 'Society's Child (Baby I've Been

Thinking)'. Her dissonant, almost detached delivery enhanced the lyricism of superior folk-rock albums, notably *For All The Seasons Of Your Mind*. Her 1975 release, *Between The Lines*, contained 'At Seventeen', Ian's sole US Top 5 entry. The artist's impetus noticeably waned during the 80s and Ian seemed to have retired from music altogether. *Breaking Silence* was an impressive comeback album which dealt with, amongst other issues, Ian's recent coming out. Although 1995's *Revenge* moved firmly into smooth pop, the lyrics remained as personal, biting and original as ever. In 1998, Ian successfully underwent surgery for a benign liver tumor. She returned in 2000 with a new studio album, *God & The FBI*.

ICE CUBE

Controversial hardcore rapper (b. O'Shea Jackson, 1969) who formerly worked with the equally inflammatory N.W.A. His debut album drew immediate mainstream attention with its controversial lyrical platform, and was attacked for its homophobia, violence and sexism. Ice Cube went on to release the excellent sets *Death Certificate*, *The Predator* and *Lethal Injection*. He also consolidated his movie career by moving into writing and production. Cube had already starred in John Singleton's 1991 hit movie, titled after his first rap, *Boyz N The Hood*, and later appeared in the same director's *Higher Learning*. His several screenplays included the 1995 comedy *Friday*. The soundtrack to his 1998 directorial debut, *The Players Club*, was a Top 10 success in the USA. Even more successful was 2000's *Next Friday*.

In 1996, Ice Cube returned to recording with Westside Connection, a hip-hop supergroup he formed with rappers Mack 10 and WC. Two years later he released his first solo set in over five years, *War & Peace, Vol. 1 (The War Disc)*, a failed attempt to recapture the intensity and shock value of his earlier albums.

ICE-T

One of the most outspoken west-coast rappers, Ice-T (b. Tracy Marrow, 1958) takes his name from black exploitation author Iceberg Slim. 'The Coldest Rapper' (1983), made him the first Los Angeles hip-hop artist. He followed it with 'Killers', but the breakthrough came with 'Ya Don't Know'. Ice-T's 1987

debut, *Rhyme Pays*, served as a mission statement: hardcore raps on street violence and survival were the order of the day. His four LPs in three years, based on his experiences as an LA gang member, created a stir in the US.

In the 90s, Ice-T contributed the title track to the gangster movie *Colors*, and starred as a cop in *New Jack City*. Ice-T's hobbies include his own thrash-metal outfit, Body Count, who released their debut album in 1992 and stirred up immeasurable controversy via one of their cuts, 'Cop Killer'. His own recording career in

the late 90s was side-tracked by his movie commitments, although he managed to find the time to record 1999's poorly received *7th Deadly Sin*.

ICICLE WORKS

The Icicle Works were formed by Ian McNabb (b. 1960; vocals, guitar), Chris Layhe (bass) and Chris Sharrock (drums). They made their recording debut in 1981 with a mini-LP, *Ascending*, before founding their Troll Kitchen label and releasing 'Nirvana'. They came to the attention of Beggars Banquet Records and 'Birds Fly (Whisper To A Scream)' was an indie hit. The following 'Love Is A Wonderful Colour' reached the UK Top 20. With producer Ian Broudie, their sound gradually shifted from subtle pop to harder rock. Layhe was replaced by Roy Corkhill (ex-Black), and Sharrock by Zak Starkey, son of Ringo Starr. This line-up prospered for a while but in 1989 McNabb assembled a new band. They signed a new contract with Epic Records and released an album, before McNabb embarked on a critically acclaimed solo career.

IDLE RACE

Dave Pritchard (guitar), Greg Masters (bass) and Roger Spencer (drums) started as the Nightriders in 1966, but when guitarist/composer Jeff Lynne (b. 1947) joined, the group took the name Idle Race. By 1967, Lynne was contributing the bulk of their original material; he also produced their second album, *Idle Race*. Public indifference led to Lynne's departure (for the **Move**).

Pritchard, Masters and Spencer recruited Mike Hopkins and Roy Collum, the latter was then replaced by Dave Walker. This reshaped quintet was responsible for *Time Is*. When Walker left, his place was taken by Birmingham veteran Steve Gibbons. When Masters left in 1971, the group became the Steve Gibbons Band.

IDOL, BILLY

While at Sussex University, UK-born Idol (b. William Michael Albert Broad, 1955) formed Chelsea. He then founded Generation X in 1976. Idol subsequently launched his solo career in New York and recorded *Don't Stop*, featuring a revival of Tommy James And The Shondells' 'Mony Mony'. In 1987, he took 'Mony Mony' to US number 1, as well as reaping hits with 'Eyes Without A Face', 'White Wedding' and 'Rebel Yell'. A motorcycle crash in February 1990 seriously damaged his leg, but he recovered remarkably quickly and the same May hit the number 2 slot in America with 'Cradle Of Love' (taken from the Andrew Dice Clay movie *The Adventures Of Ford Fairlaine*). Personal troubles curtailed Idol's hit career, however, and by the middle of the decade he had fallen out of fashion. He enjoyed a resurgence in the late 90s thanks to his cameo appearance in *The Wedding Singer*.

IFIELD, FRANK

UK-born Ifield (b. 1937) emigrated to Australia as a child. In 1957, he came to prominence with 'Whiplash', a song about the 1851 Australian goldrush. Shortly afterwards, he reached UK number 1 with 'I Remember You', the first million-selling record in England. In 1962, Ifield was back at number 1 with 'Lovesick Blues' and then with Gogi Grant's 'The Wayward Wind'. 'Confessin'' was his fourth UK chart-topper, but the beat boom put an end to his success. He continued his career, playing in pantomime and stage productions, before reverting to cabaret work. In the 90s, Ifield relocated to Australia. He now works as a country music radio presenter.

IGGY POP

'Godfather Of Punk', Iggy Pop (b. James Newell Osterberg, 1947) first joined bands as a drummer. He picked up the nickname Iggy while with the Iguanas (1964). In 1965 he joined Prime Movers, changing his name to Iggy Stooge. Inspired by seeing the **Doors**, he formed the Psychedelic Stooges with Ron Asheton. Iggy was vocalist and guitarist, Asheton played bass with Asheton's brother Scott later joining on drums. They debuted in Michigan, October 1967. Dave Alexander joined on bass, and 'Psychedelic' was dropped from their name. Ron switched to guitar, leaving Iggy free to concentrate on singing and showmanship. The Stooges signed to Elektra Records in 1968

for two albums (the first produced by John Cale) *The Stooges* and *Fun House*, but the band broke up in the early 70s.

Stooges fan David Bowie helped Iggy record *Raw Power* in 1972. When no suitable British musicians could be found, Williamson, Scott Thurston and the Ashetons were flown in. The resultant album (as Iggy And The Stooges) included 'Search And Destroy'. Bowie's involvement continued as Iggy sailed through stormy seas (including self-admission to an asylum). His live performances were legendary: self-mutilation, sex acts and an invitation to a local gang to kill him onstage.

After *Raw Power* there were sessions for *Kill City*, which was not released until 1978. The arrival of punk stirred Iggy's interest. (Television recorded the tribute 'Little Johnny Jewel'). In 1977 Bowie produced two classic Iggy Pop albums – *The Idiot* and *Lust For Life*. Key tracks from these included 'Night Clubbin'', 'The Passenger' and 'China Girl', and Iggy guested on backing vocals for Bowie's *Low*.

In the late 70s, Iggy signed to Arista Records, releasing rather average albums with occasional assistance from Glen Matlock (ex-Sex Pistols) and Ivan Kral. He went into vinyl exile after 1982's autobiography and the Chris Stein-produced *Zombie Birdhouse*. During his time out of the studio he cleaned up his drug problems and married. He also developed his acting career, appearing in *Sid And Nancy*, *The Color Of Money*, *Hardware*, and on television in *Miami Vice*. His big return came in 1986 with the Bowie-produced *Blah Blah Blah* and his first-ever UK hit single, a cover of Johnny O'Keefe's 'Real Wild Child'. *American Caesar* from its jokily self-aggrandizing title onwards, revealed continued creative growth. *Avenue B* was a stylistic oddity, a reflective, semi-acoustic set informed by the singer turning 50 and his recent divorce. Throughout he has remained the consummate live performer, setting a benchmark for at least one generation of rock musicians.

IGLESIAS, ENRIQUE

The son of global superstar **Julio Iglesias**, Enrique (b. 1975) recorded his self-titled debut album of Latin-influenced pop in 1995. The album's release saw him catapulted to superstar status in the Spanish-speaking music world. His follow-up collection, *Vivir*, won a Grammy Award, and by 1997 the two albums were credited with global sales in excess of eight million. Iglesias was even more successful in 1999, the commercial breakthrough year for Latin music, with 'Bailamos' topping the US pop charts in September and breaking into the UK Top 5. 'Be With You' also topped the US singles chart the following June. Iglesias enjoyed further success with his Interscope Records debut *Escape* and the Top 5 single, 'Hero'. The latter provided Iglesias with a UK chart-topper in January 2002.

IGLESIAS, JULIO

Spanish singer Iglesias (b. Julio José Iglesias de la Cueva, 1943) studied law at Madrid University and played football (goalkeeper) for Real Madrid before suffering severe injuries in a 1963 car accident. While recuperating, he learned guitar and began to write songs. After continuing his studies in Cambridge, England, he entered the 1968 Festivalde la Canción in Benidorm, where he won first prize and soon afterwards signed a recording contract with the independent Discos Columbia. Iglesias represented Spain in the Eurovision Song Contest, and during the next few years he toured widely in Europe and Latin America, scoring international hits with 'Manuela' (1974) and 'Hey' (1979). His global reach was increased in 1978 when he signed to CBS Records International and soon had hits in French and Italian. The first big English-language success came in 1982 when his version of 'Begin The Beguine' topped the UK charts. This was followed by the multi-language compilation album *Julio*, which sold a million in America. A later duet (and international hit) was 'My Love' with **Stevie Wonder** in 1988. By the end of the 90s, Iglesias had sold in excess of 220 million albums in seven languages, making him one of the most successful artists ever in the history of popular music.

IMBRUGLIA, NATALIE

One of 1998's surprise pop successes, Imbruglia (b. 1975) made her acting debut playing Beth in the popular Australian soap opera *Neighbours*. She had originally started out as a singer, turning to acting later. A move to England in 1996 was followed by a recording contract with RCA Records. *Left Of The Middle* sold strongly on the back of the success of her debut single, 'Torn', a massive hit throughout Europe, and the number-one airplay hit in America for over 10 weeks. The album reached number 10 on the US album chart. Subsequent UK hit singles, 'Big Mistake', 'Wishing I Was There' and 'Smoke' repeated the highly melodic indie-rock formula of her debut. *White Lilies Island* attempted to push Imbruglia into edgier territory on such tracks as 'That Day' and 'Do You Love?', although she enjoyed greater success with the more traditional 'Wrong Impression'.

INCREDIBLE STRING BAND

Scottish folk group formed in 1965, featuring Mike Heron (b. 1942), Robin Williamson (b. 1943) and Clive Palmer. In 1966, they completed *The Incredible String Band*, a unique blend of traditional and original material, but broke up upon its completion. Heron and Williamson reunited in 1967 to record *5000 Spirits Or The Layers Of The Onion*. Two further releases, *The Hangman's Beautiful Daughter* and *Wee Tam And The Big Huge*, consolidated their position and saw Williamson, in particular, contribute several lengthy, memorable compositions. *Changing Horses* and *I Looked Up* demonstrated a transformation to a rock-based perspective, although *U* reflected something of their earlier charm. Malcolm Le Maistre joined for *Liquid Acrobat As Regards The Air* and Gerald Dott (woodwinds, keyboard) joined for *No Ruinous Feud*. By this point, the two founding members were becoming estranged, both musically and socially. In 1974, they ended their partnership.

INCUBUS

This metal funk crossover band was formed in Calabasas, California, USA in 1991 by school friends Brandon Boyd (b. 1976; vocals), Mike Einziger (b. 1976; guitar), Alex Katunich (b. 1976; bass), and José Pasillas (b. 1976; drums). They later recruited DJ Lyfe (b. Gavin Koppel), who added a hip-hop element to their already eclectic mix. After the independent release of *Fungus Amongus*, they signed to Immortal Records in 1995. In January 1997, they released the six-track *Enjoy Incubus* EP and collaborated with DJ Greyboy on the *Spawn* movie soundtrack. Later that year *S.C.I.E.N.C.E.* was released. During a US tour to promote the album the band dispensed with the services of DJ Lyfe and replaced him with DJ Kilmore (b. Chris Kilmore, 1973). Two years later, after almost continual touring, *Make Yourself* was released. The single 'Pardon Me' was a significant US hit. In 2000, the band was featured on the Ozzfest, prior to recording their most successful album to date, *Morning View*.

INDIA, ARIE

This Atlanta, Georgia, USA-based singer-songwriter made an immediate impact on the neo-soul scene with the release of her debut *Acoustic Soul* in 2001. She first started playing guitar while studying jewellery-making at the Savannah College of Art and Design, and gradually became involved in the local urban music scene, helping form the artist's collective Groovement/ Earthseed. Her first songs appeared on the collective's independently released CD. A recording contract with Motown Records was signed the following year. 'In My Head' created a buzz when it was featured on the soundtrack to Spike Lee's *Bamboozled* in 2000. Her debut was nominated for several Grammy Awards.

INDIGO GIRLS

Amy Ray (b. 1964; vocals, guitar) and Emily Saliers (b. 1963; vocals, guitar) met while at school in Georgia, USA. They started to perform together, initially as the B Band, then as Saliers And Ray. As Indigo Girls, they released *Strange Fire* before signing to Epic Records in 1988. *Indigo Girls*, featuring Michael Stipe and **Hothouse Flowers**, included 'Closer To Fine', went gold and won a Grammy. *Rites Of Passage* featured traditional songs such as 'The Water Is Wide' alongside a cover version of **Dire Straits**' 'Romeo And Juliet'. *Swamp Ophelia* (1993) saw the duo swap acoustic for electric guitars. *Shaming Of The Sun* and *Come On Now Social* broke no new ground, but the duo's songwriting remains as dependable as ever.

INSANE CLOWN POSSE

Formed in Detroit, Michigan, USA, Insane Clown Posse's highly shocking rap/metal fusion and spectacular live performances earned them both public notoriety and commercial success. Violent J. (b. Joseph Bruce) and Shaggy 2 Dope (b. Joey Ulster) originally performed as the Inner City Posse in the late 80s, releasing the hardcore gangsta rap *Dog Beats* in 1991. Bruce and Ulster changed their name to Insane Clown Posse and underwent a startling change of image, adopting **Kiss**-style clown make-up and rapping about the apocalypse. The duo released several albums on their own Psychopathic Records imprint, and roused the public ire of several local politicians and moral and religious campaigners. Jive Records signed the duo and released *The Riddle Box* in 1995, but the album failed to sell. Hollywood Records signed

the band a year later, but their debut for the label, *The Great Milenko*, was recalled only six hours after it was released. Island Records bought out the Hollywood contract, and re-released the album later in the year with Insane Clown Posse still a permanent fixture in the media pages. Their Island debut, *The Amazing Jeckel Brothers*, broke into the US Top 5 in 1999. The following November the duo assaulted the US public with two separate releases, the confusingly titled *Bizaar* and *Bizzar*.

INSPIRAL CARPETS

UK indie pop band Inspiral Carpets was formed by Graham Lambert (guitar) and Stephen Holt (vocals), with drummer Craig Gill, organist Clint Boon and bass player David Swift. Boon's **Doors**-influenced playing later became the band's trademark. After their debut EP, *Planecrash*, they were asked to record a John Peel session for BBC Radio 1. In 1988, Holt and Swift were replaced by Tom Hingley and Martin Walsh and the band signed with Mute Records. 'This Is How It Feels' was a hit and Life was critically acclaimed, although further singles had less impact. The band were released from Mute in 1995 with their former company issuing an epitaph, *The Singles*. Boon set up the highly enjoyable the Clint Boon Experience, while Hingley recorded a solo album and started his own record label Newmemorabilia.

INXS

Formed in Sydney, Australia in 1977 and initially named the Farriss Brothers, INXS comprised Tim (b. 1957; guitar), Jon (b. 1961; drums) and Andrew Farriss (b. 1959; keyboards), Michael Hutchence (b. 1960, d. 1997; lead vocals), Kirk Pengilly (b. 1958; guitar, saxophone, vocals) and Garry Beers (b. 1957; bass, vocals). Their recording career began in 1980 with 'Simple Simon'. Their second album, *Underneath The Colours*, sold well, and the following *Shabooh Shoobah* reached the Australian Top 5.

'Original Sin' (1985) and the accompanying *The Swing*, reached Australian number 1 and *Listen Like Thieves* consolidated their worldwide success, although the UK proved a problematic market. They toured the USA and Europe constantly, and the overwhelming success of *Kick* brought a transatlantic hit with 'Need You Tonight' in 1988. Before the release of *X*, all members had a 12-month break. Their 1993 set, *Full Moon, Dirty Hearts*, included the single 'The

Gift' and a Hutchence/Chrissie Hynde (the Pretenders) duet, 'Kill The Pain'.

Hutchence embarked on a highly publicized relationship with Paula Yates, being cited in her divorce from Bob Geldof. Tragically, Hutchence was found hanged in his hotel room in Sydney, Australia, on 22 November 1997. The remaining members resumed live work in 2001.

IRON BUTTERFLY

Iron Butterfly was formed in the USA by Doug Ingle (b. 1946; organ, vocals) who added Ron Bushy (b. 1941; drums), Eric Brann (b. 1950; guitar), Lee Dorman (b. 1945; bass, vocals) and, briefly, Danny Weiss. *In-A-Gadda-Da-Vida (In The Garden Of Eden)* became a multi-million seller and the record industry's first platinum disc. The follow-up, *Ball*, was a lesser success. Brann was later replaced by two guitarists, Larry 'Rhino' Reinhardt (b. 1948) and Mike Pinera (b. 1948), but *Metamorphosis* was a confused collection recorded as the band was disintegrating. They re-formed in the mid-70s, delivering two disappointing albums. Another re-formation, this time in 1992, was masterminded by Pinera. A new version of 'In-A-Gadda-Da-Vida' was recorded and Pinera recruited

Dorman and Bushy for extensive touring in the USA. By 1993, their legendary second album had sold an astonishing 25 million copies and in 1995 the band re-formed once more for an anniversary tour.

IRON MAIDEN

Formed in London, England, in 1976, by Steve Harris (b. 1957; bass), Iron Maiden were the foremost band in the new wave of British heavy metal. After several personnel changes, their debut EP featured Harris, Dave Murray (b. 1958; guitar), Paul Di'Anno (b. 1959; vocals) and Doug Sampson (drums). In 1979, guitarist Tony Parsons joined for *Metal For Muthas*, however he was replaced shortly by Dennis Stratton (b. 1954); Sampson was then replaced by Clive Burr (b. 1957). *Iron Maiden*, a roughly produced album, reached UK number 4 after a tour with **Judas Priest**. The superior *Killers* saw Stratton replaced by Adrian Smith (b. 1957). The release of *Number Of The Beast* was crucial to the band's development; it was also the debut of Di'Anno's replacement Bruce Dickinson (b. Paul Bruce Dickinson, 1958). *Piece Of Mind* continued their success, reaching US number 14. *Powerslave* was heavily criticized, but their reputation was saved by *Live After Death*, a double-album package of their best-loved material recorded live on their 11-month world tour. *Somewhere In Time* was a slight departure, featuring more melody than before, and heralding the use of guitar synthesizers. After a brief hiatus, the concept album *Seventh Son Of A Seventh Son* was released.

After another world trek, the band announced a year's break, during which Dickinson released the solo *Tattooed Millionaire* and a book, *The Adventures Of Lord Iffy Boatrace*. The band planned a return to the old style (which saw Adrian Smith leave, replaced by Janick Gers) and the live show was to be scaled down in a return to much smaller venues. *No Prayer For The Dying* was reminiscent of mid-period Iron Maiden, and was well received, bringing enormous UK hits with 'Holy Smoke' and 'Bring Your Daughter To The Slaughter' (their first UK number 1). Another world tour followed and, despite being denounced 'satanists' in Chile, 1992 saw the band debut at UK number 1 with *Fear Of The Dark*.

Despite this, Dickinson left shortly afterwards. His replacement was Blaze Bayley (b. 1963), who debuted on *X-Factor*. In February 1999 it was announced that Dickinson and Smith had rejoined the band, restoring the classic 80s line-up. To the great delight of their loyal followers; an excellent new studio album, *Brave New World*, was not long in following.

ISAACS, GREGORY

Jamaican superstar Isaacs (b. 1951) began with Rupie Edwards' Success Records in the early 70s. He set up his own African Museum shop and label in 1973 and, by 1980, had signed to Front Line, becoming the number-one star in the reggae world. A new contract with Charisma Records' Pre label set up the UK release of two further classic albums by the self-styled 'Cool Ruler'. He was, however, beset by personal and legal problems in the mid-80s and was even jailed in Kingston's notorious General Penitentiary. His release was celebrated with *Out Deh*. Rumours abound about Gregory's rude-boy lifestyle, but he would claim he has to be tough to maintain his position within Kingston's notorious musical industry.

ISAAK, CHRIS

Californian Isaak (b. 1956) started out in rockabilly band Silvertone, with James Calvin Wilsey (guitar), Rowland Salley (bass) and Kenney Dale Johnson (drums). All remained with Isaak as his permanent backing band. His debut *Silvertone* was raw and diverse, while the self-titled follow-up saw him hone his style to sophisticated R&B. He finally achieved a major hit in 1990 with 'Wicked Game'. His later releases have failed to recreate this commercial peak, but in a music scene frequently dominated by synthesized, frantic pop, his simple approach has proved refreshing.

Isaac also starred in his own US cable television series *The Chris Isaak Show*, which was launched in March 2001.

ISLEY BROTHERS

Three brothers, O'Kelly (b. 1937, d. 1986), Rudolph (b. 1939) and Ronald Isley (b. 1941), began singing gospel in their home town of Cincinnati, USA, in the early 50s, accompanied by their brother Vernon, who died in a car crash around 1957. Moving to New York, the trio issued one-off singles before being signed by RCA Records. The Isleys had already developed a tight vocal unit, with Rudolph and O'Kelly supporting Ronald's strident tenor leads. The self-composed 'Shout' epitomized this approach. The group switched labels to Wand in 1962, where they enjoyed a major hit with a cover version of the Top Notes' 'Twist And Shout', an arrangement that was subsequently copied by the **Beatles**.

A brief spell with Atlantic Records in 1964 produced a classic R&B record, 'Who's That Lady?', but with little commercial success. Tired of the lack of control over their recordings, the Isleys formed their own company, T-Neck Records, in 1964 – an unprecedented step for black performers. The label's first release, 'Testify', showcased their young lead guitarist, **Jimi Hendrix**, and allowed him free rein to display his virtuosity and range of sonic effects. However, the record's experimental sound went unnoticed at the time, and the Isleys were forced to abandon both T-Neck and Hendrix, and sign a contract with Motown Records. They were allowed little involvement in the production of their records and the group were teamed with the Holland/Dozier/Holland partnership, who effectively treated them as an extension of the **Four Tops**, fashioning songs for them accordingly.

Tired of the formula and company power games, the Isleys reactivated T-Neck in 1969, along with a change of image from the regulation mohair suits to a freer, funkier west-coast image, reflected in their choice of repertoire. At this point they recruited their two younger brothers, Ernie (b. 1952; guitar) and Marvin (bass), as well as a cousin, Chris Jasper (keyboards). While their mid-60s recordings were enjoying overdue success in Britain, the Isleys were scoring enormous US hits with their new funk-influenced releases, notably 'It's Your Thing' and 'I Turned You On'. They issued a succession of ambitious albums in this vein between 1969 and 1972, among them a live double set that featured extended versions of their recent hits.

In the early 70s, the Isleys incorporated into their repertoire a variety of rock material by composers such as **Bob Dylan**, **Stephen Stills** and **Carole King**. Their dual role as composers and interpreters reached a peak in 1973 on *3+3* – the first album issued via a distribution agreement with CBS Records. Ernie's powerful, sustained guitar-work, strongly influenced by Hendrix, became a vital ingredient in the Isleys' sound, and was featured heavily on the album's 'That Lady'. Throughout the rest of the 70s, the Isleys issued a succession of slick, impressive soul albums, divided between startlingly tough funk numbers and subdued ballads. *The Heat Is On*

(1975) represented the pinnacle of both genres and 'Harvest For The World' (1976) proved to be one of their most popular recordings in Britain. 'It's A Disco Night', a UK hit in 1980, demonstrated their command of the idiom, but a growing sense of self-parody infected the Isleys' music in the early 80s.

Ernie and Marvin Isley and Chris Jasper left in 1984 to form the successful Isley, Jasper, Isley combination. The original trio soldiered on, but the sudden death of O'Kelly from a heart attack on 31 March 1986 brought their 30-year partnership to an end. Ronald and Rudolph dedicated *Smooth Sailin'* to him.

The artistic innovations of the new Isley Brothers belie the conservatism of their releases since the late 70s. Their 1996 release *Mission To Please* attempted to move them into the same smooth urban soul territory as **Keith Sweat** and **Babyface**. In 2001 they were awarded over $5 million in a lawsuit, to be paid by singer **Michael Bolton** for plagiarism of their song 'Love Is A Wonderful Thing'. Later in the year, their new album *Eternal* proved their enduring appeal when it debuted in the US Top 5. For a third time the Isley Brothers had managed to reinvent themselves.

IT'S A BEAUTIFUL DAY

This San Francisco, USA-based unit centered on the virtuoso skills of violinist David LaFlamme. Patti Santos (b. 1949, d. 1989; vocals), Hal Wagenet (guitar), Linda LaFlamme (b. 1941; keyboards), Mitchell Holman (bass) and Val Fluentes (drums) completed the line-up, which won a major recording contract in the wake of its appearance on **Cream**'s farewell concert bill. *It's A Beautiful Day* was marked by 'White Bird' with which the group is inexorably linked. Subsequent releases, *Marrying Maiden*, *Choice Quality Stuff* and *Live At Carnegie Hall* showed a pot-pourri of musical influences. LaFlamme later abandoned his creation after a protracted lawsuit. Late-period members Bud Cockrell (bass) and David Jenkins (guitar) resurfaced in Pablo Cruise, while Linda and Santos enjoyed low-key solo careers. The violinist briefly resuscitated the band in 1978 as It Was A Beautiful Day.

JA RULE

A rival to DMX as the leading post-millennial hardcore rap artist, Ja Rule (b. Jeffrey Atkins, 1976) made his name on several tracks by his mentor Jay-Z, most noticeably 'Can I Get A ... '. His distinctively gruff voice and loping flow helped make his debut *Venni Vetti Vecci* (an adaptation of the Latin saying 'he came, he saw, he conquered') a classic of its kind. Radio favourites such as 'Holla Holla', 'It's Murda' and 'World's Most Dangerous' hooked the hardcore audience, and the album became a multi-platinum success. *The Irv Gotti Presents Murderers* and a movie debut in Robert Adetuyi's *Turn It Up* followed. Despite lacking some of the rawness of his debut, *Rule 3:36* went straight to the top of the US album chart in October 2000, a feat repeated by the following year's *Pain Is Love*. He also enjoyed his first US chart-topping solo single when 'Always On Time' (featuring Ashanti) climbed to number 1 in February 2002. It was replaced at the top by his collaboration with **Jennifer Lopez**, 'Ain't It Funny'.

JACKSONS

Jackie (b. Sigmund Esco Jackson, 1951), Tito (b. Toriano Adaryll Jackson, 1953), Marlon (b. 1957), Michael Jackson (b. 1958) and Randy Jackson (b. Steven Randall Jackson, 1962) changed from the Jackson Five to the Jacksons in 1976, following their departure from Motown Records. At the same time, Randy replaced his brother Jermaine. They had difficulty continuing their former incarnation's success, although 'Blame It On The Boogie' caught the mood of the burgeoning disco market. The Jacksons' 1981 US tour emphasized Michael's dominance over the group, and the resulting *Live* included many of his solo hits. Between 1981 and the release of *Victory* in

1984, Michael issued *Thriller*. By now media and public attention was focused firmly on Michael and after internal arguments he eventually left the group. It was five years before the Jacksons' next project was complete. *2300 Jackson Street* highlighted their dilemma: once the media realized that Michael was not involved, they lost interest.

JACKSON, ALAN

Jackson (b. 1958) became the first artist to be signed to Arista Records' Nashville division. He wrote most of his 1990 debut album, *Here In The Real World*, which remained on the US country album chart for over a year. 'Blue Blooded Woman' was an immediate success, and four more singles from the album topped the US country charts – 'Here In The Real World', 'Wanted', 'Chasin' That Neon Rainbow' and 'I'd Love You All Over Again'. *Don't Rock The Jukebox* confirmed that his initial success was no fluke, spawning five number 1 singles: 'Don't Rock The Jukebox', 'Someday', 'Midnight In Montgomery', 'Dallas' and 'Love's Got A Hold On You'. Further number 1 hits have followed, including 'She's Got The Rhythm And I Got The Blues', 'Tonight I Climbed The Wall', 'Chattahoochee', 'Who Says You Can't Have It All', 'Summertime Blues', 'Livin' On Love', 'Gone Country' and 'I Don't Even Know Your Name'.

By the end of the 90s Jackson was breaking into the mainstream pop and rock charts. His 1998 set *High Mileage* debuted at number 4 on the *Billboard* Hot 200 chart. The following year's *Under The Influence* featured cover versions of songs by artists who had influenced Jackson over the years. Three years later Jackson finally reached the top of the mainstream US album chart with *Drive*.

JACKSON, JANET

Janet (b. 1966) is the youngest of the family that produced the **Jackson Five**. She signed to A&M Records in 1982, recording her self-titled debut album, followed by *Dream Street*. Both albums sold only moderately. Jackson's breakthrough came with 1986's *Control*, which reached number 1 and produced five US Top 10 singles (including the chart-topping 'When I Think Of You'). **Janet Jackson**'s *Rhythm Nation 1814* was even more successful, yielding the US chart-toppers 'Miss You Much', 'Escapade', 'Black Cat' and 'Love Will Never Do (Without You)'. By the end of the year she had scooped eight Billboard awards.

Jackson's commercial peak continued into the 90s with her Virgin Records' debut *Janet* entering the US album chart at number 1. Further US chart-topping singles included 'That's The Way Love Goes' (number 1 for eight weeks) and 'Again', which were also UK bestsellers. The compilation album *Design Of A Decade* was another huge seller, and followed her collaboration with brother **Michael Jackson** on 'Scream'. Performing as simply Janet, she released her first studio set in four years, *The Velvet Rope*, a deeply personal album that dealt frankly with her much publicised emotional breakdown. A collaboration with BLACKstreet, 'I Get Lonely', was a US/UK Top 5 hit. 'Doesn't Really Matter', a song featured in the soundtrack to *Nutty Professor 2: The Klumps*, rose to the top of the US charts in August 2000. *All For You* was premiered the following April by its chart-topping title track.

JACKSON, JERMAINE

Jermaine (b. 1954) was a member of the **Jackson Five**. Besides playing bass, he acted as vocal counterpoint to his younger brother **Michael Jackson**. Like

his brothers Michael and Jackie, Jermaine was singled out by Motown Records for a solo career, and had an immediate US Top 10 hit with 'Daddy's Home', in 1972. When the other members of the Jackson Five decided to leave Motown in 1975, he elected to remain. **Stevie Wonder** wrote and produced 'Let's Get Serious' in 1979. 'You Like Me Don't You' brought him another hit as did 'Let Me Tickle Your Fancy', an unlikely collaboration with **Devo**. In 1984, he joined the Jacksons on the *Victory* album and tour. He has continued to work with his family group and as a soloist since then.

JACKSON, JOE

UK-born Jackson (b. 1954) was signed by A&M Records in 1978. His debut, 'Is She Really Going Out With Him?' was not an immediate hit, but by the time *Look Sharp* was released, the song had become one of the stand-out numbers of his live shows. The reggaefied *Beat Crazy* began a trend of changing musical direction. *Jumpin' Jive* was a throwback to the music of the 40s. One of his most satisfying works came in 1982 with *Night And Day*, which included the memorable hit 'Steppin' Out'. *Body And Soul* was also critically acclaimed, but after this Jackson's commercial fortunes began to decline. In 1991 he signed to Virgin Records, releasing *Laughter And Lust*. Having demonstrated that film scores and orchestral works were well within his boundaries, Jackson was signed to Sony Classical in 1997. The same year's *Heaven And Hell* served as a prelude to his first symphony, released in 1999. The recording won the 2001 Grammy Award for Best Pop Instrumental Album.

JACKSON, LATOYA

LaToya (b. 1956) served as a backing vocalist to the **Jacksons** before embarking on a solo career with Polydor Records in 1980. She failed to match the commercial success of her more famous siblings, with her highest chart position being the US number 56 single 'Hearts Don't Lie' (1984). She later exacerbated family relations with a scurrilous autobiography in 1991.

JACKSON, MICHAEL

Jackson (b. 1958) was a founder member of the **Jackson Five** at the age of four, and soon became the group's lead vocalist. The Jackson Five were signed to Motown Records at the end of 1968. Their early releases, including chart-toppers 'I Want You Back' and 'I'll Be There', illustrated the young Michael's remarkable maturity.

Michael Jackson's first solo release was 'Got To Be There', a major US and UK hit. His revival of Bobby Day's 'Rockin' Robin' (1972) reached US number 2, and the sentimental film theme 'Ben' went one position further the following year. As the Jackson Five's sales slipped in the mid-70s, Michael's solo career was put on hold. He continued to reserve his talents for the group after they were reborn as the Jacksons in 1976. He re-entered the public eye with a starring role in the film musical *The Wiz*, collaborating on the soundtrack album with **Quincy Jones**. Their partnership was renewed in 1979 when Jones produced the sparkling *Off The Wall*, which topped the charts in the UK and USA, and contained two US number 1s, 'Don't Stop 'Til You Get Enough' and 'Rock With You'.

Jackson continued to tour and record with the Jacksons after this solo success, but media speculation was growing about his private life; he was increasingly portrayed as a figure trapped in eternal childhood. In 1982

Thriller, Jackson's second album with Quincy Jones, was released, and has become one of the most commercially successful albums of all time. It produced a run of successful hit singles, each accompanied by a ground-breaking promotional video. Amidst this run of hits, he slotted in 'Say Say Say', a chart-topping duet with **Paul McCartney**.

Jackson had by now become an almost mythical figure: a group of Jehovah's Witnesses announced that he was the Messiah; he was said to be taking drugs to change his skin colour to white; it was claimed that he had undergone extensive plastic surgery to alter his appearance; and photographs were published that suggested he slept in a special chamber to prevent himself ageing. More prosaically, Jackson began 1985 by co-writing and performing on the international number 1 USA For Africa benefit single 'We Are The World'. *Bad*, again with Quincy Jones, sold in multi-millions, but in comparison with *Thriller*, it was deemed disappointing. Unabashed, Jackson undertook a lengthy world concert tour to promote the album, and published his autobiography, *Moonwalker*. The long-awaited *Dangerous* justifiably scaled the charts, and 'Black And White' was a transatlantic chart-topper.

In 1993, the world was shocked by allegations of child sexual abuse directed at Jackson. No charges were made, but Jackson briefly left the USA and went into hiding. In May 1994, he married Lisa Marie Presley; the marriage collapsed just 19 months later, giving further rise to media allegations that it was merely a set-up to improve his soiled image. He did, however, enhance his reputation with *HIStory: Past, Present And Future – Book 1*. One half of the double set chronicled his past hits, but there was the equivalent of a new album forming the second half.

An unexpected second marriage (which ended in October 1999) and the birth of two children brought further media interest in Jackson. In 2001 the singer celebrated his 30th anniversary as a solo artist, reuniting with the Jackson Five on stage and breaking a long recording silence in August with his new single 'You Rock My World'. The attendant *Invincible* paired Jackson with hotshot urban producer Rodney Jerkins, but was let down by a surfeit of weak ballad material. Nevertheless, the album went straight to the top of the US and UK charts following its November release.

JACKSON, MILLIE

US-born Jackson's (b. 1944) controversial singing career began professionally in 1964. 'Hurts So Good' was a big hit and her subsequent direction was shaped in 1974 with the release of *Caught Up*. The sexual element in her work embraced either the pose of adultress or of wronged wife. *Still Caught Up* continued the saga, but Jackson's style later verged on self-parody. She possesses one of soul's outstanding voices, yet sadly chooses to limit its obvious potential.

JACKSON FIVE

The Jackson Five – brothers Jackie (b. Sigmund Esco Jackson, 1951), Tito (b. Toriano Adaryll Jackson, 1953), Jermaine (b. 1954), Marlon (b. 1957) and Michael Jackson (b. 1958) – began playing local Indiana clubs in 1962, with Michael as lead vocalist and signed to Motown Records in 1968. Their debut single, 'I Want You Back', became the fastest-selling record in the company's history and three of their next five singles also reached US number 1. By 1973, they had dropped the teenage stylings of their early hits, and perfected a harder brand of funk. In 1975 they signed to Epic Records, leading Motown boss Berry Gordy to sue them for alleged breach of contract. The case was settled in 1980, with the brothers paying Gordy $600,000, and allowing Motown all rights to the 'Jackson Five' name.

JAH WOBBLE

An innovative bass player, London-born Wobble (b. John Wardle) began his career with **Public Image Limited**. By 1980, Wobble had gone solo, and recorded with Holger Czukay and **U2**'s The Edge for *Snake Charmer* in addition to playing with the Human Condition. A bleak period as a London Underground employee was broken in 1987 when Wobble met guitarist Justin Adams and they put together Invaders Of The Heart. Wobble was in demand again, notably as collaborator with **Sinéad O'Connor** and **Primal Scream**. This was quickly followed by Invaders Of The Heart's *Rising Above Bedlam*, which featured the club hit 'Visions Of You'. Wobble's creative renaissance continued into the 90s with a series of infectious, upbeat albums for Island Records. He later released a series of concept albums on his own 30 Hertz label, exploring subjects as diverse as William Blake and Celtic poetry. Wobble also teamed up with ex-Pil bandmate Martin Atkins, Geordie Walker (ex-**Killing Joke**), and Chris Connelly (ex-**Ministry**) in the Damage Manual.

JAM

This UK trio – Paul Weller (b. 1958; vocals, guitar), Bruce Foxton (b. 1955; bass, vocals) and Rick Buckler (b. Paul Richard Buckler, 1955; drums) – were signed to Polydor Records in 1977. Although emerging at the peak of punk, the Jam seemed divorced from the movement, with their musical influences firmly entrenched in the mod style. Their debut, 'In The City', was a high-energy outing and the follow-up, 'All Around The World', infiltrated the UK Top 20.

For the next year, they registered only minor hits. A turning point in their fortunes occurred with the release of 'Down In The Tube Station At Midnight' (1978). This song saw them emerge as social commentators *par excellence*. *All Mod Cons* was widely acclaimed and thereafter the Jam rose to extraordinary heights. With *Setting Sons*, Weller fused visions of British colonialism with urban decay. Its superbly constructed 'Eton Rifles' (1979) gave the Jam their first UK Top 10 single. In 1980, they secured their first UK

number 1 with 'Going Underground'. While they continued to log number 1s with 'Start' and 'Town Called Malice', the US market remained untapped.

In 1982, the trio's run of UK chart-toppers was interrupted by 'The Bitterest Pill (I Ever Had To Swallow)', which peaked at number 2. Weller then announced that they were disbanding. Their final single, 'Beat Surrender', entered the UK chart at number 1, an extraordinary conclusion to a remarkable but brief career. Weller went on to found the **Style Council**.

JAMES

Timothy Booth (b. 1960; vocals), James Glennie (b. 1963; bass), Larry Gott (guitar) and Gavan Whelan (drums) signed with Manchester's Factory Records in 1983. They relocated to Sire Records in 1985 and released *Stutter*. Dave Baynton-Power later replaced Whelan and the band was augmented by Saul Davies (guitar, violin), Mark Hunter (keyboards) and Andy Diagram (trumpet). Fontana Records re-released an earlier track, 'Sit Down', which reached UK number 2 in 1991. *Seven* marked a change of direction and an emphasis on unconventional song structures. The upshot was a fall-off in commercial viability in their home market. *Laid* and its hit single was the first to make an impression in the USA. The move into ambient electronics on *Wah Wah* had been signposted by the 1993 Sabres Of Paradise remix of 'Jam J'.

Tim Booth recorded an album with American composer Angelo Badalamenti as Booth And The Bad Angel before, in 1997, James broke a three-year silence with the well-received *Whiplash* and the hit single 'She's A Star'. The recordings featured new guitarist Adrian Oxaal, who replaced founder-member Gott. A remix of 'Sit Down' reached UK number 7 in November 1998 on the back of the commercial success of their compilation album. The excellent *Millionaires* benefited from the creative input of Hunter and Davies and the production wiles of **Brian Eno**, employed by the band for the first time since *Laid*. They returned in 2001 with another strong release, *Pleased To Meet You*. This was to be Booth's final recording with the band.

JAMES GANG

Formed in 1967 in Cleveland, Ohio, USA, the embryonic James Gang comprised Glenn Schwartz (guitar, vocals), Tom Kriss (bass, vocals) and Jim Fox (drums, vocals). Schwartz left in 1969 but Joe Walsh (b. 1947) proved a competent replacement on *Yer Album*. Kriss was replaced by Dale Peters for *The James Gang Rides Again*. *Thirds* was another quality album, but Walsh then quit to pursue solo ambitions. Roy Kenner (vocals) and Dom Troiano (guitar) joined Fox and Peters for *Straight Shooter* and *Passin' Thru*. Troiano was then replaced by Tommy Bolin (b. 1951, d. 1976) who provided new bite and purpose, and *Bang* was a marked improvement. *Miami* coincided with Bolin's departure to **Deep Purple**, following which the James Gang was dissolved. Fox and Peters resurrected the name the following year, adding Bubba Keith (vocals) and Richard Shack (guitar) for the undistinguished *Jesse Come Home*. Various reunions have taken place.

JAMES, ELMORE

Mississippi legend Elmore James (b. 1918, d. 1963) is chiefly recalled for his debut release, 'Dust My Broom', which was marked by his unfettered vocals and searing electric slide guitar. James moved to Chicago, where he formed the Broomdusters. Subsequent recordings, including 'Bleeding Heart' and 'Shake Your Moneymaker', were later adopted by **Jimi Hendrix** and **Fleetwood Mac** and James's distinctive 'bottleneck' style resurfaced in countless British blues bands. John Mayall's 'Mr. James' was a thoughtful tribute to this significant performer, who suffered a fatal heart attack in May 1963.

JAMES, ETTA

James's (b. Jamesetta Hawkins, 1938) 'Roll With Me Henry', later retitled 'The Wallflower' in an effort to disguise its risqué lyrics, became an R&B number 1. Having secured a contract with Chess Records, Californian James unleashed a series of powerful songs, including 'All I Could Do Was Cry' (1960) and 'Pushover' (1963). In 1967 Chess Records took her to the Fame studios and the resultant *Tell Mama* was a triumph. *Etta James* earned her a US Grammy nomination. *Etta Is Betta Than Evah* completed her Chess contract in 1977, and she moved to Warner Brothers Records. The live *Late Show* albums were followed by *Seven Year Itch*, her first album for Island Records. This, and the subsequent *Stickin' To My Guns*, found her back on form. Following the use in a television advertisement of her version of Muddy Waters' 'I Just Want To Make Love To You', she found herself near the top of the UK charts in 1996. Her extraordinary voice has been showcased to great effect on her recent Private releases, including *Love's Been Rough On Me*, *Matriarch Of The Blues* and *Blue Gardenia*. The latter, a smooth album demonstrating James' love of jazz ballads, rewarded the singer by rising to the top of the jazz chart.

JAMES, RICK

The nephew of **Temptations** vocalist Melvin Franklin, James (b. James Johnson, 1948) pioneered a crossover style between R&B and rock in the mid-60s. In 1965, he formed the Mynah Birds with **Neil Young** and Motown Records signed the band, but their career was aborted when James was arrested for draft evasion.

In the early 70s, James formed the funk combo Main Line and he rapidly evolved a more individual style, which he labelled 'punk funk'. *Street Songs* was a Grammy-nominated record that catapulted James into the superstar bracket. His drift towards a more conservative image was heightened when he duetted with **Smokey Robinson** on 'Ebony Eyes'. After releasing *The Flag* in 1986, he signed to Reprise Records, where he immediately achieved a soul number 1 with 'Loosey's Rap'. Impeded by drug problems, James was jailed in 1991 for various offences. He was released in 1996.

JAMES, TOMMY, AND THE SHONDELLS

This US band, comprising Tommy James (b. 1947), Larry Coverdale (guitar), Craig Villeneuve (keyboards), Larry Wright (bass) and Jim Payne (drums), secured a deal with the local Snap label in 1962. Their first release, 'Hanky Panky' eventually sold in excess of one million copies and reached number 1. Signing to Roulette Records, James assembled a new Shondells, which settled around a nucleus of Eddie Gray (guitar), Ronnie Rossman (keyboards), Mike Vale (bass) and Pete Lucia (drums). The addition of production/songwriting team Ritchie Cordell and Bo Gentry resulted in a string of hits, including 'I Think We're Alone Now', 'Mirage' and 'Out Of The Blue' (1968). 'Mony Mony' (1968) was a UK number 1. James then wrote, arranged and produced the atmospheric 'Crimson And Clover', which topped the US chart and garnered sales of over five million copies. This desire to experiment continued with the album *Cellophane Symphony*. In 1970, the group and singer parted on amicable terms. An exhausted James retired to a farm before launching a solo career. 'Draggin' The Line' (1971) provided a US Top 5 hit, although subsequent releases from the early 70s failed to broach the Top 30. In 1980 the singer had another million-seller with 'Three Times In Love', since when he has continued to record, albeit with less success.

JAMIROQUAI

Highly successful UK funk outfit fronted by Jason 'Jay' Kay (b. 1969). Kay was signed to Sony Records on the strength of the single 'When You Gonna Learn?'. Inspired by 60s funksters Sly Stone and Roy Ayers, Kay integrated those influences into a 90s pop format that also combined new-age mysticism. His 1993 debut entered the UK chart at number 1. Backed by a regular band comprising Stuart Zender (b. 1974; bass), Toby Smith (b. 1970; keyboards), Wallis Buchanan (didgeridoo, vibes) and Derrick McKenzie (b. 1962; drums), Jamiroquai's second album was a considerable creative improvement, with songs such as 'Kids', and 'Morning Glory' giving Kay's obvious vocal talents better service. *Travelling Without Moving* confirmed Jamiroquai as a highly commercial act, selling over seven million copies worldwide and winning four trophies at the 1997 MTV Awards.

Following a string of UK hit singles, including 'Virtual Insanity', 'Cosmic Girl' and 'Alright', the band achieved their first UK chart-topper when 'Deeper Underground', taken from the soundtrack of the movie *Godzilla*, topped the charts in August 1998. Kay's long-serving bass player Zender left during the recording of the following year's *Synkronized*. At the end of the year it was confirmed that, after the **Spice Girls** and **Oasis**, Jamiroquai were the biggest-selling UK group of the decade. Kay's high-profile relationship with television presenter Denise Van Outen informed his first album of the new millennium, *A Funk Odyssey*.

JAN AND DEAN

Students at Emerson Junior High School, Los Angeles, Jan Berry (b. 1941) and Dean Torrence (b. 1940) formed the Barons, but its original members gradually drifted away, leaving Berry, Torrence and singer Arnie Ginsburg. In 1958, the trio recorded 'Jennie Lee', which became a surprise hit, although Torrence was drafted prior to its success. Berry and Torrence went on to enjoy a Top 10 entry with 'Baby Talk'. In 1963 they released 'Linda', which was redolent of the **Beach Boys**, linking the futures of the two groups. Brian Wilson co-wrote 'Surf City', Jan And Dean's first number 1 hit. In 1966, Berry crashed his sports car, incurring severe brain damage, but although recovery was slow, the singer did complete a few singles during the early 70s. Torrence kept the Jan And Dean name alive, but failed to recapture the duo's success. However, the pair were reunited in 1978 when they undertook the support slot for that year's Beach Boys tour.

JANE'S ADDICTION

Formed in Los Angeles, USA, in 1986, by vocalist Perry Farrell (b. Perry Bernstein, 1959), with the addition of guitarist Dave Navarro, bass player Eric Avery and drummer Stephen Perkins. Jane's Addiction incorporated elements of punk, rock, folk and funk into a unique and unpredictable soundscape. They debuted with a live album which received widespread acclaim. In the USA, because of censorship, *Ritual De Lo Habitual* was released in a plain envelope with the text of the First Amendment written on it. Farrell split the band in 1992 and formed **Porno For Pyros**. In the summer of 1997, the original band reunited and two new tracks appeared on a compilation of live material, demos and out-takes.

JAPAN

Formed in London in early 1974, this UK band comprised David Sylvian (b. David Batt, 1958; vocals), his brother Steve Jansen (b. Steven Batt, 1959; drums), Richard Barbieri (b. 1957; keyboards) and Mick Karn (b. Anthony Michaelides, 1958; saxophone). A second guitarist, Rob Dean, joined later. Their derivative pop style hampered their prospects during 1978, and they suffered a number of hostile reviews. Joining Virgin Records in 1980, their fortunes improved thanks to the emergence of the New Romantic movement and they registered three UK Top 20 hits. Disagreements between Karn and Sylvian undermined the band's progress and they split in late 1982. The members diversified into collaborative work and solo careers, reuniting (minus Dean) in 1991 for a project under the moniker of Rain Tree Crow.

JARRE, JEAN-MICHEL

French-born Jarre's (b. 1948) first full-scale electronic opus, *Oxygene*, reached number 2 in the UK charts, signalling his arrival as a commercial force. The subsequent *Equinoxe* explored the emotive power of orchestrated electronic rhythms and melody. With *Magnetic Fields* Jarre undertook his first tour to China. *Music For Supermarkets* proved his most elusive release; just one copy was pressed and auctioned for charity before the masters were destroyed. *Zoolook* was unfavourably received and prompted a two-year absence from recording. *Revolutions* appeared in the shops shortly after a London Docklands concert in 1988. *Waiting For Cousteau* earned a world record for attendance at a music concert, when two million people crammed in to Paris on Bastille Day. On July 14 1995, in his newly appointed role as UNESCO's 'goodwill ambassador', Jarre staged the 'Concert pour la Tolerance' to celebrate the United Nations 50th Anniversary and the Year For Tolerance. The performance in front of the Eiffel Tower was attended by over one-and-a-half million people.

Oxygene 7-13, released in 1997, showed Jarre had been listening closely to recent developments in electronic music. His credibility rose in the late 90s when he achieved a UK number 12 chart hit in July 1998 with 'Rendez-vous 98', a collaboration with Apollo 440 that was used as the theme music to ITV's coverage of the soccer World Cup. To commemorate the millennium, Jarre staged *The Twelve Dreams Of The Sun* spectacular at the Great Pyramids in Egypt. His first completely vocal album, *Metamorphoses*, was released two months later.

JARREAU, AL

Jarreau's (b. 1940) vocal style displays many influences, including jazz, the work of Jon Hendricks and African and Oriental music. More commercially successful than most jazz singers, Jarreau's work in the 70s and 80s consistently appealed to young audiences attuned to fusions in popular music. *Breakin' Away* (1981) won Grammy Awards in the pop and jazz fields. Further R&B and pop hits followed, including the theme tune to the television series *Moonlighting*. In 1996, he appeared in the Broadway production of *Grease* and released a compilation album. He subsequently signed a deal with GRP Records, releasing *Tomorrow Today* in 2000.

JASON AND THE SCORCHERS

This country rock 'n' roll-styled US band was formed in the early 80s by Jason Ringenberg (b. 1959; vocals, guitar, harmonica), Warner Hodges (b. 1959; guitar), Jeff Johnson (bass) and Perry Bags (b. 1962; drums). After four albums the Scorchers split up, with Ringenberg embarking on a solo career. He subsequently re-formed his old band, recording prolifically for Mammoth Records before setting up his own Courageous Chicken label.

JAY AND THE AMERICANS

This New York, USA-based act was formed in 1961 when former Mystics vocalist John 'Jay' Traynor (b. 1938) joined ex-Harbor Lites duo Kenny Rosenberg, aka Vance, and Sandy Yaguda, aka Deane. Howie Kane (b. Howard Kerschenbaum) completed the line-up. Jay And The Americans scored a US Top 5 hit with their second single 'She Cried', but in 1962 Traynor left. The remaining trio recruited David 'Jay' Black (b. David Blatt, 1938) who introduced fifth member Marty Saunders (guitar) to the band, and the following year established his new role with the powerful 'Only In America'. 'Come A Little Bit Closer' became a US Top 3 entry. Further hits followed, but by the end of the decade the band's impetus had waned. Black continues to perform on the nostalgia circuit.

JAY-Z

Raised in Brooklyn, Jay-Z (b. Shawn Corey Carter, 1969) first started releasing records in the late 80s, part-financing his music by hustling. He scored an underground hit single with 1995's 'In My Lifetime', and set-up his own Roc-A-Fella imprint with entrepreneur Damon Dash and Kareem 'Biggs' Burke. His debut set, *Reasonable Doubt*, went on to achieve gold sales and produced the US number 50 pop single 'Ain't No Nigga'/'Dead Presidents'. The album attracted fans with a mixture of hard-hitting street lyrics and rhymes, epitomized by the collaboration with Notorious B.I.G. on 'Brooklyn's Finest'. The follow-up *In My Lifetime, Vol. 1* was released in the aftermath of Notorious B.I.G.'s murder, and debuted at US number 3. Jay-Z then became a major star with the hit singles, 'Can I Get A ... ' and 'Hard Knock Life (Ghetto Anthem)', the latter built around a line from the musical *Annie*. The album of the same name diluted Jay-Z's hard-hitting lyrical edge in an attempt to corner the crossover market. *Vol. 2 ... Hard Knock Life* easily succeeded in its aim, staying at US number 1 for five weeks. *Vol. 3 ... Life And Times Of S. Carter* confirmed his status as one of hip-hop's most popular artists when it topped the album charts. *The Dynasty: Roc La Familia* 2000 and 2001's *The Blueprint* continued Jay-Z's remarkable creative and commercial success. The same December he was sentenced to three years probation for stabbing record producer Lance 'Un' Rivera at a New York nightclub two years previously. A duo album with R. Kelly was released in 2002.

JAYHAWKS

Hailing from Minneapolis, Minnesota, USA, the Jayhawks' line-up on their 1986 debut comprised Mark Olson (vocals, guitar), Gary Louris (vocals, guitar), Marc Perlman (bass), and Norm Rogers (drums). Subsequent releases continued the debut's blend of rugged country imagery with harsh, rough-hewn bar blues. Olson left the band in 1996 leaving Louris as the main songwriter. *Sound Of Lies* related to the break-up of his marriage. *Smile* was released on Columbia Records in 2000.

JEAN, WYCLEF

Despite the **Fugees** becoming the biggest rap crossover success of the 90s thanks to the multi-platinum worldwide success of *The Score*, Wyclef Jean (b. 1972) still found time to release a solo album in 1997. Long regarded as the production mastermind behind the Fugees' intoxicating blend of rap, soul and Haitian music, Wyclef Jean is also active as a remixer and producer to the R&B and dance music communities. In 1999, he teamed up with **U2**'s Bono to record 'New Day', the official song for the Net Aid charity concert. His

sophomore release, *The Ecleftic: 2 Sides II A Book*, was a sprawling mess, only partially redeemed by stand-out tracks such as '911' and 'It Doesn't Matter'.

JEFFERSON AIRPLANE

This US group was formed in 1965 by Marty Balin (b. Martyn Jerel Buchwald, 1942; vocals, guitar) with Paul Kantner (b. 1941; guitar, vocals) and Jorma Kaukonen (b. 1940; guitar, vocals). Bob Harvey and Jerry Peloquin gave way to Alexander 'Skip' Spence and Signe Anderson (b. 1941), later replaced by Spencer Dryden (b. 1938; drums) and Jack Casady (b. 1944). Anderson departed shortly after the release of their debut *Jefferson Airplane Takes Off* and was replaced by Grace Slick (b. Grace Barnett Wing, 1939; vocals). Slick was already well-known with her former band, the Great Society, and donated two of their songs, 'White Rabbit' and 'Somebody To Love', to Jefferson Airplane. Both titles became US Top 10 hits. This national success continued with *After Bathing At Baxters* and *Crown Of Creation*. They maintained a busy schedule and released a live album, *Bless Its Pointed Little Head* in 1969. *Volunteers* was an

excellent album, but it marked the decline of Balin's role in the band. Additionally, Dryden departed and the offshoot Hot Tuna began to take up more of Casady and Kaukonen's time. Kantner released a concept album, *Blows Against The Empire*, bearing the name Paul Kantner And The Jefferson Starship.

Following a greatest-hits selection, *Worst Of*, and the departure of Balin, the band released the cleverly packaged *Bark* on their own Grunt label. The disappointing *Long John Silver* was followed by a gutsy live outing, *30 Seconds Over Winterland*. This was the last album to bear their name. The Airplane title was resurrected in 1989 when Slick, Kaukonen, Casady, Balin and Kantner re-formed and released **Jefferson Airplane** to an indifferent audience.

JEFFERSON STARSHIP

This band evolved from Jefferson Airplane after Paul Kantner (b. 1941; guitar, vocals) had previously released *Blows Against The Empire* in 1970, billed as Paul Kantner And The Jefferson Starship. The official debut was *Dragonfly* (1974), which was an immediate success. Joining Kantner on this album were Grace Slick (b. Grace Barnett Wing, 1939; vocals), Papa John Creach (b. 1917, d. 1994; violin), David Freiberg (b. 1938; vocals, keyboards), Craig Chaquico (b. 1954; lead guitar), John Barbata (drums) and Pete Sears (bass, keyboards). Marty Balin joined in 1975 and the ensuing *Red Octopus* became their most successful album. *Spitfire* and *Earth* continued their success, although the band had now become a hard-rock outfit. Balin's lighter 'Count On Me' was a US Top 10 hit in 1978.

Slick and Balin both left the band, the latter replaced by Mickey Thomas. Drummer Aynsley Dunbar (b. 1946) also joined. The tension broke in 1985 when, following much acrimony over ownership of the band's name, Kantner was paid off and took with him half the band's moniker. His former group became Starship. Both Thomas and Freiberg left during these antagonistic times. *Knee Deep In The Hoopla* in 1985 became their most successful album since *Red Octopus*. Two singles from the album, 'We Built This City' (written by Bernie Taupin) and 'Jane', both reached US number 1 and, the following year, they reached the top spot on both sides of the Atlantic with the theme from the film *Mannequin*, 'Nothing's Gonna Stop Us Now'. After Starship broke up in the early 90s, Kantner revived the Jefferson Starship name. New vocalist Diana Mangano was featured on *Windows Of Heaven*.

JENNINGS, WAYLON

When only 12 years old, Jennings (b. Wayland Arnold Jennings, 1937, d. 2002) started as a radio disc jockey and then, in Lubbock, befriended an aspiring **Buddy Holly**. In 1958, Holly produced his debut single 'Jole Blon' and they co-wrote 'You're The One', a Holly demo that surfaced after his death. Jennings played bass on Holly's last tour, relinquishing his seat for that fatal plane journey to the **Big Bopper**.

After Holly's death, Jennings returned to radio work in Lubbock, before moving to Phoenix and forming his own group, the Waylors. They began a two-year residency at a new Phoenix club, J. D.'s, in 1964. Jennings recorded for A&M Records and RCA Records, enjoying a string of country hits. However, he was uncomfortable with session men, feeling that the arrangements were overblown.

When Jennings was ill with hepatitis, he considered leaving the business, but his drummer Richie Albright talked him into staying on. Jennings recorded some excellent Shel Silverstein songs for the soundtrack of *Ned Kelly*, which starred **Mick Jagger**, and the new Jennings fell into place with his 1971 album, *Singer Of Sad Songs*, which was sympathetically produced by Lee Hazlewood. Like the album sleeve, the music was darker and tougher, and the beat was more pronounced. The cover of *Honky Tonk Heroes* showed the new Jennings and the company he was keeping. The new pared-down, bass-driven, no-frills-allowed sound continued on *The Ramblin' Man* and on his best album, *Dreaming My Dreams*.

Wanted! The Outlaws and its hit single 'Good Hearted Woman' transformed both **Willie Nelson** and Jennings' careers, making them huge media personalities in the USA. The two artists will be remembered for shaking the Nashville establishment by assuming artistic control and heralding a new era of grittier and more honest songs, although Jennings was tired of his mean and macho image even before it caught on with the public. Jennings often recorded with his wife, Jessi Colter, and he and **Johnny Cash** had a hit with 'There Ain't No Good Chain Gang' and made an underrated album, *Heroes*. His albums with Nelson, Cash and **Kris Kristofferson** as the Highwaymen were also highly successful.

Ill-health hampered Jennings during the latter part of his career, and in December 2001 his left foot was amputated because of an infection related to diabetes. He died two months later.

JESUS AND MARY CHAIN

Formed in East Kilbride, Scotland, this indie band was formed by William Reid (vocals, guitar), Jim Reid (vocals, guitar), Douglas Hart (bass) and Murray Dalglish (drums). The quartet moved to London in 1984 and signed to Creation Records, where their debut, 'Upside Down' became a hit. Soon afterwards, Dalglish was replaced on drums by **Primal Scream** vocalist Bobby Gillespie, who returned to his former group the following year. The Jesus And Mary Chain then signed to Blanco y Negro. The Reid Brothers issued their highly acclaimed debut, *Psychocandy*. Their second album, *Darklands*, was followed by a tempestuous tour of Canada and America. By the arrival of

Automatic, the band was effectively just a duo using programmed synth drums. *Honey's Dead* housed a powerful lead single in 'Reverence', which brought the band back to the charts in February 1992. For the self-produced *Stoned & Dethroned*, the brothers swapped feedback for an acoustic, singer-songwriter approach. The brothers rejoined Creation Records at the end of 1997 and issued 'Cracking Up'. It was followed by *Munki*, on which the Reid brothers experimented with a motley collection of different styles. The band officially split up the following year, with William Reid electing to work on his Lazycame solo project and Jim Reid forming Freeheat.

JETHRO TULL

Jethro Tull was formed in Luton, England, in 1967 when Ian Anderson (b. 1947; vocals, flute) and Glenn Cornick (b. 1947; bass), joined up with Mick Abrahams (b. 1943; guitar, vocals) and Clive Bunker (b. 1946; drums). A residency at London's Marquee club and a sensational appearance at the 1968 Sunbury Blues Festival confirmed a growing reputation. Their debut LP, *This Was*, reached the UK Top 10, largely on the strength of Tull's live reputation. For many spectators, Jethro Tull was the name of the extrovert frontman Anderson – the

other musicians were merely his underlings. This impression gained credence through the band's internal ructions. Mick Abrahams left in 1968 and Martin Barre (b. 1946) joined for *Stand Up*. The band was then augmented by John Evan (b. 1948; keyboards). *Benefit* duly followed and this period also included three UK Top 10 singles, 'Living In The Past', 'Sweet Dream' (both 1969) and 'The Witch's Promise' (1970). Cornick then quit and Jeffrey Hammond-Hammond (b. 1946), was brought in for the transatlantic hit album *Aqualung*. Clive Bunker left in 1971, replaced by Barriemore Barlow (b. 1949). *Thick As A Brick* topped the US chart and reached UK number 5, but critics began questioning Anderson's reliance on obtuse concepts and *A Passion Play* was labelled pretentious. *War Child*, a US number 2, failed to chart in the UK, although *Minstrel In The Gallery* proved more popular. *Too Old To Rock 'N' Roll, Too Young To Die* marked the departure of Hammond-Hammond in favour of John Glascock (b. 1953, d. 1979), and David Palmer was added as a second keyboards player. From here Jethro Tull embarked on another successful phase which lasted until Glascock's death.

In 1980, Anderson began a projected solo album, retaining Barre and new bass player Dave Pegg (ex-**Fairport Convention**). The finished product, *A*, was ultimately issued under the Jethro Tull banner, and was followed by two more group selections. Since then Jethro Tull has continued to record and perform live, using a nucleus of Anderson, Barre and Pegg.

JETT, JOAN, AND THE BLACKHEARTS

Producer Kim Fowley took US-born Jett (b. Joan Larkin, 1960) and her group under his wing and named it the Runaways. They recorded three punk-tinged hard-rock albums which were successful in Japan and England, where they recorded their swansong, *And Now ... The Runaways*. After the group split, Jett moved to New York where her first solo album became a bestselling US independent record. With her group the Blackhearts (guitarist Ricky Byrd, bassist Gary Ryan and drummer Lee Crystal), Jett recorded *I Love Rock 'N' Roll*. The title track spent seven weeks at US number 1 in 1982. *Glorious Results Of A Misspent*

Youth again retreated to Jett's past with the Runaways. After *Good Music* Crystal and Ryan left. *Up Your Alley* brought another hit with 'I Hate Myself For Loving You', before 1990's *The Hit List*. *Notorious* saw her hook up with Paul Westerberg of the Replacements while *Pure And Simple* featured a guest appearance from **L7**, emphasizing Jett's influence on a new generation of female rockers.

JEWEL

Singer-songwriter Jewel (b. Jewel Kilcher, 1974) left her home in Alaska at the age of 16 to study opera in Michigan, Illinois. Regular concerts at the Innerchange coffee shop quickly attracted several major-label A&R staff. Warner Brothers Records won her signature and released her debut album, *Pieces Of You*, in 1995. A slow-burning success, the album eventually achieved multi-platinum status. She also signed a $2 million dollar publishing deal with HarperCollins. Her book of poetry, *A Night Without Armor*, sold over two million copies in America alone. *Spirit*, her eagerly awaited follow-up album, debuted at US number 3 in 1998, and included the Top 10 single 'Hands'. The following year the singer made her acting debut in Ang Lee's acclaimed civil war drama *Ride With The Devil*. She also released the seasonal *Joy* prior to the mediocre *This Way*.

JIMMY EAT WORLD

This Mesa, Arizona, USA-based band was formed in 1994 by Jim Adkins (guitar, vocals), Tom Linton (guitar, vocals), Mitch Porter (bass) and Zach Lind (drums). Their major-label debut, 1996's *Static Prevails*, featured a more polished take on the debut's melodic hardcore. Lead vocals on the album were shared between Adkins and Linton. On the band's second major-label release, *Clarity*, Adkins' lead vocals added a perfect sheen to the band's intense power pop. The quartet signed a new recording contract with DreamWorks for the release of 2001's *Bleed American*. The album placed them at the forefront of the new wave of so-called emo (emotional hardcore) bands breaking into the mainstream.

JODECI

Among the more eloquent practitioners of 'new jack swing' or swingbeat, Jodeci enjoyed huge success in the USA during the 90s. The band was formed by two pairs of brothers: Joel **JoJo** (b. 1971) and Cedric **K-Ci** Hailey (b. 1969), and 'Mr' Dalvin and Donald 'DeVante Swing' DeGrate Jnr. Their silky, soulful vocals were stretched over sparse hip-hop beats on their 1991 debut album. It sold two million copies and earned Jodeci numerous accolades. *Diary Of A Mad Band*, much in the vein of their debut, also went multi-platinum. For 1995's third album the band slightly altered their musical backdrop, adopting the G-funk beats made prevalent by Dr. Dre. K-Ci And JoJo were featured on 2Pac's US number 1 single 'How Do U Want It' in 1996, before breaking away on their own as a successful chart act.

JOEL, BILLY

Joel (b. 1949), a classically trained pianist from Hicksville, USA, joined his first group, the Echoes, in 1964, before moving on to the Hassels. A demo of Joel's original compositions led to the release of his debut album, *Cold Spring Harbor*, in 1971. Columbia Records then signed Joel to a long-term contract. The title track to *Piano Man* became a US Top 30 single in 1973. After *Street Life Serenade* and *Turnstiles*, his fortunes flourished with the release of *The Stranger*, which included the Grammy Award-winning 'Just The Way You Are'. *52nd Street* spawned another smash single, 'My Life', while the singer's first US number 1, 'It's Still Rock 'N' Roll To Me', came from a subsequent release, *Glass Houses*. *The Nylon Curtain* featured two notable 'protest' compositions, 'Allentown' and 'Goodnight Saigon'. However, he returned to simpler matters with 1983's *An Innocent Man*, which included the effervescent bestseller 'Uptown Girl'. Less prolific in the 90s, Joel continued to achieve respectable sales and remains

one of America's bestselling solo artists of all time. A perfectionist by nature, he also indicated a desire to pursue a wider musical style, and in 1997 announced that he would not be writing any pop songs in the foreseeable future, concentrating instead on classical scores.

JOHN, ELTON

John (b. Reginald Kenneth Dwight, 1947) formed his first band, Bluesology, in the early 60s and turned professional in 1965. In 1966, **Long John Baldry** joined the band, which included Elton Dean (saxophone) and Caleb Quaye (guitar). John eventually began to explore the possibilities of a music publishing contract; the shy John soon met Bernie Taupin and, realizing they had similar musical tastes, they began to write together.

In 1968, John, adopting a new name taken from the first names of his former colleagues Dean and Baldry, and Taupin were signed by Dick James as staff writers for his new company DJM. In 1969, *Empty Sky* was released; over the next few months, John played on sessions with the **Hollies** and made budget recordings for cover versions released in supermarkets. His long wait for recognition ended the following year when Gus Dudgeon produced the outstanding *Elton John*, which included 'Border Song' and the UK number 2 hit 'Your Song'. The momentum was maintained with *Tumbleweed Connection* and over the next few years Elton John became a superstar. Between 1972 and 1975 he had seven consecutive number 1 albums, variously spawning memorable hits including 'Rocket Man', 'Daniel', 'Saturday Night's Alright For Fighting', 'Goodbye Yellow Brick Road', 'Candle In The Wind' and 'Someone Saved My Life Tonight'.

In 1976 he topped the UK charts with 'Don't Go Breaking My Heart' (a duet with Kiki Dee), and released a further two million-selling albums, *Here And There* and *Blue Moves*. By 1979 the John/Taupin partnership went into abeyance as Taupin moved to Los Angeles and John started writing with Gary Osborne. The partnership produced few outstanding songs other than the solo 'Song For Guy'. Elton John's albums during the early 80s were patchy, and only when he started working exclusively with Taupin again did his record sales pick up. The first renaissance album was *Too Low For Zero*, which scaled the charts. During 1985 he appeared at **Wham!**'s farewell concert, and at Live Aid. He completed the year with another massive album, *Ice On Fire*. In 1986, he and Taupin contested a lengthy and expensive court case for back royalties against DJM. In 1988, he released *Reg Strikes Back* and the fast-tempo 'I Don't Want To Go On With You Like That'. At the end of the decade, he released two more strong albums *Sleeping With The Past* and *The One*.

In 1991, the *Sunday Times* announced that John had entered the list of the top 200 wealthiest people in Britain. In 1993, an array of guest musicians appeared on John's *Duets*, including **Bonnie Raitt**, **Paul Young**, **k.d. lang**, **Little Richard** and **George Michael**. Five new songs by the artist graced the soundtrack to 1994's Disney blockbuster *The Lion King*. In 1995 John produced one of his best albums, *Made In England*, which scaled the charts worldwide.

Alongside the **Beatles** and **Rolling Stones**, Elton John is Britain's most successful artist of

all time. In 1997 he sang at the funeral of Diana, Princess Of Wales, where his performance of 'Candle In The Wind '97' was seen by an estimated two billion people. Buoyed by the publicity, John's 1997 album, *The Big Picture*, was another commercial success, and at the end of the year he was awarded a knighthood by Queen Elizabeth II. In 1999, John duetted with American country star **LeAnn Rimes** on 'Written In The Stars'. The single was taken from an ambitious stage adaptation of *Aida* by John and Tim Rice. The two men teamed up again the following year, with composer Hans Zimmer, to create the soundtrack to DreamWorks animated adventure *The Road To El Dorado*.

His first studio album of the new millennium, *Songs From The West Coast*, was hailed as a return to the standards set by his classic early 70s material.

JOHNSON, LINTON KWESI

Jamaican-born Johnson's (b. 1952) family emigrated to London in 1963. After taking a degree in sociology in 1973 he published two books, *Voices Of The Living And The Dead* (1974) and *Dread Beat And Blood* (1975). Johnson also wrote about reggae for *Black Music*, and experiments with reggae bands culminated in 1977's *Dread Beat An' Blood*, recorded as **Poet And The Roots.** In 1978, Johnson issued *Forces Of Victory*, this time under his own name, followed by *Bass Culture*. *LKJ In Dub* was release in 1980, the same year as *Inglan Is A Bitch*, his third book, was published. He finally returned to the studio in 1990 to record *Tings An' Times*. Writing commitments meant another recording hiatus before 1998's *More Time*.

JOHNSON, ROBERT

Blues artist Johnson (b. Robert Leroy Johnson, 1911, d. 1938) was one of the first performers to make creative use of others' recorded efforts, adapting and augmenting their ideas to bring originality to the compositions they inspired. Johnson recorded 29 tracks between November 1936 and June 1937 and the power and precision of his guitar playing are evident from the first. Eight titles were recorded over two days, including 'Walkin' Blues' and 'Cross Road Blues', the song an echo of the legend that Johnson had sold his soul to the Devil to achieve his musical skill. He was poisoned by a jealous husband while performing in a jook joint in Mississippi. His influence is such that it hardly strains credulity to suggest that Johnson was the fulcrum upon which post-war Chicago blues turned.

JONES, HOWARD

Synth-pop maestro Jones (b. John Howard Jones, 1955) was offered a session by BBC disc jockey John Peel which led to tours with **OMD** and China Crisis. He charted in the UK with his first single, 1983's 'New Song'. His debut **Human's Lib** topped the UK charts. Hits followed with 'What Is Love', 'Hide And Seek' and 'Like To Get To Know You Well'. He continues to record sporadically and even joined the unplugged with *Live Acoustic America* in 1996.

JONES, JIMMY

Jones (b. 1937) who had spent a long apprenticeship singing in R&B doo-wop groups, became a rock 'n' roll star in the early 60s. In 1956, he formed the Savoys, which was later renamed the Pretenders. Success finally came when Jones launched a solo career, hitting with his debut 'Handy Man' and following up with 'Good Timin''. In 1960 'Handy Man' reached number 2 'Good Timin'' number 3 in the US pop charts. The latter topped the UK charts.

JONES, PAUL

Jones (b. 1942) began his singing career while studying at Oxford University. Starting with the trailblazing Blues Incorporated, he subsequently joined the Mann Hugg Blues Brothers, which evolved into **Manfred Mann** in 1963. He left the line-up in 1966, enjoying two UK Top 5 hits with 'High Time' (1966)

and 'I've Been A Bad, Bad Boy' (1967). Stage and film appearances then took precedence over his music career. In 1979, he rekindled his first musical love with the formation of the Blues Band. He has continued to lead this popular unit whenever acting commitments allow.

JONES, QUINCY

Jones (b. Quincy Delight Jones Jnr., 1933) began playing the trumpet as a child. When he joined Lionel Hampton in 1951 it was as both performer and writer. Leaving Hampton in 1953, Jones wrote arrangements for many musicians, including, Count Basie and Tommy Dorsey. He worked with **Frank Sinatra**, Johnny Mathis and **Ray Charles**. As a record producer, Jones became the first black vice-president of Mercury's New York division. Later, he spent 12 years with A&M Records before starting up his own label, Qwest.

In the 70s and 80s, in addition to many film soundtracks, he produced successful albums for George Benson (*Give Me The Night*), while for **Michael Jackson** he helped to create *Off The Wall* and *Thriller*. A major film documentary, *Listen Up: The Lives Of Quincy Jones*, was released in 1990. *Q's Jook Joint* was a retrospective of his 50 years in the music business. He published his autobiography in 2001.

JONES, RICKIE LEE

US singer-songwriter Jones (b. 1954) emerged in 1979 with a buoyant debut album lyrically indebted to beat and jazz styles, including 'Chuck E.'s In Love', a US Top 5 single. Although *Rickie Lee Jones* garnered popular success, the singer refused to be rushed into a follow-up. Two years later, *Pirates* revealed a hitherto hidden emotional depth. *Girl At Her Volcano*, a collection of old standards, marked time until the release of *The Magazine* in 1984, which confirmed the artist's imaginative talent. However, it was six years before a further album, *Flying Cowboys*, was issued. The set marked a fruitful collaboration with Glasgow group the **Blue Nile**. *Pop Pop* returned to the *Girl At Her Volcano* format. *Traffic From Paradise* revealed Jones' muse to be in fine working order, although her cover of David Bowie's 'Rebel Rebel' was the standout track. *Naked Songs*, her contribution to the 'unplugged' phenomenon, was followed by the stridently modern *Ghostyhead*, on which Jones embraced the rhythms of contemporary dance music. *It's Like This*, another cover-versions album, was in marked contrast.

JONES, TOM

Jones (b. Thomas Jones Woodward, 1940) began his musical career in 1963 as vocalist in the Welsh group Tommy Scott And The Senators. After signing with former Viscounts vocalist Gordon Mills he changed his name to Tom Jones. His first single, 'Chills And Fever', failed to chart but, early in 1965, Jones' second release 'It's Not Unusual', composed by Mills and Les Reed, reached UK number 1. Meanwhile, Mills astutely ensured that his star was given first choice for film theme songs, and 'What's New Pussycat?' became a major US/UK hit. By 1966, however, Jones' chart fortunes were in decline. Mills took drastic action by regrooming his protégé for an older market. By Christmas 1966, Jones was effectively relaunched owing to the enormous success of 'Green Green Grass Of Home', which topped the UK charts for seven weeks. In 1967, he enjoyed one of his biggest UK hits with the intense 'I'll Never Fall In Love Again', which climbed to number 2. The hit run continued with 'I'm Coming Home' and 'Delilah'.

As the 60s reached their close, Mills took his star to America, where he hosted the highly successful television show *This Is Tom Jones*. Although Jones logged a handful of hits in the UK during the early 70s, his future lay in the lucrative Las Vegas circuit. It was not until after the death of Mills, when his son Mark Woodward took over his management, that the star elected to return to recording. Jones' continued credibility was emphasized when he reached number 2 in 1987 with 'The Boy From Nowhere', and the following year collaborated with the **Art Of Noise** on a kitsch version of **Prince**'s 'Kiss'. At the end of the following decade, Jones asserted his remarkable durability when an album of duets and collaborations recorded with a host of contemporary artists topped the UK charts.

JOPLIN, JANIS

US singer Joplin (b. 1943, d. 1970) developed a brash, uncompromising vocal style. In 1962, she joined the Waller Creek Boys, but made her name as the singer with Big Brother And The Holding Company. Her reputation blossomed following the Monterey Pop Festival. *Cheap Thrills* contained two Joplin 'standards' 'Piece Of My Heart' and 'Ball And Chain'. Mike Bloomfield helped assemble a new act, Janis And The Joplinaires, later known as the Kozmic Blues Band. Sam Andrew (guitar, vocals), Terry Clements (saxophone), Marcus Doubleday (trumpet), Bill King (organ), Brad Campbell (bass) and Roy Markowitz (drums) made up the initial line-up. *I Got Dem Ol' Kozmic Blues Again Mama* was coolly received, but contained several excellent Joplin vocals. Live shows grew increasingly erratic as her addiction to drugs and alcohol deepened. A slimmed-down group, the Full Tilt Boogie Band, was unveiled in 1970. The debut album sessions were all but complete when Joplin died of a heroin overdose at her Hollywood hotel. The posthumous *Pearl* remains her most consistent work.

JORDANAIRES

A renowned harmony-vocal quartet best-known for its lengthy working relationship with **Elvis Presley**. Lead vocalist Gordon Stoker (b. 1924) was subsequently featured on Presley's first recordings for RCA Victor, while the remaining trio – Neal Matthews (b. 1929, d. 2000; tenor), Hoyt Hawkins (b. 1927, d. 1982; baritone) and Hugh Jarrett (b. 1929; bass) – joined him on the session producing 'Hound Dog' and 'Don't Be Cruel'. The quartet, featuring new bass singer Ray Walker (b. 1934), continued to accompany Presley throughout the 50s and 60s, although they were absent from the 'comeback' NBC-TV spectacular, *Elvis* in 1968. The recordings in Nashville during June and September 1970, marked the end of the Jordanaires' relationship with Presley. In 1972 they contributed to *The Guitar That Changed The World*, the solo debut by Presley's long-time guitarist Scotty Moore. The Jordanaires' own recording career has mainly focused on their favoured gospel material.

JOURNEY

This US rock band was formed in 1973 by ex-**Santana** members Neil Schon (b. 1954; guitar) and Gregg Rolie (b. 1948; keyboards), with Ross Valory (b. 1949; bass) and Prairie Prince (b. 1950; drums). George Tickner was added later as rhythm guitarist and lead vocalist. Prince was later replaced by Aynsley Dunbar (b. 1946), and Tickner by vocalist Steve Perry (b. 1953). The switch to highly sophisticated pump rock occurred with the recording of *Infinity*. Dunbar quit and was replaced by Steve Smith (b. 1954). *Evolution* followed and brought the band their first US Top 20 hit, 'Lovin', Touchin', Squeezin'', followed by a live double album, *Captured*. Rolie departed after its release, replaced by Jonathan Cain (b. 1950). *Escape* reached number 1 and stayed in the chart for over a year, spawning three US Top 10 singles. The follow-up, *Frontiers*, was also successful, and 'Separate Ways' reached the Top 10. The band reduced to a three-man nucleus of Schon, Cain and Perry to record *Raised On Radio*. This was Journey's last album before Schon and Cain joined forces with John Waite's Bad English in 1988. A

full-scale reunion occurred in 1996 when Perry, Schon, Smith, Cain and Valory released the Top 5 album *Trial By Fire*. The following year Deen Castronovo replaced Smith, and vocalist Steve Augeri was also drafted into the line-up.

JOY DIVISION

Originally known as Warsaw, this Manchester, England-based outfit comprised Ian Curtis (b. 1956, d. 1980; vocals), Bernard Dicken/Albrecht (b. 1956; guitar, vocals), Peter Hook (b. 1956; bass) and Steven Morris (b. 1957; drums). Joy Division's debut for Factory Records, *Unknown Pleasures*, was a raw, intense affair, with Curtis at his most manically arresting in 'She's Lost Control'. The charismatic Curtis was renowned for his neurotic choreography, but by the autumn of 1979, he was suffering epileptic seizures and blackouts on stage. The 1980 single 'Love Will Tear Us Apart', released the same year that Curtis killed himself, was a haunting account of a fragmented relationship. *Closer* displayed the band at the zenith of their powers. The following year, a double album, *Still*, collected the remainder of the band's material, most of it in primitive form. Within months of Curtis's death, the remaining members sought a fresh start as **New Order**.

JUDAS PRIEST

UK heavy-metal band formed in Birmingham, in 1969, by guitarist K. K. Downing (b. Kenneth Downing) and bass player Ian Hill. They played their first gig in Essington in 1971, with Alan Atkins (vocals) and John Ellis (drums). Vocalist Rob Halford (b. 1951) and drummer John Hinch joined the unit along with second guitarist Glenn Tipton (b. 1948). In 1974, the band made their debut with *Rocka Rolla*. *Sin After Sin* was a strong collection, with Simon Philips on drums. The band then visited America for the first time, with new drummer Les Binks, who appeared on *Stained Class*. *Killing Machine* featured shorter, punchier, but still-familiar rock songs. *Unleashed In The East* was recorded on the 1979 Japanese tour, and in the same year Binks was replaced on drums by Dave Holland. *British Steel* smashed into the UK album charts at number 3 and *Point Of Entry* was followed by sell-out UK and US tours. The period surrounding *Screaming For Vengeance* and *Defenders Of The Faith* offered a potent brand of headstrong metal. *Turbo*, though, was poorly received. *Ram It Down* saw a return to pure heavy metal, but by this time Judas Priest's popularity was waning. Dave Holland was replaced by Scott Travis for the return to form that was *Painkiller*.

The band were taken to court in 1990 following the suicide attempts of two fans in 1985. Both CBS Records and Judas Priest were accused of inciting suicide through their 'backwards messages' in their recording of 'Better By You, Better By Me', but were exonerated. Soon after, Halford became disheartened with the band and left to form his own outfit, Fight. Judas Priest returned to recording with 1997's *Jugulator*, featuring new vocalist Tim 'Ripper' Owens.

K-CI AND JOJO

The Hailey brothers, Cedric (b. 1969) and Joel (b. 1971), were founder members of **Jodeci**, the sexually provocative swingbeat outfit who enjoyed several US chart hits during the mid-90s. The duo featured prominently on **2Pac**'s number 1 single 'How Do U Want It' in 1996, before breaking away from Jodeci with *Love Always*. The album, which reached the US Top 10 and went multi-platinum, included April 1998's chart-topping single 'All My Life'. The duo repeated the debut album's winning formula on 1999's *It's Real*, which went platinum within two weeks of release.

KALEIDOSCOPE (USA)

Formed in 1966, this innovative US band originally comprised guitarists David Lindley and Chris Darrow, Solomon Feldthouse (vocals, oud), John Vidican (drums) and Charles Chester Crill (violin, organ, harmonic, vocals). *Side Trips* revealed a unit of enthralling imagination. Blues, jazz, folk and ethnic styles abounded as the quintet forged a fascinating collection. *A Beacon From Mars* marked the end of this particular line-up as Darrow then opted to join the **Nitty Gritty Dirt Band**. Vidican also left the band, and newcomers Stuart Brotman (bass) and Paul Lagos (drums) were featured on *Incredible Kaleidoscope*, which in turn offered a tougher, less acid-folk perspective. Further changes in the line-up ensued with the departure of Brotman. His replacement, Ron Johnson, introduced a funk-influenced element to the unit's sound, while a second newcomer, Jeff Kaplan, surprisingly took most of the lead vocals. The departures of Feldthouse and Crill in 1970, and Kaplan's death from a drugs overdose, signalled the demise of Kaleidoscope.

Darrow subsequently rejoined Feldthouse, Brotman, Lagos and Crill in the re-formed unit, completing *When Scopes Collide* which, although lacking the innovation of old, was nonetheless entertaining. The same line-up reconvened to complete 1991's equally meritorious *Greetings From Kartoonistan ... (We Ain't Dead Yet)*.

KANSAS

US rock band formed in 1974 by David Hope (b. 1949; bass), Steve Walsh (keyboards, vocals), Phil Ehart, (drums, percussion), Kerry Livgren (b. 1949; guitar, vocals), Robert Steinhardt (violin, vocals), and Richard Williams (guitar). Their second and third albums went gold, guaranteeing them a high US profile. By 1977 the band had tired of the progressive-rock pigeonhole into which the music press was forcing them, and decided to try a more commercial approach. The ballad 'Dust In The Wind' broke into the US Top 10. In the early 80s Walsh was replaced by John Elefante, who wrote four of the songs on *Vinyl Confessions*. The band split in 1983 after two unsuccessful albums. Livgren and Hope had become born-again Christians, and the former went on to record prolifically with AD.

In 1986, Walsh, Ehart and Williams re-formed Kansas with guitarist Steve Morse (b. 1954) and Billy Greer (bass), recording two hard-rocking albums. Morse subsequently left to form the Steve Morse Band, and Greg Robert (keyboards) and David Ragsdale (violin, guitar) joined the remaining members. This line-up recorded a live album and 1995's *Freaks Of Nature*, before Ragsdale and Robert both quit. Steinhardt returned to the line-up to help record *Always Never The Same*. All six original members regrouped in 2000 to record *Somewhere To Elsewhere*.

KATRINA AND THE WAVES

Anglo-American pop group formed in 1982 by Katrina Leskanich (b. 1960; vocals), Kimberley Rew (guitar; ex-**Soft Boys**), Vince De La Cruz (bass) and Alex Cooper (drums). They enjoyed a major UK hit in 1985 with 'Walking On Sunshine' but struggled through the rest of the decade. A series of reunion gigs in the 90s led to the band being nominated by the British public as the UK entry for the 1997 Eurovision Song Contest. 'Love Shine A Light' became the clear winner, and obligatory chart success followed. Leskanich then became a presenter on BBC Radio 2.

KC AND THE SUNSHINE BAND

Formed in Florida in 1973 by Harry Wayne 'KC' Casey (b. 1951; vocals, keyboards) and Richard Finch (b. 1954; bass), the other key members of this US funk-pop band included Jerome Smith (b. 1953, d. 2000; guitar) and Robert Johnson (b. 1953; drums). Casey and Finch wrote, arranged and

produced their own material, which included three consecutive US number 1s with the funky 'Get Down Tonight', 'That's The Way (I Like It)' (both 1975) and '(Shake, Shake, Shake), Shake Your Booty' (1976). Transatlantic hits followed with 'I'm Your Boogie Man', 'Please Don't Go' and 'Give It Up', the latter a UK chart-topper. Casey and Finch subsequently seemed to lose the art of penning radio-friendly soul/pop.

KEITA, SALIF

Albino vocalist/composer Keita (b. 1949) is from one of Mali's most distinguished families. He formed a trio before joining the Rail Band in 1970, but three years later switched to main rivals Les Ambassadeurs. With guitarist Kante Manfila, he extended the band's range, incorporating traditional Malian rhythms and melodies into their Afro-Cuban repertoire. Keita went solo in 1987, debuting with the rock-flavoured Soro. Keita's marriage of traditional Malian music and western instrumentation was subsequently heard to great effect on such landmark releases as *Ko-Yan* (1990), *Folon* (1995) and *Moffou* (2002).

KELIS

Kelis (b. Kelis Rogers, 1980) made a dramatic impact in 1999 with 'Caught Out There'. The single was dubbed the modern equivalent of **Gloria Gaynor**'s 'I Will Survive' and popularly perceived as 'I Hate You So Much Right Now' – from the screamed invective/chorus that disrupted the staccato, futuristic R&B track. The attendant *Kaleidoscope* was a similarly strident and lavishly styled collection of visionary R&B, funk, soul and hip-hop. Unfortunately, support had drifted considerably by the time of *Wanderland*'s release, which failed to ignite any sales sparks.

KELLY, R.

A leading figure on America's urban scene, Kelly (b. 1969) worked as musical co-ordinator and producer for a number of acts before making his first impact in 1991 with his band Public Announcement. His second album reached the top of the R&B charts in 1993, and spawned the hits 'Sex Me (Parts I & II)'

and 'Bump 'N Grind'. 'She's Got That Vibe', a reissue from his debut album, became a big club and chart hit in England at the same time. Kelly's next big success was in 1997 with 'I Believe I Can Fly', the theme for the movie *Space Jam*. The increasingly prolific Kelly, whose writing and production credits also include work for **Whitney Houston** and **Boyz II Men**, then released the sprawling double album *R*, which debuted at number 2 on the US album chart in 1998. Responding to the challenge of rivals **D'Angelo** and **Puff Daddy**, the clumsily titled *TP-2.Com* shot straight to the top of the US chart. The singer enjoyed a transatlantic hit single at the start of 2002 with his tribute to Muhammad Ali, 'The World's Greatest'. He also released a disappointing album with rap superstar **Jay-Z**.

KERSHAW, NIK

UK pop singer Kershaw (b. 1958) enjoyed a string of hits in the early- to mid-80s with 'I Won't Let The Sun Go Down On Me', 'Wouldn't It Be Good', 'The Riddle' and 'Don Quixote'. In the 90s, Kershaw returned as a songwriter of note behind other acts, notably Chesney Hawkes' massive hit 'The One And Only'. He also resumed recording as a solo artist.

KEYS, ALICIA

US singer-songwriter Keys (b. 1981) is a classically trained pianist and former student at Manhattan's Professional Performance Arts School, After contributing 'Dah Dee Dah (Sexy Thing)' to Columbia Records' *Men In Black* soundtrack, she moved to J Records. The exotic fusion of urban R&B, hip-hop and blues on the chart-topping *Songs In A Minor*, released in 2001 and featuring the transatlantic hit single 'Fallin'', helped establish the album as a minor classic of modern soul. Keys was rewarded with five trophies at the following year's Grammy Awards.

KHAN, CHAKA

US soul singer Chaka Khan (b. Yvette Marie Stevens, 1953) enjoyed a string of hit singles with Rufus in the mid-70s before releasing the solo 'I'm Every Woman', a US R&B chart-topper in 1978. Subsequent releases, 'What Cha' Gonna Do For Me' (1981) and 'Got To Be There' (1982), consolidated her position and a cover of **Prince**'s 'I Feel For You' (US number 3/UK number 1 in 1984) established her internationally. It led to a platinum-selling album and won a Grammy for Best R&B Female Performance. 'This Is My Night', 'Eye To Eye' (both 1985), and a remixed 'I'm Every Woman' (1989) were UK solo hits, but Khan enjoyed more success in her homeland with a series of collaborations with artists such as **Quincy Jones** ('I'll Be Good To You'), **Peter Cetera** ('Feels Like Heaven') and **Gladys Knight**, Brandy and Tamia ('Missing You'). She formed her own label, Earth Song, in 1998, debuting with the **Prince**-produced *Come 2 My House*.

KID CREOLE AND THE COCONUTS

A relatively exciting entry into the UK charts at the height of New Romanticism in the early 80s, Kid Creole And The Coconuts introduced many to the dynamic pulse of Latin pop. The Coconuts were formed by Kid Creole (b. Thomas August Darnell Browder, 1950), his brother Stony Browder Jnr., 'Sugar Coated' Andy Hernandez (aka Coati Mundi) and several multi-instrumentalists. They found commercial success with *Tropical Gangsters* (known as *Wise Guy* outside the UK), which included three UK Top 10 hits: 'I'm A Wonderful Thing, Baby', 'Stool Pigeon' and 'Annie, I'm Not Your Daddy'. Kid Creole had become King Creole by the advent of 1985's *In Praise Of Older Women And Other Crimes*. The follow-up, *I, Too, Have Seen The Woods*, featured female vocalist Haitia Fuller but failed to halt a sales decline. Subsequent albums were released in the Japanese and European markets. In 1999, Kid Creole appeared in the West End production of *Oh! What A Night*.

KID ROCK

White rapper Kid Rock (b. Bob Ritchie) made his debut for Jive Records with 1990's *Grits Sandwiches For Breakfast*. Aiming for a stylistic niche somewhere between the **Beastie Boys** and **2 Live Crew**, the pro-cunnilingus single 'Yo-Da-Lin In The Valley' generated little chart success. Continuing his association with the emergent gangsta-rap genre, Kid Rock supported **Ice Cube** and Too $hort on tour. He relocated to Brooklyn, New York and released two poorly received albums for Continuum Records. He then turned his efforts to running his own independent Top Dog imprint from the basement of his Michigan home, releasing and distributing *Early Mornin' Stoned Pimp*. This was a foray into a west coast G-funk sound, albeit filtered through his ever-present rock influences. On *Devil Without A Cause*, timing and major-label promotional muscle finally combined to deliver his confident fusion of a bewildering range of rap, country and hard-rock influences to a wider audience, causing the album to climb into the US Top 5 in the process. His relationship with actress Pamela Anderson helped keep Kid Rock in the public eye prior to the release of *Cocky*.

KIDD, JOHNNY, AND THE PIRATES

Kidd (b. Frederick Heath, 1939, d. 1966), is now rightly revered as an influential figure in the birth of British rock. The Pirates were formed in 1959 by Kidd, Alan Caddy (b. 1940, d. 2000; lead guitar), Tony Docherty (rhythm guitar), Johnny Gordon (bass) and Ken McKay (drums), plus backing singers Mike West and Tom Brown. They debuted with the compulsive 'Please Don't Touch'. By 1960, Kidd and Caddy were fronting a new rhythm section featuring Brian Gregg (bass) and Clem Cattini (b. 1939; drums). Their first single, 'Shakin' All Over' reached UK number 1, but its inspiration to other musicians was equally vital. Defections resulted in the formation of a third line-up – Kidd, Johnny Spence (bass), Frank Farley (drums) and Johnny Patto (guitar) – although the last was replaced by Mick Green. Two 1963 hits, 'I'll Never Get Over You' and 'Hungry For Love', owed a substantial debt to Merseybeat at the expense of the unit's own identity. The following year, Green left to join the **Dakotas**, precipitating a succession of replacements, and a depressed Kidd talked openly of retirement. However, he re-emerged in 1966, fronting the New Pirates, but his renewed optimism ended in tragedy when, on 7 October, he was killed in a car crash. The best-known line-up, Green, Spence and Farley, successfully re-established the Pirates name during the late 70s.

KIHN, GREG

In 1975, US songwriter Kihn (b. 1952; vocals, guitar) provided two solo songs for a compilation album on Beserkley Records. He later signed to the label, adding backing vocals on **Jonathan Richman**'s 'Road Runner' and then putting together a band for a series of well-received power pop releases. 'The Breakup Song (They Don't Write 'Em)' reached the US Top 20 in 1981 and *Kihntinued*, which housed it, became the Kihn band's biggest selling album. They managed a US number 2 in 1983 with the disco-styled 'Jeopardy', before Kihn dropped the band title and recorded solely as Greg Kihn. In later years, in addition to recording, Kihn has worked as a rock radio presenter and written a novel.

KILBURN AND THE HIGH ROADS

An important link between UK 'pub rock' and punk, Kilburn And The High Roads were formed in 1970 by **Ian Dury** (b. 1942, d. 2000; vocals) and Russell Hardy (b. 1941; piano). The initial line-up included Ted Speight (guitar), Terry Day (drums), George Khan (saxophone) and Charlie Hart (bass), but by 1973 it had changed to Dury, Hardy, Keith Lucas (b. 1950; guitar), Davey Payne (b. 1944; saxophone), David Newton-Rohoman (b. 1948; drums) and Humphrey Ocean (bass), although the latter was soon replaced by Charlie Sinclair. They completed an album for the Raft label, unfortunately cancelled after the label went bankrupt (the sessions were released as *Wotabunch* in the wake of Dury's solo success). Hardy was replaced by Rod Melvin, but the subsequent *Handsome* captured little of the excitement of their live work. Dury and Melvin went on to greater success with Ian Dury And The Blockheads.

KILLING JOKE

Powerful post-punk UK rock band formed by Jaz Coleman (b. Jeremy Coleman; vocals, keyboards), Paul Ferguson (drums), 'Geordie' (b. K. Walker; guitar) and Youth (b. Martin Glover, 1960; bass). The quartet debuted with the *Almost Red* EP. Via Island Records, the band set up their own Malicious Damage label and a succession of singles followed. They recorded three albums, after which the band disintegrated when Coleman, believing that the apocalypse was imminent, fled to Iceland. He was followed by Youth. The latter returned to begin work with Ferguson on a new project, *Brilliant*, until Ferguson himself left for Iceland, taking bass player Paul Raven with him. Subsequent Killing Joke output included 1985's *Night Time* (including the UK Top 20 hit 'Love Like Blood'), *Outside The Gate* (basically a Coleman solo album) and their best album for years, 1990's *Extremities, Dirt & Various Repressed Emotions*. However, the band broke up again, acrimoniously. Coleman continued with the name, reuniting with Youth and Geordie on 1994's *Pandemonium*, which yielded two UK Top 20 singles, 'Millennium' and 'Pandemonium'. In 1996, they released *Democracy*, since when Coleman has embarked on a classical career as composer-in-residence for the New Zealand Symphony Orchestra. Youth has established himself as one of the UK's top producers.

KING CRIMSON

English progressive-rock band formed in 1969 by Robert Fripp (b. 1946; guitar), Mike Giles (b. 1942; drums), Ian McDonald (b. 1946; keyboards) and Greg Lake (b. 1948; vocals, bass). Pete Sinfield supplied lyrics to Fripp's compositions. The band's debut *In The Court Of The Crimson King* drew ecstatic praise, but their brief period of critical popularity ended with *In The Wake Of Poseidon*. The album masked internal strife, which saw McDonald and Giles depart to work as a duo and Lake leave to found **Emerson, Lake And Palmer**. Fripp completed the album with various musicians including Gordon Haskell (b. 1946; bass, vocals) and Mel Collins (b. 1947; saxophone), both of whom remained for *Lizard*. Drummer Andy McCullough completed this line-up, but both he and Haskell left when the sessions terminated. Boz Burrell (b. Raymond Burrell, 1946; bass, vocals) and Ian Wallace (drums) featured on *Islands* and the live selection *Earthbound*. Fripp then recruited a more radical line-up with John Wetton (b. 1949; bass, vocals), Bill Bruford (b. 1948; drums), Jamie Muir (percussion) and David Cross (b. 1949; violin). *Larks' Tongues In Aspic* resulted, but only Fripp, Wetton and Bruford remained for the superior *Red*.

In 1974, Fripp went solo, but in 1981 resurrected the King Crimson name for himself, Bruford, Tony Levin (b. 1946; bass) and Adrian Belew (b. 1949; guitar). The adventurous albums *Discipline*, *Beat* and *Three Of A Perfect Pair* were just a temporary interlude, however, and Fripp subsequently resumed his solo career and established a new unit, the League Of Gentlemen. True to form, he reconvened King Crimson in 1994 to record *Thrak* with Belew, Trey Gunn (stick, backing vocals), Levin, Bruford and Pat Mastelotto (b. 1955; acoustic/electric percussion). He recorded with the same musicians as part of the ongoing *ProjeKcts* series, and oversaw a series of collectors' releases on his own Discipline Global Mobile label. Fripp retained Belew, Gunn and Mastelotto for the first King Crimson album of the new millennium, *The ConstruKction Of Light*.

KING CURTIS

American saxophonist and session musician Curtis (b. Curtis Ousley, 1934, d. 1971) appeared on countless releases, particularly on the Atlantic Records label. A former member of Lionel Hampton's band, Curtis scored a US R&B number 1 with 'Soul Twist', billed as King Curtis And The Noble Knights. The same group released 'The Monkey' (1963) and 'Soul Serenade' (1964), but the singer took solo credit. Curtis continued his session work alongside establishing his own career, putting together a superb studio group: Richard Tee, Cornell Dupree, Jerry Jemmott and Bernard 'Pretty' Purdie. This illustrious career was tragically ended when Curtis was stabbed to death outside his New York apartment.

KING, ALBERT

Mississippi, USA-born King (b. Albert Nelson, 1923, d. 1992) released the solo recording 'Bad Luck Blues' (1953), but it was not until the end of the decade that he embarked on a full-time career. His early work fused his distinctive fretwork to big-band influenced arrangements and included his first successful single, 'Don't Throw Your Love On Me Too Strong'. In 1966, he signed to Stax Records and began working with **Booker T. And The MGs**. However, this period is best remembered for 'Born Under A Bad Sign' (1967) and 'The Hunter' (1968), two performances that became an essential part of many repertoires, including those of **Free** and **Cream**. King became a central part of the late 60s 'blues boom', touring the college and concert circuit. His classic album, *Live Wire/Blues Power*, introduced his music to the white-rock audience. King continued to record up until his death in 1992.

KING, B. B.

Legendary US blues guitarist King (b. Riley B. King, 1925) sang in gospel groups from childhood. He began adult life working on a Mississippi plantation. Aged 20, he went to Memphis, where he busked, and lived with his cousin, Bukka White. He eventually secured work with radio station KWEM, and then with WDIA, which led to DJing on the *Sepia Swing Show*. Here he was billed as 'The Beale Street Blues Boy', later amended to 'Blues Boy King', and then 'B. B. King'.

Radio exposure promoted King's live career, performing with a band whose personnel varied according to availability. At this stage, he was still musically untutored. After recording for Bullet Records in 1949, he was signed to Modern Records, with whom he recorded for 10 years. In 1952, he reached US R&B number 1 with 'Three O'Clock Blues'. Through the 50s, King embarked on his gruelling trail of one-nighters, touring with a 13-piece band. His sound consisted chiefly of a synthesis of the bottleneck styles of the delta blues with the jazzy electric guitar of **T-Bone Walker**. To Walker's flowing, crackling music, King added finger vibrato, his own substitute for the slide. The result was a fluid guitar sound in which almost every note was bent and/or sustained. He named his beautiful black, gold-plated, pearl-inlaid Gibson 335 (or 355) guitar 'Lucille'.

In 1960, King moved to ABC Records, but by the mid-60s his career seemed in decline. Revitalization came with the discovery of the blues by young whites and, in 1968, King played the Fillmore West with **Johnny Winter** and **Mike Bloomfield**. His revival of Roy Hawkins' 'The Thrill Is Gone', which made innovatory use of strings, provided the crucial pop crossover and, in 1970, he recorded his first collaboration with rock musicians, produced by **Leon Russell**.

King's career has been smooth sailing ever since: in demand for commercials, movie soundtracks, television theme tunes, and guest appearances. Despite a workaholic schedule, he worked unobtrusively to provide entertainment for prisoners (co-founding the Foundation for the Advancement of Inmate Rehabilitation and Recreation in 1972). In 1995, King announced that, as he had turned 70, he would be drastically reducing his performing schedule: instead of a regular 300 or more gigs a year, he would be winding down to 200! He continues to record prolifically, however. Between 1999 and 2000 he released three albums including *Let The Good Times Roll*, an excellent tribute to Louis Jordan, and *Riding With The King*, a collaboration with **Eric Clapton**.

King is a giant of the blues and R&B, and a titanic figure in popular music over the last half-century.

KING, BEN E.

US soul singer Ben E. King (b. Benjamin Earl Nelson, 1938) started out in doo-wop group the Four B's, before joining the Five Crowns, who in 1959 became the **Drifters**. King was the lead vocalist on several of their recordings including 'There Goes My Baby' and 'Save The Last Dance For Me'. Going solo in 1960, he recorded the US Top 10 hit 'Spanish Harlem' (1961). 'Stand By Me' was even more successful and was followed by hits including 'Amor', 'Don't Play That Song', 'I Could Have Danced All Night' and 'What Is Soul?'. His commercial standing declined at the end of the 60s, but he bounced back in 1975 when 'Supernatural Thing Part 1' hit the US Top 5. In 1977, a collaboration with the **Average White Band** resulted in two R&B chart entries and *Benny And Us*. In 1986, 'Stand By Me' was included in the movie of the same name, reaching the US Top 10 and number 1 in the UK, thereby briefly revitalizing the singer's career.

KING, CAROLE

King (b. Carole Klein, 1942) was a prolific songwriter by her early teens. She later married fellow lyricist **Gerry Goffin** and completed a handful of solo singles, including 'The Right Girl' (1958) and 'Queen Of The Beach' (1959), prior to recording 'Oh Neil' (1960), a riposte to **Neil Sedaka**'s 'Oh Carol'. King and Goffin scored success in the 60s with the **Shirelles** ('Will You Still Love Me Tomorrow'), **Bobby Vee** ('Take Good Care Of My Baby') and the **Drifters** ('Up On The Roof') and were responsible for much of the early output on the Dimension Records label. They wrote, arranged and produced hits for **Little Eva** ('The Loco-Motion') and the Cookies ('Chains' and 'Don't Say Nothin' Bad (About My Baby)'). 'It Might As Well Rain Until September' (1962) provided King with a solo hit. Their later compositions included '(You Make Me Feel Like) A Natural Woman' (**Aretha Franklin**), 'Goin' Back' (**Dusty Springfield** and the **Byrds**) and 'Pleasant Valley Sunday' (the **Monkees**).

King moved to Los Angeles and recorded with the City before going solo in 1970 with *Writer*, then *Tapestry*, which contained 'You've Got A Friend' (US number 1 for **James Taylor**), 'It's Too Late', a US chart-topper for King, and 'So Far Away'. *Music* and *Rhymes And Reasons* went gold, as did *Fantasy*, *Wrap Around Joy* (including US number 1, 'Jazzman') and *Thoroughbred*. The last marked the end of King's tenure at Ode Records and she has since failed to reap the same commercial success.

By the early 90s, she had relocated to Ireland. Her recordings also became more measured and, if *Speeding Time*, *Colour Of Your Dreams* or *City Streets* lacked the cultural synchronization *Tapestry* enjoyed with the post-Woodstock audience, her songwriting skills were still in evidence. After a number of years keeping a relatively low profile, King released *Love Makes The World* on her own Rockingale label.

KING, FREDDIE

Blues performer King (b. Billy Myles, 1934, d. 1976) started out in several blues bands. In 1960, he recorded six titles under his own name, all on the same day, including the instrumental hit 'Hideaway'. He left his current label, King Federal, for the Atlantic Records subsidiary Cotillion, but the following albums failed to capture him at his best; nor did his work with **Leon Russell**

on his Shelter Records label. However, King also made many outstanding recordings during this period. *Getting Ready* included the original version of the much-covered 'Going Down'. Tragically, this new relationship was cut short when King died of heart failure aged 43. His last stage appearance had taken place three days earlier in his home-town of Dallas.

KING, JONATHAN

British songwriter King (b. Kenneth George King, 1944) hit the charts in the mid-60s with his plaintive protest song 'Everyone's Gone To The Moon'. Hedgehoppers Anonymous gave him his second protest hit with 'It's Good News Week'. As Decca Records' talent-spotter, King discovered **Genesis**, producing their first album. He was also heavily involved in studio novelty numbers such as the Piglets' 'Johnny Reggae', Sakkarin's 'Sugar Sugar' and St. Cecilia's 'Leap Up And Down (Wave Your Knickers In The Air)'.

In 1972, King launched UK Records, best remembered for **10cc**. He also had a hit in his own name during 1975 with 'Una Paloma Blanca'. King maintained a high-media profile via newspaper columns, radio appearances and his BBC television programme, *Entertainment USA*. His career collapsed in November 2000 when he was arrested and charged with various sexual offences against minors dating back to the early 70s. The following November King was found guilty and sentenced to seven years' imprisonment.

KINGSMEN

US musicians Jack Ely (vocals, guitar), Mike Mitchell (guitar) Bob Nordby (bass) and Lynn Easton (drums) began working as the Kingsmen in 1958. Don Gallucci (keyboards) joined in 1962. The band's debut single, 'Louie Louie', was released the following year. The song was composed and originally recorded by Richard Berry in 1956, and its primitive, churning rhythm was later adopted by several north-west state bands. Internal ructions led to Ely and Norby walking out. Norm Sundholm (bass) and Gary Abbot (drums) joined in their places, but the crucial alteration came in 1967 when Easton left the group. Numerous half-hearted reincarnations aside, his departure brought the Kingsmen to an end.

KINGSTON TRIO

US folk revivalist group formed in 1957 by Bob Shane (b. 1934), Nick Reynolds (b. 1933) and Dave Guard (b. 1934, d. 1991). The trio had limited singles success and are most remembered for 1958's US chart-topper 'Tom Dooley'. *The Kingston Trio* also reached US number 1 and in 1959, *From The Hungry i*, a live recording, reached number 2. *The Kingston Trio At Large* and *Here We Go Again* both reached number 1, as did *Sold Out* and *String Along*. Guard went solo, replaced by John Stewart (b. 1939) in 1961. *Close-Up* was the first release featuring Stewart, and this line-up continued until 1967.

Shane later re-formed the group, as the New Kingston Trio, with Roger Gambill and George Grove. Their output was prolific, but only marginally successful, and they disbanded in 1968. A 1981 television reunion brought all six members together for the first time. Shane continues to lead various Kingston Trio line-ups on the oldies circuit.

KINKS

UK band formed in 1963 as the Ravens by songwriter Ray Davies (b. 1944; vocals, guitar, piano), his brother Dave (b. 1947; guitar, vocals) and Peter Quaife (b. 1943; bass). Joined by Mick Avory (b. 1944; drums) the band debuted with 'Long Tall Sally'. It failed to sell, but their third single, 'You Really Got Me', reached UK number 1, boosted by a performance on the UK television show *Ready, Steady, Go!*. This and its successor, 'All Day And All Of The Night', provided a blueprint for hard-rock guitar.

Over the next two years Ray Davies emerged as a songwriter of startling originality and his band was rarely out of the bestsellers list. The Kinks returned to UK number 1 with 'Tired Of Waiting For You' (1965). 'Dedicated Follower Of Fashion' brilliantly satirized Carnaby Street narcissism; 'Sunny Afternoon' (UK number 1) dealt with capitalism and class and 'Dead End Street' (1966) was about poverty. Their early albums had contained a staple diet of R&B standards and harmless Davies originals. With *Face To Face* and *Something Else*, however, he set about redefining the English character, with sparkling wit and steely nerve. One of his greatest songs was *Something Else*'s final track, 'Waterloo Sunset', a simple but emotional *tour de force*. It narrowly missed the top of the charts, as did the following 'Autumn Almanac'.

By 1968, the Kinks had fallen from UK popularity, despite remaining critically well-respected. Two superb concept albums, *The Kinks Are The Village Green Preservation Society* and *Arthur (Or The Decline And Fall Of The British Empire)*, inexplicably failed to sell, despite containing some of Davies' finest songs. Quaife left in 1969, replaced by John Dalton (ex-**Creation**). The band returned to the UK bestsellers lists with 'Lola' (1970), an irresistible fable of transvestism. This marked the beginning of their US breakthrough, reaching the Top 10. The band now embarked on a series of huge American tours and rarely performed in Britain, although their business operation centre and recording studio, Konk, was based in London.

Having signed a new contract with RCA Records in 1971, the band had now enlarged to incorporate a brass section. Following the country-influenced *Muswell Hillbillies*, however, they suffered a barren period. Ray Davies experienced drug and marital problems, and their live performances revealed a man bereft of his driving, creative enthusiasm. Throughout the early 70s a series of average, over-ambitious concept albums appeared as Davies' main outlet. In 1976, Dalton departed, as their unhappy and comparatively unsuccessful years with RCA ended. A new contract with

MONO

FACE TO FACE
KINKS

Arista Records engendered a remarkable change in fortunes, and both *Sleepwalker* and *Misfits* were excellent, successful albums. Although still spending most of their time playing to vast US audiences, the Kinks were adopted by the British new wave, and were cited by many punk bands as a major influence. Both the **Jam** ('David Watts') and the **Pretenders** ('Stop Your Sobbing') provided reminders of Davies' 60s songwriting skill, while in 1983 they unexpectedly appeared in the UK singles chart with 'Come Dancing'.

In 1990, they were inducted into the Rock And Roll Hall of Fame, at the time only the fourth UK act to take the honour, behind the **Beatles**, the **Rolling Stones** and the **Who**.

Quaife and Avory were present at the ceremony. Later that year they received the Ivor Novello Award for 'outstanding services to British music'. After the comparative failure of *UK Jive* the band left London Records, and after some time without a recording contract, signed with Sony in 1991. *Phobia* was a commercial failure and the band was soon dropped, releasing *To The Bone* on their own Konk label.

Ray Davies has made his mark under the Kinks' banner as one of the most perceptive popular songwriters of our time.

KISS

US hard-rock band formed in 1972 by Paul Stanley (b. Paul Eisen, 1950; rhythm guitar, vocals), Gene Simmons (b. Chaim Witz, 1949; bass, vocals), Peter Criss (b. Peter Crisscoula, 1947; drums, vocals) and Ace Frehley (b. Paul

Frehley, 1951; lead guitar, vocals). In just over a year, Kiss had released their first three albums with a modicum of success. In 1975, their fortunes changed with the release of *Alive!*, which spawned their first US hit single, 'Rock And Roll All Nite'. *Alive!* became their first certified platinum album in the USA. *Destroyer* proved just as successful, and gave them their first US Top 10 single, 'Beth'. *Rock And Roll Over, Love Gun* and *Alive II* confirmed Kiss as major recording artists. By 1977 the group had topped the prestigious Gallup poll as the most popular act in the USA. They had become a marketing dream: Kiss merchandise included make-up kits, masks, board games and pinball machines.

After the release of *Dynasty*, which featured the worldwide hit, 'I Was Made For Lovin' You', cracks appeared in the ranks. Criss left, replaced by session player Anton Fig. Fig played drums on *Unmasked* until a permanent replacement was found in the form of Eric Carr (b. 1950, d. 1991). *Music From The Elder* represented a radical departure from traditional Kiss music and included several ballads, an orchestra and a choir. Frehley, increasingly disenchanted with the musical direction of the band, left in 1983. By this time the popularity of the band was waning and drastic measures were called for. The legendary make-up which had concealed their true identities for almost 10 years was removed on MTV in the USA.

Vinnie Vincent (b. Vincent Cusano) made his first official appearances on *Creatures Of The Night* and *Lick It Up*. The resurgence of the band continued with *Animalize*. Vincent had been replaced by Mark St. John (b. Mark Norton). His association with the band was short-lived, however, as he was struck down by Reiters Syndrome. Bruce Kulick, the brother of long-time Kiss cohort Bob, was drafted in and subsequently became a permanent member. Further commercial success was achieved with *Asylum* and *Crazy Nights*, the latter featuring their biggest UK hit, 'Crazy Crazy Nights'. *Hot In The Shade* included the US Top 10 single 'Forever'.

Carr died of cancer in 1991. Replacement drummer Eric Singer featured on the US Top 5 album, *Revenge*. A stable unit with Bruce Kulick (guitar) and Singer together with Simmons and Stanley appeared to be on the cards, but Frehley and Criss returned for a reunion tour. So successful was the tour that Kulick and Singer were naturally somewhat annoyed and both quit. Their irritation was further exacerbated by the fact that a new studio album, *Carnival Of Souls*, featured both of them. *Psycho Circus* marked the return of the original line-up to the studio, and became the band's highest-charting US album when it debuted at number 3 in October 1998.

KITT, EARTHA

US singer Kitt (b. 1927) was born in South Carolina but raised in Harlem, New York. She started out in Katharine Dunham's famed dancing troupe and appeared on Broadway in *New Faces Of 1952*. Her other Broadway shows included *Mrs. Patterson* (1954) and *Shinbone Alley* (1957). She continued to work in cabaret, theatre, television and films, playing leading roles in *St. Louis Blues* (1958) and an all-black version of *Anna Lucasta* (1958).

Although her highly mannered presentation of songs is best seen rather than merely heard, Kitt has made some songs virtually her own property, among them 'I Want To Be Evil', 'An Englishman Needs Time', 'Santa Baby' and 'I'm Just An Old-Fashioned Girl'. She remains in demand on the stage and in Hollywood, and in 2000 provided the voice for Yzma in Disney's *The Emperor's New Groove*.

KLAATU

Canadian rock trio formed in 1975 by vocalist, songwriter and drummer Terry Draper, along with John Woloschuk and Dee Long. The band's sound closely resembled that of the latter-day **Beatles** and a US journalist surmised that they might very well *be* the Beatles. The trio did nothing to stem the rumours and the hype aided sales of their debut. Their song 'Calling Occupants Of Interplanetary Craft' attained US and UK chart status in 1977 through a **Carpenters**' cover version, and is now classified as 'The Recognized Anthem Of World Contact Day'. Klaatu meanwhile, carried on working until 1981 when, after releasing four further albums, they eventually disbanded.

KLF

Since 1987, the KLF have operated under a series of guises, only gradually revealing their true nature to the public at large. Their principal spokesman is Bill Drummond (b. William Butterworth, 1953). As co-founder of the Zoo label in the late 70s, he introduced and later managed **Echo And The Bunnymen** and the **Teardrop Explodes**. Later he joined forces with Jimmy Cauty. Their first project was under the title *JAMS (Justified Ancients Of Mu Mu)*. The provocatively titled *1987 (What The Fuck Is Going On?)* was released as KLF (Kopyright Liberation Front).

In the wake of the emerging house scene, they sampled the theme tune to British television show *Doctor Who*, adding a strong disco beat and **Gary Glitter** yelps – 'Doctorin' The Tardis' was an instant number 1 in 1988, under the title Time-lords. The originators also wrote a book, *How To Have A Number One The Easy Way*. Returning as the KLF, they branched out into ambient music with the pioneering *Chill Out* album. Back in the pop charts the duo enjoyed worldwide success with their *Stadium House Trilogy*. The first instalment, 'What Time Is Love (Live At Trancentral)', reached the UK Top 5 in autumn 1990. The duo reached their commercial peak at the start of 1991 when the soulful house of '3 AM Eternal' topped the UK charts and broke into the US Top 5. The final instalment, 'Last Train To Transcentral', reached UK number 2 and the attendant *The White Room* was also a bestseller. 'Justified And Ancient' featured the unmistakable voice of Tammy Wynette. They were voted Top British Group by the BPI, and, typically, at the awards party announced that the KLF were no more.

Since that time, Drummond and Cauty have made several pseudonymous returns to the singles charts, and also engaged in several art-terrorist projects under the K Foundation banner.

KMFDM

Nihilistic industrial band originally formed in Hamburg, Germany, but who later enjoyed cult success in the USA. The band's name is an acronym of Kein Mehrheit Für Die Mitleid, a piece of German wordplay translating as No Pity For The Majority. KMFDM was formed in 1984 by electronics expert Sascha Konietzko, En Esch (vocals, drums) and Englishman Raymond 'Pig' Watts to play experimental electronic music, characterised by mechanistic beats and sampled vocals. Their first releases for the American label Wax Trax! were *Don't Blow Your Top* and *UAIOE*. The band's angst-ridden lyrics allied to graphic artist Brute!'s album covers saw them pick up a cult following in the USA, where both Konietzko and Esch, the only remaining original members, based themselves from the early 90s. *Angst*, released in 1993, perfected the band's aggressive fusion of pounding electro rhythms and screeching guitars. Konietzko and Esch returned, with Watts in tow, for 1995's dark, impenetrable *Nihil*. Further albums followed before Konietzko and Esch broke up the band at the start of 1999. Konietzko subsequently formed MDFMK with latter-day KMFDM member Tim Skold. Konietzko, Watts and Skold re-formed KMFDM three years later to record *Attak*.

KNACK

Formed in Los Angeles, USA, in 1978 by Doug Fieger (vocals, guitar), Prescott Niles (bass), Berton Averre (guitar) and Bruce Gary (drums), the Knack attempted to revive the spirit of the 60s beat boom with matching suits, and short songs boasting solid, easily memorable riffs. Their million-selling debut single 'My Sharona' reached US number 1 and the UK Top 10. *The Knack* proved an instant hit, selling five million copies. At the height of a critical backlash, they issued ... *But The Little Girls Understand*, but both the sales and the songs were less impressive and by the time of *Round Trip*, their power-pop style seemed decidedly outmoded. At the end of 1981 they voluntarily disbanded. They have reunited several times since, with drummers Billy Ward and Terry Bozzio completing the line-up.

KNIGHT, GLADYS, AND THE PIPS

Gladys Knight (b. 1944), her brother Merald 'Bubba' (b. 1942), sister Brenda and cousins Elenor and William Guest (b. 1941) formed their first vocal group, the Pips, in their native Atlanta, USA, in 1952. They recorded for Brunswick Records in 1958, with another cousin, Edward Patten (b. 1939). Langston George joined in 1959 when Brenda and Elenor left. Three years elapsed before a version of Johnny Otis's 'Every Beat Of My Heart' was leased to Vee Jay Records and went on to top the US R&B charts.

George retired in the early 60s, leaving the quartet line-up that survived into the 80s. In 1966, Gladys Knight and The Pips were signed to Motown's Soul subsidiary and teamed with producer/songwriter Norman Whitfield. In 1967, they had a major hit with the original release of 'I Heard It Through The Grapevine'. In the early 70s, the group slowly moved away from their original blues-influenced sound towards a more MOR harmony blend. Their new approach brought them success in 1972 with 'Neither One Of Us (Wants To Be The First To Say Goodbye)'. Knight and The Pips left Motown when the label moved to Hollywood. At Buddah Records, they found immediate success with the US chart-topper 'Midnight Train To Georgia', followed by major hits such as 'I've Got To Use My Imagination' and 'The Best Thing That Ever Happened To Me'. In 1975 the title track of *I Feel A Song* gave them another soul number 1. The same year they began hosting their own US television series.

Legal problems then forced Knight and The Pips to record separately until 1980. Subsequent releases alternated between the group's R&B and MOR modes. 'Love Overboard' earned them a Grammy for the Best R&B performance in 1989, after which Knight and The Pips split. Knight's subsequent work has alternated between gospel and mainstream pop.

KNOPFLER, MARK

Knopfler (b. 1949) made his name as guitarist and lead singer with **Dire Straits**, one of the most successful UK bands of the 80s. He inaugurated a parallel solo career in 1983 with the film score for *Local Hero*. Further soundtracks included *Cal*, *Comfort And Joy* and *The Princess Bride*. After playing on **Bob Dylan**'s *Slow Train Coming*, Knopfler produced the artist's *Infidels* (1983). He was also in demand as a session guitarist, working for **Steely Dan**, **Phil Lynott**, **Van Morrison** and **Bryan Ferry** among others. In 1989, he and old friends Brendan Croker and Steve Phillips formed the Notting Hillbillies for an album and tour. With Dire Straits winding down in the mid-90s, Knopfler released his 'official' debut solo album, *Golden Heart*, in 1996. He then returned to soundtrack work with

contributions to *Wag The Dog*, *Metroland*, and *A Shot At Glory*. His belated follow-up album, *Sailing To Philadelphia*, was released in 2000.

KOOL AND THE GANG

Originally formed as a quartet (the Jazziacs) by Robert 'Kool' Bell (b. 1950; bass), Robert 'Spike' Mickens (trumpet), Robert 'The Captain' Bell (b. 1951; saxophone, keyboards) and Dennis 'D.T.' Thomas (b. 1951; saxophone), they were later joined by Charles 'Claydes' Smith (b. 1948; guitar) and 'Funky' George Brown (b. 1949; drums). In 1969, they settled on the name Kool And The Gang. The group crossed over into the US pop chart in 1973 and initiated a run of 19 US Top 40 hits on their De-Lite label, including 'Funky Stuff', 'Jungle Boogie' and 'Hollywood Swinging'. In 1979, they added vocalists James 'J. T.' Taylor (b. 1953) and Earl Toon Jnr, leading to a new era of success for the group with US hits such as 'Ladies Night', 'Too Hot' and 1980's chart-topping 'Celebration'. They proved similarly popular worldwide and in the UK, 'Get Down On It' (1981), 'Joanna' (1984) and 'Cherish' (1985) all reached the Top 5. The original six members remained in the line-up into the late 80s and although newcomer Toon left, Taylor blossomed into an ideal frontman. This core was later supplemented by several auxiliaries, Clifford Adams (trombone) and Michael Ray (trumpet).

Taylor departed in 1988 and he was replaced by three singers, former **Dazz Band** member Skip Martin plus Odeen Mays and Gary Brown. Taylor rejoined in 1995, but subsequent releases indicated a group well past their sell-by date.

KOOPER, AL

Kooper (b. 1944) started out in 1959 as guitarist in the Royal Teens. He became a noted New York session musician and later forged a successful songwriting partnership with Bobby Brass and Irwin Levine. In 1965, Kooper attended a **Bob Dylan** session on organ, an instrument with which he was barely conversant. Dylan nonetheless loved his instinctive touch which breathed fire into 'Like A Rolling Stone' and the album *Highway 61 Revisited*.

The organist then joined the **Blues Project**, but left in 1967 to found **Blood, Sweat And Tears**. He stayed with them for just one album. He accepted a production post at Columbia Records, before recording *Super Session* with **Mike Bloomfield** and **Stephen Stills**. Kooper's solo career was effectively relaunched with *I Stand Alone*, a promising but inconsistent set. *You Never Know Who Your Friends Are* and *New York City (You're A Woman)* were among his most popular releases, but Kooper remains best-known for his role as a catalyst. He appeared on *Electric Ladyland* (**Jimi Hendrix**) and *Let It Bleed* (the **Rolling Stones**) and produced the debut albums by **Nils Lofgren** and the Tubes. He established his own label, Sounds Of The South, in Atlanta, Georgia, and secured international success with early protégé **Lynyrd Skynyrd**. He has also been active in recording soundtrack music.

KORN

This hardcore rock band was formed in the early 90s in Bakersfield, California, USA. Subsequently based in Huntington Beach in California, the quintet, comprising Jonathan Davis (vocals), Reggie Fieldy Arvizu (bass), James Munky Shaffer (guitar), Brian Welch (guitar/vocals) and David Silveria (drums), released their first single, 'Blind', which was widely shown on late-night MTV shows. The album gave them their commercial breakthrough. *Life Is Peachy* was another ferocious set, although further breakthrough success was limited by the explicit lyrics liberally laced throughout. In late 1997, Korn established their own label, Elementree. The eagerly anticipated *Follow The Leader* was a commercial and critical success, debuting at US number 1 in September 1998. Highlights included 'It's On' and first single 'Got The Life'. Their *Family Values* touring show also established itself as one of the most successful live ventures of the 90s. The band's prominence on the hugely popular US alternative scene was confirmed by the chart-topping success of 1999's Issues.

KORNER, ALEXIS

An inspirational figure in British music circles, Korner (b. 1928, d. 1984) was already versed in black music when he met Cyril Davies at the London Skiffle Club. Together they transformed the venue into the London Blues And Barrelhouse Club, where they performed together and showcased visiting US bluesmen. When jazz trombonist Chris Barber introduced R&B into his live repertoire, he employed Korner (guitar) and Davies (harmonica). Inspired, the pair formed Blues Incorporated in 1961, establishing the Ealing Rhythm And Blues Club in 1962. Blues Incorporated included Charlie Watts (drums), Art Wood (vocals) and Keith Scott (piano), later featuring **Long John Baldry**, **Jack Bruce**, Graham Bond and **Ginger Baker**. The name Blues Incorporated was dropped when Korner went solo, punctuated by the formation of several temporary groups, including Free At Last, New Church and Snape. While the supporting cast on such ventures remained fluid, including for a short time **Robert Plant**, the last two units featured Peter Thorup, who also collaborated with Korner on CCS; they scored notable hits

with 'Whole Lotta Love' (1970), 'Walkin'' and 'Tap Turns On The Water' (both 1971). Korner also began broadcasting for BBC radio, but continued to perform live. In 1981, he began a 13-part television documentary on the history of rock, but his premature death from cancer left this, and many other projects, unfulfilled.

KOSSOFF, PAUL

British guitarist Kossoff (b. 1950, d. 1976) was initially a member of blues band Black Cat Bones, with drummer Simon Kirke. In 1968, the duo became founding members of **Free** and later worked together in Kossoff, Kirke, Tetsu And Rabbit, a spin-off project which completed a lone album in 1971. From 1972, Kossoff was beset by recurring drug and related health problems. Often absent on tour, Kossoff finally went solo. *Back Street Crawler* was excellent, but it was two years before he was well enough to play live. He assembled a new group, Back Street Crawler, in 1975. The quintet completed one album before Kossoff suffered a near-fatal heart attack. Specialists forbade an immediate return, but in March 1976 Kossoff died in his sleep on a flight from Los Angeles to New York.

KOTTKE, LEO

Inventive US guitarist (b. 1945) whose career did not fully flourish until 1971 with *Six And Twelve String Guitar*. Kottke's desire to expand his repertoire led to *Mudlark*, which included instrumental and vocal tracks. Prodigious touring enhanced Kottke's reputation as one of America's finest acoustic 12-string guitarists, although commercial success still eludes him.

KRAFTWERK

German music students Ralf Hütter (b. 1946; organ) and Florian Schneider-Esleben (b. 1947; woodwind) drew on the influence of experimental electronic forces to create minimalist music on synthesizers, drum machines and tape recorders. After a debut album with Organisation (*Tone Float*), the duo formed Kraftwerk with drummers Andreas Hohmann and Klaus Dinger and recorded a self-titled debut. Guitarist Michael Rother and bass player Eberhard Krahnemann were subsequently recruited, but during the recording of *Kraftwerk 2*, Dinger and Homann left to form Neu!. After releasing a duo set, *Ralf Und Florian*, Hütter and Schneider-Esleben were joined by Wolfgang Flür (electronic drums) and Klaus Roeder (guitar, violin, keyboards).

Autobahn established Kraftwerk as purveyors of hi-tech, computerized music. An edited version of the title track reached the US/UK Top 10. In 1975, Roeder was replaced by Karl Bartos who made his debut on *Radioactivity*. The ensuing *Trans Europe Express* and *The Man-Machine* were pioneering electronic works which strongly influenced a generation of English electro-pop acts. Kraftwerk spent three years building their own Kling Klang studios in the late 70s, complete with – inevitably – scores of computers. The single 'The Model', from *The Man-Machine*, gave the band a surprise hit when it topped the UK charts in 1982, and it led to a trio of hits, including 'Tour De France', which became the theme for the cycling event of the same name in 1983. *Electric Cafe* was a disappointment, but Kraftwerk were now cited as a major influence on a host of electro artists. **Afrika Bambaataa** and producer Arthur Baker built their pioneering 1982 'Planet Rock' single around samples of both 'Trans Europe Express' and 'Numbers'.

Hütter and Schneider-Esleben remained enigmatically quiet following *Electric Cafe*. In 1990, a frustrated Flür departed, to be replaced by Fritz Hijbert. They made a surprise return to live performance with a headline appearance at the UK's Tribal Gathering in the summer of 1997. In December 1999, Hütter and Schneider-Esleben recorded a new single, 'Expo 2000', to promote Expo 2000 in Hannover.

KRAMER, BILLY J., AND THE DAKOTAS

UK singer Kramer (b. William Howard Ashton, 1943) originally fronted Merseybeat combo the Coasters, before signing to Brian Epstein's management agency and being teamed with the Dakotas – Mike Maxfield (b. 1944; lead guitar), Robin McDonald (b. 1943; rhythm guitar), Ray Jones (b. 1939, d. 2000; bass) and Tony Mansfield (b. Anthony Bookbinder, 1943; drums). A UK number 1 with the Beatles' 'Do You Want To Know A Secret' (1963), was followed by a run of John Lennon/Paul McCartney songs, including 'Bad To Me' (number 1), 'I'll Keep You Satisfied' and 'From A Window'. 'Little Children' (1964), by US writers Mort Shuman and John McFarland, was their third UK number 1 and reached the US Top 10. Their chart reign ended with **Burt Bacharach**'s 'Trains And Boats And Planes'. Kramer went solo in 1967, but having failed to find a new audience, sought solace on the cabaret and nostalgia circuit.

KRAUSS, ALISON

Krauss (b. 1971) is unique among the new crop of female country singers to emerge in the 90s in that she leans strongly towards more traditional forms of country music, especially bluegrass. She began learning classical music on violin at the age of five and during her teens played with John Pennell's Silver Rail before moving on to Classified Grass. Krauss then returned to Pennell's group, which had changed its name to Union Station, replacing their fiddler Andrea Zonn. In 1987, she recorded *Too Late To Cry* with them. Union Station again joined her for the Grammy-nominated follow-up album. Inspired by Ricky Skaggs, who had brought bluegrass back into contemporary country music's mainstream, she worked hard to achieve similar acclaim. *Though I've Got That Old Feeling* was subsequently awarded a Grammy as best bluegrass recording of 1990, she insisted on maintaining her links with Union Station and remained with the independent Rounder Records label despite offers from several major labels. She has also recorded albums of gospel songs with the Cox Family, and added harmony vocals and fiddle to recordings by **Dolly Parton** and **Michelle Shocked** among others. *So Long So Wrong*, her first new album with Union Station in five years,

was followed by the melancholy solo collection *Forget About It*. Krauss and Union Station made sparkling contributions to the soundtrack of the Coen Brothers' *O Brother, Where Art Thou?*, with Dan Tyminski providing the singing voice for George Clooney's character. The next Krauss and Union Station release, 2001's *New Favorite*, was buoyed by the remarkable success of the soundtrack album.

KRAVITZ, LENNY

US rock artist Kravitz (b. 1964) made his breakthrough in the late 80s with his Virgin America debut, *Let Love Rule*. The album proved highly popular and Kravitz went on to even greater success when **Madonna** recorded his 'Justify My Love'. *Mama Said* spawned the US Top 5 hit 'It Ain't Over 'Til It's Over'. The prolific Kravitz then wrote an entire album for French chanteuse Vanessa Paradis, and collaborated with artists as diverse as **Curtis Mayfield**, **Aerosmith** and **Mick Jagger**. The hard rocking title track of *Are You Gonna Go My Way?* was another worldwide success. *Circus* was a stripped down version of his overall sound and one that displayed his talent as a writer of more contemporary songs. The singer topped the UK charts in February 1999 with 'Fly Away', thanks to extensive media exposure on a Peugeot car advertisement.

KRISTOFFERSON, KRIS

Texan singer-songwriter Kristofferson (b. 1936) began his career in Europe, studying at Oxford University, and joined the US Army while continuing to perform his own material. **Jerry Lee Lewis** became the first to record one of his songs, 'Once More With Feeling'. **Johnny Cash**, a fan of Kristofferson's work, persuaded Roger Miller to record 'Me And Bobby McGee' (co-written with Fred Foster) in 1969. Sammi Smith (and later **Gladys Knight**) scored with 'Help Me Make It Through The Night'.

Kristofferson's own hits began with 'Lovin' Her Was Easier (Than Anything I'll Ever Do Again)' and 'Why Me'. In 1973, Kristofferson married **Rita Coolidge** and they recorded three albums before divorcing in 1979. Kristofferson also inaugurated a successful acting career, appearing in *The Last Movie*, *Pat Garrett And Billy The Kid*, and opposite Barbra Streisand in *A Star Is Born*, among others. He returned to country music with *The Winning Hand*, and *Highwayman* (with Johnny Cash, **Willie Nelson** and **Waylon Jennings**) headed the country chart in 1985. His recording career took an upturn with the release of *A Moment Of Forever* in 1995. He took another break from his exhausting acting schedule to revisit some of his best-known songs on 1999's *The Austin Sessions*.

KRS-ONE

The kingpin of Boogie Down Productions and a genuine hip-hop pioneer, KRS-One (b. Lawrence Krisna Parker, 1965) began a solo career following the death of his erstwhile partner, Scott LaRock (whose violent exit in 1987 played a significant role in KRS-One's anti-violence tracts). His first album to be released outside the Boogie Down Productions banner was 1993's *Return Of The Boom Bap*, but by the mid-90s a new rap hierarchy had already superseded the old-school style of MCing represented by KRS-One. His commercial and creative decline during the 90s should not, however, detract from the importance, quality and influence of his early work.

KULA SHAKER

UK retro-rock band formed in 1994 by Crispian Mills (b. 1963; vocals), Paul Winter-Hart (drums), Alonza Bevan (bass) and Jay Darlington (keyboards). Their debut single, 'Grateful When You're Dead', entered the UK Top 40 in 1996, and following Top 5 singles with 'Tattva' and 'Hey Dude', *K* entered the album chart at number 1. A frenetic cover version of Joe South's 'Hush' reached number 2 in 1997. *Peasants Pigs & Astronauts* followed in 1999, but failed to match the success of its predecessor. After all the swagger and column inches, the band was no more, with Mills leaving to concentrate on solo work.

KURSAAL FLYERS

UK band formed by Paul Shuttleworth (vocals), Graeme Douglas (guitar), Vic Collins (guitar, vocals), Richie Bull (bass, vocals) and Will Birch (drums), who enjoyed brief commercial success in the mid-70s. *Chocs Away* and *The Great Artiste* were praised, and the Kursaals became a popular live attraction. After enjoying a UK Top 20 hit in 1975 with 'Little Does She Know', the band struggled to find a suitable follow-up. Barry Martin replaced Douglas when the latter joined Eddie And The Hot Rods, but the unit disintegrated following *Five Live Kursaals*. Birch reunited the Kursaal Flyers in 1988 for *Former Tour De Force Is Forced To Tour*.

KUTI, FELA

Nigerian singer-songwriter Kuti (b. Fela Anikulapo Kuti, 1938, d. 1997) was a primary influence behind the invention and development of Afro-Beat, the west-African fusion of agit-prop lyrics and dance rhythms. Kuti began leading his highlife-meets-jazz group Koola Lobitos while studying music in London, England. Returning to Nigeria, he devoted himself entirely to a career as a bandleader. By 1968, Kuti was calling the music Koola Lobitos played 'Afro-Beat', as a retort to the slavish relationship most other local bandleaders had with black American music. He changed the name of Koola Lobitos to Afrika 70, and in 1971 enjoyed a big local hit with 'Jeun Ko'ku'. He also founded the Shrine Club in Lagos, which was to become the focus for his music and political activity.

By 1972, Kuti had become one of the biggest stars in west Africa. He rejected the traditional African bandleader stance of promoting local politicians and their policies, choosing instead to articulate the anger and aspirations of the urban poor. In the process he became a figurehead and hero for street people throughout Nigeria, Ghana and neighbouring countries. Not surprisingly, the Nigerian establishment did not enjoy hearing songs like these, nor did they approve of Kuti's high-profile propaganda on behalf of igbo (Nigerian marijuana), and after a series of personal attacks he went into voluntary exile in Ghana in 1977. Unfortunately, he was deported back to Lagos.

Kuti did not drop his revolutionary profile in subsequent years. He continued to keep himself and his band (renamed Egypt 80 in 1979) at the forefront of west-African roots culture, while continuing to struggle with the Nigerian authorities. In 1984 Kuti was jailed in Nigeria on what were widely regarded as trumped-up currency smuggling charges. During his 27-month incarceration, leading New York funk producer **Bill Laswell** was brought in to complete the production of the outstanding *Army Arrangement* album. On release from prison in 1987, Kuti issued the Wally Badarow-produced *Teacher Don't Teach Me Nonsense*. He died of an AIDS-related complication in 1997, but his son Femi Kuti has carried on in his father's footsteps.

L.A. GUNS

US heavy-rock band formed in 1987 by guitarist Tracii Guns (ex-**Guns N'Roses**) and vocalist Paul Black, although the latter was soon replaced by Phil Lewis. Mick Cripps (guitar), Kelly Nickels (bass) and Steve Riley (drums) completed the line-up. Their third album, 1991's *Hollywood Vampires*, saw them diversifying musically, but despite a successful European tour supporting **Skid Row**, the group disintegrated. Guns put together a new outfit, Killing Machine and Lewis formed Filthy Lucre, but L.A. Guns was re-formed when both bands failed. *Vicious Circle* was a strong comeback, but subsequent releases have failed to maintain the high standard.

L7

Formed in 1985 by guitarist/vocalists Donita Sparks (b. 1963) and Suzi Gardner (b. 1960), with Jennifer Finch (b. 1966; bass, vocals) and Demetra 'Dee' Plakas (b. 1960; drums) completing the line-up. Sup Pop Records released *Smell The Magic*, a raucous, grunge-flavoured album. *Bricks Are Heavy* brought major success, with the surprisingly poppy 'Pretend We're Dead' becoming a transatlantic hit. Finch departed in 1996 and was replaced by Gail Greenwood (b. 1960; ex-**Belly**), who in turn left following the release of the tour film *The Beauty Process*. The remaining members returned to their indie roots for the following year's *Slap-Happy*, released on their own Wax Tadpole label.

LA'S

This indie pop band was formed in 1984 in Liverpool, England, by Mike Badger (b. 1962), but his departure two years later left a line-up comprising Lee Mavers (b. 1962; guitar, vocals), John Power (b. 1967; bass), Paul Hemmings (guitar) and John Timson (drums). After a well-received debut single, 'Way Out', which hallmarked the band's effortless, 60s-inspired pop, they took a year out before issuing the wonderfully melodic 'There She Goes'. When this too eluded the charts, the La's line-up changed, with Lee's brother Neil (b. 1971) taking up drums and guitarist Cammy (b. Peter James Camell, 1967) joining the line-up. In the meantime, 'There She Goes' became a massive underground favourite, prompting a reissue two years on (after another single, 'Timeless Melody'). It reached the UK Top 20, and an invigorating and highly melodic debut album was released (much to the perfectionist Mavers' disapproval). Power departed to set up Cast in 1995, fed up with delays to the La's second album.

LABELLE, PATTI

The former leader of LaBelle, part-time actress Patti LaBelle (b. Patricia Holte, 1944) went solo in 1976, but did not enjoy commercial success until the mid-80s. Two tracks from 1984's hit movie *Beverly Hills Cop*, 'New Attitude' and 'Stir It Up', reached the US charts, followed by 'On My Own', a sentimental duet with **Michael McDonald** which reached number 1 in 1986. LaBelle continued to release strong albums throughout the 90s.

LADYSMITH BLACK MAMBAZO

The success of **Paul Simon**'s *Graceland* project gave a high profile to this South African choral group, founded by Joseph Shabalala (b. 1941) in 1960. Until 1975, most of Ladysmith Black Mambazo's album output concentrated on traditional folk songs, some of them with new lyrics which offered

necessarily coded, metaphorical criticisms of the apartheid regime. After 1975, and Shabalala's conversion to Christianity, religious songs were included. In 1987, after *Graceland*, the group released *Shaka Zulu* (produced by Paul Simon). In 1990, *Two Worlds One Heart* marked a radical stylistic departure for the group. On 10 December 1991, Joseph's brother and fellow founder member was shot dead in Durban. The group soldiered on and were back on a major label for 1997's *Heavenly*. Bolstered by the appearance of 'Inkanyezi Nezazi' on a Heinz television commercial, the following year's 'best of' compilation was a surprise bestseller in the UK, climbing to number 2.

LAMBCHOP

Led by singer, guitarist and former art student Kurt Wagner (b. 1958), this Nashville, Tennessee, USA-based ensemble was originally known as Poster Child, before a legally required change saw them adopting their new moniker in 1993. Lambchop's instrumentation is highly unique within the popular music tradition. Wagner's world-weary vocals are backed by an ever-changing sprawling jugband orchestra featuring clarinet, lap steel guitar, saxophone, trombone, organ, cello and 'open-end wrenches'. Lambchop made their mainstream breakthrough with 2000's *Nixon*, a record of breathtaking

magnitude and heartbreaking beauty. The same July Wagner was able to give up his day job – laying and sanding hardwood floors in Nashville.

LANE, RONNIE

A founder-member of the **Small Faces** and **Faces**, Lane (b. 1946, d. 1997) went solo in 1973. He formed a backing group, Slim Chance, and had UK hits with 'How Come?' and 'The Poacher'. A new line-up of Slim Chance was later convened around Brian Belshaw (bass), Steve Simpson (guitar, mandolin), Ruan O'Lochlainn (keyboards, saxophone), Charlie Hart (keyboards, accordion), and Glen De Fleur and Colin Davey (drums). The excellent *Ronnie Lane's Slim Chance* and *One For The Road* followed, but this unit disbanded in 1977, although several ex-members appeared on *Rough Mix* (Ronnie's collaboration with Pete Townshend). Although Lane completed *See Me*, his progress was blighted by multiple sclerosis. His condition deteriorated considerably and money was raised for him through rock benefits. Despite his illness, he still managed to tour the USA and embarked on a Japanese tour during 1990. He finally lost his battle against the disease in 1997.

LANG, JONNY

Blues guitarist/singer Jonny Lang (b. Johnny Langseth, 1981) was signed to A&M Records before his sixteenth birthday. He became the leader of Kid

Jonny Lang And The Big Bang. *Smokin'* sold 25,000 copies, despite being independently produced. By the time A&M stepped in, Lang had played alongside such blues greats as **Luther Allison**, Lonnie Brooks and **Buddy Guy**. *Lie To Me* was an impressive major label debut. *Wander This World* broadened the musical range even further, emphasizing Lang's mastery of rock and soul styles. The album broke into the US Top 30 in 1998. Later in the year, he made a cameo appearance in the film *Blues Brothers 2000*.

LANG, K. D.

A skilled pianist and guitarist, this Canadian artist (b. Kathryn Dawn Lang, 1961) scratched a living in the performing arts, classical and *avant garde* music, before choosing to sing country. After 1984's *A Truly Western Experience*, she signed to Sire Records. *Angel With A Lariat* was favoured by influential rock journals, but many country radio stations refused to play it, prejudiced by Lang's spiky haircut, vegetarianism and ambiguous sexuality. Nevertheless, she charted via 'Crying', a duet with **Roy Orbison** for 1987's *Hiding Out* soundtrack. In 1988, *Shadowland* was rendered agreeable to country consumers through a Nashville production by Owen Bradley.

In 1992, Lang released the acclaimed pop album *Ingénue* and made her debut as an actress in *Salmonberries*. The following year she provided the soundtrack to Gus Van Sant's adaptation of Tom Robbins' *Even Cowgirls Get The Blues*. Since *Ingénue*, her commercial profile has waned, although she has continued to produce quality albums. The covers album *Drag* included a highly original interpretation of **Steve Miller**'s 'The Joker'. *Invincible Summer* was a much better album and contained some of her most interesting compositions since *Ingénue*.

LANOIS, DANIEL

This esteemed Canadian producer rose to fame during the late 80s, contributing to major releases by **Peter Gabriel** (*So*) and U2 (*The Unforgettable Fire* and *The Joshua Tree*, both with **Brian Eno**). He subsequently produced *Robbie Robertson*, the widely-acclaimed 'comeback' album by the former leader of the **Band**, and in 1989 undertook **Bob Dylan**'s *Oh Mercy*. Lanois also released his own album, *Acadie*, a haunting tapestry combining the jauntiness of New Orleans' music with soundscape instrumentals. A follow-up was released in 1993. Lanois was also instrumental in redirecting **Emmylou Harris**'s career with *Wrecking Ball*, and in 1997 teamed up with Dylan on his excellent *Time Out Of Mind*.

LASWELL, BILL

US bass player Laswell (b. 1955) has organized some of the most challenging bands in recent popular music, including Material, Curlew (with Tom Cora, Nicky Skopelitis and George Cartwright), Praxis, Arcana (with Derek Bailey and Tony Williams) and Last Exit (with Sonny Sharrock, Peter Brötzmann and Ronald Shannon Jackson). Laswell has also established several adventurous record labels, including OAO, Celluloid and Axiom. The latter was formed in 1990 to facilitate the release of Laswell's experiments in ambient and techno. His collaborations in this field include work with such artists as Pete Namlook, Klaus Schulze, Buckethead and DJ Spooky. In the late 90s, Laswell began to explore drum 'n' bass, including the trance dub vehicle Sacred System. He also inaugurated his 'reconstruction and mix translation' series, applying the concept to such artists as **Bob Marley**, **Miles Davis** and **Santana**.

LAUPER, CYNDI

US singer Lauper (b. Cynthia Lauper, 1953) met pianist John Turi in 1977. They formed Blue Angel and released a self-titled album. After splitting with Turi in 1983, Lauper began working on her solo debut, *She's So Unusual*. It

provided four hit singles, including 'Girls Just Want To Have Fun' and 'Time After Time' (US number 1). She was awarded a Grammy as Best New Artist. *True Colors* did not have the same commercial edge as its predecessor, yet the title track reached US number 1. In 1987, she acted in the poorly-received movie *Vibes*. Three years later she made a brief return to the charts with 'I Drove All Night' from *A Night To Remember*, before making another lacklustre acting appearance in *Off And Running*. Her new album *Hat Full Of Stars* was overshadowed by a reworked version of one of her biggest hits, retitled 'Hey Now (Girls Just Want To Have Fun)', which reached the UK Top 5 in 1994. Subsequent releases failed to restore Lauper to the charts.

LED ZEPPELIN

Pivotal heavy-rock quartet formed in 1968 by British guitarist Jimmy Page (b. James Patrick Page, 1944) following the demise of the **Yardbirds**. John Paul Jones (b. John Baldwin, 1946; bass, keyboards) was recruited, but intended vocalist **Terry Reid** was unable to join, so **Robert Plant** (b. 1948) was chosen, alongside drummer John Bonham (b. 1948, d. 1980). The quartet completed outstanding commitments under the name New Yardbirds, before becoming Led Zeppelin. Signed to Atlantic Records, the group toured the USA supporting **Vanilla Fudge** before releasing *Led Zeppelin*. They were already a headline act, drawing sell-out crowds across the USA, when *Led Zeppelin II* confirmed an almost peerless position. The introductory track, 'Whole Lotta Love', has since become a classic. A greater subtlety was revealed on *Led Zeppelin III* and a pastoral atmosphere permeated the set.

Led Zeppelin IV included the anthemic 'Stairway To Heaven' and was subsequently revered as one of the greatest hard-rock albums of all time. The praise was more muted for *Houses Of The Holy*, critically queried for its musically diverse selection. A US tour broke all previous attendance records, and helped finance an in-concert film, *The Song Remains The Same*, and the formation of their own record label, Swan Song. *Physical Graffiti*, a double set, included material ranging from compulsive hard-rock ('Custard Pie' and 'Sick Again') to pseudo-mystical experimentation ('Kashmir'). Sell-out appearances in the UK followed the release, but rehearsals for a projected world tour had to be abandoned in August 1975 when Plant sustained multiple injuries in a car accident. After his recovery, *Presence* was recorded. Advance orders alone assured platinum status, yet it was regarded as a disappointment and UK sales were noticeably weaker.

After a year of inactivity, *In Through The Out Door* was a strong collection on which John Paul Jones emerged as the unifying factor. Rehearsals were then undertaken for another US tour, but in September 1980 Bonham was found dead following a lengthy drinking bout. On 4 December, Swan Song announced that the band had officially retired, although a collection of archive material, *Coda*, was subsequently issued. In 1994, Page and Plant (minus John Paul Jones) released *Unledded*, and cemented the relationship four years later with an album of new material.

LEE, ALBERT

English-born country rock guitarist Lee (b. 1943) joined the R&B-influenced **Chris Farlowe** And The Thunderbirds. He departed in 1967 to undertake session work. He joined honky-tonk band Country Fever, before recording as Poet And The One Man Band with Chas Hodges (later of Chas And Dave). They became the country-rock band Heads Hands And Feet. In 1975, he joined **Emmylou Harris**'s Hot Band, replacing **James Burton**. Lee also performed with **Eric Clapton**, **Jackson Browne**, **Jerry Lee Lewis** and **Dave Edmunds**. He played a major part in the historic reunion of the **Everly Brothers** at London's Royal Albert Hall in 1983. He has made several solo albums which are impressive showcases for one of the UK's most versatile guitarists.

LEE, BRENDA

Even in adolescence, Lee's (b. Brenda Mae Tarpley, 1944) voice could slip from anguished intimacy through sleepy insinuation to raucous lust. 'Let's Jump The Broomstick' and other jaunty classics kept her in the charts for a decade. By 1956, she was ensured enough airplay for her first single, a revival of **Hank Williams**' 'Jambalaya', to crack the US country chart. Her US Hot 100 debut came with 1957's 'One Step At A Time'. The next decade brought a greater proportion of heartbreak ballads, such as 'I'm Sorry' and 'Too Many Rivers', plus a role in the movie *The Two Little Bears*. Lee cut back on touring and recorded only intermittently after *Bye Bye Blues*. In 1971, she resurfaced with a huge country hit in **Kris Kristofferson**'s 'Nobody Wins', and she has continued to enjoy success in this genre with subsequent releases.

LEFT BANKE

Formed in 1965 by pianist/composer Michael Brown (b. Michael Lookofsky, 1949), he was joined in the original line-up of this US psychedelic curio by Steve Martin (vocals), Tom Finn (bass) and George Cameron (drums). The band reached the US Top 5 in 1966 with 'Walk Away Renee', although the song is more readily associated with the following year's **Four Tops** version. Jeff Winfield (guitar) was added to the line-up on the hit 'Pretty Ballerina', but internal ructions saw Brown completing a third release, 'Ivy Ivy', with session musicians. The band was reunited for 'Desiree', their final chart entry. Brown later formed Stories, although Finn, Cameron and Martin recorded a second album and were coaxed back into the studios in 1978.

LEFTFIELD

Progressive UK house act which originally comprised just Neil Barnes. He released a solo track, 'Not Forgotten', before recruiting Paul Daley. Unable to record due to contractual restraints, Leftfield embarked on a career as remixers for artists including Ultra Naté and Inner City. Later remixes for **David Bowie**, Renegade Soundwave and Yothu Yindi would follow, but by now the duo had already established their Hard Hands imprint. This debuted with the reggae-tinted 'Release The Pressure' (featuring Earl Sixteen), then the more trance-based chart entry 'Song Of Life', which gave them a minor chart success in 1992. They subsequently teamed up with John Lydon (the **Sex Pistols**) for the crossover success 'Open Up'.

Gaining favour with a mainstream audience, 1995's groundbreaking *Leftism* paved the way for the later crossover success of the **Chemical Brothers** and the **Prodigy**. Daley and Barnes, who had already produced a soundtrack for 1994's *Shallow Grave*, gained further exposure through their contribution ('A Final Hit') to the cult UK movie *Trainspotting*.

The duo spent three years recording and re-recording the follow-up, *Rhythm And Stealth*, which debuted at number 1 in the UK album chart in 1999. Stand-out track 'Africa Shox' featured guest

vocals by electro pioneer *Afrika Bambaataa*. The end of Leftfield came in March 2002, when Daley and Barnes announced they were concentrating on solo projects.

LEIBER AND STOLLER

Jerry Leiber (b. 1933) and Mike Stoller (b. 1933) began their songwriting and production partnership at the age of 17. They provided songs for Los Angeles' R&B artists during the early 50s. 'Hard Times' (Charles Brown) was the first Leiber and Stoller hit, but their biggest songs were 'Hound Dog' and 'K.C. Lovin''. In 1954, the duo set up their Spark label to release material by the Robins (soon to become the Coasters). Songs like 'Smokey Joe's Cafe', 'Searchin'', 'Yakety Yak' and 'Charlie Brown' bridged the gap between R&B and rock 'n' roll, selling millions in the 50s, while Leiber And Stoller's innovative production techniques widened the scope of the R&B record. They wrote 'Lucky Lips' for Ruth Brown and 'Saved' for LaVern Baker, but their most notable productions were for the **Drifters** and **Ben E. King**. Among these were 'On Broadway', 'Spanish Harlem', 'There Goes My Baby', 'I (Who Have Nothing)' and 'Stand By Me'. Leiber and Stoller also supplied **Elvis Presley** with songs like 'Jailhouse Rock', 'Baby I Don't Care', 'Loving You', 'Treat Me Nice' and 'His Latest Flame' and wrote hits for **Perry Como**, **Peggy Lee** and **Dion**. In 1964, the duo set up the Red Bird and Blue Cat record labels. In 1972, the duo returned to the pop world to produce albums for UK acts including **Stealer's Wheel** and **Elkie Brooks**. They went into semi-retirement, developing stage shows and appearing at award ceremonies, including their induction into the Rock And Roll Hall Of Fame in 1987. Their work inspired 1995's hit musical *Smokey Joe's Café: The Songs Of Leiber And Stoller*.

LEMONHEADS

From their origins in the sweaty back-street punk clubs of the Boston hardcore scene, the Lemonheads and their photogenic singer/guitarist Evan Dando (b. 1967) came full circle to achieve a number of hit singles. Dando, Jesse Peretz (bass) and Ben Deily (guitar, drums) made their debut EP in 1985 with *Laughing All The Way To The Cleaners*. By 1987, Dando had recruited drummer Doug Trachten, but he stayed permanent only for their debut album, *Hate Your Friends*. After *Lick*, Deily – Dando's long-time co-writer – left and the band split immediately after their acclaimed major-label debut, *Lovey*.

Dando later re-formed the Lemonheads with David Ryan (b. 1964), Byron Hoagland (drums), and Peretz. Adopting a more pop-orientated approach, their cover version of **Simon And Garfunkel**'s 'Mrs Robinson' charted and *It's A Shame About Ray* proved to be one of the year's best-loved albums. *Come On Feel The Lemonheads* continued Dando's purple songwriting patch. The less successful *Car Button Cloth* came in the wake of Dando cleaning himself up and contained some of his most mellow songs to date. Dando embarked on some well-received live dates in the new millennium.

LENNON, JOHN

Following the collapse of the **Beatles**, Lennon (b. 1940, d. 1980) and his wife **Yoko Ono** attempted to transform the world through non-musical means. Their bed-ins in Amsterdam and Montreal, black-bag appearances on stage, flirting with political activists and radicals; all received massive media attention.

Lennon's solo career began with the *avant-garde* recording *Unfinished Music No. 1 – Two Virgins*. Three months later came the equally bizarre *Unfinished Music No. 2 – Life With The Lions*. The peace anthem 'Give Peace A Chance' restored Lennon to the charts, and was followed by 'Cold Turkey', a raw rock song about heroin withdrawal. The release of *John Lennon – Plastic Ono Band* was a shock to the system for most Beatles' fans. Following psychotherapy, Lennon poured out much of his bitterness from his childhood and adolescence, neat and undiluted. More than any other work in the Lennon canon, this brilliant album was a farewell to the past.

After the strong single 'Power To The People', Lennon moved to New York and released his best-known album, *Imagine*. A Christmas single, 'Happy Christmas (War Is Over)', was another song destined for immortality. *Sometime In New York City* was a double set containing a number of political songs, and was written during the peak of Lennon's involvement with hippy-radical, Jerry Rubin. The following year he embarked on his struggle against deportation and the fight for his famous 'green card'.

At the end of 1973, Lennon released *Mind Games*, an album that highlighted problems between him and Yoko. *Walls And Bridges* contained more marital material and a surprise US number 1 hit, 'Whatever Gets You Through The Night'. In November 1974 he made his last-ever concert appearance, onstage at Madison Square Garden with **Elton John**. The following year's *Rock 'N' Roll* was a tight and energetic celebration of many of his favourite songs, including a superb version of 'Stand By Me'.

Following the birth of their son Sean, Lennon became a house husband, while Ono looked after their not-inconsiderable business interests. In November 1980, *Double Fantasy* was released and went straight to number 1 virtually worldwide. Tragically, the following month, while walking home with Yoko after a recording session, John Lennon was murdered by a gunman outside his Manhattan apartment building. The whole world reacted with unprecedented mourning.

LENNON, JULIAN

The son of **John Lennon**, Julian (b. John Charles Julian Lennon, 1963) made his debut in 1984 with the transatlantic hit singles 'Valotte' and 'Too Late For Goodbyes'. Subsequent albums failed to build on this auspicious start, although the environmental ballad 'Salt Water' made the UK Top 10 in 1991.

LENNOX, ANNIE

Following the dissolution of the **Eurythmics** in 1991, Scottish vocalist Annie Lennox (b. 1954) embarked on a highly successful solo career. *Diva* shot to UK number 1 and generated the hit singles 'Why' and 'Walking On Broken Glass'. In 1993, Lennox reached the UK Top 5 with 'Little Bird'/'Love Song For A Vampire', taken from the soundtrack of *Bram Stoker's Dracula*. *Medusa* offered a wide-ranging selection of cover versions, mainly of songs previously aired by male vocalists including 'A Whiter Shade Of Pale', 'No More I Love You's' and 'Downtown Lights'. In 1996, Lennox released the limited-edition *Live In Central Park*. Two years later she re-formed the Eurythmics with **David A. Stewart**.

LETTERMEN

US close-harmony pop trio formed by Bob Engemann (b. 1936), Tony Butala (b. 1940) and

Jim Pike (b. 1938). After two unsuccessful singles, the trio joined Capitol Records and charted in 1961 with 'The Way You Look Tonight'. During the 60s, they had 24 US chart albums, 10 of which reached the Top 40. They also had another 19 chart singles including the US Top 10 hits 'When I Fall In Love' (1961) and 'Goin' Out Of My Head'/'Can't Take My Eyes Off You' (1967). In 1968, Jim's brother Gary replaced Engemann, and six years later their brother Donny replaced Jim. The group has continued to enjoy success on the club circuit.

LEVEL 42

UK pop-funk band formed in 1980 by Mark King (b. 1958; bass, vocals), Phil Gould (b. 1957; drums), Boon Gould (b. 1955; guitar) and Mark Lindup (b. 1959; keyboards). Their Mike Vernon-produced album, a collection of dance and modern soul orientated numbers, made the UK Top 20. Most of their early singles were minor hits until 1984's 'The Sun Goes Down (Living It Up)' reached the UK Top 10. Their worldwide breakthrough came with *World Machine*, and a string of hit singles including 'Something About You', 'Lessons In Love' and 'Running In The Family'. After the release of *Running In The Family*, Boon and Phil Gould were replaced by Alan Murphy (b. 1953, d. 1989) and Gary Husband (b. 1960). Further line-up changes ensued, and despite the return of Phil Gould on *Forever Now*, the band's career had faltered by the mid-90s. They played their final show on 14 October 1994.

LEVELLERS

Formed in Brighton, England by Mark Chadwick (lead vocals, guitar, banjo), Jonathan Sevink (fiddle), Alan Miles (vocals, guitars, mandolin, harmonica), Jeremy Cunningham (bass, bouzouki) and Charlie Heather (drums), the Levellers combined folk instrumentation with rock and punk ethics, releasing the *Carry Me* EP in 1989. After their debut album, they recruited Simon Friend (guitar, vocals) and signed to China Records. *Levelling The Land* was a mixture of English and Celtic folk with powerful guitar-driven rock. The album broke into the UK Top 20. The band were disappointed with the lack of progress *The Levellers* demonstrated (the album still reached UK number 2) and it was two years before the next studio album was released. *Zeitgeist* featured the hit singles 'Hope Street' and 'Fantasy' and topped the UK charts. The Levellers' popularity was confirmed by further hits with 'Just The One' and 'What A Beautiful Day'. They announced the world's first Carbon Neutral Tour in 1998, pledging to plant trees to offset the damage caused by their transport vehicles.

LEVERT, GERALD

The son of **O'Jays** founder Eddie LeVert, Gerald LeVert (b. 1966) has a fine vocal technique, first heard in 1985 with the release of the debut album by his band, LeVert. He also established a production career before embarking on a solo project in 1991 with *Private Line*. Further work with LeVert (the band) preceded 1994's *Groove On* and the following year's international hit single 'Answering Service'. The same year also produced a well-received collection of duets performed with his father, titled *Father And Son*. In 1997, Gerald teamed-up with **Keith Sweat** and Johnny Gill for the 'soul supergroup' album *Levert Sweat Gill*. His new solo album *Love & Consequences* featured the Top 20 singles, 'Thinkin' Bout It' and 'Taking Everything'. The follow-ups *G* and *Gerald's World*, though lesser works, maintained LeVert's commercial presence.

LEWIS, GARY, AND THE PLAYBOYS

US pop group formed by Gary Lewis (b. Gary Levitch, 1946; vocals, drums), Alan Ramsey (b. 1943; guitar), John West (b. 1939; guitar), David Costell (b. 1944; bass) and David Walker (b. 1943; keyboards). Their debut, 'This Diamond Ring', reached US number 1 in 1965, and was followed by a run

of Top 10 hits. Their popularity dwindled when Lewis joined the US military in 1967. After his release in 1968, he returned to the charts with a remake of **Brian Hyland**'s 'Sealed With A Kiss'. The group disbanded at the end of the 60s. Lewis later assembled a new version of the Playboys for cabaret dates.

LEWIS, HUEY, AND THE NEWS

US AOR band formed in California in 1980, by ex-**Clover** members Huey Lewis (b. Hugh Anthony Cregg III, 1950; vocals, harmonica) and Sean Hopper (keyboards). They recruited Johnny Colla (guitar, saxophone), Mario Cipollina (bass), Bill Gibson (drums) and Chris Hayes (lead guitar). A debut album included 1982's US Top 10 hit 'Do You Believe In Love'. The band's

easy-going rock/soul fusion reached its peak with *Sports*, which provided five US Top 20 hits including 'Heart & Soul', 'If This Is It' and 'I Want A New Drug'. Lewis sued Ray Parker Jnr. over the latter, claiming it had been plagiarized for the *Ghostbusters* theme. From 1985–86, three Lewis singles headed the US charts: 'The Power Of Love' (theme tune to the movie *Back To The Future*), 'Stuck With You' and 'Jacob's Ladder'. 'Perfect World' (1988) was also a success, although *Hard At Play* did less well.

The band maintained a lower musical profile in the 90s, with Lewis electing to concentrate on his acting career instead. *Four Chords And Several Years Ago*, a tour of the band's musical mentors, was released in 1994. The soulful *Plan B* broke a long recording silence in 2001.

LEWIS, JERRY LEE

The personification of 50s rock 'n' roll at its best, Lewis (b. 1935) first recorded on *The Louisiana Hayride* in 1954. His version of 'Crazy Arms' was his Sun Records debut, but it was his second single, a revival of Roy Hall's 'Whole Lotta Shakin' Goin' On' (1957) that brought him international fame. The record, which was initially banned as obscene, narrowly missed the top of the US chart and went on to hit number 1 on the R&B and country charts. He stole the show from many other stars in the movie *Jamboree* in which he sang 'Great Balls Of Fire' (UK number 1/US number 2).

When he arrived in Britain for a tour in 1958 accompanied by his third wife, Myra, who was also his 13-year-old second cousin, the UK media went crazy. The tour was cancelled after only three concerts. When his version of **Ray Charles**' 'What'd I Say' hit the UK Top 10 in 1960 it looked like a revival was on the way, but it was not to be.

In 1968, Lewis decided to concentrate on country material. This changeover was an instant success and over the next 13 years Lewis became one of country's top-selling artists, topping the chart with records such as 'There Must Be More To Love Than This' (1970), 'Would You Take Another Chance On Me?' (1971) and a revival of 'Chantilly Lace' (1972). His behaviour became increasingly erratic, however. He accidentally shot his bass player in the chest – the musician survived and sued him – and, in 1976, was arrested for waving a gun outside **Elvis Presley**'s Graceland home. Two years later, Lewis signed to Elektra Records. Unfortunately, his association with the company ended with much-publicized lawsuits.

In 1981, Lewis was hospitalized by a haemorrhaged ulcer, but he survived and was soon back on the road. In 1982, his fourth wife drowned in a swimming pool. The following year, his fifth wife was found dead at his home from a methodone overdose. A sixth marriage followed, along with more bleeding ulcers and a period in the Betty Ford Clinic. Despite his personal problems, Lewis was one of the first people inducted into the Rock And Roll Hall Of Fame in 1986.

LEWIS, RAMSEY

Pianist Lewis (b. 1935) began his career as a church accompanist before joining the Clefs, a seven-piece dance band. In 1956, he formed a jazz trio with the Clefs' rhythm section Eldee Young (bass) and Redd Holt (drums). 'The In Crowd', an instrumental cover version, reached US number 5 in 1965, selling over a million copies. 'Hang On Sloopy' reached number 11 and sold another million and the classic 'Wade In The Water' (1966) was a major hit. Lewis never recaptured this commercial peak, although he continued securing US Top 100 hits well into the 70s. He later worked with Grover Washington Jnr. and Omar Hakim in the Urban Knights.

LIGHTFOOT, GORDON

Canadian singer-songwriter Lightfoot (b. 1938) provided songs for several acts, notably Ian And Sylvia, **Peter, Paul And Mary**, **Bob Dylan**, **Johnny Cash**, **Elvis Presley** and **Jerry Lee Lewis**. As a singer, he debuted in 1966 with *Lightfoot*, followed by *The Way I Feel* and *Did She Mention My Name*, but it was not until 1970 that he made a significant commercial breakthrough with *Sit Down Young Stranger*. The album brought a US Top 5 hit with 'If You Could Read My Mind'; it also included the first recording of **Kris Kristofferson**'s 'Me And Bobby McGee'. In 1974, Lightfoot reached US number 1 with 'Sundown', and two years later 'The Wreck Of The Edmund Fitzgerald' peaked at number 2. Although Lightfoot continued to record mature singer-songwriter-styled material, his increasing reliance on easy-listening perspectives proved unattractive to a changing rock audience. Recording infrequently, his profile lessened quite considerably during the 80s and 90s.

LIGHTHOUSE FAMILY

This UK pop band comprises the Newcastle-based duo of Tunde Baiyewu, a vocalist of Nigerian descent, and songwriter and musician Paul Tucker. The duo made their debut in 1995 with *Ocean Drive*, which included the UK hit singles 'Lifted', 'Ocean Drive', 'Goodbye Heartbreak' and 'Loving Every Minute'. 'Lifted' was later adopted as the theme song by the UK Labour Party for the 2001 general election. Detractors took great satisfaction in attacking the duo's brand of 'soul-lite' pop, but the 1997 follow-up, *Postcards From Heaven*, confirmed Lighthouse Family's status as one of Britain's most successful new bands. The album featured the UK Top 10 singles 'Raincloud', 'High' and 'Lost In Space'. An extended hiatus was broken at the end of 2001 by *Whatever Gets You Through The Day*.

LIGHTNING SEEDS

Formed by UK musician Ian Broudie (b. 1958), who had produced such acts as **Echo And The Bunnymen**, the **Fall**, and the **Icicle Works**, the **Lightning Seeds** was an opportunity for Broudie to expand his songwriting talents. His first single, 'Pure', reached the UK Top 20 in 1990. *Cloudcuckooland* followed, encapsulating Broudie's notion of the perfect, sweet pop song. *Sense* and *Jollification* were commercial successes and Broudie put together a full touring band. In 1996, Broudie composed England's football anthem 'Three Lions', recorded with comedians David Baddiel and Frank Skinner. The track topped the UK charts (two years later he repeated the success with 'Three Lions 98'). The following year's *Tilt* was an alarming commercial failure.

LIL' KIM

This US rapper (b. Kimberly Jones, 1975) was initially aided by the **Notorious B.I.G.**, who helped her team up with the New York rap collective Junior

M.A.F.I.A. A strong response to her contributions on their 1995 debut single, 'Player's Anthem', and the ensuing *Conspiracy*, earned her acclaim for her adept microphone skills. Lil' Kim launched her own career in 1996 with *Hard Core*. This sexually explicit hardcore rap album came as something of a shock in the male-dominated world of hip-hop, but it still reached the US Top 20. She also established an acting career, appearing in 1999's hit comedy *She's All That*. Her sophomore album was released the following June.

LIMP BIZKIT

Led by Fred Durst (b. William Frederick Durst, 1971), this US hard-rock/hip-hop fusion band was formed in 1994 by Durst, Wes Borland (guitar), Sam Rivers (bass) and John Otto (drums). The line-up was further augmented in 1996 by the services of DJ Lethal (b. Leor DiMant) when his former employers House Of Pain ran aground. The band made its debut with *Three Dollar Bill, Y'all$* in 1997, a record that went on to notch up sales in excess of 1.5 million as it was adopted by a new generation of MTV rock fans.

Limp Bizkit returned in 1999 with *Significant Other*, with a guest rap from **Method Man** affirming the band's hip-hop credentials. The album debuted at number 1 on the US album chart, confirming the band as one of the leading alternative acts in America. The following year they achieved a big transatlantic hit with 'Take A Look Around', the theme song for the Tom Cruise movie *Mission: Impossible 2*. They capitalized on their high profile with the release of *Chocolate Starfish And The Hot Dog Flavored Water*, which went straight to number 1 on the US charts. The band also spearheaded the 'nu-metal' breakthrough in Europe, with 'Rollin'' topping the UK singles chart for two weeks in 2001. Borland, who had earlier recorded an album with his side-project Big Dumb Face, left the band in October.

LINDISFARNE

Formed in Newcastle, England by Alan Hull (b. 1945, d. 1995; vocals, guitar, piano), Simon Cowe (b. 1948; guitar), Ray Jackson (b. 1948; harmonica, mandolin), Rod Clements (b. 1947; bass, violin) and Ray Laidlaw (b. 1948; drums). The group were originally known as the Downtown Faction, becoming Lindisfarne in 1968. Their folk-rock debut, *Nicely Out Of Tune*, was followed by the popular *Fog On The Tyne*. Its attendant single, 'Meet Me On The Corner' (1972), reached the UK Top 5. *Dingly Dell* was disappointing, and, in 1973, Laidlaw, Cowe and Clements left to form Jack The Lad. Kenny Craddock (keyboards), Charlie Harcourt (guitar), Tommy Duffy (bass) and Paul Nichols (drums) were recruited but this line-up lacked its predecessor's charm and was overshadowed by Hull's concurrent solo career. *Happy Daze* offered some promise, but Lindisfarne disbanded in 1975.

The original quintet later resumed working together, reaching the UK Top 10 with 'Run For Home' in 1978. Twelve years later Lindisfarne were back in the UK charts, backing the England international footballer and fellow Geordie Paul Gascoigne on a reworked version of 'Fog On The Tyne'. Until his sudden death in 1995, Hull maintained an independent solo career. The remaining members have continued to record new material.

LINKIN PARK

This California, USA-based outfit have earned the rather dubious distinction of becoming nu-metal's first pin-ups. Originally known as Xero, the band was formed in 1996 by Mike Shinoda (b. 1970, USA;

MC/vocals), Brad Delson (guitar), Rob Bourdon (b. 1979, USA; drums), Phoenix (bass) and DJ Joseph Hahn (b. 1977, USA). Minus the departing Phoenix, the band was joined by lead singer Chester Bennington (b. 1976) and changed their name to Hybrid Theory, but for legal reasons swiftly adopted the Linkin Park moniker. Their debut album, [Hybrid Theory], introduced a highly eclectic fusion of metal, hip-hop, industrial and pop styles. Aided by the heavy radio rotation of 'One Step Closer' the album debuted in the US Top 20 in 2000. By this time, founding member Phoenix had returned to the line-up. The band's popularity grew steadily over the next two years, with [Hybrid Theory] reaching the US Top 5 and the track 'In The End' climbing to number 2 on the singles chart.

LITTLE ANTHONY AND THE IMPERIALS
US vocal group formed in New York in 1957 by 'Little' Anthony Gourdine (b. 1940), Ernest Wright Jnr. (b. 1941), Clarence Collins (b. 1941), Tracy Lord and Glouster Rogers (b. 1940). They had their first hit with 'Tears On My Pillow' (1958), followed by 'So Much' (1959) and 'Shimmy Shimmy Ko-Ko-Bop' (1960). In 1964, Gourdine formed a 'new' Imperials around Wright, Collins and Sammy Strain (b. 1940). Their first hit, 'I'm On The Outside (Looking In)', showcased Gourdine's dazzling falsetto. 'Goin' Out Of My Head' and 'Hurt So Bad' both reached the US Top 10, but the line-up later drifted apart. Collins later formed his own Imperials.

LITTLE EVA
Discovered by songwriters **Carole King** and **Gerry Goffin**, Little Eva (b. Eva Narcissus Boyd, 1943) shot to fame in 1962 with the international hit 'The Loco-Motion'. She continued to record until 1965, but her only other substantial hit was 'Swinging On A Star', a duet with Big Dee Irwin. She made a UK chart comeback in 1972 with a reissue of 'The Loco-Motion', which peaked at number 11.

LITTLE FEAT
Little Feat combined elements of country, folk, blues, soul and boogie to create their mesmerizing sound. Lowell George (b. 1945, d. 1979; vocals), Roy Estrada (b. 1943; bass), Bill Payne (b. 1949; keyboards) and Richard Hayward (drums) recorded two poor-selling albums for Warner Brothers Records at the start of the 70s. Estrada then left and the line-up was augmented by Paul Barr're (b. 1948; guitar), Kenny Gradney (bass) and Sam Clayton (percussion). *Dixie Chicken* introduced their fluid musical interplay, and their fourth album (*Feats Don't Fail Me Now*) finally charted in the USA. However, George was over-indulging with drugs, and his contribution to *The Last Record Album* and *Time Loves A Hero* was minimal. Following the live *Waiting For Columbus*, the band disintegrated and George started work on his solo album, *Thanks I'll Eat It Here*. During a solo tour to promote the album George died from a heart attack. The remaining band re-formed for a benefit concert for his widow and released *Down On The Farm*.

In 1988, the band re-formed for the successful *Let It Roll*. Fred Tackett (guitar, mandolin) and Craig Fuller (ex-**Pure Prairie League**) took George's place, and the musical direction was guided by the faultless keyboard playing of Bill Payne. Fuller departed in 1994 and was replaced by female lead singer, Shaun Murphy.

LITTLE RICHARD
Little Richard (b. Richard Wayne Penniman, 1935) first recorded in 1951, cutting eight urban blues tracks with his mentor Billy Wright's orchestra. In 1955, after unsuccessful recordings, he recorded a dozen tracks with producer **Robert 'Bumps' Blackwell**. The classic 'Tutti Frutti' was among them and gave him his first R&B and pop hit in the USA. The following 'Long Tall Sally', topped the R&B chart and was the first of three US Top 10 hits. Richard's string of Top 20 hits continued with the double-sider 'Rip It Up'/'Ready Teddy', while his frantic, performance of 'Long Tall Sally' and 'Tutti Frutti' in the movie *Don't Knock The Rock* helped push his UK single into the Top 3.

His next film and single was *The Girl Can't Help It*, while the remainder of 1957 saw him notch up transatlantic hits with the rock 'n' roll classics 'Lucille', 'Keep A Knockin'' and 'Jenny Jenny', and a Top 20 album, *Here's Little Richard*. In 1962, Richard toured the UK for the first time. In 1964, he signed with Vee Jay Records where he re-recorded all his hits, revived a few oldies and cut some new rockers, but sales were unimpressive.

The 70s was spent jumping from label to label, recording and touring. In 1986, Richard was one of the first artists inducted into the Rock And Roll Hall of Fame and he acted in the movie *Down And Out In Beverly Hills*. Renewed interest spurred WEA Records to sign him and he released *Lifetime Friend*, which included the chart record 'Operator'. The leader of rebellious 50s rock 'n' roll, and the man who shook up the music business and the parents of the period, is now a much-loved personality.

LITTLE RIVER BAND
Australian rock band formed by Beeb Birtles (b. Gerard Birtlekamp, 1948; guitar), Graham Goble (b. 1947; guitar), Derek Pellicci (drums) and Glen Shorrock (b. 1944; vocals). Guitarist Rick Formosa (replacing Graham Davidge) and Roger McLachlan (bass) joined later. They had immediate Australian success with their first single and album and began aiming overseas. By 1976 they had enjoyed their first appearance in the US charts with 'It's A Long Way There'. Formosa and McLachlan were then replaced by David Briggs (b. 1951) and George McArdle (b. 1954). *Diamantina Cocktail* went gold in the USA in 1977, the first time for an Australian act. *Sleeper Catcher* was also hugely successful, and contained the US Top 5 hit 'Reminiscing'. McCardle left before the release of *First Under The Wire*, which broke into the US Top 10 and also generated the US hit Top 10 hit singles, 'Lady' and 'Lonesome Loser'. Wayne Nelson was brought in as the new bass player on *Time Exposure*, which contained two further US Top 10 hits 'The Night Owls' and 'Take It Easy On Me'. Briggs was replaced by Steve Housden (b. 1951) following the sessions for *Time Exposure*. Not long afterwards John Farnham (b. 1949), one of Australia's most popular singers, was recruited as lead singer, but he could do little to halt their commercial decline. Pellicci and Birtles were replaced by Steve Prestwich (drums) and David Hirschfelder (keyboards) were brought in as replacements Farnham left in 1986 to pursue his solo career. Further personnel changes have dogged the band, which has been content to play their old hits on world tours. By the late 90s Housden was the only remaining long-term member in the line-up.

LITTLE STEVEN

This US musician (b. Steve Van Zandt, 1950) toured as backing guitarist to the Dovells before passing briefly through the ranks of **Southside Johnny And The Asbury Jukes**, whose first three albums he supervised. He also contributed several compositions to these, some written with **Bruce Springsteen**, with whose E Street Band he served on and off from 1975 to 1984. Overcoming inhibitions about his singing, Van Zandt, also known as 'Miami Steve' or 'Little Steven', next led Little Steven And The Disciples Of Soul. Theirs was a body of recorded work that, lyrically, reflected Van Zandt's increasing preoccupation with world politics. After a fact-finding expedition to South Africa, he masterminded Sun City, a post-Live Aid project that raised over $400,000 for anti-apartheid movements in Africa and the Americas. Without a record contract for most of the 90s, Van Zandt's profile was raised at the end of the decade when he landed the role of Silvo Dante in HBO's acclaimed Mafia drama series *The Sopranos*, and toured with the reunited E Street Band.

LIVE

US alternative rock band formed as First Aid in the mid-80s by Patrick Dahlheimer (bass), Chad Taylor (guitar) and Chad Gracey (drums). They changed their name to Public Affection with the addition of Ed Kowalcyzk (vocals), releasing an album in 1989. Another name change (to Live) preceded *Mental Jewelry*, an intense, spiritual recording. *Throwing Copper* was an unexpected success, selling six million copies in the USA alone by 1996. *Secret Samadhi* was an altogether bleaker-sounding record, which nevertheless attained double-platinum status. *The Distance To Here* largely eschewed the experimental approach of its predecessor.

LIVING COLOUR

Highly acclaimed US rock band formed by Vernon Reid (b. 1958; guitar), Muzz Skillings (bass) and William Calhoun (b. 1964; drums) in 1984. Vocalist Corey Glover (b. 1964) joined shortly afterwards. Fusing jazz, blues and soul, alongside commercial hard rock, their 1988 debut *Vivid* reached the US Top 10. The follow-up *Time's Up* won a Grammy award, but Skillings left and was replaced by Doug Wimbish (b. 1956; ex-Tackhead) on *Stain*. An excellent retrospective, *Pride*, was released following the band's demise in 1995. Reid released a solo album in 1996 while Calhoun went on to record with his jazz quintet. The band reformed in 2001.

LL COOL J

Long-running star of the rap scene, LL Cool J (b. James Todd Smith, 1969) made his debut in 1984 on 'I Need A Beat'. However, it was 'I Just Can't Live Without My Radio' and 'I Need Love' which established him. Musically, LL Cool J (the moniker stands for Ladies Love Cool James) is probably best sampled on his 1990 triple-platinum set *Mama Said Knock You Out*. Like many of rap's senior players, he has also sustained an acting career, with appearances in *The Hard Way* and *Toys*, playing a cop in the former and a military man in the latter. *Phenomenon* and the US chart-topping *G.O.A.T.* celebrated Cool's remarkable longevity on the rap scene.

LOFGREN, NILS

In the late 60s, Chicago, USA-born guitarist Lofgren (b. 1951) recorded as Paul Dowell And The Dolphins before forming Grin with Bob Gordon and Bob Berberich. He also briefly teamed up with **Neil Young**'s backing group **Crazy Horse** for their debut album. Lofgren's association with Young continued on the *Tonight's The Night* tour. It was widely speculated that Lofgren might replace Mick Taylor in the **Rolling Stones**. Instead, he signed to A&M Records and recorded a self-titled album. The follow-up *Cry Tough* displayed Lofgren's power as a writer, arranger and musician, and was a transatlantic bestseller. When Lofgren's reputation as a solo artist declined, he embarked on Neil Young's *Trans* tour (1983), followed by a stint with **Bruce Springsteen**'s E Street Band. His solo work in the 80s and 90s appeared on several independent labels. In 1999 Lofgren reunited with Springsteen and the E Street Band for a world tour.

LOGGINS, KENNY

US artist Loggins (b. 1948) came to prominence in the 70s in **Loggins And Messina**. After going solo, he specialized in rock ballads such as the US Top 5 hit 'Whenever I Call You Friend'. Subsequent success came with the solo 'This Is It' and 'What A Fool Believes', a million-selling US number 1 for the Doobie Brothers, co-written with **Michael McDonald**. During the 80s, Loggins came to prominence as a writer and performer of theme songs: 'I'm Alright' (*Caddyshack*, 1980), 'Footloose' (*Footloose*, 1984) and 'Danger Zone' (*Top Gun*, 1986). This was followed by music for *Caddyshack II*, including another hit, 'Nobody's Fool'. He had a minor hit with 'Conviction Of The Heart' in 1991.

His most successful recordings in recent years have been two children's albums named after his first-ever hit song, 'House At Pooh Corner', which the **Nitty Gritty Dirt Band** took into the US charts in 1971.

LOGGINS AND MESSINA

The 70s partnership of **Kenny Loggins** (b. 1948) and Jim Messina (b. 1947; ex-Poco) saw nine albums reaching high US chart positions and spawned several hit singles including 'Your Mama Don't Dance' and 'My Music'. Following an amicable split after six years, Loggins went solo. Messina, following three solo albums, instigated the re-formation of Poco in 1989.

LONE JUSTICE

US country-rockers formed by **Maria McKee** (b. 1964), Ryan Hedgecock (guitar), Don Heffington (drums) and Marvin Etzioni (bass). Following the release of their 1985 debut, Etzioni and Heffington were replaced by new members Shayne Fontayne (guitar), Bruce Brody (keyboards), Greg Sutton (bass) and Rudy Richman (drums). In 1985, Feargal Sharkey had a UK number 1 with McKee's 'A Good Heart'. Lone Justice split in 1987, with McKee going solo.

LONESTAR

US country rock band formed by Richie McDonald (b. 1962; vocals, guitar), John Rich (b. 1974; vocals, bass), Michael Britt (b. 1966; guitar), Keech Rainwater (b. 1963; drums) and Dean Sams (b. 1966; keyboards). They made their debut in January 1995 when BNA Records released the *Lonestar Live* EP. A well-received debut followed, but Rich had left for a solo career by the time 'Come Cryin' To Me' and 'Everything's Changed' provided the band with two chart-toppers. Both singles were taken from 1997's *Crazy Nights*. The excellent *Lonely Grill* plumped for the middle ground between the straightforward country of their debut and the pop stylings of *Crazy Nights*. The ballad 'Amazed' spent eight weeks at number 1 on the country singles chart before crossing over to top the US Hot 100 in March 2000.

LONG RYDERS

Formed in 1981, Long Ryders were part of the Los Angeles, USA-based 'paisley underground' movement. Sid Griffin (guitar, vocals), Barry Shank (bass, vocals) and Matt Roberts (drums) were initially joined by Steve Wynn, but the guitarist was soon replaced by Stephen McCarthy. A mini-album, *The Long Ryders*, was completed with Des Brewer (bass) and Greg Sowders (drums), before Tom Stevens replaced Brewer. *Native Sons* suggested a promising future, but, unable to repeat its balance of melody and purpose, they broke up in 1987.

LONGPIGS

Formed in Sheffield, England, in 1993 by Crispin Hunt (vocals, guitar), Richard Hawley (guitar), Simon Stafford (bass) and Dee Boyle (bass). After major problems with their first record company, the Longpigs signed a new contract with **U2**'s Mother Records and re-recorded their debut album. *The Sun Is Often Out* was finally released in 1996. Songs such as 'She Said' (a chart hit), 'Lost Myself' and 'Sally Dances' confirmed the promise of the earlier singles. Boyle left before the recording of the follow-up *Mobile Home*, which mixed trip-hop beats into the band's indie-rock formula. The closure of Mother the day after the album was released resulted in the band's demise.

Hawley went on to work with **Pulp** and release acclaimed solo material.

LOPEZ, JENNIFER

Of Puerto Rican descent, Lopez (b. 1970) enjoyed great success as an actress before emerging in the late 90s as one of the new wave of Latin pop stars. Lopez made her film debut as a 16-year-old in the movie *My Little Girl*, before appearing in the series *In Living Color*, *Second Chances*, *Hotel Malibu* and *South Central*. She made her first major big-screen appearance in 1995's *Money Train*, before landing the high-profile roles of murdered Tejano star **Selena** in the 1997 biopic *Selena* and the following year's *Out Of Sight*.

Her recording debut *On The 6* was one of the great successes of 1999. The first single 'If You Had My Love' topped the US charts for five weeks. The follow-up, 'Waiting For Tonight', was also a transatlantic hit. Lopez remained in the media spotlight through her troubled romantic dalliance with **Sean 'Puffy' Combs**. Her chart-topping sophomore set *J.Lo* was premiered by the transatlantic hit single, 'Love Don't Cost A Thing'. Further hit singles lifted from the album included 'Play' and a remix of 'I'm Real' featuring rapper **Ja Rule**. The following year's remix album was promoted by the US chart-topping collaboration with Ja Rule on 'Ain't It Funny'.

LOS LOBOS

Tex-Mex band formed in 1974 in Los Angeles, USA, by Cesar Rosas (vocals, guitar, mandolin), David Hidalgo (vocals, guitar, accordion), Luis (Louie) Perez (drums, guitar, quinto), Conrad Lozano (vocals, bass, guitarron) and Steve Berlin. Leaders of the Tex-Mex brand of rock 'n' roll, *Just Another Band From East LA* was a critical success, as was 1984's *How Will The Wolf Survive?*. In 1987, their title single to the movie *La Bamba* became an international number 1 and the first song in Spanish to top the pop charts. Hidalgo and Perez have also recorded with

their sideline project, the Latin Playboys, while Rosas worked with the all-star Tex-Mex outfit Los Super Seven and released his solo debut, *Soul Disguise*. The main group re-formed in 1999 for their Hollywood Records debut, *This Time*.

LOUISE

After two successful years with UK vocal group **Eternal**, Louise (b. Louise Nurding, 1974) took the risky step of embarking on a solo career when Eternal were at their chart-topping peak. The gamble paid off with a string of UK hit singles, including 'Light Of My Life', 'Naked', 'Undivided Love' and 'One Kiss From Heaven'. *Woman In Me* included the hit singles 'Arms Around The World' and a cover version of the **Average White Band**'s 'Let's Go Round Again'. Her third album, the curiously titled *Elbow Beach*, was released to a muted reception in August 2000. The singer subsequently embarked on a career in television.

LOVE

This fêted Los Angeles, USA-based band was formed in 1965 by Arthur Lee (b. Arthur Taylor Porter, 1945; guitar, vocals), Bryan MacLean (b. 1946, d. 1998; guitar, vocals), John Echols (guitar), Don Conka (drums) and John Fleckenstein, although the latter two were soon replaced by Alban 'Snoopy' Pfisterer and Ken Forssi (d. 1998). Their debut single was a version of **Burt Bacharach** and **Hal David**'s 'My Little Red Book'. Love were an instant sensation on the LA club scene and the furiously energetic 'Seven & Seven Is' (1966) became their second hit. Line-up changes saw drummer Michael Stuart and flautist/saxophonist Tjay Cantrelli (b. John Berberis) joining, while Pfisterer moved to harpsichord and organ. Although *Da Capo* pointed to a new direction, it was *Forever Changes* that put them in the history books. This was Lee's finest work and marked the end of the partnership with MacLean.

A new Love featuring Lee, Frank Fayad (bass), Jay Donnellan (guitar) and drummers George Suranovich and Darren Theaker lasted for two albums. *False Start*, recorded by Lee, Fayad, Suranovich, Nooney Rickett (guitar, vocals) and Gary Rowles (guitar), featured a few memorable moments, including a guitar solo from **Jimi Hendrix** on 'The Everlasting First'. Lee released a solo album in 1972 before reviving the Love name for the truly wretched *Reel To Real*, following which the band faded into cult status. In the late 90s Lee was given an eight-year prison sentence for illegal possession of a firearm (he was eventually released in December 2001).

LOVE AFFAIR

Formed in 1966 in London, England by Steve Ellis (vocals), Morgan Fisher (keyboards), Rex Brayley (guitar), Mick Jackson (bass) and Maurice Bacon (drums). Fisher was briefly replaced by Lynton Guest and the following year

Ellis, backed by session musicians, recorded a cover of Robert Knight's 'Everlasting Love'. In 1968, the single hit UK number 1 and Love Affair became instant pop stars. Four more UK Top 20 hits followed – 'Rainbow Valley', 'A Day Without Love', 'One Road' and 'Bringing On Back The Good Times' – but by the end of the 60s, Steve Ellis left to form the group Ellis. The remaining quartet recruited new vocalist Gus Eadon (b. Auguste Eadon) and unsuccessfully attempted to steer the band in a more progressive direction. A line-up of the Love Affair featuring no original members went on to issue obscure singles, before plundering the band's name for cabaret/revivalist bookings.

LOVERBOY

Canadian hard-rock outfit formed in 1978 by Mike Reno (b. Joseph Michael Rynoski, 1955; vocals), Paul Dean (b. 1946; guitar), Doug Johnson (b. 1957; keyboards), Scott Smith (b. Donald Scott Smith, 1955; bass) and Matthew Frenette (b. 1954; drums). Their self-titled debut was an American-styled melodic hard-rock collection that included the hits 'Turn Me Loose' and 'The Kid Is Hot Tonite'. The following *Get Lucky* sold over two million copies, buoyed by the US Top 30 success of 'Working For The Weekend' and 'When It's Over'. After touring, they released the multi-platinum *Keep It Up*, from which 'Hot Girls In Love' reached the US Top 20. *Lovin' Every Minute Of It* proved their least successful album, though it still sold over a million copies and the title track and 'This Could Be The Night' broke into the US Top 10. Further hits followed with 'Heaven In Your Eyes' (from *Top Gun*), but by the 1989 the band had ground to a halt as Dean and Reno embarked on solo careers. The parent band re-formed for a benefit gig in 1992, and the following May resumed playing as a full-time unit. Several US tours followed before Johnson decided to leave the band in December 1996. The remaining quartet released a new album on the CMC International label in 1997.

LOVETT, LYLE

Texan singer-songwriter and former journalism and languages student, Lovett (b. 1957) began writing songs in the late 70s. He sang on two of Nanci Griffith's early albums, *Once In A Very Blue Moon* (1984) and *Last Of The True Believers* (1985). His self-titled debut for Curb Records was idiosyncratic, and his acceptance was slow in US country music circles, although it fared better in Europe. *Pontiac* made it clear that Lovett was rather more than a folk or country artist. *Lyle And His Large Band* included an insidiously straight version of the Tammy Wynette standard 'Stand By Your Man', and a version of the R&B oldie 'The Glory Of Love'. In 1992, Lovett supported **Dire Straits** on their world tour, but it did little to extend his cult following despite the excellence of the albums *Joshua Judges Ruth* and *I Love Everybody*. He acted in the movie *The Player* (the first of many films) and performed 'You've Got A Friend In Me' with **Randy Newman** for the soundtrack of the movie *Toy Story*. The Road To Ensenada mixed Lovett's razor wit with pathos for a past relationship. *On Step Inside This House* Lovett performed revelatory cover versions of 21 favourite Texan songs.

LOVIN' SPOONFUL

US pop band formed in 1965 by **John Sebastian** (b. 1944; vocals, guitar, harmonica) and Canadian Zalman Yanovsky (b. 1944; guitar, vocals), who had previously played together in the Mugwumps, and Steve Boone (b. 1943; bass) and Joe Butler (b. 1943; drums, vocals). Their unique blend of jug-band, folk, blues and rock 'n' roll was termed 'electric good-time music' and in two years the band notched up 10 US Top 20 hits, all composed by Sebastian and including 'Do You Believe In Magic?', 'Daydream' and 'Summer In The City'. Sebastian also wrote the music for two movies, Woody Allen's *What's Up, Tiger Lily?* and Francis Ford Coppola's *You're A Big Boy Now*, the latter featuring the beautiful 'Darling Be Home Soon'. Sadly the non-stop party came to an end in 1967 following the departure of Yanovsky and the arrival, albeit briefly, of Jerry Yester. Sebastian's departure the following year was the final nail in the coffin, although the remaining members squeezed out two minor hit singles before disbanding.

In 1991, Boone, Butler and Jerry and Jim Yester announced the re-formation of the band. The latter left in 1993, but with the recruitment of younger members Lena Beckett (keyboards) and Mike Arturi (drums) the band has continued plying their trade on the nostalgia circuit.

LOWE, NICK

Lowe (b. 1949) began as bass player and vocalist with British band Kippington Lodge, which evolved into **Brinsley Schwarz**. He then went into producing, working with the **Kursaal Flyers**, **Dr. Feelgood**, **Elvis Costello**, the **Damned**, **Clover** and Dave Edmunds. In 1976 he co-founded Stiff Records, and the following year was involved with Rockpile. His own singles were unsuccessful, but he was critically applauded for the catchy 'So It Goes' and 'What's So Funny 'Bout (Peace Love And Understanding)'. His own debut, *Jesus Of Cool* (US title: *Pure Pop For Now People*), was a critics' favourite. In 1979, he produced the **Pretenders**' 'Stop Your Sobbing', and released the excellent *Labour Of Lust*. He married Carlene Carter and in the early 80s and, as well as continuing his work with Costello, produced albums with **John Hiatt**, **Paul Carrack**, and the **Fabulous Thunderbirds**. In 1992, Lowe formed Little Village with Ry Cooder, Jim Keltner and John Hiatt, but their debut album received a lukewarm response. Much better was 1994's *The Impossible Bird*, which contained some of his best lyrics in years. He continued this renaissance with two fine albums, *Dig My Mood*, a dark lyrical odyssey of infidelity and sadness, and *The Convincer*.

LUDACRIS

One of the new wave of southern hip-hop artists to cross over to mainstream success at the turn of the new millennium, Ludacris (b. Chris Bridges, 1977) began rapping at an early age. He landed a production job at Atlanta's Hot 97.5 station, where as Chris Luva Luva he made his mark rapping over promos on the night show. Adopting the Ludacris moniker he released *Incognegro* on his own Disturbing Tha Peace Entertainment label. Signing with Def Jam Records' new South imprint, he recorded several new tracks with leading urban producers for a remixed version of *Incognegro*. Renamed *Back For The First Time*, the album spawned the national radio hit 'Southern Hospitality'.

LULU

Lulu (b. Marie MacDonald McLaughlin Lawrie, 1948) started out as a Scottish beat-group vocalist with the Luvvers. She came to prominence, aged 15, with a version of the **Isley Brothers**' 'Shout', but over the next two years only two of her eight singles charted. Abandoning the Luvvers, a cover of **Neil Diamond**'s 'The Boat That I Row' (1967) saw an upsurge in her career which was punctuated by an acting part in the film *To Sir With Love*. The theme tune gave her a million-selling US number 1 hit. Lulu represented Britain in the Eurovision Song Contest in 1969: 'Boom-Bang-A-Bang' tied for first place and provided her highest UK chart placing – number 2. After two albums and several flop singles, **David Bowie** intervened to produce and arrange her hit version of 'The Man Who Sold The World'. She later developed her career as an all-round entertainer, with stage appearances in *Guys And Dolls*, *Song And Dance* and regular slots on UK television. She occasionally returns to recording.

LUSH

UK indie pop band formed by Miki Berenyi (b. 1967; vocals, guitar), Emma Anderson (b. 1967; guitar, vocals), Steve Rippon (bass) and Christopher Acland (b. 1966, d. 1996; drums). Their debut mini-album *Scar* topped the independent charts in 1989. *Spooky* was a disappointment to many, but the album still reached the national Top 20. In 1992, Rippon left, replaced by Phil King (b. 1960). The critical reception that awaited *Split* was fervent. Although *Lovelife* failed to a certain degree in putting Lush in the premier league of pop bands, it did contain two classic pop songs 'Single Girl' and '500 (Shake Baby Shake)'. Tragically, Acland committed suicide in October 1996, and the band split up the following year.

LYMON, FRANKIE, AND THE TEENAGERS

Often billed as the 'boy wonder', US singer Lymon (b. 1942, d. 1968) joined all-vocal quartet the Premiers – Jimmy Merchant (b. 1940), Sherman Garnes (b. 1940, d. 1977), Herman Santiago (b. 1941) and Joe Negroni (b. 1940, d. 1978) – in 1954. They soon became the Teenagers. Their debut, 'Why Do Fools Fall In Love?', reached the US Top 10 and UK number 1, and sold over two million copies. Further hits followed with 'I Want You To Be My Girl', 'I Promise To Remember' and 'I'm Not A Juvenile Delinquent'. In 1957, Lymon split from the Teenagers, and his career prospects plummeted. Despite recording a strong album, his novelty appeal waned when his voice broke.

By 1961, the teenager was a heroin addict on a drug rehabilitation programme. Although he tried to reconstruct his career, his drug habit remained. In 1964, he was convicted of possessing narcotics. In February 1968, at the age of 25, he was discovered dead on the bathroom floor of his grandmother's New York apartment. His former group continued to record sporadically and in the 80s, surviving members Santiago and Merchant formed a new Teenagers and Pearl McKinnon took Lymon's part. They were inducted into the Rock And Roll Hall Of Fame in 1993.

LYNNE, JEFF

Lynne (b. 1947) joined the Nightriders in 1966. They changed their name to **Idle Race** and, under Lynne's guidance, became a leading exponent of classic late-60s UK pop. He joined the **Move** in 1970. Together with guitarist **Roy Wood**, Lynne attempted to form a more experimental outlet for their talents. This resulted in the launch of the **Electric Light Orchestra**, or ELO, of which Lynne took full control upon Wood's early departure and steered towards pop stardom.

Lynne abandoned his creation in 1986, moving into production and winning praise for his work with **George Harrison**, **Randy Newman**, **Roy Orbison** and **Tom Petty**. Lynne also joined the **Traveling Wilburys**, an informal 'supergroup' completed by Orbison, Harrison, Petty and **Bob Dylan**. In 1990, Lynne unveiled his solo debut, *Armchair Theatre*. He produced the **Beatles'** lost tapes, notably 'Free As A Bird' and 'Real Love', and co-produced **Paul McCartney**'s *Flaming Pie* in 1997. In 2001, he recorded a new album with ELO.

LYNNE, SHELBY

US singer Lynne (b. Shelby Lynn Moore, 1968) was raised in Jackson, Alabama, and her life reads like a soap opera: there were long arguments with her father, who had her jailed on a trumped-up charge, and later, she saw her father shoot her mother dead and then commit suicide. Her 1989 debut included the country standards 'I Love You So Much It Hurts' and 'I'm Confessin''. *Temptation* was a radical album, employing a full horn section, and sounded closer to **Harry Connick Jnr.** than country music. *Restless* marked something of a return to traditional country, although there were still jazz and R&B overtones. Despite her talent she has yet to win over US radio stations, a problem highlighted by the fact that 1999's excellent *I Am Shelby Lynne* was primarily targeted at the European market. Lynne earned belated recognition in her homeland when she won the Best New Artist Grammy award in February 2001. 'Killin' Kind', featured on the *Bridget Jones's Diary* soundtrack, gave a taste of the soulful pop direction of *Love, Shelby*.

LYNOTT, PHIL

Having enjoyed considerable success in **Thin Lizzy**, Lynott (b. 1949, d. 1986) first recorded solo in 1980. His debut, 'Dear Miss Lonely Hearts', reached the UK Top 40 and was followed by *Solo In Soho*. In 1982, 'Yellow Pearl' (UK Top 20) was used as the theme tune to the television show *Top Of The Pops*. In 1983, Thin Lizzy broke up and Lynott joined Grand Slam. In 1985, he partnered **Gary Moore** on the UK Top 5 hit, 'Out In The Fields'. He played his last gig with Grand Slam at the Marquee in London on 3 December 1985. Shortly afterwards he died of heart failure, exacerbated by pneumonia.

LYNYRD SKYNYRD

US hard-rock band formed in Florida in 1964 by Ronnie Van Zant (b. 1948, d. 1977; vocals), Allen Collins (b. 1952, d. 1990; guitar), Gary Rossington (b. 1951; guitar), Larry Jungstrom (bass) and Bob Burns (drums). The quintet played under various names and released one single, 'Need All My Friends' (1968), before changing their name to Lynyrd Skynyrd. Leon Wilkeson (b. 1952, d. 2001; bass) replaced Jungstrom and **Al Kooper** produced the band's debut album, *Pronounced Leh-Nerd Skin-Nerd*, which also featured guitarist Ed King and Billy Powell (b. 1952; keyboards). Support slots with the **Who** were followed by their momentous anthem 'Free Bird'. In 1974, the band enjoyed their biggest US hit with 'Sweet Home Alabama', an amusing and heartfelt response to **Neil Young**'s 'Southern Man'. After the release of *Second Helping*, Burns was replaced by Artimus Pyle (b. 1948) and King retired. *Gimme Back My Bullets* was produced by Tom Dowd. In 1976 Rossington was injured in a car crash, and Steve Gaines (b. 1949, d. 1977; guitar) became King's replacement. Tragedy struck in October 1977: Van Zant, Gaines, his sister Cassie (one of three backing singers) and manager Dean Kilpatrick were killed in a plane crash en route to Louisiana. Rossington, Collins, Powell and Wilkeson were all seriously injured, but recovered. The new album, *Street Survivors*, was withdrawn as the sleeve featured an unintentionally macabre design of the band surrounded by flames.

In 1987, Lynyrd Skynyrd was revived for a 'reunion' tour featuring Rossington, Powell, Pyle, Wilkeson and King, with Ronnie's brother Johnny Van Zant (vocals) and Randell Hall (guitar). Collins had been paralyzed, and his girlfriend killed, during an automobile accident in 1986 and he died in 1990 from pneumonia. However, members continued to perform and record after disentangling themselves from legal complications over the use of the name caused by objections from Van Zant's widow. The Rossington led line-up, which also features Rick Medlocke (guitar, vocals; ex-Blackfoot), Hugh Thomasson (guitar, vocals; ex-**Outlaws**), and Michael Cartellone (drums; ex-Damn Yankees), has continued to release worthy recordings, and remains a huge draw on the live circuit.

M PEOPLE

UK group founded by former Haçienda DJ Mike Pickering (b. 1958; keyboards, programming), with vocalist Heather Small (b. 1965) and Paul Heard (b. 1960; keyboards, programming). They achieved club success in 1991 with 'How Can I Love You More' and their debut album, *Northern Soul*. In 1993, on the back of major UK hits such as 'One Night In Heaven', 'Moving On Up', they were awarded a BRIT Award for Best UK Dance Act. The album *Elegant Slumming* won them the Mercury Prize for Best UK Act in any category the following year. Meanwhile, their highly polished, commercial sound (omnipresent on car stereos and commercial radio) was being cited as the perfect example of 'handbag house', a term the band themselves despised. *Bizarre Fruit* and the attendant UK Top 10 singles 'Sight For Sore Eyes', 'Open Your Heart' and 'Search For The Hero', were greeted with mild disappointment. With the addition of bongo/percussion player Shovell, the group embarked on a world tour. *Bizarre Fruit II* compiled several remixes and edits as a prelude to *Fresco*, featuring the stand-out single 'Just For You'. A lazily compiled 'best of' selection and Small's solo debut, *Proud*, are the only products to have subsequently emerged from the M People camp.

M.C. HAMMER

This popular US rap artist (b. Stanley Kirk Burrell, 1963) synthesized the street sounds of black cultural alienation, or his interpretation thereof, to great commercial gain in the early 90s. Hammer (named after his likeness to Oakland A's big hitter Henry 'Hammerin' Hank' Aaron) joined the US Navy for three years. Together with a backing band, he cut a 1987 debut set, *Feel My Power*. A minor hit, it did enough to bring Hammer to the attention of Capitol Records. After contracts were completed, including a reported advance of $750,000 (unheard of for a rap artist), the album was reissued under the title *Let's Get It Started*. Such success was overshadowed, however, by that of the follow-up, 1990's *Please Hammer Don't Hurt 'Em*. The album began a residency at the top of the US charts for a record-breaking 21-week run. The US/UK Top 5 single, 'U Can't Touch This', embodied his appeal, with near-constant rotation on pop channel MTV, and dance routines that were the equal of **Michael Jackson**. The single sampled **Rick James**'s 'Super Freak', creating a precedent for follow-ups 'Have You Seen Her' (the **Chi-Lites**) and 'Pray' (**Prince**'s 'When Doves Cry'), the latter achieving his highest chart position when it reached US number 2.

The follow-up, *Too Legit To Quit*, was released under the name Hammer. Despite a soundtrack hit with 'Addams Groove', heavily promoted in *The Addams Family* movie, Hammer's fortunes declined. By 1994, there was a huge image switch, from harem pants and leather catsuits to dark glasses and a goatee beard, and a lame adoption of the gangsta-rap sound. Hammer reverted to using the M.C. prefix for 1995's *Inside Out*, but following its release concentrated on his work as a born-again preacher. He returned to the music scene in November 2001 with a new studio album, *Active Duty*.

MacCOLL, KIRSTY

A change of label from Stiff Records to Polydor Records brought UK singer MacColl (b. 1959, d. 2000) a Top 20 success in 1981 with the witty 'There's A Guy Works Down The Chip Shop Swears He's Elvis'. Her country and pop influences was discernible on her strong debut, *Desperate Characters*. In 1984, MacColl returned to the UK charts with a stirring version of **Billy Bragg**'s 'A New England'. MacColl then balanced session work with family commitments (two children by producer Steve Lillywhite). In December 1987, she reached the number 2 slot duetting with Shane MacGowan on the **Pogues**' 'Fairytale Of New York'. Two years later she returned to recording solo with the excellent *Kite*. The album included the powerful 'Free World' and a cover version of the **Kinks**' 'Days', which brought her back to the UK Top 20. *Electric Landlady* was

another strong album that demonstrated MacColl's diversity and songwriting talent. Her career was sympathetically compiled on *Galore*.

MacColl returned over five years later with the sparkling Latin American collection, *Tropical Brainstorm*. Her revived career was cut short by a tragic accident in December 2000. The singer was hit and killed by a speedboat while swimming with her children off the coast of Mexico. She had recently finished recording a series on Cuba for BBC Radio 2.

MADNESS

This fondly regarded UK ska/pop band was formed in 1979 by Suggs (b. Graham McPherson, 1961; vocals), Mark Bedford (b. 1961; bass), Mike Barson (b. 1958; keyboards), Chris Foreman (b. 1958; guitar), Lee Thompson (b. 1957; saxophone), Chas Smash (b. Cathal Smythe, 1959; vocals, trumpet) and Dan Woodgate (b. 1960; drums). They issued a one-off single on 2-Tone Records, 'The Prince', a tribute to blues-beat maestro **Prince Buster** (whose song 'Madness' had inspired the band's name). The single reached the UK

Top 20 and the follow-up, 'One Step Beyond' (a Buster composition) did even better, peaking at number 7 – the first result of their new contract with Stiff Records.

Over the next two years, the group enjoyed an uninterrupted run of UK Top 10 hits, including 'My Girl', 'Baggy Trousers', 'Embarrassment', 'Shut Up' and 'It Must Be Love'. In

1982, they finally topped the charts with their twelfth chart entry, 'House Of Fun'. More UK hits followed, including 'Wings Of A Dove' and 'The Sun And The Rain', but in late 1983 the band suffered a setback when Barson quit. They continued to release exceptional work in 1984, including 'Michael Caine' and 'One Better Day'. They formed the label, Zarjazz, that year. Its first release was **Feargal Sharkey**'s 'Listen To Your Father' (written by Madness), which reached the UK Top 30. In the autumn of 1986, the band announced that they were splitting up. Seventeen months later, they reunited as a four-piece under the name The Madness, but failed to find success.

In 1992, the original Madness re-formed for two open-air gigs in Finsbury Park, London, which resulted in *Madstock*, a 'live' document of the event. Four UK chart entries followed; three reissues, 'It Must Be Love', 'House Of Fun' and 'My Girl', and 'The Harder They Come'. Following further Madstock concerts, the original line-up returned to the studio in the late 90s to record new material. 'Lovestruck' indicated their enduring popularity when it entered the UK singles chart at number 10 in 1999. A credible new album, *Wonderful*, followed in September.

MADONNA

An icon for female pop stars thanks to her proven ability to artistically reinvent herself while still retaining complete control of her career, Madonna (b. Madonna Louise Ciccone, 1958) is also one of the most commercially successful artists in the history of popular music.

Born in Bay City, Michigan, USA, this former dance and drama student played with a number of New York-based club bands before signing a recording contract with Sire Records. She broke out from the dance scene into mainstream pop with 1983's 'Holiday'. It reached the US Top 20 and was a Top 10 hit across Europe in 1984. The first of her US number 1 hits came with 'Like A Virgin' in 1984. From 1985-87, she turned out a string of transatlantic hit singles. 'Crazy For You, 'Into The Groove', 'Dress You Up', 'Live To Tell', 'Papa Don't Preach', 'True Blue', 'Open Your Heart', 'La Isla Bonita' and 'Who's That Girl'. She also inaugurated a film career, appearing in the acclaimed *Desperately Seeking Susan* and the critically slammed *Shanghai Surprise* (alongside then-husband Sean Penn).

Madonna continued to attract controversy when, in 1989, the video for 'Like A Prayer', made explicit links between religion and eroticism. The adverse publicity helped the album of the same title become a global bestseller. In 1990 the extravagant staging of the Blond Ambition world tour were the apotheosis of Madonna's *mélange* of sexuality, song, dance and religiosity. Among her hits of the early 90s were 'Vogue', 'Justify My Love' and 'Rescue Me'. Madonna's reputation as a strong businesswoman, in control of each aspect of her career, was confirmed in 1992 when she signed a multi-million dollar deal with the Time-Warner conglomerate, parent company of Sire. This guaranteed the release of albums, films and books created by her own Maverick production company. She also published the controversial *Sex*, a graphic and erotic coffee-table book, and released two dance-inflected albums, *Erotica* and *Bedtime Stories*.

In 1996, her need to shock mellowed considerably with a credible movie portrayal of Eva Péron in Alan Parker's *Evita*. Later that year she gave birth to Lourdes Maria Ciccone Leon. She returned to music with 1998's acclaimed *Ray Of Light*, collaborating with producer **William Orbit**. The album generated several transatlantic hit singles, including 'Frozen' (a UK chart-topper), 'Ray Of Light', 'Drowned World (Substitute For Love)', 'The Power Of Good-bye', and 'Nothing Really Matters'. 'Beautiful Stranger', taken from the soundtrack to the Mike Myers' movie *Austin Powers: The Spy Who Shagged Me*, reached number 2 in the UK charts in June 1999. She worked with Orbit and French dance producer Mirwais on her next collection, *Music*, the title track of which was a transatlantic chart-topper in 2000. Shortly before the release of the album, on 11 August, the singer gave birth to her second child, Rocco. On 22 December, she married the UK film director Guy Ritchie in Scotland.

MAGAZINE

Ex-**Buzzcocks**' vocalist Howard Devoto (b. Howard Trafford) began writing songs with John McGeoch (b. 1955) in mid-1977. They formed Magazine that year with Devoto (vocals), McGeoch (guitar), **Barry Adamson** (b. 1958; bass), Bob Dickinson (keyboards), and Martin Jackson (drums). Their moody, cold keyboards and harsh rhythms were in contrast to the mood of the day. They were signed to Virgin Records but Dickinson left in November, and their debut, 'Shot By Both Sides', was recorded by the remaining members. Dave Formula was recruited in time to play on *Real Life*. Next to leave was Jackson, replaced by John Doyle in 1978. Only their first single and 1980's 'Sweetheart Contract' reached the UK charts. As the latter was released, McGeoch left to join **Siouxsie And The Banshees** and Robin Simon was brought in. A tour of the USA and Australia led to Simon's departure and Ben Mandelson came in for the band's last months. The departure of Devoto in 1981 signalled the end for this underrated band.

MAGNUM

UK hard-rock band formed in 1972 by Tony Clarkin (guitar), Bob Catley (vocals), Kex Gorin (drums) and Dave Morgan (bass). In 1978 they won a contract with Jet Records, and in the next three years the band released three albums to moderate success. *Chase The Dragon* (1982), with Mark Stanway (keyboards), gave them their first UK Top 20 album. Following the release of *Eleventh Hour*, problems began. Clarkin became ill, and a dispute with Jet ensued. FM Revolver signed the band in 1985 for *On A Storyteller's Night*. Its Top 40 success prompted Polydor Records to offer a long-term contract. A Top 30 album and a sell-out UK tour followed, both featuring new drummer Mickey Barker. *Wings Of Heaven* (1988) gave the band their first gold album and UK Top 10 hit. Top 40 single success came with 'Days Of No Trust', 'Start Talkin' Love' and 'It Must Have Been Love'. The Keith Olsen-produced *Goodnight L.A.* enjoyed Top 10 status and another Top 40 success was achieved with, 'Rocking Chair'. A new contract with EMI Records began with 1994's *Rock Art*. Clarkin and Catley left Magnum in 1996 to work on their Hard Rain project. They reunited with their former colleagues to record 2002's well-received *Breath Of Life*.

MAHAVISHNU ORCHESTRA

Led by UK guitarist John McLaughlin, (b. 1942), between 1972–76, the Mahavishnu Orchestra played a leading part in the creation of jazz-rock fusion. The first line-up included musicians who had played on McLaughlin's solo album *The Inner Mounting Flame*. The high-energy music created by Jan Hammer (keyboards), Jerry Goodman (violin), Rick Laird (bass) and Billy

Cobham (drums) made *Birds Of Fire* a US Top 20 hit. After releasing *Between Nothingness And Eternity*, McLaughlin split the group. A year later he re-formed it with new personnel. Jean-Luc Ponty replaced Goodman and Narada Michael Walden replaced Cobham, while Gayle Moran (keyboards, vocals) and a four-piece string section also featured. This group made *Apocalypse* with producer **George Martin**. In 1975, Ponty left and Stu Goldberg (keyboards) played on the group's final albums.

MALMSTEEN, YNGWIE

Influenced by **Jimi Hendrix**, **Ritchie Blackmore** and **Eddie Van Halen**, Swedish-born Malmsteen (b. 1963) recorded a series of demos at the age of 14, one of which was picked up by producer and guitarist Mike Varney. Malmsteen joined Steeler and Alcatrazz before being offered a solo deal by Polydor. He released the self-produced *Rising Force* in 1984. He then formed Rising Force as a band and recorded two albums. Following an 18-month break, Rising Force was resurrected and *Odyssey* was released in 1988. The album reached number 40 on the US *Billboard* album chart. *Eclipse* emerged in 1990 with weak vocals and a restrained Malmsteen on guitar. He switched back to his old style on *No Mercy*, however, which featured classical material and a string orchestra. In 1996 he joined with Jeff Scott Soto as Human Clay to issue their self-titled debut, before resuming solo work.

MAMAS AND THE PAPAS

Formed in Los Angeles, USA, in 1965, by John Phillips (b. 1935, d. 2001), his wife Michelle (b. Holly Michelle Gilliam, 1944), and former Mugwumps' members Denny Doherty (b. 1941) and Mama 'Cass' Elliot (b. Ellen Naomi Cohen, 1941, d. 1974). Their debut single, 'California Dreamin'', was originally recorded by **Barry McGuire**, whose voice was erased and replaced by Doherty's. The song reached the US Top 5. The richly harmonic follow-up, 'Monday, Monday' (US number 1) also established the band in the UK. Further hit singles followed, including 'I Saw Her Again' and a revival of the **Shirelles**' 'Dedicated To The One I Love'.

The quartet's albums went gold, but marital problems between John and Michelle eroded the stability of the band and she was fired in 1966 and temporarily replaced by Jill Gibson. The original quartet reconvened for *Deliver*, another strong album, which was followed by the autobiographical 'Creeque Alley'. In the winter of 1967, UK concerts at London's Royal Albert Hall were cancelled amid rumours of a split. The quartet managed to complete one last album, *The Papas & The Mamas*, before embarking on solo careers.

Three years later, the Mamas And The Papas briefly re-formed for *People Like Us*, but their individual contributions were taped separately and the results were disappointing. Elliot's burgeoning solo career was cut short by her sudden death in 1974. In 1982 Phillips and Doherty re-formed the band. The new line-up featured Phillips' actress daughter Laura McKenzie (McKenzie Phillips) and Elaine 'Spanky' McFarlane of Spanky And Our Gang. Doherty left when the band began touring full-time, and was replaced by **Scott McKenzie** for an attraction that steadfastly retains its popularity. The original group was inducted into the Rock And Roll Hall Of Fame in 1998. John Phillips died of heart failure three years later.

MAN

Man evolved from the Bystanders, a Swansea, Wales-unit specializing in close-harmony pop. Micky Jones (b. 1946; lead guitar, vocals), Deke Leonard (b. Roger Leonard; guitar), Clive John (guitar, keyboards), Ray Williams (bass) and Jeff Jones (drums) completed Man's debut, *Revelation*, a concept album based on evolution. Man abandoned much of *Revelation*'s gimmicky frills for *2ozs Of Plastic With A Hole In The Middle*. The first in a flurry of line-up changes began when Martin Ace (b. 1945; bass) and Terry Williams (b. 1948;

drums) joined. *Man* and *Do You Like It Here Now, Are You Settling In Alright?* contained several established stage favourites, but the band only prospered with *Live At The Padgett Rooms, Penarth*.

On the departure of Deke Leonard, Jones, Williams, John, Will Youatt (b. Michael Youatt, 1950; bass, vocals) and Phil Ryan (b. 1946; keyboards) released what is generally considered to be Man's most popular album, the live set, *Be Good To Yourself At Least Once A Day*. The next album, *Back To The Future* (with Tweke Lewis replacing John) gave Man their highest UK album position, which was almost matched the following year by *Rhinos, Winos + Lunatics*, which also saw the return of Leonard alongside new members Ken Whaley (bass) and Malcolm Morley (guitar, keyboards, vocals). Following the band's success in the USA promoting *Slow Motion*, which was recorded without Morley, an ill-fated project with **Quicksilver**'s John Cippolina resulted in the unsatisfactory *Maximum Darkness*.

The band's initial demise came in 1976 when, after the release of *Welsh Connection* (featuring Jones, Leonard, Williams, the returning Ryan and new bass player John McKenzie), they lost their momentum and ground to a halt. In 1983, Jones, Leonard, Ace and drummer John 'Pugwash' Weathers (b. 1947; ex-**Gentle Giant**) resuscitated the Man name, regularly appearing on the UK pub/club circuit and throughout Europe. In 1993 the unit released their first studio album in 16 years, *The Twang Dynasty*. Weathers left after the recording of 1995's *Call Down The Moon*. Williams briefly rejoined the band before Bob Richards took over the drum stool in the late 90s. Ryan rejoined shortly afterwards, making the band a quintet for the first time since the late 70s. This line-up recorded 2000's *Endangered Species*.

MANCHESTER, MELISSA

A former staff writer at Chappell Music, Manchester (b. 1951) launched her career in 1973 with *Home To Myself*. Her intimate style showed a debt to New York singer-songwriters, but her self-titled third album was more direct. This collection yielded her first major hit, 'Midnight Blue' (US Top 10), and set her subsequent direction. 'Whenever I Call You Friend', co-written with **Kenny Loggins**, was a bestselling single for him in 1978, while in 1979 Manchester's second US Top 10 was achieved with 'Don't Cry Out Loud'. Three years later she had another hit with 'You Should Hear How She Talks About You'. Although she has since diversified into scriptwriting and acting, Manchester remains a popular recording artist.

MANFRED MANN

This UK band was formed as the Mann-Hugg Blues Brothers by South African Manfred Mann (b. Manfred Lubowitz, 1940; keyboards) and Mike Hugg (b. 1942; drums, vibraphone). They became Manfred Mann shortly after adding **Paul Jones** (b. Paul Pond, 1942; harmonica, vocals). The line-up was completed by Mike Vickers (b. 1941; flute, guitar, saxophone) and Tom McGuinness (b. 1941; bass). '5-4-3-2-1' provided the band with their first UK Top 10 hit in early 1964. By the summer, they had their first UK number 1 with the catchy 'Do Wah Diddy Diddy'. Over the next two years, they charted regularly with hits such as 'Sha La La', and **Bob Dylan**'s 'If You Got To Go, Go Now'. In 1966, they returned to UK number 1 with 'Pretty Flamingo'. It was the last major hit on which Jones appeared. He was replaced by Michael D'Abo (b. 1944; ex-**A Band Of Angels**). By this time Vickers had been replaced by **Jack Bruce**, who in turn was replaced by Klaus Voormann, with Tom McGuinness moving to lead guitar and Henry Lowther (trumpet) and Lyn Dobson (saxophone) added to the line-up. D'Abo's debut with Manfred Mann was another hit rendering of a Dylan song, 'Just Like A Woman', their first for Fontana Records.

Along with the **Byrds**, Manfred Mann were generally regarded as the best interpreters of Dylan. This was emphasized in 1968, when they registered their third UK number 1 with Dylan's 'Mighty Quinn'. They ended the 60s with a final flurry of Top 10 hits, including 'My Name Is Jack', 'Fox On The Run' and 'Raggamuffin Man'. Mann went on to form the jazz/rock band Chapter Three and the highly successful **Manfred Mann's Earth Band**.

In the 90s the majority of the band, including Jones and D'Abo, performed regularly as the Manfreds. Without Manfred Mann they could not use the original name, but in his place they recruited Benny Gallagher (bass, vocals) and ex-**Family** drummer Rob Townsend.

MANFRED MANN'S EARTH BAND

The fourth incarnation of Manfred Mann has survived for almost 30 years. The original Earth Band was formed after Mann's bold attempt at fusion with Manfred Mann Chapter Three had proved financially disastrous. The new band comprised Mann (b. Manfred Lubowitz, 1940; keyboards), Mick Rogers (vocals, guitar), Colin Pattenden (bass) and Chris Slade (drums). They debuted in 1971 with the **Bob Dylan** song 'Please Mrs Henry', but it was not until their third offering, 1973's *Messin'* (*Get Your Rocks Off* in the US), that both success and acclaim arrived. The band hit the mark with a superb interpretation of Holst's *Jupiter*, entitled 'Joybringer'. It became a UK Top 10 hit in 1973 and helped establish the band as a viable commercial attraction.

Rogers departed in 1976 and was replaced by Chris Thompson, while new guitarist Dave Flett was brought in to augment the band's sound. They had a transatlantic hit (US number 1) and worldwide sales of over two million with a version of **Bruce Springsteen**'s 'Blinded By The Light' with vocals from Thompson. *The Roaring Silence* became the band's biggest-selling album, and other hits followed, including the **Robbie Robertson**/John Simon composition 'Davy's On The Road Again' in 1978, while Thompson enjoyed two US Top 20 hits of his own with the sextet Night. Further personnel changes saw the arrival of bass player Pat King, ex-**Wings** drummer Geoff Britton, and guitarist Steve Waller. *Chance* featured new drummer John Lingwood, while Matt Irving (guitar, bass) joined in time for Mann's homage to his former homeland, *Somewhere In Afrika*. After a lengthy absence, the band made the US chart in 1984 with 'Runner', featuring the vocals of the returning Mick Rogers.

Mann put the band on hold in the late 80s and early 90s to work on his solo collection, *Plains Music*. Noel McCalla took over lead vocals when the Earth Band began touring again. After a nine-year recording hiatus they returned with 1996's *Soft Vengeance*, featuring Thompson and McCalla on lead vocals and ex-**Jethro Tull** drummer Clive Bunker. The Earth Band remains highly popular in Europe, in particular Germany.

MANHATTAN TRANSFER

Formed in 1969 as a jug band outfit, by 1972 the only surviving member of the Manhattan Transfer was Tim Hauser. He was joined by vocalists Laurel Masse, Alan Paul and Janis Siegel. An unlikely pop act, they nonetheless charted on both sides of the Atlantic. It was symptomatic of their lack of crossover appeal that the hits were different in the UK and the USA, and indeed their versatility splintered their audience. Fans of the emotive ballad 'Chanson D'Amour', were unlikely to go for the brash gospel song 'Operator', or a jazz tune like 'Tuxedo Junction'.

In 1979, Cheryl Bentyne replaced Masse without noticeably affecting the vocal sound. Arguably the Manhattan Transfer's greatest moment remains 1985's Grammy Award-winning *Vocalese*, featuring the lyrics of vocal master Jon Hendricks, although their later work for Atlantic Records, including 2000's *The Spirit Of St. Louis*, is not without merit.

MANIC STREET PREACHERS

This Welsh band have risen from cult-punk revivalists to stadium-conquering rockers. They were formed in Blackwood, Gwent, by James Dean Bradfield (b. 1969; vocals, guitar), Richey Edwards (b. 1966; rhythm guitar), Nicky Wire (b. Nick Jones, 1969; bass) and Sean Moore (b. 1970; drums). The quartet's calculated insults at a wide variety of targets, particularly their peers, had already won them infamy following the release of their 1990 debut on the Damaged Goods label, the *New Art Riot* EP (a previous single, 'Suicide Alley', featuring original rhythm guitarist Flicker, had been a limited pressing distributed at gigs and to journalists only). Their personal manifesto was explicit: rock bands should cut down the previous generation, release one explosive album, then disappear.

The band's 1992 debut album included the singles 'You Love Us', 'Stay Beautiful' and 'Love's Sweet Exile', and revealed a band beginning to approach in power what they had always had in vision. The polished, less caustic approach of *Gold Against The Soul* saw moments of sublime lyricism, but *The Holy Bible* was a bleak, nihilistic work reflecting the mental state of main lyricist Richey Edwards. Success seemed somehow irrelevant following Edwards' unexplained disappearance on 1 February 1995 (his body has never been found).

The following year the remaining members released *Everything Must Go*, an outstanding and highly commercial album. They culminated their finest year by winning three BRIT Awards, and enjoying a UK number 2 hit with 'A Design For Life'. Two years later they reached the top of the UK charts with 'If You Tolerate This Your Children Will Be Next' and the attendant *This Is My Truth Tell Me Yours*. Underlying their popularity, the band played a sell-out concert in Cardiff, Wales on New Year's Eve. A month later they

topped the UK charts with the limited edition *Masses Against The Classes* EP, an abrasive response to critics who had accused the band of selling out.

In February 2001, the Manic Street Preachers became the first major western rock band to play a concert in Cuba. Shortly afterwards, the band released two new singles on the same day, 'So Why So Sad' and 'Found That Soul'. The remaining tracks on *Know Your Enemy* adopted a hardline political stance that harked back to the band's early period.

MANILOW, BARRY

Manilow (b. Barry Alan Pincus, 1946) studied music at the Juilliard School and worked as an arranger for CBS-TV. During the 60s, he also became a skilled

composer of advertising jingles. In 1972 he served as accompanist to Bette Midler, then a cult performer in New York's gay bath-houses. Manilow subsequently arranged Midler's first two albums and gained his own recording contract with Bell. After an unsuccessful debut album, Manilow took the powerful ballad 'Mandy' to US number 1 in 1974. This was the prelude to 10 years of remarkable transatlantic success. Among the biggest hits were 'Could It Be Magic' (1975), 'I Write The Songs' (1976), 'Tryin' to Get The Feeling Again' (1976), 'Looks Like We Made It' (1977), 'Can't Smile Without You' (1978), 'Copacabana (At The Copa)' (1978), 'Somewhere In The Night' (1979), 'Ships' (1979) and 'I Made It Through The Rain' (1980).

Two albums, *2:00 AM Paradise Café* and *Swing Street*, marked a change of direction as Manilow emphasized his jazz credentials in collaborations with Gerry Mulligan and Sarah Vaughan. He also appeared on Broadway in two one-man shows including *Showstoppers* (1991). In 1994, the stage musical *Copacabana*, for which Manilow composed the music, opened in London. In the same year, he was the supervising composer and collaborated on several of the songs for the animated feature *Thumbelina*. His last album for Arista, released in 1998, was a strongly jazz flavoured recording on which he sang Sinatra classics. It was no great surprise that he signed to Concord Jazz the following year.

MANN, AIMEE

This US artist achieved recognition as the lead vocalist of the critically acclaimed 'Til Tuesday but left to go solo in 1990. Her 1993 debut *Whatever* was a remarkable set, demonstrating Mann's literate songwriting skills and featuring musical contributions from guitarist **Roger McGuinn**. Imago Records fell apart after *Whatever* appeared, and after a lengthy battle with the label, Mann signed to Geffen Records. Her major-label debut, *I'm With Stupid*, was a more mellow and relaxed affair.

In 1998, Mann married songwriter Michael Penn, made a walk-on appearance in the Coen brothers' *The Big Lebowski*, and completed the recording of her new album. She escaped the corporate clutches of the new Universal empire by buying back the rights to her album and gaining a release from her contract. In 1999, she released the limited-edition *Bachelor No. 2* EP, a taster for the following year's album of the same name. Nine of her new songs also featured heavily on the soundtrack to Paul Thomas Anderson's *Magnolia*.

MANSUN

One of the most hotly touted UK indie bands of the mid-90s, Mansun was formed in 1995 by Paul Draper (b. 1972; guitar, vocals), Dominic Chad (b. 1973; guitar) and Stove King (b. 1974; bass). The trio was augmented by Andie Rathbone (b. 1971; drums) on their debut album, *Attack Of The Grey Lantern*, which included the Top 20 hit 'Stripper Vicar'. In 1997, the band released an EP, *Closed For Business*, and continued their endless touring schedule. The follow-up, *Six*, was an outrageously ambitious, maverick rock album, which, if not always entirely successful, served to distance Mansun from other run-of-the-mill indie bands. *Little Kix* eschewed the experimentalism of their second album in favour of elegant, understated rock songs such as 'I Can Only Disappoint U' and 'We Are The Boys'.

MAR-KEYS

Formed in Memphis, Tennessee, USA, and originally known as the Royal Spades, the line-up of this instrumental unit comprised **Steve Cropper** (b. 1941; guitar), Donald 'Duck' Dunn (b. 1941; bass), Charles 'Packy' Axton (tenor saxophone), Don Nix (b. 1941; baritone saxophone), Wayne Jackson (trumpet), Charlie Freeman (guitar), Jerry Lee 'Smoochy' Smith (organ) and Terry Johnson (drums). In the summer of 1961, their debut hit, 'Last Night' (US number 3), established Satellite, its label. Within months, Satellite had changed its name to Stax Records and the Mar-Keys became the label's house band.

Initially all-white, two black musicians, **Booker T. Jones** (b. 1944; organ) and Al Jackson Jnr. (b. 1934, d. 1975; drums), had replaced Smith and Johnson by 1962. The newcomers, along with Cropper and Dunn, also worked as **Booker T. And The MGs**. Freeman left prior to the recording of 'Last Night' (but would later return for live work), Nix and Axton also quit, while Joe Arnold and Bob Snyder joined on tenor and baritone saxophone. They, in turn, were replaced by Andrew Love and Floyd Newman respectively. Although commercial success under their own name was limited, the group provided the backbone to sessions by **Otis Redding**, **Sam And Dave**, **Wilson Pickett**, Carla Thomas and many others. Jackson, Love and Newman, meanwhile, continued the Mar-Keys' legacy with releases on Stax and elsewhere, while simultaneously forging a parallel career as the **Memphis Horns**.

MARILLION

Front-runners of the short-lived UK progressive-rock revival of the early 80s, Marillion survived unfavourable comparisons with **Genesis** to become an enduring and inventive rock band. The band was formed by Doug Irvine (bass), Mick Pointer (b. 1956; drums), Steve Rothery (b. 1959; guitar) and Brian Jellyman (keyboards). After recording the instrumental demo, 'The Web', the band recruited **Fish** (b. Derek William Dick, 1958; vocals) and Diz Minnett (bass). Before recording their debut single, 'Market Square Heroes', Jellyman and Minnett were replaced by Mark Kelly (b. 1961) and Pete Trewavas (b. 1959). Fish wrote all the lyrics for 1983's debut album *Script For A Jester's Tear* and became the band's focal point. Pointer was sacked the same year, with Ian Mosley (b. 1953) being brought in as his long-term replacement. Marillion's second album embraced a hard-rock sound and yielded two UK hits, 'Assassing' and 'Punch And Judy'. The chart-topping *Misplaced Childhood* featured 'Kayleigh', a romantic ballad which rose to number 2 in the UK singles chart. Following the release of *Clutching At Straws* and the live *The Thieving Magpie*, Fish left to go solo. Marillion recruited new vocalist Steve Hogarth (b. 1959), who made his debut on *Seasons End*.

The 90s found Marillion as popular as ever, with the ghost of Fish receding into the background. With Hogarth fronting the band, consistent success continued, including UK Top 30 chart status for 'Sympathy', 'The Hollow Man' and 'Beautiful'. The best of the decade's albums was 1995's *Afraid Of Sunlight*, which tackled the subject of fame, with references to **John Lennon**, O. J. Simpson and the recently deceased **Kurt Cobain**. The band's first studio work of the new millennium, *Anoraknophobia*, was funded by fans who paid for the record a year before its release, a novel venture which raised a few eyebrows in the music industry.

MARILYN MANSON

Controversial by design rather than accident, this Florida, USA-based artist formed Marilyn Manson And The Spooky Kids in 1989 with the express intention of 'exploring the limits of censorship'. The original line-up consisted of part-time journalist Manson (b. Brian Warner, 1969; vocals), Daisy Berkowitz (guitar), Olivia Newton-Bundy (bass) and Zsa Zsa Speck (keyboards), later joined by Sara Lee Lucas (drums). Newton-Bundy and Speck were replaced at the end of 1989 by Gidget Gein and Madonna Wayne Gacy (b. Steve Bier) respectively. This line-up began to gain local recognition and signed to Trent Reznor's Nothing Records label. Gein was replaced by Twiggy Ramirez (b. Jeordie Francis White, 1971) prior to the release of the band's debut album in 1994. Further

line-up changes saw the departure of Lucas and Berkowitz, replaced by Ginger Fish (b. Kenny Wilson) and Zim Zum (b. Mike Nastasi) respectively. Antichrist Superstar contained the American hit single, 'The Beautiful People' and reached the Top 5.

By 1998, Marilyn Manson had become one of the biggest artists in the USA, assuming virtual cult status, a position aided as much by their notoriety and propensity for upsetting US right-wing and Christian groups as by their music. *Mechanical Animals* was a huge American chart-topper that also placed the band in the UK Top 10 for the first time. During the recording of the album, Zim Zum left and was replaced by Johnnie 5. The highly articulate Manson was forced to morally defend himself when, in April 1999, two alleged fans, Dylan Klebold and Eric Harris, murdered 15 of their classmates at Colombine High School in Denver, Colorado; the suggestion being that Manson's lyrics incited violence. Manson addressed many of the issues raised by the Colombine shootings on *Holly Wood (In The Shadow Of The Valley Of Death)*.

MARLEY, BOB, AND THE WAILERS

This legendary Jamaican group, formed in 1963, originally comprised six members: Robert Nesta Marley (b. 1945, d. 1981), Bunny Wailer (b. Neville O'Riley Livingston, 1947), **Peter Tosh** (b. Winston Hubert McIntosh, 1944, d. 1987), Junior Braithwaite (b. Franklin Delano Alexander Braithwaite, 1949, d. 1999), Beverley Kelso, and Cherry Smith. After tuition with vocalist Joe Higgs, they began their recording career in 1963 for **Coxsone Dodd** (Marley had also made two singles for producer Leslie Kong, 'Judge Not' and 'One Cup Of Coffee', in 1962). Between 1963–66, the Wailers made over 70 tracks for Dodd (over 20 of which were local hits) covering a wide stylistic base, from covers of US soul to the newer, 'rude-boy' sounds.

In late 1965 Braithwaite left for America, and Kelso and Smith also departed. On 10 February 1966, Marley married the vocalist Rita Anderson. The next day he left for America, returning to Jamaica that October. By the end of that year the Wailers, now a vocal trio, were making demos for Danny Sims, the manager of **Johnny Nash**. They also began recording for Leslie Kong. By the end of 1969, wider commercial success still eluded them, but the trio began a collaboration with **Lee Perry** that proved crucial to their future. They worked with fellow Jamaicans the Barrett brothers: Aston 'Familyman' (b. 1946) and Carlton (b. 1950, d. 1987), who became an integral part of the Wailers' sound.

The music made with Perry during 1969–71 stands as a zenith in Jamaican music. It was also the blueprint for Marley's international success. The group continued to record for their own Tuff Gong label after the Perry sessions and came to the attention of Chris Blackwell, then owner of Island Records. Their first album for the company, 1973's *Catch A Fire*, sold well enough to warrant the issue of *Burnin'* (featuring new member Earl 'Wire' Lindo). Just as the band was poised on the brink of wider success, internal differences caused Tosh and Bunny Wailer to depart. The new Wailers,

formed mid-1974, included Marley, the Barrett brothers and Bernard 'Touter' Harvey on keyboards, with vocal harmonies by the I-Threes: Marcia Griffiths, Rita Marley and Judy Mowatt. In 1975 the release of the massively successful *Natty Dread* was followed by a series of rapturously received concerts at the London Lyceum. At the end of the year Marley achieved his first UK chart hit with 'No Woman No Cry'. He also released his first live album, taken from the Lyceum concerts.

Marley survived an assassination attempt on 3 December 1976, leaving Jamaica for 18 months in early 1977. In July he had an operation in Miami to remove cancer cells from his right toe. His next albums *Exodus* and *Kaya* enjoyed massive international sales, and in 1978 he played the One Love Peace Concert in Kingston. The album *Survival* was released to critical acclaim, being particularly successful in Africa. Tragically, Marley's cancer began to spread and he collapsed at Madison Square Garden during a concert in 1980. Marley died on 11 May 1981 in Miami, Florida. His career did much to focus the attention of the world on Jamaican music and to establish credibility for it.

MARMALADE

Originally known as Dean Ford And The Gaylords, this Glasgow-based quintet enjoyed success on the Scottish club circuit in the early 60s. Eventually they changed their name to Marmalade. The line-up then comprised Dean Ford (b. Thomas MacAleese, 1946; vocals), Graham Knight (b. 1946; bass), Pat Fairley (b. 1946; rhythm guitar, bass), Junior Campbell (b. William Campbell, 1947; guitar, piano, vocals) and Alan Whitehead (b. 1946; drums). The band reached the UK charts in 1968 with a cover version of the Grass Roots' 'Lovin' Things' and enjoyed a number 1 with an opportunist cover of the **Beatles**' 'Ob-La-Di, Ob-La-Da'. The moving 'Reflections Of My Life' and 'Rainbow', both UK number 3 singles, were more serious works which ably displayed their underused compositional skills.

In 1971, Marmalade suffered a severe setback when Campbell, their producer and main songwriter, quit to attend the Royal College of Music. With replacement Hughie Nicholson (formerly of the Poets), they enjoyed several more UK Top 10 hits, including 'Cousin Norman', 'Radancer' and 'Falling Apart At The Seams'. The latter proved a prophetic title, for the band was dogged by line-up changes during the 70s. With Knight and Whitehead surviving from the original line-up, Marmalade was resuscitated for cabaret purposes later in the decade.

MARRIOTT, STEVE

In 1961, Decca Records engaged former child actor Marriott (b. 1947, d. 1991) as an **Adam Faith** soundalike for two unsuccessful singles. He then had another miss in the USA with a cover version of the **Kinks**' 'You Really Got Me'. In 1964, he met fellow mod **Ronnie Lane** (bass) with whom he formed the **Small Faces**. Marriott emerged as the outfit's public face, attacking the early hits such as 'Sha La La La Lee' and 'My Mind's Eye' with a strangled passion.

On leaving the Small Faces in 1969, Marriott joined **Humble Pie**. By 1975, when Humble Pie disbanded, they had earned hard-rock stardom in the USA. Marriott recorded a solo album before re-forming the Small Faces, but poor sales of two 'comeback' albums blighted their progress. A new line-up of Humble Pie also released two albums but, from the early 80s, Marriott was heard mostly on the European club circuit fronting Packet Of Three, the Next Band and the DT's. Shortly before he perished in a fire in his Essex home in April 1991, Marriot had been attempting to reconstitute Humble Pie with **Peter Frampton**.

MARSHALL TUCKER BAND

Formed in 1971 in South Carolina, USA, this southern-rock style unit enjoyed national popularity from the early to late 70s. The band was formed by Toy Caldwell (b. 1948, d. 1993; lead guitarist), his brother Tommy (b. 1950, d. 1980; bass), Doug Gray (vocals, keyboards), George McCorkle (rhythm guitar), Jerry Eubanks (saxophone, flute) and Paul Riddle (drums). The band signed with Capricorn Records and released a string of gold or platinum-selling albums. Their highest-charting album, *Searchin' For A Rainbow*, came in 1975, and 1977's 'Heard It In A Love Song' was their bestselling single. Following their 1978 *Greatest Hits* album, the band switched to Warner Brothers Records and released three final chart albums through 1981.

The band continued to perform after the death of Tommy Caldwell in an auto crash on 28 April 1980, but never recaptured their 70s success. (Caldwell was replaced by Franklin Wilkie). Though the original line-up disbanded in 1983, various members have kept the band's name alive and continue to record new material.

MARTHA AND THE MUFFINS

Canadian new-wave band who came together in 1977 when Martha Johnson (organ, vocals) joined up with Mark Gane (guitar), Carl Finkle (bass), Andy Haas (saxophone) and Tim Gane (drums). They were later joined by Martha Ladly (initially guitar, then keyboards and trombone). The band signed with DinDisc Records, releasing their debut single, 'Insect Love', in 1978. Success followed in 1980 with the UK Top 10 hit 'Echo Beach'. Follow-ups fared less well and, in 1981, Ladly left to work with the **Associates** and Jocelyne Lanois replaced Finkle. Following Haas' departure the band released *Danseparc*, before wife-and-husband team Johnson and Mark Gane formed M+M, who enjoyed a major US hit with 'Black Stations, White Stations'. They later released two albums as a duo, *Mystery Walk* and *The World Is A Ball*, before moving to the UK. The duo revived the Martha And The Muffins name for 1992's *Modern Lullaby*, but their label went bankrupt shortly after its release. They have also recorded a children's album together, *Songs From The Tree House*.

MARTHA AND THE VANDELLAS

Martha Reeves (b. 1941), with Annette Sterling Beard, Gloria Williams and Rosalind Ashford, formed the US vocal group Del-Phis in 1960. They were offered a one-off single release on Motown Records' Melody subsidiary, but Williams left when the single, credited to the Vels, flopped. Renamed Martha And The Vandellas, the group divided their time between backing other Motown artists and recording in their own right. They had a US Top 30 success in 1963 with 'Come And Get These Memories', but it was 'Heat Wave', 'Quicksand' and 'Dancing In The Street' (US number 2) that represented the pinnacle of their sound. The irresistible 'Nowhere To Run' introduced a new member, Betty Kelly, who replaced Beard. This line-up scored further Top 10 hits with 'I'm Ready For Love' and the infectious 'Jimmy Mack'. Reeves was taken seriously ill in 1968, resulting in the group disbanding. By 1970, she was able to resume her career, recruiting her sister Lois and Sandra Tilley, to form a new line-up. No major

US hits were forthcoming, but in the UK they were able to capitalize on the belated 1969 success of 'Dancing In The Street', and had several Top 30 entries in the early 70s. Reeves went solo in 1972. The group was inducted into the Rock And Roll Hall Of Fame in 1995.

MARTIN, GEORGE

Martin (b. 1926) became the world's most famous record producer through his work with the **Beatles**. Born in London and classically trained at the Guildhall School of Music, Martin was put in charge of the Parlophone Records label in 1955. He signed the Beatles in the early 60s, beginning a relationship which lasted until their demise in 1970. Martin's main contribution to the band's music lay in his ability to put their more adventurous ideas into practice.

In 1965, Martin left EMI and set up his own studios, AIR London, with fellow producers Ron Richards and John Burgess. Four years later the partnership created another studio on the Caribbean island of Montserrat, which became a favoured recording centre for artists. In the 70s Martin produced a series of hit albums by **America**. He also maintained the Beatles connection and prepared the 1977 release of the live recording *At The Hollywood Bowl* and produced two of **Paul McCartney**'s solo efforts, *Tug Of War* (1981) and *Pipes Of Peace* (1983).

During the late 80s, he was less prolific as a producer, but his work in remastering the Beatles for compact disc created remarkable results. In the mid-90s he was a major part of the Beatles' *Anthology* series. He received the Grammy Trustees Award in 1995 and was granted a knighthood in 1996. In 1997, Martin staged the Music For Montserrat charity concert, and produced Elton John's 'Candle In The Wind '97', which went on to become the biggest-selling single of all time. In 1998 he released his final album, *In My Life*, a collection of Beatles' cover versions by guest vocalists.

MARTIN, RICKY

Formerly a member of the perennially youthful boy band Menudo, Puerta Rican Martin (b. Enrique Martin Morales, 1971) established himself as one of the leading Latin pop stars of the 90s and by the end of the decade he had also enjoyed crossover success.

Martin joined Latin teen-idols Menudo in 1984, and continued to record and tour with them until the late 80s (to ensure the band's youthful image, members were required to leave when they reached the age of 16). Martin spent a short period in New York before moving to Mexico, where he gained a regular slot in the Mexican soap opera *Alcanzar Una Estrella II*. His recording career also took off when his self-titled debut and *Me Amaras* achieved gold status in several countries. Martin broke into the North American television

market playing singing bartender Miguel Morez in the long-running soap opera *General Hospital*. He performed 'No Importa La Distancia' for the Spanish-language version of Walt Disney's *Hercules*, and landed the role of Marius in the Broadway production of *Les Misérables*. 'La Copa De La Vida', the official song of the 1998 soccer World Cup, was highly successful when released as a single, reaching number 1 in several countries.

Martin won the 1999 Grammy Award for Best Latin Pop Performance. He exploited the hype to the full with the release of the lively 'Livin' La Vida Loca', which reached number 1 in the US Hot 100 in May 1999, and stayed at the top for five weeks. In the process, it became Columbia Records' biggest-selling number 1 single of all time. His self-titled English-language debut, produced by Rosa and Desmond

Child, entered the US album chart at number 1 at the end of the month. In July, 'Livin' La Vida Loca' entered the UK singles chart at number 1. Martin's follow-up single, 'She's All I Ever Had', climbed to US number 2 in September. Another transatlantic hit single, 'She Bangs', served as an effective launch-pad for *Sound Loaded*.

MARTYN, JOHN

After arriving in London in the mid-60s, singer-songwriter and guitarist Martyn (b. Iain McGeachy, 1948) was signed by Island Records. His first album was the jazz-tinged *London Conversation* (1968). The jazz influence was confirmed when, only nine months later, *The Tumbler* was released. Soon afterwards, Martyn married singer Beverly Kutner, and as John and Beverly Martyn they produced two well-received albums, *Stormbringer* and *Road To Ruin*. It was the release of the excellent solo albums *Bless The Weather* and *Solid Air*, however, that established Martyn as a concert-hall attraction. *Inside Out* and *Sunday's Child* both confirmed his standing, although commercial success still eluded him.

Frustrated by the music business, Martyn's alcohol and drug intake began taking their toll. *One World* (1977) has subtle references to this, but Martyn was going through serious problems and would not produce new work until three years later when, following the end of his marriage, he delivered *Grace & Danger*, a painfully emotional work. Following this collection, Martyn changed labels to WEA Records and delivered *Glorious Fool* and *Well Kept Secret*, which moved him firmly into the rock category. Following the live album *Philentropy*, Martyn returned to Island Records. The world's first commercially released CD single was Martyn's 'Angeline', a superbly crafted love song to his new wife, which preceded the album *Piece By Piece* in 1986.

Enjoying cult status but little commercial success, Martyn slid into another alcoholic trough, returning in 1990 with *The Apprentice*. A series of lesser albums preceded a move to Go! Discs, for whom he recorded 1996's superior *And*. Martyn's 2000 release, *Glasgow Walker*, was the first album he had written on a keyboard rather than guitar. In 2001, Martyn reunited for a tour with his old sparring partner, bass player Danny Thompson.

MARVELETTES

Despite enjoying several major US hits, this girl-group were unable to sustain a consistent line-up, which made it difficult to overcome their anonymous image. The group was formed in the late 50s in Michigan, USA, by Gladys Horton, Georgeanna Marie Tillman (d. 1980), Wanda Young, Katherine Anderson and Juanita Grant. They were spotted at a school talent show by Robert Bateman, who co-produced their early releases with Brian Holland. This led to success with 'Please Mr Postman', a US number 1 in 1961, and Motown Records' biggest-selling record up to that point. **Smokey Robinson** produced a series of hit singles for the group, the most successful being 'Don't Mess With Bill' in 1966. Gladys Horton, the Marvelettes' lead singer, left in 1967, to be replaced by Anne Bogan. They continued to achieve minor soul hits for the remainder of the decade, most notably 'When You're Young And In Love', before splitting up in 1970.

In 1989, original members Wanda Rogers (née Young) and Gladys Horton, plus Echo Johnson and Jean McLain, recorded for the Motor City label. Johnson and McLain were replaced by Jackie and Regina Holleman for subsequent releases.

MARVIN, HANK B.

UK guitarist Marvin (b. Brian Rankin, 1941) was originally asked to join Bruce Welch's Railroaders in his native Newcastle, before the duo relocated to London to perform as the Geordie Boys. They enlisted in an outfit called the **Drifters**, which evolved into the **Shadows**. While backing and, later, composing songs for **Cliff Richard**, the quartet recorded independently and became generally acknowledged as Britain's top instrumental act. Marvin's metallic, echoed picking on a red Fender Stratocaster (with generous employment of tremolo arm) was the inspirational source of the fretboard pyrotechnics of **Jeff Beck**, **Ritchie Blackmore** and many other lead guitarists who began in groups imitating the Shadows.

After their first disbandment in 1968, Marvin's solo career commenced with 'Goodnight Dick' and a self-titled album. Marvin's affinity with Cliff Richard continued via their hit duets with 'Throw Down A Line' and 'Joy Of Living'. In the early 70s, Marvin amalgamated with Welch and John Farrar for two albums dominated by vocals, and another with Farrar alone. This project was abandoned, partly through Marvin's personal commitments – notably his indoctrination as a Jehovah's Witness in 1973 – and the gradual reformation of the Shadows.

After moving to Australia, Marvin turned out for the Shadows' annual tour and studio album and continued to record as a solo artist. In 1982, he charted with 'Don't Talk' from *Words & Music*, which contained only one instrumental. After working with the Shadows during the late 80s Marvin went on to record profilically during the following decade, much to the delight of his loyal fanbase.

MASON, DAVE

UK guitarist Mason (b. 1945) met **Steve Winwood** when he was employed as a road manager for the **Spencer Davis Group**. In 1967 Winwood, together with Mason, left to form **Traffic**. Mason joined and left the band on numerous occasions throughout the 60s. He subsequently settled in America in 1969 and enjoyed success as a solo artist. His excellent debut album, *Alone Together*, proved to be his most acclaimed work. By 1973, Mason had settled permanently in America and signed a contract with CBS Records, the first album being *It's Like You Never Left*. Following a surprise US hit single with 'We Just Disagree', Mason's albums became dull, with 1980's *Old Crest On A New Wave* the nadir.

Mason kept a relatively low profile during the 80s, releasing two poor albums in the latter part of the decade. In 1993 he joined **Fleetwood Mac**, contributing to the poorly received *Time*. He left in 1995 and resumed solo work. He toured with former Traffic partner **Jim Capaldi** in 1999.

MASSIVE ATTACK

This UK dance/rap collective was formed by rapper '3D' (b. Robert Del Naja), Daddy G (b. Grant Marshall) and Mushroom (b. Andrew Vowles). They started in 1988, having previously released records under the Wild Bunch moniker. Contacts with **Neneh Cherry** led to a meeting with Cameron McVey, who produced Massive Attack's debut album. The resultant *Blue Lines*, featuring vocal contributions from Cherry, former Wild Bunch associate **Tricky**, and Shara Nelson, boasted three UK hit singles; 'Daydreaming', 'Unfinished Sympathy' and

'Safe From Harm'. 'Unfinished Sympathy' remains a perennial club favourite, and the album was subsequently regarded as a landmark 90s recording.

Forced into a temporary name-change during the Gulf War, the trio returned to the charts in 1994 with *Protection*, which featured vocals by Tricky, Nicolette, Tracey Thorn and Horace Andy. Apart from a dub remix of *Protection* recorded with the Mad Professor, little was heard from Massive Attack until 'Risingson' was released in autumn 1997. The single's menacing atmosphere was a taster for the downbeat grooves of *Mezzanine*, which was released to widespread critical acclaim in April 1998, and also became their first UK chart-topper. Guest vocalists included Andy, newcomer Sara Jay, and Elizabeth Fraser of the **Cocteau Twins**, the latter featuring on the wondrous 'Teardrop', which deservedly broke into the UK Top 10, aided by a stunning video. Rumours of personality clashes were confirmed when Mushroom left to pursue solo interests the following year.

MASTER P

The founder of the highly successful US hip-hop label No Limit Records, Master P (b. Percy Miller, 1970), one of the biggest commercial sensations of the late 90s.

Miller grew up in New Orleans, but studied business in Oakland. Left a substantial sum of money by his grandfather in the late 80s, he invested it in a music store in Richmond, California, No Limit, before starting the label of the same name in 1990. Master P and his production team Beats By The Pound began churning out cheaply produced records characterized by their use of lifted hooklines and rather clichéd G-funk backing. Scoring an underground hit with his solo debut, 1994's *Ghetto's Tryin' To Kill Me!*, he formed Tru with his brothers C-Murder and Silkk The Shocker, providing the label with its mainstream breakthrough when their debut album entered the R&B Top 30. Further Master P albums, *99 Ways To Die*, *Ice Cream Man* and the chart-topping *Ghetto D* established the highly successful No Limit practice of using an album to promote its roster of rappers and advertise future releases. With a support cast including Mia X, Mystikal and Young Bleed, No Limit was by now firmly established as one of hip-hop's most popular labels. Master P's self-produced and self-financed auto-biographical movie *I'm Bout It*, was another showcase for No Limit's gangsta-rap and G-funk fixations. The chart-topping Master P album, *MP Da Last Don* preceded the new **Snoop Doggy Dogg** album, *Da Game Is To Be Sold, Not To Be Told*, under the rapper's new moniker Snoop Dogg. The indefatigable Master P's other interests include a clothing line, a sports-management agency, and personal forays into basketball and pro-wrestling.

No Limit was rechristened New No Limit following its transition from Priority to Universal Records in 2001. The label's new partnership was inaugurated with the release of Master P's *Gameface* in December.

MATCHBOX 20

This US rock band comprises German-born Rob Thomas (b. 1971; vocals), Kyle Cook (b. 1975; guitar), Adam Gaynor (b. 1964; guitar), Brian Yale (b. 1968; bass), and Paul Doucette (b. 1972; drums). Thomas, Doucette and Yale formed Tabitha's Secret in 1995, but quickly left that band to join forces with Cook and Gaynor. The band's 1996 debut, *Yourself Or Someone Like You*, quickly gained a tenacious foothold in the *Billboard* Hot 200, eventually peaking at

number 5 and achieving multi-platinum status. Thomas enjoyed even greater success as the featured vocalist on **Santana**'s US chart-topper 'Smooth', the surprise hit single of 1999. Undergoing a slight name change (from Matchbox 20 to Matchbox Twenty), the band released their sophomore collection *Mad Season* the following May. 'Bent', a shining example of the band's inoffensive mature rock sound, climbed to the top of the Hot 100 two months later.

MATTHEWS SOUTHERN COMFORT

UK band formed in 1969 by former **Fairport Convention** singer and guitarist Iain Matthews (b. Iain Matthews McDonald, 1946), and named after his debut album. Matthews was joined by Mark Griffiths (guitar), Carl Barnwell (guitar), Gordon Huntley (pedal-steel guitar), Andy Leigh (bass) and Ray Duffy (drums). After signing to EMI Records, their debut *Second Spring* reached the UK Top 40 and was followed by their UK chart-topping cover version of **Joni Mitchell**'s 'Woodstock'. Unfortunately, success was followed by friction within the band and, two months later, Matthews announced his intention to pursue a solo career. One more album followed after which the band truncated their name to Southern Comfort. After two further albums, they disbanded in the summer of 1972.

MATTHEWS, DAVE, BAND

Matthews alternated between his native South Africa and America as a child, before finally settling in Charlottesville, Virginia, where he assembled his self-titled, multiracial rock band in 1990. Matthews (guitar, vocals), Leroi Moore (reeds, saxophone), Boyd Tinsley (violin), Steffan Lessard (bass), and Carter Beauford (drums) built a formidable reputation on the back of a punishing touring schedule, which helped sales of their self-produced and financed debut, *Remember Two Things*. Their major label debut, *Under The Table And Dreaming*, broke into the US Top 40, while its follow-up, *Crash*, immediately went to number 2, confirming their arrival as one of the most successful rock acts of the 90s. *Before These Crowded Streets* debuted at US number 1, but showed little sign of any creative progress. Their popularity was confirmed when *Live At Luther College*, a 1996 recording by Matthews and collaborator Tim Reynolds, debuted at number 2 in 1999. *Everyday* rather predictably went straight in at number 1 on the US charts in 2001.

MAVERICKS

Country-rock band formed in Miami, Florida, USA, by Raul Malo (b. 1965; vocals, guitar), Robert Reynolds (b. 1962; bass) and Paul Deakin (b. 1959; drums). The band independently released a 13-song album in 1990. Their debut for MCA Nashville, *From Hell To Paradise*, featured their new lead guitarist David Lee Holt and was a minor success. It was with 1994's *What A Crying Shame*, however, that they made their breakthrough (the same year that Reynolds married country star **Trisha Yearwood**). The album steadily racked up sales, eventually going platinum in spring 1995. The band replaced Holt with Nick Kane (b. 1954) shortly after the album's release. In 1995, they won a CMA award and released the excellent *Music For All Occasions*, another bestselling and critically acclaimed album. They received a further CMA award in 1996. The band's bold genre-hopping was in further evidence on 1998's *Trampoline*, with a four-piece horn section bolstering the songs. They also gained a surprise crossover UK hit with the catchy single 'Dance The Night Away', which spent several weeks in the

Top 20 before peaking at number 4 in May. Both Kane and Malo have recorded solo albums.

MAXWELL

Of mixed West Indian and Puerto Rican parentage, soul singer Maxwell (b. 1973) had to suffer the ignominy of his record company sitting on his debut album for a year. Finally released in 1996, Maxwell's *Urban Hang Suite* was a concept album about monogamy that eschewed male braggadocio to explore old-fashioned, romantic love. The album proved to be an unexpected critical and commercial success, going platinum and being nominated for a Grammy. Maxwell collaborated with guitarist Stuart Matthewman again for the 1998 follow-up, *Embrya*, slowing the pace down to create a wonderfully sensual and dreamlike record. The following year Maxwell enjoyed a huge US hit single with 'Fortunate', taken from the soundtrack of *Life*. His third album, *Now*, provided the singer with his first US chart-topper in 2001.

MAYALL, JOHN

The career of England's premier white blues exponent and father of British blues has now spanned five decades and much of that time has been unintentionally spent acting as a musical catalyst. Mayall (b. 1933) formed his first band, the Powerhouse Four, in 1955. He then moved to London to form his Blues Syndicate, the forerunner to his legendary Bluesbreakers. The astonishing number of musicians who subsequently passed through his bands include John McVie, **Eric Clapton**, **Jack Bruce**, Aynsley Dunbar, **Peter Green** and Mick Taylor.

His 1965 debut, *John Mayall Plays John Mayall*, was a live album. The follow-up *Bluesbreakers With Eric Clapton* is now regarded as a classic of white blues. *A Hard Road* featured guitar from future **Fleetwood Mac** founder Peter Green, while *Crusade* offered a brassier, fuller sound. The jazz-tinged *Bare Wires*, released in 1968, is arguably Mayall's finest work. The similarly packaged *Blues From Laurel Canyon* marked the end of the Bluesbreakers name and, following the departure of Mick Taylor to the **Rolling Stones**, Mayall pioneered a drumless acoustic band featuring Jon Mark (acoustic guitar), Johnny Almond (tenor saxophone, flute) and Stephen Thompson (string bass). The subsequent live album, *The Turning Point*, proved to be his biggest-selling album.

Following the double reunion *Back To The Roots*, Mayall's work lost its bite. Following a run of albums that had little or no exposure, Mayall stopped recording, playing only infrequently close to his base in California. Renewed activity and interest occurred in the 90s following the release of his finest album in many years, *A Sense Of Place*. The follow-up, 1993's *Wake Up Call*, became his biggest-selling album for over two decades. Mayall has since released a string of acclaimed albums, including 1997's *Blues For The Lost Days* and 2001's *Along For The Ride*.

MAYFIELD, CURTIS

As songwriter and vocalist with the Impressions, Mayfield (b. 1942, d. 1999) penned a succession of exemplary singles between 1961 and 1971, including 'Gypsy Woman' (1961), 'It's All Right' (1963), 'People Get Ready' (1965), 'We're A Winner' (1968) and 'Choice Of Colors' (1969).

In 1970, Mayfield began his solo career with '(Don't Worry) If There's A Hell Below We're All Going To Go'. The following year he enjoyed his biggest UK success with 'Move On Up' (number 12), one of his most enduring songs, which surprisingly did not chart in the US. His ascendancy was maintained with 'Freddie's Dead' (US number 4) and the theme from the blaxploitation movie *Superfly* (1972), but his commercial success tailed off in the late 70s.

In 1981, Mayfield joined the Boardwalk Records label and recorded *Honesty*, his strongest album

since the early 70s. Sadly, the death of the label's managing director Neil Bogart left an insurmountable gap, and Mayfield's career was then blighted by music-industry indifference. The singer nonetheless remained a highly popular live attraction, particularly in Britain where '(Celebrate) The Day After You', a collaboration with the **Blow Monkeys**, became a minor hit.

In 1990, a freak accident, in which part of a public address rig collapsed on top of him during a concert, left Mayfield permanently paralyzed from the neck down. At the end of 1996, a new album, *New World Order*, was released to excellent reviews. During the recording Mayfield had to lie on his back in order to give some gravitational power to his singing. Mayfield's contribution to soul music remains immense, whatever the limitations of his disability brought to his last years. He died in hospital on December 26, 1999.

MAZE (FEATURING FRANKIE BEVERLY)

US singer Beverly (b. 1946) formed Raw Soul in the early 1970s. They moved to San Francisco, where they became the house band at a local club. Discovered by a girlfriend of **Marvin Gaye**, it was he who suggested the name change. So the septet, which featured Wayne aka Wuane Thomas (guitar), Sam Porter (keyboards), Robin Duhe (bass), Roame Lowry (congas, vocals), McKinley Williams (percussion, vocals), Joe Provost (drums) plus Beverly, became Maze. Their debut album was issued in January 1977, the first of eight albums for Capitol Records the pick of which was 1983's *We Are One*. Personnel changes saw drummers Ahaguna Sun and Billy Johnson, keyboard players Kevin Burton and Phillip Woo, and guitarist Ron Smith brought in to the line-up.

Maze finally reached the top of the R&B charts in 1985 with 'Back In Stride', taken from the same year's *Can't Stop The Love* which was recorded with new musicians Wayne Thomas (guitar), Wayne Linsey and Sam Porter (both keyboards), Tony St. James and Ricky Lawson (both drums), and additional bass player Randy Jackson. A final album for Capitol was recorded live in Los Angeles, and featured yet another drummer, Mike White. Their debut for Warner Brothers Records, *Silky Soul*, featured the nucleus of Beverly, Williams, Lowry and Duhe. The album generated their second R&B chart-topper 'Can't Get Over You', while the title track reached the Top 5. Although they are no longer a fixture on the charts, Maze remain one of soul's most consistent live attractions.

MAZZY STAR

Highly regarded US duo featuring Hope Sandoval (vocals) and David Roback (guitar), who adopted the name Mazzy Star for their sessions together, which eventually resulted in a critically lauded debut album in 1990. They released a comeback album on Capitol Records in 1993 after an absence that was mourned by many rock critics. Various musicians were employed, but the core of the project remained Roback and Sandoval. Their third release *Among My Swan* was a lo-fi excursion with Sandoval and Roback's latest songs sounding like a cross between the **Cowboy Junkies** and **Neil Young**. In the late 90s Sandoval worked with Colm O'Ciosoig (ex-**My Bloody Valentine**) on the Warm Inventions side project.

MC5

Formed in 1964 in Detroit, Michigan, USA, and originally known as the Motor City Five, the band split the following year when its rhythm section left in protest over a radical new song, 'Back To Comm'. Michael Davis (bass) and Dennis Thompson (drums) joined founder-members Rob Tyner (b. Robert Derminer, 1944, d. 1991; vocals), Wayne Kramer (guitar) and Fred 'Sonic' Smith (b. 1949, d. 1994; guitar). A recording contract with Elektra Records resulted in the seminal *Kick Out The Jams*. Recorded live at the city's Grande Ballroom, this turbulent set captured the quintet's extraordinary sound, which, although loud, was never reckless.

MC5 later emerged anew on Atlantic Records with *Back In The USA* and *High Time*. The departure of Davis and Tyner in 1972, brought the MC5 to an end. Their reputation flourished during the punk phenomenon, and while both Kramer and Tyner attempted to use the MC5 name for several unrelated projects, they wisely abandoned such practices, leaving intact the legend of one of rock's most uncompromising and exciting acts.

McBRIDE, MARTINA

One of the leaders in contemporary US country music, McBride (b. Martina Mariea Schiff, 1966) debuted in 1992 with *The Time Has Come*. The album impressed with its treatment of material such as 'Cheap Whiskey' and 'That's Me'. Her breakthrough came after two singles in 1993, 'My Baby Loves Me The Way That I Am' and 'Independence Day'. Sales of her second album, *The Way That I Am*, climbed to the half-million mark. In 1995 RCA Records launched her third album, *Wild Angels*. 'Safe In The Arms Of Love' was a hit, although for many, her revival of Delbert McClinton's 'Two More Bottles Of Wine' was a stronger track. The opening song on 1997's *Evolution*, 'I'm Little But I'm Loud', featured the recorded talents of a seven-year-old McBride, but overall the album strayed too close to slick MOR. *Emotion* contained a number of excellent compositions that saw McBride moving further away from country towards the crossover audience targeted by **LeAnn Rimes** and **Shania Twain**.

McCARTNEY, PAUL

Although commitments to the **Beatles** took precedence in the 60s, Liverpool, England-born McCartney (b. James Paul McCartney, 1942) pursued several outside projects, ranging from production work for Cliff Bennett, Paddy, Klaus And Gibson and the **Bonzo Dog Doo-Dah Band** to appearances on sessions by **Donovan**, **Paul Jones** and **Steve Miller**. However, despite this well-documented independence, the artist ensured a critical backlash by timing the release of his solo debut *McCartney* to coincide with that of the Beatles' *Let It Be* and his announced departure from the group. *Ram*, credited to McCartney and his wife Linda (b. Linda Eastman, 1942, d. 1998), was also maligned, but nonetheless spawned 'Uncle Albert/Admiral Halsey' (US number 1), and an attendant single, 'Another Day', (UK number 2).

Denny Seiwell (drums), was invited to join a group later enhanced by former **Moody Blues**' member Denny Laine. The quartet, dubbed **Wings**, then completed *Wild Life*. Having brought in Henry McCullough (guitar), they released several singles and *Red Rose Speedway*. McCullough and Seiwell left shortly afterwards, but the remaining trio emerged triumphant with *Band On The Run*. A reconstituted Wings, which now included Jimmy McCulloch (b. 1953, d. 1979; guitar; ex-**Thunderclap Newman**) and Joe English (drums), completed *Venus And Mars*, *Wings At The Speed Of Sound* and the on-tour collection, *Wings Over America*. Although McCulloch and English left, Wings enjoyed its greatest success with 'Mull Of Kintyre' (1977). *London Town* included the US number 1 'With A Little Luck' (US number 1), while newcomers Laurence Juber (guitar) and Steve Holly (drums) added weight to *Back To The Egg*.

McCartney's solo recordings, 'Wonderful Christmastime' (1979), 'Coming Up' (1980) and *McCartney II*, already heralded a new phase. His 1984 feature film, *Give My Regards To Broad Street*, was maligned, although 'No More Lonely Nights' reached UK number 2. The 'oldies' collection *Choba B CCCP* provided a respite, before a collaboration with **Elvis Costello** produced material for the superior *Flowers In The Dirt*. A number of esoteric collaborations in the 90s included the classical *Liverpool Oratorio*, a dance project with producer Youth under the pseudonym The Fireman, but the solo *Off The Ground* received only lukewarm reviews. The success in the mid-90s of the *Beatles At The BBC* and the magnificent *Anthology* series led to McCartney's knighthood for services to music. *Flaming Pie*, his 1997 solo release, was a magnificent return to form, but was overshadowed by Linda's death from cancer the following year.

In the late 90s McCartney released another classical piece, *Standing Stone*, and collaborated with Youth on another dance project. In 1999 he was inducted into the Rock And Roll Hall Of Fame as a solo artist, and later in the year released a back-to-basics collection of 50s rock 'n' roll. In December he played a set at the rebuilt Cavern Club. McCartney released the ambitious *Liverpool Sound Collage* and published books of his paintings and poetry before releasing his first proper album of new songs since Linda's death, *Driving Rain*.

McCOYS

Formed in Union City, Indiana, USA, in 1962, this beat group initially comprised Rick Zehringer (b. 1947; guitar), his brother Randy (b. 1951; drums), Dennis Kelly (bass) and later Ronnie Brandon (organ). They became the McCoys soon after Randy Hobbs replaced Kelly. The group's debut was the US chart-topper 'Hang On Sloopy' (1965). They discarded their bubblegum image with the progressive *Infinite McCoys*. When the group disbanded Zehringer joined Edgar Winter before going solo (as Rick Derringer).

McDONALD, COUNTRY JOE

In 1964, McDonald (b. 1942) made a low-key album with fellow performer Blair Hardman and later founded the radical pamphlet *Rag Baby*. An early copy included a four-track record featuring the original version of the singer's anti-Vietnam War song, 'I-Feel-Like-I'm-Fixin'-To-Die-Rag'. In 1965, he formed the Instant Action Jug Band, which later evolved into the influential acid-rock band **Country Joe And The Fish**, but by 1969, McDonald had resumed his solo career. Two tribute albums, *Thinking Of Woody Guthrie* and *Tonight I'm Singing Just For You* presaged his first original set, *Hold On, It's Coming*. This was followed by the film soundtrack *Quiet Days In Clichy* and *War, War, War*. The acclaimed *Paris Sessions* was a critical success, but subsequent releases lacked the artist's early purpose. McDonald has remained a popular live attraction and his commitment to political and environmental causes is undiminished, as exemplified on a 1989 release *Vietnam Experience*.

McDONALD, MICHAEL

Following his departure from the **Doobie Brothers** in 1982, US soul singer McDonald (b. 1952) went solo. During the 80s, his compositions were recorded by numerous artists, including **Aretha Franklin**, **Millie Jackson** and **Carly Simon**, and he almost made the top of the US charts in 1982 with 'I Keep Forgettin' (Every Time You're Near)'. His 'Yah Mo B There', recorded with James Ingram in 1984, is regarded as a modern soul classic. The 1985 album *No Lookin' Back* was followed by his US number 1 hit with **Patti LaBelle**, 'On My Own'. During that year, he enjoyed international success with 'Sweet Freedom', the theme from the movie *Running Scared*.

McDonald's commercial profile declined in the 90s and with Reprise Records losing interest he joined the re-formed Doobie Brothers. In 1999, McDonald inaugurated the Ramp Records label with the support of actor Jeff Bridges and Chris Pelonis. The following February he released *Blue Obsession*.

McENTIRE, REBA

US country artist McEntire (b. 1955) sang with her sister Susie and brother Pake McEntire as the Singing McEntires, and in 1972, they recorded for the small Boss label. She signed a recording contract with Mercury Records two years later, and her first single, 'I Don't Want To Be A One Night Stand', made the US country charts in 1976. A number of minor successes were followed by the US country Top 10 hits '(You Lift Me) Up To Heaven' and 'Today All Over Again', and in 1982, a number 1 single with 'Can't Even Get The Blues'. She had another chart-topper in 1983 with 'You're The First Time I've Thought About Leaving'. Her string of country hits continued on MCA Records with 'Just A Little Love', 'He Broke Your Memory Last Night',

'Have I Got A New Deal For You', and the number 1 hits 'How Blue' and 'Somebody Should Leave'.

McEntire won numerous country music awards during the decade, but her 1988 album *Reba*, although very successful, irritated traditionalists, who questioned her revival of a pop hit, 'A Sunday Kind Of Love', and her version of **Otis Redding**'s 'Respect'. On 16 March 1991, tragedy struck when seven of the nine members of McEntire's band died in a plane crash shortly after taking off from San Diego. She dedicated her next album, *For My Broken Heart*, to her friends and colleagues.

During the 90s McEntire began to establish herself as a film actress, playing alongside **Kenny Rogers** in *The Gambler Returns: The Luck Of The Draw* and Bruce Willis in *North*. In 1995, she looked to her roots for an album of her favourite songs, *Starting Over*. The follow-up, *What If It's You*, featured the excellent singles 'The Fear Of Being Alone' and 'I'd Rather Ride Around With You'. Following further album releases, McEntire moved to the stage to appear as Annie Oakley in the Broadway revival of *Annie Get Your Gun*.

McGARRIGLE, KATE AND ANNA

Kate (keyboards, guitar, vocals), and her sister Anna (keyboards, banjo, vocals), were brought up in Quebec, Canada, learning to sing and perform in both French and English. The sisters became members of the Mountain City Four, before they went their separate ways at college. The sisters came to public notice when **Linda Ronstadt** and Maria Muldaur began recording their material, and they recorded a superb album in 1975 for Muldaur's label.

Apart from *Dancer With Bruised Knees*, which made the Top 40 in the UK, none of their subsequent releases has had any significant impact in the charts in either the USA or the UK. However, they have retained a strong following and their concerts, albeit on a smaller scale, consistently sell out. Their early promise has never been realized, but they still command respect and a loyal following. *Heartbeats Accelerating* and *Matapedia*, their two album releases in the 90s, were mature and seasoned song collections.

McGRAW, TIM

US country singer McGraw (b. 1967) signed to Curb Records in 1990 but charted first in 1992 with 'Welcome To The Club'. In 1994 his career took off with the single 'Indian Outlaw' (country number 1). The attendant *Not A Moment Too Soon*, entered the *Billboard* country chart at number 1. The following album, *All I Want*, also amassed huge sales. His run of success continued with *Everywhere* in 1997 reaching number 2 on the *Billboard* pop album chart in 1997, and a CMA Award for Vocal Event Of The Year on 'It's Your Love' (with his wife Faith Hill). McGraw broke into the US pop Top 10 in May 1999 with 'Please Remember Me', and topped the album charts with *A Place In The Sun*. Since then his popularity has widened way beyond the country market, with *Set This Circus Down* and attendant singles such as 'Angry All The Time' becoming huge hits.

McGRIFF, JIMMY

McGriff (b. James Herrell, 1936) is a multi-instrumentalist who plays piano, bass, vibes, drums and saxophone. After US military service he began moonlighting as a bassist, backing blues stars such as Big Maybelle. His musical career took off with the single 'I Got A Woman' in 1962, and he had a string of hits released through the Sue label. His memorable 'All About My Girl' remains one of his finest compositions. He helped to popularize a jazz-flavoured style of R&B that was influential in the UK with the rise of the 60s beat and R&B scene. Three decades later he enjoyed a revival in London clubland's 'acid jazz' circles.

McGUINN, ROGER

After playing at folk clubs in Chicago, US guitarist McGuinn (b. James Joseph McGuinn, 1942) briefly joined the Limeliters before becoming accompanist in the Chad Mitchell Trio in 1960. He played on two of their albums, *Mighty Day On Campus* and *Live At The Bitter End*, before leaving. At the Troubadour in Hollywood he formed the Jet Set with Gene Clark and **David Crosby**. Following the recruitment of Chris Hillman (bass) and Michael Clarke (drums), the quintet emerged as the **Byrds**. McGuinn became the focal point thanks largely to his 12-string Rickenbacker guitar playing and Dylanesque vocal style. He changed his name to Roger before recording the celebrated *The Notorious Byrd Brothers*. By 1968, he was the last original group member left but he kept the Byrds going until 1973. He went solo that same year, launching his solo career with a self-titled album. His second album, *Peace On You* (1974) was typical in style, but a third album *Thunderbyrd* (1977) was patchy. It did, however, coincide with a UK tour which brought together three ex-Byrds in different groups. Within a year, the trio united as McGuinn, Clark And Hillman.

For virtually the whole of the 80s McGuinn performed solo without recording. Later, he won a contract with Arista Records and set about recording his comeback album, *Back From Rio*. The album charted on both sides of the Atlantic. Still a popular live performer, McGuinn's first in-concert album was issued in 1996.

McGUIRE, BARRY

After leaving the New Christy Minstrels, US artist McGuire (b. 1935) signed to Dunhill Records and was assigned to staff writers P. F. Sloan and Steve Barri. At the peak of the 60s folk-rock boom, they wrote the rabble-rousing protest song 'Eve Of Destruction' (US number 1). McGuire continued to pursue the protest route on the albums *Eve Of Destruction* and *This Precious Time*, but by 1967 he was branching out into acting. After the meagre sales of *The World's Last Private Citizen*, McGuire ceased recording. In 1971 he returned with former **Mamas And The Papas** sideman Eric Hord on *Barry McGuire And The Doctor*. Soon afterwards, McGuire became a Christian evangelist and thereafter specialized in gospel albums.

McKEE, MARIA

Before her solo career McKee (b. 1964) was the singer with US roots act **Lone Justice**. After the band broke up McKee released a solo album which was boosted by 1990's UK number 1 hit, 'Show Me Heaven', taken from the soundtrack of *Days Of Thunder*. McKee then moved to Ireland and recorded the UK club hit 'Sweetest Child'. She returned to Los Angeles in 1992, the result being *You Gotta Sin To Get Saved*, which reunited three-quarters of the original line-up of Lone Justice: Marvin Etzioni, Don Heffington and Bruce Brody, alongside Gary Louris and Mark Olsen of the **Jayhawks**. McKee seemed more comfortable with the return to rootsy material as highlighted on 1996's *Life Is Sweet*.

McKENZIE, SCOTT

US singer McKenzie (b. Philip Blondheim, 1944) began his career in the early 60s folk group Journeymen. The singer was later invited by fellow ex-member John Phillips to join him in Los Angeles. The pairing flourished on the success of 'San Francisco (Be Sure To Wear Some Flowers In Your Hair)', an altruistic hippy anthem penned by Phillips which topped the UK charts and reached the US Top 5. The follow-ups, 'Like An Old Time Movie' and 'Holy Man', failed to emulate such success. McKenzie briefly re-emerged with the low-key

Sidebar

McKNIGHT, BRIAN
🎵 **Albums**
I Remember You (Mercury 1995)★★★★
➤ p.383 for full listings
Connections
Take 6

McLACHLAN, SARAH
🎵 **Albums**
Fumbling Towards Ecstasy (Arista 1994)★★★★
➤ p.383 for full listings
Connections
Lilith Fair

McLEAN, DON
🎵 **Albums**
American Pie (United Artists 1971)★★★★
➤ p.383 for full listings

McNABB, IAN
🎵 **Albums**
Head Like A Rock (This Way Up 1994)★★★★
➤ p.383 for full listings
Collaborators
Crazy Horse ➤ p.103
Connections
Icicle Works ➤ p.187

McTELL, RALPH
🎵 **Albums**
You Well-Meaning Brought Me Here (Famous 1971)★★★★
Not Until Tomorrow (Reprise 1972)★★★★
➤ p.383 for full listings
Further References
Book: *Angel Laughter: Autobiography Volume One*, Ralph McTell

MEAT LOAF
🎵 **Albums**
Bat Out Of Hell (Epic 1977)★★★★
Bat Out Of Hell II: Back Into Hell (Virgin 1993)★★★
➤ p.384 for full listings
Collaborators
Cher ➤ p.86
John Parr
Jim Steinman
Further References
Book: *To Hell And Back: An Autobiography*, Meat Loaf with David Dalton
Films: *Wayne's World* (1992)
Fight Club (1999)

MEAT PUPPETS
🎵 **Albums**
Mirage (SST 1987)★★★★
➤ p.384 for full listings
Connections
Nirvana ➤ p.250

Main text

Stained Glass Morning, but remained out of the public eye until the 80s, when he joined Phillips in a rejuvenated **Mamas And The Papas**.

McKNIGHT, BRIAN

The younger brother of Claude V. McKnight of *a cappella* gospel outfit Take 6, this US R&B singer (b. 1969) enjoyed his first mainstream success in 1993 with the Top 5 hit 'Love Is', a duet with Vanessa Williams taken from the television series *Beverly Hills, 90210*. His second album, *I Remember You*, sold more than half a million copies and included five Top 20 R&B singles. The star-studded *Anytime* was rewarded with a US Top 20 chart placing. McKnight switched to Motown Records for the Christmas album, *Bethlehem* and 1999's highly successful *Back At One*. The title track spent several weeks at number 2 on the US Hot 100 chart.

McLACHLAN, SARAH

Singer-songwriter McLachlan (b. 1968) made her name on the Canadian folk scene before breaking through with a series of international hits in the late 90s. Her third album, 1994's *Fumbling Towards Ecstasy*, blended her pastoral and reflective mood with a high-tech production by Pierre Marchand. In 1997, McLachlan inaugurated the Lilith Fair touring festival, a hugely successful showcase for female artists. 'Adia', taken from her US number 2 album *Surfacing*, proved to be an enduring radio hit, eventually climbing to number 3 on the singles chart in August 1998. Less successful in the UK, McLachlan nevertheless enjoyed a big club and pop hit in October 2000 with 'Silence', a four-year-old collaboration with electronica duo Delerium.

McLEAN, DON

US singer-songwriter McLean (b. 1945) began his recording career in New York in the early 60s. His 1970 debut *Tapestry* was issued by Mediarts but failed to sell. United Artists Records picked up his contract and issued 'American Pie', a lengthy paean to **Buddy Holly** which reached US number 1 and UK number 2 and is now regarded as a classic. The album of the same name was also an enormous success, while 'Vincent' (a tribute to painter Vincent Van Gogh) reached the top of the UK charts. In 1973 McLean successfully covered Holly's 'Everyday', but his career foundered until 1980 when he returned to the charts with a cover version of **Roy Orbison**'s 'Crying' (UK number 1/US number 2). As the 80s progressed, McLean moved into the country market, but in 1991 'American Pie' unexpectedly returned to the UK Top 20, once again reviving interest in his back catalogue.

McNABB, IAN

UK guitarist and singer-songwriter McNabb (b. 1960) failed to earn the commercial rewards he deserved with the **Icicle Works**, and his 1993 debut solo album, *Truth And Beauty*, failed to generate much interest outside his loyal fanbase. The follow-up, *Head Like A Rock*, was recorded over three weeks in Los Angeles with help from **Crazy Horse** and earned a Mercury Music Prize nomination. The follow-up *Merseybeast* did not build on the critical success of the previous album. McNabb decamped to South Wales for the follow-up, an engaging acoustic set, but in marked contrast, his self-titled fifth album favoured power chords and guitar solos. McNabb returned to familiar ground in 2001 with a self-titled album but, like most of the work by this underrated artist, it was virtually ignored.

McTELL, RALPH

McTell (b. 1944) emerged in the late 60s as one of Britain's leading folk singers with his first two albums, *Eight Frames A Second* and *Spiral Staircase*. The latter was notable for 'Streets Of London', a UK number 2 hit when re-released in 1974 and now firmly established as a folk classic. Its popularity obscured McTell's artistic development from acoustic troubadour to thoughtful singer-songwriter, exemplified on 1971's *You Well-Meaning Brought Me Here*. Ultimately, McTell was unable to escape the cosy image bestowed upon him by his most successful song. During the 80s he pursued a successful career in children's television. Touring occasionally, McTell is still able to comfortably fill concert halls.

MEAT LOAF

US singer Meat Loaf (b. Marvin Lee Aday, 1951) began his career in 1969 with a role in *Hair*, where he met soul vocalist Stoney. The duo recorded a self-titled album in 1971, which spawned the minor US hit, 'What You See Is What You Get'. *Hair* closed in 1971, and Meat Loaf joined **Rainbow** and then *More Than You Deserve!*, a musical by Jim Steinman. After appearing in the 1975 film version of *The Rocky Horror Picture Show*, Meat Loaf began working with Steinman on a rock opera. Epic Records and producer **Todd Rundgren** were sympathetic to the demos and they recorded *Bat Out Of Hell* in 1977. After a six-month wait the album rocketed to the top of the charts in several countries. It stayed in the UK and US album charts for 395 and 88 weeks respectively, and sold in excess of 30 million copies worldwide, making it one of the biggest-selling album releases of all time.

After a three-year gap Meat Loaf released *Dead Ringer* (UK number 1). The title song made the Top 5 in the UK but the album only reached the bottom of the US Top 50. Concentrating on European tours helped both *Midnight At The Lost And Found* and *Bad Attitude* into the UK Top 10. However, Meat Loaf signed a new deal with Virgin Records in 1990, and the Steinman-written and produced *Bat Out Of Hell II: Back Into Hell* roared to the top of the US and UK charts. The lead single 'I'd Do Anything For Love (But I Won't Do That)' was also a transatlantic chart-topper. Steinman was noticeably absent from 1995's *Welcome To The Neighborhood*, apart from two old compositions. Meat Loaf has subsequently concentrated on his burgeoning movie career.

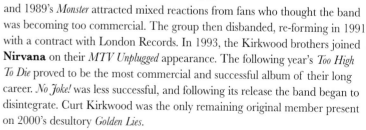

MEAT PUPPETS

Formed in Arizona, USA, Curt Kirkwood (b. 1959; guitar, vocals), Cris Kirkwood (b. 1960; bass, vocals) and Derrick Bostrom (b. 1960; drums) released their 1982 long-playing debut *Meat Puppets* on the influential label SST Records. The album offered a mix of thrash punk with hints of country. *Meat Puppets II* was marked by shifts in mood, while *Up On The Sun* showed the trio moving towards neo-psychedelic melodies. *Mirage* was another critically acclaimed set, but both 1987's *Huevos* and 1989's *Monster* attracted mixed reactions from fans who thought the band was becoming too commercial. The group then disbanded, re-forming in 1991 with a contract with London Records. In 1993, the Kirkwood brothers joined **Nirvana** on their *MTV Unplugged* appearance. The following year's *Too High To Die* proved to be the most commercial and successful album of their long career. *No Joke!* was less successful, and following its release the band began to disintegrate. Curt Kirkwood was the only remaining original member present on 2000's desultory *Golden Lies*.

MEDESKI, MARTIN AND WOOD

Progressive jazz fusionists MMW, an acronym for Medeski, Martin and Wood, were formed in New York, USA, in the early 90s by John Medeski (keyboards), Billy Martin (drums, percussion) and Chris Wood (bass). As a testament to the trio's wide-ranging appeal, they have supported rock acts such as **Phish**, **Los Lobos** and **Morphine**, while members have contributed to studio projects by Biz Markie and **Rickie Lee Jones**. A series of albums for Gramavision cemented MMW's rise and confirmed the viability of their intentions to popularize contemporary jazz. The trio subsequently signed to Blue Note Records, releasing the excellent *Combustication* and the live acoustic set *Tonic*. The more *avant-garde* textures of *The Dropper* and *Uninvisible* demonstrated their willingness to experiment, mixing acid jazz, funk, gospel and turntablism to great effect.

MEDICINE HEAD

This UK band was formed by John Fiddler (b. 1947; guitar, vocals) and Peter Hope-Evans (b. 1947; harmonica, Jew's harp). Their 1970 debut, *Old Bottles New Medicine*, offered atmospheric songs and rumbustious R&B, as did a second set, *Heavy On The Drum*. '(And The) Pictures In The Sky' reached UK number 22 in 1971, but Hope-Evans then left. Keith Relf joined Fiddler and John Davies (drums) for the band's third album, *Dark Side Of The Moon*. Hope-Evans and Fiddler teamed up again in 1972 on *One And One Is One*. The title track reached UK number 3 in 1973, while a second single, 'Rising Sun', reached number 11. As a result, the line-up was expanded with Roger Saunders (b. 1947; guitar), Ian Sainty (bass) and Rob Townsend (b. 1947; drums). Further ructions followed the release of *Thru' A Five* and by 1976 Medicine Head was again reduced to the original duo. *Two Man Band* (1976) marked the end of their collaboration.

MEGADETH

Founded in San Francisco, USA, by guitarist Dave Mustaine (b. 1961) after he left **Metallica** in 1983. Recruiting Dave Ellefson (b. 1964; bass), Chris Poland (guitar) and Gar Samuelson (drums), Mustaine signed to the Combat label. They produced *Killing Is My Business ... And Business Is Good!* in 1985. Capitol Records then signed them, and *Peace Sells ... But Who's Buying?* proved a marked improvement. In 1986, Mustaine fired Poland and Samuelson, bringing in Jeff Young and Chuck Behler as replacements before the recording of *So Far, So Good ... So What!*. *Rust In Peace* featuring Marty Friedman (b. 1962; guitar) and Nick Menza (drums), was released to critical acclaim in 1990. *Countdown To Extinction* dealt with ecological disaster and included two UK Top 20 singles, 'Skin O' My Teeth' and 'Symphony Of Destruction'. Reports of Mustaine's drug problems overshadowed sessions for their sixth album, *Youthanasia*. Following the release of *Cryptic Writings*, drummer Nick Menza left the band due to 'health problems'; he was replaced by Jimmy Degrasso. A 'clean' Mustaine steered the band in an even more melodic direction on 1999's *Risk*. Along with **Slayer**, Metallica and **Anthrax**, Megadeth remain at the forefront of the thrash-metal genre, despite the vulnerability of their central creative force.

MEKONS

The UK-based Mekons made their recording debut for the Fast Product label in 1978. After two singles, they were signed to Virgin Records where a line-up of Andy Corrigan (vocals), Mark White (vocals), Ross Allen (bass), Jon Langford (drums, later guitar, vocals), Kevin Lycett (guitar) and Tom Greenhalgh (guitar), completed *The Quality Of Mercy Is Not Strnen*. Despite personnel changes and a brief break-up in 1982, the Mekons have retained a sense of naïve adventurism, embracing world music, folk and roots along the way. In the 90s, three of the core members, Greenhalgh, Langford and Sarah Corina (violin), who joined in 1991, relocated to Chicago, USA, where the band signed to Quarterstick Records. Other important contributors to the Mekons' legacy include Sally Timms, vocalist and full-time member since the late 80s, accordion player Rico Bell, and drummer Steve Goulding.

The Mekons' first release for over three years, 1996's *King Of The Pirates*, was a bizarre collaboration with American writer Kathy Acker. *Me* was another challenging, conceptual work, but the Mekons' devoted followers were rewarded by the follow-up *Journey To The End Of The Night*'s seamless fusion of the band's eclectic musical tastes.

MELANIE

Melanie (b. Melanie Safka, 1947) emerged during the singer-songwriter boom of the early 70s. Her first US hit, the powerful 'Lay Down (Candles In The Rain)' (1970), featured backing by the Edwin Hawkins Singers. In Britain, she broke through with an original version of the **Rolling Stones**' 'Ruby Tuesday'. *Candles In The Rain* was a transatlantic bestseller and 'What Have They Done To My Song, Ma?' gave her another minor hit, outselling a rival version from the **New Seekers**. Her last major success came in 1971 with 'Brand New Key' (US number 1). The same year, Melanie founded Neighborhood Records with her husband Peter Schekeryk. Marginalized as a stylized singer-songwriter, she found it difficult to retrieve past glories. Sporadic releases continued, however, and she is often seen playing charity shows and benefit concerts.

MELLENCAMP, JOHN

Mellencamp (b. 1951) survived a phase as a glam-rocker to become one of America's most successful mainstream rock singers. In 1976, his name was changed to *Johnny Cougar*, and he released *Chestnut Street Incident*. His first charting album was *John Cougar*, which included the US Top 30 single 'I Need A Lover' in 1979. In 1982 *American Fool* headed the US album chart, while both 'Hurts So Good' and 'Jack And Diane' (US number 1) were million-sellers. The following year he became John Cougar Mellencamp, eventually dropping 'Cougar' in 1989. Many of his songs were now dealing with social problems, and Mellencamp was one of the organisers of the Farm Aid series of benefit concerts. His rock hits during the decade included 'Small Town', 'R.O.C.K. In The USA', 'Paper In Fire' and 'Cherry Bomb'. *Lonesome Jubilee* used fiddles and accordions to illustrate America in recession, while 'Pop Singer' from *Big Daddy* expressed Mellencamp's disillusionment with the music business. He continued to hit the US charts with amazing rapidity and despite the relative failure of 1993's *Human Wheels*, Mellencamp made a strong comeback with *Dance Naked* and the attendant Top 10 cover version of **Van Morrison**'s 'Wild Night'.

Mellencamp suffered a major heart attack shortly after the release of *Dance Naked*, and following this scare was sidelined for over a year. He returned in 1996 with *Mr. Happy Go Lucky*, on which his sound was augmented by the work of noted dance music producer Junior Vasquez. A more traditional self-titled set, his first for new label Columbia Records, was released in 1998, earning Mellencamp his best reviews in years. In 2000, Mellencamp teamed up with novelist Stephen King to write a full-length ghost story stage musical.

MELVIN, HAROLD, AND THE BLUE NOTES

Formed in Philadelphia, USA, in 1954, the Blue Notes – Harold Melvin (b. 1939, d. 1997), Bernard Wilson, Jesse Gillis Jnr., Franklin Peaker and Roosevelt Brodie

235

– began as a doo-wop group. Despite several excellent singles, they failed to make a breakthrough. By the end of the 1960s only Melvin and Wilson remained. Then Theodore **'Teddy' Pendergrass** (b. 1950), drummer in the Blue Notes' backing band, was brought out as the featured vocalist. Singer Lloyd Parkes also joined the group, which was then signed by producers Gamble And Huff. Pendergrass was best heard on the US Top 5 hit 'If You Don't Know Me By Now' (1972). 'The Love I Lost' (1973) and 'Where Are All My Friends' (1974) enhanced Pendergrass's reputation and led to his demand for equal billing. Melvin's refusal resulted in the singer's departure, and Melvin And The Blue Notes, with new singer David Ebo, moved to ABC Records. Despite securing a UK Top 5 hit with 'Don't Leave Me This Way' and a US R&B Top 10 hit with 'Reaching For The World' in 1977, the group failed to recapture its earlier success. They signed to Philly World in 1984, achieving minor UK hit singles the same year with 'Don't Give Me Up' and 'Today's Your Lucky Day'.

MELVINS

US alternative rock band formed in 1984 by King Buzzo (b. Buzz Osbourne, 1960; vocals, guitar), Lori Black (bass) and Dale Crover (drums). The Melvins' albums went largely unheralded until **Nirvana**'s Kurt Cobain described them as his favourite rock band, and guested on and co-produced 1993's major-label debut, *Houdini*. Their second release for Atlantic Records, *Stoner Witch*, saw Crover and Osbourne joined by Mark Deutrom (bass). The band moved to an Atlantic subsidiary for *Stag*, before retreating further away from the mainstream in the late 90s with two albums on the independent Amphetamine Reptile label. New material has subsequently appeared on the Ipecac and Man's Ruin labels.

MEMPHIS HORNS

The Memphis Horns, an offshoot of the **Mar-Keys**, always had a fluid line-up. The mainstays, Wayne Jackson (trumpet) and Andrew Love (tenor saxophone), guided the group during their time at the Stax Records and Hi Records studios. Augmented by James Mitchell (d. 2001; baritone saxophone), Jack Hale (trombone) and either Ed Logan or Lewis Collins (tenor saxophone), the Memphis Horns appeared on releases by **Al Green**, Ann Peebles, and Syl Johnson among others. During the mid-70s, the Horns secured four US R&B hits including 'Get Up And Dance' and 'Just For Your Love'.

Love and Jackson maintained the Memphis Horns name throughout the 80s and made appearances on **U2**'s *Rattle And Hum* and **Keith Richards**' *Talk Is Cheap* (both 1988). They continue to perform live throughout Europe and the USA.

MERCHANT, NATALIE

US singer Merchant (b. 1963) joined the highly regarded **10,000 Maniacs** in 1981. She finally left the group in 1992, three years before she made her solo bow. Merchant wrote all the lyrics and music, as well as producing, her debut album, *Tigerlily*, which reached the US Top 20 in 1995. The ambitious follow-up, *Ophelia*, was a semi-successful attempt by Merchant to broaden her musical and lyrical horizons. The album was another commercial success, however, reaching the US Top 10 in 1998. An enjoyable live album preceded the release of Merchant's third solo album, *Motherland*.

MERCURY REV

Hailing from Buffalo, USA, Mercury Rev was formed by Jonathan Donahue (vocals, guitar), David Fridmann (bass), Jimmy Chambers (drums), Sean 'Grasshopper' Mackowiak (guitar), Suzanne Thorpe (flute) and David Baker (vocals, guitar). Their album, *Yerself Is Steam*, although ignored in their native US, created press acclaim in the UK. Their second album, *Boces*, followed the traditions of left-field art rockers such as **Wire** and **Pere Ubu**. The

unpredictable Baker was fired in 1994, but *See You On The Other Side* showed no reduction in the band's talents.

Growing disillusionment, brought on by the lack of record-company support for their experimental music, saw the band's original members reduced to a core of Mackowiak and Donahue by the time they signed to V2 Records in 1997. Mackowiak had used the spare time to retire to a monastery and then record a solo album, *The Orbit Of Eternal Grace*, featuring new Mercury Rev members Jason and Justin Russo. The band returned with the haunting *Deserter's Songs* in 1998. Engineered by Fridmann, the album also featured contributions from Levon Helm and Garth Hudson of the **Band**. The acclaim for this album was matched by the follow-up *All Is Dream*, a work of sobering, sumptuous beauty.

MERSEYBEATS

Originally called the Mavericks, this Liverpool, England-based quartet comprised Tony Crane (vocals, lead guitar), Billy Kinsley (vocals, bass), David Ellis (rhythm guitar) and Frank Sloan (drums). In 1962, they became the Merseybeats. In early line-up changes Ellis and Sloan were replaced by Aaron Williams and John Banks. The Merseybeats' biggest UK hit was 'I Think Of You', which reached number 5 in 1964. Kinsley left but returned in time for their third major hit, 'Wishin' And Hopin''. Other members included Bob Garner, who was replaced by Johnny Gustafson from the Big Three. There were two more minor hits, 'I Love You, Yes I Do' and 'I Stand Accused'. In 1966, the group split, paving the way for hit duo the Merseys. Crane reactivated the group in later years, performing on the cabaret circuit.

MESSINA, JO DEE

US singer-songwriter Messina announced herself with the US country hit 'Heads Carolina, Tails California' in 1996. Two years later, 'Bye Bye' performed well on country radio before she triumphed once again with 'I'm Alright' in August, which spent two weeks atop *Billboard*'s Hot Country Singles & Tracks chart. An excellent album of the same title followed. Her third album, *Burn*, featured a full production with rock guitars and rousing choruses. Messina may have strayed away from country, but the commercial appeal of her music was undeniably great, with *Burn* hitting the number 1 position in the country album chart in August 2000.

METALLICA

The most innovative US metal band of the late 80s and early 90s were formed in 1981 by Lars Ulrich (b. 1963, Denmark; drums) and James Alan Hetfield (b. 1963; guitar, vocals). They recorded their first demo, *No Life Til' Leather*, with Lloyd Grand (guitar), who was replaced in 1982 by David Mustaine (b. 1961). Jef Warner (guitar) and Ron McGovney (bass) each joined for a brief spell, and, at the end of 1982, Clifford Lee Burton (b. 1962, d. 1986; bass) arrived, and Mustaine was replaced by Kirk Hammett (b. 1962; guitar). The Ulrich, Hetfield, Burton and Hammett line-up endured until a tour bus accident killed Burton.

Metallica put thrash metal on the map with their 1983 debut, *Kill 'Em All*. Although *Ride The Lightning* was not without distinction, *Master Of Puppets* revealed an appetite for the epic. After the death of Buron, the remaining three members recruited Jason Newsted (b. 1963; bass). The new line-up's first recording was the covers set *The $5.98 EP – Garage Days Re-Revisited*. The 1988 opus, *...And Justice For All*, included the breakthrough single 'One'. Three years

later, 'Enter Sandman' and 'Nothing Else Matters' broke the band on a stadium level, while the attendant *Metallica* topped the US and UK charts.

The follow-up, *Load*, entered the US charts at number 1 in 1996, but marked a change in image for the band, who began to court the alternative-rock audience. The following year's *Reload* collected together more tracks recorded at the *Load* sessions. *Garage Inc.* collected assorted cover versions, while the following year's *S&M*, recorded live with the San Francisco Symphony Orchestra, evoked the worst excesses of heavy-rock icons **Deep Purple**. In January 2001, Newsted announced he was leaving after almost 15 years service with the band.

METHENY, PAT

Although classed as a jazz guitarist, US-born Metheny (b. 1954) has bridged the gap between jazz and rock music in the same way that Miles Davis did in the late 60s and early 70s. Metheny (b. 1954), together with his musical partner Lyle Mays (keyboards), initiated a rock-group format that has produced albums of melodious jazz/rock which regularly reach the mainstream US pop charts. He also recorded the transatlantic hit 'This Is Not America' with **David Bowie**.

METHOD MAN

Method Man (b. Clifford Smith, 1971) rose to acclaim as one of the leading members of Staten Island, USA's hip-hop collective, **Wu-Tang Clan**. His smoky, flowing vocals were a prominent feature of 1993's landmark Wu-Tang debut *Enter The Wu-Tang (36 Chambers)*. His own *Tical* set, released the following year, reached the US Top 5, while the single 'Bring The Pain' broke into the national Top 50. Method Man was involved in two highly successful collaborations in 1995. His Grammy-winning duet with **Mary J. Blige** on 'I'll Be There For You'/'You're All I Need To Get By' was a US number 3 hit in June, and was followed by the 'How High' single with **Redman**. Following further work with the Wu-Tang Clan, and a screen appearance in Hype Williams' *Belly*, Method Man released his sophomore effort, *Tical 2000: Judgement Day*, in 1998. The rapper then joined forces with Redman to record the following year's *Blackout!*.

MICHAEL, GEORGE

Michael (b. Georgios (Yorgos) Kyriacos Panayiotou, 1963) served his pop apprenticeship in the million-selling UK duo **Wham!**. His solo career was foreshadowed in 1984's UK chart-topper 'Careless Whisper'. When Wham! split in 1986, Michael went solo. He cut the chart-topping 'A Different Corner', revealing his talent as a singer-songwriter and unveiling a new image. The same year he teamed up with **Aretha Franklin** for the uplifting 'I Knew You Were Waiting (For Me)'. *Faith* followed in 1988 and sold in excess of 10 million copies, topping the charts in both the UK and US. The album spawned four US number 1 hit singles, including the title track, 'Father Figure', 'One More Try' and 'Monkey'. In 1990, he released his second album, *Listen Without Prejudice, Vol. 1*. The first single from the album, 'Praying For Time', reached the top of the US charts. A duet with **Elton John** on 'Don't Let The Sun Go Down On Me' revived his UK chart fortunes, reaching number 1 in December 1991, and also topping the US charts.

Michael sought to free himself from record label Sony during 1993, arguing that his contract made him a 'pop slave', but the judge ruled in favour

of Sony and the singer's buy-out had to be financed by David Geffen's media empire, Dreamworks, and Virgin Records. His first album for his new label, *Older*, was a slickly produced collection featuring the UK chart-toppers 'Jesus To A Child' and 'Fastlove'.

On April 7 1998, the singer was arrested for 'lewd behaviour' in a toilet cubicle at the Will Rogers Memorial Park in Beverly Hills, California. Michael later confirmed his long-rumoured homosexuality and was sentenced to perform community service. He bounced back with two UK Top 5 hits, 'Outside' and a cover version of **Stevie Wonder**'s 'As' featuring **Mary J. Blige**. At the end of the year Michael released *Songs From The Last Century*, a motley selection of cover versions that drew a bemused response from most critics. he returned to the UK charts in 2002 with the one-off single 'Freeek!', which was accompanied by a controversial £1 million video.

MICRODISNEY

This indie-pop band was formed in Cork, Eire, in 1980 by Cathal Coughlan (vocals) and Sean O'Hagan (guitar). Their early singles were collected on *We Hate You White South African Bastards*, which was followed by their first album, 1984's *Everybody Is Fantastic*. Their Virgin Records debut, 'Town To Town', reached the UK charts and was quickly followed by *Crooked Mile*. The band's accessible pop sound was offset by Coughlan's bitter lyricism. Their near-hit 'Singer's Hampstead Home', was an attack on Virgin's fallen idol, **Boy George**. Microdisney bowed out with *39 Minutes*. O'Hagan went on to form the **High Llamas**, while Coughlan's **Fatima Mansions** did much to spice up the late 80s and early 90s.

MIDNIGHT OIL

Formed in Sydney, Australia, in 1975, the nucleus of this strident rock band comprises Martin Rotsey (guitar), Rob Hirst (drums), Jim Moginie (guitar), Dwayne 'Bones' Hillman (bass), and Peter Garrett (vocals). Having signed a contract with CBS/Columbia, it was the band's fourth album *10,9,8,7,6,5,4,3,2,1* that gained mainstream radio airplay. Featuring songs about the environment, anti-nuclear sentiments, anti-war songs and powerful anthems of anti-establishment, it also propelled the band into the international market place. *Red Sails In The Sunset* (1985), *Diesel And Dust* (1987) and *Blue Sky Mining* (1990) established the band in the US and UK markets. Later studio releases failed to reach the peaks of these albums, but the band remain a potent live force.

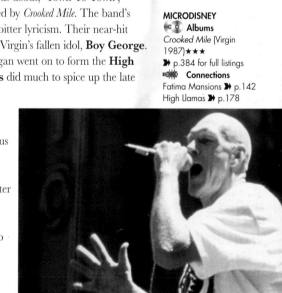

MIKE AND THE MECHANICS

Mike Rutherford (b. 1950; bass) of **Genesis** formed the Mechanics in 1985 during a lull in his parent-band's activities. The line-up comprised **Paul Carrack** (b. 1951; vocals, keyboards), Paul Young (b. 1947, d. 2000; vocals), and established session musicians Peter Van Hooke and Adrian Lee. The band's first hit was 'Silent Running (On Dangerous Ground)' in 1986, which reached the US Top 10, as did the follow-up, 'All I Need Is A Miracle'.

In early 1989 the band reached US number 1 and UK number 2 with the poignant 'The Living Years'.

After an extended hiatus working on their own projects, Mike And The Mechanics returned in 1995 with *Beggar On A Beach Of Gold*, which included the UK Top 20 hit 'Over My Shoulder'. The band continues to be as fluid as possible, with a new album appearing in 1999, although the death of Young the following year was a great shock.

MILES, BUDDY

In 1967, US drummer Miles (b. George Miles, 1945) was asked to join **Electric Flag** by guitarist **Mike Bloomfield**, whose departure left Miles in control. Miles retained its horn section for his next venture, the Buddy Miles Express. Their first album, *Expressway To Your Skull*, found a fan in **Jimi Hendrix**. In 1969, Miles joined Hendrix in the ill-fated Band Of Gypsies. The drummer subsequently formed the Buddy Miles Band and released *Them Changes*. Having participated in a doomed Electric Flag reunion, the drummer continued his prolific rock/soul output with a variety of releases. He was the guiding musical force behind the successful California Raisins, a cartoon band inspired by television advertising. In the mid-90s Miles reappeared with an accomplished album on Rykodisc Records.

MILLER, FRANKIE

With **Brinsley Schwarz** as his backing group, Scottish singer Miller recorded his first solo album, *Once In A Blue Moon*, in 1972. He worked with **Allen Toussaint** on the follow-up, *High Life*. By 1975, Miller had formed a band featuring Henry McCullough, Mick Weaver, Chrissie Stewart and Stu Perry. Their album, *The Rock*, met with middling sales. With a new band comprising Ray Minhinnit (guitar), Charlie Harrison (bass), James Hall (keyboards) and Graham Deacon (drums), Miller recorded *Full House* before he went solo for *Perfect Fit*. The latter included 1978's UK Top 10 hit, 'Darlin''. Miller remained more popular as a live performer than a studio artist, but a brain haemorrhage in 1994 curtailed his career. He has managed to rehabilitate himself enough as to begin writing songs. (NB: Not to be confused with the American honky-tonk singer).

MILLER, STEVE

US guitarist Miller (b. 1943) moved to Chicago in 1964, where he joined up with Barry Goldberg in the Goldberg Miller Blues Band. By 1967, after a move to San Francisco, he signed with Capitol Records as the Steve Miller Band. The band at that time included **Boz Scaggs**, Lonnie Turner, Jim Peterman and Tim Davis, and it was this line-up that recorded *Children Of The Future*. The album was a success but it was *Sailor* later that year that became his *pièce de résistance*. Scaggs and Peterman departed after this album, and Miller added **Nicky Hopkins** (keyboards) for *Brave New World*. Turner and Hopkins left at the end of 1969, with Bobby Winkleman coming in as a replacement. A string of poor albums followed, with Miller's commercial fortunes declining.

Miller returned to form in 1973 with the US chart-topping single 'The Joker'. The accompanying album was a similar success, (US number 2), but Miller took an extended hiatus before re-emerging in style with *Fly Like An Eagle*. Almost as successful was the sister album *Book Of Dreams* (1977). After another lengthy lay-off Miller returned in 1981 with *Circle Of Love*. Six months later, the catchy 'Abracadabra' topped the US charts. The momentum was lost over the next few years, and Miller opted out of the mainstream with the excellent *Born 2B Blue* in 1989. In the UK Levi's had used 'The Joker' for one of

their television advertisements. Capitol quickly released it, and astonishingly, Miller found himself with his first UK number 1. *Wide River* in 1993 was a return to his basic rock formula, and since then only Miller's collaboration with **Paul McCartney** on the latter's *Flaming Pie* has been of any note.

MINISTRY

Alain Jourgensen (b. 1958, Cuba) began producing music under the Ministry name in Chicago, USA, in the early 80s, but was unhappy with the Euro-pop direction of their 1983 debut *With Sympathy*. He was happier with 'Twitch', which featured his own guitar, vocals and keyboards as well as Paul Barker (b. 1958; bass, keyboards) and Bill Rieflin (drums). The band evolved their brand of guitar-based industrial metal on *The Land Of Rape And Honey* and *In Case You Didn't Feel Like Showing Up (Live)*. Ministry achieved major success with 1992's *Psalm 69* (subtitled *The Way To Succeed And The Way To Suck Eggs*), helped by the popularity on MTV of 'Jesus Built My Hotrod'. In 1994, Rieflin was replaced by Rey Washam. Following the release of *Filth Pig*, Ministry took a lengthy lay-off before returning in 1999 with *Dark Side Of The Spoon*, which reasserted their credentials as leading industrial noise terrorists. Jourgensen and Barker have also recorded as Lard (with Jello Biafra) and Revolting Cocks.

MINOGUE, KYLIE

A former Australian soap star, Minogue's (b. 1968) work with hit producers **Stock, Aitken And Waterman** moulded her wholesome image to their brand of radio-centred pop. 'I Should Be So Lucky' reached UK number 1 in 1988, presaging an impressive chart run of instantly hummable UK hits, including 'Got To Be Certain', 'Hand On Your Heart' (number 1), 'Wouldn't Change A Thing', 'Never Too Late', 'Tears On My Pillow' (number 1) and 'Better The Devil You Know'. Her solo success enhanced by duets with former Neighbours co-star Jason Donovan, including the UK number 1 'Especially For You'.

Minogue drastically changed her image in the 90s, adopting a sexier persona, recording for dance label Deconstruction Records, and duetting with **Nick Cave** in 1996 on the single 'Where The Wild Roses Grow'. A new deal with Parlophone Records returned her to the top of the UK charts in 2000 with 'Spinning Around'. The highly catchy 'Can't Get You Out Of My Head' spent several weeks at UK number 1 the following year, and even broke into the US Top 10.

MIRACLES

The Miracles were founded in Michigan, USA, in 1955 by **Smokey Robinson** (b. William Robinson, 1940), Emerson Rogers, Bobby Rogers (b. 1940), Ronnie White (b. 1939, d. 1995) and Warren 'Pete' Moore (b. 1939). Emerson Rogers left in 1956, and was replaced by his sister Claudette. After recordings with producer Berry Gordy, the Miracles signed to Gordy's Motown label in 1960. Recognizing Robinson's talent, Gordy allowed the group freedom in the studio, resulting in 'Way Over There'. 'Shop Around', then broke both the Miracles and Motown to a national audience. Robinson later scaled down his writing for the group, when they briefly worked with **Holland/ Dozier/Holland**. Robinson wrote their most ambitious and enduring songs including 'Tracks Of My Tears', 'The Tears Of A Clown', 'The Love I Saw In You Was Just A Mirage' and 'I Second That Emotion' in 1967. Guitarist Marv Tarplin, who co-wrote several of their hits, was incorporated as an unofficial Miracle in the mid-60s.

In 1971, Robinson announced he was leaving the Miracles and launched a solo career in 1973. His replacement was William 'Bill' Griffin (b. 1950). The group responded with *Renaissance*, and the following year, they re-established their position with 'Do It Baby' and 'Don'tcha Love It'. In 1975, 'Love Machine' became the Miracles' first US number 1, while the concept album *City Of Angels* was acclaimed. This twin success proved to be the Miracles' last gasp. In 1977, they lost Griffin, and since then have existed on the oldies circuit in various guises.

MISFITS

A US cult punk band, the Misfits were formed in New Jersey in 1977 by Jerry Only (bass) and Glenn Danzig (b. 1959; vocals), later adding Bobby Steele (guitar) and Joey Image (drums). Later that year the band's first single, 'Cough Cool', appeared on their own Plan 9 label. A four-track EP, *Bullet*, was recorded before their debut album, and was followed by 'Horror Business'. A third single, 'Night Of The Living Dead', surfaced in 1979. Steele left, replaced by Only's brother Doyle, while drummer Googy (aka Eerie Von) was also drafted in to the line-up. The Misfits grounded to a halt in the mid-80s, with Danzig going on to establish himself as a metal artist. In 1997, the band re-formed, with Danzig replaced by Michale Graves.

MISSION

This UK rock band evolved from the **Sisters Of Mercy**, with Wayne Hussey (b. Jerry Wayne Hussey, 1958) and Craig Adams joining up with Mick Brown (drums) and Simon Hinkler (guitar). After two successful independent singles on *Chapter 22*, they signed to Mercury Records in 1986. Their major-label debut, 'Stay With Me', entered the UK singles charts. *God's Own Medicine* was followed by the number 2 hit album, *Children*. *Carved In Sand* revealed a more sophisticated songwriting approach, but Hinkler left soon afterwards. After signing to Vertigo Records, Hussey, Adams and Brown recorded the dance-influenced *Masque*. Adams was replaced by Andy Cousin (ex-Sisters Of Mercy), while keyboard player Rik Carter and guitarist Mark Gemini Thwaite expanded the line-up. The band returned to a guitar-based sound for two subsequent releases on their own label. Soon after issuing 1996's *Blue* the band announced they were splitting-up. They were resurrected in 2002 with the surprisingly strong album *Aura*.

MISUNDERSTOOD

One of the 60s finest psychedelic bands, the Misunderstood originated in California, USA. Originally known as the Blue Notes, Greg Treadway (guitar), George Phelps (guitar) and Rick Moe (drums), Rick Brown (vocals) and Steve Whiting (bass) adopted their new name in 1965. Phelps was then replaced by Glenn Ross 'Fernando' Campbell (steel guitar). The quintet completed, 'You Don't Have To Go'/'Who's Been Talkin'?', before leaving for the UK. Treadway was later drafted and replaced by Englishman Tony Hill. 'I Can Take You To The Sun' was their only contemporary release, although 'Children Of The Sun' was issued after their break-up, in 1968. Campbell later re-established the name with several British musicians.

MITCHELL, JONI

After art college, this Canadian singer-songwriter (b. Roberta Joan Anderson, 1943) moved to Toronto, where she married Chuck Mitchell. The two performed together, playing several of her originals including 'The Circle Game'. Following her divorce in 1967, Joni Mitchell moved to New York. She was first discovered by manager Elliot Roberts at New York's Cafe Au Go-Go, and shortly

afterwards in Coconut Grove, Florida, by **David Crosby**. She and Crosby became lovers, and he went on to produce her debut album *Joni Mitchell* aka *Songs To A Seagull*. There were signs of important songwriting developments on *Clouds* and *Ladies Of The Canyon*, and the extent of Mitchell's commercial acceptance was demonstrated on the humorous 'Big Yellow Taxi', a UK Top 20 hit.

Following a sabbatical, Mitchell returned with her most introspective work to date, Blue. The follow-up, *For The Roses*, featured elaborate horn and woodwind sections. 'You Turn Me On, I'm A Radio' gave Mitchell a US Top 30 entry, but a 15-month gap ensued before the mesmerising *Court And Spark* appeared in 1974. The sweeping 'Help Me' brought huge commercial success, and he quality of Mitchell's live performances was captured on the live album *Miles Of Aisles*.

In 1975, Mitchell produced the startling *The Hissing Of Summer Lawns*, which not only displayed her increasing interest in jazz, but also world music. Although *Hejira* was equally adventurous, it was noticeably less ornate. The move into jazz territory through 1978–79, first with the double album, *Don Juan's Reckless Daughter*, culminated in her collaboration with Charlie Mingus on *Mingus*. A live double album, *Shadows And Light*, followed before Mitchell signed a long-term contract with Geffen Records. The first fruits of this deal were revealed on the uneven *Wild Things Run Fast* in 1982. The **Thomas Dolby**-produced *Dog Eat Dog* was critically underrated and represented the best of her 80s work. *Chalk Mark In A Rainstorm* continued in a similar vein, but there was a change of perspective on the stripped-down *Night Ride Home*, issued in 1991 following a three-year gap.

The creatively quiet decade that followed did little to detract from her status as Mitchell pursued her painting talents. She returned to recording with *Turbulent Indigo*, which won a Grammy in 1995 for Best Pop Album. Two contrasting compilations were released the following year, chronicling the commercial and non-commercial sides of the artist's oeuvre. Mitchell subsequently returned to the studio to record *Taming The Tiger*, a lush, textured album which echoed the sound of her mid-70s work.

MOBY

US DJ Moby (b. Richard Melville Hall, 1965) recorded several early albums for the Instinct label, but made his commercial breakthrough in 1991 when he took the theme of *Twin Peaks* into the Top 10, recording under the Go moniker. The release of 'I Feel It'/'Thousand' in 1993 was even more bizarre, with the latter classified as the fastest single ever. Moby signed to leading independent Mute Records in 1993, and the following year released 'Hymn', a transcendental religious techno odyssey. The track was included on his eclectic major label debut, *Everything Is Wrong*. He moved away from his dance base in 1996 with the thrash rock of *Animal Rights*. His 'James Bond Theme' reached the UK Top 10 the following year. The attendant *I Like To Score* was an uneasy experiment in soundtrack work. Another change of style was apparent on 1999's *Play*, on which several tracks were based around sampled field recordings made by folklorist Alan Lomax in the earlier part of the century. The album was an unexpected multi-platinum success, thanks in part to every track being licensed for commercial use. The follow-up, *18*, was released in 2002.

MOBY GRAPE

This iconoclastic US psychedelic band was formed in 1966, with the seminal line-up featuring Alexander 'Skip' Spence (b. 1946,

d. 1999; guitar, vocals), Jerry Miller (b. 1943; guitar, vocals), Bob Mosley (b. 1942; bass, vocals), Don Stevenson (b. 1942; drums) and Peter Lewis (b. 1945; guitar, vocals). They became the centre of a huge marketing campaign by CBS Records, whereupon 10 tracks (five singles plus B-sides) were released simultaneously. Only 'Omaha' reached the US charts. The resulting debut, *Moby Grape*, contained all these 10 tracks plus an additional three, and it reached the US Top 30. Their follow-up, *Wow*, made the Top 20 chart but was the final release by the original line-up. Spence had departed with drug and mental problems by the release of *Moby Grape '69*, and Mosley left after a European tour. The fourth album, *Truly Fine Citizen* was badly received. The band disintegrated, unable to use the name which was owned by manager Matthew Katz. The original five reunited for an undistinguished album in 1971, and reunited from time to time in subsequent decades. Spence succumbed to lung cancer in 1999.

MOCK TURTLES

UK band formed by Martin Coogan (guitar, vocals), Steve Green (bass), Krzysztof Korab (keyboards) and Steve Cowen (drums). The band's first 12-inch EP, *Pomona*, was issued in 1987 after which Martin Glyn Murray (guitar) joined. Andrew Stewardson and Joanne Gent replaced Green and Korab in 1989. In 1990 'Lay Me Down' arrived and hot on its heels came a well-received debut, *Turtle Soup*. Their first major-label single was a rework of the B-side of 'Lay Me Down', 'Can You Dig It?'. The single was a surprise UK Top 20 hit, but subsequent hits failed to match its profile. The band dissolved when Coogan formed a new band, Ugli, with Stewardson and Gent. The trio reunited with Murray in 1999 and resurrected the Mock Turtles name.

MODERN LOVERS

Formed in Boston, USA, the Modern Lovers revolved around singer-songwriter **Jonathan Richman** (b. 1951), who was joined by Jerry Harrison (b. 1949; guitar), Ernie Brooks (bass) and David Robinson (drums). Their individual style attracted the interest of **John Cale**, then a staff producer at Warner Brothers Records. Having completed a series of demos, a disillusioned Richman disbanded the line-up. In 1976, the unfinished tracks were purchased by Beserkley Records which released them as *The Modern Lovers*. The company also signed Richman, whose new album, *Jonathan Richman And The Modern Lovers*, was issued within months. The Modern Lovers enjoyed two surprise UK hits in 1977 with 'Roadrunner' and 'Egyptian Reggae' (numbers 11 and 5 respectively). The Modern Lovers name was dropped the following year when the singer began a solo tour.

MOGWAI

Scottish lo-fi post-rock band formed in 1995 by Stuart Braithwaite (guitar, vocals), Dominic Aitchison (bass), John Cummings (guitar) and Martin Bulloch (drums). Their debut single 'Tuner'/'Lower' appeared in 1996 on their own Rock Action label. After signing to Chemikal Underground, and with former Teenage Fanclub drummer Brendan O'Hare as a temporary member, the band released the excellent *Young Team*, which confirmed their brash claims to greatness. The remix collection *Kicking A Dead Pig* featured contributions from Alec Empire, Kid Loco and Arab Strap. Their follow-up album, *Come On Die Young*, featuring multi-instrumentalist Barry Burns, was recorded in America with **Mercury Rev** producer David Fridmann. *Rock Action* eschewed the abrasive instrumental edge of their earlier releases for a more contemplative approach, employing extensive vocals (from Braithwaite) for the first time.

MOLLY HATCHET

The initial line-up of this US blues-rock outfit comprised guitarists Dave Hlubek, Steve Holland and Duane Roland, plus Banner Thomas (bass), Danny Joe Brown (vocals) and Bruce Crump (drums). Their 1978 debut album was an instant success. Brown was replaced by Jimmy Farrar in 1980, before the recording of *Beatin' The Odds*. In 1982, Brown rejoined the band, while Thomas was replaced by Riff West. *No Guts ... No Glory* marked a return to their roots, but flopped. Steve Holden quit and keyboardist John Galvin was recruited for *The Deed Is Done*, a lightweight pop-rock album. Hlubek was then replaced by Bobby Ingram prior to the release of the band's Capitol Records debut, *Lightning Strikes Twice*. Brown, who had been plagued by diabetes, left in 1996. Ingram and Galvin continue to lead Molly Hatchett.

MONEY, ZOOT

Money (b. George Bruno Money, 1942) played in several UK rock 'n' roll acts before forming the Big Roll Band in 1961. By 1963, the line-up had changed to comprise Andy Somers aka Andy Summers (guitar), Nick Newall (saxophone) and Colin Allen (drums). The Big Roll Band secured a residency at London's Flamingo Club, and added Paul Williams (bass, vocals) and Clive Burrows (saxophone). In 1965, the band released its first album, *It Should've Been Me*. A second album, *Zoot!* introduced newcomer Johnny Almond, who replaced Burrows, but only one of their singles, 'Big Time Operator' (1966), broached the UK Top 30.

Money, Somers and Allen embraced psychedelic music in the short-lived Dantalion's Chariot, before both Money and Somers joined **Eric Burdon** in the New Animals. When the group failed Money completed *Welcome To My Head* and returned to London for Zoot Money. He continued with Centipede, and Grimms and Ellis, before joining Somers in the **Kevin Coyne** and **Kevin Ayers** bands. Since then he has played on numerous sessions and enjoyed a new career as a character actor in television drama, but was back on the road by 1995.

MONKEES

In 1965 US television producers Bob Rafelson and Bert Schneider began auditions for a show about a pop group. The final choice paired two musicians, **Michael Nesmith** (b. Robert Michael Nesmith, 1942; guitar, vocals) and folk singer Peter Tork (b. Peter Halsten Thorkelson, 1942; bass, vocals), with two budding actors and former child stars, UK-born Davy Jones (b. 1945; vocals) and Mickey Dolenz (b. George Michael Dolenz, 1945; drums, vocals).

On 12 September 1966, the first episode of *The Monkees* was aired. Attendant singles 'Last Train To Clarksville' (US number 1) and 'I'm A Believer' (US and UK number 1), and a million-selling debut album confirmed the band as the latest teenage phenomenon. However, news that the quartet did not play on their records but simply overdubbed vocals fuelled controversy. TV executive Don Kirshner also later called in staff songwriters, infuriating the Monkees' two musicians, in particular Nesmith, who described *More Of The Monkees* as 'the worst album in the history of the world'. Sales in excess of five million copies exacerbated tension, but after 'A Little Bit Me, A Little Bit You' was issued, without band approval, Kirshner was ousted. Two further 1967 singles, 'Pleasant Valley Sunday' and 'Daydream Believer', achieved gold record status. *Headquarters*, the first Monkees album on which the band members played, was a commercial and artistic success, as was *Pisces, Aquarius, Capricorn & Jones Ltd*. It was followed by the disappointing *The Birds, The Bees & The Monkees* and its accompanying single, 'Valleri'. The appeal of their series had waned, and the final episode was screened in the USA on 25 March 1968.

Peter Tork left following the release of their ambitious feature film *Head*, but although the remaining trio continued, their commercial decline was as spectacular as its ascendancy. Nesmith left for a solo career in 1969, and the following year the Monkees' name was dissolved in the wake of Dolenz/Jones recording *Changes*. However, in 1975, the latter-day duo joined their erstwhile songwriting team in Dolenz, Jones, Boyce And Hart which toured under the banner 'The Great Golden Hits Of The Monkees Show'.

Although Nesmith demurred, Dolenz, Jones and Tork embarked on a highly successful, 20th anniversary world tour which engendered a live album and a new studio set, *Pool It!*. They then disbanded as members pursued contrasting interests. They reunited (with Nesmith) in 1996 to record *Justus*, which was followed by their first tour of the UK as a quartet.

MONOCHROME SET

During late 1976, Andy Warren (bass), Lester Square (guitar) and Bid (guitar, vocals) were playing in the B-Sides with **Adam Ant**. When the B-Sides became **Adam And The Ants**, Bid and Lester Square left and formed the Monochrome Set in 1978. With Warren, Jeremy Harrington (bass) and John Haney (drums), the band began recording for Rough Trade Records. Their debut, *Strange Boutique*, skirted the UK charts. A second album, *Love Zombies*, followed before drummer Morris Windsor joined for the release of the 'The Mating Game', in 1982. The memorable *Eligible Bachelors* followed, by which time Carrie Booth had joined on keyboards while Nick Wesolowski (drum) and Foz (guitar) came into the line-up shortly afterwards. Disheartened by the lack of a breakthrough hit, the band split up in 1985. Four years later the band re-formed to record *Dante's Casino*, with Bid, Lester Square and Warren joined by Orson Presence (guitar, keyboards). From there on they concentrated primarily on their cult following in the Far East, with frequent tours there.

MONTEZ, CHRIS

US singer Montez (b. Christopher Montanez, 1943) was discovered by impresario Jim Lee in 1961, and enjoyed an international hit the following year with 'Let's Dance', which sold over one million copies. A follow-up, 'Some Kinda Fun', reached the UK Top 10 in 1963, while 'The More I See You' gave Montez a second UK Top 5 entry. Minor US successes followed with 'There Will Never Be Another You' and 'Time After Time'. Re-released in the UK in 1972, 'Let's Dance' confirmed its timeless appeal by reaching the UK Top 10. Montez

subsequently disappeared into obscurity, although he briefly resurfaced with an album on A&M's Spanish-language imprint in the mid-80s.

MOODY BLUES

This popular UK band was formed in 1964 by Denny Laine (b. Brian Hines, 1944; vocals, harmonica, guitar), Mike Pinder (b. 1942; piano, keyboards), Ray Thomas (b. 1942; flute, vocals, harmonica), Graeme Edge (b. 1941; drums) and Clint Warwick (b. 1940; bass). They established a strong London following, and soon received their big break performing live on the influential UK television show *Ready, Steady, Go!*. A few months later their Bessie Banks cover, 'Go Now' topped the UK charts and made the US Top 10. Their excellent debut *The Magnificent Moodies* combined traditional white R&B standards with originals. Warwick and Laine departed in 1966 to be replaced by Justin Hayward (b. 1946) and John Lodge (b. 1945).

The new line-up adopted a more progressive approach, debuting with Hayward's classic, 'Nights In White Satin'. The accompanying *Days Of Future Passed* was a huge success and started a run of hit albums. During this period the Moody Blues also founded Threshold Records, but split up in 1974 to follow spin-off projects. They reunited in 1978 for the hugely successful *Octave*, although shortly after its release Pinder left. Patrick Moraz (b. 1948) joined the band who went on to top the US album chart with 1981's *Long Distance Voyager*. They enjoyed another commercial renaissance in 1986 when 'Your Wildest Dreams' and *The Other Side Of Life* both reached the US Top 10. Moraz left the band in 1990 prior to the recording of *Keys Of The Kingdom*. The remaining members continue to record and tour into the new millennium.

MOORE, CHRISTY

Irish singer-songwriter Moore (b. 1945) began playing the club circuit in Eire and England in the 60s. It was in England, in 1969, that he recorded his first album, a collaboration with Dominic Behan, *Paddy On The Road*. His first solo album led to the forming of **Planxty**, where he stayed until 1974. Having once again embarked on a solo career, he became involved in the mid-70s with the Anti-Nuclear Roadshow. After a brief reunion with Planxty in the late 70s, Moore and fellow Planxty member Donal Lunny split in 1981 to form Moving Hearts. He returned to solo work in 1982. Since that time, he has continued to mix traditional songs with contemporary observations of social and political aspects of Irish life. His standing in Irish folk music is unparalleled, and his influence has spilled over into the field of pop and rock.

MOORE, GARY

A talented, blues-influenced singer and guitarist, Moore (b. 1952, Northern Ireland) formed his first major band, **Skid Row**, at the age of 16 – initially with **Phil Lynott**, who left after a few months to form **Thin Lizzy**. Skid Row continued with Brendan Shiels (bass) and Noel Bridgeman (drums), but after just two albums they disbanded, leaving Moore to form the Gary Moore Band. Their debut, *Grinding Stone*, appeared in 1973, but progress stopped in 1974 while Moore assisted Thin Lizzy. Moore subsequently moved into session work before joining Colosseum II in 1976. He made three albums with them but finally became a full-time member of Thin Lizzy. At the same time he completed the solo set *Back On The Streets*, which featured 1979's UK Top 10 single 'Parisienne Walkways', an atmospheric ballad that featured uncredited vocals by Lynott.

Moore later resumed his solo career, cutting a series of commercially ignored albums until he scored hit singles in 1985 with 'Empty Rooms' and 'Out In The Fields' with Phil Lynott. The hard-rocking *Wild Frontier* broke into the UK Top 10 in 1987. A series of blues-based albums earned the artist critical acclaim in the 90s, although he took time time out to collaborate with **Jack Bruce** and **Ginger Baker** in BBM. Moore switched tactics for 1997's rock/pop effort *Dark Days In Paradise* and 1999's dance-inflected *A Different Beat*. He returned to his roots in 2001 on the aptly-titled *Back To The Blues*.

MORCHEEBA

UK trio comprising Paul Godfrey, Ross Godfrey and Skye Edwards. The Godfrey brothers began working together, drawing on a number of influences, including 30s blues and 90s hip-hop. They met Edwards at a party in Greenwich, London, and she was enlisted to add her debonair vocals to their recording sessions. In the winter of 1995 they released their debut, 'Trigger Hippie' a huge underground hit. The success of the single led to the release of *Who Can You Trust?*. Further crossover hits followed with 'Tape Loop' and 'Shoulder Holster' before the sublime *Big Calm* was released in 1998. 'Part Of The Process' provided the trio with their biggest UK hit and has since become established as a classic track in the 'chill-out' genre. *Fragments Of Freedom* followed in 2000.

MORISSETTE, ALANIS

Morissette (b. Nadine Morissette, 1974) enjoyed considerable public acclaim in her native Canada before achieving international success in the mid-90s. Her third album, *Jagged Little Pill*, reached US number 1 and heralded a new wave of aggressive female singer-songwriters. After disappearing from the music scene for a period, during which she travelled in India, Morissette returned with *Supposed Former Infatuation Junkie*. Overlong, verbose and with an irritating line in faux-spirituality, the album nevertheless included the worldwide hit single 'Thank U', and debuted at number 1 on the US album chart in 1998. The following year, Morissette made her acting debut in Kevin Smith's controversial *Dogma*, playing a female God, and released the low-key *MTV Unplugged* in November. She returned to the studio to record *Under Rug Swept*, which was released in February 2002. The album, which was also produced by Morissette, marked a return to the AOR rock style of *Jagged Little Pill*.

MORPHINE

Addictive, offbeat and totally original, this guitarless US trio was formed by Mark Sandman (b. 1952, d. 1999; bass, vocals), Dana Colley (baritone saxophone) and Jerome Deupree (drums), although the latter was soon replaced by Billy Conway (from Sandman's previous group, Treat Her Right). The trio played a few tentative gigs then released their debut album, *Good*, in 1992. They came of age with *Yes* in 1995. The follow-up, *Like Swimming*, was gentle, surreal and lyrically fascinating. Morphine had completed a new album for the DreamWorks label when Sandman collapsed on stage at a concert outside Rome and died shortly afterwards. *The Night* was issued posthumously.

MORRISON, VAN

At the age of 12, Morrison (b. George Ivan Morrison, 1945) joined Deannie Sands And The Javelins, a skiffle group based in his native Belfast, Northern Ireland, but within two years was an integral part of the Monarchs. The experience Morrison garnered – he took up vocals, saxophone and harmonica – proved invaluable when he returned to Belfast to become one of the founder members of **Them**. This group scored two notable hit singles with 'Baby Please Don't Go' and 'Here Comes The Night' (both 1965), while the former's b-side 'Gloria', is revered as a classic of the garage-band genre. The group dissolved in 1966 following an arduous US tour, but within months the singer had returned to New York at the prompting of producer Bert Berns. Their partnership resulted in 'Brown Eyed Girl'. The single deservedly reached the US Top 10, in turn inspiring the hurriedly issued *Blowin' Your Mind*. Berns' premature death brought this period to a sudden end, and for the ensuing 12 months Morrison punctuated live performances by preparing his next release, *Astral Weeks*, recorded with jazz session musicians.

The follow-up album, *Moondance*, employed tighter, punchier arrangements to form the platform for the singer's still-soaring inflections. *His Band And The Street Choir* and *Tupelo Honey* were lesser works, although each generated a US hit single ('Domino' and 'Wild Night' respectively). Morrison's

vocals shone on *Saint Dominic's Preview*, but the follow-up *Hard Nose The Highway* proved disappointing. He reclaimed his position with 1974's enthralling *It's Too Late To Stop Now*, an in-concert selection on which he was backed by the Caledonia Soul Orchestra. It was succeeded by the pastoral *Veedon Fleece*, a set inspired by a sabbatical in Ireland during 1973.

A three-year hiatus ended with the release of *A Period Of Transition*, an undistinguished set on which the singer collaborated with **Dr. John**. *Wavelength* and *Into The Music* were more commercial, with the latter including the noticeably buoyant 'Bright Side Of The Road', the singer's first solo – albeit minor – UK chart entry. On *Common One* Morrison resumed his introspective path with a series of meandering jazz-inflected songs. A greater sense of discipline was seen on his mid-80s work, with *Beautiful Vision* and *No Guru, No Method, No Teacher* of particular note. *Irish Heartbeat*, a festive collaboration with traditional act the **Chieftains**, offered a more joyous perspective.

By this time Morrison had returned from his long domicile in America and resettled in London. He invited R&B vocalist/organist **Georgie Fame** to join his touring revue and enhanced his commercial status when 'Whenever God Shines His Light On Me', a duet with **Cliff Richard**, reached the UK Top 20 in 1989. *Too Long In Exile* revisited his R&B roots and included a reworked 'Gloria' with **John Lee Hooker**. *Days Like This*, released in 1995, was Morrison at his most accessible, while *How Long Has This Been Going On* reflected his interest in jazz. He continued in this vein with Fame, Ben Sidran and one of his idols, Mose Allison, with a tribute album to the latter in 1996. The same year, Morrison was awarded the OBE for his services to music. He returned to the UK Top 40 in 1999 with the catchy 'Precious Time', and the following year recorded an album with Linda Gail Lewis.

MORRISSEY

Morrissey (b. Steven Patrick Morrissey, 1959) began his career as a music reviewer with *Record Mirror*. In 1982 he was approached by guitarist **Johnny Maher** (later Marr) with the idea of forming a songwriting team – they developed into the **Smiths**, the most important and critically acclaimed UK band of the 80s.

In 1987, the Smiths disbanded and Morrissey went solo. He issued his solo debut, 'Suedehead', the following year. The subsequent *Viva Hate* hit UK number 1 soon after. A further UK Top 10 single came with 'Everyday Is Like Sunday'. A projected 1989 album, *Bona Drag*, was delayed then cancelled, although the title served for a formidable hits and b-side compilation. In 1991, Morrissey issued the long-awaited *Kill Uncle*, and embarked on a world tour, backed by a rockabilly group. The fruits of this collaboration were revealed on *Your Arsenal*, a neat fusion of 50s rockabilly influences and 70s glam-rock.

Beethoven Was Deaf, a live album, was a dismal failure. Morrissey, however, began to cultivate a US following, which offered welcome succour at a time when UK critics were predicting his imminent downfall after a controversial appearance at Madstock in support of the re-formed **Madness**.

The singer reasserted his credentials with the UK chart-topper *Vauxhall And I*. He moved to RCA-Victor Records for 1995's disappointing *Southpaw Grammar*. The delayed *Maladjusted* was released on Island Records two years later. Morrissey, one of the UK's most revered singers, has remained quiet since the album's release.

MOTELS

Formed in California, USA, in the early 70s, the Motels' central figure was songwriter Martha Davis (b. 1951; vocals). By the late 70s, the line-up had stabilized around Davis, Jeff Jourard (guitar), his brother Martin (keyboards, saxophone), Michael Goodroe (bass) and Brian Glascock (drums). In 1979, their debut album was issued by Capitol Records. The album was buoyed by the success of the hit ballad 'Total Control'. Davis's boyfriend Tim McGovern replaced Jeff Jourard during sessions for *Careful*. The band's third album, *All Four One*, marked the Motels' commercial zenith. In their homeland they enjoyed two Top 10 hits with 'Only The Lonely' and 'Suddenly Last Summer'. Following two further albums, Davis announced the end of the Motels in early 1987. She embarked on an abortive solo career, and later worked as a songwriter. She established a new line-up of the Motels in 1998.

MOTHERS OF INVENTION – *SEE* ZAPPA, FRANK

MÖTLEY CRÜE

This outrageous US heavy-rock band was formed in 1980 by Nikki Sixx (b. Frank Feranno, 1958; bass), Tommy Lee (b. Thomas Bass, 1962; drums) and Vince Neil (b. Vince Neil Wharton, 1961; vocals). Mick Mars (b. Bob Deal, 1956; guitar) was later added to the line-up. Their first single, 'Stick To Your Guns'/'Toast Of The Town', was issued in 1981 on their own Leathür label, followed by their self-produced debut, *Too Fast For Love*. The band signed to Elektra Records in 1982, and the album was remixed and reissued that August. The following year they recorded a new set, *Shout At The Devil*, with producer Tom Werman. He stayed at the helm for the two albums, which broke them to a much wider audience in the USA, *Theatre Of Pain* (which sold more than two million copies) and 1987's *Girls, Girls, Girls*. The band topped the US charts in 1989 with *Dr. Feelgood*, which yielded two Top 10 singles with the title track and 'Without You'.

Vince Neil was sacked in 1992. His replacement for 1994's self-titled album was John Corabi, although the band's problems continued with a record label/management split and disastrous North American tour. Neil was working with the band again in autumn 1996, after Corabi was also sacked. Lee became the focus of much press attention as a result of his explosive marriage to actress Pamela Anderson, helping boost interest in *Generation Swine*. Lee eventually left the band in 1999 to concentrate on his new outfit, Methods Of Mayhem. He was replaced by Randy Castillo (d. 2002), who debuted on the following year's *New Tattoo*.

MOTÖRHEAD

After being sacked from **Hawkwind** in 1975, Lemmy (b. Ian Kilmister, 1945; vocals, bass) formed Motörhead with Larry Wallis (guitar) and Lucas Fox (drums), but the latter soon left and was replaced by 'Philthy' Phil Taylor (b. 1954). Taylor's friend 'Fast' Eddie Clarke (b. 1950; guitar) completed the line-up, although Wallis left within a month. The band made their debut with the eponymous 'Motörhead'/'City Kids'. A similarly-titled debut album charted, before the trio moved over to Bronze Records. *Overkill* and *Bomber* firmly established Motörhead's style: a fearsome barrage of instruments topped off by Lemmy's hoarse vocals. Their reputation as a great live band was enhanced by the release of the UK chart-topping *No Sleep 'Til Hammersmith*.

In 1982, Clarke left, citing musical differences, and was replaced by Brian Robertson (b. 1956). This combination released *Another Perfect Day*, but Robertson was replaced in 1983 by Wurzel (b. Michael Burston, 1949; guitar) and Philip Campbell (b. 1961; guitar). Two months later Taylor left and was replaced by ex-**Saxon** drummer Pete Gill. Gill remained with the band until 1987 and played on several fine albums including *Orgasmatron*. Taylor rejoined and the line-up remained unchanged for another five years. Wurzel left in 1996, but Lemmy and his colleagues have continued to release albums on a regular basis on the SPV label.

MOTT THE HOOPLE

The founding members of this UK rock band were Overend Watts (b. Peter Watts, 1947; vocals, bass), Mick Ralphs (b. 1947; vocals, guitar), Verden Allen (b. 1944; organ) and Dale Griffin (b. 1948; vocals, drums). They were on the point of dissolving when they auditioned a promising singer named **Ian Hunter** (b. 1946; vocals, keyboards, guitar). Rechristened Mott The Hoople by producer Guy Stevens, their self-titled 1969 debut album revealed a very strong **Bob Dylan** influence, most notably in Hunter's nasal vocal inflexions and visual image. Their next three albums were disappointing, however. In March 1972, following the departure of Allen, the rest of the band quit in disillusionment. **David Bowie** convinced them to carry on and presented them with a stylish UK hit, 'All The Young Dudes'. The catchy 'Honaloochie Boogie' maintained the momentum but then Ralphs quit to form **Bad Company**. With new members Morgan Fisher and Ariel Bender (b. Luther Grosvenor, 1949), Mott The Hoople enjoyed a run of further UK hits including 'All The Way From Memphis' and 'Roll Away The Stone'. During their final phase, Bowie's sideman **Mick Ronson** (b. 1945, d. 1993) joined the band in place of Grosvenor (who had departed to join Widowmaker). When rumours circulated that Hunter had signed a deal instigating a solo career, with Ronson working alongside, the upheaval led to an irrevocable rift within the band resulting in a stormy demise. Watts, Griffin and Fisher carried on as the short-lived Mott.

MOULD, BOB

The former guitarist, vocalist and co-composer in leading US alternative band Hüsker Dü, Mould (b. 1960), surprised many with his reflective solo debut, *Workbook*, released in 1989. Jane Scarpantoni (cello) contributed to its air of melancholy, while two members of **Pere Ubu**, Tony Maimone (bass) and Anton Fier (drums), added sympathetic support. Maimone and Fier also provided notable support on *Black Sheets Of Rain*, which marked a return to the uncompromising power of the guitarist's previous band. Mould abandoned his solo career in 1993, reverting to the melodic hardcore trio format with **Sugar**. By 1995 he had reverted once again to his solo career. *Bob Mould* was an excellent album, as was *The Last Dog And Pony Show*. Mould's first album of the new millennium, *Modulate*, placed less emphasis on his trademark guitar sound, incorporating tape loops and beats to great effect on tracks such as '180 Rain' and 'Lost Zoloft'.

MOUNTAIN

Mountain were formed by guitarist Leslie West (b. Leslie Weinstein, 1945) and bass player Felix Pappalardi (b. 1939, d. 1983) in New York, USA, in 1968. Augmented by drummer N. D. Smart and Steve Knight on keyboards, they played Woodstock in 1970, releasing *Mountain Climbing!* shortly afterwards. Their next two albums built on this foundation, as the band refined their hard-rocking style. *Nantucket Sleighride* and *Flowers Of Evil* made the upper regions of the US charts. A live album followed, but was poorly received and the group temporarily disbanded to follow separate projects.

In 1974, Mountain rose again with Alan Schwartzberg and Bob Mann replacing Laing and Knight to record *Twin Peaks* live in Japan. This line-up was short-lived as Laing rejoined for the recording of the disappointing studio album *Avalanche*. The band collapsed once more and West concentrated on his solo career. West and Laing resurrected the band with bass player Mark Clarke and released *Go For Your Life*. They toured with **Deep Purple** throughout Europe in 1985, but kept a low profile for the remainder of the decade. They recorded two new songs with ex-**Jimi Hendrix** bass player Noel Redding for a 1995 anthology. Suitably inspired, West, Laing and Clarke released *Man's World* the following year.

MOVE

Formed in late 1965 the original line-up of this UK band comprised Roy Wood (b. 1946; vocals, guitar), Carl Wayne (b. 1943; vocals), Chris 'Ace' Kefford (bass), Trevor Burton (guitar) and Bev Bevan (b. Beverley Bevan, 1945; drums). Their first two UK hit singles were the classically inspired 'Night Of Fear' and the upbeat psychedelia of 'I Can Hear The Grass Grow'. In 1967, they signed to the reactivated Regal Zonophone Records label, which was launched with the fashionably titled 'Flowers In The Rain'. The single was the first record played on BBC Radio 1 and was promoted with a saucy postcard depicting Harold Wilson (the band was sued for libel).

In 1968, the Move returned with the high energy 'Fire Brigade'. Soon afterwards, Kefford and Wayne departed, leaving the Move to carry on as a trio. The heavy-rock sound of 'Brontosaurus' and 'When Alice Comes Down To The Farm' broadened their diverse hit repertoire. The recruitment of **Jeff Lynne** (b. 1947) from the **Idle Race** encouraged them to experiment with cellos and oboes while simultaneously pursuing their career as an increasingly straightforward pop act. The final flurry of Move hits ('Tonight', 'Chinatown' and 'California Man') were bereft of the old invention, which was henceforth to be discovered in their grand offshoots, the **Electric Light Orchestra** (ELO) and **Wizzard**.

MUD

Originally formed in 1966, this UK pop outfit comprised Les Gray (b. 1946; vocals), Dave Mount (b. 1947; drums, vocals), Ray Stiles (b. 1946; bass, vocals) and Rob Davis (b. 1947; guitar, vocals). In early 1973, they broke through in the UK with 'Crazy' and 'Hypnosis'. There followed an impressive run of 12 more UK Top 20 hits during the next three years, including three number 1 hits: 'Tiger Feet', 'Lonely This Christmas' and 'Oh Boy'. The band continued in cabaret, but their membership atrophied after the hits had ceased. Gray attempted a solo career with little success, while Stiles turned up unexpectedly in 1988 as a latterday member of the **Hollies**. Davis went on to establish himself as an in-demand writer on the UK pop scene in the late 90s, co-authoring material for Spiller ('Groovejet (If This Ain't Love)') and **Kylie Minogue** ('Can't Get You Out Of My Head') among others.

MUDDY WATERS

One of the dominant figures of post-war US blues, Muddy Waters (b. McKinley Morganfield, 1915, d. 1983) was raised in a rural Mississippi town and began performing and touring the south. Having already mastered the rudiments of the guitar, Waters began performing and this early, country blues period was later documented by Alan Lomax. Touring the south making field recordings for the Library Of Congress, this renowned archivist taped Waters on three occasions between 1941-42.

In 1943, Waters moved to Chicago and by 1948 had begun using electric instruments and signed a recording contract with the newly founded Aristocrat label (later Chess Records). Waters' second release, 'I Feel Like Goin' Home'/'I Can't Be Satisfied', was a minor R&B hit and its understated accompaniment from bass player Big Crawford set a pattern for several further singles. By 1951 the guitarist was using a full backing band and the talent he used here ensured that the Muddy Waters Band was Chicago's most influential unit, with a score of seminal recordings, including 'Hoochie Coochie Man', 'I've Got My Mojo Working', 'Mannish Boy', 'You Need Love' and 'I'm Ready'.

Although criticized for his use of amplification, Waters' effect on a new generation of white enthusiasts was incalculable. Paradoxically, while these new groups enjoyed commercial success, Waters struggled against indifference. Deemed 'old-fashioned' in the wake of soul music, he was obliged to update his sound and repertoire, resulting in such misjudged releases as *Electric Mud*. *The London Sessions* kept Waters in the public eye at the start of the 70s, as did his appearance in the **Band**'s *The Last Waltz* later in the decade, but it was a series of collaborations with guitarist Johnny Winter that signalled a dramatic rebirth. This pupil produced and arranged four albums that bestowed a sense of dignity to this musical giant's legacy. Waters died of heart failure in 1983.

MUDHONEY

Forged from a host of US bands, Mudhoney can lay claim to the accolade 'godfathers of grunge' more legitimately than most. The band, formed by brothers Mark Arm (b. 1962; vocals) and Steve Turner (b. 1965; guitar), plus Matt Lukin (b. 1964; bass) and Dan Peters (b. 1967; drums), were the first to import the sound of Sub Pop Records to wider shores. In 1988, they released 'Touch Me I'm Sick', one of the defining moments in grunge, followed shortly by their debut mini-album Their first album proper (Mudhoney) was greeted as a disappointment by many. *Every Good Boy Deserves Fudge* was a departure, with Hammond organ intruding into the band's rock formula.

After much speculation, Mudhoney moved to Reprise Records in the early 90s, debuting with 1993's average *Piece Of Cake*. Released two years later, *My Brother The Cow* revealed a band nearly back to its best. Released after extensive worldwide touring with **Pearl Jam**, highlights included 'Into Your Schtich', which reflected on the passing of Kurt Cobain. Mark Arm also played with the trashy Australian garage rock band Bloodloss, who released their major label debut, *Live My Way*, in 1995. He returned to Mudhoney for their 1998 release, *Tomorrow Hit Today*.

MUDVAYNE

US nu-metal outfit formed in 1996 by Gurrg (b. Greg Tribbett; guitar), Kud (b. Matthew McDonough; drums), Spag (b. Chad Gray; vocals), with Ryknow (b. Ryan Martinie; bass) added to the line-up two years later. The band developed bizarre stage identities, while their sound (dubbed 'math metal' in an attempt to explain its intricacies) was characterised by challenging arrangements and with influences ranging from new wave, electro to metal. The band's debut *L.D. 50* received largely excellent reviews in the rock press, although some critics suggested that the band was no more than a calculated attempt to capitalise on **Slipknot**'s success.

MUMBA, SAMANTHA

This highly talented Irish singer (b. 1983) attended Dublin's Billie Barry Stage School, but her education was interrupted in September 1998 when she landed the lead role in an adaptation of Gilbert And Sullivan's *The Hot Mikado*. Mumba wrote and recorded her debut album in several countries, but the end product sounded distinctly American in its adoption of a slickly produced, pop/R&B sound. 'Gotta Tell You' shot to the top of the Irish charts, but more importantly broke into the upper regions of the UK and US charts in 2000. 'Body II Body', built around a hypnotic sample of **David Bowie**'s 'Ashes To Ashes', repeated the success. Mumba inaugurated her acting career with a role in Simon Wells' adaptation of *The Time Machine*.

MY BLOODY VALENTINE

My Bloody Valentine's roots lay in Dublin, Eire, where singer/guitarist Kevin Shields joined drummer Colm O'Ciosoig in the short-lived Complex. Forming My Bloody Valentine in 1984, the pair were joined by vocalist Dave Conway (vocals) and Tina (keyboards). A mini-album, *This Is Your Bloody Valentine*, made little impression so the band moved to London and recruited Debbie Googe (bass). A string of independent releases followed, including *The New Record By My Bloody Valentine* EP, which meshed bubblegum pop with buzzsaw guitars.

The departure of Conway signalled a change in musical direction, reinforced by the arrival of vocalist Bilinda Butcher and a move to Creation Records. Enticing melodic structures contrasted with a snarling, almost unworldly collage of noise on the pivotal *Isn't Anything*. My Bloody Valentine's increasing maturity saw the meticulously produced *Loveless* album reinforce their reputation as one of the prime influences on the late 80s UK independent scene. However, the massive studio bills run up during that time saw My Bloody Valentine leave Creation, moving instead to Island Records. No new material has been forthcoming, although Shields has contributed to many outside projects, including 1996's *Experimental Audio Research* album Beyond The Pale. O'Ciosoig and Googe eventually tired of waiting for their errant leader, forming Clear Spot and Snowpony respectively.

MYSTIKAL

Before starting a music career, rapper Mystikal (b. Michael Tyler) had a spell in the US army, which included service in the Gulf conflict. Though he would become better known for his association with the No Limit Records label, Tyler released his debut as Mystikal on the independent Big Boy label in 1995. The record brought him to the attention of Jive Records, who signed the rapper for *Mind Of Mystikal*, an updated version of his debut. His No Limit debut, *Unpredictable*, debuted at US number 3 in 1997. The follow-up, *Ghetto Fabulous*, was another commercial success, debuting at US number 5 in 1999. By now, Mystikal's high-energy approach had become bogged down by the low budget/no frills approach to recording that blighted most No Limit product. Mystikal's bold decision to leave No Limit was rewarded when *Let's Get Ready* debuted at number 1 on the US album chart, buoyed by the radio success of the single 'Shake Ya Ass'.

'N SYNC

US vocal group formed in Orlando, Florida in 1995 by JC Chasez (b. Joshua Scott Chasez, 1976), Justin Timberlake (b. 1981), Chris Kirkpatrick (b. 1971), Joey Fatone (b. 1977) and James Lance Bass (b. 1979). Their debut album was originally released through BMG Ariola Munich, and the band became an instant success in Europe before 'I Want You Back' broke into the US Top 20 in May 1998. Further hit singles followed with 'I Want You Back', '(God Must Have Spent) A Little More Time On You' and 'Music Of My Heart'. The group's debut for Jive Records, 2000's *No Strings Attached*, became the first album in US chart history to sell more than 2 million copies in its first week of sales. The album also generated the US chart-topping single, 'It's Gonna Be Me'. Further hit singles preceded the release of the following July's *Celebrity*, the group's hugely successful fourth album.

N'DOUR, YOUSSOU

N'Dour (b. 1959) is one of Senegal's greatest musical pioneers. Along with the Star Band, N'Dour began the fusion of western electric instrumentation and traditional Wolof rhythms and lyrics that became known as mbalax. In 1979 N'Dour left the Star Band, setting up Etoile De Dakar, which he re-formed in 1982 as Super Etoile De Dakar. Ten cassette releases, starting with *Tabaski* in 1981, displayed an increasing fullness and power of arrangement. Outside Senegal his music received wider attention with the western release of two classic albums, *Immigres* and *Nelson Mandela*. In 1987 N'Dour supported **Peter Gabriel** on a US tour, returning to Dakar to record and explore the traditional sounds of Senegal. The results were heard on *The Lion* and its 1990 follow-up *Set*. For purists in the west, the albums showed rather too much western influence, but his Senegalese audience received them enthusiastically. While *Eyes Open* led some to believe N'Dour had lost his edge, *The Guide* pronounced his talent undiminished and was the first album to be conceived, recorded and produced in Senegal. '7 Seconds', a duet with **Neneh Cherry**, reached number 3 in the UK charts in 1994, only furthering N'Dour's status as a genuine crossover artist. He subsequently concentrated on his home market, releasing several cassette-only albums and appearing live every weekend at his Thiossane club. *Joko*, his long-awaited return to the international fold, was released in 2000.

N.W.A.

The initials stand for Niggers With Attitude, which was the perfect embodiment of these Los Angeles, USA-based rappers outlook. Formed by **Dr. Dre** (b. Andre Young, 1965), DJ Yella (b. Antoine Carraby), MC Ren (b. Lorenzo Patterson), Eazy-E (b. Eric Wright, 1963, d. 1995) and **Ice Cube** (b. O'Shea Jackson, 1969).

N.W.A.'s first single was 'Boyz 'N The Hood', marking out their lyrical territory as guns, violence and 'bitches'. Though *N.W.A. And The Posse* was their debut album, they only performed four of the raps on it, and to all intents and purposes, 1989's *Straight Outta Compton* counts as their first major release. A landmark release, in its aftermath rap became polarized into two distinct factions: traditional liberal (reflecting the ideas of Martin Luther King) and a black militancy redolent of Malcolm X, albeit much less focused and reasoned. Ice Cube left before the recording of *Efil4zaggin* (Niggaz4life spelt backwards), which made US number 1 and surpassed the outrage factor of its predecessor by addressing gang rape and paedophilia, in addition to the established agenda of oral sex, cop killing and prostitution.

Dr. Dre and Ice Cube enjoyed the most success following the disbandment of N.W.A., with the former going on to enjoy huge success both as an influential artist and producer with Death Row Records.

NAPALM DEATH

This Birmingham, England-based grindcore quintet was formed in 1981. Side one of their debut, *Scum*, featured Justin Broadrick (guitar), Mick Harris (drums) and Nick Bullen (bass, vocals), while side two featured Bill Steer (guitar), Jim Whitely (bass) and Lee Dorrian (vocals), with Harris the only survivor from the first inception. Dorrian and Steer left in 1989, being replaced by vocalist Mark 'Barney' Greenway and US guitarist Jesse Pintado. They embarked on the European *Grindcrusher* tour before playing US dates. A second guitarist, Mitch Harris, was added for *Harmony Corruption* and 'Suffer The Children' saw Napalm Death retreat to a purer death-metal sound. In 1992 Danny Herrara replaced Harris on drums. Subsequent albums confirmed that Napalm Death remain the antithesis of style, melody and taste – the punk concept taken to its ultimate extreme.

NAS

Nas (b. Nasir Jones, 1973), a former member of Main Source, made his name as a highly skilled rapper with the double whammy of 1994's *Illmatic* and 1996's *It Was Written*. The latter debuted at number 1 on the US album chart. The following year he collaborated with **Foxy Brown**, AZ and **Dr. Dre** on the 'supergroup' project, the Firm. Although it demonstrated signs of a creative impasse, *I Am . . .* , which revealed the new Nas Escobar alias, showed no sign of his commercial popularity having diminished when it debuted at US number 1 in 1999. Nas launched his Ill Will Records imprint in autumn 2000 with the debut release by his rap supergroup QB Finest, who enjoyed a national hit single with the salacious 'Oochie Wally'.

NASH, JOHNNY

US singer Nash (b. 1940) gained his first chart entry in 1957 with a cover of Doris Day's, 'A Very Special Love'. He had a Top 5 hit in 1965 with 'Let's Move And Groove Together'. Nash went to Jamaica to promote this hit, and was exposed to ska. Sessions with Byron Lee And The Dragonaires resulted in 'Cupid', 'Hold Me Tight' and 'You Got Soul'.

After a period in the doldrums, Nash's career was revived when the **Bob Marley**-penned 'Stir It Up' reached the UK Top 20 in 1972. Other hits followed with 'I Can See Clearly Now', 'Ooh What A Feeling' and 'There Are More Questions Than Answers', but the further he drifted from reggae the less successful the single. His career was again revived when he recorded 'Tears

On My Pillow' in Jamaica, reaching UK number 1 in 1975. He also reached the UK chart with 'Let's Be Friends' and '(What) A Wonderful World' before choosing to devote more energy to films and his West Indian recording complex.

NAZARETH

Formed in 1968 in Scotland, this hard rock band originally comprised Dan McCafferty (vocals), Manny Charlton (guitar), Pete Agnew (bass) and Darrell Sweet (b. 1947, d. 1999; drums). *Nazareth* and *Exercises* showed promise, while *Razamanaz* spawned two UK Top 10 singles – 'Broken Down Angel' and 'Bad Bad Boy' (both 1973). Cover versions of **Joni Mitchell**'s 'This Flight Tonight' and Tomorrow's 'My White Bicycle' were UK hits, while *Hair Of The Dog* established Nazareth internationally. They remained popular throughout the 70s, and added guitarist Zal Cleminson for *No Mean City*. Cleminson left after *Malice In Wonderland* and was replaced by former **Spirit** keyboard player, John Locke. Guitarist Billy Rankin later joined the band, but dissatisfaction with touring led to Locke's departure following *2XS*.

Although Nazareth remained popular in the US and Europe, their stature in the UK was receding. Bereft of a major recording deal, they suspended their career during the late 80s while McCafferty pursued solo ambitions. *No Jive* was an impressive comeback album in 1992, but they failed to capitalize on its critical success. McCafferty and Agnew continue to front this durable rock band.

NELLY

Nelly (b. Cornell Haynes Jnr) grew up in St. Louis, Missouri, where he formed

the St. Lunatics rap crew with high school friends Kyjuan (b. Robert Cleveland), City Spud (b. Lavell Webb), Big Lee (b. Ali Jones), Murphy Lee (b. Tohri Harper), and Slow Down (b. Corey Edwards). The St. Lunatics enjoyed a local underground hit in 1996 with 'Gimme What Ya Got', but in 1999 Nelly opted to pursue a solo career and was signed to Universal Records. The regional popularity of his singles translated into national success when *Country Grammar*, his debut collection, rose to the top of the US album charts. Nelly's rhyming style offered an interesting new angle with a smooth flow tailor made for the crossover urban R&B market, with the big radio-friendly hooks on tracks such as 'Country Grammar (Hot Shit)', 'Ride Wit Me', and 'St. Louie' offering the real clue to Nelly's unexpected popularity. The St. Lunatics crew released their debut album in 2001.

NELSON, BILL

Although noted for his guitar work with UK progressive rock band **Be-Bop Deluxe**, Nelson (b. William Nelson, 1948) has earned more critical acclaim for his keyboard-driven solo work. He fronted Be-Bop Deluxe for most of the 70s before assembling Bill Nelson's Red Noise. *Sound On Sound* (1979) was an agitated and confused debut. Following a short-lived contract with Mercury Records he continued to release introspective, chiefly home-recorded albums on the Cocteau label, which Nelson co-founded in 1980. Many of his releases throughout the 80s were of a whimsical, self-indulgent nature and missed the input of other musicians. Numerous albums were issued via his fan club but the quality was rarely matched by the prolificacy. Nelson also records with Roger Eno and Kate St. John as Channel Light Vessel.

NELSON, RICK

In 1957 New Jersey, USA-born Nelson (b. Eric Hilliard Nelson, 1940, d. 1985) embarked on a recording career in the mid-50s with the million-selling 'I'm

Walking'/'A Teenager's Romance'. He had further success with 'Be-Bop Baby' on the Imperial label. In 1958 Nelson formed a full-time group for live work and recordings, which included **James Burton** (guitar). Early that year Nelson (as Ricky Nelson) enjoyed his first transatlantic hit with 'Stood Up' and his first US chart-topper with 'Poor Little Fool'. Songs such as 'Believe What You Say', 'Never Be Anyone Else But You', 'Sweeter Than You' and 'I Wanna Be Loved' showed Nelson's ability at singing both ballads and up-tempo material. His issue of the million-selling 'Travelin' Man' (1961) was one of his greatest moments as a pop singer.

Pop became less popular with the emergence of the beat boom and in 1966 he switched to country music. In 1969 Nelson formed the Stone Canyon Band. A version of **Bob Dylan**'s 'She Belongs To Me' brought Nelson back into the US charts, and a series of strong albums followed. His sarcastic 'Garden Party' showed his determination to go his own way, as his audiences at the time were more interested in hearing his early material. This was his last hit, selling a million copies. After parting with the Stone Canyon Band in 1974, Nelson's recorded output declined, but he continued to tour. On 31 December 1985, he died in a plane crash near De Kalb, Texas.

NELSON, SANDY

US drummer Nelson (b. Sander L. Nelson, 1938) began his career as a member of the Kip Tyler Band. He became an in-demand session musician during the 50s, and played on the Teddy Bears' million-selling 'To Know Him Is To Love Him'. He and Bruce Johnston reached the US and UK Top 10 in 1959 with an early demo of 'Teen Beat'. He released a bevvy of singles, including 'Let There Be Drums', but the appeal quickly waned and 'Teen Beat '65' (1964) was his last chart entry. Despite being tempted into occasional, informal recordings, Nelson has remained largely inactive in professional music since 1978, although instrumental aficionados still marvel at the drummer's extensive catalogue.

NELSON, WILLIE

US country giant Nelson (b. 1933) was writing songs by the age of seven. His first recording, 'Lumberjack', written by Leon Payne, was recorded in Vancouver, Washington in 1956. He sold his song 'Night Life' for $150; Ray Price made it a country hit and there have now been over 70 other recordings. Nelson moved to Nashville, where his offbeat, nasal phrasing and dislike of rhinestone trimmings made him radically different from other country musicians.

In 1961, three of Nelson's country songs crossed over to the US pop charts: **Patsy Cline**'s 'Crazy', Faron Young's 'Hello Walls' and Jimmy Elledge's 'Funny How Time Slips Away'. In 1963, Nelson had his first country hits as a performer, first in a duet with Shirley Collie, 'Willingly', and then on his own with 'Touch Me'. Among his tracks for Liberty Records were 'Half A Man' and 'River Boy'. When Liberty dropped their country performers, Nelson moved to Monument Records. He and Ray Price joined forces for an album, and Chet Atkins also produced some fine albums for Nelson, including *Texas In My Soul*.

During the 1970s, Nelson toured extensively and his bookings at a rock venue in Austin showed the possibility of a new audience. **Waylon Jennings**' hit with 'Ladies Love Outlaws' indicated a market for 'outlaw country' music. The term separated them from more conventional country artists, and, with his pigtail and straggly beard, Nelson no longer looked like a country performer. In 1975, Nelson signed with Columbia Records and recorded *Red Headed Stranger*, which has since become a country classic. 'Blue Eyes Crying In The Rain' was a number 1 country hit and also made number 21 on the US pop charts in 1975. RCA Records then compiled *Wanted! The Outlaws* with Jennings, Nelson, Jessi Colter and Tompall Glaser. It became the first country album to go platinum. The first *Waylon And Willie* album included 'Mammas, Don't Let Your Babies Grow Up To Be Cowboys', and two beautiful Nelson performances, 'If You Can

Touch Her At All' and 'A Couple More Years'. Nelson and Jennings later joined with **Johnny Cash** and **Kris Kristofferson** for tours and albums as the Highwaymen.

Nelson has recorded numerous country songs, but more significant is his love of standards. *Stardust* (1978) took country fans by surprise, with the contents resembling a Bing Crosby album. Nelson's record label, Lone Star, founded in 1978 with Steven Fromholz and the Geezinslaw Brothers, was not a commercial success, but he later developed a recording studio and golf course at Pedernales, Texas. He has organized several Farm Aid benefits, and he and **Kenny Rogers** represented country music on 1985's USA For Africa single, 'We Are The World'.

Nelson began writing prolifically during the 90s, partly in response to the Internal Revenue Service's claim for $16 million in back-taxes. *Just One Love* and *Teatro* were the high points of this period. *Milk Cow Blues*, Nelson's first release of the new millennium, was a straightforward blues album.

NEPTUNES

Part of the new generation of superstar US hip-hop writer/producers, Chad Hugo and Pharrell Williams shot to fame at the end of the 90s owing to their work on bestselling tracks by artists such as Ol' Dirty Bastard, **Mystikal**, **Kelis** and **Jay-Z**, and by the end of 2001 were to be found working with mainstream pop artists such as **Backstreet Boys**, **No Doubt**, **'N Sync** and **Britney Spears**. Hugo and Williams' high profile afforded them the opportunity to work on their own album project. Adopting the moniker N*E*R*D (No-one Ever Really Dies), they recorded *In Search Of . . .* with vocalist Sheldon 'Shay' Haley.

N*E*R*D - SEE NEPTUNES

NESMITH, MICHAEL

Best-known as a member of the **Monkees**, Nesmith (b. Robert Michael Nesmith, 1942) recorded an instrumental album in 1968 but his independent aspirations did not flourish until he formed the First National Band in 1970. He was joined by John London (bass), Orville 'Red' Rhodes (pedal steel) and John Ware (drums), on three excellent country rock albums. The Second National Band, in which Nesmith and Rhodes were accompanied by Johnny Meeks (bass) and Jack Panelli (drums), completed *Tantamount To Treason*. The acoustic solo set, *And the Hits Just Keep On*

Comin', and *Pretty Much Your Standard Ranch Stash* ended Nesmith's tenure with RCA Records, and he subsequently founded Pacific Arts. His commercial status was reasserted with 1977's 'Rio'. The attendant video signalled a growing interest in the visual arts, and in the same year Nesmith launched a television chart show called *Popclips*. The idea was subsequently bought by Warner and reinvented as MTV. *Infinite Rider On The Big Dogma* proved to be Nesmith's biggest-selling US album, and also his last music release for a considerable time as his interest in video flourished. In 1982 the innovative *Elephant Parts* won the first ever Grammy for a video, while considerable acclaim was engendered by the movies *Repo Man* and *Timerider*, which the artist financed through Pacific Arts.

Nesmith continues to pursue his various diverse interests, but only occasionally returns to the studio to record new material. He rejoined the Monkees on their 30th anniversary album release, *Justus*, and the subsequent UK tour.

NEW KIDS ON THE BLOCK

Formed in 1984, this vocal group from Boston, USA, featured Joe McIntyre (b. 1972), Jordan Knight (b. 1970), Jonathan Knight (b. 1968), Daniel Wood (b. 1969) and Donald Wahlberg (b. 1969). Their self-titled album fused rap and pop, bringing them popularity among a predominately white teenage audience. They broke into the US charts in 1988 with 'Please Don't Go Girl'

and in 1989–90 became the biggest-selling group in America, topping the charts with 'I'll Be Loving You (Forever)', 'Hangin' Tough' and 'Step By Step'. A reissue of 'You Got It (The Right Stuff)' and 'Hangin' Tough' reached number 1 in the UK. In 1992 they shortened their name to NKOTB, but their commercial fortunes had waned. The group split-up in 1994.

NEW MODEL ARMY

Formed in Bradford, England, in 1980, New Model Army was led by Justin 'Slade The Leveller' Sullivan (guitar, vocals) with Jason 'Moose' Harris (bass, guitar) and Robb Heaton (drums, guitar). Their brand of punk and folk rock attracted a loyal cult following, and for a period between 1985 and 1991 they managed to place 12 singles in the UK chart, an impressive feat for such an uncompromisingly political unit. This underrated band has continued to record new albums and tour into the new millennium.

NEW ORDER

When **Joy Division**'s Ian Curtis committed suicide in May 1980 the three remaining members, Bernard Sumner (b. Bernard Dicken/Albrecht, 1956;

guitar, vocals), Peter Hook (b. 1956; bass) and Stephen Morris (b. 1957; drums) continued under the name New Order. Later that year they recruited Morris' girlfriend, Gillian Gilbert (b. 1961; keyboards, guitar) and wrote their debut, *Movement*, released in 1981. Their first single, 'Ceremony' was a UK Top 40 hit. *Power, Corruption & Lies* contained many surprises and memorable songs, and saw the band beginning to experiment with dance rhythms. 'Blue Monday' combined an infectious dance beat with Sumner's cool vocal. Released at this time in 12-inch format only, it went on to become the biggest-selling 12-inch single of all time in the UK.

By this time New Order were joint owners of the Haçienda nightclub in Manchester, which quickly became known for its pioneering sponsorship of American house music. The band's subsequent collaboration with New York producer Arthur Baker spawned 'Confusion' (1983) and 'Thieves Like Us' (1984). *Low-Life* marked a creative high point for New Order, although the magnificent single 'The Perfect Kiss' deserved a higher chart placing. Their next album, 1986's *Brotherhood*, was overshadowed by the following year's UK Top 5 single, 'True Faith'. *Technique*, recorded in Ibiza, was their most ambitious fusion of rock and dance with wholesale adoptions of the popular Balearic style.

In summer 1990 New Order reached the UK number 1 slot with 'World In Motion', accompanied by the England World Cup Squad. Rather than exploiting their recent successes with endless tours, they branched out into various spin-off ventures. Hook formed the hard-rocking Revenge, Sumner joined former **Smiths** guitarist Johnny Marr in **Electronic** and Morris/Gilbert recorded an album together as the Other Two. In 1991 they reconvened for an album which was eventually released in 1993. *Republic* met with mixed reviews and the band members returned to solo projects, with Hook forming Monaco in 1996.

In 1998, after five years' silence, the four members reconvened for live appearances and to record new material. The first new track to appear, 'Brutal', was featured on the soundtrack of *The Beach*. The band returned to the UK charts in August 2001 with the sparkling Top 10 single, 'Crystal'. The new studio album, *Get Ready*, followed in October.

NEW RIDERS OF THE PURPLE SAGE

Formed in 1969, New Riders Of The Purple Sage was envisaged as a spin-off from the **Grateful Dead**. Group members **Jerry Garcia** (b. 1942, d. 1995; guitar), Phil Lesh (b. Philip Chapman, 1940; bass) and Mickey Hart (drums) were joined by John Dawson (guitar, vocals) and David Nelson (guitar). They secured a recording contract in 1971, by which time Dave Torbert had replaced Lesh and Spencer Dryden (b. 1938) was installed as permanent drummer. *New Riders Of The Purple Sage* blended country rock with hippie idealism, but the final link with the Grateful Dead was severed when Garcia made way for Buddy Cage. *Powerglide* and *The Adventures Of Panama Red* brought commercial rewards. Torbert left following *Home, Home On The Road* and was replaced by Skip Battin (b. 1934). In 1978 Dryden took over as manager, while Dawson and Nelson remained at the helm until 1981. The band dissolved following *Feelin' Alright*, although Nelson subsequently resurrected the name with Gary Vogenson (guitar) and Rusty Gautier (bass).

NEW SEEKERS

This popular MOR band originally comprised Eve Graham (b. 1943; vocals), Sally Graham (vocals), Chris Barrington (bass, vocals), Laurie Heath (guitar, vocals) and Marty Kristian (b. 1947; guitar, vocals). They recorded *The New Seekers* before Heath, Barrington and Graham were replaced by Lyn Paul (b. 1949), Peter Doyle (b. 1949, d. 2001) and Paul Layton (b. 1947). 'Look What They've Done To My Song, Ma' and 'Beautiful People' rose high up the US charts, while 'I'd Like To Teach The World To Sing (In Perfect Harmony)' was their greatest international success. 'You Won't Find Another Fool Like Me' reached UK number 1 in 1973. Doyle was subsequently replaced by Peter Oliver (b. 1952; guitar, vocals), but the five disbanded with a farewell tour of Britain.

The lure of a CBS Records contract brought about a re-formation two years later, minus Lyn Paul and with Oliver replaced by Danny Finn, but they disbanded once more in 1978 after a series of failed singles.

NEW YORK DOLLS

One of the most influential rock bands of the last 20 years, the New York

Dolls predated the punk and sleaze metal movements that followed and offered a crash course in rebellion with style. The line-up stabilised in 1972 around David Johansen (b. 1950; vocals), **Johnny Thunders** (b. John Anthony Genzale Jnr., 1952, d. 1991; guitar), Arthur Harold Kane (bass), Sylvain Sylvain (guitar, piano) and Jerry Nolan (d. 1992; drums). Their self-titled debut received critical acclaim, but this never transferred to commercial success.

Too Much Too Soon indicated that alcohol and drugs were beginning to take their toll and they split after bad reviews. Johansen embarked on a solo career and Thunders and Dolan formed the **Heartbreakers**.

NEWMAN, RANDY

One of the great middle American songwriters, Newman (b. 1943) made his name writing hit songs, including: 'Nobody Needs Your Love' and 'Just One Smile' for **Gene Pitney**, 'I Don't Want To Hear It Anymore' for **Dusty Springfield** and **P. J. Proby**, 'I Think It's Going To Rain Today' for **Judy Collins**, 'I've Been Wrong Before' for **Cilla Black**, 'Simon Smith And His Amazing Dancing Bear' for **Alan Price**, and 'Mama Told Me Not To Come' for **Three Dog Night**.

Newman's debut album came in 1968 but failed to sell. In 1970 he contributed to the *Performance* soundtrack and that year **Harry Nilsson** recorded an album of his songs. During the 70s Newman released acclaimed albums such as *Sail Away*, *Good Old Boys* and *Little Criminals*, which gained commercial as well as critical acceptance. He enjoyed a surprise US Top 5 single in 1977 with the controversial 'Short People', while 'I Love Love L.A.' was used to promote the Los Angeles Olympic Games in 1984.

During the 80s and 90s, however, Newman concentrated on soundtrack work (a family tradition – his uncle was a noted Hollywood composer). One of the first examples of his soundtrack work had come as early as 1971, with the movie *Cold Turkey*. More movie scores followed, such as *Ragtime*, *The Natural*, *Parenthood*, *Avalon*, *The Paper* and *Maverick*. He scored the music for the hugely successful Walt Disney movie *Toy Story* in 1995, and other recent credits had included *A Bug's Life*, *Toy Story 2* and *Monsters, Inc.*. With 16 Oscar nominations to his credit, Newman was finally rewarded when he won the Best Original Song trophy in March 2002 for 'If I Didn't Have You', which was featured in *Monsters, Inc.*.

Newman's sporadic studio releases during this period included the semi-autobiographical *Land Of Dreams*, the ambitious *Faust* (featuring **Elton John**, **James Taylor**, **Bonnie Raitt** and **Don Henley**), and *Bad Love*.

NEWTON-JOHN, OLIVIA

Newton-John (b. 1948) was born in England but raised in Australia. She returned to London after winning a television talent show, and recorded her 1966 debut single, 'Till You Say You'll Be Mine'. Newton-John then recorded with Toomorrow before re-establishing her solo career in the early 70s. Her 1971 debut album included a UK Top 10 arrangement of **Bob Dylan**'s 'If Not For You'. In contrast, her country pop recording 'Let Me Be There' won a controversial Grammy for Best Female Country Vocal. She performed in 1974's Eurovision Song Contest, and moved to North America where her standing in pop circles improved considerably with the chart-topper 'I Honestly Love You'. She became renowned for her duets with other artists, notably in *Grease* in which she and John Travolta sang 'You're The One That I Want', one of the most successful singles in UK pop history, topping the charts for nine weeks. 'Summer Nights' was also a UK number 1 in 1978. 'Xanadu', recorded with the **Electric Light Orchestra**, was another global number 1.

During the 80s Newton-John adopted a more raunchy image with singles like 'Physical' (1981) and the 1985 album *Soul Kiss*, but much of the late 80s and early 90s was spent running her Australian-styled clothing business, Blue Koala. The award of an OBE preceded her new marriage, although her life was clouded in 1992 when her fashion empire crashed, and it was announced that she was undergoing treatment for cancer. She subsequently revealed that she had won her battle with the disease, and in 1994 released an album that she had written, produced and paid for herself. At the same time, it was estimated that in a career spanning over 30 years, this showbusiness evergreen had sold more than 50 million records worldwide.

NICE

The Nice, originally **P.P. Arnold**'s back-up band comprised Keith Emerson (b. 1944; keyboards), Brian 'Blinky' Davison (b. 1942; drums), Lee Jackson (b. 1943; bass, vocals) and David O'List (b. 1948; guitar). After leaving Arnold in October 1967, they quickly built a reputation as a visually exciting band, but their debut, *The Thoughts of Emerlist Davjack*, came nowhere near reproducing their live sound. *Ars Longa Vita Brevis*, containing 'America' from *West Side Story*, was released before O'List departed and they continued as a trio. They did not break into the US charts, despite UK chart success with *Nice* and *Five Bridges Suite*. The former contained an excellent reading of **Tim Hardin**'s 'Hang On To A Dream'; the latter was a semi-orchestral suite about working-class life in Newcastle-upon-Tyne and also contained versions of 'Intermezzo From The Karelia Suite' by Sibelius, and Tchaikovsky's 'Pathetique'. The band's attempt at fusing classical music and rock was admirable, and much of what Emerson later achieved with the huge success of **Emerson, Lake And Palmer** should be credited to the brief but valuable career of the Nice.

NICKELBACK

This melodic hard rock band was formed in 1996 in Vancouver, Canada, by brothers Chad (vocals, guitar) and Mike Kroeger (bass), their cousin Brandon (drums), and Ryan Peake (guitar, vocals). In the same year they released the *Hesher* EP and their long-playing debut *Curb*. Ryan Vikedal was installed as drummer on *The State*. The album was originally released on the band's own label, but their burgeoning popularity was rewarded by a major recording contract with EMI Canada and heavy metal label Roadrunner Records in the USA. 'How You Remind Me' from 2001's *Silver Side Up* became a staple on American rock radio. The track eventually climbed to the top of the Hot 100 in December, and also broached the UK Top 5.

NICKS, STEVIE

US singer Nicks (b. Stephanie Nicks, 1948) made her debut in 1973 with Buckingham-Nicks, recorded with her boyfriend **Lindsey Buckingham**. The album was subsequently used to demonstrate studio facilities to Mick Fleetwood, and within weeks the duo were invited to join **Fleetwood Mac**. Nicks provided many of the band's best-known and successful songs, including 'Rhiannon' and 'Dreams'.

Her solo debut, *Bella Donna*, was released in 1981. It spawned two US Top 10 singles – 'Stop Draggin' My Heart Around', a duet with **Tom Petty**, and 'Leather And Lace', with **Don Henley**. *The Wild Heart* produced the hits 'Stand Back' and 'Nightbird', but *Rock A Little*, was less successful, artistically and commercially. She rejoined Fleetwood Mac for their successful comeback album, *Tango In The Night*, before resuming solo activities with 1989's *The Other Side Of The Mirror*. She rejoined Buckingham in Fleetwood Mac when the *Rumours* line-up reconvened in 1997. A solo box set was released the following year. The star-studded but anodyne *Trouble In Shangri-La* returned Nicks to the US Top 10 in 2001.

NICO

Nico (b. Christa Paffgen (Pavolsky), 1938, d. 1988) met **Rolling Stones'** guitarist Brian Jones during a visit to London in the mid-60s, making her

recording debut with 'I'm Not Saying'. She was introduced to Andy Warhol in New York and starred in *Chelsea Girls*, before joining his protégés, the **Velvet Underground**. Nico contributed to their debut album, but resumed a solo career in 1967 with *Chelsea Girl* which included three compositions by a young **Jackson Browne**. Former bandmates **Lou Reed** and **John Cale** also provided memorable contributions, and Cale produced her subsequent three albums. In 1974 she appeared in a brief tour of the UK with ACNE (**Kevin Ayers**, John Cale and **Brian Eno**). After *The End*, she ceased recording, but re-emerged in the post-punk era. Signs of an artistic revival followed treatment for drug addiction, but she died in Ibiza in July 1988, after suffering a cerebral haemorrhage while cycling in intense heat.

NILSSON

While working in banking in Los Angeles, USA, Nilsson (b. Harry Edward Nelson III, 1941, d. 1994) touted demos of his early compositions around the city's publishing houses. In 1967 the **Yardbirds** recorded his 'Ten Little Indians', and he gave up his banking upon hearing the **Monkees'** version of 'Cuddly Toy'. He secured a contract with RCA Records (having released some unsuccessful singles for the Tower label) and made his album debut with *Pandemonium Shadow Show*. His compositions were still popular with other acts, with the **Turtles'** recording 'The Story Of Rock 'N' Roll' and **Three Dog Night** enjoying a US chart-topper and gold disc with 'One'. Nilsson's first US Top 10 hit came after he covered Fred Neil's 'Everybody's Talking', the theme to the movie *Midnight Cowboy*. A series of critically acclaimed but uncommercial albums

followed, before Nilsson enjoyed his greatest success with *Nilsson Schmilsson* and its attendant single, a cover version of **Badfinger's** 'Without You', which sold in excess of one million copies, topping both the US and UK charts and winning a Grammy in 1972. After *Son Of Schmilsson*, Nilsson confounded expectations with *A Little Touch Of Schmilsson In The Night*, containing standards including 'Makin' Whoopee' and 'As Time Goes By'. Drinking buddy **John Lennon** produced the erratic *Pussy Cats* (1974), comprised largely of pop classics.

By the 80s Nilsson had retired from music altogether to pursue business interests. RCA released *A Touch More Schmilsson In The Night* in 1988 offering the singer's renditions of more popular favourites including 'It's Only A Paper Moon' and 'Over The Rainbow'. Nilsson's health began to fail in the 90s, and in 1994 he suffered a massive heart attack. The paradox of his career is that despite achieving recognition as a superior songwriter, his best-known and most successful records were penned by other acts.

NINE INCH NAILS

US multi-instrumentalist Trent Reznor (b. 1965) began recording as Nine Inch Nails in 1988. *Pretty Hate Machine*, written, played and co-produced by Reznor, was largely synthesizer-based, but was transformed onstage by a ferocious wall of guitars. Buoyed by the radio success of the track 'Head Like A Hole', the album achieved platinum status. *The Downward Spiral's* blend of synthesizer textures and guitar fury provided a soundscape for Reznor's exploration of sex, drugs, violence, depression and suicide. The album debuted at US number 2. The first non-Nine Inch Nails releases on Reznor's Nothing label appeared in 1994 (beginning with **Marilyn Manson**), and the band also found time to construct an acclaimed soundtrack for Oliver Stone's movie *Natural Born Killers*. During 1996, Reznor worked with film director David Lynch on the music score for *Lost Highway*, and produced Manson's *Antichrist Superstar*. He returned to his own music in autumn 1999 with the acclaimed 2-CD set, *The Fragile*, which debuted at US number 1.

1910 FRUITGUM COMPANY

This US group were at the forefront of a brief wave of bubblegum-pop in the late 60s. Created by producers Jeff Katz and Jerry Kasenetz, writer Joey Levine was the voice behind the hits such as the 1968 nursery game anthem 'Simon Says', '1, 2, 3, Red Light', 'Goody Goody Gumdrops' and 'Special Delivery'. Levine hastily assembled a touring troupe and kept this manufactured group alive until the end of the decade.

NIRVANA (UK)

Songwriters Patrick Campbell-Lyons (b. Eire) and George Alex Spyropoulos (b. Greece) met in London. They established instant rapport and formed a group, adding Ray Singer (guitar), Brian Henderson (bass), Michael Coe (viola, french horn) and Sylvia Schuster (cello). The quintet, dubbed Nirvana, secured a recording deal with Island Records, making their debut in 1968 with the ambitious *The Story Of Simon Simopath*. Despite their innovative singles, they fell tantalizingly short of a major breakthrough. Campbell-Lyons and Spyropoulos then disbanded the group format and completed a second set as a duo. This featured several of Nirvana's finest songs, including 'Tiny oddess' and 'Rainbow Chaser', the latter becoming a minor UK hit in 1968. Their following albums were considerably more low-key, and Campbell-Lyons completed their fourth album on his own. Campbell-Lyons subsequently issued solo albums before reuniting with Spyropoulos in 1980 to write a musical, and on a more permanent basis in the following decade.

NIRVANA (USA)

Formed in Washington, USA, in 1988, by Kurt Cobain (b. 1967, d. 1994; guitar, vocals), Krist Novoselic (b. 1965; bass) and Chad Channing (drums).

Having signed to Sub Pop Records, they completed their debut single, 'Love Buzz'/'Big Cheese'. Second guitarist Jason Everman was added prior to ¡Bleach¡, although he took no part in the actual recording. The set quickly attracted Nirvana a cult following. Channing left the band following a European tour, and Dan Peters from **Mudhoney** stepped in temporarily. He was featured on 'Sliver', Nirvana's sole 1990 release. Dave Grohl (b. 1969) reaffirmed a sense of stability and the new look trio secured a contract with Geffen Records. The startling *Nevermind* broke the band worldwide and almost single-handedly brought the 'grunge' subculture overground. It topped the US charts early in 1992, while the opening track, 'Smells Like Teen Spirit', reached the US and UK Top 10, confirming that Nirvana now combined critical and popular acclaim.

In early 1992 Cobain and Courtney Love of **Hole** married, but it was obvious that Cobain was struggling with his new role as 'spokesman for a generation'. Press interviews ruminated on the difficulties of recording a follow-up album, also of Cobain's using drugs to stem the pain from a stomach complaint. The trio's follow-up album *In Utero* was produced by Steve Albini. When the record was finally released the effect was not as immediate as *Nevermind*, although Cobain's songwriting remained inspired on 'Penny Royal Tea', 'All Apologies' and 'Rape Me'. His descent into self-destruction accelerated in 1994 as he went into a coma during dates in Italy, before returning to Seattle to shoot himself on 5 April 1994. *MTV Unplugged In New York* offered some small comfort for Cobain's fans, with the singer's understated delivery on various cover versions and Nirvana standards enduring as one of the most emotive sights and sounds of the 90s. Grohl went on to form the **Foo Fighters**, while Novoselic inaugurated the short-lived Sweet 75 in 1997.

NITTY GRITTY DIRT BAND

Formed in California in 1965, this enduring US band originally comprised Jeff Hanna (b. 1947; guitar, vocals), Bruce Kunkel (guitar, vocals), Glen Grosclose (drums), Dave Hanna (guitar, vocals), Ralph Barr (guitar) and Les Thompson (bass, vocals). Grosclose and Dave Hanna quickly made way for Jimmie Fadden (drums, guitar) and **Jackson Browne** (guitar, vocals). Although Browne only remained for a matter of months – he was replaced by John McEuen – his songs remained in the group's repertoire throughout their early career. *Nitty Gritty Dirt Band* comprised jug-band, vaudeville and pop material. *Ricochet* maintained this balance, following which Chris Darrow, formerly of **Kaleidoscope**, replaced Kunkel.

The group completed two further albums before disbanding in 1969. They reconvened the following year around Jeff Hanna, McEuen, Fadden, Thompson and newcomer Jim Ibbotson. The acclaimed *Uncle Charlie And His Dog Teddy* included Jerry Jeff Walker's 'Mr. Bojangles', a US Top 10 hit in 1970. *Will The Circle Be Unbroken* was an expansive collaboration with the group's traditional music mentors, but Thompson departed following its release. The remaining quartet continued with *Stars And Stripes Forever* and *Dreams*. In 1976 the group dropped its 'Nitty Gritty' prefix and undertook a pioneering USSR tour the following year. By 1982 the Dirt Band were an American institution with an enduring international popularity. 'Long Hard Road (Sharecropper Dreams)' and 'Modern Day Romance' topped the country charts in 1984 and 1985, respectively, but the following year McEuen retired from the line-up. Bernie Leadon augmented the group for *Working Band*, but left again upon its completion. Still active in the new millennium, the Dirt Band have continued to maintain their remarkable enthusiasm with several new studio releases and frequent tours.

NO DOUBT

This California-based outfit, comprising Gwen Stefani (b. 1969; vocals), Tom Dumont (b. 1968; guitar), Tony Kanal (b. 1970; bass) and Adrian Young (b. 1969; drums), took America by storm in 1996 following the release of their third album, *Tragic Kingdom*. Formed in December 1986 by Stefani's keyboard-playing brother Eric, the band's original singer John Spence took his own life a year later. With Kanal, Dumont and Young on board, the band signed a deal with Interscope Records in 1991. Their ska-influenced debut sold poorly and Eric Stefani left the band two years later to work as an animator. *Tragic Kingdom* was released in October, but sales only began to pick up when the single 'Just A Girl' broke into the Top 30 on the back of constant radio play. The band ended 1996 at a peak with their album spending nine weeks at the top of the US album chart, and the power ballad 'Don't Speak' all over US and UK radio.

The highly photogenic and media friendly Stefani kept the band's name in the spotlight during a lengthy break from recording. A new single, 'Ex-Girlfriend', was released in 2000 in advance of the laboured *Return Of Saturn*. Much better was the following year's dancehall and new wave-influenced *Rock Steady*, featuring the transatlantic hit single 'Hey Baby'.

NOTORIOUS B.I.G.

A large, imposing figure in contemporary rap before his murder in 1997, the Notorious B.I.G. (b. Christopher Wallace, 1972, d. 1997) grew up in Brooklyn, New York. He first rapped, under the name Biggie Smalls, as part of the neighbourhood group the Old Gold Brothers. He came to the attention of **Sean 'Puffy' Combs** of Bad Boy Entertainment, and made his recording debut in 1993 backing **Mary J. Blige** on 'Real Love'. His 1994 debut album *Ready To Die* became a major hit thanks to the inclusion of singles such as 'Juicy', 'One More Chance' and 'Big Poppa', the latter a US Top 10 hit. He formed M.A.F.I.A. with some of his former hustler colleagues, releasing an album, *Conspiracy*, in 1995.

Wallace became involved in a running feud with rapper **2Pac**, and their disagreement soon festered into a bitter feud between the east and west coast American rap scenes. When 2Pac was murdered, the Notorious B.I.G.'s non-attendance at a rap peace summit in Harlem was widely criticized. Instead he began work on a second album, entitled, prophetically, *Life After Death*. Its cover featured the rapper standing next to a hearse with the number plate B.I.G. He never lived to see its official release. He was gunned down after leaving a party in California in March 1997. Subsequent conjecture indicated that his murder may have been in retaliation for 2Pac's killing. Issued three weeks later, *Life After Death* went straight to the top of the US charts. Two years later the Notorious B.I.G. was back at the top of the charts with *Born Again*, a motley collection of unreleased material.

NUCLEUS

The doyen of British jazz-rock groups, Nucleus was formed in 1969 by Ian Carr (trumpet), Chris Spedding (guitar), John Marshall (drums) and Karl Jenkins (keyboards). This line-up released *Elastic Rock* and *We'll Talk About It Later*, but Spedding's subsequent departure heralded a bewildering succession of changes, undermining their potential. In 1972 Jenkins and Marshall left to join fellow fusion act, **Soft Machine**, and Nucleus became an inadvertent nursery for this 'rival' ensemble. Subsequent albums lacked the innovation of those first releases and Nucleus dissolved during the early 80s.

NUGENT, TED

Nugent (b. 1948), assembled the Chicago, USA-based Amboy Dukes in 1964, assuming increasing control as original members dropped out. In 1974 a revitalized unit ñ dubbed Ted Nugent And The Amboy Dukes – completed the first of two albums, but in 1976 the guitarist embarked on a solo career. Derek St. Holmes (guitar), Rob Grange (bass) and Cliff Davies (drums) joined him for *Ted Nugent* and *Free For All*, both maintaining the high-energy rock of previous incarnations. It was as a live attraction that Nugent made his mark. Ear-piercing guitar and vocals were accompanied by a 'wild man' image. Charlie Huhn (guitar) and John Sauter (bass) replaced St. Holmes and Grange for *Weekend Warriors*, with the same line-up remaining for *State Of Shock* and *Scream Dream*.

In 1982 Nugent established a new unit which included St. Holmes and Carmine Appice (drums) but successive solo releases offered little innovation. In 1989 Nugent teamed up with Tommy Shaw (vocals, guitar; ex-**Styx**), Jack Blades (bass; ex-Night Ranger) and Michael Cartellone (drums) to form the successful 'supergroup', Damn Yankees. In 1994, Nugent resumed his solo career with *Spirit Of The Wild*.

NUMAN, GARY

London, England-born Numan (b. Gary Anthony James Webb, 1958) enjoyed enormous success in the UK in the late 70s. Originally recording as Tubeway Army, Numan topped the UK charts in 1979 with 'Are Friends Electric?' Numan abandoned the group pseudonym for 'Cars' which also topped the UK charts and reached the US Top 10, while *The Pleasure Principle* and *Telekon* entered the UK charts at number 1. His science-fiction orientated lyrics and synthesizer-based rhythms brought further Top 10 successes with 'We Are Glass', 'I Die: You Die' and 'She's Got Claws'. As the decade progressed his record sales declined and his glum-robotic persona was replaced by that of a debonair man-about-town. Despite an atrophied reputation amongst music critics, his fan base remained solid and his recordings continue to reach the lower placings in the UK charts. His career took an upturn in 1996 following the use of 'Cars' in a television advertisement.

NYRO, LAURA

The daughter of a US jazz trumpeter, Nyro's (b. Laura Nigro, 1947, d. 1997) main influences ranged from **Bob Dylan** to John Coltrane, but her 1967 debut *More Than A New Discovery* (aka *The First Songs*) revealed a talent akin to **Carole King** and Ellie Greenwich. Empathy with soul and R&B enhanced her individuality, and artists such as Barbra Streisand, **Blood, Sweat And Tears** and **5th Dimension** covered her material. *Eli And The Thirteenth Confession* and *New York Tendaberry* revealed Nyro's growing introspection and dramatic intonation. *Gonna Take A Miracle*, a collaboration with producers **Kenny Gamble** and **Leon Huff**, acknowledged the music which provided much of the artist's inspiration.

Nyro retired from music altogether before re-emerging in 1975 upon the disintegration of her marriage. Over the next decade she balanced her music career with parenthood, but *Walk The Dog And Light The Light* was her only new release of the 90s. *Stoned Soul Picnic* was a fitting retrospective, but only weeks after its release Nyro succumbed to cancer.

O'CONNOR, SINÉAD

O'Connor (b. 1966) signed with Ensign Records in 1985. She provided the vocals to **U2** guitarist The Edge's film soundtrack for *The Captive* and debuted with 'Troy' (1987). The following year's *The Lion And The Cobra* sold well on the strength of her Top 20 hit 'Mandinka'. To promote her second solo album, O'Connor chose **Prince**'s 'Nothing Compares 2 U'. The track was a transatlantic number 1, and the attendant *I Do Not Want What I Haven't Got* saw similar global success. Her 1990 tour of the USA prompted the first stirrings of a backlash: in New Jersey she refused to go onstage after 'The Star Spangled Banner' was played. Her third album, 1992's *Am I Not Your Girl?*, was a surprising collection of standards and torch songs which received mixed reviews. Further controversy ensued later in the year when O'Connor tore up a photograph of the Pope on US television. Her appearance at the **Bob Dylan** celebration concert shortly afterwards was highly charged as she defied numerous hecklers by staring them out. *Universal Mother* found only marginal success. In 1997, she appeared as an Irish Virgin Mary in Neil Jordan's *The Butcher Boy*, and released the low-key *Gospel Oak* EP. In April 1999, she was ordained as a Catholic priest in an unofficial ceremony in Lourdes, France. The new Mother Bernadette Marie was immediately denounced by the Vatican. The following year's *Faith And Courage* met with a warmer reception.

O'JAYS

Eddie LeVert (b. 1942) and Walter Williams (b. 1942) sang together as a gospel duo before forming the doo-wop-influenced Triumphs in 1958. They recruited William Powell, Bill Isles and Bobby Massey and recorded as the Mascots before becoming the O'Jays. Signing to Imperial Records in 1963, they secured their first hit with 'Lonely Drifter', and achieved their R&B Top 10 debut four years later with 'I'll Be Sweeter Tomorrow (Than I Was Today)'. Isles then left, followed in 1972 by Massey. After **Gamble And Huff** signed them to Philadelphia International Records, 'Back Stabbers' (US Top 3) established the group's style. 'Love Train' introduced the protest lyrics that would feature on their later releases. In 1975, Sammy Strain joined when ill health forced Powell to retire from live performances. Powell continued to record until his death in 1976. 'Message In Our Music' and 'Use Ta Be My Girl' were further hits, and *So Full Of Love* went platinum, but the early 80s were commercially fallow for the O'Jays. *Love Fever* and 1987's 'Lovin' You' resurrected their career. *Love You To Tears* was their best album in many years, echoing the sound of their heyday. Williams and LeVert, whose son Gerald is also a popular soul artist, continue to lead the O'Jays in the new millennium.

O'SULLIVAN, GILBERT

Irish-born singer-songwriter O'Sullivan (b. Raymond O'Sullivan, 1946) signed to CBS Records, releasing a single as Gilbert, before being launched by Gordon Mills on his new MAM label. He debuted in the UK charts with the Top 10 hit 'Nothing Rhymed' (1970). Early UK successes included 'We Will' and 'Alone

Again (Naturally)', with the latter reaching US number 1 and selling over a million copies. *Himself* included the radio favourite 'Matrimony', and was followed by two consecutive UK number 1s, 'Clair' and 'Get Down'. *Back To Front* reached UK number 1 but, despite further hits, his appeal declined.

After a spectacular falling out with Mills, O'Sullivan left MAM and returned to CBS. He became embroiled in a High Court battle against Mills and MAM in 1982. The judge not only awarded O'Sullivan substantial damages and had all agreements with MAM set aside, but decreed that all the singer's master tapes and copyrights should be returned. The case made legal history and had enormous repercussions for the British music publishing world. Nevertheless, O'Sullivan has failed to re-establish his career as a major artist. A series of albums appeared on the Park label and Sullivan now caters for a small but loyal following, enjoying particular success in Japan.

OAKENFOLD, PAUL
UK DJ and remixer who was active in club promotions from the early 80s and became one of the most successful DJs and remixers of the 90s. He worked in New York for a number of record companies, before returning to the UK where he became famed for his sets at Future and Spectrum. In 1989, he set up the label Perfecto Records and remixed the **Happy Mondays'** 'Wrote For Luck' with his musical collaborator Steve Osborne. The pair subsequently remixed for a variety of artists including **Arrested Development**, **Massive Attack**, **M People**, **New Order**, the **Shamen**, **Simply Red**, the **Stone Roses** and U2, and recorded under a number of names including Grace, Virus, the Perfecto Allstars and Wild Colour. Oakenfold also compiled a number of compilation albums for the Ministry Of Sound.

During the late 90s, Oakenfold helped to popularize the trance sound and established himself as one of the best-known DJs in the world, graduating from house towards a melodic, commercial style of trance, particularly through his residency at the UK's Cream. In 1999, Oakenfold found his name in *The Guinness Book Of Records* as The World's Most Successful Club DJ. He also became Director of Music at Home, London's new superclub.

OASIS
From Manchester, England, Oasis became overnight sensations in 1994. The band's creative axis is the Gallagher brothers, Liam (b. 1972; vocals) and Noel (b. 1967; guitar, vocals). Noel worked as a guitar technician for the **Inspiral Carpets** on worldwide tours. Meanwhile Liam joined the band Rain, with Paul 'Bonehead' Arthurs (b. 1965; guitar), Tony McCarroll (drums) and Paul 'Guigsy' McGuigan (b. 1971; bass), who then became Oasis. Noel joined the band in 1992 as lead guitarist and songwriter. The following year, Oasis supported 18 Wheeler in Glasgow. Their five songs were enough to hypnotize Alan McGee, head of Creation Records, who offered them a contract there and then.

The band immediately attracted a torrent of press coverage, much of it focusing on their errant behaviour – punch-ups and violent bickering between the Gallaghers guaranteed full media coverage. High-profile dates ensured that expectations for their debut album were phenomenal. *Definitely Maybe* entered the UK charts at number 1, while 'Live Forever', 'Cigarettes And Alcohol' and 'Whatever' reached the UK Top 10. In 1995, McCarroll left and Alan White (b. 1972) sessioned on their second album. The eagerly anticipated *(What's The Story) Morning Glory?* was rich and assured. 'Some Might Say' debuted at

UK number 1, the acoustic ballad 'Wonderwall' became a staple of UK and US radio, while the plaintive 'Don't Look Back In Anger' provided the band with their second UK chart-topper. The album has gone on to become one of the bestselling UK albums of all time.

The greatly anticipated third album was introduced by the band's third UK number 1 single, 'D'You Know What I Mean?', and sold 800,000 copies in the UK within 24 hours. It received mixed reviews, however, and instigated a period of personal upheaval for the band and the Gallagher brothers. Arthurs and McGuigan left in August 1999, and were replaced by Gem and Andy Bell (ex-**Ride**). The band released their fourth album, *Standing On The Shoulder Of Giants*, through their own Big Brother label. Though it was premiered by February 2000's chart-topping single, 'Go Let It Out', the album was poorly received. Two years later, the band's fifth UK number 1, 'The Hindu Times', and the attendant *Heathen Chemistry* were regarded as a return to form.

OCEAN COLOUR SCENE
This Birmingham, England-based band survived several lean years in the early 90s to triumph in the Britpop era with a string of hugely popular retro-rock hit singles. Simon Fowler (b. 1965; vocals), Steve Cradock (guitar), Damon Minchella (bass) and Oscar Harrison (drums) peddled a generic indie-guitar sound on their 1992 debut for the Fontana Records label. Ocean Colour Scene subsequently walked out on the contract.

Cradock and Minchella worked in **Paul Weller**'s backing band, before Ocean Colour Scene's 'The Riverboat Song' (1996), was heavily promoted on radio, reaching the UK Top 20. The band secured a new contract with MCA Records and released *Moseley Shoals*. The album spawned the UK Top 10 hits 'You've Got It Bad', 'The Day We Caught The Train' and 'The Circle'. *Marchin' Already* was released to unexpected critical disapproval, but generated the hits 'Hundred Mile High City', 'Travellers Tune' and 'Better Day'. *One From The Modern* was less successful, although Cradock enjoyed solo success when he collaborated with Liam Gallagher on the **Jam** tribute single, 'Carnation', a UK Top 10 hit. *Mechanical Wonder* was snuck out with little fanfare in 2001.

OCEAN, BILLY
Raised in England, Trinidad-born singer Ocean (b. Leslie Sebastian Charles, 1950) worked as a session musician before going solo. His mid-70s UK hits included 'Love Really Hurts Without You' and 'Red Light Spells Danger'. Subsequent releases fared less well, but he began to win a US audience and moved there shortly afterwards. After several R&B successes, 'Caribbean Queen (No More Love On The Run)' was his first US pop number 1, selling over a million copies in 1984. A following run of hits included two more US number 1s, 'There'll Be Sad Songs (To Make You Cry)' (1986) and 'Get Outta My Dreams, Get Into My Car' (1988). Despite a UK number 1 with 'When The Going Gets Tough, The Tough Get Going', Ocean's luck in Britain constantly fluctuated. Ocean's commercial fortunes waned in both the US and UK during the following decade.

OCHS, PHIL
US singer-songwriter Ochs (b. 1940, d. 1976) started out with folk act the Sundowners, before moving to Greenwich Village. His early work led to his involvement with the *Broadside* magazine movement. After signing to Elektra Records in the early 60s, he achieved popular acclaim when **Joan Baez** took 'There But For Fortune' into the charts. Ochs moved to A&M Records in 1967 and *Pleasures Of The Harbor* emphasized a greater use of orchestration, as well as an increasingly rock-based perspective. Both *Rehearsals For Retirement* and the sardonically

titled *Phil Ochs' Greatest Hits* showed an imaginative performer bereft of focus. Ochs' later years were marked by tragedy. An attempted strangulation attack permanently impaired his singing voice and, beset by chronic writers' block, Ochs sought solace in alcohol, before succumbing to schizophrenia. He was found hanged at his sister's home in 1976.

OFFSPRING

Although they achieved commercial fortune in the mid-90s, the Offspring had been a staple of the southern Californian punk community since 1984. Bryan 'Dexter' Holland (b. 1966; vocals, guitar) and Greg Kriesel (b. 1965; bass) were initially joined in Manic Subsidal by Doug Thompson (vocals) and Jim Benton (drums). When Thompson left, Holland took over vocals, while Benton was replaced by James Lilja. Kevin 'Noodles' Wasserman (b. 1963; guitar) joined later. Manic Subsidal was rechristened the Offspring in 1985. By 1987, Lilja had been replaced by Ron Welty (b. 1971). Their debut studio album introduced the band's blend of hardcore and pop melodies, but they did not make a commercial breakthrough until the mid-90s. *Smash* achieved multi-platinum status on the back of the MTV hit 'Come Out And Play (Keep 'Em Separated)'. The transatlantic hit single 'Pretty Fly (For A White Guy)' helped boost sales of 1999's *Americana*. The follow-up *Conspiracy Of One* did not deviate from the band's tried and trusted formula.

OHIO EXPRESS

This US bubblegum outfit evolved from the Ohio-based Rare Breed. Joey Levine (lead vocals), Dale Powers (lead guitar), Doug Grassel (rhythm guitar), Jim Pflayer (keyboards), Dean Krastan (bass) and Tim Corwin (drums) debuted with 'Beg, Borrow And Steal' in 1967. The following year they reached the US and UK Top 5 with 'Yummy Yummy Yummy'. By the end of 1969 they had charted on six more occasions, the final time with 'Sausalito (Is The Place To Go)', sung by Graham Gouldman, later of **10cc** fame. The group carried on until 1972.

OLDFIELD, MIKE

British born multi-instrumentalist Oldfield (b. 1953) will forever be remembered for 1973's *Tubular Bells*, which topped the US and UK charts and went on to become a worldwide bestseller.

Oldfield began his career providing acoustic-guitar accompaniment to folk songs sung by his older sister, Sally, but left to join **Kevin Ayers** And The Whole World. *Tubular Bells*, a 49-minute instrumental piece, was released on the new Virgin Records label. Excerpts from it were used in the horror movie, *The Exorcist*, and a shortened version was released as a single, reaching number 7 on the US chart in 1974. The follow-up *Hergest Ridge* reached UK number 1, but did not chart in the USA. *Ommadawn* featured Paddy Moloney playing uillean pipes, and a team of African drummers. Oldfield also had two consecutive Christmas hits with 'In Dulce Jubilo' (1975) and 'Portsmouth' (1976).

Around 1977/8, the shy, withdrawn Oldfield underwent a programme of self-assertiveness, and the result was a complete reversal of personality. *Incantations* drew strongly on disco influences, but *Platinum*, *QE2* and *Five Miles Out* caught Oldfield slightly out of step with his contemporaries. **Hall And Oates** recorded a version of 'Family Man' which became a UK Top 20 hit in 1983. By now Oldfield was working with soprano Maggie Reilly, who sang on his UK number 5 hit 'Moonlight Shadow' from the Top 10 album *Crises*. After *Discovery* he wrote the music for the award-winning film *The Killing Fields*.

Accepting that *Tubular Bells* will always overshadow most of his other work, Oldfield was drawn back to his debut in 1992, working with Trevor

Horn on *Tubular Bells II* to mark the 20th anniversary of the original album. The album topped the UK album chart. Oldfield's subsequent albums predictably failed to make the same commercial impact, and in 1998 he returned to *Tubular Bells* with a third instalment which introduced dance rhythms into the mix. The insipid *The Millennium Bell* was premiered with a typically grandiose live show in Berlin on New Year's Eve 1999.

OMD

This UK synth-pop act was formed by Paul Humphreys (b. 1960) and Andy McCluskey (b. 1959; vocals, guitar). McCluskey and Humphreys, together with Paul Collister, first performed live in 1978 under their full title Orchestral Manoeuvres In The Dark. The success of 'Electricity' allowed the duo to recruit Malcolm Holmes and Dave Hughes. They made their breakthrough in 1980 with the UK Top 10 hit, 'Enola Gay'. *Organisation* followed, with Martin Cooper replacing Hughes shortly afterwards. The more sophisticated *Architecture & Morality* showed a new romanticism, particularly in the UK Top 5 singles 'Souvenir', 'Joan Of Arc' and 'Maid Of Orleans'. *Dazzle Ships* and *Junk Culture* were less successful. Crush saw the permanent insertion of Graham and Neil Weir into the line-up. The band enjoyed a surprise US Top 5 hit in 1986 with 'If You Leave', taken from the soundtrack of the movie *Pretty In Pink*. Following the release of *The Pacific Age*, the Weir brothers and then Holmes, Cooper and Humphreys left the band.

McCluskey retained the name and, after a long restorative period, resurfaced in 1991 with the UK Top 5 hit 'Sailing On The Seven Seas', and the Top 10 follow-up 'Pandora's Box'. McCluskey continued to release records under the OMD moniker into the 1990s, though failing to match the commercial success he enjoyed during the mid-80s. He resurfaced in the new millennium as the musical mastermind behind girl group, **Atomic Kitten**.

ONO, YOKO

Japanese-born Yoko Ono (b. 1933) moved to the USA, becoming immersed in the New York *avant garde* milieu. A reputation as a film-maker and conceptual artist preceded her marriage to **John Lennon** in 1969. Their early collaborations, *Two Virgins*, *Life With The Lions* and *Wedding Album*, were self-indulgent and wilfully obscure, but with the formation of the Plastic Ono Band they forged an exciting musical direction. Unfairly blamed for the **Beatles**' demise, Ono emerged with a series of excellent compositions, including 'Don't Worry Kyoto'. *Yoko Ono / The Plastic Ono Band* was equally compulsive listening and a talent to captivate or confront was also prevalent on *Fly*, *Approximately Infinite Universe* and *Feeling The Space*. The couple's relationship continued to undergo public scrutiny, and the birth of their son Sean resulted in a prolonged retirement.

The Lennons re-emerged in 1980 with *Double Fantasy*. They were returning home from completing a new Yoko Ono single on the night Lennon was shot dead. The resultant track, 'Walking On Thin Ice', was thus imbued with a certain poignancy, but Ono's ensuing albums have failed to match its intensity. After a ten-year hiatus, Ono returned to music in 1995, recording *Rising* together with Sean and his band Ima.

ORANGE JUICE

Scottish pop group formed in the late-70s by **Edwyn Collins** (b. 1959; vocals, guitar), James Kirk (vocals, rhythm guitar), David McClymont (bass) and Steven

Daly (drums). They began their career on Postcard Records, with singles including 'Falling And Laughing'. After signing to Polydor Records they issued the acclaimed *You Can't Hide Your Love Forever*. Kirk and Daly were then replaced by Malcolm Ross and Zeke Manyika. *Rip It Up* was another strong work, and the title track reached the UK Top 10 in 1982. The band, reduced to Collins and Manyika, completed the energetic *Texas Fever*, and an eponymous third album. Collins subsequently went solo, while Ross joined **Aztec Camera**.

ORB

The Orb revolves around Alex Paterson (b. Duncan Robert Alex Paterson). He formed the Orb in 1988 with Jimmy Cauty, and their first release proper came with the following year's *Kiss* EP. This was completely overshadowed by 'A Huge Ever-Growing Pulsating Brain That Rules From The Centre Of The Ultraworld', a marriage of progressive-rock trippiness and a centre point sample of Minnie Riperton's 'Loving You'.

The band signed with Big Life Records, but Cauty departed in 1990. In the event the ethereal 'Little Fluffy Clouds', with co-writer Youth, was the next Orb release, though that too ran into difficulties when the sample of **Rickie Lee Jones** attracted the artist's displeasure. The debut album was fully in tune with, and in many ways anticipative of, the blissed-out rave sub-culture of the early 90s, mingled with dashes of early 70s progressive rock. The Orb, now featuring Paterson and Thrash (b. Kristian Weston), confirmed their popularity when *U.F.Orb* soared to the top of the UK charts in 1992, and the 39 minute single 'Blue Room' reached the Top 10.

Their first studio set for new label Island Records, *Pomme Fritz*, saw Paterson recording with German technoist Thomas Fehlmann and steering the Orb's sound away from ambient house. Following its release Weston left, allowing Fehlmann to adopt a more prominent role on 1995's *Orbus Terrarum*. Critics were more impressed by the follow-up *Orblivion*'s return to the ambient house style of the Orb's earlier work. The album was recorded by Paterson, Fehlmann and new musical partner, Andy Hughes, who was also present on the delayed follow-up *Cydonia*.

ORBISON, ROY

One of the leading US singers of the 60s, Orbison (b. 1936, d. 1988) began as a staff writer for Acuff-Rose Music. He later signed with the Monument Records label and, shortly afterwards, charted in the US with 'Up Town' (1960). A few months later, his 'Only The Lonely' was rejected by **Elvis Presley** and the **Everly Brothers**, and Orbison decided to record it himself. The song topped the UK charts and narrowly missed US number 1.

The shy and quiet-spoken Orbison donned a pair of dark-tinted glasses to cover up his chronic astigmatism. Over the next five years he enjoyed unprecedented transatlantic success, repeating his formula with further stylish but melancholy ballads, including 'Blue Angel', 'Running Scared', 'Crying', 'Dream Baby', 'Blue Bayou' and 'In Dreams'. He had two UK number 1 singles, 'It's Over' and 'Oh Pretty Woman'. Tragically, in 1966, his wife Claudette was killed falling from the back of his motorcycle, and in 1968 a fire destroyed his home, taking the lives of his two sons.

Orbison's musical direction understandably faltered in the following decade. He bounced back in 1980, winning a Grammy for his duet with **Emmylou Harris** on 'That Lovin' You Feelin' Again' from the movie *Roadie*. Six years later David Lynch used 'In Dreams' to haunting effect in his chilling *Blue Velvet* in 1986.

The following year, he was inducted into the Rock And Roll Hall Of Fame. He then joined the **Traveling Wilburys**, and their hit debut album owed much to Orbison's major input. Less than a month after its critically acclaimed release, Orbison suffered a fatal heart attack. The posthumously released *Mystery Girl* was his most successful album.

ORBIT, WILLIAM

Although he has been recording under various guises since 1983, it was only in the late 90s that UK DJ Orbit (b. William Wainwright) became a household name because of his acclaimed production and writing work on **Madonna**'s *Ray Of Light* and **Blur**'s *13*.

In his early twenties Orbit formed Torch Song with Laurie Mayer, Grant Gilbert and Rico Conning, who released *Wish Thing*, *Ecstasy*, *Exhibit A* and *Toward The Unknown* between 1984 and 1995. For his solo debut, 1987's *Orbit*, he continued to work with Mayer as his co-writer and brought in Peta Nikolich as vocalist. As Bassomatic, Orbit enjoyed his first UK Top 10 single in 1990 with the club anthem 'Fascinating Rhythm'. Alongside his work as Bassomatic, Orbit had been recording ambient soundscape albums, beginning with 1987's *Strange Cargo*. In the early 90s, Orbit worked with **Beth Orton** as Spill and recorded *Superpinkymandy* but this was released only in Japan under Orton's name.

In 1995, as the Electric Chamber, Orbit released an album of reinterpreted modern classical pieces, *Pieces In A Modern Style*, but the album was quickly withdrawn when it was discovered that the estates of two of the composers had not given permission for him to record the works. The album was effectively re-released in 2000 by WEA Records with several new tracks and recordings. The album reached number 2 in the UK. Orbit also worked with Madonna on the hit single 'Beautiful Stranger' and the soundtrack for the movie *The Next Best Thing*, and produced the **All Saints**' hit 'Pure Shores'.

ORBITAL

This UK techno outfit have done much to deliver the possibilities of improvisation to live electronic music. Formed by brothers Paul (b. 1968) and Phillip Hartnoll (b. 1964), Orbital debuted in 1990 with the UK Top 20 hit 'Chime'. They also worked on releases by artists such as the **Shamen** and **EMF**, and broke through to a wider audience with 1994's *Snivilisation*, a largely instrumental political concept album. The exquisitely dense rhythms on *In Sides* emphasized the Hartnoll's ability to blend the experimental with the accessible. Having first experimented with the use of film soundtracks on *Snivilisation*, they reworked the theme of *The Saint* for the movie remake of the cult 60s television programme and enjoyed a UK number 3 hit. Their 1999 release, *The Middle Of Nowhere*, marked a return to a more 'danceable' sound. The duo's sixth studio set, *The Altogether*, drew on a diverse range of influences from the dance and pop worlds.

ORTON, BETH

UK singer Orton (b. 1970) pulled off the unlikely task of making folk-influenced music hip among mid-90s clubbers. Orton was originally more interested in an acting career than in being a singer, but when **William Orbit** recruited her to record some spoken text for his *Strange Cargo* project. She made further guest appearances with Orbit, recording the extremely rare *Superpinkymandy* for the Japanese market in 1993. She then worked

with Red Snapper and the **Chemical Brothers**, singing the sublime 'Alive: Alone' on the latter's highly acclaimed 1995 debut, *Exit Planet Dust*. Her debut album proper, *Trailer Park*, was rivalled only by **Portishead**'s *Dummy* as a prime choice chillout album.

In 1997, Orton appeared on the Chemical Brothers' massively successful *Dig Your Own Hole* singing the chillout classic, 'Where Do I Begin?'. *The Best Bit* EP, released the same December, featured Orton duetting with her musical hero Terry Callier on a cover version of Fred Neil's 'Dolphins'. Callier appeared on Orton's eagerly anticipated follow-up, *Central Reservation*, an album which replicated the ramshackle charm of her debut.

OSBORNE, JEFFREY

US singer Osborne (b. 1948) appeared with L.T.D. (Love, Togetherness And Devotion) from 1970 until its disbandment 12 years later. Under George Duke's supervision, Osborne recorded the US Top 40 hit 'I R Wings Of Love'. The latter was a 'sleeper' hit in the UK, after 'Don't You Get So Mad' and the title track of 1983's *Stay With Me Tonight* had made headway there. *Emotional* was a strong album, as were the subsequent singles, one of which, 'You Should Be Mine (The Woo Woo Song)', reached the US Top 20. For two years, Osborne chose, perhaps unwisely, to rest on his laurels, although 'Love Power', a duet with **Dionne Warwick**, climbed to US number 12 in 1987. In 1990, Osborne transferred to Arista Records. Airplay for his increasingly predictable output was no longer automatic, however, and he was unable to restore his commercial profile. He left Arista in 1994 and recorded a Christmas album in 1997. He resurfaced in 2000 with a new album for Windham Hill Records.

OSBORNE, JOAN

US artist Osborne (b. 1962) began her singing career at the Abilene blues bar in New York, USA. The live album *Soul Show* was released on her own Womanly Hips Records in 1991 and an EP, *Blue Million Miles*, followed in 1993. Her major label debut *Relish* featured Eric Bazilian (guitar, ex-Hooters), who wrote the infectious US Top 5 single 'One Of Us'. Critical praise included one magazine describing Osborne as 'one of the most distinct voices in rock'. While recording the follow-up to *Relish*, Osborne toured with Lilith Fair. The eclectic *Righteous Love* was released in 2000 by Interscope Records.

OSBOURNE, OZZY

In 1979, UK rock vocalist Osbourne (b. John Osbourne, 1948) left **Black Sabbath**. His own band was set up with Lee Kerslake (drums), Bob Daisley (bass) and Randy Rhoads (b. Randall William Rhoads, 1956, d. 1982; guitar). Their debut was *Blizzard Of Oz*. By their second album, Daisley and Kerslake had been replaced by drummer Tommy Aldridge and bass player Rudy Sarzo. Osbourne constantly courted publicity, famously having to undergo treatment for rabies after biting the head off a bat. In 1982, the talented Rhoads was killed in an air crash; his replacement was Brad Gillis. Following a tour which saw Sarzo and Gillis walk out, Osbourne was forced to rethink the line-up; Daisley rejoined, along with guitarist Jake E. Lee. Aldridge left following *Bark At The Moon* and was replaced by Carmine Appice (b. 1946). This combination was short-lived, however, with Randy Castillo replacing Appice, and Phil Soussan joining on bass. The 1988 release, *No Rest For The Wicked*, also featured US guitarist Zakk Wylde, who would form an important part of the Osbourne band for the next seven years.

In the late 80s, Osbourne went on trial in America for allegedly using his lyrics to incite youngsters to commit suicide; he was eventually cleared. In 1989, he enjoyed a US Top 10 hit with a duet with Lita Ford, 'Close My Eyes Forever'. He embarked on a farewell tour in 1992, but predictably, neither retirement nor atonement sat too comfortably with the man, and in 1995 he released the excellent *Ozzmosis*.

Osbourne subsequently inaugurated the Ozz-Fest, a heavy metal tour package featuring himself and other hard rock bands. The tour proved to be a huge success, and remains a lucrative concern into the new millennium. At the end of the 90s Osbourne rejoined the original line-up of Black Sabbath for a series of highly successful live shows. His family life was also featured on a US television show, *The Osbournes*.

OSIBISA

Formed in London, England in 1969, by three Ghanaian and three Caribbean musicians, Osibisa played a central role in developing an awareness of African

music in the 70s. The Ghanaian members – Teddy Osei (saxophone), Sol Amarfio (drums) and Mac Tontoh (trumpet) – were joined by Spartacus R (b. Grenada; bass), Robert Bailey (b. Trinidad; keyboards) and Wendel Richardson (b. Antigua; lead guitar). Ghanaian percussionist Darko Adams (b. 1932, d. 1995) joined soon after.

Osibisa proved to be an immediate success, with the single 'Music For Gong Gong' a substantial UK hit in 1970 (three other singles later made the British Top 10: 'Sunshine Day', 'Dance The Body Music' and 'Coffee Song'). *Woyaya* reached UK number 11, and its title track was later covered by **Art Garfunkel**. During the late 70s Osibisa spent much of their time on world tours, playing to particularly large audiences in Japan, India, Australia and Africa. By this time, however, their star was in decline in Europe and America. The band continued touring and releasing records, but to steadily diminishing audiences. Effectively disbanded, Osibisa occasionally staged reunion concerts before Osei put together a new line-up for 1996's *Monsore*.

OSMOND, DONNY

The most successful solo artist to emerge from the family group, the **Osmonds**, Donny's (b. Donald Clark Osmond, 1957) first solo success came in 1971 with a version of Billy Sherrill's 'Sweet And Innocent', which reached the US Top 10. In 1972, Osmondmania reached Britain, and a revival of **Paul Anka**'s 'Puppy Love' gave Donny his first UK number 1. The American singer's clean-cut good looks and perpetual smile brought him massive coverage in the pop press. His material appeared to concentrate on the pangs of adolescent love, which made him the perfect teenage idol for the period. In 1974, Donny began a series of duets with his sister Marie, which included more UK Top 10 hits.

After the break-up of the Osmonds in 1980, Donny went on to star in the 1982 revival of the musical *Little Johnny Jones*. A decade later, a rugged Osmond returned with 'I'm In It For Love' and the more successful 'Soldier Of Love' which reached the US Top 30. Osmond proved his versatility again in the 90s by playing the lead in Canadian and North American productions of Andrew Lloyd Webber and Tim Rice's musical *Joseph And The Amazing Technicolor Dreamcoat*. He reunited with Marie in 1998 to co-host the television talk show, *Donny And Marie*. Donny Osmond returned to the studio in the new millennium to record a collection of Broadway hits.

OSMONDS

This famous family all-vocal group from Utah, USA, comprised Alan Osmond (b. 1949), Wayne Osmond (b. 1951), Merrill Osmond (b. 1953), Jay Osmond (b. 1955) and **Donny Osmond** (b. 1957). The group first appeared in the late 60s on the top-rated *Andy Williams Show*. Initially known as the Osmond Brothers they recorded for Williams' record label Barnaby. In 1971, they recorded 'One Bad Apple', which topped the US charts for five weeks. As a group, they enjoyed a string of hits, including 'Yo Yo' and 'Down By The Lazy River'. By the time Osmondmania hit the UK in 1972, the group peaked with their ecologically conscious 'Crazy Horses'. Further hits included 'Going Home', 'Let Me In' and 'I Can't Stop'. Their sole UK number 1 as a group was 'Love Me For A Reason', composed by Johnny Bristol. The individual members continued to prosper in varying degrees, but the family group disbanded in 1980. Two years later, the older members of the group re-formed without Donny, and moved into the country market. The second generation of the Osmonds began performing and recording during the 90s.

OTWAY, JOHN

This enigmatic UK singer-songwriter (b. 1952) first came to prominence in the early 70s with his guitar/fiddle-playing partner Wild Willy Barrett. Extensive gigging, highlighted by crazy stage antics, won Otway and Barrett a loyal collegiate following and finally a minor hit with 'Really Free' in 1977. Although Otway (with and without Barrett) soldiers on, he remains a cult item.

OUTKAST

US rap duo comprising 'Dre' (b. Andre Benjamin, 1975) and 'Big Boi' (b. Antoine Patton, 1975), who first met while studying at Atlanta's Tri-City high school. The duo broke big with 1994's 'Player's Ball', produced by Organized Noise. The track featured on the duo's platinum-selling debut, *Southernplayalisticadillacmuzik*. 'Elevators (Me & You)' became a major rap chart success in July 1996 and broke into the US Top 20, while the attendant *ATLiens* debuted at number 2 on the album chart. The musically diverse and mystically inclined *Aquemini* repeated the success of its predecessor. *Stankonia*'s mindbending fusion of funk and hip-hop soundtracked a wickedly satirical examination of the state of the constitution. This superb album also featured the US chart-topper 'Ms. Jackson'.

OUTLAWS

Formed in Florida, USA in 1974, by Billy Jones (guitar), Henry Paul (b. 1949; guitar), Hugh Thomasson (guitar), Monte Yoho (drums) and Frank O'Keefe (bass), the Outlaws earned respect for their unreconstructed country rock. First signing to Arista Records, their 1975 debut album reached the US Top 20. A coast-to-coast tour in 1976 saw the arrival of second drummer, David Dix. Further personnel changes saw O'Keefe replaced by Harvey Arnold, while *Bring It Back Alive* was the first album without Paul (replaced by Freddy Salem). His resignation was followed by those of Yoho and Arnold. In 1981, the band was on the edge of the US Top 20 with the title track of *Ghost Riders*, but they disbanded shortly after *Los Hombres Malo*. Paul later rejoined Thomasson in a re-formed Outlaws who issued 1986's *Soldiers Of Fortune*. Paul went on to form Blackhawk.

P. M. DAWN

This US hip-hop act, who enjoyed huge crossover success in the early 90s, was formed by brothers Prince Be (b. Attrell Cordes, 1970) and DJ Minute Mix (b. Jarrett Cordes, 1971). After signing to Gee Street Records, they took the name P.M. Dawn, indicating 'the transition from dark to light'. 'A Watcher's Point Of View', broke into the UK Top 40, introducing their melodic hip-hop to a larger audience. 'Set Adrift On Memory Bliss', based around a sample of **Spandau Ballet**'s 'True', hit number 3 in the UK charts, but was even more successful in their native country, where it topped the Hot 100. *Of The Heart, Of The Soul And Of The Cross: The Utopian Experience* emerged in September 1991 to rave reviews. Further hits followed with 'Reality Used To Be A Friend Of Mine', 'I'd Die Without You' (from the soundtrack to the Eddie Murphy movie *Boomerang*) and 'Looking Through Patient Eyes' (based around a sample of **George Michael**'s 'Father Figure'). Minute Mix, meanwhile, had changed his name to J.C. The Eternal, and Prince Be had become The Nocturnal. The duo's subsequent releases have failed to match the commercial ascendancy of their earlier work.

PAGE, JIMMY

A gifted UK rock guitarist, Page (b. James Patrick Page, 1944) began his career during the early 60s. A member of several groups, he became a respected

session musician, playing on releases by **Lulu** and **Them**, and on sessions for the **Kinks** and the **Who**. After releasing 'She Just Satisfies' (1965), he produced singles for **Nico** and **John Mayall**. Page joined the **Yardbirds** in 1966, staying with them until they split in 1968. He formed **Led Zeppelin**, for whom his riffs established the framework on tracks including 'Whole Lotta Love', 'When The Levee Breaks' and 'Achilles Last Stand'. His acoustic technique is featured on 'Black Mountain Side' and 'Tangerine'.

Page's post-Led Zeppelin recordings have been ill-focused. He contributed to the soundtrack of *Death Wish II*, and collaborated with **Paul Rodgers** in Firm. *Outrider* (1988) did much to re-establish his reputation with contributions from **Robert Plant** and Jason Bonham. *Coverdale/Page* (1993) was a successful but fleeting partnership with the former **Whitesnake** singer, but it was his reunion with Plant for the ironically titled *Unledded* project, and an album of new material in 1998, that really captured the public's imagination. Page also achieved an unlikely UK hit single the same year, collaborating with **Puff Daddy** on 'Come With Me', from the *Godzilla* soundtrack. In 2000, Page teamed up with the **Black Crowes** for a series of highly-praised US concerts. The two final shows at the L.A. Amphitheater were captured for posterity on *Live At The Greek*.

PALMER, ROBERT

Britian's leading blue-eyed soul singer, Palmer (b. Alan Palmer, 1949) joined the Mandrake Paddle Steamer in the late 60s, then the Alan Bown Set, followed by Dada, a jazz/rock unit featuring **Elkie Brooks**. Out of Dada came Vinegar Joe, with which he made three albums. His solo debut *Sneakin' Sally Through The Alley* (1974) featured backing from the Meters and Lowell George, while **Little Feat** appeared on *Pressure Drop*. Now based in America, Palmer enjoyed his first US hit in 1979 with 'Bad Case Of Loving You'. 'Johnny And Mary' and 'Some Guys Have All The Luck' made the UK charts

before Palmer joined the Power Station in 1985. *Riptide* gave him his biggest solo success, and featured the worldwide hits 'Addicted To Love' and 'I Didn't Mean To Turn You On'. He returned to the UK Top 10 periodically over the next few years, including 'She Makes My Day' and a cover version of **Bob Dylan**'s 'I'll Be Your Baby Tonight'. Palmer remains a respected artist, songwriter and the possessor of an excellent voice.

PANTERA

Texas, USA-based heavy-metal quartet formed in 1981 by Terry Glaze (guitar, vocals), Darrell Abbott (b. 1966; guitar), Vincent Abbott (b. 1964; drums) and Rex Rocker (b. Rex Brown, 1964; bass). They debuted with *Metal Magic* in 1983. *Projects In The Jungle* indicated that they were building their own sound, and was followed by a number of name changes: Glaze became Terence Lee, Darrell Abbott switched to Diamond (later Dimebag) Darrell, and brother Vince emerged as Vinne Paul. *Power Metal* was the first album with Phil Anselmo on lead vocals, and marked the conversion to their trademark heavy thrash sound. *Cowboys From Hell* and the following *Vulgar Display Of Power* and *Far Beyond Driven* were all major transatlantic hits. Their influence on the new wave of alternative metal bands that emerged in the late 90s, such as **Korn** and **Fear Factory**, should also be noted. Anselmo indulged his love of black metal in the side project, *Viking Crown*, debuting with 1999's *Unorthodox Steps Of Ritual*.

PAPA ROACH

Originating from California, this US nu-metal outfit was formed in 1993 by high school friends Jacoby Shaddix aka Coby Dick (b. 1976; vocals), Dave Buckner (b. 1976; drums) and Will James (bass), with Jerry Horton (b. 1975; guitar) joining shortly afterwards. The quartet named themselves after Shaddix's grandfather, and adopted the cockroach as an abiding symbol of resilience and longevity. The band's debut long-player, *Potatoes For Christmas*, was released on their own label in 1994. In 1996 Tobin Esperance (b. 1980) was brought in to replace James. Their second album, *Old Friends From Young Years*, established a prominent hip-hop influence, with Coby Dick often rapping entire verses of songs. Their major label debut, *Infest*, perfected the band's ferocious rap-metal hybrid. The suicide anthem 'Last Resort' hit an instant chord with many young Americans, helping *Infest* climb into the US Top 5.

PARADISE LOST

Formed in Yorkshire, England, in 1981, this death metal quintet took their name from John Milton's poem. They originally comprised Nick Holmes (b. 1970), Gregor Mackintosh (b. 1970; guitar), Aaron Aedy (b. 1969; guitar), Stephen Edmondson (b. 1969; bass) and Matthew Archer (b. 1970; drums). *Lost Paradise* and *Gothic* established the band's sound, before they found a wider audience with *Shades Of God* and gained a strong foothold on MTV with the release of 1993's *Icon*. Archer was replaced by Lee Morris, who joined in time for *Draconian Times*. Following the release of the disappointing, experimental *One Second*, the band signed to EMI Records and attempted to reaffirm their metal credentials with *Host* and *Believe In Nothing*.

PARIS, MICA

Having worked with heavyweights including **Prince**, Paris (b. Michelle Wallen, 1969) remains an underrated UK soul talent. She debuted in 1989 with *So Good*, but it wasn't until 1998's *Black Angel*, that Paris came close to fulfilling her promise.

PARKER, GRAHAM

UK artist Parker (b. 1950) came to prominence in the mid-70s with his backing group the Rumour, featuring **Brinsley Schwarz** (guitar, vocals), Bob Andrews (keyboards, vocals), Martin Belmont (guitar, vocals), Andrew Bodnar (bass) and

Steve Goulding (drums). Radio London DJ Charlie Gillett helped engender a recording deal with Vertigo Records and *Howlin' Wind* and *Heat Treatment* received great acclaim. Despite enjoying success with 'Hold Back The Night' (1978), Parker's momentum stalled after divided critical opinion of *Stick To Me* and *The Parkerilla*. *Squeezing Out Sparks*, reclaimed former glories, but *The Up Escalator* marked the end of Parker's partnership with the Rumour.

The remainder of the 80s was spent rebuilding his career and personal life in the USA. *The Mona Lisa's Sister* and *Human Soul* marked a return to form, and indicated Parker's desire to expand the perimeters of his style. Into the 90s, Parker proved fully capable, and confident, of performing to large audiences solo, with acoustic guitar or with full backing. The well-received *12 Haunted Episodes* was released in 1995, but the follow-up, *Acid Bubblegum*, showed little signs of any artistic progress. Parker, however, retains his cult following and published his first collection of short stories in 2000.

PARLIAMENT

This US group was formed in 1955 as vocal quintet the Parliaments by **George Clinton** (b. 1940), Raymond Davis (b. 1940), Calvin Simon (b. 1942), Clarence 'Fuzzy' Haskins (b. 1941) and Grady Thomas (b. 1941). Clinton fashioned the group after the influential **Frankie Lymon And The Teenagers**. 'I Wanna Testify' reached the US Top 20 in 1967, but record company problems prevented the group from building on the success of the single.

Clinton preferred to abandon the Parliaments' name altogether in order to be free to sign elsewhere. He took the existing line-up and its backing group to Westbound Records, where the entire collective recorded as **Funkadelic**. The same musicians were signed to the Invictus label as Parliament. This group unleashed the experimental and eclectic *Osmium* before securing an R&B hit with the irrepressible 'Breakdown'. For the next three years the 'Parliafunkadelicament Thang' would concentrate on Funkadelic releases, but disagreements with the Westbound hierarchy inspired Parliament's second revival. Signed to the Casablanca label in 1974, some 40 musicians were now gathered together under the P. Funk banner, including several refugees from the **James Brown** camp including **Bootsy Collins**, Fred Wesley and Maceo Parker. Parliament's success within the R&B chart continued with 'Give Up The Funk (Tear The Roof Off The Sucker)' (1976), and two 1978 bestsellers, 'Flashlight' and 'Aqua Boogie (A Psychoalphadiscobetabioaquadoloop)', where the group's hard-kicking funk was matched by the superlative horn charts and their leader's unorthodox vision. Their last chart entry was in 1980 with 'Agony Of Defeet', after which Clinton decided to shelve Parliament once again. He has periodically revived the name for recording purposes.

PARSONS, ALAN

UK recording engineer Parsons (b. 1949) attracted attention for his work on the **Beatles**' album, *Abbey Road*. His reputation was established by production work on **Pink Floyd**'s landmark recording *Dark Side Of The Moon*. Parsons subsequently forged a partnership with songwriter Eric Woolfson, creating the Alan Parsons Project. *Tales Of Mystery And Imagination*, inspired by Edgar Allen Poe, set the pattern for future releases examining specific themes: science fiction (*I Robot*) and mysticism (*Pyramid*). Parsons and Woolfson created crafted, if sterile, work, calling on session men and guest performers. However, despite enjoying a US Top 5 single in 1982 with 'Eye In The Sky', the Alan Parsons Project's subsequent recordings have failed to repeat the commercial success of those early releases. Parsons became the head of EMI studio interests in June 1997.

PARSONS, GRAM

Parsons' (b. Ingram Cecil Connor III, 1946, d. 1973) brief but influential career began in high school band, the Pacers before he joined the Shilos in 1963. The quartet moved to New York's Greenwich Village, but Parsons left in 1965. Inspired by the folk-rock boom, he founded the International Submarine Band with John Nuese (guitar), Ian Dunlop (bass) and Mickey Gauvin (drums). After two singles and a relocation to Los Angeles, Parsons was signed by producer Lee Hazelwood, but with Dunlop and Gauvin now absent from the line-up, Bob Buchanan (guitar) and Jon Corneal (drums) joined for *Safe At Home*. This album is viewed as a landmark of country rock's development, blending standards with Parsons originals. By the time of its 1968 release, Parsons had accepted an offer to join the **Byrds**. His induction resulted in *Sweetheart Of The Rodeo*, which followed *Safe At Home*'s mould. Although Parsons' role as vocalist was later diminished by Hazelwood's court injunction – the producer claimed it breached their early contract – his influence was undeniable, as exemplified on the stellar 'Hickory Wind'.

Parsons left the Byrds in protest over a South African tour, and formed the **Flying Burrito Brothers** with Chris Hillman, 'Sneaky' Pete Kleinow and Chris Ethridge. The excellent *The Gilded Palace Of Sin* drew inspiration from southern

soul and urban-country music, but the follow-up *Burrito Deluxe* failed to scale the same heights and Parsons was fired in 1970 due to his growing drug dependency. In 1972 Parsons was introduced to **Emmylou Harris** and they completed *GP*. A tour leading the Fallen Angels followed, but Parsons' self-destructive appetite remained. Sessions for a second set, *Grievous Angel*, blended favourites with original songs. Parsons' death in 1973 as a result of 'drug toxicity' and his desert cremation added to his legend. Parsons' influence on a generation of performers, from the **Eagles** to **Elvis Costello**, is a fitting testament to his talent.

PARTON, DOLLY

After childhood appearances as a singing guitarist on local radio, US country singer-songwriter Parton (b. 1946) left school in 1964. She signed to Monument Records in 1966, yielding a C&W hit, 'Dumb Blonde', as well as enlistment in the *Porter Wagoner Show*. Her country hits during this period included the autobiographical 'Coat Of Many Colours', as well as a number of duets with Wagoner.

Parton resigned from the show in 1974 after pop success with the solo 'Jolene'. Her post-1974 repertoire was less overtly country, with 1979's 'Baby I'm Burning' a lucrative stab at disco. She also ventured into film acting, starring in *9 To 5* (the title song reached the top of the US charts), *Best Little Whorehouse In Texas*, *Rhinestone* and *Steel Magnolias*. She teamed up with **Kenny Rogers** in 1983 on 'Islands in the Stream', a **Bee Gees** composition, reaching the top of the US singles chart. *Trio*, with **Linda Ronstadt** and **Emmylou Harris**, won a Grammy for best country album (1987).

Parton continued to record prolifically during the 90s. In 1992 **Whitney Houston** had a massive international hit with Parton's composition 'I Will Always Love You'. *Treasures* paid tribute to singer-songwriters of the 60s and 70s. In a busy 1999, Parton reunited with Harris and Ronstadt for a second *Trio* album, and released her first ever bluegrass collection, *The Grass Is Blue*. *Little Sparrow*, in a similar style was even better.

PAUL, LES

Paul (b. 1915) began broadcasting on US radio in the early 30s and by 1936 was leading his own trio. Although his work had a strong country leaning, Paul was highly adaptable, frequently sitting in with jazz musicians. Dissatisfied with the sound of the guitars he played, he developed and designed a solid-bodied instrument at his own expense. Paul's dissatisfaction extended beyond the instrument and into the recording studios. Eager to experiment with a multi-tracking concept, he played multi-track guitar on a succession of recordings, among them 'Brazil' and 'Whispering'. During the 50s Paul continued with similar recordings, while his wife, Mary Ford (b. 1928, d. 1977), sang multiple vocal lines. 'How High The Moon' and 'Vaya Con Dios' reached US number 1.

Paul retired in the early 1960s, returning in the late 70s for two successful albums of duets with Chet Atkins, but by the end of the decade he had retired again. In 1984 he made a comeback to performing and has continued to make sporadic appearances.

PAVEMENT

Formed in California, USA, in 1989, Pavement were originally a duo with Stephen Malkmus (vocals, guitar) and Scott 'Spiral Stairs' Kannberg (guitar). They extended to a five-piece, adding Gary Young (percussion), Bob Nastanovich (drums) and Mark Ibold (bass). The attraction on their debut, *Slay Tracks (1933–69)*, the first in a series of EPs for the Drag City label, was Malkmus' free-ranging, observational lyrics. The band's eclectic stew of musical styles was heard to great effect on their debut long-player, *Slanted And Enchanted*. Steve West replaced Young in 1993, but they continued rising to the top of the US alternative scene. By the time of *Brighten The Corners*, they were identified as an important influence on the new lo-fi direction of **Blur**. *Terror Twilight* earned the band an unlikely UK Top 20 placing, but Pavement was subsequently put on indefinite hold, allowing Malkmus to work on his self-titled solo debut.

Kannberg's *All This Sounds Gas* was recorded under the moniker Preston School Of Industry.

PAXTON, TOM

US singer-songwriter Paxton (b. 1937) moved to New York in the early 60s, becoming an aspiring performer on Greenwich Village's coffee-house circuit. Two topical song publications, *Sing Out!* and *Broadside*, published his compositions which bore a debt to Pete Seeger and Bob Gibson. Paxton signed to Elektra Records for whom he recorded his best-known work, *Ramblin' Boy*, which included the enduring ballad 'The Last Thing On My Mind'. Subsequent releases continued this mixture of romanticism, social protest and children's songs. Paxton left Elektra during the early 70s. He has subsequently concentrated on writing songs and books for children. Although he was never fêted in the manner of his early contemporaries **Bob Dylan**, **Phil Ochs** and Eric Andersen, his work reveals a thoughtful, perceptive craftsmanship.

PEARL JAM

Jeff Ament (b. 1963; bass) and Stone Gossard (b. 1965; rhythm guitar) formed this rock quintet in Seattle, USA, in the early 90s. Gossard and Ament played with Mother Love Bone, fronted by Andrew Wood who later died from a heroin overdose. Mike McCready (b. 1966; guitar), Eddie Vedder (b. Edward Louis Seversen II, 1964; vocals) and Dave Krusen (drums) hooked up with Ament and Gossard to become Pearl Jam. They signed to Epic in 1991, debuting with *Ten*, by which time Krusen had left the band (he was later replaced by Dave Abbruzzese). The album remained in the US Top 20 a year and a half after its release. Dynamic live performances and a subtle commercial edge to their material catapulted them from obscurity to virtual superstars overnight, as the Seattle scene debate raged and Kurt Cobain of **Nirvana** accused them of 'jumping the alternative bandwagon'.

The eagerly awaited *Vs* seemed overtly concerned with re-establishing the band's grassroots credibility. There were also numerous references to the death of Cobain. Abbruzzese left the band in 1994, and was eventually replaced by Jack Irons. The new line-up appeared on **Neil Young**'s *Mirror Ball* and then released the semi-acoustic *No Code*. Hailed as a return to their roots, the hard rocking *Yield* was not a great commercial success despite reaching number 2 on the US album chart, with the effects of the band's long-term

feud with Ticketmaster cutting into their fanbase. Irons was replaced later in the year by Matt Cameron, who featured on the concert album *Live: On Two Legs*. The band bounced back in summer 1999, reaching number 2 in the US singles chart with their cover version of Wayne Cochran's 'Last Kiss'.

The year 2000 proved to be an extraordinary one for Pearl Jam. In addition to a new studio album *Binaural*, they issued an unprecedented 25 separate double albums of live concerts from their recent European tour. A further series of albums was released, this time documenting their American tour.

PEEBLES, ANN

An impromptu appearance at the Rosewood Club in Memphis, led to Peebles (b. 1947) securing a recording contract. Producer Willie Mitchell fashioned an impressive debut single, 'Walk Away' (1969). Her work matured with 'I'm Gonna Tear Your Playhouse Down' and the immortal 'I Can't Stand The Rain'. 'If You Got The Time (I've Got The Love)' (1979) was her last R&B hit, but her work nonetheless remains amongst the finest in 70s soul. She performed gospel in the mid-80s, before returning to her Memphis-sound with *Full Time Love* (1992) and *Fill This World With Love* (1996).

PENDERGRASS, TEDDY

US soul singer Pendergrass (b. Theodore Pendergrass, 1950) joined **Harold Melvin And The Blue Notes** in 1969 as drummer, becoming feature vocalist within a year. His ragged, passionate interpretations brought distinction to such releases as 'I Miss You' and 'If You Don't Know Me By Now'. Clashes with Melvin led to a split and in 1976 Pendergrass embarked on a solo career. 'The Whole Town's Laughing At Me' (1977) and 'Turn Off The Lights' (1979) stand among the best of his early work. A near-fatal car accident in 1982 left him confined to a wheelchair, although his voice remains intact. In 1991, 'It Should Have Been You' did much to reinstate him in people's minds as a major artist. He moved to a new label in 1996 after a lengthy gap in his career.

PENTANGLE

Pentangle was formed in 1967 by folk musicians Bert Jansch (b. 1943) and John Renbourn, with Jacqui McShee (vocals), Danny Thompson (b. 1939; bass) and Terry Cox (drums). *The Pentangle* captured their talents, where the acoustic interplay between Jansch and Renbourn was underscored by Thompson's sympathetic support and McShee's soaring intonation. Their eclecticism was expanded on *Sweet Child*, while they enjoyed commercial success with *Basket Of Light*. Pentangle disbanded in 1972, following which Thompson began a partnership with **John Martyn**. They reconvened the following year for a European tour and *Open The Door*. McShee, Cox and Jansch were joined by Nigel Portman-Smith and Mike Piggott for 1985's *In The Round*. Gerry Conway and Rod Clements replaced Cox and Piggott for *So Early In The Spring* (1988), while *Think Of Tomorrow*, saw Clements make way for guitarist Peter Kirtley. This line-up completed *One More Road* and *Live*. Jansch became distracted by solo projects and in later shows was replaced by Alun Davies. The unit later became known as Jacqui McShee's Pentangle.

PERE UBU

Formed in Cleveland, Ohio, USA, in 1975, Pere Ubu's initial line-up comprised David Thomas (b. 1953; vocals), Peter Laughner (d. 1977; guitar), Tom Herman (guitar, bass, organ), Tim Wright (guitar, bass), Allen Ravenstine (synthesizer, saxophone) and Scott Krauss (drums), who completed the compulsive '30 Seconds Over Tokyo'. Ravenstine, Wright and Laughner left, but bass player Tony Maimone joined Thomas, Herman and Krauss before Ravenstine returned to complete the most innovative version of Pere Ubu.

The Modern Dance was an exceptional debut. Rhythmically, the unit was reminiscent of **Captain Beefheart**'s Magic Band, while Thomas' vocal gymnastics were compelling. *Dub Housing* and *New Picnic Time* maintained this sense of adventure. Guitarist Mayo Thompson replaced Herman in 1979. *The Age Of Walking* was deemed obtuse, and a dissatisfied Krauss left. Anton Fier (ex-Feelies) joined Pere Ubu for 1982's desultory *Song Of The Bailing Man*.

Thomas took the opportunity to establish his solo career, and by 1985 Maimone and Raventine were working with his new group, the Wooden Birds. Krauss sparked a Pere Ubu reunion, appearing for an encore during a Cleveland concert, and by late 1987 the Pere Ubu name was reinstated. Jim Jones (guitar) and Chris Cutler (drums) completed the new line-up for the exceptional *The Tenement Year*. Cutler and Ravenstine left after *Cloudland*, the latter being replaced by Eric Drew Feldman. *Ray Gun Suitcase* was the first album to be produced by Thomas himself, and featured new band members Michele Temple and Robert Wheeler. The band's unique vision was again evident on 1998's *Pennsylvania*.

PERKINS, CARL

American Carl Perkins (b. 1932, d. 1998) was author of 'Blue Suede Shoes' and one of the most renowned rockabilly artists recording for Sun Records in the 50s. In 1953 Carl, brothers Jay and Clayton and drummer W.S. 'Fluke' Holland formed a hillbilly band, playing in Tennessee bars. His technique, borrowed from black musicians, set Perkins apart from many contemporary country guitarists. After hearing an **Elvis Presley** record in 1954, Perkins decided to pursue a musical career and the Perkins brothers travelled to Memphis to audition for **Sam Phillips** at Sun. Although not initially impressed, he saw their potential. After Phillips sold Presley's Sun contract to RCA Records, he decided to push Perkins' single, 'Blue Suede Shoes'. It entered the US chart on 3 March 1956 (the day Presley's first single entered the chart), by which time several cover versions had been recorded by various artists. Perkins' version became a huge hit, being the first country record to appear on both R&B and pop charts, in addition to the country chart. As Perkins began enjoying the fruits of his labour, he and his band were involved in a severe road accident, and as Perkins was unable to promote the record, the momentum was lost – none of his four future chart singles climbed as high. 'Blue Suede Shoes' was Perkins' only chart single in the UK, being upstaged commercially by Presley's cover.

Perkins continued recording for Sun until mid-1958, but 'Boppin' The Blues' only reached number 70, and 'Your True Love', number 67. While at Sun, Perkins recorded numerous rockabilly tracks: 'Everybody's Trying To Be

My Baby' and 'Matchbox', both covered by the **Beatles**. In December 1956, Perkins, **Jerry Lee Lewis** and Presley joined in an impromptu jam session at Sun, released two decades later as 'The Million Dollar Quartet'. In 1958, Perkins signed with Columbia Records with whom he recorded some good songs, although only 'Pink Pedal Pushers' and 'Pointed Toe Shoes' had any chart success. Later that year Jay Perkins died of a brain tumour and Carl became an alcoholic.

Perkins signed with Decca Records in 1963, touring outside of the USA and meeting with the Beatles while in Britain. In 1967, he joined **Johnny Cash**'s band as guitarist and was allotted a guest singing spot during all Cash's concerts and television shows. By 1970, Perkins was back on Columbia, before signing with Mercury Records in 1974. Late that year, Clayton committed suicide and their father died. Perkins left Cash in 1976, going on tour with a band consisting of his two sons, with whom he was still performing in the 90s. In the 80s, Perkins recorded *The Survivors* with Cash and Lewis, and another with Cash, Lewis and **Roy Orbison** in 1986. In 1987, Perkins was elected to the Rock And Roll Hall Of Fame. Perkins was unwell for much of the 90s and suffered from a heart condition that took its toll in January 1998.

PERRY, LEE

Perry (b. Rainford Hugh Perry, 1936) is a giant of reggae music. He began his career working for producer **Coxsone Dodd** during the late 50s and early 60s, organizing recording sessions and supervising auditions at Dodd's record shop in Kingston, Jamaica. By 1963 Perry had released his own vocal record, a bluesy, declamatory vocal style over superb backing from the Skatalites, setting a pattern from which Perry rarely deviated.

In 1966 Perry fell out with Dodd and began working with other producers including JJ Johnson, Clancy Eccles and Joe Gibbs, for whom he wrote songs and produced artists such as Errol Dunkley, and the Pioneers. On parting with Gibbs, Perry set up his own Upsetter label in Jamaica, and had hits with David Isaacs ('Place In The Sun') and the Untouchables ('Tighten Up'). Perry's first UK success was with tenor saxophonist Val Bennett's 'Return Of Django', which spent three weeks at number 5 in the charts during 1969. He also began producing the **Wailers** on records including 'Small Axe', 'Duppy Conqueror' and 'Soul Rebel'.

From 1972–74 Perry consolidated his position as one of Jamaica's leading musical innovators, releasing instrumentals like 'French Connection', 'Black Ipa', and DJ tracks by artists including U-Roy, Dillinger, Dr. Alimantado, I Roy and Charlie Ace. In 1974 Perry opened a studio (the Black Ark) in Jamaica, scoring a hit with Junior Byles' 'Curly Locks'. His production of Susan Cadogan's 'Hurt So Good' reached number 4 in the UK charts (1975). From 1975 he began to employ studio technology, phase shifters and rudimentary drum machines, producing an instantly recognizable style. By 1976, Island began to release the fruits of this phase, including the Heptones' (*Party Time*), **Bob Marley** And The Wailers ('Jah Live', 'Punky Reggae Party'), George Faith (*To Be A Lover*), Junior Murvin (*Police & Thieves*) and the Upsetters (*Super Ape*).

Perry's behaviour became increasingly strange and bewildering due to infrequent commercial success, and in 1980 he destroyed his studio and left for Britain. Since then he has made a long series of eccentric solo albums, with his earlier work receiving critical and cult attention at the same time. Whatever the future holds, he has made one of the most individual contributions to the development of Jamaican music, both as producer/arranger/writer, and simply as a singularly powerful guiding force during several crucial phases.

PET SHOP BOYS

Formed in 1981, this UK pop duo features Neil Tennant (b. 1954; vocals) and Chris Lowe (b. 1959; keyboards). Lowe had previously played in cabaret act, One Under The Eight, while Tennant was employed as a journalist on UK

pop magazine *Smash Hits*. In 1984, they issued 'West End Girls', which passed unnoticed. After being dropped from Epic Records, they were picked up by Parlophone. In 1986, the re-released 'West End Girls' topped the UK and US charts. *Please* and the hits 'Opportunities (Let's Make Lots Of Money)' and 'Suburbia' consolidated their position during the year. The duo returned to the UK number 1 slot in 1987 with 'It's A Sin'. By this time, they were being critically fêted as one of the more interesting bands of their time, with an engaging love of pop irony, camp imagery and arch wordplay. The quality of their melodies was evident in the successful collaboration with **Dusty Springfield** on 'What Have I Done To Deserve This?'

By the end of the year the duo were back at the top in their home country with a cover version of the **Elvis Presley** hit, 'Always On My Mind', also a US Top 5 single. A fourth UK number 1 with 'Heart' was followed by *Introspective*, which spawned further UK Top 10 hits in 'Domino Dancing', 'Left To My Own Devices', and 'It's Alright'. A surprise collaboration in 1989 with Liza Minnelli gave her a UK Top 10 hit with 'Losing My Mind'. The duo's own inventive wit was again in evidence on the UK Top 5 hit 'So Hard', the laconic 'Being Boring', and an odd fusion of **U2**'s 'Where The Streets Have No Name' and **Frankie Valli**'s 'Can't Take My Eyes Off You'. The attendant *Behaviour* was a downbeat, slightly disappointing album.

Tennant also enjoyed UK hits with Johnny Marr and Bernard Sumner in **Electronic**, but returned to the Pet Shop Boys for 1993's *Very*. Later in the year they enjoyed a UK number 2 hit with a bold cover version of the Village People's gay anthem, 'Go West'. *Bilingual* experimented with Latin rhythms, while *Nightlife* highlighted their remarkable creativity.

Tennant and Lowe subsequently collaborated with writer Jonathan Harvey on the West End musical, *Closer To Heaven*, which opened at the Arts Theatre in May 2001 but closed after only four months. Lowe and Tennant returned to music in 2002 with *Release*, which featured a more guitar-orientated sound.

PETER AND GORDON

Peter Asher (b. 1944) and Gordon Waller (b. 1945) had a crucial advantage over their 60s contemporaries – **Paul McCartney**'s patronage (McCartney was then dating Peter's sister, Jane). Their cover of McCartney's 'A World Without Love' quickly became a transatlantic chart-topper, and two more 1964 McCartney compositions, 'Nobody I Know' and 'I Don't Want To See You Again', brought further success. The duo also covered **Buddy Holly**'s 'True Love Ways' and the Teddy Bears' retitled 'To Know You Is To Love You'. Although the partnership was strained by late 1966, the saucy 'Lady Godiva' provided a new direction and was followed by similarly quaint novelty numbers. One year later, they split. Waller subsequently pursued an unsuccessful solo career and appeared as the Pharoah in *Joseph And The Amazing Technicolor Dreamcoat*. Asher moved to Los Angeles and emerged as a formidable record producer and manager.

PETER, PAUL AND MARY

US folk trio Peter Yarrow (b. 1938), Noel Paul Stookey (b. 1937) and Mary Allin Travers (b. 1937) began performing together in 1961. Their versions of **Bob Dylan**'s 'Blowin' In The Wind' and 'Don't Think Twice, It's All Right' both made the US Top 10. They were also renowned for singing children's songs, 'Puff The Magic Dragon' being the most memorable. Their greatest success was 'Leaving On A Jet Plane' (1969) which reached number 1 in the US and number 2 in the UK, but by then the individual members were going in different directions. Yarrow was the primary force behind *You Are What You Eat*, an eccentric hippie film and in 1970 he, Travers and Stookey embarked on solo careers. They reunited briefly in 1972 for a George McGovern Democratic Party rally, and again in 1978. Following several albums for the short-lived Gold Castle label in the late 80s, the trio returned to Warner Brothers Records in the 90s.

PETTY, TOM, AND THE HEARTBREAKERS

The Heartbreakers were formed from the ashes of Petty's first professional band, Mudcrutch, in 1971. Petty (b. 1953; guitar) was joined by Mike Campbell (b. 1954; guitar), Benmont Tench (b. 1954; keyboards), Stan Lynch (b. 1955; drums) and Ron Blair (b. 1952; bass). With a Rickenbacker guitar and a **Roger McGuinn** voice, Tom Petty And The Heartbreaker's eponymous debut was accepted more in England where anything **Byrds**-like would find an audience. *You're Gonna Get It* and *Damn The Torpedoes* followed, during which time Petty filed for bankruptcy. His cash-flow soon improved as the album went platinum.

Subsequent albums have been similarly satisfying although not as successful. In 1981 Petty duetted with **Stevie Nicks** on the US hit 'Stop Draggin' My Heart Around', and in 1985 the Heartbreakers had another major hit with 'Don't Come Around Here No More'. The attendant *Southern Accents* became another million-seller. In 1988 Petty, **Jeff Lynne**, **George Harrison**, **Roy Orbison** and **Bob Dylan**, formed the highly successful **Traveling Wilburys** supergroup. The following year's *Full Moon Fever*, a Petty solo project, included the sublime Top 10 hit 'Free Fallin''.

He reunited with the Heartbreakers on *Into The Great Wide Open*, and has since combined solo work and band projects.

PHAIR, LIZ

Phair (b. 1967) was brought up in Chicago, Illinois, USA. At college in Ohio she became involved in the local music scene, soon moving to San Francisco with guitarist friend Chris Brokaw. Phair signed with Matador Records in the summer of 1992. Ignoring traditional song structures, her approach allowed her to empower her confessional, and occasionally abusive, lyrics. *Exile In Guyville* was a sprawling and powerful double album that inspired a new generation of bluntly articulate female singer-songwriters. *Whip-Smart* was a more polished set, lacking some of her previous eccentricities. It was still, however, a genuinely exciting and turbulent album, welcomed once again by critics and fans alike. The same reception was not given to *Juvenilia*, a stopgap collection of her early recordings. With motherhood preoccupying her Phair remained quiet for nearly five years, although she did appear on **Sarah McLachlan**'s high profile Lilith Fair touring show. *Whitechocolatespaceegg* adopted a more subtle approach, eschewing the abrasiveness of her earlier recordings.

PHILLIPS, SAM

Phillips (b. 1923) was a US radio DJ before opening Sam's Memphis Recording Studio in 1950. His main ambition was to record local blues acts and license the resultant masters. **Howlin' Wolf** and **B.B. King** were among the many acts Phillips produced. Phillips founded Sun Records in 1952, which flourished when Rufus Thomas scored a hit with 'Bear Cat'. Phillips looked to expand the label's horizons by recording country acts, and his wish to find a white singer comfortable with R&B was answered with **Elvis Presley**'s arrival in 1954. The singer's five Sun singles rank among pop's greatest achievements, and helped Phillips further the careers of **Carl Perkins** and **Jerry Lee Lewis**.

Phillips' simple recording technique defined classic rockabilly, but by the beginning of the 60s new Memphis-based studios, Stax and Hi Records, challenged Sun's pre-eminent position. In 1969 he sold the entire Sun empire to country entrepreneur Shelby Singleton.

PHISH

Comprising Trey Anastasio (vocals, guitar), Page McConnell (keyboards, vocals), Mike Gordon (bass, vocals) and Jon Fishman (drums, vocals), Phish were founded in 1983 in New England, USA. The band only really took shape in 1985 after the recruitment of McConnell and the departure of second guitarist Jeff Holdsworth. Drawing from jazz, funk, bluegrass, country, punk and pop, their music soon attracted a loyal following. Their own-label debut *Junta* captured the free-flowing improvisations, while *Lawn Boy* featured improved production. *After A Picture Of Nectar*, their 1992 debut for Elektra Records, several critics drew comparisons with the **Grateful Dead**. By 1994 (and *Hoist*), Phish had become both a major live attraction and important figures in the mainstream of American music. Membership of their fan newsletter had grown to over 80,000, while their Internet service, phish.net, was one of the most active throughout the USA. The 1998 studio set, *The Story Of The Ghost*, featured the major radio hit 'Birds Of A Feather', and debuted at number 8 on the US album chart.

Anastasio also records with an 11-piece fusion ensemble called Surrender To The Air, featuring alto saxophonist Marshall Allen and trumpeter Michael Ray from the Sun Ra Arkestra, and guitarist Marc Ribot. In a surprise move, the band wound down their operation in 2000, and at present their future is in abeyance.

PICKETT, BOBBY 'BORIS'

Pickett (b. 1940) moved to Los Angeles in 1961 and joined a singing group called the Cordials. Pickett and the Cordials' Leonard Capizzi wrote the song

'Monster Mash' to cash in on the dance craze that Dee Dee Sharp's 'Mashed Potato Time' launched in 1962. 'Monster Mash', credited to Bobby 'Boris' Pickett And The Crypt-Kickers, reached the top of the US charts in time for Halloween 1962, but did not reach the UK charts until 1973, when it reached number 3. Pickett had two other minor US chart singles in 1962–63, including the Top 30 'Monster's Holiday', but he is indelibly linked with the classic novelty number.

PICKETT, WILSON

US soul singer Pickett (b. 1941) sang in several Detroit R&B groups before joining the Falcons (already established by the million-selling 'You're So Fine'). Pickett wrote and sang lead on their 1962 hit 'I Found A Love', after which he launched his solo career. In 1964 he signed to Atlantic Records, forming a partnership with guitarist **Steve Cropper** on the classic hits 'In The Midnight Hour', 'Land Of 1,000 Dances', 'Mustang Sally' and 'Funky Broadway'. Other collaborators included **Bobby Womack** (1968's *The Midnight Mover* contained six songs featuring Womack's involvement). A version of the **Beatles**' 'Hey Jude', with Duane Allman on guitar, was the highlight of recording sessions at Fame's Muscle Shoals studio. The hits, 'Engine Number 9' (1970) and 'Don't Let The Green Grass Fool You' (1971), resulted from working with producers **Gamble And Huff**. Pickett switched to RCA Records in 1972, but his previous success was hard to regain. He returned in 1999 with his first new studio album in 12 years.

PINK FLOYD

One of the most predominant and celebrated rock bands of all time, the origins of Pink Floyd developed at Cambridge High School in England, where **Syd Barrett** (b. Roger Keith Barrett, 1946; guitar, vocals), **Roger Waters** (b. 1944; bass, vocals) and David Gilmour (b. 1944; guitar, vocals) were pupils and friends. On leaving, Waters formed R&B-based Sigma 6 with Nick Mason (b. 1945; drums) and Rick Wright (b. 1945; keyboards). Barrett, Waters, Mason and Wright eventually came together in 1965 as the Pink Floyd Sound, a name inspired by Georgia blues musicians Pink Anderson and Floyd Council.

By December 1966 the quartet, having dropped the superfluous 'sound' suffix, was appearing regularly at London's UFO Club, spearheading Britain's psychedelic movement with improvised sets and a highly visual lightshow. A recording deal was struck with EMI Records. Their singles were surprisingly different to their live sound, featuring Barrett's quirky melodies and lyrics. 'Arnold Layne' and 'See Emily Play' reached the UK Top 20 in 1967, while *The Piper At The Gates Of Dawn* perfectly encapsulated Britain's 'Summer of Love'. A disastrous US tour wrought unbearable pressure on Barrett's fragile psyche. His indulgence in hallucinogenic drugs exacerbated such problems and his colleagues brought Gilmour into the line-up in 1968. Plans for Barrett to maintain a backroom role failed and he left the following April.

The realigned Pink Floyd completed *Saucerful Of Secrets*. It featured Barrett's 'Jugband Blues', as well as two songs which became an integral part of their live concerts, the title track and 'Set The Controls For The Heart Of The Sun'. A film soundtrack, *More*, allowed Waters to flex his compositional muscles. *Atom Heart Mother* was an experiment, partially written with composer Ron Geesin. It featured the first in a series of impressive album covers, designed by the Hipgnosis studio.

The more coherent *Meddle* featured 'One Of These Days' and 'Echoes', but Pink Floyd's talent finally exploded in 1973 with *Dark Side Of The Moon*. It became one of the biggest-selling records of all time. Its run on the US album chart spanned over a decade, ridding the band of the spectre of Barrett's era.

The moving eulogy to Barrett, 'Shine On You Crazy Diamond', was one of the high points of the follow-up *Wish You Were Here*. *Animals* featured a scathing attack on the UK's 'clean-up television' campaigner, Mary Whitehouse, while the cover photograph of an inflatable pig over Battersea power station, has passed into Pink Floyd folklore. *The Wall* (1979) was a Waters-dominated epic which contained 'Another Brick In The Wall', the band's sole UK number 1 hit. The commercial success did not stop Pink Floyd's growing inter-personnel problems, and Wright left in 1979. Waters totally dominated *The Final Cut*, which comprised songs originally written for *The Wall*. Mason's contributions were negligible, Gilmour showed little interest and Pink Floyd's fragmentation was evident to all.

In 1987 Mason and Gilmour decided to work together under the Pink Floyd banner and Wright returned. Waters instigated an injunction, which was over-ruled. *A Momentary Lapse Of Reason* sounded more like a Pink Floyd album than its sombre 'predecessor'. A live set, *Delicate Sound Of Thunder* followed, and touring rekindled Wright and Mason's confidence. In 1994 they released the accomplished *The Division Bell*, the UK's biggest selling album of the year. *Pulse* cashed in on the success of the tours and was a perfectly recorded live album. The legacy of those 'faceless' record sleeves is irrefutable; Pink Floyd's music is somehow greater than the individuals creating it.

PITNEY, GENE

American-born Pitney (b. 1941) began recording in 1959, finding success as a songwriter, providing **Roy Orbison** with 'Today's Teardrops' and **Bobby Vee** with 'Rubber Ball'. His solo recording career took off in 1961 with 'Town Without Pity' and 'The Man Who Shot Liberty Valance'. Throughout this period, he was still writing for other artists, creating big hits for **Ricky Nelson** ('Hello Mary Lou') and the **Crystals** ('He's A Rebel'). In 1963, Pitney toured Britain where his 'Twenty Four Hours From Tulsa' reached the Top 10. Despite the onslaught of the beat groups, Pitney's big ballads remained popular. Hits from this era included 'I'm Gonna Be Strong' and 'Something's Gotten Hold Of My Heart'. In addition, Pitney recorded albums in Italian and Spanish, and there were also country music albums with George Jones and Melba Montgomery. By the late 60s, his popularity in America had waned but he continued to tour in Europe, having the occasional hit like 'Maria Elena' (1969), 'Shady Lady' (1970) and 'Blue Angel' (1974).

In 1989, Pitney had unexpected success when he sang on a revival of 'Something's Gotten Hold Of My Heart' with **Marc Almond**, which topped the UK charts. He continues to tour regularly, and is especially popular in the UK and Italy.

PIXIES

This highly influential US alternative rock band was formed in Boston, Massachusetts by room-mates Charles Thompson IV aka Black Francis (vocals, guitar) and Joey Santiago (guitar). Kim Deal (b. 1961) joined as bass player, introducing drummer David Lovering. Originally known as Pixies In Panoply, they secured a recording contract with 4AD Records. Their 1987 debut *Come On Pilgrim* introduced an abrasive sound and Francis' oblique lyrics. *Surfer Rosa* exaggerated its predecessor's fury, while *Doolittle* even managed to scale the UK Top 10, aided and abetted by the band's most enduring single, 'Monkey Gone To Heaven'. *Bossanova* blended pure pop and sheer ferocity and broke into the UK Top 5. *Trompe Le Monde* was even harsher than preceding albums. Following the rechristened **Frank Black**'s departure in early 1993 the band effectively folded, but their reputation continues to outshine any of the membership's concurrent or subsequent projects.

PJ HARVEY

UK artist Harvey (b. Polly Jean Harvey, 1970) joined the Somerset-based Automatic Dlamini, contributing saxophone, guitar and vocals, before moving to London, where she worked with bass player Ian Olliver and drummer and backing vocalist Rob Ellis (b. 1962). They first played live in 1991, using the name PJ Harvey. Too Pure Records financed their debut single 'Dress'. Olliver was replaced by Stephen Vaughan (b. 1962) on 'five-string fretless bass', after the record's release. Harvey's startling debut *Dry* caught Island Records' attention, although many expressed doubts that this evocative and disturbing songwriter would ever appeal to a mass audience. *Rid Of Me* was a vicious stew of rural blues produced by Steve Albini. Harvey's voice and guitar sounding almost animalized by the production, its title track centrepiece offered one of the most fearsome declarations ('You're not rid of me') ever articulated in rock music.

Its follow-up was forced to lower the extremity threshold. *For To Bring You My Love*, Harvey (now officially a solo artist) introduced a haunting ambience. Her band now consisted of multi-instrumentalist John Parish, Jean-Marc Butty (drums), Nick Bagnall (keyboards, bass), Joe Gore (guitar) and Eric Feldman (keyboards). In 1996 Harvey collaborated with Parish on the theatrical *Dance Hall At Louse Point*. That album's oblique musical reference points informed 1998's starkly beautiful *Is This Desire?* . The same year she made her acting debut in Hal Hartley's *The Book Of Life*. Her sixth album, the aptly-titled *Stories From The City, Stories From The Sea*, juxtaposed thrashy alternative rock with dark, sensual ballads. The album was awarded the UK's Mercury Music Prize in September 2001.

PLACEBO

A cosmopolitan trio comprising Brian Molko (b. 1972, USA; vocals, guitar), Stefan Olsdal (b. 1974, Sweden; bass) and Robert Schultzberg (b. Switzerland; drums), the seeds of Placebo were sown when Molko met Olsdal at school in Luxembourg. The duo reunited in the mid-90s to form Placebo. Their music slowly evolved from art-rock to an offbeat punk/new wave base, a transition that was aided considerably by the recruitment of drummer Schultzberg. They made their debut at the end of 1995 with a single, 'Bruise Pristine', for the independent record label Fierce Panda Records. The band's profile was subsequently heightened by the success of the UK Top 5 hit 'Nancy Boy' and media interest in Molko's androgynous image. English drummer Steve Hewitt then replaced Schultzberg. The UK Top 5 hits 'Pure Morning' and 'You Don't Care About Us' introduced

Without You I'm Nothing, on which Molko's songwriting achieved a more assured, reflective tone. The band members also made cameo appearances in Todd Haynes' glam rock tribute movie, *Velvet Goldmine*. Their third album, *Black Market Music*, met with a critical backlash.

PLANT, ROBERT

This UK rock singer's early career was spent in several Midlands-based R&B bands. In 1965 Plant (b. 1948) joined Listen, a Motown-influenced act, and signed to CBS Records. He started his solo career with 'Laughing, Crying, Laughing' and 'Long Time Coming' (both 1967), before forming the short-lived Band Of Joy. Guitarist **Jimmy Page** invited him to join **Led Zeppelin**. Plant's reputation was forged during this time, but he renewed his solo career following drummer John Bonham's death in 1980. *Pictures At Eleven* unveiled a new partnership with Robbie Blunt (guitar), Paul Martinez (bass) and Jezz Woodroffe (keyboards). *The Principle Of Moments* contained the UK/US Top 20 hit, 'Big Log' (1983). Plant featured in the Honeydrippers, an ad hoc R&B group which included Page, **Jeff Beck** and Nile Rodgers. Plant fashioned the less conventional *Shaken 'N' Stirred*, before returning to form with *Now And Zen*, *Manic Nirvana* and *Fate Of Nations*. He reunited with Page in the mid-90s for the *No Quarter* and *Walking Into Clarksdale* projects, satisfying those who would never have the vocalist forget his past. In 1999, Plant formed the folk-rock quintet Priory Of Brion with former Band Of Joy bandmate Kevyn Gammon. Two years later he began touring larger venues with his new band, Strange Sensation.

PLANXTY

This Irish band featured **Christy Moore** (b. 1945; guitar, vocals), Donal Lunny (guitar, bouzouki, synthesizer), Liam O'Flynn (uillean pipes) and Andy Irvine (guitar, mandolin, bouzouki, vocals). After two groundbreaking albums that fused traditional music with modern folk, Lunny was replaced by Johnny Moynihan (bouzouki). In 1974, Moore left and was replaced by another highly talented singer/songwriter, **Paul Brady** (b. 1947; vocals, guitar). The band split-up shortly afterwards, with Moynihan going on to join De Dannan. The original band re-formed in 1978, this time with ex-Bothy Band flautist Matt Molloy. Keyboard player Bill Whelan, who later created the highly successful *Riverdance* revue, played on *The Woman I Loved So Well* and *Words & Music*. Moore and Lunny departed once more in 1981 to form Moving Hearts. By the time *The Best Of Planxty Live* emerged, the band had split-up for a second time.

PLATTERS

The Platters, for a short time, were the most successful American vocal group in the world. Buck Ram (b. 1907, d. 1991) formed them in 1953, his talent for composing and arranging enabling them to make a lasting impression upon

POCO

Albums
Crazy Eyes (Epic 1973)★★★★
Rose Of Cimarron (ABC 1976)★★★★
Poco: The Forgotten Trail 1969-1974 (Epic/Legacy 1990)★★★★
➤ p.388 for full listings
Connections
Buffalo Springfield ➤ p.311
Eagles ➤ p.128
Influences
Flying Burrito Brothers ➤ p.146

POGUES

Albums
Rum, Sodomy & The Lash (Stiff 1985)★★★★
If I Should Fall From Grace With God (Stiff 1988)★★★★
➤ p.388 for full listings
Collaborators
Elvis Costello ➤ p.100
Kirsty MacColl ➤ p.222
Connections
Shane MacGowan
Further References
Books: *The Pogues: The Lost Decade*, Ann Scanlon
A Drink With Shane MacGowan, Victoria Mary Clarke and Shane MacGowan

POINTER SISTERS

Albums
Energy (Planet 1978)★★★
➤ p.388 for full listings

POISON

Albums
Flesh & Blood (Capitol 1990)★★★★
➤ p.388 for full listings
Further References
Video: *Greatest Video Hits* (Capitol Video 2001)

POLICE

Albums
Regatta De Blanc (A&M 1979)★★★★
Synchronicity (A&M 1983)★★★★
➤ p.388 for full listings
Connections
Curved Air ➤ p.109
Sting ➤ p.316
Stewart Copeland
Andy Summers
Further References
Video: *Every Breath You Take: The Videos* (PolyGram Video 1986)
Book: *The Police*, Lynn Goldsmith

popular music. Their original line-up, Tony Williams (b. 1928, d. 1992; lead tenor), David Lynch (b. 1929, d. 1981; tenor), Alex Hodge (baritone) and Herb Reed (b. 1931; bass), recorded unsuccessfully in 1954. Paul Robi (b. 1931, d. 1989) replaced Hodge, and Zola Taylor (b. 1934; contralto) then joined. Signed to Mercury Records, their first hit was 1955's 'Only You', reaching the US Top 5. That set the pattern for subsequent releases, including 'The Great Pretender', 'My Prayer' and 'Twilight Time', each of which reached number 1 in the US charts. 'Smoke Gets In Your Eyes' was an international number 1 hit single in 1958–59. Lead singer Williams left for a solo career in 1961, and Sandra Dawn and Nate Nelson replaced Taylor and Robi. With Sonny Turner as the featured voice, the group began embracing a more contemporary direction, evidenced in such occasional pop hits as 'I Love You 1000 Times' (1966) and 'With This Ring' (1967).

During the late 60s, and for a long time afterwards, personnel changes brought much confusion as to who were the legitimate Platters. Turner and Reed formed their own version, while Tony Williams did likewise. The group were inducted into the Rock And Roll Hall Of Fame in 1990, but Ram died the following year.

POCO

This US country-rock band was formed as Pogo in 1968 by Richie Furay (b. 1944; vocals, guitar), Randy Meisner (b. 1946; vocal, bass), George Grantham (b. 1947; drums, vocals), Jim Messina (b. 1947; vocals, guitar) and Rusty Young (b. 1946; vocals, pedal-steel guitar). They became Poco after complaints from the copyright owner of the Pogo cartoon character. *Pickin' Up The Pieces* was more country than rock and made Poco leaders of the genre. Meisner departed (later co-founding the **Eagles**) but *Poco* was released to critical applause. *Deliverin'* made the US Top 30, the band having added Timothy B. Schmit (b. 1947; bass, vocals) and Paul Cotton (b. 1943; vocals, guitar). *From The Inside* was followed by the excellent *A Good Feelin' To Know*, but Furay left after the release of *Crazy Eyes*.

During the mid-70s the line-up of Cotton, Schmit, Grantham and Young released three albums, *Head Over Heels*, *Rose Of Cimarron* and *Indian Summer*, before Schmit and Grantham departed. Charlie Harrison (bass, vocals), Steve Chapman (drums, vocals) and Kim Bullard (keyboards) were added to the line-up on 1978's million-selling *Legend*, which included the hit singles 'Crazy Love' and 'Heart Of The Night'. This line-up made a further four albums with gradually declining success. The band then disappeared, but in 1989 Furay, Messina, Meisner, Grantham and Young returned with *Legacy*. In 2000, another tour was arranged, with a line-up comprising Cotton, Young, Grantham and Jack Sundrad.

POGUES

The Pogues (originally Pogue Mahone) were formed by singer Shane MacGowan (b. 1957), Peter 'Spider' Stacy (tin whistle), Jem Finer (banjo, mandolin), James Fearnley (guitar, piano, accordion), Cait O'Riordan (bass) and Andrew Ranken (drums). After complaints they changed their name (Pogue Mahone is 'kiss my arse' in Gaelic) and attracted the **Clash**'s attention, who asked them to be their opening act. In 1984 they signed to Stiff Records and recorded *Red Roses For Me*. **Elvis Costello** produced *Rum, Sodomy & The Lash*, on which Philip Chevron replaced the temporarily absent Finer. Multi-instrumentalist Terry Woods (a co-founder of **Steeleye Span**) joined and Cait O'Riordan was replaced by Darryl Hunt on *If I Should Fall From Grace With God*. 'Fairytale Of New York', a duet by MacGowan and **Kirsty MacColl**, was a Christmas UK number 2 hit in the UK in 1987. *Peace And Love* featured songs written by nearly every member of the group and its eclectic nature saw them picking up the hurdy-gurdy, the cittern and the mandola. While the rest of the group were strong players, it was widely accepted that MacGowan was the most

talented songwriter. His output had always been highly sporadic but there were now fears that the drinking that fuelled his earlier creativity may have slowed him to a standstill. In 1991 MacGowan left the band and was replaced by the former Clash singer Joe Strummer. This relationship lasted until June 1992 when Stacy replaced Strummer as lead vocalist. MacGowan later re-emerged with his new band, the Popes, while his erstwhile colleagues continued to tour heavily, recording competent new material that lacked the flair of old. The band eventually called it a day in 1996. They reunited with the errant MacGowan in 2001 to play several live dates.

POINTER SISTERS

Sisters Anita (b. 1948), Bonnie (b. 1951), Ruth (b. 1946) and June (b. 1954), first sang together in the West Oakland Church of God, California, where their parents were ministers. Bonnie, June and Anita worked as backing singers with several of the region's acts before Ruth joined them in 1972, a year before their debut album was released. Their varied repertoire included a version of **Allen Toussaint**'s 'Yes We Can Can'. They broke up briefly in 1977, but while Bonnie left the remaining trio regrouped and **Bruce Springsteen** crafted the million-selling 'Fire'(1979). Their progress continued with two further gold discs, 'He's So Shy' and the sensual 'Slow Hand', while two 1984 releases, 'Jump (For My Love)' and 'Automatic', won Grammy Awards. Although 'Dare Me' was another major hit in 1985, their subsequent work lacked the sparkle of earlier achievements. In 1995 they appeared in a revival performance of the musical *Ain't Misbehavin'*.

POISON

This heavy-metal band was formed in Pennsylvania, USA, in 1983 by Bret Michaels (b. Bret Sychak, 1962; vocals), Rikki Rockett (b. Alan Ream, 1959; drums), Bobby Dall (b. Harry Kuy Kendall, 1958; bass) and Matt Smith (guitar). They worked as Paris, before moving to Los Angeles and changing their name. Smith left the band and was replaced by C.C. DeVille (b. Bruce Anthony Johannesson, 1963; guitar). Their 1986 debut went double platinum in America. *Open Up And Say . . . Ahh!* produced their first US number 1, 'Every Rose Has Its Thorn'. Several US hits followed before Richie Kotzen replaced DeVille in 1991. *Native Tongue* established them as purveyors of image-conscious hard melodic rock. Blues Saraceno replaced Kotzen in 1995. With Poison on hold, Michaels instigated an acting career the following year, taking a major role in *A Letter From Death Row*, which he also wrote and co-produced. A companion solo album was also released, and at the same time DeVille rejoined the band. Their 1999 reunion tour was successful and shortly afterwards the band released the live *Power To The People*.

POLICE

This highly successful UK trio comprised **Sting** (b. Gordon Sumner, 1951; bass, vocals) Stewart Copeland (b. 1952; drums, vocals) and Andy Summers (b. Andrew Somers, 1942; guitar). The experienced trio bonded so well that original guitarist Henry Padovani was given no alternative but to leave.

Their 1977 debut single 'Roxanne' failed to chart on its original release, but the heavily reggae-influenced *Outlandos D'Amour* and *Regatta De Blanc* dominated

the UK charts for most of 1979 and contained such chart-toppers as 'Message In A Bottle' and 'Walking On The Moon'. *Zenyatta Mondatta* was their big break-through in America, Europe, Japan, and indeed, the rest of the world. The band's third UK number 1, 'Don't Stand So Close To Me', was closely followed by the lyrically rich yet simply titled 'De Do Do Do, De Da Da Da'. *Ghost In The Machine* featured the hit singles 'Spirits In The Material World', 'Invisible Sun' and 'Every Little Thing She Does Is Magic', which provided their fourth UK chart-topper.

The trio concentrated on solo projects in 1982. Copeland released *Klark Kent*, and wrote the music for the film *Rumblefish*. Summers made an album with **Robert Fripp**, while Sting appeared in the television adaptation of Dennis Potter's *Brimstone And Treacle*. The obsessive 'Every Breath You Take', probably their greatest song, stayed at number 1 in the UK for four weeks, and for twice as many weeks in the USA, while the album stayed at the top of the US chart for an astonishing 17 weeks. The trio played their final live shows in June 1986, sharing top billing with **U2** on Amnesty International's 25th anniversary tour. A month later they reconvened for the final time to record an updated version of 'Don't Stand So Close To Me' for a compilation album. Greatest hits packages and a live album have periodically rekindled interest in the band, while each member has enjoyed a successful solo career.

POOLE, BRIAN, AND THE TREMELOES

Formed by vocalist Brian Poole (b. 1941) in the late 50s, this UK pop group debuted in 1960. They signed to Decca Records in 1962 in favour of the **Beatles**. A cover of the **Isley Brothers**' 'Twist And Shout' brought them a UK Top 10 hit in 1963. The follow-up, 'Do You Love Me?', was number 1 in the UK and 15 other countries. After two further UK hits, 'Someone Someone' and 'The Three Bells', their popularity waned and Poole moved into cabaret. He retired to the family butcher business, later resurfacing with a record and publishing company. The Tremeloes went on to achieve enormous chart success under their own name. In later decades, Poole and most of his original Tremeloes were back ploughing the rich vein of 60s nostalgia tours.

POP WILL EAT ITSELF

This UK indie band emerged in 1986 with a line-up comprising Clint Mansell

(b. 1963; vocals, guitar), Adam Mole (b. 1962; keyboards), Graham Crabb (b. 1964; drums, later vocals) and Richard Marsh (b. 1965; bass). Their initial recordings displayed their mix of guitar pop with sampling. In 1988 they played in the USSR, signing to RCA Records soon afterwards. Their second album was a minor hit and during 1990 they achieved mainstream acclaim with 'Touched By The Hand Of Cicciolina'. The band recruited a full-time drummer in 1992 when Fuzz (b. Robert Townshend, 1964) joined, but following *Weird's Bar & Grill* RCA dropped the band and they bowed out in the mid-90s. Crabb released an album as Golden Claw Musics. March went on to form big beat mavericks Bentley Rhythm Ace, while Mansell worked on film soundtracks.

PORNO FOR PYROS

This theatrical rock act was formed by **Perry Farrell** (b. Perry Bernstein, 1959) in 1992. Following the demise of his previous act **Jane's Addiction** he enlisted former bandmate Stephen Perkins (b. 1967; drums), Martyn LeNoble (b. 1969; bass) and Peter DiStefano (b. 1965; guitar). With Farrell's input and Perkins' talents, similarities between the two bands were inevitable, although Porno For Pyros' shows were more a carnival than traditional rock shows. Farrell had become a real star and great media fodder by the time their breakthrough album, *Good God's Urge*, was issued. DiStefano was diagnosed as having cancer in 1996, and the band cancelled all work while he underwent chemotherapy. In 1997, Farrell announced the resurrection of Jane's Addiction for live dates, and not long afterwards it was reported that Porno For Pyros had disbanded.

PORTISHEAD

Portishead were named after the port in south-west England where Geoff Barrow spent his teens. Barrow started out as a tape operator, working with **Massive Attack** and **Neneh Cherry**. He recruited jazz guitarist and musical director Adrian Utley, drummer/programmer Dave MacDonald and vocalist Beth Gibbons. They recorded a soundtrack and film, *To Kill A Dead Man* before signing to Go! Beat. 'Numb' and 'Sour Times' received good press reaction, but Barrow and Gibbons were reluctant interviewees with no initial interest in playing live. 'Glory Box' entered the UK Top 20 in 1995, after several 'album of the year' awards for *Dummy*. Their sound, a mixture of blues, jazz and hip-hop, became known as 'trip-hop'. They won the Mercury Music Prize for best album the same year. The follow-up was delayed when Barrow reached a creative impasse that almost destroyed the band. His perseverance paid off. *Portishead* was released in 1997 to excellent reviews. A perfunctory live album followed in 1998.

POSIES

John Auer (vocals, guitar) and Ken Stringfellow (vocals, guitar) were part of the original 'industrial noise' line-up of Sky Cries Mary, before forming this US indie-pop band in the late 80s. Their debut was recorded in 1988 and introduced the duo's penchant for sanguine, everyday lyrical topics. They signed to Geffen Records, and enlisted a rhythm section (Dave Fox and Mike Musburger) and brought in John Leckie to produce their major label debut. Their third album, *Frosting On The Beater* was produced by Don Fleming, and attracted wide acclaim. The band supported their heroes

Big Star on European tours, and Auer and Stringfellow both took part in their re-formation. The Posies released one final album, *Success*, before disbanding. In 2000, an excellent compilation of their Geffen material spurred Auer and Stringfellow into reuniting for an acoustic tour of America. The live documentary *In Case You Didn't Feel Like Plugging In* was released in August.

PREFAB SPROUT

The creation of literate UK songwriter Paddy McAloon (b. 1957; guitar, vocals), Prefab Sprout was formed in 1982 by McAloon, his brother Martin (b. 1962; bass), Wendy Smith (b. 1963; vocals, guitar) and Neil Conti (b. 1959). Following the self-pressed 'Lions In My Own Garden', the band attracted the attention of the Kitchenware Records label. *Swoon* made the national chart, but their real breakthrough came with 1985's *Steve McQueen* (titled *Two Wheels Good* in the US) which included the hit single 'When Love Breaks Down'. The follow-up *From Langley Park To Memphis* was a major success worldwide, and 'The King Of Rock 'N' Roll' became their biggest hit to date. McAloon unleashed the ambitious *Jordan: The Comeback* in 1990, and for many it was the album of the year. McAloon spent the next few years tinkering with various new projects, paying the bills by writing songs for actor/singer Jimmy Nail. A new album, *Andromeda Heights*, finally appeared in 1997. Sophisticated mood music, it met with a polite response from critics still entranced by McAloon's intricate musical and lyrical conceits. Another lengthy gap ensued before *The Gunman And Other Stories* was released.

PRESIDENTS OF THE UNITED STATES OF AMERICA

Formed in Seattle, USA, this trio broke into the US and UK charts in 1995. Chris Ballew (vocals, two-string bass) formed the band in 1994 with Dave Dederer (three-string guitar) and Jason Finn (drums). After their eponymous debut, they signed to Columbia Records and MTV gave 'Lump' rotation play. By 1996 the album had sold over one and a half million copies in the USA, and generated further hit singles with 'Peaches' and 'Kitty'. A second album capitalized on this momentum, but their brand of jokey alternative rock was beginning to wear thin and they disbanded in 1997. The trio re-formed at the end of the decade, initially under the self-deprecatory name the Quitters, to record the excellent *Freaked Out And Small*.

PRESLEY, ELVIS

Elvis Aaron Presley (b. 1935, d. 1977) is the most celebrated popular music phenomenon of his era and, for many, the purest embodiment of rock 'n' roll. His earliest musical influence came from psalms and gospel songs, and he also had a strong grounding in country and blues. These styles combined to provide his unique musical identity.

While a truck driver, Presley visited Sun Records to record a version of the Ink Spots' 'My Happiness' as a birthday present for his mother. The studio manager, Marion Keisker, informed Sun's owner/producer **Sam Phillips** of his potential. Phillips nurtured him before pairing him with country guitarist Scotty Moore and bassist **Bill Black**. Early sessions showed considerable promise, with Presley beginning to alternate his low-key delivery with a high-pitched whine. Presley's debut with Sun was 'That's All Right (Mama)', a showcase for his multi-textured vocal dexterity. The b-side, 'Blue Moon Of Kentucky', was a country song but the arrangement showed that Presley was threatening to slip closer to R&B. Response to these performances was encouraging, with 20,000 copies sold. Presley recorded Roy Brown's 'Good Rockin' Tonight' backed by 'I Don't Care If The Sun Don't Shine' and performed on the *Grand Old Opry* and *The Louisiana Hayride* radio programmes. A series of live dates commenced in 1955 with drummer D. J. Fontana added to the ranks. Presley toured clubs in Arkansas, Louisiana and Texas, billed as 'The King Of Western Bop' and 'The Hillbilly Cat'. Audience reaction verged

on the fanatical, a result of Presley's semi-erotic performances. The final Sun single was a cover of Junior Parker's 'Mystery Train'.

Colonel Tom Parker, who managed several country artists, persuaded Sam Phillips to release Presley. RCA Records paid Sun $35,000, and two days after his 21st birthday, Presley recorded his first major label tracks, including 'Heartbreak Hotel'. This stayed at US number 1 for eight weeks and reached UK number 2. Presley also made his national television debut, his sexually enticing gyrations subsequently persuading producers to film him exclusively from the waist upwards. Having outsold former Sun colleague **Carl Perkins** with 'Blue Suede Shoes', Presley released a debut album containing several songs he had previously recorded with Phillips.

After reaching number 1 with the ballad 'I Want You, I Need You, I Love You', Presley released the most commercially successful double-sided single in pop history, 'Hound Dog'/'Don't Be Cruel'. The former, composed by **Leiber And Stoller**, featured his backing group the **Jordanaires**. It remained at US number 1 for 11 weeks and both sides of the record were massive hits in the UK.

Celluloid fame beckoned next with *Love Me Tender*. Presley's movie debut received mixed reviews but was a box office smash, while the title track topped the US charts for five weeks. After rumours that Presley would be drafted into the US Army, RCA, Twentieth Century Fox and Colonel Parker stepped up the work-rate and release schedules. Three major films were completed in the next two-and-a-half years, including *Jailhouse Rock*. The Leiber And Stoller title track was an instant classic which topped the US charts for seven weeks and entered the UK listings at number 1.

By the time *King Creole* was released in 1958, Elvis had joined the US Forces and flown to Germany. In America, Colonel Parker kept his reputation intact via a series of films, record releases and merchandising. Hits including 'Wear My Ring Around Your Neck', 'Hard Headed Woman', 'One Night' and 'A Big Hunk O' Love' filled the two-year gap and when Presley reappeared he assumed the mantle of an all-round entertainer. 'It's Now Or Never' revealed 'the King' as an operatic crooner, and 'Are You Lonesome Tonight?' allowed him to spout Shakespeare. On celluloid, *GI Blues* played upon his recent Army exploits and showed off his knowledge of German in 'Wooden Heart'. 'Surrender' completed this phase of big ballads in the old-fashioned style. After the 1963 number 1 'Devil In

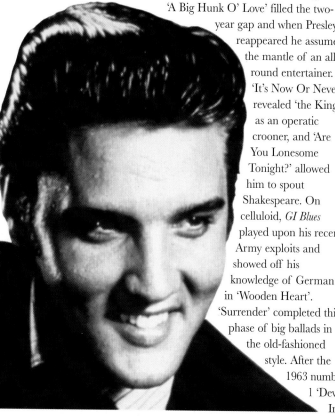

Disguise', a bleak period followed in which songs such as 'Bossa Nova Baby', 'Kiss Me Quick' and 'Blue Christmas' became the rule rather than the exception. Significantly, his biggest success of the mid-60s, the gospel song 'Crying In The Chapel', had been recorded five years before.

In the wake of the **Beatles**' rise to fame and the beat-boom explosion Presley seemed a figure out of time, and he continued to grind out pointless movies such as *Double Trouble, Speedway* and *Live A Little, Love A Little*. 'Guitar Man' and 'US Male' (both 1968) proved a spectacular return to form, and he also appeared in the one-hour Christmas show *Elvis TV Special*. Designed to capture Presley at his rock 'n' rollin' best, the film has become one of the most celebrated moments in pop broadcasting history. The critical acclaim for his television special prompted Presley to undertake his most significant recordings in years and he released *From Elvis In Memphis* and *From Memphis To Vegas/From Vegas To Memphis*. On the singles front, Presley was also back on top, most notably with 'In The Ghetto' which hit the US and UK Top 5, and the glorious 'Suspicious Minds' became his first US chart-topper since 1962. Even his final few films seemed less disastrous than expected, and Presley returned as a live performer with a strong backing group including guitarist **James Burton**. His comeback was well-received and one of the live songs, 'The Wonder Of You' (1970), stayed at UK number 1 for six weeks.

During the early 70s, Presley continued his live performances, but suffered the same atrophy that had bedevilled his celluloid career. He relied  on some rather patchy albums rather than record any fresh material. The backdrop to Presley's final years was a sordid slump into drug dependency, reinforced by the unreality of a pampered lifestyle in his fantasy home, Graceland. The dissolution of his marriage to Priscilla Presley in 1973 coincided with further decline and a tendency to gain weight. Remarkably, he continued to undertake live appearances, mainly in Las Vegas, covering up his bloated frame with brightly coloured jump suits and an enormous, ostentatiously jewelled belt. He collapsed on-stage on a couple of occasions and, on 16 August 1977, his burnt-out body expired. The official cause of death was a heart attack, no doubt brought on by long-term barbiturate usage. In the weeks after his death, his record sales rocketed and 'Way Down' reached the top of the UK charts.

PRESTON, BILLY

Preston (b. 1946) began his musical career playing organ with gospel singer Mahalia Jackson. He also worked with **Sam Cooke** and **Little Richard** and met the **Beatles** during his 1962 European tour. After relocating to Britain as part of the **Ray Charles** revue, he signed to Apple Records in 1969. **George Harrison** produced his UK hit 'That's The Way God Planned It', while Preston contributed keyboards to the Beatles' final album *Let It Be*. He moved to A&M Records, and had a run of hits, including 'Outa-Space' and the US number 1s 'Will It Go Round In Circles' and 'Nothing From Nothing'. His compositional talents were also evident on 'You Are So Beautiful', a US Top 10 hit for **Joe Cocker**. A duet with Syreeta, 'With You I'm Born Again', was an international hit in 1980. In 1989 Preston toured with **Ringo Starr**'s All Star Band and recorded for Ian Levine's Motor City label the following year. He was arrested on a morals charge in the USA during 1991 and his life continued a downward spiral when he was sentenced to three years for a drugs possession offence in 1997.

PRETENDERS

Ohio, USA-born Chrissie Hynde (b. 1951) came to England during the early 70s. After meeting with *New Musical Express* writer Nick Kent she joined the paper, gaining entry into the world of rock. By the time she assembled the

Pretenders in 1978, Hynde had gained a great deal of experience. The classic Pretenders line-up comprised: Pete Farndon (b. 1952, d. 1983; bass), James Honeyman-Scott (b. 1956, d. 1982; guitar) and Martin Chambers (b. 1951; drums). Their debut was a cover version of the **Kinks**' 'Stop Your Sobbing', and 'Kid' and 'Brass In Pocket' followed (the latter reaching number 1 in the UK). Their debut album was a *tour de force* and remains their finest work. *Pretenders II* followed in 1982, but in June of that year, Farndon was fired as a result of his drug problem. Two days later Honeyman-Scott was found dead from a concoction of heroin and cocaine. Nine months later Hynde gave birth

to a daughter; the father was the Kinks' Ray Davies. Two months later Farndon died from a drug overdose.

The new full-time Pretenders were Robbie McIntosh on lead guitar, and bass player Malcolm Foster. *Learning To Crawl* included 'Back On The Chain Gang', a poignant tribute to Honeyman-Scott. In 1984, Hynde married Jim Kerr of **Simple Minds** and duetted with **UB40** on the remake of **Sonny And Cher**'s 'I Got You Babe'. Following the birth of another daughter, Hynde dismantled the band for a period. *Get Close*, released at the end of 1987, included the UK hits 'Don't Get Me Wrong' and 'Hymn To Her'. In 1990 she returned with *Packed!*, still as the Pretenders. *Last Of The Independents* was released in 1994, with Hynde and Chambers joined by Adam Seymour (guitar) and Andy Hobson (bass). In 1995, in the company of **Cher**, **Neneh Cherry** and **Eric Clapton**, Hynde topped the UK charts with the charity single 'Love Can Build A Bridge'. The same year's *The Isle Of View* saw Hynde performing an acoustic set of Pretenders material backed by a string quartet. She returned to the band format with 1999's *¡Viva El Amor!*, a passionate record that spoke volumes about Hynde's undying commitment to rock music.

PRETTY THINGS

This UK R&B band was formed in 1963 by Dick Taylor (b. 1943; guitar), Phil May (b. 1944; vocals), Brian Pendleton (b. 1944, d. 2001; rhythm guitar), John Stax (b. 1944; bass) and Peter Kitley (drums), who was quickly replaced by Viv Andrews and then Viv Prince. Their brash approach to R&B flourished with 'Don't Bring Me Down' and 'Honey I Need'. Their first album offered much of the same. Skip Alan (b. Alan Skipper, 1948) replaced Prince in 1965, and although the Pretty Things' commercial standing subsequently declined, 'Midnight To Six Man' and 'Come See Me' were arguably their finest works. Pendleton and Stax then left and *Emotions* was completed with Wally Allen (bass, vocals) and John Povey (b. 1944; keyboards, vocals).

By late 1967 the quintet was immersed in the emergent underground scene, and their new-found confidence flourished on 1968's concept album *S.F. Sorrow*. Dick Taylor's departure in 1969 was highly damaging, and following

the release of *Parachute* the Pretty Things collapsed in 1971. May, Povey and Skip Alan re-formed to complete *Freeway Madness*. May left for a solo career in 1976, but the *Emotions* line-up plus guitarist Peter Tolson (b. 1951) managed to complete *Cross Talk*. In 1996 after dozens of changes of personnel and image the line-up was the same as the unit that recorded the stunning 'Come See Me': May, Taylor, Alan, Allan and Povey. *S.F. Sorrow* was given its live premiere at Abbey Road studios in September 1998. A new studio album followed.

PRICE, ALAN

This UK artist's first major band, the Alan Price Rhythm And Blues Combo, became the **Animals**, but despite commercial success Price (b. 1941) found the pressure of touring too much and left the band in 1965. That year he appeared in the movie *Don't Look Back* as one of **Bob Dylan**'s entourage. The Alan Price Set debuted in 1965 with 'Any Day Now'. In 1967 he had two major hits written by **Randy Newman**; 'Simon Smith And His Amazing Dancing Bear' and 'The House That Jack Built'. Three years later he and **Georgie Fame** had a hit with 'Rosetta'. Price was commissioned to write the music for Lindsay Anderson's *O Lucky Man!* in 1973, for which he won a BAFTA. The following year Price hit the charts with 'Jarrow Song'.

Price starred in *Alfie Darling* in 1975, winning the Most Promising New British Actor award. In addition to writing stage musicals like *Andy Capp* and *Who's A Lucky Boy?* he took part in two abortive Animals reunions in 1977 and 1983. He recorded a new album in 1995 with his Electric Blues Company which was a return to his R&B club days in Newcastle.

PRICE, LLOYD

US rock 'n' roll singer Price (b. 1933) formed his own band in New Orleans in 1949 and three years later signed with Specialty Records. 'Lawdy Miss Clawdy', established his career in the R&B field and he followed with four more Top 10 hits. In 1956 he settled in Washington, DC, setting up a record company with Harold Logan. Price regained his place on the chart in 1957 with 'Just Because' (US R&B number 3 and pop Top 30). Signed to ABC-Paramount Records, the company transformed him into a rock 'n' roll hit-maker for the new teen market. He and Logan revamped an old blues, 'Stack-O-Lee', and made it one of his biggest successes (US R&B and pop number 1). Price's chart career peaked in 1959, with such hits as 'Where Were You (On Our Wedding Day)', 'Personality' and 'I'm Gonna Get Married', all of which were similarly successful in the UK. The hits continued, to a lesser extent, the following year with 'Lady Luck' and 'Question'. Three years later Price resurfaced on the Double-L label (owned by Price and Logan), briefly making an impact on the emerging soul market with his reworking of jazz standards 'Misty' and 'Bill Bailey' (as 'Billy Baby'). Price's last chart record was in 1976 on the LPG label, a label he formed in partnership with the notorious boxing promoter Don King.

PRIEST, MAXI

This UK reggae singer (b. Max Elliot, 1962) took his new name upon conversion to Rastafarianism. He went on tour with Saxon International, the UK's premier reggae assembly, rubbing shoulders with Peter King and Smiley Culture. He made his name and reputation as a 'singing' DJ, soon progressing to a more soulful style captured on his 1985 debut *You're Safe*. Priest had a run of UK hits in the 80s, including 'Strollin' On', 'Crazy Love', 'Some Guys Have All The Luck' and 'Wild World'. In 1996 Priest enjoyed a Top 20 hit in the UK with 'That Girl', in combination with **Shaggy**.

PRIMAL SCREAM

The line-up that achieved so much success in 1991 comprised Bobby Gillespie (b. 1962; vocals), Andrew Innes (guitar), Robert Young (guitar), Henry Olsen (bass), Philip 'Toby' Tomanov (drums), Martin Duffy (organ) and backing vocalist Denise Johnson (b. 1966), but Primal Scream had been a fluctuating affair since the early 80s. The line-up of Gillespie (ex-**Jesus And Mary Chain**), Beattie, Young (bass), Tom McGurk (drums) and Martin St John (percussion) released 'All Fall Down' on Creation Records in 1985. Further line-up changes ensued before guitarist Innes was brought in to play on 1987's poorly received *Sonic Flower Groove*, a collection of melodic pop songs which was released on the short-lived Elevation label.

Beattie left in 1988 as the band began to veer towards rock territory, releasing a self-titled album and revealing a penchant for leather trousers, wild guitars and idol-worshipping. The band then developed an interest in the burgeoning dance music scene and reinvented themselves, with the aid of name remixers such as **Andrew Weatherall**, into a groove machine. The 'Loaded' single was the first proof of the band's transformation, stealing from rock's heritage and cult biker movies (Peter Fonda's *Wild Angels*) yet invading Britain's dancefloors to become a Top 20 hit in the UK charts in 1990, and inspiring a legion of other indie/dance crossovers. The following year's *Screamadelica* emphasized the band's cultural diversities and won the inaugural Mercury Music Prize.

The follow-up, produced by veteran Atlantic Records soul man Tom Dowd, revealed a stylistic debt to the **Rolling Stones** rather than the dance scene. Though the critical reception was frosty, Gillespie had once again reinvented himself and his band, and was able to enjoy his first UK Top 10 single with 'Rocks'. Ex-**Stone Roses** bass player Gary 'Mani' Mounfield joined the band in 1996 and the new line-up recorded *Vanishing Point*, a timely return to the rhythms of *Screamadelica* but with a far darker edge than the blissed out sentiments of the earlier album. Drummer Paul Mulreany was replaced by Darrin Mooney on *Xtrmntr*, an angry, uncommercial album that served as a welcome antidote to the increasingly bland products of the UK's music industry.

PRINCE

Prince (b. Prince Rogers Nelson, 1958) was named after the Prince Roger Trio, of whom his father, John Nelson, was a member. Brought up in Minneapolis, USA, Prince secured a long-term contract with Warner Brothers Records in the late 70s. He sent shock waves through his new sponsors by spending double his advance on the production of his debut, *Prince For You*. Despite spending considerably less time and money on it than its predecessor, Prince charted (US number 22) and boasted two successful singles, 'Why You Wanna Treat Me So Bad?' and 'I Wanna Be Your Lover'. *Dirty Mind*, *Controversy* and *1999* were released within 18 months of each other. The promotional tour featured a special revue troupe, Prince And The Revolution, replacing his original backing band. 'Little Red Corvette' gained significant airplay on MTV as Prince began work on the *Purple Rain* film, a glamourized auto-biographical piece in which he would star. 'When Doves Cry', from the soundtrack, became the first Prince song to grace the top of the US charts. 'Let's Go Crazy' and 'Purple Rain' (numbers 1 and 2, respectively) further established him as an 80s figurehead.

After the end of a huge and successful tour, Prince returned to the studio to record the quasi-psychedelic *Around The World In A Day*. He also founded the Minneapolis-based studio/label complex Paisley Park. As work began on a second movie, *Under The Cherry Moon*, 'Kiss' was released, becoming his third US number 1, pipping the **Bangles**' 'Manic Monday' (written by Prince) to the top slot. He then set out on the *Parade* tour to promote the number 1 album of the same name. The shows were spectacular even by Prince's standards, but his backing band the Revolution were disbanded at the end of the tour.

In 1987 Prince instituted a new line-up for the latest live engagements, retaining the backbone of the Revolution and adding Sheila E.. After the excellent *Sign 'O' The Times'* came *Lovesexy* and the soundtrack album for *Batman*, the latter topping the US charts for six weeks. In 1990 he released *Graffiti Bridge*, accompanying a film of the same title, but the album was his first commercial let-down for some time, peaking at number 6 in the USA (although it made number 1 in the UK). Prince, as usual, was busy putting together new projects. These included his latest backing outfit, the New Power Generation. They were in place in time for the sessions for *Diamonds And Pearls*, released in 1991. Greeted by critics as a return to form, the New Power Generation were considered his most able and vibrant collaborators since the mid-80s. Taken from it, 'Cream' became a US number 1. Both 'Sexy MF' and 'My Name Is Prince' were included on the *Love Symbol Album*, which introduced the cryptic 'symbol' that he would legally adopt as his name in 1993. Much of the attention subsequently surrounding the artist concerned his protracted battle against his record company, Warner Brothers. In October he abandoned the symbol moniker, becoming instead 'The Artist Formerly Known As Prince'.

In 1995, he released *The Gold Experience*, which included the smoothly accessible 'The Most Beautiful Girl In The World', his bestselling single for many years. Following the release of *Chaos And Disorder* in 1996, he sacked the New Power Generation and announced that he would not be touring, preferring to spend more time with his wife and new baby (who tragically died months after birth). He celebrated his release from the Warner Brothers contract with the sprawling *Emancipation*. Another 4-CD set, *Crystal Ball*, was initially sold over the Internet before being released to distributors. In May 2000, Prince announced he had reverted back to using his original moniker.

PRINCE BUSTER

Jamican-born Buster (b. Cecil Bustamante Campbell, 1938) began his career as a boxer, but soon found himself being put to use as a minder for Coxsone Dodd's Down Beat sound system. He claims, like many others, to have invented the ska sound. His first recording session produced one of the all-time classics of Jamaican music, 'Oh Carolina'. Buster released countless records both by himself and other top acts which were subsequently released in the UK on the Blue Beat imprint. He toured the UK in the mid-60s, appeared on *Ready, Steady, Go!* and enjoyed chart success with 'Al Capone' and 'Madness'.

Throughout the rest of the 70s and on into the 80s Buster lived on his shops, his juke-boxes and his past glories, but he returned to live work in the latter half of the 80s. In 1992, he even started, for the first time in years, to record new music again. 'Whine & Grine' was used as a soundtrack to a Levi's commercial, resulting in a return to the UK charts in 1998.

PRINE, JOHN

US singer-songwriter Prine (b. 1946) began his career singing in Chicago clubs, signing to Atlantic Records in 1971. His debut album contained the excellent

Vietnam veteran song 'Sam Stone'. Following the album's release, Prine went on to achieve cult status, his songs being increasingly covered by other artists, but failed to make a commercial breakthrough. During the 80s he released several albums on his own Oh Boy label, but it was 1991's *The Missing Years* which re-established his name and won a Grammy award for Best Contemporary Folk Album. In keeping with his career upswing, 1995's *Lost Dogs & Mixed Blessings* was another strong work. Since then Prine has beaten cancer, having had surgery in its earliest stage, and released the excellent *In Spite Of Ourselves*.

PROBY, P.J.

This iconoclastic US singer (b. James Marcus Smith, 1938) spent his early career in Hollywood, recording demos for song publishing houses. Several low-key singles ensued, credited to Jett Powers before the Proby appellation surfaced on 'So Do I' (1963). An ebullient revival of 'Hold Me', originally a gentle ballad, brought Proby a UK Top 3 hit, while the similarly raucous 'Together' reached number 8. Proby completely changed direction following a move to Liberty Records and, again, reached the UK Top 10 with a memorable version of 'Somewhere' from *West Side Story*. This record started a series of epic ballads featuring Proby's strong but affected vocal. Both 'I Apologise' and 'Maria' became big hits.

Following a 'split trousers' incident, Proby was accused of obscenity by the UK media. He then made an act of regularly splitting his crushed blue velvet jumpsuit. His chart career suddenly floundered and Proby was relegated to the cabaret circuit. Although he continued to record, the press were more interested in his tax problems and subsequent bankruptcy. In 1970, Proby took the role of Iago in *Catch My Soul*, but his subsequent work was more sporadic. He appeared on the UK nightclub circuit, played **Elvis Presley** in the stage production *Elvis On Stage* until he was sacked, and continued to court publicity for erratic behaviour. Years of apparent self-abuse have robbed the singer of his powers of old, but he retains the ability to enthral and infuriate with further stage appearances and occasional recording sessions.

PROCLAIMERS

This Scottish folk-pop duo comprises identical twins Craig and Charlie Reid. They had an early UK hit in 1987 with the **Gerry Rafferty**-produced 'Letter From America'. Follow-ups included the typically boisterous 'Make My Heart Fly' and 'I'm Gonna Be (500 Miles)'. The duo took a two-year sabbatical following the release of *Sunshine On Leith*. They reappeared in 1990 with the *King Of The Road* EP. The title track, a cover of the old Roger Miller song, came from the movie *The Crossing*. On the back of the unexpected success of 'I'm Gonna Be (500 Miles)', which reached the US Top 5 in 1993 after featuring prominently in the movie *Benny & Joon*, their comeback album *Hit The Highway* enjoyed commercial success in America. Following that they once again disappeared from the public's immediate view. Seven years were to pass before their next album was released.

PROCOL HARUM

This UK progressive rock band was formed from the ashes of R&B band the Paramounts by Gary Brooker (b. 1945; piano, vocals), Matthew Fisher (b. 1946; organ), Bobby Harrison (b. 1939; drums), Ray Royer (b. 1945; guitar) and Dave Knights (b. 1945; bass). Their debut, the Bach-influenced 'A Whiter Shade Of Pale', made them one of the biggest successes of 1967. It was followed by the Top 10 hit 'Homburg'. By the time a hastily thrown-together debut album was released, the band were falling apart. Harrison and Royer departed to be replaced by B.J. Wilson (b. Barrie James Wilson, 1947, d. 1990) and **Robin Trower** (b. 1945), respectively. The other unofficial member of the band was lyricist Keith Reid (b. 1946).

A Salty Dog was released to critical acclaim before Fisher and Knights departed and the circle was completed when Chris Copping (b. 1945; organ, bass) became the last former member of the Paramounts to join the band. Trower's **Jimi Hendrix**-influenced guitar patterns on *Broken Barricades* began to give the band a heavier image, not compatible with Reid's fantasy sagas. This was resolved by Trower's departure, the recruitment of Dave Ball (b. 1950) and the addition of Alan Cartwright (bass). The band pursued a more symphonic direction on the million-selling *Live In Concert With The Edmonton Symphony Orchestra*. Further line-up changes ensued with Ball departing and Mick Grabham (b. 1948) joining in 1972. This line-up became the band's most stable and they enjoyed four successful and busy years during which they released three albums. By the time their final album was released in 1977 the musical climate had dramatically changed and Procol Harum were one of the first casualties of punk.

In August 1991, Brooker, Trower, Fisher and Reid got back together, with Mark Brzezicki (b. 1957; ex-**Big Country**) replacing the recently deceased Wilson. Unlike many re-formed 'dinosaurs' the result was a well-received album *The Prodigal Stranger*. Brooker has continued to lead various line-ups of Procol Harum ever since.

PRODIGY

Based in Essex, England, the Prodigy was formed by MC Maxim Reality (b. Keith Palmer, 1967), Liam Howlett (b. 1971), Keith Flint (b. 1969) and Leeroy Thornhill (b. 1968). Howlett, a former breakdancer and DJ, handles most of the compositions and governs the band's style. The Prodigy signed to XL Records in 1990 and, in February the following year, released their first EP, *What Evil Lurks*, which proved highly popular on the underground rave scene. Their next record, 'Charly', which used samples of the famous public information road safety advertisement, climbed to number 3 on the UK charts, bringing the Prodigy to the attention of a wider audience. Its success spawned a number of similar 'toytown' techno releases.

The Prodigy differed from many anonymous dance acts by presenting a frenetic live show, with Flint and Thornhill dancing and Maxim on vocals. Their mainstream success continued with a series of Top 20 hits, which were included on their debut album, released in 1992. The Top 5 single 'No Good (Start the Dance)' preceded the album *Music For The Jilted Generation*, which entered the UK album chart at number 1. Two more singles, 'Voodoo People' and 'Poison', continued their commercial success. While they retained some elements of their original hardcore sound (notably the breakbeats), musical mastermind Howlett had broadened their sound with 'radio-friendly' elements.

In 1996, they achieved their first UK number 1 single with 'Firestarter'. Towards the end of the year, 'Breathe' became their second UK number 1 single and confirmed their popularity with a mainstream rock audience both at home and abroad. In June 1997, *Fat Of The Land* entered the UK album chart at number 1. The album moved towards a punk and thrash-style, blending techno and breakbeat sounds with guitar, live drums and vocals to create a distinctive, futuristic hybrid of rock and dance. They invoked media outrage with the release of the controversial 'Smack My Bitch Up' and its 'pornographic' promotional video. The following year Howlett released an acclaimed mix album under the Prodigy name. Thornill

subsequently left the band to release *Beyond All Reasonable Doubt* under the Flightcrank pseudonym.

PSYCHEDELIC FURS

Until they recruited drummer Vince Ely in 1979, Richard Butler (b. 1956; vocals), Roger Morris (guitar), John Ashton (b. 1957; guitar), Duncan Kilburn (woodwinds) and Tim Butler (b. 1958; bass) had difficulty finding work. Under Steve Lillywhite's direction, their bleak debut album was followed by minor singles chart entries with 'Dumb Waiter' and 'Pretty In Pink', both selections from 1981's more tuneful and enduring *Talk Talk Talk*. Philip Calvert (ex-**Birthday Party**) replaced Ely in 1982, and they released *Mirror Moves* which included UK Top 30 hit, 'Heaven'. 'Pretty In Pink' became a transatlantic hit when it featured in the 1986 movie of the same title. By 1990, Ashton and the Butler brothers were all that remained of the band. Three years later Richard Butler moved on to Love Spit Love, but reunited with his brother and John Ashton at the end of the decade.

PUBLIC ENEMY

Hugely influential and controversial New York, USA-based rap act, frequently referred to as 'The Black Sex Pistols', Public Enemy's legacy extends beyond rap, and has attained a massive cultural significance within black communities. Their origins can be traced to the college radio station at Adelphi University, New York in 1982. DJ **Chuck D** (b. Carlton Douglas Ridenhour, 1960) and Hank Shocklee were joined by Flavor Flav (b. William Drayton, 1959). By 1987 they had signed to Rick Rubin's Def Jam label and increased their line-up for musical and visual purposes – Professor Griff (b. Richard Griffin), DJ Terminator X (b. Norman Rogers) and a four-piece words/dance/martial arts back-up section (Security Of The First World). Their debut *Yo! Bum Rush The Show* was a raw-edged debut, but *It Takes A Nation Of Millions To Hold Us Back* signified a clear division between them and the gangsta rappers. Public Enemy were beginning to ask questions, and if America's white mainstream audience chose to fear rap, the invective expressed within 'Black Steel In The Hour Of Chaos', 'Prophets Of Rage' and 'Bring The Noise' gave them excellent cause. That anxiety was cleverly exploited in the title of the band's third set, *Fear Of A Black Planet*, recorded without Griff who had been ousted in 1989 for anti-Semitic statements. *Apocalypse 91 . . . The Enemy Strikes Black* was almost as effective, the band hardly missing a beat musically or lyrically with 'Bring The Noise', performed with thrash metal outfit **Anthrax**.

In the early 90s several members of the band embarked on solo careers, while Hank Shocklee and his brother Keith established Shocklee Entertainment in 1993. Public Enemy released their first album in three years in 1994 with *Muse Sick-N-Hour Mess Age*. Following its release, Flav was charged with possession of cocaine and a firearm in November 1995, while Chuck D. became a noted media pundit. In 1998 the original line-up regrouped for a new album, which also served as the soundtrack for Spike Lee's *He Got Game*. Public Enemy terminated their 12-year association with Def Jam shortly afterwards, a series of disagreements ending with an argument over the band's decision to post their new single, 'Swindler's Lust', on the Internet. They then signed up with an Internet record company and became the first mainstream band to release an album online.

PUBLIC IMAGE LIMITED

Public Image Ltd (PiL) was the 'company' formed by John Lydon (b. 1956) after leaving the **Sex Pistols** in 1978. With Keith Levene (guitar), **Jah Wobble** (b. John

Wardle; bass) and Canadian Jim Walker (drums), they released their debut single, the epic 'Public Image', later in the year. In 1979 ex-**Raincoats** drummer Richard Dudanski replaced Walker. *Metal Box* came out later that year. One of the era's most radical albums, it blended Lydon's antagonism and Levene's abrasive guitar work. Dudanski left and **Fall** drummer Karl Burns was enlisted until Martin Atkins (b. 1959) joined in time to tour the USA in 1980. *Paris Au Printemps* was recorded after which Wobble and Atkins left. After *Flowers Of Romance* Pete Jones (b. 1957) became bass player, and Atkins returned on drums. In 1983 Jones and Levene left as 'This Is Not A Love Song' became a UK Top 5 hit. Their 1986 release *Album* featured **Ginger Baker**'s drumming talents on the hit single 'Rise'. Lydon assembled a permanent band the following year, drawing on guitarists John McGeoch and Lu Edmunds, bass player Allan Dias and drummer Bruce Smith. The band fell into inactivity in the 90s, with Lydon concentrating on his autobiography and other musical projects.

PULP

From Sheffield, England, Jarvis Cocker (b. 1963) put the first version of Pulp together whilst at school, recording a John Peel radio session in 1981. That line-up boasted Cocker (vocals, guitar), Peter Dalton (keyboards), Jamie Pinchbeck (bass) and Wayne Furniss (drums). After the mini-album *It*, the first real evidence of Cocker's abilities as a lyricist arrived with tracks such as 'Little Girl (With Blue Eyes)' and 'They Suffocate At Night'.

It took a third chapter in the band's history, and a new line-up, to provide the commercial impetus. By 1992 the band's steady line-up comprised Cocker, Russell Senior (guitar, violin), Candida Doyle (keyboards), Stephen Mackay (bass) and Nicholas Banks (drums). Their 1994 single, 'Do You Remember The First Time?', was accompanied by a short film in which famous celebrities were quizzed on the loss of their virginity. The song appeared on their major-label debut, *His 'N' Hers*. The album was later nominated for the 1994 Mercury Music Prize. *Different Class* offered a supreme evocation of the 'behind the net curtains' sexual mores of working class Britons, with the sardonic hit single 'Common People' becoming one of the anthems of the year. Cocker became the darling of the music press in 1995, but during the following year's BRIT Awards he was arrested after invading **Michael Jackson**'s grandiose stage show. There was a spurious charge of actual bodily harm, but all charges were eventually dropped.

Russell Senior left the band in February 1997 (later forming Venini), and in November of that year, Pulp returned with a new single, 'Help The Aged'. It was followed by the sexually charged *This Is Hardcore*, a difficult album that alienated some of the band's new fans and suffered commercially as a result. A long hiatus ensued during which Cocker indulged his other artistic interests, including a series of UK television documentaries on 'outsider artists'. The band returned to the studio in the new millennium, with the reclusive American singer **Scott Walker** acting as producer on the excellent *We Love Life*.

PURE PRAIRIE LEAGUE

Formed in 1971, this US country rock group comprised Craig Lee Fuller (vocals, guitar), George Powell (vocals, guitar), John Call (pedal steel guitar), Jim Lanham (bass) and Jim Caughlin (drums). *Bustin' Out*, recorded by Fuller and Powell with session musicians, proved their masterwork, and is one of the most underrated country rock records. Fuller left in 1975 to form American Flyer and Powell continued with bass player Mike Reilly, lead guitarist Larry Goshorn and pianist Michael Connor. Several minor albums followed and the band achieved a surprise US Top 10 hit in 1980 with 'Let Me Love You Tonight'. Fuller later joined the revamped Little Feat, while latterday guitarist **Vince Gill**, who joined Pure Prairie League in 1979, became a superstar in the country market in the 90s. At the end of the 90s Fuller had returned and was performing with O'Connor, Gerry House, Reilly and songwriter Gary Burr.

QUATRO, SUZI

With older sister, Patti (later of Fanny), US singer Suzi Quatro (b. 1950) formed the all-female Suzi Soul And The Pleasure Seekers in 1964 and toured army bases in Vietnam. In 1971, Mickie Most persuaded her to record for his RAK Records label in England. Backed by UK musicians Alastair McKenzie (keyboards), Dave Neal (drums) and her future husband, Len Tuckey (guitar), a second RAK single, 1973's 'Can The Can', topped worldwide charts at the zenith of the glam-rock craze. The team's winning streak with the likes of '48 Crash', 'Daytona Demon' and 'Devil Gate Drive' – a second UK number 1 – faltered when 'Your Mama Won't Like Me' stuck outside the Top 30. More satisfying than tilting for hit records, however, was her development as a singing

actress, albeit in character as 'Leather Tuscadero' in seven episodes of *Happy Days* during 1977. Quatro landed the role of the quick-drawing heroine in the 1986 London production of Irving Berlin's *Annie Get Your Gun*, and went on to write and star in *Tallulah Who?* By the late 90s she was concentrating on touring and recording once more and carving a career as a broadcaster on BBC radio.

QUEEN

One of the UK's most successful rock groups of the 70s and 80s, Queen were formed as a glam-rock unit in 1971 by Brian May (b. 1947; guitar), Roger Taylor (b. Roger Meddows-Taylor, 1949; drums), Freddie Mercury (b. Frederick Bulsara, 1946, d. 1991; vocals) and John Deacon (b. 1951; bass).

Signed to EMI Records, Queen's self-titled album was an interesting fusion of 70s British glam and late 60s heavy rock. A second album fulfilled their early promise by reaching the UK Top 5. Soon after, 'Seven Seas Of Rhye' gave them their first hit single, while *Sheer Heart Attack* consolidated their commercial standing. In 1975, after touring the Far East, they completed the epic 'Bohemian Rhapsody'. The track remained at UK number 1 for nine weeks, and is now established as one of the most popular songs of all time. *A Night At The Opera* and *A Day At The Races* confirmed Queen's commercial ascendancy. The pomp and circumstance of their live act was embodied in the outrageously camp theatrics of the satin-clad Mercury, who was swiftly emerging as one of rock's most notable showmen.

The rock 'n' roll pastiche 'Crazy Little Thing Called Love' and the disco-influenced 'Another One Bites The Dust' both reached US number 1 in the late 70s, while *The Game* topped the US album chart in 1980. The band's soundtrack for the movie *Flash Gordon* was another success. In 1981, Queen were back at UK number 1 with 'Under Pressure' (a collaboration with **David Bowie**). After a flurry of solo ventures, they returned in fine form with the satirical 'Radio Gaga' (1984). A performance at 1985's Live Aid displayed Queen at their most professional and many acclaimed them the stars of the day (though there were others who accused them of hypocrisy for breaking the boycott of apartheid-locked South Africa).

By the time of 1991's UK chart-topper *Innuendo*, Queen had become an institution. Tragically, the band's ascendancy was stopped by the AIDS-related death of Freddie Mercury on 24 November 1991. A memorial concert took place at London's Wembley Stadium in May 1992, featuring an array of stars. A new Queen album was released in 1995, featuring Mercury vocals recorded during his last year of life.

QUEEN LATIFAH

Rap's first lady, Queen Latifah (b. Dana Owens, 1970) began working alongside female rapping crew Ladies Fresh, before releasing her debut single, 'Wrath Of My Madness', in 1988. Her first two albums enjoyed favourable reviews. By *Black Reign*, she had moved from Tommy Boy to Motown Records, and revealed a shift from soul and ragga tones to sophisticated, sassy hip-hop. Following a lengthy hiatus owing to acting commitments, Latifah returned to recording with 1998's *Order In The Court*.

QUEENS OF THE STONE AGE

California, USA-based heavy rock band formed from the ashes of Kyuss in 1995. Guitarist Joshua Homme began writing songs with former bandmate Alfredo Hernandez, and cooked up the provocative Queens Of The Stone Age moniker. Original Kyuss bass player Nick Oliveri, who had been playing with the Dwarves, joined up in time to help record the Queens Of The Stone Age's self-titled 1998

debut album. A minimalist update on Kyuss' acid-tinged desert rock sound, the album included the US alternative radio hit, 'If Only'. Hernandez left before the release of *Rated R*, which was recorded with a fluctuating line-up including drummers Gene Troutman and Nicky Lucero, pianist/lap steel guitarist Dave Catching, and guest vocalists Mark Lanegan and Rob Halford.

QUEENSRŸCHE

Hard rock band formed in Seattle, USA, by Geoff Tate (vocals), Chris DeGarmo (guitar), Michael Wilton (guitar), Eddie Jackson (bass) and Scott Rockenfield (drums). In 1983, the band launched their own 206 Records label to house the

songs on a self-titled 12-inch EP. EMI Records then offered them a seven-album deal. Their debut, *The Warning*, was comparatively disappointing. *Rage For Order* saw the band creating a more distinctive style, making full use of modern technology. *Operation: Mindcrime*, a George Orwell-inspired concept album, was greeted with acclaim, and worldwide sales of over one million lifted the band into rock's first division. *Empire* boasted a stripped-down but still dream-like rock aesthetic, best sampled on 'Silent Lucidity', a US Top 10 hit in 1991. *Promised Land* continued the band's tradition of dramatic song structures, but 1997's experimental *Hear In The New Frontier* confused both critics and record buyers. DeGarmo left the band the following year and was replaced by Kelly Gray. The new line-up made a short-lived move to Atlantic Records, resulting in 1999's studio set *Q2K*.

? AND THE MYSTERIANS

Formed in 1963 in Michigan, USA, as XYZ, ? And The Mysterians ultimately comprised Mexican vocalist ? (b. Rudy Martinez), Frankie Rodriguez Jnr (b. 1951; keyboards), Robert Lee 'Bobby' Balderrama (guitar), Francisco Hernandez 'Frank' Lugo (b. 1947; bass) and Eduardo Delgardo 'Eddie' Serrato (drums). The garage-rock classic '96 Tears' was initially intended as the B-side of their debut single, but after being popularized by Michigan DJs, Cameo Records took it to US number 1 in 1966. ? And The Mysterians never again came close to recapturing their brief moment of fame. Further low-key releases appeared sporadically through the 70s and 80s, and in 1997 the band re-formed to re-record the best of their classic 60s material for the Collectables label.

QUICKSILVER MESSENGER SERVICE

Of all the bands that came out of the San Francisco, USA area during the late 60s, Quicksilver Messenger Service typified most the style, attitude and sound of that era. The band was formed in 1964 by Dino Valenti (b. 1943, d. 1994; vocals), John Cipollina (b. 1943, d. 1989; guitar), David Freiberg (b. 1938; bass, vocals), Jim Murray (vocals, harmonica) and Casey Sonoban (drums). In 1965, Sonoban left and Gary Duncan (b. Gary Grubb, 1946; guitar) and Greg Elmore (b. 1946; drums) joined. Murray departed after the band's appearance at the Monterey Pop Festival in 1967. The quartet of Cipollina, Duncan, Elmore and Freiberg recorded the first two albums, marked by the twin lead guitars of Cipollina and Duncan. The second collection, *Happy Trails*, is now regarded as a classic. Duncan left and was replaced by UK session pianist **Nicky Hopkins** (b. 1944, d. 1994). *Just For Love* showed a further decline, with Valenti, now back with the band, becoming overpowering and self-indulgent. Cipollina departed, as did Freiberg following his arrest in 1971 for drug possession. Various incarnations have appeared over the years with little or no success. As recently as 1987, Duncan recorded an album carrying the band's name.

RADIOHEAD

UK rock band formed in 1991. Thom Yorke (b. 1968; vocals, guitar), Ed O'Brien (b. 1968; guitar), Colin Greenwood (b. 1969; bass), Phil Selway (b. 1967; drums) and Colin's brother Jonny (b. 1971; guitar, keyboards) were originally known as On A Friday. They became Radiohead in 1991. 'Creep' then became the alternative rock song of 1993. Ignored when first released in 1992, its re-release sparked enormous interest as the band toured with Kingmaker and **James**, and reached the UK Top 10 and US Top 40. *Pablo Honey* was followed by *The Bends* in 1995. By the end of the year *The Bends* had been universally acclaimed, winning Radiohead a BRIT Awards nomination as the best band of the year. Two years later, the band unveiled its follow-up, *OK Computer*, which received spectacular reviews.

Three years later, *Kid A* delivered a challenging electronic set, almost free of guitars. Reviews were initially mixed, but the fact that it entered both the UK and US charts at number 1 cannot be ignored. The equally challenging *Amnesiac* followed barely eight months later. The commercial success of both albums and the phenomenal speed with which tickets for their subsequent US tour sold out, owed a lot to the band's willingness to exploit their Internet presence in favour of conventional promotional methods.

RAE AND CHRISTIAN

UK hip-hop duo comprising Mark Rae, co-founder of the Grand Central label, and Steve Christian. Their 1998 debut *Northern Sulphuric Soul*, recorded with female vocalist Veba, fulfilled their early promise. Production and remix work with **Texas**, **Simply Red**, **Natalie Imbruglia** and the **Manic Street Preachers** pushed their reputation beyond underground circles. The duo's second album brought in veterans such as **Bobby Womack**, Tania Maria, and the Congos to add a new dimension to their sound.

RAFFERTY, GERRY

Scottish singer-songwriter Rafferty (b. 1947) began his career with the Humblebums in 1968. After its demise, Transatlantic Records offered him a solo contract. *Can I Have My Money Back?* blended folk and gentle pop music, but it was a commercial failure. After four years with **Stealers Wheel**, he went solo again with *City To City* in 1978. The charming 'Baker Street' became a hit single and a multi-million seller. The follow-up, *Night Owl*, was also a commercial success. Since then Rafferty's output has been sparse and of varying quality.

RAGE AGAINST THE MACHINE

This US alternative band's music is an aggressive blend of metal guitar and hip-hop rhythms that address their concerns about inner-city deprivation, racism, censorship and propaganda. Formed in Los Angeles in 1991 by guitarist Tom Morello and vocalist Zack De La Rocha, with Tim Commerford (bass) and Brad Wilk (drums), Rage Against The Machine's self-titled debut was a hit on both sides of the Atlantic, scoring single success with 'Killing In The Name'. *Evil Empire* was more successful, reaching US number 1, and 'Bulls On Parade' providing the band with a transatlantic hit single. After another long hiatus, the band returned in 1999 with *The Battle Of Los Angeles*. Hardly deviating from the blueprint of their previous two records, the album was warmly received by their supporters but dismissed by detractors who felt the

band had nothing new left to say. La Rocha left the following year, making his final appearance with the band on the cover versions set, *Renegades*.

RAIN PARADE

Part of Los Angeles' rock renaissance of the early 80s, the Rain Parade drew from late 60s influences to forge a new brand of psychedelia-tinged rock. After a promising debut single, 'What She's Done To Your Mind', the band – David Roback (vocals, guitar, percussion), brother Steve (vocals, bass), Matthew Piucci (vocals, guitar, sitar), Will Glenn (keyboards, violin) and Eddie Kalwa (drums) – issued *Emergency Third Rail Power Trip* (1983) to critical acclaim. A contract with Island Records followed, with David Roback replaced by John Thoman and new drummer Mark Marcum featuring on 1985's *Beyond The Sunset*. The band's final album, *Crashing Dream*, emerged later in the year, but some of Rain Parade's otherworldly, evocative nature had been lost.

RAINBOW

In 1975 **Ritchie Blackmore** (b. 1945; guitar) formed Rainbow with Ronnie James Dio (b. Ronald Padavona, 1940; vocals), Mickey Lee Soule (keyboards), Craig Gruber (bass) and Gary Driscoll (drums). Their debut, *Ritchie Blackmore's Rainbow*, was released in 1975. The constant turnover of personnel reflected Blackmore's quest for the ultimate line-up and sound. Jimmy Bain took over from Gruber, and Cozy Powell (b. Colin Powell, 1947, d. 1998) replaced Driscoll. With Tony Carey (b. 1953) on keyboards, *Rainbow Rising* was released. Shortly after, Bob Daisley and David Stone replaced Bain and Carey. After difficulties with Blackmore, Dio departed in 1978. His replacement was Graham Bonnet. *Down To Earth*, which saw the return of Roger Glover on bass, was a marked departure from the Dio days, but featured the enduring hit single, 'Since You've Been Gone'. Bonnet and Powell soon became victims of another reorganization of Rainbow's line-up. Bobby Rondinelli (drums) and Joe Lynn Turner (vocals) brought an American feel to the band, and a commercial sound was introduced on *Difficult To Cure*, the album which produced 'I Surrender', their biggest hit. Thereafter the band went into decline and, in 1984, the popular **Deep Purple** reunion marked its end. The band played its last gig on 14 March 1984 in Japan, accompanied by a symphony orchestra, as Blackmore adapted Beethoven's 'Ninth Symphony'. Since then, the name has been resurrected in a number line-ups, with a new studio recording issued in 1995.

RAINCOATS

Formed in London, England, in 1976 by Gina Birch and Ana Da Silva, with the flexible line-up at times including Vicky Aspinall, Shirley O'Loughlin and Palmolive (b. Paloma Romero). The Raincoats' debut, 'Fairytale In The Supermarket', appeared on Rough Trade Records in 1979. A self-titled album the same year boasted a similarly distinctive punk sound. *Odyshape* followed in 1981. The Raincoats delivered their swansong in 1984 with *Moving*.

The band's name was resurrected by Kurt Cobain of **Nirvana**, who asked the Raincoats to support his band on upcoming UK dates (he would also write sleeve-notes for the CD reissues of their albums). The 1994 model Raincoats featured Da Silva and Birch joined by violinist Anne Wood (violin) and Steve Shelley (drums). A new album, *Looking In The Shadows*, featured Da Silva and Birch augmented by Heather Dunn (drums) and Anne Wood (violin).

RAITT, BONNIE

US artist Raitt (b. 1949) established her reputation with live appearances throughout the east coast circuit. The somewhat reverential *Bonnie Raitt*, released in 1971, was replaced by the contemporary perspective of *Give It Up* and *Taking My Time*. Subsequent releases followed a similar pattern, and although *Streetlights* was a disappointment, *Home Plate*, reasserted her talent. The success of 1977's *Sweet Forgiveness* was a natural progression on which its

follow-up, *The Glow*, failed to capitalize.

After *Green Light* and *Nine Lives*, Raitt was dropped by Warner Brothers. She bounced back in 1989 with the acclaimed bestseller *Nick Of Time*; the album won a Grammy Award. *Luck Of The Draw* and *Longing In Their Hearts* were also multi-million-sellers. Raitt made a conscious effort to limit her guest appearances in the late 90s, as she felt that her own career was beginning to suffer. Both *Fundamental* and *Silver Lining* marked a noticeable return to form.

RAMMSTEIN

Formed in 1994 in Berlin, Germany, this confrontational alternative rock band comprises former Olympic swimmer Till Lindemann (b. 1963; vocals), Richard Kruspe (b. 1967; guitar), Paul Landers (b. 1964; guitar), Christoph Schneider (b. 1966; drums), Oliver Riedel (b. 1971; bass) and 'Flake' Lorenz (b. Christian Lorenz, 1966; keyboards). They made their debut the following year with *Herzeleid*, which sold in excess of half a million copies in Germany alone, and established the band as a potent commercial force. By the time *Sehnsucht* followed in 1997, they had extended their popularity via a clutch of headlining appearances at European festivals. Following US film director David Lynch's inclusion of two Rammstein songs on the soundtrack to his 1996 movie *Lost Highway*, US gore-metal fans, who followed bands such as **Marilyn Manson** and **KMFDM**, were also won over. Although they sing in German, all the band's lyrics are translated in accompanying liner notes, adding to their international appeal.

RAMONES

US band formed by Johnny Ramone (b. John Cummings, 1948; guitar), Dee Dee Ramone (b. Douglas Colvin, 1951, d. 2002; bass, vocals) and Joey Ramone (b. Jeffrey Hyman, 1951, d. 2001; drums), made their debut at New York's Performance Studio on 30 March 1974. Two months later, manager Tommy Ramone (b. Tommy Erdelyi, 1952) replaced Joey on drums, who switched to vocals. With a residency at the renowned CBGB's club, they were leading proponents of punk rock. *Ramones* was a startling first album. Its high-octane assault drew from 50s kitsch and 60s garage bands, while leather jackets, ripped jeans and an affected dumbness enhanced the music's cartoon quality. The band's debut in London in 1976 influenced a generation of British punk musicians. *The Ramones Leave Home*, which included 'Suzy Is A Headbanger' and 'Gimme Gimme Shock Treatment', confirmed the sonic attack of its predecessor. *Rocket To Russia* produced 'Sheena Is A Punk Rocker', their first UK Top 30 hit.

In 1978 Tommy Ramone left for a career in production and Marky Ramone (b. Marc Bell, 1956) replaced him for *Road To Ruin*. The band took a starring role in the trivial movie *Rock 'N' Roll High School*, which led to collaboration with **Phil Spector**. The resultant release, *End Of The Century*, was a

curious hybrid, but contained a sympathetic cover version of the **Ronettes'** 'Baby, I Love You', which became the band's biggest UK hit single when it reached the Top 10.

The Ramones entered the 80s looking increasingly anachronistic, and *Pleasant Dreams*, produced by Graham Gouldman, revealed a band outshone by the acts they had inspired. However, *Subterranean Jungle* showed a renewed purpose that was maintained sporadically on *Animal Boy* and *Halfway To Sanity*. Richie Ramone (b. Richie Reinhardt, 1957) occupied the drum stool from 1983 to 1987 before the return of Marky. Dee Dee, meanwhile, had adopted the name Dee Dee King and left the band to pursue an ill-fated rap career. Although increasingly confined to pop's fringes, a revitalized line-up – Joey, Johnny, Marky and new bass player C.J. (b. Christopher John Ward, 1965) – undertook a 1990 US tour. They announced their final gig on 6 August 1996 at The Palace club in Hollywood. Joey Ramone succumbed to lymphatic cancer in April 2001. The following year the Ramones were inducted into the Rock And Roll Hall Of Fame. Dee Dee Ramone was found dead after a suspected drugs overdose in June 2002.

RANCID

Matt Freeman (bass), Tim 'Lint' Armstrong (vocals, guitar) and Brett Reed (drums) formed this US punk band in 1989. They made their debut in 1992 with a five-track single, 'I'm Not The Only One', before adding Lars Frederiksen (guitar) to the line-up. Rancid's self-titled debut was released in April 1993, featuring more variety and composure than their debut single. *Let's Go* achieved platinum status, alerting the major labels to Rancid's presence. The band eventually stayed with Epitaph. They returned to the studio in 1995, with . . . *And Out Come The Wolves* the result. Returning to a punk/ska sound, it was a major seller, featuring the two radio hits, 'Time Bomb' and 'Ruby Soho'. The ska theme continued on 1998's *Life Won't Wait*, with two tracks recorded in Jamaica. The album featured a collaboration with Mighty Mighty Bosstones' Dicky Barrett.

RANKS, SHABBA

Ranks (b. Rexton Rawlston Gordon, 1965) recorded his debut 'Heat Under Sufferers Feet' in 1985. Despite an album shared with Chaka Demus (*Rough And Rugged*), he could not establish himself and, in 1988, left King Jammys for Bobby Digital's new label and Heatwave sound system, scoring immediately with 'Mama Man', 'Peanie Peanie' and then 'Wicked In Bed'. Mike 'Home T' Bennett teamed Ranks with Cocoa Tea and his vocal group, Home T4, for 'Who She Love' then 'Stop Spreading Rumours'. They took the formula to Gussie Clarke who produced *Holding On* and big hits including 'Pirate's Anthem', 'Twice My Age' (with Krystal) and 'Mr Loverman'.

Epic Records signed Ranks to a major label contract in late 1990. Their faith was rewarded when remixed versions of 'Mr Loverman' and 'Housecall', the latter a duet with **Maxi Priest**, and 'Slow And Sexy', became major crossover hits during the 90s. Ranks' first album for Epic, *As Raw As Ever*, earned him a US Grammy. The follow-up, *X-Tra Naked*, saw Ranks become the first DJ to win two consecutive Grammy Awards. His subsequent work has switched between dancehall and loverman styles.

RARE EARTH

Saxophonist Gil Bridges and drummer Pete Rivera (Hoorelbeke) formed their first R&B band, the Sunliners, in Detroit, USA, in 1961. John Parrish (bass), Rod Richards (guitar), Kenny James (keyboards), Ralph Terrana (keyboards), Russ Terrana (guitar) and Fred Saxon (saxophone) were later added to the line-up. After years of unspectacular records the band signed to Verve Records and released *Dreams And Answers*. They signed to Motown Records in 1969, where a progressive-rock label was named after them, and enjoyed immediate success with a rock-flavoured version of the **Temptations**' hit 'Get Ready', which reached the US Top 10. Another Temptations' classic, '(I Know) I'm

Losing You', brought them success in 1970, as did original material such as 'Born To Wander' and 'I Just Want To Celebrate'. Despite personnel changes, the band continued to record and tour into the 80s and 90s, enjoying particular success in Europe.

RASPBERRIES

Formed in 1970, the original line-up of this US pop band was **Eric Carmen** (b. 1949; vocals, guitar, keyboards), Marty Murphy (guitar) and Jim Bonfanti (b. 1948; drums). Murphy was quickly replaced by Wally Bryson (b. 1949), who introduced John Aleksic. The latter was replaced by Dave Smalley (b. 1949; guitar, bass). The Raspberries' love of the **Beatles** was apparent on their debut 'Don't Wanna Say Goodbye'. Its melodic flair set the tone of 'Go All The Way', which rose to number 5 in the US chart. The band's talents really blossomed on *Fresh*. The follow-up *Side 3* reflected a growing split between Carmen and the Bonfanti/Smalley team who were fired in 1973. Scott McCarl (guitar) and Michael McBride (drums) completed the new line-up which debuted the following year with the gloriously ambitious 'Overnight Sensation (Hit Record)'. The attendant album, *Starting Over*, contained several memorable songs, but Carmen clearly required a broader canvas for his work. He disbanded the Raspberries in 1975 and embarked on a solo career. Bryson, Smalley and McCarl reunited in the mid-90s to record the mini-album *Refreshed*.

RAY, JOHNNIE

Ray (b. 1927, d. 1990) was also known as the Prince of Wails, the Nabob of Sob and the Howling Success because of his highly emotional singing and apparent ability to cry at will. Of North American Indian origin, he was signed by Columbia Records in 1951. His first record, 'Whiskey And Gin', was followed by the US chart-topping 'Cry'. Always acknowledging his gospel roots, Ray recorded several tracks associated with black artists, including the **Drifters**' R&B hit 'Such a Night' (1954) and 'Just Walkin' In the Rain' (1956), which climbed to US number 2. Three of his US hits reached UK number 1, including 'Yes Tonight Josephine' (1957). In the early 60s, suffering from financial problems and alcoholism, and left behind as the musical climate rapidly changed, he turned to cabaret in the USA. He died of liver failure in 1990 in Los Angeles.

REA, CHRIS

UK rock artist Rea (b. 1951) made his breakthrough in 1978 with 'Fool (If You Think It's Over)', which reached the Top 20 in the US and was later successfully covered in Britain by **Elkie Brooks**. Throughout the early 80s, he gained in popularity across Europe, notably with 'I Can Hear Your Heartbeat' from 1983's *Water Sign*. In Britain, the breakthrough was 1985's *Shamrock Diaries*, which featured the hit 'Stainsby Girls'. In 1989, *The Road To Hell* reached number 1. *Auberge* also topped the UK chart, while its title track reached the UK Top 20. Rea seriously overreached himself with 1996's misguided film project, *La Passione*. He sensibly returned to easily accessible, crafted MOR on *The Blue Cafe*. The following year he took the lead role in Michael Winner's black comedy *Parting Shots*, and released the disappointing *The Road To Hell Part 2*. In summer 2000, Rea enjoyed an unlikely club hit in Ibiza with José Padilla's remix of 'All Summer Long', taken from his new album *King Of The Beach*.

READER, EDDI

After eight years as a session singer, Scottish-born Reader (b. Sadenia Reader, 1959) reached UK number 1 with **Fairground Attraction**'s 'Perfect' (1988). After their disbandment, Reader embarked on a solo career. Her debut album, *Mirmama*, failed to match RCA Record's expectations. A second album followed for Blanco y Negro in 1994 which included the Top 40 hit 'Patience Of Angels'.

In 1996 a change of image revealed a 50s glamour queen. She returned to a more straightforward style for 1998's *Angels & Electricity*. Reader left Blanco y Negro shortly after completing a promotional tour. She debuted on Rough Trade Records with the low-key *Simple Soul*.

RED HOT CHILI PEPPERS

Led by 'Antwan The Swan' (b. Anthony Kiedis, 1962; vocals), this US band's original line-up also featured 'Flea' (b. Michael Balzary, 1962; bass), Hillel Slovak (b. 1962, d. 1988; guitar) and Jack Irons (drums). The band acquired a contract with EMI America and the **Gang Of Four**'s Andy Gill produced their 1984 debut. Slovak returned to guitar for the second album, this time produced by **George Clinton**. Their third album shifted back to rock from the soul infatuation of its predecessors. The *Abbey Road* EP (1988) featured a pastiche of the famous **Beatles**' album pose on the cover (the band were totally naked save for socks covering their genitalia). Slovak took an accidental heroin overdose and died in June. Deeply upset, Irons left, and the band recruited John Frusciante (b. 1970; guitar) and Chad Smith (b. 1962; drums). After the release of *Mother's Milk*, 'Knock Me Down' was issued as a tribute to Slovak. *Blood Sugar Sex, Magik*, produced by **Rick Rubin**, was their most commercial excursion, and featured the US hit single 'Under The Bridge'.

Frusciante was replaced in 1992, with Dave Navarro (b. 1967; ex-**Jane's Addiction**) joining to participate in recording *One Hot Minute*. Navarro left the band in 1998 and was replaced by ex-member Frusciante. Having endured various personal upheavals, it was encouraging to hear the band in such good shape on 1999's US/UK Top 5 album, *Californication*, featuring stand-out tracks such as 'Scar Tissue' (a US Top 10 single), 'Parallel Universe', and 'Easily'.

RED SNAPPER

David Ayers (guitar), Ali Friend (double bass) and Richard Thair (drums) form the creative core of Red Snapper, one of a number of bands who in the mid-90s began creating instrumental music from textures and beats. The trio formed the band in London in 1993 after a varied musical background that included working in a number of jazz and rock outfits in the 80s. The three EPs the band signed to Warp Records who in 1995 collected the first three releases on *Reeled And Skinned*. The *Mooking* and *Loopascoopa* EPs accompanied their debut album *Prince Blimey* in 1996. The follow-up, *Making Bones*, featured contributions from

rapper MC Det, vocalist Alison David and trumpeter Byron Wallen. The mordant title of 2000's *Our Aim Is To Satisfy Red Snapper* reflected the album's difficult gestation period, with the vibrant bounce of their earlier work usurped by an unsettling dance-funk hybrid. In January 2002, the trio announced that following the release of a final EP and mix album they would no longer be working together under the Red Snapper moniker.

REDDING, OTIS

Redding (b. 1941, d. 1967) began recording for local independents and 'She's Alright', credited to Otis And The Shooters, was quickly followed by 'Shout Ba Malama'. 'These Arms Of Mine' crept into the American Hot 100 in 1963. He remained a cult figure until 1965 and the release of *Otis Blue*, in which original material nestled beside the **Rolling Stones**' 'Satisfaction' and two songs by **Sam Cooke**. Redding's version of the **Temptations**' 'My Girl' became a UK hit and 'Tramp', a duet with Carla Thomas, also provided success. A triumphant appearance at the Monterey Pop Festival suggested that Redding was about to attract a wider following, but tragedy struck on 10 December 1967. The light aircraft in which he was travelling plunged into Lake Monona, Madison, Wisconsin, killing Redding and four members of the **Bar-Kays**. The wistful '(Sittin' On) The Dock Of The Bay', which he had recorded three days earlier, became his only million-seller and US pop number 1. Redding's emotional drive remains compelling, and the songs he wrote, often with guitarist **Steve Cropper**, remain some of soul's most enduring moments.

REDDY, HELEN

A big-voiced interpreter of rock ballads, Australian Helen Reddy (b. 1941) had already starred in her own television show before winning a trip to New York in an Australian talent contest in 1966. There, an appearance on the *Tonight Show* led to a contract with Capitol and the 1971 hit single 'I Don't Know How To Love Him' from *Jesus Christ Superstar*. The following year, 'I Am Woman', co-written with Peter Allen, went to number 1 in the US and sold over a million copies. A dozen more hit singles followed. Her 1976 hit, 'I Can't Hear You No More', was composed by **Carole King** and **Gerry Goffin**, while Reddy's final Top 20 record (to date) was a revival of **Cilla Black**'s 1964 chart-topper, 'You're My World', co-produced by Kim Fowley. During the 80s she performed infrequently, but made her first major showcase in years at the Westwood Playhouse, Los Angeles, in 1986. In 1995 she played the lead in the hit musical *Blood Brothers* on Broadway.

REDMAN

Inventive and witty US rapper (b. Reggie Noble) whose 1992 debut *Whut? Thee Album* broke into the US Top 50. Subsequent albums saw him developing into the complete article, earning a reputation as one of rap's leading lyricists. By the time of 1998's stylish *Doc's Da Name 2000*, Redman was emulating several of his contemporaries by becoming involved in all aspects of a project, from co-production duties to marketing and A&R. The following year he collaborated with **Method Man** on the light hearted *Blackout!* The two rappers had previously recorded 1995's US Top 20 single, 'How High'.

REED, JIMMY

Reed (b. Mathis James Reed, 1925, d. 1976) was the most successful US blues singer of the 1950s. Contracted by Vee Jay Records in 1953, his 'You

Don't Have To Go' of 1955 was followed by a string of hits such as 'Ain't That Lovin' You Baby', 'You've Got Me Dizzy', 'Bright Lights Big City', 'I'm Gonna Get My Baby' and 'Honest I Do'. Much of this success must be attributed to his friend Eddie Taylor, who played on most of Reed's sessions, and his wife, Mama Reed, who wrote many of his songs. Reed's later years were marred by his unreliability, illness (he was an epileptic) and the bottle. On his visit to Europe in the early 60s it was obvious all was not well. He gained control over his drink problem, but died of respiratory failure. Reed's songs have influenced countless artists.

REED, LOU

Reed (b. Lewis Allen Reed, 1942) made his US recording debut with the Shades in 1957, later becoming a contract songwriter with Pickwick Records. His many compositions from this era include 'The Ostrich' (1965), which so impressed the label hierarchy that Reed formed the Primitives to promote it as a single. The group also included **John Cale**, thus sowing the seeds of the **Velvet Underground**. Reed left the band to go solo, releasing *Lou Reed* in 1972. Recorded in London with British musicians, the set had some excellent songs but was marred by indistinct production. **David Bowie**, a long-time Velvet Underground aficionado, oversaw *Transformer*. Although uneven, it included the classic hit 'Walk On The Wild Side', but with *Berlin* Reed returned to the dark side of his talents. A back-up band, built around guitarists Dick Wagner and Steve Hunter, provided muscle on the live *Rock 'N' Roll Animal*, but the subsequent *Sally Can't Dance* showed an artist bereft of direction. The unlistenable experimental electronic album *Metal Machine Music* was followed by the sedate *Coney Island Baby*, the inherent charm of which was diluted on the inconsequential *Rock 'N' Roll Heart*. However, its successor, *Street Hassle*, displayed a rejuvenated power, and although *The Bells* and *Growing Up In Public* failed to scale similar heights, they showed new maturity.

Reed entered the 80s a stronger, more incisive performer. However, despite the promise of selections such as *The Blue Mask*, few were prepared for 1989's *New York*. This splendid return to form created considerable interest in Reed's back-catalogue. The following year Reed collaborated with John Cale on the Andy Warhol tribute, *Songs For 'Drella*. In 1993, Reed joined his legendary colleagues for a high-profile but brief Velvet Underground reunion. *Set The Twilight Reeling* saw Reed in light-hearted mood, perhaps inspired by a romantic partnership with **Laurie Anderson**. The latter was one of the guest singers on a cover version of Reed's 'Perfect Day', released in 1997 to promote BBC Radio and Television and raise money for charity. *Ecstasy* received some favourable reviews, although the ultimate result was a patchy album.

REEF

UK rock band comprising Kenwyn House (b. 1970; guitar), Gary Stringer (b. 1973; vocals), Dominic Greensmith (b. 1970; drums) and Jack Bessant (b. 1971; bass). They rose to fame via an advert for the Sony Mini-Disc portable stereo system. Their first release was 'Good Feeling' in late 1994. *Replenish* (1995) was well received, although comparisons to **Pearl Jam** were widespread. *Glow* put them in the spotlight as a potentially major act, helped by the chart success of 'Place Your Hands'. The band returned in 1999 with the UK Top 5 album, *Rides*, although little creative development was evident in the band's sound. *Getaway* suffered from the same problem.

REEVES, JIM

Reeves' (b. James Travis Reeves, 1923, d. 1964) first singing work was with Moon Mullican's band in his native Texas. In 1952, Reeves moved to KWKH in Shreveport, where his duties included hosting *The Louisiana Hayride*. He stood in as a performer for **Hank Williams** and was signed immediately to Abbott. In 1953, Reeves received gold discs for 'Mexican Joe' and 'Bimbo'.

In 1955, he joined the *Grand Ole Opry* and began recording for RCA Records, his first hit being 'Yonder Comes A Sucker'. 'Four Walls' (1957) became an enormous US hit, crossing over to the pop market and becoming a template for his future work. Reeves swapped his western outfit for a suit and tie, and, following his hit 'Blue Boy', his group, the Wagonmasters, became the Blue Boys. Having established a commercial format, 'Gentleman Jim' had success with 'You're The Only Good Thing', 'Adios Amigo', 'Welcome To My World' and 'Guilty'. Reeves disliked flying and to avoid commercial airlines obtained his own daytime pilot's licence. On 31 July 1964, Reeves and his pianist/manager, Dean Manuel, died when their single-engine plane crashed outside Nashville during a storm. Posthumously, Reeves became a best-selling artist with *40 Golden Greats* topping the album charts in 1975.

REEVES, MARTHA

US singer Reeves (b. 1941) was schooled in both gospel and classical music, but it was vocal group R&B that caught her imagination. Performing as Martha Lavaille, she joined the fledgling Motown Records in 1961. Berry Gordy offered her the chance to record as **Martha And The Vandellas**. From 1963 they were one of Motown's most successful recording outfits and from 1967 Reeves was given individual credit in front of the group before ill health forced her to retire. She signed a solo contract with MCA Records in 1973. *Martha Reeves* (1974) earned critical acclaim but was disappointing commercially. Moving to Arista Records in 1977, she was submerged by the late 70s disco boom on a series of albums that allowed her little room to display her talents. Her subsequent recording contracts have proved unproductive, and, since the early 80s, she has found consistent work on package tours. During the late 80s she toured with a 'fake' Vandellas before being reunited with the original group (Annette Sterling and Rosalind Holmes) on Ian Levine's Motor City label.

REID, TERRY

This UK singer-songwriter (b. 1949) released his debut single, 'The Hand Don't Fit The Glove', in 1967, but greater recognition came in a trio with Pete Solley (keyboards) and Keith Webb (drums). Reid became a popular figure in the USA following a tour supporting **Cream**. His debut *Bang Bang You're Terry Reid*, produced by Mickie Most, emphasized the artist's vocal talent and impassioned guitar style. Reid's own compositions included 'Friends', which became a hit for Arrival. Following a long period out of the limelight, he re-established his recording career in 1991 with *The Driver*.

R.E.M.

R.E.M. played their first concert in Athens, Georgia, USA, on 19 April 1980. The line-up was Michael Stipe (b. 1960; vocals), Peter Buck (b. 1956; guitar), Mike Mills (b. 1958; bass) and Bill Berry (b. 1958; drums). Their debut single, 'Radio Free Europe', won considerable praise from critics, as did *Chronic Town*, a mini-LP. *Murmur* and *Reckoning*. Although received enthusiastically by critics, *Fables Of The Reconstruction* was a stark, morose album, mirroring despondency within the band. *Lifes Rich Pageant* (1986) showed the first signs of a politicization within the band that would come to a head in the late 80s.

The band's major label debut,

Green (1988), sold slowly but steadily in the USA. The attendant single 'Stand' reached the US Top 10, while 'Orange Crush' entered the UK Top 30. The band re-emerged in 1991 with *Out Of Time*. Ostensibly their first album to contain 'love' songs, it was unanimously hailed as a masterpiece, topping both US and UK album charts soon after. The accompanying singles, 'Losing My Religion', 'Shiny Happy People', 'Near Wild Heaven' and 'Radio Song', gave them further hits. *Automatic For The People* was released in 1992 to universal favour, reaching the top of the charts in the USA and UK. *Monster* showed the band in grunge-like mode, showing fans and critics alike that they had not gone soft.

In 1996 the band re-signed with Warner Brothers for the largest recording contract advance in history at the time: $80 million was guaranteed for a five-album contract. *New Adventures In Hi-Fi* was released in September. In 1997 Bill Berry (who had suffered a ruptured aneurysm on stage two years earlier) announced he would be leaving R.E.M. after 17 years. The remaining trio returned the following year with *Up*. After releasing the soundtrack for the Andy Kaufman biopic *Man On The Moon*, the band completed recording sessions for their acclaimed new studio album, *Reveal*.

REMBRANDTS

US pop band formed by Danny Wilde and Phil Solem, the Rembrandts rose to prominence in 1995 with 'I'll Be There For You', their theme song to the hit series *Friends*. Their 1990 self-titled debut, had included a US Top 20 hit, 'Just The Way It Is, Baby', but was overshadowed by the later success of 'I'll Be There For You'. Solem subsequently broke up the partnership to concentrate on his new project, Thrush. Wilde recorded 1998's *Spin This* as Danny Wilde And The Rembrandts. Solem and Wilde reunited as the Rembrandts to record 2001's *Lost Together*.

REO SPEEDWAGON

US rock band formed in 1970 when Neal Doughty (b. 1946; piano) and Alan Gratzer (b. 1948; drums) were joined by Gary Richrath (b. 1949; guitar). Barry Luttnell (vocals) and Greg Philbin (bass) completed the line-up for *REO Speedwagon*, but the former was quickly replaced by Kevin Cronin (b. 1951). Although *REO Two* and *Ridin' The Storm Out* eventually achieved gold status, disputes about direction culminated in the departure of their second vocalist. Michael Murphy replaced him in 1974, but when ensuing albums failed to generate interest, Cronin rejoined his former colleagues. Bruce Hall (b. 1953; bass) was also brought in. The live summary, *You Get What You Play For*, became

the band's first platinum disc, a distinction shared by its successor, *You Can Tune A Piano, But You Can't Tuna Fish*. *Nine Lives* gave the impression that the band had peaked, a view banished by *Hi Infidelity* (1980), a self-confident collection which topped the US album charts and spawned a series of successful singles (including the US number 1 hit 'Keep On Lovin' You'). *Wheels Are Turning* recaptured the zest of *Hi Infidelity* and brought a second US number 1 with 'Can't Fight This Feeling'. *Life As We Know It* and its successor, *The Earth, A Small Man, His Dog And A Chicken*, emphasized the band's professionalism with a line-up of Cronin, Doughty, Hall, Dave Amato (b. 1953; lead guitar), Bryan Hitt (b. 1954; drums) and Jesse Harms (b. 1952; keyboards). Though their commercial heyday seems to have long passed, the band remains a popular concert attraction.

REPLACEMENTS

US pop-punk band formed in 1979 by Paul Westerberg (b. 1960; guitar, vocals), Tommy Stinson (b. 1966; bass), Bob Stinson (b. 1959, d. 1995; guitar) and Chris Mars (b. 1961; drums). Their 1981 debut album showcased their power-trash style. Beloved by critics, the band appeared on the verge of mainstream success in America with the release of 1987's *Pleased To Meet Me*. However *All Shook Down* was rather subdued and the group disbanded in 1990. Westerberg went on to enjoy a mixed solo career, while Bob Stinson died in 1995 of a suspected drug overdose.

REPUBLICA

Republica formed in London, England, in 1994 when Tim Dorney (b. 1965; keyboards), teamed up with Andy Todd (keyboards, bass) and Saffron (b. Samantha Sprackling, 1968; vocals). The trio began creating a sound which gave club rhythms a radio-friendly, adult-pop sheen, before adding David Barbarossa (drums; ex-**Bow Wow Wow**) and Johnny Male (b. 1963; guitar). The US market pounced upon their 1996 single 'Ready To Go', which was followed by the equally impressive 'Drop Dead Gorgeous' and a solid debut album. Musical differences led to the departure of Todd the same year. *Speed Ballads* was recorded with the band's first permanent drummer, Pete Riley. While it contained trademark pop songs such as the debut single 'From Rush Hour With Love', the album also indicated a general maturing of the band's songwriting talents.

RESIDENTS

Despite a recording career spanning four decades, the Residents have successfully – and deliberately – achieved an air of wilful obscurity. Mindful of the cult of personality, they studiously retain an anonymity and refuse to name personnel, thus ensuring total artistic freedom. In 1972 the band launched Ralph Records as an outlet for their work. *Meet The Residents* established their unconventional style, matching bizarre reconstructions of 60s pop favourites with original material. The Residents' strength lies in interpretation and use of cultural icons as templates for their idiosyncratic vision. The collective have continued to mine this vision into the new millennium, increasingly drawing on digital technology to pursue their aims. The religious-themed *Wormwood: Curious Stories From The Bible* demonstrated that the Residents have not lost the capacity to shock.

REVERE, PAUL, AND THE RAIDERS

Formed in 1961, this US group comprised Paul Revere (piano), Mark Lindsay (b. 1942; vocals, saxophone), Drake Levin (guitar), Mike Holliday (bass) and

Michael Smith (drums). Their version of 'Louie Louie' was issued in 1963, but it was local rivals the **Kingsmen** who secured the national hit. In 1965 the Raiders hit their commercial stride with 'Steppin' Out', followed by a series of US hits including 'Just Like Me', 'Hungry' and 'Good Things'. The Raiders' slick stage routines and Revolutionary War garb – replete with thigh-

boots, tights, frilled shirts and three-cornered hats – was frowned upon by the emergent underground audience. Later members Freddy Weller (guitar), Keith Allison (bass) and Joe (Correro) Jnr. (drums) appeared on *Hard 'N' Heavy (With Marshmallow)* and *Collage*. In 1969, Lindsay embarked on a concurrent solo career, but although 'Arizona' sold over one million copies, later releases were less successful. Two years later, the Raiders had a US chart-topper with 'Indian Reservation', previously a UK hit for Don Fardon, but it proved their final Top 20 hit. Weller and Lindsay departed, but Revere became the act's custodian, presiding over occasional releases for independent outlets with a new line-up.

REZILLOS

Formed in Scotland in 1976, the Rezillos initially comprised Eugene Reynolds (b. Alan Forbes; vocals), Fay Fife (b. Sheila Hynde; vocals), Luke Warm aka Jo Callis (lead guitar), Hi Fi Harris (b. Mark Harris; guitar), Dr. D.K. Smythe (bass), Angel Patterson (b. Alan Patterson; drums) and Gale Warning (backing vocals). Their irreverent repertoire consisted of pre-beat favourites and glam-rock staples. Harris, Smythe and Warning left, while auxiliary member William Mysterious (b. William Donaldson; bass, saxophone) joined on a permanent basis. Signed to Sire Records, the quintet enjoyed a UK Top 20 hit in 1978 with the satirical 'Top Of The Pops'. *Can't Stand The Rezillos* also charted, before internal pressures pulled them apart in 1978. Fife and Reynolds formed the Revillos, while the rest of the band became Shake. In the 90s the Revillos/Rezillos re-formed for tours in Japan.

RICHARD, CLIFF

Richard (b. Harry Roger Webb, 1940), born in India but raised in England, began his career as a rock 'n' roll performer in 1957. Fascinated by **Elvis Presley**, he joined a skiffle group before teaming up with Terry Smart (drums) and Norman Mitham (guitar) in the Drifters. Ian Samwell (lead guitar) joined later. In 1958, they were seen by theatrical agent George Ganyou who financed a demo tape. EMI producer Norrie Paramor auditioned the quartet and, with a couple of session musicians, they recorded 'Schoolboy Crush'; however the B-side, 'Move It', proved more popular, reaching UK number 2. Meanwhile Richard made his debut on television's *Oh Boy!*, and rapidly replaced **Marty**

Wilde as Britain's premier rock 'n' roll talent. Samwell left the Drifters to become a professional songwriter, and by the end of 1958 a new line-up emerged featuring **Hank B. Marvin** and Bruce Welch. The group also changed its name to the **Shadows**, to prevent confusion with the American Drifters.

In 1959, Richard's recording of Lionel Bart's 'Living Doll' gave him a UK number 1. Three months later he returned to the top with 'Travellin' Light'. He also starred in two films within 12 months. *Serious Charge*, a non-musical drama, caused controversy because it dealt with homosexual blackmail. *Expresso Bongo* was a cinematic pop landmark. From 1960 Richard's career progressed well. Hits such as 'Please Don't Tease' (number 1), 'Nine Times Out Of Ten' and 'Theme For A Dream' demonstrated his range, and in 1962 came 'The Young Ones'. A pop anthem to youth, with striking guitar work from Hank Marvin, the song proved one of his most memorable hits. The film of the same name broke box office records and spawned a series of similar movies from its star. His run of UK Top 10 hits continued until 1965, including 'Bachelor Boy', 'Summer Holiday', 'On The Beach' and 'I Could Easily Fall'.

In 1966 Richard almost retired after converting to fundamentalist Christianity, but chose to use his career as an expression of his faith. In the swiftly changing cultural climate of the late 60s, Richard's hold on the pop charts could not be guaranteed. In the 1968 Eurovision Song Contest the jury placed him a close second with 'Congratulations', which proved one of the biggest UK number 1s of the year. Immediately thereafter, Richard's chart progress declined until a second shot at the Eurovision Song Contest with 'Power To All Our Friends' brought his only other Top 10 success of the period.

In 1976 Bruce Welch of the Shadows was assigned to produce Richard, resulting in the best-selling *I'm Nearly Famous*, which included two major hits, 'Miss You Nights' and 'Devil Woman'. The latter gave Richard a rare US chart success. Richard adopted a more contemporary sound on *Rock 'N' Roll Juvenile*, but the most startling breakthrough was the attendant single 'We Don't Talk Anymore'; it gave Richard his first UK number 1 in over a decade and reached the US Top 10. The 'new' Richard sound brought further well-arranged hits, such as 'Carrie' and 'Wired For Sound', and ensured he was a chart regular throughout the 80s.

Throughout his six decades in the pop charts, Richard has displayed a valiant longevity. He parodied one of his earliest hits with comedy quartet the Young Ones, registering another UK number 1, and he celebrated his 50th birthday with the anti-war hit 'From A Distance'. He appeared in *Time* and in John Farrar and Tim Rice's hugely successful *Heathcliff* (his own *Songs From Heathcliff* was drawn from the show). In 1995, Richard was knighted for his services to popular music. During the 80s and 90s he enjoyed a string of hit Christmas singles, including 'Mistletoe And Wine', 'Saviours Day', and 'The Millennium Prayer'.

RICHIE, LIONEL

Richie (b. 1949) formed a succession of R&B groups in the mid-60s. In 1968 he became the lead singer and saxophonist with the **Commodores**, America's most popular 70s soul group. In 1981, he duetted with **Diana Ross** on the theme song for the movie *Endless Love*. Issued as a single, the track topped the UK and US charts, and became one of Motown Records' biggest hits to date. Its success encouraged Richie to follow a solo career in 1982. His debut, *Lionel Richie*, produced the chart-topping 'Truly', which continued the style of his ballads with the Commodores. In 1983 he released *Can't Slow Down*, which eventually sold more than 15 million copies worldwide. Several Top 10 hits followed, the most successful of which was 'Hello', a sentimental love song far from his R&B roots. In 1986 came *Dancing On The Ceiling*, another phenomenally popular album that produced a run of US and UK hits. Since then, he has kept recording and live work to a minimum. He broke the silence in 1996 with *Louder Than Words*. *Time* featured several more of Richie's trademark ballads,

but was disappointingly bland. *Renaissance*, initially only available on the European market, was a marked improvement.

RICHMAN, JONATHAN

Richman (b. 1951) became prominent in the early 70s as leader of the **Modern Lovers**. Drawing inspiration from 50s pop and the **Velvet Underground**, the group offered a garage-band sound, as evinced on their UK hit 'Roadrunner' and the infectious instrumental 'Egyptian Reggae' in 1977. However, Richman increasingly distanced himself from electric music and disbanded the group in 1978 to pursue a solo career. He exhumed the Modern Lovers name in the 80s without any alteration to his style and continues to enjoy considerable cult popularity. In the 90s he made cameo appearances in the movies *Kingpin* and *There's Something About Mary*.

RIDE

Formed in 1988 by Mark Gardener (vocals, guitar), Andy Bell (guitar, vocals), Stephan Queralt (bass) and Laurence Colbert (drums), this UK indie band enjoyed success in the early 90s with *Going Blank Again*, *Carnival Of Light* and *Tarantula*. Following the release of the latter, Ride split up. Bell went on to enjoy moderate success with Hurricane #1 before joining **Oasis** at the end of 1999.

RIGHT SAID FRED

Camp UK pop trio formed by the Fairbrass brothers Richard (b. 1953; vocals) and Fred (b. Christopher Fairbrass, 1956), with the addition of Rob Manzoli (b. 1954). The band is named after the novelty 1962 Bernard Cribbins' hit. Their initial success was embedded in 1991's kitsch classic 'I'm Too Sexy' (UK number 2/US number 1), with similar follow-ups 'Deeply Dippy' and 'Don't Talk Just Kiss'. In 1991, they sold more singles than any other artist in the UK, excluding **Bryan Adams**, but their second album sold disappointingly. The brothers formed their own Happy Valley record label in 1995, releasing *Smashing!* the following year, their final recording with Manzoli. They continue to tour even though Richard Fairbrass has become a media personality, appearing on various UK game shows and co-hosting the BBC2 show *Gaytime TV*. They returned to the UK charts in 2001 with the single, 'You're My Mate'.

RIGHTEOUS BROTHERS

Despite the name, US vocalists Bill Medley (b. 1940) and Bobby Hatfield (b. 1940) are not related. A series of excellent singles, notably 'Little Latin Lupe Lu', introduced the duo to the charts in the early 60s. **Phil Spector** signed the act to his Philles label. The magnificent 'You've Lost That Lovin' Feelin'' topped the US and UK charts, but the relationship between performers and mentor rapidly soured. The Righteous Brothers moved outlets in 1966, but despite a gold disc for

'(You're My) Soul And Inspiration', they could not sustain their success. They split in 1968, with Medley going solo and Hatfield retaining the name with new partner Jimmy Walker (ex-Knickerbockers). The collaboration was short-lived. The original pair were reunited in 1974 for an appearance on *The Sonny And Cher Comedy Hour*. They scored a US Top 3 hit that year with 'Rock 'n' Roll Heaven', but could not regain former glories. A reissue of 'Unchained Melody', a hit for the Righteous Brothers in 1965, topped the UK chart in 1990 after it featured in the movie *Ghost*.

RIMES, LEANN

Rimes (b. 1982) recorded *All That*, aged 11. One track, an aching ballad, 'Blue', had been written by Bill Mack for **Patsy Cline**, who died before recording it. It was an instant US hit. Her second country number 1 came with the up-tempo 'One Way Ticket (Because I Can)'. *Blue* also topped the country albums chart. At the 1997 Grammy Awards, Rimes won Best New Artist, Best Female Country and Best Country Song for 'Blue'. A move towards the AOR market, which was confirmed by the international success of the single 'How Do I Live' and *Sittin' On Top Of The World*, an album firmly in the **Celine Dion** mould. In October 1998, 'How Do I Live' became the most successful US single of all-time completing 69 straight weeks on the *Billboard* chart (with a peak position of number 2). It also stayed in the UK Top 40 for 30 weeks.

Rimes returned to her country roots on the following year's *LeAnn Rimes*. The following year Rimes topped the UK singles chart with 'Can't Fight The Moonlight', taken from the soundtrack of *Coyote Ugly*.

RIVERS, JOHNNY

US singer Rivers (b. John Ramistella, 1942) enjoyed a succession of hits in the 60s and 70s, initially by covering R&B songs and eventually with his own compositions. In 1958 top disc jockey **Alan Freed** gave the singer his new name, Johnny Rivers. His first single, 'Baby Come Back', was issued that year. At 17, Rivers moved to Nashville, where he wrote songs with Roger Miller, and recorded demo records for **Elvis Presley**, **Johnny Cash** and **Ricky Nelson**, who recorded Rivers' 'Make Believe' in 1960. His first album for Imperial Records, *Johnny Rivers At The Whisky A Go Go* (where he was performing), was released in 1964 and yielded his first hit, **Chuck Berry**'s 'Memphis', which reached number 2. Other hits during 1964–65 included Berry's 'Maybelline', Harold Dorman's 'Mountain Of Love', the traditional folk song 'Midnight Special', **Willie Dixon**'s 'Seventh Son' and Pete Seeger's 'Where Have All The Flowers Gone'. Rivers also launched his own Soul City label in 1966, signing the popular **5th Dimension**. Rivers had hits in 1967 with two Motown cover versions, 'Baby I Need Your Lovin'' and 'The Tracks Of My Tears'.

Early 70s albums such as *Slim Slo Slider*, *Home Grown* and *LA Reggae* were critically lauded but not commercially successful, although the latter gave Rivers a Top 10 single with Huey 'Piano' Smith's 'Rockin' Pneumonia And The Boogie Woogie Flu'. A version of the **Beach Boys**' 'Help Me Rhonda' was a minor success in 1975, and two years later Rivers landed his final Top 10 single, 'Swayin' To The Music (Slow Dancin')'. Rivers recorded a handful of albums in the 80s, but none reached the charts.

ROBERTSON, ROBBIE

Robertson's (b. Jaime Robbie Robertson, 1943) professional career began in 1960 when he replaced guitarist James Evans in **Ronnie Hawkins**' backing group, the Hawks. The group left Hawkins and first as the Canadian Squires, then as Levon And The Hawks, recorded some singles, including Robertson's 'The Stones I Throw'. The Hawks' backing sessions for blues singer John Hammond led to their association with **Bob Dylan**. Robertson's raging guitar work helped complete the one-time folk singer's transformation from acoustic sage to electric guru. At the same time Robertson's lyrics assumed a greater depth, while the music of the group, now dubbed the **Band**, drew its inspiration from rural styles and soul music peers.

The Band broke up in 1976 following a farewell concert which was captured in the celebratory film *The Last Waltz*, directed by Martin Scorsese,

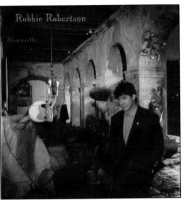

which in turn inspired Roberston's cinematic ambitions. *Carny*, which he also produced, provided his sole starring role to date, although he maintained a working relationship with Scorsese, scoring several of his movies, including *Raging Bull* and *The Color Of Money*.

A 1983 collaboration, *King Of Comedy*, was notable for Robertson's solo track, 'Between Trains'. *Robbie Robertson* (1987) was an exceptional collection and offered state-of-the-art production and notable guest contributions by **U2**, **Peter Gabriel**, **Daniel Lanois** and Gil Evans. *Storyville*, however, was a disappointment. Robertson did not join the re-formed Band in 1993. His most interesting project to date is a recording with the Red Road Ensemble, a group of native Americans. *Contact From The Underworld Of Redboy* was a bold fusion of native American tribal chants and contemporary dance beats. Robertson also achieved a surprise hit in gay clubs with the Howie B. track 'Take Your Partner By The Hand'. He joined DreamWorks Records in the capacity of A&R director in 1998.

ROBINSON, SMOKEY

A founding member of the **Miracles** in 1955, Robinson's (b. William Robinson, 1940) flexible tenor voice made him the group's lead vocalist. In 1957 he met Berry Gordy, who produced a series of Miracles singles in 1958 and 1959, all of which featured Robinson as composer and lead singer. In 1960 he signed the Miracles to Motown Records and began grooming Robinson as his second-in-command. Soon, he was charged with developing the talents of **Mary Wells** and the **Supremes**. Between 1962 and 1964 Robinson wrote and produced a series of hit singles for Wells. Robinson could not turn the Supremes into a hit-making act, but had no such problem with the **Temptations**. Between 1964 and 1965, Robinson was responsible for the records that established their reputation. Throughout the 60s, he combined this production and A&R work with his own career as leader of the Miracles, turning out a succession of high-quality songs. From 1967, Robinson was given individual credit on the Miracles' releases. Two years of commercial decline were righted when their 1965 recording of 'The Tracks Of My Tears' became a major hit in the UK, and the four-year-old 'The Tears Of A Clown' achieved similar success on both sides of the Atlantic in 1970.

In 1971 Robinson announced that he would leave the Miracles the following year to concentrate on his role as vice-president of Motown. A year later, Robinson launched his solo career with *Smokey*. He maintained a regular release schedule through the mid-70s, with one new album each year. They made little impact, although Robinson's songwriting was as consistent as ever. In 1979 with 'Cruisin', he had his biggest chart success since 'The Tears Of A Clown'. Two years later, he gained his first UK number 1 with 'Being With You', a love song that was almost as successful in the US. Throughout the 80s and 90s Robinson followed a relaxed release schedule with regular small hits

and consistent album sales. He was inducted into the Rock And Roll Hall Of Fame in 1988.

ROBINSON, TOM

UK singer-songwriter Robinson (b. 1950) formed his first group, Davanq in 1971. Two years later, Robinson formed Café Society, which in turn evolved into the Tom Robinson Band. *TRB's Power In The Darkness* included the UK Top 40 hit '2-4-6-8 Motorway'. The quartet's *Rising Free EP*, which followed the disappointing *TRB2*, contained the singalong anthem 'Glad To Be Gay'. Robinson led the short-lived Section 27 and began songwriting collaborations with **Elton John** and **Peter Gabriel**. By 1981, he was in Berlin to record *North By Northwest* and work in alternative cabaret and fringe theatre. This period produced 1983's strident UK hit 'War Baby'. *Still Loving You* produced no equivalent, and Robinson has subsequently pursued a low-key recording career. He has also enjoyed success as a radio presenter for the BBC and GLR.

ROCHES

Sisters Maggie (b. 1951) and Terre Roche (b. 1953) began singing a mixture of traditional, doo-wop and barbershop quartet songs in New York clubs in the late 60s. Their first recording was as backing singers on **Paul Simon**'s, *There Goes Rhymin' Simon*. Through Simon, the duo recorded an unsuccessful album for CBS Records in 1975. The following year, younger sister Suzzy joined and the Roches became a trio. Throughout the 80s and 90s the Roches continued to perform in New York and appear occasionally at European folk festivals, while recording critically revered albums. Suzzy Roche released her debut solo album in 1997.

ROCKET FROM THE CRYPT

With a visual image denoted by 50s silk shirts, tattoos and sideburns, this US rock group was formed in 1990 by John 'Speedo' Reis (vocals, guitar), N. D. (guitar), Petey X (bass), Sean (drums), and Elaina (backing vocals). Reis, N. D. and Petey X were joined on their second album by Apollo 9 (saxophone) and Atom (drums). After a series of low-key recordings they took a break to concentrate on their alter-ego band, *Drive Like Jehu*. Augmented by trumpeter JC 2000 the band's most productive phase began in 1995 with *The State Of Art Is On Fire* and *Hot Charity*. By 1996, the group had completed the recording of *Scream, Dracula, Scream!*, their major label debut. The album included the UK Top 20 hit, 'On A Rope'. *RTFC* and *Group Sounds* opted for a more old-fashioned sound.

RODGERS, PAUL

UK vocalist Rodgers (b. 1949) began his career in **Free**, after which he became a founder member of **Bad Company**. Later he was co-founder of the Firm (with **Jimmy Page**), but his solo career has never risen above cult status, although few would deny he possesses one of the most powerful and recognizable voices in post-60s rock music.

ROE, TOMMY

US vocalist Roe (b. 1942) began his career with high school act, the Satins. The group performed several of his compositions, notably 'Sheila', which they recorded in 1960. Though unsuccessful, Roe revived the song two years later upon securing a solo deal. This **Buddy Holly**-influenced rocker topped the US chart and reached the Top 3 in Britain. Roe scored two Top 10 hits in 1963 with 'The Folk Singer' and 'Everybody' and, although not a major chart entry, 'Sweet Pea' garnered considerable airplay thanks to pirate radio. The song reached the US Top 10, as did its follow-up, 'Hooray For Hazel', but Roe's biggest hit came in 1969 when 'Dizzy' topped the charts on both sides of the Atlantic. It returned to the top of the UK charts in 1992 in a version by the **Wonder Stuff** and Vic Reeves.

ROGERS, KENNY

US-born Rogers (b. 1938) started out in doo-wop group, the Scholars. In 1957 he recorded 'That Crazy Feeling' (as Kenneth Rogers) for a small Houston label. He also recorded 'For You Alone' for the Carlton label as Kenny Rogers The First. After recording solo for Mercury Records, Rogers joined the New Christy Minstrels while forming a splinter group, The First Edition, with other Minstrels. They signed with Reprise Records and Rogers sang lead on their first major hit, 'Just Dropped In (To See What Condition My Condition Was In)'. The group had further US success with 'Ruby, Don't Take Your Love To Town', 'Tell It All Brother' and 'Heed The Call', but broke up in 1974.

The following year Rogers signed with United Artists Records as a solo artist. Impotence was an extraordinary subject for a hit record, but 'Lucille' (US number 5, UK number 1) established Rogers as a country star. Rogers toured the UK with **Crystal Gayle**, and formed a successful partnership with Dottie West. 'You Decorated My Life' was another US hit and then came 'Coward Of The County' (US number 3, UK number 1), which became a successful television movie, and the album *Kenny* sold five million copies. Having sold 35 million albums for United Artists, Rogers moved to RCA Records in 1983. *Eyes That See In The Dark* was produced by Barry Gibb and featured the **Bee Gees**. It included 'Islands In The Stream', a US number 1 duet with **Dolly Parton**. Rogers briefly returned to Reprise in the late 80s, before relocating to the Magnatone label. He now records for his own independent label Dreamcatcher Records, and unexpectedly found himself with a huge hit in 2000. 'Buy Me A Rose', featuring both Billy Dean and Alison Krauss on harmony vocals, topped the US country chart.

ROLLING STONES

Originally billed as the Rollin' Stones, the first line-up of this highly successful UK band was Mick Jagger (b. Michael Philip Jagger, 1943; vocals), Keith Richard (b. Keith Richards, 1943; guitar), Brian Jones (b. Lewis Brian Hopkin-Jones, 1942, d. 1969; rhythm guitar) and Ian Stewart (b. 1938, d. 1985; piano). Their patron, **Alexis Korner**, arranged their debut gig at London's Marquee club on 21 July 1962.

In 1962, Bill Wyman (b. William Perks, 1936; bass) joined, as did Charlie Watts (b. 1941; drums) in 1963. Andrew Loog Oldham became their manager, and within weeks Decca Records' Dick Rowe signed the group. Oldham selected **Chuck Berry**'s 'Come On' as their debut and fired Ian Stewart as not sufficiently pop star-like. After supporting the **Everly Brothers**,

Little Richard, **Gene Vincent** and **Bo Diddley** on a UK package tour, the Rolling Stones released 'I Wanna Be Your Man', which entered the Top 10 in 1964. A flurry of recording activity saw the release of an EP and an album both titled *The Rolling Stones*. The third single, 'Not Fade Away', fused **Buddy Holly**'s quaint original with a chunky Bo Diddley beat that highlighted Jagger's vocal. With the momentum increasing, Oldham over-reached himself by organizing a US tour which proved premature and disappointing. After returning to the UK, the Stones released a decisive cover of the **Valentinos**' 'It's All Over Now', which gave them their first number 1. In 1964, 'Little Red Rooster' was released and entered the *New Musical Express* chart at number 1.

The Rolling Stones' international breakthrough came in 1965. 'The Last Time' saw them emerge with their own distinctive rhythmic style and America finally succumbed to their spell with '(I Can't Get No) Satisfaction'. 'Get Off Of My Cloud' completed their trilogy of 1965 hits. Allen Klein replaced Eric Easton as Oldham's co-manager and the Stones consolidated their success by renegotiating their Decca contract. 'Mother's Little Helper' and the Elizabethan-style 'Lady Jane', released as US-only singles, effectively displayed their contrasting styles. Both songs were included on *Aftermath*. The recording revealed the Rolling Stones as accomplished rockers and balladeers, while their writing potential was emphasized by **Chris Farlowe**'s chart-topping cover of 'Out Of Time'. Back in the singles chart, the band's success continued with '19th Nervous Breakdown' and 'Paint It Black'.

In 1967 the Stones confronted an establishment crackdown. The year began with an accomplished double A-sided single, 'Let's Spend The Night Together'/'Ruby Tuesday' which narrowly failed to reach UK number 1. The accompanying album, *Between The Buttons*, trod water and was also Oldham's final production. On 12 February, Jagger and Richard were arrested at Richard's home and charged with drugs offences. Three months later, Brian Jones was raided and charged with similar offences. The Jagger/Richard trial in June culminated in the duo receiving heavy fines and a salutary prison sentence, although the sentences were quashed on appeal. Three months later, Brian Jones faced a nine-month sentence and suffered a nervous breakdown before having his imprisonment rescinded at the end of the year.

The year ended with *Their Satanic Majesties Request*, the Rolling Stones' apparent answer to the **Beatles**' *Sgt Peppers Lonely Hearts Club Band*. The album of psychedelic/cosmic experimentation was bereft of the R&B grit that had previously characterized the Rolling Stones' sound. The revitalization of the band was demonstrated in 1968 with 'Jumpin' Jack Flash', a single that rivalled the best of their previous output. The succeeding album, *Beggars Banquet*, included the socio-political 'Street Fighting Man' and the brilliantly macabre 'Sympathy For The Devil'. While the Stones were re-establishing themselves, Brian Jones was falling deeper into drug abuse. A conviction in late 1968 prompted

doubts about his availability for US tours and he became increasingly jealous of Jagger's leading role in the band. The crisis came in June 1969 when Jones officially left. The following month he was found dead in the swimming pool of his home. The band played out the last months of the 60s with the sublime 'Honky Tonk Women'. The new album, *Let It Bleed*, was an exceptional work and a promising debut from Mick Taylor (b. 1948), **John Mayall**'s former guitarist who had replaced Jones weeks before his death.

After concluding their Decca contract with a live album, *Get Yer Ya-Ya's Out!*, the Rolling Stones established their own self-titled label. The first release was a three-track single, 'Brown Sugar'/'Bitch'/'Let It Rock', which contained some of their best work, but narrowly failed to reach UK number 1. The new

album, *Sticky Fingers*, was as consistent as it was accomplished, and within a year the group returned with the magnificent double album, *Exile On Main Street*.

The Rolling Stones' slide into the 70s mainstream began with the patchy *Goat's Head Soup*, while 1974's 'It's Only Rock 'N' Roll' proved a better song title than a single, and the album of the same name was undistinguished. Mick Taylor departed at the end of 1974, to be replaced by Ron Wood (b. 1947; ex-**Faces**) who appeared on their next release, *Black And Blue*. However, by 1977, the British music press had taken punk to its heart and the Rolling Stones were dismissed as champagne-swilling old men, out of touch with their audience. The band responded to the challenge of their younger critics with a comeback album of remarkable power. *Some Girls* was their most consistent work in years. Later that year Keith Richard escaped a jail sentence in Toronto for drugs offences, being fined and ordered to play a couple of charity concerts. As if to celebrate his release and reconciliation with his father, he reverted to Richards, his original family name.

The Rolling Stones reconvened in 1980 for *Emotional Rescue*, a lightweight album dominated by Jagger's falsetto and overuse of disco rhythms. Nevertheless, the album gave them their first UK number 1 since 1973 and the title track was a Top 10 hit on both sides of the Atlantic. *Tattoo You* was surprisingly strong and featured the excellent single 'Start Me Up'.

A three-year silence on record was broken by *Dirty Work* in 1986, which saw the Rolling Stones sign to CBS Records and team up with producer Steve Lillywhite, but increasingly they were concentrating on individual projects. However, they reconvened in 1989 and announced that they would be working on a new album and commencing a world tour. Later that year the hastily recorded *Steel Wheels* appeared to generally good critical reception. After nearly 30 years, the Rolling Stones began the 90s with the biggest grossing international tour of all time, and reiterated their intention of playing on indefinitely. *Voodoo Lounge* (1994) was a fine recording, lyrically daring and musically fresh. Riding a crest after an extraordinarily active 1995, *Stripped* dynamically emphasized just how great the Jagger/Richards songwriting team is. *Bridges To Babylon* was a particularly fresh-sounding album, with Charlie Watts anchoring the band's sound like never before.

ROLLINS, HENRY

US vocalist Henry Rollins (b. Henry Garfield, 1961) quickly returned to action after the break-up of hardcore favourites **Black Flag**, releasing *Hot Animal Machine*, followed by the *Drive-By Shooting* EP. He formed the Rollins Band in 1987 with Chris Haskett (guitar), Andrew Weiss (bass) and Sim Cain (drums). The group developed their own brand of hard rock, with blues and jazz influences, while Rollins' lyrics dealt with social and political themes. The multi-talented Rollins also runs a publishing company, 2.13.61, and a music publishing enterprise, Human Pitbull, and has established a concurrent acting career.

RONETTES

Veronica 'Ronnie' Bennett (b. 1943), her sister Estelle (b. 1944) and cousin Nedra Talley (b. 1946) began their career as a dance act, the Dolly Sisters. The trio's first single, 'I Want A Boy', was credited to Ronnie And The Relatives, but when 'Silhouettes' followed in 1962, the Ronettes name was in place. They recorded four singles before signing with **Phil Spector**. Their first collaboration, 'Be My Baby', defined the girl-group sound as Spector constructed a cavernous accompaniment around Ronnie's plaintive, nasal voice. The single reached the Top 5 in the USA and UK, succeeded by the equally worthwhile 'Baby I Love You'. The producer's infatuation with Ronnie – the couple later married – resulted in some of his finest work being reserved for her, including 'The Best Part of Breaking Up', 'Walking In The Rain' and 'Is This What I Get For Loving You'. She separated from Spector in 1973, founding a new group with vocalists Denise Edwards and Chip Fields. Ronnie And The Ronettes made their debut that year with 'Lover Lover', before changing their name to Ronnie Spector and the Ronettes. The group's name was then dropped as its lead singer pursued her solo ambitions. The long-running litigation between the Ronettes and Phil Spector came to a close in July 2000, when they were finally awarded $2.6 million in overdue payment of royalties dating back to 1963.

RONSON, MICK

UK guitarist Ronson (b. 1945, d. 1993) was a member of **David Bowie**'s backing group, Hype, (later renamed the Spiders From Mars) in 1970. Ronson played lead on Bowie's pivotal albums, *The Man Who Sold The World*, *Hunky Dory*, *The Rise And Fall Of Ziggy Stardust And The Spiders From Mars* and *Aladdin Sane*. After a brief and unsuccessful solo career, Ronson joined **Mott The Hoople** in 1974 and when lead vocalist **Ian Hunter** departed for a solo career, Ronson followed. He subsequently appeared with **Bob Dylan** in the Rolling Thunder Revue. The Hunter-Ronson partnership lasted over 15 years, but it was only on *YUI Orta* that Ronson received equal billing on the sleeve. In 1991 Ronson was treated for cancer, but died two years later.

RONSTADT, LINDA

US vocalist Ronstadt (b. 1946) first sang in the Three Ronstadts with her sisters. She and guitarist Bob Kimmel moved to Los Angeles, where they were joined by songwriter Kenny Edwards. As the Stone Poneys the trio had a US Top 20 hit with 'Different Drum'. Ronstadt embarked on a solo career in 1968. Her early solo albums, *Hand Sown . . . Home Grown* and *Silk Purse*, signalled a move towards country-flavoured material. Her third album featured a core of musicians who subsequently formed the **Eagles**. *Don't Cry Now* was undistinguished, while 1974's *Heart Like A Wheel* was excellent. This platinum-selling set included 'You're No Good', a US number 1 pop hit, and a dramatic version of **Hank Williams**' 'I Can't Help It', which won Ronstadt a Grammy.

In the 80s her performance in *The Pirates Of Penzance* drew favourable reviews, although her role in the more demanding *La Boheme* was less impressive. Ronstadt also undertook a series of releases with Nelson Riddle, which resulted in three albums of popular standards. In 1987, a duet with **James Ingram** produced 'Somewhere Out There', the theme to the film *An American*

Tail. This gave her a number 2 US (UK Top 10) hit, while that same year her collaboration with **Dolly Parton** and **Emmylou Harris**, *Trio*, and a selection of mariachi songs, *Canciones De Mi Padre*, showed an artist determined to challenge preconceptions. Her 1989 set, *Cry Like A Rainstorm*, included the number 2 hit 'Don't Know Much', a haunting duet with Aaron Neville. In 1996 she was firmly in the middle of the road with *Dedicated To The One I Love*, an album of lullabies and love songs, although this was redressed in 1998 with the more familiar *We Ran*. The following year Ronstadt reunited with Parton and Harris for a second *Trio* album, and with the latter for a duo album.

ROOMFUL OF BLUES

Formed as a seven-piece band in the late 60s, Roomful Of Blues quickly established a national reputation in the USA with their big band R&B, before breaking into the international scene in the 80s. The main successful alumni include the act's founder members Duke Robillard (b. Michael Robillard, 1948; guitar) and Al Copley (piano), alongside Ronnie Earl (b. Ronald Earl Horvath, 1953), Curtis Salgado (vocals), and Greg Piccolo (saxophone). Other long-serving members include Rich Lataille (b. 1952; saxophone), who joined in 1970, Bob Enos (b. 1947; trumpet) who was recruited in 1981, and Chris Vachon (b. 1957; guitar), who joined in 1990. Despite personnel changes, the group continues to work regularly. When *Turn It On! Turn It Up!* was released on 13 October 1995, the Governor of Rhode Island announced an annual Roomful Of Blues day for the state.

ROSE ROYCE

Formed in the USA as a multi-purpose backing group, the original nine-piece worked under a variety of names. In 1973, Kenji Brown (guitar), Victor Nix (keyboards), Kenny Copeland and Freddie Dunn (trumpets), Michael Moore (saxophone), Lequient 'Duke' Jobe (bass), Henry Garner and Terrai Santiel (drums) backed **Edwin Starr** as Total Concept Limited, before supporting Yvonne Fair as Magic Wand. This line-up became the regular studio band behind the Undisputed Truth and **Temptations**, before embarking on their own recording career with Gwen Dickey. The group took the name Rose Royce in 1976 when they recorded the successful soundtrack to *Car Wash*, the title song of which was a platinum-selling single. Two further songs from the movie reached the R&B Top 10 before the band joined producer Norman Whitfield's label. 'Wishing On A Star' and 'Love Don't Live Here Anymore', reached the Top 5 in the UK. In 1977 'Is It Love You're After' was another UK Top 20 record, but was their last chart success.

ROSE, TIM

US singer-songwriter Rose (b. 1940) began his professional career playing guitar with the Journeymen, a folk group active in the early 60s featuring John Phillips and Scott McKenzie. . He joined 'Mama' Cass Elliot and James Hendricks in the Big Three, before going solo in 1964. A series of singles, including 'Hey Joe' (1966) and 'Morning Dew' (1967), followed. *Tim Rose* was assembled from different sessions, but the presence of session musicians provided continuity. The set included a dramatic reading of 'I'm Gonna Be Strong', previously associated with **Gene Pitney**, and the haunting anti-war anthem 'Come Away Melinda'. *Through Rose Coloured Glasses* was disappointing. *After Love - A Kind Of Hate Story*, another album, also entitled *Tim Rose*, proved commercially unsuccessful. Resident in London, Rose undertook a short series of live concerts with fellow exile **Tim Hardin**. *The Musician*, released in 1975, revealed a voice which retained its distinctive power, but an artist without direction. In 1976, Rose was recording a country-tinged album which was finally released in 1991 as *The Gambler*. He returned to New York in the late 70s, but little was heard from him before he released a new album, *Haunted*, in 1997, which successfully mixed old material with recent interpretations.

ROSS, DIANA

Ross (b. 1944) was the fourth and final member of the Primettes. They signed to Motown Records in 1961, changing their name to the **Supremes**. She was a backing vocalist on their early releases until Berry Gordy insisted she become the lead singer. In 1970 Ross began a long series of successful solo releases with the US chart-topping 'Ain't No Mountain High Enough'. In 1972, she starred in Motown's film biography of Billie Holiday, *Lady Sings The Blues*, winning an Oscar nomination. Subsequent starring roles in *Mahogany* (1975) and *The Wiz* (1978) drew a mixed critical response. In 1973, Ross released an album of duets with **Marvin Gaye**. She enjoyed further US number 1 singles with 'Touch Me In The Morning', the theme song from *Mahogany* ('Do You Know Where You're Going To'), and 'Love Hangover'. The latter was a move into the disco field, a shift of direction consolidated on the 1980 album *Diana*, produced by Nile Rodgers and Bernard Edwards of **Chic**. 'Upside Down' was a major transatlantic hit, topping the US charts and reaching UK number 2. A collaboration with **Lionel Richie** in 1981 produced the US chart-topping title track to the movie *Endless Love*.

Ross formed her own production company in 1981 and further hits included reworkings of **Frankie Lymon**'s 'Why Do Fools Fall In Love' and **Michael Jackson**'s 'Muscles'. In Britain, 'Chain Reaction', an affectionate recreation of her days with the Supremes, written and produced by the **Bee Gees**, was a number 1 hit in 1986. She won more publicity for her epic live performances, notably an open-air concert in New York's Central Park in a torrential storm, than for her sporadic releases of new material, which continue to occupy the lighter end of the black music market. She continued to be more successful in the UK, reaching number 2 in late 1991 with 'When You Tell Me That You Love Me'. In 1999, 'Not Over You Yet', an attempt to replicate the sound of **Cher**'s international hit single 'Believe', reached the UK Top 10. The following year's Supremes reunion tour, featuring Ross as the only original member, was cancelled after only a few dates due to poor ticket sales.

ROXETTE

Sweden's first pop export of the 90s, Marie Fredriksson (b. Gun-Marie Fredriksson, 1958) and Per Håkan Gessle (b. 1959) enjoyed international success

thanks to a highly commercial combination of a striking image and catchy pop/rock melodies. The duo first conquered Sweden, with 1988's *Look Sharp!* becoming the second best-selling album in Swedish history. They broke through in America in early 1989 with the number 1 single 'The Look', which also reached the UK Top 10. Subsequent singles 'Dressed For Success', 'Listen To Your Heart' (number 1) and 'Dangerous' continued the band's phenomenal US success. The ballad 'It Must Have Been Love', which was used on the soundtrack of the movie *Pretty Woman*, became the band's third US chart-topper in 1990, and also reached UK number 3. 'Joyride' topped the US chart in spring 1991, was a number 1 single throughout mainland Europe, and reached the UK Top 5. Subsequent singles failed to match the band's early 90s purple patch.

After a five-year absence, the band returned in 1999 with the single 'Wish I Could Fly' and a respectable new album. Their undiminished European popularity was confirmed by the success of *Room Service*, their first album of the new millennium.

ROXY MUSIC

Influential UK band formed in 1971 by **Bryan Ferry** (b. 1945; vocals, keyboards), **Brian Eno** (b. Brian Peter George St Baptiste de la Salle Eno, 1948; electronics, keyboards), Graham Simpson (bass) and Andy Mackay (b. 1946). By early 1972 Paul Thompson (b. 1951; drums) and Phil Manzanera (b. Philip Targett Adams, 1951; guitar) had joined. Roxy Music's self-titled 1972 album for Island Records had Ferry's 50s-tinged vocals alongside distinctive 60s rhythms and 70s electronics. The UK hit single 'Virginia Plain', combined Ferry's cinematic interests and love of surrealistic art. The band scored a second UK Top 10 hit with 'Pyjamarama' and released *For Your Pleasure*. Another arresting work, the album featured 'Do The Strand', arguably their most effective rock workout. On 1973, Eno left and was replaced by Eddie Jobson (ex-**Curved Air**). After a break to record a solo album, Ferry took Roxy Music on tour to promote the excellent *Stranded*. 'Street Life', the first album track to be issued as a single, proved another Top 10 hit. Following his second solo album, Ferry completed work on *Country Life*, which ranged from the uptempo single 'All I Want Is You' to the aggressive 'The Thrill Of It All'. In spite of a challenging pilot single, 'Love Is The Drug', *Siren* was a disappointment. The 1979 comeback, *Manifesto*, included two hit singles, 'Angel Eyes' and the fatalistic 'Dance Away'. The succeeding *Flesh And Blood* included two UK hit singles, 'Over You' and 'Oh Yeah (On The Radio)'. In 1981 Roxy achieved their first number 1 single with 'Jealous Guy', an elegiac tribute to **John Lennon**. The following year, they released their final album *Avalon*, which topped the album charts and won much praise. Rumours of a reunion were rife in the summer of 1999, but it was not until February 2001 that Ferry, Manzanera and Mackay confirmed a world tour.

ROYAL TRUX

The drug-addled, chemically-fuelled dirty rock habits of Neil Hagerty (vocals, guitar) and Jennifer Herrema (vocals, sundry instruments) did much to brighten up the US alternative rock scene during Royal Trux's prolonged existence. The duo debuted with an untitled 1988 album, and a declared ambition of retracing the US noise scene back to its primal roots. Two further albums essayed the couple's heroin fixation/trials. Their major label debut, *Thank You*, saw them backed by a more permanent band. *Sweet Sixteen* was another credible album, even though the subject matter continued to be dubious, including excretion and bestiality, and succeeded in getting the band removed from their Virgin Records contract. Flush with Virgin's money, they returned to independent status in the late 90s with two elegantly wasted masterpieces, *Accelerator* and *Veterans Of Disorder*. After one final album in 2000 the duo unexpectedly announced that they were putting Royal Trux on hiatus. Hagerty released his solo debut, *Neil Michael Hagerty*, in 2001.

RUBETTES

Former songwriters of the Pete Best Four, Wayne Bickerton and Tony Waddington created the Rubettes from session musicians after their composition, 'Sugar Baby Love', was rejected by existing acts. A fusion of 50s revivalism and glam rock, it topped the UK charts and entered the US Top 40 in 1974. The song was promoted in concert by Alan Williams, Tony Thorpe, Bill Hurd, Mick Clarke and John Richardson. The five stayed together for another three years. The Rubettes' last UK hit was 1977's countrified 'Baby I Know', and by the early 80s their career had effectively faded. They were revived by success on the nostalgia circuit, and by the early 90s Williams, Clarke and Richardson had resumed recording. The latter also established himself as a popular new age recording artist.

RUBIN, RICK

Rubin's (b. Frederick Rubin) first production was 'It's Yours' by T. La Rock (1984), but it was the formation of Def Jam Records with Russell Simmons that enabled him to create the rap/metal, black/white synthesis he wanted. Uniting Simmons' brother's act, **Run-DMC**, with Rubin's adolescent heroes, **Aerosmith**, really put Def Jam on the map. 'Walk This Way' and its parent album, *Raising Hell*, was pivotal in introducing black rap to white audiences. The label ranged from the rap of **LL Cool J** and **Public Enemy**, the soul of Oran 'Juice' Jones to the speed metal of **Slayer**. At the end of the 80s Rubin left to form Def American (later American Recordings) and a successful production career, though nothing was as groundbreaking as early Def Jam material.

RUFFIN, JIMMY

Originally a gospel singer, Ruffin (b. 1939) became a session singer in the early 60s, joining Motown Records in 1961. In 1966 his 'What Becomes Of The Brokenhearted' was a major US and UK hit. Success in the USA was hard to sustain, so Ruffin concentrated on the British market. In 1980 'Hold On To My Love' brought him his first US Top 30 hit for 14 years.

RUN-DMC

New York, USA-based rappers Joe Simmons (b. 1966), Darryl 'D.M.C.' McDaniels (b. 1964) and DJ 'Jam Master Jay' (b. Jason Mizell, 1965) were originally Orange Crush, becoming Run-DMC in 1982. They had a US underground hit with 'It's Like That'. However, it was the single's b-side, 'Sucker MCs', which created the stir. Many critics signpost the single as the birth of modern hip-hop, with its stripped down sound and fashion image. Their debut album went gold in 1984, a first for a rap act. They cemented their position with appearances in Krush Groove, a fictionalized film biography of Russell Simmons (Joe's brother), joint-head of Def Jam with **Rick Rubin**. They broke into the mainstream with the heavy metal/rap collision 'Walk This Way' (featuring Steve Tyler and Joe Perry of **Aerosmith**). By 1987, *Raisin' Hell* had sold three million copies in the US.

In the 90s Daniels and Simmons experienced religious conversion, after the former succumbed to alcoholism and the latter was accused of rape. Despite making a comeback with *Down With The King*, Run-DMC seemed a spent force. However, they hit number 1 in the UK in 1998 with 'It's Like That', a collaboration with remixer Jason Nevins. Their extended studio hiatus was ended in 2001 with the release of the star-studded *Crown Royal*.

RUNAWAYS

Formed in 1975, the Runaways were initially the product of producer/svengali Kim Fowley and teenage lyricist Kari Krome. The original line-up was **Joan Jett** (b. Joan Larkin, 1960; guitar, vocals), Micki Steele (bass) and Sandy West (drums), but was quickly bolstered by Lita Ford (b. 1959; guitar, vocals) and Cherie Currie (vocals). Steele's departure brought several replacements, the

last being Jackie Fox (b. Jacqueline Fuchs). Although originally viewed as a vehicle for compositions by Fowley and Mars Bonfire, material by Jett and Krome helped assert the quintet's independence. *The Runaways* showed a group indebted to the 'glam-rock' of the **Sweet** and punchy pop of **Suzi Quatro**, and included the salutary 'Cherry Bomb'. *Queens Of Noise* repeated the pattern, but the strain of touring caused Fox to leave, as it did Currie. Subsequent releases lacked the appeal of the band's early work. The Runaways split in 1980. In 1985, Fowley resurrected the name with new personnel. This opportunistic concoction split up on completing *Young And Fast*.

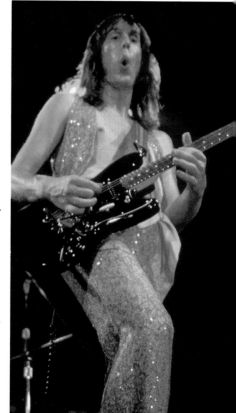

RUNDGREN, TODD

One of US rock's eccentric talents, Rundgren (b. 1948) began his career in local bar-band Woody's Truck Stop, before forming the Nazz in 1967. This US quartet completed three albums of anglophile pop/rock before disintegrating in 1970. Rundgren became an engineer – his credits included *Stage Fright* by the **Band** – before recording *Runt*. This exceptionally accomplished album spawned a US Top 20 hit in 'We Got To Get You A Woman' and led to the equally charming *The Ballad Of Todd Rundgren. Something/Anything?* contained some of Rundgren's most popular songs, including 'I Saw The Light' and 'It Wouldn't Have Made Any Difference'. *A Wizard, A True Star* offered a similarly dazzling array of styles. *Todd*, a second double-set, was equally ambitious, although less accessible.

In the mid-70s Rundgren formed Utopia, a progressive rock ensemble, who were a popular live attraction. Rundgren aficionados regretted Utopia's unrepentant self-indulgence when it encroached into the artist's 'solo' work, notably on *Initiation. Faithful* reflected a return to pop with 'Love Of The Common Man' and 'The Verb To Love'. Having already established himself as a producer with the **New York Dolls**, **Grand Funk Railroad** and **Hall And Oates**, Rundgren commenced work on **Meat Loaf**'s *Bat Out Of Hell*, which went on to become one of the bestselling albums of all time. Further solo and Utopia releases failed to revive Rundgren's commercial fortunes.

Starting with 1992's *No World Order*, however, Rundgren has devoted himself to experimenting with CD-ROM technology and interactive discs and live shows, unwilling to trade on past glories and even renaming himself TR-i (Todd Rundgren Interactive). In the late 90s he concentrated on developing his Internet presence. To this end he formed the Waking Dreams collective to hatch creative ideas online, and developed PatroNet, a device which allowed subscribers to access music directly from his web site.

RUNRIG

This Scottish outfit with a folk background was formed in 1973. Initially a trio featuring brothers Rory MacDonald (b. 1949; guitar, bass, vocals), Calum

MacDonald (b. 1953; drums, percussion, vocals) and Blair Douglas (accordion), the trio was joined by Donnie Munro (b. 1953; vocals, guitar) in 1974. *Play Gaelic* saw Robert MacDonald coming in for Douglas, although Malcolm Jones (b. 1959; guitar, mandolin, accordion) soon replaced the newcomer. *Highland Connection* emphasized electric styles and, in 1980, Iain Bayne (b. 1960) became drummer. The music still retained its rural traditions, but the sound took Runrig beyond the traditional arena. Richard Cherns (keyboard) joined the band for its first European tour, but following the release of *Heartland* he was replaced by Peter Wishart (b. 1962). After the release of *The Cutter & The Clan*, Runrig enjoyed a string of UK hit albums including *Searchlight*, *The Big Wheel* and *Amazing Things*. Donnie Munro stood as a Labour candidate at the 1997 General Election, and left the band for a political career. Bruce Guthro (b. 1961) was recruited as the band's new vocalist, and made his recording debut on 1999's *In Search Of Angels*.

RUSH

Canadian heavy rock band formed by Geddy Lee (b. Gary Lee Weinrib, 1953; keyboards, bass, vocals), Alex Lifeson (b. Alex Zivojinovich, 1953; guitar) and John Rutsey (drums). In 1973, they recorded a version of **Buddy Holly**'s 'Not Fade Away' as their debut release. Neil Peart (b. 1952; drums), who became the band's main songwriter, replaced Rutsey. *2112* (1976) was based on the work of novelist/philosopher Ayn Rand. Their most popular 70s offerings, *A Farewell To Kings* and *Hemispheres*, saw Peart finally dispense with his 'epic' songwriting style. In 1980 their hit single 'The Spirit Of Radio' took them beyond their loyal following, and in live shows Lifeson and Lee added keyboards for a fuller sound. *Moving Pictures* was a fusion of technological rock and musical craft, but subsequently inspiration waned. With *Hold Your Fire* (1987) they proved they could still scale their former heights. In 1994 the band agreed to a break for the first time in their career, during which Lifeson worked on his *Victor* side project. They returned in 1996 with *Test For Echo* and remain one of Canada's leading rock attractions.

RUSH, OTIS

Rush's (b. 1934) impassioned singing and playing on 'I Can't Quit You Baby' brought a Top 10 R&B hit in 1956. He influenced British guitarists such as **Peter Green**, **Eric Clapton** and Mick Taylor. **John Mayall** opened the pivotal *Bluesbreakers With Eric Clapton* with 'All Your Love' and continued by making Rush better known in the UK with recordings of 'So Many Roads', 'I Can't Quit You Baby' and 'Double Trouble'. *Right Place Wrong Time* (1969) was issued on the independent Bullfrog label. Rush is a guitarist's guitarist – his influence greater than his commercial standing. On 1994's *Ain't Enough Comin' In*, his best work in many years, Rush demonstrated total confidence. *Any Place I'm Going* continued the good run with some excellent brass backing adding a thick layer to Rush's blend of soul and blues.

RUSH, TOM

US folk artist Rush (b. 1941) began performing in 1961. *Got A Mind To Ramble* and *Blues Songs And Ballads* showcased an intuitive interpreter. *Tom Rush*, his first release for Elektra Records, was one of the era's finest folk/blues sets. *Take A Little Walk With Me* contained 'Galveston Flood', but its high points were six electric selections drawn from songs by **Bo Diddley**, **Chuck Berry** and **Buddy Holly**. *The Circle Game* contained material by **Joni Mitchell**, **James Taylor** and **Jackson Browne**, each of whom had yet to record in their own right. The recording also included the singer's own poignant 'No Regrets', later recorded by the **Walker Brothers** and **Midge Ure**. *Wrong End Of The Rainbow* and *Merrimack County* had much material written by Rush alone or with guitarist Trevor Veitch. By contrast, a new version of 'No Regrets' was the sole original on *Ladies Love Outlaws* (1974). It was 1982 before a new set, *New Year*, was released. Recorded live, it celebrated the artist's 20th anniversary, while a second live album, *Late Night Radio*, followed two years later. This cultured artist subsequently moved to Wyoming, but little was heard from him during the rest of the 90s. The owner of one of music's most expressive voices returned to the recording studio at the end of the decade to record a new track, 'River Song', for a CD retrospective of his career.

RUSSELL, LEON

Russell (b. 1941) is the archetypal American singer-songwriter, producer, arranger, entrepreneur, record company executive and multi-instrumentalist. His career began playing with **Ronnie Hawkins** and **Jerry Lee Lewis** in the late 50s. He was a regular session pianist on most of the classic **Phil Spector** singles, including the **Ronettes**, **Crystals** and the **Righteous Brothers**, and appeared on hundreds of major singles, including ones by **Frank Sinatra**, **Bobby Darin**, the **Byrds** and **Paul Revere**. He formed **Asylum Choir** in 1968 with Marc Benno. He befriended **Delaney And Bonnie** and created the famous Mad Dogs And Englishmen tour, which included **Joe Cocker**, who recorded Russell's 'Delta Lady' with great success. Russell founded his own label, Shelter, and released his self-titled debut to critical acclaim. His own session players included **Steve Winwood**, **George Harrison**, **Eric Clapton**, Charlie Watts, Bill Wyman and **Ringo Starr**. Following further session work, including playing with **Bob Dylan** and Dave Mason, he appeared at the Concert for Bangladesh in 1971. His country album, *Hank Wilson's Back*, acknowledged his debt to classic country singers. Three years later he received a Grammy for 'This Masquerade', which made the US Top 10 the previous year for **George Benson**. A partnership with **Willie Nelson** produced a country album in 1979 that became one of his biggest albums. Following *Hank Wilson's Volume II* in 1984, Russell became involved with his own video production company. He returned to recording in the 90s with a series of poorly received albums.

RYAN, PAUL AND BARRY

The Ryan twins, Paul (b. Paul Sapherson 1948, d. 1992) and Barry (b. Barry Sapherson, 1948), had success with their debut single, 'Don't Bring Me Your Heartaches', which reached the UK Top 20 in 1965, followed by other hits. 'Have You Ever Loved Somebody' (1966) and 'Keep It Out Of Sight' (1967) were penned, respectively, by the **Hollies** and **Cat Stevens**. They split amicably in 1968 with Paul embarking on a songwriting career while Barry recorded as a solo act. Together they created 'Eloise', the latter's impressive number 2 hit and subsequent million seller.

RYDELL, BOBBY

In 1958 Rydell (b. Robert Ridarelli, 1942), probably the most musically talented of the late 50s Philadelphia school of clean-cut teen-idols, joined the Cameo label and 'Kissin' Time' became the first of his 18 US Top 40 hits. His best-known transatlantic hits are 'Wild One', 'Sway' and 'Volare', all in 1960, and 'Forget Him', a song written and produced in Britain by Tony Hatch in 1963. Rydell starred in the movie *Bye Bye Birdie* and moved into cabaret. He returned to the studio in 1995 to re-record all his greatest hits as *The Best Of Bobby Rydell*.

RYDER, MITCH, AND THE DETROIT WHEELS

Ryder (b. William Levise Jnr, 1945) formed Billy Lee And The Rivieras in 1963. Jim McCarty (lead guitar), Joe Cubert (rhythm guitar), Earl Elliott (bass) and 'Little' John Badanjek (drums) completed the group's early line-up. The quintet was then given a sharper name – Mitch Ryder And The Detroit Wheels – and in 1965 secured their biggest hit with the frenzied 'Jenny Take A Ride', a raw and earthy performance, which set new standards in 'blue-eyed' soul, with Ryder successfully capturing the power of his black inspirations. The formula became predictable and the Wheels were fired in 1967. A union with guitarist **Steve Cropper** resulted in the excellent *Detroit/Memphis Experiment*. In 1971, Levise formed Detroit, a hard-edged rock band, but then abandoned music until the late 70s. In the 90s, Ryder was still a major concert attraction. A primary influence on **Bruce Springsteen**, the MC5 and the Stooges, Ryder's talent should not be underestimated.

S CLUB 7

The highly photogenic mixed-gender line-up of this UK pop group comprises Bradley McIntosh (b. 1981), Hannah Spearritt (b. 1981), Jon Lee (b. 1982), Jo O'Meara (b. 1979), Paul Cattermole (b. 1977), Rachel Stevens (b. 1978) and Tina Barrett (b. 1976). Their debut single, 'Bring It All Back', debuted at UK number 1 in June 1999. 'S Club Party' narrowly failed to repeat the debut single's success, stalling at number 2, the same position reached by their Christmas single, 'Two In A Million'/'You're My Number One'. Their television series *Miami 7* aka *S Club 7 In Miami*, which updated **The Monkees** format for the 90s, proved to be a highly successful export. The group continued to enjoy UK success throughout 2000, culminating in December's chart-topping charity single 'Never Had A Dream Come True'. The following March, their squeaky clean image was dented when McIntosh, Cattermole and Lee received a formal caution for possession of cannabis. Nevertheless, their next single 'Don't Stop Movin'' debuted at number 1 the following month, and 'Never Had A Dream Come True' broke into the US Top 10. The group notched up their fourth UK chart-topper with the charity single 'Have You Ever'.

S*M*A*S*H

Formed in Hertfordshire, England, this indie trio comprising Ed Borrie (vocals, guitar), Rob Haigh (drums) and Salvador Alessi (bass), were briefly fashionable as part of the New Wave Of The New Wave movement. Censorship proved a problem over '(I Want To) Kill Somebody', which reached the UK Top 30 despite being on sale for only one day. Their debut album was issued in 1994, but by 1995 the band had been dropped by Hi-Rise Records after a series of poorly received live performances. Following the 'Rest Of My Life' single they decided to split up.

SAD CAFÉ

Formed in 1976, this UK band comprised Paul Young (b. 1947, d. 2000; vocals), Ian Wilson (guitar), Mike Hehir (guitar), Lenni (saxophone), Vic Emerson (keyboards), John Stimpson (bass) and David Irving (drums). *Fanx Ta Ra* introduced a blend of hard-rock riffs and adult pop, but it was *Misplaced Ideals* which brought them international success when 'Run Home Girl' became a US hit. *Facades* contained 'Every Day Hurts' (UK Top 3, 1979) and two further Top 40 entries in 1980, 'Strange Little Girl' and 'My Oh My'. Despite some further minor hits, Sad Café were unable to sustain their early success. Young later enjoyed success as vocalist with **Mike And The Mechanics**.

SADE

Nigerian-born Sade (b. Helen Folasade Adu, 1959) sang with London-based Arriva and funk band Pride, but left the latter in 1983 to form her own band, taking Stewart Matthewman (saxophone), Andrew Hale (keyboards) and Paul Denman (bass) with her. In 1984 'Your Love Is King' was a UK Top 10 hit. This was followed by *Diamond Life*, which sold over six million copies worldwide and broke her into the US market on the back of the Top 5 single 'Smooth Operator'. Sade's next album topped both the UK and US charts, and included transatlantic hits 'The Sweetest Taboo' and 'Never As Good As The First Time'. She took her time in delivering *Love Deluxe*, which included hit singles in 'No Ordinary Love' and 'Feel No Pain', but the British public were lukewarm. It only reached the UK Top 30, but was a million-seller in the US, peaking at number 3. A greatest hits package was released in 1994, while the male members of the band recorded separately as Sweetback. In 1996, Sade gave birth to her first child. She made her long-awaited return to the music scene in 2000 with the single 'By Your Side' and *Lovers Rock*, enjoying particular success on the US market. She was awarded an OBE in 2002's New Year's Honours List.

SAINT ETIENNE

Pete Wiggs (b. 1966) and music journalist Bob Stanley (b. 1965) from Croydon, Surrey, England, formed Saint Etienne in 1988. They recruited Moira Lambert for a dance/reggae cover version of **Neil Young**'s 'Only Love Can Break Your Heart' (1990), which fared well in the nightclubs. Another cover version, 'Kiss And Make Up', was given a similar overhaul for their second single, fronted this time by New Zealand vocalist Donna Savage. 1991's 'Nothing Can Stop Us' benefited from Sarah Cracknell's (b. 1967) dreamy vocals, as would *Foxbase Alpha*, released in the autumn. 'Only Love Can Break Your Heart' was reissued and provided them with a minor chart hit. *So Tough* revealed a rich appreciation of the vital signs of British pop, and *Tiger Bay* transcended a variety of musical genres. Their biggest UK hit, reaching number 11, was 'He's On The Phone' which promoted the excellent compilation set *Too Young To Die*.

The band recorded *Good Humor*, in Sweden. Despite being another quality, pop-orientated release the album met with an indifferent commercial response. They returned in late 1999 with the vinyl only EP, *Places To Visit*. To Rococo Rot contributed some minimalist arrangements to the following year's *Sound Of Water*, an edgy and ambitious return to form.

SAINTE-MARIE, BUFFY

US singer-songwriter Sainte-Marie (b. 1941) signed to Vanguard Records in 1964. Her debut *It's My Way!* introduced a remarkable compositional and performing talent. 'Now That The Buffalo's Gone', a plea for Indian rights, reflected her native-American parentage and was one of several stand-out tracks. Her second selection included 'Until It's Time For You To Go', a song later recorded by **Elvis Presley**. Her versatility was also apparent on *I'm Gonna Be A Country Girl Again* and *Illuminations*, which featured an electronic score on several tracks. Sainte-Marie secured an international hit in 1971 with the theme song to the movie, *Soldier Blue*, but subsequent releases failed to capitalize on this success. She retired to raise her family and concentrate on her work for children's foundations, which included regular appearances on *Sesame Street*. Her later credits included co-composing, with lyricist Will Jennings, the 1982 **Joe Cocker/Jennifer Warnes'** hit, 'Up Where We Belong' which featured in the movie *An Officer And A Gentleman*.

Her welcome return to the music scene in 1992 produced the warmly received *Coincidence And Likely Stories*, which displayed her interest in computer technology (Sainte-Marie is a prominent digital artist). *Up Where We Belong*, released in 1996, included several new recordings of her old material.

SALT-N-PEPA

US rappers Cheryl 'Salt' James (b. 1964) and Sandra 'Pepa' Denton (b. 1969) grew up in New York City. Their break came when producer Hurby 'Luv Bug' Azor asked them to rap for his group the Super Lovers. They started recording as Salt-N-Pepa under Azor's guidance and released singles such as 'I'll Take Your Man', 'It's My Beat' and 'Tramp'. Joined by DJ Spinderella (b. Deidre Roper, 1971), their big break came in 1988 when 'Push It' reached UK number 2 and the US Top 20. Later that year a remake of the **Isley Brothers**' 'Twist And Shout' also went into the UK Top 5. Their most confrontational release was 1991's transatlantic hit 'Let's Talk About Sex'. They returned in 1994 with the US Top 5 hit 'Shoop' and 'Whatta Man', a collaboration with **En Vogue**. After a lengthy absence, during which they contributed tracks to several soundtracks, they returned in 1997 with *Brand New*, which saw the trio struggling to assert themselves against the brasher style of the new rap queens.

SAM AND DAVE

Samuel David Moore (b. 1935) and David Prater (b. 1937, d. 1988) first performed together in 1961 at Miami's King Of Hearts club. They later signed to Atlantic Records and released 'You Don't Know Like I Know', 'Hold On I'm Comin'' (both 1966), 'Soul Man' (1967) and 'I Thank You' (1968). By 1968 though, their personal relationship was disintegrating. 'Soul Sister, Brown Sugar' (1969) delayed the slide, but the duo split briefly in 1970 when Sam began his own career. They were reunited by a contract with United Artists Records. Despite the late 70s success of the *Blues Brothers* with 'Soul Man', Moore and Prater faltered when the differences between the two men proved irreconcilable. By 1981, Moore was again pursuing an independent direction. Prater found a new foil in the 'Sam' of Sam & Bill, but before they were able to consolidate this new partnership, Prater died in a car crash in April 1988. Moore has continued working as a solo artist.

SAM THE SHAM AND THE PHARAOHS

Backed by the Pharaohs – Ray Stinnet (guitar), Butch Gibson (saxophone), David Martin (bass) and Jerry Patterson (drums) – Texas-born Sam (b. Domingo Samudio aka Sam Samudio) had a US chart-topper in 1965 with 'Wooly Bully', which became the act's sole UK Top 20 hit. They enjoyed further success in the USA with 'Lil' Red Riding Hood', number 2 in 1966. The group later mutated into the Sam The Sham Revue, but the singer dissolved the venture in 1970 to embark on a solo career under his own name.

SANTANA

This important US group pioneered Afro-Latin rock and, as such, remains head and shoulders above all pretenders to their throne. Formed in 1966, they

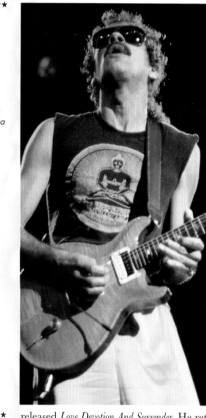

rapidly transcended the late 60s San Francisco new wave scene from which they emerged, and, over the past 30 years, Mexican guitarist Carlos Santana (b. 1947) introduced jazz and funk into their unique blend of polyrhythmic music. The original line-up consisted of Santana, Gregg Rolie (keyboards, vocals), Michael Shrieve (drums), David Brown (b. 1947), Marcus Malone and Mike Carabello. Later important members were Neal Schon (b. 1954, guitar), José Chepito Areas, Tom Coster, and Coke Escovedo.

Outstanding examples of the genre, *Santana*, *Abraxas* and *Santana III* spent months high in the US charts, and they enjoyed hit singles with 'Evil Ways', 'Black Magic Woman', 'Oyo Como Va' and 'Everybody's Everything'. *Caravanserai* marked a change of style as Rolie departed to form **Journey**. After befriending fellow guitarist John McLaughlin, Carlos Santana released *Love Devotion And Surrender*. He returned to hard Latin rock with the excellent *Amigos* in 1977, but a string of lesser releases over the following decades saw Santana retreating from critical and commercial approval.

After almost 30 years with Columbia Records, the guitarist relocated to Arista Records for 1999's highly acclaimed *Supernatural*, which included the US number 1 hit single 'Smooth' (featuring **Matchbox 20** singer Rob Thomas, it stayed at the top of the US chart for 12 weeks) and 'Put Your Lights On' (with **Everlast**). 'Maria Maria', featuring The Product G&B, followed 'Smooth' to the top of the US singles chart the following April. This unprecedented success resulted in him winning a staggering eight Grammy awards in 2000.

SATRIANI, JOE

US-born Satriani originally formed the Squares, but they folded in 1984 through lack of commercial recognition, giving Satriani the opportunity to concentrate on his guitar playing. The outcome of this was the EP *Joe Satriani*. Following a spell with the **Greg Kihn** band, Satriani released *Not Of This Earth*, an album which was less polished than its successor, *Surfing With The Alien*. This set was a major seller and brought mainstream respect. *Time Machine* contained a mixture of new and previously unreleased tracks, and live material from his 1993 world tour. The guitarist then replaced **Ritchie Blackmore** in **Deep Purple**, before resuming his solo career with further albums.

SAVAGE GARDEN

Australian pop duo Savage Garden formed in Brisbane at the end of 1996. Singer Darren Hayes and multi-instrumentalist Englishman Daniel Jones, met while playing in bar bands. Their self-titled debut album was recorded in Sydney in 1996. 'I Want You' climbed to US number 4 the following year, and they enjoyed a huge transatlantic hit during the early months of 1998 with 'Truly Madly Deeply', the single topping the US charts and spending

several weeks in the UK Top 10. On the back of their singles success, *Savage Garden* rose to number 3 on the US album chart. The follow-up single, 'To The Moon And Back', climbed to number 3 in the UK chart. The duo's follow-up, *Affirmation*, was recorded in San Francisco, and included the huge US chart-topper, 'I Knew I Loved You'. The duo split up in October 2001 shortly after Hayes completed work on his debut solo album. *Spin* was released the following spring.

SAW DOCTORS

Originating in Tuam, County Galway, Eire, the Saw Doctors – Leo Moran (vocals), Davy Carton (guitar), John 'Turps' Burke (mandolin, vocals), Pearse Doherty (bass) and John Donnelly (drums) – continue the practice of rock reacquainting itself with traditional Gaelic music. They signed to WEA Records in 1992 for *All The Way From Tuam*, having made their mark with an independent debut featuring 'I Useta Love Her'. The latter became Eire's biggest-selling single of all time. They had been joined at this juncture by Tony Lambert (keyboards, piano, accordion). They were also featured in a UK television documentary, *Sing A Powerful Song*. The band subsequently formed their own Shamtown label, and broke into the UK Top 30 with the *Small Bit Of Love* EP. Even more success followed with the Top 20 hit 'World Of Good', and the Top 10 album *Same Oul' Town*. They also remain a huge concert draw in the USA, a recognition of their status as the ultimate 'people's band'. A compilation set was followed in 1998 by *Songs From Sun Street*, their first album of all-new material to be released in America.

SAXON

UK heavy metal band formed in the late 70s by Peter 'Biff' Byford (vocals), Graham Oliver (guitar), Paul Quinn (guitar), Steve Dawson (bass) and Pete Gill (drums). Their first album was a heavy rock outing, but the release of *Wheels Of Steel* saw them embracing metal. Saxon's popularity soared, earning themselves two UK Top 20 hits with 'Wheels Of Steel' and '747 (Strangers In The Night)'. They capitalized on this with the release of *Strong Arm Of The Law*. A further Top 20 hit arrived with 'And The Bands Played On', from the following year's *Denim And Leather*. By *The Eagle Has Landed* (UK Top 5) the band were at their peak. Gill was then replaced by Nigel Glockler. *Power And The Glory* enforced their credentials as a major rock band. The follow-up, *Innocence Is No Excuse*, was a more polished and radio-friendly production but only reached the Top 40. The departure of Dawson contributed to their malaise.

In 1990 Saxon returned to the public eye with a UK tour that featured a set-list built on their popular older material. *Solid Ball Of Rock* was their most accomplished album for some time, but in early 1995 Oliver, Dawson and Gill played live together while contesting the rights to the name Saxon with Byford. The issue was soon resolved, however, and Byford was back in place for *Dogs Of War*, with Oliver having taken his leave. Oliver, Dawson and Gill formed Son Of A Bitch before winning the right to adopt the Oliver/Dawson Saxon moniker. Byford and Quinn remain at the helm of the official Saxon.

SAYER, LEO

In 1971, UK singer-songwriter Sayer (b. Gerard Hugh Sayer, 1948) formed Patches, but was soon singled out for solo work. After a miss with 'Why Is Everybody Going Home', Sayer reached UK number 1 with 1973's 'The Show Must Go On'. After 'One Man Band' and 'Long Tall Glasses', Sayer achieved a US million-seller in 'You Make Me Feel Like Dancing'. From 1977's *Endless Flight* the ballad, 'When I Need You', marked Sayer's UK commercial peak. After the title track of *Thunder In My Heart* halted just outside the UK Top 20, hits became harder to come by. 'I Can't Stop Lovin' You (Though I Try)' and revivals of **Buddy Holly**'s 'Raining In My Heart' and **Bobby Vee**'s 'More Than I Can Say' were the only smashes as his

1983 chart swansong (with 'Till You Come Back To Me') loomed nearer.

By the late 80s, Sayer was without a recording contract. His recording career re-commenced in 1990 after he was reunited with producer Alan Tarney. He undertook a major tour in 1998, buoyed by a bizarre UK media campaign (led by The *Sun* newspaper) to reinstate Sayer as a living legend.

SCAGGS, BOZ

Scaggs (b. William Royce Scaggs, 1944) was raised in Dallas, Texas, where he joined fellow guitarist **Steve Miller** in a high-school group, the Marksmen. Boz then formed an R&B unit, the Wigs, but the group broke up and the guitarist headed for mainland Europe where he became a folk-singer. This exile ended in 1967 when he received an invitation from his erstwhile colleague to join the fledgling Steve Miller Band. Scaggs recorded two albums with them but left for a solo career in 1968. *Boz Scaggs* was a magnificent offering and over the next five years, Scaggs pursued an exemplary soul/rock direction with *My Time* and *Slow Dancer*. A slick session band enhanced some of Scaggs' finest compositions on *Silk Degrees*, including 'Lowdown' (US number 3), 'What Can I Say?' and 'Lido Shuffle'. The singer's career then faltered and despite enjoying several hit singles during 1980, Scaggs maintained a low profile during the subsequent decade. It was eight years before a new selection, *Other Roads*, appeared and a further six before *Some Change*. Scaggs moved back to his roots with 1997's *Come On Home*, an earthy collection of R&B classics. *Dig* was a more contemporary release which found Scaggs attempting hip-hop and jazz flavoured material.

SCORPIONS

German hard rock band formed in 1971 by guitarists Rudolf (b. 1948) and **Michael Schenker** (b. 1955), with Klaus Meine (b. 1948; vocals), Lothar Heimberg (bass) and Wolfgang Dziony (drums). Soon after *Lonesome Crow* was released, Heimberg, Dziony and Schenker left, the latter joining **UFO**. Francis Buchholz and Jurgen Rosenthal stepped in on bass and drums, for *Fly To The Rainbow*. Ulrich Roth was recruited as Schenker's replacement in 1974 and Rudy Lenners took over from Rosenthal the following year. *In Trance* and *Virgin Killer* epitomized the Scorpions' new-found confidence. *Taken By Force* saw Herman Rarebell replace Lenners, with the band branching out into anthemic power-ballads, after which Roth quit. Matthias Jabs (b. 1956) replaced him, but had to step down temporarily when Michael Schenker returned to contribute to 1979's *Lovedrive*. He was replaced by Jabs permanently after collapsing on stage. *Blackout* made the US Top 10, as did *Love At First Sting*. *World Wide Live* captured the band at their best and peaked at US number 14. *Savage Amusement* marked a slight change in emphasis, adopting a more restrained approach. Their 1990 release *Crazy World* became their most successful album, and the ballad 'Wind Of Change' their first million-seller. Buchholz was sacked and replaced by Ralph Rieckermann (b. 1962) in 1992. Rarebell was later replaced by James Kottak (b. 1962). Kottak appeared on the band's 1999 recording, *Eye II Eye*.

SCOTT, JILL

This modern US R&B singer toured with the Roots and **Erykah Badu** before embarking on a solo career, after striking a deal with the Hidden Beach label. Her other credits include co-writing the Roots' Grammy Award-winning single 'You Got Me'. Her sophisticated sound combines rap, poetry, hip-hop, jazz and blues. The enigmatically titled debut, *Who Is Jill Scott? Words And Sounds Vol. 1*, won universal praise from critics who saw Scott as part of the new wave of female singers somewhat clumsily described as 'neo-soul'. A sprawling double album, *Experience: Jill Scott*, was released in 2001.

SCOTT-HERON, GIL

Scott-Heron (b. 1949) formed the Midnight Band with Brian Jackson in 1972, playing their original blend of jazz, soul and prototype rap music. *Small Talk At 125th And Lenox* was mostly an album of poems, but later albums showed Scott-Heron developing into a skilled songwriter whose work was soon covered by other artists. In 1973 he had a minor hit with 'The Bottle', and 'The Revolution Will Not Be Televised' and 'Home Is Where The Hatred Is' were covered by other artists. *Winter In America* and *The First Minute Of A New Day* were both heavily jazz-influenced, but later sets saw Scott-Heron exploring more pop-oriented formats, and in 1976 he scored a hit with 'Johannesburg'. Scott-Heron's later albums continued to confront issues such as nuclear power, apartheid and poverty, although his personal life was often a mess. He was imprisoned in 2001 for cocaine possession.

SCREAMING TREES

Rock band from Seattle, USA, formed by brothers Gary Lee Conner (b. 1962; guitar) and Van Conner (b. 1967; bass), Mark Lanegan (b. 1964; vocals) and Mark Pickerell (drums). The latter was replaced in 1991 by Barrett Martin (b. 1967; drums). The same year's major label debut *Uncle Anaesthesia* fine-tuned the band's blend of punk aggression and 60s mysticism, which had only intermittently succeeded over four previous albums. *Sweet Oblivion* and *Dust* confirmed their critical status, but following the release of the latter in 1996, Lanegan opted to concentrate on his increasingly successful and acclaimed solo career.

SCRITTI POLITTI

Founded by a group of Leeds, England-based art students in 1978, by the time of their first single, 'Skank Bloc Bologna', the nucleus of the band was Green Gartside (b. 'Green' Strohmeyer-Gartside, 1956; vocals, guitar), Matthew Kay (keyboards), Tom Morley (drums) and Nial Jinks (bass). The group was explicitly political, encouraging listeners to create their own music in the face of the corporate record industry. This early *avant-garde* phase gave way to a sound that brought together elements of pop, jazz, soul and reggae on songs such as 'The Sweetest Girl' and 'Asylums In Jerusalem'/'Jacques Derrida', from their debut album. Morley quit the group in 1982, by which time Gartside was Scritti Politti. After moving to Virgin Records, Green linked up with New York musicians David Gamson (keyboards, programming) and Fred Maher (drums), who formed the basis of the group that made a series of UK hits in the years 1984 to 1988. These included 'Wood Beez (Pray Like Aretha Franklin)' and 'The Word Girl'. A three-year silence was broken by 'Oh Patti (Don't Feel Sorry For Loverboy)', lifted from *Provision*. In 1991, a revival of the **Beatles'** 'She's A Woman', featuring **Shabba Ranks**, reached the UK Top 20.

Another extended lay-off was eventually broken with the release of 1999's eclectic *Anomie & Bonhomie*. The album reflected Gartside's infatuation with hip-hop.

SEAL

After a chance encounter with rap artist Chester, London-born Seal (b. Sealhenry Samuel, 1963) was introduced to techno wizard Adamski. Seal contributed lyrics

to his embryonic dance track, 'Killer', which took the UK's dance floors by storm in 1990. However, the partnership did not last and Seal released his debut solo, 'Crazy'. The lyrics were imbued with the sort of new age mysticism given vent by 90s dance culture. Seal then recorded a magnificent album which sold 3 million copies worldwide. His second album was another eponymous affair, and once again a worldwide success. The startling 'Kiss From A Rose' was used as the soundtrack theme for the movie *Batman Forever*. At the 1996 Grammys he gathered an armful of awards including, Record Of The Year, Song Of The Year and Best Pop Vocal Performance. He ended that year with a major US hit, a version of **Steve Miller**'s 'Fly Like An Eagle'. *Human Being* was another polished collection of material, although it lacked any of the dramatic highlights found on the previous two albums. The record's commercial performance, failing to break into the US Top 20, was a surprise and Seal has subsequently maintained a fairly low profile.

SEARCHERS

One of the premier groups from the mid-60s' Merseybeat explosion, the Searchers were formed in 1960 by Chris Curtis (b. Christopher Crummey, 1941; drums), Mike Pender (b. Michael John Prendergast, 1942; lead guitar), Tony Jackson (b. 1940; vocals, bass) and John McNally (b. 1941; rhythm guitar). They signed to Pye Records in 1963. Their debut 'Sweets For My Sweet' (UK number 1) was a memorable tune with strong harmonies. *Meet The Searchers* revealed the group's R&B pedigree on such standards as 'Farmer John'. Meanwhile, the follow-up, 'Sugar And Spice', just failed to reach number 1. Their third single, 'Needles And Pins' topped the UK charts and reached the US Top 20. It was followed with further US successes, including 'Ain't That Just Like Me', 'Sugar And Spice' and 'Someday We're Gonna Love Again'.

Tony Jackson, whose falsetto vocals had contributed much to the group's early sound, departed and was replaced by Frank Allen (b. Francis Renaud McNeice, 1943). A strident reading of **Jackie DeShannon**'s 'When You Walk In The Room' was another highlight of 1964. A return to the 'old' Searchers sound with the plaintive 'Goodbye My Love', took them back into the UK Top 5 in early 1965. They enjoyed further US success when their cover of the **Clovers**' 'Love Potion Number 9' was a Top 10 hit. This continued with 'Bumble Bee and 'Goodbye My Love'. 'He's Got No Love' showed that they could write their own hit material but this run could not be sustained. Their last UK hit was a version of the **Hollies**' 'Have You Ever Loved Somebody'. They threatened a resurgence in 1979 when Sire Records issued a promising comeback album. The attempt was unsuccessful, however, and after the lesser *Play For Today* (titled *Love's Melodies* in the USA), the group returned to the cabaret circuit.

SEBADOH

Based in Boston, Massachusetts, USA, Sebadoh are led by Lou Barlow (vocals, guitar). Barlow's first success came in partnership with J. Mascis in **Dinosaur Jr**, but friendships within the band began to fray, and they split in 1989. Barlow began to record four-track demos with drumming friend Eric Gaffney. These cassette releases were dwarfed by the impact of 1991's *Sebadoh III*, at which time the duo was expanded by bass player/vocalist Jason Loewenstein.

The UK-issued *Rockin The Forest* saw the band adopt a rock/pop sound and *Sebadoh Vs Helmet* included two **Nick Drake** covers. In 1994 Eric Gaffney was replaced by Bob Fay. In 1996 Barlow made a surprise entry into the US Top 40 with 'Natural One' a song written with John Davis under the Folk Implosion moniker. The new Sebadoh album *Harmacy* seemed like an unintentional bid for pop stardom and was peppered with catchy riffs. A new drummer, Russ Pollard, was brought into the line-up on 1998's *The Sebadoh*.

SEBASTIAN, JOHN

US artist Sebastian (b. 1944) is best known for his seminal jug band/rock fusion with **Lovin' Spoonful** in the 60s. In 1969 his solo performance was one of the highlights of the Woodstock Festival, and this elevated him to star status. *John B. Sebastian* included the evocative 'How Have You Been' and 'She's A Lady'. Sebastian faltered with the uneven *The Four Of Us*. His 1974 release *Tarzana Kid* sold poorly. Two years later Sebastian was asked to write the theme song for a US comedy television series, *Welcome Back Kotter*. The result was a number 1 hit, 'Welcome Back'.

Although he continued to tour, a new Sebastian studio album did not appear until 1992, when a Japanese label released his most recent songs. Together with the J-Band, which featured Jimmy Vivino, Fritz Richmond and James Wormworth, Sebastian released the jug band session *I Want My Roots* in 1996. Another J-Band release came in 1999, a live album with Geoff Muldaur in the line-up.

SEDAKA, NEIL

New York-born pianist Sedaka (b. 1939) began his songwriting career with lyricist Howard Greenfield in the early 50s. Sedaka's first major hit success came with 'Stupid Cupid', an international smash for **Connie Francis**. The following year, Sedaka signed to RCA Records as a recording artist and enjoyed a minor US hit with 'The Diary'. The frantic follow-up, 'I Go Ape', was a strong novelty record, followed by one of his most famous songs, 'Oh Carol', a lament directed at former girlfriend **Carole King**. This was succeeded by a string of early 60s hits, including 'Stairway To Heaven', 'Calendar Girl', 'Happy Birthday Sweet Sixteen' and 'Breaking Up Is Hard To Do'.

With the decline of the clean-cut teen balladeer however, there was an inevitable lull in Sedaka's fortunes. He continued writing a fair share of hits over the next 10 years, though. Sedaka relaunched his solo career with *Emergence* and relocated to the UK. By 1973, he was back in the British charts with 'That's When The Music Takes Me'. *The Tra-La Days Are Over* was highly regarded and included 'Our Last Song Together', dedicated to Howard Greenfield. With *Laughter In The Rain*, Sedaka extended his appeal to his homeland: the title track topped the US charts in 1975. That same year, **Captain And Tennille** took Sedaka's 'Love Will Keep Us Together' to the US number 1 spot and the songwriter followed suit with 'Bad Blood'. The year ended with a reworking of 'Breaking Up Is Hard To Do' which provided another worldwide smash. He enjoyed his last major hit during 1980 in the company of his daughter Dara on 'Should've Never Let You Go'. Sedaka still tours and records on a regular basis.

SEEDS

Formed in 1965, this US band provided a pivotal link between garage/punk rock and the emergent underground styles. They were led by Sky Saxon (b. Richard Marsh), with Jan Savage (guitar), Darryl Hooper (keyboards) and Rick Andridge (drums). They had a US hit the following year with the compulsive 'Pushin' Too Hard'. Its raw, simple riff and Saxon's howling, half-spoken intonation established a pattern that remained almost unchanged throughout the band's career. The Seeds enjoyed minor chart success with 'Mr. Farmer' and 'Can't Seem To Make You Mine', while their first two albums, *The Seeds* and *A Web Of Sound*, were also well received. The quartet embraced 'flower-power' with *Future*, and this release was followed by a curious interlude wherein the group, now dubbed the Sky Saxon Blues Band, recorded *A Full Spoon Of Seedy Blues*. Subsequent singles charted a collapsing unit and psyche, although Saxon later re-emerged as Sky Sunlight, fronting several aggregations known variously as Stars New Seeds or the Universal Stars Band.

SEEKERS

Founded in Australia in 1963, the Seekers comprised Athol Guy (b. 1940; vocals, double bass), Keith Potger (b. 1941; vocals, guitar), Bruce Woodley (b. 1942; vocals, guitar) and Ken Ray (lead vocals, guitar). A year later Athol Guy recruited Judith Durham (b. 1943) as the new lead singer. Following a visit to London in 1964, the group were signed to the Grade Agency, where Tom Springfield offered his services as songwriter/producer. A trilogy of hits – 'I'll Never Find Another You', 'A World Of Our Own' and 'The Carnival Is Over' – widened their appeal. In 1967, the breezy 'Georgy Girl' was a transatlantic Top 10 hit but thereafter, apart from 'When Will The Good Apples Fall' and 'Emerald City', the group were no longer chart regulars, and in 1969 they disbanded.

Potger oversaw the formation of the **New Seekers** before moving into record production. The Seekers briefly re-formed in 1975 with teenage Dutch singer Louisa Wisseling replacing Durham. 'The Sparrow Song' topped the Australian charts. In 1990 the Seekers reunited and played a series of 100 dates across Australia and New Zealand. The quartet has continued to tour throughout the world and also recorded their first studio album for 30 years, *Future Road*.

SEGER, BOB

US-born Seger (b. 1945) made his recording debut with the Beach Bums, with 'The Ballad Of The Yellow Beret'. The act then became known as Bob Seger and the Last Heard and released 'East Side Story' (1966) and 'Heavy Music' (1967). Seger was signed by Capitol Records in 1968 and the Bob Seger System enjoyed a US Top 20 hit that year with 'Ramblin' Gamblin' Man'. Numerous releases followed, but the artist was unable to repeat his early success and they disbanded in 1971.

Seger returned to music with his own label, Palladium and three unspectacular albums ensued. He garnered considerable acclaim for his 1974 single, 'Get Out Of Denver', now a much-covered classic. Seger achieved commercial success with *Beautiful Loser*. Now fronting the Silver Bullet Band, Seger reinforced his in-concert popularity with *Live Bullet*, in turn followed by *Night Moves*, his first platinum disc. The title track reached the US Top 5 in 1977, a feat 'Still The Same' repeated the following year. His triple-platinum album, *Stranger In Town*, included 'Hollywood Nights', 'Old Time Rock 'N' Roll' and

'We've Got Tonight'. *Against The Wind* also topped the US album charts. Among his later hit singles were 'Shame On The Moon', 'Understanding', and the number 1 hit 'Shakedown'. Seger released his first studio album for five years in 1991, which became a Top 10 hit in the USA. *It's A Mystery* ploughed typical Seger territory. He followed the success of the album with a box-office record-breaking tour of America in 1996. Ticketmaster claimed that the concert in his hometown sold 100,000 tickets in 57 minutes.

SELECTER

When Coventry, England's **Specials** needed a b-side for their own debut, 'Gangsters', they approached fellow local musician Neol Davies. With the assistance of John Bradbury aka Prince Rimshot (drums) and Barry Jones (trombone), Davies concocted the instrumental track 'The Selecter'. The single took off with both sides receiving airplay. This meant that a band had to be formed to tour, so Davies assembled the Selecter Mk II, consisting of Pauline Black (vocals), Crompton Amanor (drums, vocals), Charles H. Bainbridge (drums), Gappa Hendricks, Desmond Brown (keyboards) and Charlie Anderson (bass). They managed a string of successful singles such as 'On My Radio', 'Three Minute Hero' and 'Missing Words'. The group re-formed in the 90s and released their first new material for over a decade.

SELENA

In her short and tragic career Selena (b. Selena Quintanilla-Pérez, 1971, d. 1995) became the popular figurehead for the growth in popularity of Tejano and Latino music. Her father was a renowned vocalist with Tejano combo Los Dinos, and Selena made her first record in 1983, with Los Dinos as her backing band. She signed a major recording contract with EMI Latin in 1989, and was rapidly embraced by Hispanic communities the world over for her singing talent and endearing personality. She made her acting debut appearing in the romantic comedy *Don Juan De Marco*. The singer was recording her first English language album when she was shot by the president of her fan club. However, she achieved a major landmark when *Dreaming Of You* raced to number 1 on the US pop chart in July 1995, a huge achievement given that it was sung predominantly in Spanish. Following Selena's death, the biopic *Selena*, starring **Jennifer Lopez**, was released in 1997.

SENSATIONAL ALEX HARVEY BAND

Formed in 1972 when vocalist **Alex Harvey** (b. 1935, d. 1982) teamed with Glasgow group, Tear Gas. Zal Cleminson (b. 1949; guitar), Hugh McKenna (b. 1949; keyboards), Chris Glen (b. 1950; bass) and Ted McKenna (b. 1950; drums) completed the line-up. *Framed* was accompanied by a period of frenetic live activity. The quintet continued their commercial ascendancy with *Next*, *The Impossible Dream* and *Tomorrow Belongs To Me*, while enhancing their in-concert reputation. *Live* encapsulated this era, while their exaggerated reading of **Tom Jones**' hit 'Delilah' gave the band a UK Top 10 single. They enjoyed another hit single with 'Boston Tea Party' (1976), but the rigorous schedule extracted a toll on their vocalist. He entered

hospital to attend to a recurring liver problem, during which time the remaining members recorded *Fourplay*. Tommy Eyre then replaced McKenna and in 1977 Harvey rejoined to complete *Rock Drill*, only to walk out three months later. His solo career was curtailed by a fatal heart attack in 1982. In 1992 members of the original band were reunited as the Sensational Party Boys. They officially changed their name in 1993 back to the Sensational Alex Harvey Band with the original line-up joined by Stevie Doherty (b. 1959).

SEPULTURA

Formed in Belo Horizonte, Brazil, in 1984 by brothers Igor (b. 1970; drums) and Max Cavalera (b. 1969; vocals, guitar), with Paulo Jnr. (b. 1969; bass) and guitarist Jairo T, who was replaced in 1987 by Andreas Kisser (b. 1968). *Morbid Visions* was followed by *Schizophrenia*. The music on both was typified by speed, aggression and anger, much of which stemmed from the band's preoccupations with the poor social conditions in their native land. American label Roadrunner Records brought the band to international notice in 1989 when they released *Beneath The Remains*. The bestselling *Arise* followed. The sessions for *Chaos A.D.* saw the band strip down their music to a style which mirrored the punk ethos. *Roots* was considered their finest album, so it came as a shock when Cavalera left to form **Soulfly**. His replacement was American Derrick Green, who featured prominently on 1998's *Against* and 2001's *Nation*.

SEX PISTOLS

This UK punk band came together under the aegis of entrepreneur Malcolm McLaren and comprised Steve Jones (b. 1955; guitar), Paul Cook (b. 1956; drums), Glen Matlock (b. 1956; bass) and Johnny Rotten (b. John Lydon, 1956; vocals). By 1976 they had a reputation for violence, which reached a peak when a girl was blinded in a glass-smashing incident involving the band's most fearful follower, Sid Vicious. They signed to EMI Records later that year and released 'Anarchy In The UK'. The single suffered distribution problems and bans from shops, and eventually peaked at number 38 in the UK charts. Soon afterwards, the group was dropped from EMI Records in a blaze of publicity. By 1977,

Matlock had been replaced by punk caricature Sid Vicious (b. John Ritchie, 1957, d. 1979). After reluctantly signing to Virgin Records, the band issued 'God Save The Queen'. The single tore into the heart of British nationalism when the populace was celebrating the Queen's Silver Jubilee. Despite a daytime radio ban the single rose to number 1 in the *New Musical Express* chart (number 2 in the 'official' chart). A third single, the melodic 'Pretty Vacant' proved their most accessible and restored them to the Top 10. By the winter the band hit again with 'Holidays In The Sun' and issued *Never Mind The Bollocks – Here's The Sex Pistols*. It was a patchy affair, containing a preponderance of previously released material which indicated that the band was running short of ideas, and in early 1978, Rotten announced that he was leaving. McLaren, meanwhile, took the band members to Brazil so they could be filmed playing with the train robber Ronnie Biggs. McLaren promoted Biggs as the band's new lead singer and another controversial single emerged, 'Cosh The Driver', later retitled 'No One Is Innocent (A Punk Prayer)'. Vicious died of a heroin overdose in February 1979.

Virgin continued to issue the fragments of Sex Pistols work that they had on catalogue, including the compilation *Flogging A Dead Horse*. After years of rumour, the original band re-formed in 1996 for a tour of Europe and the US.

SEXSMITH, RON

Formerly a motorcycle messenger, Canadian Sexsmith released 1991's cassette only *Grand Opera Lane*. Four years lapsed before Sexsmith teamed up with producer Mitchell Froom to record a proper debut, which achieved almost universal press acclaim by critics attracted to the nakedness and intimacy of Sexsmith's songwriting. The follow-up, 1997's *Other Songs*, proffered another suite of strangely hesitant, downbeat narratives. *Whereabouts* received excellent reviews and was an assured recording. *Blue Boy* comprised markedly livelier material.

SHA NA NA

Spearheading the US rock 'n' roll revivalism that began in the late 60s, Sha Na Na emerged from Columbia University in 1968 with a repertoire derived exclusively from the 50s. The line-up in their early years included vocalists Robert Leonard, Alan Cooper, Scott Powell, Johnny Contardo, Frederick 'Denny' Greene (b. 1949), Donny York and Richard 'Ritchie' Joffe; guitarists Chris Donald aka Vinnie Taylor (d. 1974), Elliot Cahn and Henry Gross; pianists Joseph Witkin, Screamin' Scott Simon and John 'Bauzer' Bauman (b. 1947), plus Bruce Clarke (bass), Jack Marcellino (drums) and – the only musician with a revered past – saxophonist Leonard Baker (ex-**Danny And The Juniors**). Surprisingly, there were few personnel changes until a streamlining to a less cumbersome 10-piece in 1973, when bass player and singer David 'Chico' Ryan (d. 1998) was brought into the line-up. The band were launched internationally by an appearance at the Woodstock Festival in 1969. From 1972's *The Night Is Still Young*, 'Bounce In Your Buggy' was the closest the outfit ever came to a hit. By 1974, however, their act had degenerated to a dreary repetition that took its toll in unresolvable internal problems. The group bounced back in the late 70s, hosting their own syndicated television show from 1976–81 and appearing in the 1978 hit movie *Grease*. Various line-ups of the group have continued to tour and record in subsequent decades.

SHADOWS

UK instrumental group the Shadows evolved from the Five Chestnuts to become **Cliff Richard**'s backing group, the Drifters. By late 1958 the line-up had settled and comprised **Hank B. Marvin** (b. Brian Robson Rankin, 1941;

lead guitar), Bruce Welch (b. 1941; rhythm guitar), Jet Harris (b. Terence Hawkins, 1939; bass) and Tony Meehan (b. Daniel Meehan, 1943; drums). Soon after backing Richard on his debut, they were signed as a group by EMI Columbia. After two singles under their old name, they issued the vocal 'Saturday Dance', which failed to sell. In 1960 singer/songwriter Jerry Lordan presented them with 'Apache', which dominated the UK number 1 position for six weeks. A wealth of evocative instrumentals followed, including four UK number 1 hits – 'Kon-Tiki', 'Wonderful Land', 'Dance On' and 'Foot Tapper'. Despite such successes, the group underwent personnel shifts. Both Meehan and Harris left the group to be replaced by Brian Bennett (b. 1940) and Brian Locking, later replaced by John Rostill (b. 1942, d. 1973).

The Shadows continued to chart during 1963–64, but the Merseybeat boom had lessened their appeal. At the end of 1968, the group announced that they intended to split. In late 1969, a streamlined Shadows featuring Marvin, Rostill, Bennett and pianist Alan Hawkshaw toured Japan. In 1974, the Shadows reconvened for *Rockin' With Curly Leads*. Several live performances followed and the group then achieved a UK Top 20 hit with 'Let Me Be The One'. The stupendous success of an accompanying *20 Golden Greats* compilation effectively revitalized their career. By 1978, they were back in the UK Top 10 for the first time since 1965 with an instrumental reading of 'Don't Cry For Me Argentina'. That feat was repeated several months later with 'Theme From The Deer Hunter (Cavatina)'. Regular tours and compilations followed and in 1983, the group received an Ivor Novello Award from the British Academy of Songwriters, Composers and Authors to celebrate their 25th anniversary.

SHADOWS OF KNIGHT

Formed in Chicago, USA in 1965, the original line-up comprised Jim Sohns (vocals), Warren Rogers (lead guitar), Jerry McGeorge (rhythm guitar), Norm Gotsch (bass) and Tom Schiffour (drums). Their debut single, a cover version of **Them**'s 'Gloria', was the climax to the quintet's stage act, and gave them a US Top 10 hit. By this point Gotsch had been replaced, with Rogers switching to lead to accommodate new guitarist Joe Kelly. Their best-known line-up now established, the Shadows Of Knight enjoyed another minor chart entry with 'Oh Yeah', before completing their debut album *Gloria*. Two excellent group originals, 'Light Bulb Blues' and 'It Happens That Way', revealed an underused talent. *Back Door Men* offered a slightly wider perspective. Dave 'The Hawk' Wolinski replaced Warren Rogers in late 1966. This was the prelude to wholesale changes when, in 1967, Sohns fired the entire group. The singer subsequently reappeared fronting a new line-up – John Fisher, Dan Baughman, Woody Woodfuff and Kenny Turkin. 'Shake' gave the group a final US Top 50 entry. Further releases proved equally disappointing.

SHAGGY

Jamaican Shaggy (b. Orville Richard Burrell, 1968) is, effectively, the man who put New York reggae on the map, thanks to his worldwide hit, 'Oh Carolina'. The same record helped to start the ragga boom of 1993.

Burrell moved to America with his parents at the age of 18, and at 19 joined the Marines. Following active service in the Gulf War, Shaggy began to record singles for a variety of labels.

'Mampie', 'Big Up' and 'Oh Carolina' all reached the top of the reggae charts. At the end of 1992, Greensleeves Records picked up 'Oh Carolina' for UK release, and by spring 1993 Shaggy had achieved a pop chart hit all over Europe, with the song reaching number 1 in the UK and several other countries. He returned to the pop charts in 1995 with the UK number 5 single 'In The Summertime' (featuring Rayvon) and 'Boombastic', which topped the UK and US singles charts following frequent exposure (in England) as the soundtrack to an animated television advertisement for Levi's jeans. *Midnite Lover* was a lesser album, although the featured duet with Marsha, 'Piece Of My Heart', became another crossover hit. Jimmy Jam and Terry Lewis helped out on 2000's *Hot Shot*, the singer's debut for MCA Records. This quality collection of smooth pop-orientated dancehall music featured two huge transatlantic hits, 'It Wasn't Me' and 'Angel'.

SHAKATAK

One of the original benefactors of the early 80s UK jazz/funk boom, alongside contemporaries **Level 42**, the group comprised Bill Sharpe (keyboards), Steve Underwood (bass), Keith Winter (guitar), Roger Odell (drums) and Nigel Wright (keyboards, synthesizers). Between 1980 and 1987, Shakatak had 14 UK chart singles, including 'Feels Like The First Time', 'Easier Said Than Done', 'Night Birds', 'Dark Is The Night' (1983) and 'Down On The Street'. By this point a number of personnel changes had taken place, with Underwood replaced by George Anderson in 1982 and the introduction of female lead vocalist, Jill Saward, on 1984's *Down On The Street*.

The latter half of the 80s showed Shakatak honing their jazz influences and building on their enormous popularity in Japan. The band released several exclusive instrumental albums for the Japanese market during this period, but parted company with founder member Winter due to ill health. During the 90s Shakatak consolidated their reputation in both Europe and the USA, where they regularly place albums high on the Contemporary Jazz chart.

SHAKESPEARS SISTER

Formed by Siobhan Marie Deidre Fahey-Stewart (b. 1958) and Marcella Detroit (b. Marcella Levy, 1959) with producer and writer Richard Feldman. They took their name from a **Smiths**' song and kept the spelling mistake made by a designer. Their debut, 'Break My Heart (You Really)', was not a hit. However, 'You're History' reached the UK Top 10, while the debut album made number 9. The follow-up, *Hormonally Yours*, was released in 1991. The following year, *Shakespears Sister* achieved a UK number 1 coup with 'Stay', and followed it with the hits 'I Don't Care', 'Goodbye Cruel World' and 'Hello (Turn Your Radio On)'. The group was disbanded by Fahey, without warning to Detroit, live on stage at an awards ceremony in 1993.

SHAKIRA

This Colombian singer (b. Shakira Isabel Mebarak Ripoll, 1977) first broke into the Latin Music charts in 1995, and has since established herself as a crossover star with her groundbreaking blend of pop and rock styles. She released her debut album in 1991, but despite indicating a precocious talent (all the tracks were self-written) neither this nor the follow-up *Peligro* enjoyed much commercial success. She branched out into acting, appearing on the Colombian soap-opera *El Oasis*. Her breakthrough album, the rock-orientated *Pies Descalzos*, was released in 1996. The follow-up *Dónde Están Los Ladrones?* and an *MTV Unplugged* recording session were equally successful, and in 2000 Shakira won a Grammy for Best Female

Pop Vocal Performance ('Ojos Asi') at the inaugural Latin Grammy Awards. The following year's *Laundry Service*, her first album to include English language songs, affirmed the singer's superstar status when it broke into the Top 5 of the mainstream US pop chart.

SHAM 69

Formed in London, England, in 1976, this skinhead/punk-influenced band comprised Jimmy Pursey (vocals), Albie Slider (bass), Neil Harris (lead guitar), Johnny Goodfornothing (rhythm guitar) and Billy Bostik (drums). Pursey was a fierce, working-class idealist, who ironically sacked most of the above line-up within a year due to their lack of commitment. A streamlined aggregation featuring Dave Parsons (guitar), Dave Treganna (bass) and Mark Cain (drums) helped Pursey reach the UK charts in the late 70s with a series of anthemic hits including 'Angels With Dirty Faces', 'If The Kids Are United', 'Hurry Up Harry' and 'Hersham Boys'. After a troubled couple of years, Pursey went solo, but his time had passed. The group re-formed in the early 90s, performing at punk nostalgia/revival concerts and releasing new material.

SHAMEN

Formed in Scotland by Colin Angus (b. 1961; bass), Peter Stephenson (b. 1962), Keith McKenzie (b. 1961) and Derek McKenzie (b. 1964; guitar), the Shamen's debut *Drop*, captured a sense of their colourful psychedelic rock and sealed the first chapter of the band's career. Soon after, Colin Angus became fascinated by the nascent underground hip-hop movement. Will Sinnott (b. 1960, d. 1991; bass) then replaced McKenzie and further encouraged the Shamen's move towards the dancefloor. In 1988 the band relocated to London and slimmed down to the duo of Angus and Sinnott. By 1990 the Shamen's influence was vividly realized as the much-touted indie-dance crossover saw bands fuse musical cultures. However, just as the group prospered, Will Sinnott drowned off the coast of Gomera, one of the Canary Islands. The Shamen persevered with a remix of 'Move Any Mountain' which climbed into the UK Top 10. Mr C (b. Richard West, 1964) had joined the band for a section of this single and his rhymes founded the springboard for UK chart success. 'LSI', followed by the number 1 'Ebeneezer Goode', which was accused in many quarters of extolling the virtues of Ecstasy. The Shamen moved on with the release of *Boss Drum*. Such innovative work reinforced the Shamen's position as the wild cards of the UK dance music scene, although later recordings suffered from a lack of fresh ideas or even any further hit singles. The Shamen finally bowed out with 1998's *UV*.

SHANGRI-LAS

The Shangri-Las comprised two pairs of sisters, Mary-Ann and Margie Ganser (d. 1996) and Betty and Mary Weiss. They were discovered in 1963 by George 'Shadow' Morton and recorded two singles under the name Bon Bons before signing to the newly-formed Red Bird label. Relaunched as the Shangri-Las, they secured a worldwide hit with 'Remember (Walkin' In The Sand)'. The sound of a revving motorbike engine opened their distinctive follow-up, 'Leader Of The Pack', which was even more successful. By 1966, Margie Ganser had left the group, but they had already found a perfect niche, specializing in the doomed romanticism of American teenage life.

SHANNON, DEL

Shannon's (b. Charles Westover, 1934, d. 1990) debut 'Runaway' was a spectacular affair that reached the top of the charts in the USA and UK in 1961. Over the next few years Shannon produced and wrote his own material with great success, especially in Britain, where his run of 10 consecutive hits ended with 'Sue's Gotta Be Mine' in 1963. Shannon worked steadily for the next 25 years, enjoying a few more hit singles including a cover version of Bobby Freeman's 'Do You Wanna Dance'. Throughout the 60s and 70s Shannon was a regular visitor to

Britain where he found a smaller but more appreciative audience. His 1981 release *Drop Down And Get Me* was well received but sold poorly. Ironically, he received a belated hit in America with 1982's 'Sea Of Love'. This led to a brief renaissance for him in the USA. Ultimately, however, he was branded to rock 'n' roll revival tours that finally took their toll in February 1990, when a severely depressed Shannon shot himself.

SHAPIRO, HELEN

London-born Shapiro (b. 1946) drew considerable attention when, at 14, she scored a UK Top 3 hit with 'Don't Treat Me Like A Child'. By the end of 1961 she had scored two chart-topping singles with 'You Don't Know' and 'Walkin' Back To Happiness'. This success was maintained the following year with 'Tell Me What He Said' (number 2) and 'Little Miss Lonely' (number 8). Although she was younger than many beat group members, Shapiro was perceived as belonging to a now outmoded era and, despite a series of excellent singles, Shapiro was eclipsed by 'newcomers' **Cilla Black** and **Dusty Springfield**. The late 60s proved more fallow still and, barring one pseudonymous release, Shapiro did not record at all between 1970–5. 'Can't Break The Habit' became a minor hit in Europe during 1977 and in turn engendered *All For The Love Of The Music*. Since then she has maintained a media profile through radio, television and live appearances. In 2002 she announced that she would be retiring from live performances, apart from her gospel singing.

SHAW, SANDIE

Discovered by singer **Adam Faith**, Essex-born Shaw (b. Sandra Goodrich, 1947) was launched as a teenage pop star in 1964. Her first single, 'As Long As You're Happy', proved unsuccessful but the follow-up, '(There's) Always Something There To Remind Me' reached number 1 in the UK. Shaw's star shone for the next three years with a series of hits, mainly composed by her songwriter/producer Chris Andrews. His style, specializing in jerky rhythms and plaintive ballads served Sandie well, especially on 'Long Live Love', which provided her second UK number 1 in 1965. Chosen to represent Britain in the

1967 Eurovision Song Contest, Shaw triumphed with 'Puppet On A String', which gave her a third UK number 1.

Attempts to launch Shaw as a family entertainer were hampered by salacious newspaper reports and she effectively retired. In the early 80s she was rediscovered by BEF, and recorded a version of 'Anyone Who Had A Heart'. The Shaw resurgence was completed when she was heavily promoted by **Smiths** vocalist **Morrissey**. Shaw enjoyed a brief chart comeback with 'Hand In Glove' in 1984. In 1986, she reached the lower regions of the UK chart with a cover of **Lloyd Cole**'s 'Are You Ready To Be Heartbroken?'. In 1996, Shaw withdrew from performing and recording to set up the Arts Clinic. This specialist counselling service, run by Shaw under her married name of Powell, uses her experience in the music business to help artists combat problems of stress, drug dependency and eating disorders.

SHED SEVEN
Formed in York, England, Shed Seven comprises Rick Witter (vocals), Tom Gladwin (bass), Paul Banks (guitar) and Alan Leach (drums). Together they brought a flash of anti-glamour to the independent scene of the mid-90s. Signing to Polydor Records, they made their debut with 'Mark'. They achieved two Top 30 singles and a Top 20 album in 1994. The band's second album, including their Top 20 UK hit 'Getting Better', was released in 1996 to mixed reviews. They returned to the post-Britpop music scene in 1998 with the defiantly brash single 'She Left Me On A Friday' and *Let It Ride*. Banks left the band in 2000, and was replaced by original guitarist Joe Johnson. The band's new album, *Truth Be Told*, appeared on the Artful label.

SHERIDAN, TONY
British-born Sheridan (b. Anthony Sheridan McGinnity, 1940) joined Vince Taylor And The Playboys in early 1959. The group soon evolved into the Beat Brothers with a line-up of Sheridan (vocals, guitar), Ken Packwood (guitar), Rick Richards (guitar), Colin Melander (bass), Ian Hines (keyboards) and Jimmy Doyle (drums), although this changed almost constantly. Some of the more interesting personnel to pass through the Beat Brothers in these nebulous days at the Kaiserkeller were **John Lennon**, **Paul McCartney**, **George Harrison**, Stuart Sutcliffe and Pete Best. This line-up undertook a recording session in 1961, recording 'My Bonnie' and 'The Saints' among other songs. By 1962 the Beat Brothers had been joined by **Ringo Starr**, Roy Young (keyboards) and Rikky Barnes (saxophone). However, with the Hamburg beat boom all but over by 1964, Sheridan travelled to Vietnam to play US army bases. He eventually returned to Hamburg to turn solo in 1968, where his cult status has not diminished despite converting to the Sannyasin religion.

SHIRELLES
Formed in Passaic, New Jersey, this archetypal US girl group comprised Shirley Owens (b. 1941), Beverly Lee (b. 1941), Doris Kenner (b. 1941, d. 2000) and Addie 'Micki' Harris (b. 1940, d. 1982). They signed to Tiara and secured their first minor hit 'I Met Him On A Sunday'. This inspired the inauguration of a second outlet, Scepter, where the Shirelles gained pop immortality with 'Will You Love Me Tomorrow'. This was followed by a series of hits, 'Mama Said' (1961), 'Baby It's You' (1962) and 'Foolish Little Girl' (1963). The quartet's progress declined when producer and arranger Luther Dixon left and newer acts assumed the quartet's prime. By the time the Shirelles were free to move to another label, they were already confined to the 'oldies' circuit. They were inducted into the Rock And Roll Hall Of Fame in 1996.

SHOCKED, MICHELLE
This US-born roots singer/songwriter (b. Michelle Johnston, 1962) originally came to prominence via a Walkman recorded gig, taped around a campfire.

Her 1988 follow-up, *Short Sharp Shocked*, highlighted more varied and less self-conscious stylings than the more mainstream **Suzanne Vega/Tracy Chapman** school. *Captain Swing* was her 'big band' record, where she was joined by a plethora of famous extras. The recording of *Arkansas Traveller* was completed by travelling across the US and further afield with a portable studio. In the summer of 1995 Shocked filed a suit to be released from her contract with PolyGram Records following a number of accusations from both parties. *Kind Hearted Woman*, which Shocked had been selling at her gigs since 1994, was finally given a general release two years later. The independently produced follow-up was recorded with Fiachna O'Braonain of **Hothouse Flowers**. *Good News* and *Deep Natural* followed in 1998 and 2002 respectively.

SHOCKING BLUE
Formed in 1967 by guitarist Robbie van Leeuwen, this Dutch quartet originally featured lead vocalist Fred de Wilde, bass player Klassje van der Wal and drummer Cornelius van der Beek. After one minor hit in their homeland, 'Lucy Brown Is Back In Town', the band's management replaced de Wilde with female vocalist Mariska Veres. Veres brought the group a sexy image and another Netherlands hit 'Send Me A Postcard Darling'. Next came 'Venus', a massive European hit, which went on to top the US charts in 1970. They enjoyed a minor UK hit with 'Mighty Joe', which had reached number 1 in Holland. Personnel upheaval saw van der Wal replaced by Henk Smitskamp in 1971, and van Leeuwen withdrawing from many group activities two years later with Martin van Wijk brought in as cover. The band split-up the following year when Veres embarked on a solo career. The occasional Shocking Blue reunion led to a more permanent arrangement in the 90s, with Veres leading a new line-up on the festival circuit.

SHONEN KNIFE
Japanese sisters Atsuko Yamano and Naoko Yamano joined up with Michie Nakatani to form this **Ramones**-influenced punk group in 1981. Their sporadic recording career starting in Osaka before relocating to the west coast of America. There they came to the attention of US punk pop fans in general, and **Nirvana** in particular. The latter took them under their wing, and brought them international recognition. They attempted a comeback in the late 90s with *Brand New Knife* and *Happy Hour*.

SHOWADDYWADDY
When two promising Leicestershire, England-based groups fused their talents in 1973, the result was an octet comprising Dave Bartram (b. 1952; vocals),

Buddy Gask (vocals), Russ Field (guitar), Trevor Oakes (guitar), Al James (b. Geoffrey Betts; bass), Rod Deas (b. 1948; bass), Malcolm Allured (b. 1945; drums) and Romeo Challenger (drums). Showaddywaddy charted steadily, but after reaching number 2 in 1975 with **Eddie Cochran**'s 'Three Steps To Heaven', the cover version game began. Fifteen of their singles reached the UK Top 20 during the late 70s, including the chart-topping 'Under The Moon Of Love', but the seemingly foolproof hit formula eventually ran dry when the rock 'n' roll revival had passed. Ray Martinez replaced Field in 1985, and was in turn replaced by Danny Wilson 10 years later. Showaddywaddy are now regulars on the cabaret circuit, although a dispute over the ownership of the name in the mid-90s threatened to sour relationships between the original members.

SIBERRY, JANE

Canadian singer-songwriter Siberry (b. 1955) debuted in 1980 with an independently produced album. *No Borders Here* included 'Mimi On The Beach', an underground hit in Canada where *The Speckless Sky* later went gold. Siberry made her first live appearance in Europe following *The Walking*. Subsequent releases *Bound By The Beauty* and *When I Was A Boy* were critically acclaimed, but in 1996, after one further record for Warners, Siberry launched her own Sheeba label, on which she has pursued her increasingly esoteric muse.

SIFFRE, LABI

UK singer-songwriter Siffre (b. 1945) played his first gigs with a trio of like-minded youngsters, before taking up a residency at Annie's Rooms. His tenure completed, he travelled to Cannes, France, and played with a variety of soul musicians and bands. He returned to the UK in the late 60s and enjoyed solo hits with 'It Must Be Love' (1976) and 'Crying, Laughing, Loving, Lying'. Although 'Watch Me' in 1972 was his last hit of the 70s, he made a spectacular comeback in 1987 with the anthemic '(Something Inside) So Strong'. In recent years Siffre has devoted most of his time to his poetry and has shown a sensitive and intelligent grasp of world issues, campaigning against homophobia and racism.

SILVERCHAIR

When Australian rock trio Silverchair arrived in Europe in 1995, each member was just 15 years old. However, Chris Joannou (bass), Daniel Johns (vocals, guitar) and Ben Gillies (drums) seemed quite capable of producing a noise in the best adult traditions of their primary influences, **Pearl Jam** and **Nirvana**. Their debut, *frogstomp*, quickly achieved double platinum status in Australia. In the USA, where the album sold over two million, they were often thought to be another band from Seattle. In an unlikely development, the band collaborated with classical pianist David Helfgott on a track called 'Emotion Sickness', taken from 1999's *Neon Ballroom*.

SIMON AND GARFUNKEL

US folk-rock duo **Paul Simon** (b. 1941) and **Art Garfunkel** (b. Arthur Garfunkel, 1941) first enjoyed a US hit in 1958 under the name Tom And Jerry with the rock 'n' roll styled 'Hey, Schoolgirl'. They also completed an album which was later reissued after their rise to international prominence in the 60s. Garfunkel subsequently returned to college and Simon pursued a solo career before the duo reunited in 1964 for *Wednesday Morning, 3AM*, but the album did not sell well and they split. The break came when producer Tom Wilson decided to overdub 'The Sound Of Silence' with electric instrumentation, and within weeks the song (retitled 'The Sounds Of Silence') was US number 1, and Simon and Garfunkel were hastily reunited. The album was rush-released early in 1966. Among its major achievements was 'Homeward Bound', which went on to become a transatlantic hit. 'The

Dangling Conversation', was too esoteric for the Top 20, but the work testified to their artistic courage and boded well for the release of *Parsley, Sage, Rosemary And Thyme*. After two strong but uncommercial singles, 'At The Zoo' and 'Fakin' It', the duo contributed to the soundtrack of the 1968 movie, *The Graduate*. The key song, 'Mrs. Robinson', provided the duo with a huge international seller. *Bookends* was a superbly-crafted work, ranging from the serene 'Save The Life Of My Child' to the personal odyssey 'America'.

In 1969 the duo released 'The Boxer', a long single that found commercial success on both sides of the Atlantic. This classic single reappeared on their next album, the celebrated *Bridge Over Troubled Water*. One of the bestselling albums of all time (303 weeks on the UK chart), the work's title track became a standard. While at the peak of their commercial success, however, the duo became irascible and their partnership abruptly ceased.

A reunion occurred on Simon's hit single 'My Little Town' in 1975. Six years later they performed in front of half a million fans at New York's Central Park. In 1993 Simon and Garfunkel settled their differences long enough to complete 21 sell-out dates in New York.

SIMON, CARLY

In the early 60s US-born Simon (b. 1945) played Greenwich Village clubs with her sister Lucy. As the Simon Sisters they had one minor hit with 'Winkin' Blinkin' And Nod'. After the duo split, Carly Simon concentrated on song-writing with film critic Jacob Brackman. In 1971, two of their songs, the wistful 'That's The Way I've Always Heard It Should Be' and 'Anticipation' were US hits. Her third album included her most famous song, 'You're So Vain', whose target was variously identified as Warren Beatty and/or Mick Jagger. Simon's next Top 10 hit was 'Mockingbird' on which she duetted with **James Taylor** to whom she was married from 1972–83. Their marriage was given enormous coverage in the US media, and their divorce received similar treatment as Carly found solace with Taylor's drummer Russell Kunkel.

During the 80s, Simon released two albums of pre-war Broadway standards (*Torch* and *My Romance*) and increased her involvement with films. Her UK hit 'Why' (1982) was used in the movie *Soup For One*, but her biggest achievement of the decade was to compose and perform two memorable film themes, 'Coming Around Again' (from *Heartburn*) and 'Let The River Run' (from *Working Girl*). In 1990, her career came full circle when Lucy Simon was a guest artist on *Have You Seen Me Lately?*. After a lengthy gap in recording she released *Letters Never Sent*. Recent years have not been kind to Simon. She was diagnosed with breast cancer in 1997, and a bout of writer's block and lack of confidence persisted up to the release of *The Bedroom Tapes* in 2000.

SIMON, PAUL

New Jersey-born Simon (b. 1941) first entered the music business with partner **Art Garfunkel** in the duo Tom And Jerry, but they split after one album. Simon enjoyed a couple of minor US hits during 1962–3 as Tico And The Triumphs ('Motorcycle') and Jerry Landis ('The Lone Teen-Ranger'). In 1964, he signed to CBS Records and was reunited with Garfunkel. Between 1965 and 1970, **Simon And Garfunkel** became one of the most successful recording duos in the history of popular music, but the partnership eventually ended amid musical disagreements.

Simon prepared a stylistically diverse solo album, *Paul Simon*. The work spawned the hit singles 'Mother And Child Reunion' and 'Me And Julio Down By The Schoolyard'. A year later, he returned with the more commercial *There*

SIMONE, NINA

US-born Simone's (b. Eunice Waymon, 1933) jazz credentials were established in 1959 when she secured a hit with 'I Loves You Porgy'. Her influential 60s work included 'Gin House Blues', 'Forbidden Fruit' and 'I Put A Spell On You', while another of her singles, 'Don't Let Me Be Misunderstood', was later covered by the **Animals**. 'Ain't Got No – I Got Life', reached UK number 2, while 'To Love Somebody' reached number 5. In America, her own composition, 'To Be Young, Gifted And Black', reflected Simone's growing militancy. 'My Baby Just Cares For Me' pushed the singer back into the commercial spotlight when it reached UK number 5 in 1987. Tired of an America she perceived as uncaring, Simone has settled in France where her work continues to flourish.

SIMPLE MINDS

Scottish band formed in 1978 by Jim Kerr (b. 1959; vocals), Charlie Burchill (b. 1959; guitar), Tony Donald (bass) and Brian McGee (drums), later augmented by guitarist Duncan Barnwell and keyboard player Michael MacNeil (b. 1958). Derek Forbes (b. 1956) subsequently replaced Donald and Barnwell departed. Simple Minds signed to Zoom, an independent label marketed by Arista Records. 'Life In A Day' broached the UK charts in 1979 while the attendant album reached number 30. Within weeks the quintet embarked on a more radical direction, and *Real To Real Cacophony* won unanimous music press approbation. *Empires And Dance* fused the flair of its predecessor to a newly established love of dance music, most notably on 'I Travel'.

Now free of Arista, Simple Minds signed to Virgin Records in 1981, and recorded two albums, *Sons And Fascination* and *Sister Feelings Call*, initially released together. They resulted in three minor hit singles with 'The American', 'Love Song' and 'Sweat In Bullet'. In 1981 McGee left and was replaced by Kenny Hyslop, who featured on the UK Top 20 hit 'Promised You A Miracle'. Mel Gaynor (b. 1960) then became the quintet's permanent drummer. The excellent *New Gold Dream (81, 82, 83, 84)* peaked at UK number 3. *Sparkle In The Rain* united the quintet with producer Steve Lillywhite. 'Waterfront' and 'Speed Your Love To Me', prefaced its release, and the album entered the UK chart at number 1.

The band, with new bass player John Giblin, contributed the non-original 'Don't You (Forget About Me)' to the soundtrack of the movie *The Breakfast Club*. They remained ambivalent about the song, but it paradoxically became a US number 1 when issued as a single. *Once Upon A Time*, despite international success, drew considerable criticism for its bombastic approach. Three tracks, 'Alive And Kicking', 'Sanctify Yourself' and 'All The Things She Said' nonetheless reached the UK Top 10. *Street Fighting Years* drew further criticism, and this period closed with the rancorous departure of MacNeil and Giblin.

Simple Minds entered the 90s with only Kerr and Burchill remaining from the original line-up. *Real Life* saw the band re-introducing more personal themes to their songwriting after the political concerns of previous albums. The highly commercial 'She's A River' came in advance of *Good News From The Next World*. After another lengthy hiatus, Kerr, Burchill and a returning Derek Forbes released *Néapolis*, an album that marked a determined effort to recreate the edgy, electronic style of their early 80s work. In 2001 they were signed by Eagle Records, and released *Neon Lights*, an album of cover versions.

SIMPLY RED

This soul-influenced UK band was formed by Manchester-born vocalist Mick Hucknall (b. 1960) in 1983 after the demise of the Frantic Elevators. After signing to Elektra Records the band found a settled line-up featuring Hucknall, Tony Bowers (bass), Fritz McIntyre (b. 1958; keyboards), Tim Kellett (brass), Sylvan Richardson (guitar) and Chris Joyce (drums). *Picture Book* climbed to number 2 in the UK charts, while their version of the Valentine Brothers' 'Money's Too Tight To Mention' was a Top 20 hit. They continued with a

Goes Rhymin' Simon, which enjoyed massive chart success. In 1975, the chart-topping *Still Crazy After All These Years* won several Grammy awards. The wry '50 Ways To Leave Your Lover', taken from the album, provided Simon with his first solo number 1.

A five-year hiatus followed during which Simon released a *Greatest Hits* package featuring the catchy 'Slip Slidin' Away' and switched labels from CBS to Warner Brothers Records. In the wake of *One Trick Pony*, from the movie of the same name, Simon suffered a period of writer's block, which was to delay the recording of his next album. Meanwhile, a double-album live reunion of Simon And Garfunkel was issued. It was intended to preview a studio reunion, but the sessions were scrapped. Instead, Simon concentrated on his next album, *Hearts And Bones*, but it sold poorly. The situation altered with *Graceland*, one of the most commercially successful albums of the decade. Simon utilized musical contributions from **Ladysmith Black Mambazo**, **Los Lobos**, **Linda Ronstadt** and Rockin' Dopsie, but the project and subsequent tour was bathed in controversy due to accusations that Simon had broken the cultural boycott against South Africa. Simon continued his pan-cultural investigations with *The Rhythm Of The Saints*, which incorporated African and Brazilian musical elements.

Simon then began work on his ambitious Broadway musical *The Capeman*, based on the true story of Salvador Agron, a Puerto Rican gang member imprisoned for his part in the murder of two white teenagers in New York in 1959. The musical was withdrawn on 28 March 1998 after only 68 regular performances following savage reviews and protests from the surviving relatives of Agron's victims. Simon and his fellow investors were reported to have lost a record $11 million. The singer retreated to the studio to work on his first album in 10 years, *You're The One*.

sterling re-recording of the Frantic Elevators' 'Holding Back The Years' which peaked at number 2. Further hits followed with 'The Right Thing', 'Infidelity' and a reworking of the Cole Porter standard, 'Ev'ry Time We Say Goodbye'. Simply Red finally scaled the album chart summit in 1989 with *A New Flame*. The album coincided with another hit, 'It's Only Love', which was followed by a reworking of 'If You Don't Know Me By Now'. The 1991 album *Stars* topped the British charts, and proved to be one of the most successful UK albums of the 90s. The long-awaited follow-up *Life* was also a big seller, and featured the band's first chart-topping single, 'Fairground'. The band returned in 1996 and 1997 with cover versions of **Aretha Franklin**'s 'Angel' and **Gregory Isaacs**' 'Night Nurse'. *Blue* followed in 1998. The disappointing *Love And The Russian Winter*, which was pilloried in the press, broke the band's run of UK chart-toppers.

SINGH, TALVIN

Singh (b. 1970) is one of the first artists to help bring traditional Indian tabla music to the mainstream, combining it with the rhythmic surges of drum 'n' bass. Head of the Omni Records label, based in south London, Singh is a virtuoso tabla player and an accomplished composer and arranger. The arrival of ambient and drum 'n' bass music in the early 90s inspired Singh to begin producing material, and in 1996 he released the ultra-rare *Calcutta Cyber Cafe* disc. Through projects such as the compilation album *Anokha: Soundz Of The Asian Underground*, he helped establish other Asian artists, and defined the vibrant Asian club scene. Anokha, meaning 'unique' in Urdu, is the weekly club night Singh hosts at the Blue Note club in London's East End.

Before launching his solo career in 1997, Singh found time to produce a percussion-based album, *One World, One Drum*, and appeared on **Björk**'s world tour. His major label debut *OK* was an adventurous and vibrant work that fulfilled Singh's vow to challenge and re-define traditional musical categories. He was rewarded the following September when the album won the Mercury Music Prize. The belated follow-up built upon the *OK* blueprint, albeit with a more club-focused direction.

SIOUXSIE AND THE BANSHEES

Siouxsie Sioux (b. Susan Dallion, 1957) was part of the 'Bromley contingent', which followed the **Sex Pistols** in their early days. Siouxsie put together her backing group the Banshees, featuring Pete Fenton (guitar), Steve Severin (bass) and Kenny Morris (drums). By mid-1977 Fenton was replaced by John McGeoch, and in 1978, the group signed to Polydor Records. They released 'Hong Kong Garden', which reached the UK Top 10. Less commercial offerings ensued with 'The Staircase (Mystery)' and 'Playground Twist', followed by *Join Hands*. During a promotional tour, Morris and McKay abruptly left, to be replaced by Budgie (b. Peter Clark, 1957) and temporary Banshee Robert Smith, from the **Cure**. Siouxsie's Germanic influences were emphasized on the stark 'Mittageisen (Metal Postcard)', which barely scraped into the Top 50. Both 'Happy

House' and 'Christine' had greater commercial success. Another Top 10 album, *Juju*, was followed by a break.

The band reconvened in 1983 and a version of the **Beatles**' 'Dear Prudence' provided them with their biggest UK hit, reaching number 3. Early in 1984 'Swimming Horses' maintained their high profile, while further personnel changes ensued with the enlistment of John Carruthers from Clock DVA. He, in turn, was replaced by Jon Klein. Siouxsie then tackled **Bob Dylan**'s 'This Wheel's On Fire' (UK Top 20), and an entire album of cover versions followed. A change of direction with *Peep Show* saw the band embrace a more sophisticated sound. They returned to the charts in 1991 with the evocative 'Kiss Them For Me' and *Superstition*. Arguably their greatest achievement of the 90s, however, was the much-delayed *The Rapture*. Some criticism was received that the album was a sell-out and the band announced in April 1996 that they were 'going out with dignity'. Siouxsie and Budgie continued with their electronic side-project, Creatures.

SIR DOUGLAS QUINTET

Formed in 1964, this US quintet was fashioned by Houston-based producer, Huey P. Meaux, and former teenage prodigy, Doug Sahm (b. 1941, d. 1999). Augie Meyers (b. 1940; organ), Francisco (Frank) Morin (b. 1946; horns), Harvey Kagan (b. 1946; bass) and John Perez (b. 1942; drums) completed the line-up. They had an international hit with 'She's About A Mover' and a cover of the **Beatles**' 'She's A Woman'. This style continued on further singles and *The Best Of The Sir Douglas Quintet*. After a two year break the band released *Honky Blues*, although only Sahm and Morin were retained from the earlier unit. The original Quintet was reconstituted for *Mendocino*, whose title track became the band's sole million-seller. Despite delivering several further excellent albums, the unit broke up in 1972, although they have been resurrected on several occasions. Sahm suffered a fatal heart attack in 1999.

SISQO

This distinctive silver-haired singer (b. Mark Andrews, 1978) established his performing credentials as a founding member of highly successful urban R&B quartet Dru Hill. Sisqo was the first member to branch out, releasing *Unleash The Dragon* in 1999. The risqué single, 'Thong Song', was only one of many provocative tracks on an album which dealt candidly with sex and the male psyche. He subsequently made his acting debut in *Get Over It* and confirmed his pop superstar status with *Return Of Dragon*.

SISTER SLEDGE

US-born sisters Debra (b. 1954), Joan (b. 1956), Kim (b. 1957) and Kathy Sledge (b. 1959) started their recording career in 1971. They made their breakthrough in 1979 when they entered a working relationship with **Chic** masterminds Nile Rodgers and Bernard Edwards that resulted in several transatlantic hit singles, including 'He's The Greatest Dancer', 'We Are Family' and 'Lost In Music'. They began to produce their own material in 1981. Although success in the USA waned, the quartet retained their UK popularity with 'Frankie', which reached number 1 in 1985. The hits subsequently dried up and Kathy Sledge left for a solo career in 1989, but the remaining trio continues to perform on the concert circuit and released an excellent comeback album, *African Eyes*, in 1998.

SIZE, RONI

Reprazent, a Bristol, England drum 'n' bass collective, came to national prominence in 1997 when its founder and leader, Roni Size, was awarded that year's Mercury Prize. Much of the acclaim centred around Size's melding of the new with the old– the propulsive jungle beats accompanied by live drums and double bass. The band – Size (compositions/programming), DJ Krust, Onallee (vocals), MC Dynamite and rapper Bahmadia – came together on Bristol's highly fertile and disparate club scene. As a result, Reprazent's sleek, highly musical take on drum 'n' bass is equally informed by hip-hop, funk, soul and house. The mainstream break-through of *New Forms* was the most significant for jungle since **Goldie**'s debut. Size subsequently teamed up with DJ Die and Leonie Laws in Breakbeat Era, before returning to Reprazent to record 2000's uncompromising *In The Mode*.

SKELLERN, PETER
UK performer Skellern (b. 1947) recorded a country-pop album with Harlan County before they disbanded in 1971. He then struck lucky with a self-composed UK number 3 hit, 'You're A Lady'. Another hit single with the title track to *Hold On To Love* established Skellern as a purveyor of wittily-observed love songs. In 1984, he formed Oasis with Julian Lloyd Webber, Mary Hopkin and guitarist Bill Lovelady, but the group's recordings failed to make a major impact. In 1985, he joined Richard Stilgoe for *Stilgoe And Skellern Stompin' At The Savoy*. This led to the duo working together on several successful tours. In 1995, Skellern issued his first album for nearly eight years.

SKID ROW (EIRE)
Blues-based rock band, formed by guitarist **Gary Moore** (b. 1952) in Dublin, Eire, in 1968. Recruiting **Phil Lynott** (vocals, bass), Eric Bell (guitar) and Brian Downey (drums) the initial line-up only survived 12 months. Brendan Shiels replaced Lynott, and Noel Bridgeman replaced Bell. The band completed two singles, 'New Places, Old Faces' and 'Saturday Morning Man'. Their albums were well received, but Moore's growing reputation outstripped the band's musical confines and he left in 1971. Although Paul Chapman proved an able replacement, Skid Row's momentum faltered and the trio disbanded the following year.

SKID ROW (USA)
US heavy rock band formed in New Jersey, in 1986, by Dave 'The Snake' Sabo (b. 1964; guitar), Rachel Bolan (b. 1964; bass), Sebastian 'Bach' Bierk (b. 1968; vocals), Scott Hill (b. 1964; guitar) and Rob Affuso (b. 1963; drums). They were picked up by **Bon Jovi**'s management and offered the support slot on their 1989 US stadium tour. They released their debut album the same year, which peaked at number 6 on the US chart and spawned two US Top 10 singles, '18 And Life' and 'I Remember You'. *Slave To The Grind* surpassed all expectations, debuting at number 1 in the US charts. Afterwards, however, progress was halted by squabbling that broke the band apart following 1994's desultory *Subhuman Race*. Sebastian Bach embarked on a solo career.

SKIP BIFFERTY
This UK band – John Turnbull (guitar, vocals), Mickey Gallagher (keyboards), Colin Gibson (bass) and Tommy Jackman (drums), Graham Bell (vocals) – made their

debut in 1967 with 'On Love'. Two more singles followed, both memorable examples of pop psychedelia. The band's potential withered under business entanglements and a conflict with their proprietorial manager Don Arden. Although they tried to forge an alternative career as Heavy Jelly, litigation over the rights to the name brought about their demise.

SKUNK ANANSIE
London, England-based rock quartet, formed in 1994, and led by singer Skin (b. Deborah Dyer), Martin 'Ace' Kent (guitar), Robbie French (drums) and Richard 'Cass' Lewis (bass). Their debut single, 'Little Baby Swastikkka', was available only through mail order. The controversial 'Selling Jesus' was followed by 'I Can Dream' and 'Charity'. Featuring new drummer Mark Richardson (ex-Little Angels), *Stoosh* was a harder-edged collection, characterized by metal-edged guitars. Skin's anger on the excellent opening track, 'Yes It's Fucking Political', was almost tangible. The band also reaped the rewards with four UK Top 30 singles in 1996, 'Weak', a reissue of 'Charity', 'All I Want' and 'Twisted (Everyday Hurts)'. *Post Orgasmic Chill* was premiered by the thunderous clatter of UK Top 20 single, 'Charlie Big Potato', but the album's indifferent reception hastened Skunk Anansie's demise.

SLADE
Originally recording as the 'N Betweens, this UK quartet comprised Noddy Holder (b. Neville Holder, 1946; vocals, guitar), Dave Hill (b. 1946; guitar), Jimmy Lea (b. 1949; bass) and Don Powell (b. 1946; drums). They signed with Fontana Records, which insisted they change their name to Ambrose Slade and it was under that moniker that they recorded *Beginnings*. They next signed up with Chas Chandler, who abbreviated their name to Slade and oversaw their new incarnation as a skinhead group for 'Wild Winds Are Blowing'. Slade persevered with their skinhead phase until 1970 when they began to cultivate a more colourful image. 'Coz I Luv You' took them to number 1 in the UK in late 1971, precipitating an incredible run of chart success, including 'Take Me Bak 'Ome', 'Mama Weer All Crazee Now', 'Cum On Feel The Noize' and 'Skweeze Me Pleeze Me'. Their finest moment was 1977's 'Merry Xmas Everybody', one of the great festive rock songs, but by the mid-70s they were yesterday's teen heroes. The hits subsequently dried up and in the late 80s the original quartet, while never officially splitting up, began working on other projects. They last appeared together in February 1992. Slade II (minus Holder and Lea) emerged in the mid-90s. Holder has become a popular all-round television personality, and was awarded an MBE in the Millennium New Year's Honours List.

SLAYER
This death/thrash metal quartet was formed in Los Angeles, USA, during 1982. Comprising Tom Araya (b. 1961; bass, vocals), Kerry King (b. 1964; guitar), Jeff Hanneman (b. 1964; guitar) and Dave Lombardo (b. 1963; drums), the band released their first two albums on Metal Blade Records. Featuring 10 tracks in just 28 minutes *Reign In Blood* took the concept of thrash to its ultimate conclusion. *Hell Awaits* opened the band up to a wider audience and *Seasons In The Abyss* pushed them to the forefront of the thrash metal genre. A double live album followed, capturing the band at their best. However, it saw the permanent departure of Lombardo. Paul Bostaph (b. 1964) was

his replacement, but was in turn replaced by Jon Dette in 1996. Bostaph rejoined the band for 1998's *Diabolus In Musica*.

SLEATER-KINNEY

This potent feminist punk rock band was formed in 1994 in Olympia, Washington, by Carrie Brownstein (guitar, vocals) and Corin Tucker (guitar, vocals). Having established themselves as an explosive live act, the band recorded two albums (with drummers Lora McFarlane and Toni Gogin) that explored the struggle of women to establish their identity in a male-dominated culture. Their highly praised Kill Rock Stars debut, *Dig Me Out*, was recorded with new drummer Janet Weiss. Less overtly preachy, the album was a highly personal expression of female desire and frustration that cemented the band's progress. *The Hot Rock* was a proficient but unremarkable set that lacked some of the raw charm of their earlier work. The trio bounced back to form with the following year's *All Hands On The Bad One*, their most assured and melodic effort to date.

SLEDGE, PERCY

Recommended to Quin Ivy, owner of the Norala Sound studio, US soul artist Sledge (b. 1941) arrived with a rudimentary draft of 'When A Man Loves A Woman'. Released in 1966, it was a huge international hit. A series of emotional, poignant ballads followed, but none achieved a similar commercial profile. Having left Atlantic Records, Sledge re-emerged on Capricorn with *I'll Be Your Everything*. Two collections of re-recorded hits, *Percy* and *Wanted Again*, confirmed the singer's intimate yet unassuming delivery. Released in Britain following the runaway success of a resurrected 'When A Man Loves A Woman' (the song reached number 2 in 1987 after featuring in a Levi's advertisement), they are not diminished by comparison. In 1994 Sledge recorded *Blue Night*, which capitalized on the Sledge 'strong suit', the slow-burning countrified soul-ballad.

SLEEPER

The provocative statements of lead vocalist and guitarist Louise Wener (b. 1966) first launched UK-based Sleeper into the mainstream in 1994. She was joined by Jon Stewart (guitar), Andy McClure (drums) and Diid Osman (bass). 'Inbetweener' finally brought them to the UK Top 20 in 1995. 'Vegas' and 'What Do I Do Now?' also rose high in the charts, before a second album in autumn 1995. 'Sale Of The Century', 'Nice Guy Eddie' and 'Statuesque' all reached the Top 20. A critical backlash greeted 'She's A Good Girl' and *Pleased To Meet You*. Dan Kaufman replaced Osman in 1997, but the following year the band had ceased working together.

SLINT

Formed in Kentucky, USA, Slint comprised former members of local legends Squirrel Bait – Brian McMahan (vocals, guitar), Ethan Buckler (bass) and Britt Walford (drums) – plus David Pajo (guitar). Informed by a typically brutal Steve Albini production, the band's 1989 debut featured loud guitar-playing and muted vocals. The abrasive edge was toned down somewhat for 1991's *Spiderland*, which saw a number of changes. Buckler had left to form King Kong while producer Brian Paulson engendered a more sympathetic sound that made the album a popular item within the American alternative rock scene. However, afterwards progress stalled, and only one further desultory single was issued in 1994.

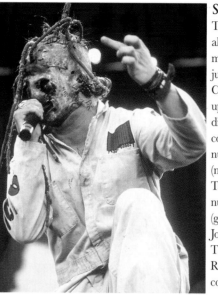

SLIPKNOT

This highly provocative, Des Moines, Iowa, USA-based alternative metal outfit, whose shock rock values are masked by their anonymous stage wear of matching jump suits and horror masks, was founded by Shawn Crahan (percussion) and Paul Grey (bass). The early line-up of Slipknot released the independently recorded and distributed *Mate. Feed. Kill. Repeat* in 1996. The band, comprising nine members, subsequently adopted a lucky number to wear on their jump suits. Alongside Crahan (number 6) and Grey (number 2), was number 8 Corey Taylor (vocals), number 7 Mick Thompson (guitar), number 5 Craig Jones (samples), number 4 James Root (guitar), number 3 Chris Fehn (percussion), number 1 Joey Jordison (drums), and number 0 Sid Wilson (DJ). They recorded their self-titled major label debut with Ross Robinson. Both *Slipknot* and *Iowa* were huge commercial successes.

SLITS

UK feminist punk band formed in 1976 with a line-up featuring Ari-Up (b. Arianna Foster; vocals), Kate Korus (b. Katherine Corris; guitar), Palmolive (b. Paloma Romero; drums) and Suzi Gutsy (bass). Korus and Gutsy both quit shortly afterwards, and were replaced by Viv Albertine and Tessa Pollitt. By the time they made their recording debut, Palmolive had been ousted and replaced by Budgie (b. Peter Clark, 1957). Signed to Island Records, they released the dub influenced *Cut*. The departure of Budgie to **Siouxsie And The Banshees** (replaced by Bruce Smith) coincided with the arrival of reggae musician Prince Hammer and trumpeter Don Cherry. A series of singles followed, but by 1981 the Slits had lost much of their original cutting edge and they disbanded at the end of the year.

SLY AND ROBBIE

Sly Dunbar (b. Lowell Charles Dunbar, 1952; drums) and Robbie Shakespeare (b. 1953; bass). Dunbar, nicknamed 'Sly' because of his fondness for **Sly And The Family Stone**, was an established figure in Skin Flesh And Bones when he met Shakespeare. The pair quickly became Jamaica's leading rhythm section. They not only formed their own label Taxi, which produced many hit records for scores of well-known artists, but also found time to do session work for just about every important name in reggae. In the early 80s they were among the first to use the burgeoning 'new technology'. Sly And Robbie's mastery of the digital genre coupled with their abiding love and respect for the music's history placed them at the forefront of Kingston's producers of the early 90s. Sly And Robbie were one of the first artists to move with Chris Blackwell when he founded the Palm Pictures label in 1998.

SLY AND THE FAMILY STONE

US multiracial group formed in San Francisco, California, in 1967, by Sly Stone (b. Sylvester Stewart, 1944), Freddie Stone (b. 1946; guitar), Rosie Stone (b. Rosemery Stewart, 1945; piano), Cynthia Robinson (b. 1946; trumpet), Jerry Martini (b. 1943; saxophone), Larry Graham (b. 1946; bass) and Greg Errico (b. 1946; drums). Sly joined Autumn Records as a songwriter/house-producer, and secured a success with Bobby Freeman's 'C'mon And Swim' in 1964. His own single, 'I Just Learned How To Swim', was less fortunate, though. In 1966 Sly formed the Stoners, a short-lived group that included Robinson. The following year Sly And The Family Stone made its debut with 'I Ain't Got Nobody'. The group then signed to Epic Records, and released *A Whole New Thing*. In 1968 'Dance To The Music' became a transatlantic

Top 10. 'Everyday People' topped the US chart early the following year, and Sly's talent was fully established on *Stand!*. Two million copies were sold, while tracks including the title song, 'I Want To Take You Higher' and 'Sex Machine', transformed black music forever. The new decade began with a double-sided hit, 'Thank You (Falettinme Be Mice Elf Agin)'/'Everybody Is A Star', an R&B and pop number 1, but the optimism suddenly clouded. *There's A Riot Goin' On* (US number 1) was dark, mysterious and brooding, but nonetheless provided three successful singles, 'Family Affair', 'Running Away' and 'Smilin''. Graham then left and Andy Newmark replaced Errico. However, the real undermining factor was the leader's drug dependency, a constant stumbling block to Sly's recurrent 'comebacks'.

SMALL FACES

Formed in London, England during 1965, this mod-influenced band initially comprised **Steve Marriott** (b. 1947, d. 1991; vocals, guitar), **Ronnie Lane** (b. 1946, d. 1997; bass), Jimmy Winston (b. James Langwith, 1945; organ) and Kenny Jones (b. 1948; drums). They signed to Don Arden's Contemporary Records and were licensed to Decca Records. 'Whatcha Gonna Do About It', brought them into the UK Top 20, but within weeks Smith was replaced by Ian McLagan (b. 1945). 'I Got Mine', failed to chart and Arden responded to this setback by recruiting hit songwriters Kenny Lynch and Mort Shuman, whose catchy 'Sha La La La Lee' gave the band a UK Top 3 hit. 'Hey Girl' reinforced their chart credibility, which reached its apogee with 'All Or Nothing'. The festive 'My Mind's Eye' was followed by disagreements with their record company.

A final two singles for Decca, 'I Can't Make It' and 'Patterns', proved unsuccessful. They signed to Immediate Records and became a quasi-psychedelic ensemble. The drug-influenced 'Here Comes The Nice' was followed by the experimental 'Itchycoo Park'. With their Top 10 status reaffirmed, the band returned to their blues style with 'Tin Soldier'. For 'Lazy Sunday' they combined cockney charm with a paean to hippie indolence, elements reflected on the chart-topping *Ogden's Nut Gone Flake*. They bowed out with the chaotic 'The Universal' and the posthumous hit 'Afterglow Of Your Love'. Successful reissues of 'Itchycoo Park' and 'Lazy Sunday' in the mid-70s persuaded Marriott, Jones, McLagan and new boy Rick Wills to revive the Small Faces name for a series of albums.

SMASH MOUTH

Formed in San Jose, California, USA, alternative rock band Smash Mouth originally comprised Steve Harwell (vocals), Greg Camp (guitar), Paul De Lisle (bass) and Kevin Coleman (drums). They were given an initial boost by the success of 'Walkin' On The Sun', the first single to be extracted from 1997's *Fush Yu Mang*. It was originally designed as a drumming 'exercise track' for Coleman, until he persuaded the rest of the band of its melodic possibilities. In truth, this light-hearted pop ditty was wholly unrepresentative of the rest of the band's canon of acerbic punk songs. The far more accessible follow-up, *Astro Lounge*, broke into the US Top 10, bolstered by the Top 5 success of the highly catchy 'All Star'. The band's self-titled third album featured new drummer Michael Urbano.

SMASHING PUMPKINS

Once widely viewed as poor relations to **Nirvana**'s major label alternative rock, Chicago, USA's Smashing Pumpkins, led by Billy Corgan (b. 1967; vocals, guitar) persevered to gradually increasing commercial acceptance and press veneration. Corgan was joined by D'Arcy Wretzky (b. 1968; bass), James Iha (b. 1968; guitar) and Jimmy Chamberlain (b. 1964; drums). The quartet released 'I Am The One' in 1990, bringing them to the attention of influential Seattle label Sub Pop Records, for which they also released 'Tristessa'/'La Dolly Vita', before moving to Caroline Records. *Gish* announced the band to both indie and metal audiences and *Siamese Dream* reached the US Top 10 *Mellon Collie And The Infinite Sadness* was a bold project, yet the band managed to pull it off. *Adore* debuted at US number 2 in 1998. Wretzky was replaced by Melissa Auf Der Maur (ex-**Hole**) on the follow-up, *MACHINA/The Machines Of God*. The album was a major disappointment and, after the initial sales burst, a commercial failure. It came as no surprise that Corgan announced that the band would split-up after their farewell tour. In one final defiant act, he made *MACHINA II/The Friends And Enemies Of Modern Music* available as an MP3 download only.

SMITH, ELLIOTT

Acclaimed US singer-songwriter Smith first recorded with alternative rockers Heatmiser. Feeling happier recording acoustic material on his home four-track set-up, Smith released his solo debut, *Roman Candle*, in 1994. Later releases appeared on the independent label Kill Rock Stars, as Smith balanced his solo career with his continuing involvement in Heatmiser. By 1997's *Either/Or*, however, Heatmiser had split and Smith relocated to Brooklyn. His big break came about when cult film director and long-time fan Gus Van Sant used six of Smith's songs on the soundtrack to his acclaimed *Good Will Hunting*. The stand-out track 'Miss Misery' was nominated for an Oscar for Best Original Song. Any worries that a major label would choke his independent spirit and songwriting skills were dispelled when the superb *XO* was released. The album confirmed that Smith had developed into one of the finest songwriters of the 90s. His second DreamWorks album, *Figure 8*, was also impressive.

SMITH, PATTI

US-born Smith's (b. 1946) first major recording was a version of a **Jim Morrison** poem on Ray Manzarek's solo album. In 1971, Smith formed a liaison with guitarist Lenny Kaye and the duo was later joined by Richard Sohl (piano) in the first Patti Smith Group. Their debut recording was 'Hey Joe'/'Piss Factory'. Ivan Kral (bass) and J. D. Daugherty (drums) were then added to the line-up featured on the acclaimed *Horses*. *Radio Ethiopia* was perceived as self-indulgent and the artist's career was undermined when she

incurred a broken neck upon falling off the stage early in 1977. Smith re-emerged the following year with the commercially successful *Easter*. 'Because The Night' from this reached the UK Top 5, but *Wave* failed to sustain such acclaim.

Patti then married former **MC5** guitarist Fred 'Sonic' Smith, and retired from active performing for much of the 80s. She resumed recording in 1988 with *Dream Of Life*. Following a series of tragic events in her life, triggered by the death of her husband she released what was seen as an exhortation album, *Gone Again*. *Peace And Noise*, released the following year, reunited Smith with Kaye and Daugherty, alongside co-writer and guitarist Oliver Ray and bass player Tony Shanahan, and marked a return to the spiky sound of her earlier material. She retained the same musicians on the excellent *Gung Ho*.

SMITH, WILL

Rap music's most successful crossover artist, Smith (b. 1968) started his career as one half of **DJ Jazzy Jeff And The Fresh Prince**. The duo's inoffensive, bubblegum rap made them a mainstream success. Smith's inventive and charming rapping style brought him to the attention of NBC, who cast him in the starring role of *The Fresh Prince Of Bel-Air*. Smith shone as the streetwise tough suffering culture shock in affluent Beverly Hills, and the situation comedy went on to become one of the station's most successful series, running until 1996. Movie stardom beckoned, with Smith making his debut in 1992's *Where The Day Takes You*. He gained further acclaim for his role in 1993's *Six Degrees Of Separation*. A string of acting roles followed which pushed Smith into the superstar league, beginning with 1995's *Bad Boys* and reaching a new high with *Independence Day* (1996) and *Men In Black* (1997). Smith also recorded under his own name for the first time, topping the US and UK charts with the infectious theme tune from *Men In Black*. He also found the time to release his solo debut, *Big Willie Style*, a smooth pop-rap production which featured 'Gettin' Jiggy Wit It', another ridiculously catchy hit single which topped the US Hot 100 chart. The album took up a long residency at the top end of the US charts. In 1999, the theme tune from Smith's new movie *Wild Wild West*, based around **Stevie Wonder**'s 'I Wish' and featuring vocal contributions from Dru Hill, topped the US charts. Released, predictably enough, at the end of the millennium, 'Will 2K' and *Willennium*, were also huge US and UK successes.

SMITHEREENS

The Smithereens formed in New Jersey, USA in 1980. Members Jim Babjak (guitar) and Dennis Diken (drums) had played together since 1971. Mike Mesaros (bass) was recruited in 1976 and Pat DiNizio (vocals) completed the line-up. In 1986 the quartet released *Especially For You*, which fared well, as did the single 'Blood And Roses'. *Smithereens 11* was their biggest selling album, reaching US number 41, but their career faltered with the early 90s albums *Blow Up* and *A Date With The Smithereens*. With the band unable to secure a new recording contract, DiNizio took the opportunity to release a solo debut in 1997. The Smithereens subsequently signed to Koch Records, and released *God Save The Smithereens*.

SMITHS

Acclaimed by many as the most important UK band of the 80s, the Smiths were formed in Manchester, England in 1982 by **Morrissey** (b. Steven Patrick Morrissey, 1959) and Johnny Marr (b. John Maher, 1963), and were later joined by Mike Joyce (b. 1963; drums) and Andy Rourke (bass). They signed to Rough Trade Records in 1983 and commenced work on their debut album. Their second single, 'This Charming Man' (1983), finally infiltrated the UK Top 30. The quartet began 1984 with the notably rockier 'What Difference Does It Make?' (UK number 12). A series of college gigs throughout Britain established the group as a cult favourite. A collaboration with **Sandie Shaw** saw a hit with 'Hand In Glove', while Morrissey dominated music press interviews. The singer's celebrated miserabilism was reinforced by the release of the autobiographical 'Heaven Knows I'm Miserable Now'. Another Top 20 hit followed with 'William, It Was Really Nothing'. While the Smiths commenced work on their next album, Rough Trade issued the interim *Hatful Of Hollow*. The Smiths now found themselves fêted as Britain's best group by various factions in the music press. The release of 'How Soon Is Now?' justified much of the hyperbole and this was reinforced by the power of their next album, *Meat Is Murder*. Their fortunes in the singles charts, however, were relatively disappointing. 'Shakespeare's Sister' stalled at number 26, amid rumours that the band were dissatisfied with their record label. A dispute with Rough Trade delayed the release of the next album, which was preceded by 'Big Mouth Strikes Again'. *The Queen Is Dead* won immediate critical acclaim for its diversity and unadulterated power. A stadium tour of the USA followed and during the band's absence they enjoyed a formidable Top 20 hit with 'Panic'. After 'Shoplifters Of The World Unite' the Smiths completed what would prove to be their final album. They announced their split in 1987. *Strangeways, Here We Come* was issued posthumously, and a belated live album, *Rank*, was issued the following year.

SNOOP DOGGY DOGG

Doggystyle was the most eagerly anticipated album in rap history, and the first debut album to enter the US chart at number 1. Dogg (b. Calvin Broadus, 1972) first appeared in 1990 when helping out **Dr. Dre** on a track called 'Deep Cover'. During UK touring commitments to support the album and single, 'Gin And Juice', he made the front page of the *Daily Star* with the headline: 'Kick This Evil Bastard Out!' A more serious impediment to Snoop's career was the trial on charges of accessory to the murder of Phillip Woldermariam, shot by his bodyguard McKinley Lee. The verdict acquitted Dogg and McKinley Lee of both murder charges and the manslaughter cases were dropped. The trial had not overtly damaged his record sales; his debut topped 7 million copies worldwide, and the follow up *Tha Doggfather* entered the USA album chart at number 1.

A subsequent falling out with the ailing Death Row Records saw Dogg transferring to **Master P**'s highly successful gangsta label, No Limit Records. Now known as Snoop Dogg, he released *Da Game Is To Be Sold, Not To Be Told* in 1998. Repeating the success of his first two albums, it debuted at US number 1. *No Limit Top Dogg* reached US number 2. The following year Snoop tried on the role of corporate mentor for size, adding guest raps and acting as executive producer on the debut album by his protégés Tha Eastsidaz. In December he released *Tha Last Meal*, his final album for No Limit.

SOFT BOYS

Cult UK singer-songwriter **Robyn Hitchcock** (b. 1953) started out as a solo performer and member of various groups, before joining Dennis And The Experts which became the Soft Boys in 1976. The line-up was Hitchcock (vocals, guitar, bass), Alan Davies (guitar), Andy Metcalfe (bass), and Morris Windsor aka Otis Fagg (drums). The original sessions remain unreleased but the same line-up also recorded a three-track single, after which Kimberley Rew replaced Davies. They released '(I Wanna Be An) Anglepoise Lamp', to little success and after *Can Of Bees* they replaced Metcalfe with Matthew Seligman. Their remaining releases included *Underwater Moonlight*, which ranks among Hitchcock's finest moments. They broke up early in 1981. The Soft Boys have periodically re-formed to play reunion gigs, including an extensive transatlantic tour in 2001.

SOFT CELL

Formed in Leeds, England, in 1980 this duo featured vocalist **Marc Almond** (b. Peter Marc Almond, 1956) and David Ball (b. 1959; synthesizer). Entrepreneur Stevo negotiated a licensing deal with Phonogram Records in Europe and Sire Records in the USA. 'Memorabilia' became an underground hit, paving the way for the celebrated 'Tainted Love' (UK number 1). This became the bestselling British single of the year and remained in the US charts for 43 weeks. Subsequent hit singles included 'Bedsitter', 'Say Hello Wave Goodbye', 'Torch' and 'What', but Almond and Ball were never happy with the pop machinery of which it had become a part, and *The Art Of Falling Apart* indicated how close they were to ending their hit collaboration. They disbanded after *This Last Night In Sodom*. Almond embarked on a solo career, while Ball would eventually become one half of the Grid. The duo reunited in the late 90s and began working on new material.

SOFT MACHINE

Founded in England in 1966, the original line-up was **Robert Wyatt** (b. 1945; drums, vocals), **Kevin Ayers** (b. 1944; vocals), Daevid Allen, Mike Ratledge and, very briefly, guitarist Larry Nolan. By 1967 the classic line-up of the Soft Machine's art-rock period (Ayers, Wyatt and Ratledge) had settled. They toured with **Jimi Hendrix**, who, with his producer Chas Chandler facilitated the recording of their first album. Ayers left at the end of 1968 and until 1970 the personnel was in a state of flux. *Volume Two* and *Third* contained their most intriguing and exciting performances. By the mid-1970s the second definitive line-up (Ratledge, Wyatt, Hugh Hopper and Elton Dean) was finally in place, but in autumn 1971, Wyatt left and John Marshall became the permanent drummer. For the next few years the Soft Machine were the standard against which all jazz-rock fusions were measured. However, with Ratledge's departure in 1976, the band began to lose their unique sound, lacking the edge of earlier incarnations. Their first three albums contain the best of their work.

SONIC YOUTH

US avant garde rock band Sonic Youth was formed by Thurston Moore (b. 1958; guitar), Lee Ranaldo (b. 1956; guitar) and Kim Gordon (b. 1953; bass), and first performed together on Glenn Branca's *Symphony No. 3*. Their own debut was recorded live at New York's Radio City Music Hall in 1981. Three further collections, *Confusion Is Sex*, *Sonic Death* and a mini-album, *Kill Yr Idols*, completed their formative period. Jim Sclavunos replaced original drummer Richard Edson, but was quickly succeeded by Bob Bert on *Bad Moon Rising*. Bert was then replaced by Steve Shelley (b. 1962). *Evol* refined their ability to mix melody with menace, particularly on the outstanding 'Shadow Of A Doubt'. In 1990 Sonic Youth signed with Geffen

Records, establishing a reputation as godfathers to the alternative US rock scene with powerful albums such as *Goo*, *Dirty* and *A Thousand Leaves*. They are now one of the nation's best-known underground bands.

SONIQUE

This UK DJ (b. Sonia Clarke) began her musical career with the club hit 'Let Me Hold You'. However, it was as the singer for Mark Moore's S'Express that she first entered the limelight, featuring on the minor hits 'Nothing To Lose' and 'Find 'Em, Fool 'Em, Forget 'Em' in 1990 and 1992, respectively. She has since made her mark as a DJ, partly helped by her unique improvised singing over her own up-tempo house sets. She enjoyed two club and dance chart hits with 'I Put A Spell On You' and 'It Feels So Good'. The latter was a mainstream hit in the US, breaking into the national Top 10, and belatedly gave her a UK chart-topper in 2000.

SONNY AND CHER

In 1964 Sonny Bono (b. Salvatore Bono, 1935, d. 1998) married **Cher** (b. Cherilyn Sarkisian La Pierre, 1946) whom he had met while recording with producer **Phil Spector**. Although the duo recorded a couple of singles under the exotic name Caeser And Cleo, it was as Sonny And Cher that they found fame with the transatlantic number 1, 'I Got You Babe'. During late 1965, they dominated the charts as both a duo and soloists with such hits as 'Baby Don't Go', 'All I Really Want To Do', 'Laugh At Me', 'Just You' and 'But You're Mine'. Although their excessive output resulted in diminishing returns, their lean periods were punctuated by further hits, most notably 'Little Man' and 'The Beat Goes On'. They had a brief resurgence as MOR entertainers in the 70s, although by that time they had divorced. Eventually, extra-curricular acting activities ended their long-standing musical partnership.

SOUL ASYLUM

This Minnesota, USA-based rock band centred around Dave Pirner (b. 1964; vocals, guitar) and Dan Murphy (b. 1962; guitar), with Karl Mueller (b. 1963; bass) and Pat Morley (drums). Morley left in 1984, replaced by Grant Young (b. 1964) on 1986's *Made To Be Broken*. *Hang Time*, saw them move into the hands of a new production team. *Soul Asylum And The Horse They Rode In On* was another splendid album, and the single 'Somebody To Shove' was heavily promoted on MTV. The US Top 5 hit 'Runaway Train' and *Grave Dancers Union* were even more successful. In 1995, the band announced that their next studio sessions would avoid the commercial textures of their previous album, although reviews of *Let Your Dim Light Shine* were mixed. They also recruited drummer, Stirling Campbell, to replace Young. *Candy From A Stranger* was the band's most relaxed and intimate recording.

SOUL II SOUL

This UK rap/soul/dance crossover group was formed by Jazzie B (b. Beresford Romeo, 1963), Nellee Hooper and Philip 'Daddae' Harvey. Following the release of 'Fairplay' and 'Feel Free', the band's profile grew. 'Keep On Movin'' reached UK number 5 in 1989. The follow-up, 'Back To Life (However Do You Want Me)', featuring Caron Wheeler, was taken from their acclaimed debut *Club Classics Vol. One*. 'Get A Life' was an expansion on the influential, stuttering rhythms that the band had employed on previous singles. The band's second album included Courtney Pine and Kym Mazelle in its star-studded cast. Despite entering the charts at number 1 it was given a frosty reception by some critics who saw it as conservative. Although *Volume III, Just Right* made its debut at UK number 3, it proffered no substantial singles successes. The group's fourth studio album was not available until 1995, as Wheeler returned to the fold. The band was dropped by Virgin in 1996, but signed up to Island Records for the release of *Time For Change*. In 1999, Virgin released a 10th anniversary special edition of *Club Classics Vol. One*.

SOULWAX

This Belgian rock band was formed in 1994 by brothers Stephen (b. 1970; vocals, keyboards, percussion) and David Dewaele (b. 1975; guitar). The brothers were initially joined in Soulwax by Stefaan Van Leuven (bass) and Piet Dierickx (drums). The quartet's four-track debut, *2nd Handsome Blues*, was released in 1995 on the Play It Again Sam label, following which the band travelled to Los Angeles to record their hard-rocking debut album. After collaborating with **Einstürzende Neubauten** on their *Ende Neu* project, Soulwax returned to LA to record their second album. An eclectic mix of rock, funk, electronica and hip-hop, *Much Against Everyone's Advice* was a marked improvement on their debut and earned favourable comparisons with fellow Belgians dEUS. The Dewaele brothers were joined on the album by Van Leuven, Stephane Misseghers (drums) and Inge Flipts (keyboards). The Dewaeles are equally renowned for their Djing prowess, holding residencies in Antwerp, Amsterdam and London under the moniker the Flying Dewaele Brothers.

SOUNDGARDEN

This Seattle, USA-based quartet fused influences as diverse as **Led Zeppelin**, the **Stooges**, **Velvet Underground** and, most particularly, early UK and US punk bands into a dirty, sweaty, sexually explicit and decidedly fresh take on rock 'n' roll. Formed by Chris Cornell (b. 1964; vocals, guitar), Kim Thayil (b. 1960; guitar), Hiro Yamamoto (b. 1968; bass) and Matt Cameron (b. 1962; drums), Soundgarden's early releases attracted the attention of A&M Records who released *Louder Than Love*, one of the most offbeat rock albums of 1989. Yamamoto was replaced by Jason Everman (ex-**Nirvana**), though he only recorded one track, a cover version of the **Beatles**' 'Come Together', before leaving. His replacement was Ben 'Hunter' Shepherd (b. 1968). *Badmotorfinger* built on the band's successful formula but added the grinding but melodious guitar sound that would come to define 'grunge'. *Superunknown* debuted at number 1 on the US chart in 1994 and sold over three million copies. *Down*

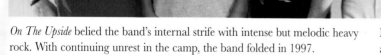

On The Upside belied the band's internal strife with intense but melodic heavy rock. With continuing unrest in the camp, the band folded in 1997.

SOUTHSIDE JOHNNY AND THE ASBURY JUKES

US R&B fanatic Southside Johnny (b. John Lyon, 1948; vocals) formed the Asbury Jukes with school friends Billy Rush (b. 1952; guitar), Kevin Kavanaugh (b. 1951; keyboards), Kenneth Pentifallo (b. 1940; bass) and Alan 'Doc' Berger (b. 1949; drums). Popular in the parochial clubs, they sought a wider audience via a 1976 promotional album, *Live At The Bottom Line*, which led to a contract with Epic Records. This led to two albums, *I Wanna Go Home* and *This Time It's For Real*. After *Hearts Of Stone* failed to reach a mass public, Epic let the band go with the valedictory *Havin' A Party With Southside Johnny*. A sensational horn section was added to the line-up, and the band's debut for Mercury Records, *The Jukes*, sold moderately as did the follow-up *Love Is A Sacrifice*. *Reach Out And Touch The Sky* halted a commercial decline that resumed with later studio efforts. The band only occasionally returns to the studio these days, opting instead to tour constantly along the eastern coast of America and sometimes venturing further afield. Widely regarded as 'The World's Greatest Bar Band', they continue to attract star guests including **Bruce Springsteen** (an early champion) and **Jon Bon Jovi**.

SPACE

UK band formed in 1993 and comprising Tommy Scott (b. 1967; vocals, bass), Andy Parle (drums), Jamie Murphy (vocals, guitar) and Franny Griffiths (keyboards). The sound of their singles lurched from the sparse ska and socio-pathic lyrics of 'Neighbourhood' to the stylish MOR noir of 'Female Of The Species'. *Spiders* showed they were capable of sustaining their eclecticism across a whole album and making it commercially viable as well, entering the UK charts at number 5. Space set off on a sell-out UK tour in 1998, with Parle replaced by Leon Caffrey. The year also brought further chart success, most notably 'Avenging Angels' and a collaboration with **Catatonia**'s Cerys Hughes on 'The Ballad of Tom Jones', both from *Tin Planet*.

SPANDAU BALLET

UK new romantic band founded in 1979 by Gary Kemp (b. 1959; guitar), his brother Martin (b. 1961; bass), Tony Hadley (b. 1960; vocals), John Keeble (b. 1959; drums) and Steve Norman (b. 1960; rhythm guitar, saxophone, percussion). Their powerful debut, 'To Cut A Long Story Short', reached the UK Top 5, but over the next year their singles 'The Freeze' and 'Musclebound' were average rather than exceptional. The insistent 'Chant Number 1 (I Don't Need This Pressure On)' revealed a more interesting soul/funk direction, and reached the UK Top 5, but again was followed by a relatively fallow period.

By 1983 the band were pushing their lead singer as a junior Frank Sinatra. The new approach was demonstrated most forcibly on 'True', which topped the UK charts and reached the US Top 5. The follow-up 'Gold' reached UK number 2. They continued to chart regularly with such hits as 'Only When You Leave', 'I'll Fly For You', 'Highly Strung' and 'Round And Round'. The politically-conscious *Through The Barricades* and its attendant hit singles 'Fight For Yourselves' and the title track partly re-established their standing. The Kemp brothers eventually turned to acting and Hadley embarked on a solo career. In May 1999, Hadley, Norman and Keeble lost their fight to reclaim a share of £1 million in royalties from the band's songwriter Gary Kemp. They continue to tour although they are unable to use the Spandau Ballet name.

SPARKLEHORSE

Mark Linkous made an innocuous start to his music career, recording two albums in the mid-80s with the US indie-rock band the Dancing Hoods. Linkous recorded many of the instrumental parts for Sparklehorse's 1995 debut himself. His brand of neo-Gothic acoustic alienation began to impress critics in the UK and it was after a London gig that Linkous mixed his prescription drugs and collapsed in his hotel bathroom, trapping his legs beneath his body.

He was only found 12 hours later, by which time he had suffered a heart attack and caused bad damage to his leg muscles. He made a steady recovery, performing from a wheelchair with his touring band. A quantum leap was made with Sparklehorse's excellent second album, *Good Morning Spider*. The *Distorted Ghost* EP, released in 2000, featured the winsome 'My Yoke Is Heavy' and served as an effective stopgap while Linkous worked on *It's A Wonderful Life*. Another superlative recording, the album marked Sparklehorse out as one of the most interesting bands on the contemporary music scene.

SPARKS

Vocalist Russell Mael (b. Dwight Russell Day, 1953) and his elder brother Ron (b. Ronald Day, 1948; keyboards) formed this US band in 1971 with Earle Mankey (guitar), Jim Mankey (bass) and Harley Fernstein (drums). Despite a regional US hit in 'Wonder Girl,' Sparks' debut album sold poorly, as did the subsequent *A Woofer In Tweeter's Clothing*. A club tour of Europe found them a cult following in England, where the Maels emigrated in 1973, signing to Island Records and enlisting a new Sparks from native players. This Anglo-American incarnation of Sparks had eight UK chart entries, starting with 1974's number 2 hit 'This Town Ain't Big Enough For Both Of Us' from *Kimono My House*. *Propaganda* was a stylistic departure but the basic formula was unaltered, and this, combined with an unsteady stage act provoked fading interest in further merchandise. Sparks engineered a transient comeback to the British Top 20 in 1979 with two singles from *Number One In Heaven*.

Following some more experimental albums in the late 80s the Maels made an abortive foray into the world of cinema. They returned to music in the 90s on the back of a Sparks revival orchestrated by several UK dance acts. The duo rose to the occasion by releasing one of their finest albums, *Gratuitous Sax And Senseless Violins*. For their next project, *Plagiarism*, they reworked the best of their back catalogue

SPEARS, BRITNEY

One of the last teenage US pop superstars of the 20th century, Spears (b. 1981) enjoyed her breakthrough success at the end of 1998. A veteran of television's *The Mickey Mouse Club*, Spears was expensively groomed by Jive Records. They employed top R&B writer Max Martin to produce her debut single, '. . . Baby, One More Time', and an album of the same title. The careful planning paid off when her debut album and single went on to top the American charts at the start of 1999. The album and single enjoyed similar success in the UK and Europe. The ballad 'Sometimes' and the funky '(You Drive Me) Crazy' were also substantial transatlantic hits, and 'Born To Make You Happy' topped the UK charts in January 2000. The demand for new Spears material was satisfied when her sophomore set, *Oops! . . . I Did It Again*, was released in May.

Spears' self-titled third album was a laboured attempt by the singer to cultivate a more mature image. Although its initial sales were not as strong as her previous two albums, Britney shot straight to the top of the US album chart on its release in November 2001 for a brief stay. Spears' mainstream film debut, *Crossroads*, was released the following February.

SPECIALS

Formed in 1977 as the Special AKA, this ska-influenced UK pop band comprised Jerry Dammers (b. Gerald Dankin, 1954; keyboards), Terry Hall (b. 1959; vocals), Neville Staples (vocals, percussion), Lynval Golding (b. 1951; guitar), Roddy Radiation (b. Rodney Byers; guitar), Sir Horace Gentleman (b. Horace Panter; bass) and John Bradbury (drums). They set up the 2-Tone label and issued 'Gangsters', which reached the UK Top 10. After signing their label over to Chrysalis Records, the group abbreviated their name to the Specials. Their debut album was an exuberant effort which included 'A Message To You, Rudi' (UK Top 10). EP *The Special AKA Live* saw the Specials at their peak and the track 'Too Much Too Young', propelled them to number 1 in the UK charts. Further Top 10 hits with 'Rat Race', 'Stereotype' and 'Do Nothing' followed. The Specials' ability to 'capture the moment' in pop was most persuasively felt with 'Ghost Town', which topped the charts during the summer of 1981 while Britain was enduring inner-city riots. At this new peak of success, the group fragmented. Staples, Hall and Golding formed **Fun Boy Three**, while Dammers reverted to the old name the Special AKA and released the protest hit, 'Nelson Mandela'. Later revivals of the Specials have failed to match the brilliance of their late 70s and early 80s peak.

SPECTOR, PHIL

Born in New York, Spector (b. Harvey Phillip Spector, 1940) became involved in music upon moving to California in 1953. There he joined a community of young aspirants, including **Sandy Nelson**, who played drums on Spector's debut recording, 'To Know Him Is To Love Him'. This million-selling single for the Teddy Bears topped the US chart in 1958. Local entrepreneur Lester Sill recommended Phil's talents to New York production team **Leiber And Stoller**, with whom he co-wrote 'Spanish Harlem' and 'Young Boy Blues' for **Ben E. King**. Spector's first major success as a producer came with Ray Petersen's version of 'Corrina Corrina' (US Top 10, 1960), and Curtis Lee's 'Pretty Little Angel Eyes' (US number 7, 1961).

In 1961 Spector formed Philles Records with Lester Sill, but within months he bought his partner out, and there followed a string of classic recordings for the **Crystals** and **Ronettes** including 'He's A Rebel' (1962), 'Then He Kissed Me', 'Be My Baby' and 'Baby I Love You' (all 1963). Spector's releases also featured some of the era's finest songwriting teams – **Gerry Goffin** and **Carole King**, Barry And Greenwich and Barry Mann and Cynthia Weil – the last of which composed 'You've Lost That Lovin' Feelin'' for the **Righteous Brothers**, the producer's stylistic apogee. Several critics also cite 'River Deep – Mountain High' (1966) by **Ike And Tina Turner** as Spector's greatest moment. It represented his most ambitious production, but barely scraped the US Hot 100 and a dispirited Spector folded his label and retired from music for several years.

He re-emerged in 1969 with a series of releases for A&M Records which included Sonny Charles And The Checkmates' 'Black Pearl' (US Top 20). After working on the **Beatles'** *Let It Be*, Spector became installed at their Apple Records label. However, his behaviour grew increasingly erratic and as the 70s progressed, he became a recluse. He re-emerged to produce albums by **Leonard Cohen** (*Death Of Ladies Man* – 1977) and the **Ramones** (*End Of The Century* – 1980). Spector remained largely detached from music throughout the 80s, although he was inducted into the Rock And Roll Hall Of Fame in 1989.

SPENCER, JON, BLUES EXPLOSION

When Washington, DC, USA-based noiseniks Pussy Galore ended their five-year reign of terror, singer/guitarist Jon Spencer realigned with Russell Simins (drums) and Judah Bauer (guitar) to form a trio that would bend the rules of alternative rock while demonstrating an obvious devotion to the music's basic R&B roots. Each successive album added new elements of blues, soul and rockabilly. Parallel with JSBE work, Spencer was playing in the more conventionally alt-rock Boss Hog with his wife (and fellow Pussy Galore survivor) Cristina Martinez and drummer Charlie Ondras. A move to London-based Mute Records was predicted by some to herald a tailing-off of the band's R&B experiments but 1996's *Now I Got Worry* featured 'Chicken Dog', a collaboration with the seminal Rufus Thomas. They remain part of a select coterie, alongside **Beck**, the **Beastie Boys** and few others, who can fuse roots and indie sounds to the satisfaction of both camps.

SPICE GIRLS

The Spice Girls – Victoria Adams aka Posh Spice (b. 1975), Melanie Brown aka Mel B/Scary Spice (b. 1975), Emma Bunton aka Baby Spice (b. 1976), Melanie Chisholm aka Mel C/Sporty Spice (b. 1974) and **Geraldine Halliwell** aka Geri/Ginger Spice (b. 1972) – met at various unsuccessful auditions for film and dance jobs. They ended up sharing a house in Berkshire, England, in 1993, where they began writing and demoing songs before finding manager Simon Fuller in 1995. A deal with Virgin Records followed and by 1996, the single 'Wannabe', an expression of their 'Girl Power' philosophy, made UK number 1. In 1997, 'Wannabe' made US number 1 and they became the first UK act ever to reach the top of the chart with their debut album. They made history when their first six hits all reached UK number 1, with songs ranging from ballads such as 'Say You'll Be There' and '2 Become 1' to the upbeat and exotic 'Spice Up Your Life'.

Towards the end of 1997 they unceremoniously dumped Fuller. The commercial success of their debut movie *Spiceworld – The Movie*, premiered on 26 December 1997, indicated otherwise. The Motown-pastiche 'Stop', only reached number 2 in the UK charts, breaking the group's run of chart-toppers. A potentially terminal threat to the future of the Spice Girls came at the end of May 1998, when Geri Halliwell announced she had left the group. Nevertheless, 'Viva Forever', the first single issued since Halliwell's departure (although her vocals appeared on the single), proved that the Spice Girls phenomenon lived on when it entered the UK charts at number 1 in August 1998. The group then became the first artists to enjoy three consecutive UK number 1 Christmas singles since the **Beatles**, when 'Goodbye' emulated the success of 'Too Much' and '2 Become 1'.

The individual members were starting to branch out into solo work by this point, and in 1999 Adams married soccer star David Beckham, a union which created *the* celebrity couple of the decade. The girls reunited in 2000 to record *Forever* with leading R&B producer Rodney Jerkins. The album was premiered in October by their ninth UK number 1, a double a-side comprising the urban-oriented 'Holler' and 'Let Love Lead The Way'. The album's disappointing sales in all territories led to many rumours concerning the future of the group.

SPIN DOCTORS

This US rock band was formed in 1989 when vocalist Christopher Barron (b. 1968) and guitarist Eric Schenkman (b. 1963) met drummer Aaron Comess (b. 1968) and bass player Mark White (b. 1962). *Pocket Full Of Kryptonite* was a varied collection of well-crafted, tuneful rock songs, including the hits 'Little Miss Can't Be Wrong' and 'Two Princes', and subsequently became a massive-selling album. A live set, *Homebelly Groove*, was released to satisfy the new demand. Schenkman was ousted in favour of Anthony Krizan in 1994. Sales of *Turn It Upside Down* proved disappointing, and when two further albums also failed it was confirmed that the Spin Doctors had ceased to be a commercial proposition.

SPIRIT

This US rock band arrived in 1968 with their self-titled debut album. The band comprised Randy California (b. Randolph Wolfe, 1951, d. 1997; guitar), Ed 'Mr Skin' Cassidy (b. 1931; drums), John Locke (b. 1943; keyboards), Jay Ferguson (b. 1947; vocals) and Mark Andes (b. 1948; bass). Their debut album fared well, and *The Family That Plays Together* was a greater success, spawning a US Top 30 hit single, 'I Got A Line On You'. *Twelve Dreams Of Dr Sardonicus*, showed Ferguson and California's songwriting reaching a peak, but soon afterwards, Spirit had their legendary album *Potatoland* rejected. Tensions within the band mounted and Ferguson, Andes and California all departed. Further personnel changes ensued before a nucleus of California and Cassidy toured widely and built up a loyal following in Britain and Germany, but the albums sold poorly and the band became despondent. The original five members reunited in 1984 for *The Thirteenth Dream*. Cassidy and California continued into the 90s with varied line-ups, before the latter's tragic death by drowning in 1997.

SPIRITUALIZED

This dark, neo-psychedelic UK band, who sometimes use the sub-title Electric Mainline, was formed by Jason Pierce (b. 1965; vocals, guitar) after his messy break-up from former writing partner and Spacemen 3 cohort Pete Kember. Pierce took the remnants of that band with him (Mark Refoy (guitar), Will Carruthers (bass) and John Mattock (drums)) and added his girlfriend Kate Radley (organ). Headliners at ICA's Irn Bru Rock Week, their familiar **Velvet Underground** guitar noise/dream pop found favour with old Spacemen 3 fans as well as new converts, and their debut album, *Lazer Guided Melodies*, was widely regarded as one of the best of 1992.

With the core of the band reduced down to Pierce, Radley and new bass player Sean Cook, *Pure Phase* finally arrived in 1995 to the usual critical fanfare. The line-up by late 1997 featured Pierce, Mike Mooney (guitar), Tim Jeffries (keyboards), Damon Reece (drums) and Ray Dickaty (saxophone). The aptly-titled *Ladies And Gentlemen We Are Floating In Space* was Pierce's finest distillation yet of his wide range of styles, an ambitious sonic experiment that even found room for the piano work of **Dr. John** on the epic closing track 'Cop Shoot Cop'. Following the release of a live album, the notoriously fickle Pierce dismissed most of his former bandmates. While Mooney, Cook and Reece regrouped as Lupine Howl, Pierce returned to the studio to record the sumptuous *Let It Come Down* with a new line-up of musicians augmented by choristers, gospel singers and full brass and string sections.

SPLIT ENZ

Formed in Auckland, New Zealand, in 1972 around the duo of Tim Finn (b. 1952; vocals, piano) and Jonathan 'Mike' Chunn (bass, keyboards). Having established themselves in their homeland, they moved to Australia and recorded their first album for Mushroom. Signed to Chrysalis Records in Europe, Phil Manzanera recorded the band's second album. Returning to Australia in 1977, Split Enz recruited Tim Finn's brother Neil (b. 1958). Their 1980 album *True Colours* contained their most successful single, Neil Finn's 'I Got You' (UK number 12). Follow-up releases saw the band reach modest positions in the US album charts, but they lost momentum, eventually dissolving in 1985 after the release of *Conflicting Emotions*. Neil Finn went on to form the successful **Crowded House**.

SPOOKY TOOTH

Formed in 1967, this UK progressive rock band comprised Gary Wright (b. 1945; keyboards, vocals), Mike Kellie (b. 1947; drums), Luther Grosvenor (b. 1949; guitar), Mike Harrison (b. 1945; vocals) and Greg Ridley (b. 1947; bass). *It's All About* was a fine debut. Although not a strong seller it contained club favourite 'Tobacco Road' and their debut single 'Sunshine Help Me'. It was *Spooky Two*, however, that put them on the map. *Ceremony* was a change of direction that found few takers. *The Last Puff* saw a number of personnel changes: Ridley, Gary Wright and Grosvenor left, replaced by Henry McCullough, Chris Stainton and Alan Spenner, and the band broke up shortly after its release, although various members eventually regrouped for three further albums. The original line-up of Spooky Tooth, minus Gary Wright, regrouped in 1999 to record a worthy album for the German Ruf label.

SPOTNICKS

Originally this Swedish instrumental group consisted of Bo Winberg (b. 1939; guitar), Bob Lander (b. Bo Starander, 1942; guitar), Bĵrn Thelin (b. 1942; bass) and Ove Johansson (drums), and they had several hit singles in their homeland. They were signed to Oriole in the UK in 1962 and had a hit with a novelty version of 'Orange Blossom Special' in 1962.

Further UK hits included 'Rocket Man', 'Hava Nagila' and 'Just Listen To My Heart'. Johansson left in 1963 and was replaced by London musician Derek Skinner (b. 1944), in turn replaced by Jimmy Nicol. In 1965 they added organist Peter Winsnes to the line-up. Nicol left in early 1967 and was replaced by Tommy Tausis (b. 1946). Thelin and Winsnes were later replaced by Magnus Hellsberg and Göran Samuelsson.

The group eventually broke up in 1970, but Winberg was persuaded to re-form the band the following year to record a Japanese album. Several further line-up changes occurred over the following years as the band continued to tour and record prolifically in Europe. Winberg was the only constant member although Lander was normally in the band until he left to form the Viking Truckers.

SPRINGFIELD, DUSTY

Springfield (b. Mary Isabel Catherine Bernadette O'Brien, 1939, d. 1999) began as a member of 50s UK pop trio the Lana Sisters, before joining her brother Tom (Dion O'Brien) and Tim Field in the Springfields. Her debut solo came in 1963 with 'I Only Want To Be With You', and over the next three years she was constantly in the chart with a string of hits. During this time she campaigned

on behalf of the then little-known black American soul, R&B and Motown artists.

Worldwide success came with an English-language version of the Italian hit 'Io Che Non Vivo (Senzate)' – 'You Don't Have To Say You Love Me'. This proved her sole UK chart-topper in 1966, and, by the end of 1967 she was becoming disillusioned with showbusiness. Her BBC television series attracted healthy viewing figures, but it was anathema to the sudden change in the pop scene. She departed for Memphis, Tennessee, and recorded her finest work, *Dusty In Memphis*. 'Son Of A Preacher Man' became a major hit, but the album failed in the UK and fared little better in the USA.

For the next few years she recorded sporadically, preferring to spend her time with friends and to campaign for animal rights. Following the release of *It Begins Again*, some five years after her previous release, she was propelled towards a comeback, which failed, although the album did garner respectable sales. Her return towards the end of the 80s was due entirely to the **Pet Shop Boys**, who persuaded her to duet with them on their hit 'What Have I Done To Deserve This?' (1987).

In 1994, having returned to Britain, treatment for breast cancer delayed the release and promotion of *A Very Fine Love*. Springfield was inducted into the Rock And Roll Hall Of Fame in 1999, too late and too ill to attend. She was also awarded an OBE in the 1999 New Year Honours list, but barely four weeks after receiving the honour at a private gathering she finally succumbed to cancer.

SPRINGSTEEN, BRUCE

Springsteen (b. 1949) began playing in a number of New Jersey bands, before settling as the Bruce Springsteen Band with David Sancious (keyboards), Gary Tallent (bass), Clarence Clemons (saxophone), Steven Van Zandt (guitar), Danny Federici (keyboards) and Vini Lopez (drums). CBS Records signed Springsteen as a solo artist, sensing a future **Bob Dylan**. Instead, Springsteen set about recording his debut with his band. *Greetings From Asbury Park N. J.* sold poorly, as did the follow-up, *The Wild, The Innocent & The E. Street Shuffle*. His musicians were re-named the E. Street Band after the latter album's release.

Born To Run (1975) was Springsteen's break-though album and a transatlantic hit, and is still regarded as one of rock's finest albums. His recording career was then held up for three years as he and manager Landau entered into litigation with Mike Appel. Meanwhile, **Manfred Mann's Earth Band** released a version of his 'Blinded By The Light', and **Patti Smith** recorded their co-written 'Because The Night'. With the successful completion of the lawsuits came the anti-climactic *Darkness On The Edge Of Town*, an edgy and unsettling work.

The double-set *The River* contained the hit singles 'Hungry Heart', 'The River' and 'Fade Away'. In marked contrast, *Nebraska*, a stark acoustic set, was recorded solo, directly on to a cassette recorder. It is raw Springsteen, uncompromising and some-times painful.

Springsteen became a bona fide rock super-star with his next release, 1984's *Born In The USA*. The album sold over 12 million copies, spawned numerous hit singles and stayed in the UK charts for two-and-a-half years. Springsteen then released a

five-album boxed set at the end of 1986. The superbly recorded *Live 1975-1985* entered the US charts at number 1. The following year the excellent *Tunnel Of Love* shot to number 1 on the day of release in the UK and USA, and received glowing reviews despite its painful meditations on love and loss.

In 1989, at the age of 40, Springsteen split the E. Street Band. Three years later, he issued two albums simultaneously: *Human Touch* and *Lucky Town*. Both scaled the charts but received mixed reviews. Springsteen received better reviews for 'Streets Of Philadelphia', the emotionally charged title track for the movie *Philadelphia* in 1994. *The Ghost Of Tom Joad* was a solo acoustic album, warm, mellow and sad. Sounding a lot like Dylan, Springsteen no longer sounded angry or energetic; merely philosophical.

In 1999 Springsteen embarked on a rapturously well-received world tour with the rejuvenated E. Street Band. The following June, Springsteen unveiled a new song, 'American Skin', at a performance at Madison Square Garden. A scathing comment on the police shooting of the unarmed Bronx resident Amadou Diallo, the song prompted NYPD calls for a boycott of the concerts. In 2002 he released the chart-topping album *The Rising*.

SQUEEZE

This popular UK pop band was formed in 1974 by Chris Difford (b. 1954; guitar, lead vocals), Glenn Tilbrook (b. 1957; guitar, vocals) and Jools Holland (b. Julian Holland, 1958; keyboards). With Harry Kakoulli (bass), and session drummer Gilson Lavis, Squeeze released the *Packet Of Three* EP. It led to a major contract with A&M Records and a UK Top 20 hit in 1978 with 'Take Me I'm Yours'. Minor success with 'Bang Bang' and 'Goodbye Girl' that same year was followed by two number 2 hits, 'Cool For Cats' and 'Up The Junction'. *Argy Bargy* spawned the singles 'Another Nail In My Heart' (UK Top 20) and 'Pulling Mussels (From The Shell)'.

In 1980, Holland left for a solo career and was replaced by singer/pianist Paul Carrack (b. 1951). *East Side Story*, which included 'Labelled With Love' (UK Top 5) became the band's most successful to date. Carrack departed soon afterwards and was replaced by Kenyan-born Don Snow (b. 1957). At the height of their success, Difford and Tilbrook dissolved the group, only to re-form in 1985 with Lavis, Holland and new bass player, Keith Wilkinson. *Cosi Fan Tutti Frutti* was hailed as a return to form. In 1987 'Hourglass' reached UK number 16 and gave the band their first US Top 40 hit. After *Frank*, Holland departed again. With Matt Irving joining as a second keyboard player, Squeeze released a live album, *A Round And A Bout*, before signing a new contract with Warner Brothers Records. *Play* confirmed Difford and Tilbrook's reputation, and *Some Fantastic Place* and *Ridiculous* saw them reunited with A&M. Following the demise of their record label, the band issued 1998's *Domino* on their own Quixotic Records label. Sadly, Difford and Tilbrook disbanded Squeeze not long afterwards.

STAIND

The line-up of this US alternative metal act, comprising Aaron Lewis (vocals), Mike Mushok (guitar), Johnny April (bass) and Jon Wyscoki (drums), came together in 1995. The following year the band recorded and distributed their debut, *Tormented*. A contract with Fred Durst's Flip Records ensued in early 1998. The songs on *Dysfunction* eschewed the overt hip-hop influence of **Limp Bizkit** for a more traditional style of hard rock rooted in the early 90s sound of **Alice In Chains**. The band's second album, *Break The Cycle*, debuted at the top of the US album charts in 2001. The ballad 'Outside' enjoyed extensive radio play.

STANDELLS

Tony Valentino (guitar, vocals) and Larry Tamblyn (organ) formed the Standells in 1962. The early line-up included drummer Gary Leeds, Gary Lane (bass) and Dick Dodd (drums). The quartet became a leading teen-based attraction

but then fashioned a series of angst-cum-protest punk anthems in 'Sometimes Good Guys Don't Wear White', 'Why Pick On Me' and 'Dirty Water' (US number 11, 1966). Lane left the band during a tour of Florida. Unfashionable in the face of San Francisco's acid rock, the band's career was confined to the cabaret circuit. Several members re-formed in 1999 for a live show at the Cavestomp festival, later released as *Ban This!*.

STANSFIELD, LISA

Manchester-born Stansfield (b. 1966) teamed up with Andy Morris and Ian Devaney to form the white-soul group, Blue Zone in 1983. With backing from Arista Records, the group released *Big Thing* (1986), and several singles on Rockin' Horse, but achieved little success outside the club circuit. In 1989, they were invited to record 'People Hold On', which reached the UK Top 20 and prompted manager Jazz Summers to sign Stansfield as a solo act, with Morris and Devaney as composers, musicians and producers. 'This Is The Right Time' reached number 13 in the UK chart while the follow-up, 'All Around This World' climbed to number 1 in the UK. *Affection* eventually sold five million copies worldwide. While 'Live Together' was peaking at number 10 in the UK,

plans were afoot to break into the US chart. 'All Around The World' then reached US number 3, while *Affection* reached the Top 10. She had further UK hits in late 1991 with 'Change' (number 10) and 'All Woman' (number 20). 'In All The Right Places' put Stansfield back into the UK Top 10 in 1993.

After a long break she returned with *Lisa Stansfield* in 1997, which featured 'Never, Never Gonna Give You Up', a song originally recorded by her musical hero **Barry White**. In 1999, Stansfield starred in the movie *Swing*, a romantic comedy following the exploits of a swing band formed in Liverpool, England. In 2001 she returned with a strong set of upbeat white soul music.

STARDUST, ALVIN

London-born Stardust (b. Bernard William Jewry, 1942) first sang during the early 60s as Shane Fenton. He re-emerged in 1973 as Alvin Stardust and returned to the charts with 'My Coo-Ca-Choo' (UK number 2). It was followed by the chart-topping 'Jealous Mind' and two further UK Top 10 hits with 'Red Dress' and 'You You You' before his chart career petered out. The indomitable Stardust revitalized his career once more during the early 80s with 'Pretend' (Top 10) and the commemorative ballad 'I Feel Like Buddy Holly'. He remains a popular star on the British showbusiness scene and in recent years, as a born-again Christian, has performed with Christian pop and rock acts.

STARR, EDWIN

US performer Edwin Starr (b. Charles Hatcher, 1942) formed the Future Tones vocal group in 1957, and recorded one single before being drafted into the US Army. His service completed, he was offered a solo contract with Ric Tic in 1965. 'Agent Double-O-Soul', was a US Top 30 hit. 'Stop Her On Sight (SOS)' repeated this success, and brought Starr a cult following in Britain. When Motown Records took over Ric Tic in 1967, Starr was initially overlooked, but he re-emerged in 1969 with '25 Miles' (Top 10). An album of duets with Blinky brought some critical acclaim, before Starr resumed his solo career with the politically outspoken 'War' (US number 1, 1970). In the 80s, Starr was based in the UK, where he enjoyed a run of club hits, most notably 'It Ain't Fair' in 1985. Between 1989 and 1991, Starr worked with Motor City Records. He remains a hugely entertaining live performer.

STARR, RINGO

Drummer Starr (b. Richard Starkey, 1940) succeeded Pete Best in the **Beatles**, upon his firing in 1962. Although overshadowed musically, a deadpan sense of humour helped establish his individuality and each album contained a Starr vocal. The most notable of these was 'Yellow Submarine', a million-selling single in 1966. His solo career started with 1969's *Sentimental Journey*, a collection of standards, and *Beaucoups Of Blues*, a country selection. Starr's debut single, 'It Don't Come Easy', co-written with **George Harrison**, topped the US charts and sold in excess of one million copies. *Ringo* featured songs and contributions from each of his former colleagues. 'You're Sixteen' topped the US chart in 1974, but despite further success with 'Oh My My', 'Snookeroo' and 'Only You', Starr's momentum waned, although he enjoyed brief success as an actor.

The 80s signalled his return to active performing, but an album recorded with US producer Chips Moman in 1987 was abandoned when sessions were blighted by excessive imbibing. Starr then reasserted his musical career with the highly popular All-Starr Band. Levon Helm, **Billy Preston**, **Joe Walsh** and **Dr. John** were among those joining the drummer for his 1989 US tour. The band continued to tour, with various personnel, throughout the following decade.

STARSAILOR

Taking their name from a **Tim Buckley** album and a fair amount of inspiration from the cult US singer-songwriter, Starsailor emerged in 2000 as the most promising of a new wave of melodic UK rock bands. Formed in Lancashire, England by James Walsh (guitar, vocals), James Stelfox (bass), Ben Byrne (drums), and Barry Westhead (keyboards), the quartet enjoyed a remarkable rise to major label status. They played their first concert in April 2000 and were snapped up by EMI Records a few months later. Extensive radio-play and a supportive music press helped their *Fever* EP break into the UK Top 20 the following March. 'Good Souls' and 'Alcoholic' also made the upper reaches of the UK charts prior to the release of the quartet's debut album, *Love Is Here*.

STATUS QUO

Founder members of UK group the Spectres, Francis Rossi (b. 1949; guitar, vocals) and Alan Lancaster (b. 1949; bass) led the act from its inception in 1962 until 1967, by which time Roy Lynes (b. 1943; organ) and John Coghlan (b. 1946; drums) completed its line-up. The singles proved commercially unsuccessful, but the band was buoyed by the arrival of Rick Parfitt (b. 1948; guitar, vocals), and the revamped unit became Status Quo in 1967. The following year, 'Pictures Of Matchstick Men', soared to number 7. The group enjoyed another UK Top 10 hit with 'Ice In The Sun', but subsequent recordings struggled to emulate such success, and despite reaching number 12 with 'Down The Dustpipe', they were increasingly viewed as a *passé* novelty.

The departure of Lynes brought the unit's guitar work to the fore. Now signed to Vertigo Records, Status Quo scored a UK Top 10 hit that year with 'Paper Plane' but more importantly, reached number 5 in the album charts with *Piledriver*. *Hello*, entered at number 1, confirming the band's emergence as a major attraction. Each of their 70s albums reached the Top 5, while a consistent presence in the singles' chart included entries such as 'Caroline' (1973), 'Down Down' (a chart topper in 1974), 'Whatever You Want' (1979) and 'Lies'/'Don't Drive My Car' (1980). The band also proved adept at adapting outside material, as evinced by their version of John Fogerty's 'Rockin' All Over The World' (1977).

Coghlan left in 1982 and Pete Kircher (b. 1948) took his place, but there was a growing estrangement between Lancaster and Rossi and Parfitt. Rossi and Parfitt secured the rights to the name and re-formed the act around John Edwards (b. 1953; bass), Jeff Rich (b. 1953; drums) and keyboard player Andy Bown (b. 1946). Despite such traumas Status Quo continued to enjoy commercial approbation with Top 10 entries 'Dear John' (1982), 'Marguerita Time' (1983), 'In The Army Now' (1986) and 'Burning Bridges (On And Off And On Again)' (1988), while *1+9+8+2* was their fourth chart-topping album. They achieved another number 1 single in 1994 with 'Come On You Reds', a musically dubious reworking of their own 'Burning Bridges' recorded with soccer club Manchester United. In 1996 they attempted to sue BBC Radio 1

for not playlisting the single 'Fun Fun Fun' (with the **Beach Boys**) or their latest album *(Don't Stop)*. Parfitt had a health scare in April 1997 when he was rushed into hospital for a quadruple heart bypass, but has since made an excellent recovery. In 1999 the band played a short tour of UK pubs. Rich was replaced by Matthew Letley (b. 1961) the following year.

STEALERS WHEEL

UK band formed by vocalist **Gerry Rafferty** (b. 1947), Joe Egan, Rab Noakes, Ian Campbell and Roger Brown. They signed to A&M Records in the early 70s, but the band had split before they entered the studio. Paul Pilnick (guitar), Tony Williams (bass) and Rod Coombes (drums) bailed out Rafferty and Egan and the result was a surprising success. 'Stuck In The Middle With You' was a transatlantic Top 10 hit in 1973. Rafferty then departed and was replaced by Luther Grosvenor. Rafferty had returned by the second album, but the musical chairs continued as all the remaining members left the band. *Ferguslie Park* was a failure commercially and the two leaders set about completing their contractual obligations and recording their final work *Right Or Wrong*. The album failed and disillusioned Rafferty and Egan buried the name forever.

STEELEYE SPAN

English folk-rock group comprising Ashley Hutchings (b. 1945; bass), Terry Woods (vocals, guitar, mandolin), Gay Woods (vocals, concertina, autoharp), Tim Hart (b. 1948; vocals, guitar, dulcimer, harmonium) and Maddy Prior (b. 1947; vocals). They began extensive rehearsals before recording *Hark! The Village Wait*. The Woods then left to pursue their own career and were replaced by **Martin Carthy** (b. 1940; vocals, guitar) and Peter Knight (vocals, fiddle) for *Please To See The King* and *Ten Man Mop*. They toured extensively, but the departure of Hutchings signalled a dramatic realignment in the Steeleye Span camp. Carthy resumed his solo career and Bob Johnson (guitar) and Rick Kemp (bass) were brought in. Both *Below The Salt* and *Parcel Of Rogues* displayed an electric content and tight dynamics, while *Now We Are Six*, emphasized the terse drumming of newcomer Nigel Pegrum. They enjoyed two UK hit singles with 'Gaudete' (1973) and 'All Around My Hat' (UK Top 5, 1975), but the group was 'rested' following the disappointing *Rocket Cottage*. They reconvened for *Storm Force Ten*, although John Kirkpatrick (accordion) and the prodigal Martin Carthy took Knight and Johnson's places. Their formal disbanding was announced in 1978, although Steeleye Span has been resurrected on subsequent occasions. Prior announced she was finally leaving the band in July 1997.

STEELY DAN

The seeds of this much-respected rock band were sewn at New York's Bard College where founder members *Donald Fagen* (b. 1948; keyboards, vocals) and Walter Becker (b. 1950; bass, vocals) enjoyed a contemporaneous association with pop/harmony act Jay And The Americans, members of whom joined the pair for the soundtrack record, *You Gotta Walk It Like You Talk It (Or You'll Lose That Beat)*. Denny Dias (guitar) contributed to these sessions and soon after the trio was expanded by David Palmer (vocals), Jeff 'Skunk' Baxter (b. 1948; guitar) and Jim Hodder (d. 1990; drums). *Can't Buy A Thrill* was completed within weeks, but drew praise for its immaculate musicianship. The title track and 'Do It Again' reached the US Top 20 and this new-found fame inspired the sarcasm of 'Show Biz Kids' on *Countdown To Ecstasy*.

After Palmer had left the line-up, *Pretzel Logic* became Steely Dan's first US Top 10 album. It included the US Top 5 hit 'Rikki Don't Lose That Number'. Steely Dan's final live appearance was in July 1974 and ensuing strife resulted in the departures of both Baxter and Hodder. Dias joined newcomers **Michael McDonald** (keyboards, vocals) and Jeff Porcaro (drums) for *Katy Lied*. *The Royal Scam* included 'Haitian Divorce', the band's lone Top 20 hit in Britain. *Aja* continued in a similar vein, with an array of quality jazz

musicians bringing a painstaking meticulousness to the set. A similar pattern was unveiled on *Gaucho*, which achieved platinum sales and an attendant single, 'Hey Nineteen', reached the US Top 10.

Becker and Fagen had now tired of their creation and in June 1981 they announced the break-up of their partnership. The duo collaborated together on a number of solo projects in subsequent years. Nothing gels quite like the two working together as Steely Dan, however, and their much vaunted studio reunion *Two Against Nature* eventually saw the light of day in 2000. The duo's triumphant comeback was sealed when they won a Grammy for Album Of The Year the following February.

STEPPENWOLF

German-born John Kay (b. Joachim F. Krauledat, 1944; vocals), Michael Monarch (b. 1950; lead guitar), Goldy McJohn (b. 1945; keyboards), Rushton Moreve (bass) and Jerry Edmonton (b. 1946; drums) formed Steppenwolf in 1967. John Morgan replaced Moreve prior to recording. The band's debut album included 'Born To Be Wild' (US number 2). Steppenwolf actively cultivated a menacing, hard-rock image, and successive collections mixed this heavy style with blues. 'Magic Carpet Ride' and 'Rock Me' were also US Top 10 singles. Newcomers Larry Byrom (guitar) and another German, Nick St. Nicholas (b. 1943; bass), featured on 1969's *Monster*, Steppenwolf's most cohesive set. Continued personnel changes undermined their stability and John Kay dissolved the band in 1972, but within two years he was leading a reconstituted Steppenwolf. The singer has left and re-formed his creation several times over the ensuing years, but has been unable to repeat former glories.

STEPS

A collaboration between svengali Pete Waterman and promotions veteran Steve Jenkins that produced one of the UK pop sensations of the late 90s. The five members of Steps – Lisa Scott-Lee, Claire Richards, Faye Tozer, Lee Latchford and Ian 'H' Watkins – were recruited through an advertisement placed in *Stage* in 1997 by manager Tim Byrne. Inspired by the concurrent line-dancing fad, '5,6,7,8' was released in late 1997, and spent 17 weeks in the UK Top 40. 'Last Thing On My Mind', memorably described by Waterman as 'Abba on speed', reached the UK Top 10 the following year. Further hits followed with 'One For Sorrow', 'Heartbeat/Tragedy' (number 1), 'Better Best Forgotten', 'Love's Got A Hold On My Heart', 'After The Love Has Gone' and 'Stomp' (number 1), before, in December 2001, the group announced they would be pursuing separate careers. Watkins and Richards announced they would be continuing to record as a duo.

STEREO MC'S

This UK crossover outfit's commercial breakthrough in the early 90s was the result of both sustained hard work and an original talent. Their initial line-up revolved around Rob Birch (b. 1961; vocals), Nick 'The Head' Hallam (b. 1 1962; synthesizers, computers, scratching), and Owen If (b. Ian Frederick Rossiter, 1959; percussion). The Stereo

MC's first recording was 'Move It', released before Hallam and Birch recruited Italian-British DJ Cesare, and formed their alter-ego remix team, Ultimatum. Cesare left stating that he was unhappy with the band's direction and financial arrangements, but the band pressed on, recording *Supernatural* with Baby Bam of the Jungle Brothers. Their first crossover hit was 1991's 'Lost In Music'. 'Elevate Your Mind' gave the group a US Top 40 hit. *Connected* was released to mounting acclaim and included the UK hit title track.

In its wake the Stereo MC's collared the Best Group category at the 1994 BRIT Awards ceremony, which celebrated the band's pre-eminence within the commercial dance music field to the detriment of their hip-hop roots. The band's failure to release a follow-up proved to be one of the biggest disappointments of the decade. An excellent mix album did appear in 2000 as part of Studio !K7's *DJ-Kicks* series. The session also provided the creative impetus for the band to finally complete work on their new album, which was released to mixed reviews the following May.

STEREOLAB

UK outfit led by Tim Gane (b. 1964) and his girlfriend Laetitia Sadier. By the time of the 'Low-Fi' 10-inch in 1992, Mary Hansen had arrived to lend keyboard and vocal support. The acclaimed mini-album *The Groop Played Space Age Bachelor Pad Music* saw further line-up changes. *Transient Random Noise-Bursts With Announcements* straddled both indie and dance markets. This maintained their reputation not only as a rock outfit, but also as an important fixture of the experimental dance music axis. *Music For The Amorphous Body Study Centre* continued to embrace subjects outside pop music convention, and *Emperor Tomato Ketchup* confirmed Stereolab as one of the most rewarding UK acts to emerge from the 90s. Ever prolific, they have released several albums including the dance-orientated *Dots And Loops* and *Cobra And Phases Group Play Voltage In The Milky Night*, indicating a willingness to experiment with their established sound.

STEREOPHONICS

Famed for being the first ever signings to Richard Branson's new music label, V2 Records, this Welsh trio have gone on to become arguably the UK's most popular rock band of the new millennium. The band comprises three friends: songwriter Kelly Jones (b. 1974; guitar, vocals), Richard Jones (b. 1974; bass) and Stuart Cable (b. 1970; drums), grew up with each other in the small Welsh village of Cwmaman. Adopting the name Stereophonics, their 1997 debut featured the minor hits 'Local Boy In The Photograph' and 'A Thousand Trees' and reached the UK Top 10. 'The Bartender And The Thief' and 'Just Looking' both reached the Top 5, and were followed by the chart-topping *Performance And Cocktails*. Jones embarked on a low-key solo tour the following year, premiering material to be featured on the band's third album. Provisionally titled *J.E.E.P.*, the band was forced to alter the title to *Just Enough Education To Perform* after the automotive manufacturer Chrysler threatened legal action. The album met with a mixed reaction upon its release in April 2001. It was reissued several months later with the addition of a cover version of Mike D'Abo's 'Handbags And Gladrags'.

STEVENS, CAT

In 1966, producer Mike Hurst spotted this London-born singer-songwriter (b. Steven Georgiou, 1947) performing at the Hammersmith College, London and subsequently arranged to record him and his song, 'I Love My Dog'. Tony Hall at Decca Records was similarly impressed and Stevens became the first artist on the new Deram label. The record and its b-side 'Portobello Road' showed great promise and over the next two years Stevens delivered many perfect pop songs. His own hits, 'Matthew And Son', 'I'm Gonna Get Me A Gun' and 'Bad Night', were equalled by the quality of his songs for others; the soulful 'The First Cut Is The Deepest' by **P.P. Arnold** and the addictive 'Here Comes My Baby' by the **Tremeloes**.

After recovering from a serious bout of tuberculosis, Stevens returned with the introspective *Mona Bone Jakon*. This album was followed by two hugely successful works: *Tea For The Tillerman* and *Teaser And The Firecat*. These let the listener into Stevens' private thoughts, aspirations and desires, and featured classic tracks such as 'Wild World', 'Peace Train' and 'Moon Shadow'. In 1979, Stevens became a devout Muslim and retired from the music business. He returned to the studio in 1995 under the name of Yusef Islam with *Mohammed - The Life Of The Prophet*. In his time Stevens had eight consecutive gold albums and 10 hit singles in the UK and 14 in the USA.

STEVENS, SHAKIN'

In the late 60s Welshman Stevens (b. Michael Barratt, 1948) was lead singer with the Backbeats, later Shakin' Stevens And The Sunsets, who recorded several unsuccessful albums before disbanding in 1976. Stevens' solo career began in 1977 with an album for Track Records, followed by unsuccessful revivals of 50s hits. A change of producer to Stuart Colman in 1980 brought Stevens' first Top 20 hit, 'Marie Marie', and the following year Colman's arrangement of 'This Ole House' topped the UK chart. Over the next seven years, Stevens had over twenty Top 20 hits in the UK, including three number 1s – 'Green Door' (1981), 'Oh Julie' (1982) and 'Merry Christmas Everyone' (1985). By the end of the decade, Stevens' hold over British audiences was faltering and he failed to resurrect his commercial fortunes in the 90s.

STEWART, AL

Glasgow-born Stewart (b. 1945) signed to Decca Records in 1966 and released one unsuccessful single, 'The Elf'. The following year, he joined CBS Records and released the acoustic, string-accompanied *Bedsitter Images*. The succeeding *Love Chronicles* was most notable for the lengthy title track. Stewart's interest in acoustic folk continued on *Zero She Flies*, which featured the historical narrative 'Manuscript'. *Orange* contained the impressive 'Night Of The 4th Of May' and was followed by the ambitious concept album, *Past, Present And Future*. A considerable gap ensued before the release of *Modern Times*.

After leaving CBS and signing to RCA Records, Stewart surprised many by the commercial power of his celebrated *Year Of The Cat* (US Top 10). Another switch of label to Arista Records preceded *Time Passages*, which suffered by comparison with its predecessor. *24 P Carrots* was succeeded by a part studio/part live album, which merely consolidated his position. With *Russians And Americans*, Stewart embraced a more political stance, but the sales were disappointing. Legal and contractual problems deterred him from recording for four years until the welcome *Last Days Of The Century*.

In the 90s, Stewart toured extensively as a solo artist or with pianist/guitarist Peter White, a partnership captured on the live *Rhymes In Rooms*. Stewart now records with ex-**Wings** guitarist Laurence Juber, although releases are few and far between.

STEWART, ROD

Rod Stewart (b. 1945) started his career roaming Europe with folk artist Wizz Jones, but later returned to his native Britain to play harmonica for Jimmy Powell And The Five Dimensions in 1963. He was soon hired by **Long John Baldry** in his band the Hoochie Coochie Men. Without significant success outside the club scene, the band evolved into the Steampacket, with Baldry, Stewart, Brian Auger, Julie Driscoll, Mickey Waller and Rick Brown. In 1965, he joined the blues-based Shotgun Express as joint lead vocalist with Beryl Marsden, but it was joining the **Jeff Beck** Group that gave him national exposure. During his tenure with Beck he recorded two important albums, *Truth* and *Cosa Nostra-Beck Ola*.

When the group broke up Stewart and Ron Wood joined the **Faces**, and Stewart was simultaneously signed as a solo artist to Phonogram Records. His first album sold only moderately and it was *Gasoline Alley* that made the breakthrough. Stewart became a superstar on the strength of his next two albums, *Every Picture Tells A Story* and *Never A Dull Moment*. *Atlantic Crossing* was his last critical success for many years and included the number 1 hit, 'Sailing'. His albums throughout the second half of the 70s, although phenomenally successful, were patchy affairs.

The 80s saw Stewart jet-setting all over the world and his talents surfaced throughout the decade with numbers like 'How Long' and 'Some Guys Have All The Luck'. *Unplugged And Seated* in 1993 boosted his credibility with an exciting performance of familiar songs. In 1998, he re-entered both the single and album charts with *When We Were The New Boys* and embarked on an extensive tour. Stewart subsequently moved to Atlantic Records, although his debut for the label, *Human*, was delayed by voice-threatening throat surgery. In February 2002 Stewart left the WEA conglomerate after 25 years, signing a new recording contract with J Records.

STIFF LITTLE FINGERS

In 1977, Jake Burns (vocals, lead guitar) led Henry Cluney (rhythm guitar), Ali McMordie (bass) and Brian Falloon (drums) as Ireland's first new wave band to enjoy mainstream success. Rough Trade Records quickly picked up the distribution, and released the band's third single, 'Alternative Ulster'. *Inflammable Material* featured songs concentrating on personal experiences in the politically charged climate of Northern Ireland. The release marked the departure of Falloon who was replaced by Jim Reilly. The follow-up, *Nobody's Heroes*, branched out into dub, reggae and pop. *Go For It!* saw the band at the peak of their abilities and popularity. Reilly left for the USA with Brian 'Dolphin' Taylor drafted as his replacement. *Now Then* embraced songs of a more pop-rock nature, but the departure of Burns in 1983 spelled the end of the band. In 1990 they re-formed on a permanent basis, and have continued to record new material.

STILLS, STEPHEN

Texan-born Stills (b. 1945) is best known for his work with **Buffalo Springfield**, and his association with **David Crosby**, Graham Nash and **Neil Young**. His solo career began during one of **Crosby, Stills And Nash**'s many hiatuses. Stills enlisted a team of musical heavyweights to play on his self-titled debut which reached the US Top 5 in 1970, and spawned the hit single 'Love The One You're With'. *Stephen Stills 2* was a similar success containing 'Change Partners' and a brass reworking of Buffalo Springfield's 'Bluebird'. His superbly eclectic double album with *Manassas*, and its consolidating follow-up, made Stills an immensely important figure, but ultimately he was unable to match his opening pair of albums. His nadir came in 1978 with *Thoroughfare Gap*. No official solo release came until 1984, when Stills put out the AOR-orientated *Right By You*. Since then he has continued his stop-go career with Crosby, Nash, and occasionally Young.

STING

Formerly lead singer and bass player with the **Police**, UK-born Sting's (b. Gordon Sumner, 1951) solo career began in 1982, when he starred in the film *Brimstone And Treacle*, and released a version of 'Spread A Little Happiness'. By 1985, Sting had formed a touring band, the Blue Turtles, including leading jazz figures such as Branford Marsalis (alto saxophone), Kenny Kirkland (keyboards) and Omar Hakim (drums). *Dream Of The Blue Turtles* brought him three international hits: 'If You Love Somebody Set Them Free', 'Fortress Around Your Heart' and 'Russians'. His second album included minor hits with 'We'll Be Together' and 'Fragile', although a remixed 'An Englishman In New York' belatedly hit the Top 40 in 1990. Sting returned in 1991 with the autobiographical *The Soul Cages* from which 'All This Time' was a US Top 5 hit. He continued in a similar vein with *Ten Summoner's Tales*, which contained further quality hit singles including 'If I Ever Lose My Faith In You' and 'Fields Of Gold'. 'All For Love', a collaboration with **Bryan Adams** and **Rod Stewart** for the movie *The Three Musketeers*, topped the US charts in November 1993, and reached number 2 in the UK in January 1994. A compilation set generated two new UK hits, 'When We Dance' and 'This Cowboy Song'. *Mercury Falling* was very much a marking-time album, but good enough to placate most reviewers. *Brand New Day* lacked the punch of his more recent work, but struck a chord in America where it enjoyed a long residency on the charts. Similarly low-key and slightly subdued was . . . *All This Time*, a live album recorded on the fateful 11 September 2001.

STOCK, AITKEN AND WATERMAN

Mike Stock (b. 1951), Matt Aitken (b. 1956), and Pete Waterman (b. 1947) first designed records for the thriving British disco scene, having their first hits with singles by **Dead Or Alive** ('You Spin Me Round (Like A Record)', UK number 1, 1985) and Sinitta ('So Macho', 1986). The team gained further UK number 1s in 1987 with 'Respectable' by Mel And Kim and **Rick Astley**'s 'Never Gonna Give You Up'. In that year, they released a dance single under their own names, 'Roadblock', which reached the UK Top 20. In 1988, they launched the PWL label and shifted their attention to the teenage audience. Their main vehicles were Australian soap opera stars **Kylie Minogue** and Jason Donovan. Minogue's 'I Should Be So Lucky' was the first of over a dozen Top 10 hits in four years. The formula was applied to numerous other artists but by 1991, a change of direction was apparent and the SAW team came to an end with the departure of main songwriter Aitken. Stock and Aitken became independent producers, while Waterman stayed busy as PWL branched into three new labels, PWL America, PWL Continental and PWL International. In the late 90s he found even greater success as producer of **Steps**.

STONE ROSES

Formed in 1985, this Manchester, England-based band was formed by **Ian Brown** (b. Ian George Brown, 1963; vocals), John Squire (b. 1962; guitar), Reni (b. Alan John Wren, 1964; drums), Andy Couzens (guitar) and Pete Garner (bass). By 1987 Couzens had left, and Garner followed soon after, allowing Gary 'Mani' Mounfield (b. 1962) to take over on bass. By the end of the year the foursome were packing out local venues, but finding it difficult to attract national attention. A contract with Silvertone Records in 1988 produced 'Elephant Stone', influenced by classic 60s pop. Their debut album was hailed in all quarters as a guitar/pop classic. In 1990 'One Love' reached the UK Top 10, but the media was mainly concerned with the Stone Roses' rows with their previous and present record companies. They tried to leave Silvertone, who prevented any further Stone Roses material from being released. The band eventually won their case and signed to Geffen Records, but it was not until 1995 that *Second Coming* was released. Almost inevitably, it failed to meet expectations. They also lost drummer Reni, who was replaced within weeks of its release by Robbie Maddix. Promotional gigs seemed less relaxed, and it was not too great a shock when Squire announced his departure in 1996. Brown decided to recruit new members, Aziz Ibrahim (guitar) and Nigel Ippinson (keyboards), but ultimately made the right decision in 1996 by announcing the demise of the Stone Roses.

STONE TEMPLE PILOTS

A songwriting partnership between Scott Weiland (b. 1967; vocals) and Robert DeLeo (b. 1966; bass) led to the formation of this US band, with Eric Kretz (b. 1966; drums) and DeLeo's guitarist brother Dean (b. 1961). The band started playing club shows and developed hard rock material, given an alternative edge by their varied influences. 'Sex Type Thing' deals with sexual harassment from a male viewpoint. *Core* reached the US Top 20, eventually selling over four million copies in the USA. The 1994 follow-up *Purple* debuted at US number 1. *Tiny Music . . . Songs from The Vatican Gift Shop* was powerful, but its success was tainted by Weiland being confined to a drug rehabilitation centre. By the end of 1996, he was clean and the band were back on the road, but this tour was blighted by Weiland's returning drug problems. Shortly afterwards, however, he was arrested in New York and charged with heroin possession, leading to a jail sentence. Despite their singer's incarceration, the band went ahead and released *No. 4* the following year. Following his release from jail, Weiland rejoined his colleagues to record *Shangri-La Dee Da*.

STONE, ANGIE

This gospel-trained soul singer first appeared with the mid-80s prototype female rap trio Sequence. She later appeared with **Lenny Kravitz** and **D'Angelo**, and wrote material for **Mary J. Blige**, but for all her efforts was forced to endure mundane day jobs to feed her young family. Her big break came when she was signed to Arista Records as a solo artist. *Black Diamond*, released in 1999, was a classic soul record, reminiscent of both old school singer **Gladys Knight** and contemporary neo-soul artists **Lauryn Hill** and **Erykah Badu**. *Mahogany Soul* followed in 2001.

STOOGES

The Stooges were led by James Newel Osterberg (aka Iggy Stooge and **Iggy Pop**, b. 1947). Iggy formed the Psychedelic Stooges with guitarist Ron Asheton, Scott Asheton (drums) and Dave Alexander (bass). By 1967, the group had become the Stooges and achieved a notoriety through the on stage behaviour of its uninhibited frontman. Their **John Cale**-produced debut album matched its malevolent, garage-band sneer with the air of nihilism prevalent in the immediate post-summer of love era. *Funhouse* documented a contemporary live set closing with the anarchic 'LA Blues', but proved uncommercial and the Stooges were dropped by their label. A second guitarist, Bill Cheatham joined in 1970, while over the next few months two bassists, Zeke Zettner and Jimmy Recca, passed through the ranks as replacements for Dave Alexander. Cheatham was then ousted in favour of James Williamson. *Raw Power* became the Stooges' most successful release, containing 'Gimme Danger' and 'Search And Destroy'. However, the quartet – Iggy, Williamson and the Asheton brothers – were dropped from the new Mainman label for alleged drug dependence. In 1973, Scott Thurston (keyboards) was added to the line-up, but their impetus was waning. The Stooges made their final live appearance in February 1974.

STRANGLERS

In 1976, the first full line-up of the Stranglers emerged in Guildford, England, comprising Hugh Cornwell (b. 1949; vocals, guitar), Jean Jacques Burnel (b. 1952; vocals, bass), Jet Black (b. Brian Duffy, 1943; drums) and Dave Greenfield (keyboards). Their debut, '(Get A) Grip (On Yourself)' (UK number 44), displayed Cornwell's gruff vocal to strong effect. *Rattus Norvegicus*, was greeted with enthusiasm by the rock press and sold well. The women-baiting second single, 'Peaches' was banned by BBC radio, but still charted thanks to airplay for the b-side, 'Go Buddy Go'. The band subsequently compounded the felony by introducing strippers at a London concert. Journalists were treated in an even more cavalier fashion. The public kept faith, however, and ensured that the Stranglers enjoyed a run of hits over the next few years. Their cover version of the **Burt Bacharach**/Hal David standard, 'Walk On By', reached number 21 in spite of the fact that 100,000 copies of the record had already been issued gratis with *Black And White*. Equally effective was 'Duchess', which displayed the Stranglers' plaintive edge to surprising effect. Their albums also revealed a new diversity, from *The Raven* to the genuinely strange *The Meninblack*. *La Folie* spawned the band's biggest hit, 'Golden Brown', with its startling, classical-influenced harpsichord arrangement.

Their subsequent albums failed to attract serious critical attention. Perpetual derision by the press finally took its toll on Cornwell, and in 1990 he

announced his departure. The band recruited vocalist Paul Roberts (b. 1959) and guitarist John Ellis. *Stranglers In The Night* was a return to form, but still failed to recapture old glories. A second set with the band's new line-up emerged in 1995, but Cornwell's absence was felt in the unadventurous songwriting. The band celebrated their 21st anniversary with a concert at London's Royal Albert Hall, incongruously backed by a string section. Baz Warne replaced Ellis on guitar in March 2000.

STRAWBERRY ALARM CLOCK

The Strawberry Alarm Clock enjoyed a US number 1 in 1967 with 'Incense And Peppermints'. The group ñ Mark Weitz (organ), Ed King (lead guitar), Lee Freeman (rhythm guitar), Gary Lovetro (bass) and Randy Seol (drums) – added a second bassist, George Bunnell, prior to recording their debut album, which coupled hippie trappings with enchanting melodies and imaginative instrumentation. Such features were maintained on successive albums, while 'Tomorrow' and 'Sit With The Guru' continued their reign as chart contenders. Lovetro left the line-up prior to *Wake Up It's Tomorrow*, and several subsequent changes undermined the band's direction. *Good Morning Starshine* introduced a reshaped band where Jimmy Pitman (guitar) and Gene Gunnels (drums) joined Weitz and King. Although they remained together until 1971, the Strawberry Alarm Clock was unable to regain its early profile.

STRAWBS

British unit formed in 1967 by guitarists Dave Cousins (b. 1945; guitar, banjo, piano, recorder) and Tony Hooper. The founding duo added Ron Chesterman on bass prior to the arrival of singer **Sandy Denny**. *Strawbs*, featuring 'The Battle', was acclaimed by both folk and rock audiences. *Dragonfly* was less well received, prompting a realignment in the band. The original duo was joined by John Ford (b. 1948; bass, acoustic guitar) and Richard Hudson (b. 1948; drums, guitar, sitar), plus Rick Wakeman (keyboards). The Strawbs embraced electric rock with *Just A Collection Of Antiques And Curios*. Such plaudits continued on *From The Witchwood* but the pianist grew frustrated and was replaced by Derek 'Blue' Weaver (b. 1949). Despite the commercial success generated by *Grave New World*, tension mounted, and in 1972 Hooper was replaced by Dave Lambert (b. 1949). Relations between Cousins and Hudson and Ford were also deteriorating by the time 'Lay Down' and the jocular 'Part Of The Union' broke into the upper reaches of the UK charts. Cousins presided over several fluctuating line-ups and continued to record into the 80s despite a shrinking popularity. In 1987, Cousins, Hooper And Hudson reunited for the *Don't Say Goodbye* album. They continue to play together on a regular basis.

STROKES

Formed in New York City in 1999, by the end of the following year the Strokes were being hyped as the most important US rock band of the new millennium. Julian Casablancas (vocals), Nick Valensi (guitar) and Fabrizio Moretti (drums) first began playing together at prep-school in Manhattan. Film school student Albert Hammond Jnr. (guitar), the son of singer-songwriter Albert Hammond, and Nikolai Fraiture (bass) completed the line-up. The band's demo was picked up by Rough Trade Records and released in January 2001 as a three-song EP called *The Modern Age*. Despite being forced to remove a track called 'New York City Cops' from the US version of the

album, in the wake of the terrorist attacks on the World Trade Center, the band's debut *Is This It* was enthusiastically received by the music press on both sides of the Atlantic.

STYLE COUNCIL

Founded in England in 1983 by **Paul Weller** (b. 1958) and Mick Talbot (b. 1958). Weller had been lead singer of the **Jam** and his avowed aim with the Style Council was to merge his twin interests of soul music and social comment. The continuing popularity of the Jam ensured that Style Council's first four releases in 1983 were UK hits. They included the EP *Paris*, 'Speak Like A Child' and 'Long Hot Summer'. 'My Ever Changing Moods' was the first of three UK Top 10 hits in 1984 and the band's only US hit. There were continuing British hits, notably 'The Walls Come Tumbling Down' (1985), 'Have You Ever Had It Blue' and 'Wanted' (1987). Their 1988 album was less of a commercial success and by 1990, the Style Council was defunct.

STYLISTICS

Formed in 1968 by Russell Thompkins Jnr (b. 1951), Airrion Love (b. 1949), James Smith (b. 1950), Herbie Murrell (b. 1949) and James Dunn (b. 1950), US group the Stylistics' debut single, 'You're A Big Girl Now' became a national hit. A series of immaculate singles, including 'You Are Everything' (1971), 'Betcha By Golly Wow' and 'I'm Stone In Love With You' (both 1972) followed. Their style reached its apogee in 1974 with 'You Make Me Feel Brand New' (UK and US number 2). Although their American fortunes waned, the Stylistics continued to enjoy success in the UK with 'Sing Baby Sing', 'Can't Give You Anything (But My Love)' (both 1975) and '16 Bars' (1976). Ill health forced Dunn to retire in 1978. Two years later they were signed to TSOP/Philadelphia International, but problems within the company undermined the group's progress. Subsequent singles took the Stylistics into the lower reaches of the R&B chart, but their halcyon days seemed to be over.

STYX

The line-up comprised Dennis De Young (vocals, keyboards), James Young (guitar, vocals), Chuck Panozzo (bass), John Panozzo (b. 1947, d. 1996; drums) and John Curulewski (guitar). *Styx II*, originally released in 1973, spawned the US Top Ten hit 'Lady' in 1975. The album then made similar progress, eventually peaking at number 20. After signing to A&M Records in 1975, Curulewski departed with the release of *Equinox*, to be replaced by Tommy Shaw. *The Grand Illusion* was Shaw's first major success, peaking at number 6. It also featured the hit 'Sail Away'. *Pieces Of Eight* and *Cornerstone* consolidated their success, the latter containing 'Babe', the band's first US number 1 single. *Paradise Theater* was the Styx's *tour de force*, generating two further US Top 10 hits in 'The Best Of Times' and 'Too Much Time On My Hands'. *Kilroy Was Here* followed, but they disbanded shortly after the uninspired *Caught In The Act*. Styx re-formed in 1990 with the original line-up, except for pop-rock funkster Glenn Burtnick, who replaced Shaw. *Edge Of The Century* indicated that the band still had something to offer. With Shaw back on board, but without the late John Panozzo, Styx have continued on the nostalgia circuit into the new millennium.

SUEDE

This UK indie band broke through in 1993 by merging the lyrical perspective of **Morrissey** with the posturings of **David Bowie** and the glam set. Brett Anderson (b. 1967; vocals) had a rare gift for evocative mood swings and much was made of guitarist Bernard Butler's similarities to Johnny Marr (**Smiths**,

Electronic). The initial line-up also featured Matt Osman (b. 1967; bass) and Simon Gilbert (drums). 'The Drowners' arrived in 1992, and the b-side 'My Insatiable One' was a brooding low-life London tale. By this time, the mainstream music media had latched on to the band. Their appearance at the 1993 BRIT Awards gave them massive exposure and their debut album reached UK number 1. Butler left on the eve of the second album, replaced by 17-year-old 'unknown' Richard Oakes (b. 1976). In 1996, Neil Codling (keyboards) was recruited. Great pressure preceded their third album. Any fears were dispelled by *Coming Up*, a stunning collection of crafted, concise songs. In 1999, the band premiered their new album with the UK number 5 single 'Electricity'. The following month *Head Music* entered the UK album chart at number 1, although it soon dropped down. In March 2001 it was announced that Codling, who suffers from chronic fatigue syndrome, would be replaced in the line-up by Alex Lee.

SUGAR

In the aftermath of **Nirvana**'s commercial breakthrough, **Bob Mould** (b. 1960; guitar, vocals) found himself subject to the somewhat unflattering representation 'Godfather of Grunge'. With Sugar he seemed set to continue to justify the critical plaudits that have followed his every move. Joined by David Barbe (b. 1963; bass, vocals) and Malcolm Travis (b. 1953; drums), he found another powerful triumvirate. Sugar's breakthrough came with *Copper Blue* in 1992. Singles such as 'Changes' tied the band's musical muscle to a straightforward commercial skeleton. Mould responded a few months later with *Beaster* in which the melodies and hooks were buried under layers of harsh feedback. *F.U.E.L.* offered a hybrid of the approaches on the two previous albums. Afterwards, however, Mould ruminated widely about the long-term future of Sugar, suggesting inner-band tensions between the trio. They disbanded in 1995, after which Mould began a solo career.

SUGAR RAY

One of an increasing number of US bands in the 90s to combine hip-hop beats with hard rock riffs, Orange County, California-based Sugar Ray was formed by Mark McGrath (vocals), Rodney Sheppard (guitar), Murphy Karges (bass), Stan Frazier (drums). Heavily promoted by their record company on both sides of the ocean, the band have gone on to great success, charting with the memorable

Top 40 radio hit 'Fly' and three bestselling albums. *14:59* included the US number 3 hit, 'Every Morning', and the follow-up Top 10 single, 'Someday'.

SUGARCUBES

Offbeat pop band formed in Reykjavik, Iceland, in 1986. The line-up featured **Björk** Gudmundsdottir (b. 1965; vocals, keyboards), Bragi Olaffson (bass), Einar Orn Benediktsson (vocals, trumpet), Margret 'Magga' Ornolfsdottir (keyboards), Sigtryggur 'Siggi' Baldursson (drums) and Thor Eldon (guitar). After early stage appearances Björk completed her first album at the age of 11. She was also the singer for prototype groups Tappi Tikarrass then Theyr, alongside Baldursson. Björk, Einar and Siggi then went on to form Kukl, who toured Europe and released two records on Crass, establishing a link with the UK anarcho-punk scene. The Sugarcubes' debut single, 'Birthday', and album, *Life's Too Good*, saw the band championed in the UK press almost immediately. *Here Today, Tomorrow, Next Week*, was a more elaborate album. The third found them back in favour with the music press and back in the charts with 'Hit', but shortly afterwards Björk left for a rewarding solo career.

SUM 41

This Canadian pop punk quartet was formed in Ajax, Ontario in 1997 by teenagers Deryck Whibley (vocals, guitar), Steve Jocz (drums), Dave Baksh (guitar) and Cone McCaslin (b. Jay McCaslin; bass). They took their unusual moniker from the fact that they were formed 41 days into the summer. Their 2000 debut, *Half Hour Of Power*, helped establish their reputation for snappy pop melodies and puerile lyrics. *All Killer No Filler* repeated the formula, albeit with a better production sound, and was buoyed by the success of single 'Fat Lip' on US radio.

SUMMER, DONNA

US star Summer's (b. Ladonna Gaines, 1948) first records were 'Hostage' and 'Lady Of The Night' for Giorgio Moroder's Oasis label in Munich. They were local hits but it was 'Love To Love You Baby' (1975) that made her an international star. The track sold a million copies in the USA on Neil Bogart's Casablanca label. In 1977, a similar formula took 'I Feel Love' to the top of the UK chart, and 'Down Deep Inside' was a big international success. Her film debut came the next year in *Thank God It's Friday*, in which she sang another million-seller, 'Last Dance'. She achieved four more US number 1s in 1978–9. In 1980 she signed to David Geffen's new company and her work took on a more pronounced soul and gospel flavour. Some of her major US hits during the early 80s were 'On The Radio', 'The Wanderer', 'She Works Hard For The Money' and 'Love Is In Control (Finger On The Trigger)'. Summer returned in 1987 and enjoyed another hit with 'Dinner With Gershwin'. Her best-selling 1989 album for Warner Brothers was written and produced by **Stock, Aitken And Waterman** while Clivilles And Cole worked on *Love Is Gonna Change*. The 90s proved only moderately successful for her.

SUPER FURRY ANIMALS

Founded in Cardiff, Wales, indie band Super Furry Animals comprises Gruff Rhys (b. 1970; vocals, guitar), Dafydd Ieuan (b. 1969; drums), Cian Ciaran (b. 1976; electronics), Guto Pryce (b. 1972; bass) and Huw 'Bunf' Bunford (b. 1967; guitar/vocals). The first evidence of the band's distinctive, scabrous pop came with the release of the *Welsh Concept* EP. Creation Records invited them to submit some of their English-language material, resulting in a long-term development contract. Their debut album showcased their ambitions to 'push technology to the limit'. It included their debut single for Creation, 'Hometown Unicorn' and 'God! Show Me Magic'. Critical approval as well as a growing fan base confirmed their breakthrough. Further late 90s shenanigans were apparent with the lighter *Radiator* and *Guerilla*. After the collapse of Creation the band inaugurated their own record label, releasing their first Welsh-language album

in May 2000. *Rings Around The World*, their debut for Epic Records, was a wildly ambitious concept album about global communication. A DVD version, featuring specially commissioned individual film shorts, was released simultaneously.

SUPERGRASS

UK indie pop band comprising Danny Goffey (drums), Gary Coombes (vocals, guitar) and Mickey Quinn (bass). Debut single 'Caught By The Fuzz' brought them to public attention, though not before it had been released on three separate occasions. Parlophone Records re-released it in 1994, when it climbed to number 42 in the UK charts. They also toured with **Shed Seven** and supported **Blur**, before the release of a second single, 'Man Size Rooster', in early 1995. Their debut album was produced with Mystics singer Sam Williams, while the band also contributed to the Sub Pop Records Singles Club with 'Lose It'. However, all was eclipsed by the astonishing success of 'Alright', which shot to the top of the UK charts and made instant celebrities of the band. The resultant interest in Supergrass pushed *I Should Coco* to number 1 in the UK album chart. In 1997, the band rose to the pressure of producing a follow-up with *In It For The Money*. They returned in May 1999 with a punchy new single, 'Pumping On Your Stereo', taken from their self-titled third album, although ultimately this release did not enjoy the commercial success of their previous efforts.

SUPERTRAMP

Supertramp were financed by Dutch millionaire Stanley August Miesegaes, which enabled Richard Davies (b. 1944; vocals, keyboards) to recruit Roger Hodgson (b. 1950; guitar), Dave Winthrop (b. 1948; saxophone), Richard Palmer (guitar) and Bob Miller (drums). *Supertramp* was an unspectacular affair and *Indelibly Stamped* was similarly unsuccessful. The band were in dire straits when Miesegaes departed, along with Winthrop and Palmer. They recruited John Helliwell (b. 1945), Dougie Thompson (b. 1951) and Bob Benberg and had a remarkable change in fortune as *Crime Of The Century* became one of the top-selling albums of 1974. 'Dreamer' was taken from the album, while 'Bloody Well Right' was a Top 40 hit in the USA, but the subsequent *Crisis? What Crisis?* and *Even In The Quietest Moments* were lesser works. 'Give A Little Bit', with its infectious acoustic guitar introduction was a minor transatlantic hit in 1977. Supertramp were elevated to rock's first division with *Breakfast In America*. Four of the tracks became hits, 'The Logical Song', 'Take The Long Way Home', 'Goodbye Stranger' and the title track. The album stayed on top of the US charts for six weeks. The obligatory live album was followed by the R&B-influenced *Famous Last Words*. Hodgson left shortly afterwards. Supertramp's recent releases, however, have only found minor success.

SUPREMES

America's most successful female vocal group of all time was formed by four Detroit schoolgirls in the late 50s. **Diana Ross** (b. 1944), Betty Hutton, Florence Ballard (b. 1943, d. 1976) and Mary Wilson (b. 1944) issued a solitary single on a small local label, then signed to Berry Gordy's Motown Records label. When Diana Ross supplanted Florence Ballard as the group's regular lead vocalist, the Supremes broke into the US charts. 'When The Lovelight Starts Shining In His Eyes', was the group's first hit in 1963. The follow-up single flopped, but 'Where Did Our Love Go' topped the US charts and was also a hit in Britain. There followed a remarkable run of successes for the group and their producers, **Holland/Dozier/Holland**, as their next four releases – 'Baby Love', 'Come See About Me', 'Stop! In The Name Of Love' and 'Back In My Arms Again' – all topped the US singles charts. 'Nothing But Heartaches' broke the chart-topping sequence, which was immediately restored by the more ambitious 'I Hear A Symphony'. As Holland/Dozier/ Holland moved into their prime, the group's repertoire grew more mature. The hits kept coming, but behind the scenes, the group's future was in some jeopardy. Florence Ballard was unhappy with her supporting role, and she was forced out in mid-1967, replaced by Cindy Birdsong. Ross's prime position in the group's hierarchy was then confirmed in public, and in 1968 they formed a successful recording partnership with the **Temptations**, exemplified by the hit single 'I'm Gonna Make You Love Me'.

In 1969, rumours that Berry Gordy was about to launch Diana Ross on a solo career, were confirmed when the Supremes staged a farewell performance, and Ross bade goodbye to the group with the elegiac 'Someday We'll Be Together'. Ross was replaced by Jean Terrell and the new line-up found immediate success with 'Up The Ladder To The Roof' in early 1970, while 'Stoned Love' became the group's biggest UK hit for four years. Gradually, the momentum was lost, and the group finally petered out in the late 70s, although their have been occasional revivals led by former members. In 1988, the Supremes were inducted into the Rock And Roll Hall Of Fame.

SURFARIS

Formed in Glendora, California, in 1962, the Surfaris – Jim Fuller (lead guitar), Jim Pash (guitar), Bob Berryhill (guitar), Pat Connolly (bass) and Ron Wilson (drums) – achieved international success with 'Wipe Out', now recognised as one of the definitive surfing anthems. *Hit City '64* introduced a partnership with producer Gary Usher, who employed a team of experienced session musicians on ensuing Surfaris releases. In 1965 the group turned to folk rock. Wilson had become an accomplished lead singer and with Ken Forssi replacing Connolly on bass, the Surfaris completed the promising *It Ain't Me Babe*. However, Usher then severed his relationship with the band and they broke up when Jim Pash left the line-up. The Surfaris name was resurrected in 1981 for live performances.

SUTHERLAND BROTHERS (AND QUIVER)

Basically a duo from the outset, comprising Scottish brothers Iain (b. 1948; vocals, guitar, keyboards) and Gavin Sutherland (b. 1951; bass, guitar, vocals). They had been signed to Island Records, releasing *The Sutherland Brothers Band* in 1972. The Sutherland Brothers needed a band, and Quiver needed new songs, so the Sutherland Brothers And Quiver were born, comprising Iain and Gavin, Tim Renwick (b. 1949; guitar, vocals, flute), Willie Wilson (b. John Wilson, 1947; drums, vocals, percussion), Bruce Thomas (b. 1948; bass), Cal Batchelor (vocals, guitar, keyboards), and Pete Wood (d. 1994; keyboards). Within a few months they released *Lifeboat*. After recording, Cal Batchelor left. Bruce Thomas departed shortly after *Dream Kid*, and further personnel changed undermined the band's progress. Gavin Sutherland later worked as a music writer.

SWAN, BILLY

US-born Swan (b. 1942) grew up listening to country stars and 50s rock 'n' rollers. At the age of 16, he wrote 'Lover Please', which **Elvis Presley**'s bass player, **Bill Black**, recorded with his Combo in 1960. Swan later moved to Memphis to write for Bill Black's Combo. He also worked as a janitor at Columbia's studios. He quit while **Bob Dylan** was recording *Blonde On Blonde*, offering his job to **Kris Kristofferson** who was looking for work. Swan worked as a roadie before meeting Tony Joe White and producing demos of his 'swamp rock' including *Black And White*. Swan then joined Kinky Friedman in the Texas Jewboys. Shortly afterwards, producer Chip Young invited him to record for Monument. The first single was a revival of **Hank Williams**' 'Wedding Bells', followed by 'I Can Help' (US number 1). The subsequent album was a cheerful affair, and included the single 'I'm Her Fool'.

In 1975, Elvis Presley recorded a version of 'I Can Help', which became a UK hit in 1983. Billy Swan released three more albums for Monument and then one each for A&M and Epic, but failed to recapture the overall quality of his first. Swan and Kristofferson co-wrote 'Nobody Loves Anybody Anymore' on Kristofferson's *To The Bone* and Swan also played on albums by **Harry Chapin** among others. He worked briefly with Randy Meisner of the **Eagles** in a country rock band, Black Tie, releasing *When The Night Falls* in 1986. Since then, Swan has continued to tour with Kristofferson.

SWEAT, KEITH

A veteran of contemporary R&B, Sweat (b. Keith 'Sabu' Crier, 1961) has presided over a musical style that has evolved enormously since his double-platinum debut album, *Make It Last Forever*, was released in 1987. In the 90s Sweat established his own Keia Productions management agency and constructed the Sweat Shop recording studio in his home base of Atlanta, Georgia. In 1997 he joined with **Gerald LeVert** and Johnny Gill for the 'soul supergroup' album, *Levert Sweat Gill*. The Top 10 solo set, *Still In The Game*, maintained his strong commercial profile. The album included the hit single 'Come And Get With Me', featuring **Snoop Doggy Dogg**.

SWEET

Mick Tucker (b. 1949, d. 2002) and vocalist Brian Connolly (b. 1945, d. 1997), formed Sweetshop, later shortened to Sweet, with Steve Priest (b. 1950; bass) and Frank Torpey (guitar). After releasing four unsuccessful singles on Fontana and EMI, Torpey was replaced by Andy Scott (b. 1951) and the new line-up signed to RCA Records. The band were introduced to the writing partnership of Chinn And Chapman, and their initial success was down to bubblegum pop anthems such as 'Funny, Funny', 'Co-Co', 'Poppa Joe' and 'Little Willy'. However, the band were writing their own hard-rock numbers on the b-sides of these hits. Sweet decided to take greater control of their own destiny in 1974, and recorded the album *Sweet Fanny Adams* without the assistance of Chinn and Chapman. The album charted at number 27, but disappeared again after just two weeks. 'Set Me Free', 'Restless' and 'Sweet F.A.' epitomized their no-frills hard-rock style. *Desolation Boulevard* included the self-penned 'Fox On The Run' (UK number 2). However, the hit singles began to dry up; 1978's 'Love Is Like Oxygen' being their last Top 10 hit. Following a move to Polydor Records, they cut four albums with each release making less impact than its predecessor. Since

1982, various incarnations of the band have appeared from time to time, although both Connolly and Tucker have now passed away.

SWEET, MATTHEW

Before the critical success of 1992's *Girlfriend*, US-born Sweet (b. 1964) had been best known for his work in the late 80s with the Golden Palominos. *Inside*, his debut solo album under his own name, followed in 1986 and featured contributions from the **Bangles** and Chris Stamey. *Son Of Altered Beast* remixed the best track from *Altered Beast*, 'Devil With The Green Eyes', and added five live tracks. *100% Fun* and *Blue Sky On Mars* were both crammed with appealing hooks, but none with the mark of 'a truly great pop song'. *In Reverse* was a sumptuous follow-up that was his finest album since *Girlfriend*.

SWINGING BLUE JEANS

Liverpool skiffle group founded in 1958, comprising singer and lead guitarist Ray Ennis (b. 1942), rhythm guitarist Ray Ellis (b. 1942), bass player Les Braid (b. 1941), drummer Norman Kuhlke (b. 1942) and Paul Moss (banjo). They signed with EMI's HMV label and had a minor hit with 'It's Too Late Now', but it was the group's third single, 'Hippy Hippy Shake', that provided their biggest success (number 2). Their version of 'Good Golly Miss Molly' peaked at number 11, while the reflective rendition of Betty Everett's 'You're No Good' reached number 3. It was, however, the quartet's last substantial hit. Several personnel changes ensued, including the induction of two former Escorts, Terry Sylvester and Mike Gregory, but this did not make any difference to their fortunes. The revival of interest in 60s music persuaded Ennis to re-form the group for the nostalgia circuit.

SWV

Acronym for Sisters With Voices, this US urban R&B trio comprised the talents of Coko (b. Cheryl Gamble), Taj (b. Tamara Johnson) and Lelee (b. Leanne Lyons). Their 1993 debut also encompassed both rap and *a cappella* vocal stylings, and included three massive crossover US hit singles, 'I'm So Into You' (number 6), the chart-topping 'Weak' and 'Right Here'/'Human Nature' (number 2). Nominated for a Grammy in 1995 they repeated the formula with *A New Beginning* and *Release Some Tension*. The trio broke up in 1998, with Coko releasing her solo debut the following year.

SYSTEM OF A DOWN

This Los Angeles, California, USA-based alternative metal band comprises three members of Armenian heritage, Serj Tankian (vocals), Daron Malakian (guitar) and Shavo Odadjian (bass), and John Dolmayan (drums). Tankian, Malakian and Odadjian first played together in 1993 as Soil, renaming themselves System Of A Down, from a poem by Malakian, in 1995. The band's heady fusion of alternative metal and programmed beats was augmented by subtle Eastern European influences and a highly political lyrical agenda. They confirmed their status as one of the leading rock acts of the new millennium with *Toxicity*.

T. REX

Originally known as Tyrannosaurus Rex, this UK band was formed by Londoner **Marc Bolan** (b. Mark Feld, 1947, d. 1977; vocals, guitar) with Steve 'Peregrine' Took (b. 1949, d. 1980; percussion) in 1967. 'Debora', their debut single, broached the UK Top 40, while a follow-up, 'One Inch Rock', reached number 28, but Tyrannosaurus Rex found a wider audience with their quirky albums, *My People Were Fair And Had Sky In Their Hair But Now They're Content To Wear Stars On Their Brows* and *Prophets, Seers, Sages, The Angels Of The Ages*. *Unicorn* introduced a much fuller sound as Tyrannosaurus Rex found a wider popularity. Long-time producer Tony Visconti (b. 1944) emphasized the supporting instruments – organ, harmonium, bass guitar and drum kit. Took left in 1970 and was replaced by Mickey Finn (b. 1947). *A Beard Of Stars* completed the transformation into a fully-fledged electric group. The duo's name was truncated to T. Rex in 1970. Commercial success was established by 'Ride A White Swan', which hit number 2. Steve Currie (b. 1947, d. 1981; bass) and Bill (Fifield) Legend (b. 1944; drums), were added to the line-up for 'Hot Love', 'Get It On', and the album *Electric Warrior*, all of which topped the charts. The renamed 'Bang A Gong (Get It On)' provided Bolan with his only US Top 10 single. A series of big hits followed and a documentary, *Born To Boogie*, captured this frenetic period, but by 1973 their success was waning. Bolan's relationship with Visconti was severed following 'Truck On (Tyke)' and a tired predictability crept into the singer's work. Changes were made to the line-up, including American soul singer Gloria Jones, Herbie Flowers (bass) and Tony Newman (drums). Tragically, however, on 16 September 1977, Marc Bolan was killed in a car accident. His death was followed by those of Took and Currie.

TAJ MAHAL

The son of a West Indian jazz arranger, Taj Mahal (b. Henry Saint Clair Fredericks, 1940) developed his early interest in black music by studying its origins while at the University of Massachusetts. After graduating with a BA in Agriculture, he began performing in Boston clubs, before moving to the west coast in 1965. The artist was a founder-memeber of the legendary Rising Sons, a respected folk-rock group that also included guitarist **Ry Cooder** and **Spirit** drummer Ed Cassidy. Mahal's 1968 debut album was a powerful compendium of electrified country blues. A similarly styled second album, *The Natch'l Blues*, was followed by *Giant Step/De Ole Folks At Home*, a double album comprising a traditional-styled acoustic album and rock selection. His pursuit of ethnic styles resulted in the African-American persuasion of *Happy Just To Be Like I Am* and the West Indian influence of *Mo' Roots*. Mahal has maintained his chameleon-like quality over a succession of cultured releases during the subsequent decades. He has also branched out into composing movie and television scores, and has recorded albums of children's music. He remains a popular live attraction, performing with a fluctuating backing group, known initially as the Intergalactic Soul Messengers, then later as the International Rhythm Band. In the 90's, Mahal's music veered more closely towards soul and R&B. His interpretations of 'Doc Pomus', 'Lonely Avenue' and the **Dave Bartholomew/Fats Domino** classic 'Let the Four Winds Blow' were particularly noteworthy on *Phantom Blues*.

TAKE THAT

Formed in Manchester, England, Take That comprised vocalists Gary Barlow (b. 1971), Mark Anthony Owen (b. 1972), Howard Paul Donald (b. 1968), Jason Thomas Orange (b. 1970) and **Robbie Williams** (b. 1974). The band released its debut single, 'Do What U Like' in 1991. 1992 brought a cover of the Tavares' 'It Only Takes A Minute' which reached number 7 and founded a fanatical following. The ensuing album *Take That And Party* debuted at UK number 5. The *A Million Love Songs* EP, led by its powerful title-track also reached number7. By the following year the group's debut album had climbed up to UK number 2, following their successful cover of **Barry Manilow**'s 'Could It Be Magic'. 'Pray' became their first UK number 1 in 1993, a feat repeated with 'Relight My Fire', featuring a guest appearance from **Lulu**. *Everything Changes* debuted at UK number 1 and the group's huge success continued throughout 1994. 'Everything Changes', 'Sure', 'Back For Good' and 'Never Forget' earned them four more UK number 1 placings. 'Back For Good' demonstrated much more substance than their usual lightweight pop, and was also a US Top 10 hit. Fans were shocked when Williams announced his departure for a solo career in 1995. It was confirmed in 1996 that the band were going their separate ways.

TALK TALK

Formed in 1981 by Mark Hollis (b. 1955; vocals), Lee Harris (drums), Paul Webb (bass) and Simon Brenner (keyboards). This UK group enjoyed a number of early hit singles including, 'Talk Talk', 'It's My Life' and 'Today'. Keen to lose their 'new romantic' image, Hollis spent a couple of years writing new material: the experimental *The Colour Of Spring* and *Spirit Of Eden* showed their true musical preferences, but their poor showing led to EMI Records dropping the band. A greatest hits compilation was issued giving them three more hit singles. Hollis broke his musical silence in 1997 with an astonishing solo album.

TALKING HEADS

After graduating from the Rhode Island School of Design, students **David Byrne** (b. 1952; vocals, guitar), Chris Frantz (b. Charlton Christopher Frantz, 1951; drums) and Tina Weymouth (b. Martina Weymouth, 1950; bass) relocated to New York and formed Talking Heads in 1975. Sire Records eventually signed the group and early in 1976 the line-up was expanded to include pianist Jerry Harrison (b. Jeremiah Harrison, 1949). *Talking Heads '77* was an exhilarating first album; the highlight of the set was the insistent 'Psycho Killer'. **Brian Eno** produced *More Songs About Buildings And Food* and his services were retained for *Fear Of Music*, which included the popular 'Life During Wartime'. During the early 80s, the group's extra-curricular activities increased and while Byrne explored ballet on *The Catherine Wheel*, Frantz and Weymouth found success with their spin-off project, Tom Tom Club. The live double *The Name Of This Band Is Talking Heads* served as a stopgap until *Speaking In Tongues*. *Little Creatures* was a more accessible offering providing three strong singles, including their biggest UK hit 'Road To Nowhere'. In 1986, Byrne moved into movies with *True Stories*, for which Talking Heads provided the soundtrack; it was two more years before the group re-convened for their final album *Naked*.

In 1996, Weymouth, Frantz and Harrison launched the Heads. The original Talking Heads buried the hatchet for long enough to perform at their inauguration into the Rock And Roll Hall Of Fame in March 2002.

TANGERINE DREAM

Since this German band's formation in 1968, it has been led by Edgar Froese (b. 1944; guitar). He was joined by Volker Hombach (flute, violin), Kurt Herkenber (bass) and Lanse Hapshash (drums), but they split the following year. Froese recruited Steve Jollife (electric flute), who left soon after, only to rejoin later. Konrad Schnitzler and Klaus Schulze (b. 1947) were added for their debut album. Jazz drummer Christoph Franke and organist Steve Schroyder joined in 1973. This line-up recorded *Alpha Centauri*. Peter Baumann replaced Schroyder, and this became the band's first stable line-up, staying together until 1977.

Zeit incorporated new synthesizer technology, while *Atem* focused on atmospheric, restrained passages. *Phaedra* established their biggest foothold in the UK market, but then their attentions turned to a series of film soundtracks. *Stratosfear* was their most commercial album so far. Baumann was replaced by former member Jollife, and drummer Klaus Krieger also joined. *Cyclone* featured vocals and lyrics for the first time, although they returned to instrumental work with *Force Majeure*. In 1985 Schmoelling departed and was replaced by classically trained Paul Haslinger. Three years later Chris Franke, after 17 years service, also left for a solo career. Ralf Wadephal took his place but when he left, Froese and Haslinger elected to continue as a duo until the latter was replaced by the former's son, Jerome, in 1991. The father and son partnership has continued to work at a prolific rate, issuing remixed versions of old recordings alongside new material on their own TDI label.

TASTE

Taste was formed in Cork, Eire in 1966 when Eric Kittringham (bass) and Norman Damery (drums) joined guitarist **Rory Gallagher** (b. 1949, d. 1995). In 1968, Gallagher replaced the original rhythm section with Charlie McCracken (bass) and John Wilson (ex-**Them**) on drums. *Taste*, was one of the era's most popular releases, featuring 'Same Old Story' and 'Sugar Mama' and *On The Boards* was another commercial success. The unit broke up in 1970 following arguments between Gallagher and his colleagues. The guitarist then began a fruitful solo career until his death in 1995.

TATE, HOWARD

A former member of the Gainors with Garnet Mimms, US-born Tate (b. 1943) also sang with Bill Doggett's band. A solo act by 1962, Howard secured four US R&B hits between 1966 and 1968. Tate's work provided material for several acts, most notably **Janis Joplin**, who recorded 'Get It While You Can'. After releasing two singles in 1969 and 1970, Tate moved to Atlantic Records. From there he moved on to various other labels, but with little success.

TAYLOR, JAMES

James Taylor (b. 1948), the epitome of the American singer-songwriter, was frail and troubled from an early age, suffering from mental problems and heroin addiction by the age of 18. He travelled to London, where he signed to Apple Records. *James Taylor* was not a success, despite classic songs like 'Carolina On My Mind' and 'Something In The Way She Moves'. Taylor secured a deal with Warner Brothers Records and released *Sweet Baby James*. The album eventually spent two years in the US charts. The follow-up *Mud Slide Slim And The Blue Horizon* consolidated the previous success and contained

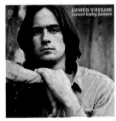

the definitive reading of **Carole King**'s 'You've Got a Friend'. In 1972, now free of drugs, Taylor worked with the **Beach Boys**' Dennis Wilson on the movie *Two Lane Blacktop* and released *One Man Dog* which contained another hit 'Don't Let Me Be Lonely Tonight'. Taylor married **Carly Simon** and they duetted on 'Mockingbird' which made the US Top 5 in 1974.

Ironically most of his subsequent hits were non-originals: **Holland Dozier Holland**'s 'How Sweet It Is', Otis Blackwell's 'Handy Man', Goffin And King's 'Up On The Roof'. In recent years Taylor has continued to add his harmony vocals to all and sundry as a session singer, in addition to regularly touring. *Hourglass* in 1997 was well received by critics, and received a Grammy Award.

TAYLOR, JOHNNIE

Taylor (b. 1938) surfaced as part of several American gospel groups. From there he joined the Soul Stirrers, replacing **Sam Cooke**. Taylor switched to secular music in 1961. In 1965, he signed with Stax Records and had several R&B hits before 'Who's Making Love' (1968) reached Billboard's Top 5. 'Disco Lady' (1976) was the first single to be certified platinum by the RIAA, but although subsequent releases reached the R&B chart they fared less well with the wider audience. *This Is The Night* (1984), reaffirmed his gritty, blues-edged approach, a feature consolidated on *Wall To Wall*, *Lover Boy* and *Crazy 'Bout You*. In 1996, Taylor experienced something of a revival when his Malaco album *Good Love!* became a huge hit and reached the top of the Billboard blues chart.

TEARDROP EXPLODES

This Liverpool, England-based band, assembled by vocalist **Julian Cope** (b. 1957), emerged in late 1978 with a line-up featuring Cope, Michael Finkler (guitar), Paul Simpson (keyboards) and Gary Dwyer (drums). They signed to Zoo and issued several singles; 'Treason (It's Just A Story)' was unlucky not to chart. The release of *Kilimanjaro* displayed the band as one of the most inventive and intriguing of their era. A repromoted/remixed version of 'Treason' belatedly charted, as did 'Passionate Friend'. In 1981, Cope recruited new members including Alfie Agius and Troy Tate. *Wilder* further displayed Cope's talent, but in 1984 he embarked on an erratic solo career.

TEARS FOR FEARS

UK schoolfriends Roland Orzabal (b. 1961) and Curt Smith (b. 1961) formed Tears For Fears after they had spent their teenage years in groups together. Their third single, 'Mad World', made UK number 3 in 1982 and *The Hurting* topped the UK charts. By *Songs From The Big Chair*, Orzabal was handling most of the vocal duties and had taken on the role of chief songwriter. 'Shout' and 'Everybody Wants To Rule The World' were number 1 hits in the US. In 1989, after a four-year break, they released *The Seeds Of Love*. Both the album and the title single were Top 10 hits in the US, but did not receive the same approval in the UK. Smith left the band in the early 90s to begin a solo career. Retaining the name of the band, Orzabal released *Elemental*, the first album after Smith's departure. A muted response greeted *Raoul And The Kings Of Spain* in 1995, and by the new millennium Orzabal had begun working with Smith again.

TEENAGE FANCLUB

Scotland-based Teenage Fanclub originally comprised Norman Blake (b. 1965; guitar, vocals), Raymond McGinley (b. 1964; guitar, vocals), Francis MacDonald (b. 1970; drums) and Gerard Love (b. 1967; bass, vocals). Shortly afterwards, MacDonald made way for Brendan O'Hare (b. 1970). Teenage Fanclub stamped their mark on 1990 with a series of drunken live shows and the erratic rock debut *A Catholic Education*. 1991's *Bandwagonesque* suggested a band ready to outgrow their humble independent origins, but a sense of disappointment accompanied the release of *Thirteen*. The majestic power pop classic *Grand Prix* saw the introduction of new drummer Paul Quinn. The

follow-up *Songs From Northern Britain* contained some of their finest moments. They signed to Columbia Records for 2000's *Howdy!*, but their next project was a collaboration with maverick US performer Jad Fair.

TELEVISION

Lead guitarist/vocalist **Tom Verlaine** (b. Thomas Miller, 1949) worked with bassist **Richard Hell** (b. Richard Meyers, 1949) and drummer Billy Ficca as the Neon Boys. In 1973, they recruited rhythm guitarist Richard Lloyd and reunited as Television. In 1974 they were at the forefront of New York's new wave explosion. Hell was replaced by bass player Fred Smith. The new line-up recorded *Marquee Moon* – it was largely ignored in their homeland, but elicited ecstatic reviews in the UK. Adventure was a lesser work and the group broke up in 1978. In 1991, Verlaine, Lloyd, Smith and Ficca revived Television and rehearsed for a comeback album. They returned to Britain and appeared at the 1992 Glastonbury Festival. They re-formed once again in 2001 for live dates.

TEMPTATIONS

Formed in 1961 in Detroit, Michigan, USA, the Temptations were made up of Eddie Kendricks (b. 1939) and Paul Williams (b. 1939, d. 1973) who both sang with the Primes, Melvin Franklin (b. David English, 1942, d. 1995), Eldridge Bryant and Otis Williams (b. Otis Miles 1941) who came from the Distants. Berry Gordy signed them to Motown Records in 1961 and the group's classic line-up was established in 1963, when Bryant was replaced by David Ruffin (b. 1941, d. 1991). 'The Way You Do The Things You Do' was the Temptations' first major hit, a simple rhythm number featuring a typically cunning series of lyrical images. 'My Girl' in 1965, the group's first US number 1, brought Ruffin's vocals to the fore for the first time. 'Get Ready' embodied all the excitement of the Motown rhythm factory, blending an irresistible melody with a stunning vocal arrangement. Norman Whitfield became the Temptations' producer in 1966 and introduced a new rawness into their sound.

The peak of Whitfield's initial phase with the group was 'I Wish It Would Rain'. The record gave the Temptations their sixth R&B number 1 in three years. It also marked the end of an era, as David Ruffin elected to leave for a solo career. He was replaced by ex-Contour Dennis Edwards (b. 1943). Over the next four years, Whitfield and the Temptations pioneered the concept of psychedelic soul. 'Runaway Child, Running Wild' examined the problems of teenage rebellion; 'I Can't Get Next To You' reflected the fragmentation of personal relationships (and topped the US charts with the group's second number 1 hit); and 'Ball Of Confusion' bemoaned the disintegrating fabric of American society. The new direction alarmed Eddie Kendricks, who left in 1971, after another US number 1, 'Just My Imagination'. He was replaced first by Richard Owens, then in 1971 by Damon Harris. This line-up recorded the 1972 number 1, 'Papa Was A Rolling Stone', which remains one of Motown's finest achievements.

After that, everything was an anti-climax. Paul Williams left the group in 1971, to be replaced by Richard Street. Whitfield's partnership with Strong was broken the same year, and although he continued to rework the 'Papa Was A Rolling Stone' formula, the commercial and artistic returns were smaller. The Temptations still had hits, and 'Masterpiece', 'Let Your Hair Down' (both 1973) and 'Happy People' (1975) all topped the soul charts; but they were no longer a leading creative force in black music. Williams was the sole remaining founder member left on 1998's *Phoenix Rising*, astonishingly their first platinum album.

10,000 MANIACS

This US group was formed by vocalist **Natalie Merchant** (b. 1963) and backed by John Lombardo (guitar), Robert Buck (b. 1958,

d. 2000; guitar), Dennis Drew (keyboards) and Steven Gustafson (bass). The group started playing together in 1981, with drummer Jerome Augustyniak added to the line-up shortly afterwards. They were signed to Elektra Records in 1985 and after a UK tour recorded *The Wishing Chair*, following which Lombardo departed. Peter Asher produced the popular *In My Tribe* and *Blind Man's Zoo*. *Our Time In Eden*, included the lilting 'Noah's Dove' and the punchy 'Few And Far Between'. In 1993, Merchant departed to pursue her solo career. 10,000 Maniacs persevered by recruiting former member John Lombardo and new lead singer Mary Ramsey. This line-up recorded two pleasant but unremarkable folk rock collections before Buck succumbed to liver disease in December 2000.

10CC

Experienced UK musicians Eric Stewart (b. 1945; vocals, guitar, keyboards), Lol Creme (b. Lawrence Creme, 1947; vocals, guitar, keyboards), Kevin Godley (b. 1945; vocals, drums) and Graham Gouldman (b. 1946; vocals, bass) formed 10cc in 1970 and launched their recording career with 'Donna'. The song reached UK number 2, spearheading a run which continued almost uninterrupted until the end of the decade. The chart-topping 'Rubber Bullets', the high school romp 'The Dean And I', the sardonic 'Wall Street Shuffle', zestful 'Silly Love' and mock-philosophical 'Life Is A Minestrone' were all delightful slices of 70s pop. In 1975, the band reached number 1 with the tragi-comic 'I'm Not In Love', but internal strife began to undermine progress. In 1976, the group split, with **Godley and Creme** striking out on their own. Stewart and Gouldman toured as 10cc with a line-up comprising Tony O'Malley (keyboards), Rick Fenn (guitar) and Stuart Tosh (drums) and charted with 'The Things We Do For Love' and 'Dreadlock Holiday'. The hits ceased after 1982 and Stewart and Gouldman went on to pursue other ventures until 1992 when the duo issued a new album as 10cc. One further album limped out before the 10cc name was put on hold once more.

TEN YEARS AFTER

Formed in Nottingham, England, the quartet of Alvin Lee (b. 1944; guitar, vocals), Chick Churchill (b. 1949; keyboards), Ric Lee (b. 1945; drums) and Leo Lyons (b. 1943; bass) played an exciting mixture of rock 'n' roll and blues. *Undead* (1968) showed that Lee was an outstanding guitarist and over the next two years they delivered four chart albums, of which *Ssssh*, was the strongest. By the time of *Rock 'N' Roll Music To The World* the band were jaded and they rested from touring to work on solo projects. When they reconvened, their spark had all but gone. After months of rumour, Lee admitted that the band had broken up. In 1989 the original band re-formed and released *About Time*. They remained active in the following decade.

TERRORVISION

This quartet from Bradford, England formed in 1986 as Spoilt Bratz, fusing rock, funk and thrash influences to great effect. Singer Tony Wright (b. 1968), guitarist Mark Yates (b. 1968), bass player Leigh Marklew (b. 1968) and drummer Shutty (b. 1967) were signed by EMI Records. *Formaldehyde* produced minor hits in 'American TV' and 'New Policy One', while 1994 saw their UK Top 30 breakthrough with 'My House'. *How To Make Friends And Influence People* entered the UK Top 20 and produced four more Top 30 singles. Terrorvision finally made the big screen with *Regular Urban Survivors*, which included the UK Top 5 single 'Perseverance'. They maintained their commercial momentum with *Shaving Peaches*, and their highest-charting UK single, 'Tequila', which reached number 2 in January 1999. Shortly afterwards, however, they left long-standing label EMI. Their new album, *Good To Go*, marked a return to the rough and ready exuberance of their earlier material, but shortly afterwards the band announced they were to split up.

TEX, JOE

Tex (b. Joseph Arrington Jnr, 1933, d. 1982) won first place in a 1954 talent contest at the Apollo and duly secured a record deal. **James Brown**'s version of 'Baby You're Right' (1962) became a US R&B number 2, and Tex was signed by Buddy Killen. In 1965, 'Hold On To What You've Got' was a US Top 5 hit. Later releases were less successful. A fallow period ended with 'I Gotcha' (1972), but Tex chose this moment to retire. He returned to music in 1975 and in 1977 he enjoyed a 'comeback' hit with 'Ain't Gonna Bump No More (With No Big Fat Woman)'. In 1982, this underrated US soul singer died following a heart attack.

TEXAS

The Scottish guitar pop band with the American name originally consisted of Italian-descended Sharleen Spiteri (vocals, guitar), Ally McErlaine (guitar), Johnny McElhone (b. 1963; bass) and Stuart Kerr (drums). The band were formed in 1986 around McElhone who formerly played bass in **Altered Images** and Hipsway, though Spiteri and McErlaine quickly became the focal point. 'I Don't Want A Lover', the very first song main songwriters Spiteri and McElhone had written together, reached the UK Top 10 in 1989. *Southside* sold over two million copies worldwide. Richard Hynd replaced Kerr on drums in 1991 and the band was also augmented by the presence of Eddie Campbell on keyboards. *Mother's Heaven* failed to repeat the success of their debut, though the band achieved their second UK Top 20 hit in 1992 with a version of **Al Green**'s 'Tired Of Being Alone'. *Ricks Road* was completed with new producer Paul Fox.

In 1997, after a lengthy hiatus, they returned in style with the UK Top 10 hit 'Say What You Want'. Their dramatic comeback continued with the remarkable UK success of *White On Blonde*, an album which demonstrated the band's mastery of a number of musical styles. The oriental-styled 'In Our Lifetime' debuted at UK number 4 in April 1999, and was followed by the chart-topping *The Hush*, another bestselling collection of note-perfect white soul. Mykie Wilson replaced Hynd shortly afterwards. The following year's compilation included several new tracks.

THAT PETROL EMOTION

This Irish band was originally formed when the O'Neill brothers – Sean (b. 1957; guitar) and Damian (b. Stephen Damian O'Neill, 1961; bass) – parted from the **Undertones**. They added Ciaran McLaughlin (b. 1962; drums), Reámann O'Gormain (b. 1961; guitar), and Seattle-born frontman Steve Mack (b. 1963; vocals). Both their pop-based debut and *Babble* were dominated by frantic guitar and Mack's wholehearted delivery. *End Of The Millenium Psychosis Blues* included the controversial ballad 'Cellophane'. Sean O'Neill elected to give family matters more prominence and returned to Derry. His brother switched to guitar with John Marchini (b. 1960) taking over on bass. *Chemicrazy* was exceptionally strong, especially on singles 'Hey Venus' and 'Sensitize'. After one more album on their own Koogat label with new bass player Brendan Kelly, the band split in 1994.

THE THE

Formed in 1979, this UK band centred on the activities of singer-songwriter Matt Johnson. Initially the line-up featured Johnson alone. The The's first single, 'Controversial Subject', was issued in 1979 by 4AD Records. Two years later, they signed with Stevo's Some Bizzare Records and released 'Cold Spell Ahead'. Johnson issued *Burning Blue Soul* for them under his own name. A projected album, *The Pornography Of Despair*, was vetoed by the

uncompromising Johnson. It was eventually replaced by the superb *Soul Mining*, one of the most critically acclaimed albums of 1983. Three years passed before the release of the compelling *Infected*, a harrowing commentary on the sexual, spiritual, political and economic malaise of 80s Britain.

In 1988, Johnson established a new version of The The featuring ex-**Smiths** guitarist Johnny Marr, bass player James Eller and drummer Dave Palmer for the bombastic *Mind Bomb*. The bizarre *Hanky Panky* saw Johnson deliver 11 cover versions of **Hank Williams**' songs to coincide with the publication of a biography on the subject. After relocating to New York, Johnson left Epic after they rejected 1997's experimental *Gun Sluts*. He returned in 2000 with the typically uncompromising *Naked Self*.

THEM

The original line-up of this Irish band – **Van Morrison** (b. George Ivan Morrison, 1945; vocals, harmonica), Billy Harrison (guitar), Eric Wrixen (keyboards), Alan Henderson (bass) and Ronnie Millings (drums) – forged an uncompromising brand of 60s R&B. They moved to London from Belfast and issued their debut single, 'Don't Start Crying Now', which flopped. Brothers Patrick and Jackie McAuley had replaced Wrixen and Millings by the time Them's second single, a version of Big Joe Williams' 'Baby Please Don't Go', reached the UK Top 10 in 1965. It was backed by the Morrison-penned 'Gloria', a paean to teenage lust hinged to a hypnotic riff. The follow-up, Bert Berns' 'Here Comes The Night', peaked at UK number 2. **Peter Bardens** (b. 1945, d. 2002) replaced Jackie McAuley for the band's excellent debut album. By the release of *Them Again*, the unit had been recast around Morrison, Henderson, Jim Armstrong (guitar), Ray Elliott (saxophone, keyboards) and John Wilson (drums). This set boasted several highlights, including a cover of **Bob Dylan**'s 'It's All Over Now, Baby Blue'. Dave Harvey then replaced Wilson, but this version of Them disintegrated in 1966 following a US tour.

Morrison began a highly prolific solo career, leaving the McAuley brothers to re-emerge with a unit known variously as Them, Them Belfast Gypsies or the Belfast Gypsies. Meanwhile, Kenny McDowell (vocals) joined Henderson, Armstrong, Elliott and Harvey in a reconstituted Them. Two further albums appeared following which Henderson maintained a new line-up for a period before retiring from music. He reunited with Harrison in 1979 to record *Shut Your Mouth*, after which the Them appellation was again laid to rest.

THERAPY?

Northern Irish hard rock unit formed by Michael McKeegan (b. 1971; bass), Andy Cairns (b. 1965; guitar, vocals) and Fyfe Ewing (drums). Their debut, 'Meat Abstract'/'Punishment Kiss', was added to new material for a mini-album, *Babyteeth*. This was followed by a second abbreviated set, *Pleasure Death*. Therapy? signed to A&M Records in 1992, and collected a much bigger budget for a new album, *Nurse*. In 1993, 'Screamager' made the UK Top 10. Almost a year later *Troublegum* was unveiled, which returned to more familiar Therapy? elements – buzzsaw guitar, harsh but persistent melodies and musical adrenalin. In 1995, *Infernal Love* offered the trademark grinding hardcore sound alongside ballads, string quartets and upbeat lyrics. Ewing was replaced by Graham Hopkins in 1996, and the band was further augmented by cellist Martin McCarrick. After a protracted absence they released *Semi-Detached*, an excellent album that returned the band to their roots. Following the collapse of the UK's A&M operation, the band returned to their independent label roots for *Suicide Pact – You First*, another powerful collection of old school metal.

THEY MIGHT BE GIANTS

John Flansburgh and John Linnell formed this New York, USA-based act in 1984, taking their name from a George C. Scott movie. With MTV picking up on their quirky visual appeal, *Lincoln* became the biggest-selling independent album of 1989 in the USA. *Flood* fine-tuned their obtuse lyrical approach; the UK hit single 'Birdhouse In Your Soul' was a beautifully crafted pop song highlighting the band's affection for the naïve charm of the 60s ballad. While *Apollo 18* brought minor hits in 'The Statue Got Me High' and 'The Guitar (The Lion Sleeps Tonight)', John Henry saw them introduce a full band for the first time. In 1995 the band contributed 'Sensurround' to the soundtrack of *Mighty Morphin Power Rangers*. In 1999, Flansburgh and Linnell attracted media attention by making their new album, *The Long Tall Weekend*, available exclusively via the Internet.

THIN LIZZY

Formed in Dublin, Eire, in 1969 by **Phil Lynott** (b. 1949, d. 1986; vocals, bass), Eric Bell (b. 1947; guitar) and Brian Downey (b. 1951; drums). After two early albums and no success, they recorded a version of the Irish traditional song, 'Whiskey In The Jar', which became a UK hit and changed their fortunes. *Vagabonds Of The Western World* cemented their reputation as a creative hard rock band and when Bell quit and rising new guitarist **Gary Moore** (b. 1952) took his place, progress seemed assured. However, Moore was not to last either. Andy Gee and John Cann floated in and out before the most successful group of Lynott, Downey, Californian Scott Gorham (b. 1951) and Brian Robertson (b. 1956) came together. They had worldwide hits in 1976 with the anthemic 'The Boys Are Back In Town' and *Jailbreak*. Problems hit when Lynott was struck down with hepatitis just before they released *Johnny The Fox*, and after when Robertson badly injured his hand in a fight and was replaced by the returning Moore. Another UK Top 20 hit followed with the scathing 'Don't Believe A Word', drawn from *Johnny The Fox*. Moore then returned to Colosseum and the recovered Robertson took his place. Both 'Dancin' In The Moonlight (It's Caught Me In The Spotlight)' and *Bad Reputation* were UK Top 10 hits and were soon followed by the excellent double album, *Live And Dangerous*.

The torturous line-up changes continued apace. Robertson left and Moore returned to help record *Black Rose*, but within a year was replaced by **Midge Ure**. The following year saw the band scaling new commercial heights with such Top 20 singles as 'Waiting For An Alibi' and 'Do Anything You Want To', plus the bestselling *Black Rose*. By late 1979, the peripatetic Ure had moved on to **Ultravox** and was replaced by Snowy White. After recording some solo work, Lynott reunited with Thin Lizzy for *Chinatown*, which included the controversial Top 10 single, 'Killer On The Loose'. The heavily promoted *Adventures Of Thin Lizzy* maintained their standing, before White bowed out on *Renegade*. He was replaced by John Sykes. One more album, *Thunder And Lightning*, followed before Lynott split up the band in the summer of 1984. Two years later he died of heart failure and pneumonia after a drugs overdose. The 90s found Brian Robertson touring with tribute band, Ain't Lizzy.

THIRD EYE BLIND

Formed in San Francisco, California, USA, contemporary rock band Third Eye Blind are led by singer-songwriter Stephan Jenkins (b. 1963). After numerous personnel changes he was joined in 1995 by Arion Salazar (b. 1970; bass), Kevin Cadogan (b. 1970; guitar) and Brad Hargreaves (b. 1971; drums).

Their first single, 'Semi-Charmed Life', became a number 1 hit on *Billboard*'s Modern Rock chart. Their self-titled debut album easily broke into the US Top 30 following its release in 1997. The band enjoyed further mainstream success when 'How's It Going To Be' reached the US Top 10 in 1998, and 'Jumper' climbed to number 5 the following January. *Blue* failed to capture the imagination of the public, and after initial strong sales quickly faded from view. Cadogan was fired from the band in January 2000, and was replaced by touring guitarist and original member Tony Fredianelli.

13TH FLOOR ELEVATORS

Formed in Texas, USA, in 1965, the original line-up of this influential psychedelic rock band included Stacy Sutherland (guitar), Benny Thurman (bass), John Ike Walton (drums) and Max Rainey (vocals). The latter was soon replaced by **Roky Erickson** (b. Roger Erkynard Erickson, 1947; vocals, guitar). Lyricist and jug player Tommy Hall (b. 1943) also joined and they changed their name from the Lingsmen to the 13th Floor Elevators. They made their recording debut with 'You're Gonna Miss Me', following which new bass player Ronnie Leatherman was recruited. *The Psychedelic Sounds Of The 13th Floor Elevators* combined off-beat spiritualism with R&B. After a brief break-up in 1967, Hall, Erickson and Sutherland regrouped to record *Easter Everywhere* with Dan Galindo (d. 2001) and Danny Thomas. Studio outtakes were overdubbed with fake applause to create *Live*, while a final collection, *Bull Of The Woods*, coupled partially completed performances with older, unissued masters. The 13th Floor Elevators disintegrated when Erickson and Sutherland were both busted for drug offences. To avoid being sent to prison, Erickson claimed to be a Martian and was committed to Rusk State Hospital for the criminally insane. Sutherland was not so lucky and was imprisoned in Huntsville, the Texas state prison. Sutherland was shot dead by his wife in 1978.

THOMPSON TWINS

Formed in 1977, the original line-up of this UK synth-pop group featured Tom Bailey (b. 1956; vocals, keyboards, percussion), Peter Dodd (b. 1953; guitar), John Roog (guitar, vocals, percussion) and drummer Chris Bell. In 1981 their line-up expanded to include Joe Leeway (b. 1955; percussion. vocals), New Zealand-born Alannah Currie (b. 1958; percussion. saxophone), and Matthew Seligman (bass, ex-**Soft Boys**). *A Product Of . . .* showed a band struggling to make the transition from stage to studio. Producer Steve Lillywhite took them in hand for *Set*, and the Bailey-penned 'In The Name Of Love' saw them achieve their first UK/US hit. Four of the band were jettisoned, leaving just Bailey, Currie and Leeway. *Quick Step & Side Kick* rose to UK number 2 in 1983. 'We Are Detective', 'Hold Me Now', 'Doctor! Doctor!' and 'You Take Me Up' put them firmly in the first division of UK pop acts, and their fourth album *Into The Gap* topped the UK charts. Leeway left at the end of 1986, leaving Bailey and Currie to carry on as a duo. Jettisoning the Thompson Twins name, they formed the dance-orientated Babble in 1994.

THOMPSON, RICHARD

Thompson (b. 1949) forged his reputation as guitarist, vocalist and composer with **Fairport Convention**. He left the band in 1971 and completed *Henry The Human Fly*. He then forged a professional partnership with his wife, Linda Peters and, as **Richard And Linda Thompson**, recorded a series of excellent albums.

The Thompsons separated in 1982, although the guitarist had completed his second solo album, the instrumental *Strict Tempo!*, the previous year. He recorded an in-concert set, *Small Town Romance*, followed by *Hand Of Kindness* and *Across The Crowded Room*. In 1986, Thompson promoted *Daring Adventures*, leading a group which included Clive Gregson and Christine Collister. He then completed the soundtrack to *The Marksman*, a BBC television series,

before joining John French, Fred Frith and Henry Kaiser for the experimental *Live, Love, Larf & Loaf*.

In 1988 he switched outlets to Capitol Records, teaming up with *Daring Adventures* producer Mitchell Froom once again to record the over-cooked *Amnesia*. Froom's production was also a problem on the 1991 follow-up *Rumor And Sigh*, although some of the material ('Read About Love', 'I Feel So Good', 'I Misunderstood', '1952 Vincent Black Lightning') was among the finest of his career. Thompson recorded with the **Golden Palominos**, and performed with **David Byrne** during the same year. The 1993 3-CD compilation *Watching The Dark* collected many unreleased live performances, and helped to put into perspective Thompson's remarkable contribution to rock music from his debut with Fairport Convention onwards.

If *Watching The Dark* was his past, the double CD set *You? Me? Us?* and *Mock Tudor* represent his future. In musical terms nothing has changed. Thompson's lyrics remain as dark and bleak as ever, and the guitar playing is exemplary as usual.

THOMPSON, RICHARD AND LINDA

This husband-and-wife folk-rock duo began performing together officially in 1972. **Richard Thompson** (b. 1949; guitar, vocals) and Linda (b. Linda Peters) began a professional, and personal, relationship, introduced on the compelling *I Want To See The Bright Lights Tonight*. A third album, *Pour Down Like Silver*, reflected the couple's growing interest in the Sufi faith. A three-year hiatus was broken by the lesser *First Light* and *Sunnyvista*. The superb *Shoot Out The Lights* was nominated by *Rolling Stone* as the best album of 1982. Their marriage disintegrated, however, and later that year the duo made their final appearance together. Richard Thompson then resumed his solo career, while Linda went on to record *One Clear Moment* in 1985.

THOROGOOD, GEORGE

US blues guitarist George Thorogood (b. 1952) formed the Destroyers in Delaware in 1973 before moving them to Boston, where they backed visiting blues stars. The Destroyers comprised Thorogood (guitar), Michael Lenn (bass) and Jeff Simon (drums), Ron Smith played guitar on-and-off to complete the quartet. Their debut album was completed with new bass player Bill Blough. The band opened for the **Rolling Stones** at several of their American gigs and continued to record throughout the 80s. In 1985 they appeared at Live Aid playing with blues legend **Albert Collins**. Thorogood and the Destroyers continued to record throughout the 90s.

3 COLOURS RED

UK hard rock band 3 Colours Red were formed in London, in 1994. Comprising Pete Vuckovic (b. 1971; vocals, bass, ex-Diamond Head), Chris McCormack (b. 1973; guitar), Ben Harding (b. 1965; guitar, ex-Senseless Things) and Keith Baxter (b. 1971; drums), their early stage show combined the earnest ferocity of garage rock with memorable pop hooklines. Their debut album *Pure*, attempted to consolidate on the modest success of their chart singles. They achieved mainstream success in 1999 when the powerful ballad 'Beautiful Day' debuted at UK

number 11. On the back of the single, *Revolt* became a considerable success. Surprisingly, the band then announced they were splitting-up, citing musical differences. Vuckovic and Baxter later teamed up in Elevation.

THREE DEGREES

This Philadelphia, USA-based group comprised Fayette Pickney, Linda Turner and Shirley Porter. They scored a US hit with their first single, 'Gee Baby (I'm Sorry)', in 1965. Sheila Ferguson and Valerie Holiday then joined the line-up in place of Turner and Porter. They shared vocals with MFSB on 'TSOP', the theme song to television's successful *Soul Train* show. This US number 1 preceded the trio's international hits, 'Year Of Decision' and 'When Will I See You Again?' (1974). 'Take Good Care Of Yourself', 'Woman In Love' and 'My Simple Heart' were later UK hits. Fêted by royalty – Prince Charles stated they were his favourite group after booking them for his 30th birthday party – the 80s saw the group resident in the UK where they were a fixture on the variety and supperclub circuit.

THREE DOG NIGHT

This US harmony rock trio formed in 1968 with a line-up comprising Danny Hutton (b. 1942), Cory Wells (b. 1942) and Chuck Negron (b. Charles Negron, 1942). They were backed by Jim Greenspoon (b. 1948; organ), Joe Schermie (b. 1948; bass), Mike Allsup (b. 1947; guitar) and Floyd Sneed (b. 1943; drums). They had 21 US Top 40 hits between 1969–75. Both **Nilsson** and **Laura Nyro** first glimpsed the Top 10 courtesy of Three Dog Night's covers of 'One' and 'Eli's Coming', respectively. The risqué 'Mama Told Me Not To Come' provided the same service for **Randy Newman** while also giving the band their first number 1 in 1970. The departure of Danny Hutton precipitated the group's decline and disbandment. During 1981, they reunited briefly with Hutton but failed to revive past glories.

THROWING MUSES

Indie-pop unit formed in Providence, Rhode Island, USA, by step-sisters Kristin Hersh (b. 1966; vocals, guitar) and Tanya Donelly (b. 1966; vocals, guitar), with Elaine Adamedes (bass) and David Narcizo (drums). Adamedes was replaced by Leslie Langston, who, in turn, was replaced by Fred Abong for 1991's *The Real Ramona*. Donelly then announced her permanent departure from the Throwing Muses, although she stayed on for the subsequent tour. After this the core of the band comprised Hersh, Narcizo and Bernard Georges (bass). This line-up recorded the critically acclaimed *Red Heaven*, but they broke up the following year. They regrouped in 1994 and released *University*. However, the poor sales of this album and the follow-up *Limbo* convinced Hersh to finally leave the band and concentrate on her solo career. Narcizo recorded ambient electronica as Lakuna.

THUNDERCLAP NEWMAN

Although singer/composer Speedy Keen (b. John Keen, 1945) wrote much of this short-lived band's material, its impact was derived from the quirky, old-fashioned image of pianist Andy Newman. Guitarist Jimmy McCulloch

(b. 1953, d. 1979) completed the original line-up responsible for 'Something In The Air', a soaring, optimistic song which hit UK number 1 in 1969. After a solitary album *Hollywood Dream* Thunderclap Newman broke up.

THUNDERS, JOHNNY

Johnny Thunders (b. John Anthony Genzale Jnr, 1952, d. 1991) first gained recognition as a member of the **New York Dolls**. Genzale, now renamed Johnny Thunders left the band in 1975 and along with drummer Jerry Nolan and **Richard Hell** formed the **Heartbreakers**. He earned a reputation for his shambling stage performances owing to an excess of drugs and alcohol. His first solo collection, *So Alone*, found him supported by many leading UK musicians. Thunders was found dead in a hotel room in New Orleans in 1991.

TIKARAM, TANITA

German-born but raised in the UK, Tikaram's (b. 1969) intense lyrics brought her instant commercial success at the age of 19. She began writing songs as a teenager and in 1987 played her first gig. *Ancient Heart* (1988) included the UK hits 'Good Tradition' and 'Twist In My Sobriety'. Most of 1989 was spent on tour before releasing her second album, *The Sweet Keeper*. Further releases failed to restore her commercial status. Following a three-year sabbatical in the mid-90s during which she acted and travelled, Tikaram returned in 1998 with a different image and an atmospheric new album, *The Cappuccino Songs*.

TIMBALAND

Timbaland (b. Tim Mosley, 1971) rapidly established himself as one of the hottest producers in contemporary US music thanks to his highly acclaimed work with hip-hop and R&B artists including **Aaliyah**, **Missy 'Misdemeanor' Elliott** and **Ginuwine**. Since the late 80s he has worked on and off with rapper Magoo, a fellow Virginian.

Timbaland's concerted efforts to break into the music business bore its first fruits with **Jodeci**, but his real breakthrough came in autumn 1996, when he worked on Aaliyah's *One In A Million*. On a roll, he then wrote and produced hits for **Ginuwine** ('Pony') and **SWV** ('Can We'), before hooking up with Elliott, his other long-term musical partner. Timbaland and Magoo's major contributions to Elliott's *Supa Dupa Fly* introduced a new sound to the record-buying public. The funky syncopated beats on the hugely popular single 'Rain (Supa Dupa Fly)' confirmed the arrival of a new southern dynamic to rival the traditional east coast/west coast hip-hop axis.

Timbaland built on his success with 1997's *Welcome To Our World*, a joint effort with Magoo. By now Timbaland was heavily in-demand as a producer, and he also worked on the soundtracks for *Can't Hardly Wait*, *Dr. Dolittle* and *Why Do Fools Fall In Love*. He contributed to **Jay-Z**'s chart-topping *Vol. 2 . . . Hard Knock Life* and, in November 1998, released his debut set *Tim's Bio*, the soundtrack to a purported movie about his life and music.

By now Timbaland's trademark sound was dominating the US mainstream, establishing him as one of the priciest producers in rap and urban music. Acclaimed work with Ginuwine and Elliott preceded a second collaboration with Magoo.

TINDERSTICKS

Formed in Nottingham, England, Tindersticks revolve around the melancholic tones of singer Stuart Staples. Dickon Hinchcliffe (violin), Dave Boulter (keyboards), Neil Fraser (guitar), Mark Colwill (bass) and Al McCauley (drums) completed the act, which was previously known as the Asphalt Ribbons. The sextet made its debut in 1992 with 'Patchwork', released on their own Tippy Toe label. Their self-titled debut album received rapturous acclaim from the UK press. The *Kathleen* EP then gave the band its first chart hit. Their second studio album featured Terry Edwards of Gallon Drunk and Carla Togerson of the Walkabouts, and a second live album was recorded with a full 28-piece orchestra. The stable line-up remained for *Curtains*.

Simple Pleasure failed to satisfy the band's new label Island Records, but was an intriguing collection which brought their previously underplayed soul influence to the fore. A cover version of the **Four Tops**' 'What Is A Man?', their first release for new label Beggars Banquet Records, was used as the theme to the highly acclaimed BBC1 series *The Sins* and preceded the excellent *Can Our Love . . . .*

TLC

Urban R&B female trio from Atlanta, Georgia, USA, formed by Lisa 'Left Eye' Lopes (b. 1971, d. 2002), Rozonda 'Chilli' Thomas (b. 1971) and T-Boz (b. Tionne Watkins, 1970). They found immediate US chart success in 1992 with 'Ain't 2 Proud 2 Beg', 'Baby-Baby-Baby' and 'What About Your Friends'. *CrazySexyCool* went quadruple platinum in America and the sublime singles 'Creep' and 'Waterfalls' topped the singles chart, but nevertheless the trio was forced to file for bankruptcy in 1995. The previous year Lopes was sentenced to five years probation for setting fire to her boyfriend's house. Ongoing contractual negotiations ensured a lengthy delay before the release of 1999's US chart-topper *Fanmail*. The single 'No Scrubs' climbed to the top of the US Hot 100, and spent several weeks in the UK Top 10. 'Unpretty' followed 'No Scrubs' to the top of the US charts in September. Lopes embarked on solo work, but was killed in a car accident in Honduras in April 2002.

TOAD THE WET SPROCKET

This US rock band was formed in the mid-80s in Santa Barbara, California, by Dean Dinning (bass, keyboards), Randy Guss (drums), Todd Nichols (guitar, vocals) and Glen Phillips (vocals, guitar, keyboards). Made for just $650, their debut album sold at local stores and gigs. It allowed them to finance the release of a second set, before signing to Columbia Records in 1988. The band's major label debut, *Fear*, followed in 1991. *Dulcinea* took its title from the love of Don Quixote's life – the idea of unattainable perfection was central to the album's concept. On 1997's *Coil* the band abandoned their pop format and went for a harder-edged sound with deeper lyrics. The following year they announced they were splitting up.

TONE-LOC

Playful US rapper (b. Anthony T. Smith, 1966) whose stage name is derived from his Spanish nickname, Antonio Loco. His debut album featured the two worldwide 1990 hits, 'Wild Thing' and 'Funky Cold Medina', both built on sparse rock samples. The songs were written by Marvin Young, aka Young MC, with 'Wild Thing' going on to become America's second biggest-selling single of all time. *Loc-ed After Dark* made the US number 1 spot, only the second rap album to do so. 'All Through The Night', the first single from his follow-up album, featured the **Brand New Heavies** in support. However, its failure to crack the Top 20 indicated a reversal in his fortunes and he moved into a more productive voiceover career.

TONY! TONI! TONÉ!

R&B trio from Oakland, California, formed by brothers Dwayne (b. 1963; lead vocals, guitar) and Raphael Wiggins (b. 1966; lead vocals, bass), and their cousin Timothy Christian (b. 1965; drums). Their name (pronounced 'Tony' on each of the three occurrences) was taken from a character they invented when they went out shopping to buy vintage clothing. The trio remained at their most successful when moving, unceremoniously, from tight, gospel-tinged harmonics to assured, laconic hip-hop, as on 1990's hit, 'It Never Rains In Southern California'. After four albums of high-quality, modern R&B the trio split-up to concentrate on solo projects. Dwayne Wiggins was the first member to release a solo album with 2000's *Eyes Never Lie*. His brother, going under the name of Raphael Saadiq, teamed up with DJ Ali Shaheed Muhammad (ex-**A Tribe Called Quest**) and Dawn Robinson (ex-**En Vogue**) in the R&B 'supergroup' Lucy Pearl.

TOOL

One of the leading US alternative metal acts to emerge in the 90s, Tool was formed in Los Angeles in 1990 by Adam Jones (guitar), Maynard James Keenan (b. James Herbert Keenan, 1964; vocals), Paul D'Amour (bass) and Danny Carey (drums). The mini-album, *Opiate*, was a powerful introduction to Tool's densely rhythmic style. Their increased confidence was evident on *Undertow*, which featured a guest vocal from **Henry Rollins** on 'Bottom'. The album reached platinum status as the band toured extensively, including a stint on the 1993 Lollapalooza tour. *Aenima*, featuring new bass player Justin Chancellor, was their most assured and most successful album, narrowly missing the top of the US album chart in November 1996. Keenan later formed **A Perfect Circle** with guitarist Billy Howerdel, who helped record *Aenima*, while continuing to play with Tool. In December 2000 the band released the limited edition *Salival*. Five months later, *Lateralus* debuted at the top of the US charts.

TOPLOADER

The retro rock sensibilities of this East Sussex, England-based quintet found a surprisingly appreciative audience on the new millennium's UK music scene. The band, formed in 1997, comprises Joseph Washbourn (b. 1975; keyboards, vocals), Dan Hipgrave (b. 1975; guitar), Matt Knight (b. 1972; bass), Rob Green (b. 1969; drums), and Julian Deane (b. 1971; guitar). The band signed to the Sony S2 label the following year. After achieving two minor UK hits in summer 1999, the soaring power ballad 'Achilles Heel' and 'Let The People Know', the band teamed up with American producer George Drakoulias to record a cover version of **King Harvest**'s 1973 US hit 'Dancing In The Moonlight'. The perfect feel-good anthem for a feel-good band, the single provided Toploader with their breakthrough UK Top 20 hit. Even better was to follow when a re-released 'Achilles Heel' broke into the Top 10. *Onka's Big Moka* was an enjoyable album, although the band adds little to the sum of their influences. On 20 August 2000 Toploader, as support for **Bon Jovi**, became the last British band to play at the original Wembley Stadium before it was rebuilt.

TORNADOS

The only serious challengers to the **Shadows** as Britain's top instrumental unit, the Tornados lasted only as long as their console svengali, independent record producer Joe Meek. Meek recruited Alan Caddy (b. 1940, d. 2000; guitar) and drummer Clem Cattini (b. 1939). George Bellamy (b. 1941; guitar) and Roger Lavern (b. Roger Jackson, 1938; keyboards) were session players while German Heinz Burt (b. 1942, d. 2000) on bass was one of Meek's own protégés. The Tornados made the big time with a second single, 'Telstar'. In 1962, it topped the domestic hit parade in the UK and the US. The following year saw 'Globetrotter', 'Robot' and 'The Ice Cream Man' all cracking the UK Top 20. The exit of Burt, coupled with the levelling blow of the beat boom and its emphasis on vocals rendered the Tornados passé. Following the departure of Cattini, the last original Tornado, there came further desperate strategies until Meek's suicide and the outfit's disbandment. Cattini has periodically revived the name with a new line-up.

TORTOISE

Experimental US band formed in Chicago, in 1990, by Douglas McCombs (bass) and John Herndon (drums). By 1994, they had recruited John McEntire (drums, vibraphone), Bundy K. Brown (bass) and Dan Bitney (percussion), and set about work on their self-titled debut album. A richly formulated collection of atmospheric collages, combining dub reggae bass, electronic, jazz, ambient and classical movements, it saw them become the toast of a number of US and UK magazines. *Rhythms, Resolutions & Clusters*, a remix project drawing principally on the debut, was released the following year. David Pajo (b. Texas, USA; ex-**Slint**) replaced Brown for the band's second album, *Millions Now Living Will Never Die*. Released early in 1996, the album fairly exploded with audacious ideas and daring experiments with song structures, epitomised by the 20-minute plus 'Djed'. *TNT* was less experimental, concentrating on meandering jazz-fusion. The following year they worked with Brazilian guitarist Tom Zé. *Standards* saw the band returning to a more compact and aggressive approach to song construction.

TOSH, PETER

Tosh (b. Winston Hubert McIntosh, 1944, d. 1987) first gained recognition in **Bob Marley**'s Wailers. He was the first to emerge from the morass of doo-wop wails and chants that constituted the Wailers' early records, recording as Peter Tosh or Peter Touch And The Wailers on 'Hoot Nanny Hoot', 'Shame And Scandal', and 'Maga Dog'. He also made records without the Wailers and with Rita Anderson, Marley's future wife.

Despite contributing 'Get Up, Stand Up' to the Wailer's *Burnin'*, Tosh quit the group in 1973. His two albums for Virgin Records (*Legalize It* and *Equal Rights*) did not sell well, but the patronage of Mick Jagger nearly gave him a chart hit with a cover of the **Temptations**' 'Don't Look Back'. His first album for the Rolling Stones label, *Bush Doctor*, sold well, but *Mystic Man* and *Wanted, Dread & Alive*, did not. Tosh also released three albums with EMI Records; the last, *No Nuclear War*, was his best since *Legalize It*. The record won the first best reggae album Grammy Award in 1988, but by then Tosh was dead, shot in a robbery at his home in Kingston.

TOTO

The Los Angeles, USA-based session team of Bobby Kimball (b. Robert Toteaux, 1947; vocals), Steve Lukather (b. 1957; guitar), David Paich (b. 1954; keyboards, vocals), Steve Porcaro (b. 1957; keyboards, vocals), David Hungate (bass) and Jeff Porcaro (b. 1954, d. 1992; drums) decided in 1978 to perform in their own right after years of supporting others on tour and disc. *Toto* was attended by a transatlantic hit in 'Hold The Line', but the band's most commercial period was 1982–3 when the Grammy Award-winning *Toto IV* spawned two international hits with 'Africa' and 'Rosanna', as well as the US Top 10 single, 'I Won't Hold You Back'. The following year, Kimball and Hungate were replaced by Dave Fergie Frederikson (b. 1951) and Mike Porcaro (b. 1955). Sales of *Isolation* and the soundtrack to the movie *Dune* were poor. With a new lead singer, Joseph Williams, Toto made the big time again with 1986's 'I'll Be Over You'. Two years later, they re-entered the US Top 30 with 'Pamela'. Jeff Porcaro died after a heart attack and his replacement on subsequent British dates was session drummer Simon Phillips. In 1995 the band released the blues-tinged *Tambu*, which attempted to steer their sound away from mainstream pop/rock. Kimball returned in 1999, although the subsequent *Mindfields* was disappointing.

TOURÉ, ALI FARKA

Mali-born guitarist Touré plays in a style uncannily close to the original Delta blues of **Robert Johnson** and his successors. This coincidence, picked up on by adventurous British world-music critics and broadcasters in the late 80s, gave him a brief flush of popularity in Europe and the USA. His career took a dramatic turn in 1994 when, after a meeting with **Ry Cooder** in 1992 they recorded the album *Talking Timbuktu* together. The result was a success musically, artistically and commercially. Touré returned to his home village to record 1999's *Niafunké*.

TOURISTS

The Tourists were notable as the first setting in which the David A. Stewart/**Annie Lennox** partnership came into the spotlight. The band grew out of an earlier duo formed by guitarist Stewart (b. 1952) with fellow Sunderland singer-songwriter Pete Coombes. They met Lennox (b. 1954), and as Catch they made one single, 'Black Blood' (1977), before re-forming as the five-strong Tourists with Jim Toomey (drums) and Eddie Chin (bass). Success came with a revival of the 1963 **Dusty Springfield** hit 'I Only Want To Be With You' (1979) and 'So Good To Be Back Home Again' (1980), which both reached the UK Top 10. *Luminous Basement* sold poorly and after a final UK tour they disbanded. Lennox and Stewart re-emerged the following year as the **Eurythmics**.

TOUSSAINT, ALLEN

Allen Toussaint (b. 1938) first came to prominence as the touring piano player with Shirley And Lee. His solo debut came in 1958 with Wild Sounds Of New Orleans, which included 'Java', later a hit single for trumpeter Al Hirt. Toussaint's 'Ooh Poo Pah Doo – Part II', was a US Top 30 hit in 1960. He then worked with Irma Thomas, Aaron Neville, Ernie K-Doe and Lee Dorsey, and formed a partnership with fellow producer Marshall Sehorn. Toussaint's solo career continued with 1971's self-titled album whose highlight was the excellent 'From A Whisper To A Scream'. *Life, Love And Faith* was uninspired, but *Southern Nights* (1975) was much stronger and featured the original version of 'What Do You Want The Girl To Do?'.

Despite his inability to master a consistent solo path, Allen's gifts as a songwriter and producer were continually in demand during the 70s. The **Band**, **Dr. John** and **Paul Simon** were only a handful of those who called upon his talents. Toussaint spent most of the 80s working as a composer and musical director for stage and film productions. His importance in New Orleans' music circles was confirmed by his involvement in 1994's *Crescent City Gold* project. In the same decade, Toussaint made a welcome return to the studios to record *Connected* and *A Taste Of New Orleans*.

TOWER OF POWER

Formed in 1967 in Oakland, California, USA, this durable funky soul group originally comprised Rufus Miller (vocals), Greg Adams (trumpet), Emilio 'Mimi' Castillo (saxophone), Steve Kupka (saxophone), Lenny Pickett (saxophone), David Padron (trumpet), Mic Gillette (horns), Willie Fulton (guitar), Francis Prestia (bass), Brent Byers (percussion) and David Garibaldi (drums). Tower Of Power's 1969 debut album, *East Bay Grease* followed several popular appearances at San Francisco's Fillmore auditorium. Their next two albums, *Bump City* and *Tower Of Power* produced a hit single each in 'You're Still A Young Man' and 'So Very Hard To Go'. Miller was then replaced, firstly by Rick Stevens and then Lenny Williams (b. 1945). Other members passing through were Chester Thompson (vocals, organ), Skip Mesquite (saxophone, flute), Ken Balzell (trumpet) and Bruce Conte (guitar, vocals). Curiously, the horn section stayed intact and was much in demand for session work, a factor that doubtlessly kept the parent group intact despite dwindling commercial fortunes. 'Don't Change Horses (In The Middle Of A Stream)' (1974) was their last US Top 30 single.

TOWNSHEND, PETE

The son of singer Betty Dennis and saxophonist Cliff Townshend, Pete (b. 1945) served his apprenticeship playing banjo in a dixieland jazz band. He joined the Detours, which also featured Roger Daltrey and John Entwistle and was a vital stepping-stone to the formation of the **Who**.

Townshend began a solo career in 1970 with contributions to *Happy Birthday*, a collection devoted to spiritual guru Meher Baba. A second set, *I Am*, appeared in 1972 and although not intended for public consumption, the albums featured material which also found its way into the Who lexicon. *Who Came First*, the guitarist's first official solo release reflected a gentler, pastoral side to the artist's work and was followed by *Rough Mix*, a collaboration with former **Small Faces** bass player **Ronnie Lane**.

Townshend subsequently founded a record label and publishing company, both named Eel Pie, and his solo work did not flourish fully until the release of *Empty Glass* in 1980. 'Let My Love Open The Door' reached the US Top 10. The abstract *All The Best Cowboys Have Chinese Eyes* was a marked disappointment. *Scoop*, a collection of home-produced demos, marked time until the release of *White City* which promised more than it fulfilled. During this period Townshend became a consultant editor at the London publishing house, Faber & Faber. He ended the 80s with *Iron Man*, a musical adaptation of Ted Hughes' children's story. In 1993, Townshend launched his new 'pop opera', *Psychoderelict*. During the remainder of the decade he worked on his revitalised 'pop opera' *Tommy*, and played with the Who. In 1999, his infamous *Lifehouse* project, extracts from which had appeared on *Who's Next* and *Who Came First*, finally saw the light of day as a BBC Radio Play. The work's vision of a future world of virtual living bore certain similarities to the Internet, a medium which Townshend actively promoted on the interactive section of the attendant *Lifehouse* box set.

TRAFFIC

Formed in 1967, this UK band comprised **Steve Winwood** (b. 1948; keyboards, guitar, bass, vocals), Chris Wood (b. 1944, d. 1983; saxophone, flute), **Jim Capaldi** (b. 1944; drums, percussion, vocals) and **Dave Mason** (b. 1945;

guitar, vocals). Their first single, the psychedelic 'Paper Sun' was an instant hit, closely followed by 'Hole In My Shoe' and the film theme 'Here We Go Round The Mulberry Bush'. Mason left at the end of an eventful year, just as the first album, *Mr. Fantasy* was released. From then on Traffic ceased to be a singles band, and built up a large following, especially in the USA. Their second album, *Traffic*, showed refinement and progression. Dave Mason had returned briefly and two of his songs were particularly memorable, 'You Can All Join In' and 'Feelin' Alright'.

Last Exit was a fragmented affair and during its recording Mason departed once more. At this point the band disintegrated. Following a brief spell as a member of **Blind Faith**, Winwood embarked on a solo project, to be called *Mad Shadows*. He enlisted the help of Wood and Capaldi, and this became Traffic once again. The resulting album was the well-received *John Barleycorn Must Die*. Ric Grech, formerly of **Family** also joined the band. In 1971, *Welcome To The Canteen* appeared with Dave Mason rejoining for a third time. Drummer Jim Gordon (from **Derek And The Dominos**) and Reebop Kwaku Baah (b. 1944, d. 1982) joined in 1971. The excellent *The Low Spark Of The High Heeled Boys* was followed by *Shoot Out At The Fantasy Factory*. The latter saw the substitution of David Hood and Roger Hawkins for Grech and Gordon. The final Traffic album was *When The Eagle Flies* in 1974, another fine collection with Rosko Gee on bass and Capaldi back behind the drum kit.

Traffic did not so much break up as fizzle out, although they did record together again when Capaldi became involved on Winwood's later solo work. Twenty years after they dissolved, the name was used again by Capaldi and Winwood. *Far From Home* was warmly received and they followed it with a major tour.

TRAIN

A **Counting Crows**-styled rock band formed in 1994 in San Francisco, USA, by Patrick Monahan (vocals, percussion), Jimmy Stafford (guitar), Rob Hotchkiss (guitar), Charlie Colin (bass) and Scott Underwood (drums). The band self-released their debut album in 1996, but soon afterwards landed a joint deal with the Chicago independent label Aware and Columbia Records. A reworked version of Train's album was released in 1998. Propelled by the success of singles 'Free' and 'Meet Virginia', the latter a tribute to independent-thinking women, the album became a slow-burn success. The follow-up *Drops Of Jupiter*, another rather ordinary collection of modern rock songs, proved equally successful on the US charts. The band earned a Grammy Award for the title track, which has become a staple of US rock radio.

TRAVELING WILBURYS

This group was formed in 1988 by accident, as **George Harrison** attempted to make a new solo album after enlisting the production talent of **Jeff Lynne**. Only **Bob Dylan**'s garage was available to rehearse in, and **Tom Petty** and **Roy Orbison** dropped by. The result was not a Harrison solo but *Handle With Care*, credited to the Traveling Wilburys. The outing proved to be a major success, bringing out the best of each artist. In particular this was a marvellous swan song for Roy Orbison who tragically died soon afterwards. *Volume 3* was released in 1990 and received similar plaudits. The band were then under pressure to tour, but they were able to resist this, leaving open the possibility of future collaboration if this were mutually convenient at some point.

TRAVERS, PAT, BAND

Canadian guitarist Pat Travers (b. 1954) worked with Peter 'Mars' Cowling (bass) and Roy Dyke (drums) on his 1976 debut. Pat Thrall (guitar) and Tommy Aldridge (drums) were recruited to work on Travers' fourth album, *Heat In The Street*. Their relationship with the band was short-lived, however. After the tour to support *Crash And Burn*, Thrall and Aldridge departed in order to work with **Ozzy Osbourne**. Subsequent recordings featured Sandy Gennaro and Michael Shrieve, and were notable for their solid, blues-like sound. In 1984 the line-up of Pat Marchino (drums), Barry Dunaway (bass), Jerry Riggs (guitar) and Travers released *Hot Shot*, an album that was not a commercial success. There was then a lengthy break in Travers' recording career until 1990 when he released *School Of Hard Knocks*. The following year Travers was working again with Thrall, Aldridge and Cowling, touring Japan along with Jerry Riggs and Scott Zymowski. After this came a series of blues-orientated albums for the Blues Bureau label, including the well-received *Blues Tracks* and *Blues Magnet*.

TRAVIS

Travis were formed in Glasgow, Scotland from the ashes of local act Glass Onion. The line-up comprises Francis Healy (vocals), Neil Primrose (drums), Andy Dunlop (guitar) and Dougie Payne (bass), the latter the last to join in 1996. A support slot for **Oasis** heralded a debut album, on which Healy's dramatic and often Lennonesque vocals drew attention away from their average songwriting. The excellent *The Man Who* built on the band's reputation as a charismatic live act. Released in May 1999 it proved to be one of the summer's surprise hit records, with 'Why Does It Always Rain On Me?' providing the band with a UK Top 10 single. A surge in sales following a hugely successful performance at the UK's V99 festival resulted in *The Man Who* finally topping the album charts and becoming one of the major successes of the year. It also inspired a new wave of UK-based acoustic rock bands, with **Coldplay** and **Starsailor** the most successful challengers to the chart dominance of urban and dance acts. Travis' difficult third album arrived in 2001 to mixed, but largely favourable reviews.

TREMELOES

When UK chart-toppers Brian Poole And The Tremeloes parted company in 1966, the relaunched Tremeloes went it alone. In 1966, the line-up comprised Rick West (b. Richard Westwood, 1943; guitar), Alan Blakely (b. 1942, d. 1995; rhythm guitar), Dave Munden (b. 1943; drums) and Alan Howard (b. 1941; bass). In 1966, Howard was replaced by Mike Clark and later Len 'Chip' Hawkes (b. 1946), whose lead vocals and boyish looks gave the group a stronger visual identity. Their third release 'Here Comes My Baby' smashed into the Top 10 on both sides of the Atlantic. The follow-up, 'Silence Is Golden', gave them their only UK number 1. Their first self-penned single, '(Call Me) Number One', reached UK number 2. Their progressive phase was encapsulated in the album *Master*, which provided a final Top 20 single, 'Me And My Life'. Thereafter, they turned increasingly to cabaret where their strong live performances were well appreciated. They were still active in the new millennium, with Munden and West joined by Joe Gillingham (keyboards, vocals) and Davey Freyer (bass, vocals).

TRICKY

Formerly of UK trip-hop crew **Massive Attack**, Tricky (b. Adrian Thaws) rapped on 'Daydreaming' and 'Five Man Army' on their Blue Lines debut. In 1993, he released his first solo single 'Aftermath', which came after informal sessions with Mark Stewart (ex-Pop Group). *Maxinquaye* was one of the critical successes of 1995, an atmospheric and unsettling record exploring the darker recesses of its creator's mind. *Nearly God* saw Tricky collaborating with guest vocalists including Björk, **Neneh Cherry** and Terry Hall. After moving to New York City he continued to pursue a busy remixing schedule while writing tracks for his second album, and even found the time to make his big-screen debut in *The Fifth Element*. *Pre-Millennium Tension* made for even more uneasy listening, but by 1998's *Angels With Dirty Faces*, however, Tricky had begun to sound like a pastiche of himself as song after song stooped further into dark isolation against a relentlessly droning musical backdrop.

The following year's *Juxtapose*, a collaboration with DJ Muggs (**Cypress Hill**) and **DMX** producer Grease, was a timely return to form. It proved to be his last release on Island Records, with whom the artist parted company at the end of the year. He subsequently signed to the hip Anti imprint of Epitaph Records and spoke candidly about being cured of a debilitating physical disease. The excellent *Blowback* was heralded as his best album since *Maxinquaye*.

TRIFFIDS

This Western Australian group was formed in 1980 by David McComb (b. 1962, d. 1999; vocals, guitar, keyboards), Jill Birt (keyboards/vocals), his brother Robert (violin, guitar, vocals), and Alsy MacDonald (b. 1961; drums, vocals). Martyn Casey (bass) and Jill Birt (keyboards, vocals) completed the line-up on 1983's *Treeless Plain*. The band's biggest success was 1986's *Born Sandy Devotional*, recorded with steel guitarist 'Evil' Graham Lee. The follow-up found the Triffids producing a collection of Australian C&W/folk-blues songs. Adam Peters (guitar) joined on

Calenture, and McComb's lyrics reached new peaks on *The Black Swan*. Disillusioned by their lack of commercial success the band split, with McComb going solo, although ill-health curtailed his musical activities and he underwent a heart transplant in 1995. His untimely death in February 1999 was apparently the result of complications following a car accident.

TROGGS

The original Troglodytes were an ill-starred early 60s band from Hampshire, England, who suddenly found themselves reduced to two members: vocalist Dave Wright and bass player Reginald Ball (b. 1943). Another local group, Ten Foot Five, featuring bass player Peter Staples (b. 1944) and guitarist Chris Britton (b. 1945), were suffering similar personnel upheavals. They amalgamated, with Ball emerging as the new lead vocalist. Wright soon moved on and the revitalized Troggs found a drummer, Ronnie Bond (b. Ronald Bullis, 1943, d. 1992). After signing with producer/manager Larry Page, and with Ball changing his name to Reg Presley, the Troggs recorded 'Lost Girl'. After switching to the Page One label, they found success with a cover of Chip Taylor's 'Wild Thing', which reached UK number 2 in 1966. The follow-up, 'With A Girl Like You', went one better. Stateside success was equally impressive with 'Wild Thing' topping the charts. While clearly at home with basic rockers like 'Give It To Me', the band also tinkered with counter-culture subject matter on 'Night Of The Long Grass' and 'Love Is All Around', and their albums also occasionally veered towards the psychedelic market.

Any hopes of sustaining their hit career were lost when they fell out with Larry Page in a High Court action. During the 70s they achieved a certain cult status thanks to the 'Troggs Tapes', a notorious bootleg recording of an abortive session, consisting mainly of a stream of swear words. They continued to record, however, and 1992's **R.E.M.**-linked *Athens Andover* took many observers by surprise. Two years later, **Wet Wet Wet**'s version of 'Love Is All Around' took up residency at the top of the UK charts. Chris Britton and Reg Presley, now an enthusiastic crop-circle investigator and UFO watcher, has kept the Troggs going as a live act.

TUBES

Never short of personnel, the Tubes comprised bass player Rick Anderson (b. 1947), Michael Cotten (b. 1950; keyboards), Prairie Prince (b. 1950; drums), Bill 'Sputnick' Spooner (b. 1949; guitar), Roger Steen (b. 1949; guitar), Re

Styles (b. 1950; dancer, vocals), Fee Waybill (b. John Waldo, 1950; vocals) and Vince Welnick (b. 1951; keyboards). Their 1975 debut album included the UK Top 30 hit 'White Punks On Dope'. The band's alleged sexism was tempered somewhat during the late 70s as they toned down their live shows in a misguided attempt to focus on their musical abilities. The band's satirical thrust declined due to over-familiarity but prior to their demise, they enjoyed their greatest commercial success with the US Top 10 hit 'She's A Beauty' in 1983. Both Spooner and Waybill released solo material, while the latter also established himself as a songwriter and actor.

Waybill, Steen, Anderson and Prince re-formed the band in 1993, recording a new album and carrying the Tubes name into the new millennium.

2PAC

The controversy-laced gangsta rapper 2Pac (b. Tupac Amaru Shakur, 1971, d. 1996) studied at the Baltimore School Of Arts, before he moved to Marin City, California with his family and began hustling on the streets. His first appearance on the hip-hop scene came with a brief spell as part of Digital Underground, but it was with his 1991 debut *2Pacalypse Now* that he announced himself as one of rap's newest talents. He gained his first crossover success in 1993 with 'I Get Around' and the platinum-selling *Strictly 4 My N.I.G.G.A.Z.*. In 1994, Shakur collaborated with his older brother Mopreme, Syke, Macadoshis and the Rated R on the short-lived Thug Life project, releasing the morbid and violent *Volume 1*. By this time his acting career was also burgeoning, following a memorable performance as Bishop in Ernest Dickerson's *Juice*. After appearing in director John Singleton's movie *Poetic Justice*, he was dropped from the same director's *Higher Learning*. Shakur took things into his own hands when he was also removed from the set of Allen Hughes' *Menace II Society* when he attacked the director, for which he received a 15-day jail sentence in February 1994. He did however, make it on to the final cut of the basketball movie *Above The Rim*.

Shakur's run-ins with the police had escalated in line with his profile as a prominent black artist. Shakur was found guilty of the sexual assault of a female fan in November 1994, but the following day (30 November) was shot and robbed in the lobby of Quad Studios in New York's Times Square. Shakur later accused Biggie Smalls (the **Notorious B.I.G.**), Andre Harrell and **Sean 'Puffy' Combs** of involvement in the shooting, directly leading to the east coast/west coast feud that would eventually result in the deaths of both the Notorious B.I.G. and Shakur himself.

Following the shooting incident, Shakur was sentenced to four and a half years in jail on 7 February 1995. The epic *Me Against The World* was released while he was serving his sentence, but still debuted at number 1 in the US charts. Meanwhile, Marion 'Suge' Knight, president of hip-hop's most successful label Death Row Records, had arranged parole for Shakur, who eventually served only eight months of his sentence. Newly signed to Death Row, Shakur released 1996's sprawling double set *All Eyez On Me*, which entered the US chart at number 1. The album sold over six million in its first year, and generated a hit single with the **Dr. Dre** duet 'California Love'. During the same year, Shakur began concentrating on his acting career again, appearing in *Bullet* and *Gridlock'd*. Further drama came when he was gunned down in Las Vegas on 8 September after watching the Mike Tyson-Bruce Seldon fight at the MGM Grand, and died five days later. The east coast/west coast rivalry continued after his death, leading to the Notorious B.I.G.'s murder in similar circumstances six months later. In a further twist, Orlando Anderson, the chief suspect in Shakur's murder, was shot dead on 29 May 1998.

Since his death Shakur's recorded legacy has generated several posthumous releases and hit singles, amid ugly squabbling over his estate.

TURNER, IKE AND TINA

This duo comprised Ike Turner (b. Izear Luster Turner Jnr, 1931) and **Tina Turner** (b. Annie Mae Bullock, 1939). Ike Turner formed his Kings Of Rhythm during the late 40s. This influential group was responsible for 'Rocket 88', a 1950 release often named as the first rock 'n' roll recording but confusingly credited to its vocalist, Jackie Brenston. This group were later augmented by a former gospel singer, Annie Mae Bullock. Originally billed as 'Little Ann', she gradually became the core of the act, particularly following her marriage to Ike in 1958. Their debut release as Ike And Tina Turner came two years later. 'A Fool In Love' preceded several excellent singles. Producer **Phil Spector** constructed his 'wall-of-sound' around Tina's impassioned voice, but the resultant single, 'River Deep –

Mountain High', was an unaccountable miss in the USA, although in the UK charts it reached the Top 3. Ike, unhappy at relinquishing the reins, took the duo elsewhere when further releases were less successful. A support slot on the **Rolling Stones**' 1969 North American tour introduced the Turners to a wider, generally white, audience. Their version of John Fogerty's 'Proud Mary' was a gold disc in 1971, while the autobiographical 'Nutbush City Limits' (1973) was also an international hit. The Turners became increasingly estranged and the couple were finally divorced in 1976.

TURNER, TINA

Turner (b. Annie Mae Bullock, 1939) was a regular performer in St. Louis' nightclubs when she was discovered by guitarist Ike Turner in 1956. She joined his group as a backing singer, before going on to enjoy hits as **Ike And Tina Turner**. Tina left their professional and personal relationship in 1975, and appeared in the film version of the **Who**'s *Tommy*.

Her career was rejuvenated in 1983 when she was invited to participate in the UK electronic project BEF; she contributed a raucous version of the **Temptations** 'Ball Of Confusion'. Her reading of **Al Green**'s 'Let's Stay Together' reached the UK Top 10, while *Private Dancer* spawned another major hit in the Grammy Award-winning 'What's Love Got To Do With It'. The title track was also a transatlantic hit. In 1984, Tina accepted a role in the movie *Mad Max Beyond Thunderdome*, whose theme 'We Don't Need Another Hero', was another international hit. Her 1985 autobiography was filmed in 1993 as *What's Love Got To Do With It*, which also gave its title to a bestselling album. She released the title track from the James Bond movie *Goldeneye* in 1995. The **Trevor Horn**-produced *Wildest Dreams* was a solid rock album, laying her strong R&B roots to history. Turner returned to the UK Top 10 in October 1999, days short of her sixtieth birthday, with 'When The Heartache Is Over'. This preceded the disappointing *Twenty Four Seven*, following which Turner announced she was retiring from live performance.

TURTLES

This Los Angeles, USA-based sextet switched from surf instrumentals to beat music during 1964 in imitation of the **Beatles**. The line-up consisted of Howard Kaylan (b. Howard Kaplan, 1947; vocals, saxophone) and Mark Volman (b. 1947; vocals, saxophone), backed by Al Nichol (b. 1945; piano, guitar), Jim Tucker (b. 1946; guitar), Chuck Portz (b. 1945; bass) and Don Murray (b. 1945, d. 1996; drums). A **Bob Dylan** cover ('It Ain't Me Babe') reached the US Top 10 in 1965. The psychedelic boom saw a change in the band's image and coincided with line-up fluctuations resulting in the induction of drummer John Barbata and successive bass players Chip Douglas and Jim Pons. The exuberant 'Happy Together' revitalized their chart fortunes, reaching number 1 in the US and also charting in the UK. The follow-up 'She'd Rather Be With Me' (US/UK Top 5) established the Turtles as pop craftsmen. The mid-tempo 'You Know What I Mean' and 'Elenore' were also impressive. The Turtles ended their hit career by returning to their folk-rock roots, courtesy of 'You Showed Me'. Volman and Kaylan later revived the band as the Turtles . . . Featuring Flo And Eddie, the names they adopted after joining the **Mothers Of Invention**.

TWAIN, SHANIA

This glamorous Canadian country-pop star (b. Eilleen Regina Edwards, 1965) grew up in the mining town of Timmins. Before her musical career began she planted trees with her Native American stepfather as part of a forest crew. Both the tragedy of her parents' death (they were both killed in an automobile accident in November 1987) and their musical legacy were explored on her 1993 debut. Elsewhere the single 'Dance With The One That Brought You', a staple of Country MTV, directed by Sean Penn, provoked comparisons with **Trisha Yearwood**. The follow-up album saw a rare non-rock outing for her producer,

songwriting partner and husband Robert 'Mutt' Lange. *The Woman In Me* was an extraordinary crossover success in the USA, not only when it was first released, but over a year later, when it went back to the top of the album charts for another six months. *Come On Over* was predominantly a pop collection, with Twain's country roots buried beneath Lange's glossy production. 'You're Still The One' was a crossover pop hit, peaking at number 2, and the album became a permanent fixture in both the US and UK Top 10. 'From This Moment On', 'That Don't Impress Me Much' and 'Man! I Feel Like A Woman' were also huge US/UK hit singles the following year, and by March 2000 the album was confirmed as both the bestselling album in country music history, and the bestselling album ever by a female artist.

TWISTED SISTER

Formed in 1976, this US heavy metal quintet originally featured Dee Snider (b. Daniel Snider, 1955; vocals), Eddie Ojeda (guitar), Mark 'The Animal' Mendoza (bass; ex-Dictators), Jay Jay French (guitar) and Tony Petri (drums). They combined sexually provocative lyrics and dumb choruses with metallic rock 'n' roll. A. J. Pero (drums) joined before the recording of their 1982 debut *Under The Blade*. *Stay Hungry* included the UK Top 20 hit 'I Am, I'm Me', but *Come Out And Play* was a flop. Pero quit and was replaced by Joey 'Seven' Franco. Snider steered the band in a more melodic direction on *Love Is For Suckers*, but they imploded in 1987. Snider went on to form Desperado, with ex-Gillan guitarist Bernie Tormé (subsequently evolving, more permanently, into Widowmaker), before finding belated success as a heavy metal DJ. Twisted Sister briefly reunited to record a new song for the 1998 movie *Strangeland*, which was written by and starred Snider.

TYLER, BONNIE

Welsh-born Tyler's (b. Gaynor Hopkins, 1951) powerful voice was a perfect vehicle for the quasi-operatic imagination of producer Jim Steinman. A throat operation in 1976 gave her voice an extra huskiness which attracted writer/producers Ronnie Scott and Steve Wolfe. Tyler successfully recorded their compositions 'Lost In France' and 'It's A Heartache', a million-seller in the USA. In 1981 Tyler was teamed with **Meat Loaf** producer Steinman. He created 'Total Eclipse Of The Heart', which reached number 1 on both sides of the Atlantic. 'Faster Than The Speed Of Night' also topped the UK charts. After duetting with Shakin' Stevens on 'A Rockin' Good Way', recording the film themes 'Holding Out For A Hero' (from *Footloose*) and 'Here She Comes' (from Giorgio Moroder's *Metropolis*), Steinman paired Tyler with **Todd Rundgren** on 'Loving You's A Dirty Job But Someone's Got To Do It' (1986). Songwriter Desmond Child was brought in to produce *Hide Your Heart* in 1988. *Bitterblue*, on the Hansa label, was a big hit in Europe. Her new contract with East West brought her together again with Jim Steinman for 1995's lacklustre *Free Spirit*.

U2

Indisputably one of the most popular rock acts in the world, Irish unit U2 began their musical career at school in Dublin back in 1977. Bono (b. Paul David Hewson, 1960; vocals), The Edge (b. David Evans, 1961; guitar), Adam Clayton (b. 1960; bass) and Larry Mullen Jnr (b. Laurence Mullen, 1961; drums) initially played as Feedback and the Hype. They came under the wing of manager Paul McGuinness and were subsequently signed to CBS Records Ireland. 'Out Of Control' (1979) propelled them to number 1 in the Irish charts. They repeated that feat with 'Another Day' (1980). Their UK debut '11 O'Clock Tick Tock', released by Island Records, was well received but failed to chart.

Boy received critical approbation, which was reinforced by the live shows that U2 were undertaking throughout the country. Bono's impassioned vocals and the band's rhythmic tightness revealed them as the most promising live unit of 1981. 'Fire' and 'Gloria' were followed by the strident *October*. In February 1983 the band reached the UK Top 10 with 'New Year's Day', a song of hope inspired by the Polish Solidarity Movement. *War* followed soon afterwards to critical plaudits, and included live favourite 'Sunday Bloody Sunday'. The live *Under A Blood Red Sky* reached number 2 in the UK, and broke into the US Top 30.

By the summer of 1984, U2 were about to enter the vanguard of the rock elite. *The Unforgettable Fire* and the attendant single, 'Pride (In The Name Of Love)', revealed a new maturity and improved their commercial and critical standing in the US charts. The band's commitment to their ideals was further underlined by their appearances at Live Aid and Ireland's Self Aid. During this same period, U2 embarked on a world tour and completed work on their next album. *The Joshua Tree* emerged in March 1987 and confirmed U2's standing,

now as one of the most popular groups in the world. The album topped both the US and UK charts and revealed a new, more expansive sound that complemented their soul-searching lyrics. The following year ended with the double-live album and film, *Rattle And Hum*. The band also belatedly scored their first UK number 1 single with the R&B-influenced 'Desire'.

In late 1991, 'The Fly' entered the UK charts at number 1, emulating the success of 'Desire'. *Achtung Baby* was an impressive work that captured the majesty of its predecessor, yet also stripped down the sound to provide a greater sense of spontaneity. Although the critics were less than generous with *Zooropa* and the dance-orientated *Pop* the band remained one of the most popular 'stadium' attractions in the world during the 90s.

In the mid-90s Bono established himself as a highly respected and shrewd political advocate for a number of causes, most particularly the singer's tireless work in helping to solve the financial and health crisis in Africa. In 1999 he joined the Jubilee 2000 (later renamed Drop The Debt) and met with Pope John Paul II, US president George W. Bush and former US president Bill Clinton among other world leaders. In 2002, he founded DATA (Debt, Aid, Trade for Africa)

In 2000, the Bono-scripted movie *The Million Dollar Hotel* was released. The soundtrack included 'The Ground Beneath Her Feet', featuring lyrics by novelist Salman Rushdie. *All That You Can't Leave Behind* eschewed the band's preoccupation with electronica to return to the epic rock sound they championed in the late 80s. The album's enduring appeal was confirmed when the band won seven Grammy awards between 2001 and 2002.

UB40

Named after the form issued to unemployed people in the UK to receive benefit, UB40 are the most long-lasting proponents of crossover reggae in the UK. The multiracial band was formed around the brothers Robin (b. 1954; guitar) and Ali Campbell (b. 1959; vocals, guitar). Other founder-members included Earl Falconer (b. 1957; bass), Mickey Virtue (b. 1957; keyboards), Brian Travers (b. 1959; saxophone), Jim Brown (b. 1957; drums), and Norman Hassan (b. 1958; percussion). Reggae toaster Astro (b. Terence Wilson, 1957) joined UB40 to record 'Food For Thought'. Their 1980 debut album, *Signing Off*, boasted an album sleeve with a 12-inch square replica of the notorious, bright yellow unemployment card. The following year, the group formed their own label, DEP International, on which they released 'One In Ten', an impassioned protest about unemployment. *Labour Of Love*, a collection of cover versions, signalled a return to the reggae mainstream and it brought UB40's first number 1 in 'Red Red Wine' (1983). The follow-up, *Geffrey Morgan* supplied the group with the Top 10 hit 'If It Happens Again'. 'I Got You Babe' (1986) was a different kind of cover version, as Ali Campbell and Chrissie Hynde of the **Pretenders** duetted on the **Sonny And Cher** hit. The same team had a further hit in 1988 with a revival of Lorna Bennett's 1969 reggae song 'Breakfast In Bed'. Promotion in the USA resulted in the single reaching the number 1 spot.

The group had further transatlantic singles success with the **Chi-Lites'** 'Homely Girl' (1989), Lord Creator's 'Kingston Town' (1990, **Bob Dylan**'s 'I'll Be Your Baby Tonight' (with **Robert Palmer**), the **Temptations'** 'The Way You Do The Things You Do', and 'I Can't Help Falling In Love With You'. In 1994 they backed Pato Banton on his worldwide hit cover version of the **Equals'** 'Baby Come Back'. In 1998 they backed various reggae 'chatters' on *UB40 Present The Dancehall Album*, recorded at Ali Campbell and Brian Travers' new Jamaican studio. *Labour Of Love III* included the band's biggest UK hit since 1993, a cover version of Johnny Osbourne's 'Come Back Darling' reaching number 10 in October 1998.

U2

Albums
The Joshua Tree (Island 1987) ★★★★
Achtung Baby (Island 1991) ★★★
All That You Can't Leave Behind (Island 2000) ★★★★
➤ p.397 for full listings
Collaborators
Brian Eno ➤ p.134
Daniel Lanois ➤ p.212
Further References
Video: *The Best Of 1980-1990* (PolyGram Music Video 1999)
Book: *U2: The Complete Encyclopedia*, Mark Chatterton
Film: *Rattle And Hum* (1988)

UB40

Albums
Labour Of Love (DEP 1983) ★★★★
UB40 (DEP 1988) ★★★★
➤ p.397 for full listings
Collaborators
Robert Palmer ➤ p.258
Pato Banton
Chrissie Hynde
Further References
Video: *Live In The New South Africa* (PMI 1995)

UFO

This UK heavy rock band formed in 1969 when Andy Parker (b. 1952; drums) joined Phil Mogg (b. 1948; vocals), Pete Way (b. 1951; bass) and Mick Bolton (b. 1950; guitar) in Hocus Pocus. With a name change to UFO, they released three albums on the Nova-Beacon label. In 1974 Bolton quit, to be replaced by Larry Wallis, followed by Bernie Marsden and finally German ace Michael Schenker (b. 1955). Schenker's presence helped to forge their new sound, and a series of strong albums followed. The band expanded to a five-piece in 1976, with the addition of a keyboard player, initially Danny Peyronel and later Paul Raymond. After long-running internal disagreements, Schenker quit in 1978 and was replaced by Paul Chapman (b. 1954). A string of uninspiring albums followed. Raymond was replaced by Neil Carter (b. 1958) in 1980, and Way left in 1982.

A farewell UK tour was undertaken in 1983, but two years later Mogg resurrected the name with Raymond and Gray, plus bass player Paul Gray (b. 1958), drummer Jim and Japanese guitarist Atomik Tommy M (b. Thomas McClendon, 1954). Success eluded this line-up, and Mogg and Way subsequently got back together, recruiting guitarist Laurence Archer (b. 1962) and drummer Clive Edwards, to record 1992's *High Stakes & Desperate Men*. In 1995 the band's 'classic line-up' (Mogg, Schenker, Way, Raymond and Parker) re-formed to record *Walk On Water*. Mogg, Way and Schenker were joined by drummer Aynsley Dunbar (b. 1946) on 2000's *Covenant*.

UGLY KID JOE

US rock band formed in California in 1989 by Whitfield Crane (vocals), Klaus Eichstadt (guitar), Mark Davis (drums), Roger Lahr (guitar) and Cordell Crockett (bass), Ugly Kid Joe made their debut with a mini-album, *As Ugly As They Wanna Be*, which was an almost instant success, on the back of the poppy transatlantic hit 'Everything About You'. Shannon Larkin (drums) and Dave Fortman (ex-Sugartooth) were brought in for *America's Least Wanted*, which produced further hits in the shape of 'Neighbor' and 'Cats In The Cradle'. Following the release of *Menace To Sobriety* the band returned to independent status, releasing *Motel California* on their own Evilution label, but split-up shortly afterwards.

UK SUBS

This London, England-based band was formed in 1976 by veteran R&B singer Charlie Harper (b. David Charles Perez, 1944). The initial line-up included Nicky Garratt (guitar), Steve Slack (bass) and Rory Lyons (drums), although the latter pair were soon replaced by Paul Slack and Pete Davies. The UK Subs specialized in shambolic sub-three-minute bursts of alcohol-driven rock 'n' roll, including the minor hit singles 'I Live In A Car', 'Stranglehold' and 'Tomorrow's

Girls'. *Crash Course* was their most successful chart, but was the last release to feature Slack and Davies. The band's line-up has rarely been stable, with only Harper surviving each new incarnation. He continues to lead the UK Subs in the new millennium.

ULTRAMAGNETIC MC'S

This New York, USA-based crew earned their reputation at the forefront of late 80s rap, pioneering the use of the sampler in hip-hop. The band comprised: Maurice Smith (aka PJ Mo Love; DJ), Keith Thornton (aka Kool Keith; lead MC), Trevor Randolph (aka TR Love; rapper) and Cedric Miller (aka Ced Gee; MC). Their 1988 debut served as a direct influence on the 'Daisy Age' rap of

subsequent acts such as **De La Soul** and **P. M. Dawn**. Following the group's split Kool Keith collaborated with the **Prodigy**, who sampled the Ultramagnetic MC's 'Give The Drummer Some', and set up his own Funky Ass label. In 1998, the original members re-formed to record a new album.

ULTRAVOX

Formed in 1974, initially as Tiger Lily, the early line-up of this UK band comprised John Foxx (b. Dennis Leigh; vocals), Steve Shears (guitar), Warren Cann (b. 1952; drums), Chris Cross (b. Christopher Allen, 1952; bass) and Billy Currie (b. 1950; keyboards, synthesizer, violin). Although their early albums made little impact on the record buying public, their influence on a growing movement of British synthesizer music was later acknowledged. Shears was replaced by Robin Simon in 1978, but after *Systems Of Romance* both Simon and main songwriter Foxx left to pursue solo careers.

Currie and Cross re-formed the band as a more pop-orientated unit with **Midge Ure** (b. James Ure, 1953; vocals, guitar). Their new direction brought minor chart success with 'Sleepwalk' and 'Passing Strangers', but in 1981 they broke through with the atmospheric 'Vienna' (number 2). A string of UK hits followed during the next three years, including 'All Stood Still' and 'The Voice' (1981), 'Reap The Wild Wind' (1982), 'We Came To Dance' (1983), 'Dancing With Tears In My Eyes' and 'Love's Great Adventure' (1984). While Ure's simultaneous solo work proved, for a short time, successful, the group projects became less cohesive as their vocalist achieved greater fame. Cann was replaced by Mark Brzezicki on 1986's *U-Vox*, but by the following year Ultravox had disbanded. Billy Currie carried on with U-Vox and then Humania, before winning a legal battle to use the Ultravox name in 1991. He teamed up with singer Tony Fennell on *Revelation*, and with Sam Blue (vocals), Vinny Burns (guitar), Gary Williams (bass), and Tony Holmes (drums) on *Ingenuity*, before resuming his solo career.

UNCLE KRACKER

Born Matt Shafer, Michigan, USA. Shafer's association with multi-platinum selling rap artist **Kid Rock** helped sales of his debut album, *Double Wide*, which enjoyed transatlantic success in 2000. The 13-year-old Shafer first met up with Kid Rock in 1987, and (as Kracker) soon became an integral part of Kid Rock's band, co-writing and performing on all his albums. *Double Wide* was recorded on Kid Rock's tour bus as it travelled America, with the aid of Rock and the Twisted Brown Trucker Band, and mined a similar rock/hip-hop groove to Kid Rock's material. The melodic 'Follow Me' reached the US and UK Top 10.

UNCLE TUPELO

Formed in Illinois, USA in 1987, Uncle Tupelo revolved around songwriters Jeff Tweedy and Jay Farrar. Primarily influenced by punk, blue-collar folk and country, they released two independent albums before a Reprise Records contract arrived in 1992. *March 16-20, 1992* and Anodyne featured cranked-up rock blow-outs alternating with **Gram Parsons**-styled laments. The band broke up in 1994 just as their marriage of bluegrass and pop was being recognized as a touchstone in the re-emergence of roots rock, with their first album giving its name to the alternative country movement of the late 90s. Tweedy teamed up with his fellow Uncle Tupelo travellers John Stirratt, Ken Coomer and Max Johnson to form **Wilco**, while drummer Mike Heidorn joined Farrar in Son Volt.

UNDERTONES

Formed in Londonderry, Northern Ireland, in 1975, this much-loved punk/pop quintet comprised Feargal Sharkey (b. Sean Feargal Sharkey, 1958; vocals), John O'Neill (b. 1957; guitar), Damian O'Neill (b. Stephen Damian O'Neill, 1961; guitar), Michael Bradley (b. 1959; bass) and Billy Doherty (b. 1958;

drums). Their debut EP, *Teenage Kicks*, was heavily promoted by the influential BBC disc jockey John Peel. The band were still without a manager, so Sharkey took on responsibility for arranging a five-year contract with Sire Records. By the spring of 1979, the band had entered the UK Top 20 with the infectious 'Jimmy Jimmy' and gained considerable acclaim for their debut album. *Hypnotised* was a more accomplished work, and featured the UK hit singles 'My Perfect Cousin' and 'Wednesday Week'. The band were released from their Sire contract, setting up their own label, Ardeck Records, licensed through EMI Records. *Positive Touch* indicated a new-found maturity, but 'It's Going To Happen!' and the gorgeous 'Julie Ocean' were only minor successes.

Following one further album, *The Sin Of Pride*, the band ended their association in June 1983. Sharkey went on to team up with Vince Clarke in the short-lived Assembly, before finding considerable success as a soloist and latterly an A&R man. The O'Neill brothers subsequently formed **That Petrol Emotion**. The Undertones re-formed on a temporary basis in the late 90s minus Sharkey, who was replaced by new singer Paul McLoon.

UNDERWORLD

Based in Romford, Essex, England, Underworld arose from the ashes of Freur in the late 80s. Two funk rock-based albums followed, before key members Karl Hyde (guitar, vocals) and Rick Smith (keyboards) brought this line-up to an abrupt end during a 1990 tour. The duo re-formed Underworld as a predominantly dance music-orientated band with DJ Darren Emerson. They had their first success in early 1993 with 'Mmm Skyscraper . . . I Love You' and later that year with 'Rez', both of which became popular with the dance fraternity. *Dubnobasswithmyheadman* mixed elements of what were unreconcilable styles including ambient, house, techno and dub with pop sensibilities. Much of the sound from this innovative album continued to have resonance in music produced into the late 90s. In 1995 they released a single 'Born Slippy', which gained mass exposure on the soundtrack to the movie *Trainspotting* and was subsequently re-issued in 1996 when it became a chart hit. *Second Toughest In The Infants*, which introduced breakbeats and elements of drum 'n' bass into the sound, was even more successful than its predecessor.

Hyde and Smith became involved with the art and design collective Tomato before returning to the studio to record 1999's *Beaucoup Fish*. The following April Emerson announced his decision to leave the band to work on solo projects.

URE, MIDGE

Scottish vocalist Ure (b. James Ure, 1953) began his professional career as guitarist/vocalist with Salvation, a popular Glasgow-based act that evolved into Slik in 1974. Despite enjoying a UK chart-topping single ('Forever And Ever'), Ure subsequently opted to join the Rich Kids, a punk/pop act, centred on former **Sex Pistols** bass player Glen Matlock. He then founded **Visage** with Steve Strange (vocals) and Rusty Egan (drums), but left to join **Ultravox**, who rose from cult status to become one of the most popular UK acts of the early 80s. In 1982, Ure enjoyed a UK Top 10 solo hit with his version of 'No Regrets'. Two years later he set up Band Aid with **Bob Geldof**. Their joint composition, the multi-million-selling 'Do They Know It's Christmas?', featured an all-star cast of pop contemporaries. Ure was also heavily involved in the running of 1985's spectacular rock concert, Live Aid. He resumed his solo career later in the same year with *The Gift*, which spawned a number 1 single, 'If I Was'. *Answers To Nothing*, recorded when Ultravox had eventually fizzled out in 1987, proved less successful. *Pure* demonstrated that Ure had not lost his touch for melody, and he returned to the UK Top 20 in 1991 with 'Cold, Cold Heart'. Although his recent work has been undistinguished and largely ignored in England, Ure continues to maintain a healthy following on the European market.

URGE OVERKILL

US alternative rock band formed in 1986 in Illinois, by National 'Nash' Kato (b. 1965; vocals), Blackie 'Black Caesar' Onassis (b. Johnny Rowan, 1967; vocals, drums) and Eddie 'King' Roeser (b. 1969; bass). Urge Overkill recorded four albums for seminal Chicago punk label Touch & Go Records, but constantly railed against their punk rock influences. *Saturation*, their major-label debut, once again revealed a much more gaudy, vaudeville and escapist outlook than other Chicago bands. Their cover version of 'Girl, You'll Be A Woman Soon' became a chart hit in 1994 as a result of its use on the soundtrack to Quentin Tarantino's *Pulp Fiction*. Roeser, who had grown increasingly dismayed by Onassis' drug problems, left the band and was replaced by Nils St. Cyr at the end of 1996, but soon afterwards the band split-up to concentrate on their own projects.

URIAH HEEP

UK heavy rock band who deserve most credit for continuing despite almost 30 personnel changes and two deaths along the way. David Byron (b. David Garrick, 1947, d. 1985; vocals) formed Uriah Heep with Mick Box (b. 1947; lead guitar, vocals) and Ken Hensley (b. 1945; guitar, keyboards, vocals). Numerous drummers came and went in the band's early days. Their debut, *Very 'eavy . . . Very 'umble*, was released in 1970. *Salisbury* was a drastic development from the debut, with many lengthy, meandering solos. *Look At Yourself*, their debut for Bronze Records, became the band's first UK charting album. Gary Thain (b. 1948, d. 1975) took over on bass, and the stability of the new line-up enabled the band to enter their most successful period during the early 70s. *Demons And Wizards* was their first album to enter the US charts. John Wetton replaced Thain on bass in March 1975, but lasted barely a year. After a power struggle with Hensley, Byron was forced to leave the following year.

The singer's position underwent further changes during the late 70s and 80s as the band found themselves playing to a cult. Hensley left the band, leaving original member Mick Box to pick up the pieces. Despite seeming out of time with all other developments in hard rock, Uriah Heep have continued to record albums and tour into the new millennium.

USHER

US R&B star Usher (b. Usher Raymond) released his self-titled debut in 1994, but had to wait three years before making his breakthrough with the US Top 10 album *My Way*. The first single to be taken from the album, 'You Make Me Wanna', was typical of the smooth ballads on offer. More unusual was the experimental, hip-hop-styled 'Nice 'N' Slow', a US chart-topper in March 1998. Usher returned to the top of the US charts in July 2001 with 'U Remind Me', which premiered the hit album *8701*. The single 'U Got It Bad' also reached the US number 1 position in 2002.

UTAH SAINTS

Formed in Leeds, England, Utah Saints comprises DJs Jez Willis (b. 1963) and Tim Garbutt (b. 1969). Both were formerly members of electro outfit MDMA. The duo's move to house music, using samples and a driving backbeat, proved much more successful than the efforts of their former incarnation. They enjoyed two UK Top 10 hits in 1991 with 'What Can You Do For Me' (featuring a **Eurythmics** sample) and 'Something Good' (featuring a **Kate Bush** sample). Utah Saints sold over a quarter of a million copies in the USA (where it was released first) in addition to its UK success. Their first release in over a year, 'Ohio', arrived in 1995, but a projected album was never released due to a dispute with their record label. The duo's work as Utah Saints then took a back seat to other commitments. Garbutt's busy DJing schedule took in a stint at New York's The Tunnel, while Willis continued to work as a remixer. 'Love Song', the new Utah Saints single, finally appeared in 2000. Their second album, succinctly titled *Two*, followed in October.

VALENS, RITCHIE

Valens (b. Richard Steve Valenzuela, 1941, d. 1959) was the first major Hispanic-American rock star, the artist who popularized the classic 50s hit 'La Bamba'. It was while attending school in California that Valens was first exposed to R&B music and rock 'n' roll. His first single, the original 'Come On, Let's Go', reached number 42 in the USA, and following its release the singer went on an 11-city US tour. In October 1958 the single 'Donna'/'La Bamba' was issued. The ballad 'Donna' was the bigger hit, reaching number 2. 'La Bamba', the b-side, only reached number 22 in the USA but has proved to be the more fondly remembered song. Embarking on a winter tour in 1959 with **Buddy Holly** and the **Big Bopper**, the three performers were killed in an aeroplane crash following a concert in Clear Lake, Iowa. Valens' status grew in the years following his death, culminating in the 1987 film *La Bamba*, a dramatized version of Valens' brief life and stardom.

VALENTINOS

Formed in the 50s and originally known as the Womack Brothers, this US group's line-up featured **Bobby Womack** (b. 1944), Friendly Womack Jnr, Harry Womack, Curtis Womack and Cecil Womack. They were later renamed the Valentinos. One of Bobby's gospel songs, 'Couldn't Hear Nobody Pray', was reshaped into the secular 'Looking For A Love', a Top 10 R&B single in 1962. Another original, 'Somewhere There's A God', became 'Somewhere There's A Girl', but the Valentinos' next chart entry came in 1964 with the bubbling 'It's All Over Now'. Their own version was overshadowed by that of the **Rolling Stones**. Disillusioned, the brothers drifted apart and Bobby Womack began his solo career. However, the Valentinos did briefly reunite for two 70s singles, 'I Can Understand It' and 'Raise Your Hand In Anger'.

VALLI, FRANKIE

Originally a solo singer recording under the name Frankie Valley, Valli (b. Francis Castelluccio, 1937) joined the Variatones in 1954. They made their first records as the Four Lovers but achieved lasting success when they became the **Four Seasons** in 1962. Although he was lead singer with the group, Valli also had a solo recording career, starting with '(You're Gonna) Hurt Yourself' in late 1965. He scored a million-seller in 1967 with 'Can't Take My Eyes Off You'. From the same album came further US hits, 'I Make A Fool Of Myself', and 'To Give (The Reason I Live)'. Valli had his first solo number 1 in 1975 with 'My Eyes Adored You', followed by 'Swearin' To God' and a revival of Ruby And The Romantics' 'Our Day Will Come'. In 1978 he sold two million copies of the Barry Gibb-composed theme song from *Grease*. He subsequently rejoined the Four Seasons. In 1990, the Four Seasons were inducted into the Rock And Roll Hall Of Fame, and for the rest of the decade Valli continued to lead the group on the lucrative oldies circuit.

VAN DER GRAAF GENERATOR

This inventive UK rock band was formed in 1967 by Chris Judge-Smith (drums), Nick Peame (keyboards) and **Peter Hammill** (b. 1948; vocals). With the enlistment of Keith Ellis (ex-Koobas) on bass, and the substitution of Smith for Guy Evans, and Peame by Hugh Banton, the band recorded a single, 'People You Were Going To', before breaking up. However, Hammill's intended solo album, *The Aerosol Grey Machine*, evolved into a band effort. By then Hammill had developed a manic, but clear vocal style and a fatalistic line as a wordsmith. David Jackson (woodwinds) joined the line-up and almost upstaged Hammill on the band's best album, 1971's *Pawn Hearts*. Hammill then resumed his solo career before re-forming the band in 1975. A more raw sound pervaded their albums, thanks to the recruitment of String-Driven Thing's violinist Graham Smith when Banton and Jackson departed in 1976. Hammill continued as a soloist when, unable to expand commercially beyond a loyal cult market, Van Der Graaf Generator finally broke up after 1978's in-concert double, *Vital*.

VAN HALEN

One of America's most successful heavy metal bands, Van Halen were originally known as Mammoth when Eddie Van Halen (b. 1957; guitar, keyboards), Alex Van Halen (b. 1955; drums), Michael Anthony (b. 1955; bass) and flamboyant singer David Lee Roth (b. 1955) formed the band in 1973. Rechristened Van Halen, the quartet signed to Warner Brothers Records and recorded their self-titled debut in 1978. The album featured a unique fusion of energy, sophistication and virtuosity through Eddie Van Halen's extraordinary guitar lines and Roth's self-assured vocal style. Within 12 months it had sold two million units, peaking at number 19 in the *Billboard* chart; over the years this album has continued to sell and by 1996 it had been certified in the USA alone at 9 million sales. The follow-up, simply titled *Van Halen II*, kept to the same formula and was equally successful. *Women And Children First* and *Fair Warning* were marked departures from earlier releases, but still went platinum, as did the weak *Diver Down*. Eddie Van Halen was also a guest on **Michael Jackson**'s 'Beat It', a US number 1 in February 1983.

Van Halen returned to form with *1984*, which was spearheaded by 'Jump', a US number 1 and UK Top 10 hit single, the album lodged at number 2 in the US chart for a full five weeks during its one-year residency. Roth upset the apple cart by quitting in 1985 to concentrate on his solo career, and ex-Montrose vocalist Sammy Hagar (b. 1947) eventually filled the vacancy. The new line-up released *5150* in 1986. The lead-off single, 'Why Can't This Be Love', reached number 3 in the US chart, while the album became their first US number 1. Subsequent albums attained platinum status, and the band rode into the 90s on a commercial high. Hagar departed in 1996 after rumours persisted that he was at loggerheads with the other members. The vacancy went to Gary Cherone (b. 1961) soon after his band **Extreme** announced their formal disbanding in October 1996. The first album to feature Cherone, 1998's *Van Halen III*, was universally slated. The singer left the following year and had not been replaced by the time the band parted company with Warners in January 2002.

VANDROSS, LUTHER

One of the leading US soul singers of the late 80s and early 90s, Vandross (b. 1951) started out as a solo singer, performing with **David Bowie**, **Chaka Khan**, **Ringo Starr**, Barbra Streisand and **Donna Summer**. Two mid-70s releases with the specially put-together vocal group Luther flopped, and Vandross drifted back to session work. His performance as guest singer with the studio group Change on 1980's *The Glow Of Love* earned two UK Top 20 hits in 'Glow Of Love' and 'Searching'. This led to the re-launch of a higher profile solo career, with the singles 'Never Too Much', 'Stop To Love' (1986) and a duet with Gregory Hines, 'There's Nothing Better Than Love' (1987), doing well on the US R&B charts. 'Give Me The Reason', 'Here And Now', 'Power Of Love'/'Love Power' and 'Don't Want To Be A Fool' crossed over to become major pop hits. 'Endless Love', a duet with **Mariah Carey**, reached UK number 3 in 1994. A decline in sales during the mid-90s saw the termination of his Sony contract. *I Know* marked his debut for EMI Records, but he subsequently relocated to J Records.

VANGELIS

A child prodigy, Greek instrumentalist Vangelis (b. Evanghelos Odyssey Papathanassiou, 1943) made his name in his home country in the mid-60s with beat outfit Formix, before going on to enjoy international success with **Aphrodite's Child**. When the latter disbanded following 1972's ambitious *666: The Apocalypse Of John*, Vangelis turned to the newly minted synthesizer as his main compositional tool. His albums during this period developed a fusion of electronic and acoustic sound, as well as experimenting with vocal samples and Eastern instrumentation.

In the early 80s, Vangelis joined forces with **Yes** vocalist Jon Anderson, and as Jon And Vangelis they had international success with 'I Hear You Now' (1980) and 'I'll Find My Way Home' (1981). He resumed his activities as a film music composer with the award-winning *Chariots Of Fire*, which scooped the Oscar for Best Original Score at the 1982 Academy Awards. The title-track was a worldwide hit. This was followed by impressive scores for Ridley Scott's *Blade Runner* and Costas-Gravas' *Missing*. In 1988, Vangelis released *Direct*, the first in a series of improvised albums which he composed, arranged and recorded simultaneously with MIDI sequencers. In 1991 he reunited with Anderson on *Page Of Life*, and enjoyed further soundtrack success with Roman Polanski's *Bitter Moon* (1992) and Ridley Scott's *1492: Conquest Of Paradise* (1993). In 1995 'Conquest Of Paradise' became an unexpected German radio hit.

VANILLA FUDGE

This US rock band was formed in 1966 by Mark Stein (b. 1947; organ), Vince Martell (b. 1945; guitar), Tim Bogert (b. 1944; bass) and Joey Brennan (drums), although the latter was soon replaced by Carmine Appice (b. 1946). Dubbed Vanilla Fudge by their record label, the quartet scored an immediate success with an atmospheric revival of the **Supremes**' hit, 'You Keep Me Hangin' On'. A flawed concept album, *The Beat Goes On*, proved over-ambitious, while further selections showed a band unable to create original material of the calibre of their debut. Subsequent records relied on simpler, hard-edged rock. The unit re-formed in 1983, releasing *Mystery* which failed to make any impact.

VANILLA ICE

Controversial white rapper (b. Robert Van Winkle, 1968) who borrowed liberally from **M. C. Hammer**'s blueprint for commercial success, and scored a UK/US number 1 in 1990 with 'Ice Ice Baby'. In a desperate attempt to catch up with the gangsta set, *Mindblowing* was a blueprint hardcore rap album. Ice disappeared from the music scene for several years before returning with 1998's *Hard To Swallow*.

VEE, BOBBY

US singer Vee (b. Robert Thomas Velline, 1943) made his chart debut with a revival of the **Clovers**' 1956 hit 'Devil Or Angel', before finding transatlantic success via the infectious, if lyrically innocuous, 'Rubber Ball'. Between 1961 and 1962, he peaked with a series of infectious hits including 'More Than I Can Say', 'How Many Tears', 'Take Good Care Of My Baby' (a US number 1), 'Run To Him', 'Please Don't Ask About Barbara', 'Sharing You' and 'A Forever Kind Of Love'. The imaginatively titled 'The Night Has A Thousand Eyes' proved his most enduring song. Like many American teen-orientated artists, Vee's appeal waned following the arrival of the **Beatles** and the beat group explosion. In 1967 he returned to the US Top 10 with 'Come Back When You Grow Up'. An attempt to fashion a more serious image prompted Vee to revert to his real name for *Nothing Like A Sunny Day*. The experiment was short-lived, however, and Vee later contented himself with regular appearances at rock 'n' roll revival shows.

VEGA, SUZANNE

Vega (b. 1959) is a highly literate US singer-songwriter who enjoyed international success in the late 80s and early 90s. Her 1985 debut album included the hit 'Marlene On The Wall'. In 1987 'Luka' grabbed even more attention with its evocation of the pain of child abuse told from the victim's point of view. In 1990, the serendipitous 'Tom's Diner' from *Solitude Standing* became a hit in Britain after being sampled by the production duo, D.N.A. Vega's commercial presence faded during the 90s, although her critical standing continued to remain high. After a five-year absence, during which she raised her daughter and published her first book, Vega returned to the recording scene in 2001 with *Songs In Red And Gray*.

VELVET UNDERGROUND

The antithesis of late-60s west coast love and peace, New York, USA's the Velvet Underground portrayed a darker side to that era's hedonism. The band was formed by **Lou Reed** (b. 1942; guitar, vocals), Welshman **John Cale** (b. 1942; viola, bass, organ), Sterling Morrison (b. 1942, d. 1995; guitar) and Angus MacLise (d. 1979), who suggested they adopt the name 'The Velvet Underground', the title of a contemporary pulp paperback. MacLise was subsequently replaced by Maureen 'Mo' Tucker (b. 1945). Pop-art celebrity Andy Warhol invited them to join the Exploding Plastic Inevitable, a theatrical mixture of music, films, light-shows and dancing, and also suggested adding German actress/singer **Nico** (b. Christa Paffgen, 1938, d. 1988) to the line-up. The band recorded their debut album in the spring of 1966 but the completed master was rejected by several major companies, fearful of both its controversial content and lengthy tracks. *The Velvet Underground & Nico* was eventually issued by Verve Records the following year. This powerful collection introduced Reed's decidedly urban infatuations, a fascination for street culture and amorality bordering on voyeurism.

Nico left for a solo career in 1967 and the remaining quartet then parted from Warhol's patronage. Sessions for a second album, *White Light/White Heat*, exacerbated other internal conflicts and its six compositions were marked by a raging intensity. The 17-minute tour de force 'Sister Ray' offers some of John Cale's most inspired atonal instrumental work. This pivotal figure was then removed from the band and replaced by an orthodox bass player, Doug Yule. A third album, entitled simply *The Velvet Underground*, unveiled a pastoral approach, gentler and more subtle, but retaining the chilling, disquieting aura of previous releases. *Loaded*, an album of considerable commercial promise, emphasized their new-found perspective. Released in 1970, this unfettered collection contained one of Reed's most popular compositions, 'Sweet Jane'. Paradoxically, by the time *Loaded* was issued, Lou Reed had abandoned the group he had created and Yule now took control, leading several variations on the Velvet Underground name.

The Velvet Underground has since become regarded as one of rock music's most influential acts. Their regrouping in 1993 for a major tour was greeted with great excitement. Old wounds were opened between Cale and Reed and no further plans were imminent other than a one-off appearance together following their induction to the Rock And Roll Hall Of Fame in 1996. Morrison died only a few months before the latter event.

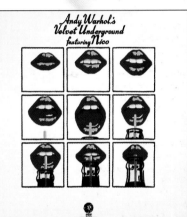

VENTURES

This pivotal instrumental group was formed in Tacoma, USA, in 1959 by Don Wilson (b. 1937, USA; rhythm guitar) and Bob Bogle (b. 1937, USA; lead guitar). They began performing together as the Impacts, using a pick-up rhythm section, before Nokie Edwards (b. 1939, USA; bass) and Skip Moore (drums) completed a line-up redubbed the Ventures. The quartet re-recorded 'Walk, Don't Run', initially a jazz instrumental, in a surf-rock style and reached number 2 in the US charts with sales in excess of one million copies, a distinction matched by its follow-up, 'Perfidia'. At this point Moore had been replaced by Howie Johnson (d. 1988), who in turn retired following a major car accident. Drummer Mel Taylor (b. 1934, d. 1996) was then added to the group.

Other notable Ventures singles included 'The 2,000 Pound Bee (Part 2)' (1962), 'The Savage' (1963), 'Diamond Head' (1965). The Ventures' continued appeal lay in an ability to embrace contemporary fashion, and they also survived several personnel changes. In 1969 the Ventures had their last major US hit when 'Hawaii Five-O', the theme tune to a popular detective series, reached US number 4. They remain a popular attraction, particularly in Japan, where the group is the subject of almost fanatical reverence.

VERLAINE, TOM

US guitarist Verlaine (b. Thomas Miller, 1949) made his name as a member of **Television**. Their debut, *Marquee Moon*, was acclaimed a classic, although a lukewarm reception for the ensuing *Adventure* exacerbated inner tensions and the quartet was disbanded in 1978. Verlaine began a solo career which failed to re-establish him as a commercial force. Nevertheless, Verlaine's gifted lyricism and brittle, shimmering guitar work has ensured a reputation as one of rock's most innovative and respected talents. In 1991 a decision was made to re-form the original Television line-up and the following year was spent recording a disappointing third album. Following its release, Verlaine continued with his solo career.

VERTICAL HORIZON

This endearingly popular US 'modern rock' outfit was formed in 1991 by Keith Kane and Matthew Scannell. Two low-key albums followed before the duo recruited Ed Toth as their full-time drummer. Bass player Sean Hurley became the fourth member of the band in 1998. Shortly afterwards they signed a major label deal with RCA Records and released *Everything You Want*. The album proved to be a slow-burning commercial success. It climbed steadily up the US charts during the year buoyed by the radio success of singles such as the chart-topping title track and 'We Are'.

VERVE

UK rock band formed by Peter Salisbury (b. 1971; drums), Richard Ashcroft (b. 1971; vocals), Simon Jones (b. 1972; bass) and Nick McCabe (b. 1971;

guitar). After a run of singles their erratic debut album arrived in 1993. On the back of this rise to prominence the band had come to the attention of the Verve Records jazz label, who insisted on copyright of the name. Failing to accept a compromise 'Verv' spelling, after a two-year battle the band were re-named The Verve. *A Northern Soul* was greeted with strong reviews, but Ashcroft left the band during 1995 to form his own version of the Verve and the band officially broke up in August, only to announce in early 1997 that they had re-formed. Their new material stormed the bestsellers in the UK. Accompanied by a memorable promotional video, 'Bitter Sweet Symphony' made the UK Top 5, despite legal wranglings over the use of a **Rolling Stones** instrumental sample (the Verve were obliged to hand over the single's royalties to Allen Klein and credit Keith Richards and Mick Jagger as songwriters). The song also broke the band in the USA, reaching number 12. 'The Drugs Don't Work' reached UK number 1 on the week of release. *Urban Hymns* then received rave critical reviews and entered the UK album chart at number 1. McCabe opted out of subsequent live work, however, hinting at new tensions between the members. This was confirmed in April 1999 when the band announced they were splitting-up. Ashcroft embarked on a solo career.

VILLAGE PEOPLE

The Village People from New York City, USA, were a concept before they were a group. The brainchild of French record producer Jacques Morali, the troupe was assembled in 1977 and featured Felipe Rose, Alexander Briley, Randy Jones, David Hodo, Glenn Hughes (b. 1950, d. 2001) and lead singer Victor Willis. Each member of the group was outfitted to cash in on the homosexual 'macho' stereotyping; in addition to the American Indian (Rose) there was a cowboy (Jones), a policeman (Willis), a hard-hat construction worker (Hodo), a biker (Hughes) and a G.I. (Briley). The group first charted in the UK with the Top 50 single, 'San Francisco (You've Got Me)' in 1977, but their first major US hit was the Top 30 'Macho Man' in 1978, followed by two international hits, 'Y.M.C.A.' and 'In The Navy'. In the UK their success continued with the Top 20 singles, 'Go West' (1979) and 'Can't Stop The Music' (1980). The latter was the theme song to an ill-timed film excursion. Willis had quit the group two days before filming began and was replaced by Ray Simpson. With anti-disco fever prevalent in the USA, the failure of the critically panned movie virtually killed off the group's chart career.

Attempts to resurface with new personnel and new styles did not aid their sagging fortunes. Simpson, Rose, Hodo, Hughes, Briley and Olson re-formed the group in the late 80s, and continue to earn a tidy living on the live circuit. In 1995, an ill Hughes dropped out of performing, but was present to help the group celebrate their 20th anniversary two years later. He was replaced by Eric Anzalone, and died of lung cancer in 2001.

VINCENT, GENE

One of the original bad boys of rock 'n' roll, the self-destructive Vincent (b. Vincent Eugene Craddock, 1935, d. 1971) was involved in a motorcycle crash in July 1955 and his left leg was permanently damaged. Discharged from the US Navy, he began appearing on country music radio. His debut recording 'Be-Bop A-Lula' was completed in 1956 with the backing of the Blue Caps; Cliff Gallup (lead guitar), Jack Neal (upright bass), Willie Williams (b. 1936, d. 1999; acoustic guitar) and Dickie Harrell (drums). Weeks later, 'Be-Bop-A-Lula' stormed the charts, temporarily providing Capitol Records with their own version of **Elvis Presley**. Vincent's image was brooding, inarticulate and menacing and with such rock 'n' roll authenticity he was not easily marketable in the USA. His second single, 'Race With The Devil', failed to chart in his homeland, but proved successful in the UK, where he attracted a devoted following. Vincent rapidly lost the impetus that had thrust him to the centre stage as a rock 'n' roll icon, and even an appearance in the movie *The Girl Can't Help It* failed to arrest his commercial decline. Vincent's alcoholism and buccaneering road life made him a liability to promoters and by the late 50s, his career seemed in ruins.

He relocated to England, where Jack Good exacerbated his rebel image by dressing him in black leather and encouraging the star to accentuate his limp. A comeback album of sorts, *I'm Back And I'm Proud*, lacked sufficient punch to revitalize his career and he continued playing with pick-up groups, churning out his old repertoire. The often intolerable pain he suffered due to his festering leg merely exacerbated his alcoholism, which in turn devastated his health. On 12 October 1971, his abused body finally succumbed to a bleeding ulcer and rock 'n' roll lost one of its genuinely great rebellious spirits.

VIRGIN PRUNES

This Irish performance-art/*avant-garde* musical ensemble was originally formed in 1976. Fionan Hanvey, better known under his pseudonym Gavin Friday, was joined by Guggi (Derek Rowen) and Dave-id (b. David Watson; vocals), Strongman (b. Trevor Rowen; bass), Dik Evans (guitar) and Pod (b. Anthony Murphy; drums). Early gigs were very much performance events, with audiences bemused by the expectations placed on them. As a manifestation of their unconventional approach their first album was initially released as a set of 7-, 10- and 12-inch singles, with component parts making up *A New Form Of Beauty*. Further experimental works followed before 1986's *The Moon Looked Down And Laughed* witnessed another change in direction, consisting largely of ballads and melodic pop. However, following the continued lack of response from the record-buying public, Friday called a halt to his involvement with the band and embarked on a varied solo career.

VISAGE

A synthesizer 'jamming' band fronted by Steve Strange (b. Steve Harrington, 1959), with other members including **Midge Ure** (b. James Ure, 1953; guitar), Rusty Egan (b. 1957), Billy Currie (b. William Lee Currie, 1950; violin), Dave Formula (keyboards), John McGeoch (b. 1955; guitar) and **Barry Adamson** (b. 1958; bass). Polydor Records picked up on the band and were rewarded with a massive UK Top 10 hit in late 1980/early 1981 with 'Fade To Grey', which fitted in with the burgeoning synthesizer pop scene of the early 80s. Visage eventually fizzled out in the mid-80s.

VOICE OF THE BEEHIVE

Formed by sisters Tracey Bryn (b. 1962) and Melissa Brooke Belland (b. 1966), this unusual indie pop band also included guitarist Mike Jones, Dan Woodgate (b. 1960; drums) and Mark Bedford (b. 1961; bass). The singles, 'Just A City', 'I Say Nothing' and 'I Walk The Earth' followed before Bedford was replaced by Martin Brett, who arrived in time to assist with the band's 1988 debut album. *Let It Bee* was a pleasant, witty pop confectionery, which included the

UK Top 20 single 'Don't Call Me Baby'. The appealing pop of Voice Of The Beehive climaxed in the summer of 1991 with the release of *Honey Lingers*. Reduced to a duo of Bryn and Belland, the band quietly broke up after 1995's disappointing *Sex & Misery*.

W.A.S.P.

US shock-rock troupe formed in 1982 in Los Angeles. Famed for outrageous live performances, the band – Blackie Lawless (b. 1956; bass, vocals), Chris Holmes (b. 1961; guitar), Randy Piper (guitar) and Tony Richards (drums) – were snapped up by Capitol Records. On legal advice, the label refused to release their debut single, 'Animal (Fuck Like A Beast)', released later independently. *W.A.S.P.* was an adequate basic metal debut, while *The Last Command*, with new drummer Steve Riley, produced the excellent 'Wild Child' and 'Blind In Texas'. W.A.S.P. became a major US concert draw, albeit with a toned-down stage show. *Inside The Electric Circus* saw the debut of bass player Johnny Rod with Lawless replacing Piper on rhythm guitar. Lawless, a tireless free-speech campaigner, moved the band towards a serious stance on *The Headless Children*; with Frankie Banali replacing Riley. Holmes left soon afterwards. Lawless used session musicians to record *The Crimson Idol*, a concept effort, and toured with Rod, Doug Blair (guitar) and Stet Howland (drums). In 1993, he announced the end of W.A.S.P. but his solo album, *Still Not Black Enough*, was nevertheless issued under the W.A.S.P. name. Lawless reunited with Holmes in 1996 and elected to carry on recording and touring as W.A.S.P.. The forgettable *Kill, Fuck, Die*, featured new bass player Mike Duda. *Unholy Terror* proved the band was still capable of producing quality work in the studio.

WAH!

Melodramatic UK pop band formed by Pete Wylie (b. 1958; guitar, vocals) in the early-80s. Wylie had been part of Crucial 3 with **Julian Cope** and Ian McCulloch. The albums Wah! left behind are remarkably inconsistent, and a more informed purchase would be a compilation of the band's singles, including 'Come Back' and 'Hope', plus their major UK chart success, 'The Story Of The Blues'. Wylie went solo in 1987 with *Sinful*. A serious back injury sidelined Wylie for several years, but he made a triumphant return in early 2000 with the euphoric guitar pop of *Songs Of Strength & Heartbreak*, featuring the anthemic 'Heart As Big As Liverpool'.

WAINWRIGHT, LOUDON, III

US singer-songwriter Wainwright (b. 1946) began playing folk clubs in New York and Boston, before signing to Atlantic Records. His first albums featured his high-pitched voice and guitar almost exclusively, and his intense, sardonic songs were about himself. His songs included 'Glad To See You've Got Religion', 'Motel Blues' and 'Be Careful, There's A Baby In The House'. Wainwright's third album included a surprise US Top 20 pop hit in 'Dead Skunk'. He wrote 'A.M. World' about his success and, almost defiantly, followed it with the uncommercial *Attempted Mustache*. *Unrequited*, partly recorded live, was a return to form and included the hilarious, but controversial, 'Rufus Is A Tit Man'.

Wainwright appeared in a few episodes of the television series *M*A*S*H* and acted on stage in *The Birthday Party* and *Pump Boys And Dinettes*. He is best known in the UK, where he lived during the mid-80s, for his performance of specially written topical songs on the Jasper Carrott television series. Wainwright reached top form on four 80s albums – *Fame And Wealth*, *I'm Alright*, *More Love Songs*, and *Therapy*. He enjoyed middling success on the Virgin Records label in the following decade, before re-establishing his credentials on his first album of the new millennium, *Last Man On Earth*.

WAITE, JOHN

Waite (b. 1952) has found greater fame in the US than in his native England. After playing in various bands, he formed the Babys with Mike Corby, Tony Brock and Walter Stocker, in 1976. They were signed to Chrysalis Records, but their brand of rock had become unfashionable in the UK and they relocated to the USA.

When the Babys split in 1981, Waite went solo. 'Missing You', from his second album, reached US number 1. Waite formed the No Brakes band to promote the new album, but did not scale the same heights again. He formed the ill-fated Bad English in 1989, before resuming his solo career in the mid-90s. In 1995, he charted with the power ballad 'How Did I Get By Without You'.

WAITS, TOM

Gifted lyricist, composer and raconteur, Tom Waits (b. 1949) began performing in the late 60s. He was signed by manager Herb Cohen and by Asylum Records. *Tom Waits* was somewhat unfocused, however it did contain 'Ol' 55', later covered by the **Eagles**. *The Heart Of Saturday Night* was more accomplished, sung in a razor-edged, rasping voice, and infused with beatnik prepossessions. Waits' ability to paint blue-collar American life is encapsulated in its haunting, melodic title track. *Nighthawks At The Diner* and *Small Change*, closed his first era. *Foreign Affairs* unveiled a widening perspective and a duet with Bette Midler, 'I Never Talk To Strangers', provided the impetus for his soundtrack to *One From The Heart*. *Blue Valentine* was marked by its balance between lyrical ballads and up-front R&B, a contrast maintained on *Heartattack And Vine*.

In 1983, Waits moved to Island Records, signalling a new musical direction with the radical *Swordfishtrombones* (exotic instruments, sound textures and offbeat rhythms). He came close to having a hit with the evocative 'In The Neighbourhood'. He also inaugurated an acting career, starring in *Rumble Fish*, *Down By Law* and *Ironweed*. The album *Rain Dogs*, which featured support from Keith Richard on 'Big Black Mariah', included 'Downtown Train', later a hit for **Rod Stewart**. Waits continued in films with roles in *Candy Mountain* and *Cold Feet* and in 1989 made his theatrical debut in *Demon Wine*. 'Good Old World (Waltz)' was the stand-out track from his 1992 soundtrack to Jim Jarmusch's *Night On Earth*. His rhythmic experimentation came to fruition the same year on *Bone Machine*, which was for many his finest album. The following year's *The Black Rider* featured music from Waits' stage play of the same name, co-written with William Burroughs.

This perplexing genius remains a cult figure, and made further acting roles in *Short Cuts* and Francis Ford Coppola's *Dracula*. After signing to independent label Epitaph Records, Waits released *Mule Variations* in 1999. Astonishingly, the album broke into the UK Top 10 and won a Grammy Award. Waits released two follow-ups in May 2002.

WAKEMAN, RICK

Master UK keyboardist Wakeman (b. 1949) made a series of ambitious, conceptual, classical rock albums after leaving **Yes** in 1973: *The Six Wives Of Henry VIII*, *Journey To The Centre Of The Earth* and *The Myths And Legends Of King Arthur And The Knights Of The Round Table* (staged using a full orchestra and 50-strong choir). All three albums were hugely successful. During the 80s, he contributed to Kevin Peeks' *Awakening*, co-wrote a musical version of George Orwell's *1984* with Tim Rice, and created sensitive film scores for *Lisztomania* and *The Burning*.

Having overcome his alcoholism with the help of his new partner Nina Carter, Wakeman signed a new recording contract with President Records and began to make an impact on the New Age charts. In the late-80s, he rejoined his former Yes bandmates for a tour. In 1990, he formed another label, Ambient Records, and worked with Norman Wisdom on a series of relaxation cassettes. By 1992, his son Adam was performing with him. Wakeman's prodigious recording and touring schedule was maintained during the rest of the decade, alternating new age, religious and solo piano work with commitments to Wakeman With Wakeman and Yes.

WALKER BROTHERS

Originally named the Dalton Brothers, **Scott Walker** (b. Noel Scott Engel, 1944), John Walker (b. John Maus, 1943) and Gary Walker (b. Gary Leeds, 1944), changed their name to the Walker Brothers in 1964, and left the USA for the UK. In 1965, they met manager Maurice King and were signed to Philips Records, debuting with 'Pretty Girls Everywhere' followed by 'Love Her' (1965, UK Top 20). Scott was the chosen 'a-side' main vocalist, with Maus providing the strong high harmony. The Walkers' film star looks meant they were adopted as teen idols. On album, they played a contrasting selection of ballads, soul standards and occasional upbeat pop, but for the singles they specialized in high melodrama, brilliantly augmented by the string arrangements of Johnny Franz.

The lachrymose **Burt Bacharach**/Hal David ballad 'Make It Easy On Yourself' gave them a UK number 1, while 'My Ship Is Coming In' reached the Top 3. Their version of the Bob Crewe/Bob Gaudio composition, 'The Sun Ain't Gonna Shine Anymore' reached UK number 1/US Top 20. Thereafter, there was immense friction in the band and their second EP *Solo Scott, Solo John*, neatly summarized their future intentions. Later singles seemed a weak follow-up to their grandiose number 1 and commenced their gradual commercial decline. In 1967, the group broke up. Their farewell single, 'Walking In The Rain', surprisingly did not reach number 1.

Unexpectedly, the trio reunited in 1975, for *No Regrets*. The title track returned them to the Top 10. The following *Lines* was similar in style to its predecessor, but for their swansong, the self-penned *Nite Flights*, the trio produced a brave, experimental work, with oblique, foreboding lyrics and unusual arrangements. Sadly it was a commercial failure.

WALKER, JUNIOR, AND THE ALL STARS

As a teenager, US saxophonist Walker (b. Autry DeWalt II, 1931, d. 1995) formed the Jumping Jacks, adopting the stage name Junior Walker. By 1961, he had achieved a prominent local reputation and was signed to the Harvey label, where he recorded a series of raw saxophone-led instrumentals. In 1964, Walker moved to Motown Records. 'Shotgun' (1965) typified his blend of raunchy R&B and Detroit soul and established Walker as the label's prime exponent of traditional R&B. **Holland/Dozier/Holland** also encouraged Walker to record instrumental versions of hits they had written for other Motown artists. Walker's style became progressively more lyrical, a development that reached its peak on the 1969 US Top 5 hit, 'What Does It Take (To Win Your Love)?' However, subsequent attempts to repeat the winning formula failed and from 1972 onwards the All Stars recorded only sporadically. *Hot Shot* marked a move towards the disco market, confirmed on two further albums and Walker's first as a solo artist. In 1979, he moved to Whitfield Records, but returned to Motown in 1983, issuing *Blow The House Down*. The novelty single 'Sex Pot' rekindled memories of his classic hits, although Walker's greatest commercial success in the 80s came when he guested with **Foreigner**, playing the magnificent saxophone solo on their hit 'Urgent'. Walker died after a two-year battle with cancer.

WALKER, SCOTT

Scott (b. Noel Scott Engel, 1944) briefly recorded as Scotty Engel before joining the Routers as bassist. He then teamed up with singer John Maus as the Dalton Brothers, later becoming the **Walker Brothers**. When the group broke up in 1967, Scott was regarded as a sex symbol and potential solo superstar, yet he was known for his moody reclusiveness. The classic pop existentialist, Walker was trapped in a system that regarded him as a contradiction. His manager Maurice King encouraged a straightforward showbusiness career involving regular television appearances and cabaret. Walker, a devotee of French composer **Jacques Brel**, included several of Brel's songs on his debut solo album, *Scott*. He was also displaying immense talent as a songwriter, with poetic, brooding songs like 'Such A Small Love' and 'Always Coming Back To You'. The album was rendered unique by Walker's distinctive, deep, crooning tone and strong vibrato. However, Walker remained uneasy about his career; at one point, he reverted to his real surname, and announced that he would no longer be issuing singles. While the brilliant *Scott 4* contained solely original material and might have heralded the re-evaluation of Walker as a serious songwriter, the BBC chose that very same period to issue the MOR *Scott Sings Songs From His Television Series*. He then bowed to popular demand, recording an album of cover versions, *The Moviegoer*, followed by a series of Walker Brothers albums. Thereafter Scott retreated from the music business, returning in 1984 for the critically acclaimed *Climate Of Hunter*. Eleven years later he released the startling *Tilt*, which received mixed reviews. In the late 90s, Walker contributed new recordings to several movie soundtracks. He also embarked on his first production job, overseeing **Pulp**'s *We Love Life*.

WALKER, T-BONE

Walker (b. Aaron Thibeaux Walker, 1910, d. 1975) was raised in Dallas, amidst blues musicians. During the 20s he toured Texas as a musician/comedian/dancer, before joining a travelling revue. By 1929, he had made a country blues record for Columbia as 'Oak Cliff T-Bone'. He then travelled to Oklahoma City, where he was taught by Chuck Richardson. In 1934, Walker joined 'Big' Jim Wynn's band. His popularity grew steadily and in 1940 he joined Les Hite's Orchestra. Upon arriving in New York with Hite, Varsity Records recorded the orchestra, and Walker's feature, 'T-Bone Blues', became a great success. Leaving Hite, Walker co-led a band with Big Jim Wynn.

In 1942–4, Walker recorded for Capitol Records with Freddie Slack's band. Slack then supported Walker on his first solo release. The two tracks, 'Mean Old World' and 'I Got A Break Baby', became standards. During 1945–6 Walker played Chicago clubs; upon his return to the west coast, he was in great demand, both in concert and for his new records. These included 'I'm Gonna Find My Baby', 'T-Bone Shuffle' and 'Call It Stormy Monday'. The latter melancholic ballad, also known as 'Stormy Monday' and 'Stormy Monday Blues', has since been the subject of numerous interpretations by artists as disparate as **Chris Farlowe**, Bobby Bland and the **Allman Brothers Band**.

In 1950, he signed with Imperial Records where he demonstrated a harder, funkier style of blues, utilizing T. J. Fowler's band and **Dave Bartholomew**'s band, as well as his own working unit from LA. These experiments continued after moving to Atlantic Records (1955–9), where he

worked with blues harmonica player Junior Wells and modern jazz guitarist Barney Kessel. Walker continued to record prolifically, but by the early 70s his powers were diminished through ill health. In 1974, he suffered a severe stroke from which he never recovered.

WALLFLOWERS

The vast majority of the initial attention surrounding US alternative rock band the Wallflowers concerned the fact that one Jakob Dylan (b. 1970), the son of **Bob Dylan**, was their songwriter, singer and guitarist. Despite

good reviews, their 1992 album failed to translate critical approval into sales. They subsequently signed to Interscope Records, with Dylan reassembling a new line-up around founding members Rami Jaffe (keyboards) and Greg Richling (bass), with the addition of Michael Ward (guitar) and Mario Calire (drums). *Bringing Down The Horse* elevated the band following its success in the USA. *(Breach)*, the band's delayed third album, confirmed Dylan's status as one of US contemporary rock's most assured songwriters.

WALSH, JOE

US guitar hero Walsh (b. 1947) started his career in 1965 with the G-Clefs joining the **James Gang** in 1969. He left in 1972 and formed Barnstorm with Joe Vitale (drums) and Kenny Passarelli (bass). Their self-titled album made a respectable showing in the US charts. Despite the follow-up being credited to Walsh, *The Smoker You Drink, The Player You Get* was still Barnstorm, although the band broke up that year. *Smoker* became his first gold album, featuring 'Meadows' and 'Rocky Mountain Way'. *So What?* went gold and featured the classic, 'Turn To Stone'. He then performed at London's Wembley Stadium with the **Beach Boys**, **Elton John** and the **Eagles**. Five months later Walsh joined the Eagles, replacing Bernie Leadon. His distinctive tone contributed greatly to *Hotel California*, including the title track. Walsh's highly successful career continued with further solo albums including the excellent *But Seriously Folks . . .*. In 1980, he contributed to the bestselling soundtrack *Urban Cowboy* and was rewarded with a US Top 20 hit 'All Night Long'. Subsequent solo releases failed to maintain his profile, although Walsh continued to prosper as a session player. In 1995 he joined the reunited Eagles.

WAR

Leroy 'Lonnie' Jordan (b. 1948; keyboards), Howard Scott (b. 1946; guitar), Charles Miller (b. 1939; flute, saxophone), Morris 'B.B.' Dickerson (b. 1949; bass) and Harold Brown (b. 1946; drums) had made several records in the US under different names. In 1969, they became Nightshift, and were adopted by UK vocalist **Eric Burdon** as his backing band. Renamed War, the ensemble was completed by Lee Oskar (b. Oskar Levetin Hansen, 1948; harmonica) and 'Papa' Dee Allen (b. 1931, d. 1988; percussion).

After two albums, the group broke away from Burdon. War's potent fusion of funk, R&B, rock and latin styles produced a progressive soul sound and they enjoyed significant US chart success with 'The Cisco Kid' (1973), 'Why Can't We Be Friends?' (1975) and 'Summer' (1976), all of which went gold. In the UK they earned two Top 20 hits with 'Low Rider' (1976) and 'Galaxy' (1978). Despite early promise and a move to MCA, the group's sales dipped and Oskar went solo. Two 1982 singles, 'You Got The Power' and 'Outlaw', were not followed up until 1987's remake of 'Low Rider', which crept into the R&B chart. The band struggled on in the 90s, although most of the original members had departed.

WARNES, JENNIFER

US singer Warnes (b. 1947) established herself as a part of the Los Angeles club scene. She also took a leading role in the west coast production of *Hair*. As a solo artist Warnes recorded unsuccessfully until signing with Arista Records in 1975. There she had a Top 10 hit with 'Right Time Of The Night' (1977) followed by 'I Know A Heartache When I See One' (1979). In 1980, Warnes' film theme 'It Goes Like It Goes' won an Oscar for Best Original Song. She performed **Randy Newman**'s 'One More Hour' on the soundtrack of *Ragtime* before scoring a US number 1 with 'Up Where We Belong' (from the movie *An Officer And A Gentleman*), a duet with **Joe Cocker**. Warnes reached number 1 again when she teamed up with Bill Medley for the *Dirty Dancing* theme, '(I've Had) The Time Of My Life' (1987). The previous year, she recorded a selection of **Leonard Cohen** compositions, *Famous Blue Raincoat*. Warnes had first worked with Cohen in 1973 and had created vocal arrangements for his *Recent Songs*. Warnes co-produced her own 1992 album for *Private Music* as well as co-writing most of the songs. She subsequently resumed work as a session vocalist, before making a long overdue return to the studio to record *The Well*.

WARWICK, DIONNE

US singer Warwick (b. Marie Dionne Warrick, 1940) sang in a church choir, before forming the Gospelaires with her sister, Dee Dee and aunt Cissy Houston. Increasingly employed as backing singers, Warwick came into contact with songwriters **Burt Bacharach** and Hal David. Her first solo single, 'Don't Make Me Over' (1963), was a fragile slice of 'uptown R&B' and set the tone for such classic collaborations as 'Anyone Who Had A Heart' and 'Walk On By'. Although many of her singles charted, few were Top 10 hits, so Dionne

moved closer to the mainstream with such successes as 'I Say A Little Prayer' (1967) and 'Do You Know The Way To San José?' (1968). In 1971, Warwick signed to Warner Brothers Records, but despite several promising releases, the relationship floundered. Her biggest hit came with the **Detroit Spinners** on 'Then Came You' (1974). Warwick moved to Arista Records in 1979 where work with **Barry Manilow** rekindled her commercial standing. *Heartbreaker* (with the **Bee Gees**) resulted in several hit singles and since then she has been paired with **Luther Vandross**, **Elton John**, **Gladys Knight**, **Stevie Wonder** and **Jeffrey Osborne** among others.

WATERBOYS

UK rock band formed in the late 70s by vocalist Mike Scott (b. 1958) with John Caldwell (guitar). Scott recruited Anthony Thistlethwaite (b. 1955; saxophone) and Karl Wallinger (b. 1957; keyboards, percussion, vocals) and work was completed on 'A Girl Called Johnny'. Their debut album was a solid work, emphasizing Scott's singer-songwriter ability. 'December' was an excellent Christmas single but, like their debut, failed to chart. Kevin Wilkinson (drums), Roddy Lorimar (trumpet) and Tim Blanthorn (violin) joined and the Waterboys completed *A Pagan Place*. For *This Is The Sea*, Scott recruited drummer Chris Whitten and fiddler Steve Wickham. The attendant 'The Whole Of The Moon' reached UK number 28 (it hit the Top 10 when reissued in 1990).

When Wallinger left to form **World Party**, Wickham took on a more prominent role. Three years passed before the distinctively folk-flavoured *Fisherman's Blues* was released. Scott's assimilation of traditional Irish music produced a work of considerable charm and power. *Room To Roam* retained the folk sound, but within days of the album's release, Wickham left, forcing Scott to reconstruct the Waterboys' sound once more. In 1992, Thistlethwaite also left the band. Following the release of the disappointingly mainstream *Dream Harder*, Scott concentrated on his solo career for several years, before re-forming the band to record the excellent comeback album, *A Rock In The Weary Land*.

WATERS, ROGER

UK songwriter Waters (b. 1944) was a co-founder of **Pink Floyd**. His lyrics

often focused on the death of his father during World War II, and addressed his increasing conflict with the pressures of rock stardom and alienation with the audience. The introspective nature of these often led to accusations of indulgence, which in part led to the break-up of Pink Floyd in 1983. His first official solo album was *The Pros And Cons Of Hitchhiking*. Waters also wrote and performed the soundtrack to the anti-nuclear animated film, *When The Wind Blows* (1986). *Radio K.A.O.S.* followed together with the excellent single 'The Tide Is Turning (After Live Aid)'. In 1990, as part of a project in aid of the Leonard Cheshire Memorial Fund For Disaster Relief, Waters masterminded a massive televised performance of *The Wall* alongside the remains of the Berlin Wall. Refusing to stray from his familiar themes, Waters dedicated 1992's *Amused To Death* to the memory of a late World War II soldier. During this time Waters was in bitter litigation with other members of his former group as he unsuccessfully tried to stop them using the Pink Floyd name. Although no new recordings were in sight Waters did tour the USA during the summer of 1999. Several of the performances were later compiled on *In The Flesh*.

WATSON, JOHNNY 'GUITAR'

Watson (b. 1935, d. 1996) started playing piano in the Chuck Higgins band, billed as 'Young John Watson'. Switching to guitar, he recorded 'Space Guitar', an instrumental far ahead of its time in the use of reverberation and feedback, and 'Motorhead Baby' (with the Amos Milburn band) with an enthusiasm that was to become his trademark. Watson then toured and recorded with the Olympics, Don And Dewey and **Little Richard**. In 1955, he had immediate success with a bluesy ballad, 'Those Lonely, Lonely Nights' (US R&B Top 10). In 1957, the novelty 'Gangster Of Love' gave him a minor hit. Watson did not return to the charts until 1962, when 'Cuttin' In' reached US R&B number 6. The following year he recorded *I Cried For You*, a 'cocktail-lounge' album with hip renditions of 'Polkadots And Moonbeams' and 'Witchcraft'. A partnership with Larry Williams was particularly successful and in 1965 they toured England and recorded an album.

Watson recorded two soulful funk albums, *Listen* and *I Don't Want To Be Alone, Stranger*, with keyboardist Andre Lewis. **Frank Zappa** was a great admirer of Watson and recruited him to play on *One Size Fits All*. Watson also produced and played bass, keyboards and drums on *Ain't That A Bitch*, a brilliant marriage of 50s rockin' R&B, Hollywood schmaltz and futuristic funk. In 1981, Watson signed with A&M Records, but the production diluted his unique sound and the record was a failure. After a brief retirement Watson re-emerged with *Strike On Computers*. In the 90s his music was sampled by **Snoop Doggy Dogg** and **Dr. Dre**, and the album *Bow Wow* made the US charts. Watson died of a heart attack on 17 May 1996 while performing at the Yokohama Blues Cafe in Japan.

WAYNE, JEFF

US musician Wayne was a member of early 60s group the Sandpipers, although not at the time they had their worldwide hit with 'Guantanamera'. He also worked as an arranger for the **Righteous Brothers** before travelling to London in 1966 and establishing himself as a jingle writer. He then became involved with the career of **David Essex**, producing most of his early hits. Wayne sprang to the public's attention with his concept album based on H. G. Wells's *War Of The Worlds*. Written by Wayne and featuring the talents of Essex, actor Richard Burton, Justin Hayward, **Phil Lynott**, Chris Thompson and Julie Covington, the album was a huge success. Living off its royalties, Wayne kept a low profile in the 80s. In 1992 his next project, *Spartacus*, featuring Anthony Hopkins, Jimmy Helms, and **Ladysmith Black Mambazo** among others, was premiered to a lacklustre response.

WEATHER REPORT

The highly accomplished Weather Report was one of the groups credited with inventing jazz-rock fusion music in the 70s. Founded by Joe Zawinul (keyboards) and Wayne Shorter (reeds), they recruited Airto Moreira (percussion) and Miroslav Vitous (bass). Eric Gravatt (drums) and Um Romao (percussion) joined for the bestselling *I Sing The Body Electric*. During the mid-70s, the group adopted more elements of rock rhythms and electronic technology, a process which reached its peak on *Black Market* (featuring electric bassist Jaco Pastorius). In the late 70s and early 80s, the group featured drummer Peter Erskine (replaced by Omar Hakim in 1982), Pastorius and the two founder members. *Procession* featured vocals by Janis Siegel. During the mid-80s, Zawinul and Shorter made solo albums before dissolving Weather Report in 1986.

WEATHERALL, ANDREW

UK dance music magnate Weatherall (b. 1963) began with residencies at the Shoom and Spectrum clubs in the acid house boom of 1988. Afterwards he founded the *Boy's Own* fanzine with Terry Farley and Steve Mayes, which concentrated on club music, fashion and football. When *Boy's Own* became a record label, he appeared, as guest vocalist, on a Bocca Juniors track. He made his name, however, by remixing **Primal Scream**'s 'Loaded'. The likes of **James**, the **Happy Mondays**, **That Petrol Emotion**, **Saint Etienne**, **Orb**, **Jah Wobble**, **Björk**, **Yello**, **Stereo MC's** and **New Order** followed. His landmark achievement, however, remains his supervising role on Primal Scream's *Screamadelica*. He also enjoyed a stint as DJ on Kiss-FM, before his eclectic, anarchic tastes proved too much for programmers. He subsequently set up a further label, recording and remix operation under the title Sabres Of Paradise. By the mid-90s he had begun to distance himself from the mainstream dance scene. Going back to his punk roots he has subsequently recorded with Keith Tenniswood as the Two Lone Swordsmen, releasing several mail order only singles and three albums of esoteric techno.

WEBB, JIMMY

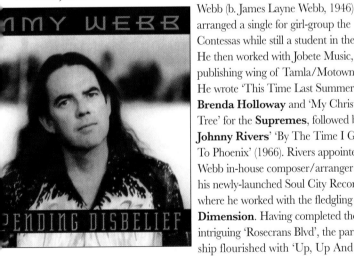

Webb (b. James Layne Webb, 1946) arranged a single for girl-group the Contessas while still a student in the US. He then worked with Jobete Music, the publishing wing of Tamla/Motown. He wrote 'This Time Last Summer' for **Brenda Holloway** and 'My Christmas Tree' for the **Supremes**, followed by **Johnny Rivers**' 'By The Time I Get To Phoenix' (1966). Rivers appointed Webb in-house composer/arranger for his newly-launched Soul City Records where he worked with the fledgling **5th Dimension**. Having completed the intriguing 'Rosecrans Blvd', the partnership flourished with 'Up, Up And Away', which sold over one million copies.

Eventually Webb issued a single, 'Love Years Coming', credited to the Strawberry Children. **Glen Campbell** then exhumed 'By The Time I Get To Phoenix', which won a Grammy as the Best Vocal Performance of 1967. In 1968, Richard Harris scored a major international smash with 'MacArthur Park' followed by 'Didn't We'. Webb arranged and composed material for Harris' albums *A Tramp Shining* and *The Yard Went On Forever*, but was dismayed when his own solo debut, *Jimmy Webb Sings Jimmy Webb*, was issued – it featured early demo recordings, overdubbed and orchestrated without his consent. Further success for Campbell with 'Wichita Lineman' (1968) demonstrated Webb's songwriting ability.

After a series of solo albums, Webb rekindled partnerships with Campbell and the **5th Dimension**, and also wrote and/or produced material for **Cher**, **Joan Baez**, **Joe Cocker**, Frank Sinatra and **Art Garfunkel**. He also continued to score film soundtracks, including *Voices* and *Hanoi Hilton*, and two musicals, *The Children's Crusade* and *Dandelion Wine*. Webb ceased recording following the release of 1982's *Angel Heart*. He undertook several live shows in 1988 and released the studio albums *Suspending Disbelief* and *Ten Easy Pieces* during the 90s.

WEDDING PRESENT

Formed in Leeds, England, in 1985 by David Gedge (b. 1960; guitar, vocals) with Keith Gregory (bass), Peter Salowka (guitar) and Shaun Charman (drums). The Wedding Present staked their musical claim with a ferocious blend of implausibly fast guitars and lovelorn lyrics over a series of much-lauded singles. Before *Seamonsters* was released, Salowka was replaced by Paul Dorrington, instead remaining on the business side of the band and formed the Ukranians. In 1992, the Wedding Present released a single every month, throughout the year. Each single reached the UK Top 30. Their relationship with RCA Records ended following the *Hit Parade* compilations. They signed to Island, minus Keith Gregory. *Mini* and *Saturnalia* enhanced their place as influential indie popsters, but in 1998 Gedge laid the band to rest and teamed up with Sally Murrell in Cinerama.

WEEZER

US guitar pop artisans from Los Angeles, USA. Rivers Cuomo (b. 1970; vocals, guitar), Brian Bell (b. 1968; guitar), Matt Sharp (bass) and Patrick Wilson (b. 1969; drums) signed to DGC Records in 1993. On the back of offbeat singles, 'Undone – The Sweater Song' and 'Buddy Holly' and seven months' touring the country, their self-titled debut album sold nearly a million copies. Their preference for goofy garage aesthetics were distinctive, along with their fuzzboxes and Sharp's falsetto harmonies. The title of *Pinkerton* infuriated the security company Pinkerton Service, who issued legal proceedings shortly after its release. Wilson and Sharp also recorded with the Rentals; the latter left Weezer in 1998 to concentrate on this new outfit. His replacement was Mikey Welsh (b. 1971). The *Green Album* was a sparkling return to the infectious heavy pop of their debut.

WELCH, GILLIAN

The daughter of Hollywood television composers, Welch attended the Berklee College Of Music in Boston, where she met her musical and songwriting partner David Rawlings. They began playing bluegrass clubs as a duo, gradually incorporating original material into a set consisting of traditional country songs. *Revival* (marketed under Welch's name, but essentially a duo album with Rawlings) featured 'By The Mark', a surprise favourite on American alternative radio. **Emmylou Harris** provided Welch with her first success when she covered 'Orphan Girl' on her acclaimed *Wrecking Ball*. The critically acclaimed *Hell Among The Yearlings* featured just Welch and Rawlings on a collection of songs marked by their melancholic beauty. In 2000, her music was featured in the hit movie *O Brother, Where Art Thou?*. Welch released *Time (The Revelator)*, on her own Acony imprint.

WELLER, PAUL

Weller (b. John William Weller, 1958) started out with UK band the **Jam**, then formed the **Style Council**. By 1990, he found himself without either a band or a recording contract for the first time in 13 years. Returning to early influences, he became inspired to write new material and set up a new band, the Paul Weller Movement. Weller released his first solo single, 'Into Tomorrow', on his own Freedom High label, before contributing seven compositions to wife D. C. Lee's Slam Slam project. His debut album was initially released on Pony Canyon in Japan, six months before a UK issue on Go! Discs. Second single 'Uh Huh, Oh Yeh' reached the UK Top 20. Weller's renaissance continued with 'Sunflower' and the bestselling *Wild Wood*, which demonstrated a love of 70s folk rock. Live favourites 'The Weaver' and 'Hung Up' reached the charts.

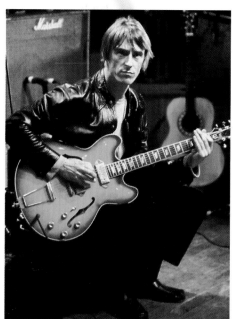

Stanley Road featured **Oasis**' Noel Gallagher on a cover version of **Dr. John**'s 'Walk On Gilded Splinters', and the endearing 'You Do Something To Me'. *Heavy Soul* and *Heliocentric* lacked the punch and sparkle of previous efforts.

WELLS, MARY

At the age of 17, Mary Wells (b. 1943, d. 1992) composed 'Bye Bye Baby'. Producer Berry Gordy offered her a contract with Motown, and Wells' rendition of her song became one of the company's first Top 50 hits in 1960. **Smokey Robinson** masterminded all her subsequent Motown releases. 'The One Who Really Loves You', 'You Beat Me To The Punch' and 'Two Lovers' were all Top 10 hits. The pinnacle of the Robinson/Wells partnership, however, was 'My Guy' (1964, US number 1/UK Top 5). It introduced the Motown sound to a worldwide audience. Gordy encouraged her to record an album of duets with **Marvin Gaye**, from which 'Once Upon A Time' was another major hit. Just as Wells' career reached its peak, she chose to leave Motown, tempted by a film offer from 20th Century Fox. Without Robinson, she was unable to capture her hit form, and she left Fox the following year. In 1966, she married Cecil Womack and moved to Atco Records, where she scored minor hits with 'Dear Lover', 'Such A Sweet Thing' and 'The Doctor'. Subsequent sessions for a variety of US labels proved less than successful, and she was reduced to re-recording her Motown hits in the 80s, she also continued touring and recording. Sadly Wells died of throat cancer in 1992.

WESTLIFE

This Irish boy band, originally known as Westside, emerged in the late 90s as the highly successful protégés of Ronan Keating of **Boyzone**. Kian Egan (b. 1980), Shane Filan (b. 1979), Mark Feehily (b. 1980), Nicky Byrne (b. 1978) and Bryan McFadden (b. 1980) made their debut in 1999 with 'Swear It Again'. The track was an Irish and UK chart-topper. 'If I Let You Go', 'Flying Without Wings', 'I Have A Dream'/'Seasons In The Sun', 'Fool Again', 'Against All Odds' (with **Mariah Carey**) and 'My Love', were consecutive UK number 1s in 1999–2000, breaking all chart records. Their Christmas single 'What Makes A Man'/'My Girl' was pipped to the coveted number 1 slot by children television's character Bob The Builder. The group bounced back to the top in March 2001 with their cover version of Billy Joel's 'Uptown Girl', released for the Comic Relief charity. 'Queen Of My Heart' and 'World Of Our Own' also reached number 1.

WET WET WET

Formed in 1982, this Scottish pop group comprised Graeme Clark (bass, vocals), Neil Mitchell (keyboards), Marti Pellow (b. Mark McLoughlin, 1966; vocals) and Tom Cunningham (drums). After live performances, they were signed by Phonogram Records in 1985. In 1987, 'Wishing I Was Lucky' reached the UK Top 10, followed by the even more successful 'Sweet Little Mystery'. The group's agreeable blue-eyed soul was evident on their debut *Popped In Souled Out*. Further hits followed with 'Angel Eyes (Home And Away)' and 'Temptation'. In 1988, the group's profile was increased when they reached UK number 1 with a reading of the **Beatles**' 'With A Little Help From My Friends'. In 1992, 'Goodnight Girl' remained at UK number 1 for several weeks. Two years later they enjoyed staggering UK success with a cover of the **Troggs**' 'Love Is All Around', the theme song to the hit movie *Four Weddings And A Funeral*. It stayed at UK number 1 for 15 weeks. Following 1997's *10*, drummer Cunningham left

the group. A more serious defection followed in 1999, when Pellow announced he was embarking on a solo career following the admission of a drug habit. His debut, *Smile*, was released in 2001.

WHAM!

Wham! was formed in 1982 by school friends **George Michael** (b. Georgios (Yorgos) Kyriacos Panayiotou, 1963; vocals) and Andrew Ridgeley (b. 1963; guitar). They completed their debut single 'Wham! Rap' which had been intended as a disco parody. What emerged was an exhilarating dance number with intriguing double-edged lyrics. The song initially failed to chart. The following 'Young Guns' (1982) reached the UK Top 10, as did a remixed 'Wham! Rap'. The duo then signed to Epic Records and achieved their first UK number 1 with 'Wake Me Up Before You Go Go', quickly followed by 'Careless Whisper' (credited to George Michael). *Make It Big* zoomed to number 1 and by the end of 1984 the group had two further major successes 'Freedom' and 'Last Christmas'/'Everything She Wants'. In 1985, they toured China and enjoyed considerable success in America. On 28 June 1986, they played a farewell concert before 72,000 fans at London's Wembley Stadium. After the split George Michael's solo career blossomed, notably in the USA where he was taken more seriously as an AOR artist. Ridgeley predictably struggled to establish his own music career.

WHEATUS

New York, USA-based guitar pop outfit created by songwriter Brendan B. Brown (b. 1973; guitar, vocals), and joined by his younger brother Peter (b. 1976; drums), multi-instrumentalist Phil A. Jimenez (b. 1975), and Rich Leigey (bass) on Wheatus' 2000 debut. Tracks such as the hit single 'Teenage Dirtbag', 'Sunshine' and 'Truffles' displayed a fine understanding of the rudiments of power pop. Leigey was replaced by Mike McCabe shortly before the album was released.

WHISKEYTOWN

North Carolina, USA-based alternative country band led by songwriter **Ryan Adams** (b. David Ryan Adams, 1974; vocals, guitar, banjo). Adams formed Whiskeytown in 1994 with Phil Wandscher (guitar, vocals), Caitlin Cary (violin, vocals), Eric 'Skillet' Gilmore (drums, vocals) and Steve Grothman (bass). Their debut *Faithless Street* appeared in 1996. Adams' abrasive and reckless vocal style was reminiscent of Paul Westerberg, although Cary contributed the album's most affecting vocal on 'Matrimony'. Adams, Wandscher, Cary, and new rhythm section Jeff Rice (bass) and Steve Terry (drums) recorded the material for their major label debut *Strangers Almanac*, although Wandscher left shortly afterwards. Adams and Cary were then joined by Ed Crawford (guitar, vocals, ex-**fIREHOSE**), Mike Daly (keyboards, guitar), Jenni Snyder (bass), with founder member Gilmore returning on drums. A revised line-up featuring Adams, Cary, Daly, Brad Rice (guitar), Richard Causon (keyboards), Jennifer Condos (bass) recorded the final Whiskeytown album, following which Adams and Cary embarked on solo careers. The final Whiskeytown album, *Pneumonia*, was released in 2001.

WHITE STRIPES

One of a new breed of back-to-basics rock acts to emerge from Detroit, Michigan, USA, the White Stripes comprises enigmatic duo Jack White (b. John White; guitar, vocals) and Meg White (drums). The Whites, variously assumed to be brother and sister or husband and ex-wife, but both denied, formed their new band in 1997. Their striking stage presence, dressed in minimalist red and white outfits, is allied to their thrilling grasp of the rudiments of timeless rock music. Their self-titled long-playing debut garnered immediate praise, mixing astute cover versions (**Robert Johnson**'s 'Stop Breaking Down Blues' and **Bob Dylan**'s 'One More Cup Of Coffee') with originals. By the time of the following year's *De Stijl*, named after the Dutch abstract art movement, the media buzz surrounding the White Stripes had reached new heights. Of particular note was the duo's incredible reception in the UK, where their music was lauded by a wide range of media outlets. The Whites went some way to justifying the media hype surrounding them when they released an excellent third album, *White Blood Cells*.

WHITE ZOMBIE

Theatrical metal band formed in 1985 in New York, USA, by **Rob Zombie** (b. Robert Cummings, 1966), Sean Yseult (bass), Ivan DePlume (drums) and Tom Guay (guitar). They released two albums of noisy metal on their own labels. John Ricci replaced Guay for *Make Them Die Slowly*, but was in turn replaced by Jay Yuenger for the *God Of Thunder* EP. They toured the USA ceaselessly, receiving continuous MTV coverage. As *La Sexorcisto: Devil Music Vol. 1* took off, DePlume was replaced by Philo, then by John Tempesta. *Astro Creep 2000* was greeted with enthusiasm, selling over a million US copies in a few weeks. 'More Human Than Human', also became a major hit, appearing on mainstream radio. *Supersexy Swingin' Sounds* in 1996 was very well received, although as a marketing tool the 60s easy listening hammock style cover was a total contradiction to the music within. Rob Zombie released his solo debut, *Hellbilly Deluxe*, in 1998, retaining Tempesta on drums. The album debuted at US number 5 in September, shortly before White Zombie announced they were splitting-up.

WHITE, BARRY

At age 11, US-born White (b. 1944) played piano on Jesse Belvin's hit, 'Goodnight My Love'. He made several records during the early 60s, as 'Barry Lee', and as a member of various bands, alongside guiding the careers of, amongst others, Felice Taylor and Viola Wills. In 1969, White put together Love Unlimited, a female vocal trio made up of Diana Taylor, Glodean James (his future wife) and her sister Linda. He also founded the Love Unlimited Orchestra. Love Unlimited's success with 'Walkin' In The Rain With The One I Love' (1972), featuring White's gravelly, passion-soaked voice, rejuvenated his career, scoring major US and UK hits with 'I'm Gonna Love You Just A Little More Baby', 'Never, Never Gonna Give Ya Up' (both 1973), 'Can't Get Enough Of Your Love, Babe' and 'You're The First, The Last, My Everything' (both 1974). White's lyrics grew more sexually explicit and, although his pop hits lessened towards the end of the 70s, he remained the idolatry subject of live performances. His last major hit was in 1978 with **Billy Joel**'s 'Just The Way You Are', although he returned to the UK Top 20 in 1987 with 'Sho' You Right'. During the 90s, a series of commercially successful albums proved White's status as more than just a cult figure.

WHITESNAKE

UK-based heavy rock band led by former **Deep Purple** vocalist David Coverdale (b. 1951; ex-Deep Purple). Coverdale had recorded two solo albums, *Whitesnake* and *Northwinds*, before forming a touring band from musicians who

had played on those records: Micky Moody (guitar), Bernie Marsden (guitar), Brian Johnston (keyboards), Neil Murray (bass) and David Dowell (drums). Severeal personnel changes saw ex-Deep Purple members Jon Lord and Ian Paice joining on keyboards and drums. Whitesnake's first British hit was 'Fool For Your Loving' (1980), and the double album *Live In The Heart Of The City* reached the Top 10. After a temporary hiatus, Whitesnake re-formed in 1982 but only Coverdale, Lord and Moody remained from the earlier line-up. The new members were Mel Galley (guitar), Colin Hodgkinson (bass) and Cozy Powell (drums). By 1984, Moody and Lord had also left, but despite further personnel changes the band remained one of the leading exponents of heavy rock and frequent tours brought a million-selling album in the USA with *Whitesnake*. Coverdale's bluesy ballad style brought transatlantic Top 10 hits with 'Is This Love' and 'Here I Go Again'. Coverdale put the group on ice in 1990 and went on join forces with **Jimmy Page** for *Coverdale/Page* in early 1993. Coverdale returned in 1997 with a new Whitesnake album, *Restless Heart*.

WHO

Formed in London, England, in 1964 by **Pete Townshend** (b. 1945; guitar, vocals), Roger Daltrey (b. 1944; vocals) and John Entwistle (b. 1944; bass). They recruited drummer Keith Moon (b. 1946, d. 1978) and were adopted by manager/publicist Peter Meadon, who changed their name to the High Numbers, dressed them in stylish clothes and determinedly courted a mod audience, through their single, 'I'm The Face'. Two budding film directors, Kit Lambert and Chris Stamp, then assumed management responsibilities and re-named them the Who.

Their in-person violence matched an anti-social attitude and despite a successful residency at London's Marquee club, the Who were shunned by major labels. Eventually they signed with American Decca Records. 'I Can't Explain' (1965) reached UK Top 10, followed by 'Anyway, Anyhow, Anywhere' and 'My Generation'. The Who's debut album was delayed to accommodate new Townshend originals at the expense of now passé cover versions. The Who continued to chart, although Townshend's decidedly English perceptions initially precluded a sustained international success. The Who's popularity in the USA flourished only in the wake of their appearance at the 1967 Monterey Pop Festival.

They returned to the UK Top 10 in 1967 with the powerful 'I Can See For Miles'. However, the band failed to achieve a number 1 hit on either side of the Atlantic. They embraced the album market fully with *Tommy*, an extravagant rock opera which became a staple part of their increasingly in demand live appearances. The set spawned a major hit in 'Pinball Wizard' but, more crucially, established the Who as a serious act courting critical respectability. The propulsive *Live At Leeds* was a sturdy concert souvenir.

Townshend's next project, *Lighthouse*, was later aborted, although several of its songs were incorporated into the highly successful *Who's Next*. A series of specifically created singles came next – 'Let's See Action' (1971), 'Join

Together' (1972), 'Relay' (1973) – which marked time as Townshend completed work on another concept album, *Quadrophenia*.

Commitments to solo careers then undermined the band's progress and *The Who By Numbers* was low-key. They re-emerged with the confident *Who Are You*, but its release was sadly overshadowed when, on 23 August 1978, Keith Moon died following an overdose of medication taken to alleviate alcohol addiction. His madcap behaviour and idiosyncratic, exciting drumming had been an integral part of the Who fabric. A retrospective film, *The Kids Are Alright*, enhanced a sense of finality, but the Who resumed recording in 1979 with former **Small Faces/Faces** drummer Kenny Jones (b. 1948). *Neither Face Dances* nor *It's Hard* recaptured previous artistic heights. A farewell tour was undertaken in 1982–3 and although the band reunited for Live Aid, they remained estranged until 1989, when Townshend agreed to undertake a series of US dates for their 25th anniversary (with drummer Simon Phillips).

In 1996, the band performed *Quadrophenia* at London's Hyde Park, in front of 200,000 people, with Zak Starkey on drums. They toured the USA and the UK later that year. A major tour also took place in 2000.

WIDESPREAD PANIC
The **Allman Brothers Band** of the 90s, Georgia, USA-based Widespread Panic were formed at the University of Georgia in the mid-80s by John Bell (vocals, guitar), Michael Houser (guitar) and Dave Schools (bass). This trio recorded a single, 'Coconut Image', before Todd Nance (drums) joined in 1986, and with the addition of temporary member Domingo Ortiz (percussion), the new line-up toured extensively. A poorly recorded debut album appeared on the independent Landslide label in 1988. Tee Lavitz (ex-Dixie Dregs) appeared on their self-titled Capricorn debut. The band's final line-up came about when Ortiz joined full time and John 'JoJo' Herman replaced Lavitz. The band gained a higher profile with their appearances on the first two HORDE tours (Horizons Of Rock Developing Everywhere). Their Capricorn albums faithfully replicate their loose, jamming live sound. They have also recorded two albums with songwriter Vic Chesnutt as Brute.

WILCO
This US quintet was initially viewed as part of the 'No Depression' movement of neo-country rock acts in the early 90s. Formed by ex-**Uncle Tupelo** member Jeff Tweedy (vocals, guitar), their 1995 debut album sold modestly. It was followed by the double *Being There*, with the band agreeing to take a cut in their royalties in order to facilitate its release. The ever productive Tweedy has also recorded two albums with Golden Smog, a side project involving, among others, members of the **Jayhawks** and **Soul Asylum**. In 1998, the whole band worked with English singer-songwriter **Billy Bragg** on the acclaimed *Mermaid Avenue* project, adding music to lyrics bequeathed by American folk legend **Woody Guthrie** (a second volume was released two years later). In contrast, *Summer Teeth* was an album swimming in the lush pop sounds of synthesizers, mellotrons and brass. *Yankee Hotel Foxtrot* was delayed following a dispute with Reprise Records. The album was eventually released in 2002 on Nonesuch Records.

WILDE, KIM
The daughter of 50s pop idol **Marty Wilde**, UK born Kim (b. Kim Smith, 1960) was signed to Mickie Most's Rak Records in 1980. Her first single, 'Kids In America', reached UK number 2. Further singles success followed and *Kim Wilde* fared well in the album charts. While 'View From A Bridge' maintained her standing at home, 'Kids In America' reached the US Top 30. An energetic reworking of the **Supremes**' 'You Keep Me Hangin' On' took her back to UK number 2. In 1988, the dance-orientated 'You Came' was followed by further Top 10 hits 'Never Trust A Stranger' and 'Four Letter Word'. Later she scored a Christmas novelty hit 'Rockin' Around The Christmas Tree' with comedian Mel Smith. Her 90s singles gained lowly chart positions, and in 1999 Wilde put her recording career behind her to present a series of television gardening programmes.

WILDE, MARTY
UK rock 'n' roll singer Wilde (b. Reginald Leonard Smith, 1936) was spotted by songwriter Lionel Bart, and signed to entrepreneur Larry Parnes. Parnes arranged a record deal with Philips Records, but Wilde's initial singles failed to chart. Nevertheless, Wilde was promoted vigorously, culminating in a hit recording of Jody Reynolds' 'Endless Sleep' (1957). Soon afterwards, Wilde became the resident star of new television programme *Oh Boy!* – until he was replaced by **Cliff Richard**. After considerable success with such songs as 'Donna', 'Teenager In Love', 'Sea Of Love' and his own composition 'Bad Boy', Wilde veered away from rock 'n' roll to concentrate on Frank Sinatra-style ballads. His last major success was with a lacklustre version of **Bobby Vee**'s 'Rubber Ball' in 1961. Wilde also enjoyed songwriting success, with hits like **Status Quo**'s 'Ice In The Sun'. By the 70s, he was managing his son Ricky, who later achieved songwriting success for his sister, **Kim Wilde**.

WILLIAMS, HANK
Hank (b. Hiram Williams, 1923, d. 1953) learned guitar from an elderly black musician, Teetot (Rufe Payne), and as a result, a strong blues thread runs through his work. After winning a talent contest, Williams formed the Drifting Cowboys. In 1946, Williams made his first recordings for the small Sterling label before signing to MGM Records, where 'Move It On Over' sold several thousand copies. He joined the radio show *The Louisiana Hayride* in 1948 and was featured on its concert tours. His revival of 'Lovesick Blues' topped the US country charts for 16 weeks. *The Grand Ole Opry* invited him to perform the song, leading to an unprecedented six encores. He and the Drifting Cowboys became regulars, commanding $1,000 for concert appearances. 'Wedding Bells' made number 2, as did 'I'm So Lonesome I Could Cry'. In 1950, he had three country number 1s, 'Long Gone Lonesome Blues', 'Why Don't You Love Me?' and 'Moanin' The Blues'. The following year, he had two further chart-toppers with 'Cold, Cold Heart' and 'Hey, Good Lookin'. In 1952, Williams reached number 1 with 'Jambalaya'.

Williams drank too much, took drugs and permanently lived in conflict. His songs articulated real life and love; he also recorded melodramatic monologues as Luke The Drifter. Williams' wife, 'Miss Audrey', also made solo records, but she was frustrated by her own lack of success and many of Williams' songs stemmed from their quarrels. They were divorced in 1952.

In the same year, Williams was fired from the *Grand Ole Opry* due to his drinking. His earnings fell and he was reduced to playing small clubs with pick-up bands. Scrabbling for security, he married the 19-year-old Billie Jean Jones. His biggest booking for some time was on New Year's Day, 1953 with Hawkshaw Hawkins and Homer And Jethro in Canton, Ohio. Because of a blizzard, Williams' plane was cancelled and an 18-year-old taxi driver, Charles Carr, was hired to drive Williams' Cadillac. Williams, having devoured a bottle of whiskey, sank into a deep sleep. Five hours later, Carr discovered that his passenger was dead, officially due to 'severe heart attack with haemorrhage' – his current number 1 was 'I'll Never Get Out Of This World Alive'.

WILLIAMS, HANK, JNR

Williams Jnr (b. Randall Hank Williams Jnr, 1949), the son of **Hank Williams**, performed as a child, and had a high school band, Rockin' Randall And The Rockets. He copied his father's style for the soundtrack of the film biography of his father, *Your Cheatin' Heart* (1964), and starred in the inferior *A Time To Sing*. In 1974, Hank recorded *Hank Williams Jr. And Friends*, with Charlie Daniels and other top-class southern country rockers. In 1975, he fell 500 feet down a Montana mountain face and almost died. He had to learn to speak (and sing) all over again. Williams' rowdy image did not fit in well with the clean-cut 'hat acts' of the early 90s, and his record sales and airplay faltered. However he remains a sell-out concert draw.

WILLIAMS, ROBBIE

After his controversial split from **Take That** in 1995, UK singer Williams (b. 1974) hit the tabloid headlines as a result of occasional wild behaviour. He signed to Chrysalis Records in 1996, and released 'Freedom', a **George Michael** cover. It was badly received critically, despite reaching UK number 2. *Life Thru A Lens*, his autobiographical debut co-written with Guy Chambers of **World Party**, was released to critical acclaim but slow sales. The Christmas single 'Angels' almost single-handedly revived his ailing career. His album, which had slumped, entered the UK Top 10 for the first time and eventually climbed to number one 28 weeks after it was first released. His renaissance continued with 'Millennium' entering the UK singles chart at number 1 in 1998, and *I've Been Expecting You* topping the album chart two months later. Williams was also announced to be the biggest selling album artist of 1998.

In 1999, Williams set about trying to woo America, touring in support of *The Ego Has Landed*, a selection of the best tracks from both albums. In November, he returned to the top of the UK charts with the double a-side, 'She's The One'/'It's Only Us'. The former song was written and previously recorded by Karl Wallinger of World Party. *Sing When You're Winning* proved beyond all doubt that Williams had won over the UK tabloids, music press and record buying public. Of more dubious musical value was the Frank Sinatra-worshipping *Swing When You're Winning*. Nevertheless, an entertaining collaboration with actress Nicole Kidman on 'Somethin' Stupid' reached number 1 and the album was a huge commercial success.

WILSON, BRIAN

Brian Wilson (b. 1942) was the spiritual leader of the **Beach Boys**, but this 'musical genius' was dogged by mental health problems during much of the 60s and 70s. He released the solo 'Caroline No' in 1966, but it has since been absorbed into the Beach Boys canon. His 1988 debut *Brian Wilson* was released to excellent reviews with Wilson bravely appearing for the major publicity that ensued, but by commercial standards it was a flop. After the rest of the Beach Boys had taken him to court, Wilson successfully contested the ownership of his back catalogue, which had been sold by his father. Immediately after this, Mike Love issued a writ claiming he had co-written 79 of Wilson's songs and demanding royalties. To crown this, Sire Records rejected Wilson's *Sweet Insanity* as 'pathetic'. However, in 1993 he was working with Van Dyke Parks and Andy Paley on further new songs, and was once again writing songs with Mike Love. The television documentary *I Just Wasn't Made For These Times* was the first in-depth interview with Wilson. The accompanying Don Was-produced album failed to ignite, but *Orange Crate Art* (recorded with Van Dyke Parks) was more cohesive. Wilson worked long and hard on *Imagination*, although sales were modest. He undertook a tour of the USA in 1999. The following year he embarked on the Pet Sounds Symphony tour, backed by a 55-piece orchestra.

WILSON, JACKIE

When parental pressure thwarted his boxing ambitions, Wilson (b. 1934, d. 1984) took to singing in small local clubs. He sang with the Thrillers, recorded some solo tracks for **Dizzy Gillespie**'s Dee Gee label (as Sonny Wilson) and joined Billy Ward And The Dominoes in 1953. He went solo in 1957, releasing 'Reet Petite'. It was a comparative failure in the USA; in the UK, however, it soared to number 6. 'Reet Petite' had been written by Berry Gordy and Tyran Carlo (Roquel 'Billy' Davis), who went on to compose several of Wilson's subsequent releases, including 'Lonely Teardrops' (1958).

In 1960, Wilson enjoyed two R&B number 1 hits with 'Doggin' Around' and 'A Woman, A Lover, A Friend'. His musical direction then grew increasingly erratic. There were still obvious highlights such as 'Baby Workout' (1963), 'Squeeze Her Please Her' (1964), 'No Pity (In The Naked City)' (1965), but all too often his wonderfully fluid voice was wasted on cursory, quickly dated material. The artist's live appearances, however, remained exciting.

Wilson's career was rejuvenated in 1966 with 'Whispers (Gettin' Louder)'. However, 'This Love Is Real (I Can Feel Those Vibrations)' (1970) proved to be his last Top 10 R&B entry. In 1975, Wilson suffered a heart attack on-stage at New Jersey's Latin Casino. He struck his head on falling and the resulting brain damage left him comatose. He remained hospitalized until his death. Fate provided a final twist in 1987, when an imaginative video using Plasticene animation, propelled 'Reet Petite' to number 1 in the UK charts. Wilson was inducted into the Rock And Roll Hall Of Fame the same year.

WINCHESTER, JESSE

Evading the US draft, Winchester (b. 1944) moved to Canada. His self-titled debut album was followed by 'Brand New Tennessee Waltz', which was covered by a number of artists including the **Everly Brothers**. *Third Down, 110 To Go* was produced by **Todd Rundgren**, but in spite of its solid quality failed to sell. On *Learn To Love* he was assisted by several members of the Amazing Rhythm Aces. By 1976, Winchester was touring the USA, having received an amnesty from President Carter. His songs have been covered by **Elvis Costello**, **Tim Hardin** and **Joan Baez**.

WINGS

Wings was formed in 1971 by **Paul McCartney** (b. 1942) and his wife Linda (b. Linda Eastman, 1942, d. 1998; percussion, vocals) with Denny Laine (b. Brian Hines, 1944; guitar, vocals, ex-Moody Blues), and Denny Seiwell (drums). Guitarist Henry McCullough joined in 1971, and 1972 was taken up by the famous 'surprise' college gigs around the UK. Notoriety was achieved at about the same time by the BBC's banning of 'Give Ireland Back To The Irish'. Later that year 'Hi,Hi,Hi' (doubled with 'C Moon') also offended the censors for its 'overt sexual references', though it penetrated the US and UK Top 10. In 1973, Wings scored a double number 1 in the USA with *Red Rose Speedway* and 'My Love'.

Shortly before the next album, McCullough and Seiwell quit. Ironically, the result was the band's most acclaimed album, *Band On The Run*, with McCartney taking a multi-instrumental role. It topped the UK and US charts, and kicked off 1974 by yielding two transatlantic Top 10 singles in 'Jet' and 'Band On The Run'. In 1974, Jimmy McCulloch (b. 1953, d. 1979; guitar, vocals) and Joe English (drums) joined. The new line-up got off to a strong start with *Venus And Mars* (UK/US number 1), the single 'Listen To What The Man Said' also topped the US charts. After *Wings At The Speed Of Sound* (UK number 2/US number 1), they embarked on a massive US tour. The resulting live triple *Wings Over America* became their fifth consecutive US number 1 album and the biggest-selling triple of all time.

McCulloch and English left in 1977 and the remaining Wings cut the maudlin 'Mull Of Kintyre', which stayed at UK number 1 for 9 weeks. Laurence Juber and Steve Holly were recruited following the release of *London Town*, but *Back To The Egg* failed to impress, with 'Getting Closer' not even hitting the UK chart. Shortly afterwards McCartney went solo.

WINTER, JOHNNY

Blues guitarist Winter (b. 1944) made his recording debut in 1960, fronting Johnny and the Jammers. By 1968, he was leading Tommy Shannon (bass) and John Turner (drums) in Winter. The group recorded a single for Sonobeat, subsequently issued by United Artists Records as *The Progressive Blues Experiment*. *Johnny Winter* ably demonstrated his exceptional dexterity, while *Second Winter*, which included rousing versions of 'Johnny B. Goode' and 'Highway 61 Revisited', suggested a new-found emphasis on rock. Heroin addiction forced Winter into partial retirement and it was two years before he re-emerged with *Still Alive And Well*. Subsequent work was bedevilled by indecision until the artist returned to his roots with the late 70s albums *Nothing But The Blues* and *White Hot And Blue*. Winter also produced and arranged a series of acclaimed albums for **Muddy Waters**. His contribution to the blues should not be underestimated; he remains an exceptional talent.

WINWOOD, STEVE

UK artist Winwood (b. 1948) first achieved 'star' status with the **Spencer Davis Group**. In 1967 he left to form **Traffic**, and briefly played with the supergroup **Blind Faith**. Traffic ground to a halt in 1974, but the eagerly anticipated solo album did not appear until 1977, and it displayed a relaxed Winwood performing only six numbers. In 1980, the majestic *Arc Of A Diver* was an unqualified and unexpected triumph, going platinum in the USA. The

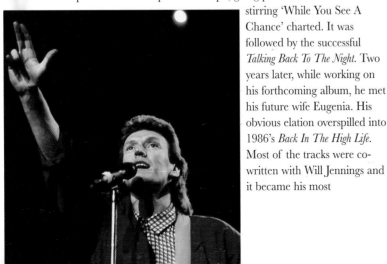

stirring 'While You See A Chance' charted. It was followed by the successful *Talking Back To The Night*. Two years later, while working on his forthcoming album, he met his future wife Eugenia. His obvious elation overspilled into 1986's *Back In The High Life*. Most of the tracks were co-written with Will Jennings and it became his most commercially successful record so far. The album spawned three hits including 'Higher Love' (US number 1).

The single 'Roll With It' preceded the album of the same name. Both reached US number 1. In 1990, *Refugees Of The Heart* became his least successful album, although it contained another major US hit with the Winwood/**Jim Capaldi** composition 'One And Only Man'. In 1994, Traffic re-formed, but *Far From Home* sounded more like a Winwood solo album than any Traffic project. His next studio album, 1997's *Junction 7*, was a bitter disappointment.

WIRE

Punk-influenced UK band formed in 1976 by Colin Newman (b. 1954; vocals, guitar), Bruce Gilbert (b. 1946; guitar), Graham Lewis (b. 1953; bass, vocals), Robert Gotobed (b. Mark Field; drums) and lead guitarist George Gill. The latter was dismissed preceding the band's appearance on *The Roxy, London, WC2*. Wire's impressive debut, *Pink Flag*, featured 21 tracks ranging from the furious 'Field Day For The Sundays' and 'Mr Suit' to the more brittle 'Mannequin', their first single. *Chairs Missing* was similar to its predecessor, but more mature. *154* contained several exceptional moments, including 'A Touching Display' and the haunting 'A Mutual Friend'. However, the album marked the end of Wire's Harvest Records contract and musical differences led to the band splitting. *Document And Eyewitness* chronicled Wire's final concert at London's Electric Ballroom in 1980.

In 1985, the band began recording again with *The Ideal Copy* which topped the independent chart. *A Bell Is A Cup (Until It Is Struck)* maintained the new-found balance between art and commercial pop. In 1990, they abandoned the 'beat combo' concept of 1985 and utilized computer and sequencer technology. *Manscape* showed a dramatic sound change. Gotobed left shortly afterwards and the remaining trio changed their name to Wir. Their first release, *The First Letter*, showed a harder edge than their 80s work. Although this was their final release, the band subsequently became the subject of renewed interest in the mid-90s when indie darlings **Elastica** not only name-checked but also borrowed liberally from their back-catalogue. The original quartet re-formed in 1999.

WISHBONE ASH

In 1966, Steve Upton (drums) joined Martin Turner (bass, vocals) and Glen Turner (guitar) in the UK band, Empty Vessels. They became Tanglewood. Glen Turner departed, and Ted Turner (b. David Alan Turner; guitar) joined. Andy Powell (guitar) also joined and they took the name Wishbone Ash. The hallmark of this progressive rock band was the powerful sound of twin lead guitars. Their biggest commercial success was 1972's *Argus*, a set preoccupied with historical themes, complex instrumentals and folk-rock. Personnel changes saw Ted Turner replaced by Laurie Wisefield in 1974, Martin Turner by John Wetton in 1980, and Wetton himself by Trevor Bolder. In 1987, after several further line-up changes, the original quartet recorded *Nouveau Calls*. They continue to perform.

WITHERS, BILL

After several years of trying to sell his songs, US artist Withers (b. 1938) was signed to Sussex Records in 1971. He secured an immediate hit with his debut 'Ain't No Sunshine', produced by Booker T. Jones. 'Lean On Me' and 'Use Me' (both 1972) followed – all three were million-sellers. Withers continued to score success with 'Make Love To Your Mind' (1975), 'Lovely Day' (1977) and 'Just The Two Of Us' (1981). The latter, a duet with saxophonist Grover Washington Jnr, won a Grammy in 1982 for Best R&B Performance. 'Lovely Day' reached the UK Top 5 in 1988.

WITNESS

This Greater Manchester, England-based band was formed by long time friends Gerard Starkie (vocals) and Ray Chan (guitar). Joined by bass player Dylan

Keeton and drummer John Langley, they recorded 1999's excellent *Before The Calm*. The album's melancholic soundscapes evoked memories of early **R.E.M.** and **American Music Club**.

WIZZARD

Formed in 1972 by **Roy Wood** (b. Ulysses Adrian Wood, 1946) with Rick Price (vocals, bass), Hugh McDowell (cello), Bill Hunt (keyboards), Mike Burney (saxophone), Mike Burney (saxophone), Nick Pentelow (saxophone), Keith Smart (drums) and Charlie Grima (drums). They debuted at the 1972 Wembley Rock 'n' Roll Festival and hit the charts with 'Ball Park Incident' (1972). Wood was at his peak as a producer during this period and his **Phil Spector**-like 'wall of sound' pop experiments produced two memorable UK number 1s ('See My Baby Jive', 'Angel Fingers') and a perennial festive hit ('I Wish It Could Be Christmas Every Day'). Much of Wizzard's charm came from the complementary pop theatrics of Roy Wood, who covered himself with war paint, painted stars on his forehead and sported an unruly mane of multi-coloured hair. By the mid-70s Wizzard had folded, with Wood going on to form the short-lived Wizzo Band before concentrating on solo work.

WOMACK AND WOMACK

One of modern soul's most successful duos, comprising husband and wife team Cecil Womack (b. Cleveland, Ohio, USA) and Linda Cooke Womack. They worked as a writing team for Philadelphia International, numbering the **O'Jays** and **Patti LaBelle** among their clients. They achieved notable success with 'Love TKO', a 1980 soul hit for **Teddy Pendergrass** and the Womack's first US chart entry. The duo's fortunes prospered in the USA and UK, including the club favourite 'Love Wars' (1984) and 'Teardrops' (1988). In the early 90s, they journeyed to Nigeria, where they discovered ancestral ties to the Zekkariyas tribe. They consequently adopted the names Zeriiya (Linda) and Zekkariyas (Cecil).

WOMACK, BOBBY

A founder member of the **Valentinos**, US musician Womack (b. 1944) also worked as a guitarist for **Sam Cooke**. Womack's early solo singles, 'Nothing You Can Do' and 'I Found A True Love', were all but shunned and he reverted to session work. He became a fixture at Chips Moman's American Recording Studio and worked with **Wilson Pickett**, who recorded 17 Womack songs. Womack meanwhile resurrected his solo career and began a string of R&B hits, including 'It's Gonna Rain', 'How I Miss You Baby' (both 1969) and 'More Than I Can Stand' (1970). *The Womack Live* introduced the freer, more personal direction he would undertake in the 70s. The strong *Understanding* yielded impressive singles that achieved high positions in the R&B charts: 'That's The Way I Feel About Cha' (number 2), 'Woman's Gotta Have It' (number 1) and 'Harry Hippie' (number 8). In 1981, Womack recorded the powerful *The Poet*. His single, 'If You Think You're Lonely Now', reached the US R&B Top 5. *The Poet II* featured three duets with **Patti LaBelle**, one of which, 'Love Has Finally Come At Last', was another hit. Womack remained fairly quiet during the 90s, although he returned to the recording studio in 1999 with his first ever gospel set, *Back To My Roots*.

WONDER STUFF

UK indie band formed in 1986 by Miles Hunt (vocals, guitar), Malcolm Treece (guitar), Rob Jones (b. 1964, d. 1993; bass; replacing original member Chris Fradgley) and drummer Martin Gilks. They released their debut EP, *It's A Wonderful Day*, to favourable small press coverage. 'Give Give Give Me More More More' offered a minor hit in 1988, the perfect precursor to the Wonder Stuff's vital *The Eight Legged Groove Machine*, which reached the UK charts. 'It's Yer Money I'm After Baby', also from the album, continued to mine Hunt's cynical furrow and began a string of UK Top 40 hits. *Hup*, aided by fiddle, banjo and keyboard player Martin Bell, contrasted a harder, hi-tech sound with a rootsy, folk feel. The band's well-documented internal wrangles came to a head with the departure of Rob Jones at the end of the decade (he died of heart failure in 1993). 'Circlesquare' introduced new bass player Paul Clifford, and was followed by 1991's UK Top 10 hit 'The Size Of A Cow'. This was quickly followed by 'Caught In My Shadow' and *Never Loved Elvis*. Gone were the brash, punk-inspired three-minute classics, replaced by a richer musical and song-writing content. In 1991, in conjunction with comedian Vic Reeves, they topped the UK charts with a revival of **Tommy Roe**'s 'Dizzy'. The band made a swift return to the Top 10 in 1992 with the *Welcome To The Cheap Seats* EP followed by *Construction For The Modern Idiot*, but split in 1994.

Former members of the band (Treece, Clifford and Gilks) briefly regrouped in 1995 as Weknowwhereyoulive. Hunt also gave up his job as host of MTV's *120 Minutes* to put together a new band known as Vent 414. Following the break-up of both these ventures the four surviving original members of the Wonder Stuff reunited in late 2000 to perform a number of live shows in London. Hunt subsequently began recording with the Miles Hunt Club, releasing an eponymous album in 2002.

WONDER, STEVIE

Despite being blind almost from birth, US musician Wonder (b. Steveland Judkins, 1950) had mastered piano, drums and harmonica by the age of nine. In 1961, he was discovered by Ronnie White (**Miracles**), who arranged an audition at Motown Records. In 1963 the release of the live recording 'Fingertips (Part 2)' established his commercial success. Wonder's career was placed on hold while his voice was breaking, but he re-emerged in 1965 with a typically Motown sound, scoring a worldwide hit with the dance-orientated 'Uptight (Everything's Alright)'. This began a run of US Top 40 hits that continued for over six years.

From 1965-70, Stevie Wonder was marketed like other Motown stars, recording material chosen for him by the label's executives, and issuing albums that mixed conventional soul compositions with pop standards. He co-wrote almost all his singles from 1967 onwards, and began to collaborate on releases by other Motown artists. His contract with Motown expired in 1971. Rather than re-signing immediately, as the label expected, Wonder financed the recording of two albums of his own material, playing almost all the instruments himself, experimenting with the synthesizer and widening his lyrical concerns to take in racial problems and spiritual questions. He then used these recordings as a lever to persuade Motown to offer him total artistic control, plus the opportunity to hold the rights to the music publishing. He celebrated the signing of the deal with the release of the solo recordings, *Where I'm Coming From* and *Music Of My Mind*.

Talking Book combined the artistic advances of recent albums with major commercial success, producing hit singles with 'Superstition' and 'You Are The Sunshine Of My Life'. *Innervisions* consolidated his growth, bringing further hits with the socially aware 'Living For The City' and 'Higher Ground'. Later that year, Wonder was seriously injured in a car accident; his subsequent work was tinged with the awareness of mortality, fired by his spiritual beliefs. *Fulfillingness' First Finale* epitomized this more austere approach. The double album *Songs In The Key Of Life* was widely greeted as his most ambitious and satisfying work to date.

No new recordings surfaced for over three years, as Wonder concentrated on the disappointing soundtrack music to the documentary film, *The Secret Life Of Plants*. Wonder quickly delivered the highly successful *Hotter Than July*, which included a tribute song to Martin Luther King, 'Happy Birthday'. Soundtrack music for the movie, *The Woman In Red*, included his biggest-selling single to date, the sentimental ballad 'I Just Called To Say I Loved You'. *In Square Circle* and *Characters* heralded a return to the accessible, melodic music of the previous decade, but critical and public response was disappointing.

Wonder's status was boosted by his campaign in the early 80s to have Martin Luther King's birthday celebrated as a national holiday in the USA. This request was granted by President Reagan, and the first Martin Luther King Day was celebrated on 15 January 1986, with a concert at which Wonder topped the bill. In the 90s, he contributed to the film soundtrack of *Jungle Fever* and released the disappointingly average *Conversation Peace*.

WOOD, ROY

As a teenager, Wood (b. 1946) was an itinerant guitarist, moving steadily through a succession of minor UK groups. Later he pooled his talents with some of the best musicians on the Birmingham beat scene to form the **Move**. Wood emerged as their leading songwriter. By 'Fire Brigade' (1967), Wood was their lead singer and it was his fertile imagination which took the group through a plethora of musical styles, ranging from psychedelia to rock 'n' roll revivalism, classical rock and heavy metal. Wood then launched the **Electric Light Orchestra**, but survived as their frontman for only one single and album before a personality clash with Jeff Lynne prompted his departure in 1972. He soon returned with **Wizzard**. He also enjoyed a parallel solo career and although his two albums were uneven, they revealed his many areas of creative energy (multi-instrumentalist, engineer, producer and sleeve designer). Wood the soloist also scored several UK hit singles including the majestic 'Forever'. By the late 70s, Wood was ploughing less commercial ground with the Wizzo Band, Rock Brigade and the Helicopters.

WORLD PARTY

Founded on the talents of ex-**Waterboys** member Karl Wallinger (b. 1957), who recorded the first two World Party albums practically single-handed. *Bang!*, released in 1993, saw him joined by Chris Sharrock (drums) and Dave Catlin-Birch (guitars, keyboards) and was World Party's most successful release. This has been revitalized on his subsequent, sterling work, although some of the reviews for *Egyptology* and *Dumbing*

Up were lesser albums, although the former indirectly gave Wallinger a worthy chart-topping single, when **Robbie Williams**' cover version of 'She's The One' reached the top of the UK singles chart in 1999.

WRAY, LINK

Guitarist Wray (b. 1929) formed his first group in 1942, and subsequently forming the Raymen with Shorty Horton (bass) and Doug Wray (drums). They enjoyed a million-seller with 'Rumble' (1958), a pioneering instrumental on which the artist's frenzied style and distorted tone invoked a gang-fight. The single incurred bans on technical grounds and for its subject matter, but is now recognized as one of pop's most innovative releases. Wray scored another gold disc for 'Rawhide' (1959), but ensuing releases failed to emulate this. He continued to record, and 1971's *Link Wray* received critical acclaim. In the late 70s, he forged a fruitful partnership with new-wave rockabilly singer Robert Gordon, before resurrecting his solo career. He continues to record and tour into his seventies.

WU-TANG CLAN

Highly influential US hip-hop crew formed by Raekwon (b. Corey Woods), **Method Man** (b. Clifford Smith, 1971), Inspectah Deck aka Rebel INS (b. Jason Hunter), Ol' Dirty Bastard (b. Russell Jones, 1968), U-God, Ghostface Killah (b. Dennis Coles, 1970), the Genius aka GZA (b. Gary Grice), and producer RZA aka Prince Rakeem (b. Robert Diggs). Their 1993 debut album was divided into two sides, Shaolin and Wu-Tang Sword, to symbolize the combat-like disciplines they apply to their rapping. Their musical armoury centres around old-school rhyming and trickery, while the musical backing is one of stripped-down beats, with samples culled from kung-fu movies. The ranks of the Wu-Tang Clan have been swelled with the addition of the ninth and tenth official members, Masta Killa and Cappadonna.

The crew regrouped for 1997's chart-topping *Wu-Tang Forever*, a long sprawling record that rarely matched the quality of their debut or GZA's exceptional solo collection, *Liquid Swords*. Further releases from the Wu-Tang Clan stable took their place in an ever-expanding business empire that now includes the Wu-Wear clothes line and video games. The various members of the crew somehow managed to find the time to record *The W*, an excellent return to form that marked something of a departure by including guest appearances from non-Clan members.

WYATT, ROBERT

Wyatt (b. 1945) was the drummer, vocalist and guiding spirit of the original **Soft Machine**. His first solo album, 1970's *The End Of An Ear*, received a muted reception. He then formed the ill-fated Matching Mole. A planned relaunch was forcibly abandoned following a tragic fall, which left Wyatt confined to a wheelchair. *Rock Bottom* was a heartfelt, deeply personal collection marked by an aching vulnerability that successfully avoided any hint of self-pity. It was succeeded by a UK hit single with the **Monkees**, 'I'm A Believer'. *Ruth Is Stranger Than Richard* was a more open collection, and balanced original pieces with outside material.

Although Wyatt, a committed Marxist, made frequent guest appearances, his own career was shelved until 1980 when a single of two South American liberation songs were released. These performances were subsequently compiled on *Nothing Can Stop Us*, which also featured 'Shipbuilding' (1983), a haunting anti-Falklands War composition, specifically written for Wyatt by **Elvis Costello**. Wyatt's more recent recordings, *Dondestan* and *Shleep*, are as brilliantly idiosyncratic as anything he has recorded.

X

Formed in Los Angeles, USA, in 1977, X originally comprised Exene Cervenka (b. Christine Cervenka, 1956; vocals), Billy Zoom (b. Tyson Kindale; guitar), John Doe (b. John Nommensen; bass) and Mick Basher (drums), although the last-named was quickly replaced by D.J. (Don). The quartet achieved a considerable live reputation for their imaginative blend of punk, rockabilly and blues. Former **Doors** organist Ray Manzarek produced *Los Angeles* and *Wild Gift*, the latter of which established X as a major talent. Dave Alvin replaced Billy Zoom following the release of *Ain't Love Grand* and X was subsequently augmented by guitarist Tony Gilkyson. However, Alvin left for a solo career on the completion of *See How We Are* and the band was soon dissolved. Doe and Cervenka reunited in 1993 with a new recording contract for *Hey Zeus!*. Zoom rejoined the band for a series of concerts in 1998.

X-RAY SPEX

One of the most inventive, original and genuinely exciting UK groups to appear during the punk era, X-Ray Spex were the brainchild of Poly Styrene (b. Marion Elliot, London, England), Lora Logic (b. Susan Whitby), later replaced by Glyn Johns (saxophone), Jak Stafford (guitar), Paul Dean (bass) and B.P. Hurding (drums). The group began performing in 1977 and a series of extraordinary singles including 'Germ Free Adolescence', 'Oh Bondage, Up Yours', 'The Day The World Turned Dayglo' and 'Identity' followed. Always ambivalent about her pop-star status, Poly Styrene dismantled the group in 1979. During the 90s the band re-formed, releasing their second studio album, *Conscious Consumer*, on which Elliot was joined by founding members Lora Logic and Paul Dean.

XTC

This widely beloved UK pop unit made their debut with a line-up comprising Colin Moulding (b. 1955), Terry Chambers (b. 1955), Andy Partridge (b. 1953; guitar, vocals), Johnny Perkins (keyboards) and Barry Andrews (b. 1956). The band's sparkling debut, *White Music*, revealed a keener hearing for pop than the energetic new wave sound with which they were often aligned. Shortly after the release of *Go2*, Andrews was replaced by Dave Gregory (b. 1952). *Drums And Wires* was a major step forward from the pure pop of the first two albums. 'Making Plans For Nigel' exposed them to a new and eager audience. Singles were regularly taken from their subsequent albums and they continued reaching the UK charts with high-quality pop songs, including 'Sgt Rock (Is Going To Help Me)' and 'Senses Working Overtime'. Partridge subsequently fell ill through exhaustion and nervous breakdowns, and announced that XTC would continue only as recording artists. Subsequent albums found only limited success, with those of the Dukes Of Stratosphear, their alter ego, reputedly selling more copies.

Mummer, *The Big Express*, *Skylarking*, *Oranges & Lemons* and *Nonsuch* were critically acclaimed but commercial failures. After almost showing a profit the band decided to go on strike in 1992. They were finally released from Virgin Records in 1996. Following the departure of Gregory, who had tendered his resignation from the team, Partridge and Moulding broke their recording silence in 1999 with the majestic *Apple Venus Volume 1*. The following year's *Wasp Star (Apple Venus Volume 2)* was even better.

YARDBIRDS

This pivotal UK R&B group was formed in London in 1963 when Keith Relf (b. 1943, d. 1976; vocals, harmonica) and Paul Samwell-Smith (b. 1943; bass) joined forces with Chris Dreja (b. 1944; rhythm guitar), Tony 'Top' Topham (lead guitar) and Jim McCarty (b. 1943; drums). Topham was soon replaced by **Eric Clapton** (b. Eric Clapp, 1945). Two enthusiastic, if low-key singles, 'I Wish You Would' and 'Good Morning Little Schoolgirl', attracted critical interest, but the quintet's fortunes flourished with the release of *Five Live Yardbirds*. Clapton emerged as the unit's focal point, but a desire for musical purity led to his departure in March 1965 in the wake of a magnificent third single, 'For Your Love'. **Jeff Beck** (b. 1944) joined the Yardbirds as the single rose to number 1 in the UK's New Musical Express chart. The new line-up's desire for experimentation prevailed in the raga-rock of 'Shapes Of Things', the chaotic 'Over Under Sideways Down' and the excellent *Roger The Engineer*. Samwell-Smith departed in 1966. Respected session guitarist **Jimmy Page** (b. James Patrick Page, 1944) was brought into a line-up that, with Dreja switching to bass, now adopted a devastating twin-lead guitar format. The experimental 'Happenings Ten Years Time Ago' confirmed such hopes, but within six months Beck had departed during a gruelling USA tour. The Yardbirds remained a quartet but, despite a growing reputation on the American 'underground' circuit, their appeal as a pop attraction waned. Two bizarre successes in America, 'Ha Ha Said The Clown' and **Nilsson**'s 'Ten Little Indians', followed, but when Relf and McCarty announced a desire to pursue a folk-based direction, the band folded in July 1968.

In 1992, McCarty and Dreja performed a series of reunion concerts in London to commemorate the Yardbirds election to the Rock And Roll Hall Of Fame. The two men reunited once more in 1996, this time on a more permanent basis.

353

YAZOO

This UK electro-pop group was formed at the beginning of 1982 by former **Depeche Mode** keyboard player Vince Clarke (b. 1961) and vocalist Alison Moyet (b. 1961). Their debut single, 'Only You', climbed to number 2 in the UK charts in May. Yazoo enjoyed an almost equally successful follow-up with 'Don't Go', which climbed to number 3. A tour of the USA saw the duo change their name to Yaz in order not to conflict with an American record company of the same name. The duo enjoyed further hits with 'The Other Side Of Love' and 'Nobody's Diary' before parting in 1983. Moyet enjoyed considerable success as a solo singer, while Clarke maintained his high profile with the Assembly and particularly, **Erasure**.

YEARWOOD, TRISHA

US country singer Yearwood (b. 1964) became the first female singer to top the US country charts with her debut single, 1991's sparkling 'She's In Love With The Boy'. Further singles such as 'Like We Never Had A Broken Heart', 'That's What I Like About You', 'The Woman Before Me' and 'Wrong Side Of Memphis' quickly established her as a major new talent in contemporary country music. Married to the **Mavericks**' bass player Robert Reynolds in 1995, Yearwood won the CMA Award in 1997 and 1998 for Best Female Vocalist, and received the 1998 Grammy for Best Country Female Vocal Performance for the highly successful single 'How Do I Live'. The same year's *Where Your Road Leads* was a pop-orientated collection. *Real Live Woman* was released in the aftermath of her divorce from Reynolds.

YELLO

This Swiss electronic band is led by Dieter Meier (b. 4 March 1945) and Boris Blank (b. 1938). The duo originally joined up with tape manipulator Carlos Peron to form Yello, debuting with 'Bimbo' and the album *Solid Pleasure* in 1980. In the UK they signed to the Do It label, launching their career with 'Bostich', a track which had already become an underground club classic in America. Chart success in the UK began after a move to Stiff Records in 1983 where they released *You Gotta Say Yes To Another Excess*, the last album to feature Peron. In the mid-80s, Meier and Blank released the highly popular albums *Stella* and *One Second*. On the latter they worked closely with **Shirley Bassey** and Billy MacKenzie (the **Associates**). Meier and Blank also enjoyed major success with the UK Top 10 single, 'The Race' (from 1988's *Flag*). The Yello blueprint, on which Meier mumbled his bizarrely imaginative lyrics over Blank's inventive electronic beats, proved highly popular in London dance clubs. By the early 90s their albums had begun to move into the realm of self-parody, and both Meier and Blank subsequently became more and more embroiled in soundtrack work. They also founded Solid Pleasure, the innovative Swiss dance label.

YES

During the progressive music boom of the early 70s, Yes were rivalled only by fellow UK bands **Emerson, Lake And Palmer** and **Genesis**. They were formed in 1968 by Jon Anderson (b. John Roy Anderson, 1944; vocals), Chris Squire (b. 1948; bass), Bill Bruford (b. William Scott Bruford, 1949; drums), Peter Banks (b. Peter Brockbanks, 1947) and Tony Kaye (b. Anthony John Selvidge, 1946). Neither their debut *Yes* nor *Time And A Word* made much of an impression beyond their growing following. Banks was replaced in the spring of 1970 by guitar virtuoso Steve Howe (b. 1947), and the new look band created major interest and strong sales with the accomplished and dynamic *The Yes Album*. Kaye then and was replaced by keyboard wizard, **Rick Wakeman** (b. 1949). *Fragile* was another success, and was a landmark in that it began a series of Roger Dean's Tolkien-inspired fantasy covers, integrated with his custom-calligraphed Yes logotype. The album spawned a surprise US hit single, 'Roundabout'. Shortly afterwards Bruford departed and was replaced by Alan White (b. 1949). Later that year Yes released what now stands up as their finest work, *Close To The Edge*.

Now Yes were a major band, and they confidently issued a triple live album *Yessongs*, followed by a double, the overlong and indulgent *Tales From Topographic Oceans*. Both were huge successes, with the latter reaching number 1 in the UK. Artistically, the band now started to decline, and Wakeman was replaced by Patrick Moraz (b. 1948). Following *Relayer* the band fragmented to undertake solo projects. When the band reconvened, Wakeman rejoined in place of Moraz. *Going For The One* moved the band back into the realms of rock music. Another hit single, 'Wonderous Stories', made the UK Top 10 in 1977.

Internal problems were rife, however, resulting in the second departure of Wakeman, immediately followed by Anderson. Astonishingly their replacements were Trevor Horn (b. 1949) and Geoffrey Downes (b. 1952; keyboards) who, as **Buggles** had topped the UK charts the previous year with 'Video Killed The Radio Star'. This bizarre marriage lasted a year, spawning Drama, before Yes finally said 'no' and broke up in 1981.

All the members enjoyed successful solo careers, while Howe and Downes moved on to the supergroup **Asia**, and it came as a surprise in 1983 to find a re-formed Yes (Anderson, Kaye, Squire, White and South African guitarist Trevor Rabin (b. Trevor Charles Rabinowitz, 1955)), topping the UK singles chart with the excellent Trevor Horn-produced 'Owner Of A Lonely Heart'. The subsequent *90125* showed a rejuvenated band with short contemporary pop songs that fitted with 80s fashion. No new Yes output came until four years later with the desultory *Big Generator*, and in 1989 *Anderson, Bruford, Wakeman, Howe* was released by four Yes members during a lengthy legal dispute.

With the ownership problem solved, Yes announced a major tour in 1991, and the composite line-up of Anderson, Howe, Wakeman, Squire, Kaye, White, Rabin and Bruford were once again in the US Top 10 with their new album *Union*. The follow-up *Talk* was recorded by Anderson, Kaye, Squire, Rabin and White. Wakeman had by now departed, this time due to his health, although he vowed this would be for the last time. Anderson, Howe, Squire, White and Igor Khoroshev (b. 1965) completed the disappointing *Open Your Eyes* and *The Ladder*. The follow-up, *Magnification*, was their first recording without a keyboard player following the departure of Khoroshev.

YO LA TENGO

New Jersey, USA-based alternative rock band revolving around husband and wife duo Ira Kaplan (vocals, guitar) and Georgia Hubley (drums, vocals), plus various associates including regular member James McNew (bass). Their 1986 debut included a cover version of Ray Davies' 'Big Sky'. The oft-stated comparisons between Kaplan's vocals and those of **Lou Reed** were further endorsed by a version of the latter's 'It's Alright (The Way That You Live)' on the subsequent *New Wave Hot Dogs* collection. Two live songs from a CBGB's set were included on the band's best early recording, 1989's *President Yo La Tengo*. McNew joined up in time for 1992's *May I Sing With Me*, which featured lead vocals from Hubley for the first time. *Painful* contained the usual assortment of beautiful pop moments, notably 'Nowhere Near' and 'The Whole Of The Law'. Both the melodic indie-pop outing *I Can Hear The Heart Beating As One* and the coyly romantic and mellow follow-up, *And Then Nothing Turned Itself Inside-Out*, gained excellent reviews.

YOAKAM, DWIGHT

Much of Yoakam's (b. 1956) hip honky-tonk music paved the way for rock audiences accepting country music in the 90s. In 1984, the release of a self-financed mini-album on the Enigma label led to him signing for Warner/Reprise Records. Two years later, following the release of his excellent debut *Guitars, Cadillacs, Etc., Etc.*, he registered Top 5 US country chart hits with Johnny Horton's 'Honky Tonk Man' and his own 'Guitars, Cadillacs'. A string of country hits culminated in 1988 with a US number 1 with his self-penned 'I Sang Dixie'. He would also make the top of the country charts with 'The Streets Of Bakersfield', duetting with veteran 60s superstar Buck Owens. Yoakam's straight country style is his most effective work, even though he attempted to cross over into the mainstream rock market with *La Croix D'Amour*. He also turned his hand to acting, appearing in a Los Angeles stage production, *Southern Rapture* (he has gone on to become a Hollywood regular). Yoakam came back in 1993 with the hardcore country of *This Time*. The album included the number 1 country hit 'Ain't That Lonely Yet', which won a Grammy Award for Best Country Vocal Performance. After more than

fifteen years of commercial success, Yoakam has firmly established his staying power as one of the leading artists of the new era of country music.

YOUNG RASCALS

One of America's finest pop/soul ensembles, the Young Rascals were formed in 1965 by Felix Cavaliere (b. 1943; organ, vocals), Eddie Brigati (b. 1946; vocals, percussion), Dino Danelli (b. 1945; drums) and Gene Cornish (b. 1946; vocals, guitar). The quartet enjoyed a minor hit with 'I Ain't Gonna Eat Out My Heart Anymore' before securing a US number 1 with the energetic 'Good Lovin''. The Young Rascals secured their biggest hit with 'Groovin''. This melancholic performance became an international hit, signalling a lighter, more introspective approach, and although Brigati was featured on the haunting 'How Can I Be Sure', a US Top 5 entry, Cavaliere gradually became the band's focal point. In 1968 the band dropped its 'Young' prefix and enjoyed a third US number 1 with 'People Got To Be Free'. The quartet later began exploring jazz-based compositions, and although remaining respected, lost much of their commercial momentum. Brigati and Cornish left in 1971, and although newcomers Buzzy Feiten (guitar), Ann Sutton (vocals) and Robert Popwell (drums) contributed to final albums, *Peaceful World* and *The Island Of Real*, the Rascals broke up the following year. Cavaliere, Danelli, Cornish were reunited in 1988 for an extensive US tour.

YOUNG, NEIL

Canadian Young (b. 1945) began his enigmatic career as a member of the Squires, whose indebtedness to the UK instrumental combo the **Shadows** was captured on Young's composition 'Aurora'/'The Sultan'. Young then joined the Mynah Birds, a pop-soul attraction that also featured Rick James, but this act folded prematurely upon the latter's arrest for draft evasion. Group bass player Bruce Palmer accompanied Young on a subsequent move to California where they teamed with Stephen Stills and Richie Furay to form the Buffalo Springfield. Young's tenure in this seminal 'west coast' act was tempered by several 'sabbaticals', but two luxurious, atmospheric compositions, 'Broken Arrow' and 'Expecting To Fly', established the highly sculptured, orchestral-tinged sound prevalent on his debut solo record, 1969's *Neil Young*. Following his first album, Young was joined by Danny Whitten (guitar), Billy Talbot (bass) and Ralph Molina (drums) – three former members of the Rockets – in a new backing group dubbed **Crazy Horse**. The classic *Everybody Knows This Is Nowhere* captured a performer liberated from a previous self-consciousness with the extended 'Down By The River' and 'Cowgirl In The Sand', allowing space for his stutteringly simple, yet enthralling, guitar style. An attendant tour confirmed the strength of the Young/Crazy Horse partnership, while Young also secured acclaim as a member of **Crosby, Stills, Nash And Young**.

After The Goldrush provided a commercial breakthrough and included several of Young's best-known compositions, including the haunting title track, 'Only Love Can Break Your Heart', and the fiery 'Southern Man'. The highly commercial *Harvest* confirmed this new found ascendancy and spawned a US chart-topper in 'Heart Of Gold'. This commercial peak ended abruptly with *Journey Through The Past*, a highly indulgent soundtrack to a rarely screened autobiographical film. The deaths of Whitten and road crew member Bruce Berry inspired the harrowing *Tonight's The Night*, on which Young's bare-nerved emotions were expounded over his bleakest songs to date. *On The Beach*, released prior to *Tonight's The Night*, was equally bleak.

Young next chose to team up Crazy Horse again – Talbot, Molina and new guitarist Frank Sampedro – for *Zuma*. 'Like A Hurricane', was the pivotal feature of *American Stars 'N' Bars*, an otherwise piecemeal collection drawn from extant masters and newer, country-oriented recordings. The latter direction was maintained on *Comes A Time*, Young's most accessible set since

Harvest. Characteristically, Young chose to follow this up by rejoining Crazy Horse for the excellent *Rust Never Sleeps*. The album was preceded by a Young movie of the same name and was followed by the double live album, *Live Rust*.

During the 80s the artist became increasingly unpredictable as each new release rejected the musical directions suggested by its predecessor. The underrated *Hawks And Doves* was followed by excursions through electric R&B (*Re-Ac-Tor*), electro-pop (*Trans*) and rockabilly (*Everybody's Rockin'*), before embracing ol' timey country (*Old Ways*), hard rock (*Landing On Water*) and R&B (*This Note's For You*). The last-named achieved notoriety when a video for the title song, which attacked the intertwining of rock with corporate sponsorship, was banned by MTV. *Freedom* was an artistic and commercial triumph which garnered positive reviews and assuaged those viewing its creator as merely eccentric. Young affirmed this regeneration with *Ragged Glory*, a blistering collaboration with Crazy Horse. An ensuing in-concert set, *Weld* (accompanied by an album of feedback experimentation, *Arc*), was rightly applauded as another milestone in Young's often contrary oeuvre. Following this, Young made a return to his *Harvest*-period with *Harvest Moon*. Less than a year later he produced *Unplugged*, which was a confident live set recorded for MTV. *Sleeps With Angels* mixed some of his dirtiest guitar with some frail and winsome offerings.

A collaboration with Pearl Jam produced a good album in 1995. *Dead Man* was a challenging and rambling guitar soundtrack to a Jim Jamursch movie, and neither a commercial nor a listenable excursion. *Broken Arrow* received a less than positive reception from the critics. In 1999, Young reunited with his CSN colleagues for a lucrative tour and an album. The lacklustre contributions he made to their album spilled over to *Silver & Gold*. *Are You Passionate?* marked a partial return to form, with Young spurred on by the presence of soul veterans Booker T. Jones and Donald Dunn in his studio band.

YOUNG, PAUL

Prior to his major success as a solo artist, UK vocalist Young (b. 1956) was a former member of Streetband, who made the UK charts in 1978 with the novelty record 'Toast'. He was then part of the much-loved Q-Tips, a band that did much to preserve an interest in 60s soul and R&B. Young then signed as a solo artist with CBS Records. Following two flop singles, his smooth soul

voice captured the public's imagination with a superb chart-topping version of **Marvin Gaye**'s 'Wherever I Lay My Hat (That's My Home)'. The following *No Parlez* was a phenomenally triumphant debut, reaching number 1 in the UK and staying in the charts for well over two years.

After touring to support the album, Young experienced a recurring problem with his voice which would continue to plague his career. It was two years before he was able to record *The Secret Of Association*. This album also topped the UK chart and produced three top 10 singles including 'Everything Must Change' and a cover of Daryl Hall's 'Every Time You Go Away'. *Between Two Fires* was a below-par album, after which Young went into hibernation before returning in 1990 with *Other Voices*. His next album was buoyed by the Top 20 success of 'Now I Know What Made Otis Blue', but following the relative commercial failure of his self-titled 1997 release, Young was dropped by East West Records.

YOUNGBLOODS

Formed in 1965 in Massachusetts, USA, the Youngbloods was formed by folk singers Jesse Colin Young (b. Perry Miller, 1944) and Jerry Corbitt who together completed a single, 'My Babe', prior to the arrival of drummer Joe Bauer (b. 1941) and guitarist/pianist Lowell Levinger III, better known simply as Banana. The quartet took the name 'Youngbloods' from the singer's second solo album. Their debut, *The Youngbloods*, eloquently encapsulated folk-rock and the band's reading of Dino Valenti's 'Get Together' subsequently became a hit in California. *Elephant Mountain*, their most popular album, reflected a new-found peace of mind and included several of the band's best-known songs, including 'Darkness, Darkness' and 'Sunlight'. Corbitt had left the line-up during the early stages of recording. The Youngbloods gained complete artistic freedom with their own label, Raccoon, but their final releases were marred by inconsistency. Michael Kane, joined the band in the spring of 1971, but they split the following year when Young resumed his solo career. Banana, Bauer and Kane continued as Banana And The Bunch, but this occasional venture subsequently folded.

ZAPPA, FRANK

In 1964 Zappa (b. 1940, d. 1993), who had been working in a local studio, recording spoof doo-wop singles and composing scores for b-movies, joined a local R&B outfit called the Soul Giants, whose line-up included vocalist Ray Collins (b. 1937), bass player Roy Estrada (b. 1943), and drummer Jimmy Carl Black (b. 1938). Zappa changed their name to the Mothers, but 'Of Invention' was later added at the insistence of their label, Verve Records. With the addition of Elliott Ingber, the **Mothers Of Invention** debuted with *Freak Out!*. They made great play of their hair and ugliness, becoming the perfect counter-cultural icons. Ingber left to form the Fraternity Of Man before the recording of the band's second album, *Absolutely Free*. Zappa chose to expand the Mothers Of Invention with the addition of second drummer Billy Mundi, keyboardist Don Preston (b. 1932, USA), and horn players Bunk Gardner and Jim 'Motorhead' Sherwood.

Tours and releases followed, including the solo *Lumpy Gravy* and *We're Only In It For The Money*, (with its brilliant parody of the **Beatles**' *Sgt. Peppers Lonely Hearts Club Band* record cover) a scathing satire on hippiedom and the reactions to it in the USA. In stark contrast, *Cruising With Ruben & The Jets* paid excellent homage to the doo-wop era. British fans were particularly impressed with *Hot Rats*, a solo Zappa record that ditched the sociological commentary for barnstorming jazz-rock. Collins had quit in April 1968, and the Mothers Of Invention would eventually disintegrate the following August. Both *Uncle Meat* and *Hot Rats* appeared on Zappa's own Bizarre Records label which, together with his other outlet Straight Records, released a number of highly regarded albums that were nevertheless commercial flops.

Eager to gain a 'heavier' image than the band that had brought them fame, the Turtles' singers Mark Volman (b. 1947) and Howard Kaylan (b. Howard Kaplan, 1947), aka Flo And Eddie, joined up with Zappa for the movie *200 Motels* and three further albums. The newly re-christened Mothers now included George Duke (b. 1946; keyboards, trombone), Ian Underwood (keyboards, saxophone), Aynsley Dunbar (b. 1946; drums), and Jeff Simmons (bass, vocals), although the latter was quickly replaced by Jim Pons (b. 1943).

In December 1971, Zappa was pushed off-stage at London's Rainbow theatre, crushing his larynx (lowering his voice a third), damaging his spine and keeping him wheelchair-bound for the best part of a year. He spent 1972 developing an extraordinary new species of big band fusion (*Waka/Jawaka* and *The Grand Wazoo*). *Over-Nite Sensation* announced fusion-chops, salacious lyrics and driving rhythms. *Apostrophe (')*, *Roxy & Elsewhere* and *One Size Fits All* furthered Zappa's reputation. In 1975, **Captain Beefheart** joined Zappa for a tour and despite an earlier rift, sang on *Bongo Fury*. After the mid-70s interest in philosophical concepts and band in-jokes, Zappa's music in the 80s became more political. *Tinseltown Rebellion* and *You Are What You Is* commented on the growth of the fundamentalist Right. He also enjoyed an unexpected hit in 1982 with 'Valley Girl', which featured his daughter Moon Unit satirizing the accents of young moneyed Hollywood people. Of his prolific mid-80s period, *Does Humor Belong In Music?* and *Meets The Mothers Of Prevention* were effective responses to the rise of powerful censor groups in America; renowned French composer Pierre Boulez conducted Zappa's work on *The Perfect Starnger*; he released a rock album *Them Or Us*, which widened still further the impact of his scurrilously inventive guitar; *Thing Fish* was a 'Broadway Musical' about AIDS, homophobia and racism; and he unearthed an eighteenth-century composer named Francesco Zappa and recorded his work on a synclavier.

Zappa's next big project materialised in 1988: a 12-piece band playing covers, instrumentals and a brace of new political songs (collected respectively as *Broadway The Hard Way*, *The Best Band You Never Heard In Your Life*, and *Make A Jazz Noise Here*). As well as the retrospective series *You Can't Do That On Stage Anymore*, Zappa released his most popular bootlegs in two instalments as part of his 'Beat The Boots' campaign. In Czechoslovakia, where he had long been a hero of the cultural underground, he was appointed as the country's Cultural Liaison Officer with the West. In 1991 he announced he would be standing as an independent candidate in the 1992 US presidential election, but in November it was confirmed that he was suffering from cancer of the prostate. He succumbed to the disease in 1993.

Although much of his oeuvre can easily be dismissed as flippant, history will certainly recognize Zappa as a sophisticated, serious composer and a highly accomplished master of music.

ZEVON, WARREN

After moving to the west coast of America, where he sought work as a song-writer in the mid-60s, Zevon (b. 1947) wrote songs for the Turtles and Nino Tempo And April Stevens. His inauspicious debut, *Zevon: Wanted Dead Or Alive*, was produced by Kim Fowley. One track from the album, 'She Quit Me', was featured in the movie *Midnight Cowboy*. After a spell as musical director to the Everly Brothers, Zevon finally released his long-awaited second album in 1976. *Warren Zevon* was a highly accomplished work, which revealed its creator's songwriting power to an exceptional degree. The follow-up *Excitable Boy* was released two years later, and the range of material proved even more fascinating. He even enjoyed a US hit with the jaunty satire of 'Werewolves Of London'. A superb trilogy of Zevon albums was completed with *Bad Luck Streak In Dancing School* which was most notable for its inventive use of orchestration.

Although Zevon seemed likely to establish himself as one of the prominent singer-songwriters of the 80s, personal problems would soon undo his progress. The much neglected *The Envoy* was his last major work for five years. During the interim, he became an alcoholic and underwent counselling and therapy. He returned in 1987 with *Sentimental Hygiene*, a welcome return to top form which featured an array of guest stars. The finely-produced *Transverse City* and *Mr Bad Example* completed his rehabilitation, and Zevon also formed a band with Peter Buck, Mike Mills and Bill Berry of **R.E.M.** under the name Hindu Love Gods, who issued a self-titled album in 1990. Zevon's next album, 1995's *Mutineer*, featured two songs ('Rottweiler Blues' and 'Seminole Bingo') co-written with the American crime writer, Carl Hiaasen. *Life'll Kill Ya* and *My Ride's Here* revealed a mature songwriter at the height of his powers.

ZOMBIE, ROB

The lead vocalist of controversial hard rock band White Zombie, Rob Zombie (b. Robert Cummings, 1966) delivered his US Top 5 debut album in 1998. The contents would have proved no surprise to Zombie's existing fans, with horror and gore-inspired lyrics predominating and abrasive hard rock the dominant musical motif. The album was remixed the following year by various members of Nine Inch Nails, Rammstein and Limp Bizkit, by which time White Zombie had split-up. Zombie released his sophomore album, *The Sinister Urge*, in 2001.

ZOMBIES

Rod Argent (b. 1945; piano), **Colin Blunstone** (b. 1945; vocals), Paul Atkinson (b. 1946; guitar), Paul Arnold (bass) and Hugh Grundy (b. 1945; drums) formed this UK band in 1963, although Chris White (b. 1943) replaced Arnold within weeks of

their inception. The Zombies' debut single, 'She's Not There', rose to number 12 in the UK, but proved more popular still in America, where it reached number 2. Although 'Tell Her No' was another US Top 10 entrant, it fared much less well at home while later releases, including 'Whenever You're Ready' and 'Is This The Dream' unaccountably missed out altogether. The group, not unnaturally, grew frustrated and broke up in 1967 on completion of *Odessey & Oracle*. Its closing track, 'Time Of The Season', became a massive US hit, but despite several overtures, the original line-up steadfastly refused to reunite. Argent and Grundy were subsequently joined by bass player Jim Rodford (b. 1941) and Rick Birkett (guitar) and this reshaped ensemble was responsible for the Zombies' final single, 'Imagine The Swan'. Despite the label credit, this release was ostensibly the first recording by the keyboard player's new venture, Argent. Colin Blunstone, meanwhile, embarked on a stop-start solo career. The original band reconvened to record *New World* in 1991, which on release received respectable reviews.

ZORN, JOHN

Saxophonist Zorn (b. 1953) is a leading representative of the US avant garde. His initial recordings saw him working with Eugene Chadbourne, Derek Bailey, Bill Frisell and George Lewis. In 1985 he made a commercial breakthrough with *The Big Gundown*, which interpreted Ennio Morricone's film. Declaring that hardcore rock music had the same intensity as 60s free jazz, he championed England's **Napalm Death** and recorded hardcore versions of Ornette Coleman's tunes on the provocative *Spy Vs Spy* (1989). *Naked City* (Frisell – guitar, Horvitz – keyboards, Fred Frith – bass, Joey Baron – drums) became his vehicle for skipping between sleaze-jazz, surf rock and hardcore. They continued to record challenging work throughout the 90s (with Boredoms' vocalist Yamatsuka Eye recruited as a full-time member). In 1991 he formed Pain Killer with bass player/producer **Bill Laswell** and Mick Harris (the drummer from Napalm Death). In the mid-90s he inaugurated Masada to explore his fascination with Jewish history and music.

ZZ TOP

ZZ Top's original line-up – Billy Gibbons (b. 1949; guitar, vocals), Lanier Greig (bass) and Dan Mitchell (drums) – was also the final version of the Moving Sidewalks. This initial trio completed ZZ Top's debut single, 'Salt Lick', before Greig was

fired. He was replaced by Bill Ethridge. Mitchell was then replaced by Frank Beard (b. 1949; drums), while Dusty Hill (b. Joe Hill, 1949; bass, vocals) subsequently joined in place of Ethridge. The trio's initial recording were firmly within the southern boogie genre, but *Rio Grande Mud* indicated a greater flexibility. Their third album, *Tres Hombres*, featured the band's first national hit with 'La Grange' and was their first platinum album. In 1974, the band's first annual 'Texas-Size Rompin' Stompin' Barndance And Bar-B-Q' was held at the Memorial Stadium at the University Of Texas. 85,000 people attended.

After a brief hiatus, the trio resumed their career in 1979 with the superb *Deguello*, by which time both Gibbons and Hill had grown lengthy beards (without each other knowing!). The transitional *El Loco* followed in 1981 and although it lacked the punch of its predecessor, the set introduced the growing love of technology that marked their subsequent releases. *Eliminator* was fuelled by a series of memorable, tongue-in-cheek videos, and included the international hit singles 'Gimme All Your Lovin', 'Sharp Dressed Man' and 'Legs'. The follow-up, *Afterburner*, featured more hits in 'Sleeping Bag', 'Rough Boy' and 'Velcro Fly'. The band's studio work during the 90s failed to match the commercial and critical success of the previous decade, although 1996's *Rhythmeen* demonstrated a willingness to experiment with their trademark sound.

A

A FLOCK OF SEAGULLS
ALBUMS: A Flock Of Seagulls (Jive 1982)★★★, Listen (Jive 1983)★★★, The Story Of A Young Heart (Jive 1984)★★, Dream Come True (Jive 1986)★★, The Light At The End Of The World (Sava 1995)★★.
COMPILATIONS: The Best Of A Flock Of Seagulls (Jive 1987)★★★, 20 Classics Of The '80s (Emporio 1995)★★★, Greatest Hits Remixed (Cleopatra 1999)★★★.

A TRIBE CALLED QUEST
ALBUMS: People's Instinctive Travels And The Paths Of Rhythm (Jive 1990)★★★, The Low-End Theory (Jive 1991)★★★★, Revised Quest For The Seasoned Traveller remix album (Jive 1992)★★, Midnight Marauders (Jive 1993)★★★, Beats, Rhymes And Life (Jive 1996)★★★★, The Love Movement (Jive 1998)★★★.
COMPILATIONS: The Anthology (Jive 1999)★★★★.

A-HA
ALBUMS: Hunting High And Low (Warners 1985)★★★★, Scoundrel Days (Warners 1986)★★, Stay On These Roads (Warners 1988)★★★, East Of The Sun, West Of The Moon (Warners 1990)★★★, Memorial Beach (Warners 1993)★★, Minor Earth/Major Sky (Warners 2000)★★★.
COMPILATIONS: Headlines And Deadlines: The Hits Of A-Ha (Warners 1991)★★★.
VIDEOS: Headlines And Deadlines: The Hits Of A-Ha (Warner Music Video 1991), Live In South America (Warner Music Video 1993).

A1
ALBUMS: Here We Come (Columbia 1999)★★★, The A List (Columbia 2000)★★★.
VIDEOS: A1 In The Picture (Columbia Music Video 2000).

AALIYAH
ALBUMS: Age Ain't Nothing But A Number (Blackground/Atlantic 1994)★★★, One In A Million (Blackground/Atlantic 1996)★★★, Aaliyah (Blackground/Virgin 2001)★★★.
FILMS: Romeo Must Die (2000), Queen Of The Damned (2002).

ABBA
ALBUMS: as Bjorn & Benny, Agnetha & Frida Ring Ring (Epic 1973)★★, Waterloo (Epic 1974)★★, Abba (Epic 1975) ★★★, Arrival (Epic 1976)★★★, The Album (Epic 1977) ★★★, Voulez-Vous (Epic 1979)★★★, Super Trouper (Epic 1980)★★★, Gracias Por La Musica (Epic 1980)★★, The Visitors (Epic 1981)★★★, Abba Live (Polydor 1986)★★.
COMPILATIONS: Honey Honey (Polydor 1974)★★★, Greatest Hits (Epic 1976)★★★★, Greatest Hits Vol. 2 (Epic 1979)★★★, The Magic Of Abba US only (K-Tel 1980) ★★★, The Singles: The First Ten Years (Epic 1982)★★★★, The Love Songs (Pickwick 1982)★★★, Abba International (Polydor 1982)★★★, Thank You For The Music: A Collection (Epic 1983)★★★, Energhighs (Epic 1983)★★, The Abba Special (Epic 1983)★★★, The Best Of Abba US only (Silver Eagle 1984)★★★, I Love Abba US only (Atlantic 1984) ★★★, From Abba With Love (Polydor 1984)★★, The Best Of Abba 5-LP box set (Readers Digest 1986)★★★, The Collection (Castle 1987)★★★, Abba: The Hits (Pickwick 1987)★★★, Abba: The Hits 2 (Pickwick 1988)★★, Abba: The Hits 3 (Pickwick 1988)★★, The Collection Vol. 2 (Castle 1988)★★, Absolute Abba (Telstar 1988)★★★, Abba Gold: Greatest Hits (Polydor 1992)★★★★, More Abba Gold: More Abba Hits (Polydor 1993)★★★, Thank You For The Music 4-CD box set (Polydor 1994)★★★, The Music Still Goes On (Spectrum 1996)★★★, Forever Gold (Polydor 1996)★★★★, Love Stories (PolyGram 1998)★★★, Singles Collection box set (Polydor 1999)★★★, The Definitive Collection (Polydor 2001)★★★★.
VIDEOS: Story Of Abba (MGM 1986), Video Biography 1974-1982 (Virgin Vision 1987), Abba: The Movie (MGM/UA 1988), Abba: The Video Hits (Screen Legends 1988), More Video Hits Of Abba (Screen Legends 1988), Abba Gold: Greatest Hits (PolyGram Music Video 1993), Thank You Abba (PolyGram Music Video 1995), Forever Gold (PolyGram Music Video 1996), More Abba Gold (PolyGram Music Video 1996), The Winner Takes It All: The Abba Story (VVL 1999).
FURTHER READING: Abba: The Ultimate Pop Group, Marianne Lindwall. Abba By Abba (originally called The Abba Phenomenon), Christer Borg. Abba, Harry Edington and Peter Himmelstrand. Abba For The Record: The Authorized Story In Words And Pictures, John Tobler. Abba In Their Own Words, Rosemary York. Abba: A Lyrical Collection 1972-1982, Bjorn Ulvaeus. Abba Gold: The Complete Story, John Tobler. The Name Of The Game, A. Oldham, T. Calder and C. Irwin. Abba: The Complete Recording Sessions, Carl Magnus Palm. Abba: The Music Still Goes On, Paul Snaith. As I Am: Abba Before And Beyond, Agnetha Fältskog with Brita Åhman. Abba: The Book, Jean-Marie Potiez. From Abba To Mamma Mia! The Official Book, Anders Hanser, Carl Magnus Palm. Bright Lights, Dark Shadows: The Real Story Of Abba, Carl Magnus Palm.
FILMS: Abba: The Movie (1977).

ABC
ALBUMS: The Lexicon Of Love (Neutron/Mercury 1982) ★★★★★, Beauty Stab (Neutron/Mercury 1983)★★★, How To Be A ... Zillionaire! (Neutron/Mercury 1985)★★★, Alphabet City (Neutron/Mercury 1987)★★★, Up (Neutron/Mercury 1989)★★★, Abracadabra (Parlophone/MCA 1991)★★, Skyscraping (Blatant/Deconstruction 1997)★★★, Lexicon Of Live (Blatant 1999)★★★.
COMPILATIONS: Absolutely (Neutron/Mercury 1990) ★★★, The Remix Collection (Connoisseur 1993)★★★, The Best Of ABC: The Millennium Collection (Mercury 2000) ★★★, Hello! An Introduction To ABC (Mercury 2001)★★★, Look Of Love: The Very Best Of ABC (Mercury 2001)★★★★.
VIDEOS: Mantrap (Hendring Music Video 1983), Absolutely (PolyGram Music Video 1990).

AC/DC
ALBUMS: High Voltage Australia only (Albert 1975)★★, T.N.T. Australia only (Albert 1976)★★, Dirty Deeds Done Dirt Cheap (Atlantic 1976)★★★, Let There Be Rock (Atlantic 1977)★★★★, Powerage (Atlantic 1978)★★★, If You Want Blood You've Got It (Atlantic 1978)★★★, Highway To Hell (Atlantic 1979)★★★★, Back In Black (Atlantic 1980) ★★★★, For Those About To Rock (We Salute You) (Atlantic 1981)★★★★, Flick Of The Switch (Atlantic 1983)★★, '74 Jailbreak mini-album (Atlantic 1984)★★, Fly On The Wall (Atlantic 1985)★★, Who Made Who (Atco 1986)★★★, Blow Up Your Video (Atlantic 1988)★★, The Razors Edge (Atco 1990)★★★, Live (Atco 1992)★★, Ballbreaker (Atlantic 1995)★★★, Stiff Upper Lip (EMI 2000)★★★.
COMPILATIONS: High Voltage (Atlantic 1976)★★, Box Set 1 (EMI 1981)★★★, Box Set 2 (EMI 1987)★★★, Bonfire 4-CD box set (EMI 1997)★★★★.
VIDEOS: Let There Be Rock (Warner Home Video 1985), Fly On The Wall (Atlantic Video 1985), Who Made Who (Atlantic Video 1986), Clipped (AVision 1991), Live At Donington (AVision 1992), No Bull (Warner Music Vision 1996), Stiff Upper Lip Live (Warner Music Vision 2001).
FURTHER READING: The AC/DC Story, Paul Ezra. AC/DC, Malcolm Dome. AC/DC: Hell Ain't No Bad Place To Be, Richard Bunton. AC/DC: An Illustrated Collectors Guide Volumes 1 & 2, Chris Tesch. AC/DC Illustrated Biography, Mark Putterford. Shock To The System, Mark Putterford. HM Photo Book, no author listed. The World's Most Electrifying Rock 'n' Roll Band, Malcolm Dome (ed.). Highway To Hell: The Life & Times Of AC/DC Legend Bon Scott, Clinton Walker. AC/DC: The World's Heaviest Rock, Martin Huxley. Get Your Jumbo Jet Out Of My Airport: Random Notes For AC/DC Obsessives, Howard Johnson. AC/DC: The Definitive History, The Kerrang! Files.

ADAM AND THE ANTS
ALBUMS: Dirk Wears White Sox (Do It 1979)★★, Kings Of The Wild Frontier (CBS/Epic 1980)★★★, Prince Charming (CBS/Epic 1981)★★, Peel Sessions (Strange Fruit 1990)★★.
COMPILATIONS: Hits (CBS 1986)★★★, Antics In The Forbidden Zone (Columbia 1990)★★★, The Collection (Castle 1991)★★★, Antmusic: The Very Best Of Adam Ant (Arcade 1993)★★★★, B-Side Babies (Epic/Legacy 1994)★★★, Super Hits (Epic/Legacy 1998)★★★, The Very Best Of Adam And The Ants (Columbia 1999)★★★★, Antbox 3-CD box set (Columbia 2000)★★★, Live At The BBC (Fuel 2000 2001)★★.
VIDEOS: Prince Charming Revue (CBS Video 1982), Live In Japan aka Live In Tokyo (CBS Video/Arcade 1982), Hits (CBS/Fox Video 1986), Antmusic: The Very Best Of Adam Ant (Arcade Video 1993), AntVideo (Columbia 2000).
FURTHER READING: Adam And The Ants, Mike West. Adam And The Ants, Chris Welch. Adam And The Ants, Fred & Judy Vermorel. Adam Ant Tribal Rock Special, Martha Rodriguez (design). The Official Adam Ant Story, James Maw. Adam And The Ants Kings: The Official Adam And The Ants Song Book, Stephen Lavers.

ADAM ANT
ALBUMS: Friend Or Foe (CBS/Epic 1982)★★★, Strip (CBS/Epic 1983)★★, Vive Le Rock (CBS/Epic 1985)★★, Manners & Physique (MCA 1990)★★, Wonderful (EMI/Capitol 1995)★★★.
COMPILATIONS: Hits (CBS 1986)★★★, Antics In The Forbidden Zone (Columbia 1990)★★★, The Collection (Castle 1991)★★★, Antmusic: The Very Best Of Adam Ant (Arcade 1993)★★★, B-Side Babies (Epic/Legacy 1994)★★★, Super Hits (Epic/Legacy 1998)★★★, The Very Best Of Adam And The Ants (Columbia 1999)★★★, Antbox 3-CD box set (Columbia 2000)★★★.
VIDEOS: Prince Charming Revue (CBS Video 1982), Live In Japan aka Live In Tokyo (CBS Video/Arcade 1982), Hits (CBS/Fox Video 1986), Antmusic: The Very Best Of Adam Ant (Arcade Video 1993), AntVideo (Columbia 2000).
FURTHER READING: Adam And The Ants, Mike West. Adam And The Ants, Chris Welch. Adam And The Ants, Fred and Judy Vermorel. Adam Ant Tribal Rock Special, Martha Rodriguez (design). The Official Adam Ant Story, James Maw. Adam And The Ants Kings: The Official Adam And The Ants Song Book, Stephen Lavers.
FILMS: Jubilee (1977), Nomads (1986), Slamdance (1987), Cold Steel (1987), World Gone Wild (1988), Spellcaster (1988), Trust Me (1989), Sunset Heat aka Midnight Heat (1991), Love Bites (1993), Acting On Impulse aka Eyes Of A Stranger (1993), Drop Dead Rock (1995), Desert Winds (1995), Cyber Bandits (1995), Lover's Knot (1996), Sweetwater (1999).

ADAMS, BRYAN
ALBUMS: Bryan Adams (A&M 1980)★★★, You Want It, You Got It (A&M 1981)★★★, Cuts Like A Knife (A&M 1983)★★, Reckless (A&M 1984)★★★★, Into The Fire (A&M 1987)★★★, Live! Live! Live! (A&M 1989)★★, Waking Up The Neighbours (A&M 1991)★★★, 18 'Til I Die (A&M 1996)★★, Unplugged (A&M 1997)★★★, On A Day Like Today (A&M 1998)★★★.
COMPILATIONS: So Far So Good (A&M 1993)★★★★, The Best Of Me (A&M 1999)★★★★.
VIDEOS: Reckless (A&M Video 1984), Waking Up The Neighbours (A&M Video 1992), So Far So Good And More (A&M Video 1994), MTV Unplugged (A&M Video 1998).
FURTHER READING: Bryan Adams: The Inside Story, Hugh Gregory. The Illustrated Biography, Sandy Robertson. Bryan Adams: A Fretted Biography, Mark Duffett. Bryan Adams: Everything He Does, Sorelle Saidman.
FILMS: Tears Are Not Enough (1985), Pink Cadillac (1989).

ADAMS, RYAN
ALBUMS: Heartbreaker (Bloodshot/Cooking Vinyl 2000)★★★★, Gold (Lost Highway 2001)★★★★.

ADAMSON, BARRY
ALBUMS: Moss Side Story (Mute 1988)★★★, Delusion film soundtrack (Mute 1991)★★★, Soul Murder (Mute 1992) ★★★★, The Negro Inside Me mini-album (Mute 1993) ★★★, Oedipus Schmoedipus (Mute 1996)★★★★, As Above, So Below (Mute 1998)★★★, with Pan Sonic Motorlab #3 (Kitchen Motors 2001)★★★.
COMPILATIONS: The Murky World Of Barry Adamson (Mute 1999)★★★★.

ADVERTS
ALBUMS: Crossing The Red Sea With The Adverts (Bright 1978)★★★, Cast Of Thousands (RCA 1979)★★, The Peel Sessions mini-album (Strange Fruit 1987)★★, Live At The Roxy Club (Receiver 1990)★★★.
COMPILATIONS: The Wonders Don't Care: The Complete Radio Recordings (New Millennium 1997)★★★, The Punk Singles Collection (Anagram 1997)★★★, Best Of The Adverts (Anagram 1998)★★★.

AEROSMITH
ALBUMS: Aerosmith (Columbia 1973)★★★, Get Your Wings (Columbia 1974)★★★, Toys In The Attic (Columbia 1975) ★★★★, Rocks (Columbia 1976)★★★★, Draw The Line (Columbia 1977)★★★, Live! Bootleg (Columbia 1978)★★★, Night In The Ruts (Columbia 1979)★★, Rock In A Hard Place (Columbia 1982)★★, Done With Mirrors (Geffen 1985) ★★★, Permanent Vacation (Geffen 1987)★★★, Pump (Geffen 1989)★★★★, Get A Grip (Geffen 1993)★★★★, Nine Lives (Columbia 1997)★★★★, A Little South Of Sanity (Geffen 1998)★★★★, Just Push Play (Columbia 2001)★★★.
COMPILATIONS: Aerosmith's Greatest Hits (Columbia 1980)★★★★, Classics Live! (Columbia 1986)★★, Classics Live II (Columbia 1987)★★★, Gems (Columbia 1988)★★★, Anthology (Raw Power/Castle 1988)★★, Pandora's Box 3-CD box set (Columbia 1991)★★★, Big Ones (Geffen 1994)★★★★, Box Of Fire 13-CD box set (Columbia 1994)★★★★, Classics Live! Complete (Columbia 1998)★★★, Young Lust: The Aerosmith Anthology (Geffen 2001)★★★★.
VIDEOS: Video Scrapbook (CBS/Fox Video 1987), Live Texxas Jam '78 (CBS Music Video Enterprises 1988), Permanent Vacation 3x5 (Geffen Home Video 1988), Things That Go Pump In The Night (Geffen Home Video 1990), The Making Of Pump (CBS Music Video Enterprises 1990), Big Ones You Can Look At (Geffen Home Video 1994).
FURTHER READING: The Fall And Rise Of Aerosmith, Mark Putterford. Live!, Mark Putterford. Toys In The Attic: The Rise, Fall And Rise Of Aerosmith, Martin Huxley. What It Takes, Dave Bowler and Brian Dray. Dream On: Living On The Edge With Steven Tyler, Cyrinda Foxe-Tyler and Danny Fields. Walk This Way: The Autobiography Of Aerosmith, Aerosmith with Stephen Davis.

AFGHAN WHIGS
ALBUMS: Big Top Halloween (Ultra Suede 1988)★★★, Up In It (Sub Pop 1990)★★★, Congregation (Sub Pop 1992) ★★★, Gentlemen (Sub Pop/Elektra 1993)★★★★, What Jail Is Like mini-album (Sub Pop/Elektra 1994)★★, Black Love (Sub Pop/Elektra 1996)★★★★, 1965 (Columbia 1998)★★★★.

AFRIKA BAMBAATAA
ALBUMS: with Shango Funk Theology (Celluloid 1984)★★★, with Soul Sonic Force Planet Rock - The Album (Tommy Boy 1986)★★★★, Beware (The Funk Is Everywhere) (Tommy Boy 1986)★★★ Death Mix Throwdown (Blatant 1987)★★★★, The Light (Capitol 1988)★★★, The Decade Of Darkness (1990-2000) (EMI 1991)★★★, Don't Stop - Planet Rock Remix (ZTT 1992)★★★, with Soul Sonic Force Lost Generation (Hot 1996)★★, Hydraulic Funk (Strictly Hype 2000)★★★★.
COMPILATIONS: Looking For The Perfect Beat 1980-1985 (Tommy Boy 2001)★★★★.

AGUILERA, CHRISTINA
ALBUMS: Christina Aguilera (RCA 1999)★★★, Mi Reflejo (RCA 2000)★★, My Kind Of Christmas (RCA 2000)★★, Just Be Free (Platinum 2001)★★.
VIDEOS: Genie Gets Her Wish (RCA 1999), Out Of The Bottle (RCA 1999), My Reflection (Aviva 2001).
FURTHER READING: Christina Aguilera: An Unauthorized Biography, Jackie Robb. Christina Aguilera, Anna Louise Golden. Christina Aguilera, Catherine Murphy. Christina Aguilera: The Unofficial Book, Molly MacDermot. Backstage Pass: Christina Aguilera, Jan Gabriel.

AIR
ALBUMS: Moon Safari (Source/Astralwerks 1998)★★★★, The Virgin Suicides film soundtrack (Source/Astralwerks 2000)★★★, 10,000 Hz Legend (Source/Astralwerks 2001)★★★★.
COMPILATIONS: Premiers Symptomes (Source/Astralwerks 1997)★★★, Everybody Hertz (Astralwerks 2002)★★★.

ALABAMA
ALBUMS: Wild Country (LSI 1977)★★★, Deuces Wild (LSI 1978)★★★, My Home's In Alabama (RCA 1980)★★★, Feels So Right (RCA 1981)★★★, Mountain Music (RCA 1982)★★★★, The Closer You Get (RCA 1983)★★★, Roll On (RCA 1984)★★★, Alabama Christmas (RCA 1985)★★, 40 Hour Week (RCA 1985)★★★, The Touch (RCA 1986)★★★, Just Us (RCA 1987)★★★, Alabama Live (RCA 1988)★★, Southern Star (RCA 1989)★★★, Pass It On Down (RCA 1990)★★★, American Pride (RCA 1992) ★★★, Gonna Have A Party ... Live (RCA 1993)★★, Cheap Seats (RCA 1993)★★★, In Pictures (RCA 1995)★★★, Alabama Christmas Volume II (RCA 1996)★★, Dancin' On The Boulevard (RCA 1997)★★★, Twentieth Century (RCA 1999)★★★, When It All Goes South (RCA 2001)★★★.
COMPILATIONS: Wild Country (LSI 1981)★★★, Greatest Hits (RCA 1986)★★★★, Greatest Hits, Volume 2 (RCA 1991)★★★, Greatest Hits, Volume 3 (RCA 1994)★★★, Super Hits (RCA 1996)★★★, Super Hits Volume 2 (RCA 1998)★★★, For The Record: 41 Number One Hits (RCA 1998)★★★★.

ALBION COUNTRY BAND
ALBUMS: as the Albion Country Band Battle Of The Field (Island 1976)★★★★; as the Albion Dance Band The Prospect Before Us (Harvest 1977)★★★; as the Albion Band: Rise Up Like The Sun (Harvest 1978)★★★, Lark Rise To Candleford (A Country Tapestry) (Charisma 1980)★★, Light Shining (Albino 1982)★★★, Shuffle Off (Making Waves 1983)★★★, Under The Rose (Spindrift 1984)★★★, A Christmas Present From The Albion Band (Fun 1985)★★, Stella Maria (Making Waves 1987)★★★, The Wild Side Of Town (Celtic Music 1987)★★, I Got New Shoes (Celtic Music 1987)★★★, Give Me A Saddle And I'll Trade You A Car (Topic 1989)★★★, 1990 (Topic 1990)★★★, BBC Radio Live In Concert (Windsong 1993)★★★, Acousticity (HTD 1994)★★★, Albion Heart (HTD 1995)★★★★, Demi Paradise (HTD 1996)★★★, The BBC Sessions (Strange Fruit 1997)★★★, Along The Pilgrim's Way (Mooncrest 1998)★★★★, Live At The Cambridge Folk Festival (Strange Fruit 1998)★★★, Before Us Stands Yesterday (HTD 1999)★★★, Christmas Album (HTD 1999)★★, Road Movies (Topic 2001)★★★.
COMPILATIONS: Songs From The Shows Volume 1 (Road Goes On Forever 1992)★★★, Songs From The Shows Volume 2 (Road Goes On Forever 1992)★★★, The Acoustic Years (HTD 1997)★★★.

ALEXANDER, ARTHUR
ALBUMS: You Better Move On (Dot 1962)★★★, Alexander The Great (Dot 1964)★★★, Arthur Alexander i (Dot 1965)★★★, Arthur Alexander ii (Warners 1972)★★, Arthur Alexander iii (Buddah 1975)★★, Lonely Just Like Me (Elektra 1993)★★★.
COMPILATIONS: A Shot Of Rhythm And Soul (Ace 1985)★★★, Soldier Of Love (Ace 1987)★★★, The Greatest (Ace 1989)★★★★, The Ultimate Arthur Alexander (Razor & Tie 1993)★★★★, Rainbow Road: The Warner Bros. Recordings (Warner Archives 1994)★★★, The Monument Years (Ace 2001)★★★.
FURTHER READING: Get A Shot Of Rhythm & Blues: The Arthur Alexander Story, Richard Younger.

ALICE COOPER
ALBUMS: Pretties For You (Straight 1969)★★, Easy Action (Straight 1970)★★★, Love It To Death (Warners 1971) ★★★★, Killer (Warners 1971)★★★, School's Out (Warners 1972)★★★★, Billion Dollar Babies (Warners 1973)★★★★, Muscle Of Love (Warners 1973)★★, Welcome To My Nightmare (Atlantic 1975)★★★, Goes To Hell (Warners 1976)★★, Lace And Whiskey (Warners 1977)H, The Alice Cooper Show (Warners 1977)★★, From The Inside (Warners 1978)★★, Flush The Fashion (Warners 1980)H, Special Forces (Warners 1981)H, Zipper Catches Skin (Warners 1982)H, Da Da (Warners 1983)★★, Live In Toronto (Breakaway 1984)H, Constrictor (MCA 1986)★★, Raise Your Fist And Yell (MCA 1987)★★, Trash (Epic 1989)★★★, Hey Stoopid (Epic 1991)★★, Live At The Whiskey A-Go-Go 1969 recording (Edsel 1992)★★, The Last Temptation (Epic 1994)★★, A Fistful Of Alice (Guardian 1997)★★, Brutal Planet (Spitfire 2000)★★★★, Billion Dollar Babies Deluxe Edition 2-CD set (Rhino 2001)★★★★, Dragon Town (Spitfire 2001)★★★, Slack Alice Live In Toronto 1969 (Yeaah! 2001)★★.
COMPILATIONS: School Days (Warners 1973)★★★, Alice Cooper's Greatest Hits (Warners 1974)★★★★, Freak Out Song (Castle 1986)★★★, The Beast Of Alice Cooper (Warners 1989)★★★★, Classicks (Epic 1995)★★★ Freedom For Frankenstein: Hits & Pieces 1984-'91 (Raven 1998) ★★★★, The Life And Crimes Of Alice Cooper 4-CD box set (Warners/Rhino 1999)★★★★, Mascara & Monsters: The Best Of Alice Cooper (Rhino 2001)★★★★, The Definitive Alice Cooper (Warners 2001)★★★★.
VIDEOS: The Nightmare Returns (Hendring Music Video 1987), Welcome To My Nightmare (Hendring Music Video 1988), Video Trash (Hendring Music Video 1989), Alice Cooper Trashes The World (CMV Enterprises 1990), Prime Cuts (PolyGram Video 1991), Brutally Live (Eagle Vision 2000).
FURTHER READING: Alice Cooper, Steve Demorest. Billion Dollar Baby, Bob Greene. Me, Alice: The Autobiography Of Alice Cooper, Alice Cooper with Steven Gaines. Rolling Stone Scrapbook: Alice Cooper, Rolling Stone. No More Mr Nice Guy: The Inside Story Of The Alice Cooper Group, Michael Bruce with Billy James. The Illustrated Collector's Guide To Alice Cooper, Dale Sherman.
FILMS: Diary Of A Mad Housewife (1970), Midsummer Rock Fest (1971), Medicine Ball Caravan aka We Have Come For Your Daughters (1971), Rock-a-bye (1973), Good To See You Again, Alice Cooper (1974), Welcome To My Nightmare (1976), This Is America Part 2 (1977), Sgt. Pepper's Lonely Hearts Club Band (1978), Sextette (1978), The Strange Case Of Alice Cooper (1979), Roadie (1980), Leviatán aka Monster Dog (1984), Alice Cooper: The Nightmare Returns (1986), Prince Of Darkness (1987), The Decline Of Western Civilization Part II: The Metal Years (1988), Freddy's Dead: The Final Nightmare (1991), Wayne's World (1992), Celebration: The Music Of Pete Townshend And The Who (1994), The History Of Rock 'N' Roll, Vol. 8 (1995), British Rock Symphony (1999), The Attic Expeditions (2000), Mayor Of Sunset Strip (2001).

ALICE IN CHAINS
ALBUMS: Facelift (Columbia 1990)★★★, Sap mini-album (Columbia 1992)★★★, Dirt (Columbia 1992)★★★★, Jar Of Flies mini-album (Columbia 1993)★★★★, Alice In Chains (Columbia 1995)★★★, MTV Unplugged Live (Sony 1996)★★★, Live (Columbia 2000)★★★.
Solo: Jerry Cantrell Boggy Depot (Columbia 1998)★★.
COMPILATIONS: Nothing Safe: The Best Of The Box (Columbia 1999)★★★★, Music Bank 3-CD box set (Columbia 1999)★★★, Greatest Hits (Columbia 2001)★★★★.
VIDEOS: Live Facelift (SMV 1994), Nona Weisbaum (Columbia 1995), The Nona Tapes (SMV 1996), MTV Unplugged (SMV 1996), Music Bank: The Videos (Columbia 2001).

ALIEN ANT FARM
ALBUMS: Greatest Hits (Chick Music 1999)★★★, ANThology (New Noize/DreamWorks 2001)★★★★.

ALL ABOUT EVE
ALBUMS: All About Eve (Mercury 1987)★★★, Scarlet And Other Stories (Mercury 1989)★★★, Touched By Jesus (Vertigo 1991)★★, Ultraviolet (MCA 1992)★★, Fairy Light Nights (Yeaah/AlmaFame 2000)★★★, Fairy Light Nights Two: Live Acoustic (Jamtart/AlmaFame 2001)★★★, Live & Electric At The Union Chapel (Jamtart 2002)★★★.
COMPILATIONS: Winter Words, Hits And Rarities (MCA 1992)★★★, The Best Of All About Eve (Spectrum 1999)★★★.
VIDEOS: Martha's Harbour (PolyGram Music Video 1988), What Kind Of Fool (PolyGram Music Video 1989), Evergreen (Channel 5 1989).

ALL SAINTS
ALBUMS: All Saints (London 1997)★★★, The Remix Album (London 1998)★★, Saints & Sinners (London 2000)★★★.
COMPILATIONS: All Hits (London 2001)★★★★.
VIDEOS: The Video (London 1998), The Videos (Warner Music Vision 2001).
FILMS: Honest (2000).

ALLISON, LUTHER
ALBUMS: Love Me Mama (Delmark 1969)★★★, Bad News Is Coming (Gordy 1973)★★★, Luther's Blues (Gordy 1974)★★★, Night Life (Gordy 1976)★★★, Love Me Papa (Black & Blue 1977)★★★, Live In Paris (Free Bird 1979)★★★, Live (Blue Silver 1979)★★★, Gonna Be A Live One In Here Tonight (Rumble 1979)★★★, Time (Paris Album 1980)★★★, South Side Safari (Red Lightnin' 1982)★★★, Lets Have A Natural Ball (JSP 1984)★★★, Serious (Blind Pig 1984)★★★, Here I Come (Encore 1985)★★★, Powerwire Blues (Charly 1986)★★★, Rich Man (Entente 1987)★★★, Life Is A Bitch (Encore 1988)★★, Love Me Mama (Delmark 1988)★★★, Let's Try It Again - Live '89 (Teldec 1989)★★, More From Berlin (Melodie 1991)★★, Hand Me Down My Moonshine (In-Akustik 1992)★★, Soul Fixin' Man (Alligator 1994)★★★, Bad Love (Ruf 1994)★★★, Blue Streak (Ruf 1995)★★★, Reckless (Ruf 1997)★★★★, Where Have You Been? Live In Montreux 1976-1994 (Ruf 1997)★★★★, Live In Paradise (Ruf 1998)★★★★, Live In Chicago (Alligator 1999)★★★★, South Side Safari (Catfish 2000)★★.
COMPILATIONS: Sweet Home Chicago (Delmark 1993)★★★.
VIDEOS: Live In Paradise (RUF 1998).

ALLMAN BROTHERS BAND
ALBUMS: The Allman Brothers Band (Capricorn 1969) ★★★★, Idlewild South (Capricorn 1970)★★★★, Live At The Fillmore East (Capricorn 1971)★★★★, Eat A Peach (Capricorn 1972)★★★, Brothers And Sisters (Capricorn 1973)★★★, Win, Lose Or Draw (Capricorn 1975)★★★, Wipe The Windows, Check The Oil, Dollar Gas (Capricorn 1976)H, Enlightened Rogues (Capricorn 1979)★★★, Reach For The Sky (Arista 1980)★★, Brothers Of The Road (Arista 1981)★★, Live At Ludlow Garage 1970 (PolyGram 1990) ★★★, Seven Turns (Epic 1990)★★★, Shades Of Two Worlds (Epic 1991)★★★, An Evening With The Allman Brothers Band (Epic 1992)★★★, The Fillmore Concerts (Polydor 1993)★★★★, Where It All Begins (Epic 1994) ★★★, 2nd Set (Epic 1995)★★, Twenty (SPV 1997)★★, Peakin' At The Beacon (Sony 2000)★★.
COMPILATIONS: The Road Goes On Forever (Capricorn 1975)★★★, The Best Of The Allman Brothers Band (Polydor 1981)★★★, Dreams 4-CD box set (Polydor 1989)★★★★, A Decade Of Hits 1969-1979 (PolyGram 1991)★★★★, Hell And High Water (Arista 1994)★★, Madness Of The West (Camden 1998)★★, Mycology: An Anthology (Epic 1998)★★, The Best Of The Allman Brothers Band Live (Spectrum 1998)★★, The Best Of The Allman Brothers Band: The Millennium Collection (Polydor 2000)★★★★.
VIDEOS: Brothers Of The Road (RCA/Columbia 1988), Live At Great Woods (Sony Music Video 1993).
FURTHER READING: The Allman Brothers: A Biography In Words And Pictures, Tom Nolan. Midnight Riders: The Story Of The Allman Brothers Band, Scott Freeman.

ALMOND, MARC
ALBUMS: Vermin In Ermine (Some Bizzare/Phonogram 1984)★★, Stories Of Johnny (Some Bizzare/Virgin 1985)★★★, A Woman's Story mini-album (Some Bizzare/Virgin 1986)★★★, Violent Silence mini-album (Virgin 1986)★★★, Mother Fist And Her Five Daughters (Some Bizzare/Virgin 1987)★★, The Stars We Are (Some Bizzare/Capitol 1988)★★★, Jacques (Some Bizzare/Rough Trade 1989)★★★, Enchanted (Some Bizzare/Capitol 1990)★★★, Tenement Symphony (Some Bizzare/Sire 1991)★★, 12 Years Of Tears: Live At The Royal Albert Hall (Some Bizzare/Sire 1993)★★★, Absinthe: The French Album (Some Bizzare 1994)★★★, Fantastic Star (Mercury 1996)★★★, Open All Night (Blue Star 1999)★★★, Stranger Things (XIII Bis 2001)★★★.
COMPILATIONS: Singles 1984-1987 (Some Bizzare/Virgin 1987)★★★, with Soft Cell Memorabilia: The Singles (Polydor 1991)★★★, A Virgin's Tale Vol. I (Some Bizzare/Virgin 1992)★★★, A Virgin's Tale Vol. II (Some Bizzare/Virgin 1992)★★★, Treasure Box (Some Bizzare/EMI 1995)★★.
VIDEOS: Marc Almond Videos: 1984 - 1987 (Virgin Vision 1987), Marc Almond Live In Concert (Windsong 1992), 12 Years Of Tears (Sire 1993).
FURTHER READING: The Angel Of Death In The Adonis Lounge, Marc Almond. The Last Star: A Biography Of Marc Almond, Jeremy Reed. Gutterheart, Paul Burston. Beautiful Twisted Night, Marc Almond. Tainted Life: The Autobiography, Marc Almond. The End Of New York, Marc Almond.

ALTERED IMAGES
ALBUMS: Happy Birthday (Epic 1981)★★★, Pinky Blue (Epic 1982)★★, Bite (Epic 1983)★★.
COMPILATIONS: Collected Images (Epic 1984)★★★, The Best Of Altered Images (Receiver 1992)★★★, I Could Be Happy: The Best Of Altered Images (Epic 1997)★★★.

AMEN
ALBUMS: Slave (Dragula 1995)★★★, Amen (I Am/Roadrunner 1999)★★★, We Have Come For Your Parents (I Am/Virgin 2000)★★★.

AMEN CORNER
ALBUMS: Round Amen Corner (Deram 1968)★★★, National Welsh Coast Live Explosive Company (Immediate 1969)★★★, Farewell To The Real Magnificent Seven (Immediate 1969)★★, Return Of The Magnificent Seven (Immediate 1976)★.
COMPILATIONS: World Of Amen Corner (Decca 1969) ★★★, Greatest Hits (Immediate 1978)★★★, The Best Of Amen Corner (Repertoire 1999)★★★, If Paradise Was Half As Nice: The Immediate Anthology (Sanctuary/Immediate 2000)★★★.

AMERICA
ALBUMS: America (Warners 1972)★★★, Homecoming (Warners 1972)★★★, Hat Trick (Warners 1973)★★, Holiday (Warners 1974)★★★, Hearts (Warners 1975) ★★★, Hideaway (Warners 1976)★★★, Harbor (Warners 1976)★★, America/Live (Warners 1977)H, Silent Letter (Capitol 1979)★★, Alibi (Capitol 1980)★★, View From The Ground (Capitol 1982)★★, Your Move (Capitol 1983)★★, Perspective (Capitol 1984)★★, In Concert (Capitol 1985)★★, The Last Unicorn (Virgin 1988)H, Hourglass (American Gramophone 1994)★★, Live On The King Biscuit Flower Hour (Strange Fruit/King Biscuit Flower Hour 1998)★★, Human Nature (Oxygen 1998)★★★.
COMPILATIONS: History: America's Greatest Hits (Warners 1975)★★★, Encore! More Greatest Hits (Rhino 1990)★★, The Best Of America (EMI 1997)★★★, Highway: 30 Years Of America 3-CD box set (Rhino 2000)★★★, The Definitive America (Rhino 2001)★★★.
VIDEOS: Live In Central Park (PMI 1986).

AMERICAN MUSIC CLUB
ALBUMS: The Restless Stranger (Grifter 1986)★★★, Engine (Grifter/Frontier 1987)★★★, California (Grifter/Frontier 1988)★★★, United Kingdom (Demon 1990)★★★, Everclear (Alias 1991)★★★★, Mercury (Reprise 1993)★★★★, San Francisco (Reprise 1994)★★★.
FURTHER READING: Wish The World Away: Mark Eitzel And The American Music Club, Sean Body.

AMON DÜÜL II
ALBUMS: Phallus Dei (Teldec/Sunset 1969)★★★, Yeti (Teldec/Liberty 1970)★★★★, Dance Of The Lemmings aka Tanz Der Lemminge (Teldec/United Artists 1971)★★★★, Carnival In Babylon (United Artists 1972)★★★, Wolf City (Teldec/United Artists 1973)★★★, Live In London (United Artists 1973)★★, Vive La Trance (United Artists 1974)★★, Hijack (Atlantic 1974)★★, Made In Germany (Nova/Atco 1975)★★, Pyragony X (Nova 1976)★★, Almost Alive (Nova 1977)★★, Only Human (Strand 1978)★★, Vortex (Telefunken 1981)★★, Hawk Meets Penguin (Illuminated 1982)★★, as Amon Düül (UK) Meetings With Menmachines (Inglorious Heroes Of The Past) aka Meetings With Menmachines (Unremarkable Heroes Of The Past) (Illuminated 1984)★★, as Amon Düül (UK) Fool Moon (Demi Monde 1989)★★, as Amon Düül (UK) Die Lösung (Demi Monde 1989)★★, Live In Concert 1973 recording (Windsong 1992)★★★, Nada Moonshine # (Faruk/Mystic 1995)★★, Live In Tokyo (Mystic 1997)★★, Live In London (Mystic 1998)★★.
COMPILATIONS: Lemmingmania (United Artists 1974)★★★, The Classic German Rock Scene (United Artists 1974)★★★, Rock In Deutschland - Vol. 1 (Strand 1981)★★★, as Amon Düül (UK) Airs On A Shoestring (Best Of) (Thunderbolt 1987)★★, Milestones (Castle 1989)★★★, Surrounded By The Bars (Spalax 1993)★★, The Greatest Hits (Vinyl 1994)★★★, Kobe (Reconstructions) (Captain Trip 1996) ★★★, Eternal Flashback (Captain Trip 1996)★★★, The Best Of 1969-1974 (Cleopatra 1997)★★★, Flawless (Mystic 1997)★★★, Drei Jahrzehnte (1968-1998) 4-CD set (East West 1997)★★★, The UA Years 1969-1974 (Cleopatra 1999)★★★, Manana (Strange Fruit 2000)★★★.

AMOS, TORI
ALBUMS: as Y Kant Tori Read Y Kant Tori Read (Atlantic 1988)★★, Little Earthquakes (East West 1992)★★★★, Under The Pink (East West 1994)★★★★, Boys For Pele (East West 1996)★★★★, From The Choirgirl Hotel (East West 1998)★★★★, To Venus And Back (East West 1999)★★★, Strange Little Girls (Atlantic 2001)★★★.
VIDEOS: Little Earthquake (A*Vision 1992), Tori Amos: Live From New York (Warner Music Vision 1997), The Complete Videos 1991-1998 (Warner Music Vision 1999).
FURTHER READING: All These Years: The Illustrated Biography, Kalen Rogers.

ANASTACIA
ALBUMS: Not That Kind (Daylight/Epic 2000)★★★★, Freak Of Nature (Daylight/Epic 2001)★★★★.

AND YOU WILL KNOW US BY THE TRAIL OF DEAD
ALBUMS: .... And You Will Know Us By The Trail Of Dead (Trance Syndicate 1998)★★★, Madonna (Merge/Domino 1999)★★★★, Source Tags & Codes (Interscope 2002)★★★.

ANDERSON, LAURIE
ALBUMS: Big Science (Warners 1982)★★★★, Mr. Heartbreak (Warners 1984)★★★, United States 5-LP set (Warners 1985)★★, Home Of The Brave (Warners 1986)★★★, Strange Angels (Warners 1989)★★★★, Bright Red (Warners 1994)★★★, The Ugly One With The Jewels And Other Stories (Warners 1995)★★★, Life On A String (Nonesuch/Warners 2001)★★★.
COMPILATIONS: Talk Normal: The Laurie Anderson Anthology (Rhino/WEA 2000)★★★★.
VIDEOS: Home Of The Brave (Warners 1986), Collected Videos (Warner Reprise 1990).

ANIMALS
ALBUMS: The Animals (Columbia 1964)★★★★, The Animals On Tour (MGM 1965)★★★, Animal Tracks (Columbia 1965) ★★★, Most Of The Animals (Columbia 1966)★★★★, Animalization (MGM 1966)★★★, Animalisms (Decca 1966)★★★, Eric Is Here (MGM 1967)★★★, Winds Of Change (MGM 1967)★★★, The Twain Shall Meet (MGM 1968)★★★, Everyone Of Us (MGM 1968)★★★, Love Is (MGM 1968)★★★, In Concert From Newcastle (DJM 1976) ★★, Before We Were Rudely Interrupted (United Artists 1977)H, The Ark (I.R.S. 1983)H, Rip It To Shreds - The Animals Greatest Hits Live! (I.R.S. 1984)★★, The Animals With Sonny Boy Williamson (Decal/Charly 1988)★★★.
COMPILATIONS: The Best Of The Animals (MGM 1966)★★★, The Best Of Eric Burdon And The Animals Volume 2 (MGM 1967)★★★, The Greatest Hits Of Eric Burdon And The Animals (MGM 1969)★★★, The EP Collection (See For Miles 1988)★★★★, The Complete Animals (EMI 1990)★★★★, Trackin' The Hits (Decal/Charly 1990)★★★, The Very Best Of The Animals (Spectrum 1998)★★★, as Eric Burdon And The New Animals Psychedelic World (Edsel 2001)★★★.
FURTHER READING: I Used To Be An Animal But I'm All Right Now, Eric Burdon. Wild Animals, Andy Blackford. The Last Poet: The Story Of Eric Burdon, Jeff Kent. Good Times: The Ultimate Eric Burdon, Dionisio Castello. Animal Tracks: The Story Of The Animals, Sean Egan.
FILMS: Get Yourself A College Girl (1964), It's A Bikini World (1967).

ANKA, PAUL
ALBUMS: Paul Anka (ABC 1958)★★★, My Heart Sings (ABC 1959)★★★, Paul Anka Swings For Young Lovers (ABC 1960)★★★★, Anka At The Copa (ABC 1960)★★★, It's Christmas Everywhere (ABC 1960)★★★, Strictly Instrumental (ABC 1961)★★, Diana (ABC 1962)★★★★, Young, Alive And In Love! (RCA Victor 1962)★★★★, Let's Sit This One Out! (RCA Victor 1962)★★★, Our Man Around The World (RCA Victor 1963)★★★, Songs I Wished I'd Written (RCA Victor 1963)★★, Excitement On Park Avenue (RCA Victor 1964)★★★, Strictly Nashville (RCA Victor 1966)★★, Paul Anka Alive (RCA Victor 1967)★★, Goodnight My Love (RCA Victor 1969)★★★, Life Goes On (RCA Victor 1969)★★★, Paul Anka (Buddah 1971)★★, Jubilation (Buddah 1972)★★, Anka (United Artists 1974)★★★, Feelings (United Artists 1975)★★★, The Painter (United Artists 1976)★★★, The Music Man (United Artists 1977)★★★, Listen To Your Heart (RCA 1978)★★, Both Sides Of Love (RCA 1981)★★★, Walk A Fine Line (Columbia 1983)★★★, Italiano (Crescent 1987)★★★, Amigos (Globo/Sony 1996)★★★, A Body Of Work (Epic 1999)★★.
COMPILATIONS: Paul Anka Sings His Big 15 (ABC 1960)★★★★, Paul Anka Sings His Big 15, Volume 2 (ABC 1961)★★★, Paul Anka Sings His Big 15, Volume 3 (ABC 1961)★★, Paul Anka's 21 Golden Hits (RCA 1963)★★★, Paul Anka Gold (Sire 1974)★★★★, Times Of Your Life (United Artists 1975)★★★, Paul Anka At His Best (United Artists 1979)★★★★, The Original Hits Of Paul Anka (Columbia 1987)★★★, 30th Anniversary Collection (Rhino 1989)★★★, The Ultimate Collection (Capitol 1992)★★★★, The Best Of United Artists Years (Capitol 1996)★★★★, The Very Best Of Paul Anka (RCA 2000)★★★★.
FILMS: Let's Rock aka Keep It Cool (1958), Girls Town aka The Innocent And The Damned (1959), The Private Life Of Adam And Eve (1961), Look In Any Window (1961), The Longest Day (1962), Lonely Boy (1962), Iskelmäprinssi

(1990), Captain Ron (1992), Ordinary Magic aka Ganesh (1993), Mr. Payback: An Interactive Movie (1995), Mad Dog Time (1996), 3000 Miles To Graceland (2001).

ANTHRAX
ALBUMS: Fistful Of Metal (Megaforce 1984)★★, Spreading The Disease (Island/Megaforce 1986)★★★★, Among The Living (Island/Megaforce 1987)★★★, State Of Euphoria (Island/Megaforce 1988)★★, Persistence Of Time (Island/Megaforce 1990)★★★★, Attack Of The Killer B's (Island/Megaforce 1991)★★★, Sound Of White Noise (Elektra 1993)★★★★, Live - The Island Years (Island 1994)★★★, Stomp 442 (Elektra 1995)★★, Volume 8 - The Threat Is Real (Ignition 1998)★★★.
COMPILATIONS: Moshers 1986-1991 (Connoisseur Collection 1998)★★★★, Return Of The Killer A's (Beyond/Spitfire 1999)★★★, Madhouse: The Very Best Of Anthrax (Island 2001)★★★★.
VIDEOS: Oidivnikufesin N.F.V. (Island Visual Arts 1988), Persistence Through Time (Island Visual Arts 1990), Through Time (PolyGram Music Video 1991), N.F.V. (PolyGram Music Video 1991).

APHEX TWIN
ALBUMS: Selected Ambient Works '85 - '92 (R&S 1992)★★★★, as Polygon Window Surfing On Sine Waves (Warp/Wax Trax! 1993)★★★, Selected Ambient Works Volume II (Warp/Sire 1994)★★★, ... I Care Because You Do (Warp/Sire 1995)★★★, Richard D. James Album (Warp/Sire 1996)★★★, Drukqs (Warp/Sire 2001)★★★★.
COMPILATIONS: Classics (R&S 1995)★★★★, as Caustic Window Compilation (Rephlex 1998)★★★.
VIDEOS: Come To Viddy (Warp 1997), Windowlicker (Warp 1999).

APHRODITE'S CHILD
ALBUMS: End Of The World/Rain And Tears (Mercury 1968)★★, It's Five O'Clock (Mercury 1969)★★, 666: The Apocalypse Of John (Vertigo 1972)★★★.
COMPILATIONS: Rain And Tears: The Best Of Aphrodite's Child (Philips 1975)★★★, Greatest Hits (Mercury 1981)★★★, The Complete Collection (Mercury 1996)★★★.

APPLE, FIONA
ALBUMS: Tidal (Clean Slate/Work Group 1996)★★★, When The Pawn ... (Clean Slate/Epic 1999)★★★.

ARGENT
ALBUMS: Argent (Columbia 1970)★★★, Ring Of Hands (Columbia 1971)★★★, All Together Now (Epic 1972)★★★, In Deep (Epic 1973)★★, Nexus (Epic 1974)★★, Encore - Live In Concert (Epic 1974)H, Circus (Epic 1975)H, Counterpoint (RCA 1975)★★, In Concert (Windsong 1995)★★★, Out Of The Shadows (Redhouse 2001)★★★.
COMPILATIONS: The Best Of Argent (Epic 1976)★★★, Anthology (Epic 1984)★★★, Music From The Spheres (Elite 1991)★★★, The BBC Sessions (Strange Fruit 1997)★★★.

ARMATRADING, JOAN
ALBUMS: Whatever's For Us (A&M 1972)★★★, Back To The Night (A&M 1975)★★★, Joan Armatrading (A&M 1976)★★★★, Show Some Emotion (A&M 1977)★★★, To The Limit (A&M 1978)★★★, Steppin' Out (A&M 1978)★★, Me Myself I (A&M 1980)★★★★, Walk Under Ladders (A&M 1981)★★★, The Key (A&M 1983)★★★, Secret Secrets (A&M 1985)★★★, Sleight Of Hand (A&M 1986)★★★, The Shouting Stage (A&M 1988)★★★★, Hearts And Flowers (A&M 1990)★★★, Square The Circle (A&M 1992)★★★, What's Inside (RCA 1995)★★★.
COMPILATIONS: Track Record (A&M 1983)★★★, The Very Best Of Joan Armatrading (A&M 1991)★★★★, Greatest Hits (A&M 1996)★★★★, The Best Of Joan Armatrading: The Millennium Collection (A&M 2000)★★★★.
VIDEOS: Track Record (A&M Sound Pictures 1989), Very Best Of Joan Armatrading (A&M Sound Pictures 1991).
FURTHER READING: Joan Armatrading: A Biography, Sean Mayes.

ARNOLD, P.P.
ALBUMS: First Lady Of Immediate (Immediate 1967)★★★, Kafunta (Immediate 1968)★★.
COMPILATIONS: Greatest Hits (Immediate 1978)★★, The P.P. Arnold Collection (See For Miles 1988)★★★, P.P. Arnold's Greatest Hits (Castle 1998)★★★, The Best Of P.P. Arnold (Repertoire 1999)★★★, The First Cut (Immediate 2001)★★★.
FILMS: Pop Pirates (1984).

ARRESTED DEVELOPMENT
ALBUMS: 3 Years, 5 Months, And 2 Days In The Life Of ... (Chrysalis 1992)★★★★, Unplugged (Chrysalis 1993)★★★, Zingalamaduni (Chrysalis 1994)★★★.
COMPILATIONS: The Best Of Arrested Development (Chrysalis 1998)★★★, Greatest Hits (EMI 2001)★★★, Classic Masters (EMD 2002)★★★.

ART OF NOISE
ALBUMS: Into Battle With The Art Of Noise mini-album (ZTT 1983)★★★, (Who's Afraid Of?) The Art Of Noise! (ZTT 1984)★★★, In Visible Silence (Chrysalis 1986)★★★, Daft (China 1987)★★★, In No Sense? Nonsense! (China 1987)★★, Below The Waste (China 1989)★★, The Ambient Collection (China 1990)★★★, Drum And Bass Collection (China 1996)★★★, State Of The Art 3-CD remix box (China 1997)★★★, The Seduction Of Claude Debussy (ZTT 1999)★★★, The Reduction (ZTT 2000)★★.
COMPILATIONS: The Best Of The Art Of Noise (China 1988)★★★★.
VIDEOS: In Visible Silence (Channel 5 1988).
FILMS: Breakdance - The Movie (1984).

ASH
ALBUMS: Trailer mini-album (Infectious 1994)★★★, 1977 (Infectious/Warners 1996)★★★★, Live At The Wireless (Death Star 1997)★★★, Nu-Clear Sounds (Infectious/DreamWorks 1998)★★★, Free All Angels (Infectious 2001)★★★★.
VIDEOS: Tokyo Blitz (Infectious 2001).
FURTHER READING: Ash '77-'97 , Charlie Porter. Ash: A Biography Of The Irish Band, Dave Bowler.

ASHFORD AND SIMPSON
ALBUMS: Gimme Something Real (Warners 1973)★★, I Wanna Be Selfish (Warners 1974)★★, Come As You Are (Warners 1976)★★, So, So Satisfied (Warners 1977) ★★★, Send It (Warners 1977)★★★, Is It Still Good To Ya? (Warners 1978)★★★, Stay Free (Warners 1979)★★★, A Musical Affair (Warners 1980)★★★, Performance (Warners 1981)★★★, Street Opera (Capitol 1982)★★★, High-Rise (Capitol 1983)★★★, Solid (Capitol 1984)★★★, Real Love (Capitol 1986)★★★, Love Or Physical (Capitol 1989)★★, with Maya Angelou Been Found (Hopsack And Silk 1996)★★★.
COMPILATIONS: The Best Of Ashford & Simpson (Capitol 1993)★★★★, The Very Best Of Ashford & Simpson (Rhino 2002)★★★★.
VIDEOS: The Ashford And Simpson Video (EMI 1982).
FILMS: Body Rock (1984).

ASIA
ALBUMS: Asia (Geffen 1982)★★★, Alpha (Geffen 1983)★★, Astra (Geffen 1985)★★, Then & Now (Geffen 1990)★★★, Live: 09-XI-90 Mockba (Cromwell/Rhino 1991)★★, Aqua (Musidisc/Pyramid 1992)★★, Aria (Intercord/I.R.S. 1994)★★, Arena (Intercord/Bulletproof 1996)★★★, Now: Live Nottingham 1990 recording (Blueprint 1997)★★, Live: Osaka - Japan - June 1992 (Blueprint 1997)★★, Live: Philadelphia - Chestnut Cabaret - 21st November 1992 (Blueprint 1997)★★, Live: Köln - Germany - 5th October 1994 (Blueprint 1997)★★, Live At The Town & Country Club 1992 recording (Resurgence 1999)★★, Live Acoustic 1997 recording (Resurgence 1999)★★, Aura (Recognition 2001)★★★, Alive In Hallowed Halls 1983 recording (Zoom Club 2001)★★.
COMPILATIONS: Archiva 1 (Resurgence 1996)★★, Archiva 2 (Resurgence 1996)★★, Anthology (Snapper 1997)★★★, Axioms (Snapper 1998)★★, Rare (Resurgence 2000)★★, The Very Best Of Asia: Heat Of The Moment (1982-1990) (Geffen 2000)★★★.
VIDEOS: Asia In Asia (Vestron Music Video 1984), Asia (Live) (Virgin Vision 1991).
FURTHER READING: The Heat Goes On, David Gallant.

ASIAN DUB FOUNDATION
ALBUMS: Facts & Fictions (Nation 1995)★★★, R.A.F.I. (Virgin France 1997)★★★★, Rafi's Revenge (London/Slash 1998)★★★★, Community Music (London 2000)★★★★.
COMPILATIONS: Frontline 93-97: Rarities And Remixes (Nation 2001)★★★.

ASLEEP AT THE WHEEL
ALBUMS: Comin' Right At Ya (Sunset 1973)★★★, Asleep At The Wheel (Epic 1974)★★★, Texas Gold (Capitol 1975)★★★★, Wheelin' And Dealin' (Capitol 1975)★★★, with various artists Texas Country (1976)★★, The Wheel (Capitol 1977)★★★★, Collision Course (Capitol 1978) ★★★, Served Live (Capitol 1979)★★★, Framed (MCA 1980)★★★, Asleep At The Wheel (MCA/Dot 1985)★★, Pasture Prime (MCA 1985)★★★★, Jumpin' At The Woodside (Edsel 1986)★★★, Ten (Epic 1987)★★★, Western Standard Time (Epic 1988)★★★, Keepin' Me Up Nights (Arista 1990)★★★, Tribute To The Music Of Bob Wills And The Texas Playboys (Liberty 1993)★★★, The Wheel Keeps On Rollin' (Capitol Nashville 1995)★★★, Back To The Future Now - Live At Arizona Charlie's, Las Vegas (Epic 1997)★★★, Merry Texas Christmas, Y'All (High Street Records 1997)★★, Ride With Bob: A Tribute To Bob Wills And The Texas Playboys (DreamWorks 1999)★★★.
COMPILATIONS: The Very Best Of Asleep At The Wheel (See For Miles 1987)★★★, Greatest Hits: Live & Kickin' (Arista 1991)★★★, Best Of (CEMA 1992)★★★, The Swinging Best Of Asleep At The Wheel (Epic 1992)★★★, 21 Country Classics (EMI 1999)★★★, The Very Best Of Asleep At The Wheel Since 1970 (Relentless 2001)★★★★.

ASSOCIATES
ALBUMS: The Affectionate Punch (Fiction 1980)★★★, Sulk (Associates/WEA 1982)★★★★, Perhaps (WEA 1985)★★, Wild And Lonely (Circa/Charisma 1990)★★★.
SOLO: Billy MacKenzie Outernational (Circa 1991)★★, Beyond The Sun (Nude 1997)★★★, with Paul Haig Memory Palace (Rhythm Of Life 1999)★★, with Steve Aungle Eurocentric (Rhythm Of Life 2001)★★★. Alan Rankine The Day The World Became Her Age (Disques du Crépuscule 1986)★★★, She Loves Me Not (Virgin 1987)★★★, The Big Picture Sucks (Disques du Crépuscule 1989)★★.
COMPILATIONS: Fourth Drawer Down (Situation 2 1981)★★★, Popera: The Singles Collection (East West 1991)★★★, The Radio 1 Sessions (Nighttracks 1994)★★★, Double Hipness (V2 2000)★★.
FURTHER READING: The Glamour Chase: The Maverick Life Of Billy MacKenzie, Tom Doyle.

ASSOCIATION
ALBUMS: And Then ... Along Comes The Association (Valiant 1966)★★★★, Renaissance (Valiant 1967)★★, Insight Out (Warners 1967)★★, Birthday (Warners 1968)★★, The Association (Warners 1969)★★, Live (Warners 1970)H, Stop Your Motor (Warners 1971)★★, Waterbeds In Trinidad (Columbia 1972)★★.
Solo: Russ Giguere Hexagram II (Warners 1971)★★.
COMPILATIONS: Greatest Hits (Warners 1968)★★★★, Golden Heebie Jeebies (Edsel 1988)★★★, Ten Best (Cleopatra 2000)★★★, Just The Right Sound: The Association Anthology (Rhino 2002)★★★★.

ASTLEY, RICK
ALBUMS: Whenever You Need Somebody (RCA 1987) ★★★, Hold Me In Your Arms (RCA 1988)★★, Free (RCA 1991)★★★, Body & Soul (RCA 1993)★★★, Keep It Turned On (Polydor 2001)★★★.
COMPILATIONS: Greatest Hits (BMG Heritage/RCA 2002)★★★★.
VIDEOS: Video Hits (BMG Video 1989).

ASWAD
ALBUMS: Aswad (Mango/Island 1975)★★★, Hulet (Grove Music 1978)★★★★, New Chapter (Columbia 1981)★★★, Not Satisfied (Columbia 1982)★★★, A New Chapter Of Dub (Mango/Island 1982)★★★, Live And Direct (Mango/Island 1983)★★★, Rebel Souls (Mango/Island 1984)★★★, Jah Shaka Meets Aswad In Addis Ababa Studio (Jah Shaka 1985)★★★, To The Top (Simba 1986)★★★★, Distant Thunder (Mango/Island 1988)★★★, Too Wicked (Mango/Island 1990)★★, Rise And Shine (Bubblin'/Mesa 1994)★★★, Rise And Shine Again! (Bubblin'/Mesa 1995)★★★, Dub: The Nex Frontier (Mesa 1995)★★★, Big Up (Atlantic 1997)★★★, Roots Revival (Ark 1999)★★, 25 Live (Universal 2000)★★.
COMPILATIONS: Showcase (Grove Music 1981)★★★, Renaissance (Stylus 1988)★★★, Crucial Tracks: The Best Of Aswad (Mango/Island 1989)★★★★, Don't Turn Around (Mango/Island 1993)★★★, Firesticks (Mango/Island 1993)★★★, Roots Rocking: The Island Anthology (Island Jamaica 1997)★★★, Reggae Greats (Spectrum 1998)★★★.
VIDEOS: Distant Thunder Concert (Island Visual Arts 1989), Always Wicked (Island Visual Arts 1990).

AT THE DRIVE-IN
ALBUMS: Acrobatic Tenement (Flipside 1997)★★★, In/Casino/Out (Fearless 1998)★★★, Vaya mini-album (Fearless 1999)★★★★, Relationship Of Command (Grand Royal 2000)★★★★.

ATLANTA RHYTHM SECTION
ALBUMS: The Atlanta Rhythm Section (Decca 1972)★★★, Back Up Against The Wall (Decca 1973)★★★, Third Annual Pipe Dream (Polydor 1974)★★★, Dog Days (Polydor 1975)★★, Red Tape (Polydor 1976)★★★, A Rock And Roll Alternative (Polydor 1977)★★★★, Champagne Jam (Polydor 1978)★★★, Underdog (Polydor 1979)★★★, Are You Ready! (Polydor 1979)★★★, The Boys From Doraville (Polydor 1980)★★, Quinella (Columbia 1981)★★, Truth In A Structured Form (Imagine 1989)★★, Partly Plugged (Southern Tracks 1997)★★★, Eufaula (Intersound 1999)★★★.
COMPILATIONS: The Best Of Atlanta Rhythm Section (Polydor 1982)★★★★, The Collection (Connoisseur 2001)★★★.

ATOMIC KITTEN
ALBUMS: Right Now (Innocent 2000)★★★.

ATOMIC ROOSTER
ALBUMS: Atomic Rooster (B&C 1970)★★, Death Walks Behind You (B&C 1970)★★★, In Hearing Of (Pegasus 1971)★★★, Made In England (Dawn 1972)★★, Nice 'N' Greasy (Dawn 1973)★, Atomic Rooster (EMI 1980)★, Headline News (Towerbell 1983)★.
COMPILATIONS: Assortment (B&C 1974)★★, Home To Roost (Mooncrest 1977)★★, The Devil Hits Back (Demi Monde 1989)★★, BBC In Concert (Windsong 1994)★★, The First 10 Explosive Years (Angel Air 1999)★★★, Live And Raw 70/71 (Angel Air 2001)★★, Rarities (Angel Air 2001)★★, The First 10 Explosive Years Volume 2 (Angel Air 2001)★★★, Heavy Soul (Sanctuary 2001)★★★.

AUTEURS
ALBUMS: New Wave (Hut 1993)★★★★, Now I'm A Cowboy (Hut 1994)★★★, After Murder Park (Hut 1996)★★★, as Baader-Meinhof Baader-Meinhof (Hut 1996)★★, How I Learned To Love The Bootboys (Hut 1999)★★★.

AVERAGE WHITE BAND
ALBUMS: Show Your Hand aka Put It Where You Want It (MCA 1973)★★★, AWB (Atlantic 1974)★★★★, Cut The Cake (Atlantic 1975)★★★, Soul Searching (Atlantic 1976)★★, Person To Person (Atlantic 1976)★★★, with Ben E. King Benny And Us (Atlantic 1977)★★★, Warmer Communications (Atlantic 1978)★★, Feel No Fret (Atlantic 1979)★★★, Shine (Arista 1980)★★, Cupid's In Fashion (Arista 1982)★★, Aftershock (Track/Polydor 1989)★★★, Live On The Test (Windsong 1995)★★, Soul Tattoo (Foundation/SPV 1997)★★★, Face To Face Live 1997 recording (Average Enterprises 1999)★★★.
COMPILATIONS: Volume VIII (Atlantic 1980)★★★, Best Of Average White Band (RCA 1984)★★★, Pickin' Up The Pieces: The Best Of Average White Band (Rhino 1992) ★★★★, The Very Best Of Average White Band (Music Club 1997)★★★, Classic Cuts (Snapper 1998)★★★.
VIDEOS: Tonight: Average White Band In Concert (Aviva International 2002).

AYERS, KEVIN
ALBUMS: Joy Of A Toy (Harvest 1969)★★★★, Shooting At The Moon (Harvest 1970)★★★★, Whatevershebringswesing (Harvest 1971)★★★, Bananamour (Harvest/Sire 1973) ★★★, The Confessions Of Dr Dream And Other Stories (Island 1974)★★★, with John Cale, Eno, Nico June 1, 1974 (Island 1974)★★★, Sweet Deceiver (Island 1975)★★★, Yes We Have No Mañanas, So Get Your Mañanas Today (Harvest/ABC 1976)★★★, Rainbow Takeaway (Harvest 1978)★★★, That's What You Get Babe (Harvest 1980)★★, Diamond Jack And The Queen Of Pain (Roadrunner/Charly 1983)★★, Deia ... Vu (Blau 1984)★★, As Close As You Think (Illuminated 1986)★★, Falling Up (Grabaciones Accidentales/Virgin 1988)★★★★, Still Life With Guitar (Permanent 1992)★★★, BBC Radio 1 Live In Concert 1972 recording (Windsong 1992)★★★, with various artists Banana Follies 1972 recording (Hux 1998)★★, with the Wizards Of Twiddly Turn The Lights Down! Live In London 1995 (Market Square 2000)★★★.
COMPILATIONS: Odd Ditties (Harvest 1976)★★★, The Kevin Ayers Collection (See For Miles 1983)★★★, Banana Productions: The Best Of Kevin Ayers (Harvest 1989) ★★★★, Document Series Presents (Connoisseur 1992) ★★★, Singing The Bruise (Band Of Joy 1996)★★★, First Show In The Appearance Business (Band Of Joy 1996) ★★★, Too Old To Die Young (Hux 1998)★★★.

AZTEC CAMERA
ALBUMS: High Land, Hard Rain (Rough Trade/Sire 1983) ★★★★, Knife (WEA/Sire 1984)★★★, Love (WEA/Sire 1987)★★★, Stray (WEA/Sire 1990)★★★, Dreamland (WEA 1993)★★★, Frestonia (WEA/Sire 1995)★★★★.
COMPILATIONS: The Best Of Aztec Camera (WEA 1999)★★★★.
VIDEOS: Aztec Camera (WEA Music Video 1989).

B

B-52'S
ALBUMS: B-52's (Warners 1979)★★★★, Wild Planet (Warners 1980)★★★, Party Mix! remix album (Warners 1981)★★★, Mesopotamia mini-album (Warners 1982)★★, Whammy! (Warners 1983)★★, Bouncing Off The Satellites (Warners 1986)★★, Cosmic Thing (Reprise 1989)★★★, Good Stuff (Warners 1992)★★.
SOLO: Fred Schneider Fred Schneider And The Shake Society (Warners 1984)★★★, Just Fred (Reprise 1996)★★★.
COMPILATIONS: Best Of The B-52's: Dance This Mess Around (Island 1990)★★★★, Party Mix-Mesopotamia (Warners 1991)★★★, Planet Claire (Spectrum 1995)★★★, Time Capsule: Songs For A Future Generation (Warners 1998)★★★★, Nude On The Moon: The B-52's Anthology (Rhino 2002)★★★★.
VIDEOS: Time Capsule: Videos For A Future Generation 1979-1998 (Warner Music Vision 1998).

B. BUMBLE AND THE STINGERS
COMPILATIONS: Best O'B Bumble (One Way 1995)★★★, Nut Rocker And All The Classics (Ace 1996)★★★.

BABES IN TOYLAND
ALBUMS: Spanking Machine (Twin Tone 1990)★★, To Mother mini-album (Reprise/WEA 1991)★★, The Peel Sessions (Strange Fruit 1992)★★★, Fontanelle (Reprise/WEA 1992)★★★★, Painkillers (Reprise/WEA 1993)★★★, Nemesisters (Reprise/WEA 1995)★★★★, Minneapolism (Cherry Red 2000)★★★, Devil (Almafame 2001)★★, Viled (Almafame 2001)★★, Live (Almafame 2001)★★★.
COMPILATIONS: Viled (Almafame 2000)★★★, The Further Adventures Of Babes In Toyland (Fuel 2000 2001)★★★.
FURTHER READING: Babes In Toyland: The Making And Selling Of A Rock And Roll Band, Neal Karlen.

BABYBIRD
ALBUMS: I Was Born A Man (Baby Bird 1995)★★★, Bad Shave (Baby Bird 1995)★★, Fatherhood (Baby Bird 1995)★★★★, The Happiest Man Alive (Baby Bird 1996)★★★, Ugly Beautiful (Echo 1996)★★★, Dying Happy (Baby Bird 1997)★★, There's Something Going On (Echo 1998)★★★, Bugged (Echo 2000)★★★.
COMPILATIONS: The Greatest Hits US only (Baby Bird 1997)★★★, Stephen Jones 1985-2001 (Easy Tiger 2001)★★★.
FURTHER READING: The Bad Book, Stephen Jones.

BABYFACE
ALBUMS: Lovers (Solar 1987)★★, Tender Lover (Solar 1989) ★★, A Closer Look (Solar 1991)★★, For The Cool In You (Epic 1993)★★★, The Day (Epic 1996)★★★, MTV Unplugged NYC 1997 (Epic 1997)★★, Christmas With Babyface (Epic 1998)★★★, Face 2 Face (Arista 2001)★★★.
COMPILATIONS: A Collection Of His Greatest Hits (Epic 2000)★★★, Love Songs (Sony/Legacy 2001)★★★, The Ultimate (Epic/Legacy 2002)★★★.
VIDEOS: Babyface: A Collection Of Videos (Epic 2000).

BACHARACH, BURT
ALBUMS: Hit Maker - Plays The Burt Bacharach Hits (London 1965)★★★, Casino Royale film soundtrack (RCA 1967) ★★★, Reach Out (A&M 1967)★★★, Make It Easy On Yourself (A&M 1969)★★, Butch Cassidy And The Sundance Kid film soundtrack (A&M 1970)★★★, Burt Bacharach (A&M 1971)★★, Living Together (A&M 1973)★★, In Concert (A&M 1974)★★, Futures (A&M 1977)★★, Woman (A&M 1979)★★, with Elvis Costello Painted From Memory: The New Songs Of Bacharach & Costello (Mercury 1998)★★★, One Amazing Night (Edel 1998)★★.
COMPILATIONS: Portrait In Music (A&M 1971)★★★, Portrait In Music Volume 2 (A&M 1973)★★★, Burt Bacharach's Greatest Hits (A&M 1974)★★★★, The Best Of Burt Bacharach (A&M 1996)★★★★, The Burt Bacharach Songbook (Varèse Sarabande 1997)★★★, A Man And His Music (Spectrum 1998)★★★, The Look Of Love: The Burt Bacharach Collection 3-CD box set (Rhino 1998)★★★★, More From The Bacharach Songbook (Varèse Vintage 1999)★★★★, The Love Songs Of Burt Bacharach (PolyGram 1999)★★★, Trains & Boats & Covers: The Songs Of Burt Bacharach (Sequel 1999)★★★★, The Look Of Love: The Burt Bacharach Collection (Warner ESP 2001)★★★★.
VIDEOS: A Tribute To Burt Bacharach & Hal David (Aviva International 2001).
FILMS: Austin Powers: International Man Of Mystery (1997), Austin Powers: The Spy Who Shagged Me (1999), Listen With Your Eyes (2000).

BACHELORS
ALBUMS: The Bachelors (Decca 1963)★★★, The Bachelors Second Album (Decca 1964)★★, Presenting: The Bachelors (Decca 1964)★★★, The Bachelors And Sixteen Great Songs (Decca 1964)★★★, No Arms Can Ever Hold You (Decca 1965)★★★, Marie (Decca 1965)★★★, More Great Song Hits From The Bachelors (Decca 1965)★★★, Hits Of The Sixties (Decca 1966)★★★, The Bachelors' Girls (Decca 1966)★★★, The Golden All-Time Hits (Decca 1967)★★★, Under & Over (16 Irish Songs) (Decca 1971)★★★, The Bachelors With Patricia Cahill (Decca 1971)★★★, Bachelors 74 (Philips 1974)★★★, Singalong Album (Philips 1975)★★, In Love With Love Songs (Bachelors 2000)★★.
COMPILATIONS: World Of The Bachelors (Decca 1968) ★★★★, World Of The Bachelors: Volume Two (Decca 1969)★★★★, World Of The Bachelors: Volume Three (Decca 1969)★★★, World Of The Bachelors: Volume Four (Decca 1970)★★★★, World Of The Bachelors: Volume Five (Decca 1970)★★, The Very Best Of The Bachelors (Decca 1974)★★★, Focus On The Bachelors (Decca 1979)★★★, 25 Golden Greats (Warwick 1979)★★★★, The Best Of The Bachelors (Decca 1981)★★★, The Bachelors Collection (Pickwick 1985)★★★, Bachelors Hits (Deram 1989)★★★, The Decca Years 1962-1972 (Decca 1999)★★★.
FILMS: It's All Over Town (1964).

BACHMAN-TURNER OVERDRIVE
ALBUMS: Bachman-Turner Overdrive (Mercury 1973)★★, Bachman-Turner Overdrive II (Mercury 1973)★★★, Not Fragile (Mercury 1974)★★★★, Four Wheel Drive (Mercury 1975)★★★, Head On (Mercury 1975)★★, Freeways (Mercury 1977)★★, B.T.O. Japan Tour (Mercury 1977)★★, as B.T.O. Street Action (Mercury 1978)H, as B.T.O. Rock N' Roll Nights (Mercury 1979)H, Bachman Turner Overdrive (CEC 1984)★★, Live-Live-Live!!! (Curb 1986)★★, Best Of Bachman-Turner Overdrive Live (Curb 1994)★★, Trial By Fire: Greatest & Latest (CMC 1996)★★, King Biscuit Flower Hour 1974 recording (King Biscuit 1998)★★★.
COMPILATIONS: Best Of B.T.O. (So Far) (Mercury 1976) ★★★, BTO's Greatest Hits (Mercury 1981)★★★, The Anthology (Mercury 1993)★★★, The Best Of B.T.O. (Remastered Hits) (Mercury 1998)★★★, The Collection (Spectrum 2001)★★★.
FURTHER READING: Bachman Turner Overdrive: Rock Is My Life, This Is My Song: The Authorized Biography, Martin Melhuish. Randy Bachman: Takin' Care Of Business, John Einarson.

BACKSTREET BOYS
ALBUMS: Backstreet Boys (Jive 1995)★★★★, Backstreet's Back (Jive 1997)★★★, Millennium (Jive 1999)★★★, Black & Blue (Jive 2000)★★★.
COMPILATIONS: The Hits: Chapter One (Jive 2001)★★★★.
VIDEOS: Live In Concert (MVD Video 1998), All Access Video (Jive Video 1998), Night Out With The Backstreet Boys (Jive Video 1998), Homecoming: Live In Orlando (Jive Video 1999), Around The World With The Backstreet Boys (Jive 2001), The Video Hits: Chapter One (Jive 2001).

BAD BRAINS
ALBUMS: Bad Brains cassette only (ROIR 1982)★★, Rock For Light (PVC 1983)★★★★, I Against I (SST 1986) ★★★★, Live (SST 1988)★★, Attitude: The ROIR Sessions (In-Effect 1989)★★★, Quickness (Caroline 1989)★★★, The Youth Are Getting Restless (Caroline 1990)★★★, Rise (Epic 1993)★★★, God Of Love (Maverick 1995)★★★, Black Dots (Caroline 1996)★★★, Omega Sessions 1980 recordings (Victory 1997)★★★.

BAD COMPANY
ALBUMS: Bad Company (Island 1974)★★★★, Straight Shooter (Island 1975)★★★, Run With The Pack (Island 1976)★★, Burnin' Sky (Island 1977)★★, Desolation Angels (Island 1979)★★★, Rough Diamonds (Swan Song 1982) ★★, Fame And Fortune (Atlantic 1986)★★, Dangerous Age (Atlantic 1988)★★, Holy Water (Atlantic 1990)★★, Here Comes Trouble (Atlantic 1992)★★, Company Of Strangers (Atlantic 1995)★★, Stories Told & Untold (Atlantic 1996)★★★.
COMPILATIONS: 10 From 6 (Atlantic 1986)★★★★, The Best Of Bad Company Live ... What You Hear Is What You Get (Atco 1993)★★★, The Original Bad Company Anthology (Elektra 1999)★★★.

BAD MANNERS
ALBUMS: Ska 'N' B (Magnet 1980)★★★, Loonee Tunes (Magnet 1981)★★★, Gosh It's ... Bad Manners (Magnet 1981)★★★★, Forging Ahead (Magnet 1982)★★★, Mental Notes (Portrait 1985)★★, Live And Loud!! (Link 1987)★★★, Eat The Beat (Blue Beat/Squale 1988)★★★, Return Of The Ugly (Blue Beat 1989)★★, Fat Sound (Pork Pie 1992)★★, Don't Knock The Bald Head (Receiver 1997)★★.
COMPILATIONS: The Height Of Bad Manners (Telstar 1983)★★★, The Collection (Cleopatra 1998)★★★★, Rare & Fatty: Unreleased Recordings 1976-1997 (Moon Ska 1999)★★, Magnetism: The Very Best Of Bad Manners (Magnet 2000)★★★★.
VIDEOS: Bad Manners (Videoform).
FURTHER READING: Bad Manners, George Marshall.

BAD RELIGION
ALBUMS: How Could Hell Be Any Worse? (Epitaph 1982) ★★★★, Into The Unknown (Epitaph 1983)★★★, Suffer (Epitaph 1988)★★★★, No Control (Epitaph 1989)★★★, Against The Grain (Epitaph 1990)★★★, Generator (Epitaph 1992)★★★, Recipe For Hate (Epitaph 1993) ★★★, Stranger Than Fiction (Atlantic 1994)★★★, The Gray Race (Atlantic 1996)★★★★, Tested (Epic 1997)★★★, No Substance (Atlantic 1998)★★, The New America (Atlantic 2000)★★★, The Process Of Belief (Epitaph 2002)★★★.
COMPILATIONS: 80-85 (Epitaph 1991)★★★, All Ages (Epitaph 1995)★★★.

BADFINGER
ALBUMS: Magic Christian Music By Badfinger (Apple 1970)★★★, No Dice (Apple 1970)★★★★, Straight Up (Apple 1971)★★★★, Ass (Apple 1973)★★, Badfinger (Warners 1974)★★★, Wish You Were Here (Warners 1974)★★★★, Airwaves (Elektra 1979)★★, Say No More (Radio 1981)★★, Badfinger Live: Day After Day 1974 recording (Rykodisc 1990)★★★, BBC In Concert 1972-73 (Strange Fruit/Fuel 2000 1997)★★★, Head First 1974 recording (Snapper 2000)★★★.
COMPILATIONS: Shine On (Edsel 1989)★★★, The Best Of Badfinger, Volume II (Rhino 1989)★★★★, The Best Of Badfinger (Apple/Capitol 1995)★★★★, The Very Best Of Badfinger (Apple/Capitol 2000)★★★★.
VIDEOS: Badfinger: A Riveting And Emotionally Gripping Saga (Director's Cut Ltd. 1997).
FURTHER READING: Without You: The Tragic Story Of Badfinger, Dan Matovina.

BADLY DRAWN BOY
ALBUMS: The Hour Of Bewilderbeast (Twisted Nerve/Beggars Banquet 2000)★★★★, About A Boy soundtrack (Twisted Nerve/XL 2002)★★★.

BADU, ERYKAH
ALBUMS: Baduizm (Kedar/Universal 1997)★★★★, Live! (Universal 1997)★★★, Mama's Gun (Motown 2000)★★★.
FILMS: Blues Brothers 2000 (1998), The Cider House Rules (1999).

BAEZ, JOAN
ALBUMS: Joan Baez (Vanguard 1960)★★★, Joan Baez 2 (Vanguard 1961)★★★, Joan Baez In Concert (Vanguard 1962)★★★★, Joan Baez In Concert Part 2 (Vanguard 1963)★★★, Joan Baez 5 (Vanguard 1964)★★★★, Farewell Angelina (Vanguard 1965)★★★★, Portrait (Vanguard 1966)★★★, Noel (Vanguard 1966)★★, Joan (Vanguard 1967)★★★, Baptism (Vanguard 1968)★★★, Any Day Now (Songs Of Bob Dylan) (Vanguard 1968) ★★★, David's Album (Vanguard 1969)★★, One Day At A Time (Vanguard 1970)★★★, Blessed Are (Vanguard 1971)★★★, Carry It On (Vanguard 1971)★★★, Sacco And Vanzetti (RCA Victor 1971)★★, Come From The Shadows (A&M 1972)★★★, Where Are You Now, My Son? (Vanguard 1973)★★, Gracias A La Vida (Here's To Life) (A&M 1974)★★, Diamonds And Rust (A&M 1975) ★★★, Live In Japan (Vanguard 1975)★★★, From Every Stage (A&M 1976)★★, Gulf Winds (A&M 1976)★★, Blowing Away (Portrait 1977)★★★, Honest Lullaby (Portrait 1979)★★, The Night They Drove Old Dixie Down (Vanguard 1979)★★★★, Country Music Album (Vanguard 1979)★★★, European Tour (Portrait 1981)★★, Live Europe 83 (Ariola 1983)★★, Recently (Gold Castle 1988)★★★, Diamonds And Rust In The Bullring (Gold Castle 1989)★★, Speaking Of Dreams (Gold Castle 1989)★★★, No Woman No Cry (Laserlight 1989)★★★, Brothers In Arms (Gold Castle 1991)★★★, Play Me Backwards (Virgin 1992) ★★★, Ring Them Bells (Grapevine 1995)★★★, Gone From Danger (Guardian 1997)★★★.
COMPILATIONS: The First Ten Years (Vanguard 1970) ★★★★, The Ballad Book (Vanguard 1972)★★★, The Contemporary Ballad Book (Vanguard 1974)★★★, The Love Song Album (Vanguard 1975)★★★, Hits Greatest And Others (Vanguard 1976)★★★, The Best Of Joan Baez (A&M 1977)★★★, Spotlight On Joan Baez (Spotlight 1980)★★★, Very Early Joan Baez (Vanguard 1983)★★★, Rare, Live And Classic 3-CD box set (Vanguard 1994)★★★★, Diamonds (PolyGram Chronicles 1996)★★★, The Best Of Joan Baez: The Millennium Collection (PolyGram 1999)★★★★.
VIDEOS: Joan Baez In Concert (Old Gold 1990).
FURTHER READING: Daybreak: An Intimate Journey, Joan Baez. The Playboy Interviews: Joan Baez, no editor listed. Joan Baez, A Bio-Disco-Bibliography: Being A Selected Guide To Material In Print, Peter Swan. Diamonds And Rust: A Bibliography And Discography Of Joan Baez, Joan Swanekamp. And A Voice to Sing With, Joan Baez. Positively 4th Street: The Lives And Times Of Joan Baez, Bob Dylan, Mimi Baez Fariña And Richard Fariña, David Hajdu.
FILMS: Don't Look Back (1967), Woodstock (1970), Carry It On aka Joan (1970), Dynamite Chicken (1971), Banjoman (1975), Renaldo And Clara (1976), In Remembrance Of Martin (1986), The Return Of Bruno (1988), The Life And Times Of Allen Ginsberg (1993).

BAKER, GINGER
ALBUMS: Stratavarious (Polydor 1972)★★, Fela Ransome Kuti Live With Ginger Baker (Regal Zonophone 1972)★★★, 11 Sides Of Baker (Mountain 1977)★★, From Humble Oranges (CDG 1983)★★, Horses And Trees (Celluloid 1986)★★★, The Album (ITM 1987)★★, No Material (ITM 1987)★★, In Concert (Onsala 1987)★★, African Force (ITM 1989)★★, Middle Passage (Axiom 1990)★★★, Unseen Rain (Daylight Music 1993)★★, with Bill Frisell, Charlie Haden Going Back Home (Atlantic 1994)★★★, with Jens Johansson, Jonas Hellborg Unseen Rain (DEM 1996)★★★, with Frisell, Haden Falling Off The Roof (Atlantic 1996) ★★★★, Coward Of The County (Atlantic 1999)★★★★.
COMPILATIONS: The Best Of Ginger Baker (RSO1973)★★.

BAKER, LAVERN
ALBUMS: LaVern (Atlantic 1956)★★★, LaVern Baker (Atlantic 1957)★★★★, Rock And Roll With LaVern (Atlantic 1957)★★★★, Sings Bessie Smith (Atlantic 1958)★★★, Blues Ballads (Atlantic 1959)★★★★, Precious Memories (Atlantic 1959)★★★, Saved (Atlantic 1961)★★★, See See Rider (Atlantic 1963)★★★, I'm Gonna Get You (C5 1966)★★, Live In Hollywood '91 (Rhino 1991)★★★★, Woke Up This Mornin' (DRG 1992)★★★.
COMPILATIONS: The Best Of LaVern Baker (Atlantic 1963)★★★★, Real Gone Gal (Charly 1984)★★★, Soul On Fire: The Best Of LaVern Baker (Atlantic 1993)★★★★, Rock & Roll (Sequel 1997)★★★★.

BALDRY, LONG JOHN
ALBUMS: as Hoochie Coochie Men Long John's Blues (United Artists 1964)★★★, Lookin' At Long John (United Artists 1966)★★★, Let The Heartaches Begin (Pye 1968)★★, Wait For Me (Pye 1969)H, It Ain't Easy (Warners 1971)★★, Everything Stops For Tea (Warners 1972)H, Good To Be Alive (GM 1976)★★, Welcome To The Club (Casablanca 1977) ★★, Baldry's Out! (A&M 1979)★★, Rock With The Best (A&M 1982)★★, Silent Treatment (Capitol 1986)★★, It Still Ain't Easy (Stony Plain 1991)★★, Right To Sing The Blues (Stony Plain 1997)★★★, Live (Stony Plain 2000)★★★, Evening Conversation 1993 recording (Hypertension 2000)★★★, Remembering Leadbelly (Stony Plain 2002)★★★.
COMPILATIONS: Let The Heartaches Begin: The Best Of John Baldry (PRT 1988)★★★, The Best Of Long John Baldry (Castle 1991)★★★★, Mexico (Spectrum 1995)★★, The Very Best Of Long John Baldry (Music Club 1997)★★★★.

BANANARAMA
ALBUMS: Deep Sea Skiving (London 1983)★★★, Bananarama (London 1984)★★★, True Confessions (London 1986)★★★, Wow! (London 1987)★★★, Pop Life (London 1991)★★, Please Yourself (London 1993)★★, Ultra Violet (Curb 1995)★★, Exotica (Fr 2001)★★★.
COMPILATIONS: The Greatest Hits Collection (London 1988)★★★★, Bunch Of Hits (London 1993)★★★, The Very Best Of Bananarama (London 2001)★★★.
VIDEOS: Bananarama (PolyGram Music Video 1984), Bananarama: Video Singles (Channel 5 1987), Love In The First Degree (PolyGram Music Video 1988), Greatest Hits: Bananarama (Channel 5 1988), And That's Not All (Channel 5 1988), Greatest Hits Collection (PolyGram Music Video 1991).

BAND
ALBUMS: Music From Big Pink (Capitol 1968)★★★★★, The Band (Capitol 1969)★★★★★, Stage Fright (Capitol 1970)★★★★, Cahoots (Capitol 1971)★★★, Rock Of Ages (Capitol 1972)★★★★, Moondog Matinee (Capitol 1973) ★★★, Northern Lights-Southern Cross (Capitol 1975) ★★★★, Islands (Capitol 1977)★★, with various artists The Last Waltz (Warners 1977)★★★, Jericho (Pyramid 1993) ★★★, Live At Watkins Glen 1973 recording (Capitol 1995) ★★★★, High On The Hog (Transatlantic 1996)★★, Jubilation (River North 1998)★★.
COMPILATIONS: The Best Of The Band (Capitol 1976) ★★★, Anthology Volume 1 (Capitol 1978)★★★, To Kingdom Come: The Definitive Collection 3-LP set (Capitol 1988)★★★★, The Collection i (Castle 1992)★★★, Across The Great Divide 3-CD box set (Capitol 1994)★★★★, The Best Of Across The Great Divide (Capitol 1994)★★★★, The Collection ii (EMI 1997)★★★, The Shape I'm In: The Very Best Of The Band (EMI 1998)★★★★, The Best Of The Band: 36 All-Time Greatest Hits (EMI 1998)★★★★, The Best Of The Band Volume II (Rhino 1999)★★★, Greatest Hits (Capitol 2000)★★★★.
VIDEOS: The Band Is Back aka Reunion Concert (Pioneer Artist Video 1983), The Last Waltz (Warner Home Video 1988), The Authorized Video Biography (ABC 1995), The Band - Live At The New Orleans Jazz Festival (Pioneer Artist Video 1996), Classic Albums: The Band – The Band (Eagle Rock 1999), Live At Loreley (Sanctuary Video Entertainment 2001).
FURTHER READING: Mystery Train: Images Of America In Rock And Roll Music, Greil Marcus. Across The Great Divide: The Band And America, Barney Hoskyns. This Wheel's On Fire: Levon Helm And The Story Of The Band, Levon Helm with Stephen Davis. Invisible Republic: Bob Dylan's Basement Tapes, Greil Marcus.
FILMS: Eat The Document (1972), The Last Waltz (1977), Man Outside aka Hidden Fear (1986).

BANGLES
ALBUMS: All Over The Place (Columbia 1985)★★★, Different Light (Columbia 1986)★★★★, Everything (Columbia 1988)★★.
COMPILATIONS: The Bangles Greatest Hits (Columbia 1991)★★★★, Twelve Inch Mixes (Columbia 1993)★★,

Eternal Flame: The Best Of (Sony 2001)★★★★.
VIDEOS: *Bangles Greatest Hits* (SMV 1990).

BAR-KAYS
ALBUMS: *Soul Finger* (Volt 1967)★★★★, *Gotta Groove* (Volt 1969)★★★, *Black Rock* (Volt 1971)★★, *Do You See What I See?* (Polydor 1972)★★★, *Cold Blooded* (Stax 1974)★★, *Too Hot To Stop* (Mercury 1976)★★, *Flying High On Your Love* (Mercury 1977)★★★, *Money Talks* (Stax 1978)★★, *Light Of Life* (Mercury 1978)★★, *Injoy* (Mercury 1979)★★, *As One* (Mercury 1980)★★★, *Nightcruising* (Mercury 1981)★★★, *Propositions* (Mercury 1982)★★, *Dangerous* (Mercury 1984)★★, *Banging The Wall* (Mercury 1985)★★, *Contagious* (Mercury 1987)★★★, *Animal* (Mercury 1989)★★★, *48 Hours* (Basix 1994)★★, *Best Of Barkays* (Curb 1996)★★.
COMPILATIONS: *The Best Of The Bar-Kays i* (Stax 1988) ★★★★, *The Best Of The Bar-Kays ii* (Mercury 1993)★★★, *The Best Of The Bar-Kays Volume 2* (Mercury 1996)★★, *Greatest Hits* (Masters 2001)★★★.
FILMS: *Breakdance - The Movie* (1984).

BARCLAY JAMES HARVEST
ALBUMS: *Barclay James Harvest* (Harvest 1970)★★, *Once Again* (Harvest 1971)★★★, *Barclay James Harvest And Other Short Stories* (Harvest 1971)★★★, *Early Morning Onwards* (Harvest 1972)★★★, *Baby James Harvest* (Harvest 1972)★★★, *Everyone Is Everybody Else* (Polydor 1974) ★★★★, *Barclay James Harvest Live* (Polydor 1974)★★, *Time Honoured Ghosts* (Polydor 1975)★★★, *Octoberon* (Polydor 1976)★★★, *Gone To Earth* (Polydor 1977)★★★, *Live Tapes* (Polydor 1978)★★, *XII* (Polydor 1978)★★, *Eyes Of The Universe* (Polydor 1979)★★, *Turn Of The Tide* (Polydor 1981)★★★, *A Concert For The People (Berlin)* (Polydor 1982)★★, *Ring Of Changes* (Polydor 1983)★★★, *Victims Of Circumstance* (Polydor 1984)★★★, *Face To Face* (Polydor 1987)★★, *Glasnost* (Polydor 1988)★★, *Welcome To The Show* (Polydor 1990)★★★, *Caught In The Light* (Polydor 1993)★★★, *River Of Dreams* (Polydor Germany 1997)★★, *Revival: Live 1999* (Eagle 2000)★★★.
SOLO: John Lees *A Major Fancy* (Harvest 1977)★★. Woolly Wolstenholme *Maestoso* (Polydor 1980)★★, *Too Late* cassette only (Swallowtail 1989)★★, *Songs From The Black Box* (Voiceprint 1994)★★.
COMPILATIONS: *The Best Of Barclay James Harvest* (Harvest 1977)★★★, *The Best Of Barclay James Harvest, Volume 2* (Harvest 1979)★★★, *The Best Of Barclay James Harvest, Volume 3* (Harvest 1981)★★, *The Compact Story Of Barclay James Harvest* (Polydor 1985)★★★, *Another Arable Parable* (EMI 1987)★★★, *Alone We Fly* (Connoisseur 1990)★★★, *The Harvest Years* 3-LP set (Harvest 1991)★★★, *The Best Of Barclay James Harvest* (Polydor 1992)★★★, *Sorcerers And Keepers* (Spectrum 1993)★★, *Endless Dream* (Connoisseur 1996)★★, *The Best Of Barclay James Harvest* (EMI 1997)★★★, *Mockingbird: The Best Of Barclay James Harvest* (EMI 2001)★★★★.
VIDEOS: *Berlin: A Concert For The People* (Channel 5 1982), *Victims Of Circumstance* (Channel 5 1985), *Glasnost* (Channel 5 1988), *The Best Of BJH Live* (Virgin Vision 1992).

BARDENS, PETER
ALBUMS: *The Answer* (Transatlantic 1970)★★, *Peter Bardens* aka *Write My Name In The Dust* (Transatlantic 1971)★★★, *Heart To Heart* (Arista 1979)★★, *Seen One Earth* (Capitol 1987)★★★, *Speed Of Light* (Capitol 1988)★★, *Water Colors* (Miramar 1991)★★★, *Further Than You Know* (Miramar 1993)★★, *Big Sky* (HTD 1995)★★★.
COMPILATIONS: *Vintage '69* (Transatlantic 1976)★★★.

BARENAKED LADIES
ALBUMS: *Gordon* (Sire 1992)★★★★, *Maybe You Should Drive* (Sire 1994)★★★, *Born On A Pirate Ship* (Reprise 1996)★★★★, *Rock Spectacle* (Reprise 1996)★★★, *Stunt* (Reprise 1998)★★★★, *Maroon* (Reprise 2000)★★.
COMPILATIONS: *All Their Greatest Hits* (Reprise 2001)★★★.
VIDEOS: *Barenaked In America: The Stunt Tour* (Aviva International 2002).

BARRETT, SYD
ALBUMS: *The Madcap Laughs* (Harvest 1970)★★★, *Barrett* (Harvest 1970)★★★, *The Peel Sessions* (Strange Fruit 1995)★★★.
COMPILATIONS: *Opel* (Harvest 1988)★★★, *Crazy Diamond* 3-CD box set (Harvest 1993)★★★, *Wouldn't You Miss Me? The Best Of Syd Barrett* (Harvest 2001)★★★.
VIDEOS: *Syd Barrett's First Trip* (Vex 1993).
FURTHER READING: *Crazy Diamond: Syd Barrett And The Dawn Of Pink Floyd*, Mike Watkinson and Pete Anderson. *Syd Barrett: The Madcap Laughs*, Pete Anderson and Mick Rock. *A Fish Out Of Water*, Luca Ferrari. *Lost In The Woods: Syd Barrett And The Pink Floyd*, Julian Palacios. *Random Precision: Recording The Music Of Syd Barrett 1965-1974*, David Parker.

BARTHOLOMEW, DAVE
ALBUMS: *Fats Domino Presents Dave Bartholomew* (Imperial 1961)★★★, *New Orleans House Party* (Imperial 1963)★★★, *Dave Bartholomew And The Maryland Jazz Band* (GHB 1995)★★★, *New Orleans Big Beat* (Landslide 1998)★★★.
COMPILATIONS: *Jump Children* (Pathé Marconi 1984)★★, *The Monkey* (Pathé Marconi 1985)★★★, *The Best Of Dave Bartholomew: The Classic New Orleans R&B Band Sound* (Stateside 1989)★★★★, *In The Alley* (Charly 1991)★★★, *The Spirit Of New Orleans: The Genius Of Dave Bartholomew* (EMI 1993)★★★★, *1947-1950* (Melodie 2001)★★★.

BASEMENT JAXX
ALBUMS: *Remedy* (XL 1999)★★★★, *Rooty* (XL/Astralwerks 2001)★★★★.

BASSEY, SHIRLEY
ALBUMS: *Born To Sing The Blues* (Philips 1958)★★★, *The Bewitching Miss Bassey* (MGM 1959)★★★, *The Fabulous Shirley Bassey* (MGM 1960)★★★, *Shirley* (Columbia 1961)★★★★, *Shirley Bassey* (United Artists 1962)★★★, *Shirley Bassey Sings The Hit From 'Oliver' (And 11 Other Musical Tunes)* (United Artists 1962)★★★, *Let's Face The Music* (Columbia 1962)★★★, *Shirley Bassey At The Pigalle* (Columbia 1965)★★★★, *Shirley Bassey Belts The Best!* (Columbia 1965)★★★, *I've Got A Song For You* (United Artists 1966)★★★, *Twelve Of Those Songs* (Columbia 1968)★★★, *Live At The Talk Of The Town* (United Artists 1970)★★★, *Something* (United Artists 1970)★★★, *Something Else* (United Artists 1971)★★★, *Big Spender* (United Artists 1971)★★★, *It's Magic* (United Artists 1971)★★★, *What Now My Love* (United Artists 1971) ★★★, *I Capricorn* (United Artists 1972)★★★, *And I Love You So* (United Artists 1972)★★★, *Never, Never, Never* (United Artists 1973)★★★, *Live At Carnegie Hall* (United Artists 1973)★★★★, *Broadway, Bassey's Way* (United Artists 1973)★★★, *Nobody Does It Like Me* (United Artists 1974)★★, *Good, Bad But Beautiful* (United Artists 1975) ★★★, *Love, Life And Feelings* (United Artists 1976)★★, *Thoughts Of Love* (United Artists 1976)★★★, *You Take My Heart Away* (United Artists 1977)★★★, *The Magic Is You* (United Artists 1979)★★★, *As Long As He Needs Me* (Ideal 1980)★★★, *As Time Goes By* (MFP 1980)★★★, *I'm In The Mood For Love* (MFP 1981)★★, *Love Songs* (Applause 1982)★★, *All By Myself* (Vogue 1984)★★, *I Am What I Am* (Towerbell 1984)★★★, *Playing Solitaire* (President 1985)★★★, *I've Got You Under My Skin* (Astan 1985) ★★★, *Sings The Songs From The Shows* (Hour Of Pleasure 1986)★★★, *Let Me Sing And I'm Happy* (EMI 1988)★★★, *Her Favourite Songs* (EMI 1988)★★, *Keep The Music Playing* (Freestyle 1991)★★★, *Sings Andrew Lloyd Webber* (Premier 1993)★★, *Sings The Movies* (PolyGram 1995) ★★★, *The Show Must Go On* (PolyGram 1996)★★★, *The Birthday Concert* (Artful 1998)★★★★.
COMPILATIONS: *Golden Hits Of Shirley Bassey* (Columbia 1968)★★★, *The Shirley Bassey Collection* (United Artists 1972)★★★, *The Shirley Bassey Singles Album* (United Artists 1975)★★★★, *25th Anniversary Album* (United Artists 1978)★★★, *21 Hit Singles* (EMI 1979)★★★, *Tonight* (MFP 1984)★★★★, *Diamonds - The Best Of Shirley Bassey* (EMI 1988)★★★, *The Best Of Shirley Bassey* (Dino 1992)★★★, *The Definitive Collection* (Magnum 1994)★★★, *The EMI/UA Years 1959-1979* 5-CD box set (EMI 1994)★★★★, *The Magic Of Shirley Bassey* (Mercury 1998)★★★, *The Diamond Collection: Greatest Hits 1958-1998* (EMI 1998)★★★, *The Remix Album ... Diamonds Are Forever* (EMI 2000)★★★, *This Is My Life: The Greatest Hits* (EMI 2000)★★★★.
VIDEOS: *Shirley Bassey Live* (Video Gems 1988), *Live In Cardiff* (BBC 1995), *Divas Are Forever* (Eagle Rock 1998).
FURTHER READING: *Shirley: An Appreciation Of The Life Of Shirley Bassey*, Muriel Burgess.
FILMS: *La Passione* (1997).

BATT, MIKE
ALBUMS: *The Mike Batt Orchestra* (Penny Farthing 1970) ★★, *Portrait Of The Rolling Stones* (Pye 1971)★★, *Portrait Of Elton John* (Pye 1971)★★, *Portrait Of Simon & Garfunkel* (Pye 1971)★★, *Portrait Of Bob Dylan* (Pye 1971)★★★, *Portrait Of Cat Stevens* (Pye 1972)★★, *Portrait Of George Harrison* (Pye 1972)★★, *Portrait Of Mike Batt* (Pye 1974)★★, with The London Symphony Orchestra *Schizophonia* (Epic 1977)★★, with The London Philharmonic Orchestra *Caravans* film soundtrack (CBS 1978)★★★★, with The London Symphony Orchestra *Tarot Suite* (Epic 1979)★★, with The Amsterdam Chamber Orchestra *Waves* (Epic 1980)★★, with The Berlin Opera Orchestra *Six Days In Berlin* (Epic 1981)★★, with The Sydney Symphonic Orchestra *Zero, Zero* (Epic 1982)★★, with The London Symphony Orchestra *The Hunting Of The Snark* (Epic 1987)★★★, with The London Philharmonic Orchestra *Songs Of Love And War* (Adventure 1988)★★, with The London Philharmonic Orchestra *The Dreamstone* film soundtrack (Adventure 1990)★★, with The National Symphony Orchestra Of London *Arabesque* (Epic 1995)★★, with The Royal Philharmonic Orchestra *Keep The Aspidistra Flying* (EMI 1998)★★★, *Bright Eyes At The Railway Hotel* (Dramatico 2000)★★★.
COMPILATIONS: *The Very Best Of Mike Batt* (Epic 1991)★★★, *The Winds Of Change: Greatest Hits* (Connoisseur 1992)★★★, *The Ride To Agadir* (Zounds 1999)★★★.
FILMS: *The Hunting Of The Snark* (1987).

BAUHAUS
ALBUMS: *In The Flat Field* (4AD 1980)★★, *Mask* (Beggars Banquet 1981)★★★, *The Sky's Gone Out* (Beggars Banquet/A&M 1982)★★★, *Press The Eject And Give Me The Tape* (Beggars Banquet 1982)★★, *Burning From The Inside* (Beggars Banquet/A&M 1983)★★, *Rest In Piece: The Final Concert* (Nemo 1992)★★, *Gotham Live 1998* (Cargo 2000)★★.
COMPILATIONS: *1979-1983* (Beggars Banquet 1985) ★★★, *Swing The Heartache: The BBC Sessions* (Beggars Banquet 1989)★★, *Crackle: The Definitive Collection* (Beggars Banquet 1998)★★★.
VIDEOS: *Shadow Of Light* (Hendring 1984), *Archive* (Beggars Banquet 1984).
FURTHER READING: *Dark Entries: Bauhaus And Beyond*, Ian Shirley.

BAY CITY ROLLERS
ALBUMS: *Rollin'* (Bell 1974)★★★, *Once Upon A Star* (Bell 1975)★★★, *Wouldn't You Like It* (Bell 1975)★★★, *Dedication* (Bell 1976)★★, *It's A Game* (Arista 1977)★★, *Strangers In The Wind* (Arista 1978)★★, as the Rollers *Richocet* (Epic 1981)★★★.
COMPILATIONS: *Bye Bye Baby: The Very Best Of Les McKeown's 70's Bay City Rollers* (Hallmark 1998) ★★★, *Shang-A-Lang* (Camden 1998)★★★, *The Definitive Collection* (Arista 2000)★★★.
VIDEOS: *Shang-A-Lang: The Very Best Of...* (Video 1993).
FURTHER READING: *The Bay City Rollers Scrapbook*, David Golumb. *Bay City Rollers*, Elkis Allen. *The Bay City Rollers*, Tam Paton. *Bye Bye Baby: My Tragic Love Affair With The Bay City Rollers*, Caroline Sullivan.

BEACH BOYS
ALBUMS: *Surfin' Safari* (Capitol 1962)★★, *Surfin' USA* (Capitol 1963)★★★, *Surfer Girl* (Capitol 1963)★★★, *Little Deuce Coupe* (Capitol 1963)★★★, *Shut Down Vol. 2* (Capitol 1964)★★★★, *All Summer Long* (Capitol 1964) ★★★★, *Beach Boys Concert* (Capitol 1964)★★★, *The Beach Boys' Christmas Album* (Capitol 1964)★★★, *The Beach Boys Today!* (Capitol 1965)★★★★, *Summer Days (And Summer Nights!!)* (Capitol 1965)★★★★, *The Beach Boys' Party!* (Capitol 1965)★★, *Pet Sounds* (Capitol 1966) ★★★★★, *Smiley Smile* (Capitol 1967)★★★★, *Wild Honey* (Capitol 1967)★★★, *Friends* (Capitol 1968)★★★★, *Stack-O-Tracks* (Capitol 1968)★★, *20/20* (Capitol 1969)★★★, *Live In London* (Capitol 1970)★★, *Sunflower* (Brother 1970) ★★★★★, *Surf's Up* (Brother 1971)★★★★★, *Carl And The Passions-So Tough* (Brother 1972)★★★, *Holland* (Brother 1973)★★★★, *The Beach Boys In Concert* (Brother 1973) ★★, *15 Big Ones* (Brother 1976)★★★, *The Beach Boys Love You* (Brother 1977)★★★, *M.I.U. Album* (Brother 1978)★, *LA (Light Album)* (Caribou 1979)★★★, *Keepin' The Summer Alive* (Caribou 1980)H, *Rarities* (Capitol 1983) ★★★, *The Beach Boys* (Caribou 1985)★★★, *Still Cruisin'* (Capitol 1989)★, *Summer In Paradise* (Brother 1992)H, *Stars And Stripes Vol. 1* (River North 1996)★, *Ultimate Christmas 1964/1977 recordings* (Capitol 1998)★★.
COMPILATIONS: *Endless Summer* (Capitol 1974)★★★★★, *Spirit Of America* (Capitol 1975)★★★★, *20 Golden Greats* (Capitol 1976)★★★★, *Sunshine Dream* (Capitol 1982)★★★, *The Very Best Of The Beach Boys* (Capitol 1983)★★★, *Made In The USA* (Capitol 1986)★★★★, *Summer Dreams* (Capitol 1990)★★★★, *Good Vibrations: Thirty Years Of The Beach Boys* 5-CD box set (Capitol 1993)★★★★★, *The Pet Sounds Sessions* 4-CD box set (Capitol 1997)★★★★★, *Endless Harmony* (Capitol 1998)★★★★, *The Greatest Hits Volume 1: 20 Good Vibrations* (Capitol 1999)★★★★★, *The Greatest Hits Volume 2: 20 More Good Vibrations* (Capitol 1999) ★★★★, *The Greatest Hits Volume Three: Best Of The Brother Years* (Capitol 2000)★★★★, *Hawthorn CA, Birthplace Of A Musical Legacy* (Capitol 2001)★★★.
VIDEOS: *Beach Boys: An American Band* (Vestron Music Video 1988), *Summer Dreams* (PolyGram Music Video 1991), *Nashville Sounds* (Feedback Fusion 1997).
FURTHER READING: *The Beach Boys: Southern California Pastoral*, Bruce Golden. *The Beach Boys: A Biography In Words & Pictures*, Ken Barnes. *The Beach Boys*, John Tobler. *The Beach Boys And The California Myth*, David Leaf. *The Beach Boys: The Authorized Illustrated Biography*, Byron Preiss. *Surf's Up!: The Beach Boys On Record, 1961 - 1981*, Brad Elliott. *The Beach Boys*, Dean Anthony. *The Beach Boys: Silver Anniversary*, John Millward. *Heroes And Villains: The True Story Of The Beach Boys*, Steven Gaines. *Look! Listen! Vibrate! SMILE*, Dominic Priore. *Denny Remembered, Dennis Wilson In Words And Pictures*, Edward L. Wincentsen. *Wouldn't It Be Nice: My Own Story*, Brian Wilson and Todd Gold. *In Their Own Words*, Nick Wise (compiler). *The Nearest Faraway Place: Brian Wilson, The Beach Boys & The Southern California Experience*, Timothy White. *The Rainbow Files: The Beach Boys On CD*, Rene Hultz and Hans Christian Skotte. *Back To The Beach: A Brian Wilson And The Beach Boys Reader*, Kingsley Abbott (ed.). *Add Some Music To Your Day: Analyzing And Enjoying The Music Of The Beach Boys*, Don Cunningham (ed.) and Jeff Bleiel (ed.). *Dennis Wilson: The Real Beach Boy*, Jon Stebbins.
FILMS: *Girls On The Beach* (1965), *Americation* (1979).

BEASTIE BOYS
ALBUMS: *Licensed To Ill* (Def Jam/Columbia 1986)★★★, *Paul's Boutique* (Capitol 1989)★★★★, *Check Your Head* (Capitol 1992)★★★★, *Ill Communication* (Grand Royal 1994)★★★★, *Root Down EP* (Grand Royal 1995)★★, *Aglio E Olio EP* (Grand Royal 1995)★★★, *The In Sound From Way Out!* (Grand Royal 1996)★★, *Hello Nasty* (Grand Royal 1998)★★★★.
COMPILATIONS: *Some Old Bullshit* (Capitol 1994)★★★, *Beastie Boys Anthology: The Sounds Of Science* (Grand Royal 1999)★★★★.
VIDEOS: *Sabotage* (1994), *The Skills To Pay The Bills* (1994), *The Beastie Boys Video Anthology* (Criterion 2000).
FURTHER READING: *Rhyming & Stealing: A History Of The Beastie Boys*, Angus Batey.

BEAT (UK)
ALBUMS: *I Just Can't Stop It* (Go-Feet 1980)★★★★, *Wha'ppen?* (Go-Feet 1981)★★★, *Special Beat Service* (Go-Feet 1982)★★★.
COMPILATIONS: *What Is Beat* (Go-Feet 1983)★★★, *BPM: The Very Best Of The Beat* (Arista 1995)★★★, *The Best Of The Beat: Beat This!* (London 2000)★★★.
FURTHER READING: *The Beat: Twist And Crawl*, Malu Halasha.

BEATLES
ALBUMS: *Please Please Me* (Parlophone 1963)★★★★, *With The Beatles* (Parlophone 1963)★★★★, *A Hard Day's Night* (Parlophone 1964)★★★★★, *Beatles For Sale* (Parlophone 1964)★★★★, *The Savage Young Beatles* (USA) (Savage 1964)H, *Ain't She Sweet* (USA) (Atco 1964)H, *The Beatles With Tony Sheridan & Their Guests & Others* (USA) (MGM 1964)H, *Meet The Beatles* (USA) (Capitol 1964)★★★, *The Beatles Second Album* (USA) (Capitol 1964)★★★, *Something New* (USA) (Capitol 1964)★★★, *Beatles '65* (USA) (Capitol 1965)★★★, *The Early Beatles* (USA) (Capitol 1965)★★, *Beatles VI* (USA) (Capitol 1965)★★, *Help!* (Parlophone 1965)★★★★★, *Rubber Soul* (Parlophone 1965)★★★★★, *Yesterday And Today* (Capitol 1966)★★★, *Revolver* (Parlophone 1966)★★★★★, *Sgt. Peppers Lonely Hearts Club Band* (Parlophone 1967)★★★★★, *Magical Mystery Tour* (Capitol 1968)★★★★, *The Beatles* (Apple 1968)★★★★★, *Yellow Submarine* (Apple 1969)★★, *Abbey Road* (Apple 1969)★★★★★, *Let It Be* (Apple 1970)★★★, *Hey Jude* (Capitol 1970)★★★, *The Beatles At The Hollywood Bowl* (Parlophone 1977)★★, *Yellow Submarine Songtrack* (Parlophone 1999)★★★★.
COMPILATIONS: *A Collection Of Beatles Oldies* (Parlophone 1966)★★★★, *The Early Years* (Contour 1971)★★, *The Beatles 1962-1966* (Apple 1973)★★★★★, *The Beatles 1967-1970* (Apple 1973)★★★★★, *Rock & Roll Music* (EMI 1976)★★★★, *Love Songs* (EMI 1977)★★★★, *Rarities* (Parlophone 1979)★★★★, *Past Masters Volume 1* (Parlophone 1988)★★★★★, *Past Masters Volume 2* (Parlophone 1988)★★★★★, *Live At The BBC* (Apple 1994)★★★★, *Anthology 1* (Apple 1995)★★★★, *Anthology 2* (Apple 1996)★★★★, *Anthology 3* (Apple 1996)★★★, *1* (Parlophone/Capitol 2000)★★★★, *Once Upon A Time In Germany* (Bear Family 2002)★★★.
CD-ROMS: *At The Movies/Scenes From A Career* (UFO 1998).
VIDEOS: *Ready Steady Go Special* (PMI 1985), *A Hard Days Night* (Vestron Video 1986), *The Compleat Beatles* (MGM 1986), *Magical Mystery Tour* (PMI 1989), *Help!* (PMI 1989), *On The Road* (MMG Video 1990), *Alone And Together* (Channel 5 1990), *The First U.S. Visit* (1993), *Beatles Firsts* (Goodtimes 1995), The *Making Of A Hard Day's Night* (VCI 1995), *The Beatles Anthology Volumes 1-8* (PMI 1996), *Alf Bicknell's Personal Beatles Diary* (Simitar Entertainment 1997), *Yellow Submarine* (MGM 1999).
FURTHER READING: There have been hundreds of books published of varying quality. Our four recommendations are: *The Complete Beatles Chronicle* by Mark Lewisohn, an accurate and definitive career and recording history by their greatest historian; *The Beatles After The Break-Up 1970-2000*, by Keith Badman; *Shout! The True Story Of The Beatles* by Philip Norman, the most readable and objective biography; *Revolution In The Head* by Ian MacDonald, a beautifully written authoritative study of every song. *The True Story Of The Beatles*, Billy Shepherd. *The Beatles Book*, Norman Parkinson and Maureen Cleave. *A Cellarful Of Noise*, Brian Epstein. *The Beatles: A Hard Day's Night*, John Burke. *Love Me Do: The Beatles' Progress*, Michael Braun. *The Beatles In Help*, Al Hine. *The Beatles: Words Without Music*, Rick Friedman. *The Beatles*, Hunter Davies. *Get Back*, Ethan Russell (photographs). *The Beatles Illustrated Lyrics Volume 2*, Alan Aldridge (ed.). *Apple To The Core: The Unmaking Of The Beatles*, Peter McCabe and Robert D. Schonfeld. *The Longest Cocktail Party*, Richard DiLello. *As Time Goes By: Living In The Sixties*, Derek Taylor. *Twilight Of The Gods: The Beatles In Retrospect*, Wilfred Mellers. *The Man Who Gave The Beatles Away*, Allan Williams. *The Beatles: An Illustrated Record*, Roy Carr and Tony Tyler. *All Together Now: The First Complete Beatles Discography 1961-1975*, Harry Castleman and Walter J. Podrazik. *The Beatles: Yesterday, Today, Tomorrow*, Rochelle Larkin. *Beatles In Their Own Words*, Miles. *The Beatles: A Day In The Life: The Day By Day Diary 1960-1970*, Tom Schultheiss. *The Boys From Liverpool: John, Paul, George, Ringo*, Nicholas Schaffner. *The Beatles Illustrated Lyrics*, Alan Aldridge (ed.). *The Beatles Apart*, Bob Woffinden. *Shout! The True Story Of The Beatles*, Philip Norman. *The Beatles: An Illustrated Discography*, Miles. *Thank U Very Much: Mike McCartney's Family Album*, (Peter) Michael McCartney. *All You Needed Was Love: The Beatles After The Beatles*, John Blake. *The Long And Winding Road: A History Of The Beatles On Record*, Neville Stannard. *Abbey Road: The Story Of The World's Most Famous Recording Studios*, Brian Southall. *The Complete Beatles Lyrics*, no author listed. *The Beatles At The Beeb 62-65: The Story Of Their Radio Career*, Kevin Howlett. *With The Beatles: The Historic Photographs*, Dezo Hoffman. *Beatles' England*, David Bacon and Norman Maslov. *Working Class Heroes: The History Of The Beatles' Solo Recordings*, Neville Stannard. *The Beatles: An Illustrated Diary*, H.V. Fulpen. *The Love You Make: An Insider's Story Of The Beatles*, Peter Brown and Steven Gaines. *John Ono Lennon 1967-1980*, Ray Coleman. *John Winston Lennon 1940-1966*, Ray Coleman. *Beatlemania: An Illustrated Filmography*, Bill Harry. *Paperback Writers: An Illustrated Bibliography*, Bill Harry. *The End Of The Beatles*, Harry Castleman and Wally Podrazik. *Beatle! The Pete Best Story*, Pete Best and Patrick Doncaster. *The Beatles Live*, Mark Lewisohn. *It Was Twenty Years Ago*, Derek Taylor. *Yesterday: The Beatles Remembered*, Alistair Taylor. *All Our Loving: A Beatle Fan's Memoir*, Carolyn Lee Mitchell and Michael Munn. *The Beatles: 25 Years In The Life*, Mark Lewisohn. *Brian Epstein: The Man Who Made The Beatles*, Ray Coleman. *The Beatles Album File And Complete Discography*, Jeff Russell. *How They Became The Beatles: A Definitive History Of The Early Years 1960-1964*, Gareth L. Pawlowski. *Complete Beatles Recording Sessions: The Official Story Of The Abbey Road Years*, Mark Lewisohn. *Day By Day*, Mark Lewisohn. *Speak Words Of Wisdom: Reflections On The Beatles*, Spencer Leigh. *In Their Own Words: The Beatles After The Break-Up*, David Bennahum. *The Complete Beatles Chronicle*, Mark Lewisohn. *Ultimate Beatles Encyclopedia*, Bill Harry. *Tomorrow Never Knows: Thirty Years Of Beatles Music & Memorabilia*, Geoffrey Giuliano. *The Ultimate Recording Guide*, Allen J. Wiener. *Beatles*, John Ewing. *It Was Thirty Years Ago Today*, Terence Spencer. *The Summer Of Love*, George Martin. *A Hard Day's Write*, Steve Turner. *Revolution In The Head: The Beatles Records And The Sixties*, Ian MacDonald. *Backbeat*, Alan Clayson and Pauline Sutcliffe. *The Essential Guide To The Music Of ...*, John Robertson. *The Beatles' London*, Piet Schreuders, Mark Lewisohn and Adam Smith. *A Day In The Life: The Music And Artistry Of The Beatles*, Mark Hertsgaard. *The Beatles: Not For Sale*, Jim Belmo. *The Encyclopedia Of Beatles People*, Bill Harry. *Beatles - From Cavern To Star Club*, Hans Olaf Gottfridsson. *The Beatles Movies*, Bob Neaverson. *Hamburg: The Cradle Of British Rock*, Alan Clayson. *The Complete Idiot's Guide To The Beatles*, Richard Buskin. *Classic Rock Albums: Abbey Road/Let It Be*, Peter Doggett. *The Beatles: A Diary*, Miles. *Beatles Undercover*, Kristofer Engelhardt. *Drummed Out! The Sacking Of Pete Best*, Spencer Leigh. *Get Back: The Beatles' Let It Be Disaster*, Doug Sulphy and Ray Schweighardt. *The Beatles: Inside The One And Only Lonely Hearts Club Band*, David Pritchard and Alan Lysaght. *The Beatles After The Break-Up: 1970-2000*, Keith Badman. *The Rocking City: The Explosive Birth Of The Beatles*, Sam Leach. *Beatletoons: The Real Story Behind The Cartoon Beatles*, Mitch Axelrod. *The Beatles' Story On Capitol Records: Beatlemania & The Singles*, Bruce Spizer (ed.). *The Beatles Anthology*, the Beatles. *The Beatles Off The Record*, Keith Badman. *The Beatles In Rishikesh*, Paul Saltzman. *The Beatles, Popular Music And Society: A Thousand Voices*, Ian Inglis (ed.). *The Beatles Uncovered: 1,000,000 Mop-Top Murders By The Fans And The Famous*, Dave Henderson. *The Beatles Mixes*, Holger Schoeler & Thorsten Schmidt. *Mania Days*, Curt Gunther (photographer). *Sgt. Pepper's Lonely Hearts Club Band: The Album Collection Vol. 8*, Azing Moltmaker. *The Quarrymen*, Hunter Davies. *The Beatles: The Dream Is Over*, Keith Badman.
FILMS: *A Hard Day's Night* (1964), *Help!* (1965), *Magical Mystery Tour* (1967), *Yellow Submarine* (1968), *Let It Be* (1970).

BEAU BRUMMELS
ALBUMS: *Introducing The Beau Brummels* (Autumn/Pye International 1965)★★★, *Beau Brummels, Volume 2* (Autumn 1965)★★★, *Beau Brummels 66* (Warners 1966)★★, *Triangle* (Warners 1967)★★★★, *Bradley's Barn* (Warners 1968)★★★★, *Volume 44* (Vault 1968)★★, *The Beau Brummels* (Warners 1975)★★.
COMPILATIONS: *The Best Of The Beau Brummels* (Vault 1967)★★★, *The Beau Brummels Sing* (Post 1972)★★★, *The Original Hits Of The Beau Brummels* (JAS 1975)★★★, *The Best Of The Beau Brummels* 1964-68 recordings (Rhino 1981)★★★, *From The Vaults* (Rhino 1982)★★★, *Autumn In San Francisco* (Edsel 1985)★★★, *The Autumn Of Their Years* (Big Beat/Nuggets From The Golden Era 1995)★★★, *San Fran Sessions* 3-CD set (Sundazed 1996)★★, *Greatest Hits* (Classic World 2000)★★★.

BEAUTIFUL SOUTH
ALBUMS: *Welcome To The Beautiful South* (Go! Discs/Elektra 1989)★★★, *Choke* (Go! Discs/Elektra 1990)★★★, *0898: Beautiful South* (Go! Discs/Elektra 1992)★★★, *Miaow* (Go! Discs 1994)★★★, *Blue Is The Colour* (Go! Discs/Ark 21 1996)★★★, *Quench* (Go! Discs 1998)★★★, *Painting It Red* (Go! Discs/Ark 21 2000)★★★★.
COMPILATIONS: *Carry On Up The Charts: The Best Of The Beautiful South* (Go! Discs/Mercury 1994)★★★★, *Solid Bronze - Great Hits* (Mercury 2001)★★★★.
VIDEOS: *The Pumpkin* (Go! Discs 1992), *Carry On Up The Charts: The Best Of The Beautiful South* (Go! Discs 1994), *Much Later With ... The Beautiful South* (PNE Video 1997).
FURTHER READING: *Last Orders At The Liars' Bar: The Official Story Of The Beautiful South*, Mike Pattenden.

BECK
ALBUMS: *A Western Harvest Field By Moonlight* 10-inch album (Fingerpaint 1993)★★, *Golden Feelings* (Sonic Enemy 1993)★★, *Mellow Gold* (Geffen 1994)★★★★, *Stereo Pathetic Soul Manure* (Flipside 1994)★★, *One Foot In The Grave* 1993 recording (K Records 1995)★★, *Odelay* (Geffen 1996)★★★★, *Mutations* (Geffen 1998) ★★★, *Midnite Vultures* (Geffen 1999)★★★★.
FURTHER READING: *Beck! On A Backwards River: The Story Of Beck*, Rob Jovanovic.

BECK, JEFF
ALBUMS: *Truth* (Columbia/Epic 1968)★★★, *Cosa Nostra Beck-Ola* (Columbia/Epic 1969)★★, *Rough And Ready* (Epic 1971)★★, *Jeff Beck Group* (Epic 1972)★★, *Blow By Blow* (Epic 1975)★★★★, *Wired* (Epic 1976)★★★, with Jan Hammer *Jeff Beck With The Jan Hammer Group Live* (CBS 1977)★★★, *There And Back* (Epic 1980)★★, *Flash* (Epic 1985)★★, with Terry Bozzio, Tony Hymas *Jeff Beck's Guitar Shop* (Epic 1989)★★, with the Big Town Playboys *Crazy Legs* (Epic 1993)★★★, *Who Else!* (Epic 1999)★★★, *You Had It Coming* (Epic 2001)★★★.
COMPILATIONS: *Beckology* CD box set (Epic 1992)★★★★.
FURTHER READING: *Jeff Beck: A Chronology Part One, 1965-1970*, Christopher Hjort. *Crazy Fingers*, Annette Carson. *Jeff's Book*, Christopher Hjort and Doug Hinman.

BEE GEES
ALBUMS: *Barry Gibb And The Bee Gees Sing And Play 14 Barry Gibb Songs* (Leedon 1965)★★, *Spicks And Specks* (Leedon 1966)★★, *The Bee Gees First* (Polydor 1967)★★★★, *Horizontal* (Polydor 1968)★★★★, *Idea* (Polydor 1968)★★★, *Odessa* (Polydor 1969)★★★, *Cucumber Castle* (Polydor 1970)★★, *Two Years On* (Polydor 1970)★★, *Trafalgar* (Polydor 1971)★★, *To Whom It May Concern* (Polydor 1972)★★, *Life In A Tin Can* (RSO 1973)★★, *Mr Natural* (RSO 1974)★★, *Main Course* (RSO 1975)★★★★, *Children Of The World* (RSO 1976)★★★, *Here At Last ... Bee Gees Live* (RSO 1977)★★, *Saturday Night Fever* film soundtrack (RSO 1977)★★★★, *Sgt. Pepper's Lonely Hearts Club Band* film soundtrack (RSO 1978)H, *Spirits Having Flown* (RSO 1979)★★★, *Living Eyes* (RSO 1981)★★, *Stayin' Alive* film soundtrack (RSO 1983)★★, *ESP* (Warners 1987)★★★, *High Civilisation* (Warners 1991)★★, *Size Isn't Everything* (Polydor 1993)★★, *Still Waters* (Polydor 1997)★★★, *Live: One Night Only* (Polydor 1998)★★★, *This Is Where I Came In* (Polydor 2001)★★★.
COMPILATIONS: *Rare Precious And Beautiful* (Polydor 1968)★★★, *Rare Precious And Beautiful Volume 2* (Polydor 1968)★★, *Rare Precious And Beautiful Volume 3* (Polydor 1969)★★, *Best Of The Bee Gees* (Polydor 1969)★★★★, *Best Of The Bee Gees Volume 2* (Polydor 1973)★★★★, *Bee Gees Gold Volume One* (RSO 1976)★★★★, *Bee Gees Greatest* (RSO 1979)★★★★, *The Early Days Volume 1* (Hallmark 1979)★★, *The Early Days Volume 2* (Hallmark 1979)★★, *The Early Days Volume 3* (Hallmark 1979)H, *Very Best Of The Bee Gees* (Polydor 1990)★★★★, *Tales From The Brothers Gibb (A History In Song)* (Polydor 1990)★★★★, *Big Chance* (ABMM 2000)★★★, *Their Greatest Hits: The Record* (Polydor 2001)★★★★.
VIDEOS: *Bee Gees: Video Biography* (Virgin Vision 1988), *Very Best Of The Bee Gees* (Video Collection 1990), *One For All Tour Volume 1* (Video Collection 1990), *One For All Tour Volume 2* (Video Collection 1990), *One Night Only* (Eagle Rock 1998), *This Is Where I Came In: The Official Story Of The Bee Gees* (Eagle Vision 2001).
FURTHER READING: *The Bee Gees: A Photo Biography*, Kim Stevens. *The Bee Gees*, Suzanne Munshower. *The Incredible Bee Gees*, Dick Tatham. *The Bee Gees*, Larry Pryce. *Bee Gees: The Authorized Biography*, Barry, Robin and Maurice Gibb as told to David Leaf. *Tales Of The Brother Gibb: The Ultimate Biography Of The Bee Gees*, Melinda Bilyeu, Hector Cook and Andrew Môn Hughes.

BELL, ARCHIE, AND THE DRELLS
ALBUMS: *Tighten Up* (Atlantic 1968)★★★★, *I Can't Stop Dancing* (Atlantic 1968)★★★, *There's Gonna Be A Showdown* (Atlantic 1969)★★★, *Dance Your Troubles Away* (TSOP 1976)★★★, *Where Will You Go, When The Party's Over* (TSOP 1976)★★, *Hard Not To Like It* (TSOP 1977)★★★.
COMPILATIONS: *Artists Showcase: Archie Bell* (DM Streetsounds 1986)★★★, *Disco Showdown* (Music Club 1998)★★★.

BELL, FREDDIE, AND THE BELLBOYS
ALBUMS: *Rock 'n' Roll All Flavours* (Mercury 1958)★★★, *Bells Are Swinging* (20th Century 1964)★★.
COMPILATIONS: *Rockin' Is Our Business* (Bear Family 1996)★★★.
FILMS: *Rock Around The Clock* (1956), *Rumble On The Docks* (1956), *Get Yourself A College Girl* aka *The Swinging Set* (1964).

BELLAMY BROTHERS
ALBUMS: *Let Your Love Flow* (Warners 1976)★★★★, *Plain And Fancy* (Warners 1977)★★★, *Beautiful Friends* (Warners 1978)★★, *The Two And Only* (Warners 1979)★★★, *You Can Get Crazy* (Warners 1980)★★★, *Sons Of The Sun* (Warners 1980)★★, *When We Were Boys* (Elektra 1982) ★★, *Strong Weakness* (1983)★★, *Restless* (MCA 1984)★★, *Howard And David* (MCA 1986)★★, *Country Rap* (MCA 1987)★★, *Crazy From The Heart* (1987)★★, *Rebels Without A Clue* (MCA 1988)★★, *Rolling Thunder* (Atlantic 1991)★★, *Rip Off The Knob* (Bellamy Brothers 1993)★★, *Heartbreak Overload* (Intersound 1994)★★, *Sons Of Beaches* (Bellamy Brothers 1995)★★, *The Bellamy Brothers Dancin'* (Bellamy Brothers 1996)★★, *A Tropical Christmas* (Bellamy Brothers 1996)★★, *Over The Line* (Bellamy Brothers 1997)★★★, *The Reggae Cowboys* (Bellamy Brothers 1998)★★★, *Lonely Planet* (Start 1999)★★, *Live At Gilley's* (Connoisseur Collection 2000)★★★.
COMPILATIONS: *The Bellamy Brothers' Greatest Hits* (MCA 1982)★★★, *Bellamy Brothers' Greatest Hits Volume 2* (MCA 1986)★★, *Bellamy Brothers' Greatest Hits Volume 3* (MCA 1989)★★, *Best Of The Best* (Intersound 1992)★★★, *Let Your Love Flow: Twenty Years Of Hits* (Bellamy Brothers/Intersound 1997)★★★.
VIDEOS: *Best Of The Best* (Start Video 1994).

BELLE AND SEBASTIAN
ALBUMS: *Tigermilk* (Electric Honey 1996)★★★, *If You're Feeling Sinister* (Jeepster/Enclave 1996)★★★★, *The Boy With The Arab Strap* (Jeepster/Matador 1998)★★★★, *Fold Your Hands Child, You Walk Like A Peasant* (Jeepster/Matador 2000)★★★.
COMPILATIONS: *Lazy Line Painter Jane* (Jeepster 2000)★★.

BELLY
ALBUMS: *Star* (Sire/4AD 1993)★★★, *King* (Sire/4AD 1995)★★.

BEN FOLDS FIVE
ALBUMS: *Ben Folds Five* (Caroline 1995)★★★★, *Whatever And Ever Amen* (Epic 1997)★★★★, *The Unauthorized Biography Of Reinhold Messner* (Epic 1999)★★★.
COMPILATIONS: *Naked Baby Photos* (Caroline 1997)★★★.

BENATAR, PAT
ALBUMS: *In The Heat Of The Night* (Chrysalis 1979)★★★, *Crimes Of Passion* (Chrysalis 1980)★★★, *Precious Time* (Chrysalis 1981)★★, *Get Nervous* (Chrysalis 1982)★★, *Live From Earth* (Chrysalis 1983)★★, *Tropico* (Chrysalis 1984)★★, *Seven The Hard Way* (Chrysalis 1985)★★★, *Wide Awake In Dreamland* (Chrysalis 1988)★★, *True Love* (Chrysalis 1991)★★, *Gravity's Rainbow* (Chrysalis 1993)★★, *Innamorata* (CMC 1997)★★★, *8-15-80* (CMC 1998)★★★.
COMPILATIONS: *Best Shots* (Chrysalis 1987)★★★, *The Very Best Of Pat Benatar: All Fired Up* (Chrysalis 1994)★★★, *16 Classic Performances* (EMI 1996)★★★, *Synchronistic Wanderings: Recorded Anthology 1979 To 1999* 3-CD set (Chrysalis 1999)★★★, *The Very Best Of Pat Benatar* (Chrysalis 2000)★★★.
VIDEOS: *Hit Videos* (RCA/Columbia 1988), *Best Shots* (Chrysalis Music Video 1988), *Benatar* (RCA/Columbia 1988).
FURTHER READING: *Benatar*, Doug Magee.
FILMS: *Union City* (1980).

BENNETT, TONY
ALBUMS: *Because Of You* (Columbia 1952)★★★, *Alone At Last With Tony Bennett* (Columbia 1955)★★, *Treasure Chest Of Songs* (1955)★★★, *Cloud Seven* (Columbia 1955)★★, *Tony* (Columbia 1957)★★★, *The Beat Of My Heart* (Columbia 1957)★★★, *Long Ago And Far Away* (Columbia 1958)★★★, with Count Basie *Basie Swings, Bennett Sings* (Roulette 1958)★★★★, *Blue Velvet* (Columbia 1959)★★★, *If I Ruled The World* (Columbia 1959)★★★★, with Basie *Tony Bennett In Person* (Columbia 1959)★★★, *Hometown, My Town* (Columbia 1959)★★★, *To My Wonderful One* (Columbia 1960)★★, *Tony Sings For Two* (Columbia 1960) ★★★, *Alone Together* (Columbia 1960)★★★, *A String Of Harold Arlen* (Columbia 1960)★★★, *My Heart Sings* (Columbia 1961)★★★, with Basie *Bennett And Basie Strike Up The Band* (Roulette 1962)★★, *Mr. Broadway* (Columbia 1962)★★★, *I Left My Heart In San Francisco* (Columbia 1962)★★★★, *On The Glory Road* (Columbia 1962)★★, *Tony Bennett At Carnegie Hall* (Columbia 1962)★★★, *I Wanna Be Around* (Columbia 1963)★★★★, *This Is All I Ask* (Columbia 1963)★★★, *The Many Moods Of Tony* (Columbia 1964)★★★, *When Lights Are Low* (Columbia 1964)★★★, *Who Can I Turn To* (Columbia 1964)★★★, *If I Ruled The World - Songs For The Jet Set* (Columbia 1965) ★★★, *The Movie Song Album* (Columbia 1966)★★★, *A Time For Love* (Columbia 1966)★★★, *The Oscar* film soundtrack (Columbia 1966)★★, *Tony Makes It Happen!* (Columbia 1967)★★, *For Once In My Life* (Columbia 1967)★★★, *Snowfall/The Tony Bennett Christmas Album* (Columbia 1968)★★★, *I've Gotta Be Me* (Columbia 1969) ★★, *Tony Sings The Great Hits Of Today!* (Columbia 1970) ★★, *Tony Bennett's 'Something'* (Columbia 1970)★★★, *Love Story* (Columbia 1971)★★★, *Get Happy With The London Philharmonic Orchestra* (Columbia 1971)★★, *Summer Of '42* (Columbia 1972)★★, *With Love* (Columbia 1972)★★★, *The Good Things In Life* (MGM/Verve 1972) ★★★, *Rodgers And Hart Songbook* (Columbia 1973)★★, with Bill Evans *The Tony Bennett/Bill Evans Album* (Original Jazz Classics 1975)★★★★, with Bill Evans *Together Again* (DRG 1976)★★★, *Chicago* (DCC 1984)★★★, *The Art Of Excellence* (Columbia 1986)★★★, *Jazz* (Columbia 1987) ★★★, *Astoria: Portrait Of The Artist* (Columbia 1990) ★★★, *Perfectly Frank* (Columbia 1992) ★★, *Steppin' Out* (Columbia 1993)★★★, *MTV Unplugged* (Columbia 1994) ★★★★, *Here's To The Ladies* (Columbia 1995)★★★, *Tony Bennett On Holiday: A Tribute To Billie Holiday* (Columbia 1997)★★★, *The Playground* (Columbia 1998)★★, *Bennett Sings Ellington Hot And Cool* (Columbia 1999)★★★★, *Playing With My Friends: Bennett Sings The Blues* (Columbia 2001)★★★.
COMPILATIONS: *Tony's Greatest Hits* (Columbia 1958) ★★★★, *More Tony's Greatest Hits* (Columbia 1960)★★★★, *Tony's Greatest Hits, Volume III* (Columbia 1965)★★★★, *A String Of Tony's Hits* (Columbia 1966)★★★★, *Tony Bennett's Greatest Hits, Volume IV* (Columbia 1969)★★★, *Tony Bennett's All-Time Greatest Hits* (Columbia 1972)★★★, *The Very Best Of Tony Bennett – 20 Greatest Hits* (Warwick 1977)★★★, *40 Years, The Artistry Of Tony Bennett* 4-CD box set (Legacy 1991)★★★★, *The Essential Tony Bennett (A Retrospective)* (Columbia 1998)★★★★.
VIDEOS: *Tony Bennett In Concert* (Mastervision 1987), *A Special Evening With Tony Bennett* (MIA 1995), *The Art Of The Singer* (SMV 1996).
FURTHER READING: *What My Heart Has Seen*, Tony Bennett. *The Good Life*, Tony Bennett.

BENSON, GEORGE
ALBUMS: with the Brother Jack McDuff Quartet *The New Boss Guitar Of George Benson* (Prestige 1964)★★★★, *It's Uptown* (Columbia 1965)★★★★, *Most Exciting* (Columbia 1966) ★★★, *Benson Burner* (Columbia 1966)★★★★, *The George Benson Cook Book* (Columbia 1967)★★★, *Giblet Gravy* (Verve 1968)★★★, *Goodies* (Verve 1969)★★★, *Shape Of Things To Come* (A&M 1969)★★, *Tell It Like It Is* (A&M 1969)★★, *The Other Side Of Abbey Road* (A&M 1970) ★★★, *Beyond The Blue Horizon* (CTI 1971)★★★, *White Rabbit* (CTI 1972)★★, *Body Talk* (CTI 1973)★★★, *Bad Benson* (CTI 1974)★★, *Supership* (CTI 1975)★★★, *Breezin'* (Warners 1976)★★★★, *Good King Bad* (CTI 1976)★★★, with Joe Farrell *Benson And Farrell* (CTI 1976)★★★, *George Benson In Concert: Carnegie Hall* (CTI 1977)★★, *In Flight* (Warners 1977)★★★★, *George Benson And Jack McDuff* (Prestige 1977)★★★, *Weekend In LA* (Warners 1978)★★, *Living Inside Your Love* (Warners 1979)★★, *Give Me The Night* (Warners 1980)★★★★, *Blue Benson* (Polydor 1983) ★★★, *In Your Eyes* (Warners 1983)★★★, *Stormy Weather* (Columbia 1984)★★, *20/20* (Warners 1985)★★, *The Electrifying George Benson* (Affinity 1985)★★★, *In Concert* (Premier 1985)★★, *Love Walked In* (Platinum 1985)★★, *While The City Sleeps* (Warners 1986)★★, with Earl Klugh *Collaboration* (Warners 1987)★★★★, *Love For Sale* (Masters 1988) ★★★, *Twice The Love* (Warners 1988)★★, *Detroit's George Benson* (Parkwood 1988)★★★, *Tenderly* (Warners 1989) ★★, with the Count Basie Orchestra *Big Boss Band* (Warners 1990)★★★, *Lil' Darlin'* (Thunderbolt 1990)★★★, *Live At The Casa Caribe Volumes 1-3* (Jazz View 1992)★★★, *Love Remembers* (Warners 1993)★★, *That's Right* (GRP 1996) ★★★, *Standing Together* (GRP 1998)★★, *Absolute Benson* (GRP 2000)★★★.
COMPILATIONS: *The George Benson Collection* (Warners 1981)★★★★, *Early Years* (CTI 1982)★★★, *Best Of George Benson* (A&M 1982)★★★, *The Wonderful Years* (Proton 1984)★★★, *The Love Songs* (K-Tel 1985)★★★★, *The Silver Collection* (Verve 1985)★★★, *Compact Jazz* (Verve 1988)★★★, *Best Of* (Epic 1992)★★, *Guitar Giants* (Pickwick 1992)★★★, *The Best Of George Benson* (Warners 1995)★★★, *Essentials: The Very Best Of George Benson* (Jive 1998)★★★, *George Benson Anthology* 2-CD box set (Rhino/Warner Archives 2000)★★★★.

BENTON, BROOK
ALBUMS: *Brook Benton At His Best* (Epic 1959)★★, *It's Just A Matter Of Time* (Mercury 1959)★★★, *Brook Benton* (Mercury 1959)★★★, *Endlessly* (1959)★★★, *So Many*

Ways I Love You (Mercury 1960)★★★, with Dinah Washington The Two Of Us (Mercury 1960)★★★★, Songs I Love To Sing (Mercury 1960)★★★, The Boll Weevil Song (& Eleven Other Great Hits) (Mercury 1961)★★★, If You Believe (Mercury 1961)★★★, Singing The Blues – Lie To Me (Mercury 1962)★★★, There Goes That Song Again (Mercury 1962)★★★, Best Ballads Of Broadway (Mercury 1963)★★, with Jesse Belvin Brook Benton And Jesse Belvin (Crown 1963)★★★, Born To Sing The Blues (Mercury 1964)★★★, That Old Feeling (RCA 1966)★★★, Laura (What's He Got That I Ain't Got) (Reprise 1967)★★, Do Your Own Thing (Cotillion 1969)★★, Brook Benton Today (Cotillion 1970)★★, Home Style (Cotillion 1970)★★★, The Gospel Truth (Cotillion 1971)★★, Something For Everyone (MGM 1973)★★, Sings A Love Story (RCA 1975)★★, Mr. Bartender (All Platinum 1976)★★, This Is Brook Benton (All Platinum 1976)★★★, Makin' Love Is Good For You (Olde Worlde 1978)★★, Ebony (Olde Worlde 1978)★★, Brook Benton Sings The Standards (RCA 1984)★★★.
COMPILATIONS: Brook Benton's Golden Hits (Mercury 1961)★★★, Golden Hits Volume Two (Mercury 1963) ★★★, Spotlight On Brook Benton (Philips 1977)★★★, The Incomparable Brook Benton: 20 Greatest Hits (Audio Fidelity 1982)★★★, Sixteen Golden Classics (Unforgettable/Castle 1986)★★★, The Brook Benton Anthology (Rhino 1986) ★★★★, His Greatest Hits (Mercury 1987)★★★, 40 Greatest Hits (Mercury 1990)★★★★, A Rainy Night In Georgia (Mainline 1990)★★★, Greatest Hits (Curb 1991) ★★★, Endlessly: The Best Of Brook Benton (Rhino 1998) ★★★★, The Essential MGM And RCA Victor Recordings (Taragon 2000)★★★, Red Hot And Blue (TKO 2001)★★★.
FILMS: Mister Rock And Roll (1957).

BERLIN
ALBUMS: Pleasure Victim (Geffen 1983)★★, Love Life (Geffen 1984)★★, Count Three And Pray (Mercury 1987)★★.
COMPILATIONS: Best Of Berlin 1979-1988 (Geffen 1988)★★★.

BERRY, CHUCK
ALBUMS: After School Session (Chess 1958)★★★★, One Dozen Berrys (Chess 1958)★★★★★, Chuck Berry Is On Top (Chess 1959)★★★★, Rockin' At The Hops (Chess 1960)★★★★, New Juke-Box Hits (Chess 1961)★★★, Chuck Berry Twist (Chess 1962)★★★, More Chuck Berry UK release (Pye 1963)★★★, Chuck Berry On Stage (Chess 1963)★★, The Latest And The Greatest (Chess 1964)★★★, You Never Can Tell (Chess 1964)★★★, with Bo Diddley Two Great Guitars (Chess 1964)★★★, St. Louis To Liverpool (Chess 1964)★★★★, Chuck Berry In London (Chess 1965) ★★★, Fresh Berry's (Chess 1965)★★★, Golden Hits new recordings (Mercury 1967)★★, Chuck Berry In Memphis (Mercury 1967)★★★, Live At The Fillmore Auditorium (Mercury 1967)★★, From St. Louis To Frisco (Mercury 1968)★★, Concerto In B. Goode (Mercury 1969)★★, Back Home (Chess 1970)★★, San Francisco Dues (Chess 1971) ★★, The London Chuck Berry Sessions (Chess 1972)★★, Bio (Chess 1973)★★, Chuck Berry (Chess 1975)★★, Live In Concert (Magnum 1978)★★★, Rockit (Atco 1979)★★★★, Rock! Rock! Rock 'N' Roll! (Atco 1980)★★, Hail! Hail! Rock 'N' Roll film soundtrack (MCA 1987)★★, Live 1982 recording (Columbia River 2000)★★.
COMPILATIONS: Chuck Berry's Greatest Hits (Chess 1964) ★★★★★, Chuck Berry's Golden Decade (Chess 1967) ★★★★★, Golden Decade, Volume 2 (Chess 1973)★★★★, Golden Decade, Volume 3 (Chess 1974)★★★★, Motorvatin' (Chess 1977)★★★, Spotlight On Chuck Berry (PRT 1980) ★★★, The Great Twenty-Eight (Chess/MCA 1982)★★★★★, Chess Masters (Chess 1983)★★★, Reelin' And Rockin' (Live) (Aura 1984)★★, Rock 'N' Roll Rarities (Chess/MCA 1986)★★, More Rock 'N' Roll Rarities (Chess/MCA 1986) ★★★, Chicago Golden Years (Vogue 1988)★★★, Decade '55 To '65 (Platinum 1988)★★★, Chess Box 3-CD box set (Chess/MCA 1989)★★★★, Missing Berries: Rarities, Volume 3 (Chess/MCA 1990)★★★, The Chess Years 9-CD box set (Charly 1991)★★★★★, On The Blues Side (Ace 1993)★★★★, Oh Yeah! (Charly 1994)★★★, Poet Of Rock 'N' Roll 4-CD box set (Charly 1995)★★★★★, His Best Volume 1 (Chess 1997)★★★★, The Best Of Chuck Berry: The Millennium Collection (PolyGram 1999)★★★★, Chuck Berry: The Anthology (MCA 2000)★★★★.
VIDEOS: The Legendary Chuck Berry (Channel 5 1987), Hail Hail Rock 'N' Roll (CIC Video 1988), Live At The Roxy (Old Gold 1990), Rock 'N' Roll Music (BMG Video 1991).
FURTHER READING: Chuck Berry: Rock 'N' Roll Music, Howard A. De Witt. Chuck Berry: Mr Rock 'N' Roll, Krista Reese. Chuck Berry: The Autobiography, Chuck Berry. Long Distance Information: Chuck Berry's Recorded Legacy, Fred Rothwell.
FILMS: Rock, Rock, Rock (1956), Mister Rock And Roll (1957), Go, Johnny, Go! (1958), Jazz On A Summer's Day (1959), Alice In Den Städten aka Alice In The Cities (1974), American Hot Wax (1978), Class Reunion (1982), Hail! Hail! Rock 'N' Roll (1987).

BERRY, DAVE
ALBUMS: Dave Berry (Decca 1964)★★★, The Special Sound Of Dave Berry (Decca 1966)★★★, One Dozen Berrys (Ace Of Clubs 1966)★★★, Dave Berry '68 (Decca 1968)★★, Hostage To The Beat (Butt 1986)★★.
COMPILATIONS: Berry's Best (Ace 1988)★★★, The Very Best Of Dave Berry (Spectrum 1998)★★★.

BERRY, RICHARD
ALBUMS: Richard Berry And The Dreamers (Crown 1963) ★★★, with the Soul Searchers Live From H.D. Hover Century Restaurant (Pam 1968)★★, with the Soul Searchers Wild Berry (Pam 1968)★★, Great Rhythm & Blues Oldies (Blues Spectrum 1977)★★★.
COMPILATIONS: Get Out Of The Car (Ace 1982)★★★★, Louie, Louie (Earth Angel 1986)★★.

BETA BAND
ALBUMS: The 3 E.P.'s (Regal/Astralwerks 1998)★★★★, The Beta Band (Regal/Astralwerks 1999)★★★, Hot Shots II (Regal/Astralwerks 2001)★★★.

BEVIS FROND
ALBUMS: Miasma (Woronzow 1987)★★★, Inner Marshland (Woronzow 1987)★★★, Triptych (Woronzow 1987)★★★, Bevis Through The Looking Glass (Reckless 1988)★★★, Acid Jam (Woronzow 1988)★★★, The Aunty Winnie Album (Reckless 1989)★★★, Any Gas Faster (Woronzow 1990)★★★★, as Bevis and Twink Magic Eye (Woronzow 1990)★★★, New River Head (Woronzow 1991)★★★★, London Stone (Woronzow 1992)★★★, It Just Is (Woronzow 1993)★★★, Sprawl (Woronzow 1994) ★★★, Superseeder (Woronzow 1995)★★★, North Circular (Woronzow 1997)★★★, Live (Woronzow 2000) ★★★, Valedictory Songs (Woronzow 2000)★★★.
COMPILATIONS: A Gathering Of Fronds (Woronzow 1992)★★★.

BHUNDU BOYS
ALBUMS: The Bhundu Boys (1981)★★★, Hupenyu Hwenasi (1984)★★★, Shabini (Discafrique 1985)★★★★, Tsvimbodzemoto (Discafrique 1987)★★★★, True Jit (WEA 1987)★★★★, Pamberi (WEA 1989)★★★, Absolute Jit! Live At King Tut's Wah Wah Hut (Discafrique 1990)★★★, Friends On The Road (Cooking Vinyl 1993)★★★, Muchiyedza (Out Of The Dark) (Cooking Vinyl 1997)★★★.
COMPILATIONS: The Shed Sessions (Sadza 2001)★★★.

BIG AUDIO DYNAMITE
ALBUMS: This Is Big Audio Dynamite (CBS 1985)★★★★, No. 10 Upping Street (CBS 1986)★★★★★, Tighten Up, Vol. 88 (CBS 1988)★★★, Megatop Phoenix (CBS 1989)★★★, as B.A.D. II Kool-Aid (CBS 1990)★★, as B.A.D. II The Globe (Columbia 1991)★★, as Big Audio Higher Power (Columbia 1994)★★, as Big Audio Looking For A Song (Columbia 1994)★★, as Big Audio Dynamite F-Punk (Radioactive 1995)★★★.
COMPILATIONS: Planet B.A.D.: Greatest Hits (Columbia 1995)★★★, Super Hits (Columbia 1999)★★★★.

BIG BLACK
ALBUMS: Atomizer (Homestead/Blast First 1986)★★★, Sound Of Impact live album (Walls Have Ears 1987)★★, Songs About Fucking (Touch And Go/Blast First 1987) ★★★, Pigpile (Blast First 1992)★★★.
COMPILATIONS: The Hammer Party (Homestead/Blast First 1986)★★★, The Rich Man's Eight-Track Tape (Homestead/Blast First 1987)★★★.

BIG BOPPER
ALBUMS: Chantilly Lace (Mercury 1959)★★★.
COMPILATIONS: Hellooo Baby! The Best Of The Big Bopper 1954-1959 (Rhino 1989)★★★.
FURTHER READING: Chantilly Lace: The Life & Times Of J.P. Richardson, Tim Knight.

BIG COUNTRY
ALBUMS: The Crossing (Mercury 1983)★★★★, Steeltown (Mercury 1984)★★★, The Seer (Mercury 1986)★★, Peace In Our Time (Mercury/Reprise 1988)★★★, No Place Like Home (Vertigo 1991)★★, The Buffalo Skinners (Compulsion 1993) ★★★, Without The Aid Of A Safety Net (Compulsion 1994) ★★, BBC Live In Concert (Windsong 1995)★★, Why The Long Face (Transatlantic 1995)★★★, Eclectic (Transatlantic 1996) ★★★, Big Country (King Biscuit Flower Hour 1997)★★★, Brighton Rock (Snapper 1997)★★, Driving To Damascus (Track 1999)★★★, Come Up Screaming (Track 2000)★★, Under Cover (Track 2001)★★★.
COMPILATIONS: Through A Big Country: Greatest Hits (Mercury 1990)★★★, The Collection (Castle 1993)★★★, Radio 1 Sessions 1982/1983 recordings (Strange Fruit 1994)★★, Restless Natives & Rarities (Mercury 1998) ★★★, Kings Of Emotion (Recall 1998)★★★, Rarities II (Track 2001)★★.
VIDEOS: Big Country Live (Channel 5 1986), King Of Emotion (PolyGram Music Video 1988), In A Big Country (PolyGram Music Video 1988), Peace In Our Time: Moscow 1988 (Channel 5 1989), Greatest Hits: Big Country (Channel 5 1990), Through A Big Country (PolyGram Music Video 1991), The Seer: Live (Virgin Vision 1991), Without The Aid Of A Safety Net - Live (PMI/EMI 1994).
FURTHER READING: Big Country: A Certain Chemistry, John May.

BIG STAR
ALBUMS: #1 Record (Ardent 1972)★★★★, Radio City (Ardent 1974)★★★★, 3rd (PVC 1978)★★★, Sister Lovers (PVC 1985)★★★, Third/Sister Lovers (Ryko 1992)★★★, Live 1974 recording (Rykodisc 1992)★★★, Columbia: Live At Missouri University 4/25/93 (Zoo 1993)★★★, Nobody Can Dance (Norton 1999)★★.
COMPILATIONS: The Best Of Big Star (Big Beat 1999)★★★★.

BIKINI KILL
ALBUMS: Bikini Kil (K Records 1992)★★★, Bikini Kill mini-album (Kill Rock Stars 1993)★★★, with Huggy Bear Yeah Yeah Yeah (Kill Rock Stars 1993)★★★, Pussy Whipped (Kill Rock Stars 1993)★★, Reject All American (Kill Rock Stars 1996)★★★.
COMPILATIONS: The Tape Version Of The First Two Albums (Kill Rock Stars 1994)★★★, The Singles (Kill Rock Stars 1998)★★★.

BIOHAZARD
ALBUMS: Biohazard (Maze 1990)★★, Urban Discipline (Roadrunner 1992)★★★, State Of The World Address (Warners 1994)★★★, Mata Leáo (Warners 1996)★★, No Holds Barred (Roadrunner 1997)★★★, New World Disorder (Mercury 1999)★★★, Uncivilization (Steamhammer 2001)★★★.
COMPILATIONS: Tales From The B-Side (Renegade 2001)★★★.

BIRKIN, JANE
ALBUMS: with Serge Gainsbourg Jane Birkin And Serge Gainsbourg (Fontana 1969)★★★, Jane B (Phonogram 1974)★★★, Di Doo Dah (Phonogram 1975)★★, Versions Jane (Discovery 1996)★★★.
COMPILATIONS: The Best Of Jane Birkin (Mercury 1997)★★★, Talent Of The Century (Universal 2000)★★★.
FILMS: Blowup (1966), Kaleidoscope aka The Bank Breaker (1966), La Piscine aka The Swimming Pool (1969), Wonderwall: The Movie (1969), Les Chemins De Katmandou aka The Road To Katmandu (1969), Cannabis aka The Mafia Wants Your Blood (1969), Trop Petit Mon Ami aka Too Small My Friend (1970), Sex Power (1970), Alba Pagana (May Morning In Oxford) (1970), Romance Of A Horsethief (1971), 19 Djevojaka I 1 Mornar (1971), Trop Jolies Pour Être Honnêtes aka Too Pretty To Be Honest (1972), Don Juan 73 (1973), Projection Privée aka Private Projection (1973), La Morte Negli Occhi Del Gatto aka Seven Deaths In The Cat's Eye (1973), Le Mouton Enragé aka The French Way Is (1974), Sérieux Comme Le Plaisir aka Serious As Pleasure (1974), La Moutarde Me Monte Au Nez aka Lucky Pierre (1974), Dark Places (1974), Comment Réussir Dans La Vie Quand On Est Con Et Pleurnichard (1974), La Course À L'Échalote aka The Wild Goose Chase (1975), Catherine Et Cie aka Catherine & Co. (1975), Sept Morts Sur Ordonnance aka Bestial Quartet (1975), Je T'Aime, Moi Non Plus aka I Love You, I Don't (1975), Le Diable Au Coeur aka The Devil In The Heart (1975), Bruciati Da Cocente Passione aka Burnt By A Scalding Passion (1976), L'Animal (1977), Death On The Nile (1978), Au Bout Du Bout Du Banc aka Make Room For Tomorrow (1978), La Miel aka Honey (1979), Melancholy Baby (1979), La Fille Prodigue (1981), Rends-Moi La Clé! (1981), Nestor Burma, Détective De Choc (1981), Egon Schile - Exzesse (1981), Evil Under The Sun (1982), Circulez Y'A Rien À Voir (1983), L'Ami De Vincent aka A Friend Of Vincent (1983), Le Garde Du Corps (1984), La Pirate (1984), L'Amour Par Terre aka Love On The Ground (1984), Dust (1985), Le Neveu De Beethoven aka Beethoven's Nephew (1985), Leave All Fair (1985), La Femme De Ma Vie aka Women Of My Life (1986), Comédie! (1987), Soigne Ta Droite aka Keep Up Your Right (1987), Kung Fu Master (1987), Jane B. Par Agnès V. (1987), Daddy Nostalgie (1990), La Belle Noiseuse aka The Beautiful Troublemaker (1991), Contre L'Oubli (1991), Les Cent Et Une Nuits (1995), Noir Comme Le Souvenir aka Black For Remembrance (1995), Between The Devil And The Deep Blue Sea voice only (1995), On Connaît La Chanson aka The Same Old Song (1997), A Soldier's Daughter Never Cries (1998), The Last September (1999).

BIRTHDAY PARTY
ALBUMS: The Birthday Party (Missing Link 1980)★★★, Prayers On Fire (Thermidor 1981)★★★, Drunk On The Pope's Blood mini-album (4AD 1982)★★★, Junk Yard (4AD 1982)★★★, It's Still Living live recording (Missing Link 1985)★★★.
COMPILATIONS: A Collection (Missing Link 1985)★★★, Hee Haw (4AD 1989)★★★, The Peel Sessions Album (Strange Fruit 1991)★★★, Hits (4AD 1992)★★★★, Definitive Missing Link Recordings 1979-1982 (Missing Link 1994)★★★★, Live 1981-82 (4AD 1999)★★★★.
VIDEOS: Pleasure Heads Must Burn (IKON 1988).

BISHOP, ELVIN
ALBUMS: The Elvin Bishop Group (Fillmore 1969)★★, Feel It (Fillmore 1970)★★, Rock My Soul (Fillmore 1972)★★, Let It Flow (Capricorn 1974)★★★, Juke Joint Jump (Capricorn 1975)★★★, Struttin' My Stuff (Capricorn 1975)★★★★, Hometown Boy Makes Good! (Capricorn 1976)★★, Live! Raisin' Hell (Capricorn 1977)★★★, Hog Heaven (Capricorn 1978)★★★, Is You Is Or Is You Ain't My Baby (Line 1982)★★, Big Fun (Alligator 1988)★★★, Don't Let The Bossman Get You Down (Alligator 1991)★★★, Ace In The Hole (Alligator 1995)★★★, The Skin I'm In (Alligator 1998)★★★, with Little Smokey Smothers That's My Partner! (Alligator 2000)★★★, King Biscuit Flower Hour Presents (King Biscuit Flower Hour 2001)★★★.
COMPILATIONS: The Best Of Elvin Bishop: Crabshaw Rising (Epic 1972)★★, Tulsa Shuffle: The Best Of Elvin Bishop (Columbia 1994)★★★★, The Best Of Elvin Bishop: The Millennium Collection (Mercury 2002)★★★★.

BISHOP, STEPHEN
ALBUMS: Careless (ABC 1976)★★★, Bish (ABC 1978) ★★★, Red Cab To Manhattan (Warners 1980)★★★, Bowling In Paris (Atlantic 1989)★★★, Blue Guitars (Foundation 1996)★★★★.
COMPILATIONS: The Best Of Bish (Rhino 1988)★★★, On & On: The Hits Of Steven Bishop (MCA 1994)★★★★.
FURTHER READING: Songs In The Rough, Stephen Bishop.
FILMS: The Kentucky Fried Movie (1977), Animal House (1978), The Blues Brothers (1980), Twilight Zone: The Movie (1983), Someone To Love (1987).

BJÖRK
ALBUMS: Björk (Fàlkinn 1977)★★★, with Trió Gudmundar Gling-Gló (Smekkleysa 1990)★★★, Debut (One Little Indian/Elektra 1993)★★★★, Post (One Little Indian/Elektra 1995)★★★★, Telegram remix album (One Little Indian 1996)★★★, Homogenic (One Little Indian/Elektra 1997) ★★★★, Selma Songs film soundtrack (One Little Indian/ Elektra 2000)★★★, Vespertine (One Little Indian/Elektra 2001)★★★★.
COMPILATIONS: The Best Remixes From The Album, Debut, For All The People Who Don't Buy White-Labels (One Little Indian 1994)★★.
VIDEOS: Björk (Propaganda 1994), Vessel (PolyGram Music Video 1994), Live In Shepherd's Bush (One Little Indian 1998), Volumen (One Little Indian 1998), Hidden Place (Elektra Entertainment 2001).
FURTHER READING: Post: The Official Björk Book, Penny Phillips. Björkgraphy, Martin Aston. Björk, Björk.
FILMS: Juniper Tree (1987), Prêt-à-Porter aka Ready To Wear (1994), Dancer In The Dark (2000).

BLACK CROWES
ALBUMS: Shake Your Money Maker (Def American 1990)★★★, The Southern Harmony And Musical Companion (Def American 1992)★★★★, Amorica (American 1994)★★★, Three Snakes And One Charm (American 1996)★★★, By Your Side (Columbia 1999)★★★, with Jimmy Page Live At The Greek (TVT/SPV 2000)★★★, Lions (V2 2001)★★★★.
COMPILATIONS: Sho' Nuff (American 1998)★★★, Greatest Hits 1990-1999: A Tribute To A Work In Progress ... (Columbia 2000)★★★★.
VIDEOS: Who Killed That Bird On Your Windowsill ... The Movie (Warner Brothers Video 1993).
FURTHER READING: The Black Crowes, Martin Black.

BLACK FLAG
ALBUMS: Damaged (SST 1981)★★★★, My War (SST 1984)★★★, Family Man (SST 1984)★★, Slip It In (SST 1984)★★★, Live '84 (SST 1984)★★, Loose Nut (SST 1985)★★, In My Head (SST 1985)★★★, Who's Got The 10 ½? (SST 1986)★★★.
COMPILATIONS: Everything Went Black (SST 1982)★★★, The First Four Years (SST 1983)★★★★, Wasted ... Again (SST 1988)★★★★.
VIDEOS: Black Flag Live (Jettisoundz 1984).

BLACK GRAPE
ALBUMS: It's Great When You're Straight ... Yeah (Radioactive 1995)★★★★, Stupid, Stupid, Stupid (Radioactive 1997)★★★.
VIDEOS: The Grape Tapes (Radioactive 1997).
FURTHER READING: Shaun Ryder: Happy Mondays, Black Grape And Other Traumas, Mick Middles. High Life 'N' Low Down Dirty: The Thrills And Spills Of Shaun Ryder, Lisa Verrico. Freaky Dancin', Bez.

BLACK OAK ARKANSAS
ALBUMS: as the Knowbody Else The Knowbody Else (Stax 1969)★★, Black Oak Arkansas (Atco 1971)★★, Keep The Faith (Atco 1972)★★, If An Angel Came To See You, Would You Make Her Feel At Home? (Atco 1972)★★, Raunch 'N' Roll Live (Atlantic 1973)★★★, High On The Hog (Atco 1973)★★, Street Party (Atco 1974)★★, Ain't Life Grand (Atco 1975)★★, X-Rated (MCA 1975)★, Live! Mutha (Atco 1976)★, Balls Of Fire (MCA 1976)H, 10 Yr Overnight Success (MCA 1977)★, Race With The Devil (Capricorn 1977)★, I'd Rather Be Sailing (Capricorn 1978)★, The Black Attack Is Back (Capricorn 1986)★, Live On The King Biscuit Flower Hour 1976 recording (King Biscuit Flower Hour 1998)★★, The Wild Bunch (Cleopatra 1999)★★.
COMPILATIONS: Early Times (Stax 1974)★★, The Best Of Black Oak Arkansas (Atco 1977)★★, Hot & Nasty: The Best Of Black Oak Arkansas (Rhino 1993)★★★.

BLACK REBEL MOTORCYCLE CLUB
ALBUMS: B.R.M.C. (Virgin 2001)★★★★.

BLACK SABBATH
ALBUMS: Black Sabbath (Vertigo 1970)★★★, Paranoid (Vertigo 1970)★★★★, Master Of Reality (Vertigo 1971) ★★★, Black Sabbath Vol. 4 (Vertigo 1972)★★★★, Sabbath Bloody Sabbath (World Wide Artists 1974)★★★, Sabotage (NEMS 1975)★★★, Technical Ecstasy (Vertigo 1976)★★★, Never Say Die! (Vertigo 1978)★★★, Heaven And Hell (Vertigo 1980)★★★★, Live At Last (NEMS 1980)★★, Mob Rules (Vertigo 1981)★★, Live Evil (Vertigo 1982)★★, Born Again (Vertigo 1983)★★, Seventh Star (Vertigo 1986)★★★, The Eternal Idol (Vertigo 1987)★★, Headless Cross (IRS 1989)★★, TYR (I.R.S. 1990)★★, Dehumanizer (I.R.S. 1992) ★★, Cross Purposes (EMI 1994)★★★, Forbidden (I.R.S. 1995)★★, Reunion (Epic 1998)★★★★.
COMPILATIONS: We Sold Our Soul For Rock 'n' Roll (NEMS 1976)★★, Greatest Hits (NEMS 1980)★★★, Collection: Black Sabbath (Castle 1985)★★★★, Blackest Sabbath (Vertigo 1989)★★, Backtrackin' (Backtrackin' 1990)★★, The Ozzy Osbourne Years 3-CD box set (Essential 1991) ★★★★, Between Heaven And Hell 1970-1983 (Raw Power 1995)★★★, Sabbath Stones (I.R.S. 1996)★★, Under Wheels Of Confusion 1970-1987 4-CD box set (Essential 1997)★★★★, The Best Of Black Sabbath (Sanctuary 2000)★★★★, The Complete 70s Replica CD Collection 1970-1978 8-CD box set (Sanctuary 2001)★★★★.
VIDEOS: Never Say Die (VCL 1986), The Black Sabbath Story Volume 1 (1970-1978) (Castle Music Pictures 1992), Under Wheels Of Confusion 1970-1987 (Castle Music Pictures 1996), The Last Supper (Sony Music Video 1999).
FURTHER READING: Black Sabbath, Chris Welch.

BLACK UHURU
ALBUMS: Love Crisis (Prince Jammys/Third World 1977) ★★★, Showcase (Taxi/Heartbeat 1979)★★★, Sinsemilla (Mango/Island 1980)★★★, Red (Mango/ Island 1981) ★★★★, Black Uhuru (Virgin 1981)★★★, Chill Out (Mango/Island 1982)★★★, Tear It Up – Live (Mango/ Island 1982)★★★, Guess Who's Coming To Dinner (Heartbeat 1983)★★★, The Dub Factor (Mango/Island 1983)★★★, Anthem (Mango/ Island 1984)★★★, Uhuru In Dub (CSA 1985)★★★, Brutal (RAS 1986)★★★★, Brutal Dub (RAS 1986)★★★, Positive (RAS 1987)★★★, Positive Dub (RAS 1987)★★★, Live In New York City (Rohit 1988)★★★, Now (Mesa 1990)★★★, Now Dub (Mesa 1990)★★★★, Iron Storm (Mesa 1991)★★, Mystical Touch (Mesa 1993)★★★, Unification (Five Star General 1999)★★★, Dynasty (RAS 2001)★★★.
COMPILATIONS: Reggae Greats (Mango/Island 1985)★★★★, Liberation: The Island Anthology 2-CD box set (Mango/Island 1993)★★★★, What Is Life? An Introduction To Black Uhuru (Island 1999)★★★, Ultimate Collection (Hip-O 2000)★★★★.
VIDEOS: Tear It Up (Channel 5 1988), Black Uhuru Live (PolyGram Music Video 1991).

BLACK, BILL
ALBUMS: Smokie (Hi 1960)★★★, Saxy Jazz (Hi 1960) ★★★, Solid And Raunchy (Hi 1960)★★★★, That Wonderful Feeling (Hi 1961)★★★, Movin' (Hi 1961)★★★, Bill Black's Record Hop (Hi 1962)★★★, Let's Twist Her (Hi 1962)★★★★, The Untouchable Sound Of Bill Black (Hi 1963)★★★, Bill Black Plays The Blues (Hi 1964)★★★, Bill Black Plays Tunes By Chuck Berry (Hi 1964)★★, Bill Black's Combo Goes Big Band (Hi 1964)★★, More Solid And Raunchy (Hi 1965)★★, All Timers (Hi 1966)★★, Black Lace (Hi 1967)★★, King Of The Road (Hi 1967)★★, The Beat Goes On (Hi 1968)★★, Turn On Your Lovelight (London 1969)★★, Solid And Raunchy The 3rd (Hi 1969)★★, Soulin' The Blues (London 1969)★★.
COMPILATIONS: Greatest Hits (Hi/London 1963)★★★, Hi Rollin': The Story Of Bill Black's Combo (1960-65) (Edsel 1998)★★★, The Best Of Bill Black's Combo: The Hi Record Years (Hi 2000)★★★.

BLACK, CILLA
ALBUMS: Cilla (Parlophone 1965)★★★, Cilla Sings A Rainbow (Parlophone 1966)★★★, Sher-oo! (Parlophone 1968)★★★, Surround Yourself With Cilla (Parlophone 1968)★★, Sweet Inspiration (Parlophone 1969)★★★, Images (Parlophone 1970)★★, Day By Day With Cilla (Parlophone 1973)★★, In My Life (EMI 1974)★★★, It Makes Me Feel Good (EMI 1976)★★, Modern Priscilla (EMI 1978)★★★, Especially For You reissued as Love Songs (K-Tel 1980)★★★, Surprisingly Cilla (Towerbell 1985)★★, Cilla's World Australia only (Virgin 1990)★★, Through The Years (Columbia 1993)★★★.
COMPILATIONS: The Best Of Cilla Black (Parlophone 1968)★★★, You're My World (Regal Starline 1970)★★★, The Very Best Of Cilla Black (EMI 1983)★★★, 25th Anniversary Album (MFP 1988)★★★, The Best Of The EMI Years (EMI 1991)★★★★, Love, Cilla (EMI 1993)★★★, 1963-1973: The Abbey Road Decade 3-CD box set (EMI 1997)★★★, The Essential Cilla Black 1963-1978 (EMI 1999)★★★★.
VIDEOS: Through The Years: The Cilla Black Story (SMV 1993).
FILMS: Ferry Across The Mersey (1965), Work Is A Four Letter Word (1965).

BLACK, FRANK
ALBUMS: Frank Black (4AD/Elektra 1993)★★★, Teenager Of The Year (4AD/Elektra 1994)★★★★, with Teenage Fanclub Frank Black & Teenage Fanclub (Strange Fruit 1995)★★★, The Cult Of Ray (American/Epic 1996)★★★, Frank Black And The Catholics (Play It Again Sam/spinART 1998)★★★, Pistolero (Play It Again Sam/spinART 1999) ★★★, Dog In The Sand (Cooking Vinyl 2001)★★★★.

BLACK, MARY
ALBUMS: Mary Black (Dara 1983)★★★, Collected (Dara 1984)★★★, Without The Fanfare (Dara 1985)★★★, with the Black Family The Black Family (Dara 1986)★★★, By The Time It Gets Dark (Dara 1987)★★★, with the Black Family Time For Touching Home (Dara 1989)★★★, No Frontiers (Dara 1989) ★★★, Babes In The Wood (Grapevine 1991)★★★★, The Holy Ground (Gifthorse 1993)★★★, Circus (Grapevine 1995)★★★, Shine (Grapevine 1997)★★★, Speaking With The Angel (Grapevine 1999)★★★.
COMPILATIONS: The Best Of Mary Black (Dara 1991) ★★★★, The Collection (Dara 1992)★★★★, Looking Back: The Best Of Mary Black (Curb 1995)★★★★, The Best Of Mary Black 1991-2001 (Grapevine 2001)★★★★.

BLACKMORE, RITCHIE
ALBUMS: as Blackmore's Night Shadow Of The Moon (HTD 1998)★★, as Blackmore's Night Under A Violet Moon (Candle Light 1999)★★, as Blackmore's Night Fires At Midnight (SPV 2001)★★★.
COMPILATIONS: Ritchie Blackmore Volume 1: Early Sessions To Rainbow (RPM 1990)★★★, Ritchie Blackmore Volume 2 (RPM 1991)★★, Session Man (RPM 1993)★★★, Take It! – Sessions 63/68 (RPM 1995)★★★.

BLACKWELL, OTIS
ALBUMS: Singin' The Blues (Davis 1956)★★, These Are My Songs (Inner City 1978)★★.

BLAINE, HAL
ALBUMS: Deuces, T's, Roadsters & Drums (RCA Victor 1963)★★, Drums! Drums! A Go Go (Dunhill 1966)★★, Psychedelic Percussion (Dunhill 1967)H, Have Fun!!! Play Drums!!! (Dunhill 1969)★★, Buh-Doom! spoken word (Acoustic Disc 1998)★★.
FURTHER READING: Hal Blaine And The Wrecking Crew, Hal Blaine.

BLASTERS
ALBUMS: American Music (Rollin' Rock 1980)★★★, The Blasters (Slash 1981)★★★★, Non Fiction (Slash 1983) ★★★, Hard Line (Slash 1985)★★★.
COMPILATIONS: The Blasters Collection (Slash 1991)★★★★.
FURTHER READING: Any Rough Times Are Now Behind You, Dave Alvin.

BLIGE, MARY J.
ALBUMS: What's The 411? (Uptown 1992)★★★★, What's The 411? - Remix Album (Uptown 1993)★★★, My Life (Uptown 1994)★★★, Share My World (MCA 1997) ★★★★, The Tour (MCA 1998)★★, Mary (MCA 1999) ★★★★, No More Drama (MCA 2001)★★★★.
FILMS: Prison Song (2000).

BLIND FAITH
ALBUMS: Blind Faith (Polydor 1969)★★★, Blind Faith – Deluxe Edition (Polydor 2001)★★★★.

BLIND MELON
ALBUMS: Blind Melon (Capitol 1993)★★★★, Soup (Capitol 1995)★★, Nico (Capitol 1997)★★.
COMPILATIONS: Classic Masters (EMD 2002)★★★.
VIDEOS: Letters From A Porcupine (Capitol 1996).

BLINK-182
ALBUMS: Cheshire Cat (Grilled Cheese/Cargo 1994)★★★, Dude Ranch (Cargo 1997)★★★, Enema Of The State (MCA 1999)★★★, The Mark, Tom & Travis Show (The Enema Strikes Back!) (MCA 2000)★★, Take Off Your Pants And Jacket (MCA 2001)★★★.
VIDEOS: The Urethra Chronicles (MCA 2000).

BLODWYN PIG
ALBUMS: Ahead Rings Out (Chrysalis 1969)★★★★, Getting To This (Chrysalis 1970)★★★, Lies (A New Day 1993)★★, All Tore Down (Indigo 1996)★★, Pig In The Middle (A New Day 1997)★★, The Full Porky: Live In London 1991 (A New Day 1992)★★, Live At The Layfayette (Indigo 1997)★★★.

BLONDIE
ALBUMS: Blondie (Private Stock 1976)★★★, Plastic Letters (Chrysalis 1978)★★★, Parallel Lines (Chrysalis 1978) ★★★★, Eat To The Beat (Chrysalis 1979)★★, Autoamerican (Chrysalis 1980)★★, The Hunter (Chrysalis 1982)★★, No Exit (Beyond 1999)★★★, Blondie Live: Philadelphia 1978/Dallas 1980 (Chrysalis 1999)★★, Livid (RCA 2000)★★.
COMPILATIONS: The Best Of Blondie (Chrysalis 1981) ★★★, Once More Into The Bleach (Chrysalis 1988)★★★, The Complete Picture: The Very Best Of Deborah Harry And Blondie (Chrysalis 1991)★★★★, Blonde And Beyond (Chrysalis 1993)★★★, The Platinum Collection (Chrysalis 1994)★★★, Beautiful: The Remix Album (Chrysalis 1995) ★★★, The Essential Collection (EMI Gold 1997)★★★★, Atomic: The Very Best Of Blondie (Chrysalis 1998)★★★★, Atomic/Atomix: The Very Best Of Blondie (Chrysalis 1999) ★★★★.
VIDEOS: Blondie - Live (CIC Video 1986), Eat To The Beat (Chrysalis Music Video 1988), Best Of Blondie (Chrysalis Music Video 1988).
FURTHER READING: Rip Her To Shreds: A Look At Blondie, Paul Sinclair. Blondie, Fred Schruers. Blondie, Lester Bangs. Making Tracks: The Rise Of Blondie, Debbie Harry, Chris Stein and Victor Bockris. New York Rocker, Gary Valentine.

BLOOD, SWEAT AND TEARS
ALBUMS: Child Is Father To The Man (Columbia 1968) ★★★, Blood, Sweat & Tears (Columbia 1969)★★★★, Blood, Sweat & Tears 3 (Columbia 1970)★★★, BS&T4 (Columbia 1971)★★★, New Blood (Columbia 1972)★★, No Sweat (Columbia 1973)★★, Mirror Image (Columbia 1974)★★, New City (Columbia 1975)★★, More Than Ever (Columbia 1976)★★, Brand New Day (ABC 1977)★★, Nuclear Blues (LAX 1980)★★, Live And Improvised (Columbia 1991)★★, Live (Rhino 1994)★★.
COMPILATIONS: Greatest Hits (Columbia 1972)★★★★, Classic B S T (Columbia 1980)★★★, What Goes Up! The Best Of (Columbia/Legacy 1995)★★★★, Super Hits (Columbia 1998)★★★.
FURTHER READING: Blood, Sweat & Tears, Lorraine Alterman.

BLOODHOUND GANG
ALBUMS: Use Your Fingers (Columbia 1995)★★★, One Fierce Beer Coaster (Republic/Geffen 1996)★★★, Hooray For Boobies (Interscope 1999)★★.

BLOOMFIELD, MIKE
ALBUMS: with Al Kooper, Stephen Stills Super Session (Columbia 1968)★★★★, The Live Adventures Of Mike Bloomfield And Al Kooper (Columbia 1969)★★★, with Barry Goldberg Two Jews Blues (Buddah 1969)★★, It's Not Killing Me (Columbia 1970)★★, with Dr. John, John Hammond Triumvirate (Columbia 1973)★★★, with KGB KGB (MCA 1976)H, with Mill Valley Bunch Mill Valley Session (Polydor 1976)★★★, If You Love These Blues, Play 'Em As You Please (Guitar Player 1976)★★★★, Analine (Takoma 1977)★★, Count Talent And The Originals (Clouds 1978)★★, Michael Bloomfield (Takoma 1978)★★, with Woody Harris Bloomfield/Harris (Kicking Mule 1979)★★, Between The Hard Place And The Ground (Takoma 1979) ★★, Livin' In The Fast Lane (Waterhouse 1980)★★, Gospel Duets (Kicking Mule 1981)★★, Cruisin' For A Bruisin' (Takoma 1981)★★, Junko Partners (Intermedia 1984)★★, I'm With You Always 1977 recording (Demon 1987)★★, Try It Before You Buy It 1973 recording (One Way 1990) ★★, Blues, Gospel And Ragtime Guitar Instrumentals (Shanachie 1994)★★★.
COMPILATIONS: Bloomfield: A Retrospective (Columbia 1983)★★★, Don't Say That I Ain't Your Man! Essential Blues 1964-1969 (Columbia/Legacy 1994)★★★, The Best Of (Takoma/Ace 1997)★★★.
FURTHER READING: The Rise And Fall Of An American Guitar Hero, Ed Ward. If You Love These Blues, Jan Mark.

BLOW MONKEYS
ALBUMS: Limping For A Generation (RCA 1984)★★★, Animal Magic (RCA 1986)★★★, She Was Only A Grocer's Daughter (RCA 1987)★★★, Whoops! There Goes The Neighbourhood (RCA 1989)★★, Choices (RCA 1989)★★.
COMPILATIONS: The Best Of (RCA 1993)★★★, For The Record (BMG 1996)★★★, Atomic Lullabies: Very Best Of The Blow Monkeys (BMG 1999)★★★.
VIDEOS: Video Magic (Hendring Music Video 1988), Digging Your Scene (RCA/Columbia 1988), Choices (BMG Video 1989).

BLUE AEROPLANES
ALBUMS: Bop Art (Abstract 1984)★★★, Tolerance (Fire 1986)★★★, Spitting Out Miracles (Fire 1987)★★★, Swagger (Ensign 1990)★★★, Beatsongs (Ensign 1991) ★★★★, Life Model (Beggars Banquet 1994)★★★, Rough Music (Beggars Banquet 1995)★★★, Cavaliers (Swarf Finger 2000)★★★.
SOLO: Gerard Langley and Ian Kearey Siamese Boyfriends mini-album (Fire 1986)★★.
COMPILATIONS: Friendloverplane (Fire 1988)★★★★, Friendloverplane 2 (Ensign 1992)★★★, Fruit (Fire 1996)★★★, Huh! The Best Of The Blue Aeroplanes 1987-1992 (Chrysalis 1997)★★★, Weird Shit (Swarf Finger 2001)★★★.

BLUE CHEER
ALBUMS: Vincebus Eruptum (Philips 1967)★★★, Outsideinside (Philips 1968)★★★, New! Improved! Blue Cheer (Philips 1969)★★, Blue Cheer (Philips 1969)★★, The Original Human Being (Philips 1970)★★★, Oh! Pleasant Hope (Philips 1971)H, The Beast Is Back (Megaforce 1985) ★, Blitzkrieg Over Nuremberg (Thunderbolt 1989)★★★, Dining With Sharks (Nibelung 1991)★★.
COMPILATIONS: The Best Of Blue Cheer (Philips 1982) ★★★, Louder Than God (Rhino 1986)★★★, Good Times Are So Hard To Find (The History Of Blue Cheer) (Mercury 1988)★★★, Highlights And Lowlives (Nibelung 1990)★★, The Beast Is Back: The Megaforce Years (Megaforce 1996) ★★, Live & Unreleased (Captain Trip 1996)★★.

BLUE NILE
ALBUMS: A Walk Across The Rooftops (Linn/Virgin 1984) ★★★★, Hats (Linn/Virgin 1989)★★★★, Peace At Last (Warners 1996)★★★.

BLUE ÖYSTER CULT
ALBUMS: Blue Öyster Cult (Columbia 1971)★★★, Tyranny And Mutation (Columbia 1973)★★★, Secret Treaties (Columbia 1974)★★, On Your Feet Or On Your Knees (Columbia 1975)★★, Agents Of Fortune (Columbia 1976) ★★★★, Spectres (Columbia 1977)★★, Some Enchanted Evening (Columbia 1978)★★, Mirrors (Columbia 1979) ★★, Cultosaurus Erectus (Columbia 1980)★★, Fire Of Unknown Origin (Columbia 1981)★★, Extraterrestial Live (Columbia 1982)H, The Revolution By Night (Columbia 1983)H, Club Ninja (Columbia 1986)★★, Imaginos (Columbia 1988)★★★, Bad Channels film soundtrack (Moonstone 1992)★★, Live 1976 (Gopaco 1994)★★★, Heaven Forbid (CMC International 1998)★★, Curse Of The Hidden Mirror (Sanctuary 2001)★★, Tales From The Psychic Wars (Burning Airlines 2001)★★.
SOLO: Donald Roeser Flat Out (Portrait 1982)★★.
COMPILATIONS: (Don't Fear) The Reaper (CBS Special Products 1989)★★★, On Flame With Rock & Roll (CBS Special Products 1990)★★★, Career Of Evil: The Metal Years (Columbia 1990) ★★★, Cult Classic (Herald 1994)★★★, Workshop Of The Telescopes (Columbia/ Legacy 1995)★★★★, Revisited (Gusto 1996)★★★, Super Hits (Columbia/Legacy 1998)★★★.
VIDEOS: Live 1976 (Castle Music Pictures 1991).

BLUE, DAVID
ALBUMS: with Richard Farina Singer/Songwriter Project (Elektra 1965)★★★, David Blue (Elektra 1966)★★★, These 23 Days In December (Elektra 1968)★★, Me, S. David Cohen (1970)★★, Stories (Asylum 1971)★★★, Nice Baby And The Angel (Asylum 1973)★★★, Com'n Back For More (Asylum 1975)★★★, Cupid's Arrow (Asylum 1976)★★★.
FILMS: Der Amerikanische Freund aka The American Friend (1977), Renaldo And Clara (1978).

BLUES BROTHERS
ALBUMS: Briefcase Full Of Blues (Atlantic 1978)★★, The Blues Brothers film soundtrack (Atlantic 1980)★★★, Made In America (Atlantic 1980)★★, as the Blues Brothers Band The Blues Brothers Band Live (Warners 1990)H, Red, White & Blues (Warners 1992)★.
COMPILATIONS: The Best Of The Blues Brothers (Atlantic 1981)★★.
VIDEOS: Live At Montreux (WEA Music Video 1990), Things We Did Last Summer (Brave World 1991).
FILMS: The Blues Brothers (1980).

BLUES MAGOOS
ALBUMS: Psychedelic Lollipop (Mercury 1966)★★★, Electric Comic Book (Mercury 1967)★★★, Basic Blues Magoos (Mercury 1968)★★, Never Goin' Back To Georgia (ABC 1969)★★, Gulf Coast Bound (ABC 1970)★★.
COMPILATIONS: Kaleidescopic Compendium: The Best Of The Blues Magoos (Mercury 1992)★★★.

BLUES PROJECT
ALBUMS: Live At The Cafe Au-Go-Go (Verve/Forecast 1966)★★★, Projections (Verve/Forecast 1967)★★★★, Live At The Town Hall (Verve/Forecast 1967)★★★, Planned Obsolescence (Verve/Forecast 1968)★★★, Flanders Kalb Katz Etc. (Verve/Forecast 1969)★★, Lazarus (Capitol

1971)★★, The Blues Project (Capitol 1972)★★, Reunion In Central Park (Capitol 1973)★★.
COMPILATIONS: The Best Of The Blues Project (Rhino 1989)★★★, Anthology (Polydor 1997)★★★★.

BLUES TRAVELER
ALBUMS: Blues Traveler (A&M 1990)★★, Travelers And Thieves (A&M 1991)★★★, On Tour Forever bonus disc given away free with copies of Travelers And Thieves (A&M 1992) ★★★, Save His Soul (A&M 1993)★★, Four (A&M 1994) ★★★★, Live From The Fall (A&M 1996)★★, Straight On Till Morning (A&M 1997)★★★, Bridge (A&M 2001)★★★.

BLUNSTONE, COLIN
ALBUMS: One Year (Epic 1971)★★★★, Ennismore (Epic 1972)★★★★, Journey (Epic 1974)★★★, Planes (Rocket 1976)★★★, Never Even Thought (Rocket 1978)★★, Late Nights In Soho Holland only (Rocket 1979)★★, with Keats Keats (EMI 1984)★★, Colin Blunstone Sings His Greatest Hits aka Greatest Hits (Essential 1991)★★★, Echo Bridge (Permanent/Renaissance 1995)★★, Live At The BBC (Windsong 1995)★★★, The Light Inside (Mystic 1998)★★, with Rod Argent Out Of The Shadows (Red House 2001)★★★.
COMPILATIONS: I Don't Believe In Miracles (CBS 1979)★★★★, Miracles (Pickwick 1983)★★★, Golden Highlights Holland only (Epic 1985)★★★, Some Years: It's The Time Of Colin Blunstone (Epic/Legacy 1995)★★★★.
FURTHER READING: The Zombies: Hung Up On A Dream, Claes Johansen.

BLUR
ALBUMS: Leisure (Food 1991)★★★★, Modern Life Is Rubbish (Food 1993)★★★, Parklife (Food 1994)★★★★, The Great Escape (Food 1995)★★★, Live At The Budokan (Food 1996)★★★, Blur (Food 1997)★★★★, Bustin' + Dronin' remixes (Food 1998)★★, 13 (Food 1999)★★★★.
Solo: Graham Coxon The Sky Is Too High (Transcopic 1998)★★★, The Golden D (Transcopic 2000)★★★, Crow Sit On Blood Tree (Transcopic 2001)★★★.
COMPILATIONS: 10th Anniversary Box Set (Food 1999)★★★, The Best Of (Food 2000)★★★★.
VIDEOS: Star Shaped (PMI 1993), Showtime (PMI 1995).
FURTHER READING: Blurbook, Paul Postle. An Illustrated Biography, Linda Holorney. Blurbook, Paul Postle. Blur: The Illustrated Story, Paul Lester. Blur: The Whole Story, Martin Roach. Blur: The Great Escape, Paul Moody. Blur In Their Own Words, Mick St Michael. 3862 Days: The Official History, Stuart Maconie.

BOB AND EARL
ALBUMS: Harlem Shuffle (Tip/Sue 1966)★★★, Bob And Earl (Crestview/B&C 1969)★★, Together (Joy 1969)★★.

BOLAN, MARC
ALBUMS: The Beginning Of Doves (Track 1974)★★★, You Scare Me To Death (Cherry Red 1981)★★, Dance In The Midnight (Marc On Wax 1983)★★, Beyond The Rising Sun (Cambra 1984)★★, Love And Death (Cherry Red 1985)★★, The Marc Shows television recordings (Marc On Wax 1989)★★★, Shadowhead (Thunderwing 2001)★★.
COMPILATIONS: Best Of The 20th Century Boy (K-Tel 1985)★★★★.
VIDEOS: On Video (Videoform 1984), Marc (Channel 5 1989), The Ultimate Collection (Telstar Video 1991), T. Rex Double Box Set (Virgin Vision 1991), Born To Boogie (PMI 1991), 20th Century Boy (PolyGram Music Video 1991), The Groover Live In Concert (MIA 1995).
FURTHER READING: The Warlock Of Love, Marc Bolan. Marc Bolan Lyric Book, no editor listed. The Marc Bolan Story, George Tremlett. Marc Bolan, Ted Dicks. Marc Bolan: Born To Boogie, Chris Welch and Simon Napier-Bell. Electric Warrior: The Marc Bolan Story, Paul Sinclair. Marc Bolan: The Illustrated Discography, John Bramley and Shan. Marc Bolan: Wilderness Of The Mind, John Willans and Caron Thomas. Twentieth Century Boy, Mark Paytress. Marc Bolan: The Legendary Years, John Bramley and Shan. Marc Bolan: The Krakenmist, no author listed. Marc Bolan: The Motivator, Dave Williams. Glam! Bowie, Bolan And The Glitter Rock Revolution, Barney Hoskyns. Marc Bolan 1947-1977: A Chronology, Cliff McLenehan.

BOLTON, MICHAEL
ALBUMS: as Michael Bolotin Michael Bolotin (RCA 1975) ★★, as Michael Bolotin Every Day Of My Life (RCA 1976) ★★, with Blackjack Blackjack (Polydor 1979)★★, with Blackjack Worlds Apart (Polydor 1980)★★, Michael Bolton (Columbia 1983)★★, Everybody's Crazy (Columbia 1985) ★★, The Hunger (Columbia 1987)★★★, Soul Provider (Columbia 1989)★★★, Time, Love And Tenderness (Columbia 1991)★★, The One Thing (Columbia 1993)★★, This Is The Time - The Christmas Album (Columbia 1996)H, All That Matters (Columbia 1997)★★★, My Secret Passion: The Arias (Sony Classical 1998)★★.
COMPILATIONS: Timeless - The Classics (Columbia 1992)★★★, Greatest Hits 1985-1995 (Sony 1995)★★★, The Early Years (RCA 1997)★★, Timeless - The Classics, Vol. 2 (Columbia 1999)★★, Love Songs (Columbia 2002)★★★.
VIDEOS: Soul Provider; The Videos (CMV Enterprises 1990), This Is Michael Bolton (SMV 1992), Decade: Greatest Hits 1985-1995 The Videos (SMV 1995).

BON JOVI
ALBUMS: Bon Jovi (Mercury 1984)★★, 7800 Degrees Fahrenheit (Mercury 1985)★★, Slippery When Wet (Mercury 1986)★★★★, New Jersey (Mercury 1988)★★★, Keep The Faith (Jambco/Mercury 1992)★★★★, These Days (Mercury 1995)★★★, These Days Tour Edition mini-album (Mercury 1996)★★, Crush (Island/Mercury 2000)★★★, One Wild Night: Live 1985-2001 (Island/Mercury 2001)★★★.
COMPILATIONS: Crossroad – The Best Of (Mercury 1994)★★★★.
VIDEOS: Breakout (PolyGram Music Video 1986), Slippery When Wet (Channel 5 1988), New Jersey (Channel 5 1989), Dead Or Alive (PolyGram Music Video 1989), Access All Areas (PolyGram Music Video 1990), Keep The Faith: An Evening With Bon Jovi (PolyGram Music Video 1993), Crossroad: The Best Of (PolyGram Music Video 1994), Live From London (PolyGram Music Video 1995), The Crush Tour (Mercury 2000).
FURTHER READING: Bon Jovi: An Illustrated Biography, Eddy McSquare. Faith And Glory, Malcolm Dome. Bon Jovi: Runaway, Dave Bowler and Bryan Dray. The Illustrated Biography, Mick Wall. The Complete Guide To The Music Of Bon Jovi, Mick Wall and Malcolm Dome. Bon Jovi, Neil Jeffries.

BONDS, GARY 'U.S.'
ALBUMS: Dance 'Til Quarter To Three (Legrand/Top Rank 1961)★★★, Twist Up Calypso (Legrand/Stateside 1962) ★★★, Dedication (EMI America 1981)★★★, On The Line (EMI America 1982)★★, Gary 'U.S.' Bonds Meets Chubby Checker (EMI 1983)★★, Standing In The Line Of Fire (Phoenix 1984)★★, At The Stone Pony, Asbury Park, NJ, November 25, 2000 (King Biscuit Flower Hour 2001)★★★.
COMPILATIONS: Greatest Hits Of Gary 'U.S.' Bonds (Legrand/Stateside 1962)★★★★, Certified Soul (Rhino 1982)★★, The School Of Rock 'n' Roll: The Best Of Gary 'U.S' Bonds (Rhino 1990)★★★★, Take Me Back To New Orleans (Ace 1995)★★★, The Best Of Gary U.S. Bonds (EMI 1996)★★★★, The Very Best Of Gary U.S. Bonds (Varèse Sarabande 1998)★★★★.
FILMS: It's Trad, Dad aka Ring-A-Ding Rhythm (1962), Blues Brothers 2000 (1998).

BONE THUGS-N-HARMONY
ALBUMS: as Bone Enterpri$es Faces Of Death (Stoney Burke 1993)★★★, E. 1999 Eternal (Ruthless/Relativity 1995)★★★★, The Art Of War (Ruthless/Relativity 1997) ★★, BTNHResurrection (Loud/Epic 2000)★★★.
SOLO: Bizzy Bone Heaven'z Movie (Ruthless/Relativity 1998)★★★, The Gift (AMC 2001)★★★. Flesh-n-Bone T.H.U.G.S. (Def Jam 1996)★★★, Fifth Dog Lets Loose (Koch 2000)★★★. Krayzie Bone Thug Mentality 1999 (Relativity 1999)★★★, Thug On Da Line (Ruthless/Loud 2001)★★★. Layzie Bone as L-Burna Thug By Nature (Epic 2001)★★.
COMPILATIONS: The Collection: Volume One (Ruthless 1998)★★★★, The Collection: Volume Two (Ruthless/Epic 2000)★★★.
VIDEOS: The Collection Volume 1 (Epic Music Video 1998).

BONEY M.
ALBUMS: Take The Heat Off Me (Atlantic 1976)★★, Love For Sale (Atlantic 1977)★★, Night Flight To Venus (Atlantic 1978)★★★, Oceans Of Fantasy (Atlantic 1979)★★, Boonoonoonoos (Atlantic 1981)★★, Christmas Album mini-album (Atlantic 1981)★, Ten Thousand Light Years (Carrere 1984)★★, Eye Dance (Carrere 1985)★★.
COMPILATIONS: The Magic Of Boney M. (Atlantic 1980) ★★★, 32 Superhits: The Best Of 10 Years (Stylus 1986) ★★, The 20 Greatest Christmas Songs (BMG 1986)★★, Greatest Hits Of All Time Remix '88 (BMG 1988)★★, Greatest Hits Of All Time Remix '89 (BMG 1989)★★, Gold: 20 Super Hits (BMG 1992)★★, More Gold (BMG 1993)★, 20th Century Hits (BMG 1999)★, Their Most Beautiful Ballads (Logic 2000)★★, Greatest Hits (BMG Heritage/RCA 2002)★★★.
VIDEOS: Gold (BMG 1992).
FURTHER READING: Boney M, John Shearlaw.

BONO, SONNY
ALBUMS: Inner Views (Atco 1967)★.
FURTHER READING: Sonny And Cher, Thomas Braun. And The Beat Goes On, Sonny Bono.
FILMS: Good Times (1967), Hairspray (1988).

BONZO DOG DOO-DAH BAND
ALBUMS: Gorilla (Liberty 1967)★★★★, The Doughnut In Granny's Greenhouse (Liberty 1968)★★★★, Tadpoles (Liberty 1969)★★★, Keynsham (Liberty 1969)★★, Let's Make Up And Be Friendly (United Artists 1972)★★.
COMPILATIONS: The History Of The Bonzos (United Artists 1974)★★★★, The Bestiality Of The Bonzo Dog Band (Liberty 1989)★★★, Cornology Volumes 1-3 (EMI 1992)★★★, New Tricks (Right Recordings 2000)★★★.
FILMS: Magical Mystery Tour (1967), Adventures Of The Son Of Exploding Sausage (1969).
FURTHER READING: Ginger Geezer: The Life Of Vivian Stanshall, Lucian Randall & Chris Welch

BOO RADLEYS
ALBUMS: Ichabod And I (Action 1990)★★, Everything's Alright Forever (Creation 1992)★★★, Giant Steps (Creation 1993)★★★★, Wake Up (Creation 1995)★★★★, C'mon Kids (Creation 1996)★★★★, Kingsize (Creation 1998)★★★.
Solo: Eggman First Fruits (Creation 1996)★★★.
COMPILATIONS: Learning To Walk (Rough Trade 1994)★★★.

BOOKER T. AND THE MGS
ALBUMS: Green Onions (Stax 1962)★★★★, Mo' Onions (Stax 1963)★★★★, Soul Dressing (Stax 1965)★★★★, My Sweet Potato (Stax 1965)★★★, And Now! (Stax 1966) ★★★, In The Christmas Spirit (Stax 1966)H, Hip Hug-Her (Stax 1967)★★★, with the Mar-Keys Back To Back (Stax 1967)★★★, Doin' Our Thing (Stax 1968)★★★, Soul Limbo (Stax 1968)★★★, Uptight film soundtrack (Stax 1969)★★, The Booker T. Set (Stax 1969)★★★, McLemore Avenue (Stax 1970)★★, Melting Pot (Stax 1971)★★, as the MGs The MGs (Stax 1973)★★, Memphis Sound (Warners 1975)★★, Time Is Tight (Warners 1976)★★, Universal Language (Asylum 1977)★.
COMPILATIONS: The Best Of Booker T. And The MGs (Atco 1968)★★★★, Booker T. And The MGs Greatest Hits (Stax 1970)★★★★, Booker T And The MGs: The Memphis Sound (Stax 1975)★★★★, Union Extended (Stax 1976)★★★★, The Best Of Booker T And The MGs (Very Best Of) (Rhino 1993)★★★★, Play The Hip Hits (Stax/Ace 1995)★★★★, Time Is Tight 3-CD box set (Stax 1998)★★★★.

BOOMTOWN RATS
ALBUMS: The Boomtown Rats (Ensign/Mercury 1977)★★★, A Tonic For The Troops (Ensign/Columbia 1978)★★★★, The Fine Art Of Surfacing (Ensign/Columbia 1979)★★★, Mondo Bongo (Mercury/Columbia 1981)★★★, V Deep (Mercury/Columbia 1982)★★, In The Long Grass (Mercury/Columbia 1984)★★.
COMPILATIONS: Greatest Hits (Mercury/Columbia 1987)★★★, Loudmouth: The Best Of The Boomtown Rats And Bob Geldof (Vertigo 1994)★★★, Great Songs Of Indifference: The Best Of Bob Geldof & The Boomtown Rats (Columbia 1997)★★★.
VIDEOS: A Tonic For The Troops (VCL 1986), On A Night Like This (Spectrum 1989).
FURTHER READING: The Boomtown Rats: Having Their Picture Taken, Peter Stone. Is That It?, Bob Geldof.

BOSTON
ALBUMS: Boston (Epic 1976)★★★★, Don't Look Back (Epic 1978)★★★, Third Stage (MCA 1986)★★★, Walk On (MCA 1994)★★.
COMPILATIONS: Greatest Hits (Epic 1997)★★★.

BOW WOW WOW
ALBUMS: Your Cassette Pet cassette only (EMI 1980) ★★★★, See Jungle! See Jungle! Go Join Your Gang, Yeah, City All Over! Go Ape Crazy! (RCA 1981)★★★, I Want Candy (RCA 1982)★★, When The Going Gets Tough, The Tough Get Going (RCA 1983)★★, Wild In The U.S.A. (Cleopatra 1999)★★★.
SOLO: Annabella Fever (RCA 1986)★★.
COMPILATIONS: The Best Of Bow Wow Wow i (Receiver 1989)★★★, Girl Bites Dog: Your Compact Disc Pet (EMI 1993)★★★, The Best Of Bow Wow Wow ii (RCA 1996) ★★★.

BOWIE, DAVID
ALBUMS: David Bowie aka The World Of David Bowie (Deram 1967)★★, David Bowie aka Man Of Words, Man Of Music/Space Oddity (RCA Victor 1969)★★★, The Man Who Sold The World (RCA Victor 1970)★★★, Hunky Dory (RCA Victor 1971)★★★★★, The Rise And Fall Of Ziggy Stardust And The Spiders From Mars (RCA Victor 1972) ★★★★★, Aladdin Sane (RCA Victor 1973)★★★★, Pin Ups (RCA Victor 1973)★★★, Diamond Dogs (RCA Victor 1974)★★★★, David Live (RCA Victor 1974)H, Young Americans (RCA Victor 1975)★★★★, Station To Station (RCA Victor 1976)★★★★, Low (RCA Victor 1977)★★★★, Heroes (RCA Victor 1977)★★★★★, Stage (RCA Victor 1978)★★, Lodger (RCA Victor 1979)★★, Scary Monsters (And Super Creeps) (RCA Victor 1980)★★★★, Rare (RCA 1983)★★, Let's Dance (EMI America 1983)★★★, Ziggy Stardust – The Motion Picture film soundtrack (RCA 1983) ★★, Tonight (EMI America 1984)H, Never Let Me Down (EMI America 1987)H, Black Tie White Noise (Arista 1993) ★★★, The Buddha Of Suburbia (Arista 1993)★★★, 1. Outside (Virgin 1995)★★, Earthling (Virgin 1997)★★, hours ... (Virgin 1999)★★★★.
COMPILATIONS: Images 1966-67 (Decca 1973)★★, Changesonebowie (RCA 1976)★★★★★, Best Of David Bowie (K-Tel 1981)★★★, Changestwobowie (RCA 1981) ★★, Golden Years (RCA 1983)★★★, Fame And Fashion (All Time Greatest Hits) (RCA 1984)★★★, Love You Til Tuesday (Deram 1984)★★, Changesbowie (EMI 1990) ★★★, The Singles Collection (EMI 1993)★★★★★, The Deram Anthology 1966-1968 (London 1997)★★, The Best Of 1969/1974 (EMI 1997)★★★, The Best Of 1974/1979 (EMI 1998)★★, I Dig Everything: The 1966 Pye Singles mini-album (Castle 1999)★★, Bowie At The Beeb: The Best Of The BBC Sessions 68-72 3-CD box set (EMI 2000)★★★★, All Saints (EMI 2001)★★★.
VIDEOS: David Bowie - Video EP (Virgin Vision 1983), Serious Moonlight (Videoform 1984), Ziggy Stardust And The Spiders From Mars (Thorn-EMI 1984), Live Video: David Bowie (Videoform 1984), Rock Idols (Video Gems 1985), Video EP: David Bowie (PMI 1986), Serious Moonlight 2 (Channel 5 1986), Jazzin' For Blue Jean (Video Collection 1987), Day In Day Out (PMI 1987), Glass Spider Volume 1 (Video Collection 1988), Glass Spider Volume 2 (Video Collection 1988), Love You Till Tuesday (Channel 5 1989), Ricochet (Virgin 1992), David Bowie: The Video Collection (PMI 1993), David Bowie: Black Tie White Noise (Arista 1993), Rebel Rebel (MasterVision 1996).
FURTHER READING: The David Bowie Story, George Tremlett. David Bowie: A Portrait In Words And Music, Vivian Claire. The David Bowie Biography, Paul Sinclair. David Bowie Black Book: The Illustrated Biography, Miles and Chris Charlesworth. Bowie In His Own Words, Miles. David Bowie: An Illustrated Discography, Stuart Hoggard. David Bowie: Profile, Chris Charlesworth. David Bowie: An Illustrated Record, Roy Carr and Charles Shaar Murray. Free Spirit Angie Bowie. David Bowie: The Pitt Report, Kenneth Pitt. David Bowie: A Chronology, Kevin Cann. David Bowie: A Rock 'N' Roll Odyssey, Kate Lynch. Bowie, Jerry Hopkins. David Bowie: The Concert Tapes, Pimm Jal de la Parra. David Bowie: The Starzone Interviews, David Currie. Stardust, Tony Zanetta. In Other Words ... David Bowie, Kerry Juby. David Bowie: The Archive, Chris Charlesworth. Alias David Bowie, Peter Gillman and Leni. Backstage Passes: Life On The Wild Side With David Bowie, Angie Bowie. The Bowie Companion, Elizabeth Thomson and David Gutman (eds.). Glam! Bowie, Bolan And The Glitter Rock Revolution, Barney Hoskyns. Strange Fascination - David Bowie: The Definitive Biography, David Buckley. Changes: The Stories Behind Every David Bowie Song 1970-1980, Chris Welch, Bowie Style, Mark Paytress and Steve Pafford. The Complete David Bowie, Nicholas Pegg.
FILMS: The Virgin Soldiers (1969), The Man Who Fell To Earth (1976), Schöner Gigolo, Armer Gigolo aka Just A Gigolo (1979), Christiane F aka We Children From Bahnhof Zoo (1981), The Hunger (1983), Merry Christmas, Mr. Lawrence (1983), Yellowbeard (1983), Ziggy Stardust And The Spiders From Mars 1973 performance (1983), Group Madness (1983), Into The Night (1985), Absolute Beginners (1986), Labyrinth (1986), The Last Temptation Of Christ (1988), The Linguini Incident (1991), Twin Peaks: Fire Walk With Me (1992), Travelling Light (1992), Basquiat aka Build A Fort, Set It On Fire (1996), Inspirations (1997), Il Mio West aka My West (1998), Everybody Loves Sunshine (1999), Mr. Rice's Secret (2000), Mayor Of Sunset Strip (2001).

BOX TOPS
ALBUMS: The Letter/Neon Rainbow (Bell 1967)★★★, Cry Like A Baby (Bell 1968)★★★, Non Stop (Bell 1968)★★★, Dimensions (Bell 1969)★★.
COMPILATIONS: The Box Tops Super Hits (Bell 1968)★★★, Greatest Hits (Rhino 1982)★★★, Ultimate Box Tops (Warners 1988)★★★, Soul Deep: The Best Of The Box Tops (Arista 1998)★★★★.

BOY GEORGE
ALBUMS: Sold (Virgin 1987)★★★, Tense Nervous Headache (Virgin 1988)★★, Boyfriend (Virgin 1989)★★, High Hat (US) (Virgin 1989)★★, Cheapness And Beauty (Virgin 1995)★★★, The Unrecoupable One Man Bandit (Back Door/Nu Gruv 1999)★★★.
COMPILATIONS: as Jesus Loves You The Martyr Mantras (More Protein/Virgin 1991)★★★, At Worst ... The Best Of Boy George And Culture Club (Virgin 1993)★★★★, as Jesus Loves You The Devil In Sister George (More Protein/Virgin 1994)★★, The Annual - Pete Tong & Boy George (MOS 1995)★★★, Dance Nation 2 - Pete Tong & Boy George (MOS 1996)★★★, The Annual II - Pete Tong & Boy George (MOS 1996)★★★★, Dance Nation 4 - Pete Tong & Boy George (MOS 1997)★★★★, Dance Nation 5 - Pete Tong & Boy George (MOS 1998)★★★, The Annual IV - Pete Tong & Boy George (MOS 1998)★★★★, Essential Mix (London/Sire 2001)★★★★, BoyGeorgeDj.com (Trust The DJ 2001)★★★★, Lucky For Some (J-Bird 2001)★★★, Classic Masters (EMD 2002)★★★.
FURTHER READING: Take It Like A Man, Boy George.

BOYZ II MEN
ALBUMS: Cooleyhighharmony (Motown 1991)★★★, II (Motown 1994)★★★★, Remix, Remake, Remember (Motown 1996)★★★★, Evolution (Motown 1997)★★★, Nathan Michael Shawn Wanya (Motown 2000)★★★.
COMPILATIONS: Legacy: The Greatest Hits Collection (Motown 2001)★★★★.
VIDEOS: Then II Now (Motown Video 1994), Music In High Places (Aviva International 2001).

BOYZONE
ALBUMS: Said And Done (Polydor 1995)★★★, A Different Beat (Polydor 1996)★★★, Where We Belong (Polydor 1998)★★.
COMPILATIONS: By Request (Polydor 1999)★★★.
VIDEOS: Said And Done (VVL 1995), Live At Wembley (Vision Video 1996), Live: Where We Belong (VVL 1998), By Request: Their Greatest Hits (Vision Video 1999), Dublin: Live By Request (Vision Video 1999), 2000 Live From The Point (VVL 2000).
FURTHER READING: Boyzone: All Talk, Anne Marcus. Ronan Keating, Courtney Myers. Boyzone ... By Request, B.P. Fallon. Boyzone: In Their Own Words, Keiran Reilly. Ronan Keating: Life Is A Rollercoaster, Ronan Keating and Eddie Rowley.

BRADY, PAUL
ALBUMS: with Andy Irvine Andy Irvine/Paul Brady (Mulligan 1976)★★★★, with Tommy Peoples The High Part Of The Road (Shanachie 1976)★★★, Welcome Here Kind Stranger (Mulligan 1978)★★★, Hard Station (Polydor 1981)★★★, True For You (Polydor 1983)★★★, Full Moon (Demon 1984) ★★★★, Back To The Centre (Mercury 1985)★★★, with Peoples, Matt Molloy Molloy, Brady, Peoples (Mulligan 1986) ★★★, Primitive Dance (Mercury 1987)★★★★, Trick Or Treat (Fontana 1990)★★★, Songs And Crazy Dreams (Fontana 1992)★★★, Spirits Colliding (Fontana 1995)★★★★, Oh What A World (Rykodisc 2000)★★★.
COMPILATIONS: Nobody Knows: The Best Of Paul Brady (Rykodisc 1999)★★★★, The Liberty Tapes (Compass 2002)★★★.
VIDEOS: Echoes And Extracts (Fontana 1991).

BRAGG, BILLY
ALBUMS: Life's A Riot With Spy Vs Spy (Utility 1983)★★★, Brewing Up With Billy Bragg (Go! Discs 1984)★★★★, Talking With The Taxman About Poetry (Go! Discs 1986) ★★★★, Workers Playtime (Go! Discs 1988)★★★, Help Save The Youth Of America - Live And Dubious US/Canada release (Go! Discs 1988)★★★, The Internationale (Utility 1990)★★★, Don't Try This At Home (Go! Discs 1991) ★★★★, William Bloke (Cooking Vinyl 1996)★★★★, with Wilco Mermaid Avenue (East West 1998)★★★★, with Wilco Mermaid Avenue Vol II (East West 2000)★★★, England, Half English (Cooking Vinyl/Elektra 2002)★★★.
COMPILATIONS: Back To Basics a repackage of the first two albums (Go! Discs 1987)★★★, The Peel Sessions Album 1983-1988 recordings (Strange Fruit 1992)★★★, Reaching To The Converted (Minding The Gaps) (Cooking Vinyl 1999)★★★.
VIDEOS: Billy Bragg Goes To Moscow And Norton, Virginia Too (ReVision 1990), with Wilco Man In The Sand (Union Productions 1999).
FURTHER READING: Midnight In Moscow, Chris Salewicz. Still Suitable For Miners: Billy Bragg - The Official Biography, Andrew Collins.

BRAN VAN 3000
ALBUMS: Glee (Audioworks/Capitol 1997)★★★, Discosis (Grand Royal/Virgin 2001)★★★.

BRAND NEW HEAVIES
ALBUMS: The Brand New Heavies (Acid Jazz 1990)★★★, The Brand New Heavies re-recorded version (PolyGram 1992)★★★, Heavy Rhyme Experience: Vol. 1 (ffrr 1992) ★★★★, Brother Sister (ffrr 1994)★★★, Shelter (London 1997)★★★.
COMPILATIONS: Original Flava (Acid Jazz 1994)★★, Excursions: Remixes & Rare Grooves (Delicious Vinyl 1995)★★, Dream Come True: The Best Of The Acid Jazz Years (Music Club 1998)★★★, Trunk Funk: The Best Of The Brand New Heavies (ffrr 1999)★★★, Put The Funk Back In It: Best Of The Acid Jazz Years (Snapper 2001)★★★, The Acid Jazz Years (Metro 2001)★★★.

BRANDY
ALBUMS: Brandy (Atlantic 1994)★★★, Never S-A-Y Never (Atlantic 1998)★★, Full Moon (Atlantic 2002)★★★.
VIDEOS: The Videos (Warner Vision 2000).
FURTHER READING: Brandy ... An Intimate Look, Karu F. Daniels.
FILMS: I Still Know What You Did Last Summer (1999).

BRAXTON, TONI
ALBUMS: Toni Braxton (LaFace/Arista 1993)★★★, Secrets (LaFace/Arista 1996)★★★, The Heat (LaFace/Arista 2000) ★★★★, Snowflakes (LaFace/Arista 2001)★★.
VIDEOS: The Home Video (Arista 1994), From Toni With Love: The Video Collection (BMG Video 2001).
FILMS: Kingdom Come (2001).

BREAD
ALBUMS: Bread (Elektra 1969)★★, On The Waters (Elektra 1970)★★, Manna (Elektra 1971)★★★, Baby I'm-A Want You (Elektra 1972)★★★, Guitar Man (Elektra 1972)★★★★, Lost Without Your Love (Elektra 1977)★★★.
COMPILATIONS: The Best Of Bread (Elektra 1972)★★★★, The Best Of Bread, Vol. II (Elektra 1974)★★, The Sound Of Bread (Elektra 1977)★★, Anthology (Elektra 1985)★★★★, The Very Best Of Bread (Pickwick 1988)★★★, Retrospective (Rhino 1996)★★★★.

BREEDERS
ALBUMS: Pod (4AD 1990)★★★, Last Splash (4AD 1993) ★★★, Live In Stockholm (Breeders' Digest 1995)★★★.

BREL, JACQUES
ALBUMS: Jacques Brel i (Philips 1954)★★★, Jacques Brel ii (Philips 1957)★★★★, Jacques Brel iii (Philips 1958)★★★★, Jacques Brel iv (Philips 1959)★★★★, Jacques Brel v (Philips 1961)★★★★, Jacques Brel vi (Philips 1962)★★★★, Jacques Brel vii (Barclay 1962)★★★, Jacques Brel viii (Barclay 1963) ★★★, Jacques Brel ix (Barclay 1964)★★★★, Olympia 64 (Barclay 1964)★★★, Jacques Brel x (Barclay 1965)★★★, Jacques Brel xi (Barclay 1967)★★★, Jacques Brel xii (Barclay 1967)★★★, Jacques Brel xiii (Barclay 1968)★★★★, L'Homme De La Mancha (Barclay 1968)★★★, L'Histoire De Babar/Pierre Et Le Loup (Barclay 1969)★★★, Jacques Brel xiv (Barclay 1972)★★★★, Brel (Barclay 1977)★★★.
COMPILATIONS: American Debut (CBS 1957)★★★★, The Complete Works Of Jacques Brel 15-CD box set (Barclay 1988)★★★★, Greatest Hits (PolyGram 1993)★★★★, various artists Ne Me Quitte Pas: Brel Songs (Irregular 1998)★★★.
FURTHER READING: Jacques Brel: The Biography, Alan Clayson.
FILMS: La Grande Peur De Monsieur Clément (1956), Les Risques Du Métier aka Risky Business (1967), Mon Oncle Benjamin aka The Adventures Of Uncle Benjamin (1969), La Bande À Bonnot (1969), Les Assassins De L'Ordre aka Law Breakers (1971), Mont-Dragon (1971), Franz (1971), L'Aventure, C'est L'Aventure (1972), La Bar De La Fourche (1972), Far West (1973), L'Emmerdeur (1973), Jacques Brel Is Alive And Well And Living In Paris (1975).

BRICKELL, EDIE
ALBUMS: Picture Perfect Morning (Geffen 1994)★★.

BRINSLEY SCHWARZ
ALBUMS: Brinsley Schwarz (United Artists 1970)★★★, Despite It All (United Artists 1970)★★★, Silver Pistol (United Artists 1972)★★★★, Nervous On The Road (United Artists 1972)★★★, Please Don't Ever Change (United Artists 1973)★★★, The New Favourites Of Brinsley Schwarz (United Artists 1974)★★★★.
COMPILATIONS: Original Golden Greats (United Artists 1974)★★★★, The Fifteen Thoughts Of Brinsley Schwarz (United Artists 1978)★★★★, Hen's Teeth (Edsel 1998)★★★, What Is So Funny About Peace, Love And Understanding? (Hux 2001)★★★.

BRONSKI BEAT
ALBUMS: The Age Of Consent (Forbidden Fruit/London 1984)★★★, Hundreds And Thousands remix album (Forbidden Fruit/London 1985)★★★, TruthDareDoubleDare (Forbidden Fruit/London 1986)★★, Rainbow Nation (ZYX 1995)★★★.
COMPILATIONS: The Very Best Of Jimmy Somerville, Bronski Beat And The Communards (Warners 2001)★★★.
VIDEOS: The First Chapter (Channel 5 1986).

BROOKS, ELKIE
ALBUMS: Rich Man's Woman (A&M 1975)★★★, Two Days Away (A&M 1977)★★★, Shooting Star (A&M 1978)★★★, Live And Learn (A&M 1979)★★★, Pearls (A&M 1981)★★★, Pearls II (A&M 1982)★★, Minutes (A&M 1984)★★, Screen Gems (EMI 1984)★★★, No More The Fool (Legend 1986) ★★, Bookbinder's Kid (Legend 1988)★★★, Inspiration (Telstar 1989)★★, Pearls III - Close To The Edge (Freestyle 1991)★★, 'Round Midnight (Castle 1993)★★, Nothing But The Blues (Castle 1994)★★★, Circles (Permanent 1995)★★, Amazing (Carlton 1996)★★★, Unfinished Business (BMG 2000)★★★.
COMPILATIONS: The Very Best Of Elkie Brooks (A&M 1986)★★★, Elkie Brooks: The Collection (Castle 1987) ★★★, The Early Years 1964-66 (C5 1987)★★, Priceless: Her Very Best (Pickwick 1991)★★★, We've Got Tonight (Spectrum 1994)★★★, The Pearls Concert (Artful 1997) ★★★, The Best Of Elkie Brooks (Spectrum 1998)★★★, Hold The Dream: Elkie Brooks Anthology (Sanctuary 2000)★★★.
VIDEOS: Pearls - The Video Show (A&M Sound Pictures 1982), We've Got Tonight (Video Collection 1987).

BROOKS, GARTH
ALBUMS: Garth Brooks (Liberty 1989)★★★★, No Fences (Liberty 1990)★★★★, Ropin' The Wind (Liberty 1991) ★★★★, The Chase (Liberty 1992)★★★★, Beyond The Season (Liberty 1992)★★, In Pieces (Liberty 1993)★★★★, Fresh Horses (Capitol Nashville 1995)★★★, Sevens (Capitol Nashville 1997)★★★, Double Live (Capitol 1998)★★★, Garth Brooks In ... The Life Of Chris Gaines (Capitol 1999) ★★★, Garth Brooks & The Magic Of Christmas (Capitol 1999)★★, Scarecrow (Capitol 2001)★★★.
COMPILATIONS: The Hits (Liberty 1994)★★★★, The Limited Series 6-CD box set (Capitol 1998)★★★.
VIDEOS: Garth Brooks (Liberty 1991), This Is Garth Brooks (Liberty 1992), The Video Collection Volume II (Capitol 1996), Garth Live From Central Park (Orion Home Video 1998).
FURTHER READING: Garth Brooks: Platinum Cowboy, Edward Morris. One Of A Kind, Workin' On A Full House, Rick Mitchell. The Road Out Of Santa Fe, Matt O'Meilia. American Thunder: The Garth Brooks Story, Jo Sgammato.

BROS
ALBUMS: Push (Columbia 1988)★★★, The Time (Columbia 1989)★★, Changing Faces (Columbia 1991)★★.
VIDEOS: Live: The Big Push Tour (CMV Enterprises 1988), Push Over (CMV Enterprises 1989).
FURTHER READING: I Owe You Nothing: My Story, Luke Goss.

BROTHERHOOD OF MAN
ALBUMS: United We Stand (Deram 1970)★★, We're The Brotherhood Of Man (Deram 1971)★★, The World Of The Brotherhood Of Man (Deram 1973)★★, Good Things Happening (Dawn 1974)★★, Love & Kisses From Brotherhood Of Man (Pye 1975)★★, B For Brotherhood (Pye 1978)★★, Singing A Song (PRT 1979)★★, Sing 20 Number One Hits (Warwick 1980)★★, Lightning Flash (Epic 1983)★★.
COMPILATIONS: The Best Of The Brotherhood Of Man (Spot 1983)★★, 20 Great Hits (Prestige 1992)★★, Golden Classics (Collectables 1994)★★.

BROUGHTON, EDGAR, BAND
ALBUMS: Wasa Wasa (Harvest 1969)★★★★, Sing Brother Sing (Harvest 1970)★★★, Edgar Broughton Band (Harvest 1971)★★★, In Side Out (Harvest 1972)★★, Oora (Harvest 1973)★★, Bandages (NEMS 1975)★★, as the Broughtons Parlez-Vous English (Infinity 1979)★★, Live Hits Harder (BB 1979)★★, Supership (Sheet 1982)★★.
COMPILATIONS: A Bunch Of 45s (Harvest 1975)★★, As Was (EMI 1988)★★, Document Series Presents ... Classic Album & Single Tracks 1969-1973 (Ace 1992)★★★, Demons At The Beeb (Hux 2000)★★★, Out Demons Out (EMI 2001)★★★.

BROWN, ARTHUR
ALBUMS: The Crazy World Of Arthur Brown (Track 1968) ★★★, Dance (Gull 1974)H, Chisholm In My Bosom (Gull 1978)H, with Vincent Crane Faster Than The Speed Of Light (Warners 1980)★★, Requiem (Remote 1982)★★, Strangelands (Reckless 1988)★★, with Jimmy Carl Black Brown, Black & Blue (Voiceprint 1991)★★★, Order From Chaos – Live 1993 (Voiceprint 1994)★★★.
FILMS: Tommy (1975), Club Paradise (1986).

BROWN, BOBBY
ALBUMS: King Of Stage (MCA 1986)★★, Don't Be Cruel (MCA 1988)★★★★, Dance! ... Ya Know It! (MCA 1989) ★★★★, Bobby (MCA 1992)★★★, Forever (MCA 1997) ★★★.
COMPILATIONS: Greatest Hits (MCA 2000)★★★★.
VIDEOS: His Prerogative (MCA 1989).
FILMS: Gojira aka Godzilla (1984), Ghostbusters II (1989), Knights (1993), Nemseis 2: Nebula (1995), Nemesis III: Prey Harder (1995), Panther (1995), A Thin Line Between Love And Hate (1996), Pecker (1998).

BROWN, FOXY
ALBUMS: Ill Na Na (Def Jam 1996)★★★★, Chyna Doll (Def Jam 1998)★★★★, Broken Silence (Def Jam 2001)★★★★.
FILMS: Woo (1998).

BROWN, IAN
ALBUMS: Unfinished Monkey Business (Polydor 1998) ★★★, Golden Greats (Polydor/Interscope 1999)★★★, Music Of The Spheres (Polydor 2001)★★★★.
COMPILATIONS: Planet Groove: The Ian Brown Session (Beechwood 2001)★★★★.

BROWN, JAMES
ALBUMS: Please Please Please (King 1959)★★★, Try Me (King 1959)★★, Think (King 1960)★★★, The Amazing James Brown (King 1961)★★★, James Brown Presents His Band/Night Train (King 1961)★★★, Shout And Shimmy (King 1962)★★★, James Brown And His Famous Flames Tour The USA (King 1962)★★, Excitement Mr Dynamite (King 1962)★★★, Live At The Apollo (King 1963) ★★★★★, Prisoner Of Love (King 1963)★★★, Pure Dynamite! Live At The Royal (King 1964)★★★, Showtime (Smash 1964)★★, The Unbeatable James Brown (King 1964)★★★, Grits And Soul (Smash 1964)★★, Out Of Sight (Smash 1964)★★★, Papa's Got A Brand New Bag (King 1965)★★★, James Brown Plays James Brown Today And Yesterday (Smash 1965)★★, I Got You (I Feel Good) (King 1966)★★★, Mighty Instrumentals (King 1966)★★, James Brown Plays New Breed (The Boo-Ga-Loo) (Smash 1966)★★, Soul Brother No. 1: It's A Man's Man's Man's World (King 1966)★★★, James Brown Sings Christmas Songs (King 1966)★★, Handful Of Soul (Smash 1966)★★, The James Brown Show (Smash 1967)★★, Sings Raw Soul (King 1967)★★★, James Brown Plays The Real Thing (Smash 1967)★★★, Live At The Garden (King 1967)★★, Cold Sweat (King 1967)★★★, James Brown Presents His Show Of Tomorrow (King 1968)★★★, I Can't Stand Myself (When You Touch Me) (King 1968)★★, I Got The Feelin' (King 1968)★★★, Live At The Apollo, Volume 2 (King 1968)★★★★, James Brown Sings Out Of Sight (King 1968)★★★, Thinking About Little Willie John And A Few Nice Things (King 1968)★★★, A Soulful Christmas (King 1968)★★, Say It Loud, I'm Black And I'm Proud (King 1969)★★★★, Gettin' Down To It (King 1969)★★★, The Popcorn (King 1969)★★★, It's A Mother (King 1969)★★★, Ain't It Funky (King 1970)★★★, Soul On Top (King 1970)★★★, It's A New Day - Let A Man Come In (King 1970)★★★, Sex Machine (King 1970)★★★, Hey America (King 1970)★★★, Super Bad (King 1971)★★, Sho' Is Funky Down Here (King 1971)★★, Hot Pants (Polydor 1971)★★, Revolution Of The Mind/Live At The Apollo, Volume 3 (Polydor 1971)★★★, There It Is (Polydor 1972)★★★, Get On The Good Foot (Polydor 1972)★★★, Black Caesar film soundtrack (Polydor 1973)★★★, Slaughter's Big Rip-Off film soundtrack (Polydor 1973)H, The Payback (Polydor 1974)★★★★, Hell (Polydor 1974)★★★, Reality (Polydor 1975)★★★, Sex Machine Today (Polydor 1975)★★★, Everybody's Doin' The Hustle And Dead On The Double Bump (Polydor 1975)★★, Hot (Polydor 1976)★★★, Get Up Offa That Thing (Polydor 1976)★★, Bodyheat (Polydor 1976)★★, Mutha's Nature (Polydor 1977)★★★, Jam/1980's (Polydor 1978)★★★, Take A Look At Those Cakes (Polydor 1979)★★★, The Original Disco Man (Polydor 1979)★★★, People (Polydor 1980)★★★, James Brown ... Live/Hot On The One (Polydor 1980)★★, Soul Syndrome (TK 1980)★★★★, Nonstop! (Polydor 1981)★★★, Live In New York (Audio Fidelity 1981)★★★, Bring It On (Churchill 1983)★★★, Gravity (Scotti Bros 1986)★★★, James Brown And Friends (Scotti Bros 1988)★★★, I'm Real (Scotti Bros 1988)★★★, Soul Session Live (Scotti Bros 1989)★★★★, Love Overdue (Scotti Bros 1991)★★★, Universal James (Scotti Bros 1993)★★, Live At The Apollo 1995 (Scotti Bros 1995) ★★★, I'm Back (Private I 1998)★★.
COMPILATIONS: James Brown Soul Classics (Polydor 1973) ★★★, Soul Classics, Volume 2 (Polydor 1974)★★★, Soul Classics, Volume 3 (Polydor 1975)★★★, Solid Gold (Polydor 1977)★★★, The Fabulous James Brown (HRB 1977)★★★, Can Your Heart Stand It? (Solid Smoke 1981) ★★★, The Best Of James Brown (Polydor 1981)★★★★, The Federal Years, Part 1 (Solid Smoke 1984)★★★★, The Federal Years, Part 2 (Solid Smoke 1984)★★★, Roots Of A Revolution (Polydor 1984)★★★, Ain't That A Groove: The James Brown Story 1966-1969 (Polydor 1984)★★★, Doing It To Death: The James Brown Story 1970-1973 (Polydor 1984)★★★, Dead On The Heavy Funk: The James Brown Story 1974-1976 (Polydor 1985)★★★, The CD Of JB: Sex Machine And Other Soul Classics (Polydor 1985) ★★★★, James Brown's Funky People (Polydor 1986) ★★★★, In The Jungle Groove (Polydor 1986)★★★, The CD Of JB II: Cold Sweat And Other Soul Classics (Polydor 1987)★★★★, James Brown's Funky People (Part 2) (Polydor 1988)★★★, Motherlode (Polydor 1988) ★★★, Messing With The Blues (Polydor 1990)★★★, 20 All-Time Greatest Hits! (Polydor 1991)★★★★, Star Time 4-CD box set (Polydor 1991)★★★★★, Sex Machine (The Very Best Of James Brown, Volume 1) (Polydor 1991)★★★★, The Greatest Hits Of The Fourth Decade (Scotti Brothers 1992) ★★★, Soul Pride (The Instrumentals 1960-1969) (Polydor 1993)★★★, Funky President (The Very Best Of James Brown, Volume 2) (Polydor 1993)★★★, 40th Anniversary Collection (Polydor 1996)★★★★, Foundations Of Funk (A Brand New Bag: 1964-1969) (Polydor 1997)★★★★★, On Stage (Charly 1997)★★★, Dead On The Heavy Funk: 1975-1983 (Polydor 1998)★★★★, James Brown's Original Funky Divas (Polydor 1998)★★★, the JBs The JBs Funky Good Time: The Anthology (Polydor 1998)★★★, Out Of Sight! The Very Best Of James Brown (Polydor 2002)★★★★.
VIDEOS: Video Biography (Virgin Vision 1988), Live In London: James Brown (Virgin Vision 1988), James Brown And Friends (Video Collection 1988), Live In Berlin (Channel 5 1989), Soul Jubilee (MMG Video 1990), Live On Stage (With Special Guest B.B. King) (Old Gold 1990), Sex Machine (The Very Best Of James Brown) (PolyGram Music Video 1991), The Lost Years (Live In Santa Cruz) (BMG Video 1991), Live In New York (Enteleky 1991), James Brown Live (MIA 1995). Live From The House Of Blues (Aviva 2001).
FURTHER READING: James Brown: The Godfather Of Soul, James Brown with Bruce Tucker. Living In America: The Soul Saga Of James Brown, Cynthia Rose. James Brown: A Biography, Geoff Brown.
FILMS: The Blues Brothers (1980).

BROWN, JOE
ALBUMS: *A Picture Of You* (Pye Golden Guinea 1962) ★★★, *Joe Brown Live* (Piccadilly 1963)★★★, *Here Comes Joe!* (Pye 1967)★★, *Joe Brown* (MCA 1968)★★★, *Browns Home Brew* (Vertigo 1972)★★★, *Together* (Vertigo 1974) ★★★, *Joe Brown Live* (Power 1977)★★★, *Come On Joe* (Power 1993)★★★, *Fifty Six & Taller Than You Think* (Demon 1997)★★★, *On A Day Like This* (Round Tower 1999)★★★★.
COMPILATIONS: *Joe Brown Collection* (Pye 1974)★★★, *Hits 'N' Pieces* (PRT 1988)★★, *The Joe Brown Story* (Sequel 1993)★★★★.
VIDEOS: *Joe Brown In Concert* (1994).
FURTHER READING: *Brown Sauce: The Life And Times Of Joe Brown*, Joe Brown.
FILMS: *What A Crazy World* (1963), *Three Hats For Lisa* (1965), *Hostile Guns* (1967), *Lionheart* (1968), *Mona Lisa* (1986).

BROWNE, JACKSON
ALBUMS: *Jackson Browne* aka *Saturate Before Using* (Asylum 1972)★★★★, *For Everyman* (Asylum 1973) ★★★★, *Late For The Sky* (Asylum 1974)★★★★, *The Pretender* (Asylum 1976)★★★★, *Running On Empty* (Asylum 1977)★★★, *Hold Out* (Asylum 1980)★★, *Lawyers In Love* (Asylum 1983)★★★, *Lives In The Balance* (Asylum 1986)★★, *Worlds In Motion* (Elektra 1989)★★, *I'm Alive* (Elektra 1994)★★★★, *Looking East* (Elektra 1996)★★.
COMPILATIONS: *The Best Of Jackson Browne* (East West 1997)★★★★.

BRUCE, JACK
ALBUMS: *Songs For A Tailor* (Polydor 1969)★★★★★, *Things We Like* (Polydor 1970)★★★, *Harmony Row* (Polydor 1971)★★★★, *Out Of The Storm* (Polydor 1974) ★★★★, *How's Tricks* (RSO 1977)★★★, *I've Always Wanted To Do This* (Epic 1980)★★★, with Robin Trower *Truce* (Chrysalis 1982)★★, *Automatic* (President 1987)★★, *A Question Of Time* (Epic 1989)★★★★, And Friends *Live At The Bottom Line* (Traditional Line 1992)★★★, *Somethin Els* (CMP 1993)★★★, *Cities Of the Heart* (CMP 1994) ★★★★, with Paul Jones *Alexis Korner Memorial Concert Volume 1* (Indigo 1995)★★★, *Live On The Old Grey Whistle Test* (Strange Fruit 1998)★★★★, *Shadows In The Air* (Sanctuary 2001)★★★★, *Doing This ... On Ice!* (Burning Airlines 2001)★★★.
COMPILATIONS: *Jack Bruce At His Best* (Polydor 1972) ★★★, *Greatest Hits* (Polydor 1980)★★★, *Willpower* (Polydor 1989)★★★★, *The Collection* (Castle 1992)★★★.

BRUFORD, BILL
ALBUMS: with Bruford *Feels Good To Me* (EG 1977)★★★, with Bruford *One Of A Kind* (EG 1978)★★, with Bruford *The Bruford Tapes* (EG 1979)★★★★, with Bruford *Gradually Going Tornado* (EG 1980)★★★, with Patrick Moraz *Music For Piano And Drums* (Editions EG 1983) ★★★, with Patrick Moraz *Flag* (EG 1985)★★★, with Earthworks *Earthworks* (EG 1987)★★★★, with Earthworks *Dig?* (Editions EG 1989)★★★, with Earthworks *All Heaven Broke Loose* (Editions EG 1991)★★★, with Earthworks *Stamping Ground* (Virgin 1994)★★, with Ralph Towner, Eddie Gomez *If Summer Had Its Ghosts* (Discipline 1997) ★★, with Tony Levin *Upper Extremities* (Papa Bear 1998) ★★★, with Earthworks *A Part, And Yet Apart* (Discipline 1999)★★★, with Earthworks *The Sound Of Surprise* (Discipline 2001)★★★★.
COMPILATIONS: *Master Strokes 1978-1985* (EG 1986)★★★, with Earthworks *Heavenly Bodies* (Virgin 1997)★★★.
VIDEOS: *Bruford & The Beat* (1982).
FURTHER READING: *When In Doubt, Roll!*, Bill Bruford.

BRYANT, BOUDLEAUX
ALBUMS: *Boudleaux Bryant's Best Sellers* (Monument 1963) ★★★, with Felice Bryant *All I Have To Do Is Dream* aka *A Touch Of Bryant* (CMH 1979)★★.

BRYANT, FELICE
ALBUMS: with Boudleaux Bryant *All I Have To Do Is Dream* aka *A Touch Of Bryant* (CMH 1979)★★.

BRYSON, PEABO
ALBUMS: *Reaching For The Sky* (Capitol 1978)★★★, *Crosswinds* (Capitol 1978)★★★, with Natalie Cole *We're The Best Of Friends* (Capitol 1979)★★★, *Paradise* (Capitol 1980)★★★, with Roberta Flack *Live And More* (Atlantic 1980)★★★, *Turn The Hands Of Time* (Capitol 1981)★★★, *I Am Love* (Capitol 1981)★★★, *Don't Play With Fire* (Capitol 1982)★★★, with Roberta Flack *Born To Love* (Capitol 1983) ★★★, *Straight From The Heart* (Elektra 1984)★★★, *Take No Prisoners* (Elektra 1985)★★★, *Quiet Storm* (Elektra 1986)★★★, *Positive* (Elektra 1988)★★★, *Can You Stop The Rain* (Columbia 1991)★★★, *Unconditional Love* (Private Music 1999)★★★.
COMPILATIONS: *The Peabo Bryson Collection* (Capitol 1984)★★★★, *I'm So Into You: The Passion Of Peabo Bryson* (EMI 1997)★★★★, *Anthology* (The Right Stuff 2001)★★★★.

BUCKCHERRY
ALBUMS: *Buckcherry* (DreamWorks 1999)★★★, *Timebomb* (DreamWorks 2001)★★★.

BUCKINGHAM, LINDSEY
ALBUMS: *Law And Order* (Asylum 1981)★★★, *Go Insane* (Elektra 1984)★★, *Out Of The Cradle* (Reprise 1992)★★.

BUCKINGHAMS
ALBUMS: *Kind Of A Drag* (USA 1967)★★★, *Time And Changes* (Columbia 1967)★★★, *Portraits* (Columbia 1968)★★★, *In One Ear And Gone Tomorrow* (Columbia 1968)★★, *Made In Chicago* (Columbia 1969)★★★, *Terra Firma* (Nation 1998)★★.
COMPILATIONS: *The Buckinghams' Greatest Hits* (Columbia 1969)★★★, *Mercy Mercy Mercy: A Collection* (Columbia 1991)★★★.

BUCKLEY, JEFF
ALBUMS: *Live At Sin-é* mini-album (Big Cat 1992)★★★, *Grace* (Sony 1994)★★★★, *Live From The Bataclan* mini-album (Columbia 1996)★★★, *Sketches (For My Sweetheart The Drunk)* (Columbia 1998)★★★, *Mystery White Boy: Live '95-'96* (Columbia 2000)★★★, *Live A L'Olympia* (Columbia 2001)★★★.
VIDEOS: *Live In Chicago* (SMV Enterprises 2000).
FURTHER READING: *Dream Brother: The Lives & Music Of Jeff And Tim Buckley*, David Browne.

BUCKLEY, TIM
ALBUMS: *Tim Buckley* (Elektra 1966)★★★, *Goodbye And Hello* (Elektra 1967)★★★, *Happy Sad* (Elektra 1968) ★★★★, *Blue Afternoon* (Straight 1969)★★★★, *Lorca* (Elektra 1970)★★★, *Starsailor* (Straight 1970)★★★, *Greetings From L.A.* (Warners 1972)★★★, *Sefronia* (DiscReet 1974)★★, *Look At The Fool* (DiscReet 1974)★★, *Dream Letter (Live In London 1968)* (Demon 1990)★★★★, *The Peel Sessions* (Strange Fruit 1991)★★★, *Live At The Troubadour 1969* (Edsel 1994)★★★, *Honeyman* 1973 live recording (Edsel 1995)★★★, *Once I Was* (Strange Fruit 1999)★★★, *Works In Progress* 1968 recordings (Rhino 1999)★★★, *The Copenhagen Tapes* 1968 recordings (PLR 2000)★★★.
COMPILATIONS: *The Best Of Tim Buckley* (Rhino 1983) ★★★, *Morning Glory: The Tim Buckley Anthology* (Rhino 2001)★★★★, *The Dream Belongs To Me: Rare And Unreleased Recordings 1968/1973* (Manifesto 2001)★★★.
FURTHER READING: *Dream Brother: The Lives & Music Of Jeff And Tim Buckley*, David Browne.

BUFFALO SPRINGFIELD
ALBUMS: *Buffalo Springfield* (Atco 1967)★★★★, *Buffalo Springfield Again* (Atco 1967)★★★★★, *Last Time Around* (Atco 1968)★★★.
COMPILATIONS: *Retrospective* (Atco 1969)★★★★, *Expecting To Fly* (Atlantic 1970)★★★★, *Buffalo Springfield* (Atco 1973)★★★★, *Buffalo Springfield* 4-CD box set (Rhino 2001)★★★★.
FURTHER READING: *Neil Young: Here We Are In The Years*, Johnny Rogan. *Crosby, Stills, Nash & Young: The Visual Documentary*, Johnny Rogan. *Crosby, Stills & Nash: The Biography*, Dave Zimmer and Henry Diltz. *For What It's Worth: The Story Of Buffalo Springfield*, John Einarson and Richie Furay. *Prisoner Of Woodstock*, Dallas Taylor.

BUFFALO TOM
ALBUMS: *Sunflower Suit* (SST 1989)★★★, *Birdbrain* (Situation 2 1990)★★★, *Let Me Come Over* (Situation 2 1992)★★★★, *Big Red Letter Day* (Beggars Banquet 1993)★★★, *Sleepy Eyed* (Beggars Banquet 1995)★★★, *Smitten* (Beggars Banquet 1998)★★★.
SOLO: Bill Janovitz *Lonesome Billy* (Beggars Banquet 1996)★★★.
COMPILATIONS: *Asides From Buffalo Tom: Nineteen: Eighty: Eight To Nineteen: Ninety: Nine* (Beggars Banquet 2000)★★★★.

BUFFETT, JIMMY
ALBUMS: *Down To Earth* (Barnaby 1970)★★, *A White Sport Coat And A Pink Crustacean* (ABC 1973)★★★, *Living And Dying In 3/4 Time* (ABC 1974)★★, *A1A* (ABC 1974)★★★, *Rancho DeLuxe* film soundtrack (United Artists 1975)★★★, *Havana Daydreaming* (ABC 1976)★★★, *High Cumberland Jubilee* 1972 recording (Barnaby 1976)★★★, *Changes In Latitudes, Changes In Attitudes* (ABC 1977) ★★★, *Son Of A Son Of A Sailor* (ABC 1978)★★★, *You Had To Be There* (ABC 1978)★★★, *Volcano* (MCA 1979)★★★, *Coconut Telegraph* (MCA 1981)★★, *Somewhere Over China* (MCA 1982)★★, *Fast Times At Ridgemont High* (Full Moon/Asylum 1982)★★, *One Particular Harbour* (MCA 1983)★★, *Riddles In The Sand* (MCA 1984)★★, *Last Mango In Paris* (MCA 1985)★★, *Floridays* (MCA 1986)★★, *Hot Water* (MCA 1988)★★, *Off To See The Lizard* (MCA 1989)★★, *Always* film soundtrack (MCA 1990)★★, *Live Feeding Frenzy* (MCA 1990)★★, *Fruitcakes* (MCA 1994)★★★★, *Barometer Soup* (Margaritaville 1995)★★★★, *Banana Wind* (Margaritaville 1996)★★★★, *Christmas Island* (Margaritaville 1996)★★★, *Carnival* (Island 1998)★★, *Beach House On The Moon* (Margaritaville 1999)★★★, *Buffett Live: Tuesdays, Thursdays, Saturdays* (Mailboat 1999)★★★, *Far Side Of The World* (Mailboat 2002)★★★.
COMPILATIONS: *Songs You Know By Heart – Greatest Hits* box set (MCA 1985)★★★★, *Boats Beaches, Bars And Ballads* 4-CD box set (MCA 1992)★★★★, *Before The Beach* reissue of Barnaby material (Margaritaville/MCA 1993)★★, *All The Great Hits* (Prism Leisure 1994)★★★.
FURTHER READING: *The Jimmy Buffett Scrapbook*, Mark Humphrey with Harris Lewine. *The Man From Margaritaville Revisited*, Steve Eng. *A Pirate Looks At 50*, Jimmy Buffett.

BUGGLES
ALBUMS: *The Age Of Plastic* (Island 1980)★★★.

BURDON, ERIC
ALBUMS: as Eric Burdon And War *Eric Burdon Declares War* (Polydor 1970)★★★, as Eric Burdon And War *Black Man's Burdon* (Liberty 1971)★★★, with Jimmy Witherspoon *Guilty!* (United Artists 1971)★★★, *Ring Of Fire* (Capitol 1974)★★★, *Sun Secrets* (Capitol 1975)★★, *Stop* (Capitol 1975)★★, *Survivor* (Polydor 1978)★★, *Darkness – Darkness* (Polydor 1980)★★, as Eric Burdon's Fire Department *The Last Drive* (Ariola 1980)★★, *Comeback* (Line 1982)★★ reissued as *The Road* (Thunderbolt 1984), as The Eric Burdon Band *Comeback* new songs from 1982 session (Blackline 1983)★★, *Power Company* aka *Devil's Daughter* new songs from 1982 session (Carrere 1983)★★, as The Eric Burdon Band *That's Live* (In-Akustik 1985)★★, *I Used To Be An Animal* (Striped Horse 1988)★★, *Wicked Man* reissue of *Comeback/Power Company* material (GNP Crescendo 1988)★★, *The Unreleased Eric Burdon* (Blue Wave 1992)★★, *Crawling King Snake* (Thunderbolt 1992) ★★, with Brian Auger *Access All Areas* (SPV 1993)★★, *Misunderstood* (Aim 1995)★★, *Live At The Roxy* 1976 recording (Magnum 1997)★★, *F#ck Me!!! I Thought I Was Dead: Greatest Hits Alive* (One Way 1999)★★, *Lost Within The Halls Of Fame* (Mooncrest 2000)★★★.
COMPILATIONS: War featuring Eric Burdon *Love Is All Around* (ABC 1976)★★, *The Touch Of Eric Burdon* (K-Tel 1983)★★, *Star Portrait* (Polydor 1988)★★★, *Sings The Animals Greatest Hits* (Avenue 1994)★★.
VIDEOS: *Finally* (Warners 1992).
FURTHER READING: *Wild Animals*, Andy Blackford. *I Used To Be An Animal But I'm All Right Now*, Eric Burdon. *The Last Poet: The Story Of Eric Burdon*, Jeff Kent. *Good Times: The Ultimate Eric Burdon*, Dionisio Castello. *Animal Tracks: The Story Of The Animals*, Sean Egan. *Don't Let Me Be Misunderstood*, Eric Burdon and J. Marshall Craig.
FILMS: *Pop Gear* aka *Go Go Mania* (1965), *Tonite Let's All Make Love In London* aka *The London Scene* (1967), *Monterey Pop* (1969), *Comeback* (1982), *The Doors* (1991), *Schee In Der Neujahrsnacht* aka *Snow On New Year's Eve* (1999), *Plaster Caster* (2001).

BURKE, SOLOMON
ALBUMS: *Solomon Burke* (Apollo 1962)★★★, *If You Need Me* (Atlantic 1963)★★★, *Rock 'N' Soul* (Atlantic 1964)★★★, *I Wish I Knew* (Atlantic 1968)★★★, *King Solomon* (Atlantic 1968)★★★, *Proud Mary* (Bell 1969)★★★★, *Electronic Magnetism* (Polydor 1972)★★, *King Heavy* (Polydor 1972) ★★, *We're Almost Home* (Polydor 1972)★★, *I Have A Dream* (Dunhill 1974)★★, *Midnight And You* (Dunhill 1975) ★★, *Music To Make Love By* (Chess 1975)★★, *Back To My Roots* (Chess 1977)★★, *Please Don't You Say Goodbye To Me* (Amherst 1978)★★★, *Sidewalks Fences & Walls* (Infinity 1979)★★, *Lord I Need A Miracle Right Now* (Savoy 1981) ★★, *Into My Life You Came* (Savoy 1982)★★, *Take Me, Shake Me* (Savoy 1983)★★, *This Is His Song* (Savoy 1984) ★★, *Soul Alive* (Rounder 1984)★★, *A Change Is Gonna Come* (Rounder 1986)★★★, *Love Trap* (PolyGram 1987)★★★, *Home Land* (Bizarre 1991)★★★, *Soul Of The Blues* (Black Top 1993)★★★, *Live At The House Of Blues* (Black Top 1994)★★★, *Definition Of Soul* (Pointblank/Virgin 1997)★★★.
COMPILATIONS: *Solomon Burke's Greatest Hits* (Atlantic 1962)★★★, *The Best Of Solomon Burke* (Atlantic 1965) ★★★★, *King Of Rock 'N' Soul/From The Heart* (Charly 1981)★★★, *Cry To Me* (Charly 1984)★★★★, *You Can Run But You Can't Hide* (Mr R&B 1987)★★★, *Hold On I'm Coming* (Atlantic 1991)★★★, *Home In Your Heart: The Best Of Solomon Burke* (Rhino 1992)★★★★, *Greatest Hits: If You Need Me* (Sequel 1997)★★★, *The Very Best Of Solomon Burke* (Rhino 1998)★★★★, *King Of Blues 'n' Soul* (Fuel 2001)★★★★.

BURNETT, T-BONE
ALBUMS: as J. Henry Burnett *The B-52 Band & The Fabulous Skylarks* (Uni 1972)★★★, *Truth Decay* (Takoma 1980)★★★, Trap Door *mini-album (Warners 1982)*★★★, Proof Through The Night *(Warners 1983)*★★★★, Behind The Trap Door *mini-album (Demon 1984)*★★★, T-Bone Burnett *(Dot 1986)*★★★, The Talking Animals *(Columbia 1987)*★★★, The Criminal Under My Own Hat *(Columbia 1992)*★★★★.
FILMS: Renaldo And Clara *(1978)*, Heaven's Gate *(1980)*, Bob *(2001)*.

BURNETTE, JOHNNY
ALBUMS: as the Johnny Burnette Trio Johnny Burnette And The Rock 'N' Roll Trio *10-inch album (Coral 1956)*★★★★, Dreamin' *(Liberty 1961)*★★★, You're Sixteen *(Liberty 1961)*★★★, Johnny Burnette *(Liberty 1961)*★★★, Johnny Burnette Sings *(Liberty 1961)*★★★, Burnette's Hits And Other Favourites *(Liberty 1962)*★★★, Roses Are Red *(Liberty 1962)*★★★.
COMPILATIONS: The Johnny Burnette Story *(Liberty 1964)*★★★★, *with the Rock 'n' Roll Trio* Tear It Up *(Solid Smoke/Coral 1968)*★★★, Tenth Anniversary Album *(United Artists 1974)*★★★, We're Having A Party *(Rockstar 1988)*★★★, Rock 'N' Roll Masters: The Best Of Johnny Burnette *(Liberty 1989)*★★★★, You're Sixteen: The Best Of Johnny Burnette *(Capitol 1992)*★★★★, 25 Greatest Hits *(MFP 1998)*★★★, Dreamin': The Very Best Of Johnny Burnette *(Collectables 1999)*★★★.
FILMS: Rock Rock Rock (1956).

BURNING SPEAR
ALBUMS: *Studio One Presents Burning Spear* (Studio One 1973)★★★, *Rocking Time* (Studio One 1974)★★★, *Marcus Garvey* (Mango/Island 1975)★★★★★, *Man In The Hills* (Fox-Wolf/Island 1976)★★★★, *Garvey's Ghost* (Mango/Island 1976)★★★★, *Dry & Heavy* (Mango/Island 1977)★★★★, *Burning Spear Live* (Island 1977)★★, *Marcus Children* aka Social Living *(Burning Spear/One Stop 1978)*★★★★★, Living Dub *(Burning Spear/Heartbeat 1979)*★★★★, Hail H.I.M. *(Burning Spear/EMI 1980)* ★★★★, Living Dub Volume 2 *(Burning Spear 1981)*★★★★, Farover *(Burning Spear/ Heartbeat 1982)*★★★, Fittest Of The Fittest *(Burning Spear/ Heartbeat 1983)*★★★, Resistance *(Heartbeat 1985)*★★★★, People Of The World *(Slash/ Greensleeves 1986)*★★★, Mistress Music *(Slash/ Greensleeves 1988)*★★, Live In Paris: Zenith '88 *(Slash/ Greensleeves 1989)*★★★, Mek We Dweet *(Mango/ Island 1990)*★★★, Jah Kingdom *(Mango/Island 1992)*★★★, The World Should Know *(Mango/Island 1993)*★★★, Rasta Business *(Heartbeat 1996)*★★★, Appointment With His Majesty *(Heartbeat 1997)*★★★, (A)live In Concert '97 *(Musidisc 1998)*★★, Calling Rastafari *(Heartbeat 1999)*★★★.
COMPILATIONS: Reggae Greats *(Island 1985)*★★★★, Selection *(EMI 1987)*★★★★, 100th Anniversary Marcus Garvey and Garvey's Ghost *(Mango/Island 1990)*★★★★, Chant Down Babylon: The Island Anthology *(Island 1996)*★★★★, Harder Than The Rest *(Island 2000)*★★★★, Ultimate Collection *(Hip-O 2001)*★★★★, Spear Burning: Burning Spear Productions 1975-1979 *(Pressure Sounds 2001)*★★★.

BURTON, JAMES
ALBUMS: with Ralph Mooney Corn Pickin' And Slick Slidin' *(Capitol 1966)*★★★, The Guitar Sound Of James Burton *(A&M 1971)*★★★.

BUSH
ALBUMS: Sixteen Stone *(Trauma/Interscope 1994)*★★★★, Razorblade Suitcase *(Trauma/Interscope 1996)*★★★★, *Deconstructed* remixes (Trauma/Interscope 1997)★★★, *The Science Of Things* (Trauma/Interscope 1999)★★★, *Golden State* (Atlantic 2001)★★★★.
VIDEOS: *Alleys And Motorways* (Universal/Interscope 1998).
FURTHER READING: *Twenty-Seventh Letter: The Official History Of Bush*, Jennifer Nine.

BUSH, KATE
ALBUMS: *The Kick Inside* (EMI 1978)★★★★, *Lionheart* (EMI 1978)★★, *Never For Ever* (EMI 1980)★★★, *The Dreaming* (EMI 1982)★★★★, *Hounds Of Love* (EMI 1985)★★★★, *The Sensual World* (EMI 1989)★★★★, *The Red Shoes* (EMI 1993)★★★★.
COMPILATIONS: *The Whole Story* (EMI 1986)★★★, *This Woman's Work* (EMI 1990)★★★★.
VIDEOS: *Live At Hammersmith Odeon* (PMI 1984), *The Whole Story* (PMI 1986), *Hair Of The Hound* (PMI 1986), *Sensual World* (PMI 1990), *The Single File* (Music Club Video 1992), *The Line, The Cross & The Curve* (PMI 1994).
FURTHER READING: *Kate Bush: An Illustrated Biography*, Paul Kerton. *Leaving My Tracks*, Kate Bush. *The Secret History Of Kate Bush (& The Strange Art Of Pop)*, Fred Vermorel. *Kate Bush: The Whole Story*, Kerry Juby. *Kate Bush: A Visual Documentary*, Kevin Cann and Sean Mayes.

BUTTERFIELD, PAUL
ALBUMS: *The Paul Butterfield Blues Band* (Elektra 1965) ★★★★, *East-West* (Elektra 1966)★★★★, *The Resurrection Of Pigboy Crabshaw* (Elektra 1968)★★★, *In My Own Dream* (Elektra 1968)★★★, *Keep On Movin'* (Elektra 1969)★★, *Live* (Elektra 1971)★★, *Sometimes I Just Feel Like Smilin'* (Elektra 1971)★★, as Better Days *It All Comes Back* (Bearsville 1973)★★, as Better Days *Better Days* (Bearsville 1973)★★★, *Put It In Your Ear* (Bearsville 1976) ★★, *North South For Bearsville* (Bearsville 1981)★★, *The Legendary Paul Butterfield Rides Again (Amherst 1986)* ★★★, Strawberry Jam *(Winner 1995)*★★, The Original Lost Elektra Sessions *1964 recordings (Rhino 1995)*★★★, East-West Live *1966/67 recordings (Winner 1997)*★★★★.
COMPILATIONS: Golden Butter – Best Of The Paul Butterfield Blues Band *(Elektra 1972)*★★★, An Anthology: The Elektra Years *(Elektra 1998)*★★★★, Bearsville Anthology *(Essential 2000)*★★.

BUTTHOLE SURFERS
ALBUMS: Butthole Surfers *(Alternative Tentacles 1983)* ★★★, Live PCPPEP *(Alternative Tentacles 1984)*★★★, Psychic ... Powerless ... Another Man's Sac *(Touch And Go 1985)*★★★, Rembrandt Pussyhorse *(Touch And Go 1986)* ★★★, Locust Abortion Technician *(Touch And Go 1987)* ★★★, Hairway To Steven *(Touch And Go 1988)*★★★, piouhgd *(Rough Trade 1991)*★★★, Independent Worm Saloon *(Capitol 1994)*★★, Electriclarryland *(Capitol 1996)* ★★★★, After The Astronaut *(Capitol 1998)*★★★, Weird Revolution *(Surfdog 2001)*★★★.
SOLO: Paul Leary The History Of Dogs *(Rough Trade 1991)*★★★.
COMPILATIONS: Double Live *(Latino Buggerveil 1989)* ★★★, The Hole Truth ... And Nothing Butt! *(Trance Syndicate 1995)*★★★, Classic Masters *(EMD 2002)*★★★.
VIDEOS: Blind Eye Sees All (Touch And Go).

BUZZCOCKS
ALBUMS: *Another Music In A Different Kitchen* (United Artists 1978)★★★★, *Love Bites* (United Artists 1978)★★★, *A Different Kind Of Tension* (United Artists/I.R.S. 1979)★★★, *Live At The Roxy Club April '77* (Absolutely Free 1989)★★★, *Entertaining Friends: Live At The Hammersmith Odeon March 1979* (I.R.S. 1992)★★★, *Trade Test Transmissions* (Essential/Caroline 1993)★★★, *French* (I.R.S. 1995)★★, *All Set* (I.R.S. 1996)★★, *Paris - Encore Du Pain* 1995 recording (Burning Airlines 1999) ★★, *Modern/A Different Kind Of Product* (EMI 1999) ★★★, *Beating Hearts* (Burning Airlines 2000)★★★.
COMPILATIONS: *Singles Going Steady* (I.R.S. 1979)★★★★, *Lest We Forget* cassette only (ROIR 1988)★★★, *Product* 3-CD box set (Restless Retro 1989)★★★, *The Peel Sessions Album* (Strange Fruit 1989)★★★, *Time's Up* 1976 recording (Document 1991)★★, *Operator's Manual: Buzzcocks Best* (I.R.S. 1991)★★★★, *Chronology* (EMI 1997)★★★, *BBC Sessions* (EMI 1998)★★★.
VIDEOS: *Auf Wiedersehen* (Ikon Video 1989), *Live Legends* (PolyGram Video 1990).
FURTHER READING: *Buzzcocks: The Complete History*, Tony McGartland.

BYRDS
ALBUMS: *Mr Tambourine Man* (Columbia 1965)★★★★, *Turn! Turn! Turn!* (Columbia 1965)★★★★, *Fifth Dimension* (Columbia 1966)★★★★, *Younger Than Yesterday* (Columbia 1967)★★★★★, *The Notorious Byrd Brothers* (Columbia 1968)★★★★★, *Sweetheart Of The Rodeo* (Columbia 1968)★★★★, *Dr Byrds & Mr Hyde* (Columbia 1969)★★★, *Ballad Of Easy Rider* (Columbia 1969)★★★, *The Byrds (Untitled)* (Columbia 1970)★★★★, *Byrdmaniax* (Columbia 1971)★★, *Farther Along* (Columbia 1972)H, *Byrds* (Asylum 1973)★★★, *Live At The Fillmore February 1969* (Columbia/Legacy 2000)★★★.
COMPILATIONS: *Greatest Hits* (Columbia 1967)★★★★, *Preflyte* (Together 1969)★★, *Greatest Hits, Volume II* (Columbia 1971)★★★, *History Of The Byrds* (Columbia 1973)★★★★, *The Byrds Play Dylan* (Columbia 1979) ★★★, *The Original Singles* (Columbia 1980)★★★★, *The Original Singles, Volume II* (Columbia 1982)★★★, *Never Before* (Murray Hill 1989)★★★, *In The Beginning* (Rhino 1989)★★★, *The Byrds Collection* (Castle 1989)★★★, *The Byrds* 4-CD box set (Columbia/Legacy 1990)★★★★, *20 Essential Tracks* (Columbia 1993)★★★★, *The Very Best Of The Byrds* (Columbia 1997)★★★★, *Sanctuary* (Sundazed 2000)★★★, *Sanctuary II* (Sundazed 2000)★★★, *Sanctuary III* (Sundazed 2001)★★★, *The Preflyte Sessions* (Sundazed 2001)★★★.
FURTHER READING: *The Byrds*, Bud Scoppa. *Timeless Flight: The Definitive Biography Of The Byrds*, Johnny Rogan. *Timeless Flight Revisited: The Sequel*, Johnny Rogan.

BYRNE, DAVID
ALBUMS: with Brian Eno *My Life In The Bush Of Ghosts* (Sire/Polydor 1981)★★★★, *The Complete Score From The Broadway Production Of "The Catherine Wheel"* soundtrack (Sire 1981)★★★★, *Music For The Knee Plays* (ECM 1985)★★★, *Sounds From True Stories* film soundtrack (Sire 1986)★★★, with Ryûichi Sakamoto, Cong Su *The Last Emperor* film soundtrack (Virgin 1988)★★★★, *Rei Momo* (Luaka Bop/Sire 1989)★★★, *The Forest* (Luaka Bop/ Warners 1991)★★★, *Uh-Oh* (Luaka Bop/Warners 1992) ★★★, *David Byrne (Luaka Bop/Warners 1994)*★★, Feelings *(Luaka Bop/Warners 1997)*★★★★, The Visible Man *remix album (Luaka Bop 1998)*★★★, In Spite Of Wishing And Wanting *dance soundtrack (Luaka Bop 1999)*★★★, Look Into The Eyeball *(Luaka Bop/Virgin 2001)*★★★★.
VIDEOS: Catherine Wheel *(Elektra Entertainment 1982)*, David Byrne: Between The Teeth *(Warner Reprise Video 1994)*.
FURTHER READING: American Originals: David Byrne, *John Howell*. Strange Ritual, *David Byrne*. Your Action World: Winners Are Losers With A New Attitude, *David Byrne*.
FILMS: Stop Making Sense *(1984)*, True Stories *(1986)*, Heavy Petting *(1988)*, Checking Out *(1989)*, Between The Teeth *(1994)*, Lulu On The Bridge *(1998)*.

C

CABARET VOLTAIRE
ALBUMS: *Mix-Up* (Rough Trade/Go 1979)★★★, *Three Mantras* mini-album (Rough Trade 1980)★★, *The Voice Of America* (Rough Trade 1980)★★, *Live At The YMCA 27.10.79.* (Rough Trade 1981)★★, *Red Mecca* (Rough Trade 1981)★★★, *Live At The Lyceum* cassette only (Rough Trade 1982)★★★, *2 x 45* (Rough Trade 1982)★★★, *Hai! Live In Japan* (Nichion/Rough Trade 1982)★★★, *Johnny YesNo* film soundtrack (Doublevision 1983)★★★, *The Crackdown* (Some Bizzare/Virgin 1983)★★★, *Micro-Phonies* (Some Bizzare/ Virgin 1984)★★★, *The Arm Of The Lord* aka *The Covenant, The Sword And The Arm Of The Lord* (Some Bizzare/Virgin 1985)★★★, *Drinking Gasoline* (Some Bizzare/Virgin 1985) ★★★, *Code* (Parlophone/EMI Manhattan 1987)★★★★, *Groovy, Laidback And Nasty* (Parlophone 1990)★★★, *Body And Soul* (Les Disques Du Crepuscule 1991)★★★, *Percussion Force* mini-album (Les Disques Du Crepuscule 1991)★★★, *Colours* mini-album (Plastex/Mute 1991)★★★, *Plasticity* (Plastex 1992)★★★, *International Language* (Plastex 1993) ★★★, *The Conversation* (Instinct/Apollo 1994)★★★.
COMPILATIONS: *74-76* cassette only (Industrial 1978)★★, *The Golden Moments Of Cabaret Voltaire* (Rough Trade 1987)★★★★, *Eight Crépescule Tracks* (Giant 1988)★★★, *Listen Up With Cabaret Voltaire* (Mute 1990)★★★, *The Living Legends* (Mute 1990)★★, *Technology: Western Re-Works 1992* (Virgin 1992)★★★, *Radiation* (New Millennium 1998)★★★, *Remixed* (EMI 2001)★★★, *Conform To Deform: '82/'90. Archive;* 3-CD box set (Virgin 2001)★★★, *The Original Sound Of Sheffield: '83/'87. Best Of;* (Virgin 2001)★★★★.
VIDEOS: *Doublevision Presents Cabaret Voltaire* (Doublevision 1983), *TV Wipeout* (Doublevision 1984), *Gasoline In Your Eye* (Doublevision/Virgin Vision 1985).
FURTHER READING: *Cabaret Voltaire: The Art Of The Sixth Sense*, M. Fish & D. Hallbery.

CALE, J.J.
ALBUMS: *Naturally* (Shelter/A&M 1971)★★★★, *Really* (Shelter/A&M 1972)★★★★, *Okie* (Shelter/A&M 1974) ★★★, *Troubadour* (Shelter 1976)★★★★, *5* (Shelter/MCA 1979)★★★★, *Shades* (Shelter/MCA 1980)★★★, *Grasshopper* (Mercury/Shelter 1982)★★, *#8* (Mercury 1983)★★, *Travel-Log* (Silvertone 1989)★★★, *Number 10* (Silvertone 1992)★★★, *Closer To You* (Virgin 1994)★★★, *Guitar Man* (Virgin 1996)★★, *Live* (Virgin 2001)★★★.
COMPILATIONS: *Special Edition* (Mercury 1984)★★★, *La Femme De Mon Pote* (Mercury 1984)★★★, *Night Riding* (Knight 1988)★★★, *Anyway The Wind Blows: The Anthology* (Mercury 1997)★★★★, *The Very Best Of J.J. Cale* (Mercury 1998)★★★, *Universal Masters Collection* (Universal 2000)★★★.

CALE, JOHN
ALBUMS: *Vintage Violence* (Columbia 1970)★★★★, with Terry Riley *Church Of Anthrax* (Columbia 1971)★★★★, *The Academy In Peril* (Reprise 1972)★★★, *Paris 1919* (Reprise 1973)★★★★, *Fear* (Island 1974)★★★, with Kevin Ayers, Eno, Nico *June 1, 1974* (Island 1974)★★, *Slow Dazzle* (Island 1975)★★★, *Helen Of Troy* (Island 1975) ★★, *Sabotage/Live* (Spy 1979)★★, *Honi Soit* (A&M 1981)★★★, *Music For A New Society* (Ze 1982)★★★★, *Caribbean Sunset* (Ze 1984)★★, *Comes Alive* (Ze 1984) ★★★, *Artificial Intelligence* (Beggars Banquet 1985)★★★, *Words For The Dying* (Opal 1989)★★★, with Lou Reed *Songs For Drella* (Warners 1990)★★★★, with Brian Eno *Wrong Way Up* (Land 1990)★★★★, *Fragments Of A Rainy Season* (Hannibal 1992)★★★, *Paris S'Eveille* (Les Disques Du Crepuscule 1993)★★★, *23 Solo Pieces For La Naissance De L'Amour* (Les Disques Du Crepuscule 1993) ★★★, with Bob Neuwirth *Last Day On Earth* (MCA 1994) ★★★, *Antártida* (Les Disques Du Crepuscule 1995)★★★, *N'Oublie Pas Que Tu Vas Mourir* (Les Disques Du Crepuscule 1995)★★★, *Walking On Locusts* (Hannibal 1996)★★★, *Eat/Kiss: Music For The Films By Andy Warhol* (Hannibal 1997)★★★, *Dance Music* (Detour 1998)★★, *Somewhere In The City* film soundtrack (Velvel 1998)★★★, *Le Vent De La Nuit*film soundtrack (Les Disques Du Crepuscule 1999)★★★, *Sun Blindness Music* (Table Of The Elements 2001)★★★, *Dream Interpretation: Inside The Dream Syndicate Volume II* (Table Of Elements 2002)★★★ *Stainless Gamelan: Inside The Dream Syndicate Volume III* (Table Of Elements 2002)★★★.
COMPILATIONS: *Guts* (Island 1977)★★★★, *Seducing Down The Door: A Collection 1970-1990* (Rhino 1994)★★★★, *The Island Years* (Island 1996)★★★, *Close Watch: An Introduction To John Cale* (Island 1999)★★★.
VIDEOS: *Songs For Drella* (Warner Music Video 1991).
FURTHER READING: *What's Welsh For Zen: The Autobiography Of John Cale*, John Cale & Victor Bockris.
FILMS: *Put More Blood Into The Music* (1987), *Words For The Dying* (1990), *Antártida* (1995), *Rhinoceros Hunting In Budapest* (1996).

CAMEO
ALBUMS: *Cardiac Arrest* (Chocolate City 1977)★★, *We All Know Who We Are* (Chocolate City 1977)★★★, *Ugly Ego* (Chocolate City 1978)★★, *Secret Omen* (Chocolate City 1979)★★, *Cameosis* (Chocolate City 1980)★★★, *Feel Me* (Chocolate City 1980)★★★, *Knights Of The Sound Table* (Chocolate City 1981)★★★, *Alligator Woman* (Chocolate City 1982)★★, *Style* (Atlanta Artists 1983)★★★, *She's Strange* (Atlanta Artists 1984)★★★, *Single Life* (Atlanta Artists/Club 1985)★★★★, *Word Up!* (Atlanta Artists/Club 1986)★★★★, *Machismo* (Atlanta Artists/Club 1988)★★★, *Real Men ... Wear Black* (Atlanta Artists 1990)★★★, *Emotional Violence* (Reprise 1992)★★★, *In The Face Of Funk* (Way 2 Funky 1994)★★, *Nasty* (Intersound 1996) ★★, *Sexy Sweet Thing* (Private I 2000)★★★.
COMPILATIONS: *The Best Of Cameo* (Phonogram 1993)★★★★, *The Best Of Cameo, Volume 2* (Phonogram 1996)★★★, *Live: Word Up* (CEMA 1998)★★★, *The Ballads Collection* (PolyGram 1998)★★★, *Cameo: The Hits Collection* (Spectrum 1998)★★★★, *Greatest Hits* (PolyGram 1998)★★★★, *The Best Of Cameo: The Millennium Collection* (PolyGram 2001)★★★★.
VIDEOS: *Cameo: The Video Singles* (Channel 5 1987), *Back And Forth* (Club 1987).

CAMPBELL, GLEN
ALBUMS: *Too Late To Worry, Too Late To Cry* (Capitol 1963) ★★★, *The Astounding 12-String Guitar Of Glen Campbell* (Capitol 1964)★★★, *The Big Bad Rock Guitar Of Glen Campbell* (Capitol 1965)★★★, *Gentle On My Mind* (Capitol 1967)★★★, *By The Time I Get To Phoenix* (Capitol 1967)★★★, *Hey, Little One* (Capitol 1968)★★★, *A New Place In The Sun* (Capitol 1968)★★★, *Bobbie Gentry And Glen Campbell* (Capitol 1968)★★★, *Wichita Lineman* (Capitol 1968)★★★, *That Christmas Feeling* (Capitol 1968) ★★, *Galveston* (Capitol 1969)★★★, *Glen Campbell – Live* (Capitol 1969)★★, *Try A Little Kindness* (Capitol 1970) ★★★, *Oh Happy Day* (Capitol 1970)★★★, *Norwood* film soundtrack (Capitol 1970)★★, *The Glen Campbell Goodtime Album* (Capitol 1970)★★★, *The Last Time I Saw Her* (Capitol 1971)★★★, *Anne Murray/Glen Campbell* (Capitol 1971)★★★, *Glen Travis Campbell* (Capitol 1972) ★★★, *I Knew Jesus (Before He Was A Star)* (Capitol 1973) ★★★, *I Remember Hank Williams* (Capitol 1973)★★, *Reunion (The Songs Of Jimmy Webb)* (Capitol 1974)★★★, *Arkansas* (Capitol 1975)★★, *Rhinestone Cowboy* (Capitol 1975)★★, *Bloodline* (Capitol 1976)★★★, *Southern Nights* (Capitol 1977)★★★, with the Royal Philharmonic Orchestra *Live At The Royal Festival Hall* (Capitol 1978)★★★, *Basic* (Capitol 1978)★★★, *Somethin' 'Bout You Baby I Like* (Capitol 1980)★★★, *It's The World Gone Crazy* (Capitol 1981)★★★★, *Old Home Town* (Atlantic 1983)★★★, *Letter To Home* (Atlantic 1984)★★★, *Just A Matter Of Time* (Atlantic 1986)★★★, *No More Night* (Word 1988)★★★, *Still Within The Sound Of My Voice* (MCA 1988)★★★, *Walkin' In The Sun* (Capitol 1990)★★★★, *Unconditional Love* (Capitol Nashville 1991)★★★, *Somebody Like That* (Capitol 1993)★★★, *The Rhinestone Cowboy Live In Concert* (Summit 1995)★★★.
COMPILATIONS: *Glen Campbell's Greatest Hits* (Capitol 1971)★★★, *The Best Of Glen Campbell* (Capitol 1976) ★★★, *20 Classic Tracks* (MFP 1981)★★, *The Very Best Of Glen Campbell* (Capitol 1987)★★★★, *The Best Of The Early Years* (Curb 1987)★★★, *Country Boy* (MFP 1988) ★★, *The Complete Glen Campbell* (Stylus 1989)★★★, *Love Songs* (MFP 1990)★★, *Greatest Country Hits* (Curb 1990) ★★★, *Classics Collection* (Liberty 1990)★★★, *Essential Glen Campbell, Volumes 1-3* (Capitol 1995)★★★, *Gentle On My Mind: The Collection* (Razor & Tie 1997)★★★★, *The Capitol Years* (Capitol 1999)★★★★, *My Hits & Love Songs* (EMI 1999)★★★★, with Jimmy Webb *Reunited With Jimmy Webb 1974-1988* (Raven 2000)★★★★.
VIDEOS: *Glen Campbell Live* (Channel 5 1988), *An Evening With* (Music Club Video 1989), *Glen Campbell* (Castle Music Pictures 1991), *Glen Campbell In Concert* (Aviva International 2002).
FURTHER READING: *The Glen Campbell Story*, Freda Kramer. *Rhinestone Cowboy: An Autobiography*, Glen Campbell with Tom Carter.
FILMS: *Baby The Rain Must Fall* (1965), *The Cool Ones* aka *Cool Baby, Cool!* (1967), *True Grit* (1969), *Norwood* (1970), *Any Which Way You Can* (1980), *Uphill All The Way* (1986), *Rock-A-Doodle* voice only (1991), *Family Prayers* (1993), *Third World Cop* (1999).

CAMPER VAN BEETHOVEN
ALBUMS: *Telephone Free Landslide Victory* (Independent Project 1985)★★★, *Take The Skinheads Bowling* mini-album (Pitch-A-Tent 1986)★★★, *II/III* (Pitch-A-Tent 1986) ★★★★, *Camper Van Beethoven* (Pitch-A-Tent 1986)★★★, *Vampire Can Mating Oven* mini-album (Pitch-A-Tent 1987) ★★★, *Our Beloved Revolutionary Sweetheart* (Virgin 1988) ★★★★, *Key Lime Pie* (Virgin 1989)★★★.
COMPILATIONS: *Camper Vantiquies* (I.R.S. 1994)★★★, *Camper Van Beethoven Is Dead, Long Live Camper Van Beethoven* (Pitch-A-Tent 2000)★★★.

CAN
ALBUMS: *Monster Movie* (United Artists 1969)★★★★, *Soundtracks* film soundtrack (United Artists 1970)★★★, *Tago Mago* (United Artists 1971)★★★★, *Ege Bamyasi* (United Artists 1972)★★★★, *Future Days* (United Artists 1973)★★★★, *Soon Over Babaluma* (United Artists 1974) ★★★★★, *Landed* (Virgin 1975)★★★, *Flow Motion* (Virgin 1976)★★★, *Saw Delight* (Virgin 1977)★★★, *Out Of Reach* (Lightning 1978)★★, *Can* aka *Inner Space* (Laser 1979)★★, *Delay 1968* (Spoon 1981)★★★, *Rite Time* (Mercury 1989) ★★★, *The Peel Sessions* (Strange Fruit 1995)★★★.
COMPILATIONS: *Limited Edition* (United Artists 1974)★★★, *Unlimited Edition* (Caroline 1976)★★★, *Opener* (Sunset 1976)★★, *Cannibalism* (United Artists 1978)★★★★★, *Incandescence* (Virgin 1981)★★, *Delay 1968* (Spoon 1981)★★★, *Onlyou* cassette only (Pure Freude 1982) ★★★★, *Prehistoric Future: June, 1968* cassette only (Tago Mago 1985)★★★, *Cannibalism 2* (Spoon 1992)★★★, *Anthology: 25 Years* (Spoon 1994)★★★★.
FURTHER READING: *Box: Book*, Hildegard Schmidt & Wolf Kampmann.

CANNED HEAT
ALBUMS: *Canned Heat* (Liberty 1967)★★★, *Livin' The Blues* (Liberty 1968)★★★, *Boogie With Canned Heat* (Liberty 1968)★★★, *Hallelujah* (Liberty 1968)★★★★, *Live In Europe* (Liberty 1970)★★, *Live At Topanga Canyon* (Wand 1970)★★★, *Future Blues* (Liberty 1970)★★★, with Memphis Slim *Memphis Heat* (Barclay 1971)★★★, with John Lee Hooker *Hooker 'N' Heat* (Liberty 1971)★★★, *Historical Figures & Ancient Heads* (United Artists 1972) ★★★, with Clarence 'Gatemouth' Brown *Gate's On Heat* (Barclay 1973)★★★, *New Age* (United Artists 1973)★★, *One More River To Cross* (Atlantic 1974)★★, *Live At The Topanga Corral* (Wand/DJM 1976)★★★, *The Human Condition* (Takoma 1978)★★, with John Lee Hooker *Hooker 'N' Heat - Live* (Rhino 1981)★★★, *Kings Of The Boogie* (Destiny 1982)★★, *The Boogie Assault: Live In Australia* (Bedrock 1987)★★★, *Reheated* (SPV/Chameleon 1988) ★★, *Live At The Turku Rock Festival* (Bear Family 1990)★★, *Internal Combustion* (River Road 1994)★★, *In Concert* 1979 recording (King Biscuit Flower Hour 1995)★★★, *Blues Band* (Mystic 1997)★★, *The Ties That Bind* 1974 recording (Navarre/Archive 1997)★★, *Canned Heat Live At The King Biscuit Flower Hour* 1979 recording (King Biscuit 1998)★★, *Canned Heat Blues Band* (Ruf/Mystic 1997)★★★, *Boogie 2000* (Ruf/Platinum 1999)★★, *Live At The Kaleidoscope 1969* (Varèse Sarabande 2000)★★.
COMPILATIONS: *Canned Heat Cookbook (The Best Of Canned Heat)* (Liberty 1969)★★★, *Vintage* (Janus 1970) ★★, *Collage* (Sunset 1971)★★★, *The Best Of Canned Heat* (EMI 1972)★★★, *The Very Best Of Canned Heat* (United Artists 1973)★★★, with John Lee Hooker *Infinite Boogie* (Rhino 1986)★★★, with John Lee Hooker *Hooker 'N' Heat Volume 2* (Rhino 1988)★★, *The Best Of Hooker 'N' Heat* (See For Miles 1988)★★★, *Let's Work Together: The Best Of Canned Heat* (Liberty 1989)★★★, *Uncanned! The Best Of Canned Heat* (Liberty 1994)★★★★, *1967-1976: The Boogie House Tapes* (Ruf 2000)★★★.
VIDEOS: *Canned Heat - Boogie Assault* (Video Music 1984).
FURTHER READING: *Living The Blues: Canned Heat's Story Of Music, Drugs, Death, Sex And Survival*, Fito de la Parra with T.W. and Marlene McGarry.

CANNON, FREDDY
ALBUMS: *The Explosive! Freddy Cannon* (Swan/Top Rank 1960)★★★★, *Happy Shades Of Blue* (Swan 1960)★★★, *Freddy Cannon's Solid Gold Hits* (Swan 1961)★★★, *Twistin' All Night Long* (Swan 1961)★★★, *Freddy Cannon*

At Palisades Park (Swan 1962)★★★, Freddy Cannon Steps Out (Swan 1963)★★, Freddy Cannon (Warners 1964)★★, Action! (Warners 1966)★★.
COMPILATIONS: Freddy Cannon's Greatest Hits (Warners 1966)★★★★, Big Blast From Boston! The Best Of Freddy Cannon (Rhino 1995)★★★, The EP Collection (See For Miles 1999)★★★.

CAPALDI, JIM
ALBUMS: Oh How We Danced (Island 1972)★★★★, Whale Meat Again (Island 1974)★★, Short Cut Draw Blood (Island 1975)★★★★, Play It By Ear (Island 1977)★★, The Contender (Polydor 1978)★★★, Electric Nights (Polydor 1979)★★, The Sweet Smell Of Success (Carrere 1980)★★, Let The Thunder Cry (Carrere 1981)★★★, Fierce Heart (Atlantic 1983)★★★, One Man Mission (Warners 1984) ★★, Some Come Running (Island 1989)★★★, with Dave Mason Live: The 40,000 Headmen Tour (Receiver 1999) ★★★, Living on The Outside (SPV 2001)★★.
FURTHER READING: Keep On Running: The Steve Winwood Story, Chris Welch. Back In The High Life: A Biography Of Steve Winwood, Alan Clayson.

CAPTAIN AND TENNILLE
ALBUMS: Love Will Keep Us Together (A&M 1975)★★★, Por Amor Viviremos (A&M 1975)★★, Song Of Joy (A&M 1976)★★, Come In From The Rain (A&M 1977)★★, Dream (A&M 1978)★★, Make Your Move (Casablanca 1979)★★, Keeping Our Love Warm (Casablanca 1980) ★★, Twenty Years Of Romance (K-Tel 1995)★★.
COMPILATIONS: Greatest Hits (A&M 1977)★★★, 20 Greatest Hits (MFP 1980)★★, The Ultimate Collection: The Complete Hits (Hip-O 2001)★★★.
FURTHER READING: Captain And Tennille, James Spada.

CAPTAIN BEEFHEART
ALBUMS: Safe As Milk (Buddah 1967)★★★★, Strictly Personal (Blue Thumb/Liberty 1968)★★★★, Trout Mask Replica (Straight 1969)★★★★★, Lick My Decals Off, Baby (Straight 1970)★★★★, The Spotlight Kid (Reprise 1972) ★★★, Clear Spot (Reprise 1972)★★★, Mirror Man (Buddah 1973)★★★, Unconditionally Guaranteed (Virgin 1974)★★, Bluejeans And Moonbeams (Virgin 1974)★★★, with Frank Zappa Bongo Fury (DiscReet 1975)★★★, Shiny Beast (Bat Chain Puller) (Virgin 1978)★★★, Doc At The Radar Station (Virgin 1980)★★★, Ice Cream For Crow (Virgin 1982)★★★, Merseytrout: Live In Liverpool 1980 (Ozit 2000)★★, I'm Going To Do What I Wanna Do 1978 live recording (Rhino 2001)★★★.
COMPILATIONS: The Alternate Captain Beefheart: I May Be Hungry But I Sure Ain't Weird (Sequel 1992)★★★, Zig Zag Wanderer: The Best Of The Buddah Years (Wooden Hill 1997)★★★, Electricity (Camden 1998)★★★★, Grow Fins 5-CD box set (Revenant 1999)★★★, The Dust Blows Forward (An Anthology) (Rhino 1999)★★★★, Dust Sucker (Ozit 2002)★★★.
FURTHER READING: The Lives And Times Of Captain Beefheart, no editor listed. Captain Beefheart: The Man And His Music, Colin David Webb. Fast And Bulbous: The Captain Beefheart Story, Ben Cruickshank. Lunar Notes: Zoot Horn Rollo's Captain Beefheart Experience, Bill Harkleroad with Billy James. Captain Beefheart, Mike Barnes.

CAPTAIN SENSIBLE
ALBUMS: Women And Captains First (A&M 1982)★★★, The Power Of Love (A&M 1983)★★, Revolution Now (Deltic 1989)★★, The Universe Of Geoffrey Brown (Deltic 1993) ★★, Live At The Milky Way (Humbug 1994)★★★★, Mad Cows & Englishmen (Scratch 1996)★★★.
COMPILATIONS: Sensible Singles (A&M 1984)★★★, A Day In The Life Of Captain Sensible (A&M 1984)★★★, Meathead (Humbug 1995)★★★, A Slice Of ... Captain Sensible (Humbug 1996)★★★, Sensible Lifestyles: The Best Of Captain Sensible (Cleopatra 1997)★★★, The Masters (Eagle 1999)★★★.

CARAVAN
ALBUMS: Caravan (Verbe 1968)★★★, If I Could Do It All Over Again, I'd Do It All Over You (Decca 1970)★★★, In The Land Of Grey And Pink (Deram 1971)★★★, Waterloo Lily (Deram 1972)★★★★, For Girls Who Grow Plump In The Night (Deram 1973)★★★, Caravan And The New Symphonia (Decca 1974)★★, Cunning Stunts (Deram 1975)★★★, Blind Dog At St. Dunstans' (BTM 1976)★★★, Better By Far (Arista 1977)★★, The Album (Kingdom 1980)★★, The Best Of Caravan Live (Kingdom 1980)★★, Back To The Front (Kingdom 1982)★★, Live (Demon 1993)★★, Cool Water (HTD 1994)★★, The Battle Of Hastings (HTD 1995)★★★, All Over You (HTD 1996)★★★, Live From The Astoria (HTD 1997)★★, BBC Live In Concert 1975 recording (Strange Fruit 1998)★★★, Surprise Supplies 1975 recording (HTD 1999)★★, All Over You ... Too (HTD 1999)★★.
COMPILATIONS: Canterbury Tales (Decca 1976)★★★★, Collection: Caravan (Kingdom 1984)★★★, And I Wish I Weren't Stoned, Don't Worry (See For Miles 1985)★★★, The Best Of Caravan (C5 1987)★★★, Canterbury Collection (Kingdom 1987)★★★, Travelling Man (Mooncrest 1998)★★★, Songs For Oblivion Fisherman (Hux 1998)★★★, Ether Way (Hux 1998)★★, Where But For Caravan Would I? An Anthology (Decca 2000)★★★★, The HTD Anthology (Castle 2001)★★★.

CARDIGANS
ALBUMS: Emmerdale (Trampolene/Stockholm 1994)★★★, Life (Trampolene/Stockholm 1995)★★★, First Band On The Moon (Stockholm 1996)★★★★, Gran Turismo (Stockholm 1998)★★★★.

CAREY, MARIAH
ALBUMS: Mariah Carey (Columbia 1990)★★★, Emotions (Columbia 1991)★★★, MTV Unplugged (Columbia 1992) ★★★, Music Box (Columbia 1993)★★★, Merry Christmas (Columbia 1994)★★, Daydream (Columbia 1995)★★★, Butterfly (Columbia 1997)★★★, with Celine Dion, Gloria Estefan, Aretha Franklin, Shania Twain Divas Live (Epic 1998) ★★, Rainbow (Columbia 1999)★★★, Glitter (Virgin 2001)★★.
COMPILATIONS: #1s (Columbia 1998)★★★★, Greatest Hits (Columbia 2001)★★★★.
VIDEOS: Mariah Carey (Columbia Music Video 1994), Fantasy: Live At Madison Square Garden (Columbia Music Video 1996), My All (Columbia Music Video 1998), with Celine Dion, Gloria Estefan, Aretha Franklin, Shania Twain Divas Live (Sony Music Video 1998), Around The World (Sony Music Video 1999), MTV Unplugged + 3 (Sony Music Video 1999), #1s (Sony Music Video 1999).
FILMS: The Bachelor (1999), Glitter (2001), Wisegirls (2002).
FURTHER READING: Mariah Carey, Marc Shapiro.

CARLISLE, BELINDA
ALBUMS: Belinda (I.R.S. 1986)★★★, Heaven On Earth (Virgin 1987)★★★, Runaway Horses (Virgin 1989)★★, Live Your Life Be Free (Virgin 1991)★★, Real (Virgin 1993) ★★, A Woman And A Man (Chrysalis 1996)★★.
COMPILATIONS: Her Greatest Hits (MCA 1992)★★★, A Place On Earth: The Greatest Hits (Virgin 1999)★★★.
VIDEOS: Belinda Live (Virgin Vision 1988), Runaway - Live (Castle Music Pictures 1990), Runaway Videos (Virgin Vision 1991), The Best Of ... Volume 1 (Virgin 1992).

CARLTON, LARRY
ALBUMS: With A Little Help From My Friends (Uni 1968)★★, Singing/Playing (Blue Thumb 1973)★★★, Larry Carlton (Warners 1978)★★, Live In Japan (Flyover 1979)★★★, Strikes Twice (MCA 1980)★★★, Sleepwalk (MCA 1981) ★★★, Eight Times Up (Warners 1983)★★★, Friends (MCA 1983)★★★, Alone But Never Alone (MCA 1986)★★★★, Discovery (MCA 1986)★★★★, Last Nite (MCA 1986)★★★★, On Solid Ground (MCA 1989)★★★, Renegade Gentleman (GRP 1991)★★★, Kid Gloves (GRP 1992)★★★, with Lee Ritenour Larry And Lee (GRP 1995)★★★★, The Gift (GRP 1996)★★★, Fingerprints (Warners 2000)★★★, with Steve Lukather No Substitutions: Live In Osaka (Favored Nations 2001)★★★★, Deep Into It (Warners 2001)★★★.
COMPILATIONS: The Collection (GRP 1990)★★★★.

CARMEN, ERIC
ALBUMS: Eric Carmen (Arista 1975)★★★, Boats Against The Current (Arista 1977)★★★★, Change Of Heart (Arista 1978)★★, Tonight You're Mine (Arista 1980)★★, Eric Carmen (Geffen 1985)★★, Winter Dreams (Pioneer 1998) ★★★, I Was Born To Love You (Pyramid 2000)★★★.
COMPILATIONS: The Best Of Eric Carmen (Arista 1988)★★★, The Definitive Collection (Arista 1997)★★★.

CARNES, KIM
ALBUMS: Rest On Me (Amos 1971)★★, Kim Carnes (A&M 1975)★★★, Sailin' (A&M 1976)★★★, St Vincent's Court (EMI America 1979)★★, Romance Dance (EMI America 1980)★★★, Mistaken Identity (EMI America 1981)★★★★, Voyeur (EMI America 1982)★★★, Cafe Racers (EMI America 1983)★★, Barking At Airplanes (EMI America 1985)★★, Light House (EMI America 1986)★★★, View From The House (MCA 1988)★★★★, Checking Out The Ghosts (Teichiku 1991)★★★.
COMPILATIONS: The Best Of You (A&M 1988)★★★, Crazy In The Night (CEMA 1990)★★★, Gypsy Honeymoon: The Best Of Kim Carnes (EMI America 1993)★★★, The Mistaken Identity Collection (Razor & Tie 1999)★★★.
FILMS: C'mon, Let's Live A Little (1967).

CARPENTER, MARY-CHAPIN
ALBUMS: Hometown Girl (Columbia 1987)★★, State Of The Heart (Columbia 1989)★★★, Shooting Straight In The Dark (Columbia 1990)★★★, Come On Come On (Columbia 1992)★★★★, Stones In The Road (Columbia 1994)★★★★, A Place In The World (Columbia 1996) ★★★, Time*Sex*Love (Columbia 2001)★★★.
COMPILATIONS: Party Doll And Other Favorites (Columbia 1999)★★★★.
VIDEOS: Shut Up And Kiss Me (Columbia Music Video 1994), 5 (Columbia Music Video 1994), My Record Company Made Me Do This! (Columbia Music Video 1995), Jubilee: Live At The Wolf Trap (Columbia Music Video 1995).

CARPENTERS
ALBUMS: Offering aka Ticket To Ride (A&M 1969)★★, Close To You (A&M 1970)★★★★, The Carpenters (A&M 1971)★★★★, A Song For You (A&M 1972)★★★, Now And Then (A&M 1973)★★, Horizon (A&M 1975)★★★, Live In Japan (A&M 1975)★★, A Kind Of Hush (A&M 1976)★★, Live At The Palladium (A&M 1976)★★, Passage (A&M 1977)★★, Christmas Portrait (A&M 1978)H, Made In America (A&M 1981)★★, Voice Of The Heart (A&M 1983)★★★, An Old Fashioned Christmas (A&M 1984)H.
Solo: Richard Carpenter Time (A&M 1987)H. Karen Carpenter Karen Carpenter (A&M 1996)★★.
COMPILATIONS: The Singles 1969-73 (A&M 1973) ★★★★, Collection (A&M 1976)★★★★, The Singles 1974-78 (A&M 1978)★★★★, Silver Double Disc Of The Carpenters (A&M 1979)★★, The Best Of The Carpenters (World 1981)★★, The Carpenters Collection: The Very Best Of The Carpenters (EMI 1984)★★★★, Lovelines (A&M 1989)★★, The Compact Disc Collection 12-CD box set (A&M 1989)★★★, From The Top (1965-82) 4-CD box set (A&M 1992)★★★★, Love Songs (A&M 1997)★★★.
VIDEOS: Yesterday Once More (A&M Sound Pictures 1986), Only Yesterday: Richard & Karen Carpenter's Greatest Hits (Channel 5 1990), Close To You: Remembering The Carpenters (MPI Home Video 1998).
FURTHER READING: The Carpenters: The Untold Story, Ray Coleman. Yesterday Once More: Memories Of The Carpenters And Their Music, Randy Schmidt (ed.).

CARR, JAMES
ALBUMS: You Got My Mind Messed Up (Goldwax 1966) ★★★★, A Man Needs A Woman (Goldwax 1968)★★★, Freedom Train (Goldwax 1968)★★★, Take Me To The Limit (Goldwax 1991)★★★, Soul Survivor (Soultrax/Ace 1993)★★★.
COMPILATIONS: At The Dark End Of The Street (Blueside 1987)★★★, The Complete James Carr, Volume 1 (Goldwax 1993)★★★★, The Essential (Razor & Tie 1995)★★★★, with the Jubilee Hummingbirds Guilty Of Serving God (Ace 1996)★★★, The Complete Goldwax Singles (Kent/Ace 2001)★★★★, 24 Karat Soul (Soultrax 2001)★★.

CARRACK, PAUL
ALBUMS: Nightbird (Vertigo 1980)★★, Suburban Voodoo (Epic 1982)★★, One Good Reason (Chrysalis 1987)★★★, Groove Approved (Chrysalis 1989)★★★, Blue Views (I.R.S. 1996)★★★★, Beautiful World (Ark 21 1997)★★★, Satisfy My Soul (Compass 2000)★★★, Groovin' (Carrack 2001)★★★.
COMPILATIONS: Ace Mechanic (Demon 1987)★★★, Carrackter Reference (Demon 1991)★★★.

CARS
ALBUMS: The Cars (Elektra 1978)★★★★, Candy-O (Elektra 1979)★★★, Panorama (Elektra 1980)★★, Shake It Up (Elektra 1981)★★★, Heartbeat City (Elektra 1984) ★★★★, Door To Door (Elektra 1987)★.
SOLO: Elliot Easton Change No Change (Elektra 1985)★★. Greg Hawkes Niagara Falls (Passport 1983)★★. Benjamin Orr The Lace (Elektra 1986)★★.
COMPILATIONS: The Cars Greatest Hits (Elektra 1985)★★★, Just What I Needed: The Cars Anthology (Elektra/Rhino 1995)★★★★, Complete Greatest Hits (Rhino 2002)★★★★.
VIDEOS: Heartbeat City (Warner Music Video 1984), Cars Live (Vestron Music Video 1988).
FURTHER READING: The Cars, Philip Kamin.

CARTER USM
ALBUMS: 101 Damnations (Big Cat 1990)★★★★, 30 Something (Rough Trade 1991)★★★, 1992 – The Love Album (Chrysalis 1992)★★★★, Post Historic Monsters (Chrysalis 1993)★★★★, Starry Eyed And Bollock Naked (Chrysalis 1994)★★★, Worry Bomb (Chrysalis 1995)★★★, A World Without Dave mini-album (Cooking Vinyl 1997)★★★, I Blame The Government (Cooking Vinyl 1997)★★★.
COMPILATIONS: Straw Donkey (Chrysalis 1995)★★★, Anytime, Anyplace, Anywhere ... The Very Best Of Carter USM (EMI 2000)★★★.
VIDEOS: In Bed With Carter (PMI 1991), What Do You Think Of The Programme So Far? (PMI 1992), Straw Donkey: The Videos (PMI 1995), Flicking The V's-Live In Croatia (1995).

CARTER, CARLENE
ALBUMS: Carlene Carter (Warners 1978)★★★, Two Sides To Every Woman (Warners 1979)★★, Musical Shapes (F-Beat 1980)★★★, Blue Nun (F-Beat 1981)★★, C'est Bon (Epic 1983)★★★, with Anita, Helen and June Carter Wildwood Flower (Mercury 1988)★★★, I Fell In Love (Reprise 1990)★★, Little Love Letters (Giant 1993)★★★, Little Acts Of Treason (Giant 1995)★★★.
COMPILATIONS: Hindsight 20/20 (Giant 1996)★★★★.
VIDEOS: Open Fire (Hendring Video 1990).

CARTHY, MARTIN
ALBUMS: Martin Carthy (Fontana 1965)★★★, Second Album (Fontana 1966)★★★, with Dave Swarbrick Byker Hill (Fontana 1967)★★★★, with Swarbrick But Two Came By (Fontana 1968)★★★, with Swarbrick Prince Heathen (Fontana 1969)★★★, with Swarbrick Selections (Pegasus 1971)★★★, Landfall (Philips 1971)★★★★, Shearwater (Topic 1972)★★★, Sweet Wivelsfield (Topic 1974)★★★, Crown Of Horn (Topic 1976)★★★, Because It's There (Topic 1979)★★★, Out Of The Cut (Topic 1982)★★★, Right Of Passage (Topic 1988)★★★★, with Swarbrick Life And Limb (Special Delivery 1990)★★★, with Swarbrick Skin & Bone (Special Delivery 1992)★★★★, with Eliza Carthy, Norma Waterson Waterson: Carthy (Topic 1995)★★★★, Signs Of Life (Topic 1998)★★★★, with Wood Wilson Carthy Wood Wilson Carthy (R.U.F. 1998)★★★, with Eliza Carthy, Norma Waterson Broken Ground (Topic 1999)★★★★.
COMPILATIONS: This Is ... Martin Carthy: The Bonny Black Hare And Other Songs (Philips 1972)★★★★, The Collection (Green Linnet 1993)★★★★, Rigs Of The Time - The Best Of Martin Carthy (Music Club 1998)★★★, A Collection (Topic 1999)★★★, The Carthy Chronicles 4-CD box set (Free Reed 2001)★★★★.
VIDEOS: with Dave Swarbrick 100 Not Out (MusikFolk 1992).

CASH, JOHNNY
ALBUMS: Johnny Cash With His Hot And Blue Guitar (Sun 1957)★★★, Johnny Cash Sings The Songs That Made Him Famous (Sun 1958)★★★, The Fabulous Johnny Cash (Columbia 1958)★★★, Hymns By Johnny Cash (Columbia 1959)H, Songs Of Our Soil (Columbia 1959)★★, Now There Was A Song (Columbia 1960)★★, Johnny Cash Sings Hank Williams And Other Favorite Tunes (Sun 1960) ★★★, Ride This Train (Columbia 1960)★★★★, Now Here's Johnny Cash (Sun 1961)★★★, The Lure Of The Grand Canyon (Columbia 1961)★★, Hymns From The Heart (Columbia 1962)H, The Sound Of Johnny Cash (Columbia 1962)★★, All Aboard The Blue Train (Sun 1963)★★★, Blood, Sweat And Tears (Columbia 1963) ★★★★, The Christmas Spirit (Columbia 1963)★★, with the Carter Family Keep On The Sunny Side (1964)★★★, I Walk The Line (Columbia 1964)★★★★, Bitter Tears (Ballads Of The American Indian) (Columbia 1964)★★★, Orange Blossom Special (Columbia 1964)★★★★, Mean As Hell (Columbia 1965)★★, The Sons Of Katie Elder film soundtrack (Columbia 1965)★★, Johnny Cash Sings Ballads Of The True West (Columbia 1965) ★★★, Ballads Of The True West, Volume 2 (Columbia 1965)★★★, Everybody Loves A Nut (Columbia 1966)H, Happiness Is You (Columbia 1966)★★, with June Carter Carryin' On (Columbia 1967)★★, From Sea To Shining Sea (Columbia 1967)★★, Old Golden Throat (Columbia 1968) ★★, Johnny Cash At Folsom Prison (Columbia 1968)★★★★, The Holy Land (Columbia 1968)H, More Of Old Golden Throat (Columbia 1969)★★, Johnny Cash At San Quentin (Columbia 1969)★★★★, Hello I'm Johnny Cash (Columbia 1970)★★★, The Johnny Cash Show (Columbia 1970)★★★, with Carl Perkins Little Fauss And Big Halsey (Columbia 1970)★★, The Man In Black (Columbia 1971)★★★, with Jerry Lee Lewis Sings Hank Williams (Sun 1971)★★, A Thing Called Love (Columbia 1972)★★, with Jerry Lee Lewis Sunday Down South (Sun 1972)★★★, Christmas And The Cash Family (Columbia 1972)★★, America (A 200-Year Salute In Story And Song) (Columbia 1972)★★, Any Old Wind That Blows (Columbia 1973)★★, The Gospel Road (Columbia 1973)★★, with June Carter Johnny Cash And His Woman (Columbia 1973)★★, Ragged Old Flag (Columbia 1974)★★, The Junkie And The Juicehead Minus Me (Columbia 1974)★★, Pa Osteraker aka Inside A Swedish Prison (Columbia 1974)★★, John R. Cash (Columbia 1975) ★★★, Look At Them Beans (Columbia 1975)★★, Strawberry Cake (Columbia 1976)★★★, One Piece At A Time (Columbia 1976)★★★★, The Last Gunfighter Ballad (Columbia 1977) ★★★, The Rambler (Columbia 1977)★★★, Gone Girl (Columbia 1978)★★★, I Would Like To See You Again (Columbia 1978)★★★, Silver (Columbia 1979)★★★, A Believer Sings The Truth (Columbia 1979)★★, Rockabilly Blues (Columbia 1980)★★★★, The Baron (Columbia 1981) ★★★, with Jerry Lee Lewis, Carl Perkins The Survivors (Columbia 1982)★★★, The Adventures Of Johnny Cash (Columbia 1982)★★, Johnny 99 (Columbia 1983)★★, Rainbow (Columbia 1985)★★★, with Kris Kristofferson, Waylon Jennings, Willie Nelson Highwayman (Columbia 1985)★★★★, with Jerry Lee Lewis, Carl Perkins, Roy Orbison The Class Of '55 (1986)★★★, with Waylon Jennings Heroes (Columbia 1986)★★★, Believe In Him (Word 1986)★★, Johnny Cash Is Back In Town (Mercury 1987)★★★, Water From The Wells Of Home (Mercury 1988)★★★★, Boom Chicka Boom (Mercury 1989)★★★, with Jennings, Kristofferson and Nelson Highwayman 2 (Columbia 1990)★★★, The Mystery Of Life (Mercury 1991)★★★, Get Rhythm (Sun 1991)★★★, American Recordings (American 1994)★★★★, with Jennings, Kristofferson, Nelson The Road Goes On Forever (Liberty 1995)★★, Unchained (American 1996)★★★, with Nelson VH1 Storytellers (American 1998)★★★★, American III: Solitary Man (American 2000)★★★.
COMPILATIONS: Johnny Cash's Greatest (Sun 1959)★★★, Ring Of Fire (The Best Of Johnny Cash) (Columbia 1963) ★★★, The Original Sun Sound Of Johnny Cash (Sun 1965)★★★, Johnny Cash's Greatest Hits, Volume 1 (Columbia 1967)★★★, Original Golden Hits, Volume 1 (Sun 1969)★★★, Original Golden Hits, Volume 2 (Sun 1969)★★★, Get Rhythm (Sun 1969)★★★, Story Songs Of The Trains And Rivers (Sun 1969)★★★, Showtime (Sun 1969)★★★, The Rough Cut King Of Country Music (Sun 1970)★★★, The Singing Story Teller (Sun 1970)★★★, The Legend (Sun 1970)★★★★, The World Of Johnny Cash (Columbia 1970)★★★★, Original Golden Hits, Volume 3 (Sun 1971)★★, Johnny Cash: The Man, The World, His Music (Sun 1971)★★★, His Greatest Hits, Volume 2 (Columbia 1971)★★★, Destination Victoria Station (Bear Family 1976)★★, Superbilly (Sun 1977)★★, Golden Souvenirs (Plantation 1977)★★★, The Unissued Johnny Cash (Bear Family 1978)★★, Greatest Hits, Volume 3 (Columbia 1978)★★★, Johnny And June (Bear Family 1980)★★, Tall Man (Bear Family 1980)★★★, Encore (Greatest Hits, Volume 4) (Columbia 1981)★★★, Biggest Hits (Columbia 1982)★★★, Johnny Cash: The Sun Years 5-LP box set (Sun 1984)★★★★, Up Through The Years, 1955-1957 (Bear Family 1986)★★★★, Johnny Cash - Columbia Records 1958-1986 (Columbia 1987)★★★★, Vintage Years: 1955-1963 (Rhino 1987)★★★, Classic Cash (Mercury 1988)★★★, The Sun Years (Rhino 1990)★★★★, I Walk The Line And Other Big Hits (Rhino 1990)★★★, The Man In Black: 1954-1958 5-CD box set (Bear Family 1990)★★★★, Come Along And Ride This Train 4-CD box set (Bear Family 1991)★★★, The Man In Black: 1959-1962 5-CD box set (Bear Family 1992)★★★★, The Essential Johnny Cash 1955-1983 3-CD box set (Columbia/Legacy 1992)★★★★, Wanted Man (Mercury 1994)★★★, The Man In Black: The Definitive Collection (Columbia 1994)★★★★, Get Rhythm: The Best Of The Sun Years (Pickwick 1995)★★★, Ring Of Fire (Spectrum 1995) ★★★, The Man In Black: 1963-1969 Plus 6-CD box set (Bear Family 1996)★★★★, All American Country (Spectrum 1997)★★★, Tennessee Top Cat Live 1955-1965 (Cotton Town Jubilee 1997)★★★★, Sings The Country Classics (Eagle 1997)★★★, Hits And Classics (Carlton 1998)★★★, The Complete Original Sun Singles (Varèse Sarabande 1999)★★★★, Love God Murder 3-CD set (American/Legacy 2000)★★★★, Wanted Man: The Very Best Of Johnny Cash (Sony 2000)★★★★, Johnny Cash, The EP Collection Plus (See For Miles 2000)★★★, The Very Best Of The Sun Years (Metro 2001)★★★, Man In Black: The Very Best Of Johnny Cash (Sony 2002)★★★★.
VIDEOS: Live In London: Johnny Cash (BBC Video 1987), In San Quentin (Vestron Video 1987), Riding The Rails (Hendring Music Video 1990), Johnny Cash Live! (1993), The Tennessee Top Cat Live 1955-1965 (Jubilee 1995), The Man, His World, The Music (1995), Johnny Cash: The Man In Black (IMC 1999).
FURTHER READING: Johnny Cash Discography And Recording History 1954-1969, John L. Smith. A Boy Named Cash, Albert Govoni. The Johnny Cash Story, George Carpozi. Johnny Cash: Winners Get Scars Too, Christopher S. Wren. The New Johnny Cash, Charles Paul Conn. Man In Black, Johnny Cash. The Johnny Cash Discography 1954-1984, John L. Smith. The Johnny Cash Record Catalogue, John L. Smith (ed.). Johnny Cash: The Autobiography, Johnny Cash with Patrick Carr. The Cash Family Scrapbook, Cindy Cash. Johnny Cash, Frank Moriarty. I've Been Everywhere: The Complete Johnny Cash Chronicle, Peter Lewry.

CASH, ROSANNE
ALBUMS: Rosanne Cash (Ariola 1978)★★, Right Or Wrong (Columbia 1979)★★★, Seven Year Ache (Columbia 1981)★★★, Somewhere In The Stars (Columbia 1982) ★★★, Rhythm And Romance (Columbia 1985)★★★, King's Record Shop (Columbia 1988)★★★, Interiors (Columbia 1990)★★★★, The Wheel (Columbia 1993)★★★, 10 Song Demo (Capitol 1996)★★★★.
COMPILATIONS: Hits 1979-1989 (Columbia 1989)★★★★, Retrospective (Columbia 1995)★★★★.
VIDEOS: Live - The Interiors Tour (1994).
FURTHER READING: Bodies Of Water, Rosanne Cash.

CASSIDY, DAVID
ALBUMS: Cherish (Bell 1972)★★, Could It Be Forever (Bell 1972)★★, Rock Me Baby (Bell 1973)★★, Dreams Are Nuthin' More Than Wishes (Bell 1973)★★, Cassidy Live! (Bell 1974)★, The Higher They Climb The Harder They Fall (RCA 1975)★★, Home Is Where The Heart Is (RCA 1976)★★★, Gettin' It In The Street (RCA 1976)★★★, Romance (Arista 1985)★★, His Greatest Hits Live (Starblend 1986)★★, David Cassidy (Enigma 1990)★★, Didn't You Used To Be ... (Scotti Bros 1992)★★★, Old Trick, New Dog (Slamajama 1998) ★★★, Then And Now (Universal TV 2001)★★★.
COMPILATIONS: David Cassidy's Greatest Hits (Bell 1974)★★★, 'I Think I Love You': Classic Songs (Curb 1996)★★★, When I'm A Rock 'N' Roll Star: The David Cassidy Collection (Razor & Tie 1996)★★★.
FURTHER READING: Meet David Cassidy, James A. Hudson. David Cassidy Annual 1974, no editor listed. The David Cassidy Story, James Gregory. David In Europe: Exclusive! David's Own Story In David's Own Words, David Cassidy. C'mon Get Happy ... Fear And Loathing On The Partridge Family Bus, David Cassidy.
FILMS: The Spirit Of '76 (1990), Instant Karma (1990).

CASSIDY, EVA
ALBUMS: with Chuck Brown Live At Blues Alley (Blix Street 1996)★★★★, Eva By Heart (Blix Street 1997)★★★★, The Other Side 1992 recordings (Biondo 1999)★★, Time After Time (Blix Street 2000)★★★★.
COMPILATIONS: Songbird (Blix Street 1998)★★★★.
FURTHER READING: Songbird: Her Story By Those Who Knew Her, Rob Burley and Jonathan Maitland.

CAST
ALBUMS: All Change (Polydor 1995)★★★★, Mother Nature Calls (Polydor 1997)★★★, Magic Hour (Polydor 1999)★★★★, Beetroot (Polydor 2001)★★.

CASTAWAYS
COMPILATIONS: Liar, Liar: The Best Of The Castaways (Plum 1999)★★★.
FILMS: It's A Bikini World (1967).

CATATONIA
ALBUMS: Way Beyond Blue (Blanco y Negro 1996)★★★, International Velvet (Blanco y Negro/Warners 1997) ★★★★, Equally Cursed And Blessed (Blanco y Negro/Atlantic 1999)★★★★, Paper Scissors Stone (Blanco y Negro 2001)★★.
COMPILATIONS: The Sublime Magic Of ... (The Songs 1994 – 1995) (Nursery 1995)★★★, The Crai EPs (Crai 1999)★★★.
FURTHER READING: Cerys, Catatonia And The Rise Of Welsh Pop, David Owens. To Hell And Back With Catatonia, Brian Wright.

CAVE, NICK
ALBUMS: From Her To Eternity (Mute 1984)★★★, The Firstborn Is Dead (Mute 1985)★★★, Kicking Against The Pricks (Mute 1986)★★★, Your Funeral, My Trial (Mute 1986)★★★, Tender Prey (Mute 1988)★★★, with Mick Harvey, Blixa Bargeld Ghosts Of The Civil Dead film soundtrack (Mute 1989)★★★, The Good Son (Mute 1990)★★★★, Henry's Dream (Mute 1992)★★★, Live Seeds (Mute 1993) ★★★, Let Love In (Mute 1994)★★★★, Murder Ballads (Mute/Reprise 1996)★★★★, with Harvey, Bargeld To Have And To Hold film soundtrack (Mute 1996)★★★, The Boatman's Call (Mute 1997)★★★★, The Secret Life Of The Love Song/The Flesh Made Word spoken word (King Mob 2000)★★★, No More Shall We Part (Mute 2001)★★★★.
COMPILATIONS: The Best Of Nick Cave & The Bad Seeds (Mute 1998)★★★★.
VIDEOS: Kings Of Independence (Studio 1989), The Road To God Knows Where (BMG Video 1990), Live At The Paradiso (Mute 1992), Ritual Habitual (PolyGram Music Video 1996), The Videos (Mute 1998).
FURTHER READING: King Ink, Nick Cave. And The Ass Saw The Angel, Nick Cave. Fish In A Barrel: Nick Cave & The Bad Seeds On Tour, Peter Milne. Hellfire: Life According To Nick Cave, Jeremy Dean. Bad Seed: The Biography Of Nick Cave, Ian Johnston. Nick Cave: The Birthday Party And Other Epic Adventures, Robert Brokenmouth. King Ink II, Nick Cave. The Complete Lyrics: 1978-2001, Nick Cave.
FILMS: Der Himmel Über Berlin aka Wings Of Desire (1987), Dandy (1987), Ghosts ... Of The Civil Dead (1988), The Road To God Knows Where (1990), Johnny Suede (1991), Jonas In The Desert (1994), Rhinoceros Hunting In Budapest (1996).

CHAD AND JEREMY
ALBUMS: Sing For You (UK) (Ember 1964)★★★, Yesterday's Gone (US) (World Artists 1964)★★★, Chad & Jeremy's Second Album (UK) (Ember 1965)★★★, Sing For You (US) (World Artists 1965)★★★, Before And After (Columbia 1965)★★★, I Don't Want To Lose You Baby (Columbia 1965)★★★, Distant Shores (Columbia 1966)★★★, Of Cabbages And Kings (Columbia 1967)★★★, The Ark (Columbia 1968)★★★★, Three In The Attic film soundtrack (Sidewalk 1969)★★, Chad Stuart & Jeremy Clyde (Rocshire 1983)★★.
COMPILATIONS: 5 + 10 = 15 Fabulous Hits (Fidu 1966)★★, The Best Of Chad & Jeremy (Capitol/Ember 1966)★★★, More Chad & Jeremy (Capitol 1966)★★★, Chad And Jeremy (Harmony 1969)★★★, The Soft Sound Of Chad & Jeremy (K-Tel 1990)★★★, Painted Dayglow Smile: A Collection (Columbia/Legacy 1992)★★★★, Yesterday's Gone (Drive Archive 1994)★★★, A Summer Song (K-Tel 1995)★★★, The Best Of Chad & Jeremy (One Way 1996)★★★, Best Of Chad And Jeremy (Quicksilver/Bulldog 1997)★★, Greatest Hits (Laserlight 1999)★★★, The Very Best Of Chad & Jeremy (Varèse Sarabande 2000)★★★★.

CHAIRMEN OF THE BOARD
ALBUMS: as the Chairmen Of The Board The Chairmen Of The Board (Invictus 1969)★★★, In Session (Invictus 1970)★★, Men Are Getting Scarce (Bittersweet) (Invictus 1972)★★, Skin I'm In (Invictus 1974)★★★, as General Johnson And The Chairmen Success (Surfside 1981)★★, A Gift Of Beach Music (Surfside 1982)★★, The Music (Surfside 1987)★★.
SOLO: General Johnson Generally Speaking (Invictus 1972)★★, General Johnson (Arista 1976)★★★. Harrison Kennedy Hypnotic Music (Invictus 1972)★★. Danny Woods Aries (Invictus 1972)★★.
COMPILATIONS: Salute The General (HDH/Demon 1983)★★★, A.G.M. (HDH/Demon 1985)★★★, Soul Agenda (HDH 1989)★★, Greatest Hits (HDH/Fantasy 1991)★★★★, The Best Of Chairmen Of The Board (Renaissance 1997)★★★★, Any Other Business: (Life As A) Chairman Of The Board (Sequel 1998)★★★★, Everthing's Tuesday: The Best Of (Castle 2000)★★★★.

CHAMBERS, KASEY
ALBUMS: The Captain (Virgin/Warners 1999)★★★★, Barricades & Brickwalls (EMI 2001)★★★★.

CHAMELEONS
ALBUMS: Script Of The Bridge (Statik/MCA 1983)★★★, What Does Anything Mean? Basically (Statik 1985)★★★★, Strange Times (Geffen 1986)★★★★, Tripping Dogs 1985 recordings (Glass Pyramid 1990)★★, Live In Toronto 1987 recording (Imaginary 1992)★★★, Free Trade Hall Rehearsal 1985 recordings (Imaginary 1993)★★, Dali's Picture (Imaginary 1993)★★, Aufführung In Berlin (Imaginary 1993)★★★, Live At The Gallery Club Manchester 18 December 1982 (Visionary 1996)★★★, Strip (Paradiso 2000)★★★, Why Call It Anything (Artful/Cleopatra 2001)★★★★.
COMPILATIONS: The Fan And The Bellows (Hybrid 1986)★★★, John Peel Sessions (Strange Fruit 1990)★★, Here Today ... Gone Tomorrow (Imaginary 1992)★★, The Radio 1 Evening Show Sessions (Nighttracks 1993)★★★, Northern Songs (Bone Idol 1994)★★★, Live Shreds (Cleopatra 1996)★★, Return Of The Roughnecks: The Best Of The Chameleons (Dead Dead Good 1997)★★★★.
VIDEOS: Live At The Camden Palace (Jettisoundz 1985), Live At The Haçienda (Jettisoundz 1994), Arsenal (Jettisoundz 1995), Live At The Gallery Club 1982 (Jettisoundz 1996).

CHANDLER, GENE
ALBUMS: The Duke Of Earl (Vee Jay 1962)★★★★, Just Be True (1964)★★★, Gene Chandler Live On Stage In '65 (Constellation 1965)★★★, The Girl Don't Care (Brunswick 1967)★★★, The Duke Of Soul (Checker 1967)★★★, There Was A Time (Brunswick 1968)★★, The Two Sides Of Gene Chandler (Brunswick 1969)★★, The Gene Chandler Situation (Mercury 1970)★★★, with Jerry Butler Gene And Jerry – One & One (Mercury 1971)★★★, Get Down (Chi-Sound 1978)★★★, When You're Number One (20th Century 1979), '80 (20th Century 1980)★★★, Here's To Love (20th Century 1981)★★, Your Love Looks Good On Me (Fastfire 1985)★★★.
COMPILATIONS: Greatest Hits By Gene Chandler (Constellation 1964)★★★, Stroll On With The Duke (Solid Smoke 1984)★★★, 60s Soul Brother (Kent/Ace 1986)★★★, Get Down (Charly 1992)★★★, Nothing Can Stop Me: Gene Chandler's Greatest Hits (Varèse Sarabande 1994)★★★, Duke Of Soul: The Brunswick Years (Brunswick 1998)★★★, Get Down With The Get Down: The Best Of The Chi-Sound Years 1978-83 (Westside 1999)★★★, The Best Of Gene Chandler: The Duke Of Earl (Collectables 2000)★★★.
FILMS: Don't Knock The Twist (1962).

CHANTAYS
ALBUMS: Pipeline (Downey 1963)★★★, Two Sides Of The Chantays (Dot 1964)★★★.

CHAPIN, HARRY
ALBUMS: Heads And Tales (Elektra 1972)★★★, Sniper And Other Love Songs (Elektra 1972)★★, Short Stories (Elektra 1974)★★★, Verities And Balderdash (Elektra 1974)★★★, Portrait Gallery (Elektra 1975)★★★, Greatest Stories – Live (Elektra 1976)★★, On The Road To Kingdom Come (Elektra 1976)★★, Dance Band On The Titanic (Elektra 1977)★★★, Living Room Suite (Elektra 1978)★★, Legends Of The Lost And Found – New Greatest Stories Live (Elektra 1979)★★, Sequel (Boardwalk 1980)★★★, The Last Protest Singer (Sequel 1989)★★, Bottom Line Encore Collection 1981 recording (Bottom Line 1998)★★.
COMPILATIONS: Anthology (Elektra 1985)★★★, Story Of A Life 3-CD box set (Elektra/Rhino 1999)★★★, Behind The Music: The Harry Chapin Collection (Warners 2001)★★★.
FURTHER READING: Taxi: The Harry Chapin Story, Peter M. Coan.

CHAPMAN, MICHAEL
ALBUMS: Rainmaker (Harvest 1969)★★★, Fully Qualified Survivor (Harvest 1970)★★★★, Window (Harvest 1971) ★★★, Wrecked Again (Harvest 1971)★★★★, Millstone Grit (Gamma Decca 1973)★★★, Deal Gone Down (Gamma Decca 1974)★★★, Pleasures Of The Street (Nova 1975) ★★★, Savage Amusement (Gamma Decca 1976)★★, The Man Who Hated Mornings (Gamma Decca 1977)★★★, Playing Guitar The Easy Way guitar tutor (Criminal 1978) ★★★, Life On The Ceiling (Criminal 1979)★★, Looking For Eleven (Criminal 1980)★★★, Almost Alone (Black Crow 1981)★★★★, with Rick Kemp Original Owners (Konnexion 1984)★★★, Heartbeat (Coda 1987)★★★, Still Making Rain (Homemade/Making Waves 1992)★★★, Navigation (Planet 1995)★★★★, Dreaming Out Loud (Demon 1997)★★★, Live In Hamburg (Mooncrest 2000)★★★, The Twisted Road (Mystic 2000)★★★, Americana (Siren 2000)★★★★.
COMPILATIONS: Lady On The Rocks (Nova 1975)★★★, Michael Chapman Lived Here From 1968-72 aka The Best Of Michael Chapman (1969 - 1971) (Cube/See For Miles 1975)★★★★, BBC Sessions 69-75 (Strange Fruit 1998)★★★, Growing Pains: Previously Unissued 1966-1980 (Mooncrest 2000)★★, Growing Pains 2 (Mooncrest 2001)★★★.
FURTHER READING: Firewater Dreams, Michael Chapman.

CHAPMAN, ROGER
ALBUMS: Chappo (Acrobat 1979)★★★, with The Shortlist Live In Hamburg (Acrobat 1979)★★★, Mail Order M.a.g.i.c (Kamera 1980)★★, Hyenas Only Laugh For Fun (Line 1981)★★, as The Shortlist The Riffburgler Album (Line 1982)★★, with The Shortlist He Was ... She Was ... You Was ... We Was (Polydor 1982)★★, as The Riffburglars Swag (Instant 1983)★★, Mango Crazy (Instant 1983)★★, The Shadow Knows (Instant 1984)★★★, Zipper (RCA 1986)★★, Techno Prisoners (RCA 1987)★★, Live In Berlin mini-album (Polydor 1989)★★, Walking The Cat (SPV 1989)★★★, Hybrid And Lowdown (Polydor 1990)★★★, Under No Obligation (Polydor 1992)★★, Kiss My Soul (Essential 1996)★★★★, with The Shortlist A Turn Unstoned? (SPV 1998)★★, with The Shortlist In My Own Time (Live) (SPV 1999)★★★, with The Shortlist Rollin' & Tumblin' (Mystic 2001)★★★.
COMPILATIONS: Strong Songs: The Best Of Roger Chapman (SPV 1990)★★★, Kick It Back (Essential 1990)★★★, King Of The Shouters: The Best Of Roger Chapman (Line 1994)★★★, Anthology 1979-1998 (Essential 1998)★★★★, Selecta (Thunderbird 2001)★★★.

CHAPMAN, TRACY
ALBUMS: Tracy Chapman (Elektra 1988)★★★★, Crossroads (Elektra 1989)★★★, Matters Of The Heart (Elektra 1992)★★, New Beginning (Elektra 1995)★★★, Telling Stories (Elektra 2000)★★★★.
COMPILATIONS: Tracy Chapman Collection (East West 2001)★★★★.

CHARLATANS (UK)
ALBUMS: Some Friendly (Situation 2 1990)★★★★, Between 10th And 11th (Situation 2 1992)★★, Up To Our Hips (Beggars Banquet 1994)★★★, Charlatans (Beggars Banquet 1995)★★★, Tellin' Stories (Beggars Banquet 1997)★★★★, Us And Us Only (Universal 1999)★★★★, Wonderland (Universal 2001)★★★, Songs From The Other Side (Beggars Banquet 2002)★★★.
COMPILATIONS: Melting Pot (Beggars Banquet 1997)★★★★.
FURTHER READING: The Charlatans: The Authorised History, Dominic Wills And Tom Sheehan.

CHARLATANS (USA)
ALBUMS: The Charlatans (Philips 1969)★★★, The Autumn Demos (Ace 1982)★★★.
COMPILATIONS: The Charlatans (Ace 1996)★★★, The Amazing Charlatans (Ace/Big Beat 1996)★★★.

CHARLES AND EDDIE
ALBUMS: Duophonic (Stateside/Capitol 1992)★★★, Chocolate Milk (Capitol 1995)★★.

CHARLES, RAY
ALBUMS: Hallelujah, I Love Her So aka Ray Charles (Atlantic 1957)★★★, The Great Ray Charles (Atlantic 1957)★★★★, with Milt Jackson Soul Brothers (Atlantic 1958)★★★★, Ray Charles At Newport (Atlantic 1958)★★★★, Yes Indeed (Atlantic 1959)★★★, Ray Charles (Hollywood 1959)★★★★, The Fabulous Ray Charles (Hollywood 1959)★★★, What'd I Say (Atlantic 1959)★★★, The Genius Of Ray Charles (Atlantic 1959)★★★★★, Ray Charles In Person (Atlantic 1960)★★★★, The Genius Hits The Road (ABC 1960) ★★★★, Dedicated To You (ABC 1961)★★★, Genius + Soul = Jazz (Impulse! 1961)★★★★★, The Genius After Hours (Atlantic 1961)★★★★, with Betty Carter Ray Charles And Betty Carter (ABC 1961)★★★★, The Genius Sings The Blues (Atlantic 1961)★★★★, with Jackson Soul Meeting (Atlantic 1961)★★★★, Do The Twist With Ray Charles (Atlantic 1961)★★★, Modern Sounds In Country And Western Music (ABC 1962)★★★★★, Modern Sounds In Country And Western Volume 2 (ABC 1962)★★★★, Ingredients In A Recipe For Soul (ABC 1963)★★★★, Sweet And Sour Tears (ABC 1964)★★★, Have A Smile With Me (ABC 1964)★★★, Ray Charles Live In Concert (ABC 1965)★★★, Country And Western Meets Rhythm And Blues aka Together Again (ABC 1965)★★★, Crying Time (ABC 1966)★★★, Ray's Moods (ABC 1966)★★★, Ray Charles Invites You To Listen (ABC 1967)★★★, A Portrait Of Ray (ABC 1968)★★★, I'm All Yours, Baby! (ABC 1969)★★, Doing His Thing (ABC 1969) ★★★, My Kind Of Jazz (Tangerine 1970)★★★, Love Country Style (ABC 1970)★★, Volcanic Action Of My Soul (ABC 1971)★★★, A Message From The People (ABC 1972) ★★★★, Through The Eyes Of Love (ABC 1972), Jazz Number II (Tangerine 1972)★★★, Ray Charles Live (Atlantic 1973)★★★, Come Live With Me (Crossover 1974)★★, Renaissance (Crossover 1975)★★, My Kind Of Jazz III (Crossover 1975)★★, Live In Japan (Atlantic 1975)★★★,

with Cleo Laine Porgy And Bess (RCA 1976)★★★, True To Life (Atlantic 1977)★★, Love And Peace (Atlantic 1978)H, Ain't It So (Atlantic 1979)★★, Brother Ray Is At It Again (Atlantic 1980)★★, Wish You Were Here Tonight (Columbia 1983)★★, Do I Ever Cross Your Mind (Columbia 1984)★★, Friendship (Columbia 1985)★★★★, The Spirit Of Christmas (Columbia 1985)★★, From The Pages Of My Mind (Columbia 1986)★★, Just Between Us (Columbia 1988)★★, Seven Spanish Angels And Other Hits (Columbia 1989)★★, Would You Believe (Warners 1990)★★, My World (Warners 1993)★★★, Strong Love Affair (Qwest/Warners 1996)★★, Berlin, 1962 (Pablo 1996)★★★★.
COMPILATIONS: The Ray Charles Story (Atlantic 1962)★★★, Ray Charles' Greatest Hits (ABC 1962)★★★★, A Man And His Soul (ABC 1967)★★★, The Best Of Ray Charles 1956-58 (Atlantic 1970)★★★★, A 25th Anniversary In Show Business Salute To Ray Charles (ABC 1971)★★★★, The Right Time (Atlantic 1987)★★★, A Life In Music 1956-59 (Atlantic 1982)★★★★, Greatest Hits Volume 1 1960-67 (Rhino 1988)★★★★, Greatest Hits Volume 2 1960-72 (Rhino 1988)★★★★, Anthology (Rhino 1989)★★★★, The Collection ABC recordings (Castle 1990)★★★, Blues Is My Middle Name 1949-52 recordings (Double Play 1991)★★★, The Birth Of Soul: The Complete Atlantic R&B '52-'59 (Rhino/Atlantic 1991)★★★★★, The Living Legend (Atlantic 1993) ★★★, The Best Of The Atlantic Years (Rhino/Atlantic 1994)★★★, Classics (Rhino 1995)★★★, Genius & Soul 5-CD box set (Rhino 1997)★★★★★, Standards (Rhino 1998)★★★★, The Complete Country & Western Recordings, 1959-1986 4-CD box set (Rhino 1998)★★★★★, The Definitive Ray Charles (WSM 2001)★★★★.
FURTHER READING: Ray Charles, Sharon Bell Mathis. Brother Ray, Ray Charles' Own Story, Ray Charles and David Ritz. Ray Charles: Man And Music, Michael Lydon.
FILMS: Blues For Lovers aka Ballad In Blue (1964), The Blues Brothers (1980).

CHEAP TRICK
ALBUMS: Cheap Trick (Epic 1977)★★★, In Color (Epic 1977)★★★, Heaven Tonight (Epic 1978)★★★★, At Budokan (Epic 1979)★★★★, Dream Police (Epic 1979) ★★★, Found All The Parts mini-album (Epic 1980)★★, All Shook Up (Epic 1980)★★, One On One (Epic 1982)★★, Next Position Please (Epic 1983)★★, Standing On The Edge (Epic 1985)★★★, The Doctor (Epic 1986)★★, Lap Of Luxury (Epic 1988)★★★, Busted (Epic 1990)★★★, Woke Up With A Monster (Warners 1994)★★, Budokan II 1978 recording (Epic/Sony 1994)★★, Cheap Trick (Red Ant 1997)★★★, Cheap Trick At Budokan: The Complete Concert (Columbia/Legacy 1998)★★★★, Music For Hangovers (Cheap Trick 1999)★★★, Silver (Cheap Trick 2001)★★★.
COMPILATIONS: The Collection (Castle 1991)★★★★, Greatest Hits (Epic 1992)★★★, Sex, America, Cheap Trick 4-CD box set (Epic 1996)★★★★, Authorized Greatest Hits (Epic 2000)★★★★.
VIDEOS: Every Trick In The Book (CMV Enterprises 1990), Silver (Image Entertainment 2001).
FURTHER READING: Reputation Is A Fragile Thing: The Story Of Cheap Trick, Mike Hayes and Ken Sharp.

CHECKER, CHUBBY
ALBUMS: Chubby Checker (Parkway 1960)★★★, Twist With Chubby Checker (Parkway 1960)★★★, For Twisters Only (Parkway 1960)★★★, It's Pony Time (Parkway 1961)★★★, Let's Twist Again (Parkway 1961)★★★★, Bobby Rydell/Chubby Checker (Parkway 1961)★★★, Twistin' Round The World (Parkway 1962)★★, For Teen Twisters Only (Parkway 1962)★★★, Don't Knock The Twist film soundtrack (Parkway 1962)★★, All The Hits (For Your Dancin' Party) (Parkway 1962)★★★, Limbo Party (Parkway 1962)★★★, Let's Limbo Some More (Parkway 1963)★★, Beach Party (Parkway 1963)★★, Chubby Checker In Person (Parkway 1963)★★, Chubby's Folk Album (Parkway 1964)H, Chubby Checker With Sy Oliver (Parkway 1964)★★, Discotheque (Parkway 1965)★★, Chequered (London 1971)★★, The Change Has Come (MCA 1982)★★, The Texas Twist (Twisted Entertainment 2001)★★★, Toward The Light (Twisted Entertainment 2001)★★★.
COMPILATIONS: Your Twist Party (Parkway 1961)★★★, Chubby Checker's Biggest Hits (Parkway 1962)★★★★, Chubby Checker's Eighteen Golden Hits (Parkway 1966)★★★★, Chubby Checker's Greatest Hits (ABKCO 1972)★★★★, Let's Twist Again (BMG 1997)★★★.
FILMS: It's Trad, Dad! aka Ring-A-Ding Rhythm (1962), Don't Knock The Twist (1962).

CHEMICAL BROTHERS
ALBUMS: Exit Planet Dust (Junior Boy's Own/Astralwerks 1995)★★★★, Dig Your Own Hole (Freestyle Dust 1997) ★★★★★, Surrender (Freestyle Dust/Astralwerks 1999)★★★★, Come With Us (Freestyle Dust/Astralwerks 2002)★★★★.
COMPILATIONS: Live At The Social: Volume One (Heavenly 1996)★★★★, Brothers Gonna Work It Out (Freestyle Dust/Astralwerks 1998)★★★.

CHER
ALBUMS: All I Really Want To Do (Imperial 1966)★★, The Sonny Side Of Cher (Imperial 1966)★★, Cher i (Imperial 1966)★★★, Backstage (Imperial 1967)★★, Sings The Hits (Springboard 1967)★★, With Love (Imperial 1967)★★, 3614 Jackson Highway (Atco 1969)★★, Gypsys, Tramps & Thieves (Kapp 1971)★★★, Foxy Lady (Kapp 1972)★★, Half Breed (MCA 1973)★★, Dark Lady (MCA 1974)★★, Bittersweet White Light (MCA 1974)★★, Stars (Warners 1975)★★, I'd Rather Believe In You (Warners 1976)★★, with Gregg Allman as Allman And Woman Two The Hard Way (Warners 1977)H, Take Me Home (Casablanca 1979)★★, Prisoner (Casablanca 1980)★★, Black Rose (Casablanca 1980)★★, I Paralyze (Columbia 1982)★★, Cher ii (Geffen 1987)★★, Heart Of Stone (Geffen 1989)★★, Love Hurts (Geffen 1991)★★★★, It's A Man's World (Warners 1995)★★★, Believe (Warners 1998)★★★, Not.com.mercial (CherDirect.Com 2000)★★★, Living Proof (Warners 2001)★★.
COMPILATIONS: Cher's Golden Greats (Imperial 1968)★★, The Best Of Cher 60s recordings (EMI America 1991)★★★, Greatest Hits (Geffen 1992)★★★, The Casablanca Years (PolyGram 1996)★★★, Bang, Bang: The Early Years (EMI 1999)★★★, Behind The Door: 1964-1974 (Raven 2000)★★★, The Way Of Love (MCA 2000)★★★.
VIDEOS: Extravaganza: Live At The Mirage (1992), Cher: Live In Concert (Warner Music Vision 1999).
FURTHER READING: Cher: Simply Cher, Linda Jacobs. Sonny And Cher, Thomas Braun. Cher, J. Randy Taraborrelli. Totally Uninhibited: The Life & Times Of Cher, Lawrence J. Quirk. Cher: In Her Own Words, Nigel Goodall. Cher: The Visual Documentary, Mick St. Michael. The First Time, Cher. Cher: If You Believe, Mark Bego.
FILMS: Wild On The Beach aka Beach House Party (1965), Good Times (1967), Chastity (1969), Come Back To The Five And Dime, Jimmy Dean, Jimmy Dean (1982), Silkwood (1983), Mask (1985), The Witches Of Eastwick (1987), Suspect (1987), Moonstruck (1987), Mermaids (1990), The Player (1992), Prêt-à-Porter aka Ready To Wear (1994), Faithful (1996), Tea With Mussolini (1999).

CHERRY, NENEH
ALBUMS: Raw Like Sushi (Circa 1989)★★★★, Homebrew (Virgin 1992)★★★, Man (Hut 1996)★★★.
VIDEOS: The Rise Of Neneh Cherry (BMG Video 1989).

CHI-LITES
ALBUMS: Give It Away (Brunswick 1969)★★★, I Like Your Lovin' (Brunswick 1971)★★★, Give More Power To The People (Brunswick 1971)★★★★, A Lonely Man (Brunswick 1972) ★★★, A Letter To Myself (Brunswick 1973)★★★, The Chi-Lites (Brunswick 1973)★★★, Toby (Brunswick 1974)★★★, Half A Love (Brunswick 1975)★★, Happy Being Lonely (Mercury 1976)★★★, The Fantastic Chi-Lites (Mercury 1977)★★★, Heavenly Body (Chi-Sound 1980)★★, Me And You (Chi-Sound 1982)★★, Bottoms Up (Larc 1983)★★★, Steppin' Out (Private I 1984)★★, Just Say You Love Me (Ichiban 1990)★★★.
SOLO: Eugene Record Welcome To My Fantasy (Warners 1979)★★.
COMPILATIONS: The Chi-Lites Greatest Hits (Brunswick 1972)★★★★, The Chi-Lites Greatest Hits Volume Two (Brunswick 1975)★★★, The Best Of The Chi-Lites (Kent 1987)★★★, Greatest Hits (Street Life 1988)★★★, Very Best Of The Chi-Lites (BR Music 1988)★★★, The Chi-Lites Greatest Hits (Rhino 1992)★★★★, Have You Seen Her? The Very Best Of ... (Pickwick 1995)★★★, Too Good To Be Forgotten 3-CD box set (Edsel 1998)★★★★, One In A Million: The Best Of The Chi-Lites (Music Club 1999)★★★.

CHIC
ALBUMS: Chic (Atlantic 1977)★★★, C'Est Chic (Atlantic 1978)★★★★, Risqué (Atlantic 1979)★★★★, Real People (Atlantic 1980)★★★★, Take It Off (Atlantic 1981)★★★★, Tongue In Chic (Atlantic 1982)★★★, Believer (Atlantic 1983)★★★, Chic-Ism (Warners 1992)★★★.
COMPILATIONS: Les Plus Grands Succès De Chic: Chic's Greatest Hits (Atlantic 1979)★★★★, Megachic: The Best Of Chic (Warners 1990)★★★★, Dance Dance Dance: The Best Of Chic (Atlantic 1991)★★★★, Everybody Dance (Rhino 1995)★★★★, The Very Best Of Chic (Rhino 2000)★★★★.

CHICAGO
ALBUMS: Chicago Transit Authority (Columbia 1969)★★★★, Chicago II (Columbia 1970)★★★, Chicago III (Columbia 1971)★★★, Chicago At Carnegie Hall (Columbia 1971)★★, Chicago V (Columbia 1972)★★★, Chicago VI (Columbia 1973)★★★, Chicago VII (Columbia 1974)★★★, Chicago VIII (Columbia 1975)★★★★, Chicago X (Columbia 1976) ★★, Chicago XI (Columbia 1977)★★, Hot Streets (Columbia 1978)★★★, Chicago 13 (Columbia 1979)★★, Chicago XIV (Columbia 1980)★★, Chicago 16 (Full Moon 1982)★★, Chicago 17 (Full Moon 1984)★★, Chicago 18 (Warners 1987)★★, Chicago 19 (Reprise 1988)★★, Chicago 21 (Reprise 1991)★★, Night And Day (Giant 1995)★★★, Chicago 25 (Chicago 1998)★★, Chicago 26 (Chicago 1999)★★.
COMPILATIONS: Chicago IX – Chicago's Greatest Hits (Columbia 1975)★★★★, Chicago – Greatest Hits, Volume II (Columbia 1981)★★★, Greatest Hits 1982-1989 (Reprise 1989)★★★, The Heart Of Chicago (Warners 1989)★★★, Group Portrait (Columbia/Legacy 1991)★★★★, The Very Best Of Chicago (Arcade 1996)★★★, The Heart Of Chicago 1967-1997 (Reprise 1997)★★★, The Heart Of Chicago 1967-1997 Volume II (Reprise 1997)★★★.
VIDEOS: And The Band Played On (Warner Reprise 1994), In Concert At The Greek Theatre (Warner Music Vision 1994).

CHICKEN SHACK
ALBUMS: Forty Blue Fingers Freshly Packed And Ready To Serve (Blue Horizon 1968)★★★★, OK Ken? (Blue Horizon 1969)★★★, 100 Ton Chicken (Blue Horizon 1969)★★★, Accept! Chicken Shack (Blue Horizon 1970)★★★, Imagination Lady (Deram 1972)★★★, Unlucky Boy (Deram 1973)★★★★, Goodbye Chicken Shack (Deram 1974)★★, The Creeper (Warners 1979)★★, Chicken Shack (Gull 1979)★★, Roadie's Concerto (RCA 1981)★★★, Chicken Shack On Air (Band Of Joy 1991)★★★, Changes (Indigo 1992)★★★, Webb's Blues (Indigo 1994)★★★, Plucking Good (Inak 1994)★★★, Stan 'The Man' Live (Indigo 1995)★★★, Imagination Lady (Indigo 1997)★★, Private Collection Vol 1 (Gygax 1999)★★, Poor Boy: In Concert 1973 & 1981 (Indigo 2000)★★★.
SOLO: Stan Webb Webb (Indigo 2001)★★.
COMPILATIONS: The Golden Era Of Pop Music (Columbia 1977)★★★, In The Can (Columbia 1980)★★★, Collection: Chicken Shack (Castle 1988)★★★, Black Night (Indigo 1997)★★★, Jersey Lightning 1975-1978 recordings (Indigo 2000)★★★.

CHICORY TIP
ALBUMS: Son Of My Father (Columbia 1972)★★.
COMPILATIONS: The Best Of Chicory Tip (Repertoire 1999)★★.

CHIEFTAINS
ALBUMS: Chieftains 1 (Claddagh 1964)★★★, Chieftains 2 (Claddagh 1969)★★★, Chieftains 3 (Claddagh 1971)★★★, Chieftains 4 (Claddagh 1973)★★★★, Chieftains 5 (Island 1975)★★★, Women Of Ireland (Island 1976)★★★, Bonaparte's Retreat (Claddagh 1976)★★★, Chieftains Live (Columbia 1977)★★★, Chieftains 7 (Claddagh 1977)★★★, Chieftains 8 (Columbia 1978)★★★, Volume 9 (Claddagh 1979)★★★, Boil The Breakfast Early (Columbia 1980)★★★★, Chieftains 10 (Claddagh 1981)★★★, Year Of The French original soundtrack (Claddagh 1983)★★★, The Chieftains In China (Shanachie 1984)★★★, Ballad Of The Irish Horse film soundtrack (Shanachie 1985)★★★, Celtic Wedding (RCA 1987)★★★, James Galway And The Chieftains In Ireland (RCA 1987)★★★, with Van Morrison Irish Heartbeat (Mercury 1988)★★★★, A Chieftains Celebration (RCA 1989)★★★★, The Celtic Connection - James Galway And The Chieftains (1990)★★★, Bells Of Dublin (RCA 1991)★★★★, An Irish Evening: Live At The Grand Opera House, Belfast (RCA 1992)★★★, Another Country (RCA 1992)★★★, with the Belfast Harp Orchestra The Celtic Harp (RCA 1993)★★★, The Long Black Veil (RCA 1995)★★★★, The Bells Of Dublin (RCA Victor 1995)★★★★, Film Cuts (RCA Victor 1996)★★★, Santiago (RCA Victor 1996)★★★, Tears Of Stone (RCA Victor 1999)★★★★, Water From The Well (RCA Victor 2000) ★★★★, The Wide World Over (RCA Vicotr 2002)★★★.
COMPILATIONS: Chieftains Collection (Claddagh 1989) ★★★★, The Best Of The Chieftains (Columbia 1992)★★★.
VIDEOS: Live In China (Hendring Music Video 1991), An Irish Evening (BMG Video 1992).

CHIFFONS
ALBUMS: He's So Fine (Laurie 1963)★★, One Fine Day (Laurie 1963)★★, Sweet Talkin' Guy (Laurie 1966)★★.
COMPILATIONS: Everything You Ever Wanted To Hear ... But Couldn't Get (Laurie 1981)★★★, Doo-Lang Doo-Lang Doo-Lang (Impact/Ace 1985)★★★, Flips, Flops And Rarities (Impact/Ace 1986)★★, Greatest Recordings (Ace 1990)★★★★, The Fabulous Chiffons (Ace 1991)★★★, One Fine Day And Other Favourites (CEMA 1992)★★★, Greatest Hits (Capitol 1996)★★★★, Best Of The Chiffons (DJ Specialist 1998)★★★.

CHILLI WILLI AND THE RED HOT PEPPERS
ALBUMS: Kings Of The Robot Rhythm (Revelation 1972)★★★, Bongos Over Balham (Mooncrest 1974)★★★.
COMPILATIONS: I'll Be Home (Proper 1997)★★★.

CHOCOLATE WATCH BAND
ALBUMS: No Way Out (Tower 1967)★★★, The Inner Mystique (Tower 1968)★★★, One Step Beyond (Tower 1969)★★, At The Love-In, Live! 1999 recording (Roir 2001)★★.
COMPILATIONS: The Best Of The Chocolate Watch Band (Rhino 1983)★★★, 44 (Big Beat/Ace 1984)★★★.

CHRISTIANS
ALBUMS: The Christians (Island 1987)★★★★, Colour (Island 1990)★★★, Happy In Hell (Island 1992)★★★.
COMPILATIONS: The Best Of The Christians (Island 1993)★★★★.
VIDEOS: The Best Of The Christians (Island 1993).

CHRISTIE, LOU
ALBUMS: Lou Christie (Roulette 1963)★★, Lightnin' Strikes (MGM 1966)★★★, Lou Christie Strikes Back (Co & Ce 1966)★★★, Lou Christie Strikes Again (Colpix 1966)★★★, Lou Christie Painter Of Hits (MGM 1966)★★, I'm Gonna Make You Mine (Buddah 1969)★★★, Paint America Love (Buddah 1971)★★, Lou Christie - Zip-A-Dee-Doo-Dah (CTI 1974)★★.
COMPILATIONS: Beyond The Blue Horizon: More Of The Best Of Lou Christie (Varèse Sarabande 1995)★★★, Gonna Make You Mine (Camden 1998)★★★, The Complete Co & Ce/Roulette Recordings (Taragon 1998)★★★.

CHUCK D.
ALBUMS: Autobiography Of Mistachuck (Mercury 1996)★★★★.
FURTHER READING: Fight The Power – Rap Race And Reality, Chuck D. with Yusuf Jah.
FILMS: Burn Hollywood Burn (1997).

CHUMBAWAMBA
ALBUMS: Pictures Of Starving Children Sell Records (Agit Prop 1986)★★★★, Never Mind The Ballots, Here's The Rest Of Your Life (Agit Prop 1987)★★★★, English Rebel Songs 1381-1914 mini-album (Agit Prop 1989)★★★, Slap! (Agit Prop 1990)★★★, Anarchy (One Little Indian 1994)★★★, Show business! Chumbawamba Live (One Little Indian 1995)★★, Swingin' With Raymond (One Little Indian 1996)★★★, Tubthumper (EMI 1997)★★★★, WYSIWYG (Chrysalis 2000)★★★.
COMPILATIONS: First 2 (Agit Prop 1993)★★★★, Uneasy Listening (EMI 1999)★★★.

CHURCH
ALBUMS: Of Skins And Heart (Parlophone/Arista 1981) ★★★, The Church US version of debut (Carrere/Capitol 1982)★★★, The Blurred Crusade (Parlophone/Carrere 1982) ★★★, Séance (Parlophone/Carrere 1983)★★★, Remote Luxury (Parlophone/Warners 1984)★★★★, Heyday (EMI/Warners 1985)★★★, Starfish (Mushroom/Arista 1988)★★★, Gold Afternoon Fix (Mushroom/Arista 1990)★★★★, Priest=Aura (Mushroom/Arista 1992)★★★, Sometime Anywhere (Mushroom/Arista 1994)★★★, Magician Among The Spirits (Deep Karma/Mushroom 1996)★★★, Hologram Of Baal (Cooking Vinyl/Thirsty Ear/Festival 1998)★★★, A Box Of Birds (Cooking Vinyl/Thirsty Ear 1999)★★★, After Everything Now This (Cooking Vinyl 2002)★★★.
SOLO: Marty Willson-Piper In Reflection (Chase 1987)★★★, Art Attack (Survival/Rykodisc 1988)★★★, Rhyme (Rykodisc/Festival 1989)★★★, Spirit Level (Rykodisc/Festival 1992) ★★★. Peter Koppes Manchild & Myth (Session/Rykodisc 1988)★★★, From The Well (TV Toons 1989)★★★, with the Well Water Rites (Worldwater 1995)★★, Love Era/Irony (Immersion/Phantom 1997)★★.
COMPILATIONS: Hindsight 1980-1987 (EMI 1987)★★★, Conception (Carrerre 1988)★★★, A Quick Smoke At Spot's (Archives 1980-1990) (Arista 1991)★★★, Almost Yesterday 1981-1990 (Raven 1994)★★★★, Under The Milky Way: The Best Of The Church (Buddah 1999)★★★★.
VIDEOS: The Church (EMI Australia 1986), Goldfish (Jokes, Magic & Souvenirs) (Arista/BMG Video 1990).

CITY HIGH
ALBUMS: City High (Booga Basement 2001)★★★.

CLANNAD
ALBUMS: Clannad (Philips 1973)★★★, Clannad 2 (Gael-Linn/Shanachie 1974)★★★, Dúlamán (Gael-Linn/Shanachie 1976)★★★, Clannad In Concert (Ogham/Shanachie 1978)★★★, Crann Ull (Ogham/Tara 1980)★★★, Fuaim (Tara 1982)★★★★, Magical Ring (RCA 1983)★★★, "Legend" (RCA 1984)★★★, Macalla (RCA 1985)★★★, Sirius (RCA 1987)★★, Atlantic Realm television soundtrack (BBC 1989)★★★, with narration by Tom Conti The Angel And The Soldier Boy (RCA 1989)★★★, Anam (RCA/Atlantic 1990)★★★, Banba (RCA/Atlantic 1993)★★★, Lore (RCA 1996)★★★, Lore/Themes (RCA 1996)★★★, Landmarks (RCA 1998)★★★.
COMPILATIONS: Clannad: The Collection (K-Tel 1986) ★★★, Past Present (RCA 1989)★★★, Themes (K-Tel/Celtic Heartbeat 1992)★★★, Rogha: The Best Of Clannad (RCA 1997)★★★, The Ultimate Collection (RCA 1997)★★★, Magic Elements: The Best Of Clannad (BMG 1998)★★★, An Diolaim: The Folk Roots Of One Of Ireland's Finest Groups (Music Club 1998)★★★★, Celtic Collection (BMG 1999)★★★, Greatest Hits (RCA 2000)★★★, The Celtic Voice (Erin 2000)★★★.
VIDEOS: Past Present (BMG Video 1989).
FURTHER READING: The Other Side Of The Rainbow, Maire Brennan.

CLAPTON, ERIC
ALBUMS: three tracks as the Powerhouse with Steve Winwood, Jack Bruce, Pete York, Paul Jones What's Shakin'? (Elektra 1966)★★★, Eric Clapton (Polydor 1970)★★★, Eric Clapton's Rainbow Concert (RSO 1973)★★★, 461 Ocean Boulevard (RSO 1974)★★★★, There's One In Every Crowd (RSO 1975)★★★, E.C. Was Here (RSO 1975)★★, No Reason To Cry (RSO 1976)★★★, Slowhand (RSO 1977) ★★★★, Backless (RSO 1978)★★★, Just One Night (RSO 1980)★★★, Another Ticket (RSO 1981)★★★, Money And Cigarettes (Duck 1983)★★★, Behind The Sun (Duck 1985) ★★★, August (Duck 1986)★★★, with Michael Kamen Homeboy television soundtrack (Virgin 1989)★★, Journeyman (Duck 1989)★★★★, 24 Nights (Duck 1991)★★, Rush film soundtrack (Reprise 1992)★★, MTV Unplugged (Sony 1992)★★★★, From The Cradle (Duck 1994)★★★, Pilgrim (Warners 1998)★★★★, with B.B. King Riding With The King (Reprise 2000)★★★, Reptile (Reprise 2001)★★★.
COMPILATIONS: Time Pieces – The Best Of Eric Clapton (RSO 1982)★★★, Time Pieces Volume II: Live In The Seventies (RSO 1983)★★★, Backtrackin' (Starblend 1984)★★★★, Crossroads 4-CD box set (Polydor 1988)★★★★★, The Cream Of Eric Clapton (Polydor 1989)★★★★, Stages (Spectrum 1993)★★★, Crossroads 2: Live In The 70s (Polydor 1996)★★★★, Blues (Polydor 1999)★★★★, Clapton Chronicles: The Best Of Eric Clapton (Reprise 1999)★★★★.
VIDEOS: Eric Clapton On Whistle Test (BBC Video 1984), Live '85 (Polygram Music Video 1986), Live At The NEC Birmingham (MSD 1987), The Cream Of Eric Clapton (Channel 5 1989), Man And His Music (Video Collection 1990), Eric Clapton In Concert (Abbey Music Video 1991), 24 Nights (Warner Music Video 1991), Unplugged (1992), Clapton Chronicles: The Best Of Eric Clapton (Warner Music Vision 1999), Eric Clapton & Friends In Concert (Warner Music 2000).
FURTHER READING: Conversations With Eric Clapton, Steve Turner. Eric Clapton: A Biography, John Pidgeon. Survivor: The Authorized Biography Of Eric Clapton, Ray Coleman. Clapton: The Complete Chronicle, Marc Roberty. Eric Clapton: The New Visual Documentary, Marc Roberty. Eric Clapton: Lost In The Blues, Harry Shapiro. Eric Clapton: The Complete Recording Sessions, Marc Roberty. The Man, The Music, The Memorabilia, Marc Roberty. Edge Of Darkness, Christopher Sandford. The Complete Guide To The Music Of, Marc Roberty. Crossroads: The Life And Music Of Eric Clapton, Michael Schumacher.
FILMS: Tommy (1975), Water (1985), Blues Brothers 2000 (1998).

CLARK, DAVE, FIVE
ALBUMS: A Session With The Dave Clark Five (Columbia 1964)★★★★, Glad All Over (Epic 1964)★★★, The Dave Clark Five Return (Epic 1964)★★★, American Tour Volume 1 (Epic 1964)★★★, Coast To Coast (Epic 1965)★★★, Weekend In London (Epic 1965)★★★, Catch Us If You Can (UK) Having A Wild Weekend (US) film soundtrack (Columbia 1965)★★★★, I Like It Like That (Epic 1965)★★★, Try Too Hard (Epic 1966)★★★, Satisfied With You (Epic 1966)★★★, You Got What It Takes (Epic 1967)★★★, Everybody Knows (Epic 1968)★★★, If Somebody Loves You (Columbia 1970)★★★, Glad All Over Again (Epic 1975)★★★.
COMPILATIONS: The Dave Clark Five's Greatest Hits (Columbia 1967)★★★★, 5x5 – Go! (Epic 1969)★★★★, The Best Of The Dave Clark Five (Regal Starline 1970)★★★★, 25 Thumping Great Hits (Polydor 1977)★★★★, The History Of The Dave Clark Five (Hollywood 1993)★★★★.
VIDEOS: Glad All Over Again (PMI 1993).
FILMS: Get Yourself A College Girl (1964), Catch Us If You Can aka Having A Wild Weekend (1965).

CLARK, GENE
ALBUMS: Echoes aka Gene Clark With The Gosdin Brothers (Columbia 1967)★★★, as Dillard And Clark The Fantastic Expedition Of Dillard And Clark (A&M 1968)★★★★, as Dillard And Clark Through The Morning, Through The Night (A&M 1969)★★★★, White Light (A&M 1971)★★★, Roadmaster (A&M 1972)★★★, No Other (Asylum 1974)★★★★, Two Sides To Every Story (RSO 1977)★★, Firebyrd aka This Byrd Has Flown (Takoma 1984)★★, with Carla Olson So Rebellious A Lover (Demon 1987)★★★, with Carla Olson Silhouetted In Light (Demon 1992)★★★.
COMPILATIONS: American Dreamer 1964-'74 (Raven 1993)★★★★, Flying High (Polydor 1998)★★★★, Gypsy Angel: The Gene Clark Demos 1983-1990 (Evangeline 2001)★★★.
FURTHER READING: The Byrds: Timeless Flight Revisited, Johnny Rogan.

CLARK, GUY
ALBUMS: Old No. 1 (RCA 1975)★★★★, Texas Cookin' (RCA 1976)★★★, Guy Clark (Warners 1978)★★★, The South Coast Of Texas (Warners 1981)★★★, Better Days (Warners 1983)★★★, Old Friends (Sugar Hill 1989)★★, Boats To Build (Asylum 1992)★★★, Dublin Blues (Asylum 1995)★★★, Keepers – A Live Recording (Sugar Hill 1997)★★★, Cold Dog Soup (Sugar Hill 1999)★★★★, with Steve Earle, Townes Van Zandt Together At The Bluebird (Catfish 2001)★★★★.
COMPILATIONS: Best Of Guy Clark (RCA 1982)★★★, Craftsman (Philo 1995)★★★, The Essential Guy Clark (RCA 1997)★★★★.
FURTHER READING: Songbuilder: The Life & Music Of Guy Clark, Nick Evans and Jeff Horne.

CLARK, PETULA
ALBUMS: Petula Clark Sings (Pye Nixa 1956)★★★, A Date With Pet (Pye Nixa 1956)★★★, You Are My Lucky Star (Pye Nixa 1957)★★★, A Christmas Carol mini-album (Pye Nixa 1958)★★★, Petula Clark In Hollywood (Pye Nixa 1959) ★★★, Tête A Tête Avec Petula Clark (Vogue 1961) ★★★, Rendez-Vous Avec Petula Clark (Vogue 1961)★★★, In Other Words (Pye 1962)★★★, Petula (Vogue 1962)★★★, Ceux Qui Ont Un Coeur (Vogue 1964)★★★, Hello Paris (Pye/Vogue 1964)★★★, Les James Dean (Pye/Vogue 1964)★★★, Downtown (Pye/Warners 1965)★★★★, Uptown With Petula Clark (Imperial 1965)★★★, I Know A Place (Pye 1965) ★★★, The International Hits! (Pye/Warners 1965)★★★, Petula '65 (Pye/Vogue 1965)★★★★, In Love! (Laurie 1965) ★★★, My Love (Pye/Warners 1966)★★★★, I Couldn't Live Without Your Love (Pye/Warners 1966)★★★★, Petula Clark (Vogue 1966)★★★, Le Palmares (Vogue 1966)★★★, Petula Clark's Hit Parade (Pye 1966)★★★, Colour My World/Who Am I? (Pye/Warners 1967)★★★, These Are My Songs (Pye/Warners/Vogue 1967)★★★, C'est Ma Chanson (Vogue 1967)★★★, C'est Le Refrain De Ma Vie (Vogue 1967)★★★, The Other Man's Grass Is Always Greener (Pye/Warners 1968)★★★★, Petula Clark (Vogue 1968)★★★, Portrait Of Petula (Pye/Warners/Vogue 1969)★★★, Just Pet (Pye/Warners/Vogue 1969)★★★, Petula Clark (Vogue 1969) ★★★, Memphis (Pye/Warners 1970)★★, The Song Of My Life UK title Warm And Tender US/French title (Pye/Warners/Vogue 1971)★★★, Today (Pye 1971)★★★, Petula '71 (Pye 1971)★★★, Live At The Royal Albert Hall 1969 recording (Pye/Vogue 1972)★★★, The Petula Clark Album (Pye 1972) ★★★★, Now (Polydor 1972)★★★, La Chanson De Marie-Madeleine (Vogue 1972)★★★, Comme Une Priere (Vogue 1972)★★★, Come On Home (Polydor 1974)★★★, Live In London (Polydor 1974)★★★, I'm The Woman You Need (Polydor 1975)★★★, Just Petula (Polydor 1975)★★★, Noël (Pet Projects 1975)★★, Beautiful Sounds (Pet Projects 1976) ★★, Je Reviens (CBS 1977)★★★, Destiny (CBS 1978)★★★, An Hour In Concert With Petula Clark And The London Philharmonic Orchestra (MFP 1983)★★★, Where The Heart Is (Connoisseur Collection 1998)★★★★, A Sign Of The Times (Varèse Sarabande 2001)★★★.
COMPILATIONS: The Best Of Petula Clark (Pye 1969)★★★★, Hits ... My Way (Warners 1970)★★★, The Best Of Petula Clark (Reader's Digest 1971)★★★, The Petula Clark Story Vol. 1 (Golden Hour 1971)★★★, 12 Succes De Petula Clark (Mondio/Vogue 1972)★★★, 12 Succes De Petula Clark, Vol. 2 (Mondio/Vogue 1973)★★★, Petula 3-LP set (RSP 1975)★★★, 20 All-Time Greatest (K-Tel 1977)★★★★, Spotlight On Petula Clark (PRT 1980)★★★, 100 Minutes Of Petula Clark (PRT 1982)★★★, 20 Greatest Hits (Vogue 1984)★★★, Greatest Hits Of Petula Clark (GNP Crescendo 1986)★★★, The Early Years (PRT 1986) ★★★, The Hit Singles Collection (PRT 1987)★★★★, Love Songs (Pickwick 1988)★★★, Downtown: The Petula Clark Collection (PRT 1988)★★★, My Greatest (MFP 1989)★★★, A Golden Hour Of Petula Clark (Knight 1990)★★★, The EP Collection (See For Miles 1990)★★★★, Downtown (Castle 1990)★★, The Special Collection (Castle 1990)★★★, A Golden Hour Of Petula Clark, Vol. 2 (Knight 1991)★★★, Portrait Of A Song Stylist (Knight 1991)★★★, The Best Of Petula Clark (Castle 1992)★★★, Treasures, Volume 1 (Scotti Bros 1992)★★★, Jumble Sale: Rarities And Obscurities 1959-1964 2-CD set (Sequel 1992)★★★★, The EP Collection Volume Two (See For Miles 1993)★★★, The Polygon Years, Volume One: 1950-1952 (RPM 1994)★★★, The Polygon Years, Volume Two: 1952-1955 (RPM 1994) ★★★, The Nixa Years, Volume One (RPM 1994)★★★★, The Nixa Years, Volume Two (RPM 1994)★★★★, I Love To Sing 3-CD box set (Sequel 1995)★★★★, Downtown: The Best Of Petula Clark (Pulse 1995)★★★, These Are My Songs (Start 1996)★★★, The Classic Collection 4-CD box set (Pulse 1997)★★★, Petula Clark – Her Greatest Hits (Snapper 1997)★★★, Sings Tony Hatch (Castle Select 1999)★★★, Showstoppers (Castle Select 1999)★★★, The International Collection 4-CD box set (Bear Family 1999)★★★★, Downtown: The Pye Anthology (Sequel 1999)★★★, The Songs Of My Life: The Very Best Of Petula Clark 3-CD box set (Reader's Digest 1999)★★★★, The Petula Clark Anthology: Downtown To Sunset B (Hip-O 2000)★★★★, The Sixties EP Collection 10-CD box set (Sequel 2000)★★★★, En Vogue (Beat En Francais) (Castle 2001)★★★★, With All My Heart: The Nixa Anthology 1956-59 (Sequel 2001)★★★.
VIDEOS: Petula Clark Spectacular (Laserlight 1996).
FURTHER READING: This Is My Song: A Biography Of Petula Clark, Andrea Kon.
FILMS: Medal For The General aka The Gay Intruders (1944), Strawberry Roan (1945), Murder In Reverse aka Query (1945), I Know Where I'm Going! (1945), London Town aka My Heart Goes Crazy (1946), Vice Versa (1948), Easy Money (1948), Here Come The Huggetts (1948), Vote For Huggett (1949), The Huggetts Abroad (1949), Don't Ever Leave Me (1949), The Romantic Age aka Naughty Arlette (1949), Dance Hall (1950), White Corridors (1951), Madame Louise (1951), The Card aka The Promoter (1952), Made In Heaven (1952), The Runaway Bus (1954), The Gay Dog (1954), The Happiness Of Three Women (1954), Track The Man Down (1955), That Woman Opposite aka City After Midnight (1957), 6.5 Special aka Calling All Cars (1958), A Couteaux Tirés aka Daggers Drawn (1964), Finian's Rainbow (1968), Goodbye, Mr. Chips (1969), Droles De Zebres (1977), Never Never Land (1982).

CLASH
ALBUMS: The Clash (CBS 1977)★★★★★, Give 'Em Enough Rope (CBS 1978)★★★, London Calling (CBS 1979)★★★★★, Sandinista! (CBS 1980)★★★, Combat Rock (CBS 1982)★★★, Cut The Crap (CBS 1985)H, From Here To Eternity Live (Columbia 1999)★★★★.
COMPILATIONS: The Story Of The Clash: Volume 1 (CBS 1988)★★★★, The Singles (Columbia 1991)★★★, Clash On Broadway 3-CD set (Columbia 1994)★★★, Super Black Market Clash (Columbia 1994)★★★.
VIDEOS: This Is Video Clash (CBS-Fox 1985), Rude Boy (Hendring Video 1987), Westway To The World (SMV 1999).
FURTHER READING: The Clash: Before & After, Pennie Smith. The Clash, Miles and John Tobler. Joe Strummer With The 101'ers & The Clash, Julian Leonard Yewdall. New Visual Documentary, James Wells. Last Gang In Town: Story Of The Clash, Marcus Gray. A Riot Of Our Own: Night And Day With The Clash, Johnny Green and Garry Barker. The Clash Retrospective, Agent Provocateur. The Clash, David Quantick. Return Of The Last Gang In Town, Marcus Gray.
FILMS: Rude Boy (1980).

CLASSICS IV
ALBUMS: Spooky (Liberty 1968)★★★, Mamas And Papas/Soul Train (Liberty 1969)★★, Traces (Liberty 1969)★★.
COMPILATIONS: Dennis Yost And The Classics IV Golden Greats Volume 1 (Liberty 1969)★★★, The Very Best Of The Classic IV (EMI 1975)★★★, Greatest Hits (CEMA 1992)★★★.

CLIFF, JIMMY
ALBUMS: Jimmy Cliff (Trojan 1969)★★★, Wonderful World, Beautiful People (A&M 1970)★★★★, Hard Road To Travel (Trojan/A&M 1970)★★★, Another Cycle (Island 1971)★★★, The Harder They Come film soundtrack (Mango/Island 1972)★★★★★, Unlimited (EMI 1973, Trojan 1990)★★★, Struggling Man (Island 1974)★★★, Brave Warrior (EMI 1975)★★★, Follow My Mind (Reprise 1976) ★★, Give Thanx (Warners 1978)★★, Oh Jamaica (EMI 1979)★★, I Am The Living (Warners 1980)★★, Give The People What They Want (Oneness/Warners 1981)★★, House Of Exile (1981)★★, Special (Columbia 1982)★★, The Power And The Glory (Columbia 1983)★★★, Can't Get Enough Of It (Veep 1984)★★★, Cliff Hanger (Dynamic/Columbia 1985)★★, Sense Of Direction (Sire 1985)★★★, Hang Fire (Dynamic/Columbia 1987)★★★, Images (Cliff Sounds 1989)★★★, Save Our Planet Earth (Musidisc 1990) ★★, Breakout (Cliff Sounds 1993)★★★, The Cool Runner Live In London (More Music 1995)★★.
COMPILATIONS: The Best Of Jimmy Cliff (Island 1974) ★★★★, The Best Of Jimmy Cliff In Concert (Reprise 1977) ★★★, The Collection (EMI 1983)★★★, Jimmy Cliff (Trojan 1983)★★★, Reggae Greats (Island 1985)★★★, Fundamental Reggae (See For Miles 1987)★★★, The Best Of Jimmy Cliff (Mango/Island 1988)★★★★, The Messenger (Metro 2001)★★★.
VIDEOS: Bongo Man (Hendring Music Video 1989).
FILMS: The Harder They Come (1972).

CLIMAX BLUES BAND
ALBUMS: Climax Chicago Blues Band (Parlophone 1969)★★, Plays On (Parlophone 1969)★★★★, A Lot Of Bottle (Harvest 1970)★★, Tightly Knit (Harvest 1971)★★★, Rich Man (Harvest 1972)★★★, FM/Live (Polydor 1973), Sense Of Direction (Polydor 1974)★★★, Stamp Album (BTM 1975)★★★, Gold Plated (BTM 1976)★★, Shine On (Warners 1978)★★★, Real To Reel (Warners 1979)★★★, Flying The Flag (Warners 1980)★★★, Lucky For Some (Warners 1981)★★, Sample And Hold (Virgin 1983)★★, Drastic Steps (Clay 1988)★★, Blues From The Attic (HTD 1994)★★★★.
COMPILATIONS: 1969-1972 (Harvest 1975)★★★, Best Of The Climax Blues Band (RCA 1983)★★★, Loosen Up (1974-1976) (See For Miles 1984)★★★, Couldn't Get It Right (C5 1987)★★, 25 Years Of The Climax Blues Band (Repertoire 1993)★★★.

CLINE, PATSY
ALBUMS: Patsy Cline (Decca 1957)★★★★, Patsy Cline Showcase (Decca 1961)★★★★, Sentimentally Yours (Decca 1962)★★★★, In Memoriam (Everest 1963)★★★★, Encores (Everest 1963)★★★, A Legend (Everest 1963)★★★, Reflections (Everest 1964)★★★, A Portrait Of Patsy Cline (Decca 1964)★★★★, That's How A Heartache Begins (Decca 1964)★★★, Today, Tomorrow, Forever (Hilltop 1964)★★★, Gotta Lot Of Rhythm In My Soul (Metro 1965)★★★, Stop The World And Let Me Off (Hilltop 1966)★★★, The Last Sessions (MCA 1980)★★★★, Try Again (Quicksilver 1982)★★★, Sweet Dreams film soundtrack (1985)★★★, Live At The Opry (MCA 1988)★★★, Live - Volume Two (MCA 1989)★★★, The Birth Of A Star (Razor & Tie 1996)★★★, Live At The Cimarron Ballroom 1961 recording (MCA 1997)★★★★.
COMPILATIONS: Patsy Cline's Golden Hits (Everest 1962)★★★, The Patsy Cline Story (Decca 1963)★★★★, Patsy Cline's Greatest Hits (Decca 1967)★★★★, Country Great (Vocalion 1969)★★★, Greatest Hits (MCA 1973) ★★★★, Golden Greats (MCA 1979)★★★★, 20 Golden Greats (Astan 1984)★★★, 20 Classic Tracks (Starburst 1987)★★★, 12 Greatest Hits (MCA 1988)★★★★, Dreaming (Platinum Music 1988)★★★, 20 Golden Hits (Deluxe 1989)★★★, Walkin' Dreams: Her First Recordings, Volume One (Rhino 1989)★★★★, Hungry For Love: Her First Recordings, Volume Two (Rhino 1989)★★★★, Rockin' Side: Her First Recordings, Volume Three (Rhino 1989)★★★★, The Patsy Cline Collection 4-CD box set (MCA 1991)★★★★★, The Definitive (MCA 1992)★★★, Discovery (Prism Leisure 1994)★★★, Premier Collection (Pickwick 1994)★★★, The Patsy Cline Story (MCA 1994)★★★★, Thinking Of You (Summit 1995)★★★, Today, Tomorrow And Forever 2-CD set (Parade 1995)★★★, Through The Eyes Of ... An Anthology (Snapper 1998)★★★★, The Ultimate Collection (UTV 2000) ★★★★, A Star Is Born (Yeaah! 2001)★★★, The Essential Collection (Universal 2001)★★★★.
VIDEOS: The Real Patsy Cline (Platinum Music 1989), Remembering Patsy (1993).
FURTHER READING: Patsy Cline: Sweet Dreams, Ellis Nassour. Honky Tonk Angel: The Intimate Story Of Patsy Cline, Ellis Nassour. Patsy: The Life And Times Of Patsy Cline, Margaret Jones. I Fall To Pieces: The Music And The Life Of Patsy Cline, Mark Bego. Singing Girl From Shenandoah Valley, Stuart E. Brown. Love Always, Patsy: Patsy Cline's Letters To A Friend, Cindy Hazen and Mike Freeman.

CLINTON, GEORGE
ALBUMS: Computer Games (Capitol 1982)★★★, You Shouldn't-Nuf Bit Fish (Capitol 1984)★★★★, with the P-Funk All Stars Urban Dance Floor Guerillas (Sony 1984) ★★★, Some Of My Best Jokes Are Friends (Capitol 1985) ★★★★, R&B Skeletons In The Closet (Capitol 1986)★★★, The Cinderella Theory (Paisley Park 1989)★★★, Sample A Bit Of Disc And A Bit Of Dat (AEM 1993)★★★, Hey Man ... Smell My Finger (Paisley Park 1993)★★★, A Fifth Of Funk (Castle Communications 1995)★★★, The Music Of Red Shoe Diaries (Wienerworld 1995)★★★, Mortal Kombat (London 1996)★★★, with the P-Funk All Stars The Awesome Power Of A Fully Operational Mothership (Epic 1996)★★★, P-Funk All Stars Live At The Beverly Theatre (Westbound 1996)★★★, with the P-Funk All Stars Live And Kickin' (Intersound 1997)★★★, with the P-Funk All Stars Dope Dogs (Dogone 1999)★★★.
COMPILATIONS: The Best Of George Clinton (Capitol 1986)★★★★, Family Series: Testing Positive 4 The Funk (Essential 1994)★★★, Greatest Funkin' Hits (Capitol 1996)★★★★, Extended Pleasure (EMI 2000)★★★, Greatest Hits (Right Stuff 2000)★★★★.
VIDEOS: Mothership Connection (Virgin Vision 1987).

CLOVER
ALBUMS: Clover (Fantasy 1970)★★, Forty-Niner (Fantasy 1971)★★★, Unavailable (Vertigo 1977)★★★, Love On The Wire (Vertigo 1977)★★★.
COMPILATIONS: Clover Chronicle: The Best Of The Fantasy Years (DJM 1979)★★★, The Best Of Clover (Mercury 1986)★★★.

CLOVERS
ALBUMS: The Clovers (Atlantic 1956)★★★★, Dance Party (Atlantic 1959)★★★★, In Clover (Poplar 1959)★★, Love Potion Number Nine (United Artists 1959)★★★, Clovers Live At CT's (1989)★★.
COMPILATIONS: The Original Love Potion Number Nine (Grand Prix 1964)★★★★, Their Greatest Recordings – The Early Years (Atco 1975)★★★★, The Best Of The Clovers: Love Potion Number Nine (EMI 1991)★★★★, Down In The Alley (Atlantic 1991)★★★, Dance Party (Sequel 1997)★★★★, The Very Best Of The Clovers (Atlantic 1998)★★★★.

COASTERS
ALBUMS: The Coasters (Atco 1957)★★★★, The Coasters' Greatest Hits (Atco/London 1959)★★★★★, One By One (Atco 1960)★★★★, Coast Along With The Coasters (Atco/London 1962)★★★, On Broadway (King/London 1973)★★★.
COMPILATIONS: That Is Rock & Roll (Clarion 1965)★★, Their Greatest Recordings: The Early Years (Atco/Atlantic 1971) ★★★★, 16 Greatest Hits (Trip 1975)★★★, 20 Great Originals (Atlantic 1978)★★★, What Is The Secret Of Your Success? (Mr. R&B 1980)★★★, The Coasters (Warners/ Pioneer 1980)★★★★, Wake Me, Shake Me (Warners/Pioneer 1981)★★★★, All About The Coasters (Warners/Pioneer 1982)★★★, Young Blood aka The Ultimate Coasters (Atlantic 1982)★★★★, Thumbin' A Ride (Edsel 1984)★★★, 20 Greatest Hits (Highland-DeLuxe 1987)★★★★, Poison Ivy: The Best Of The Coasters (Atco 1991)★★★★, 50 Coastin' Classics (Rhino/Atlantic 1992) ★★★★★, Yakety Yak (Rhino 1993) ★★★, The Very Best Of The Coasters (Rhino 1994)★★★★★, Spotlight: The Coasters & More - 20 All Time Greats (Javelin 1996)★★★, Yakety Yak: 17 Classic Tracks (MasterTone 1997) ★★★, The Coasters (Time-Life 1999)★★★, Charlie Brown aka The

Clown Princes Of Rock N Roll (Mr. R&B/Millennium 2000) ★★★★.
FURTHER READING: The Coasters, Bill Millar.

COCHRAN, EDDIE
ALBUMS: Singing To My Baby (Liberty 1957)★★★, The Eddie Cochran Memorial Album (Liberty 1960)★★★, Never To Be Forgotten (Liberty 1962)★★★, Cherished Memories (Liberty 1962)★★★★, My Way (Liberty 1964)★★★, On The Air (United Artists 1972)★★★, The Many Sides Of Eddie Cochran (Rockstar 1975)★★★, The Young Eddie Cochran (Rockstar 1982)★★★, Words And Music (Rockstar 1985)★★★, Portrait Of A Legend (Rockstar 1985)★★★, The Many Styles Of Eddie Cochran (Conifer 1985)★★★, The Hollywood Sessions (Rockstar 1986)★★★, Thinkin' About You (Rockstar 1989)★★★, with Hank Cochran Eddie And Hank: The Cochran Brothers (Rockstar 1991)★★★, L.A. Sessions (Rockstar 1992)★★★, Mighty Mean (Rockstar 1995)★★★★, Cruisin' The Drive In (Rockstar 1996)★★★, One Minute To One (Rockstar 1996)★★★, Rockin' It Country Style (Rockstar 1997)★★, Rock & Roll TV Show (Carlton 1997)★★★, Don't Forget Me (Rockstar 1998)★★★★, with Gene Vincent The Town Hall Party TV Shows (Rockstar 1999)★★.
COMPILATIONS: Summertime Blues (Sunset 1966)★★★★, The Very Best Of Eddie Cochran (Liberty 1970)★★★★, Legendary Masters (United Artists 1971)★★★★, The Very Best Of Eddie Cochran: 15th Anniversary Album (United Artists 1975)★★★, The Singles Album (United Artists 1979) ★★★★, 20th Anniversary Album 4-LP box set (United Artists 1980)★★★★, The 25th Anniversary Album (Liberty 1985)★★★★, Rock 'N' Roll Legend (Rockstar 1987)★★★, The Early Years (Ace 1988)★★★★, C'mon Everybody (Liberty 1988)★★★★, The Eddie Cochran Box Set 4-CD box set (Liberty 1988)★★★★, The EP Collection (See For Miles 1989)★★★★, Greatest Hits (Curb 1990)★★★★, Rare 'N' Rockin' (Music Club 1997)★★★, Legends Of The 20th Century (EMI 1999)★★★.
VIDEOS: The Town Hall Party TV Shows 1959 (Rockstar 2001).
FURTHER READING: The Eddie Cochran Nostalgia Book, Alan Clark. Eddie Cochran: Never To Be Forgotten, Alan Clark. The Legend Continues, Alan Clark. Don't Forget Me: The Eddie Cochran Story, Julie Mundy and Darrel Higham.
FILMS: The Girl Can't Help It (1956), Go Johnny Go (1958).

COCKBURN, BRUCE
ALBUMS: Bruce Cockburn (True North 1970)★★, High Winds White Sky (True North 1971)★★, Sunwheel Dance (True North 1972)★★, Night Vision (True North 1973)★★★, Salt Sun And Time (True North 1974)★★, Joy Will Find A Way (True North 1975)★★★, Circles In The Stream (True North 1977)★★, In The Falling Dark (True North 1977)★★, Further Adventures Of (True North 1978)★★★, Dancing In The Dragon's Jaws (True North 1980)★★★★, Rumours Of Glory (True North 1980)★★★, Humans (True North 1980) ★★★, Inner City Front (True North 1981)★★★, Trouble With Normal (True North 1983)★★★, Stealing Fire (True North 1984)★★★★, World Of Wonders (True North 1986)★★★, Big Circumstance (True North 1989)★★★, Live (True North 1990)★★★, Nothing But A Burning Light (Columbia 1992) ★★★★, Dart To The Heart (Columbia 1994)★★★, The Charity Of Night (Rykodisc 1996)★★★, You Pay Your Money And You Take Your Chance (Rykodisc 1998)★★★, Breakfast In New Orleans, Dinner In Timbuktu (Rykodisc 1999)★★★★.
COMPILATIONS: Mummy Dust/Resumé (True North 1981) ★★★★, Waiting For A Miracle singles collection (Revolver 1987)★★★★, Anything Anytime Anywhere: Singles 1979-2002 (Rounder 2002)★★★★.

COCKER, JOE
ALBUMS: With A Little Help From My Friends (Regal Zonophone 1969)★★★★, Joe Cocker! (Regal Zonophone 1970)★★★★, Mad Dogs And Englishmen (A&M 1970) ★★★★, Cocker Happy (Fly 1971)★★★★, Something To Say (Cube 1973)★★, I Can Stand A Little Rain (Cube 1974)★★, Jamaica Say You Will (Cube 1975)★★, Stingray (A&M 1976)★★★, Live In LA (Cube 1976)★★, Luxury You Can Afford (Asylum 1978)★★★, by the Crusaders Standing Tall (MCA 1981)★★, Sheffield Steel (Island 1982)★★★, Space Captain (Cube 1982)★★★, Countdown Joe Cocker (Cube 1982)★★, A Civilized Man (Capitol 1984)★★, Cocker (Capitol 1986)★★, Unchain My Heart (Capitol 1987)★★★, One Night Of Sin (Capitol 1989)★★, Joe Cocker Live (Capitol 1990)★★, Night Calls (Capitol 1992)★★, Have A Little Faith (Capitol 1994) ★★★★, Organic (Parlophone 1996)★★★★, Across From Midnight (Parlophone 1997)★★★, No Ordinary World (Parlophone 1999)★★, Standing Here (Burning Airlines 2001)★★, Respect Yourself (Parlophone 2002)★★★.
COMPILATIONS: Greatest Hits Volume 1 (Hallmark 1978) ★★★, Joe Cocker Platinum Collection (Cube 1981)★★★, The Very Best Of Joe Cocker (Telstar 1986)★★★, Joe Cocker Collection (Castle 1986)★★★, Best Of Joe Cocker (K-Tel 1988)★★★, Connoisseur's Cocker (Raven 1991)★★★, The Legend: The Essential Collection (PolyGram 1992)★★★★, The Long Voyage Home 4-CD box set (A&M 1995)★★★★, Greatest Hits (EMI 1999)★★★, Anthology (Polydor 2000) ★★★★, The Essential Joe Cocker Vol 2 (Spectrum 2001)★★.
VIDEOS: Mad Dogs And Englishmen (A&M Sound Pictures 1988), Have A Little Faith (1995), Joe Cocker Live - Across From Midnight Tour (Parlophone 1997).
FURTHER READING: Joe Cocker: With A Little Help From My Friends, J.P. Bean.
FILMS: Mad Dogs And Englishmen (1971).

COCKNEY REBEL
ALBUMS: The Human Menagerie (EMI 1973)★★★, The Psychomodo (EMI 1974)★★★, The Best Years Of Our Lives (EMI 1975)★★, Love's A Prima Donna (EMI 1976)★★, Face To Face - A Live Recording (EMI 1977)★★, Hobo With A Grin (EMI 1978)★★.
Solo: Steve Harley Poetic Justice (Castle 1996)★★, Stripped To The Bare Bone (New Millennium 1999)★★★.
COMPILATIONS: Timeless Flight (EMI 1976)★★, The Best Of Steve Harley And Cockney Rebel (EMI 1980)★★★, Mr Soft - Greatest Hits (Connoisseur 1988)★★★, Make Me Smile: The Best Of Steve Harley And Cockney Rebel (EMI 1992)★★★, More Than Somewhat: The Very Best Of Steve Harley (EMI 1998)★★★.

COCTEAU TWINS
ALBUMS: Garlands (4AD 1982)★★★, Head Over Heels (4AD 1983)★★★, Treasure (4AD 1984)★★★, Victorialand (4AD 1986)★★★, as Harold Budd, Elizabeth Fraser, Robin Guthrie, Simon Raymonde The Moon And The Melodies (4AD/Relativity 1986)★★★, Blue Bell Knoll (4AD/Capitol 1988)★★, Heaven Or Las Vegas (4AD/Capitol 1990) ★★★★, Four-Calendar Café (Fontana/Capitol 1993)★★★, Milk & Kisses (Fontana/Capitol 1996)★★★.
COMPILATIONS: The Pink Opaque (4AD/Relativity 1986)★★★, Cocteau Twins box set (Capitol 1991)★★★, BBC Sessions (Bella Union 1999)★★★★, Stars And Topsoil: A Collection (1982-1990) (4AD 2000)★★★★.

COHEN, LEONARD
ALBUMS: Songs Of Leonard Cohen (Columbia 1967) ★★★★, Songs From A Room (Columbia 1969)★★★, Songs Of Love And Hate (Columbia 1971)★★★, Live Songs (Columbia 1973)★★★, New Skin For The Old Ceremony (Columbia 1974)★★★, Death Of A Ladies' Man (Columbia 1977)★★★, Recent Songs (Columbia 1979) ★★★, Various Positions (Columbia 1985)★★★, I'm Your Man (Columbia 1988)★★★★, The Future (Columbia 1992)★★★★, Cohen Live (Columbia 1994)★★★, Field Commander Cohen: Tour Of 1979 (Columbia 2001)★★★.
COMPILATIONS: The Best Of (Columbia 1975)★★★★, various artists tribute album Tower Of Song: The Songs Of Leonard Cohen (A&M 1995)★★, More Best Of (Columbia 1997)★★★.
VIDEOS: Songs From The Life Of Leonard Cohen (CMV Enterprises 1989).
FURTHER READING: Let Us Compare Mythologies, Leonard Cohen. The Spice-Box Of Earth, Leonard Cohen. The Favorite Game, Leonard Cohen. Flowers For Hitler, Leonard Cohen. Beautiful Losers, Leonard Cohen. Parasites Of Heaven, Leonard Cohen. Selected Poems 1956-1968, Leonard Cohen. The Energy Of Slaves, Leonard Cohen. Death Of A Lady's Man, Leonard Cohen. Leonard Cohen, Stephen Scobie. Book Of Mercy, Leonard Cohen. Leonard Cohen: Prophet Of The Heart, Loranne S. Dorman & Clive L. Rawlins. So Long Leonard: Leben Und Lieder Von Leonard Cohen, Christof Graf. Leonard Cohen: In Quest Of Delight, Rod Sinclair. Stranger Music: Selected Poems And Songs, Leonard Cohen. Take This Waltz: A Celebration Of Leonard Cohen, Michael Fournier & Ken Norris (eds.). Leonard Cohen: A Life In Art, Ira Nadel. Leonard Cohen: In Every Style Of Passion, Jim Devlin. Various Positions: A Life Of Leonard Cohen, Ira B. Nadel.
FILMS: Angel (1966), Poen (1967), Dynamite Chicken (1971), Guitare Au Poing (1972), Bird On A Wire (1972), Schneeweißrosenrot aka SnowhiteRosered (1991), Heaven Before I Die (1997).

COLDPLAY
ALBUMS: Parachutes (Parlophone/Nettwerk 2000)★★★★.

COLE, LLOYD
ALBUMS: with the Commotions Rattlesnakes (Polydor 1984) ★★★★, with the Commotions Easy Pieces (Polydor 1985) ★★★, with the Commotions Mainstream (Polydor 1987)★★★, Lloyd Cole (Polydor 1989)★★★, Don't Get Weird On Me, Babe (Polydor 1991)★★★, Bad Vibes (Fontana 1993)★★, Love Story (Fontana 1995)★★★, with the Negatives The Negatives (What Are/XIII Bis 2000)★★★.
COMPILATIONS: 1984-1989 (Polydor 1989)★★★★, The Collection (Mercury 1998)★★★★, An Introduction To Lloyd Cole & The Commotions (Polydor 2001)★★★★, 2001: The Collected Recordings By Lloyd Cole 4-CD box set (Xiii Bis 2001)★★★.
VIDEOS: Lloyd Cole & The Commotions (Channel 5 Video 1986), From The Hip (PolyGram Music Video 1988), 1984-1989 (Lloyd Cole & The Commotions) (Channel 5 Video 1989).

COLE, NAT 'KING'
ALBUMS: The King Cole Trio 10-inch album (Capitol 1950)★★★, The King Cole Trio Volume 2 10-inch album (Capitol 1950)★★★, The King Cole Trio Volume 3 10-inch album (Capitol 1950)★★★, At The Piano 10-inch album (Capitol 1950)★★★, The King Cole Trio Volume 4 10-inch album (Capitol 1950)★★★, Harvest Of Hits 10-inch album (Capitol 1950)★★★, with Buddy Rich, Lester Young The Lester Young Trio 10-inch album (Mercury 1951)★★★★, Penthouse Serenade 10-inch album (Capitol 1952)★★★★, Unforgettable (Capitol 1952)★★★★, with Red Callender, Young King Cole-Lester Young-Red Callender Trio reissued as Lester Young-Nat King Cole Trio (Aladdin/Score 1953) ★★★★, Nat 'King' Cole Sings For Two In Love 10-inch album (Capitol 1953)★★★, 8 Top Pops (Capitol 1954)★★★, Tenth Anniversary Album (Capitol 1955)★★★, Vocal Classics (Capitol 1955)★★★, Instrumental Classics (Capitol 1955) ★★★, The Piano Style of Nat King Cole (Capitol 1956) ★★★, In The Beginning (Decca 1956)★★, Ballads Of The Day (Capitol 1956)★★★, After Midnight (Capitol 1957) ★★★★, Love Is The Thing (Capitol 1957)★★★★, This Is Nat 'King' Cole (Capitol 1957)★★★★, Just One Of Those Things (Capitol 1957)★★★, St. Louis Blues film soundtrack (Capitol 1958)★★, Cole Espanol (Columbia 1958)★★, The Very Thought Of You (Capitol 1958)★★★★, Welcome To The Club (Capitol 1959)★★★, To Whom It May Concern (Capitol 1959)★★★, A Mis Amigos (Capitol 1959)★★, Tell Me All About Yourself (Capitol 1960)★★★, Every Time I Feel The Spirit (Capitol 1960)★★★, Wild Is Love (Capitol 1960)★★★, The Magic Of Christmas (Capitol 1960)★★, The Touch Of Your Lips (Capitol 1961)★★★★, String Along With Nat 'King' Cole (Capitol 1961)★★★★, Nat 'King' Cole Sings/George Shearing Plays (Capitol 1962)★★★★, Ramblin' Rose (Capitol 1962)★★★, Sings The Blues (Capitol 1962)★★★, Dear Lonely Hearts (Capitol 1962)★★★, Where Did Everyone Go? (Capitol 1963)★★★, Those Lazy-Hazy-Crazy Days Of Summer (Capitol 1963)★★★, Sings The Blues Volume 2 (Capitol 1963)★★★, The Christmas Song (Capitol 1963) ★★★, I Don't Want To Be Hurt Anymore (Capitol 1964)★★★, My Fair Lady (Capitol 1964)★★★, L-O-V-E (Capitol 1965) ★★★, Songs From 'Cat Ballou' And Other Motion Pictures (Capitol 1965)★★★, Looking Back (Capitol 1965)★★★, Nat 'King' Cole At The Sands (Capitol 1966)★★★, At JATP (Verve 1966)★★★, At JATP 2 (Verve 1966)★★★, The Great Songs! 1957 recording (Capitol 1966)★★★★, with Dean Martin White Christmas (Capitol 1971)★★★, Christmas With Nat 'King' Cole (Stylus 1988)★★★.
COMPILATIONS: The Nat King Cole Story 3-LP box set (Capitol 1961)★★★★, The Best Of Nat King Cole (Capitol 1968)★★★★, 20 Golden Greats (Capitol 1978)★★★★, Greatest Love Songs (Capitol 1982)★★★★, Trio Days (Affinity 1984)★★★, The Complete Capitol Recordings Of The Nat King Cole Trio 18-CD box set (Mosiac 1990) ★★★★★, The Unforgettable Nat 'King' Cole (EMI 1991) ★★★★, The Nat King Cole Gold Collection (1993)★★★★, World War II Transcriptions (1994)★★★, The Best Of The Nat 'King' Cole Trio 3-CD set (Capitol Jazz 1998)★★★★, The Ultimate Collection (EMI 1999)★★★★.
VIDEOS: Nat King Cole (Missing In Action 1988), Unforgettable (PMI 1988), Nat King Cole Collection (Castle Music Pictures 1990), Nat King Cole 1942-1949 (Verve Video 1990), Nat King Cole (Virgin Vision 1992).
FURTHER READING: Nat King Cole: The Man And His Music, Jim Haskins & Kathleen Benson. Unforgettable: The Life And Mystique Of Nat King Cole, Leslie Gourse. Nat King Cole, Daniel Mark Epstein.

COLE, NATALIE
ALBUMS: Inseparable (Capitol 1975)★★★★, Natalie (Capitol 1976)★★★, Unpredictable (Capitol 1977)★★★, Thankful (Capitol 1977)★★★, Natalie ... Live! (Capitol 1978)★★★★, I Love You So (Capitol 1979)★★★, with Peabo Bryson We're The Best Of Friends (Capitol 1979) ★★★, Don't Look Back (Capitol 1980)★★, Happy Love (Capitol 1981)★★, with Johnny Mathis Unforgettable: A Musical Tribute To Nat 'King' Cole (Columbia 1983)★★★, I'm Ready (Epic 1983)★★, Dangerous (Modern 1985)★★, Everlasting (Manhattan 1987)★★, Good To Be Back (EMI 1989)★★, Unforgettable ... With Love (Elektra 1991) ★★★★, Take A Look (Elektra 1993)★★★★, Holly & Ivy (Elektra 1994)★★★, Stardust (Elektra 1996)★★★, with José Carreras, Placido Domingo Celebration Of Christmas (Elektra 1996)★★★, Snowfall On The Sahara (Elektra 1999)★★★, with the London Symphony Orchestra The Magic Of Christmas (Elektra 1999)★★★.
COMPILATIONS: The Natalie Cole Collection (Capitol 1988)★★★, The Soul Of Natalie Cole (1974-80) (Capitol 1991)★★★★, Greatest Hits: Volume 1 (Elektra 2000) ★★★★.
VIDEOS: Video Hits (PMI 1989), Holly & Ivy (Warner Music Vision 1995).
FURTHER READING: Angel On My Shoulder: The Autobiography Of Natalie Cole, Natalie Cole with Digby Diehl.

COLLECTIVE SOUL
ALBUMS: Hints, Allegations & Things Left Unsaid (Atlantic 1993)★★★, Collective Soul (Atlantic 1995)★★★★, Disciplined Breakdown (Atlantic 1997)★★, Dosage (Atlantic 1999)★★, Blender (Atlantic 2000)★★.
COMPILATIONS: 7even Year Itch: Greatest Hits 1994-2001 (Atlantic 2001)★★★.
VIDEOS: Music In High Places (Aviva International 2001).

COLLINS, ALBERT
ALBUMS: The Cool Sound Of (TCF Hall 1965)★★★, Love Can Be Found Anywhere, Even In A Guitar (Imperial 1968)★★★, Trash Talkin' (Imperial 1969)★★★, The Complete Albert Collins (Imperial 1969)★★★, Alive And Cool (1969)★★★, Truckin' With Albert Collins (Blue Thumb 1969)★★★, with Barrelhouse Live (Munich 1970)★★, There's Gotta Be A Change (1971)★★, Ice Pickin' (Alligator 1978)★★★★, Frostbite (Alligator 1980)★★★★, Frozen Alive! (Alligator 1981)★★★★, Don't Lose Your Cool (Alligator 1983)★★★, Live In Japan (Alligator 1984) ★★★★, with Johnny Copeland, Robert Cray Showdown! (Alligator 1985)★★★★, Cold Snap (Alligator 1986)★★★, The Ice Man (Charisma/Point Blank 1991)★★★★, Molten Ice (Red Lightnin' 1992)★★★, Live 92/93 (Pointblank 1995)★★★, Robert Cray With Albert Collins In Concert 1977 recording (Indigo 1999)★★★.
COMPILATIONS: The Complete Imperial Recordings (EMI 1991)★★★★, Collins Mix (The Best Of) (Pointblank 1993) ★★★★, Deluxe Edition (Alligator 1997)★★★★, The Ice Axe Cometh: The Collection 1978-86 (Music Club 1999)★★★.

COLLINS, BOOTSY
ALBUMS: Stretchin' Out In Bootsy's Rubber Band (Warners 1976)★★★, Ahh...The Name Is Bootsy, Baby! (Warners 1977)★★★, Bootsy? Player Of The Year (Warners 1978) ★★★, This Boot Is Made For Fonk-n (Warners 1979)★★, Ultra Wave (Warners 1980)★★★, The One Giveth, The Count Taketh Away (Warners 1982)★★★, What's Bootsy Doin'? (Columbia 1988)★★★, Jungle Bass (4th & Broadway 1990)★★★, Blasters Of The Universe (Rykodisc 1994)★★★, Fresh Outta "P" University (Warners 1997)★★★.
COMPILATIONS: Back In The Day: The Best Of Bootsy Collins (Warners 1995)★★★★, Glory B Da Funk's On Me! The Bootsy Collins Anthology (Rhino 2001)★★★★.

COLLINS, EDWYN
ALBUMS: Hope And Despair (Demon 1989)★★★, Hellbent On Compromise (Demon 1990)★★, Gorgeous George (Setanta 1994)★★★★, I'm Not Following You (Setanta 1997)★★★, Doctor Syntax (Setanta 2002)★★★.
VIDEOS: Phantasmagoria (Alternative Image 1992).

COLLINS, JUDY
ALBUMS: A Maid Of Constant Sorrow (Elektra 1961)★★★, Golden Apples Of The Sun (Elektra 1962)★★★★, Judy Collins #3 (Elektra 1964)★★★, The Judy Collins Concert (Elektra 1964)★★, Judy Collins' Fifth Album (Elektra 1965) ★★★, In My Life (Elektra 1966)★★★★, Wildflowers (Elektra 1967)★★★★, Who Knows Where The Time Goes (Elektra 1968)★★★★, Whales And Nightingales (Elektra 1970) ★★★, Living (Elektra 1971)★★★, True Stories And Other Dreams (Elektra 1973)★★★, Judith (Elektra 1975)★★★, Bread And Roses (Elektra 1976)★★★, Hard Times For Lovers (Elektra 1979)★★, Running For My Life (Elektra 1980)★★★, Times Of Our Lives (Elektra 1982)★★, Home Again (Asylum/Elektra 1984)★★, Trust Your Heart (Gold Castle 1987)★★, Sanity And Grace (Gold Castle 1989)★★, Baby's Bedtime (Lightyear 1990)★★★, Baby's Morningtime (Lightyear 1990)★★★, Fires Of Eden (Columbia 1990)★★, Judy Sings Dylan ... Just Like A Woman (Geffen 1993)★★, Come Rejoice! A Judy Collins Christmas (Mesa 1994)★★★, Shameless (Mesa 1995)★★★, Voices includes songbook and a memoir (Clarkson Potter 1995)★★★, Christmas At The Biltmore Estate (Elektra 1997)★★★, Both Sides Now (QVC 1998)★★, Broadway Classics (Intersound 1999) ★★★, Live At Wolf Trap! (Wildflower 2000)★★★.
COMPILATIONS: Recollections (Elektra 1969)★★★★, Colors Of The Day: The Best Of Judy Collins (Elektra 1972)★★★★, So Early In The Spring, The First 15 Years (Elektra 1977)★★★★, Most Beautiful Songs Of Judy Collins (Elektra 1979)★★★★, Both Sides Now (Pickwick 1981) ★★★, Amazing Grace (Telstar 1985)★★★, Her Finest Hour (Pair 1986)★★★, Wind Beneath My Wings (Laserlight 1992)★★★, Live At Newport (1959-1966) (Vanguard 1994)★★★, Forever: An Anthology (Elektra 1997)★★★★, The Very Best Of Judy Collins (Rhino 2001)★★★★.
VIDEOS: Baby's Morningtime (WEA 1990), Baby's Bedtime (WEA 1990).
FURTHER READING: The Judy Collins Songbook, Judy Collins and Herbert Haufrecht. Judy Collins, Vivian Claire. Trust Your Heart, Judy Collins. My Father, Judy Collins. Shameless, Judy Collins. Singing Lessons: A Memoir Of Love, Loss, Hope, And Healing, Judy Collins.
FILMS: La Liga No Es Cosa De Hombres (1972), Ninguno De Los Tres Se Llamaba Trinidad (1973), Busco Tonta Para Fin De Semana (1973), He Makes Me Feel Like Dancin' (1983), Junior (1994), Earl Robinson: Ballad Of An American (1994).

COLLINS, PHIL
ALBUMS: Face Value (Virgin 1981)★★★★, Hello, I Must Be Going (Virgin 1982)★★★★, No Jacket Required (Virgin 1985)★★★, ... But Seriously (Virgin 1989)★★★, Serious Hits ... Live! (Virgin 1990)★★, Both Sides (Virgin 1993)★★★, Dance Into The Light (Face Value 1996)H, Tarzan film soundtrack (Disney 1999)★★, A Hot Night In Paris (Warners 1999)★★.
COMPILATIONS: Hits (Virgin 1998)★★★.
VIDEOS: Live: Phil Collins (Thorn-EMI 1984), Video EP: Phil Collins (PMI/EMI 1986), No Ticket Required (WEA Music Video 1986), Live At Perkin's Palace (PMI/EMI 1986), You Can't Hurry Love (Gold Rushes 1987), No Jacket Required (Virgin Vision 1988), The Singles Collection (Virgin Vision 1989), Seriously Live (Virgin Vision 1990), But Seriously, The Videos (Virgin Vision 1992), Live And Loose In Paris (Warner Vision 1998).
FURTHER READING: Phil Collins Johnny Waller.

COLVIN, SHAWN
ALBUMS: Steady On (Columbia 1989)★★★★, Fat City (Columbia 1992)★★★, Cover Girl (Columbia 1994)★★, Live '88 (Plump 1995)H, A Few Small Repairs (Columbia 1996)★★★★, Holiday Songs And Lullabies (Columbia 1998)★★★, Whole New You (Columbia 2001)★★★★.

COMBS, SEAN 'PUFFY'
ALBUMS: No Way Out (Bad Boy 1997)★★★, Forever (Bad Boy 1999)★★, as P. Diddy The Saga Continues ... (Bad Boy 2001)★★.

COMMANDER CODY AND HIS LOST PLANET AIRMEN
ALBUMS: Lost In The Ozone (Paramount 1971)★★★, Hot Licks, Cold Steel And Trucker's Favourites (Paramount 1972)★★★, Country Casanova (Paramount 1973)★★★, Live From Deep In The Heart Of Texas (Paramount 1974) ★★★★, Commander Cody And His Lost Planet Airmen (Warners 1975)★★, Tales From The Ozone (Warners 1975)★★, We've Got A Live One Here! (Warners 1976) ★★★★, Let's Rock (Blind Pig 1986)★★, as the Commander Cody Band Rock 'N' Roll Again (Arista 1977)★★, as the Commander Cody Band Lose It Tonite (Line 1980)★★, Let's Rock! (Blind Pig 1986)★★★, Sleazy Roadside Stories 1973 live recording (Relix 1988)★★★, Aces High (Relix 1990) ★★, Lost In Space 1975 recording (Relix 1993)★★, Worst Case Scenario (Aim 1993)★★★, Live At Gilley's 1982 recording (Q/Atlantic 2000)★★★.
SOLO: Commander Cody Midnight Man (Arista 1977)★★.
COMPILATIONS: The Very Best Of (... plus) (See For Miles 1986)★★★★, Cody Returns From Outer Space (Edsel 1987)★★★, Too Much Fun: The Best Of Commander Cody (MCA 1990)★★★, Bar Room Classics(Aim 1994)★★★★, Relix's Best Of (Relix 1995)★★★.

COMMODORES
ALBUMS: Machine Gun (Motown 1974)★★★★, Caught In The Act (Motown 1975)★★★, Movin' On (Motown 1975) ★★★, Hot On The Tracks (Motown 1976)★★★, Commodores aka Zoom (Motown 1977)★★★, Live! (Motown 1977)★★★, Natural High (Motown 1978)★★★, Midnight Magic (Motown 1979)★★★, Heroes (Motown 1980)★★★, In The Pocket (Motown 1981)★★★, Commodores 13 (Motown 1983)★★★, Nightshift (Motown 1985)★★★, United (Polydor 1986)★★, Rock Solid (Polydor 1988)★★, Hits Vol. 1 (Commodores 1992)★★★, Hits Vol. II (Commodores 1992)★★, XX – No Tricks (Commodores 1993)★★, Christmas (Commodores 1995)★★, Live (Commodores 1997)★★.
COMPILATIONS: Commodores' Greatest Hits (Motown 1978) ★★★★, All The Great Hits (Motown 1982)★★★, Anthology (Motown 1983)★★★★, 14 Greatest Hits (Motown 1984) ★★★, The Best Of The Commodores (Telstar 1985) ★★★, All The Great Love Songs (Motown 1985)★★★, Rise Up (Magnum 1987)★★★, The Very Best Of the Commodores (Motown 1995)★★★★, The Ultimate Collection (Motown 1997)★★★★, The Best Of The Commodores: The Millennium Collection (Motown 1999)★★★★, Early Gold And New Spins (Cleopatra 2000)★★★.
VIDEOS: 1978 Platinum Tour (Motown Video 1978), Cover Story (Stylus Video 1990).

COMMUNARDS
ALBUMS: Communards (London 1986)★★★, Red (London 1987)★★★.
SOLO: Jimmy Somerville Read My Lips (London 1989) ★★★, Dare To Love (London 1995)★★, Manage The Damage (Gut 1999)★★.
COMPILATIONS: The Singles Collection, 1984-1990 includes recordings from Bronski Beat, Communards, Jimmy Somerville (London 1990)★★★★, The Very Best Of Jimmy Somerville, Bronski Beat And The Communards (Warners 2001)★★★.
VIDEOS: Communards: The Video Singles (Channel 5 1987).

CONCRETE BLONDE
ALBUMS: Concrete Blonde (I.R.S. 1986)★★, Free (I.R.S. 1989)★★★, Bloodletting (I.R.S. 1990)★★★, Walking In London (I.R.S. 1992)★★★, Mexican Moon (I.R.S. 1993) ★★★, Concrete Blonde Y Los Illegals (Ark 21 1997)★★, Group Therapy (Manifesto 2002)★★★.
COMPILATIONS: Still In Hollywood (I.R.S. 1994)★★, Recollection: The Best Of (I.R.S. 1996)★★★, Classic Masters (EMD 2002)★★★.

CONLEY, ARTHUR
ALBUMS: Sweet Soul Music (Atco 1967)★★★★, Shake, Rattle And Roll (Atco 1967)★★★, Soul Directions (Atco 1968)★★★, More Sweet Soul (Atco 1969)★★★, One More Sweet Soul Music (Warners 1988)★★, as Lee Roberts And The Sweater Soulin' (Blue Shadow 1988)★★★.
COMPILATIONS: Arthur Conley (Atlantic 1988)★★★, Sweet Soul Music: The Best Of Arthur Conley (Soul/Ichiban 1995)★★★.
FURTHER READING: Sweet Soul Music, Peter Guralnick.

CONTOURS
ALBUMS: Do You Love Me (Gordy 1962)★★★, Running In Circles (Motor City 1990)★★, A New Direction (Orchard 2000)★★.
COMPILATIONS: Baby Hit And Run (MFP 1974)★★★, The Very Best Of The Contours (Motown 1999)★★★★.

COODER, RY
ALBUMS: Ry Cooder (Reprise 1970)★★★, Into The Purple Valley (Reprise 1972)★★★★, Boomer's Story (Reprise 1972)★★★★, Paradise And Lunch (Reprise 1974)★★★★, Chicken Skin Music (Reprise 1976)★★★★, Show Time (Warners 1977)★★★, Jazz (Warners 1978)★★, Bop Till You Drop (Warners 1979)★★★, Borderline (Warners 1980)★★★, The Long Riders film soundtrack (Warners 1980)★★★, The Border film soundtrack (MCA 1981)★★★, The Slide Area (Warners 1982)★★, Paris, Texas film soundtrack (Warners 1985)★★★★, Blue City film soundtrack (Warners 1986)★★, Crossroads film soundtrack (Warners 1986)★★★, Get Rhythm (Warners 1987)★★, Johnny Handsome film soundtrack (Warners 1989)★★★, Trespass film soundtrack (Warners 1992)★★, Geronimo: An American Legend film soundtrack (Columbia 1993) ★★★, with V.M. Bhatt A Meeting By The River (Water Lily Acoustics 1993)★★★, with Ali Farka Touré Talking Timbuktu (World Circuit 1994)★★★★, Last Man Standing film soundtrack (Verve/PolyGram 1996)★★★, The End Of Violence film soundtrack (Outpost 1997)★★★, Primary Colors film soundtrack (MCA 1998)★★.
COMPILATIONS: Why Don't You Try Me Tonight? (Warners 1986)★★★, River Rescue: The Very Best Of (Warners 1994)★★★★, Music By Ry Cooder (Warners 1995)★★★.

COOKE, SAM
ALBUMS: Sam Cooke i (Keen 1958)★★★, Encore (Keen 1959)★★★, Tribute To The Lady (Keen 1959)★★★, Hit Kit (Keen 1960)★★★, I Thank God (Keen 1960)★★★, The Wonderful World Of Sam Cooke (Keen 1960)★★★, Cooke's Tour (RCA Victor 1960)★★★, Hits Of The 50's (RCA Victor 1960)★★★, Swing Low (RCA Victor 1960) ★★★, My Kind Of Blues (RCA Victor 1961)★★★★, Twistin' The Night Away (RCA Victor 1962)★★★★, Mr. Soul (RCA Victor 1963)★★★★, Night Beat (RCA Victor 1963)★★★, Ain't That Good News (RCA Victor 1964) ★★★★, Sam Cooke At The Copa (RCA Victor 1964)★★★★, Shake (RCA Victor 1965)★★★, Try A Little Love (RCA Victor 1965)★★★, Sam Cooke Sings Billie Holiday (RCA 1976) ★★★, Sam Cooke Live At The Harlem Square Club, 1963 (RCA 1985)★★★.
COMPILATIONS: The Best Of Sam Cooke (RCA Victor 1962)★★★★, The Best Of Sam Cooke, Volume 2 (RCA Victor 1965)★★★★, The Unforgettable Sam Cooke (RCA Victor 1966)★★★, The Man Who Invented Soul (RCA Victor 1968)★★★, The Gospel Soul Of Sam Cooke With The Soul Stirrers, Volume 1 (Specialty 1969)★★★★, The Gospel Soul Of Sam Cooke With The Soul Stirrers, Volume 2 (Specialty 1970)★★★★, The Two Sides Of Sam Cooke (Specialty 1970)★★★, This Is Sam Cooke (RCA 1971)★★★, That's Heaven To Me: Sam Cooke With The Soul Stirrers (Specialty 1972)★★★★, The Golden Age Of Sam Cooke (RCA 1976)★★★, The Man And His Music (RCA 1986)★★★★★, Forever (Specialty 1986)★★★, Sam Cooke ii (Déjà Vu 1987)★★★, You Send Me (Topline/Charly 1987)★★★, 20 Greatest Hits (Compact Collection 1987)★★★★, Wonderful World (Fame 1988)★★★★, The World Of Sam Cooke (Instant 1989)★★★★, Legend (EMS 1990)★★★, The Magic Of Sam Cooke (Music Club 1991)★★★, Sam Cooke With The Soul Stirrers (Specialty 1991)★★★★, Sam Cooke's Sar Records Story (ABKCO 1994)★★★, Hits! (RCA 2000) ★★★★, The Man Who Invented Soul 4-CD box set (RCA 2000)★★★★★, Keep Movin' On (ABKCO 2002)★★★.
FURTHER READING: Sam Cooke: The Man Who Invented Soul: A Biography In Words & Pictures, Joe McEwen. You Send Me: The Life And Times Of Sam Cooke, S.R. Crain, Clifton White and G. David Tenenbaum.

COOLIDGE, RITA
ALBUMS: Rita Coolidge (A&M 1971)★★★, Nice Feelin' (A&M 1971)★★, The Lady's Not For Sale (A&M 1972) ★★★, with Kris Kristofferson Full Moon (A&M 1973)★★★, Fall Into Spring (A&M 1974)★★★, with Kristofferson Breakaway (Monument 1974)H, It's Only Love (A&M 1975)★★, Anytime ... Anywhere (A&M 1977)★★★★, Love Me Again (A&M 1978)★★★, with Kristofferson Natural Act (A&M 1978)★★, Satisfied (A&M 1979)★★, Heartbreak Radio (A&M 1981)★★, Never Let You Go (A&M 1983)★★, Inside The Fire (A&M 1984)★★, Fire Me Back (Attic 1990)★★★, Dancing With An Angel (Attic 1991)★★, Love Lessons (Attic 1992)★★★, Cherokee (Permanent 1995)★★, with Walela Walela (Triloka 1997)★★★, Thinkin' About You (404 1998)★★★, with Walela Unbearable Love (Triloka 2000)★★★.
COMPILATIONS: Greatest Hits (A&M 1981)★★★, Classics, Volume 5 (A&M 1987)★★★, A&M Gold Series, Vol. 2 (A&M 1988)★★★, Out Of The Blues (Beacon 1996)★★★, The Best Of Rita Coolidge: The Millennium Collection (A&M 2000)★★★★, Classic Rita Coolidge: The Universal Masters Collection (Universal 2001)★★★.

COOLIO
ALBUMS: It Takes A Thief (Tommy Boy 1994)★★★, Gangsta's Paradise (Tommy Boy 1995)★★★★, My Soul (Tommy Boy 1997)★★★.
COMPILATIONS: Fantastic Voyage: The Greatest Hits (Tommy Boy 2001)★★★.
FILMS: Phat Beach (1996), Dear God (1996), Burn Hollywood Burn (1997), Batman & Robin (1997), Tyrone (1999), Midnight Mass (1999), Judgement Day (1999), I Know What You Screamed Last Summer (1999).

COPE, JULIAN
ALBUMS: World Shut Your Mouth (Mercury 1984)★★★, Fried (Mercury 1984)★★★, Saint Julian (Island 1987) ★★★★, My Nation Underground (Island 1988)★★★, Skellington (Capeco-Zippo 1990)★★★, Droolian (Mofoco-Zippo 1990)★★, Peggy Suicide (Island 1991)★★★★, Jehovahkill (Island 1993)★★, Autogeddon (Echo 1994)★★, Rite (Echo 1994)★★, Queen Elizabeth (Echo 1994)★★, Julian Cope Presents 20 Mothers (Echo 1995)★★★, Interpreter (Echo 1996)★★★★, Rite 2 (Head Heritage 1997)★★.
COMPILATIONS: Floored Genius - The Best Of Julian Cope And The Teardrop Explodes 1981-91 (Island 1992)★★★★, Floored Genius 2 - Best Of The BBC Sessions 1983-91 (Nighttracks 1993)★★★, The Followers Of Saint Julian (Island 1997)★★★, Leper Grin: An Introduction To Julian Cope (Island 1999)★★★★, Floored Genius 3: Julian Cope's Oddicon Of Lost Rarities & Versions (1978-98) (Head Heritage 2000)★★★, The Collection (Spectrum 2002)★★★.
VIDEOS: Copeulation (Island Visual Arts 1989).
FURTHER READING: Head-On: Memories Of The Liverpool Punk Scene And The Story Of The Teardrop Explodes (1976-82), Julian Cope. Krautrocksampler: One Head's Guide To Great Kosmische Music, Julian Cope. The Modern Antiquarian: A Pre-Millennial Odyssey Through Megalithic Britain, Julian Cope. Repossessed: Shamanic Depressions In Tamworth & London (1983-89), Julian Cope.

CORROSION OF CONFORMITY
ALBUMS: Eye For An Eye (No Core 1984)★★★, Animosity (Combat 1985)★★★, Technocracy mini-album (Combat 1987)★★★, Six Songs With Mike Singing mini-album, 1985 recording (Caroline 1988)★★, Blind (Combat 1991)★★★, Deliverance (Sony 1994)★★★, Wiseblood (Sony 1996) ★★★, America's Volume Dealer (Sanctuary 2000)★★★.

CORRS
ALBUMS: Forgiven, Not Forgotten (143/Lava 1995)★★★★, Talk On Corners (143/Lava 1997)★★★★, MTV Unplugged (143/Lava 1999)★★★, In Blue (143/Lava 2000)★★★, VH1 Presents The Corrs Live In Dublin (143/Lava 2002)★★★.
COMPILATIONS: Best Of The Corrs (143/Lava 2001)★★★.
VIDEOS: Live At The Royal Albert Hall (Warner Music Vision 1998), The Corrs Unplugged (Atlantic 1999), Live At Lansdowne Road (Warner Music Vision 2000), The Corrs Live In London (Warner Music Vision 2001).
FURTHER READING: The Corrs, Jane Cornwell.

COSTELLO, ELVIS
ALBUMS: My Aim Is True (Stiff/Columbia 1977)★★★★, with the Attractions This Year's Model (Radar/Columbia 1978)★★★★★, with the Attractions Armed Forces (Radar/Columbia 1979)★★★, with the Attractions Get Happy!! (F-Beat/Columbia 1980)★★★★, with the Attractions Trust (F-Beat/Columbia 1981)★★★★, with the Attractions Almost Blue (F-Beat/Columbia 1981)★★★, with the Attractions Imperial Bedroom (F-Beat/Columbia 1982)★★★★★, with the Attractions Punch The Clock (F-Beat/Columbia 1983) ★★★, with the Attractions Goodbye Cruel World (F-Beat/Columbia 1984)★★★, King Of America (Demon/Columbia 1986)★★★★, with the Attractions Blood & Chocolate (Demon/Columbia 1986)★★★, Spike (Warners 1989)★★★, Mighty Like A Rose (Warners 1991)★★★, with Richard Harvey G.B.H.: Original Music From The Channel Four Series (Demon Soundtracks 1991)★★★, with the Brodsky Quartet The Juliet Letters (Warners 1993)★★★★, with the Attractions Brutal Youth (Warners 1994)★★★, Kojak Variety (Warners 1995)★★, with Bill Frisell Deep Dead Blue: Live 25 June 95 (Nonesuch 1995)★★★, with Harvey Original Music From Jake's Progress (Demon Soundtracks 1996)★★, with the Attractions All This Useless Beauty (Warners 1996)★★★, with Steve Nieve Costello & Nieve (Warners 1996)★★★, with Burt Bacharach Painted From Memory: The New Songs Of Bacharach & Costello (Mercury 1998)★★★, with Anne Sofie Von Otter For The Stars (Deutsche Grammophon 2001)★★★★, When I Was Cruel (Mercury 2002)★★★.
COMPILATIONS: Taking Liberties (Columbia 1980)★★★★, Ten Bloody Marys And Ten Hows Your Fathers (Demon 1980)★★★★, The Best Of Elvis Costello - The Man (Telstar 1985)★★★★, Out Of Our Idiot (Demon 1987)★★★, Girls Girls Girls Girls (Demon 1989)★★★★★, The Very Best Of ... 1977-1986 (Demon 1994)★★★★, Extreme Honey: The Very Best Of The Warner Bros. Years (Warners 1997) ★★★★, various artists Bespoke Songs, Lost Dogs, Detours & Rendezvous: Songs Of Elvis Costello (Rhino 1998)★★★★, The Very Best Of Elvis Costello (Universal 1999)★★★★.
VIDEOS: Best Of Elvis Costello (Palace Video 1986), with Brodsky Quartet The Juliet Letters (Warner Vision 1993), The Very Best Of (1994), Live: A Case For Song (Warner Vision 1996), with Burt Bacharach Painted From Memory: The New Songs Of Bacharach & Costello (Mercury 1998).
FURTHER READING: Elvis Costello: Completely False Biography Based On Rumour, Innuendo And Lies, Krista Reese. Elvis Costello, Mick St. Michael. Elvis Costello: A Man Out Of Time, David Gouldstone. The Big Wheel, Bruce Thomas. Going Through The Motions (Elvis Costello 1982-1985), Richard Groothuizen and Kees Den Heyer. Elvis Costello: A Biography, Tony Clayton-Lea. Elvis Costello: A Bio-Bibliography, David E. Perone. Let Them All Talk: The Music Of Elvis Costello, Brian Hinton. Elvis Costello, David Sheppard.
FILMS: Americathon (1979), No Surrender (1985), Straight To Hell (1987), Spice World (1997), 200 Cigarettes (1999), Austin Powers: The Spy Who Shagged Me (1999), Sans Plomb aka Unleaded (2000), Prison Song (2000).

COUNTING CROWS
ALBUMS: August And Everything After (Geffen 1993)★★★★, Recovering The Satellites (Geffen 1996)★★★, Across A Wire: Live In New York City (Geffen 1998)★★★, This Desert Life (Geffen 1999)★★★★.

COUNTRY JOE AND THE FISH
ALBUMS: Electric Music For The Mind And Body (Vanguard 1967)★★★★, I-Feel-Like-I'm-Fixin'-To-Die (Vanguard 1967)★★★, Together (Vanguard 1968)★★, Here We Are Again (Vanguard 1969)★★★, C.J. Fish (Vanguard 1970) ★★, Reunion (Fantasy 1977)H, Live! Fillmore West 1969 (Vanguard 1994)★★★.
COMPILATIONS: Greatest Hits (Vanguard 1969)★★★, The Life And Times Of Country Joe And The Fish From Haight-Ashbury To Woodstock (Vanguard 1971)★★★, Collectors' Items - The First Three EPs (Rag Baby 1980)★★★, The Collected Country Joe And The Fish (Vanguard 1987)★★★.
FILMS: Gas! Or It Became Necessary ... (1970).

COVAY, DON
ALBUMS: Mercy! (Atlantic 1965)★★★, See Saw (Atlantic 1966)★★★★, with the Jefferson Lemon Blues Band The House Of Blue Lights (Atlantic 1969)★★★, Different Strokes (Atlantic 1970)★★, Superdude 1 (Mercury 1973)★★★, Hot Blood (Mercury 1975)★★, Travellin' In Heavy Traffic (Philadelphia International 1976)★★, Ad Lib (Cannonball 2000)★★.
COMPILATIONS: Sweet Thang (Topline 1987)★★★, Checkin' In With Don Covay (Mercury 1989)★★★, Mercy Mercy: The Definitive Don Covay (Razor & Tie 1994)★★★★.

COWBOY JUNKIES
ALBUMS: Whites Off Earth Now!! (Latent/RCA 1986)★★★, The Trinity Session (Latent/RCA 1988)★★★★, The Caution Horses (RCA 1990)★★★, Black Eyed Man (RCA 1992) ★★★, Pale Sun, Crescent Moon (RCA 1993)★★★, Lay It Down (Geffen 1996)★★★★, Miles From Our Home (Geffen 1998)★★★, Waltz Across America (Latent 2000)★★★, Open (Zöe/Cooking Vinyl 2001)★★★.
COMPILATIONS: 200 More Miles: Live Performances 1985-1994 (RCA 1995)★★★★, Selected Studio Recordings 1986-1995 (RCA 1996)★★★★, Rarities, B-Sides And Slow, Sad Waltzes (Latent 1999)★★★.

COYNE, KEVIN
ALBUMS: Case History (Dandelion 1972)★★★, Marjory Razor Blade (Virgin 1973)★★★★, Blame It On The Night (Virgin 1974)★★★★, Matching Head And Feet (Virgin 1975)★★★, Heartburn (Virgin 1976)★★★, In Living Black And White (Virgin 1977)★★★★, Dynamite Daze (Virgin 1978)★★★, Millionaires And Teddy Bears (Virgin 1979) ★★★, with Dagmar Krause Babble (Virgin 1979)★★★★, Bursting Bubbles (Virgin 1980)★★★, Sanity Stomp (Virgin 1980)★★, Pointing The Finger (Cherry Red 1981)★★★, Politicz (Cherry Red 1982)★★★, Legless In Manila (Collapse 1984)★★★, Rough (On 1985)★★★, with the Kevin Coyne Band Stumbling On To Paradise (Line 1987)★★★, with the Paradise Band Everybody's Naked (Zabo 1989)★★, with the Paradise Band Romance-Romance (Zabo 1990)★★★, with the Paradise Band Wild Tiger Love (Golden Hind/Rockport 1991)★★, Burning Head (Rockport 1992)★★★, Tough And Sweet (Golden Hind/Rockport 1993)★★★, The Adventures Of Crazy Frank (Golden Hind/Rockport 1995)

★★★, Knocking On Your Brain (Golden Hind/Rockport 1997)★★★, Live Rough And More (Golden Hind/Rockport 1997)★★★, Sugar Candy Taxi (Ruf 1999)★★★, Room Full Of Fools (Ruf 2000)★★★.
COMPILATIONS: Let's Have A Party (Virgin Ariola 1976) ★★★, Beautiful Extremes (Virgin Ariola 1977)★★★★, The Dandelion Years 3-LP box set (Butt 1981)★★★, Beautiful Extremes Et Cetera (Cherry Red 1983)★★★★, Peel Sessions (Strange Fruit 1991)★★★★, Sign Of The Times (Virgin 1994)★★★★, Elvira: Songs From The Archives 1979-83 (Golden Hind/Rockport 1994)★★★.
FURTHER READING: The Party Dress, Kevin Coyne. Paradise, Kevin Coyne. Show Business, Kevin Coyne. Tagebuch Eines Teddybären, Kevin Coyne. Ich, Elvis Und Die Anderen, Kevin Coyne.

CRACKER
ALBUMS: Cracker (Virgin 1992)★★★, Kerosene Hat (Virgin 1993)★★★, The Golden Age (Virgin 1996)★★★, Gentleman's Blues (Virgin 1998)★★★, Flash Your Sirens!!! The Cracker And Traveling Apothecary Show And Review Live (Pitch-A-Tent 2001)★★★, Forever (Virgin 2002)★★★.
COMPILATIONS: Garage D'Or (Virgin 2000)★★★, Classic Masters (EMD 2002)★★★.

CRADLE OF FILTH
ALBUMS: The Principle Of Evil Made Flesh (Cacophonous 1994)★★, Vempire: Dark Faerytales In Phallustein mini-album (Cacophonous 1996)★★★, Dusk ... And Her Embrace (Music For Nations 1996)★★, Cruelty And The Beast (Music For Nations 1998)★★★★, Midian (Music For Nations 2000)★★★, Bitter Suites To Succubi mini-album (Abra Cadaver 2001)★★★.
VIDEOS: PanDaemonAeon (Music For Nations 1999), Heavy, Left-Handed & Candid (Snapper 2001).

CRAMER, FLOYD
ALBUMS: That Honky Tonk Piano reissued as Floyd Cramer Goes Honky Tonkin' (MGM 1957)★★★, Hello Blues (RCA 1960)★★★, Last Date (RCA 1961)★★★★, On The Rebound (RCA 1961)★★★★, America's Biggest Selling Pianist (RCA 1961)★★★, Floyd Cramer Get Organ-ized (RCA 1962)★★, I Remember Hank Williams (RCA 1962) ★★★, Swing Along With Floyd Cramer (RCA 1963)★★★, Comin' On (RCA 1963)★★★, Country Piano - City Strings (RCA 1964)★★★, Cramer At The Console (RCA 1964)★★★, Hits From The Country Hall Of Fame (RCA 1965)★★★, The Magic Touch Of Floyd Cramer (RCA 1965)★★★, Class Of '65 (RCA 1965)★★★, The Distinctive Piano Styling Of Floyd Cramer (RCA 1966)★★★, The Big Ones (RCA 1966)★★★, Class Of '6 (RCA 1966)★★★, Here's What's Happening (RCA 1967)★★★, Floyd Cramer Plays The Monkees (RCA 1967)★★★, Class Of '67 (RCA 1967)★★★, Floyd Cramer Plays Country Classics (RCA 1968)★★★, Class Of '68 (RCA 1968)★★★, Floyd Cramer Plays MacArthur Park (RCA 1968)★★, Class Of '69 (RCA 1969)★★★★, More Country Classics (RCA 1969)★★★, Looking For Mr. Goodbar (RCA 1968)★★★, The Big Ones - Volume 2 (RCA 1970)★★★, Floyd Cramer With The Music City Pops (RCA 1970)★★★, Class Of '70 (RCA 1970)★★, Sounds Of Sunday (RCA 1971)★★, with Chet Atkins, 'Boots' Randolph Chet, Floyd, Boots (RCA Camden 1971)★★★, Class Of '71 (RCA 1971) ★★★, Floyd Cramer Detours (RCA 1972)★★★, Class Of '72 (RCA 1972)★★★, Super Country Hits Featuring Crystal Chandelier And Battle Of New Orleans (RCA 1973)★★, Class Of '73 (RCA 1973)★★, The Young And The Restless (RCA 1974)★★, Floyd Cramer In Concert (RCA 1974)★★, Class Of '74 And '75 (RCA 1975)★★, Floyd Cramer Country (RCA 1976)★★, with Chet Atkins, Danny Davis Chet, Floyd & Danny (RCA Victor 1977)★★★★, Floyd Cramer And The Keyboard Kick Band (RCA 1977)★★★, Superhits (RCA 1979)★★, Dallas (RCA 1980)★★, The Best Of The West (RCA 1981)★★, Country Gold (RCA 1988)★★, Just Me And My Piano! (RCA 1988)★★★, Special Songs Of Love (RCA 1988)★★, Originals (RCA 1991)★★★, Classics (RCA 1992)★★★.
COMPILATIONS: The Best Of Floyd Cramer (RCA 1964)★★★★, The Best Of Floyd Cramer - Volume 2 (RCA 1968)★★★, This Is Floyd Cramer (RCA 1970)★★★★, Plays The Big Hits (Camden 1973)★★★, Best Of The Class Of (RCA 1973)★★★, Spotlight On Floyd Cramer (1974)★★★, Piano Masterpieces 1900-1975 (RCA 1975)★★, All My Best (RCA 1980)★★★, Great Country Hits (RCA 1981)★★★, Treasury Of Favourites (1984)★★★, Country Classics (1984)★★★★, 20 Of The Best: Floyd Cramer (RCA 1986)★★★, Our Class Reunion (1987)★★★, Easy Listening Favorites (1991)★★★, Favorite Country Hits (Ranwood 1995)★★★, King Of Country Piano (Pickwick 1995)★★★, Collector's Series (RCA 1995)★★★, The Essential Floyd Cramer (RCA 1996)★★★★.

CRAMPS
ALBUMS: Songs The Lord Taught Us (Illegal/I.R.S. 1980) ★★★, Psychedelic Jungle (I.R.S. 1981)★★★, Smell Of Female (Enigma 1983)★★★, A Date With Elvis (Big Beat 1986) ★★★, Rockinnreelininaucklandnewzelandxxx (Vengeance 1987)★★★, Stay Sick (Enigma 1990)★★★, Look Mom No Head! (Big Beat 1991)★★, Flamejob (Medicine 1994)★★★, Big Beat From Badsville (Epitaph 1997)★★.
COMPILATIONS: Off The Bone (I.R.S. 1983)★★★, Bad Music For Bad People (I.R.S. 1984)★★★, Greatest Hits (BMG 1998)★★★.
FURTHER READING: The Wild Wild World Of The Cramps, Ian Johnston.

CRANBERRIES
ALBUMS: Everybody Else Is Doing It, So Why Can't We? (Island 1993)★★★★, No Need To Argue (Island 1994) ★★★★, To The Faithful Departed (Island 1996)★★★, Sa Va Bella (For Lady Legends) (Qwest/Warners 1997)★★★★, Bury The Hatchet (Island 1999)★★, Wake Up And Smell The Coffee (Island 2001)★★★.
I CD-ROMS: Doors And Windows (Philips 1995)★★.
VIDEOS: Live (Island 1994), Beneath The Skin: Live In Paris (Aviva 2001).
FURTHER READING: The Cranberries, Stuart Bailee.

CRASH TEST DUMMIES
ALBUMS: The Ghosts That Haunt Me (Arista 1991)★★, God Shuffled His Feet (Arista 1993)★★★★, A Worm's Life (Arista 1996)★★, Give Yourself A Hand (Arista 1999) ★★★, I Don't Care That You Don't Mind (Cha-Ching 2001) ★★★★.
VIDEOS: Symptomology Of A Rock Band: The Case Of Crash Test Dummies (Arista 1994).
FURTHER READING: Superman's Song: The Story Of Crash Test Dummies, Stephen Ostick.

CRAWFORD, RANDY
ALBUMS: Miss Randy Crawford (Warners 1977)★★★, Raw Silk (Warners 1979)★★★★, Now We May Begin (Warners 1980)★★★, Everything Must Change (Warners 1980)★★, Secret Combination (Warners 1981)★★★★, Windsong (Warners 1982)★★, Nightline (Warners 1983)★★★, Abstract Emotions (Warners 1986)★★★, Rich And Poor (Warners 1989)★★★, Naked And True (Bluemoon 1995) ★★★★, Every Kind Of Mood: Randy, Randi, Randee (Atlantic 1998)★★★, Permanent (Warners 2001)★★★★.
COMPILATIONS: Miss Randy Crawford - Greatest Hits (K-Tel 1984)★★★, Love Songs (Telstar 1987)★★★, The Very Best Of (Dino 1992)★★★, The Best Of (Warners 1996)★★★★.

CRAY, ROBERT
ALBUMS: Who's Been Talkin' (Tomato 1980)★★★, Bad Influence (HighTone 1983)★★★★, False Accusations (HighTone 1985)★★★, with Albert Collins, Johnny Copeland Showdown! (Alligator 1985)★★★★, Strong Persuader (Mercury 1986)★★★, Don't Be Afraid Of The Dark (Mercury 1988)★★★★, Midnight Stroll (Mercury 1990)★★★★, Too Many Cooks (Tomato 1991)★★★, I Was Warned (Mercury 1992)★★★, The Score reissue of Who's Been Talkin' (Charly 1992)★★★, Shame And A Sin (Mercury 1993)★★★, Some Rainy Morning (Mercury 1995)★★★, Sweet Potato Pie (Mercury 1997)★★★★, Take Your Shoes Off (Rykodisc 1999)★★★, Robert Cray With Albert Collins In Concert 1977 recording (Indigo 1999) ★★★, Shoulda Been Home (Rykodisc 2001)★★★★.
COMPILATIONS: Heavy Picks: The Robert Cray Band Collection (Mercury 1999)★★★★.
VIDEOS: Smoking Gun (PolyGram Music Video 1989), Collection: Robert Cray (PolyGram Music Video 1991).

CRAZY HORSE
ALBUMS: Crazy Horse (Reprise 1971)★★★★, Loose (Reprise 1972)★★★, At Crooked Lake (Epic 1973)★★★, Crazy Moon (One Way 1978)★★★, Left For Dead (Capitol 1989)★★.

CRAZY TOWN
ALBUMS: The Gift Of Game (Columbia 1999)★★★★.

CREAM
ALBUMS: Fresh Cream (Polydor 1966)★★★★, Disraeli Gears (Polydor 1967)★★★★★, Wheels Of Fire (Polydor 1968)★★★★, Goodbye (Polydor 1969)★★★, Live Cream (Polydor 1970)★★★, Live Cream, Volume 2 (Polydor 1972)★★★.
COMPILATIONS: The Best Of Cream (Polydor 1969)★★★★, Heavy Cream (Polydor 1973)★★★, Strange Brew: The Very Best Of Cream (Polydor 1986)★★★★, Those Were The Days 4-CD box set (Polydor 1997)★★★★★.
VIDEOS: Farewell Concert (Polygram Music Video 1986), Strange Brew (Warner Music Video 1992), Fresh Live Cream (PolyGram Music Video 1994).
FURTHER READING: Cream In Gear (Limited Edition), Gerard Mankowitz and Robert Whitaker (photographers). Strange Brew, Chris Welch. Cream, Chris Welch.

CREATION
ALBUMS: We Are Paintermen (Hi-Ton 1967)★★★, Lay The Ghost (Cohesion 1993)★★, Power Surge (Creation 1996) ★★.
COMPILATIONS: The Best Of Creation (Pop Schallplatten 1968)★★★, The Creation 66-67 (Charisma 1973)★★★, How Does It Feel To Feel? (Edsel 1982)★★★, The Mark Four The Creation (Eva 1983)★★★, Recreation (Line 1984) ★★, Our Music Is Red, With Purple Flashes (DiAblo/Demon 1998)★★★★, Making Time: Volume 1 (Retroactive 1998) ★★★★, Biff Bang Pow! Volume 2 (Retroactive 1998)★★★★.

CREED
ALBUMS: My Own Prison (Wind-up/Epic 1998)★★★★, Human Clay (Wind-up/Epic 1999)★★★★, Weathered (Wind-up/Epic 2001)★★★★.

CREEDENCE CLEARWATER REVIVAL
ALBUMS: Creedence Clearwater Revival (Fantasy 1968)★★★, Bayou Country (Fantasy 1969)★★★★, Green River (Fantasy 1969)★★★★, Willie And The Poor Boys (Fantasy 1969) ★★★★, Cosmo's Factory (Fantasy 1970)★★★★, Pendulum (Fantasy 1970)★★★, Mardi Gras (Fantasy 1972)★★, Live In Europe (Fantasy 1973)★★, Live At The Royal Albert Hall aka The Concert (Fantasy 1980)★★, as Creedence Clearwater Revisited Recollection (SPV 1998)★★★.
COMPILATIONS: Creedence Gold (Fantasy 1972)★★★★, More Creedence Gold (Fantasy 1973)★★★★, Chronicle: The 20 Greatest Hits (Fantasy 1976)★★★★, Greatest Hits (Fantasy 1979)★★★, Creedence Country (Fantasy 1981) ★★★, Creedence Clearwater Revival Hits Album (Fantasy 1982)★★★★, The Creedence Collection (Impression 1985)★★★, Chronicle II (Fantasy 1986)★★★★, Best Of Volume 1 (Fantasy 1988)★★★★, Best Of Volume 2 (Fantasy 1988)★★★★, At The Movies (Fantasy 2000) ★★★, Creedence Clearwater Revival 6-CD box set (Fantasy 2001)★★★★.
FURTHER READING: Inside Creedence, John Hallowell.

CRENSHAW, MARSHALL
ALBUMS: Marshall Crenshaw (Warners 1982)★★★★, Field Day (Warners 1983)★★★, Downtown (Warners 1985) ★★★, Sings Mary Jean & Nine Others (Warners 1987) ★★★, Good Evening (Warners 1989)★★★, Life's Too Short (MCA 1991)★★★, My Truck Is My Home (Razor & Tie 1994)★★★, Miracle Of Science (Razor & Tie 1996)★★★, The 9 Volt Years: Battery Powered Home Demos And Curios (Razor & Tie 1998)★★, #447 (Razor & Tie 1999)★★★, I've Suffered For My Art ... Now It's Your Turn (King Biscuit Flower Hour 2001)★★★.
COMPILATIONS: This Is Easy: The Best Of Marshall Crenshaw (Rhino 2000)★★★★.

CREW-CUTS
ALBUMS: The Crew-Cuts On The Campus (Mercury 1954) ★★★, The Crew-Cuts Go Longhair (Mercury 1956)★★★, Crew-Cut Capers (Mercury 1957)★★★, Music Ala Carte (Mercury 1957)★★★, Rock And Roll Bash (Mercury 1957) ★★★, Surprise Package (RCA Victor 1958)★★★, The Crew-Cuts Sing! (RCA Victor 1959)★★★, You Must Have Been A Beautiful Baby (RCA Victor 1960)★★★, The Crew Cuts Sing Out! (RCA Victor 1960)★★★, The Crew Cuts Have A Ball And Bowling Tips (RCA Victor 1960)★★★, The Crew Cuts (RCA Victor 1962)★★★, High School Favorites (RCA Victor 1962)★★★, Sing The Masters (RCA Victor 1962) ★★★, The Crew-Cuts Sing Folk (RCA Victor 1963)★★.

CRICKETS
ALBUMS: In Style With The Crickets (Coral 1960)★★★★, Bobby Vee Meets The Crickets (Liberty 1962)★★★, Something Old, Something New, Something Borrowed, Somethin' Else!!! (Liberty 1963)★★★★, The Crickets (Liberty 1964)★★★, Rockin' 50s Rock 'N' Roll (Barnaby 1970)★★★, Bubblegum, Bop, Ballads And Boogies (Mercury 1973)★★, Remnants (Vertigo 1974)★★, A Long Way From Lubbock (Mercury 1974)★★, Three-Piece (Rollercoaster 1988)★★, T-Shirt (CBS 1988)★★, Too Much Monday Morning (Carlton 1997)★★.
COMPILATIONS: A Collection (Liberty 1965)★★★, The Liberty Years (EMI America 1991)★★★★, Still In Style (Bear Family 1992)★★★★, The Singles Collection 1957-1961 (Pickwick 1994)★★★, 25 Greatest Hits (MFP 1998)★★★.
VIDEOS: My Love Is Bigger Than A Cadillac (Hendring Music Video 1990).
FILMS: Girls On The Beach (1965).

CROCE, JIM
ALBUMS: with Ingrid Croce Approaching Day (Capitol 1969)★★, You Don't Mess Around With Jim (ABC 1972) ★★★, Life And Times (ABC 1973)★★★, I Got A Name (ABC 1973)★★★.
COMPILATIONS: Photographs & Memories: His Greatest Hits (ABC 1974)★★★★, The Faces I've Been 1961-1971 recordings (Lifesong 1975,)★★, Time In A Bottle: Jim Croce's Greatest Love Songs (Lifesong 1977)★★, Collection (Castle 1986)★★★★, with Ingrid Croce Bombs Over Puerto Rico (Bear Family 1996)★★, Time In A Bottle: The Definitive Collection (Essential 1999)★★★★, Behind The Music: The Jim Croce Collection (Rhino 2001)★★★.
FURTHER READING: The Faces I've Been, Jim Croce. Jim Croce: The Feeling Lives On, Linda Jacobs.

CROPPER, STEVE
ALBUMS: with Albert King, 'Pops' Staples Jammed Together (Stax 1969)★★★, With A Little Help From My Friends (Stax 1971)★★, Playing My Thang (MCA 1980)★★.
FILMS: The Blues Brothers (1980), Blues Bothers 2000 (1998).

CROSBY, DAVID
ALBUMS: If I Could Only Remember My Name (Atlantic 1971)★★★★★, Oh Yes I Can (Atlantic 1989)★★★, Thousand Roads (Atlantic 1993)★★★, It's All Coming Back To Me Now (Atlantic 1995)★★★, Live On The King Biscuit Flower Hour 1989 recording (King Biscuit Flower Hour 1996)★★★★.
FURTHER READING: Long Time Gone, David Crosby and Carl Gottlieb. Timeless Flight, Johnny Rogan.

CROSBY, STILLS AND NASH
ALBUMS: Crosby, Stills And Nash (Atlantic 1969)★★★★★, CSN (Atlantic 1977)★★★★, Daylight Again (Atlantic 1982)★★★, Allies (Atlantic 1983)★★★, Live It Up (Atlantic 1990)★★, After The Storm (Atlantic 1994)★★.
COMPILATIONS: Replay (Atlantic 1980)★★★★, CSN 4-CD box set (Atlantic 1991)★★★★★.
VIDEOS: Daylight Again (CIC 1983), Acoustic (Warner Music Vision 1991), Crosby, Stills And Nash: Long Time Comin' (Wienerworld 1994).
FURTHER READING: Crosby, Stills & Nash: The Authorized Biography, Dave Zimmer and Henry Diltz. Prisoner Of Woodstock, Dallas Taylor. Crosby, Stills, Nash & Young: The Visual Documentary, Johnny Rogan.

CROSBY, STILLS, NASH AND YOUNG
ALBUMS: Déjà Vu (Atlantic 1970)★★★★★, Four Way Street (Atlantic 1971)★★★, American Dream (Atlantic 1989)★★★, Looking Forward (Atlantic 1999)★★.
COMPILATIONS: So Far (Atlantic 1974)★★★.
FURTHER READING: Prisoner Of Woodstock, Dallas Taylor. Crosby, Stills, Nash & Young: The Visual Documentary, Johnny Rogan. Crosby, Stills & Nash: The Biography, Dave Zimmer and Henry Diltz.

CROSS, CHRISTOPHER
ALBUMS: Christopher Cross (Warners 1980)★★★, Another Page (Warners 1983)★★★, Every Turn Of The World (Warners 1985)★★, Back Of My Mind (Warners 1988)★★, Rendezvous (BMG 1992)★★★, Window (BMG 1995)★★★, Walking In Avalon (CMC 1998)★★★, Red Room (CMC 1999)★★★, Greatest Hits - Live (CMC 1999)★★★.
COMPILATIONS: The Definitive Christopher Cross (Rhino 2001)★★★★.
VIDEOS: An Evening With Christopher Cross (BMG 1998).

CROW, SHERYL
ALBUMS: Tuesday Night Music Club (A&M 1993)★★★★, Sheryl Crow (A&M 1996)★★★, The Globe Sessions (A&M 1998)★★★, Sheryl Crow And Friends Live From Central Park (A&M 1999)★★★, C'Mon, C'Mon (A&M 2002)★★★.
VIDEOS: Live From The Palladium (VVL 1997), Rockin' The Globe Live (Aviva 1999).

CROWDED HOUSE
ALBUMS: Crowded House (Capitol 1986)★★★, Temple Of Low Men (Capitol 1988)★★★, Woodface (Capitol 1991) ★★★★, Together Alone (Capitol 1993)★★★.
COMPILATIONS: Recurring Dreams (Capitol 1996) ★★★★★, After Glow (Capitol 1999)★★★.
VIDEOS: Farewell To The World: Live At The Sydney Opera House (PolyGram Video 1997).
FURTHER READING: Private Universe: The Illustrated Biography, Chris Twomey and Kerry Doole. Crowded House: Something So Strong, Chris Bourke. Once Removed, Neil Finn & Mark Smith.

CROWELL, RODNEY
ALBUMS: Ain't Living Long Like This (Warners 1978)★★★★, But What Will The Neighbors Think (Warners 1980)★★★, Rodney Crowell (Warners 1981)★★★, Street Language (Columbia 1986)★★★★, Diamonds And Dirt (Columbia 1988)★★★★, Keys To The Highway (Columbia 1989) ★★★★, Life Is Messy (Columbia 1992)★★★, Let The Picture Paint Itself (MCA 1994)★★★, Soul Searchin' (Excelsior 1994)★★★, Jewel Of The South (MCA 1995)★★★, The Cicadas (Warners 1997)★★★, The Houston Kid (Sugar Hill 2001)★★★★.
COMPILATIONS: The Rodney Crowell Collection (Warners 1989)★★★★, Greatest Hits (Columbia 1993)★★★★, Super Hits (Columbia 1995)★★★.

CRYSTALS
ALBUMS: Twist Uptown (Philles 1962)★★, He's A Rebel (Philles 1963)★★★.
COMPILATIONS: The Crystals Sing Their Greatest Hits (Philles 1963)★★★, Uptown (Spectrum 1988)★★★, The Best Of The Crystals (ABKCO 1992)★★★, Greatest Hits (Classic World 2000)★★★.

CULT
ALBUMS: as Southern Death Cult The Southern Death Cult (Beggars Banquet 1983)★★, Dreamtime (Beggars Banquet 1984)★★, Dreamtime Live At The Lyceum (Beggars Banquet 1984)★★, Love (Beggars Banquet/Sire 1985)★★, Electric (Beggars Banquet/Sire 1987)★★★, Sonic Temple (Beggars Banquet/Sire 1989)★★★, Ceremony (Beggars Banquet/Sire 1991)★★, The Cult (Beggars Banquet/Sire 1994)★★, Live Cult: Marquee London MCMXCI (Beggars Banquet 1999)★★, Beyond Good And Evil (Lava 2001)★★★.
COMPILATIONS: as Southern Death Cult Complete Recordings (Situation Two 1991)★★★, Pure Cult (Beggars Banquet 1993)★★★, as Death Cult Ghost Dance (Beggars Banquet 1996)★★★, High Octane Cult (Beggars Banquet 1996)★★★, Rare Cult 6-CD box set (Beggars Banquet 2000)★★, Best Of Rare Cult (Beggars Banquet 2000)★★★.
VIDEOS: Dreamtime At The Lyceum (Beggars Banquet 1984), Electric Love (Beggars Banquet 1987), Cult: Video Single (One Plus One 1987), Sonic Ceremony (Beggars Banquet 1992), Pure Cult (Beggars Banquet 1993), Dreamtime Live At The Lyceum (Beggars Banquet 1996).

CULTURE CLUB
ALBUMS: Kissing To Be Clever (Virgin 1982)★★★, Colour By Numbers (Virgin 1983)★★★★, Waking Up With The House On Fire (Virgin 1984)★★, From Luxury To Heartache (Virgin 1986)★★★, Don't Mind If I Do (Virgin 1999)★★★.
COMPILATIONS: This Time: The First Four Years (Virgin 1987)★★★, The Best Of Culture Club (Virgin 1989)★★★, At Worst . . . The Best Of Boy George & Culture Club (Virgin 1993)★★★★, Greatest Moments (Virgin 1998)★★★★.
VIDEOS: Kiss Across The Ocean (Virgin Vision 1984), This Time: The First Four Years (Virgin Vision 1987).
FURTHER READING: Culture Club: When Cameras Go Crazy, Kasper de Graaf and Malcolm Garrett. Mad About The Boy: The Life And Times Of Boy George & Culture Club, Anton Gill. Boy George And Culture Club, Jo Dietrich. Like Punk Never Happened: Culture Club And The New Pop, Dave Rimmer.

CURE
ALBUMS: Three Imaginary Boys (Fiction 1979)★★★, Boys Don't Cry (Fiction 1979)★★, Seventeen Seconds (Fiction 1980)★★★, Faith (Fiction 1981)★★★★, Pornography (Fiction 1982)★★★★, The Top (Fiction 1984)★★★, Concert – The Cure Live (Fiction 1984)★★, Concert And Curiosity – Cure Anomalies 1977-1984 (Fiction 1984)★★, Head On The Door (Fiction 1985)★★★, Kiss Me, Kiss Me, Kiss Me (Fiction 1987)★★★★, Disintegration (Fiction 1990)★★★★, Entreat (Fiction 1991)★★★, Wish (Fiction 1992)★★★★, Show (Fiction 1993)★★★, Paris (Fiction 1993)★★★, Wild Mood Swings (Fiction 1996)★★★, Bloodflowers (Fiction 2000)★★★★.
COMPILATIONS: Japanese Whispers – The Cure Singles Nov 1982-Nov 1983 (Fiction 1983)★★★, Standing On The Beach - The Singles titled Staring At The Sea on CD (Fiction 1986)★★★★, Mixed Up (Fiction 1990)★★★, Galore - The Singles 1987-1997 (Fiction 1997)★★★, Greatest Hits (Fiction 2001)★★★.
VIDEOS: Staring At the Sea: The Images (Palace Video 1986), The Cure In Orange (PolyGram Music Video 1987), In Between Days (PolyGram Music Video 1988), Close To Me (PolyGram Music Video 1989), Cure Picture Show (PolyGram Music Video 1991), The Cure Play Out (Windsong 1991), The Cure Show (PolyGram Music Video 1993), Galore - The Videos (PolyGram Music Video 1997), Greatest Hits (Warner Music Vision 2001).
FURTHER READING: The Cure: A Visual Documentary, Dave Thompson and Jo-Anne Greene. Ten Imaginary Years, Lydia Barbarian, Steve Sutherland and Robert Smith. The Cure Songwords 1978 - 1989, Robert Smith (ed.). The Cure: Success Corruption & Lies, Ross Clarke. The Cure On Record, Daren Butler. The Cure: Faith, Dave Bowler and Bryan Dray. The Making Of: The Cure's Disintegration, Mary Elizabeth Hargrove. Catch: Robert Smith And The Cure, Daniel Patton.

CURVE
ALBUMS: Doppelgänger (AnXious/Charisma 1992)★★★, Cuckoo (AnXious/Charisma 1993)★★★, Come Clean (Universal 1998)★★★, Gift (Hip-O 2001)★★★.
SOLO: Toni Halliday Hearts And Handshakes (WTG 1989)★★.
COMPILATIONS: Pubic Fruit (AnXious/Charisma 1992)★★★★, Radio Sessions (AnXious 1993)★★★.

CURVED AIR
ALBUMS: Air Conditioning (Warners 1970)★★★, Second Album (Warners 1971)★★★, Phantasmagoria (Warners 1971)★★★, Air Cut (Warners 1973)★★, Live (Deram 1975)★★★, Midnight Wire (BTM 1975)★★, Airborne (BTM 1976)★★, Lovechild (Castle 1990)★★, Live At The BBC (Band Of Joy 1995)★★, Alive, 1990 (Mystic 2000)★★.
COMPILATIONS: The Best Of Curved Air (Warners 1976)★★★.

CYPRESS HILL
ALBUMS: Cypress Hill (Ruffhouse/Columbia 1991)★★★★, Black Sunday (Ruffhouse/Columbia 1993)★★★, III: Temples Of Boom (Ruffhouse/Columbia 1995)★★★, Unreleased & Revamped EP mini-album (Ruffhouse/Columbia 1996)★★, Cypress Hill IV (Ruffhouse/Columbia 1998)★★★, Skull & Bones (Ruffhouse/Columbia 2000)★★★, Live At The Fillmore (Columbia 2000)★★★, Stoned Raiders (Columbia 2001)★★★.
COMPILATIONS: Los Grandes Exitos En Espanol (Sony 1999)★★★.
VIDEOS: Still Smokin' (Columbia Music Video 2001).

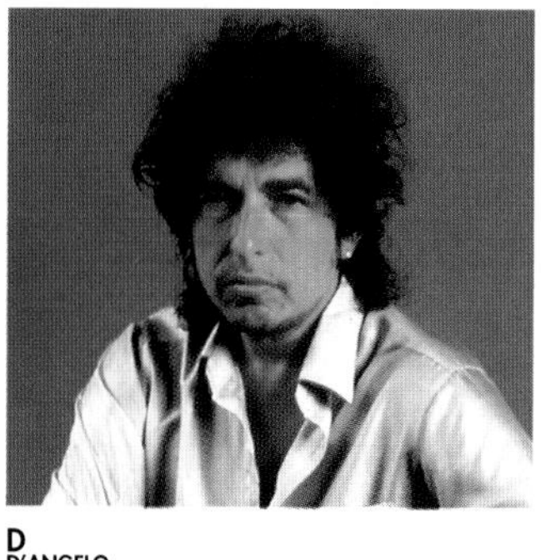

D

D'ANGELO
ALBUMS: Brown Sugar (EMI 1995)★★★★, Live At The Jazz Cafe, London (EMI 1998)★★★, Voodoo (EMI 2000)★★★.

D'ARBY, TERENCE TRENT
ALBUMS: Introducing The Hardline According To Terence Trent D'Arby (Columbia 1987)★★★★, Neither Fish Nor Flesh (Columbia 1989)★★, Symphony Or Damn: Exploring The Tension Inside The Sweetness (Columbia 1993)★★★, Vibrator (Columbia 1995)★★★.
VIDEOS: Introducing The Hardline: Live (CBS-Fox 1988).
FURTHER READING: Neither Fish Nor Flesh: Inspiration For An Album, Paolo Hewitt.

DAFT PUNK
ALBUMS: Homework (Virgin 1997)★★★★, Discovery (Virgin 2001)★★★★, Alive 1997 (Virgin 2001)★★★.

DALE, DICK
ALBUMS: Surfers' Choice (Deltone 1962)★★★, King Of The Surf Guitar (Capitol 1963)★★★, Checkered Flag (Capitol 1963)★★★, Mr. Eliminator (Capitol 1964)★★★, Summer Surf (Capitol 1964)★★★, Rock Out With Dick Dale And His Del-Tones - Live At Ciro's (Capitol 1965)★★, The Tiger's Loose (Balboa 1983)★★, Tribal Thunder (Hightone 1993)★★, Unknown Territory (Hightone 1994)★★★, Calling Up Spirits (Beggars Banquet 1996)★★, Spacial Disorientation (Sin-Drome 2002)★★★.
COMPILATIONS: Dick Dale's Greatest Hits (GNP Crescendo 1975)★★★, King Of The Surf Guitar: The Best Of Dick Dale And His Del-Tones (Rhino 1986)★★★★, Better Shred Than Dead: The Dick Dale Anthology (Rhino 1997)★★★★.
FURTHER READING: Surf Beat: The Dick Dale Story, Stephen J. McParland.
FILMS: Let's Make Love (1960), A Swingin' Affair (1963), Beach Party (1963), Muscle Beach Party (1964), Back To The Beach (1987), Treasure (1990), Liquid Stage: The Lure Of Surfing television (1994).

DAMNED
ALBUMS: Damned Damned Damned (Stiff 1977)★★★★, Music For Pleasure (Stiff 1977)★★, Machine Gun Etiquette (Chiswick 1979)★★★, The Black Album (Chiswick 1980) ★★★★, Strawberries (Bronze 1982)★★★, Phantasmagoria (MCA 1985)★★, Anything (MCA 1986)★★, Not Of This Earth (Cleopatra 1996) released in UK as I'm Alright Jack & The Beans Talk (Marble Orchid 1996)★★, Molten Lager (Musical Tragedies 2000)★★, Grave Disorder (Nitro 2001)★★★.
COMPILATIONS: The Best Of The Damned (Chiswick 1981) ★★★, Live At Shepperton (Big Beat 1982)★★, Not The Captain's Birthday Party (Stiff 1986)★★, Damned But Not Forgotten (Dojo 1986)★★, Light At The End Of The Tunnel (MCA 1987)★★, Mindless, Directionless Energy (ID 1987)★★, The Long Lost Weekend: Best Of Volumes 1 & 2 (Big Beat 1988)★★★, Final Damnation (Essential 1989)★★, Totally Damned (Live And Rare) (Dojo 1991)★★, Skip Off School To See The Damned: The Stiff Singles (Stiff 1992)★★★, School Bullies (Receiver 1993)★★, Sessions Of The Damned (Strange Fruit 1993)★★, Eternally Damned: The Very Best Of The Damned (MCI 1994)★★★, The Radio 1 Sessions (Strange Fruit 1996)★★★, The Chaos Years: Rare & Unreleased 1977-1982 (Cleopatra 1997)H, Marvellous: The Best Of The Damned (Big Beat 2000)★★, The Pleasure And The Pain: Selected Highlights 1982-1991 (Essential 2000)★★★.
VIDEOS: Light At The End Of The Tunnel (CIC Video 1987).
FURTHER READING: The Damned: The Light At The End Of The Tunnel, Carol Clerk.

DANDY WARHOLS
ALBUMS: Dandys Rule OK (Tim Kerr 1995)★★★, ... The Dandy Warhols Come Down (Tim Kerr/Capitol 1997)★★★★, Thirteen Tales From Urban Bohemia (Capitol 2000)★★★★.

DANNY AND THE JUNIORS
COMPILATIONS: Rockin' With Danny And The Juniors (MCA 1983)★★, Back To Hop (Roller Coaster 1992)★★.

DARIN, BOBBY
ALBUMS: Bobby Darin (Atco 1958)★★★★, That's All (Atco 1959)★★★, This Is Darin (Atco 1960)★★★, Darin At The Copa (Atco 1960)★★★, For Teenagers Only (Atco 1960) ★★★, The 25th Day Of December (Atco 1960)★★★, with Johnny Mercer Two Of A Kind (Atco 1961)★★★, Love Swings (Atco 1961)★★★, Twist With Bobby Darin (Atco 1962)★★★, Bobby Darin Sings Ray Charles (Atco 1962) ★★★, Things & Other Things (Atco 1962)★★★, Oh! Look At Me Now (Capitol 1962)★★★, You're The Reason I'm Living (Capitol 1963)★★★, It's You Or No One 1960 recording (Atco 1963)★★★, 18 Yellow Roses & 11 Other Hits (Capitol 1963)★★★, Earthy! (Capitol 1963)★★★, Golden Folk Hits (Capitol 1963)★★★, Winners (Atco 1964)★★★, From Hello Dolly To Goodbye Charlie (Capitol 1964)★★, Venice Blue (Capitol 1965)★★, Bobby Darin Sings The Shadow Of Your Smile (Atlantic 1966)★★, In A Broadway Bag (Atlantic 1966)★★, If I Were A Carpenter (Atlantic 1966)★★★★, Inside Out (Atlantic 1967)★★★, Bobby Darin Sings Doctor Dolittle (Atlantic 1967)H, Born Walden Robert Cassotto (Direction 1968)★★★, Commitment (Direction 1969)★★★, Bobby Darin (Motown 1972)★★.
COMPILATIONS: The Bobby Darin Story (Atco 1961)★★★★, Clementine (Clarion 1964)★★★★, The Best Of Bobby Darin (Capitol 1965)★★★, Something Special television soundtrack (Atlantic 1967)★★★, The Legendary Bobby Darin (Candlelite 1976)★★★, The Versatile Bobby Darin (Capitol 1985)★★★, The Legend Of Bobby Darin (Stylus 1985)★★★, His Greatest Hits (Capitol 1985)★★★, Bobby Darin: Collectors Series (Capitol 1989)★★★, Splish Splash: The Best Of Bobby Darin Volume One (Atco 1991)★★★, Mack The Knife: The Best Of Bobby Darin Volume 2 (Atco 1991)★★★, From Sea To Sea: Recorded Live From 1959 To 1967 (Live Gold 1992)★★★, Spotlight On Bobby Darin (Capitol 1995)★★★, As Long As I'm Singing: The Bobby Darin Collection 4-CD box set (Rhino 1995)★★★★, Roberto Cassotto: Rare, Rockin' & Unreleased (Ring Of Stars 1997)★★★, A&E Biography (Capitol 1998) ★★★, Mood Swings: The Best Of The Atlantic Years 1965-1967 (Edsel 1999)★★★★, The Capitol Years 3-CD box set (EMI 1999)★★★, Swingin' The Standards (Varèse Sarabande 1999)★★★, Wild, Cool & Swingin' (Capitol 1999)★★★, The Unreleased Capitol Sides (Collector's Choice 1999)★★★, The Very Best Of Bobby Darin 1966-1969: If I Were A Carpenter (Varèse Sarabande 1999)★★★★.
VIDEOS: Bobby Darin - Live! (Legends Of Entertainment 1999).
FURTHER READING: Borrowed Time: The 37 Years Of Bobby Darin, Al Diorio. That's All: Bobby Darin On Record, Stage And Screen, Jeff Bleiel. Dream Lovers, Dodd Darin.
FILMS: Pepe (1960), Too Late Blues (1961), Come September (1961), Pressure Point (1962), If A Man Answers (1962), State Fair (1962), Hell Is For Heroes (1962), Captain Newman, M.D. (1963), That Funny Feeling (1965), Cop-Out aka Stranger In The House (1967), Gunfight In Abilene (1967), Happy Mother's Day, Love George aka Run, Stranger, Run (1973).

DARTS
ALBUMS: Darts (Magnet 1977)★★, Everyone Plays Darts (Magnet 1978)★★, Dart Attack (Magnet 1979)★★.
COMPILATIONS: Amazing Darts (Magnet 1978)★★, Greatest Hits (Magnet 1983)★★★.

DAVE DEE, DOZY, BEAKY, MICK AND TICH
ALBUMS: Dave Dee, Dozy, Beaky, Mick And Tich (Fontana 1966)★★★, If Music Be The Food Of Love (Fontana 1967) ★★★, If No One Sang (Fontana 1968)★★★, The Legend Of Dave Dee, Dozy, Beaky, Mick And Tich (Fontana 1969) ★★, Together (Fontana 1969)★★.
COMPILATIONS: Greatest Hits (Fontana 1968)★★★, Hold Tight! The Best Of The Fontana Years (Collectables 1995)★★★, The Best Of Dave Dee, Dozy, Beaky, Mick And Tich (Spectrum 1996)★★★, The Complete Collection (Mercury 1997)★★★, Boxed 4-CD box set (BR 1999)★★★, The Singles (BR 1999)★★★.

DAVID, CRAIG
ALBUMS: Born To Do It (Wildstar 2000)★★★★.
VIDEOS: Off The Hook - Live At Wembley (Wildstar 2001).

DAVIS, SPENCER, GROUP
ALBUMS: The First Album (Fontana 1965)★★★, The Second Album (Fontana 1966)★★★, Autumn '66 (Fontana 1966) ★★★★, Here We Go Round The Mulberry Bush film soundtrack (United Artists 1967)★★★, Gimme Some Lovin' (United Artists 1967)★★★, I'm A Man (United Artists 1967)★★★★, With Their New Face On (United Artists 1968)★★, Heavies (United Artists 1969)★★, Funky recorded 1969 (Columbia 1971)★★, Gluggo (Vertigo 1973)★★★, Living In The Back Street (Vertigo 1974)★★, Catch You On The Rebop: Live In Europe (RPM 1995)★★★★.
COMPILATIONS: The Best Of The Spencer Davis Group (Island 1968)★★★★, The Best Of Spencer Davis Group (EMI America 1987)★★★, Keep On Running (Royal Collection 1991)★★★, Taking Out Time 1967-69 (RPM 1994)★★, Spotlight On Spencer Davis (Javelin 1994)★★, Live Together 1988 recordings (In Akustik 1995)H, 24 Hours Live In Germany 1988 recordings (In Akustik 1995)★, Eight Gigs A Week: The Steve Winwood Years (Island/Chronicles 1996)★★★★, Mulberry Bush (RPM 1999)★★★, Mojo Rhythms & Midnight Blues Vol. 1: Sessions 1965-1968 (RPM 2000)★★★★, Mojo Rhythms & Midnight Blues Vol. 2: Shows 1965-1968 (RPM 2000)★★★★, Live Anthology 1965-68 (Varèse Sarabande 2001)★★★★.
FURTHER READING: Keep On Running: The Steve Winwood Story, Chris Welch. Back In The High Life: A Biography Of Steve Winwood, Alan Clayson.

DAWN
ALBUMS: Candida (Bell 1970)★★★, Dawn Featuring Tony Orlando (Bell 1971)★★, Tuneweaving (Bell 1973)★★★, Dawn's New Ragtime Follies (Bell 1973)★★, Prime Time (Bell 1974)★★★, Golden Ribbons (Bell 1974)★★, He Don't Love You (Like I Love You) (Elektra 1975)★★★, Skybird (Arista 1975)★★, To Be With You (Elektra 1976)★★.
COMPILATIONS: Greatest Hits (Arista 1975)★★★, The Best Of Tony Orlando And Dawn (Rhino 1995)★★★.

DAYS OF THE NEW
ALBUMS: Days Of The New (Outpost 1997)★★★, Days Of The New II (Outpost 1999)★★★★, Days Of The New III (Outpost 2001)★★★.

DAZZ BAND
ALBUMS: Invitation To Love (Motown 1980)★★★, Let The Music Play (Motown 1981)★★★, Keep It Live (Motown 1982)★★★, On The One (Motown 1983)★★★, Joystick (Motown 1983)★★★, Jukebox (Motown 1984)★★★, Hot Spot (Motown 1985)★★, Wild And Free (Geffen 1986)★★, Rock The Room (RCA 1988)★★, Under The Streetlights (Lucky 1996)★★★, Here We Go Again (Platinum 1998)★★.

DB'S
ALBUMS: Stands For Decibels (Albion 1981)★★★★, Repercussion (Albion 1982)★★★★, Like This (Bearsville 1985)★★★★, The Sound Of Music (I.R.S. 1987)★★★.
SOLO: Will Rigby Sidekick Phenomenon (Egon 1985)★★★.
COMPILATIONS: Amplifier (Dojo 1986)★★★, The dB's Ride The Wild Tom Tom (Rhino 1993)★★★★.

DE BURGH, CHRIS
ALBUMS: Far Beyond These Castle Walls (A&M 1975)★★, Spanish Train & Other Stories (A&M 1975)★★, At The End Of A Perfect Day (A&M 1977)★★★, Crusader (A&M 1979) ★★★, Live In S.A. (A&M 1979)★★, Eastern Wind (A&M 1980)★★, The Getaway (A&M 1982)★★★, Man On The Line (A&M 1984)★★★, Into The Light (A&M 1986)★★★, Flying Colours (A&M 1988)★★★, High On Emotion: Live From Dublin (A&M 1990)★★★, Power Of Ten (A&M 1992)★★★, This Way Up (A&M 1994)★★, Beautiful Dreams (A&M 1995)★★, Love Songs (A&M 1997)★★, Quiet Revolution (Mercury 1999)★★.
COMPILATIONS: Best Moves (A&M 1981)★★★, The Very Best Of Chris De Burgh (Telstar 1984)★★★, From A Spark To A Flame: The Very Best Of Chris De Burgh (A&M 1989)★★★, The Lady In Red: The Very Best Of Chris De Burgh (Ark 21 2000)★★★, Notes From Planet Earth: The Ultimate Collection (Mercury 2001)★★★.

DE LA SOUL
ALBUMS: 3 Feet High And Rising (Tommy Boy 1989)★★★★, De La Soul Is Dead (Tommy Boy 1991)★★★, Buhloone Mindstate (Tommy Boy 1993)★★★, Stakes Is High (Tommy Boy 1996)★★★, Art Official Intelligence: Mosaic Thump (Tommy Boy 2000)★★★★, AOI: Bionix (Tommy Boy 2001)★★★★.
VIDEOS: 3 Feet High And Rising (Big Life 1989).

DEACON BLUE
ALBUMS: Raintown (Columbia 1987)★★★★, When The World Knows Your Name (Columbia 1989)★★★★, Ooh Las Vegas (Columbia 1990)★★★, Fellow Hoodlums (Columbia 1991)★★★, Whatever You Say, Say Nothing (Columbia 1993)★★, Homesick (Papillon 2001)★★★.
Solo: Ricky Ross What You Are (Epic 1996)★★★.
COMPILATIONS: Our Town: Greatest Hits (Columbia 1994)★★★★, Walking Back Home (Columbia 1999)★★★, The Very Best Of Deacon Blue (Columbia 2001)★★★★.
VIDEOS: The Big Picture Live (CMV Enterprises 1990).

DEAD BOYS
ALBUMS: Young, Loud And Snotty (Sire 1977)★★★★, We Have Come For Your Children (Sire 1978)★★, Night Of The Living Dead Boys (Bomp 1981)★★.
COMPILATIONS: Younger, Louder And Snottier (Necrophilia 1989)★★★.

DEAD CAN DANCE
ALBUMS: Dead Can Dance (4AD 1984)★★★★, Spleen And Ideal (4AD 1985)★★★, Within The Realm Of A Dying Sun (4AD 1987)★★★, The Serpent's Egg (4AD 1988) ★★★, Aion (4AD 1990)★★★, Into The Labyrinth (4AD 1993)★★★, Towards The Within (4AD 1994)★★★★, Spiritchaser (4AD 1995)★★★★.
COMPILATIONS: 1981-1998 box set (Rhino 2001)★★★.
VIDEOS: Toward The Within (Warners 1994).

DEAD KENNEDYS
ALBUMS: Fresh Fruit For Rotting Vegetables (I.R.S./Cherry Red 1980)★★★★, In God We Trust, Inc. mini-album (Alternative Tentacles/Faulty Products 1981)★★★, Plastic Surgery Disasters (Alternative Tentacles 1982)★★★, Frankenchrist (Alternative Tentacles 1985)★★★, Bedtime For Democracy (Alternative Tentacles 1986)★★★, Mutiny On The Bay: Live From The San Francisco Bay Area 1982/1986 recordings (DKD 2001)★★★.
SOLO: Klaus Flouride Cha Cha Cha With Mr. Flouride (Alternative Tentacles 1985)★★, Because I Say So (Alternative Tentacles 1988)★★, The Light Is Flickering (Alternative Tentacles 1991)★★.
COMPILATIONS: Give Me Convenience Or Give Me Death (Alternative Tentacles 1987)★★★★.
VIDEOS: Live In San Francisco (Hendring Music Video 1987), Dead Kennedys Live At DMPO's (Visionary 1998).

DEAD OR ALIVE
ALBUMS: Sophisticated Boom Boom (Epic 1984)★★, Youthquake (Epic 1985)★★★, Mad, Bad, And Dangerous To Know (Epic 1987)★★, Rip It Up (Epic 1987)★★★, Nude (Epic 1989)★★, Nukleopatra (Sony/Cleopatra 1995)★★, Fragile (Avex 2000)★★.
VIDEOS: Youthquake (CBS-Fox 1988).

DEATH IN VEGAS
ALBUMS: Dead Elvis (Concrete 1997)★★★★, The Contino Sessions (Concrete 1999)★★★★.

DEBARGE
ALBUMS: The DeBarges (Gordy 1981)★★★, All This Love (Gordy 1982)★★★, In A Special Way (Gordy 1983)★★, Rhythm Of The Night (Gordy 1985)★★, Bad Boys (Striped Horse 1988)★★.
COMPILATIONS: Greatest Hits (Motown 1986)★★★.

DEE, JOEY, AND THE STARLITERS
ALBUMS: Joey Dee And The Starliters (Scepter 1960)★★★, Doin' The Twist At The Peppermint Lounge (Roulette 1961) ★★★, The Peppermint Twist (Scepter 1961)★★★, Hey, Let's Twist film soundtrack (Roulette 1962)★★, Back At The Peppermint Lounge (Roulette 1962)★★★, All The World Is Twistin' (Roulette 1962)★★★, Two Tickets To Paris film soundtrack (Roulette 1962)★★, Joey Dee (Roulette 1963) ★★★, Dance, Dance, Dance (Roulette 1963)★★, Hitsville (Jubilee 1966)★★.
COMPILATIONS: Hey Let's Twist! The Best Of Joey Dee And The Starliters (Rhino 1990)★★★, Starbright (Westside 1999)★★★, In Hollywood (Soundies 1999)★★.
FILMS: Hey, Let's Twist (1961), Two Tickets To Paris (1962), Twist (1992).

DEE, KIKI
ALBUMS: Kiki Dee (UK) Patterns (US) (Fontana/Liberty 1968)★★★, Great Expectations (Tamla Motown 1970)★★, Loving & Free (Rocket 1973)★★★, I've Got The Music In Me (Rocket 1974)★★★, Kiki Dee (Rocket 1977)★★★, Stay With Me (Rocket 1979)★★★, Perfect Timing (Ariola/RCA 1980)★★, Angel Eyes (Columbia 1987)★★★, Almost Naked (Tickety-Boo 1995)★★★★, with Carmelo Luggeri Where Rivers Meet (Tickety-Boo 1998)★★★.
COMPILATIONS: Kiki Dee's Greatest Hits (Warwick 1980) ★★★, Spotlight On Kiki Dee: Greatest Hits (Rocket 1991) ★★★, The Very Best Of Kiki Dee (Rocket 1994)★★★, Amoureuse (Spectrum 1996)★★★.
VIDEOS: Where Rivers Meet (Tickety-Boo 1999).
FILMS: Dateline Diamonds (1965).

DEEP PURPLE
ALBUMS: Shades Of Deep Purple (Parlophone/Tetragrammoton 1968)★★, The Book Of Taliesyn (Tetragrammoton/Parlophone 1968)★★★, Deep Purple (Tetragrammoton/Harvest 1969) ★★★, Concerto For Group And Orchestra (Tetragrammoton/Harvest 1969)★★, Deep Purple In Rock (Harvest/Warners 1970)★★★★, Fireball (Warners/Harvest 1971)★★★★, Machine Head (Purple/Warners 1972)★★★★, Made In Japan (Purple/Warners 1972)★★★, Who Do We Think We Are! (Purple/Warners 1973)★★★, Burn (Purple/Warners 1974) ★★★, Stormbringer (Purple/Warners 1974)★★★, Come Taste The Band (Purple/Warners 1975)★★★, Made In Europe (Purple/Warners 1976)★★★, Last Concert In Japan (Warners 1977)★★, Live In London 1974 recording (Harvest 1982)★★, Perfect Strangers (Mercury 1984)★★★, The House Of Blue Light (Polydor/Mercury 1987)★★★, Nobody's Perfect (Polydor 1988)★★, Scandinavian Nights (UK) Live And Rare (US) 1970 recording (Connoisseur 1988)★★, Slaves And Masters (RCA 1990)★★, In The Absence Of Pink: Knebworth '85 (Connoisseur 1991)★★, Gemini Suite 1971 recording (RPM 1993)★★, Live In Japan 1972 recordings (EMI 1993)★★★, The Battle Rages On (RCA 1993)★★★, The Final Battle (RCA 1994)★★★, Come Hell Or High Water (RCA 1994)★★, King Biscuit Flower Hour Presents: Deep Purple In Concert (US) On The Wings Of A Russian Foxbat (Live In California) (UK) 1976 recordings (King Biscuit Flower Hour/Connoisseur 1995)★★★, California Jamming (UK) Live At The California Jam (US) (EMI/Mausoleum 1996)★★, Deep Purple In Concert On The King Biscuit Flower Hour (King Biscuit 1996)★★★, Purpendicular (RCA/CMC 1996)★★★, Mark III: The Final Concerts (UK) Archive Alive! (US) 1976 recordings (Connoisseur/Archive 1996)★★, Live At The Olympia '96 (EMI Thames 1997)★★★, Abandon (EMI/CMC 1998)★★, Total Abandon: Live In Australia '99 (Drew Thompson/Thames Talent 1999)★★, with the London Symphony Orchestra Live At The Royal Albert Hall (Polydor/Eagle 1999)★★, Days May Come & Days May Go 1975 recordings (Purple 2000)★★, Extended Versions 1976 recordings (BMG 2000)★★, This Time Around: Live In Tokyo 1975 recording (Purple/Sanctuary 2001)★★, Live At The Rotterdam Ahoy (Thames/Thomson 2001)★★.
COMPILATIONS: The Best Of Deep Purple (Scepter/Polydor 1970)★★, Purple Passages (Warners 1972)★★, Early Purple (Polydor 1972)★★, Mark I & II (EMI/Purple 1973) ★★★, 24 Carat Purple (Purple/Warners 1975)★★★★, Powerhouse (Purple 1977)★★★, When We Rock, We Rock And When We Roll, We Roll (Warners 1978)★★★★, Singles A's & B's (Harvest 1978)★★★, The Mark II Purple Singles (Purple 1979)★★★, Deepest Purple: The Very Best Of Deep Purple (EMI 1980)★★★★, The Anthology (EMI/Harvest 1985)★★★, The Best Of Deep Purple i (Telstar 1985)★★★, The Best Of Deep Purple ii (Creative Sounds 1990)★★, Anthology (EMI 1991)★★★, Knockin' At Your Back Door: The Best Of Deep Purple In The 80's (Polydor 1992)★★★, Best On Stage 1970-1985 3-CD box set (Connoisseur 1994)★★★, Collection (Creative Sounds 1995)★★, The Collection (EMI Gold 1997)★★★★, Purplexed (BMG 1998)★★, Smoke On The Water (PolyGram 1998)★★★, Very Best Of Deep Purple: 30th Anniversary Collection (EMI 1998)★★★★, various artists The Friends & Relatives Album (Eagle 1999)★★★, Shades 1968-1998 4-CD set (Rhino 1999)★★★, Under The Gun (Spectrum 2000)★★★, Anthems (EMI Gold 2000)★★★★, The Very Best Of Deep Purple (Rhino 2000)★★★★, On The Road 4-CD box set (Connoisseur 2001)★★★, New, Live & Rare: The Bootleg Collection 1984-2000 12-CD box set (Thompson 2001)★★, The Soundboard Series 12-CD box set (Thames/Thomson 2001)★★.
VIDEOS: Rises Over Japan (Warners 1976), Live At The California Jam (BBC Video 1981), Concerto For Group & Orchestra (BBC Video 1984), The Videosingles (PolyGram Music 1987), Bad Attitude (Polydor 1988), Doing Their Thing (Castle Music Pictures 1990), Scandinavian Nights (Live In Denmark) aka Machine Head Live 1972 (Connoisseur Collection 1990), Heavy Metal Pioneers (Warner Music Vision 1991), Come Hell Or High Water (BMG Video 1994), A Band Downunder (TMM/Thames Talent 1999), Total Abandon: Australia '99 (Drew Thompson/Thames Talent 1999), Live At The Royal Albert Hall (Eagle/Image Entertainment 2000), Around The World 1995-1999 (TMM/Thames Talent 2000), Bombay Calling: Deep Purple Live In Bombay '95 (TMM/Thames Talent 2000), New, Live & Rare: The Video Collection 1984-2000 (TMM/Thames Talent 2001).
FURTHER READING: Deep Purple: The Illustrated Biography, Chris Charlesworth.

DEF LEPPARD
ALBUMS: On Through The Night (Mercury 1980)★★★, High 'N' Dry (Mercury 1981)★★★★, Pyromania (Mercury 1983)★★★★, Hysteria (Mercury 1987)★★★★, Adrenalize (Mercury 1992)★★★, Slang (Mercury 1996)★★★, Euphoria (Bludgeon Riffola 1999)★★.
COMPILATIONS: Retro Active (Mercury 1993)★★★, Vault: Def Leppard Greatest Hits 1980-1995 (Mercury 1995)★★★★.
VIDEOS: Love Bites (PolyGram Music Video 1988), Historia (PolyGram Music Video 1988), Rocket (PolyGram Music Video 1989), Rock Of Ages (PolyGram Music Video 1989), In The Round – In Your Face (PolyGram Music Video 1989), Animal (PolyGram Music Video 1989), Visualise (PolyGram Music Video 1993), Unlock The Rock: Video Archive 1993-1995 (PolyGram Music Video 1995).
FURTHER READING: Def Leppard: Animal Instinct, David Fricke. Def Leppard, Jason Rich. Biographize: The Def Leppard Story, Dave Dickson.

DEKKER, DESMOND
ALBUMS: 007 (Shanty Town) (Beverley's 1967)★★★★, Action! (Beverley's 1968)★★★, The Israelites (Beverley's 1969)★★★★, This Is Desmond Dekker (Trojan 1969)★★★★, You Can Get It If You Really Want (Trojan 1970)★★★★, Black And Dekker (Stiff 1980)★★★, Compass Point (Stiff 1981) ★★★, Officially Live And Rare (Trojan 1987)★★, Music Like Dirt (Trojan 1992)★★★, with the Specials King Of Kings (Trojan 1993)★★★, Halfway To Paradise (Trojan 1999)★★.
COMPILATIONS: Double Dekker (Trojan 1974)★★★★, Sweet 16 Hits (Trojan 1978)★★★★, The Original Reggae Hitsound (Trojan 1985)★★★★, 20 Golden Pieces (Bulldog 1987)★★★★, Best Of And The Rest Of (Action Replay/Trojan 1989)★★★, King Of Ska (Trojan 1991)★★★★, 20 Greatest Hits (Point 2 1992)★★★★, Crucial Cuts – The Best Of Desmond Dekker (1993)★★★★, First Time For Long Time (Trojan 1997)★★★, The Writing On The Wall (Trojan 1998)★★★, Israelites: Anthology 1963-1999 (Trojan 2001)★★★★.

DEL AMITRI
ALBUMS: Del Amitri (Chrysalis 1985)★★★, Waking Hours (A&M 1989)★★★, Change Everything (A&M 1992)★★★★, Twisted (A&M 1995)★★★, Some Other Sucker's Parade (A&M 1997)★★★★, Can You Do Me Good? (A&M 2002)★★★.
COMPILATIONS: The Best Of Del Amitri: Hatful Of Rain (A&M 1998)★★★★, Lousy With Love: The B-Sides (A&M 1998)★★★.
VIDEOS: Let's Go Home (VVL 1996), The Best Of Del Amitri: Hatful Of Rain (VVL 1998).

DEL-VIKINGS
ALBUMS: Come Go With The Del Vikings (Luniverse 1957) ★★★, They Sing - They Swing (Mercury 1957)★★★, A Swinging, Singing Record Session (Mercury 1958)★★, Newies And Oldies (1959)★★★, The Del Vikings And The Sonnets (Crown 1963)★★★, Come Go With Me (Dot 1966)★★★.
COMPILATIONS: Del Vikings (Buffalo Bop 1988)★★★, Cool Shake (Buffalo Bop 1988)★★★, Collectables (Mercury 1988)★★★, In Harmony (Fireball 1998)★★★.

DELANEY AND BONNIE
ALBUMS: Accept No Substitute – The Original Delaney & Bonnie (Elektra 1969)★★★, Home (Atco 1969)★★, Delaney & Bonnie & Friends On Tour With Eric Clapton (Atco 1970)★★★★, To Bonnie From Delaney (Atco 1970)★★★, Motel Shot (Atco 1971)★★★, D&B Together (Columbia 1972)★★, Country Life (Columbia 1972)★★★.
COMPILATIONS: The Best Of Delaney & Bonnie (Atco 1973)★★★.
FILMS: Catch My Soul (1974).

DELFONICS
ALBUMS: La La Means I Love You (Philly Groove 1968)★★★, The Sound Of Sexy Soul (Philly Groove 1969)★★★, The Delfonics (Philly Groove 1970)★★★, Tell Me This Is A Dream (Philly Groove 1972)★★★, Alive And Kicking (Philly Groove 1974)★★.
COMPILATIONS: The Delfonics Super Hits (Philly Groove 1969)★★★, Symphonic Soul – Greatest Hits (Charly 1988) ★★★★, Echoes – The Best Of The Delfonics (Arista 1991) ★★★★, La-La Means I Love You (Arista 1998)★★★, The Professionals (Ace 1998)★★★, The Definitive Collection (Camden 1999)★★★.

DELLS
ALBUMS: Oh What A Nite (Vee Jay 1959)★★★, It's Not Unusual (Vee Jay 1965)★★★, There Is (Cadet 1968)★★★★, Stay In My Corner (Cadet 1968)★★★, The Dells Musical Menu/Always Together (Cadet 1969)★★★, Love Is Blue (Cadet 1969)★★★, Like It Is, Like It Was (Cadet 1970)★★★, Oh, What A Night (Cadet 1970)★★★, Freedom Means (Cadet 1971)★★★, Dells Sing Dionne Warwick's Greatest Hits (Cadet 1972)★★, Sweet As Funk Can Be (Cadet 1972) ★★★, Give Your Baby A Standing Ovation (Cadet 1973)★★★, with the Dramatics The Dells Vs The Dramatics (Cadet 1974) ★★★, The Mighty Mighty Dells (Cadet 1974)★★★, We Got To Get Our Thing Together (Cadet 1975)★★★, No Way Back (Mercury 1975)★★★, They Said It Couldn't Be Done, But We Did It (Mercury 1977)★★, Love Connection (Mercury 1977) ★★★, New Beginnings (ABC 1978)★★, Face To Face (ABC 1979)★★★, I Touched A Dream (20th Century 1980)★★★, Whatever Turns You On (20th Century 1981)★★, One Step Closer (Private I 1984)★★, The Second Time (Veteran 1988)★★, I Salute You: 40th Anniversary (Zoo 1992)★★★.
COMPILATIONS: The Dells Greatest Hits (Cadet 1969)★★★, The Best Of The Dells (JCI 1973)★★★★, Cornered (DJM 1977)★★★, Rockin' On Bandstand (Charly 1983)★★★, From Streetcorner To Soul (Charly 1984)★★★, Breezy Ballads And Tender Tunes (Solid Smoke 1985)★★★, On Their Corner: The Best Of The Dells (Chess/MCA 1992) ★★★★, Dreams Of Contentment (Vee Jay 1993)★★★, Dells, Vol. 2 (Vee Jay 1994)★★★, Passionate Breezes: The Best Of 1975-1991 (Mercury 1995)★★★, Oh What A Night! The Great Ballads (MCA 1998)★★★, Anthology (Hip-O 1999)★★★★, 20th Century Masters: The Millennium Collection (MCA 2000)★★★★.

DENNY, SANDY
ALBUMS: with Johnny Silvo Sandy And Johnny (Saga 1967)★★, The North Star Grassman And The Ravens (Island 1971)★★★, Sandy (Island 1972)★★★★, with the Bunch Rock On (Island 1972)★★★, with the Strawbs All Our Own Work (Hallmark 1973)★★★, Like An Old Fashioned Waltz (Island 1973)★★★, Rendezvous (Island 1977)★★★, The BBC Sessions 1971-1973 (Strange Fruit 1997)★★★★, Gold Dust: Live At The Royalty 1977 recording (Island 1998)★★★.
COMPILATIONS: Sandy Denny (Saga 1970)★★, The Original Sandy Denny (Mooncrest 1978)★★★, Who Knows Where The Time Goes? 3-CD box set (Island 1986)★★★★, The Best Of Sandy Denny (Island 1987)★★★, with Trevor Lucas The Attic Tracks 1972 - 1984 Outtakes And Rarities (Special Delivery 1995)★★★★, The Best Of Sandy Denny (Island 1996)★★★★, Listen Listen: An Introduction To Sandy Denny (Island 1999)★★★★, No More Sad Refrains: The Anthology (A&M 2000)★★★★.
FURTHER READING: No More Sad Refrains: The Life And Times Of Sandy Denny, Clinton Heylin.

DENVER, JOHN
ALBUMS: Rhymes & Reasons (RCA 1969)★★★, Take Me To Tomorrow (RCA 1970)★★★, Whose Garden Was This? (RCA 1970)★★★, Poems, Prayers & Promises (RCA 1971)★★★, Aerie (RCA 1972)★★★, Rocky Mountain High (RCA 1972) ★★★★, Farewell Andromeda (RCA 1974)★★★, Back Home Again (RCA 1974)★★★★, An Evening With John Denver (RCA 1975)★★★★, Windsong (RCA 1975)★★★★, Rocky Mountain Christmas (RCA 1975)★★, Live In London (RCA 1976)★★, Spirit (RCA 1976)★★★★, I Want To Live (RCA 1977)★★, Live At The Sydney Opera House (RCA 1978)★★, John Denver (RCA 1979)★★★★, with the Muppets A Christmas Together (RCA 1979)★★, Autograph (RCA 1980) ★★★, Some Days Are Diamonds (RCA 1981)★★★, with Placido Domingo Perhaps Love (Columbia 1981)★★, Seasons Of The Heart (RCA 1982)★★★, with the Muppets Rocky Mountain Holiday (RCA 1982)★★, It's About Time (RCA 1983)★★★, Dreamland Express (RCA 1985)★★, One World (RCA 1986)★★, Higher Ground (RCA 1988)★★, The Flower That Shattered The Stone (Windstar 1990)★★★, Christmas Like A Lullaby (Windstar 1990)★★, Earth Songs (Windstar 1990)★★★, Different Directions (Windstar 1991)★★★, The Wildlife Concert (Legacy 1995)★★★, All Aboard (Sony 1997)★★, Celebration Of Life/The Last Recordings (A&M 1997)★★, Live (Rivie're International 1997)★★, The Best Of John Denver Live (Legacy 1997)★★★, Forever, John (RCA 1998)★★, Live At The Sydney Opera House (RCA 1999)★★, Christmas In Concert (RCA 2001)★★.
COMPILATIONS: John Denver's Greatest Hits (RCA 1974) ★★★, John Denver's Greatest Hits, Volume 2 (RCA 1977) ★★★, The John Denver Collection (Telstar 1984)★★★, John Denver's Greatest Hits, Volume 3 (RCA 1984)★★★, Reflections: Songs Of Love & Life (RCA 1996)★★★, The Rocky Mountain Collection (BMG 1997)★★★★, The Country Roads Collection (RCA 1997)★★★★, Greatest Country Hits (RCA 1998)★★★, Love Songs & Poetry (Camden 1999)★★, Behind The Music: The John Denver Collection (RCA 2000)★★★★.
VIDEOS: A Portrait (Telstar 1994), The Wildlife Concert (Sony Music Video 1995).
FURTHER READING: John Denver, Leonore Fleischer. John Denver, David Dachs. John Denver: Rocky Mountain Wonderboy, James Martin. Take Me Home: An Autobiography, John Denver with Arthur Tobier. John Denver: Mother Nature's Son, John Collis.
FILMS: Oh, God! (1977), Fire And Ice voice only (1987), Walking Thunder (1997).

DENVER, KARL
ALBUMS: Wimoweh (Decca 1961)★★★, Karl Denver (Decca 1962)★★★, Karl Denver At The Yew Tree (Decca 1962)★★, With Love (Decca 1964)★★★, Karl Denver (Narvis 1972)★★, Just Loving You (Plaza 1993)★★★.
COMPILATIONS: The Best Of Karl Denver (Prism 2001)★★★.

DEPECHE MODE
ALBUMS: Speak & Spell (Mute/Sire 1981)★★★, A Broken Frame (Mute/Sire 1982)★★, Construction Time Again (Mute/Sire 1983)★★★, Some Great Reward (Mute/Sire 1984)★★★, Black Celebration (Mute/Sire 1986)★★★, Music For The Masses (Mute/Sire 1987)★★★, 101 (Mute/Sire 1989)★★, Violator (Mute/Sire 1990)★★★★, Songs Of Faith And Devotion (Mute/Sire 1993)★★★★, Songs Of Faith And Devotion Live (Mute/Sire 1993)★★★, Ultra (Mute/Reprise 1997)★★★, Exciter (Mute/Reprise 2001)★★★★.
COMPILATIONS: People Are People US only (Sire 1984) ★★★, Catching Up With Depeche Mode US only (Sire 1985) ★★★★, The Singles 81>85 (Mute/Reprise 1985)★★★★, The Singles 86>98 (Mute/Reprise 1998)★★★★, The Singles 81>98 3-CD box set (Mute 2001)★★★★.
VIDEOS: Some Great Videos (Virgin Vision 1986), Strange (Virgin Vision 1988), 101 (Virgin Vision 1989), Strange Too – Another Violation (BMG Video 1990), Devotional (Virgin Vision 1993), Live In Hamburg (Virgin Vision 1993), The Videos 86>98 (Mute 1998).
FURTHER READING: Depeche Mode, Dave Thomas. Depeche Mode: Strangers - The Photographs, Anton Corbijn. Depeche Mode: Some Great Reward, Dave Thompson. Depeche Mode: A Biography, Steve Malins.

DEREK AND THE DOMINOS
ALBUMS: Layla And Other Assorted Love Songs (Polydor 1970)★★★★, In Concert (Polydor 1973)★★★.

DESCENDENTS
ALBUMS: Milo Goes To College (New Alliance 1982)★★★, I Don't Want To Grow Up (New Alliance 1985)★★★, Enjoy! (New Alliance 1986)★★★, All (SST 1987)★★, Liveage! (SST 1987)★★, Hallraker Live! (SST 1989)★★, Everything Sucks (Epitaph 1996)★★★.
COMPILATIONS: Two Things At Once (SST 1988)★★★, Somery (SST 1990)★★★.

DESERT ROSE BAND
ALBUMS: The Desert Rose Band (MCA 1987)★★★, Running (MCA 1988)★★★★, Pages Of Life (MCA 1989)★★★★, True Love (Curb 1991)★★, Traditional (Curb 1993)★★, Life Goes On (Curb 1993)★★.
COMPILATIONS: A Dozen Roses: Greatest Hits (MCA 1991)★★★★, Greatest Hits (Curb 1994)★★★★.

DESHANNON, JACKIE
ALBUMS: Jackie De Shannon (Liberty 1963)★★, Breakin' It Up On The Beatles Tour! (Liberty 1964)★★, This Is Jackie De Shannon (Imperial 1965)★★★, In The Wind (Imperial 1965)★★★, Are You Ready For This? (Imperial 1966)★★★, New Image (Imperial 1967)★★, For You (Imperial 1967) ★★, Me About You (Imperial 1968)★★, What The World Needs Now Is Love (Imperial 1968)★★★, Laurel Canyon (Imperial 1968)★★★, Put A Little Love In Your Heart (Imperial 1969)★★, To Be Free (Imperial 1970)★★, Songs (Capitol 1971)★★★, Jackie (Atlantic 1972)★★, Your Baby Is A Lady (Atlantic 1974)★★★, New Arrangement (Columbia 1975) ★★, You're The Only Dancer (Amherst 1977)★★, Quick Touches (Amherst 1978)★★, You Know Me (Varèse Sarabande 2000)★★.
COMPILATIONS: You Won't Forget Me (Imperial 1965) ★★★, Lonely Girl (Sunset 1968)★★, The Very Best Of Jackie DeShannon (United Artists 1975)★★★, Good As Gold! (Pair 1990)★★★, The Best Of Jackie DeShannon (Rhino 1991)★★★★, What The World Needs Now Is Jackie De Shannon: The Definitive Collection (EMI 1993) ★★★★, The Early Years (Missing 1998)★★, Best Of ... 1958-1980: Come And Get Me (Raven 2000)★★★★.
FILMS: Surf Party (1964), Intimacy aka The Deceivers (1966), C'mon, Let's Live A Little (1967).

DESTINY'S CHILD
ALBUMS: Destiny's Child (Columbia 1998)★★★, The Writing's On The Wall (Columbia 1999)★★★★, Survivor (Columbia 2001)★★★, 8 Days Of Christmas (Columbia 2001)★★.
COMPILATIONS: This Is The Remix (Columbia 2002)★★★.
VIDEOS: The Platinum's On The Wall (Sony Music Video 2001), Survivor (Columbia Music Video 2001).

DETROIT SPINNERS
ALBUMS: Party - My Pad (Motown 1963)★★, The Original Spinners (Motown 1967)★★★, The Detroit Spinners (Motown 1968)★★★, Second Time Around (V.I.P. 1970)★★★, The (Detroit) Spinners (Atlantic 1973)★★★★, Mighty Love (Atlantic 1974)★★★★, New And Improved (Atlantic 1974)★★★, Pick Of The Litter (Atlantic 1975) ★★★★, (Detroit) Spinners Live! (Atlantic 1975)★★★, Happiness Is Being With The (Detroit) Spinners (Atlantic 1976)★★★, Yesterday, Today And Tomorrow (Atlantic 1977)★★, Spinners/8 (Atlantic 1977)★★, From Here To Eternally (Atlantic 1979)★★, Dancin' And Lovin' (Atlantic 1980)★★, Love Trippin' (Atlantic 1980)★★★, Labor Of Love (Atlantic 1981)★★, Can't Shake This Feelin' (Atlantic 1982)★★, Grand Slam (Atlantic 1983)★★, Cross Fire (Atlantic 1984)★★, Lovin' Feelings (Atco 1985)★★, Down To Business (Volt 1989)★★.
COMPILATIONS: The Best Of The Detroit Spinners (Motown 1973)★★★★, Smash Hits (Atlantic 1977)★★★★, The Best Of The Spinners (Atlantic 1978)★★★★, 20 Golden Classics – The Detroit Spinners (Motown 1980)★★★★, Golden Greats – Detroit Spinners (Atlantic 1985)★★★, A One Of A Kind Love Affair: The Anthology (Atlantic 1991)★★★★, The Essential Collection (Spectrum 2001)★★★★.

DEUS
ALBUMS: Worst Case Scenario (Island 1994)★★★, My Sister Is A Clock (Island 1995) ★★★, In A Bar Under The Sea (Island 1996)★★★★, The Ideal Crash (Island 1999)★★★★.

DEVO
ALBUMS: Q: Are We Not Men? A: We Are Devo! (Warners 1978)★★★★, Duty Now For The Future (Warners 1979) ★★★, Freedom Of Choice (Warners 1980)★★★, Dev-o Live mini-album (Warners 1981)H, New Traditionalists (Warners 1981)★★★, Oh No, It's Devo (Warners 1982) ★★★, Shout (Warners 1984)★★, Total Devo (Enigma 1988)★★, Smooth Noodle Maps (Enigma 1990)★★.
SOLO: Mark Mothersbaugh Muzik For Insomniaks Volume 1 (Enigma 1988)★★, Muzik For Insomniaks Volume 2 (Enigma 1988)★★.
COMPILATIONS: E-Z Listening Disc (Rykodisc 1987)★★, Now It Can Be Told (Enigma 1989)★★★, Greatest Hits (Warners 1990)★★★★, Greatest Misses (Warners 1990) ★★★, Hard Core Devo (Rykodisc 1990)★★, Hardcore Devo 1974-77, Volumes 1 & 2 (Fan Club 1991)★★, Live: The Mongoloid Years (Rykodisc 1992)★★, Pioneers Who Got Scalped 3-CD set (Warners 2000)★★★.

DEXYS MIDNIGHT RUNNERS
ALBUMS: Searching For The Young Soul Rebels (Parlophone/EMI America 1980)★★★★, as Kevin Rowland And Dexys Midnight Runners Too-Rye-Ay (Mercury 1982)★★★★, Don't Stand Me Down (Mercury 1985)★★★, BBC Radio One Live In Concert 1982 recording (Windsong 1994)★★★, Don't Stand Me Down: The Director's Cut (EMI 2002)★★★.
SOLO: Kevin Rowland The Wanderer (Mercury 1988)★★, My Beauty (Creation 1999)H.
COMPILATIONS: Geno (EMI 1983)★★★, The Very Best Of Dexys Midnight Runners (Mercury 1991)★★★★, 1980-1982: The Radio One Sessions (Nighttracks 1995)★★★, It Was Like This (EMI 1996)★★★★.

DIAMOND HEAD
ALBUMS: Lightning To The Nation (Woolfe 1981)★★★, Borrowed Time (MCA 1982)★★★, Canterbury (MCA 1983)★★, Behold The Beginning (Heavy Metal 1986)★★, Am I Evil (FM Revolver 1987)★★★, Death & Progress (Bronze 1993)★★★.
VIDEOS: Diamond Head (1981).

DIAMOND, NEIL
ALBUMS: The Feel Of Neil Diamond (Bang 1966)★★, Just For You (Bang 1967)★★★, Velvet Gloves And Spit (Uni 1968)★★, Brother Love's Travelling Salvation Show (Uni 1969)★★★, Touching You Touching Me (Uni 1969)★★★, Gold (Uni 1970)★★★, Shilo (Bang 1970)★★, Tap Root Manuscript (Uni 1970)★★★★, Do It! (Bang 1971)★★, Stones (Uni 1971)★★★, Moods (Uni 1972)★★★, Hot August Night (MCA 1972)★★★★, Jonathan Livingston Seagull (Columbia 1973)★★, Serenade (Columbia 1974) ★★★, Beautiful Noise (Columbia 1976)★★★★, Love At The Greek (Columbia 1977)★★★, I'm Glad You're Here With Me Tonight (Columbia 1977)★★★, You Don't Bring Me Flowers (Columbia 1978)★★★★, September Morn (Columbia 1980)★★★, The Jazz Singer film soundtrack (Capitol 1980)★★★★, On The Way To The Sky (Columbia 1981)★★★, Heartlight (Columbia 1982)★★★, Primitive (Columbia 1984)★★★, Headed For The Future (Columbia 1986)★★★, Hot August Night II (Columbia 1987)★★, The Best Years Of Our Lives (Columbia 1989)★★★, Lovescape (Columbia 1991)★★★, The Christmas Album (Columbia 1992)★★★, Up On The Roof (Songs From The Brill Building) (Columbia 1993)★★★, Live In America (Columbia 1994)★★★, Tennessee Moon (Columbia 1996)★★★★, The Movie Album: As Time Goes By (Columbia 1998)★★, Three Chord Opera (Columbia 2001)★★★.
COMPILATIONS: Neil Diamond's Greatest Hits (Bang 1968) ★★★, Double Gold (Bang 1973)★★★, Rainbow (MCA 1973) ★★★, His 12 Greatest Hits (MCA 1974)★★★★, And The Singer Sings His Song (MCA 1976)★★★, Diamonds (MCA 1981)★★, 12 Greatest Hits, Vol. II (Columbia 1982) ★★★★, Classics: The Early Years (Columbia 1983)★★★, Red Red Wine (Pickwick 1988)★★, The Greatest Hits 1966 – 1992 (Columbia 1992)★★★★, The Very Best Of Neil Diamond (Pickwick 1996) ★★★, In My Lifetime 3-CD box set (Columbia 1996)★★★★, The Essential (Legacy/Columbia 2001)★★★★, Play Me: The Complete Uni Studio Recordings ... Plus! (MCA 2002)★★★.
VIDEOS: Neil Diamond: The Christmas Special (1993), The Roof Party (Columbia 1994), Under A Tennessee Moon (SMV 1996).
FURTHER READING: Neil Diamond, Suzanne K. O'Regan. Solitary Star: Biography Of Neil Diamond, Rich Wiseman.
FILMS: The Jazz Singer (1980).

DIDDLEY, BO
ALBUMS: Bo Diddley (Checker 1957)★★★, Go Bo Diddley (Checker 1958)★★★, Have Guitar Will Travel (Checker 1959)★★★, Bo Diddley In The Spotlight (Checker 1960) ★★★, Bo Diddley Is A Gunslinger (Checker 1961)★★★, Bo Diddley Is A Lover (Checker 1961)★★★, Bo Diddley (Checker 1962)★★★, Bo Diddley Is A Twister (Checker 1962)★★★, Hey Bo Diddley (Checker 1963)★★★, Bo Diddley And Company (Checker 1963)★★★, Bo Diddley Rides Again (Checker 1963)★★★, Bo Diddley's Beach Party (Checker 1963)★★★, Bo Diddley Goes Surfing aka Surfin' With Bo Diddley (Checker 1963)★★★, Hey Good Looking (Checker 1964)★★★, with Chuck Berry Two Great Guitars (Checker 1964)★★★, 500% More Man (Checker 1965)★★★, Let Me Pass (Checker 1965)★★★, The Originator (Checker 1966)★★★, Boss Man (Checker 1967)★★★, Superblues (Checker 1968)★★★, The Super Super Blues Band (Checker 1968)★★★, The Black Gladiator (Checker 1969) ★★, Another Dimension (Chess 1971)★★★, Where It All Begins (Chess 1972)★★, The Bo Diddley London Sessions (Chess 1973)★★, Big Bad Bo (Chess 1974)★★★, Got My Own Bag Of Tricks (Chess 1974)★★★, The 20th Anniversary Of Rock 'N' Roll (RCA Victor 1976)★★, Bo's Blues (Ace 1993)★★, A Man Amongst Men (Code Blue 1996)★★.
COMPILATIONS: Chess Master (Chess 1988)★★★, EP Collection (See For Miles 1991)★★★★, The Chess Years 12-CD box set (Charly 1993)★★★★★, Collection (Castle 1995)★★★, His Best: The Chess 50th Anniversary Collection (Chess 1997)★★★★★, The Best Of Bo Diddley: The Millennium Collection (MCA 2000)★★★★.
VIDEOS: I Don't Sound Like Nobody (Hendring Music Video 1990).
FURTHER READING: Where Are You Now Bo Diddley?, Edward Kiersh. The Complete Bo Diddley Sessions, George White (ed.). Bo Diddley: Living Legend, George White.
FILMS: Rock Rock Rock (1956), Trading Places (1983), Rockula (1990), Blues Brothers 2000 (1998).

DIDO
ALBUMS: No Angel (Arista/Cheeky Records 1999)★★★★.

DIFRANCO, ANI
ALBUMS: Ani DiFranco (Righteous Babe 1990)★★★★, Not So Soft (Righteous Babe 1991)★★★, Imperfectly (Righteous Babe 1992)★★★, Puddle Dive (Righteous Babe 1993)★★★★, Out Of Range (Righteous Babe 1994)★★★★, Not A Pretty Girl (Righteous Babe 1995)★★★★, Dilate (Righteous Babe 1996) ★★★, with Utah Phillips The Past Didn't Go Anywhere (Righteous Babe 1996)★★★, Living In Clip (Righteous Babe 1997)★★★★, Little Plastic Castle (Righteous Babe 1998) ★★★★, Up Up Up Up Up Up (Righteous Babe 1999)★★★★, with Utah Phillips Fellow Workers (Righteous Babe 1999)★★★, To The Teeth (Righteous Babe 1999)★★★, Revelling/Reckoning (Righteous Babe 2001)★★★.
COMPILATIONS: Like I Said (Songs 1990-91) (Righteous Babe 1994)★★★.

DILLARD AND CLARK
ALBUMS: The Fantastic Expedition Of Dillard And Clark (A&M 1968)★★★★, Through The Morning, Through The Night (A&M 1969)★★★★.
FURTHER READING: The Byrds: Timeless Flight Revisited, Johnny Rogan.

DILLARDS
ALBUMS: Back Porch Bluegrass (Elektra 1963)★★★, The Dillards Live! Almost! (Elektra 1964)★★★, with Byron Berline Pickin' & Fiddlin' (Elektra 1965)★★★, Wheatstraw Suite (Elektra 1968)★★★★, Copperfields (Elektra 1970) ★★★, Roots And Branches (Anthem 1972)★★, Tribute To The American Duck (Poppy 1973)★★★★, The Dillards Versus The Incredible LA Time Machine (Sonet 1977)★★, Glitter-Grass From The Nashwood Hollyville Strings (1977) ★★★, Decade Waltz (Flying Fish 1979)★★, Homecoming & Family Reunion (Flying Fish 1980)★★★, Mountain Rock (Flying Fish 1980)★★★, Let It Fly (Vanguard 1990)★★★, A Long Time Ago: The First Time Live! (Varèse Sarabande 1999)★★★.
COMPILATIONS: Country Tracks (Elektra 1974)★★★, I'll Fly Away (Edsel 1988)★★★, There Is A Time (1963-1970) (Vanguard 1991)★★★★.
VIDEOS: A Night In The Ozarks (Hendring Music Video 1991).
FURTHER READING: Everybody On The Truck, Lee Grant.

DINOSAUR JR
ALBUMS: as Dinosaur Dinosaur (Homestead 1985)★★★, You're Living All Over Me (SST 1987)★★★, Bug (SST 1988)★★★★, Green Mind (Blanco y Negro/Sire 1991) ★★★, Whatever's Cool With Me mini-album (Blanco y Negro/Sire 1993)★★, Where You Been (Blanco y Negro 1993)★★★★, Without A Sound (Blanco y Negro 1994) ★★★, Hand It Over (Blanco y Negro 1997)★★★, In Session 1988 recording (Strange Fruit 1999)★★★.
SOLO: J Mascis Martin + Me (Baked Goods/Reprise 1996)★★★, as J Mascis + The Fog More Light (Ultimatum/City Slang 2000)★★★★.
COMPILATIONS: Ear Bleeding Country: The Best Of Dinosaur Jr. (Rhino 2001)★★★★.

DION
ALBUMS: with the Belmonts Presenting Dion And The Belmonts (Laurie 1959)★★★, with the Belmonts Wish Upon A Star (Laurie 1960)★★, Alone With Dion (Laurie 1961) ★★★, Runaround Sue (Laurie 1961)★★★, Lovers Who Wander (Laurie 1962)★★★★, Dion Sings His Greatest Hits (Laurie 1962)★★★, Love Came To Me (Laurie 1963)★★★, Ruby Baby (Columbia 1963)★★★, Dion Sings The 15 Million Sellers (Laurie 1963)★★★★, Donna The Prima Donna (Columbia 1963)★★★★, Dion Sings To Sandy (Laurie 1963)★★★, with the Belmonts Together (Laurie 1963)★★★, with the Belmonts Together Again (ABC 1967) ★★★, Dion (Laurie 1968)★★★★, Sit Down Old Friend (Warners 1969)★★★, You're Not Alone (Warners 1971) ★★★, Sanctuary (Warners 1971)★★★, Suite For Late Summer (Warners 1972)★★★, with the Belmonts Reunion: Live 1972 (Reprise 1973)★★, Born To Be With You (Spector 1975)★★★★, Streetheart (Warners 1976)★★★, The Return Of The Wanderer (Lifesong 1978)★★★, Inside Job (Dayspring 1980)★★, Only Jesus (Dayspring 1981)★★, I Put Away My Idols (Dayspring 1983)★★★, Seasons (Dayspring 1984)★★★, Kingdom In The Streets (Myrrh 1985)★★, Velvet And Steel (Dayspring 1986)★★★, Yo Frankie! (Arista 1989)★★★, Dream On Fire (Vision 1992) ★★★, Déjà Nu (Collectables 2000)★★★★.
COMPILATIONS: Dion's Greatest Hits (Columbia 1973) ★★★, 20 Golden Greats (K-Tel 1980)★★★★, 24 Original Classics (Arista 1984)★★★★, So Why Didn't You Do That The First Time? (Ace 1985)★★★★, Runaround Sue: The Best Of The Rest (Ace 1988)★★★, Bronx Blues: The Columbia Recordings (1962-1965) (Columbia 1990)★★★★, The Road I'm On: A Retrospective (Columbia Legacy 1997) ★★★, The Best Of The Gospel Years (Ace 1997)★★★, Bronx Blues: The Columbia Recordings (1962-1965) (Columbia 1999)★★★, King Of The New York Streets 3-CD box set (The Right Stuff 2000)★★★★, Dion: The EP Collection (See For Miles 2001)★★★.
FURTHER READING: The Wanderer, Dion DiMucci with Davin Seay.

DION, CELINE
ALBUMS: La Voix Du Bon Dieu (Disques Super Etoiles 1981)★★, Celine Dion Chante Noëel (Disques Super Etoiles 1981)★★, Tellement J'ai D'amour (Saisons 1982)★★, Les Chemins De Ma Maison (Saisons 1983)★★, Du Soleil Au Coeur (Pathe Marconi 1983)★★, Chants Et Contes De Noël (1983)★★, Mélanie (TBS 1984)★★, Les Oiseaux Du Bonheur (Pathe Marconi 1984)★★, C'est Pour Toi (TBS 1985)★★, Celine Dion En Concert (TBS 1985)★★, Incognito (Columbia 1987)★★, Unison (Epic 1990)★★, Dion Chante Plamondon/Des Mots Qui Sonnent (Epic 1991)★★★, Celine Dion (Epic 1992)★★★★, The Colour Of My Love (Epic 1993)★★★★, Celine Dion À L'Olympia (Columbia 1994)★★★, D'Eux/The French Album (Epic 1995)★★★, Falling Into You (Epic 1996)★★★★, Live À Paris (Epic 1996)★★★, Let's Talk About Love (Epic 1997) ★★★, S'il Suffisait D'Aimer (Epic 1998)★★, with Mariah Carey, Gloria Estefan, Aretha Franklin, Shania Twain Divas Live (Epic 1998)★★, These Are Special Times (Epic 1998)★★★, A New Day Has Come (Epic 2002)★★★.
COMPILATIONS: Les Plus Grands Succès De Celine Dion (TBS 1984)★★★, Les Chansons En Or (TBS 1986)★★, Vivre: The Best Of Celine Dion (Carrere 1988)★★, Les Premières Années (Versailles 1993)★★, Celine Dion Gold (Versailles 1995)★★★, Celine Dion Gold Volume 2 (Versailles 1995)★★★, C'est Pour Vivre (Eureka 1997) ★★★, All The Way ... A Decade Of Song (Epic 1999) ★★★, The Collector's Series Volume One (Epic 2000)★★★.
VIDEOS: Unison (1991), The Colour Of My Love Concert (Epic Music Video 1995), Live À Paris (1996), with Mariah Carey, Gloria Estefan, Aretha Franklin, Shania Twain Divas Live (Sony Music Video 1998), Live In Memphis – The Concert (Sony Music Video 1998), All The Way ... A Decade Of Song (Epic Music Video 2001), Au Coeur Du Stade (Sony Music Video 2002).
FURTHER READING: Celine Dion: Behind The Fairytale, Ian Halperin. Celine Dion: Falling Into You, Barry Grills. A Voice And A Dream: The Celine Dion Story, Richard Crouse. Celine: The Authorized Biography, Georges-Hébert Germain. Celine Dion, Marianne McKay. Celine Dion: The Complete Biography, Lisa Peters with Della Druick. My Story, My Dream, Celine Dion.
FILMS: Quest For Camelot voice only (1998), Passionnément (1999).

DIRE STRAITS
ALBUMS: Dire Straits (Vertigo 1978)★★★★, Communique (Vertigo 1979)★★, Making Movies (Vertigo 1980)★★★★, Love Over Gold (Vertigo 1982)★★★, Alchemy – Live (Vertigo 1984)★★, Brothers In Arms (Vertigo 1985)★★★, On Every Street (Vertigo 1991)★★★, On The Night (Vertigo 1993)★★, Live At The BBC (Windsong 1995)★★★.
COMPILATIONS: Money For Nothing (Vertigo 1988)★★★★, Sultans Of Swing: The Very Best Of Dire Straits (Mercury 1998)★★★★.
VIDEOS: Brothers In Arms (PolyGram Music Video 1988), Alchemy Live (Channel 5 1988), The Videos (PolyGram Music Video 1992).
FURTHER READING: Dire Straits, Michael Oldfield. Mark Knopfler: The Unauthorised Biography, Myles Palmer.

DISPOSABLE HEROES OF HIPHOPRISY
ALBUMS: Hypocrisy Is The Greatest Luxury (4th & Broadway 1992)★★★★, with William Burroughs Spare Ass Annie & Other Tales (4th & Broadway 1993)★★★.

DISTURBED
ALBUMS: The Sickness (Giant 2000)★★★.

DIVINE COMEDY
ALBUMS: Fanfare For The Comic Muse (Setanta 1990)★★, Liberation (Setanta 1993)★★★, Promenade (Setanta 1994) ★★★★, Casanova (Setanta 1996)★★★★, A Short Album About Love mini-album (Setanta 1997)★★★★, Fin De Siècle (Setanta 1998)★★★, Regeneration (Parlophone/Nettwerk 2001)★★★.
COMPILATIONS: A Secret History (Setanta/Red Ink 1999)★★★★.

DIXIE CHICKS
ALBUMS: Thank Heavens For Dale Evans (Crystal Clear 1990)★★★, Little Ol' Cowgirl (Crystal Clear 1992)★★★, Shouldn't A Told You That (Crystal Clear 1993)★★★, Wide Open Spaces (Monument 1998)★★★★, Fly (Monument 1999)★★★★.
FURTHER READING: Chicks Rule: The Story Of The Dixie Chicks, Scott Gray. Dixiechicks: The New Photo Biog, Kathleen Tracy.

DIXIE CUPS
ALBUMS: Chapel Of Love aka Iko Iko (Red Bird 1964)★★★, Ridin' High (ABC/Paramount 1965)★★.
COMPILATIONS: The Best Of The Dixie Cups (Delta 1997)★★★, Chapel Of Love: The Very Best Of The Dixie Cups (Collectables 1999)★★★.

DIXON, WILLIE
ALBUMS: Willie's Blues (Bluesville 1959)★★★, Memphis Slim & Willie Dixon At The Village Gate (1960)★★★★, I Am The Blues (Columbia 1970)★★★, Peace (Yambo 1971)★★★, Catalyst (Ovation 1973)★★★, Mighty Earthquake And Hurricane (Chase 1983)★★★, I Feel Like Steppin' Out (1986)★★★, Hidden Charms (Bug 1988)★★★, Blues Dixonary (1993)★★★, Across The Borderline (1993)★★★.
COMPILATIONS: Collection (Deja Vu 1987)★★★, The Chess Box box set (Chess 1988)★★★★, The Original Wang Dang Doodle - The Chess Recordings & More (MCA/Chess 1995)★★★★, Poet Of The Blues (Columbia/Legacy 1998)★★★★, The Songs Of Willie Dixon tribute album (Telarc 1999)★★.
FURTHER READING: I Am The Blues, Willie Dixon.

DJ JAZZY JEFF AND THE FRESH PRINCE
ALBUMS: Rock The House (Word Up 1987)★★, He's The DJ, I'm The Rapper (Jive 1988)★★★, And In This Corner (Jive 1990)★★★, Homebase (Jive 1991)★★★, Code Red (Jive 1993)★★★.
COMPILATIONS: Greatest Hits (Jive 1998)★★★★, Before The Willennium (BMG 2000)★★★.

DJ SHADOW
ALBUMS: Endtroducing... (Mo' Wax 1996)★★★★, with Q-Bert Camel Bob Sled Race (Q-Bert Mega Mix) mini-album (Mo' Wax 1997)★★★, Pre-emptive Strike (Mo' Wax 1998)★★★, with Cut Chemist Brainfreeze (Sixty7 1999)★★★★, with Cut Chemist Product Placement (One29 2001)★★★★.
VIDEOS: with Cut Chemist Freeze (Regeneration TV 2001).

DMX
ALBUMS: It's Dark And Hell Is Hot (Def Jam 1998)★★★★, Flesh Of My Flesh, Blood Of My Blood (Def Jam 1998)★★★, ... And Then There Was X (Def Jam 1999)★★★, The Great Depression (Def Jam 2001)★★★.
VIDEOS: Best Of DMX (MVC Video 2001), Angel (Universal 2001).
FILMS: Belly (1998), Romeo Must Die (2000), Boricua's Bond (2000), Backstage (2000), Exit Wounds (2001).

DODD, COXSONE
COMPILATIONS: All Star Top Hits (Studio One 1961)★★★★, Oldies But Goodies (Volumes 1 & 2) (Studio One 1968)★★★★, Best Of Studio One (Volumes 1, 2, & 3) (Heartbeat 1983-87)★★★★, Respect To Studio One (Heartbeat 1995)★★★.
FURTHER READING: A Scorcha From Studio One/More Scorcha From Studio One, Roger Dalke.

DOLBY, THOMAS
ALBUMS: The Golden Age Of Wireless (Venice In Peril 1982)★★★★, The Flat Earth (Parlophone 1984)★★★, Aliens Ate My Buick (Manhattan 1988)★★, Astronauts And Heretics (Virgin 1992)★★.
COMPILATIONS: Hyperactive (EMI 1999)★★★.
VIDEOS: The Gate To The Mind's Eye (Miramar Images 1994).

DOMINO, FATS
ALBUMS: Carry On Rockin' (Imperial 1955)★★★★, Rock And Rollin' With Fats (Imperial 1956)★★★★, Rock And Rollin' (Imperial 1956)★★★★, This Is Fats Domino! (Imperial 1957)★★★★, Here Stands Fats Domino (Imperial 1958)★★★★, Fabulous Mr D (Imperial 1958)★★★★, Let's Play Fats Domino (Imperial 1959)★★★★, Fats Domino Swings (Imperial 1959)★★★★★, Million Record Hits (Imperial 1960)★★★★, A Lot Of Dominos (Imperial 1960)★★★★, I Miss You So (Imperial 1961)★★★, Let The Four Winds Blow (Imperial 1961)★★★★, What A Party (Imperial 1962)★★★, Twistin' The Stomp (Imperial 1962)★★★, Just Domino (Imperial 1962)★★★, Here Comes Fats Domino (ABC-Paramount 1963)★★★, Walkin' To New Orleans (Imperial 1963)★★★★, Let's Dance With Domino (Imperial 1963) ★★★, Here He Comes Again (Imperial 1963)★★★, Fats On Fire (ABC 1964)★★★, Fats Domino '65 (Mercury 1965)★★★, Getaway With Fats Domino (ABC 1965)★★★, Fats Is Back (Reprise 1968)★★★, Cookin' With Fats (United Artists 1974)★★★, Sleeping On The Job (Sonet 1979)★★, Live At Montreux (Atlantic 1987)★★★, The Domino Effect (Charly 1989)★★★, Christmas Is A Special Day (Right Stuff/EMI 1994)★★.
COMPILATIONS: The Very Best Of Fats Domino (Liberty 1970)★★★★, Rare Domino's (Liberty 1970)★★★, Rare Domino's Volume 2 (Liberty 1971)★★★, Fats Domino – His Greatest Hits (MCA 1986)★★★, My Blue Heaven – The Best Of Fats Domino (EMI 1990)★★★★, They Call Me The Fat Man: The Legendary Imperial Recordings 4-CD box set (EMI/Imperial 1991)★★★★★, Out Of Orleans 8-CD box set (Bear Family 1993)★★★★★, The EP Collection Volume 1 (See For Miles 1995)★★★★, The Early Imperial Singles 1950-52 (Ace 1996)★★★★, The EP Collection Volume 2 (See For Miles 1997)★★★★, The Imperial Singles Volume 3 (Ace 1999)★★★★, Legends Of The 20th Century (EMI 1999)★★★.
FILMS: The Girl Can't Help It (1956), Jamboree aka Disc Jockey Jamboree (1957), The Big Beat (1957).

DONEGAN, LONNIE
ALBUMS: Showcase (Pye Nixa 1956)★★★, Lonnie (Pye Nixa 1957)★★★, Tops With Lonnie (Pye 1958)★★★★, Lonnie Rides Again (Pye 1959)★★★, More Tops With Lonnie (Pye 1961)★★★★, Sings Hallelujah (Pye 1962)★★★, The Lonnie Donegan Folk Album (Pye 1965)★★★★, Lonniepops-Lonnie Donegan Today (Decca 1970)★★★, Lonnie Donegan Meets Leineman (1974)★★, Lonnie Donegan (1975)★★, Lonnie Donegan Meets Leineman-Country Roads (1976)★★, Putting On The Style (Chrysalis 1978)★★★, Sundown (Chrysalis 1979)★★★, Jubilee Concert (Cube 1981)★★, Muleskinner Blues (BMG 1998)★★★★.
COMPILATIONS: Golden Age Of Donegan (Golden Guinea 1962)★★★★, Golden Age Of Donegan Volume 2 (Golden Guinea 1963)★★★★, Golden Hour Of Golden Hits (Golden Hour 1973)★★★, Golden Hour Of Golden Hits, Volume 2 (Golden Hour 1974)★★★, The Lonnie Donegan File (Pye 1977)★★★★, The Hits Of Lonnie Donegan (MFP 1978)★★★, Greatest Hits: Lonnie Donegan (Ditto 1983)★★★★, Rare And Unissued Gems (Bear Family 1985)★★★, Rock Island Line (Flashback 1985)★★★★, The Hit Singles Collection (PRT 1987)★★★★, The Best Of Lonnie Donegan (Pickwick 1989)★★★★, The Collection: Lonnie Donegan (Castle 1989)★★★★, The EP Collection (See For Miles 1992)★★★, Putting On The Styles 3-CD box set (1992)★★★★, More Than 'Pye In The Sky' 8-CD box set (Bear Family 1994)★★★★, Talking Guitar Blues: The Very Best Of Lonnie Donegan (Sequel 1999)★★★★.
FURTHER READING: Skiffle: The Inside Story, Chas McDevitt. The Skiffle Craze, Mike Dewe.

DONNAS
ALBUMS: The Donnas (Super*Teem 1996)★★★, American Teenage Rock 'N' Roll Machine (Lookout! 1998)★★★★, Get Skintight (Lookout! 1999)★★★, Turn 21 (Lookout! 2001)★★★.
FILMS: Jawbreaker (1999), Drive Me Crazy (1999).

DONOVAN
ALBUMS: What's Bin Did And What's Bin Hid (UK) Catch The Wind (US) (Pye/Hickory 1965)★★★★, Fairytale (Pye/Hickory 1965)★★★★, Sunshine Superman US only (Epic 1966)★★★★, Mellow Yellow US only (Epic 1967)★★★★, A Gift From A Flower To A Garden (Epic 1967)★★★, Wear Your Love Like Heaven US only (Epic 1967)★★★, For Little Ones US only (Epic 1967)★★★, Donovan In Concert (Epic/Pye 1968)★★★, The Hurdy Gurdy Man US only (Epic 1968)★★★★, Barabajagal (Epic 1969)★★★★, Open Road (Dawn/Epic 1970)★★★, HMS Donovan (Dawn 1971)★★★, Brother Sun, Sister Moon film soundtrack (EMI 1972)★★, Colours (Hallmark 1972)★★★, Cosmic Wheels (Epic 1973)★★★, Live In Japan (Sony 1973)★★★, Essence To Essence (Epic 1973)★★, 7-Tease (Epic 1974)★★★, Slow Down World (Epic 1976)★★, Donovan (RAK/Arista 1977)★★, Neutronica (Barclay/RCA 1980)★★, Love Is Only Feeling (RCA 1981)★★, Lady Of The Stars (RCA/Allegiance 1984)★★, Donovan Rising (UK) The Classics Live (US) (Permanent/Great Northern Arts 1993)★★★, Sutras (American Recordings 1996)★★★, Greatest Hits Live: Vancouver 1986 (Varèse Vintage 2001)★★★.
COMPILATIONS: The Real Donovan US only (Hickory 1966)★★★, Sunshine Superman UK only (Pye 1967)★★★★, Universal Soldier (Marble Arch 1967)★★★★, Like It Is, Was, And Evermore Shall Be (Hickory 1968)★★★, The Best Of Donovan (Epic/Pye 1969)★★★★, The Best Of Donovan (Hickory 1969)★★★, The World Of Donovan (Marble Arch 1969)★★★, Donovan P. Leitch US only (Janus 1970)★★★, Catch The Wind (Hallmark 1971)★★★, Golden Hour Of Donovan (Golden Hour 1971)★★★★, Colours (Hallmark 1972)★★★, The World Of Donovan US only (Epic 1972)★★★, Early Treasures US only (Bell 1973)★★★, Four Shades 4-LP box set (Pye 1973)★★★, Hear Me Now (Janus 1974)★★★, The Pye History Of British Pop Music: Donovan US only (Pye 1975)★★★, The Pye History Of British Pop Music: Donovan, Vol. 2 US only (Pye 1976)★★★, The Donovan File (Pye 1977)★★★, Spotlight On Donovan (PRT 1981)★★★★, Universal Soldier (Spot 1983)★★★, Catch The Wind (Showcase 1986)★★★, Colours (PRT 1987)★★★, Catch The Wind US only (Garland 1988)★★★, Greatest Hits ... And More (EMI 1989)★★★★, The EP Collection (See For Miles 1990)★★★★, The Collection (Castle 1991)★★★, The Trip (EMI 1991)★★★★, Colours (Del Rack 1991)★★★★, Troubadour: The Definitive Collection 1964-1976 2-CD box set (Epic/Legacy 1992)★★★★, The Early Years (Dojo 1993)★★★, Sunshine Superman - 18 Songs Of Love And Freedom (Remember 1993)★★★, Gold (Disky 1993)★★★, Josie (Castle 1994)★★★, Universal Soldier (Spectrum 1995)★★★★, Peace And Love Songs (Sony 1995)★★★, Catch The Wind: The Best Of Donovan (Pulse 1996)★★★, Sunshine Troubadour (Hallmark 1996)★★★, Love Is Hot, Truth Is Molten: Original Essential Recordings 1965-1973 (HMV 1998)★★★, Mellow (Snapper 1997)★★★, Catch The Wind (Laserlight 1998)★★★, Fairytales And Colours (Select 1998)★★★, Summer Day Reflection Songs (Castle 2000)★★★★.
FURTHER READING: Dry Songs And Scribbles, Donovan. She, Donovan.

DOOBIE BROTHERS
ALBUMS: The Doobie Brothers (Warners 1971)★★, Toulouse Street (Warners 1972)★★★, The Captain And Me (Warners 1973)★★★★, What Were Once Vices Are Now Habits (Warners 1974)★★★, Stampede (Warners 1975)★★★, Takin' It To The Streets (Warners 1976)★★★★, Livin' On The Fault Line (Warners 1977)★★★, Minute By Minute (Warners 1978)★★★★, One Step Closer (Warners 1980)★★, The Doobie Brothers Farewell Tour (Warners 1983)★★★, Cycles (Capitol 1989)★★, Brotherhood (Capitol 1991)H, Rockin' Down The Highway (Legacy 1996)★★★, Sibling Rivalry (Rhino/Eagle 2000)★★★.
COMPILATIONS: Best Of The Doobies (Warners 1976)★★★, Best Of The Doobies, Volume 2 (Warners 1981)★★★, Very Best Of The Doobie Brothers (Warners 1993)★★★★, Best Of The Doobie Brothers Live (Sony 1999)★★★, Long Train Runnin' 1970-2000 4-CD box set (Warners/Rhino 2000)★★★.

DOORS
ALBUMS: The Doors (Elektra 1967)★★★★★, Strange Days (Elektra 1967)★★★★, Waiting For The Sun (Elektra 1968)★★★, The Soft Parade (Elektra 1969)★★, Morrison Hotel (Elektra 1970)★★★★, Absolutely Live (Elektra 1970)★★, L.A. Woman (Elektra 1971)★★★★, Other Voices (Elektra 1971)★★, Full Circle (Elektra 1972)H, An American Prayer (Elektra 1978)★★, Alive, She Cried (Elektra 1983)★★, Live At The Hollywood Bowl 1968 recording (Elektra 1987)★★, The Doors film soundtrack (Elektra 1991)★★★, Bright Midnight: Live In America 1969/1970 recordings (Elektra 2001)★★★.
COMPILATIONS: 13 (Elektra 1970)★★★★, Weird Scenes Inside The Goldmine (Elektra 1972)★★★, The Best Of The Doors (Elektra 1973)★★★, Greatest Hits (Elektra 1980)★★★★, Classics (Elektra 1985)★★★★, The Best Of The Doors (Elektra 1985)★★★★, In Concert (Elektra 1991)★★★, Greatest Hits enhanced CD (Elektra 1996)★★★★, The Doors Box Set 4-CD box set (Elektra 1997)★★★, Box Set Part One (Elektra 1998)★★★, Box Set Part Two (Elektra 1998)★★★, The Complete Studio Recordings 7-CD box set (Elektra 1999)★★★, Essential Rarities (Elektra 2000)★★★.
VIDEOS: Dance On Fire: Classic Performances & Greatest Hits (Pioneer 1985), Live At The Hollywood Bowl (Elektra 1987), A Tribute To Jim Morrison (Warner Home Video 1988), Live In Europe 1968 (Atlantic 1989), The Soft Parade: A Retrospective (MCA 1991), The Doors Are Open (Warner Home Video 1992), The Best Of The Doors (Universal 1997), The Doors: 30 Years Commemorative Edition (Universal 2001), VH1 Storytellers - The Doors: A Celebration (Aviva International 2001).
FURTHER READING: Jim Morrison And The Doors: An Unauthorized Book, Mike Jahn. An American Prayer, Jim Morrison. The Lords & The New Creatures, Jim Morrison. Jim Morrison Au Dela Des Doors, Herve Muller. No One Here Gets Out Alive, Jerry Hopkins and Danny Sugerman. Burn Down The Night, Craig Kee Strete. Jim Morrison: The Story Of The Doors In Words And Pictures, Jim Morrison. Jim Morrison: An Hour For Magic, Frank Lisciandro. The Doors: The Illustrated History, Danny Sugerman. The Doors, John Tobler and Andrew Doe. Jim Morrison: Dark Star, Dylan Jones. Images Of Jim Morrison, Edward Wincentsen. The End: The Death Of Jim Morrison, Bob Seymore. The American Night: The Writings Of Jim Morrison, Jim Morrison. The American Night Volume 2, Jim Morrison. Morrison: A Feast Of Friends, Frank Lisciandro. Light My Fire, John Densmore. Riders On The Storm: My Life With Jim Morrison And The Doors, John Densmore. The Doors Complete Illustrated Lyrics, Danny Sugerman (ed.). Break On Through: The Life And Death Of Jim Morrison, James Riordan & Jerry Prochnicky. The Doors: Lyrics, 1965-71, no author. The Lizard King: The Essential Jim Morrison, Jerry Hopkins. The Doors: Dance On Fire, Ross Clarke. The Complete Guide To The Music Of The Doors, Peter K. Hogan. The Doors: Moonlight Drive, Chuck Crisafulli. Wild Child: Life With Jim Morrison, Linda Ashcroft. The Tragic Romance Of Pamela & Jim Morrison, Patricia Butler. Light My Fire: My Life With The Doors, Ray Manzarek.
FILMS: American Pop (1981), The Doors (1991).

DOVES
ALBUMS: Lost Souls (Heavenly/Astralwerks 2000)★★★★, The Last Broadcast (Heavenly 2002)★★★★.

DOWNLINERS SECT
ALBUMS: The Sect (Columbia 1964)★★★, The Country Sect (Columbia 1965)★★, The Rock Sect's In (Columbia 1966)★★, Showbiz (Raw 1979)★★★, Sect Appeal (Indigo 2000)★★.
COMPILATIONS: I Want My Baby Back (Charly 1978)★★★, Be A Sect Maniac (Out Line 1983)★★, Savage Return (1991)★★, The Definitive Downliners Sect – Singles A's & B's (See For Miles 1994)★★★.

DR. DRE
ALBUMS: The Chronic (Death Row 1992)★★★★, Dr. Dre 2001 (Aftermath 1999)★★★★, The Wash film soundtrack (Aftermath 2001)★★★.
COMPILATIONS: Concrete Roots (Triple X 1994)★★, Back 'N The Day (Blue Dolphin 1996)★★, First Round Knock Out (Triple X 1996)★★★, Dr. Dre Presents The Aftermath (Aftermath 1996)★★★★, The Chronicle: The Best Of ... Dr. Dre (Death Row 2001)★★★.
FILMS: The Show (1995), Set It Off (1996), Rhyme & Reason (1997), Whiteboys (1999).

DR. FEELGOOD
ALBUMS: Down By The Jetty (United Artists 1975)★★★★, Malpractice (United Artists/Columbia 1975)★★★, Stupidity (United Artists 1976)★★★, Sneakin' Suspicion (United Artists/Columbia 1977)★★, Be Seeing You (United Artists 1977)★★★, Private Practice (United Artists 1978)★★★, As It Happens (United Artists 1979)★★, Let It Roll (United Artists 1979)★★, A Case Of The Shakes (United Artists 1980)★★, On The Job (Liberty 1981)★★, Fast Women Slow Horses (Chiswick 1982)★★, Doctor's Orders (Demon 1984)★★, Mad Man Blues mini-album (ID 1985)★★★, Brilleaux (Stiff 1986)★★★, Classic (Stiff 1987)★★, Live In London (Grand 1990)★★★, Primo (Grand 1991)★★, The Feelgood Factor (Grand 1993)★★, Down At The Doctors (Grand 1994)★★, On The Road Again (Grand 1996)★★★, Chess Masters (Grand 2000)★★★.
COMPILATIONS: Casebook (Liberty 1981)★★★, Case History – The Best Of Dr. Feelgood (EMI 1987)★★★, Singles (The U.A. Years) (Liberty 1989)★★★, Looking Back 5-CD box set (EMI 1995)★★★, Twenty Five Years Of Dr Feelgood (1972-1997) (Grand 1997)★★★★, The Best Of Dr. Feelgood: Centenary Collection (EMI 1997)★★★, Live At The BBC 1974-5 (Grand 1999)★★★, The Complete BBC Sessions (Grand 2001)★★★, Singled Out (EMI 2001)★★★★.
VIDEOS: Live Legends (PolyGram Music Video 1990), Going Back Home: Dr. Feelgood Live In 1975 (Grand).
FURTHER READING: Down By The Jetty: The Dr Feelgood Story, Tony Moon.

DR. HOOK
ALBUMS: Dr. Hook And the Medicine Show (Columbia 1972)★★★, Sloppy Seconds (Columbia 1972)★★★, Belly Up (Columbia 1973)★★, Fried Face US only (Columbia 1974)★★, Bankrupt (Capitol 1975)★★, A Little Bit More (Capitol 1976)★★★, Making Love And Music (Capitol 1977)★★, Pleasure And Pain (Capitol 1978)★★★, Sometimes You Win (Capitol 1979)★★★, Rising (Casablanca 1980)★★, Live In The UK (Capitol 1981)★★, Players In The Dark (Casablanca 1982)★★, On The Run 1976 recording (Burning Airlines 2001)★★★.
COMPILATIONS: Greatest Hits (Capitol 1980)★★★, Completely Hooked-The Best Of Dr. Hook (Columbia 1992)★★★, Pleasure And Pain: The History Of Dr. Hook 3-CD box set (EMI 1996)★★★, Love Songs (EMI 1999)★★★.
VIDEOS: Completely Hooked (PMI 1992).

DR. JOHN
ALBUMS: Gris-Gris (Atlantic 1968)★★★★, Babylon (Atco 1969)★★★, Remedies (Atco 1970)★★★, The Sun, Moon & Herbs (Atco 1971)★★★, Dr. John's Gumbo (Atlantic 1972)★★★★, In The Right Place (Atlantic 1973)★★★, with Mike Bloomfield, John Hammond Triumvirate (Columbia 1973)★★★, Desitively Bonnaroo (Atlantic 1974)★★★, Hollywood Be Thy Name (United Artists 1975)★★, City Lights (Horizon 1978)★★★, Tango Palace (Horizon 1979)★★, with Chris Barber Take Me Back To New Orleans (Black Lion 1980)★★★, Dr. John Plays Mac Rebennack (Clean Cuts 1982)★★★, The Brightest Smile In Town (Clean Cuts 1983)★★★, Such A Night: Live In London (Spindrift 1984)★★★, with Hank Crawford Roadhouse Symphony (Milestone 1986)★★★, In A Sentimental Mood (Warners 1989)★★, with Art Blakey, David 'Fathead' Newman Bluesiana Triangle (Windham Hill 1990)★★★, Goin' Back To New Orleans (Warners 1992)★★★, Television (GRP 1994)★★, Afterglow (GRP 1995)★★, Trippin' Live (Eagle 1997)★★★, Anutha Zone (Parlophone 1998)★★★, Duke Elegant (Parlophone 1999)★★★★, Creole Moon (Parlophone/Blue Note 2001)★★★.
COMPILATIONS: Cut Me While I'm Hot (Anytime, Anyplace) pre-Atlantic material (DJM 1975)★★, I Been Hoodood (Edsel 1984)★★★, In The Night pre-Atlantic material (Topline 1985)★★★, Zu Zu Man pre-Atlantic material (Topline 1987)★★★, Loser For You Baby pre-Atlantic material (Thunderbolt 1988)★★★, Mos' Scocious: The Dr. John Anthology 2-CD set (Rhino 1994)★★★★, The Very Best Of Dr. John (Rhino 1995)★★★★, The Crazy Cajun Recordings (Edsel 1999)★★★, The Ear Is On Strike (Yeaah! 2001)★★★.
VIDEOS: Dr. John And Chris Barber Live At The Marquee Club (Jettisoundz 1986), Live At The Marquee (Hendring Music Video 1990), New Orleans Piano (Homespun Video 1996).
FURTHER READING: Dr. John: Under A Hoodoo Moon, Mac Rebennack with Jack Rummel.

DRAKE, NICK
ALBUMS: Five Leaves Left (Island 1969)★★★★, Bryter Layter (Island 1970)★★★★, Pink Moon (Island 1972)★★★.
COMPILATIONS: Heaven In A Wild Flower (Island 1985)★★★★, Fruit Tree 4-LP box set (Island 1979)★★★★, Time Of No Reply (Hannibal 1986)★★★, Way To Blue (Island 1994)★★★★.
FURTHER READING: Nick Drake, David Housden. Nick Drake: A Biography, Patrick Humphries.

DRIFTERS
ALBUMS: Save The Last Dance For Me (Atlantic 1961)★★★★, The Good Life With The Drifters (Atlantic 1964)★★★★, The Drifters (Clarion 1964)★★, I'll Take You Where The Music's Playing (Atlantic 1965)★★★, Souvenirs (Bell 1974)★★★, Love Games (Bell 1975)★★★, There Goes My First Love (Bell 1975)★★★, Every Night's A Saturday Night (Bell 1976)★★★, Greatest Hits Live (Astan 1984)★★, Live At Harvard University (Showcase 1986)★★, Too Hot (Columbia 1989)★★.
COMPILATIONS: Up On The Roof – The Best Of The Drifters (Atlantic 1963)★★★★, Under The Boardwalk (Atlantic 1964)★★★★, The Drifters Golden Hits (Atlantic 1968)★★★★, 24 Original Hits (Atlantic 1975)★★★★, The Collection (Castle 1987)★★★, Diamond Series: The Drifters (RCA 1988)★★★, Best Of The Drifters (Pickwick 1990)★★★, Let The Boogie Woogie Roll - Greatest Hits (1953-58) (Atlantic 1993)★★★, All Time Greatest Hits And More (1959-65) (Atlantic 1993)★★★★, Up On The Roof, On Broadway & Under The Boardwalk (Rhino/Pickwick 1995)★★★★, Rockin' And Driftin': The Drifters Box 3-CD box set (Rhino 1996)★★★★, Anthology One: Clyde & The Drifters (Sequel 1996)★★★★, Anthology Two: Rockin' & Driftin' (Sequel 1996)★★★, Anthology Three: Save The Last Dance For Me (Sequel 1996)★★★★, Anthology Four: Up On The Roof (Sequel 1996)★★★★, Anthology Five: Under The Boardwalk (Sequel 1997)★★★★, Anthology Six: The Good Life With The Drifters (Sequel 1997)★★★, Anthology Seven: I'll Take You Where The Music's Playing (Sequel 1997)★★★★.
FURTHER READING: The Drifters: The Rise And Fall Of The Black Vocal Group, Bill Millar. Save The Last Dance For Me: The Musical Legacy 1953-92, Tony Allan and Faye Treadwell.

DUBLINERS
ALBUMS: The Dubliners (Transatlantic 1964)★★★★, In Concert (Transatlantic 1965)★★★, Finnegan Wakes (Transatlantic 1966)★★★★, A Drop Of The Hard Stuff aka Seven Drunken Nights (Major Minor/Starline 1967)★★★★, More Of The Hard Stuff (Major Minor/Starline 1967)★★★, Drinkin' And Courtin' (Major Minor 1968)★★★, At It Again aka Seven Deadly Sings (Major Minor/Starline 1968)★★★, Live At The Albert Hall (Major Minor 1969)★★★, At Home With The Dubliners (Columbia 1969)★★★, Revolution (Columbia 1970)★★★, Hometown! (Columbia 1972)★★★, Double Dubliners (Columbia 1972)★★★, Plain & Simple (Polydor 1973)★★★, Live (Polydor 1974)★★★, Now (Polydor 1975)★★★, Parcel Of Rogues (Polydor 1976)★★★, 15 Years On (Polydor 1977)★★★, Live At Montreux (Intercord 1977)★★★, Together Again (Polydor 1979)★★★, 21 Years On (RTE 1983)★★★, Prodigal Sons (Polydor 1983)★★★, Live In Carré (Polydor 1985)★★, Celebration (Stylus 1987)★★★, The Dubliners' Dublin (Baycourt 1988)★★★, 30 Years A'Greying (Baycourt 1992)★★★, Further Along (Transatlantic 1996)★★★, Alive Alive O (Baycourt 1997)★★.
COMPILATIONS: The Best Of The Dubliners (Transatlantic 1967)★★★★★, A Drop Of The Dubliners (Major Minor 1969)★★★★, Drinking And Wenching (MFP 1969)★★★, It's The Dubliners (Hallmark 1969)★★★, The Patriot Game (Hallmark 1971)★★★, Very Best Of The Dubliners (EMI 1975)★★★★, The Collection (Castle 1987)★★★★, Dublin Songs (K-TEL 1988)★★★, 20 Greatest Hits: Dubliners (Sound 1989)★★★★, 20 Original Greatest Hits Volume 2 (Chyme 1989)★★★, The Collection, Volume 2 (Castle 1990)★★★, The Original Dubliners (EMI 1993)★★★, The Definitive Transatlantic Collection (Transatlantic 1997)★★★★, The Collection (Camden 1999)★★★.
VIDEOS: Dublin (Hendring Music Video 1990).
FURTHER READING: The Dubliners Scrapbook, Mary Hardy.

DURAN DURAN
ALBUMS: Duran Duran (EMI/Harvest 1981)★★★, Rio (EMI/Harvest 1982)★★★★, Seven And The Ragged Tiger (EMI/Capitol 1983)★★, Arena (Parlophone/Capitol 1984)★★, Notorious (EMI/Capitol 1986)★★★, as DuranDuran Big Thing (EMI/Capitol 1988)★★, Liberty (Parlophone/Capitol 1990)H, Duran Duran aka The Wedding Album (Parlophone/Capitol 1993)★★★, Thank You (Parlophone/Capitol 1995)★★, Medazzaland (Capitol 1997)★★★, Pop Trash (Hollywood 2000)★★★★.
COMPILATIONS: Decade (EMI/Capitol 1989)★★★★, Essential Duran Duran (Night Versions) (EMI 1998)★★★, Greatest (EMI/Capitol 1998)★★★★, Strange Behaviour (EMI 1999)★★, Girls On Film: 'The Collection' (EMI 2000)★★★, Classic Masters (EMD 2002)★★★.
VIDEOS: Duran Duran (The First 11 Videos) (PMI 1983), Dancing On The Valentine (PMI 1984), Sing Blue Silver (PMI 1984), Arena: An Absurd Notion (PMI 1984), The Making Of Arena (PMI 1985), Working For The Skin Trade (PMI 1987), Three To Get Ready (BMG/Aurora 1987), 6ix By 3hree (PMI 1988), Decade (PMI 1989), Extraordinary World (PMI 1993), Greatest: The Videos (EMI 1998).
FURTHER READING: Duran Duran: Their Story, Kasper deGraff and Malcolm Garrett. Duran Duran: An Independent Story In Words And Pictures, John Carver. Duran Duran, Maria David. Duran Duran: A Behind-The-Scenes Biography Of The Supergroup Of The Eighties, Cynthia C. Kent. Everything You Want To Know About Duran Duran, Toby Goldstein. Duran Duran, Susan Martin. Duran Duran Live, Peter Goddard & Philip Kamin. Inside Duran Duran, Robyn Flans. Duran Duran, Annette Weidner.

DURUTTI COLUMN
ALBUMS: The Return Of The Durutti Column (Factory 1980)★★★, LC (Factory 1981)★★★, Another Setting (Factory 1983)★★★, Live At The Venue, London (VU 1983)★★★, Amigos En Portugal (Fundacio Atlantica 1984)★★, Without Mercy (Factory 1984)★★★, Domo Arigato (Factory 1985)★★★, Circuses And Bread (Factory 1985)★★★, Live At The Bottom Line New York cassette only (ROIR 1987)★★★, The Guitar And Other Machines (Factory 1987)★★★, Vini Reilly (Factory 1989)★★★★, Obey The Time (Factory 1990)★★★, Lips That Would Kiss Form Prayers To Broken Stone (Factory 1991)★★★, Dry (Materiali Sonori 1991)★★★, Sex & Death (Factory Too 1994)★★★, Fidelity (Crépescule 1996)★★★, Time Was GIGANTIC ... When We Were Kids (Factory Too 1998)★★★, A Night In New York (Shellshock 1999)★★★, Rebellion (Artful 2001)★★★. Solo: Vini Reilly The Sporadic Recordings (Sporadic 1989)★★★.
COMPILATIONS: Valuable Passages (Factory 1986)★★★, The Durutti Column – The First Four Albums (Factory 1988)★★★.

DURY, IAN
ALBUMS: New Boots And Panties (Stiff 1977)★★★★, Do It Yourself (Stiff 1979)★★★, Laughter (Stiff 1980)★★, Lord Upminster (Polydor 1981)★★, 4,000 Weeks Holiday (Polydor 1984)★★★, Warts 'N' Audience (Demon 1991)★★★, The Bus Driver's Prayer And Other Stories (Demon 1992)★★★, Mr. Love Pants (RH 1998)★★★★, Straight From The Desk 1978 recording (East Central One 2002)★★★, Ten More Turnips From The Tip (Ronnie Harris 2002)★★★.
COMPILATIONS: Juke Box Dury (Stiff 1981)★★★★, Greatest Hits (Fame 1981)★★★, Sex & Drugs & Rock 'n' Roll (Demon 1987)★★★★, Reasons To Be Cheerful (Repertoire 1996)★★★★.
FURTHER READING: Sex & Drugs & Rock 'N' Roll: The Life Of Ian Dury, Richard Balls.
FILMS: Pirates (1986), Rocinante (1987), O Paradissos Anigi Me Antiklidi aka Red Ants (1987), Hearts Of Fire (1987), The Raggedy Rawney (1988), Brennende Betten (1988), The Cook The Thief His Wife & Her Lover (1989), The Rainbow Thief (1990), After Midnight (1990), Split Second (1992), Boswell & Johnson's Tour Of The Western Islands (1993), Skallagrigg (1994), Judge Dredd (1995), The Crow: City Of Angels (1996), Different For Girls (1996), Underground (1998), Middleton's Changeling (1998).

DYLAN, BOB
ALBUMS: Bob Dylan (Columbia 1962)★★★, The Freewheelin' Bob Dylan (Columbia 1963)★★★★, The Times They Are A-Changin' (Columbia 1964)★★★★, Another Side Of Bob Dylan (Columbia 1964)★★★★, Bringing It All Back Home (Columbia 1965)★★★★★, Highway 61 Revisited (Columbia 1965)★★★★★, Blonde On Blonde (Columbia 1966)★★★★★, John Wesley Harding (Columbia 1968)★★★★, Nashville Skyline (Columbia 1969)★★★, Self Portrait (Columbia 1970)★★, New Morning (Columbia 1970)★★★, Pat Garrett & Billy The Kid (Columbia 1973)★★★, Dylan (A Fool Such As I) (Columbia 1973)★, Planet Waves (Island 1974)★★★★, with The Band Before The Flood (Asylum 1974)★★★, Blood On The Tracks (Columbia 1975)★★★★★, with The Band The Basement Tapes (Columbia 1975)★★★, Desire (Columbia 1976)★★★★★, Hard Rain (Columbia 1976)★★, Street Legal (Columbia 1978)★★★, Slow Train Coming (Columbia 1979)★★★, At Budokan (Columbia 1979)★★★, Saved (Columbia 1980)H, Shot Of Love (Columbia 1981)★★, Infidels (Columbia 1983)★★★, Real Live (Columbia 1984)H, Empire Burlesque (Columbia 1985)★★, Knocked Out Loaded (Columbia 1986)★★, Down In The Groove (Columbia 1988)★, with the Grateful Dead Dylan And The Dead (Columbia 1989)★, Oh Mercy (Columbia 1989)★★★★, Under The Red Sky (Columbia 1990)★★★, Good As I Been To You (Columbia 1992)★★★, World Gone Wrong (Columbia 1993)★★, The 30th Anniversary Concert Celebration (Columbia 1993)★★★★, MTV Unplugged (Columbia 1995)★★, Time Out Of Mind (Columbia 1997)★★★★, The Bootleg Series Vol. 4: Bob Dylan Live 1966: The "Royal Albert Hall" Concert (Columbia/Legacy 1998)★★★★★, Live 1961/2000 (Columbia 2001)★★★, Love And Theft (Columbia 2001)★★★.
COMPILATIONS: Bob Dylan's Greatest Hits (Columbia 1967)★★★★★, More Bob Dylan Greatest Hits (Columbia 1972)★★★★, Biograph 5-LP box set (Columbia 1985)★★★★, The Bootleg Series, Volumes 1-3, Rare And Unreleased 1961-1991 3-LP box set (Columbia/Legacy 1991)★★★★★, Greatest Hits Volume 3 (Columbia 1994)★★★, The Best Of Bob Dylan Volume 2 (Columbia 2000)★★★, The Essential Bob Dylan (Columbia 2000)★★★★.
VIDEOS: Hard To Handle (Virgin Vision 1987), Don't Look Back (Virgin Vision 1988), 30th Anniversary Concert Celebration (1993), MTV Unplugged (1995).
FURTHER READING: Like all major artists there are many books available. The editor's recommendation would contain three essential works: No Direction Home, Robert Shelton. Song & Dance Man III, Michael Gray. Wanted Man: In Search Of Bob Dylan, John Bauldie. Others: Bob Dylan In His Own Write, Bob Dylan. Eleven Outlined Epitaphs & Off The Top Of My Head, Bob Dylan. Folk-Rock: The Bob Dylan Story, Sy and Barbra Ribakove. Don't Look Back, D.A. Pennebaker. Bob Dylan: An Intimate Biography, Anthony Scaduto. Positively Main Street: An Unorthodox View Of Bob Dylan, Toby Thompson. Bob Dylan: A Retrospective, Craig McGregor. Song And Dance Man: The Art Of Bob Dylan, Michael Gray. Bob Dylan: Writings And Drawings, Bob Dylan. Knocking On Dylan's Door, Rolling Stone editors. Rolling Thunder Logbook, Sam Shepard. On The Road With Bob Dylan: Rolling With The Thunder, Larry Sloman. Bob Dylan: The Illustrated Record, Alan Rinzler. Bob Dylan In His Own Words, Miles. Bob Dylan: An Illustrated Discography, Stuart Hoggard and Jim Shields. Bob Dylan: An Illustrated History, Michael Gross. Bob Dylan: His Unreleased Recordings, Paul Cable. Dylan: What Happened?, Paul Williams. Conclusions On The Wall: New Essays On Bob Dylan, Liz Thomson. Twenty Years Of Recording: The Bob Dylan Reference Book, Michael Krogsgaard. Voice Without Restraint: A Study Of Bob Dylan's Lyrics And Their Background, John Herdman. Bob Dylan: From A Hard Rain To A Slow Train, Tim Dowley and Barry Dunnage. No Direction Home: The Life And Music Of Bob Dylan, Robert Shelton. Bringing It All Back Home, Robbie Wolliver. All Across The Telegraph: A Bob Dylan Handbook, Michael Gray and John Bauldie (eds.). Raging Glory, Dennis R. Liff. Bob Dylan: Stolen Moments, Clinton Heylin. Jokerman: Reading The Lyrics Of Bob Dylan, Aidan Day. Dylan: A Biography, Bob Spitz. Performing Artist: The Music Of Bob Dylan Volume 1, 1960-1973, Paul Williams. Dylan Companion, Elizabeth M. Thomson and David Gutman. Lyrics: 1962-1985, Bob Dylan. Bob Dylan: Performing Artist, Paul Williams. Oh No! Not Another Bob Dylan Book, Patrick Humphries and John Bauldie. Absolutely Dylan, Patrick Humphries and John Bauldie. Dylan: Behind The Shades, Clinton Heylin. Bob Dylan: A Portrait Of the Artist's Early Years, Daniel Kramer. Wanted Man: In Search Of Bob Dylan, John Bauldie (ed.). Bob Dylan: In His Own Words, Chris Williams. Tangled Up In Tapes, Glen Dundas. Hard Rain: A Dylan Commentary, Tim Riley. Complete Guide To The Music Of Bob Dylan, Patrick Humphries. Bob Dylan Drawn Blank (Folio of drawings), Bob Dylan. Watching The River Flow (1966-1995), Paul Williams. Like The Night: Bob Dylan And The Road To The Manchester Free Trade Hall, C.P. Lee. Classic Bob Dylan 1962-69, Andy Gill. Touched By The Hand Of Bob: Epiphanal Bob Dylan Experiences From A Buick Six, Dave Henderson. Song & Dance Man III: The Art Of Bob Dylan, Michael Gray. Like A Bullet Of Light: The Films Of Bob Dylan, C.P. Lee. Encounters With Bob Dylan: If You See Him, Say Hello, Tracy Johnson (ed.). The Bob Dylan Companion: Four Decades Of Commentary, Carl Benson (ed.). Down The Highway: The Life Of Bob Dylan, Howard Sounes. Razor's Edge: Bob Dylan And The Never Ending Tour, Andrew Muir. Positively 4th Street: The Lives And Times Of Joan Baez, Bob Dylan, Mimi Baez Fariña And Richard Fariña, David Hadju. The Nightingale's Code: A Poetic Study Of Bob Dylan, John Gibbens. Isis: A Bob Dylan Anthology, Derek Barker (ed.).
FILMS: Don't Look Back (1966), Eat The Document (1971), Pat Garrett & Billy The Kid (1973), Renaldo And Clara (1978), Hearts Of Fire (1987).

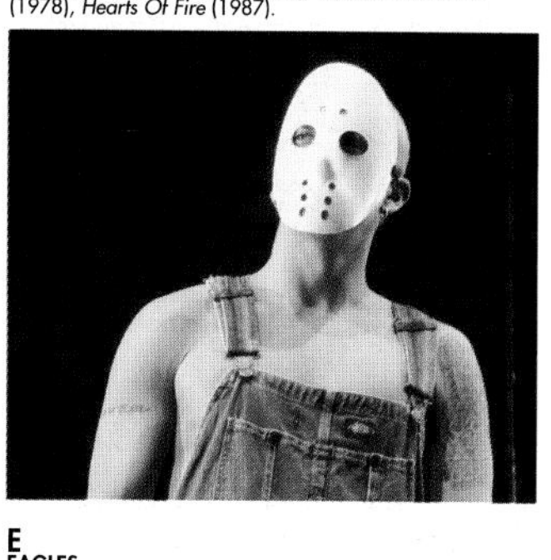

E

EAGLES
ALBUMS: The Eagles (Asylum 1972)★★★, Desperado (Asylum 1973)★★★★, On The Border (Asylum 1974)★★★★, One Of These Nights (Asylum 1975)★★★, Hotel California (Asylum 1976)★★★★, The Long Run (Asylum 1979)★★, Live (Asylum 1980)★★, Hell Freezes Over (Geffen 1994)★★★.
COMPILATIONS: Their Greatest Hits 1971-1975 (Asylum 1976)★★★★, Greatest Hits Volume 2 (Asylum 1982)★★★, Best Of The Eagles (Asylum 1985)★★★★, 1972-1999: Selected Works 4-CD box set (Elektra 2000)★★★★, The Very Best Of The Eagles (Elektra 2001)★★★★.
VIDEOS: Hell Freezes Over (Geffen Home Video 1994).
FURTHER READING: The Eagles, John Swenson. The Long Run: The Story Of The Eagles, Marc Shapiro. To The Limit: The Untold Story Of The Eagles, Marc Eliot.

EARLE, STEVE
ALBUMS: Guitar Town (MCA 1986)★★★★, Exit O (MCA 1987)★★★, Copperhead Road (MCA 1988)★★★★, The Hard Way (MCA 1990)★★★, Shut Up And Die Like An Aviator (MCA 1991)★★★★, BBC Radio 1 Live In Concert (Windsong 1992)★★★, Train A Comin' (Winter Harvest/Transatlantic 1995)★★★★, I Feel Alright (E Squared/Transatlantic 1996)★★★, El Corazón (E Squared/Warners 1997)★★★★, with the Del McCoury Band The Mountain (E Squared/Grapevine 1999)★★★★, Transcendental Blues (E Squared 2000)★★★, with Townes Van Zandt, Guy Clark Together At The Bluebird (Catfish 2001)★★★★, Sidetracks (Epic/Artemis 2002)★★★.
COMPILATIONS: Early Tracks (Epic 1987)★★★, We Ain't Ever Satisfied: Essential Steve Earle (MCA 1992)★★★★, Essential Steve Earle (MCA 1993)★★★★, This Highway's Mine (Pickwick 1993)★★★, Fearless Heart (MCA 1995)★★★, The Very Best Of Steve Earle: Angry Young Man (Nectar 1996)★★★, Ain't Ever Satisfied: The Steve Earle Collection (Hip-O 1996)★★★★, The Devil's Right Hand: An Introduction To Steve Earle (MCA 2000)★★★★, Sidetracks (E Squared/Artemis 2002)★★★.
FURTHER READING: Doghouse Roses, Steve Earle.

EARTH, WIND AND FIRE
ALBUMS: Earth, Wind And Fire (Warners 1971)★★, The Need Of Love (Warners 1972)★★, Last Days And Time (Columbia 1972)★★, Head To The Sky (Columbia 1973)★★★, Open Our Eyes (Columbia 1974)★★★★, That's The Way Of The World (Columbia 1975)★★★★, Gratitude (Columbia 1975)★★★, Spirit (Columbia 1976)★★★, All And All (Columbia 1977)★★★, I Am (ARC 1979)★★★, Faces (ARC 1980)★★★, Raise! (ARC 1981)★★★, Powerlight (Columbia 1983)★★★, Electric Universe (Columbia 1983)★★, Touch The World (Columbia 1987)★★★, Heritage (Columbia 1990)★★, Millennium (Columbia 1993)★★★, Greatest Hits Live, Tokyo Japan (Rhino 1996)★★, In The Name Of Love (Eagle 1997)★★★.
COMPILATIONS: The Best Of Earth, Wind And Fire, Volume 1 (ARC 1978)★★★★, The Collection (K-Tel 1986)★★★, The Best Of Earth, Wind And Fire, Volume 2 (Columbia 1988)★★★★, The Eternal Dance (Sony 1993)★★★, The Very Best Of Earth, Wind And Fire (Sony 1993)★★★, Ultimate Collection (Sony 1999)★★★★.
VIDEOS: The Ultimate Collection (Sony Music Video 1999), Shining Stars: The Official Story Of Earth, Wind & Fire (Evergreen Entertainment 2001).

EAST 17
ALBUMS: Walthamstow (London 1993)★★★★, Steam (London 1994)★★★, Up All Night (London 1995)★★★, as E-17 Resurrection (Telstar 1998)★★.
COMPILATIONS: Around The World – The Journey So Far (London 1996)★★★.
VIDEOS: Up All Night (PolyGram Music Video 1995), Letting Of Steam: Live (PolyGram Music Video 1995), Greatest Hits (PolyGram Music Video 1996).
FURTHER READING: East 17: Talk Back, Carl Jenkins.

EASTON, SHEENA
ALBUMS: Take My Time aka Sheena Easton (EMI 1981)★★, You Could Have Been With Me (EMI 1981)★★, Madness, Money And Music (EMI 1982)★★, Best Kept Secret (EMI 1983)★★, Todo Me Recuerda A Ti (EMI 1984)★★★, A Private Heaven (EMI 1984)★★★★, Do You (EMI 1985)★★, No Sound But A Heart (EMI 1987)★★, The Lover In Me (MCA 1988)★★★, What Comes Naturally (MCA 1991)★★★, No Strings (MCA 1993)★★★, My Cherie (MCA 1995)★★★, Freedom (SkyJay Trax/MCA 1997)★★★, Home (Universal Japan 1999)★★★, Fabulous (Universal International 2000)★★★.
COMPILATIONS: The Best Of Sheena Easton (EMI America 1989)★★★, For Your Eyes Only: The Best Of Sheena Easton

(EMI 1989)★★★, The World Of Sheena Easton: The Singles Collection (EMI America 1993)★★★★, Greatest Hits (CEMA 1995)★★★, The Best Of Sheena Easton (Disky 1996)★★★, The Gold Collection (EMI 1996)★★★, Body & Soul (Universal 1997)★★★, 20 Great Love Songs (Disky 1998)★★★.
VIDEOS: Live At The Palace, Hollywood (Sony 1982), Sheena Easton (Sony 1983), A Private Heaven (Sony 1984), Sheena Easton Act 1 (Prism 1986), Star Portraits (Gemini Vision 1992).
FILMS: Sign 'O' The Times (1987), Indecent Proposal (1993), All Dogs Go To Heaven 2 voice only (1996), An All Dogs Christmas Carol (1998).

EASYBEATS
ALBUMS: Easy (Parlophone 1965)★★, It's 2 Easy (Parlophone 1966)★★, Volume 3 (Parlophone 1966)★★★, Good Friday (United Artists 1967)★★★, Vigil (United Artists 1968)★★, Friends (Polydor 1969)★★, Live Studio And Stage (Raven 1995)★★.
COMPILATIONS: The Shame Just Drained (Alberts 1977), Absolute Anthology (Alberts 1980)★★★, Best Of The Easybeats (Rhino 1986)★★★, The Best Of The Easybeats (Repertoire 1995)★★★, Aussie Beat That Shook The World (Repertoire 1996)★★★, Gonna Have A Good Time (Sin-Drome 1999)★★★, The Definitive Anthology (Repertoire 2000)★★★.

ECHO AND THE BUNNYMEN
ALBUMS: Crocodiles (Korova 1980)★★★★, Heaven Up Here (Korova 1981)★★★, Porcupine (Korova 1983)★★★★, Ocean Rain (Korova 1984)★★★, Echo And The Bunnymen (Warners 1987)★★, Reverberation (Korova 1990)★★, Evergreen (London 1997)★★★, What Are You Going To Do With Your Life? (London 1999)★★★, Avalanche mini-album (Gimmemusic 2000)★★★, Flowers (Cooking Vinyl 2001) ★★★, Live In Liverpool (Cooking Vinyl/spinART 2002)★★★.
SOLO: Will Sergeant Themes For Grind (92 Happy Customers 1983)★★, as Glide Performance (Ochre 2000)★★.
COMPILATIONS: Songs To Learn And Sing (Korova 1985) ★★★★, Live In Concert (Windsong 1991)★★★, The Cutter (Warners 1993)★★★, The Peel Sessions (Strange Fruit 1995)★★★, Ballyhoo: The Best Of Echo And The Bunnymen (Warners 1997)★★★★, Crystal Days (1979-1999) 4-CD box set (Rhino 2001)★★★★.
VIDEOS: Porcupine (Virgin Video 1983), Live In Liverpool (Cooking Vinyl 2002).
FURTHER READING: Liverpool Explodes: The Teardrop Explodes, Echo And The Bunnymen, Mark Cooper. Never Stop: The Echo & The Bunnymen Story, Tony Fletcher. Ian McCulloch: King Of Cool, Mick Middles.

ECHOBELLY
ALBUMS: Everyone's Got One (Rhythm King 1994)★★★, On (Rhythm King 1995)★★★★, Lustra (Epic 1997)★★, People Are Expensive (Fry Up 2001)★★★.
COMPILATIONS: I Can't Imagine The World Without Me (Epic 2001)★★★.

EDDIE AND THE HOT RODS
ALBUMS: Teenage Depression (Island 1976)★★★★, Life On The Line (Island 1977)★★★, Thriller (Island 1979)★★, Fish 'N' Chips (EMI America 1980)★★, One Story Town (Waterfront 1985)★★, Gasoline Days (Creative Man 1996)★★.
COMPILATIONS: The Curse Of The Rods (Hound Dog 1990)★★★, Live And Rare (Receiver 1993)★★, The Best Of ... The End Of The Beginning (Island 1995)★★★, Do Anything You Wanna Do (Spectrum 2001)★★★.

EDDY, DUANE
ALBUMS: Have 'Twangy' Guitar Will Travel (Jamie 1958) ★★★, Especially For You (Jamie 1958)★★★★, The 'Twang's The 'Thang' (Jamie 1959)★★★★, Songs Of Our Heritage (Jamie 1960)★★★, $1,000,000 Worth Of Twang (Jamie 1960)★★★★, Girls! Girls! Girls! (Jamie 1961)★★★, $1,000,000 Worth Of Twang, Volume 2 (Jamie 1962)★★★, Twistin' And Twangin' (RCA-Victor 1962)★★★★, Twisting With Duane Eddy (Jamie 1962)★★★, Twangy Guitar-Silky Strings (RCA-Victor 1962)★★★★, Dance With The Guitar Man (RCA-Victor 1963)★★★★, Duane Eddy & The Rebels In Person (Jamie 1963)★★★, Surfin' With Duane Eddy (Jamie 1963)★★★, Twang A Country Song (RCA-Victor 1963)★★, Twanging Up A Storm! (RCA-Victor 1963)★★★, Lonely Guitar (RCA-Victor 1964)★★★, Water Skiing (RCA-Victor 1964)★★, Twangsville (RCA-Victor 1965)★★, Twangin' The Golden Hits (RCA-Victor 1965)★★★, Duane Goes Bob Dylan (RCA-Victor 1965)★★, Duane A Go Go (RCA-Victor 1965)★★, Biggest Twang Of Them All (RCA-Victor 1966) ★★, Roaring Twangies (RCA-Victor 1967)★★, Twangy Guitar (1970)★★★, Duane Eddy (1987)★★★.
COMPILATIONS: 16 Greatest Hits (Jamie 1964)★★★★, The Best Of Duane Eddy (RCA-Victor 1966)★★★★, The Vintage Years (Sire 1975)★★★, Legends Of Rock (Deram 1975)★★★, Twenty Terrific Twangies (RCA 1981)★★★, Greatest Hits (1991)★★★★, Twang Thang: The Duane Eddy Anthology (1993)★★★★, That Classic Twang 2-CD set (Bear Family 1994)★★★★, Twangin' From Phoenix To L.A. - The Jamie Years 5-CD box set (Bear Family 1995) ★★★★★, Boss Guitar (Camden 1997)★★★★, Deep In The Heart Of Twangsville: The Complete RCA Victor Recordings 6-CD box set (Bear Family 1999)★★★.
FILMS: Because They're Young (1960).

EDEN'S CRUSH
ALBUMS: Popstars (143/Sire 2001)★★★.

EDISON LIGHTHOUSE
COMPILATIONS: Love Grows: The Best Of The Edison Lighthouse (Repertoire 1999)★★★.

EDMUNDS, DAVE
ALBUMS: Subtle As A Flying Mallet (RCA 1975)★★★, Get It (Swansong 1977)★★★, Tracks On Wax (Swansong 1978) ★★★, Repeat When Necessary (Swansong 1979)★★★★, Twangin' (Arista 1981)★★★, D.E.7th (Arista 1982)★★★, Information (Arista 1983)★★, Riff Raff (Arista 1984)★★, I Hear You Rockin' (Arista 1987)★★★, Closer To The Flame (Capitol 1990)★★, Plugged In (Columbia 1994)★★★, Live On The King Biscuit Flower Hour 1980/1990 recordings (King Biscuit Flower Hour 1999)★★★, A Pile Of Rock Live (Essential 2000)★★★.
COMPILATIONS: The Best Of Dave Edmunds (Swansong 1981)★★★★, The Complete Early Edmunds (EMI 1991) ★★★, The Dave Edmunds Anthology (1968-90) (Rhino/WEA 1993)★★★★, Chronicles (Connoisseur 1995)★★★★.
FILMS: Give My Regards To Broad Street (1985).

EELS
ALBUMS: Beautiful Freak (DreamWorks 1996)★★★★, Electro-Shock Blues (DreamWorks 1998)★★★★, Daisies Of The Galaxy (DreamWorks 2000)★★★★, Oh What A Beautiful Morning (E Works 2000)★★★, Souljacker (DreamWorks 2001)★★.
SOLO: E A Man Called (E) (Polydor 1992)★★★★, Broken Toy Shop (Polydor 1993)★★★.

808 STATE
ALBUMS: Newbuild (Creed 1988)★★★, Quadrastate (Creed 1989)★★★★, Ninety (ZTT 1989)★★★★, Utd. State 90 US only (Tommy Boy 1990)★★★★, Ex:El (ZTT/Tommy Boy 1991)★★★, Gorgeous (ZTT/Tommy Boy 1993)★★★, Don Solaris (ZTT/Hypnotic 1996)★★★.
COMPILATIONS: Thermo Kings (ZTT/Hypnotic 1996)★★★, 808:88:98 (ZTT 1998)★★★★.
VIDEOS: Opti Buk (ZTT 2002).

EINSTÜRZENDE NEUBAUTEN
ALBUMS: Kollaps (Zick Zack 1981)★★★, Die Zeichnungen Des Patienten O.T. (Some Bizzare/Rough Trade 1983) ★★★★, 2x4 cassette only (ROIR 1984)★★, Halber Mensch (Some Bizzare 1985)★★★, Fünf Auf Der Nach Oben Offenen Richterskala (Some Bizzare/Relativity 1987)★★★, Haus Der Lüge (Some Bizzare/Rough Trade 1989)★★★, Die Hamletmaschine film soundtrack (Ego 1991)★★, Tabula Rasa (Mute 1993)★★★, Faustmusik film soundtrack (Ego 1996)★★, Ende Neu (Mute 1996)★★★, Ende Neu Remixes (Mute 1997)★★, Silence Is Sexy (Mute 2000)★★★.
COMPILATIONS: Strategien Gegen Architekturen 80=83 (Mute 1984)★★★, Strategies Against Architecture II (Ego/Mute 1991)★★★, Strategies Against Architecture III (Mute 2001)★★★.
VIDEOS: Halber Mensch (Doublevision/Mute 1986), Liebenslieder (Mute 1993).

EITZEL, MARK
ALBUMS: Songs Of Love Live (Demon 1992)★★★, 60 Watt Silver Lining (Virgin 1996)★★★, West (Warners 1997) ★★★★, Caught In A Trap And I Can't Back Out 'Cause I Love You Too Much Baby (Matador 1998)★★★, The Invisible Man (Matador 2001)★★★★, Music For Courage & Confidence (New West 2002)★★★.
FURTHER READING: Wish The World Away: Mark Eitzel And The American Music Club, Sean Body.

ELASTICA
ALBUMS: Elastica (Deceptive 1995)★★★★, The Menace (Deceptive/Atlantic 2000)★★★.
COMPILATIONS: The Radio One Sessions (Strange Fruit 2001)★★★.

ELBOW
ALBUMS: Asleep In The Back (V2 2001)★★★★.

ELECTRIC FLAG
ALBUMS: The Trip film soundtrack (Sidewalk 1967)★★, A Long Time Comin' (Columbia 1968)★★★★, The Electric Flag (Columbia 1969)★★, The Band Kept Playing (Atlantic 1974)★.
COMPILATIONS: The Best Of The Electric Flag (Columbia 1971)★★★, Old Glory: The Best Of Electric Flag – An American Music Band (Columbia/Legacy 1995)★★★★, Small Town Blues (Columbia River 2000)★★.

ELECTRIC LIGHT ORCHESTRA
ALBUMS: Electric Light Orchestra aka No Answer (Harvest 1971)★★, ELO II (Harvest 1973)★★, On The Third Day (Warners 1973)★★★, The Night The Lights Went On In Long Beach (Warners 1974)★★, Eldorado (Warners 1975) ★★★★, Face The Music (Jet 1975)★★★★, A New World Record (Jet 1976)★★★★, Out Of The Blue (Jet 1977) ★★★★, Discovery (Jet 1979)★★★, with Olivia Newton-John Xanadu film soundtrack (Jet 1980)★★, Time (Jet 1981)★★, Secret Messages (Jet 1983)★★, Balance Of Power (Epic 1986)★★, Electric Light Orchestra Part Two (Telstar 1991)★, as ELO 2 Moment Of Truth (Edel 1994)★, Live At Winterland '76 (Eagle/Cleopatra 1998)★★★, Live At Wembley '78 (Eagle/Cleopatra 1998)★★★, Zoom (Epic 2001)★★★.
COMPILATIONS: Showdown (Harvest 1974)★★★, Olé ELO (Jet 1976)★★★, The Light Shines On (Harvest 1976)★★★, Greatest Hits (Jet 1979)★★★★, A Box Of Their Best (Jet 1980)★★★, First Movement (Harvest 1986)★★, A Perfect World Of Music (Jet 1988)★★★★, Their Greatest Hits (Epic 1989)★★★, The Definitive Collection (Jet 1993)★★★, The Very Best Of ... (Dino 1994)★★★, Strange Magic: Best Of ELO (Sony 1995)★★★★, The Gold Collection (EMI 1996) ★★★, Light Years (Epic 1997)★★★, Friends And Relatives (Eagle/Cleopatra 1999)★★★, Complete ELO Live Collection (Cleopatra 2000)★★★, Flashback 3-CD box set (Epic 2000)★★★★.
VIDEOS: 'Out Of The Blue' Tour Live At Wembley (Eagle Rock 1999), Discovery (Eagle Rock 1999), Zoom Tour Live (Aviva International 2001).
FURTHER READING: The Electric Light Orchestra Story, Bev Bevan.

ELECTRIC PRUNES
ALBUMS: The Electric Prunes (I Had Too Much To Dream Last Night) (Reprise 1967)★★★, Underground (Reprise 1967)★★★, Mass In F Minor (Reprise 1967)★★, Release Of An Oath (Reprise 1968)★★, Just Good Old Rock 'N' Roll (Reprise 1969)H, Stockholm 67 (Heartbeat 1997)★★.
COMPILATIONS: Long Day's Flight (Demon 1986)★★★, Lost Dreams (Birdman 2001)★★★★.

ELECTRONIC
ALBUMS: Electronic (Parlophone 1991)★★★★, Raise The Pressure (Parlophone 1996)★★★, Twisted Tenderness (Parlophone/Koch 1999)★★★.

ELLIOTT, MISSY 'MISDEMEANOR'
ALBUMS: Supa Dupa Fly (East West 1997)★★★★, Da Real World (East West 1999)★★★★, Miss E ... So Addictive (The Gold Mind/Elektra 2001)★★★★.

ELLIOTT, RAMBLIN' JACK
ALBUMS: Woody Guthrie's Blues (Topic 1957)★★★, with Derroll Adams The Rambling Boys 10-inch album (Topic 1957)★★★, Jack Takes The Floor 10-inch album (Topic 1958)★★★, In London (UK) Monitor Presents Jack Elliott: Ramblin' Cowboy (US) (Columbia/Monitor 1959)★★★, Sings Songs By Woody Guthrie And Jimmy Rogers (Columbia/Monitor 1960)★★★, Sings The Songs Of Woody Guthrie (Stateside/Prestige 1961)★★★, Songs To Grow On By Woody Guthrie, Sung By Jack Elliott (Folkways 1961)★★★, Ramblin' Jack Elliott (Prestige 1961)★★★★, Jack Elliott At The Second Fret aka Hootenanny With Jack Elliott (Prestige 1962)★★★, Country Style (Prestige 1962) ★★★, Talking Woody Guthrie (Topic 1963)★★★, with Adams Roll On Buddy (Topic 1963)★★★, Muleskinner (Topic/Delmark 1964)★★★, Jack Elliott i (Everest Archive 1964)★★★, Jack Elliott ii (Vanguard/Fontana 1964)★★★, Young Brigham (Reprise 1967)★★★, Bill Durham Sacks & Railroad Tracks (Reprise 1967)★★★, with Adams Folkland Songs aka America: Folk Songs-West-Ballads 1955-1961 recordings (Joker 1969)★★★, Kerouac's Last Dream (Folk Freak 1981)★★★, with Spider John Koerner, U. Utah Phillips Legends Of Folk (Red House 1992)★★★, South Coast (Red House 1995)★★★, Friends Of Mine (Hightone 1998)★★★, Live In Japan 1974 recording (Vivid/Bellwood 1998)★★★, The Long Ride (Hightone 1999)★★★, The Ballad Of Ramblin' Jack film soundtrack (Vanguard 2000)★★★.
COMPILATIONS: The Essential Ramblin' Jack Elliott (Vanguard 1976)★★★, Hard Travelin': Songs By Woody Guthrie And Others (Fantasy/Big Beat 1989)★★★★, Talking Dust Bowl: The Best Of Ramblin' Jack Elliott (Big Beat 1989)★★★★, Sings Woody Guthrie And Jimmie Rodgers & Cowboy Songs (Monitor 1994)★★★, Me & Bobby McGee (Rounder 1995)★★★, Ramblin' Jack: The Legendary Topic Masters (Topic 1995)★★★, Country Style/Live (Fantasy 1999)★★★, The Best Of The Vanguard Years (Vanguard 2000)★★★★.
FILMS: The Ballad Of Ramblin' Jack (2000).

ELY, JOE
ALBUMS: Joe Ely (MCA 1977)★★★★, Honky Tonk Masquerade (MCA 1978)★★★★, Down On The Drag (MCA 1979)★★★★, Live Shots (MCA 1980)★★★, One Road More (Charly 1980)★★★, Musta Notta Gotta Lotta (SouthCoast 1981)★★★, Hi-Res (MCA 1984)★★★, Lord Of The Highway (Hightone 1987)★★★★, Dig All Night (HighTone 1988)★★★★, Milkshakes And Malts (Sunstorm 1988)★★★, Whatever Happened To Maria (Sunstorm 1989)★★★, Live At Liberty Lunch (MCA 1990)★★★★, Love And Danger (MCA 1992)★★★, Highways And Heartaches (1993)★★★, Letter To Laredo (Transatlantic 1995)★★★★, Twistin' In The Wind (MCA 1998)★★★★, Live At The Cambridge Folk Festival 1990 recording (Strange Fruit 1998)★★★, Live @ Antone's (Rounder 2000)★★★★.
COMPILATIONS: No Bad Talk Or Loud Talk '77 - '81 (Edsel 1995)★★★★, The Time For Travellin': The Best Of ... Volume 2 (Edsel 1996)★★★★, The Best Of Joe Ely (MCA 2000)★★★★.

EMBRACE
ALBUMS: The Good Will Out (Hut 1998)★★★★, Drawn From Memory (Hut 2000)★★★, If You've Never Been (Hut 2001)★★★.
COMPILATIONS: Fireworks (Singles 1997-2002) (Hut 2002)★★★★.

EMERSON, LAKE AND PALMER
ALBUMS: Emerson, Lake & Palmer (Island/Cotillion 1970) ★★★, Tarkus (Island/Cotillion 1971)★★★, Pictures At An Exhibition (Island/Cotillion 1971)★★★★, Trilogy (Island/Cotillion 1972)★★★, Brain Salad Surgery (Manticore 1973) ★★★, Welcome Back, My Friends, To The Show That Never Ends: Ladies And Gentlemen ... Emerson Lake & Palmer (Manticore 1974)★★, Works: Volume 1 (Atlantic 1977)★★, Works: Volume 2 (Atlantic 1977)★★, Love Beach (Atlantic 1978) ★★, Emerson, Lake & Palmer In Concert (Atlantic 1979)★★, as Emerson, Lake And Powell Emerson, Lake & Powell (Polydor 1986)★★, Black Moon (Victory 1992)★★, Live At The Royal Albert Hall (Victory 1993)★★, Works Live 1977 recording (Victory 1993)★★, In The Hot Seat (Victory 1994)★★, King Biscuit Flower Hour (King Biscuit Flower Hour 1997)★★.
COMPILATIONS: The Best Of Emerson, Lake & Palmer (Atlantic 1980)★★★, The Atlantic Years (Atlantic 1992)★★★★, The Return Of The Manticore 4-CD box set (Victory 1993)★★★★, Then & Now (Eagle 1998)★★, Extended Versions: The Encore Collection (BMG 2000)★★, Fanfare For The Common Man: The Anthology (Sanctuary 2001)★★★★, The Very Best Of Emerson, Lake & Palmer (Rhino 2001)★★★★, The Original Bootleg Series From The Manticore Vaults Vol. One 7-CD box set (Castle 2001)★★★, The Original Bootleg Series From The Manticore Vaults Vol. Two 8-CD box set (Castle 2001)★★★.
VIDEOS: Pictures At An Exhibition (Hendring Music Video 1990).
FURTHER READING: Emerson, Lake And Palmer: The Show That Never Ends, A Musical Biography, George Forrester, Martyn Hanson, Frank Askew.

EMF
ALBUMS: Schubert Dip (Parlophone 1991)★★★★, Stigma (Parlophone 1992)★★, Cha Cha Cha (Parlophone 1995) ★★★.
COMPILATIONS: The Best Of EMF: Epsom Mad Funkers (Parlophone 2001)★★★★.

EMINEM
ALBUMS: Infinite (FBT 1997)★★, The Slim Shady LP (Aftermath/Interscope 1999)★★★★, The Marshall Mathers LP (Aftermath/Interscope 2000)★★★.
VIDEOS: E (Interscope 2001), Hitz & Disses: Unauthorized (Wienerworld 2001), The Slim Shady Show (MIA 2001).
FURTHER READING: Shady Bizness: Life As Marshall Mathers' Bodyguard In An Industry Of Paper Gangsters, Byron 'Big Naz' Williams. Eminem: Crossing The Line, Martin Huxley. Eminem: Angry Blonde, Eminem.

EN VOGUE
ALBUMS: Born To Sing (Atlantic 1990)★★★, Remix To Sing (Atlantic 1991)★★★, Funky Divas (East West 1992)★★★★, Runaway Love mini-album (East West 1993)★★★, EV3 (East West 1997)★★★, Masterpiece Theatre (Elektra 2000)★★★★.
Solo: Terry Ellis Southern Gal (East West 1995)★★.
COMPILATIONS: Best Of En Vogue (East West 1998)★★★★.

ENGLAND DAN AND JOHN FORD COLEY
ALBUMS: as Southwest F.O.B. Smell Of Incense (A&M 1968)★★, England Dan And John Ford Coley (A&M 1971)★★, Fables (A&M 1971)★★, I Hear The Music (A&M 1976)★★, Nights Are Forever (Big Tree 1976)★★, Dowdy Ferry Road (Big Tree 1977)★★★, Some Things Don't Come Easy (Big Tree 1978)★★, Dr. Heckle And Mr. Jive (Big Tree 1979)★★, Just Tell Me If You Love Me (Big Tree 1980)★★.
COMPILATIONS: Best Of England Dan & John Ford Coley (Big Tree 1980)★★★, The Very Best Of England Dan & John Ford Coley (Rhino 1997)★★★.

ENID
ALBUMS: In The Region Of The Summer Stars (Buk 1976) ★★★, Aerie Faerie Nonsense (Honeybee 1977)★★★, Touch Me (Pye 1978)★★★, Six Pieces (Pye 1979)★★★, Live At Hammersmith Vol. 1 (Enid 1983)★★, Live At Hammersmith Vol. 2 (Enid 1983)★★, Something Wicked This Way Comes (Enid 1983)★★★, The Spell (Enid 1985) ★★★, Fand (Enid 1985)★★★, Salome (Enid 1986)★★★, The Seed And The Sower (Enid 1988)★★★★, Final Noise (Enid 1989)★★★, Tripping The Light Fantastic (Mantella 1994)★★★, Healing Hearts (Mantella 1996)★★★, White Goddess (Mantella 1998)★★★.
COMPILATIONS: Lovers & Fools (Dojo 1986)★★★, An Alternative History Volume 1 (Enid 1994), An Alternative History Volume 2 (Enid 1994), An Alternative History Volume 3 (Enid 1995), Sundialer (Mantella 1995)★★★, Anarchy On 45 (Mantella 1996)★★★, Members One Of Another (Mantella 1996)★★★, Tears Of The Sun (HTD 1999)★★★★.
VIDEOS: Stonehenge Free Festival (Visionary 1984), Claret Hall Farm (Visionary 1985).

ENIGMA
ALBUMS: MCMXC AD (Virgin 1990)★★★★, The Cross Of Changes (Virgin 1993)★★★★, Le Roi Est Mort, Vive Le Roi! (Virgin 1996)★★★, The Screen Behind The Mirror (Virgin 2000)★★.
COMPILATIONS: Love Sensuality Devotion: The Greatest Hits (Virgin 2001)★★★★.

ENO, BRIAN
ALBUMS: with Robert Fripp No Pussyfooting (Island/Antilles 1973)★★★, Here Come The Warm Jets (Island 1974) ★★★★, Taking Tiger Mountain (By Strategy) (Island 1974) ★★★★, with John Cale, Kevin Ayers, Nico June 1st 1974 (Island 1974)★★, Another Green World (Island 1975) ★★★★, Discreet Music (Island 1975)★★★, with Robert Fripp Evening Star (Island/Antilles 1975)★★★, Before And After Science (Polydor 1977)★★★★, with Cluster Cluster And Eno (Sky 1977)★★★, Music For Films (Polydor 1978) ★★★, Ambient 1: Music For Airports (Ambient 1978)★★★★, with Moebius, Roedelius After The Heat (Sky 1978)★★★, with Harold Budd Ambient 2: The Plateaux Of Mirror (Editions EG/Ambient 1980)★★★★, with Jon Hassell Fourth World Vol i: Possible Musics (Polydor/Editions EG 1980)★★★, with David Byrne My Life In The Bush Of Ghosts (Sire/Polydor 1981)★★★★, Ambient 4: On Land (Editions EG 1982) ★★★, with Daniel Lanois, Roger Eno Apollo: Atmospheres & Soundtracks (Editions EG 1983)★★★★, with Harold Budd, Daniel Lanois The Pearl (Editions EG 1984)★★★, Thursday Afternoon (EG 1985)★★★, with Michael Brook, Daniel Lanois Hybrid (Editions 1985)★★★, with Roger Eno Voices (Editions 1985)★★★, with John Cale Wrong Way Up (Land 1990)★★★★, Nerve Net (Opal/Warners 1992) ★★★, The Shutov Assembly (Opal/Warners 1992)★★★, Neroli (All Saints 1993)★★★, with Jah Wobble Spinner (All Saints 1995)★★★, with various artists Passengers: Original Soundtracks 1 (Island 1995)★★★, The Drop (All Saints 1997)★★, Sonora Portraits 1 (Materiali Sonori 1999)★★★ with J Peter Schwalm Drawn From Life (Venture/Astralwerks 2001)★★★.
COMPILATIONS: Working Backwards 1983-1973 (Editions EG 1983)★★★, with Moebius, Roedelius, Plank Begegnungen (Sky 1984)★★★, with Moebius, Roedelius, Plank Begegnungen II (Sky 1985)★★★, with Cluster Old Land (Sky 1985)★★★, Desert Island Selection (EG 1986)★★★★, More Blank Than Frank (EG 1986)★★★★, Box 1 – Instrumental 3-CD box set (Virgin 1993)★★★, Box II – Vocal 3-CD box set (Virgin 1993)★★★, with Robert Fripp The Essential Fripp And Eno (Venture 1993)★★★.
CD ROMS: Headcandy (Ion 1995).
VIDEOS: Thursday Afternoon (Sony 1984), Excerpt From The Khumba Mele (Hendring Video), Mistaken Memories Of Medieval Manhattan (Hendring Video), Imaginary Landscapes (Mystic Fire 1991).
FURTHER READING: Music For Non-Musicians, Brian Eno. Roxy Music: Style With Substance - Roxy's First Ten Years, Johnny Rogan. More Dark Than Shark, Brian Eno and Russell Mills. Brian Eno: His Music And The Vertical Colour Of Sound, Eric Tamm. A Year With Swollen Appendices, Brian Eno.

ENYA
ALBUMS: Enya aka The Celts (BBC 1987)★★, Watermark (WEA/Geffen 1988)★★★★, Shepherd Moons (WEA/Reprise 1991)★★★, The Memory Of Trees (WEA/Reprise 1995)★★★, A Day Without Rain (WEA/Reprise 2000)★★★.
COMPILATIONS: Paint The Sky With Stars: The Best Of Enya (WEA/Reprise 1997)★★★★, A Box Of Dreams 3-CD box-set (WEA 1997)★★★.
VIDEOS: Moonshadows (Warner Music Vision 1991), The Video Collection (Warner Music Vision 2001).
FURTHER READING: Enya: A Beginning Discography, Matt Hargreaves.

EPSTEIN, BRIAN
FURTHER READING: A Cellarful Of Noise, Brian Epstein. Brian Epstein: The Man Who Made The Beatles, Ray Coleman. The Brian Epstein Story, Deborah Geller.

EQUALS
ALBUMS: Unequalled Equals (President 1967)★★★, Equals Explosion aka Equal Sensational Equals (President 1968) ★★★, Equals Supreme (President 1968)★★★, Baby Come Back (President 1968)★★★★, Equals Strike Back (President 1969) ★★, Equals At The Top (President 1970)★★, Equals Rock Around The Clock (1974)★★, Doin' The 45s (1975) ★★★, Born Ya (Mercury 1976)★★, Mystic Synster (Ice 1978)★★.
COMPILATIONS: The Best Of The Equals (President 1969) ★★★, Greatest Hits (1974)★★★★, The Very Best Of The Equals (See For Miles 1996)★★★, Viva Equals! The Very Best Of The Equals (Music Club 1999)★★★.

ERASURE
ALBUMS: Wonderland (Mute 1986)★★★, The Circus (Mute/Sire 1987)★★★, The Two Ring Circus remix album (Mute/Sire 1988)★★★, The Innocents (Mute/Sire 1988)★★★, Wild! (Mute/Sire 1989)★★★, Chorus (Mute/Sire 1991)★★★, Abba-esque mini-album (Mute 1992)★★★, I Say, I Say, I Say (Mute 1994)★★, Erasure (Mute 1995)★★★, Cowboy (Mute/Maverick 1997)★★★, Loveboat (Mute 2000)★★★.
COMPILATIONS: Pop! – The First 20 Hits (Mute/Sire 1992)★★★★.
VIDEOS: Pop – 20 Hits (Mute 1993).

ERICKSON, ROKY
ALBUMS: Roky Erickson And The Aliens (Columbia 1980) ★★★, The Evil One (415 Records 1981)★★★, Clear Night For Love mini-album (New Rose 1985)★★, Don't Slander Me (Enigma/Pink Dust 1986 (US), Demon 1987 (UK)) ★★★, Gremlins Have Pictures (Enigma/Pink Dust 1986 (US), Demon 1987 (UK))★★, I Think Of Demons adds two tracks to Roky Erickson And The Aliens (Edsel 1987)★★★, Casting The Runes (Five Hours Back 1987)★★, The Holiday Inn Tapes (Fan Club 1987)★★, Openers (Five Hours Back 1988)★★, Live At The Ritz, 1987 (New Rose/Fan Club 1988)★★, Mad Dog (Swordfish 1992)★★, All That May Do My Rhyme (Trance Syndicate 1995)★★★.
COMPILATIONS: The Evil One (Enigma/Pink Dust 1987) ★★★, Click Your Fingers Applauding The Play (New Rose/Fan Club 1988)★★★, You're Gonna Miss Me: The Best Of Roky Erickson (Restless 1991)★★★★, Never Say Goodbye (Emperor Jones 1999)★★.

ESSEX, DAVID
ALBUMS: Rock On (CBS 1973)★★★, David Essex (CBS 1974)★★★, All The Fun Of The Fair (CBS 1975)★★, Out On The Street (CBS 1976)★★, On Tour (CBS 1976)★★, Gold And Ivory (CBS 1977)★★, Hold Me Close (CBS 1979)★★, The David Essex Album (CBS 1979)★★, Imperial Wizard (Mercury 1979)★★, Hot Love (Mercury 1980)★★, Be-Bop – The Future (Mercury 1981)★★, Stage-Struck (Mercury 1982)★★, various artists Mutiny! (Mercury 1983)★★, The Whisper (Mercury 1983)★★, This One's For You (Mercury 1984)★★, Live At The Royal Albert Hall (Mercury 1984)★★, Centre Stage (K-Tel 1986)★★, Touching The Ghost (PolyGram TV 1989)★★, Cover Shot (PolyGram TV 1993)★★, Back To Back (PolyGram TV 1994)★★, Missing You (PolyGram TV 1995)★★★, Living In England US only (Cleveland International 1995)★★★, A Night At The Movies (PolyGram TV 1997)★★★, Here We All Are Together (Lamplight 1998)★★, I Still Believe (Lamplight 1999)★★, Thank You (Own Label 2000)★★★.
COMPILATIONS: The David Essex Collection (Pickwick 1980) ★★★, The Very Best Of David Essex (TV Records 1982)★★★, His Greatest Hits (Mercury 1991), Spotlight On David Essex (Spotlight 1993)★★★, The Best Of David Essex (Columbia 1996)★★★, Greatest Hits (PolyGram TV 1998)★★★★.
VIDEOS: Live At The Royal Albert Hall (PolyGram Music Video 1984).
FURTHER READING: The David Essex Story, George Tremlett.
FILMS: Assault (1971), All Coppers Are ... (1972), That'll Be The Day (1973), Stardust (1974), The Big Bus (1976), Silver Dream Racer (1980), Journey Of Honor (1992).

ESTEFAN, GLORIA
ALBUMS: with the Miami Sound Machine Miami Sound Machine (Columbia 1976)★★★, with the Miami Sound Machine Rio (Columbia 1978)★★★, with the Miami Sound Machine Eyes Of Innocence (Columbia 1984)★★★, with the Miami Sound Machine Primitive Love (Epic 1986)★★★, with the Miami Sound Machine Let it Loose (USA) Anything For You (UK) (Epic 1987)★★★★, Cuts Both Ways (Epic 1989)★★★, Exitos De Gloria Estefan (Columbia 1990) ★★★, Into The Light (Epic 1991)★★★★, Mi Tierra (Epic 1993)★★★★, Christmas Through Your Eyes (Epic 1993) ★★, Hold Me, Thrill Me, Kiss Me (Epic 1994)★★, Abriendo Puertas (Epic 1995)★★★★, Destiny (Epic 1996)★★★, Gloria! (Epic 1998)★★★, with Mariah Carey, Celine Dion, Aretha Franklin, Shania Twain Divas Live (Epic 1998)★★, Alma Caribeñña (Epic 2000)★★★.
COMPILATIONS: with the Miami Sound Machine Greatest Hits (Epic 1992)★★★★, Greatest Hits Vol. II (Epic 2001)★★★★.
VIDEOS: Everlasting Gloria! (Sony Music Video 1995), The Evolution Tour: Live In Miami (Epic Music Video 1996), with Mariah Carey, Celine Dion, Aretha Franklin, Shania Twain Divas Live (Sony Music Video 1998), Don't Stop! (Sony Music Video 1998), Que Siga La Tradicion (Sony Music Video 2001).
FURTHER READING: Gloria Estefan, Grace Catalano.
FILMS: Music Of The Heart (1999).

ETERNAL
ALBUMS: Always And Forever (First Avenue/EMI 1994)★★, Power Of A Woman (First Avenue/EMI 1995)★★★, Before The Rain (First Avenue/EMI 1997)★★, Eternal (EMI 1999)★★★.
COMPILATIONS: Greatest Hits (EMI 1997)★★★, Essential Eternal (EMI 2001)★★★.
VIDEOS: Always And Forever (EMI 1994), The Greatest Clips (EMI 1997).

ETHERIDGE, MELISSA
ALBUMS: Melissa Etheridge (Island 1988)★★, Brave And Crazy (Island 1989)★★★, Never Enough (Island 1991) ★★★★, Yes I Am (Island 1993)★★★, Your Little Secret (Island 1995)★★★, Breakdown (Island 1999)★★, Skin (Island 2001)★★★.
FURTHER READING: Our Little Secret, Joyce Luck.

EURYTHMICS
ALBUMS: In The Garden (RCA 1981)★★, Sweet Dreams (Are Made Of This) (RCA 1983)★★★★, Touch (RCA 1983)★★★★, Touch Dance (RCA 1984)★★, 1984 (For The Love Of Big Brother) film soundtrack (Virgin 1984)★★, Be Yourself Tonight (RCA 1985)★★★★, Revenge (RCA 1986)★★★★, Savage (RCA 1987)★★★, We Too Are One (RCA 1989)★★★, Peace (RCA 1999)★★★.
COMPILATIONS: Greatest Hits (RCA 1991)★★★★, Eurythmics Live 1983-1989 (RCA 1993)★★★.
VIDEOS: Sweet Dreams (Eagle Rock 2000).
FURTHER READING: Eurythmics: Sweet Dreams: The Definitive Biography, Johnny Waller. Annie Lennox: The Biography, Bryony Sutherland & Lucy Ellis.

EVERCLEAR
ALBUMS: World Of Noise (Fire 1994)★★★, White Trash Hell mini-album (Fire 1995)★★★★, Sparkle And Fade (Capitol 1995)★★★★, So Much For The Afterglow (Capitol 1997)★★★★, Songs From An American Movie Vol. One: Learning How To Smile (Capitol 2000)★★★, Songs From An American Movie Vol. Two: Good Time For A Bad Attitude (Capitol 2000)★★★★.

EVERLAST
ALBUMS: Forever Everlasting (Warners 1990)★★, Whitey Ford Sings The Blues (Tommy Boy 1998)★★★★, Eat At Whitey's (Tommy Boy 2000)★★★★.

EVERLY BROTHERS
ALBUMS: The Everly Brothers (Cadence 1958)★★★★, Songs Our Daddy Taught Us (Cadence 1959)★★★★, The Everly Brothers' Best (Cadence 1959)★★★, It's Everly Time (Warners 1960)★★★, The Fabulous Style Of The Everly Brothers (Cadence 1960)★★★★, A Date With The Everly Brothers (Warners 1960)★★★★, Both Sides Of An Evening (Warners 1961)★★★, Folk Songs Of the Everly Brothers (Cadence 1962)★★★, Instant Party (Warners 1962)★★★, Christmas With The Everly Brothers And The Boys Town Choir (Warners 1962)★★, The Everly Brothers Sing Great Country Hits (Warners 1963)★★★, Gone Gone Gone (Warners 1965) ★★★★, Rock 'N' Soul (Warners 1965)★★★, Beat 'N' Soul (Warners 1965)★★★, In Our Image (Warners 1966)★★★, Two Yanks In England (Warners 1966)★★★, The Hit Sound Of The Everly Brothers (Warners 1967)★★★, The Everly Brothers Sing (Warners 1967)★★★, Roots (Warners 1968) ★★★★, The Everly Brothers Show (Warners 1970)★★★, End Of An Era (Barnaby/Columbia 1971)★★★, Stories We Could Tell (RCA-Victor 1972)★★★, Pass The Chicken And Listen (RCA-Victor 1973)★★, The Exciting Everly Brothers (RCA 1975)★★★, Living Legends (Warwick 1977)★★★, The New Album previously unissued Warners material (Warners 1977)★★★, The Everly Brothers Reunion Concert (Impression 1983)★★★★, Nice Guys previously unissued Warners material (Magnum Force 1984)★★, EB84 (Mercury 1984)★★★, In The Studio previously unissued Cadence material (Ace 1985)★★★, Born Yesterday (Mercury 1985)★★★, Some Hearts (Mercury 1988)★★★, Live In Paris 1963 recording (Big Beat 1997) ★★★, Live At The Olympia 10-inch album (Big Beat 1997)★★★.
SOLO: Don Everly Don Everly (A&M 1971)★★, Sunset Towers (Ode 1974)★★, Brother Juke Box (Hickory 1976) ★★★. Phil Everly Star Spangled Springer (RCA 1973)★★★, Phil's Diner (There's Nothing Too Good For My Baby) (Pye 1974)★★, Mystic Line (Pye 1975)★★, Living Alone (Elektra 1979)★★, Phil Everly (Capitol 1983)★★.
COMPILATIONS: The Golden Hits Of The Everly Brothers (Warners 1962)★★★★, 15 Everly Hits (Cadence 1963) ★★★, The Very Best Of The Everly Brothers (Warners 1964)★★★★, The Everly Brothers' Original Greatest Hits (Columbia 1970)★★★★★, The Most Beautiful Songs Of The Everly Brothers (Warners 1973)★★★, Don's And Phil's Fabulous Fifties Treasury (Janus 1974)★★★, Walk Right Back With The Everlys (Warners 1975)★★★★, The Everly Brothers Greatest Hits Collection (Pickwick 1979)★★★, The Sensational Everly Brothers (Reader Digest 1979)★★, Cathy's Clown (Pickwick 1980)★★★, The Very Best Of The Everly Brothers (Marks & Spencer 1980)★★, The Everly Brothers (Warners 1981)★★★, Rock 'N' Roll Forever (Warners 1981)★★★, Love Hurts (K-Tel 1982)★★, Rip It Up (Ace 1983)★★★, Cadence Classics (Their 20 Greatest Hits) (Rhino 1985)★★★★, The Best Of The Everly Brothers (Rhino 1985)★★★, All They Had To Do Is Dream US only (Rhino 1985)★★★, Great Recordings (Ace 1986)★★★, The Everly Brothers Collection (Castle 1988)★★★, The Very Best Of The Everly Brothers (Pickwick 1988)★★★, Hidden Gems Warners material (Ace 1989)★★★, The Very Best Of The Everly Brothers Volume 2 (Pickwick 1990)★★, Perfect Harmony box set (Knight 1990)★★★, Classic Everly Brothers 3-CD box set (Bear Family 1992)★★★★, The Golden Years Of The Everly Brothers (Warners 1993)★★★★, Heartaches And Harmonies 4-CD box set (Rhino 1995)★★★★★, Walk Right Back: On Warner Bros. 1960 To 1969 2-CD set (Warners 1996)★★★★, All I Have To Do Is Dream (Carlton 1997) ★★★, The EP Collection (See For Miles 1998)★★★, The Masters (Eagle 1998)★★★, The Very Best Of The Cadence Era (Repertoire 1999)★★★, Devoted To You: Love Songs (Varèse Sarabande 2000)★★★★, The Complete Cadence Recordings: 1957-1960 (Varèse Sarabande 2001)★★★★.
VIDEOS: Rock 'N' Roll Odyssey (MGM 1984).
FURTHER READING: Everly Brothers: An Illustrated Discography, John Hosum. The Everly Brothers: Walk Right Back, Roger White. Ike's Boys, Phyllis Karpp. The Everly Brothers: Ladies Love Outlaws, Consuelo Dodge. For-Everly Yours, Peter Aarts and Martin Alberts.

EVERYTHING BUT THE GIRL
ALBUMS: Eden (Blanco y Negro 1984)★★★★, Love Not Money (Blanco y Negro 1985)★★, Baby The Stars Shine Bright (Blanco y Negro 1986)★★, Idlewild (Blanco y Negro 1988)★★★★, The Language Of Life (Blanco y Negro 1990)★★★, World-wide (Blanco y Negro 1991)★★, Amplified Heart (Blanco y Negro 1994)★★★★, Walking Wounded (Virgin 1996)★★★★, Temperamental (Virgin 1999)★★★.
SOLO: Tracey Thorn A Distant Shore mini-album (Cherry Red 1982)★★★. Ben Watt North Marine Drive (Cherry Red 1983)★★★.
COMPILATIONS: Home Movies: The Best Of Everything But The Girl (Blanco y Negro 1993)★★★★, The Best Of Everything But The Girl (Blanco y Negro 1997)★★★★, Back To Mine (DMC/Ultra 2001)★★★★.
FURTHER READING: Patient: The History Of A Rare Illness, Ben Watt.

EXILE
ALBUMS: Exile (Wooden Nickel 1973)★★★★, Mixed Emotions (Epic 1978)★★★, All There Is (Epic 1979)★★★, Don't Leave Me This Way (Epic 1980)★★★, Heart And Soul (Epic 1981)★★★, Exile (Epic 1983)★★★, Kentucky Hearts (Epic 1984)★★, Hang On To Your Heart (Epic 1985)★★, Shelter From The Night (Epic 1987)★★★, Still Standing (Arista 1990)★★★★, Justice (Arista 1991)★★★.
COMPILATIONS: The Best Of Exile (Curb 1985)★★★★, Exile's Greatest Hits (Epic 1986)★★★, The Complete Collection (Curb 1991)★★★★, Super Hits (Epic 1993)★★★.

EXPLOITED
ALBUMS: Punk's Not Dead (Secret 1981)★★★, On Stage (Superville 1981)★★★, Troops Of Tomorrow (Secret 1982) ★★★, Let's Start A War (Said Maggie One Day) (Combat/Pax 1983)★★★, Horror Epics (Combat/ Konnexion 1985)★★★, Live At The Whitehouse (Combat Core 1985)★★, Death Before Dishonour (Rough Justice 1989)★★, The Massacre (Rough Justice 1991)★★, Beat The Bastards (Rough Justice 1996)★★.
COMPILATIONS: Totally Exploited (Dojo 1984)★★, Live On The Apocalypse Now Tour '81 (Chaos 1985)★★★, Live And Loud!! (Link 1987)★★, Inner City Decay (Snow 1987)★★★, On Stage 91/Live At The Whitehouse 1985 (Dojo 1991)★★, The Singles Collection (Cleopatra 1993)★★★, Dead Cities (Harry May 2000)★★★, Punk Singles And Rarities (Captain Oi! 2001)★★★.
VIDEOS: Live At The Palm Cove (Jettisoundz 1983), 1983-87 (Jettisoundz 1987), Sexual Favours (Jettisoundz 1987), Live In Japan (Jettisoundz 1991), Live In Buenos Aires (Jettisoundz 1993), Rock & Roll Outlaws (Jettisoundz 1995).

EXTREME
ALBUMS: Extreme (A&M 1989)★★★, Pornograffitti (A&M 1990)★★★★, III Sides To Every Story (A&M 1992)★★★, Waiting For The Punchline (A&M 1995)★★.
COMPILATIONS: The Best Of Extreme: An Accidental Collication Of Atoms? (A&M 1997)★★★, The Millennium Collection (A&M 2002)★★★.

EXTREME NOISE TERROR
ALBUMS: split with Chaos UK Radioactive (Manic Ears 1985)★★, A Holocaust In Your Head (Hurt 1987)★★, The Peel Sessions (Strange Fruit 1990)★★★, Phonophobia (Vinyl Japan 1992)★★, Retro-bution (Earache 1995)★★★, Damage 381 (Earache 1997)★★★, Being And Nothing (Candlelight 2001)★★★.
VIDEOS: From One Extreme To The Other (Jettisoundz 1989).

F

FABIAN
ALBUMS: Hold That Tiger (Chancellor 1959)★★, The Fabulous Fabian (Chancellor 1959)★★, The Good Old Summertime (Chancellor 1960)★★, Fabian Facade (Chancellor 1961)★★, Rockin' Hot (Chancellor 1961)★★, Fabian's 16 Fabulous Hits (Chancellor 1962)★★.
COMPILATIONS: The Best Of Fabian (Varèse Sarabande 1996)★★★, Turn Me Loose: Very Best Of Fabian (Collectables 1999)★★★.
FILMS: Hound-Dog Man (1959), North To Alaska aka Go North (1960), High Time (1960), Love In A Goldfish Bowl (1961), Mr. Hobbs Takes A Vacation (1962), Five Weeks In A Balloon (1962), The Longest Day (1962), Ride The Wild Surf (1964), Dear Brigitte (1965), Ten Little Indians (1966), Spie Vengono Dal Semifreddo aka Dr. Goldfoot And The Girl Bombs (1966), Fireball 500 (1966), Thunder Alley aka Hell Drivers (1967), The Wild Racers (1968), Maryjane (1968), The Devil's 8 (1969), A Bullet For Pretty Boy (1970), Little Laura And Big John (1973), The Day The Lord Got Busted aka Soul Hustler (1976), Disco Fever (1978), Kiss Daddy Goodbye aka Caution, Children At Play (1981), Get Crazy aka Flip Out (1983), Up Close & Personal (1996).

FABULOUS THUNDERBIRDS
ALBUMS: The Fabulous Thunderbirds aka Girls Go Wild (Chrysalis 1979)★★★★, What's The Word (Chrysalis 1980)★★★, Butt Rockin' (Chrysalis 1981)★★★, T-Bird Rhythm (Chrysalis 1982)★★★, Tuff Enuff (Columbia 1986)★★★, Hot Number (Columbia 1987)★★★, Powerful Stuff (Columbia 1989)★★★, Walk That Walk, Talk That Talk (Columbia 1991)★★★, Roll Of The Dice (Private Music 1995)★★, High Water (High Street 1997)★★★★, with Al Copley Good Understanding 1992 recording (Bullseye Blues 1998)★★★, Live (Sanctuary 2001)★★★.
COMPILATIONS: Portfolio (Chrysalis 1987)★★★★, Hot Stuff: The Greatest Hits (Columbia 1992)★★★★, Different Tacos (Country Town Music 1998)★★★★.
VIDEOS: Tuff Enuff (Hendring Music Video 1990).

FACES
ALBUMS: First Step (Warners 1970)★★★, Long Player (Warners 1971)★★★★, A Nod's As Good As A Wink ... To A Blind Horse (Warners 1971)★★★, Ooh La La (Warners 1973)★★★, Coast To Coast: Overture And Beginners (Mercury 1974)★★★.
COMPILATIONS: The Best Of The Faces (Riva 1977)★★★, Good Boys ... When They're Asleep: The Best Of The Faces (Warner Archives/Rhino 1999)★★★★.
FURTHER READING: Rock On Wood: The Origin Of A Rock & Roll Face, Terry Rawlings.

FAGEN, DONALD
ALBUMS: The Nightfly (Warners 1982)★★★★, Kamakiriad (Reprise 1993)★★★★.
VIDEOS: Concepts For Jazz/Rock Piano (Homespun Video 1996).

FAIRGROUND ATTRACTION
ALBUMS: The First Of A Million Kisses (RCA 1988)★★★.
COMPILATIONS: Ay Fond Kiss (RCA 1990)★★★.

FAIRPORT CONVENTION
ALBUMS: Fairport Convention (Polydor 1968)★★★, What We Did On Our Holidays (Island 1969)★★★★★, Unhalfbricking (Island 1969)★★★★, Liege And Lief (Island 1969)★★★★, Full House (Island 1970)★★★★, Angel Delight (Island 1971)★★★, Babbacombe Lee (Island 1971)★★★, Rosie (Island 1973)★★★, Nine (Island 1973)★★, Live Convention (A Moveable Feast) (Island 1974)★★, Rising For The Moon (Island 1975)★★, as Fairport Gottle O'Geer (Island 1976)H, Live At The LA Troubadour (Island 1977)★★, A Bonny Bunch Of Roses (Vertigo 1977)★★, Tipplers Tales (Vertigo 1978)★★, Farewell, Farewell (Simons 1979)★★★, Moat On The Ledge: Live At Broughton Castle (Woodworm 1981)★★★, Gladys' Leap (Woodworm 1985)★★★, Expletive Delighted (Woodworm 1986)★★★, House Full (Hannibal 1986)★★, In Real Time – Live '87 (Island 1987)★★, Red And Gold (New Routes 1989)★★, Five Seasons (New Routes 1991)★★, 25th Anniversary Concert (Wormwood 1994)★★★, Jewel In The Crown (Woodworm 1995)★★★★, Old New Borrowed Blue (Woodworm 1996)★★★, Who Knows Where The Time Goes? (Woodworm 1997)★★★, The Cropredy Box 3-CD box set (Woodworm 1998)★★★★, Close To The Wind (Mooncrest 1998)★★★, The Wood & The Wire (Woodworm 2000)★★★★, XXXV (Woodworm/Compass 2002)★★★.
COMPILATIONS: History Of Fairport Convention (Island 1972)★★★★, Heyday: The BBC Radio Sessions 1968-9 (Hannibal 1986)★★★, The Best Of Fairport Convention (Island 1988)★★★★, The Woodworm Years (Woodworm 1992)★★★, Fiddlestix: The Best Of Fairport 1972-1984 (Raven 1998)★★★, Rhythm Of The Time (Delta 1999)★★★, Meet On The Ledge: The Classic Years (1967-1975) (Island 2000)★★★★, Wishfulness Waltz (Mooncrest 2000)★★★★, The Other Boot/The Third Leg 3-CD set (Woodworm 2001)★★★, Heyday: The BBC Sessions 1968-1969/Expanded (Island 2002)★★★.
VIDEOS: Reunion Festival Broughton Castle 1981 (Videotech 1982), Cropredy 39 August 1980 (Videotech 1982), A Weekend In The Country (Videotech 1983), Cropredy Capers (Intech Video 1986), In Real Time (Island Visual Arts 1987), It All Comes Round Again (Island Visual Arts 1987), Live At Maidstone 1970 (Musikfolk 1991), Beyond The Ledge (Beckmann Visual Publishing 1999).
FURTHER READING: Meet On The Ledge: A History Of Fairport Convention, Patrick Humphries. The Woodworm Era: The Story Of Today's Fairport Convention, Fred Redwood and Martin Woodward. Richard Thompson: Strange Affair, Patrick Humphries. Fairportfolio, Kingsley Abbott. The Fairport Tour, David Hughes. No More Sad Refrains: The Life And Times Of Sandy Denny, Clinton Heylin.

FAITH NO MORE
ALBUMS: Faith No More (Mordam 1984)★★, Introduce Yourself (Slash 1987)★★★★, The Real Thing (Slash/Reprise 1989)★★★★, Live At The Brixton Academy (Slash/London 1991)★★★, Angel Dust (Slash/Reprise 1992)★★, King For A Day ... Fool For A Lifetime (Slash/Reprise 1995)★★★, Album Of The Year (Slash/Reprise 1997)★★.
COMPILATIONS: Who Cares A Lot? (Slash/Reprise 1998)★★★.
VIDEOS: Live At Brixton (London 1990), Who Cares A Lot?: The Greatest Videos (London 1998).
FURTHER READING: Faith No More: The Real Story, Steffan Chirazi.

FAITH, ADAM
ALBUMS: Adam (Parlophone 1960)★★★, Beat Girl film soundtrack (Columbia 1961)★★★, Adam Faith (Parlophone 1962)★★★, From Adam With Love (Parlophone 1963)★★★, For You (Parlophone 1963)★★★, On The Move (Parlophone 1964)★★★, Faith Alive (Parlophone 1965)★★, I Survive (Warners 1974)★★, Midnight Postcards (PolyGram 1993)★★.
COMPILATIONS: Best Of Adam Faith (Starline 1974)★★★, The Two Best Sides Of Adam Faith (EMI 1978)★★★, 20 Golden Greats (Warwick 1981)★★★, Not Just A Memory (See For Miles 1983)★★★★, The Best Of Adam Faith (MFP 1985)★★★★, The Adam Faith Singles Collection: His Greatest Hits (EMI 1990)★★★, The EP Collection (See For Miles 1991)★★★★, The Best Of The EMI Years (EMI 1994)★★★★, The Very Best Of Adam Faith (EMI Gold 1997)★★★★.
FURTHER READING: Adam, His Fabulous Year, Adam Faith. Poor Me, Adam Faith. Acts Of Faith, Adam Faith.
FILMS: Beat Girl aka Wild For Kicks (1960), Never Let Go (1960), What A Whopper! (1961), What A Carve Up! aka No Place Like Homicide (1962), Mix Me A Person (1962), Stardust (1974), Yesterday's Hero (1979), Foxes (1980), McVicar (1980).

FAITHFULL, MARIANNE
ALBUMS: Come My Way (Decca 1965)★★★, Marianne Faithfull (Decca 1965)★★★★, Go Away From My World (Decca 1965)★★★, Faithfull Forever (Decca 1966), North Country Maid (Decca 1966)★★, Loveinamist (Decca 1967)★★, Dreamin' My Dreams (Nems 1976)★★, Faithless (Immediate 1977)★★, Broken English (Island 1979)★★★★, Dangerous Acquaintances (Island 1981)★★★, A Child's Adventure (Island 1983)★★★, Strange Weather (Island 1987)★★★, Blazing Away (Island 1990)★★★, A Secret Life (Island 1995)★★, 20th Century Blues (RCA 1996)★★, The Seven Deadly Sins (RCA 1998)★★★, Vagabond Ways (It Records 1999)★★★★, Kissin' Time (Hut 2002)★★★.
COMPILATIONS: The World Of Marianne Faithfull (Decca 1969)★★★★, Marianne Faithfull's Greatest Hits (Abkco 1969)★★★, As Tears Go By (Decca 1981)★★★★, Summer Nights (Rock Echoes 1984)★★★, Rich Kid Blues (Castle 1985)★★★, The Very Best Of Marianne Faithfull (London 1987)★★★, Faithfull: A Collection Of Her Best Recordings (Island 1994)★★★, A Perfect Stranger: The Island Anthology (Island 1998)★★★★, A Stranger On Earth: An Introduction To Marianne Faithfull (Decca 2001)★★★★.
FURTHER READING: Marianne Faithfull: As Tears Go By, Mark Hodkinson. Faithfull, Marianne Faithfull and David Dalton.
FILMS: Made In U.S.A. (1966), Don't Look Back (1967), I'll Never Forget What's'isname (1967), Girl On A Motorcycle (1968), Hamlet (1969), Lucifer Rising (1973), Ghost Story (1974), Assault On Agathon (1975), The Turn Of The Screw (1992), When Pigs Fly (1993), Shopping (1994), Moondance (1995), The Rolling Stones Rock And Roll Circus (1996), Crimetime (1996), Intimacy (2000), Far From China (2001).

FAITHLESS
ALBUMS: Reverence (Cheeky 1996)★★★★, Sunday 8pm (Cheeky 1998)★★★★, Saturday 3am remix album (Cheeky 1999)★★★, Outrospective (Cheeky 2001)★★★.
COMPILATIONS: Back To Mine (DMC 2000)★★★.

FALL
ALBUMS: Live At The Witch Trials (Step Forward 1979)★★★★, Dragnet (Step Forward 1979)★★★★, Totale's Turns (It's Now Or Never) (Live) (Rough Trade 1980)★★, Grotesque (After The Gramme) (Rough Trade 1980)★★★, Slates mini-album (Rough Trade 1981)★★★, Hex Enduction Hour (Kamera 1982)★★★★, Room To Live (Kamera 1982)★★★, Perverted By Language (Rough Trade 1983)★★★, The Wonderful And Frightening World Of ... (Beggars Banquet 1984)★★★★, This Nation's Saving Grace (Beggars Banquet 1985)★★★★, Bend Sinister (Beggars Banquet 1986)★★★★, The Frenz Experiment (Beggars Banquet 1988)★★★★, I Am Kurious Oranj (Beggars Banquet 1988)★★★, Seminal Live (Beggars Banquet 1989)★★★, Extricate (Cog Sinister/Fontana 1990)★★★, Shiftwork (Cog Sinister/Fontana 1991)★★★★, Code: Selfish (Cog Sinister/Fontana 1992)★★★, The Infotainment Scan (Cog Sinister/Permanent 1993)★★★, BBC Live In Concert 1987 recording (Windsong 1993)★★★, Middle Class Revolt (Permanent 1994)★★★★, Cerebral Caustic (Permanent 1995)★★★★, The Twenty-Seven Points (Permanent 1996)★★★, The Light User Synrome (Jet 1996)★★★, In The City (Artful 1997)★★★, Levitate (Artful 1997)★★★, Live To Air In Melbourne '82 (Cog Sinister 1998)★★★★, The Marshall Suite (Artful 1999)★★★★, The Unutterable (Eagle 2000)★★★★, Liverpool 78 (Cog Sinister 2001)H, Are You Are Missing Winner (Cog Sinister 2001)★★★.
SOLO: Mark E. Smith The Post Nearly Man (Artful 1998)★★.
COMPILATIONS: 77 – Early Years – 79 (Step Forward 1981)★★★, Live At Acklam Hall, London, 1980 cassette only (Chaos 1982)★★★, Hip Priests And Kamerads (Situaton 2 1985)★★★, In Palace Of Swords Reversed (80-83) (Cog Sinister 1987)★★★★, 458489 A Sides (Beggars Banquet 1990)★★★★, 458489-B Sides (Beggars Banquet 1990)★★★, The Collection (Castle 1993)★★★, Sinister Waltz archive recordings (Receiver 1996)★★, Fiend With A Violin archive recordings (Receiver 1996)★★★, Oswald Defence Lawyer archive recordings (Receiver 1996)★★, Oxymoron (Receiver 1997)★★, The More You Look The Less You Find (Trojan 1998)★★, Slates/A Part Of America Therein, 1981 (Castle 1998)★★★, Smile ... It's The Best Of The Fall (Castle 1998)★★★, Northern Attitude: An Alternative Selection (Music Club 1998)★★, The Peel Sessions (Strange Fruit 1999)★★★, A Past Gone Mad: The Best Of The Fall 1990-2000 (Artful 2000)★★★★, Psykick Dance Hall: Classic Archive Recordings From The Fall 1977 - 1982 3-CD set (Eagle 2000)★★★, A World Bewitched: Best Of 1990-2000 (Artful 2001)★★★★.
VIDEOS: VHS8489 (Beggars Banquet 1991), Perverted By Language Bis (IKON 1992).
FURTHER READING: Paintwork: A Portrait Of The Fall, Brian Edge.

FAME, GEORGIE
ALBUMS: Rhythm And Blues At The Flamingo (Columbia 1964)★★★★, Fame At Last (Columbia 1964)★★★★, Sweet Things (Columbia 1966)★★★, Sound Venture (Columbia 1966)★★★★, Two Faces Of Fame (CBS 1967)★★★, The Third Face Of Fame (CBS 1968)★★★, Seventh Son (CBS 1969)★★, Georgie Does His Thing With Strings (CBS 1970)★★, Goin' Home (CBS 1971)★★, with Alan Price Fame And Price, Price And Fame Together (CBS 1971)★★★, All Me Own Work (Reprise 1972)★★, Georgie Fame (Island 1974)★★, Right Now! (Pye 1979)★★★, That's What Friends Are For (Pye 1979)★★★, Closing The Gap (Piccadilly 1980)★★, with Annie Ross In Hoagland '81 (Bald Eagle 1981)★★★★, No Worries (4 Leaf Clover 1988)★★, Cool Cat Blues (Go Jazz 1991)★★★★, The Blues And Me (Go Jazz 1994)★★★, with Van Morrison How Long Has This Been Going On (Verve 1995)★★★★, with Morrison, Ben Sidran, Mose Allison Tell Me Something: The Songs Of Mose Allison (Verve 1996)★★, Name Droppin': Live At Ronnie Scott's (Go Jazz 1999)★★★, Poet In New York (Go Jazz 2000)★★★, Walking Wounded: Live At Ronnie Scott's (Go Jazz 2000)★★★★, Relationships (Three Line Whip 2001)★★★★.
COMPILATIONS: Hall Of Fame (Columbia 1967)★★★★, Georgie Fame (Starline 1969)★★★★, Fame Again (Starline 1972)★★★★, 20 Beat Classics (Polydor 1982)★★★★, The First 30 Years (Connoisseur 1989)★★★, The Very Best Of Georgie Fame And The Blue Flames (Spectrum 1998)★★★★, Funny How Time Slips Away (Castle 2001)★★★.

FAMILY
ALBUMS: Music In A Doll's House (Reprise 1968)★★★★, Family Entertainment (Reprise 1969)★★★★, A Song For Me (Reprise 1970)★★★, Anyway (Reprise 1970)★★★, Fearless (Reprise 1971)★★★★, Bandstand (Reprise 1972)★★★★, It's Only A Movie (Reprise 1973)★★, Peel Sessions mini-album (Strange Fruit 1988)★★, In Concert (Windsong 1991)★★★★.
COMPILATIONS: Old Songs New Songs (Reprise 1971)★★★★, Best Of Family (Reprise 1974)★★★, Singles A's and B's (See For Miles 1991)★★★★, A Family Selection: The Best Of Family (Essential 2000)★★★★.

FANNY
ALBUMS: Fanny (Reprise 1970)★★★, Charity Ball (Reprise 1971)★★★, Fanny Hill (Reprise 1972)★★★, Mother's Pride (Reprise 1973)★★, Rock 'N' Roll Survivors (Casablanca 1974)★★.
SOLO: Nickey Barclay Diamond In A Junkyard (Ariola 1976)★★.

FARLOWE, CHRIS
ALBUMS: Chris Farlowe & The Thunderbirds aka Stormy Monday (Columbia 1966)★★★, 14 Things To Think About (Immediate 1966)★★★, The Art Of Chris Farlowe (Immediate 1966)★★★, The Last Goodbye (Immediate 1969)★★, as Chris Farlowe And The Hill From Here To Mama Rosa (Polydor 1970)★★, Live! (Polydor 1975)★★★, Out Of The Blue (Brand New 1985)★★★, Born Again (Brand New 1986)★★★, Farlowe aka Waiting In The Wings (Barsa/Line 1991)★★★, with Roy Herrington Live In Berlin (Backyard 1991)★★★, Lonesome Road (Indigo 1995)★★★, As Time Goes By (KEG 1995)★★, BBC In Concert 1969, 1976 recordings (Windsong 1996)★★★, The Voice (Citadel 1998)★★★, Glory Bound (Out Of Time 2001)★★★.
COMPILATIONS: The Best Of Chris Farlowe Volume 1 (Immediate 1967)★★★, Out Of Time (Immediate 1975)★★★★, Out Of Time – Paint It Black (Charly 1978)★★★, Greatest Hits (Immediate 1978)★★★★, Mr. Soulful (Castle 1986)★★★, Buzz With The Fuzz (Decal 1987)★★★, I'm The Greatest (See For Miles 1996)★★★★, Hits (Repertoire 1999)★★★, Dig The Buzz: First Recordings '62-'65 (RPM 2001)★★★.

FARM
ALBUMS: Spartacus (Produce 1991)★★★★, Love See No Colour (End Product 1992)★★, Hullabaloo (Sire 1994)★★★.
COMPILATIONS: The Best Of The Farm (Castle 1998)★★★, The Very Best Of The Farm (Music Club 2001)★★★.
VIDEOS: Groovy Times (Produce 1991).

FARRELL, PERRY
ALBUMS: Song Yet To Be Sung (Virgin 2001)★★★.
COMPILATIONS: Rev (WEA 1999)★★★.
FURTHER READING: Perry Farrell: The Saga Of A Hypester, Dave Thompson.
FILMS: The Doom Generation (1995).

FATBOY SLIM
ALBUMS: Better Living Through Chemistry (Skint/Astralwerks 1996)★★★, You've Come A Long Way, Baby (Skint/Astralwerks 1998)★★★★, Halfway Between The Gutter And The Stars (Skint/Astralwerks 2000)★★★.
COMPILATIONS: On The Floor At The Boutique Mixed By Fatboy Slim (Skint Brassic/Astralwerks 1998)★★★, shared with Pete Tong, Paul Oakenfold Essential Millennium (ffrr 1999)★★★★, The Fatboy Slim/Norman Cook Collection US only (Hip-O 2000)★★★★, Live On Brighton Beach (Southern Fried 2002)★★★.

FATIMA MANSIONS
ALBUMS: Against Nature mini-album (Kitchenware 1989)★★★, Viva Dead Ponies (Kitchenware 1990)★★★★, Bertie's Brochures mini-album (Radioactive/Kitchenware 1991)★★★, Valhalla Avenue (Radioactive/Kitchenware 1992)★★★★, Lost In The Former West (Radioactive 1994)★★★.
COMPILATIONS: Come Back My Children (Kitchenware 1992)★★★, Tíma Mansió Dumps The Dead (Radioactive 1992)★★★.
VIDEOS: Y'Knaa (1994).

FAUST
ALBUMS: Faust (Polydor 1972)★★★, So Far (Polydor 1972)★★★, The Faust Tapes (Virgin 1973)★★★, with Tony Conrad Outside The Dream Syndicate (Virgin 1973)★★★, Faust 4 (Virgin 1973)★★★, One (Recommended 1979)★★, Rien (Table Of The Elements 1996)★★, You Know Us (Table Of The Elements 1997)★★, Edinburgh 1997 (Klangbad 1998)★★, Faust Wakes Nosferatu (Klangbad 1998)★★★, Ravvivando (Klangbad 1999)★★★.
COMPILATIONS: Munich And Elsewhere (Recommended 1986)★★★, The Wümme Years 1970-73 5-CD box set (RER 2000)★★★, BBC Sessions (ReR 2001)★★★★.

FEAR FACTORY
ALBUMS: Soul Of A New Machine (Roadrunner 1992)★★★, Fear Is The Mind Killer mini-album (Roadrunner 1993)★★★, Demanufacture (Roadrunner 1995)★★★★, Remanufacture (Cloning Technology) (Roadrunner 1997)★★★, Obsolete (Roadrunner 1998)★★★★, Digimortal (Roadrunner 2001)★★★.
VIDEOS: Digital Connectivity (Roadrunner 2002).

FEEDER
ALBUMS: Swim mini-album (Echo 1996)★★★, Polythene (Echo 1997)★★★★, Yesterday Went Too Soon (Echo 1999)★★★, Echo Park (Echo 2001)★★★.

FELICIANO, JOSÉ
ALBUMS: The Voice And Guitar Of José Feliciano (RCA 1964)★★, A Bag Full Of Soul (RCA 1965)★★★★, Feliciano! (RCA 1968)★★★★, Souled (RCA 1969)★★★, Feliciano 10 To 23 (RCA 1969)★★, Alive Alive-O (RCA 1969)★★, Fireworks (RCA 1970)★★, That The Spirit Needs (RCA 1971)★★, José Feliciano Sings (RCA 1972)★★, Compartments (RCA 1973)★★, And The Feeling's Good (RCA 1974)★★, Just Wanna Rock 'N' Roll (RCA 1975)★★, Sweet Soul Music (RCA 1976)★★★, Jose Feliciano (Motown 1981)★★, Escenas De Amor (Latino 1982)★★, Romance In The Night (Latino 1983)★★, Los Exitos De José Feliciano (Latino 1984)★★, Sings And Plays The Beatles (RCA 1985)★★, Tu Immenso Amor (EMI 1987)★★★, I'm Never Gonna Change (EMI 1989)★★, Steppin' Out (Optimism 1990)★★★, El Americano (PolyGram 1996)★★★.
COMPILATIONS: Encore! (RCA 1971)★★★★, The Best Of José Feliciano (RCA 1985)★★★★, Portrait (Telstar 1985)★★★, And I Love Her (Camden 1996)★★★★.

FERRY, BRYAN
ALBUMS: These Foolish Things (Island 1973)★★★★, Another Time Another Place (Island 1974)★★★, Let's Stick Together (Island 1976)★★★, In Your Mind (Polydor 1977)★★★, The Bride Stripped Bare (Polydor 1978)★★★★, Boys And Girls (EG 1985)★★★, Bête Noire (Virgin 1987)★★, Taxi (Virgin 1993)★★, Mamouna (Virgin 1994)★★, As Time Goes By (Virgin 1999)★★★, Frantic (Virgin 2002)★★★.
COMPILATIONS: The Compact Collection 3-CD box set (Virgin 1992)★★★★, Slave To Love (Virgin 2000)★★★.
VIDEOS: Bryan Ferry And Roxy Music (Virgin Video 1995).
FURTHER READING: The Bryan Ferry Story, Rex Balfour. Bryan Ferry & Roxy Music, Barry Lazell and Dafydd Rees.

FIELDS OF THE NEPHILIM
ALBUMS: Dawnrazor (Situation 2 1987)★★, The Nephilim (Situation 2 1988)★★★, Elizium (Beggars Banquet 1990)★★, Earth Inferno (Beggars Banquet 1991)★★, BBC Radio 1 In Concert (Windsong 1992)★★, Revelations (Beggars Banquet 1993)★★.
COMPILATIONS: From Gehenna To Here (Jungle 2001)★★.
VIDEOS: Forever Remain (Situation 2 1988), Morphic Fields (Situation 2 1989), Earth Inferno (Beggars Banquet 1991), Visionary Heads (Beggars Banquet 1992), Revelations (Beggars Banquet 1993).

5TH DIMENSION
ALBUMS: Up Up And Away (Soul City 1967)★★★, The Magic Garden (Soul City 1967)★★★, Stoned Soul Picnic (Soul City 1968)★★★, The Age Of Aquarius (Soul City 1969)★★★, Portrait (Bell 1970)★★, Love's Lines, Angles & Rhymes (Bell 1971)★★★, Live! (Bell 1971)★★, Individually & Collectively (Bell 1972)★★, Living Together, Growing Together (Bell 1973)★★, Soul & Inspiration (Bell 1974)★★, Earthbound (ABC 1975)★★, Star Dancing (Motown 1978)★★, High On Sunshine (Motown 1978)★★, In The House (Click 1995)★★.
COMPILATIONS: The Greatest Hits (Soul City 1969)★★★, The July 5th Album (Soul City 1969)★★★, Reflections (Bell 1971)★★★, Greatest Hits On Earth (Bell 1972)★★★, Anthology (Rhino 1986)★★★, The Definitive Collection (Arista 1997)★★★, The Very Best Of 5th Dimension (Camden 1999)★★★★.

FINE YOUNG CANNIBALS
ALBUMS: Fine Young Cannibals (London 1985)★★★, The Raw And The Cooked (London 1989)★★★★, The Raw And The Remix (London 1990)★★★.
COMPILATIONS: The Finest (London 1996)★★★★.
VIDEOS: The Finest (London 1996).
FURTHER READING: The Sweet And The Sour: The Fine Young Cannibals' Story, Brian Edge.

FIREBALLS
ALBUMS: The Fireballs (Top Rank 1960)★★★, Vaquero (Top Rank 1960)★★★, Here Are The Fireballs (Warwick 1961)★★★, Torquay (Dot 1963)★★★, as Jimmy Gilmer And The Fireballs Sugar Shack (Dot 1963)★★★, The Sugar Shackers (Crown 1963)★★★, Sensational (Crown 1963)★★★, as Jimmy Gilmer And The Fireballs Buddy's Buddy (Dot 1964)★★★, as Jimmy Gilmer Lucky 'Leven (Dot 1965)★★, as Jimmy Gilmer Folk Beat (Dot 1965)★★, Campusology (Dot 1966)★★, Firewater (Dot 1968)★★, Bottle Of Wine (Atco 1968)★★★, Come On, React! (Atco 1969)★★.
COMPILATIONS: The Best Of The Fireballs (The Original Norman Petty Masters) (Ace 1992)★★★★, Blue Fire & Rarities (Ace 1993)★★★, The Best Of The Fireballs Vocals (Ace 1994)★★★, The Fireballs/Fireball Country (Calf Creek 1995)★★★, Sugar Shack: The Best Of Jimmy Gilmer And The Fireballs (Varèse Sarabande 1996)★★★, The Tex-Mex Fireball George Tomsco retrospective (Ace 1998)★★★.

FIREHOSE
ALBUMS: Ragin', Full-On (SST 1986)★★★, If'n (SST 1987)★★, fROMOHIO (SST 1989)★★★, Flyin' The Flannel (Columbia 1991)★★★, Live Totem Pole mini-album (Columbia 1992)★★, Mr. Machinery Operator (Columbia 1993)★★.

FISH
ALBUMS: Vigil In A Wilderness Of Mirrors (EMI 1990)★★, Internal Exile (Polydor 1991)★★, Songs From The Mirror (Polydor 1993)★★, Suits (Dick Bros/Renaissance 1994)★★, Sunsets On Empire (Dick Bros 1997)★★★★, Raingods With Zippos (Roadrunner 1999)★★★, Fellini Days (Chocolate Frog 2001)★★★.
COMPILATIONS: Yin (Dick Bros/Renaissance 1995)★★★, Yang (Dick Bros/Renaissance 1995)★★★, Kettle Of Fish '88-'98 (Roadrunner 1998)★★★, The Complete BBC Sessions (Voiceprint 1999)★★★.

FISHBONE
ALBUMS: Fishbone mini-album (Columbia 1985)★★, In Your Face (Columbia 1986)★★, Truth And Soul (Columbia 1988)★★★★, The Reality Of My Surroundings (Columbia 1991)★★★, Give A Monkey A Brain And He'll Swear He's The Centre Of The Universe (Columbia 1993)★★★, Chim Chim's Badass Revenge (Rowdy 1996)★★★, The Psychotic Friends Nuttwerx (Hollywood 2000)★★★.
COMPILATIONS: Singles (Sony Japan 1993)★★★, Fishbone 101 - Nuttasaurusmeg Fossil Fuelin' (Columbia/Legacy 1996)★★★.

FIVE
ALBUMS: Five (RCA/Arista 1998)★★★, Invincible (RCA 1999)★★★, Kingsize (RCA 2001)★★★.
COMPILATIONS: Greatest Hits (RCA 2001)★★★.
VIDEOS: Five Inside (BMG Video 1998).

FIVE STAR
ALBUMS: Luxury Of Life (Tent 1985)★★, Silk And Steel (Tent 1986)★★★, Between The Lines (Tent 1987)★★, Rock The World (Tent 1988)★★, Five Star (Tent 1990)★★.
COMPILATIONS: Greatest Hits (Tent 1989)★★★.

FLACK, ROBERTA
ALBUMS: First Take (Atlantic 1970)★★★★, Chapter Two (Atlantic 1970)★★★, Quiet Fire (Atlantic 1971)★★, Roberta Flack And Donny Hathaway (Atlantic 1972)★★★, Killing Me Softly (Atlantic 1973)★★, Feel Like Making Love (Atlantic 1975)★★, Blue Lights In The Basement (Atlantic 1978)★★, Roberta Flack (Atlantic 1978)★★, Roberta Flack Featuring Donny Hathaway (Atlantic 1980)★★★, with Peabo Bryson Live And More (Atlantic 1980)★★, Bustin' Loose (MCA 1981)★★, I'm The One (Atlantic 1982)★★, with Bryson Born To Love (Capitol 1983)★★★, Oasis (Atlantic 1989)★★, Set The Night To Music (Atlantic 1991)★★, Roberta (Atlantic/East West 1995)★★★.
COMPILATIONS: The Best Of Roberta Flack (Atlantic 1980)★★★, Softly With These Songs: The Best Of Roberta Flack (Atlantic 1993)★★★.
FURTHER READING: Roberta Flack: Sound Of Velvet Melting, Linda Jacobs.
FILMS: The Wiz voice only (1978), Renaldo And Clara (1978).

FLAMIN' GROOVIES
ALBUMS: Sneakers mini-album (Snazz 1968)★★, Supersnazz (Epic 1969)★★★, Flamingo (Kama Sutra 1970)★★★, Teenage Head (Kama Sutra 1971)★★★, Shake Some Action (Sire 1976)★★★★, Flamin' Groovies Now (Sire 1978)★★★, Jumpin' In The Night (Sire 1979)★★★, Slow Death, Live! aka Bucketful Of Brains (Lolita/Voxx 1983)★★★, Live At The Whiskey A Go-Go '79 (Lolita 1985)★★, One Night Stand (ABC 1987)★★, Rock Juice (National 1992)★★★.
COMPILATIONS: Still Shakin' (Buddah 1976)★★, Flamin' Groovies '68 (Eva 1983)★★, Flamin' Groovies '70 (Eva 1983)★★, The Gold Star Tapes (Skydog 1984)★★, Roadhouse (Edsel 1986)★★★, The Rockfield Sessions mini-album (Aim 1989)★★, Groovies' Greatest Grooves (Sire 1989)★★★★, A Collection Of Rare Demos & Live Recordings (Marilyn 1993)★★★, Live At The Festival Of The Sun (Aim 1995)★★, Yesterday's Numbers (Camden 1998)★★★★, Grease (Jungle 1998)★★★.
FURTHER READING: A Flamin' Saga: The Flamin' Groovies Histoire & Discographie Jea-Pierre Poncelet. Bucketfull Of Groovies Jon Storey.

FLAMING LIPS
ALBUMS: The Flaming Lips (Lovely Sorts Of Death 1985)★★★, Hear It Is (Pink Dust 1986)★★★, Oh My Gawd!!! ...The Flaming Lips (Restless 1987)★★★, Telepathic Surgery (Restless 1988)★★, Live cassette only (Lovely Sorts Of Death 1989)★★, In A Priest Driven Ambulance (Restless 1990)★★★, Hit To Death In The Future Head (Warners 1992)★★★, Transmissions From The Satellite Heart (Warners 1993)★★★, Providing Needles For Your Balloons (Warners 1995)★★, Clouds Taste Metallic (Warners 1995)★★★★, Zaireeka 4-CD set (Warners 1998)★★, The Soft Bulletin (Warners 1999)★★★★.
COMPILATIONS: A Collection Of Songs Representing An Enthusiasm For Recording ... By Amateurs ... Or The Accidental Career (Restless 1998)★★★.

FLEETWOOD MAC
ALBUMS: Fleetwood Mac (Columbia/Blue Horizon 1968)★★★★, Mr. Wonderful (Columbia/Blue Horizon 1968)★★★, English Rose (Epic 1969)★★★, Then Play On (Reprise 1969)★★★★, Blues Jam At Chess aka Fleetwood Mac In Chicago (Blue Horizon 1969)★★★, Kiln House (Reprise 1970)★★★★, Future Games (Reprise 1971)★★★, Bare Trees (Reprise 1972)★★, Penguin (Reprise 1973)★★, Mystery To Me (Reprise 1973)★★, Heroes Are Hard To Find (Reprise 1974)★★★, Fleetwood Mac (Reprise 1975)★★★★, Rumours (Warners 1977)★★★★, Tusk (Warners 1979)★★★, Fleetwood Mac Live (Warners 1980)★★, Mirage (Warners 1982)★★★, Live In Boston (Shanghai 1985)★★, London Live '68 (Thunderbolt 1986)★, Tango In The Night (Warners 1988)★★★★, Behind The Mask (Warners 1989)★★★, Live At The Marquee 1967 recording (Sunflower 1992)★, Live 1968 recording (Abracadabra 1995)H, Peter Green's Fleetwood Mac: Live At The BBC (Fleetwood/Castle 1995)★★★★, Time (Warners 1995)★, The Dance (Reprise 1997)★★★, Shrine '69 1969 recording (Rykodisc 1999)★★★.
SOLO: Mick Fleetwood The Visitor (RCA 1981)H, I'm Not Me (RCA 1983)H. Danny Kirwan Second Chapter (DJM 1976)★★, Midnight In San Juan (DJM 1976)★, Hello There Big Boy (DJM 1979)H. Jeremy Spencer Jeremy Spencer (Reprise 1970)★★, Jeremy Spencer And The Children Of God (Columbia 1973)★, Flee (Atlantic 1979)★.
COMPILATIONS: The Pious Bird Of Good Omen (Columbia/Blue Horizon 1969)★★, The Original Fleetwood Mac (Columbia/Blue Horizon 1971)★★, Fleetwood Mac's Greatest Hits (Columbia 1971)★★★★, The Vintage Years (Sire 1975)★★★, Albatross (Columbia 1977)★★★, Man Of The World (Columbia 1978)★★, Best Of (Reprise 1978)★★★, Cerurlean (Shanghai 1985)★★, Greatest Hits: Fleetwood Mac (Columbia 1988)★★★, The Blues Years (Essential 1991)★★★, The Chain CD box set (Warners 1992)★★★, The Early Years (Dojo 1992)★★, Fleetwood Mac Family Album (Connoisseur 1996)★★, The Best Of Fleetwood Mac (Columbia 1996)★★★, The Vaudeville Years Of Fleetwood Mac 1968-1970 Volume 1 (Receiver 1998)★★★, The Complete Blue Horizon Sessions 1967-1969 6-CD box set (Columbia 1999)★★★, Show-Biz Blues 1968-1970 Volume 2 (Receiver 2001)★★.
VIDEOS: Fleetwood Mac (Warners 1981), In Concert - Mirage Tour (Spectrum 1983), Video Biography (Virgin Vision 1988), Tango In The Night (Warner Music Video 1988), Peter Green's Fleetwood Mac: The Early Years 1967-1970 (PNE 1995), The Dance (Warner Video 1997).
FURTHER READING: Fleetwood Mac: The Authorized History, Samuel Graham. Fleetwood Mac: Rumours 'N' Fax, Roy Carr and Steve Clarke. Fleetwood Mac, Steve Clarke. Fleetwood: My Life And Adventures With Fleetwood Mac, Mick Fleetwood with Stephen Davis. The Crazed Story Of Fleetwood Mac, Stephen Davis. Fleetwood Mac: Behind The Masks (updated as Fleetwood Mac: The First 30 Years), Bob Brunning. Peter Green: The Biography (updated as Peter Green: Founder Of Fleetwood Mac), Martin Celmins. Fleetwood Mac: The Complete Recording Sessions 1967-1997, Peter Lewry. Fleetwood Mac Through The Years, Edward Wincentsen.

FLEETWOODS
ALBUMS: Mr. Blue (Dolton 1959)★★★★, The Fleetwoods (Dolton 1960)★★★★, Softly (Dolton 1961)★★★★, Deep In A Dream (Dolton 1961)★★★, The Best Of The Oldies (Dolton 1962)★★★★, Goodnight My Love (Dalton 1963)★★★, The Fleetwoods Sing For Lovers By Night (Dolton 1963)★★★, Before And After (Dolton 1965)★★, Folk Rock (Dolton 1966)★★.
COMPILATIONS: The Fleetwoods' Greatest Hits (Dolton 1962)★★★★, In A Mellow Mood (Sunset 1966)★★★, The Best Of The Fleetwoods (Rhino 1990)★★★★, Come Softly To Me: The Best Of The Fleetwoods (EMI 1993)★★★★.

FLICKERSTICK
ALBUMS: Welcoming Home The Astronauts (226/Epic 2000)★★★.

FLOWERPOT MEN
COMPILATIONS: Let's Go To San Francisco (C5 1988)★★★, A Walk In The Sky (RPM 2001)★★★.

FLOYD, EDDIE
ALBUMS: Knock On Wood (Stax 1967)★★★, I've Never Found A Girl (Stax 1968)★★★, You've Got To Have Eddie (Stax 1969)★★★, California Girl (Stax 1970)★★, Down To Earth (Stax 1971)★★, Baby Lay Your Head Down (Stax 1973)★★, Soul Street (Stax 1974)★★, Experience (Malaco 1977)★★, Flashback (Wilbe 1988)★★.
COMPILATIONS: Rare Stamps (Stax 1968)★★★, Chronicle (Stax 1979)★★★, Knock On Wood: The Best Of Eddie Floyd (Atlantic 1988)★★★★, Rare Stamps (Stax 1993)★★.

FLYING BURRITO BROTHERS
ALBUMS: The Gilded Palace Of Sin (A&M 1969)★★★★★, Burrito Deluxe (A&M 1970)★★★, The Flying Burrito Bros (A&M 1971)★★★, Last Of The Red Hot Burritos (A&M 1972)★★★★, Six Days On The Road: Live In Amsterdam (Bumble 1973)★★★, Flying Again (Columbia 1975)★★, Airborne (Columbia 1976)★★, Flying High (J.B. 1978)★★, Live From Tokyo (Regency 1979)★★, Burrito Country (Brian 1979)★★, as Burrito Brothers Hearts On The Line (Curb 1981)★★, as Burrito Brothers Sunset Sundown (Curb 1982)★★, Cabin Fever (Relix 1985)★★, Encore: Live From Europe (Relix 1986)★★, Skip & Sneeky In Italy Italy only (Moondance 1986)★★, as Burrito Brothers Back To The Sweethearts Of The Rodeo aka The Burrito Bros. Farewell Album (Disky 1987)★★, From Another Time (Sundown 1991)★★, Close Encounters To The West Coast (Relix 1991)★★, Sin City (Relix 1992)★★, Eye Of The Hurricane (Sundown 1993)★★★, California Jukebox (Ether/American Harvest 1997)★★, Sons Of The Golden West (Grateful Dead 1999)★★.
COMPILATIONS: Honky Tonk Heaven (A&M 1972)★★, Close Up The Honky Tonks: The Flying Burrito Bros 1968-1972 (A&M 1974)★★★★, Bluegrass Special (Ariola 1975)★★, Hot Burrito - 2 (A&M 1975)★★, with Gram Parsons Sleepless Nights (A&M 1976)★★★, with Parsons Dim Lights, Thick Smoke And Loud, Loud Music (Edsel 1987)★★★, Farther Along: The Best Of The Flying Burrito Brothers (A&M 1988)★★★★, Hollywood Nights 1979-1982 (Sundown 1990)★★★, Southern Tracks (Voodoo 1993)★★, Relix Records Best Of (Relix 1995)★★★, Out Of The Blue (Edsel 1996)★★★★, The Masters (Eagle 1999)★★★, Hot Burritos! Anthology 1969-1972 (A&M 2000)★★★★.

FOCUS
ALBUMS: In And Out Of Focus (Polydor 1971)★★★, Moving Waves (Blue Horizon 1971)★★★★, Focus III (Polydor 1972)★★★, At The Rainbow (Polydor 1973)★★, Hamburger Concerto (Polydor 1974)★★, Mother Focus (Polydor 1975)★★, Ship Of Memories (Harvest 1977)★★, Focus Con Proby (Harvest 1977)★★★.
COMPILATIONS: Greatest Hits (Fame 1984)★★, Hocus Pocus: The Best Of Focus (EMI 1994)★★★★.

FOETUS
ALBUMS: as You've Got Foetus On Your Breath Deaf (Self Immolation 1981)★★★, as You've Got Foetus On Your Breath Ache (Self Immolation 1982)★★★, as Scraping Foetus Off The Wheel Hole (Self Immolation 1984)★★★, as Scraping Foetus Off The Wheel Nail (Self Immolation/Some Bizzare 1985)★★★, as Foetus Interruptus Thaw (Self Immolation/Some Bizzare 1988)★★★, as Foetus Corruptus Rife (No Label 1989)★★★, as Foetus In Excelsis Corruptus DeLuxe Male recorded 1990 (Big Cat 1993)★★★, Gash (Columbia 1995)★★★, Boil (Cleopatra 1996)★★★, as The Foetus Symphony Orchestra York mini-album (Thirsty Ear 1997)★★★, Flow (Thirsty Ear 2001)★★★, Blow (Noise-O-Lution 2002)★★.
COMPILATIONS: as Foetus Inc Sink (Self Immolation/Wax Trax! 1989)★★★.
VIDEOS: !Male! (Visionary 1994).

FOGELBERG, DAN
ALBUMS: Home Free (Columbia 1972)★★, Souvenirs (Full Moon 1974)★★★, Captured Angel (Full Moon 1975)★★, Netherlands (Full Moon 1977)★★, with Tim Weisberg Twin Sons Of Different Mothers (Full Moon 1978)★★★★, Phoenix (Full Moon 1979)★★★★, The Innocent Age (Full Moon 1981)★★★★, Windows And Walls (Full Moon 1984)★★, High Country Snows (Full Moon 1985)★★★★, Exiles (Full Moon 1987)★★★, The Wild Places (Full Moon 1990)★★, Dan Fogelberg Live - Greetings From The West (Full Moon 1991)★★, River Of Souls (Full Moon 1993)★★★, with Tim Weisberg No Resemblance Whatsoever

(Giant 1995)★★★, The First Christmas Morning (Chicago 1999)★★, Something Old, Something New, Something Borrowed And Some Blues (Chicago 2000)★★★.
COMPILATIONS: Greatest Hits (Full Moon 1982)★★★, Portrait: The Music Of Dan Fogelberg From 1972-1997 4-CD box set (Epic 1997)★★★★, Super Hits (Epic 1998) ★★★, The Very Best Of Dan Fogelberg (Sony 2001)★★★.
VIDEOS: Greetings From The West Live (CBS Video 1991).

FONTANA, WAYNE
ALBUMS: Wayne Fontana And The Mindbenders (Fontana 1965)★★★, The Game Of Love (Fontana 1965)★★★, Eric, Rick Wayne And Bob (Fontana 1966)★★★, Wayne One (Fontana 1966)★★, Wayne Fontana (MGM 1967)★★.
COMPILATIONS: The Best Of Wayne Fontana & The Mindbenders (PolyGram 1994)★★★, The World Of Wayne Fontana & The Mindbenders (Spectrum 1996)★★★.

FOO FIGHTERS
ALBUMS: Foo Fighters (Roswell/Capitol 1995)★★★★, The Colour And The Shape (Roswell/Capitol 1997)★★★★, There Is Nothing Left To Lose (Roswell/RCA 1999)★★★★.

FORBERT, STEVE
ALBUMS: Alive On Arrival (Epic 1979)★★★, Jackrabbit Slim (Epic 1979)★★★, Little Stevie Orbit (Epic 1980)★★, Steve Forbert (Epic 1982)★★, Streets Of This Town (Geffen 1988)★★★, The American In Me (Geffen 1992)★★★, Mission Of The Crossroad Palms (Giant 1995)★★★, Rocking Horse Head (Revolution 1996)★★★, Evergreen Boy (Koch 2000)★★★.

FORD, FRANKIE
ALBUMS: Let's Take A Sea Cruise With Frankie Ford (Ace 1959)★★★, Frankie Ford (Briarmeade 1976)★★, Hot & Lonely (Ace 1995)★★, Christmas (Avanti 1999)★★.
COMPILATIONS: New Orleans Dynamo (Ace 1984)★★★, Ooh-Wee Baby! The Very Best Of Frankie Ford (Westside 1997)★★★, Sea Cruise: The Very Best Of Frankie Ford (Music Club 1998)★★★, Cruisin' With Frankie Ford: The Imperial Sides And London Sessions (Ace 1998)★★★.
FILMS: American Hot Wax (1977).

FOREIGNER
ALBUMS: Foreigner (Atlantic 1977)★★★, Double Vision (Atlantic 1978)★★★, Head Games (Atlantic 1979)★★★, 4 (Atlantic 1981)★★★★, Agent Provocateur (Atlantic 1985) ★★★, Inside Information (Atlantic 1987)★★★, Unusual Heat (Atlantic 1991)★★★, Mr Moonlight (BMG 1994)★★★.
Solo: Mick Jones Mick Jones (Atlantic 1989)★★.
COMPILATIONS: Records (Atlantic 1982)★★★★, The Very Best Of Foreigner (Atlantic 1992)★★★★, The Very Best ... And Beyond (Atlantic 1992)★★★★, Classic Hits Live (Atlantic 1993)★★★, Anthology: Jukebox Heroes (Rhino/Atlantic 2000)★★★★.
FILMS: Footloose (1984).

FORTUNES
ALBUMS: The Fortunes i (Decca 1965)★★★, That Same Old Feeling (World Pacific 1969)★★★, The Fortunes ii (Capitol 1971)★★★, Here Comes That Rainy Day Feeling Again (Capitol 1971)★★★, Storm In A Teacup (Capitol 1972)★★★.
COMPILATIONS: Remembering (Decca 1977)★★★, Best Of The Fortunes (EMI 1983)★★★, Music For The Millions (Decca 1984)★★★, Greatest Hits (BR 1985)★★★, Here It Comes Again (Deram 1996)★★★, The Singles (BR 1999)★★★.

FOUNDATIONS
ALBUMS: From The Foundations (Pye 1967)★★, Rocking The Foundations (Pye 1968)★★, Digging The Foundations (Pye 1969)★★.
COMPILATIONS: Back To The Beat (PRT 1983)★★, The Best Of The Foundations (PRT 1987)★★★, Foundations Greatest Hits (Knight 1990)★★★, Strong Foundations: The Singles And More (Music Club 1997)★★★★, Baby Now That I've Found You (Sequel 1999)★★★.
FILMS: The Cool Ones (1967).

FOUNTAINS OF WAYNE
ALBUMS: Fountains Of Wayne (Scratchie/Atlantic 1997) ★★★★, Utopia Parkway (Atlantic 1999)★★★★.

FOUR FRESHMEN
ALBUMS: Voices In Modern (Capitol 1955)★★★★, Four Freshmen And 5 Trombones (Capitol 1956)★★★★, Freshmen Favorites (Capitol 1956)★★★, 4 Freshmen And 5 Trumpets (Capitol 1957)★★★, Four Freshmen And Five Saxes (Capitol 1957)★★★, Voices In Latin (Capitol 1958) ★★, The Four Freshmen In Person (Capitol 1958)★★★, Voices In Love (Capitol 1958)★★★, Freshmen Favorites Volume 2 (Capitol 1959)★★★, Love Lost (Capitol 1959) ★★, The Four Freshmen And Five Guitars (Capitol 1960) ★★, Voices And Brass (Capitol 1960)★★, Road Show (Capitol 1960)★★★, First Affair (Capitol 1960)★★, Freshmen Year (Capitol 1961)★★, Voices In Fun (Capitol 1961)★★, Stars In Our Eyes (Capitol 1962)★★, Got That Feelin' (Capitol 1963)★★, More With 5 Trombones (Capitol 1964)★★★, Time Slips Away (Capitol 1964)★★★, Still Fresh (Pat's Gold 1999)★★★, Live In The New Millennium (Pat's Gold 2002)★★★.
COMPILATIONS: The Best Of The Four Freshmen (Capitol 1962)★★★★, The EP Collection (See For Miles 2000)★★★★.

4 NON BLONDES
ALBUMS: Bigger, Better, Faster, More! (Interscope 1993)★★★.

FOUR PREPS
ALBUMS: The Four Preps (Capitol 1958)★★★★, The Things We Did Last Summer (Capitol 1958)★★★★, Dancing And Dreaming (Capitol 1959)★★★, Early In The Morning (Capitol 1960)★★, Those Good Old Memories (Capitol 1960)★★★, Four Preps On Campus (Capitol 1961)★★★, Campus Encore (Capitol 1962)★★★, Campus Confidential (Capitol 1963)★★, Songs For A Campus Party (Capitol 1963)★★, How To Succeed In Love! (Capitol 1964)★★.
COMPILATIONS: Best Of The Four Preps (Capitol 1967) ★★★★, Capitol Collectors Series (Capitol 1989)★★★★.

FOUR SEASONS
ALBUMS: Sherry And 11 Others (Vee Jay 1962)★★★★, Ain't That A Shame And 11 Others (Vee Jay 1963)★★★, The 4 Seasons Greetings (Vee Jay 1963)★★★, Big Girls Don't Cry (Vee Jay 1963)★★★, Folk-Nanny (Vee Jay 1963)★★★, Born To Wander (Philips 1964)★★★, Dawn And 11 Other Great Songs (Philips 1964)★★★★, Stay And Other Great Hits (Vee Jay 1964)★★★, Rag Doll (Philips 1964)★★★★, We Love Girls (Vee Jay 1965)★★★, The Four Seasons Entertain You (Philips 1965)★★★, Recorded Live On Stage (Vee Jay 1965)★★, The Four Seasons Sing Big Hits By Bacharach, David And Dylan (Philips 1965)★★, Working My Way Back To You (Philips 1966)★★★, Lookin' Back (Philips 1966)★★★, Christmas Album (Philips 1967) ★★★, Genuine Imitation Life Gazette (Philips 1969)★★★, Edizione D'Oro (Philips 1969)★★★★, Chameleon (Mowest 1972)★★★, Who Loves You (Warners 1976)★★★, Helicon (Warners 1977)★★★, Reunited Live (Sweet Thunder 1981) ★★, Streetfighter (Curb 1985)★★★, Hope/Glory (Curb 1992)★★★.
COMPILATIONS: Golden Hits Of The Four Seasons (Vee Jay 1963)★★★★, More Golden Hits By The Four Seasons (Vee Jay 1964)★★★★, Gold Vault Of Hits (Philips 1965) ★★★★, Second Vault Of Golden Hits (Philips 1967) ★★★★, Seasoned Hits (Fontana 1968)★★★★, The Big Ones (Philips 1971) ★★★★, The Four Seasons Story (Private Stock 1976)★★★★, Greatest Hits (K-Tel 1976) ★★★, The Collection (Telstar 1988) ★★★★, Anthology (Rhino 1988)★★★★, Rarities Volume 1 (Rhino 1990)★★★, Rarities Volume 2 (Rhino 1990)★★★, The Very Best Of Frankie Valli And The Four Seasons (PolyGram 1992) ★★★★, In Season: Frankie Valli And The Four Seasons Anthology (Rhino 2001)★★★★, Off Season: Criminally Ignored Sides From Frankie Valli & The 4 Seasons (Rhino 2001)★★★★, The Definitive Frankie Valli & The Four Seasons (Warners 2001)★★★★.
FILMS: Beach Ball (1965).

FOUR TOPS
ALBUMS: Four Tops (Motown 1965)★★★, Four Tops No. 2 (Motown 1965)★★★★, Four Tops On Top (Motown 1966) ★★★★, Four Tops Live! (Motown 1966)★★★★, Four Tops On Broadway (Motown 1967)★★★, Four Tops Reach Out (Motown 1967)★★★★, Yesterday's Dreams (Motown 1968)★★★, Four Tops Now! (Motown 1969)★★★, Soul Spin (Motown 1969)★★★, Still Waters Run Deep (Motown 1970)★★★, Changing Times (Motown 1970)★★★, with the Supremes The Magnificent Seven (Motown 1970) ★★★★, with the Supremes The Return Of The Magnificent Seven (Motown 1971)★★, with the Supremes Dynamite (Motown 1972)★★★, Nature Planned It (Motown 1972) ★★★, Keeper Of The Castle (Dunhill 1972)★★★, Shaft In Africa film soundtrack (Dunhill 1973)★★, Main Street People (Dunhill 1973)★★, Meeting Of The Minds (Dunhill 1974)★★, Live And In Concert (Dunhill 1974)★★, Night Lights Harmony (ABC 1975)★★, Catfish (ABC 1976)★★, The Show Must Go On (ABC 1977)★★, At The Top (MCA 1978)★★, The Four Tops Tonight! (Casablanca 1981)★★, One More Mountain (Casablanca 1982)★★, Back Where I Belong (Motown 1983)★★, Magic (Motown 1985)★★, Hot Nights (Motown 1986)★★, Indestructible (Arista 1988)★★.
COMPILATIONS: Four Tops Greatest Hits (Motown 1967) ★★★★★, Four Tops Greatest Hits, Volume 2 (Motown 1971)★★★★, Four Tops Story (Motown 1973)★★★★, Four Tops Anthology (Motown 1974)★★★★★, Best Of The Four Tops (K-Tel 1982)★★★, Collection: Four Tops (Castle 1992)★★★, Early Classics (Spectrum 1996)★★★ , The Best Of The ABC Years 1972-77 (Music Club 1998)★★★, The Ultimate Collection (Motown 1998)★★★★, Breaking Through (Motown 1999)★★★, The Best Of The Four Tops: The Millennium Collection (Polydor 1999)★★★★, Fourever 4-CD box set (Hip-O 2001)★★★★.

FOURMOST
ALBUMS: First And Fourmost (Parlophone 1965)★★★.
COMPILATIONS: The Most Of The Fourmost (Parlophone 1982)★★★.
FILMS: Pop Gear (1964), Ferry Cross The Mersey (1964).

FOURPLAY
ALBUMS: Fourplay (Warners 1991)★★★★, Between The Sheets (Warners 1993)★★★, Elixir (Warners 1995)★★★, 4 (Warners 1998)★★, Snowbound (Warners 1999)★★★, Yes, Please! (Warners 2000)★★★.
COMPILATIONS: The Best Of Fourplay (Warners 1997)★★★.

FRAMPTON, PETER
ALBUMS: Wind Of Change (A&M 1972)★★★, Frampton's Camel (A&M 1973)★★★, Somethin's Happening (A&M 1974)★★, Frampton (A&M 1975)★★, Frampton Comes Alive! (A&M 1976)★★★★, I'm In You (A&M 1977)★★, Where I Should Be (A&M 1979)★★, Breaking All The Rules (A&M 1981)★★, The Art Of Control (A&M 1982)★★, Premonition (Atlantic 1986)H, When All The Pieces Fit (Atlantic 1989)★★, Peter Frampton (Relativity 1994)★★★, Acoustics (Relativity 1994)★★★, Frampton Comes Alive II (El Dorado/I.R.S. 1995)★★, Live In Detroit (CMC 2000)★★★.
COMPILATIONS: Peter Frampton's Greatest Hits (A&M 1987)★★★★, Shine On: A Collection (A&M 1992)★★★★, The Very Best Of Peter Frampton (A&M 1998)★★★, Anthology: The History Of Peter Frampton (Universal 2001)★★★★.
VIDEOS: Frampton Comes Alive II (El Dorado/I.R.S. 1995), Live In Detroit (Image Entertainment 2000).
FURTHER READING: Frampton!: An Unauthorized Biography, Susan Katz. Peter Frampton, Marsha Daly. Peter Frampton: A Photo Biography, Irene Adler.
FILMS: Son Of Dracula aka Young Dracula (1974), Sgt. Pepper's Lonely Hearts Club Band (1978), Almost Famous (2000).

FRANCIS, CONNIE
ALBUMS: Who's Sorry Now? (MGM 1958)★★★★, The Exciting Connie Francis (MGM 1959)★★★★, My Thanks To You (MGM 1959)★★★★, Christmas In My Heart (MGM 1959)★★★, Italian Favorites (MGM 1960)★★★, More Italian Favorites (MGM 1960)★★★, Rock 'N' Roll Million Sellers (MGM 1960)★★★, Country And Western Golden Hits (MGM 1960)★★, Spanish And Latin American Favorites (MGM 1960)★★★, Connie Francis At The Copa (MGM 1961)★★, Connie Francis Sings Great Jewish Favorites (MGM 1961)★★, Songs To A Swingin' Band (MGM 1961)★★, Never On Sunday And Other Title Songs From Motion Pictures (MGM 1961)★★★, Folk Song Favorites (MGM 1961)★★★, Do The Twist (MGM 1962) ★★★, Second Hand Love And Other Hits (MGM 1962)★★★, Country Music Connie Style (MGM 1962)★★★, Modern Italian Hits (MGM 1963)★★★, Follow The Boys film soundtrack (MGM 1963)★★★, German Favorites (MGM 1963) ★★, Award Winning Motion Picture Hits (MGM 1963)★★, Great American Waltzes (MGM 1963)★★★, In The Summer Of His Years (MGM 1964)★★★, Looking For Love film soundtrack (MGM 1964)★★, with Hank Williams Jnr. Great Country Favorites (MGM 1964)★★, A New Kind Of Connie (MGM 1964)★★★, Connie Francis Sings For Mama (MGM 1965)★★★, When The Boys Meet The Girls film soundtrack (MGM 1965)★★★, Movie Greats Of The Sixties (MGM 1966)★★★, Live At The Sahara In Las Vegas (MGM 1966) ★★, Love Italian Style (MGM 1967)★★★, Happiness (MGM 1967)★★, My Heart Cries For You (MGM 1967)★★★, Hawaii Connie (MGM 1968)★★, Connie And Clyde (MGM 1968)★★, Connie Sings Bacharach And David (MGM 1968) ★★★, The Wedding Cake (MGM 1969)★★★, Connie Francis Sings Great Country Hits, Volume Two (MGM 1973)★★, Sings The Big Band Hits (MGM 1977)★★, I'm Me Again - Silver Anniversary Album (MGM 1981)★★★, Connie Francis And Peter Kraus, Volumes 1 & 2 (MGM 1984)★★★, Country Store (MGM 1988)★★, Live At Trump's Castle (Click 1996)★★★.
COMPILATIONS: Connie's Greatest Hits (MGM 1960) ★★★★, More Greatest Hits (MGM 1961)★★★★, Mala Femmena And Connie's Big Hits From Italy (MGM 1963) ★★★, The Very Best Of Connie Francis (MGM 1963) ★★★★, The All Time International Hits (MGM 1965) ★★★★, 20 All Time Greats (Polydor 1977)★★★★, Connie Francis In Deutschland 8-LP box set (Bear Family 1988) ★★★★, The Very Best Of Connie Francis (Polydor 1988) ★★★, The Singles Collection (PolyGram 1993)★★★, White Sox, Pink Lipstick ... And Stupid Cupid 5-CD box set (Bear Family 1993)★★★★, Souvenirs 4-CD box set (Polydor/ Chronicles 1996)★★★★, On Guard With Connie Francis (Jazz Band 1996)★★★, Where The Boys Are: Connie Francis In Hollywood (Rhino/Turner 1997)★★★, Kissin' And Twistin': Going Where The Boys Are 5-CD box set (Bear Family 1997)★★★, The Best Of Connie Francis: The Millennium Collection (Polydor 1999)★★★★.
VIDEOS: The Legend Live (Prism Video 1990).
FURTHER READING: Who's Sorry Now?, Connie Francis.
FILMS: Jamboree aka Disc Jockey Jamboree (1957), Where The Boys Are (1960), Follow The Boys (1963), Looking For Love (1964), When The Boys Meet The Girls (1965).

FRANK AND WALTERS
ALBUMS: Trains, Boats And Planes (Go! Discs 1992)★★★, The Grand Parade (Go! Discs 1996)★★, Beauty Becomes More Than Life (Setanta 1999)★★★, Glass (Setanta 2000)★★★.

FRANKIE GOES TO HOLLYWOOD
ALBUMS: Welcome To The Pleasure Dome (ZTT 1984)★★★★, Liverpool (ZTT 1986)★★.
COMPILATIONS: Bang! The Greatest Hits Of Frankie Goes To Hollywood (ZTT 1993)★★★★, Maximum Joy (ZTT 2000)★★★, Twelve Inches (ZTT 2001)★★★.
VIDEOS: Shoot!: The Greatest Hits (ZTT 1993), Hard On (ZTT 2000).
FURTHER READING: Give It Loads: The Story Of Frankie Goes To Hollywood, Bruno Hizer. Frankie Say: The Rise Of Frankie Goes To Hollywood, Danny Jackson. A Bone In My Flute, Holly Johnson.

FRANKLIN, ARETHA
ALBUMS: Aretha (Columbia 1961)★★, The Electrifying Aretha Franklin (Columbia 1962)★★, The Tender, The Moving, The Swinging Aretha Franklin (Columbia 1962)★★, Laughing On The Outside (Columbia 1963)★★, Unforgettable (Columbia 1964)★★, Songs Of Faith (Checker 1964)★★, Runnin' Out Of Fools (Columbia 1964)★★, Yeah!!! (Columbia 1965)★★, Soul Sister (Columbia 1966)★★★, Take It Like You Give It (Columbia 1967)★★★, I Never Loved A Man The Way That I Love You (Atlantic 1967)★★★★★, Aretha Arrives (Atlantic 1967)★★★★, Take A Look early recordings (Columbia 1967) ★★★, Aretha: Lady Soul (Atlantic 1968)★★★★★, Aretha Now (Atlantic 1968)★★★★, Aretha In Paris (Atlantic 1968) ★★, Aretha Franklin: Soul '69 (Atlantic 1969)★★★★, Today I Sing The Blues (Columbia 1969)★★★★, Soft And Beautiful (Columbia 1969)★★★, This Girl's In Love With You (Atlantic 1970)★★★, Spirit In The Dark (Atlantic 1970)★★★, Aretha Live At Fillmore West (Atlantic 1971)★★★★, Young, Gifted And Black (Atlantic 1972)★★★, Amazing Grace (Atlantic 1972)★★★★, Hey Now Hey (The Other Side Of The Sky) (Atlantic 1973)★★, Let Me Into Your Life (Atlantic 1974)★★★★, With Everything I Feel In Me (Atlantic 1974)★★★, You (Atlantic 1975)★★, Sparkle film soundtrack (Atlantic 1976)★★, Sweet Passion (Atlantic 1977)★★, Almighty Fire (Atlantic 1978)★★, La Diva (Atlantic 1979)★★, Aretha (Arista 1980)★★★, Love All The Hurt Away (Arista 1981)★★, Jump To It (Arista 1982) ★★, Get It Right (Arista 1983)★★, Who's Zoomin' Who? (Arista 1985)★★★, Aretha (Arista 1986)★★★, One Lord, One Faith, One Baptism (Arista 1987)★★★, Through The Storm (Arista 1989)★★, What You See Is What You Sweat (Arista 1991)★★, A Rose Is Still A Rose (Arista 1998)★★★, with Mariah Carey, Celine Dion, Gloria Estefan, Shania Twain Divas Live (Epic 1998)★★.
COMPILATIONS: Aretha Franklin's Greatest Hits Columbia recordings 1961-66 (Columbia 1967)★★★, Aretha's Gold (Atlantic 1969)★★★★, Aretha's Greatest Hits (Atlantic 1971)★★★★, In The Beginning / The World Of Aretha Franklin 1960-1967 (Columbia 1972)★★★, The Great Aretha Franklin: The First 12 Sides (Columbia 1973)★★★, Ten Years Of Gold (Atlantic 1976)★★★★, Legendary Queen Of Soul (Columbia 1983)★★★★, Aretha's Jazz (Atlantic 1984)★★★, Aretha Sings The Blues (Columbia 1985)★★★, The Collection (Castle 1986)★★★★, Never Grow Old (Chess 1987)★★★★, 20 Greatest Hits (Warners 1987)★★★★, Aretha Franklin's Greatest Hits 1960-1965 (Columbia 1987)★★★★, Queen Of Soul: The Atlantic Recordings 4-CD box set (Rhino/Atlantic 1992)★★★★★, Aretha's Jazz (Atlantic 1993)★★★, Greatest Hits 1980-1994 (Arista 1994)★★★, Love Songs (Rhino/Atlantic 1997)★★★, This Is Jazz (Columbia Legacy 1998)★★★, Greatest Hits (Global/Warners 1998)★★★★, Amazing Grace: The Complete Recordings (Rhino 1999)★★★★, Aretha's Best (Rhino 2001)★★★★.
VIDEOS: Queen Of Soul (Music Club 1988), Live At Park West (PVE 1995), with Mariah Carey, Celine Dion, Gloria Estefan, Shania Twain Divas Live (Sony Music Video 1998).
FURTHER READING: Aretha Franklin, Mark Bego. Aretha: From These Roots, Aretha Franklin and David Ritz.
FILMS: The Blues Brothers (1980).

FRED, JOHN, AND HIS PLAYBOY BAND
ALBUMS: John Fred And His Playboys (Paula 1965)★★★, 34:40 Of John Fred And His Playboys (Paula 1966)★★★, Agnes English aka Judy In Disguise (Paula 1967)★★★, Permanently Stated (Paula 1968)★★★, Love My Soul (Universal City 1969)★★★.
COMPILATIONS: With Glasses: The Very Best Of John Fred And His Playboy Band (Westside 2001)★★★★.

FREDDIE AND THE DREAMERS
ALBUMS: Freddie And The Dreamers (Columbia 1963) ★★★, You Were Made For Me (Columbia 1964)★★★, Freddie And The Dreamers (Mercury 1965)★★★, Sing-Along Party (Columbia 1965)★★, Do The Freddie (Mercury 1965)★★, Seaside Swingers aka Everyday's A Holiday film soundtrack (Mercury 1965)★★, Frantic Freddie (Mercury 1965)★★, Freddie And The Dreamers In Disneyland (Columbia 1966)H, Fun Lovin' Freddie (Mercury 1966)★★, King Freddie And His Dreaming Knights (Columbia 1967) ★★, Oliver In The Underworld (Starline 1970)★★.
COMPILATIONS: The Best Of Freddie And The Dreamers (EMI 1982)★★★, The Hits Of Freddie And The Dreamers (EMI 1988)★★★, The Best Of Freddie And The Dreamers: The Definitive Collection (EMI 1992)★★★, The Very Best Of Freddie And The Dreamers (MFP 2001)★★★.
FILMS: What A Crazy World (1963), Cuckoo Patrol (1965).

FREE
ALBUMS: Tons Of Sobs (Island 1968)★★★, Free (Island 1969)★★★, Fire And Water (Island 1970)★★★★, Highway (Island 1970)★★★, Free Live (Island 1971)★★, Free At Last (Island 1972)★★, Heartbreaker (Island 1973)★★.
COMPILATIONS: The Free Story (Island 1974)★★★★, Completely Free (Island 1982)★★★, All Right Now (Island 1991)★★★, Molton Gold: The Anthology (Island 1993) ★★★★, Walk In My Shadow: An Introduction To Free (Island 1998)★★★★, Songs Of Yesterday 5-CD box set (Island 2000)★★★.
VIDEOS: Free (Island Visual Arts 1989).
FURTHER READING: Heavy Load: Free, David Clayton and Todd K. Smith.

FREED, ALAN
ALBUMS: The Big Beat 10-inch album (MGM 1956)★★★, Alan Freed's Rock 'N Roll Dance Party, Volume 1 (Coral 1956)★★★, Alan Freed's Rock 'N Roll Dance Party, Volume 2 (Coral 1956)★★★, Go Go Go - Alan Freed's TV Record Hop (Coral 1957)★★★, Rock Around The Block (Coral 1958)★★★, Alan Freed Presents The King's Henchmen (Coral 1958)★★★, The Alan Freed Rock & Roll Show (Brunswick 1959)★★★, Alan Freed's Memory Lane (End 1962)★★.
FURTHER READING: Big Beat Heat: Alan Freed And The Early Years Of Rock 'n' Roll, John A. Jackson.
FILMS: Rock Around The Clock (1956), Don't Knock The Rock (1956), Rock Rock Rock (1956), Mister Rock And Roll (1957), Go Johnny Go (1958).

FRIPP, ROBERT
ALBUMS: as Giles, Giles And Fripp The Cheerful Insanity Of Giles, Giles And Fripp (Deram 1968)★★★, with Brian Eno No Pussyfooting (Island/Antilles 1973)★★★, with Eno Evening Star (Island/Antilles 1975)★★★, Exposure (Polydor 1979)★★★★, God Save The Queen/Under Heavy Manners (EG/Polydor 1980)★★, Robert Fripp/The League Of Gentlemen (Editions EG 1981)★★★, Let The Power Fall (Editions EG 1981)★★★, with Andy Summers I Advance Masked (A&M 1982)★★★★, with Andy Summers Bewitched (A&M 1984)★★★, with The League Of Gentlemen God Save The King (Editions EG 1985)★★★, with Toyah The Lady Or The Tiger (Editions EG 1986)★★★, with The League Of Crafty Guitarists Live! (Editions EG 1986)★★★, Network (Editions 1987)★★★, with The League Of Crafty Guitarists Get Crafty I (Guitar Craft Services 1988)★★★, with The League Of Crafty Guitarists Live II (Guitar Craft Services 1990)★★★, with The League Of Crafty Guitarists Show Of Hands (Editions EG 1991)★★★, with David Sylvian The First Day (Virgin 1993)★★★, as the Robert Fripp String Quintet The Bridge Between (Discipline/DGM 1993)★★★, with David Sylvian Damage (Virgin 1994)★★★, 1999: Soundscapes - Live In Argentina (DGM 1994)★★★, A Blessing Of Tears: 1995 Soundscapes Volume Two - Live In California (DGM 1995)★★★, with The League Of Crafty Guitarists Intergalactic Boogie Express: Live In Europe 1991 (DGM 1995)★★★, Radiophonics: 1995 Soundscapes Volume 1– Live In Argentina (DGM 1996)★★★, with The League Of Gentlemen Thrang Thrang Gozinbulx: Official Bootleg Live In 1980 (DGM 1996)★★★, That Which Passes: 1995 Soundscapes –Live Volume 3 (DGM 1996)★★★, November Suite: Live At Green Park Station (DGM 1997)★★, The Gates Of Paradise (DGM 1997)★★★, with Trey Gunn, Bill Rieflin The Repercussions Of Angelic Behaviour (First World 1999)★★★, with Jeffrey Fayman A Temple In The Clouds (Projekt 2000)★★★.
COMPILATIONS: The Essential Fripp And Eno (Venture 1993)★★★★.
VIDEOS: Live In Japan (Discipline 1994), with David Sylvian Live In Japan (VAP 1995).
FURTHER READING: Robert Fripp: From King Crimson To Guitar Craft, Eric Tamm.

FUGAZI
ALBUMS: Fugazi EP (Dischord 1988)★★★, Margin Walker EP (Dischord 1989)★★★, Repeater (Dischord 1990) ★★★★, Steady Diet Of Nothing (Dischord 1991)★★★, In On The Killtaker (Dischord 1993)★★★, Red Medicine (Dischord 1995)★★★, End Hits (Dischord 1998)★★★, Instrument Soundtrack (Dischord 1999)★★, The Argument (Dischord 2001)★★★.
COMPILATIONS: 13 Songs first two EPs (Dischord 1988)★★★.
VIDEOS: Instrument (Dischord 1999).

FUGEES
ALBUMS: as Fugees Tranzlator Crew Blunted On Reality (Ruffhouse/Columbia 1994)★★, The Score (Ruffhouse/ Columbia 1996)★★★★, Bootleg Versions (Columbia 1996)★★★, The Complete Score (Columbia 2001)★★★★.
VIDEOS: The Score (SMV 1996).
FURTHER READING: Fugees: The Unofficial Book, Chris Roberts.

FUGS
ALBUMS: The Village Fugs aka The Fugs First Album (ESP 1965)★★★★, The Fugs (ESP 1966)★★★★, Virgin Fugs (ESP 1966)★★★★, Tenderness Junction (Reprise 1967)★★★, It Crawled Into My Hand, Honest (Reprise 1968)★★★, The Belle Of Avenue A (Reprise 1969)★★, No More Slavery (New Rose 1986)★★★, Star Peace (New Rose 1987)★★, The Real Woodstock Festival (Fugs 1995)★★.
COMPILATIONS: Golden Filth (Reprise 1969)★★★★, The Fugs 4, Rounders Score (ESP 1975)★★★, Refuse To Be Burnt Out: Live In The 1960s (New Rose 1985)★★, Live From The 60s (Fugs 1994)★★.

FULLER, BOBBY
ALBUMS: KRLA King Of The Wheels (Mustang 1965)★★★, I Fought The Law aka Memorial Album (Mustang 1966) ★★★★, Live Again (Eva 1984)★★.
COMPILATIONS: The Best Of The Bobby Fuller Four (Rhino 1981)★★★★, The Bobby Fuller Tapes, Volume 1 (Voxx 1983)★★★, Bobby Fuller Tapes Volume 2 (Voxx 1984)★★, The Bobby Fuller Instrumental Album (Rockhouse 1985)★★, Never To Be Forgotten 3-CD box set (Mustang 1998)★★★.

FUN BOY THREE
ALBUMS: Fun Boy Three (Chrysalis 1982)★★★, Waiting (Chrysalis 1983)★★★.
COMPILATIONS: Really Saying Something: The Best Of Fun Boy Three (Chrysalis 1997)★★★★.

FUN LOVIN' CRIMINALS
ALBUMS: Come Find Yourself (EMI/Chrysalis 1996)★★★★, 100% Colombian (Virgin/Chrysalis 1998)★★★★, Loco (Chrysalis 2001)★★★.
COMPILATIONS: Mimosa (Chrysalis 1999)★★★.
VIDEOS: Love Ya Back: A Video Collection (Chrysalis 2001).

FUNKADELIC
ALBUMS: Funkadelic (Westbound 1970)★★★, Free Your Mind ... And Your Ass Will Follow (Westbound 1970)★★★, Maggot Brain (Westbound 1971)★★★★, America Eats Its Young (Westbound 1972)★★★★, Cosmic Slop (Westbound 1973)★★★, Standing On The Verge Of Getting It On (Westbound 1974)★★★, Let's Take It To The Stage (Westbound 1975)★★★★, Hardcore Jollies (Warners 1976)★★★, One Nation Under A Groove (Warners 1978)★★★★, Uncle Jam Wants You (Warners 1979)★★★, Connections And Disconnections (LAX 1981)★★, The Electric Spanking Of War Babies (Warners 1981)★★★★, Live: Meadowbrook, Rochester, Michigan 12th September 1971 (Westbound 1996)★★★.
COMPILATIONS: Funkadelic's Greatest Hits (Westbound 1975)★★★, Tales Of Kidd Funkadelic (Westbound 1976) ★★★, The Best Of The Early Years – Volume One (Westbound 1977)★★★★, Music For Your Mother (Westbound 1993) ★★★★, The Best Of Funkadelic 1976-1981 (Charly 1994) ★★★★, Parliament-Funkadelic Live 1976-1993 4-CD box set (Sequel 1994)★★★, Funkadelic's Finest (Westbound 1997) ★★★★, The Complete Recordings 1976-81 (Charly 2000) ★★★, The Original Cosmic Funk Crew (Metro 2000)★★★.

FURTADO, NELLY
ALBUMS: Whoa, Nelly! (DreamWorks 2000)★★★.

FURY, BILLY
ALBUMS: Sound Of Fury 10-inch album (Decca 1960)★★★★, Billy Fury (Ace Of Clubs 1960)★★★, Halfway To Paradise (Ace Of Clubs 1961)★★★, Billy (Decca 1963)★★★, We Want Billy (Decca 1963)★★, I've Got A Horse (Decca 1965)★★★, The One And Only (Polydor 1983)★★★.
COMPILATIONS: The Best Of Billy Fury (Ace Of Clubs 1967)★★★★, The World Of Billy Fury (Decca 1972)★★★★, The Billy Fury Story (Decca 1977)★★★, The World Of Billy Fury, Volume 2 (Decca 1980)★★★, The Missing Years 1967-1980 (Red Bus 1983)★★★, The Billy Fury Hit Parade (Rock Echoes 1983)★★★, The Other Side Of Fury (See For Miles 1984)★★★★, Loving You (Magnum Force 1984)★★★, Stick 'N' Stones (Magnum Force 1985)★★★, The EP Collection (See For Miles 1985)★★★★, The Collection (Castle 1987)★★★, The Best Of Billy Fury (K-Tel 1988)★★★, The Sound Of Fury + 10 (Decca 1988)★★★, Am I Blue? (Decca 1993)★★★, The 40th Anniversary Anthology (Deram 1998)★★★.
FILMS: Play It Cool (1962), I've Gotta Horse (1965), That'll Be The Day (1973).

G

GABRIEL, PETER
ALBUMS: Peter Gabriel (Charisma/Atco 1977)★★★, Peter Gabriel (Charisma/Atlantic 1978)★★★, Peter Gabriel (Charisma/Mercury 1980)★★★★, Peter Gabriel (Security) (Charisma/Geffen 1982)★★★★, Peter Gabriel Plays Live (Charisma/Geffen 1983)★★, Birdy film soundtrack (Charisma/ Geffen 1985)★★, So (Virgin/Geffen 1986)★★★★, Passion: Music For The Last Temptation Of Christ (Virgin/Geffen 1989)★★, Us (Real World/Geffen 1992)★★★, Secret World - Live (Real World 1994)★★★, Ovo (Real World 2000)★★★.
COMPILATIONS: Shaking The Tree: Sixteen Golden Greats (Virgin/Geffen 1990)★★★★.
VIDEOS: Point Of View (Live In Athens) (Virgin Vision 1989), The Desert And Her Daughters (Hendring Music Video 1990), CV (Virgin Vision 1991), All About Us (Real World 1993), Secret World Live (Real World 1994), Computer Animation: Vol. 2. (Real World 1994).
FURTHER READING: Peter Gabriel: An Authorized Biography, Spenser Bright. In His Own Words, Mick St. Michael.

GABRIELLE
ALBUMS: Find Your Way (Go! Beat 1994)★★★, Gabrielle (Go! Beat 1996)★★★, Rise (Go! Beat 1999)★★★★.
COMPILATIONS: Dreams Can Come True: Greatest Hits Vol 1 (Go! Beat 2001)★★★★.

GALLAGHER AND LYLE
ALBUMS: Gallagher And Lyle (A&M 1972)★★, Willie And The Lap Dog (A&M 1973)★★, Seeds (A&M 1973)★★, The Last Cowboy (A&M 1974)★★★, Breakaway (A&M 1976) ★★★, Love On The Airwaves (A&M 1977)★★, Showdown (A&M 1978)★★, Gone Crazy (A&M 1979)★★, Lonesome No More (Mercury 1979)★★, Live In Concert (Strange Fruit 1999)★★.
COMPILATIONS: The Best Of Gallagher And Lyle (A&M 1980)★★★, Heart On My Sleeve (A&M 1991)★★★, The Best Of Gallagher And Lyle (Spectrum 1998)★★★.

GALLAGHER, RORY
ALBUMS: Rory Gallagher (Polydor 1971)★★★, Deuce (Polydor 1971)★★★★, Live! In Europe (Polydor 1972) ★★★, Blueprint (Polydor 1973)★★★★, Tattoo (Polydor 1973)★★★★, Irish Tour 74 (Polydor 1974)★★★★, Saint ... And Sinner (Polydor 1975)★★★, Against The Grain (Chrysalis 1975)★★★★, Calling-Card (Chrysalis 1976) ★★★★, Photo Finish (Chrysalis 1978)★★★, Top Priority (Chrysalis 1978)★★★, Stage Struck (Chrysalis 1980)★★★, Jinx (Chrysalis 1982)★★★, Defender (Demon 1987)★★, Fresh Evidence (Castle 1990)★★, BBC Sessions (RCA 1999)★★★★.
COMPILATIONS: The Best Years (Polydor 1973)★★★, In The Beginning (Emerald 1974)★★★, The Story So Far (Polydor 1976)★★★, Best Of Rory Gallagher And Taste (Razor 1988)★★★★, Edged In Blue (Demon 1992)★★★, A Blue Day For The Blues (I.R.S. 1995)★★★, Let's Go To Work 4-CD box set (Capo/RCA 2001)★★★★.
VIDEOS: Live In Cork (Castle Hendring Video 1989), Messin' With The Kid: Live At The Cork Opera House (BMG 1999).
FURTHER READING: Rory Gallagher, Jean Noel Coghe.

GANG OF FOUR
ALBUMS: Entertainment! (EMI/Warners 1979)★★★★, Solid Gold (EMI/Warners 1981)★★★, Songs Of The Free (EMI/ Warners 1982)★★★, Hard (EMI/Warners 1983)★★, At The Palace (Mercury/Phonogram 1984)★★, Mall (Polydor 1991)★★★, Shrinkwrapped (When! 1995)★★★★.
COMPILATIONS: The Peel Sessions (Strange Fruit 1990)★★★, A Brief History Of The Twentieth Century (EMI/Warners 1990)★★★★, 100 Flowers Bloom (Rhino 1998)★★★★.

GAP BAND
ALBUMS: The Gap Band (Mercury 1977)★★★, The Gap Band II (Mercury 1979)★★★★, The Gap Band III (Mercury 1980) ★★★, The Gap Band IV (Total Experience 1982)★★★★, Gap Band V - Jammin' (Total Experience 1983)★★★, The Gap Band VI (Total Experience 1985)★★★, The Gap Band VII (Total Experience 1986)★★★, The Gap Band VIII (Total Experience 1986)★★, Straight From The Heart (Total Experience 1987)★★, Round Trip (Capitol 1989)★★, Live And Well (Intersound 1996)★★, Y2K: Funkin' 'Till 2000 Comz (Mercury/Eagle 1999)★★, Love At Your Fingatips (Ark 21 2001)★★.
COMPILATIONS: Gap Gold/Best Of The Gap Band (Mercury 1985)★★★★, The 12" Collection (Mercury 1986)★★★, Greatest Hits (Spectrum 1998)★★★, Ultimate Collection (Hip-O 2001)★★★.

GARBAGE
ALBUMS: Garbage (Mushroom 1995)★★★★, Version 2.0 (Mushroom 1998)★★★, Beautifulgarbage (Mushroom 2001)★★★★.
VIDEOS: Garbage Video (Mushroom 1996), Garbage (Geffen Video 1996).

GARCIA, JERRY
ALBUMS: Hooteroll (Douglas 1971)★★, Garcia (Warners 1972)★★★★, with Merl Saunders, John Kahn, Bill Vitt Live At The Keystone (Fantasy 1973)★★★, Garcia (Compliments) (Round 1974)★★★, Reflections (Reflections 1976)★★, Cats Under The Stars (Arista 1978)★★★★, Run For The Roses (Arista 1982)★★★, with Saunders, Kahn, Vitt Keystone Encores, Volume 1 1973 recording (Fantasy 1988)★★, with Saunders, Kahn, Vitt Keystone Encores, Volume 2 1973 recording (Fantasy 1988)★★, as the Jerry Garcia Acoustic Band Almost Acoustic (Grateful Dead 1989)★★★, Jerry Garcia Band (Arista 1991)★★★★, with David Grisman Garcia/Grisman (Acoustic Disc 1991)★★★★, with Grisman Not For Kids Only (Acoustic Disc 1993)★★★, with Grisman Shady Grove (Acoustic 1996)★★★, How Sweet It Is (Grateful Dead Records 1997)★★★, with Grisman So What (Acoustic Disc 1998)★★★, with Grisman, Tony Rice The Pizza Tapes (Acoustic Disc 2000)★★★★.
COMPILATIONS: Shining Star (Arista 2001)★★★.
FURTHER READING: Garcia: A Signpost To A New Space, Charles Reich and Jann Wenner. Grateful Dead: The Music Never Stopped, Blair Jackson. Captain Trips: A Biography Of Jerry Garcia, Sandy Troy. Living With The Dead, Rock Scully with David Dalton. Sweet Chaos: The Grateful Dead's American Adventure, Carol Brightman. Garcia, Editors of Rolling Stone. Dark Star: An Oral Biography Of Jerry Garcia, Robert Greenfield. Garcia: An American Life, Blair Jackson.

GARFUNKEL, ART
ALBUMS: Angel Clare (Columbia 1973)★★★, Breakaway (Columbia 1975)★★★★, Watermark (Columbia 1977) ★★★★, Fate For Breakfast (Columbia 1979)★★★, Scissors Cut (Watermark 1981)★★★★, Lefty (Columbia 1988) ★★★, Up 'Til Now (Columbia 1993)★★, The Very Best Of – Across America (Virgin 1996)★★★, Songs From A Parent To A Child (Wonder 1997)★★.
COMPILATIONS: The Best Of Art Garfunkel (Columbia 1990)★★★.
FILMS: Catch-22 (1970), Carnal Knowledge (1971), Bad Timing (1980), Good To Go aka Short Fuse (1986), Boxing Helena (1993), 54 (1998).

GAYE, MARVIN
ALBUMS: The Soulful Moods Of Marvin Gaye (Tamla 1961) ★★★, That Stubborn Kind Of Fella (Tamla 1963)★★★★, Recorded Live: On Stage (Tamla 1964)★★★, When I'm Alone I Cry (Tamla 1964)★★★, with Mary Wells Together (Motown 1964)★★★, Hello Broadway This Is Marvin (Tamla 1965)★★, How Sweet It Is To Be Loved By You (Tamla 1965)★★★, A Tribute To The Great Nat King Cole (Tamla 1965)★★★, Moods Of Marvin Gaye (Tamla 1966)★★★, with Kim Weston Take Two (Tamla 1966)★★★, with Tammi Terrell United (Tamla 1967)★★★, In The Groove (Tamla 1968)★★★, with Terrell You're All I Need (Tamla 1968) ★★★, with Terrell, Weston, Mary Wells Marvin Gaye And His Girls (Tamla 1969)★★★, with Terrell Easy (Tamla 1969) ★★★, M.P.G. (Tamla 1969)★★★, That's The Way Love Is (Tamla 1970)★★★, What's Going On (Tamla 1971)★★★★★, Trouble Man film soundtrack (Tamla 1972)★★★, Let's Get It On (Tamla 1973)★★★★★, with Diana Ross Diana And Marvin (Motown 1973)★★★, Marvin Gaye Live! (Tamla 1974)★★, I Want You (Tamla 1976)★★★★, Marvin Gaye Live At The London Palladium (Tamla 1977)★★★, Here, My Dear (Tamla 1978)★★★★, In Our Lifetime (Tamla 1981)★★★, Midnight Love (Columbia 1982)★★★★, Romantically Yours (Columbia 1985)★★★, The Last Concert Tour (Giant 1991) ★★, Vulnerable (Motown 1997)★★★, Midnight Love & The Sexual Healing Sessions (Columbia/Legacy 1998)★★★, The Final Concert 1983 recording (Capitol 2000)★★★.
COMPILATIONS: Marvin Gaye's Greatest Hits (Tamla 1964)★★★★, Marvin Gaye's Greatest Hits Vol. 2 (Tamla 1967)★★★, with Tammi Terell Marvin Gaye & Tammi Terrell: Greatest Hits (Tamla 1970)★★★, Super Hits (Tamla 1970)★★★, Anthology (Motown 1974)★★★, Marvin Gaye's Greatest Hit (Tamla 1976)★★★★, Every Great Motown Hit Of Marvin Gaye (Motown 1983)★★★★, Dream Of A Lifetime (Columbia 1985)★★★, Motown Remembers Marvin Gaye (Tamla 1986)★★★, 18 Greatest

Hits (Motown 1988)★★★★, Love Songs (Telstar 1990) ★★★★, The Marvin Gaye Collection 4-CD box set (Tamla/Motown 1990)★★★★★, Seek And You Shall Find: More Of The Best (1963-1981) (Rhino 1993)★★★, Love Starved Heart (Motown 1994)★★★, The Master: 1961-1984 4-CD box set (Motown 1995)★★★★, Early Classics (Spectrum 1996)★★★, The Love Songs (Motown 2000) ★★★★, with Terrell The Complete Duets (Motown 2001)★★★★.
VIDEOS: Behind The Music (Eagle Vision 2002).
FURTHER READING: Divided Soul: The Life Of Marvin Gaye, David Ritz. I Heard It Through The Grapevine: Marvin Gaye, The Biography, Sharon Davis. Trouble Man: The Life And Death Of Marvin Gaye, Steve Turner. What's Going On And The Last Days Of The Motown Sound, Ben Edmunds.

GAYLE, CRYSTAL
ALBUMS: Crystal Gayle (United Artists 1975)★★★, Somebody Loves You (United Artists 1975)★★★, Crystal (United Artists 1976)★★★, We Must Believe In Magic (United Artists 1977)★★★, When I Dream (United Artists 1978)★★★★, I've Cried The Blue Right Out Of My Eyes (MCA 1978)★★★, We Should Be Together (United Artists 1979)★★★, Miss The Mississippi (Columbia 1979)★★★★, A Woman's Heart (Columbia 1980)★★★★, These Days (Columbia 1980)★★★, Hollywood, Tennessee (Columbia 1981)★★★, True Love (Elektra 1982)★★★★, with Tom Waits One From The Heart film soundtrack (Columbia 1982)★★★★, Cage The Songbird (Warners 1983)★★★, Nobody Wants To Be Alone (Warners 1985)★★★, Straight To The Heart (Warners 1986)★★★, A Crystal Christmas (Warners 1986)★★, with Gary Morris What If We Fall In Love (Warners 1987)★★, I Love Country (Columbia 1987) ★★, Nobody's Angel (Warners 1988)★★★, Ain't Gonna Worry (Capitol 1990)★★★, Three Good Reasons (Liberty 1992)★★★★, Someday (Intersound 1995)★★★, Joy And Inspiration aka He Is Beautiful! (Intersound 1997)★★★, Crystal Gayle Sings The Heart & Soul Of Hoagy Carmichael (Intersound 1999)★★★, In My Arms (Madacy 2000)★★★.
COMPILATIONS: Classic Crystal (United Artists 1979)★★★, Favorites (United Artists 1980)★★★, Crystal Gayle's Greatest Hits (Columbia 1983)★★★★, The Best Of Crystal Gayle (Warners 1987)★★★, All-Time Greatest Hits (Curb 1990)★★★, Best Always (Branson 1993)★★★, Super Hits (Sony 1998)★★★.

GAYNOR, GLORIA
ALBUMS: Never Can Say Goodbye (MGM 1975)★★★★, Experience Gloria Gaynor (MGM 1975)★★★, I've Got You (Polydor 1976)★★, Glorious (Polydor 1977)★★, Park Avenue Sound (Polydor 1978)★★★, I Have A Right (Polydor 1979)★★★, Love Tracks (Polydor 1979)★★★, Stories (Polydor 1980)★★, I Kinda Like Me (Polydor 1981) ★★, Gloria Gaynor (Polydor 1983)★★★, I Am Gloria Gaynor (Chrysalis 1984)★★, The Power Of Gloria Gaynor (Stylus 1986)★★, I Will Survive (PolyGram 1990)★★, Just Keep Thinking About You (Logic 2001)★★★.
COMPILATIONS: Greatest Hits (Polydor 1982)★★★★, The Collection (Castle 1992)★★★, I Will Survive: The Anthology (Polydor 1998)★★★, The Best Of Gloria Gaynor (Pegasus 1999)★★★, The Best Of Gloria Gaynor: The Millennium Collection (Polydor 2000)★★★★.
FURTHER READING: I Will Survive, Gloria Gaynor.

GEILS, J., BAND
ALBUMS: J. Geils Band (Atlantic 1971)★★★, The Morning After (Atlantic 1971)★★★, Live - Full House (Atlantic 1972)★★★, Bloodshot (Atlantic 1973)★★, Ladies Invited (Atlantic 1973)★★★, Nightmares ... And Other Tales From The Vinyl Jungle (Atlantic 1974)★★, Hotline (Atlantic 1975)★★★, Live - Blow Your Face Out (Atlantic 1976)★★★, Monkey Island (Atlantic 1977)★★★, Sanctuary (Atlantic 1978)★★★, Love Stinks (EMI 1980)★★★, Freeze Frame (EMI 1981)★★★, Showtime! (EMI 1982)★★★, You're Gettin' Even While I'm Gettin' Old (EMI 1984)★★.
COMPILATIONS: The Best Of The J. Geils Band (Atlantic 1979)★★★, Houseparty: The J. Geils Band Anthology (Rhino 1992)★★★.

GELDOF, BOB
ALBUMS: Deep In The Heart Of Nowhere (Mercury/Atlantic 1986)★★★, The Vegetarians Of Love (Mercury/Atlantic 1990)★★★, The Happy Club (Vertigo 1992)★★, Sex, Age & Death (Eagle 2001)★★★.
COMPILATIONS: Loudmouth: The Best Of The Boomtown Rats And Bob Geldof (Vertigo 1994)★★★, Great Songs Of Indifference: The Best Of Bob Geldof & The Boomtown Rats (Columbia 1997)★★★.
FURTHER READING: Is That It?, Bob Geldof. Bob Geldof, Charlotte Gray.
FILMS: The Wall (1982), Diana & Me (1997), Spice World (1997).

GENE
ALBUMS: Olympian (Costermonger 1995)★★★★, To See The Lights (Costermonger 1996)★★★, Drawn To The Deep End (Polydor 1997)★★★, Revelations (Polydor 1999)★★★, Rising From Sunset (Contra 2000)★★★, Libertine (Contra 2001)★★★.
COMPILATIONS: As Good As It Gets: The Best Of (Polydor 2001)★★★.

GENESIS
ALBUMS: From Genesis To Revelation (Decca 1969)★, Trespass (Charisma 1970)★★, Nursery Cryme (Charisma 1971)★★★, Foxtrot (Charisma 1972)★★★, Genesis Live (Charisma 1973)★★, Selling England By The Pound (Charisma 1973)★★★, The Lamb Lies Down On Broadway (Charisma 1974)★★★★, A Trick Of The Tail (Charisma 1976)★★★, Wind And Wuthering (Charisma 1977)★★★, Seconds Out (Charisma 1977)★★, And Then There Were Three (Charisma 1978)★★★, Duke (Charisma 1980) ★★★★, Abacab (Charisma 1981)★★★, 3 Sides Live (Charisma 1982)★★, Genesis (Charisma 1983)★★★, Invisible Touch (Charisma 1986)★★★, We Can't Dance (Virgin 1991)★★★, The Way We Walk – Volume 1: The Shorts (Virgin 1992)★★, Live The Way We Walk – Volume 2: The Longs (Virgin 1993)★★, Calling All Stations (Virgin 1997)★★.
COMPILATIONS: Archive 1967-75 4-CD box set (Virgin 1998)★★★★, Turn It On Again ... The Hits (Virgin 1999) ★★★★, Archive #2 1976-1992 3-CD box set (Virgin 2000)★★★★.
VIDEOS: Three Sides Live (Virgin 1986), Live: The Mama Tour (Virgin 1986), Visible Touch (Virgin 1987), Genesis 2 (Virgin 1988), Genesis 1 (Virgin 1988), Invisible Touch Tour (Virgin 1989), Genesis: A History 1967-1991 (Virgin 1991), Live: The Way We Walk (Virgin 1993), Songbook (Eagle Vision 2001).
FURTHER READING: Genesis: The Evolution Of A Rock Band, Armando Gallo. Genesis Lyrics, Kim Poor. Genesis: Turn It On Again, Steve Clarke. Genesis: A Biography, Dave Bowler and Brian Dray. Opening The Musical Box, Alan Hewitt. Genesis: Inside & Out, Robin Platts.

GENTLE GIANT
ALBUMS: Gentle Giant (Vertigo 1970)★★★, Acquiring The Taste (Vertigo 1971)★★★, Three Friends (Vertigo 1972) ★★★, Octopus (Vertigo 1973)★★, In A Glass House (WWA 1973)★★, The Power And The Glory (WWA 1974) ★★, Free Hand (Chrysalis 1975)★★★, In'terview (Chrysalis 1976)★★★, The Official 'Live' Gentle Giant (Playing The Fool) (Chrysalis 1977)★★★, The Missing Piece (Chrysalis 1977)★★, Giant For A Day (Chrysalis 1978)★★, Civilian (Chrysalis 1980)★★, Live-Playing The Fool (Essential 1989)★★, Live On The King Biscuit Flower Hour recorded 1975 (King Biscuit Flower Hour 1998)★★★, In A Palesport House 1973 live recording (Glasshouse 2001)★★.
COMPILATIONS: Giant Steps (The First Five Years) (Vertigo 1975)★★★, Pretentious (For The Sake Of It) (Vertigo 1977)★★, Greatest Hits (Vertigo 1981)★★★, In Concert (Windsong 1995)★★, Out Of The Woods: The BBC Sessions (Band Of Joy 1996)★★, Out Of The Fire: The BBC Concerts 1973, 1978 recordings (Hux 1998)★★, Totally Out Of The Woods: The BBC Sessions (Hux 2000)★★.

GERRY AND THE PACEMAKERS
ALBUMS: How Do You Like It (Columbia 1963)★★★★, Don't Let The Sun Catch You Crying US only (Laurie 1964) ★★★, Second Album US only (Laurie 1964)★★★, I'll Be There US only (Laurie 1964)★★★, Ferry Cross The Mersey film soundtrack (Columbia/United Artists 1965)★★★★, Girl On A Swing (Laurie 1966)★★★, 20 Year Anniversary Album (Deb 1982)★★.
SOLO: Gerry Marsden Much Missed Man (Ozit 2001)★.
COMPILATIONS: Gerry And The Pacemakers' Greatest Hits (Laurie 1965)★★★★, The Best Of Gerry And The Pacemakers (Capitol 1977)★★★★, The Very Best Of Gerry And The Pacemakers (MFP 1984)★★★★, Hit Singles Album (EMI 1986)★★★★, The EP Collection (See For Miles 1987)★★★★, The Singles Plus (EMI 1987)★★★★, All The Hits Of Gerry And The Pacemakers (Razor & Tie 1995)★★★★.
VIDEOS: In Concert (Legend 1990).
FURTHER READING: I'll Never Walk Alone, Gerry Marsden with Ray Coleman.
FILMS: Ferry Cross The Mersey (1965).

GIBBONS, STEVE
ALBUMS: Any Road Up (Goldhawk/MCA 1976)★★★, Rollin' On (Polydor/MCA 1977)★★★, Caught In The Act (Polydor/MCA 1977)★★★, Down In The Bunker (Polydor 1978)★★★★, Street Parade (RCA/Polydor 1980)★★★, Saints And Sinners (RCA 1981)★★★, On The Loose (Magnum Force 1986)★★★, Maintaining Radio Silence (Episode 1988)★★★, Ridin' Out The Dark (SPV 1990)★★★, Birmingham To Memphis (Linn 1993)★★★★, Stained Glass (Havic 1996)★★★, Live At The Robin '98 (Reckless 1998) ★★, The Dylan Project (Woodworm 1998)★★★.
COMPILATIONS: The Best Of Steve Gibbons Band: Get Up And Dance (Polydor 1980)★★★.

GILL, VINCE
ALBUMS: with David Grisman, Herb Pedersen, Jim Buchanan, Emory Gordy Here Today (Rounder 1982)★★★, Turn Me Loose mini-album (RCA 1984)★★, The Things That Matter (RCA 1985)★★★, The Way Back Home (RCA 1987) ★★★, When I Call Your Name (MCA 1989)★★★, Pocket Full Of Gold (MCA 1991)★★★, I Still Believe In You (MCA 1992)★★★★, Let There Be Peace On Earth (MCA 1993)★★, When Love Finds You (MCA 1994)★★★★, High Lonesome Sound (MCA 1996)★★★, The Key (MCA 1998)★★★★, with Patrick Williams And His Orchestra Breath Of Heaven: A Christmas Collection (MCA 1998)★★, Let's Make Sure We Kiss Goodbye (MCA 2000)★★.
COMPILATIONS: The Best Of Vince Gill (MCA 1989)★★★, I Never Knew Lonely (RCA 1992)★★★, The Essential Vince Gill (RCA 1995)★★★★, Souvenirs (MCA 1995)★★★★, Super Hits (RCA 1996)★★★, Vintage Gill (RCA 1997)★★★.
VIDEOS: I Still Believe In You (MCA Music Video 1993).
FURTHER READING: For The Music: The Vince Gill Story, Jo Sgammato.

GILLAN, IAN
ALBUMS: with Ian Gillan Band Child In Time (Oyster 1976) ★★★, with Ian Gillan Band Clear Air Turbulence (Island 1977)★★, with Ian Gillan Band Scarabus (Scarabus 1977) ★★, with Ian Gillan Band I.G.B. Live At The Budokan (Island 1978)★★, with Gillan Gillan (Eastworld 1978)★★, with Gillan Mr. Universe (Acrobat 1979)★★, Glory Road (Virgin 1980)★★★★, with Gillan Future Shock (Virgin 1981)★★★, with Gillan Double Trouble (Virgin 1982)★★★, with Gillan Magic (Virgin 1982)★★★, with Gillan Live At The Budokan (Virgin 1983)★★, with Gillan What I Did On My Vacation (Virgin 1986)★★, with Gillan Live At Reading 1980 (Raw Fruit 1990)★★, as Garth Rockett Story Of (Rock Hard 1990)★★★, Naked Thunder (East West 1990)★★★, Toolbox (East West 1991)★★★, with the Javelins Raving ... With The Javelins (RPM 1994)★★, Dreamcatcher (Carambi 1997)★★, with Gillan Dead Of Night: The BBC Tapes Volume 1 1979 (RPM 1998)★★, with Ian Gillan Band Live At The Rainbow 1977 recording (Angel Air 1998)★★, with Gillan Unchain Your Brain: The BBC Tapes Volume 2 1980 (RPM 1998)★★, Live Yubin Chokin Hall, Hiroshima 1977 (Angel Air 2001)H, with Gillan Live Tokyo 23rd October 1978, Shinjuku Koseinenkin Hall (Angel Air 2001)★★.
COMPILATIONS: with Episode Six Put Yourself In My Place (PRT 1987)★★, with Gillan/Glover Accidentally On Purpose (Virgin 1988)★★, Trouble: The Best Of (Virgin 1991)★★★, The Japanese Album (East West 1993)★★★, The Gillan Tapes Volume 2 (Angel Air 1999)★★.
VIDEOS: Gillan Live At The Rainbow 1978 (Spectrum 1988), Ian Gillan Band (Spectrum 1990), Ian Gillan Live (Castle 1992). As Garth Rockett And The Moonshiners Live (Fotodisk 1990).
FURTHER READING: Child In Time: The Life Story Of The Singer From Deep Purple, Ian Gillan with David Cohen.

GIN BLOSSOMS
ALBUMS: Dusted (San Jacinto 1989)★★★, New Miserable Experience (A&M 1992)★★★★, Congratulations I'm Sorry (A&M 1996)★★★.
COMPILATIONS: Outside Looking In: The Best Of The Gin Blossoms (A&M 1999)★★★★.

GINUWINE
ALBUMS: Ginuwine: The Bachelor (550 Music 1997)★★★★, 100% Ginuwine (550 Music 1999)★★★★, The Life (Epic 2001)★★★.

GIRLSCHOOL
ALBUMS: Demolition (Bronze 1980)★★, Hit 'N' Run (Bronze 1981)★★★, Screaming Blue Murder (Bronze 1982)★★★, Play Dirty (Bronze 1983)★★★, Running Wild (Mercury 1985)★★, Nightmare At Maple Cross (GWR 1986)★★, Take A Bite (GWR 1988)★★, Live (Communiqué 1995)★★, Race With The Devil (Live) (Receiver 1998)★★, Live On The King Biscuit Flower Hour recorded 1984 (Strange Fruit 1998)★★.
COMPILATIONS: Race With The Devil (Raw Power 1986)★★★, Cheers You Lot (Razor 1989)★★, Collection (Castle 1991)★★★, From The Vaults (Sequel 1994)★★.
VIDEOS: Play Dirty Live (1984), Bronze Rocks (1985).

GLITTER, GARY
ALBUMS: Glitter (Bell 1972)★★, Touch Me (Bell 1973)★★, Remember Me This Way (Bell 1974)★★★, Always Yours (MFP 1975)★★, GG (Bell 1975)★★, I Love You Love (Hallmark 1977)★★★, Silver Star (Arista 1978)★★, The Leader (GTO 1980)★★, Boys Will Be Boys (Arista 1984)H.
COMPILATIONS: Greatest Hits (Bell 1976)★★★, Gary Glitter's Golden Greats (GTO 1977)★★★, The Leader (GTO 1980)★★, Gary Glitter's Gangshow (Castle 1989) ★★, Rock And Roll: Greatest Hits (Rhino 1990)★★★, Many Happy Returns: The Hits (EMI 1992)★★★, The Glam Years: Part 1 (Repertoire 1995)★★★.
VIDEOS: Gary Glitter's Gangshow (Hendring Video 1989), Gary Glitter Story (Channel 5 1990), Rock'n'Roll's Greatest Show: Gary Glitter Live (PMI 1993).
FURTHER READING: The Gary Glitter Story, George Tremlett. Leader: The Autobiography Of Gary Glitter, Gary Glitter with Lloyd Bradley.
FILMS: Remember Me This Way (1974), Spiceworld (1997).

GO WEST
ALBUMS: Go West (Chrysalis 1985)★★★, Bangs And Crashes (Chrysalis 1985)★★, Dancing On The Couch (Chrysalis 1987)★★, Indian Summer (Chrysalis 1992)★★★.
COMPILATIONS: Aces And Kings: The Best Of Go West (Chrysalis 1993)★★★.
VIDEOS: Aces And Kings: The Best Of The Videos (Chrysalis 1993).

Go-Betweens
ALBUMS: Send Me A Lullaby (Missing Link/Rough Trade 1981)★★, Before Hollywood (Rough Trade 1983)★★★, Spring Hill Fair (Sire 1984)★★★★, Liberty Belle And The Black Diamond Express (Beggars Banquet 1986)★★★★, Tallulah (Beggars Banquet 1987)★★★, 16 Lovers Lane (Beggars Banquet 1988)★★★★, 78 Til 79: The Lost Album (Tag Five 1999)★★, The Friends Of Rachel Worth (Circus/Jet Set 2000)★★★★.
COMPILATIONS: Very Quick On The Eye (Man Made 1982) ★★★, Metals And Shells (PVC 1985)★★★, Go-Betweens 1978-1990 (Beggars Banquet 1990)★★★★, Bellavista Terrace: Best Of The Go-Betweens (Beggars Banquet 1999)★★★★.
VIDEOS: That Way (Visionary 1993).
FURTHER READING: The Go-Betweens, David Nichols.

GO-GO'S
ALBUMS: Beauty And The Beat (I.R.S. 1981)★★★, Vacation (I.R.S. 1982)★★★, Talk Show (I.R.S. 1984)★★, God Bless The Go-Go's (Go-Go's/Beyond 2001)★★★.
COMPILATIONS: Go-Go's Greatest (I.R.S. 1990)★★★, Return To The Valley Of The Go-Go's (I.R.S. 1995)★★★, Go-Go's Collection (A&M 2000)★★★.

GODLEY AND CREME
ALBUMS: Consequences (Mercury 1977)★★, L (Mercury 1978)★★, Freeze Frame (Polydor 1979)★★, Ismism (Polydor 1981)★★★, Birds Of Prey (Polydor 1983)★★, The History Mix Volume 1 (Polydor 1985)★★★★, Goodbye Blue Sky (Polydor 1988)★★.
COMPILATIONS: The Changing Face Of 10cc And Godley And Creme (Polydor 1987)★★★, Images (Polydor 1993)★★★.
VIDEOS: Changing Faces-The Very Best Of 10cc And Godley And Creme (PolyGram Music Video 1988), Cry (PolyGram Music Video 1988), Mondo Video (Virgin 1989).

GOFFIN, GERRY
ALBUMS: It Ain't Exactly Entertainment (Adelphi 1973)★★, Back Room Blood (Adelphi 1996)★★.
COMPILATIONS: The Goffin And King Songbook various artists interpretations of Goffin And King compositions (Columbia 1989)★★★.

GOLD, ANDREW
ALBUMS: Andrew Gold (Asylum 1975)★★★, What's Wrong With This Picture? (Asylum 1976)★★, All This And Heaven Too (Asylum 1978)★★★, Whirlwind (Asylum 1979)★★, Since 1951 (Pony Canyon 1996)★★★, Halloween Howls (Music For Little People 1996)★★, as The Fraternal Order Of The All Greetings From Planet Love (J-Bird/Dome 1997)★★★, The Spence Manor Suite (Dome 2000)★★★.
COMPILATIONS: Thank You For Being A Friend: The Best Of Andrew Gold (Rhino 1997)★★★, Leftovers (Quarkbrain 1998)★★.

GOLDEN EARRING
ALBUMS: Just Ear-rings (Polydor 1965)★★★, Winter Harvest (Polydor/Capitol 1966)★★★, Miracle Mirror (Polydor/Capitol 1968)★★★, On The Double (Polydor 1969)★★★, Eight Miles High (Polydor 1969)★★★, Golden Earring (Wall Of Dolls) (Polydor 1970)★★★, Seven Tears (Polydor 1971)★★★, Together (Polydor 1972)★★★, Moontan (Polydor/MCA 1974)★★★, Switch (Polydor 1975)★★★, To The Hilt (Polydor 1976)★★★, Contraband (Polydor 1976)★★★, Mad Love (Polydor 1977)★★★, Live (Polydor 1977)★★★, Grab It For A Second (Polydor 1978) ★★★, No Promises ... No Debts (Polydor 1979)★★★, Prisoner Of The Night (Polydor 1980)★★★, 2nd Live (Polydor 1981)★★★, Cut (21 1982)★★★, N.E.W.S. (North East West South) (21 1984)★★★, Something Heavy Going Down - Live From The Twilight Zone (21 1984)★★★, The Hole (21 1986)★★★, Keeper Of The Flame (Jaws 1989)★★★, Bloody Buccaneers (Columbia 1991)★★★, The Naked Truth (Columbia 1992)★★★, Face It (Columbia 1994)★★★, Love Sweat (Columbia 1995)★★, Naked II (Arcade 1997)★★★, Paradise In Distress (Arcade 1999) ★★, Last Blast Of The Century (Arcade 2000)★★.
SOLO: George Kooymans Jojo (Polydor 1972)★★, Solo (Ring 1987)★★. Barry Hay Only Parrots, Frogs And Angels (Polydor 1972)★★★, Victory Of Bad Taste (Ring 1987)★★. Rinus Gerritsen and Michel Van Dijk Gerritsen En Van Dijk (Atlantic 1979)★★. Cesar Zuiderwijk as Labyrinth Labyrinth (21 1985)★★.
COMPILATIONS: Hits Van De Golden Earrings (Polydor 1967)★★★, Greatest Hits (Polydor 1968)★★★★, Golden Earring Box 5-LP box set (Polydor 1970)★★★★, Greatest Hits Volume 2 (Polydor 1970)★★★, Superstarshine Vol. 1 (Polydor 1972)★★★, The Best Of Golden Earring (Polydor 1974)★★★, The Best Ten Years: Twenty Hits (Arcade 1975) ★★★, Fabulous Golden Earring (Polydor 1976)★★★, Greatest Hits Volume 3 (Polydor 1981)★★★★, Just Golden Earrings (Polydor 1990)★★★, The Complete Singles Collection 1 1965-1974 (Arcade 1992)★★★★, The Complete Singles Collection 1975-1991 (Arcade 1992)★★★★.
VIDEOS: Golden Earring Clips (Red Bullet 1984), Live From The Twilight Zone (RCA 1984), Golden Earring Video EP (Sony 1984), Twilight Zone (Musicvision 1991), The Naked Truth (Acoustic Live) (Columbia 1991), Making Face It (Sony Music Video 1995), Last Blast Of The Century (Arcade 2000).

GOLDEN PALOMINOS
ALBUMS: The Golden Palominos (OAO/Celluloid 1983) ★★★★, Visions Of Excess (Celluloid 1985)★★★★, Blast Of Silence (Celluloid 1986)★★★, A Dead Horse (Celluloid 1989)★★★, Drunk With Passion (Restless 1991)★★★★, This Is How It Feels (Restless 1993)★★★, Pure (Restless 1995)★★★, Dead Inside (Restless 1996)★★★.
COMPILATIONS: The Best Of The Golden Palominos 1983 - 1989 (Music Club 1997)★★★.

GOLDFRAPP
ALBUMS: Felt Mountain (Mute 2000)★★★★.

GOLDIE
ALBUMS: Goldie Presents Metalheadz: Timeless (London 1995)★★★★, with Rob Playford The Shadow (Moving Shadow 1997)★★★, Saturnz Return (London 1998)★★★, Goldie.co.uk (Trust The DJ 2001)★★★.
COMPILATIONS: Platinum Breakz (Metalheadz/London 1996)★★★★.
VIDEOS: Talkin' Headz: The Metalheadz Documentary (Manga Video 1998).
FILMS: Everybody Loves Sunshine aka B.U.S.T.E.D. (1999), The Ninth Gate (1999), The World Is Not Enough (1999), Snatch (2000), The Price Of Air (2000).

GOLDSBORO, BOBBY
ALBUMS: The Bobby Goldsboro Album (United Artists 1964) ★★★, I Can't Stop Loving You (United Artists 1964)★★, Little Things (United Artists 1965)★★, Broomstick Cowboy (United Artists 1965)★★, It's Too Late (United Artists 1966) ★★, Blue Autumn (United Artists 1966)★★★, The Romantic, Wacky, Soulful, Rockin', Country, Bobby Goldsboro (United Artists 1967)★★★, with Del Reeves Our Way Of Life (United Artists 1967)★★★, Honey (United Artists 1968) ★★★, Word Pictures - Autumn Of My Life (United Artists 1968)★★★, Today (United Artists 1969)★★★, Muddy Mississippi Line (United Artists 1970)★★★, We Gotta Start Lovin' (United Artists 1970) ★★★, Come Back Home (United Artists 1971)★★, California Wine (United Artists 1972)★★★, Brand New Kind Of Love (United Artists 1973)★★, Summer (The First Time) (United Artists 1973)★★★, 10th Anniversary Album (United Artists 1974)★★, Through The Eyes Of A Man (United Artists 1975)★★★, A Butterfly For Bucky (United Artists 1976)★★, Goldsboro (Epic 1977)★★, Bobby Goldsboro (Curb 1980)★★, Round Up Saloon (Curb 1982)★★, Honey (Ariola 1990)★★, Happy Holidays From Bobby Goldsboro (La Rana 1999)★★, The Greatest Hits Collection (La Rana 1999)★★.
COMPILATIONS: Solid Goldsboro: Bobby Goldsboro's Greatest Hits (United Artists 1967)★★★, Hello Summertime (United Artists 1974)★★★, Bobby Goldsboro's Greatest Hits (United Artists 1978)★★★★, Best Of Bobby Goldsboro (MFP 1983)★★★★, The Very Best Of Bobby Goldsboro (C5 1988)★★★★, All Time Greatest Hits (Curb 1990) ★★★, 22 Greatest Hits (Remember 1995)★★★, Honey: The Best Of Bobby Goldsboro (Collectables 1996)★★★, Hello Summertime: The Very Best Of Bobby Goldsboro (EMI 1999)★★★.

GOMEZ
ALBUMS: Bring It On (Hut 1998)★★★, Liquid Skin (Hut 1999)★★★★, In Our Gun (Hut 2002)★★★.
COMPILATIONS: Abandoned Shopping Trolley Hotline (Hut 2000)★★★.

GONG
ALBUMS: Magick Brother, Mystic Sister (BYG 1969)★★, Continental Circus (Philips 1971)★★★, Camembert Electrique (BYG 1971)★★★★, Radio Gnome Invisible Part 1: The Flying Teapot (Virgin 1973)★★★★, Radio Gnome Invisible Part 2: Angel's Egg (Virgin 1973)★★★, You (Virgin 1974)★★★, Shamal (Virgin 1975)★★★, Gazeuse! (UK) Expresso 1 (US) (Virgin 1976)★★, Gong Est Mort - Vive Gong (Tapioca 1977)★★, Expresso 2 (Virgin 1978) ★★, Downwind (Arista 1979)★★, Time Is The Key (Arista 1979)★★, Pierre Moerlen's Gong, Live (Arista 1980)★★, Leave It Open (Arista 1981)★★, Breakthrough (Arc/Eulenspiegel 1986)★★, Second Wind (Line 1988)★★, Floating Anarchy (Decal 1990)★★, Live Au Bataclan 1973 (Mantra 1990)★★★, Live At Sheffield 1974 (Mantra 1990)★★★, 25th Birthday Party (Voiceprint 1995)★★, The Peel Sessions (Strange Fruit 1995) ★★★, Shapeshifter + (Viceroy 1997)★★, You - Remixed (Gliss 1997)★★, Zero To Infinity (Snapper 2000)★★★, From Here To Eternitea (Snapper 2002)★★★.
SOLO: Tim Blake The Tide Of The Century (Blueprint 2000)★★★.
COMPILATIONS: Gong Live Etc. (Virgin 1977)★★, A Wingful Of Eyes (Virgin 1987)★★★, The Mystery And The History Of The Planet G**g (Demi-Monde 1989)★★★, The Best Of Gong (Nectar Masters 1995)★★★, The Best Of Gong (Reactive Masters 1998)★★★, Family Jewels (Gas 1998)★★★.
VIDEOS: Gong Maison (Voiceprint 1993).

GOO GOO DOLLS
ALBUMS: Goo Goo Dolls (Mercenary/Celluloid 1987)★★, Jed (Death/Enigma 1989)★★, Hold Me Up (Metal Blade/Warners 1990)★★★, Superstar Car Wash (Metal Blade/Warners 1993)★★★, A Boy Named Goo (Metal Blade/Warners 1995)★★★★, Dizzy Up The Girl (Warners 1998) ★★★, Gutterflower (Warners 2002)★★★.
COMPILATIONS: What I Learned About Ego, Opinion, Art & Commerce (1987-2000) (Warners 2001)★★★.

GORKY'S ZYGOTIC MYNCI
ALBUMS: Tatay (Ankst 1994)★★★, Patio mini-album (Ankst 1995)★★★, Bwyd Time (Ankst 1995)★★★, Barafundle (Fontana 1997)★★★★, Gorky 5 (Fontana 1998)★★★, Spanish Dance Troupe (Mantra/Beggars Banquet 1999) ★★★★, The Blue Trees mini-album (Mantra/Beggars Banquet 2000)★★★★, How I Long To Feel That Summer In My Heart (Mantra/Beggars Banquet 2001)★★★★.

GRAND FUNK RAILROAD
ALBUMS: On Time (Capitol 1969)★★★, Grand Funk (Capitol 1970)★★★★, Closer To Home (Capitol 1970) ★★★, Live (Capitol 1970)★★, Survival (Capitol 1971)★★, E Pluribus Funk (Capitol 1971)★★★, Phoenix (Capitol 1972)★★★, We're An American Band (Capitol 1973) ★★★, Shinin' On (Capitol 1974)★★, All The Girls In The World Beware!!! (Capitol 1974)★★, Caught In The Act (MCA 1975)★★, Good Singin', Good Playin' (MCA 1976) ★★★, Grand Funk Lives (Full Moon 1981)★★, What's Funk? (Full Moon 1983)★★.
COMPILATIONS: Mark, Don & Mel 1969-71 (Capitol 1972)★★, Grand Funk Hits (Capitol 1976)★★★, The Best Of Grand Funk Railroad (Capitol 1990)★★★, More Of The Best Of Grand Funk Railroad (Capitol 1991)★★, The Collection (Castle 1992)★★★.
FURTHER READING: An American Band: The Story Of Grand Funk Railroad, Billy James.

GRANDADDY
ALBUMS: A Pretty Mess By This One Band mini-album (Will 1995)★★, Under The Western Freeway (Will 1997) ★★★★, The Sophtware Slump (V2 2000)★★★★.
COMPILATIONS: The Broken Down Comforter Collection (Big Cat 1999)★★★.

GRANDMASTER FLASH
ALBUMS: as Grandmaster Flash And The Furious Five The Message (Sugarhill 1982)★★★★, as Grandmaster Flash And The Furious Five Greatest Messages (Sugarhill 1983) ★★★, as Grandmaster Flash And The Furious Five On The Strength (Elektra 1988)★★, They Said It Couldn't Be Done (Elektra 1985)★★, The Source (Elektra 1986)★★, Ba-Dop-Boom-Bang (Elektra 1987)★★★.
COMPILATIONS: as Grandmaster Flash And The Furious Five/Grandmaster Melle Mel Greatest Hits (Sugarhill 1989)★★★★, The Best Of ... (Rhino 1994)★★★★, The Greatest Mixes (Deepbeats 1998)★★★, Adventures On The Wheels Of Steel 3-CD set (Sequel 1999)★★★, The Official Adventures Of Grandmaster Flash (Strut 2002)★★★★.

GRANT LEE BUFFALO
ALBUMS: Fuzzy (Slash 1993)★★★★, Mighty Joe Moon (Slash 1994)★★★★, Copperopolis (Slash 1996)★★★, Jubilee (Slash 1998)★★★.
COMPILATIONS: Storm Hymnal: Gems From The Vault Of Grant Lee Buffalo (London 2001)★★★★.

GRANT, EDDY
ALBUMS: Message Man (Ice 1977)★★★, Walking On Sunshine (Ice 1979)★★★, Love In Exile (Ice 1980)★★★, Can't Get Enough (Ice 1981)★★★, Live At Notting Hill (Ice 1981)★★, Paintings Of The Soul (Ice 1982)★★★, Killer On The Rampage (Ice/RCA 1982)★★★, Can't Get Enough (Ice/RCA 1983)★★★, Going For Broke (Ice/RCA 1984)★★, Born Tuff (Ice 1987)★★, File Under Rock (Parlophone 1988) ★★★, Paintings Of The Soul (Ice 1992)★★★, Hearts And Diamonds (Ice 1999)★★★.
COMPILATIONS: All the Hits: The Killer At His Best (K-Tel 1984)★★, Hits (Starr 1988)★★, Walking On Sunshine (The Best Of Eddy Grant) (Parlophone 1989)★★★, Greatest Hits Collection (Ice/Castle 1999)★★★★, Hits From The Frontline (Music Club 1999)★★★, The Greatest Hits (Ice/East West 2001)★★★★.
VIDEOS: Live In London (PMI 1986), Walking On Sunshine (PMI 1989).

GRATEFUL DEAD
ALBUMS: The Grateful Dead (Warners 1967)★★★, Anthem Of The Sun (Warners 1968)★★★★, Aoxomoxoa (Warners 1969)★★★★, Live/Dead (Warners 1970)★★★★, Workingman's Dead (Warners 1970)★★★★★, Vintage Dead (Sunflower 1970)H, American Beauty (Warners 1970) ★★★★★, Historic Dead (Sunflower 1971)★, Grateful Dead (Warners 1971)★★★★, Europe '72 (Warners 1972)★★★, History Of The Grateful Dead, Vol. 1 (Bear's Choice) (Warners 1973)★★★, Wake Of The Flood (Grateful Dead 1973)★★★★, From The Mars Hotel (Grateful Dead 1974) ★★★★, Blues For Allah (Grateful Dead 1975)★★, Steal Your Face (Grateful Dead 1976)★★, Terrapin Station (Arista 1977)★★★★, Shakedown Street (Arista 1978)★★, Go To Heaven (Arista 1980)★, Reckoning (Arista 1981)★★★, Dead Set (Arista 1981)★★, In The Dark (Arista 1987) ★★★★, Built To Last (Arista 1989)★★, with Bob Dylan Dylan And The Dead (Columbia 1990)H, Without A Net (Arista 1990)★★, One From The Vault (Grateful Dead 1991)★★★, Infrared Roses (Grateful Dead 1991)★★, Two From The Vault (Grateful Dead 1992)★★★, Dick's Picks, Volume One: Tampa, Florida December 19 1973 (Grateful Dead 1993)★★★, Dick's Picks, Volume Two: Columbus, Ohio October 31 1971 (Grateful Dead 1995)★★★, Hundred Year Hall (Arista 1995)★★★★, Dick's Picks, Volume Three: Pembroke Pines, Florida May 22 1977 (Grateful Dead 1995)★★★, Dick's Picks, Volume Four: Fillmore East, New York 13/14 February 1970 (Grateful Dead 1996)★★★★, Dick's Picks, Volume Five: Oakland Auditorium Arena, California December 26 1979 (Grateful Dead 1996)★★★, Dozin' At The Knick (Grateful Dead/Arista 1996)★★★★, Dick's Picks, Volume Six: Hartford Civic Center October 14 1983 (Grateful Dead 1996)★★★★, Dick's Picks, Volume Seven: Alexandra Palace, London, England, September 1974 (Grateful Dead 1997)★★, Dick's Picks, Volume Eight: Harpur College, Binghamton, NY, May 2 1970 (Grateful Dead 1997)★★★, Fallout From The Phil Zone (Grateful Dead/Arista 1997)★★★★★, Dick's Picks, Volume Nine: Madison Square Garden, September 16 1990 (Grateful Dead 1997) ★★★, Fillmore East 2-11-69 (Grateful Dead 1997)★★★★, Dick's Picks, Volume Ten: Winterland Arena, December 29 1977 (Grateful Dead 1998)★★★★, Dick's Picks, Volume Eleven: Stanley Theater, Jersey City, September 27 1972 (Grateful Dead 1998)★★★, Dick's Picks, Volume Twelve: Providence Civic, June 26 1974, Boston Garden June 28 1974 (Grateful Dead 1998)★★★, Trouble Ahead, Trouble Behind: The Dead Live In Concert 1971 (Pinnacle 1999)★★, Dick's Picks, Volume Thirteen: Nassau Coliseum, New York May 6 1981 (Grateful Dead 1999)★★★★, Dick's Picks, Volume Fourteen: Boston Music Hall, 30 November & 2 December 1973 (Grateful Dead 1999)★★★★, Dick's Picks, Volume Fifteen: Englishtown, New Jersey, September 3 1977 (Grateful Dead 1999)★★★, Dick's Picks, Volume Sixteen: Fillmore Auditorium, San Francisco November 8 1969 (Grateful Dead 2000)★★★, Dick's Picks, Volume Seventeen: Boston Garden September 25 1991 (Grateful Dead 2000) ★★★★, View From The Vault Soundtrack 1990 live recording (Grateful Dead 2000)★★★, Dick's Picks, Volume Eighteen: Dane County Coliseum February 3 1978, Uni-Dome, University Of North Iowa February 5 1978 (Grateful Dead 2000)★★★, Ladies And Gentlemen ... Fillmore East: New York City, April 1971 4-CD set (Arista 2000)★★★★, Dick's Picks, Volume Nineteen: Fairgrounds Arene, Oklahoma City, OK October 19 1973 (Grateful Dead 2000)★★★, Dick's Picks, Volume Twenty 1976 Capital Centre, Landover, Maryland 25 september 1976/Onondaga County War Memorial, Syracuse, New York 28 September 1976 (Grateful Dead 2001)★★★, Dick's Picks, Volume Twenty-One: Richmond Coliseum, Richmond, Vancouver, 1 November 1985 (Grateful Dead 2001)★★★, Dick's Picks, Volume Twenty-Two: Kings Beach Bowl, Kings Beach, Lake Tahoe, 23/24 February 1968 (Grateful Dead 2001)★★★★, View From The Vault II Soundtrack 1990/1991 live recordings (Grateful Dead 2001)★★★, Nightfall Of Diamonds (Arista 2001)★★★★, Dick's Picks, Volume Twenty-Three: Baltimore Civic Center September 17 1972 (Grateful Dead 2001)★★★.
COMPILATIONS: The Best Of: Skeletons From The Closet (Warners 1974)★★★★, What A Long Strange Trip It's Been: The Best Of The Grateful Dead (Warners 1977) ★★★★, The Arista Years (Arista 1996)★★★, So Many Roads (1965-1995) 5-CD box set (Grateful Dead/Arista 1999)★★★★, The Golden Road (1965-1973) 12-CD box set (Rhino 2001)★★★★★, Postcards Of The Hanging: Grateful Dead Perform The Songs Of Bob Dylan (Grateful Dead/Arista 2002)★★★.
VIDEOS: Grateful Dead In Concert (RCA Video 1984), So Far (Virgin Vision 1988), The Grateful Dead Movie (Palace Premiere 1990), Infrared Sightings (Trigon 1995), Dead Ahead (Monterey 1995), Backstage Pass: Access All Areas (Pearson 1995), Ticket To New Year's (Monterey Home Video 1996), Tie Died: Rock 'n' Roll's Most Dedicated Fans (BMG Video 1996), Downhill From Here (Monterey 1997), Anthem To Beauty (Rhino Home Video 1998), View From The Vault II (Monterey Home Video 2001).
FURTHER READING: The Dead Book: A Social History Of The Grateful Dead, Hank Harrison. The Grateful Dead, Hank Harrison. Grateful Dead: The Official Book Of The Deadheads, Paul Grushkin, Jonas Grushkin and Cynthia Bassett. History Of The Grateful Dead, William Ruhlmann. Built To Last: Twenty-Five Years Of The Grateful Dead, Jamie Jensen. Drumming At The Edge Of Magic, Mickey Hart. Grateful Dead Family Album, Jerilyn Lee Brandelius. Sunshine Daydreams: Grateful Dead Journal, Herb Greene. Aesthetics Of The Grateful Dead, David Womack. One More Saturday Night: Reflections With The Grateful Dead, Sandy Troy. Drumming At the Edge Of Magic, Mickey Hart and Jay Stevens. Planet Drum, Mickey Hart and Fredric Lieberman. Book Of The Dead: Celebrating 25 Years With The Grateful Dead, Herb Greene. Conversations With The Grateful Dead, David Gans. Story Of The Grateful Dead, Adrian Hall. Dead Base IX: Complete Guide To Grateful Dead Song Lists, Nixon and Scot Dolgushkin. Living With The Dead, Rock Scully with David Dalton. Box Of Rain, Robert Hunter. Dead To The Core: A Grateful Dead Almanack, Eric F. Wybenga. The Music Never Stopped, Blair Jackson. Captain Trips: A Biography Of Jerry Garcia, Sandy Troy. Sweet Chaos: The Grateful Dead's American Adventure, Carol Brightman. Dark Star: An Oral Biography Of Jerry Garcia, Robert Greenfield. What A Long Strange Trip: The Stories Behind Every Grateful Dead Song 1965-1995, Stephen Peters. Garcia: An American Life, Blair Jackson.

GRAY, DAVID
ALBUMS: A Century Ends (Hut 1993)★★★, Flesh (Hut 1994)★★★, Sell, Sell, Sell (EMI/Nettwerk 1996)★★★★, White Ladder (IHT/ATO 1998)★★★★.
COMPILATIONS: Lost Songs 95-98 (IHT/RCA 2000)★★★, The EP's 92-94 (Hut/Caroline 2001)★★★.
VIDEOS: David Gray Live (Warner Music Vision 2000).
FURTHER READING: David Gray: A Biography, Michael Heatley.

GRAY, MACY
ALBUMS: On How Life Is (Epic 1999)★★★★, The ID (Epic 2001)★★★.

GREAT SOCIETY
ALBUMS: Conspicuous Only In Its Absence (Columbia 1968)★★★, How It Was (Columbia 1968)★★.
COMPILATIONS: Live At The Matrix (Sundazed 1989)★★, Born To Be Burned (Sundazed 1996)★★★.
FURTHER READING: The Jefferson Airplane And The San Francisco Sound, Ralph J. Gleeson. Grace Slick - The Biography, Barbara Rowe. Don't You Want Somebody To Love, Darby Slick.

GREEN DAY
ALBUMS: 39/Smooth (Lookout 1990)★★★, Kerplunk! (Lookout 1992)★★★, Dookie (Reprise 1994)★★★★, Insomniac (Reprise 1995)★★, Nimrod (Reprise 1997)★★★, Warning (Reprise 2000)★★★.
COMPILATIONS: 1,039/Smoothed Out Slappy Hours (Lookout 1991)★★, International Superhits (Warners 2001)★★★.
VIDEOS: International Supervideos! (Warner Music Vision 2001).

GREEN ON RED
ALBUMS: Green On Red (Down There 1982)★★★, Gravity Talks (Slash 1983)★★★, Gas Food Lodging (Demon 1985) ★★★, No Free Lunch (Mercury 1985)★★★, The Killer Inside Me (Mercury 1987)★★★★, Here Come The Snakes (Red Rhino 1989)★★★★, Live At The Town And Country Club mini-album (China/Polydor 1989)★★, This Time Around (China 1989)★★★, Scapegoats (China 1991)★★★, Too Much Fun (Off Beat 1992)★★★.
COMPILATIONS: Little Things In Life (Music Club 1991)★★★★, The Best Of Green On Red: Rock 'n' Roll Disease (China 1994)★★★, What Were You Thinking? (Normal 1998)★★★.

GREEN, AL
ALBUMS: Green Is Blues (Hi 1970)★★★, Al Green Gets Next To You (Hi 1971)★★★★, Let's Stay Together (Hi 1972)★★★★, Al Green (Bell 1972)★★★, I'm Still In Love With You (Hi 1972)★★★★, Call Me (Hi 1973)★★★★, Livin' For You (Hi 1973)★★★★, Al Green Explores Your Mind (Hi 1974)★★★★, Al Green Is Love (Hi 1975)★★★, Full Of Fire (Hi 1976)★★★, Have A Good Time (Hi 1976)★★★, The Belle Album (Hi 1977)★★★★, Truth 'N' Time (Hi 1978)★★★★, The Lord Will Make A Way (Myrrh 1980)★★★, Higher Plane (Myrrh 1981)★★★, Tokyo Live (Hi 1981)★★★★, Precious Lord (Myhh 1982)★★, I'll Rise Again (Myrrh 1983)★★★, Trust In God (Myrrh 1984) ★★★, He Is The Light (A&M 1985)★★★, Going Away (A&M 1986)★★★, White Christmas (Hi 1986)★★, Soul Survivor (A&M 1987)★★★, I Get Joy (A&M 1989)★★★, Don't Look Back (RCA 1993)★★★, In Good Hands (MCA 1995)★★★.
COMPILATIONS: Greatest Hits (Hi 1975)★★★★★, Greatest Hits, Volume 2 (Hi 1977)★★★★, The Cream Of Al Green (Hi 1980)★★★★, Spotlight On Al Green (PRT 1981)★★★★, Take Me To The River (Greatest Hits Volume 2) (Hi 1987)★★★★, Hi-Life: The Best Of Al Green (K-Tel 1988)★★★, Love Ritual: Rare & Previously Unreleased

1968-1976 (Hi 1989)★★★★, You Say It! (Hi 1990)★★★, Christmas Cheers nine tracks plus 12 by Ace Cannon (Hi 1991)★★, One In A Million (Word/Epic 1991)★★★★, The Flipside Of Al Green (Hi 1993)★★★, Hi And Mighty: The Story Of Al Green (1969-78) (Edsel 1998)★★★★, True Love: A Collection (Music Club 1999)★★★★, Greatest Gospel Hits (Right Stuff 2000)★★★★, The Hi Singles As And Bs (Hi 2000)★★★★, Listen: The Rarities (Hi 2000)★★★, Testify: The Best Of The A&M Years (A&M 2001)★★★, Love & Happiness (Hi 2001)★★★.
VIDEOS: Gospel According To Al Green (Hendring Music Video 1990).
FURTHER READING: Take Me To The River, Al Green with Davin Seay.

GREEN, PETER
ALBUMS: The End Of The Game (Reprise 1970)★★, In The Skies (PVK 1979)★★★, Little Dreamer (PVK 1980)★★★, Whatcha Gonna Do (PVK 1981)★★, Blue Guitar (Creole 1981)★★, White Sky (Headline 1982)★★, Kolors (Headline 1983)★★, Legend (Creole 1988)★★, tribute album Rattlesnake Guitar: The Music Of Peter Green (Coast To Coast 1995)★★★, Peter Green Splinter Group (Red Snapper 1997)★★, with Nigel Watson The Robert Johnson Songbook (Artisan/Snapper 1998)★★★, with the Splinter Group Soho Session (Artisan/Snapper 1999)★★★, with the Splinter Group Destiny Road (Artisan/Snapper 1999)★★★★, with the Splinter Group Hot Foot Powder (Artisan/Snapper 2000)★★★, with the Splinter Group Time Traders (Eagle/Blue Storm 2001)★★★.
COMPILATIONS: Backtrackin' (Backtrackin' 1990)★★★, The Best Of Peter Green 1977-1981 (Music Collection 1996) ★★★, Me And The Devil box set (Snapper 2001)★★★.
FURTHER READING: Peter Green: The Biography (updated as Peter Green: Founder Of Fleetwood Mac), Martin Celmins.

GREENBAUM, NORMAN
ALBUMS: Spirit In The Sky (Reprise 1970)★★, Back Home Again (Reprise 1971)H, Petaluma (Reprise 1972)★★.
COMPILATIONS: Spirit In The Sky: The Best Of Norman Greenbaum (Varèse Sarabande 1996)★★★, with Dr. West's Medicine Show And Junk Band Euphoria! The Best Of (Sundazed 1999)★★.

GRIFFITH, NANCI
ALBUMS: There's A Light Beyond These Wood (BF Deal 1978)★★, Poet In My Window (Featherbed 1982)★★, Once In A Very Blue Moon (Philo 1985)★★★, Last Of The True Believers (Philo 1986)★★★★, Lone Star State Of Mind (MCA 1987)★★★★, Little Love Affairs (MCA 1988)★★★★, One Fair Summer Evening (MCA 1988)★★★★, Storms (MCA 1989)★★★★, Late Night Grande Hotel (MCA 1991)★★★★, Other Voices, Other Rooms (Elektra 1993) ★★★★, Flyer (Elektra 1994)★★★★, Blue Roses From The Moon (East West 1997)★★★★, Other Voices, Too (A Trip Back To Bountiful) (Elektra 1998)★★★★, The Dust Bowl Symphony (Elektra 1999)★★★, Clock Without Hands (Elektra 2001)★★★★.
COMPILATIONS: The Best Of Nanci Griffith (MCA 1993) ★★★★, Wings To Fly And A Place To Be: An Introduction To Nanci Griffith (MCA 2000)★★★.
FURTHER READING: Nanci Griffith's Other Voices: A Personal History Of Folk Music, Nanci Griffith and Joe Jackson.

GROOVE ARMADA
ALBUMS: Northern Star (Tummy Touch 1998)★★★★, Vertigo (Pepper/Jive Electro 1999)★★★★, Goodbye Country (Hello Nightclub) (Pepper 2001)★★★.
COMPILATIONS: Back To Mine (DMC 2000)★★★★.

GROUNDHOGS
ALBUMS: Scratching The Surface (Liberty 1968)★★, Blues Obituary (Liberty 1969)★★★, Thank Christ For The Bomb (Liberty 1970)★★★, Split (Liberty 1971)★★★★, Who Will Save The World? (United Artists 1972)★★★, Hogwash (United Artists 1972)★★★, Solid (WWA 1974)★★, Crosscut Saw (United Artists 1976)★★, Black Diamond (United Artists 1976)★★, Razor's Edge (Conquest 1985)★★, Back Against The Wall (Demi-Monde 1987)★★, Hogs On The Road (Demi-Monde 1988)★★, as Tony McPhee's Groundhogs Who Said Cherry Red? (Indigo 1996)★★, Hogs In Wolf's Clothing (HTD 1998)★★, No Surrender/Razor's Edge Tour 1985 recording (HTD 1998)★★, Boogie With Us 70s recordings (Indigo 2000)★★, The Lost Tapes Vol 1: Live In London, December 1989 (Dragon 2001)★★, The Lost Tapes Vol 2: Live In Milan, June 1994 (Dragon 2001)★★.
COMPILATIONS: Groundhogs Best 1969-1972 (United Artists 1974)★★★, Hoggin' The Stage (Psycho 1984)★★★, Moving Fast, Standing Still, comprises McPhee solo album 2 Sides Of plus Razor's Edge (Raw Power 1986)★★, No Surrender (Total 1990)★★, The Best Of The Groundhogs (EMI Gold 1997)★★★, On Air 1970 – 1972 (Strange Fruit 1998)★★★, 54146 (Burning Islands 2001)★★.
VIDEOS: Live At The Astoria (Wienerworld 1999).

GUESS WHO
ALBUMS: Shakin' All Over (Scepter 1965)★★, A Wild Pair (King 1967)★★, Wheatfield Soul (RCA 1969)★★★, Canned Wheat Packed By The Guess Who (RCA 1969)★★★, American Woman (RCA 1970)★★, Share The Land (RCA 1970)★★★, So Long, Bannatyne (RCA 1971)★★★, Rockin' (RCA 1972)★★, Live At The Paramount (Seattle) (RCA 1972) ★, Artificial Paradise (RCA 1973)★★, #10 (RCA 1973)★★, Road Food (RCA 1974)★★, Flavours (RCA 1975)H, Power In The Music (RCA 1975)★★, Lonely One (Intersound 1995)★★.
COMPILATIONS: The Best Of The Guess Who (RCA 1971) ★★★, The Best Of The Guess Who, Volume II (RCA 1974)★★, The Greatest Of The Guess Who (RCA 1977)★★★.

GUIDED BY VOICES
ALBUMS: Devil Between My Toes (E 1987)★★, Sandbox (Halo 1987)★★, Self-Inflicted Aerial Nostalgia (Halo 1989)★★, Same Place The Fly Got Smashed (Rocket #9 1990)★★★, Propeller (Rockathon 1992)★★★, Vampire On Titus (Scat/Matador 1993)★★★, Bee Thousand (Scat/Matador 1994)★★★★, Crying Your Knife Away (Lo-Fi 1994)★★★, Alien Lanes (Matador 1995)★★★, Under The Bushes, Under The Stars (Matador 1996)★★★, Sunfish Holy Breakfast mini-album (Matador 1996)★★★, Tonics & Twisted Chasers (Rockathon 1997)★★★, Mag Earwhig! (Matador 1997)★★★★, Do The Collapse (TVT/Creation 1999)★★★, Isolation Drills (TVT 2001)★★★★.
COMPILATIONS: An Earful O' Wax (Get Happy!! 1993)★★★, Box 6-LP/5-CD box set (Scat 1995)★★★, Suitcase: Failed Experiments And Trashed Aircraft 4-CD box set (Rockathon 2000)★★★, Suitcase Abridged: Drinks And Deliveries (Rockathon 2000)★★★, Daredevil Stamp Collector: Do The Collapse B-Sides (Rockathon 2001)★★.

GUNS N'ROSES
ALBUMS: Appetite For Destruction (Geffen 1987)★★★★, G N' R Lies (Geffen 1989)★★★, Use Your Illusion I (Geffen 1991)★★★, Use Your Illusion II (Geffen 1991)★★★, The Spaghetti Incident (Geffen 1993)★★.
COMPILATIONS: Live Era '87-'93 (Geffen 1999)★★.
VIDEOS: Use Your Illusion I (Geffen Video 1992), Making Fuckin' Videos Vol. 1 (Geffen Video 1993), Making Fuckin' Videos Vol. 2 (Geffen Video 1993), The Making Of Estranged - Part IV Of The Trilogy (Geffen Video 1994), Guns N'Roses: Welcome To The Videos (Geffen Video 1998).
FURTHER READING: Guns N'Roses: The World's Most Outrageous Hard Rock Band, Paul Elliot. Appetite For Destruction: The Days Of Guns N'Roses, Danny Sugerman. The Most Dangerous Band In The World, Mick Wall. Over The Top: The True Story Of ... , Mark Putterford. In Their Own Words, Mark Putterford. The Pictures, ed. George Chin. Lowlife In The Fast Lane, Eddy McSquare. Live!, Mick St. Michael.

GUTHRIE, ARLO
ALBUMS: Alice's Restaurant (Reprise 1967)★★★★, Arlo (Reprise 1968)★★, Running Down The Road (Reprise 1969) ★★★, Alice's Restaurant film soundtrack (Reprise 1969)★★, Washington County (Reprise 1970)★★★, Hobo's Lullaby (Reprise 1972)★★★, Last Of The Brooklyn Cowboys (Reprise 1973)★★★, Arlo Guthrie (Reprise 1974) ★★★, with Pete Seeger Together In Concert (Reprise 1975)★★, Amigo (Reprise 1976)★★★★, One Night (Warners 1978)★★, Outlasting The Blues (Warners 1979)★★★★, Power Of Love (Warners 1981)★★★, with Pete Seeger Precious Friend (Warners 1982)★★★, Someday (Rising Son 1986)★★★, All Over The World (Rising Son 1991)★★★, Son Of The Wind (Rising Son 1992)★★★, Mystic Journey (Rising Son 1996)★★★.
COMPILATIONS: The Best Of Arlo Guthrie (Warners 1977)★★★.
FILMS: Alice's Restaurant (1969).

GUTHRIE, WOODY
ALBUMS: Dust Bowl Ballads 1940 recording (Folkways 1950)★★★★, More Songs By Guthrie (Meldisc 1955)★★★, Songs To Grow On (Folkways 1958)★★★, Struggle (Folkways 1958)★★★, Bound For Glory (Folkways 1958) ★★★★, Sacco & Vanzetti (Folkways 1960)★★★★, Dust Bowl Ballads 1940 recordings (Folkways 1964)★★★★, Library Of Congress Recordings 1940 recordings (Folkways 1964)★★★★, Bed On The Floor (Verve/Folkways 1965) ★★★, Woody Guthrie (Xtra 1965)★★★, Bonneville Dam And Other Columbia River Songs (Verve/Folkways 1965) ★★★, Poor Boy (Xtra 1966)★★★, This Land Is Your Land (Smithsonian/Folkways 1967)★★★★.
COMPILATIONS: The Greatest Songs Of Woody Guthrie (Vanguard 1972)★★★★, Woody Guthrie (Ember 1968) ★★★, A Legendary Performer (RCA 1977)★★★, Poor Boy (Transatlantic 1981)★★★, Columbia River Collection (Rounder 1988)★★★, Folkways: The Original Vision (Folkways 1989) ★★★★, Long Ways To Travel The Unreleased Folkways Masters 1944-1949 (Smithsonian/Folkways 1994)★★★★, Woody Guthrie Sings Folk Songs (Smithsonian/ Folkways 1995)★★★★.
VIDEOS: Vision Shared: A Tribute To Woody Guthrie (CMV Enterprises 1989).
FURTHER READING: Woody Guthrie Folk Songs, Woody Guthrie. American Folksong, Woody Guthrie. Born To Win, Woody Guthrie and Robert Shelton (ed.). A Mighty Hard Road: The Woody Guthrie Story, Henrietta Yurchenco. Bound For Glory, Woody Guthrie. Seeds Of Man: An Experience Lived And Dreamed, Woody Guthrie. Woody Guthrie: A Life, Joe Klein. Pastures Of Plenty-A Self Portrait, Woody Guthrie. Woody Guthrie: Roll On Columbia, Bill Murlin (ed.).

GUY, BUDDY
ALBUMS: A Man And The Blues (Vanguard 1968)★★★★, Coming At You (Vanguard 1968)★★★, This Is Buddy Guy (Vanguard 1968)★★★★, Blues Today (Vanguard 1968) ★★★, Hot And Cool (Vanguard 1969)★★★, First Time I Met The Blues (Python 1969)★★★, with Junior Mance, Junior Wells Buddy And The Juniors (Blue Thumb 1970) ★★★★, Hold That Plane! (Vanguard 1972)★★★, with Wells Play The Blues (Atco 1972)★★★★, Got To Use Your House (Blues Ball 1979)★★★, with Wells Alone & Acoustic (Alligator 1981)★★★★, Dollar Done Fell (JSP 1982)★★★, DJ Play My Blues (JSP 1982)★★★, with Wells Drinking' TNT 'N' Smokin' Dynamite 1974 recording (Blind Pig 1982) ★★★★, The Original Blues Brothers - Live (Blue Moon 1983)★★★, Ten Blue Fingers (JSP 1985)★★★, Live At The Checkerboard, Chicago, 1979 (JSP 1988)★★★, Breaking Out (JSP 1988)★★★, with Wells Alone & Acoustic 1981 recording (Hightone 1991)★★★★, Damn Right, I've Got The Blues (Silvertone 1991)★★★★, with Wells Alive In Montreux (Evidence 1992)★★★★, My Time After Awhile (Vanguard 1992)★★★, Feels Like Rain (Silvertone 1993) ★★★★, Slippin' In (Silvertone 1994)★★★, with G.E. Smith And The Saturday Night Live Band Buddy Guy Live: The Real Deal (Silvertone 1996)★★★★, Heavy Love (Silvertone 1998)★★★, Sweet Tea (Silvertone 2001)★★★.
COMPILATIONS: I Left My Blues In San Francisco (Chess 1967)★★★, In The Beginning (Red Lightnin' 1971)★★, I Was Walking Through The Woods (Chess 1974)★★★, Chess Masters (Charly 1987)★★★★, Stone Crazy (Alligator 1988)★★★, I Ain't Got No Money (Flyright 1989)★★★, The Best Of Buddy Guy (Rhino 1992)★★★, The Complete Chess Studio Sessions (Chess 1992)★★★★, As Good As It Gets (Vanguard 1998)★★★★, Buddy's Blues 1978-1982: The Best Of The JSP Recordings (JSP 1998)★★★, This Is Buddy Guy (VMD 1998)★★★, Buddy's Baddest: The Best Of Buddy Guy (Silvertone 1999)★★★★, The Complete Vanguard Recordings 3-CD set (Vanguard 2000)★★★★.
VIDEOS: Messin' With The Blues (BMG Video 1991), Buddy Guy Live: The Real Deal (Wienerworld 1996).
FURTHER READING: Damn Right I Got The Blues: Blues Roots Of Rock N Roll, Donald E. Wilcock and Buddy Guy.

H

H.P. LOVECRAFT
ALBUMS: H.P. Lovecraft (Philips 1967)★★★, H.P. Lovecraft II (Philips 1968)★★★, as Lovecraft Valley Of The Moon (Reprise 1970)★★, as Lovecraft We Love You Whoever You Are (Mercury 1975)★★, as H.P. Lovecraft Live - May 11, 1968 (Sundazed 1992)★★.
COMPILATIONS: At The Mountains Of Madness (Edsel 1988)★★★★.

HAGGARD, MERLE
ALBUMS: Strangers (Capitol 1965)★★★, with Bonnie Owens Just Between The Two Of Us (Capitol 1966)★★★, Swinging Doors (Capitol 1966)★★★, I'm A Lonesome Fugitive (Capitol 1967)★★★, Branded Man (Capitol 1967)★★★, Sing Me Back Home (Capitol 1968)★★★, The Legend Of Bonnie And Clyde (Capitol 1968)★★★, Mama Tried (Capitol 1968) ★★★★, Pride In What I Am (Capitol 1969)★★★, Same Train, Different Time (Capitol 1969)★★★, Close Up (Capitol 1969)★★★, Okie From Muskogee (Capitol 1969)★★★★, Introducing My Friends The Strangers (Capitol 1970)★★★, The Fightin' Side Of Me (Capitol 1970)★★★, A Tribute To The Best Damn Fiddle Player In The World (Or, My Salute To Bob Wills) (Capitol 1970)★★★★, Sing A Sad Song (Capitol 1970)★★★, High On A Hilltop (Capitol 1971)★★★, Hag (Capitol 1971)★★★, Someday We'll Look Back (Capitol 1971)★★★, The Land Of Many Churches (Capitol 1971) ★★★, Let Me Tell You About A Song (Capitol 1972)★★★, It's Not Love, But It's Not Bad (Capitol 1972)★★★, Totally Instrumental (With One Exception) (Capitol 1973)★★★, I Love Dixie Blues ... So I Recorded 'Live' In New Orleans (Capitol 1973)★★★, Merle Haggard's Christmas Present (Capitol 1973)★★, If We Make It Through December (Capitol 1974)★★, Merle Haggard Presents His 30th Album (Capitol 1974)★★, Keep Movin' On (Capitol 1975)★★★, It's All In The Movies (Capitol 1976)★★, My Love Affair With Trains (Capitol 1976)★★★, The Roots Of My Raising (Capitol 1976)★★★, A Working Man Can't Get Nowhere Today (Capitol 1977)★★★, Ramblin' Fever (MCA 1977)★★★, My Farewell To Elvis (MCA 1977)★★★, I'm Always On A Mountain When I Fall (MCA 1978)★★★, The Way It Was In 51 (Capitol 1978)★★★, Serving 190 Proof (MCA 1979) ★★★, The Way I Am (MCA 1980)★★★, Back To The Barrooms (MCA 1981)★★★, Rainbow Stew: Live At Anaheim Stadium (MCA 1981)★★★, with Johnny Paycheck Mr Hag Told My Story (Epic 1981)★★★, Songs For The Mama That Tried (MCA 1981)★★★, Big City (Epic 1981)★★★, with Willie Nelson Poncho And Lefty (Epic 1982)★★★, Going Where The Lonely Go (Epic 1982)★★★, with George Jones A Taste Of Yesterday's Wine (Epic 1982)★★★, Goin' Home For Christmas (Epic 1982)★★★, That's The Way Love Goes (Epic 1983)★★★, The Epic Collection Live (Epic 1983)★★★, It's All In The Game (Epic 1984)★★★, Kern River (Epic 1985) ★★★, Amber Waves Of Grain (Epic 1985)★★★, Out Among The Stars (Epic 1986)★★★, A Friend In California (Epic 1986)★★★, with Nelson The Seashores Of Old Mexico (Epic 1987)★★★, Chill Factor (Epic 1987)★★★, 5:01 Blues (Epic 1989)★★★, Blue Jungle (Curb 1990)★★★, A Christmas Present (Curb 1990)★★, 1994 (Curb 1994)★★★, 20 Hits (Curb 1995)★★, 1996 (Curb 1996)★★★, If I Could Only Fly (Anti 2000)★★★, Cabin In The Hills (Hag/Madacy 2000) ★★★, with Albert E. Brumley Jr. Two Old Friends (Hag/Madacy 2000)★★★, Roots Volume 1 (Anti 2001)★★★.
COMPILATIONS: The Best Of Merle Haggard (Capitol 1968)★★★, A Portrait Of Merle Haggard (Capitol 1969) ★★★, The Best Of The Best Of Merle Haggard (Capitol 1972)★★★★, Songs I'll Always Sing (Capitol 1976)★★★★, Eleven Winners (Capitol 1978)★★★★, Country Boy (Pair 1978)★★★, His Epic Hits: First Eleven To Be Continued (Epic 1984)★★★, Greatest Hits Of The 80s (Epic 1990)★★★, Best Of Country Blues (Curb 1990)★★★, Capitol Collectors Series (Capitol 1990)★★★, More Of The Best (Rhino 1990)★★★★, All Night Long (Curb 1991)★★★, Best Of The Early Years (Curb 1991)★★★, 18 Rare Classics (Curb 1991)★★★, Super Hits (Epic 1993)★★★, Greatest Hits Volume 1 (Curb 1994)★★★, Greatest Hits Volume 2 (Curb 1994)★★★, Lonesome Fugitive: The Merle Haggard Anthology (1963-1977) (Razor & Tie 1995)★★★★, Untamed Hawk 5-CD box set (Bear Family 1995)★★★★, Vintage (Capitol 1996)★★★, Down Every Road (Capitol 1996)★★★★, Poet Of The Common Man (Curb 1997)★★★★, For The Record: 43 Legendary Hits (BNA 1999)★★★★.
VIDEOS: The Best Of Merle Haggard (Curb 1989), Merle Haggard Live In Concert (Curb 1993), Poet Of The Common Man (Curb 1997).
FURTHER READING: Sing Me Back Home: My Story, Merle Haggard with Peggy Russell. Merle Haggard's My House Of Memories, Merle Haggard with Tom Carter.
FILMS: Hillbillys In A Haunted House (1967), Killers Three (1968), From Nashville With Music (1969), Bronco Billy (1980), The Legend Of The Lone Ranger (1981), Wag The Dog (1997).

HAIRCUT 100
ALBUMS: Pelican West (Arista 1982)★★★★, Paint On Paint (Arista 1984)★★.
COMPILATIONS: Best Of Nick Heyward And Haircut 100 (Ariola 1989)★★★★, The Greatest Hits Of Nick Heyward & Haircut 100 (RCA Camden 1996)★★★★.
FURTHER READING: The Haircut 100 Catalogue, Sally Payne. Haircut 100: Not A Trace Of Brylcreem, no editor listed.

HALEY, BILL, AND HIS COMETS
ALBUMS: Rock With Bill Haley And The Comets (Essex 1955)★★, Shake, Rattle And Roll 10-inch album (Decca 1955)★★★, Rock Around The Clock (Decca 1956)★★★★, with various artists Music For The Boyfriend (Decca 1956)★★, Rock 'N Roll Stage Show (Decca 1956)★★★★, Rocking The Oldies (Decca 1957)★★, Rockin' Around The World (Decca 1958)★★★, Rocking The Joint (Decca 1958)★★★, Bill Haley's Chicks (Decca 1959)★★★★, Strictly Instrumental (Decca 1960)★★, Bill Haley And His Comets (Warners 1960)★★★, Bill Haley's Jukebox (Warners 1960)★★★, Twistin' Knights At The Round Table (Roulette 1962)★★★, Bill Haley And The Comets (Vocalion 1963)★★, Rip It Up (MCA 1968)★★★, Scrapbook/Live At The Bitter End (Kama Sutra 1970)H, Travelin' Band (Janus 1970)★★★, Golden King Of Rock (Hallmark 1972)★★★, Just Rock And Roll Music (Sonet 1973)★★★, Live In London '74 (Atlantic 1974)★★, Rock Around The Country (Hallmark 1974)★★.
COMPILATIONS: Bill Haley's Greatest Hits (Decca 1967) ★★★, King Of Rock (Ember 1968)★★★, Mister Rock 'n' Roll (Ember 1969)★★★, The Bill Haley Collection (Pickwick 1976)★★★, R-O-C-K (Sonet 1976)★★★, Armchair Rock 'N' Roll (MCA 1978)★★★, Everyone Can Rock 'N' Roll (Sonet 1980)★★★, A Tribute To Bill Haley (MCA 1981) ★★★, The Essential Bill Haley (Charly 1984)★★★, Hillbilly Haley (Rollercoaster 1984)★★★, Boogie With Bill Haley (Topline 1985)★★★, Greatest Hits (MCA 1985)★★★, Golden Greats (MCA 1985)★★★, From The Original Master Tapes (MCA 1985)★★★, The Original Hits '54-'57 (Hallmark 1987)★★★, Greatest Hits (Connoisseur 1988) ★★★, Rip It Up Rock 'N' Roll (Connoisseur 1988)★★★, Golden CD Collection (Bulldog 1989)★★★, Bill Haley's Rock 'N' Roll Scrapbook (Sequel 1990)★★★, The Decca Years And More 5-CD box set (Bear Family 1991)★★★.
FURTHER READING: Sound & Glory, John Von Hoelle and John Haley.
FILMS: Don't Knock The Rock (1956).

HALF MAN HALF BISCUIT
ALBUMS: Back In The DHSS (Probe Plus 1985)★★★★, McIntyre, Treadmore And Davitt (Probe Plus 1991)★★★, This Leaden Pall (Probe Plus 1993)★★★, Some Call It Godcore (Probe Plus 1995)★★★, Voyage To The Bottom Of The Road (Probe Plus 1997)★★★, Four Lads Who Shook The Wirral (Probe Plus 1998)★★★, Trouble Over Bridgwater (Probe Plus 2000)★★★.
COMPILATIONS: Back Again In The DHSS (Probe Plus 1987)★★★, ACD (Probe Plus 1988)★★★.
VIDEOS: Live (Alternative Image 1993).

HALL AND OATES
I ALBUMS: Whole Oats (Atlantic 1972)★★★, Abandoned Luncheonette (Atlantic 1973)★★★★, War Babies (Atlantic 1974)★★, Daryl Hall & John Oates (RCA 1975)★★, Bigger Than Both Of Us (RCA 1976)★★★, Beauty On A Back Street (RCA 1977)★★★, Livetime (RCA 1978)★★, Along The Red Ledge (RCA 1978)★★★, X-Static (RCA 1979)★★, Voices (RCA 1980)★★★, Private Eyes (RCA 1981)★★★★, H2O (RCA 1982)★★★★, Big Bam Boom (RCA 1984)★★★, with David Ruffin, Eddie Kendrick Live At The Apollo (RCA 1985)★★★★, Ooh Yeah! (Arista 1988)★★, Change Of Season (Arista 1990)★★, Marigold Sky (Push 1997)★★★, Ecstasy On The Edge 1979 recording (Burning Airlines 2001)★★.
COMPILATIONS: No Goodbyes (Atlantic 1977)★★★, Greatest Hits: Rock 'N Soul Part 1 (RCA 1983)★★★★, 2Gether (Delta 1987)★★, The Best Of Daryl Hall + John Oates: Looking Back (Arista 1991)★★★, Really Smokin' (Thunderbolt 1993)★★, The Early Years (Javelin 1994)★★, The Best Of Times: Greatest Hits (Arista 1995)★★★, The Atlantic Collection (Rhino 1996)★★★, Greatest Hits (Razor & Tie 1997)★★★, With Love From ... Hall & Oates: The Best Of The Ballads (BMG 1998)★★★, Past Times Behind (Legacy 1998)★★, Rich Girl (Camden 1999)★★, Backtracks (Renaissance 1999)★★, Master Hits (Arista 1999)★★★, The Very Best Of Daryl Hall And John Oates (RCA 2001)★★★★, The Essential Collection (BMG 2001)★★★★, Behind The Music: The Daryl Hall And John Oates Collection (BMG 2002)★★★★.
VIDEOS: Rock 'N Soul Live (RCA 1984), The Daryl Hall & John Oates Video Collection: 7 Big Ones (RCA 1984), The Liberty Concert (RCA 1986), Live At The Apollo (RCA 1987), Sara Smile (Master Tone 1995), The Best Of MusikLaden Live (Encore Music Entertainment 1999).
FURTHER READING: Dangerous Dances, Nick Tosches.

HALLIWELL, GERI
ALBUMS: Schiz-ophonic (EMI 1999)★★★, Scream If You Wanna Go Faster (EMI 2001)★★.
FURTHER READING: If Only, Geri Halliwell.
FILMS: Spiceworld - The Movie (1997).

HALLYDAY, JOHNNY
ALBUMS: Johnny Hallyday Sings America's Rockin' Hits (Philips 1961)★★★, Johnny A Nashville - La Fantastique Epopee Du Rock (Philips 1962)★★★, Generation Perdue (Philips 1966)★★, Olympia 1967 (Philips 1967)★★★, Que Je T'Aime (Philips 1969)★★, Je Suis Ne Dans La Rue (Philips 1969)★★★, Vie (Philips 1970)★★★, Flagrant Delit (Philips 1971)★★★, Country Folk Rock (Philips 1972)★★★, Insolitude (Philips 1973)★★★, Derriere L'Amour (Philips 1976)★★★, C'Est La Vie (Philips 1977)★★★, Solitudes A Deux (Philips 1978)★★★, Hollywood (Philips 1979)★★★, Drôle De Métier (Philips 1984)★★★, Rock 'N' Roll Attitude (Philips 1985)★★★, Gang (Philips 1986)★★★, Trift De Rattles (Philips 1986)★★★★, Les Grands Success De Johnny Hallyday (Philips 1988)★★★, La Peur (Philips 1988) ★★★, Cadillac (Philips 1989)★★★, Ça Ne Change Pas Un Homme (Philips 1991)★★★, Parc Des Princes 1993 (Philips 1993)★★, Lorada (Philips 1995)★★★, Ce Que Je Sais (Mercury 1998)★★★, Sang Pour Sang (Mercury 1999) ★★★, Tour Eiffel (Mercury 2000)★★.
COMPILATIONS: La Nuit Johnny 42-CD box set (Philips 1993)★★★, Ballades (Mercury 1999)★★★.
FILMS: Les Diaboliques aka The Fiends (1955), Dossier 1413 aka Secret File 1413 (1961), Les Parisiennes aka Tales Of Paris (1962), Cherchez L'Idole aka The Chase (1963), D'Où Viens-Tu L'Idole (1964), A Tout Casser aka Breaking It Up (1967), Les Poneyttes (1967), Visa De Censure (1968), Gli Specialisti aka Drop Them Or I'll Shoot (1969), Point De Chute (1970), Malpertuis: Histoire D'Une Maison Maudite (1971), L'Aventure, C'Est Aventure aka Money Money Money (1972), J'Ai Tout Donné (1972), L'Animal aka The Animal (1977), Le Jour Se Lève Et Les Conneries Commencement (1981), Détective (1985), Terminus (1986), Le Conseil De Famille aka Family Business (1986), The Iron Triangle (1989), La Gamine (1991), Paparazzi (1998), Porquoi Pas Moi? (1999), Love Me (2000), Eau Et Gaz A Tous Les Etages (2000).

HAMMILL, PETER
ALBUMS: Fool's Mate (Charisma 1971)★★★★, Chameleon In The Shadow Of Night (Charisma 1973)★★★, The Silent Corner And The Empty Stage (Charisma 1974)★★★, In Camera (Charisma 1974)★★, Nadir's Big Chance (Charisma 1975)★★★, Over (Charisma 1977)★★★, The Future Now (Charisma 1978)★★★, ph7 (Charisma 1979)★★★, A Black Box (S Type 1980)★★★, Sitting Targets (Virgin 1981)★★★, Enter K (Naive 1982)★★★, Patience (Naive 1983)★★★, Loops And Reels (Sofa 1983)★★★, The Love Songs (Charisma 1984)★★★, The Margin - Live (Foundry 1985)★★★, Skin (Foundry 1986)★★★, And Close As This (Virgin 1986) ★★★★, In A Foreign Town (Enigma 1988)★★★, with Guy Evans Spur Of The Moment (Red Hot 1988)★★, Out Of Water (Enigma 1990)★★★, Room Temperature Live (Fie! 1990) ★★★, The Fall Of The House Of Usher (World Chief 1991)★, Fireships (Fie! 1992)★★, The Noise (Fie! 1993)★★, with Guy Evans Spur Of The Moment (Red Hot 1993)★★★, There Goes The Daylight (Fie! 1994)★★★, Peter Hammill And The K Group The Margin, Roaring Forties (Fie! 1994)★★★, The Peel Sessions (Windsong 1995)★★★, X My Heart (Fie! 1996) ★★★, The Union Chapel Concert (Fie! 1996)★★, Everyone You Hold (Fie! 1997)★★★, Sonix: Hybrid Experiments 1994-1996 (Fie! 1998)★★, This (Fie! 1999)★★★, with Roger Eno The Given Hour (Fie! 1999)★★, Typical (Fie! 1999)★★★, None Of The Above (Fie! 2000)★★★, What Now (Fie! 2001)★★.
COMPILATIONS: The Love Songs (Charisma 1984)★★★, The Calm After The Storm (Virgin 1993)★★★, After The Show (Virgin 1996)★★★, Past Go (Fie! 1997)★★★.
VIDEOS: In The Passionskirche, Berlin MVMXCII (Studio 1993).
FURTHER READING: The Lemming Chronicles, David Shaw-Parker. Killers, Angels, Refugees, Peter Hammill. Mirrors, Dreams And Miracles, Peter Hammill.

HAMMOND, ALBERT
ALBUMS: It Never Rains In Southern California (Mum 1973) ★★, Free Electric Band (Mum 1973)★★★, Albert Hammond (Mum 1974)★★.

HANCOCK, HERBIE
ALBUMS: Takin' Off (Blue Note 1962)★★★★, My Point Of View (Blue Note 1963)★★★★, Inventions And Dimensions (Blue Note 1963)★★★, Empyrean Isles (Blue Note 1964) ★★★★, Maiden Voyage (Blue Note 1965)★★★★, Speak Like A Child (Blue Note 1968)★★★, The Prisoner (Blue Note 1969)★★★, Fat Albert Rotunda (Warners 1970)★★★, Mwandishi (Warners 1971)★★★★, Crossings (Warners 1972)★★★★, Sextant (Columbia 1973)★★★★, Head Hunters (Columbia 1974)★★★★★, Thrust (Columbia 1974)★★★, Man-Child (Columbia 1975)★★★★, V.S.O.P. (Columbia 1976)★★★★, Secrets (Columbia 1976)★★, V.S.O.P: The Quintet (Columbia 1977)★★★★, Sunlight (Columbia 1978)★★★, An Evening With Herbie Hancock And Chick Corea (Columbia 1979)★★★, with Chick Corea Homecoming: Corea And Hancock (Polydor 1979)★★★, Feets Don't Fail Me Now (Columbia 1979)★★, Mr. Hands (Columbia 1980)★★★, Monster (Columbia 1980)★★, Magic Windows (Columbia 1981)★★, Quartet (Columbia 1982)★★★, Lite Me Up (Columbia 1982)★★, Future Shock (Columbia 1983)★★★★, Hot And Heavy (Premier 1984) ★★, Herbie Hancock And The Rockit Band (Columbia 1984)★★★, Sound-System (Columbia 1984)★★, with Dexter Gordon 'Round Midnight film soundtrack (Columbia 1986)★★★, with Wayne Shorter, Ron Carter, Wallace Roney, Tony Williams A Tribute To Miles (Qwest/Reprise 1994)★★★, Dis Is Da Drum (Mercury 1994)★★★, The New Standard (Verve 1996)★★★★, with Wayne Shorter 1+1 (Verve 1997)★★★★, with various artists Gershwin's World (Verve 1998)★★★★, Return Of The Headhunters! (Hancock/Verve Forecast 1998)★★, Future 2 Future (Transparent 2001)★★★.
COMPILATIONS: Greatest Hits (Columbia 1980)★★★, The Best Of Herbie Hancock: The Blue Note Years (Blue Note 1988)★★★★, A Jazz Collection (Columbia 1991)★★★, The Collection (Castle 1991)★★★, The Very Best Of Herbie Hancock (Sony 1991)★★★★, The Best Of Vol. 2 (Sony 1992)★★★, Mwandishi: The Complete Warner Bros. Recordings (Warners 1994)★★★, Jazz Profile (Blue Note 1997)★★★★, This Is Jazz (Columbia/Legacy 1998)★★★, The Complete Blue Note Sixties Sessions 6-CD box set (Blue Note 1998)★★★★.
VIDEOS: Herbie Hancock And The Rockit Band (Columbia 1984).

HANOI ROCKS
ALBUMS: Bangkok Shocks, Saigon Shakes, Hanoi Rocks (Johanna 1981)★★★, Oriental Beat (Johanna 1981)★★★, Back To Mystery City (Johanna 1983)★★★, All Those Wasted Years! (Johanna 1984)★★, Two Steps From The Move (Johanna/CBS 1984)★★★, Rock 'N' Roll Divorce (Lick 1985)★★, Lean On Me (Lick 1992)★★.
COMPILATIONS: Self Destruction Blues (Johanna 1982)★★★, The Best Of Hanoi Rocks (Johanna 1985)★★★, Dead By Christmas (Raw Power 1985)★★, Tracks From A Broken Dream (Lick 1990)★★★, Decadent Dangerous Delicious (Essential 2000)★★★★.
VIDEOS: All Those Wasted Years: Live At The Marquee (Mercury 1984), Up Around The Bend aka The Nottingham Tapes (Mercury 1990).

HANSON
ALBUMS: Middle Of Nowhere (Mercury 1997)★★★, Snowed In For Christmas (Mercury 1997)H, Live From Albertane (Mercury 1998)★★★, This Time Around (Mercury 2000)★★★★.
COMPILATIONS: 3 Car Garage: The Indie Recordings '95-'96 (Mercury 1998)★★★.
VIDEOS: Hanson: Tulsa, Tokyo And The Middle Of Nowhere (PolyGram Music Video 1997), Hanson Tour '98: Road To Albertane (Polygram Video 1998).

HAPPY MONDAYS
ALBUMS: Squirrel And G-Man Twenty Four Hour Party People Plastic Face Carnt Smile (White Out) (Factory 1987)★★★, Bummed (Factory 1988)★★★★, Pills 'N' Thrills And Bellyaches (Factory 1990)★★★★, Live (Factory 1991)★★, Yes Please! (Factory 1992)★★, The Peel Sessions (Strange Fruit 1996)★★.
COMPILATIONS: Loads – The Best Of (London 1995)★★★, Loads More limited edition (London 1995)★★, Greatest Hits (London 1999)★★★.
FURTHER READING: Shaun Ryder: Happy Mondays, Black Grape And Other Traumas, Mick Middles. High Life 'N' Low Down Dirty: The Thrills And Spills Of Shaun Ryder, Lisa Verrico. Freaky Dancin', Bez. Hallelujah! The Extraordinary Return Of Shaun Ryder And Happy Mondays, John Warburton with Shaun Ryder.

HARDCASTLE, PAUL
ALBUMS: Paul Hardcastle (Chrysalis 1985)★★★, Rain Forest US only (Profile 1985)★★★, No Winners (Chrysalis 1988)★★, as the Jazzmasters The Jazzmasters (Push 1991) ★★★★, Hardcastle (Push 1994)★★★, as the Jazzmasters The Jazzmasters II (Push 1995)★★★, Hardcastle 2 (Push 1996)★★, as the Jazzmasters The Jazzmasters III (Push 1999)★★★.
COMPILATIONS: The Definitive Collection (K-Tel 1993) ★★★, Cover To Cover: A Musical Autobiography (Push 1997)★★★, as the Jazzmasters The Greatest Hits (New Note 2000)★★★.

HARDIN, TIM
ALBUMS: Tim Hardin 1 (Verve Forecast 1966)★★★★, Tim Hardin 2 (Verve Forecast 1967)★★★★, This Is Tim Hardin (Atco 1967)★★, Tim Hardin 3 Live In Concert (Verve Forecast 1968)★★★, Tim Hardin 4 (Verve Forecast 1969)★★★★, Suite For Susan Moore And Damion – We Are – One. One, All In One (Columbia 1969)★★★, Golden Archive Series (MGM 1970)★★★, Bird On A Wire (Columbia 1971)★★, Painted Head (Columbia 1972)★★, Archetypes (MGM 1973)★★★, Nine (GM/Antilles 1974)★★★, The Shock Of Grace (Columbia 1981)★★★, The Homecoming Concert (Line 1981)★★★★.
COMPILATIONS: Best Of Tim Hardin (Verve Forecast 1969)★★★★, Memorial Album (Polydor 1981)★★★, Reason To Believe (The Best Of) (Polydor 1987)★★★★, Hang On To A Dream: The Verve Recordings (Polydor 1994)★★★★, Simple Songs Of Freedom: The Tim Hardin Collection (Columbia 1996)★★★★, Person To Person: The Essential Classic Hardin 1963-1980 (Raven 2000)★★★★, The Best Of Tim Hardin: The Millennium Collection (Polydor 2002)★★★★.

HARPER, BEN
ALBUMS: Welcome To The Cruel World (Virgin 1994) ★★★★, Fight For Your Mind (Virgin 1995)★★★, with the Innocent Criminals The Will To Live (Virgin 1997)★★★★, with the Innocent Criminals The Will To Live – Bonus Live EP Edition (Virgin 1998)★★★★, with the Innocent Criminals Burn To Shine (Virgin 1999)★★★, with the Innocent Criminals Live From Mars (Virgin 2001)★★★★.
COMPILATIONS: 3 CD box set (Virgin 1999)★★★.

HARPER, ROY
ALBUMS: The Sophisticated Beggar aka Legend (Strike 1966)★★, Come Out Fighting Genghis Smith aka The Early Years (Columbia 1968)★★★, Folkjokeopus (Liberty 1969) ★★, Flat, Baroque And Berserk (Harvest 1970)★★★, Stormcock (Harvest 1971)★★★★, Lifemask (Harvest 1973) ★★★★, Valentine (Harvest 1974)★★★, Flashes From The Archives Of Oblivion (Harvest 1974)★★★, HQ aka When An Old Cricketer Leaves The Crease (Harvest 1975)★★★, Bullinamingvase aka One Of Those Days In England (Harvest 1977)★★★★, The Unknown Soldier (Harvest 1980)★★, Work Of Heart (Public 1982)★★★, Born In Captivity (Hardup/Awareness 1984)★★★, with Jimmy Page Whatever Happened To Jugula? (Beggars Banquet 1985)★★★, In Between Every Line (Harvest 1986)★★, Descendants Of Smith aka Garden Of Uranium (EMI 1988)★★★, Loony On The Bus (Awareness 1988)★★, Once (Awareness 1990)★★★, Burn The World (Awareness 1990)★★★★, Death Or Glory? (Awareness 1992)★★★, Born In Captivity II aka Unhinged (Hard Up/Science Friction 1992)★★★, Live At Les Cousins 1969 live recording (Blueprint 1996)★★★, Poems, Speeches, Thoughts & Doodles spoken word (Science Friction 1997)★★★, The Dream Society (Science Friction 1998)★★★, The Green Man (Science Friction 2000)★★★★.
COMPILATIONS: An Introduction To ... Roy Harper (Griffin 1976)★★★★, Harper 1970-1975 (Harvest 1978)★★★★, The BBC Tapes Vol. 1 1969-73 recordings (Science Friction 1997)★★★★, The BBC Tapes Vol. 2 1974 live recording (Science Friction 1997)★★★★, The BBC Tapes Vol. 3 1974 recordings (Science Friction 1997)★★★★, The BBC Tapes Vol. 4 1975 live recording (Science Friction 1997)★★★, The BBC Tapes Vol. 5 1975-78 recordings (Science Friction 1997)★★★★, The BBC Tapes Vol. 6 1978 live recording (Science Friction 1997)★★, East Of The Sun: A Collection Of Love Songs (Science Friction 2001)★★★★.

HARPERS BIZARRE
ALBUMS: Feelin' Groovy (Warners 1967)★★★, Anything Goes (Warners 1967)★★, The Secret Life Of Harpers Bizarre (Warners 1968)★★, Harpers Bizarre 4 (Warners 1969)★★, As Time Goes By (Forest Bay 1976)★.
COMPILATIONS: Feelin' Groovy: The Best Of Harpers Bizarre (Warner Archives 1997)★★★.

HARRIS, EMMYLOU
ALBUMS: Gliding Bird (Jubilee 1970)★★, Pieces Of The Sky (Reprise 1975)★★★★, Elite Hotel (Reprise 1975)★★★, Luxury Liner (Warners 1977)★★★★, Quarter Moon In A Ten Cent Town (Warners 1978)★★★★, Blue Kentucky Girl (Warners 1979)★★★★, Light Of The Stable: The Christmas Album (Warners 1979)★★★, Roses In The Snow (Warners 1980)★★★★, Evangeline (Warners 1981)★★★, Cimmaron (Warners 1981)★★★★, Last Date (Warners 1982)★★★, White Shoes (Warners 1983)★★★, The Ballad Of Sally Rose (Warners 1985)★★★, Thirteen (Warners 1986)★★★, Angel Band (Warners 1987)★★★, with Dolly Parton, Linda Ronstadt Trio (Warners 1987)★★★★, Bluebird (Reprise 1989)★★★, Brand New Dance (Reprise 1990)★★★★, Emmylou Harris And The Nash Ramblers At The Ryman (Reprise 1992)★★★, Cowgirl's Prayer (Asylum 1993)★★★, Wrecking Ball (Asylum/Grapevine 1995)★★★★, Spyboy (Eminent/Grapevine 1998)★★★★, with Parton, Ronstadt Trio II (Asylum 1999)★★★, with Ronstadt Western Wall/The Tucson Sessions (Asylum 1999)★★★, Red Dirt Girl (Grapevine 2000)★★★.
COMPILATIONS: Profile (The Best Of Emmylou Harris) (Warners 1978)★★★★, Her Best Songs (K-Tel 1980)★★★, Profile II (The Best Of Emmylou Harris) (Warners 1984) ★★★, Duets (Reprise 1988)★★★★, Songs Of The West (Warners 1994)★★★, Portraits 3-CD box set (Reprise Archives 1996)★★★★, Singin' With Emmylou (Raven 2000)★★★★, Anthology: The Warner/Reprise Years (Rhino 2001)★★★★.
VIDEOS: At The Ryman (Warner Video 1992), Spyboy: Live From The Legendary Exit/In (Eminent 1998).

HARRIS, JET, AND TONY MEEHAN
COMPILATIONS: Remembering: Jet Harris And Tony Meehan (Decca 1976)★★★★, Diamonds (Decca 1983)★★★, Diamonds And Other Gems (Deram 1989)★★★★, The Best Of Jet Harris & Tony Meehan (Spectrum 2000)★★★.

HARRISON, GEORGE
ALBUMS: Wonderwall (Apple 1968)★★, Electronic Sound (Apple 1969)★★, All Things Must Pass (Apple 1970) ★★★★, with other artists The Concert For Bangla Desh (Apple 1971)★★★★, Living In The Material World (Apple 1973)★★★, Dark Horse (Apple 1974)★, Extra Texture

(Read All About It) (Apple 1975)★★, *Thirty Three & 1/3* (Dark Horse 1976)★★★, *George Harrison* (Dark Horse 1979)★★★, *Somewhere In England* (Dark Horse 1981) ★★★, *Gone Troppo* (Dark Horse 1982)H, *Cloud Nine* (Dark Horse 1987)★★★★, *Live In Japan* (Dark Horse/Warners 1992)★★.
COMPILATIONS: *The Best Of George Harrison* (Parlophone/Capitol 1976)★★★, *Best Of Dark Horse 1976-1989* (Dark Horse/Warners 1989)★★★.
FURTHER READING: *George Harrison Yesterday And Today*, Ross Michaels. *I Me Mine*, George Harrison. *Fifty Years Adrift*, George Harrison and Derek Taylor. *Dark Horse: The Secret Life Of George Harrison*, Geoffrey Giuliano. *The Quiet One: A Life Of George Harrison*, Alan Clayson. *The Illustrated George Harrison*, Geoffrey Giuliano.
FILMS: *A Hard Day's Night* (1964), *Help!* (1965), *Magical Mystery Tour* (1967), *Yellow Submarine* (1968), *Let It Be* (1970), *Life Of Brian* (1979), *Water* (1985), *Shanghai Surprise* (1986).

HARRISON, WILBERT
ALBUMS: *Kansas City* (Sphere Sound 1965)★★★, *Let's Work Together* (Sue 1970)★★★, *Shoot You Full Of Love* (Juggernaut 1971)★★, *Anything You Want* (Wet Soul 1971)★★, *Wilbert Harrison* (Buddah 1971)★★, *Soul Food Man* (Chelsea 1976)★★, *Lovin' Operator* (Charly 1985) ★★, *Small Labels* (Krazy Kat 1986)★★, *Listen To My Song* (Savoy Jazz 1987)★★.
COMPILATIONS: *Kansas City* (Relic 1990)★★★★.

HARVEY, ALEX
ALBUMS: *Alex Harvey And His Soul Band* (Polydor 1964) ★★★, *The Blues* (Polydor 1964)★★★, *Hair Rave Up Live From The Shaftesbury Theatre* (Pye 1969)★★, *Roman Wall Blues* (Fontana 1969)★★, *Alex Harvey Narrates The Loch Ness Monster* (K-Tel 1977)★★, *The Mafia Stole My Guitar* (RCA 1979)★★, *The Soldier On The Wall* (Power Supply 1983)★★★.
COMPILATIONS: *The Collection* (Castle 1986)★★★, *Delilah: The Very Best Of Alex Harvey* (PolyGram 1998) ★★★, *Alex Harvey And His Soul Band* 1963, 1964 recordings (Bear Family 1999)★★★, *Faith Healer: An Introduction To The Sensational Alex Harvey Band* (Universal 2002)★★★.

HATFIELD, JULIANA
ALBUMS: *Hey Babe* (Mammoth 1992)★★, *Become What You Are* (Mammoth 1993)★★★, *Only Everything* (Mammoth 1995)★★★, *Bed* (Zoe 1998)★★, *Beautiful Creature* (Zoe 2000)★★★★, *Total System Failure* (Zoe 2000)★★.

HAVENS, RICHIE
ALBUMS: *Mixed Bag* (Verve/Forecast 1967)★★★★, *Richie Havens Record* (Douglas 1968)★★, *Electric Havens* (Douglas 1968)★★, *Something Else Again* (Forecast 1968)★★★, *Richard P. Havens 1983* (Forecast 1969)★★★★, *Stonehenge* (Stormy Forest 1970)★★, *Alarm Clock* (Stormy Forest 1971) ★★★, *The Great Blind Degree* (Stormy Forest 1971)★★, *Richie Havens On Stage* (Stormy Forest 1972)★★★, *Portfolio* (Stormy Forest 1973)★★★, *Mixed Bag II* (Stormy Forest 1974)★★, *The End Of The Beginning* (A&M 1976)★★, *Mirage* (A&M 1977)★★, *Connections* (Elektra 1980)★★, *Common Ground* (Connexion 1984)★★, *Simple Things* (RBI 1987)H, *Richie Havens Sings The Beatles And Dylan* (Rykodisc 1987)★★, *Live At The Cellar Door* (Five Star 1990)★★★, *Now* (Solar/Epic 1991)★★★, *Cuts To The Chase* (Rhino/Forward 1994)★★★, *Wishing Well* (Evangeline 2002)★★★★.
COMPILATIONS: *Resumé* (Rhino 1993)★★★★, *The Best Of Richie Havens – The Millennium Collection* (PolyGram 2000)★★★★.
FILMS: *Woodstock* (1970), *Catch My Soul* (1974), *Greased Lightning* (1977), *The Boss' Son* (1978), *Hearts Of Fire* (1987), *Street Hunter* (1990).

HAWKINS, 'SCREAMIN' JAY'
ALBUMS: *At Home With Screamin' Jay Hawkins* (Epic 1958)★★★, *I Put A Spell On You* (Epic 1959)★★★★, *The Night & Day Of Screamin' Jay Hawkins* (Planet 1965) ★★★, *What That Is* (Philips 1969)★★, *Screamin' Jay Hawkins* (Philips 1970)★★★, *A Portrait Of A Man & His Woman* (Hot Line 1972)★★★, *Frenzy* (Edsel 1982)★★, *Real Life* (Charly 1983)★★, *Live And Crazy* (Midnight Music 1986)★★★, *Feast Of The Mau Mau* (Edsel 1988) ★★, *Real Life* (Charly 1989)★★★, *Black Music For White People* (Demon 1991)★★★, *Stone Crazy* (Demon 1993) ★★★, *Somethin' Funny Goin' On* (Demon 1994)★★★, *At Last* (Last Call 1998)★★★★, *Live Olympia, Paris 1998* (Last Call 1999)★★★.
COMPILATIONS: *I Put A Spell On You* (Direction 1969)★★★, *Screamin' The Blues* (Red Lightnin' 1982)★★★★, *Frenzy* (Edsel 1986)★★★, *I Put A Spell On You* (Charly 1989)★★★, *Spellbound! 1955-1974* (Bear Family 1990)★★★★, *Voodoo Jive: The Best Of Screamin' Jay Hawkins* (Rhino 1990)★★★, *Cow Fingers & Mosquito Pie* (Epic 1991)★★★★, *1952-1955* (Magpie 1991)★★★, *From Gotham And Grand* (SJH 1992) ★★★, *Portrait Of A Man: A History Of Screamin' Jay Hawkins* (Edsel 1995)★★★, *Alligator Wine* (Music Club 1997)★★★, *Best Of The Bizarre Sessions: 1990-1994* (Manifesto 2000)★★★.
FILMS: *Mister Rock And Roll* (1957), *American Hot Wax* (1978), *Joey* (1985), *Two Moon Junction* (1988), *Mystery Train* (1989), *A Rage In Harlem* (1991), *Perdita Durango* aka *Dance With The Devil* (1997), *Peut-être* aka *Maybe* (1999).

HAWKINS, RONNIE
ALBUMS: *Ronnie Hawkins* (Roulette 1959)★★, *Mr. Dynamo* (Roulette 1960)★★, *The Folk Ballads Of Ronnie Hawkins* (Roulette 1960)★★, *Ronnie Hawkins Sings The Songs Of Hank Williams* (Roulette 1960)★★, *Ronnie Hawkins* (Cotillion 1970)★★, *Arkansas Rock Pile* (Roulette 1970)★★, *The Hawk i* (Cotillion 1971)★★, *Rock 'N' Roll Resurrection* (Monument 1972)★★, *The Giant Of Rock And Roll* (Monument 1974) ★★, *The Hawk ii* (United Artists 1979)★★, *Rrrracket Time* (Charly 1979)★★, *A Legend In His Spare Time* (Quality 1981)★★, *The Hawk And Rock* (Trilogy 1982)★★, *Making It Again* (Epic 1984)★★, *Hello Again ... Mary Lou* (Epic 1987)★★.
COMPILATIONS: *The Best Of Ronnie Hawkins & His Band* (Roulette 1970)★★★, *The Best Of Ronnie Hawkins And The Hawks* (Rhino 1990)★★★, *The Roulette Years* (Sequel 1994)★★★.
VIDEOS: *The Hawk In Concert* (MMG Video 1988), *This Country's Rockin' - Reunion Concert* (1993).
FURTHER READING: *The Hawk: The Story Of Ronnie Hawkins & The Hawks*, Ian Wallis.
FILMS: *The Last Waltz* (1978), *Renaldo And Clara* (1978), *Heaven's Gate* (1980), *Meatballs III* (1987), *Boozecan* (1994), *Red Green: Duct Tape Forever* (2001).

HAWKWIND
ALBUMS: *Hawkwind* (Liberty 1970)★★★★, *In Search Of Space* (United Artists 1971)★★★★, *Doremi Fasol Latido* (United Artists 1972)★★, *Space Ritual* (United Artists 1973)★★★★, *Hall Of The Mountain Grill* (United Artists 1974)★★★, *Warrior On The Edge Of Time* (United Artists 1975)★★★, *Astounding Sounds, Amazing Music* (Charisma 1976)★★★, *Quark, Strangeness And Charm* (Charisma 1977)★★, as Hawklords *25 Years On* (Charisma 1978)★★, *PXR5* (Charisma 1979)★★★, *Live 79* (Bronze 1980)★★, *Levitation* (Bronze 1980)★★★, *Sonic Attack* (RCA 1981) ★★★, *Church Of Hawkwind* (RCA 1982)★★, *Choose Your Masques* (RCA 1982)★★★, *Zones* (Flicknife 1983)★★★, *Stonehenge: This Is Hawkwind Do Not Panic* (Flicknife 1984)★★, *Bring Me The Head Of Yuri Gagarin* 1973 recording (Demi-Monde 1985)★, *Space Ritual Volume 2* (American Phonograph 1985)★★★, *Chronicle Of The Black Sword* (Flicknife 1985)★★★, *Ridicule* (Obsession 1985) ★★★, *Live Chronicles* (GWR 1986)★★★, *Out & Intake* (Flicknife 1987)★★, *The Xenon Codex* (GWR 1988)★★★, *Space Bandits* (GWR 1990)★★★, *Palace Springs* (GWR 1991)★★, *BBC Radio 1 Live In Concert* (Windsong 1991) ★★★, *The Friday Rock Show Sessions: Live At Reading '86* (Raw Fruit 1992)★★, *Electric Tepee* (Castle 1992)★★★, *It Is The Business Of The Future To Be Dangerous* (Castle 1993) ★★★, *The Business Trip: Live* (Emergency Broadcast Systems 1994)★★, *California Brainstorm* (Iloki/Cyclops 1995)★★★, *Future Reconstructions: Ritual Of The Solstice* (Emergency Broadcast Systems 1996)★★★, *1999 Party – Live At The Chicago Auditorium March 21 1974* (EMI 1997)★★★, *The Weird Tapes No 1: Dave Brock, Sonic Assassins* (Hawkwind 2000)★★★, *The Weird Tapes No 2: Hawkwind Live/Hawklords Studio* (Hawkwind 2000)★★★, *The Weird Tapes No 3: Free Festival* (Hawkwind 2000)★★, *The Weird Tapes No 4: Live '78* (Hawkwind 2000)★★, *The Weird Tapes No 5: Live '76 And '77* (Hawkwind 2000)★★★, *Atomhenge* (Hawkwind 2001)★★★, *Family Tree* (Hawkwind 2001)★★, *Spacebrock* (Hawkwind 2001)★★, *Yule Ritual: London Astoria 29.12.00* (Hawkwind 2001)★★★.
COMPILATIONS: *Road Hawks* (United Artists 1976)★★★, *Masters Of The Universe* (United Artists 1977)★★★, *Repeat Performance* (Charisma 1980)★★★, *Hawkwind, Friends And Relations* (Flicknife 1982)H, *Twice Upon A Time: Hawkwind, Friends And Relations Volume 2* (Flicknife 1983)★★, *The Text Of Festival (Hawkwind Live 1970-72)* (Illuminated 1983)★★, *Independent Days* mini-album (Flicknife 1984)★★, *Hawkwind, Friends And Relations Volume 3* (Flicknife 1985)★★, *Live 70/73* (Castle/Dojo 1985)★★, *In The Beginning* (Demi-Monde 1985)★★, *Utopia 84* (Mausoleum 1985)★★, *Anthology Volume 1* (Samurai 1985)★★★, *Welcome To The Future* (Mausoleum 1985)★★, *Anthology Volume 2* (Samurai 1986)★★★, *Anthology Volume 3* (Samurai 1986)★★, *Hawkfan 12* (Hawkfan 1986)★★★, *The Hawkwind Collection* (Castle 1986)★★★★, *Angels Of Death* (RCA 1986)★★★, *Independent Days Volume 2* (Flicknife 1986)★★, *Approved History Of Hawkwind* 3-LP set (Samurai 1986)★★★, British Tribal Music (Start 1987)★★, *Early Daze (Best Of Hawkwind)* (Thunderbolt 1987)★★, *Spirit Of The Age* (Virgin 1988) ★★★, *Best Of Hawkwind, Friends And Relations* (Flicknife 1988)★★★, *Ironstrike* (Avanti 1989)★★, *Night Of The Hawk* (Powerhouse 1989)★★★, *The Best Of And The Rest Of Hawkwind Live* (Action Replay 1990)★★, *Night Riding* (Knight 1990)★★, *Stasis: The UA Years 1971-1975* (EMI 1990)★★★, *Masters Of The Universe* not 1977 UA release (Marble Arch 1991)★★, *Spirit Of The Age* not 1988 Virgin release (Elite 1991)★★, *Anthology* 3-CD set (Castle 1991) ★★★, *Mighty Hawkwind Classics 1980-1985* (Anagram 1992)★★★, *The Psychedelic Warlords* (Cleopatra 1992) ★★★, *Lord Of Light* (Cleopatra 1993)★★★, *Hawkwind, Friends And Relations, The Rarities* (Anagram 1995)★★★, *Sonic Boom Killers: Best Of Singles A's And B's From 1970 To 1980* (Repertoire 1999)★★★, *Epocheclipse: The Ultimate Best Of* (EMI 1999)★★★, *Epocheclipse* 3-CD box set (EMI 1999)★★.
VIDEOS: *Night Of The Hawks* (Jettisoundz 1984), with Enid, Roy Harper *Stonehenge 84* (Jettisoundz 1984), *Chronicle Of The Black Sword* (Jettisoundz 1986), *Live Legends* (Castle 1990), *Promo Collection* (Castle 1992), *Hawkwind: The Solstice At Stonehenge 1984* (1993), *Love In Space 1995* (Visionary 1996).
FURTHER READING: *This Is Hawkwind, Do Not Panic*, Kris Tait.

HAYES, ISAAC
ALBUMS: *Presenting Isaac Hayes* later reissued as *In The Beginning* (Stax 1967)★★, *Hot Buttered Soul* (Enterprise 1969)★★★★, *The Isaac Hayes Movement* (Enterprise 1970)★★, *To Be Continued* (Enterprise 1970)★★, *Shaft* film soundtrack (Enterprise 1971)★★★★, *Black Moses* (Enterprise 1971)★★, *Live At The Sahara Tahoe* (Enterprise 1973)★★★, *Joy* (Enterprise 1973)★★, *Tough Guys* film soundtrack (Enterprise 1974)★★, *Truck Turner* film soundtrack (Enterprise 1974)★★, *Chocolate Chip* (HBS 1975)★★★, *Use Me* (Enterprise 1975)★★, *Disco Connection* (HBS 1976)★★, *Groove-A-Thon* (HBS 1976)H, *Juicy Fruit (Disco Freak)* (HBS 1976)H, with Dionne Warwick *A Man And A Woman* (HBS 1977)★★★, *New Horizon* (Polydor 1977)H, *Hot Bed* (Stax 1978)★★, *For The Sake Of Love* (Polydor 1978)H, *Don't Let Go* (Polydor 1979)★★, with Millie Jackson *Royal Rappin's* (Polydor 1979)★★, *And Once Again* (Polydor 1980)★★, *A Lifetime Thing* (Polydor 1981)★★, *U Turn* (Columbia 1984) ★★, *Love Attack* (Columbia 1988)★★, *Branded* (PointBlank 1995)★★, *Raw And Refined* (PointBlank 1995)★★.
COMPILATIONS: *The Best Of Isaac Hayes* (Enterprise 1975)★★★, *Enterprise: His Greatest Hits* (Stax 1980) ★★★★, *Best Of Isaac Hayes, Volumes 1 & 2* (Stax 1986)★★★, *Isaac's Moods* (Stax 1988)★★★, *Greatest Hit Singles* (Stax 1991)★★★, *The Collection* (Connoisseur Collection 1995)★★★, *Wonderful* (Stax/Ace 1997)★★★, *The Man! The Ultimate Isaac Hayes 1969-1977* (Stax/Ace 2001)★★★★.

HEALEY, JEFF
ALBUMS: *See The Light* (Arista 1989)★★★★, *Hell To Pay* (Arista 1990)★★, *Feel This* (Arista 1992)★★★, *Cover To Cover* (Arista 1995)★★★, *Get Me Some* (Forte 2000)★★★★.
COMPILATIONS: *The Very Best Of* (Camden 1998)★★★, *The Master Hits* (Arista 1999)★★★.
FILMS: *Roadhouse* (1989).

HEAR'SAY
ALBUMS: *Popstars* (Polydor 2001)★★, *Everybody* (Polydor 2001)★★.
VIDEOS: *Popstars: The Video* (Granada Media 2001).
FURTHER READING: *Popstars: The Making Of Hear'Say*, Maria Malone. *Hear'Say*, Suzie Russell. *Hear'Say: Our Story*, Maria Malone.

HEART
ALBUMS: *Dreamboat Annie* (Mushroom 1976)★★★★, *Little Queen* (Portrait 1977)★★★, *Dog And Butterfly* (Portrait 1978)★★★★, *Magazine* (Mushroom 1978)★★, *Bebe Le Strange* (Portrait 1980)★★★, *Greatest Hits/Live* (Portrait 1981)★★★, *Private Audition* (Epic 1982)★★, *Passionworks* (Epic 1983)★★, *Heart* (Capitol 1985)★★, *Bad Animals* (Capitol 1987)★★, *Brigade* (Capitol 1990)★★, *Rock The House Live!* (Capitol 1991)★★, *Desire Walks On* (Capitol 1993)★★, *The Road Home* (Capitol 1995)★★★.
SOLO: Nancy Wilson *Live At McCabes Guitar Shop* (Epic 1999)★★.
COMPILATIONS: *Heart Box Set* (Capitol 1990)★★, *Greatest Hits* (Capitol 1997)★★★.
VIDEOS: *If Looks Could Kill* (PMI/EMI 1988), *The Road Home* (Capitol 1995).

HEARTBREAKERS
ALBUMS: *L.A.M.F.* (Track 1977)★★★★, *Live At Max's Kansas City* (Max's Kansas City 1979)★★, *D.T.K. Live At The Speakeasy* (Jungle 1982)★★, *Live At The Lyceum Ballroom 1984* (ABC 1984)★★, *L.A.M.F. Revisited* remixed version of their debut (Jungle 1984)★★★.
COMPILATIONS: *D.T.K. - L.A.M.F.* (Jungle 1984)★★★.

HEATWAVE
ALBUMS: *Too Hot To Handle* (Epic 1977)★★★★, *Central Heating* (Epic 1978)★★★, *Hot Property* (Epic 1979)★★, *Candles* (Epic 1980)★★★, *Current* (Epic 1982)★★.
COMPILATIONS: *Best Of* (Epic 1993)★★★★.

HEAVEN 17
ALBUMS: *Penthouse And Pavement* (Virgin 1981)★★★, *Heaven 17* (Virgin 1983)★★★, *The Luxury Gap* (Virgin 1983)★★★, *How Men Are* (BEF 1984)★★, *Endless* (Virgin 1986)★★, *Pleasure One* (Virgin 1987)★★★, *Teddy Bear, Duke & Psycho* (Virgin 1988)★★★, *Bigger Than America* (Warners 1996)★★, *How Live Is* (Almafame 1999)★★.
COMPILATIONS: *Higher & Higher (The Very Best Of Heaven 17)* (Virgin 1993)★★★, *Retox/Detox* (Eagle 1998)★★.

HELL, RICHARD
ALBUMS: with the Voidoids *Blank Generation* (Sire 1977)★★★★, with the Voidoids *Destiny Street* (Red Star 1982)★★★, *Go Now* spoken word (Codex 1995)★★.
COMPILATIONS: *R.I.P.* (ROIR 1984)★★★, with the Voidoids *Funhunt* (ROIR 1989)★★★, *Time* (Matador 2002)★★★.
VIDEOS: *Smithereens* (Merlin 1983), *Blank Generation* (Hendring Music Video 1991).
FURTHER READING: *Artifact*, Richard Hell. *The Voidoid*, Richard Hell. *Go Now: A Novel*, Richard Hell. *Hot And Cold*, Richard Hell.
FILMS: *Blank Generation* (1979), *Smithereens* (1982), *Geek Maggot Bingo* aka *The Freak From Suckweasel Mountain* (1983), *Desperately Seeking Susan* (1985).

HELLOWEEN
ALBUMS: *Helloween* mini-album (Noise 1985)★★, *Walls Of Jericho* (Noise 1986)★★, *Keeper Of The Seven Keys Part I* (Noise 1987)★★★, *Keeper Of The Seven Keys Part II* (Noise 1988)★★★, *Live In The UK* (Noise 1989)★★, *Pink Bubbles Go Ape* (EMI 1991)★★, *Chameleon* (EMI 1993)★★, *The Master Of The Rings* (Raw Power 1994)★★★, *The Time Of The Oath* (Raw Power 1996)★★★, *High Live* (Raw Power 1996)★★, *Better Than Raw* (Raw Power 1998)★★★, *Metal Jukebox* (Raw Power 1999)★★, *The Dark Ride* (Nuclear Blast 2000)★★★.
COMPILATIONS: *The Best The Rest The Rare* (Noise 1991) ★★★.

HENDRIX, JIMI
ALBUMS: *Are You Experienced?* (Track 1967)★★★★★, *Axis: Bold As Love* (Track 1967)★★★★★, *Electric Ladyland* (Track 1968)★★★★, *Band Of Gypsies* (Track 1970)★★★, shared with Otis Redding *Monterey International Pop Festival* (Reprise 1970)★★★★, *Cry Of Love* (Polydor 1971)★★★, *Experience* (Ember 1971)★★, *Isle Of Wight* (Polydor 1971)★★, *Rainbow Bridge* (Reprise 1971)★★, *Hendrix In The West* (Polydor 1971)★★★, *More Experience* (Ember 1972)H, *War Heroes* (Polydor 1972)★★, *Loose Ends* (Polydor 1974)★★, *Crash Landing* (Polydor 1975) ★★, *Midnight Lightnin'* (Polydor 1975)★★, *Nine To The Universe* (Polydor 1980)★★, *The Jimi Hendrix Concerts* (Columbia 1982)★★★, *Jimi Plays Monterey* (Polydor 1986) ★★★, *Live At Winterland* (Polydor 1987)★★★, *Radio One* (Castle 1988)★★★★, *Live And Unreleased* (Castle 1989) ★★★, *First Rays Of The New Rising Sun* (Experience/MCA 1997)★★★, *South Saturn Delta* (Experience 1997)★★★, *Original Soundtrack To The Motion Picture 'Experience'* (Charly 1998)★★, *Live At The Fillmore East* (MCA 1999) ★★★★, *Live At Woodstock* (MCA 1999)★★★, *The Albert Hall Experience* (Charly 2001)★★.
COMPILATIONS: *Smash Hits* (Track 1968)★★★★, *The Essential Jimi Hendrix* (Polydor 1978)★★★★, *The Essential Jimi Hendrix Volume Two* (Polydor 1979)★★★, *The Singles Album* (Polydor 1983)★★★★, *Kiss The Sky* (Polydor 1984) ★★★, *Cornerstones* (Polydor 1990)★★★, *Blues* (Polydor 1994)★★★, *Exp Over Sweden* (Univibes 1993)★★, *Jimi In Denmark* (Univibes 1995)★★, *BBC Sessions* (Experience/MCA 1998)★★★★, *Experience Hendrix: The Best Of Jimi Hendrix* (Experience/MCA 1998)★★★★, *The Jimi Hendrix Experience* 4-CD box set (Experience/MCA 2000)★★★★, *The Summer Of Love Sessions* (Freud 2001)★★, *Voodoo Child: The Jimi Hendrix Collection* (Universal 2001)★★★★.
VIDEOS: *Jimi Hendrix Plays Berkeley* (Palace Video 1986), *Jimi Plays Monterey* (Virgin Vision 1986), *Jimi Hendrix* (Warner Home Video 1986), *Experience* (Palace Video 1987), *Rainbow Bridge* (Hendring Video 1988), *Live At The Isle Of Wight 1970* (Rhino Home Video 1990), *Jimi Hendrix Live At Monterey* (1994), *Jimi At Woodstock* (BMG 1995), *Jimi At The Atlanta Pop Festival* (BMG 1995), *Jimi Hendrix Experience* (BMG 1995), *Jimi Hendrix Plays The Great Pop Festivals* (BMG 1995).
FURTHER READING: *Jimi: An Intimate Biography Of Jimi Hendrix*, Curtis Knight. *Jimi Hendrix*, Alain Dister. *Jimi Hendrix: Voodoo Child Of The Aquarian Age*, David Henderson. *Scuze Me While I Kiss The Sky: The Life Of Jimi Hendrix*, David Henderson. *Hendrix: A Biography*, Chris Welch. *Hendrix: An Illustrated Biography*, Victor Sampson. *The Jimi Hendrix Story*, Jerry Hopkins. *Crosstown Traffic: Jimi Hendrix And Post-War Pop*, Charles Shaar Murray. *Jimi Hendrix: Electric Gypsy*, Harry Shapiro and Caesar Glebbeek. *Are You Experienced?*, Noel Redding and Carole Appleby. *The Hendrix Experience*, Mitch Mitchell and John Platt. *And The Man With The Guitar*, Jon Price and Gary Geldeart. *The Jimi Hendrix Experience In 1967 (Limited Edition)*, Gerard Mankowitz and Robert Whitaker (photographers). *Jimi Hendrix: A Visual Documentary, His Life, Loves And Music*, Tony Brown. *Jimi Hendrix: Starchild*, Curtis Knight. *Hendrix: Setting The Record Straight*, John McDermott with Eddie Kramer. *The Illustrated Jimi Hendrix*, Geoffrey Guiliano. *Cherokee Mist - The Lost Writings Of Jimi Hendrix*, Bill Nitopi (compiler). *Voodoo Child: The Illustrated Legend Of Jimi Hendrix*, Martin L. Green and Bill Sienkiewicz. *The Ultimate Experience*, Adrian Boot and Chris Salewicz. *The Lost Writings Of Jimi Hendrix*, Jimi Hendrix. *The Complete Studio Recording Sessions 1963-1970*, John McDermott. *Complete Guide To The Music Of*, John Robertson. *The Inner World Of Jimi Hendrix*, Monika Dannemann. *Jimi Hendrix Experience*, Jerry Hopkins. *Jimi Hendrix: Voices From Home*, Mary Willix. *The Man, The Music, The Memorabilia*, Caesar Glebbeek and Douglas Noble. *Eye Witness: The Illustrated Jimi Hendrix Concerts*, Ben Valkhoff. *Hendrix: The Final Days*, Tony Brown. *The Jimi Hendrix Companion*, Chris Potash (ed.). *Through Gypsy Eyes: My Life, The Sixties And Jimi Hendrix*, Kathy Etchingham. *Eyewitness Hendrix*, Johnny Black. *Jimi Hendrix Concert Files*, Tony Brown.

HENLEY, DON
ALBUMS: *I Can't Stand Still* (Asylum 1982)★★★★, *Building The Perfect Beast* (Geffen 1984)★★★★, *The End Of The Innocence* (Geffen 1989)★★★, *Inside Job* (Warners 2000)★★.
COMPILATIONS: *Actual Miles: Henley's Greatest Hits* (Geffen 1995)★★★.
VIDEOS: *Live: Inside Job* (Aviva International 2001).

HERD
ALBUMS: *Paradise Lost* (Fontana 1968)★★★, *Lookin' Thru You* US only (Fontana 1968)★★★, *Nostalgia* (Bumble 1972)★★★.
COMPILATIONS: *An Anthology* (Music Club 1998)★★★, *I Can Fly: The Very Best Of The Herd* (Collectables 1998)★★★.

HERMAN'S HERMITS
ALBUMS: *Herman's Hermits* (Columbia 1965)★★★, *Introducing Herman's Hermits* (Columbia 1965)★★★, *Herman's Hermits On Tour* (Columbia 1965)★★★, *Hold On!* film soundtrack (Columbia 1966)★★, *Both Sides Of Herman's Hermits* (Columbia 1966)★★★, *There's A Kind Of Hush* (Columbia 1967)★★★, *Mrs Brown You've Got A Lovely Daughter* (Columbia 1968)★★★, *Blaze* (Columbia 1967)★★★, as Sourmash *A Whale Of A Tale!* 1972 recording (Pluto 2001)★★.
COMPILATIONS: *The Best Of Herman's Hermits* (Columbia 1969)★★★, *The Most Of Herman's Hermits* (MFP 1971) ★★★, *The Most Of Herman's Hermits, Volume 2* (MFP 1972)★★★, *Twenty Greatest Hits* (K-Tel 1977)★★★, *The Very Best Of Herman's Hermits* (MFP 1984)★★★, *The Collection* (Castle 1990)★★★, *The EP Collection* (See For Miles 1990)★★★★, *The Best Of The EMI Years, Volume 1* (EMI 1991)★★★★, *The Best Of The EMI Years, Volume 2* (EMI 1992)★★★, *Golden Legends* (Direct Source 2000)★★★.
FILMS: *When The Boys Meet The Girls* (1965), *Hold On!* aka *There's No Place Like Space* (1966).

HEYWARD, NICK
ALBUMS: *North Of A Miracle* (Arista 1983)★★★, *Postcards From Home* (Arista 1986)★★, *I Love You Avenue* (Warners 1988)★★, *From Monday To Sunday* (Epic 1992)★★, *Tangled* (Epic 1995)★★★★, *The Apple Bed* (Creation 1998)★★★.
COMPILATIONS: *Best Of Nick Heyward And Haircut 100* (Ariola 1989)★★★★, *The Greatest Hits Of Nick Heyward & Haircut 100* (RCA Camden 1996)★★★★.
FURTHER READING: *The Haircut 100 Catalogue*, Sally Payne. *Haircut 100: Not A Trace Of Brylcreem*, no editor listed.

HIATT, JOHN
ALBUMS: *Hanging Around The Observatory* (Epic 1974) ★★★, *Overcoats* (Epic 1975)★★★, *Slug Line* (Epic 1979) ★★★, *Two Bit Monsters* (MCA 1980)★★★, *All Of A Sudden* (MCA 1982)★★, *Riding With The King* (Geffen 1983)★★★★, *Warming Up To The Ice Age* (Geffen 1985)★★★, *Bring The Family* (A&M 1987)★★★★, *Slow Turning* (A&M 1988)★★★, *Stolen Moments* (A&M 1990)★★★, *Perfectly Good Guitar* (A&M 1993)★★★★, with the Guilty Dogs *Hiatt Comes Alive At Budokan?* (A&M 1994)★★★, *Walk On* (Capitol 1995) ★★★★, *Little Head* (Capitol 1997)★★★, *Crossing Muddy Waters* (Vanguard/Sanctuary 2000)★★★★, *The Tiki Bar Is Open* (Vanguard/Sanctuary 2001)★★★.
COMPILATIONS: *Y'All Caught?: The Ones That Got Away 1979-1985* (Geffen 1991)★★★, *The Best Of John Hiatt* (Parlophone 1998)★★★, *Greatest Hits: The A&M Years '87-'94* (A&M 1998)★★★★, *Anthology* (Hip-O 2001)★★★★.

HICKS, DAN
ALBUMS: *The Original Recordings* (Epic 1969)★★★, *Where's The Money?* (Blue Thumb 1971)★★★, *Striking It Rich!* (Blue Thumb 1972)★★★★, *Last Train To Hicksville ... The Home Of Happy Feet* (Blue Thumb 1973)★★, *It Happened One Bite* (Warners 1978)★★★, with the Acoustic Warriors *Shootin' Straight* (Private Music 1994)★★★, *Beatin' The Heat* (Surfdog 2000)★★★.
COMPILATIONS: *Rich & Happy In Hicksville: Very Best Of Dan Hicks And His Hot Licks* (See For Miles 1985)★★★, *Return To Hicksville: The Best Of Dan Hicks And His Hot Licks (The Blue Thumb Years 1971-1973)* (Hip-O 1997)★★★★, *Early Muses* (Big Beat 1998)★★★.

HIGH LLAMAS
ALBUMS: as Sean O'Hagan *High Llamas* (Demon 1990) ★★★, *Apricots* mini-album (Plastic 1992)★★, *Santa Barbara* (Vogue/Mute 1994)★★★, *Gideon Gaye* (Target 1994) ★★★★, *Hawaii* (Alpaca Park 1996)★★★★, *Cold And Bouncy* (Alpaca Park 1997)★★★, *Lollo Rosso* remix album (V2 1998)★★★, *Snowbug* (V2 1999)★★★, *Buzzle Bee* (Duophonic 2000)★★.

HILL, FAITH
ALBUMS: *Take Me As I Am* (Warners 1993)★★★, *It Matters To Me* (Warners 1995)★★★★, *Faith* (US) *Love Will Always Win* (UK) (Warners 1998)★★★★, *Breathe* (Warners 1999)★★★.
VIDEOS: *Piece Of My Heart* (Deaton Flanigen 1994).

HILL, LAURYN
ALBUMS: *The Miseducation Of Lauryn Hill* (Columbia 1998)★★★★.
FILMS: *King Of The Hill* (1993), *Sister Act 2: Back In The Habit* (1993), *Rhyme & Reason* (1997), *Hav Plenty* (1997), *Restaurant* (1998).

HILLAGE, STEVE
ALBUMS: *Fish Rising* (Virgin 1975)★★★, *L* (Virgin 1976) ★★★, *Motivation Radio* (Virgin 1977)★★★, *Green* (Virgin 1978)★★★, *Live Herald* (Virgin 1979)★★★, *Open* (Virgin 1979)★★★, *Rainbow Dome Musick* (Virgin 1979)★★★, *For To Next/And Not Or* (Virgin 1983)★★★.

HITCHCOCK, ROBYN
ALBUMS: *Black Snake Diamond Role* (Armageddon 1981) ★★★, *Groovy Decay* (Albion 1982)★★, *I Often Dream Of Trains* (Midnight Music 1984)★★★, with the Egyptians *Fegmania!* (Midnight Music/Slash 1985)★★★★, with the Egyptians *Gotta Let This Hen Out!* (Midnight Music/Relativity 1985)★★★★, *Groovy Decoy* original demos of *Groovy Decay* (Midnight Music 1985)★★★, with the Egyptians *Element Of Light* (Glass Fish/Relativity 1986) ★★★★, with the Egyptians *Globe Of Frogs* (A&M 1988) ★★★, with the Egyptians *Queen Elvis* (A&M 1989)★★, *Eye* (Glass Fish/Twin/Tone 1990)★★★, with the Egyptians *Perspex Island* (Go! Discs/A&M 1991)★★★, with the Egyptians *Respect* (A&M 1993)★★★, *Mossy Liquor (Outtakes And Prototypes)* vinyl-only release (Warners 1996)★★★, *Moss Elixir* (Warners 1996)★★★, with the Egyptians *Live At The Cambridge Folk Festival* (Strange Fruit 1998)★★★, *Storefront Hitchcock* (Warners 1998)★★★, *Jewels For Sophia* (Warners 1999)★★★, *A Star For Bram* (Editions PAF! 2000) ★★★.
COMPILATIONS: *Invisible Hitchcock* (Glass Fish/Relativity 1986)★★★, *Robyn Hitchcock And The Egyptians: The Kershaw Sessions* (Strange Roots 1994)★★★, *You & Oblivion* (Rhino/Sequel 1995)★★★, *Robyn Hitchcock* (Sequel 1995)★★★, *Gravy Deco* (Rhino 1995)★★★, with the Egyptians *Greatest Hits* (A&M 1996)★★★, *Uncorrected Personality Traits* (Rhino/Sequel 1997)★★★★.
VIDEOS: *Gotta Let This Hen Out!* (Jettisoundz 1985), *Brenda Of The Lightbulb Eyes* (A&M 1990).

HOLE
ALBUMS: *Pretty On The Inside* (City Slang 1991)★★★, *Live Through This* (Geffen 1994)★★★★, *Celebrity Skin* (Geffen 1998)★★★.
COMPILATIONS: *My Body The Hand Grenade* (City Slang 1997)★★★.
FURTHER READING: *Courtney Love*, Nick Wise. *Queen Of Noise: A Most Unauthorised Biography*, Melissa Rossi. *Look Through This*, Susan Wilson. *Courtney Love: The Real Story*, Poppy Z. Brite.
FILMS: *The People Vs Larry Flynt* (1997), *Kurt & Courtney* (1998).

HOLLAND/DOZIER/HOLLAND
COMPILATIONS: *Hot Wax Greatest Hits* (Hot Wax 1972) ★★★, *The Very Best Of The Invictus Years* (Deep Beats 1997)★★★, *Invictus Unconquered: The Best Of Invictus Records Vol. 1* (Deep Beats 1998)★★★, *Cherish What Is Dear To You: Invictus Unconquered Volume Two* (Deep Beats 1998)★★★, *Molten Gold: The Best Of Hot Wax Records* (Deep Beats 1998)★★★, *Invictus Chartbusters* (Sequel 1999)★★★, *Why Can't We Be Lovers* (Castle 2000)★★★.

HOLLIES
ALBUMS: *Stay With The Hollies* (Parlophone 1964)★★★★, *Here I Go Again* US only (Imperial 1964)★★★★, *In The Hollies Style* (Parlophone 1964)★★★★, *Hollies* aka *Reflection* (Parlophone 1965)★★★★, *Hear! Here!* US only (Imperial 1965)★★★★, *Beat Group!* US only (Imperial 1966)★★★★, *Would You Believe?* (Parlophone 1966) ★★★★, *Bus Stop* US only (Imperial 1966)★★★★, *For Certain Because ...* aka *Stop! Stop! Stop!* (Parlophone 1966)★★★★, Stop! Stop! Stop! US only (Imperial 1967) ★★★★, *Evolution* aka *The Hollies* (Parlophone/Epic 1967) ★★★, *Butterfly* (Parlophone 1967)★★★, *Dear Eloise/King Midas In Reverse* US only (Epic 1967)★★★, *The Hollies Sing Dylan* (UK) *Words And Music By Bob Dylan* (US) (Parlophone/Epic 1969)★★, *Hollies Sing Hollies* (Parlophone 1969)★★, *He Ain't Heavy, He's My Brother* US only (Epic 1969)★★, *Confessions Of The Mind* (Parlophone 1970)★★, *Moving Finger* US only (Epic 1970)★★, *Distant Light* (Parlophone/Epic 1971)★★, *Romany* (Polydor/Epic 1972)★★, *Out On The Road* (Hansa 1973)★★, *Hollies* (Polydor/Epic 1974)★★, *Another Night* (Polydor/Epic 1975)★★, *Write On* (Polydor 1976)★★, *Russian Roulette* (Polydor 1976)★★, *Live Hits* (Polydor 1977)★★, *Clarke, Hicks, Sylvester, Calvert, Elliott* US only (Epic 1977)★★, *A Crazy Steal* (Polydor/Epic 1978)★★, *Five Three One-Double Seven O Four* (Polydor 1979)★★, *Buddy Holly* (Polydor 1980)★★, *What Goes Around* (WEA/Atlantic 1983)★★.
COMPILATIONS: *The Hollies' Greatest Hits* US only (Imperial 1967)★★★★, *Hollies' Greatest* (Parlophone 1968)★★★★, *Hollies' Greatest Vol. 2* (Parlophone 1972)★★★, *The Hollies' Greatest Hits* US only (Epic 1973)★★★★, *The Very Best Of The Hollies* US only (United Artists 1975)★★★, *The History Of The Hollies* (EMI 1975)★★★, *The Hollies Volume 1* US only (Realm 1976)★★★, *Everything You Always Wanted To Hear By The Hollies But Were Afraid To Ask* US only (Epic 1977)★★★, *20 Golden Greats* (EMI 1978) ★★★★, *The Best Of The Hollies EP's* (Parlophone 1978) ★★★★, *The Other Side Of The Hollies* (Parlophone 1978) ★★★, *Up Front* (St. Michael 1979)★★★, *Long Cool Woman In A Black Dress* (MFP 1979)★★★, *Hollies' Greatest* US only (Capitol 1980)★★★, *The Air That I Breathe* (Polydor 1980) ★★★, *The Hollies* (MFP 1985)★★★, *Not The Hits Again* (See For Miles 1986)★★★★, *All The Hits And More: The Definitive Collection* (EMI 1988)★★★★, *Rarities* (EMI 1988) ★★★★, *The Hollies* US only (CBS 1989)★★★, *Love Songs* (MFP 1990)★★★, *The Hollies Epic Anthology* US only (Epic 1990)★★★★, *The Air That I Breathe: The Best Of The Hollies* (EMI 1993)★★★, *30th Anniversary Collection 1963-1993* 3-CD box set (EMI 1993)★★★★, *Singles A's And B's 1970-1979* (MFP 1993)★★★★, *Four Hollies Originals* 4-CD box set (EMI 1994)★★★, *Legendary Top Tens 1963-1988* (Avon 1994)★★★, *The Best Of The Hollies* (MFP 1995)★★★, *Four More Hollies Originals* 4-CD box set (EMI 1996)★★★, *20 Classic Tracks* (EMI 1996)★★★, *The Best Of The Hollies* (EMI 1997)★★★★, *At Abbey Road 1963 To 1966* (EMI 1997) ★★★★, *A Special Collection* 3-CD box set (MFP 1997) ★★★, *At Abbey Road 1966 To 1970* (EMI 1998)★★★★, *The Essential Collection* (MFP 1998)★★★, *At Abbey Road 1973 To 1989* (EMI 1998)★★★, *Orchestral Heaven* (EMI 2000)★★, *Classic Masters* (EMD 2002)★★★★.
FILMS: *It's All Over Town* (1964).

HOLLOWAY, BRENDA
ALBUMS: *Every Little Bit Hurts* (Tamla 1964)★★★, *The Artistry Of Brenda Holloway* (Motown 1968)★★★, *Together* (KRL 1999)★★★.
COMPILATIONS: *Greatest Hits & Rare Classics* (Motown 1991)★★★, *The Very Best Of Brenda Holloway* (Motown 1999)★★★★.

HOLLY, BUDDY
ALBUMS: *The 'Chirping' Crickets* (Brunswick 1957)★★★★, *Buddy Holly* (Coral 1958)★★★★, *That'll Be The Day* (Decca 1958)★★★★, *The Buddy Holly Story* (Coral 1959)★★★★, *The Buddy Holly Story, Volume 2* (Coral 1960)★★★★, *Buddy Holly And The Crickets* (Coral 1963)★★★★, *Reminiscing* (Coral 1963)★★★★, *Showcase* (Coral 1964) ★★★★, *Holly In The Hills* (Coral 1965)★★★★, *The Great Buddy Holly* (Vocalion 1967)★★★★, *Giant* (Coral 1969) ★★★★, *Remember* (Coral 1971)★★★, *Good Rockin'* (Vocalion 1971)★★★, *A Rock And Roll Collection* (Decca 1972)★★★, *The Nashville Sessions* (MCA 1975)★★★★, *Western And Bop* (Coral 1977)★★★, *For The First Time Anywhere* (MCA 1983)★★★, *From The Original Master Tapes* (MCA 1985)★★★★, *Something Special From Buddy Holly* (Rollercoaster 1986)★★★, Buddy Holly And The Picks *Original Voices Of The Crickets* (Ace 1993)★★.
COMPILATIONS: *The Best Of Buddy Holly* (Coral 1966) ★★★★, *Buddy Holly's Greatest Hits* (Coral 1967)★★★, *Rave On* (MFP 1975)★★★, *20 Golden Greats* (MCA 1978) ★★★★★, *The Complete Buddy Holly* 6-LP box set (Coral 1979)★★★★, *Love Songs* (MCA 1981)★★★, *Legend* (MCA 1985)★★★★, *Buddy Holly Rocks* (Charly 1985)★★★, *Buddy Holly* (Castle 1986)★★★, *True Love Ways* (Telstar 1989) ★★★★, *Words Of Love* (PolyGram 1993)★★★★, *The Singles Collection 1957-1960* (Pickwick 1994)★★★, *The Very Best Of Buddy Holly* (Dino 1996)★★★★, *The Ultimate EP Collection* (See For Miles 2001)★★★★.
FURTHER READING: *Buddy Holly*, Dave Laing. *Buddy Holly: A Biography In Words Photographs And Music*, Elizabeth Peer and Ralph Peer. *Buddy Holly: His Life And Music*, John Goldrosen. *The Buddy I Knew*, Larry Holley. *The Buddy Holly Story*, John Goldrosen. *Buddy Holly And The Crickets*, Alan Clark. *Buddy Holly: 30th Anniversary Memorial Series No 1*, Alan Clark. *The Legend That Is Buddy Holly*, Richard Peters. *Buddy Holly, Alan Mann's A-Z*, Alan Mann. *Buddy Holly: A Biography*, Ellis Amburn. *Remembering Buddy*, John Goldrosen and John Beecher. *Buddy The Biography* (UK) *Rave On* (USA), Phillip Norman. *Memories Of Buddy Holly*, Jim Dawson and Spencer Leigh.

HOLLYWOOD ARGYLES
ALBUMS: *The Hollywood Argyles* (Lute 1960)★★★.

HOLMES, DAVID
ALBUMS: *This Film's Crap, Let's Slash The Seats* (Go! Discs 1995)★★★★, *Let's Get Killed* (Go! Beat 1997)★★★★, *Stop Arresting Artists* (Go! Beat 1998)★★★, *Out Of Sight OS* film soundtrack (Jersey/MCA 1998)★★★★, *Bow Down To The Exit Sign* (Go! Beat/1500 Records 2000)★★★★, *Ocean's Eleven* film soundtrack (Warners 2002)★★★★.
COMPILATIONS: *Essential Mix* (ffrr 1998)★★★★, as David Holmes Introducing Free Association *Come Get It I Got It* (13 Amp 2002)★★★.

HONEYCOMBS
ALBUMS: *The Honeycombs* (Pye 1964)★★★, *All Systems Go* (Pye 1965)★★★, *Here Are The Honeycombs* (Vee Jay 1964)★★★.
COMPILATIONS: *Meek And Honey* (PRT 1983)★★★, *It's The Honeycombs/All Systems Go* (Sequel 1990)★★★, *The Best Of The Honeycombs* (Sequel 1993)★★★.

HOOKER, JOHN LEE
ALBUMS: with Sticks McGhee *Highways Of Blues* (Audio Lab 1959)★★, *The Folk Blues Of John Lee Hooker* (Riverside 1959)★★★★, *I'm John Lee Hooker* (Vee Jay 1959)★★★★, *Travelin'* (Vee Jay 1960)★★★★, *Sings The Blues* (King 1960)★★★★, *Thats My Story* (Riverside 1960) ★★★★, *House Of The Blues* (Chess 1960)★★★★, *The Blues* (Crown 1960)★★★, *The Country Blues Of John Lee Hooker* (Riverside 1960)★★★★, *The Folk Lore Of John Lee Hooker* (Vee Jay 1961)★★★★, *Burnin'* (Vee Jay 1962) ★★★, *John Lee Hooker On Campus* (Vee Jay 1963)★★★, *The Great John Lee Hooker* (Crown 1963)★★, *The Big Soul Of John Lee Hooker* (Vee Jay 1963)★★★, *Don't Turn Me From Your Door* (Atco 1963)★★★, *John Lee Hooker At Newport* (Vee Jay 1964)★★★★, Burning Hell (Riverside/Fontana 1964)★★★★, *I Want To Shout The Blues* (Stateside 1964)★★★, *John Lee Hooker And Seven Nights* (Verve/Folkways 1965)★★★, *Real Folk Blues* (Chess 1966) ★★★★, *It Serve You Right To Suffer* (Impulse! 1966)★★★, *Live At The Cafe Au Go Go* (Bluesway 1966)★★★★, *Urban Blues* (Bluesway 1967)★★★, *Simply The Truth* (Bluesway 1968)★★★, *You're Leaving Me Baby* (Riverside 1969)★★★★, Tupelo Blues (Riverside 1969), with Earl Hooker *If You Miss 'Im ... I Got 'Im* (Bluesway 1970)★★★, *Moanin' And Stompin' Blues* (King 1970)★★★, *That's Where It's At* (Stax 1969)★★, with Canned Heat *Hooker 'N' Heat* (Liberty 1971)★★★★, *Endless Boogie* (ABC 1971)★★★, *Never Get Out Of These Blues Alive* (ABC 1972)★★★, *Live At Soledad Prison* (ABC 1972)★★★★, *John Lee Hooker's Detroit* (United Artists 1973)★★★, *Live At Kabuki Wuki* (Bluesway 1973)★★, *Mad Man's Blues* (Chess 1973)★★★, *John Lee Hooker With The Groundhogs* (New World 1973)★★, *Born In Mississippi, Raised Up In Tennessee* (ABC 1973)★★, *Whiskey And Wimmen* (Trip 1973)★★, *Slim's Stomp* (Polydor 1973)★★, *Mad Man's Blues* (Chess 1973)★★★, *Free Beer And Chicken* (ABC 1974)★★, *Blues Before Sunrise* (Bulldog 1976)★★★, *Alone* (Tomato 1976)★★★★, *No Friend Around* (Charly 1979) ★★, *This Is Hip* (Charly 1980)★★★, *Black Snake Blues* (Fantasy 1980)★★★, *Moanin' The Blues* (Charly 1982) ★★★, *Lonesome Mood* (MCA 1983)★★★, *Solid Sender* (Charly 1984)★★, *Jealous* (Pointblank 1986)★★★, *The Healer* (Chameleon 1989)★★★★★, *The Detroit Lion* (Demon 1990)★★, *Boogie Awhile* (Krazy Kat 1990)★★★, *More Real Folk Blues: The Missing Album* (Chess 1991) ★★★★, *Mr Lucky* (Charisma 1991)★★★★, *Boom Boom* (Pointblank 1992)★★★, *Chill Out* (Pointblank 1995) ★★★★, with the Groundhogs *Hooker & The Hogs* 1965 recording (Indigo 1996)★★, *The First Concert – Alone* 1976 recording (Blues Alliance 1996)★★★, *Don't Look Back* (Silvertone 1997)★★★, *The Unknown John Lee Hooker* (Interstate 2000)★★★.
COMPILATIONS: *The Best Of John Lee Hooker* (Vee Jay 1962)★★★, *Collection: John Lee Hooker – 20 Blues Greats* (Déjà Vu 1985)★★★, *The Ultimate Collection 1948-1990* (Rhino 1992)★★★★, *The Best Of John Lee Hooker 1965 To 1974* (MCA 1992)★★★★, *Blues Brother: Sensation Recordings* (Ace 1992)★★★★, *The Legendary Modern Recordings 1948-54* (Ace 1993)★★★★, *Helpless Blues* (Realisation 1994)★★★, *Original Folk Blues ... Plus* (Ace 1994)★★★★, *The Rising Sun Collection* (Just A Memory 1994)★★★, *Live At The Café Au Go Go (And Soledad Prison)* (MCA 1996)★★★★, *The EP Collection Plus* (See For Miles 1995)★★★, *The Early Years* (Tomato 1995)★★★★, *I Feel Good* (Jewel 1995)★★★, *Alternative Boogie: Early Studio Recordings 1948-1952* (Capitol 1996)★★★, *The Complete 50s Chess Recordings* (Chess 1998)★★★★, *Best Of Friends* (Pointblank 1998)★★★★, *House Rent Boogie* (Ace 2001)★★★, *Boogie Chillen: The Essential Recordings Of John Lee Hooker* (Indigo 2001)★★★.
VIDEOS: *Survivors – The Blues Today* (Hendring Music

Video 1989), John Lee Hooker/Lowell Fulson/Percy Mayfield (1992), John Lee Hooker And Friends 1984-1992 (Vestapol Video 1996), Rare Performances 1960-1984 (Vestapol Video 1996).
FURTHER READING: Boogie Chillen: A Guide To John Lee Hooker On Disc, Les Fancourt. Boogie Man: The Adventures Of John Lee Hooker In The American Twentieth Century, Charles Shaar Murray.
FILMS: The Blues Brothers (1980).

HOOTIE AND THE BLOWFISH
ALBUMS: Cracked Rear View (East West 1994)★★★★, Fairweather Johnson (Atlantic 1996)★★, Musical Chairs (Atlantic 1998)★★★, Scattered, Smothered & Covered (Atlantic 2000)★★★.
VIDEOS: Summer Camp With Trucks (Warners 1995), A Series Of Short Trips (Atlantic Video 1996).

HOPKINS, LIGHTNIN'
ALBUMS: Strums The Blues (Score 1958)★★★★, Lightnin' And The Blues (Herald 1959)★★★, The Roots Of Lightnin' Hopkins (Folkways 1959)★★★, Down South Summit Meeting (1960)★★★★, Mojo Hand (Fire 1960)★★★★, Country Blues (Tradition 1960)★★★, Lightnin' In New York (Candid 1961)★★★, Autobiography In Blues (Tradition 1961)★★★, Lightnin' (Bluesville 1961)★★★, with Sonny Terry Last Night Blues (Bluesville 1961)★★★★, Blues In My Bottle (Bluesville 1962)★★★★, Lightnin' Strikes Again (Dart 1962)★★★, Sings The Blues (Crown 1962)★★★, Lightnin' Hopkins (Folkways 1962)★★★★, Fast Life Woman (Verve 1962)★★★, On Stage (Imperial 1962)★★, Walkin' This Street (Bluesville 1962)★★★★, Lightnin' And Co (Bluesville 1963)★★★, Smokes Like Lightnin' (Bluesville 1963)★★★, First Meetin' (World Pacific 1963)★★★, Lightnin' And The Blues (Imperial 1963)★★★, Goin' Away (Bluesville 1963) ★★★, Hootin' The Blues (Folklore 1964)★★★, Down Home Blues (Bluesville 1964)★★★★, The Roots Of Lightnin' Hopkins (Verve/Folkways 1965)★★★★, Soul Blues (Prestige 1966)★★★, Something Blue (Verve/Folkways 1967)★★★, Free Form Patterns (International Artists 1968)★★★, California Mudslide (Vault/Rhino 1969)★★★.
COMPILATIONS: Legacy Of The Blues Volume Twelve (Sonet 1974)★★★★, The Best Of Lightnin' Hopkins (Tradition 1964) ★★★, The Gold Star Sessions - Volumes 1&2 (Arhoolie 1990)★★★★, The Complete Prestige/Bluesville Recordings 7-CD box set (Prestige/Bluesville 1992)★★★★, The Complete Aladdin Recordings (EMI 1992)★★★★, Sittin' In With Lightnin' Hopkins (Mainstream 1992)★★★, Mojo Hand: The Lightnin' Hopkins Anthology (Rhino 1993)★★★★, Coffee House Blues 1960-62 recordings (Charly 1993) ★★★★, Po' Lightnin' (Arhoolie 1995)★★★★, Blue Lightnin' (Jewel 1995)★★★, Hootin' The Blues (Prestige 1995)★★★★, The Rising Sun Collection (Just A Memory 1995)★★★★, Autobiography In Blues (Tradition 1996)★★★★, Country Blues (Tradition 1996)★★★★, Shake It Baby (Javelin 1996) ★★★, Jake Head Boogie (Ace 1999)★★★, The Remaining Titles Vol 1: 1950-1961 (Document 1999)★★★★, Rainy Day In Houston (Indigo 2000)★★★★, Lightnin' And The Blues: The Herald Sessions (Buddha 2001)★★★.
VIDEOS: Rare Performances 1960-1979 (Vestapol 1995).
FURTHER READING: Lightnin' Hopkins: Blues', M. McCormick.

HOPKINS, NICKY
ALBUMS: The Revolutionary Piano Of Nicky Hopkins (CBS 1966)★★, The Tin Man Was A Dreamer (Columbia 1973) ★★, No More Changes (Mercury 1976)★★.

HORNSBY, BRUCE, AND THE RANGE
ALBUMS: The Way It Is (RCA 1986)★★★, Scenes From The South Side (RCA 1988)★★★★, Night On The Town (RCA 1990)★★★, Harbor Lights (RCA 1993)★★★★, Hot House (RCA 1995)★★★, Spirit Trail (RCA 1998)★★★★, Here Come The Noise Makers (RCA 2000)★★★.

HORSLIPS
ALBUMS: Happy To Meet, Sorry To Part (Oats/RCA 1972) ★★★, The Táin (Horslips/RCA 1973)★★★, Dancehall Sweethearts (Oats/RCA 1974)★★★, The Unfortunate Cup Of Tea (Oats/RCA 1975)★★★, Drive The Cold Winter Away (Horslips 1975)★★★, Live (Horslips 1976)★★★, The Book Of Invasions: A Celtic Symphony (Oats/DJM 1976)★★★, Aliens (Horslips/DJM 1977)★★★, The Man Who Built America (Horslips/DJM 1978)★★★, Short Stories Tall Tales (Horslips/Mercury 1979)★★★, The Belfast Gigs (Horslips/Mercury 1980)★★.
COMPILATIONS: Tracks From The Vaults (Horslips 1977) ★★★, The Best Of Horslips (Oats 1982)★★★★, Folk Collection (Stoic 1984)★★★, Horslips History 1972-1975 (1983)★★★★, Horslips History 1976-1980 (1983)★★★★, Straight From The Horse's Mouth: The Horslips Story (Homespun 1989)★★★★, Celtic Collection (K-Tel 1997)★★★, The Best Of Horslips (Edsel 2001)★★★★.

HOT CHOCOLATE
ALBUMS: Cicero Park (Rak 1974)★★, Hot Chocolate (Rak 1975)★★, Man To Man (Rak 1976)★★, Every 1's A Winner (Rak 1978)★★★, Going Through The Motions (Rak 1979)★★, Class (Rak 1980)★★, Mystery (Rak 1982)★★, Love Shot (Rak 1983)★★.
COMPILATIONS: Hot Chocolate's Greatest Hits (Rak 1976) ★★, 20 Hottest Hits (EMI 1979)★★★, The Very Best Of Hot Chocolate (EMI 1987)★★★, Their Greatest Hits (EMI 1993) ★★★, 14 Greatest Hits (EMI 1996)★★★, The Full Monty: The Ultimate Hot Chocolate Collection (EMI 1999)★★★.
VIDEOS: Greatest Hits (Video Collection 1985), Very Best Of (Video Collection 1987).

HOT TUNA
ALBUMS: Hot Tuna (RCA 1970)★★★★, First Pull Up Then Pull Down (RCA 1971)★★★, Burgers (Grunt 1972)★★★★, The Phosphorescent Rat (Grunt 1973)★★, America's Choice (Grunt 1975)★★★, Yellow Fever (Grunt 1975)★★, Hoppkorv (Grunt 1976)★★★★, Double Dose (Grunt 1978)★★★, Final Vinyl (Grunt 1979)★★★, Splashdown 1975 recording (Relix 1985)★★, Historic Hot Tuna 1971 recording (Relix 1985) ★★★, Pair A Dice Found (Epic 1991)★★, Live At Sweetwater (Relix 1992)★★, Live At Sweetwater Two (Relix 1993)★★, Historic (Relix 1993)★★, Classic Electric 1971 recording (Relix 1996)★★★, Classic Acoustic 1971 recording (Relix 1996)★★★, Splashdown Two (Relix 1997)★★, Live In Japan: At Stove's Yokohoma City 02/20/97 (Relix 1998)★★.
COMPILATIONS: Trimmed And Burning (Edsel 1994) ★★★★, Hot Tuna In A Can 5-CD tin (Rhino 1996)★★★★.

HOTHOUSE FLOWERS
ALBUMS: People (London 1988)★★★, Home (London 1990)★★, Songs From The Rain (London 1993)★★★, Born (London 1998)★★.
COMPILATIONS: The Best Of (London 2000)★★★.

HOUSE OF LOVE
ALBUMS: The House Of Love (Creation/Relativity 1988)★★★★, Fontana (Fontana/PolyGram 1990)★★★, Babe Rainbow (Fontana 1992)★★★, Audience With The Mind (Fontana 1993)★★.
COMPILATIONS: A Spy In The House Of Love (Fontana 1990)★★, Best Of (Fontana/Mercury 1998)★★★★, The John Peel Sessions 1988:1989 (Strange Fruit 2000)★★★, 1986-1988: The Creation Recordings (PLR 2001)★★★.

HOUSEMARTINS
ALBUMS: London 0 Hull 4 (Go! Discs 1986)★★★★, The People Who Grinned Themselves To Death (Go! Discs 1987)★★.
COMPILATIONS: Now That's What I Call Quite Good! (Go! Discs 1988)★★★★.
FURTHER READING: The Housemartins, Tales From Humberside, Nick Swift.

HOUSTON, WHITNEY
ALBUMS: Whitney Houston (Arista 1985)★★★★, Whitney (Arista 1987)★★★★, I'm Your Baby Tonight (Arista 1990) ★★★, various artists The Bodyguard film soundtrack (Arista 1992)★★★, The Preacher's Wife film soundtrack (Arista 1996)★★, My Love Is Your Love (Arista 1998)★★★.
COMPILATIONS: Whitney: The Greatest Hits (Arista 2000) ★★★★, Love, Whitney (Arista 2001)★★★.
VIDEOS: The Greatest Hits (Arista 2000).
FILMS: The Bodyguard (1992), The Preacher's Wife (1996).

HOWLIN' WOLF
IALBUMS: Moaning In The Moonlight (Chess 1959)★★★★, Howlin' Wolf aka The Rocking Chair Album (Chess 1962) ★★★★, Howlin' Wolf Sings The Blues (Crown 1962)★★★, The Real Folk Blues (Chess 1966)★★★★, Big City Blues (Custom 1966)★★★, Original Folk Blues (Kent 1967)★★★, More Real Folk Blues (Chess 1967)★★★★, This Is Howlin' Wolf's New Album aka The Dog Shit Album (Cadet 1969) ★★, Evil (Chess 1969)★★★, Message To The Young (Chess 1971)★★, The London Sessions (Chess 1971)★★★, Live And Cookin' At Alice's Revisited (Chess 1972)★★, Howlin' Wolf AKA Chester Burnett (Chess 1972)★★★, The Back Door Wolf (Chess 1973)★★★★, Change My Way (Chess 1975)★★★, Ridin' In The Moonlight (Ace 1982)★★★, Live In Europe 1964 (Sundown 1988)★★★, Memphis Days Volume 1 (Bear Family 1989)★★★, Memphis Days Volume 2 (Bear Family 1990)★★★, Howlin' Wolf Rides Again (Ace 1991)★★★.
COMPILATIONS: Going Back Home (Chess 1970)★★★, Chess Blues Masters (Chess 1976)★★★★★, The Legendary Sun Performers (Charly 1977)★★★, Chess Masters (Chess 1981)★★★★, Chess Masters 2 (Chess 1982)★★★★, Chess Masters 3 (Chess 1983)★★★, The Wolf (Blue Moon 1984)★★★, Golden Classics (Astan 1984)★★★, The Howlin' Wolf Collection (Deja Vu 1985)★★★★, His Greatest Hits (Chess 1986)★★★, Cadillac Daddy: Memphis Recordings, 1952 (Rounder 1987)★★★, Howlin' For My Baby (Sun 1987)★★★, Shake For Me – The Red Rooster (Vogue 1988)★★★, Smokestack Lightnin' (Vogue 1988)★★★, Red Rooster (Joker 1988)★★★, Moanin' And Howlin' (Charly 1988)★★★, Howlin' Wolf 5-LP box set (Chess 1991)★★★★, Going Down Slow 5-CD box set (Roots 1992)★★★★, Gold Collection (1993)★★★, The Wolf Is At Your Door (Fan 1994)★★★, The Complete Recordings 1951-1969 7-CD box set (Charly 1994) ★★★★, The Genuine Article – The Best Of (MCA 1994)★★★★, The Very Best Of Howlin' Wolf 3-CD set (Charly 1995)★★★★, His Best (Chess 1997)★★★★, various artists A Tribute To Howlin' Wolf (Telarc 1998)★★★.

HUMAN LEAGUE
ALBUMS: Reproduction (Virgin 1979)★★, Travelogue (Virgin 1980)★★, Dare! (Virgin 1981)★★★★, Love And Dancing (Virgin 1982)★★★, Hysteria (Virgin 1984)★★, Crash (Virgin 1986)★★, Romantic (Virgin 1990)★★, Octopus (East West 1995)★★★, Secrets (Papillon/Ark 21 2001)★★★★.
COMPILATIONS: Human League's Greatest Hits (Virgin 1988)★★★★, Greatest Hits (Virgin 1995)★★★★.
VIDEOS: Greatest Video Hits (Warners 1995).
FURTHER READING: The Story Of A Band Called The Human League, Alaska Ross and Jill Furmanovsky. The Human League: Perfect Pop, Peter Nash.

HUMBLE PIE
ALBUMS: As Safe As Yesterday Is (Immediate 1969)★★★★, Town And Country (Immediate 1969)★★★, Humble Pie (A&M 1970)★★★, Rock On (A&M 1971)★★★, Performance – Rockin' The Fillmore (A&M 1972)★★, Smokin' (A&M 1972) ★★, Eat It (A&M 1973)★★, Thunderbox (A&M 1974)★, Street Rats (A&M 1975)H, On To Victory (Jet 1980)★, Go For The Throat (Jet 1981)H, Humble Pie Live On The King Biscuit Flower Hour 1973 recording (King Biscuit 1998)★★, Live At The Whiskey-A-Go-Go 1969 (Castle 2001)★★★★, Back On Track (Sanctuary 2002)★★.
COMPILATIONS: Crust Of Humble Pie (EMI 1975)★★, The Humble Pie Collection (Castle 1994)★★★, Natural Born Boogie (BBC 1998)★★★, Running With The Pack (Burning Airlines 1999)★★, Natural Born Bugie: The Immediate Anthology (Sanctuary/Immediate 2000)★★★★.

HUNTER, IAN
ALBUMS: Ian Hunter (CBS 1975)★★★, All American Alien Boy (CBS 1976)★★, Overnight Angels (CBS 1977)★★, You're Never Alone With A Schizophrenic (Chrysalis 1979)★★★, Welcome To The Club (Chrysalis 1980)★★★, Short Back 'N' Sides (Chrysalis 1981)★★★, All Of The Good Ones Are Taken (CBS 1983)★★★, with Mick Ronson YUI Orta (Mercury 1989)★★★, as Ian Hunter's Dirty Laundry Ian Hunter's Dirty Laundry (Norsk 1995)★★★, as the Hunter Ronson Band BBC Live In Concert (Strange Fruit 1995)★★★, The Artful Dodger (Citadel 1997)★★★, Missing In Action (New Millennium 2000)★★★, Rant (Papillon/Fuel 2000 2001)★★★.
COMPILATIONS: Shades Of Ian Hunter (Columbia 1980) ★★★★, The Very Best Of Ian Hunter (Columbia 1990) ★★★, The Collection (Castle 1991)★★★, Once Bitten Twice Shy (Sony 2000)★★★★.
FURTHER READING: Diary Of A Rock 'N' Roll Star, Ian Hunter. Reflections Of A Rock Star, Ian Hunter. All The Way To Memphis, Phil Cato. Mott The Hoople And Ian Hunter: All The Young Dudes, Campbell Devine.

HÜSKER DÜ
ALBUMS: Land Speed Record (New Alliance 1981)★★, Everything Falls Apart (Reflex 1982)★★, Metal Circus mini-album (Reflex/SST 1983)★★★, Zen Arcade (SST 1984) ★★★★, New Day Rising (SST 1985)★★★, Flip Your Wig (SST 1985)★★★★, Candy Apple Grey (Warners 1986)★★★★, Warehouse: Songs And Stories (Warners 1987)★★★★, The Living End 1987 recording (Warners 1994)★★★.
COMPILATIONS: Everything Falls Apart And More (Warners 1993)★★★★.

HYLAND, BRIAN
ALBUMS: The Bashful Blonde (Kapp 1960)★★, Let Me Belong To You (ABC 1961)★★, Sealed With A Kiss (ABC 1962)★★★, Country Meets Folk (ABC 1964)H, Here's To Our Love (Philips 1964)★★, Rockin' Folk (Philips 1965)★★, The Joker Went Wild (Philips 1966)★★★, Tragedy (Dot 1969)★★, Stay And Love Me All Summer (Dot 1969)★★, Brian Hyland (Uni 1970)★★.
COMPILATIONS: Greatest Hits (Rhino 1994)★★★, Brian's 21 Big Ones (Connoisseur 2001)★★★.

I

IAN, JANIS
ALBUMS: Janis Ian (Verve Forecast 1967)★★, A Song For All The Seasons Of Your Mind (Verve Forecast 1968)★★★, The Secret Life Of J. Eddy Fink (Verve Forecast 1968)★★, Who Really Cares (Verve Forecast 1969)★★, Present Company (Capitol 1971)★★, Stars (Columbia 1974)★★★, Between The Lines (Columbia 1975)★★★★, Aftertones (Columbia 1976) ★★★, Miracle Row (Columbia 1977)★★, Janis Ian (Columbia 1978)★★, Night Rains (Columbia 1979)★★★, Restless Eyes (Columbia 1981)★★, Uncle Wonderful Australia only (Festival 1984)★★★, Breaking Silence (Morgan Creek 1993)★★★★, Live On The Test 1976 (Nighttracks/Windsong 1995)★★, Revenge (Beacon/ Grapevine 1995)★★★, Hunger (Windham Hill 1997) ★★★, The Bottom Line Encore Collection 1980 recording (Bottom Line 1999)★★★, God & The FBI (Windham Hill 2000)★★★.
COMPILATIONS: The Best Of Janis Ian (Columbia 1980) ★★★, Society's Child: The Verve Recordings (Polydor 1995)★★★.
FURTHER READING: Who Really Cares?, Janis Ian.

ICE CUBE
ALBUMS: AmeriKKKa's Most Wanted (Priority 1990)★★★★, Kill At Will mini-album (Priority 1990)★★★, Death Certificate (Priority 1991)★★★, The Predator (Lench Mob/Priority 1992)★★★, Lethal Injection (Lench Mob/Priority 1993) ★★★, War & Peace, Vol. 1 (The War Disc) (Priority 1998)★★, War & Peace, Vol. 2 (The Peace Disc) (Priority 2000)★★★★.
COMPILATIONS: Bootlegs & B-Sides (Lench Mob/Priority 1994)★★, Featuring ... Ice Cube (Priority 1997)★★★, Greatest Hits (Priority 2001)★★★.
FILMS: Boyz N The Hood (1991), Trespass (1992), CB4 (1993), The Glass Shield (1994), Higher Learning (1995), Friday (1995), Dangerous Ground (1997), Anaconda (1997), The Players Club (1998), I Got The Hook Up (1998), Thicker Than Water (1999), Three Kings (1999), Next Friday (2000).

ICE-T
ALBUMS: Rhyme Pays (Sire 1987)★★★, Power (Sire 1988) ★★, The Iceberg/Freedom Of Speech ... Just Watch What You Say (Sire 1989)★★★, OG (Original Gangster) (Syndicate/Sire 1991)★★★★, Home Invasion (Priority 1993)★★★, Born Dead (Priority 1994)★★★, VI: Return Of The Real (Priority 1996)★★, 7th Deadly Sin (Roadrunner 1999)★★.
COMPILATIONS: Greatest Hits: The Evidence (Atomic Pop 2000)★★★★.
VIDEOS: OG: The Original Gangster Video (Sire 1991).
FURTHER READING: The Ice Opinion, Ice-T and Heidi Seigmund.
FILMS: Breakin' (1984), Rappin' (1985), Listen Up: The Lives Of Quincy Jones (1990), New Jack City (1991), Ricochet (1991), Trespass (1992), Who's The Man (1993), CB4 (1993), Surviving The Game (1994), The Legend Of Dolemite (1994), Mr Payback: An Interactive Movie (1995), Tank Girl (1995), Johnny Mnemonic (1995), Mean Guns (1997), Below Utopia (1997), Rhyme & Reason (1997), The Deli (1997), Crazy Six (1998), Stealth Fighter (1999).

ICICLE WORKS
ALBUMS: The Icicle Works (Beggars Banquet 1984)★★★, The Small Price Of A Bicycle (Beggars Banquet 1985)★★★, If You Want To Defeat Your Enemy Sing His Song (Beggars Banquet 1987)★★★, Blind (Beggars Banquet 1988)★★★, Permanent Damage (Epic 1990)★★★, BBC Radio One Live In Concert 1987 recording (Windsong 1994)★★.
COMPILATIONS: Seven Singles Deep (Beggars Banquet 1986)★★, The Best Of (Beggars Banquet 1992)★★★.

IDLE RACE
ALBUMS: The Birthday Party (Liberty 1968)★★★, Idle Race (Liberty 1969)★★★, Time Is (Regal Zonophone 1971)★★.
COMPILATIONS: On With The Show (Sunset 1973)★★★, Back To The Story (Premier 1996)★★★★.

IDOL, BILLY
ALBUMS: Billy Idol (Chrysalis 1981)★★★, Don't Stop (Chrysalis 1981)★★★, Rebel Yell (Chrysalis 1984)★★★★, Whiplash Smile (Chrysalis 1986)★★★, Charmed Life (Chrysalis 1990)★★, Cyberpunk (Chrysalis 1993)★★, VH1 Storytellers (Capitol 2002)★★★.
COMPILATIONS: Vital Idol (Chrysalis 1986)★★★, Idol Sings: 11 Of The Best (Chrysalis 1988)★★★, Greatest Hits (Chrysalis 2001)★★★.
FURTHER READING: Billy Idol: Visual Documentary, Mike Wrenn.
FILMS: The Doors (1991), The Wedding Singer (1998).

IFIELD, FRANK
ALBUMS: I'll Remember You (Columbia 1963)★★★, Born Free (Columbia 1963)★★★, Blue Skies (Columbia 1964) ★★★, Portrait In Song (Columbia 1965)★★★, Up Jumped A Swagman film soundtrack (Columbia 1965)★★★, Someone To Give My Love To (Spark 1973)★★, Barbary Coast (Fir 1978)★★, Sweet Vibrations (Fir 1980)★★, If Love Must Go (Fir 1982)★★, At The Sandcastle (Fir 1983)★★.
COMPILATIONS: Greatest Hits (Columbia 1964)★★★, Best Of The EMI Years (Columbia 1991)★★★★, The EP Collection (See For Miles 1991)★★★★, Frank Ifield Collection (HMV Easy 2001)★★★★.
FILMS: Up Jumped A Swagman (1965).

IGGY POP
ALBUMS: The Idiot (RCA 1977)★★★★, Lust For Life (RCA 1977)★★★★★, TV Eye Live (RCA 1978)★★, New Values (Arista 1979)★★, Soldier (Arista 1980)★★, Party (Arista 1981)★★, Zombie Birdhouse (Animal 1982)★★, Blah Blah Blah (A&M 1986)★★★, Instinct (A&M 1988)★★, Brick By Brick (Virgin 1990)★★★, American Caesar (Virgin 1993) ★★★, Naughty Little Doggie (Virgin 1996)★★★, Heroin Hates You 1979 recording (Other People's Music 1997)★★★, Live On The King Biscuit Flower Hour 1988 recording (King Biscuit 1998)★★★, Avenue B (Virgin 1999)★★★, Beat 'Em Up (Virgin 2001)★★★.
COMPILATIONS: Choice Cuts (RCA 1984)★★★, Compact Hits (A&M 1988)★★★, Suck On This! (Revenge 1993)★★, Live NYC Ritz '86 (Revenge 1993)★★, Best Of Iggy Pop Live (MCA 1996)★★, Nude & Rude: The Best Of Iggy Pop (Virgin 1996)★★★★, Pop Music (BMG/Camden 1996)★★★, Nuggets (Jungle 1999)★★, Night Of The Iguana 4-CD set (Remedy 2000)★★★.
FURTHER READING: The Lives And Crimes Of Iggy Pop, Mike West. I Need More: The Stooges And Other Stories, Iggy Pop with Anne Wehrer. Iggy Pop: The Wild One, Per Nilsen and Dorothy Sherman. Iggy Pop: Collection, Connie Ambrosch. Neighbourhood Threat: On Tour With Iggy Pop, Alvin Gibbs. Raw Power: Iggy And The Stooges 1972, Mick Rock.
FILMS: Rock & Rule voice only (1983), Sid And Nancy (1986), The Color Of Money (1986), Hardware aka M.A.R.K. 13 (1990), Cry-Baby (1990), Coffee And Cigarettes III (1993), Tank Girl (1995), Dead Man (1995), Atolladero (1995), The Crow: City Of Angels (1996), Private Parts (1997), The Rugrats Movie voice only (1998), Snow Day (2000).

IGLESIAS, ENRIQUE
ALBUMS: Enrique Iglesias (Fonovisa 1995)★★★, Vivir (Fonovisa 1997)★★★★, Cosas Del Amor (Fonovisa 1998) ★★★, Enrique (Fonovisa 1999)★★★, Escape (Interscope 2001)★★★.
COMPILATIONS: The Best Hits (Fonovisa 2000)★★★★.

IGLESIAS, JULIO
ALBUMS: Yo Canto (Columbia 1969)★★★, Todos Los Dias Un Dia (Columbia 1969)★★★, Soy (Columbia 1970)★★, Gwendolyne (Columbia 1970)★★, Como El Alamo Al Camino (Columbia 1971)★★, Rio Rebelde (Columbia 1972) ★★, Asi Nacemos (Columbia 1973)★★, A Flor De Piel (Columbia 1974)★★, El Amor (Columbia 1975)★★, A Mexico (Columbia 1975)★★, America (Columbia 1976)★★, En El Olympia (Columbia 1976)★★, A Mis 33 Años (Columbia 1977)★★, Mi Vida En Canciones (Columbia 1978)★★, Emociones (Columbia 1979)★★, Hey! (Columbia 1980)★★, De Niña A Mujer (Columbia 1981)★★, Begin The Beguine (Columbia 1981)★★★, Momentos (Columbia 1981) ★★, En Concierto (Columbia 1982)★★, Amor (Columbia 1982)★★, Julio (Columbia 1983)★★★, 1100 Bel Air Place (Columbia 1984)★★★, Libra (Columbia 1985)★★, Un Hombre Solo (Columbia 1987)★★, Non Stop (Columbia 1988)★★, Sentimental (Columbia 1988)★★, Raices (Columbia 1989)★★, Starry Night (Columbia 1990)★★★, Calor (Columbia 1992)★★, La Carreterra (Columbia 1995)★★★, Tango (Columbia 1996)★★, Noche De Cuatro Lunas (Columbia 2000)★★★.
COMPILATIONS: My Life: The Greatest Hits (Columbia 1998) ★★★.
FURTHER READING: Julio!, Jeff Rovin.
FILMS: La Vida Sigue Igual (1969), Me Olvidé De Vivir (1980).

IMBRUGLIA, NATALIE
ALBUMS: Left Of The Middle (RCA 1997)★★★, White Lilies Island (RCA 2001)★★.

INCREDIBLE STRING BAND
ALBUMS: The Incredible String Band (Elektra 1966)★★★, 5000 Spirits Or The Layers Of The Onion (Elektra 1967) ★★★★, The Hangman's Beautiful Daughter (Elektra 1968) ★★★★, Wee Tam And The Big Huge (Elektra 1968)★★★, Changing Horses (Elektra 1969), I Looked Up (Elektra 1970) ★★, U (Elektra 1970)★★, Be Glad For The Song Has No Ending (Island 1971)★★, Liquid Acrobat As Regards The Air (Island 1971)★★, Earthspan (Island 1972)★★, No Ruinous Feud (Island 1973)★★, Hard Rope And Silken Twine (Island 1974)★★, In Concert (Windsong 1992)★★★, The Chelsea Sessions (Pig's Whisker 1997)★★★, The First Girl I Loved (Mooncrest 1998)★★★.
COMPILATIONS: Relics Of The Incredible String Band (Elektra 1971)★★★, Seasons They Change (Island 1976)★★★, The Best Of 1966-1970 (Elektra 2001)★★★, 'Here Till Here Is There': An Introduction To The Incredible String Band (Island 2001)★★★.
VIDEOS: Be Glad For The Song Has No Ending (Island 1994).

INCUBUS
ALBUMS: Fungus Amongus (Own Label 1995)★★, S.C.I.E.N.C.E. (Immortal/Epic 1997)★★★, Make Yourself (Immortal/Epic 1999)★★★★, When Incubus Attacks Vol 1 mini-album (Immortal/Epic 2000)★★★, Morning View (Immortal/Epic 2001)★★★.
VIDEOS: When Incubus Attacks Vol 2 (Epic 2001).

INDIA.ARIE
ALBUMS: Acoustic Soul (Motown 2001)★★★★.

INDIGO GIRLS
ALBUMS: as the B Band Tuesday's Children cassette only (Unicorn 1981)★★, Blue Food cassette only (J Ellis 1985) ★★★, Strange Fire (Indigo 1987)★★, Indigo Girls (Epic 1989)★★★, Nomads*Indians*Saints (Epic 1990)★★★, Indigo Girls Live: Back On The Bus, Y'All mini-album (Epic 1991)★★, Rites Of Passage (Epic 1992)★★★★, Swamp Ophelia (Epic 1994)★★★, Shaming Of The Sun (Epic 1997)★★★, Come On Now Social (Epic 1999)★★★, Become You (Daemon/Epic 2002)★★★.
Solo: Amy Ray Color Me Grey cassette only (No Label 1985)★★, Stag (Daemon 2001)★★★.
COMPILATIONS: 1200 Curfews (Epic 1995)★★★, Retrospective (Epic 2000)★★★★.
VIDEOS: Watershed (Columbia Music Video 1995).

INSANE CLOWN POSSE
ALBUMS: Carnival Of Carnage (Psychopathic 1992)★★★, The Ringmaster (Psychopathic 1994)★★, The Riddle Box (Battery 1995)★★, The Great Milenko (Hollywood 1997) ★★★, The Amazing Jeckel Brothers (Island 1999)★★★, Bizzar (Island 2000)★★★.
COMPILATIONS: Forgotten Freshness (PSY 1995)★★, Forgotten Freshness Volumes 1 & 2 (Island 1998)★★★.
VIDEOS: Shockumentary (PolyGram Music Video 1998), Big Money Hustla$ (Psychopathic Video 2001).
FILMS: Big Money Hustla$ (1999).

INSPIRAL CARPETS
ALBUMS: Life (Mute 1990)★★★, The Beast Inside (Mute 1991)★★★, Revenge Of The Goldfish (Mute 1992)★★★, Devil Hopping (Mute 1994)★★★.
COMPILATIONS: The Singles (Mute 1995)★★★, Radio 1 Sessions (Strange Fruit 1999)★★★.

INXS
ALBUMS: INXS (Deluxe 1980)★★, Underneath The Colours (RCA 1981)★★, Shabooh Shoobah (Mercury 1982)★★★, The Swing (Mercury 1984)★★★, Listen Like Thieves (Mercury 1985)★★★, Kick (Mercury 1987)★★★, X (Mercury 1990) ★★, Live Baby Live (Mercury 1991)★★, Welcome To Wherever You Are (Mercury 1992)★★★, Full Moon, Dirty Hearts (Mercury 1993)★★★, Elegantly Wasted (Mercury 1997)★★.
Solo: Max Q Max Q (Mercury 1989)★★★. Absent Friends Here's Looking Up Your Address (Roo Art 1990)★★.
COMPILATIONS: The Greatest Hits (Mercury 1994)★★★★, Shine Like It Does: The Anthology (1979-1997) (Rhino 2001)★★★★.
VIDEOS: Truism (PMI/EMI 1991), The Best Of INXS (PMI/EMI 1994).
FURTHER READING: INXS: The Official Story Of A Band On The Road, St John Yann Gamblin (ed.). The Final Days Of Michael Hutchence, Mike Gee.

IRON BUTTERFLY
ALBUMS: Heavy (Atco 1968)★★★, In-A-Gadda-Da-Vida (Atco 1968)★★★★, Ball (Atco 1969)★★★, Iron Butterfly Live (Atco 1970)H, Metamorphosis (Atco 1970)★★, Scorching Beauty (MCA 1975)★★, Sun And Steel (MCA 1976)★★★.
COMPILATIONS: The Best Of Iron Butterfly: Evolution (Atco 1971)★★★, Star Collection (Atlantic 1973)★★★, Light And Heavy: The Best Of Iron Butterfly (Rhino 1993)★★★.

IRON MAIDEN
ALBUMS: Iron Maiden (EMI 1980)★★★, Killers (EMI 1981)★★, Number Of The Beast (EMI 1982)★★★★, Piece Of Mind (EMI 1983)★★★, Powerslave (EMI 1984)★★, Live After Death (EMI 1985)★★★, Somewhere In Time (EMI 1986)★★★, Seventh Son Of A Seventh Son (EMI 1988) ★★★★, No Prayer For The Dying (EMI 1990)★★★, Fear Of The Dark (EMI 1992)★★★, A Real Live One (Volume One) (EMI 1993)★★★, A Real Dead One (EMI 1993)★★, Live At Donington '92 (EMI 1993)★★, The X Factor (EMI 1995)★★★, Virtual XI (EMI 1998)★★★, Brave New World (EMI 2000)★★★★, Rock In Rio (EMI 2002)★★★.
COMPILATIONS: The Best Of The Beast (EMI 1996)★★★, Ed Hunter (EMI 1999)★★★★.
VIDEOS: Live At The Rainbow (PMI/EMI 1984), Behind The Iron Curtain Video EP (PMI/EMI 1986), Live After Death (PMI/EMI 1986), Run To The Hills (Video Collection 1987), Twelve Wasted Years (PMI/EMI 1987), Maiden England (PMI/EMI 1989), The First Ten Years (The Videos) (PMI/EMI 1990), Raising Hell (PMI/EMI 1993), Donington Live 1992 (PMI/EMI 1994).
FURTHER READING: Running Free: The Official Story Of Iron Maiden, Garry Bushell and Ross Halfin. Iron Maiden: A Photographic History, Ross Halfin. What Are We Doing This For?, Ross Halfin. Run To The Hills, Iron Maiden: The Official Biography, Mick Wall, The Iron Maiden Companion, Marco Gamba & Nicola Visintini.

ISAACS, GREGORY
ALBUMS: Gregory Isaacs Meets Ronnie Davis (Plant 1970) ★★★, In Person (Trojan 1975)★★★, All I Have Is Love (Trojan 1976)★★★, Extra Classic (Conflict 1977)★★★, Mr Isaacs (Earthquake 1977)★★★★, Slum Dub (Burning Sounds 1978)★★★★, Best Of Volume 1 not compilation (GG's 1976)★★★, The Cool Ruler (Front Line 1978)★★★★, Soon Forward (Front Line 1979)★★★★, Showcase (Taxi 1980) ★★★, The Lonely Lover (Pre 1980)★★★, For Everyone (Success 1980)★★★, Best Of Volume 1 not compilation (GG's 1981)★★★, More Gregory (Pre 1981)★★★, Night Nurse (Mango/Island 1982)★★★, The Sensational Gregory Isaacs (Vista 1982)★★★, Out Deh! (Mango/Island 1983) ★★★★, Reggae Greats (Live) (Mango/Island 1984)★★★, Live At The Academy Brixton (Rough Trade 1984)★★★, with Dennis Brown Two Bad Superstars Meet (Burning Sounds 1984)★★★, Judge Not (Greensleeves 1984)★★★, with Jah Mel Double Explosive (Andys 1984)★★★, Private Beach Party (RAS 1985)★★★, Easy (Tad's 1985)★★★, All I Have Is Love, Love Love (Tad's 1986)★★★, with Sugar Minott Double Dose (Blue Mountain 1987)★★★, Victim (C&E 1987)★★★, Watchman Of The City (Rohit 1988)★★★, Sly And Robbie Presents Gregory Isaacs (RAS 1988)★★★, Talk Don't Bother Me (Skengdon 1988)★★★, Come Along (Live & Love 1988)★★★, Encore (Kingdom 1988)★★★, Red Rose For Gregory (Greensleeves 1988)★★★, I.O.U. (RAS 1989) ★★★, No Contest (Music Works 1989)★★★, Call Me Collect (RAS 1990)★★★, Dancing Floor (Heartbeat 1990) ★★★, Come Again Dub (ROIR 1991)★★★, Can't Stay Away (1992)★★★, Pardon Me (1992)★★★, No Luck (1993)★★★, Absent (Greensleeves 1993)★★★, Over The Bridge (Musidisc/I&I Sound 1994)★★★, Reggae Greats – Live 1982 recording (1994)★★★, Midnight Confidential (Greensleeves 1994)★★★, Mr Love (Virgin Front Line 1995)★★★★, Memories (Musidisc 1995)★★★, Dem Talk Too Much (Trojan 1995)★★★, with Dennis Brown, Glen Washington Reggae Trilogy (Jet Star 2000)★★★, Rat Patrol (Jet Star 2001)★★★.
COMPILATIONS: The Early Years (Trojan 1981)★★★, Lover's Rock double album comprising The Lonely Lover and More Gregory (Pre 1982)★★★, Crucial Cuts (Virgin 1983) ★★★, My Number One (Heartbeat 1990)★★★, Love Is Overdue (Network 1991)★★★, The Cool Ruler Rides Again - 22 Classics From 1978-81 (Music Club 1993)★★★, Loving Pauper (Trojan 1998)★★★, The Prime Of Gregory Isaacs (Music Club 1998)★★★★, Reasoning With The Almighty (Trojan 2001)★★★, All I Have Is Love – Anthology (Trojan 2001)★★★.

ISAAK, CHRIS
ALBUMS: Silvertone (Warners 1985)★★, Chris Isaak (Warners 1987)★★★, Heart Shaped World reissued as Wicked Game (Reprise 1989)★★★, San Francisco Days (Reprise 1993)★★★, Forever Blue (Reprise 1995)★★, Baja Sessions (Reprise 1996)★★, Speak Of The Devil (Reprise 1998)★★, Always Got Tonight (Reprise 2002)★★★.
VIDEOS: Wicked Game (Warner Music Video 1991).
FILMS: Married To The Mob (1988), Let's Get Lost (1988), The Silence Of The Lambs (1991), Twin Peaks: Fire Walk With Me (1992), Little Buddha (1993), Grace Of My Heart (1996), That Thing You Do! (1996), Blue Ridge Fall (1999).

ISLEY BROTHERS
ALBUMS: Shout (RCA Victor 1959)★★★, Twist And Shout (Wand 1962)★★★★, The Fabulous Isley Brothers-Twisting And Shouting (Wand 1964)★★, Take Some Time Out-The Famous Isley Brothers (United Artists 1964)★★, This Old Heart Of Mine (Tamla 1966)★★, Soul On The Rocks (Tamla 1967)★★, It's Our Thing (T-Neck 1969)★★★, Doin' Their Thing (Tamla 1969)★★★, The Brothers: Isley (T-Neck 1969)★★★, with Brooklyn Bridge and Edwin Hawkins Live At Yankee Stadium (T-Neck 1969)★★, Get Into Something (T-Neck 1970)★★★, Givin' It Back (T-Neck 1971)★★★, Brother Brother Brother (T-Neck 1972)★★★, The Isleys Live (T-Neck 1973)★★★, 3+3 (T-Neck 1973)★★★★, Live It Up (T-Neck 1974)★★★, The Heat Is On (T-Neck 1975)★★★★, Harvest For The World (T-Neck 1976)★★★, Go For Your Guns (T-Neck 1977)★★★, Showdown (T-Neck 1978)★★★, Winner Takes All (T-Neck 1979)★★★, Go All The Way (T-Neck 1980)★★★, Grand Slam (T-Neck 1981)★★★, Inside You (T-Neck 1981)★★★, The Real Deal (T-Neck 1982) ★★★, Between The Sheets (T-Neck 1983)★★★, Masterpiece (Warners 1985)★★★, Smooth Sailin' (Warners 1987)★★★, as Isley Brothers Featuring Ronald Isley Spend The Night (Warners 1989)★★, Tracks Of Life (Warners 1992)★★★, Live (Elektra 1993)★★, Mission To Please (Island 1996)★★, Eternal (DreamWorks 2001)★★★.
COMPILATIONS: In The Beginning: With Jimi Hendrix (T-Neck 1970)★★, Isleys' Greatest Hits (T-Neck 1973)★★★★, Rock Around The Clock (Camden 1975)★★, Super Hits (Motown 1976)★★★, Forever Gold (T-Neck 1977)★★★★, The Best Of The Isley Brothers (United Artists 1978)★★★, Timeless (Epic 1979)★★★, Let's Go (Stateside 1986)★★, Greatest Motown Hits (Motown 1987)★★★, The Complete UA Sessions (EMI 1990)★★★, The Isley Brothers Story/Volume 1: The Rockin' Years (1959-1968) (Rhino 1991) ★★★, The Isley Brothers Story/Volume 2: T-Neck Years (1968-1985) (Rhino 1991)★★★★, Beautiful Ballads (Epic Legacy 1995)★★, Funky Family (Epic Legacy 1995)★★, Early Classics (Spectrum 1996)★★★, Shout! (Camden 1998)★★★, It's Your Thing: The Story Of The Isley Brothers 3-CD set (Epic 1999)★★★★, The Ultimate Isley Brothers (Epic 2000)★★★.

IT'S A BEAUTIFUL DAY
ALBUMS: It's A Beautiful Day (Columbia 1969)★★★★, Marrying Maiden (Columbia 1970)★★★, Choice Quality Stuff/Anytime (Columbia 1971)★★, It's A Beautiful Day At Carnegie Hall (Columbia 1972)★★, It's A Beautiful Day ... Today (Columbia 1973)H, 1001 Nights (Columbia 1974)★★.
COMPILATIONS: It's A Beautiful Day (Columbia 1979)★★★.

J

JA RULE
ALBUMS: Venni Vetti Vecci (Murder Inc/Def Jam 1999) ★★★★, Rule 3:36 (Murder Inc/Def Jam 2000)★★★, Pain Is Love (Murder Inc/Def Jam 2001)★★★.
FILMS: Turn It Up (2000), Backstage (2000), Da Hip Hop Witch (2000), The Fast And The Furious (2001), Crime Partners 2000 (2001).

JACKSON FIVE
ALBUMS: Diana Ross Presents The Jackson 5 (Motown 1970)★★★, ABC (Motown 1970)★★★★, Third Album (Motown 1970)★★★, Christmas Album (Motown 1970) ★★, Maybe Tomorrow (Motown 1971)★★, Goin' Back To Indiana (Motown 1971)★★, Lookin' Through The Windows (Motown 1972)★★★, Skywriter (Motown 1973)★★★★, Get It Together (Motown 1973)★★★, Dancing Machine (Motown 1974)★★★, Moving Violation (Motown 1975) ★★★, Joyful Jukebox Music (Motown 1976)★★★.
COMPILATIONS: Jackson 5 Greatest Hits (Motown 1971) ★★★★, Jackson Five Anthology 3-LP set (Motown 1976) ★★★★, Soulstation! - 25th Anniversary Collection 4-CD box set (Motown 1995)★★★★, Early Classics (Spectrum 1996) ★★★, The Ultimate Collection (Motown 1998)★★★★, The Steeltown Sessions 1965 recordings (Almafame 1999)★★★.
FURTHER READING: Jackson Five, Charles Morse. The

Jacksons, Steve Manning. Pap Joe's Boys: The Jacksons' Story, Leonard Pitts. The Magic And The Madness, J. Randy Taraborrelli. The Record History: International Jackson Record Guide, Ingmar Kuliha.

JACKSON, ALAN
ALBUMS: Here In The Real World (Arista 1990)★★★, Don't Rock The Jukebox (Arista 1991)★★★★, A Lot About Livin' (And A Little 'Bout Lovin) (Arista 1992)★★★★, Honky Tonk Christmas (Arista 1993)★★, Who I Am (Arista 1994)★★★, Everything I Love (Arista 1996)★★★★, High Mileage (Arista 1998)★★★, Under The Influence (Arista 1999) ★★★, When Somebody Loves You (Arista 2000)★★★★, Drive (Arista 2002)★★★.
COMPILATIONS: The Greatest Hits Collection (Arista 1995)★★★★.
VIDEOS: Here In The Reel World (Arista 1990), Livin', Lovin', And Rockin' That Jukebox (Arista 1994), Who Says You Can't Have It All (DNA 1994), The Greatest Video Hits Collection (6 West Home Video 1995).

JACKSON, JANET
ALBUMS: Janet Jackson (A&M 1982)★★, Dream Street (A&M 1984)★★★, Control (A&M 1986)★★★★, Control: The Remixes (A&M 1987)★★★, Janet Jackson's Rhythm Nation 1814 (A&M 1989)★★★★, Janet (Virgin 1993) ★★★★, Janet Remixed (Virgin 1993)★★★, as Janet The Velvet Rope (Virgin 1997)★★★, as Janet All For You (Virgin 2001)★★★.
COMPILATIONS: Design Of A Decade 1986/1996 (A&M 1995)★★★★.
VIDEOS: Janet (Virgin 1994), Design Of A Decade 86-96 (VVL 1995), Rhythm Nation Compilation (A&M Video 2001), All For You (Virgin Video 2001).
FURTHER READING: Out Of The Madness (The Strictly Unauthorised Biography Of ...), Andrew Bart and J Randy Taraborrelli (eds.).
FILMS: Poetic Justice (1993).

JACKSON, JERMAINE
ALBUMS: Jermaine (Motown 1972)★★, Come Into My Life (Motown 1973)★★, My Name Is Jermaine (Motown 1976) ★★, Feel The Fire (Motown 1977)★★, Frontier (Motown 1978)★★, Let's Get Serious (Motown 1980)★★★, Jermaine (Motown 1980)★★, I Like Your Style (Motown 1981)★★, Let Me Tickle Your Fancy (Motown 1982)★★, Jermaine Jackson (USA) Dynamite (UK) (Arista 1984)★★★, Precious Moments (Arista 1986)★★, Don't Take It Personal (Arista 1989)★★, You Said (La Face 1991)★★.
COMPILATIONS: Greatest Hits & Rare Classics (Motown 1991)★★★, Ultimate Collection (Hip-O 2001)★★★★.

JACKSON, JOE
ALBUMS: Look Sharp! (A&M 1979)★★★★, I'm The Man (A&M 1979)★★★★, Beat Crazy (A&M 1980)★★, Joe Jackson's Jumpin' Jive (A&M 1981)★★★★, Night And Day (A&M 1982)★★★★, Mike's Murder film soundtrack (A&M 1983)★★, Body And Soul (A&M 1984)★★★★, Big World (A&M 1986)★★, Will Power (A&M 1987)★★★, Joe Jackson - Live (A&M 1988)★★★, Tucker: Original Soundtrack (A&M 1988)★★, Blaze Of Glory (A&M 1989)★★, Laughter And Lust (Virgin 1991)★★, Night Music (Virgin 1994)★★★, Heaven And Hell (Sony Classical 1997)★★★★, Symphony No. 1 (Sony Classical 1999)★★★★, Summer In The City (Manticore/Sony Classical 2000)★★★, Night And Day II (Manticore/Sony Classical 2000)★★★, Two Rainy Nights (Manticore 2002)★★★.
COMPILATIONS: Steppin' Out: The Very Best Of Joe Jackson (A&M 1990)★★★, This Is It: The A&M Years (A&M 1997)★★★★, The Best Of Joe Jackson: The Millennium Collection (Chronicles 2001)★★★★.
FURTHER READING: A Cure For Gravity: A Musical Journey, Joe Jackson.

JACKSON, LATOYA
ALBUMS: LaToya Jackson (Polydor 1980)★★, My Special Love (Polydor 1981)★★, Heart Don't Lie (Private Stock 1984)★★, Imagination (Private Stock 1985)★★, You're Gonna Get Rocked (RCA 1988)★★.
FURTHER READING: LaToya Jackson, LaToya Jackson with Patricia Romanowski.

JACKSON, MICHAEL
ALBUMS: Got To Be There (Motown 1971)★★★, Ben (Motown 1972)★★★, Music And Me (Motown 1973)★★★, Forever, Michael (Motown 1975)★★★, Off The Wall (Epic 1979)★★★★★, One Day In Your Life (Motown 1981) ★★★, Thriller (Epic 1982)★★★★★, ET – The Extra Terrestrial (MCA 1983)★★, Farewell My Summer Love 1973 recording (Motown 1984)★★★, Looking Back To Yesterday (Motown 1986)★★★, Bad (Epic 1987)★★★, Dangerous (Epic 1991)★★★★, HIStory: Past, Present And Future – Book 1 (Epic 1995)★★★★, Blood On The Dance Floor – HIStory In The Mix (Epic 1997)★★★, Invincible (Epic 2001)★★.
COMPILATIONS: The Best Of Michael Jackson (Motown 1975)★★★, Michael Jackson 9 Single Pack (Epic 1983) ★★★, The Michael Jackson Mix (Stylus 1987)★★★, Anthology (Motown 1993)★★★★, The Best Of Michael Jackson: The Millennium Collection (Polydor 2000)★★★★, Love Songs (Motown 2002)★★★.
VIDEOS: Moonwalker (CBS 1988), The Making Of Thriller (Vestron Music Video 1986), The Legend Continues (Video Collection 1988), Dangerous – The Short Films (SMV 1993), HIStory, Volume 1 (SMV 1995), HIStory On Film, Vol. 2 (SMV 1997).
FURTHER READING: Michael Jackson, Stewart Regan. The Magic Of Michael Jackson, no editor listed. Michael Jackson, Doug Magee. The Michael Jackson Story, Nelson George. Michael In Concert, Phyl Garland. Michael Jackson: Body And Soul: An Illustrated Biography, Geoff Brown. Michael!: The Michael Jackson Story, Mark Bego. On The Road With Michael Jackson, Mark Bego. Sequins & Shades: The Michael Jackson Reference Guide, Carol D. Terry. Michael Jackson: Electrifying, Greg Quill. Moonwalk, Michael Jackson, Michael Jackson: The Magic And The Madness, J. Randy Taraborrelli. Michael Jackson : The Man In The Mirror, Todd Gold. Live And Dangerous, Adrian Grant. Michael Jackson: The King Of Pop, Lisa D. Campbell. Michael Jackson: In His Own Words, Michael Jackson. The Visual Documentary, Adrian Grant. Michael Jackson Unauthorized, Christopher Andersen. The Many Faces Of Michael Jackson, Lee Pinkerton.
FILMS: The Love Machine (1971), Save The Children (1973), Free To Be ... You & Me (1974), The Wiz (1978), Captain EO (1986), Moonwalker (1988), HIStory (1994), Ghosts aka Michael Jackson's Ghosts (1997).

JACKSON, MILLIE
ALBUMS: Millie Jackson (Spring 1972)★★★, It Hurts So Good (Spring 1973)★★★, Caught Up (Spring 1974) ★★★★, Soul Believer (Spring 1974)★★★, Still Caught Up (Spring 1975)★★★, Free And In Love (Spring 1976)★★★, Lovingly Yours (Spring 1977)★★★, Feelin' Bitchy (Spring 1977)★★★★, Get It Out 'Cha System (Spring 1978)★★★, A Moment's Pleasure (Spring 1979)★★★, with Isaac Hayes Royal Rappin's (Polydor 1979)★★, Live And Uncensored (Spring 1979)★★★, For Men Only (Spring 1980)★★★, I Had To Say It (Spring 1981)★★, Just A Lil' Bit Country (Spring 1981)★★, Live And Outrageous (Spring 1982)★★, Hard Times (Spring 1982)★★, E.S.P. (Extra Sexual Persuasion) (Sire 1984)★★, An Imitation Of Love (Jive 1986)★★★, The Tide Is Turning (Jive 1988)★★★, Back To The S**t! (Jive 1989)★★, Young Man, Older Woman (Jive 1991)★★, Between The Sheets (7N 1999)★★★, Not For Church Folk! (Weird Wrekuds 2001)★★★.
COMPILATIONS: Best Of Millie Jackson (Spring 1976) ★★★★, 21 Of The Best (Southbound/Ace 1994)★★★★, The Very Best! Of Millie Jackson (Jive 1994)★★★, Totally Unrestricted! The Millie Jackson Anthology (Atlantic/Rhino 1997)★★★★.

JACKSONS
ALBUMS: The Jacksons (Epic 1976)★★★, Goin' Places (Epic 1977)★★★, Destiny (Epic 1978)★★★★, Triumph (Epic 1980)★★★, The Jacksons Live (Epic 1981)★★★, Victory (Epic 1984)★★★, 2300 Jackson Street (Epic 1989)★★.
COMPILATIONS: Greatest Hits (Epic 1995)★★★.

JAH WOBBLE
ALBUMS: The Legend Lives On ... Jah Wobble In 'Betrayal' mini-album (Virgin 1980)★★, with Holger Czukay On The Way To The Peak Of Normal (EMI 1982)★★★★, Jah Wobble's Bedroom Album (Lago 1983)★★, with Czukay, the Edge Snake Charmer (Island 1983)★★★, with Czukay, Jaki Liebezeit Full Circle (Virgin 1983)★★★, with Ollie Manland Neon Moon (Island 1985)★★★, with Manland Tradewinds (Lago 1986)★★★, Psalms (Wob 1987)★★★, with Invaders Of The Heart Without Judgement (KK 1989)★★★★, with Invaders Of The Heart Rising Above Bedlam (Oval 1991)★★★★, with Invaders Of The Heart Take Me To God (Island 1994)★★★★, with Eno Spinner (All Saints 1995)★★★, Heaven & Earth (Island 1995) ★★★, The Inspiration Of William Blake (All Saints 1996) ★★★, with Invaders Of The Heart The Celtic Poet (30 Hertz 1997)★★★, Requiem (30 Hertz 1997)★★★, The Light Programme (30 Hertz 1997)★★, Umbra Sumus (30 Hertz 1998)★★★, with Zi Lan Liao The Five Tone Dragon (30 Hertz 1998)★★★, Deep Space (30 Hertz 1999)★★, with Invaders Of The Heart Full Moon Over The Shopping Mall (30 Hertz 1999)★★, with Deep Space Beach Fervour Spare (30 Hertz 2000)★★★, with Invaders Of The Heart Molam Dub (30 Hertz 2000)★★, with Evan Parker Passage To Hades (30 Hertz 2001)★★★, with Bill Laswell Radioaxiom: A Dub Transmission (Palm Pictures 2001)★★★★.
COMPILATIONS: 30 Hertz: A Collection Of Diverse Workings From A Creative Genius (Eagle 2000)★★★★.

JAM
ALBUMS: In The City (Polydor 1977)★★★★, This Is The Modern World (Polydor 1977)★★★, All Mod Cons (Polydor 1978)★★★★, Setting Sons (Polydor 1979) ★★★★, Sound Affects (Polydor 1980)★★★★, The Gift (Polydor 1982)★★★, Dig The New Breed (Polydor 1982) ★★★, Live Jam (Polydor 1993)★★★.
COMPILATIONS: Snap! (Polydor 1983)★★★★, Greatest Hits (Polydor 1991)★★★★, Extras (Polydor 1992)★★★, The Jam Collection (Polydor 1996)★★★★, Direction, Reaction, Creation 4-CD box set (Polydor 1997)★★★★, Beat Surrender (Spectrum 2000)★★★, The Singles 1977-79 box set (Polydor 2001)★★★★. The Singles 1980-82 box set (Polydor 2001)★★★★.
VIDEOS: Video Snap! (PolyGram Music Video 1983)★★★, Transglobal Unity Express (Channel 5 1988)★★★, Greatest Hits (PolyGram Music Video 1991)★★★, Little Angels: Jam On Film (PolyGram Music Video 1994)★★★.
FURTHER READING: The Jam: The Modern World By Numbers, Paul Honeyford. Jam, Miles. The Jam: A Beat Concerto, The Authorized Biography, Paolo Hewitt. About The Young Idea: The Story Of The Jam 1972-1982, Mike Nicholls. Our Story, Bruce Foxton and Rick Buckler with Alex Ogg. Keeping The Flame, Steve Brookes. The Complete Guide To The Music Of Paul Weller And The Jam, John Reed.

JAMES
ALBUMS: Stutter (Sire 1986)★★★★, Strip Mine (Sire 1988) ★★★, One Man Clapping (Rough Trade 1989)★★★, Gold Mother (Fontana 1990)★★★★, Seven (Fontana 1992)★★★★, Laid (Fontana 1993)★★★, Wah Wah (Fontana 1994)★★, Whiplash (Fontana 1997)★★★, Millionaires (Fontana 1999) ★★★★, Pleased To Meet You (Fontana 2001)★★★.
COMPILATIONS: James: The Best Of (Fontana 1998) ★★★★, B-Sides Ultra (Fontana 2001)★★★.
VIDEOS: Come Home Live (PolyGram Music Video 1991), Seven - The Live Video (PolyGram Music Video 1992).
FURTHER READING: Folklore: The Official History, Stuart Maconie.

JAMES GANG
ALBUMS: Yer Album (BluesWay 1969)★★★, The James Gang Rides Again (ABC 1970)★★★★, Thirds (ABC 1971)★★★, James Gang Live In Concert (ABC 1971)★★★, Straight Shooter (ABC 1972)★★, Passin' Thru' (ABC 1972)★★, Bang (Atco 1974)★★, Miami (Atco 1974)★★, Newborn (Atco 1975)★★, Jesse Come Home (Atco 1976)★★.
COMPILATIONS: The Best Of The James Gang Featuring Joe Walsh (ABC 1973)★★★, 16 Greatest Hits (ABC 1973)★★★, The True Story Of The James Gang (See For Miles 1987)★★★, The Best Of James Gang (Repertoire 1998)★★★.

JAMES, ELMORE
COMPILATIONS: Blues After Hours (Crown 1961)★★★★, Original Folk Blues (Kent 1964)★★★★, The Sky Is Crying (Sphere Sound 1965)★★★, The Best Of Elmore James (Sue 1965)★★★★, I Need You (Sphere Sound 1966)★★★, The Elmore James Memorial Album (Sue 1966)★★★★, Something Inside Of Me (Bell 1968)★★★, The Late Fantastically Great Elmore James (Ember 1968)★★★, To Know A Man (Blue Horizon 1969)★★★, Whose Muddy Shoes (Chess 1969) ★★★, Elmore James (Bell 1969)★★★, Blues In My Heart, Rhythm In My Soul (1969)★★★, The Legend Of Elmore James (United Artists 1970)★★★, Tough (Blue Horizon 1970)★★★, Cotton Patch Hotfoots (Polydor 1974)★★★, All Them Blues (DJM 1976)★★★, with Robert Nighthawk Blues In D'Natural (1979)★★★★, The Best Of Elmore James (Ace 1981)★★★, Got To Move (Charly 1981)★★★, King Of The Slide Guitar (Ace 1983)★★★★, Red Hot Blues (Blue Moon 1983)★★★, The Original Meteor And Flair Sides (Ace 1984)★★★★, Come Go With Me (Charly 1984)★★★, One Way Out (Charly 1985)★★★, The Elmore James Collection (Déjà Vu 1985)★★★★, Let's Cut It (Ace 1986)★★★, King Of The Bottleneck Blues (Crown 1986)★★★★, Shake Your Moneymaker (Charly 1986)★★★★, Pickin' The Blues (Castle 1986)★★★, Greatest Hits (Blue City 1988)★★★, Chicago Golden Years (Vogue 1988)★★★, Dust My Broom (Instant 1990)★★★★, Rollin' And Tumblin' - The Best Of (Relic 1992)★★★★, Elmore James Box Set (Charly 1992)★★★★, The Classic Early Recordings 1951-56 3-CD box set (Flair/Ace 1993)★★★★, The Best Of Elmore James: The Early Years (Ace 1995) ★★★★, Rollin' And Tumblin' (Recall 1999)★★★★, Shake Your Moneymaker: The Best Of The Fire Sessions (Buddha 2001)★★★.

JAMES, ETTA
ALBUMS: Miss Etta James (Crown 1961)★★★★, At Last! (Argo 1961)★★★★, Second Time Around (Argo 1961) ★★★★, Twist With Etta James (Crown 1962)★★★★, Etta James (Argo 1962)★★★★, Etta James Sings For Lovers (Argo 1962)★★★★, Etta James Top Ten (Argo 1963)★★★, Etta James Rocks The House (Argo 1964)★★★, The Queen Of Soul (Argo 1965)★★★★, Call My Name (Cadet 1967) ★★★, Tell Mama (Cadet 1968)★★★★★, Etta James Sings Funk (Cadet 1970)★★★, Losers Weepers (Cadet 1971)★★★, Etta James (Chess 1973)★★★, Come A Little Closer (Chess 1974)★★★, Etta Is Betta Than Evah! (Chess 1977)★★★, Deep In The Night (Warners 1978)★★★★, Changes (MCA 1980)★★★, with Eddie 'Cleanhead' Vinson Blues In The Night: The Early Show (Fantasy 1986)★★★, Blues In The Night: The Late Show (Fantasy 1986)★★★, Seven Year Itch (Island 1989)★★★, Stickin' To My Guns (Island 1990) ★★★★, Something's Gotta Hold On Me (Etta James Volume 2) (Roots 1992)★★★, The Right Time (Elektra 1992)★★★, Mystery Lady: Songs Of Billie Holiday (Private 1994)★★★, Love's Been Rough On Me (Private 1997) ★★★★, Life, Love & The Blues (Private 1998)★★★, 12 Songs Of Christmas (Private 1998)★★, Heart Of A Woman (Private 1999)★★★, Matriarch Of The Blues (Private 2000)★★★★, Blue Gardenia (Private 2001)★★★★.
COMPILATIONS: The Best Of Etta James (Crown 1962) ★★★★, The Soul Of Etta James (Ember 1968)★★★★, Golden Decade (Chess 1972)★★★★, Peaches (Chess 1973)★★★★, Good Rockin' Mama (Ace 1981)★★★★, Chess Masters (Chess 1981)★★★, Tuff Lover (Ace 1983) ★★★★, Juicy Peaches (Chess 1985)★★★, R&B Queen (Crown 1986)★★★, Her Greatest Sides, Volume One (Chess/MCA 1987)★★★★, R&B Dynamite reissued as Hickory Dickory Dock (Ace 1987)★★★★, Rocks The House (Charly 1987)★★★★, The Sweetest Peaches: The Chess Years, Volume 1 (1960-1966) (Chess/MCA 1988)★★★★, The Sweetest Peaches: The Chess Years, Volume 2 (1967-1975) (Chess/MCA 1988)★★★★, Tell Mama (1988)★★★★, Chicago Golden Years (Vogue 1988)★★★, Come A Little Closer (Charly 1988)★★★, Juicy Peaches (Charly 1989) ★★★★, The Gospel Soul Of Etta James (AJK 1990)★★★, Legendary Hits (Jazz Archives 1992)★★★, Back In The Blues (Zillion 1992)★★★, The Soulful Miss Peaches (Charly 1993) ★★★★, I'd Rather Go Blind - The World Of Etta James (Trace 1993)★★★, Something's Got A Hold (Charly 1994)★★★, Blues In The Night, The Early Show (Fantasy 1994)★★★, Blues In The Night, The Late Show (Fantasy 1994)★★★, Miss Peaches Sings The Soul (That's Soul 1994)★★★, Live From San Francisco '81 (Private Music 1994)★★★, The Genuine Article: The Best Of (MCA/Chess 1996)★★★★, Her Best (MCA/Chess 1997)★★★★, The Chess Box 3-CD box set (MCA 2000)★★★★, Love Songs (Chess 2001)★★★★, The Best Of Etta James (Spectrum 2001)★★★.
VIDEOS: Live At Montreux (Island Visual Arts 1990), Live At Montreux: Etta James (PolyGram Music Video 1992).
FURTHER READING: Rage To Survive, Etta James and David Ritz.

JAMES, RICK
ALBUMS: Come Get It! (Gordy 1978)★★★, Bustin' Out Of L Seven (Gordy 1979)★★★, Fire It Up (Gordy 1979)★★★, In 'n' Out (Gordy 1980)★★, Garden Of Love (Gordy 1980) ★★, Street Songs (Gordy 1981)★★★★, Throwin' Down (Gordy 1982)★★★, Cold Blooded (Gordy 1983)★★, Glow (Gordy 1985)★★, The Flag (Gordy 1986)★★, Wonderful (Reprise 1988)★★, Urban Rapsody (Higher Source 1997)★★★.
COMPILATIONS: Reflections: All The Great Hits (Gordy 1984)★★★★, Greatest Hits (Motown 1993)★★★, Bustin' Out: The Best Of Rick James (Motown 1994)★★★, Greatest Hits (Spectrum 1996)★★★, The Ultimate Collection (Motown 1997)★★★★, The Best Of Rick James: The Millennium Collection (Universal 2000)★★★★.

JAMES, TOMMY, AND THE SHONDELLS
ALBUMS: Hanky Panky (Roulette 1966)★★★, It's Only Love (Roulette 1967)★★★, I Think We're Alone Now (Roulette 1967)★★★, Gettin' Together (Roulette 1968)★★, Mony Mony (Roulette 1968)★★★, Crimson & Clover (Roulette 1968)★★★, Cellophane Symphony (Roulette 1969)★★, Travelin' (Roulette 1970)★★★.
COMPILATIONS: Something Special! The Best Of Tommy James And The Shondells (Roulette 1968)★★★, The Best Of Tommy James And The Shondells (Roulette 1969)★★★, Anthology (Rhino 1990)★★★★, The Best Of Tommy James And The Shondells (Rhino 1994)★★★★, It's A New Vibration: An Ultimate Anthology (Westside 1997)★★★★.

JAMIROQUAI
ALBUMS: Emergency On Planet Earth (Sony 1993)★★★, The Return Of The Space Cowboy (Sony 1994)★★★★, Travelling Without Moving (Sony 1996)★★★★, Synkronized (Sony 1999)★★★★, A Funk Odyssey (Sony 2001)★★★.

JAN AND DEAN
ALBUMS: Jan And Dean (Dore 1960)★★★, Jan And Dean Take Linda Surfin' (Liberty 1963)★★★, Surf City (And Other Swinging Cities) (Liberty 1963)★★★, Drag City (Liberty 1964)★★★, Dead Man's Curve/New Girl In School (Liberty 1964)★★★, Ride The Wild Surf (Liberty 1964)★★★, The Little Old Lady From Pasadena (Liberty 1964)★★★, Command Performance - Live In Person (Liberty 1965)H, Folk 'N Roll (Liberty 1966)★★, Filet Of Soul - A 'Live' One (Liberty 1966)H, Jan And Dean Meet Batman (Liberty 1966)★★, Popsicle (Liberty 1966)★★, Save It For A Rainy Day (J&D 1967)★★.
COMPILATIONS: Jan And Dean's Golden Hits (Liberty 1962)★★★, Golden Hits Volume 2 (Liberty 1965)★★★, Gotta Take That One Last Ride (One Way 1973)★★★, Ride The Wild Surf (Hits From Surf City, USA) (EMI 1976)★★★★, Teen Suite 1958-1962 (Varèse Sarabande 1995)★★★★, Surf City (The Very Best Of Jan And Dean) (EMI 1999)★★★.
FURTHER READING: Jan And Dean, Allan Clark.

JANE'S ADDICTION
ALBUMS: Jane's Addiction (Triple X 1987)★★★, Nothing's Shocking (Warners 1988)★★★★, Ritual De Lo Habitual (Warners 1991)★★★.
COMPILATIONS: Kettle Whistle (Warners 1997)★★★.
FURTHER READING: Perry Farrell: The Saga Of A Hypester, Dave Thompson.

JAPAN
ALBUMS: Adolescent Sex (Ariola-Hansa 1978)★★, Obscure Alternatives (Ariola-Hansa 1978)★★, Quiet Life (Ariola-Hansa 1980)★★★, Gentlemen Take Polaroids (Virgin 1980)★★★, Tin Drum (Virgin 1981)★★★, Oil On Canvas (Virgin 1983)★★.
COMPILATIONS: Assemblage (Hansa 1981)★★★, Exorcising Ghosts (Virgin 1984)★★★, In Vogue (Camden 1997)★★★.
FURTHER READING: A Tourist's Guide To Japan, Arthur A. Pitt.

JARRE, JEAN-MICHEL
ALBUMS: Deserted Palace (Sam Fox/Polydor 1972)★★★, Les Granges Brulées film soundtrack (Eden 1973)★★, Oxygene (Dreyfus/Polydor 1976)★★★★, Paris By Night film soundtrack (Barclay 1977)★★★, Equinoxe (Dreyfus/Polydor 1978)★★★★, Les Chants Magnetiques aka Magnetic Fields (Dreyfus/Polydor 1981)★★★, Les Concerts En Chine aka The Concerts In China (Dreyfus/Polydor 1982)★★★, Musique Pour Supermarche aka Music For Supermarkets (Dreyfus 1983)★★★, Zoolook (Dreyfus/Polydor 1984)★★★, Rendez-vous (Dreyfus/Polydor 1986) ★★, En Concert: Houston/Lyon (Dreyfus/Polydor 1987)★★, Revolutions (Dreyfus/Polydor 1988)★★★, Jarre Live (Dreyfus/Polydor 1989)★★, En Attendant Cousteau aka Waiting For Cousteau (Dreyfus/Polydor 1990)★★, Chronologie (Disques Dreyfus/Polydor 1993)★★, Hong Kong (Dreyfus 1994)★★, Oxygene 7-13 (Dreyfus/Epic 1997)★★★, Metamorphoses (Dreyfus/Epic 2000)★★★.
COMPILATIONS: Musik Aus Zeit Und Raum (Drefus 1983) ★★★, The Essential Jean-Michel Jarre (PolyGram 1983) ★★★, The Essential 1976-1986 (Dreyfus/Polydor 1985)★★★, Anniversary 8-CD box set (Polydor 1987)★★★, Images: The Best Of Jean-Michel Jarre (Disques Dreyfus 1991)★★★, Jarremix remix album (Dreyfus 1995)★★★, Complete Oxygene (Dreyfus/Epic 1997)★★★, Odyssey Through O2 remix album (Epic 1998)★★★.
VIDEOS: Les Concerts En Chine (PolyGram 1982), Rendez-Vous Houston: A City In Concert (Dreyfus/PolyGram 1986), Rendez-Vous Lyon: A Concert For The Pope (PolyGram 1987), Destination Docklands (PolyGram 1989), Paris La Defense - A City In Concert (Genesis 1990), Images: The Best Of Jean-Michel Jarre (PolyGram 1991), Europe In Concert - Barcelona (PolyGram 1994), Oxygen In Moscow (SMV 1998).
FURTHER READING: Jean-Michel Jarre, Jean-Louis Remilleux. The Unofficial Jean-Michel Jarre Biography, Graham Needham.

JARREAU, AL
ALBUMS: 1965 (Bainbridge 1965)★★★, We Got By (Reprise 1975)★★★, Glow (Reprise 1976)★★, Look To The Rainbow: Live In Europe (Warners 1977)★★★, All Fly Home (Warners 1978)★★★★, This Time (Warners 1980) ★★★, Breakin' Away (Warners 1981)★★★★, Jarreau (Warners 1983)★★★, High Crime (Warners 1984)★★, Al Jarreau In London (Warners 1984)★★★, You (Platinum 1985)★★★, L Is For Lover (Warners 1986)★★★, Heart's Horizon (Reprise 1988)★★★, Heaven And Earth (Reprise 1992)★★★★, Tenderness (Warners 1994)★★, Tomorrow Today (GRP 2000)★★★★.
COMPILATIONS: Best Of Al Jarreau (Warners 1996)★★★★.

Jason And The Scorchers
ALBUMS: as Jason And The Nashville Scorchers Fervor (Praxis 1983)★★★, Lost & Found (EMI 1985)★★★, Still Standing (EMI 1986)★★★, Thunder And Fire (A&M 1989) ★★★, A Blazing Grace (Mammoth 1995)★★★, as Jason And The Nashville Scorchers Reckless Country Soul 1982 recordings (Mammoth 1996)★★★★, Clear Impetuous Morning (Mammoth 1996)★★★, Midnight Roads & Stages Seen (Mammoth 1998)★★★, Rock On Germany (Courageous Chicken 2001)★★★.
COMPILATIONS: Essential Jason And The Scorchers: Are You Ready For The Country (EMI 1992)★★★★, Both Sides Of The Line (EMI 1996)★★★★, Wildfires + Misfires: Two Decades Of Outtakes And Rarities (Courageous Chicken/Yep Roc 2002)★★★.
VIDEOS: Midnight Roads And Stages Seen (Mammoth 1998).

JAY AND THE AMERICANS
ALBUMS: She Cried (United Artists 1962)★★★, Jay And The Americans At The Cafe Wha? (United Artists 1963)★★, Come A Little Bit Closer (United Artists 1964)★★★, Blockbusters (United Artists 1965)★★, Sunday And Me (United Artists 1966)★★★, Livin' Above Your Head (United Artists 1966)★★★, Try Some Of This (United Artists 1967) ★★, Sands Of Time (United Artists 1969)★★, Wax Museum (United Artists 1970)★★.
COMPILATIONS: Jay And The Americans' Greatest Hits (United Artists 1965)★★★, Jay And The Americans' Greatest Hits Volume Two (United Artists 1966)★★★, The Very Best Of Jay And The Americans (United Artists 1975) ★★★, Come A Little Bit Closer : The Best Of Jay And The Americans (United Artists 1990)★★★, All-Time Greatest Hits (Rhino 1995)★★★★.

JAY-Z
ALBUMS: Reasonable Doubt (Roc-A-Fella 1996)★★★, In My Lifetime, Vol. 1 ... (Roc-A-Fella/Def Jam 1997)★★★★, Vol. 2 ... Hard Knock Life (Roc-A-Fella/Def Jam 1998) ★★★, Vol. 3 ... Life And Times Of S. Carter (Roc-A-Fella/Def Jam 1999)★★★★, The Dynasty: Roc La Familia 2000 (Roc-A-Fella/Def Jam 2000)★★★★, The Blueprint (Roc-A-Fella/Def Jam 2001)★★★★, MTV Unplugged (Roc-A-Fella/Def Jam 2001)★★★, with R. Kelly The Best Of Both Worlds (Def Jam/Jive 2002)★★.
FILMS: Backstage (2000).

JAYHAWKS
ALBUMS: The Jayhawks (Bunkhouse 1986)★★★, The Blue Earth (Twin/Tone 1989)★★★★, Hollywood Town Hall (Def American 1992)★★★, Tomorrow The Green Grass (American 1995)★★★★, Sound Of Lies (American 1997) ★★★, Smile (Columbia 2000)★★★★.

JEAN, WYCLEF
ALBUMS: Wyclef Jean Presents The Carnival Featuring The Refugee Allstars (Columbia 1997)★★★, The Ecleftic: 2 Sides II A Book (Columbia 2000)★★★.
FILMS: Rhyme & Reason (1997), Shottas (2001).

JEFFERSON AIRPLANE
ALBUMS: Jefferson Airplane Takes Off (RCA 1966)★★, Surrealistic Pillow (RCA 1967)★★★★, After Bathing At Baxter's (RCA 1967)★★★, Crown Of Creation (RCA 1968)★★★★, Bless Its Pointed Little Head (RCA 1969) ★★★, Volunteers (RCA 1969)★★★★, Bark (Grunt 1971) ★★★, Long John Silver (Grunt 1972)★★★, 30 Seconds Over Winterland (Grunt 1973)★★★, Jefferson Airplane (Epic 1989)H, Live At The Fillmore East 1968 recording (RCA 1998)★★★.
COMPILATIONS: Worst Of Jefferson Airplane (RCA 1970) ★★★, Early Flight (Grunt 1974)★★★, featuring Jefferson Airplane and Jefferson Starship Flight Log (1966-1976) (Grunt 1977)★★★★, The Best Of Jefferson Airplane (RCA 1980)★★★★, 2400 Fulton Street: An Anthology (RCA 1987)★★★★, Collection (Castle 1988)★★★, White Rabbit & Other Hits (RCA 1990)★★, Jefferson Airplane Loves You 3-CD box set (RCA 1992)★★★, Journey: The Best Of Jefferson Airplane (Camden 1996)★★★, Through The Looking Glass (Almafame 1999)★★, Ignition 4-CD box set (RCA 2001)★★★.
FURTHER READING: The Jefferson Airplane And The San Francisco Sound, Ralph J. Gleason. Grace Slick – The Biography, Barbara Rowe.

JEFFERSON STARSHIP
ALBUMS: Dragonfly (Grunt 1974)★★★, Red Octopus (Grunt 1975)★★★★, Spitfire (Grunt 1976)★★★, Earth (Grunt 1978)★★, Freedom At Point Zero (Grunt 1979)★★, Modern Times (RCA 1981)★★, Winds Of Change (Grunt 1982)★★, Nuclear Furniture (Grunt 1984)★★, as Starship Knee Deep In The Hoopla (RCA 1985)★★, as Starship No Protection (RCA 1987)★★, as Starship Love Among The Cannibals (RCA 1989)H, Deep Space/Virgin Sky (Intersound 1995)H, Live: Miracles (EMI 1997)H, Windows Of Heaven (SPV 1998)H.
COMPILATIONS: featuring Jefferson Airplane and Jefferson Starship Flight Log (1966-1976) (Grunt 1977)★★★★, Gold (Grunt 1979)★★★★, Jefferson Starship: At Their Best (RCA 1993)★★★, Collection (Griffin 1995)★★.

JENNINGS, WAYLON
ALBUMS: Waylon Jennings: Live At J.D's (Bat 1964)★★★, Don't Think Twice (A&M 1965)★★, Waylon Jennings – Folk/Country (RCA 1966)★★, Leaving Town (RCA 1966) ★★, Nashville Rebel (RCA 1966)★★★, Waylon Sings Ol' Harlan (RCA 1967)★★, The One And Only Waylon Jennings (Camden 1967)★★★, Love Of The Common People (RCA 1967)★★, Hangin' On (RCA 1968)★★, Only The Greatest (RCA 1968)★★★, Jewels (RCA 1968)★★★★, Waylon Jennings (Vocalion 1969)★★★, with the Kimberlys Country Folk (RCA 1969)★★★, Just To Satisfy You (RCA 1969)★★★, Ned Kelly film soundtrack (United Artists 1970)★★, Waylon (RCA 1970)★★★, Singer Of Sad Songs (RCA 1970)★★★, The Taker/Tulsa (RCA 1971)★★★, Cedartown, Georgia (RCA 1971)★★, Good Hearted Woman (RCA 1972)★★★, Ladies Love Outlaws (RCA 1972)★★★, Lonesome, On'ry And Mean (RCA 1973) ★★★, Honky Tonk Heroes (RCA 1973)★★★★, Nashville Rebel film soundtrack (RCA 1973)★★★, This Time (RCA 1974)★★★, The Ramblin' Man (RCA 1974)★★, Dreaming My Dreams (RCA 1975)★★★★, Mackintosh And T.J. (RCA 1976)★★★, with Willie Nelson, Jessi Colter, Tompall Glaser Wanted! The Outlaws (RCA 1976)★★★★, Are You Ready For The Country? (RCA 1976)★★★, Waylon 'Live' (RCA 1976)★★, Ol' Waylon (RCA 1977)★★★, with Nelson Waylon And Willie (RCA 1978)★★★★, with Colter, John Dillon, Steve Cash White Mansions (RCA 1978)★★★, I've Always Been Crazy (RCA 1978)★★★, The Early Years (RCA 1979)★★, What Goes Around Comes Around (RCA 1979)★★★, Waylon Music (RCA 1980)★★★, Music Man (RCA 1980)★★, with Colter Leather And Lace (RCA 1981) ★★★, with Nelson WWII (RCA 1982)★★★★, with Colter The Pursuit Of D.B. Cooper film soundtrack (RCA 1982)★★, Black On Black (RCA 1982)★★, It's Only Rock & Roll (RCA 1983)★★★, Waylon And Company (RCA 1983)★★, with Nelson Take It To The Limit (Columbia 1983)★★★, Never Could Toe The Mark (RCA 1984)★★, Turn The Page (RCA 1985)★★, Will The Wolf Survive? (MCA 1985)★★★★, with Nelson, Johnny Cash, Kris Kristofferson, Highwayman (Columbia 1985)★★★★, with Cash Heroes (Columbia 1986)★★★, Hangin' Tough (MCA 1987)★★★, A Man Called Hoss (MCA 1987)★★, Full Circle (MCA 1988)★★★, with Cash, Kristofferson, Nelson Highwayman 2 (Columbia 1990)★★★, The Eagle (Epic 1990)★★★, with Nelson Clean Shirt (Epic 1991)★★, Too Dumb For New York City - Too Ugly For L.A. (Epic 1992)★★★, Cowboys, Sisters, Rascals & Dirt (Epic 1993)★★★, Waymore's Blues (Part II) (Epic 1994)★★, with Nelson, Cash, Kristofferson The Road Goes On Forever (Liberty 1995)★★, Ol' Waylon Sings Ol' Hank (WJ 1995)★★★, Right For The Time (Justice 1996) ★★★, with Nelson, Colter, Glaser Wanted! The Outlaws (1976-1996, 20th Anniversary) (RCA 1996)★★★★, Closing In On The Fire (Ark 1998)★★★, with Bobby Bare, Jerry Reed, Mel Tillis Old Dogs (Atlantic 1999)★★, with the Waymore Blues Band Never Say Die, Live (Lucky Dog 2000)★★★★.
COMPILATIONS: Greatest Hits (RCA 1979)★★★★, Greatest Hits, Volume 2 (RCA 1985)★★★, Waylon: Best Of Waylon Jennings (RCA 1985)★★★, New Classic Waylon (MCA 1989)★★★, Silver Collection (RCA 1992)★★★, Only Daddy That'll Walk The Line: The RCA Years (RCA 1993)★★★, The Essential Waylon Jennings (RCA 1996) ★★★★, Super Hits (RCA 1998)★★★, Greatest Hits (Camden 1998)★★★★, with Willie Nelson The Masters (Eagle 1998)★★★, The Journey: Destiny's Child 6-CD box set (Bear Family 1999)★★★★, The Journey: Six Strings Away 6-CD box set (Bear Family 2000)★★★★, Phase One: The Best Of 1959-1964 (Hip-O 2002)★★★.
VIDEOS: Renegade Outlaw Legend (Prism 1991), The Lost Outlaw Performance (Prism 1991), America (Prism 1992).
FURTHER READING: Waylon Jennings, Albert Cunniff. Waylon – A Biography, R. Serge Denisoff. Waylon And Willie, Bob Allen. The Waylon Jennings Discography, John L. Smith (ed.). Waylon: An Autobiography, Waylon Jennings with Lenny Kaye.
FILMS: Nashville Rebel (1966), The Road To Nashville (1967), Travelin' Light (1971), Moonrunners (1974), Sesame Street Presents Follow That Bird (1985), Maverick (1994).

JESUS AND MARY CHAIN
ALBUMS: Psychocandy (Blanco y Negro 1985)★★★★, Darklands (Blanco y Negro 1987)★★★, Automatic (Blanco y Negro 1989)★★, Honey's Dead (Blanco y Negro 1992) ★★★, Stoned & Dethroned (Blanco y Negro 1994)★★★, Munki (Creation 1998)★★★.
COMPILATIONS: Barbed Wire Kisses (Blanco y Negro 1988)★★★, The Sound Of Speed (Blanco y Negro 1993) ★★★, The Complete John Peel Sessions (Strange Fruit 2000)★★★.
FURTHER READING: The Jesus and Mary Chain: A Musical Biography, John Robertson.

JETHRO TULL
ALBUMS: This Was (Chrysalis 1968)★★★★, Stand Up (Chrysalis 1969)★★★★, Benefit (Chrysalis 1970)★★★, Aqualung (Chrysalis 1971)★★★★, Thick As A Brick (Chrysalis 1972)★★★, A Passion Play (Chrysalis 1973) ★★, War Child (Chrysalis 1974)★★, Minstrel In The Gallery (Chrysalis 1975)★★★, Too Old To Rock 'N' Roll Too Young To Die (Chrysalis 1976)★★★, Songs From The Wood (Chrysalis 1977)★★★★, Heavy Horses (Chrysalis 1978)★★★, Live - Bursting Out (Chrysalis 1978)★★, Storm Watch (Chrysalis 1979)★★★, A (Chrysalis 1980)★★, The Broadsword And The Beast (Chrysalis 1982)★★, Under Wraps (Chrysalis 1984)★★, Crest Of A Knave (Chrysalis 1987)★★★, Rock Island (Chrysalis 1989)★★, as the John Evan Band Live '66 (A New Day 1990)★★, Live At Hammersmith (Raw Fruit 1990)★★, Catfish Rising (Chrysalis 1991)★★, A Little Light Music (Chrysalis 1992)★★, Nightcap (Chrysalis 1993)★★, In Concert (Windsong 1995)★★★, Roots To Branches (Chrysalis 1995)★★, J-Tull Dot Com (Papillon 1999)★★★.
SOLO: Ian Anderson Walk Into Light (Chrysalis 1983)★★, Divinities: Twelve Dances With God (EMI 1995)★★, The Secret Language Of Birds (Papillon 2000)★★★.
COMPILATIONS: Living In The Past (Chrysalis 1972)★★★★, M.U.: Best Of Jethro Tull (Chrysalis 1976)★★★, Repeat, The Best Of Jethro Tull - Volume II (Chrysalis 1977)★★★, Original Masters (Chrysalis 1985)★★★, 20 Years Of Jethro Tull 3-CD box set (Chrysalis 1988)★★★★, 25th Anniversary Box Set 4-CD box set (Chrysalis 1992)★★★★, The Anniversary Collection (Chrysalis 1993)★★★, The Very Best Of Jethro Tull (Chrysalis 2001)★★★★.
VIDEOS: Slipstream (Chrysalis 1981), 20 Years Of Jethro Tull (Virgin Video 1988), 25th Anniversary Video (PMI 1993).
FURTHER READING: Minstrels In The Gallery: A History Of Jethro Tull, David Rees. Flying Colours: The Jethro Tull Reference Manual, Greg Russo.

JETT, JOAN, AND THE BLACKHEARTS
ALBUMS: Joan Jett aka Bad Reputation (Blackheart 1980) ★★★, I Love Rock 'n' Roll (Boardwalk 1981)★★★★, Album (MCA/Blackheart 1983)★★★, Glorious Results Of A Misspent Youth (MCA/Blackheart 1984)★★★, Good Music (Columbia/Blackheart 1986)★★★, Up Your Alley (Columbia/Blackheart 1988)★★★, The Hit List (Columbia/Blackheart 1990)★★★, Notorious (Epic/Blackheart 1991)★★★, Pure And Simple (Blackheart/Warners 1994)★★★.
COMPILATIONS: Flashback (Blackheart 1993)★★★★, Fit To Be Tied (Mercury 1997)★★★, Fetish (Blackheart 1999)★★.

JEWEL
ALBUMS: Pieces Of You (Atlantic 1995)★★★★, A Night Without Armor spoken word (Atlantic 1998)★★, Spirit (Atlantic 1998)★★★, Joy: A Holiday Collection (Atlantic 1999)★★★, Chasing Down The Dawn spoken word (Atlantic 2000)★★, This Way (Atlantic 2001)★★★.
VIDEOS: Joy: A Holiday Collection (Atlantic 1999), A Life Uncommon (Atlantic 1999).
FURTHER READING: A Night Without Armor, Jewel. Angel Standing By: The Story Of Jewel, P.J. McFarland. Scrapbook, Jewel. Chasing Down The Dawn, Jewel.
FILMS: Ride With The Devil (1999).

JIMMY EAT WORLD
ALBUMS: Jimmy Eat World (Wooden Blue 1994)★★, Static Prevails (Capitol 1996)★★★, Bleed American (DreamWorks 2001)★★★.
COMPILATIONS: The Singles (Big Wheel Recreation 2000) ★★★.

JODECI
ALBUMS: Forever My Lady (Uptown/MCA 1991)★★★★, Diary Of A Mad Band (Uptown/MCA 1993)★★★, The Show, The After Party, The Hotel (Uptown/MCA 1995)★★★.

JOEL, BILLY
ALBUMS: Cold Spring Harbor (Family 1971)★★, Piano Man (Columbia 1973)★★, Street Life Serenade (Columbia 1975)★★, Turnstiles (Columbia 1976)★★★, The Stranger (Columbia 1977)★★★★, 52nd Street (Columbia 1978) ★★★, Glass Houses (Columbia 1980)★★★, Songs In The Attic (Columbia 1981)★★★, The Nylon Curtain (Columbia 1982)★★★, An Innocent Man (Columbia 1983)★★★, The Bridge (Columbia 1986)★★★, Kohyept - Live In Leningrad (Columbia 1987)★★, Storm Front (Columbia 1989)★★★, River Of Dreams (Columbia 1993)★★★★, 2000 Years: The Millennium Concert (Columbia 2000)★★★, Fantasies & Delusions: Music For Solo Piano (Columbia 2001)★★★.
COMPILATIONS: Greatest Hits Volumes 1 & 2 (Columbia 1985)★★★★, Greatest Hits 3 (Columbia 1997)★★★, The Complete Hits Collection 1973-1997 4-CD box set (Columbia 1997)★★★★, The Ultimate Collection (Columbia 2001)★★★★.
VIDEOS: Video Album Volume 1 (Fox Video 1986), Live At Long Island (CBS-Fox 1988), Storm Front (CMV Enterprises 1990), Live At Yankee Stadium (SMV 1992), Live From Leningrad (SMV 1992), A Matter Of Trust (SMV 1992), Shades Of Grey (SMV 1994), Video Album Volume 2 (SMV 1994), The Essential Video Collection (Sony 2001).
FURTHER READING: Billy Joel: A Personal File, Peter Gambaccini.

JOHN, ELTON
ALBUMS: Empty Sky (DJM/MCA 1969)★★, Elton John (DJM/Uni 1970)★★★★, Tumbleweed Connection (DJM/Uni 1970)★★★★, 17-11-70 (UK) 11-17-70 (US) (DJM/Uni 1971)★★, Friends film soundtrack (Paramount 1971)H, Madman Across The Water (DJM/Uni 1971)★★★, Honky Chateau (DJM/Uni 1972)★★★★, Don't Shoot Me I'm Only The Piano Player (DJM/MCA 1973)★★★, Goodbye Yellow Brick Road (DJM/MCA 1973)★★★★, Caribou (DJM/MCA 1974)★★★, Captain Fantastic And The Brown Dirt Cowboy (DJM/MCA 1975)★★★, Rock Of The Westies (DJM/MCA 1975)★★★★, Here And There aka London & New York (DJM/MCA 1976)★★, Blue Moves (Rocket/MCA 1976)★★, A Single Man (Rocket/MCA 1978)★★★, Victim Of Love (Rocket/MCA 1979)★★, 21 At 33 (Rocket/MCA 1980)★★, Lady Samantha (DJM 1980)★★★, The Fox (Rocket/Geffen 1981)★★, Jump Up (Rocket/Geffen 1982)★★, Too Low For Zero (Rocket/Geffen 1983)★★★, Breaking Hearts (Rocket/ Geffen 1984)★★, Ice On Fire (Rocket/Geffen 1985)★★★, Leather Jackets (Rocket/Geffen 1986)★★, Live In Australia With The Melbourne Symphony Orchestra (Rocket/MCA 1987)★★, Reg Strikes Back (Rocket/MCA 1988)★★★, Sleeping With The Past (Rocket/MCA 1989)★★★, The One (Rocket/MCA

1992)★★★, Duets (Rocket/MCA 1993)★★, Made In England (Rocket/Island 1995)★★★★, The Big Picture (Rocket/Island 1997)★★★, Live At The Ritz (Rocket/ Island 1999)★★★, Elton John And Tim Rice's Aida (Rocket/ Island 1999)★★★, The Muse film soundtrack (Rocket/Island 1999)★★, Elton John's The Road To El Dorado film soundtrack (Dreamworks 2000)★★, One Night Only: The Greatest Hits (Rocket/Island 2000)★★★, Songs From The West Coast (Rocket/Island 2001)★★★★.
COMPILATIONS: Greatest Hits (DJM/MCA 1974)★★★★, Elton John's Greatest Hits Volume II (DJM/MCA 1977) ★★★, Candle In The Wind (St Michael 1978)★★★, The Elton John Live Collection (Pickwick 1979)★★, Elton John 5-LP box set (DJM 1979)★★★, The Very Best Of Elton John (K-Tel 1980)★★★, Milestones (1970-1980 A Decade Of Gold) (K-Tel 1980)★★★, The Album (Pickwick 1981)★★, The Best Of Elton John Volume One (CBS 1981)★★★, The Best Of Elton John Volume Two (CBS 1981)★★★, Love Songs (TV 1982)★★★★, The New Collection (Everest 1983)★★★, The New Collection Volume Two (Everest 1983)★★, The Superior Sound Of Elton John (1970-1975) (DJM 1984)★★★, Your Songs (MCA 1985)★★★, Greatest Hits Volume III (1979-1987) (Geffen 1987)★★★, The Complete Thom Bell Sessions (MCA 1989)★★★, The Collection (Pickwick 1990)★★★, To Be Continued ... 4-CD box set (MCA/Rocket 1990)★★★★, The Very Best Of Elton John (Rocket 1990)★★★★, Love Songs (Pickwick 1991)★★★, Song Book (Pickwick 1992)★★, Greatest Hits 1976-1986 (MCA 1992)★★★, Rare Masters (Polydor 1992)★★, Reg Dwight's Piano Goes Pop aka Chartbusters Go Pop (RPM/Cleopatra 1994)★★, Love Songs (Rocket/MCA 1995)★★★.
VIDEOS: The Afternoon Concert (Vestron Music Video 1984), Night Time Concert (Vestron Music Video 1984), The Video Singles (PolyGram/Spectrum 1984), Live In Central Park - New York (VCL 1986), Live In Australia 1 & 2 (Virgin Vision 1988), Very Best Of Elton John (Channel 5 1990), Single Man In Concert (4 Front 1991), Live In Barcelona (Warner Music Vision 1992), Live - World Tour 1992 (1993), Live In Australia (J2 Communications 1995), Love Songs (PolyGram Music Video 1995), Tantrums And Tiaras (VVL 1996), An Audience With ... Elton John (1998), One Night Only (Universal 2001).
FURTHER READING:. Elton John, Cathi Stein. A Conversation With Elton John And Bernie Taupin, Paul Gambaccini. Elton John, Dick Tatham and Tony Jasper. Elton John Discography, Paul Sobieski. Elton John: A Biography In Words & Pictures, Greg Shaw. Elton John: Reginald Dwight & Co, Linda Jacobs. Elton: It's A Little Bit Funny, David Nutter. The Elton John Tapes: Elton John In Conversation With Andy Peebles, Elton John. Elton John: The Illustrated Discography, Alan Finch. Elton John 'Only The Piano Player': The Illustrated Elton John Story, Chris Charlesworth. Elton John: A Biography, Barry Toberman. Two Rooms: A Celebration Of Elton John & Bernie Taupin, Elton John and Bernie Taupin. A Visual Documentary, Nigel Goodall. Candle In The Wind, no author listed. Elton John: The Biography, Philip Norman. The Many Lives Of Elton John, Susan Crimp and Patricia Burstein. The Complete Lyrics Of Elton John And Bernie Taupin, no author listed. Elton John: 25 Years In The Charts, John Tobler. Rocket Man: The Encyclopedia Of Elton John, Claude Bernardin and Tom Stanton. His Song: The Musical Journey Of Elton John, Elizabeth J. Rosenthal.
FILMS: Born To Boogie (1972), Tommy aka The Who's Tommy (1975), To Russia ... With Elton (1979), The Return Of Bruno (1988), Spice World (1997), The Road To El Dorado voice only (2000).

JOHNSON, LINTON KWESI
ALBUMS: as Poet And The Roots Dread Beat An' Blood (Front Line 1977)★★★, Forces Of Victory (Island 1979) ★★★★, Bass Culture (Island 1980)★★★★, LKJ In Dub (Island 1980)★★★, Making History (Island 1984)★★★★, Linton Kwesi Johnson Live (Rough Trade 1985)★★★, In Concert With The Dub Band (LKJ 1986)★★★, Tings An' Times (LKJ 1990)★★★★, LKJ In Dub Volume 2 (1992)★★★, A Cappella Live (LKJ 1997)★★★, More Time (LKJ 1998)★★★.
COMPILATIONS: Reggae Greats (Island 1985)★★★★, Independent Intavenshan: The Island Anthology (Island 1998)★★★★.

JOHNSON, ROBERT
COMPILATIONS: King Of The Delta Blues Singers (Columbia 1961)★★★★★, King Of The Delta Blues Singers, Volume 2 (Columbia 1970)★★★★★, Robert Johnson Delta Blues Legend (Charly 1992)★★★★★, Hellhound On My Trail: The Essential Recordings (Indigo 1995)★★★★★, The Complete Recordings (Columbia Legacy 1996)★★★★★, with various artists Beg, Borrow Or Steal (Catfish 1998)★★★★, Steady Rollin' Man (Recall 1999)★★★★.
VIDEOS: The Search For Robert Johnson (Columbia 1992).
FURTHER READING: Searching For Robert Johnson, Peter Guralnick. The Devil's Son-in-Law, P. Garon. Love In Vain: Visions Of Robert Johnson, Alan Greenberg. King Of The Delta Blues: Transcriptions & Details Lessons For 29 Songs, Dave Rubin.

JONES, HOWARD
ALBUMS: Human's Lib (WEA 1984)★★★★, The 12 Inch Album (WEA 1984)★★, Dream Into Action (WEA 1985) ★★★, One To One (WEA 1986)★★, Cross That Line (WEA 1989)★★★, In The Running (WEA 1992)★★, Live Acoustic America (Plump 1996)★★★, People (Dtox/Ark 21 1998)★★.
COMPILATIONS: The Best Of Howard Jones (WEA 1993)★★★.

JONES, JIMMY
ALBUMS: Good Timin' (MGM 1960)★★★.
COMPILATIONS: Handy Man: The Anthology (Sequel 2002)★★★.

JONES, PAUL
ALBUMS: My Way (HMV 1966)★★★, Privilege film soundtrack (HMV 1967)★★★, Love Me Love My Friends (HMV 1968)★★, Come Into My Music Box (Columbia 1969)★★, Crucifix On A Horse (Vertigo 1971)★★, Drake's Dream film soundtrack (President 1974)★★, with Jack Bruce Alexis Korner Memorial Concert Vol. 1 (Indigo 1995)★★★.
COMPILATIONS: Hits And Blues (One-Up 1980)★★, The Paul Jones Collection: Volume One: My Way (RPM 1996) ★★★, The Paul Jones Collection: Volume Two: Love Me, Love My Friend (RPM 1996)★★, The Paul Jones Collection: Volume Three: Come Into My Music Box (RPM 1998)★★.

JONES, QUINCY
ALBUMS: Quincy Jones With The Swedish/U.S. All Stars (Prestige 1953)★★★, This Is How I Feel About Jazz (ABC-Paramount 1957)★★★, Go West, Man! (ABC-Paramount 1957)★★★, The Birth Of A Band (Mercury 1959)★★★, The Great Wide World Of Quincy Jones (Mercury 1960) ★★, Quincy Jones At Newport '61 (Mercury 1961)★★★★, I Dig Dancers (Mercury 1961)★★★, Around The World (Mercury 1961)★★★, The Quintessence (Impulse! 1961) ★★★, Billy Eckstine & Quincy Jones At Basin St. East (Mercury 1962)★★★, Big Band Bossa Nova (Mercury 1962)★★★, Quincy Jones Plays Hip Hits (Mercury 1963) ★★, Quincy's Got A Brand New Bag (Mercury 1964)★★, Quincy Jones Explores The Music Of Henry Mancini (Mercury 1964)★★★, Golden Boy (Mercury 1964)★★★, The Pawnbroker (Mercury 1964)★★★, Quincy Plays For Pussycats (Mercury 1965)★★★, Walk Don't Run (Mainstream 1966)★★, The Slender Thread (Mercury 1966)★★★, The Deadly Affair (Verve 1967)★★★, Enter Laughing (Liberty 1967)★★★, In The Heat Of The Night film soundtrack (United Artists 1967)★★★★, In Cold Blood film soundtrack (Colgems 1967)★★★, For The Love Of Ivy (ABC 1968)★★, MacKennas Gold (RCA 1969)★★★, The Italian Job film soundtrack (Paramount 1969)★★★★, Bob & Carol & Ted & Alice (Bell 1969)★★★, John And Mary (A&M 1969)★★★, Walking In Space (A&M 1969)★★, Gula Matari (A&M 1970)★★★, The Out Of Towners (United Artists 1970)★★★, Cactus Flower (Bell 1970)★★★, They Call Me Mr Tibbs (United Artists 1970)★★★, Smackwater Jack (A&M 1971) ★★★, Dollar (Reprise 1971)★★★, The Hot Rock (Prophesy 1972)★★★, Ndeda (Mercury 1972) ★★★, with Donny Hathaway Come Back, Charleston Blue film soundtrack (Atco 1972)★★, You've Got It Bad Girl (A&M 1973)★★, Body Heat (A&M 1974)★★★★, This Is How I Feel About Jazz (Impulse! 1974)★★★, Mellow Madness (A&M 1975)★★★, I Heard That! (A&M 1976) ★★★, Roots (A&M 1977)★★★, Sounds ... And Stuff Like That (A&M 1978)★★, The Wiz (MCA 1978)★★★, The Dude (A&M 1981)★★★, The Color Purple film soundtrack (Qwest 1985)★★★★, Back On The Block (Qwest 1989)★★★, Listen Up, The Lives Of Quincy Jones (Qwest 1990)★★★, with Miles Davis Live At Montreux 1991 recording (Reprise 1993)★★★★, Q's Jook Joint (Qwest 1995)★★★★, From Q, With Love (Qwest 1999)★★★, Go West, Man! reissue (Chessmates 1999)★★★, Big Band Bossa Nova reissue (Verve 1999) ★★★, with Sammy Nestico Basie & Beyond (Qwest 2000)★★★★.
COMPILATIONS: Compact Jazz: Quincy Jones (Phillips/PolyGram 1989)★★★★, Pure Delight: The Essence Of Quincy Jones And His Orchestra (1953-1964) (Razor & Tie 1995)★★★, Greatest Hits (A&M 1996)★★★, Best Of Quincy Jones (Spectrum 1998)★★★, Straight No Chaser: The Many Faces Of Quincy Jones (Universal 2000)★★★★, Quincey Jones: Talkin' Verve (Verve 2001)★★★, Q: The Musical Biography Of Quincy Jones 4-CD box set (Rhino 2001)★★★★.
VIDEOS: Miles Davis And Quincy Jones: Live At Montreux (1993).
FURTHER READING: Quincy Jones, Raymond Horricks. Q: The Autobiography Of Quincy Jones, Quincy Jones.
FILMS: Listen Up: The Lives Of Quincy Jones (1990).

JONES, RICKIE LEE
ALBUMS: Rickie Lee Jones (Warners 1979)★★★★, Pirates (Warners 1981)★★★★, Girl At Her Volcano mini-album (Warners 1982)★★, The Magazine (Warners 1984)★★★, Flying Cowboys (Geffen 1990)★★★, Pop Pop (Geffen 1991)★★★, Traffic From Paradise (Geffen 1993)★★★, Naked Songs: Live And Acoustic (Warners 1995)★★★, Ghostyhead (Warners 1997)★★★, It's Like This (Artemis 2000)★★★, Live At Red Rocks (Artemis 2001)★★★.
VIDEOS: Naked Songs (Warner Music Vision 1996).
FILMS: Pinocchio And The Emperor Of The Night voice only (1987), Tricks (2000).

JONES, TOM
ALBUMS: Along Came Jones (Decca 1965)★★★, It's Not Unusual US only (Parrot 1965)★★★, What's New Pussycat? US only (Parrot 1965)★★★, A-Tom-Ic Jones (Decca 1966) ★★★★, Green, Green Grass Of Home (Decca/Parrot 1966)★★★★, From The Heart (Decca 1966)★★★, Tom Jones Live! At The Talk Of The Town (Decca/Parrot 1967) ★★★, 13 Smash Hits (Decca 1967)★★★, The Tom Jones Fever Zone (Parrot 1968)★★★, Delilah (Decca 1968)★★★, Help Yourself (Decca/Parrot 1968)★★★★, Tom Jones Live! (Parrot 1969)★★★, This Is Tom Jones (Decca/Parrot 1969) ★★★, Tom Jones Live In Las Vegas (Decca 1969)★★★, Tom (Decca/Parrot 1970)★★★, I (Who Have Nothing) (Decca/ Parrot 1970)★★★, Tom Jones Sings She's A Lady (Decca/ Parrot 1971)★★★, Tom Jones Live At Caesar's Palace, Las Vegas (Decca/Parrot 1971)★★★, Close Up (Decca/Parrot 1972)★★★, The Body And Soul Of Tom Jones (Decca/ Parrot 1973)★★★, Something 'Bout You Baby I Like (Decca 1974) ★★, Memories Don't Leave Like People Do (Decca 1975) ★★★, Say You'll Stay Until Tomorrow (Epic 1977)★★, Do You Take This Man (EMI 1979)★★★, Rescue Me (Columbia 1980)★★★, Darlin' (Polydor 1981)★★★, Matador: The Musical Life Of El Cordobes cast recording (Epic 1987)★★★, At This Moment (Jive 1989)★★★, After Dark (Stylus 1989) ★★, Carrying A Torch (Dover 1991)★★★, The Lead And How To Swing It (ZTT 1994)★★★★, Reload (Gut 1999)★★★★.
COMPILATIONS: Greatest Hits (Decca/Parrot 1973) ★★★★, Tom Jones: 20 Greatest Hits (Decca 1975)★★★★, The World Of Tom Jones (Decca 1975)★★★★, Tom Jones Sings 24 Great Standards (Decca 1976)★★★★, What A Night (EMI 1978)★★★, I'm Coming Home (Lotus 1978)★★★, Super Disc Of Tom Jones (A&M 1979)★★★, Tom Jones Sings The Hits (EMI 1979)★★★, The Very Best Of Tom Jones (EMI 1979)★★★, The Golden Hits (Decca 1980)★★★, 16 Love Songs (Contour 1983)★★★, The Tom Jones Album (Decca 1983)★★★, The Soul Of Tom Jones (Decca 1986) ★★★, Love Songs (Arcade 1986)★★★, The Great Love Songs (Contour 1987)★★★, Tom Jones: The Greatest Hits (Telstar 1987)★★★, It's Not Unusual: His Greatest Hits (Decca 1987)★★★★, The Complete Tom Jones (The Hit Label 1992)★★★, The Ultimate Hit Collection: 1965-1988 (Repertoire 1995)★★★, Collection (Spectrum 1996)★★★, In Nashville (Spectrum 1996)★★★, At His Best (Pulse 1997)★★★, The Best Of ... Tom Jones (Deram 1998)★★★, The Ultimate Performance (Reactive 1998)★★, She's A Lady (Castle 2001)★★.
VIDEOS: One Night Only (Watchmaker Productions 1997), The Ultimate Collection (Prism Leisure Video 1999).
FURTHER READING: Tom Jones: Biography Of A Great Star, Tom Jones. Tom Jones, Stafford Hildred and David Griffen. Tom Jones, Chris Roberts. Close Up, Lucy Ellis and Bryony Sutherland.

JOPLIN, JANIS
ALBUMS: I Got Dem Ol' Kozmic Blues Again Mama! (Columbia 1969)★★★, Pearl (Columbia 1971)★★★★, Janis Joplin In Concert (Columbia 1972)★★★, with Big Brother And The Holding Company Live At Winterland '68 (Columbia 1998)★★★.
COMPILATIONS: Greatest Hits (Columbia 1973)★★★★, Janis film soundtrack including live and rare recordings (1975)★★★★, Anthology (Columbia 1980)★★★, Farewell Song (Columbia 1982)★★★, Janis 3-CD box-set (Columbia/Legacy 1995)★★★★, 18 Essential Songs (Columbia 1995)★★★, Box Of Pearls: The Janis Joplin Collection 5-CD box set (Columbia 1999)★★★★, Love, Janis: The Songs, The Letters, The Soul Of Janis Joplin (Columbia 2001)★★★★.
FURTHER READING: Janis Joplin: Her Life And Times, Deborah Landau. Going Down With Janis, Peggy Caserta as told to Dan Knapp. Janis Joplin: Buried Alive, Myra Friedman. Janis Joplin: Piece Of My Heart, David Dalton. Love, Janis, Laura Joplin. Pearl: The Obsessions And Passions Of Janis Joplin, Ellis Amburn. Scars Of Sweet Paradise: The Life And Times Of Janis Joplin, Alice Echols.
FILMS: American Pop (1981).

JORDANAIRES
ALBUMS: Beautiful City 10-inch album (RCA Victor 1953) ★★★, Peace In The Valley aka Church In The Wildwood (Decca/Vocalion 1957)★★★★, Heavenly Spirit! (Capitol 1958)★★★, Gloryland (Capitol 1959)★★★★, Of Rivers And Plains (Sesac 1959)★★★, with Tennessee Ernie Ford A Friend We Have In Jesus (Capitol 1960)★★★, Land Of Jordan (Capitol 1960)★★★★, To God Be The Glory (Capitol 1961)★★★, Spotlight On The Jordanaires (Capitol 1962)★★★, with Tennessee Ernie Ford Great Gospel Songs (Capitol 1964)★★★★, This Land (Columbia 1964)★★★, The Big Country Hits (Columbia 1965)★★★, Beyond This Day (Worldwide 1966)★★★, Monster Makers (Stop 1969) ★★★, We'd Like To Teach The World To Sing (Ember 1972) ★★★, with Tennessee Ernie Ford Swing Wide Your Golden Gate (Word 1978)★★★★, The Jordanaires Sing Elvis's Gospel Favourites (Magnum Force 1986)★★★, The Jordanaires Sing Elvis's Favourite Spirituals (Rockhouse 1990)★★★, 40th Anniversary (Worldwide 1990)★★★, With Friends, Denmark (Worldwide 1991)★★★.
COMPILATIONS: Will The Circle Be Unbroken (CEMA 1985)★★★, Golden Gospel Greats (Time/Life 1993)★★★★.
FILMS: Jailhouse Rock (1957), G.I. Blues (1960), Blue Hawaii (1961), Girls Girls Girls (1962), Fun In Acapulco (1963), Elvis – The Movie (1979).

JOURNEY
ALBUMS: Journey (Columbia 1975)★★★, Look Into The Future (Columbia 1976)★★★, Next (Columbia 1977)★★★, Infinity (Columbia 1978)★★★★, Evolution (Columbia 1979)★★★, Departure (Columbia 1980)★★★, Captured (Columbia 1981)★★★, Escape (Columbia 1981)★★★★, Frontiers (Columbia 1983)★★★, Raised On Radio (Columbia 1986)★★★, Trial By Fire (Columbia 1996)★★, Arrival (Columbia 2000)★★★.
SOLO: Gregg Rolie Roots (Sanctuary 2001)★★★.
COMPILATIONS: In The Beginning (Columbia 1979)★★, Greatest Hits/Best Of Journey (Columbia 1988)★★★★, Time 3-CD box set (Columbia 1992)★★★★, Greatest Hits Live (Columbia 1998)★★, The Essential (Legacy 2001)★★★.
VIDEOS: Live: 2001 (Sony Music Video 2001).

JOY DIVISION
ALBUMS: Unknown Pleasures (Factory 1979)★★★★, Closer (Factory 1980)★★★★, Still (Factory 1981)★★★, Preston 28 February 1980 (Burning Airlines 1999)★★★, Les Bains Douches 18 December 1979 (Burning Airlines 2001)★★.
COMPILATIONS: Substance 1977-1980 (Factory 1988) ★★★★, Peel Sessions (Strange Fruit 1990)★★★, Permanent (London 1995)★★★★, Heart And Soul 4-CD box set (London 1997)★★★, The Complete BBC Recordings (Strange Fruit 2000)★★★.
VIDEOS: Here Are The Young Men (Factory 1982).
FURTHER READING: An Ideal For Living: An History Of Joy Division, Mark Johnson. Touching From A Distance, Deborah Curtis. New Order & Joy Division, Claude Flowers.

JUDAS PRIEST
ALBUMS: Rocka Rolla (Gull 1974)★★, Sad Wings Of Destiny (Gull 1976)★★, Sin After Sin (Columbia 1977) ★★★, Stained Class (Columbia 1978)★★★, Killing Machine (Columbia 1978)★★, Live – Unleashed In The East (Columbia 1979)★★★★, British Steel (Columbia 1980) ★★★★, Point Of Entry (Columbia 1981)★★★, Screaming For Vengeance (Columbia 1982)★★★, Defenders Of The Faith (Columbia 1984)★★★, Turbo (Columbia 1986)★★, Priest Live (Columbia 1987)★★, Ram It Down (Columbia 1988)★★★, Painkiller (Columbia 1990)★★★, Jugulator (SPV 1997)★★★, Concert Classics (Ranch Life 1998)★★, Meltdown: '98 Live (SPV 1998)★★, Demolition (SPV 2001)★★.
COMPILATIONS: Best Of (Gull 1978)★★, Hero Hero (Telaeg 1987)★★, Collection (Castle 1989)★★★, Metal Works '73 – '93 (Columbia 1993)★★★★, Living After Midnight (Columbia 1997)★★★.
VIDEOS: Fuel Of Life (Columbia Music Video 1986), Judas Priest Live (Virgin Vision 1987), Painkiller (Sony Music Video 1990), Metal Works 73-93 (Columbia Music Video 1993), Classic Albums: British Steel (Eagle Vision 2001).
FURTHER READING: Heavy Duty, Steve Gett.

K

K-CI AND JOJO
ALBUMS: Love Always (MCA 1997)★★★, It's Real (MCA 1999)★★★, X (MCA 2000)★★★.

KALEIDOSCOPE
ALBUMS: Side Trips (Epic 1967)★★★, A Beacon From Mars (Epic 1968)★★★, Incredible Kaleidoscope (Epic 1969)★★★, Bernice (Epic 1970)★★, When Scopes Collide (Island 1976)★★★★, Greetings From Kartoonistan ... (We Ain't Dead Yet) (Curb 1991)★★★.
COMPILATIONS: Bacon From Mars (Edsel 1983)★★★, Rampe Rampe (Edsel 1984)★★★, Egyptian Candy (Legacy 1990)★★★, Blues From Baghdad: The Very Best Of Kaleidoscope (Edsel 1993)★★★, Infinite Colours Infinite Patterns: The Best Of Kaleidoscope (Edsel 2000)★★★.

KANSAS
ALBUMS: Kansas (Kirshner 1974)★★★, Song For America (Kirshner 1975)★★★, Masque (Kirshner 1975)★★★, Leftoverture (Kirshner 1976)★★★, Point Of Know Return (Kirshner 1977)★★★★, Two For The Show (Kirshner 1978) ★★★, Monolith (Kirshner 1979)★★★, Audio-Visions (Kirshner 1980)★★★, Vinyl Confessions (Kirshner 1982)★★, Drastic Measures (Columbia 1983)★★, Power (MCA 1986) ★★★★, In The Spirit Of Things (MCA 1988)★★, Live At The Whisky (Intersound 1992)★★, Freaks Of Nature (Intersound 1995)★★, Always Never The Same (River North 1998)★★★, Live On The King Biscuit Flower Hour 1989 recording (King Biscuit Flower Hour 1998)★★, Somewhere To Elsewhere (Magna Carta 2000)★★★.
COMPILATIONS: The Best Of Kansas (Columbia 1984) ★★★, Box Set (Sony 1994)★★★.

KATRINA AND THE WAVES
ALBUMS: Walking On Sunshine (Canada 1983)★★★, Katrina And The Waves 2 (Canada 1984)★★, Katrina And The Waves (Capitol 1985)★★, Waves (Capitol 1985)★★, Break Of Hearts (SBK 1989)★★, Walk On Water (Eternal 1997)★★.
COMPILATIONS: Anthology (One Way 1995)★★★, Walking On Sunshine: The Greatest Hits (EMI 1999)★★★.

KC AND THE SUNSHINE BAND
ALBUMS: Do It Good (TK 1974)★★★, KC And The Sunshine Band (TK 1974)★★★, as the Sunshine Band The Sound Of Sunshine (TK 1975)★★, Part 3 (TK 1976)★★★★, I Like To Do It (Jay Boy 1977)★★★, Who Do Ya (Love) (TK 1978) ★★, Do You Wanna Go Party (TK 1979)★★, The Painter (Epic 1981)★★, All In A Night's Work (Epic 1983)★★, Oh Yeah! (ZYX 1993)★★, Get Down Live! (Intersound 1995)★★.
SOLO: Wayne Casey/KC Space Cadet (Epic 1981)★★, KC Ten (Meca 1984)★★.
COMPILATIONS: Greatest Hits (TK 1980)★★★, The Best Of KC And The Sunshine Band (Rhino 1990)★★★★, Get Down Tonight: The Very Best Of (EMI 1998)★★★, 25th Anniversary Collection (Rhino 1999)★★★.

KEITA, SALIF
ALBUMS: Soro (Stern's 1987)★★★★, Ko-Yan (Mango 1990)★★, Amen (Mango 1991)★★, Folon (Mango 1995) ★★★★, Sosie (MSS 1997)★★★, Papa (Metro Blue 1999)★★★, Moffou (EMarcy 2002)★★★★.
COMPILATIONS: The Mansa Of Mali (Mango 1993)★★★, The Golden Voice: The Best Of Salif Keita (Wrasse 2001)★★★★.
VIDEOS: Salif Keita Live (Mango 1991).

KELIS
ALBUMS: Kaleidoscope (Virgin 1999)★★★★, Wanderland (Virgin 2001)★★.

KELLY, R.
ALBUMS: with Public Announcement Born Into The 90's (Jive 1992)★★★, 12 Play (Jive 1993)★★★★, R. Kelly (Jive 1995)★★★, R (Jive 1998)★★★★, TP-2.Com (Jive 2000) ★★★, with Jay-Z The Best Of Both World (Def Jam/Jive 2002)★★.
VIDEOS: 12 Play-The Hit Videos Vol. 1 (Jive 1994), Top Secret Down Low Videos (6 West 1996), TP-2.Com: The Videos (Jive/Zomba 2001).

KERSHAW, NIK
ALBUMS: Human Racing (MCA 1984)★★★, The Riddle (MCA 1984)★★★, Radio Musicola (MCA 1986)★★, The Works (MCA 1990)★★, 15 Minutes (Eagle 1999)★★★★, To Be Frank (Eagle 2001)★★★★.
COMPILATIONS: The Collection (MCA 1991)★★★★, The Essential (Spectrum 2000)★★★★.
FURTHER READING: Spilling The Beans On ... Making It In Music, Nik Kershaw.

KEYS, ALICIA
ALBUMS: Songs In A Minor (J 2001)★★★★.

KHAN, CHAKA
ALBUMS: Chaka (Warners 1978)★★★, Naughty (Warners 1980)★★★, What Cha' Gonna Do For Me (Warners 1981)★★★, Echoes Of An Era (Elektra 1982)★★★, Chaka Khan (Warners 1982)★★★, I Feel For You (Warners 1984) ★★★, Destiny (Warners 1986)★★, CK (Warners 1988) ★★★, Life Is A Dance - The Remix Project (Warners 1989) ★★, The Woman I Am (Warners 1992)★★★, Come 2 My House (Earth Song/NPG 1998)★★★.
COMPILATIONS: Epiphany: The Best Of ... Volume 1 (Reprise 1996)★★★★, I'm Every Woman: The Best Of (Warners 1999)★★★.
I VIDEOS: The Jazz Channel Presents Chaka Khan (Image Entertainment 2001).

KID CREOLE AND THE COCONUTS
ALBUMS: Off The Coast Of Me (Ze 1980)★★★, Fresh Fruit In Foreign Places (Ze 1981)★★★, Tropical Gangsters aka Wise Guy (Ze 1982)★★★, Doppelganger (Ze 1983)★★★, In Praise Of Older Women And Other Crimes (Sire 1985) ★★★, I, Too, Have Seen The Woods (Sire 1987)★★, Private Waters In The Great Divide (Columbia 1990)★★, You Shoulda Told Me You Were ... (Columbia 1991)★★, To Travel Sideways (Ascot/Hot 1994)★★, Kiss Me Before The Light Changes (Victor/Hot 1994)★★, The Conquest Of You (SPV 1997)★★, Live (Brilliant 2000)★★★.
COMPILATIONS: Cre-Ole: The Best Of Kid Creole & The Coconuts (Ze 1984)★★★★, Redux (Sire 1992)★★★★, The Best Of Kid Creole And The Coconuts (Island 1996)★★★★, Wonderful Thing (Spectrum 2000)★★★.
VIDEOS: Live: The Leisure Tour (Embassy 1986).

KID ROCK
ALBUMS: Grits Sandwiches For Breakfast (Jive 1990)★★, The Polyfuze Method (Continuum 1993)★★★, Fire It Up mini-album (Continuum 1995)H, Early Mornin' Stoned Pimp (Top Dog 1996)★★★, Devil Without A Cause (Lava/ Atlantic 1998)★★★★, Cocky (Lava/Atlantic 2001)★★★.
COMPILATIONS: The History Of Rock (East West 2000)★★★.

KIDD, JOHNNY, AND THE PIRATES
COMPILATIONS: Shakin' All Over (Regal Starline 1971) ★★★, Johnny Kidd - Rocker (EMI France 1978)★★★, The Best Of Johnny Kidd And The Pirates (EMI 1978)★★★, Rarities (See For Miles 1983)★★★, The Classic And The Rare (See For Miles 1990)★★★, The Complete Johnny Kidd (EMI 1992)★★★★, 25 Greatest Hits (MFP 1998)★★★★.
FURTHER READING: Shaking All Over, Keith Hunt.

KIHN, GREG
ALBUMS: Greg Kihn (Beserkley 1975)★★, Greg Kihn Again (Beserkley 1977)★★★, Next Of Kihn (Beserkley 1978)★★, With The Naked Eye (Beserkley 1979)★★★, Glass House Rock (Beserkley 1980)★★, Rockihnroll (Beserkley 1981) ★★★★, Kihntinued (Beserkley 1982)★★★, Kihnspiracy (Beserkley 1983)★★★★, Kihntageous (Beserkley 1984) ★★★, Citizen Kihn (EMI 1985)★★, Love And Rock And Roll (EMI 1986)★★★, Unkihntrollable (Rhino 1989)★★★, Kihn Of Hearts (FR 1992)★★★, Mutiny (Clean Cuts 1994)★★★, Live: King Biscuit Flower Hour (King Biscuit Flower Hour 1996)★★★, Horror Show (Clean Cuts 1996)★★★, All The Right Reasons (Castle 2000)★★★.
COMPILATIONS: Kihnsolidation: The Best Of Greg Kihn (Rhino 1989)★★★★, Kihnspicuous: The Best Of Greg Kihn (Snapper 1998)★★★★.
FURTHER READING: Horror Show, Greg Kihn.

KILBURN AND THE HIGH ROADS
ALBUMS: Handsome (Dawn 1975)★★, Wotabunch (Warners 1978)★★.
COMPILATIONS: The Best Of Kilburn And The High Roads (Warners 1977)★★★.
FURTHER READING: Sex & Drugs & Rock 'n' Roll: The Life Of Ian Dury, Richard Balls.

KILLING JOKE
ALBUMS: Killing Joke (Malicious Damage/EG 1980) ★★★★, what's THIS for ... ! (Malicious Damage/EG 1981) ★★★, Revelations (Malicious Damage/EG 1982)★★★, Ha! EP10 (Malicious Damage/EG 1982)★★★, Fire Dances (EG 1983)★★★★, Night Time (EG/Polydor 1985)★★★, Brighter Than A Thousand Suns (EG/Virgin 1986)★★★, Outside The Gate (EG/Virgin 1988)★★★, Extremities, Dirt & Various Repressed Emotions (Noise International/RCA 1990)★★★★, Pandemonium (Big Life/Zoo 1994)★★★, BBC In Concert (Strange Fruit/Windsong 1995)★★★, Democracy (Zoo 1996)★★★, No Way Out But Forward Go 1985 live recordings (Burning Airlines 2001)★★★.
COMPILATIONS: An Incomplete Collection (EG 1990)★★★, Laugh? I Nearly Bought One! (EG/Caroline 1992)★★★, Wilful Days (Blue Plate 1995)★★★.

KING CRIMSON
ALBUMS: In The Court Of The Crimson King ... An Observation By King Crimson (Island/Atlantic 1969) ★★★★, In The Wake Of Poseidon (Island/Atlantic 1970) ★★★, Lizard (Island/Atlantic 1970)★★★, Islands (Island/ Atlantic 1971)★★, Earthbound (Island 1972)★★, Larks' Tongues In Aspic (Island/Atlantic 1973)★★★★, Starless And Bible Black (Island/Atlantic 1974)★★★, Red (Island/ Atlantic 1974)★★★★, USA (Island/Atlantic 1975)★★★, Discipline (EG/Warners 1981)★★★, Beat (EG/Warners 1982)★★★, Three Of A Perfect Pair (EG/Warners 1984) ★★★, Thrak (DGM/Virgin 1995)★★★, B'Boom: Official Bootleg - Live In Argentina (DGM 1995)★★, THRaKaTTak (DGM 1996)★★★, Epitaph: Live In 1969 (DGM 1997) ★★★, The Nightwatch: Live At The Amsterdam Concertgebouw (DGM 1997)★★★, Absent Lovers: Live In Montreal 1984 (DGM 1998)★★★, Live At The Marquee 1969 (DGM 1998) ★★★, Live At Jacksonville 1972 (DGM 1998)★★★, The Beat Club Bremen 1972 (DGM 1999)★★★, Live At Cap D'Adge, 1982 (DGM 1999)★★★, On Broadway: Live In NYC 1995 (DGM 1999)★★★, Live In Mexico City 1996 (DGM 1999) ★★★, The Vrooom Sessions 1994 (DGM 2000)★★, Live At Summit Studios, 1972 (DGM 2000)★★★, Live In Central Park, NYC, 1974 (DGM 2000)★★★, Live At Moles Club, Bath, 1981 (DGM 2000)★★★, The ConstruKction Of Light (DGM 2000) ★★★, Heavy ConstuKction 3-CD box set (DGM 2000)★★★, Vroom Vroom 1996 live recordings (DGM 2001)★★★.
COMPILATIONS: The Young Persons' Guide To King Crimson (Island 1976)★★★, The Compact King Crimson (EG 1986)★★★, King Crimson 1989 4-CD box set (EG 1989)★★★, The Essential King Crimson: Frame By Frame 4-CD box set (EG 1991)★★★★, The Abbreviated King Crimson: Heartbeat (EG 1991)★★★, The Great Deceiver: Live 1973-1974 4-CD box set (Discipline 1992)★★★, The First Three 3-CD box set (Virgin/Caroline 1993)★★★, Sleepless: The Concise King Crimson (Caroline 1993) ★★★★, Cirkus: The Young Persons' Guide To King Crimson Live (Virgin 1999)★★★, The ProjeKcts 4-CD box set (DGM 1999)★★★, The Deception Of The Thrush: A Beginners Guide To ProjeKcts (DGM 1999)★★★, A Beginners' Guide To The King Crimson Collectors' Club (DGM 2000)★★★.
I VIDEOS: The Noise: Frejus 1982 (EG 1984), Three Of A Perfect Pair: Live In Japan (EG 1984), Live In Japan: 1995 (DGM 1996), Deja Vrooom (Ryko 1999).
FURTHER READING: Robert Fripp: From King Crimson To Guitar Craft, Eric Tamm. In The Court Of King Crimson, Sid Smith.

KING CURTIS
ALBUMS: Have Tenor Sax, Will Blow (Atco 1959)★★★, The New Scene Of King Curtis (New Jazz 1960)★★★, Azure (Everest 1961)★★★, Trouble In Mind King Curtis Sings The Blues (Tru-Sound 1961)★★★★, Old Gold (Tru-Sound 1961)★★, Doin' The Dixie Twist (Tru-Sound 1962)★★★, It's Party Time With King Curtis (Tru-Sound 1962)★★★★, Soul Meeting (Prestige 1962)★★★, Arthur Murray's Music For Dancing: The Twist (RCA Victor 1962)★★, Soul Twist (Enjoy 1962)★★★, Country Soul (Capitol 1963)★★, The Great King Curtis (Clarion 1964)★★, Soul Serenade (Capitol 1964)★★★, King Curtis Plays The Hits Made Famous By Sam Cooke (Capitol 1965)★★★, That Lovin' Feelin' (Atco 1966)★★★, Live At Small's Paradise (Atco 1966)★★★, Plays The Great Memphis Hits (Atco 1967)★★★, King Size Soul (Atco 1967)★★, Sax In Motion (Atco 1968)★★, Sweet Soul (Atco 1968)★★★, Instant Groove (Atco 1969) ★★, Eternally Soul (Atco 1970)★★★, Everybody's Talkin' (Atco 1970)★★, Get Ready (Atco 1970)★★★, Blues At Montreux (Atco 1970)★★★, Live At Fillmore West (Atco 1971)★★★, Mr. Soul (Ember 1972)★★★.
COMPILATIONS: Best Of King Curtis (Capitol 1968) ★★★★, Didn't He Play! (Red Lightnin' 1988)★★★, The Capitol Years 1962-65 (EMI 1993)★★★★, Instant Soul: The Legendary King Curtis (Razor & Tie 1994)★★★★, The Best Of King Curtis (Collectables 1996)★★★.

KING, ALBERT
ALBUMS: The Big Blues (King 1962)★★★, Born Under A Bad Sign (Atlantic 1967)★★★★, King Of The Blues Guitar (Atlantic 1968)★★★★, Live Wire/Blues Power (King 1968) ★★★★, with Steve Cropper, 'Pops' Staples Jammed Together (Stax 1969)★★★, Years Gone By (Stax 1969)★★★★, King, Does The King's Thing (Stax 1970)★★★, Lovejoy (Stax 1971) ★★, I'll Play The Blues For You (Stax 1972)★★, Live At Montreux/Blues At Sunrise (Stax 1973)★★★, I Wanna Get Funky (Stax 1974)★★, The Pinch (Stax 1976)★★, Albert (Utopia 1976)★★★, Truckload Of Lovin' (Utopia 1976)★★, Albert Live (Utopia 1977)★★★, King Albert (1977)★★★, New Orleans Heat (Tomato 1978)★★★, San Francisco '83 (Stax 1983)★★★, I'm In A 'Phone Booth, Baby (Stax 1984) ★★★, with John Mayall The Lost Session recorded 1971 (Stax 1986)★★, Red House (Essential 1991)★★★, Blues At Sunset (Stax 1996)★★★, with Stevie Ray Vaughan In Session 1983 recording (Fantasy/Stax 1999)★★★.
COMPILATIONS: shared with Otis Rush Door To Door (Chess 1969)★★★, Laundromat Blues (Edsel 1984)★★★, The Best Of Albert King (Stax 1986)★★★, I'll Play The Blues For You: The Best Of Albert King (Stax 1988)★★★, Let's Have A Natural Ball 1959-63 recordings (Modern Blues Recordings 1989)★★★, Wednesday Night In San Francisco (Live At The Fillmore) and Thursday Night In San Francisco (Live At The Fillmore) (Stax 1990)★★, Live On Memory Lane (Monad 1995)★★★, Hard Bargain (Stax 1996)★★★★, The Best Of Albert King (Stax 1998)★★★, The Very Best Of Albert King (Rhino 1999)★★★★.

KING, B.B.
ALBUMS: Singin' The Blues (Crown 1957)★★★★, The Blues (Crown 1958)★★★, B.B. King Wails (Crown 1959)★★★, B.B. King Sings Spirituals (Crown 1960)★★, The Great B.B. King (Crown 1961)★★★, King Of The Blues (Crown 1961)★★★, My Kind Of Blues (Crown 1961)★★★, More B.B. King (Crown 1962)★★★, Twist With B.B. King (Crown 1962)★★, Easy Listening Blues (Crown 1962)★★★, Blues In My Heart (Crown 1962)★★★, B.B. King (Crown 1963) ★★★, Mr. Blues (ABC 1963)★★★, Rock Me Baby (Kent 1964)★★★★, Live At The Regal (ABC 1965)★★★★★, Confessin' The Blues (ABC 1965)★★★, Let Me Love You (United 1965)★★★, B.B. King Live On Stage (United 1965)★★★, The Soul Of B.B. King (United 1966)★★★, The Jungle (Kent 1967)★★★, Blues Is King (Bluesway 1967) ★★★★, Blues On Top Of Blues (Bluesway 1968)★★★, Lucille (Bluesway 1968)★★★★, Live And Well (MCA 1969)★★★★, Completely Well (MCA 1969)★★★, Back In The Alley (MCA 1970)★★★, Indianola Mississippi Seeds (MCA 1970)★★★★, Live In Cook County Jail (MCA 1971)★★★★, In London (MCA 1971)★★★, L.A. Midnight (ABC 1972)★★★, Guess Who (ABC 1972)★★★, To Know You Is To Love You (ABC 1973)★★★, with Bobby Bland Together For The First Time ... Live (MCA 1974)★★★★, Friends (ABC 1974)★★★, Lucille Talks Back (MCA 1975) ★★★★, with Bobby Bland Together Again ... Live (MCA 1976)★★★, King Size (MCA 1977)★★★, Midnight Believer (MCA 1978)★★★, Take It Home (MCA 1979)★★★, Now Appearing At Ole Miss (MCA 1980)★★, There Must Be A Better World Somewhere (MCA 1981)★★★★, Love Me Tender (MCA 1982)★★, Blues 'N' Jazz (MCA 1983)★★, Six Silver Strings (MCA 1985)★★, Do The Boogie (Ace 1988) ★★★, Lucille Had A Baby (Ace 1989)★★, Live At San Quentin (MCA 1990)★★★★, Live At The Apollo (GRP 1991)★★★, Singin' The Blues & The Blues (Ace 1991)★★★, There's Always One More Time (MCA 1992)★★★★, Blues Summit (MCA 1993)★★★★, with Diane Schuur Heart To Heart (GRP 1994)★★, Lucille And Friends (MCA 1995) ★★★, Deuces Wild (MCA 1997)★★★★, Blues On The Bayou (MCA 1998)★★★★, Let The Good Times Roll (MCA 1999)★★★★, Makin' Love Is Good For You (MCA 2000) ★★★, with Eric Clapton Riding With The King (Reprise 2000)★★★, A Christmas Celebration Of Hope (MCA 2001) ★★.
COMPILATIONS: The Best Of B.B. King (Galaxy 1962)★★, His Best – The Electric B.B. King (Kent 1968)★★★, The Incredible Soul Of B.B. King (Kent 1970)★★★, The Best Of B.B. King (MCA 1973)★★★★, The Rarest King (Blues Boy 1980)★★★, The Memphis Master (Ace 1982)★★★, B.B. King - 20 Blues Greats (Déjà Vu 1985)★★★, Introducing (1969-85) (MCA 1987)★★★, Across The Tracks (Ace 1988)★★★, My Sweet Little Angel (Ace 1992)★★★★, King Of The Blues 4-CD box set (MCA 1993)★★★★, Gold Collection (MCA 1993)★★, King Of The Blues (Pickwick 1994)★★, Heart & Soul: A Collection Of Blues Ballads (Pointblank Classic 1995)★★★, The Collection: 20 Master Recordings (Castle 1995)★★★, How Blue Can You Get Classic Live Performances 1964-1994 (MCA 1996)★★★★, He's Dynamite! (Ace 1998)★★★★, The RPM Hits 1951-1957 (Ace 1999)★★★★, His Definitive Greatest Hits (PolyGram 1999)★★★★, Anthology (MCA 2000)★★★★, Forever Gold (St Clair 2000)★★★, Best Of B.B. King: The Millennium Collection (MCA 2000)★★★★, Here & There: The Uncollected B.B. King (Hip-O 2001)★★★, Classic Masters (EMD 2002)★★★.
CD-ROM: On The Road With B.B. King (MCA 1996)★★★★.
VIDEOS: Live At Nick's (Hendring Music Video 1987), A Blues Session (Video Collection 1988), Live In Africa (BMG Video 1991), Blues Master, Highlights (Warner Music Video 1995), The Blues Summit Concert (MCA 1995), B.B. King: Ralph Gleason's Jazz Casual (Rhino Home 2000), The Jazz Channel Presents B.B. King (Aviva International 2001).

FURTHER READING: The Arrival Of B.B. King: The Authorized Biography, Charles Sawyer. B.B. King, Sebastian Danchin. Blues All Around Me: The Autobiography Of B.B. King, B.B. King and David Ritz.

KING, BEN E.
ALBUMS: Spanish Harlem (Atco 1961)★★★, Ben E. King Sings For Soulful Lovers (Atco 1962)★★★, Don't Play That Song (Atco 1962)★★★, Young Boy Blues (Clarion 1964), Seven Letters (Atco 1965)★★★, What Is Soul (Atco 1967) ★★★, Rough Edges (Maxwell 1970)★★★, Supernatural (Atco 1975)★★★, I Had A Love (Atco 1976)★★, with the Average White Band Benny And Us (Atlantic 1977)★★★, Let Me Live In Your Life (Atco 1978)★★, Music Trance (Atlantic 1980)★★, Street Tough (Atlantic 1981)★★, Save The Last Dance For Me (EMI 1988)★★★, Shades Of Blue (Half Note 1999)★★★.
COMPILATIONS: Greatest Hits (Atco 1964)★★★, Beginning Of It All (Mandala 1971)★★★, Here Comes The Night (Edsel 1984)★★★, The Ultimate Collection: Ben E. King (Atlantic 1987)★★★★, Anthology One: Spanish Harlem (RSA 1996)★★★, Anthology Two: For Soulful Lovers (RSA 1996)★★★, Anthology Three: Don't Play That Song (RSA 1996)★★★, Anthology Four: Seven Letters (RSA 1997) ★★★, Anthology Five: What Is Soul? (RSA 1997)★★★, Anthology Six: Supernatural (RSA 1997)★★★, Anthology Seven: Benny And Us (RSA 1997)★★, The Very Best Of Ben E. King (Rhino 1998)★★★★.
VIDEOS: The Jazz Channel Presents Ben E. King (Aviva 2001).

KING, CAROLE
ALBUMS: Writer (Ode 1970)★★★, Tapestry (Ode 1971) ★★★★, Music (Ode 1971)★★★, Rhymes And Reasons (Ode 1972)★★★, Fantasy (Ode 1973)★★★★, Wrap Around Joy (Ode 1974)★★★, Really Rosie (Ode 1975) ★★★, Thoroughbred (Ode 1976)★★★, Simple Things (Capitol 1977)★★, Welcome Home (Avatar 1978)★★, Touch The Sky (Capitol 1979)★★, Pearls (Songs Of Goffin And King) (Capitol 1980)★★, One To One (Atlantic 1982) ★★, Speeding Time (Atlantic 1984)★★★, City Streets (Capitol 1989)★★, Colour Of Your Dreams (Valley 1993) ★★★, In Concert (Quality 1994)★★, The Carnegie Hall Concert 1971 (Sony 1996)★★★, Love Makes The World (Rockingale 2001)★★★★.
COMPILATIONS: Her Greatest Hits (Ode 1973)★★★, A Natural Woman: The Ode Collection 1968-1976 (Legacy 1995)★★★★, Goin' Back (Sony 1996)★★★, Natural Woman: The Very Best Of Carole King (Sony 2000)★★★★.
VIDEOS: In Concert (Wienerworld 1994).
FURTHER READING: Carole King, Paula Taylor. Carole King: A Biography In Words & Pictures, Mitchell S. Cohen.

KING, FREDDIE
ALBUMS: Freddie King Sings The Blues (King 1961)★★★, Let's Hideaway And Dance Away (King 1961)★★★★, Boy-Girl-Boy (King 1962)★★★, Bossa Nova And Blues (King 1962)★★, Freddie King Goes Surfing (King 1963)★★, Freddie King Gives You A Bonanza Of Instrumentals (King 1965)★★★, 24 Vocals And Instrumentals (King 1966) ★★★, Hide Away (King 1969)★★★★, Freddie King Is A Blues Master (Atlantic 1969)★★★, My Feeling For The Blues (Atlantic 1970)★★★, Getting Ready (Shelter 1971) ★★★★, Texas Cannonball (Shelter 1972)★★★, Woman Across The Water (Shelter 1973)★★★, Burglar (RSO 1974) ★★★, Larger Than Life (RSO 1975)★★★, Live At The Electric Ballroom 1974 (Black Top 1996)★★★.
COMPILATIONS: The Best Of Freddie King (Shelter 1974) ★★★★, Rockin' The Blues – Live (Crosscut 1983)★★★, Takin' Care Of Business (Charly 1985)★★★, Live In Antibes, 1974 (Concert 1988)★★★, Live In Nancy, 1975 Volume 1 (Concert 1989)★★★, Blues Guitar Hero: The Influential Early Sessions (EMI 1993)★★★, King Of The Blues (EMI/Shelter 1996)★★★★, Key To The Highway (Wolf 1995)★★★, Stayin' Home With The Blues RSO material (Spectrum 1998)★★★, The Ultimate Collection (Hip-O 2001)★★★★.
VIDEOS: Freddie King Jan 20 1973 (Vestapol Music Video 1995), Freddie King In Concert (Vestapol Music Video 1995), Freddie King: The !!!!Beat 1966 (Vestapol Music Video 1995), Live At The Sugarbowl, 1972 (Vestapol Music Video 1998).

KING, JONATHAN
ALBUMS: Or Then Again (Decca 1965)★★, Try Something Different (Decca 1972)★★, A Rose In A Fisted Glove (UK 1975)★★, JK All The Way (UK 1976)★★, Anticloning mini-album (Revolution 1992)★★.
COMPILATIONS: King Size King (PRT 1982)★★, The Butterfly That Stamped (Castle 1989)★★, The Many Faces Of Jonathan King (Castle 1993)★★.

KINGSMEN
ALBUMS: The Kingsmen In Person (Wand 1963)★★, The Kingsmen, Volume 2 (More Great Sounds) (Wand 1964) ★★, The Kingsmen, Volume 3 (Wand 1965)★★, The Kingsmen On Campus (Wand 1965)★★, Up Up And Away (Wand 1966)★★.
COMPILATIONS: 15 Great Hits (Wand 1966)★★, The Kingsmen's Greatest Hits (Wand 1967)★★, Louie Louie/ Greatest Hits (Charly 1986)★★★, The Very Best Of The Kingsmen (Varèse Vintage 1998)★★★.
FILMS: How To Stuff A Wild Bikini (1965).

KINGSTON TRIO
ALBUMS: The Kingston Trio (Capitol 1958)★★★, From The Hungry i (Capitol 1959)★★★, The Kingston Trio At Large (Capitol 1959)★★★★, Here We Go Again! (Capitol 1959)★★★★, Sold Out (Capitol 1960)★★★, String Along (Capitol 1960)★★★, Stereo Concert (Capitol 1960)★★★, The Last Month Of The Year (Capitol 1960)★★★, Make Way! (Capitol 1961)★★★, Goin' Places (Capitol 1961) ★★★, Close-Up (Capitol 1961)★★★, College Concert: The Kingston Trio Recorded In Live Performance (Capitol 1962) ★★★, Something Special (Capitol 1962)★★★, New Frontier (Capitol 1962)★★★, #16 (Capitol 1963)★★, Sunny Side! (Capitol 1963)★★, Sing A Song With The Kingston Trio (Capitol 1963)★★, Time To Think (Capitol 1963)★★★, Back In Town (Capitol 1964)★★★, Nick Bob John (Decca 1964)★★, Stay Awhile (Decca 1965)★★, Somethin' Else (Decca 1965)★★, Children Of The Morning (Decca 1966)★★, Once Upon A Time 1966 live recording (Tetragammatron 1969)★★★, American Gold (Longines 1973)★★★★, Best Of The Best (Proarté 1986)★★.
COMPILATIONS: Encores (Capitol 1961)★★★★, The Best Of The Kingston Trio (Capitol 1962)★★★★, The Folk Era 3-LP box set (Capitol 1964)★★★, The Best Of The Kingston Trio Volume 2 (Capitol 1965)★★★★, The Best Of The Kingston Trio Volume 3 (Capitol 1966)★★★, The Historic Recordings Of The Kingston Trio (Capitol 1975)★★★★, Rediscover The Kingston Trio (1985)★★★, The Very Best Of The Kingston Trio (Capitol 1987)★★★★, Capitol Collectors Series (Capitol 1991)★★★, Greatest Hits (Curb 1991)★★★, The EP Collection (See For Miles 1997)★★★★, The Guard Years 10-CD box set (Bear Family 1998)★★★, The Stewart Years 10-CD box set (Bear Family 2000)★★★.
FURTHER READING: The Kingston Trio On Record, Kingston Korner.

KINKS
ALBUMS: Kinks (UK) You Really Got Me (US) (Pye/Reprise 1964)★★★, Kinks-Size US only (Reprise 1965)★★★, Kinda Kinks (Pye/Reprise 1965)★★★, Kinkdom US only (Reprise 1965)★★★, The Kink Kontroversy (Pye/Reprise 1966)★★★★, Face To Face (Pye/Reprise 1966)★★★★, Live At Kelvin Hall (UK) The Live Kinks (US) (Pye/Reprise 1968)H, Something Else (Pye/Reprise 1967)★★★★★, Are The Village Green Preservation Society (Pye/Reprise 1968) ★★★★★, Arthur (Or The Decline And Fall Of The British Empire) (Pye/Reprise 1969)★★★★, Lola Versus Powerman And The Moneygoround, Part One (Pye/Reprise 1970) ★★★, Percy film soundtrack (Pye 1971)★★, Muswell Hillbillies (RCA 1971)★★★★, Everybody's In Show-Biz (RCA 1972)★★★ Preservation Act 1 (RCA 1973)★★, Preservation Act 2 (RCA 1974)★★, Soap Opera (RCA 1975)★★, Schoolboys In Disgrace (RCA 1975)★★★, Sleepwalker (Arista 1977)★★★, Misfits (Arista 1978) ★★★★, Low Budget (Arista 1979)★★★, One For The Road (Arista 1980)★★★★, Give The People What They Want (Arista 1981)★★★, State Of Confusion (Arista 1983)★★★, Word Of Mouth (Arista 1984)★★, Think Visual (London/MCA 1986)★★, Live: The Road (London/ MCA 1987)★★, UK Jive (London/MCA 1989)★★, Phobia (Columbia 1993)★★★, To The Bone (UK) (Konk 1994) ★★★★, To The Bone (USA) (Guardian 1996)★★★★.
COMPILATIONS: Well Respected Kinks (Marble Arch 1966) ★★★★, Greatest Hits! US only (Reprise 1966)★★★★, Then Now And Inbetween US only (Reprise 1969)★★★★, The Kinks (Pye 1970)★★★★, The Kink Kronikles US only (Reprise 1971)★★★★, The Great Lost Kinks Album US only (Reprise 1973)★★★, Lola, Percy And The Apeman Come Face To Face With The Village Green Preservation Society ... Something Else (Golden Hour 1973)★★★★, All The Good Times 4-LP box set (Pye 1973)★★★★, Celluloid Heroes: Greatest Hits (RCA 1976)★★★★, The Kinks File (Pye 1977)★★★★, Second Time Around US only (RCA 1980)★★, Dead End Street: Greatest Hits (PRT 1983) ★★★★, Come Dancing With The Kinks US only (Arista 1986)★★★, Are Well Respected Men (PRT 1987)★★★★, Greatest Hits (Rhino 1989)★★★★★, Fab Forty: The Singles Collection: 1964-1970 (Decal 1990)★★★★, The EP Collection (See For Miles 1990)★★★★, The EP Collection Vol. Two (See For Miles 1991)★★★, The Complete Collection (Castle 1991)★★★★, Lost & Found (1986-89) (MCA 1991)★★, The Best Of The Ballads (BMG 1993) ★★★, Tired Of Waiting For You (Rhino 1995)★★★, Remastered 3-CD set (Castle 1995)★★★★, The Singles Collection/Waterloo Sunset (Castle 1997)★★★★★, Kinks reissue (Castle 1998)★★★, Kinda Kinks reissue (Castle 1998)★★★, The Kink Kontroversy reissue (Castle 1998) ★★★★, Face To Face reissue (Castle 1998)★★★★, Something Else reissue (Castle 1998)★★★★★, The Songs We Sang For Auntie: BBC Sessions 1964 - 1977 (Sanctuary 2001)★★★★, The Marble Arch Years 3-CD box set (Castle 2001)★★★★.
VIDEOS: The Kinks: One For The Road (Time Live 1980), Come Dancing With The Kinks (Columbia Pictures Home Video 1986), Shindig! Presents The Kinks (Rhino Home Video 1992).
FURTHER READING: The Kinks: The Sound And The Fury, Johnny Rogan. The Kinks: The Official Biography, Jon Savage. The Kinks Part One: You Really Got Me - An Illustrated World Discography Of The Kinks, 1964-1993, Doug Hinman with Jason Brabazon. X-Ray, Ray Davies. Kink: An Autobiography, Dave Davies. The Kinks: Well Respected Men, Neville Marten and Jeffrey Hudson. Waterloo Sunset, Ray Davies. The Complete Guide To The Music Of The Kinks, Johnny Rogan.

KISS
ALBUMS: Kiss (Casablanca 1974)★★★, Hotter Than Hell (Casablanca 1974)★★, Dressed To Kill (Casablanca 1975) ★★★, Alive! (Casablanca 1975)★★★, Destroyer (Casablanca 1976)★★★★, Rock And Roll Over (Casablanca 1976)★★, Love Gun (Casablanca 1977)★★★, Alive II (Casablanca 1977)★★★, Dynasty (Casablanca 1979)★★, Unmasked (Casablanca 1980)★★, Music From The Elder (Casablanca 1981)★★, Creatures Of The Night (Casablanca 1982)★★, Lick It Up (Vertigo 1983)★★, Animalize (Vertigo 1984)★★, Asylum (Vertigo 1985)★★, Crazy Nights (Vertigo 1987)★★★, Hot In The Shade (Vertigo 1989)★★, Revenge (Mercury 1992)★★★, Alive III (Mercury 1993)★★, MTV Unplugged (Mercury 1996)★★★, Carnival Of Souls: The Final Sessions (Mercury 1997)★★, Psycho Circus (Mercury 1998)★★★.
COMPILATIONS: The Originals 3-LP set (Casablanca 1976)★★★, Originals II 3-LP set (Casablanca 1978)★★★, Double Platinum (Casablanca 1978)★★★, Killers (Casablanca 1982)★★★, Smashes, Thrashes & Hits (Vertigo 1988)★★★, Revenge (Mercury 1992)★★, You Wanted The Best, You Got The Best (Mercury 1996)★★★★, Greatest Kiss (Mercury 1996)★★★, Kiss 5-CD box set (Mercury 2001)★★★.
VIDEOS: Kiss Animalize Live – Uncensored (Embassy Home Video 1984), The Phantom Of The Park (IVS 1987), Kiss Exposed (PolyGram Music Video 1987), Crazy, Crazy Nights (Channel 5 1988), Age Of Chance (Virgin Vision 1988), X-Treme Close Up (1992), Konfidential (PolyGram Music Video 1993), Kiss My A** (PolyGram Music Video 1994), Unplugged (PolyGram Music Video 1996), Psycho Circus (PolyGram Video 1998), The Second Coming (PolyGram Video 1998), UnAuthorised (Wienerworld 2000).
FURTHER READING: Kiss, Robert Duncan. Goldmine Kiss Collectables Price Guide, Tom Shannon. Kiss: The Greatest Rock Show On Earth, John Swenson. Kiss: The Real Story Authorized, Peggy Tomarkin. Kiss Live, Mick St. Michael. Black Diamond: The Unauthorised Biography Of Kiss, Dale Sherman. Kiss And Sell: The Making Of A Supergroup, C.K. Lendt. Kiss And Make-Up, Gene Simmons.

KITT, EARTHA
ALBUMS: New Faces Of 1952 original cast (RCA Victor 1952)★★★, Songs 10-inch album (RCA Victor 1953)★★★, That Bad Eartha 10-inch album (RCA Victor 1953)★★★★, Down To Eartha (RCA Victor 1955)★★★, Thursday's Child (RCA Victor 1956)★★★, St. Louis Blues (RCA Victor 1958) ★★★, The Fabulous Eartha Kitt (Kapp 1959)★★★, Eartha Kitt Revisited (Kapp 1960)★★★, Bad But Beautiful (MGM 1962)★★★, Eartha Kitt Sings In Spanish (Decca 1965)★★★, C'est Si Bon (IMS 1983)★★★, I Love Men (Record Shack 1984)★★★, Love For Sale (Capitol 1984)★★, The Romantic Eartha Kitt (Pathe Marconi 1984)★★, St. Louis Blues (RCA Germany 1985)★★★, That Bad Eartha (RCA Germany 1985)★★★, Eartha Kitt In Person At The Plaza (GNP 1988) ★★★★, I'm A Funny Dame (Official 1988)★★★, My Way (Caravan 1988)★★★, I'm Still Here (Arista 1989)★★★, Live In London (Arista 1990)★★★★, Thinking Jazz (ITM 1992) ★★★, Back In Business (ITM 1994)★★★.
COMPILATIONS: At Her Very Best (RCA 1982)★★★, Songs (RCA 1983)★★★, Diamond Series: Eartha Kitt (Diamond 1988)★★★, Best Of Eartha Kitt (MCA 1990)★★★, The Best Of Eartha Kitt: Where Is My Man (Hot 1995)★★★, Purr-Fect: Greatest Hits (Buddah 1999)★★★★.
FURTHER READING: Thursday's Child, Eartha Kitt. Alone With Me: A New Biography, Eartha Kitt. I'm Still Here, Eartha Kitt.
FILMS: Casbah (1948), New Faces (1954), The Mark Of The Hawk aka Accused (1957), St. Louis Blues (1958), Anna Lucasta (1958), Saint Of Devil's Island aka Seventy Times Seven (1961), Synanon aka Get Off My Back (1965), Onkel Toms Hütte aka Uncle Tom's Cabin (1969), Up The Chastity Belt aka Naughty Knights (1971), Friday Foster (1975), All By Myself (1982), The Serpent Warriors (1985), The Pink Chiquitas (1987), Erik The Viking (1989), Master Of Dragonard Hill (1989), Living Doll (1990), Ernest Scared Stupid (1991), Boomerang (1992), Fatal Instinct (1993), Unzipped (1995), Harriet The Spy (1996), Ill Gotten Gains voice only (1997), I Woke Up Early The Day I Died (1998), The Emperor's New Groove voice only (2000).

KLAATU
ALBUMS: Klaatu (Capitol 1976)★★★, Hope (Capitol 1977) ★★, Sir Army Suit (Capitol 1978)★★, Endangered Species (Capitol 1980)★★, Magentalane (Permanent 1981)★★.
COMPILATIONS: Peaks (Attic 1993)★★★.

KLF
ALBUMS: Towards The Trance (KLF Communications 1988)★★★★, The What Time Is Love Story (KLF Communications 1989)★★★★, The White Room (KLF Communications/Arista 1990)★★★, Chill Out (KLF Communications/Wax Trax! 1990)★★★★.
VIDEOS: Stadium House (PMI 1991).
FURTHER READING: Justified And Ancient: The Unfolding Story Of The KLF, Pete Robinson. Bad Wisdom, Mark Manning and Bill Drummond.

KMFDM
ALBUMS: Don't Blow Your Top (Wax Trax 1988)★★★, UAIOE (Wax Trax 1989)★★★, Naïve (Wax Trax 1992) ★★★, Money (Wax Trax 1992)★★★, Angst (Wax Trax 1993) ★★★★, Naïve: Hell To Go (Wax Trax 1994)★★★, Nihil (Wax Trax 1995)★★★, Xtort (Wax Trax 1996)★★★, Symbols (Wax Trax 1997)★★★, Adios (Wax Trax 1999)★★★.
Solo: En Esch Cheesy (TVT 1993)★★★.
COMPILATIONS: What Do You Know, Deutschland? (Z/ Skysaw 1986)★★★, Retro (Wax Trax 1998)★★★★, Agogo (TVT 1998)★★★.

KNACK
ALBUMS: Get The Knack (Capitol 1979)★★★, ... But The Little Girls Understand (Capitol 1980)★★, Round Trip (Capitol 1981)★★, Serious Fun (Charisma 1991)★★, Zoom (Rhino 1998)★★★, Normal As The Next Guy (Image 2001)★★.
COMPILATIONS: Retrospective: The Best Of The Knack (Capitol 1992)★★★, The Very Best Of The Knack (Rhino 1998)★★★.

KNIGHT, GLADYS, AND THE PIPS
ALBUMS: Letter Full Of Tears (Fury 1961)★★, Gladys Knight And The Pips (Maxx 1964)★★, Everybody Needs Love (Soul 1967)★★★, Feelin' Bluesy (Soul 1968)★★★, Silk 'N' Soul (Soul 1969)★★★, Nitty Gritty (Soul 1969) ★★★, All In A Knight's Work (Soul 1970)★★★, If I Were Your Woman (Soul 1971)★★★, Standing Ovation (Soul 1972)★★★, Neither One Of Us (Soul 1973)★★★★, All I Need Is Time (Soul 1973)★★★, Imagination (Buddah 1973)★★★★, Knight Time (Soul 1974)★★, Claudine (Buddah 1974)★★★, I Feel A Song (Buddah 1974)★★★, A Little Knight Music (Soul 1975)★★★, Second Anniversary (Buddah 1975)★★★, Bless This House (Buddah 1976)★★, Pipe Dreams film soundtrack (Buddah 1976)★★, Still Together (Buddah 1977)★★★, The One And Only (Buddah 1978)★★★, About Love (Columbia 1980)★★★, Touch (Columbia 1981)★★★, That Special Time Of Year (Columbia 1982)★★, Visions (Columbia 1983)★★★, Life (Columbia 1985)★★★, All Our Love (MCA 1987)★★★.
SOLO: Gladys Knight Miss Gladys Knight (Buddah 1979) ★★, A Good Woman (MCA 1991)★★★, Many Different Roads (Many Roads 1999)★★★, At Last (MCA 2001) ★★★. The Pips At Last - The Pips (Casablanca 1979)★★, Callin' (Casablanca 1979)★★.
COMPILATIONS: Gladys Knight And The Pips Greatest Hits (Soul 1970)★★★★, Anthology (Motown 1974)★★★★, The Best Of Gladys Knight And The Pips (Buddah 1976) ★★★★, 30 Greatest (K-Tel 1977)★★★, The Collection – 20 Greatest Hits (1984)★★★, The Best Of Gladys Knight And The Pips: The Columbia Years (Columbia 1988)★★★, Every Beat Of My Heart: The Greatest Hits (Chameleon 1989)★★★, The Singles Album (PolyGram 1989)★★★, Soul Survivors: The Best Of Gladys Knight And The Pips (Rhino 1990)★★★★, 17 Greatest Hits (1992)★★★, The Greatest Hits (Camden 1998)★★★, The Ultimate Collection (Motown 1998)★★★, Essential Collection (Hip-O/Universal 1999)★★★, Behind The Music: Gladys Knight & The Pips Collection (Buddah/BMG 2000)★★★.
FURTHER READING: Between Each Line Of Pain And Glory -- My Life Story, Gladys Knight.

KNOPFLER, MARK
ALBUMS: Local Hero film soundtrack (Vertigo/Warners 1983)★★★, Cal film soundtrack (Vertigo/PolyGram 1984)★★★, Comfort And Joy (Vertigo 1984)★★, The Princess Bride film soundtrack (Vertigo/Warners 1987)★★, Last Exit To Brooklyn film soundtrack (Vertigo/Warners 1989)★★, with Chet Atkins Neck And Neck (Columbia 1990)★★★, Golden Heart (Vertigo/Warners 1996)★★★, Wag The Dog mini-album film soundtrack (Vertigo/ PolyGram 1998)★★, Sailing To Philadelphia (Mercury/ Warners 2000)★★★, A Shot At Glory film soundtrack (Mercury 2001)★★★.
COMPILATIONS: Screenplaying (Vertigo/Warners 1993)★★★.
FURTHER READING: Mark Knopfler: An Unauthorised Biography, Myles Palmer. Mark Knopfler, Wolf Marshall.

KOOL AND THE GANG
ALBUMS: Kool And The Gang (De-Lite 1969)★★, Live At The Sex Machine (De-Lite 1971)★★, Live At P.J.s (De-Lite 1971)★★, Music Is The Message (De-Lite 1972)★★, Good Times (De-Lite 1973)★★★, Wild And Peaceful (De-Lite 1973)★★★, Light Of Worlds (De-Lite 1974)★★★, Spirit Of The Boogie (De-Lite 1975)★★, Love And Understanding (De-Lite 1976)★★, Open Sesame (De-Lite 1976)★★, The Force (De-Lite 1977)★★, Everbody's Dancin' (1978)★★, Ladies' Night (De-Lite 1979)★★★, Celebrate! (De-Lite 1980)★★★, Something Special (De-Lite 1981)★★, As One (De-Lite 1982)★★, In The Heart (De-Lite 1983)★★★★, Emergency (De-Lite 1984)★★, Victory (Curb 1986)★★, Forever (Mercury 1986)★★, Sweat (Mercury 1989)★★, Kool Love (Telstar 1990)★★, State Of Affairs (Curb 1996) ★★, All The Best (Curb 1998)★★, Gangland (Eagle 2001)★★.
COMPILATIONS: The Best Of Kool And The Gang (De-Lite 1971)★★, Kool Jazz (De-Lite 1974)★★, Kool And The Gang Greatest Hits! (De-Lite 1975)★★★, Spin Their Top Hits (De-Lite 1978)★★★★, Kool Kuts (De-Lite 1982)★★★, Twice As Kool (De-Lite 1983)★★★★, The Singles Collection (De-Lite 1988)★★★★, Everything's Kool And The Gang: Greatest Hits And More (Mercury 1988)★★★★, Great And Remixed 91 (Mercury 1992)★★★, The Collection (Spectrum 1996)★★★.

KOOPER, AL
ALBUMS: with Mike Bloomfield, Stephen Stills Super Session (Columbia 1968)★★★★, The Live Adventures Of Al Kooper And Mike Bloomfield (Columbia 1969)★★, I Stand Alone (Columbia 1969)★★★, You Never Know Who Your Friends Are (Columbia 1969)★★, with Shuggie Otis Kooper Session (Columbia 1970)★★, Easy Does It (Columbia 1970)★★★★, Landlord film soundtrack (1971)★★, New York City (You're A Woman) (Columbia 1971)★★★, A Possible Projection Of The Future/Childhood's End (Columbia 1972)★, Naked Songs (Columbia 1973)★★, Unclaimed Freight (Columbia 1975)★★, Act Like Nothing's Wrong (United Artists 1977)★★, Championship Wrestling (Columbia 1982)★★, Rekooperation (Music Masters 1994)★★★, Live: Soul Of A Man (Music Masters 1995)★★★.
COMPILATIONS: Al's Big Deal (Columbia 1989)★★★, Rare & Well Done: The Greatest And Most Obscure Recordings 1964-2001 (Legacy 2001)★★★.
FURTHER READING: Backstage Passes & Backstabbing Bastards, Al Kooper.

KORN
ALBUMS: Korn (Immortal/Epic 1994)★★★★, Life Is Peachy (Immortal/Epic 1996)★★★, Follow The Leader (Epic 1998) ★★★★, Issues (Epic 1999)★★★★.
VIDEOS: Who Then Now? (SMV 1997).
FURTHER READING: Korn: Life In The Pit, Leah Furman.

KORNER, ALEXIS
ALBUMS: with Blues Incorporated R&B From The Marquee (Ace Of Clubs 1962)★★★★, with Blues Incorporated Alexis Korner's Blues Incorporated (Ace Of Clubs 1964)★★★, with Blues Incorporated Red Hot From Alex aka Alexis Korner's All Star Blues Incorporated (Transatlantic 1964) ★★★★, with Blues Incorporated At The Cavern (Oriole 1964)★★★, with Blues Incorporated Sky High (Spot 1966) ★★, with Blues Incorporated Blues Incorporated (Wednesday Night Prayer Meeting) (Polydor 1967)★★★★, I Wonder Who (Fontana 1967)★★★, A New Generation Of Blues aka What's That Sound I Hear (Transatlantic 1968)★★★, Both Sides Of Alexis Korner (Metronome 1969)★★★, Alexis (Rak 1971)★★★, Mr. Blues (Toadstool 1974)★★★, Alexis Korner (Polydor 1974)★★★, Get Off My Cloud (Columbia 1975)★★★, Just Easy (Intercord 1978)★★★, Me (Jeton 1979)★★★, The Party Album (Intercord 1980)★★★, Juvenile Delinquent (1984)★★, Live In Paris: Alexis Korner (Magnum 1988)★★★; by New Church The New Church (Metronome 1970); by Snape Accidentally Born In New Orleans (Transatlantic 1973)★★★, Snape Live On Tour (Brain 1974)★★★.
COMPILATIONS: Bootleg Him (Rak 1972)★★★, Profile (Teldec 1981)★★★, with Cyril Davies Alexis 1957 (Krazy Kat 1984)★★★, with Colin Hodgkinson Testament (Thunderbolt 1985)★★★, Alexis Korner 1961-1972 (Castle 1986)★★★, Hammer And Nails (Thunderbolt 1987)★★★, The Alexis Korner Collection (Castle 1988)★★★, And .... (Castle 1994)★★, On The Move (Castle 1996)★★, The Best Of Alexis Korner (Castle 2000)★★★.
VIDEOS: Eat A Little Rhythm And Blues (BBC Video 1988).
FURTHER READING: Alexis Korner: The Biography, Harry Shapiro.

KOSSOFF, PAUL
ALBUMS: Back Street Crawler (Island 1973)★★★, Live In Croydon, June 15th 1975 (Repertoire 1995)★★.
COMPILATIONS: Koss (DJM 1977)★★★, The Hunter (Street Tunes 1983)★★, Leaves In The Wind (Street Tunes 1983) ★★, Blue Soul (Island 1986)★★★, The Collection (Hit Label 1995)★★★, Stone Free (Carlton Sounds 1997)★★★, Blue Blue Soul: The Best Of Paul Kossoff 1969-1976 (Music Club 1998)★★★.

KOTTKE, LEO
ALBUMS: 12-String Blues: Live At The Scholar Coffee House (Oblivion 1968)★★★, 6- And 12-String Guitar (Takoma/ Sonet 1969)★★★, Circle Round The Sun (Symposium 1970) ★★★, Mudlark (Capitol 1971)★★★, Greenhouse (Capitol 1972)★★★★, My Feet Are Smiling (Capitol 1973) ★★★★, Ice Water (Capitol 1974)★★★★, John Fahey, Leo Kottke, Peter Lang (Takoma 1974)★★★, Dreams And All That Stuff (Capitol 1975)★★, Chewing Pine (Capitol 1975) ★★★, Leo Kottke (Chrysalis 1976)★★★★, Burnt Lips (Chrysalis 1979) ★★★, Balance (Chrysalis 1979)★★, Leo Kottke Live In Europe (Chrysalis 1980), Guitar Music (Chrysalis 1981)★★★, Time Step (Chrysalis 1983)★★★★, A Shout Towards Noon (Private Music 1986)★★★, Regards From Chuck Pink (Private Music 1988)★★★★, My Father's Face (Private Music 1989)★★★, That's What (Private Music 1990)★★★, Great Big Boy (Private Music 1991)★★★, Peculiaroso (Private Music 1994)★★★, Live (Private Music 1995)★★★, Standing In My Shoes (Private Music 1997) ★★★★, One Guitar No Vocals (Private Music 1999)★★★.
COMPILATIONS: Leo Kottke 1971-1976: Did You Hear Me? (Capitol 1976)★★★, The Best (Capitol 1977)★★★, The Best Of Leo Kottke (EMI 1979)★★★, Essential Leo Kottke (Chrysalis 1991)★★★★, The Leo Kottke Anthology (Rhino 1997)★★★★.

KRAFTWERK
ALBUMS: Kraftwerk (Philips 1970)★★, Kraftwerk 2 (Philips 1971)★★, Ralf Und Florian (Philips/Vertigo 1973)★★★, Autobahn (Philips/Vertigo 1974)★★★★, Radioaktivität aka Radioactivity (Kling Klang/Capitol 1975)★★★, Trans Europe Express (Kling Klang/Capitol 1977)★★★★★, Die Mensch Maschine aka The Man-Machine (Kling Klang/ Capitol 1978)★★★★, Computerwelt aka Computer World (Kling Klang/EMI 1981)★★★★, Electric Cafe (Kling Klang/ EMI 1986)★★★, Concert Classics 1975 recording (Ranch Life 1998)★★★.
COMPILATIONS: Kraftwerk a UK compilation of the first two releases (Vertigo 1972)★★, The Best Of Kraftwerk: Exceller 8 (Vertigo 1975)★★★, Highrail (Fontana 1979)★★★, Elektro Kinetik (Vertigo 1981)★★★, The Mix (Kling Klang/ EMI 1991)★★★★.
FURTHER READING: Kraftwerk: Man, Machine & Music, Pacal Bussy. From Düsseldorf To The Future (With Love), Tim Barr. Kraftwerk: I Was A Robot, Wolfgang Flür.

KRAMER, BILLY J., AND THE DAKOTAS
ALBUMS: Listen – To Billy J. Kramer (Parlophone 1963) ★★★, Little Children (Imperial 1963)★★★, I'll Keep You Satisfied (Imperial 1964)★★★, Trains & Boats & Planes (Imperial 1965)★★.
COMPILATIONS: The Best Of Billy J. Kramer (Capitol 1979)★★★, The EMI Years (EMI 1991)★★★, The EP Collection (See For Miles 1995)★★★, At Abbey Road 1963-1966 (EMI 1998)★★★★, Golden Legends (Direct Source 2000)★★★.

KRAUSS, ALISON
ALBUMS: with Union Station Too Late To Cry (Rounder 1987)★★★, with Union Station Two Highways (Rounder 1989)★★★, with Union Station I've Got That Old Feeling (Rounder 1990)★★★, with Union Station Every Time You Say Goodbye (Rounder 1992)★★★★, with the Cox Family Everybody's Reaching Out For Someone (Rounder 1993) ★★★, with the Cox Family I Know Who Holds Tomorrow (Rounder 1994)★★★, with the Cox Family Beyond The City (Rounder 1995)★★★, with Union Station So Long So Wrong (Rounder 1997)★★★★, Forget About It (Rounder 1999)★★★★, with Union Station New Favorite (Rounder 2001)★★★★.
COMPILATIONS: Now That I've Found You: A Collection (Rounder 1995)★★★★.

KRAVITZ, LENNY
ALBUMS: Let Love Rule (Virgin 1989)★★★, Mama Said (Virgin 1991)★★★★, Are You Gonna Go My Way? (Virgin 1993)★★★, Circus (Virgin 1995)★★★, 5 (Virgin 1998) ★★★, Lenny (Virgin 2001)★★★.
COMPILATIONS: Greatest Hits (Virgin 2000)★★★★.
VIDEOS: Alive From Planet Earth (Virgin 1994)★★★.

KRISTOFFERSON, KRIS
ALBUMS: Kristofferson (Monument 1970)★★, The Silver-Tongued Devil And I (Monument 1971)★★★★, Me And Bobby McGee (Monument 1971)★★★, Border Lord (Monument 1972)★★★, Jesus Was A Capricorn (Monument 1972)★★★, with Rita Coolidge Full Moon (A&M 1973) ★★★, Spooky Lady's Sideshow (Monument 1974)★★, with Coolidge Breakaway (A&M 1974)H, Who's To Bless ... And Who's To Blame (Monument 1975)★★, Surreal Thing (Monument 1976)★★, Easter Island (Monument 1977)★★, with Coolidge Natural Act (A&M 1978)★★, Shake Hands With The Devil (Monument 1979)★★★, To The Bone (Monument 1981)★★, with Dolly Parton, Brenda Lee, Willie Nelson The Winning Hand (Monument 1983)★★★, with Nelson Music From Songwriter film soundtrack (Columbia 1984)★★★, with Nelson, Johnny Cash, Waylon Jennings Highwayman (Columbia 1985)★★★★, Repossessed (Mercury 1986)★★, Third World Warrior (Mercury 1990)★★, with Nelson, Cash, Jennings Highwayman 2 (Columbia 1990)★★★, Live At The Philharmonic (Monument 1992)★★★, with Nelson, Cash, Jennings The Road Goes On Forever (Liberty 1995)★★, A Moment Of Forever (Justice 1995)★★★★, The Austin Sessions (Atlantic 1999)★★★.
COMPILATIONS: The Songs Of Kristofferson (Monument 1977)★★★, Country Store (Starblend 1988)★★★, The Legendary Years (Connoisseur Collection 1990)★★★, Singer/Songwriter (Monument 1991)★★★, The Best Of Kris Kristofferson (Sony 1995)★★★★, The Country Collection (Spectrum 1998)★★, Super Hits (Sony 1999)★★★, All-Time Greatest Hits (Varèse Sarabande 2001)★★★.
FURTHER READING: Kris Kristofferson, Beth Kalet.
FILMS: The Last Movie (1971), Cisco Pike (1972), The Gospel Road (1973), Blume In Love (1973), Pat Garrett And Billy The Kid (1973), Free to Be ... You & Me (1974), Alice Doesn't Live Here Any More (1974), Bring Me The Head Of Alfredo Garcia (1974), Vigilante Force (1976), A Star Is Born (1976), The Sailor Who Fell From Grace With The Sea (1976), Convoy (1978), Semi-Tough (1978), Heaven's Gate (1980), Rollover (1981), Songwriter (1984), Flashpoint (1984), Trouble In Mind (1985), Big Top Pee-Wee (1988), Welcome Home (1989), Millennium (1989), Sandino (1990), Night Of The Cyclone (1990), Original Intent (1992), No Place To Hide (1992), Paper Hearts (1993), Knights (1993), Pharaoh's Army (1995), Lone Star (1996), Fire Down Below (1997), A Soldier's Daughter Never Cries (1998), Girls' Night (1998), Blade (1998), Dance With Me (1998), Limbo (1999), The Joyriders (1999), Payback (1999), Molokai: The Story Of Father Damien (1999).

KRS-ONE
ALBUMS: Return Of The Boom Bap (Jive 1993)★★★★, KRS-One (Jive 1995)★★★, with MC Shan The Battle For Rap Supremacy (Cold Chillin' 1996)★★★, I Got Next (Jive 1997)★★, The Sneak Attack (Koch 2001)★★★, Spiritual Minded (Koch 2002)★★★.
COMPILATIONS: A Retrospective (Jive 2000)★★★★.

KULA SHAKER
ALBUMS: K (Columbia 1996)★★★★, Peasants Pigs & Astronauts (Columbia 1999)★★★.
FURTHER READING: Kula Shaker, Nigel Cross.

KURSAAL FLYERS
ALBUMS: Chocs Away (UK 1975)★★★, The Great Artiste (UK 1975)★★★, Golden Mile (Columbia 1976)★★★, Five Live Kursaals (Columbia 1977)★★, Former Tour De Force Is Forced To Tour (Waterfront 1988)★★.
COMPILATIONS: The Best Of The Kursaal Flyers (Teldec 1983)★★★, In For A Spin (Edsel 1985)★★★.

KUTI, FELA
ALBUMS: Fela's London Scene (HNLX 1970)★★★, Live With Ginger Baker (Regal Zonophone 1972)★★★, Shakara (EMI 1972)★★★, Gentleman (NEMI 1973) ★★★★, He Miss Road (NEMI 1973)★★★, Alagbon Close (JILP 1974)★★★★, Expensive Shit (SWS 1975)★★★, Open & Close (SWS 1975)★★★★, Yellow Fever (Decca West Africa 1976)★★★, Zombie (CRLP 1977)★★★, Kalakuta Show (CRLP 1978)★★★★, Coffin For Head Of State (KALP 1979)★★★★, VIP Vagabonds In Power (KILP 1979)★★★, with Roy Ayers Africa, Center Of The World (Polydor 1981)★★★, with Lester Bowie Perambulator (LIR 1983)★★★, Army Arrangement (Celluloid 1985)★★★, Teacher Don't Teach Me Nonsense (London 1987)★★★★, I Go Shout Plenty (Decca 1987)★★★★, with Roy Ayers 2000 Blacks (Justin 1988)★★★, Beasts Of No Nation (JDEUR 1988)★★★, Us (Stern's 1992)★★★, Underground System (Stern's 1993)★★★, The '69 Los Angeles Sessions (Stern's 1993)★★★.
COMPILATIONS: Fela Kuti Volumes 1 & 2 (EMI 1977) ★★★, The Best Of Fela Kuti (MCA 1999)★★★★.
VIDEOS: Teacher Don't Teach Me Nonsense (London 1984), Fela Live (London 1984).

L

L.A. Guns
ALBUMS: L.A. Guns (PolyGram 1988)★★, Cocked And Loaded (PolyGram 1989)★★★, Hollywood Vampires (PolyGram 1991)★★★, Vicious Circle (PolyGram 1994) ★★★, Shrinking Violet (Axe Killer 1999)★★, Man In The Moon (Eagle 2001)★★★.
COMPILATIONS: Greatest Hits And Black Beauties (Deadline 1999)★★★.
VIDEOS: One More Reason (1989), Love, Peace & Geese (1990).

L7
ALBUMS: L7 (Epitaph 1988)★★★, Smell The Magic mini-album (Sup Pop 1990)★★★, Bricks Are Heavy (Slash/ Reprise 1992)★★★★, Hungry For Stink (Slash/Reprise 1994)★★★, The Beauty Process: Triple Platinum (Slash/ Reprise 1997)★★★, Live Omaha To Osaka (Man's Ruin 1998)★★, Slap-Happy (Wax Tadpole/Bongload 1999)★★★.
COMPILATIONS: The Best Of The Slash Years (Slash 2000) ★★★.

LA'S
ALBUMS: The La's (Go! Discs 1990)★★★★.
COMPILATIONS: Lost La's 1984-1986: Breakloose (Viper 1999)★★★, Lost La's 1986-1987: Callin' All (Viper 2001)★★★.

LABELLE, PATTI
ALBUMS: Patti LaBelle (Epic 1977)★★★, Tasty (Epic 1978) ★★★, It's Alright With Me (Epic 1979)★★★, Released (Epic 1980)★★★, The Spirit's In It (Philadelphia International 1981)★★★, I'm In Love Again (Philadelphia International 1983)★★★, Patti (Philadelphia International 1985)★★★, The Winner In You (MCA 1986)★★★, Be Yourself (MCA 1989)★★, Starlight Christmas (MCA 1990)★★★, Burnin' (MCA 1991)★★★, Live! (MCA 1992)★★, Gems (MCA 1994)★★★, Flame (MCA 1997)★★★, Live! One Night Only (MCA 1998)★★, When A Woman Loves (MCA 2000)★★★.
COMPILATIONS: Best Of ... (Epic 1986)★★★, Greatest Hits (MCA 1996)★★★.
VIDEOS: Live! One Night Only (MCA Music Video 1998).

LADYSMITH BLACK MAMBAZO
ALBUMS: Amabutho (BL 1973)★★★, Isitimela (BL 1974) ★★★, Amaghawe (BL 1976)★★★, Ulwandle Oluncgwele (BL 1977)★★★, Umthombo Wamanzi (BL 1982)★★★, Ibhayibheli Liyindlela (BL 1984)★★★, Induku Zethu (Shanachie 1984)★★★, Inala (Shanachie 1986)★★★, Ezulwini Siyakhona (Shanachie 1986)★★★, Shaka Zulu (Warners 1987)★★★★, Journey Of Dreams (Warners 1988)★★★★, with Danny Glover How The Leopard Got His Spots (Windham Hill 1989)★★★, Two Worlds One Heart (Warners 1990)★★★★, Inkanyezi Nezazi (Flame Tree 1992)★★★, Liph' Iqiniso (Flame Tree 1994)★★★, Gift Of The Tortoise (Flame Tree 1995)★★★, Thuthukani Ngoxolo (Let's Develop In Peace) (Shanachie 1996)★★★, Heavenly (A&M 1997)★★, In Harmony (Wrasse 1999)★★.
COMPILATIONS: Classic Tracks (Shanachie 1991)★★★★, Best Of Ladysmith Black Mambazo (Shanachie 1992) ★★★★, Spirit Of South Africa (Nascente 1997)★★★★, The Star And Wiseman: The Best Of Ladysmith Black Mambazo (PolyGram 1998)★★★, Gospel Songs (Wrasse 1999)★★★★.

LAMBCHOP
ALBUMS: I Hope You're Sitting Down/Jack's Tulips (Merge 1994)★★★, How I Quit Smoking (Merge 1996)★★★★, Thriller (Merge/City Slang 1996)★★★★, What Another Man Spills (Merge/City Slang 1998)★★★, Nixon (Merge/ City Slang 2000)★★★★, Is A Woman (Merge/City Slang 2002)★★★.
COMPILATIONS Tools In The Dryer (Merge 2001)★★★.

LANE, RONNIE
ALBUMS: Anymore For Anymore (GM 1974)★★★, Ronnie Lane's Slim Chance (GM 1975)★★★★, One For The Road (GM 1976)★★★★, with Ron Wood Mahoney's Last Stand (Atlantic 1976)★★★, with Pete Townshend Rough Mix

(Polydor 1977)★★★★, *See Me* (Gem 1979)★★★.
COMPILATIONS: with Slim Chance *You Never Can Tell: The BBC Sessions* (Burning Airlines 1997)★★★, *Kuschty Rye: The Singles 1973-1980* (Burning Airlines 1997)★★★, *Plonk* 4-CD box set (Burning Airlines 1999)★★★, *April Fool* (Burning Airlines 1999)★★★★, *Tin & Tambourine* (Burning Airlines 1999)★★★, with Steve Marriott *The Legendary Majic Mijits* (Burning Airlines 2000)★★, *Live In Austin* (Sideburn 2000)★★★, *Rocket 69* (Burning Airlines 2001)★★★.

LANG, JONNY
ALBUMS: *Smokin'* (Own Label 1996)★★, *Lie To Me* (A&M 1997)★★★★, *Wander This World* (A&M 1998)★★★.
FILMS: *Blues Brothers 2000* (1998).

LANG, K.D.
ALBUMS: *A Truly Western Experience* (Bumstead 1984)★★, *Angel With A Lariat* (Sire 1987)★★★, *Shadowland* (Sire 1988)★★★★, *Absolute Torch And Twang* (Sire 1989)★★★, *Ingénue* (Sire/Warners 1992)★★★★, *Even Cowgirls Get The Blues* film soundtrack (Sire/Warners 1993)★★, *All You Can Eat* (Warners 1995)★★★, *Drag* (Warners 1997)★★★, *Invincible Summer* (Warners 2000)★★★★, *Live By Request* (Warners 2001)★★★.
VIDEOS: *Harvest Of Seven Years* (Warner Music Video 1992), *Live In Sydney* (Warner Music Video 1998), *Live By Request* (Warner Music Video 2001).
FURTHER READING: *Carrying The Torch*, William Robertson. *k.d. lang, In Her Own Words*, David Bennahum. *All You Get Is Me*, Victoria Starr. *An Illustrated Biography*, David Bennahum. *k.d. lang*, Rose Collis.
FILMS: *Salmonberries* (1991), *Teresa's Tattoo* (1994), *Eye Of The Beholder* (1999).

LANOIS, DANIEL
ALBUMS: *Acadie* (Opal 1989)★★★★, *For The Beauty Of Wynona* (Warners 1993)★★★.

LASWELL, BILL
ALBUMS: *Baselines* (OAO/Celluloid 1984)★★★, with Peter Brötzmann *Lowlife* (Celluloid 1987)★★★, *Hear No Evil* (Virgin 1988)★★★, with Pete Namlook *Psychonavigation* (FAX/Subharmonic 1994)★★★★, with Jonah Sharp *Visitation* (Subharmonic 1994)★★★, with Tetsu Inoue *Cymatic Scan* (FAX/Subharmonic 1994)★★★, *Outer Dark* (FAX 1994)★★★, with Namlook *Outland* (FAX 1994) ★★★★, with Terre Thaemlitz *Web* (Subharmonic 1995) ★★★, with Nicholas James Bullen *Bass Terror* (Subsonic/Sub Rosa 1995)★★★, with M.J. Harris *Somnific Flux* (Subharmonic 1995)★★★, with Atom Heart, Tetsu Inoue *Second Nature* (FAX/Sub Meta 1995)★★★, *Silent Recoil* (Low 1995)★★★, with Namlook *Psychonavigation 2* (FAX/Subharmonic 1995) ★★★★, with Sacred System *Chapter One (Book Of Entrance)* (ROIR 1996)★★★, with Namlook, Klaus Schulze *The Dark Side Of The Moog IV* (FAX/Ambient World 1996)★★★, with Haruomi Hosono *Interpieces Organization* (Teichiku/Baidis 1996)★★★, with Namlook *Outland 2* (FAX 1996)★★★, *Oscillations* (Sub Rosa 1996)★★★, with Namlook, Schulze *The Dark Side Of The Moog V* (FAX 1996)★★★, with Namlook *Psychonavigation III* (FAX 1997)★★★, *City Of Lights* (Sub Rosa 1997)★★★, with Namlook, Schulze *The Dark Side Of The Moog VI* (FAX 1997)★★★, with Style Scott *Bill Laswell Meets Style Scott Inna Dub Meltdown* (WordSound 1997)★★★, *Dreams Of Freedom: Ambient Translations Of Bob Marley In Dub* (Axiom/Island 1997)★★★★, with Sacred System *Sacred System: Chapter Two* (ROIR 1997)★★★, *Panthalassa: The Music Of Miles Davis 1969-1974* (Sony/Columbia 1997) ★★★★, with Namlook *Outland 3* (FAX 1998)★★★, *Oscillations 2* (SubRosa 1998)★★★, with Percy Howard, Charles Hayward, Fred Frith *Meridiem* (Materiali Sonori 1998)★★★, *Jazzonia* (Douglas 1998)★★★, with Namlook, Schulze *The Dark Side Of The Moog VII* (FAX 1998)★★★, *Invisible Design* (Tzadik 1999)★★★, with Namlook *Psychonavigation 4* (FAX 1999)★★★, *Imaginary Cuba: Deconstructing Havana* (Wicklow/BMG 1999)★★★★, *Broken Vessels* film soundtrack (VelVel/Koch 1999)★★★, *Permutation* (Ion 1999)★★★, *Dub Chamber 3* (ROIR 2000)★★★, with Namlook *Outland 4* (FAX 2000)★★★, *Emerald Aether: Shape Shifting* (Shanachie 2000)★★★★, *Lo-Def Pressure* (Sub Rosa 2000)★★★, with Toshinori Kondo *Life/Space/Death* (MusicDeli/Spiritual Nature 2000)★★★, *Cyclops* aka *Points Of Order* (Cyclops/Points Of Order 2001)★★★, with Jah Wobble *Radioaxiom: A Dub Transmission* (Palm Pictures 2001)★★★★, *Divine Light: The Music Of Carlos Santana* (Sony 2001)★★★★.
COMPILATIONS: *Material & Friends* (Celluloid 1984) ★★★★, *Deconstruction: The Celluloid Recordings* (Celluloid/Metronome 1994)★★★★, *Ambient Compendium* (M.I.L. Multimedia 1996)★★★, *Filmtracks 2000* (Tzadik 2001)★★★★.

LAUPER, CYNDI
ALBUMS: as Blue Angel *Blue Angel* (Polydor 1980)★★★, *She's So Unusual* (Portrait 1984)★★★★, *True Colors* (Portrait 1986)★★★, *A Night To Remember* (Epic 1989) ★★, *Hat Full Of Stars* (Epic 1993)★★, *Sisters Of Avalon* (Epic 1997)★★★, *Merry Christmas ... Have A Nice Life* (Epic 1998)★★★.
COMPILATIONS: *12 Deadly Cyns* (Epic 1994)★★★★, *Time After Time: The Best Of Cyndi Lauper* (Epic 2001)★★★★.
VIDEOS: *Twelve Deadly Cyns ... And Then Some* (Epic 1994).

LED ZEPPELIN
ALBUMS: *Led Zeppelin* (Atlantic 1969)★★★★, *Led Zeppelin II* (Atlantic 1969)★★★★, *Led Zeppelin III* (Atlantic 1970)★★★★, *Led Zeppelin IV* (Atlantic 1971)★★★★★, *Houses Of The Holy* (Atlantic 1973)★★★★, *Physical Graffiti* (Swan Song 1975)★★★★, *Presence* (Swan Song 1976)★★★, *The Song Remains The Same* film soundtrack (Swan Song 1976)★★, *In Through The Out Door* (Swan Song 1979)★★★, *Coda* (Swan Song 1982)★★, *BBC Sessions* (Atlantic 1997)★★★★.
COMPILATIONS: *Led Zeppelin* 4-CD box set (Swan Song 1991)★★★★, *Remasters* (Swan Song 1991)★★★★, *Remasters II* (Swan Song 1993)★★★, *Early Days: The Best Of Led Zeppelin Volume One* (Atlantic 1999)★★★★, *Latter Days: The Best Of Led Zeppelin Volume II* (Atlantic 2000)★★★★.
VIDEOS: *The Song Remains The Same* (Warner Home Video 1986).
FURTHER READING: *Led Zeppelin*, Michael Gross and Robert Plant. *The Led Zeppelin Biography*, Ritchie Yorke. *Led Zeppelin*, Howard Mylett. *Led Zeppelin: In The Light 1968-1980*, Howard Mylett and Richard Bunton. *Led Zeppelin: A Celebration*, Dave Lewis. *Led Zeppelin In Their Own Words*, Paul Kendall. *Led Zeppelin: A Visual Documentary*, Paul Kendall. *Led Zeppelin: The Book*, Jeremy Burston. *Jimmy Page: Tangents Within A Framework*, Howard Mylett. *Led Zeppelin: The Final Acclaim*, Dave Lewis. *Hammer Of The Gods: The Led Zeppelin Saga*, Stephen Davis. *Illustrated Collector's Guide To Led Zeppelin*, Robert Godwin. *Led Zeppelin: Heaven & Hell*, Charles Cross and Erik Flannigan. *Stairway To Heaven*, Richard Cole with Richard Trubo. *Led Zeppelin: Breaking And Making Records*, Ross Clarke. *Led Zeppelin: The Definitive Biography*, Ritchie Yorke. *On Tour With Led Zeppelin*, Howard Mylett (ed.). *Led Zeppelin*, Chris Welch. *The Complete Guide To The Music Of ...*, Dave Lewis. *Led Zeppelin Live: An Illustrated Exploration Of Underground Tapes*, Luis Rey. *The Making Of: Led Zeppelin IV*, Robert Godwin. *The Photographer's Led Zeppelin*, Ross Halfin (ed.). *The Led Zeppelin Concert File*, Dave Lewis and Simon Pallett. *Led Zeppelin - Dazed And Confused*, Chris Welch. *From Early Days To Page And Plant*, Ritchie Yorke. *Follow The Legend Volume 1: Albion There And Back*, Shannon MacBay & Karol Rhys-Gruffydd. *Peter Grant: The Man Who Led Zeppelin*, Chris Welch. *John Bonham: A Thunder Of Drums*, Chris Welch and Geoff Nicholls. *In The Houses Of The Holy: Led Zeppelin And The Power Of Rock Music*, Susan Fast.
FILMS: *The Song Remains The Same* (1976).

LEE, ALBERT
ALBUMS: *Hiding* (A&M 1979)★★★★, *Albert Lee* (Polydor 1982)★★★, *Speechless* (MCA 1987)★★★, *Gagged But Not Bound* (MCA 1988)★★, *Black Claw And Country Fever* (Line 1991)★★, with Hogan's Heroes *Live At Montreux* 1992 recording (Round Tower 1994)★★, *Undiscovered - The Early Years* (Diamond 1998)★★★.
COMPILATIONS: *Country Guitar Man* (Magnum 1986)★★★.

LEE, BRENDA
ALBUMS: *Grandma, What Great Songs You Sang* (Decca 1959)★★, *Brenda Lee* (Decca 1960)★★★★, *This Is ... Brenda* (Decca 1960)★★★★, *Miss Dynamite* (Brunswick 1961)★★★★, *Emotions* (Decca 1961)★★★, *All The Way* (Decca 1961)★★★, *Sincerely Brenda Lee* (Decca 1962) ★★★★, *Brenda, That's All* (Decca 1962)★★★★, *All Alone Am I* (Decca 1963)★★★, *Let Me Sing* (Decca 1963)★★★, *Sings Songs Everybody Knows* (Decca 1964)★★★, *By Request* (Decca 1964)★★★, *Merry Christmas From Brenda Lee* (Decca 1964)★★★, *Top Teen Hits* (Decca 1964)★★★, *The Versatile Brenda Lee* (Decca 1965)★★★, *Too Many Rivers* (Decca 1965)★★★, *Bye Bye Blues* (Decca 1965) ★★★, *Coming On Strong* (Decca 1966)★★★, *Call Me Brenda* (Decca 1967)★★★, *Reflections In Blue* (Decca 1967)★★★, *Good Life* (Decca 1967)★★★, with Tennessee Ernie Ford *The Show For Christmas Seals* (Decca 1968) ★★★, with Pete Fountain *For The First Time* (Decca 1968) ★★★, *Johnny One Time* (Decca 1969)★★★, *Memphis Portrait* (Decca 1970)★★★, *Let It Be Me* (Vocalion 1970) ★★★, *A Whole Lotta* (MCA 1972)★★★, *Brenda* (MCA 1973)★★★, *New Sunrise* (MCA 1974)★★★, *Brenda Lee Now* (MCA 1975)★★★, *The LA Sessions* (MCA 1977) ★★★, *Even Better* (MCA 1980)★★★, *Take Me Back* (MCA 1981)★★★, *Only When I Laugh* (MCA 1982)★★★, with Dolly Parton, Kris Kristofferson, Willie Nelson *The Winning Hand* (Monument 1983)★★★, *Feels So Right* (MCA 1985) ★★★, *Brenda Lee* (Warners 1991)★★★, *A Brenda Lee Christmas* (Warners 1991)★★★, *Greatest Hits Live* (MCA 1992)★★★, *Coming On Strong* (Muskateer 1995)★★★.
COMPILATIONS: *10 Golden Years* (Decca 1966)★★★, *The Brenda Lee Story – Her Greatest Hits* (MCA 1973)★★★★, *Little Miss Dynamite* (MCA 1976)★★★★, *Greatest Country Hits* (MCA 1982)★★★, *25th Anniversary* (MCA 1984) ★★★★, *The Early Years* (MCA 1984)★★★, *The Golden Decade* (Charly 1985)★★★★, *The Best Of Brenda Lee* (MCA 1986)★★★★, *Love Songs* (MCA 1986)★★★, *Brenda's Best* (Ce De 1989)★★★★, *Very Best Of Brenda Lee Volume 1* (MCA 1990)★★★★, *Very Best Of Brenda Lee Volume 2* (MCA 1990)★★★, *The Brenda Lee Anthology Volume One, 1956-1961* (MCA 1991)★★★★, *The Brenda Lee Anthology Volume Two, 1962-1980* (MCA 1991)★★★, *Little Miss Dynamite* 4-CD box set (Bear Family 1996)★★★★, *The EP Collection* (See For Miles 1996) ★★★★, *The Best Of Brenda Lee: The Millennium Collection* (MCA 1999)★★★★.

LEFT BANKE
ALBUMS: *Walk Away Renee/Pretty Ballerina* (Smash 1967) ★★★★, *The Left Banke Too* (Smash 1968)★★, *Voices Calling* UK title *Strangers On A Train* US title (Bam-Caruso/Camerica 1986)★★★.
COMPILATIONS: *And Suddenly It's The Left Banke* (Bam-Caruso 1982)★★★★, *The History Of The Left Banke* (Rhino 1985)★★★★, *Walk Away Renee* mini-album (Bam-Caruso 1986)★★★, *There's Gonna Be A Storm: The Complete Recordings 1966-1969* (Mercury 1992)★★★★.

LEFTFIELD
ALBUMS: *Leftism* (Hard Hands/Columbia 1995)★★★★★, *Rhythm And Stealth* (Hard Hands/Higher Ground 1999) ★★★★.

LEIBER AND STOLLER
COMPILATIONS: *Leiber & Stoller Present The Spark Records Story* (Ace 2001)★★★.
FURTHER READING: *Baby, That Was Rock & Roll: The Legendary Leiber And Stoller*, Robert Palmer.

LEMONHEADS
ALBUMS: *Hate Your Friends* (Taang! 1987)★★, *Creator* (Taang! 1988)★★, *Lick* (Taang! 1989)★★★, *Lovey* (Atlantic 1990)★★, *Favorite Spanish Dishes* mini-album (Atlantic 1990)★★, *It's A Shame About Ray* (Atlantic 1992)★★★★, *Come On Feel The Lemonheads* (Atlantic 1993)★★★★, *Car Button Cloth* (Atlantic 1996)★★★. Solo Evan Dando: *Live At The Brattle Theatre* (Modular 2001)★★★.
COMPILATIONS: *Create Your Friends* (Taang! 1989)★★, *The Best Of The Atlantic Years* (Atlantic 1998)★★★.
VIDEOS: *Two Weeks In Australia* (Atlantic 1993).
FURTHER READING: *The Illustrated Story*, Everett True. *The Lemonheads*, Mick St. Michael.

LENNON, JOHN
ALBUMS: *Unfinished Music No 1 - Two Virgins* (Apple 1968)★, *Unfinished Music No 2 - Life With The Lions* (Zapple 1969)★, *The Wedding Album* (Apple 1969)★, *The Plastic Ono Band; Live Peace In Toronto 1969* (Apple 1970)★★★, *John Lennon Plastic Ono Band* (Apple 1971)★★★★★, *Imagine* (Apple 1971)★★★★, *Sometime In New York City* (Apple 1972)★★★, *Mind Games* (Apple 1973)★★★, *Walls And Bridges* (Apple 1974)★★★, *Rock 'N' Roll* (Apple 1975)★★★★, *Double Fantasy* (Geffen 1980)★★★, *Heartplay - Unfinished Dialogue* (Polydor 1983)★, *Milk And Honey* (Polydor 1984)★★, *Live In New York City* (Capitol 1986)★★, *Menlove Ave* (Capitol 1986)★★, *The Last Word* (Baktabak 1988)★, *Imagine – Music From The Motion Picture* (Parlophone 1988)★★, *John & Yoko: The Interview* (BBC 1990)★.
COMPILATIONS: *Shaved Fish* (Apple 1975)★★★★, *The John Lennon Collection* (Parlophone 1982)★★★★★, *The Ultimate John Lennon Collection* (Parlophone 1990)★★★★, *Lennon Legend* (Parlophone 1997)★★★★★, *The John Lennon Anthology* 4-CD box set (Parlophone 1998)★★★★, *Wonsaponatime* (Parlophone 1998)★★★★.
VIDEOS: *The Bed-In* (PMI 1991), *The John Lennon Video Collection* (PMI 1992), *One To One* (BMG 1993), *John Lennon: Imagine* (PMI 1997).
FURTHER READING: many books have been written about Lennon, many are mediocre. The essential three are Ray Coleman's biography, Lennon's own *A Spaniard In The Works/In His Own Write* and *The Ballad Of John And Yoko*, from *Rolling Stone*.
The full list: *In His Own Write*, John Lennon. *The Penguin John Lennon*, John Lennon. *Lennon Remembers: The Rolling Stone Interviews*, Jann Wenner. *The Lennon Factor*, Paul Young. *The John Lennon Story*, George Tremlett. *John Lennon: One Day At A Time: A Personal Biography Of The Seventies*, Anthony Fawcett. *A Twist Of Lennon*, Cynthia Lennon. *John Lennon: The Life & Legend*, editors of *Sunday Times*. *John Lennon In His Own Words*, Miles. *A Spaniard In The Works*, John Lennon. *Lennon: What Happened!*, Timothy Green (ed.). *Strawberry Fields Forever: John Lennon Remembered*, Vic Garbarini and Brian Cullman with Barbara Graustark. *John Lennon: Death Of A Dream*, George Carpozi. *The Lennon Tapes: Andy Peebles In Conversation With John Lennon And Yoko Ono*, Andy Peebles. *The Ballad Of John And Yoko*, Rolling Stone Editors. *The Playboy Interviews With John Lennon And Yoko Ono*, John Lennon. *John Lennon: In My Life*, Peter Shotton and Nicholas Schaffner. *Loving John*, May Pang. *Dakota Days: The Untold Story Of John Lennon's Final Years*, John Green. *The Book Of Lennon*, Bill Harry. *John Ono Lennon 1967-1980*, Ray Coleman. *John Winston Lennon 1940-1966*, Ray Coleman. *Come Together: John Lennon In His Own Time*, Jon Wiener. *John Lennon: For The Record*, Peter McCabe and Robert D. Schonfeld. *The Lennon Companion: 25 Years Of Comment*, Elizabeth M. Thomson and David Gutman. *Imagine John Lennon*, Andrew Solt and Sam Egan. *Skywriting By Word Of Mouth*, John Lennon. *The Lives Of John Lennon*, Albert Goldman. *John Lennon My Brother*, Julia Baird. *The Other Side Of Lennon*, Sandra Shevey. *Days In The Life: John Lennon Remembered*, Philip Norman. *The Murder Of John Lennon*, Fenton Bresler. *The Art & Music Of John Lennon*, John Robertson. *In My Life: John Lennon Remembered*, Kevin Howless and Mark Lewisohn. *John Lennon: Living On Borrowed Time*, Frederic Seaman. *Let Me Take You Down: Inside The Mind Of Mark Chapman*, Jack Jones. *The Immortal John Lennon 1940-1980*, Michael Heatley. *John Lennon*, William Ruhlmann. *AI: Japan Through John Lennon's Eyes (A Personal Sketchbook)*, John Lennon. *The Art & Music Of John Lennon*, John Robertson. *We All Shine On*, Paul Du Noyer. *Gimme Some Truth: The John Lennon FBI Files*, Jon Wiener. *Nowhere Man: The Final Days Of John Lennon*, Robert Rosen. *All We Are Saying: The Last Major Interview With John Lennon And Yoko Ono*, David Sheff.
FILMS: *A Hard Day's Night* (1964), *Help!* (1965), *How I Won The War* (1967), *Magical Mystery Tour* (1967), *Yellow Submarine* (1968), *Let It Be* (1970), *Diaries, Notebooks And Sketches* (1970), *Eat The Document* (1972), *Imagine* (1973), *Fire In The Water* (1977).

LENNON, JULIAN
ALBUMS: *Valotte* (Virgin 1984)★★★, *The Secret Value Of Daydreaming* (Virgin 1986)★★, *Mr Jordan* (Virgin 1989)★★, *Help Yourself* (Virgin 1991)★★, *Photograph Smile* (Music From Another Room 1998)★★★★.
COMPILATIONS: *Behind The Music* (Rhino 2001)★★★.

LENNOX, ANNIE
ALBUMS: *Diva* (RCA 1992)★★★★, *Medusa* (RCA 1995) ★★★, *Live In Central Park* (Arista 1996)★★★.
VIDEOS: *In The Park* (BMG 1996).
FURTHER READING: *Annie Lennox*, Lucy O'Brien. *Annie Lennox: The Biography*, Bryony Sutherland & Lucy Ellis.
FILMS: *Revolution* (1985), *Brand New Day* (1987), *Naissance D'un Golem* (1991), *Edward II* (1991).

LETTERMEN
ALBUMS: *A Song For Young Love* (Capitol 1962)★★★, *Once Upon A Time* (Capitol 1962)★★★, *Jim, Tony And Bob* (Capitol 1962)★★★, *College Standards* (Capitol 1963)★★★, *The Lettermen In Concert* (Capitol 1963)★★, *A Lettermen Kind Of Love* (Capitol 1964)★★, *The Lettermen Look At Love* (Capitol 1964)★★★, *She Cried* (Capitol 1964)★★★, *Portrait Of My Love* (Capitol 1965)★★★, *The Hit Sounds Of The Lettermen* (Capitol 1965)★★, *You'll Never Walk Alone* (Capitol 1965)★★★, *More Hit Sounds Of The Lettermen!* (Capitol 1966)★★, *A New Song For Young Love* (Capitol 1966)★★★, *For Christmas This Year* (Capitol 1966)★★, *Warm* (Capitol 1967)★★★, *Spring!* (Capitol 1967)★★★, *The Lettermen!!! ... And Live!* (Capitol 1967)★★, *Goin' Out Of My Head* (Capitol 1968)★★★, *Special Request* (Capitol 1968)★★, *Put Your Head On My Shoulder* (Capitol 1968)★★★, *I Have Dreamed* (Capitol 1969)★★★, *Hurt So Bad* (Capitol 1969)★★★, *Traces/Memories* (Capitol 1970)★★★, *Reflections* (Capitol 1970)★★, *Everything's Good About You* (Capitol 1971) ★★★, *Feelings* (Capitol 1971)★★★, *Love Book* (Capitol 1971)★★★, *Lettermen 1* (Capitol 1972)★★★, *"Alive" Again ... Naturally* (Capitol 1973)★★, *Evergreen* (Alfa Omega 1985)★★.
COMPILATIONS: *The Best Of The Lettermen* (Capitol 1966)★★★, *The Best Of The Lettermen, Vol. 2* (Capitol 1969)★★★, *All-Time Greatest Hits* (Capitol 1974)★★★, *Memories: The Very Best Of The Lettermen* (Collectables 1999)★★★.

LEVEL 42
ALBUMS: *Level 42* (Polydor 1981)★★★, *Strategy* (Elite 1981)★★★, *The Early Tapes: July-August 1980* (Polydor 1981)★★, *The Pursuit Of Accidents* (Polydor 1982)★★★, *Standing In The Light* (Polydor 1983)★★★, *True Colours* (Polydor 1984)★★★★, *A Physical Presence* (Polydor 1985)★★, *World Machine* (Polydor 1985)★★★★, *Running In The Family* (Polydor 1987)★★★, *Staring At The Sun* (Polydor 1988)★★, *Guaranteed* (RCA 1991)★★, *Forever Now* (RCA 1994)★★.
SOLO: Mark King *Influences* (Polydor 1993)★★, *One Man* (Eagle 1998)★★.
COMPILATIONS: *Level Best* (Polydor 1989)★★★★, *The Remixes* (Polydor 1992)★★★, *The Very Best Of Level 42* (Polydor 1998)★★★.
VIDEOS: *Live At Wembley* (Channel 5 1987), *Family Of Five* (Channel 5 1988), *Level Best* (Channel 5 1989), *Fait Accompli* (PolyGram Music Video 1989).
FURTHER READING: *Level 42: The Definitive Biography*, Michael Cowton.

LEVELLERS
ALBUMS: *A Weapon Called The Word* (Musidisc 1990) ★★★, *Levelling The Land* (China/Elektra 1991)★★★, *The Levellers* (China/Elektra 1993)★★★★, *Zeitgeist* (China/Elektra 1995)★★★, *Best Live: Headlights, White Lines, Black Tar Rivers* (China 1996)★★, *Mouth To Mouth* (China 1997)★★★, *Hello Pig* (China 2000)★★★, with McDermott's 2 Hours *The World Turned Upside Down* (Hag 2001)★★★.
COMPILATIONS: *See Nothing, Hear Nothing, Do Something* (China/Elektra 1993)★★★, *One Way Of Life: Best Of The Levellers* (China 1998)★★★★, *Special Brew* (Hag 2001)★★★.
VIDEOS: *The Great Video Swindle (Live At Glasgow Barrowlands)* (China 1992), *Best Live: Headlights, White Lines, Black Tar Rivers* (Warner Home Video 1996).
FURTHER READING: *Dance Before The Storm: The Official Story Of The Levellers*, George Berger.

LEVERT, GERALD
ALBUMS: *Private Line* (Atlantic 1991)★★★★, *Groove On* (Atlantic 1994)★★★, as Levert Sweat Gill *Levert Sweat Gill* (East West 1997)★★, *Love & Consequences* (East West 1998)★★★★, *G* (East West 1999)★★★, *Gerald's World* (East West 2001)★★★.

LEWIS, GARY, AND THE PLAYBOYS
ALBUMS: *This Diamond Ring* (Liberty 1965)★★★, *Everybody Loves A Clown* (Liberty 1965)★★★, *She's Just My Style* (Liberty 1966)★★★★, *Hits Again!* (Liberty 1966) ★★★, *You Don't Have To Paint Me A Picture* (Liberty 1967) ★★, *New Directions* (Liberty 1967)★★, *Now!* (Liberty 1968)★★, *Close Cover Before Playing* (Liberty 1968)★★, *Rhythm Of The Rain* (Liberty 1969)★★, *I'm On The Road Right Now* (Liberty 1969)★★.
COMPILATIONS: *Golden Greats* (Liberty 1966)★★★, *More Golden Greats* (Liberty 1968)★★, *Twenty Golden Greats* (Liberty 1979)★★★, *Greatest Hits: Gary Lewis And The Playboys* (Rhino 1986)★★★★, *Legendary Masters* (Capitol 1990)★★★, *Greatest Hits* (Curb 1994)★★★.

LEWIS, HUEY, AND THE NEWS
ALBUMS: *Huey Lewis & The News* (Chrysalis 1980)★★, *Picture This* (Chrysalis 1982)★★★★, *Sports* (Chrysalis 1983)★★★★, *Fore!* (Chrysalis 1986)★★, *Small World* (Chrysalis 1988)★★, *Hard At Play* (EMI 1991)★★, *Four Chords And Several Years Ago* (Elektra 1994)★★★, *Plan B* (Silvertone 2001)★★★.
COMPILATIONS: *The Heart Of Rock & Roll: The Best Of Huey Lewis & The News* (Chrysalis 1992)★★★, *Time Flies: The Best Of Huey Lewis & The News* (East West 1996) ★★★, *The Heart Of Rock & Roll* (EMI Gold 2000)★★★, *Classic Masters* (EMD 2002)★★★.

LEWIS, JERRY LEE
ALBUMS: *Jerry Lee Lewis* (Sun 1957)★★★★, *Jerry Lee Lewis And His Pumping Piano* (London 1958)★★★, *Jerry Lee's Greatest* (Sun 1961)★★★★, *Rockin' With Jerry Lee Lewis* (Design 1963)★★★, *The Greatest Live Show On Earth* (Smash 1964)★★★, with the Nashville Teens *Live At The Star Club, Hamburg* (Philips 1965)★★, *The Return Of Rock* (Smash 1965)★★★, *Country Songs For City Folks* (Smash 1965)★★★, *Whole Lotta Shakin' Goin' On* (London 1965)★★★★, *Memphis Beat* (Smash 1966)★★★, *By Request - More Greatest Live Show On Earth* (Smash 1966)★★★, *Breathless* (London 1967)★★★, *Soul My Way* (Smash 1967)★★★, *Got You On My Mind* (Fontana 1968)★★★, *Another Time, Another Place* (Mercury 1969)★★★, *She Still Comes Around* (Mercury 1969)★★★, *I'm On Fire* (Mercury 1969)★★★, *Jerry Lee Lewis' Rockin' Rhythm And Blues* (Sun 1969)★★★, with Linda Gail Lewis *Together* (Mercury 1970)★★★, *She Even Woke Me Up To Say Goodbye* (Mercury 1970)★★★, *A Taste Of Country* (Sun 1970)★★★, *There Must Be More To Love Than This* (Mercury 1970)★★★, *Johnny Cash And Jerry Lee Lewis Sing Hank Williams* (Sun 1971)★★★, *Touching Home* (Mercury 1971)★★★, *In Loving Memories* (Mercury 1971) ★★★, *Would You Take Another Chance On Me* (Mercury 1972)★★★, *The Killer Rocks On* (Mercury 1972)★★★, *Old Tyme Country Music* (Sun 1972)★★★, with Johnny Cash *Sunday Down South* (Sun 1972)★★, *The Session* (Mercury 1973)★★★, *Live At The International, Las Vegas* (Mercury 1973)★★★, *Great Balls of Fire* (Hallmark 1973)★★★, *Southern Roots* (Mercury 1974)★★★, *Rockin' Up A Storm* (Sun 1974)★★★, *Rockin' And Free* (Sun 1974)★★★, *I'm A Rocker* (Mercury 1975)★★★, *Odd Man In* (Mercury 1975)★★★, *Jerry Lee Lewis* (Elektra 1979) ★★★, *Killer Country* (Elektra 1980)★★★, *When Two Worlds Collide* (Elektra 1980)★★★, with Johnny Cash, Carl Perkins *The Survivors* (Columbia 1982)★★★, *My Fingers Do The Talking* (MCA 1983)★★★, *I Am What I Am* (MCA 1984)★★★, with Webb Pierce, Mel Tillis, Faron Young *Four Legends* (1985)★★★, with Johnny Cash, Carl Perkins, Roy Orbison *Class Of '55* (America 1986)★★★, *Interviews From The Class Of '55 Recording Sessions* (America 1986)★★, *Keep Your Hands Off It* (Zu Zazz 1987)★★★, *Don't Drop It* (Zu Zazz 1988)★★★, *Live In Italy* (Magnum Force 1989)★★, *Great Balls Of Fire!* film soundtrack (Polydor 1989)★★★, with Carl Perkins, Elvis Presley *The Million Dollar Quartet* (RCA 1990)★★★, *Rocket* (Instant 1990)★★★, *Live At The Vapors Club* (Ace 1991)★★★, *Young Blood* (Sire/Elektra 1995)★★★, *Jerry Lee Lewis At Hank Cochran's* 1987 recording (Trend 1996)★★★, *Live At Gilley's* (Connoisseur Collection 2000)★★.
COMPILATIONS: *Golden Hits* (Smash 1964)★★★★, *Country Music Hall Of Fame Hits Volume 1* (Smash 1969)★★★★, *Country Music Hall Of Fame Hits Volume 2* (Smash 1969)★★★★, *Original Golden Hits Volume 1* (Sun 1969)★★★★, *Original Golden Hits Volume 2* (Sun 1969) ★★★, *The Best Of Jerry Lee Lewis* (Smash 1970)★★★★, *Original Golden Hits Volume 3* (Sun 1971)★★★, *Monsters* (Sun 1971)★★★, *Rockin' With Jerry Lee Lewis* (Mercury 1972)★★★★, *Fan Club Choice* (Mercury 1974)★★★, *Whole Lotta Shakin' Goin' On* (Hallmark 1974)★★★★, *Good Rockin' Tonight* (Hallmark 1975)★★★, *Jerry Lee Lewis And His Pumping Piano* (Charly 1975)★★★, *Rare Jerry Lee Lewis Volume 1* (Charly 1975)★★★, *Rare Jerry Lee Lewis Volume 2* (Charly 1975)★★★, *The Jerry Lee Lewis Collection* (Hallmark 1976)★★★★, *Golden Hits* (Mercury 1976)★★★★, *The Original Jerry Lee Lewis* (Charly 1976)★★★★, *Nuggets* (Charly 1977)★★★★, *Nuggets Volume 2* (Charly 1977)★★★, *The Essential Jerry Lee Lewis* (Charly 1978)★★★★, *Shakin' Jerry Lee* (Arcade 1978)★★★, *Back To Back* (Mercury 1978)★★★, *Duets* (Sun 1979)★★★, *Jerry Lee Lewis* (Hammer 1979)★★★, *Good Golly Miss Molly* (Bravo 1980)★★★, *Trio Plus* (Sun 1980)★★★, *Jerry Lee's Greatest* (Charly 1981)★★★★, *Killer Country i* (Elektra 1981)★★★★, *Jerry Lee Lewis* (Mercury 1981)★★★, *The Sun Years* 12-LP box set (Sun 1984)★★★★, *18 Original Sun Greatest Hits* (Rhino 1984) ★★★★, *Milestones* (Rhino 1985)★★★★, *The Collection* (Deja Vu 1986)★★★★, *The Pumpin' Piano Cat* (Sun 1986) ★★★, *Great Balls Of Fire* (Sun 1986)★★★★, *The Wild One* (Sun 1986)★★★, *At The Country Store* (Starblend 1987)★★★, *The Very Best Of Jerry Lee Lewis* (Philips 1987)★★★★, *The Country Sound Of Jerry Lee Lewis* (Pickwick 1988)★★, *The Classic Jerry Lee Lewis* 8-CD box set (Bear Family 1989)★★★★, *The Classic Jerry Lee Lewis* (Ocean 1989)★★★, *Killer's Birthday Cake* (Sun 1989) ★★★, *Killer's Rhythm And Blues* (Sun 1989)★★★★, *Killer: The Mercury Years, Volume One, 1963-1968* (Mercury 1989)★★★, *Killer: The Mercury Years, Volume Two, 1969-1972* (Mercury 1989)★★★, *Killer: The Mercury Years, Volume Three, 1973-1977* (Mercury 1989)★★★★, *Great Balls Of Fire* (Pickwick 1989)★★, *The EP Collection* (See For Miles 1990)★★★★, *The Jerry Lee Lewis Collection* (Castle 1990)★★★, *The Best Of Jerry Lee Lewis* (Curb 1991)★★★, *Rockin' My Life Away* (Warners 1991)★★★★, *Pretty Much Country* (Ace 1992)★★★, *All Killer, No Filler: The Anthology* (Rhino 1993)★★★★, *The Complete Palomino Club Recordings* (1993)★★★, *The EP Collection Volume 2 ... Plus* (See For Miles 1994)★★★★, *The Locust Years . . . And The Return To The Promised Land* 8-CD box set (Bear Family 1995)★★★★, *Sun Classics* (Charly 1995)★★★★, *Killer Country ii* (Mercury 1995)★★★, *The Country Collection* (Eagle 1997)★★★, *Sings The Rock 'N' Roll Classics* (Eagle 1997)★★★, *The Killer Collection* (Spectrum 1998)★★★, *Mercury Smashes ... And Rockin' Sessions* 10-CD box set (Bear Family 2001)★★★★.
VIDEOS: *Carl Perkins & Jerry Lee Lewis Live* (BBC Video 1987), *Jerry Lee Lewis* (Fox Video 1989), *I Am What I Am* (Charly Video 1990), *The Killer* (Telstar Video 1991), *Killer Performance* (Virgin Vision 1991), *The Jerry Lee Lewis Show* (MMG Video 1991).
FURTHER READING: *Jerry Lee Lewis: The Ball Of Fire*, Allan Clark. *Jerry Lee Lewis*, Robert Palmer. *Whole Lotta Shakin' Goin' On: Jerry Lee Lewis*, Robert Cain. *Hellfire: The Jerry Lee Lewis Story*, Nick Tosches. *Great Balls Of Fire: The True Story Of Jerry Lee Lewis*, Myra Lewis. *Rockin' My Life Away: Listening To Jerry Lee Lewis*, Jimmy Guteman. *Killer!*, Jerry Lee Lewis And Charles White. *The Devil, Me, And Jerry Lee*, Linda Gail Lewis with Les Pendleton.
FILMS: *Jamboree* aka *Disc Jockey Jamboree* (1957), *Beach Ball* (1964), *Be My Guest* (1965), *American Hot Wax* (1976).

LEWIS, RAMSEY
ALBUMS: *Down To Earth* (EmArcy 1958)★★★, *Gentleman Of Swing* (Argo 1958)★★★, *Gentlemen Of Jazz* (Argo 1958)★★★, *An Hour With The Ramsey Lewis Trio* (Argo 1959)★★★, *Stretching Out* (Argo 1960)★★★, *The Ramsey Lewis Trio In Chicago* (Argo 1961)★★★, *More Music From The Soil* (Argo 1961)★★★, *Sound Of Christmas* (Argo 1961)★★★, *The Sound Of Spring* (Argo 1962)★★★, *Country Meets The Blues* (Argo 1962)★★★, *Bossa Nova* (Argo 1962)★★★, *Pot Luck* (Argo 1962)★★★, *Barefoot Sunday Blues* (Argo 1963)★★★, *The Ramsey Lewis Trio At The Bohemian Caverns* (Argo 1964)★★★, *Bach To The Blues* (Argo 1964)★★★, *More Sounds Of Christmas* (Argo 1964)★★★, *You Better Believe It* (Argo 1965)★★★★, *The In Crowd* (Argo 1965)★★★★, *Hang On Ramsey!* (Cadet 1965)★★★★, *Swingin'* (Cadet 1966)★★★★, *Wade In The Water* (Cadet 1966)★★★★, *Goin' Latin* (Cadet 1967)★★, *The Movie Album* (Cadet 1967)★★, *Dancing In The Street* (Cadet 1967)★★★, *Up Pops Ramsey Lewis* (Cadet 1968) ★★★, *Maiden Voyage* (Cadet 1968)★★★, *Mother Nature's Son* (Cadet 1969)★★, *Another Voyage* (Cadet 1969)★★, *Ramsey Lewis: The Piano Player* (Cadet 1970)★★★, *Them Changes* (Cadet 1970)★★★, *Back To The Roots* (Cadet 1971)★★★, *Upendo Ni Pamoja* (Columbia 1972)★★★, *Funky Serenity* (Columbia 1973)★★, *Sun Goddess* (Columbia 1974)★★★, *Don't It Feel Good* (Columbia 1975)★★★, *Salongo* (Columbia 1976)★★★, *Love Notes* (Columbia 1977)★★★, *Tequila Mockingbird* (Columbia 1977)★★★, *Legacy* (Columbia 1978)★★★, *Routes* (Columbia 1980) ★★★, *Three Piece Suite* (Columbia 1981)★★★, *Live At The Savoy* (Columbia 1982)★★★, *Chance Encounter* (Columbia 1983)★★, with Nancy Wilson *The Two Of Us* (Columbia 1984)★★★, *Reunion* (Columbia 1984)★★★, *Keys To The City* (Columbia 1987)★★, *Classic Encounter* (Columbia 1988) ★★, with Billy Taylor *We Meet Again* (Columbia 1989)★★★, *Urban Renewal* (Columbia 1989)★★★, *Electric Collection* (Columbia 1991)★★★, *Ivory Pyramid* (GRP 1992)★★, *Between The Keys* (GRP 1996)★★, *Dance Of the Soul* (GRP 1998)★★★, *Appassionata* (Narada 1999)★★★★, with Wilson *Meant To Be* (Narada 2002)★★★.
COMPILATIONS: *Choice! The Best Of The Ramsey Lewis Trio* (Cadet 1965)★★★, *The Best Of Ramsey Lewis* (Cadet 1970)★★★, *Ramsey Lewis' Newly Recorded All-Time, Non-Stop Golden Hits* (Columbia 1973)★★★, *The Greatest Hits Of Ramsey Lewis* (Chess 1988)★★★★, *Collection* (More Music 1995)★★★, *The Ramsey Lewis Trio In Person 1960-1967* (Chess 1998)★★★★, *Priceless Jazz Collection* (GRP 1998)★★★, *This Is Jazz* 80s recordings (Song 1998)★★★, *The Best Of Ramsey Lewis: The Millennium Collection* (Chess 2002)★★★★.
FILMS: *Gonks Go Beat* (1965).

LIGHTFOOT, GORDON
ALBUMS: *Lightfoot* (United Artists 1966)★★★, *Early Lightfoot* (United Artists 1966)★★★, *The Way I Feel* (United Artists 1967)★★★, *Did She Mention My Name* (United Artists 1968)★★★, *Back Here On Earth* (United Artists 1969)★★, *Sunday Concert* (United Artists 1969)★★★, *Sit Down Young Stranger* aka *If You Could Read My Mind* (Reprise 1970)★★★★, *Summer Side Of Life* (Reprise 1971)★★, *Don Quixote* (Reprise 1972)★★★, *Old Dan's Records* (Reprise 1972)★★, *Sundown* (Reprise 1974)★★★, *Cold On The Shoulder* (Reprise 1975)★★, *Summertime Dream* (Reprise 1976)★★★, *Endless Wire* (Warners 1978) ★★, *Dream Street Rose* (Warners 1980)★★, *Shadows* (Warners 1982)★★, *Salute* (Warners 1983)★★★, *East Of Midnight* (Warners 1986)★★★, *Waiting For You* (Reprise 1993)★★, *A Painter Passing Through* (Warners 1998)★★★.
COMPILATIONS: *The Very Best Of Gordon Lightfoot* (United Artists 1974)★★★, *Gord's Gold* (Reprise 1975)★★★, *The Best Of Gordon Lightfoot* (Warners 1981)★★★, *Gord's Gold, Volume 2* (Warners 1988)★★, *Songbook* 4-CD box set (Warner Archives 1999)★★★★, *Complete Greatest Hits* (Warner Archives 2002)★★★★.
FURTHER READING: *Gordon Lightfoot*, Alfrieda Gabiou. *If You Could Read My Mind*, Maynard Collins.

LIGHTHOUSE FAMILY
ALBUMS: *Ocean Drive* (Wild Card/Polydor 1995)★★★★, *Postcards From Heaven* (Wild Card/Polydor 1997)★★★, *Whatever Gets You Through The Day* (Polydor 2001)★★★.

LIGHTNING SEEDS
ALBUMS: *Cloudcuckooland* (Epic 1990)★★★, *Sense* (Epic 1992)★★★, *Jollification* (Epic 1994)★★★★, *Dizzy Heights* (Epic 1996)★★★★, *Tilt* (Epic 1999)★★★.
COMPILATIONS: *Pure Lightning Seeds* (Virgin 1996)★★★, *Like You Do* (Epic 1997)★★★★.
VIDEOS: *Like You Do - The Greatest Hits* (SMV 1997).

LIL' KIM
ALBUMS: *Hard Core* (Undeas/Big Beat 1996)★★★, *Notorious K.I.M.* (Undeas/Atlantic 2000)★★★.
FILMS: *She's All That* (1999).

LIMP BIZKIT
ALBUMS: *Three Dollar Bill, Y'all$* (Flip/Interscope 1997) ★★★, *Significant Other* (Flip/Interscope 1999)★★★★, *Chocolate Starfish And The Hot Dog Flavored Water* (Flip/Interscope 2000)★★★.
COMPILATIONS: *New Old Songs* remix album (Flip/Interscope 2001)★★★.
FURTHER READING: *Limp Bizkit*, Colin Devenish. *The Story Of Limp Bizkit*, Doug Small.

LINDISFARNE
ALBUMS: *Nicely Out Of Tune* (Charisma 1970)★★★★, *Fog On The Tyne* (Charisma 1971)★★★★, *Dingly Dell* (Charisma 1972)★★★, *Lindisfarne Live* (Charisma 1973)★★, *Roll On Ruby* (Charisma 1973)★★, *Happy Daze* (Warners 1974) ★★★, *Back And Fourth* (Mercury 1978)★★★, *Magic In The Air* (Mercury 1978)★★, *The News* (Mercury 1979)★★, *Sleepless Night* (LMP 1982)★★, *LindisfarneTastic Live* (LMP 1984)★★, *LindisfarneTastic Volume 2* (LMP 1984)★★, *Dance Your Life Away* (River City 1986)★★, *C'mon Everybody* (Stylus 1987)★★, *Peel Sessions* (Strange Fruit 1988)★★★, *Amigos* (Black Crow 1989)★★, *Elvis Lives On The Moon* (Essential 1993)★★, *Another Fine Mess* (Grapevine 1995) ★★, *The Cropredy Concert* 1994 recording (Mooncrest 1998)★★★, *Untapped & Acoustic* (Park 1998)★★, *Here Comes The Neighbourhood* (Park 1998)★★, *Live At The Cambridge Folk Festival* (Strange Fruit 1999)★★★, *BT3* (Buried Treasure 2001)★★, *Promenade* (Park 2002)★★★. Solo: Ray Jackson *In The Night* (Mercury 1980)★★. Rod Clements with Bert Jansch *Leather Launderette* (Black Crow 1988)★★.
COMPILATIONS: *Take Off Your Head* (Rubber 1974)★★, *Finest Hour* (Charisma 1975)★★★, *The Best Of Lindisfarne* (Virgin 1989)★★★, *Buried Treasures Volume 1* (Virgin 1993)★★, *Buried Treasures Volume 2* (Virgin 1993)★★, *On Tap* (Essential 1994)★★, *City Songs* 1971/1972 recordings (New Millennium 1998)★★★, *BT3: Rare And Unreleased 1969-2000* (Siren 2001)★★.
VIDEOS: *Rock Of The North* (Park Video 2000).
FURTHER READING: *Fog On The Tyne: The Official History Of Lindisfarne*, Dave Ian Hill.

LINKIN PARK
ALBUMS: *Hybrid Theory* (Warners 2000)★★★★.
VIDEOS: *Frat Party At The Pankake Festival* (Warner Music Vision 2001).

LITTLE ANTHONY AND THE IMPERIALS
ALBUMS: *We Are The Imperials* (End 1959)★★★, *Shades Of The 40's* (End 1961)★★★, *I'm On The Outside Looking In* (DCP 1964)★★★, *Goin' Out Of My Head* (DCP 1965) ★★★, *Paying Our Dues* (Veep 1967)★★★, *Reflections* (Veep 1967)★★, *Movie Grabbers* (Veep 1968)★★, *Out Of Sight, Out Of Mind* (United Artists 1969)★★, *On A New Street* (Avco 1974)★★.
SOLO: Anthony Gourdine *Daylight* (Songbird 1980)★★.
COMPILATIONS: *Little Anthony And The Imperials Greatest Hits* (Roulette 1965)★★★, *The Best Of Little Anthony And The Imperials* (DCP 1966)★★★, *The Best Of Little Anthony And The Imperials* (Rhino 1989)★★★, *25 Greatest Hits* (MFP 1998)★★★.

LITTLE EVA
ALBUMS: *L-L-L-L-Loco-Motion* (Dimension 1962)★★, *Back On Track* (Malibu 1989)★★★.
COMPILATIONS: *Lil' Loco'Motion* (Rock Echoes 1982)★★, *L L L L Little Eva: The Complete Dimension Recordings* (Westside 1998)★★★, *The Original* (Disky 1998)★★★.

LITTLE FEAT
ALBUMS: *Little Feat* (Warners 1971)★★★★, *Sailin' Shoes* (Warners 1972)★★★★, *Dixie Chicken* (Warners 1973) ★★★★, *Feats Don't Fail Me Now* (Warners 1974)★★★★, *The Last Record Album* (Warners 1975)★★★, *Time Loves A Hero* (Warners 1977)★★★, *Waiting For Columbus* (Warners 1978)★★★★, *Down On The Farm* (Warners 1979)★★★, *Let It Roll* (Warners 1988)★★★, *Representing The Mambo* (Warners 1990)★★, *Shake Me Up* (Morgan Creek 1991)★★, *Ain't Had Enough Fun* (Zoo 1995)★★, *Live From Neon Park* (Zoo 1996)★★★, *Under The Radar* (CMC 1998)★★, *Chinese Work Songs* (CMC 2000)★★, *Late Night Truck Stop* 1973 live recording (Burning Airlines 2001)★★★.
COMPILATIONS: *Hoy-Hoy!* (Warners 1981)★★★, *As Time Goes By: The Best Of Little Feat* (Warners 1986)★★★★, *Hotcakes & Outtakes: 30 Years Of Little Feat* 4-CD box set (Warner Archives/Rhino 2000)★★★.

LITTLE RICHARD
ALBUMS: *Little Richard* (Camden 1956)★★★, *Here's Little Richard* (Specialty 1957)★★★★★, *Little Richard Volume 2* (Specialty 1957)★★★★★, *The Fabulous Little Richard* (Specialty 1958)★★★★★, *Sings Gospel* (20th Century 1959)★★, *It's Real* (Mercury 1961)★★, *Little Richard Sings Freedom Songs* (Crown 1963)★★, *Coming Home* (Coral 1963)★★, *King Of The Gospel Singers* (Wing 1964)★, *Little Richard Is Back* (Vee Jay 1965)★★, *The Explosive Little Richard* (Columbia 1967)★★★, *Good Golly Miss Molly* (Specialty 1969)★★★, *The Little Richard Story* (Joy 1970)★★★, *Well Alright* (Specialty 1970)★★★, *Rock Hard Rock Heavy* (Specialty 1970)★★, *You Can't Keep A Good Man Down* (Union Pacific 1970)★★, *The Rill Thing* (Reprise 1970)★★, *Mr Big* (Joy 1971)★★, *Cast A Long Shadow* (Epic 1971)★★, *King Of Rock 'n' Roll* (Reprise 1971)★★★, *The Original Little Richard* (Specialty 1972)★★★, *The Second Coming* (Warners 1973)★★★, *Rip It Up* (Joy 1973)★★, *Slippin' And Slidin'* (Joy 1973)★★, *Good Golly Miss Molly* (Hallmark 1974)★★★, *Greatest Hits Recorded Live* (Embassy 1974)★★★, *Keep A Knockin'* (Rhapsody 1975)★★, *Dollars Dollars* (Charly 1975)★★, *The Great Ones* (MFP 1976)★★, *Little Richard And Jimi Hendrix Together* (Ember 1977)★, *Whole Lotta Shakin' Goin' On* (DJM 1977)★★★, *Little Richard Now* (Creole 1977)★★, *The Georgia Peach* (Charly 1980)★★★, *Little Richard And His Band* (Specialty 1980)★★, *Ooh! My Soul* (Charly 1982)★★★, *Whole Lotta Shakin'* (Bulldog 1982)★★★, *Get Down With It* (Edsel 1982)★★, *The Real Thing* (Magnum Force 1983)★★★, *Little Richard* (Cambra 1983)★★★, *He's Got It* (Topline 1984)★★, *Lifetime Friend* (Warners 1986) ★★★, *Black Diamond: Live In Boston – 1970* (Fireball 1998)★★.

COMPILATIONS: His Biggest Hits (Specialty 1963)★★★★, Little Richard's Greatest Hits (Vee Jay 1965)★★★★, Little Richard's Greatest Hits (OKeh 1967)★★★★, Little Richard's Greatest Hits (Joy 1968)★★★, Little Richard's Grooviest 17 Original Hits (Specialty 1968)★★★★, 20 Original Greatest Hits (Specialty 1976)★★★★, The Essential Little Richard (Specialty 1985)★★★★, 18 Greatest Hits (Rhino 1985) ★★★★, 20 Classic Cuts (Ace 1986)★★★★, Shut Up! A Collection Of Rare Tracks (1951 - 1964) (Rhino 1988) ★★★, The Collection (Castle 1989)★★★★, The Specialty Sessions 6-CD box set (Specialty 1990)★★★★★, The Formative Years, 1951-53 (Bear Family 1989)★★★, The EP Collection (See For Miles 1993)★★★★★, King Of Rock 'N' Roll (ABM 1999)★★★, Talkin' Bout Soul (RPM 2001)★★.
FURTHER READING: The Life And Times Of Little Richard: The Quasar Of Rock, Charles White.
FILMS: The Girl Can't Help It (1956), Don't Knock The Rock (1956), Catalina Caper (1967).

LITTLE RIVER BAND
ALBUMS: Little River Band (Harvest 1976)★★★, Diamantina Cocktail (Harvest 1977)★★★, Sleeper Catcher (Harvest 1978)★★★, First Under The Wire (Capitol 1979)★★, Backstage Pass (Capitol 1980)★★, Time Exposure (Capitol 1981)★★★★, The Net (Capitol 1983)★★, Playing To Win (Capitol 1984)★★, No Reins (Capitol 1986)★★★, Monsoon (MCA 1988)★★★, Get Lucky (MCA 1990)★★, Live Classics (MCA 1992)★★, Where We Started From (Scream 2001)★★.
COMPILATIONS: Greatest Hits (Capitol 1982)★★★, To Late To Load (Capitol 1986)★★★, Worldwide Love (Curb 1991)★★★, The Classic Collection (Capitol 1992)★★★, Reminiscing: The Twentieth Anniversary Collection (Rhino 1995)★★★★, Premium Gold Collection (EMI Electrola 1996)★★★, The Best Of The Little River Band (EMI 1997)★★★.
VIDEOS: Live Exposure (PMI 1981).

LITTLE STEVEN
ALBUMS: as Little Steven And The Disciples Of Soul Men Without Women (EMI America 1982)★★★, Voice Of America (EMI America 1984)★★★, Freedom No Compromise (Manhattan 1987)★★★, Revolution (RCA 1989)★★★, Born Again Savage (Renegade Nation 1999) ★★.
COMPILATIONS: Greatest Hits (EMI 1999)★★★.
FILMS: American Flyers (1985).

LIVE
ALBUMS: Mental Jewelry (Radioactive 1991)★★, Throwing Copper (Radioactive 1994)★★★★, Secret Samadhi (Radioactive 1997)★★★, The Distance To Here (Radioactive 1999)★★★★, V (Radioactive 2001)★★★.

LIVING COLOUR
ALBUMS: Vivid (Epic 1988)★★★★, Time's Up (Epic 1990) ★★★★, Stain (Epic 1993)★★★, Dread Japanese live release (Epic 1993)★★★.
COMPILATIONS: Pride (Epic 1995)★★★★.

LL COOL J
ALBUMS: Radio (Columbia 1985)★★★, Bigger And Deffer (Def Jam 1987)★★, Walking With A Panther (Def Jam 1989) ★★★, Mama Said Knock You Out (Def Jam 1990)★★★★, 14 Shots To The Dome (Def Jam 1992)★★★, Mr. Smith (Def Jam 1995)★★★, Phenomenon (Def Jam 1997)★★★★, G.O.A.T. Featuring James T. Smith: The Greatest Of All Time (Def Jam 2000)★★★.
COMPILATIONS: All World Greatest Hits (Def Jam 1996)★★★.
FILMS: Krush Groove (1985), Wildcats aka First And Goal (1986), The Hard Way (1991), Toys (1992), Out-Of-Sync (1995), Touch (1997), B*A*P*S (1997), Caught Up (1998), Woo (1998), Halloween H20: Twenty Years Later aka Halloween 7 (1998), Deep Blue Sea (1999), In Too Deep (1999), Any Given Sunday (1999), Charlie's Angels (2000).

LOFGREN, NILS
ALBUMS: Nils Lofgren (A&M 1975)★★★★, Cry Tough (A&M 1976)★★★, I Came To Dance (A&M 1977)★★★, Night After Night (A&M 1978)★★, Nils (A&M 1979)★★★, Night Fades Away (Backstreet 1981)★★, Wonderland (Backstreet 1983)★★★, Flip (Columbia 1985)★★★, Code Of The Road (A&M 1986)★★★, Silver Lining (Rykodisc 1991)★★★, Crooked Line (Rykodisc 1992)★★, Everybreath film soundtrack (Stampede 1993)★★★, Live On The Test (Windsong 1993)★★★, Damaged Goods (Pure 1995) ★★★★, Acoustic Live (Vision/Demon 1997)★★★★, Break Away Angel (Vision 2001)★★★.
COMPILATIONS: The Best Of Nils Lofgren (A&M 1981)★★★, A Rhythm Romance (A&M 1982)★★★, Classics Volume 13 (A&M 1987)★★★, The Best Of Nils Lofgren: Don't Walk, Rock (Connoisseur 1990)★★, Shine Silently (Spectrum 1995) ★★, Soft Fun, Tough Tears 1971-1979 (Raven 1995)★★★★, Steal Your Heart (A&M 1996)★★★, Code Of The Road: Greatest Hits Live (Capitol 1997)★★★, The Best Of Nils Lofgren & Grin: The A&M Years (Spectrum 1998)★★★★, New Lives (Hux 1998)★★, Ultimate Collection (Hip-O 1999) ★★★★, Bootleg 1975 recording (Vision Music 2001)★★★★.
VIDEOS: How To Play Guitar (Hot Licks 1989), Nils Lofgren Band Live At Town And Country Club (Castle 1991), Live & Raw (Vision Music 2001).

LOGGINS AND MESSINA
ALBUMS: Kenny Loggins With Jim Messina Sittin' In (Columbia 1972)★★★★, Loggins And Messina (Columbia 1972)★★★★, Full Sail (Columbia 1973)★★, On Stage (Columbia 1974)★★★, Mother Lode (Columbia 1974)★★, So Fine (Columbia 1975)★★, Native Sons (Columbia 1976)★★, Finale (Columbia 1977)★★.
COMPILATIONS: The Best Of Friends (Columbia 1976)★★★.

LOGGINS, KENNY
ALBUMS: Celebrate Me Home (Columbia 1977)★★★, Nightwatch (Columbia 1978)★★★, Keep The Fire (Columbia 1979)★★★★, Alive (Columbia 1980)★★★, High Adventure (Columbia 1982)★★★, Vox Humana (Columbia 1985)★★, Back To Avalon (Columbia 1988)★★, Leap Of Faith (Columbia 1991)★★, Outside From The Redwoods – An Acoustic Afternoon (Columbia 1993)★★★, Return To Pooh Corner (Sony Wonder 1994)★★★, The Unimaginable Life (Sony 1997)★★, December (Sony 1998)★★★, More Songs From Pooh Corner (Sony Wonder 2000)★★★.
COMPILATIONS: At His Best (Hollywood 1992)★★★, Yesterday, Today, Tomorrow: The Greatest Hits Of Kenny Loggins (Columbia 1997)★★★.
VIDEOS: Alive (CBS/Fox 1981), Outside From The Redwoods (Sony Music Video 1993), Return To Pooh Corner (Sony Wonder 1996).
FURTHER READING: The Unimaginable Life: Lessons Learned On The Path Of Love, Kenny And Julia Loggins.

LONE JUSTICE
ALBUMS: Lone Justice (Geffen 1985)★★★, Shelter (Geffen 1987)★★, Radio One Live In Concert 1986 recording (Windsong 1993)★★.
COMPILATIONS: This World Is Not My Home (Geffen 1999)★★★.

LONESTAR
ALBUMS: Lonestar (BNA 1995)★★★, Crazy Nights (BNA 1997)★★★, Lonely Grill (BNA 1999)★★★★, This Christmas Time (BNA 2000)★★, I'm Already There (BNA 2001)★★★.

LONG RYDERS
ALBUMS: The Long Ryders aka 10.5.60 mini-album (PVC 1983)★★★, Native Sons (Frontier/Zippo 1984)★★★★, State Of Our Union (Island 1985)★★★, Two-Fisted Tales (Island 1987)★★, BBC Radio One In Concert (Windsong 1994)★★★.
COMPILATIONS: Metallic B.O. early recordings (Overground 1990)★★, Best Of The Long Ryders (PolyGram 1998) ★★★★.

LONGPIGS
ALBUMS: The Sun Is Often Out (Mother 1996)★★★, Mobile Home (Mother 1999)★★★.

LOPEZ, JENNIFER
ALBUMS: On The 6 (Work/Epic 1999)★★★, J.Lo (Epic 2001)★★, J To Tha L-O! The Remixes (Epic 2002)★★★.
VIDEOS: Feelin' So Good (Epic 2000).
FILMS: My Little Girl (1986), My Family, Mi Familia (1995), Money Train (1995), Jack (1996), Blood And Wine (1997), Selena (1997), Anaconda (1997), U Turn (1997), Out Of Sight (1998), Antz voice only (1998), Thieves (1999), The Cell (2000), The Wedding Planner (2001), Angel Eyes (2001).

LOS LOBOS
ALBUMS: Si Se Puede! (Pan American 1976)★★★, Just Another Band From East LA (New Vista 1978)★★★, And A Time To Dance (Slash 1983)★★★, How Will The Wolf Survive? (Slash 1984)★★★★, By The Light Of The Moon (Slash 1987)★★★★, La Bamba (Slash 1987)★★★, La Pistola Y El Corazon (Slash 1988)★★★, The Neighbourhood (Slash 1990)★★★★, Kiko (Slash 1992)★★★★, Papa's Dream (Warners 1995)★★★, Colossal Head (Warners 1996)★★★, This Time (Hollywood 1999)★★★★.
SOLO: Cesar Rosas Soul Disguise (Rykodisc 1999)★★★.
COMPILATIONS: Just Another Band From East L.A: A Collection (Warners 1993)★★★★, El Cancionero Mas Y Mas: La Historia De La Banda Del Este De Los Angeles 4-CD box set (Rhino/WEA 2000)★★★★.

LOUISE
ALBUMS: Naked (EMI 1996)★★★, Woman In Me (EMI 1997)★★★, Elbow Beach (EMI 2000)★★.
COMPILATIONS: Changing Faces – The Best Of Louise: The Hits And Mixes (EMI 2001)★★★.

LOVE
ALBUMS: Love (Elektra 1966)★★★, Da Capo (Elektra 1967) ★★★★, Forever Changes (Elektra 1967)★★★★★, Four Sail (Elektra 1969)★★★★, Out Here (Blue Thumb 1969)★★, False Start (Blue Thumb 1970)★★★, Reel To Real (RSO 1974)H, Love Live 1978 recording (Rhino 1982)★★, Studio/Live (MCA 1982)★★, Electrically Speaking: Live In Concert (Yeaah! 2001) ★★, The Last Wall Of The Castle 1966 demos (Deep Six 2001)★★.
COMPILATIONS: Revisited (Elektra 1970)★★★, Masters (Elektra 1973)★★★, Best Of Love (Rhino 1980)★★★, Out There (Big Beat 1988)★★★, Comes In Colours (Big Beat 1993)★★★★, Love Story: 1966-1972 (Rhino 1995)★★★★.
FURTHER READING: Arthur Lee: Love Story, Ken Brooks. Arthur Lee: Alone Again Or, Barney Hoskyns.

LOVE AFFAIR
ALBUMS: The Everlasting Love Affair (CBS 1968)★★★, as LA New Day (CBS 1971)★★, as Steve Ellis' Love Affair Plugged In: Live At The Cavendish aka Love That's Everlasting (Tring/Javelin 1997)★★.
COMPILATIONS: No Strings (Angel Air 2001)★★, The Best Of The Good Times (Columbia 2001)★★★.

LOVERBOY
ALBUMS: Loverboy (Columbia 1980)★★★, Get Lucky (Columbia 1981)★★★, Keep It Up (Columbia 1983)★★★, Lovin' Every Minute Of It (Columbia 1985)★★★, Wildside (Columbia 1987)★★★, Six aka VI (CMC 1997)★★.
COMPILATIONS: Big Ones (Columbia 1989)★★★★, Classics (Columbia 1994)★★★, Temperature's Rising (Sony 1994)★★★, Super Hits (Sony 1997)★★★.
VIDEOS: Loverboy In Concert (Vestron Video 1985), Any Way You Look At It (CBO 1986).

LOVETT, LYLE
ALBUMS: Lyle Lovett (MCA/Curb 1986)★★★★, Pontiac (MCA/Curb 1987)★★★★, Lyle Lovett And His Large Band (MCA/Curb 1989)★★★, Joshua Judges Ruth (MCA/Curb 1992)★★★★, I Love Everybody (MCA/Curb 1994) ★★★★, The Road To Ensenada (MCA/Curb 1996)★★★, Step Inside This House (MCA/Curb 1998)★★★, Live In Texas (MCA/Curb 1999)★★★★.
COMPILATIONS: Anthology Volume One: Cowboy Man (MCA 2001)★★★★.
FILMS: The Player (1992), Short Cuts (1993), Luck, Trust & Ketchup: Robert Altman In Carver Country (1993), Prêt-à-Porter aka Ready To Wear (1994), Bastard Out Of Carolina (1996), Fear And Loathing In Las Vegas (1998), The Opposite Of Sex (1998), Cookie's Fortune (1999), 3 Days Of Rain (2000), The New Guy (2001).

LOVIN' SPOONFUL
ALBUMS: Do You Believe In Magic (Kama Sutra 1965) ★★★★, Daydream (Kama Sutra 1966)★★★★★, What's Up, Tiger Lily? film soundtrack (Kama Sutra 1966)★★, Hums Of The Lovin' Spoonful (Kama Sutra 1966)★★★★, You're A Big Boy Now film soundtrack (Kama Sutra 1967) ★★, Everything Playing (Kama Sutra 1967)★★★, Revelation: Revolution '69 (Kama Sutra 1968)H, Live At The Hotel Seville (Varèse Sarabande 1999)★★.
COMPILATIONS: The Best Of The Lovin' Spoonful (Kama Sutra 1967)★★★★, The Best Of The Lovin' Spoonful Volume Two (Kama Sutra 1968)★★★, 24 Karat Hits (Kama Sutra 1968)★★★, John Sebastian Song Book Vol. 1 (Kama Sutra 1970)★★★, The Very Best Of The Lovin' Spoonful (Kama Sutra 1970)★★★★, Once Upon A Time (Kama Sutra 1971)★★★, The Best ... Lovin' Spoonful (Kama Sutra 1976)★★★★, The Collection (Castle 1988)★★★★, The EP Collection (See For Miles 1988)★★★★, Anthology (Rhino 1990)★★★★, Summer In The City (Spectrum 1995)★★★, The Very Best Of Lovin' Spoonful (Camden 1998)★★★★, Collector's Edition 3-CD set (Platinum 1999)★★★.

LOWE, NICK
ALBUMS: Jesus Of Cool aka Pure Pop For Now People (Radar 1978)★★★★, Labour Of Lust (Radar 1978)★★★★, Nick The Knife (F-Beat 1982)★★★, The Abominable Showman (F-Beat 1983)★★★, Nick Lowe And His Cowboy Outfit (RCA 1984)★★★, as Nick Lowe And His Cowboy Outfit Rose Of England (RCA 1985)★★★, Pinker And Prouder Than Previous (Demon 1988)★★★, Party Of One (Reprise 1990)★★★, The Impossible Bird (Demon 1994) ★★★★, Dig My Mood (Demon 1998)★★★★, The Convincer (Proper/Yep Roc 2001)★★★.
COMPILATIONS: 16 All Time Lowes (Demon 1984)★★★★, Nick's Knack (Demon 1986)★★★, Basher: The Best Of Nick Lowe (Demon 1989)★★★★, The Wilderness Years (Demon 1991)★★★, The Doings (The Solo Years) 4-CD box set (Edsel 1999)★★★.
FILMS: Americation (1979).

LUDACRIS
ALBUMS: Incognegro (Disturbing Tha Peace 2000)★★★, Back For The First Time (Def Jam South 2000)★★★★, Word Of Mouf (Def Jam South 2001)★★★.

LULU
ALBUMS: Something To Shout About (Decca 1965)★★★★, Love Loves To Love Lulu (Columbia 1967)★★★, Lulu's Album (Columbia 1969)★★★, New Routes (Atco 1970)★★, Melody Fair (Atco 1971)★★, Don't Take Love For Granted (Rocket 1979)★★★, Lulu (Alfa 1981)★★★, Take Me To Your Heart Again (Alfa 1982)★★★, Shape Up And Dance With Lulu (Life Style 1984)★★, The Man Who Sold The World (Start 1989)★★★, Independence (Dome 1993)★★★.
COMPILATIONS: The World Of Lulu (Decca 1969)★★★★, The World Of Lulu Volume 2 (Decca 1970)★★★, The Most Of Lulu (MFP 1971)★★★★, The Most Of Lulu Volume 2 (MFP 1972)★★★, The Very Best Of Lulu (Warwick 1980) ★★★★, Shout (MFP 1983)★★★, I'm A Tiger (MFP 1989) ★★★, From Crayons To Perfume: The Best Of ... (Rhino 1995)★★★, Supersneakers (Sundazed 1997)★★★, The Man Who Sold The World (Sequel 1999)★★★.
FILMS: Gonks Go Beat (1965).

LUSH
ALBUMS: Spooky (4AD/Reprise 1992)★★, Split (4AD/Reprise 1994)★★★, Lovelife (4AD/Reprise 1996)★★★.
COMPILATIONS: Gala (4AD/Reprise 1990)★★★, Ciao! Best Of Lush (4AD 2001)★★★★.

LYMON, FRANKIE, AND THE TEENAGERS
ALBUMS: The Teenagers Featuring Frankie Lymon (Gee 1957)★★★, The Teenagers At The London Palladium (Roulette 1958)★★, Rock 'N' Roll Party With Frankie Lymon (Guest 1959)★★★.
COMPILATIONS: Frankie Lymon And The Teenagers 61-track set (Murray Hill 1987)★★★, The Best Of Frankie Lymon And The Teenagers (Roulette 1990)★★★, Not Too Young To Dream: Undiscovered Rarities (Fireball 1998)★★★, The Very Best Of (Rhino 1998)★★★.

LYNNE, JEFF
ALBUMS: Armchair Theatre (Reprise 1990)★★.
COMPILATIONS: Message From The Country (The Jeff Lynne Years 1968-1973) (Harvest 1979)★★★.

LYNNE, SHELBY
ALBUMS: Sunrise (Epic 1989)★★★, Tough All Over (Epic 1990)★★★★, Soft Talk (Epic 1991)★★★, Temptation (Morgan Creek 1993)★★★, Restless (Magnatone 1995) ★★★, I Am Shelby Lynne (Mercury 1999)★★★★, Love, Shelby (Mercury 2001)★★★★.
COMPILATIONS: This Is Shelby Lynne: The Best Of The Epic Years (Epic 2000)★★★.

LYNOTT, PHIL
ALBUMS: Solo In Soho (Vertigo 1981)★★★, The Phillip Lynott Solo Album (Vertigo 1992)★★.
FURTHER READING: Phillip Lynott: The Rocker, Mark Putterford. Songs For While I'm Away, Phillip Lynott, My Boy: The Phillip Lynott Story, Philomena Lynott.

LYNYRD SKYNYRD
ALBUMS: Pronounced Leh-Nerd Skin-Nerd (Sounds Of The South/MCA 1973)★★★★, Second Helping (Sounds Of The South/MCA 1974)★★★★, Nuthin' Fancy (MCA 1975) ★★★, Gimme Back My Bullets (MCA 1976)★★, One More From The Road (MCA 1976)★★★★, Street Survivors (MCA 1977)★★★★, Skynyrd's First And ... Last 1970-72 recordings (MCA 1978)★★★, Southern By The Grace Of God Tribute Tour 1987 (MCA 1988)★★★, Lynyrd Skynyrd 1991 (Atlantic 1991)★★★, The Last Rebel (Atlantic 1993)★★★, Endangered Species (Capricorn 1994)★★★, Southern Knights (CBH 1996)★★★, Twenty (CMC/SPV 1997)★★, Lyve From Steel Town (CMC/SPV 1998)★★★, Skynyrd's First: The Complete Muscle Shoals Album (MCA 1998)★★★★, Edge Of Forever (CMC/SPV 1999)★★★, Then And Now (CMC 2000)★★, Christmas Time Again (CMC 2000)★★, Collectybles (MCA 2000)★★★★.
COMPILATIONS: Gold & Platinum (MCA 1979)★★★★, Best Of The Rest (MCA 1982)★★★, Legend (MCA 1987) ★★★, Anthology (Raw Power 1987)★★★, Skynyrd's Innyrds (MCA 1989)★★, Definitive 3-CD box set (MCA 1991)★★★★, The Essential Lynyrd Skynyrd (MCA 1998) ★★★★, The Best Of Lynyrd Skynyrd: The Millennium Collection (MCA 1999)★★★★, Solo Flytes (MCA 1999) ★★★, All Time Greatest Hits (MCA 2000)★★★★, Lynyrd Skynyrd: The Collection (Spectrum 2001)★★★★.
VIDEOS: Freebird: The Movie (Cabin Fever 1997), Lynyrd Skynyrd Live: The Concert Video (CMC Video 1998), Lyve From Steel Town (CMC Video 1998).
FURTHER READING: Lynyrd Skynyrd: An Oral History, Lee Ballinger.

M

M PEOPLE
ALBUMS: Northern Soul (Deconstruction 1992)★★★, Elegant Slumming (Deconstruction 1993)★★★★, Bizarre Fruit (Deconstruction 1994)★★★, Bizarre Fruit II (Deconstruction 1995)★★, Fresco (BMG 1997)★★, Testify US only (Epic 1999)★★★.
COMPILATIONS: The Best Of M People (BMG 1998)★★★.
VIDEOS: Elegant TV (BMG Video 1994), Come Again (BMG Video 1995), One Night In Heaven (Game Entertainment 1998).

M.C. HAMMER
ALBUMS: Feel My Power (Bustin' 1987)★★★, Let's Get It Started (Capitol 1988)★★★, Please Hammer Don't Hurt 'Em (Capitol 1990)★★★, as Hammer Too Legit To Quit (Capitol 1991)★★, as Hammer The Funky Headhunter (RCA 1994)★★, Inside Out (Giant 1995)★★, Active Duty (World Hit 2001)★★.
COMPILATIONS: Greatest Hits (Capitol 1996)★★★★, Back To Back Hits (CEMA 1998)★★★, The Hits (EMI Gold 2000)★★★.
I FURTHER READING: M.C. Hammer: U Can't Touch This, Bruce Dessau.

MACCOLL, KIRSTY
ALBUMS: Desperate Characters (Polydor 1981)★★★, Kite (Virgin 1989)★★★★, Electric Landlady (Virgin 1991)★★★, Titanic Days (ZTT 1994)★★, Tropical Brainstorm (V2 2000) ★★★★.
COMPILATIONS: Galore (Virgin 1995)★★★★, What Do Pretty Girls Do? (Hux 1998)★★★, The One And Only (Metro 2001)★★★.

MADNESS
ALBUMS: One Step Beyond (Stiff 1979)★★★★, Absolutely (Stiff 1980)★★★, Madness 7 (Stiff 1981)★★★, The Rise And Fall (Stiff 1982)★★★★, Madness (1983)★★★★, Keep Moving (Stiff 1984)★★★, Mad Not Mad (Zarjazz 1985)★★, as the Madness The Madness (Virgin 1988)★★, Madstock (Go! Discs 1992)★★★, Wonderful (Virgin 1999)★★★.
COMPILATIONS: Complete Madness (Stiff 1982)★★★, Utter Madness (Zarjazz 1986)★★★, The Peel Sessions (Strange Fruit 1986)★★, Divine Madness (Virgin 1992)★★★★, The Business: The Definitive Singles Collection (Virgin 1993) ★★★★, The Heavy Heavy Hits (Virgin 1998)★★★★, The Lot box set (Virgin 1999)★★★.
VIDEOS: Complete Madness (Stiff 1984), Utter Madness (Virgin Vision 1988), Complete And Utter Madness (Virgin Vision 1988), Divine Madness (Virgin Vision 1992).
FURTHER READING: A Brief Case Of Madness, Mark Williams. Total Madness, George Marshall.

MADONNA
ALBUMS: Madonna (Sire 1983)★★★, Like A Virgin (Sire 1984)★★★, True Blue (Sire 1986)★★★★, Who's That Girl film soundtrack (Sire 1987)★★, You Can Dance remix album (Sire 1987)★★★, Like A Prayer (Sire 1989)★★★★, I'm Breathless (Sire 1990)★★★, Erotica (Maverick 1992)★★★, Bedtime Stories (Maverick 1994)★★★★, Evita film soundtrack (Warners 1996)★★★, Ray Of Light (Maverick/Warners 1998)★★★★, Music (Maverick/Warners 2000)★★★★.
COMPILATIONS: The Immaculate Collection (Sire 1990) ★★★★★, Best Of The Rest Volume 2 (Sire 1993)★★★, Something To Remember (Maverick 1995)★★★★, The Early Years: Give It To Me (Sanctuary 2001)★★★, GHV2 (Maverick 2001)★★★★.
VIDEOS: The Virgin Tour (Warner Music Video 1986), Ciao Italia - Live From Italy (Sire 1988), Immaculate Collection (Warner Music Video 1990), Justify My Love (Warner Music Video 1991), The Real Story (Wienerworld Video 1991), Madonna Video EP (Warner Music Video 1991), In Bed With Madonna (Video Collection 1991), Madonna: The Unauthorised Biography (MIA Video 1994), Ray Of Light (Warner Home Video 1998), The Video Collection 93:99 (Warner Vision 1999), What It Feels Like For A Girl (Warner Reprise Video 2001), Drowned World Tour 2001 (Warner Music Vision 2001).
FURTHER READING: Madonna: Her Story, Michael McKenzie. Madonna: The New Illustrated Biography, Debbi Voller. Madonna: In Her Own Words, Mick St Michael. Madonna: The Biography, Robert Matthew-Walker. Madonna, Marie Cahill. Madonna: The Style Book, Debbi Voller. Like A Virgin: Madonna Revealed, Douglas Thompson. Sex, Madonna. Madonna Unauthorized, Christopher Anderson. I Dream Of Madonna: Women's Dreams Of The Goddess Of Pop, Kay Turner (compiler). The I Hate Madonna Handbook, Ilene Rosenzweig. Madonna: The Girlie Show, Glenn O'Brien. Deconstructing Madonna, Fran Lloyd. Live!, no author listed. The Madonna Scrapbook, Lee Randall. Madonna: An Intimate Biography, J. Randy Taraborrelli. Madonna: Queen Of The World, Douglas Thompson. Madonna, Andrew Morton.
FILMS: A Certain Sacrifice (1979), Desperately Seeking Susan (1985), Vision Quest (1985), Shangai Surprise (1986), Who's That Girl? (1987), Bloodhounds Of Broadway (1989), Dick Tracy (1990), Madonna: Blond Ambition World Tour '90 (1990), Madonna: Truth Or Dare (1991), A League Of Their Own (1992), Shadows And Fog (1992), Body Of Evidence (1993), Dangerous Game (1993), Blue In The Face (1995), Four Rooms (1995), Girl 6 (1996), Evita (1996), The Next Best Thing (2000).

MAGAZINE
ALBUMS: Real Life (Virgin 1978)★★★★, Secondhand Daylight (Virgin 1979)★★★★, The Correct Use Of Soap (Virgin 1980)★★★, Play (Virgin/I.R.S. 1980)★★★, Magic, Murder And The Weather (Virgin/I.R.S. 1981)★★★.
COMPILATIONS: After The Fact (Virgin/I.R.S. 1982)★★★, Rays & Hail 1978-81 (Virgin 1987)★★★, Scree: Rarities 1978-1981 (Virgin/Blue Plate 1990)★★, BBC Radio 1 Live In Concert (Windsong 1993)★★★, (Maybe It's Right To Be Nervous Now) 3-CD box set (Virgin 2000)★★★, (Where The Power Is) (Virgin 2000)★★★★.

MAGNUM
ALBUMS: Kingdom Of Madness (Jet 1978)★★★, Magnum II (Jet 1979)★★★, Marauder (Jet 1980)★★★, Chase The Dragon (Jet 1982)★★★, The Eleventh Hour (Jet 1983) ★★★, On A StoryTeller's Night (Polydor 1985)★★★, Vigilante (Polydor 1986)★★★, Wings Of Heaven (Polydor 1988)★★★★, Goodnight L.A. (Polydor 1990), Invasion - Magnum Live (Receiver 1990)★★★, The Spirit (Polydor 1991)★★★, Sleepwalking (Polydor 1992)★★★, Rock Art (EMI 1994)★★★, Firebird (Spectrum/PolyGram 1995) ★★★, Breath Of Life (SPV 2002)★★★.
COMPILATIONS: Anthology (Raw Power 1986)★★★★, Collection (Castle 1990)★★★★, Box Set (Castle 1992)★★★, Chapter And Verse: Best Of (Polydor 1993)★★★, Uncorked (Jet 1994)★★★.
VIDEOS: The Sacred Hour Live (1986), On The Wings Of Heaven (1988), From Midnight To LA (1990).

MAHAVISHNU ORCHESTRA
ALBUMS: The Inner Mounting Flame (Columbia 1972) ★★★★, Birds Of Fire (Columbia 1973)★★★★, Between Nothingness And Eternity (Columbia 1973)★★★, Apocalypse (Columbia 1974)★★, Visions Of The Emerald Beyond (Columbia 1975)★★★, Inner Worlds (Columbia 1976)★★★, Adventures In Radioland (Relativity 1987) ★★★, The Lost Trident Sessions 1973 recording (Columbia/Legacy 1999)★★★★.
FURTHER READING: John McLaughlin And The Mahavishnu Orchestra, John McLaughlin.

MALMSTEEN, YNGWIE
ALBUMS: Yngwie Malmsteen's Rising Force (Polydor 1984) ★★★, Marching Out (Polydor 1985)★★★, Trilogy (Polydor 1986)★★★, Odyssey (Polydor 1988)★★★, Live In Leningrad (Polydor 1989)★★, Eclipse (Polydor 1990)★★, Fire & Ice (Elektra 1992)★★, Seventh Sign (Elektra 1994)★★★, No Mercy (CMC International 1994)★★★, Facing The Animal (Ranch Life 1998)★★, Live!! (Dream Catcher 1998)★★, Alchemy (Dream Catcher 1999)★★, War To End All Wars (Spitfire 2000)★★★.
COMPILATIONS: Archives 8-CD box set (Pony Canyon 2001)★★★.
VIDEOS: Rising Force Live 85 (1989), Trial By Fire (1989), Collection (1992), Live!! (Dreamcatcher 1998).

MAMAS AND THE PAPAS
ALBUMS: If You Can Believe Your Eyes And Ears (Dunhill/RCA Victor 1966)★★★★, The Mamas And The Papas aka Cass, John, Michelle, Denny (Dunhill/RCA Victor 1966) ★★★★, Deliver (Dunhill/RCA Victor 1967)★★★★, The Papas & The Mamas (Dunhill/RCA Victor 1968)★★★★, People Like Us (Dunhill 1971)★.
COMPILATIONS: Farewell To The First Golden Era (Dunhill 1967)★★★★, Golden Era Volume 2 (Dunhill 1968)★★★★, 16 Of Their Greatest Hits (MCA 1969)★★★★, A Gathering Of Flowers (Dunhill 1971)★★★, 20 Golden Hits (Dunhill 1973)★★★★, The ABC Collection: Greatest Hits (ABC 1976)★★★, Creeque Alley: The History Of The Mamas And Papas (MCA 1991)★★★★, California Dreamin' – The Very Best Of The Mamas And The Papas (PolyGram 1995) ★★★★, All The Leaves Are Brown: The Golden Era Collection (MCA 2001)★★★★.
FURTHER READING: Papa John, John Phillips with Jim Jerome. California Dreamin' - The True Story Of The Mamas And Papas, Michelle Phillips.

MAN
ALBUMS: Revelation (Pye 1969)★★★★, 2ozs Of Plastic With A Hole In The Middle (Dawn 1969)★★★, Man aka Man 1970 (Liberty 1971)★★, Do You Like It Here Now, Are You Settling In? (United Artists/Liberty 1971)★★, with Hawkwind, Brinsley Schwarz Greasy Truckers Party (United Artists 1972)★★★, Live At The Padgett Rooms Penarth (United Artists 1972)★★★, Be Good To Yourself At Least Once A Day (United Artists 1972)★★★★, Back Into The Future (United Artists 1973)★★, Rhinos, Winos + Lunatics (United Artists 1974)★★★, Slow Motion (United Artists 1974)★★★, Maximum Darkness (United Artists 1975)★★, Welsh Connection (MCA 1976)★★, All's Well That Ends Well (MCA 1977)★★, Friday 13th (Picasso 1984)★★★, Live At The Rainbow 1972 (WWR 1990)★★★, The Twang Dynasty (Road Goes On Forever/Point 1992)★★, Live At Reading '83 (Raw Fruit 1993)★★, Deke Leonard's Iceberg and Man BBC Radio One Live In Concert 1973 recording (Windsong 1993)★★★, Live: Official Bootleg (The Welsh Connection/Point 1994)★★★, Call Down The Moon (Hypertension/Point 1995)★★★, The 1999 Party Tour 1974 live recording (Point 1998)★★, 1998 At The Star Club (P+O 1998)★★, Endangered Species (Evangeline 2000)★★★, Undrugged (Point 2002)★★★.
COMPILATIONS: Golden Hour Of (Pye 1973)★★, Green Fly (Latymer 1986)★★★, Perfect Timing: The UA Years (EMI 1991)★★★, The Early Years (Dojo 1993)★★, The Dawn Of Man (Recall 1997)★★★, The Definitive Collection (Castle 1998)★★★, Rare (Point/IMC 1999)★★, 3 Decades Of Man: The Best Of The 70's, 80's & 90's (Eagle 2000) ★★★, Many Are Called But Few Get Up (Receiver 2001)★★★★.
FURTHER READING: Mannerisms, Martin Mycock. Mannerisms II, Martin Mycock. Rhinos, Winos & Lunatics: The Legend Of Man A Rock 'n' Roll Band, Deke Leonard. Maybe I Should've Stayed In Bed? The Flip Side Of The Rock 'n' Roll Dream, Deke Leonard.

MANCHESTER, MELISSA
ALBUMS: Home To Myself (Bell 1973)★★, Bright Eyes (Bell 1974)★★, Melissa (Arista 1975)★★★★, Better Days And Happy Endings (Arista 1976)★★★, Help Is On The Way (Arista 1976)★★★, Singin' (Arista 1977)★★, Don't Cry Out Loud (Arista 1978)★★, Melissa Manchester (Arista 1979)★★, For The Working Girl (Arista 1980)★★, Hey Ricky (Arista 1982)★★★, Emergency (Arista 1983)★★, Mathematics (MCA 1985)★★.
COMPILATIONS: Greatest Hits (Arista 1983)★★★★, The Definitive Collection (Arista 1997)★★★.

MANFRED MANN
ALBUMS: The Manfred Mann Album (Ascot 1964)★★★★, The Five Faces Of Manfred Mann (HMV 1964)★★★★, Mann Made (HMV 1965)★★★★, My Little Red Book Of Winners (Ascot 1965)★★★★, As Is (Fontana 1966)★★★, Pretty Flamingo (United Artists 1966)★★★, What A Mann (Fontana 1968)★★★, The Mighty Garvey (Fontana 1968) ★★★, as the Manfreds 5-4-3-2-1 (Camden 1998)★★, as the Manfreds Maximum Manfreds (Manfreds 2002)★★★.
COMPILATIONS: Mann Made Hits (HMV 1966)★★★★, Manfred Mann's Greatest Hits (United Artists 1966)★★★★, Soul Of Mann (HMV 1967)★★★, What A Mann (Fontana 1968)★★★★, Semi-Detached Suburban (EMI 1979)★★★, The Singles Plus (See For Miles 1987)★★★★, The EP Collection (See For Miles 1989)★★★★, The Collection (Castle 1990)★★★, Ages Of Mann: 22 Classic Hits Of The 60s (PolyGram 1992)★★★★, Best Of The EMI Years (EMI 1993)★★★★, Groovin' With The Manfreds (EMI 1996)★★★★, Singles In The Sixties (BR Music 1997)★★★, The Very Best Of The Fontana Years (Spectrum 1998)★★★, BBC Sessions (EMI 1998)★★★, The Very Best Of Manfred Mann (MFP 1998)★★★, All Manner Of Menn: 1963-1969 And More ... (Raven 2000)★★★.
FURTHER READING: Mannerisms: The Five Phases Of Manfred Mann, Greg Russo.

MANFRED MANN'S EARTH BAND
ALBUMS: Manfred Mann's Earth Band (Philips/Polydor 1972)★★, Glorified Magnified (Philips 1972)★★★, Messin' (UK) Get Your Rocks Off (US) (Vertigo/Polydor 1973)★★★★, Solar Fire (Bronze/Warners 1973)★★★, The Good Earth (Bronze/Warners 1974)★★★★, Nightingales & Bombers (Bronze/Warners 1975)★★★, The Roaring Silence (Bronze/Warners 1976)★★★★, Watch (Bronze/Warners 1978)★★★, Angel Station (Bronze/Warners 1979)★★★, Chance (Bronze/Warners 1980) ★★★, Somewhere In Afrika (Bronze/Arista 1982)★★★, Live In Budapest (Bronze 1984)★★★, Criminal Tango (10 1986)★★★, Masque: Songs And Planets (10 1987)★★★, Soft Vengeance (Grapevine 1996)★★, Mann Alive (RMG 1998)★★★, Wired 1977 radio recording (NMC Pilot 2001)★★.
COMPILATIONS: The New Bronze Age (Bronze 1977)★★★, 20 Years Of Manfred Mann's Earth Band: 1971-1991 (Cohesion 1991)★★★, Manfred Mann's Earth Band 13-CD box set (Cohesion 1992)★★★, Blindin': A Stunning Collection Of Powerful Rock Masterpieces 1973-1982 (MCI 2000)★★★.
FURTHER READING: Mannerisms: The Five Phases Of Manfred Mann, Greg Russo.

MANHATTAN TRANSFER
ALBUMS: Jukin' (Capitol 1971/75)★★, Manhattan Transfer (Atlantic 1975)★★★★, Coming Out (Atlantic 1976)★★★, Pastiche (Atlantic 1978)★★★, Live (Atlantic 1978)★★, Extensions (Atlantic 1979)★★★, Mecca For Moderns (Atlantic 1981)★★★, Bodies And Souls (Atlantic 1983) ★★★, Bop Doo-Wop (Atlantic 1985)★★★, Vocalese (Atlantic 1985)★★★★, Live In Tokyo (Atlantic 1987)★★★, Brasil (Atlantic 1987)★★, The Offbeat Of Avenues (Columbia 1991)★★★, Tonin' (Atlantic 1995)★★★, Swing (Atlantic 1997)★★★, The Spirit Of St. Louis (Atlantic 2000)★★★★.
COMPILATIONS: Best Of Manhattan Transfer (Atlantic 1981)★★★, The Christmas Album (Columbia 1992)★★, The Very Best Of ... (Rhino 1993)★★★★.

MANIC STREET PREACHERS
ALBUMS: Generation Terrorists (Columbia 1992)★★★★, Gold Against The Soul (Columbia 1993)★★★★, The Holy Bible (Columbia 1994)★★★, Everything Must Go (Epic 1996)★★★★★, This Is My Truth Tell Me Yours (Epic/Virgin 1998)★★★★, Know Your Enemy (Epic/Virgin 2001)★★★.
VIDEOS: Everything Live (SMV 1997), Leaving The 20th Century: Cardiff Millennium Stadium 1999/2000 (SMV 2000), Live In Cuba: Louder Than War (SMV 2001).
FURTHER READING: Design For Living, Paula Shutkever. Manic Street Preachers, Sweet Venom, Martin Clarke. Everything (A Book About Manic Street Preachers), Simon Price. Manic Street Preachers, Mick Middles.

MANILOW, BARRY
ALBUMS: Barry Manilow (Bell 1972)★★★, Barry Manilow II (Bell 1973)★★★, Tryin' To Get The Feeling (Arista 1975) ★★★, This One's For You (Arista 1976)★★★, Live (Arista 1977)★★★, Even Now (Arista 1978)★★★, One Voice (Arista 1979)★★★, Barry (Arista 1980)★★★, If I Should Love Again (Arista 1981)★★, Oh, Julie! (Arista 1982)★★, Here Comes The Night (Arista 1982)★★, Barry Live In Britain (Arista 1982)★★★, Swing Street (Arista 1984)★★★, 2:00 AM Paradise Café (Arista 1985)★★★, Songs To Make The Whole World Sing (Arista 1989)★★, Live On Broadway (Arista 1990)★★★, Because It's Christmas (Arista 1990)★★, Showstoppers (Arista 1991)★★★, Hidden Treasures (Arista 1993)★★★, Singin' With The Big Bands (Arista 1994) ★★★, Summer Of '78 (Arista 1996)★★★, Manilow Sings Sinatra (Arista 1998)★★★, Here At The Mayflower (Concord Jazz 2001)★★★.
COMPILATIONS: Greatest Hits (Arista 1978)★★★, Greatest Hits Volume II (Arista 1983)★★★, The Songs 1975-1990 (Arista 1990)★★★, The Complete Collection And Then Some 4-CD box set (Arista 1992)★★★, Greatest Hits: The Platinum Collection (Arista 1999)★★★, Ultimate Manilow (Arista 2002)★★★★.
VIDEOS: In Concert At The Greek (Guild Home Video 1984), Live On Broadway (Arista 1990), The Greatest Hits ... And Then Some (Arista 1994), Manilow Live! (Image 2000).
FURTHER READING: Barry Manilow, Ann Morse. Barry Manilow: An Autobiography, Barry Manilow with Mark Bego. Barry Manilow, Howard Elson. The Magic Of Barry Manilow, Alan Clarke. Barry Manilow For The Record, Simon Weir. The Barry Manilow Scrapbook: His Magical World In Works And Pictures, Richard Peters. Barry Manilow, Tony Jasper. Barry Manilow: The Biography, Patricia Butler.

MANN, AIMEE
ALBUMS: Whatever (Imago 1993)★★★★, I'm With Stupid (Geffen 1995)★★★, Magnolia film soundtrack (Reprise 1999)★★★, Bachelor No. 2 (Or The Last Remains Of The Dodo) (Superego 2000)★★★★.
COMPILATIONS: Ultimate Collection (Hip-O 2000)★★★★.
FILMS: The Big Lebowski (1998).

MANSUN
ALBUMS: Attack Of The Grey Lantern (Parlophone/Epic 1997)★★★★, Six (Parlophone/Epic 1998)★★★, Little Kix (Parlophone 2000)★★★★.
FURTHER READING: Tax-Loss Lovers From Chester, Mick Middles.

MAR-KEYS
ALBUMS: Last Night (Atlantic 1961)★★★, Do The Popeye With The Mar-Keys (London 1962)★★★, The Great Memphis Sound (Atlantic 1966)★★★, with Booker T. And The MGs Back To Back (Stax 1967)★★★, Mellow Jello (Atlantic 1968)★★★, Damifiknow (Stax 1969)★★, Memphis Experience (1971)★★.

MARILLION
ALBUMS: Script For A Jester's Tear (EMI/Capitol 1983) ★★★, Fugazi (EMI/Capitol 1984)★★★, Real To Reel mini-album (EMI 1984)★★, Misplaced Childhood (EMI/Capitol 1985)★★★★, Brief Encounter mini-album (Capitol 1986)H, Clutching At Straws (EMI/Capitol 1987)★★★, The Thieving

Magpie (La Gazza Ladra) (EMI/Capitol 1988)★★, Seasons End (EMI/Capitol 1989)★★★, Holidays In Eden (EMI 1991)★★★, Brave (EMI/I.R.S. 1994)★★★, Afraid Of Sunlight (EMI/I.R.S. 1995)★★★★, Made Again (EMI/Intact 1996)★★, This Strange Engine (Intact/Velvel 1997)★★★, Radiation (Raw Power/Velvel 1998)★★, Marillion.com (Intact 1999)★★★, Anoraknophobia (Racket 2001)★★★.
COMPILATIONS: B'Sides Themselves (EMI 1988)★★, A Singles Collection 1982-1992 UK title Six Of One, Half-Dozen Of The Other US title (EMI/I.R.S. 1992)★★★, Essential Collection (EMI 1996)★★★, The Best Of Both Worlds (EMI 1997)★★★★, Kayleigh: The Essential Collection (EMI 1998)★★★, The CD Singles '82-'88 (EMI 2000)★★★, Refracted! (Racket 2001)★★.
VIDEOS: Recital Of The Script (EMI 1983), 1982-86 The Videos (EMI 1986), Live From Loreley (EMI 1987), From Stoke Row To Ipanema (EMI 1990), A Singles Collection (EMI 1992), Brave The Movie (EMI 1995).
FURTHER READING: Marillion: In Words And Pictures, Carol Clerk. Market Square Heroes: The Authorized Story Of Marillion, Mick Wall. Marillion: The Script, Clive Gifford.

MARILYN MANSON
ALBUMS: Portrait Of An American Family (Nothing/Interscope 1994)★★, Smells Like Children (Nothing/Interscope 1995)★★, Antichrist Superstar (Nothing/Interscope 1996) ★★★★, Remix And Repent (Nothing/Interscope 1998)★★★, Mechanical Animals (Nothing/Interscope 1998)★★★, The Last Tour On Earth (Nothing/Interscope 1999)★★★, Holly Wood (In The Shadow Of The Valley Of Death) (Nothing/Interscope 2000)★★★.
VIDEOS: Dead To The World (Nothing/Interscope 1998), Demystifying The Devil: An Unauthorised Biography (Wienerworld 2000).
FURTHER READING: The Story Of Marilyn Manson, Doug Small. Marilyn Manson: Smells Like White Trash, Susan Wilson. Marilyn Manson: The Unauthorized Biography, Kalen Rogers. Marilyn Manson: The Long Hard Road Out Of Hell, Marilyn Manson with Neil Strauss. Marilyn Manson, Kurt Reighley. Marilyn Manson: In His Own Words, Chuck Weiner. Dissecting Marilyn Manson, Gavin Baddeley.

MARLEY, BOB
ALBUMS: Wailing Wailers (Studio One 1965)★★★, The Best Of The Wailers (Beverley's 1970)★★★, Soul Rebels (Trojan/Upsetter 1970)★★★, Catch A Fire (Island 1973) ★★★★★, Burnin' (Island 1973)★★★★, African Herbsman (Trojan 1974)★★★, Rasta Revolution (Trojan 1974)★★★, Natty Dread (Island 1975)★★★★★, Live! aka Live At The Lyceum (Island 1975)★★★★, Rastaman Vibration (Island 1976)★★★★, Exodus (Island 1977)★★★★, Kaya (Island 1978)★★★★, Babylon By Bus (Island 1978)★★★, Survival (Tuff Gong/Island 1979)★★★★, Uprising (Tuff Gong/Island 1980)★★★★, Marley, Tosh Livingston & Associates (Studio One 1980)★★★, Catch A Fire deluxe edition (Tuff Gong 2001)★★★★★.
COMPILATIONS: In The Beginning (Psycho/Trojan 1979) ★★★, Chances Are (Warners 1981)★★★, Bob Marley - The Boxed Set 9-LP box set (Island 1982)★★★, Confrontation (Tuff Gong/Island 1983)★★★, Legend (Island 1984)★★★★★, Mellow Mood (Topline 1984)★★, Reggae Greats (Island 1985)★★★, Soul Revolution I & II the first UK release of the 70s Jamaican double album (Trojan 1988)★★★, Interviews (Tuff Gong 1988)★★, One Love: Bob Marley And The Wailers At Studio One (Heartbeat 1991)★★★, Talkin' Blues (Tuff Gong 1991)★★★, All The Hits (Rohit 1991)★★★, Upsetter Record Shop Parts 1 & 2 (Esoldun 1992)★★★, Songs Of Freedom 4-CD box set (Island 1992)★★★★, Never Ending Wailers (RAS 1993)★★★, Natural Mystic: The Legend Continues (Island 1995)★★★★, Power (More Music 1995) ★★★, Soul Almighty: The Formative Years Volume 1 (JAD 1996)★★★, Roots Of A Legend (Trojan 1997)★★★, The Complete Bob Marley & The Wailers 1967-1972 Part 1 3-CD set (JAD/Koch 1998)★★★★, Trench Town Rock 4-CD set (Charly 1998)★★★★, Rainbow Country: Rare & Instrumental Material 1969-1972 (Orange Street 1999)★★★, various artists Chant Down Babylon (Tuff Gong 1999)★★★, The Complete Upsetter Collection 6-CD box set (Trojan 2000) ★★★★, Climb The Ladder (Heartbeat 2001)★★, One Love: The Very Best Of Bob Marley & The Wailers (Tuff Gong/Island 2001)★★★★, Natty Rebel (Universal 2001)★★★, Small Axe (Universal 2001)★★★, Trenchtown Days: Birth Of A Legend (Columbia 2001)★★★.
VIDEOS: One Love Peace Concert (Hendring Music Video 1988), Live At The Rainbow (Channel 5 Video 1988), Caribbean Nights (Island Video 1988), Legend (Island Video 1991), Time Will Tell (1992), The Bob Marley Story (Island Video 1994), Rebel Music: The Bob Marley Story (Palm Pictures 2001).
FURTHER READING: Bob Marley: Music, Myth & The Rastas, Henderson Dalrymple. Bob Marley: The Roots Of Reggae, Cathy McKnight and John Tobler. Bob Marley: Soul Rebel – Natural Mystic, Adrian Boot and Vivien Goldman. Bob Marley: The Biography, Stephen Davis. Catch A Fire, The Life Of Bob Marley, Timothy White. Bob Marley: Reggae King Of The World, Malika Lee Whitney. Bob Marley: In His Own, Ian McCann. Bob Marley: Conquering Lion Of Reggae, Stephen Davis. So Much Things To Say: My Life As Bob Marley's Manager, Don Taylor. The Illustrated Legend 1945-1981, Barry Lazell. Spirit Dancer, Bruce W. Talamon, The Complete Guide To The Music Of ... , Ian McCann. Bob Marley: An Intimate Portrait By His Mother, Cedella Booker with Anthony Winkler, Bob Marley: A Rebel Life, Dennis Morris.

MARMALADE
ALBUMS: There's A Lot Of It About (Columbia 1968)★★★, Reflections Of The Marmalade (Decca 1970)★★★, Songs (Decca 1971)★★★, Our House Is Rockin' (EMI 1974)★★, Only Light On My Horizon Now (Target 1977)★★, Doing It All For You (Skyclad 1979)★★.
COMPILATIONS: The Best Of The Marmalade (Columbia 1970)★★★, The Definitive Collection (Castle 1996)★★★★, I See The Rain: The CBS Years (Sequel 2000)★★★★, Rainbow: The Decca Years (Sequel 2000)★★★★, Reflections Of The Marmalade: The Anthology (Sanctuary 2001)★★★★.

MARRIOTT, STEVE
ALBUMS: Marriott (A&M 1975)★★, 30 Seconds To Midnite (Trax 1989)★★, with Packet Of Three Live 23rd October 1985 (Zeus 1996)★★, with the Next Band Live In Germany 1985 (Castle 2000)★★★, with the D.T.s Sing The Blues: Live 1988 (Castle 2001)★★★.
COMPILATIONS: Clear Through The Night (New Millennium 1999)★★, with Ronnie Lane The Legendary Majic Mijit (Burning Airlines 2000)★★.
FILMS: Heavens Above (1962), Night Cargoes (1962), Live It Up (1963), Be My Guest (1963).

MARSHALL TUCKER BAND
ALBUMS: The Marshall Tucker Band (Capricorn 1973)★★★★, A New Life (Capricorn 1974)★★★, Where We All Belong (Capricorn 1974)★★★, Searchin' For A Rainbow (Capricorn 1975)★★★★, Long Hard Ride (Capricorn 1976)★★★, Carolina Dreams (Capricorn 1977)★★★, Together Forever (Capricorn 1978)★★★, Running Like The Wind (Warners 1979)★★★, Tenth (Warners 1980)★★★, Dedicated (Warners 1981)★★★, Tuckerized (Warners 1981)★★★, Just Us (Warners 1983)★★, Greetings From South Carolina (Warners 1983)★★, Still Holdin' On (Mercury 1988)★★, Southern Spirit (Capitol 1990)★★, Still Smokin' (Cabin Fever 1992)★★, Walk Outside The Lines (Cabin Fever 1993) ★★★, Country Tucker (K-Tel 1996)★★, M.T. Blues (K-Tel 1997)★★★, Face Down In The Blues (K-Tel 1998)★★★.
COMPILATIONS: Greatest Hits (Capricorn 1978)★★★.
VIDEOS: This Country's Rockin' (Cabin Fever 1993), Then And Now (Cabin Fever 1993).

MARTHA AND THE MUFFINS
ALBUMS: Metro Music (DinDisc/Virgin 1980)★★★, Trance And Dance (DinDisc/Virgin 1980)★★★, This Is The Ice Age (DinDisc/Virgin 1981)★★★, Danseparc (Current/RCA 1982)★★, as M+M Mystery Walk (Current/RCA 1984) ★★★, as M+M The World Is A Ball (Current/RCA 1985) ★★★, Modern Lullaby (Intrepid 1992)★★★.
COMPILATIONS: Far Away In Time (Plan/Virgin 1988)★★★, Then Again: A Retrospective (Muffin/EMI 1998)★★★★.

MARTHA AND THE VANDELLAS
ALBUMS: Come And Get These Memories (Gordy 1963) ★★★, Heat Wave (Gordy 1963)★★★, Dance Party (Gordy 1965)★★★, Watchout! (Gordy 1967)★★, Martha & The Vandellas Live! (Gordy 1967)H, as Martha Reeves And The Vandellas Ridin' High (Gordy 1968)★★, Sugar 'n' Spice (Gordy 1969)★★, Natural Resources (Gordy 1970)★★, Black Magic (Gordy 1972)★★.
COMPILATIONS: Greatest Hits (Gordy 1966)★★★★, Anthology (Motown 1974)★★★★, Compact Command Performances (Motown 1992)★★★, 24 Greatest Hits (Motown 1992)★★★★, Live Wire, 1962-1972 (Motown 1993)★★★★, Milestones (Motown 1995)★★★★, Early Classics (Spectrum 1996)★★★, The Ultimate Collection (Motown 1998)★★★★, Universal Masters Collection (Universal 2000)★★★★.

MARTIN, GEORGE
ALBUMS: Off The Beatle Track (Parlophone 1964)★★★, George Martin (United Artists 1965)★★★, George Martin Scores Instrumental Versions Of The Hits (1965)★★★, Plays Help! (Columbia 1965)★★, Salutes The Beatle Girls (United Artists)★★★, And I Love Her (Studio Two 1966)★★★, By George! (1967)★★★, The Family Way film soundtrack (1967)★★★, British Maid (United Artists 1968)★★★, with the Beatles Yellow Submarine (Parlophone 1969)★★★, Live And Let Die (United Artists 1973)★★★, Beatles To Bond And Bach (Polydor 1974)★★★, In My Life (Echo 1998)★★★.
COMPILATIONS: Produced By George Martin: 50 Years In Recording 6-CD box set (EMI 2001)★★★★.
FURTHER READING: All You Need Is Ears, George Martin. Summer Of Love: The Making Of Sgt Pepper, George Martin.
FILMS: Give My Regards To Broad Street (1985).

MARTIN, RICKY
ALBUMS: Ricky Martin (Sony Discos 1991)★★, Me Amaras (Sony Discos 1993)★★, A Medio Vivir (Sony Discos 1995) ★★★, Vuelve (Sony Discos 1998)★★★, Ricky Martin (C2/Columbia 1999)★★★, Sound Loaded (C2/Columbia 2000)★★★.
COMPILATIONS: La Historia (Sony Discos 2001)★★★, The Best Of Ricky Martin (Columbia 2001)★★★.
VIDEOS: The Ricky Martin Video Collection (SMV 1999), One Night Only (SMV 1999).

MARTYN, JOHN
ALBUMS: London Conversation (Island 1967)★★, The Tumbler (Island 1968)★★, with Beverley Martyn Stormbringer (Island 1970)★★★, with Beverley Martyn The Road To Ruin (Island 1970)★★★, Bless The Weather (Island 1971)★★★, Solid Air (Island 1973)★★★★, Inside Out (Island 1973)★★★, Sunday's Child (Island 1975)★★★, Live At Leeds (Own Label 1975)★★★, One World (Island 1977)★★★★, Grace & Danger (Island 1980)★★★★, Glorious Fool (WEA 1981) ★★★★, Well Kept Secret (WEA 1982)★★★★, Philentropy (Body Swerve/Castle 1983)★★★, Sapphire (Island 1984) ★★★★, Piece By Piece (Island 1986)★★★★, Foundations (Island 1987)★★★, The Apprentice (Permanent 1990)★★★, Cooltide (Permanent 1991)★★, BBC Radio 1 Live In Concert (Windsong 1992)★★★, Couldn't Love You More (Permanent 1992)★★, No Little Boy (Permanent 1993)★★★, Live aka Dirty, Down And Live 1990 recording (Griffin 1995)★★★, And (Go! Discs 1996)★★★★, The Church With One Bell (Independiente 1998)★★, Live At Bristol 1991: Official Bootleg (Voiceprint 1998)★★★, Glasgow Walker (Independiente 2000)★★★, The New York Session (Voiceprint 2000)★★, with Danny Thompson Live In Germany 1986 (One World 2001) ★★★, with Danny Thompson The Brewery Arts Centre Kendal 1986 (One World 2001)★★★, Sweet Certain Surprise (One World 2002)★★★.
COMPILATIONS: So Far So Good (Island 1977)★★★, The Electric John Martyn (Island 1982)★★★, Sweet Little Mysteries: The Island Anthology (Island 1994)★★★★, The Hidden Years (Artful 1996)★★★, The Very Best Of John Martyn (Artful 1997)★★★, The Best Of The Rest (Artful 1997)★★★, Serendipity: An Introduction To John Martyn (Island 1998)★★★★, Another World (Voiceprint 1999) ★★★, Classics (Artful 2000)★★★, The Best Of John Martyn Live '91 (Eagle 2000)★★★, Patterns In The Rain (Mooncrest 2001)★★★★.
VIDEOS: In Vision 1973-1981 (BBC Video 1982), Live From London (PolyGram Music Video 1984), John Martyn: Tell Them I'm Somebody Else .... (Pulse 2001).

MARVELETTES
ALBUMS: Please Mr Postman (Tamla 1961)★★★★, The Marvelettes Sing Smash Hits Of 1962 (Tamla 1962)★★★, Playboy (Tamla 1962)★★★, The Marvellous Marvelettes (Tamla 1963)★★★★, Recorded Live: On Stage (Tamla 1963)★★, The Marvelettes (Tamla 1967)★★★, Sophisticated Soul (Tamla 1968)★★★, In Full Bloom (Motown 1969)★★, The Return Of The Marvelettes (Motown 1970)★★, Now (Motor City 1990)★★.
COMPILATIONS: The Marvelettes Greatest Hits (Tamla 1963)★★★★, Anthology (Motown 1975)★★★★, Compact Command Performances - 23 Greatest Hits (Motown 1992) ★★★★, Deliver The Singles 1961-1971 (Motown 1993) ★★★★, The Very Best (Essential Gold 1996)★★★, The Ultimate Collection (Motown 1998)★★★★, The Best Of The Marvelettes: The Millennium Collection (Motown 2000)★★★★.

MARVIN, HANK B.
ALBUMS: Hank Marvin (Columbia 1969)★★, The Hank Marvin Guitar Syndicate (EMI 1977)★★, Words & Music (Polydor 1982)★★, All Alone With Friends (Polydor 1983) ★★, Into The Light (Polydor 1992)★★, Heartbeat (Polydor 1993)★★, Hank Plays Cliff (Polydor 1995)★★★, Hank Plays Holly (Polydor 1996)★★★, Hank Plays Live (PolyGram 1997)★★★, Marvin At The Movies (Universal 2000)★★★.
COMPILATIONS: The Best Of Hank Marvin And The Shadows (Polydor 1994)★★★, Handpicked (Polydor 1995)★★★, Another Side Of Hank Marvin (Spectrum 1998)★★, The Very Best Of Hank Marvin & The Shadows: The First 40 Years (Polydor 1998)★★★.
FURTHER READING: A Guide To The Shadows And Hank Marvin On CD, Malcolm Campbell.
FILMS: Expresso Bongo (1959), Summer Holiday (1962), Wonderful Life (1964), Finders Keepers (1966).

MASON, DAVE
ALBUMS: Alone Together (Blue Thumb 1970)★★★★, with 'Mama' Cass Elliot Dave Mason And Mama Cass (Blue Thumb 1971)★★, Headkeeper (Blue Thumb 1972)★★, Dave Mason Is Alive! (Blue Thumb 1973)★★, It's Like You Never Left (Columbia 1973)★★★, Dave Mason (Columbia 1974)★★★, Split Coconut (Columbia 1975)★★, Certified Live (Columbia 1976)★★, Let It Flow (Columbia 1977)★★, Mariposa De Oro (Columbia 1978)★★, Old Crest On A New Wave (Columbia 1980)★★, Some Assembly Required (Maze 1987)H, Two Hearts (MCA 1988)H, with Jim Capaldi Live: The 40,000 Headmen Tour (Receiver 1999)★★★.
COMPILATIONS: The Best Of Dave Mason (Blue Thumb 1974)★★, Dave Mason At His Best (Blue Thumb 1975)★★, The Very Best Of Dave Mason (ABC 1978)★★★, The Best Of Dave Mason (Columbia 1981)★★★, Long Lost Friend: The Best Of Dave Mason (Sony 1995)★★★, Ultimate Collection (PolyGram 1999)★★★.

MASSIVE ATTACK
ALBUMS: Blue Lines (Wild Bunch/EMI 1991)★★★★★, Protection (EMI 1994)★★★, as Massive Attack Vs The Mad Professor No Protection (Circa 1995)★★★, Mezzanine (Virgin 1998)★★★★.
COMPILATIONS: The Singles Box 11-CD box set (Virgin 1998)★★★★.
VIDEOS: 11 Promos (Virgin 2001).

MASTER P
ALBUMS: Ghetto's Tryin' To Kill Me! (No Limit 1994)★★★, 99 Ways To Die (No Limit 1995)★★★, Ice Cream Man (No Limit 1996)★★★, Ghetto D (No Limit 1997)★★★, MP Da Last Don (No Limit 1998)★★★, Only God Can Judge Me (No Limit 1999)★★★, Ghetto Postage (No Limit 2000) ★★★, Gameface (New No Limit 2001)★★.
COMPILATIONS: Master P Presents ... West Coast Bad Boyz Vol. 1 (No Limit 90s)★★★, Master P Presents ... West Coast Bad Boyz II (No Limit 1997)★★★, No Limit Soldiers Compilation: We Can't Be Stopped (No Limit 1998)★★★.
VIDEOS: Master P Presents No Limit Records Video Compilation Vol. 1 (Ventura 1999).
FILMS: Rhyme & Reason (1997), No Tomorrow (1998), I Got The Hook-Up (1998), Takedown (1999), Lock Down (1999), Hot Boyz (1999), Foolish (1999).

MATCHBOX 20
ALBUMS: Yourself Or Someone Like You (Lava/Atlantic 1996)★★★, Mad Season (Lava/Atlantic 2000)★★★.

MATTHEWS SOUTHERN COMFORT
ALBUMS: Matthews Southern Comfort (UNI 1970)★★★, Second Spring (UNI 1970)★★★, Later That Same Year (UNI 1970)★★, as Southern Comfort Southern Comfort (1971)★★, as Southern Comfort Frog City (1971)★★, as Southern Comfort Stir Don't Shake (1972)★★, Scion 1970 recordings (Band Of Joy 1994)★★.
COMPILATIONS: Best Of Matthews Southern Comfort (MCA 1974)★★★, The Essential Collection (Half Moon 1997)★★★.

MATTHEWS, DAVE, BAND
ALBUMS: Remember Two Things (Bama Rags 1993)★★★, Under The Table And Dreaming (RCA 1994)★★★★, Crash (RCA 1996)★★★★, Live At Red Rocks 8.15.95 (RCA 1997)★★, Before These Crowded Streets (RCA 1998) ★★★, with Tim Reynolds Live At Luther College (Bama Rags/RCA 1999)★★★, Listener Supported (RCA 1999) ★★★, Everyday (RCA 2001)★★, Live In Chicago 12.19.98 At The United Center (RCA 2001)★★★.
VIDEOS: Listener Supported (BMG Video 1999), The Videos: 1994-2001 (BMG Video 2001).

MAVERICKS
ALBUMS: The Mavericks (Y&T 1990)★★★, From Hell To Paradise (MCA 1992)★★★, What A Crying Shame (MCA 1994)★★★★, Music For All Occasions (MCA 1995) ★★★★, Trampoline (MCA 1998)★★★★.
SOLO: Nick Kane Songs In The Key Of E (Demon 1999)★★★. Raul Malo Today (Higher Octave 2001)★★★.
COMPILATIONS: The Best Of The Mavericks (Mercury 1999)★★★★, 'O What A Thrill' An Introduction To The Mavericks (Island 2001)★★★.
VIDEOS: Live At The Royal Albert Hall (VVL 1999).

MAXWELL
ALBUMS: Maxwell's Urban Hang Suite (Columbia 1996) ★★★★, Embrya (Columbia 1998)★★★★, Now (Columbia 2001)★★★.

MAYALL, JOHN
ALBUMS: John Mayall Plays John Mayall (Decca 1965) ★★★★, Bluesbreakers With Eric Clapton (Decca 1966) ★★★★★, A Hard Road (Decca 1967)★★★★, Crusade (Decca 1967)★★★, The Blues Alone (Ace Of Clubs 1967)★★★★★, Diary Of A Band Vol. 1 (Decca 1968)★★★, Diary Of A Band Vol. 2 (Decca 1968)★★★, Bare Wires (Decca 1968)★★★★★, Blues From Laurel Canyon (Decca 1968)★★★★, Turning Point (Polydor 1969)★★★★, Empty Rooms (Polydor 1970)★★★★, USA Union (Polydor 1970)★★★, Back To The Roots (Polydor 1971)★★★, Beyond The Turning Point (Polydor 1971)★★★, Memories (Polydor 1971)★★★, Jazz Blues Fusion (Polydor 1972)★★★, Moving On (Polydor 1973)★★, Ten Years Are Gone (Polydor 1973)★★, Down The Line (London US 1973) ★★, The Latest Edition (Polydor 1975)★★, New Year, New Band, New Company (ABC 1975)★★, Time Expired, Notice To Appear (ABC 1975)★★, John Mayall (Polydor 1976)★★, A Banquet Of Blues (ABC 1976)★★, Lots Of People (ABC 1977) ★★, A Hard Core Package (ABC 1977)★★, Primal Solos (London 1977)★★★, Blues Roots (Decca 1978)★★, Last Of The British Blues (MCA 1978)★★, Bottom Line (DJM 1979)★★, No More Interviews (DJM 1979)★★★, Roadshow Blues (DJM 1980)★★, Last Edition (Polydor 1983)★★, Behind The Iron Curtain (PRT 1986)★★, Chicago Line (Island 1988)★★, Archives To Eighties (Polydor 1989)★★★, A Sense Of Place (Island 1990)★★★★, Wake Up Call (Silvertone 1993)★★★★, The 1982 Reunion Concert (Repertoire 1994)★★, Spinning Coin (Silvertone 1995)★★, Blues For The Lost Days (Silvertone 1997)★★★★, Padlock On The Blues (Eagle 1999)★★★, Rock The Blues 1970-71 recordings (Indigo 1999)H, Along For The Ride (Eagle 2001)★★★.
COMPILATIONS: Looking Back (Decca 1969)★★★★, World Of John Mayall (Decca 1970)★★★★, World Of John Mayall Volume 2 (Decca 1971)★★★★, Thru The Years (Decca 1971)★★★, The John Mayall Story Volume 1 (Decca 1983)★★★★, The John Mayall Story Volume 2 (Decca 1983)★★★, London Blues 1964-1969 (PolyGram 1992)★★★★, Room To Move 1969-1974 (PolyGram 1992)★★★★, As It All Began 1964-1969 (Deram 1998)★★★★, Silver Tones: The Best Of John Mayall & The Bluesbreakers (Silvertone 1998)★★★, Blues Power (Snapper 1999)★★★, Drivin' On: The ABC Years 1975-1982 (MCA 1999)★★, Reaching For The Blues '79 To '81 (Cleopatra 2000)★★★, Steppin' Out: An Introduction To John Mayall (Decca 2001)★★★.
VIDEOS: John Mayall's Bluesbreakers: Blues Alive (PVE 1995).
FURTHER READING: John Mayall: Blues Breaker, Richard Newman.

MAYFIELD, CURTIS
ALBUMS: Curtis (Buddah 1970)★★★, Curtis/Live! (Buddah 1971)★★★, Roots (Buddah 1971)★★★★, Superfly film soundtrack (Buddah 1972)★★★★★, Back To The World (Buddah 1973)★★★★, Curtis In Chicago (Buddah 1973)★★★, Sweet Exorcist (Buddah 1974)★★★, Got To Find A Way (Buddah 1974)★★★, Claudine film soundtrack (Buddah 1975)★★, Let's Do It Again (Curtom 1975)★★★, There's No Place Like America Today (Curtom 1975)★★★, Sparkle film soundtrack (Curtom 1976)★★, Give, Get, Take And Have (Curtom 1976)★★, Short Eyes film soundtrack (Curtom 1977)★★, Never Say You Can't Survive (Curtom 1977)★★, A Piece Of The Action film soundtrack (Curtom 1978)★★, Do It All Night (Curtom 1978)★★★, Heartbeat (RSO 1979)★★★, with Linda Clifford The Right Combination (RSO 1980)★★, Something To Believe In (RSO 1980)★★, Love Is The Place (Boardwalk 1981)★★, Honesty (Boardwalk 1983)★★★★, We Come In Peace With A Message Of Love (CRC 1985)★★★, Live In Europe (Ichiban 1988)★★★, People Get Ready (Essential 1990)★★★, Take It To The Streets (Curtom 1990)★★★★, BBC Radio 1 Live In Concert (Windsong 1994)★★, New World Order (Warners 1996)★★★★, Live At Ronnie Scott's 1988 recording (Sanctuary 2000)★★★.
COMPILATIONS: Of All Time (Curtom 1990)★★★, Tripping Out (Charly 1994)★★★, Living Legend (Curtom Classics 1995)★★★, People Get Ready: The Curtis Mayfield Story 3-CD box set (Rhino 1996)★★★★, Love Peace And Understanding 3-CD box set (Sequel 1997)★★★, Curtis: The Very Best Of (Beechwood 1998)★★★★, Gospel (Rhino 1999)★★★, Move On Up: The Singles Anthology 1970-90 (Sequel 1999)★★★★.
VIDEOS: Curtis Mayfield At Ronnie Scott's (Hendring Music Video 1988).
FILMS: Superfly (1972), The Groove Tube (1974).

MAZE (FEATURING FRANKIE BEVERLY)
ALBUMS: Maze Featuring Frankie Beverly (Capitol 1977) ★★★★, Golden Time Of Day (Capitol 1978)★★★★, Inspiration (Capitol 1979)★★★, Joy And Pain (Capitol 1980)★★★, Live In New Orleans (Capitol 1981)★★★★, We Are One (Capitol 1983)★★★★, Can't Stop The Love (Capitol 1985)★★★, Live In Los Angeles (Capitol 1986)★★★★, Silky Soul (Warners 1989)★★★, Back To Basics (Warners 1993)★★★.
COMPILATIONS: LifeLines: The Greatest Hits Of Maze Featuring Frankie Beverly (Capitol 1989)★★★★, Southern Girl (CEMA 1995)★★★, Anthology (Capitol 1996)★★★★, Greatest Slow Jams (Capitol 1998)★★★★.
VIDEOS: Live In New Orleans (Capitol 2001).

MAZZY STAR
ALBUMS: She Hangs Brightly (Rough Trade 1990)★★★, So Tonight That I Might See (Capitol 1993)★★★, Among My Swan (Capitol 1996)★★★.

MC5
ALBUMS: Kick Out The Jams (Elektra 1969)★★★★, Back In The USA (Elektra 1970)★★★, High Time (Elektra 1971)★★, Do It (Revenge 1987)★★, Live Detroit 68/69 (Revenge 1988)H, Motor City Is Burning (Castle 1999)H.
COMPILATIONS: Babes In Arms cassette only (ROIR 1983)★★★, Looking At You (Receiver 1994)★★★, Power Trip (Alive 1994)★★★, Thunder Express (Jungle 1999)★★★, '66 Breakout (Total Energy 1999)★★, The Big Bang! Best Of The MC5 (Rhino 2000)★★★.

McBRIDE, MARTINA
ALBUMS: The Time Has Come (RCA 1992)★★★, The Way That I Am (RCA 1993)★★★★, Wild Angels (RCA 1995) ★★★★, Evolution (RCA 1997)★★★, White Christmas (RCA 1998)★★, with Sara Evans, Mindy McCready, Lorrie Morgan Girls' Night Out (BNA 1999)★★★, Emotion (RCA 1999)★★★★.
COMPILATIONS: Greatest Hits (RCA 2001)★★★★.
VIDEOS: Independence Day (1994), Greatest Hits Video Collection (BMG 2001).

McCARTNEY, PAUL
ALBUMS: McCartney (Apple 1970)★★★, Ram (Apple 1971)★★★, McCartney II (Parlophone/Columbia 1980)★★, Tug Of War (Parlophone/Columbia 1982)★★, Pipes Of Peace (Parlophone/Columbia 1983)★★, Give My Regards To Broad Street film soundtrack (Parlophone/Columbia 1984)★, Press To Play (Parlophone/Capitol 1986)★★, Choba B CCCP (Melodiya 1988)★★★, Flowers In The Dirt (Parlophone/Capitol 1989)★★★, Tripping The Live Fantastic (Parlophone/Capitol 1990)★★, Tripping The Live Fantastic - Highlights! (Parlophone/Capitol 1990)★★★, Unplugged (The Official Bootleg) (Parlophone/Capitol 1991)★★★, Paul McCartney's Liverpool Oratorio (EMI Classics 1991)★★★, Choba B CCCP (The Russian Album) (Parlophone/Capitol 1991)★★★, Off The Ground (Parlophone/Capitol 1992) ★★, Paul Is Live (Parlophone/Capitol 1993)★★, as The Fireman Strawberries Oceans Ships Forest (Parlophone/Capitol 1994)★★★, Flaming Pie (Parlophone/Capitol 1997)★★★★, Paul McCartney's Standing Stone (EMI Classics 1997)★★, as The Fireman Rushes (Hydra/Capitol 1998)★★★, Run Devil Run (Parlophone 1999)★★★★, Working Classical (EMI Classics 1999)★★★, Liverpool Sound Collage (Hydra/Capitol 2000)★★★, Driving Rain (Parlophone/Capitol 2001)★★.
COMPILATIONS: All The Best! (Parlophone/Capitol 1987)★★★★.
VIDEOS: The Paul McCartney Special (Music Club 1987), Once Upon A Video (CMV 1987), Put It There (CMV 1989), Get Back (M 1991), Movin' On (MPI 1993), Paul Is Live In Concert On The New World Tour (PMI 1994), In The World Tonight (PNV/Rhino 1997), Live At The Cavern Club! (Image Entertainment 2001), Paul McCartney & Friends: The PETA Concert For Party Animals (Aviva International 2001), Wingspan (Hits & History) (Capitol Video 2001).
FURTHER READING: Body Count, Francie Schwartz. The Paul McCartney Story, George Tremlett. Paul McCartney In His Own Words, Paul Gambaccini. Paul McCartney: A Biography In Words & Pictures, John Mendelsohn. Paul McCartney: Composer/Artist, Paul McCartney. Paul McCartney: The Definitive Biography, Chris Welch. McCartney, Chris Salewicz. McCartney: The Biography, Chet Flippo. Blackbird: The Life And Times Of Paul McCartney, Geoffrey Giuliano. Paul McCartney: Behind The Myth, Ross Benson. McCartney: Yesterday & Today, Ray Coleman. Roadworks, Linda McCartney. Paul McCartney: Many Years From Now, Barry Miles, Linda McCartney: The Biography, Danny Fields. Paintings, Paul McCartney. I Saw Him Standing There, Jorie B. Gracen. Blackbird Singing: Poems And Lyrics 1965-1999, Paul McCartney.
FILMS: A Hard Day's Night (1964), Help! (1965), Magical Mystery Tour (1967), Yellow Submarine (1968), Let It Be (1970), Give My Regards To Broad Street (1984), Eat The Rich (1987), Get Back (1991).

McCOYS
ALBUMS: Hang On Sloopy (Bang 1965)★★★, You Make Me Feel So Good (Bang 1966)★★★, Infinite McCoys (Mercury 1968)H, Human Ball (Mercury 1969)★.
COMPILATIONS: Psychedelic Years (One Way 1994)★★★, Hang On Sloopy: The Best Of The McCoys (Legacy 1995)★★★★.

McDONALD, COUNTRY JOE
ALBUMS: Country Joe And Blair Hardman (No Label 1964) ★★, Thinking Of Woody Guthrie (Vanguard 1969)★★★, Tonight I'm Singing Just For You (Vanguard 1970)★★★, Quiet Days In Clichy film soundtrack (Sonet 1970)★★, Hold On It's Coming (Vanguard 1971)★★, War, War, War (Vanguard 1971)★★, Incredible! Live! (Vanguard 1972)★★, The Paris Sessions (Vanguard 1973)★★★, Country Joe (Vanguard 1974)★★★, Paradise With An Ocean View (Fantasy 1975) ★★, Love Is A Fire (Fantasy 1976)★★, Goodbye Blues (Fantasy 1977)★★, Rock 'N' Roll Music From The Planet Earth (Fantasy 1978)★★, Leisure Suite (Fantasy 1979)★★, On My Own (Rag Baby 1981)★★, Animal Tracks (Animus 1983)★★, Into The Fray (Sweet Thunder 1982)★★, Child's Play (Rag Baby 1983) ★★, Peace On Earth (Line 1989)★★, Vietnam Experience (Line 1989)★★.
COMPILATIONS: The Best Of Country Joe McDonald (Vanguard 1973)★★★, The Essential Country Joe McDonald (Vanguard 1975)★★★, A Golden Hour Of Country Joe McDonald (Pye 1977)★★, Classics (Big Beat 1989)★★★, Something Borrowed, Something New (Big Beat 1998)★★★.

McDONALD, MICHAEL
ALBUMS: If That's What It Takes (Warners 1982)★★★★, No Lookin' Back (Warners 1985)★★★, Lonely Talk (Warners 1989)★★★, Take It To Heart (Reprise 1990)★★★, Blink Of An Eye (Reprise 1993)★★, Blue Obsession (Ramp 2000) ★★★, In The Spirit: A Christmas Album (MCA 2001)★★.
COMPILATIONS: That Was Then: The Early Recordings Of Michael McDonald (Arista 1982)★★, Sweet Freedom: Best Of Michael McDonald (Warners 1986)★★★, The Very Best Of Michael McDonald (Rhino 2001)★★★★.
VIDEOS: A Gathering Of Friends (Aviva International 2001).

McENTIRE, REBA
ALBUMS: Reba McEntire (Mercury 1977)★★, Out Of A Dream (Mercury 1979)★★★, Feel The Fire (Mercury 1980) ★★★, Heart To Heart (Mercury 1981)★★★, Unlimited (Mercury 1982)★★★, Behind The Scene (Mercury 1983) ★★★, Just A Little Love (MCA 1984)★★★, Have I Got A Deal For You (MCA 1985)★★★, My Kind Of Country (MCA 1986)★★★, Whoever's In New England (MCA 1986)★★★, Reba Nell McEntire (MCA 1986)★★★, What Am I Gonna Do About You (MCA 1986)★★★, The Last One To Know (MCA 1987)★★★, So So So Long (MCA 1988)★★★, Merry Christmas To You (MCA 1988)★★★, Reba (MCA 1988) ★★★, Sweet Sixteen (MCA 1989)★★★, Live (MCA 1989) ★★★, Rumour Has It (MCA 1990)★★★★, For My Broken Heart (MCA 1991)★★★, It's Your Call (MCA 1992)★★★★, Read My Mind (MCA 1994)★★★★, Starting Over (MCA 1995)★★★★, What If It's You (MCA 1996)★★★, If You See Him (MCA 1998)★★★★, So Good Together (MCA 1999)★★★, Secret Of Giving: A Christmas Collection (MCA 1999)★★.
COMPILATIONS: The Best Of Reba McEntire (Mercury 1985)★★★★, The Very Best Of Reba McEntire (Country Store 1987)★★★, Greatest Hits (MCA 1987)★★★★, Greatest Hits Volume 2 (MCA 1993)★★★★, Moments & Memories: The Best Of Reba McEntire (Universal 1998)★★★★, I'll Be (MCA 2000)★★★, Greatest Hits Volume III: I'm A Survivor (MCA 2001)★★★.
VIDEOS: Reba In Concert (1992), For My Broken Heart (1993), Greatest Hits (MCA 1994), Why Haven't I Heard From You (Picture Vision 1994), Reba Live (MCA 1995), And Still (MCA 1995), Reba Celebrating 20 Years (MCA 1996), The Video Collection (MCA Video 1999).
FURTHER READING: Reba: Country Music's Queen, Don Cusic. Reba - My Story, Reba McEntire with Tom Carter. Comfort From A Country Quilt, Reba McEntire.
FILMS: Tremors (1990), The Gambler Returns: The Luck Of The Draw (1991), North (1994), The Little Rascals (1994).

McGARRIGLE, KATE AND ANNA
ALBUMS: Kate And Anna McGarrigle (Warners 1975) ★★★★, Dancer With Bruised Knees (Warners 1977)★★★★, Pronto Monto (Warners 1978)★★★, French Record (Hannibal 1980)★★★★, Love Over And Over (Polydor 1982)★★★★, Heartbeats Accelerating (Private Music 1990)★★★★, Matapedia (Hannibal 1996)★★★★, with various artists The McGarrigle Hour (Hannibal 1998)★★★★.

McGRAW, TIM
ALBUMS: Tim McGraw (Curb 1993)★★★, Not A Moment Too Soon (Curb 1994)★★★★, All I Want (Curb/Hit 1995)★★★★, Everywhere (Curb 1997)★★★★, A Place In The Sun (Curb 1999)★★★, Set This Circus Down (Curb 2001)★★★.
COMPILATIONS: Greatest Hits (Curb 2000)★★★★.
VIDEOS: Indian Outlaw (Curb 1994), Refried Dreams (Curb 1995), An Hour With Tim (Curb 1995), It's Your Love (Curb 1997).

McGRIFF, JIMMY
ALBUMS: I've Got A Woman (Sue 1962)★★★, One Of Mine (Sue 1963)★★★, Jimmy McGriff At The Apollo (Sue 1963)★★★, Jimmy McGriff At The Organ (Sue 1963) ★★★★, Topkapi (Sue 1964)★★★, One Of Mine (Sue 1964)★★★, Blues For Mister Jimmy (Sue 1965)★★★★, The Big Band Of Jimmy McGriff (Solid State 1966)★★★★, Tribute To Count Basie (LRC 1966)★★★, A Bag Full Of Soul (Solid State 1966)★★★★, Cherry (Solid State 1967)★★★, Honey (Solid State 1968)★★★, The Worm (Solid State 1968)★★★★, A Thing To Come By (Solid State 1969)★★, Electric Funk (Blue Note 1969)★★, Groove Grease (Groove Merchant 1971)★★★, Black And Blues (Groove Merchant 1971)★★★, Let's Stay Together (Simitar 1972)★★★, Fly Dude (Groove Merchant 1972)★★★, Come Together (Groove Merchant 1973)★★★, Main Squeeze (Groove Merchant 1974)★★★, City Lights (Jazz America 1981)★★, Movin' Upside The Blues (Jazz America 1982)★★★, The Countdown (Milestone 1983)★★★, Skywalk (Milestone 1985)★★★, Steppin' Up (Milestone c.1985)★★★, State Of The Art (Milestone 1986)★★★, with Hank Crawford Soul Survivors (Milestone 1986)★★★★, The Starting Five (Milestone 1987)★★★, Blue To The Bone (Milestone 1988) ★★, On The Blue Side (Milestone 1990)★★★, You Ought To Think About Me (Headfirst 1990)★★★, In A Blue Mood (Headfirst 1991)★★, Right Turn On Blues (Telarc 1994)★★★, with Crawford Blues Groove (Telarc 1996)★★★★, The Dream Team (Milestone 1997)★★★★, Straight Up (Milestone 1999)★★, with Crawford Crunch Time (Milestone 1999) ★★★, McGriff's House Party (Milestone 2000)★★★★, Feelin' It (Milestone 2001)★★★.
COMPILATIONS: A Toast To Jimmy McGriff's Golden Classics (Collectable 1989)★★★, Georgia On My Mind 60s, 70s recordings (LRC 1990)★★★★, The Funkiest Little Band In The Land 1968-74 recordings (LRC 1992)★★★, Pullin' Out The Stops! The Best Of Jimmy McGriff (Blue Note 1994)★★★★.

McGUINN, ROGER
ALBUMS: Roger McGuinn (Columbia 1973)★★★★, Peace On You (Columbia 1974)★★★, Roger McGuinn And Band (Columbia 1975)★★★, Cardiff Rose (Columbia 1976) ★★★★, Thunderbyrd (Columbia 1977)★★★, Back From Rio (Arista 1990)★★★, Live From Mars (Hollywood 1996)★★, Treasures From The Folk Den (Appleseed 2001)★★★.
COMPILATIONS: Born To Rock 'n' Roll (Columbia Legacy 1992)★★★★.
VIDEOS: The 12-String Guitar Of Roger McGuinn (Homespun Video 1996).
FURTHER READING: Timeless Flight: The Definitive Biography Of The Byrds, Johnny Rogan. Timeless Flight Revisited: The Sequel, Johnny Rogan.

McGUIRE, BARRY
ALBUMS: The Barry McGuire Album (Horizon 1963)★★★, Star Folk With Barry McGuire (Surrey 1965)★★, Eve Of Destruction (1965)★★★, This Precious Time (Dunhill 1966) ★★★, Star Folk With Barry McGuire Vol. 2 (Surrey 1966) ★★, Star Folk With Barry McGuire Vol. 3 (Surrey 1966)★★, Star Folk With Barry McGuire Vol. 4 (Surrey 1966)★★, Barry McGuire Featuring Eve of Destruction (Dunhill 1966) ★★★, The Eve Of Destruction Man (Ember 1966)H, The World's Last Private Citizen (Dunhill 1968)★★, Barry McGuire And The Doctor (Ode 1971)★★, Seeds (Myrrh 1973)★★, Narnia (Myrrh 1974)★★, Lighten Up (Myrrh 1975)★★★, C'mon Along (Sparrow 1976)★★, Have You Heard (Sparrow 1976)★★★, Cosmic Cowboy (Sparrow 1979)★★, To The Bride (Myrrh 1982)★★.
COMPILATIONS: The Best Of Barry McGuire (Sparrow 1982)★★, Anthology (One Way 1994)★★★.

McKEE, MARIA
ALBUMS: Maria McKee (Geffen 1989)★★★, You Gotta Sin To Get Saved (Geffen 1993)★★★, Life Is Sweet (Geffen 1996)★★★★.

McKENZIE, SCOTT
ALBUMS: The Voice Of Scott McKenzie (Ode/Columbia 1967)★★, Stained Glass Morning (1970)★★.

McKNIGHT, BRIAN
ALBUMS: Brian McKnight (Mercury 1992)★★, I Remember You (Mercury 1995)★★★★, Anytime (Mercury 1997) ★★★★, Bethlehem (Motown 1998)★★★, Back At One (Motown 1999)★★★, Superhero (Motown 2001)★★★.
VIDEOS: Music In High Places (Aviva International 2001).

McLACHLAN, SARAH
ALBUMS: Touch (Arista 1988)★★★, Solace (Arista 1992)★★★, Fumbling Towards Ecstasy (Arista 1994) ★★★★, The Freedom Sessions (Nettwerk/Arista 1995)★★, Surfacing (Arista 1997)★★★★, Mirrorball (Arista 1999)★★★.
COMPILATIONS: Remixed (Nettwerk 2001)★★★.
VIDEOS: Mirrorball (BMG Video 1999).

McLEAN, DON
ALBUMS: Tapestry (Mediarts 1970)★★, American Pie (United Artists 1971)★★★★, Don McLean (United Artists 1972)★★★, Playin' Favorites (United Artists 1973)★★, Homeless Brother (United Artists 1974)★★, Solo (United Artists 1976)★★★, Prime Time (Arista 1977)★★, Chain Lightning (Millennium 1980)★★, Believers (Millennium 1981)★★, Dominion (Millennium 1983)★★★, For The Memories, Vols. 1 & 2 (Gold Castle 1989)★★, Christmas (Curb 1991)★★, The River Of Love (Curb 1996)★★, Christmas Dreams (Hip-O 1997)★★, Greatest Hits Live 1980 recording (Hip-O 1997)★★.
COMPILATIONS: The Very Best Of Don McLean (United Artists 1980)★★, Don McLean's Greatest Hits: Then And Now (EMI 1987)★★★, Love Tracks (Capitol 1987)★★, The Best Of Don McLean (EMI 1991)★★★, Classics (Curb 1992)★★★, Favorites & Rarities (EMI 1992)★★★★, American Pie: The Greatest Hits (EMI 2000)★★★.

McNABB, IAN
ALBUMS: Truth And Beauty (This Way Up 1993)★★★★, Head Like A Rock (This Way Up 1994)★★★, Merseybeast (This Way Up 1996)★★★★, A Party Political Broadcast On Behalf Of The Emotional Party (Fairfield 1998)★★★, Ian McNabb (Sanctuary 2001)★★★★, Live At Life (Castle 2001)★★★.
COMPILATIONS: Waifs & Strays (Evangeline 2001)★★★.

McTELL, RALPH
ALBUMS: Eight Frames A Second (Transatlantic 1968)★★★, Spiral Staircase (Transatlantic 1969)★★★, My Side Of Your Window (Transatlantic 1970)★★★, You Well-Meaning Brought Me Here (Famous 1971)★★★★, Not Until Tomorrow (Reprise 1972)★★★★, Easy (Reprise 1974)★★★, Streets (Warners 1975)★★★, Right Side Up (Warners 1976)★★★, Ralph, Albert & Sydney (Warners 1977)★★★, Slide Away The Screen (Warners 1979)★★★, Love Grows (Mays

1982)★★★, Water Of Dreams (Mays 1982)★★★, Weather The Storm (Mays 1982)★★★, Songs From Alphabet Zoo (Mays 1983)★★★, The Best Of Alphabet Zoo (MFP 1984) ★★★, At The End Of A Perfect Day (Telstar 1985)★★★, Tickle On The Tum (Mays 1986)★★★, Bridge Of Sighs (Mays 1987)★★★, The Ferryman (Mays 1987)★★★, Blue Skies, Black Heroes (Leola 1988)★★★, Stealin' Back. (Essential 1990)★★★, The Boy With The Note (Leola 1992)★★★, Alphabet Zoo (The Road Goes On Forever 1994)★★★, Sand In Your Shoes (Transatlantic 1995)★★★, Travelling Man (Leola 1999)★★★, Red Sky (Leola 2000)★★★.
COMPILATIONS: Ralph McTell Revisited (Transatlantic 1970) ★★★, The Ralph McTell Collection (Pickwick 1978)★★★, Streets Of London (Transatlantic 1981)★★★, 71/72 (Mays 1982)★★, Ralph McTell At His Best (Cambra 1985)★★★, From Clare To Here: The Songs Of Ralph McTell (Red House 1996)★★★★, The Definitive Transatlantic Collection (Essential 1997)★★★★, Spiral Staircase: Classic Songs (Snapper 1998)★★★.
FURTHER READING: Streets Of London: The Official Biography Of Ralph McTell, Chris Hockenhull. Angel Laughter: Autobiography Volume One, Ralph McTell.

MEAT LOAF
ALBUMS: Meat Loaf & Stoney (Rare Earth 1971)★★, Bat Out Of Hell (Epic 1977)★★★★, Dead Ringer (Epic 1981) ★★★, Midnight At The Lost And Found (Epic 1983)★★★, Bad Attitude (Arista/RCA 1984)★★, Blind Before I Stop (Arista 1986)★★★, Meat Loaf Live (Arista 1987)★★★, Bat Out Of Hell II: Back Into Hell (Virgin 1993)★★★, Alive In Hell (Pure Music 1994)★★★, Welcome To The Neighborhood (Virgin 1995)★★★, Live Around The World (Tommy Boy 1996)★★★.
COMPILATIONS: Hits Out Of Hell (Epic 1984)★★★, Rock'n'Roll Hero (Pickwick 1994)★★★, Definitive Collection (Alex 1995) ★★, The Very Best Of Meat Loaf (Virgin 1998)★★★.
VIDEOS: Live At Wembley (Videoform 1984), Hits Out Of Hell (Epic 1985), Bad Attitude Live! (Virgin Vision 1986), Meat Loaf Live (RCA 1992), Bat Out Of Hell II: Picture Show (MCA 1994), The Very Best Of Meat Loaf (SMV 1998).
FURTHER READING: Meatloaf: Jim Steinman And The Phenomenology Of Excess, Sandy Robertson. To Hell And Back: An Autobiography, Meat Loaf with David Dalton.
FILMS: The Rocky Horror Picture Show (1975), Scavenger Hunt (1979), Americathon (1979), Roadie (1980), Der Formel Eins Film (1985), Out Of Bounds (1986), The Squeeze (1987), Dead Ringer (1991), Motorama (1992), Leap Of Faith (1992), Wayne's World (1992), The Gun In Betty Lou's Handbag (1992), Spice World (1997), The Mighty (1998), Gunshy (1998), Black Dog (1998), Outside Ozona (1998), The Hurdy Gurdy Man (1999), Fight Club (1999), Crazy In Alabama (1999).

MEAT PUPPETS
ALBUMS: Meat Puppets (SST 1982)★★, Meat Puppets II (SST 1983)★★★, Up On The Sun (SST 1985)★★★, Mirage (SST 1987)★★★★, Huevos (SST 1987)★★★, Monsters (SST 1989)★★★, Forbidden Places (London 1991)★★★, Too High To Die (London 1994)★★★, No Joke! (London 1995)★★★, Live In Montana 1988 recording (Rykodisc 1999)★★★, Golden Lies (Breaking/Atlantic 2000)★★, Live At Maxwell's (DCN 2002)★★.
COMPILATIONS: No Strings Attached (SST 1990)★★★.

MEDESKI, MARTIN AND WOOD
ALBUMS: Notes From The Underground (Accurate 1992)★★★, It's A Jungle In Here (Gramavision/Rykodisc 1993)★★★★, Friday Afternoon In The Universe (Gramavision/Rykodisc 1995)★★★★, Shack-man (Gramavision/Rykodisc 1996)★★★, Combustication (Blue Note 1998)★★★★, Tonic (Blue Note 2000)★★★, The Dropper (Blue Note 2000)★★★, Uninvisible (Blue Note 2002)★★★.
COMPILATIONS: Last Chance To Dance Trance (Perhaps), Best Of (1991-1996) (Gramavision 1999)★★★★.

MEDICINE HEAD
ALBUMS: Old Bottles New Medicine (Dandelion 1970) ★★★, Heavy On The Drum (Dandelion 1971)★★★, Dark Side Of The Moon (Dandelion 1972)★★★, One And One Is One (Polydor 1973)★★★, Thru' A Five (Polydor 1974) ★★, Two Man Band (Polydor 1976)★★, Timepeace, Live In London 1975 (Red Steel 1995)★★.
COMPILATIONS: Medicine Head (Polydor 1976)★★★, Best Of Medicine Head (Polydor 1981)★★★.

MEGADETH
ALBUMS: Killing Is My Business ... And Business Is Good! (Combat/Megaforce 1985)★★, Peace Sells ... But Who's Buying? (Capitol 1986)★★★, So Far, So Good ... So What! (Capitol 1988)★★★, Rust In Peace (Capitol 1990) ★★★★, Countdown To Extinction (Capitol 1992)★★★, Youthanasia (Capitol 1994)★★★, Cryptic Writings (Capitol 1997)★★★, Risk (Capitol 1999)★★★, The World Needs A Hero (Sanctuary 2001)★★★, Rude Awakening (Sanctuary 2002)★★.
COMPILATIONS: Hidden Treasures (Capitol 1995)★★★, Capitol Punishment: The Megadeth Years (Capitol 2000)★★★★.
VIDEOS: Rusted Pieces (EMI 1991), Exposure Of A Dream (PMI 1993), Evolver: The Making Of Youthanasia (Capitol 1995), VH1 Behind The Music (Extended) (BMG Video 2001).

MEKONS
ALBUMS: The Quality Of Mercy Is Not Strnen (Virgin 1979)★★★, Mekons aka Devil Rats And Piggies A Special Message From Godzilla (Red Rhino 1980)★★★, Fear And Whiskey (Sin 1985)★★★, The Edge Of The World (Sin 1986)★★★, The Mekons Honky Tonkin' (Sin/Cooking Vinyl 1987)★★★, So Good It Hurts (Sin/Cooking Vinyl 1988) ★★★, Rock N' Roll (Blast First/A&M 1989)★★★, The Curse Of The Mekons (Blast First/Mute 1991)★★★, I Love Mekons (Quarterstick/Touch And Go 1993)★★★, Retreat From Memphis (Quarterstick 1994)★★★, with Kathy Acker Pussy, King Of The Pirates (Scout 1996)★★★, Mekons United CD/Novel (Quarterstick 1996)★★, Me (Quarterstick 1998)★★★, Journey To The End Of The Night (Quarterstick 2000)★★★★.
COMPILATIONS: It Falleth Like Gentle Rain From Heaven: The Mekons Story (CNT Productions 1982)★★★, New York cassette only (ROIR 1987)★★★, Original Sin (Rough Trade/TwinTone 1989)★★★, I Have Been To Heaven And Back: Hen's Teeth And Other Lost Fragments Of Unpopular Culture Vol. 1 (Quarterback 1999)★★★, Where Were You?: Hen's Teeth And Other Lost Fragments Of Unpopular Culture Vol. 2 (Quarterback 1999)★★★, New York On The Road 86-87 (ROIR 2001)★★★.
FURTHER READING: Mekons United, no author listed.

MELANIE
ALBUMS: Born To Be reissued as My First Album (Buddah 1969)★★, Affectionately Melanie (Buddah 1969)★★, Candles In The Rain (Buddah 1970)★★★, Leftover Wine (Buddah 1970)★★★, The Good Book (Buddah 1971)★★★, Gather Me (Neighborhood 1971)★★★, Garden In The City (Buddah 1971)★★, Stoneground Words (Neighborhood 1972)★★, Melanie At Carnegie Hall (Neighborhood 1973)★★, Please Love Me (Buddah 1973)★★, Madrugada (Neighborhood 1974)★★, As I See It Now (Neighborhood 1974)★★, Sunset And Other Beginnings (Neighborhood 1975)★★, Photograph (Atlantic 1976)★★, Phonogenic - Not Just Another Pretty Face (Midsong 1978)★★★, Ballroom Streets (Tomato 1979)★★, Arabesque (Blanche 1982)★★, Seventh Wave (Neighborhood 1983)★★, Am I Real Or What (Amherst 1985)★★, Cowabonga (Food For Thought 1989)★★, Freedom Knows My Name (Lonestar 1993)★★, Old Bitch Warrior (Creastars/BMG 1995)★★★, Unchained Melanie (VTM 1996)★★, Her Greatest Hits Live & New (Laserlight 1996)★★, On Air (Strange Fruit 1997) ★★, Antlers (Blue Moon 1997)★★.
COMPILATIONS: The Four Sides Of Melanie (Buddah 1972) ★★★, The Very Best Of Melanie (Buddah 1973)★★★, The Best Of Melanie (Rhino 1990)★★★, Best Of The Rest Of Melanie: The Buddah Years (Sequel 1992)★★, Oldie Giant (Spectrum 1997)★★, Acoustic Blue: The Very Best Of Melanie (Laserlight 1997)★★★, The Encore Collection (BMG 1997)★★★, The Very Best Of Melanie (Camden 1998) ★★★, Ring The Living Bell: A Collection (Renaissance 1999)★★★, Beautiful People: The Greatest Hits Of Melanie (Buddah 1999)★★★.

MELLENCAMP, JOHN
ALBUMS: Chestnut Street Incident (MainMan 1976)★★, The Kid Inside (Castle 1977)★★, A Biography (Riva 1978)★★, John Cougar (Riva 1979)★★★, Nothing Matters And What If It Did (Riva 1981)H, American Fool (Riva 1982)★★★, Uh-Huh (Riva 1983)★★★, Scarecrow (Riva 1985)★★★, The Lonesome Jubilee (Mercury 1987)★★★, Big Daddy (Mercury 1989) ★★★, Whenever We Wanted (Mercury 1991)★★★, Human Wheels (Mercury 1993)★★★, Dance Naked (Mercury 1994) ★★★, Mr. Happy Go Lucky (Mercury 1996)★★★, John Mellencamp (Columbia 1998)★★★★, Cuttin' Heads (Columbia 2001)★★★.
COMPILATIONS: Early Years (Rhino 1986)★★, The John Cougar Collection (Castle 1986)★★★, The Best That I Could Do 1978-1988 (Mercury 1997)★★★, Rough Harvest (Mercury 1999)★★★.
VIDEOS: John Cougar Mellencamp: Ain't That America (Embassy 1984).
FURTHER READING: American Fool: The Roots And Improbable Rise Of John Cougar Mellencamp, Torgoff. Mellencamp: Paintings And Reflections, John Mellencamp.
FILMS: Falling From Grace (1992).

MELVIN, HAROLD, AND THE BLUE NOTES
ALBUMS: Harold Melvin & The Blue Notes (Philadelphia International 1972)★★★, Black & Blue (Philadelphia International 1973)★★★★, To Be True (Philadelphia International 1975)★★★★, Wake Up Everybody (Philadelphia International 1975)★★★★, Reaching For The World (ABC 1977)★★★★, Now Is The Time (ABC 1977)★★, The Blue Album (Source 1980)★★, All Things Happen In Time (MCA 1981)★★, Talk It Up (Tell Everybody) (Philly World 1984)★★.
COMPILATIONS: All Their Greatest Hits! (Philadelphia International 1976)★★★★, Greatest Hits (Columbia 1985)★★★, Satisfaction Guaranteed: The Best Of Harold Melvin And The Blue Notes (Philadelphia International 1992)★★★, If You Don't Know Me By Now: The Best Of Harold Melvin & The Blue Notes (Epic/Legacy 1995) ★★★★, Blue Notes & Ballads (Sony 1998)★★★★.

MELVINS
ALBUMS: Gluey Porch Treatments (Alchemy 1987)★★★, Ozma (Boner 1989)★★, Bullhead (Boner 1990)★★, 10 Songs (C/Z/ 1991)★★, Melvins aka Lysol (Boner/Tupelo 1992)★★★, Houdini (Atlantic 1993)★★★★, as Snivlem Prick (Amphetamine Reptile 1994)H, Stoner Witch (Atlantic 1994)★★★, Live (X-mas 1996)★★, Stag (Mammoth/Atlantic 1996)★★★★, Honky (Amphetamine Reptile 1997)★★, Live At The F*cker Club: Australia (Amphetamine Reptile 1998)★★, The Maggot (Ipecac 1999)★★★★, The Bootlicker (Ipecac 1999)★★★, The Crybaby (Ipecac 2000)★★, Electroretard (Man's Ruin 2001)★★★, Colossus Of Destiny (Ipecac 2001)★★.
COMPILATIONS: Singles 1-12 (Amphetamine Reptile 1997)★★★.

MEMPHIS HORNS
ALBUMS: Memphis Horns (Cotillion 1970)★★★, Horns For Everything (Million 1972)★★★, High On Music (RCA 1976)★★, Get Up And Dance (RCA 1977)★★, Memphis Horns Band II (RCA 1978)★★★, Welcome To Memphis (RCA 1979)★★, Flame Out (Lucky 7 1992)★★★.

MERCHANT, NATALIE
ALBUMS: Tigerlily (Elektra 1995)★★★★, Ophelia (Elektra 1998)★★★, Live In Concert New York City June 12, 1999 (Elektra 1999)★★★, Motherland (Elektra 2001)★★★.
VIDEOS: Live In Concert New York City June 12, 1999 (Elektra 1999).

MERCURY REV
ALBUMS: Yerself Is Steam (Rough Trade/Mint Films 1991) ★★★, Boces (Columbia/Beggars Banquet 1993)★★, See You On The Other Side (Work/Beggars Banquet 1995) ★★★, Deserter's Songs (V2 1998)★★★★, All Is Dream (V2 2001)★★★★.

MERSEYBEATS
ALBUMS: The Merseybeats (Fontana 1964)★★★★.
COMPILATIONS: Greatest Hits (Look 1977)★★★, The Merseybeats; Beat And Ballads (Edsel 1982)★★★★, The Very Best Of The Merseybeats (Spectrum 1997)★★★★.

MESSINA, JO DEE
ALBUMS: Jo Dee Messina (Curb 1996)★★★, I'm Alright (Curb 1998)★★★★, Burn (Curb 2000)★★★★.

METALLICA
ALBUMS: Kill 'Em All (Megaforce 1983)★★★, Ride The Lightning (Megaforce 1984)★★★, Master Of Puppets (Elektra 1986)★★★★, And Justice For All (Elektra 1988) ★★★, Metallica (Elektra 1991)★★★★, Live Shit: Binge & Purge 3-CD/video set (Elektra 1993)★★★★, Load (Mercury 1996)★★★★, Reload (Vertigo 1997)★★★, Garage Inc. (Vertigo 1998)★★★, S&M (Vertigo 1999)★★.
VIDEOS: Cliff 'Em All (C.hannel 5 1988), 2 Of One (Channel 5 1989), A Year And A Half In The Life Of Metallica (PolyGram Music Video 1992), Metal Up Your Ass: The Interview Sessions (Startalk 1996), Cunning Stunts (PolyGram Music Video 1998), S&M (Elektra Entertainment 1999), Classic Albums: Metallica (Eagle Vision 2001).
FURTHER READING: A Visual Documentary, Mark Putterford. In Their Own Words, Mark Putterford. Metallica Unbound, K.J. Doughton. Metallica's Lars Ulrich: An Up-Close Look At The Playing Style Of ..., Dino Fauci. Metallica Unbound, K.J. Doughton. Metallica Live!, Mark Putterford. Metallica: The Frayed Ends Of Metal, Chris Crocker. The Making Of: Metallica's Metallica, Mick Wall and Malcolm Dome. From Silver To Black, Ross Halfin.

METHENY, PAT
ALBUMS: Bright Size Life (ECM 1976)★★★★, Watercolors (ECM 1977)★★★, Pat Metheny Group (ECM 1978)★★★★, New Chautauqua (ECM 1979)★★★★, American Garage (ECM 1979)★★★★, 80/81 (ECM 1980)★★★, with Lyle Mays As Falls Wichita, So Falls Wichita Falls (ECM 1981) ★★★★, Offramp (ECM 1982)★★★★, Travels (ECM 1983) ★★★★, with Charlie Haden, Billy Higgins Rejoicing (ECM 1983)★★★, First Circle (ECM 1984)★★★, The Falcon And The Snowman film soundtrack (EMI America 1985)★★, with Ornette Coleman Song X (Geffen 1986)★★★, Still Life (Talking) (Geffen 1987)★★★★, Letter From Home (Geffen 1989)★★★, with Gary Burton Reunion (Geffen 1989) ★★★★, Question And Answer (Geffen 1990)★★★★, Secret Story (Geffen 1992)★★★★, The Road To You: Recorded Live In Europe (Geffen 1993)★★★, with John Scofield I Can See Your House From Here (Blue Note 1994)★★★, Zero Tolerance For Silence (Geffen 1994)★, We Live Here (Geffen 1995)★★★★, Quartet (Geffen 1997)★★★, Beyond The Missouri Sky (Short Stories By Charlie Haden & Pat Metheny) (Verve 1997)★★★★, Imaginary Day (Warners 1997)★★★★, with Derek Bailey, Gregg Bendian, Paul Wertico The Sign Of 4 3-CD set (Knitting Factory Works 1997)★★★★, with Burton, Chick Corea, Roy Haynes, Dave Holland Like Minds (Concord Jazz 1998)★★★★, Jim Hall & Pat Metheny (Telarc 1999)★★★, A Map Of The World (Warners 1999)★★★★, Trio 99-00 (Warners 2000)★★★★, Trio - Live (Warners 2000)★★★★, Speaking Of Now (Warners 2002)★★★.
COMPILATIONS: Works (ECM 1983)★★★★, Works II (ECM 1988)★★★★.
VIDEOS: More Travels (Geffen 1993).

METHOD MAN
ALBUMS: Tical (Def Jam 1994)★★★, Tical 2000: Judgement Day (Def Jam 1998)★★★, with Redman Blackout! (Def Jam 1999)★★★.
FILMS: The Show (1995), The Great White Hype (1996), Rhyme & Reason (1997), One Eight Seven (1997), Cop Land (1997), Belly (1998), P.I.G.S. (1999), Black And White (1999), Boricua's Bond (2000).

MICHAEL, GEORGE
ALBUMS: Faith (Epic 1987)★★★★, Listen Without Prejudice, Vol. 1 (Epic 1990)★★★, Older (Virgin 1996)★★★, Songs From The Last Century (Aegean/Virgin 1999)★★.
COMPILATIONS: Ladies & Gentlemen: The Best Of George Michael (Epic 1998)★★★★.
CD-ROM: Older/Upper (Aegean/Virgin 1998)★★★.
VIDEOS: Faith (CMV Enterprises 1988), George Michael (CMV Enterprises 1990), The Video Selection (SMV 1998).
FURTHER READING: Wham! (Confidential) The Death Of A Supergroup, Johnny Rogan. George Michael: The Making Of A Super Star, Bruce Dessau. Bare, George Michael with Tony Parsons. In His Own Words, Nigel Goodall. Older: The Unauthorised Biography Of George Michael, Nicholas and Tim Wapshott.

MICRODISNEY
ALBUMS: Everybody Is Fantastic (Rough Trade 1984)★★★, We Hate You White South African Bastards mini-album (Rough Trade 1984)★★, The Clock Comes Down The Stairs (Rough Trade 1985)★★★, Crooked Mile (Virgin 1987) ★★★, 39 Minutes (Virgin 1988)★★★.
COMPILATIONS: Peel Sessions (Strange Fruit 1989)★★★★, Big Sleeping House (Virgin 1995)★★★★.

MIDNIGHT OIL
ALBUMS: Midnight Oil (Powderworks 1978)★★, Head Injuries (Powderworks 1979)★★★, Place Without A Postcard (Columbia 1981)★★★, 10,9,8,7,6,5,4,3,2,1 (Columbia 1982)★★★, Red Sails In The Sunset (Columbia 1985) ★★★★, Diesel And Dust (Columbia 1987)★★★★, Blue Sky Mining (Columbia 1990)★★★★, Scream In Blue-Live (Columbia 1992)★★★, Earth And Sun And Moon (Columbia 1993) ★★★, Breathe (Columbia 1996)★★★, Redneck Wonderland (Columbia 1998)★★★, Capricornia (Liquid 8 2002)★★★.
COMPILATIONS: 20,000 Watts R.S.L.: The Collection (Columbia 1997)★★★★.
FURTHER READING: Strict Rules, Andrew McMillan.

MIKE AND THE MECHANICS
ALBUMS: Mike + The Mechanics (WEA 1985)★★, Living Years (WEA 1988)★★★★, Word Of Mouth (Virgin 1991)★★★, Beggar On A Beach Of Gold (Virgin 1995)★★, Mike And The Mechanics (Virgin 1999)★★★.
COMPILATIONS: Hits (Virgin 1996)★★★.
VIDEOS: Hits (Warner Music Vision 1996).

MILES, BUDDY
ALBUMS: as the Buddy Miles Express Expressway To Your Skull (Mercury 1968)★★★★, as the Buddy Miles Express Electric Church (Mercury 1969)★★★, as the Buddy Miles Band Them Changes (Mercury 1970)★★★, as the Buddy Miles Band We Got To Live Together (Mercury 1970)★★★, as the Buddy Miles Band A Message To The People (Mercury 1971)★★★, as the Buddy Miles Band Buddy Miles Live (Mercury 1971)★★, Carlos Santana And Buddy Miles! Live! (Columbia 1972)★★, as the Buddy Miles Band Chapter VII (Columbia 1973)★★, as the Buddy Miles Express Booger Bear (Columbia 1973)★★, All The Faces Of Buddy Miles (Epic 1974)★★★, More Miles Per Gallon (Casablanca 1975)★★, Bicentennial Gathering Of The Tribes (Casablanca 1976)★★, Sneak Attack (Atlantic 1981)★★, Hell And Back (Ryko 1994)★★★, Tribute To Jimi Hendrix (Pavement 1997)★★★, Miles Away From Home (EFA 1997)★★★.
COMPILATIONS: The Best Of Buddy Miles (PolyGram 1997)★★★★.

MILLER, FRANKIE
ALBUMS: Once In A Blue Moon (Chrysalis 1972)★★★, High Life (Chrysalis 1973)★★★, The Rock (Chrysalis 1975)★★★, Full House (Chrysalis 1977)★★★, Double Trouble (Chrysalis 1978)★★★, Falling In Love (Chrysalis 1979)★★★, Perfect Fit (Chrysalis 1979)★★★, Easy Money (Chrysalis 1980)★★★, Standing On The Edge (Capitol 1982)★★★, Dancing In The Rain (Vertigo 1986)★★★.
COMPILATIONS: Best Of Frankie Miller (1992)★★★, BBC Radio One Live In Concert 1977-1979 recordings (Windsong 1994)★★★.

MILLER, STEVE
ALBUMS: Children Of the Future (Capitol 1968)★★★★, Sailor (Capitol 1968)★★★★★, Brave New World (Capitol 1969)★★★★, Your Saving Grace (Capitol 1969)★★★, Revolution film soundtrack 3 tracks only (United Artists 1969)★★, Number 5 (Capitol 1970)★★★★, Rock Love (Capitol 1971)★★, Recall The Beginning ... A Journey From Eden (Capitol 1972)★★★★, The Joker (Capitol 1973) ★★★, Fly Like An Eagle (Capitol 1976)★★★★, Book Of Dreams (Capitol 1977)★★★★, Circle Of Love (Capitol 1981)★★★, Abracadabra (Capitol 1982)★★★, Steve Miller Band - Live! (Capitol 1983)★★★, Italian X Rays (Capitol 1984)★★★, Living In The 20th Century (Capitol 1986)★★★, Born 2B Blue (Capitol 1988)★★★, Wide River (Polydor 1993)★★.
COMPILATIONS: Anthology (Capitol 1972)★★★★, Living In The U.S.A. (Capitol 1973)★★★, Greatest Hits (1974-1978) (Capitol 1978)★★★★, The Best Of 1968-1973 (Capitol 1990)★★★★, Box Set 3-CD box set (Capitol 1994)★★★★, Greatest Hits (PolyGram 1998)★★★★.
VIDEOS: Steve Miller Band Live (Video Collection 1988).

MINISTRY
ALBUMS: With Sympathy aka Work For Love (Arista 1983)★★, Twitch (Sire 1986)★★★, The Land Of Rape And Honey (Sire 1988)★★★, The Mind Is A Terrible Thing To Taste (Sire 1989)★★★, In Case You Didn't Feel Like Showing Up (Live) mini-album (Sire 1990)★★★, Psalm 69: The Way To Succeed And The Way To Suck Eggs (Sire/Warners 1992)★★★, Filth Pig (Warners 1996)★★★, Dark Side Of The Spoon (Warners 1999)★★★★, Sphinctour (Sanctuary 2002)★★★.
SOLO: Paul Barker as Lead Into Gold Age Of Reason (Wax Trax! 1992)★★.
COMPILATIONS: Twelve Inch Singles 1981-1984 (Wax Trax! 1987)★★★, Greatest Fits (Warners 2001)★★★★.
VIDEOS: In Case You Didn't Feel Like Showing Up (Live) (Warner Music 1990), Tapes Of Wrath (Warner Reprise Video 2000).

MINOGUE, KYLIE
ALBUMS: Kylie (PWL 1988)★★★, Enjoy Yourself (PWL 1989)★★★, Rhythm Of Love (PWL 1990)★★★★, Let's Get To It (PWL 1991)★★, Kylie Minogue i (Deconstruction 1994)★★, Kylie Minogue ii (Deconstruction 1998)★★★, Light Years (Parlophone 2000)★★★★, Fever (Parlophone/Capitol 2001)★★★★.
COMPILATIONS: The Kylie Collection (Mushroom 1988) ★★★, Kylie's Remixes (Alfa/PWL 1989)★★, Remixed And Official 1990 (PWL 1990)★★, Kylie's Remixes Vol. 2 (PWL 1992)★★, Celebration: Greatest Hits (PWL 1992)★★★, Greatest Remix Hits Vol. 1 (WEA/Mushroom 1993)★★★, Kylie Non Stop History 50 + 1 (Mushroom 1993)★★★, Greatest Remix Hits Vol. II (WEA/Mushroom 1993)★★★, Greatest Remix Hits Vol. 3 (Mushroom 1998)★★★, Greatest Remix Hits Vol. 4 (Mushroom 1998)★★, Hits+ (Deconstruction 2000)★★★.
VIDEOS: On A Night Like This: Live In Sydney (Parlophone 2001).
FURTHER READING: Kylie Minogue: An Illustrated Biography, Sasha Stone. The Superstar Next Door, Sasha Stone.
FILMS: The Delinquents (1989), Street Fighter (1994), Hayride To Hell (1995), Misfit (1996), Bio-Dome (1996), Diana & Me (1997), Cut (2000), Sample People (2000), Moulin Rouge! (2001).

MIRACLES
ALBUMS: Hi, We're The Miracles (Tamla 1961)★★★, Cookin' With The Miracles (Tamla 1962)★★★★, I'll Try Something New (Tamla 1962)★★★, The Fabulous Miracles (Tamla 1963)★★★, Recorded Live: On Stage (Tamla 1963)★★, Christmas With The Miracles (Tamla 1963)★★, The Miracles Doin' 'Mickey's Monkey' (Tamla 1963)★★★, Going To A Go-Go (Tamla 1965)★★★★, I Like It Like That (Tamla 1965)★★★, Away We A Go-Go (Tamla 1966)★★★, Make It Happen (Tamla 1967)★★★, Special Occasion (Tamla 1968)★★★, Live! (Tamla 1969)★★, Time Out For Smokey Robinson And The Miracles (Tamla 1969)★★★, Four In Blue (Tamla 1969)★★★, What Love Has Joined Together (Tamla 1970)★★★, A Pocket Full Of Miracles (Tamla 1970)★★★, The Season For Miracles (Tamla 1970)★★★, One Dozen Roses (Tamla 1971)★★★, Flying High Together (Tamla 1972)★★★, Renaissance (Tamla 1973)★★★, Do It Baby (Tamla 1974)★★★, Don't Cha Love It (Tamla 1975) ★★, City Of Angels (Tamla 1975)★★★, The Power Of Music (Tamla 1976)★★, Love Crazy (Columbia 1977)★★, The Miracles (Columbia 1978)★★.
COMPILATIONS: Greatest Hits From The Beginning (Tamla 1965)★★★★, Greatest Hits Volume 2 (Tamla 1968)★★★★, 1957-72 (Tamla 1972)★★★★, Smokey Robinson And The Miracles' Anthology (Motown 1973)★★★★, Compact Command Performances (Motown 1987)★★★★, The Greatest Hits (Motown 1992)★★★★, The 35th Anniversary Collection 4-CD box set (Motown Masters 1994)★★★★, Early Classics (Spectrum 1996)★★★, The Ultimate Collection (Motown 1998)★★★★, Along Came Love (Motown 1999)★★★.
FURTHER READING: Smokey: Inside My Life, Smokey Robinson and David Ritz.

MISFITS
ALBUMS: Walk Among Us (Ruby 1982)★★★, Evilive mini-album (Plan 9 1982)★★★, Earth A.D./Wolfsblood (Plan 9 1983)★★★, American Psycho (Geffen 1997)★★★, Famous Monsters (Roadrunner 1999)★★★.
COMPILATIONS: Legacy Of Brutality (Plan 9 1985)★★★, The Misfits (Plan 9 1986)★★★★, Evilive expanded version of 1981 mini-album (Plan 9 1987)★★★, The Misfits 4-CD box set (Caroline 1996)★★★★, Static Age (Caroline 1997) ★★★★, Cuts From The Crypt (Roadrunner 2001)★★★.

MISSION
ALBUMS: God's Own Medicine (Mercury 1986)★★, The First Chapter (Mercury 1987)★★★, Children (Mercury 1988)★★★, Carved In Sand (Mercury 1990)★★★, Grains Of Sand (Mercury 1990)★★, Masque (Vertigo 1992)★★★, Live: No Snow, No Show For The Eskimo (Windsong 1993)★★, Neverland (Equator 1995)★★, Blue (Equator 1996)★★, Aura (Playground 2002)★★★★.
COMPILATIONS: Magnificent Pieces 4-CD box set (PHCR 1991)★★★, Sum And Substance (Vertigo 1994)★★★, Salad Daze: Radio 1 Sessions (Nighttracks 1994)★★, Tower Of Strength (Spectrum 2000)★★★★.
VIDEOS: Crusade (Channel 5 1987), From Dusk To Dawn (PolyGram Music Video 1988), South America (MISH Productions 1989), Waves Upon The Sand (PolyGram Music Video 1991), Sum And Substance (PolyGram Music Video 1994).
FURTHER READING: The Mission: Names Are For Tombstones Baby, Martin Roach with Neil Perry.

MISUNDERSTOOD
COMPILATIONS: The Legendary Goldstar Album Plus Golden Glass (Cherry Red 1984)★★★, Before The Dream Faded (Cherry Red 1992)★★★★.

MITCHELL, JONI
ALBUMS: Joni Mitchell aka Song To A Seagull (Reprise 1968)★★★, Clouds (Reprise 1969)★★★, Ladies Of The Canyon (Reprise 1970)★★★★, Blue (Reprise 1971) ★★★★★, For The Roses (Asylum 1972)★★★★, Court And Spark (Asylum 1974)★★★★★, Miles Of Aisles (Asylum 1974)★★★, The Hissing Of Summer Lawns (Asylum 1975) ★★★★, Hejira (Asylum 1976)★★★★, Don Juan's Reckless Daughter (Asylum 1977)★★★, Mingus (Asylum 1979) ★★★★, Shadows And Light (Asylum 1980)★★★★, Wild Things Run Fast (Geffen 1982)★★★, Dog Eat Dog (Geffen 1985)★★★, Chalk Mark In A Rainstorm (Geffen 1988) ★★★, Night Ride Home (Geffen 1991)★★★★, Turbulent Indigo (Warners 1994)★★★, Taming The Tiger (Warners 1998)★★★, Both Sides Now (Reprise 2000)★★★★.
COMPILATIONS: Joni Mitchell Hits (Reprise 1996)★★★, Joni Mitchell Misses (Reprise 1996)★★★.
VIDEOS: Painting With Words And Music (ILC/Eagle Entertainment 1999).
FURTHER READING: Joni Mitchell, Leonore Fleischer. Both Sides Now, Brian Hinton. A Memoir, Joni Mitchell. Complete Poems And Lyrics, Joni Mitchell. Shadows And Light: The Definitive Biography, Karen O'Brien.

MOBY
ALBUMS: Moby (Instinct 1992)★★★, Early Underground (Instinct 1993)★★★, Ambient (Instinct 1993)★★, Everything Is Wrong (Mute/Elektra 1995)★★★★, Everything Is Wrong (DJ Mix Album) (Mute 1996)★★★, Animal Rights (Mute/Elektra 1996)★★★, I Like To Score (Mute/Elektra 1997) ★★★, Play (Mute/Virgin 1999) ★★★★, 18 (Mute/Virgin 2002)★★★.
COMPILATIONS: The Story So Far (Equator 1993)★★★, Rare: The Collected B-Sides (Instinct 1996)★★★, Songs: 1993-1998 (Elektra 1999)★★★.
VIDEOS: Play (Mute Films 2001).
FURTHER READING: Moby Replay: His Life And Times, Martin James.

MOBY GRAPE
ALBUMS: Moby Grape (Columbia 1967)★★★★★, Wow (Columbia 1967)★★★, Grape Jam (Columbia 1967)★★★, Moby Grape '69 (Columbia 1969)★★★★, Truly Fine Citizen (Columbia 1969)★★★, 20 Granite Creek (Reprise 1971)★★★★, Live Grape (Escape 1978)★★★, Moby Grape (San Francisco Sound 1983)★★.
SOLO: Bob Mosley Bob Mosley (Warners 1972)★★. Peter Lewis Peter Lewis (Taxim 1996)★★★.
COMPILATIONS: Great Grape (Columbia 1973)★★★, Vintage Grape 2-CD box set with unreleased material and alternate takes (Columbia/Legacy 1993)★★★★★.

MOCK TURTLES
ALBUMS: Turtle Soup (Imaginary 1990)★★★, Two Sides (Two Sides 1991)★★★★.
COMPILATIONS: 87-90 (Imaginary 1991)★★★.

MODERN LOVERS
ALBUMS: The Modern Lovers (Beserkley 1976)★★★★, as Jonathan Richman And The Modern Lovers Jonathan Richman And The Modern Lovers (Beserkley 1977)★★★, as Jonathan Richman And The Modern Lovers Rock 'N' Roll With The Modern Lovers (Beserkley 1977)★★★, The Modern Lovers Live (Beserkley 1977)★★.
COMPILATIONS: The Original Modern Lovers early recordings (Bomp! 1981)★★★, The Beserkley Years: The Best Of Jonathan Richman And The Modern Lovers (Beserkley/Rhino 1987)★★★, Jonathan Richman And The Modern Lovers: 23 Great Recordings (Beserkley/Castle 1990)★★★★, Home Of The Hits! (Castle 1999)★★★★.
FURTHER READING: There's Something About Jonathan: Jonathan Richman And The Modern Lovers, Tim Mitchell.

MOGWAI
ALBUMS: Young Team (Chemikal Underground 1997)★★★★, Kicking A Dead Pig remixes (Eye-Q 1998)★★★, Come On Die Young (Chemikal Underground/Matador 1999)★★★★, Rock Action (Southpaw/Matador 2001)★★★★.
COMPILATIONS: Ten Rapid (Rock Action/Jetset 1997) ★★★, EP + 6 (Chemikal Underground 2001)★★★.

MOLLY HATCHET
ALBUMS: Molly Hatchet (Epic 1978)★★★, Flirtin' With Disaster (Epic 1979)★★★, Beatin' The Odds (Epic 1980) ★★, Take No Prisoners (Epic 1981)★★, No Guts ... No Glory (Epic 1983)★★★, The Deed Is Done (Epic 1984)★★, Double Trouble Live (Epic 1985)★★, Lightning Strikes Twice (Capitol 1989)★★, Devil's Canyon (SPV/Mayhem 1996) ★★, Silent Reign Of Heroes (SPV/CMC 1998)★★, Live At The Agora Ballroom 1979 recording (Phoenix 1999)★★★, Kingdom Of XII (SPV/CMC 2000)★★.
COMPILATIONS: Greatest Hits (Epic 1985)★★★, Cut To The Bone (Sony 1995)★★★, Super Hits (Epic 1998)★★★.

MONEY, ZOOT
ALBUMS: It Should've Been Me (Columbia 1965)★★★, Zoot! Live At Klook's Kleek (Columbia 1966)★★★, Transition (Direction 1968)★★, Welcome To My Head (1969)★★, Zoot Money (Polydor 1970)★★, Mr. Money (Magic Moon 1980)★★, with Chris Farlowe Alexis Korner Memorial Concert Volume 2 (Indigo 1995)★★★, Were You There? Live 1966 (Indigo 1999)★★★★, Fully Clothed & Naked (Indigo 2000)★★.

MONKEES
ALBUMS: The Monkees (Colgems 1966)★★★★, More Of The Monkees (Colgems 1967)★★★★, Headquarters (Colgems 1967)★★★, Pisces, Aquarius, Capricorn & Jones Ltd. (Colgems 1967)★★, The Birds, The Bees & The Monkees (Colgems 1968)★★, Head film soundtrack (Colgems 1968)★★, Instant Replay (Colgems 1969)★★★, The Monkees Present (Colgems 1969)★★★, Changes (Colgems 1970)★★★, 20th Anniversary Tour 1986 (No Label 1987)★★, Live 1967 (Rhino 1987)★★★, Pool It! (Rhino 1987)★★, Justus (Rhino 1996)★★.
COMPILATIONS: Greatest Hits (Colgems 1969)★★★★, Golden Hits (Colgems 1970)★★★, Barrel Full Of Monkees (Colgems 1970)★★★★, Re-focus (Bell 1973)★★★, The Monkees (Laurie House 1976)★★★, Monkeemania: 40 Timeless Hits From The Monkees Australia only (Arista 1979)★★★, Monkeeshines (Zilch 1981)★★★, The Monkees Golden Story (Arista 1981)★★★★, More Greatest Hits Of The Monkees (Arista 1982)★★★, Monkee Business (Rhino 1982)★★★, Tails Of The Monkees (Silhouette 1983)★★, Monkee Flips: Best Of The Monkees, Volume Four - 14 Swinging Songs (Rhino 1984)★★★, Hey-Hey-It's The Monkees: 20 Smash Hits (Circa 1985)★★★, Hit Factory (Pair 1985)★★★, The Best Of The Monkees (Silver Eagle 1986)★★★★, Then & Now ... The Best Of The Monkees (Arista 1986)★★★★, Missing Links (Rhino 1987)★★★, Missing Links Volume Two (Rhino 1990)★★★, Listen To The Band 4-CD box set (Rhino 1991)★★★, Greatest Hits (Rhino 1995)★★★★, Missing Links Volume 3 (Rhino 1996)★★, 30th Anniversary Collection (Rhino 1996)★★★, Here They Come ... The Greatest Hits Of The Monkees (Warners/Telstar 1997)★★★★, Anthology (Rhino 1997)★★★★, Music Box 4-CD box set (Rhino 2001) ★★★★, The Definitive Monkees 2-CD set (Warners 2001) ★★★★.
CD ROMS: Hey Hey We're The Monkees (nu.millennia 1996).
VIDEOS: The Monkees Collection box set (Rhino 1995), 33 1/3 Revolutions Per Monkee (Rhino Home Video 1996).
FURTHER READING: Love Letters To The Monkees, Bill Adler. The Monkees Tale, Eric Lefcowitz. The Monkees Scrapbook, Ed Finn and T. Bone. Monkeemania, Glenn A. Baker. The Monkees: A Manufactured Image, Ed Reilly, Maggie McMannus and Bill Chadwick. I'm A Believer: My Life Of Monkees, Music And Madness, Mickey Dolenz and Mark Bego.
FILMS: Head (1968).

MONOCHROME SET
ALBUMS: Strange Boutique (DinDisc 1980)★★, Love Zombies (DinDisc 1980)★★, Eligible Bachelors (Cherry Red 1982)★★★, The Lost Weekend (Blanco y Negro 1985) ★★★, Dante's Casino (Vinyl Japan 1990)★★★, Jack (Honeymoon 1991)★★, Charade (Cherry Red 1993)★★★, Misère (Cherry Red 1994)★★★, Trinity Road (Cherry Red 1995)★★★.
COMPILATIONS: Volume, Contrast, Brilliance ... Sessions & Singles Vol. 1 (Cherry Red 1983)★★★, Fin (El 1986)★★★, Colour Transmission (Virgin 1987)★★★, Westminster Affair (Cherry Red 1988)★★, What A Whopper! (Cherry Red 1991)★★★, Black & White Minstrels (Cherry Red 1995) ★★★, Tomorrow Will Be Too Long: The Best Of The Monochrome Set (Caroline 1995)★★★, Chaps (Recall 1997)★★★.
VIDEOS: Destiny Calling (Visionary 1994).

MONTEZ, CHRIS
ALBUMS: Let's Dance And Have Some Kinda Fun!!! (Monogram 1963)★★★, The More I See You/Call Me (A&M 1966)★★★, Time After Time (A&M 1966)★★★, Foolin' Around (A&M 1967)★★, Watch What Happens (A&M 1968)★★.
COMPILATIONS: Let's Dance! All-Time Greatest Hits (Digital Compact Classics 1991)★★★, The Hits (Repertoire 1999)★★★.

MOODY BLUES
ALBUMS: The Magnificent Moodies (UK) Go Now/Moody Blues #1 (US) (Decca/London 1965)★★★★, Days Of Future Passed (Deram 1967)★★★★, In Search Of The Lost Chord (Deram 1968)★★★, On The Threshold Of A Dream (Deram 1969)★★★★, To Our Children's Children's Children (Threshold 1969)★★★★, A Question Of Balance (Threshold 1970)★★★, Every Good Boy Deserves Favour (Threshold 1971)★★★, Seventh Sojourn (Threshold 1972)★★★★, Caught Live + 5 (Decca 1977)★★, Octave (Decca 1978) ★★, Long Distance Voyager (Threshold 1981)★★★★, The Present (Threshold 1983)★★★, The Other Side Of Life (Polydor 1986)★★★, Sur La Mer (Polydor 1988)★★★, Keys Of The Kingdom (Polydor 1991)★★, A Night At Red Rocks With The Colorado Symphony Orchestra (Polydor 1993)★★, Strange Times (Threshold/Universal 1999)★★, Hall Of Fame (Threshold/Universal 2000)★★★.
COMPILATIONS: This Is The Moody Blues (Threshold 1974) ★★★★, Out Of This World (K-Tel 1979)★★★, Voices In The Sky: The Best Of The Moody Blues (Threshold 1984)★★★, Prelude (Polydor 1987)★★, The Magnificent Moodies expanded edition of debut album (London 1988)★★★★, Greatest Hits (Polydor 1989)★★★, Time Traveller 5-CD box set (Polydor 1994)★★★, The Very Best Of The Moody Blues (PolyGram 1996)★★★, The Best Of The Moody Blues (Polydor 1997)★★★, Anthology (Polydor 1998)★★★★.
VIDEOS: Cover Story (Stylus 1990), The Story Of The Moody Blues ... Legend Of A Band (PolyGram Music Video 1990), Star Portrait (Gemini Vision 1991), A Night At Red Rocks With The Colorado Symphony Orchestra (PolyGram Music Video 1993).

MOORE, CHRISTY
ALBUMS: Paddy On The Road (Mercury 1969)★★★, Prosperous (Trailer 1972)★★★, Whatever Tickles Your Fancy (Polydor 1975)★★★, Christy Moore (Polydor 1976) ★★★, The Iron Behind The Velvet (Tara 1978)★★★, Live In Dublin (Tara 1979)★★★, The Time Has Come (WEA 1983)★★★, Ride On (WEA 1984)★★★, The Spirit Of Freedom 1983 recording (WEA 1985)★★★, Ordinary Man (WEA 1985)★★★, Nice 'N' Easy (Polydor 1986) ★★★, Unfinished Revolution (WEA 1987)★★★, Voyage (WEA 1989)★★★, Smoke & Strong Whiskey (Newberry 1991)★★★, King Puck (Grapevine 1993)★★★, Live At The Point (Grapevine 1994)★★★, Graffiti Tongue (Grapevine 1996)★★★★, Traveller (Columbia 1999)★★★, This Is The Day (Columbia 2001)★★★.
COMPILATIONS: The Christy Moore Folk Collection i (Tara 1972)★★★, The Christy Moore Folk Collection ii (Tara 1978)★★★, The Christy Moore Folk Collection iii (Tara 1978)★★★, The Christy Moore Collection '81-'91 (WEA 1991)★★★★, Collection Part Two (Grapevine 1997)★★★.
VIDEOS: Christy (SMV 1995).
FURTHER READING: One Voice: My Life In Song, Christy Moore.

MOORE, GARY
ALBUMS: as the Gary Moore Band Grinding Stone (Columbia 1973)★★, Back On The Streets (MCA 1979)★★★★, Corridors Of Power (Virgin 1982)★★★, Dirty Fingers (Jet 1983)★★, Live At The Marquee (Jet 1983)★★★, Victims Of The Future (10 1984)★★★★, We Want Moore! (10 1984)★★★, Run For Cover (10 1985)★★★, Rockin' Every Night - Live In Japan (10 1986)★★★, Wild Frontier (10 1987)★★, After The War (Virgin 1989)★★★, Still Got The Blues (Virgin 1990)★★★★, After Hours (Virgin 1992)★★★, Blues Alive (Virgin 1993) ★★★★, Blues For Greeny (Virgin 1995)★★★★, Dark Days In Paradise (Virgin 1997)★★, A Different Beat (Raw Power 1999) ★★, Back To The Blues (Sanctuary 2001)★★★.
COMPILATIONS: Anthology (Raw Power 1986)★★★, The Collection (Castle 1990)★★★, CD Box Set (Virgin 1991) ★★★, Ballads + Blues 1982-1994 (Virgin 1994)★★★★, Out In The Fields: The Very Best Of (Virgin 1998)★★★, The Best Of The Blue (Virgin 2002)★★★★.

VIDEOS: Emerald Aisles (Virgin Vision 1986), Video Singles: Gary Moore (Virgin Vision 1988), Gary Moore: Live In Sweden (Virgin Vision 1988), Evening Of The Blues (Virgin Vision 1991), Live Blues (1993), Ballads And Blues 1982-1994 (1995), Blues For Greeny Live (Warner Music Video 1996).

MORCHEEBA
ALBUMS: Who Can You Trust (Indochina 1996)★★★, Big Calm (Indochina 1998)★★★★, Fragments Of Freedom (Indochina 2000)★★★★.
COMPILATIONS: Who Can You Trust/Beats And B Sides (Indochina 1997)★★★, Back To Mine (DMC 2001)★★★.

MORISSETTE, ALANIS
ALBUMS: Alanis (MCA Canada 1990)★★, Now Is The Time (MCA Canada 1992)★★, Jagged Little Pill (Maverick/Reprise 1995)★★★★, Supposed Former Infatuation Junkie (Maverick 1998)★★★, MTV Unplugged (Maverick 1999)★★★, Under Rug Swept (Maverick 2002)★★★.
FURTHER READING: Alanis Morissette: Death Of Cinderella, Stuart Coles. Ironic – Alanis Morissette: The True Story, Barry Grills.
FILMS: Dogma (1999).

MORPHINE
ALBUMS: Good (Accurate/Distortion 1992)★★★, Cure For Pain (Rykodisc 1993)★★★, Yes (Rykodisc 1995)★★★★, Like Swimming (Rykodisc 1997)★★★★, The Night (DreamWorks 2000)★★★★, Bootleg Detroit (Rykodisc 2000)★★★★.
COMPILATIONS: B-Sides And Otherwise (Rykodisc 1997)★★★★.

MORRISON, VAN
ALBUMS: Blowin' Your Mind (Bang 1967)★★, Astral Weeks (Warners 1968)★★★★★, Moondance (Warners 1970) ★★★★, His Band And The Street Choir (Warners 1970) ★★★, Tupelo Honey (Warners 1971)★★★★, Saint Dominic's Preview (Warners 1972)★★★★, T.B. Sheets (Bang 1973)★★, Hard Nose The Highway (Warners 1973)★★, It's Too Late To Stop Now (Warners 1974)★★★★, Veedon Fleece (Warners 1974)★★★★, A Period Of Transition (Warners 1977)★★★, Wavelength (Warners 1978)★★★, Into The Music (Vertigo 1979)★★★, Common One (Mercury 1980)★★, Beautiful Vision (Mercury 1982)★★★, Inarticulate Speech Of The Heart (Mercury 1983)★★, Live At The Grand Opera House, Belfast (Mercury 1984)★★, A Sense Of Wonder (Mercury 1984) ★★★★, No Guru, No Method, No Teacher (Mercury 1986) ★★★★, Poetic Champions Compose (Mercury 1987)★★★★, with the Chieftains Irish Heartbeat (Mercury 1988)★★★★, Avalon Sunset (Mercury 1989)★★★★, Enlightenment (Mercury 1990)★★★, Hymns To The Silence (Polydor 1991)★★★, Too Long In Exile (Polydor 1993)★★, A Night In San Francisco (Polydor 1994)★★, Days Like This (Polydor 1995)★★★, with Georgie Fame How Long Has This Been Going On (Verve 1995)★★★, with Fame, Mose Allison, Ben Sidran Tell Me Something: The Songs Of Mose Allison (Verve 1996)★★, The Healing Game (Polydor 1997)★★★, Back On Top (PointBlank 1999)★★★★, The Skiffle Sessions: Live In Belfast (Exile 1999) ★★★, with Linda Gail Lewis You Win Again (PointBlank 2000) ★★★, Down The Road (Polydor 2002)★★★.
COMPILATIONS: The Best Of Van Morrison (Bang 1971)★★, This Is Where I Came In (Bang 1977)★★, The Best Of Van Morrison (Polydor 1990)★★★★★, Bang Masters (Legacy 1991)★★★, The Best Of Volume 2 (Polydor 1992)★★★★, New York Sessions '67 (Burning Airlines 1997)★★, The Philosopher's Stone (Polydor 1998)★★★.
VIDEOS: The Concert (Channel 5 1990).
FURTHER READING: Van Morrison: Into The Music, Ritchie Yorke. Van Morrison: A Portrait Of The Artist, Johnny Rogan. Van Morrison: The Mystic's Music, Howard A. DeWitt. Van Morrison: Too Late To Stop Now, Steve Turner. Van Morrison: Inarticulate Speech Of The Heart, John Collis. Celtic Crossroads: The Art Of Van Morrison, Brian Hinton.

MORRISSEY
ALBUMS: Viva Hate (HMV/Sire 1988)★★★★, Kill Uncle (HMV/Sire 1991)★★, Your Arsenal (HMV/Sire 1992) ★★★★, Beethoven Was Deaf (HMV 1993)★★, Vauxhall And I (Parlophone/Sire 1994)★★★★, Southpaw Grammar (RCA Victor/Reprise 1995)★★★, Maladjusted (Island 1997)★★★.
COMPILATIONS: Bona Drag (HMV/Sire 1990)★★★★, The World Of Morrissey (Parlophone/EMI 1995)★★, Suedehead: The Best Of (EMI 1997)★★★, The CD Singles '88-'91 (EMI 2000)★★★, The CD Singles '91-'95 (EMI 2001)★★★, The Best Of Morrissey (Rhino 2001)★★★★.
VIDEOS: Hulmerist (PMI/EMI 1990), Live In Dallas (Warner Music Video 1992), Introducing Morrissey (Warner Music Video 1996), ¡Oye Esteban! (Reprise 2000).
FURTHER READING: Morrissey In His Own Words, John Robertson. Morrissey Shot, Linder Sterling. Morrissey & Marr: The Severed Alliance, Johnny Rogan. Peepholism: Into The Art Of Morrissey, Jo Slee. Landscapes Of The Mind, David Bret.

MOTELS
ALBUMS: Motels (Capitol 1979)★★★★, Careful (Capitol 1980)★★★, All Four One (Capitol 1982)★★★, Little Robbers (Capitol 1983)★★, Shock (Capitol 1985)★★.
SOLO: Martha Davis Policy (Capitol 1987)★★★.
COMPILATIONS: No Vacancy: The Best Of The Motels (Capitol 1990)★★★★, Anthologyland (Oglio 2001)★★★★, Classic Masters (EMD 2002)★★★.

MOTHERS OF INVENTION
ALBUMS: Comprising the entire Frank Zappa catalogue. With The Mothers Of Invention Freak Out! (Verve 1966) ★★★★, with The Mothers Of Invention Absolutely Free (Verve 1967)★★★★, with The Mothers Of Invention We're Only In It For The Money (Verve 1968)★★★★, Lumpy Gravy (Verve 1968)★★★★, with The Mothers Of Invention Cruising With Ruben & The Jets (Verve 1968)★★★, with The Mothers Of Invention Uncle Meat (Bizarre 1969) ★★★★, Hot Rats (Bizarre 1969)★★★★, with The Mothers Of Invention Burnt Weeny Sandwich (Bizarre 1970)★★★, with The Mothers Of Invention Weasels Ripped My Flesh (Bizarre 1970)★★★★, Chunga's Revenge (Bizarre 1970) ★★★★, with The Mothers Fillmore East, June 1971 (Bizarre 1971)★★★, Frank Zappa's 200 Motels (United Artists 1971)★★, with The Mothers Just Another Band From L.A. (Bizarre 1972)★★★, Waka/Jawaka (Bizarre 1972)★★★, with The Mothers The Grand Wazoo (Bizarre 1972)★★★, with The Mothers Over-Nite Sensation (DiscReet 1973) ★★★, Apostrophe (') (DiscReet 1974)★★★★, with The Mothers Roxy & Elsewhere (DiscReet 1974)★★★, with The Mothers Of Invention One Size Fits All (DiscReet 1975) ★★★★, with Captain Beefheart Bongo Fury (DiscReet 1975)★★★, Zoot Allures (Warners 1976)★★★★, Zappa In New York (DiscReet 1978)★★★, Studio Tan (DiscReet 1978)★★★, Sleep Dirt (DiscReet 1979)★★, Sheik Yerbouti (Zappa 1979)★★★★, Orchestral Favorites (DiscReet 1979) ★★★, Joe's Garage Act I (Zappa 1979)★★★★, Joe's Garage Acts II & III (Zappa 1979)★★★★, Tinseltown Rebellion (Barking Pumpkin 1981)★★★, Shut Up 'N Play Yer Guitar (Zappa 1981)★★★, Shut Up 'N Play Yer Guitar Some More (Zappa 1981)★★★, Return Of The Son Of Shut Up 'N Play Yer Guitar (Zappa 1981)★★★, You Are What You Is (Barking Pumpkin 1981)★★★, Ship Arriving Too Late To Save A Drowning Witch (Barking Pumpkin 1982)★★★, Baby Snakes (Barking Pumpkin 1982)★★★, The Man From Utopia (Barking Pumpkin 1983)★★★, Baby Snakes film soundtrack (Barking Pumpkin 1983)★★, The London Symphony Orchestra Vol. I (Barking Pumpkin 1983)★★★★, Boulez Conducts Zappa: The Perfect Stranger (Angel 1984) ★★★, Them Or Us (Barking Pumpkin 1984)★★★, Thing-Fish (Barking Pumpkin 1984)★★★★, Francesco Zappa (Barking Pumpkin 1984)★★★, Meets The Mothers Of Prevention (Barking Pumpkin/EMI 1985)★★★, Does Humor Belong In Music? (EMI 1986)★★★, Jazz From Hell (Barking Pumpkin 1986)★★★, London Symphony Orchestra Vol. II (Barking Pumpkin 1987)★★★, Guitar (Barking Pumpkin 1988)★★★, Broadway The Hard Way (Barking Pumpkin 1988)★★★, The Best Band You Never Heard In Your Life (Barking Pumpkin 1991)★★★★, Make A Jazz Noise Here (Barking Pumpkin 1991)★★★, with The Mothers Of Invention Ahead Of Their Time 1968 live recording (Barking Pumpkin 1993)★★★, with Ensemble Modern The Yellow Shark (Barking Pumpkin 1993)★★★, Civilization Phaze III (Barking Pumpkin 1994)★★★, Everything Is Healing Nicely 1991 recording (Barking Pumpkin 1999)★★★.
Beat The Boots I: with The Mothers Of Invention 'Tis The Season To Be Jelly 1967 recording (Foo-Eee 1991)★★★, with The Mothers Of Invention The Ark 1969 recording (Foo-Eee 1991)★★★, Freaks And Motherf*#@%! 1970 recordings (Foo-Eee 1991)★★★, with The Mothers Piquantique 1973/1974 recordings (Foo-Eee 1991)★★★, Unmitigated Audacity 1974 recording (Foo-Eee 1991)★★★, Saarbrücken 1978 (Foo-Eee 1991)★★★, Anyway The Wind Blows 1979 recording (Foo-Eee 1991)★★★, As An Am 1981/1982 recordings (Foo-Eee 1991)★★★.
Beat The Boots II: Disconnected Synapses 1970 recording (Foo-Eee 1992)★★★, Tengo Na Minchia Tanta 1970 recordings (Foo-Eee 1992)★★★, Electric Aunt Jemima 1968 recordings (Foo-Eee 1992)★★★, At The Circus 1978 recording (Foo-Eee 1992)★★★, Swiss Cheese/Fire! 1971 recordings (Foo-Eee 1992)★★★, Our Man In Nirvana 1968 recording (Foo-Eee 1992)★★★, Conceptual Continuity 1976 recording (Foo-Eee 1992)★★★.
COMPILATIONS: with The Mothers Of Invention Mothermania: The Best Of The Mothers (Verve 1969)★★★, The Old Masters Box One (Barking Pumpkin 1985)★★★, The Old Masters Box Two (Barking Pumpkin 1986)★★★, The Old Masters Box Three (Barking Pumpkin 1987)★★★, You Can't Do That On Stage Anymore Vol. 1 (Rykodisc 1988)★★★★, You Can't Do That On Stage Anymore Vol. 2: The Helsinki Concert (Rykodisc 1988) ★★★★, You Can't Do That On Stage Anymore Vol. 3 (Rykodisc 1989)★★★★, You Can't Do That On Stage Anymore Vol. 4 (Rykodisc 1991)★★★★, You Can't Do That On Stage Anymore Vol. 5 (Rykodisc 1992)★★★★, You Can't Do That On Stage Anymore Vol. 6 (Rykodisc 1992)★★★★, with The Mothers Of Invention Playground Psychotics 1970/1971 recordings (Barking Pumpkin 1992) ★★★, Strictly Commercial: The Best Of Frank Zappa (Rykodisc 1995)★★★, The Lost Episodes (Rykodisc 1996)★★★, Läther (Rykodisc 1996)★★★★, Plays The Music Of Frank Zappa: A Memorial Tribute (Barking Pumpkin 1996)★★★, Have I Offended Someone? (Rykodisc 1997)★★★, Strictly Genteel: A "Classical" Introduction To Frank Zappa (Rykodisc 1997)★★★, Cheap Thrills (Rykodisc 1998)★★★, Cucamonga (Del-Fi 1998)★★, Mystery Disc (Rykodisc 1998)★★, Son Of Cheep Thrills (Rykodisc 1999)★★. The entire reissued catalogue is currently available on Rykodisc.
VIDEOS: The Dub Room Special (Barking Pumpkin 1982), Frank Zappa's 200 Motels (Warner Home Video 1984), Does Humor Belong In Music? (MPI Home Video 1985), The Amazing Mr. Bickford (MPI/Honker Home Video 1987), Video From Hell (Honker Home Video 1987), Uncle Meat: The Mothers Of Invention Movie (Barfko-Swill 1987), Baby Snakes (Honker Home Video 1987), The True Story Of Frank Zappa's 200 Motels (Barfko-Swill 1989).
FURTHER READING: Frank Zappa: Over Het Begin En Het Einde Van De Progressieve Popmuziek, Rolf-Ulrich Kaiser. No Commercial Potential: The Saga Of Frank Zappa & The Mothers Of Invention, David Walley. Good Night Boys And Girls, Michael Gray. Frank Zappa Et Les Mothers Of Invention, Alain Dister. No Commercial Potential: The Saga Of Frank Zappa Then And Now, David Walley. Zappalog The First Step Of Zappology, Norbert Obermanns. Them Or Us (The Book), Frank Zappa. Mother! Is The Story Of Frank Zappa, Michael Gray. Viva Zappa, Dominique Chevalier. Zappa: A Biography, Julian Colbeck. The Real Frank Zappa Book, Frank Zappa with Peter Occhiogrosso. Frank Zappa: A Visual Documentary, Miles (ed.). Frank Zappa In His Own Words, Miles. Mother! The Frank Zappa Story, Michael Gray. Frank Zappa: The Negative Dialectics Of Poodle Play, Ben Watson. Being Frank: My Time With Frank Zappa, Nigey Lennon. Zappa: Electric Don Quixote, Neil Slaven. Frank Zappa: A Strictly Genteel Genius, Ben Cruickshank. Cosmik Debris: The Collected History And Improvisations Of Frank Zappa, Greg Russo. Necessity Is ... The Early Years Of Frank Zappa & The Mothers Of Invention, Billy James.
FILMS: Head (1968), 200 Motels (1971), Baby Snakes (1979).

MÖTLEY CRÜE
ALBUMS: Too Fast For Love (Leathür 1981)★★, Shout At The Devil (Elektra 1983)★★, Theatre Of Pain (Elektra 1985)★★, Girls, Girls, Girls (Elektra 1987)★★★, Dr. Feelgood (Elektra 1989)★★★, Mötley Crüe (Elektra 1994)★★★, Generation Swine (Elektra 1997)★★★, New Tattoo (Motley 2000)★★.
COMPILATIONS: Raw Tracks (Elektra 1988)★★★, Decade Of Decadence '81 - '91 (Elektra 1991)★★★★, Greate$t Hit$ (Motley 1998)★★★, Live: Entertainment Or Death (Motley 1999)★★★, Supersonic & Demonic Relics (Motley 1999)★★.
VIDEOS: Uncensored (WEA Music Video 1987), Dr. Feelgood, The Videos (Warner Music Video 1991), Decade Of Decadence '81 - '91 (Warner Music Video 1992), Lewd Crüed & Tattooed (Aviva International 2001).
FURTHER READING: Lüde, Crüde And Rüde, Sylvie Simmons and Malcolm Dome. The Dirt: Confessions Of The World's Most Notorious Rock Band, Tommy Lee, Mick Mars, Vince Neil and Nikki Sixx with Neil Strauss.

MOTÖRHEAD
ALBUMS: Motörhead (Chiswick 1977)★★★, Overkill (Bronze 1979)★★★, Bomber (Bronze 1979)★★★, On Parole (United Artists 1979)★★★, Ace Of Spades (Bronze 1980)★★★★, No Sleep 'Til Hammersmith (Bronze 1981) ★★★★, Iron Fist (Bronze 1982)★★★★, What's Words Worth? 1978 recording (Big Beat 1983)★★★, Another Perfect Day (Bronze 1983)★★, Orgasmatron (GWR 1986) ★★★★, Rock'N'Roll (GWR 1987)★★★, Eat The Rich film soundtrack (GWR 1987)★★★, No Sleep At All (GWR 1988)★★★, Blitzkreig On Birmingham Live '77 (Receiver 1989)★★, The Birthday Party (GWR 1990)★★, 1916 (Epic 1991)★★★, March Or Die (Epic 1992)★★★, Bastards (ZYX 1993)★★★, I (SPV 1996)★★, Overnight Sensation (SPV 1996)★★★, Snake Bite Love (SPV 1998)★★★, Live On The King Biscuit Flower Hour 1983 recording (King Biscuit 1998)★★, Everything Louder Than Everyone Else (SPV 1999)★★, We Are Motörhead (SPV 2000)★★, Hammered (SPV 2002)★★.
COMPILATIONS: No Remorse (Bronze 1984)★★★★, Anthology (Raw Power 1986)★★, Born To Lose (Castle 1986)★★, Dirty Love (Receiver 1990)★★, Welcome To The Bear Trap (Castle 1990)★★, Best Of Motörhead (Action Replay 1990)★★, Lock Up Your Daughters (Receiver 1990) ★★, From The Vaults (Knight 1990)★★, Meltdown 3-CD box set (Castle 1991)★★★, All The Aces (Castle 1993)★★, The Best Of Motörhead (Castle 1993)★★★★, Protect The Innocent 4-CD box set (Essential 1997)★★★, Born To Lose, Live To Win: The Bronze Singles 1978-1983 10-CD box set (Castle 1999)★★★★, The Best Of Motörhead (Metal-Is 2000)★★★★, The Chase Is Better Than The Catch: The Singles A's & B's (Castle 2001)★★★, Over The Top: The Rarities (Castle 2001)★★★, Motörhead (Ace 2001)★★★.
VIDEOS: Live In Toronto (Avatar 1984), Deaf Not Blind (Virgin Vision 1984), The Birthday Party (Virgin Vision 1986), The Best Of Motorhead (Castle Music Pictures 1991), Everything Louder Than Everything Else (Sony Music Video 1991), 25 & Alive: Boneshaker (SPV 2001).
FURTHER READING: Motörhead: Born To Lose, Live To Win, Alan Burridge. Motörhead, Giovanni Dadomo.

MOTT THE HOOPLE
ALBUMS: Mott The Hoople (Island 1969)★★★, Mad Shadows (Island 1970)★★★, Wild Life (Island 1971)★★, Brain Capers (Island 1971)★★★, All The Young Dudes (Columbia 1972)★★★, Mott (Columbia 1973)★★★★, The Hoople (Columbia 1974)★★★★, Live (Columbia 1974) ★★★, Original Mixed Up Kids: The BBC Recordings (Windsong 1996)★★★, All The Way From Stockholm To Philadelphia: Live 71/72 (Angel Air 1998)★★★, Two Miles Live From Heaven 1971-1974 recordings (Angel Air 2001)★★.
COMPILATIONS: Rock And Roll Queen (Island 1972)★★, Greatest Hits (Columbia 1975)★★★★, Shades Of Ian Hunter: The Ballad Of Ian Hunter And Mott The Hoople (Columbia 1979)★★★★, Two Miles From Heaven (Island 1981)★★★, All The Way From Memphis (Hallmark 1981) ★★★, Greatest Hits (Columbia 1981)★★★★, Backsliding Fearlessly (Rhino 1994)★★★, All The Young Dudes: The Anthology 3-CD box set (Sony 1998)★★★★, The Best Of The Island Years 1969-1972 (Spectrum 1998)★★★, Friends And Relatives (Eagle 1999)★★.
VIDEOS: Mott The Hoople 1st Annual Convention Souvenir Video (Jerkin Crocus 2001).
FURTHER READING: The Diary Of A Rock 'N' Roll Star, Ian Hunter. All The Way To Memphis, Phil Cato. Mott The Hoople And Ian Hunter: All The Young Dudes, Campbell Devine.

MOULD, BOB
ALBUMS: Workbook (Virgin 1989)★★★, Black Sheets Of Rain (Virgin 1990)★★★, Bob Mould (Creation/Rykodisk 1996)★★★★, The Last Dog And Pony Show (Creation 1998)★★★, Modulate (Granary 2002)★★★.
COMPILATIONS: Poison Years (Virgin 1994)★★★★.

MOUNTAIN
ALBUMS: Mountain Climbing! (Windfall 1970)★★★, Nantucket Sleighride (Windfall 1971)★★★, Flowers Of Evil (Windfall 1971)★★★★, Mountain Live (The Road Goes Ever On) (Windfall 1972)★★, Twin Peaks (Columbia 1974)★★, Avalanche (Columbia 1974)★★, Go For Your Life (Scotti Brothers 1985)★★, Man's World (Viceroy 1996)★★★.
COMPILATIONS: The Best Of Mountain (Columbia 1973) ★★★, Over The Top (Columbia/Legacy 1995)★★★, Super Hits (Sony 1998)★★★.

MOVE
ALBUMS: The Move (Regal Zonophone 1968)★★★★, Shazam (Regal Zonophone 1970)★★★★, Looking On (Fly 1970)★★★, Message From The Country (Harvest 1971) ★★★, California Man (Harvest 1974)★★★.
COMPILATIONS: The Collection (Castle 1986)★★★, The Early Years (Dojo 1992)★★★, The BBC Sessions (Band Of Joy 1995)★★, Movements: 30th Anniversary Anthology 3-CD box set (Westside 1997)★★★★, Looking Back ... The Best Of The Move (Music Club 1998)★★★, Omnibus: The 60s Singles As And Bs (Edsel 1999)★★★, Hits & Rarities Singles A's & B's (Repertoire 1999)★★★★.

MUD
ALBUMS: Mud Rock (RAK 1974)★★★, Mud Rock Vol. 2 (RAK 1975)★★, Use Your Imagination (Private Stock 1975) ★★, It's Better Than Working (Private Stock 1976)★★, Mudpack (Private Stock 1978)★★, Rock On (RCA 1979) ★★, As You Like It (RCA 1980)H, Mud (Runaway 1983)★.
COMPILATIONS: Mud's Greatest Hits (RAK 1975)★★★, Let's Have A Party (EMI 1990)★★, L-L-Lucy (Spectrum 1995)★★, The Gold Collection (EMI 1996)★★, The Singles '67-'78 (Repertoire)★★★.

MUDDY WATERS
ALBUMS: Muddy Waters Sings Big Bill Broonzy (Chess 1960)★★★, Muddy Waters At Newport, 1960 (Chess 1963)★★★★, Muddy Waters, Folk Singer (Chess 1964) ★★★★, Muddy, Brass And The Blues (Chess 1965)★★, Down On Stovall's Plantation (Testament 1966)★★★, Blues From Big Bill's Copacabana (Chess 1968)★★★, Electric Mud (Cadet 1968)★★, Fathers And Sons (Chess 1969)★★★, After The Rain (Cadet 1969)★★, Sail On (Chess 1969) ★★★, The London Sessions (Chess 1971)★★★, Live At Mister Kelly's (1971)★★★, Experiment In Blues (1972)★★★, Can't Get No Grindin' (Chess 1973)★★★, Mud In Your Ear (Musicor 1973)★★★, London Revisited (Chess 1974)★★, The Muddy Waters Woodstock Album (Chess 1975)★★, Unk In Funk (Chess 1977)★★, Hard Again (Blue Sky 1977)★★★, I'm Ready (Blue Sky 1978)★★★, Muddy Mississippi Waters Live (Blue Sky 1979)★★★, King Bee (Blue Sky 1981)★★★, Paris 1972 (Pablo 1997)★★★, Goin' Way Back 1967 recording (Just A Memory 1998)★★★.
COMPILATIONS: The Best Of Muddy Waters (Chess 1957) ★★★★★, The Real Folk Blues Of Muddy Waters (Chess 1966)★★★★, More Real Folk Blues (Chess 1967)★★★★, Vintage Mud (Sunnyland 1970)★★★, They Call Me Muddy Waters (Chess 1970)★★★, McKinley Morganfield aka Muddy Waters (Chess 1971)★★★★, Back In The Early Days (Red Lightnin' 1977)★★★, Chess Masters 3 volumes (Chess 1981-83)★★★★, Rolling Stone (Chess 1982)★★★, Rare And Unissued (Chess 1984)★★★, Trouble No More: Singles 1955-1959 (Chess/MCA 1989)★★★, Muddy Waters 6-LP box set (Chess 1989)★★★★★, The Chess Box 1947-67 9-CD box set (Chess/MCA 1990)★★★★★, Blues Sky (Columbia/Legacy 1992)★★★★, The Complete Plantation Recordings (Chess/MCA 1993)★★★★, The King Of Chicago Blues (Charly 1995)★★★★, His Best: 1947 To 1955 (Chess/MCA 1997)★★★★, His Best: 1956 To 1964 (Chess/MCA 1997)★★★★, King Of The Electric Blues (Columbia/Legacy 1998)★★★, The Lost Tapes (Blind Pig 1999)★★★★, Best Of Muddy Waters: 20th Century Masters (MCA 1999)★★★★, Mojo: The Live Collection (MCI 2000)★★★, The Best Of Muddy Waters: The Millennium Collection (MCA 2000)★★★★, Rollin' Stone: The Golden Anniversary Collection (MCA 2000)★★★★.
VIDEOS: Messin' With The Blues (BMG 1991), Live (BMG 1993), Got My Mojo Working: Rare Performances 1968-1978 (Yazoo 2000).
FURTHER READING: The Complete Muddy Waters Discography, Phil Wight and Fred Rothwell. Muddy Waters Biographie, Francis Hofstein. Muddy Waters: Mojo Man, Sandra B. Tooze.

MUDHONEY
ALBUMS: Superfuzz Bigmuff mini-album (Sub Pop 1988) ★★★, Mudhoney (Sub Pop 1989)★★, Every Good Boy Deserves Fudge (Sub Pop 1991)★★★, Piece Of Cake (Reprise 1993)★★★, Five Dollar Bob's Mock Cooter Stew mini-album (Reprise 1993)★★, My Brother The Cow (Reprise 1995)★★★, Tomorrow Hit Today (Reprise 1998)★★★.
COMPILATIONS: Superfuzz Bigmuff Plus Early Singles (Sub Pop 1991)★★★, March To Fuzz: Best Of & Rarities (Sub Pop 2000)★★★.
VIDEOS: Absolutely Live (Pinnacle 1991), No. 1 Video In America This Week (Warner Music Video 1995).

MUDVAYNE
ALBUMS: L.D. 50 (Epic 2000)★★★, The Beginning Of All Things To End (Epic 2001)★★.
VIDEOS: Dig (Epic Music Video 2001), L(IVE)D)OSAGE) 50 Live In Peoria (Epic Music Video 2001).

MUMBA, SAMANTHA
ALBUMS: Gotta Tell You (Wild Card/Polydor 2000)★★★.

MUSE
ALBUMS: Showbiz (Mushroom/Maverick 1999)★★★, Origin Of Symmetry (Mushroom 2001)★★★.

MY BLOODY VALENTINE
ALBUMS: This Is Your Bloody Valentine mini-album (Tycoon 1984)★★, Ecstasy mini-album (Lazy 1987)★★, Isn't Anything (Creation 1988)★★★★, Loveless (Creation 1991)★★★.

MYSTIKAL
ALBUMS: Mystikal (Big Boy 1995)★★★, Mind Of Mystikal (Jive 1995)★★★, Unpredictable (No Limit 1997)★★★, Ghetto Fabulous (No Limit 1998)★★, Let's Get Ready (Jive 2000)★★★, Tarantula (Jive 2001)★★★.
VIDEOS: Mardi Raw: Close Up And Personal (BMG Video 2001).

N

'N SYNC
ALBUMS: 'N Sync (BMG/RCA 1998)★★★★, Home For Christmas (RCA 1998)★★, No Strings Attached (Jive 2000) ★★★, Celebrity (Jive 2001)★★★★.
VIDEOS: The Ultimate 'N Sync Party! (MVP Home Entertainment 1999), Live At Madison Square Garden (Jive/Zomba Video 2000), 'N The Mix: The Official Home DVD (BMG Video 2000), Making The Tour (Jive/Zomba Video 2001).

N'DOUR, YOUSSOU
ALBUMS: Show A Abidjan (ED 1983)★★, Diongoma (MP 1983)★★★, Immigrés (Celluloid/Earthworks 1984)★★★★, Nelson Mandela (ERT 1985)★★★★, The Lion (Virgin 1989)★★★, Set (Virgin 1990)★★, Eyes Open (40 Acres 1992)★★, Wommat: The Guide (Columbia 1994)★★★★, with Yandé Codou Sène Gainde - Voices From The Heart Of Africa (World Network 1995)★★★, Lii! cassette only (Jololi 1997)★★★, Spéécial Fin D'Année (Jololi 1999)★★★★, Joko (The Link) (Columbia/Nonesuch 2000)★★★★, Le Grand Bal Vol 1 & 2 (Jololi 2000)★★★.
COMPILATIONS: Hey You! The Best Of (Music Club 1993) ★★★, Live: Bir Sorano Juin '93, Vols. 1 & 2 (Studio 1993)★★★.

N.W.A.
ALBUMS: N.W.A. And The Posse (Ruthless 1987)★★★, Straight Outta Compton (Ruthless 1989)★★★★★, Efil4zaggin (Ruthless 1991)★★.
COMPILATIONS: Greatest Hits (Virgin 1996)★★★, The N.W.A. Legacy Volume 1, 1988-1998 (Priority/Virgin 1999)★★★★.

NAPALM DEATH
ALBUMS: Scum (Earache 1986)★★, From Enslavement To Obliteration (Earache 1988)★★★, The Peel Sessions mini-album (Strange Fruit 1989)★★★, Harmony Corruption (Earache/Combat 1990)H, Live Corruption (Earache 1990)★, Utopia Banished (Earache/Relativity 1992)★★, Fear, Emptiness, Despair (Earache/Columbia 1994)★★, Diatribes (Earache 1996)★★, Inside The Torn Apart (Earache 1997)★★, Breed To Breathe mini-album (Earache 1997)★★, Bootlegged In Japan (Earache 1998)★★, Words From The Exit Wound (Earache 1998)★★★, Leaders Not Followers mini-album (Dream Catcher/Relapse 1999)★★, Enemy Of The Music Business (Dream Catcher/Spitfire 2000)★★★.
COMPILATIONS: Death By Manipulation (Earache/Relativity 1991)★★, The Complete Radio One Sessions (Strange Fruit/Fuel 2000)★★★.
VIDEOS: Live Corruption (Fotodisk 1990), The DVD (Earache 2001).

NAS
ALBUMS: Illmatic (Columbia 1994)★★★★, It Was Written (Columbia 1996)★★★★, I Am ... (Columbia 1999)★★★, Nastradamus (Columbia 1999)★★, Stillmatic (Columbia 2001)★★★.
FILMS: Rhyme & Reason (1997), Belly (1998), In Too Deep (1999).

NASH, JOHNNY
ALBUMS: A Teenager Sings The Blues (ABC 1957)★★★, I Got Rhythm (ABC 1959)★★★, Hold Me Tight (JAD 1968) ★★★, Let's Go Dancing (Columbia 1969)★★★, I Can See Clearly Now (Columbia 1972)★★★, My Merry Go Round (Columbia 1973)★★, Celebrate Life (Columbia 1974) ★★★, Tears On My Pillow (Columbia 1975)★★★, What A Wonderful World (Columbia 1977)★★, Johnny Nash Album (Columbia 1980)★★★, Stir It Up (Hallmark 1981)★★, Here Again (London 1986)★★.
COMPILATIONS: Greatest Hits (Columbia 1975)★★★, The Johnny Nash Collection (Epic 1977)★★★, The Reggae Collection (Columbia 1993)★★★, The Best Of (Columbia 1996)★★★.

NAZARETH
ALBUMS: Nazareth (Mooncrest 1971)★★★, Exercises (Mooncrest 1972)★★★, Razamanaz (Mooncrest 1973) ★★★★, Loud 'N' Proud (Mooncrest 1974)★★★, Rampant (Mooncrest 1974)★★★, Hair Of The Dog (Mooncrest 1975) ★★★★, Close Enough For Rock 'N' Roll (Mountain 1976) ★★★, Play 'N' The Game (Mountain 1976)★★, Expect No Mercy (Mountain 1977)★★, No Mean City (Mountain 1978) ★★, Malice In Wonderland (Mountain 1980)★★, The Fool Circle (NEMS 1981)★★★, 'Snaz (NEMS 1981)★★, 2XS (NEMS 1982)★★, Sound Elixir (Vertigo 1983)★★, The Catch (Vertigo 1984)★★, Cinema (Vertigo 1986)★★, Snakes & Ladders (Vertigo 1990)★★, No Jive (Mainstream 1992)★★★, Nazareth At The Beeb (Reef 1998)★★★, Boogaloo (SPV 1998)★★★.
COMPILATIONS: Greatest Hits (Mountain 1975)★★★, 20 Greatest Hits: Nazareth (Sahara 1985)★★★, Anthology: Nazareth (Raw Power 1988)★★★, Greatest Hits Volume 2 (Castle 1998)★★★, Back To The Trenches: Live 1972-1984 (Receiver 2001)★★★, The Very Best Of Nazareth (Eagle 2001)★★★★, Back To The Trenches: Live 1972-1984 (Receiver 2001)★★★.
VIDEOS: Razamanaz (Hendring Music Video 1990).

NELLY
ALBUMS: Country Grammar (Fo' Reel/Universal 2000)★★★.

NELSON, BILL
ALBUMS: Northern Dream (Smile 1971)★★★, as Bill Nelson's Red Noise Sound On Sound (Harvest 1979)★★★, Quit Dreaming And Get On The Beam (Mercury 1981) ★★★★, Sounding The Ritual Echo (Mercury 1981)★★★, Das Kabinet (Cocteau 1981)★★★, The Love That Whirls (Diary Of A Thinking Heart) (Cocteau/PVC 1982)★★★, La Belle Et La Bete (Cocteau/PVC 1982)★★★, Chimera mini-album (Mercury 1983)★★★, Savage Gestures For Charms Sake (Cocteau 1983)★★★, Vistamix expanded re-release of Chimera (Portrait 1984)★★★, A Catalogue Of Obsessions (Cocteau 1984)★★★, The Summer Of God's Piano (Cocteau 1984)★★★, as Bill Nelson's Orchestra Arcana Iconography (Cocteau 1986)★★, Getting The Holy Ghost Across (UK) On A Blue Wing (US) (Portrait 1986)★★★, Chamber Of Dreams (Cocteau 1986)★★★, Map Of Dreams television soundtrack (Cocteau 1987)★★★, Chance Encounters In The Garden Of Lights (Cocteau 1987)★★★, as Bill Nelson's Orchestra Arcana Optimism (Cocteau 1988)★★, Pavilions Of The Heart And Soul (Cocteau 1989)★★★, Demonstrations Of Affection (Cocteau 1989)★★★, Altar Pieces cassette only (The Orpheus Organisation 1990)★★★, Simplex (Cocteau 1990)★★★, Luminous (Imaginary 1991)★★★, Blue Moons & Laughing Guitars (Virgin Venture/Caroline 1992)★★★, Crimsworth (Flowers, Stones, Fountains And Flames) (Resurgence 1995)★★★, Practically Wired (Or How I Became ... Guitar Boy!) (All Saints/Gyroscope 1995)★★★, After The Satellite Sings (Resurgence/Gyroscope 1996)★★★, with Culturemix Culturemix With Bill Nelson (Resurgence 1996)★★★, Buddha Head (Populuxe/Blueprint 1997)★★★, Electricity Made Us Angels (Populuxe/Blueprint 1997)★★★, Deep Dream Decoder (Populuxe/Resurgence 1997)★★★, Atom Shop (Discipline 1998)★★★.
COMPILATIONS: Trial By Intimacy (The Book Of Splendours) 4-LP box set (Cocteau 1984)★★★, The Two Fold Aspect Of Everything (Cocteau 1984)★★★, The Strangest Things Sampler (Cocteau 1989)★★★, Duplex: The Best Of Bill Nelson (Cocteau 1989)★★★, Demonstrations Of Affection 4-CD box set (Cocteau 1990)★★★, My Secret Studio: Music From The Great Magnetic Back Of Beyond 4-CD box set (Resurgence/Gyroscope 1995)★★★, Confessions Of A Hyperdreamer (My Secret Studio, Volume 2) (Populuxe/Resurgence 1997)★★★, What Now, What Next? (Discipline 1998)★★★, Whistling While The World Turns (Lenin 2000)★★★.

NELSON, RICK
ALBUMS: with various artists Teen Time (Verve 1957)★★, Ricky (Imperial 1957)★★, Ricky Nelson (Imperial 1958) ★★, Ricky Sings Again (Imperial 1959)★★, Songs By Ricky (Imperial 1959)★★★, More Songs By Ricky (Imperial 1960) ★★, Rick Is 21 (Imperial 1961)★★, Album Seven By Rick (Imperial 1962)★★, Best Sellers By Rick Nelson (Imperial 1962)★★, It's Up To You (Imperial 1962)★★★, A Long Vacation (Imperial 1963)★★, Million Sellers By Rick Nelson (Imperial 1963)★★★★, For Your Sweet Love (Decca 1963) ★★, Rick Nelson Sings For You (Decca 1963)★★★, Rick Nelson Sings 'For You' (Decca 1963)★★★★, The Very Thought Of You (Decca 1964)★★, Spotlight On Rick (Decca 1964)★★★, Best Always (Decca 1965)★★, Love And Kisses (Decca 1965)★★, Bright Lights And Country Music (Decca 1966)★★★★, On The Flip-Side film soundtrack (Decca 1966)H, Country Fever (Decca 1967)★★★★, Another Side Of Rick (Decca 1968)★★, Perspective (Decca 1968)H, Ricky Nelson In Concert (Decca 1970)★★★, Rick Sings Nelson (Decca 1970)★★★, Rudy The Fifth (Decca 1971)★★★, Garden Party (Decca 1972)★★★★, Windfall (1974)★★, Intakes (Epic 1977)★★, Playing To Win (Capitol 1981)★★★, Memphis Sessions (Epic 1986)★★★, Live 1983-1985 (Rhino 1989)★★★.
COMPILATIONS: The Very Best Of Rick Nelson (Decca 1970) ★★★★, Legendary Masters (United Artists 1971)★★★★
The Singles Album 1963-1976 (United Artists 1977)★★★★, The Singles Album 1957-63 (United Artists 1977)★★★★, Greatest Hits (Rhino 1984)★★★, Rockin' With Ricky (Ace 1984)★★★★, String Along With Rick (Charly 1984)★★★, All My Best (MCA 1985)★★★★, Best Of 1963-1975 (MCA 1990)★★★★, Best Of Rick Nelson, Volume 2 (Capitol 1991) ★★★★, 1969-1976 (Edsel 1995)★★★, The Best Of The Later Years 1963-1975 (Ace 1997)★★★, 25 Greatest Hits (MFP 1998)★★★, with the Stone Canyon Band The Essential Collection (Half Moon 1998)★★★, Anthology (Charly 1998) ★★★, Legacy 4-CD box set (Capitol 2000)★★★★.
FURTHER READING: The Ricky Nelson Story, John Stafford and Iain Young. Ricky Nelson: Idol For A Generation, Joel Selvin. Ricky Nelson: Teenage Idol, Travelin' Man, Philip Bashe.

NELSON, SANDY
ALBUMS: Teen Beat (Imperial 1960)★★★, He's A Drummer Boy aka Happy Drums (Imperial 1960)★★★, Let There Be Drums (Imperial 1961)★★★, Drums Are My Beat! (Imperial 1962)★★★, Drummin' Up A Storm (Imperial 1962)★★★, Golden Hits aka Sandy Nelson Plays Fats Domino (Imperial 1962)★★, On The Wild Side aka Country Style (Imperial 1962)★★, Compelling Percussion aka And Then There Were Drums (Imperial/London 1962)★★★, Teenage House Party (Imperial 1963)★★★, Beat That Drum (Imperial 1963)★★, Be True To Your School (Imperial 1963)★★, Live! In Las Vegas (Imperial 1964)★★, Teen Beat '65 (Imperial 1965)★★★, Drum Discotheque (Imperial 1965)★★, Drums A Go-Go (Imperial 1965)★★, Boss Beat (Imperial 1966)★★, 'In' Beat (Imperial 1966)★★, Superdrums (Imperial 1966)★★, Beat That #!!&* Drum (Imperial 1966)★★, Cheetah Beat (Imperial 1967)★★, The Beat Goes On (Imperial 1967)★★, Soul Drums (Imperial 1968)★★, Boogaloo Beat (Imperial 1968)★★, Rock 'N' Roll Revival (Imperial 1968)★★, Golden Pops (Imperial 1968)★★, Rebirth Of The Beat (Imperial 1969)★★, Manhattan Spiritual (Imperial 1969)★★, Groovy! (Imperial 1969)★★, Keep On Rockin' (United Artists 1972)★★, Roll Over Beethoven aka Hocus Pocus (EMI 1973)★★, Let The Good Times Rock (1974)★★, Bang Bang Rhythm (1975)★.
COMPILATIONS: Best Of The Beats (Imperial 1963)★★★, Best Of Sandy Nelson (Liberty 1974)★★★, The Very Best Of Sandy Nelson (United Artists 1974)★★★, 20 Rock 'N' Roll Hits: Sandy Nelson (EMI 1983)★★★, King Of The Drums: His Greatest Hits (See For Miles 1995)★★★.

NELSON, WILLIE
ALBUMS: And Then I Wrote (Liberty 1962)★★★, Here's Willie Nelson (Liberty 1963)★★★, Country Willie – His Own Songs (RCA Victor 1965)★★★, Country Favorites Willie Nelson Style (RCA Victor 1966)★★★, Country Music Concert (Live At Panther Hall) (RCA Victor 1966)★★★, Make Way For Willie Nelson (RCA Victor 1967)★★★, The Party's Over (RCA Victor 1967)★★★, Texas In My Soul (RCA Victor 1968)★★★, Good Times (RCA Victor 1968)★★★, My Own Peculiar Way (RCA Victor 1969)★★★, Both Sides Now (RCA Victor 1970)★★★, Laying My Burdens Down (RCA Victor 1970)★★★, Willie Nelson And Family (RCA Victor 1971)★★★, Yesterday's Wine (RCA Victor 1971)★★★, The Words Don't Fit The Picture (RCA Victor 1972)★★★, The Willie Way (RCA Victor 1972) ★★★, Shotgun Willie (Atlantic 1973)★★★★, Phases And Stages (Atlantic 1974)★★★, What Can You Do To Me Now (RCA 1975)★★, Red Headed Stranger (Columbia 1975) ★★★★★, with Waylon Jennings, Jessi Colter, Tompall Glaser Wanted! The Outlaws (RCA 1976)★★★★, The Sound In Your Mind (Columbia 1976)★★★★, Phases And Stages 1964 recording (Atlantic 1976)★★, Willie Nelson - Live (RCA 1976)★★, The Troublemaker (Columbia 1976)★★★, Before His Time (RCA 1977)★★, To Lefty From Willie (Columbia 1977)★★★, Stardust (Columbia 1978)★★★★, Face Of A Fighter 1961 recording (Lone Star 1978)★★★, Willie And Family Live (Columbia 1978)★★★, with Jennings Waylon And Willie (RCA 1978)★★★★, with Leon Russell One For The Road (Columbia 1978)★★★★, The Electric Horseman (Columbia 1979)★★★★, Willie Nelson Sings Kristofferson (Columbia 1979)★★, Pretty Paper (Columbia 1979)H, Sweet Memories (RCA 1979)★★★, Danny Davis And Willie Nelson With The Nashville Brass (RCA 1980)★★★, with Ray Price San Antonio Rose (Columbia 1980)★★★, Honeysuckle Rose (Columbia 1980)★★★★, Family Bible (MCA Songbird

1980) ★★★, Somewhere Over The Rainbow (Columbia 1981)★★★, Minstrel Man (RCA 1981)★★, with Roger Miller Old Friends (Columbia 1982)★★★, Always On My Mind (Columbia 1982)★★★★, with Jennings WWII (RCA 1982)★★★★, with Webb Pierce In The Jailhouse Now (Columbia 1982)★★★, with Kris Kristofferson, Brenda Lee, Dolly Parton The Winning Hand (Monument 1982)★★★, with Merle Haggard Poncho And Lefty (Epic 1982)★★★, Without A Song (Columbia 1983)★★, Tougher Than Leather (Columbia 1983)★★★, My Own Way (RCA 1983)★★★, with Jennings Take It To The Limit (Columbia 1983)★★★, with Jackie King Angel Eyes (Columbia 1984)★★, Slow Down Old World (1984)★★★★, City Of New Orleans (Columbia 1984)★★, with Kristofferson Music From Songwriter film soundtrack (Columbia 1984)★★★, with Faron Young Funny How Time Slips Away (Columbia 1984)★★★, with Johnny Cash, Jennings, Kristofferson Highwayman (Columbia 1985)★★★★, with Hank Snow Brand On My Heart (Columbia 1985)★★★, Me And Paul (Columbia 1985)★★★, Half Nelson (Columbia 1985)★★, The Promiseland (Columbia 1986)★★, Partners (Columbia 1986)★★★, Island In The Sea (Columbia 1987)★★★, with Haggard Seashores Of Old Mexico (Epic 1987)★★★, with J.R. Chatwell Jammin' With J.R. And Friends (1988)★★★, What A Wonderful World (Columbia 1988) ★★★, A Horse Called Music (Columbia 1989)★★★, with Cash, Jennings, Kristofferson Highwayman 2 (Columbia 1990) ★★★, Born For Trouble (Columbia 1990)★★★, with Jennings Clean Shirt (Epic 1991)★★, Who'll Buy My Memories - The IRS Tapes (Columbia 1991)★★★, Across The Borderline (Columbia 1993)★★★★, Healing Hands Of Time (Liberty 1994)★★★, Moonlight Becomes You (Justice 1994)★★, with Curtis Porter Six Hours At Pedernales (Step One 1994)★★, with Don Cherry Augusta (Coast To Coast 1995)★★, with Cash, Jennings, Kristofferson The Road Goes On Forever (Liberty 1995)★★, Just One Love (Transatlantic 1995)★★★, Spirit (Island 1996) ★★★★, with Jennings, Colter, Glaser Wanted! The Outlaws (1976-1996, 20th Anniversary) (RCA 1996)★★★★, with Bobbie Nelson How Great Thou Art (Finer Arts 1996)★★, with Bobbie Nelson Hill Country Christmas (Finer Arts 1997)★★, with Cash VH1 Storytellers (American 1998)★★★★, Teatro (Mercury/Island 1998)★★★, Night And Day (Pedernales 1999)★★, Milk Cow Blues (Mercury/Island 2000)★★★, with Larry Butler Memories Of Hank Williams Sr. (BSW 2000)★★★, with the Offenders Me And The Drummer (Luck 2000)★★, with King The Gypsy (FreeFalls 2001)★★★, Rainbow Connection (Mercury/Island 2001)★★★, The Great Divide (Lost Highway 2002)★★★.
COMPILATIONS: The Best Of Willie Nelson (United Artists 1973)★★★, Willie Nelson's Greatest Hits (And Some That Will Be) (Columbia 1981)★★★, 20 Of The Best (RCA 1982) ★★★, Country Willie (Capitol 1987)★★★, The Collection (Castle 1988)★★★, Nite Life: Greatest Hits And Rare Tracks, 1959-1971 (Rhino 1990)★★★★, 45 Original Tracks (EMI 1993)★★★, The Early Years (Scotti Bros 1994) ★★★, The Early Years: The Complete Liberty Recordings Plus More 2-CD set (Liberty 1994)★★★, Super Hits (Columbia 1994)★★★, A Classic And Unreleased Collection 3-CD box set (Rhino 1995)★★★, Revolutions Of Time: The Journey 1975-1993 (Columbia/Legacy 1995) ★★★★, The Essential Willie Nelson (RCA 1995)★★★, 20 Country Classics (EMI 1998)★★★, Sings The Country Hits (Eagle 1998)★★★, My Songs (Eagle 1998)★★★★, with Waylon Jennings The Masters (Eagle 1998) ★★★★, Nashville Was The Roughest ... 8-CD box set (Bear Family 1998)★★★★, 16 Biggest Hits (Legacy 1998)★★★★.
VIDEOS: with Ray Charles First Time Together, My Life – Biography, Willie Nelson And Family In Concert (CBS-Fox 1988), The Best Of (Vestron Video 1990), The Original Outlaw/On The Road Again (Hughes Leisure 1994), Nashville Superstar (Magnum Music 1997), Live In Amsterdam (Aviva International 2001).
FURTHER READING: Willie Nelson Family Album, Lana Nelson Fowler (ed.). Willie Nelson: Country Outlaw, Lola Socbey. Willie, Michael Bane. I Didn't Come Here And I Ain't Leavin', Willie Nelson with Bud Shrake. Heartworn Memories: A Daughter's Personal Biography Of Willie Nelson, Susie Nelson. Willie: An Autobiography, Willie Nelson and Bud Shrake. Willie Nelson Sings America, Steven Opdyke. Behind The Music, Clint Richmond. The Facts Of Life And Other Dirty Jokes, Willie Nelson.
FILMS: The Electric Horseman (1979), Bob & Ray, Jane, Laraine & Gilda (1979), Honeysuckle Rose (1980), Thief (1981), Barbarosa (1982), Hell's Angels Forever (1983), Songwriter (1984), Red Headed Stranger (1986), Dust To Dust (1994), Big Country (1994), Starlight (1996), Gone Fishn' (1997), Anthem (1997), Wag The Dog (1997), Half Baked (1998), Dill Scallion (1999), Austin Powers: The Spy Who Shagged Me (1999).

NEPTUNES
ALBUMS: as N*E*R*D In Search Of ... (Virgin 2001)★★★.

NESMITH, MICHAEL
ALBUMS: Mike Nesmith Presents The Wichita Train Whistle Sings (Dot 1968)★★, Magnetic South (RCA 1970)★★★, Loose Salute (RCA 1971)★★★★, Nevada Fighter (RCA 1971)★★★★, Tantamount To Treason (RCA 1972)★★, And The Hits Just Keep On Comin' (RCA 1972)★★★★, Pretty Much Your Standard Ranch Stash (RCA 1973)★★★★, The Prison (Pacific Arts 1975)★★, From A Radio Engine To The Photon Wing (Pacific Arts 1977)★★★, Live At The Palais (Pacific Arts 1978)★★, Infinite Rider On The Big Dogma (Pacific Arts 1979)★★★, Tropical Campfire's ... (Pacific Arts 1992)★★★, The Garden (Rio Royal 1994)★★, Live At The Britt Festival (Cooking Vinyl 1999)★★★.
COMPILATIONS: The Best Of Mike Nesmith (RCA 1977) ★★★, The Newer Stuff (Awareness 1989)★★★, The Older Stuff (Rhino 1992)★★★★, Complete (Pacific Arts 1993) ★★★, Listen To The Band (Camden 1997)★★★.
VIDEOS: Elephant Parts (Pacific Arts 1981).
FURTHER READING: The Long Sandy Hair Of Neftoon Zamora: A Novel, Michael Nesmith.
FILMS: Head (1968).

NEW KIDS ON THE BLOCK
ALBUMS: New Kids On The Block (Columbia 1986)★★, Hangin' Tough (Columbia 1988)★★★, Merry, Merry Christmas (Columbia 1989)H, Step By Step (Columbia 1990)★★, No More Games/The Remix Album (Columbia 1990)★★, Face The Music (Columbia 1994)★★★.
COMPILATIONS: H.I.T.S (Columbia 1991)★★★, Greatest Hits (Sony 1999)★★★.
FURTHER READING: New Kids On The Block: The Whole Story By Their Friends, Robin McGibbon. New Kids On The Block, Lynn Goldsmith.

NEW MODEL ARMY
ALBUMS: Vengeance (Abstract 1984)★★★, No Rest For The Wicked (EMI 1985)★★★, The Ghost Of Cain (EMI 1986)★★, New Model Army mini-album (EMI 1987)★★, Radio Sessions 83 - 84 (Abstract 1988)★★, Thunder And Consolation (EMI 1989)★★★, Impurity (EMI 1990)★★★, Raw Melody Men (EMI 1990)★★★, The Love Of Hopeless Causes (Epic 1993) ★★★, BBC Radio One: Live In Concert (Windsong 1994)★★, Strange Brotherhood (EMI 1998) ★★★, & Nobody Else (Attack 1999)★★★, Eight (Attack 2000)★★.
COMPILATIONS: The Independent Story (Abstract 1987) ★★★, History (EMI 1992)★★★, B-Sides & Abandoned Tracks (EMI 1998)★★★, All Of This: The 'Live' Rarities (EMI 1999)★★.
VIDEOS: History: The Videos 85-90 (PMI 1993).

NEW ORDER
ALBUMS: Movement (Factory 1981)★★★, Power, Corruption & Lies (Factory 1983)★★★, Low-Life (Factory/Qwest 1985)★★★★, Brotherhood (Factory/Qwest 1986)★★★★, Technique (Factory/Qwest 1989)★★★, Republic (London 1993)★★★★, Get Ready (London/Reprise 2001)★★★.
COMPILATIONS: Substance (Factory/Qwest 1987)★★★★, The Peel Sessions (Strange Fruit 1990)★★★, Live In Concert (Windsong 1992)★★★, (The Best Of) New Order (London 1995)★★★★★, (The Rest Of) New Order (London 1995)★★★.
VIDEOS: Taras Schevenko (Factory 1983), Pumped Full Of Drugs (Factory 1986), Academy (Palace Video 1989), Substance 1989 (Factory/Virgin 1989), New Order Story (PolyGram Video 1993), (The Best Of) New Order (PolyGram Video 1994), New Order 3 16 (Warner Music Vision 2001).
FURTHER READING: New Order & Joy Division: Pleasures And Wayward Distractions, Brian Edge. New Order & Joy Division: Dreams Never End, Claude Flowers.

NEW RIDERS OF THE PURPLE SAGE
ALBUMS: N.R.P.S. (Columbia 1971)★★★★, Powerglide (Columbia 1972)★★★, Gypsy Cowboy (Columbia 1972)★★, The Adventures Of Panama Red (Columbia 1973)★★★, Home, Home On The Road (Columbia 1974)★★, Brujo (Columbia 1974)★★, Oh, What A Mighty Time (Columbia 1975)★★, New Riders (MCA 1976)★★, Who Are These Guys? (MCA 1977) ★★, Marin County Line (MCA 1978)★★, Feelin' Alright (A&M 1981)H, Friend Of The Devil (Relix 1991)★★, Live In Japan (Relix 1994)★★, Live 1982 recording (Avenue 1995)★★.
COMPILATIONS: The Best Of The New Riders Of The Purple Sage (Columbia 1976)★★★, Before Time Began (Relix 1976)★★, Vintage NRPS (Relix 1988)★★, Wasted Tasters (Raven 1998)★★.

NEW SEEKERS
ALBUMS: The New Seekers (Philips 1969)★★★, Keith Potger & The New Seekers (Philips 1970)★★, New Colours (Polydor 1971)★★★, Beautiful People (Philips 1971)★★, We'd Like To Teach The World To Sing (Polydor 1972)★★, Live At The Royal Albert Hall (Polydor 1972)★★, Never Ending Song Of Love (Polydor 1972)★★, Circles (Polydor 1972)★★, Now (Polydor 1973)★★, Pinball Wizards (Polydor 1973)★★, Together (Polydor 1974)★★, Farewell Album (Polydor 1974) ★★, Together Again (Columbia 1976)★★.
COMPILATIONS: Look What They've Done To My Song, Ma (Contour 1972)★★, 15 Great Hits (Orbit 1983)★★, The Best Of The New Seekers (Contour 1985)★★★, Greatest Hits (Object 1987)★★, The Very Best Of The New Seekers (Spectrum 1998)★★★.

NEW YORK DOLLS
ALBUMS: New York Dolls (Mercury 1973)★★★★, Too Much Too Soon (Mercury 1974)★★★, Red Patent Leather (New Rose 1984)★★, I'm A Human Being (Live) (Receiver 1998)★★, Live In Concert: Paris 1974 (Castle 1999)★★★, A Hard Night's Day (Norton 2000)★★.
COMPILATIONS: Lipstick Killers (ROIR 1981)★★★, Best Of The New York Dolls (Mercury 1985)★★★, Night Of The Living Dolls (Mercury 1986)★★★, Rock 'N' Roll (Mercury 1994)★★★★.
FURTHER READING: New York Dolls, Steven Morrissey. The New York Dolls: Too Much Too Soon, Nina Antonia.

NEWMAN, RANDY
ALBUMS: Randy Newman (Reprise 1968)★★★, 12 Songs (Reprise 1970)★★★★, Randy Newman/Live (Reprise 1971) ★★★, Sail Away (Reprise 1972)★★★★, Good Old Boys (Reprise 1974)★★★★, Little Criminals (Warners 1977) ★★★★, Born Again (Warners 1979)★★★, Ragtime film soundtrack (Elektra 1981)★★, Trouble In Paradise (Warners 1983)★★★, The Natural film soundtrack (Atlantic 1984)★★★, Land Of Dreams (Reprise 1988)★★★★, Parenthood film soundtrack (Reprise 1989)★★, Awakenings film soundtrack (Warners 1990)★★, The Paper film soundtrack (Reprise 1994)★★★, Maverick film soundtrack (Reprise 1994)★★, Toy Story film soundtrack (Disney 1995)★★★, Faust (Reprise 1995)★★★, A Bug's Life film soundtrack (Disney 1998)★★★, Bad Love (Dreamworks 1999)★★★★, Toy Story 2 film soundtrack (Disney 1999)★★★, Meet The Parents film soundtrack (Dreamworks 2000)★★★, Monsters, Inc. film soundtrack (Disney 2002)★★★.
COMPILATIONS: Randy Newman Retrospect (Warners 1983)★★★, Lonely At The Top: The Best Of Randy Newman (Warners 1987)★★★★, Guilty: 30 Years Of Randy Newman 4-CD box set (Rhino 1998)★★★★, The Best Of Randy Newman (Rhino 2001)★★★★.
VIDEOS: Randy Newman At The Odeon (Warner Music Vision 2001)

NEWTON-JOHN, OLIVIA
ALBUMS: Olivia Newton-John aka If Not For You (Pye/Festival 1971)★★★, Olivia (Festival/Pye 1972)★★, Music Makes My Day aka Let Me Be There (Pye/Festival 1974)★★, Long Live Love (EMI/Festival 1974)★★, Have You Never Been Mellow (MCA/ EMI 1975)★★★, Clearly Love (MCA/EMI 1975)★★, Come On Over (MCA/EMI 1976)★★, Don't Stop Believin' (MCA/EMI 1976)★★, Making A Good Thing Better (MCA/EMI 1977)★★, Totally Hot (MCA/EMI 1978)★★★, Love Performance 1976 recording (EMI 1980)★★, Physical (MCA/EMI 1981)★★★, Soul Kiss (MCA/Mercury 1985)★★, The Rumour (MCA/Mercury 1988)★★, Warm And Tender (Geffen/Mercury 1989)★★, Gaia: One Woman's Journey (Festival/Pinnacle 1994)★★, Back With A Heart (MCA Nashville 1998)★★★, The Christmas Collection (Hip-O 2001)★★.
COMPILATIONS: Let Me Be There US only (MCA 1973)★★★, Crystal Lady Japan only (EMI 1974)★★★, If You Love Me Let Me Know US only (MCA 1974)★★★, First Impressions (EMI 1974)★★★, Olivia Newton-John's Greatest Hits (MCA/EMI 1977)★★★, Olivia's Greatest Hits (EMI 1982)★★★, Olivia's Greatest Hits Vol. 2 (MCA 1982)★★★, Early Olivia (EMI 1989)★★★, Back To Basics: The Essential Collection 1971-1992 (Festival/Mercury 1992)★★★, 48 Original Tracks (EMI 1994)★★★, Country Girl (EMI 1998)★★★, The Best Of Olivia Newton-John (EMI 1999)★★★, The Best Of Olivia Newton-John: The Millennium Collection (EMI 2002)★★★.
VIDEOS: Physical (PMI 1984), Twist Of Fate (MCA Home Video 1984), Olivia In Concert aka Olivia Newton-John Live (MCA Home Video/Channel 5 Video 1986), Soul Kiss (MCA Home Video 1986), Olivia Down Under (PolyGram Video 1989).
FURTHER READING: Olivia Newton-John: Sunshine Supergirl, Linda Jacobs. Olivia Newton-John, Ann Morse. Olivia Newton-John, Peter Ruff. A Pig Tale, Olivia Newton-John and Brian Seth Hurst. Olivia - More Than Physical: A Collector's Guide, Gregory Branson-Trent. Olivia: One Woman's Story, Darren Mason.
FILMS: Funny Things Happen Down Under (1966), Toomorrow (1970), The Wandering Minstrel Show (1973), Grease (1978), Xanadu (1980), Two Of A Kind (1983), She's Having A Baby (1988), It's My Party (1996), The Main Event (1999).

NICE
ALBUMS: The Thoughts Of Emerlist Davjack (Immediate 1967)★★★, Ars Longa Vita Brevis (Immediate 1968)★★★, The Nice (Immediate 1969)★★★★, Five Bridges (Charisma 1970)★★★★, Elegy (Charisma 1971)★★, The Swedish Radio Sessions (Castle/Sanctuary 2001)★★.
COMPILATIONS: The Best Of The Nice (Essential 1998)★★★, Collection (Castle 1998)★★★, All The Nice (Repertoire 1999)★★★, Here Come The Nice: The Immediate Anthology 3-CD box set (Castle 2000)★★★★.

NICKELBACK
ALBUMS: Curb (Own Label 1996)★★★, The State (EMI Canada/Roadrunner 1999)★★★★, Silver Side Up (EMI Canada/Roadrunner 2001)★★★★.

NICKS, STEVIE
ALBUMS: with Lindsey Buckingham Buckingham-Nicks (Polydor 1973)★★, Bella Donna (Warners 1981)★★★★, The Wild Heart (Warners 1983)★★★, Rock A Little (Modern 1985)★★, The Other Side Of The Mirror (EMI 1989)★★★, Street Angel (EMI 1994)★★, Trouble In Shangri-La (Warners 2001)★★.
COMPILATIONS: Timespace: The Best Of Stevie Nicks (EMI 1991)★★★, The Enchanted Works Of Stevie Nicks 3-CD box set (Atlantic 1998)★★★.
VIDEOS: In Concert (CBS-Fox 1983), Live At Red Rocks (Sony Entertainment 1987), I Can't Wait (Weaver-Finch 1996).

NICO
ALBUMS: Chelsea Girl (Verve 1967)★★, The Marble Index (Elektra 1969)★★★★, Desertshore (Reprise 1971)★★★, with Kevin Ayers, John Cale, Brian Eno June 1 1974 (Island 1974)★★, The End (Island 1974)★★★, Drama Of Exile (Aura 1981)★★★, Do Or Die! Nico In Europe, 1982 Diary (Reach Out 1983)★★★, Camera Obscura (Beggars Banquet 1985)★★, The Blue Angel (Aura 1986)★★, Behind The Iron Curtain (Dojo 1986)★★, Live In Tokyo (Dojo 1987)★★, Live In Denmark (Vu 1987)★★, En Personne En Europe (One Over Two 1988)★★★, Live Heroes (Performance 1989)★★, Hanging Gardens (Emergo 1990)★★, Icon (Cleopatra 1996)★★, Janitor Of Lunacy (Cherry Red 1996)★★, Nico's Last Concert: Fato Morgana (SPV 1996)★★★.
COMPILATIONS: Innocent & Vain: An Introduction To Nico (Universal 2002)★★★, Femme Fatale (Jungle 2002)★★.
VIDEOS: An Underground Experience (Wide Angle/Visionary 1993).
FURTHER READING: The Life And Lies Of An Icon, Richard Witts. Songs They Never Play On The Radio: Nico, The Last Bohemian, James Young.

NILSSON
ALBUMS: Pandemonium Shadow Show (RCA Victor 1967) ★★★, Aerial Ballet (RCA 1968)★★★, Harry (RCA 1969) ★★★★, Skidoo film soundtrack (RCA 1969)★★, Nilsson Sings Newman (RCA 1970)★★★★, The Point (RCA 1971)★★★, Nilsson Schmilsson (RCA 1971)★★★★, Son Of Schmilsson (RCA 1972)★★, A Little Touch Of Schmilsson In The Night (RCA 1973)★★★★, Son Of Dracula (Rapple 1974)★★, Pussy Cats (RCA 1974)★★★, Duit On Mon Dei (RCA 1975)★★, The Sandman (RCA 1975)★★, That's The Way It Is (RCA 1976) ★★★, Knillssonn (RCA 1977)★★, Night After Night (RCA 1979)★★★, Flash Harry (Mercury 1980)★★, A Touch More Schmilsson In The Night (RCA 1988)★★.
COMPILATIONS: Early Years (One Up 1972)★★, Ariel Pandemonium Ballet (RCA 1973)★★★, Early Tymes (DJM 1977)H, Nilsson's Greatest Music (RCA 1978)★★★, Diamond Series: Nilsson (Diamond Series 1988)★★★, Nilsson '62 - The Debut Sessions (Retro 1996)★★, As Time Goes By ... The Complete Schmilsson In The Night (Camden 1997)★★★, The Masters (Eagle 1998)★★★.

NINE INCH NAILS
ALBUMS: Pretty Hate Machine (TVT 1989)★★★, Broken mini-album (TVT 1992)★★, Fixed mini-album (TVT 1992) ★★, The Downward Spiral (Nothing/TVT 1994)★★★★, Further Down The Spiral remix mini-album (TVT/Island 1995)★★★, The Fragile (Nothing/Island 1999)★★★★, Things Falling Apart remix mini-album (Nothing/Island 2000)★★★, And All That Could Have Been (Nothing 2002)★★★.
VIDEOS: Closure (Nothing/Interscope Video 1997), And All That Could Have Been (Nothing/Interscope Video 2002).
FURTHER READING: Nine Inch Nails, Martin Huxley.

1910 FRUITGUM COMPANY
ALBUMS: Simon Says (Buddah 1968)★★, 1, 2, 3 Red Light (Buddah 1968)★★, Indian Giver (Buddah 1969)★★, 1910 Fruitgum Company And Ohio Express (Buddah 1969)★★★.

NIRVANA (UK)
ALBUMS: The Story Of Simon Simopath (Island 1968)★★★, All Of Us (Island 1968)★★, To Markos 3 (Pye 1969)★★, Local Anaesthetic (Vertigo 1971)★★★, Songs Of Love And Praise (Philips 1972)★★, Orange And Blue (Demon 1996)★★★.
COMPILATIONS: Secret Theatre (Edsel 1987)★★, Chemistry 3-CD box set (Edsel 1999)★★★.

NIRVANA (USA)
ALBUMS: "Bleach" (Sub Pop 1989)★★★, Nevermind (Geffen 1991)★★★★★, In Utero (Geffen 1993)★★★★, MTV Unplugged In New York (Geffen 1994)★★★★.
COMPILATIONS: Incesticide (Geffen 1992)★★★, Singles (Geffen 1995)★★★★, From The Muddy Banks Of The Wishkah (Geffen 1996)★★★★.
VIDEOS: Live! Tonight! Sold Out!! (Geffen 1994), Teen Spirit: The Tribute To Kurt Cobain (Labyrinth 1996).
FURTHER READING: Route 666: On The Road To Nirvana, Gina Arnold. Nirvana And The Sound Of Seattle, Brad Morrell. Come As You Are, Michael Azerrad. Nirvana: An Illustrated Biography, Suzi Black. Nirvana: Tribute, Suzi Black. Never Fade Away, Dave Thompson. Kurt Cobain, Christopher Sandford. Teen Spirit: The Stories Behind Every Nirvana Song, Chuck Crisafulli. Nirvana: Nevermind, Susan Wilson. Who Killed Kurt Cobain?, Ian Halperin and Max Wallace. The Nirvana Companion, John Rocco. The Cobain Dossier, Martin Clarke and Paul Woods (ed.). Eyewitness Nirvana: The Day-By-Day Chronicle, Carrie Borzillo. Nirvana, Steve Gullick and Stephen Sweet (photographers). Heavier Than Heaven: The Biography Of Kurt Cobain, Charles R. Cross.
FILMS: Kurt & Courtney (1998).

NITTY GRITTY DIRT BAND
ALBUMS: The Nitty Gritty Dirt Band (Liberty 1967)★★★, Ricochet (Liberty 1967)★★★, Rare Junk (Liberty 1968)★★, Alive (Liberty 1969)★★, Uncle Charlie And His Dog Teddy (Liberty 1970)★★★★, All The Good Times (United Artists 1972)★★★, Will The Circle Be Unbroken triple album (United Artists 1972)★★★★, Stars And Stripes Forever (United Artists 1974)★★, Dreams (United Artists 1975)★★★, as Dirt Band The Dirt Band (United Artists 1978)★★, An American Dream (United Artists 1979)★★★, Make A Little Magic (United Artists 1980)★★, Jealousy (United Artists 1981)★★, Let's Go (United Artists 1983)★★, Plain Dirt Fashion (Warners. 1984)★★★, Partners, Brothers And Friends (Warners 1985)★★★, Hold On (Warners 1987) ★★★, Workin' Band (Warners. 1988)★★★, Will The Circle Be Unbroken Volume II (Warners 1989)★★★★, The Rest Of The Dream (MCA 1991)★★★, Live Two Five (Liberty 1991) ★★★, Not Fade Away (Liberty 1992)★★, Acoustic (Liberty 1994)★★★, The Christmas Album (Rising Tide 1997)★★, Bang Bang Bang (Dreamworks 1998)★★★.
COMPILATIONS: Pure Dirt (Liberty UK 1968)★★, Dead And Alive (Liberty UK 1969)★★, Dirt, Silver And Gold (United Artists 1976)★★★, Gold From Dirt (United Artists UK 1980)★★★, Early Dirt 1967-1970 (Decal UK 1986) ★★★, Twenty Years Of Dirt (Warners 1987)★★★★, Country Store: The Nitty Gritty Dirt Band (Country Store 1987)★★, The Best Of The Nitty Gritty Dirt Band Volume 2 (Atlantic 1988)★★, More Great Dirt: The Best Of The Nitty Gritty Dirt Band, Volume 2 (Warners 1989)★★.

NO DOUBT
ALBUMS: No Doubt (Interscope 1992)★★★, The Beacon Street Collection (Beacon Street 1995)★★★★, Tragic Kingdom (Interscope 1995)★★★★, Return Of Saturn (Interscope 2000)★★, Rock Steady (Interscope 2001)★★★.
VIDEOS: Live In The Tragic Kingdom (Interscope 1997).

NOTORIOUS B.I.G.
ALBUMS: Ready To Die (Bad Boy/Arista 1994)★★★, Life After Death (Bad Boy/Arista 1997)★★★★, Born Again (Bad Boy/Arista 1999)★★★.
VIDEOS: Notorious B.I.G.: Bigger Than Life (IMC/Scimitar 1998).
FURTHER READING: The Notorious B.I.G. - The Murder Of Biggie Smalls, Cathy Scott.

NUCLEUS
ALBUMS: Elastic Rock (Vertigo 1970)★★★★, We'll Talk About It later (Vertigo 1970)★★★, Solar Plexus (Vertigo 1971)★★★★, Belladonna (Vertigo 1972)★★★, Labyrinth (Vertigo 1973)★★★, Roots (Vertigo 1973)★★★, Under The Sun (Vertigo 1974)★★★, Snake Hips Etcetera (Vertigo 1975)★★★, Direct Hits (Vertigo 1976)★★★, In Flagrante Delicto (Capitol 1978)★★★, Out Of The Long Dark (Capitol 1979)★★, Awakening (Mood 1980)★★, Live At The Theaterhaus (1985)★★★.

NUGENT, TED
ALBUMS: Ted Nugent (Epic 1975)★★★, Free For All (Epic 1976)★★★, Cat Scratch Fever (Epic 1977)★★★★, Double Live Gonzo (Epic 1978)★★★, Weekend Warriors (Epic 1978)★★★, State Of Shock (Epic 1979)★★★, Scream Dream (Epic 1980)★★★, Intensities In Ten Cities (Epic 1981)★★★, Nugent (Atlantic 1982)★★, Penetrator (Atlantic 1984)★★, Little Miss Dangerous (Atlantic 1986)★★, If You Can't Lick 'Em ... Lick 'Em (Atlantic 1988)★★, Spirit Of The Wild (Atlantic 1995)★★, Live At Hammersmith '79 (Sony 1997)★★, Full Bluntal Nudity (Spitfire 2001)★★.
COMPILATIONS: Great Gonzos! The Best Of Ted Nugent (Epic 1981)★★★★, Anthology: Ted Nugent (Raw Power 1986)★★★, Out Of Control (Epic 1993)★★★.
VIDEOS: New Year's Eve Whiplash Bash (Atlantic 1991).
FURTHER READING: The Legendary Ted Nugent, Robert Holland.

NUMAN, GARY
ALBUMS: as Tubeway Army Tubeway Army (Beggars Banquet 1979)★★, as Tubeway Army Replicas (Beggars Banquet 1979)★★, The Pleasure Principle (Beggars Banquet 1979)★★★, Telekon (Beggars Banquet 1980)★★★, Living Ornaments 1979-80 (Beggars Banquet 1981)★★, Dance (Beggars Banquet 1981)★★, I Assassin (Beggars Banquet 1982)★★, Warriors (Beggars Banquet 1983)★★, The Plan (Beggars Banquet 1984)★★, Berserker (Numa 1984)★★, White Noise - Live (Numa 1985)★★, The Fury (Numa 1985)★★, Strange Charm (Numa 1986)★★, Exhibition (Beggars Banquet 1987)★★, Metal Rhythm (Illegal 1988)★★, The Skin Mechanic (I.R.S. 1989)★★, Outland (I.R.S. 1991)★★, Machine + Soul (Numa 1992)★★, Dream Corrosion (Numa 1994)★★, Pure (Eagle 2000)★★★.
COMPILATIONS: New Man Numan: The Best Of Gary Numan (TV 1982)★★★, Document Series Presents (Document 1992) ★★, The Best Of Gary Numan (Beggars Banquet 1993) ★★★★, The Premier Hits (PolyGram 1996) ★★★★, The Best Of Gary Numan (Emporio 1997)★★★, Archive (Rialto 1997) ★★, tribute album Random various artists (Beggars Banquet 1997)★★★, The Radio One Sessions (Strange Fruit 1999) ★★★, Down In The Park: The Alternative Anthology (Castle 1999)★★★, New Dreams For Old (Eagle 1999)★★★.
VIDEOS: Dream Corrosion (Numa 1994).
FURTHER READING: Gary Numan By Computer, Fred and Judy Vermorel. Gary Numan: The Authorized Biography, Ray Coleman, Praying To The Aliens, Gary Numan with Steve Malins.

NYRO, LAURA
ALBUMS: More Than A New Discovery aka The First Songs (Verve/Forecast 1967)★★★, Eli And The Thirteenth Confession (Columbia 1968)★★★★, New York Tendaberry (Columbia 1969)★★★★, Christmas And The Beads Of Sweat (Columbia 1970)★★★, Gonna Take A Miracle (Columbia 1971)★★★, Smile (Columbia 1976)★★★, Season Of Lights (Columbia 1977)★★★, Nested (Columbia 1979)★★★, Mother's Spiritual (Columbia 1985)★★, Live At The Bottom Line (Columbia 1990)★★, Walk The Dog And Light The Light (Columbia 1993)★★, Live From Mountain Stage 1990 recording (Blue Plate 2000)★★★, Angel In The Dark (Rounder 2001)★★★.
COMPILATIONS: Impressions (Columbia 1980)★★★★, Stoned Soul Picnic: The Best Of Laura Nyro (Columbia/Legacy 1997)★★★★, various artists Time And Love: The Music Of Laura Nyro (Astor Place 1997)★★★, Time And Love: The Essential Masters (Columbia/Legacy 2000)★★★.

O

O'CONNOR, SINÉAD
ALBUMS: The Lion And The Cobra (Ensign/Chrysalis 1987) ★★★, I Do Not Want What I Haven't Got (Ensign/Chrysalis 1990)★★★★, Am I Not Your Girl? (Ensign/Chrysalis 1992) ★★★, Universal Mother (Ensign/Chrysalis 1994)★★, Faith And Courage (Atlantic 2000)★★★.
COMPILATIONS: So Far ... The Best Of Sinéad O'Connor (Chrysalis 1997)★★★.
VIDEOS: The Value Of Ignorance (PolyGram Music Video 1989), The Year Of The Horse (PolyGram Music Video 1991).
FURTHER READING: Sinéad O'Connor: So Different, Dermott Hayes. Sinéad: Her Life And Music, Jimmy Guterman.
FILMS: Hush-A-Bye-Baby (1990), Wuthering Heights (1992), The Butcher Boy (1997).

O'JAYS
ALBUMS: Comin' Through (Imperial 1965)★★★, Soul Sounds (Imperial 1967)★★★, O'Jays (Minit 1967)★★★, Full Of Soul (Minit 1968)★★★, Back On Top (Bell 1968)★★★, The O'Jays In Philadelphia (Neptune 1969)★★★, Back Stabbers (Philadelphia International 1972)★★★★, Ship Ahoy (Philadelphia International 1973)★★★★, The O'Jays Live In London (Philadelphia International 1974)★★, Survival (Philadelphia International 1975) ★★★, Family Reunion (Philadelphia International 1975)★★, with the Moments The O'Jays Meet The Moments (Philadelphia International 1975)★★★, Message In The Music (Philadelphia International 1976)★★★, Travelin' At The Speed Of Thought (Philadelphia International 1977)★★, So Full Of Love (Philadelphia International 1978)★★★, Identify Yourself (Philadelphia International 1979)★★★, The Year 2000 (TSOP 1980)★★, Peace (Phoenix 1981)★★, My Favorite Person (Philadelphia International 1982)★★, When Will I See You Again (Epic 1983) ★★, Love And More (Philadelphia International 1984)★★★, Love Fever (Philadelphia International 1985)★★★, Close Company (Philadelphia International 1985)★★★, Let Me Touch You (EMI Manhattan 1987)★★★, Serious (EMI 1989)★★, Emotionally Yours (EMI 1991)★★, Heartbreaker (EMI 1993)★★, Love You To Tears (Global Soul/BMG 1997)★★★★, For The Love ... (MCA 2001)★★★.
COMPILATIONS: Collectors' Items: Greatest Hits (Philadelphia International 1977)★★★, Greatest Hits (Philadelphia International 1984)★★★★, From The Beginning (Chess 1984)★★★, Working On Your Case (Stateside 1985)★★★, Reflections In Gold 1973-1982 (Charly 1988)★★★, Love Train: The Best Of ... (Columbia/Legacy 1995)★★★★, The Classic Philadelphia Years (Music Club 1998)★★★, Best Of The O'Jays: 1976-1991 (The Right Stuff 1999)★★★, Significant Singles: The R&B Chart Hits & Flips 1976-87 (Westside 2000)★★★, The Bell Sessions 1967-1969 (Sundazed 2002)★★★.

O'SULLIVAN, GILBERT
ALBUMS: Himself (MAM 1971)★★★, Back To Front (MAM 1973)★★★★, I'm A Writer Not A Fighter (MAM 1973)★★★, A Stranger In My Own Back Yard (MAM 1974)★★, Southpaw (MAM 1977)★★, Off Centre (CBS 1980)★★, Life & Rhymes (CBS 1982)★★, Frobisher Drive (Ultraphone 1987)★★, In The Key Of G (Dover 1989)★★, Sounds Of The Loop (Toshiba/Park 1991)★★, The Little Album (Kitty 1992)★★, Tomorrow Today: Live In Japan '93 (Toshiba 1993)★★, By Larry (Park 1994)★★, Every Song Has Its Play (Park 1995)★★, Singer Sowing Machine (Park 1997)★★, Irish (Kitty 2000)★★.
COMPILATIONS: Greatest Hits (MAM 1976)★★★, 20 Golden Greats (K-Tel 1981)★★★, 20 Of The Very Best (Hallmark 1981)★★★, 20 Golden Pieces (Bulldog 1985)★★★, Unforgettable: 16 Golden Classics (Castle 1987)★★★, Nothing But The Best (Castle 1991)★★★, The Best Of Gilbert O'Sullivan (Rhino 1991)★★★★, Rare Tracks (Kitty 1992)★★, Original Collection 1971 —1977 (Kitty 1990)★★★.

OAKENFOLD, PAUL
COMPILATIONS: Sessions 2 - Paul Oakenfold (MOS 1994) ★★★, Perfection - A Perfecto Compilation (Perfecto 1995) ★★★, Global Underground 004 - Oslo (Boxed 1997)★★★, Global Underground 007 - New York (Boxed/Thrive 1998) ★★★, Tranceport (Kinetic/Reprise 1998)★★★, Resident: Two Years Of Oakenfold At Cream (Virgin 1999)★★★★, shared with Pete Tong, Fatboy Slim Essential Millennium (ffrr 1999) ★★★★, Perfecto Presents Another World (ffrr/Sire 2000) ★★★, Travelling (Perfecto 2000)★★★, A Voyage Into Trance (Hypnotic 2001)★★★, Perfecto Presents Ibiza (Perfecto 2001) ★★★, Bust A Groove (Hypnotic 2002)★★★.

OASIS
ALBUMS: Definitely Maybe (Creation/Epic 1994)★★★★, (What's The Story) Morning Glory? (Creation/Epic 1995) ★★★★★, Be Here Now (Creation/Epic 1997)★★, Standing On The Shoulder Of Giants (Big Brother/Epic 2000)★★★, Familiar To Millions (Big Brother/Epic 2000)★★★.
COMPILATIONS: The Masterplan (Creation/Epic 1998)★★★.
VIDEOS: Live By The Sea (PMI 1995), There And Then (SMV 1996), Familiar To Millions (Big Brother 2000).
FURTHER READING: Oasis: How Does It Feel, Jemma Wheeler. Oasis: The Illustrated Story, Paul Lester. The World On The Street: The Unsanctioned Story Of Oasis, Eugene Masterson. Oasis Definitely, Tim Abbot. Oasis, Mick St. Michael. Oasis '96, Pat Gilbert. Oasis: What's The Story, Ian Robertson. Oasis: Round Their Way, Mick Middles. Brothers: From Childhood To Oasis: The Real Story, Paul Gallagher and Terry Christian. Oasis: The Story, Paul Mathur. Getting High: The Adventures Of Oasis, Paolo Hewitt. Don't Look Back In Anger: Growing Up With Oasis, Chris Hutton and Richard Kurt. Forever The People: Six Months On The Road With Oasis, Paolo Hewitt.

OCEAN COLOUR SCENE
ALBUMS: Ocean Colour Scene (Fontana 1992)★★, Moseley Shoals (MCA 1996)★★★★, Marchin' Already (MCA 1997)★★★, One From The Modern (Island 1999) ★★★, Mechanical Wonder (Island 2001)★★★.
COMPILATIONS: B-Sides, Seasides & Freerides (MCA 1997)★★, Songs For The Front Row (Island 2001)★★★.
VIDEOS: Travellers Tunes/Live At Stirling Castle August 1998 (Universal 1999).

OCEAN, BILLY
ALBUMS: Billy Ocean (GTO 1977)★★, City Limit (GTO 1980)★★, Nights (Feel Like Getting Down) (GTO 1981) ★★★, Inner Feelings (GTO 1982)★★★, Suddenly (Jive 1984)★★★, Love Zone (Jive 1986)★★, Tear Down These Walls (Jive 1988)★★, Time To Move On (Jive 1993)★★, Life (Jive 1997)★★.
COMPILATIONS: Greatest Hits (Jive 1989)★★★, Lover Boy (Spectrum 1993)★★★.

OCHS, PHIL
ALBUMS: All The News That's Fit To Sing (Elektra 1964) ★★★★, I Ain't Marching Any More (Elektra 1965)★★★★, Phil Ochs In Concert (Elektra 1966)★★★, Pleasures Of The Harbor (A&M 1967)★★★★, Tape From California (A&M 1968)★★★, Rehearsals For Retirement (A&M 1969) ★★★★, Phil Ochs Greatest Hits (A&M 1970)★★★, Gunfight At Carnegie Hall (A&M 1971)★★, There And Now: Live In Vancouver (Rhino 1991)★★★.
COMPILATIONS: Phil Ochs - Chords Of Fame (A&M 1976) ★★★★, A Toast To Those Who Are Gone (Archives Alive 1986)★★★, The War Is Over: The Best Of Phil Ochs (A&M 1988)★★★★, There But For Fortune (Elektra 1989)★★★★, The Broadside Tapes: 1 (Folkways 1989)★★★, American Troubadour (A&M 1997)★★★, Farewells & Fantasies 3-CD box set (Elektra/Rhino 1997)★★★★, Live At Newport 1963/1964/1966 recordings (Vanguard 1998)★★★, The Early Years (Vanguard 2000)★★★★, The Best Of Phil Ochs: The Millennium Collection (A&M 2002)★★★★.
FURTHER READING: Phil Ochs: Death Of A Rebel, Marc Elliott. There But For Fortune: The Life Of Phil Ochs, Michael Schumacher.

OFFSPRING
ALBUMS: Offspring (Nemesis 1989)★★, Ignition (Epitaph 1992)★★★, Smash (Epitaph 1994)★★★, Ixnay On The Hombre (Columbia 1997)★★★★, Americana (Columbia 1998)★★★, Conspiracy Of One (Columbia 2000)★★★.
VIDEOS: The Offspring Presents Americana (Columbia 1999), Huck It (Columbia 2001).

OHIO EXPRESS
ALBUMS: Beg, Borrow And Steal (Cameo 1968)★★, Ohio Express (Buddah 1968)★★★, Salt Water Taffy (Buddah 1968)★★, Chewy, Chewy (Buddah 1969)★★★, Mercy (Buddah 1969)★★.
COMPILATIONS: Very Best Of The Ohio Express (Buddah 1970)★★★, The Super K Kollection (Collectables 1994)★★★.

OLDFIELD, MIKE
ALBUMS: Tubular Bells (Virgin 1973)★★★★, Hergest Ridge (Virgin 1974)★★★, with the Royal Philharmonic Orchestra The Orchestral Tubular Bells (Virgin 1975)★★★, Ommadawn (Virgin 1975)★★★, Incantations (Virgin 1978)★★, Exposed (Virgin 1979)★★, Platinum (Virgin 1979)★★, QE2 (Virgin 1980)★★, Five Miles Out (Virgin 1982)★★, Crises (Virgin 1983)★★, Discovery (Virgin 1984)★★, The Killing Fields film soundtrack (Virgin 1984)★★, Islands (Virgin 1987)★★, Earth Moving (Virgin 1989)★★, Amarok (Virgin 1990)★★, Heaven's Open (Virgin 1991)★★, Tubular Bells II (Warners 1992)★★★, The Songs Of Distant Earth (Warners 1994)★★, Voyager (Warners 1996)★★, Tubular Bells III (Warners 1998)★★★, Guitars (Warners 1999)★★, The Millennium Bell (Warners 1999)★★.
COMPILATIONS: Boxed (Virgin 1976)★★★, The Complete Mike Oldfield (Virgin 1985)★★★, Elements: The Best Of Mike Oldfield (Virgin 1993)★★★, The Best Of Tubular Bells (Virgin 2001)★★★.
VIDEOS: The Wind Chimes (Virgin Vision 1988), Essential Mike Oldfield (Virgin Vision 1988), Elements (Virgin Vision 1993), Tubular Bells III Live (Warner Music Vision 1998), The Millennium Bell: Live In Berlin (Warner Music Vision 2001).
FURTHER READING: True Story Of The Making Of Tubular Bells, Richard Newman. Mike Oldfield: A Man And His Music, Sean Moraghan.

OMD
ALBUMS: Orchestral Manoeuvres In The Dark (DinDisc 1980)★★★, Organisation (DinDisc 1980)★★★, Architecture & Morality (DinDisc 1981)★★★, Dazzle Ships (Virgin 1983) ★★, Junk Culture (Virgin 1984)★★★, Crush (Virgin 1985) ★★★, The Pacific Age (Virgin 1986)★★, Sugar Tax (Virgin 1991)★★, Liberator (Virgin 1993)★★★, Universal (Virgin 1996)★★★.
COMPILATIONS: The Best Of OMD (Virgin 1988)★★★★, The OMD Singles (Virgin 1998)★★★★, The Peel Sessions 1979-1983 (Virgin 2000)★★★, Navigation: The OMD B-Sides (Virgin 2001)★★★.
FURTHER READING: Orchestral Manoeuvres In The Dark, Mike West.

ONO, YOKO
ALBUMS: Yoko Ono/The Plastic Ono Band (Apple 1970) ★★★, Fly (Apple 1971)★★★, Approximately Infinite Universe (Apple 1973)★★★, Feeling The Space (Apple 1973)★★, Season Of Glass (Geffen 1981)★★★★, It's Alright (I See Rainbows) (Polydor 1982)★★, Starpeace (Polydor 1985)★★, with Ima Rising (Capitol 1995)★★★, Rising Remixes (Capitol 1996)★★★★, A Story 1974 recording (Rykodisc 1997)★★, Blueprint For A Sunrise (Capitol 2001)★★★.
COMPILATIONS: The Ono Box (Rykodisc 1992)★★★, Walking On Thin Ice (Rykodisc 1992)★★★★.
VIDEOS: The Bed-In (PMI 1991).
FURTHER READING: Grapefruit: A Book Of Instructions And Drawings, Yoko Ono. Yoko Ono: A Biography, Jerry Hopkins. Yoko Ono - Arias And Objects, Barbara Haskell and John G. Hanhardt. All We Are Saying: The Last Major Interview With John Lennon And Yoko Ono, David Sheff.

ORANGE JUICE
ALBUMS: You Can't Hide Your Love Forever (Polydor 1982)★★★, Rip It Up (Polydor 1982)★★★★, Texas Fever mini-album (Polydor 1984)★★★, The Orange Juice (Polydor 1984)★★★, Ostrich Churchyard (Postcard 1992)★★.
SOLO: Zeke Manyika Call And Response (Polydor 1985)★★★, Mastercrime (Some Bizzare/ Parlophone 1989)★★★.
COMPILATIONS: In A Nutshell (Polydor 1985)★★★, The Very Best Of Orange Juice (Polydor 1992)★★★★, The Heather's On Fire (Postcard 1993)★★★.
VIDEOS: Dada With Juice (Hendring Music Video 1989).

ORB
ALBUMS: The Orb's Adventures Beyond The Ultraworld (Big Life/Mercury 1991)★★★★, Peel Sessions (Strange Fruit 1991)★★★★, Aubrey Mixes: The Ultraworld Excursions (Big Life/Caroline 1992)★★★, U.F.Orb (Big Life/Mercury 1992)★★★★, Live 93 (InterModo/Island 1993)★★, Pomme Fritz (InterModo/Island 1994)★★★, Orbus Terrarum (Island 1995)★★★, Orblivion (Island 1997)★★★, Cydonia (Island 2001)★★★.
COMPILATIONS: Peel Sessions 92-95 (Strange Fruit 1996)★★★, Auntie Aubrey's Excursions Beyond The Call Of Duty (Deviant 1996)★★★★, U.F. Off: The Best Of The Orb (Island 1998)★★★★, Auntie Aubrey's Excursions Beyond The Call Of Duty: The Orb Remix Project 2 (Deviant 2001)★★★.
VIDEOS: The Orb's Adventures Beyond The Ultraworld - Patterns And Textures (Big Life 1992), U.F. Off – The Best Of The Orb (Island/Vision Video 1998).

ORBISON, ROY
ALBUMS: Lonely And Blue (Monument 1961)★★, Exciting Sounds Of Roy Orbison (Roy Orbison At The Rockhouse) (Sun 1961)★★, Crying (Monument 1962)★★★, In Dreams (Monument 1963)★★★, Oh Pretty Woman (1964)★★★★, Early Orbison (Monument 1964)★★, There Is Only One Roy Orbison (MGM 1965)★★, Orbisongs (Monument 1965)★★, The Orbison Way (MGM 1965)★★, The Classic Roy Orbison (MGM 1966)★★, Roy Orbison Sings Don Gibson (MGM 1966)★★★, Cry Softly, Lonely One (MGM 1967)★★, The Fastest Guitar Alive (MGM 1968)H, Roy Orbison's Many Moods (MGM 1969)★★, The Big O (MGM 1970)★★, Hank Williams: The Roy Orbison Way (MGM 1970)★★, Roy Orbison Sings (MGM 1972)★★, Memphis (MGM 1972)★★, Milestones (MGM 1973)★★, I'm Still In Love With You (Mercury 1975)★★, Regeneration (Monument 1976)★★, Laminar Flow (Asylum 1979)★★, with Johnny Cash, Jerry Lee Lewis, Carl Perkins The Class Of '55 (1986)★★★, Black & White Night (Virgin 1987)★★★, Mystery Girl (Virgin 1989)★★★★, Rare Orbison (Monument 1989)★★★, King Of Hearts (Virgin 1992)★★★★, Combo Concert: 1965 Holland (Orbison/Demon 1997)★★★.
COMPILATIONS: Roy Orbison's Greatest Hits (Monument 1962)★★★★, More Of Roy Orbison's Greatest Hits (Monument 1964)★★★, The Very Best Of Roy Orbison (Monument 1965)★★★★, The Great Songs Of Roy Orbison (Monument 1970)★★★★, All-Time Greatest Hits Of Roy Orbison, Volumes 1 & 2 (Monument 1976)★★★, Golden Days (Monument 1981)★★★, My Spell On You (Hits Unlimited 1982)★★★, Big O Country (Decca 1983)★★, Problem Child (Zu Zazz 1984)★★, In Dreams: The Greatest Hits (Virgin 1987)★★★★, The Legendary Roy Orbison (Sony 1988)★★★, For The Lonely: A Roy Orbison Anthology 1956-1965 (Rhino 1988)★★★★, The Classic Roy Orbison (1965-1968) (Rhino 1989)★★★, Sun Years (Rhino 1989)★★★★, Our Love Song (Monument 1989)★★★, Singles Collection (PolyGram 1989)★★★, The Sun Years 1956-58 (Bear Family 1989)★★★, The Legendary Roy Orbison (Columbia 1990)★★★★, The Gold Collection (Tristar 1996)★★★, The Very Best Of Roy Orbison (Virgin 1996)★★★★, The Big Roy Orbison: The Original Singles Collection (Monument 1998)★★★, Love Songs (Virgin 2001)★★★★, Orbison 1955-1965 7-CD box set (Bear Family 2001)★★★.
VIDEOS: A Black & White Night: Roy Orbison And Friends (Image Entertainment 2001), Roy Orbison: The Anthology (Kultur/White Star 1999), Double Feature: The Man His Music His Life (Wienerworld 1999).
FURTHER READING: Dark Star, Ellis Amburn. Only The Lonely: The Roy Orbison Story, Alan Clayson. Only The Lonely: The Roy Orbison Story (10th Anniversary Special Edition), Alan Clayson.
FILMS: The Fastest Guitar Alive (1966).

ORBIT, WILLIAM
ALBUMS: Orbit (I.R.S. 1987)★★★★, Strange Cargo (I.R.S. 1987)★★★★, Strange Cargo II (I.R.S. 1990)★★★, Strange Cargo 3 (I.R.S. 1993)★★★, Strange Cargo ? Hinterland (N-Gram 1995)★★★, Pieces In A Modern Style i (N-Gram 1995)★★, Pieces In A Modern Style ii (WEA 2000)★★★.
COMPILATIONS: Strange Cargos (I.R.S. 1996)★★★★.

ORBITAL
ALBUMS: Untitled 1 (Internal/ffrr 1991)★★★, Untitled 2 (Internal/ffrr 1993)★★★★, Peel Session (Internal/ffrr 1994)★★★, Snivilisation (Internal/ffrr 1994)★★★★, In Sides (London/ffrr 1996)★★★★, with Michael Kamen Event Horizon film soundtrack (London 1997)★★, The Middle Of Nowhere (ffrr/PolyGram 1999)★★★★, The Altogether (ffrr 2001)★★★.
VIDEOS: The Altogether (Warner Vision 2001).

ORTON, BETH
ALBUMS: Superpinkymandy (Toshiba/EMI 1993)★★★, Trailer Park (Heavenly 1996)★★★★, Central Reservation (Heavenly 1999)★★★★.

OSBORNE, JEFFREY
ALBUMS: Jeffrey Osborne (A&M 1982)★★★, Stay With Me Tonight (A&M 1983)★★★, Don't Stop (A&M 1984)★★★, Emotional (A&M 1986)★★★, One Love – One Dream (A&M 1988)★★, Only Human (Arista 1990)★★★, Something Warm For Christmas (Modern 1997)★★, That's For Sure (Private/Windham Hill 2000)★★★.
VIDEOS: The Jazz Channel Presents Jeffrey Osborne (Image Entertainment 2001).

OSBORNE, JOAN
ALBUMS: Soul Show (Womanly Hips 1991)★★, Relish (Blue Gorilla/Mercury 1995)★★★★, Righteous Love (Interscope 2000)★★★.
COMPILATIONS: Early Recordings (Mercury 1996)★★.

OSBOURNE, OZZY
ALBUMS: Blizzard Of Oz (Jet 1980)★★★, Diary Of A Madman (Jet 1981)★★★, Talk Of The Devil (Jet 1982)★★★, Bark At The Moon (Jet 1983)★★, The Ultimate Sin (Epic 1986)★★, Tribute (Epic 1987)★★★, No Rest For The Wicked (Epic 1988)★★, Just Say Ozzy (Epic 1990)★★, No More Tears (Epic 1991)★★★, Live & Loud (Epic 1993)★★, Ozzmosis (Epic 1995)★★★★, Down To Earth (Epic 2001)★★★.
COMPILATIONS: Ten Commandments (Priority 1990)★★, The Ozz Man Cometh (Epic 1997)★★★★.
VIDEOS: The Ultimate Ozzy (Virgin Vision 1987), Wicked Videos (CIC Videos 1988), Bark At The Moon (Hendring Music Video 1990), Don't Blame Me (Sony Music Video 1992), Live & Loud (Sony Music Video 1993), Ozzy Osbourne: The Man Cometh (SMV 1997).
FURTHER READING: Ozzy Osbourne, Garry Johnson. Diary Of A Madman: The Uncensored Memoirs Of Rock's Greatest Rogue, Mick Wall.

OSIBISA
ALBUMS: Osibisa (MCA 1971)★★★, Woyaya (MCA 1972)★★★★, Heads (MCA 1972)★★★, Happy Children (Warners 1973)★★, Superfly TNT (Buddah 1974)★★, Osibirock (Warners 1974)★★★, Welcome Home (Bronze 1976)★★, Ojah Awake (Bronze 1976)★★★, Black Magic Night: Live At The Royal Festival Hall (Bronze 1977)★★★★, Mystic Energy (Calibre 1980)★★, Celebration (Bronze 1983)★★, Unleashed: Live In India 1981 (Magnet 1983)★★, Live At The Marquee (Premier 1984)★★★, Monsore (Red Steel 1996)★★★.
COMPILATIONS: The Best Of Osibisa (MCA 1974)★★★, The Best Of Osibisa (BBC 1990)★★★★, Sunshine Day: The Pye/Bronze Anthology (Sequel 1999)★★★★.
VIDEOS: Warrior (Hendring Music Video 1990).

OSMOND, DONNY
ALBUMS: The Donny Osmond Album (MGM 1971)★★★, To You With Love, Donny (MGM 1971)★★, Portrait Of Donny (MGM 1972)★★★, Too Young (MGM 1972)★★, Alone Together (MGM 1973)★★, A Time For Us (MGM 1973)★★, Donny (MGM 1974)★★★, with Marie Osmond I'm Leaving It All Up To You (MGM 1974)★★★, with Marie Osmond Featuring Songs From Their Television Show (Polydor 1975)★★★, with Marie Osmond Make The World Go Away (MGM 1975)★★★, Disco Train (Polydor 1976)★★, Donald Clark Osmond (Polydor 1977)★★, with Marie Osmond New Season (Polydor 1977)★★, with Marie Osmond A Winning Combination (Polydor 1977)★★, with Marie Osmond I'm Leaving It All Up To You (Polydor 1977)★★, with Marie Osmond Goin' Coconuts (Polydor 1978)★★ Donny Osmond (Capitol/Virgin 1989)★★★, Eyes Don't Lie (Capitol 1990)★★★, Christmas At Home (Epic/Legacy 1997)★★, This Is The Moment (Decca 2001)★★★.
COMPILATIONS: My Best To You (MGM 1972)★★★, Superstar (K-Tel 1973)★★★, Greatest Hits (Curb 1992)★★★, Best Of Donny Osmond (Curb 1994)★★★, 25 Hits (Curb 1995)★★★, The Best Of Donny Osmond (Excelsior 1996)★★★.
FURTHER READING: Life Is Just What You Make It: My Life So Far, Donny Osmond and Patricia Romanowski.
FILMS: Goin' Coconuts (1978), Mulan voice only (1998).

OSMONDS
ALBUMS: as the Osmond Brothers Songs We Sang On The Andy Williams Show (MGM 1963)★★, as the Osmond Brothers We Sing You A Merry Christmas (MGM 1963)★★, as the Osmond Brothers The Osmond Brothers Sing The All Time Hymn Favorites (MGM 1964)★★, as the Osmond Brothers The New Sound Of The Osmond Brothers: Singing More Songs They Sang On The Andy Williams Show (MGM 1965)★★, Osmonds (MGM 1970)★★★, Homemade (MGM 1971)★★★, Phase-III (MGM 1972)★★★, The Osmonds "Live" (MGM 1972)H, Crazy Horses (MGM 1972)★★★, The Plan (MGM 1973)★★, Our Best To You (MGM 1974)★★, Love Me For A Reason (MGM 1974)★★, I'm Still Gonna Need You (MGM 1975)★★, The Proud One (MGM 1975)★★, Around The World – Live In Concert (MGM 1975)H, Brainstorm (Polydor 1976)★★, Christmas Album (Polydor 1976)★★, Steppin' Out (Mercury 1979)★★, The Osmond Brothers (Elektra 1982)★★, America Fest (Osmond 1983)★★, One Way Rider (Warners 1985)★★, Today (Range 1985)★★, with Marie Osmond Our Best To You (United 1985)★★.
COMPILATIONS: The Osmonds Greatest Hits (Polydor 1978)★★★, Greatest Hits (Curb 1992)★★★, 21 Hits: Special Collection (Curb 1995)★★★, The Very Best Of The Osmonds (Polydor 1996)★★★.
VIDEOS: Very Best Of (Wienerworld 1996), The Very Best Of The Osmonds (Wienerworld 1999).
FURTHER READING: At Last ... Donny!, James Gregory. The Osmond Brothers And The New Pop Scene, Richard Robinson. Donny And The Osmonds Backstage, James Gregory. The Osmond Story, George Tremlett. The Osmonds, Monica Delaney. On Tour With Donny & Marie And The Osmonds, Lynn Roeder. Donny And Marie Osmond: Breaking All The Rules, Constance Van Brunt McMillan. The Osmonds: The Official Story Of The Osmond Family, Paul H. Dunn. Donny And Marie, Patricia Mulrooney Eldred.

OTWAY, JOHN
ALBUMS: with Wild Willy Barrett John Otway & Wild Willy Barrett (Extracked/Polydor 1977)★★★, with Wild Willy Barrett Deep And Meaningless (Polydor 1978)★★★, Where Did I Go Right? (Polydor 1979)★★★, with Barrett Way & Bar (Polydor 1980)★★, with Wild Willy Barrett I Did It Otway mini-album (Stiff America 1981)★★★, All Balls & No Willy (Empire 1982)★★, with Wild Willy Barrett The Wimp And The Wild (VM 1989)★★, with Attila The Stockbroker Cheryl - A Rock Opera (Strikeback 1991)★★★, Under The Covers And Over The Top (Otway Records 1992)★★, John Otway And The Big Band Live! (Amazing Feet 1993)★★★, Premature Adulation (Amazing Feet 1995)★★★, with the Big Band The Set Remains The Same (Otway Records 2000)★★★.
COMPILATIONS: with Wild Willy Barrett Gone With The Bin Or The Best Of Otway & Barrett (Polydor 1981)★★★, John Otway's Greatest Hits (Strike Back 1986)★★★, Cor Baby That's Really Me! (Strike Back 1990)★★★★.
VIDEOS: John Otway And Wild Willie Barrett (ReVision 1990).
FURTHER READING: Cor Baby, That's Really Me! Rock And Roll's Greatest Failure!, John Otway.

OUTKAST
ALBUMS: Southerplayalisticadillacmuzik (LaFace 1994)★★★★, ATLiens (LaFace 1996)★★★, Aquemini (LaFace 1998)★★★, Stankonia (LaFace 2000)★★★★.
COMPILATIONS: Big Boi & Dre Present ... Outkast (La Face 2001)★★★★.

OUTLAWS
ALBUMS: The Outlaws (Arista 1975)★★★★, Lady In Waiting (Arista 1976)★★★, Hurry Sundown (Arista 1977)★★, Bring It Back Alive (Arista 1978)★★★, Playin' To Win (Arista 1978)★★, In The Eye Of The Storm (Arista 1979)★★, Ghost Riders (Arista 1980)★★★, Los Hombres Malo (Arista 1982)★★, Soldiers Of Fortune (Pasha 1986)★★.
COMPILATIONS: Greatest Hits Of The Outlaws/High Tides Forever (Arista 1982)★★★★, On The Run Again (Raw Power 1986)★★, Best Of The Outlaws: Green Grass And High Tides (Arista 1998)★★★★.

P

P.M. DAWN
ALBUMS: Of The Heart, Of The Soul And Of The Cross: The Utopian Experience (Gee Street 1991)★★★★, The Bliss Album? (Vibrations Of Love And Anger And The Ponderance Of Life And Existence) (Gee Street 1993)★★★, Jesus Wept (Gee Street 1995)★★★, Dearest Christian, I'm So Very Sorry For Bringing You Here. Love, Dad (Gee Street 1998)★★★.

PAGE, JIMMY
ALBUMS: Death Wish II film soundtrack (Swan Song 1982)★★, with Roy Harper Whatever Happened To Jugula (Beggars Banquet 1985)★★★, Outrider (Geffen 1988)★★, with David Coverdale Coverdale/Page (EMI 1993)★★★, with Robert Plant Unledded/No Quarter (Fontana 1994)★★★★, with Plant Walking Into Clarksdale (Atlantic 1998)★★★★, with the Black Crowes Live At The Greek (TVT/SPV 2000)★★★, with John Paul Jones Lovin' Up A Storm (Columbia River 2000)★★★, with John Paul Jones, John Bonham Rock And Roll Highway (Thunderbolt 2000)★★.
COMPILATIONS: Jam Session (Charly 1982)★★, No Introduction Necessary (Thunderbolt 1984)★★, Smoke And Fire (Thunderbolt 1985)★★, Jimmy Page And His Heavy Friends: Hip Young Guitar Slinger (Sequel 2000)★★★★, Guitar For Hire (Castle 2001)★★★.
VIDEOS: with Robert Plant No Quarter (Atlantic 1995).
FURTHER READING: Mangled Mind Archive: Jimmy Page, Adrian T'Vell.

PALMER, ROBERT
ALBUMS: Sneakin' Sally Through The Alley (Island 1974)★★★, Pressure Drop (Island 1975)★★, Some People Can Do What They Like (Island 1976)★★, Double Fun (Island 1978)★★, Secrets (Island 1979)★★, Clues (Island 1980)★★★, Maybe It's Live (Island 1982)★★, Pride (Island 1983)★★, Riptide (Island 1985)★★★★, Heavy Nova (EMI 1988)★★★★, Don't Explain (EMI 1990)★★, Ridin' High (EMI 1992)★★, Honey (EMI 1994)★★★, Rhythm & Blues (Eagle 1999)★★★.
COMPILATIONS: The Early Years (C5 1987)★★, Addictions, Volume 1 (Island 1989)★★★★, Addictions, Volume 2 (Island 1992)★★★, Woke Up Laughing (EMI 1999)★★★, The Essential Collection (EMI Gold 2000)★★★, Some Guys Have All The Luck (Spectrum 2001)★★★.
VIDEOS: Some Guys Have All The Luck (Palace Video 1984), Super Nova (PMI 1989), Video Addictions (PolyGram Music Video 1992), Robert Palmer: The Very Best Of (PMI 1995).

PANTERA
ALBUMS: Metal Magic (Metal Magic 1983)★★★, Projects In The Jungle (Metal Magic 1984)★★★, I Am The Night (Metal Magic 1985)★★★, Power Metal (Metal Magic 1988)★★, Cowboys From Hell (Atco 1990)★★★★, Vulgar Display Of Power (Atco 1992)★★★★, Far Beyond Driven (East West 1994)★★★★, Driven Downunder Tour '94 Souvenir Collection (East West 1995)★★, The Great Southern Trendkill (East West 1996)★★★, Official Live: 101 Proof (East West 1997)★★, Reinventing The Steel (East West 2000)★★★.
VIDEOS: Vulgar Video (A*Vision 1993), 3 - Watch It Go (East West 1998).

PAPA ROACH
ALBUMS: Potatoes For Christmas (Own Label 1994)★★, Old Friends From Young Years (Own Label 1997)★★★, Infest (DreamWorks 2000)★★★★.

PARADISE LOST
ALBUMS: Lost Paradise (Peaceville 1990)★★★, Gothic (Peaceville 1991)★★★, Shades Of God (Music For Nations 1992)★★★, Icon (Music For Nations 1993)★★★★, Draconian Times (Music For Nations 1995)★★★★, One Second (Music For Nations 1997)★★, Host (EMI 1999)★★★, Believe In Nothing (EMI 2001)★★★.
COMPILATIONS: The Singles Collection 5-CD box set (Music For Nations 1997)★★★★, Reflection (Music For Nations 1998)★★★.
VIDEOS: Harmony Breaks (Music For Nations 1994), One Second Live (Paradise Lost 1999).

PARIS, MICA
ALBUMS: So Good (4th & Broadway 1989)★★★, Contribution (4th & Broadway 1990)★★, Black Angel (Cooltempo 1998)★★★★.
VIDEOS: Mica Paris (Island Visual Arts 1991).

PARKER, GRAHAM
ALBUMS: Howlin' Wind (Vertigo/Mercury 1976)★★★★, Heat Treatment (Vertigo/Mercury 1976)★★★★, Stick To Me (Vertigo/Mercury 1977)★★★, The Parkerilla (Vertigo/Mercury 1978)★ Squeezing Out Sparks (Vertigo/Arista 1979)★★★★, The Up Escalator (Stiff/Arista 1980)★★★, Another Grey Area (RCA/Arista 1982)★★★, The Real Macaw (RCA 1983)★★★, Steady Nerves (Elektra 1985)★★, The Mona Lisa's Sister (Demon/RCA 1988)★★★★, Live! Alone In America (Demon/RCA 1989)★★★★, Human Soul (Demon/RCA 1989)★★★, Struck By Lightning (Demon/RCA 1991)★★★, Burning Questions (Demon/Capitol 1992)★★★★, Live Alone! Discovering Japan (Demon 1993)★★★, Live On The Test 1977/1978 recordings (Windsong 1994)★★★, 12 Haunted Episodes (Razor & Tie/Grapevine 1995)★★★, Live From New York, NY (Nectar/Rock The House 1996)★★★, Acid Bubblegum (Razor & Tie/Essential! 1996)★★★, The Last Rock 'N' Roll Tour (Razor & Tie 1997)★★★, Not If It Pleases Me 1976/1977 recordings (Hux 1998)★★★, Deepcut To Nowhere (Razor & Tie/Evangeline 2001)★★★, King Biscuit Flower Hour Presents Graham Parker 1983 recording (King Biscuit Flower Hour 2002)★★★.
COMPILATIONS: The Best Of Graham Parker And The Rumour i (Vertigo 1980)★★★, It Don't Mean A Thing If You Ain't Got That Swing (Vertigo 1984)★★★, Look Back In Anger: Classic Performances (Arista 1985)★★★, Pourin' It All Out: The Mercury Years (Mercury 1985)★★★, The Best Of Graham Parker And The Rumour ii (Vertigo 1992)★★★★, The Best Of Graham Parker 1988-1991 (RCA 1992)★★★, Passion Is No Ordinary Word: The Graham Parker Anthology 1976-1991 (Rhino 1993)★★★★, BBC Live In Concert (Windsong 1996)★★★, No Holding Back 3-CD box set (Demon 1996)★★★, Vertigo (Vertigo 1996)★★★★, Temporary Beauty (Camden 1997)★★★, Hold Back The Night (Rebound 1998)★★★, Loose Monkeys (Up Yours 1999)★★★, Stiffs & Demons (A Collection 1980-93) (Music Club 1999)★★★, Master Hits (Arista 1999)★★★, The Ultimate Collection (Hip-O 2001)★★★★, That's When You Know: The Acoustic Demos & Live At Marble Arch (Universal 2001)★★★, You Can't Be Too Strong: An Introduction To Graham Parker & The Rumour (Decca 2001)★★★.
VIDEOS: Graham Parker Live (Castle Music Video 1982).
FURTHER READING: Carp Fishing On Valium, Graham Parker.

PARLIAMENT
ALBUMS: Osmium (Invictus 1970)★★★, Up For The Down Stroke (Casablanca 1974)★★★★, Chocolate City (Casablanca 1975)★★★, Mothership Connection (Casablanca 1976)★★★★, The Clones Of Doctor Funkenstein (Casablanca 1976)★★★★, Parliament Live - P. Funk Earth Tour (Casablanca 1977)★★★, Funkentelechy Vs The Placebo Syndrome (Casablanca 1977)★★★★, Motor-Booty Affair (Casablanca 1978)★★★★, Gloryhallastoopid (Or Pin The Tale On The Funky) (Casablanca 1979)★★★, Trombipulation (Casablanca 1980)★★★, Dope Dogs (Hot Hands 1995)★★★.
COMPILATIONS: Parliament's Greatest Hits (Casablanca 1984)★★★★, The Best Of Parliament (Club 1986)★★★, Rhenium (Demon 1990)★★★, Tear The Roof Off 1974-80 (Casablanca 1993)★★★★, Parliament-Funkadelic Live 1976-93 4-CD box set (Sequel 1994)★★★★, The Early Years (Deep Beats 1997)★★★, Get Funked Up! The Ultimate Collection (Spectrum 2000)★★★, Osmium (The Complete Invictus Recordings) (Sequel 2001)★★★.

PARSONS, ALAN
ALBUMS: Tales Of Mystery And Imagination (Charisma 1975)★★★, I Robot (Arista 1977)★★★, Pyramid (Arista 1978)★★★, Eve (Arista 1979)★★★★, The Turn Of A Friendly Card (Arista 1980)★★★, Eye In The Sky (Arista 1982)★★★, Ammonia Avenue (Arista 1984)★★★, Vulture Culture (Arista 1985)★★, Stereotomy (Arista 1985)★★, Gaudi (Arista 1987)★★, Try Anything Once (Arista 1993)★★, On Air (Tot 1997)★★, The Time Machine (Arcade/Miramar 1999)★★★.
COMPILATIONS: The Best Of The Alan Parsons Project (Arista 1983)★★★, Limelight: The Best Of The Alan Parsons Project Volume 2 (Arista 1988)★★, Instrumental Works (Arista 1988)★★★, The Definitive Collection (Arista 1997)★★★.

PARSONS, GRAM
ALBUMS: GP (Reprise 1972)★★★★, Grievous Angel (Reprise 1973)★★★★, Gram Parsons & The Fallen Angels: Live 1973 (Sierra 1981)★★★, Cosmic American Music: The Rehearsal Tapes 1972 demos (Sundown 1995)★★★.
COMPILATIONS: with the Flying Burrito Brothers Sleepless Nights (A&M 1976)★★★, Gram Parsons (Warners 1982)★★★, The Early Years 1963-1965 (Sierra/Briar 1984)★★★, with the Flying Burrito Brothers Dim Lights, Thick Smoke And Loud, Loud Music (Edsel 1987)★★★, Warm Evenings, Pale Mornings, Bottled Blues 1963-1973 (Raven 1992)★★★, Another Side Of This Life: The Lost Recordings Of Gram Parsons 1965-1966 (Sundazed 2000)★★★, Sacred Hearts/Fallen Angels: The Gram Parsons Anthology (Rhino 2001)★★★★.
FURTHER READING: Gram Parsons: A Music Biography, Sid Griffin (ed.). Hickory Wind: The Life And Times Of Gram Parsons, Ben Fong-Torres.

PARTON, DOLLY
ALBUMS: Hello, I'm Dolly (Monument 1967)★★, with Porter Wagoner Just Between You And Me (RCA Victor 1968)★★★, with George Jones Dolly Parton And George Jones (Starday 1968)★★, Just Because I'm A Woman (RCA 1968)★★★, with Wagoner Just The Two Of Us (RCA Victor 1968)★★★★, with Wagoner Always, Always (RCA Victor 1969)★★★, My Blue Ridge Mountain Boy (RCA 1969)★★★, with Wagoner Porter Wayne And Dolly Rebecca (RCA Victor 1970)★★★, A Real Live Dolly (RCA 1970)★★★, with Wagoner Once More (RCA Victor 1970)★★★, with Wagoner Two Of A Kind (RCA Victor 1971)★★★, Coat Of Many Colours (RCA 1971)★★★★, with Wagoner The Right Combination (RCA Victor 1972)★★★, with Wagoner Together Always (RCA Victor 1972)★★★, with Wagoner Love And Music (RCA Victor 1973)★★★, with Wagoner We Found It (RCA Victor 1973)★★★, My Tennessee Mountain Home (RCA 1973)★★★★, with Wagoner Porter 'N' Dolly (RCA 1974)★★★, Love Is Like A Butterfly (RCA 1974)★★★★, Jolene (RCA 1974)★★★★, with Wagoner Say Forever You'll Be Mine (RCA 1975)★★★, The Bargain Store (RCA 1975)★★★★, Dolly (RCA 1976)★★★, All I Can Do (RCA 1976)★★★, New Harvest ... First Gathering (RCA 1977)★★★★, Here You Come Again (RCA 1977)★★, Heartbreaker (RCA 1978)★★, Dolly Parton And Friends At Goldband (1979)★★, Great Balls Of Fire (RCA 1979)★★, with Wagoner Porter Wagoner & Dolly Parton (RCA 1980)★★★★, Dolly Dolly Dolly (RCA 1980)★★, 9 To 5 And Odd Jobs (RCA 1980)★★★, Heartbreak Express (RCA 1982)★★, The Best Little Whorehouse In Texas film soundtrack (MCA 1982)★★, with Kris Kristofferson, Brenda Lee, Willie Nelson The Winning Hand (Monument 1983)★★★, Burlap And Satin (RCA 1983)★★, The Great Pretender (RCA 1984)★★, Rhinestone film soundtrack (RCA 1984)★★, with Kenny Rogers Once Upon A Christmas (RCA 1984)★★★, Real Love (RCA 1985)★★★, with Emmylou Harris, Linda Ronstadt Trio (Warners 1987)★★★★, Rainbow (Columbia 1987)★★, White Limozeen (Columbia 1989)★★★, Eagle When She Flies (Columbia 1991)★★★, Straight Talk film soundtrack (Hollywood 1992,)★★, Slow Dancing With The Moon (Columbia 1993)★★★, with Wagoner Sweet Harmony (RCA 1993)★★, with Tammy Wynette, Loretta Lynn Honky Tonk Angels (Columbia 1993)★★★★, Heartsongs - Live From Home (Columbia 1994)★★★, Something Special (Columbia 1995)★★★, Treasures (Rising Tide 1996)★★★, Hungry Again (MCA Nashville 1998)★★★, with Harris, Ronstadt Trio II (Asylum 1999)★★★, The Grass Is Blue (Sugar Hill/Blue Eye 1999)★★★★, Little Sparrow (Sugar Hill/Sanctuary 2001)★★★★.
COMPILATIONS: with Porter Wagoner The Best Of Porter Wagoner And Dolly Parton (RCA Victor 1971)★★★★, The Best Of Dolly Parton (RCA 1973)★★★★, The Best Of Dolly Parton Volume 2 (RCA 1975)★★★★, with Wagoner Hits Of Dolly Parton And Porter Wagoner (RCA 1977)★★★★, The Dolly Parton Collection (Pickwick 1979)★★★, The Very Best Of Dolly Parton (RCA 1981)★★★★, The Dolly Parton Collection (Monument 1982)★★★, Greatest Hits (RCA 1982)★★, Collector's Series (RCA 1985)★★★, The World Of Dolly Parton, Volume 1 (Monument 1988)★★★, The World Of Dolly Parton, Volume 2 (Monument 1988)★★★, Greatest Hits Volume 2 (RCA 1989)★★, Anthology (Connoisseur 1991)★★★, The RCA Years 1967-1986 2-CD set (RCA 1993)★★★★, The Essential Dolly Parton - Volume One (RCA 1995)★★★, The Greatest Hits (Telstar 1995)★★★, with Wagoner The Essential Porter And Dolly (RCA 1996)★★★★, I Will Always Love You And Other Greatest Hits (Columbia 1996)★★★, The Essential Dolly Parton - Volume Two (RCA 1997)★★★, The Ultimate Dolly Parton (BMG 1997)★★★, A Life In Music: The Ultimate Collection (BMG 1999)★★★, Mission Chapel Memories 1971-1975 (Raven 2001)★★★★.
VIDEOS: Dolly Parton In London (RCA/Columbia 1988), with Kenny Rogers Real Love (RCA/Columbia 1988), Blue Valley Songbird (Aviva International 2001).
FURTHER READING: Dolly Parton: Country Goin' To Town, Susan Saunders. Dolly Parton, Otis James. The Official Dolly Parton Scrapbook, Connie Berman. Dolly, Alanna Nash. Dolly Parton (By Scott Keely), Scott Keely. Dolly Parton, Robert K. Krishef. Dolly, Here I Come Again, Leonore Fleischer. My Story, Dolly Parton.
FILMS: Nine To Five (1980), The Best Little Whorehouse In Texas (1982), Rhinestone (1984), Steel Magnolias (1989), Straight Talk (1992), The Beverly Hillbillies (1993), Heartsong (1995).

PAUL, LES
ALBUMS: with Mary Ford Hawaiian Paradise (Decca 1949)★★, Galloping Guitars (Decca 1952)★★★, with Ford New Sound, Volume 1 & 2 (Capitol 1950)★★★, Bye, Bye Blues (Capitol 1952)★★★★, with Ford The Hitmakers (Capitol 1955)★★★, Les And Mary (Capitol 1955)★★★★, with Ford Time To Dream (Capitol 1957)★★★, More Of Les (Decca 1958)★★★, with Ford Lover's Luau (Columbia 1959)★★★, with Ford Warm And Wonderful (Columbia 1962)★★★, with Ford Bouquet Of Roses (Columbia 1962)★★★, with Ford Swingin' South (Columbia 1963)★★★, Les Paul Now (Decca 1968)★★★, with Chet Atkins Chester & Lester (RCA Victor 1975)★★★, with Atkins Guitar Monsters (RCA Victor 1978)★★★.
COMPILATIONS: The Hits Of Les And Mary (Capitol 1960)★★★★, The Fabulous Les Paul And Mary Ford (Columbia 1965)★★★, The Very Best Of Les Paul And Mary Ford (1974)★★★★, with Ford The Capitol Years (Capitol 1989)★★★★, The Legend And The Legacy 4-CD box set (Capitol 1991)★★★★, with Ford Blowing The Smoke Away From A Trail Of Hits (Jasmine 2000)★★, with Ford The Collection ... Plus (See For Miles 2001)★★★.
VIDEOS: He Changed The Music (Excalibur 1990), Living Legend Of The Electric Guitar (BMG 1995).
FURTHER READING: Les Paul: An American Original, Mary Alice Shaughnessy. Gibson Les Paul Book: A Complete History Of Les Paul Guitars, Tony Bacon and Paul Day.

PAVEMENT
ALBUMS: Perfect Sound Forever mini-album (Drag City 1991)★★★, Slanted And Enchanted (Matador 1992)★★★★, Crooked Rain, Crooked Rain (Matador 1994)★★★★, Wowee Zowee! (Matador 1995)★★, Brighten The Corners (Matador 1997)★★★, Terror Twilight (Matador 1999)★★★★.
COMPILATIONS: Westing (By Musket And Sextant) (Drag City 1993)★★★.

PAXTON, TOM
ALBUMS: I'm The Man That Built The Bridges (Gaslight 1962)★★, Ramblin' Boy (Elektra 1964)★★★★, Ain't That News (Elektra 1965)★★★, Outward Bound (Elektra 1966)★★★, Morning Again (Elektra 1967)★★★, The Things I Notice Now (Elektra 1968)★★★★, #6 (Elektra 1970)★★★, How Come The Sun (Reprise 1971)★★★, Peace Will Come (Reprise 1972)★★★, New Songs For Old Friends (Reprise 1973)★★★, Children's Song Book (Bradleys 1974)★★, Something In My Life (Private Stock 1975)★★★, Saturday Night (MAM 1976)★★★, New Songs From The Briarpatch (Vanguard 1977)★★★, Heroes (Vanguard 1978)★★★, Up & Up (Mountain Railroad 1979)★★★, The Paxton Report (Mountain Railroad 1980)★★★, Bulletin (Hogeye 1983)★★★, Even A Gray Day (Flying Fish 1983)★★★, The Marvellous Toy And Other Gallimaufry (Flying Fish 1984)★★★, One Million Lawyers And Other Disasters (Flying Fish 1985)★★★, And Loving You (Flying Fish 1986)★★★, Balloon-Alloon-Alloon (Sony Kids 1987)★★★, Politics Live (Flying Fish 1988)★★, It Ain't Easy (Flying Fish 1991)★★★, A Child's Christmas (Sony Kids 1992)★★★, Peanut Butter Pie (Sony Kids 1992)★★★, Suzy Is A Rocker (Sony Kids 1992)★★★, Wearing The Time (Sugar Hill 1994)★★★, Live For The Record (Sugar Hill 1996)★★★, A Car Full Of Songs (Sony Kids 1997)★★★, Goin' To The Zoo (Rounder 1997)★★★, I've Got A Yo-Yo (Rounder 1997)★★★, Live In Concert (Strange Fruit 1998)★★★, Fun Animal Songs (Delta 1999)★★★, Fun Food Songs (Delta 1999)★★★, A Car Full Of Fun Songs (Delta 1999)★★★, Live From Mountain Stage (Blue Plate 2001)★★★, with Anne Hills Under American Skies (Appleseed/Koch 2001)★★★.
COMPILATIONS: The Compleat Tom Paxton (Elektra 1970)★★★, A Paxton Primer (Pax 1986)★★★, The Very Best Of Tom Paxton (Flying Fish 1988)★★★, Storyteller (Start 1989)★★★, I Can't Help But Wonder Where I'm Bound: The Best Of Tom Paxton (Rhino 1999)★★★★, Best Of The Vanguard Years (Vanguard 2000)★★★.
FURTHER READING: Englebert The Elephant, Tom Paxton and Steven Kellogg. Belling The Cat And Other Aesop's Fables, Tom Paxton and Robert Rayevsky. The Story Of The Tooth Fairy, Tom Paxton. Going To The Zoo, Tom Paxton.

PEARL JAM
ALBUMS: Ten (Epic 1991)★★★★, Vs (Epic 1993)★★★★, Vitalogy (Epic 1994)★★★★, No Code (Epic 1996)★★★★, Yield (Epic 1998)★★★, Live: On Two Legs (Epic 1998)★★★, Binaural (Epic 2000)★★★, 23/5/00: Estadio Do Restelo, Lisbon, Portugal (Epic 2000)★★★, 25/5/00: Palau Sant Jordi, Barcelona, Spain (Epic 2000)★★★, 26/5/00: Velodromo Anoeta, San Sebastian, Spain (Epic 2000)★★, 29/5/00: Wembley Arena, London, England (Epic 2000)★★★, 30/5/00: Wembley Arena, London, England (Epic 2000)★★★, 01/6/00: The Point Theater, Dublin, Ireland (Epic 2000)★★★, 03/6/00: SE+CC Arena, Glasgow, Scotland (Epic 2000)★★★, 04/6/00: Manchester Evening News Arena, Manchester, England (Epic 2000)★★★, 06/6/00: Cardiff International Arena, Cardiff, Wales (Epic 2000)★★★, 08/6/00: Bercy, Paris, France (Epic 2000)★★★, 09/6/00: Nürburg Ring, Eifel, Germany (Epic 2000)★★★, 11/6/00: Nürnberg, Germany (Epic 2000)★★★, 12/6/00: Pinkpop, Heerden, Holland (Epic 2000)★★★, 14/6/00: Paegas Arena, Praha, Czech Republic (Epic 2000)★★★, 15/6/00: Spodek, Katowice, Poland (Epic 2000)★★, 16/6/00: Spodek, Katowice, Poland (Epic 2000)★★★★, 18/6/00: Salzburg City Square, Salzburg, Austria (Epic 2000)★★★, 19/6/00: Hala Tivoli, Ljubljana, Slovenia (Epic 2000)★★★, 20/6/00: Arena Di Verona, Verona, Italy (Epic 2000)★★★, 22/6/00: Fila Forum Arena, Milan, Italy (Epic 2000)★★★, 23/6/00: Hallenstadion, Zurich, Switzerland (Epic 2000)★★★, 25/6/00: Parkbühne Wuhlheide, Berlin, Germany (Epic 2000)★★★, 26/6/00: Sporthalle, Hamburg, Germany (Epic 2000)★★★, 28/6/00: Maritime Museum, Stockholm, Sweden (Epic 2000)★★★, 29/6/00: Spectrum, Oslo, Norway (Epic 2000)★★★, August 3 2000: Virginia Beach, Virginia (Epic 2001)★★★, August 4 2000: Charlotte, North Carolina (Epic 2001)★★★, August 6 2000: Greensboro, North Carolina (Epic 2001)★★★, August 7 2000: Atlanta, Georgia (Epic 2001)★★★, August 9 2000: West Palm Beach, Florida (Epic 2001)★★★, August 10 2000: West Palm Beach, Florida (Epic 2001)★★★, August 12 2000: Tampa, Florida (Epic 2001)★★★, August 14 2000: New Orleans, Louisiana (Epic 2001)★★★, August 15 2000: Memphis, Tennessee (Epic 2001)★★★★, August 17 2000: Nashville, Tennessee (Epic 2001)★★★, August 18 2000: Indianapolis, Indiana (Epic 2001)★★★★, August 20 2000: Cincinnati, Ohio (Epic 2001)★★★, August 21 2000: Columbus, Ohio (Epic 2001)★★★, August 23 2000: Jones Beach, New York (Epic 2001)★★★, August 24 2000: Jones Beach, New York (Epic 2001)★★★, August 25 2000: Jones Beach, New York (Epic 2001)★★★★, August 27 2000: Saratoga, New York (Epic 2001)★★★, August 29 2000: Boston, Massachusetts (Epic 2001)★★★★, August 30 2000: Boston, Massachusetts (Epic 2001)★★★, September 1 2000: Philadelphia, Pennsylvania (Epic 2001)★★★★, September 2 2000: Philadelphia, Pennsylvania (Epic 2001)★★★, September 4 2000: Washington, DC (Epic 2001)★★★, September 5 2000: Pittsburgh, Pennsylvania (Epic 2001)★★★★, October 4 2000: Montreal, Canada (Epic 2001)★★★, October 5 2000: Toronto, Canada (Epic 2001)★★★, October 7 2000: Detroit, Michigan (Epic 2001)★★★, October 8 2000: East Troy, Wisconsin (Epic 2001)★★★, October 9 2000: Chicago, Illinois (Epic 2001)★★★, October 11 2000: St Louis, Missouri (Epic 2001)★★★, October 12 2000: Kansas City, Missouri (Epic 2001)★★★, October 14 2000: Houston, Texas (Epic 2001)★★★, October 15 2000: Houston, Texas (Epic 2001)★★★, October 17 2000: Dallas, Texas (Epic 2001)★★★, October 18 2000: Lubbock, Texas (Epic 2001)★★★, October 20 2000: Albuquerque, New Mexico (Epic 2001)★★★, October 21 2000: Phoenix, Arizona (Epic 2001)★★★, October 22 2000: Las Vegas, Nevada (Epic 2001)★★★★, October 24 2000: Los Angeles, California (Epic 2001)★★★, October 25 2000: San Diego, California (Epic 2001)★★★, October 27 2000: Fresno, California (Epic 2001)★★★, October 28 2000: San Bernardino, California (Epic 2001)★★★, October 30 2000: Sacramento, California (Epic 2001)★★★, October 31 2000: San Francisco, California (Epic 2001)★★★, November 2 2000: Portland, Oregon (Epic 2001)★★★, November 3 2000: Boise, Idaho (Epic 2001)★★★, November 5 2000: Seattle, Washington (Epic 2001)★★★★, November 6 2000: Seattle, Washington (Epic 2001)★★★.
Solo: Stone Gossard Bayleaf (Epic 2001)★★.
VIDEOS: Single Video Theory (Sony Music Video 1998), Touring Band 2000 (Sony Music Video 2001).
FURTHER READING: Pearl Jam: The Illustrated Biography, Brad Morrell. Pearl Jam Live!, Joey Lorenzo (compiler). The Illustrated Story, Allan Jones. Pearl Jam & Eddie Vedder: None Too Fragile, Martin Clarke. Five Against One: The Pearl Jam Story, Kim Neely.

PEEBLES, ANN
ALBUMS: This Is Ann Peebles (Hi 1969)★★★, Part Time Love (Hi 1971)★★★, Straight From The Heart (Hi 1972)★★★, I Can't Stand The Rain (Hi 1974)★★★★, Tellin' It (Hi 1976)★★★, If This Is Heaven (Hi 1978)★★★, The Handwriting On The Wall (Hi 1979)★★★, Call Me (Waylo 1990)★★★, Full Time Love (Rounder/Bullseye 1992)★★★, Fill This World With Love (Bullseye Blues 1996)★★★.
COMPILATIONS: I'm Gonna Tear Your Playhouse Down (Hi 1985)★★★★, 99 lbs (Hi 1987)★★★, Greatest Hits (Hi 1988)★★★★, Lookin' For A Lovin' (Hi 1990)★★★, The Best Of Ann Peebles: The Hi Records Years (Capitol 1996)★★★, U.S. R&B Hits '69-'79 (Hi 1996)★★★, St. Louis Woman 4-CD box set (Hi 1996)★★★★, The Hi Masters (Hi 1998)★★★, How Strong Is A Woman - The Story Of Ann Peebles (1969-80) (Hi 1998)★★★.

PENDERGRASS, TEDDY
ALBUMS: Teddy Pendergrass (Philadelphia International 1977)★★★, Life Is A Song Worth Singing (Philadelphia International 1978)★★★, Teddy (Philadelphia International 1979)★★★★, Teddy Live! (Coast To Coast) (Philadelphia International 1979)★★, T.P. (Philadelphia International 1980)★★★★, It's Time For Love (Philadelphia International 1981)★★★, This One's For You (Philadelphia International 1982)★★★, Heaven Only Knows (Philadelphia International 1983)★★★, Love Language (Asylum 1984)★★, Workin' It Back (Asylum 1985)★★★, Joy (Elektra 1988)★★★, Truly Blessed (Elektra 1991)★★★, A Little More Magic (Elektra 1993)★★★, You And I (Surefire 1997)★★★, This Christmas (I'd Rather Have Love) (Surefire 1998)★★.
COMPILATIONS: Greatest Hits (Philadelphia International 1984)★★★★, The Philly Years (Repertoire 1995)★★★★, The Best Of Teddy Pendergrass: Turn Off The Lights (Music Club 1998)★★★, Significant Singles: The R&B Chart Hits & Flips 1977-84 (Westside 2000)★★★, Somebody Loves You Back: The Mixes (Cleopatra 2002)★★★.
VIDEOS: Teddy Pendergrass Live (CBS-Fox 1988).
FURTHER READING: Truly Blessed, Teddy Pendergrass and Patricia Romanowski.

PENTANGLE
ALBUMS: The Pentangle (Transatlantic 1968)★★★★, Sweet Child (Transatlantic 1968)★★★★, Basket Of Light (Transatlantic 1969)★★★★, Cruel Sister (Transatlantic 1970)★★★, Reflection (Transatlantic 1971)★★★★, Solomon's Seal (Reprise 1972)★★★, Open The Door (Making Waves 1983)★★★, In The Round (Making Waves 1985)★★★, So Early In The Spring (Park 1988)★★★, Think Of Tomorrow (Ariola/Hypertension 1991)★★★, One More Road (Permanent 1993)★★★, Live At The BBC (Strange Fruit 1994)★★★★, Live 1994 (Hypertension 1995)★★, On Air (Strange Fruit 1998)★★★, as Jacqui McShee's Pentangle Passe-Avant (Park 1998)★★★, as Jacqui

McShee's Pentangle *At The Little Theatre* (Park 2001)★★★.
COMPILATIONS: *History Book* (Transatlantic 1972)★★★★, *Pentangling* (Transatlantic 1973)★★★★, *The Pentangle Collection* (Transatlantic 1975)★★★★, *Anthology* (Transatlantic 1978)★★★★, *The Essential Pentangle Volume 1* (Transatlantic 1987)★★★★, *The Essential Pentangle Volume 2* (Transatlantic 1987)★★★, *Early Classics* (Shanachie 1992)★★★, *People On The Highway 1968 - 1971* (Demon 1993)★★★★, *Light Flight: The Anthology* (Essential 2000)★★★, *The Pentangle Family* (Transatlantic 2000)★★★★.

PERE UBU
ALBUMS: *The Modern Dance* (Blank 1978)★★★★, *Dub Housing* (Chrysalis 1978)★★★★, *New Picnic Time* (Rough Trade 1979)★★★, *The Art Of Walking* (Rough Trade 1980)★★★, *390 Degrees Of Simulated Stereo - Ubu Live: Volume 1* (Rough Trade 1981)★★★, *Song Of The Bailing Man* (Rough Trade 1982)★★, *The Tenement Year* (Enigma 1988)★★★★, *One Man Drives While The Other Man Screams - Live Volume 2: Pere Ubu On Tour* (Rough Trade 1989)★★, *Cloudland* (Fontana 1989)★★★, *Worlds In Collision* (Fontana 1991)★★★, *Story Of My Life* (Imago 1993)★★★, *Ray Gun Suitcase* (Tim/Kerr 1995)★★★, *Pennsylvania* (Cooking Vinyl 1998)★★★, *Apocalypse Now* 1991 recording (Cooking Vinyl 1999)★★★.
COMPILATIONS: *Terminal Tower: An Archival Collection* (Twin/Tone 1985)★★★★, *Datapanik In The Year Zero* 5-CD box set (Geffen 1996)★★★★.

PERKINS, CARL
ALBUMS: *The Dance Album Of Carl Perkins* (Sun 1957) ★★★★, *Whole Lotta Shakin'* (Columbia 1958)★★★, *Country Boy's Dream* (Dollie 1967)★★★, *Blue Suede Shoes* (Sun 1969)★★★, *Carl Perkins On Top* (Columbia 1969)★★★, with the NRBQ *Boppin' The Blues* (Columbia 1970)★★★, *My Kind Of Country* (Mercury 1973)★★★, *The Carl Perkins Show* (Suede 1976)★★★, *Ol' Blue Suede's Back* (Jet 1978)★★, *Rock 'N' Gospel* (Koala 1979)★★, *Sing A Song With Me* (Koala 1979)★★, *Country Soul* (Koala 1979)★★, *Cane Creek Glory Church* (Koala 1979)★★, *Live At Austin City Limits* (Suede 1981)★★★, with Jerry Lee Lewis, Johnny Cash *The Survivors* (Columbia 1982)★★★, *Carl Perkins* (Dot 1985)★★★, *Turn Around* Decca demos (Culture Press 1985)★★★, with Jerry Lee Lewis, Johnny Cash, Roy Orbison *Class Of '55* (America 1986)★★★, *Interviews From The Class Of '55 Recording Sessions* (America 1986)★★, *Born To Rock* (Universal/MCA 1989)★★★, with Elvis Presley and Jerry Lee Lewis *The Million Dollar Quartet* (RCA 1990)★★★, *Friends, Family & Legends* (Platinum 1992)★★★, with Scotty Moore *706 Reunion – A Sentimental Journey* cassette only (Belle Meade 1993)★★★, *Hound Dog* (Muskateer 1995)★★★, with various artists *Go Cat Go!* (Dinosaur 1996)★★★, *Live At Gilley's* (Connoisseur Collection 2000)★★★★★.
COMPILATIONS: *King Of Rock* (Columbia 1968)★★★, *Carl Perkins' Greatest Hits* re-recorded Sun material (Columbia 1969)★★, *Original Golden Hits* (Sun 1970)★★★, *Blue Suede Shoes* (Sun 1971)★★★, *Carl Perkins* (Harmony 1970)★★★, *The Sun Years* 3-LP box set (Sun 1982)★★★★, *Carl Perkins* (Cambra 1983)★★★, *The Heart And Soul Of Carl Perkins* (Allegiance 1984)★★★, *Dixie Fried* (Charly 1986)★★★, *Up Through The Years, 1954-1957* (Bear Family 1986)★★★★, *Original Sun Greatest Hits* (Rhino 1986)★★★★, *The Country Store Collection* (Country Store 1988)★★, *Honky Tonk Gal: Rare And Unissued Sun Masters* (Rounder 1989)★★, *Matchbox* (Tring 1990)★★, *Jive After Five: Best Of Carl Perkins (1958-1978)* (Rhino 1990)★★★, *The Classic Carl Perkins* 5-CD box set (Bear Family 1990) ★★★★, *Restless: The Columbia Recordings* (Columbia 1992)★★★, *Country Boy's Dream: The Dollie Masters* (Bear Family 1994)★★★, *Best Of Carl Perkins* (Castle 1995) ★★★, *Boppin' Blue Suede Shoes* (Charly 1995)★★★, *The Rockabilly King* (Charly 1995)★★★, *The Unissued Carl Perkins* (Charly 1995)★★, *The Masters* (Eagle 1997)★★★, *The Definitive Collection* (Charly 1998)★★★, *Back On Top* 4-CD box set (Bear Family 2000)★★★.
VIDEOS: *Rockabilly Session* (Virgin Vision 1986), *Carl Perkins & Jerry Lee Lewis Live* (BBC Video 1987), *This Country's Rockin'* (1993).
FURTHER READING: *Disciple In Blue Suede Shoes*, Carl Perkins. *Go, Cat, Go: Life And Times Of Carl Perkins The King Of Rockabilly*, Carl Perkins with David McGee.
FILMS: *Jamboree* aka *Disc Jockey Jamboree* (1957).

PERRY, LEE
ALBUMS: as Lee Perry/Lee Perry And The Upsetters: *The Upsetter* (Trojan 1969)★★★★, *Many Moods Of The Upsetter* (1970)★★★, *Scratch The Upsetter Again* (1970)★★★★, with Dave Barker *Prisoner Of Love: Dave Barker Meets The Upsetters* (Trojan 1970)★★★★, *Africa's Blood* (1972)★★★, *Battle Axe* (1972)★★★, *Cloak & Dagger* (Rhino 1972)★★★, *Double Seven* (Trojan 1973)★★★, *Rhythm Shower* (Upsetter 1973)★★★★, *Blackboard Jungle* (Upsetter 1973)★★★★, *Return Of Wax* (Upsetter 1974)★★★, *Musical Bones* (Upsetter 1974)★★★, *Kung Fu Meets The Dragon* (D.I.P. 1974)★★★, *D.I.P. Presents The Upsetter* (D.I.P. 1974)★★★, *Revolution Dub* (Cactus 1975)★★★★, *Super Ape* (Mango/Island 1976) ★★★★, with Prince Jazzbo *Natty Passing Through* aka *Ital Corner* (Black Wax 1976)★★★★, with Jah Lion, as producer *Colombia Collie* (Island 1977)★★★★, *Return Of The Super Ape* (Lion Of Judah/Mango 1977)★★★, *Roast Fish, Collie Weed & Corn Bread* (Lion Of Judah 1978)★★★, *Scratch On The Wire* (Island 1979)★★★, *Scratch And Company: Chapter 1* (Clocktower 1980)★★★, *Return Of Pipecock Jackson* (Black Star 1981)★★★, *Mystic Miracle Star* (Heartbeat 1982)★★★, *History Mystery & Prophecy* (Mango/Island 1984)★★★, *Black Ark Volumes 1 & 2* (Black Ark 1984)★★★, *Black Ark In Dub* (Black Ark 1985)★★★, *Battle Of Armagideon: Millionaire Liquidator* (Trojan 1986)★★★, with Dub Syndicate *Time Boom X De Devil Dead* (On-U-Sound 1987)★★★, *Satan Kicked The Bucket* (Wackies 1988)★★★, *Scratch Attack* (RAS 1988) ★★★, *Chicken Scratch* (Heartbeat 1989)★★★, *Turn And Fire* (Anachron 1989)★★★, with Aura *Full Experience* (Blue Moon/Mesa 1990)★★★, with Bullwackie *Lee 'Scratch' Perry Meets Bullwackie - Satan's Dub* (ROIR 1990)★★★, *From The Secret Laboratory* (Mango/Island 1990)★★★, *Message From Yard* (Rohit 1990)★★★, *Blood Vapour* (La/Unicorn 1990) ★★★, *Magnetic Mirror Master Mix* (Anachron 1990)★★★, with Mad Professor *Lee Scratch Perry Meets The Mad Professor, Volumes 1 & 2* (Ariwa 1990)★★★, with Mad Professor *Lee 'Scratch' Perry Meets The Mad Professor In Dub, Volumes 1 & 2* (Angella 1991)★★★, *Spiritual Healing* (Black Cat 1991) ★★★, *God Muzick* (Network/Kook Kat 1991)★★★, *The Upsetter And The Beat* (Heartbeat 1992)★★★, *Soundz From The Hot Line* (Heartbeat 1993)★★★, *Technomajikal* (ROIR 1997)★★★, *On The Wire* 1988 recording (Trojan 2000) ★★★★, *Station Underground Report* (Trojan 2001)★★, *Jamaican E.T.* (Trojan/Sanctuary 2002)★★★.
COMPILATIONS: *Reggae Greats* (Island 1984)★★★, *Best Of* (Pama 1984)★★★★, *The Upsetter Box Set* (Trojan 1985) ★★★★, *Some Of The Best* (Heartbeat 1986)★★★, *The Upsetter Compact Set* (1988)★★★★, *All The Hits* (Rohit 1989)★★★★, *Larks From The Ark* (Nectar Masters 1995) ★★★, *Voodooism* (Pressure Sounds 1996)★★★. As Lee Perry And Friends: *Give Me Power* (Trojan 1988)★★★, *Open The Gate* (Trojan 1989)★★★, *Shocks Of Mighty 1969-1974* (Attack 1989)★★★, *Build The Ark* (Trojan 1990)★★★, *Public Jestering* (Attack 1990). As the Upsetters *The Upsetter Collection* (Trojan 1981)★★★★, *Version Like Rain* (Trojan 1990)★★★, *Upsetters A Go Go* (Heartbeat 1996)★★★. Various Artists: *Heart Of The Ark, Volume 1* (Seven Leaves 1982)★★★★, *Heart Of The Ark, Volume 2* (Seven Leaves 1983)★★★, *Megaton Dub* (Seven Leaves 1983)★★★, *Megaton Dub 2* (Seven Leaves 1983)★★★, *Turn & Fire: Upsetter Disco Dub* (1989)★★★, *Words Of My Mouth* (Trojan 1996)★★★★, *Arkology* 3-CD box set (Island/Chronicles 1997)★★★★★, *Dry Acid: Lee Perry Productions 1968-69* (Trojan 1998)★★★★, *Lost Treasures Of The Ark* 3-CD box set (Jet Star 1999)★★★, *The Upsetter Shop, Volume 2: 1969 To 1973* (Heartbeat 1999)★★★, *Chapter Two Of Words* (Trojan 1999)★★★, *The Complete Upsetter Singles Collection Vol. 3* (Trojan 2000)★★★★, *Chapter 3: Live As One* (Trojan 2001) ★★★, *Born In The Sky* (Motion 2001)★★★★, *Upsetter At The Controls: 1969-1975, Born In The Sky* (Motion Records 2001) ★★★★, *The Complete UK Upsetter Singles Collection Vol. 4* (Trojan 2000)★★★★.
VIDEOS: *The Ultimate Destruction* (1992).
FURTHER READING: *People Funny Boy: The Genius Of Lee "Scratch" Perry*, David Katz. *The Almost Complete Album Discography 1969-1999*, Gary Simons. *Give Me Power: A Complete Discography*, Dave Katz & Jeremy Collingwood.

PET SHOP BOYS
ALBUMS: *Please* (Parlophone 1986)★★★★, *Disco* (Parlophone 1986)★★★, *Actually* (Parlophone 1987)★★★★, *Introspective* (Parlophone 1988)★★★, *Behaviour* (Parlophone 1990)★★★, *Very* (Parlophone 1993)★★★★, *Disco 2* (Parlophone 1994)★★, *Bilingual* (Parlophone 1996)★★★, *Bilingual Remixed* (Parlophone 1997)★★★, *Nightlife* (Parlophone 1999)★★★★, *Release* (Parlophone 2002)★★★.
COMPILATIONS: *Discography: The Complete Singles Collection* (Parlophone 1991)★★★★★, *Alternative* (Parlophone 1995)★★★★, *Essential Pet Shop Boys* (EMI 1998)★★★.
VIDEOS: *Highlights: Pet Shop Boys On Tour* (PMI 1990), *Videography: The Singles Collection On Video* (PMI 1991), *Performance* (PMI 1992), *Projections* (PMI 1993), *Various* (PMI 1994), *Discovery: Live In Rio* (PMI 1995), *Somewhere: Pet Shop Boys In Concert* (Game Entertainment 1997), *Montage: The Nightlife Tour* (PMI 2001).
FURTHER READING: *Pet Shop Boys, Literally*, Chris Heath. *Pet Shop Boys: Introspective*, Michael Crowton. *Pet Shop Boys Versus America*, Chris Heath and Pennie Smith.
FILMS: *It Couldn't Happen Here* (1987).

PETER AND GORDON
ALBUMS: *Peter & Gordon* (UK) *A World Without Love* (US) (Columbia/Capitol 1964)★★★, *In Touch With Peter And Gordon* UK only (Columbia 1964)★★★, *I Don't Want To See You Again* US only (Capitol 1964)★★★, *I Go To Pieces* (Columbia 1965)★★★, *True Love Ways* US only (Capitol 1965)★★★, *Hurtin' 'N' Lovin'* UK only (Columbia 1965)★★★, *Peter And Gordon Sing And Play The Hits Of Nashville, Tennessee* US only (Capitol 1966)★★, *Woman* (Capitol/Columbia 1966)★★★, *Somewhere* UK only (Columbia 1966)★★★, *Lady Godiva* (Capitol/Columbia 1967)★★, *A Knight In Rusty Armour* (Capitol 1967)★★, *In London For Tea* (Capitol 1967)★★, *Hot, Cold And Custard* (Capitol 1968)★★.
COMPILATIONS: *Greatest Hits* (Columbia 1966)★★★, *The Best Of Peter & Gordon* (EMI 1977)★★★, *The Hits And More* (EMI 1986)★★★, *Peter & Gordon: The Best Of The EMI Years* (EMI 1991)★★★, *The Best Of Peter & Gordon* (Rhino 1991) ★★★, *The EP Collection* (See For Miles 1995)★★★.

PETER, PAUL AND MARY
ALBUMS: *Peter, Paul And Mary* (Warners 1962)★★★★, *In The Wind* (Warners 1963)★★★★, *In Concert* (Warners 1964)★★★★, *A Song Will Rise* (Warners 1965)★★★★, *See What Tomorrow Brings* (Warners 1965)★★★, *Peter, Paul And Mary Album* (Warners 1966)★★★★, *Album 1700* (Warners 1967)★★★, *Late Again* (Warners 1968)★★★, *Peter, Paul And Mommy* (Warners 1969)★★★, *Reunion* (Warners 1978)★★★, *Such Is Love* (Warners 1983)★★, *No Easy Walk To Freedom* (Gold Castle 1986)★★, *A Holiday Celebration* (Gold Castle 1988)★★★, *Flowers And Stones* (Gold Castle 1990)★★, *Peter, Paul & Mommy, Too* (Warners 1993)★★, *LifeLines* (Warners 1995)★★, *LifeLines Live* (Warners 1996)★★.
SOLO: Paul Stookey *Paul And* (Warners 1971)★★★, *One Night Stand* (Warners 1973)★★, *Real ToReel* (1977)★★, *Something New And Fresh* (1978)★★, *Band & Bodyworks* (Myrrh 1980)★★, *Wait'll You Hear This!* (1982)★★, *State Of The Heart* (1985)★★, *In Love Beyond Our Lives* (Gold Castle 1990)★★. Mary Travers *Mary* (Warners 1971)★★, *Morning Glory* (Warners 1972)★★, *All My Choices* (Warners 1973)★★, *Circles* (Warners 1974)★★, *It's In Everyone Of Us* (Chrysalis 1978)★★. Peter Yarrow *Peter* (Warners 1972)★★★, *That's Enough For Me* (Warners 1973)★★, *Hard Times* (Warners 1975)★★.
COMPILATIONS: *(Ten) Years Together: The Best Of Peter, Paul And Mary* (Warners 1970)★★★★, *Around The Campfire* (Warners 1998)★★★, *The Collection: Their Greatest Hits & Finest Performances* (Reader's Digest 1998)★★★, *Songs Of Conscience & Concern* (Warners 1999)★★★, *Weave Me This Sunshine* (ABX 1999)★★★.
VIDEOS: *25th Anniversary Concert* (Rhino Home Video 1986), *Holiday Concert* (Rhino Home Video 1988), *Peter, Paul & Mommy, Too* (Warner Reprise Video 1993), *LifeLines Live* (Warner Reprise Video 1996).

PETTY, TOM, AND THE HEARTBREAKERS
ALBUMS: *Tom Petty And The Heartbreakers* (Shelter 1976)★★★, *You're Gonna Get It* (Shelter 1978)★★★★, *Damn The Torpedoes* (MCA 1979)★★★★, *Hard Promises* (MCA 1981)★★★★, *Long After Dark* (MCA 1982)★★★, *Southern Accents* (MCA 1985)★★★★, *Pack Up The Plantation: Live!* (MCA 1985)★★★, *Let Me Up (I've Had Enough)* (MCA 1987)★★★★, *Full Moon Fever* (MCA 1989)★★★★, *Into The Great Wide Open* (MCA 1991) ★★★★, *Wildflowers* (Warners 1994)★★★★, *She's The One* (Warners 1996)★★★, *Echo* (Warners 1999)★★★.
COMPILATIONS: *Greatest Hits* (MCA 1993)★★★★, *Playback* 6-CD box set (MCA 1995)★★★★, *Anthology: Through The Years* (Universal 2000)★★★★.
VIDEOS: *Playback* (MCA Music Video 1995), *High Grass Dogs: Live From The Fillmore* (Warner Reprise Video 1999).

PHAIR, LIZ
ALBUMS: *Exile In Guyville* (Matador 1993)★★★★, *Whip-Smart* (Matador 1994)★★★★, *Juvenilia* (Matador 1995) ★★, *Whitechocolatespaceegg* (Matador 1999)★★★.

PHISH
ALBUMS: *Junta* (Own Label 1988)★★, *Lawn Boy* (Absolute A Go Go 1990)★★★, *A Picture Of Nectar* (Elektra 1992)★★★, *Rift* (Elektra 1993)★★★, *(Hoist)* (Elektra 1994)★★★, *A Live One* (Elektra 1995)★★★★, *Billy Breathes* (Elektra 1996) ★★★★, *Slip Stitch And Pass* (Elektra 1997)★★, *The Story Of The Ghost* (Elektra 1998)★★★, *Hampton Comes Alive* 6-CD set (Elektra 1999)★★★, *Farmhouse* (Elektra 2000)★★★★, *The Siket Disc* 1997 recording (Elektra 2000)★★★, *Live Phish 01: 12.14.95 - Binghamton, New York* (Elektra 2001)★★★, *Live Phish 02: 7.16.94 - North Fayston, Vermont* (Elektra 2001)★★★, *Live Phish 03: 9.14.00 - Darien Center, New York* (Elektra 2001)★★★, *Live Phish 04: 6.14.00 - Fukuoka, Japan* (Elektra 2001)★★★, *Live Phish 05: 7.8.00 - East Troy, Wisconsin* (Elektra 2001)★★★, *Live Phish 06: 11.27.98 - Worcester, Massachusetts* (Elektra 2001)★★★.
COMPILATIONS: *Stash* (Elektra 1996)★★★.
VIDEOS: *Bittersweet Motel* (Image Entertainment/Aviva 2001).
FURTHER READING: *The Phishing Manual: A Compendium To The Music Of Phish*, Dean Budnick. *Mike's Corner: Daunting Literary Snippets From Phish's Bassist*, Mike Gordon. *Go Phish*, Dave Thompson. *The Pharmer's Almanac: The Unofficial Guide To The Band Phish*, Andy Bernstein (ed.). *The Phish Book*, Richard Gehr and Phish. *The Phish Companion: A Guide To The Band And Their Music*, Tom Marshall and The Mockingbird Foundation. *Run Like An Antelope: On The Road With Phish*, Sean Gibbon.

PICKETT, BOBBY 'BORIS'
ALBUMS: *The Original Monster Mash* (Garpax 1962)★★.

PICKETT, WILSON
ALBUMS: *It's Too Late* (Double-L 1963)★★, *In The Midnight Hour* (Atlantic 1965)★★★★, *The Exciting Wilson Pickett* (Atlantic 1966)★★★★, *The Wicked Pickett* (Atlantic 1966) ★★★★, *The Sound Of Wilson Pickett* (Atlantic 1967)★★★★, *I'm In Love* (Atlantic 1968)★★★, *The Midnight Mover* (Atlantic 1968)★★★, *Hey Jude* (Atlantic 1969)★★★, *Right On* (Atlantic 1970)★★★, *Wilson Pickett In Philadelphia* (Atlantic 1970)★★, *If You Need Me* (Joy 1970)★★, *Don't Knock My Love* (Atlantic 1971)★★, *Mr. Magic Man* (RCA 1973)★★, *Miz Lena's Boy* (RCA 1973)★★, *Tonight I'm My Biggest Audience* (RCA 1974)★★, *Live In Japan* (1974)★★, *Pickett In Pocket* (RCA 1974)★★, *Join Me & Let's Be Free* (RCA 1975)★★, *Chocolate Mountain* (Wicked 1976)★★, *A Funky Situation* (Wicked 1978)★★, *I Want You* (EMI America 1979)★★, *The Right Track* (EMI America 1981)★★, *American Soul Man* (Motown 1987)★★, *It's Harder Now* (Bullseye Blues 1999)★★★.
COMPILATIONS: *The Best Of Wilson Pickett* (Atlantic 1967) ★★★★, *The Best Of Wilson Pickett Vol. 2* (Atlantic 1971) ★★★★, *Wilson Pickett's Greatest Hits i* (Atlantic 1973)★★★★, *Collection* (Castle 1992)★★★, *A Man And A Half: The Best Of Wilson Pickett* (Rhino/Atlantic 1992)★★★★★, *Take Your Pleasure Where You Find It: Best Of The RCA Years* (Camden 1998)★★★.

PINK FLOYD
ALBUMS: *The Piper At The Gates Of Dawn* (EMI Columbia 1967)★★★★, *Saucerful Of Secrets* (EMI Columbia 1968) ★★★★, *More* film soundtrack (EMI Columbia 1969)★★, *Ummagumma* (Harvest 1969)★★★, *Atom Heart Mother* (Harvest 1970)★★★, *Meddle* (Harvest 1971)★★★★, *Obscured By Clouds* film soundtrack (Harvest 1972)★★, *Dark Side Of The Moon* (Harvest 1973)★★★★★, *Wish You Were Here* (Harvest 1975)★★★★, *Animals* (Harvest 1977)★★★★, *The Wall* (Harvest 1979)★★★★, *The Final Cut* (Harvest 1983)★★, *A Momentary Lapse Of Reason* (EMI 1987)★★★, *Delicate Sound Of Thunder* (EMI 1988)★★★, *In London 1966-1967* (See For Miles 1990)★★★, *The Division Bell* (EMI 1994)★★★, *Pulse* (EMI 1995)★★, *Is Anybody Out There? The Wall Live* (EMI 2000)★★★.
SOLO: Rick Wright *Wet Dream* (Harvest 1978)★★, with Dave Harris *Zee* (Harvest 1984)★★, *Broken China* (EMI 1996)★★.
COMPILATIONS: *Relics* (Harvest 1971)★★★★, *A Nice Pair* (Harvest 1974)★★★★, *First Eleven* 11-LP box set (EMI 1977)★★★, *A Collection Of Great Dance Songs* (Harvest 1981)★★, *Works* (Capitol 1983)★★★, *Shine On* 8-CD box set (EMI 1992)★★★, *Echoes: The Best Of Pink Floyd* (EMI 2001)★★★★.
VIDEOS: *Pink Floyd: London '66-'67* (See For Miles 1994), *Delicate Sound Of Thunder* (Columbia 1994), *Live At Pompeii* (4 Front 1995), *Pulse: 20,10,94* (PMI/EMI 1995).
FURTHER READING: *The Pink Floyd*, Rick Sanders. *Pink Floyd*, Jean Marie Leduc. *Pink Floyd: The Illustrated Discography*, Miles. *The Wall*, Roger Waters and David Appleby. *Pink Floyd Lyric Book*, Roger Waters. *Pink Floyd: Another Brick*, Miles. *Pink Floyd: Bricks In The Wall*, Karl Dallas. *Pink Floyd: A Visual Documentary*, Miles and Andy Mabbett. *Crazy Diamond: Syd Barrett And The Dawn Of Pink Floyd*, Mike Watkinson and Pete Anderson. *Saucerful Of Secrets: The Pink Floyd Odyssey*, Nicholas Schaffner. *Pink Floyd Back-Stage*, Bob Hassall. *Pink Floyd*, William Ruhlmann. *Syd Barrett: The Madcap Laughs*, Pete Anderson and Mick Rock. *Complete Guide To The Music Of*, Andy Mabbett. *Echoes: The Stories Behind Every Pink Floyd Song*, Cliff Jones. *Pink Floyd Through The Eyes Of ... The Band, Its Fans, Friends And Foes*, Bruno MacDonald (ed.). *Mind Over Matter: The Images Of Pink Floyd*, Storm Thorgenson. *Pink Floyd: In The Flesh (The Complete Performance History)*, Glenn Povey and Ian Russell. *Lost In The Woods: Syd Barrett And The Pink Floyd*, Julian Palacios, *Through The Eyes Of The Band, It's Fans, Friends And Foes*, ed. Bruno McDonald. *The Pink Floyd Encyclopedia*, Vernon Fitch. *Which One's Pink? An Analysis Of The Concept Albums Of Roger Waters & Pink Floyd*, Phil Rose. *Embryo: A Pink Floyd Chronology 1966-1971*, Nick Hodges and Ian Priston. *The Press Reports 1966-1983*, Vernon Fitch.

PITNEY, GENE
ALBUMS: *The Many Sides Of Gene Pitney* (Musicor 1962) ★★★, *Only Love Can Break A Heart* (Musicor 1962)★★★, *Gene Pitney Sings Just For You* (Musicor 1963)★★★, *Gene Pitney Sings World-Wide Winners* (Musicor 1963)★★★, *Blue Gene* (Musicor 1963)★★★★, *Gene Pitney Meets The Fair Young Ladies Of Folkland* (Musicor 1964)★★, *Gene Italiano* (Musicor 1964)★★, *It Hurts To Be In Love* (Musicor 1964) ★★★★, with George Jones *For The First Time Ever! Two Great Singers* (Musicor 1965)★★, *I Must Be Seeing Things* (Musicor 1965)★★★★, *It's Country Time Again!* (Musicor 1965)★★, *Looking Through The Eyes Of Love* (Musicor 1965)★★★★, *Espanol* (Musicor 1965)★★, with Melba Montgomery *Being Together* (Musicor 1965)★★, *Famous Country Duets* (Musicor 1965)H, *Backstage (I'm Lonely)* (Musicor 1966)★★★, *Nessuno Mi Puo Giudicare* (Musicor 1966)★★, *The Gene Pitney Show* (Musicor 1966)★★★, *The Country Side Of Gene Pitney* (Musicor 1966)H, *Young And Warm And Wonderful* (Musicor 1966)★★★★, *Just One Smile* (Musicor 1967)★★★★, *Sings Burt Bacharach* (Musicor 1968)★★★, *She's A Heartbreaker* (Musicor 1968)★★, *This Is Gene Pitney* (Musicor 1970)★★, *Ten Years After* (Musicor 1971)★★, *Pitney '75* (Bronze 1975)★★, *Walkin' In The Sun* (1979)★★.
COMPILATIONS: *Big Sixteen* (Musicor 1964)★★★★, *More Big Sixteen, Volume 2* (Musicor 1965)★★★, *Big Sixteen, Volume 3* (Musicor 1966)★★★, *Greatest Hits Of All Time* (Musicor 1966)★★★, *Golden Greats* (Musicor 1967)★★★, *Spotlight On Gene Pitney* (Design 1967)★★★, *The Gene Pitney Story* double album (Musicor 1968)★★★, *The Greatest Hits Of Gene Pitney* (Musicor 1969)★★★★, *The Man Who Shot Liberty Valance* (Music Disc 1969)★★★, *Town Without Pity* (Music Disc 1969)★★★, *Twenty Four Hours From Tulsa* (Music Disc 1969)★★★, *Baby I Need Your Lovin'* (Music Disc 1969)★★★, *The Golden Hits Of Gene Pitney* (Musicor 1971)★★★, *The Fabulous Gene Pitney* double album (Columbia 1972)★★★, *The Pick Of Gene Pitney* (West-52 1979)★★★, *Anthology 1961-68* (Rhino 1986)★★★★, *Best Of* (K-Tel 1988)★★★, *All The Hits* (Jet 1990)★★★, *Greatest Hits* (Pickwick 1991)★★★, *The Original Hits 1961-70* (Jet 1991)★★★, *The EP Collection* (See For Miles 1991)★★★, *The Heartbreaker* (Repertoire 1994)★★★, *More Greatest Hits* (Varese Sarabande 1995)★★★, *The Gold Collection: 15 Classic Hits* (Summit 1996)★★★, *The Great Recordings* (Tomato 1996)★★★, *The Definitive Collection* (Charly 1997)★★★, *The Hits And More* (Eagle 1998)★★★★, *25 All-Time Greatest Hits* (Varese Sarabande 1999)★★★★, *Being Together/The Country Side Of Gene Pitney* (Sequel 1999)★★, *Geno Italiano/Nessuno Mi Puo Giudicare* (Sequel 1999)★★, *Looking Through Gene Pitney: The Ultimate Collection* (Sequel 2000)★★★★.

PIXIES
ALBUMS: *Come On Pilgrim* (4AD 1987)★★★, *Surfer Rosa* (4AD 1988)★★★★, *Doolittle* (4AD/Elektra 1989)★★★★, *Bossanova* (4AD/Elektra 1990)★★★, *Trompe Le Monde* (4AD/Elektra 1991)★★★.
COMPILATIONS: *Death To The Pixies 1987-1991* (4AD 1997)★★★★, *Pixies At The BBC* (4AD/Elektra 1998)★★★, *Complete B-Sides* (4AD 2001)★★★★.

PJ HARVEY
ALBUMS: *Dry* (Too Pure 1992)★★★★, *Demonstration* 'demo' album given away with initial copies of *Dry* (Too Pure 1992) ★★★, *Rid Of Me* (Island 1993)★★★★, *4-Track Demos* (Island 1993)★★, *To Bring You My Love* (Island 1995)★★★★, with John Parish *Dance Hall At Louse Point* (Island 1996) ★★★, *Is This Desire?* (Island 1998)★★★★, *Stories From The City, Stories From The Sea* (Island 2000)★★★★.
COMPILATIONS: *B-Sides* (Island 1995)★★★.
VIDEOS: *Reeling* (PolyGram Music Video 1994).
FILMS: *The Book Of Life* (1998).

PLACEBO
ALBUMS: *Placebo* (Hut 1996)★★★, *Without You I'm Nothing* (Hut 1998)★★★★, *Black Market Music* (Hut 2000)★★.

PLANT, ROBERT
ALBUMS: *Pictures At Eleven* (Swan Song/Atlantic 1982) ★★★, *The Principle Of Moments* (Es Paranza/Atlantic 1983)★★★, *Shaken 'N' Stirred* (Es Paranza/Atlantic 1985)★★, *Now And Zen* (Es Paranza/Atlantic 1988) ★★★★, *Manic Nirvana* (Es Paranza/Atlantic 1990)★★★, *Fate Of Nations* (Fontana/Atlantic 1993)★★★★, with Jimmy Page *No Quarter* (Fontana/Atlantic 1994)★★★★, with Page *Walking Into Clarksdale* (Mercury/Atlantic 1998)★★★★.
VIDEOS: *Mumbo Jumbo* (Atlantic 1989), with Page *No Quarter* (Atlantic 1995).
FURTHER READING: *Robert Plant*, Michael Gross. *Led Zeppelin's Robert Plant Through The Mirror*, Mike Randolph.

PLANXTY
ALBUMS: *Planxty* (Polydor 1972)★★★★, *The Well Below The Valley* (Polydor 1973)★★★★, *Cold Blow And The Rainy Night* (Polydor 1974)★★★, *After The Break* (Tara 1979) ★★★, *The Woman I Loved So Well* (Tara 1980)★★★, *Words & Music* (WEA 1983)★★★, *Aris!* (Polydor 1984)★★.
COMPILATIONS: *The Planxty Collection* (Polydor 1976)★★★★, *The Best Of Planxty Live* (1987)★★.

PLATTERS
ALBUMS: *The Platters* (Federal 1955)★★★★ also released on King as *Only You* and Mercury labels, *The Platters, Volume 2* (Mercury 1956)★★★★, *The Flying Platters* (Mercury 1957) ★★★, *The Platters On Parade* (Mercury 1959)★★★, *Flying Platters Around The World* (Mercury 1959)★★★, *Remember When* (Mercury 1959)★★★, *Reflections* (Mercury 1960) ★★★, *Encore Of Golden Hits* (Mercury 1960)★★★, *More Encore Of Golden Hits* (Mercury 1960)★★★, *The Platters* (Mercury 1960)★★★, *Life Is Just A Bowl Of Cherries* (Mercury 1961)★★★, *The Platters Sing For The Lonely* (Mercury 1962)★★★, *Encore Of The Golden Hits Of The Groups* (Mercury 1962)★★★, *Moonlight Memories* (Mercury 1963)★★★, *Platters Sing All The Movie Hits* (Mercury 1963)★★, *Platters Sing Latino* (Mercury 1963)★★, *Christmas With The Platters* (Mercury 1963)★★★, *New Soul Campus Style Of The Platters* (Mercury 1965)★★, *I Love You 1000 Times* (Musicor 1966)★★, *Going Back To Detroit* (Musicor 1967)★★★, *I Get The Sweetest Feeling* (Musicor 1968) ★★★, *Sweet Sweet Lovin'* (Musicor 1968)★★, *Our Way* (Pye International 1971)★★★, *Encore Of Broadway Golden Hits* (1972)★★★, *Live* (Contour 1974)★★.
COMPILATIONS: *The Original Platters - 20 Classic Hits* (Mercury 1978)★★★, *Platterama* (Mercury 1982)★★★, *Smoke Gets In Your Eyes* (Charly 1991)★★★, *The Magic Touch: An Anthology* (Mercury 1992)★★★★, *The Very Best Of The Platters 1966-1969* (Varèse 1997)★★★★, *Enchanted: The Best Of The Platters* (Rhino 1998)★★★★.
FILMS: *Carnival Rock* (1957), *Girl's Town* aka *The Innocent And The Damned* (1959).

POCO
ALBUMS: *Pickin' Up The Pieces* (Epic 1969)★★★, *Poco* (Epic 1970)★★★, *Deliverin'* (Epic 1971)★★★, *From The Inside* (Epic 1971)★★★★, *A Good Feelin' To Know* (Epic 1972)★★★★, *Crazy Eyes* (Epic 1973)★★★★, *Seven* (Epic 1974)★★★, *Cantamos* (Epic 1974)★★, *Head Over Heels* (ABC 1975)★★★★, *Live* (Epic 1976)★★, *Rose Of Cimarron* (ABC 1976)★★★★, *Indian Summer* (ABC 1977)★★★★, *Legend* (ABC 1978)★★★, *Under The Gun* (MCA 1980)★★, *Blue And Gray* (MCA 1981)★★, *Cowboys And Englishmen* (MCA 1982)★★, *Ghost Town* (Atlantic 1982)★★, *Inamorata* (Atlantic 1984)★★★, *Legacy* (RCA 1989)★★★★.
COMPILATIONS: *The Very Best Of Poco* (Epic 1975)★★★, *Songs Of Paul Cotton* (Epic 1980)★★★, *Songs Of Richie Furay* (Epic 1980)★★★, *Backtracks* (MCA 1983)★★★, *Crazy Loving: The Best Of Poco 1975-1982* (RCA 1989)★★★, *Poco: The Forgotten Trail 1969-1974* (Epic/Legacy 1990)★★★★, *The Very Best Of* (Beat Goes On 1998)★★★★.

POGUES
ALBUMS: *Red Roses For Me* (Stiff 1984)★★★, *Rum, Sodomy & The Lash* (Stiff 1985)★★★★, *If I Should Fall From Grace With God* (Stiff 1988)★★★★, *Peace And Love* (Warners 1989)★★★, *Hell's Ditch* (Pogue Mahone 1990)★★★, *Waiting For Herb* (PM 1993)★★, *Pogue Mahone* (Warners 1995)★★, *Streams Of Whiskey* 1991 recording (Sanctuary 2002)★★.
COMPILATIONS: *The Best Of The Pogues* (PM 1991)★★★★, *The Rest Of The Best* (PM 1992)★★★, *The Very Best Of ...* (Warners 2001)★★★★.
VIDEOS: *Live At The Town And Country* (Virgin 1988), *Completely Pogued* (Start 1988), *Poguevision* (WEA 1991).
FURTHER READING: *The Pogues: The Lost Decade*, Ann Scanlon. *Poguetry: The Lyrics Of Shane MacGowan*, John Hewitt and Steve Pyke (illustrators). *Shane MacGowan: Last Of The Celtic Soul Rebels*, Ian O'Doherty. *A Drink With Shane MacGowan*, Victoria Mary Clarke and Shane MacGowan. *Life & Music ... Shane MacGowan*, Joe Merrick.

POINTER SISTERS
ALBUMS: *The Pointer Sisters* (Blue Thumb 1973)★★★, *That's A Plenty* (Blue Thumb 1974)★★, *Live At The Opera House* (Blue Thumb 1974)★★, *Steppin'* (Blue Thumb 1975)★★, *Havin' A Party* (Blue Thumb 1977)★★, *Energy* (Planet 1978)★★★, *Priority* (Planet 1979)★★★, *Special Things* (Planet 1980)★★★, *Black And White* (Planet 1981)★★★, *So Excited!* (Planet 1982)★★★, Break Out (Planet 1983)★★★, Contact (RCA 1985)★★★, *Hot Together* (RCA 1986)★★, *Sweet & Soulful* (RCA 1987)★★, *Serious Slammin'* (RCA 1988)★★, *Right Rhythm* (Motown 1990)★★, *Only Sisters Can Do That* (Capitol 1993)★★.
SOLO: Anita Pointer *Love For What It Is* (RCA 1987)★★. June Pointer *Baby Sitter* (Planet 1983)★★.
COMPILATIONS: *The Best Of The Pointer Sisters* (Blue Thumb 1976)★★★★, *Greatest Hits* (Planet 1982)★★★, *Jump: The Best Of The Pointer Sisters* (RCA 1989)★★★★, *The Collection* (RCA 1993)★★★, *Fire: The Very Best Of The Pointer Sisters* (RCA 1996)★★★★, *Yes We Can Can: The Best Of The Blue Thumb Recordings* (Hip-O 1997)★★★.

POISON
ALBUMS: *Look What The Cat Dragged In* (Capitol 1986) ★★★, *Open Up And Say ... Ahh!* (Capitol 1988)★★★★, *Flesh & Blood* (Capitol 1990)★★★★, *Swallow This Live* (Capitol 1991)★★★, *Native Tongue* (Capitol 1993)★★★, *Crack A Smile - And More!* (Capitol 2000)★★★★, *Power To The People* (CMI 2000)★★★.
COMPILATIONS: *Poison's Greatest Hits 1986-1996* (Capitol 1996)★★★.
VIDEOS: *Sight For Sore Ears* (Enigma Music Video 1989), *Flesh, Blood & Videotape* (Capitol Music Video 1991), *7 Days Live* (Capitol Music Video 1994), *Greatest Video Hits* (Capitol Video 2001).

POLICE
ALBUMS: *Outlandos D'Amour* (A&M 1978)★★★★, *Regatta De Blanc* (A&M 1979)★★★★, *Zenyatta Mondatta* (A&M 1980)★★★, *Ghost In The Machine* (A&M 1981) ★★★, *Synchronicity* (A&M 1983)★★★★, *Live!* 1979 recording (A&M 1995)★★.
COMPILATIONS: *Every Breath You Take: The Singles* (A&M 1986)★★★★, *Greatest Hits* (A&M 1992)★★★★, *Message In A Box* 3-CD box set (A&M 1993)★★★, *Every Breath You Take: The Classics* (A&M 1995)★★★★, *The Very Best Of Sting & The Police* (A&M 1997)★★★★.
VIDEOS: *Around The World* (Thorn EMI Video 1981), *Synchronicity Concert* (PolyGram Video 1983), *Every Breath You Take: The Videos* (PolyGram Video 1986), *Outlandos To Synchronicities: A History Of The Police Live!* (PolyGram Video 1995).
FURTHER READING: *The Police Released*, no editor listed. *Message In A Bottle*, Rossetta Woolf. *The Police: L'Historia Bandido*, Phil Sutcliffe and Hugh Fielder. *The Police: A Visual Documentary*, Miles. *The Police*, Lynn Goldsmith. *Complete Guide To The Music Of The Police And Sting*, Chris Welch.

POOLE, BRIAN, AND THE TREMELOES
ALBUMS: *Twist And Shout With Brian Poole And The Tremeloes* (Decca 1963)★★★★, *Big Hits Of '62* (Ace of Clubs 1963)H, *It's About Time* (Decca 1965)★★★.
COMPILATIONS: *Remembering Brian Poole And The Tremeloes* (Decca 1977)★★★★, *Twist And Shout* (Decca 1982)★★★, *Do You Love Me* (Deram 1991)★★★, *The Very Best Of* (Spectrum 1998)★★★.
FURTHER READING: *Talkback: An Easy Guide To British Slang*, Brian Poole.

POP WILL EAT ITSELF
ALBUMS: *Box Frenzy* (Chapter 22 1987)★★, *Now For A Feast!* early recordings (Rough Trade 1989)★★★, *This Is The Day, This Is The Hour, This Is This!* (RCA 1989)★★★, *The Pop Will Eat Itself Cure For Sanity* (RCA 1990)★★, *The Looks Or The Lifestyle* (RCA 1992)★★★, *Weird's Bar & Grill* (RCA 1993)★★, *Dos Dedos Mes Amigos* (Infectious 1994)★★★, *Two Fingers My Friends!* remixes (Infectious 1995)★★★.
COMPILATIONS: *There Is No Love Between Us Anymore* (Chapter 22 1992)★★★, *16 Different Flavours Of Hell* (RCA/BMG 1993)★★★, *Wise Up Suckers* (BMG 1996)★★★.

PORNO FOR PYROS
ALBUMS: *Porno For Pyros* (Warners 1993)★★★, *Good God's Urge* (Warners 1996)★★★.
FURTHER READING: *Perry Farrell: The Saga Of A Hypester*, Dave Thompson.

PORTISHEAD
ALBUMS: *Dummy* (Go! Beat 1994)★★★★, *Portishead* (Go! Beat 1997)★★★, *P. Live In NYC* (Go! Beat 1998)★★★.
VIDEOS: *PNYC* (Go! Beat 1998).

POSIES
ALBUMS: *Failure* (23/PopLlama 1988)★★★, *Dear 23* (DGC 1990)★★★★, *Frosting On The Beater* (DGC 1993)★★★★, *Amazing Disgrace* (DGC 1996)★★★, *Success* (PopLlama 1998)★★★, *Alive Before The Iceberg* (Houston Party 2000) ★★★, *In Case You Didn't Feel Like Plugging In* (Casa Recording 2000)★★★, *Nice Cheekbones And A Ph.D.* mini-album (Badman/Houston Party 2001)★★★.
COMPILATIONS: *The Best Of The Posies: Dream All Day* (DGC 2000)★★★★, *At Least At Last* 4-CD box set (Not Lame Arch 2000)★★★.

PREFAB SPROUT
ALBUMS: *Swoon* (Kitchenware 1984)★★★, *Steve McQueen* (Kitchenware 1985)★★★★, *From Langley Park To Memphis* (Kitchenware 1988)★★★, *Protest Songs* (Kitchenware 1989)★★★, *Jordan: The Comeback* (Kitchenware 1990) ★★★★, *Andromeda Heights* (Columbia 1997)★★★, *The Gunman And Other Stories* (Columbia 2001)★★★.
COMPILATIONS: *A Life Of Surprises: The Best Of* (Kitchenware 1992)★★★★, *38 Carat Collection* (Columbia 1999)★★★★.
VIDEOS: *A Life Of Surprises: The Video Collection* (SMV 1997).
FURTHER READING: *Myths, Melodies & Metaphysics, Paddy McAloon's Prefab Sprout*, John Birch.

PRESIDENTS OF THE UNITED STATES OF AMERICA
ALBUMS: *The Presidents Of The United States Of America* (PopLlama/Columbia 1995)★★★★, *II* (Columbia 1996) ★★★, *Freaked Out And Small* (MusicBlitz 2000)★★★.
COMPILATIONS: *Pure Frosting* (Columbia 1998)★★.

PRESLEY, ELVIS
ALBUMS: *Elvis Presley* (RCA Victor 1956)★★★★, *Elvis* (RCA Victor 1956)★★★★★, *Rock 'N' Roll* UK release (HMV 1956) ★★★★, *Rock 'N' Roll No. 2* UK release (HMV 1957)★★★★, *Loving You* film soundtrack (RCA Victor 1957)★★★★, *Elvis' Christmas Album* (RCA Victor 1957)★★★, *King Creole* film soundtrack (RCA Victor 1958)★★★★, *For LP Fans Only* (RCA Victor 1959)★★★★, *A Date With Elvis* (RCA Victor 1959) ★★★★, *Elvis Is Back!* (RCA Victor 1960)★★★★, *G.I. Blues* film soundtrack (RCA Victor 1960)★★★, *His Hand In Mine* (RCA Victor 1961)★★★, *Something For Everybody* (RCA Victor 1961)★★★, *Blue Hawaii* (RCA Victor 1961)★★★, *Pot Luck* (RCA Victor 1962)★★★, *Girls! Girls! Girls!* film soundtrack (RCA Victor 1963)★★★, *It Happened At The World's Fair* film soundtrack (RCA Victor 1963)★★, *Fun In Acapulco* film soundtrack (RCA Victor 1963)★★, *Kissin' Cousins* film soundtrack (RCA Victor 1964)★★, *Roustabout* film soundtrack (RCA Victor 1964)★★, *Girl Happy* film soundtrack (RCA Victor 1965)★★, *Harem Scarum* film soundtrack (RCA Victor 1965) ★★, *Frankie And Johnny* film soundtrack (RCA Victor 1966)★★, *Paradise, Hawaiian Style* film soundtrack (RCA Victor 1966)★★, *Spinout* film soundtrack (RCA Victor 1966)★★, *How Great Thou Art* (RCA Victor 1967)★★★, *Double Trouble* film soundtrack (RCA Victor 1967)★★, *Clambake* film soundtrack (RCA Victor 1967)★★, *Speedway* film soundtrack (RCA Victor 1968)★★, *Elvis - TV Special* (RCA Victor 1968)★★★, *From Elvis In Memphis* (RCA Victor 1969)★★★★, *From Memphis To Vegas/From Vegas To Memphis* (RCA Victor 1969)★★★, *On Stage February 1970* (RCA Victor 1970)★★★★, *Elvis Back In Memphis* (RCA Victor 1970)★★★, *That's The Way It Is* (RCA 1970)★★★, *Elvis Country (I'm 10,000 Years Old)* (RCA 1971) ★★★, *Love Letters From Elvis* (RCA 1971)★★★, *Elvis Sings The Wonderful World Of Christmas* (RCA 1971)★★★, *Elvis Now* (RCA 1972)★★★, *He Touched Me* (RCA 1972)★★★, *Elvis As Recorded At Madison Square Garden* (RCA 1972)★★★, *Aloha From Hawaii Via Satellite* (RCA 1973)★★★, *Elvis* (RCA 1973) ★★★, *Raised On Rock/For Ol' Times Sake* (RCA 1973)★★★, *Good Times* (RCA 1974)★★★, *Elvis Recorded Live On Stage In Memphis* (RCA 1974)★★★★, *Having Fun With Elvis On Stage* (RCA 1974)H, *Promised Land* (RCA 1975)★★★, *Elvis Today* (RCA 1975)★★★, *From Elvis Presley Boulevard, Memphis, Tennessee* (RCA 1976)★★★, *Welcome To My World* (RCA 1977)★★★, *Moody Blue* (RCA 1977)★★★, *Guitar Man* (RCA 1980)★★★, *The Ultimate Performance* (RCA 1981) ★★★, *The Sound Of Your Cry* (RCA 1982)★★★, *The First Year* (Sun 1983)★★★, *Jailhouse Rock/Love In Las Vegas* (RCA 1983)★★★, *Elvis: The First Live Recordings* (Music Works 1984)★★★, *The Elvis Presley Interview Record: An Audio Self-Portrait* (RCA 1984)★★, with Carl Perkins and Jerry Lee Lewis *The Million Dollar Quartet* (RCA 1990)★★★, *The Lost Album* (RCA 1991)★★★, *If Every Day Was Like Christmas* (RCA 1994)★★★, *Elvis Presley '56* (RCA 1996)★★★★★, *Essential Elvis, Volume 4: A Hundred Years From Now* (RCA 1996)★★★, *Essential Elvis, Volume 5: Rhythm And Country* (RCA 1998) ★★★, *Tiger Man* 1968 recording (RCA 1998)★★★★, *Essential Elvis, Volume 6: Such A Night* (RCA 2000)★★★.
COMPILATIONS: *The Best Of Elvis* UK release (HMV 1957) ★★★★, *Elvis' Golden Records* (RCA Victor 1958)★★★★★, *50,000,000 Elvis Fans Can't Be Wrong: Golden Records, Volume 2* (RCA Victor 1960)★★★★★, *Elvis' Golden Records, Volume 3* (RCA Victor 1963)★★★★, *Elvis For Everyone!* (RCA Victor 1965)★★★, *Elvis' Golden Records, Volume 4* (RCA Victor 1968)★★★★, *Elvis Sings 'Flaming Star' And Other Hits From His Movies* (RCA Camden 1969)★★, *Let's Be Friends* (RCA Camden 1970)★★★★, *Almost In Love* (RCA Camden 1970)★★, *Worldwide 50 Gold Award Hits, Volume 1 - A Touch Of Gold* 4-LP box set (RCA Victor 1970)★★★★★, *You'll Never Walk Alone* (RCA Camden 1971)★★★, *C'mon Everybody* (RCA Camden 1971)★★★, *The Other Sides – Worldwide 50 Gold Award Hits, Volume 2* 4-LP box set (RCA Victor 1971)★★★★, *I Got Lucky* (RCA Camden 1971)★★★, *Elvis Sings Hits From His Movies, Volume 1* (RCA Camden 1972)★★★, *Burning Love And Hits From His Movies, Volume 2* (RCA Camden 1972)★★★, *Separate Ways* (RCA Camden 1973)★★★, *Elvis - A Legendary Performer, Volume 1* (RCA 1974)★★★★, *Hits Of The 70s* (RCA 1974)★★★, *Pure Gold* (RCA 1975)★★★, *Easy Come Easy Go* (RCA Camden 1975) ★★★, *The U.S. Male* (RCA Camden 1975)★★★, *Elvis Presley's Greatest Hits* 7-LP box set (Readers Digest 1975)★★★, *Pictures Of Elvis* (RCA Starcall 1975)★★, *Elvis - A Legendary Performer, Volume 2* (RCA 1976)★★★★, *Sun Sessions* (RCA 1976) ★★★★★, *Elvis In Demand* (RCA 1977)★★★, *The Elvis Tapes* interview disc (Redwood 1977)★★, *He Walks Beside Me* (RCA 1978)★★★, *Elvis Sings For Children And Grownups Too!* (RCA 1978)★★★, *Elvis - A Canadian Tribute* (RCA 1978)★★★, *The '56 Sessions, Volume 1* (RCA 1978)★★★★, *Elvis' 40 Greatest* (RCA 1978)★★★★★, *Elvis - A Legendary Performer, Volume 3* (RCA 1979)★★★★, *Our Memories Of Elvis* (RCA 1979)★★★, *Our Memories Of Elvis Volume 2* (RCA 1979)★★★, *The '56 Sessions, Volume 2* (RCA 1979)★★★★, *Elvis Presley Sings Leiber And Stoller* (RCA 1979)★★★★, *Elvis - A Legendary Performer, Volume 4* (RCA 1980)★★★★, *Elvis Aaron Presley* 8-LP box set (RCA 1980)★★★, *This Is Elvis* (RCA 1981)★★★, *Elvis - Greatest Hits, Volume 1* (RCA 1981)★★, *The Elvis Medley* (RCA 1982)★★★, *I Was The One* (RCA 1983)★★★★, *Elvis' Golden Records, Volume 5* (RCA 1984)★★★★, *Elvis: A Golden Celebration* 6-LP box set (RCA 1984)★★★, *Rocker* (RCA 1984) ★★★★, *Reconsider Baby* (RCA 1985)★★★★, *A Valentine Gift For You* (RCA 1985)★★★, *Always On My Mind* (RCA 1985) ★★★★, *Return Of The Rocker* (RCA 1986)★★★, *The Number One Hits* (RCA 1987)★★★★★, *The Top Ten Hits* (RCA 1987) ★★★★, *The Complete Sun Sessions* (RCA 1987)★★★★★, *Essential Elvis* (RCA 1988)★★★★, *Stereo '57 (Essential Elvis Volume 2)* (RCA 1988)★★★★, *Known Only To Him: Elvis Gospel: 1957-1971* (RCA 1989)★★★★, *Hits Like Never Before: Essential Elvis, Volume 3* (RCA 1990)★★★, *Collector's Gold* (RCA 1991)★★★★, *The King Of Rock 'n' Roll: The Complete '50s Masters* 5-CD box set (RCA 1992)★★★★★, *From Nashville To Memphis: The Essential '60s Masters* 5-CD box set (RCA 1993)★★★★★, *Amazing Grace: His Greatest Sacred Songs* (RCA 1994)★★★★, *Heart And Soul* (RCA 1995)★★, *Walk A Mile In My Shoes: The Essential '70s Masters* 5-CD box set (RCA 1995)★★★★, *Presley - The All Time Greats* (RCA 1996)★★★★, *Great Country Songs* (RCA 1997)★★★, *Platinum: A Life In Music* 4-CD box set (RCA 1997)★★★★, *Love Songs* (Camden 1999)★★★★, *Sunrise*

(RCA 1999)★★★★, Suspicious Minds: The Memphis 1969 Anthology (RCA 1999)★★★★, The Home Recordings (RCA 1999)★★, Artist Of The Century 3-CD set (RCA 1999)★★★★★, Can't Help Falling In Love: The Hollywood Hits (RCA 1999)★★★, The Legend Begins (Manifest 2000)★★★, Peace In The Valley 3-CD box set (RCA 2000)★★★★, The 50 Greatest Hits (RCA 2000)★★★★★, The Live Greatest Hits (RCA 2001)★★★★, Elvis: Live In Las Vegas 4-CD box set (RCA 2001)★★★★.
VIDEOS: Elvis On Tour (MGM/UA 1984), Elvis Presley In Concert (Mountain Films 1986), 68 Comeback Special (Virgin Vision 1986), One Night With You (Virgin Vision 1986), Aloha From Hawaii (Virgin Vision 1986), '56 In the Beginning (Virgin Vision 1987), Memories (Vestron Music Video 1987), This Is Elvis (Warner Home Video 1988), Graceland (Video Gems 1988), Great Performances Volume 1 (Buena Vista 1990), Great Performances Volume 2 (Buena Vista 1990), Young Elvis (Channel 5 1990), Sun Days With Elvis (MMG Video 1991), Elvis: A Portrait By His Friends (Qube Pictures 1991), The Lost Performances (BMG 1992), Private Elvis (1993), Elvis In Hollywood (1993), The Alternate Aloha Concert (Lightyear 1996), Elvis 56 - The Video (BMG 1996), Elvis - That's The Way It Is (1996), Private Moments (Telstar 1997), The Great Performances (Wienerworld 1997), The Legend Lives On (Real Entertainment 1997), Collapse Of The Kingdom (Real Entertainment 1997), The King Comes Back (Real Entertainment 1997), Wild In Hollywood (Real Entertainment 1997), Rocket Ride To Stardom (Real Entertainment 1997), Elvis: All The Kings Men (Real Entertainment 1997), NBC T.V. Special (Lightyear 1997).
FURTHER READING: To begin to wade through the list of books about Elvis is daunting. Many are appalling, some are excellent. In reality you only need two, and both were written in recent years by Peter Guralnick. Last Train To Memphis and Careless Love are historically accurate, objective and beautifully written.
I Called Him Babe: Elvis Presley's Nurse Remembers, Marian J. Cocke. The Three Loves Of Elvis Presley: The True Story Of The Presley Legend, Robert Holmes. A Century Of Elvis, Albert Hand. The Elvis They Dig, Albert Hand. Operation Elvis, Alan Levy. The Elvis Presley Pocket Handbook, Albert Hand. All Elvis: An Unofficial Biography Of The 'King Of Discs', Philip Buckle. The Elvis Presley Encyclopedia, Roy Barlow. Elvis: A Biography, Jerry Hopkins. Meet Elvis Presley, Favius Friedman Elvis Presley, Paula Taylor. Elvis, Jerry Hopkins. The Elvis Presley Scrapbook 1935-1977, James Robert Paris. Elvis And The Colonel, May Mann. Recording Sessions 1954-1974, Ernst Jorgensen and Erik Rasmussen. Elvis Presley: An Illustrated Biography, W.A. Harbinson. Elvis: The Films And Career Of Elvis Presley, Steven Zmijewsky and Boris Zmijewsky. Presley Nation, Spencer Leigh. Elvis, Peter Jones. Presley: Entertainer Of The Century, Antony James. Elvis And His Secret, Maria Gripe. On Stage, Elvis Presley, Kathleen Bowman. The Elvis Presley American Discography, Ron Barry. Elvis: What Happened, Red West, Sonny West and Dave Hebler. Elvis: Tribute To The King Of Rock, Dick Tatham. Elvis Presley, Todd Slaughter. Elvis: Recording Sessions, Ernst Jorgensen, Erick Rasmussen and Johnny Mikkelsen. The Life And Death Of Elvis Presley, W.A. Harbinson. Elvis: Lonely Star At The Top, David Hanna. Elvis In His Own Words, Mick Farren and Pearce Marchbank. Twenty Years Of Elvis: The Session File, Colin Escott and Martin Hawkins. Starring Elvis, James W. Bowser. My Life With Elvis, Becky Yancey and Cliff Lindecker. The Real Elvis: A Good Old Boy, Vince Staten. The Elvis Presley Trivia Quiz Book, Helen Rosenbaum. A Presley Speaks, Vester Presley. The Graceland Gates, Harold Lloyd. The Boy Who Dared To Rock: The Definitive Elvis, Paul Lichter. Eine Illustrierte Dokumentation, Bernd King and Heinz Plehn. Elvis Presley Speaks, Hans Holzer. Elvis: The Legend Lives! One Year Later, Martin A. Grove. Private Elvis, Diego Cortez. Bill Adler's Love Letters To Elvis, Bill Adler. Elvis: His Life And Times In Poetry And Lines, Joan Buchanan West. Elvis '56: In The Beginning, Alfred Wertheimer. Elvis Presley: An Illustrated Biography, Rainer Wallraf and Heinz Plehn. Even Elvis, Mary Ann Thornton. Elvis: Images & Fancies, Jac L. Tharpe. Elvis In Concert, John Reggero. Elvis Presley: A Study In Music, Robert Matthew-Walker. Elvis; Portrait Of A Friend, Marty Lacker, Patsy Lacker and Leslie E. Smith. Elvis Is That You?, Holly Hatcher. Elvis: Newly Discovered Drawings Of Elvis Presley, Betty Harper. Trying To Get To You: The Story Of Elvis Presley, Valerie Harms. Love Of Elvis, Bruce Hamilton and Michael L. Liben. To Elvis With Love, Lena Canada. The Truth About Elvis, Jess Stearn. Elvis: We Love You Tender, Dee Presley, David Rick and Billy Stanley. Presleyana, Jerry Osborne and Bruce Hamilton. Elvis: The Final Years, Jerry Hopkins. When Elvis Died, Nancy Gregory and Joseph. All About Elvis, Fred L. Worth and Steve D. Tamerius. Elvis Presley: A Reference Guide And Discography, John A. Whisle. The Illustrated Discography, Martin Hawkins and Colin Escott. Elvis: Legend Of Love, Marie Greenfield. Elvis Presley: King Of Rock 'N' Roll, Richard Wooton. The Complete Elvis, Martin Torgoff. Elvis Special 1982, Todd Slaughter. Elvis, Dave Marsh. Up And Down With Elvis Presley, Marge Crumbaker with Gabe Tucker. Elvis For The Record, Maureen Covey. Elvis: The Complete Illustrated Record, Roy Carr and Mick Farren. Elvis Collectables, Rosalind Cranor. Jailhouse Rock: The Bootleg Records Of Elvis Presley 1970, Lee Cotten and Howard A. DeWitt. Elvis The Soldier, Rex and Elisabeth Mansfield. All Shook Up: Elvis Day-By-Day, 1954-1977, Lee Cotten. Elvis, John Townson, Gordon Minto and George Richardson. Priscilla, Elvis & Me, Michael Edwards. Elvis On The Road To Stardom: 1955-1956, Jim Black. Return To Sender, Howard F. Banney. Elvis: His Life From A To Z, Fred L. Worth and Steve D. Tamerius. Elvis And The Colonel, Dirk Vallenga with Mick Farren. Elvis: My Brother, Bill Stanley with George Erikson. Long Lonely Highway: 1950's Elvis Scrapbook, Ger J. Rijff. Elvis In Hollywood, Gerry McLafferty. Reconsider Baby: Definitive Elvis Sessionography, E. Jorgensen. Elvis '69, The Return, Joseph A. Tunzi. The Death Of Elvis: What Really Happened, Charles C. Thompson and James P. Cole. Elvis For Beginners, Jill Pearlman. Elvis, The Cool King, Bob Morel and Jan Van Gestel. The Elvis Presley Scrapbooks 1955-1965, Peter Haining (ed.). The Boy Who Would Be King. An Intimate Portrait Of Elvis Presley By His Cousin, Earl Greenwood and Kathleen Tracy. Elvis: The Last 24 Hours, Albert Goldman. The Elvis Files, Gail Brewer-Giorgio. Elvis, My Dad, David Adler and Ernest Andrews. The Elvis Reader: Texts And Sources On The King Of Rock 'n' Roll, Kevin Quain (ed.). Elvis Bootlegs Buyer's Guide, Pts 1 & 2, Tommy Robinson. Elvis: The Music Lives On - The Recording Sessions 1954-1976, Richard Peters. The King Forever, no author listed. Dead Elvis: A Chronicle Of A Cultural Obsession, Greil Marcus. Elvis People: Cult Of The King, Ted Harrison. In Search Of The King, Craig Gelfand, Lynn Blocker-Krantz and Rogerio Noguera. Aren Med Elvis, Roger Ersson and Lennart Svedberg. Elvis And Gladys, Elaine Dundy. King And I: Little Gallery of Elvis Impersonators, Kent Barker and Karin Pritikin. Elvis Sessions: The Recorded Music Of Elvis Aaron Presley 1953-1977, Joseph A. Tunzi. Elvis: The Sun Years, Howard A. DeWitt. Elvis In Germany: The Missing Years, Andreas Schroer. Graceland: The Living Legend Of Elvis Presley, Chet Flippo. Elvis: The Secret Files, John Parker. The Life And Cuisine Of Elvis Presley, David Adler. Last Train To Memphis: The Rise Of Elvis Presley, Peter Guralnick. In His Own Words, Mick Farren. Elvis: Murdered By The Mob, John Parker. The Complete Guide To The Music Of ..., John Robertson. Elvis' Man Friday, Gene Smith. The Hitchhiker's Guide To Elvis, Mick Farren. Elvis, The Lost Photographs 1948-1969, Joseph Tunzi and O'Neal. Elvis Aaron Presley: Revelations From The Memphis Mafia, Alanna Nash. The Elvis Encyclopaedia, David E. Stanley. E: Reflections On The Birth Of The Elvis Faith, John E. Strausbaugh. Elvis Meets The Beatles: The Untold Story Of Their Entangled Lives, Chris Hutchins and Peter Thompson. Elvis, Highway 51 South, Memphis, Tennessee, Joseph A. Tunzi. Elvis In The Army, William J. Taylor Jnr. Everything Elvis, Pauline Bartel. Elvis In Wonderland, Bob Jope. Elvis: Memories And Memorabilia, Richard Bushkin. Elvis Sessions II: The Recorded Music Of Elvis Aaron Presley 1953-1977, Joseph A. Tunzi. The Ultimate Album Cover Book, Paul Dowling. The King Of The Road, Robert Gordon. That's Alright, Elvis, Scotty Moore and James Dickerson. Raised On Rock: Growing Up At Graceland, David A. Stanley and Mark Bego. Elvis: In The Twilight Of Memory, June Juanico. The Rise And Fall And Rise Of Elvis, Aubrey Dillon-Malone. In Search Of Elvis: Music, Race, Art, Religion, Vernon Chadwick (editor). The Complete Idiot's Guide To Elvis, Frank Coffey. The Elvis Encyclopedia: An Impartial Guide To The Films Of Elvis, Eric Braun. Essential Elvis, Peter Silverton. Talking Elvis, Trevor Cajiao. A Life In Music: The Complete Recording Sessions, Ernst Jorgensen. Careless Love: The Unmaking Of Elvis Presley, Peter Guralnick. Elvis For CD Fans Only, Dale Hampton. Double Trouble: Bill Clinton And Elvis Presley In The Land Of No Alternatives, Greil Marcus. A Life In Music: The Complete Recording Sessions, Ernst Jorgensen. Elvis Day By Day: The Definitive Record Of His Life And Music, Peter Guralnick and Ernst Jorgensen. Elvis: The King On Film, Chutley Chops (ed.). Colonel Tom Parker: The Curious Life Of Elvis Presley's Eccentric Manager, James L. Dickerson.
FILMS: Love Me Tender (1956), Loving You (1957), Jailhouse Rock (1957), King Creole (1958), G.I. Blues (1960), Flaming Star (1960), Wild In The Country (1961), Blue Hawaii (1961), Kid Galahad (1962), Girls Girls Girls (1962), Follow That Dream (1962), It Happened At The World's Fair (1963), Fun In Acapulco (1963), Roustabout (1964), Viva Las Vegas (1964), Kissin' Cousins (1964), Tickle Me (1965), Harem Scarum aka Harem Holiday (1965), Girl Happy (1965), Spinout (1966), Paradise Hawaiian Style (1966), Frankie And Johnny (1966), Easy Come Easy Go (1967), Clambake (1967), Live A Little Love A Little (1968), Speedway (1968), Stay Away Joe (1968), Double Trouble (1968), The Trouble With Girls (1969), Charro! (1969), Change Of Habit (1969), This Is Elvis compilation (1981).

PRESTON, BILLY
ALBUMS: Gospel In My Soul (1962)★★, 16 Year Old Soul (Derby 1963)★★, The Most Exciting Organ Ever (Vee Jay 1965)★★★, Early Hits Of 1965 (Vee Jay 1965)★★, The Wildest Organ In Town! (Vee Jay 1966)★★★, That's The Way God Planned It (Apple 1969)★★★, Greazee Soul (Apple 1969)★★★, Encouraging Words (Apple 1970)★★, I Wrote A Simple Song (A&M 1972)★★★, Music Is My Life (A&M 1972)★★★, Everybody Likes Some Kind Of Music (A&M 1973)★★, The Kids & Me (A&M 1974)★★★, Live European Tour (A&M 1974)★★, It's My Pleasure (A&M 1975)★★★, Do What You Want (A&M 1976)★★, Billy Preston (A&M 1976)★★, A Whole New Thing (A&M 1977)★★, Soul'd Out (A&M 1977)★★, with Syreeta Fast Break film soundtrack (Motown 1979)★★, Late At Night (Motown 1980)★★★, Behold (Myrrh 1980)★★, The Way I Am (Motown 1981)★★, with Syreeta Billy Preston & Syreeta (Motown 1981)★★, Pressin' On (Motown 1982)★★, Billy's Back (NuGroov 1995)★★.
COMPILATIONS: The Best Of Billy Preston (A&M 1988)★★★, Collection (Castle 1989)★★★.

PRETENDERS
ALBUMS: Pretenders (Real/Sire 1980)★★★★, Pretenders II (Real/Sire 1981)★★★★, Learning To Crawl (Real/Sire 1984)★★★★, Get Close (WEA/Sire 1986)★★, Packed! (WEA/Sire 1990)★★, Last Of The Independents (WEA 1994)★★★, The Isle Of View (WEA 1995)★★★, ¡Viva El Amor! (WEA 1999)★★★.
COMPILATIONS: The Singles (WEA/Sire 1987)★★★★, Greatest Hits (WEA 2000)★★★★.
VIDEOS: The Isle Of View (Warner Music Vision 1995).
FURTHER READING: Pretenders, Miles. The Pretenders, Chris Salewicz. The Pretenders: With Hyndesight, Mike Wrenn.

PRETTY THINGS
ALBUMS: The Pretty Things (Fontana 1965)★★★★, Get The Picture? (Fontana 1965)★★★★, Emotions (Fontana 1967) ★★, S.F. Sorrow (EMI 1968)★★★★, Parachute (Harvest 1970)★★★★, Freeway Madness (Warners 1972)★★★, Silk Torpedo (Swan Song 1974)★★★, Savage Eye (Swan Song 1976)★★★, Live '78 (Jade 1978)★★, Cross Talk (Warners 1980)★★, Live At The Heartbreak Hotel (Ace 1984)★★, Out Of The Island (Inak 1988)★★, On Air (Band Of Joy 1992)★★, Rage Before Beauty (Madfish 1999)★★★, Resurrection (Worldwidetribe 1999)★★★.
The group also completed several albums of background music suitable for films: Electric Banana (De Wolfe 1967)★★, More Electric Banana (De Wolfe 1968)★★, Even More Electric Banana (De Wolfe 1969)★★, Hot Licks (De Wolfe 1973)★★, Return Of The Electric Banana (De Wolfe 1978)★★.
COMPILATIONS: Greatest Hits 64-67 (Philips 1975) ★★★★, The Vintage Years (Sire 1976)★★★★, Singles A's And B's (Harvest 1977)★★★, Electric Banana: The Seventies (Butt 1979)★★, Electric Banana: The Sixties (Butt 1980)★★, The Pretty Things 1967-1971 (See For Miles 1982)★★★★, Cries From The Midnight Circus: The Best Of The Pretty Things 1968-1971 (Harvest 1986)★★★, Let Me Hear The Choir Sing (Edsel 1986)★★★, Closed Restaurant Blues (Bam Caruso 1987)★★★, Unrepentant 2-CD box set (Fragile 1995)★★★, Latest Writs Greatest Hits: The Best Of Pretty Things (Snapper 2000)★★★★.
FURTHER READING: The Pretty Things: Their Own Story And The Downliners Sect Story, Mike Stax.

PRICE, ALAN
ALBUMS: The Price To Play (Decca 1966)★★★, A Price On His Head (Decca 1967)★★★, The Price Is Right (Parrot 1968) ★★★, with Georgie Fame Fame And Price, Price And Fame Together (CBS 1971)★★★, O Lucky Man! film soundtrack (Warners 1973)★★★, Between Today And Yesterday (Warners 1974)★★★★, Metropolitan Man (Polydor 1974)★★★, Performing Price (Polydor 1975)★★★, Shouts Across The Street (Polydor 1976)★★★, Rainbows End (Jet 1977)★★, Alan Price (Jet 1977)★★, England My England (Jet 1978)★★★, Rising Sun (Jet 1980)★★★, A Rock And Roll Night At The Royal Court (Key 1981)★★★, Geordie Roots And Branches (MWM 1983)★★★, Travellin' Man (Trojan 1986)★★★, Liberty (Ariola 1989)★★★, Live In Concert (1993)★★, with The Electric Blues Company A Gigster's Life For Me (Indigo 1995)★★.
COMPILATIONS: The World Of Alan Price (Decca 1970)★★★, Profile: Alan Price (Teldec 1983)★★, 16 Golden Classics (Unforgettable 1986)★★, Greatest Hits (K-Tel 1987)★★, The Best Of Alan Price (MFP 1987)★★★, The Best Of And The Rest Of (Action Replay 1989)★★★, Anthology: The Best Of Alan Price (Repertoire 1999)★★★, I Put A Spell On You: The Singles As & Bs (Edsel 2001)★★★★.
FURTHER READING: Wild Animals, Andy Blackford. Animal Tracks: The Story Of The Animals, Sean Egan

PRICE, LLOYD
ALBUMS: Lloyd Price (Specialty 1959)★★★★, The Exciting Lloyd Price (ABC-Paramount 1959)★★★★, Mr. Personality (ABC-Paramount 1959)★★★★, Mr. Personality Sings The Blues (ABC-Paramount 1960)★★★★, The Fantastic Lloyd Price (ABC-Paramount 1960)★★★, Lloyd Price Sings The Million Sellers (ABC-Paramount 1961)★★★, Cookin' With Lloyd Price (ABC-Paramount 1961)★★, The Lloyd Price Orchestra (Double-L 1963)★★, Misty (Double-L 1963)★★, Lloyd Swings For Sammy (Monument 1965)★★, Lloyd Price Now (Jad 1969)★★, To The Roots And Back (1972)★★, The Nominee (1978)★★.
COMPILATIONS: Mr. Personality's Big 15 (ABC-Paramount 1960)★★★★, The Best Of Lloyd Price (1970)★★★★, Lloyd Price's 16 Greatest Hits (ABC 1972)★★★★, Original Hits (1972)★★★, The ABC Collection (ABC 1976)★★★★, Mr. Personality Revisited (Charly 1983)★★★, Lloyd Price (Specialty 1986)★★★, Personality Plus (Specialty 1986) ★★★, Walkin' The Track (Specialty 1986)★★, Lawdy! (Specialty 1991)★★★, Stagger Lee & All His Other Greatest Hits (1993)★★★★, Greatest Hits (MCA 1995)★★★★.

PRIEST, MAXI
ALBUMS: You're Safe (Virgin 1985)★★, Intentions (Virgin 1986)★★, Maxi (Ten 1987)★★, Bona Fide (Ten 1990) ★★★, Fe Real (Ten 1992)★★, Man With The Fun (Virgin 1996)★★, Live In Concert 1986 recording (Strange Fruit 1999)★★★, Combination (Virgin 1999)★★★.
COMPILATIONS: The Best Of Me (Ten 1991)★★★.

PRIMAL SCREAM
ALBUMS: Sonic Flower Groove (Elevation 1987)★★, Primal Scream (Creation 1989)★★★, Screamadelica (Creation 1991)★★★★, Give Out But Don't Give Up (Creation 1994)★★★, Vanishing Point (Creation 1997)★★★★, Echodek remixes (Creation 1997)★★★, Xtrmntr (Creation 2000)★★★★.
FURTHER READING: Higher Than The Sun, Grant Fleming.

PRINCE
ALBUMS: Prince - For You (Warners 1978)★★★, Prince (Warners 1979)★★★, Dirty Mind (Warners 1980)★★★, Controversy (Warners 1981)★★★, 1999 (Warners 1982) ★★★★, Purple Rain film soundtrack (Warners 1984)★★★★, Around The World In A Day (Paisley Park 1985)★★★, Parade - Music From Under The Cherry Moon film soundtrack (Paisley Park 1986)★★★, Sign 'O' The Times (Paisley Park 1987)★★★★, Lovesexy (Paisley Park 1988)★★★, Batman film soundtrack (Warners 1989)★★★, Graffiti Bridge (Paisley Park 1990)★★, Diamonds And Pearls (Paisley Park 1991)★★★, Symbol (Paisley Park 1993)★★★, Come (Paisley Park 1994)★★, The Gold Experience (Warners 1995)★★★, Chaos And Disorder (Warners 1996)★★, Emancipation (New Power Generation 1996)★★, Crystal Ball 4-CD set (New Power Generation 1998)★★★, New Power Soul (NPG 1998)★★, Rave Un2 The Joy Fantastic (Arista/NPG 1999)★★★, The Rainbow Children (NPG 2001)★★★.
COMPILATIONS: The Hits: Volume I & II (Paisley Park/Warners 1993)★★★★, The Vault ... Old Friends 4 Sale (Warners 1999)★★★★, The Very Best Of Prince (Rhino 2001)★★★★.
VIDEOS: Double Live (PolyGram Music Video 1986), Prince And The Revolution; Live (Channel 5 Video 1987), Sign O' The Times (Palace Video 1988), Lovesexy Part 1 (Palace Video 1989), Lovesexy Part 2 (Palace Video 1989), Get Off (Warner Music Video 1991), Prince: The Hits Collection (Warner Music Video 1993), 3 Chains O' Gold (Warner Reprise 1994), Billboards (Warner Vision 1994).
FURTHER READING: Prince: Imp Of The Perverse, Barney Hoskyns. Prince: A Pop Life, Dave Hill. Prince By Controversy, The 'Controversy' Team. Prince: A Documentary, Per Nilsen. Prince: An Illustrated Biography, John W. Duffy. Prince, John Ewing. Dancemusicsexromance - Prince: The First Decade, Per Nilsen.

PRINCE BUSTER
ALBUMS: with various artists I Feel The Spirit (Blue Beat 1963)★★★★, with various artists Pain In My Belly (Islam/Blue Beat 1966)★★★★, On Tour (1966)★★★, Judge Dread Rock Steady (Blue Beat 1967)★★★, Wreck A Pum Pum (Blue Beat 1968)★★★★, She Was A Rough Rider (Melodisc 1969)★★★★, Big Five (Melodisc 1972)★★★.
COMPILATIONS: Prince Buster's Fabulous Greatest Hits (Fab 1967)★★★★, Original Golden Oldies Volumes 1 & 2 (Prince Buster 1989)★★★★, Fabulous Greatest Hits (Diamond Range 1998)★★★★.

PRINE, JOHN
ALBUMS: John Prine (Atlantic 1972)★★★★, Diamonds In The Rough (Atlantic 1972)★★★, Sweet Revenge (Atlantic 1973)★★★★, Common Sense (Atlantic 1975)★★★, Bruised Orange (Asylum 1978)★★★, Pink Cadillac (Asylum 1979)★★★, Storm Windows (Asylum 1980)★★★, Aimless Love (Oh Boy 1985)★★★, German Afternoons (Oh Boy 1987)★★★, John Prine Live (Oh Boy 1988)★★★, The Missing Years (Oh Boy 1991)★★★★, Live (Oh Boy 1993)★★★★, Lost Dogs & Mixed Blessings (Oh Boy 1995)★★★, Live On Tour (Oh Boy 1997)★★★, In Spite Of Ourselves (Oh Boy 1999)★★★★, Souvenirs: Fifteen New Recordings Of Classic Songs (Oh Boy 2000)★★★.
COMPILATIONS: Prime Prine: The Best Of John Prine (Atlantic 1977)★★★, Anthology: Great Days (Rhino 1993)★★★★.
VIDEOS: Live From Sessions At West 54th (Oh Boy 2001).

PROBY, P.J.
ALBUMS: I Am P.J. Proby (Liberty 1964)★★★★, P.J. Proby (Liberty 1965)★★★★, P.J. Proby In Town (Liberty 1965) ★★★, Enigma (Liberty 1966)★★★, Phenomenon (Liberty 1967)★★, Believe It Or Not (Liberty 1968)★★, Three Week Hero (Liberty 1969)★★, I'm Yours (Ember 1973)★★, The Hero (Palm 1981)★★, Clown Shoes (1987)★★, The Savoy Sessions (Savoy 1995)★★, Legend (EMI 1996)★★, Lord Horror (Savoy 1999)★★.
COMPILATIONS: as Jet Powers California License (Liberty 1969)H, Somewhere (Sunset 1975)★★★, The Legendary P.J. Proby At His Very Best (See For Miles 1986)★★★★, The Legendary P.J. Proby At His Very Best, Volume 2 (See For Miles 1987)★★★★, The EP Collection (See For Miles 1996)★★★★, The Very Best Of P.J. Proby (EMI 1998)★★★★.

PROCLAIMERS
ALBUMS: This Is The Story (Chrysalis 1987)★★★, Sunshine On Leith (Chrysalis 1988)★★★★, Hit The Highway (Chrysalis 1994)★★★, 'Persevere' (Nettwerk 2001)★★★.

PROCOL HARUM
ALBUMS: Procol Harum aka A Whiter Shade Of Pale (Deram/A&M 1967)★★★, Shine On Brightly (Regal Zonophone/A&M 1968)★★★, A Salty Dog (Regal Zonophone/A&M 1969)★★★★, Home (Regal Zonophone/A&M 1970)★★★, Broken Barricades (Chrysalis/A&M 1971)★★★, Live In Concert With The Edmonton Symphony Orchestra (Chrysalis/A&M 1972)★★★★, Grand Hotel (Chrysalis 1973)★★★, Exotic Birds And Fruit (Chrysalis 1974)★★★, Procol's Ninth (Chrysalis 1975)★★★, Something Magic (Chrysalis 1977)★★, The Prodigal Stranger (Zoo 1991)★★★, with various artists The Long Goodbye aka Symphonic Music Of Procol Harum (RCA Victor 1995)★★.
COMPILATIONS: The Best Of Procol Harum (A&M 1972) ★★★★, Platinum Collection (Cube 1981)★★★★, The Collection (Castle 1985)★★★★, The Chrysalis Years 1973-1977 (Chrysalis 1989)★★★★, Chapter One: Turning Back The Page 1967-1991 (Zoo 1991)★★★★, The Early Years (Griffin 1992)★★★, Homburg And Other Hats: Procol Harum's Best (Essential 1995)★★★★, Halycon Daze (Music Club 1997)★★★, 30th Anniversary Anthology 3-CD set (Westside 1998)★★★★.
FURTHER READING: Beyond The Pale, Claes Johansen.

PRODIGY
ALBUMS: The Prodigy Experience (XL 1992)★★★, Music For The Jilted Generation (XL 1994)★★★★, Fat Of The Land (XL 1997)★★★★, Prodigy Present The Dirtchamber Sessions Volume One (XL 1999)★★★★.
VIDEOS: Electronic Punks (XL Recordings 1995), Evolution (Visual 1997).
FURTHER READING: Electronic Punks: The Official Story, Martin Roach. Prodigy: Exit The Underground, Lisa Verrico. Prodigy: The Fat Of The Land, no author listed. Adventures With The Voodoo Crew, Martin James. Prodigy – An Illustrated Biography, Stuart Coles.

PSYCHEDELIC FURS
ALBUMS: Psychedelic Furs (Columbia 1980)★★★, Talk Talk Talk (Columbia 1981)★★★, Forever Now (Columbia 1982)★★★, Mirror Moves (Columbia 1984)★★★, Midnight To Midnight (Columbia 1987)★★, Book Of Days (Columbia 1989)★★, World Outside (Columbia 1991)★★, Radio 1 Sessions (Strange Fruit 1997)★★★.
COMPILATIONS: All Of This And Nothing (Columbia 1988) ★★★★, Crucial Music: The Collection (Columbia 1989)★★★, Should God Forget: A Retrospective (Columbia/Legacy 1997)★★★, Greatest Hits (Columbia/Legacy 2001)★★★.

PUBLIC ENEMY
ALBUMS: Yo! Bum Rush The Show (Def Jam 1987)★★★, It Takes A Nation Of Millions To Hold Us Back (Def Jam 1988)★★★★, Fear Of A Black Planet (Def Jam 1990)★★★★, Apocalypse '91 ... The Enemy Strikes Black (Def Jam 1991) ★★★, Muse Sick-N-Hour Mess Age (Def Jam 1994)★★★, He Got Game film soundtrack (Def Jam 1998)★★★, There's A Poison Goin On ... (Atomic Pop 1999)★★★★.
COMPILATIONS: Greatest Misses features six 'new' tracks (Def Jam 1992)★★★★, Twelve Inch Mixes (Def Jam 1993)★★★.
VIDEOS: Public Enemy Live From House Of Blues (Aviva International 2001).
FURTHER READING: Fight The Power – Rap, Race And Reality, Chuck D. with Yusuf Jah.

PUBLIC IMAGE LIMITED
ALBUMS: Public Image (Virgin 1978)★★★, Metal Box UK title Second Edition US title (Virgin 1979)★★★★, Paris Au Printemps (Virgin 1980)★★, Flowers Of Romance (Virgin 1981)★★, Live In Tokyo (Virgin 1983)★★, Commercial Zone (PiL/Virgin 1983)★★, This Is What You Want, This Is What You Get (Virgin 1984)★★★, Album (Virgin 1986)★★★, Happy? (Virgin 1987)★★★, 9 (Virgin 1989)★★, That What Is Not (Virgin 1992)★★.
COMPILATIONS: Greatest Hits ... So Far (Virgin 1990) ★★★, Plastic Box 4-CD box set (Virgin 1999)★★★.
VIDEOS: Live In Tokyo (Virgin Video 1983), Videos (Virgin Video 1986).
FURTHER READING: Public Image Limited: Rise Fall, Clinton Heylin.

PULP
ALBUMS: It mini-album (Red Rhino 1983)★★, Freaks (Fire 1986)★★, Separations 1989 recording (Fire 1992)★★★, His 'N' Hers (Island 1994)★★★★, Different Class (Island 1995)★★★★, This Is Hardcore (Island 1998)★★★, We Love Life (Island 2001)★★★.
COMPILATIONS: Pulpintro: The Gift Recordings (Island 1993)★★, Masters Of The Universe: Pulp On Fire 1985-86 (Fire 1995)★★★, Countdown 1992-83 (Nectar 1996)★★, Primal ... The Best Of The Fire Years 1983-1992 (Music Club 1998)★★★, Pulped 83-92 4-CD box set (Cooking Vinyl 1999)★★★.
VIDEOS: Pulp - Sorted For Films And Vids (VVL 1995), Pulp – A Feeling Called Love (VVL 1996), The Park Is Mine (VVL 1998).
FURTHER READING: Pulp, Martin Aston.

PURE PRAIRIE LEAGUE
ALBUMS: Pure Prairie League (RCA 1972)★★★, Bustin' Out (RCA 1975)★★★★, Two Lane Highway (RCA 1975)★★★★, If The Shoe Fits (RCA 1976)★★★, Dance (RCA 1976)★★★, Live!! Takin' The Stage (RCA 1977)★★, Just Fly (RCA 1978) ★★, Can't Hold Back (RCA 1979)★★, Firin' Up (Casablanca 1980)★★, Something In The Night (Casablanca 1981)★★, Songs Of Pure Harmony 1974 live recording (Pilot 2001)★★.
COMPILATIONS: Pure Prairie Collection (RCA 1981)★★★, Mementoes 1971-1987 (Rushmore 1987)★★★, Best Of Pure Prairie League (Mercury Nashville 1995)★★★★, Anthology (Camden 1998)★★★.

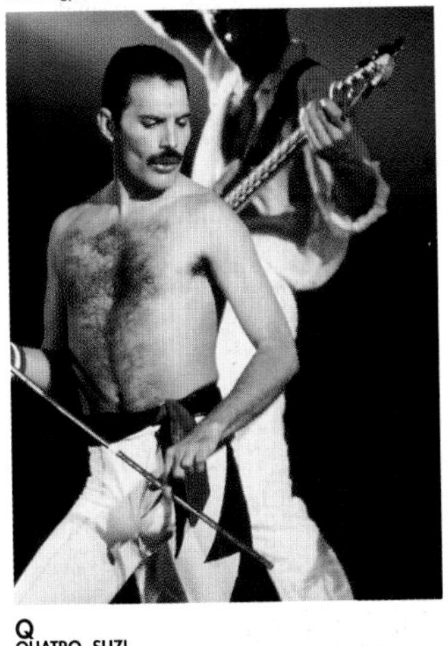

Q

QUATRO, SUZI
ALBUMS: Suzi Quatro (Rak 1973)★★★, Quatro (Rak 1974) ★★, Your Mama Won't Like Me (Rak 1975)★★, Aggro-Phobia (Rak 1977)★★, Live 'N' Kickin' (EMI Japan 1977) ★★, If You Knew Suzi (Rak 1978)★★, Suzi And Other Four Letter Words (Rak 1979)★★, Rock Hard (Dreamland 1981) ★★, Main Attraction (Polydor 1983)★★, Saturday Night Special (Biff 1987)★★, Rock 'Til Ya Drop (Biff 1988) ★★, Oh, Suzi Q (Bellaphon 1991)★★, What Goes Around: Greatest & Latest (CMC 1995)★★★, Unreleased Emotion 1983 recording (Connoisseur 1998)★★.
COMPILATIONS: The Suzi Quatro Story (Rak 1975)★★, Suzi Quatro's Greatest Hits (Rak 1980)★★★, The Wild One (The Greatest Hits) (EMI 1990)★★★, Greatest Hits (EMI 1996)★★★.
FURTHER READING: Suzi Quatro, Margaret Mander.

QUEEN
ALBUMS: Queen (EMI 1973)★★★, Queen II (EMI 1974) ★★★★, Sheer Heart Attack (EMI 1974)★★★★, A Night At The Opera (EMI 1975)★★★★, A Day At The Races (EMI 1976)★★★, News Of The World (EMI 1977)★★, Jazz (EMI 1978)★★, Live Killers (EMI 1979)★★, The Game (EMI 1980) ★★★, Flash Gordon film soundtrack (EMI 1980)★★, Hot Space (EMI 1982)H, The Works (EMI 1984)★★★, A Kind Of Magic (EMI 1986)★★★★, Live Magic (EMI 1986)★★, The Miracle (EMI 1989)★★, Queen At The Beeb (Band Of Joy 1989)H, Innuendo (EMI 1991)★★★, Live At Wembley '86 (EMI 1992)★★, Made In Heaven (EMI 1995)★★★.
COMPILATIONS: Greatest Hits (EMI 1981)★★★★★, The Complete Works 14-LP box set (EMI 1985)★★★, Greatest Hits II (EMI 1991)★★★, Queen Rocks (EMI 1997)★★★, Queen + Greatest Hits III (EMI 1999)★★★.
VIDEOS: Queen's Greatest Flix (PMI 1984), We Will Rock You (Peppermint Music Video 1984), The Works Video EP (PMI 1984), Live In Rio (PMI 1985), Live In Budapest (PMI 1987), The Magic Years Volume One: Foundations (PMI 1987), The Magic Years Volume Two: Live Killers In The Making (PMI 1987), The Magic Years Volume Three: Crowning Glory (PMI 1987), Rare Live: A Concert Through Time And Space (PMI 1989), The Miracle EP (PMI 1989), Queen At Wembley (PMI 1990), Greatest Flix II (PMI 1991), Box Of Flix (PMI 1991), Champions Of The World (PMI 1995), Rock You (Music Club 1995), Made In Heaven: The Films (Wienerworld 1996), Queen Rocks: The Video (Queen Films 1998), Greatest Flix III (PMI 1999).
FURTHER READING: Queen, Larry Pryce. The Queen Story, George Tremlett. Queen: The First Ten Years, Mike West. Queen's Greatest Pix, Jacques Lowe. Queen: An Illustrated Biography, Judith Davis. Queen: A Visual Documentary, Ken Dean. Queen: Greatest Pix 2, Richard Gray (ed.). A Kind Of Magic: A Tribute To Freddie Mercury, Ross Clarke. Freddie Mercury: This Is The Real Life, David Evans and David Minns. The Show Must Go On: The Life Of Freddie Mercury, Rick Sky. Queen: As It Began, Jacky Gun and Jim Jenkins. Queen Unseen, Michael Putland. Mercury And Me, Jim Hutton with Tim Wapshott. Queen And I, The Brian May Story, Laura Jackson. Queen: The Early Years, Mark Hodkinson. The Complete Guide To The Music Of Queen, Peter Hogan. Mercury: The King Of Queen, Laura Jackson. Queen Live: A Concert Documentary, Greg Brooks. Freddie Mercury: More Of The Real Life, David Evans and David Minns. Queen Live: A Concert Documentary, Greg Brooks. Freddie Mercury: The Definitive Biography, Lesley Ann Jones. The Ultimate Queen, Peter Lewry and Nigel Goodall. Living On The Edge: The Freddie Mercury Story, David Bret. Queen: The Definitive Biography, Laura Jackson.

QUEEN LATIFAH
ALBUMS: All Hail The Queen (Tommy Boy 1989)★★★★, Nature Of A Sista (Tommy Boy 1991)★★★, Black Reign (Motown 1993)★★★, Order In The Court (Flavor Unit 1998)★★★.
FILMS: Jungle Fever (1991), House Party 2 (1991), Juice (1992), Who's The Man (1993), My Life (1993), Set It Off (1996), Hoodlum (1997), The Wizard Of Oz (1998), Living Out Loud (1998), Sphere (1998), The Bone Collector (1999).

QUEENS OF THE STONE AGE
ALBUMS: Queens Of The Stone Age (Loosegroove 1998) ★★★, Rated R (Interscope 2000)★★★★.

QUEENSRŸCHE
ALBUMS: The Warning (EMI 1984)★★, Rage For Order (EMI 1986)★★, Operation: Mindcrime (EMI 1988)★★★★, Empire (EMI 1990)★★★, Promised Land (EMI 1994)★★★, Hear In The New Frontier (EMI 1997)★★★, Q2K (Atlantic 1999)★★★, Live Evolution (Sanctuary 2001)★★.
COMPILATIONS: Queensrÿche includes Queensrÿche and Prophecy EPs (EMI 1988)★★★.
VIDEOS: Live In Tokyo (PMI 1985), Video Mindcrime (PMI 1989), Operation Livecrime (PMI 1991/93), Building Empires (PMI 1993), Live Evolution (Sanctuary 2001).

? AND THE MYSTERIANS
ALBUMS: 96 Tears (Cameo 1966)★★★, Action (Cameo 1967)★★★, Dallas Reunion Tapes cassette only (ROIR 1984)★★, Question Mark & The Mysterians (Collectables 1997)★★★, More Action (Cavestomp 1999)★★★.
COMPILATIONS: Feel It! The Very Best Of ? And The Mysterians (Varèse Vintage 2001)★★★.

QUICKSILVER MESSENGER SERVICE
ALBUMS: Quicksilver Messenger Service (Capitol 1968) ★★★★, Happy Trails (Capitol 1969)★★★★★, Shady Grove (Capitol 1969)★★, Just For Love (Capitol 1970)★★, What About Me (Capitol 1971)★★, Quicksilver (Capitol 1971)★★, Comin' Thru (Capitol 1972)★★, Solid Silver (Capitol 1975)★★, Maiden Of The Cancer Moon 1968 recording (Psycho 1983)★★, Peace By Piece (Capitol 1987)★★.
COMPILATIONS: Anthology (Capitol 1973)★★★, The Best Of Quicksilver Messenger Service (Capitol 1990)★★★, Sons Of Mercury (1968-1975) (Rhino 1991)★★★★, The Best Of Quicksilver Messenger Service (CEMA 1992)★★★, Classic Masters (EMD 2002)★★★.

R

R.E.M.
ALBUMS: Chronic Town mini-album (I.R.S. 1982)★★★, Murmur (I.R.S. 1983)★★★★, Reckoning (I.R.S. 1984)★★★, Fables Of The Reconstruction (I.R.S. 1985)★★★, Lifes Rich Pageant (I.R.S. 1986)★★★★, Document (I.R.S. 1987)★★★, Green (Warners 1988)★★★★, Out Of Time (Warners 1991)★★★★, Automatic For The People (Warners 1992) ★★★★, Monster (Warners 1994)★★★, New Adventures In Hi-Fi (Warners 1996)★★★★, Up (Warners 1998)★★, Reveal (Warners 2001)★★★★.
COMPILATIONS: Dead Letter Office (I.R.S. 1987)★★★, Eponymous (I.R.S. 1988)★★★★, The Best Of R.E.M. (I.R.S. 1991)★★★, In The Attic: Alternative Recordings 1985-1989 (Capitol/EMI 1997)★★★.
VIDEOS: Athens, Ga – Inside/Out (A&M Video 1987), Succumbs (A&M Video 1987), Pop Screen (Warner Reprise Video 1990), Tourfilm (Warner Reprise Video 1990), This Film Is On (Warner Reprise Video 1991), Parallel (Warner Reprise Video 1995), Roadmovie (Warner Reprise Video 1996).
FURTHER READING: REMarks: The Story Of R.E.M., Tony Fletcher. R.E.M.: Behind The Mask, Jim Greer. R.E.M.: File Under Water, The Definitive Guide To 12 Years Of Recordings And Concerts, Jon Storey. REMnants: The R.E.M. Collector's Handbook, Gary Nabors. It Crawled From The South: An R.E.M. Companion, Marcus Gray. Talk About The Passion: R.E.M. An Oral History, Denise Sullivan. R.E.M. The "Rolling Stone" Files: The Ultimate Compendium Of Interviews, no editor listed. R.E.M. Documental, Dave Bowler and Bryan Dray. R.E.M. Inside Out, Craig Rosen. The R.E.M. Companion, John Platt (ed.). Adventures In Hi-Fi: The Complete R.E.M., Rob Jovanovic and Tim Abbott.

RADIOHEAD
ALBUMS: Pablo Honey (Parlophone/Capitol 1993)★★★, The Bends (Parlophone/Capitol 1995)★★★★, OK Computer (Parlophone/Capitol 1997)★★★★, Kid A (Parlophone/Capitol 2000)★★★, Amnesiac (Parlophone/Capitol 2001) ★★★, I Might Be Wrong: Live Recordings (Parlophone 2001)★★★.
VIDEOS: 27/5/94 The Astoria London Live (PMI 1995), 7 Television Commercials (Parlophone 1998), Meeting People Is Easy (Parlophone 1998).
FURTHER READING: Radiohead: An Illustrated Biography, Nick Johnstone. Coming Up For Air, Steve Malins. From A Great Height, Jonathan Hale. Radiohead: Hysterical & Useless, Martin Clarke. Radiohead: Standing On The Edge, Alex Ogg. Exit Music, Mac Randall.

RAE AND CHRISTIAN
ALBUMS: Northern Sulphuric Soul (Grand Central/Smile 1998)★★★★, Sleepwalking (Grand Central/!K7 2001) ★★★★, Nocturnal Activity: Sleepwalking Remixed (Grand Central/!K7 2002)★★★.
COMPILATIONS: Blazing The Crop (MML 1999)★★★, Anotherlatenight (Azuli 2001)★★★.

RAFFERTY, GERRY
ALBUMS: Can I Have My Money Back? (Transatlantic 1971) ★★★★, City To City (United Artists 1978)★★★★, Night Owl (United Artists 1979)★★★★, Snakes And Ladders (United Artists 1980)★★★, Sleepwalking (Liberty 1982)★★, North And South (Polydor 1988)★★, On A Wing And A Prayer (Polydor 1992)★★, Over My Head (Polydor 1995)★★.
COMPILATIONS: Early Collection (Transatlantic 1986)★★★, Blood And Glory (Transatlantic 1988)★★, Right Down The Line: The Best Of Gerry Rafferty (EMI 1991)★★★, One More Dream - The Very Best Of Gerry Rafferty (PolyGram 1995)★★★★, Can I Have My Money Back: The Best Of Gerry Rafferty (Essential 2000)★★★★.

RAGE AGAINST THE MACHINE
ALBUMS: Rage Against The Machine (Epic 1992)★★★★, Evil Empire (Epic 1996)★★★★, The Battle Of Los Angeles (Epic 1999)★★★, Renegades (Epic 2000)★★.
VIDEOS: Home Movie (Sony Music Video 1997), Rage Against The Machine (Epic Music Video 1998), The Battle Of Mexico City (Epic Music Video 2001).

RAIN PARADE
ALBUMS: Emergency Third Rail Power Trip (Enigma 1983) ★★★, Explosions In The Glass Palace mini-album (Zippo 1984)★★★★, Beyond The Sunset (Restless 1985)★★★, Crashing Dream (Island 1985)★★★.

RAINBOW
ALBUMS: Ritchie Blackmore's Rainbow (Oyster 1975)★★★, Rainbow Rising (Polydor 1976)★★★★, On Stage (Polydor 1977)★★, Long Live Rock 'N' Roll (Polydor 1978)★★★, Down To Earth (Polydor 1979)★★★, Difficult To Cure (Polydor 1981)★★, Straight Between The Eyes (Polydor 1982)★★, Bent Out Of Shape (Polydor 1983)★★, Stranger In Us All (RCA 1995)★★.
COMPILATIONS: Best Of (Polydor 1983)★★★, Finyl Vinyl (Polydor 1986)★★.
VIDEOS: The Final Cut (PolyGram Music Video 1986), Live Between The Eyes (Channel 5 1988).
FURTHER READING: Rainbow, Peter Makowski.

RAINCOATS
ALBUMS: The Raincoats (Rough Trade 1979)★★★, Odyshape (Rough Trade 1981)★★, The Kitchen Tapes cassette only (ROIR 1983)★★★, Moving (Rough Trade 1984)★★★, Looking In The Shadows (Geffen 1996)★★★.
COMPILATIONS: Fairytales (Tim/Kerr 1995)★★★.

RAITT, BONNIE
ALBUMS: Bonnie Raitt (Warners 1971)★★★, Give It Up (Warners 1972)★★★, Takin' My Time (Warners 1973) ★★★★, Streetlights (Warners 1974)★★★, Home Plate (Warners 1975)★★, Sweet Forgiveness (Warners 1977) ★★★, The Glow (Warners 1979)★★★, Green Light (Warners 1982)★★★, Nine Lives (Warners 1986)★★, Nick Of Time (Capitol 1989)★★★★, Luck Of The Draw (Capitol 1991)★★★★, Longing In Their Hearts (Capitol 1994) ★★★, Road Tested (Capitol 1995)★★, Fundamental (Capitol 1998)★★★★, Silver Lining (Capitol 2002)★★★★.
COMPILATIONS: The Bonnie Raitt Collection (Warners 1990)★★★★.
VIDEOS: The Video Collection (PMI 1992), Road Tested (Capitol 1995).
FURTHER READING: Just In The Nick Of Time, Mark Bego.

RAMMSTEIN
ALBUMS: Herzeleid (Motor Music/Eureka 1995)★★★, Sehnsucht (Motor Music/Slash 1997)★★★★, Live Aus Berlin (Motor Music/Mercury 1999)★★★, Mutter (Motor Music/Republic 2001)★★★.
VIDEOS: Rammstein: Live Aus Berlin (Universal/Island 1999).
FURTHER READING: Rammstein, Gert Hohf.

RAMONES
ALBUMS: Ramones (Sire 1976)★★★★, Leave Home (Sire 1977)★★★★, Rocket To Russia (Sire 1977)★★★★, Road To Ruin (Sire 1978)★★★★, It's Alive (Sire 1979)★★★, End Of The Century (Sire 1980)★★★, Pleasant Dreams (Sire 1981) ★★★, Subterranean Jungle (Sire 1983)★★★, Too Tough To Die (Sire/Beggars Banquet 1984)★★★★, Animal Boy (Sire/ Beggars Banquet 1986)★★★, Halfway To Sanity (Sire/ Beggars Banquet 1987)★★, Brain Drain (Sire 1989) ★★, Loco Live (Sire/Chrysalis 1992)★★, Mondo Bizarro (Radioactive/Chrysalis 1992)★★, Acid Eaters (Radioactive/ Chrysalis 1993)★★, ¡Adios Amigos! (Radioactive/Chrysalis 1995) ★★★, We're Outta Here! (Radioactive/Eagle 1997)★★★.
COMPILATIONS: Mania (Sire 1988)★★★, All The Stuff And More: Volume One (Sire 1990)★★★★, All The Stuff And More: Volume Two (Sire 1991)★★★, End Of The Decade (Beggars Banquet 1990)★★★★, Greatest Hits Live (Radioactive 1996)★★★, Anthology: Hey Ho Let's Go! (Rhino/Warners 1999)★★★★.
VIDEOS: Lifestyles Of The Ramones (Warner-Reprise Video 1990), The Ramones: Around The World (Rhino Video 1998).
FURTHER READING: The Ramones: An Illustrated Biography, Miles. Ramones: An American Band, Jim Bessman. Poison Heart: Surviving The Ramones, Dee Dee Ramone with Veronica Kofman.
FILMS: Rock 'n' Roll High School (1979).

RANCID
ALBUMS: Rancid i (Epitaph 1993)★★★, Let's Go (Epitaph 1994)★★★, And Out Come The Wolves (Epitaph 1995) ★★★, Life Won't Wait (Epitaph 1998)★★★, Rancid ii (Hellcat 2000)★★★.

RANKS, SHABBA
ALBUMS: with Chaka Demus Rough And Rugged (Jammys 1988)★★★, Best Baby Father (Blue Mountain 1989)★★★★, with Home T, Cocoa Tea Holding On (Greensleeves 1989) ★★★, Just Reality (Blue Mountain 1990)★★★, Star Of The 90s (Jammys 1990)★★★★, Golden Touch (Two Friends/ Greensleeves 1990)★★★★, As Raw As Ever (Epic 1991) ★★★, Rough & Ready Vol. 1 (Epic 1992)★★★★, X-Tra Naked (Epic 1992)★★★, Rough & Ready Vol. 2 (Epic 1993)★★★, A Mi Shabba (Epic 1995)★★★, Get Up Stand Up (Artists Only 1998)★★★.
COMPILATIONS: Rappin' With The Ladies (Greensleeves 1990)★★★, Mr Maximum (Greensleeves 1992)★★★, King of Dancehall (Celluloid 1998)★★★, Shabba Ranks And Friends (Epic 1999)★★★★.

RARE EARTH
ALBUMS: Dreams And Answers (Verve 1968)★★★, Get Ready (Rare Earth 1969)★★★, Ecology (Rare Earth 1970)★★★, One World (Rare Earth 1971)★★★, Rare Earth In Concert (Rare Earth 1971)★★, Willie Remembers (Rare Earth 1972)★★★, Ma (Rare Earth 1973)★★★, Back To Earth (Rare Earth 1975)★★★, Midnight Lady (Rare Earth 1976)★★, Rare Earth (Prodigal 1977)★★, Band Together (Prodigal 1978)★★, Grand Slam (Prodigal 1978)★★, Made In Switzerland (Line 1989)★★, Different World (Koch 1993)★★.
COMPILATIONS: The Best Of Rare Earth (Rare Earth 1972) ★★★, Rare Earth: Superstars Series (Motown 1981)★★★, Greatest Hits And Rare Classics (Motown 1991)★★★, Earth Tones: The Essential Rare Earth (Motown 1994)★★★, Anthology (Motown 1995)★★★.

RASPBERRIES
ALBUMS: Raspberries (Capitol 1972)★★★, Fresh (Capitol 1972)★★★★, Side 3 (Capitol 1973)★★★, Starting Over (Capitol 1974)★★★.
COMPILATIONS: Raspberries' Best Featuring Eric Carmen (Capitol 1976)★★★, Overnight Sensation: The Very Best Of The Raspberries (Zap 1987)★★★, Collectors Series (Capitol 1991)★★★, Power Pop: Volume One (RPM 1996)★★★★, Power Pop: Volume Two (RPM 1996)★★★.
FURTHER READING: Overnight Sensation: The Story Of The Raspberries, Ken Sharp.

RAY, JOHNNIE
ALBUMS: Johnnie Ray 10-inch album (Columbia 1952) ★★★, At The London Palladium 10-inch album (Philips 1954)★★★, I Cry For You 10-inch album (Columbia 1955) ★★★, Johnnie Ray 10-inch album (Epic 1955)★★★, The Voice Of Your Choice 10-inch album (Philips 1955)★★★, Sings The Big Beat (Columbia/Philips 1957)★★★★, At The Desert Inn In Las Vegas (Columbia/Philips 1958)★★★, Showcase Of Hits (Philips 1958)★★★★, A Sinner Am I (Philips 1959)★★, 'Til Morning (Columbia 1959)★★, On The Trail (Columbia/Philips 1959)★★, Johnnie Ray (Liberty 1962)★★, Yesterday, Today And Tomorrow (Celebrity 1980)★★.
COMPILATIONS: Johnnie Ray's Greatest Hits (Columbia 1959)★★★★, The Best Of Johnny Ray (Realm 1966) ★★★★, An American Legend (Columbia 1978)★★★★, Portrait Of A Song Stylist (Masterpiece 1989)★★★★, Greatest Hits (Pickwick 1991)★★★, Cry 5-CD box set (Bear Family 1998) ★★★★, Yes Tonight Josephine 5-CD box set (Bear Family 1999)★★★★.
FURTHER READING: The Johnnie Ray Story, Ray Sonin.

REA, CHRIS
ALBUMS: Whatever Happened To Benny Santini (Magnet 1978)★★★, Deltics (Magnet 1979)★★, Tennis (Magnet 1980)★★, Chris Rea (Magnet 1982)★★, Water Sign (Magnet 1983)★★, Wired To The Moon (Magnet 1984)★★, Shamrock Diaries (Magnet 1985)★★★, On The Beach (Magnet 1986)★★★★, Dancing With Strangers (Magnet 1987)★★★★, The Road To Hell (Warners 1989)★★★★, Auberge (Atco 1991)★★★★, God's Great Banana Skin (East West 1992)★★★, Espresso Logic (East West 1993)★★★, La Passione film soundtrack (East West 1996)★★, The Blue Cafe (East West 1998)★★★, The Road To Hell Part 2 (East West 1999)★★, King Of The Beach (East West 2000)★★★.
COMPILATIONS: New Light Through Old Windows (Warners 1988)★★★, The Very Best Of (East West 2001)★★★★.
FILMS: La Passione (1996), Parting Shots (1999).

READER, EDDI
ALBUMS: with the Patron Saints Of Imperfection Mirmama (RCA 1992)★★★, Eddi Reader (Blanco y Negro/Reprise 1994)★★★★, Candyfloss And Medicine (Blanco y Negro/ Reprise 1996)★★, Angels & Electricity (Blanco y Negro 1998)★★★, Simple Soul (Rough Trade/Compass 2001)★★★.

RED HOT CHILI PEPPERS
ALBUMS: The Red Hot Chili Peppers (EMI America 1984) ★★★★, Freaky Styley (EMI America 1985)★★★, The Uplift Mofo Party Plan (EMI Manhattan 1987)★★★, Mother's Milk (EMI America 1989)★★★, Blood Sugar Sex Magik (Warners 1991)★★★★, One Hot Minute (Warners 1995)★★★, Californication (Warners 1999)★★★★.
COMPILATIONS: What Hits!? (EMI 1992)★★★, Plasma Shaft (Warners 1994)★★★, Out In L.A. (EMI 1994)H, Greatest Hits (CEMA/EMI 1995)★★★, Essential Red Hot Chili Peppers: Under The Covers (EMI 1998)★★.
VIDEOS: Funky Monks (Warner Music Vision 1991), What Hits!? (EMI Video 1992), Off The Map (Warner Music Vision 2002).
FURTHER READING: True Men Don't Kill Coyotes, Dave Thompson. Sugar And Spice, Chris Watts. The Complete Story, Spike Harvey. Body Parts: On The Road With The Red Hot Chili Peppers, Grier Govorko.

RED SNAPPER
ALBUMS: Prince Blimey (Warp 1996)★★★★, Making Bones (Warp/Matador 1998)★★★, Our Aim Is To Satisfy Red Snapper (Warp/Matador 2000)★★★★.
COMPILATIONS: Reeled And Skinned (Warp 1995)★★★★, It's All Good (Keep Diggin' 2002)★★★.

REDDING, OTIS
ALBUMS: Pain In My Heart (Atco 1964)★★★★, The Great Otis Redding Sings Soul Ballads (Volt 1965)★★★★, Otis Blue/Otis Redding Sings Soul (Volt 1965)★★★★★, The Soul Album (Volt 1966)★★★★, Complete And Unbelievable: The Otis Redding Dictionary Of Soul (Volt 1966)★★★★, with Carla Thomas The King & Queen (Stax 1967)★★★★, Live In Europe (Volt 1967)★★★★, The Dock Of The Bay (Volt 1968)★★★, The Immortal Otis Redding (Atco 1968)★★★, In Person At The Whisky A Go Go (Atco 1968)★★★, Love Man (Atco 1969)★★★★, Tell The Truth (Atco 1970)★★★, shared with Jimi Hendrix Monterey International Pop Festival (Reprise 1970)★★★★, Live Otis Redding (Atlantic 1982) ★★★, Good To Me: Recorded Live At The Whiskey A Go Go, Vol. 2 (Stax 1993)★★★.
COMPILATIONS: The History Of Otis Redding (Volt 1967)★★★★, Here Comes Some Soul From Otis Redding And Little Joe Curtis pre-1962 recordings (Marble Arch 1968)H, Remembering (Atlantic 1970)★★★, The Best Of Otis Redding (Atco 1972)★★★★, Pure Otis (Atlantic 1979)★★★, Come To Me (Charly 1984)★★, Dock Of The Bay: The Definitive Collection (Atlantic 1987)★★★★, The Otis Redding Story 4-LP box set (Atlantic 1989)★★★★, Remember Me US title It's Not Just Sentimental UK title (Stax 1992)★★★, Otis!: The Definitive Otis Redding 4-CD box set (Rhino 1993)★★★★★, The Very Best Of Otis Redding (Rhino 1993)★★★★, The Very Best Of Otis Redding, Vol. 2 (Rhino 1995)★★★, Love Songs (Rhino 1998)★★★★, Dreams To Remember: The Anthology (Rhino 1998)★★★★.
VIDEOS: Remembering Otis (Virgin 1990).
FURTHER READING: The Otis Redding Story, Jane Schiesel, Try A Little Tenderness, Geoff Brown.

REDDY, HELEN
ALBUMS: I Don't Know How To Love Him (Capitol 1970)★★★, Helen Reddy (Capitol 1970)★★★, I Am Woman (Capitol 1972)★★★, Long Hard Climb (Capitol 1973)★★, Love Song For Jeffrey (Capitol 1974)★★, Free And Easy (Capitol 1974) ★★★, Ain't No Way To Treat A Lady (Capitol 1975)★★★, Music, Music (Capitol 1976)★★, Ear Candy (Capitol 1977) ★★★, We'll Sing In The Sunshine (Capitol 1978)★★, Live In London (Capitol 1978)★★★, Reddy (Capitol 1979)★★, Take What You Find (Capitol 1980)★★, Play Me Out (MCA 1981) ★★, Imagination (MCA 1983)★★, Feel So Young (Own Label 1990)★★★, Center Stage (Varèse Sarabande 1998)★★★, The Best Christmas Ever (Home Shopping Network 2000)★★.
COMPILATIONS: Helen Reddy's Greatest Hits (Capitol 1975)★★★, Helen Reddy's Greatest Hits (And More) (Capitol 1987)★★★, All Time Greatest Hits (CEMA 1991) ★★★, The Best Of Helen Reddy (Staff 1995)★★★, I Am Woman: The Essential Helen Reddy Collection (Razor & Tie 1998)★★★★, The Helen Reddy Collection (HMV 2001)★★★.
FILMS: Airport 1975 (1974), Pete's Dragon (1977), Sgt. Pepper's Lonely Hearts Club Band (1978), Disorderlies (1987).

REDMAN
ALBUMS: Whut? Thee Album (RAL 1992)★★★, Dare Iz A Darkside (RAL/Def Jam 1994)★★★, Muddy Waters (Def Jam 1996)★★★★, Doc's Da Name 2000 (Def Jam 1998)★★★★, with Method Man Blackout! (Def Jam 1999)★★★, Malpractice (Def Jam 2001)★★★.
FILMS: Rhyme & Reason (1997), Ride (1998), P.I.G.S. (1999), Boricua's Bond (2000).

REED, JIMMY
ALBUMS: I'm Jimmy Reed (Vee Jay 1958)★★★★, Rockin' With Reed (Vee Jay 1959)★★★★, Found Love (Vee Jay 1960)★★★★, Now Appearing (Vee Jay 1960)★★★★, At Carnegie Hall (Vee Jay 1961)★★★, Just Jimmy Reed (Vee Jay 1962)★★★★, T'ain't No Big Thing ... But He Is! (Vee Jay 1963)★★★, The Best Of The Blues (Vee Jay 1963)★★★, The 12-String Guitar Blues (Vee Jay 1963)★★★★, Jimmy Reed At Soul City (Vee Jay 1964)★★★, The Legend, The Man (Vee Jay 1965)★★★, The New Jimmy Reed Album (Bluesway 1967)★★★, Soulin' (Bluesway 1967)★★★, Big Boss Man (Bluesway 1968)★★★, Down In Virginia (Bluesway 1969) ★★★, As Jimmy Is (Roker 1970)★★★, Let The Bossman Speak! (Blues On Blues 1971)★★★.
COMPILATIONS: The Best Of Jimmy Reed (Vee Jay 1962) ★★★★, More Of The Best Of Jimmy Reed (Vee Jay 1964) ★★★★, The Soulful Sound Of Jimmy Reed (Upfront 1970) ★★★, I Ain't From Chicago (Bluesway 1973)★★★, The Ultimate Jimmy Reed (Bluesway 1973)★★★★, Cold Chills (Antilles 1976)★★★, Jimmy Reed Is Back (Roots 1980)★★★, Hard Walkin' Hanna (Versatile 1980)★★★, Greatest Hits (Hollywood 1992)★★★, Speak The Lyrics To Me, Mama Reed (Vee Jay 1993)★★★, Cry Before I Go (Drive Archive 1995)★★★, The Classic Recordings Volumes 1-3 (Tomato/ Rhino 1995)★★★★, Big Legged Woman (Collectables 1996)★★★★, All Night Boogie (Javelin 1996)★★.

REED, LOU
ALBUMS: Lou Reed (RCA 1972)★★, Transformer (RCA 1972)★★★★, Berlin (RCA 1973)★★★★, Rock n Roll Animal (RCA 1974)★★★, Sally Can't Dance (RCA 1974)★★★, Metal Machine Music (RCA 1975)H, Lou Reed Live (RCA 1975)★★, Coney Island Baby (RCA 1976)★★★★, Rock 'N' Roll Heart (Arista 1976)★★, Street Hassle (Arista 1978) ★★★★, Live - Take No Prisoners (RCA 1978)★★, The Bells (Arista 1979)★★★, Growing Up In Public (Arista 1980)★★, The Blue Mask (RCA 1982)★★★, Legendary Hearts (RCA 1983)★★★, New Sensations (RCA 1984)★★★★, Live In Italy (RCA 1984)★★, Mistrial (RCA 1986)★★, New York (Sire 1989)★★★★, with John Cale Songs For 'Drella (Warners 1990)★★★, Magic And Loss (Sire 1992)★★★★, Set The Twilight Reeling (Warners 1996)★★★, Perfect Night In London (Reprise 1998)★★★, Ecstasy (Warners 2000)★★★, American Poet 1972 recording (Burning Airlines 2001)★★.
COMPILATIONS: Walk On The Wild Side – The Best Of Lou Reed (RCA 1977)★★★, Rock 'N' Roll Diary 1967-1980 (Arista 1980)★★★, I Can't Stand It (RCA 1983)★★, New York Superstar (Fame 1986)★★, Between Thought And Expression 3-CD box set (RCA 1992)★★★★, Perfect Day (Camden 1997)★★★, The Very Best Of Lou Reed (Camden 1999)★★★★, The Definitive Collection (Arista 1999)★★★★.
VIDEOS: The New York Album (Warner Music Video 1990), Songs For Drella (Warner Music Video 1991), A Night With Lou Reed (PNE 1996), Rock And Roll Heart (IMC 1998).
FURTHER READING: Lou Reed & The Velvets, Nigel Trevena. Rock 'N' Roll Animal, no author listed. Lou Reed: Words & Music, Barry Miles. The Velvet Underground & Lou Reed, Mike West. Lou Reed & The Velvet Underground, Diana Clapton. Lou Reed: Growing Up In Public, Peter Doggett. Between Thought And Expression, Lou Reed. Between The Lines, Michael Wrenn. Waiting For the Man: A Biography Of Lou Reed, Jeremy Reed. Lou Reed: The Biography, Victor Bockris. Transformer: The Lou Reed Story, Victor Bockris. Pass Thru Fire: The Collected Lyrics, Lou Reed.

REEF
ALBUMS: Replenish (Sony 1995)★★★, Glow (Sony 1996) ★★★★, Rides (Sony 1999)★★★, Getaway (Sony 2000)★★★.

REEVES, JIM
ALBUMS: Jim Reeves Sings (Abbott 1956)★★, Singing Down The Lane (RCA Victor 1956)★★★, Bimbo (RCA Victor 1957)★★★, Jim Reeves (RCA Victor 1957)★★★, Girls I Have Known (RCA Victor 1958)★★★, God Be With You (RCA Victor 1958)★★★, Songs To Warm The Heart (RCA Victor 1959)★★★, He'll Have To Go (RCA Victor 1960)★★★★, According To My Heart (Camden 1960)★★★, The Intimate Jim Reeves (RCA Victor 1960)★★★★, Talking To Your Heart (RCA Victor 1961)★★★, Tall Tales And Short Tempers (RCA Victor 1961)★★★, The Country Side Of Jim Reeves (RCA Victor 1962)★★★, A Touch Of Velvet (RCA Victor 1962) ★★★, We Thank Thee (RCA Victor 1962)★★★, Good 'N' Country (Camden 1963)★★★★, Diamonds In The Sand (Camden 1963)★★★, Gentleman Jim (RCA Victor 1963) ★★★★, The International Jim Reeves (RCA Victor 1963) ★★★, Twelve Songs Of Christmas (RCA Victor 1963)★★★, Moonlight And Roses (RCA Victor 1964)★★★★, Have I Told You Lately That I Love You? (RCA Victor 1964)★★★, Kimberley Jim (RCA Victor 1964)★★, The Jim Reeves Way (RCA Victor 1965)★★★, Distant Drums (RCA Victor 1966) ★★★★, Yours Sincerely, Jim Reeves (RCA Victor 1966)★★★, Blue Side Of Lonesome (RCA Victor 1967)★★★, My Cathedral (RCA Victor 1967)★★★, A Touch of Sadness (RCA Victor 1968)★★★, Jim Reeves On Stage (RCA Victor 1968) ★★★, Jim Reeves - And Some Friends (RCA Victor 1969) ★★★, Jim Reeves Writes You A Record (RCA Victor 1971) ★★★, Something Special (RCA Victor 1971)★★★, Young And Country (RCA Victor 1971)★★★, My Friend (RCA Victor 1972)★★★, Missing You (RCA Victor 1972)★★★, Am I That Easy To Forget (RCA Victor 1973)★★★, Great Moments With Jim Reeves (RCA Victor 1973)★★, I'd Fight The World (RCA Victor 1974)★★★, Songs Of Love (RCA Victor 1975)★★, I Love You Because (RCA Victor 1976)★★, It's Nothin' To Me (RCA Victor 1977)★★★★, Jim Reeves (RCA Victor 1978)★★★, with Deborah Allen Don't Let Me Cross Over (RCA Victor 1979)★★, There's Always Me (RCA Victor 1980)★★, with Patsy Cline Greatest Hits (RCA Victor 1981)★★, Dear Hearts & Gentle People (1992)★★★, Jim Reeves (Summit 1995)★★★.
COMPILATIONS: The Best Of Jim Reeves (RCA Victor 1964)★★★, The Best Of Jim Reeves, Volume 2 (RCA Victor 1966)★★★, The Best Of Jim Reeves, Volume 3 (RCA Victor 1969)★★★, The Best Of Jim Reeves Sacred Songs (RCA Victor 1975)★★★, Abbott Recordings, Volume 1 (1982) ★★★, Abbott Recordings, Volume 2 (1982)★★, Live At The Grand Ole Opry (CMF 1987)★★★, Four Walls - The Legend Begins (RCA 1991)★★★★, The Definitive Jim Reeves (RCA 1992)★★★, Welcome To My World: The Essential Jim Reeves Collection (RCA 1993)★★★★, Welcome To My World 16-CD box set (Bear Family 1994)★★★★, The Essential Jim Reeves (RCA 1995)★★★★, The Ultimate Collection (RCA 1996)★★★★, Jim Reeves And Friends Radio Days Volume 1 4-CD box set (Bear Family 1998) ★★★★, The Unreleased Hits Of Jim Reeves (BMG 2000) ★★, Jim Reeves And Friends Radio Days Volume 2 4-CD box set (Bear Family 2001)★★★.
FURTHER READING: The Saga Of Jim Reeves: Country And Western Singer And Musician, Pansy Cook. Like A Moth To A Flame: The Jim Reeves Story, Michael Streissguth.

REEVES, MARTHA
ALBUMS: Martha Reeves (MCA 1974)★★★, The Rest Of My Life (Arista 1977)★, We Meet Again (Milestone 1978)★, Gotta Keep Moving (Fantasy 1980)★.
COMPILATIONS: Early Classics (Spectrum 1996)★★.

REID, TERRY
ALBUMS: Bang Bang You're Terry Reid (Epic 1968)★★★★, Terry Reid (Epic 1969)★★★, River (Atlantic 1973)★★★, Seed Of Memory (ABC 1976)★★★, Rogue Waves (Capitol 1979)★★, The Driver (Warners 1991)★★.
COMPILATIONS: The Most Of Terry Reid (1971)★★, The Hand Don't Fit The Glove (See For Miles 1985)★★★★.

REMBRANDTS
ALBUMS: Rembrandts (Atco 1990)★★★, Untitled (Atco 1992)★★, L.P. (East West 1995)★★★, as Danny Wilde And The Rembrandts Spin This (Elektra 1998)★★★, Lost Together (J-Bird 2001)★★★.

REO SPEEDWAGON
ALBUMS: REO Speedwagon (Epic 1971)★★★, REO Two (Epic 1972)★★★, Ridin' The Storm Out (Epic 1974)★★★, Lost In A Dream (Epic 1974)★★, This Time We Mean It (Epic 1975)★★, REO (Epic 1976)★★, REO Speedwagon Live/You Get What You Play For (Epic 1977)★★, You Can Tune A Piano But You Can't Tuna Fish (Epic 1978)★★, Nine Lives (Epic 1979)★★, Hi Infidelity (Epic 1980)★★★, Good Trouble (Epic 1982)★★, Wheels Are Turning (Epic 1984) ★★, Life As We Know It (Epic 1987)★★, The Earth, A Small Man, His Dog And A Chicken (Epic 1990)★★, Building The Bridge (Essential 1996)★★, with Styx Live At Riverport (Sanctuary 2000)★★★, REO Speedwagon Live Plus (Sanctuary 2001)★★★.
COMPILATIONS: A Decade Of Rock 'N' Roll 1970-1980 (Epic 1980)★★★, Best Foot Forward (Epic 1985)★★, The Hits (Epic 1988)★★★, The Second Decade Of Rock 'N' Roll 1981-1991 (Epic 1991)★★, The Ballads (Epic 2000)★★.
VIDEOS: Wheels Are Turnin' (Virgin Vision 1987), REO Speedwagon (Fox Video 1988).

REPLACEMENTS
ALBUMS: Sorry Ma, Forgot To Take Out The Trash (Twin/ Tone 1981)★★, Hootenanny (Twin/Tone 1983)★★★, Let It Be (Twin/Tone 1984)★★★★, The Shit Hits The Fans cassette only (Twin/Tone 1985)★★, Tim (Sire 1985)★★★, Pleased To Meet Me (Sire 1987)★★★★, Don't Tell A Soul (Sire 1989)★★★, All Shook Down (Sire 1990)★★★.
COMPILATIONS: Boink!! (Glass 1986)★★★, All For Nothing/Nothing For All (Reprise 1997)★★★.

REPUBLICA
ALBUMS: Republica (Deconstruction/RCA 1997)★★★, Speed Ballads (Deconstruction 1998)★★★.

RESIDENTS
ALBUMS: Meet The Residents (Ralph 1974)★★★★, The Third Reich 'N' Roll (Ralph 1976)★★★, Fingerprince (Ralph 1977)★★★, Not Available (Ralph 1978)★★★, Duck Stab/Buster And Glen (Ralph 1978)★★★★, Eskimo (Ralph 1979)★★★, The Commercial Album (Ralph/Pre 1980) ★★★★, Mark Of The Mole (Ralph 1981)★★★, The Tunes Of Two Cities (Ralph 1982)★★, Intermission mini-album (Ralph 1982)★★, with Renaldo And The Loaf Title In Limbo (Ralph 1983)★★★, The Mole Show Live At The Roxy (Ralph 1983)★★, George And James (Ralph/Korova 1984)★★★, Whatever Happened To Vileness Fats? (Ralph 1984)★★, Assorted Secrets cassette only (Ralph 1984)★★, The Census Taker (Episode 1985)★★, The Big Bubble (Ralph 1985)★★, The 13th Anniversary Show (Ralph 1986)★★, Live In The USA/The 13th Anniversary Tour (Ralph 1986)★★, Stars & Hank Forever (Ralph 1986)★★, For Elsie (Cryptic 1987)★★, The 13th Anniversary Show: Live In Holland (Torso 1987)★★, God In Three Persons (Rykodisc 1988)★★, God In Three Persons: Original Soundtrack Recording (Rykodisc 1988)★★, The King And Eye (Enigma 1989)★★, Buckaroo Blues & Black Barry cassette only (Ralph 1989)★★, Stranger Than Supper (UWEB 1990) ★★★, Cube-E: Live In Holland (Enigma 1990)★★, Freak Show (Ralph 1990)★★★, Daydream B-Liver (UWEB 1991)★★, Our Finest Flowers (East Side Digital 1992)★★, Poor Kaw-Liga's Pain (EuroRalph 1994)★★, Gingerbread Man (EuroRalph/East Side Digital 1994)★★, Hunters (Milan 1995)★★, Have A Bad Day (EuroRalph/East Side Digital 1996)★★, Pollex Christi (Ralph 1997)★★, Live At The Fillmore (Ralph 1998)★★, Residue Deux (East Side Digital 1998)★★, Wormwood: Curious Stories From The Bible (EuroRalph/East Side Digital 1998)★★★.
COMPILATIONS: Nibbles (Virgin 1979)★★★, Residue (Ralph 1983)★★, Ralph Before '84 Volume 1 (Korova 1984)★★★, Ralph Before '84 Volume 2 (Ralph 1985)★★★, Heaven? (Rykodisc 1986)★★★, Hell! (Rykodisc 1986)★★★, Liver Music (UWEB 1990)★★★, Uncle Willie's Highly Opinionated Guide To The Residents (Ralph 1993)★★★, Our Tired, Our Poor, Our Huddled Masses (EuroRalph/Rykodisc 1997)★★★★.
VIDEOS: Ralph Volume One (Ralph 1984), The Mole Show/Whatever Happened To Vileness Fats? (Ralph 1986), Video Voodoo (Ralph 1987), The Eyes Scream (Palace/Torso 1991), Twenty Twisted Questions (Ralph 1993), Freak Show (Ralph 1995), Disfigured Night (Cryptic Corporation 1997), Icky Flix (East Side Digital 2001).
FURTHER READING: Meet The Residents: America's Most Eccentric Band, Ian Shirley.

REVERE, PAUL, AND THE RAIDERS
ALBUMS: Like, Long Hair (Gardena 1961)★★★, Paul Revere And The Raiders aka In The Beginning (Jerden 1961)★★, Here They Come! (Columbia 1965)★★★, Just Like Us! (Columbia 1966)★★★, Midnight Ride (Columbia 1966) ★★★, The Spirit Of '67 aka Good Thing (Columbia 1967) ★★★, Revolution! (Columbia 1967)★★★, A Christmas Present ... And Past (Columbia 1967)★★★, Goin' To Memphis (Columbia 1968)★★★, Something Happening (Columbia 1968)★★★, Hard 'N' Heavy (With Marshmallow) (Columbia 1969)★★, Alias Pink Puzz (Columbia 1969)★★, Collage (Columbia 1970)★★★, Indian Reservation (Columbia 1971)★★★, Country Wine (Columbia 1972)★★, We Gotta All Get Together (Realm 1976)★★, Featuring Mark Lindsay's Arizona (Realm 1976)★★.
COMPILATIONS: Greatest Hits (Columbia 1967)★★★, Greatest Hits, Vol. 2 (Columbia 1971)★★★, All-Time Greatest Hits (Columbia 1972)★★★, Kicks (Edsel 1983)★★★, The Legend Of Paul Revere (Columbia/Legacy 1990)★★★★, The Essential Ride '63-'67 (Columbia/Legacy 1995)★★★★, Mojo Workout! (Sundazed 2000)★★★.

REZILLOS
ALBUMS: Can't Stand The Rezillos (Sire 1978)★★★, Mission Accomplished ... But The Beat Goes On (Sire 1979)★★, Live And On Fire In Japan (Vinyl Japan 1995)★★.
COMPILATIONS: Can't Stand The Rezillos, The (Almost) Complete Rezillos (Sire 1995)★★★.

RICHARD, CLIFF
ALBUMS: Cliff (Columbia 1959)★★★, Cliff Sings (Columbia 1959)★★★★, Me And My Shadows (Columbia 1960) ★★★★, Listen To Cliff (Columbia 1961)★★★, 21 Today (Columbia 1961)★★★, The Young Ones (Columbia 1961)★★★, 32 Minutes And 17 Seconds With Cliff Richard (Columbia 1962)★★★★, Summer Holiday (Columbia 1963)★★★, Cliff's Hit Album (Columbia 1963)★★★★, When In Spain (Columbia 1963)★★★, Wonderful Life (Columbia 1964)★★★, Aladdin And His Wonderful Lamp (Columbia 1964)★★★, Cliff Richard (Columbia 1965)★★★, More Hits By Cliff (Columbia 1965)★★★, When In Rome (Columbia 1965)★★, Love Is Forever (Columbia 1965)★★★, Kinda Latin (Columbia 1966)★★★, Finders Keepers (Columbia 1966) ★★, Cinderella (Columbia 1967)★★, Don't Stop Me Now (Columbia 1967)★★★, Good News (Columbia 1967)★★★, Cliff In Japan (Columbia 1968)★★★, Two A Penny (Columbia 1968)★★★, Established 1958 (Columbia 1968)★★★, Sincerely Cliff (Columbia 1969)★★★, It'll Be Me (Regal Starline 1969)★★★, Cliff 'Live' At The Talk Of The Town (Regal Starline 1970)★★★, All My Love (MFP 1970)★★★, About That Man (Columbia 1970)★★★, Tracks 'N' Grooves (Columbia 1970)★★★, His Land (Columbia 1970)★★★, Cliff's Hit Album stereo reissue of 1963 album (EMI 1971) ★★★★, Take Me High (EMI 1973)★★★, Help It Along (EMI 1974)★★★, The 31st Of February Street (EMI 1974)★★★, Everybody Needs Someone (MFP 1975)★★★, I'm Nearly Famous (EMI 1976)★★★, Cliff Live (MFP 1976)★★★, Every Face Tells A Story (EMI 1977)★★★, Small Corners (EMI 1977)★★★, Green Light (EMI 1978)★★★, Thank You Very Much (EMI 1979)★★★, Rock 'N' Roll Juvenile (EMI 1979) ★★★, Rock On With Cliff (MFP 1980)★★★, Listen To Cliff (MFP 1980)★★★, I'm No Hero (EMI 1980)★★★, Love Songs (EMI 1981)★★★, Wired For Sound (EMI 1981)★★★, Now You See Me, Now You Don't (EMI 1982)★★★, Dressed For The Occasion (EMI 1983)★★★, Silver (EMI 1983)★★★, Cliff In The 60s (MFP 1984)★★★, Cliff And The Shadows (EMI 1984)★★★, Thank You Very Much (MFP 1984)★★★, The Rock Connection (EMI 1984)★★★, Walking In The Light (Myrrh 1985)★★★, Time (EMI 1986)★★★, Hymns And Inspirational Songs (Word 1986)★★★, Always Guaranteed (EMI 1987)★★★, Stronger (EMI 1989)★★★, From A Distance ... The Event (EMI 1990)★★★, Together With Cliff (EMI 1991)★★★, The Album (EMI 1993)★★★, Songs From Heathcliff (EMI 1995)★★★, Real As I Wanna Be (EMI 1998)★★★, Wanted (Papillon 2001)★★★.
COMPILATIONS: The Best Of Cliff (Columbia 1969)★★★★, The Best Of Cliff Volume 2 (Columbia 1972)★★★★, The Cliff Richard Story 6-LP box set (WRC 1972)★★★, 40 Golden Greats (EMI 1979)★★★★, The Cliff Richard Songbook 6-LP box set (WRC 1980)★★★★, Private Collection 1979-1988 (EMI 1988)★★★, 20 Original Greats (EMI 1989)★★★, The Hit List (EMI 1994)★★★★, At The Movies 1959-1974 (EMI 1996)★★★, The Rock 'N' Roll Years 1958-1963 4-CD box set (EMI 1997)★★★, On The Continent 5-CD box set (Bear Family 1998)★★★, 1960s (EMI 1998)★★★, 1970s (EMI 1998)★★★, 1980s (EMI 1998)★★★, The Whole Story: His Greatest Hits (EMI 2000)★★★★.
VIDEOS: Two A Penny (1978), The Video Connection (PMI 1984), Together (PMI 1984), Thank You Very Much (Thorn-EMI 1984), Rock In Australia (PMI 1986), We Don't Talk Anymore (Gold Rushes 1987), Video EP (PMI 1988), The Young Ones (1988), Summer Holiday (1988), Wonderful Life (1988), Take Me High (Warner Home Video 1988), Private Collection (PMI 1988), Always Guaranteed (PMI 1988), Live And Guaranteed (PMI 1989), From A Distance ... The Event Volumes 1 and 2 (PMI 1990), Together With Cliff Richard (PMI 1991), Expresso Bongo (1992), Cliff- When The Music Stops (1993), Access All Areas (1993), The Story So Far (1993), The Hit List (PMI 1995), The Hit List Live (PMI 1995), Finders Keepers (1996), Cliff At The Movies (PolyGram Music Video 1996), The 40th Anniversary Concert (VCI 1998), An Audience With (VCI 2000).
FURTHER READING: Driftin' With Cliff Richard: The Inside Story Of What Really Happens On Tour, Jet Harris and Royston Ellis. Cliff, The Baron Of Beat, Jack Sutter. It's Great To Be Young, Cliff Richard. Me And My Shadows, Cliff Richard. Top Pops, Cliff Richard. Cliff Around The Clock, Bob Ferrier. The Wonderful World Of Cliff Richard, Bob Ferrier. Questions: Cliff Answering Reader And Fan Queries, Cliff Richard. The Way I See It, Cliff Richard. The Cliff Richard Story, George Tremlett. New Singer, New Song: The Cliff Richard Story, David Winter. Which One's Cliff?, Cliff Richard with Bill Latham. Happy Christmas From Cliff, Cliff Richard. Cliff In His Own Words, Kevin St. John. Cliff, Patrick Doncaster and Tony Jasper. Cliff Richard, John Tobler. Silver Cliff: A 25 Year Journal 1958-1983, Tony Jasper. Cliff Richard, Single-Minded, no author listed. Cliff Richard: The Complete Recording Sessions, 1958-1990, Peter Lewry and Nigel Goodall. Cliff: A Biography, Tony Jasper. Cliff Richard, The Complete Chronicle, Mike Read, Nigel Goodall and Peter Lewry. Cliff Richard: The Autobiography, Steve Turner. Ultimate Cliff, Peter Lewry and Nigel Goodall. A Celebration: The Official Story Of 40 Years In Show Business, André Deutsch.
FILMS: Serious Charge (1959), Expresso Bongo (1960), The Young Ones (1961), Summer Holiday (1962), Wonderful Life (1964), Thunderbirds Are Go! (1966), Finders Keepers (1966), Two A Penny (1968), Take Me High (1973).

RICHIE, LIONEL
ALBUMS: Lionel Richie (Motown 1982)★★★, Can't Slow Down (Motown 1983)★★★★, Dancing On The Ceiling (Motown 1986)★★★, Back To Front (Motown 1992)★★, Louder Than Words (Mercury 1996)★★, Time (Mercury 1998)★★, Renaissance (Mercury/Island 2000)★★★.
COMPILATIONS: Truly: The Love Songs (Motown 1998)★★★.
VIDEOS: All Night Long (RCA/Columbia 1986), Dancing On The Ceiling (Hendring Music Video 1988).
FURTHER READING: Lionel Richie: An Illustrated Biography, David Nathan.
FILMS: The Preacher's Wife (1996).

RICHMAN, JONATHAN
ALBUMS: as The Modern Lovers The Modern Lovers (Beserkley 1976)★★★★, as Jonathan Richman And The Modern Lovers Jonathan Richman And The Modern Lovers (Beserkley 1977)★★★, as Jonathan Richman And The Modern Lovers Rock 'N' Roll With The Modern Lovers (Beserkley 1977)★★★, as The Modern Lovers The Modern Lovers Live (Beserkley 1977)★★, Back In Your Life (Beserkley 1979)★★★, The Jonathan Richman Songbook (Beserkley 1980)★★★, Jonathan Sings! (Sire 1983)★★★, Rockin' And Romance (Twin Tone 1985)★★, as Jonathan Richman And The Modern Lovers Its Time For Jonathan Richman And The Modern Lovers (Upside 1986)★★, with Barence Whitfield Jonathan Richman & Barence Whitfield (Rounder 1988), Modern Lovers 88 (Rounder 1988)★★, Jonathan Richman (Rounder 1989)★★, Jonathan Goes Country (Rounder 1990)★★, Having A Party (Cheree 1991)★★★, I, Jonathan (Rounder 1992)★★★, Jonathan Tu Vas A Emoncionar (Rounder 1993)★★, Plea For Tenderness (Nectar Masters 1994)★★, You Must Ask The Heart (Rounder 1995)★★, Surrender To Jonathan (Vapor 1996)★★★, I'm So Confused (Vapor 1998)★★★, Her Mystery Not Of High Heels And Eyeshadow (Vapor 2001)★★★.
COMPILATIONS: as The Modern Lovers The Original Modern Lovers early recordings (Bomp 1981)★★★, The Beserkley Years: The Best Of Jonathan Richman And The Modern Lovers (Beserkley/Rhino 1987)★★★, Jonathan Richman And The Modern Lovers: 23 Great Recordings (Beserkley/Castle 1990)★★★★, I Must Be King: The Best Of (Cooking Vinyl 1999)★★★, Home Of The Hits! (Castle 1999)★★★★, Action Packed (Rounder 2002)★★★★.
FURTHER READING: There's Something About Jonathan: Jonathan Richman And The Modern Lovers, Tim Mitchell.
FILMS: Kingpin (1996), There's Something About Mary (1998).

RIDE
ALBUMS: Smile US only (Sire/Reprise 1990)★★★, Nowhere (Creation/Sire 1990)★★★, Going Blank Again (Creation/ Sire 1992)★★★★, Carnival Of Light (Creation/Sire 1994) ★★, Live Light 1994 recording (Mutiny 1995)★★★, Tarantula (Creation/Sire 1996)★★★.
COMPILATIONS: OX4 - The Best Of Ride (Ignition 2001)★★★.

RIGHT SAID FRED
ALBUMS: Up (Tug/Charisma 1992)★★★, Sex And Travel (Tug/Charisma 1993)★★★, Smashing! (Happy Valley 1996)★★, Fredhead (Kingsize 2001)★★★.
VIDEOS: Up The Video (Tug 1992).
FURTHER READING: The Official Right Said Annual.

RIGHTEOUS BROTHERS
ALBUMS: The Righteous Brothers - Right Now! (Moonglow 1963)★★, Some Blue-Eyed Soul (Moonglow 1965)★★, You've Lost That Lovin' Feelin' (Philles 1965)★★★★, Just Once In My Life (Philles 1965)★★★★, Back To Back (Philles 1965)★★★★, This Is New! (Moonglow 1965)★★, In Action (Sue 1966)★★, Soul And Inspiration (Verve 1966)★★★★, Go Ahead And Cry (Verve 1966)★★★, Sayin' Somethin' (Verve 1967)★★★, Souled Out (Verve 1967)★★★, Standards (Verve 1967)★★★, One For The Road (Verve 1968)★★★, Rebirth (Verve 1970)★★, Give It To The People (Haven 1974)★★, The Sons Of Mrs Righteous (Haven 1975)★★, Reunion (Hit 1999)★★★.
COMPILATIONS: The Best Of The Righteous Brothers (Moonglow 1966)★★, Greatest Hits (Verve 1967)★★★★, Greatest Hits Volume 2 (Verve 1969)★★★, 2 By 2 (MGM 1973)★★★, Best Of The Righteous Brothers (Verve 1987) ★★★★, Anthology (1962-1974) (Rhino 1989)★★★★, Best Of The Righteous Brothers (Curb 1990)★★★, Unchained Melody: The Very Best Of The Righteous Brothers (PolyGram 1990)★★★★, The Moonglow Years (PolyGram 1991)★★★.
VIDEOS: 21st Anniversary Celebration (Old Gold 1990).
FILMS: Beach Ball (1964).

RIMES, LEANN
ALBUMS: All That (Nor Va Jak 1993)★★, Blue (Curb 1996)★★★★, Unchained Melody/The Early Years (Curb 1997)★★, You Light Up My Life/Inspirational Songs (Curb 1997)★★★, Sittin' On Top Of The World (Curb 1998) ★★★★, LeAnn Rimes (Curb 1999)★★★, I Need You (Curb 2001)★★★, God Bless America (Curb 2001)★★.
FILMS: Dill Scallion (1999).

RIVERS, JOHNNY
ALBUMS: Johnny Rivers At The Whisky A Go Go (Imperial 1964)★★★★, The Sensational Johnny Rivers (Capitol 1964)★★★★, Go, Johnny, Go (1964)★★★, Here We A-Go-Go Again (Imperial 1964)★★★, Johnny Rivers In Action! (Imperial 1965)★★★, Meanwhile Back At The Whisky A Go Go (Imperial 1965)★★★★, Johnny Rivers Rocks The Folk (Imperial 1965)★★, And I Know You Wanna Dance (Imperial 1966)★★★, Changes (Imperial 1966)★★★, Rewind (Imperial 1967)★★★, Realization (Imperial 1968)★★★, Johnny Rivers (Sunset 1968)★★★, A Touch Of Gold (Imperial 1969)★★★, Slim Slo Slider (Imperial 1970)★★★, Rockin' With Johnny Rivers (Sunset 1971)★★★, Non-Stop Dancing At The Whisky A Go Go (United Artists 1971)★★★, Home Grown (United Artists 1971)★★★, L.A. Reggae (United Artists 1972)★★★, Johnny Rivers (United Artists 1972)★★★, Blue Suede Shoes (United Artists 1973)★★★, Last Boogie In Paris (Atlantic 1974)★★★, Rockin' Rivers (1974)★★★, Road (Atlantic 1975)★★★, New Lovers And Old Friends (Epic 1975) ★★★, Help Me Rhonda (Epic 1975)★★★, Wild Night (United Artists 1976)★★★, Outside Help (Big Tree 1978)★★, Borrowed Time (RSO 1980)★★, The Johnny Rivers Story (1982)★★★, Portrait Of (1982)★★★, Not A Through Street (Priority 1983)★★.
COMPILATIONS: Johnny Rivers' Golden Hits (Imperial 1966)★★★, The History Of Johnny Rivers (Liberty 1971)★★★, Go Johnny Go (Hallmark 1971)★★★, Greatest Hits re-recordings (MCA 1985)★★, The Best Of Johnny Rivers (EMI America 1987)★★★, Anthology 1964-1977 (Rhino 1991)★★★★.

ROBERTSON, ROBBIE
ALBUMS: Robbie Robertson (Geffen 1987)★★★★, Storyville (Geffen 1991)★★★, with the Red Road Ensemble Music For The Native Americans (Capitol 1994)★★★, Contact From The Underworld Of Redboy (Capitol 1998)★★★★.
FILMS: Eat The Document (1972), The Last Waltz (1978), Carny (1980), Visiting Hours (1982), The Crossing Guard (1995), Dakota Exile narrator (1996), Wolves narrator (1999).

ROBINSON, SMOKEY
ALBUMS: Smokey (Tamla 1973)★★★, Pure Smokey (Tamla 1974)★★★, A Quiet Storm (Tamla 1975)★★★, Smokey's Family Robinson (Tamla 1976)★★★, Deep In My Soul (Tamla 1977)★★★, Big Time (Tamla 1977)★★★, Love Breeze (Tamla 1978)★★★, Smokin' (Tamla 1978)★★★, Where There's Smoke (Tamla 1979)★★★, Warm Thoughts (Tamla 1980)★★★★, Being With You (Tamla 1981)★★★★, Yes It's You Lady (Tamla 1982)★★★, Touch The Sky (Tamla 1983)★★★, Blame It On Love (Tamla 1983)★★★, Essar (Tamla 1984)★★★, Smoke Signals (Tamla 1985)★★★, One Heartbeat (Motown 1987)★★★, Love, Smokey (Motown 1990)★★★, Double Good Everything (SBK 1991)★★, Intimate (Motown 1999)★★★.
COMPILATIONS: with the Miracles The Greatest Hits (Motown 1992)★★★★, with the Miracles The 35th Anniversary Collection 4-CD box set (Motown Masters 1994)★★★★, Early Classics (Spectrum 1996)★★★★, The Ultimate Collection (Motown 1998)★★★.
FURTHER READING: Smokey: Inside My Life, Smokey Robinson and David Ritz.

ROBINSON, TOM
ALBUMS: with the Tom Robinson Band Power In The Darkness (EMI 1978)★★★★, with the Tom Robinson Band TRB Two (EMI 1979)★★, with Sector 27 Sector 27 (Fontana 1980) ★★, North By Northwest (Fontana 1982)★★★, Cabaret '79 (Panic 1982)★★★, Hope And Glory (Castaway 1984)★★★, Still Loving You (RCA 1986)★★★, Last Tango: Midnight At The Fringe (Line 1988)★★, with Jakko Jakszyk We Never Had It So Good (Musidisc 1990)★★★, with the Tom Robinson Band The Winter Of 89 (1992)★★★, Living In A Boom Time (Cooking Vinyl 1992)★★★, Love Over Rage (Cooking Vinyl

1994)★★★★, *Having It Both Ways* (Cooking Vinyl 1996) ★★★, *Home From Home* (Oyster 1999)★★★, *Castaway Club Vol. 8 Smelling Dogs* (Castaway Northwest 2001)★★.
COMPILATIONS: *The Collection 1977-'87* (EMI 1987)★★★★, *The Undiscovered* (Castaway Northwest 1996)★★★, *Rising Free: The Very Best Of TRB* (EMI 1997)★★★★.

ROCHES
ALBUMS: *Seductive Reasoning* (Columbia 1975)★★, *The Roches* (Warners 1979)★★★★, *Nurds* (Warners 1980)★★★, *Keep On Doing* (Warners 1982)★★★, *Another World* (Warners 1985)★★★, *No Trespassing* (Rhino 1986)★★, *Crossing Delancey* soundtrack (Varèse Sarabande 1988) ★★★, *Speak* (MCA/Paradox 1989)★★★, *Three Kings* (MCA 1990)★★★, *A Dove* (MCA 1992)★★, *Will You Be My Friend* (Baby Boom 1994)★★, *Can We Go Home Now?* (Rykodisc 1995)★★★, Suzzy And Maggie Roche *Zero Church* (Red House 2002)★★★.

ROCKET FROM THE CRYPT
ALBUMS: *Paint As A Fragrance* (Headhunter 1991)★★, *Circa: Now!* (Headhunter 1992)★★★, *The State Of Art Is On Fire* mini-album (Sympathy For The Record Industry 1995) ★★★, *Hot Charity* mini-album (Perfect Sound/Elemental 1995)★★, *Scream, Dracula, Scream!* (Interscope/Elemental 1996)★★★★, *RFTC* (Interscope/Elemental 1998)★★★, *Group Sounds* (Vagrant 2001)★★★.
COMPILATIONS: *All Systems Go!* (Toy's Factory/Headhunter 1993)★★★, *All Systems Go 2* (Swami 1999)★★★.

RODGERS, PAUL
ALBUMS: *Cut Loose* (Atlantic 1983)★★, *Muddy Water Blues* (Victory 1993)★★★★, *The Hendrix Set* (Victory 1993)★★★, *Live* (SPV 1996)★★★, *Now* (SPV 1997)★★★, Electric (SPV 1999)★★★.

ROE, TOMMY
ALBUMS: *Sheila* (ABC 1962)★★★, *Something For Everybody* (ABC 1964)★★★, *Everybody Likes Tommy Roe* (HMV 1964)★★★, *Ballads And Beat* (HMV 1965)★★★, *It's Now Winters Day* (ABC 1967)★★, *Phantasy* (ABC 1967) ★★, *Dizzy* (ABC 1969)★★★, *We Can Make Music* (ABC 1970)★★, *Beginnings* (ABC 1971)★★, *Energy* (Monument 1976)★★, *Full Bloom* (Monument 1977)★★.
COMPILATIONS: *Sweet Pea* (ABC 1966)★★★, *12 In A Roe: A Collection Of Tommy Roe's Greatest Hits* (ABC 1970)★★★, *Tommy Roe's Greatest Hits* (Stateside 1970) ★★★, *16 Greatest Hits* (ABC 1971)★★★, *Greatest Hits* (MCA 1993)★★★, *Greatest Hits* (Curb 1994)★★, *Dizzy: The Best Of Tommy Roe* (Music Club 1998)★★★, *Tommy's 22 Big Ones* (Connoisseur 2001)★★★.

ROGERS, KENNY
ALBUMS: with the First Edition *The First Edition* (Reprise 1967)★★, with the First Edition *The First Edition's 2nd* (Reprise 1968)★★, with the First Edition *The First Edition '69* (Reprise 1969)★★, with the First Edition *Ruby, Don't Take Your Love To Town* (Reprise 1969)★★★, with the First Edition *Something's Burning* (Reprise 1970)★★★★, with the First Edition *Tell It All Brother* (Reprise 1971)★★★, with the First Edition *Transition* (Reprise 1971)★★★, with the First Edition *The Ballad Of Calico* (Reprise 1972)★★★, with the First Edition *Backroads* (Jolly Rogers 1972)★★★, with the First Edition *Monumental* (Jolly Rogers 1973)★★★, with the First Edition *Rollin'* (Jolly Rogers 1974)★★, *Love Lifted Me* (United Artists 1976)★★★, *Kenny Rogers* (United Artists 1976)★★★, *Daytime Friends* (United Artists 1977)★★★, with Dottie West *Every Time Two Fools Collide* (United Artists 1978)★★★, *Love Or Something Like It* (United Artists 1978)★★★, *The Gambler* (United Artists 1978)★★★★, with West *Classics* (United Artists 1979)★★, *Kenny* (United Artists 1979) ★★★★, *Gideon* (United Artists 1980)★★★, *Share Your Love* (Liberty 1981)★★★, *Christmas* (Liberty 1981)★★, *Love Will Turn You Around* (Liberty 1982)★★★, *We've Got Tonight* (Liberty 1983)★★★★, *Eyes That See In The Dark* (RCA 1983)★★★★, with Dottie West, Kim Carnes, Sheena Easton *Duets* (Liberty 1984)★★★, *What About Me?* (RCA 1984) ★★★, with Dolly Parton *Once Upon A Christmas* (RCA 1984)★★★, *Love Is What We Make It* (Liberty 1985)★★, *The Heart Of The Matter* (RCA 1985)★★, *They Don't Make Them Like They Used To* (RCA 1986)★★, *I Prefer The Moonlight* (RCA 1987)★★, *Something Inside So Strong* (Reprise 1989)★★, *Christmas In America* (Reprise 1989)★★, *Love Is Strange* (Reprise 1990)★★★, *Back Home Again* (Reprise 1991)★★★, *If Only My Heart Had A Voice* (Reprise 1993)★★★, *The Gift* (Magnatone 1996)★★★, *Across My Heart* (Magnatone 1997)★★★, *Christmas From The Heart* (Dreamcatcher 1998)★★, *With Love* (ONQ 1999)★★, *She Rides Wild Horses* (Dreamcatcher 1999)★★★, *All The Hits & All New Love Songs* (EMI 1999)★★★, *There You Go Again* (Dreamcatcher 2000)★★★, *Live By Request* (Dreamcatcher 2001)★★★.
COMPILATIONS: with the First Edition *Greatest Hits* (Reprise 1971)★★★, *Ten Years Of Gold* (United Artists 1978)★★★, *Kenny Rogers' Greatest Hits* (Liberty 1980)★★★★, *Twenty Greatest Hits* (Liberty 1983)★★★, *25 Greatest Hits* (EMI 1987)★★★, *The Very Best Of Kenny Rogers* (Warners 1990)★★★, *All Time Greatest Hits* 3-CD box set (CEMA 1996)★★★, as Kenny Rogers And The First Edition *The Best Of* (Half Moon 1998)★★★, *Islands In The Stream* (Music Club 1999)★★★, *Through The Years: A Retrospective* 4-CD box set (Capitol 1999)★★★, *Love Songs: Volume 2* (Capitol 2000)★★★.
VIDEOS: with Dolly Parton *Real Love* (RCA/Columbia 1988), *Going Home* (Weinerworld 1999).
FURTHER READING: *Making It In Music*, Kenny Rogers and Len Epand. *Gambler, Dreamer, Lover: The Kenny Rogers Story*, Martha Hume.
FILMS: *Six Pack* (1982).

ROLLING STONES
ALBUMS: *The Rolling Stones* (London/Decca 1964)★★★★, *12X5* (London 1964)★★★★, *The Rolling Stones* (London/Decca 1965)★★★★, *The Rolling Stones Now!* (London 1965)★★★★, *December's Children (And Everybody's* (London 1965)★★★★, *Out Of Our Heads* (Decca/London 1965) ★★★★, *Aftermath* (Decca/London 1966)★★★★, *Got Live If You Want It* (London 1966)★★★, *Between The Buttons* (London/Decca 1967)★★★, *Their Satanic Majesties Request* (Decca/London 1967)★★★, *Flowers* (London 1967)★★★, *Beggars Banquet* (London 1968)★★★★★, *Let It Bleed* (London/Decca 1969)★★★★★, *'Get Yer Ya-Ya's Out!'* (Decca/London 1970)★★★★, *Sticky Fingers* (Rolling Stones 1971)★★★★, *Exile On Main Street* (Rolling Stones 1972) ★★★★★, *Goat's Head Soup* (Rolling Stones 1973)★★★, *It's Only Rock 'N' Roll* (Rolling Stones 1974)★★★, *Black And Blue* (Rolling Stones 1976)★★★, *Love You Live* (Rolling Stones 1977)★★★, *Some Girls* (Rolling Stones 1978)★★★, *Emotional Rescue* (Rolling Stones 1980)★★, *Tattoo You* (Rolling Stones 1981)★★★, *Still Life (American Concerts 1981)* (Rolling Stones 1982)★★, *Undercover* (Rolling Stones 1983)★★, *Dirty Work* (Rolling Stones 1986)★★★, *Steel Wheels* (Rolling Stones 1989)★★★, *Flashpoint* (Rolling Stones 1991)★★★, *Voodoo Lounge* (Virgin 1994)★★★★, *Stripped* (Virgin 1995)★★★, *Bridges To Babylon* (Virgin 1997)★★★★, *No Security* (Virgin 1998)★★★★.
COMPILATIONS: *Big Hits (High Tide And Green Grass)* (London 1966)★★★★, *Through The Past, Darkly* (London 1969)★★★★, *Hot Rocks 1964-1971* (London 1972)★★★★, *More Hot Rocks (Big Hits And Fazed Cookies)* (London 1972)★★★★, *The Rolling Stones Singles Collection: The London Years* 3-CD box set (Abko/London 1989)★★★★★, *Jump Back: The Best Of The Rolling Stones 1971-1993* (Virgin 1993)★★★★. Many other compilation and archive albums have also been issued.
CD ROM: *Voodoo Lounge* (Virgin 1995).
VIDEOS: *The Stones In The Park* (BMG 1993), *Gimme Shelter* (1993), *Live At The Max* (PolyGram Music Video 1994), *25 x 5 The Continuing Adventures Of The Rolling Stones* (1994), *Sympathy For The Devil* (BMG 1995), *Voodoo Lounge* (Game Entertainment 1995), *One Plus One* (Connoisseur 1998), *Bridges To Babylon 1998: Live In Concert* (Game Entertainment 1998).
FURTHER READING: *The Rolling Stones File*, Tim Hewat. *The Stones*, Philip Carmelo Luce. *Uptight With The Rolling Stones*, Richard Elman. *Rolling Stones: An Unauthorized Biography In Words, Photographs And Music*, David Dalton. *Mick Jagger: The Singer Not The Song*, J. Marks. *Mick Jagger: Everybody's Lucifer*, Anthony Scaduto. *A Journey Through America With The Rolling Stones*, Robert Greenfield. *Les Rolling Stones*, Philippe Contantin. *The Rolling Stones Story*, George Tremlett. *The Rolling Stones*, Cindy Ehrlich. *The Rolling Stones*, David Dalton. *The Rolling Stones: A Celebration*, Nik Cohn. *The Rolling Stones*, Tony Jasper. *The Rolling Stones: An Illustrated Record*, Roy Carr. *The Rolling Stones*, Jeremy Pascall. *The Rolling Stones On Tour*, Annie Leibowitz. *Up And Down With The Rolling Stones*, Tony Sanchez with John Blake. *The Rolling Stones: An Annotated Bibliography*, Mary Laverne Dimmick. *Keith Richards*, Barbara Charone. *Rolling Stones In Their Own Words*, Rolling Stones. *The Rolling Stones: An Illustrated Discography*, Miles. *The Rolling Stones In Their Own Words*, David Dalton and Mick Farren. *The Rolling Stones: The First Twenty Years*, David Dalton. *Mick Jagger In His Own Words*, Miles. *The Rolling Stones In Concert*, Linda Martin. *The Rolling Stones: Live In America*, Philip Kamin and Peter Goddard. *Death Of A Rolling Stone: The Brian Jones Story*, Mandy Aftel. *Jagger*, Carey Schofield. *The Rolling Stones: The Last Tour*, Philip Kamin and James Karnbac. *The Rolling Stones A To Z*, Sue Weiner and Lisa Howard. *The Rolling Stones*, Robert Palmer. *The Stones*, Philip Norman. *Satisfaction: The Rolling Stones*, Gered Mankowitz. *The Rolling Stones*, Dezo Hoffman. *On The Road With The Rolling Stones*, Chet Flippo. *The True Adventures Of The Rolling Stones*, Stanley Booth. *Heart Of Stone: The Definitive Rolling Stones Discography*, Felix Aeppli. *Yesterday's Papers: The Rolling Stones In Print*, Jessica MacPhail. *The Life And Good Times Of The Rolling Stones*, Philip Norman. *Stone Alone*, Bill Wyman and Ray Coleman. *The Rolling Stones 25th Anniversary Tour*, Greg Quill. *Blown Away: The Rolling Stones And The Death Of The Sixties*, A.E. Hotchner. *The Rolling Stones: Complete Recording Sessions 1963-1989*, Martin Elliott. *The Rolling Stones Story*, Robert Draper. *The Rolling Stones Chronicle: The First Thirty Years*, Massimo Bonanno. *Rolling Stones: Images Of The World Tour 1989-1990*, David Fricke and Robert Sandall. *The Rolling Stones' Rock 'N' Roll Circus*, no author listed. *The Rolling Stones: Behind The Buttons (Limited Edition)*, Gered Mankowitz and Robert Whitaker (Photographers). *Golden Stone: The Untold Life And Mysterious Death Of Brian Jones*, Laura Jackson. *Rolling Stones: Das Weissbuch*, Dieter Hoffmann. *Not Fade Away: Rolling Stones Collection*, Geoffrey Giuliano. *Keith Richards: The Unauthorised Biography*, Victor Bockris. *The Rolling Stones: The Complete Works Vol.1 1962-75*, Nico Zentgraf. *Street Fighting Years*, Stephen Barnard. *Paint It Black: The Murder Of Brian Jones*, Geoffrey Giuliano. *Brian Jones: The Inside Story Of The Original Rolling Stone*, Nicholas Fitzgerald. *Who Killed Christopher Robin*, Terry Rawlings. *A Visual Documentary*, Miles. *Not Fade Away*, Chris Eborn. *Complete Guide To The Music Of*, James Hector. *The Stones By Krüger*, Stefan Krüger. *The Rolling Stones 1962-1995; The Ultimate Guide*, Felix Aeppli. *The Rolling Stones Chronicle*, Massimo Bonanno. *Good Times Bad Times: The Definitive Diary Of The Rolling Stones 1960-1969*, Terry Rawlings and Keith Badman. *It's Only Rock 'N' Roll*, Steve Appleford. *The Rolling Stones: A Life On The Road. Pleased To Meet You*, Michael Putland (photographer). *Brian Jones: The Last Decadent*, Jeremy Reed. *The Murder Of Brian Jones: The Secret Story Of My Love Affair With The Murdered Rolling Stone*, Anna Wohlin with Christine Lindsjöo. *Rock On Wood: The Origin Of A Rock & Roll Face*, Terry Rawlings.

ROLLINS, HENRY
ALBUMS: *Hot Animal Machine* (Texas Hotel 1986)★★, *Big Ugly Mouth* spoken word (Texas Hotel 1987)★★★, *Sweat Box* spoken word (Texas Hotel 1989)★★, *The Boxed Life* spoken word (Imago 1993)★★★, as The Rollins Band *Live* (Eksakt 1987)★★★, *Life Time* (Texas Hotel 1988)★★★, *Do It* (Texas Hotel 1988), *Hard Volume* (Texas Hotel 1989)★★★, *Turned On* (Quarterstick 1990)★★★, *The End Of Silence* (Imago 1992)★★★, *Weight* (Imago 1994)★★★, *Get In The Van* (Imago 1994)★★★, *Everything* (Thirsty Ear 1996)★★, *Come In And Burn* (DreamWorks 1997)★★, *Think Tank* spoken word (DreamWorks 1998)★★★, *Get Some Go Again* (DreamWorks 2000)★★★, *A Rollins In The Wry* spoken word (Quarterstick 2001)★★★, as The Rollins Band*Nice* (Sanctuary/SPV 2001)★★★.
VIDEOS: *You Saw Me Up There* (Sanctuary 2001).
FURTHER READING: *High Adventures In The Great Outdoors aka Bodybag*, Henry Rollins. *Pissing In The Gene Pool*, Henry Rollins. *Bang!*, Henry Rollins. *Art To Choke Hearts*, Henry Rollins. *One From None*, Henry Rollins. *Black Coffee Blues*, Henry Rollins. *Letters To Rollins*, R.K. Overton. *Get In The Van: On The Road With Black Flag*, Henry Rollins. *Eye Scream*, Henry Rollins. *See A Grown Man Cry, Now Watch Him Die*, Henry Rollins. *The Portable Henry Rollins*, Henry Rollins. *Solipist*, Henry Rollins. *Do I Come Here Often? (Black Coffee Blues Pt. 2)*, Henry Rollins. *Turned On: A Biography Of Henry Rollins*, James Parker. *Smile, You're Traveling, (Black Coffee Blues Pt. 3)*, Henry Rollins.
FILMS: *The Right Side Of My Brain* (1985), *Jugular Wine: A Vampire Odyssey* (1994), *The Chase* (1994), *Johnny Mnemonic* (1995), *Heat* (1995), *Lost Highway* (1997), *Jack Frost aka Frost* (1998), *You Saw Me Up There* (1998), *Morgan's Ferry* (1999), *Live Freaky Die Freaky* voice only (1999), *Desperate But Not Serious* (1999), *Scenes Of The Crime* (2001), *Past Tense* (2001).

RONETTES
ALBUMS: *Presenting The Fabulous Ronettes Featuring Veronica* (Philes 1964)★★★.
COMPILATIONS: *The Ronettes Sing Their Greatest Hits* (Phil Spector International 1975)★★★, *Their Greatest Hits - Volume II* (1981)★★, *The Colpix Years 1961-63* (Murray Hill 1987)★★★, *The Best Of* (ABKCO 1992)★★★, *The Ultimate Collection* (Marginal 1997)★★★★.

RONSON, MICK
ALBUMS: *Slaughter On Tenth Avenue* (RCA 1974)★★★, *Play Don't Worry* (RCA 1975)★★★, with Ian Hunter *YUI Orta* (Mercury 1989)★★★, *Heaven And Hull* (Epic 1994) ★★, *Just Like This* 1976 recording (New Millennium 1999) ★★★, *Indian Summer* soundtrack (NMC 2000)★★.
COMPILATIONS: *Showtime* (New Millennium 1999)★★★.
FURTHER READING: *Mick Ronson Discography*, Sven Gusevik.

RONSTADT, LINDA
ALBUMS: *Hand Sown ... Home Grown* (Capitol 1969)★★, *Silk Purse* (Capitol 1970)★★, *Linda Ronstadt* (Capitol 1971)★★, *Don't Cry Now* (Asylum 1973)★★★, *Heart Like A Wheel* (Capitol 1974)★★★★, *Prisoner In Disguise* (Asylum 1975)★★★, *Hasten Down The Wind* (Asylum 1976)★★★, *Simple Dreams* (Asylum 1977)★★★, *Living In The USA* (Asylum 1978)★★, *Mad Love* (Asylum 1980)★★, *Get Closer* (Asylum 1982)★★, *What's New* (Asylum 1983)★★★, *Lush Life* (Asylum 1984)★★★, *For Sentimental Reasons* (Asylum 1986)★★★, with Emmylou Harris, Dolly Parton *Trio* (Warners 1987)★★★★, *Canciones De Mi Padre* (Elektra 1987)★★★, *Cry Like A Rainstorm - Howl Like The Wind* (Elektra 1989) ★★★, *Mas Canciones* (Elektra 1991)★★★, *Frenesi* (Elektra 1992)★★★, *Winter Light* (Elektra 1993) ★★★, *Feels Like Home* (Warners 1995)★★★, *Dedicated To The One I Love* (Elektra 1996)H, *We Ran* (Elektra 1998) ★★, with Emmylou Harris, Dolly Parton *Trio II* (Asylum 1999) ★★★, with Emmylou Harris *Western Wall/The Tucson Sessions* (Asylum 1999)★★★, *Merry Little Christmas* (Elektra 2000)★★, *Cristal: Glass Music Through The Ages* (Sony Classical 2002)★★★.
COMPILATIONS: *Different Drum* includes five Stone Poneys tracks (Capitol 1974)★★, *Greatest Hits: Linda Ronstadt* (Asylum 1976)★★★★, *A Retrospective* (Capitol 1977)★★★, *Greatest Hits: Linda Ronstadt Volume 2* (Asylum 1980)★★★, *Linda Ronstadt* 4-CD box set (Elektra 1999)★★★.
FURTHER READING: *Linda Ronstadt: A Portrait*, Richard Kanakaris. *The Linda Ronstadt Scrapbook*, Mary Ellen Moore. *Linda Ronstadt*, Vivian Claire. *Linda Ronstadt: An Illustrated Biography*, Connie Berman. *Linda Ronstadt: It's So Easy*, Mark Bego.

ROOMFUL OF BLUES
ALBUMS: *The First Album* (Island 1977)★★, *Let's Have A Party* (Antilles 1979)★★, *Hot Little Mama* (Blue Flame 1981)★★★, *Eddie 'Cleanhead' Vinson And Roomful Of Blues* (Muse 1982)★★★★, *Blues Train/Big Joe Turner & Roomful Of Blues* (Muse 1983)★★★, *Dressed Up To Get Messed Up* (Rounder 1984)★★★, *Live At Lupo's Heartbreak Hotel* (Rounder 1986)★★★, with Earl King *Glazed* (Black Top 1988)★★★, *Dance All Night* (Rounder 1994)★★★, *Turn It On! Turn It Up!* (Bullseye Blues 1995)★★★★, *Under One Roof* (Bullseye Blues 1997)★★★, *There Goes The Neighborhood* (Bullseye Blues 1998)★★, *Watch You When You Go* (Bullseye 2001)★★★.
COMPILATIONS: *Roomful Of Blues With Joe Turner/Roomful Of Blues With Eddie Cleanhead Vinson* (32 Blues 1997)★★★★, *Swingin' & Jumpin'* (32 1999)★★★, *Blues'll Make You Happy Too* (Bullseye Blues 2000)★★★★.

ROSE ROYCE
ALBUMS: *Car Wash* (MCA 1976)★★★★, *Rose Royce II/In Full Bloom* (Whitfield 1977)★★★★, *Rose Royce III/Strikes Again!* (Whitfield 1978)★★★, *Rose Royce IV/Rainbow Connection* (Whitfield 1979)★★, *Golden Touch* (Whitfield 1981)★★, *Jump Street* (Warners 1981)★★, *Stronger Than Ever* (Epic 1982)★★, *Music Magic* (Streetwave 1984)★★, *The Show Must Go On* (Streetwave 1985)★★, *Fresh Cut* (Carrere 1987)★★.
COMPILATIONS: *Greatest Hits* (Whitfield 1980)★★★★, *Is It Love You're After* (Blatant 1988)★★★.

ROSE, TIM
ALBUMS: *Tim Rose* (Columbia 1967)★★★★, *Through Rose Coloured Glasses* (Columbia 1969)★★★, *Love - A Kind Of Hate Story* (Capitol 1970)★★, *Tim Rose* (Dawn 1972)★★, *The Musician* (Atlantic 1975)★★, *The Gambler* (President 1991)★★, *Tim Rose/Through Rose Coloured Glasses* (BGO 1998)★★★★, *Haunted* (Best Dressed 1997)★★★★, *American Son* (Mystic 2002)★★★.
COMPILATIONS: *Hide Your Love Away* (Flying Thorn 1998) ★★★.

ROSS, DIANA
ALBUMS: *Diana Ross* (Motown 1970)★★★, *Everything Is Everything* (Motown 1970)★★★, *Diana!* television soundtrack (Motown 1971)★★★, *Surrender* (Motown 1971)★★★, *Lady Sings The Blues* film soundtrack (Motown 1972)★★★★, *Touch Me In The Morning* (Motown 1973)★★★, with Marvin Gaye *Diana And Marvin* (Motown 1973)★★★, *Last Time I Saw Him* (Motown 1973)★★★, *Diana Ross Live At Caesar's Palace* (Motown 1974)★★★, *Mahogany* (Motown 1975)★★, *Diana Ross* (Motown 1976)★★★, *An Evening With Diana Ross* (Motown 1977)★★★, *Baby It's Me* (Motown 1977)★★★, *Ross* (Motown 1978)★★★, *The Boss* (Motown 1979)★★★, *Diana* (Motown 1980)★★★★, *To Love Again* (Motown 1981)★★★, *Why Do Fools Fall In Love* (RCA 1981)★★★, *Silk Electric* (RCA 1982)★★, *Ross* (RCA 1983)★★, *Swept Away* (RCA 1984) ★★, *Eaten Alive* (RCA 1985)★★, *Red Hot Rhythm 'N' Blues* (RCA 1987)★★★, *Workin' Overtime* (Motown 1989)★★, *Greatest Hits Live* (EMI 1989)★★, *The Force Behind The Power* (Motown 1991)★★, *Diana Ross Live: The Lady Sings ... Jazz And Blues/Stolen Moments* (Motown 1993)★★★, with José Carreras, Placido Domingo *Christmas In Vienna* (Sony Classical 1993)★★★, *Take Me Higher* (Motown 1995)★★, *Every Day Is A New Day* (Motown 1999)★★★.
COMPILATIONS: *Diana Ross' Greatest Hits* (Motown 1976)★★★★, *All The Great Hits* (Motown 1981)★★★★, *Diana's Duets* (Motown 1982)★★★★, *Diana Ross Anthology* (Motown 1983)★★★★, *14 Greatest Hits* (Motown 1984) ★★★, *All The Great Love Songs* (Motown 1986)★★★, *One Woman - The Ultimate Collection* (EMI 1993)★★★, *Forever Diana: Musical Memoirs* 4-CD box set (Motown 1993)★★★, *Diana Extended - The Remixes* (Motown 1994)★★, *Greatest Hits: The RCA Years* (RCA 1997)★★★, *Love & Life : The Very Best Of Diana Ross* (EMI 2001)★★★★.
VIDEOS: *The Visions Of Diana Ross* (RCA/PMI 1985), with José Carreras, Placido Domingo *Christmas In Vienna* (Sony Classical 1993), *One Woman - The Video Collection* (PMI 1993), *Diana Ross Live: Stolen Moments* (PMI/Motown 1993).
FURTHER READING: *Diana Ross*, Leonore K. Itzkowitz. *Diana Ross*, Patricia Mulrooney Eldred. *Diana Ross: Supreme Lady*, Connie Berman. *I'm Gonna Make You Love Me: The Story Of Diana Ross*, James Haskins. *Diana Ross: An Illustrated Biography*, Geoff Brown. *Call Her Miss Ross*, J. Randy Taraborrelli. *Secrets Of The Sparrow*, Diana Ross.
FILMS: *Lady Sings The Blues* (1972), *Mahogany* (1975), *The Wiz* (1978).

ROXETTE
ALBUMS: *Pearls Of Passion* (EMI Sweden 1986)★★, *Dance Passion* (EMI Sweden 1987)★★, *Look Sharp!* (EMI 1988) ★★★, *Joyride* (EMI 1991)★★, *Tourism* (EMI 1992)★★★, *Crash! Boom! Bang!* (EMI 1994)★★★, *Baladas En Español* (EMI 1996)★★, *Have A Nice Day* (EMI 1999)★★★, *Room Service* (EMI 2001)★★★.
COMPILATIONS: *Roxette Rarities* (EMI 1995)★★, *Don't Bore Us - Get To The Chorus! Roxette's Greatest Hits* (EMI 1995)★★★★.
VIDEOS: *Roxette Sweden Live* (EMI 1989), *Look Sharp Live* (EMI 1989), *Roxette: The Videos* (EMI 1991), *Live-Ism* (EMI 1992), *Don't Bore Us – Get To The Chorus! Roxette's Greatest Video Hits* (EMI 1995), *Crash! Boom! Live!* (EMI 1995).
FURTHER READING: *Join The Joyride*, Andreas Kraatz and Manfred Gillig. *Roxette Music Star aka Roxette V.I.P.*, Katja Röcker. *Roxette The Book: Den Auktoriserade Biografin*, Larz Lundgren and Jan-Owe Wikström. *Debe Haber Sido Amor*, Estheban Reynoso. *Roxette*, Darío Vico.

ROXY MUSIC
ALBUMS: *Roxy Music* (Island 1972)★★★★, *For Your Pleasure* (Island 1973)★★★★, *Stranded* (Island 1973) ★★★★, *Country Life* (Island 1974)★★★, *Siren* (Island 1975)★★★, *Viva! Roxy Music* (Island 1976)★★★, *Manifesto* (Polydor 1979)★★★, *Flesh And Blood* (Polydor 1980)★★★, *Avalon* (EG 1982)★★★★, *The High Road* (EG 1983)★★★, *Heart Still Beatin'* (Virgin 1990)★★, *Concert Classics* (Ranch Life 1998)★★, *Vintage* (Burning Airlines 2001)H, *Concerto - Live* 1979 recording (Burning Airlines 2001)★★.
COMPILATIONS: *Greatest Hits* (Polydor 1977)★★★, *The Atlantic Years 1973-1980* (EG 1983)★★★, *Street Life: 20 Great Hits* (EG 1986)★★★★, *The Ultimate Collection* (EG 1988)★★★★, *The Compact Collection* 3-CD box set (Virgin 1992)★★★, *The Thrill Of It All* 4-CD box set (Virgin 1995) ★★★, Bryan Ferry And Roxy Music *More Than This: The Best Of* (Virgin 1995)★★★★, *The Early Years* (Virgin 2000) ★★★★, *The Best Of Roxy Music* (Virgin 2001)★★★★.
VIDEOS: *Total Recall* (Virgin Video 1990).
FURTHER READING: *The Bryan Ferry Story*, Rex Balfour. *Bryan Ferry & Roxy Music*, Barry Lazell and Dafydd Rees. *Roxy Music: Style With Substance - Roxy's First Ten Years*, Johnny Rogan. *Unknown Pleasures: A Cultural Biography Of Roxy Music*, Paul Stump.

ROYAL TRUX
ALBUMS: *Royal Trux* (Royal 1988)★★, *Twin Infinitives* (Drag City 1990)★★, *Royal Trux* (Drag City 1992)★★★, *Cats And Dogs* (Drag City 1993)★★★, *Thank You* (Hut/Virgin 1995) ★★★, *Sweet Sixteen* (Virgin 1997)★★★, *Accelerator* (Drag City 1998)★★★★, *Veterans Of Disorder* (Drag City 1999) ★★★, *Pound For Pound* (Drag City 2000)★★★.
SOLO: Neil Hagerty *Neil Michael Hagerty* (Domino 2001)★★.
COMPILATIONS: *Singles Live Unreleased* (Drag City 1997)★★.

RUBETTES
ALBUMS: *Wear It's At* (Polydor 1974)★★★, *We Can Do It* (State 1975)★★★, *Rubettes* (State 1975)★★, *Sign Of The Times* (State 1976)★★, *Baby I Know* (State 1977)★★, *Sometime In Oldchurch* (Polydor 1978)★★, *Still Unwinding* (Polydor 1979)★★, *Riding On A Rainbow* (Dice 1992)★★, *20th Anniversary* (Dice 1994)★★, *Smile* (Royal River 1994)★★, *Making Love In The Rain* (Dice 1995)★★.
COMPILATIONS: *The Best Of The Rubettes* (Polydor 1976) ★★★, *The Singles Collection 1974 - 1979* (Dice 1992) ★★★, *Juke Box Jive* (Smart Art 1994)★★, *I Can Do It* (Dice 1993)★★, *Sugar Baby Love* (Legend 1993)★★★, *The Very Best Of The Rubettes* (Polydor 1999)★★★.
FURTHER READING: *The Rubettes Story*, Alan Rowett.

RUFFIN, JIMMY
ALBUMS: *Top Ten* (Soul 1967)★★★, *Ruff'n'Ready* (Soul 1969)★★, *The Groove Governor* (Soul 1970)★★, with David Ruffin *I Am My Brother's Keeper* (Motown 1970)★★, *Jimmy Ruffin* (1973)★★, *Love Is All We Need* (Polydor 1975)★★, *Sunrise* (RSO 1980)★★★.
COMPILATIONS: *Greatest Hits* (Tamla Motown 1974)★★★, *20 Golden Classics* (Motown 1981)★★★, *Greatest Motown Hits* (Motown 1989)★★★, *Early Classics* (Spectrum 1996)★★.

RUN-DMC
ALBUMS: *Run-D.M.C.* (Profile 1984)★★★★, *King Of Rock* (Profile 1985)★★★★, *Raising Hell* (Profile 1986)★★★★, *Tougher Than Leather* (Profile 1988)★★★, *Back From Hell* (Profile 1990)★★★, *Down With The King* (Profile 1993) ★★★, *Crown Royal* (Profile 2001)★★★.
COMPILATIONS: *Together Forever: Greatest Hits 1983-1991* (Profile 1991)★★★★, *Together Forever: Greatest Hits 1983-1998* (Profile 1998)★★★★.
VIDEOS: *Kings Of Rap* (Visual Entertainment 1998).
FURTHER READING: *Run-DMC*, B. Adler.
FILMS: *Krush Groove* (1985), *Tougher Than Leather* (1988).

RUNAWAYS
ALBUMS: *The Runaways* (Mercury 1976)★★★, *Queens Of Noise* (Mercury 1977)★★, *Live In Japan* (Mercury 1977)★★, *Waitin' For The Night* (Mercury 1977)★★, *And Now ... The Runaways* (Phonogram 1979)★★, *Young And Fast* (Allegiance 1987)H.
COMPILATIONS: *Rock Heavies* (Mercury 1979)★★★, *Flamin' Schoolgirls* (Phonogram 1982)★★, *The Best Of The Runaways* (Mercury 1982)★★, *I Love Playing With Fire* (Laker 1982)★★.

RUNDGREN, TODD
ALBUMS: *Runt* (Bearsville 1970)★★★, *The Ballad Of Todd Rundgren* (Bearsville 1971)★★★★, *Something/Anything?* (Bearsville 1972)★★★★★, *A Wizard, A True Star* (Bearsville 1973)★★★★, *Todd* (Bearsville 1974)★★★, *Initiation* (Bearsville 1975)H, *Faithful* (Bearsville 1976)★★★, *Hermit Of Mink Hollow* (Bearsville 1978)★★★★, *Back To The Bars* (Bearsville 1978)★★, *Healing* (Bearsville 1981)★★★, *The Ever Popular Tortured Artist Effect* (Lamborghini 1983)★★, *A Cappella* (Warners 1985)★★, *Nearly Human* (Warners 1989)★★★, *2nd Wind* (Warners 1991)★★, as TR-i *No World Order* (Pony Canyon/Philips 1992)★★★, as TR-i *No World Order Lite* (Pony Canyon/Philips 1994)★★★, as TR-i *The Individualist* (Pony Canyon/Digital 1995)★★, *Up Against It* (Pony Canyon 1997)★★, *With A Twist* (Guardian EMI 1997)★★, *Live In Tokyo 1979* (Pony Canyon 1999)★★★, *Live In NYC 1978* (Pony Canyon 1999)★★★, *Live In Chicago 1981* (Pony Canyon 1999)★★★, *One Long Year* (Artemis 2000)★★★, *King Biscuit Flower Hour Presents Todd Rundgren Live* (King Biscuit Flower Hour 2000)★★★, *Reconstructed* (Cleopatra 2000)★★.
COMPILATIONS: *The Collection* (Castle 1988)★★★★, *Anthology 1968-1985* (Rhino 1989)★★★★, *The Rundgren Collection* (Pony Canyon 1996)★★★, *The Very Best Of Todd Rundgren* (Rhino 1997)★★★, *I Saw The Light And Other Hits* (Flashback 1997)★★★, *Singles* (Bearsville/Victor 1998)★★★★, *The Best Of Todd Rundgren: Go Ahead. Ignore Me* (Castle 1999)★★★★, *I Saw The Light: Best Of Todd Rundgren* (Essential 2000)★★★, *Demos And Lost Albums* (Nippon Crown/Rhino 2001)★★★.
VIDEOS: *The Ever Popular Tortured Artist Effect* (BMG Video 1986), *2nd Wind Live Recording Sessions* (Rhino Home Video), *Nearly Human* (Warner-Pioneer).
FURTHER READING: *Music For The Eye*, Todd Rundgren with David Levine.

RUNRIG
ALBUMS: *Play Gaelic* (Neptune/Lismor 1978)★★★, *Highland Connection* (Ridge 1979)★★★, *Recovery* (Ridge 1981)★★★, *Heartland* (Ridge 1985)★★★, *The Cutter & The Clan* (Ridge 1987)★★★, *Once In A Lifetime* (Chrysalis 1988)★★★, *Searchlight* (Chrysalis 1989)★★★, *The Big Wheel* (Chrysalis 1991)★★★★, *Amazing Things* (Chrysalis 1993)★★★, *Transmitting Live* (Chrysalis 1994)★★★, *Mara* (Chrysalis 1995)★★, *In Search Of Angels* (Ridge 1999)★★★, *Live At Celtic Connections 2000* (Ridge 2000)★★★, *The Stamping Ground* (Ridge 2001)★★★.
COMPILATIONS: *Long Distance: The Best Of Runrig* (Chrysalis 1996)★★★★, *Beat The Drum* (EMI 1998) ★★★★, *The Gaelic Collection 1973-1998* (Ridge 1998) ★★★, *BBC Session And Live At The Royal Concert Hall, Glasgow '96* (EMI 1999)★★★.
VIDEOS: *City Of Lights* (PolyGram Video 1990), *Wheel In Motion* (PolyGram Video 1992), *Runrig Live At Stirling Castle: Donnie Munro's Farewell* (PolyGram Video 1997), *Live In Bonn* (2000).
FURTHER READING: *Going Home: The Runrig Story*, Tom Morton.

RUSH
ALBUMS: *Rush* (Moon 1974)★★, *Fly By Night* (Moon 1975)★★, *Caress Of Steel* (Mercury 1975)★★, *2112* (Mercury 1976)★★★, *All The World's A Stage* (Mercury 1976)★★, *A Farewell To Kings* (Mercury 1977)★★, *Hemispheres* (Mercury 1978)★★, *Permanent Waves* (Mercury 1980)★★★, *Moving Pictures* (Mercury 1981)★★★, *Exit: Stage Left* (Mercury 1981)★★★, *Signals* (Mercury 1982)★★★, *Grace Under Pressure* (Mercury 1984)★★, *Power Windows* (Mercury 1985)★★, *Hold Your Fire* (Mercury 1987)★★, *A Show Of Hands* (Mercury 1989)★★, *Presto* (Atlantic 1989)★★, *Roll The Bones* (Atlantic 1991)★★, *Counterparts* (Mercury 1993)★★, *Test For Echo* (Atlantic 1996)★★.
COMPILATIONS: *Archives* 3-CD set (Mercury 1978)★★★, *Rush Through Time* (Mercury 1980)★★, *Chronicles* (Mercury 1990)★★★, *Retrospective 1 (1974-1980)* (Mercury 1997) ★★★, *Retrospective 2 (1981-1987)* (Mercury 1997)★★★, *Different Stages: Live* 3-CD set (East West 1998)★★★.
VIDEOS: *Grace Under Pressure* (1986), *Exit Stage Left* (1988), *Thru' The Camera's Eye* (1989), *A Show Of Hands* (1989), *Chronicles* (1991).
FURTHER READING: *Rush*, Brian Harrigan. *Rush Visions: The Official Biography*, Bill Banasiewicz.

RUSH, OTIS
ALBUMS: *Chicago – The Blues – Today !* (Chess 1964)★★★, *This One's A Good Un* (Blue Horizon 1968)★★★, *Mourning In The Morning* (Cotillion 1969)★★★, *Chicago Blues* (Blue Horizon 1970)★★★, *Groaning The Blues* (Python 1970) ★★, *Cold Day In Hell* (Delmark 1975)★★★, *Right Place, Wrong Time* (Bulldog 1976)★★, *So Many Roads - Live In Concert* (1978)★★★, *Troubles, Troubles* (Sonet 1978)★★★, *Screamin' And Cryin'* (1979)★★, *Tops* (Blind Pig 1988) ★★★, *Lost In The Blues* (Alligator 1991)★★★, *Ain't Enough Comin' In* (This Way Up 1994)★★★★, *Blues Interaction Live In Japan 1986* (Sequel 1996)★★★★, *Live And Awesome* (Genes 1996)★★, *Any Place I'm Going* (House Of Blues 1999)★★★★.
COMPILATIONS: *Blues Masters Volume 2* (Blue Horizon 1968)★★★, shared with Albert King *Open The Door* (Chess 1969)★★★, *Double Trouble: Charly Blues Masterworks Volume 24* (Charly 1992)★★★★, *Good 'Un's: The Classic Cobra Recordings 1956-1958* (Westside 2000) ★★★.

RUSH, TOM
ALBUMS: *Live At The Unicorn* (Own Label 1962)★★, *Got A Mind To Ramble* aka *Mind Rambling* (Folklore 1963)★★, *Blues Songs And Ballads* (Prestige 1964)★★, *Tom Rush* (Elektra 1965)★★★★, *Take A Little Walk With Me* aka *The New Album* (Elektra 1966)★★★★, *The Circle Game* (Elektra 1968)★★★★, *Tom Rush* (Columbia 1970)★★★★, *Wrong End Of The Rainbow* (Columbia 1970)★★★, *Merrimack County* (Columbia 1972)★★★, *Ladies Love Outlaws* (Columbia 1974)★★★, *New Year* (Night Light 1982)★★, *Late Night Radio* (Night Light 1984)★★.
COMPILATIONS: *Classic Rush* (Elektra 1970)★★★★, *The Best Of Tom Rush* (Columbia 1975)★★★★, *The Very Best Of Tom Rush: No Regrets* (Sony 1999)★★★★.

RUSSELL, LEON
ALBUMS: *Leon Russell* (Shelter 1970)★★★★, *Leon Russell And The Shelter People* (Shelter 1971)★★★★, *Carney* (Shelter 1972)★★★★, *Leon Live* (Shelter 1973)★★★, *Hank Wilson's Back, Vol. 1* (Shelter 1973)★★★, *Stop All That Jazz* (Shelter 1974)★★, *Will O' The Wisp* (Shelter 1975)★★, *Wedding Album* (Paradise 1976)★★, *Make Love To The Music* (Paradise 1977)★★, *Americana* (Paradise 1978)★★, with Willie Nelson *One For The Road* (Columbia 1979)★★★, with the New Grass Revival *The Live Album* (Paradise 1981) ★★★, *Hank Wilson Vol. II* (1984)★★, *Anything Can Happen* (Virgin 1992)★★, *Legend In My Time: Hank Wilson, Vol. III* (Ark 21 1998)★★★, *Face In The Crowd* (Sagestone 1999)★★.
COMPILATIONS: *Best Of Leon* (Shelter 1976)★★★★, *The Collection* (Castle 1992)★★★, *Gimme Shelter!: The Best Of Leon Russell* (EMI 1996)★★★★, *Retrospective* (The Right Stuff/Shelter 1997)★★★.
VIDEOS: with Edgar Winter *Main Street Cafe* (Hendring Music Video 1990).

RYAN, PAUL AND BARRY
ALBUMS: *The Ryans Two Of A Kind* (Decca 1967)★★★, *Paul And Barry Ryan* (MGM 1968)★★★.
COMPILATIONS: *The Best Of Paul & Barry Ryan* (Popumentary 1998)★★★.

RYDELL, BOBBY
ALBUMS: *We Got Love* (Cameo 1959)★★★, *Bobby Sings* (Cameo 1960)★★, *Bobby Rydell Salutes The Great Ones* (Cameo 1961)★★, *Rydell At The Copa* (Cameo 1961)★★, *Bobby Rydell/Chubby Checker* (Cameo-Parkway 1961)★★★, *Bye Bye Birdie* (Cameo 1963)★★, *Wild Wood Days* (Cameo 1963)★★, *The Top Hits Of 1963* (Cameo 1964)★★, *Forget Him* (Cameo 1964)★★.
COMPILATIONS: *Bobby's Biggest Hits* (Cameo 1961)★★★, *All The Hits* (Cameo 1962)★★★, *Biggest Hits, Volume 2* (Cameo 1962)★★, *16 Golden Hits* (Cameo 1965)★★, *Best Of Bobby Rydell* (K-Tel 1995)★★, *The Best Of Bobby Rydell* (Prestige 2000)★★★, *The Complete Bobby Rydell On Capitol* (Collectors Choice 2001)★★★.
FILMS: *Because They're Young* (1960).

RYDER, MITCH, AND THE DETROIT WHEELS
ALBUMS: with the Detroit Wheels *Take A Ride* (New Voice 1966)★★★★, *Breakout ... !!!* (New Voice 1966)★★★, *Sock It To Me!* (New Voice 1967)★★★.
Mitch Ryder solo *What Now My Love?* (Dyno Voice 1967) ★★, *Mitch Ryder Sings The Hits* (New Voice 1968)★★, *The Detroit-Memphis Experience* (Dot 1969)★★★, *How I Spent My Vacation* (Line 1979)★★★, *Naked But Not Dead* (Line 1980)★★★, *Live Talkies* (Line 1981)★★★, *Got Change For A Million* (Line 1981)★★★, *Smart Ass* (Line 1982)★★★, *Never Kick A Sleeping Dog* (Line 1983)★★★, *Red Blood, White Mink* (Line 1988)★★★, *In The China Shop* (Line 1988)★★★, *La Gash* (Line 1992)★★, *Rite Of Passage* (Line 1994)★★.
COMPILATIONS: *All Mitch Ryder Hits!* (New Voice 1967)★★★, *All The Heavy Hits* (Crewe 1967)★★★, *Mitch Ryder And The Detroit Wheels' Greatest Hits* (Bellaphon 1972)★★★, *Rev Up: The Best Of Mitch Ryder And The Detroit Wheels* (Rhino 1990)★★★, *Detroit Breakout! An Ultimate Anthology* (Westside 1997)★★★.

S

S CLUB 7
ALBUMS: *S Club 7* (Polydor 1999)★★, *'7'* (Polydor 2000)★★, *Sunshine* (Polydor 2001)★★.
VIDEOS: *It's An S Club Thing* (Warner Music Vision 1999), *S Club 7 In Miami: Volume One* (Fox Home Entertainment 1999), *S Club 7 In Miami: Volume Two* (Fox Home Entertainment 1999).
FURTHER READING: *S Club 7: The Unofficial Book*, Michael Roberts. *S Club 7*, Anna Louise Golden.

S*M*A*S*H
ALBUMS: *S*M*A*S*H* mini-album (Hi-Rise 1994)★★★, *Self Abused* (Hi-Rise 1994)★★★.

SAD CAFÉ
ALBUMS: *Fanx Ta Ra* (RCA 1977)★★★, *Misplaced Ideals* (RCA 1978)★★★★, *Facades* (RCA 1979)★★, *Sad Café* (RCA 1980)★★★, *Live* (RCA 1981)★★, *Ole* (Polydor 1981)★★, *The Politics Of Existing* (Legacy 1986)★★★, *Whatever It Takes* (Legacy 1989)★★.
COMPILATIONS: *The Best Of Sad Café* (RCA 1985)★★★, *Everyday Hurts: The Very Best Of Sad Café* (Camden 2000)★★★, *The Masters* (Eagle 2000)★★★.

SADE
ALBUMS: *Diamond Life* (Epic/Portrait 1984)★★★★, *Promise* (Epic/Portrait 1985)★★★★, *Stronger Than Pride* (Epic 1988)★★★★, *Love Deluxe* (Epic 1992)★★, *Lovers Rock* (Epic 2000)★★★★, *Lovers Live* (Epic 2002)★★★.
COMPILATIONS: *The Best Of Sade* (Epic 1994)★★★★.
VIDEOS: *Diamond Life* (SMV 1985), *Life Promise Pride Love* (SMV 1993), *Sade Live* (SMV 1994).
FILMS: *Absolute Beginners* (1986).

SAINT ETIENNE
ALBUMS: *Foxbase Alpha* (Heavenly 1991)★★★, *So Tough* (Heavenly 1993)★★★, *Tiger Bay* (Heavenly 1994)★★★★, *Good Humor* (Creation 1998)★★★, *Sound Of Water* (Mantra 2000)★★★★.
COMPILATIONS: *You Need A Mess Of Help To Stand Alone* (Heavenly 1993)★★★, *Too Young To Die: The Singles* (Heavenly 1995)★★★★, *Casino Classics* (Heavenly 1996)★★★, *Smash The System: Singles And More* (Columbia 2001)★★★★.
VIDEOS: *Too Young To Die* (Wienerworld 1995).

SAINTE-MARIE, BUFFY
ALBUMS: *It's My Way!* (Vanguard 1964)★★★, *Many A Mile* (Vanguard 1965)★★★★, *Little Wheel Spin And Spin* (Vanguard 1966)★★★, *Fire & Fleet & Candlelight* (Vanguard 1967)★★★, *I'm Gonna Be A Country Girl Again* (Vanguard 1968)★★★★, *Illuminations* (Illuminations 1969)★★★, *She Used To Wanna Be A Ballerina* (Vanguard 1971)★★★★, *Moonshot* (Vanguard 1972)★★★, *Quiet Places* (Vanguard 1973)★★, *Buffy* (MCA 1974)★★, *Changing Woman* (MCA 1975)★★, *Sweet America* (ABC 1976)★★, *Coincidence And Likely Stories* (Chrysalis 1992)★★★, *Up Where We Belong* (EMI 1996)★★★.
COMPILATIONS: *The Best Of Buffy Sainte-Marie* (Vanguard 1970)★★★★, *Native North American Child: An Odyssey* (Vanguard 1974)★★★, *The Best Of Buffy Sainte-Marie, Volume 2* (Vanguard 1974)★★★.

SALT-N-PEPA
ALBUMS: *Hot Cool & Vicious* (Next Plateau 1987)★★★, *A Salt With A Deadly Pepa* (Next Plateau 1988)★★★, *Blacks' Magic* (Next Plateau 1990)★★★, *Rapped In Remixes* (Next Plateau 1992)★★★, *Very Necessary* (Next Plateau/London 1993)★★★★, *Brand New* (London/Red Ant 1997)★★★.
COMPILATIONS: *A Blitz Of Salt 'N' Pepa Hits* (Next Plateau 1991)★★, *The Greatest Hits* (London 1991)★★★★.

SAM AND DAVE
ALBUMS: *Sam And Dave i* (Roulette/King 1966)★★, *Hold On, I'm Comin'* (Stax 1966)★★★★, *Double Dynamite* (Stax 1967)★★★★, *Soul Men* (Stax 1967)★★★★, *I Thank You* (Atlantic 1968)★★★, *Double Trouble* (Stax 1969)★★★, *Back At 'Cha* (United Artists 1976)★★, *Sam And Dave ii* 1962-63 recordings (Edsel 1994)★★.
COMPILATIONS: *The Best Of Sam And Dave* (Atlantic 1969) ★★★★, *Can't Stand Up For Falling Down* (Edsel 1984)★★★, *Greatest Hits* (Castle 1986)★★★, *Wonderful World* (Topline 1987)★★★, *Sweet Funky Gold* (Gusto 1988)★★★, *Sweat 'N'*

Soul: Anthology 1968 - 1971 (Rhino 1993)★★★★, The Very Best Of Sam & Dave (Rhino 1995)★★★★.

SAM THE SHAM AND THE PHARAOHS
ALBUMS: Sam The Sham And Wooly Bully (MGM 1965) ★★★, Their Second Album (MGM 1965)★★, Sam The Sham And The Pharaohs On Tour (MGM 1966)★★, Lil' Red Riding Hood (MGM 1966)★★, The Sam The Sham Revue/ Nefertiti (MGM 1967)★★, Ten Of Pentacles (MGM 1968)★★.
COMPILATIONS: The Best Of Sam The Sham And The Pharoahs (MGM 1967)★★★, Pharaohization: The Best Of Sam The Sham And The Pharaohs (Rhino 1999)★★★.
FILMS: The Fastest Guitar Alive (1966).

SANTANA
ALBUMS: Santana (Columbia 1969)★★★★, Abraxas (Columbia 1970)★★★★, Santana III (Columbia 1971)★★★★, Caravanserai (Columbia 1972)★★★★, Carlos Santana And Buddy Miles! Live! (Columbia 1972)★★, Love Devotion Surrender (Columbia 1973)★★★, Welcome (Columbia 1973) ★★★, Borboletta (Columbia 1974)★★★, with Alice Coltrane Illuminations (Columbia 1974)★★★★, Lotus (Columbia 1975) ★★★, Amigos (Columbia 1976)★★★★, Festival (Columbia 1977)★★★, Moonflower (Columbia 1977)★★★, Inner Secrets (Columbia 1978)★★, Marathon (Columbia 1979)★★★, Oneness: Silver Dreams, Golden Reality (Columbia 1979)★★, The Swing Of Delight (Columbia 1980)★★, Zebop! (Columbia 1981)★★★★, Shango (Columbia 1982)★★★, Havana Moon (Columbia 1983)★★, Beyond Appearances (Columbia 1985) ★★★, La Bamba (Columbia 1986)★★, Freedom (Columbia 1987)★★★, Blues For Salvador (Columbia 1987)★★★, Persuasion (Thunderbolt 1989)★★, Spirits Dancing In The Flesh (Columbia 1990)★★, Milagro (Polydor 1992)★★★, Sacred Fire: Live In South America (Columbia 1993)★★, with the Santana Brothers Santana Brothers (Island 1994)★★, Live At The Fillmore 1968 (Columbia/Legacy 1997)★★, Supernatural (Arista 1999)★★★.
COMPILATIONS: Greatest Hits (Columbia 1974)★★★★, Viva Santana: The Very Best (Columbia 1988)★★★★, The Very Best Of Santana, Volumes 1 And 2 (Arcade 1988)★★★★, Dance Of The Rainbow Serpent 3-CD box set (Columbia/ Legacy 1995)★★★★, Awakenings (Charly 1998)★★★, The Ultimate Collection (Sony 1998)★★★★, Tropical Spirits Parts I & II (Cleopatra 2000)★★★, Mystical Spirits (Cleopatra 2000)★★★, The Best Of Santana Volume 2 (Sony 2000)★★★.
VIDEOS: Influences (DCI 1995), Viva Santana! (Columbia 1995), Lightdance (Miramar Images 1995), Supernatural Live: An Evening With Carlos Santana And Friends (Aviva 2000), Sacred Fire: Live In Mexico (Island 2001).
FURTHER READING: Soul Sacrifice: The Santana Story, Simon Leng.

SATRIANI, JOE
ALBUMS: Not Of This Earth (Relativity 1986)★★★, Surfing With The Alien (Relativity 1987)★★★★, Dreaming 11 (Relativity 1988)★★★, Flying In A Blue Dream (Relativity 1989)★★★, Time Machine (Relativity 1993)★★★, Joe Satriani (Epic 1995)★★★, with Eric Johnson, Steve Vai G3 Live In Concert (Epic 1997)★★★★, Crystal Planet (Epic 1998)★★★, Engines Of Creation (Epic 2000)★★★, Live In San Francisco (Epic 2001)★★.
COMPILATIONS: The Extremist (Relativity 1992)★★★.
VIDEOS: Reel Satriani (Dream Catcher 1998), Live In San Francisco (Epic Music Video 2001).

SAVAGE GARDEN
ALBUMS: Savage Garden (JDM 1996)★★★, Affirmation (Columbia 1999)★★★.
VIDEOS: The Video Collection (SMV 1998).

SAW DOCTORS
ALBUMS: If This Is Rock 'n' Roll I Want My Old Job Back (Solid 1991)★★★, All The Way From Tuam (Solid/Grapevine 1992)★★★★, Same Oul' Town (Shamtown 1996)★★, Songs From Sun Street (Shamtown 1998)★★★, Villians? (Shamtown 2001)★★★.
COMPILATIONS: Sing A Powerful Song (Paradigm 1997)★★★.

SAXON
ALBUMS: Saxon (Saxon Carrere 1979)★★★, Wheels Of Steel (Saxon Carrere 1980)★★★, Strong Arm Of The Law (Carrere 1980)★★★, Denim And Leather (Carrere 1981) ★★★, The Eagle Has Landed (Carrere 1982)★★★, Power And The Glory (Carrere 1983)★★★, Crusader (Carrere 1984)★★★, Innocence Is No Excuse (Parlophone 1985) ★★, Rock The Nations (EMI 1986)★★, Destiny (EMI 1988) ★★★, Rock 'N' Roll Gypsies (Roadrunner 1990)★★, Solid Ball Of Rock (Virgin 1991)★★★, Dogs Of War (HTD/ Virgin 1995)★★, Metalhead (SPV 1999)★★, Killing Ground (SPV 2001)★★★.
COMPILATIONS: Anthology (Raw Power 1988)★★★, Back On The Streets (Connoisseur 1990)★★★, Greatest Hits Live (Essential 1990)★★, Best Of (EMI 1991)★★★★, BBC Sessions/Live At The Reading Festival '86 (EMI 1998)★★★, Diamonds And Nuggets (Angel Air 2000)★★★.
VIDEOS: Live Innocence (PMI/EMI 1986), Power & The Glory – The Video Anthology (PMI/EMI 1989), Saxon Live (Spectrum/PolyGram 1989), Greatest Hits Live (Castle Music Pictures 1990).

SAYER, LEO
ALBUMS: Silver Bird (Chrysalis 1973)★★★, Just A Boy (Chrysalis 1974)★★★, Another Year (Chrysalis 1975)★★, Endless Flight (Chrysalis 1976)★★★, Thunder In My Heart (Chrysalis 1977)★★, Leo Sayer (Chrysalis 1978)★★, Here (Chrysalis 1979)★★, Living In A Fantasy (Chrysalis 1980) ★★, World Radio (Chrysalis 1982)★★, Have You Ever Been In Love (Chrysalis 1983)★★, Cool Touch (EMI 1990) ★★, Live In London (ABM 1999)★★★.
COMPILATIONS: The Very Best Of Leo Sayer (Chrysalis 1979)★★★, All The Best (East West 1993)★★★, The Show Must Go On: The Anthology (Rhino 1997)★★★, The Definitive Hits Collection (PolyGram 1999)★★★.

SCAGGS, BOZ
ALBUMS: Boz (1966)★★, Boz Scaggs (Atlantic 1969)★★★, Moments (Columbia 1971)★★★, Boz Scaggs And Band (Columbia 1971)★★★, My Time (Columbia 1972)★★★, Slow Dancer (Columbia 1974)★★★, Silk Degrees (Columbia 1976)★★★★, Down Two Then Left (Columbia 1977)★★, Middle Man (Columbia 1980)★★★, Other Roads (Columbia 1988)★★★, Some Change (Virgin 1994)★★, Come On Home (Virgin 1997)★★★★, Dig (Virgin 2001)★★★.
COMPILATIONS: Hits! (Columbia 1980)★★★, My Time: A Boz Scaggs Anthology (1969-1987) (Columbia 1997)★★★★.

SCORPIONS
ALBUMS: Action/Lonesome Crow (Metronome/Brain 1972)★★★, Fly To The Rainbow (RCA 1974)★★★, In Trance (RCA 1975)★★★★, Virgin Killer (RCA 1976)★★, Taken By Force (RCA 1977)★★, Tokyo Tapes (RCA 1978) ★★, Lovedrive (EMI 1979)★★, Animal Magnetism (EMI 1980)★★, Blackout (EMI 1982)★★★, Love At First Sting (EMI 1984)★★★★, World Wide Live (EMI 1985)★★★, Savage Amusement (EMI 1988)★★★, Crazy World (Vertigo 1990)★★★, Face The Heat (Mercury 1993)★★, Live Bites (Mercury 1995)★★, Pure Instinct (East West 1996)★★, Eye II Eye (Coalition 1999)★★.
SOLO: Herman Rarebell Nip In The Bud (Harvest 1981)★★.
COMPILATIONS: The Best Of The Scorpions (RCA 1979)★★★, The Best Of The Scorpions, Volume 2 (RCA 1984)★★, Gold Ballads (EMI 1985)★★, Best Of Rockers 'N' Ballads (EMI 1989)★★, CD Box Set (EMI 1991)★★, Deadly Sting: The Mercury Years (EMI 1995)★★★, One And Only Power Ballads (Mercury 1997)★★★.
VIDEOS: First Sting (PMI 1985), World Wide Live (PMI 1985), Crazy World Tour (PMI 1991), Acoustica (Warners 2001).

SCOTT, JILL
ALBUMS: Who Is Jill Scott? Words And Sounds Vol. 1 (Hidden Beach/Epic 2000)★★★★, Experience: Jill Scott (Hidden Beach/Epic 2001)★★★.

SCOTT-HERON, GIL
ALBUMS: Small Talk At 125th And Lenox (Flying Dutchman 1972)★★★, Free Will (Flying Dutchman 1972)★★★, Pieces Of A Man (Flying Dutchman 1973)★★★, Winter In America (Strata East 1974)★★★, The First Minute Of A New Day (Arista 1975)★★★, From South Africa To South Carolina (Arista 1975)★★★, It's Your World (Arista 1976)★★★, Bridges (Arista 1977)★★★, Secrets (Arista 1978)★★★, 1980 (Arista 1980)★★★, Real Eyes (Arista 1980)★★★, Reflections (Arista 1981)★★★, Moving Target (Arista 1982)★★★, Spirits (TVT Records 1994)★★★.
COMPILATIONS: The Revolution Will Not Be Televised (Flying Dutchman 1974)★★★★, The Mind Of Gil Scott-Heron (Arista 1979)★★★, The Best Of Gil Scott-Heron (Arista 1984)★★★★, Tales Of Gil (Essential 1990)★★★, Glory: The Gil Scott-Heron Collection (Arista 1990)★★★, Ghetto Style (Camden 1998)★★★★, Evolution & Flashback: The Very Best Of Gil Scott-Heron (RCA 1999)★★★★.
VIDEOS: Tales Of Gil (Essential Video 1990).

SCREAMING TREES
ALBUMS: Clairvoyance (Velvetone 1986)★★, Even If And Especially When (SST 1987)★★★, Invisible Lantern (SST 1988)★★★, Buzz Factory (SST 1989)★★, Uncle Anaesthesia (Epic 1991)★★★, Sweet Oblivion (Epic 1992)★★★, Change Has Come mini-album (Epic 1993)★★★, Dust (Epic 1996) ★★★★.
COMPILATIONS: Anthology: SST Years 1985-1989 (SST 1995)★★★.

SCRITTI POLITTI
ALBUMS: Songs To Remember (Rough Trade 1982)★★★, Cupid And Psyche (Virgin 1985)★★★, Provision (Virgin 1988)★★, Anomie & Bonhomie (Virgin 1999)★★★.
VIDEOS: Scritti Politti (Virgin 1985), Boom! There She Was (Virgin 1988).

SEAL
ALBUMS: Seal i (WEA 1991)★★★★, Seal ii (WEA 1994) ★★★★, Human Being (Warners 1998)★★★.

SEARCHERS
ALBUMS: Meet The Searchers (UK) (Pye 1963)★★★★, Meet The Searchers/Needles And Pins (US) (Kapp 1963)★★★, Sugar And Spice (UK) (Pye 1963)★★★, Hear! Hear! (US) (Mercury 1964)★★★, It's The Searchers (UK) (Pye 1964) ★★★, Bumble Bee: The New Searchers LP (US) (Kapp 1964)★★★, This Is Us (US) (Kapp 1964)★★★, Sounds Like Searchers (UK) The Searchers No. 4 (US) (Pye/Kapp 1965) ★★★, Take Me For What I'm Worth (Pye/Kapp 1965)★★★, Second Take (RCA 1972)★★, The Searchers (Sire 1979) ★★★, Play For Today aka Love's Melodies (Sire 1981)★★, Hungry Hearts (Coconut 1989)★★.
COMPILATIONS: Greatest Hits (Rhino 1985)★★★★, Silver Searchers (PRT 1986)★★★★, The Searchers Hit Collection (Castle 1987)★★★★, The EP Collection (See For Miles 1989)★★★★, 30th Anniversary Collection (Sequel 1992) ★★★★, The EP Collection Volume 2 (See For Miles 1992) ★★★, Rare Recordings (See For Miles 1993)★★★, The Definitive Collection (Castle 1998)★★★, The Pye Anthology 1963-1967 (Sequel 2000)★★★★.
FURTHER READING: Travelling Man - On The Road With The Searchers, Frank Allen.

SEBADOH
ALBUMS: Freed Man (Homestead 1989)★★★, Weed Forestin (Homestead 1990)★★★, Sebadoh III (Homestead 1991)★★★, Rockin The Forest (20/20 1992)★★, Sebadoh Vs Helmet (20/20 1992)★★★, Smash Your Head On The Punk Rock (Sub Pop 1992)★★★, Bubble And Scrape (Sub Pop 1993)★★★, 4-Songs (Domino 1994)★★★, Bakesale (Sub Pop/Domino 1994)★★★★, In Tokyo (Bolide 1995) ★★, Harmacy (Sub Pop 1996)★★★★, The Sebadoh (Domino 1998)★★★.
COMPILATIONS: Freed Weed (Homestead 1990)★★★.

SEBASTIAN, JOHN
ALBUMS: John B. Sebastian (Reprise/MGM 1969)★★★★, Live (MGM 1970)★★, Cheapo-Cheapo Productions Presents Real Live John Sebastian (Reprise 1971)★★★, The Four Of Us (Reprise 1971)★★, Tarzana Kid (Reprise 1974)★★★★, Welcome Back (Warners 1976)★★★, Tar Beach (Shanachie 1992)★★★, with the J-Band I Want My Roots (Music Masters 1996)★★, John Sebastian Live On The King Biscuit Flower Hour 1979 recording (King Biscuit 1996)★★★, with the J-Band Chasin' Gus' Ghost (Hollywood 1998)★★.
COMPILATIONS: The Best Of John Sebastian (Rhino 1989) ★★★, Faithful Virtue: The Reprise Recordings 3-CD set (Rhino 2002)★★★★.
FURTHER READING: John Sebastian Teaches Beginning Blues Harmonica, John Sebastian.

SEDAKA, NEIL
ALBUMS: Neil Sedaka (RCA Victor 1959)★★★★, Circulate (RCA Victor 1961)★★★, Sings Little Devil And His Other Hits (RCA Victor 1961)★★★★, Sings His Greatest Hits (RCA Victor 1962)★★★★, Emergence (Kirshner 1971)★★★, The Tra-La Days Are Over (MGM 1973)★★★★, Solitaire (Kirshner 1974)★★★, Laughter In The Rain (Polydor 1974)★★★, Live At The Royal Festival Hall (Polydor 1974)★★★, Overnight Success (Polydor 1975)★★, The Hungry Years (Rocket 1975) ★★, On Stage (RCA 1976)★★, Steppin' Out (Rocket 1976) ★★, A Song (Elektra/Polydor 1977)★★, All You Need Is The Music (Elektra 1978)★★, In The Pocket (Elektra 1980)★★, Now (Elektra/Polydor 1981)★★, Come See About Me (MCA 1984)★★, The Good Times (PRT 1986)★★, Love Will Keep Us Together: The Singer And His Songs (Polydor 1992)★★★, Classically Sedaka (Telstar 1995)★★★, Tales Of Love And Other Passions (Artful 1998)★★★.
COMPILATIONS: Sedaka's Back (Rocket 1974)★★★★, Laughter And Tears: The Best Of Neil Sedaka Today (Polydor 1976)★★★, Me And My Friends (Polydor 1986)★★★, Timeless: The Very Best Of Neil Sedaka (Polydor 1991)★★★, Laughter In The Rain: The Best Of Neil Sedaka 1974-1980 (Varèse Vintage 1994)★★★★, Tuneweaver (Varèse Vintage 1995)★★★★.
FURTHER READING: Breaking Up Is Hard To Do, Neil Sedaka.
FILMS: Sting Of Death (1965), Playgirl Killer aka Portrait Of Fear (1966).

SEEDS
ALBUMS: The Seeds (Crescendo 1966)★★★, A Web Of Sound (Crescendo 1966)★★★, Future (Crescendo 1967) ★★, A Full Spoon Of Seedy Blues (Crescendo 1967)★★, Raw And Alive At Merlin's Music Box (Crescendo 1967) ★★★.
COMPILATIONS: Fallin' Off The Edge (GNP 1977)★★★, Evil Hoodoo (Bam Caruso 1988)★★★, A Faded Picture (Diablo 1991)★★★, Flower Punk 3-CD set (Demon 1996)★★★, Raw & Alive & Rare Seeds (Diablo 2001)★★★.

SEEKERS
ALBUMS: Introducing The Seekers aka The Seekers (W&G/ Decca 1963)★★★, The Seekers aka Roving With The Seekers (W&G 1964)★★★, Hide & Seekers aka The Four And Only Seekers (WRC 1965)★★★, A World Of Our Own (EMI 1965)★★★, Come The Day aka Georgy Girl (EMI/Capitol 1966)★★★, Seen In Green (EMI/Capitol 1967)★★★, Live At The Talk Of The Town (EMI 1968)★★, Future Road (EMI 2000)★★.
COMPILATIONS: The Best Of The Seekers (EMI 1968)★★★, Golden Collection aka The Seekers Sing (Philips 1969)★★★, A World Of Their Own (EMI 1969)★★★, The Seekers Greatest Hits (EMI 1988)★★★, A Carnival Of Hits (EMI 1994)★★★.
FURTHER READING: Colours Of My Life, Judith Durham.

SEGER, BOB
ALBUMS: Ramblin' Gamblin' Man (Capitol 1969)★★★, Noah (Capitol 1969)★★★, Mongrel (Capitol 1970)★★★, Brand New Morning (Capitol 1971)★★★, Back In '72 (Palladium 1973)★★★, Smokin' O.P.'s (Palladium 1973)★★★, Seven (Palladium 1974)★★★, Beautiful Loser (Capitol 1975)★★★, Live Bullet (Capitol 1976)★★★★, Night Moves (Capitol 1976)★★★★, Stranger In Town (Capitol 1978)★★★★, Against The Wind (Capitol 1980)★★★, Nine Tonight (Capitol 1981)★★★, The Distance (Capitol 1982)★★★, Like A Rock (Capitol 1986)★★★, The Fire Inside (Capitol 1991)★★★, It's A Mystery (Capitol 1995)★★★.
COMPILATIONS: Bob Seger And The Silver Bullet Band Greatest Hits (Capitol 1994)★★★★.
FILMS: American Pop (1981).

SELECTER
ALBUMS: Too Much Pressure (2-Tone 1980)★★★★, Celebrate The Bullet (Chrysalis 1981)★★★, Out On The Streets: Live In London (Triple X 1992)★★, The Happy Album (Triple X 1994)★★★, Hairspray (Triple X 1995)★★★, Live At Roskilde Festival (Magnam Music 1997)★★, Cruel Britannia (Madfish/Snapper 1998)★★, Perform The Trojan Songbook (Receiver 1999)★★★, My Perfect World: Live (Receiver 1999)★★, Perform The Trojan Songbook Vol 2 (Receiver 2000)★★★.
COMPILATIONS: Prime Cuts (Magnum 1995)★★★, Selecterized: The Best Of The Selecter 1991-1996 (Dojo 1997)★★★, BBC Sessions/Live At The Paris Theatre '79 (EMI 1998)★★★, Too Much Pressure (Harry May 1999)★★★.

SELENA
ALBUMS: with Los Dinos Selena Y Los Dinos (Freddie 1984)★★, with Los Dinos Alpha (GP 1986)★★★, with Los Dinos Meñequito De Trapo (GP 1986)★★★, with Los Dinos And The Winner Is ... (GP 1987)★★, with Los Dinos Preciosa (RP 1988)★★★, with Los Dinos Dulce Amor (RP 1988)★★★, with Los Dinos Selena (EMI 1989)★★★, Ven Conmigo (EMI 1990)★★★, Entre A Mi Mundo (EMI Latin 1992)★★★★, with Los Dinos Baila Esta Cumbia (EMI 1992)★★★, with Los Dinos Quiero ... (EMI 1993)★★★, Live (EMI Latin 1993)★★★, Amor Prohibido (EMI Latin 1994)★★★★, with Los Dinos Mis Primeras Grabaciones 1984 recording (Freddie 1995)★★, Dreaming Of You (EMI Latin 1995)★★★, Siempre Selena (EMI Latin 1996)★★★, Selena Live: The Last Concert (EMI Latin 2001)★★.
COMPILATIONS: with Los Dinos Personal Best (CBS 1990) ★★★, with Los Dinos 16 Super Exitos (Capitol EMI 1990) ★★★, Mis Mejores Canciones: 17 Super Exitos (EMI 1993) ★★★, 12 Super Exitos (EMI Latin 1994)★★★, Anthology (EMI Latin 1998)★★★★, All My Hits: Todos Mis Exitos (EMI Latin 1999)★★★★, All My Hits: Todos Mis Exitos Vol. 2 (EMI Latin 2000)★★★.
VIDEOS: Selena: The Final Notes (Simitar 1995), Selena Remembered (EMI Latin 1995).
FURTHER READING: Remembering Selena: A Tribute In Pictures And Words aka Recordando Selena: Un Tributo En Palabras Y Fotos, Himilce Novas And Rosemary Silva. Selena! The Phenomenal Life And Tragic Death Of The Tejana Music Queen, Clint Richmond. Selena: Como La Flor, Joe Nick Patoski. Selena's Secret: The Revealing Story Behind Her Tragic Death, María Celeste Arrarás.
FILMS: Don Juan DeMarco (1995).

SENSATIONAL ALEX HARVEY BAND
ALBUMS: Framed (Vertigo 1972)★★, Next (Vertigo 1973) ★★★★, The Impossible Dream (Vertigo 1974)★★★, Tomorrow Belongs To Me (Vertigo 1975)★★★, Live (Vertigo 1975)★★★, The Penthouse Tapes (Vertigo 1976)★★★, SAHB Stories (Mountain 1976)★★★, Rock Drill (Mountain 1978)★★, Live In Concert (Windsong 1991)★★★, Live On The Test (Windsong 1994)★★★.
COMPILATIONS: Big Hits And Close Shaves (Vertigo 1977) ★★★, Collectors Items (Mountain 1980)★★★, The Best Of The Sensational Alex Harvey Band (RCA 1982)★★★★, The Legend (Sahara 1985)★★★, Collection - Alex Harvey (Castle 1986)★★★, Delilah (Spectrum 1998)★★★, The Gospel According To Harvey 1972-77 recordings (New Millennium 1998)★★★, Faith Healer: An Introduction To The Sensational Alex Harvey Band (Universal 2002)★★★.
VIDEOS: Live On The Test (Windsong 1994).

SEPULTURA
ALBUMS: Bestial Devastation with Overdose (Cogumelo 1985)★★★, Morbid Visions (Cogumelo 1986)★★★, Schizophrenia (Cogumelo 1987)★★★, Beneath The Remains (Roadrunner 1989)★★★, Arise (Roadracer 1991)★★★, Chaos A.D. (Roadrunner 1993)★★★. Max Cavalera in Nailbomb Point Blank (Roadrunner 1994)★★★, Roots (Roadrunner 1996)★★★★, Against (Roadrunner 1998)★★, Nation (Roadrunner 2001)★★★.
COMPILATIONS: Blood-Rooted (Roadrunner 1997)★★★.
VIDEOS: Third World Chaos (Roadrunner 1995), We Are What We Are (Roadrunner 1997).

SEX PISTOLS
ALBUMS: Never Mind The Bollocks – Here's The Sex Pistols (Virgin 1977)★★★★★, Filthy Lucre Live (Virgin 1996)★★★.
COMPILATIONS: The Great Rock 'n' Roll Swindle (Virgin 1979)★★★, Some Product - Carri On Sex Pistols (Virgin 1979)★★, Flogging A Dead Horse (Virgin 1980)★★, No Future (Virgin 1989)★★, Kiss This (Virgin 1992)★★, Alive (Essential 1996)★★, This Is Crap double CD reissue with Never Mind The Bollocks (Virgin 1996)★★★, There Is No Future (Essential 1999)★★, Live At Winterland 1978 (Sanctuary 2001)★★.
VIDEOS: The Great Rock 'n' Roll Swindle (Virgin Video 1982), Sid And Nancy (BMG Video 1996), Live At Longhorns (Pearson New Entertainment 1996), Live In Winterland (Pearson New Entertainment 1996), The Filth And The Fury: A Sex Pistols Film (VCI 2000).
FURTHER READING: Sex Pistols Scrap Book, Ray Stevenson. Sex Pistols: The Inside Story, Fred and Judy Vermorel. Sex Pistols File, Ray Stevenson. The Great Rock 'N' Roll Swindle: A Novel, Michael Moorcock. The Sid Vicious Family Album, Anne Beverley. The Sex Pistols Diary, Lee Wood. I Was A Teenage Sex Pistol, Glen Matlock. 12 Days On The Road: The Sex Pistols And America, Neil Monk and Jimmy Guterman. Chaos: The Sex Pistols, Bob Gruen. England's Dreaming: Sex Pistols And Punk Rock, Jon Savage. Never Mind The B*ll*cks: A Photographed Record Of The Sex Pistols, Dennis Morris. Sex Pistols: Agents Of Anarchy, Tony Scrivener. Sid's Way: The Life & Death Of Sid Vicious, Alan Parker and Keith Bateson. Rotten: No Irish, No Blacks, No Dogs, Johnny Rotten. Sex Pistols Retrospective, no author listed. Sid Vicious Rock 'N' Roll Star, Malcolm Butt. Sid Vicious: They Died Too Young, Tom Stockdale. Classic Rock Albums: Never Mind The Bollocks, Clinton Heylin. Destroy, Dennis Morris. Satellite, Paul Burgess and Alan Parker. The Complete Guide To The Music Of The Sex Pistols, Mark Paytress.
FILMS: The Great Rock 'n' Roll Swindle (1979), The Filth And The Fury (2000).

SEXSMITH, RON
ALBUMS: Grand Opera Lane cassette only (1991)★★★, Ron Sexsmith (Interscope/Atlantic 1995)★★★★, Other Songs (Interscope/Atlantic 1997)★★★, Whereabouts (Geffen 1999)★★★★, Blue Boy (spinART/Cooking Vinyl 2001)★★★★.

SHA NA NA
ALBUMS: Rock & Roll Is Here To Stay! (Kama Sutra 1969) ★★★, Sha Na Na (Kama Sutra 1971)★★★★, The Night Is Still Young (Kama Sutra 1972)★★★★, The Golden Age Of Rock 'N' Roll (Kama Sutra 1973)★★, From The Streets Of New York (Kama Sutra 1973)★★★, Hot Sox (Kama Sutra 1974)★★, Sha Na Now (Kama Sutra 1975)★★, Rock 'N' Roll Revival (Pye 1977)★★, Havin' An Oldies Party With (K-Tel 1980)★★, Remember Then (Accord 1981)★★★, Rock 'N' Roll Dance Party (Gold 1997)★★, Live In Japan (Sony 2000)★★.
COMPILATIONS: 20 Greatest Hits (Black Tulip 1989)★★★, Whole Lotta Sha-Na-Na: The Encore Collection (BMG 1997)★★★.
FILMS: Grease (1978).

SHADOWS
ALBUMS: The Shadows (Columbia 1961)★★★★, Out Of The Shadows (Columbia 1962)★★★★, Dance With The Shadows (Columbia 1964)★★★★, The Sound Of The Shadows (Columbia 1965)★★★★, Shadow Music (Columbia 1966)★★★, Jigsaw (Columbia 1967)★★★, From Hank, Bruce, Brian And John (Columbia 1967)★★★, with Cliff Richard Established 1958 (Columbia 1968)★★★, Shades Of Rock (Columbia 1970)★★★, Rockin' With Curly Leads (EMI 1973)★★★, Specs Appeal (EMI 1975)★★★, Live At The Paris Olympia (EMI 1975)★★, Tasty (EMI 1977)★★★, with Cliff Richard Thank You Very Much (EMI 1979)★★★, Change Of Address (Polydor 1980)★★, Hits Right Up Your Street (Polydor 1981)★★, Life In The Jungle/Live At Abbey Road (Polydor 1982)★★, XXV (Polydor 1983)★★★, Guardian Angel (Polydor 1984)★★, Moonlight Shadows (Polydor 1986)★★★, Simply Shadows (Polydor 1987)★★★, Steppin' To The Shadows (Roll Over Records 1989)★★★, Reflections (Polydor 1991)★★★.
COMPILATIONS: The Shadows' Greatest Hits (Columbia 1963)★★★★, More Hits! (Columbia 1965)★★★★, Somethin' Else (Regal Starline 1969)★★★, 20 Golden Greats (EMI 1977)★★★★, The Shadows At The Movies (MFP 1978)★★★, String Of Hits (EMI 1979)★★★★, Rock On With The Shadows (MFP 1980)★★, Another String Of Hot Hits (EMI 1980)★★★, The Shadows 6-LP box set (WRC 1981)★★★★, The Shadows Live! (MFP 1981)★★★, The Shadows' Silver Album (Tellydisc 1983)★★★, The Shadows' Vocals (EMI 1984)★★★, At Their Very Best (Polydor 1989)★★★★, Themes And Dreams (Roll Over Records 1991)★★★, The Early Years 1959-1966 6-CD box set (EMI 1991)★★★★, The Best Of Hank Marvin And The Shadows (Polydor 1994)★★★, The First 20 Years At The Top (EMI 1995)★★★★, Hank Marvin And The Shadows Play The Music Of Andrew Lloyd Webber And Tim Rice (Polydor 1997)★★★, The Very Best Of Hank Marvin & The Shadows: The First 40 Years (Polydor 1998)★★★★, 50 Golden Greats (EMI 2000)★★★, The Shadows Collection (HMV Easy 2001)★★★.
FURTHER READING: The Shadows By Themselves, Shadows. Foot Tapping: The Shadows 1958-1978, George Thomson Geddes. The Shadows: A History And Discography, George Thomson Geddes. The Story Of The Shadows: An Autobiography, Shadows as told to Mike Reed. Rock 'N' Roll: I Gave You The Best Years Of My Life: A Life In The Shadows, Bruce Welch. Funny Old World: The Life And Times Of John Henry Rostill, Rob Bradford. A Guide To The Shadows And Hank Marvin On CD, Malcolm Campbell. The Shadows At EMI: The Vinyl Legacy, Malcolm Campbell.
FILMS: Carnival Rock (1957), Expresso Bongo (1960), Finders Keepers (1966).

SHADOWS OF KNIGHT
ALBUMS: Gloria (Dunwich 1966)★★★, Back Door Men (Dunwich 1967)★★★, The Shadows Of Knight (Super-K 1969)★★★, Raw And Alive At The Cellar, Chicago 1966! (Sundazed 1992)★★.
COMPILATIONS: Gee-El-O-Are-I-Ay (Gloria) (Radar 1979) ★★★, Dark Sides: The Best Of The Shadows Of Knight (Rhino 1994)★★★.

SHAGGY
ALBUMS: Pure Pleasure (Virgin 1993)★★★, Boombastic (Virgin 1995)★★★★, Midnite Lover (Virgin 1997)★★★, Hot Shot (MCA 2000)★★★.
COMPILATIONS: Mr Lover Lover: The Best Of Shaggy, Part One (Virgin 2002)★★★.
FILMS: The Reggae Movie (1995).

SHAKATAK
ALBUMS: Drivin' Hard (Polydor 1981)★★★, Nightbirds (Polydor 1982)★★★★, Invitations (Polydor 1982)★★★, Out Of This World (Polydor 1983)★★★, Down On The Street (Polydor 1984)★★★, Live! (Polydor 1985)★★, Day By Day/City Rhythm (Polydor 1985)★★★, Into The Blue Japan only (Polydor 1986)★★★, Golden Wings Japan only (Polydor 1987)★★★, Never Stop Your Love aka Manic & Cool (Polydor 1987)★★★★, Da Makani Japan only (Polydor 1988)★★★, Niteflite Japan only (Polydor 1989) ★★★, Fiesta Japan only (Polydor 1990)★★★, Bitter Sweet (Polydor 1991)★★★, Utopia Japan only (Polydor 1991) ★★★, Street Level (Inside Out 1993)★★★, Under The Sun (Inside Out 1993)★★★, The Christmas Album (Inside Out 1993)★★★, Full Circle (Inside Out 1994)★★★, Let The Piano Play (Inside Out 1997)★★★, Live At Ronnie Scott's (Indigo 1998)★★★★, View From The City aka Magic (Inside Out/Instinct 1999)★★★.
COMPILATIONS: Coolest Cuts (Polydor 1988)★★★★, Greatest Grooves (Connoisseur 1990)★★★★, Perfect Smile (Polydor 1990)★★★, Night Moves (Pickwick 1990)★★★, Open Your Eyes (Polydor 1991)★★★, The Remix Best Album (Polydor 1991)★★, The Collection Vol. 1 (Spectrum 1998)★★★, Shinin' On (Instinct 1998)★★★, Jazz In The Night (Inside Out 1999)★★★, The Collection Vol. 2 (Spectrum 2000)★★★, The Magic Of Shakatak (Inside Out 2000)★★★★.

SHAKESPEARS SISTER
ALBUMS: Sacred Heart (London 1989)★★★, Hormonally Yours (London 1991)★★★.

SHAKIRA
ALBUMS: Magia (Sony Discos 1991)★★, Peligro (Sony Discos 1993)★★★, Pies Descalzos (Sony Discos 1996) ★★★★, Dónde Están Los Ladrones? (Sony Discos 1998) ★★★, MTV Unplugged (Sony Discos 2000)★★★, Laundry Service (Sony Discos 2001)★★★.
COMPILATIONS: The Remixes (Sony Discos 1997)★★★.

SHAM 69
ALBUMS: Tell Us The Truth (Polydor/Sire 1978)★★★, That's Life (Polydor 1978)★★, The Adventures Of Hersham Boys (Polydor 1979)★★★, The Game (Polydor 1980)★★, Volunteer (Legacy 1988)★★, Sham's Last Stand (Link 1989)★★, Live At The Roxy 1977 recording (Receiver 1990)★★, Live At CBGB's 1988 (Dojo 1991)★★, Information Libre (Rotate 1992)★★, Live In Japan (Dojo 1993)★★, BBC Radio 1 Live In Concert (Windsong 1993)★★, Kings & Queens (Creative Man 1993)★★, Soapy Water And Mister Marmalade (Plus Eye 1995)H, The A Files (Scratch/Cleopatra 1997)★★, Live In Italy (Essential 1999)H, Green Eggs And Sham (Big Ear 1999)H, Direct Action: Day 21 (Store For Music 2001)★★.
COMPILATIONS: The First, The Best And The Last (Polydor 1980)★★★, The Complete Sham 69 Live (Castle 1983)★★, Angels With Dirty Faces: The Best Of Sham 69 (Receiver 1986)★★★, Live And Loud (Link 1987)★★, Live And Loud Vol. 2 (Link 1988)H, The Best Of & The Rest Of Sham 69 Live (Receiver 1989)★★★, The Best Of Sham 69 (Essential 1995)★★★, The Very Best Of The Hersham Boys (Castle 1998)★★★, Punk Singles Collection 1977-1980 (Cleopatra 1998)★★★, The Masters (Eagle 1998)★★★, Angels With Dirty Faces (Castle 1999)★★★, Laced Up Boots & Corduroys (Delta 2000)★★★, Rarities 1977-80 (Captain Oi! 2000)★★.
VIDEOS: Live In Japan (Visionary 1993).

SHAMEN
ALBUMS: Drop (Moshka 1987)★★★, In Gorbachev We Trust (Demon 1989)★★★, Phorward (Moshka 1989)★★★, En-Tact (One Little Indian 1990)★★★, En-Tek (One Little Indian 1990)★★★, Progeny (One Little Indian 1991)★★★, Boss Drum (One Little Indian 1992)★★★★, Different Drum (One Little Indian 1992)★★★, The Shamen On Air (Band Of Joy 1993)★★, Axis Mutatis (One Little Indian 1995)★★, Hempton Manor (One Little Indian 1996)★★, UV (Moksha 1998)★★★.
COMPILATIONS: Collection (One Little Indian 1997)★★★, The Remix Collection (Stars On 45) (One Little Indian 1997)★★★.

SHANGRI-LAS
ALBUMS: Leader Of The Pack (Red Bird 1965)★★★, '65 (Red Bird 1965)★★★.
COMPILATIONS: Golden Hits (Mercury 1966)★★★, The Best Of the Shangri-La's (Bac-Trac 1985)★★★, Myrmidons Of Melodrama (RPM 1994)★★★, The Best Of The Shangri-Las (Merury 1996)★★★, The Very Best Of The Shangri-Las (Cleopatra 2000)★★★.
FURTHER READING: Girl Groups: The Story Of A Sound, Alan Betrock.

SHANNON, DEL
ALBUMS: Runaway With Del Shannon (Big Top/London 1961)★★★★, Hats Off To Del Shannon (London 1963) ★★★★, Little Town Flirt (Big Top 1963)★★★★, Handy Man (Amy 1964)★★★★, Del Shannon Sings Hank Williams (Amy 1965)★★, One Thousand Six Hundred Sixty Seconds With Del Shannon (Amy 1965)★★★, This Is My Bag (Liberty 1966)★★, Total Commitment (Liberty 1966) ★★, The Further Adventures Of Charles Westover (Liberty 1968)★★★, Del Shannon Live In England (United Artists 1973)★★, Drop Down And Get Me (Network 1981)★★★, Rock On! (Silvertone 1991)★★.
COMPILATIONS: The Best Of Del Shannon (Dot 1967)★★★★, The Vintage Years (Sire 1975)★★★★, The Del Shannon Collection (Line 1987)★★★★, Runaway Hits (Edsel 1990) ★★★★, I Go To Pieces (Edsel 1990)★★★★, Looking Back, His Biggest Hits (Connoisseur 1991)★★★★, Greatest Hits (Charly 1993)★★★★, A Complete Career Anthology 1961-1990 (Raven 1998)★★★★, The Definitive Collection (Recall 1998) ★★★★, The EP Collection (See For Miles 1998)★★★, The Best Of Del Shannon (Repertoire 1999)★★★, The Definitive Collection (Recall 2000)★★★, 25 All-Time Greatest Hits (Varèse Sarabande 2001)★★★★, Runaway: The Very Best Of Del Shannon (Collectables 2002)★★★★.
FILMS: It's Trad, Dad! aka Ring-A-Ding Rhythm (1962).

SHAPIRO, HELEN
ALBUMS: Tops With Me (Columbia 1962)★★★★, Helen's Sixteen (Columbia 1963)★★★★, Helen In Nashville (Columbia 1963)★★, Helen Hits Out (Columbia 1964) ★★★, All For The Love Of The Music (1977)★★★, Straighten Up And Fly Right (Oval 1983)★★★, Echoes Of The Duke (1985)★★★, The Quality Of Mercer (Calligraph 1987)★★★★, Nothing But The Best (1995)★★★, Sing, Swing Together (Calligraph 1999)★★★.
COMPILATIONS: Hits And A Miss Helen Shapiro (Encore 1965)★★★, Twelve Hits And A Miss Shapiro (Encore 1967)★★★, The Very Best Of Helen Shapiro (Columbia 1974)★★★★, The 25th Anniversary Album (MFP 1986) ★★★★, The EP Collection (See For Miles 1989)★★★★, Sensational! The Uncollected Helen Shapiro (RPM 1995) ★★★★, Original Hits (Musicrama 1997)★★★, Abbey Road 1961-1967 (EMI 1998)★★★★.
FURTHER READING: Walking Back To Happiness, Helen Shapiro. Helen Shapiro: Pop Princess, John S. Janson.
FILMS: It's Trad, Dad aka Ring-A-Ding Rhythm (1962).

SHAW, SANDIE
ALBUMS: Sandie Shaw (Pye 1965)★★★, Me (Pye 1965) ★★★, Puppet On A String (Pye 1967)★★, Love Me, Please Love Me (Pye 1967)★★, The Sandie Shaw Supplement (Pye 1968)★★, Reviewing The Situation (Pye 1969)★★, Hello Angel (Rough Trade 1988)★★.
COMPILATIONS: Golden Hits Of Sandie Shaw (Golden Guinea 1965)★★★★, Sandie Sings (Golden Guinea 1967) ★★★★, The Golden Hits Of Sandie Shaw (Marble Arch 1968)★★★★, A Golden Hour Of Sandie Shaw - Greatest Hits (Golden Hour 1974)★★★★, 20 Golden Pieces (Bulldog 1986)★★★, The Sandie Shaw Golden CD Collection (K-Tel 1989)★★★, The EP Collection (See For Miles 1991)★★★★, Nothing Less Than Brilliant: The Best Of Sandie Shaw (Virgin 1994)★★★★, Cover To Cover (Emporio 1995)★★★, Cool About You - The BBC Sessions 1984/88 (RPM 1998)★★★, Princess Of Britpop (Sequel 1998)★★★, The Pye Anthology 64/67 (Sequel 2000)★★★★.
VIDEOS: Live In London (Channel 5 1989).
FURTHER READING: The World At My Feet, Sandie Shaw.

SHED SEVEN
ALBUMS: Change Giver (Polydor 1994)★★★, A Maximum High (Polydor 1996)★★★★, Let It Ride (Polydor 1998) ★★★, Truth Be Told (Artful 2001)★★★.
COMPILATIONS: Going For Gold: The Best Of (Polydor 1999)★★★.
VIDEOS: Go And Get Stuffed (PolyGram Music Video 1997).

SHERIDAN, TONY
ALBUMS: My Bonnie (Polydor 1962)★★, The Beatles' First Featuring Tony Sheridan (Polydor 1964)★★, Just A Little Bit Of Tony Sheridan (Polydor 1964)★★, The Best Of Tony Sheridan (Polydor 1964)★★, Meet The Beat (Polydor 1965)★★, Rocks On (Metronome 1974)★★, Worlds Apart (Antagon 1978)★★.
COMPILATIONS: with the Beatles Once Upon A Time In Germany (Bear Family 2002)★★★.
FURTHER READING: Hamburg: The Cradle Of British Rock, Alan Clayson.

SHIRELLES
ALBUMS: Tonight's The Night (Scepter 1961)★★★, The Shirelles Sing To Trumpets And Strings (Scepter/Top Rank 1961)★★★, Baby It's You (Scepter/Stateside 1962)★★★★, Twist Party (Scepter 1962)★★★, Foolish Little Girl (Scepter 1963)★★★, It's A Mad Mad Mad Mad World (Scepter 1963)★★, The Shirelles Sing The Golden Oldies (Scepter 1964)H, with King Curtis Eternally Soul (Wand 1970)★★★, Tonight's The Night (Wand 1971)★★★, Happy In Love (RCA 1972)★★, The Shirelles (RCA 1973)★★, Let's Give Each Other Love (RCA 1976)★★, Spontaneous Combustion (Scepter 1997)★★.
SOLO: Shirley Alston [Owens] With A Little Help From My Friends (Strawberry 1975)★★, Lady Rose (Strawberry 1977)★★.
COMPILATIONS: The Shirelles Hits (Scepter/Stateside 1963)★★★★, The Shirelles Greatest Hits Volume 2 (Scepter 1967)★★★, Remember When Volume 1 (Wand 1972)★★★, Remember When Volume 2 (Wand 1972)★★★, Golden Hour Of The Shirelles (Golden Hour 1973)★★★, Juke Box Giants (Audio Fidelity 1981)★★★, The Shirelles Anthology (1959-1967) (Rhino 1984)★★★★, Soulfully Yours (Kent/Ace 1985)★★★, Sha La La (Impact/Ace 1985)★★★, The Shirelles Anthology (1959-1964) (Rhino 1986)★★★★, Lost And Found (Impact/Ace 1987)★★★, Greatest Hits (Impact/ Ace 1987)★★★★, 16 Greatest Hits (Gusto 1988)★★★★, The Collection (Castle 1990)★★★★, The Best Of (Ace 1992)★★★★, Lost And Found: Rare And Unissued (1994) ★★★, The Very Best Of The Shirelles (Rhino 1994)★★★★, The World's Greatest Girls Group (Tomato/Rhino 1995) ★★★★, The EP Collection (See For Miles 1999)★★★.
FURTHER READING: Girl Groups: The Story Of A Sound, Alan Betrock.

SHOCKED, MICHELLE
ALBUMS: The Texas Campfire Tapes (Cooking Vinyl 1986) ★★★, Short Sharp Shocked (Mercury/Cooking Vinyl 1988) ★★★, Captain Swing (Mercury/Cooking Vinyl 1989)★★, Arkansas Traveller (Mercury/London 1992)★★★, Kind Hearted Woman (Mood Swing/Private 1994)★★★, with Fiachna O'Braonain Artists Make Lousy Slaves (Private 1996)★★★, Good News (Mood Swing 1998)★★★, Deep Natural (Mighty Sound 2002)★★★.
COMPILATIONS: Mercury Poise: 1988-1995 (Mercury 1996)★★★.

SHOCKING BLUE
ALBUMS: Beat With Us (Polydor 1968)★★★, At Home (Pink Elephant 1969)★★★, Scorpio's Dance (Pink Elephant 1970)★★★, Third Album aka Shocking You (Pink Elephant 1971)★★, Inkpot (Pink Elephant 1972)★★, Live In Japan (Pink Elephant 1972)★★, Attila aka Eve And The Apple (Pink Elephant/Polydor 1972)★★★, Dream On Dreamer aka Ham (Polydor/Pink Elephant 1973)★★, Good Times (Pink Elephant 1974)★★.
COMPILATIONS: The Very Best Of Shocking Blue (Red Bullet 1990)★★★, The Shocking Blue (Castle 1990)★★★, The Best Of Shocking Blue (Connoisseur 1994)★★★, The Gold Collection (Castle 1995)★★★, Singles A's And B's (Repertoire 1998)★★★★, Golden Collection 2000 (Lighthouse 2000)★★★.

SHONEN KNIFE
ALBUMS: Burning Farm mini-album (Zero 1982)★★★, Yamano Atchan mini-album (Zero 1984)★★★, Pretty Little Baka Guy mini-album (Zero 1986)★★★, 712 (Nippon Crown 1991)★★★, Let's Knife (MCA Victor 1992)★★★, Rock Animals (August Records 1993)★★, Brand New Knife (MCA 1996)★★, Happy Hour (Universal 1998)★★.
COMPILATIONS: Shonen Knife (Giant 1990)★★★, The Birds And The B Sides (Virgin America 1996)★★★.

SHOWADDYWADDY
ALBUMS: *Showaddywaddy* (Bell 1974)★★★, *Step Two* (Bell 1975)★★★, *Trocadero* (Bell 1976)★★, *Red Star* (Arista 1977)★★, *Crepes & Drapes* (Arista 1979)★★★, *Bright Lights* (Arista 1980)★★, *Good Times* (Bell 1981)★★, *Living Legends* (RCA 1983)★★, *The Best Steps To Heaven* (Tiger 1987)★★, *Jump Boogie & Jive* (President 1991)★★, *The One & Only* (CMC 1997)★★.
COMPILATIONS: *Greatest Hits* (Arista 1976)★★★, *Greatest Hits (1976-1978)* (Arista 1978)★★★, *The Very Best Of Showaddywaddy* (Arista 1981)★★★, *25 Steps To The Top* (Repertoire 1991)★★★, *20 Greatest Hits* (Tring 1992)★★★, *Hey Rock 'N' Roll: The Very Best Of Showaddywaddy* (Music Club 1999)★★★, *The Bell Singles* (Cherry Red 2002)★★★.

SIBERRY, JANE
ALBUMS: *Jane Siberry* (Street 1980)★★★, *No Borders Here* (Open Air 1984)★★★, *The Speckless Sky* (Reprise 1985)★★★, *The Walking* (Duke Street 1987)★★, *Bound By The Beauty* (Reprise 1989)★★★★, *When I Was A Boy* (Reprise 1993)★★★, *Maria* (Warners 1995)★★★, *Teenager* (Sheeba 1996)★★★, A Day In The Life (Sheeba 1997)★★, *Tree: Music For Films And Forests* (Sheeba 1997)★★, *Lips: Music For Saying It* (Sheeba 1998)★★, *Child: Music For the Christmas Season* (Sheeba 1999)★★, *Hush* (Sheeba 2000)★★★, *City* (Sheeba 2001)★★★.
COMPILATIONS: *Summer In The Yukon* (Reprise 1992)★★★, *A Collection 1984-1989* (Duke Street 1993)★★★, *New York Trilogy* 4-CD box set (Sheeba 1999)★★★.

SIFFRE, LABI
ALBUMS: *Labi Siffre* (Pye 1970)★★★, *Singer And The Song* (Pye 1971)★★★, *Crying, Laughing, Loving, Lying* (Pye 1972)★★★, *Remember The Song* (Pye 1975)★★★, *So Strong* (China 1988)★★★, *Make My Day* (China 1989) ★★★, *Man Of Reason* (China 1991)★★★, *The Last Songs* (Labi 1998)★★★.
COMPILATIONS: *The Labi Siffre Collection* (Conifer 1986)★★★.
FURTHER READING: *Nigger*, Labi Siffre. *Blood On The Page*, Labi Siffre. *Deathwrite*, Labi Siffre. *Monument*, Labi Siffre.

SILVERCHAIR
ALBUMS: *frogstomp* (Murmur/Epic 1995)★★★, *Freak Show* (Epic 1997)★★★★, *Neon Ballroom* (Columbia 1999)★★★.
COMPILATIONS: *The Best Of Volume 1* (Murmur/Columbia 2000)★★★.
FURTHER READING: *Silverchair*, Matthew Reid.

SIMON AND GARFUNKEL
ALBUMS: *Wednesday Morning, 3AM* (Columbia 1965)★★, *The Sound Of Silence* (Columbia 1966)★★★★, *Parsley, Sage, Rosemary And Thyme* (Columbia 1966)★★★★, *The Graduate* film soundtrack (Columbia 1968)★★, *Bookends* (Columbia 1968)★★★★, *Bridge Over Troubled Water* (Columbia 1970)★★★★, *The Concert In Central Park* (Warners 1982)★★★.
COMPILATIONS: *Simon And Garfunkel's Greatest Hits* (Columbia 1972)★★★★, *The Simon And Garfunkel Collection* (Columbia 1981)★★★★, *The Definitive Simon And Garfunkel* (Columbia 1992)★★★★, *Old Friends* 4-CD box set (Columbia 1997)★★★★, *The Very Best Of Simon & Garfunkel: Tales From New York* (Columbia 1999)★★★★, *Two Can Dream Alone* (Burning Airlines 2000)★★★, *The Columbia Studio Recordings 1964-1970* 5-CD box set (Columbia/Legacy 2001)★★★★.
FURTHER READING: *Simon & Garfunkel: A Biography In Words & Pictures*, Michael S. Cohen. *Paul Simon: Now And Then*, Spencer Leigh. *Paul Simon*, Dave Marsh. *Simon And Garfunkel*, Robert Matthew-Walker. *Bookends: The Simon And Garfunkel Story*, Patrick Humphries. *The Boy In The Bubble: A Biography Of Paul Simon*, Patrick Humphries. *Paul Simon*, Patrick Humphries. *Simon And Garfunkel: Old Friends*, Joseph Morella and Patricia Barey. *Simon And Garfunkel: The Definitive Biography*, Victoria Kingston.

SIMON, CARLY
ALBUMS: as the Simon Sisters *The Simon Sisters* (Kapp 1964)★★, as the Simon Sisters *Cuddlebug* (Kapp 1965) ★★, *Carly Simon* (Elektra 1971)★★, *Anticipation* (Elektra 1971)★★★★, *No Secrets* (Elektra 1972)★★★★, *Hotcakes* (Elektra 1974)★★★, *Playing Possum* (Elektra 1975)★★★, *Another Passenger* (Elektra 1976)★★★, *Boys In The Trees* (Elektra 1978)★★★, *Spy* (Elektra 1979)★★★, *Come Upstairs* (Warners 1980)★★, *Torch* (Warners 1981)★★, *Hello Big Man* (Warners 1983)★★★, *Spoiled Girl* (Epic 1985)★★★, *Coming Around Again* (Arista 1987)★★, *Greatest Hits Live* (Arista 1988)★★★, *My Romance* (Arista 1990)★★, *Have You Seen Me Lately?* (Arista 1990)★★★, *Letters Never Sent* (Arista 1994)★★★, *Film Noir* (Arista 1997)★★, *The Bedroom Tapes* (Arista 2000)★★★.
COMPILATIONS: *The Best Of Carly Simon* (Elektra 1975) ★★★, *Clouds In My Coffee* 3-CD box set (Arista 1995) ★★★, *Nobody Does It Better: The Very Best Of Carly Simon* (Global 1998)★★★.
VIDEOS: *Live At Grand Central* (PolyGram Music Video 1996).
FURTHER READING: *Carly Simon*, Charles Morse.
FILMS: *Taking Off* (1971), *In Our Hands* (1984), *Perfect* (1985).

SIMON, PAUL
ALBUMS: *The Paul Simon Songbook* (CBS 1965)★★★, *Paul Simon* (CBS 1972)★★★★, *There Goes Rhymin' Simon* (CBS 1973)★★★★, *Paul Simon In Concert: Live Rhymin'* (CBS 1974)★★, *Still Crazy After All These Years* (CBS 1975) ★★★★, *One-Trick Pony* film soundtrack (Warners 1980)★★, *Hearts And Bones* (Warners 1983)★★★★, *Graceland* (Warners 1986)★★★★, *The Rhythm Of The Saints* (Warners 1990)★★★, *Paul Simon's Concert In The Park* (Warners 1991)★★★, *Songs From The Capeman* (Warners 1997) ★★★, *You're The One* (Warners 2000)★★★★.
COMPILATIONS: *Greatest Hits, Etc.* (CBS 1977)★★★★, *Negotiations And Love Songs 1971-1986* (Warners 1988)★★★★★, *Paul Simon: 1964/1993* 3-CD box set (Warners 1993)★★★, *Greatest Hits: Shining Like A National Guitar* (Warners 2000)★★★.
VIDEOS: *The Paul Simon Special* (Pacific Arts 1977), *Paul Simon In Concert* (Warner Home Video 1981), *Graceland: The African Concert* (Warner Reprise Video 1987), *Paul Simon's Concert In The Park* (Warner Home Video 1991), *Paul Simon: Born At The Right Time* (Warner Home Video 1992), *You're The One In Concert* (Warner Reprise Video 2001).FURTHER READING: *Paul Simon: Now And Then*, Spencer Leigh. *Paul Simon*, Dave Marsh. *Paul Simon*, Patrick Humphries. *The Boy In The Bubble: A Biography Of Paul Simon*, Patrick Humphries.
FILMS: *Annie Hall* (1977), *One-Trick Pony* (1980).

SIMONE, NINA
ALBUMS: *Little Girl Blue* (Bethlehem 1959)★★, *Nina Simone And Her Friends* expanded reissue of first album (Bethlehem 1959)★★, *The Amazing Nina Simone* (Colpix 1959)★★★★, *Nina Simone At The Town Hall* (Colpix 1959)★★★, *Nina Simone At Newport* (Colpix 1960) ★★★★, *Forbidden Fruit* (Colpix 1961)★★★, *Nina Simone At The Village Gate* (Colpix 1961)★★★, *Nina Simone Sings Ellington* (Colpix 1962)★★★, *Nina's Choice* (Colpix 1963)★★★, *Nina Simone At Carnegie Hall* (Colpix 1963) ★★★★, *Folksy Nina* (Colpix 1964)★★★, *Nina Simone In Concert* (Philips 1964)★★★, *Broadway ... Blues ... Ballads* (Philips 1964)★★★, *I Put A Spell On You* (Philips 1965) ★★★, *Tell Me More* (Philips 1965)★★★, *Pastel Blues* (Philips 1965)★★★, *Let It All Out* (Philips 1966)★★★, *Wild Is The Wind* (Philips 1966)★★★, *Nina With Strings* (Colpix 1966)★★★, *High Priestess Of Soul* (Philips 1966)★★★★, *Nina Simone Sings The Blues* (RCA Victor 1967)★★★★, *Silk And Soul* (RCA Victor 1967)★★★, *'Nuff Said* (RCA Victor 1968)★★★, *Black Gold* (RCA 1969)★★★, *Nina Simone And Piano!* (RCA Victor 1969)★★★, *To Love Somebody* (RCA 1971)★★★, *Here Comes The Sun* (RCA 1971)★★★, *Heart And Soul* (RCA 1972)★★★, *Emergency Ward* (RCA 1973)★★★, *It Is Finished* (RCA 1974)★★★, *Gifted And Black* (Mojo 1974)★★★, *I Loves You Porgy* (CBS 1977)★★★, *Baltimore* (CTI 1978)★★★, *Cry Before I Go* (Manhattan 1980)★★★, *Nina Simone* (Dakota 1982) ★★★, *Fodder On My Wings* (IMS 1982)★★★, *Nina's Back* (VPI 1985)★★★, *Live At Vine Street* (Verve 1987)★★★, *Live At Ronnie Scott's* (Windham Hill 1988)★★★, *Live* (Zeta 1990)★★, *The Blues* (Novus/RCA 1991)★★★, *A Single Woman* (Elektra 1993)★★★, *The Great Show Of Nina Simone: Live In Paris* (Accord 1996)★★.
COMPILATIONS: *The Best Of Nina Simone* (Philips 1966) ★★★★, *The Best Of Nina Simone* (RCA 1970)★★★★, *Fine And Mellow* (Golden Hour 1975)★★★, *The Artistry Of Nina Simone* (RCA 1982)★★★, *Music For The Millions* (Phillips 1983)★★★, *My Baby Just Cares For Me* (Charly 1984) ★★★★, *Lady Midnight* (Connoisseur 1987)★★★, *The Nina Simone Collection* (Deja Vu 1988)★★★★, *The Nina Simone Story* (Deja Vu 1989)★★★, *16 Greatest Hits* (1993)★★★★, *Anthology: The Colpix Years* (Rhino 1997) ★★★★, *Saga Of The Good Life And Hard Times* 1968 sessions (RCA 1997) ★★★★, *The Great Nina Simone* (Music Club 1997)★★★, *Ultimate Nina Simone* (Verve 1997)★★★★, *Blue For You: The Very Best Of Nina Simone* (Global 1998)★★★★, *Sugar In My Bowl: The Very Best Of 1967-1972* (RCA 1998)★★★★, *At Newport, At The Village Gate, And Elsewhere ...* (Westside 1999)★★★★, *Nina Simone's Finest Hour* (Verve 2000)★★★, *Gin House Blues: Nina Simone In Concert* (Castle Pie 2000)★★★.
VIDEOS: *Live At Ronnie Scott's* (Hendring Music Video 1988).
FURTHER READING: *I Put A Spell On You: The Autobiography Of Nina Simone*, Nina Simone with Stephen Cleary.

SIMPLE MINDS
ALBUMS: *Life In A Day* (Zoom 1979)★★, *Real To Real Cacophony* (Arista 1979)★★★, *Empires And Dance* (Arista 1980)★★, *Sons And Fascination/Sister Feelings Call* (Virgin 1981)★★★, *New Gold Dream (81, 82, 83, 84)* (Virgin/A&M 1982)★★★★, *Sparkle In The Rain* (Virgin/A&M 1984) ★★★★, *Once Upon A Time* (Virgin/A&M 1985)★★★★, *Live In The City Of Light* (Virgin/A&M 1987)★★, *Street Fighting Years* (Virgin/A&M 1989)★★, *Real Life* (Virgin/A&M 1991)★★★, *Good News From The Next World* (Virgin 1995)★★★, *Néapolis* (Chrysalis 1998)★★★, *Neon Lights* (Eagle 2001)★★, *Cry* (Eagle 2002)★★★.
COMPILATIONS: *Themes For Great Cities: Definitive Collection 79-81* US only (Stiff 1981)★★, *Celebration* (Arista 1982)★★★, *Glittering Prize 81/92* (Virgin/A&M 1992)★★★★, *The Early Years: 1977-1978* (Mindmood 1998)★★, *Original Gold* (Disky 1999)★★★, *The Best Of Simple Minds* (Virgin 2001)★★★.
VIDEOS: *Verona* (Virgin Music Video 1990), *Glittering Prize 81/92* (Vision Video 1992).
FURTHER READING: *Simple Minds: The Race Is The Prize*, Alfred Bos. *Simple Minds: Glittering Prize*, Dave Thomas. *Simple Minds*, Adam Sweeting. *Simple Minds: Street Fighting Years*, Alfred Bos. *Simple Minds: A Visual Documentary*, Mike Wrenn.

SIMPLY RED
ALBUMS: *Picture Book* (Elektra 1985)★★★★, *Men And Women* (Warners 1987)★★, *A New Flame* (Warners 1989)★★★, *Stars* (East West 1991)★★★★, *Life* (East West 1995)★★★, *Blue* (East West 1998)★★★, *Love And The Russian Winter* (East West 1999)★★.
COMPILATIONS: *Greatest Hits* (East West 1996)★★★, *It's Only Love* (East West 2000)★★★.
VIDEOS: *Greatest Video Hits* (Warner Music Vision 1996), *Simply Red: Live At The Lyceum* (Warner Music Vision 1998).
FURTHER READING: *Simply Mick: Mick Hucknall Of Simply Red. The Inside Story*, Robin McGibbon and Rob McGibbon. *The First Fully Illustrated Biography*, Mark Hodkinson.

SINGH, TALVIN
ALBUMS: *Calcutta Cyber Cafe* (Omni 1996)★★★, *OK* (Omni 1998)★★★★, *Ha* (Omni 2001)★★★, with Rakesh Chaurasia *Vira* (Sona Rupa 2002)★★★.
COMPILATIONS: *Talvin Singh Presents Anokha: Soundz Of The Asian Underground* (Mango 1997)★★★★, *Back To Mine* (DMC 2001)★★★★.

SIOUXSIE AND THE BANSHEES
ALBUMS: *The Scream* (Polydor 1978)★★★, *Join Hands* (Polydor 1979)★★★, *Kaleidoscope* (Polydor 1980)★★★, *Juju* (Polydor 1981)★★★, *A Kiss In The Dreamhouse* (Polydor 1982)★★★, *Nocturne* (Polydor 1983)★★★, *Hyaena* (Polydor 1984)★★★, *Tinderbox* (Polydor 1986)★★★, *Through The Looking Glass* (Polydor 1987)★★, *Peep Show* (Polydor 1988)★★★, *Superstition* (Polydor 1991)★★★, *The Rapture* (Polydor 1995)★★★.
COMPILATIONS: *Once Upon A Time - The Singles* (Polydor 1981)★★★★, *The Peel Sessions* (Strange Fruit 1991)★★★, *Twice Upon A Time* (Polydor 1992)★★★.
VIDEOS: *Greetings From Zurich* (1994).
FURTHER READING: *Siouxsie And The Banshees*, Mike West. *Entranced: The Siouxsie & The Banshees Story*, Brian Johns.
FILMS: *Jubilee* (1978).

SIR DOUGLAS QUINTET
ALBUMS: *The Best Of Sir Douglas Quintet* (Tribe 1965)★★★, *Sir Douglas Quintet + 2 = Honkey Blues* (Smash 1968)★★★, *Mendocino* (Smash 1969)★★★★, *Together After Five* (Smash 1970)★★★, *1+1+1 = 4* (Philips 1970)★★, *The Return Of Doug Saldaña* (Philips 1971)★★★, as Doug Sahm With The Sir Douglas Quintet *Rough Edges* (Mercury 1973)★★, as the Sir Douglas Band *Texas Tornado* (Atlantic 1973)★★, with Freddy Fender *Re-union Of The Cosmic Brothers* (Crazy Cajun 1976)★★★, as Sir Douglas Quintet, Doug Sahm And Augie Meyers *Live Love* reissued as *Wanted Very Much Alive* (TRC 1977)★★★, *The Tracker* (Crazy Cajun 1977)★★, *Border Wave* (Takoma 1981)★★★, *Quintessence* (Sonet/Varrick 1982)★★, *Back To The 'Dillo* (Sonet 1983)★★★, *Midnight Sun* (Sonet/Stony Plain 1983)★★★, *Live: Texas Tornado* (Takoma 1983)★★★, *Rio Medina* (Sonet/Stony Plain 1984)★★, *Luv Ya' Europa* (Sonet 1985)★★★, *Day Dreaming At Midnight* (Elektra 1994)★★★★.
COMPILATIONS: *The Best Of The Sir Douglas Quintet* (Takoma 1980)★★★★, *The Collection* (Castle 1986)★★★★, *Sir Doug's Recording Trip* (Edsel 1989)★★★, *The Best Of Doug Sahm And The Sir Douglas Quintet* (Mercury 1990)★★★★, *The Crazy Cajun Recordings* (Crazy Cajun 1998)★★★.

SISQO
ALBUMS: *Unleash The Dragon* (Def Jam 1999)★★★★, *Return Of Dragon* (Def Jam 2001)★★★.
VIDEOS: *The Thong Song* (Urban Edge 2000), *24 Hours With Sisqo* (2001).
FILMS: *Get Over It* (2001), *Winterdance* (2001).

SISTER SLEDGE
ALBUMS: *Circle Of Love* (Atco/Atlantic 1975)★★, *Together* (Cotillion/Atlantic 1977)★★, *We Are Family* (Cotillion/Atlantic 1979)★★★, *Love Somebody Today* (Cotillion/Atlantic 1980)★★★, *All American Girls* (Cotillion/Atlantic 1981) ★★★, *The Sisters* (Cotillion/Atlantic 1982)★★, *Bet Cha Say That To All The Girls* (Cotillion/Atlantic 1983)★★, *When The Boys Meet The Girls* (Atlantic 1985)★★, *Live In Concert* (Prime Cuts 1995)★★, *African Eyes* (Farenheit 1998)★★★.
COMPILATIONS: *Greatest Hits* (Atlantic 1986)★★★, *The Best Of Sister Sledge (1973-1985)* (Rhino 1992)★★★★, *The Very Best Of Sister Sledge (1973-1993)* (Atlantic 1993)★★★★, *Free Soul: The Classics Of Sister Sledge* (WEA 2000)★★★.

SIZE, RONI
ALBUMS: as Reprazent *New Forms* (Full Cycle/Talkin' Loud 1997)★★★★, with Reprazent *In The Mode* (Talkin' Loud/Island 2000)★★★★.

SKELLERN, PETER
ALBUMS: *Peter Skellern* (Decca 1972)★★★, *Not Without A Friend* (Decca 1974)★★★, *Holding My Own* (Decca 1974) ★★, *Hold On To Love* (Decca 1975)★★★, *Hard Times* (Island 1975)★★, *Kissing In The Cactus* (Mercury 1977)★★, *Skellern* (Mercury 1978)★★★, *Astaire* (Mercury 1979) ★★★, *Still Magic* (Mercury 1980)★★, *Happy Endings* (BBC 1981)★★★, *A String Of Pearls* (Mercury 1982)★★★, *Ain't Life Something* (Elite 1984)★★, *Lovelight* (Sonet 1987)★★★, *Stardust Memories* (Warners 1995)★★★.
COMPILATIONS: *Right From The Start* (Elite 1981)★★★, *The Best Of Peter Skellern* (Decca 1985)★★★, *The Singer And The Song* (Spectrum 1993)★★★.

SKID ROW (EIRE)
ALBUMS: *Skid* (Columbia 1970)★★★, *34 Hours* (Columbia 1971)★★★, *Alive And Kicking* (Columbia 1978)★★.
COMPILATIONS: *Skid Row* (Columbia 1987)★★★.

SKID ROW (USA)
ALBUMS: *Skid Row* (Atlantic 1989)★★, *Slave To The Grind* (Atlantic 1991)★★★, *B-Side Ourselves* mini-album (Atlantic 1992)★★, *Subhuman Race* (Atlantic 1994)★★.
COMPILATIONS: *40 Seasons: The Best Of Skid Row* (Atlantic 1998)★★★.
VIDEOS: *Oh Say Can You Scream?* (Atlantic 1991), *No Frills Video* (Atlantic 1993), *Roadkill* (Atlantic 1993).

SKIP BIFFERTY
ALBUMS: *Skip Bifferty* (RCA 1968)★★★★.

SKUNK ANANSIE
ALBUMS: *Paranoid And Sunburnt* (One Little Indian 1995) ★★★, *Stoosh* (One Little Indian 1996)★★★★, *Post Orgasmic Chill* (Virgin 1999)★★★.
FURTHER READING: *Skunk Anansie: Skin I'm In*, Steve Malins.

SLADE
ALBUMS: as Ambrose Slade *Beginnings* (UK) *Ballzy* (US) (Fontana 1969)★★, *Play It Loud* (Polydor/Cotillion 1970) ★★, *Alive!* (Polydor 1972)★★★★, *Slayed?* (Polydor 1972) ★★★, *Old, New, Borrowed And Blue* (UK) *Stomp Your Hands, Clap Your Feet* (US) (Polydor/Warners 1974)★★★, *In Flame* film soundtrack (Polydor/Warners 1974)★★★★, *Nobody's Fools* (Polydor/Warners 1976)★★★, *Whatever Happened To Slade* (Barn 1977)★★★★, *Slade Alive Vol. Two* (Barn 1978)★★, *Return To Base ...* (Barn 1979)★★, *We'll Bring The House Down* (Cheapskate 1981)★★, *Till Deaf Do Us Part* (RCA 1981)★★, *On Stage* (RCA 1982) ★★★, *Slade Alive* (Polydor 1983)★★, *The Amazing Kamikazee Syndrome* (UK) *Keep Your Hands Off My Power Supply* (US) (RCA/CBS Assoc. 1983)★★★, *Rogues Gallery* (RCA/CBS Assocs. 1985)★★, *Crackers – The Christmas Party Album* (Telstar/Castle 1985)★★, *You Boyz Make Big Noize* (RCA/CBS Assocs. 1987)★★, as Slade II *Keep On Rockin'* (Total 1996)★★.
COMPILATIONS: *Sladest* (Polydor/Reprise 1973)★★★, *Beginnings Of Slade* (Contour 1975)★★, *The Story Of Slade* (Barn 1977)★★★, *Smashes* (Polydor 1980)★★★, *Slade's Greats* (Polydor 1984)★★★, *The Slade Collection 81-87* (RCA 1991)★★★, *Wall Of Hits* (Polydor 1991)★★★, *The Slade Collection, Vol. 2 79-87* (RCA 1993)★★★, *Greatest Hits: Feel The Noize* (Polydor 1997)★★★★, *The Genesis Of Slade: A Compilation Of Rare Recordings - 1964 To 1966 - By Groups Featuring Members Of Slade* (TMC/Cherry Red 1997)★★.
VIDEOS: *Slade In Flame* (3M Video 1983), *Wall Of Hits* (PolyGram Music Video 1991).
FURTHER READING: *The Slade Story*, George Tremlett. *Slade In Flame*, John Pidgeon. *Slade: Feel The Noize*, Chris Charlesworth. *Who's Crazee Now? My Autobiography*, Noddy Holder.
FILMS: *Flame* (1975)

SLAYER
ALBUMS: *Show No Mercy* (Metal Blade 1983)★★, *Live Undead* (Metal Blade 1985)★★, *Hell Awaits* (Metal Blade 1985)★★, *Reign In Blood* (Def Jam 1986)★★★★, *South Of Heaven* (Def Jam 1988)★★★, *Seasons In The Abyss* (Def American 1990)★★★, *Live: Decade Of Aggression* (Def American 1991)★★★★, *Divine Intervention* (American 1994)★★★, *Undisputed Attitude* (American 1996)★★★, *Diabolus In Musica* (American 1998)★★★★, *God Hates Us All* (American 2001)★★★.
VIDEOS: *Live Intrusion* (American Visuals 1995).

SLEATER-KINNEY
ALBUMS: *Sleater-Kinney* (Chainsaw/Villa Villakula 1995) ★★★, *Call The Doctor* (Chainsaw 1996)★★★, *Dig Me Out* (Kill Rock Stars 1997)★★★★, *The Hot Rock* (Kill Rock Stars 1999)★★★, *All Hands On The Bad One* (Kill Rock Stars 2000)★★★★.

SLEDGE, PERCY
ALBUMS: *When A Man Loves A Woman* (Atlantic 1966) ★★★★, *Warm And Tender Soul* (Atlantic 1966)★★★★, *The Percy Sledge Way* (Atlantic 1967)★★★, *Take Time To Know Her* (Atlantic 1968)★★★, *I'll Be Your Everything* (Capricorn 1974)★★★, *If Loving You Is Wrong* (Charly 1986)★★★, *Percy!* (Monument 1987)★★★, *Wanted Again* (Demon 1989)★★, *Blue Night* (Sky Ranch 1994)★★★★.
COMPILATIONS: *The Best Of Percy Sledge* (Atlantic 1969) ★★★★, *The Golden Voice Of Soul* (Atlantic 1975)★★★, *Any Day Now* (Charly 1984)★★★, *Warm And Tender Love* (Blue Moon 1986)★★★, *When A Man Loves A Woman (The Ultimate Collection)* (Atlantic 1987)★★★★, *It Tears Me Up: The Best Of Percy Sledge* (Rhino 1992)★★★★, *The Very Best Of Percy Sledge* (Rhino 1998)★★★★.

SLEEPER
ALBUMS: *Smart* (Indolent 1995)★★★, *The It Girl* (Indolent 1996)★★★★, *Pleased To Meet You* (Indolent 1997)★★.

SLINT
ALBUMS: *Tweez* (Jennifer Hartman 1989)★★★, *Spiderland* (Touch & Go 1991)★★★★.

SLIPKNOT
ALBUMS: *Mate. Feed. Kill. Repeat* (Independent 1996)★★, *Slipknot* (Roadrunner 1999)★★★★, *Iowa* (Roadrunner 2001)★★★.
COMPILATIONS: *Maggot Corps Box* (Paperbox 2001)H.
VIDEOS: *Welcome To Our Neighbourhood* (Roadrunner Video 1999).
FURTHER READING: *Slipknot: Inside The Sickness, Behind The Masks*, Jason Arnopp. *Barcode Killers: The Slipknot Story*, Mark Crampton. *Slipknot: Unmasked*, Joel McIver.

SLITS
ALBUMS: *Cut* (Island/Antilles 1979)★★★★, *Bootleg Retrospective* (Rough Trade 1980)★★★, *Return Of The Giant Slits* (CBS 1981)★★.
COMPILATIONS: *The Peel Sessions* (Strange Fruit 1989) ★★, *In The Beginning (A Live Anthology)* (Jungle 1997)★★.

SLY AND ROBBIE
ALBUMS: *Disco Dub* (Gorgon 1978)★★, *Gamblers Choice* (Taxi 1980)★★★, *Raiders Of The Lost Dub* (Mango/Island 1981)★★★, *60s, 70s Into The 80s* (Mango/Island 1981) ★★★, *Dub Extravaganza* (CSA 1984)★★★, *A Dub Experience* (Island 1985)★★★, *Language Barrier* (Island 1985)★★★, *Electro Reggae* (Island 1986)★★★, *The Sting* (Taxi 1986)★★★, *Rhythm Killers* (4th & Broadway 1987) ★★★★, *Dub Rockers Delight* (Blue Moon 1987)★★★, *The Summit* (RAS 1988)★★★, *Silent Assassin* (4th & Broadway 1989)★★★, *Friends* (East West 1997)★★, *Drum & Bass Strip To The Bone By Howie B* (Palm Pictures 1998)★★★.
COMPILATIONS: *Present Taxi* (Taxi 1981)★★★★, *Crucial Reggae* (Taxi 1984)★★★, *Taxi Wax* (Taxi 1984)★★★, *Taxi Gang* (Taxi 1984)★★★, *Reggae Greats* (Island 1985)★★★, *Taxi Connection Live In London* (Taxi 1986)★★★, *Taxi Fare* (Taxi 1987)★★★, *Two Rhythms Clash* (RAS 1990)★★★, *DJ Riot* (Mango/Island 1990)★★★, *Hits 1987-90* (Sonic Sounds 1991)★★★★, *Present Sound Of Sound* (Musidisc 1994)★★★, *Present Ragga Pon Top* (Musidisc 1994)★★★.

SLY AND THE FAMILY STONE
ALBUMS: *A Whole New Thing* (Epic 1967)★★★, *Dance To The Music* (Epic 1968)★★★★, *Life* (USA) *M'Lady* (UK) (Epic/Direction 1968)★★★★, *Stand!* (Epic 1969)★★★★, *There's A Riot Going On* (Epic 1971)★★★★, *Fresh* (Epic 1973)★★★, *Small Talk* (Epic 1974)★★★, *High On You* (Epic 1975)★★, *Heard Ya Missed Me, Well I'm Back* (Epic 1976)★★, *Back On The Right Track* (Warners 1979)★★★, *Ain't But The One Way* (Warners 1982)★★.
COMPILATIONS: *Greatest Hits* (Epic 1970)★★★★, *High Energy* (Epic 1975)★★★★, *Ten Years Too Soon* (Epic 1979) ★★, *Anthology* (Epic 1981)★★★★, *Takin' You Higher: The Best Of Sly And The Family Stone* (Sony 1992)★★★★, *Precious Stone: In The Studio With Sly Stone 1963-1965* (Ace 1994)★★, *Three Cream Crackers And A Dog Biscuit* (Almafame 1999)★★.

SMALL FACES
ALBUMS: *The Small Faces* (Decca 1966)★★★, *Small Faces* (Immediate 1967)★★★, *There Are But Four Faces* US only (Immediate 1968)★★★, *Ogden's Nut Gone Flake* (Immediate 1968)★★★★, *Playmates* (Atlantic 1977)★★, *78 In The Shade* (Atlantic 1978)H.
COMPILATIONS: *From The Beginning* (Decca 1967)★★★, *The Autumn Stone* (Immediate 1969)★★★★, *In Memoriam (Small Faces Live)* Germany only (Immediate 1969)★★★, *Archetypes* US only (MGM 1970)★★★, *Wham Bam* (Immediate 1970)★★★, *Early Faces* US only (Pride 1972) ★★★, *The History Of Small Faces* US only (Pride 1972) ★★★, *Magic Moments* (Immediate/Nems 1976)★★★, *Rock Roots: The Decca Singles* (Decca 1977)★★★, *Greatest Hits* (Immediate/Nems 1978)★★★, *Profile* (Teldec 1979) ★★★, *Small Faces, Big Hits* (Virgin 1980)★★★, *For Your Delight, The Darlings Of Wapping Wharf Launderette* (Virgin 1980)★★★, *Sha La La La Lee* (Decca 1981)★★★, *Historia De La Musica Rock* (Decca Spain 1981)★★★, *By Appointment* (Accord 1982)★★★, *Big Music: A Compleat Collection* (Compleat 1984)★★, *Sorry She's Mine* (Platinum 1985)★★, *The Collection* (Castle 1985)★★★, *Quite Naturally* (Castle 1986)★★★, *20 Greatest Hits* (Big Time 1988)★★, *Nightriding: Small Faces* (Knight 1988)★★, *The Ultimate Collection* (Castle 1990)★★★, *Singles A's And B's* (See For Miles 1990)★★★★, *Lazy Sunday* (Success 1990)★★, *25 Greatest Hits* (Repertoire 1992)★★, *It's All Or Nothing* (Spectrum 1993)★★, *Itchycoo Park* (Laserlight 1993)★★★, *Small Faces' Greatest Hits* (Charly 1993) ★★★, *Here Comes The Nice* (Laserlight 1994)★★★, *Greatest Hits* (Arc 1994) ★★, *The Best Of The Small Faces* (Summit 1995)★★, *The Small Faces Boxed: The Definitive Anthology* (Repertoire 1995)★★★★, *The Immediate Years* 4-CD box set (Charly 1995)★★★★, *The Very Best Of The Small Faces* (Charly 1998)★★★, *The Singles Collection* 6-CD box set (Castle 1999)★★★★, *The Darlings Of Wapping Wharf Launderette: The Immediate Anthology* (Sequel 1999)★★★★, *Me You And Us Too: Best Of The Immediate Years* (Repertoire 1999)★★★.
VIDEOS: *Big Hits* (Castle 1991).
FURTHER READING: *The Young Mods' Forgotten Story*, Paolo Hewitt. *Happy Boys Happy*, Roland Schmidt and Uli Twelker. *Quite Naturally*, Keith Badman and Terry Rawlins. *A Fortnight Of Furore: The Who And The Small Faces Down Under*, Andrew Neil. *All The Rage*, Ian McLagan. *Rock On Wood: The Origin Of A Rock & Roll Face*, Terry Rawlings.
FILMS: *Dateline Diamonds* (1965).

SMASH MOUTH
ALBUMS: *Fush Yu Mang* (Interscope 1997)★★★, *Astro Lounge* (Interscope 1999)★★★★, *Smash Mouth* (Interscope 2001)★★★.
COMPILATIONS: *The East Bay Session* (Red Clay 1999)★★★.

SMASHING PUMPKINS
ALBUMS: *Gish* (Caroline 1991)★★★, *Siamese Dream* (Virgin 1993)★★★★, *Mellon Collie And The Infinite Sadness* (Virgin 1995)★★★★, *Zero* (Hut 1996)★★, *Adore* (Hut 1998)★★★★, *MACHINA/The Machines Of God* (Hut 2000)★★, *MACHINA II/The Friends And Enemies Of Modern Music* (Constantinople 2000)★★★★.
SOLO: James Iha *Let It Come Down* (Hut 1998)★★★.
COMPILATIONS: *Pisces Iscariot* (Virgin 1994)★★, *The Aeroplane Flies High* 5 CD-box set (Virgin 1996)★★★, *Greatest Hits (Rotten Apples)* (Virgin 2001)★★★★.
VIDEOS: *Vieuphoria* (Virgin Music Video 1994), *1991-2000 Greatest Hits Video Collection* (Virgin 2001).
FURTHER READING: *Smashing Pumpkins*, Nick Wise.

SMITH, ELLIOTT
ALBUMS: *Roman Candle* (Cavity Search 1994)★★★, *Elliott Smith* (Kill Rock Stars 1995)★★★, *Either/Or* (Kill Rock Stars 1997)★★★★, *XO* (DreamWorks 1998)★★★★, *Figure 8* (DreamWorks 2000)★★★★.
VIDEOS *Strange Parallel* (DreamWorks 1998).

SMITH, PATTI
ALBUMS: *Horses* (Arista 1975)★★★★, *Radio Ethiopia* (Arista 1976)★★★, *Easter* (Arista 1978)★★★, *Wave* (Arista 1979)★★, *Dream Of Life* (Arista 1988)★★, *Gone Again* (Arista 1996)★★★, *Peace And Noise* (Arista 1997) ★★★, *Gung Ho* (Arista 2000)★★★★.
COMPILATIONS: *Land (1975-2002)* (Arista 2002)★★★★.
FURTHER READING: *A Useless Death*, Patti Smith. *The Tongue Of Love*, Patti Smith. *Seventh Heaven*, Patti Smith. *Kodak*, Patti Smith. *Witt*, Patti Smith. *Babel*, Patti Smith. *The Night*, Patti Smith and Tom Verlaine. *Ha! Ha! Houdini!*, Patti Smith. *Patti Smith: Rock & Roll Madonna*, Dusty Roach. *Patti Smith: High On Rebellion*, Muir. *Early Work: 1970-1979*, Patti Smith. *The Coral Sea*, Patti Smith. *Patti Smith: A Biography*, Nick Johnston. *Patti Smith: An Unauthorized Biography*, Victor Bockris and Roberta Bayley. *Patti Smith Complete: Lyrics, Notes And Reflections*, Patti Smith.

SMITH, WILL
ALBUMS: *Big Willie Style* (Columbia 1997)★★★, *Willennium* (Columbia 1999)★★★.
VIDEOS: *The Will Smith Story* (MVP Home Video 1999), *The Will Smith Music Video Collection* (Sony 1999).
FILMS: *Where The Day Takes You* (1992), *Six Degrees Of Separation* (1993), *Bad Boys* (1995), *Independence Day* (1996), *Men In Black* (1997), *Enemy Of The State* (1998), *Wild Wild West* (1999).

SMITHEREENS
ALBUMS: *Especially For You* (Enigma 1986)★★★, *Green Thoughts* (Capitol 1988)★★★★, *Smithereens 11* (Enigma 1990)★★★★, *Blow Up* (Capitol 1991)★★, *A Date With The Smithereens* (RCA 1994)★★, *God Save The Smithereens* (Koch 1999)★★★.
SOLO: Pat DiNizio *Songs & Sounds* (Velvel 1997)★★★.
COMPILATIONS: *Blown To Smithereens* (Capitol 1995) ★★★★, *Attack Of The Smithereens* (Capitol 1995)★★.

SMITHS
ALBUMS: *The Smiths* (Rough Trade 1984)★★★, *Meat Is Murder* (Rough Trade 1985)★★★★, *The Queen Is Dead* (Rough Trade 1986)★★★★, *"Strangeways, Here We Come"* (Rough Trade 1987)★★★, *"Rank"* (Rough Trade 1988)★★.
COMPILATIONS: *Hatful Of Hollow* (Rough Trade 1984) ★★★, *The World Won't Listen* (Rough Trade 1987)★★★, *Louder Than Bombs* (Rough Trade 1987)★★★, *The Peel Sessions* (Strange Fruit 1988)★★, *Best ... I* (WEA 1992) ★★★, *Best ... II* (WEA 1992)★★, *Singles* (WEA 1995) ★★★★, *The Very Best Of* (WEA 2001)★★★★.
VIDEOS: *The Complete Picture* (WEA 1993).
FURTHER READING: *The Smiths*, Mick Middles. *Morrissey & Marr: The Severed Alliance*, Johnny Rogan. *The Smiths: The Visual Documentary*, Johnny Rogan. *The Smiths: All Men Have Secrets*, Tom Gallagher, M. Chapman and M. Gillies. *The Smiths And Beyond: Images*, Kevin Cummins.

SNOOP DOGGY DOGG
ALBUMS: *Doggystyle* (Death Row 1993)★★★★, *Tha Doggfather* (Death Row 1996)★★★★, as Snoop Dogg *Da Game Is To Be Sold, Not To Be Told* (No Limit 1998)★★★, as Snoop Dogg *No Limit Top Dogg* (No Limit 1999)★★, as Snoop Dogg *Tha Last Meal* (No Limit 2000)★★★.
COMPILATIONS: *Dead Man Walkin'* (D3 2000)★★★, *Death Row's Greatest Hits* (Death Row 2001)★★★★.
VIDEOS: *Murder Was The Case* (Warners 1994), *Game Of Life* (Priority Video 1998), *Doggystyle* (MVD 2001).
FILMS: *The Show* (1995), *Half Baked* (1998), *Caught Up* (1998), *Ride* (1998), *I Got The Hook Up* (1998), *The Wizard Of Oz* (1998), *Urban Menace* (1999), *Whiteboys* (1999), *The Wrecking Crew* (1999), *Hot Boyz* (1999), *Tha Eastsidaz* (2000), *Baby Boy* (2001), *Training Day* (2001), *Bones* (2001), *The Wash* (2001), *Crime Partners* (2001).

SOFT BOYS
ALBUMS: *A Can Of Bees* (Two Crabs 1979)★★★, *Underwater Moonlight* (Armageddon 1980)★★★★, *Two Halves For The Price Of One* (Armageddon 1981)★★★, *Invisible Hits* (Midnight Music 1983)★★★, *Live At The Portland Arms* cassette only (Midnight Music 1987)★★★.
COMPILATIONS: *Raw Cuts* mini-album (Overground 1989)★★, *The Soft Boys 1976-81* (Rykodisc 1994)★★★★.

SOFT CELL
ALBUMS: *Non-Stop Erotic Cabaret* (Some Bizzare 1981) ★★★, *Non-Stop Ecstatic Dancing* (Some Bizzare 1982)★★, *The Art Of Falling Apart* (Some Bizzare 1983)★★, *This Last Night In Sodom* (Some Bizzare 1984)★★.
COMPILATIONS: *The Singles 1981-85* (Some Bizzare 1986)★★★, *Their Greatest Hits* (Some Bizzare 1988)★★★, *Memorabilia: The Singles* (Polydor 1991)★★★, *Say Hello To Soft Cell* (Spectrum 1996)★★, *The Twelve Inch Singles* 3-CD set (Some Bizzare 2001)★★★.
FURTHER READING: *Soft Cell*, Simon Tebbutt. *The Last Star: A Biography Of Marc Almond*, Jeremy Reed. *Tainted Life: The Autobiography*, Marc Almond.

SOFT MACHINE
ALBUMS: *Soft Machine* (Probe 1968)★★★, *Volume Two* (Probe 1969)★★★★, *Third* (CBS 1970)★★★★, *Fourth* (CBS 1971)★★★, *Fifth* (CBS 1972)★★★, *Six* (CBS 1973)★★★, *Seven* (CBS 1973)★★, *Bundles* (Harvest 1975)★★★, *Softs* (Harvest 1976)★★, *Alive & Well Recorded In Paris* (Harvest 1978)★★, *Land Of Cockayne* (EMI 1981)★★, *Live At The Proms 1970* (Reckless 1988)★★, *The Peel Sessions* (Strange Fruit 1990)★★★★, *BBC Radio 1 Live In Concert* 1971 recording (Windsong 1993)★★★, *BBC Radio 1 Live In Concert* 1972 recording (Windsong 1994)★★★, *Rubber Riff* (Voiceprint 1994)★★, *Live In France* (One Way 1995) ★★, *Live At The Paradiso 1969* (Voiceprint 1995)★★, *Spaced* 1968 recording (Cuneiform 1996)★★★, *Virtually* (Cuneiform 1997)★★, *Live 70* (Blueprint 1998)★★★, *Noisette* 1970 live recording (Cuneiform 2000)★★★, *Turns On Volume 1* (Voiceprint 2001)★★, *Turns On Volume 2* (Voiceprint 2001)★★.
COMPILATIONS: *Faces & Places Vol. 7* 1967 recordings (BYG 1972)★★★, *Triple Echo* 3-LP box set (Harvest 1977) ★★★, *Jet Propelled Photographs* 1967 recordings (Get Back 1989)★★★, *The Best Of Soft Machine: Harvest Years* (See For Miles 1995)★★★, *Man In A Deaf Corner: Anthology 1963-1970* (Mooncrest/Sanctuary 2001)★★★.
FURTHER READING: *Gong Dreaming*, Daevid Allen.

SONIC YOUTH
ALBUMS: *Confusion Is Sex* (Neutral 1983)★★★, *Kill Yr Idols* mini-album (Zensor 1983)★★, *Sonic Death: Sonic Youth Live* cassette only (Ecstatic Peace! 1984)★★, *Bad Moon Rising* (Homestead 1985)★★★, *EVOL* (SST 1986) ★★★★, *Sister* (SST 1987)★★★★, *Daydream Nation* (Blast First 1988)★★★★, *Goo* (Geffen 1990)★★★, *Dirty* (Geffen 1992)★★★★, *Experimental Jet Set, Trash And No Star* (Geffen 1994)★★★, *Washing Machine* (Geffen 1995) ★★★, *Made In USA* film soundtrack 1986 recording (Rhino/Warners 1995)★★, *Syr 1* mini-album (Syr 1997) ★★★, *Syr 2* mini-album (Syr 1997)★★★, with Jim O'Rourke *Syr 3* mini-album (Syr 1997)★★★, *A Thousand Leaves* (Geffen 1998)★★★★, *Goodbye 20th Century* (Syr 1999)★★, *NYC Ghosts & Flowers* (Geffen 2000)★★★.
COMPILATIONS: *Screaming Fields Of Sonic Love* (Blast First 1995)★★★.
VIDEOS: *Goo* (DGC 1991).
FURTHER READING: *Confusion Is Next: The Sonic Youth Story*, Alec Foege.

SONIQUE
ALBUMS: *Hear My Cry* (Universal 2000)★★★.
COMPILATIONS: *The Serious Sound Of Sonique* (Serious/Virgin 2000)★★★★, *Club Mix* (Virgin 2001)★★★.

SONNY AND CHER
ALBUMS: *Look At Us* (Atco 1965)★★, *The Wondrous World Of Sonny & Cher* (Atco 1966)★★, *In Case You're In Love* (Atco 1967)★★, *Good Times* (Atco 1967)★★, *Sonny & Cher Live* (Kapp 1971)H, *All I Ever Need Is You* (Kapp 1972)★★, *Mama Was A Rock And Roll Singer, Papa Used To Write All Her Songs* (MCA 1973)H, *Live In Las Vegas Vol. 2* (MCA 1973)★.
COMPILATIONS: *Greatest Hits* (Atco 1967)★★★, *Greatest Hits* (MCA 1974)★★★, *All I Ever Need: The Kapp/MCA Anthology* (MCA 1996)★★★.
FURTHER READING: *Sonny And Cher*, Thomas Braun.
FILMS: *Good Times* (1967), *Chastity* (1969).

SOUL ASYLUM
ALBUMS: *Say What You Will* (Twin Tone 1984)★★★, *Made To Be Broken* (Twin Tone 1986)★★★, *While You Were Out* (Twin Tone 1986)★★★, *Hang Time* (Twin Tone/A&M 1988)★★★, *Clam Dip And Other Delights* mini-album (What Goes On 1989)★★★, *Soul Asylum And The Horse They Rode In On* (Twin Tone/A&M 1990)★★★★, *Grave Dancers Union* (A&M 1993)★★★, *Let Your Dim Light Shine* (A&M 1995)★★★, *Candy From A Stranger* (Columbia 1998)★★★.
COMPILATIONS: *Time's Incinerator* cassette only (Twin Tone 1984)★★★, *Say What You Will Clarence, Karl Sold The Truck* (Twin Tone 1989)★★★, *Black Gold: The Best Of Soul Asylum* (Columbia 2000)★★★★.

SOUL II SOUL
ALBUMS: *Club Classics Vol. I* (Ten 1989)★★★★, *Volume II: 1990 A New Decade* (Ten 1990)★★★, *Volume III, Just Right* (Ten 1992)★★★, *Volume V - Believe* (Virgin 1995) ★★★, *Time For Change* (Island 1997)★★★.
COMPILATIONS: *Volume IV - The Classic Singles 88-93* (Virgin 1993)★★★★.

SOULWAX
ALBUMS: *Leave The Story Untold* (Play It Again Sam 1996) ★★★, *Much Against Everyone's Advice* (Play It Again Sam/Almo 1998)★★★★.

SOUNDGARDEN
ALBUMS: *Ultramega OK* (SST 1988)★★★, *Louder Than Love* (A&M 1989)★★★, *Screaming Life/Fopp* (Sub Pop 1990)★★, *Badmotorfinger* (A&M 1991)★★★★, *Superunknown* (A&M 1994)★★★★, *Down On The Upside* (A&M 1996)★★★.
COMPILATIONS: *A-sides* (A&M 1997)★★★★.
VIDEOS: *Motorvision* (A&M 1993).
FURTHER READING: *Soundgarden: New Metal Crown*, Chris Nickson.

SOUTHSIDE JOHNNY AND THE ASBURY JUKES
ALBUMS: *Live At The Bottom Line* (Epic 1976)★★★★, *I Don't Want To Go Home* (Epic 1976)★★★★, *This Time It's For Real* (Epic 1977)★★★, *Hearts Of Stone* (Epic 1978) ★★★★, *The Jukes* (Mercury 1979)★★, *Love Is A Sacrifice* (Mercury 1980)★★, *Reach Up And Touch The Sky: Southside Johnny And The Asbury Jukes Live!* (Mercury 1981)★★★★, *Trash It Up!* (Mirage 1983)★★★, *In The Heat* (Mirage 1984)★★, *At Least We Got Shoes* (Atlantic 1986)★★, *Better Days* (Impact 1991)★★★, *Spittin Fire* (Grapevine 1997)★★★, *Live! At The Paradise Theater, Boston, Massachusetts, December 23, 1978* (Phoenix Gems 2000)★★★, *Messin' With The Blues* (Leroy 2000)★★★.
SOLO: Southside Johnny *Slow Dance* (Cypress 1988) ★★★.
COMPILATIONS: *Havin' A Party With Southside Johnny* (Epic 1979)★★★★, *The Best Of Southside Johnny And The Asbury Jukes* (Epic 1992)★★★★, *All I Want Is Everything: The Best Of Southside Johnny & The Asbury Jukes* (Rhino 1993)★★★★, *Restless Heart* (Rebound 1998)★★★, *Super Hits* (Sony 2001)★★★★.
VIDEOS: *Having A Party* (Channel 5 1984).

SPACE
ALBUMS: *Spiders* (Gut 1996)★★★, *Tin Planet* (Gut 1998)★★★★.
COMPILATIONS: *Invasion Of The Spiders – Remixed & Unreleased Tracks* (Gut 1997)★★★.
VIDEOS: *Tin Planet Live* (Warner Vision 1998).

SPANDAU BALLET
ALBUMS: Journey To Glory (Reformation 1981)★★, Diamond (Reformation 1982)H, True (Reformation 1983) ★★★, Parade (Reformation 1984)★★, Through The Barricades (Reformation 1986)★★★, Heart Like A Sky (CBS 1989)★★.
COMPILATIONS: The Singles Collection (Chrysalis 1985) ★★★, The Best Of Spandau Ballet (Chrysalis 1991)★★★, Gold: The Best Of Spandau Ballet (Chrysalis 2000)★★★.

SPARKLEHORSE
ALBUMS: Vivadixiesubmarinetransmissionplot (Slow River/ Parlophone 1995)★★★, Good Morning Spider (Parlophone 1998)★★★★, It's A Wonderful Life (Capitol 2001)★★★★.

SPARKS
ALBUMS: Halfnelson aka Sparks (Bearsville 1971)★★, A Woofer In Tweeter's Clothing (Bearsville 1972)★★★, Kimono My House (Island 1974)★★★, Propaganda (Island 1974) ★★★, Indiscreet (Island 1975)★★, Big Beat (Columbia 1976)★★, Introducing Sparks (Columbia 1977)★★, No.1 In Heaven (Elektra 1979)★★★, Terminal Jive (Virgin 1979)★★, Whomp That Sucker (Why-Fi/RCA 1981)★★, Angst In My Pants (Atlantic 1982)★★, Sparks In Outer Space (Atlantic 1983)★★★, Pulling Rabbits Out Of A Hat (Atlantic 1984) ★★, Music That You Can Dance To (Curb 1986)★★, Interior Design (Fine Art 1988)★★, Gratuitous Sax And Senseless Violins (Logic/Arista 1994)★★★, Plagiarism (Roadrunner 1997)★★★, Balls (Oglio/Recognition 2000)★★★.
COMPILATIONS: Best Of Sparks (Island 1979)★★★, Mael Intuition: The Best Of Sparks 1974-1976 (Island 1990) ★★★, Profile: The Ultimate Sparks Collection (Rhino 1991) ★★★, 12" Mixes (Oglio 1996)★★.

SPEARS, BRITNEY
ALBUMS: Baby, One More Time (Jive 1998)★★★, Oops! ... I Did It Again (Jive 2000)★★★, Britney (Jive 2001)★★.
VIDEOS: The Britney Spears Story: Unauthorised (Creative Media 1999), Time Out With Britney Spears (Jive/Zomba 1999), Britney In Hawaii: Live And More! (Jive/Zomba 2001), Britney: The Videos (Jive/Zomba 2001), Britney Spears Live From Las Vegas (Jive/Zomba 2002).
FILMS: Crossroads (2002).

SPECIALS
ALBUMS: The Specials (2-Tone/Chrysalis 1979)★★★, More Specials (2-Tone/Chrysalis 1980)★★★, as the Special AKA In The Studio (2-Tone/Chrysalis 1984)★★★, with Desmond Dekker King Of Kings (Trojan 1993)★★★, Today's Specials (Kuff 1995)★★★, Guilty Til Proved Innocent (MCA 1998) ★★, Ghost Town Live 1995 recording (Receiver 1999)★★, The Conquering Ruler: 15 Skanking Trojan Classics (Receiver 2001)★★★.
COMPILATIONS: Singles (Chrysalis 1991)★★★★, The Selecter & The Specials: Live In Concert (Windsong 1993)★★, Too Much Too Young (EMI 1996)★★★, BBC Sessions (EMI 1998)★★★, Stereo-Typical A's, B's And Rarities 3-CD set (EMI 2000)★★★.

SPECTOR, PHIL
COMPILATIONS: Today's Hits (Philles 1963)★★★, A Christmas Gift For You (Philles 1963)★★★★, Phil Spector Wall Of Sound, Volume 1: The Ronettes (Phil Spector International 1975)★★★★, Phil Spector Wall Of Sound, Volume 2: Bob B. Soxx And The Blue Jeans (Phil Spector International 1975) ★★★★, Phil Spector Wall Of Sound, Volume 3: The Crystals (Phil Spector International 1975)★★★★, Phil Spector Wall Of Sound, Volume 4: Yesterday's Hits Today (Phil Spector International 1976)★★★★, Phil Spector Wall Of Sound, Volume 5: Rare Masters (Phil Spector International 1976)★★★, Phil Spector Wall Of Sound, Volume 6: Rare Masters Volume 2 (Phil Spector International 1976)★★★, The Phil Spector Story (1976)★★★, Echoes Of The Sixties (1977)★★★, Phil Spector 1974-1979 (1979)★★★★, Wall Of Sound (1981)★★★, Phil Spector: The Early Productions 1958-1961 (Rhino 1984)★★★, Twist And Shout: Twelve Atlantic Tracks Produced By Phil Spector (1989)★★★, Back To Mono 4-CD box set (Rhino 1991)★★★★★.
FURTHER READING: The Phil Spector Story: Out Of His Head, Richard Williams. The Phil Spector Story, Rob Finnis. He's A Rebel: Phil Spector, Rock And Roll's Legendary Producer, Mark Ribowsky. Collecting Phil Spector: The Man, The Legend, The Music, Jack Fitzpatrick and James E. Fogerty.

SPENCER, JON, BLUES EXPLOSION
ALBUMS: Crypt Style (Crypt 1992)★★, The Jon Spencer Blues Explosion (Caroline 1992)★★, Extra Width (Matador 1993)★★, Mo Width (Au-Go-Go 1994)★★, Orange (Matador 1994)★★★, Remixes (Matador 1995)★★, Now I Got Worry (Mute 1996)★★★★, Acme (Mute 1998) ★★★★, with Dub Narcotic Sound System Sideways Soul (K 1999)★★★, Plastic Fang (Mute 2002)★★★.
COMPILATIONS: Acme-Plus (Mute 1999)★★★.

SPICE GIRLS
ALBUMS: Spice (Virgin 1996)★★★★, Spiceworld (Virgin 1997)★★★, Forever (Virgin 2000)★★.
VIDEOS: Spice Power (Visual), Spice – Official Video Volume 1 (Virgin Video 1997), One Hour Of Girl Power (Warner Home Video 1997), Spice Exposed: Too Hot! (Quantum Leap 1998), Spiceworld - The Movie (PolyGram Music Video 1998), Girl Power! Live In Istanbul (Virgin Music Video 1998), Spice Girls Live At Wembley Stadium (Virgin Music Video 1998), Spice Girls In America: A Tour Story (Virgin Music Video 1999).
FURTHER READING: Girl Power, Spice Girls. Spice Power: The Inside Story, Rob McGibbon. Spiceworld: The Official Book Of The Movie, Dean Freeman (photographer). Spiced Up! My Mad Year With The Spice Girls, Muff Fitzgerald. If Only, Geri Halliwell. Learning To Fly: The Autobiography, Victoria Beckham.
FILMS: Spiceworld - The Movie (1997).

SPIN DOCTORS
ALBUMS: Pocket Full Of Kryptonite (Epic 1991)★★★★, Homebelly Groove (Epic 1992)★★, Turn It Upside Down (Epic 1994)★★, You've Got To Believe In Something (Epic 1996)★★, Here Comes The Bride (Universal 1999)★★.
COMPILATIONS: Just Go Ahead Now: A Retrospective (Epic 2000)★★★.

SPIRIT
ALBUMS: Spirit (Ode 1968)★★★★, The Family That Plays Together (Ode 1969)★★★★, Clear (Ode 1969)★★★, Twelve Dreams Of Dr. Sardonicus (Epic 1970)★★★★★, Feedback (Epic 1972)★★, Spirit Of '76 (Mercury 1975) ★★★★, Son Of Spirit (Mercury 1975)★★★, Farther Along (Mercury 1976)★★★, Future Games (A Magical Kahuna Dream) (Mercury 1977)★★★★, Live Spirit (Potato 1978) ★★★, The Adventures Of Kaptain Kopter & Commander Cassidy In Potatoland 1974 recording (Rhino/Beggars Banquet 1981)★★★, The Thirteenth Dream aka Spirit Of '84 (Mercury 1984)★★, Rapture In The Chambers (I.R.S. 1989)★★, Tent Of Miracles (Dolphin 1990)★★, Live At La Paloma (W.E.R.C. C.R.E.W. 1995)★★★, California Blues (W.E.R.C. C.R.E.W. 1996)★★★, Live At The Rainbow 1978 (Past & Present 1999)★★.
COMPILATIONS: The Best Of Spirit (Epic 1973)★★★, Time Circle (1968-1972) (Epic/Legacy 1991)★★★★, Chronicles 1967-1992 (W.E.R.C. C.R.E.W. 1991)★★★★, The Mercury Years (Mercury 1997)★★★★, Cosmic Smile (Phoenix Media 2000)★★★, The Very Best Of Spirit: 100% Proof (Sony 2000)★★.

SPIRITUALIZED
ALBUMS: Lazer Guided Melodies (Dedicated 1992)★★★★, Fucked Up Inside (Dedicated 1993)★★, Pure Phase (Dedicated 1995)★★★★, Ladies And Gentlemen We Are Floating In Space (Dedicated/Arista 1997)★★★★, Live At The Royal Albert Hall: October 10 1997 (Deconstruction/ Arista 1998)★★★, Let It Come Down (Arista 2001)★★★★.

SPLIT ENZ
ALBUMS: Mental Notes (Mushroom 1975)★★, Second Thoughts (Chrysalis 1976)★★, Dizrhythmia (Chrysalis 1977)★★★★, Frenzy (Mushroom 1979)★★★, True Colours (A&M 1980)★★★★, Waiata (A&M 1981)★★★, Time And Tide (A&M 1982)★★★, Conflicting Emotions (A&M 1984)★★, See Ya Round (Mushroom 1984)★★, The Livin' Enz (Mushroom 1985)★★.
COMPILATIONS: The Beginning Of The Enz (Chrysalis 1980)★★★, Anniversary (Mushroom 1995)★★★★, Other Enz: Split Enz And Beyond (Raven 1999)★★★.

SPOOKY TOOTH
ALBUMS: It's All About (UK) Tobacco Road (US) (Island/ Mala 1968)★★★, Spooky Two (Island/A&M 1969)★★★★, with Pierre Henry Ceremony (Island/A&M 1970)★★, The Last Puff (Island/A&M 1970)★★★★, You Broke My Heart So I Busted Your Jaw (Island/A&M 1973)★★, Witness (Island 1973)★★, The Mirror (Good Ear/Island 1974)★★, Cross Purpose (Ruf/Brilliant 1999)★★★.
COMPILATIONS: with Gary Wright That Was Only Yesterday (Island/A&M 1976)★★★, The Best Of Spooky Tooth (Island 1976)★★★★.

SPOTNICKS
ALBUMS: Out-A Space: In London (Karusell 1962)★★★, In Paris: Dansons Avec Les Spotnicks (Karusell 1963)★★★, In Spain: Bailemos Con Los Spotnicks (SweDisc 1963)★★★, In Stockholm (SweDisc 1964)★★★, In Berlin (SweDisc 1964) ★★★, At Home In Gothenburg (SweDisc 1965)★★, In Tokyo (SweDisc 1966)★★, Around The World (SweDisc 1966)★★★, In Winterland (SweDisc 1966)★★, Live In Japan (SweDisc 1967)★★, In Acapulco, Mexico (SweDisc 1967)★★★, In The Groove (SweDisc 1968)★★★, By Request (SweDisc 1968)★★, Back In The Race (Polydor 1970)★★, Ame No Ballad (Canyon 1971)★★, Something Like Country (Polydor 1972)★★★, Bo Winberg & The Spotnicks Today (Polydor 1973)★★★, Live In Berlin '74 (Polydor 1974)★★, Feelings - 12 Brand New Songs (Polydor 1976)★★, Charttoppers Recorded 77 (Polydor 1977)★★, The Great Snowman (Marianne 1978)★★, Never Trust Robots (Polydor 1978)★★, Saturday Night Music (Marianne 1979)★★, Pink Lady Super Hits (SweDisc 1979) ★★, 20th Anniversary Album (Polydor 1980)★★, We Don't Wanna Play Amapola No More (Mill 1982)★★, In The Middle Of The Universe (Mill 1983)★★, Highway Boogie (Mill 1985) ★★, In Time (Mill 1986)★★, Love Is Blue (Europa 1987)★★, Happy Guitar (Imtrat 1987)★★, Unlimited (Mill 1989)★★, The Spotnicks/Bo Winberg #1 (BMG 1993)★★, Tracks (BMG 1995)★★★, The Spotnicks 1997 (Riverside 1997)★★★.
COMPILATIONS: The Best Of The Spotnicks (Chrysalis 1978)★★★, The Very Best Of The Spotnicks (Air 1981) ★★★, 16 Golden World Hits (Koch 1987)★★★.
FILMS: Just For Fun (1963).

SPRINGFIELD, DUSTY
ALBUMS: A Girl Called Dusty (Philips 1964)★★★★, Ev'rything's Coming Up Dusty (Philips 1965)★★★★, Where Am I Going (Philips 1967)★★★★, Dusty ... Definitely (Philips 1968)★★★★, Dusty In Memphis (Philips 1969)★★★★★, A Brand New Me (From Dusty With Love) (Philips 1970)★★★★, See All Her Faces (Philips 1972)★★★, Cameo (Philips 1973) ★★★, Dusty Sings Burt Bacharach And Carole King (Philips 1975)★★★, It Begins Again (Mercury 1978)★★★, Living Without Your Love (Mercury 1979)★★★, White Heat (Casablanca 1982)★★★★, Reputation (Parlophone 1990) ★★★, A Very Fine Love (Columbia 1995)★★.
COMPILATIONS: Golden Hits (Philips 1966)★★★★, Stay Awhile (Wing 1968)★★★★, This Is Dusty Springfield (Philips 1971)★★★★, This Is Dusty Springfield Volume 2: The Magic Garden (Philips 1973)★★★★, Greatest Hits (Philips 1979)★★★★, The Very Best Of Dusty Springfield (K-Tel 1981)★★★★, Dusty: Love Songs (Philips 1983)★★★★, The Silver Collection (Philips 1988)★★★★★, Dusty's Sounds Of The 60's (Pickwick 1989)★★★★, Love Songs (Pickwick 1989) ★★★★, Dusty Springfield Songbook (Pickwick 1990)★★★★★, Blue For You (1993)★★★★, Goin' Back: The Very Best Of Dusty Springfield (Philips 1994)★★★★★, Dusty, The Legend Of Dusty Springfield 4-CD box set (Philips 1994)★★★★, Something Special (Mercury 1996)★★★★, Songbooks (Philips 1998)★★★★, The Very Best Of Dusty Springfield (Mercury 1998)★★★★, Simply Dusty: The Definitive Dusty Springfield Collection 4-CD box set (Mercury 2000)★★★★★, Beautiful Soul: The ABC/Dunhill Collection (Hip-O 2001)★★★.
FURTHER READING: Dusty, Lucy O'Brien. Scissors And Paste: A Collage Biography, David Evans. Dancing With Demons, Penny Valentine and Vicki Wickham. The Complete Dusty Springfield, Paul Howes.

SPRINGSTEEN, BRUCE
ALBUMS: Greetings From Asbury Park N.J. (Columbia 1973)★★★, The Wild, The Innocent & The E Street Shuffle (Columbia 1973)★★★★, Born To Run (Columbia 1975) ★★★★★, Darkness On The Edge Of Town (Columbia 1978)★★★★, The River (Columbia 1980)★★★★, Nebraska (Columbia 1982)★★★★, Born In The USA (Columbia 1984)★★★, Tunnel Of Love (Columbia 1987)★★★★, Human Touch (Columbia 1992)★★★, Lucky Town (Columbia 1992) ★★★, In Concert - MTV Plugged (Columbia 1993)★★★, The Ghost Of Tom Joad (Columbia 1995)★★★★, with The E Street Band Live In New York City (Columbia 2001)★★★.
COMPILATIONS: with The E Street Band Live/1975-85 box set (Columbia 1986)★★★, Greatest Hits (Columbia 1995) ★★★★, Tracks 4-CD box set (Columbia 1998)★★★★, 18 Tracks (Columbia 1999)★★★★.
VIDEOS: Video Anthology 1978-1988 (Columbia Music Video 1989), Blood Brothers (Columbia Music Video 1996), The Complete Video Anthology: 1978-2000 (Columbia Music Video 2000), Bruce Springsteen & The E Street Band Live In New York City (SMV Enterprises 2001).
FURTHER READING: Springsteen: Born To Run, Dave Marsh. Bruce Springsteen, Peter Gambaccini. Springsteen: Blinded By The Light, Patrick Humphries and Chris Hunt. Springsteen: No Surrender, Kate Lynch. Bruce Springsteen Here & Now, Craig MacInnis. The E. Street Shuffle, Clinton Heylin and Simon Gee. Glory Days, Dave Marsh. Backstreets: Springsteen - The Man And His Music, Charles R. Cross (ed.). Down Thunder Road, Mark Eliot. Bruce Springsteen In His Own Words, John Duffy. Rolling Stone Files, editors of Rolling Stone. The Complete Guide To The Music Of: Bruce Springsteen, Patrick Humphries. Born In The USA: Bruce Springsteen And The American Tradition, Jim Cullen. Songs, Bruce Springsteen. Springsteen: Point Blank, Christopher Sandford. It Ain't No Sin To Be Glad You're Alive: The Promise Of Bruce Springsteen, Eric Alterman. Springsteen, Access All Areas, Lynn Goldsmith.

SQUEEZE
ALBUMS: Squeeze (A&M 1978)★★★, Cool For Cats (A&M 1979)★★★★, Argybargy (A&M 1980)★★★★, East Side Story (A&M 1981)★★★★, Sweets From A Stranger (A&M 1982)★★, Cosi Fan Tutti Frutti (A&M 1985)★★★, Babylon And On (A&M 1987)★★★, Frank (A&M 1989)★★★, A Round And A Bout (Deptford Fun City/I.R.S. 1990)★★, Play (Reprise 1991)★★, Some Fantastic Place (A&M 1993) ★★★, Ridiculous (A&M/Ark 21 1995)★★★★, Domino (Quixotic/Valley 1998)★★★★.
SOLO: Glenn Tilbrook The Incomplete Glenn Tilbrook (Quixotic 2001)★★★.
COMPILATIONS: Singles 45's And Under (A&M 1982) ★★★★, Greatest Hits (A&M 1992)★★★, Excess Moderation (A&M 1996)★★★, Piccadilly Collection (A&M 1996)★★★, Six Of One box set (A&M 1997)★★★★, Up The Junction (Spectrum 2000)★★★.

STAIND
ALBUMS: Dysfunction (Flip/Elektra 1999)★★★★, Break The Cycle (Flip/Elektra 2001)★★★.

STANDELLS
ALBUMS: The Standells Live At PJs (Liberty 1964)★★★, Live And Out Of Sight (Sunset 1966)★★★, Dirty Water (Tower 1966)★★★, Why Pick On Me (Tower 1966)★★, The Hot Ones (Tower 1966)★★, Try It (Tower 1967)★★, Ban This! (Live From Cavestomp) (Varèse Sarabande 2000)★★.
COMPILATIONS: The Best Of The Standells (Rhino 1984) ★★★, Very Best Of The Standells (Hip-O 1998)★★★.
FILMS: Get Yourself A College Girl (1964), Riot On Sunset Strip (1967).

STANSFIELD, LISA
ALBUMS: Affection (Arista 1989)★★★, Real Love (Arista 1991)★★★, So Natural (Arista 1993)★★, Lisa Stansfield (Arista 1997)★★★, The Number 1 Remixes mini-album (Arista 1998)★★★, Face Up (Arista 2001)★★★.
VIDEOS: Lisa Live (PMI 1993).
FILMS: Swing (1999).

STARDUST, ALVIN
ALBUMS: The Untouchable (Magnet 1974)★★★, Alvin Stardust (Magnet 1974)★★, Rock With Alvin (Magnet 1975)★★, I'm A Moody Guy (Magnet 1982)★★, I Feel Like ... Alvin Stardust (Chrysalis 1984)★★.
COMPILATIONS: Greatest Hits: Alvin Stardust (Magnet 1977)★★★, 20 Of The Best (Object 1987)★★★.
FURTHER READING: The Alvin Stardust Story, George Tremlett.

STARR, EDWIN
ALBUMS: Soul Master (Gordy 1968)★★★, 25 Miles (Gordy 1969)★★★, with Blinky Just We Two (Gordy 1969)★★★, War And Peace (Gordy 1970)★★★, Involved (Gordy 1971)★★★, Hell Up In Harlem film soundtrack (Gordy 1974)★★★, Free To Be Myself (1975)★★★, Edwin Starr (1977)★★, Afternoon Sunshine (GTO 1977)★★★, Clean (20th Century 1978)★★, HAPPY Radio (20th Century 1979)★★★, Stronger Than You Think I Am (20th Century 1980)★★, Where Is The Sound (Motor City 1991)★★.
COMPILATIONS: The Hits of Edwin Starr (Tamla Motown 1972)★★★, 20 Greatest Motown Hits (Motown 1986)★★★, Early Classics (Spectrum 1996)★★★, The Essential Collection (Spectrum 2001)★★★.

STARR, RINGO
ALBUMS: Sentimental Journey (Apple 1969)★★, Beaucoups Of Blues (Apple 1970)★★, Ringo (Apple 1973)★★★, Goodnight Vienna (Apple 1974)★★, Ringo's Rotogravure (Polydor/Atlantic 1976)★★, Ringo The 4th (Polydor/ Atlantic 1977)★★, Bad Boy (Polydor/Portrait 1977)★★, Stop And Smell The Roses (RCA/Boardwalk 1981)★★, Old Wave (Bellaphon/RCA 1983)H, Ringo Starr And His All-Starr Band (Rykodisc 1990)★★★, Time Takes Time (Arista/ Private 1992)★★, Ringo Starr And His All-Starr Band Live From Montreux (Rykodisc 1993)★★, Ringo Starr And His Third All-Starr Band (Blockbuster 1997)★★, Vertical Man (Mercury 1998)★★★, VH1 Storytellers (Mercury 1998)★★, I Wanna Be Santa Claus (Mercury 1999)★★.
COMPILATIONS: Blast From Your Past (Apple 1975)★★★, Starr Struck: Best Of Ringo Starr, Vol. 2 (Rhino 1989)★★★, The Anthology ... So Far (Megaworld 2001)★★★.
VIDEOS: Ringo Starr And His Fourth All-Star Band (MPI Home Video 1998), The Best Of Ringo Starr And His All Starr Band So Far ... (Aviva International 2001).
FURTHER READING: Ringo Starr: Straight Man Or Joker?, Alan Clayson.
FILMS: A Hard Day's Night (1964), Help! (1965), Magical Mystery Tour (1967), Yellow Submarine (1968), Candy (1968), The Magic Christian (1969), Let It Be (1970), 200 Motels (1971), Blindman aka Il Cieco (1971), Born To Boogie (1972), That'll Be The Day (1973), Son Of Dracula aka Young Dracula (1974), Lisztomania (1975), Sextette (1978), Caveman (1981), Give My Regards To Broad Street (1984), Water (1985), To The North Of Katmandu (1986), Walking After Midnight (1988).

STARSAILOR
ALBUMS: Love Is Here (Chrysalis/Capitol 2001)★★★.

STATUS QUO
ALBUMS: Picturesque Matchstickable Messages From The Status Quo (Pye 1968)★★★, Messages From The Status Quo US only (Cadet 1968)★★★, Spare Parts (Pye 1969) ★★, Ma Kelly's Greasy Spoon (Pye 1970)★★★★, Dog Of Two Head (Pye 1971)★★★, Piledriver (Vertigo 1972) ★★★★, Hello! (Vertigo 1973)★★★, Quo (Vertigo 1974)★★★, On The Level (Vertigo 1975)★★★, Blue For You (Vertigo 1976)★★, Live! (Vertigo 1977)★★, Rockin' All Over The World (Vertigo 1977)★★★, If You Can't Stand The Heat ... (Vertigo 1978)★★★, Whatever You Want (Vertigo 1979)★★★, Just Supposin' (Vertigo 1980)★★★, Never Too Late (Vertigo 1981)★★, 1+9+8+2 (Vertigo 1982)★★, Live At The N.E.C. (Vertigo 1982)★★, Back To Back (Vertigo 1983)★★, In The Army Now (Vertigo 1986) ★★★, Ain't Complaining (Vertigo 1988)★★★, Perfect Remedy (Vertigo 1989)★★, Rock 'Til You Drop (Vertigo 1991)★★, Live Alive Quo (Vertigo 1993)★★, Thirsty Work (Polydor 1994)★★, Don't Stop (PolyGram TV 1996)★★, Under The Influence (Eagle 1999)★★, Famous In The Last Century (Universal Music TV 2000)★★.
COMPILATIONS: Status Quo-tations (Marble Arch 1969) ★★★, The Best Of Status Quo (Pye 1973)★★★, The Golden Hour Of Status Quo (Golden Hour 1973)★★★, Down The Dustpipe (Golden Hour 1975)★★★, The Rest Of Status Quo (Pye 1976)★★, The Status Quo File (Pye 1977) ★★★, The Status Quo Collection (Pickwick 1978)★★★, 12 Gold Bars (Vertigo 1980)★★★★, Spotlight On Status Quo Volume 1 (PRT 1980)★★★, Fresh Quota (PRT 1981)★★★, 100 Minutes Of Status Quo (PRT 1982)★★★, Spotlight On Status Quo Volume 2 (PRT 1982)★★★, "From The Makers Of ..." (Phonogram 1983)★★★, Works (PRT 1983)★★★, To Be Or Not To Be (Contour 1983)★★★, 12 Gold Bars Volume II (Vertigo 1984)★★★, Na Na Na (Flashback 1985)★★★, Collection: Status Quo (Castle 1985)★★★, Quotations Vol. 1: The Beginning (PRT 1987)★★★, Quotations: Vol. 2 (PRT 1987)★★★, From The Beginning (PRT 1988)★★★, C.90 Collector (Legacy 1989)★★★, B-Sides And Rarities (Castle 1990)★★★, The Early Works 1968 - '73 CD box set (Essential 1990)★★★, Rocking All Over The Years (Vertigo 1991)★★★★, The Other Side Of Status Quo (Connoisseur 1995)★★★, Whatever You Want: The Very Best Of Status Quo (PolyGram TV 1997)★★★★, The Singles Collection 1966-73 (Castle 1999)★★★★, Matchstickmen: The Psychedelic Years (Select 1999)★★★, The Technicolor Dreams Of The Status Quo: The Complete 60s Recordings (Castle 2001)★★★, Down The Dustpipe (Sanctuary 2001)★★★, The 70s Singles Box (Sanctuary 2001)★★★, Rockers Rollin': Quo In Time 1972-2000 4-CD box set (Mercury 2001)★★★.
VIDEOS: Off The Road (VCL 1980), Live At The N.E.C. (PolyGram Music Video 1983), End Of The Road '84 (Videoform 1984), More From The End Of The Road (Videoform 1985), Preserved (Heron 1985), Rocking Through The Years (Channel 5 1986), The Status Quo Video Box (Channel 5 1989), Rocking All Over The Years (Channel 5 1990), Anniversary Waltz (Castle Music Pictures 1991), Rock 'Til You Drop (PolyGram Music Video 1991), One To One - Rossi & Parfitt (Video Collection 1991), Knebworth '90 (Castle Music Pictures 1991), Live Alive Quo (PolyGram Music Video 1992), Don't Stop (PolyGram Music Video 1996), Famous In The Last Century (Universal 2001).
FURTHER READING: Status Quo: The Authorized Biography, John Shearlaw. Status Quo: The Authorized Biography - The 20th Anniversary Edition, John Shearlaw. Status Quo, Tom Hibbert. Again And Again, Bob Young and John Shearlaw Status Quo: Rockin' All Over The World, Neil Jeffries. Status Quo: The Authorized Biography - The 25th Anniversary Edition, John Shearlaw. Just For The Record: The Autobiography Of Status Quo, Francis Rossi and Rick Parfitt with Cindy Blake and Roger Kasper. Quotographs: Celebrating 30 Years Of Status Quo, Bob Young. Rockers Rollin': The Story Of Status Quo, Dave Oxley.

STEALERS WHEEL
ALBUMS: Stealers Wheel (A&M 1972)★★★★, Ferguslie Park (A&M 1973)★★★★, Right Or Wrong (A&M 1975)★★★.
COMPILATIONS: The Best Of Stealers Wheel (A&M 1978) ★★★, Stuck In The Middle With You: The Hits Collection (Spectrum 1998)★★★.

STEELEYE SPAN
ALBUMS: Hark! The Village Wait (RCA 1970)★★★★, Please To See The King (B&C 1971)★★★★, Ten Man Mop, Or Mr. Reservoir Strikes Again (Chrysalis 1971)★★★, Below The Salt (Chrysalis 1972)★★★, Parcel Of Rogues (Chrysalis 1973)★★★, Now We Are Six (Chrysalis 1974) ★★★, Commoners Crown (Chrysalis 1975)★★★, All Around My Hat (Chrysalis 1975)★★★, Rocket Cottage (Chrysalis 1976)★★, Storm Force Ten (Chrysalis 1977) ★★★, Live At Last! (Chrysalis 1978)★★, Sails Of Silver (Chrysalis 1980)★★★, Recollections Australia only (Chrysalis 1981)★★, On Tour Australia only (Chrysalis 1983)★★, Back In Line (Flutterby 1986)★★★, Tempted And Tried (Dover 1989) ★★★, Tonight's The Night Live (Park 1992)★★, Steeleye Span In Concert (Park 1994)★★, Time (Park 1996)★★★, Horkstow Grange (Park 1998)★★★, The Journey 1995 recording (Park 1999)★★★, Bedlam Born (Park 2000)★★★.
COMPILATIONS: Individually And Collectively (Charisma 1972)★★★, Steeleye Span Almanack (Charisma 1973) ★★★, Original Masters (Chrysalis 1977)★★★, Time Span (Mooncrest 1977)★★, Steeleye Span Volume One (Chrysalis 1978)★★★, Adam Catched Eve (Boulevard 1979)★★, Steeleye Span (Pickwick 1980)★★, The Best Of Steeleye Span (Chrysalis 1984)★★★★, Steeleye Span (Cambra 1984)★★★, Portfolio (Chrysalis 1988)★★★, Steeleye Span: The Early Years (Connoisseur 1989)★★, The Collection (Castle 1991)★★★, Spanning The Years (Chrysalis 1995) ★★★, A Stack Of Steeleye Span (Their Finest Folk Recordings 1973-1975) (Emporio 1996)★★, The King: The Best Of Steeleye Span (Mooncrest 1996)★★★, Original Masters (BG 1996)★★★★, The Hills Of Greenmore (Snapper 1998)★★★, A Rare Collection (Raven 1999)★★★.
VIDEOS: Time (Park 1996).

STEELY DAN
ALBUMS: You Gotta Walk It Like You Talk It (Or You'll Lose That Beat) film soundtrack (Spark 1970)★★, Can't Buy A Thrill (ABC 1972)★★★★, Countdown To Ecstasy (ABC 1973)★★★★, Pretzel Logic (ABC 1974)★★★★, Katy Lied (ABC 1975)★★★, The Royal Scam (ABC 1976)★★★★, Aja (ABC 1977)★★★★, Gaucho (MCA 1980)★★★, Alive In America 1993, 1994 recordings (Giant/BMG 1995)★★, Two Against Nature (Giant 2000)★★★.
COMPILATIONS: Greatest Hits (ABC 1978)★★★, Gold (MCA 1982)★★★, A Decade Of Steely Dan (MCA 1985) ★★★★, Berry Town (Bellaphon 1986)★★, Sun Mountain (Showcase 1986)★★, Reelin' In The Years: The Very Best Of Steely Dan (Telstar 1987)★★★★, Old Regime (Thunderbolt 1987)★★, Stone Piano (Thunderbolt 1988)★★, Gold (Expanded Edition) (MCA 1991)★★★, Citizen Steely Dan, 1972-80 4-CD box set (MCA 1993)★★★★, Remastered: The Best Of (MCA 1994)★★★★, Forward Into The Past: Becker & Fagen: The Early Years (Beacon 1997)★★, Showbiz Kids: The Steely Dan Story 1972-1980 (MCA 2000)★★★★.
VIDEOS: Two Against Nature (Aviva 2000).
FURTHER READING: Steely Dan: Reelin' In The Years, Brian Sweet.

STEPPENWOLF
ALBUMS: Steppenwolf (Dunhill 1968)★★★, The Second (Dunhill 1968)★★★, Steppenwolf At Your Birthday Party (Dunhill 1969)★★★, Early Steppenwolf (Dunhill 1969)★★, Monster (Dunhill 1969)★★★★, Steppenwolf 'Live' (Dunhill 1970)★★, Steppenwolf 7 (Dunhill 1970)★★, For Ladies Only (Dunhill 1971)★★★, Slow Flux (Mums 1974)★★, Hour Of The Wolf (Epic 1975)★★, Skullduggery (Epic 1976)★★, Live In London (Attic 1982)★★, Wolf Tracks (Attic 1982)★★, Rock & Roll Rebels (Qwil 1987)★★, Rise And Shine (I.R.S. 1990)★★.
SOLO: John Kay: The Lost Heritage Tapes (Macola 1998) ★★, Heretics And Privateers (Cannonball 2001)★★★.
COMPILATIONS: Steppenwolf Gold (Dunhill 1971)★★★, Rest In Peace (Dunhill 1972)★★★, 16 Greatest Hits (Dunhill 1973)★★★★, Masters Of Rock (Dunhill 1975)★★★, Golden Greats (MCA 1985)★★★, Born To Be Wild: Retrospective (MCA 1991)★★★, All Time Greatest Hits (MCA 1999)★★★★.

STEPS
ALBUMS: Step One (Jive 1998)★★★, Steptacular (Jive 1999)★★, Buzz (Jive 2000)★★.
COMPILATIONS: Gold: Greatest Hits (Jive 2001)★★★.
VIDEOS: The Video (Zoo 1998), The Steps Story: Unauthorised (Visual Entertainment 1999), The Next Step: Live (Jive 2000).

STEREO MC'S
ALBUMS: 33, 45,78 (4th & Broadway 1989)★★★, Supernatural (4th & Broadway 1990)★★★, Connected (4th & Broadway 1992)★★★★, Deep Down & Dirty (Island 2001)★★★.
COMPILATIONS: DJ-Kicks (Studio !K7 2000)★★★★.
VIDEOS: Connected (4th & Broadway 1993).

STEREOLAB
ALBUMS: Peng! (Too Pure 1992)★★★, The Groop Played Space Age Bachelor Pad Music mini-album (Too Pure 1993) ★★★★, Transient Random Noise-Bursts With Announcements (Duophonic 1993)★★★, Mars Audiac Quintet (Duophonic 1994)★★★★, Music For The Amorphous Body Study Centre mini-album (Duophonic 1995)★★★, Emperor Tomato Ketchup (Duophonic 1996)★★★★, Dots And Loops (Duophonic 1997)★★★★, Cobra And Phases Group Play Voltage In The Milky Night (Duophonic 1999)★★★★, The First Of The Microbe Hunters mini-album (Duophonic 2000)★★★, Sound-Dust (Duophonic 2001)★★★.
COMPILATIONS: Switched On (Too Pure 1992)★★★, Refried Ectoplasm (Switched On Volume 2) (Duophonic 1995)★★★, Aluminium Tunes (Switched On Volume 3) (Duophonic 1998)★★★.

STEREOPHONICS
ALBUMS: Word Gets Around (V2 1997)★★★★, Performance And Cocktails (V2 1999)★★★★, Just Enough Education To Perform (V2 2001)★★★.
VIDEOS: Word Gets Around (PAL 1998), Cwmaman Feel The Noize: Live At Cardiff Castle (Visual Entertainment 1999), Performance And Cocktails Live At Morfa Stadium (Visual Entertainment 1999), Call Us What You Want But Don't Call Us In The Morning: The Performance & Cocktails Video Collection (Visual Entertainment 2000).
FURTHER READING: High Times & Headlines: The Story Of Stereophonics, Mike Black. Stereophonics: Just Enough Evidence To Print, Danny O'Connor

STEVENS, CAT
ALBUMS: Matthew & Son (Deram 1967)★★★, New Masters (Deram 1968)★★★, Mona Bone Jakon (Island 1970)★★★, Tea For The Tillerman (Island 1970)★★★★, Teaser & The Firecat (Island 1971)★★★★, Catch Bull At Four (Island 1972)★★★★, Foreigner (Island 1973)★★, Buddha And The Chocolate Box (Island 1974)★★, Numbers (Island 1975)H, Izitso (Island 1977)★, Back To Earth (Island 1978)★★. As Yusuf Islam The Life Of The Last Prophet (Mountain Of Light 1995)★, Prayers Of The Last Prophet (Mountain Of Light 1997)★, A Is For Allah (Mountain Of Light 1999)★.
COMPILATIONS: Very Young And Early Songs (Deram 1972)★★, View From The Top (Deram 1974)★★, Greatest Hits (Island 1975)★★★★, The Very Best Of Cat Stevens (Island 1990)★★★★, Remember Cat Stevens: The Ultimate Collection (Island 1999)★★★★, The Very Best Of Cat Stevens (UTV 2000)★★★★, On The Road To Find Out 4-CD box set (Island 2001)★★★.
VIDEOS: Tea For The Tillerman Live – The Best Of (Island 1993).
FURTHER READING: Cat Stevens, Chris Charlesworth.

STEVENS, SHAKIN'
ALBUMS: with the Sunsets A Legend (Parlophone 1970)★★, with the Sunsets I'm No J.D. (Columbia 1971)★★★, with the Sunsets Rockin' And Shakin' (Contour 1972)★★, with the Sunsets Shakin' Stevens And The Sunsets (Emerald 1973)★★, Shakin' Stevens (Track 1977)★★, Take One! (Epic 1979) ★★★, This Ole House (Epic 1981)★★★, Shaky (Epic 1981) ★★★★, Give Me Your Heart Tonight (Epic 1982)★★, The Bop Won't Stop (Epic 1983)★★, Lipstick, Powder And Paint (Epic 1985)★★★, Let's Boogie (Epic 1987)★★, A Whole Lotta Shaky (Epic 1988)★★, Rock 'N' Roll (Telstar 1990)★★, Merry Christmas Everyone (Epic 1991)★.
COMPILATIONS: Greatest Hits (Epic 1984)★★★, with the Sunsets The Collection (Castle 1986)★★, The Track Years (MFP 1986)★★, with the Sunsets Good Rockin' Tonight (Pickwick 1987)★★, with the Sunsets Outlaw Man (Spectrum 1988)★★, The Epic Years (Epic 1992)★★★, Greatest Hits (Rhino 1995)★★★★, The Very Best Of Shakin' Stevens released in Norway only (Epic 1999)★★★.
VIDEOS: Shakin' Stevens Video Show Volumes 1&2 (CMV 1989).

STEWART, AL
ALBUMS: Bedsitter Images (CBS 1967)★★★, Love Chronicles (CBS/Epic 1969)★★★★, Zero She Flies (CBS 1970)★★★, The First Album (Bedsitter Images) (CBS 1970)★★★, Orange (CBS 1972)★★★, Past, Present And Future (CBS/Janus 1973)★★★, Modern Times (CBS/Janus 1975)★★★, Year Of The Cat (RCA/Janus 1976)★★★★, Time Passages (RCA/ Arista 1978)★★, 24 P/Carrots (RCA/Arista 1980)★★★, Indian Summer/Live (RCA/Arista 1981)★★★, Russians And Americans (RCA/Passport 1984)★★★, Last Days Of The Century (Enigma 1988) ★★★, with Peter White Rhymes In Rooms (EMI/Mesa 1992)★★★, Famous Last Words (Permanent/Mesa 1993) ★★★, with Laurence Juber Between The Wars (EMI/Mesa 1995)★★★, Seemed Like A Good Idea At The Time (Acoustic 1996)★★, Down In The Cellar (Miramar 2001)★★★.
COMPILATIONS: The Early Years (RCA/Janus 1977)★★★, The Best Of Al Stewart (RCA/Arista 1985)★★★, Chronicles (Fame/EMI 1991)★★★★, To Whom It May Concern: Al Stewart 1966-1970 (EMI 1993)★★★.

STEWART, ROD
ALBUMS: An Old Raincoat Won't Ever Let You Down (Vertigo 1970)★★★★, Gasoline Alley (Vertigo 1970)★★★★, Every Picture Tells A Story (Mercury 1971)★★★★, Never A Dull Moment (Mercury 1972)★★★★, Smiler (Mercury 1974) ★★★, Atlantic Crossing (Warners 1975)★★★, A Night On The Town (Riva 1976)★★★★, Foot Loose And Fancy Free (Riva 1977)★★, Blondes Have More Fun (Riva 1978)★★, Foolish Behaviour (Riva 1980)H, Tonight I'm Yours (Riva 1981)★★, Absolutely Live (Riva 1982)H, Body Wishes (Warners 1983)H, Camouflage (Warners 1984)H, Out Of Order (Warners 1988)★★, Vagabond Heart (Warners 1991) ★★★, Unplugged And Seated (Warners 1993)★★★★, A Spanner In The Works (Warners 1995)★★★, If We Fall In Love Tonight (Warners 1996)★★★, When We Were The New Boys (Warners 1998)★★★★, Human (Atlantic 2001)★★★★.
COMPILATIONS: Sing It Again Rod (Mercury 1973)★★★★, The Vintage Years (Mercury 1976)★★★, Recorded Highlights And Action Replays (Philips 1976)★★★, The Best Of Rod Stewart (Mercury 1977)★★★★, The Best Of Rod Stewart Volume 2 (Mercury 1977)★★★, Rod Stewart's Greatest Hits Volume 1 (Riva 1979)★★★, Hot Rods (Mercury 1980)★★, Maggie May (Pickwick 1981)★★, Jukebox Heaven (Pickwick 1987)★★, The Best Of Rod Stewart (Warners 1989)★★★★, Storyteller (Warners 1989)★★★★, The Early Years (Warners 1992)★★★, Lead Vocalist (Warners 1993)★★★, The Very Best Of Rod Stewart (Mercury 1998)★★★★, 1964-1969 (Pilot 2000)★★★, A Little Misunderstood: The Sixties Sessions (Yeaah! 2001)★★★, Voice: The Very Best Of Rod Stewart (Rhino 2001)★★★★, The Story So Far: The Very Best Of (Warners 2001)★★★★.
FURTHER READING: The Rod Stewart Story, George Tremlett. Rod Stewart And The Faces, John Pidgeon. Rod Stewart: A Biography In Words & Pictures, Richard Cromelin. Rod Stewart, Tony Jasper. Rod Stewart: A Life On The Town, Peter Burton. Rod Stewart, Gerd Rockl and Paul Sahner. Rod Stewart, Paul Nelson and Lester Bangs. Rod Stewart: A Biography, Tim Ewbank and Stafford Hildred. Rod Stewart: Vagabond Heart, Geoffrey Guiliano.

STIFF LITTLE FINGERS
ALBUMS: Inflammable Material (Rough Trade 1979)★★★, Nobody's Heroes (Chrysalis 1980)★★★, Hanx! (Chrysalis 1980)★★, Go For It! (Chrysalis 1981)★★★, Now Then (Chrysalis 1982)★★, Flags And Emblems (Essential 1991) ★★, Fly The Flag (Essential 1993)★★, Get A Life (Castle 1994)★★, Pure Fingers Live - St. Patrix 1993 (Dojo 1995) ★★, Tinderbox (Abstract 1997)★★★, And Best Of All .../Hope Street (EMI 1999)★★★.
COMPILATIONS: All The Best (Chrysalis 1983)★★★, Live And Loud (Link 1988)★★, No Sleep Till Belfast (Kaz 1988)★★, See You Up There (Virgin 1989)★★, Live In Sweden (Limited Edition 1989)★★, The Peel Sessions (Strange Fruit 1989)★★, Greatest Hits Live (Link 1991)★★, Alternative Chartbusters (Link 1991)★★, Tin Soldiers (Harry May 1999)★★.

STILLS, STEPHEN
ALBUMS: with Mike Bloomfield, Al Kooper Super Session (Columbia 1968)★★★★, Stephen Stills (Atlantic 1970) ★★★★★, Stephen Stills 2 (Atlantic 1971)★★★★, Stills (Columbia 1975)★★★★, Stephen Stills Live (Atlantic 1975) ★★★, Illegal Stills (Columbia 1976)★★, Thoroughfare Gap (Columbia 1978)H, Right By You (Atlantic 1984)★★★, Stills Alone (Gold Hill 1991)★★★.
COMPILATIONS: Still Stills (Atlantic 1976)★★★.
FURTHER READING: Crosby, Stills, Nash & Young: The Visual Documentary, Johnny Rogan. Crosby, Stills & Nash: The Biography, Dave Zimmer and Henry Diltz. For What It's Worth: The Story Of Buffalo Springfield, John Einarson and Richie Furay. Prisoner Of Woodstock, Dallas Taylor.

STING
ALBUMS: Dream Of The Blue Turtles (A&M 1985)★★★, Bring On The Night (A&M 1986)★★, ... Nothing Like The Sun (A&M 1987)★★★★, Nado Como El Sol mini-album (A&M 1988)★★★, The Soul Cages (A&M 1991)★★★, Acoustic Live In Newcastle mini-album (A&M 1991)★★★, Ten Summoner's Tales (A&M 1993)★★★★, Mercury Falling (A&M 1996)★★★, Brand New Day (A&M 1999)★★★, ... All This Time (A&M 2001)★★.
COMPILATIONS: Fields Of Gold 1984-1994 (A&M 1994) ★★★★, The Best Of Sting/The Police (A&M 1997)★★★★.
VIDEOS: Bring On The Night (A&M Sound Pictures 1987), Sting: The Videos (A&M Sound Pictures 1988), The Soul Cages Concert (A&M Video 1991), Live At The Hague (PolyGram Music Video 1991), Unplugged (A&M Video 1992), Ten Summoner's Tales (A&M Video 1993), The Best Of Sting: Fields Of Gold 1984-94 (A&M Video 1994), The Brand New Day Tour: Live From The Universal Amphitheatre (PolyGram Music Video 2000), ... All This Time (Universal 2002).
FURTHER READING: Sting: A Biography, Robert Sellers. The Secret Life Of Gordon Sumner, Wensley Clarkson. Complete Guide To The Music Of: The Police And Sting, Chris Welch. Demolition Man, Christopher Sandford.
FILMS: Quadrophenia (1979), Radio On (1980), Artemis '81 (1980), Brimstone And Treacle (1982), Dune (1984), Plenty (1985), Bring On The Night (1985), Stormy Monday (1988), Julia Julia (1988), Lock, Stock And Two Smoking Barrels (1998).

STOCK, AITKEN AND WATERMAN
COMPILATIONS: Hit Factory (PWL 1987)★★★, Hit Factory, Volume 2 (PWL 1988)★★★, Hit Factory, Volume 3 (PWL 1989)★★★, The Best Of Stock, Aitken And Waterman (PWL 1990)★★★.
VIDEOS: Roadblock (Touchstone Video 1988).
FURTHER READING: I Wish I Was Me, Pete Waterman.

STONE ROSES
ALBUMS: The Stone Roses (Silvertone 1989)★★★★, Second Coming (Geffen 1995)★★★.
COMPILATIONS: Turns Into Stone (Silvertone 1992)★★★, The Complete Stone Roses (Silvertone 1995)★★★, Garage Flower (Silvertone 1996)★★, The Remixes (Silvertone 2000)★★.
VIDEOS: The Complete Stone Roses (Wienerworld 1995).
FURTHER READING: The Stone Roses And The Resurrection Of British Pop, John Robb. Breaking Into Heaven: The Rise And Fall Of The Stone Roses, Mick Middles.

STONE TEMPLE PILOTS
ALBUMS: Core (Atlantic 1992)★★★, Purple (Atlantic 1994)★★★★, Tiny Music ... Songs From The Vatican Gift Shop (Atlantic 1996)★★★, No. 4 (Atlantic 1999)★★, Shangri-La Dee Da (Atlantic 2001)★★★.
SOLO: Scott Weiland 12 Bar Blues (East West 1998)★★★.
FURTHER READING: Stone Temple Pilots, Mike Wall and Malcolm Dome.

STONE, ANGIE
ALBUMS: Black Diamond (Arista 1999)★★★★, Mahogany Soul (J 2001)★★★.

STOOGES
ALBUMS: The Stooges (Elektra 1969)★★★★, Funhouse (Elektra 1970)★★★★, as Iggy And The Stooges Raw Power (Columbia 1973)★★★★, Metallic KO 1974 recording (SkyDog 1976)★★★, Rubber Legs rare recordings from 1973/1974 (Fan Club 1988)★★, Open Up And Bleed (Bomp 1996)★★, Metallic KO reissue featuring additional 1973 concert (Jungle 1998)★★★.
COMPILATIONS: as Iggy Pop And James Williamson Kill City (Bomp 1977)★★, No Fun (Elektra 1980)★★, as Iggy And The Stooges I'm Sick Of You (Line 1981)★★, I Gotta Right (Invasion 1983)★★.
FURTHER READING: Raw Power: Iggy And The Stooges 1972, Mick Rock.

STRANGLERS
ALBUMS: Rattus Norvegicus (United Artists 1977)★★★★, No More Heroes (United Artists 1977)★★★★, Black And White (United Artists 1978)★★★, Live (X Cert) (United Artists 1978)★★, The Raven (United Artists 1979)★★★, IV US only (I.R.S. 1980)★★★, The Meninblack (Liberty 1981)★★★, La Folie (Liberty 1981)★★★★, Feline (Epic 1983)★★★, Aural Sculpture (Epic 1984)★★★, Dreamtime (Epic 1986)★★, All Live And All Of The Night (Epic 1988)★★, 10 (Epic 1990)★★, Stranglers In The Night (Psycho 1992)★★, Death & Night & Blood (Receiver 1994)★★, About Time (When! 1995)★★, The Stranglers And Friends: Live In Concert 1980 recording (Receiver 1995)★★★, Written In Red (When! 1997)★★, Friday The Thirteenth: Live At The Royal Albert Hall (Eagle 1997)★★★, Live At The Hammersmith Odeon '81 (EMI 1998)★★, Coup De Grace (Eagle 1998)★★, 5 Live 01 (SPV 2001)★★★★.
COMPILATIONS: The Collection 1977-82 (Liberty 1982) ★★★, Off The Beaten Track (Liberty 1986)★★, Singles (The U.A. Years) (EMI 1989)★★★★, Greatest Hits: 1977-1990 (Epic 1990)★★★★, All Twelve Inches (Epic 1992)★★, The Early Years: 74-75-76 Rare, Live & Unreleased (Newspeak 1992)H, The Old Testament (The UA Recordings 1977-1982) 4-CD box set (EMI 1992)★★★★, Saturday Night Sunday Morning (Castle 1993)★★, Strangled: From Birth And Beyond (SIS 1993)★★, The Hit Men (EMI 1997)★★★★, The Collection (EMI 1997)★★★, The Epic Years (Epic 1997) ★★★, The Masters (Eagle 1998)★★, The Collection (Disky 1998)★★, Hits Collection (EMI 1999)★★★, Hits And Heroes (EMI 1999)★★★.
VIDEOS: The Video Collection (EMI 1982), Screentime (CBS/Fox 1986), The Meninblack In Colour 1983-1990 (SMV 1991), The Old Testament (PMI 1992), Saturday Night Sunday Morning (Castle 1993), Friday The Thirteenth (Eagle Rock 1997), The Stranglers - Live At Alexandra Palace (Castle 2000).
FURTHER READING: Inside Information, Hugh Cornwell. Much Ado About Nothing, Jet Black. No Mercy: The Authorised And Uncensored Biography Of The Stranglers, David Buckley. The Stranglers Song By Song, Hugh Cornwell with Jim Drury.

STRAWBERRY ALARM CLOCK
ALBUMS: Incense And Peppermints (Uni 1967)★★★, Wake Up It's Tomorrow (Uni 1967)★★, The World In A Seashell (Uni 1968)★★, Good Morning Starshine (Uni 1969)★★.
COMPILATIONS: The Best Of The Strawberry Alarm Clock (Uni 1970)★★★, Changes (Vocalion 1971)★★.

STRAWBS
ALBUMS: Strawbs (A&M 1969)★★★★, Dragonfly (A&M 1970)★★★, Just A Collection Of Antiques And Curios (A&M 1970)★★★, From The Witchwood (A&M 1971)★★★, Grave New World (A&M 1972)★★★★, as Sandy Denny And The Strawbs All Our Own Work (A&M 1973)★★★, Bursting At The Seams (A&M 1973)★★★, Hero And Heroine (A&M 1974)★★★, Ghosts (A&M 1975)★★★, Nomadness (A&M 1976)★★★, Deep Cuts (Oyster 1976)★★★, Burning For You (Oyster 1977)★★★, Dead Lines (Arista 1978)★★★, Don't Say Goodbye (Toots 1987)★★★.
COMPILATIONS: Strawbs By Choice (A&M 1974)★★★, Best Of The Strawbs (A&M 1978)★★★, A Choice Collection (1992)★★★, Uncanned Preserves (Road Goes On Forever 1992)★★★, Greatest Hits Live (Road Goes On Forever 1994)★★, Heartbreak Hill (Road Goes On Forever 1995)★★★, In Concert (Windsong 1995)★★★, Halcyon Days: The Very Best Of The Strawbs (A&M 1997)★★★.

STROKES
ALBUMS: Is This It (Rough Trade/RCA 2001)★★★★.

STYLE COUNCIL
ALBUMS: Introducing The Style Council mini-album (Polydor 1983)★★★, Caféé Bleu (UK) My Ever Changing Moods (US) (Polydor/Geffen 1984)★★★, Our Favourite Shop (UK) Internationalists (US) (Polydor/Geffen 1985)★★★★, Live! The Style Council, Home & Abroad (Polydor/Geffen 1986)★★, The Cost Of Loving (Polydor 1987)★★, Confessions Of A Pop Group (Polydor 1988)★★.
COMPILATIONS: The Singular Adventures Of The Style Council: Greatest Hits Vol. 1 (Polydor 1989)★★★★, Here's Some That Got Away (Polydor 1993)★★, The Style Council Collection (Polydor 1996)★★★, The Style Council In Concert (Polydor 1998)★★, The Complete Adventures Of The Style Council 5-CD box set (Polydor 1998)★★★, Greatest Hits (Polydor 2000)★★★★, The Collection (Spectrum 2001)★★★.
VIDEOS: What We Did On Our Holidays (PolyGram Music Video 1983), Far East & Far Out: Council Meeting In Japan (PolyGram Music Video 1984), What We Did The Following Year (PolyGram Music Video 1985), Showbiz!, The Style Council Live (PolyGram Music Video 1986), JerUSAlem (Palace Video 1987), Confessions Of A Pop Group (Channel 5 Video 1988), The Video Adventures Of The Style Council (Channel 5/PolyGram Music Video 1989).
FURTHER READING: Mr Cool's Dream – The Complete History Of The Style Council, Ian Munn.

STYLISTICS
ALBUMS: The Stylistics (Avco 1971)★★★, Round 2: The Stylistics (Avco 1972)★★★, Rockin' Roll Baby (Avco 1973) ★★★★, Let's Put It All Together (Avco 1974)★★★★, Heavy (US) From The Mountain (UK) (Avco 1974)★★★, Thank You Baby (Avco 1975)★★★, You Are Beautiful (Avco 1975) ★★★, Fabulous (H&L 1976)★★★, Once Upon A Juke Box (H&L 1976)★★★, Sun And Soul (H&L 1977)★★★, Wonder Woman (H&L 1978)★★★, In Fashion (H&L 1978)★★★, Black Satin (H&L 1979)★★★, Love Spell (Mercury 1979)★★★, Live In Japan (Flyover 1979)★★, Hurry Up This Way Again (TSOP/Philadelphia International 1980)★★★★, Closer Than Close (TSOP/Philadelphia International 1981)★★★, 1982 (TSOP/Philadelphia International 1982)★★★, Some Things Never Change (Streetwise 1985)★★, Love Talk (Amherst 1991)★★, Christmas (Amherst 1992)★★, Love Is Back In Style (Marathon 1996)★★.
COMPILATIONS: The Best Of The Stylistics (Avco 1975) ★★★★, Spotlight On The Stylistics (Spotlight 1977)★★★★, All About Love (Contour 1981)★★★, Very Best Of The Stylistics (H&L 1983)★★★★, The Great Love Hits (Contour 1983)★★★.

STYX
ALBUMS: Styx (Wooden Nickel 1972)★★, Styx II (Wooden Nickel 1973)★★★, The Serpent Is Rising (Wooden Nickel 1973)★★★, Man Of Miracles (Wooden Nickel 1974)★★★, Equinox (A&M 1975)★★★, Crystal Ball (A&M 1976)★★★, The Grand Illusion (A&M 1977)★★★, Pieces Of Eight (A&M 1978)★★★, Cornerstone (A&M 1979)★★★, Paradise Theatre (A&M 1980)★★★★, Kilroy Was Here (A&M 1983) ★★★, Caught In The Act/Live (A&M 1984)★★, Edge Of The Century (A&M 1990)★★★, Return To Paradise (CMC International 1997)★★, Brave New World (CMC 1999)★★, with REO Speedwagon Live At Riverport (Sanctuary 2000) ★★★, Styxworld Live 2001 (Sanctuary 2001)★★★.
COMPILATIONS: The Best Of Styx (A&M 1979)★★★, Classics Volume 15 (A&M 1987)★★★.
VIDEOS: Caught In The Act (A&M Video 1984), Return To Paradise (BMG 1997).

SUEDE
ALBUMS: Suede (Nude 1993)★★★★, Dog Man Star (Nude 1994)★★★, Coming Up (Nude 1996)★★★★, Head Music (Nude 1999)★★★.
COMPILATIONS: Sci-Fi Lullabies (Nude 1997)★★★★.
VIDEOS: Love & Poison (Nude 1993), Bootleg 1 (Nude 1993), Introducing The Band (Nude 1995), Lost In TV (Nude 2001).
FURTHER READING: Suede: The Illustrated Biography, York Membrey.

SUGAR
ALBUMS: Copper Blue (Creation 1992)★★★★, Beaster mini-album (Creation 1993)★★★★, F.U.E.L. (File Under Easy Listening) (Creation 1994)★★.
COMPILATIONS: Besides (Rykodisk 1995)★★.

SUGAR RAY
ALBUMS: Lemonade And Brownies (Atlantic 1995)★★, Floored (Atlantic 1997)★★★, 14:59 (Atlantic 1999)★★★, Sugar Ray (Atlantic 2001)★★★.

SUGARCUBES
ALBUMS: Life's Too Good (One Little Indian 1988)★★★★, Here Today, Tomorrow, Next Week (One Little Indian 1989) ★★, Stick Around For Joy (One Little Indian 1992)★★★, It's It remixes (One Little Indian 1992)★★.
COMPILATIONS: The Great Crossover Potential (One Little Indian 1998)★★★.

SUM 41
ALBUMS: Half Hour Of Power (Aquarius/Island 2000) ★★★, All Killer No Filler (Aquarius/Island 2001)★★★★.

SUMMER, DONNA
ALBUMS: Love To Love You Baby (Oasis 1975)★★★, A Love Trilogy (Oasis 1976)★★, Four Seasons Of Love (Casablanca 1976)★★, I Remember Yesterday (Casablanca 1977)★★★, Once Upon A Time (Casablanca 1977)★★★, Live And More (Casablanca 1978)★★, Bad Girls (Casablanca 1979) ★★★★, The Wanderer (Geffen 1980)★★★★, Donna Summer (Geffen 1982)★★★, She Works Hard For The Money (Mercury 1983)★★★★, Cats Without Claws (Geffen 1984)★★, All Systems Go (Geffen 1987)★★, Another Place And Time (Warners 1989)★★, Love Is Gonna Change (Atlantic 1990)★★, Mistaken Identity (Atlantic 1991)★★, This Time I Know It's For Real (Alex 1993)★★, I'm A Rainbow 1981 recording (PolyGram 1996)★★★, VH1 Presents Live And More Encore! (Epic 1999)★★★.
COMPILATIONS: On The Radio: Greatest Hits, Volumes 1 And 2 (Casablanca 1979)★★★★, Walk Away: Collector's Edition (The Best Of 1977-1980) (Casablanca 1980)★★★, The Best Of Donna Summer (East West 1990)★★★★, The Donna Summer Anthology (Casablanca 1993)★★★, Endless Summer: Donna Summer's Greatest Hits (Mercury 1994)★★★, Greatest Hits (PolyGram 1998)★★★.
FURTHER READING: Donna Summer: An Unauthorized Biography, James Haskins.

SUPER FURRY ANIMALS
ALBUMS: Fuzzy Logic (Creation/Sony 1996)★★★★, Radiator (Creation/Flydaddy 1997)★★★★, Guerilla (Creation/Flydaddy 1999)★★★★, Mwng (Ankst 2000)★★★, Rings Around The World (Epic 2001)★★★★.
COMPILATIONS: Out Spaced (Creation 1998)★★★.

SUPERGRASS
ALBUMS: I Should Coco (Parlophone/Capitol 1995) ★★★★, In It For The Money (Parlophone/Capitol 1997) ★★★★, Supergrass (Parlophone/Island 1999)★★★.
FURTHER READING: Supergrass, Linda Holorny.

SUPERTRAMP
ALBUMS: Supertramp (A&M 1970)★★, Indelibly Stamped (A&M 1971)★★, Crime Of The Century (A&M 1974)★★★★, Crisis? What Crisis? (A&M 1975)★★★★, Even In The Quietest Moments (A&M 1977)★★★, Breakfast In America (A&M 1979)★★★★, Paris (A&M 1980)★★, Famous Last Words (A&M 1982)★★★, Brother Where You Bound (A&M 1985)★★, Free As A Bird (A&M 1987)★★, Supertramp Live 88 (A&M 1988)★★, Some Things Never Change (Chrysalis 1997)★★★, It Was The Best Of Times (EMI 1999)★★★, Is Everybody Listening 1976 live recording (Burning Airlines 2001)★★.
COMPILATIONS: The Autobiography Of Supertramp (A&M 1986)★★★, The Very Best Of Supertramp (A&M 1992) ★★★★.
FURTHER READING: The Supertramp Book, Martin Melhuish.

SUPREMES
ALBUMS: Meet The Supremes (Motown 1963)★★★, Where Did Our Love Go? (Motown 1964)★★★, A Bit Of Liverpool (Motown 1964)★★, The Supremes Sing Country, Western And Pop (Motown 1964)H, We Remember Sam Cooke (Motown 1965)★★★, More Hits By The Supremes (Motown 1965)★★★, Merry Christmas (Motown 1965)★★★, The Supremes At The Copa (Motown 1965)★★★, I Hear A Symphony (Motown 1966)★★★, The Supremes A-Go-Go (Motown 1966)★★★, The Supremes Sing Holland, Dozier, Holland (Motown 1967)★★★★, The Supremes Sing Rodgers And Hart (Motown 1967)★★, Right On (Motown 1970) ★★★, with the Four Tops The Magnificent Seven (Motown 1970)★★★★, New Ways But Love Stays (Motown 1970) ★★★, Touch (Motown 1971)★★, with the Four Tops The Return Of The Magnificent Seven (Motown 1971)★★, with the Four Tops Dynamite (Motown 1971)★★★, Floy Joy (Motown 1972)★★★, The Supremes (Motown 1975)★★, High Energy (Motown 1976)★★, Mary, Scherrie And Susaye (Motown 1976)★★★. As Diana Ross And The Supremes: Reflections (Motown 1968)★★★, Diana Ross And The Supremes Sing And Perform 'Funny Girl' (Motown 1968)H, Diana Ross And The Supremes Live At London's Talk Of The Town (Motown 1968)★★★, with the Temptations Diana Ross And The Supremes Join The Temptations (Motown 1968) ★★★, Love Child (Motown 1968)★★★, with the Temptations TCB (Motown 1968)★★★, Let The Sunshine In (Motown 1969)★★, with the Temptations Together (Motown 1969) ★★★, Cream Of The Crop (Motown 1969)★★, with the Temptations Diana Ross And The Supremes On Broadway (Motown 1969)★★, Farewell (Motown 1970)★★.
COMPILATIONS: Diana Ross And The Supremes Greatest Hits (Motown 1967)★★★★, Diana Ross And The Supremes Greatest Hits, Volume 2 (Motown 1967)★★★★, Diana Ross And The Supremes Greatest Hits, Volume 3 (Motown 1969) ★★★, Anthology 1962-69 (Motown 1974)★★★★, Supremes At Their Best (Motown 1978)★★★, 20 Greatest Hits (Motown 1986)★★★★, 25th Anniversary (Motown 1986)★★★★, Early Classics (Spectrum 1996)★★★, The Ultimate Collection (Motown 1998)★★★★, The Supremes 5-CD box set (Motown 2000)★★★★.
FURTHER READING: Reflections, Johnny Bond. Dreamgirl: My Life As A Supreme, Mary Wilson. Supreme Faith: Someday We'll Be Together, Mary Wilson with Patricia Romanowski. All That Glittered: My Life With The Supremes, Tony Turner and Barbara Aria.
FILMS: Beach Ball (1965).

SURFARIS
ALBUMS: Wipe Out (Dot 1963)★★★, The Surfaris Play Wipe Out And Others (Decca 1963)★★★, Hit City '64 (Decca 1964)★★★, Fun City, USA (Decca 1964)★★, Hit City '65 (Decca 1965)★★, It Ain't Me Babe (Decca 1965) ★★★, Surfaris Live (1983)★★.
COMPILATIONS: Yesterday's Pop Scene (Coral 1973)★★★, Surfers Rule (Decca 1976)★★★, Gone With The Wave (Decca 1977)★★★, Wipe Out! The Best Of The Surfaris (Varèse Sarabande 1994)★★★, Surfaris Stomp (Varèse Sarabande 1995)★★★.

SUTHERLAND BROTHERS (AND QUIVER)
ALBUMS: The Sutherland Brothers Band (Island 1972)★★★. With Quiver Lifeboat (Island 1972)★★★, Dream Kid (Island 1974)★★★★, Beat Of The Street (Island 1974)★★★, Reach For The Sky (Columbia 1975)★★★, Slipstream (Columbia 1976)★★★, Down To Earth (Columbia 1977)★★★, When The Night Comes Down (Columbia 1978)★★.
SOLO: Gavin Sutherland Diamonds And Gold (Corazong 2000)★★.
COMPILATIONS: Sailing (Island 1976)★★★.
FURTHER READING: The Whaling Years, Peterhead 1788-1893, Gavin Sutherland.

SWAN, BILLY
ALBUMS: I Can Help (Monument 1974)★★★★, Rock 'N' Roll Moon (Monument 1975)★★★, Billy Swan (Monument 1976)★★★★, Billy Swan – Four (Monument 1977)★★★, You're OK, I'm OK (A&M 1978)★★, I'm Into Lovin' You (Epic 1981)★★, Bop To Be (Elite 1995)★★★, Like Elvis Used To Do (Castle Select 1999)★★★.
COMPILATIONS: Billy Swan At His Best (Monument 1978)★★★.

SWEAT, KEITH
ALBUMS: Make It Last Forever (Vintertainment/Elektra 1987)★★★, I'll Give All My Love To You (Vintertainment/Elektra 1990)★★★★, Keep It Comin' (Elektra 1991)★★★, Get Up On It (Elektra 1994)★★★, Keith Sweat (Elektra 1996)★★★, as Levert Sweat Gill Levert Sweat Gill (East West 1997)★★, Still In The Game (Elektra 1998)★★, Didn't See Me Coming (Elektra 2000)★★★.
COMPILATIONS: Just A Touch (Elektra 1997)★★★.

SWEET
ALBUMS: Funny How Sweet Co Co Can Be (RCA 1971)★★, Sweet (RCA 1973)★★, Sweet Fanny Adams (RCA 1974) ★★★, Desolation Boulevard (RCA 1974)★★★, Strung Up (RCA 1975)★★★, Give Us A Wink (RCA 1976)★★, Off The Record (RCA 1977)★★, Level Headed (Polydor 1978) ★★, Cut Above The Rest (Polydor 1979)★★★, Water's Edge (Polydor 1980)★★, Identity Crisis (Polydor 1982)★★, Live At The Marquee (SPV/Maze 1989)H, Blockbusters (RCA 1989)★★.
COMPILATIONS: Biggest Hits (RCA 1972)★★, Sweet's Golden Greats (RCA 1977)★★★, Sweet 16 - It's, It's The Sweet's Hits (Anagram 1984)★★, Hard Centres - The Rock Years (Zebra 1987)★★, The Collection (Castle Communications 1989) ★★★★, Ballroom Blitz – Live 1973 (Dojo 1993)★★, Love Is Like Oxygen – The Singles Collection 1978-1982 (Pseudonym 1993)★★★, Platinum Rare (Repertoire 1995)★★, Hit Singles: The Complete A And B Sides (Repertoire 1996)★★★, Ballroom Hitz: The Very Best Of Sweet (PolyGram 1996) ★★★, Solid Gold Sweet (Snapper 1998)★★, Sweet Originals: The Best 37 Glamrock Originals Ever (RCA 1999)★★★★.
FURTHER READING: The Not Even Close To Complete Sweet Encyclopedia, Christer Nilsson.

SWEET, MATTHEW
ALBUMS: as Buzz Of Delight Sound Castles mini-album (DB 1984)★★, Inside (Columbia 1986)★★, Earth (A&M 1989) ★★★, Girlfriend (Zoo 1992)★★★★, Altered Beast (Zoo 1993)★★★, Son Of Altered Beast mini-album (Zoo 1994) ★★, 100% Fun (Zoo 1995)★★★, Blue Sky On Mars (Zoo 1997)★★★, In Reverse (Zomba 1999)★★★★.
COMPILATIONS: Time Capsule: The Best Of Matthew Sweet 90/00 (Volcano 2000)★★★★.

SWINGING BLUE JEANS
ALBUMS: Blue Jeans A' Swinging aka Swinging Blue Jeans aka Tutti Frutti (HMV 1964)★★★, The Swinging Blue Jeans: La Voce Del Padrone (HMV 1966)★★★, Hippy Hippy Shake (Imperial 1973)★★★, Brand New And Faded (Dart 1974)★★, Live Sharin' (Prestige 1990)★★.
COMPILATIONS: Shake: The Best Of The Swinging Blue Jeans (EMI 1986)★★★, All The Hits Plus More (Prestige 1992)★★★, The EMI Years (EMI 1992)★★★★, At Abbey Road (EMI 1998)★★★.

SWV
ALBUMS: It's About Time (RCA 1993)★★★, A New Beginning (RCA 1996)★★★, Release Some Tension (RCA 1997)★★.
COMPILATIONS: Greatest Hits (RCA 1999)★★★.

SYSTEM OF A DOWN
ALBUMS: System Of A Down (American 1998)★★★★, Toxicity (American 2001)★★★★.

T

T. REX
ALBUMS: T. Rex (Fly 1970)★★★, Electric Warrior (Fly 1971) ★★★★★, The Slider (EMI 1972)★★★, Tanx (EMI 1973) ★★★, Zinc Alloy And The Hidden Riders Of Tomorrow Or A Creamed Cage In August (EMI 1974)★★, Bolan's Zip Gun (EMI 1975)★★★, Futuristic Dragon (EMI 1976)★★, Dandy In The Underworld (EMI 1977)★★★, T. Rex In Concert: The Electric Warrior Tour 1971 (Marc 1981)★★★.
COMPILATIONS: The Best Of T. Rex contains Tyrannosaurus Rex material (Fly 1971)★★★, Bolan Boogie (Fly 1972)★★★, Great Hits (EMI 1973)★★★★, Light Of Love (Casablanca 1974)★★, Marc: The Words And Music 1947-1977 (Cube 1978)★★, Solid Gold T. Rex (EMI 1979)★★★, The Unobtainable T. Rex (EMI 1980)★★, Children Of Rarn Suite (Marc On Wax 1982) ★★, Across The Airwaves (Cube 1982)★★, Billy Super Duper (Marc 1982)★★, Dance In The Midnight (Marc On Wax 1983)★★, Beyond The Rising Sun (Cambra 1984)★★, The Best Of The 20th Century Boy (K-Tel 1985)★★★, Till Dawn (Marc On Wax 1985)★★, The T. Rex Collection (Castle 1986)★★★★, A Crown Of Jewels (Dojo 1986)★★★, The Singles Collection (Marc On Wax 1987)★★★, The Marc Shows (Marc On Wax 1989)★★★, The Ultimate Collection (Telstar 1991)★★★★, Great Hits 1972-1977: The A-Sides (Edsel 1994)★★★★, Great Hits 1972-1977: The B-Sides (Edsel 1994)★★, Rabbit Fighter (The Alternate Slider) (Edsel 1994)★★★, Left Hand Luke (The Alternate Tanx) (Edsel 1994)★★★, Unchained: Unreleased Recordings Volumes 1-4 (Edsel 1995)★★, Change (The Alternate Zinc Alloy) (Edsel 1995)★★, Precious Star (The Alternate Bolan's Zip Gun (Edsel 1996)★★, A BBC History (Band Of Joy 1996)★★★★, Electric Warrior Sessions (New Millennium 1996)★★★, Unchained: Unreleased Recordings Volumes 5 & 6 (Edsel 1996)★★, Unchained: Unreleased Recordings Volume 7 (Edsel 1996)★★, Dazzling Raiment (The Alternate Futuristic Dragon) (Edsel 1997)★★, The BBC Recordings 1970 - 1976 (Pilot 1998)★★★, Extended Play (New Millennium 1998)★★, Prince Of Players (The Alternate Dandy In The Underworld) (Edsel 1998)★★, The Very Best Of T. Rex, Vol. 2 (Music Club 1999)★★★, Solid Gold: The Best Of T. Rex (Repertoire 1999)★★★.
FURTHER READING: Glam! Bowie, Bolan And The Glitter Rock Revolution, Barney Hoskyns.

TAJ MAHAL
ALBUMS: Taj Mahal (Columbia 1968)★★★★, The Natch'l Blues (Columbia 1968)★★★★, Giant Step/De Ole Folks At Home (Columbia 1969)★★★★, The Real Thing (Columbia 1971)★★★, Happy Just To Be Like I Am (Columbia 1971) ★★, Recycling The Blues & Other Related Stuff (Columbia 1972)★★★, Sounder film soundtrack (Columbia 1972) ★★★, Oooh So Good 'N Blues (Columbia 1973)★★★, Mo' Roots (Columbia 1974)★★★, Music Keeps Me Together (Columbia 1975)★★, Satisfied 'N Tickled Too (Columbia 1976)★★, Music Fuh Ya (Warners 1977)★★, Brothers film soundtrack (Warners 1977)★★, Evolution (The Most Recent) (Warners 1977)★★, Take A Giant Step (Magnet 1983)★★★, Taj (Sonet 1986)★★★, with the International Rhythm Band Live & Direct (Teldec 1987) ★★★, Shake Sugaree: Taj Mahal Plays And Sings For Children (Music For Little Children 1988)★★★, The Hot Spot film soundtrack (Antilles 1990)★★★, Big Blues: Taj Mahal Live At Ronnie Scott's London (Essential 1990)★★★, with Danny Glover Brer Rabbit And The Wonderful Tar Baby (Windham Hill 1991)★★★★, Mule Bone soundtrack (Gramavision 1991)★★★, Like Never Before (Private Music 1991)★★★, with Cedella Marley-Booker Smilin' Island Of Song: Reggae & Calypso Music For Children (Music For Little People 1993)★★★, Dancing The Blues (Private Music/BMG 1994)★★★, An Evening Of Acoustic Music (Tradition & Moderne/Topic 1995)★★★, Phantom Blues (Private 1996)★★★★, with V.M. Bhatt, N. Ravikiran Mumtaz Mahal (Water Lily Acoustics 1996)★★★★, An Evening Of Acoustic Music (Ruf 1997)★★★, Señor Blues (Private Music/BMG 1997)★★★, with the Hula Blues Band Sacred Island (Tradition & Moderne 1998) ★★★, with Toumani Diabaté Kulanjan (Hannibal 1999) ★★★★, Shoutin' In Key (Hannibal 2000)★★★, Live At Ronnie Scott's (Castle 2001)★★★.
COMPILATIONS: Going Home (Columbia 1980)★★★★, The Best Of Taj Mahal (Sony 1981)★★★★, The Taj Mahal Collection (Castle 1987)★★★, Taj's Blues (Columbia/Legacy 1992)★★★, World Music (Columbia/Legacy 1993)★★★, The Very Best Of Taj Mahal (Global 1998)★★★★, In Progress & In Motion 1965-1998 3-CD box set (Columbia/Legacy 1998)★★★★.
VIDEOS: At Ronnie Scott's 1988 (Hendring Music Video 1989).
FURTHER READING: Taj Mahal: Autobiography Of A Bluesman, Taj Mahal with Stephen Foehr.

TAKE THAT
ALBUMS: Take That And Party (RCA 1992)★★★, Everything Changes (RCA 1993)★★★, Nobody Else (RCA 1995)★★★.
COMPILATIONS: Greatest Hits (RCA 1996)★★★.
VIDEOS: Take That And Party (BMG 1992), Take That: The Party-Live At Wembley (BMG 1993), Greatest Hits (BMG 1995), From Zeros To Heroes (Wienerworld 1995), Everything Changes (BMG 1995), Hometown: Live At Manchester G-Mex (BMG 1995), Berlin (BMG 1995), Nobody Else: The Movie (BMG 1996).
FURTHER READING: Take That: Our Story, Piers Morgan. The Unofficial Biography, Mick St. Michael. Everything Changes, Take That. Talk Back, Luke Taylor.

TALK TALK
ALBUMS The Party's Over (EMI 1982)★★, It's My Life (EMI 1984)★★★, It's My Mix (EMI 1984)★★, The Colour Of Spring (EMI 1986)★★★★, Spirit Of Eden (Parlophone 1988)★★★★, Laughing Stock (Verve 1991)★★★, Hammersmith 1986 recording (Pond Life 1999)★★★.
SOLO: Mark Hollis Mark Hollis (Polydor 1997)★★★.
COMPILATIONS: Natural History: The Very Best Of Talk Talk (Parlophone 1990)★★★, History Revisited: The Remixes (Parlophone 1991)★★, The Very Best Of Talk Talk (EMI 1997)★★★, Asides And Besides (EMI 1998)★★, The Collection (EMI Gold 2000)★★★, Remixed (EMI 2001)H.

TALKING HEADS
ALBUMS: Talking Heads: 77 (Sire 1977)★★★★, More Songs About Buildings And Food (Sire 1978)★★★★, Fear Of Music (Sire 1979)★★★, Remain In Light (Sire 1980) ★★★★★, The Name Of This Band Is Talking Heads (Sire 1982)★★★, Speaking In Tongues (Sire/EMI 1983)★★★, Stop Making Sense (Sire/EMI 1984)★★★★, Little Creatures (Sire/EMI 1985)★★★★, True Stories (Sire/EMI 1986)★★★, Naked (Sire/EMI 1988)★★★, as the Heads No Talking Just Head (Radioactive/MCA 1996)★★★, Stop Making Sense: Special New Edition (EMI 1999)★★★★.
COMPILATIONS: The Best Of: Once In A Lifetime (Sire/EMI 1992)★★★★, Popular Favorites: Sand In The Vaseline (Sire/EMI 1992)★★★★, 12x12 Original Remixes (EMI 1999)★★.
VIDEOS: Stop Making Sense (PMI 1985), True Stories (PMI 1986), Storytelling Giant (PMI 1988), Stop Making Sense: Special New Edition (Palm Pictures 1999).
FURTHER READING: Talking Heads, Miles. The Name Of This Book Is Talking Heads, Krista Reese. Talking Heads: The Band And Their Music, David Gans. Talking Heads: A Biography, Jerome Davis. This Must Be The Place: The Adventures Of Talking Heads In The 20th Century (US) Fa Fa Fa Fa Fa Fa: The Adventures Of Talking Heads In The 20th Century (UK), David Bowman.
FILMS: Stop Making Sense (1984).

TANGERINE DREAM
ALBUMS: Electronic Meditation (Ohr 1970)★★★, Alpha Centauri (Ohr 1971)★★★, Zeit (Largo In Four Movements) (Ohr 1972)★★★, Atem (Ohr 1973)★★★, Phaedra (Virgin 1974)★★★★, Rubycon (Virgin 1975)★★★, Ricochet (Virgin 1975)★★★, Stratosfear (Virgin 1976)★★★★, Encore (Virgin 1977)★★, Sorcerer film soundtrack (MCA 1977)★★, Cyclone (Virgin 1978)★★★, Force Majeure (Virgin 1979)★★★, Thief film soundtrack (Virgin 1980)★★, Tangram (Virgin 1980) ★★★, Quichotte reissued as Pergamon (Amiga 1980)★★★, Exit (Virgin 1981)★★★, White Eagle (Virgin 1982)★★★, Logos: Live At The Dominion (Virgin 1983)★★, Wavelength film soundtrack (Varese Sarabande 1983)★★, Risky Business film soundtrack (Virgin 1983)★★, Hyperborea (Virgin 1983) ★★, Firestarter film soundtrack (MCA 1984)★★★, Flashpoint film soundtrack (EMI 1984)★★, Poland: The Warsaw Concert (Jive Electro 1984)★★, Heartbreakers film soundtrack (Virgin 1985)★★, Le Parc (Jive Electro 1985)★★, Legend film soundtrack (MCA 1986)★★, Underwater Sunlight (Jive Electro 1986)★★, Near Dark film soundtrack (Silva Screen 1987) ★★, Tyger (Jive Electro 1987)★★, Three O'Clock High film soundtrack (Varese Sarabande 1987)★★, Shy People film soundtrack (Varese Sarabande 1987)★★, Live Miles (Jive Electro 1988)★★, Optical Race (Private 1988)★★★, Lily On The Beach (Private 1989)★★, Miracle Mile film soundtrack (Private 1989)★★, Melrose (Private 1990)★★, Rockoon (Miramar 1992)★★, Quinona fan club only (Volt 1992)★★★, 220 Volt (Miramar 1993)★★★, Turn Of The Tides (Miramar 1994)★★, Tyranny Of Beauty (Miramar 1995)★★, Goblin's Club (Sequel 1996)★★★, Ambient Monkeys (TDI 1997)★★, Dream Encores (TDI 1998)★★★, Oasis film soundtrack (TDI 1997)★★★, Tournado: Live In Europe (TDI 1998)★★★, Transsiberia film soundtrack (TDI 1998)★★, Valentine Wheels: The Shepherds Bush Empire Concert London 1997 (TDI 1999)★★, Soho Man: Live In Sydney 1982 (TDI 1999)★★, What A Blast film soundtrack (TDI 1999)★★, Mars Polaris (TDI 1999)★★★, Soundmill Navigator: Live At The Philharmonic 1976 (EFA 1999)★★★, Great Wall Of China film soundtrack (EFA 2000)★★★, The Seven Letters From Tibet (EFA 2000) ★★★.
COMPILATIONS: Tangerine Dream '70-'80 4-LP box set (Virgin 1980)★★★, Dream Sequence 3-LP box set (Virgin 1985)★★★, The Collection (Castle 1987)★★★, Tangents 5-CD box set (Virgin 1994)★★★, Book Of Dreams (Essential 1995)★★★, Dream Mixes One (TDI 1995)★★★, The Dream Roots Collection 5-CD box set (Essential 1996)★★★, TimeSquare: Dream Mixes II (TDI 1997)★★★, The Hollywood Years Vol. 1 (TDI 1998)★★★, The Hollywood Years Vol. 2 (TDI 1998)★★★, Atlantic Bridges (TDI 1998)★★★, Atlantic Walls (TDI 1998)★★★, The Best Of Tangerine Dream - The Pink Years (Castle 1998)★★★, The Best Of Tangerine Dream - The Blue Years (Castle 1998)★★★, Tang-Go: The World Of Tangerine Dream (EFA 1999)★★★, Antique Dreams (EFA 1999)★★★, i-Box 1970-1990 6-CD box set (EFA 2000)★★★.
VIDEOS: Three Phase (Miramar 1993), The Video Dream Mixes (Castle 1996), Oasis (Camera One 1996), Luminous Vision (Sony 1998), Architecture In Motion (Unapix/Miramar 1999).
FURTHER READING: Digital Gothic: A Critical Discography Of Tangerine Dream, Paul Stump.

TASTE
ALBUMS: Taste (Polydor 1969)★★★, On The Boards (Polydor 1970)★★★★, Live Taste (Polydor 1971)★★, Live At The Isle Of Wight (Polydor 1972)★★.
COMPILATIONS: The Greatest Rock Sensation (Polydor 1985)★★★.

TATE, HOWARD
ALBUMS: Get It While You Can (Verve 1967)★★★★, Howard Tate (Atlantic 1972)★★★.
COMPILATIONS: Get It While You Can: The Legendary Sessions (Mercury 1995)★★★★.

TAYLOR, JAMES
ALBUMS: James Taylor (Apple 1968)★★★, Sweet Baby James (Warners 1970)★★★★★, James Taylor And The Original Flying Machine - 1967 (Euphoria 1970)H, Mud Slide Slim And The Blue Horizon (Warners 1971)★★★★, One Man Dog (Warners 1972)★★★, Walking Man (Warners 1974)★★★, Gorilla (Warners 1975)★★★, In The Pocket (Warners 1976)★★, JT (Columbia 1977)★★★★, Flag (Columbia 1979)★★, Dad Loves His Work (Columbia 1981)★★, That's Why I'm Here (Columbia 1985)★★★★, Never Die Young (Columbia 1988)★★★, New Moon Shine (Columbia 1991)★★★, Live In Rio 1985 recording (Columbia 1992)★★★, Live (Columbia 1993)★★★★, Hourglass (Columbia 1997)★★★.
COMPILATIONS: Greatest Hits (Warners 1976)★★★★, Classic Songs (CBS/WEA 1987)★★★★★, The Best Of James Taylor: The Classic Years (WEA 1990)★★★★, Greatest Hits Volume 2 (Columbia 2000)★★★.
VIDEOS: James Taylor In Concert (SMV 1991), Squibnocket (SMV 1993), James Taylor Live At The Beacon Theatre (SMV 1998).
FURTHER READING: Fire And Rain: The James Taylor Story, Ian Halperin. Long Ago And Far Away, James Taylor, His Life And Music, Timothy White.
FILMS: Two Lane Blacktop (1971), No Nukes (1979), In Our Hands (1984).

TAYLOR, JOHNNIE
ALBUMS: Wanted: One Soul Singer (Stax 1967)★★★★, Who's Making Love ... (Stax 1968)★★★★, Raw Blues (Stax 1968)★★★, The Johnnie Taylor Philosophy Continues (Stax 1969)★★★, Rare Stamps (Stax 1970)★★★, One Step Beyond (Stax 1971)★★★, Taylored In Silk (Stax 1973) ★★★★, Super Taylor (Stax 1974)★★★, Eargasm (Columbia 1976)★★★, Rated Extraordinaire (Columbia 1977)★★, Disco 9000 (Columbia 1977)★★, Ever Ready (Columbia 1978)★★, Reflections (Columbia 1979)★★, She's Killing Me (Columbia 1979)★★, A New Day (Columbia 1980)★★, Just Ain't Good Enough (Beverly Glen 1982)★★★, This Is Your Night (Malaco 1984)★★★, Wall To Wall (Malaco 1985) ★★★, Lover Boy (Malaco 1987)★★★, In Control (Malaco 1988)★★, Crazy 'Bout You (Malaco 1989)★★★, I Know It's Wrong, But I ... Just Can't Do Right (Malaco 1991)★★★, Real Love (Malaco 1994)★★★, Good Love! (Malaco 1996)★★★★, Taylored To Please (Malaco 1998)★★★, Gotta Get The Groove Back (Malaco 1999)★★★★.
COMPILATIONS: The Roots Of Johnnie Taylor (Sar 1969) ★★★, Johnnie Taylor's Greatest Hits Vol. 1 (Stax 1970) ★★★★, The Johnnie Taylor Chronicle (1968-1972) (Stax 1978)★★★★, The Johnnie Taylor Chronicle (1972-1974) (Stax 1978)★★★, The Best Of Johnnie Taylor (Columbia 1981)★★, Little Bluebird (Stax 1991)★★★, The Best Of Johnnie Taylor ... On Malaco Vol. 1 (Malaco 1994)★★★, The Best Of Johnnie Taylor: Rated X-Traordinaire (Columbia/Legacy 1996)★★★, Funksoulbrother (Fuel 2000)★★★, Lifetime 3-CD box set (Stax 2000)★★★★.

TEARDROP EXPLODES
ALBUMS: Kilimanjaro (Mercury 1980)★★★, Wilder (Mercury 1981)★★★★, Everybody Wants To Shag The Teardrop Explodes (Fontana 1990)★★.
COMPILATIONS: Piano (Document 1990)★★★, The Greatest Hit (Mercury 2001)★★★.

TEARS FOR FEARS
ALBUMS: The Hurting (Mercury 1983)★★★, Songs From The Big Chair (Mercury 1985)★★★★, The Seeds Of Love (Fontana 1989)★★★, Elemental (Mercury 1993)★★, Raoul And The Kings Of Spain (Epic 1995)★★.
SOLO: Curt Smith Soul On Board (Mercury 1993)★, as Mayfield Mayfield (Zerodisc 1998)★. Roland Orzabal Tom Cats Screaming Outside (Eagle 2001)★★★★.
COMPILATIONS: Tears Roll Down (Greatest Hits 82-92) (Fontana 1992)★★★★, Saturnine Martial & Lunatic (Fontana 1996)★★★, The Best Of Tears For Fears: The Millennium Collection (Universal 2000)★★★★, The Working Hour: An Introduction To Tears For Fears (Mercury 2001)★★★, Shout: The Very Best Of Tears For Fears (Mercury 2001)★★★.
VIDEOS: Scenes From The Big Chair (4 Front Video 1991).
FURTHER READING: Tears For Fears, Ann Greene.

TEENAGE FANCLUB
ALBUMS: A Catholic Education (Paperhouse 1990)★★★, The King (Creation 1991)★★, Bandwagonesque (Creation/Geffen 1991)★★★★, Thirteen (Creation 1993)★★, Grand Prix (Creation/Geffen 1995)★★★★, Songs From Northern Britain (Creation/Sony 1997)★★★★, Howdy! (Columbia/Thirsty Ear 2000)★★★, with Jad Fair Words Of Wisdom And Hope (Geographic/Alternative Tentacles 2002)★★★.
COMPILATIONS: Deep Fried Fanclub (Paperhouse/Fire 1995)★★.

TELEVISION
ALBUMS: Marquee Moon (Elektra 1977)★★★★, Adventure (Elektra 1978)★★★, The Blow Up 1978 live recording (ROIR/Danceteria 1982)★★, Television (Capitol 1992)★★.

TEMPTATIONS
ALBUMS: Meet The Temptations (Gordy 1964)★★★★, The Temptations Sing Smokey (Gordy 1965)★★★★, Temptin' Temptations (Gordy 1965)★★★★, Gettin' Ready (Gordy 1966)★★★★, Temptations Live! (Gordy 1967)★★, With A Lot O' Soul (Gordy 1967)★★★, The Temptations In A Mellow Mood (Gordy 1967)★★★, Wish It Would Rain (Gordy 1968)★★★★, Diana Ross And The Supremes Join The Temptations (Motown 1968)★★★, with Diana Ross And The Supremes TCB (Motown 1968)★★★, Live At The Copa (Gordy 1968)★★, Cloud Nine (Gordy 1969)★★★★, The Temptations' Show (Gordy 1969)★★★, Puzzle People (Gordy 1969)★★★, with Diana Ross And The Supremes Together (Motown 1969)★★★, with Diana Ross And The Supremes On Broadway (Motown 1969)★★★, Psychedelic Shack (Gordy 1970)★★★★, Live At London's Talk Of The Town (Gordy 1970)★★★, The Temptations Christmas Card (Gordy 1970)H, Sky's The Limit (Gordy 1971)★★★, Solid Rock (Gordy 1972)★★★, All Directions (Gordy 1972) ★★★, Masterpiece (Gordy 1973)★★★, 1990 (Gordy 1973)★★★, A Song For You (Gordy 1975)★★★, House Party (Gordy 1975)★★, Wings Of Love (Gordy 1976)★★, The Temptations Do The Temptations (Gordy 1976)★★, Hear To Tempt You (Atlantic 1977)★★, Bare Back (Atlantic 1978) ★★, Power (Gordy 1980)★★, Give Love At Christmas (Gordy 1980)H, The Temptations (Gordy 1981)★★, with Jimmy Ruffin, Eddie Kendricks Reunion (Gordy 1982)★★★, Surface Thrills (Gordy 1983)★★, Back To Basics (Gordy 1984)★★★, Truly For You (Gordy 1984)★★, Touch Me (Gordy 1985)★★, To Be Continued ... (Gordy 1986)★★★, Together Again (Motown 1987)★★★, Special (Motown 1989)★★, Milestone (Motown 1991)★★, Phoenix Rising (Motown 1998)★★★★★, Ear-Resistable (Motown 2000)★★★, Awesome (Motown 2001)★★★.
COMPILATIONS: The Temptations Greatest Hits (Gordy 1966)★★★★, Temptations Greatest Hits, Volume 2 (Gordy 1970)★★★★, Anthology (Motown 1973)★★★★, All The Million Sellers (Gordy 1981)★★★, Best Of The Temptations (Telstar 1986)★★, 25 Anniversary (Motown 1986)★★★★, Compact Command Performances (Motown 1989)★★★, Hum Along And Dance: More Of The Best 1963-1974 (Rhino 1993)★★★, The Original Lead Singers Of The Temptations (1993)★★★, Emperors Of Soul 5-CD box set (Motown 1994)★★★★, Early Classics (Spectrum 1996)★★★, The

Ultimate Collection (Motown 1998)★★★★, You've Got To Earn It (Motown 1999)★★★, Psychedelic Soul (Spectrum 2000)★★★★, At Their Very Best (Universal 2001)★★★.
VIDEOS: Get Ready (PMI 1988), Temptations And The Four Tops (Video Collection 1988), Live In Concert (Old Gold 1990).
FURTHER READING: Temptations, Otis Williams with Patricia Romanowski.

10CC
ALBUMS: 10cc (UK 1973)★★★, Sheet Music (UK 1974)★★★, The Original Soundtrack (Mercury 1975)★★★★, How Dare You (Mercury 1976)★★★, Deceptive Bends (Mercury 1977)★★★, Live And Let Live (Mercury 1977)★★, Bloody Tourists (Mercury/Polydor 1978)★★, Look Hear (Mercury/Warners 1980)★★, Ten Out Of 10 (Mercury 1981)★★, In Concert 1977 recording (Pickwick 1982)★★, Windows In The Jungle (Mercury 1983)★★, Meanwhile (Polydor 1992)★★, Alive (Jade/Creative Man 1993)H, Mirror Mirror (Avex/Critique 1995)★★, In Concert 1975 recording (King Biscuit Flower Hour 1996)★★★.
COMPILATIONS: 100cc: Greatest Hits Of 10cc (Decca/UK 1975)★★★, Greatest Hits 1972-1978 (Mercury/Polydor 1979)★★★★, Changing Faces: The Best Of 10cc And Godley & Creme (Polydor1987)★★★★, The Collection (Castle 1989)★★★, The Best Of The Early Years (Music Club 1993)★★★, The Very Best Of 10cc (PolyGram 1997)★★★★, The Singles (PolyGram 1998)★★★★, Two From Ten (Snapper 2000)★★★, Good News: An Introduction To 10cc (Decca 2001)★★★.
VIDEOS: Live In Concert (VCL 1986), Live At The International Music Show (VCL 1987), Changing Faces: The Best Of 10cc And Godley & Creme (Channel 5 1988), 10cc Alive: The Classic Hits Tour (Wienerworld 2001).
FURTHER READING: The 10cc Story, George Tremlett. The Worst Band In The World: The Definitive Biography Of 10cc, Liam Newton.

10,000 MANIACS
ALBUMS: Human Conflict Number Five mini-album (Mark 1982)★★, Secrets Of The I Ching (Christian Burial 1983)★★★, The Wishing Chair (Elektra 1985)★★, In My Tribe (Elektra 1987)★★★★, Blind Man's Zoo (Elektra 1989)★★★, Our Time In Eden (Elektra 1992)★★★, MTV Unplugged (Elektra 1993)★★★, Love Among The Ruins (Geffen 1997)★★, The Earth Pressed Flat (Bar/None 1999)★★★.
COMPILATIONS: Hope Chest: The Fredonia Recordings 1982-1983 (Elektra 1990)★★.
VIDEOS: MTV Unplugged (Elektra 1994).

TEN YEARS AFTER
ALBUMS: Ten Years After (Deram 1967)★★★, Undead (Deram 1968)★★★★, Stonedhenge (Deram 1969)★★★, Ssssh (Deram 1969)★★★★, Cricklewood Green (Deram 1970)★★★★, Watt (Deram 1970)★★★, A Space In Time (Chrysalis 1971)★★★, Rock 'N' Roll Music To The World (Chrysalis 1972)★★, Recorded Live (Chrysalis 1973)★★, Positive Vibrations (Chrysalis 1974)★★, About Time (Chrysalis 1989)★★, Live 1990 (Demon 1994)★★, Live At The Fillmore East 1970 (EMI 2001)★★★★.
COMPILATIONS: Alvin Lee & Company (Deram 1972)★★★, Goin' Home! - Their Greatest Hits (Deram 1975)★★★, The Essential (Chrysalis 1992)★★★★, Solid Rock (Chrysalis 1997)★★★.
FURTHER READING: Alvin Lee & Ten Years After: A Visual History, Herb Staehr.

TERRORVISION
ALBUMS: Formaldehyde (Total Vegas 1992)★★★, How To Make Friends And Influence People (Total Vegas 1994)★★★★, Regular Urban Survivors (Total Vegas 1996)★★★★, Shaving Peaches (Total Vegas 1998)★★★, Good To Go (Total Vegas/Papillon 2001)★★★★.
COMPILATIONS: Whales & Dolphins: The Best Of Terrorvision (EMI 2001)★★★★.
VIDEOS: Fired Up And Lairy (PMI 1995).

TEX, JOE
ALBUMS: Hold On (Checker 1964)★★★, Hold What You've Got (Atlantic 1965)★★★, The New Boss (Atlantic 1965)★★★★, The Love You Save (Atlantic 1966)★★★, I've Got To Do A Little Better (Atlantic 1966)★★★★, Live And Lively (Atlantic 1968)★★, Soul Country (Atlantic 1968)★★★, You Better Believe It (Atlantic 1969)★★★, Buying A Book (Atlantic 1969)★★★, Sings With Strings And Things (Atlantic 1970)★★★, From The Roots Came The Rapper (Atlantic 1972)★★, I Gotcha (Dial 1972)★★, Spills The Beans (Dial 1973)★★, Another Man's Woman (Powerpak 1974)★★, Bumps And Bruises (Epic 1977)★★, Rub Down (Epic 1978)★★, He Who Is Without Funk Cast The First Stone (Dial 1979)★★.
COMPILATIONS: The Best Of Joe Tex (King 1965)★★★, The Very Best Of Joe Tex (Atlantic 1967)★★★★, Greatest Hits (Atlantic 1967)★★★★, The Very Best Of Joe Tex - Real Country Soul ... Scarce As Hen's Teeth (Rhino 1988)★★★, I Believe I'm Gonna Make It: The Best Of Joe Tex 1964-1972 (Rhino 1988)★★★★, Different Strokes (Charly 1989)★★★, I Gotcha (His Greatest Hits) (BMG 1993)★★★, Skinny Legs And All: The Classic Early Dial Sides (Kent 1994)★★★, You're Right Joe Tex! (Kent 1995)★★★, The Very Best Of Joe Tex (Rhino 1996)★★★★, I Gotcha: Greatest Hits (BMG 1998)★★★, 25 All Time Greatest Hits (Varèse Sarabande 2000)★★★★, Oh Boy Classics Presents Joe Tex (Oh Boy 2001)★★★.

TEXAS
ALBUMS: Southside (Mercury 1989)★★★, Mother's Heaven (Mercury 1991)★★, Ricks Road (Vertigo 1993)★★★, White On Blonde (Mercury 1997)★★★★, The Hush (Mercury 1999)★★★★.
COMPILATIONS: The Greatest Hits (Mercury 2000)★★★★.
VIDEOS: Texas, Paris (Mercury 2001).

THAT PETROL EMOTION
ALBUMS: Manic Pop Thrill (Demon 1986)★★★, Babble (Polydor 1987)★★★★, End Of The Millennium Psychosis Blues (Virgin 1988)★★★, Peel Sessions Album (Strange Fruit 1989)★★★, Chemicrazy (Virgin 1990)★★★★, Fireproof (Koogat 1993)★★★, Final Flame 1994 live recording (Sanctuary 2000)★★★.

THE THE
ALBUMS: Soul Mining (Some Bizzare 1983)★★★★, Infected (Epic 1986)★★★★, Mind Bomb (Epic 1989)★★, Dusk (Epic 1993)★★★, Hanky Panky (Epic 1995)★★, Naked Self (Nothing/Universal 2000)★★★.
VIDEOS: Infected (CBS-Fox 1987), Versus The World (Sony Music Video 1991), From Dawn 'Til Dusk (1993).

THEM
ALBUMS: Them aka The Angry Young Them (Decca 1965)★★★★, Them Again (Decca 1966)★★★★, Now And Them (Tower 1968)★★★, Time Out, Time In For Them (Tower 1968)★★★, Them (Happy Tiger 1970)★★★, In Reality (Happy Tiger 1971)★★★, Shut Your Mouth (Teldec 1979)★★★.
SOLO: Billy Harrison Billy Who? (Vagabound 1980)★★.
COMPILATIONS: The World Of Them (Decca 1970)★★★★, Them Featuring Van Morrison, Lead Singer (Decca 1973)★★★, Backtrackin' With Them (London 1974)★★★, Rock Roots: Them (Decca 1976)★★★★, One More Time (Decca 1984)★★★, The Them Collection (Castle 1986)★★★, The Singles (See For Miles 1987)★★★★, The Story Of Them (Deram 1997)★★★★.
FURTHER READING: Van Morrison: A Portrait Of The Artist, Johnny Rogan.

THERAPY?
ALBUMS: Babyteeth mini-album (Wiiija 1991)★★, Pleasure Death mini-album (Wiiija 1992)★★★, Nurse (A&M 1992)★★★, Troublegum (A&M 1994)★★★★, Infernal Love (A&M 1995)★★, Semi-Detached (A&M 1998)★★★, Suicide Pact - You First (Ark 21 1999)★★★, Shameless (Ark 21 2001)★★★.
COMPILATIONS: So Much For The Ten Year Plan: A Retrospective 1990-2000 (Ark 21 2000)★★★.

THEY MIGHT BE GIANTS
ALBUMS: They Might Be Giants self-released cassette (TMB Music 1985), They Might Be Giants (Bar/None 1986)★★★, Lincoln (Bar/None 1989)★★★, Don't Let's Start (Elektra 1989)★★★, Flood (Elektra 1990)★★, Apollo 18 (Elektra 1992)★★, John Henry (Elektra 1994)★★★, Factory Showroom (Elektra 1996)★★★, Severe Tire Damage (Cooking Vinyl 1998)★★, The Long Tall Weekend (GoodNoise 1999)★★★, Mink Car (Restless 2001)★★★.
COMPILATIONS: Don't Let's Start (One Little Indian 1989)★★★, Miscellaneous T (Bar/None 1991)★★★, Then: The Earlier Years (Restless 1997)★★★.
VIDEOS: They Might Be Giants (Warner Music Video 1991).

THIN LIZZY
ALBUMS: Thin Lizzy (Decca 1971)★★, Shades Of A Blue Orphanage (Decca 1972)★★, Vagabonds Of The Western World (Decca 1973)★★★, Night Life (Vertigo 1974)★★★, Fighting (Vertigo 1975)★★★, Jailbreak (Vertigo 1976)★★★★, Johnny The Fox (Vertigo 1976)★★★, Bad Reputation (Vertigo 1977)★★★, Live And Dangerous (Vertigo 1978)★★★★, Black Rose (Vertigo 1979)★★★, Renegade (Vertigo 1981)★★★, Thunder And Lightning (Vertigo 1983)★★, Life-Live double album (Vertigo 1983)★★, BBC Radio 1 Live In Concert 1983 recording (Windsong 1992)★★★, One Night Only (CMC 2000)★★.
COMPILATIONS: Remembering - Part One (Decca 1976)★★, The Continuing Saga Of The Ageing Orphans (Decca 1979)★★, Rockers (Decca 1981)★★, Adventures Of Thin Lizzy (Vertigo 1981)★★★, Lizzy Killers (Vertigo 1983)★★★, The Collection (Castle 1985)★★★, The Best Of Phil Lynott And Thin Lizzy (Telstar 1987)★★★, Dedication: The Very Best Of Thin Lizzy (Vertigo 1991)★★★★, The Peel Sessions (Strange Fruit 1994)★★, Wild One: The Very Best Of Thin Lizzy (Mercury 1995)★★★★, Whiskey In The Jar (Spectrum 1998)★★★, Vagabonds Kings Warriors Angels 4-CD box set (Vertigo 2001)★★★★.
VIDEOS: Live And Dangerous (VCL 1986), Dedication (PMV 1991), The Boys Are Back In Town (Eagle Rock Entertainment 1998).
FURTHER READING: Songs For While I'm Away, Philip Lynott. Thin Lizzy, Larry Pryce. Philip, Philip Lynott. Thin Lizzy: The Approved Biography, Chris Salewicz. Phil Lynott: The Rocker, Mark Putterford. My Boy: The Philip Lynott Story, Philomena Lynott with Jackie Hayden. The Ballad Of The Thin Man, Stuart Bailie.

THIRD EYE BLIND
ALBUMS: Third Eye Blind (Elektra 1997)★★★★, Blue (Elektra 1999)★★★.

13TH FLOOR ELEVATORS
ALBUMS: The Psychedelic Sounds Of The 13th Floor Elevators (International Artists 1966)★★★★, Easter Everywhere (International Artists 1967)★★★, Live (International Artists 1968)H, Bull Of The Woods (International Artists 1968)★★, I've Seen Your Face Before live recording (Big Beat 1988)★★★, Out Of Order: Live At The Avalon Ballroom 1966 recording (Magnum 1993)★★★.
COMPILATIONS: Epitaph For A Legend (International Artists 1980)★★★, Fire In My Bones (Texas Archive 1985)★★, Elevator Tracks (Texas Archive 1987)★★, The Original Sound Of The 13th Floor Elevators (USA) Demos Everywhere (UK) (13th Hour 1988)H, The Collection 4-CD set (Decal 1991)★★★, The Interpreter (Thunderbolt 1996)★★★, The Best Of ... Manicure Your Mind (Eva 1997)★★★, All Time Highs (Music Club 1998)★★★, The Legendary Group At Their Best (Collectables 2001)★★★, The Psychedelic World Of The 13th Floor Elevators 3-CD box set (Charly 2002)★★★★.

THOMPSON TWINS
ALBUMS: A Product Of ... (Hansa/T 1981)★★, Set (T 1982)★★, In The Name Of Love US only (Arista 1982)★★, Quick Step & Side Kick (UK) SideKicks (US) (Arista 1983)★★★★, Into The Gap (Arista 1984)★★★, Here's To Future Days (Arista 1985)★★, Close To The Bone (Arista 1987)★★, Big Trash (Warners 1989)★★, Queer (Warners 1991)★★.
COMPILATIONS: Take Two (Arista 1983)★★, Greatest Mixes: The Best Of Thompson Twins (Arista 1988)★★★, The Greatest Hits (Stylus 1990)★★★, The Best Of Thompson Twins (Old Gold 1991)★★★, Love, Lies, And Other Strange Things: Greatest Hits (Arista 1996)★★★, Singles Collection (Camden 1996)★★★, Master Hits (Arista 1999)★★★.
VIDEOS: SideKicks: The Movie (Thorn EMI 1983), Into The Gap Live (Arista Video 1984), Single Vision (Arista Video 1985).
FURTHER READING: The Thompson Twins: An Odd Couple, Rose Rousse. Thompson Twin: An '80s Memoir, Michael White.

THOMPSON, RICHARD
ALBUMS: see also Fairport Convention, Richard And Linda Thompson entries. Henry The Human Fly (Island 1972)★★★, Strict Tempo! (Elixir 1981)★★★, Hand Of Kindness (Hannibal 1983)★★★★, Small Town Romance (Hannibal 1984)★★★★, Across A Crowded Room (Polydor 1985)★★★, Daring Adventures (Polydor 1986)★★★★, with John French, Fred Frith, Henry Kaiser Live, Love, Larf & Loaf (Rhino/Demon 1987)★★★★, with Peter Filleul The Marksman film soundtrack (BBC 1987)★★, Amnesia (Capitol 1988)★★★, with French, Frith, Kaiser Invisible Means (Windham Hill/Demon 1990)★★★, with Filleul Hard Cash film soundtrack (Special Delivery 1990)★★★, Sweet Talker film soundtrack (Capitol 1991)★★, Rumor And Sigh (Capitol 1991)★★★★, Mirror Blue (Capitol 1994)★★★★, with Danny Thompson Live At Crawley 1993 (Whatdisc 1995)★★★, You? Me? Us? (EMI 1996)★★★, Two Letter Words 1994 recording (Fly 1996)★★★, with Thompson Industry (Parlophone 1997)★★★, with Philip Pickett The Bones Of All Men (Hannibal 1998)★★★, Celtschmerz (Flypaper 1998)★★★, Mock Tudor (Capitol 1999)★★★★.
COMPILATIONS: (Guitar, Vocal) (Island 1976)★★★★, Live (More Or Less) US only (Island 1977)★★★★, Doom & Gloom From The Tomb cassette only (Fly 1985)★★★, The Guitar Of Richard Thompson cassette only (Homespun 1986)★★★, Doom & Gloom II - Over My Dead Body cassette only (Fly 1991)★★★, Watching The Dark 3-CD box set (Hannibal 1993)★★★★★, Action Packed: The Best Of The Capitol Years (Capitol 2001)★★★★.
VIDEOS: Across A Crowded Room (Sony 1983).
FURTHER READING: Richard Thompson: 21 Years Of Doom & Gloom, Clinton Heylin. Gypsy Love Songs & Sad Refrains: The Recordings Of Richard Thompson & Sandy Denny, Clinton Heylin. Richard Thompson: Strange Affair, The Biography, Patrick Humphries.

THOMPSON, RICHARD AND LINDA
ALBUMS: I Want To See The Bright Lights Tonight (Island 1974)★★★★, Hokey Pokey (Island 1975)★★★★, Pour Down Like Silver (Island 1975)★★★★, First Light (Chrysalis 1978)★★★, Sunnyvista (Chrysalis 1979)★★, Shoot Out The Lights (Hannibal 1982)★★★★.

THOROGOOD, GEORGE
ALBUMS: George Thorogood And The Destroyers (Rounder 1977)★★★, Move It On Over (Rounder 1978)★★★, Better Than The Rest (Rounder 1979)★★, More George Thorogood And The Destroyers (Rounder 1980)★★, Bad To The Bone (Capitol 1982)★★★★, Maverick (Capitol 1985)★★, Live (Capitol 1986)★★, Born To Be Bad (Capitol 1988)★★, Boogie People (Capitol 1991)★★, Haircut (EMI 1993)★★, Let's Work Together (EMI 1995)★★, Rockin' My Life Away (EMI 1997)★★, Half A Boy/Half A Man (SPV 1999)★★★.
COMPILATIONS: The Baddest (EMI 1992)★★★★, Anthology (Capitol 2000)★★★★.

3 COLOURS RED
ALBUMS: Pure (Creation 1997)★★★, Revolt (Creation 1999)★★★.

THREE DEGREES
ALBUMS: Maybe (Roulette 1970)★★★, Three Degrees (Philadelphia International 1974)★★★, International (Philadelphia International 1975)★★★, So Much Love (Roulette 1975)★★, Take Good Care Of Yourself (Philadelphia International 1975)★★, The Three Degrees Live (Philadelphia International 1975)★★, Three Degrees Live In Japan (Columbia 1975)★★, Standing Up For Love (Philadelphia International 1977)★★, The Three Degrees (Ariola 1978)★★, New Dimensions (Ariola 1978)★★, 3-D (Ariola 1979)★★, ... And Holding (Ichiban 1989)★★.
COMPILATIONS: Gold (K-Tel 1980)★★, Hits Hits Hits (Hallmark 1981)★★, 20 Golden Greats (Epic 1984)★★★, The Roulette Years (Sequel 1995)★★, A Collection Of Their 20 Greatest Hits (Columbia 1996)★★★.

THREE DOG NIGHT
ALBUMS: Three Dog Night (Dunhill 1969)★★★, Suitable For Framing (Dunhill 1969)★★, Captured Live At The Forum (Dunhill 1969)★★, It Ain't Easy (Dunhill 1970)★★★★, Naturally (Dunhill 1970)★★, Golden Bisquits (Dunhill 1971)★★★★, Harmony (Dunhill 1971)★★★, Seven Separate Fools (Dunhill 1972)★★★, Around The World With Three Dog Night (Dunhill 1973)★★, Cyan (Dunhill 1973)★★, Hard Labor (Dunhill 1974)★★, Coming Down Your Way (ABC 1975)★★, American Pastime (ABC 1976)★★, It's A Jungle (Lamborghini 1983)★.
COMPILATIONS: Joy To The World: Their Greatest Hits (Dunhill 1975)★★★★, The Best Of (Dunhill 1989)★★★, Celebrate: The Three Dog Night Story (MCA 1993)★★, That Ain't The Way To Have Fun: Greatest Hits (Connoisseur Collection 1995)★★★.

THROWING MUSES
ALBUMS: Throwing Muses (4AD 1986)★★★, The Fat Skier mini-album (Sire/4AD 1987)★★★, House Tornado (Sire/4AD 1988)★★★, Hunkpapa (Sire/4AD 1989)★★, The Real Ramona (Sire/4AD 1991)★★★★, Red Heaven (Sire/4AD 1992)★★★ University (Sire/4AD 1995)★★★★, Limbo (4AD 1996)★★★.
COMPILATIONS: In A Doghouse (4AD 1998)★★★.

THUNDERCLAP NEWMAN
ALBUMS: Hollywood Dream (Track 1970)★★★.

THUNDERS, JOHNNY
ALBUMS: So Alone (Real 1978)★★★★, In Cold Blood (New Rose 1983)★★★, Too Much Junkie Business cassette only (ROIR 1983)★★★, Hurt Me (New Rose 1984)★★★, Que Sera Sera (Jungle 1985)★★★, Stations Of The Cross cassette only (ROIR 1987)★★, with Patti Palladin Copy Cats (Restless 1988)★★★, with Wayne Kramer Gang War (Zodiac 1990)H, Bootlegging The Bootleggers (Jungle 1990)★★, Live At Max's Kansas City '79 (ROIR 1996)★★★, Have Faith (Mutiny 1996)★★, with Sylvain Sylvain Sad Vacation 1984 recordings (Receiver 1999)★★★, Belfast Nights (Amsterdamned 2000)★★, Live And Wasted: Unplugged 1990 (Receiver 2000)★★★.
COMPILATIONS: Hurt Me (Dojo 1995)★★★, The Studio Bootlegs (Dojo 1996)★★, Born Too Loose: The Best Of Johnny Thunders (Jungle 1999)★★★.
FURTHER READING: Johnny Thunders: In Cold Blood, Nina Antonia. Johnny Thunders Discography.

TIKARAM, TANITA
ALBUMS: Ancient Heart (Warners 1988)★★★★, The Sweet Keeper (East West 1990)★★, Everybody's Angel (East West 1991)★★, Eleven Kinds Of Loneliness (East West 1992)★★, Lovers In The City (East West 1995)★★★, The Cappuccino Songs (Mother 1998)★★★.

TIMBALAND
ALBUMS: with Magoo Welcome To Our World (Blackground/Atlantic 1997)★★★★, Tim's Bio: From The Motion Picture: Life From Da Bassment (Blackground/Atlantic 1998)★★★, with Magoo Indecent Proposal (Blackground/Virgin 2001)★★★.

TINDERSTICKS
ALBUMS: Tindersticks (This Way Up 1993)★★★★, Amsterdam February '94 10-inch album (This Way Up 1994)★★, The Second Tindersticks Album (This Way Up 1995)★★★★, The Bloomsbury Theatre 12.3.95 10-inch album (This Way Up 1995)★★, Nénette Et Boni film soundtrack (This Way Up 1996)★★★, Curtains (This Way Up 1997)★★★★, Simple Pleasure (Island 1999)★★★, Can Our Love ... (Beggars Banquet 2001)★★★★, Trouble Every Day film soundtrack (Beggars Banquet 2001)★★★.
COMPILATIONS: Donkeys '92-'97 (Island 1998)★★★★.

TLC
ALBUMS: Oooooohhh ... On The TLC Tip (LaFace/Arista 1992)★★, TLC (LaFace/Arista 1993)★★★★, CrazySexyCool (LaFace/Arista 1995)★★★★, Fanmail (Arista 1999)★★★★.
SOLO: Lisa 'Left Eye' Lopes Supernova (Arista 2001)★★★.
VIDEOS: Crazy Video Cool (BMG Video 1995).

TOAD THE WET SPROCKET
ALBUMS: Bread And Circus (Abe's 1986)★★★, Pale (Abe's 1988)★★, Fear (Columbia 1991)★★, Dulcinea (Columbia 1994)★★★, In Light Syrup (Columbia 1995)★★, Coil (Columbia 1997)★★★.

TONE-LOC
ALBUMS: Loc-ed After Dark (Delicious Vinyl 1989)★★★, Cool Hand Loc (Delicious Vinyl 1991)★★★.
FILMS: The Adventures Of Ford Fairlaine (1990), The Return Of Superfly (1990), FernGully: The Last Rainforest voice only (1992), Bebe's Kids voice only (1992), Surf Ninjas (1993), Posse (1993), Poetic Justice (1993), Car 54, Where Are You? (1994), Blank Check (1994), Ace Ventura: Pet Detective (1994), Heat (1995), Spy Hard (1996), Fakin' Da Funk (1997), Freedom Strike (1998), Whispers: An Elephant's Tale voice only (2000), Titan A.E. voice only (2000), Deadly Rhapsody (2001).

TONY! TONI! TONÉ!
ALBUMS: Who? (Wing 1988)★★★, The Revival (Wing/Mercury 1990)★★★, Sons Of Soul (Wing/Mercury 1993)★★★, House Of Music (Mercury 1996)★★★★.
COMPILATIONS: Hits (Mercury 1997)★★★★.

TOOL
ALBUMS: Opiate mini-album (Zoo 1992)★★, Undertow (Zoo 1993)★★★, Aenima (RCA 1996)★★★★, Salival (Tool Dissectional 2000)★★★, Lateralus (Tool Dissectional/Music For Nations 2001)★★★★.
VIDEOS: Salival (BMG Video 2000).

TOPLOADER
ALBUMS: Onka's Big Moka (S2/Epic 2000)★★★.

TORNADOS
ALBUMS: Away From It All (Decca 1963)★★★.
COMPILATIONS: The World Of The Tornados (Decca 1972)★★★, Remembering ... The Tornados (Decca 1976)★★★, The Original 60s Hits (Music Club 1994)★★★, The EP Collection (See For Miles 1996)★★★★, The Very Best Of The Tornados (Music Club 1997)★★★, Telstar: The Complete (Repertoire 1998)★★★, Satellites And Sound Effects (Connoisseur 2000)★★★.

TORTOISE
ALBUMS: Tortoise (Thrill Jockey/City Slang 1994)★★★, Rhythms, Resolutions & Clusters (Thrill Jockey/City Slang 1995)★★★, Millions Now Living Will Never Die (Thrill Jockey/City Slang 1996)★★★★, TNT (Thrill Jockey/City Slang 1998)★★★, Standards (Thrill Jockey/Warp 2001)★★★.

TOSH, PETER
ALBUMS: Legalize It (Virgin 1976)★★★★, Equal Rights (Virgin 1977)★★★★, Bush Doctor (Rolling Stones 1978)★★★★, Mystic Man (Rolling Stones/EMI 1979)★★★, Wanted, Dread & Alive (Rolling Stones/Dynamic 1981)★★★, Mama Africa (Intel Diplo/EMI 1983)★★★, Captured Live (EMI 1984)★★★, No Nuclear War (EMI 1987)★★★, Live & Dangerous Boston 1976 (Columbia/Legacy 2001)★★★★.
COMPILATIONS: The Toughest (Parlophone 1988)★★★, The Gold Collection (EMI 1996)★★★, Honorary Citizen 3-CD box set (Legacy 1997)★★★★, Scrolls Of The Prophet: The Best Of Peter Tosh (Columbia 1999)★★★★, Arise Black Man (Trojan 2000)★★★★, Arise! The Best Of Peter Tosh (Music Club 2001)★★★★.
VIDEOS: Live (PMI 1986), Downpresser Man (Hendring Music Video 1988), Stepping Razor - Red X (1993).

TOTO
ALBUMS: Toto (Columbia 1978)★★★, Hydra (Columbia 1979)★★, Turn Back (Columbia 1981)★★, Toto IV (Columbia 1982)★★★★, Isolation (Columbia 1984)★★, Dune film soundtrack (Columbia 1984)★★, Fahrenheit (Columbia 1986)★★, The Seventh One (Columbia 1988)★★, Kingdom Of Desire (Columbia 1992)★★, Absolutely Live (Columbia 1993)H, Tambu (Columbia 1995)★★★, Mindfields (Columbia 1999)★★.
COMPILATIONS: Past To Present 1977-1990 (Columbia 1990)★★★, Toto XX (Columbia 1998)★★★.
VIDEOS: Past To Present 1977-1990 (Sony Music Video 1990).

TOURÉ, ALI FARKA
ALBUMS: Bandolobourou (Son Afrique 1974)★★, Ali Farka Touré (Son Afrique 1976)★★★★, Special (Son Afrique 1976)★★★, Bienelle (Son Afrique 1977)★★★, Yer Sabou Yerkoy (Son Afrique 1977)★★★, Banga (Son Afrique 1979)★★★, La Drogue (Disques Esperance 1984)★★★, Ali Farka Touré (World Circuit 1987)★★★★, Sidy Gouro (Disques Esperance 1988)★★★, The River (World Circuit 1990)★★★, The Source (World Circuit 1993)★★★, with Ry Cooder Talking Timbuktu (World Circuit 1994)★★★★, Radio Mali (World Circuit 1996)★★★, Niafunké (World Circuit 1999)★★★.

TOURISTS
ALBUMS: The Tourists (Logo 1979)★★, Reality Effect (Logo 1979)★★★★, Luminous Basement (RCA 1980)★★★.
COMPILATIONS: Should Have Been Greatest Hits (Epic 1984)★★★, Greatest Hits (Camden 1997)★★★.
FURTHER READING: Annie Lennox: The Biography, Bryony Sutherland & Lucy Ellis.

TOUSSAINT, ALLEN
ALBUMS: originally released under the name of Al Tousan The Wild Sounds Of New Orleans (RCA 1958)★★★, Toussaint (Reprise 1971)★★★, Life Love And Faith (Reprise 1972)★★★, Southern Nights (Reprise 1975)★★★★, Motion (Reprise 1978)★★★, Connected (Nyno 1996)★★★, as Allen Toussaint And Friends A Taste Of New Orleans (Nyno 1999)★★★.
COMPILATIONS: The Allen Toussaint Collection (Warners 1991)★★★★, The Wild Sound Of New Orleans: The Complete 'Tousan' Sessions (Bear Family 1992)★★★★, Mr. New Orleans (Charly 1994)★★★, The Allen Toussaint Touch (RPM/Shout 2000)★★★.
FILMS: Eve's Bayou (1997).

TOWER OF POWER
ALBUMS: East Bay Grease (San Francisco 1969)★★★, Bump City (Warners 1971)★★★, Tower Of Power (Warners 1973)★★★★, Back To Oakland (Warners 1974)★★★★, Urban Renewal (Warners 1975)★★★★, In The Slot (Warners 1975)★★★, Live And In Living Color (Warners 1976)★★★★, Ain't Nothin' Stoppin' Us Now (Columbia 1976)★★★, We Came To Play! (Columbia 1978)★★★, Back On The Streets (Columbia 1979)★★★, Direct (Sheffield Lab 1981)★★★, Power (Cypress 1987)★★★, Monster On A Leash (Epic 1991)★★★, T.O.P. (Epic 1993)★★★, Souled Out (Epic 1995)★★★, Rhythm & Business (Epic 1997)★★★, Dinosaur Tracks 1982 recording (Rhino Handmade 1999)★★★.
COMPILATIONS: What Is Hip? (Edsel 1986)★★★★, What Is Hip? The Tower Of Power Anthology (Warners/Rhino 1999)★★★★, The Very Best Of Tower Of Power: The Warner Years (Rhino 2001)★★★★, Soul With A Capital 'S': The Best Of (Epic/Legacy 2002)★★★★.

TOWNSHEND, PETE
ALBUMS: Who Came First (Track 1972)★★★, with Ronnie Lane Rough Mix (Polydor 1977)★★★★, Empty Glass (Atco 1980)★★★, All The Best Cowboys Have Chinese Eyes (Atco 1982)★★, Scoop (Polydor 1983)★★, White City (Atco 1985)★★, Pete Townshend's Deep End - Live (Atco 1986)★★, Another Scoop (Atco 1987)★★, Iron Man (Atlantic 1989)★★, Psychoderelict (Atlantic 1993)★★★, Pete Townshend Live: A Benefit For Maryville Academy (Platinum 1999)★★★, Live > The Fillmore 1996 (Eel Pie 2000)★★★, Live > The Empire 1998 (Eel Pie 2000)★★★, Live > Sadler's Wells 2000 (Eel Pie 2000)★★★, with Raphael Rudd The Oceanic Concerts (Warners/Rhino 2001)★★★, 22/06/01: Live > La Jolla Playhouse 2001 (Eel Pie 2001)★★★, 23/06/01: Live > La Jolla Playhouse 2001 (Eel Pie 2001)★★★, Scoop 3 (Eel Pie 2002)★★★.
COMPILATIONS: The Best Of Pete Townshend (East West 1996)★★★, The Lifehouse Chronicles 6-CD box set (Eel Pie 2000)★★★, Lifehouse Elements (Eel Pie 2000)★★★.
VIDEOS: Music From Lifehouse (Aviva International 2001).
FURTHER READING: The Horses Neck, Pete Townshend. A Life Of Pete Townshend: Behind Blue Eyes, Geoffrey Guiliano. Lifehouse, Pete Townshend with Jeff Young.

TRAFFIC
ALBUMS: Mr. Fantasy (Island 1967)★★★★, Traffic (Island 1968)★★★★★, Last Exit (Island 1969)★★, John Barleycorn Must Die (Island 1970)★★★★, Welcome To The Canteen (Island 1971)★★★, The Low Spark Of High Heeled Boys (Island 1971)★★★★, Shoot Out At The Fantasy Factory (Island 1973)★★★, On The Road (Island 1973)★★, When The Eagle Flies (Island 1974)★★★, Far From Home (Virgin 1994)★★★.
COMPILATIONS: Best Of Traffic (Island 1970)★★★★, Heavy Traffic (Island 1975)★★★★, More Heavy Traffic (Island 1975)★★★, Smiling Phases 2-CD set (Island 1991)★★★★, Heaven Is In Your Mind: An Introduction To Traffic (Island 1998)★★★, The Best Of Traffic (Spectrum 2001)★★★.
FURTHER READING: Keep On Running: The Steve Winwood Story, Chris Welch. Back In The High Life: A Biography Of Steve Winwood, Alan Clayson.

TRAIN
ALBUMS: Train (Aware/Columbia 1998)★★★, Drops Of Jupiter (Aware/Columbia 2001)★★★.
VIDEOS: Midnight Moon (Sony 2001).

TRAVELING WILBURYS
ALBUMS: Volume 1 (Wilbury 1988)★★★★, Volume 3 (Wilbury 1990)★★★★.

TRAVERS, PAT, BAND
ALBUMS: Pat Travers (Polydor 1976)★★★, Makin' Magic (Polydor 1977)★★★, Puttin' It Straight (Polydor 1977)★★★, Heat In The Street (Polydor 1978)★★★, Live! Go For What You Know (Polydor 1979)★★★, Crash & Burn (Polydor 1980)★★★, Radio Active (Polydor 1981)★★★, Black Pearl (Polydor 1982)★★★, Hot Shot (Polydor 1984)★★★, School Of Hard Knocks (Episode 1990)★★★, Blues Tracks (Blues Bureau 1992)★★★, Just A Touch (Blues Bureau 1993)★★★, Blues Magnet (Blues Bureau 1994)★★★, Halfway To Somewhere (Blues Bureau 1995)★★★, Lookin' Up (Blues Bureau 1996)★★★, King Biscuit Flower Hour 1984 live recording (King Biscuit Flower Hour 1997)★★★, Blues Tracks 2 (Blues Bureau 1998)★★★.
COMPILATIONS: Boom Boom: The Best Of Pat Travers (Polydor 1983)★★★★, Anthology Volume 1 (Polydor 1990)★★★★, Anthology Volume 2 (Polydor 1990)★★★★.
VIDEOS: Boom Boom (Essential 1991).

TRAVIS
ALBUMS: Good Feeling (Independiente 1997)★★★, The Man Who (Independiente 1999)★★★★, The Invisible Band (Independiente 2001)★★★.
VIDEOS: More Than Us: Live From Glasgow (Independiente 2001).
FURTHER READING: Closer Every Year: The Story Of Travis, Mike Black.

TREMELOES
ALBUMS: Here Comes The Tremeloes (CBS 1967)★★★★, Chip, Dave, Alan And Rick (CBS 1967)★★★, Here Comes My Baby US only (Epic 1967)★★★★, Even The Bad Times Are Good US only (Epic 1967)★★★, Suddenly You Love Me US only (Epic 1968)★★★, World Explosion 58/68 US only (Epic 1968)★★★, Live In Cabaret (CBS 1969)★★, Master (CBS 1970)★★, Shiner (DJM 1974)★★, Don't Let The Music Die (DJM 1976)★★, May Morning 1970 film soundtrack (Castle 2000)★★★.
COMPILATIONS: Greatest Hits (Pickwick 1981)★★★, The Ultimate Collection (Castle 1990)★★★, The Best Of The Tremeloes (Rhino 1992)★★★★, Silence Is Golden (Spectrum 1995)★★★, Tremendous Hits (Music Club 1997)★★★, The Definitive Collection (Castle 1998)★★★, Good Day Sunshine: Singles A's & B's (Castle 1999)★★★★.

TRICKY
ALBUMS: Maxinquaye (4th & Broadway 1995)★★★★★, as Nearly God Nearly God (Durban Poison 1996)★★★, Pre-Millennium Tension (Island 1996)★★★, Angels With Dirty Faces (Island 1998)★★, with DJ Muggs, Grease Juxtapose (Island 1999)★★★, Blowback (Anti/Hollywood 2001)★★★★.
FILMS: The Fifth Element (1997).

TRIFFIDS
ALBUMS: Treeless Plain (Hot/Rough Trade 1983)★★★, Raining Pleasure mini-album (Hot/Rough Trade 1984)★★★, Field Of Glass (Hot/Rough Trade 1985)★★★, Born Sandy Devotional (Hot/Rough Trade 1986)★★★★, In The Pines (Hot/Rough Trade 1986)★★★, Calenture (Island 1987)★★★★, The Black Swan (Island 1989)★★★, Stockholm (MNW 1990)★★★.
SOLO: David McComb Love Of Will (Mushroom 1994)★★★★.
COMPILATIONS: Love In Bright Landscapes Dutch release (Hot/Megadisc 1986)★★★, Australian Melodrama (Mushroom 1994)★★★★.

TROGGS
ALBUMS: From Nowhere ... The Troggs (Fontana 1966)★★★★, Trogglodynamite (Page One 1967)★★★★, Cellophane (Page One 1967)★★★★, Mixed Bag (Page One 1968)★★★, Trogglomania (Page One 1969)★★★, Contrasts (DJM 1970)★★, With A Girl Like You (DJM 1975)★★, The Original Troggs Tapes (DJM 1976)★, Live At Max's Kansas City (President 1981)★, Black Bottom (RCA 1982)★★, Rock It Up (Action Replay 1984)★★, Au (New Rose 1989)★★, Athens Andover (Page One 1992)★★★.
COMPILATIONS: The Best Of The Troggs (Page One 1967)★★★★, The Best Of The Troggs Volume 2 (Page One 1968)★★★, Wild Things (DJM 1975)★★★, 14 Greatest Hits (Spectrum 1988)★★★★, The Troggs Hit Singles Anthology (Fontana 1991)★★★, Archaeology 1966 - 1976 (Fontana 1992)★★★, Greatest Hits (PolyGram 1994)★★★★, The EP Collection (See For Miles 1996)★★★★.
FURTHER READING: Rock's Wild Things: The Troggs Files, Alan Clayson and Jacqueline Ryan.

TUBES
ALBUMS: The Tubes (A&M 1975)★★★, Young And Rich (A&M 1976)★★★, Now (A&M 1977)★★★, What Do You Want From Live (A&M 1978)★★, Remote Control (A&M 1979)★★, The Completion Backward Principle (Capitol 1981)★★, Outside Inside (Capitol 1983)★★★, Love Bomb (Capitol 1985)★★, Genius Of America (Popular 1996)★★, The Tubes Infomercial: How To Become Tubular 1981 recording (Hux 2000)★★, TWT 2001 (CMC/Sanctuary 2000)★★★.
COMPILATIONS: T.R.A.S.H. (Tubes Rarities And Smash Hits) (A&M 1981)★★★, The Best Of The Tubes 1981-1987 (Capitol 1991)★★★, The Best Of The Tubes (Capitol 1992)★★★, Goin' Down (A&M 1996)★★★, Dawn Of The Tubes: Demo Daze And Radio Waves (Phoenix Gems 2000)★★★, The Best Of The Tubes: The Millennium Collection (A&M 2000)★★★.
VIDEOS: The Tubes Live At The Greek (Monterey Video 1976), The Tubes Video (Cannon 1982).

2PAC
ALBUMS: 2Pacalypse Now (TNT/Interscope 1991)★★★, Strictly 4 My N.I.G.G.A.Z. (TNT/Interscope 1993)★★★, Me Against The World (Out Da Gutta/Interscope 1995)★★★★, All Eyez On Me (Death Row/Interscope 1996)★★★★, as Makaveli The Don Killuminati: The 7 Day Theory (Death Row/Interscope 1996)★★, In His Own Words (Mecca 1998)★★, with Outlawz Still I Rise (Interscope 1999)★★★, The Rose That Grew From Concrete (Interscope 2000)★★★★.
COMPILATIONS: R U Still Down? (Remember Me) (Amaru 1997)★★★, Greatest Hits (Interscope 1998)★★★★, as Makaveli Volume 8: The Remix Album (Cochise 2000)★★, Until The End Of Time (Amaru/Death Row 2001)★★★.
VIDEOS: Thug Immortal: The Tupac Shakur Story (Xenon Entertainment 1998), Words Never Die (IMC/Scimitar 1998).
FURTHER READING: Tupac Shakur, editors of Vibe. Rebel For The Hell Of It: The Life Of Tupac Shakur, Armond White. Got Your Back: Life As Tupac Shakur's Bodyguard In The Hardcore World Of Gangsta Rap, Frank Alexander with Heidi Siegmund Cuda. The Rose That Grew From Concrete, Tupac Shakur. The Killing Of Tupac Shakur, Cathy Scott, Holler If You Hear Me: Searching For Tupac Shakur, Michael Eric Dyson.
FILMS: Nothing But Trouble (1991), Juice aka Angel Town 2 (1992), Poetic Justice (1993), Above The Rim (1994), Bullet (1996), Gridlock'd (1997), Rhyme & Reason (1997), Gang Related (1997).

TURNER, IKE AND TINA
ALBUMS: The Soul Of Ike And Tina Turner (Sue 1960)★★, Dance With The Kings Of Rhythm (Sue 1960)★★★, Dance With Ike And Tina Turner (Sue 1962)★★★, Festival Of Live Performances (Kent 1962)★★, Dynamite (Sue 1963)★★★★, Don't Play Me Cheap (Sue 1963)★★★, It's Gonna Work Out Fine (Sue 1963)★★★★, Please Please Please (Kent 1964)★★★, The Soul Of Ike And Tina Turner (Kent 1964)★★★, The Ike And Tina Show Live (Loma 1965)★★★★, The Ike And Tina Turner Show Live (Warners 1965)★★★★, River Deep - Mountain High (London 1966)★★★★, So Fine (Pompeii 1968)★★★★, In Person (Minit 1968)★★★★, Cussin', Cryin' And Carrying On (Pompeii 1969)★★★, Get It Together! (Pompeii 1969)★★★★, A Black Man's Soul (Pompeii 1969)★★★, Outta Season (Liberty 1969)★★★, In Person (Minit 1969)★★★, River Deep - Mountain High (A&M/London 1969)★★★★, Come Together (Liberty 1970)★★★, The Hunter (Harvest 1970)★★★★, Workin' Together (Liberty 1971)★★★, Her Man, His Woman (Capitol 1971)★★★, Live In Paris (Liberty 1971)★★★★, Live At Carnegie Hall - What You Hear Is What You Get (Liberty 1971)★★★, 'Nuff Said (United Artists 1972)★★, Feel Good (United Artists 1972)★★, Let Me Touch Your Mind (United Artists 1973)★★, Nutbush City Limits (United Artists 1973)★★★★, Strange Fruit (1974)★★★, Sweet Island Rhode Red (United Artists 1974)★★, Delilah's Power (United Artists 1977)★★, Airwaves (1978)★★.
COMPILATIONS: Ike And Tina Turner's Greatest Hits (Sue 1965)★★★, Ike And Tina Turner's Greatest Hits (Warners 1969)★★★★, Tough Enough (Liberty 1984)★★★, Fingerpoppin' -The Warner Brothers Years (Warners 1988)★★★, Proud Mary: The Best Of Ike And Tina Turner (EMI 1991)★★★★, Feel It! (Carlton 1998)★★★.
FURTHER READING: I Tina, Tina Turner with Kurt Loder. The Tina Turner Experience, Chris Welch. Takin' Back My Name, Ike Turner with Nigel Cawthorne.

TURNER, TINA
ALBUMS: The Country Of Tina Turner (Connoisseur)★★★, Acid Queen (United Artists 1975)★★★, Rough (United Artists 1978)★★, Love Explosion (United Artists 1979)★★★, Private Dancer (Capitol 1984)★★★★, Break Every Rule (Capitol 1986)★★★, Live In Europe: Tina Turner (Capitol 1988)★★, Foreign Affair (Capitol 1989)★★★, What's Love Got To Do With It? film soundtrack (Parlophone 1993)★★★, Wildest Dreams (Parlophone/Virgin 1996)★★★, Twenty Four Seven (Parlophone 1999)★★.
COMPILATIONS: Simply The Best (Capitol 1991)★★★★, Tina Turner: The Collected Recordings, 60s To 90s (Capitol 1994)★★★★.
VIDEOS: Nice 'N' Rough (EMI 1982), Private Dancer Video EP (PMI 1985), Private Dancer Tour (PMI 1985), What You See Is What You Get (PMI 1987), Break Every Rule (PMI

1987), *Rio 88* (PolyGram Music Video 1988), *Foreign Affair* (PMI 1990), *Do You Want Some Action* (Channel 5 1990), *Simply The Best* (PMI 1991), *Wild Lady Of Rock* (Hendring Music Video 1992), *What's Love Live* (1994), *The Girl From Nutbush* (Strand 1995), *Wildest Dreams* (Feedback Fusion 1996), *Live In Amsterdam* (Castle Music Pictures 1997), *One Last Time Live In Concert* (Eagle Vision 2001).
FURTHER READING: *I, Tina*, Tina Turner with Kurt Loder. *The Tina Turner Experience*, Chris Welch. *Takin' Back My Name*, Ike Turner and Nigel Cawthorne.
FILMS: *Tommy* (1975), *Sgt. Pepper's Lonely Hearts Club Band* (1978), *Mad Max Beyond Thunderdome* (1985), *What's Love Got To Do With It* (1993), *Last Action Hero* (1993).

TURTLES
ALBUMS: *It Ain't Me Babe* (White Whale 1965)★★★, *You Baby* (White Whale 1966)★★, *Happy Together* (White Whale 1967)★★★, *The Battle Of The Bands* (White Whale 1968)★★, *Turtle Soup* (White Whale 1969)★★, *Wooden Head* (White Whale 1971)★★, *Happy Together Again* (Sire 1974)★★.
COMPILATIONS: *Golden Hits Vol. I* (White Whale 1967)★★★, *Golden Hits Vol. II* (White Whale 1968)★★★, *20 Greatest Hits* (Rhino 1983)★★★, *20 Golden Classics* (Mainline 1990)★★★, *Happy Together: The Very Best Of The Turtles* (Music Club 1991)★★★, *Happy Together: 30 Years Of Rock & Roll* 5-CD box set (Laserlight 1995)★★★, *Solid Zinc* (Rhino 2002)★★★★.

TWAIN, SHANIA
ALBUMS: *Shania Twain* (Mercury 1993)★★★, *The Woman In Me* (Mercury 1995)★★★★, *Come On Over* (Mercury 1997)★★★, with Mariah Carey, Celine Dion, Gloria Estefan, Aretha Franklin *Divas Live* (Epic 1998)★★.
VIDEOS: *Any Man Of Mine* (Mercury 1995), *The Complete Woman In Me* (PolyGram Music Video 1996), with Mariah Carey, Celine Dion, Gloria Estefan, Aretha Franklin *Divas Live* (Sony Music Video 1998), *Live* (USA Home Entertainment/Universal 1999).
FURTHER READING: *Shania Twain*, Peter Kane. *Shania Twain: Still The One*, Jim Brown.

TWISTED SISTER
ALBUMS: *Under The Blade* (Secret 1982)★★, *You Can't Stop Rock 'N' Roll* (Atlantic 1983)★★, *Stay Hungry* (Atlantic 1984)★★, *Come Out And Play* (Atlantic 1985)★★, *Love Is For Suckers* (Atlantic 1987)★★, *Live At Hammersmith* (Music For Nations/CMC 1994)★★.
COMPILATIONS: *Big Hits & Nasty Cuts: The Best Of Twisted Sister* (Atlantic 1992)★★★, *Club Daze Volume 1: The Studio Sessions* (Spitfire 1999)★★, *Club Daze Volume 2: Never Say Never* (Spitfire 2001)★★, *Disco Sucks* (Snapper 2001)★.
VIDEOS: *Stay Hungry* (Virgin 1984), *Come Out And Play* (Atlantic 1985).
FILMS: *Pee-Wee's Big Adventure* (1985).

TYLER, BONNIE
ALBUMS: *The World Starts Tonight* (RCA 1977)★★, *Natural Force (It's A Heartache USA)* (RCA 1978)★★★, *Diamond Cut* (RCA 1979)★★★, *Goodbye To The Island* (RCA 1981)★★, *Faster Than The Speed Of Night* (Columbia 1983)★★★, *Secret Dreams And Forbidden Fire* (Columbia 1986)★★, *Hide Your Heart* (Columbia 1988)★★, *Bitterblue* (Hansa 1991)★★, *Free Spirit* (East West 1995)★★.
COMPILATIONS: *The Very Best Of Bonnie Tyler* (RCA 1981)★★★, *Greatest Hits* (Telstar 1986)★★★, *The Best* (Columbia 1993)★★★, *Greatest Hits* (Sanctuary 2001)★★★.
FILMS: *Footloose* (1984).

U
U2
ALBUMS: *Boy* (Island 1980)★★★★, *October* (Island 1981)★★★, *War* (Island 1983)★★★★, *The Unforgettable Fire* (Island 1984)★★★★, *Wide Awake In America* (Island 1985)★★★, *The Joshua Tree* (Island 1987)★★★★, *The Joshua Tree Singles* (Island 1987)★★★★, *Rattle And Hum* (Island 1988)★★★, *Achtung Baby* (Island 1991)★★★★, *Zooropa* (Island 1993)★★★, *Pop* (Island 1997)★★★, *All That You Can't Leave Behind* (Island 2000)★★★★.
COMPILATIONS: *The Best Of 1980-1990* (Island 1998)★★★.
VIDEOS: *Under A Blood Red Sky (Live At Red Rocks)* (PolyGram Music Video 1983), *The Unforgettable Fire Collection* (PolyGram Music Video 1985), *Rattle And Hum* (PolyGram Music Video 1988), *Achtung Baby* (PolyGram Music Video 1992), *Zoo TV: Live From Sydney* (PolyGram Music Video 1994), *PopMart: Live From Mexico City* (PolyGram Music Video 1998), *The Best Of 1980-1990* (PolyGram Music Video 1999), *Classic Albums: U2 - Joshua Tree* (Eagle Rock Entertainment 1999), *Elevation 2001: U2 Live From Boston* (Universal 2001).
FURTHER READING: *U2: Touch The Flame: An Illustrated Documentary*, Geoff Parkyn. *Unforgettable Fire: The Story Of U2*, Eamon Dunphy. *Rattle And Hum*, Peter Williams and Steve Turner. *U2: Stories For Boys*, Dave Thomas. *U2: The Early Days: Another Time, Another Place*, Bill Graham. *U2: Three Chords & The Truth*, Niall Stokes. *Wide Awake In America*, Alan Carter. *U2: A Conspiracy Of Hope*, Dave Bowler and Brian Dray. *U2: The Story So Far*, Richard Seal. *U2: Burning Desire: The Complete Story*, Sam Goodman. *U2 Live: A Concert Documentary*, Pimm Jal De La Perra. *Race Of Angels: The Genesis Of U2*, John Waters. *U2, The Rolling Stones File*, editors of Rolling Stone. *U2 At The End Of The World*, Bill Flanagan. *U2 Faraway So Close*, B.P. Fallon. *The Complete Guide To The Music Of U2*, Bill Graham. *The Making Of U2's Joshua Tree*, Dave Thompson. *Bono: The Biography*, Laura Jackson. *Into The Heart: The Stories Behind Every Song*, Niall Stokes. *U2: The Complete Encyclopedia*, Mark Chatterton.
FILMS: *Rattle And Hum* (1988).

UB40
ALBUMS: *Signing Off* (Graduate 1980)★★★★, *Present Arms* (DEP 1981)★★★, *Present Arms In Dub* (DEP 1981)★★★★, *UB44* (DEP 1982)★★★, *UB40 Live* (DEP 1983)★★★, *Labour Of Love* (DEP 1983)★★★, *Geffrey Morgan* (DEP 1984)★★★★, *Baggariddim* (DEP 1985)★★★, *Rat In Mi Kitchen*

(DEP 1986)★★★★, *UB40* (DEP 1988)★★★★, *Labour Of Love II* (DEP 1989)★★★★, *Promises And Lies* (DEP 1993)★★★, *Guns In The Ghetto* (Virgin 1997)★★★, with various artists *UB40 Present The Dancehall Album* (Virgin 1998)★★★, *Labour Of Love III* (Virgin 1998)★★★, *Cover Up* (Virgin 2001)★★★★.
SOLO: Ali Campbell *Big Love* (Virgin 1995)★★★.
COMPILATIONS: *The Singles Album* (Graduate 1982)★★★, *The UB40 File* double album (Graduate 1985)★★★, *The Best Of UB40 Volume 1* (DEP 1987)★★★, *UB40 Box Set* (Virgin 1991)★★★★, *The Best Of UB40 Volume 2* (DEP 1995)★★★, *The Very Best Of 1980-2000* (Virgin 2000)★★★★.
VIDEOS: *Labour Of Love* (Virgin Vision 1984), *Best Of UB40* (Virgin Vision 1987), *CCCP: The Video Mix* (Virgin Vision 1987), *UB40 Live* (Virgin Vision 1988), *Dance With The Devil* (Virgin Vision 1988), *Labour Of Love II* (Virgin Vision 1990), *A Family Affair Live In Concert* (Virgin Vision 1991), *Live In The New South Africa* (PMI 1995).

UFO
ALBUMS: *UFO 1* (Nova-Beacon 1970)★★, *UFO 2: Flying One Hour Space Rock* (Nova-Beacon 1971)★★, *UFO Live* (Nova-Beacon 1972)★★★, *Phenomenon* (Chrysalis 1974)★★★★, *Force It* (Chrysalis 1975)★★★, *No Heavy Petting* (Chrysalis 1976)★★, *Lights Out* (Chrysalis 1977)★★★★, *Obsession* (Chrysalis 1978)★★★, *Strangers In The Night* (Chrysalis 1979)★★★, *No Place To Run* (Chrysalis 1979)★★★, *The Wild The Willing And The Innocent* (Chrysalis 1981)★★, *Mechanix* (Chrysalis 1982)★★, *Making Contact* (Chrysalis 1983)★★, *Misdemeanor* (Chrysalis 1985)★★, *Ain't Misbehavin'* (FM Revolver 1988)★★, *High Stakes & Desperate Men* (Essential 1992)★★★, *BBC Radio 1 Live In Concert* (Windsong 1992)★★, *Lights Out In Tokyo — Live* (Victor 1992)★★★, *Walk On Water* (Zero 1995)★★★, *On With The Action: Live At The Roundhouse 1976 Zoom* (Zoom 1997)★★★, *Werewolves Of London* (Zoom 1999)★★, *Covenant* (Shrapnel/Koch 2000)★★.
COMPILATIONS: *The Best Of UFO* (Nova-Beacon 1973)★★★, *Headstone: The Best Of UFO* (Chrysalis 1983)★★★, *The Collection Part 1* (Castle 1985)★★★, *Anthology* (Raw 1987)★★★, *The Best Of The Rest* (Chrysalis 1988)★★★, *Essential UFO* (Chrysalis 1992)★★★★, *The Decca Years* (Repertoire 1993)★★★, *Too Hot To Handle: The Best Of UFO* (Music Club 1993)★★★, *TNT* (Castle 1994)★★, *Doctor, Doctor* (Spectrum/Polydor 1995)★★★, *Champions Of Rock* (Disky 1996)★★, *The X Factor: Out There ... And Back!* (Recall 1997)★★★, *Time To Rock: Best Of Singles A's & B's* (Repertoire 1998)★★★, *In Session And Live In Concert* (EMI 1999)★★★★.
VIDEOS: *UFO Live!*, *The Misdemeanor Tour* (Embassy 1986), *History Of UFO* (with Michael Schenker) (Toshiba 1992).

UGLY KID JOE
ALBUMS: *As Ugly As They Wanna Be* mini-album (Stardog 1992)★★★, *America's Least Wanted* (Stardog 1992)★★★, *Menace To Sobriety* (Mercury 1995)★★★, *Motel California* (Evilution 1996)★★.
COMPILATIONS: *As Ugly As It Gets: The Very Best Of* (Mercury 1998)★★★.

UK SUBS
ALBUMS: *Another Kind Of Blues* (Gem 1979)★★★, *Brand New Age* (Gem 1980)★★★, *Crash Course* (Gem 1980)★★★, *Diminished Responsibility* (Gem 1981)★★, *Endangered Species* (NEMS 1981)★★, *Flood Of Lies* (Fall Out/Jungle 1983)★★, *Gross Out USA* (Fall Out 1985)★★, *Huntington Beach* (RFB 1986)★★, *In Action* (RFB 1986)★★, *Japan Today* (Fall Out/Jungle 1987)H, *Killing Time* (New Red Archives 1988)H, *Live In Paris* (Released Emotions 1989)★★, *Mad Cow Fever* (Fall Out/Jungle 1990)★★, *Normal Service Resumed* (Fall Out/Jungle 1993)★★, *Occupied* (Fall Out/Jungle 1996)H, *Quintessentials* (Fall Out 1997)★★★, *Riot* (Cleopatra 1997)★★, *The Revolution's Here* (Combat 2001)★★, *Timewarp Greatest Hits* (Anagram 2001)★★★.
COMPILATIONS: *Live Kicks 1977* recordings (Stiff 1979)★★★, *Recorded 1979-1981* (Abstract 1982)★★, *Danger UK Subs Live* cassette only (Chaos 1982)★★, *Demonstration Tapes* (Konexion 1984)★★, *Raw Material* (Killerwatt 1986)★★, *Left For Dead: Alive In Holland '86* cassette only (ROIR 1986)★★, *Subs Standards* (Dojo 1986)H, *A.W.O.L.* (New Red Archives 1987)H, *Europe Calling* (Released Emotions 1989)★★, *Down On The Farm (A Collection Of The Less Obvious)* (Streetlink 1991)★★, *The Singles 1978-1982* (Abstract 1991)★★★, *Scum Of The Earth: The Best Of* (Music Club 1993)★★, *Punk Can Take It* (Cleopatra 1995)★★, *Self Destruct* (Cleopatra 1996)★★, *Peel Sessions 1978-79* (Fall Out/Jungle 1997)★★★, *The Punk Is Back* (Cleopatra 1997)★★, *Punk Rock Rarities* (Captain Oi! 1998)★★, *Warhead* (Harry Mary 1999)★★, *Sub Mission: The Best Of UK Subs 1982-1998* (Fall Out 1999)★★, *In Action (Tenth Anniversary)* (R 'N' B Recordings 1999)★★★.
VIDEOS: *Live At Peterless Leisure Centre Friday 10th June 1994* (Barn End 1994).
FURTHER READING: *Neighbourhood Threat*, Alvin Gibbs.

ULTRAMAGNETIC MC'S
ALBUMS: *Critical Beatdown* (Next Plateau 1988)★★★★, *Funk Your Head Up* (Mercury 1992)★★★, *The Four Horsemen* (Wild Pitch 1993)★★★.
COMPILATIONS: *The Basement Tapes 1984-1990* (Tuff City 1994)★★.

ULTRAVOX
ALBUMS: *Ultravox!* (Island 1977)★★, *Ha! Ha! Ha!* (Island 1977)★★, *Systems Of Romance* (Island 1978)★★★, *Vienna* (Chrysalis 1980)★★★, *Rage In Eden* (Chrysalis 1981)★★★, *Quartet* (Chrysalis 1982)★★, *Monument - The Soundtrack* (Chrysalis 1983)★★, *Lament* (Chrysalis 1984)★★, *U-Vox* (Chrysalis 1986)★★, *BBC Radio 1 Live In Concert 1981* recording (Windsong 1992)★★, *Revelation* (Deutsche Schallatten 1993)★★, *Ingenuity* (Intercord 1994)★★, *Future Picture Receiver* 1995)★★.
COMPILATIONS: *Three Into One* (Island 1980)★★★, *The Collection* (Chrysalis 1984)★★★, *If I Was: The Very Best Of Midge Ure & Ultravox* (Chrysalis 1993)★★★, *Rare* (Chrysalis 1993)★★, *Rare Volume 2* (Chrysalis 1994)★★, *Slow Motion* (Ultravox 1994)★★, *Dancing With Tears In My Eyes* (EMI 1995)★★★, *The Voice: The Best Of Ultravox* (Monument 1997)★★★, *Extended Ultravox* (EMI 1998)★★, *Original Gold* (Disky 1998)★★★, *The Island Years* (Disky 1999)★★★, *The Very Best Of Midge Ure & Ultravox* (Chrysalis 2001)★★★.
VIDEOS: *The Collection* (Chrysalis 1984).
FURTHER READING: *The Past, Present & Future Of Ultravox*, Drake and Gilbert.

UNCLE KRACKER
ALBUMS: *Double Wide* (Top Dog/Lava 2000)★★★★.

UNCLE TUPELO
ALBUMS: *No Depression* (Rockville 1990)★★★★, *Still Feel Gone* (Rockville 1991)★★★, *March 16-20, 1992* (Sire 1992)★★★★, *Anodyne* (Sire 1993)★★★★.
COMPILATIONS: *89/93: An Anthology* (Columbia/Legacy 2002)★★★★.

UNDERTONES
ALBUMS: *The Undertones* (Sire 1979)★★★★, *Hypnotised* (Sire 1980)★★★★, *Positive Touch* (Ardeck 1981)★★★★, *The Sin Of Pride* (Ardeck 1983)★★★.
COMPILATIONS: *All Wrapped Up* (Ardeck 1983)★★★★, *Cher O'Bowlies: The Pick Of The Undertones* (Ardeck 1986)★★★, *The Peel Sessions Album* (Strange Fruit 1989)★★★, *The Best Of The Undertones: Teenage Kicks* (Castle 1993)★★★, *True Confessions (Singles = A's + B's)* (Essential 1999)★★★, *The Singles Box Set* (Essential 2000)★★★★.

UNDERWORLD
ALBUMS: *Underneath The Radar* (Sire 1988)★★, *Change The Weather* (Sire 1989)★★★, *Dubnobasswithmyheadman* (Junior Boy's Own 1993)★★★★, *Second Toughest In The Infants* (Junior Boy's Own 1996)★★★, *Beaucoup Fish* (V2 1999)★★★, *Everything, Everything* (Junior Boy's Own 2000)★★★.
VIDEOS: *Everything, Everything* (Junior Boy's Own 2000).

URE, MIDGE
ALBUMS: with Chris Cross *The Bloodied Sword* film soundtrack (Chrysalis 1983)★★★, *The Gift* (Chrysalis 1985)★★★, *Answers To Nothing* (Chrysalis 1988)★★, *Pure* (Arista 1991)★★, *Breathe* (RCA 1996)★★, *Move Me* (Arista/Curb 2000)★★.
COMPILATIONS: *If I Was: The Very Best Of Midge Ure & Ultravox* (Chrysalis 1993)★★★, *If I Was* (Disky 1997)★★★, *No Regrets: The Very Best Of Midge Ure* (EMI Gold 2000)★★★, *The Very Best Of Midge Ure & Ultravox* (Chrysalis 2001)★★★.

URGE OVERKILL
ALBUMS: *Jesus Urge Superstar* (Touch & Go 1989)★★, *Americruiser* (Touch & Go 1990)★★, *The Supersonic Storybook* (Touch & Go 1991)★★★, *Stull* mini-album (Touch & Go 1992)★★, *Saturation* (Geffen 1993)★★★, *Exit The Dragon* (Geffen 1995)★★★.

URIAH HEEP
ALBUMS: *Very 'eavy... Very 'umble (UK)*, *Uriah Heep (USA)* (Vertigo 1970)★★★, *Salisbury* (Vertigo 1971)★★★, *Look At Yourself* (Bronze 1971)★★★, *Demons And Wizards* (Bronze 1972)★★★★, *The Magician's Birthday* (Bronze 1972)★★★, *Live: January 1973* (Bronze 1973)★★★, *Sweet Freedom* (Bronze 1973)★★, *Wonderworld* (Bronze 1974)★★★, *Return To Fantasy* (Bronze 1975)★★, *High And Mighty* (Bronze 1976)★★, *Firefly* (Bronze 1977)★★, *Innocent Victim* (Bronze 1977)★★, *Fallen Angel* (Bronze 1978)★★, *Conquest* (Bronze 1980)★★, *Abominog* (Bronze 1982)★★★, *Head First* (Bronze 1983)★★, *Equator* (Portrait 1985)★★★, *Live At Shepperton '74* (Castle 1986)★★, *Live: Right Here Live In Moscow* (Legacy 1988)★★, *Raging Silence* (Legacy 1989)★★, *Different World* (Legacy 1991)★★, *Sea Of Light* (HTD 1995)★★★, *Spellbinder 1994* live recording (CBH 1996)★★★, *Live On The King Biscuit Flower Hour 1974* recording (King Biscuit 1997)★★, *Sonic Origami* (Eagle 1998)★★★, *Acoustically Driven* (Phantom 2001)★★★.
COMPILATIONS: *The Best Of ...* (Bronze 1975)★★★, *The Best Of Uriah Heep* (Mercury 1976)★★★★, *Anthology* (Raw Power 1985)★★★, *Anthology Volume One* (Legacy 1986)★★★, *The Collection* (Castle 1989)★★★, *Trainkiller: 14 Rock Hard Hits* (Anwil 1989)★★, *Milestones* (Castle 1989)★★, *Still 'Eavy, Still Proud: Two Decades Of Uriah Heep* (Legacy 1990)★★★, *Two Decades In Rock* (Essential 1990)★★, *Echoes In The Dark* (Elite 1991)★★, *Rarities From The Bronze Age* (Sequel 1991)★★★, *The Lansdowne Tapes* (Red Steel 1993)★, *A Time Of Revelation: 25 Years On* 4-CD box set (Essential 1996)★★, *The Best Of ... Part 2* (Essential 1997)★★★, *Classic Heep: An Anthology* (Mercury 1998)★★★, *Travellers In Time: Anthology Vol 1* (Castle 2000)★★★, *Easy Livin'* (Delta 2000)★★★, *Blood On Stone: Anthology Volume II* (Castle 2001)★★★, *Empty The Vaults: The Rarities* (Castle 2001)★★★, *Come Away Melinda: A Collection Of Classic Uriah Heep Ballads* (Castle 2001)★★★, *Two Sides Of Uriah Heep* (CRL 2001)★★★, *Remasters: The Official Anthology* (Classic Rock Legends 2002)★★★.
VIDEOS: *Easy Livin': A History Of Uriah Heep* (Virgin Video 1985), *Raging Through The Silence* (Fotodisk Video 1989), *Uriah Heep: Live Castle Music Pictures* (1990), *Gypsy aka Live In London* (Hendring Music Video 1990), *Live In Moscow* (Syncrown 1995), *The Legend Continues ... A Celebration Of Thirty Years In Rock* (Cromwell Productions 2000), *Acoustically Driven* (2001), *Sailing The Sea Of Light* (2001).
FURTHER READING: *Uriah Heep: Golden Years*, Alexander Krispin and Stefan Eickhoff.

USHER
ALBUMS: *Usher* (LaFace 1994)★★★, *My Way* (LaFace 1997)★★★, *Live* (LaFace 1999)★★, *8701* (LaFace 2001)★★★.

UTAH SAINTS
ALBUMS: *Utah Saints* (London/ffrr 1992)★★★★, *Two* (Echo 2000)★★★.

V

VALENS, RITCHIE
ALBUMS: *Ritchie Valens* (Del Fi 1959)★★★★, *Ritchie* (Del Fi 1959)★★★, *Ritchie Valens In Concert At Pacoima Junior High* (Del Fi 1960)★★.
COMPILATIONS: *His Greatest Hits* (Del Fi 1963)★★★★, *His Greatest Hits Volume 2* (Del Fi 1965)★★, *I Remember Ritchie Valens* (President 1967)★★★, *The Best Of Ritchie Valens* (Rhino 1987)★★★, *The Best Of Ritchie Valens* (Ace 1992)★★★, *The Ritchie Valens Story* (Del Fi 1993)★★★, *The Very Best Of Ritchie Valens* (Music Club 1995)★★★, *Best In Space* (RCA 1994)★★★, *Come On Let's Go!* 3-CD box set (Del-Fi 1998)★★★★.
FURTHER READING: *Ritchie Valens: The First Latino Rocker*, Beverly Mendheim. *Ritchie Valens 1941-1959: 30th Anniversary Memorial Series No. 2*, Alan Clark.
FILMS: *Go Johnny Go* (1958).

VALENTINOS
ALBUMS: one side only *Double Barrelled Soul* (Sar 1968)★★, *Bobby Womack And The Valentinos* (Clifton 1984)★★.

VALLI, FRANKIE
ALBUMS: *Solo* (Philips 1967)★★★, *Timeless* (Philips 1968)★★★, *Close Up* (Private St. 1975)★★, *Our Day Will Come* (Private St. 1975)★★, *Frankie Valli Is The Word* (Warners 1978)★★, *Heaven Above Me* (MCA 1980)★★.
COMPILATIONS: *Gold* (Private St. 1975)★★★, *The Collection –The 20 Greatest Hits* (Telstar 1988)★★★, *The Very Best Of*

VAN HALEN
ALBUMS: *Van Halen* (Warners 1978)★★★★, *Van Halen II* (Warners 1979)★★★★, *Women And Children First* (Warners 1980)★★★, *Fair Warning* (Warners 1981)★★★, *Diver Down* (Warners 1982)★★★, *1984 (MCMLXXXIV)* (Warners 1984)★★★★, *5150* (Warners 1986)★★★★, *OU812* (Warners 1988)★★★, *For Unlawful Carnal Knowledge* (Warners 1991)★★★★, *Live: Right Here Now* (Warners 1993)★★★, *Balance* (Warners 1995)★★★, *Van Halen III* (Warners 1998)★★.
COMPILATIONS: *Best Of Volume 1* (Warners 1996)★★★.
VIDEOS: *Live Without A Net* (WEA 1987), *Live: Right Here Now* (1993), *Video Hits Volume 1* (Warner Music Video 1996).
FURTHER READING: *Van Halen*, Michelle Craven. *Excess All Areas*, Malcolm Dome.

VANDROSS, LUTHER
ALBUMS: *Never Too Much* (Epic 1981)★★★, *Forever, For Always, For Love* (Epic 1982)★★★, *Busy Body* (Epic 1983)★★★, *The Night I Fell In Love* (Epic 1985)★★★, *Give Me The Reason* (Epic 1986)★★★, *Any Love* (Epic 1988)★★★, *Power Of Love* (Epic 1991)★★★★, *Never Let Me Go* (Epic 1993)★★★, *Songs* (Epic 1994)★★★, *Your Secret Love* (Epic 1996)★★★, *I Know* (Virgin/EMI 1998)★★★, *Luther Vandross* (J 2001)★★★.
COMPILATIONS: *The Best Of Luther Vandross ... The Best Of Love* (Epic 1989)★★★, *Greatest Hits 1981-1995* (Epic 1995)★★★, *One Night With You: The Best Of Love Volume 2* (Epic 1997)★★, *Always & Forever: The Classics* (Epic 1998)★★★, *Greatest Hits* (Legacy 1999)★★★, *Super Hits* (Epic 2000)★★★, *The Essential Luther Vandross* (Epic 2002)★★★.
VIDEOS: *An Evening Of Songs* (Epic 1994), *Always And Forever* (Epic 1995).

VANGELIS
ALBUMS: *Sex Power* film soundtrack (Philips 1970)★★, *Fais Que Ton Rêve Soit Plus Long Que La Nuit* (Poème Symphonique De Vangelis Papathanassiou) (Reprise 1972)★★★, *Earth* (Vertigo 1973)★★, *L'Apocalypse Des Animaux* television soundtrack (Polydor 1973)★★★★, *Heaven And Hell* (RCA 1975)★★★, *Albedo 0.39* (RCA 1976)★★★, *Spiral* (RCA 1977)★★, as Vangelis Papahanassiou *Entends-tu Les Chiens Aboyer?* (BASF 1977)★★, *Ignacio* film soundtrack (Egg 1977)★★★, *Beaubourg* (RCA 1978)★★, *China* (Polydor 1979)★★★, *Opera Sauvage* television soundtrack (Polydor 1979)★★★, *See You Later* (Polydor 1980)★★★, *Chariots Of Fire* film soundtrack (Polydor 1981)★★★★, *To The Unknown Man* (RCA 1982)★★★, *Antarctica* film soundtrack (Polydor 1983)★★, *Soil Festivities* (Polydor 1984)★★, *Invisible Connections* (Deutsche Grammophon 1985)★★, *Mask* (Polydor 1985)★★★, *Direct* (Arista 1988)★★★, *Antarctica* 1991 soundtrack (Polydor 1988)★★★, *The City* (East West 1990)★★★, *1492: Conquest Of Paradise* film soundtrack (East West 1992)★★, *Blade Runner* film soundtrack (East West 1994)★★★, *Foros Timis Ston Greko (A Tribute To El Greco)* Greece only, reissued 1998 (Warners/East West 1995)★★★, as Jon And Vangelis: *Short Stories* (Polydor 1980)★★★, *The Friends Of Mr. Cairo* (Polydor 1981)★★, *Private Collection* (Polydor 1983)★★, *Page Of Life* (Arista 1991)★★.
COMPILATIONS: *Best Of Vangelis* (Ariola 1975)★★★, *The Best Of Vangelis* (RCA 1978)★★★, *Magic Moments* cassette only (RCA 1984)★★★, *Themes* (Polydor 1989)★★★, *Reprise 1990-1999* (East West 1999)★★.
As Jon And Vangelis: *The Best Of Jon And Vangelis* (Polydor 1984)★★★.

VANILLA FUDGE
ALBUMS: *Vanilla Fudge* (Atco 1967)★★★, *The Beat Goes On* (Atco 1968)★★, *Renaissance* (Atco 1968)★★★, *Near The Beginning* (Atco 1969)★★, *Rock & Roll* (Atco 1970)★★, *Mystery* (Atco 1984)★★★.
COMPILATIONS: *The Best Of The Vanilla Fudge* (Atco 1982)★★★, *Psychedelic Sundae: The Best Of* (Rhino 1993)★★★.

VANILLA ICE
ALBUMS: *To The Extreme* (SBK 1990)★★, *Extremely Live* (SBK 1991)★★, *Mindblowing* (SBK 1994)★★, *Hard To Swallow* (Republic/Universal 1998)★★★.

VEE, BOBBY
ALBUMS: *Bobby Vee Sings Your Favorites* (Liberty 1960)★★★, *Bobby Vee* (Liberty 1961)★★★, *Bobby Vee With Strings And Things* (Liberty 1961)★★★, *Bobby Vee Sings Hits Of The Rockin' 50's* (Liberty 1961)★★, *Take Good Care Of My Baby* (Liberty 1961)★★★, *Bobby Vee Meets The Crickets* (Liberty 1962)★★★, *A Bobby Vee Recording Session* (Liberty 1962)★★, *The Night Has A Thousand Eyes* (Liberty 1963)★★, with the Ventures *Bobby Vee Meets The Ventures* (Dolton 1963)★★, *I Remember Buddy Holly* (Liberty 1963)★★, *Bobby Vee Sings The New Sound From England!* (Liberty 1964)★★, *Bobby Vee Live On Tour* (Liberty 1965)★★, *C'mon Let's Live A Little* film soundtrack (1966)★★, *Look At Me Girl* (Liberty 1966)★★, *Come Back When You Grow Up* (Liberty 1967)★★, *Just Today* (Liberty 1968)★★, *Do What You Gotta Do* (Liberty 1968)★★, *Gates, Grills And Railings* (Liberty 1969)★★, *Nothing Like A Sunny Day* (1972)★★, with the Shadows *The Early Rockin' Years* (K-tel 1995)★★, *Down The Line* 1996 recording (Rollercoaster 1998)★★.
COMPILATIONS: *Bobby Vee's Golden Greats* (Liberty 1962)★★★★, *Bobby Vee's Golden Greats, Volume Two* (Liberty 1966)★★★, *A Forever Kind Of Love* (Sunset 1969)★★★, *Legendary Masters* (United Artists 1973)★★, *The Best Of Bobb Vee* (EMI 1985)★★★, *The EP Collection* (See For Miles 1991)★★★, *Greatest Hits* (Curb 1994)★★★, *Essential & Collectable* (EMI 1999)★★★.
FILMS: *C'mon Let's Live A Little* (1967).

VEGA, SUZANNE
ALBUMS: *Suzanne Vega* (A&M 1985)★★★, *Solitude Standing* (A&M 1987)★★★★, *Days Of Open Hand* (A&M 1990)★★, *99.9F°* (A&M 1992)★★★, *Nine Objects Of Desire* (A&M 1996)★★★, *Songs In Red And Gray* (Interscope 2001)★★★.
COMPILATIONS: *Tried And True: The Best Of Suzanne Vega* (A&M 1998)★★★.
FURTHER READING: *The Passionate Eye: The Collected Writings Of Suzanne Vega*, Suzanne Vega.

VELVET UNDERGROUND
ALBUMS: *The Velvet Underground & Nico* (Verve 1967)★★★★★, *White Light/White Heat* (Verve 1968)★★★★★, *The Velvet Underground* (MGM 1969)★★★★, *Loaded* (Cotillion/Atlantic 1970)★★★★, *Live At Max's Kansas City* (Cotillion/Atlantic 1972)H, *Squeeze* (Polydor 1973)★★, *1969: Velvet Underground Live* (Mercury 1974)★★★, *Live MCMXCIII* (Sire/Warners 1993)★★★, *Loaded (Fully Loaded)* (Rhino 1997)★★★★.
COMPILATIONS: *The Best Of Velvet Underground (Golden Archive Series 1970)★★★, *Andy Warhol's Velvet Underground Featuring Nico* (MGM 1971)★★★, *Lou Reed And The Velvet Underground aka That's The Story Of My Life* (Pride 1973)★★★, *VU* (Verve PolyGram 1985)★★★, *Another View* (Verve PolyGram 1986)★★★, *The Velvet Underground 5-LP box set* (Polydor 1986)★★★, *The Best Of The Velvet Underground* (Verve 1989)★★★, *The Best Of Lou Reed & The Velvet Underground* (Global Television 1995)★★★★, *Peel Slowly And See 5-CD box set* (Polydor 1995)★★★, *The Best Of The Velvet Underground: The Millennium Collection* (Polydor 2000)★★★, *Rock & Roll: An Introduction To The Velvet Underground* (Polydor 2001)★★★, *Bootleg Series Volume 1: The Quine Tapes 3-CD set* (Polydor 2001)★★★, *Final V.U. 1971-1973* 4-CD box set (Captain Trip 2001)★★★.
VIDEOS: *Velvet Redux - Live MCMXCIII* (Warner Music Vision 1993).
FURTHER READING: *Lou Reed & The Velvets*, Nigel Trevena. *The Velvet Underground & Lou Reed*, Mike West. *Up-Tight: The Velvet Underground Story*, Victor Bockris & Gerard Malanga. *Lou Reed and The Velvet Underground*, Diana Clapton. *Beyond The Velvet Underground*, Dave Thompson. *The Velvet Underground Handbook*, M.C. Kostek. *Warhol's Factory: The Velvet Years 1965-1967*, Stephen Shore & Lynne Tillman. *'69 Live: Velvet Underground Photographs*, Doug Yule. *The Velvet Underground Companion: Four Decades Of Commentary*, Albin Zak III. *The Complete Guide To The Music Of The Velvet Underground*, Peter Hogan.
FILMS: *Venus In Furs* (1965), *Andy Warhol's Exploding Plastic Inevitable* (1966), *The Velvet Underground And Nico (A Symphony Of Sound)* (1966), *Walden aka Diaries, Notes and Sketches* (1968), *Scenes From The Life Of Andy Warhol* (1990).

VENTURES

ALBUMS: *Walk, Don't Run* (Dolton 1960)★★★, *The Ventures* (Dolton 1961)★★★, *Another Smash* (Dolton 1961)★★, *The Colorful Ventures* (Dolton 1961)★★★, *Twist With The Ventures aka Dance* (Dolton 1962)★★, *Twist Party Volume 2 aka Dance With The Ventures* (Dolton 1962)★★, *Mashed Potatoes And Gravy aka The Ventures' Beach Party* (Dolton 1962)★★, *Going To The Ventures' Dance Party* (Dolton 1962)★★★, *The Ventures Play 'Telstar' And 'Lonely Bull'* (Dolton 1963)★★, with Bobby Vee *Bobby Vee Meets The Ventures* (Liberty 1963)★★, *Surfin'* (Dolton 1963)★★, *The Ventures Play The Country Classics aka I Walk The Line* (Dolton 1963)★★, *Let's Go!* (Dolton 1963)★★★, *In Space* (Dolton 1964)★★, *The Fabulous Ventures* (Dolton 1964)★★, *Walk, Don't Run, Volume 2* (Dolton 1964)★★★, *Knock Me Out!* (Dolton 1965)★★★, *In Japan* (Liberty 1965)★★★, *On Stage* (Dolton 1965)★★★, *A-Go-Go* (Dolton 1965)★★★, *The Christmas Album* (Dolton 1965)★★, *Where The Action Is* (Dolton 1966)★★★, *Play Guitar With The Ventures* (Dolton 1966)★★★, *The "Batman" Theme* (Dolton 1966)★★★, *In Japan, Volume 2* (Liberty 1966)★★★, *Go With The Ventures* (Dolton 1966)★★★, *Wild Thing!* (Dolton 1966)★★, *Blue Sunset* (Liberty 1966)★★★, *On Stage Encore* (Liberty 1967)★★, *Guitar Freakout aka Revolving Sounds* (Liberty 1967)★★, *Wonderful Ventures* (Liberty 1967)★★, *Super Psychedelics aka Changing Times* (Liberty 1967)★★★, *Pops In Japan* (Liberty 1967)★★, *Ventures Deluxe* (Liberty 1967)★★, *$1,000,000 Weekend* (Liberty 1967)★★, *The Versatile Ventures* (Liberty 1967)★★, *Flights Of Fantasy* (Liberty 1968)★★★, *Pops In Japan No. 2* (Liberty 1968)★★, *Pops Sound* (Liberty 1968)★★, *The Horse aka On The Scene* (Liberty 1968)★★, *Best Of Surfing* (Liberty 1968)★★, *In Tokyo '68* (Liberty 1968)★★, *Underground Fire* (Liberty 1969)★★★, *Colourful Ventures* (Liberty 1969)★★, *Swamp Rock* (Liberty 1969)★★, *10th Anniversary Album* (Liberty 1970)★★, *Hawaii Five-O* (Liberty 1969)★★★, *Theme From The Moon* (Liberty 1969)★★, *More Golden Pops* (Liberty 1970)★★★, *Live* (Liberty 1970)★★★, *New Testament* (United Artists 1971)★★, *Pops In Japan '71* (Liberty 1971)★★★, *Theme From "Shaft"* (United Artists 1972)★★, *Pops In Japan '71* (United Artists 1972)★★, *Joy: The Ventures Play The Classics* (United Artists 1972)★★, *Rock And Roll Forever* (United Artists 1972)★★, *On Stage '72* (Liberty 1972)★★, *Pops In Japan '73* (Liberty 1973)★★, *On Stage '73* (Liberty 1973)★★, *Only Hits* (United Artists 1973)★★★, *The Jim Croce Songbook* (United Artists 1974)★★, *On Stage '74* (Liberty 1974)★★, *The Carpenters* (United Artists 1974)★★, *On Stage '75* (Liberty 1975)★★★, *Hollywood: Yuya Uchida Meets The Ventures* (Liberty 1976)★★, *On Stage '76* (Liberty 1976)★★★, *TV Themes* (United Artists 1977)★★, *Live In Japan '77* (King 1977)★★, *In Space '78* (King 1978)★★, *Surfin' USA '78* (King 1978)★★, *Pops Best 20* (King 1978)★★★, *On Stage '79* (King 1979)★★, *Latin Album* (East World 1979)★★, *Original Four* (East World 1979)★★, *Chameleon* (East World 1980)★★, *Super Live '80* (East World 1980)★★, *'60s Pops* (East World 1981)★★, *Pops In Japan '81* (East World 1981)★★★, *Latin Album '82* (St. Louis Memory* (East World 1982)★★, *The Ventures Today* (Valentine 1983)★★, *Surfin' Deluxe* (EMI 1984)★★, *Radical Guitars* (Iloki 1987)★★, *Walk Don't Run '88* (Teichiku 1989)★★, *Play Southern All Stars* (Toshiba 1990)★★, *Live In Japan '90* (Toshiba 1990)★★★, *Flyin'*

High (Toshiba 1992)★★★, Wild Again: The Ventures Play Heavy Hitters (Toshiba 1996)★★★, Wild Again II: Tribute To Mel Taylor (Toshiba 1997)★★★, Wild Again Concert '97 (Toshiba 1998)★★★, V-Gold (M&I 1999)★★★, Walk, Don't Run 2000 (M&I 1999)★★★, V-Gold Live '99 (M&I 1999)★★, V-Gold II (M&I 2000)★★, Acoustic Rock (M&I 2000)★★, In Japan Live 2000 (M&I 2000)★★★, V-Gold III (M&I 2001)★★, Play Southern All Stars – Tsunami (M&I 2001)★★★.
COMPILATIONS: Original Hits (Liberty 1964)★★★, Best Of The Ventures (Liberty 1965)★★★, Best Of The Ventures, Volume 2 (Liberty 1966)★★★, Running Strong (Sunset 1966)★★★, Golden Greats (Liberty 1967)★★★, Golden Original Hits (Liberty 1967)★★★, Guitar Genius Of The Ventures (Sunset 1968)★★★, Deluxe Double, Volume 1 (Liberty 1968)★★★, Deluxe Double, Volume 2 (Liberty 1969)★★★, This Is The Ventures, Volume 1 (Liberty 1969) ★★★, This Is The Ventures, Volume 2 (Liberty 1969)★★★, Super Group (Sunset 1969)★★★, More Golden Greats (Liberty 1970)★★★, A Decade With The Ventures (Liberty 1971)★★★, Superpak (United Artists 1971)★★★, Very Best Of The Ventures (United Artists 1975)★★★, 15 Years Of Japanese Pop (Liberty 1975)★★★, Now Playing (United Artists 1975)★★★, Early Sounds (Liberty 1976)★★★, 20 Greatest Hits (Tee Vee 1977)★★★★, Special Deluxe Edition 8-LP set (United Artists 1979)★★★, Greatest Hits (Tridex 1980)★★★, Rare Collection (King 1980)★★★, Walk, Don't Run: The Best Of The Ventures (EMI 1990)★★★★, The Collection: Ventures Forever (East World 1981)★★★, Best Of Live '65-'69 (Toshiba 1991)★★★, Live Box, Volume 1 4-CD box set (Toshiba 1992)★★★, History Box, Volume 1 4-CD box set (Toshiba 1992)★★★, History Box, Volume 2 4-CD box set (Toshiba 1992)★★★, History Box, Volume 3 4-CD box set (Toshiba 1992)★★★, History Box, Volume 4 4-CD box set (Toshiba 1992)★★★, History Box, Volume 5 4-CD box set (Toshiba 1992)★★★, Live Box, Volume 2 4-CD box set (Toshiba 1992)★★★, Pops In Japan Box 4-CD box set (Toshiba 1992)★★★, Live Box, Volume 3 4-CD box set (Toshiba 1993)★★★, EP Box 4-CD box set (Toshiba 1994)★★★, In The Vaults (Ace 1997)★★★, In The Vaults, Volume 2 (Ace 1999)★★★, Best Collection Box Set 8-CD box set (EMI 2000)★★★, The Ultimate Collection (See For Miles 2001)★★★, The Ventures Play The Greatest Surfin' Hits Of All Time (Varèse Vintage 2001)★★★.

VERLAINE, TOM
ALBUMS: Tom Verlaine (Elektra 1979)★★★★, Dreamtime (Warners 1981)★★★, Words From The Front (Virgin/Warners 1982)★★★, Cover (Virgin/Warners 1984)★★★★, Flashlight (Fontana/I.R.S. 1987)★★★, The Wonder (Fontana 1990)★★★, Warm And Cool (Rough Trade/Rykodisc 1992)★★★.
COMPILATIONS: The Miller's Tale: A Tom Verlaine Anthology (Virgin 1996)★★★★.

VERTICAL HORIZON
ALBUMS: There And Back Again (Rythmic 1993)★★★, Running On Ice (Rythmic 1995)★★★, Live Stages (Rythmic 1996)★★★★, Everything You Want (RCA 1999)★★★★.

VERVE
ALBUMS: Storm In Heaven (Hut 1993)★★★, A Northern Soul (Hut 1995)★★★★, Urban Hymns (Hut 1997)★★★★.
COMPILATIONS: No Come Down (Virgin 1994)★★★.
VIDEOS: Some Bitter - Some Sweet: Unauthorised Biography (Talking Heads Video 1998), The Verve: The Video 96-98 (Hut 1999).
FURTHER READING: The Verve: Bitter Sweet, Peter Wilding. The Verve: Crazed Highs + Horrible Lows, Martin Clarke. The Verve: Star Sail, Sean Egan.

VILLAGE PEOPLE
ALBUMS: Village People (Casablanca/DJM 1977)★★, Macho Man (Casablanca/DJM 1978)★★, Cruisin' (Casablanca/ Mercury 1978)★★, Go West (Casablanca/ Mercury 1979) ★★★, Live And Sleazy (Casablanca/ Mercury 1979)★, Can't Stop The Music film soundtrack (Casablanca/Mercury 1980) ★, Renaissance (RCA/ Mercury 1981)★, Fox On The Box aka In The Street (Ariola 1982)★★, Sex Over The Phone (Ariola 1985)★.
COMPILATIONS: Greatest Hits (Groove & Move 1988) ★★★, The Hits (Music Club 1991)★★★, The Best Of Village People (Bell 1993)★★★, The Best Of Village People (Casablanca 1994)★★★, Greatest Hits (Wrasse 1999)★★★.
VIDEOS: The Best Of ... (1994).
FILMS: Can't Stop The Music (1980).

VINCENT, GENE
ALBUMS: Bluejean Bop! (Capitol 1956)★★★★, Gene Vincent And The Blue Caps (Capitol 1957)★★★, Gene Vincent Rocks! And The Bluecaps Roll (Capitol 1958)★★★, A Gene Vincent Record Date (Capitol 1958)★★★, Sounds Like Gene Vincent (Capitol 1959)★★★, Crazy Times! (Capitol 1960)★★★, The Crazy Beat Of Gene Vincent (Capitol 1963)★★★, Shakin' Up A Storm (Columbia 1964)★★★, Bird Doggin' reissued as Ain't That Too Much (London 1967)★★★, Gene Vincent (London 1967)★★, I'm Back And I'm Proud reissued as The Bop They Couldn't Stop (Dandelion 1970)★★, If Only You Could See Me Today (UK) The Day The World Turned Blue (USA) (Karma Sutra 1971)★★, The Be-Bop Boogie Boy (Stomper Time 2001)★★.
COMPILATIONS: The Best Of Gene Vincent (Capitol 1967) ★★★, The Best Of Gene Vincent Volume 2 (Capitol 1968) ★★★, Gene Vincent's Greatest (Capitol 1969)★★★, Pioneers Of Rock Volume One (Regal Starline 1972)★★★, The King Of Fools (Regal Starline 1974)★★★, The Bop That Just Won't Stop (Capitol 1974)★★★, Greatest Hits (Capitol 1977)★★★, Greatest Hits Volume 2 (Capitol 1979)★★★, Rock On With Gene Vincent (MFP 1980)★★★, The Gene Vincent Singles Album (Capitol 1981)★★★, Dressed In Black (Magnum Force 1982)★★★, Gene Vincent's Greatest Hits (Fame 1982)★★★, From LA To 'Frisco (Magnum Force 1983)★★★, For Collectors Only (Magnum Force 1984) ★★★, Forever Gene Vincent (Rollin' Rock 1984)★★★, Born To Be A Rolling Stone (Topline 1985)★★★, Gene Vincent: The Capitol Years 10-LP box set (Charly 1987) ★★★★, Into The Seventies (See For Miles 1988)★★★, The EP Collection (See For Miles 1989)★★★, The Gene Vincent Box Set 6-CD box set (EMI 1990)★★★★, His 30 Original Hits (Entertainers 1992)★★★, Rebel Heart Volume 1 (Magnum 1992)★★★, Be-Bop-A-Lula (Charly 1993)★★★, Ain't That Too Much: The Complete Challenge Sessions (Hollowbody/Sundazed 1994)★★★, Rebel Heart Volume 2 (Magnum 1995)★★, Rebel Heart Volume 3 (Magnum 1996)★★, 500 Miles (Camden 1998)★★★, The EP Collection Volume 2 (See For Miles 1998)★★★.
FURTHER READING: Wild Cat: A Tribute To Gene Vincent, Eddie Muir. Gene Vincent & The Blue Caps, Rob Finnis and Bob Dunham. I Remember Gene Vincent, Alan Vince. Gene Vincent: The Screaming End, Alan Clark. The Day The World Turned Blue, Britt Hagerty. Gene Vincent: A Discography, Derek Henderson. Race With The Devil: Gene Vincent's Life In The Fast Lane, Susan Vanhecke.
FILMS: The Girl Can't Help It (1956), Hot Rod Gang aka Fury Unleashed (1958), It's Trad, Dad! aka Ring-A-Ding Rhythm (1961).

VIRGIN PRUNES
ALBUMS: A New Form Of Beauty (Rough Trade 1981)★★, If I Die ... I Die (Rough Trade 1982)★★★, Heresie (L'invitation Au Suicide 1982)★★, The Moon Looked Down And Laughed (Baby 1986)★★★, The Hidden Lie (Live In Paris 6/6/86) (Baby 1986)★★. As the Prunes Lite Fantastik (Baby 1988)★★, Nada (Baby 1989)★★.

VISAGE
ALBUMS: Visage (Polydor 1980)★★, The Anvil (Polydor 1982)★★, Beat Boy (Polydor 1984)★★.
COMPILATIONS: Fade To Grey: The Singles Collection (Polydor 1983)★★★, Fade To Grey: Dance Mix Album (Polydor 1983)★★, The Damned Don't Cry (Spectrum 2000)★★★.
VIDEOS: The Visage Videos (PolyGram Music Video 1986).

VOICE OF THE BEEHIVE
ALBUMS: Let It Bee (London 1988)★★★, Honey Lingers (London 1991)★★★★, Sex & Misery (East West 1995)★★.

W

W.A.S.P.
ALBUMS: W.A.S.P. (Capitol 1984)★★, The Last Command (Capitol 1985)★★★, Inside The Electric Circus (Capitol 1986)★★★, Live ... In The Raw (Capitol 1987)★★, The Headless Children (Capitol 1989)★★, The Crimson Idol (Parlophone/Capitol 1992)★★★, Still Not Black Enough (Castle 1995)★★★, Kill, Fuck, Die (Castle 1997)★★, Double Live Assassins (CMC/Snapper 1998)★★★, Helldorado (CMC/Apocalypse 1999)★★, The Sting (Snapper 2000)★★, Unholy Terror (Metal-Is 2001)★★★.
COMPILATIONS: First Blood ... Last Cuts (Capitol 1993)★★★, The Best Of The Best (Apocalypse 2000)★★★★.
VIDEOS: Live At The Lyceum, London (PMI 1984), Videos ... In The Raw (PMI 1988), First Blood ... Last Visions ... (PMI 1993), The Sting: Live At The Key Club, L.A. (Snapper 2001).

WAH!
ALBUMS: Nah! Poo! The Art Of Bluff (Eternal 1981)★★, as Mighty Wah! A Word To The Wise Guy (Beggars Banquet 1984)★★★, as Pete Wylie Sinful (Virgin 1987)★★★, Infamy! Or I Didn't Get Where I Am Today (1991)★★★, as Pete Wylie Is The Mighty Wah! Songs Of Strength & Heartbreak (When! 2000)★★★★.
COMPILATIONS: The Maverick Years '80 -'81 (Wonderful World 1982)★★, as Mighty Wah! The Way We Wah! (Warners 1984)★★★, The Handy Wah! Whole: Songs From The Repertwah!: The Maverick Years 2000 (Essential 2000)★★★★.

WAINWRIGHT, LOUDON, III
ALBUMS: Loudon Wainwright III (Atlantic 1970)★★★, Album II (Atlantic 1971)★★★, Album III (Columbia/CBS 1972) ★★★, Attempted Mustache (Columbia/CBS 1974)★★, Unrequited (Columbia/CBS 1975)★★★, T Shirt (Arista 1976)★★★, Final Exam (Arista 1978)★★, A Live One (Rounder/Radar 1979) ★★★, Fame And Wealth (Rounder/ Demon 1983)★★★, I'm Alright (Rounder/Demon 1985) ★★★, More Love Songs (Rounder/Demon 1986)★★★, Therapy (Silvertone 1989) ★★★, History (Virgin/Charisma 1992)★★★, Career Moves (Virgin 1993)★★★, Grown Man (Virgin 1995)★★★, Little Ship (Virgin 1997)★★★, Social Studies (Hannibal 1999) ★★★, Last Man On Earth (Red House 2001)★★★★.
COMPILATIONS: One Man Guy: The Best Of Loudon Wainwright 1982-1986 (Music Club 1994)★★★★, The BBC Sessions (Strange Fruit 1998)★★★, The Atlantic Recordings (Rhino 2000)★★★.
FILMS: The Slugger's Wife (1985), Jacknife (1989), 28 Days (2000).

WAITE, JOHN
ALBUMS: Ignition (Chrysalis 1982)★★, No Brakes (EMI America 1984)★★★, Mask Of Smiles (Capitol 1985)★★, Rover's Return (EMI America 1987)★★, Temple Bar (Imago 1995)★★★, When You Were Mine (Pure 1997)★★, Figure In A Landscape (Gold Circle 2001)★★★.
COMPILATIONS: Essential (Chrysalis 1992)★★★, Falling Backwards: The Complete John Waite (EMI 1996)★★★.

WAITS, TOM
ALBUMS: Closing Time (Asylum 1973)★★★, The Heart Of Saturday Night (Asylum 1974)★★★, Nighthawks At The Diner (Asylum 1975)★★★, Small Change (Asylum 1976) ★★★★, Foreign Affairs (Asylum 1977)★★★, Blue Valentine (Asylum 1978)★★★★, Heartattack And Vine (Asylum 1980)★★★★, with Crystal Gayle One From The Heart (Columbia 1982)★★★★, Swordfishtrombones (Island 1983)★★★★, Rain Dogs (Island 1985)★★★★, Frank's Wild Years (Island 1987)★★★, Big Time (Island 1988) ★★★, Night On Earth film soundtrack (Island 1992)★★★, Bone Machine (Island 1992)★★★★, The Black Rider (Island 1993)★★★, Mule Variations (Epitaph 1999)★★★★, Blood Money (Anti 2002)★★★★, Alice (Anti 2002)★★★★.
COMPILATIONS: Bounced Checks (Asylum 1981)★★★, Asylum Years (Asylum 1986)★★★★, The Early Years (Bizarre/Straight 1991)★★★, The Early Years Vol. 2 (Bizarre/Straight 1992)★★, Beautiful Maladies: The Island Years (Island 1998)★★★★, Used Songs (1973-1980) (Rhino 2001)★★★★.
FURTHER READING: Small Change: A Life Of Tom Waits, Patrick Humphries. Tom Waits, Cath Carroll. Wild Years: The Music And Myth Of Tom Waits, Jay S. Jacobs.
FILMS: Paradise Alley (1978), Wolfen (1981), Poetry In Motion (1982), Rumble Fish (1983), The Outsiders (1983), The Cotton Club (1984), Down By Law (1986), Ironweed (1987), Candy Mountain (1987), Big Time (1988), Cold Feet (1989), Bearskin: An Urban Fairytale (1989), Mystery Train voice only (1989), The Two Jakes (1990), Queens Logic (1991), The Fisher King (1991), At Play In The Fields Of The Lord (1991), Dracula (1992), Coffee And Cigarettes III (1993), Short Cuts (1993), Guy Maddin: Waiting For Twilight (1997), Mystery Men (1999), In The Boom Boom Room (2000), Cadillac Tramps (2000).

WAKEMAN, RICK
ALBUMS: Piano Vibrations (Polydor 1971)★★★, The Six Wives Of Henry VIII (A&M 1973)★★★, Journey To The Centre Of The Earth (A&M 1974)★★, The Myths And Legends Of King Arthur And The Knights Of The Round Table (A&M 1975)★★★, Lisztomania film soundtrack (A&M 1975)★★★, No Earthly Connection (A&M 1976)★★★, Rick Wakeman's Criminal Record (A&M 1977)★★★, White Rock film soundtrack (A&M 1977)★★, Rhapsodies (A&M 1979)★★, 1984 (Charisma 1981)★★★, The Burning film soundtrack (Charisma 1981)★★, Rock N' Roll Prophet (Moon 1982)★★, Cost Of Living (Charisma 1983)★★★, G'Olé! film soundtrack (Charisma 1983)★★, Silent Nights (President 1985)★★, Live At Hammersmith (President 1985)★★, Crimes Of Passion film soundtrack (President 1986)★★, Country Airs (Coda 1986)★★★★, The Gospels (Stylus 1987)★★, The Family Album (President 1987)★★, with Ramon Remedios A Suite Of Gods (President 1988)★★, with Tony Fernandez Zodiaque (President/ Relativity 1988)★★, Time Machine (President 1988)★★, with Mario Fasciano Black Knights At The Court Of Ferdinand IV (Ambient 1989)★★★, Sea Airs (President 1989)★★★, In The Beginning (Asaph 1990)★★, Night Airs (President 1990)★★★, Phantom Power film soundtrack (Ambient 1990)★★, Aspirant Sunrise (President 1991) ★★★, Softsword: King John And The Magna Charter (President 1991)★★, African Bach (President 1991)★★★, 2000 A.D. Into The Future (President 1991)★★, The Classical Connection (President 1991)★★★, Aspirant Sunset (President 1991)★★★, Aspirant Sunshadows (President 1991)★★★, The Classical Connection 2 (President 1992)★★, with Adam Wakeman Wakeman With Wakeman (President 1993)★★, Heritage Suite: A Tribute To The Unique Heritage Of The Isle Of Man (President 1993)★★★, with Adam Wakeman No Expense Spared (President 1993)★★★, Prayers (Hope 1993)★★★, Classic Tracks (Zazoo 1993)★★★, Unleashing The Tethered One: The 1974 North American Tour (Mellow 1994)★★, with the English Rock Ensemble Live On The Test 1976 recording (Windsong 1994)★★★, The Stage Collection (Nota Blu 1994)★★, with Adam Wakeman Lure Of The Wild (Nota Blue 1994)★★, with Adam Wakeman The Official Bootleg (Cyclops 1994)★★★, Rick Wakeman's Greatest Hits (Herald 1994)★★, with Adam Wakeman Wakeman With Wakeman Live (Zero 1994)★★, Rock & Pop Legends (Disky 1995)★★★, The Piano Album (Castle 1995) ★★★★, Cirque Surreal: State Circus Of Imagination (Pinnacle 1995)★★★, with Adam Wakeman Romance Of The Victorian Age (President 1995)★★★, Visions (President 1995)★★★, The Seven Wonders Of The World (West Coast 1995)★★, Rick Wakeman In Concert 1975 recording (King Biscuit Flower Hour 1995)★★, Almost Live In Europe (Griffin 1995)★★, Can You Hear Me? (Hope 1996)★★★, with Adam Wakeman Tapestries (President 1996)★★★, The Word And Music (Hope 1996)★★, The New Gospels (Hope 1996)★★, Fields Of Green (Griffin/Music Fusion 1996)★★, Orisons (Hope 1996)★★, with Adam Wakeman Vignettes (President 1996)★★★, Simply Acoustic: The Music (Asaph 1997)★★★, Tribute (RPM 1997)★★★, Themes (President 1998)★★★, Official Live Bootleg: Live In Buenos Aires 1993 recording (Music Fusion 1998)★★★, with Mario Fasciano Stella Bianca Alla Corte Di Re Ferdinando (MP 1999)★★★, Art In Music Trilogy (Music Fusion 1999)★★★, The Natural World Trilogy (Music Fusion 1999)★★★, White Rock II rescored film soundtrack (Music Fusion 1999)★★, Return To The Centre Of The Earth (EMI Classics 1999)★★, Chronicles Of Man (President 2000)★★★, Christmas Variations (Music Fusion 2000)★★★, The Legend: Live In Concert 2000 (Pinnacle 2000)★★★, Morning Has Broken (Kevin Mayhew 2000)★★★, Preludes To A Century (President 2000)★★.
COMPILATIONS: Best Known Works (A&M 1978)★★, 20th Anniversary Limited Edition (A&M 1989)★★★, Best Works Collection (Jimco 1992)★★★, The Private Collection (President 1995)★★★, Voyage: The Very Best Of Rick Wakeman (A&M 1996)★★★★, Master Series (A&M 1998)★★★, The Masters (Eagle 1999)★★★, Recollections: The Very Best Of Rick Wakeman (A&M 2000)★★★★, The Caped Collection (Snapper 2000)★★★, Greatest Hits (Disky 2001)★★★, Tales Of Future And Past (Purple Pyramid 2001)★★★★.
VIDEOS: The Word & The Gospels (Beckmann Home Video 1988), The Classical Connection (Beckmann Home Video 1991), The Very Best Of The Rick Wakeman Chronicles (Griffin 1994), Simply Acoustic: An Evening Of Solo Grand Piano (Hope Vision 1996), The New Gospels: A Modern Oratoria By Rick Wakeman (Hope Vision 1996), The Piano Tour Live (Hope Vision 1997), Live (Castle Communications 1998), An Evening With Rick Wakeman (Pinnacle 2000).
FURTHER READING: Rick Wakeman: The Caped Crusader, Dan Wooding. Say Yes!, Rick Wakeman.

WALKER BROTHERS
ALBUMS: Take It Easy With The Walker Brothers (Philips 1965)★★★★, Portrait (Philips 1966)★★★★, Images (Philips 1967)★★★, No Regrets (GTO 1975)★★★, Lines (GTO 1977)★★, Nite Flights (GTO 1978)★★★★, The Walker Brothers In Japan 1968 recording (Bam Caruso 1987)★★.
COMPILATIONS: After The Lights Go Out: The Best Of 1965-1967 (Fontana 1990)★★★★, No Regrets: The Best Of The Walker Brothers (Fontana 1991)★★★★, The Collection (Spectrum 1996)★★★★, If You Could Hear Me Now (Sony 2001)★★★.
FILMS: Beach Ball (1965).

WALKER, JUNIOR, AND THE ALL STARS
ALBUMS: Shotgun (Soul/Tamla Motown 1965)★★★★, Soul Session (Tamla Motown 1966)★★★★, Road Runner (Tamla Motown 1966)★★★★, Live! (Tamla Motown 1967)★★★, Home Cookin' (Tamla Motown 1969)★★★, Gotta Hold On To This Feeling (Soul 1969)★★★, What Does It Take To Win Your Love? (Soul 1969)★★★, A Gassssssss (Soul 1970)★★★, Rainbow Funk (Soul 1971)★★★, Moody Jr. (Soul 1971) ★★★, Peace And Understanding Is Hard To Find (Soul 1973) ★★, Hot Shot (Soul 1976)★★, Sax Appeal (Soul 1976)★★★, Whopper Bopper Show Stopper (Soul 1976)★★, Smooth (Soul 1978)★★, Back Street Boogie (Whitfield 1979)★★, Blow The House Down (Motown 1983)★★.
COMPILATIONS: Greatest Hits (Soul 1969)★★★★, Anthology (Motown 1981)★★★★, Junior Walker's Greatest Hits (Motown 1982)★★★★, 19 Greatest Hits (Motown 1987)★★★★, Shake And Fingerpop (Blue Moon 1989) ★★★, Compact Command Performance - 19 Greatest Hits (Motown 1992)★★★★, The Ultimate Collection (Motown 1997)★★★★, 20th Century Masters: The Millennium Collection (Motown 2000)★★★★.

WALKER, SCOTT
ALBUMS: Scott (Philips 1967)★★★, Scott 2 (Philips 1968) ★★★★, Scott 3 (Philips 1969)★★★★, Scott Walker Sings Songs From His TV Series (Philips 1969)★★, Scott 4 (Philips 1969)★★★★★, 'Til The Band Comes In (Philips 1970) ★★★, The Moviegoer (Philips 1972)★★, Any Day Now (Philips 1973)★★, Stretch (CBS 1973)★★★, We Had It All (CBS 1974)★★, Climate Of Hunter (Virgin 1984)★★★★, Tilt (Fontana/Drag City 1995)★★★.
COMPILATIONS: Looking Back With Scott Walker (Ember 1968)★★★, The Romantic Scott Walker (Philips 1969) ★★★, The Best Of Scott Walker (Philips 1970)★★★, This Is Scott Walker (Philips 1971)★★★★, This Is Scott Walker, Volume 2 (Philips 1972)★★★, Spotlight On Scott Walker (Philips 1976)★★★, Fire Escape In The Sky: The Godlike Genius Of Scott Walker (Zoo 1981)★★★★, Scott Walker Sings Jacques Brel (Philips 1981)★★★★, Boy Child: The Best Of 1967-1970 (Fontana 1990)★★★★, When Is A Boy A Man? Early Years Of Scott Walker (A-Side 1995)★★, It's Raining Today: The Scott Walker Story (1967-70) (Razor & Tie 1996)★★★★.
FURTHER READING: Scott Walker: A Deep Shade Of Blue, Mike Watkinson and Pete Anderson. Butterfly: The Music Of Scott Walker. Another Tear Falls, Jeremy Reed. Scott Walker, Ken Brooks.

WALKER, T-BONE
ALBUMS: Classics In Jazz 10-inch album (Capitol 1953) ★★★, Sings The Blues (Imperial 1959)★★★★, T-Bone Blues (Atlantic 1960)★★★★, Singing The Blues (Imperial 1960)★★★★, I Get So Weary (Imperial 1961)★★★★, The Great Blues, Vocals And Guitar (Capitol 1963)★★★★, I Want A Little Girl (Delmark 1967)★★★, Stormy Monday Blues (Wet Soul 1967)★★★★, The Truth (Brunswick 1968)★★★, Blue Rocks (Charly 1968)★★★, Funky Town (Bluesway 1968)★★★, Feeling The Blues (B&B 1969)★★★, Very Rare (Reprise 1973)★★★, Dirty Mistreater (Bluesway 1973)★★★, Good Feelin' 1968 recording (Polydor 1982)★★★, Hot Leftovers (Pathé Marconi 1985)★★★, Low Down Blues (Charly 1986)★★★★, with 'Big' Joe Turner Bosses Of The Blues (Bluebird 1989)★★★, Back On The Scene: Texas 1966 (Indigo 2001)★★★.
COMPILATIONS: The Blues Of T-Bone Walker (1965)★★★★, Classics Of Modern Blues (Blue Note 1975)★★★★, Stormy Monday Blues (Charly 1978)★★★★, T-Bone Jumps Again (Charly 1980)★★★, Plain Ole Blues (Charly 1982)★★★, The Natural Blues (Charly 1983)★★★, Collection - T-Bone Walker (Déjà Vu 1985)★★★, I Don't Be Jivin' (Bear Family 1987)★★★, The Inventor Of The Electric Guitar Blues (Blues Boy 1983)★★★★, The Bluesway Sessions (Charly 1988) ★★★★, The Talkin' Guitar (Blues Encore 1990)★★★, The Hustle Is On: Imperial Sessions, Volume 1 (Sequel 1990) ★★★★, The Complete 1940 - 1954 Recordings Of T-Bone Walker (Mosaic 1990)★★★, The Complete Imperial Recordings, 1950-54 (EMI 1991)★★★★, T-Bone Blues recorded 1955-57 (Sequel 1994)★★★★, The Complete Capitol Black And White Recordings 3-CD set (Capitol 1995)★★★★, T-Bone Standard Time: The Crazy Cajun Recordings (Edsel 1999)★★★, The Essential Recordings Of T-Bone Walker 1942-47 recordings (Indigo 2000)★★★★, The Very Best Of T-Bone Walker (Rhino 2000)★★★★.
FURTHER READING: Stormy Monday, Helen Oakly Dance.

WALLFLOWERS
ALBUMS: The Wallflowers (Virgin 1992)★★, Bringing Down The Horse (Interscope 1996)★★★★, (Breach) (Interscope 2000)★★★★.

WALSH, JOE
ALBUMS: Barnstorm (ABC 1972)★★★, The Smoker You Drink, The Player You Get (ABC 1973)★★★★, So What? (ABC 1975)★★★★, You Can't Argue With A Sick Mind (ABC 1976)★★, But Seriously Folks ... (Asylum 1978) ★★★, There Goes The Neighborhood (Asylum 1981)★★, You Bought It, You Name It (Warners 1983)★★, The Confessor (Warners 1985)★★, Got Any Gum? (Warners 1987)★★, Ordinary Average Guy (Epic 1991)★★, Songs For A Dying Planet (Epic 1992)★★.
COMPILATIONS: The Best Of Joe Walsh (ABC 1978)★★★, All The Best (Pickwick 1994)★★, Look What I Did! The Joe Walsh Anthology (MCA 1995)★★★, Joe Walsh's Greatest Hits: Little Did He Know ... (MCA 1997)★★★★, 20th Century Masters: The Millennium Collection (MCA 2000)★★★.

WAR
ALBUMS: with Eric Burdon Eric Burdon Declares War (MGM 1970)★★★, with Burdon The Black Man's Burdon (MGM 1970)★★, War (United Artists 1971)★★★, All Day Music (United Artists 1971)★★★, The World Is A Ghetto (United Artists 1972)★★★★, Deliver The Word (United Artists 1973)★★★, War Live! (United Artists 1974)★★, Why Can't We Be Friends? (United Artists 1975)★★★★, Galaxy (MCA 1977)★★★, Youngblood (United Artists 1978)★★★, The Music Band (MCA 1979)★★, The Music Band 2 (MCA 1979)★★, Outlaw (RCA 1982)★★, Life (Is So Strange) (RCA 1983)★★, Where There's Smoke (Coco Plum 1984)★★, Peace Sign (RCA/Avenue 1994)★★.
COMPILATIONS: with Eric Burdon Love Is All Around (ABC 1976)★★, Greatest Hits (United Artists 1976)★★★★, Platinum Jazz (Blue Note 1977)★★, Best Of The Music Band (MCA 1994)★★★★, Anthology 1970-1994 (Avenue/Rhino 1995)★★★★, The Best Of War And More: Vol. 2 (Avenue/Rhino 1997)★★★, Grooves & Messages: The Greatest Hits Of War (Avenue 1999)★★★.

WARNES, JENNIFER
ALBUMS: ... I Can Remember Everything (Parrot 1968)★★, See Me, Feel Me, Touch Me Heal Me (Parrot 1969)★★, Jennifer (Reprise 1972)★★★, Jennifer Warnes (Arista 1977)★★, Shot Through the Heart (Arista 1979)★★, Famous Blue Raincoat (Cypress 1986)★★★★, The Hunter (Private 1992)★★★, The Well (Sin-Drome 2001)★★★.
COMPILATIONS: The Best Of Jennifer Warnes (Arista 1982)★★★, Just Jennifer (Deram 1992)★★.

WARWICK, DIONNE
ALBUMS: Presenting Dionne Warwick (Scepter 1963)★★★, Anyone Who Had A Heart (Scepter 1964)★★★★, Make Way For Dionne Warwick (Scepter 1964)★★★★, The Sensitive Sound Of Dionne Warwick (Scepter 1965)★★★★, Here I Am (Scepter 1966)★★★★, Dionne Warwick In Paris (Scepter 1966)★★★, Here Where There Is Love (Scepter 1967)★★★, Dionne Warwick Onstage And In The Movies (Scepter 1967)★★★, The Windows Of The World (Scepter 1968)★★★, Dionne In The Valley Of The Dolls (Scepter 1968)★★★★, The Magic Of Believing (Scepter 1968)★★★, Promises Promises (Scepter 1968)★★★★, Soulful (Scepter 1969)★★★, Dionne Warwick's Greatest Motion Picture Hits (Scepter 1969)★★★, I'll Never Fall In Love Again (Scepter 1970)★★★, Very Dionne (Scepter 1970)★★, The Love Machine (Scepter 1971)★★★★, The Dionne Warwick Story - Live (Scepter 1971)★★, From Within (Scepter 1972)★★, Dionne (Warners 1972)★★, Just Being Myself (Warners 1973)★★, Then Came You (Warners 1975)★★★, Track Of The Cat (Warners 1975)★★★, with Isaac Hayes A Man And A Woman (HBS 1977)★★★, Only Love Can Break A Heart (Musicor 1977)★★★, Love At First Sight (Warners 1979)★★, Dionne (Arista 1979)★★★★, No Night So Long (Arista 1980)★★, Hot! Live And Otherwise (Mobile Fidelity 1981) ★★★, Friends In Love (Arista 1982)★★★, Heartbreaker (Arista 1982)★★★, How Many Times Can We Say Goodbye (Arista 1983)★★, Friends (Arista 1985)★★★, Finder Of Lost Loves (Arista 1985)★★★ Without Your Love (Arista 1985) ★★★, Reservations For Two (Arista 1988)★★★, Dionne Warwick Sings Cole Porter (Arista 1989)★★★, Friends Can Be Lovers (Arista 1993)★★★, Aquarela Do Brazil (Arista 1995) ★★★, Dionne Sings Dionne (River North 1998)★★★.
COMPILATIONS: Dionne Warwick's Golden Hits, Part 1 (Scepter 1967)★★★★, Dionne Warwick's Golden Hits, Part 2 (Scepter 1969)★★★★, The Best Of Dionne Warwick (Pye 1983)★★★★, The Dionne Warwick Collection: Her All-Time Greatest Hits (Rhino 1989)★★★★★, Greatest Hits 1979-1990 (Arista 1989)★★★★, The Essential Collection (Global 1996)★★★★, Walk On By: The Definitive Dionne Warwick Collection (Warners 2000)★★★★.

WATERBOYS
ALBUMS: The Waterboys (Chicken Jazz 1983)★★★, A Pagan Place (Ensign 1984)★★★, This Is The Sea (Ensign 1985)★★★★, Fisherman's Blues (Ensign 1988)★★★★, Room To Roam (Ensign 1990)★★★, Dream Harder (Geffen 1993)★★, A Rock In The Weary Land (RCA/Razor & Tie 2000)★★★★.
COMPILATIONS: The Best Of 1981-90 (Ensign 1991)★★★, The Secret Life Of The Waterboys: 1981-1985 (Ensign 1994)★★, The Live Adventures Of The Waterboys (New Millennium 1998)★★★, The Whole Of The Moon: The Music Of Mike Scott And The Waterboys (EMI 1998) ★★★★, Too Close To Heaven: The Unreleased Fisherman's Blues Sessions (RCA 2001)★★★.

WATERS, ROGER
ALBUMS: with Ron Geesin Music From The Body film soundtrack (Harvest 1970)★★, The Pros And Cons Of Hitch Hiking (Harvest 1984)★★★, When The Wind Blows film soundtrack (Virgin 1986)★★, Radio K.A.O.S (EMI 1987) ★★, The Wall: Live In Berlin (Mercury 1990)★★, Amused To Death (Columbia 1992)★★, In The Flesh (Columbia 2000)★★.
VIDEOS: In The Flesh - Live (SMV Enterprises 2002).

WATSON, JOHNNY 'GUITAR'
ALBUMS: Gangster Of Love (King 1958)★★★★, Johnny Guitar Watson (King 1963)★★★, The Blues Soul Of Johnny Guitar Watson (Chess 1964)★★★★, Bad (Chess 1966) ★★★★, with Larry Williams Two For The Price Of One (OKeh 1967)★★★★, Johnny Watson Plays Fats Waller In The Fats Bag (OKeh 1968)★★★, Listen (Fantasy 1974) ★★★, I Don't Want To Be Alone, Stranger (Fantasy 1975) ★★★, Captured Live (DJM 1976)★★★, Ain't That A Bitch (DJM 1976)★★★★, A Real Mother For Ya (DJM 1977)★★, Funk Beyond The Call Of Duty (DJM 1977)★★, Gangster Of Love (DJM 1977)★★★, Giant (DJM 1978)★★, with Papa John Creach Inphasion (DJM 1978)★★, What The Hell Is This? (DJM 1979)★★, Love Jones (DJM 1980)★★, Johnny 'Guitar' Watson And The Family Clone (DJM 1981) ★★, That's What Time It Is (A&M 1981)★★, Strike On Computers (Valley Vue 1984)★★, Bow Wow (Bellmark 1995)★★.
COMPILATIONS: The Very Best Of Johnny 'Guitar' Watson (DJM 1981)★★★★, I Heard That! (Chess 1985)★★★★, Hit The Highway (Ace 1985)★★★★, Gettin' Down With Johnny 'Guitar' Watson (Chess 1987)★★★, Three Hours Past Midnight (Flair 1991)★★★, Gangster Of Love (Charly 1991)★★★★, Listen/I Don't Want To Be Alone, Stranger (Ace 1992)★★★, Gangster Of Love: The Best Of Johnny 'Guitar' Watson (Castle 1995)★★★★, Hot Just Like TNT (Ace 1996)★★★★, The Very Best Of Johnny Guitar Watson (Rhino 1999)★★★★.

WAYNE, JEFF
ALBUMS: The War Of The Worlds (Columbia 1978)★★★, The War Of The Worlds - Highlights (Columbia 1981) ★★★, Spartacus (Columbia 1992)★★★.
COMPILATIONS: ULLAdubULLA The Remix Album (2000)★★.

WEATHER REPORT
ALBUMS: Weather Report i (Columbia 1971)★★★, I Sing The Body Electric (Columbia 1972)★★★★, Sweetnighter (Columbia 1973)★★★, Mysterious Traveller (Columbia 1974)★★★★, Tail Spinnin' (Columbia 1975)★★★, Black Market (Columbia 1976)★★★★, Heavy Weather (Columbia 1977)★★★★, Mr. Gone (Columbia 1978), 8:30 (Columbia 1979)★★★, Night Passages (Columbia 1980) ★★★, Weather Report ii (Columbia 1982)★★★, Procession (Columbia 1983)★★★, Domino Theory (Columbia 1984)★★★, Sportin' Life (Columbia 1985) ★★★, This Is This (Columbia 1986) ★★★, New Album (Columbia 1988)★★★, Live In Tokyo recorded 1972 (Sony 1998)★★★.
COMPILATIONS: Heavy Weather: The Collection (Columbia 1990)★★★★, The Jaco Years 1975-80 recordings (Columbia 1990)★★★, The Weather Report Selection 3-CD box set (Columbia 1992)★★★.

WEATHERALL, ANDREW
COMPILATIONS: with Richard Fearless Heavenly Presents Live At The Social Volume 3 (React 1999)★★★★, Nine O'Clock Drop (Nuphonic 2000)★★★★, Hypercity Force Tracks (Force Tracks 2001)★★★.

WEBB, JIMMY
ALBUMS: Jimmy Webb Sings Jimmy Webb (Epic 1968)★★, Words And Music (Reprise 1970)★★★, And So: On (Reprise 1971)★★★, Letters (Reprise 1972)★★★★, Land's End (Asylum 1974)★★★★, El Mirage (Asylum 1977)★★★, Voices soundtrack (Planet 1979)★★, Angel Heart (Columbia/ Lorimar 1982)★★★, Hanoi Hilton soundtrack (1987)★★, Suspending Disbelief (Warners 1993)★★★, Ten Easy Pieces (Guardian 1996)★★★.
COMPILATIONS: Archive (Warners 1993)★★★★, And Someone Left The Cake Out In The Rain: The Classic Songs Of Jimmy Webb (Debutante Deluxe 1998)★★★★, Up, Up & Away: The Songs Of Jimmy Webb (Sequel 1999)★★★★, with Glen Campbell Reunited With Jimmy Webb 1974-1988 (Raven 2000)★★★★.
FURTHER READING: Tunesmith: Inside The Art Of Songwriting, Jimmy Webb.

WEDDING PRESENT
ALBUMS: George Best (Reception 1987)★★★, Ukrainski Vistupi V Johna Peela mini-album (RCA 1989)★★, Bizarro (RCA 1989)★★, Seamonsters (RCA 1991)★★★, Watusi (Island 1994)★★★, Mini (Cooking Vinyl 1996)★★, Saturnalia (Cooking Vinyl 1996)★★★.
COMPILATIONS: Tommy (Reception 1988)★★★, The BBC Sessions (Strange Fruit 1988)★★, The Hit Parade Part One (RCA 1992)★★★, The Hit Parade Part Two (RCA 1993)★★, John Peel Sessions 1987-1990 (Strange Fruit 1993)★★★, Evening Sessions 1986-1994 (Strange Fruit 1997)★★★, Singles 1989-1991 (Manifesto 1999)★★★, Singles 1995-97 (Cooking Vinyl 1999)★★.
FURTHER READING: The Wedding Present: Thank Yer, Very Glad, Mark Hodkinson.

WEEZER
ALBUMS: Weezer (DGC 1994)★★★★, Pinkerton (DGC 1996)★★★, The Green Album (DGC 2001)★★★★, Maladroit (Geffen 2002)★★★.

WELCH, GILLIAN
ALBUMS: Revival (Almo 1996)★★★★, Hell Among The Yearlings (Almo 1998)★★★★, Time (The Revelator) (Acony 2001)★★★.
FILMS: O Brother, Where Art Thou? (2000), Down From The Mountain (2000).

WELLER, PAUL
ALBUMS: Paul Weller (Go! Discs 1992)★★, Wild Wood (Go! Discs 1994)★★★★, Live Wood (Go! Discs 1994)★★★, Stanley Road (Go! Discs 1995)★★★★, Heavy Soul (Island 1997)★★★★, Heliocentric (Island 2000)★★, Days Of Speed (Independiente 2001)★★★.
COMPILATIONS: Modern Classics (Island 1998)★★★★.
VIDEOS: The Paul Weller Movement Live At Brixton Academy (Video Collection 1991), Live Wood (PolyGram Music Video 1994), Highlights & Hang Ups (PolyGram Music Video 1994), Live At The Royal Albert Hall (Warner Music Vision 2000).
FURTHER READING: Days Lose Their Names And Time Slips Away: 1992-95, Lawrence Watson and Paulo Hewitt. Paul Weller: My Ever Changing Moods, John Reed. The Unauthorised Biography, Steve Malins. Paul Weller: In His Own Words, Michael Heatley. The Complete Guide To The Music Of Paul Weller And The Jam, John Reed.

WELLS, MARY
ALBUMS: Bye Bye Baby, I Don't Want To Take A Chance (Motown 1961)★★★, The One Who Really Loves You (Motown 1962)★★★, Two Lovers And Other Great Hits (Motown 1963)★★★, Recorded Live On Stage (Motown 1963)★★★, Second Time Around (Motown 1963)★★★, with Marvin Gaye Together (Motown 1964)★★★, Mary Wells Sings My Guy (Motown 1964)★★★★, Mary Wells (20th Century 1965)★★★, Mary Wells Sings Love Songs To The Beatles (20th Century 1965)★★★, Vintage Stock (Motown 1966)★★★, The Two Sides Of Mary Wells (Atco 1966)★★★, Ooh! (Movietone 1966)★★★, Servin' Up Some Soul (Jubilee 1968)★★, In And Out Of Love (EPK 1981)★★, Keeping My Mind On Love (Motor City 1990)★★.
COMPILATIONS: Greatest Hits (Motown 1964)★★★, The Old, The New And The Best Of Mary Wells (Allegiance 1984)★★★, Compact Command Performances (Sequel 1993)★★★, The Complete Jubilee Sessions (Sequel 1993)★★★, Ain't It The Truth: The Best Of Mary Wells 1964-82 (Varèse Sarabande 1993)★★★, Looking Back 1961-64 (Motown 1993)★★★, Dear Lover: The Atco Sessions (Ichiban 1995)★★★, Early Classics (Spectrum 1996)★★★, Never, Never Leave Me: The 20th Century Sides (Ichiban 1997)★★★, 20th Century Masters: The Millennium Collection (Motown 1999)★★★★.
FILMS: Catalina Caper (1967).

WESTLIFE
ALBUMS: Westlife (RCA 1999)★★★, Coast To Coast (RCA 2000)★★, World Of Our Own (RCA 2001)★★★.
VIDEOS: The Westlife Story (BMG Video 2000).
FURTHER READING: Westlife: In Our Own Words, Eugene Masterson. Westlife: Our Story, Rob McGibbon. Westlife: In Real Life, Lisa Hand. Westlife: Backstage Pass, Michael-Anne Johns and Christopher Patrick. Westlife On Tour, Eddie Rowley.

WET WET WET
ALBUMS: Popped In Souled Out (Precious 1987)★★★, The Memphis Sessions (Precious 1988)★★, Holding Back The River (Precious 1989)★★★, as Maggie Pie And The Imposters Cloak And Dagger (1990)★★★, Live cassette only (1991)★★, High On The Happy Side (Precious 1991)★★, Live At The Royal Albert Hall (Precious 1993)★★, Picture This (Mercury 1995)★★, 10 (Mercury 1997)★★. Solo Marti Pellow Smile (Mercury 2001)★★.
COMPILATIONS: End Of Part One (Precious 1993)★★★.
FURTHER READING: Wet Wet Wet Pictured, Simon Fowler and Alan Jackson.

WHAM!
ALBUMS: Fantastic (Inner Vision 1983)★★, Make It Big (Epic 1984)★★★, The Final (Epic 1986)★★★.

COMPILATIONS: If You Were There - The Best Of Wham (Epic 1997)★★★★.
VIDEOS: Wham! The Video (CBS-Fox 1985), The Best Of Wham! (VCI 1997).
FURTHER READING: Wham! (Confidential) The Death Of A Supergroup, Johnny Rogan. Bare, George Michael.

WHEATUS
ALBUMS: Wheatus (Columbia 2000)★★★.

WHISKEYTOWN
ALBUMS: Faithless Street (Mood Food 1996)★★★, Strangers Almanac (Outpost 1997)★★★★, Faithless Street expanded/remastered version (Outpost 1998)★★★, Pneumonia (Lost Highway 2001)★★★.
COMPILATIONS: Rural Free Delivery (Mood Food 1997)★★★.

WHITE, BARRY
ALBUMS: I've Got So Much To Give (20th Century 1973)★★★, Stone Gon' (20th Century/Pye 1973)★★★, Can't Get Enough (20th Century 1974)★★★★, Just Another Way To Say I Love You (20th Century 1975)★★★, Let The Music Play (20th Century 1976)★★★, Is This Whatcha Wont? (20th Century 1976)★★★, Barry White Sings For Someone You Love (20th Century 1977)★★★, Barry White The Man (20th Century 1978)★★★, The Message Is Love (Unlimited Gold 1979)★★★, I Love To Sing The Songs I Sing (20th Century 1979)★★, Barry White's Sheet Music (Unlimited Gold 1980)★★, The Best Of Our Love (Unlimited Gold 1981)★★, with Glodean James Barry And Glodean (Unlimited Gold 1981)★★★, Change (Unlimited Gold 1982)★★, Dedicated (Unlimited Gold 1983)★★, The Right Night And Barry White (A&M/Breakout 1987)★★, The Man Is Back! (A&M 1989)★★, Put Me In Your Mix (A&M 1991)★★★, The Icon Is Love (A&M 1994)★★, Staying Power (Private 1999)★★★.
COMPILATIONS: Barry White's Greatest Hits (20th Century 1975)★★★★, Barry White's Greatest Hits Volume 2 (20th Century 1977)★★★, Heart And Soul (K-Tel 1985)★★, Satin & Soul (Connoisseur 1987)★★★, The Collection (Polydor/Mercury 1988)★★★★, Satin & Soul Vol. 2 (Connoisseur 1990)★★, Just For You 3-CD box set (A&M 1992)★★★, All-Time Greatest Hits (PolyGram 1995)★★★, Boss Soul: The Genius Of Barry White (Del-Fi 1998)★★★, Soul Seduction (Spectrum 2000)★★★, The Ultimate Collection (Universal 2000)★★★★.
FURTHER READING: Love Unlimited: Insights On Life & Love, Barry White with Marc Eliot.
FILMS: Coonskin aka Streetfight (1974), Why Colors? voice only (1992).

WHITE STRIPES
ALBUMS: The White Stripes (Sympathy For The Record Industry 1999)★★★, De Stijl (Sympathy For The Record Industry 2000)★★★, White Blood Cells (Sympathy For The Record Industry/XL 2001)★★★★.

WHITE ZOMBIE
ALBUMS: Psycho-Head Blowout (Silent Explosion 1986)★★, Soul Crusher (Silent Explosion 1987)★★★, Make Them Die Slowly (Caroline 1989)★★★, La Sexorcisto: Devil Music Vol. 1 (Geffen 1992)★★★★, Astro Creep 2000: Songs Of Love, Destruction And Other Synthetic Delusions Of The Electric Head (Geffen 1995)★★★★, Supersexy Swingin' Sounds (Geffen 1996)★★★.

WHITESNAKE
ALBUMS: Trouble (United Artists 1978)★★★, Love Hunter (United Artists 1979)★★★, Live At Hammersmith Japanese release (United Artists 1980)★★, Ready An' Willing (United Artists 1980)★★★, Live ... In The Heart Of The City (United Artists 1980)★★★, Come An' Get It (Liberty 1981)★★★, Saints & Sinners (Liberty 1982)★★, Slide It In (Liberty 1984)★★★, Whitesnake (Liberty 1987)★★★★, Slip Of The Tongue (EMI 1989)★★★, Restless Heart (EMI 1997)★★★.
COMPILATIONS: Best Of (EMI 1988)★★★★, Greatest Hits (MCA 1994)★★★★.
VIDEOS: Fourplay (PMI/EMI 1984), Whitesnake Live (PMI/EMI 1984), Trilogy (PMI/EMI 1988).
FURTHER READING: Illustrated Biography, Simon Robinson. Whitesnake, Tom Hibbert.

WHO
ALBUMS: My Generation (Brunswick 1965)★★★★, The Who Sings My Generation (Decca 1966)★★★★, A Quick One (Reaction 1966)★★★★, The Who Sell Out (Track 1967)★★★★, Happy Jack (Decca 1967)★★★, Magic Bus - The Who On Tour (Decca 1968)★★★, Tommy (Track 1969)★★★★, Live At Leeds (Track 1970)★★★★★, Who's Next (Track 1971)★★★★★, Quadrophenia (MCA 1973)★★★★, The Who By Numbers (Polydor 1975)★★★, Who Are You (Polydor 1978)★★, The Kids Are Alright film soundtrack (Polydor 1979)★★★, Quadrophenia film soundtrack (Polydor 1979)★★★★, Face Dances (Polydor 1981)★★, It's Hard (Polydor 1982)★★, Join Together (Virgin 1990)★★★, Live At The Isle Of Wight Festival 1970 (Essential 1996)★★★★, Live At Leeds Deluxe Edition (Polydor 2001)★★★★★.
COMPILATIONS: Magic Bus (Decca 1967)★★★, Direct Hits (Decca 1968)★★★, Meaty, Beaty, Big & Bouncy (Polydor 1971)★★★★★, Odds & Sods (Track 1974)★★★★, The Story Of The Who (Polydor 1976)★★★, Hooligans (MCA 1981) ★★★, Rarities Volume 1 (1966-1968) (Polydor 1983)★★★, Rarities Volume 2 (1970-1973) (Polydor 1983)★★★, The Singles (Polydor 1984)★★★, Who's Last (MCA 1984)★★, Who's Missing (MCA 1985)★★, Who's Better Who's Best (Polydor 1988)★★★★, The Who Collection (Stylus 1988) ★★★, Thirty Years Of Maximum R&B 4-CD box set (Polydor 1994)★★★★★, My Generation - The Very Best Of The Who (Polydor 1996)★★★★★, BBC Sessions (Polydor 2000)★★★★.
VIDEOS: The Kids Are Alright (PolyGram Music Video 1984), Thirty Years Of Maximum R&B Live (PolyGram Music Video 1994), The Who Live At The Isle Of Wight Festival 1970 (Warner Music Vision 1996), Live, Featuring The Rock Opera Tommy (Sony Music Video 1996), Classic Albums: Who's Next (Eagle Rock 1999), The Who & Special Guests Live At The Royal Albert Hall (Aviva International 2001).
FURTHER READING: The Who, Gary Herman. The Who, Jeff Stein and Chris Johnston. Les Who, Sacha Reins. The Who ... Through The Eyes Of Pete Townshend, Conner McKnight and Caroline Silver. The Who, George Tremlett. The Who: Ten Great Years, Cindy Ehrlich. The Who Generation, Nik Cohn. A Decade Of The Who: An Authorized History In Music, Paintings, Words And Photo, Steve Turner. The Story Of Tommy, Richard Barnes and Pete Townshend. Whose Who? A Who Retrospective, Brian Ashley and Steve Monnery. Keith Moon: The Life And Death Of A Rock Legend, Ivan Waterman. The Who: Britain's Greatest Rock Group, John Swenson. The Who File, Pearce Marchbank. Quadrophenia, Alan Fletcher. The Who In Their Own Words, Steve Clarke. Mods!, Richard Barnes. The Who, Paul Sahner and Thomas Veszelits. The Who, Giacomo Mazzone. The Who: An Illustrated Discography, Ed Hanel. Moon The Loon: The Amazing Rock And Roll Life Of Keith Moon, Late Of The Who, Dougal Butler with Chris Trengove and Peter Lawrence. The Who: The Illustrated Biography, Chris Charlesworth. Full Moon: The Amazing Rock & Roll Life Of Keith Moon, Late Of The Who, Dougal Butler. The Who Maximum R & B: An Illustrated Biography, Richard Barnes. Before I Get Old: The Story Of The Who, Dave Marsh. The Who: The Farewell Tour, Philip Kamin and Peter Goddard. The Complete Guide To The Music Of ..., Chris Charlesworth. The Who In Sweden, Ollie Lunden (ed.). The Who Concert File, Joe McMichael and Irish Jack Lyones. Dear Boy: The Life Of Keith Moon, Tony Fletcher. A Fortnight Of Furore: The Who And The Small Faces Down Under, Andrew Neill. Meaty, Beaty, Big And Bouncy, John Perry. The Who On Record: A Critical History 1963-1998, John Atkins. Eyewitness The Who, Johnny Black.
FILMS: Tommy (1975), The Kids Are Alright (1978), Quadrophenia (1979).

WIDESPREAD PANIC
ALBUMS: Space Wrangler (Landslide 1988)★★, Widespread Panic (Capricorn 1991)★★★, Everyday (Capricorn 1993)★★★, Ain't Life Grand (Capricorn 1994)★★★, with Vic Chesnutt Brute: Nine High A Pallet (Capricorn 1995)★★, Bombs & Butterflies (Capricorn 1997)★★★, Panic In The Streets (Capricorn 1998)★★★, Light Fuse, Get Away (Capricorn 1998)★★★, 'Til The Medicine Takes (Capricorn 1999)★★★, with The Dirty Dozen Brass Band Another Joyous Occasion (Widespread 2000)★★★, Don't Tell The Band (Sanctuary 2001)★★★, with Chesnutt Brute: Co-Balt (Widespread 2002)★★★.
VIDEOS: Live From The Georgia Theatre (Capricorn 1992), Live At Oak Mountain (BMG 2001).

WILCO
ALBUMS: A.M. (Reprise 1995)★★★, Being There (Reprise 1996)★★★, with Billy Bragg Mermaid Avenue (East West 1998)★★★★, Summer Teeth (Reprise 1999)★★★★, with Billy Bragg Mermaid Avenue Vol II (East West 2000)★★★, Yankee Hotel Foxtrot (Nonesuch 2002)★★★.
VIDEOS: with Billy Bragg Man In The Sand (Union Productions 1999).

WILDE, KIM
ALBUMS: Kim Wilde (RAK 1981)★★★, Select (RAK 1982)★★, Catch As Catch Can (RAK 1983)★★, Teases And Dares (MCA 1984)★★, Another Step (MCA 1986) ★★, Close (MCA 1988)★★★★, Love Moves (MCA 1990) ★★, Love Is (MCA 1992)★★★, Now And Forever (MCA 1995)★★.
COMPILATIONS: The Very Best Of Kim Wilde (RAK 1985) ★★★, The Singles Collection 1981-1993 (MCA 1993) ★★★, The Gold Collection (EMI 1996)★★★, The Collection (Spectrum 2001)★★★, The Very Best Of Kim Wilde (EMI 2001)★★★.
VIDEOS: Video EP: Kim Wilde (MCA 1987), Close (MCA 1989), Another Step (Closer To You) (MCA 1990), The Singles Collection 1981-1993 (MCA 1993).

WILDE, MARTY
ALBUMS: Wilde About Marty (Philips 1959)★★★, Bad Boy (Epic 1960)★★★, Showcase (Philips 1960)★★★, The Versatile Mr. Wilde (Philips 1960)★★★, Diversions (Philips 1969)★★, Rock 'N' Roll (Philips 1970)★★, Good Rocking - Then And Now (Philips 1974)★★★.
COMPILATIONS: Wild Cat Rocker (Jan 1981)★★★, The Hits Of Marty Wilde (Philips 1984)★★★.

WILLIAMS, HANK
ALBUMS: Hank Williams Sings 10-inch album (MGM 1951) ★★★★, Moanin' The Blues (MGM 1952/56)★★★★, Hank Williams Memorial Album (MGM 1953/55)★★★★, Hank Williams as Luke The Drifter overdubbed as Beyond The Sunset MGM 1963 (MGM 1953/55)★★★, Honky Tonkin' (MGM 1954/57)★★★, I Saw The Light (MGM 1954/56) ★★★, Ramblin' Man (MGM 1954/55)★★★, Sing Me A Blue Song (MGM 1957)★★★, The Immortal Hank Williams overdubbed as First Last And Always MGM 1969 (MGM 1958)★★★, The Unforgettable Hank Williams overdubbed MGM 1968 (MGM 1959)★★★, Lonesome Sound Of Hank Williams (MGM 1960)★★★, Wait For The Light To Shine overdubbed MGM 1968 (MGM 1960)★★★, Let Me Sing A Blue Song overdubbed 1968 (MGM 1961)★★★, Wanderin' Around overdubbed 1968 (MGM 1961)★★★, I'm Blue Inside overdubbed MGM 1968 (MGM 1961)★★★, The Spirit Of Hank Williams overdubbed MGM 1969 (MGM 1961)★★★, On Stage-Live Volume 1 (MGM 1962)★★★, On Stage Volume II (MGM 1963)★★★, Lost Highways & Other Folk Ballads (MGM 1964)★★★, Father And Son overdubbed (MGM 1965)★★★, Kawliga And Other Humorous Songs some overdubbed (MGM 1965)★★★, Hank Williams With Strings overdubbed (MGM 1966)★★★, Hank Williams, Hank Williams Jr. Again (MGM 1966)★★★, Movin' On - Luke The Drifter overdubbed (MGM 1966)★★★, Mr & Mrs Hank Williams (With Audrey) (Metro 1966)★★★, More Hank Williams And Strings (MGM 1967)★★★, I Won't Be Home No More overdubbed (MGM 1967)★★★, Hank Williams And Strings, Volume III (MGM 1968)★★★, In The Beginning (MGM 1968)★★★, Life To Legend Hank Williams (MGM 1970)★★★, The Last Picture Show Film Soundtrack (MGM 1971)★★★, Hank Williams/Hank Williams Jr. Legend In Story And Song (MGM 1973)★★★, Hank Williams/Hank Williams Jr. Insights In Story And Song (MGM 1974)★★★, A Home In Heaven (MGM 1975)★★★, Live At The Grand Ole Opry (MGM 1976)★★★★, Hank Williams And The Drifting Cowboys On Radio (Golden Country 1982)★★★★, Early Country Live Volume 1 (Hank Williams On Radio Shows Plus Others) (ACM 1983)★★★★, Rare Takes And Radio Cuts (Polydor 1984)★★★, Early Country Live Volume 2 (Hank Williams On Radio Shows) (ACM 1984)★★★★, Early Country Music Live Volume 3 (Hank Williams On Radio Shows) (ACM 1985)★★★★, Just Me And My Guitar (CMF 1985)★★★, Hank Williams – The First Recordings (CMF 1985)★★★★, Hank Williams – On The Air (Polydor 1985)★★★, Hank Williams: I Ain't Got Nothin' But Time December 1946-August 1947 (Polydor 1985)★★★★, Hank Williams: Lovesick Blues – August 1947-December 1948 (Polydor 1985)★★★★, Hank Williams: Lost Highway – December 1948-March 1949 (Polydor 1986)★★★, Hank Williams: I'm So Lonesome I Could Cry –March 1949-August 1949 (Polydor 1986)★★★★, Hank Williams: Long Gone Lonesome Blues - August 1949-December 1950 (Polydor 1987)★★★★★, Hank Williams: Hey, Good Lookin' – December 1950-July 1951 (Polydor 1987)★★★★, Hank Williams: Let's Turn Back The Years, July 1951-June 1952 (Polydor 1987)★★★★, Hank Williams: I Won't Be Home No More, June 1952-September 1952 (Polydor 1987)★★★★, There's Nothing As Sweet As My Baby (Mount Olive 1988)★★★, Hank Williams - Jambalaya (Creative Sounds 1992)★★★, Health And Happiness Shows (Mercury 1993)★★★, Alone And Forsaken (Mercury 1995)★★★, with Hank Williams, Hank Williams Jnr. Three Hanks, Men With Broken Hearts (Curb 1996)★★★.
COMPILATIONS: Greatest Hits (Polydor 1963)★★★, The Very Best Of Hank Williams (Polydor 1963)★★★, 24 Of Hank Williams' Greatest Hits (MGM 1970)★★★★, 24 Greatest Hits, Volume 2 (Polydor 1976)★★, 40 Greatest Hits (Polydor 1978)★★★★, The Collectors' Edition 8-LP box set of Polydor albums listed above (Polydor 1987)★★★★, Rare Demos: First To Last (CMF 1990)★★★, The Original Singles Collection Plus 3-CD box set (Polydor 1990) ★★★★★, Low Down Blues (PolyGram 1996)★★★, Best Of Hank Williams (Spectrum 1998)★★★★, The Complete Hank Williams 10-CD box set (Mercury 1998)★★★★★, various artists Songwriter To Legend (Bear Family 1998) ★★★★, Live At The Grand Ole Opry (Mercury 1999) ★★★★, The Hank Williams Story 4-CD box set (Chrome Dreams 2000)★★★, Alone With His Guitar (Mercury 2000)★★★★.
VIDEOS: The Hank Williams Story (1994).
FURTHER READING: Hank Williams: From Life To Legend, Jerry Rivers. Sing A Sad Song: The Life Of Hank Williams, Roger M. Williams. I Saw The Light: The Gospel Life Of Hank Williams, Al Bock. Hank Williams: Country Music's Tragic King, Jay Caress. The First Outlaw: Hank Williams, Jim Arp. Your Cheating Heart: A Biography Of Hank Williams, Chet Flippo. Hank Williams: A Bio-Bibliography, George William Koon. Still In Love With You: The Story Of Hank And Audrey Williams, Lycrecia Williams. Ain't Nothin' As Sweet As My Baby: The Story Of Hank Williams' Lost Daughter, Jett Williams and Pamela Thomas. Hank Williams: The Complete Lyrics, Don Cusic. The Life And Times Of Hank Williams, Arnold Rogers and Bruce Gidoll. Hank Williams: The Biography, Colin Escott. The Essential Hank Williams, Richard Courtney. Hank Williams: Snapshots From The Lost Highway, Colin Escott and Kira Florita.

WILLIAMS, HANK, JNR.
ALBUMS: Hank Williams Jr. Sings The Songs Of Hank Williams (MGM 1963)★★★, Connie Francis And Hank Williams Jr. Sing Great Country Favorites (MGM 1964)★★★, Your Cheatin' Heart film soundtrack (MGM 1964)★★, Ballad Of The Hills And Plains (MGM 1965)★★★, Father And Son - Hank Williams Sr And Hank Williams Jr. Again (MGM 1965)★★★, Blue's My Name (MGM 1966)★★★, Country Shadows (MGM 1966)★★★, In My Own Way (MGM 1967)★★★, My Songs (MGM 1968)★★★, A Time To Sing film soundtrack (MGM 1968)★★, Luke The Drifter Jr. (MGM 1969)★★★, Songs My Father Left Me (MGM 1969)★★★, Live At Cobo Hall, Detroit (MGM 1969)★★★★, Luke The Drifter Jr., Volume 2 (MGM 1969)★★★, Sunday Morning (MGM 1970)★★★, Singing My Songs (MGM 1970)★★★, Luke The Drifter Jr., Volume 3 (MGM 1970)★★★, with Louis Johnson Removing The Shadow (MGM 1970)★★, All For The Love Of Sunshine (MGM 1970)★★★, I've Got A Right To Cry/They All Used To Belong To Me (MGM 1971), Sweet Dreams (MGM 1971)★★★, Eleven Roses (MGM 1972)★★, with Johnson Send Me Some Lovin'/Whole Lotta Lovin' (MGM 1972)★★★, After You/Pride's Not Hard To Swallow (MGM 1973)★★★, Hank Williams/Hank Williams Jr: The Legend In Story And Song a double album in which Hank Jr. narrates his father's life (MGM 1973)★★★, Just Pickin' – No Singing (MGM 1973)★★★, The Last Love Song (MGM 1973)★★★, Hank Williams/Hank Williams Jr. Insights In Story And Song (MGM 1974)★★★, Bocephus (MGM 1975)★★, Hank Williams Jr. And Friends (MGM 1975)★★★★, One Night Stands (Warners/Curb 1977)★★★★, The New South (Warners 1978)★★★★, Family Tradition (Elektra/Curb 1979)★★★★, Whiskey Bent And Hell Bound (Elektra/Curb 1979)★★★★, Habits Old And New (Elektra/Curb 1980) ★★★, Rowdy (Elektra/Curb 1981)★★★★, The Pressure Is On (Elektra/Curb 1981)★★★★, High Notes (Elektra/Curb 1982)★★★, Strong Stuff (Elektra/Curb 1983)★★★, Man Of Steel (Warners/Curb 1983)★★★★, Major Moves (Warners/Curb 1984)★★★★, Five-O (Warners/Curb 1985)★★★★, Montana Cafe (Warners/Curb 1986)★★★★, Hank Live (Warners/Curb 1987)★★★, Born To Boogie (Warners/Curb 1987)★★★★, Wild Streak (Warners/Curb 1988)★★★★, Lone Wolf (Warners/Curb 1990)★★, America – The Way I See It (Warners/Curb 1990)H, Pure Hank (Warners/Curb 1991)★★★, Maverick (Curb/Capricorn 1992)★★★★, Out Of Left Field (Curb/Capricorn 1993)★★★, Hog Wild (MCG/Curb 1995)★★★, AKA Wham Bam Sam (MCG/Curb 1996)★★, with Hank Williams, Hank Williams III Three Hanks, Men With Broken Hearts (Curb 1996)★★★, Stormy (Curb 1999)★★★★, Almeria Club (Curb 2002)★★★.
COMPILATIONS: The Best Of Hank Williams Jr. (MGM 1967)★★★, Living Proof: The MGM Recordings 1963 - 1975 (Mercury 1974)★★★★, 14 Greatest Hits (Polydor 1976)★★★, Hank Williams Jr.'s Greatest Hits (Warners/Curb 1982)★★★, Greatest Hits Volume Two (Warners/Curb 1985)★★★★, The Early Years 1976-1978 (Warners/Curb 1986)★★★, Country Store (Country Store 1988) ★★★, Standing In The Shadows (Polydor 1988)★★★★, Greatest Hits Volume 3 (Warners/Curb 1989)★★★★, The Bocephus Box: Hank Williams Jr. Collection '79 - 92 (Capricorn 1992)★★★, The Best Of, Volume 1: Roots And Branches (Mercury 1992)★★★, Hank Williams Jr.'s Greatest Hits (Curb 1994)★★★, The Early Years Part One (Curb 1998)★★★, The Early Years Part Two (Curb 1998) ★★★, The Complete Hank Williams Jr. 3-CD set (Curb 1999)★★★, The Bocephus Box Set (1979-1999) 3-CD box set (Curb 2000)★★★.
FURTHER READING: Living Proof, Hank Williams Jnr. with Michael Bane.

WILLIAMS, ROBBIE
ALBUMS: Life Thru A Lens (Chrysalis 1997)★★★★, I've Been Expecting You (Chrysalis 1998)★★★★, Sing When You're Winning (Chrysalis/Capitol 2000)★★★, Swing When You're Winning (Chrysalis 2001)★★★.
COMPILATIONS: The Ego Has Landed US only (EMI 1999)★★★★.
VIDEOS: Live In Your Living Room (Chrysalis 1998), Where Egos Dare (Chrysalis 2000), Live At The Albert (Chrysalis 2001).
FURTHER READING: Robbie Williams: Let Me Entertain You, Jim Parton. Robbie Williams: Somebody Someday, Robbie Williams & Mark McCrum.

WILSON, BRIAN
ALBUMS: Brian Wilson (Sire 1988)★★★★, I Just Wasn't Made For These Times (MCA 1995)★★, with Van Dyke Parks Orange Crate Art (Warners 1995)★★★, Imagination (Giant 1998)★★★, Live At The Roxy Theatre (BriMel/Oglio 2000)★★★.
VIDEOS: I Just Wasn't Made For These Times (WEA Video 1995).
FURTHER READING: Heroes And Villains: The True Story Of The Beach Boys, Steven Gaines. Wouldn't It Be Nice: My Own Story, Brian Wilson. The Nearest Faraway Place: Brian Wilson, The Beach Boys & The Southern California Experience, Timothy White. Back To The Beach: A Brian Wilson And The Beach Boys Reader, Kingsley Abbott (ed.).

WILSON, JACKIE
ALBUMS: He's So Fine (Brunswick 1958)★★★, Lonely Teardrops (Brunswick 1959)★★★★, Doggin' Around (Brunswick 1959)★★★, So Much (Brunswick 1960)★★★, Night (Brunswick 1960)★★★, Jackie Wilson Sings The Blues (Brunswick 1960)★★★★, A Woman A Lover A Friend (Brunswick 1961)★★★★, Try A Little Tenderness (Brunswick 1961)★★★, You Ain't Heard Nothing Yet (Brunswick 1961) ★★★, By Special Request (Brunswick 1961)★★★, Body And Soul (Brunswick 1962)★★★, Jackie Wilson At The Copa (Brunswick 1962)★★★, Jackie Wilson Sings The World's Greatest Melodies (Brunswick 1962)★★★, Baby Workout (Brunswick 1963)★★★★, Merry Christmas From Jackie Wilson (Brunswick 1963)★★, with Linda Hopkins Shake A Hand (Brunswick 1963)★★, Somethin' Else (Brunswick 1964)★★★★, Soul Time (Brunswick 1965)★★★★, Spotlight On Jackie Wilson (Brunswick 1965)★★★, Soul Galore (Brunswick 1966)★★★, Whispers (Brunswick 1967)★★★, Higher And Higher (Brunswick 1967)★★★★, with Count Basie Manufacturers Of Soul (Brunswick 1968)★★★, I Get The Sweetest Feeling (Brunswick 1968)★★★★, Do Your Thing (Brunswick 1970)★★★, This Love Is Real (Brunswick 1970) ★★★, You Got Me Walking (Brunswick 1971)★★, Beautiful Day (Brunswick 1973)★★, Nowstalgia (Brunswick 1974)★★, Nobody But You (Brunswick 1976)★★.
COMPILATIONS: My Golden Favourites (Brunswick 1960)★★★, My Golden Favourites – Volume 2 (Brunswick 1964)★★★, Jackie Wilson's Greatest Hits (Brunswick 1969)★★★, It's All Part Of Love (Brunswick 1969)★★★, Classic Jackie Wilson (Skratch 1984)★★★, Reet Petite (Ace 1985)★★★★, The Soul Years (Kent 1985)★★★★, The Soul Years Volume 2 (Kent 1986)★★★, Higher And Higher i (Kent 1986)★★★, Through The Years (Rhino 1987)★★★, The Very Best Of Jackie Wilson (Ace 1987)★★★, Mr Excitement! 3-CD box set (Rhino 1992)★★★★★, The Very Best Of Jackie Wilson (Rhino 1994)★★★★, A Portrait Of Jackie Wilson (Essential Gold/Pickwick 1995)★★★★, Higher And Higher (Rhino 1995)★★★★, The Hit Collection (Carlton 1997)★★★, The Titan Of Soul 3-CD box set (Edsel 1998)★★★★, Sweetest Feelin': The Very Best Of Jackie Wilson (Music Club 1999)★★★.
FURTHER READING: Lonely Teardrops: The Jackie Wilson Story, Tony Douglas. Jackie Wilson: The Man, The Music, The Mob, Tony Douglas.
FILMS: Go Johnny Go (1958).

WINCHESTER, JESSE
ALBUMS: Jesse Winchester (Ampex 1970)★★★★, Third Down, 110 To Go (Bearsville 1972)★★★, Learn To Love It (Bearsville 1974)★★★, Let The Rough Side Drag (Bearsville 1976)★★★, Nothin' But A Breeze (Bearsville 1977)★★★, A Touch On The Rainy Side (Bearsville 1978)★★★, Talk Memphis (Bearsville 1981)★★★, Humour Me (Sugar Hill 1988)★★★, Gentleman Of Leisure (Sugar Hill 1999)★★★.
COMPILATIONS: The Best Of Jesse Winchester (See For Miles 1988)★★★★, Anthology (Bearsville 1999)★★★★.

WINGS
ALBUMS: Wild Life (Apple 1971)★★, as Paul McCartney And Wings Red Rose Speedway (Apple 1973)★★★, as Paul McCartney And Wings Band On The Run (Apple 1973) ★★★★, Venus And Mars (Apple/Capitol 1975)★★★★, Wings At The Speed Of Sound (Apple/Capitol 1976)★★★, Wings Over America (Parlophone/Capitol 1976)★★★, London Town (Parlophone/Capitol 1978)★★★, Back To The Egg (Parlophone/Columbia 1979)★★★.
COMPILATIONS: Wings' Greatest Hits (Parlophone/Capitol 1978)★★★, Wingspan: Paul McCartney, Hits And History (Parlophone 2001)★★★★.
VIDEOS: Wingspan (Hits & History) (Capitol Video 2001).
FURTHER READING: The Facts About A Rock Group, Featuring Wings, David Gelly. Paul McCartney & Wings, Tony Jasper. Paul McCartney: Beatle With Wings, Martin A. Grove. Hands Across The Water: Wings Tour USA, no author listed. The Ocean View: Paintings And Drawings Of Wings American Tour April To June 1976, Humphrey Ocean, Body Count, Francie Schwartz. The Paul McCartney Story, George Tremlett. Paul McCartney In His Own Words, Paul Gambaccini. Paul McCartney: A Biography In Words & Pictures, John Mendelsohn. Paul McCartney: Composer/Artist, Paul McCartney. Paul McCartney: The Definitive Biography, Chris Welch. McCartney, Chris Salewicz. McCartney: The Biography, Chet Flippo. Blackbird: The Life And Times Of Paul McCartney, Geoffrey Giuliano. Paul McCartney: Behind The Myth, Ross Benson. McCartney: Yesterday & Today, Ray Coleman. Roadworks, Linda McCartney. Paul McCartney: Many Years From Now, Barry Miles, Linda McCartney: The Biography, Danny Fields.

WINTER, JOHNNY
ALBUMS: The Progressive Blues Experiment (Sonobeat/Imperial 1969)★★★, Johnny Winter (Columbia 1969) ★★★★, Second Winter (Columbia 1969)★★★, Johnny Winter And (Columbia 1970)★★★★, Johnny Winter And Live (Columbia 1971)★★★, Still Alive And Well (Columbia 1973)★★★, Saints And Sinners (Columbia 1974)★★★, John Dawson Winter III (Blue Sky 1974)★★★, Captured Live! (Blue Sky 1976)★★★, with Edgar Winter Together (Blue Sky 1976)★★★★, Nothin' But The Blues (Blue Sky 1977)★★★, White Hot And Blue (Blue Sky 1978)★★, Raisin' Cain (Blue Sky 1980)★★, Raised On Rock (Blue Sky 1981)★★, Guitar Slinger (Alligator 1984)★★★, Serious Business (Alligator 1985)★★★, Third Degree (Alligator 1986)★★★, Winter Of '88 (MCA 1988)★★, Let Me In (Virgin/PointBlank 1991)★★★, Jack Daniels Kind Of Day (Thunderbolt 1992)★★★, Hey, Where's Your Brother? (PointBlank 1992)★★★, Live In NYC '97 (PointBlank 1998)★★, Back In Beaumont (Magnum 2000)★★★.
COMPILATIONS: The Johnny Winter Story (GRT 1969)★★★, First Winter (Buddah 1970)★★★, Early Times (Janus 1971)★★, About Blues (Janus 1972)★★, Before The Storm (Janus 1972)★★★, Austin Texas (United Artists 1972)★★★, The Johnny Winter Collection (Castle 1986)★★★★, Birds Can't Row Boats (Relix 1988)★★★, Scorchin' Blues (Epic/Legacy 1992)★★★, A Rock N'Roll Collection (Columbia/Legacy 1994)★★★★, Winter Heat (Columbia 1998)★★★★.
VIDEOS: Johnny Winter Live (Channel 5 1989).

WINWOOD, STEVE
ALBUMS: Steve Winwood (Island 1977)★★★★, Arc Of A Diver (Island 1980)★★★★, Talking Back To The Night (Island 1983)★★★, Back In The High Life (Island 1986) ★★★★, Roll With It (Virgin 1988)★★★★, Refugees Of The Heart (Virgin 1990)★★★, Junction 7 (Virgin 1997)★.
COMPILATIONS: Chronicles (Island 1987)★★★★, The Finer Things 4-CD box set (Island 1995)★★★★.
FURTHER READING: Back In The High Life: A Biography Of Steve Winwood, Alan Clayson. Keep On Running: The Steve Winwood Story, Chris Welch.

WIRE
ALBUMS: Pink Flag (Harvest 1977)★★★★, Chairs Missing (Harvest 1978)★★★★, 154 (Harvest 1979)★★★★, Document And Eyewitness (Rough Trade 1981)★★, The Ideal Copy (Mute 1987)★★★★, A Bell Is A Cup (Until It Is Struck) (Mute 1988)★★, It's Beginning To And Back Again (Mute 1989)★★★, The Peel Sessions (Strange Fruit 1989) ★★★, Manscape (Mute 1990)★★, The Drill (Mute 1991) ★★, as Wir The First Letter (Mute 1991)★★★.
COMPILATIONS: And Here It Is ... Again ... Wire (Sneaky Pete 1984)★★★, Wire Play Pop (Pink 1986)★★★, On Returning (Harvest 1989)★★★★.
FURTHER READING: Wire ... Everybody Loves A History, Kevin S. Eden.

WISHBONE ASH
ALBUMS: Wishbone Ash (MCA/Decca 1970)★★★, Pilgrimage (MCA/Decca 1971)★★, Argus (MCA 1972) ★★★, Wishbone Four (MCA 1973)★★★, Live Dates (MCA 1973)★★★, There's The Rub (MCA 1974)★★, Locked In (MCA/ Atlantic 1976)★★, New England (MCA/Atlantic 1976)★★, Front Page News (MCA 1977)★★, No Smoke Without Fire (MCA 1978)★★, Live In Tokyo (MCA 1978) ★★, Just Testing (MCA 1979)★★★, Live Dates Volume Two (MCA 1980)★★, Number The Brave (MCA 1981)★★, Twin Barrels Burning (Fantasy 1982)★★, Raw To The Bone (Neat 1985)★★★, Nouveau Calls (I.R.S. 1987)★★★, Here To Hear (I.R.S. 1989) ★★, Strange Affair (I.R.S. 1991)★★, BBC Radio 1 Live In Concert 1972 recording (Windsong/Griffin 1991)★★★, Live In Chicago (Permanent/Griffin 1992)★★, Live In Geneva (Hengest 1996)★★, Illuminations (HTD/Renaissance 1996) ★★, Live - Timeline 1991 recording (Receiver 1997)★★, Trance Visionary (Invisible Hands/Resurgence 1998)★★★, Psychic Terrorism (Dreamscape/Ration 1998)★★★, Bare Bones (HTD 1999) ★★, Live Dates 3 (Eagle 2001)★★.
COMPILATIONS: Classic Ash (MCA 1977)★★★, Best Of Wishbone Ash (MCA 1982)★★★, Hot Ash (MCA 1981)★★, Time Was: The Wishbone Ash Collection (MCA 1993)★★★, The Very Best Of Wishbone Ash: Blowin' Free (Nectar 1994)★★★, From The Archives Vol. 1 (Dr. John/Powerbright 1994)★★★, Archives Vol. II (USASH/Powerbright 1995)★★, Live At The BBC aka On Air 1971/1972 recordings (Windsong 1995)★★★, Archives Volume Three (USASH/Powerbright 1996)★★, Distillation 4-CD box set (Repertoire 1997)★★★, The Best Of Wishbone Ash (MCA 1997)★★★, Outward Bound (BMG 1998)★★★, The King Will Come – Live 1973/1976 recordings (Receiver 1999)★★, Blowin' Free: An Introduction To Wishbone Ash (Universal 2001)★★★.
VIDEOS: Phoenix (Hengest 1990), Wishbone Ash Live (BMG 1990).
FURTHER READING: The Illustrated Collector's Guide To Wishbone Ash, Andy Powell. Blowin' Free: Thirty Years Of Wishbone Ash, Mark Chatterton and Gary Carter.

WITHERS, BILL
ALBUMS: Just As I Am (Sussex 1971)★★★★, Still Bill (Sussex 1972)★★★★, Live At Carnegie Hall (Sussex 1973)★★, +'Justments (Sussex 1974)★★★, Making Music (Columbia 1975)★★★, Naked And Warm (Columbia 1976)★★★, Menagerie (Columbia 1977)★★★, 'Bout Love (Columbia 1979)★★★, Watching You Watching Me (Columbia 1985)★★★.
COMPILATIONS: The Best Of Bill Withers (Sussex 1975) ★★★★, Bill Withers' Greatest Hits (Columbia 1981)★★★, Lean On Me: The Best Of Bill Withers (Columbia/Legacy 1995)★★★, Lovely Day: The Best Of Bill Withers (Columbia/Legacy 1998)★★★.

WITNESS
ALBUMS: Before The Calm (Island 1999)★★★, "Under A Sun" (Island 2001)★★★★.

WIZZARD
ALBUMS: Wizzard Brew (Harvest 1973)★★★, Introducing Eddy And The Falcons (Warners 1974)★★★, Main Street 1976 recording (West Side 2000)★★★.
COMPILATIONS: See My Baby Jive (Harvest 1974)★★★.

WOMACK AND WOMACK
ALBUMS: Love Wars (Elektra 1983)★★★, Radio M.U.S.I.C. Man (Elektra 1985)★★★, Starbright (Manhattan/EMI 1986)★★★, Conscience (4th & Broadway 1988)★★, Family Spirit (Arista 1991)★★, Transformation To The House Of Zekkariyas (Warners 1993)★★.
COMPILATIONS: Greatest Hits (Spectrum 1998)★★★.

WOMACK, BOBBY
ALBUMS: Fly Me To The Moon (Minit 1968)★★★, My Prescription (Minit 1969)★★★, with Gabor Szabó High Contrast (Blue Thumb 1970)★★★, The Womack Live (United Artists 1970)★★★, Communication (United Artists 1971)★★★, Understanding (United Artists 1972)★★★, Across 110th Street film soundtrack (United Artists 1972) ★★, Facts Of Life (United Artists 1973)★★★, Looking For A Love Again (United Artists 1974)★★★, I Don't Know What The World Is Coming To (United Artists 1975)★★★, Safety Zone (United Artists 1976)★★★, BW Goes C&W (United Artists 1976)★★, Home Is Where The Heart Is (Columbia 1976)★★, Pieces (Columbia 1977)★★, Roads Of Life (Arista 1979)★★, The Poet (Beverly Glen 1981) ★★★, The Poet II (Beverly Glen 1984)★★, Someday We'll All Be Free (Beverly Glen 1985)★★, So Many Rivers (MCA 1985)★★, Womagic (MCA 1986)★★, The Last Soul Man (MCA 1987)★★, Back To My Roots (The Right Stuff 1999) ★★★, Traditions (Capitol 1999)★★★.
COMPILATIONS: Bobby Womack's Greatest Hits (United Artists 1974)★★★★, Somebody Special (Liberty 1984) ★★★, Check It Out (Stateside 1986)★★★, Womack Winners 1968-1975 (Charly 1989, 1993)★★★, Midnight Mover: The Bobby Womack Collection (EMI 1993)★★★★, Lookin' For A Real Love: The Best Of Bobby Womack (Razor & Tie 1994)★★★, I Feel A Groove Comin' On (Charly 1995)★★★, Only Survivor: The MCA Years (MCA 1996) ★★★, The Soul Of Bobby Womack: Stop On By (EMI 1997)★★★, Greatest Hits (Charly 1998)★★★, The Best Of The Poets (Sequel 1999)★★★.
VIDEOS: The Jazz Channel Presents Bobby Womack (Aviva International 2000).

WONDER STUFF
ALBUMS: The Eight Legged Groove Machine (Polydor 1988)★★★★, Hup (Polydor 1989)★★★, Never Loved Elvis (Polydor 1991)★★★, Construction For The Modern Idiot (Polydor 1993)★★, Live In Manchester (Windsong 1995) ★★, Cursed With Insincerity (Eagle 2001)★★★.
COMPILATIONS: If The Beatles Had Read Hunter ... The Singles (Polydor 1994)★★★★, Love Bites And Bruises (Polydor 2000)★★★.
VIDEOS: Eleven Appalling Promos (PolyGram Music Video 1990), Welcome To The Cheap Seats (PolyGram Music Video 1992), Greatest Hits Finally Live (PolyGram Music Video 1994).

WONDER, STEVIE
ALBUMS: Tribute To Uncle Ray (Tamla 1962)★★★, The Jazz Soul Of Little Stevie (Tamla 1962)★★★, The 12-Year-Old Genius Recorded Live (Tamla 1963)★★★, With A Song In My Heart (Tamla 1963)★★, Stevie At The Beach (Tamla 1964)★★, Up-Tight (Everything's Alright) (Tamla 1966) ★★★, Down To Earth (Tamla 1966)★★★, I Was Made To Love Her (Tamla 1967)★★★★, Someday At Christmas (Tamla 1967)★★, For Once In My Life (Tamla 1968) ★★★★, My Cherie Amour (Tamla 1969)★★★★, Stevie Wonder Live (Tamla 1970)★★, Stevie Wonder Live At The Talk Of The Town (Tamla 1970)★★★, Signed Sealed & Delivered (Tamla 1970)★★★★, Where I'm Coming From (Tamla 1971)★★★★, Music Of My Mind (Tamla 1972) ★★★★, Talking Book (Tamla Motown 1972)★★★★★, Innervisions (Tamla Motown 1973)★★★★★, Fulfillingness' First Finale (Tamla Motown 1974)★★★, Songs In The Key Of Life (Motown 1976)★★★★★, Stevie Wonder's Journey Through The Secret Life Of Plants (Motown 1979)★★, Hotter Than July (Motown 1980)★★★, The Woman In Red soundtrack (Motown 1984)★★, In Square Circle (Motown 1985)★★, Characters (Motown 1987)★★, Conversation Peace (Motown 1995)★★, Natural Wonder (Motown 1995)★★.
COMPILATIONS: Greatest Hits (Tamla 1968)★★★★, Greatest Hits Vol. 2 (Tamla 1971)★★★★, Anthology aka Looking Back 1962-71 recordings (Motown 1977)★★★★, Stevie Wonder's Original Musiquarium I (Motown 1982) ★★★★, Song Review: A Greatest Hits Collection (Motown 1998)★★★, At The Close Of A Century 4-CD box set (Motown 1999)★★★★, Ballad Collection (Motown 2000) ★★★.
FURTHER READING: Stevie Wonder, Sam Hasegawa. The Story Of Stevie Wonder, Jim Haskins. Stevie Wonder, Ray Fox-Cumming. Stevie Wonder, Constanze Elsner. The Picture Life Of Stevie Wonder, Audrey Edwards. Stevie Wonder, C. Dragonwagon. Stevie Wonder, Beth P. Wilson. The Stevie Wonder Scrapbook, Jim Haskins with Kathleen Benson. Stevie Wonder, Rick Taylor. Innervisions: The Music Of Stevie Wonder, Martin E. Horn.
FILMS: Bikini Beach (1964).

WOOD, ROY
ALBUMS: Boulders (Harvest 1973)★★★, Mustard (Jet 1975)★★★, with the Roy Wood Wizzo Band Super Active (Warners 1977)★★★, On The Road Again (Warners 1979)★★, Starting Up (Legacy 1986)★★.
COMPILATIONS: The Roy Wood Story (Harvest 1976)★★★, The Singles (Speed 1982)★★★, The Best Of Roy Wood 1970-1974 (MFP 1985)★★★, Singles (Repertoire 1995) ★★★, Through The Years: The Best Of Roy Wood (EMI 1997)★★★, Exotic Mixture: Best Of Singles A's & B's (Repertoire 1999)★★★.

WORLD PARTY
ALBUMS: Private Revolution (Ensign 1987)★★, Goodbye Jumbo (Ensign 1990)★★★★, Thank You World mini-album (Ensign 1991)★★★, Bang! (Ensign 1993)★★★, Egyptology (Chrysalis 1997)★★★★, Dumbing Up (Papillon 2000)★★★.

WRAY, LINK
ALBUMS: Link Wray And The Raymen (Epic 1959)★★★★, Jack The Ripper (Swan 1963)★★★★, Great Guitar Hits (Vermillion 1963)★★★, Sings And Plays Guitar (Vermillion 1964)★★★, Yesterday And Today (Record Factory 1969)★★★, Link Wray (Polydor 1971)★★★, Be What You Want To Be (Polydor 1972)★★★, Beans And Fatback (Virgin 1973)★★★, The Link Wray Rumble (Polydor 1974)★★★, Interstate 10 (Virgin 1975)★★★, Stuck In Gear (Virgin 1976)★★★, with Robert Gordon Robert Gordon With Link Wray (Private Stock 1977)★★★, with Robert Gordon Fresh Fish Special (Private Stock 1978) ★★★, Bullshot (Charisma 1979)★★★, Live At The Paradiso (Magnum Force 1980)★★★, Live In '85 (Big Beat 1986) ★★★, Indian Child (Creation 1993)★★★, Shadowman (Ace/Hip-O 1997)★★★, Walking Down A Street Called Love: The Rumble Man Live In London And Manchester (Cleopatra 1997)★★★, Barbed Wire (Ace 2000)★★★.
COMPILATIONS: There's Good Rockin' Tonight (Union Pacific 1971)★★★, Rockin' And Handclappin' (Epic 1973)★★★, Rock 'N' Roll Rumble (Charly 1974)★★★★, Early Recordings (Ace 1979)★★★★, Good Rocking' Tonight (Chiswick 1983)★★★★, Link Wray And The Wraymen (Edsel 1985)★★★★, Growlin' Guitar (Ace 1987)★★★, Hillbilly Wolf: Missing Links Volume 1 (Norton 1990)★★★, Big City After Dark: Missing Links Volume 2 (Norton 1990)★★★, Some Kinda Nut: Missing Links Volume 3 (Norton 1990)★★★, Rumble! The Best Of Link Wray (Rhino 1993)★★★★, Mr. Guitar: Original Swan Recordings (Norton 1995)★★★★, Guitar Preacher: The Polydor Years (Polydor 1995)★★★, Streets Of Chicago: Missing Links Volume 4 (Norton 1997)★★★, Slinky! The Epic Sessions (Sundazed 2002)★★★.
VIDEOS: Link Wray: The Rumble Man (Visionary/Cleopatra 1996).

WU-TANG CLAN
ALBUMS: Enter The Wu-Tang (36 Chambers) (Loud/RCA 1993)★★★★, Wu-Tang Forever (Loud/RCA 1997)★★★, The W (Loud/RCA 2000)★★★★, Iron Flag (Loud 2001) ★★★.
COMPILATIONS: Wu-Chronicles (Priority 1999)★★★.
VIDEOS: Da Mystery Of Kung-Fu (MIA 1998), Gravel Pit (Epic Music Video 2001).

WYATT, ROBERT
ALBUMS: The End Of An Ear (Columbia 1970)★★★, Rock Bottom (Virgin 1974)★★★★, Ruth Is Stranger Than Richard (Virgin 1975)★★★, Nothing Can Stop Us (Rough Trade 1982)★★★★, Animals film soundtrack (Rough Trade 1984)★★★, Old Rotten Hat (Rough Trade 1985)★★★, Dondestan (Rough Trade 1991)★★★, A Short Break mini-

album (Rough Trade 1992)★★★, *Shleep* (Hannibal/Thirsty Ear 1997)★★★★, *Dondestan Revisited* (Hannibal 1998)★★★.
COMPILATIONS: *Going Back A Bit: A Little History Of Robert Wyatt* (Virgin Universal 1994)★★★, *Flotsam Jetsam* (Rough Trade 1994)★★, various artists *Soupsongs: The Music Of Robert Wyatt* (Voiceprint 2000)★★★.
FURTHER READING: *Wrong Movements: A Robert Wyatt History*, Michael King.

X
ALBUMS: *Los Angeles* (Slash 1980)★★★, *Wild Gift* (Slash 1981)★★★★, *The Decline ... Of Western Civilization* film soundtrack (Slash 1981)★★★, *Under The Big Black Sun* (Elektra 1982)★★★, *More Fun In The New World* (Elektra 1983)★★, *Ain't Love Grand* (Elektra 1985)★★★, *See How We Are* (Elektra 1987)★★★, *Live At The Whiskey A Go-Go On The Fabulous Sunset Strip* (Elektra 1988)★★★, *Major League* film soundtrack (Curb 1989)★★, *Hey Zeus!* (Big Life/Mercury 1993)★★★, *Unclogged* (Infidelity 1995)★★★.
SOLO: John Doe *Meet John Doe* (DGC 1990)★★★, *Freedom Is ...* (spinART 2000)★★★. Exene Cervenka with Wanda Coleman *Live At McCabe's* (Freeway 1985)H, *Old Wives' Tales* (Rhino 1989)★★★, *Running Scared* (RNA 1990)★★. Exene Cervenkova *Surface To Air Serpents* (Year One 1995)★★★. *Surface To Air Serpents* (Year One 1995)★★★.
COMPILATIONS: *Beyond & Back: The X Anthology* (Elektra 1997)★★★★.

X-RAY SPEX
ALBUMS: *Germ Free Adolescents* (EMI 1978)★★★, *Live At The Roxy* (Receiver 1991)★★, *Conscious Consumer* (Receiver 1995)★★.
COMPILATIONS: *Obsessed With You: The Early Years* (Receiver 1991)★★, *Germ Free Adolescents: The Anthology* (Castle 2002)★★★.

XTC
ALBUMS: *White Music* (Virgin 1978)★★★, *Go2* (Virgin 1978)★★★, *Drums And Wires* (Virgin 1979)★★★★, *Black Sea* (Virgin 1980)★★★, *English Settlement* (Virgin 1982)★★★, *Mummer* (Virgin 1983)★★★, *The Big Express* (Virgin 1984)★★★, *Skylarking* (Virgin 1986)★★★★, *Oranges & Lemons* (Virgin 1989)★★★, *Explode Together: The Dub Experiments 78-80* (Virgin 1990)★★★, *Rag And Bone Buffet* (Virgin 1990)★★★, *Nonsuch* (Virgin 1992)★★★★, *Apple Venus Volume 1* (Idea/Cooking Vinyl 1999)★★★, *Wasp Star (Apple Venus Volume 2)* (Idea/Cooking Vinyl 2000)★★★, *Homegrown* (Idea/TVT 2001)★★★.
SOLO: Andy Partridge *Take Away (The Lure of Salvage)* (Virgin 1980)★★★.
COMPILATIONS: *Waxworks: Some Singles 1977-1982* originally released with free compilation, *Beeswax, a collection of b-sides* (Virgin 1982)★★★, *Beeswax* (Virgin 1983)★★, *The Compact XTC – The Singles 1985-1985* (Virgin 1986)★★★★, *Live In Concert 1980* (Windsong 1992)★★★, *Drums And Wireless - BBC Radio Sessions 77-89* (Nighttracks 1995)★★★, *Fossil Fuel: The Singles 1977-92* (Virgin 1996)★★★, *Transistor Blast: The Best Of The BBC Sessions 4-CD box set* (Cooking Vinyl 1998)★★★, *A Coat Of Many Cupboards 4-CD box set* (Virgin 2002)★★★★.
FURTHER READING: *Chalkhills And Children*, Chris Twomey. *XTC: Song Stories*, XTC and Neville Farmer.

Y
YARDBIRDS
ALBUMS: *Five Live Yardbirds* (Columbia 1964)★★★★, *For Your Love* US only (Epic 1965)★★★, *Having A Rave Up With The Yardbirds* US only (Epic 1965)★★★, *Roger The Engineer aka Over Under Sideways Down* (Epic 1966)★★★, *Little Games* (Epic 1967)★★★, *The Yardbirds Reunion Concert* (Renaissance 1992)★★★.
COMPILATIONS: *The Yardbirds With Sonny Boy Williamson* 1963 recordings (Fontana 1966)★★★, *The Yardbirds' Greatest Hits* (Epic 1967)★★★, *The Yardbirds Featuring*

Performances By Jeff Beck, Eric Clapton, Jimmy Page (Epic 1970)★★★★, *Remember The Yardbirds* (Regal 1971)★★★, *Live Yardbirds* (Epic 1971)★★★, *Yardbirds Featuring Eric Clapton* (Charly 1977)★★★, *Yardbirds Featuring Jeff Beck* (Charly 1977)★★★, *Shapes Of Things* (Collection 3-LP box 1984)★★★, *The First Recordings* (Charly 1982)★★★, *The Studio Sessions* (Charly 1989)★★★, *Yardbirds ... On Air* (Band Of Joy 1991)★★★, *Smokestack Lightning* (Sony 1991)★★★★, *Blues, Backtracks And Shapes Of Things* (Sony 1991)★★★, *Train Kept A Rollin': The Complete Giorgio Gomelsky Recordings 4-CD box set* (Charly 1993)★★★, *Honey In Your Hips 1963-66 recordings* (Charly 1994)★★★, *The Best Of The Yardbirds* (Rhino 1994)★★★, *Good Morning Little Schoolgirl* (Essential Gold 1995)★★★, *Where The Action Is!* (New Millennium/Caroline 1997)★★★, *The Complete BBC Sessions* (Get Back 1998)★★★, *The Best Of The Yardbirds* (Charly 1998)★★★, *Cumular Limit* (Burning Airlines 2000)★★★, *Ultimate!* (Rhino 2001)★★★.
VIDEOS: *Yardbirds* (Delilah Music Pictures 1991)★★★.
FURTHER READING: *Blues In The Night: The Yardbirds' Story*, James White. *Yardbirds*, John Platt. *Yardbirds World*, Richard MacKay and Michael Ober. *Yardbirds: The Ultimate Rave-up*, Greg Russo.

YAZOO
ALBUMS: *Upstairs At Eric's* (Mute/Sire 1982)★★★, *You And Me Both* (Mute/Sire 1983)★★.
COMPILATIONS: *Only Yazoo: The Best Of Yazoo* (Mute 1999)★★★.

YEARWOOD, TRISHA
ALBUMS: *Trisha Yearwood* (MCA 1991)★★★, *Hearts In Armor* (MCA 1992)★★★, *The Song Remembers When* (MCA 1993)★★★, *The Sweetest Gift* (MCA 1994)★★★, *Thinkin' Bout You* (MCA 1995)★★★, *Everybody Knows* (MCA 1996)★★★, *Where Your Road Leads* (MCA 1998)★★★, *Real Live Woman* (MCA 2000)★★★, *Inside Out* (MCA 2001)★★★.
COMPILATIONS: *Songbook: A Collection Of Hits* (MCA 1997)★★★★.
FURTHER READING: *Get Hot Or Go Home: The Making Of A Nashville Star*, Lisa Rebecca Gubernick.

YELLO
ALBUMS: *Solid Pleasure* (Ralph/Do It 1980)★★★, *Claro Que Si* (Ralph/Do It 1981)★★★, *You Gotta Say Yes To Another Excess* (Elektra/Stiff 1983)★★★, *Stella* (Elektra 1985)★★★, *One Second* (Mercury 1987)★★★, *Flag* (Mercury 1988)★★★, *Baby* (Mercury 1991)★★★, *Zebra* (Mercury/4th & Broadway 1994)★★★, *Pocket Universe* (Mercury 1997)★★★, *Motion Picture* (Mercury 1999)★★.
COMPILATIONS: *Yello 1980-1985: The New Mix In One Go* (Mercury 1986)★★★, *Essential* (Smash/Mercury 1992)★★★, various artists *Hands On Yello: The Remixes* (Polydor 1995)★★★, *Eccentric Remixes* (Mercury 1999)★★.
VIDEOS: *The Video Race* (Mercury 1988), *Yello Live At The Roxy N.Y. Dec '83* (Mercury 1989), *Essential Video* (Mercury 1992).

YES
ALBUMS: *Yes* (Atlantic 1969)★★★, *Time And A Word* (Atlantic 1970)★★★, *The Yes Album* (Atlantic 1971)★★★★, *Fragile* (Atlantic 1971)★★★★, *Close To The Edge* (Atlantic 1972)★★★★, *Yessongs* (Atlantic 1973)★★★, *Tales From Topographic Oceans* (Atlantic 1973)H, *Relayer* (Atlantic 1974)★★★, *Going For The One* (Atlantic 1977)★★★, *Tormato* (Atlantic 1978)H, *Drama* (Atlantic 1980)★★, *Yesshows* (Atlantic 1980)★★, *90125* (Atco 1983)★★★, *90125 Live-The Solos* (Atco 1985)H, *Big Generator* (Atlantic 1987)★★, *Union* (Arista 1991)★★, *Talk* (Victory 1994)★★★, *Keys To Ascension* (CMC/BMG 1996)★★, *Keys To Ascension 2* (Castle/Cleopatra 1997)★★, *Open Your Eyes* (Eagle/Beyond 1997)★★, *The Ladder* (Eagle/Beyond 1999)★★★, *House Of Yes: Live From House Of Blues* (Eagle/Beyond 2000)★★★, *Magnification* (Eagle/Beyond 2001)★★★.
COMPILATIONS: *Yesterdays* (Atlantic 1975)★★, *Classic Yes* (Atlantic 198)★★★, *Yesyears 4-CD box set* (Atlantic 1991)★★★, *Highlights: The Very Best Of Yes* (Atlantic 1993)★★★, *Something's Coming reissued as Beyond & Before: BBC Recordings 1969-1970* (Pilot 1998)★★★, *Friends And Relatives* (Cleopatra 1998)★★★, *Friends And Relatives Volume Two* (Cleopatra 2001)★★★, *Keystudio* (Sanctuary 2001)★★★, *Today* (Snapper 2002)★★★.
VIDEOS: *90125 Live: The Solos* (Atlantic 1985), *Greatest Hits* (Atlantic 1991), *Yesyears: A Retrospective* (Atlantic 1991), *House Of Yes: Live From House Of Blues* (BMG 2000).
FURTHER READING: *Yes: The Authorized Biography*, Dan Hedges. *Music Of Yes: Structure And Vision In Progressive Rock*, Bill Martin. *Yesstories: Yes In Their Own Words*, Tim Morse. *Close To The Edge: The Story Of Yes*, Chris Welch. *Yes! Perpetual Change - Thirty Years Of Yes*, David Watkinson.

YO LA TENGO
ALBUMS: *Ride The Tiger* (Coyote/Twin Tone 1986)★★★, *New Wave Hot Dogs* (Coyote/Twin Tone 1987)★★★, *President Yo La Tengo* (Coyote 1989)★★★, *Fakebook* (Bar/None 1990)★★★, *May I Sing With Me* (Alias 1992)★★★, *Painful* (City Slang 1993)★★★, *Electr-O-Pura* (City Slang 1995)★★★, *I Can Hear The Heart Beating As One* (Matador 1997)★★★, with Jad Fair *Strange But True* (Matador 1998)★★★, *And Then Nothing Turned Itself Inside-Out* (Matador 2000)★★★, *Danelectro* mini-album (Matador 2000)★★★.
COMPILATIONS: *Genius + Love = Yo La Tengo* (Matador 1996)★★★.

YOAKAM, DWIGHT
ALBUMS: *Guitars, Cadillacs, Etc., Etc.* (Reprise 1986)★★★★, *Hillbilly DeLuxe* (Reprise 1987)★★★★, *Buenas Noches From A Lonely Room* (Reprise 1988)★★★, *If There Was A Way* (Reprise 1990)★★★, *La Croix D'Amour* (Reprise 1992)★★★, *This Time* (Reprise 1993)★★★, *Dwight Live* (Reprise 1995)★★, *Gone* (Reprise 1995)★★★, *Under The Covers* (Reprise 1997)★★★, *Come On Christmas* (Reprise 1997)★★, *A Long Way Home* (Reprise 1998)★★★, *dwightyoakamacoustic.net* (Reprise 2000)★★★, *Tomorrow's Sounds Today* (Reprise 2000)★★★, *South Of Heaven West Of Hell* film soundtrack (Warners 2001)★★★.
COMPILATIONS: *Just Lookin' For A Hit* (Reprise 1989)★★★★, *Last Chance For A Thousand Years: Greatest Hits From The 90s* (Reprise 1999)★★★.
VIDEOS: *Dwight Yoakam, Just Lookin' For A Hit* (Reprise 1989), *Fast As You* (Reprise 1993), *Pieces Of Time* (Reprise 1994), *Live On Stage* (Magnum Video 1994).
FURTHER READING: *A Long Way Home (12 Years Of Words)*, Dwight Yoakam.
FILMS: *Red Rock West* (1992), *The Little Death* (1995), *Sling Blade aka Reckoning* (1996), *Painted Hero aka Shadow Of The Past* (1996), *The Newton Boys* (1998), *Ozzie And Harriet: The Adventures Of America's Favorite Family* (1998), *The Minus Man* (1999), *South Of Heaven, West Of Hell* (2000), *Panic Room* (2002).

YOUNG RASCALS
ALBUMS: *The Young Rascals* (Atlantic 1966)★★★, *Collections* (Atlantic 1966)★★, *Groovin'* (Atlantic 1967)★★★★, as The Rascals *Once Upon A Dream* (Atlantic 1968)★★★, as The Rascals *Freedom Suite* (Atlantic 1969)★★★, as The Rascals *Search And Nearness* (Atlantic 1969)★★★, as The Rascals *See* (Atlantic 1970)★★, as The Rascals *Peaceful World* (Columbia 1971)★★, as The Rascals *The Island of Real* (Columbia 1972)★★.
COMPILATIONS: *Timepeace: The Rascals' Greatest Hits* (Atlantic 1968)★★★★, *Star Collection* (WEA 1973)★★★, *Searching For Ecstasy: The Rest Of The Rascals 1969-1972* (Rhino 1988)★★★, *Anthology (1965-1972)* (Rhino 1992)★★★★, *The Very Best Of The Rascals* (Rhino 1994)★★★, *All I Really Need: The Atlantic Recordings*

YOUNG, NEIL
1965-1971 (Rhino Handmade 2000)★★★.
ALBUMS: *Neil Young* (Reprise 1969)★★★, *Everybody Knows This Is Nowhere* (Reprise 1969)★★★, *After The Goldrush* (Reprise 1970)★★★★, *Harvest* (Reprise 1972)★★★, *Journey Through The Past* film soundtrack (Reprise 1972)H, *Time Fades Away* (Reprise 1973)★★, *On The Beach* (Reprise 1974)★★★, *Tonight's The Night* (Reprise 1975)★★★★, *Zuma* (Reprise 1975)★★★★, *American Stars 'N' Bars* (Reprise 1977)★★★, *Comes A Time* (Reprise 1978)★★★, *Rust Never Sleeps* (Reprise 1979)★★★★, *Live Rust* (Reprise 1979)★★★, *Hawks And Doves* (Reprise 1980)★★★, *Re-Ac-Tor* (Reprise 1981)★★★, *Trans* (Geffen 1983)★★★, *Everybody's Rockin'* (Geffen 1983)★★, *Old Ways* (Geffen 1985)★★★, *Landing On Water* (Geffen 1986)H, *Life* (Geffen 1987)★★, *This Note's For You* (Reprise 1988)★★★, *Eldorado* mini-album (Reprise 1989)★★★, *Freedom* (Reprise 1989)★★★, *Ragged Glory* (Reprise 1990)★★★, *Weld* (Reprise 1991)★★★, *Arc/Weld* (Reprise 1991)★★★, *Harvest Moon* (Reprise 1992)★★★, *Unplugged* (Reprise 1993)★★★, *Sleeps With Angels* (Reprise 1994)★★★, *Mirror Ball* (Reprise 1995)★★★, *Dead Man* film soundtrack (Vapor 1996)H, *Broken Arrow* (Reprise/Vapor 1996)★★, *The Year Of The Horse* (Reprise 1997)★★★, *Silver & Gold* (Reprise 2000)★★, *Road Rock V. 1* (Reprise 2000)★★★, *Are You Passionate?* (Reprise 2002)★★★.
COMPILATIONS: *Decade* (Reprise 1977)★★★★, *Greatest Hits* (Reprise 1985)★★, *Lucky Thirteen* (Geffen 1992)★★★.
VIDEOS: *Neil Young & Crazy Horse: Rust Never Sleeps* (RCA 1984), *Berlin* (Channel 5 1988), *Freedom* (Warner Music Video 1990), *Ragged Glory* (Warner Music Video 1991), *Weld* (Warner Music Video 1991), *Unplugged* (Warner Music Video 1993), *The Complex Sessions* (Warner Music Video 1994), *Human Highway* (Warner Music Video 1995), *Silver & Gold* (Warner Music Video 2000).
FURTHER READING: *Neil Young*, Carole Dufrechou. *Neil Young: The Definitive Story Of His Musical Career*, Johnny Rogan. *Neil and Me*, Scott Young. *Neil Young: Een Portret*, Herman Verbeke and Lucien van Diggelen. *Neil Young: Complete Illustrated Bootleg Discography*, Bruno Fisson and Alan Jenkins. *Aurora: The Story Of Neil Young And The Squires*, John Einarson. *Don't Be Denied: The Canadian Years*, John Einarson. *The Visual Documentary*, John Robertson. *His Life And Music*, Michael Heatley. *A Dreamer Of Pictures: Neil Young - The Man And His Music*, David Downing. *Neil Young And Broken Arrow: On A Journey Through The Past*, Alan Jenkins. *Ghosts On The Road: Neil Young In Concert*, Pete Long. *Love To Burn: Neil Young*, Paul Williams. *Neil Young, Alex Petridis. *Neil Young: Zero To Sixty*, Johnny Rogan. *Neil Young: Reflections In Broken Glass*, Sylvie Simmons.
FILMS: *Journey Through The Past* (1973), *Human Highway* (1982), *Year Of The Horse* (1998).

YOUNG, PAUL
ALBUMS: *No Parlez* (CBS 1983)★★★★, *The Secret Of Association* (CBS 1985)★★★, *Between Two Fires* (CBS 1986)★★, *Other Voices* (CBS 1990)★★, *The Crossing* (Columbia 1993)★★, *Reflections* (Vision 1994)★★★, *Acoustic Paul Young* mini-album (Columbia 1994)★★★, *Paul Young* (East West 1997)★★.
COMPILATIONS: *From Time To Time: The Singles Collection* (Columbia 1991)★★★★, *Love Songs* (Columbia

Z
ZAPPA, FRANK
ALBUMS: with The Mothers Of Invention *Freak Out!* (Verve 1966)★★★★, with The Mothers Of Invention *Absolutely*

Free (Verve 1967)★★★★, with The Mothers Of Invention *We're Only In It For The Money* (Verve 1968)★★★★, *Lumpy Gravy* (Verve 1968)★★★, with The Mothers Of Invention *Cruising With Ruben & The Jets* (Verve 1968)★★★, with The Mothers Of Invention *Uncle Meat* (Bizarre 1969)★★★, *Hot Rats* (Bizarre 1969)★★★★, with The Mothers Of Invention *Burnt Weeny Sandwich* (Bizarre 1970)★★★, with The Mothers Of Invention *Weasels Ripped My Flesh* (Bizarre 1970)★★★★, *Chunga's Revenge* (Bizarre 1970)★★★, with The Mothers *Fillmore East, June 1971* (Bizarre 1971)★★★, *Frank Zappa's 200 Motels* (United Artists 1971)★★, with *The Mothers Just Another Band From L.A.* (Bizarre 1972)★★★, *Waka/Jawaka* (Bizarre 1972)★★★, with The Mothers *The Grand Wazoo* (Bizarre 1972)★★★, with The Mothers *Over-Nite Sensation* (DiscReet 1973)★★★, *Apostrophe (')* (DiscReet 1974)★★★★, with The Mothers *Roxy & Elsewhere* (DiscReet 1974)★★★, with The Mothers *One Size Fits All* (DiscReet 1975)★★★, with Captain Beefheart *Bongo Fury* (DiscReet 1975)★★★, *Zoot Allures* (Warners 1976)★★★, *Zappa In New York* (DiscReet 1978)★★★, *Studio Tan* (DiscReet 1978)★★, *Sleep Dirt* (DiscReet 1979)★★★, *Sheik Yerbouti* (Zappa 1979)★★★, *Orchestral Favorites* (DiscReet 1979)★★, *Joe's Garage Act I* (Zappa 1979)★★★, *Joe's Garage Acts II & III* (Zappa 1979)★★★, *Tinseltown Rebellion* (Barking Pumpkin 1981)★★★, *Shut Up 'N Play Yer Guitar* (Barking Pumpkin 1981)★★★, *Shut Up 'N Play Yer Guitar Some More* (Zappa 1981)★★★, *Return Of The Son Of Shut Up 'N Play Yer Guitar* (Zappa 1981)★★★, *You Are What You Is* (Barking Pumpkin 1981)★★★, *Ship Arriving Too Late To Save A Drowning Witch* (Barking Pumpkin 1982)★★★, *The Man From Utopia* (Barking Pumpkin 1983)★★★, *Baby Snakes* film soundtrack (Barking Pumpkin 1983)★★★, *The London Symphony Orchestra Vol. 1* (Barking Pumpkin 1983)★★★★, *Boulez Conducts Zappa: The Perfect Stranger* (Angel 1984)★★★, *Them Or Us* (Barking Pumpkin 1984)★★★, *Thing-Fish* (Barking Pumpkin 1984)★★★, *Francesco Zappa* (Barking Pumpkin 1984)★★, *Meets The Mothers Of Prevention* (Barking Pumpkin/EMI 1985)★★★, *Does Humor Belong In Music?* (EMI 1986)★★★, *Jazz From Hell* (Barking Pumpkin 1986)★★★, *London Symphony Orchestra Vol. II* (Barking Pumpkin 1987)★★★, *Guitar* (Barking Pumpkin 1988)★★★, *Broadway The Hard Way* (Barking Pumpkin 1988)★★★, *The Best Band You Never Heard In Your Life* (Barking Pumpkin 1991)★★★, *Make A Jazz Noise Here* (Barking Pumpkin 1991)★★★, with The Mothers *Ahead Of Their Time* 1968 live recording (Barking Pumpkin 1993)★★★, with Ensemble Modern *The Yellow Shark* (Barking Pumpkin 1993)★★★, *Civilization Phaze III* (Barking Pumpkin 1994)★★★, *Everything Is Healing Nicely* 1991 recording (Barking Pumpkin 1999)★★★.
Beat The Boots I: With The Mothers Of Invention 'Tis The Season To Be Jelly 1967 recording (Foo-Eee 1991)★★, with The Mothers Of Invention *The Ark* 1969 recording (Foo-Eee 1991)★★★, *Freaks And Mother*#@%! 1970 recordings (Foo-Eee 1991)★★, with The Mothers *Piquantique 1973/1974 recordings* (Foo-Eee 1991)★★, *Unmitigated Audacity* 1974 recording (Foo-Eee 1991)★★, *Saarbrücken 1978* (Foo-Eee 1991)★★, *Anyway The Wind Blows 1979 recording* (Foo-Eee 1991)★★, *As An Am 1981/1982 recordings* (Foo-Eee 1991)★★★.
Beat The Boots II: Disconnected Synapses 1970 recording (Foo-Eee 1992)★★, *Tengo Na Minchia Tanta 1970 recordings* (Foo-Eee 1992)★★, *Electric Aunt Jemima 1968 recordings* (Foo-Eee 1992)★★, *At The Circus 1978 recording* (Foo-Eee 1992)★★, *Swiss Cheese/Fire! 1971 1968 recordings* (Foo-Eee 1992)★★, *Our Man In Nirvana 1968 recording* (Foo-Eee 1992)★★, *Conceptual Continuity 1976 recording* (Foo-Eee 1992)★★.
COMPILATIONS: with The Mothers Of Invention *Mothermania: The Best Of The Mothers* (Verve 1969)★★★, *The Old Masters Box One* (Barking Pumpkin 1985)★★★, *The Old Masters Box Two* (Barking Pumpkin 1986)★★★, *The Old Masters Box Three* (Barking Pumpkin 1987)★★★, *You Can't Do That In Stage Anymore Vol. 1* (Rykodisc 1988)★★★, *You Can't Do That On Stage Anymore Vol. 2: The Helsinki Concert* (Rykodisc 1988)★★★, *You Can't Do That On Stage Anymore Vol. 3* (Rykodisc 1989)★★★, *You Can't Do That On Stage Anymore Vol. 4* (Rykodisc 1991)★★★, *You Can't Do That On Stage Anymore Vol. 5* (Rykodisc 1992)★★★, *You Can't Do That On Stage Anymore Vol. 6* (Rykodisc 1992)★★★, with The Mothers Of Invention *Playground Psychotics 1970/1971 recordings* (Barking Pumpkin 1992)★★★, *Strictly Commercial: The Best Of Frank Zappa* (Rykodisc 1995)★★★, *The Lost Episodes* (Rykodisc 1996)★★★, *Lather* (Rykodisc 1996)★★★, *Plays The Music Of Frank Zappa: A Memorial Tribute* (Barking Pumpkin 1996)★★★, *Have I Offended Someone?* (Rykodisc 1997)★★★, *Strictly Genteel: A Classical Introduction To Frank Zappa* (Rykodisc 1997)★★★, *Cheap Thrills* (Rykodisc 1998)★★★, *Cucamonga* (Del-Fi 1998)★★★, *Mystery Disc* (Rykodisc 1998)★★★, *Son Of Cheep Thrills* (Rykodisc 1999)★★★. The entire reissued catalogue is currently available on Rykodisc.
VIDEOS: *The Dub Room Special* (Barking Pumpkin 1982), *Frank Zappa's 200 Motels* (Warner Home Video 1984), *Does Humor Belong In Music?* (MPI Home Video 1985), *The Amazing Mr. Bickford* (MPI/Honker Home Video 1987), *Video From Hell* (Honker Home Video 1987), *Uncle Meat: The Mothers Of Invention Movie* (Barfko-Swill 1987), *Baby Snakes* (Honker Home Video 1987), *The True Story Of Frank Zappa's 200 Motels* (Barfko-Swill 1989).
FURTHER READING: *Frank Zappa: Over Het Begin En Het Einde Van De Progressieve Popmuziek*, Roll-Ulrich Kaiser. *No Commercial Potential: The Saga Of Frank Zappa & The Mothers Of Invention*, David Walley. *Good Night Boys And Girls*, Michael Gray. *Frank Zappa Et Les Mothers Of Invention*, Alain Dister. *No Commercial Potential: The Saga Of Frank Zappa Then And Now*, David Walley. *Zappalog: The First Step Of Zappology*, Norbert Obermanns. *Them Or Us (The Book)*, Frank Zappa. *Mother! Is The Story Of Frank Zappa*, Michael Gray. *Viva Zappa!*, Dominique Chevalier. *Zappa: A Biography*, Julian Colbeck. *The Real Frank Zappa Book*, Frank Zappa with Peter Occhiogrosso. *Frank Zappa: A Visual Documentary*, Miles (ed.). *Frank Zappa In His Own Words*, Miles. *Mother! The Frank Zappa Story*, Michael Gray. *Frank Zappa: The Negative Dialectics Of Poodle Play*, Ben Watson. *Being Frank: My Time With Frank Zappa*, Nigey Lennon. *Zappa: Electric Don Quixote*, Neil Slaven. *Frank Zappa: A Strictly Genteel Genius*, Ben Cruickshank. *Cosmik Debris: The Collected History And Improvisations of Frank Zappa*, Greg Russo. *Necessity Is ...: The Early Years of Frank Zappa & The Mothers Of Invention*, Billy James.
FILMS: *Head* (1968), *200 Motels* (1971), *Baby Snakes* (1979).

ZEVON, WARREN
ALBUMS: *Zevon: Wanted Dead Or Alive* (Imperial 1969)★★, *Warren Zevon* (Asylum 1976)★★★, *Excitable Boy* (Asylum 1978)★★★★, *Bad Luck Streak In Dancing School* (Asylum 1980)★★★, *Stand In The Fire* (Asylum 1980)★★★, *The Envoy* (Asylum 1982)★★★, *Sentimental Hygiene* (Virgin 1987)★★★, *Transverse City* (Virgin 1989)★★★, *Mr Bad Example* (Giant 1991)★★★, *Learning To Flinch* (Giant 1993)★★★, *Mutineer* (Giant 1995)★★★, *Life'll Kill Ya* (Artemis 2000)★★★, *My Ride's Here* (Artemis 2002)★★★.
COMPILATIONS: *A Quiet Normal Life: The Best Of Warren Zevon* (Asylum 1986)★★★, *I'll Sleep When I'm Dead (An Anthology)* (Rhino 1996)★★★.

ZOMBIE, ROB
ALBUMS: *Hellbilly Deluxe* (Geffen 1998)★★★★, *American Made Music To Strip By* remix album (Geffen 1999)★★★, *The Sinister Urge* (Geffen 2001)★★★.

ZOMBIES
ALBUMS: *Begin Here* (Decca 1965)★★★, *Odessey & Oracle* (Columbia 1968)★★★★, *Early Days* (London 1969)★★, *The Zombies Live On The BBC 1965-1967* (Rhino 1985)★★★, *Meet The Zombies* (Razor 1989)★★★, *New World* (USE 1991)★★.
COMPILATIONS: *The World Of The Zombies* (Decca 1970)★★★, *Time Of The Zombies* (Epic 1973)★★, *Rock Roots* (Decca 1976)★★★, *The Best And The Rest Of The Zombies* (Back Trac 1984)★★★, *Greatest Hits* (DCC 1990)★★★, *Best Of The Zombies* (Music Club 1991)★★★, *The*

EP Collection (See For Miles 1992)★★★, *The Zombies 1964-67* (More Music 1995)★★★, *Zombie Heaven 4-CD box set* (Ace 1997)★★★★.
FURTHER READING: *The Zombies: Hung Up On A Dream*, Claes Johansen.

ZORN, JOHN
ALBUMS: with Eugene Chadbourne *School* (Parachute 1978)★★★, *Pool* (Parachute 1980)★★★, *Archery* (Parachute 1982)★★★, *Locus Solus* (Rift 1983)★★★, with Derek Bailey, George Lewis *Yankees* (Celluloid 1983)★★★, *The Classic Guide To Strategy, Volume One* (Lumina 1983)★★★, with Chadbourne *The Great Duo Live* (The Beast From 20,000 Fathoms (Parachute 1984)★★★, with Michihiro Sato *Ganryu* (Yukon 1985)★★★, *The Classic Guide To Strategy, Volume Two* (Lumina 1986)★★★, with Steve Beresford, David Toop, Tonie Marshall *Deadly Weapons* (Nato 1986)★★★, *The Big Gundown* (Icon 1986)★★★, *Cobra 1985 recording* (hatART 1987)★★★, *Spillane* (Elektra/Nonesuch 1987)★★★, with George Lewis, Bill Frisell *News For Lulu* (hatART 1988)★★★, *Spy Vs Spy: The Music Of Ornette Coleman* (Elektra/Musician 1989)★★★, *Cynical Hysterie Hour aka Filmworks VII* (CBS/Tzadik 1989)★★★, *Naked City* (Elektra/Nonesuch 1990)★★★, with Pain Killer *The Guts Of A Virgin* 1989 recording (hatART 1992)★★★, with Lewis, Frisell *More News For Lulu* 1989 recording (hatART 1992)★★★, with Pain Killer *Buried Secrets* (Earache 1992)★★★, *Elegy* (Eva 1992)★★★, *Kristallnacht* (Eva 1993)★★★, *Radical Jewish Culture In Japan* (Toy's Factory 1993)★★★, with Pain Killer *Rituals: Live In Ground* (Subharmonic 1994)★★★, with Masada *Masada 1 aka Alef* (DIW 1994)★★★, with Masada *Masada 2 aka Beit* (DIW 1995)★★★, with Fred Frith *Art Of Memory* (Incus 1995)★★★, *Cobra Live At The Knitting Factory 1992 recordings* (KFW 1995)★★★, *Redbird* (Tzadik 1995)★★★, *The Book Of Heads* (Tzadik 1995)★★★, with Masada *Masada Live Jazz Door 1995)★★★, *Filmworks II: Music For An Untitled Film By Walter Hill 1992 recording* (Toy's Factory 1995)★★★, with Masada *Masada 7 aka Zayin* (DIW 1996)★★★, *Filmworks V: Tears Of Ecstasy* (Tzadik 1996)★★★, *Filmworks VI: 1996* (Tzadik 1996)★★★, *New Traditions In East Asian Bar Bands* (Tzadik 1997)★★★, *Filmworks IV: S/M + More* (Tzadik 1997)★★★, *Duras: Duchamp* (Tzadik 1997)★★★, with Masada *Masada 8 aka Het* (Tzadik 1997)★★★, with Bobby Previte *Euclid's Nightmare* (Depth Of Field 1997)★★★, *Angelus Novus* (Tzadik 1998)★★★, with Masada *Masada 9 aka Tet* (DIW 1998)★★★, *Filmworks VII: 1997* (Tzadik 1998)★★★, *The Circle Maker* (Tzadik 1998)★★★, with Wayne Horvitz, Elliott Sharp, Bobby Previte *Downtown Lullaby* (Depth Of Field 1998)★★★, with Masada *Masada 10 aka Yod* (Tzadik 1998)★★★, *Aporias* (Tzadik 1998)★★★, *The Bribe* (Tzadik 1998)★★★, *Music Romance Volume 1: Music For Children* (Tzadik 1998)★★★, with Masada *Live In Jerusalem* (Tzadik 1999)★★★, with Masada *Live In Taipei 1995* (Tzadik 1999)★★★, *The String Quartets* (Tzadik 1999)★★★, *Godard/Spillane* (Tzadik 1999)★★★, *Taboo And Exile* (Tzadik 1999)★★★, with Masada *Live In Middelheim* (Tzadik 1999)★★★, *Lacrosse 1978* (Tzadik 2000)★★★, with Masada *Live In Sevilla* (Tzadik 2000)★★★, *Xu Feng* (Tzadik 2000)★★★, with Masada *Live At Tonic 2001* (Tzadik 2001)★★★.
COMPILATIONS: *Film Works: 1986-1990* (Wave/Elektra 1991)★★★, *First Recordings 1973* (Tzadik 1995)★★★, *The Parachute Years 1977-1980 7-CD set* (Tzadik 1997)★★★, with Eugene Chadbourne *Sonora (1977-1981)* (Materiali Sonori 1998)★★★.

ZZ TOP
ALBUMS: *ZZ Top's First Album* (London 1971)★★★, *Rio Grande Mud* (London 1972)★★★, *Tres Hombres* (London 1973)★★★★, *Fandango!* (London 1975)★★★, *Tejas* (London 1976)★★, *Dequello* (Warners 1979)★★★, *El Loco* (Warners 1981)★★, *Eliminator* (Warners 1983)★★★★, *Afterburner* (Warners 1985)★★★, *Recycler* (Warners 1990)★★★, *Antenna* (RCA 1994)★★★, *Rhythmeen* (RCA 1996)★★★, *XXX* (RCA 1999)★★.
COMPILATIONS: *The Best Of ZZ Top* (London 1977)★★★, *Greatest Hits* (Warners 1991)★★★, *One Foot In The Blues* (Warners 1994)★★★.
VIDEOS: *Greatest Hits Video Collection* (Warner Music Video 1992).
FURTHER READING: *Elimination: The ZZ Top Story*, Dave Thomas.